WINNERS

Revised Edition

The Blue Ribbon Encyclopedia of Awards

WINNERS

Revised Edition

The Blue Ribbon Encyclopedia of Awards

By Claire Walter

Indexed by Felice D. Levy and Cynthia Crippen

Facts On File
460 Park Avenue South, New York, N.Y. 10016

WINNERS
Revised Edition
The Blue Ribbon Encyclopedia of Awards

Published by Facts On File, Inc.,
460 Park Avenue South, New York, N.Y. 10016

Library of Congress Cataloging in Publication Data

Walter, Claire
Winners, the blue ribbon encyclopedia of awards, (Revised Edition).
Includes index.
1. Rewards (Prizes, etc.)—Directories. I. Facts on File, inc., New York. II. Title.
AS8.W34 1981 929.8′1 80-22177
ISBN 0-87196-386-8

9 8 7 6 5 4 3 2 1
PRINTED IN
THE UNITED STATES OF AMERICA

Contents

Preface

When a book such as WINNERS: THE BLUE RIBBON ENCYCLOPEDIA OF AWARDS is issued, some words of explanation are required on how the volume was compiled, what has been included and what—perhaps—has been left out.

Every topical reference book must have a cutoff date, even though the story may be incomplete. For almost all of the awards and prizes included in this volume, the last word can never be written: there are, of course, new winners year after year. It is Facts On File's intention to issue an updated revised edition of WINNERS every three years. The present second edition includes new winners for the awards which were in the original data bank and new awards and any significant prizes that might have been overlooked in the first edition. We welcome suggestions for additions, supplementary information, corrections and the names of subsequent award winners. Such information should be sent to: Awards Editor, Facts On File Publications, 460 Park Ave. South, New York, N.Y. 10016.

WINNERS fills a gap in reference material by compiling and indexing available information about awards, the organizations that give them and the people or institutions that have received them. Obviously, it has been impossible to include all the world's awards and prizes. We have concentrated on major American honors in various fields of endeavor, as well as important awards given abroad, particularly those of international scope. Humorous as well as serious honors are included.

WINNERS comprises awards given on the basis of judgment rather than for measurable or objectively defined achievements. Therefore, we have included books which have won literary prizes but not those that topped the best seller list, the baseball star voted the Most Valuable Player in the league rather than the athlete with the highest batting average, movies and people in the film industry honored with an Oscar or at Cannes but not a list of the highest grossing pictures at the box office and people cited for public service achievements rather than those who won elections. Most, but not all, halls of fame have been excluded. This decision was based in part on necessity: there are literally thousands of halls of fame covering every field of endeavor imaginable. Another factor in this decision was that the process of selection by ballot or election differs markedly from that used to determine the winners of most awards. We have, however, included a few halls of fame where in our judgment the selection process or the nature of the honor is more similar to those of awards than to those commonly associated with halls of fame. This was particularly true where the sponsoring organization itself describes or treats such an honor as comparable to its other awards. Significance also affected our decision on whether or not a hall of fame should be included.

We contacted by mail, phone or both thousands of award-giving organizations, asking them to describe the selection process for their major awards, what the individual honored receives (plaque, trophy, statuette, amount of money, etc.), a complete chronological list of all winners from the inception of the award through 1980 and, if possible, in each case the achievement for which the honor was granted. Every effort was made to track down information on awards whose sponsors chose not to reply to our series of questionnaires as well as to answer questions raised by discrepancies in the material we had received.

The vast majority of the material included in WINNERS has as its original source the organizations that gave the award. We have taken their word on spellings of names of individuals they have honored, except when the recipients were public figures whose names could be cross-checked in other reference sources. In most cases the year listed is the year in which the award was won. In the case of a few honors, an award for a particular year is issued at a later date. In all cases, we have followed the practice of the sponsors of the awards in our listings.

For the sake of consistency, given the scores of languages involved, we have eliminated all accent marks in foreign names and words rather than mislead readers by including some and omitting others. Except for awards of valor, where the recipient's death was one reason for the honor, we have deleted all references as to whether the award was made posthumously or whether the recipient is alive at this writing. Again for reasons of consistency, we have eliminated the titles "Dr." and "Professor." Where available, we have kept military rank, titles of nobility, clerical designations and, frequently, indications of elective office—all at the time of presentation of the award. When an honor included an expense-paid trip to an organization's meeting to accept the honor, or to present an address, we have not included this information in the descriptions of what the winner received except when these facts were especially significant.

We have organized the awards in what we believe are logical categories. In many cases, an individual award could have been placed logically in any one of several chapters. For example, an award to an author of a work of history might be included either in the "Books & Literature" chapter or in the chapter encompassing "Humanities & the Social Sciences." In such cases, we have asked ourselves—and at times the sponsor whether the award is made *primarily* on the basis of literary merit, historical significance, the quality of scholarship or all three. On this basis, the National Book Award and the Pulitzer Prize for history were placed in the chapter on "Books & Literature," while those awards made by the American Historical Association to the authors of various historical works were placed in the chapter on the "Humanities & the Social Sciences." Inevitably, the final placement of some borderline cases reflects subjective judgments by the author and editor. We have attempted to compensate for this by cross-referencing and inclusion of an extensive index.

Within the chapters established, we have tried to group awards into logical packages, not alphabetically or by the name of the granting organization or of the award. For instance, sports awards are grouped first for general athletic achievement ("Athlete of the Year"-type honors) and then by sport. Within these categories and sub-categories, which are spelled out at the opening of each section, we attempted to alphabetize by the key word. Therefore, the order will sometimes be by the award's official name, sometimes by a well-known nickname and occasionally by the organization that grants it. Discrepancies between our judgment and that of the reader on what constitutes the key word will be reconciled by the index. We opted for ease of use rather than for a rigidly disciplined organizational approach.

In addition to the assistance granted us by hundreds of people who took the time to answer our queries, we would like to acknowledge several publications we found useful in doublechecking information about award-giving organizations and the people they honored: *Awards, Honors and Prizes* by Paul Wasserman and Krystyna Wasserman published by Gale Research Company, *Literary and Library Prizes* published by R.R. Bowker Company and Sandra Lee Stuart's *Who Won What* published by Lyle Stuart.

Claire Walter
Hoboken, New Jersey
August 1981

G

eneral Achievement

Contents

Related Awards

Boy of the Year

BOYS' CLUBS OF AMERICA
771 First Ave., New York, N.Y. 10017 (212/557-8593)

The "Boy of the Year" is an honor for demonstrated leadership and service to "home, church, community, school and Boys' Club" by a youngster between the ages of 13 and 18. Supported by the Reader's Digest Foundation and carrying a $5,000 scholarship award, the Boy-of-the-Year presentation is traditionally made by the President of the United States. A system of regional and national nomination and judging is used to select the winner.

1963 **Ignacio Chavez**
1964 **Michael Rapinchuck**
1965 **Edwin Bassemier**
1966 **Peter Arroyo**
1967 **Gerald Simila**
1968 **William Beigl**
1969 **Perry Ludy**
1970 **James Heath**
1971 **Pelton Stewart**
1972 **Rodrigo Guerra, Jr.**
1973 **Gilbert Baez**
1974 **George Clark**
1975 **Kenneth Ivory**
1976 **Robert Fisher**
1977 **Gregory Baron**
1978 **Ray Anthony Owens**
1979 **Danny Rollet**
1980 **Jace Smith**

Cosmos Club Award

COSMOS CLUB
2121 Massachusetts Ave. NW, Washington, D.C. 20008
(202/387-7783)

The Cosmos Club Award is given annually to further the Club's cultural objectives and honors significant contributions in science, literature, the learned professions or public service. The award consists of $1,000 and a citation. The winner is selected by the Board of Management from nominations by the Awards Committee.

1964 **Elvin C. Stakman,** Biologist
1965 **Henry Allen Moe,** Humanitarian
1966 **Merle Antony Tuve,** Geophysicist
1967 **McGeorge Bundy,** Foundation Executive
1968 **Samuel Eliot Morison,** Historian
1969 **Robert D. Calkins,** Economist
1970 **Edwin Herbert Land,** Scientist
1971 **Kenneth Mackenzie Clark,** Art Historian
1972 **Howard A. Rusk,** Physician
1973 **Louis B. Wright,** Historian
1974 **Horace M. Albright,** Conservationist
1975 **Helen Hayes,** Performing Arts
1976 **Roger Tory Peterson,** Ornithologist-Artist
1977 **Archibald MacLeish,** Poet
1978 **Caryl P. Haskins,** Biologist
1979 **Bernard MacGregor Walker Knox,** Classical Scholar
1980 **John William Gardner,** Foundation Executive

Award of Merit

DECALOGUE SOCIETY OF LAWYERS
180 W. Washington St., Chicago, Ill. 60602 (312/263-6493)

The Award of Merit, which consists of a scroll, annually honors contributions to the Jewish community, the nation and the world through achievements in the arts, science, culture, public service or leadership.

1941 **Barnet Hodes**
1942 **Marshall Field**
1943 **Col. Frank Knox**
1944 **Wendell L. Willkie**
1945 **Leo Lerner**
1946 **Bartley C. Crum**
1947 **Bishop Bernard J. Sheil**
1948 **Rabbi Stephen S. Wise**
1949 **Col. Jacob M. Arvey**
1950 **Percy L. Julian**
1951 **Judge Harry M. Fisher**
1952 **Gov. Adlai E. Stevenson**
1953 **Albert Einstein**
1954 **Hon. Harry S. Truman**
1955 **Sen. Herbert Lehman**
1956 **Edward J. Sparling**
1957 **Eleanor Roosevelt**
1958 **Judge Simon E. Sobeloff**
1959 **Philip M. Klutznick**
1960 **Judge Julius H. Miner**
1961 **Hon. Arthur J. Goldberg**
1962 **Sen. Jacob K. Javits**
1963 **Hon. Michael A. Musmanno**
1964 **Rabbi Mordecai M. Kaplan**
1965 **Albert B. Sabin**
1966 **Hon. Paul H. Douglas**
1967 **Hon. Abraham L. Marovitz**
1968 **Sen. Charles H. Percy**
1969 **Rene Cassin**
1970 **Ramsey Clark**
1971 **Sir Georg Solti**
1972 **Hon. Sidney R. Yates**
1973 **Justice William O. Douglas**
1974 **No award**
1975 **Saul Bellow**
1976 **Hon. Samuel B. Epstein**
1977 **Simon Wiesenthal**
1978 **Linus Pauling**
1979 **Isaac Bashevis Singer**
1980 **A.N. Pritzker**

Encyclopaedia Britannica Award

ENCYCLOPAEDIA BRITANNICA
425 N. Michigan Ave., Chicago, Ill. 60611 (312/321-7000)

The Encyclopaedia Britannica Awards, which consist of medallions, are given annually to honor up to nine individuals for significant contributions to society and for exemplifying the encyclopedia's "ideals of authority, excellence and human achievement." The Board of Editors selects the winners.

1978 **Ellen Burstyn**, Theater
John M. Goddard, Exploration
Marchese Antonio Guadigni, Over-all achievements
Peter Hurd, Arts
Ruby S. Murchison, Education
Peter C. Newman, Journalism
David Packard, Business
Hans Selye, Science and medicine

LeRoy T. Walker, Sports
1979 **Hank Aaron**, Sports
Steve Allen, Television
Pearl Bailey, Performing arts
Lucille Ball, Entertainment
Jim Bishop, Journalism
Ernest Boyer, Education
Hubert H. Humphrey, Public service
Robert S. Ingersoll, Foreign service
Irving Layton, Literature
1980 **Frank Borman**, Exploration and business
Michael E. deBakey, Science and medicine
Hugh Downs, Television
Ella Fitzgerald, Performing arts
Benny Goodman, Music
Leonard "Red" Kelly, Sports
James A. Michener, Literature
Edmund D. Pellegrino, Education

Antonio Feltrinelli Prizes: Italian Citizens Award International Prize Gold Medal

ACCADEMIA NAZIONALE DEI LINCEI
Via Della Lungara 10, 00165-Rome, Italy

The Academy annually gives Antonio Feltrinelli prizes in rotation for accomplishments in moral and historical sciences; physical, natural and mathematical sciences; letters; the arts; medicine; and, as merited, for exceptional humanitarian or moral achievement. Substantial cash honoraria are made, the amount varying according to the year's income from the Antonio Feltrinelli Fund, which supports the awards. Members of the National Academy, presidents of other Italian academies and, in the case of the international awards, presidents of foreign academies may make nominations for consideration by a five-member committee convened to vote on the recipient.

ITALIAN CITIZENS AWARD

1950 **Paola Zancani Montuoro and Umberto Zanotti Bianco,** Archeology
1951 **Gleb Wataghin,** Mathematics, astronomy and physics
Vincenzo Diamare, Biology
1952 **Marino Moretti,** Narrative prose
Emilio Cecchi, Letters
Ferdinando Neri, Criticism and history
1953 **Filippo de Pisis,** Painting
Giacomo Manzu, Sculpture
Mario Ridolfi, Architecture
Lorenzo Perosi, Music
Fausto Torrefranca, Art criticism
1954 **Alberto Ascoli,** Medicine
Luigi Califano, Medicine
Vittorio Erspamer, Medicine
Massimiliano Aloisi, Medicine
1955 **Gianfranco Contini,** Philology and history
Francesco Gabrieli, Philology and history
Federico Chabod, History
Nicola Turchi, History
Tullio Ascarelli, Jurisprudence
Salvatore Pugliatti, Jurisprudence
Augusta Guzzo, Philosophy
Bruno Nardi, Philosophy
Gaetano Pieraccini, Economics and social science
Livio Livi, Economics and social science
1956 **Beppo Levi,** Mathematics
Bruno Finzi, Mechanical science
Livio Gratton, Astronomy
Antonio Rostagni, Physics
Pietro Caloi, Geodesics and geophysics
Gino Bozza, Chemistry
Giovanni Merla, Geology and paleontology
Paolo Gallitelli, Minerology
Francesco D'Amato, Botany
Giuseppe Moruzzi, Physiology
1957 **Antonio Baldini,** Letters
Virgilio Giotti, Letters
Vasco Pratolini, Letters
1958 **Mirko Basaldella,** Sculpture
Giovanni Michelucci, Architecture
1959 **Angelo Bairati,** Medicine
Giovanni di Guglielmo, Medicine
Alessandro Rossi-Fanelli, Medicine
1960 **Mario Praz,** Philology, history and literary criticism
Arnaldo Momigliano, Historical science
Guido Calogero, Philosophical science
1961 **Francesco G. Tricomi,** Mathematics and mechanics
Giampietro Puppi, Astronomy, geology and geophysics
Livio Trevisan, Geology, paleontology and minerology
1962 **Bruno Cicognani,** Letters
Giuseppe de Robertis, Letters
Carlo Emilio Gadda, Letters
Camillo Sbarbaro, Letters
1963 **Mino Maccari,** Painting
Giorgio Federico Ghedini, Music
Luchino Visconti, Cinematography
1964 **Antonio Ascenzi,** Morphology
Luigi Musajo, Physiology and biochemistry
Enrico Ciaranfi, Pathology
1965 **Giuseppe Billanovich,** Philology
1966 **Guido Stampacchia,** Mathematics, mechanics and their application
Luigi Radicati di Brozolo, Physics, chemistry and their application
Vittorio Capraro, Biological science and its application
1967 **Carlo Betocchi,** Poetry
Giacomo Debenedetti, Essay
Quintino Cataudella and Ezio Raimondi, Criticism and history
1968 **Pericle Fazzini,** Sculpture
Luigi Moretti, Architecture
Francesco Arcangeli, Art criticism
Gian Francesco Malipiero, Music
1969 **Giovanni Moruzzi,** Medicine
Giacomo Mottura, Medicine
Oreste Pinotti, Medicine
Giulio Raffaele, Medicine
1970 **Giorgio Petrocchi,** Linguistics and philology
Eugenio Garin, Philosophical science
Giuseppe de Meo, Social and political science
1971 **Aldo Andreotti,** Mathematics, mechanics and their application
Giuseppe Colombo, Astronomy, geology, geophysics and their application
Adriano Gozzini, Geology, paleontology, minerology and their application
Pasquale Pasquini, Biological science and its application
1972 **Italo Calvino,** Fiction
Italo Siciliano, History and literary criticism

Gianfranco Folena, Theory and history of linguistics
Vittorio Sereni, Poetry
1973 **Alberto Burri,** Graphics
Pier Luigi Cervellati, City planning
Luigi Dallapiccola, Music
Umberto Mastroianni, Sculpture
1974 **Emilio Agostoni,** Medicine
Eraldo Antonini, Medicine
Luigi Donato, Medicine
Ottavio Pompeiano, Medicine
Gaetano Salvatore, Medicine
1975 **Dinu Adamestreanu,** Archeology
Fabrizio Sergio Donadoni, Archeology
Rolando Quadri, Jurisprudence
Giulio Capodaglio, Social and political science
Giuseppi di Nardi, Social and political science
Maria Floriani Squarciapino, Archeology (unpublished work)
1976 **Enrico Bombieri,** Mathematics, mechanics and their application
Gaetano Fichera, Mathematics, mechanics and their application
Michele Caputo, Astronomy, geology, geophysics and their application
Ferdinando Amman, Physics, chemistry and their application
Massimilla Baldo Ceolin, Physics, chemistry and their application
Raffaello Fusco, Physics, chemistry and their application
Ezio Tongiorgi, Geology, paleontology and their application
Giorgio Forti, Biological science and its application
Emanuele Padoa, Biological science and its application
Leo Pardi, Biological science and its application
1977 **Diego Fabbri,** Theater
Giovanni Macchia, Literary history
1978 **Fausto Melotti**, Sculpture
Raffaello Monterosso, Art criticism and history of art
Luciano Baldassari, Architecture
1979 **Giovanni Bussolati**, Medicine
Mario Umberto Dianzani, Medicine
Guido Giulio Guidotti, Medicine
Vittorio Marinozzi, Medicine
1980 **Cesare Brandi**, Criticism of art and poetry
Franco Venturi, History
Sofia Vanni Rovishi, Philosophy of science
Giovanni Pugliese, Judicial science

INTERNATIONAL PRIZE

1951 **Jacques Hadamard,** Mathematics and astronomy
1952 **Thomas Mann,** Letters
Ramon Menedez Pidal, History and criticism
1953 **Ludwig Mies van der Rohe,** Architecture
Igor Stravinsky, Music
1954 **Alfred Blalock and Helen Taussig,** Medicine
H.R. Griffith and A.R. MacIntyre, Medicine
1955 **Leo Spitzer,** Philology and literary history
Gaetano Salvemini, History
Ernst Rabel, Jurisprudence
Werner Jaeger, Philosophy
A.C. Pigou, Economics and social science
1956 **Solomon Lefschetz,** Mathematics, mechanics and their application
Sydney Chapman, Astronomy, geology, geophysics and their application
Giuseppe P.S. Occhialini, Physics, Philology and literary history
Bruno Sander, Geology, paleontology, minerology and their application
Ross Granville Henderson, Biological science and its application
1957 **Wystan Hugh Auden,** Letters
Aldo Palazzeschi, Letters
1958 **Georges Braque,** Painting
Ildebrando Pizzetti, Music
1959 **Gaston Ramon,** Medicine
1960 **Hans Kelsen,** Jurisprudence
1961 **Pierre Auger,** Physics and chemistry
John Burdon Sanderson Haldane, Biological science
1962 **Eugenio Montale,** Letters
1963 **Henry Moore,** Sculpture
1964 **Wallace O. Fenn,** Experimental medicine
Albert Bruce Sabin, Medical science and surgical application
1965 **John Davidson Beazley,** Archeology
1966 **Harry Hammond Hess,** Geology
1967 **John Dos Passos,** Fiction
1968 **Pier Luigi Nervi,** Architecture
1969 **Rita Levi Montalcini,** Medicine
1970 **Claudio Sanchez Albornoz,** History, historical geography and anthropology
1971 **Jean Leray,** Mathematics and its application
Bruno Rossi, Physics and astrophysics
1972 **Eduardo de Filippo,** Theater
1973 **Richard Krautheimer,** Criticism and art history
1974 **Hugh Esmore Huxley,** Medicine
1975 **Alfred Verdross,** Jurisprudence
1976 **Edgar Bright Wilson, Jr.,** Chemistry
1977 **Jorge Guillen,** Poetry
1978 **Gofredo Petressi**, Music
Jean Miro, Painting
1979 **Roderic Alfred Gregory**, Medicine
1980 **Roman Jakobson**, Philosophy and Linguistics
Gottried Haberler, Economics

PRIZE FOR OUTSTANDING HIGH MORAL OR HUMANITARIAN DEEDS

1954 **Assn. Nazionale per gli Interessi del Mezzogiorno d'Italia** (Assn. for the Interests of the Mezzogiorno of Italy)
1959 **Unione Nazionale per la Lotta Contro l'Analfabetismo** (National Union for the Fight Against Illiteracy)
1969 **Coretta Scott King**
1975 **Piccola Casa della Divina Providenza "Il Cottolengo"** (Il Cottolengo, Little House of the Divine Providence)
1980 **Giorgio Cini Foundation**

GOLD MEDAL

1969 **Comitato Internazionale Croce Rossa** (International Committee of the Red Cross)
Rubrica "Specchio dei Tempi" ("Mirror of Time" Directory)
Danilo Dolci

Hall of Fame Induction

HALL OF FAME FOR GREAT AMERICANS

Mailing Address: c/o New York University Public Affairs Dept., 21 Washington Place, New York, N.Y. 10013
(212/598-7733 or 212/220-6450)

The Hall of Fame Colonnade is a museum, open to the public, on the campus of the Bronx Community College, that commemorates achievements of American citizens of historical significance in the arts, sciences, humanities, government, business or labor. The public is invited to propose names for nomination and selection by the Electors of the Hall of Fame, which is now done every three years. To be nominated, a candidate must be dead at least 25 years. The dates to the left below indicate the years of selection.

1900 **John Adams** (1735-1826), Second President of the U.S.
John James Audubon (1785?-1851), Ornithologist and artist
Henry Ward Beecher (1813-87), Theologian
William Ellery Channing (1780-1842), Theologian
Henry Clay (1777-1852), Statesman
Peter Cooper (1791-1883), Philanthropist
Jonathan Edwards (1703-58), Theologian
Ralph Waldo Emerson (1803-82), Poet and essayist
David Glasgow Farragut (1801-70), Naval commander
Benjamin Franklin (1706-90), Statesman and inventor
Robert Fulton (1765-1815), Inventor
Ulysses S. Grant (1822-85), Union general and 18th President of the U.S.
Asa Gray (1810-88), Botanist
Nathaniel Hawthorne (1804-64), Author
Washington Irving (1783-1859), Author and diplomat
Thomas Jefferson (1743-1826), Third President of the U.S.
James Kent (1763-1847), Jurist
Robert E. Lee (1807-70), Confederate general
Abraham Lincoln (1809-65), Sixteenth President of the U.S.
Henry Wadsworth Longfellow (1807-82), Poet
Horace Mann (1796-1859), Educator
John Marshall (1755-1835), Chief Justice, U.S. Supreme Court
Samuel F.B. Morse (1791-1872), Inventor
George Peabody (1795-1869), Financier and philanthropist
Joseph Story (1779-1845), Jurist and Associate Justice, U.S. Supreme Court
Gilbert Stuart (1755-1845), Painter
George Washington (1732-99), Revolutionary War general and first President of the U.S.
Daniel Webster (1782-1852), Statesman
Eli Whitney (1765-1825), Inventor

1905 **John Quincy Adams** (1767-1848), Sixth President of the U.S.
James Russell Lowell (1819-91), Poet, critic and editor
Mary Lyon (1797-1849), Educator
James Madison (1751-1836), Fourth President of the U.S.
Maria Mitchell (1818-89), Astronomer
John Greenleaf Whittier (1807-92), Poet
William Tecumseh Sherman (1820-91), Union general
Emma Willard (1787-1870), Educator

1910 **George Bancroft** (1800-91), Historian and diplomat
Philip Brooks (1835-93), Theologian
William Cullen Bryant (1794-1878), Poet and editor
James Fenimore Cooper (1789-1842), Novelist
Oliver Wendell Holmes (1809-94), Essayist and poet
Andrew Jackson (1767-1845), Statesman and seventh President of the U.S.
John Lothrop Motley (1814-77), Historian
Edgar Allen Poe (1809-49), Poet, writer and critic
Harriet Beecher Stowe (1811-96), Author and humanitarian
Frances Elizabeth Willard (1839-98), Social reformer

1915 **Louis Agassiz** (1807-73), Naturalist
Daniel Boone (1734-1820), Frontiersman
Rufus Choate (1799-1859), Lawyer and legislator
Charlotte Cushman (1816-75), Actress
Alexander Hamilton (1755?-1804), Statesman
Joseph Henry (1797-1878), Physicist
Mark Hopkins (1802-87), Educator
Elias Howe (1819-67), Inventor
Francis Parkman (1823-93), Historian

1920 **Samuel Langhorne Clemens (Mark Twain,** 1835-1910), Novelist
James Eads (1820-87), Engineer
Patrick Henry (1736-99), Statesman
William Morton (1819-68), Dentist
Alice Palmer (1855-1902), Educator
Augustus Saint-Gaudens (1848-1907), Sculptor
Roger Williams (1603?-83), Colonial leader and theologian

1925 **Edwin Booth** (1833-93), Actor
John Paul Jones (1747-92), Naval commander

1930 **Matthew Fontaine Maury** (1806-73), Naval officer and oceanographer
James Monroe (1758-1831), Fifth President of the U.S.
James A. McNeill Whistler (1834-1903), Painter
Walt Whitman (1819-92), Poet

1935 **Grover Cleveland** (1837-1908), Twenty-second and 24th President of the U.S.
Simon Newcomb (1835-1909), Astronomer
William Penn (1644-1718), Colonial leader and statesman

1940 **Stephen Foster** (1826-64), Composer

1945 **Sidney Lanier** (1842-81), Poet and musician
Thomas Paine (1737-1809), Political writer and pamphleteer
Walter Reed (1851-1902), Physician
Booker T. Washington (1856-1915), Educator

1950 **Susan B. Anthony** (1820-1906), Social reformer
Alexander Graham Bell (1848-1922), Inventor and scientist
Josiah Gibbs (1839-1903), Physicist
William Crawford Gorgas (1854-1920), Physician and scientist
Theodore Roosevelt (1858-1919), Twenty-sixth President of the U.S.
Woodrow Wilson (1856-1924), Twenty-eighth President of the U.S.

1955 **Thomas J. (Stonewall) Jackson** (1824-63), Confederate general
George Westinghouse (1846-1914), Inventor
Wilbur Wright (1867-1912), Inventor

1960 **Thomas Alva Edison** (1847-1931), Inventor
Edward Alexander McDowell (1861-1908), Composer
Henry David Thoreau (1817-62), Poet and essayist

1965 **Jane Addams** (1860-1935), Social reformer
Oliver Wendell Holmes, Jr. (1841-1935), Associate Justice, U.S. Supreme Court
Sylvanus Thayer (1785-1872), Soldier
Orville Wright (1871-1948), Inventor

1970 **Albert Michelson** (1852-1931), Physicist
Lillian Wald (1867-1940), Social worker

1973 **Louis D. Brandeis** (1856-1941), Jurist
George Washington Carver (1859?-1943), Agricultural chemist

Franklin Delano Roosevelt (1882-1945), Thirty-second President of the U.S.
John Philip Sousa (1854-1932), Composer
1976 **Clara Barton** (1821-1912), Founder of the American Red Cross
Luther Burbank (1849-1926), Horticulturalist
Andrew Carnegie (1835-1919), Steel-maker and philanthropist

Alexander Hamilton Medal

COLUMBIA COLLEGE ALUMNI ASSOCIATION
Hamilton Hall, Columbia University, New York, N.Y. 10027
(212/280-1754)

The Alexander Hamilton Medal, which is of bronze, is awarded annually to a distinguished alumnus or past or present faculty member for service and accomplishment in any field of endeavor. (Class year in parentheses.)

1947 **Nicholas Murray Butler** ('82)
1948 **Frank Diehl Fackenthal** ('06)
1949 **Vi Kyuin Wellington Koo** ('09)
1950 **William Joseph Donovan** ('05)
1951 **Harry James Carman**
1952 **Carlton Joseph Huntley Hayes** ('04)
1953 **Arthur Hays Sulzberger** ('13)
1954 **Frank Smithwick Hogan** ('24)
1955 **Frederick Coykendall** ('95)
Marcellus Hartley Dodge ('03)
1956 **Richard Rodgers** ('23)
Oscar Hammerstein 2nd ('16)
1957 **Grayson Kirk**
1958 **Edmund Astley Prentis** ('06)
1959 **Mark Van Doren**
1960 **Ward Melville** ('09)
1961 Columbia College's Nobel Prize-winning Faculty Members and Alumni:
Edward Charles Kendall ('08)
Polykarp Kush
Willis Eugene Lamb, Jr.
Joshua Lederburg ('44)
Hermann Joseph Muller ('10)
John Howard Northrop ('12)
Isidor Isaac Rabi
Harold Clayton Urey
1962 **John Allen Krout**
1963 **Dwight David Eisenhower**
1964 **William Towson Taylor ('21)**
1965 **Peter Grimm** ('11)
1966 **Alfred A. Knopf** ('12)
1967 **Benjamin J. Buttenwieser** ('19)
1968 **Allan Nevins**
1969 **Arthur F. Burns** ('25)
Joseph Wood Krutch
1970 **Andrew W. Cordier**
1971 **Lionel Trilling** ('25)
1972 **No award**
1973 **Emanuel Celler** ('10)
1974 **Nicholas McD. McKnight** ('21)
1975 **Meyer Schapiro** ('24)
1976 **Arthur B. Krim** ('30)
1977 **George E. Jonas** ('19)
1978 **George T. Delacorte**
1979 **William J. Magill**
1980 **Herman Wouk**

Harvey Prize

TECHNION—ISRAEL INSTITUTE OF TECHNOLOGY
Technion City, Haifa, 32000-Israel (Tel: 227 111)

The $35,000 Harvey Prize is awarded annually for excellence in science, technology or human health, for advancement of peace in the Middle East or for a literary work with profound insight into the life and mores of the Middle Eastern peoples. Two awards are made annually, based on a selection by the Harvey Prize Council, the Technion Senate and the American Society for Technion.

1972 **William J. Kolff,** U.S.A., Invention of artificial kidney
Claude E. Shannon, U.S.A., Mathematical theory of communication known as Information Theory
1973 **No award**
1974 **Alan Howard Cottrell,** Great Britain, Comprehensive theories concerning the medical properties of materials
Gershom Scholem, Israel, Illuminating studies of Jewish mysticism
1975 **George Klein,** Sweden, Discoveries in cancer immunology
Edward Teller, U.S.A., Discoveries in atomic, nuclear and solid state physics and their practical application for the production of energy
1976 **Saul Lieberman,** U.S.A., Investigations into the civilizations of the peoples of the Middle East in the Hellenistic and Roman periods, and commentaries on the sources of Talmudic literature
Herman F. Mark, U.S.A., Research in polymers and plastics
1977 **Seymour Benzer,** U.S.A., Discoveries in molecular genetics and behavior
Freeman John Dyson, U.S.A., Studies in quantum electrodynamics, ferromagnetism, field theory, statistical mechanics and stability of matter
1978 **Bernard Lewis,** U.S.A. (born in Great Britain), Literature and insights into the life and mores of the people of the Middle East
Isaak Wahl, Israel, Research and techniques in the improvement of cereal grains, which have inspired scientists seeking to provide adequate food supplies for an ever-growing world population
1979 **Edwin Herbert Land,** U.S.A. original work in the field of polarized light with applications in many fields of Science and technology; imaginative inventions, which have advanced the science of photography; and pioneering studies in the nature of color vision.
Ephraim Racker, U.S.A., Contributions to the understanding of the complex process by which living beings harness energy, and the application of this knowledge to the correction of metabolic aberrations found in the diseased cell
1980 **Shlomo Dov Goitein,** U.S.A.-Israel, Monumental work on the everyday life, culture, society and economy of Jews and non-Jews in Moslem countries in the Middle Ages, and numerous contributions in the field of Jewish and Arab History
Michael O. Rabin Israel, His ground-breaking work in Computer Theory serves as a source of inspiration to computer scientists

Lessing Prize

CITY OF HAMBURG
Rathaus, D-2000 Hamburg-1, Federal Republic of Germany

The Lessing Prize of the Free Hanseatic City of Hamburg is awarded every two years for meritorious achievement. The amount of the honorarium is not available.

1971 **Werner Haftmann,** Achievements as museum director and art historian
1973 **Hannah Arendt,** Work in political thought and philosophy
1975 **Gustave Heinemann,** Political writings
1977 **Jean Amery,** Author
1979 **No award**

Mademoiselle Awards

MADEMOISELLE MAGAZINE
350 Madison Ave., New York, N.Y. 10017 (212/692-5500)

The editors of *Mademoiselle* magazine annually select up to 14 women to receive Mademoiselle Awards honoring outstanding career achievement. Winners are recognized editorially in the magazine and receive a trophy. The award was discontinued in 1978.

1943 **Agnes de Mille**
Lena Horne
1944 **Lauren Bacall**
1945 **Barbara Bel Geddes**
Blanche Thebom
1946 **Judy Holliday**
Ceil Chapman
1947 **Santha Rama Rau**
Carson McCullers
1948 **No award**
1949 **Margot Fonteyn**
Julie Harris
1950 **Marguerite Higgins**
Florence Chadwick
Anne Fogarty
1951 **Maria Tallchief**
Shelley Winters
Maureen Stapleton
1952 **Geraldine Page**
Melissa Hayden
1953 **Audrey Hepburn**
Maria Callas
1954 **Eva Marie Saint**
Anne Klein
1955 **Kim Stanley**
Leontyne Price
Francoise Sagan
1956 **Julie Andrews**
Doris Day
1957 **Althea Gibson**
Carol Lawrence
1958 **Anne Bancroft**
1959 **Ingrid Thulin**
Gael Greene
1960 **Elaine May**
Wilma Rudolph
1961 **Monica Vitti**
Joan Baez
1962 **Barbara Harris**
Edna O'Brian
Margaret Court Smith
1963 **Deanna Littell**
Susan Sontag
Barbra Streisand
1964 **Shirley Knight**
Renata Adler
Emmanuelle Khanh
Patricia McBride
1965 **Suzanne Farrell**
Lesley Ann Warren
1966 **Betsey Johnson**
Jane Marsh
1967 **Cecelia Holland**
Bobbie Gentry
Faye Dunaway
Frances FitzGerald
1968 **Jacqueline du Pre**
Sondra Locke
Laura Nyro
Joyce Carol Oates
Wyomia Tyus
1969 **Bernadette Devlin**
Ali MacGraw
Kay Mazzo
Stephanie Mills
Blythe Danner
Liza Minelli
Joan Murray
Bernadette Peters
Gloria Rojas
The Urban Corps
1970 **Marion Edey**
Peggy Cooper
Alice Tepper
Bonnie Sherk
Florette Angel
Eva Jefferson
Mary Breasted
1971 **Alicia Bay Laurel**
Nikki Giovanni
Marjorie Crow
Sherri Winter Kaplan
Glenda Copes
Susan Davis
Pamela Gentry
1972 **Cynthia Buchanan**
Suzy Chaffee
Judy Chicago
Micki Grant
Barbara Haskell
Elizabeth Holtzman
Brenda Itta
Bobbie Greene Kilberg
Lesley Oelsner
Amalie R. Rothschild
National Theatre of the Deaf actresses
1973 **Kathryn Burkhart**
Lisa Connolly
Karol Hope
Sharon Curtin
Mary Emmons
Mary Beth Sheak
Anne Grant
Bette Midler
Carol Ruckdeschel
Claudia Weill
Laura X
Boston Women's Health Book Collective
1974 **Rachel Scott**
Leslie Crocker Snyder
Thea Lammers
Francine Prose
Sylvia Law

Karen Petersen
J. J. Wilson
Jill Godmilow
Judy Collins
Donna Karan
Colleen Myers
Carol Vittert
1975 Ruth Welting
Twyla Tharp
Louise McAllister Merritt
Susan Brownmiller
Diana Nyad
Gayl Jones
Pamela Zekman
First Women's Bank founders
1976 Lynn Sherr
Martha Coolidge
Ntozake Shange
Trazana Beverley
Lynn B. Jordan
Kristina Nordstrom
Lea Laiman
Eve Sonneman
Clamma Dale
Barbara Kopple
Meryl Streep
Kristina Mailliard
1977 Maxine Hung Kingston
France Moore Lappe
Karen Sauvigne
Susan Meyer
Anne Sutherland Harris
Linda Nochlin
Carol Bellamy
Elizabeth Swados
Marcia Tucker
Lynn Meadow
Linda Weir-Enegren
Carole Brill
Gilda Radner

Man of the Year

TIME MAGAZINE
Time-Life Bldg., 1271 Ave. of the Americas, New York, N.Y. 10019 (212/586-1212)

The editors of *Time* annually select the individual who has had the greatest influence on the course of the previous year as its Man of the Year. A portrait of this person appears on the magazine's year-end cover. The concept of great influence does not always imply praise. Occasionally, groups have also been selected for year-end review.

1927 Charles A. Lindbergh
1928 Walter P. Chrysler
1929 Owen D. Young
1930 Mohandas K. Gandhi
1931 Pierre Laval
1932 Franklin D. Roosevelt
1933 Hugh S. Johnson
1934 Franklin D. Roosevelt
1935 Haile Selassie
1936 Wallis Warfield Simpson
1937 General and Mme. Chiang Kai-Shek
1938 Adolf Hitler
1939 Joseph Stalin
1940 Winston Churchill
1941 Franklin D. Roosevelt
1942 Joseph Stalin
1943 George C. Marshall
1944 Dwight D. Eisenhower
1945 Harry S. Truman
1946 James F. Byrnes
1947 George C. Marshall
1948 Harry S. Truman
1949 Winston Churchill
1950 G.I. Joe
1951 Mohammed Mossadegh
1952 Queen Elizabeth II
1953 Konrad Adenauer
1954 John Foster Dulles
1955 Harlow Curtice
1956 Hungarian Freedom Fighter
1957 Nikita Khrushchev
1958 Charles de Gaulle
1959 Dwight D. Eisenhower
1960 Top U.S. Scientists (15)
1961 John F. Kennedy
1962 Pope John XXIII
1963 Martin Luther King
1964 Lyndon B. Johnson
1965 Gen. William Westmoreland
1966 Youth, 25 years and under
1967 Lyndon B. Johnson
1968 Astronauts Anders, Borman and Lovell
1969 Middle Americans
1970 Willy Brandt
1971 Richard Nixon
1972 Richard Nixon and Henry Kissinger
1973 Judge John Sirica
1974 King Faisal
1975 Women of the Year (12)
1976 Jimmy Carter
1977 Anwar Sadat
1978 Teng Hsiao-Ping
1979 Ayatollah Ruhallah Khomeini
1980 Ronald Wilson Reagan

Molson Prizes

CANADA COUNCIL
151 Sparks St., Box 1047, Ottawa, Ont. K1P 5V8, Canada (613/237-3400)

The Molson Prizes now each carry a $20,000 honorarium from the Molson Foundation and annually recognize cultural achievement and contributions to the arts, social sciences, the humanities and national unity in Canada.

1963 Donald Creighton
Alain Grandbois
1964 No award
1965 Jean Gascon
Frank Scott
1966 Rev. Georges-Henri Levesque
Hugh McLennan
1967 Arthur Erickson
Anne Hebert
Marshall McLuhan
1968 Glenn Gould
Jean Le Moyne
1970 Jean-Paul Audet
Morley Callaghan
Arnold Spohr
1971 Maureen Forrester
Rina Lasnier
Norman McLaren

1972 **John James Deutsch**
Alfred Pellan
George Woodcock
1973 **Celia Franca**
W. A. C. H. Dobson
Jean-Paul Lemieux
1974 **Alex Colville**
Pierre Dansereau
Margaret Laurence
1975 **Denise Pelletier**
Oxford String Quartet (Andrew Dawes, Terrence Helmer, Kenneth Perkins and Marcel St.-Cyr)
Jon Vickers
1976 **John Hirsch**
Bill Reid
Jean-Louis Roux
1977 **Jack Shadboldt**
George Story
Gabrielle Roy
1978 **Betty Oliphant**
Michael Snow
Jean Duceppe
1979 **Lois Marshall**
Robert Weaver
Michael Brault
1980 **Not available at press time**

Omega Achievers Award

SAMSONITE CORPORATION
1120 E. 45th Ave., Denver, Colo. 80239 (303/344-6262)

As a Bicentennial gesture, 10,000 editors, Congressmen and educators were polled to choose American nominees in 16 categories for the Omega Achievers Award. The award consisted of a sculpture and a commemorative attache case. The awards were made in 1977 "as America enters its third century."

Frank Borman, Aerospace
Norman Borlaug, Agriculture
R. Buckminster Fuller, Architecture
Henry Ford, Sr., Business and Industry
Margaret Mead, Education
Levi Strauss, Fashion
Earl Warren, Law
Alex Haley, Literature
Beverly Sills, Performing Arts
Robert Woodward and Carl Bernstein, The Press
Harry Truman, Public Service
Martin Luther King, Religion
James Cash Penney, Retailing
Jonas Salk, Science and Medicine
General David Sarnoff, Television/Radio
Lowell Thomas, Travel

Orden pour le Merite

MINISTRY OF THE INTERIOR
Graurheindorferstrasse 198, D-5300 Bonn, Federal Republic of Germany

The insignia of the Orden pour le Merite fuer Wissenschaften und Kuenste is given each year to several individuals for outstanding achievement in art or science. They may be Germans or foreigners.

1974 **W. Gentner,** Physics
T.G. Georgiades, Music history
Fritz Lippmann, Biochemistry
Sir Ronald Syme, History
1975 **Pierre Boulez,** Composition and conducting
Richard Ettinghausen, Art history
Gyoorg Ligeti, Composition
Kenzo Tange, Architecture
1976 **Peter Huchel,** Writing
George F. Kennan, History and diplomacy
Heinz Maier-Leibnitz, Physics
1977 **Hansjochem Autrum,** Zoology
Sir Ernst Gombrich, Art History
Hans Hartung, Painting
Friedrich August von Havek, National Economics
Bruno Snell, Classical philology
1978 **Gerd Meyer-Schwiockerath,** Opthamology
Victor Friedrich Weisskopf, Physics
1979 **Fritz Schalk,** Novels
Felix Bloch, Physics
Elias Cannetti, Writing
1980 **Wolfgang Paul,** Physics
Werner Reichardt, Biology
Leopold Reidemeister, Art history
Sir Karl Popper, Scientific theory

Presidential Medal of Freedom

UNITED STATES EXECUTIVE OFFICE OF THE PRESIDENT
The White House, Washington, D.C. 20015 (202/456-1414)

The Presidential Medal of Freedom, which is of gold, is the highest civilian honor given in the United States and recognizes contributions to the national interest or security of the United States, the advancement of world peace or endeavors in the field of culture or other public or private endeavors beneficial to the nation. The Medal is presented in White House ceremonies. The award was established in 1963, replacing the Medal of Freedom. The first group of candidates was selected by the administration of John F. Kennedy but received their awards after his death from President Lyndon B. Johnson, who added posthumous honors both for his predecessor and for Pope John XXIII. Other posthumous honors have subsequently been made.

AWARDS BY PRESIDENT KENNEDY

1963 **Marian Anderson,** singer
Ralph J. Bunche, United Nations undersecretary
Ellsworth Bunker, diplomat
Pablo Casals, cellist
Genevieve Caulfield, educator
James B. Conant, educator
John F. Enders, bacteriologist
Felix Frankfurter, jurist
Karl Holton, youth authority
Pope John XXIII
John F. Kennedy, President of U.S.
Robert J. Kiphuth, athletic director
Edwin H. Land, inventor
Herbert H. Lehman, statesman
Robert A. Lovett, statesman
J. Clifford MacDonald, educator
John J. McCloy, banker and statesman
George Meany, labor leader
Alexander Meiklejohn, philosopher
Ludwig Mies van der Rohe, architect
Jean Monnet, European statesman

Luis Munoz-Marin, Governor, Puerto Rico
Clarence B. Randall, industrialist
Rudolf Serkin, pianist
Edward Steichen, photographer
George W. Taylor, educator
Alan T. Waterman, scientist
Mark S. Watson, journalist
Annie D. Wauneka, public health worker
E. B. White, author
Thornton Wilder, author
Edmund Wilson, author and critic
Andrew N. Wyeth, artist

AWARDS BY PRESIDENT JOHNSON

1964 **Dean Acheson,** statesman
Detlev W. Bronk, neurophysiologist
Aaron Copland, composer
Willem de Kooning, painter
Walt Disney, animated cartoonist and film producer
J. Frank Dobie, author
Lena F. Edwards, physician and humanitarian
Thomas Stearns Eliot, poet
Lynn Fontanne, actress
John W. Gardner, educator
Rev. Theodore M. Hesburgh, educator
Clarence L. Johnson, aircraft engineer
Frederick R. Kappel, telephone executive
Helen A. Keller, educator and author
John L. Lewis, labor leader
Walter Lippmann, journalist
Alfred Lunt, actor
Ralph Emerson McGill, journalist
Samuel Eliot Morison, historian
Lewis Mumford, urban planner and critic
Edward R. Murrow, radio-TV commentator
Reinhold Niebuhr, theologian
Leontyne Price, soprano
A. Philip Randolph, labor leader
Carl Sandburg, poet and biographer
John Steinbeck, author
Helen B. Taussig, pediatrician
Carl Vinson, legislator
Thomas J. Watson, Jr., industrialist
Paul Dudley White, physician
1967 **Ellsworth Bunker,** diplomat
Eugene M. Locke, diplomat
Robert W. Komer, government official
1968 **Robert S. McNamara,** government official
James Webb, NASA administrator
1969 **Eugene R. Black,** banker
McGeorge Bundy, government official
Clark M. Clifford, statesman
Michael E. DeBakey, surgeon
David Dubinsky, labor leader
Henry Ford II, industrialist
Ralph Ellison, author
W. Averell Harriman, statesman
Bob Hope, comedian
Edgar Kaiser, industrialist
Mary Lasker, philanthropist
John W. Macy, Jr., government official
Gregory Peck, actor
Laurance S. Rockefeller, conservationist
Walt W. Rostow, government official
Dean Rusk, statesman
Merriman Smith, journalist
Cyrus R. Vance, government official
William S. White, journalist
Roy Wilkins, social welfare executive
Whitney M. Young, social welfare executive

AWARDS BY PRESIDENT NIXON

1969 **Col. Edwin E. Aldrin, Jr.,** astronaut
Neil A. Armstrong, astronaut
Lt. Col. Michael Collins, astronaut
Duke Ellington, musician
1970 **Apollo 13 Mission Operations Team**
Earl Charles Behrens, journalist
Edward T. Folliard, journalist
Fred Wallace Haise, Jr., astronaut
William M. Henry, journalist
Arthur Krock, journalist
David Lawrence, journalist
George Gould Lincoln, journalist
James A. Lovell, Jr., astronaut
Raymond Moley, journalist
Eugene Ormandy, conductor
Adela Rogers St. Johns, journalist
John Leonard Swigert, Jr., astronaut
1971 **Samuel Goldwyn,** film producer
Manlio Brosio, NATO Secretary General
William J. Hopkins, White House executive clerk
1972 **Lila and DeWitt Wallace,** founders of *Reader's Digest*
John Paul Vann, adviser in Vietnam war
1973 **John Ford,** film director
William P. Rogers, diplomat
1974 **Melvin R. Laird,** government official
Charles L. Lowman, orthopedist
Paul G. Hoffman, statesman
1975 **No award**

AWARDS BY PRESIDENT FORD

1976 **David K.E. Bruce,** diplomat
Martha Graham, dancer and choreographer
Jesse Owens, track and field champion
Arthur Rubinstein, pianist
1977 **I. W. Abel,** labor leader
John Bardeen, physicist
Irving Berlin, composer
Norman Borlaug, agricultural scientist
Omar N. Bradley, national security
Arleigh Burke, national security
Alexander Calder, sculptor
Bruce Catton, historian
Joseph P. DiMaggio, baseball star
Ariel Durant, author
Will Durant, author
Arthur Fiedler, conductor
Henry J. Friendly, jurist
Claudia "Lady Bird" Johnson, service to U.S. scenic beauty
Henry A. Kissinger, statesman
Archibald MacLeish, poet
James A. Michener, author
Georgia O'Keeffe, artist
Nelson A. Rockefeller, for government service
Norman Rockwell, illustrator
Donald H. Rumsfeld, for government service
Katherine Filene Shouse, for service to the performing arts
Lowell Thomas, radio-TV commentator and author
James D. Watson, biochemist

AWARDS BY PRESIDENT CARTER

1977 **Rev. Martin Luther King, Jr.,** civil rights leader
Jonas Salk, medical researcher
1978 **No Award**
1979 **Margaret Mead,** anthropologist
1980 **Ansel Adams,** photographer

Rachel Carson, naturalist and conservationist
Lucia Chase, performing arts and dance
Hubert H. Humphrey, statesman and Vice President
Arthur J. Goldberg, statesman and diplomat
Archbishop Iakovas, religious leader
Lyndon B. Johnson, statesman and President
Clarence Mitchell, civil rights leader
Roger Tory Peterson, ornithologist and author
Adm. Hyman Rickover, military leader and scientist
Beverly Sills, performing arts and opera
Robert Penn Warren, novelist and poet
John Wayne, actor
Eudora Welty, novelist
Tennessee Williams, playwright

Smithson Medal

SMITHSONIAN INSTITUTION
1000 Jefferson Dr. SW, Washington, D.C. 20560
(202/357-1300)

The Smithson Medal is the Smithsonian's highest honor and recognizes outstanding contributions to art, science, history, education or technology. The golden medal, which is awarded as merited, carries an honorarium "when appropriate."

1965 **Royal Society of London,** For outstanding contributions "to the increase and diffusion of knowledge among men"
1968 **Edgar P. Richardson,** Former director of the Detroit Institute of Arts and Henry Francis duPont Winterthur Museum and chairman of the Smithsonian Art Commission, "for helping to shape the course of art scholarship in this country, interweaving the two streams of history and men into effective unity"
1975 **Nancy Hanks,** Chairman of the National Endowment for the Arts and the National Council on the Arts, "for her effective leadership . . . in increasing the interest and support of both the Congress and the public in cultural programs for all Americans"
1976 **Ralph E. Becker,** Washington attorney, in recognition of his donation to the Smithsonian of his valuable collection of political campaign materials, as well as other services to the Institution
1979 **Pope John-Paul II**

Spingarn Medal
Walter White Award

NATIONAL ASSOCIATION FOR THE ADVANCEMENT OF COLORED PEOPLE
1790 Broadway, New York, N.Y. 10019 (212/245-2100)

The Spingarn Medal is awarded annually for the "highest or noblest achievement by an American Negro" for the preceeding year or years. A Committee of Award selects the winner in a scientific, spiritual, commercial, educational, artistic or other field of endeavor. The medal is presented at the NAACP annual convention by a distiguished citizen.

1915 **Ernest D. Just,** Head of Department of Physiology, Howard University, for research in biology
1916 **Maj. Charles Young,** U.S. Army, for services organizing the Liberian constabulary and developing roads in the Republic of Liberia
1917 **Harry T. Burleigh,** Composer, pianist and singer, for excellence in creative music
1918 **William Stanley Braithwaite,** Poet, literary critic and editor, for distinguished achievement in literature
1919 **Archibald H. Grimke,** Former U.S. Consul to Santo Domingo, for distinguished service to his race and country
1920 **W. E. B. DuBois,** Author, editor, for the founding and calling of the Pan-African Congress
1921 **Charles S. Gilpin,** Actor, for his performance in the title role of *The Emperor Jones* by Eugene O'Neill
1922 **Mary B. Talbert,** Former president of the National Assn. of Colored Women, for service to the women of her race and for restoration of the Frederick Douglass Home
1923 **George Washington Carver,** Head, Department of Research, Tuskegee Institute, for distinguished research in agricultural chemistry
1924 **Roland Hayes,** Singer, for his interpretations of Negro folk music and work as a soloist with the Boston Symphony Orchestra
1925 **James Weldon Johnson,** Former U.S. Consul in Venezuela and Nicaragua, former editor and secretary of the NAACP, for distinguished achievements
1926 **Carter G. Woodson,** Historian, founder of the Assn. for the Study of Negro Life and editor, for 10 years' service in collecting and publishing records of the Negro in America
1927 **Anthony Overton,** Businessman, president of Victory Life Insurance Co., for his successful business career
1928 **Charles W. Chesnutt,** Author, for his pioneer work depicting the life and struggle of the American Negro
1929 **Mordecai Wyatt Johnson,** President, Howard University, for his successful administration as the first Negro president of the University and for his success in securing federal appropriations for the University
1930 **Henry A. Hunt,** Principal, Fort Valley High School, for devotion in the education of Negroes in rural Georgia
1931 **Richard Berry Harrison,** Actor, for his "fine and reverent characterization of the Lord" in *The Green Pastures* and for his long achievement interpreting English drama "for the mass of colored people"
1932 **Robert Russa Moton,** Principal, Tuskegee Institute, for his leadership at home, his stand on education in Haiti, his support of equal opportunity for the Negro in the American public school system and his expression of the best ideals of the Negro in his book, *What the Negro Thinks*
1933 **Max Yergan,** Missionary, for his 10 years as American YMCA secretary among the native students of South Africa and his efforts toward interracial understanding
1934 **William Taylor Burwell Williams,** Dean, Tuskegee Institute, for his long service in Negro education
1935 **Mary McLeod Bethune,** Founder and president of Bethune-Cookman College, for surmounting difficulties in creating an educational institution in Daytona Beach, Fla.
1936 **Howard Hope,** President, Atlanta University, for his leadership and distinguished role in education
1937 **Walter White,** Executive secretary of the NAACP, for his personal investigation of 41 lynchings and eight race riots and for lobbying for a federal anti-lynching bill
1938 **No award**
1939 **Marian Anderson,** Singer, for her special achievement in music and for "her magnificent dignity as a human being"
1940 **Louis T. Wright,** Surgeon, for his contributions and high standards as a medical man

1941 **Richard Wright,** Author, for his depiction of the effects of proscription, segregation and denial of opportunities of the American Negro in his books, *Uncle Tom's Children* and *Native Son*
1942 **A. Philip Randolph,** Labor leader and international president of the Brotherhood of Sleeping Car Porters
1943 **Wiliam H. Hastie,** Jurist and educator, for being an uncompromising champion of equal justice
1944 **Charles R. Drew,** Scientist, for his outstanding work with blood plasma
1945 **Paul Robeson,** Singer and actor, for his achievement in theater and on the concert stage
1946 **Thurgood Marshall,** Special counsel of the NAACP, for his service as a lawyer before many courts, especially in the Texas Primary Case, which influenced the end of disenfranchisement because of race
1947 **Percy L. Julian,** Research chemist, for his technical skill and for his discoveries to benefit mankind
1948 **Channing H. Tobias,** "For his consistent role as a defender of fundamental civil liberties" and his contributions to the President's Council on Civil Liberties
1949 **Ralph J. Bunche,** International civil servant, for his service as U.N. mediator in Palestine, his distinguished scholarship, his contributions in fashioning sections of the U.N. Charter and his efforts as director of the Trusteeship Council
1950 **Charles Hamilton Houston,** Chairman, NAACP Legal Committee, for his championship of equal rights
1951 **Mabel Keaton Staupers,** Leader National Assn. of Colored Graduate Nurses, for spearheading the integration of Negro nurses into American life
1952 **Henry T. Moore,** NAACP leader in Florida; "a martyr in the crusade for freedom"; assassinated by a bomb in his home, Christmas Eve 1951
1953 **Paul R. Williams,** Architect
1954 **Theodore K. Lawless,** Physician, educator and philanthropist
1955 **Carl Murphy,** Editor, publisher and civic leader
1956 **Jackie Robinson,** Athlete
1957 **Martin Luther King, Jr.,** "Dedicated and selfless clergyman," for creative contributions and outstanding leadership in the Montgomery bus boycott
1958 **Daisy Bates and the Little Rock Nine,** For "their pioneer role in upholding the basic ideals of American democracy in the face of continuing harassment"
1959 **Edward Kennedy (Duke) Ellington,** Composer and orchestra leader
1960 **Langston Hughes,** Poet, author and playwright
1961 **Kenneth B. Clark,** Professor of Psychology at the College of the City of New York; founder and director of the Northside Center for Child Development
1962 **Robert C. Weaver,** Administrator, Housing and Home Finance Agency
1963 **Medgar Wiley Evers,** NAACP Field Secretary for Mississippi; World War II veteran; "hero and martyr felled by an assassin's bullet" on June 12, 1963
1964 **Roy Wilkins,** Executive Director of the NAACP, "for the militancy of his leadership, the integrity of his performance, his determined and persistent pursuit of clearly perceived goals, his dedication and intelligence"
1965 **Leontyne Price,** Metropolitan Opera star
1966 **John H. Johnson,** Founder and president of the Johnson Publishing Co.
1967 **Edward W. Brooke III,** "First Negro to win popular election to the United States Senate"
1968 **Sammy Davis, Jr.,** Broadway and Hollywood star, civil rights activist
1969 **Clarence M. Mitchell, Jr.,** Director, NAACP Washington Bureau; lobbyist; specifically for role in passage of the Civil Rights Act of 1968 with its fair housing provisions
1970 **Jacob Lawrence,** Artist, teacher and humanitarian
1971 **Leon Howard Sullivan,** Clergyman, activist and prophet
1972 **Gordon Alexander Buchanan Parks,** "Twentieth Century Renaissance Man"
1973 **Wilson C. Riles,** Educator who achieved national stature in the field and has remained devoted "to the best principles of education for integrated living in a multiracial society"
1974 **Damon J. Keith,** Jurist, "in tribute to his steadfast defense of constitutional principles as revealed in a series of memorable decisions handed down as a U.S. District Court judge"
1975 **No Award**
1975 **Hank Aaron**, Athlete "in recognition of his singular achievement in the sport which symbolizes America - baseball," especially for his home-run record
1977 **Alvin Ailey**, Dancer, choreographer and artistic director "in recognition of his international pre-eminence in the field of dance"
Alexander Palmer Haley, author, biographer and lecturer "in recognition of the incomparable, exhaustive research and literary skill which was combined in *Roots*"
1978 **Andrew Jackson Young**, Minister Plenipotentiary and Extraordinary United States Ambassador to the United Nations, diplomat and Cabinet member, civil rights activist and minister
1979 **Rosa L. Parks**, community activist "in tribute to her quiet courage and determination" in 1955 "when she refused to surrender her seat on a Montgomery, Ala., bus to a white male passenger, ultimately bringing about desegregation of the buses in that city
1980 **Rayford W. Logan**, "educator and historian "for his prodigious efforts to set before the world black American's continuing struggle against the forces of oppression and inhumanity and for his equally penetrating monographs on conditions which adversely affect the people of Africa and Haiti"

The Walter White Award named for the NAACP's former executive director, is anb equivalent to the Spingarn but open to individuals of all ethnic backgrounds. it is given for outstanding contributions to the NAACP. The award is an original sculpture designed by Judith Brown.

1978 **Hubert Horatio Humphrey**, for more than three decades a force in shaping and enactment of civil-rights legislation
1979 **Buell Gordon Gallagher**, theologian, educator, author and civil libertarian
Julius Waites Waring, attorney, politcal activist, federal judge and guardian of civil rights
1980 **Lyndon Baines Johnson**, for the late President's role as the prime force behind the Civil Richts Act of 1964 and for appointing Turgood Marshall as the first black Supreme Court Justice

UCLA Alumnus of the Year Award
Professional Achievement Award

UCLA ALUMNI ASSOCIATION
405 Hilgard Dr., Los Angeles, Calif. 90024 (213/825-3901)

The Alumnus of the Year Award, honors a graduate who has "rendered a special and outstanding service to

UCLA, or who, by personal achievement, has brought honor and distinction to the University." The Alumni Awards Selection Committee picks the winner from nominations of alumni and friends. (Class year in parentheses.)

1946 **M. Philip Davis** ('28)
1947 **William C. Ackerman** ('24)
1948 **Frederick F. Houser** ('26)
1949 **Ralph Bunche** ('27)
1950 **Victor Hansen** ('26)
1951 **Bruce Russell** ('26)
1952 **Glenn T. Seaborg** ('34)
1953 **Agnes DeMille** ('26)
1954 **Edward W. Carter** ('32)
1955 **Wilbur C. Johns** ('25)
1956 **John E. Canaday** ('27)
1957 **Cyril C. Nigg** ('27)
1958 **Saul Winstein** ('34)
1959 **Warren H. Crowell** ('27)
1960 **Charles I. Schottland** ('27)
1961 **Thomas J. Cunningham** ('28)
1962 **Jack R. Robinson** ('42)
1963 **Waldo E. Lyon** ('36)
1964 **Arjay R. Miller** ('37)
1965 **Jerome Hines** ('43)
1966 **Louis Banks** ('37)
1967 **William E. Forbes** ('28)
1968 **Carol Burnett** ('54)
1969 **W. Thomas Davis** ('31)
1970 **H.R. Haldeman** ('48)
1971 **John V. Vaughn** ('32)
1972 **M.J. Frankovich** ('34)
1973 **John R. Wooden** (Honorary Alumnus)
1974 **Thomas Bradley** ('41)
1975 **Francis Ford Coppola MFA** ('67)
1976 **Fred L. Whipple** ('27)
1977 **E. Cardon Walker** ('38)
1978 **Frank T. Cary** ('43)
1979 **Lawrence E. Irell** ('32)
1980 **J.D. Morgan** ('41)

Professional Achievement Awards honor the distinguished career achievement of UCLA alumni. Selection is made by a subcommittee of the Alumni Awards Selection Committee from nominations, and awards are given in more than a dozen fields, although not all fields are represented in any given year. (Class year in parentheses.)

1962 **Dudley E. Browne** ('34) Business
Dean E. McHenry ('32) Education
Ernest H. Martin ('42) Entertainment
Frank S. Balthis ('26) Judiciary
1963 **William P. Gray** ('34) Law
Louise Seyler Geyer ('27), MA ('38), Ph.D. ('45) Education
1964 **Glenn M. Anderson** ('36) Government
Thomas P. Phelan ('29) Business
Hale Sparks ('30) Education
1965 **Scribner Birlenbach** ('28) Business
Jules Gregory Charney ('38), MS ('40), Ph. D. ('46) Science
John D. French, MD ('33) Medicine
Augustus F. Hawkins ('31) Government
Lt. Gen. William R. Peers ('37) Military
Charles E. Rickershauser, Jr. ('49), LLB ('57) Public Service
Robert Waterfield ('45) Athletics
Charles Wellman ('37) Finance
1966 **Walter Dunbar** ('38) Public Service
Kenneth Kroehler ('39) Business
Maj. Gen. Edward G. Lansdale ('30) Military
J.D. Morgan ('41) Athletics
Bertram L. Perkins ('47) Business
Maxwell L. Rafferty ('38) Education
Judge David W. Williams ('34) Jurisprudence
Elliot McKay See, Jr. ('62) Special Professional Achievement Award, Astronaut
1967 **Maj. Gen. Norman J. Anderson** ('34) Military
M.J. Frankovich ('34) Business and Entertainment
Chancellor Glenn S. Dumke ('42) Education
John D. Roberts ('41), MD ('44) Science
1968 **Vincent M. Barnett, Jr.** ('35) Education
Congressman James S. Corman ('42) Government
Maurice J. Dahlem ('34) Business
1969 **Walter Cunningham** MA ('61) Astronaut
Maj. Gen. Salve H. Matheson ('42) Military
Dorothy Wright Nelson ('50), LLB ('53) Law and Education
1970 **Joseph Blatchford** ('56) Government
Madeline C. Hunter ('36), M.Ed. ('51), Ed.D. ('66) Education
Donn D. Moomaw (N.A.), Ministry
1971 **Frank T. Cary** ('43) Business
Lawrence E. Irell ('32) Law
Joseph Jerome Kaufman ('42) Medicine
Chauncey J. Medberry III ('38) Finance
Maj. Gen. John Kirk Singlaub ('58) Military
Sen. Ted Stevens ('47) Government
1972 **Jeanne Quint Benoliel,** D.N.S., M.S. ('55) Nursing
Thomas Bradley ('41) Government
Rita Milaw Lawrence ('40) Business
E. Cardon Walker ('38) Entertainment
Harold M. Williams ('46) Business and Education
1973 **Gladys Ancrum,** M.P.H. ('65), Dr. P.H. ('68) Nursing
Josephine Miles ('32) Education
Paul Ichira Terasaki ('50), MA ('52), Ph. D. ('56) Medicine
1974 **Arthur Ashe, Jr.** ('66) Athletics
Yvonne Braithwaite Burke ('53) Government
R. Bruce Merrifield ('43), Ph.D. ('49) Science
Robert W. Rand ('45), Ph.D., M.D. Medicine
Donald M. Small M.D. ('60) Medicine
1975 **Ralph E. Crump** ('50) Science
Lamont Johnson (1942-43) Entertainment
Judge Joan Dempsey Klein, LL.B ('55) Law
1976 **Ross M. Blakely** ('40) Finance
William Frederickson, Jr. ('31) Recreation
Bernard S. Jefferson ('31) Judiciary
Elias George Theros ('47), MD ('57) Medicine
1977 **Howard L. Berman** ('62), LLB ('65) Government
Roy Huggins ('39) Entertainment
William B. Keene ('49), LLB ('52) Judiciary
Walter H. Munk Ph. D. ('47) Science
1978 **Kareem Abdul Jabbar** ('69), Athletics
d'Arcy Hayman ('49), M.A. ('52), Arts
William Coweoin Jones ('49), Government
Abraham Kaplan Ph.D. ('42), Philosophy and education
Hoyt S. Pardee ('41), Business
Edward Rubin ('33), Law
1979 **Michele C. Bergerac** M.B.A. ('55), Business
Adrienne Hall (N.A.), Advertising

Jack Morrison ('34), M.A. ('51), Arts and education
Louis B. Perry ('38), M.A. ('40) Ph.D. ('50), Business and education
Marianna Pfaelzer J.D. ('57), Judiciary
George C. Pimentel ('43), Science
1980 **Harlan Amstutz** ('53), M.D. ('56), Medicine
Edmund D. Edelman ('54), L.L.B. ('58), Government
Melville B. Nimmer ('41-42, '46), Law

International Prize

JENNY AND ANTTI WIHURI FOUNDATION
Arkadiankatu 21 B 25, 00100-Helsinki 10, Finland (Tel: 444 145)

The Foundation awards prizes as merited for contributions to art, culture, science and economics, as determined by the organization and its Research Institute in consultation with experts from the field where appropriate.

1958 **Rolf Nevanlinna**
1961 **Pentti Halonen**
Vaino Hovi
Joonas Kokkonen
1968 **John McMichael**
Lars Ahlfors
1971 **P. B. Hirsh**
1976 **Georg Henrik von Wright**
Jaakko Hintikka
1979 **Derrick B. Jelliffe**

Woman of Conscience Award

NATIONAL COUNCIL OF WOMEN OF THE U.S.
777 United Nations Plaza, 12th Floor, New York, N.Y. 10017 (212/697-1278)

The $1,500 Woman of Conscience Award, which is funded by Clairol and administered by the National Council of Women, honors achievements in which women responded to a compelling community problem, demonstrated courage or made an unusual contribution. The winner is selected by a committee consisting of some members of the Council's Executive Committee and additional judges.

1963 **Rachel Carson,** Author
1964 **Hazel Brannon Smith,** Mississippi newspaper editor
1965 **Virginia Sanders,** Minnesota Plan author and advocate of education for women
1966 **Judge Florence M. Kelley,** New York City Family Court
1967 **Ellen Jackson,** Creative community program leadership
1968 **Dorothy Ainsworth**
Mrs. Andrew Brown
Mary S. Calderone
Mrs. Edward Carter
Mme. Marcel De Gallaix
Mrs. D. Joe Hendrickson
Florence Smith Jacobsen
May Hall James
Mrs. Martin Luther King, Jr.
Dorothy M. Lewis
Margaret Moore
Jan Papenek
Mamie B. Reese
Mrs. Harold E. Rodden
Mrs. Dean Rusk
Dorothea W. Sitley
Hilda Torrop
Mrs. Raphael Tuorover
Helen F. Winfield
Mrs. William Volker
Lt. Violet Hill Whyte
1969 **Annie May Bankhead,** Black leader
1970 **Ellen Sulzberger Straus,** Creator of *Call for Action,* New York radio program
1971 **No award**
1972 **Sister Ruth Dowd,** Educator of teenagers in Harlem
1973 **Patricia Smith,** Hospital and medical work in Vietnam
1974 **Frances F. Pauley,** Civil Rights worker
1975 **Margaret Mead,** Anthropologist
1976 **Barbara Jordan,** Congresswoman
1977 **Nancy Hanks,** Chairman, National Endowment for the Arts
1978 **Frances Lehman Loeb,** Outstanding achievements in volunteerism
1979 **Mary Allen Engle,** Pioneering research on and treatment of cardiovascular disease in children
1980 **Elise Boulding,** Chairman, Sociology Dept., Dartmouth College; author and lecturer on the peaceful solution of conflict

Woman of the Year
Woman of the Decade

LADIES' HOME JOURNAL
641 Lexington Ave., New York, N.Y. 10022 (212/935-6160)

Selection as a Ladies' Home Journal Woman of the Year gives recognition to women in various fields who are United States citizens for involved and accomplished leadership that provides an inspiring example to other women. The readers of *Ladies' Home Journal* return a ballot to the magazine for selections reviewed by a jury panel. Women selected receive a gold pin studded with a diamond "W."

1973 **Helen Hayes,** Arts and Humanities
Shirley Chisholm, Public Affairs
Katharine Graham, Economy and Business
Nikki Giovanni, Youth Leadership
Ellen Sulzberger Straus, Voluntary Action
LaDonna Harris, Human Rights
Mary Lasker, Quality of Life
Virginia Apgar, Science and Research
1974 **Martha W. Griffiths,** Public Affairs
Patricia Roberts Harris, Business and Professions
Dorothy Height, Human Rights
Katharine Hepburn, Creative Arts
Billie Jean King, Sports
Barbara McDonald, Community Service
Dixy Lee Ray, Science and Research
Barbara Walters, Communications
1975 **Maj. Gen. Jeanne M. Holm,** Government and Diplomacy
Barbara Jordan, Political Life
Sylvia Porter, Business and Economics
Joan Ganz Cooney, Education
Helen Thomas, Communications

Lillian Hellman, Creative Arts
Lady Bird Johnson, Quality of Life
LaRue Diaforli, Humanitarian and Community Service

1976 **Betty Furness,** Business and Economics
Margaret Mead, Science and Research
Beverly Sills, Performing Arts
Capt. Micki King, Sports
Shirley Hufstedler, Government and Diplomacy
Gov. Ella Grasso, Political Life
Maya Angelou, Communications
Annie Dodge Wauneka, Educational Leadership
Betty Ford, Humanitarian and Community Service

1977 **Ruth C. Clusen,** Political Life
Elisabeth Kubler-Ross, Science and Research
Gloria Scott, Humanitarian and Community Service
Liz Carpenter, Government and Public Affairs
Elizabeth Drew, Communications
Margaret McNamara, Education
Addie Wyatt, Business and Economy
Marian Anderson, Creative Arts
Sheila Young Ochowicz, Sports

1978 **Anne Bancroft**, New Performing Arts
Carol Bellamy, New Politics and government
Rosalynn Carter, New Social Responsibility
Natalie Cole, New Music—Popular Artists
Chris Evert, New Sports Equality
Margaret Hillis, New Music—Classical Artists
Roberta S. Karmel, New Business Leadership
Juanita Kreps, New Politics and Government—National
Cicely Tyson, New Performing Arts—Acting

Late in 1979 *Ladies' Home Journal* announced its Women of the Decade list, compiled from the Woman of the Year honors since their inception. The magazine intends to resume Woman of the Year honors in 1981.

1979-80 **Margaret Meade**, Science and Research
Katharine Hepburn, Creative Arts
Barbara Walters, Communications
Helen Hayes, Arts and Humanities
Marian Anderson, Creative Arts
Betty Ford, Inspirational Leadership
Elizabeth Kubler-Ross, Science and Research
Barbara Jordan, Political Life
Sylvian Porter, Business and Economics
Joan Ganz Cooney, Education
Beverly Sills, Performing Arts

Contents

GENERAL

Books & Literature

Related Awards

Grand Prix du Roman

ACADEMIE FRANCAISE INSTITUT DE FRANCE
23 Quai de Conti, 75006-Paris, France (Tel: 326-02-92)

Of the dozens of literary prizes awarded by the Academy, the 30,000-franc Grand Prix du Roman is one of the most important. In annually honors an author or poet of a body of work displaying notable style and significant thought. A committee chooses the winner.

1915 **Paul Acker,** Collected works
1916 **Avesnes,** *L'ile hereuse*
1917 **Charles Geniaux,** Collected works
1918 **Camille Mayran,** *Gotton*
1919 **Pierre Benoit,** *L'Atlantide*
1920 **Andre Corthis,** *Pour moi seul*
1921 **Pierre Villetard,** *Monsieur Bille dans la tourmente*
1922 **Francis Carco,** *L'homme traque*
1923 **Alphonse de Chateaubriant,** *La Briere*
1924 **Emile Henriot,** *Aricie Brun ou les Vertus*
1925 **Francois Dourourcau,** *L'Enfant de la Victoire*
1926 **Francois Mauriac,** *Le Desert de l'amour*
1927 **Joseph Kessel,** *Les Captifs*
1928 **Jean Balde,** *Reine d'Arbieu*
1929 **Andre Demaison,** *Le Livre des betes qu'on appelle sauvages*
1930 **Jacques de Lacretelle,** *Amour nuptial*
1931 **Henri Pourrat,** *Gaspard des montagnes*
1932 **Jacques Chardonne,** *Claire*
1933 **Roger Chacvire,** *Mademoiselle de Bois-Dauphin*
1934 **Paul Regnier,** *L'Abbaye d'Evolayne*
1935 **Albert Touchard,** *La Guepe*
1936 **Georges Bernanos,** *Journal d'un cure de campagne*
1937 **Guy de Poutales,** *La Peche miraculeuse*
1938 **Jean de la Varende,** *Le Centaure de Dieu*
1939 **Antoine de Saint-Exupery,** *Terre des hommes*
1940 **Edouard Peisson,** *Le Voyage d'Edgar*
1941 **Robert Bourget-Pailleron,** *La Folie d'Hubert*
1942 **Jean Blanzat,** *L'Orage du matin*
1943 **J.H. Louwyck,** *Danse pour ton ombre*
1944 **Pierre de Lagarde,** *Valmaurie*
1945 **Marc Blancpain,** *Le Solitaire*
1946 **Jean Orieux,** *Fontagre*
1947 **Philippe Heriat,** *La Famille Bousardel*
1948 **Yves Gandon,** *Ginevre*
1949 **Yvonne Pagniez,** *Evasion*
1950 **Joseph Jolinon,** *Les Provinciaux*
1951 **Bernard Barbey,** *Chevaux abandonnes sur le champ de bataille*
1952 **Henri Castillou,** *Le Feu de l'Eina*
1953 **Jean Hougron,** *Mort en fraude*
1954 **Pierre Moinot,** *La Chasse royale*
1955 **Michel de Saint-Pierre,** *Les Aristocrates*
1956 **Paul Guth,** *Le Naif localaire*
1957 **Jacques de Bourbon-Busset,** *Le Silence et la Joie*
1958 **Henri Queffelec,** *Un royaume sous la mer*
1959 **Gabriel d'Aubarede,** *La Foi de notre enfance*
1960 **Christian Marciaux,** *Notre Dame de Desempaies*
1961 **Pham Van Ky,** *Perdre la demeure*
1962 **Michel Mohrt,** *La prison maritime*
1963 **Robert Margerit,** *La Revolution*
1964 **Michel Droit,** *Le Retour*
1965 **Jean Husson,** *Le Cheval d'Herbeleau*
1966 **Francois Nourissier,** *Une histoire*
1967 **Michel Tourier,** *Vendredi ou les Limbes du Pacifique*
1968 **Albert Cohen,** *Belle du Seigneur*
1969 **Pierre Moustiers,** *La Parole*
1970 **Bertrand Poirot-Delpech,** *La Folle de Lituanie*
1971 **Jean d'Ormesson,** *La Gloire de l'Empire*
1972 **Patrick Modiano,** *Les Boulevards de ceinture*
1973 **Michel Deon,** *Un taxi mauve*
1974 **Kleber Headens,** *Adios*
1975 **No award**
1976 **Pierre Schoendoerffer,** *Le crabe-tambour*
1977 **Camille Bourniquel,** *Tempo*
1978 **Alain Bosquet,** *Une mere russe*
Pascal Jardin, *Le Nain jaune*
1979 **Henri Coulonges,** *L'adieu a la femme sauvage*
1980 **Louis Gardel,** *Fort Saganne*

Jane Addams Children's Book Award

JANE ADDAMS PEACE ASSOCIATION
777 United Nations Plaza, New York, N.Y. 10017
(212/682-8830)

The Jane Addams Children's Book Award is given annually by the Jane Addams Peace Association and the Women's International League for Peace and Freedom to honor the book that most effectively promotes peace, social justice and world community in the eyes of a committee of judges drawn from individuals concerned with children's books. A scroll goes to the recipient.

1953 **Eva Knox,** *People Are Important*
1954 **Jean Ketchum,** *Stick-In-The-Mud*
1955 **Elizabeth Yates,** *Rainbow Around The World*
1956 **Arna Bontemps,** *Story Of The Negro*
1957 **Margot Benary-Isbert,** *Blue Mystery*
1958 **William O. Steele,** *The Perilous Road*
1959 **No award**
1960 **Edith Patterson Meyer,** *Champions Of Peace*
1961 **Shirley L. Arora,** *What Then, Raman?*
1962 **Aimee Sommerfelt,** *The Road To Agra*
1963 **Ryerson Johnson,** *Monkey And The Wild, Wild Wind*
1964 **John F. Kennedy,** *Profiles In Courage*
1965 **Duane Bradley,** *Meeting With A Stranger*
1966 **Emily Cheney Neville,** *Berries Goodman*
1967 **Robert Burch,** *Queenie Peavy*
1968 **Erik Christian Haugaard,** *The Little Fishes*
1969 **Esther Hautzig,** *The Endless Steppe*
1970 **No award**
1971 **Cornelia Meigs,** *Jane Addams: Pioneer Of Social Justice*
1972 **Betty Underwood,** *The Tamarack Tree*
1973 **S. Carl Hirsch,** *The Riddle Of Racism*
1974 **Nicholasa Mohr,** *Nilda*
1975 **Charlotte Pomerantz,** *The Princess And The Admiral*
1976 **Eloise Greenfield,** *Paul Robeson*
1977 **Milton Meltzer,** *Never To Forget: The Jews Of The Holocaust*
1978 **Lawrence Yep,** *Children of the Owl*
1979 **Jamake Highwater,** *Many Smokes, Many Moons*
1980 **David Kherdian,** *The Road from Home*

The Age Book of the Year Award

THE AGE
250 Spencer St., Melbourne, Vic. 3000, Australia (600421))

The A$3,000 Book of the Year Award given by *The Age* honors the work which best expresses Australia's identity and prevailing concerns and is of outstanding literary merit. A four-judge panel selects the winner.

1974 **Manning Clark**, *A History of Australia, Vol. III*
David Foster, *The Pure Land*
1975 **Thea Astley**, *A Kindness Cup*
1976 **Hugh Stretton**, *Capitalism, Socialism and the Environment*
Alec Hope, *A Late Picking*
1977 **Graham Freudenberg**, *A Certain Grandeur*
1978 **Patsy Adam-Smith**, *The Anzacs*
C.J. Koch, *The Year of Living Dangerously*
1979 **Roger McDonald**, *1915*
1980 **David Ireland**, *A Woman of the Future*
Murray Bail, *Homesickness*

Academy-Institute Awards

AMERICAN ACADEMY AND INSTITUTE OF ARTS AND LETTERS
633 W. 155th St., New York, N.Y. 10032 (212/368-5900)

To encourage qualified writers and help them continue their creative work, the Institute annually gives cash awards currently $5,000 each to non-members. These Academy Institute Awards, formerly called Arts and Letters Awards, may not be applied for. Similar awards are given in art and music.

In addition to these specific literature awards, the American Academy and Institute of Arts and Letters gives several awards for achievements in various arts and belles lettres, which will be found on pp. 37, 38, 42, and 46.

1941
Mary M. Colum **Jesse Stuart**

1942
Hermann Broch **Norman Corwin**
Edgar Lee Masters **Muriel Rukeyser**

1943
Virgil Geddes **Carson McCullers**
Jose Garcia Villa **Joseph Wittlin**

1944
Hugo Ignotus **Jeremy Ingalls**
Thomas Sancton **Karl Shapiro**
Eudora Welty **Tennessee Williams**

1945
Kenneth Fearing **Feike Feikema**
Alexander Greendale **Norman Rosten**
Jean Stafford **Marguerite Young**

1946
Gwendolyn Brooks **Kenneth Burke**
Malcolm Cowley **Peter DeVries**
Langston Hughes **Arthur Laurents**
Marianne Craig Moore **Arthur Schlesinger, Jr.**
Irwin Shaw

1947
Nelson Algren **Eleanor Clark**
Lloyd Frankenberg **Robert Lowell**
Elizabeth Parsons **James Still**

1948
Bertolt Brecht **Dudley Fitts**
Harry Levin **James F. Powers**
Genevieve Taggard **Allen Tate**

1949
Leonie Adams **James Agee**
Joseph Campbell **Alfred Kazin**
Vincent McHugh **James Stern**

1950
John Berryman **Paul Bowles**
Maxwell David Geismar **Caroline Gordon**
Shirley Graham **Hyam Plutzik**

1951
Newton Arvin **Elizabeth Bishop**
Louise Bogan **Brendan Gill**
Randall Jarrell **Vladimir Nabokov**

1952
Saul Bellow **Alfred Hayes**
Theodore Roethke **Elizabeth Spencer**
Peter Taylor **Yvor Winters**

1953
Eric Bentley **Isabel Bolton**
Richard Chase **Francis Fergusson**
Paul Goodman **Delmore Schwartz**

1954
Hannah Arendt **Ray Bradbury**
Richmond Lattimore **David Riesman**
Ruthven Todd **C. Vann Woodward**

1955
Richard Eberhart **Robert Horan**
Chester Kallman **William Krasner**
Milton Lott **Morton D. Zabel**

1956
James Baldwin **John Cheever**
Henry Russel Hitchcock **Joseph Kerman**
Josephine Miles **Priscilla Robertson**
Frank Rooney

1957
Leslie Fiedler **Robert Fitzgerald**
Mary McCarthy **W.S. Merwin**
Flannery O'Connor **Robert Pack**

1958
Joseph Frank **Herbert Gold**
R.W.B. Lewis **William Maxwell**
William Meredith **James Purdy**
Francis Steegmuller

1959
Truman Capote **Leon Edel**
Charles Jackson **Stanley J. Kunitz**
Conrad Richter **Isaac Bashevis Singer**
James Wright

1960
Irving Howe **Norman Mailer**
Wright Morris **Adrienne Rich**
Philip Roth **W.D. Snodgrass**
May Swenson

1961
Edward Dahlberg
Mark Harris
Warren Miller
Howard Nemerov
Jean Garrigue
David McCord
Brian Moore

1962
Daniel Fuchs
Galway Kinnell
Frank O'Connor
John A. Williams
John Hawkes
Edwin O'Connor
Joan Williams

1963
Richard Bankowsky
Joseph Heller
William Humphrey
Richard Yates
William Gaddis
John Hollander
Peter Matthiessen

1964
Lionel Abel
Norman Fruchter
Eric Hoffer
Kenneth Rexroth
Dorothy Baker
Thom Gunn
David Ignatow

1965
Ben Belitt
J. V. Cunningham
Joseph Mitchell
Henry Roth
Robert Bly
Denise Levertov
P. M. Pasinetti
Harvey Swados

1966
William Alfred
James Dickey
Josephine Herbst
Gary Snyder
John Barth
Shirley Hazzard
Edwin Honig
M. B. Tolson

1967
Philip Booth
Daniel Hoffman
Stanley Edgar Hyman
David Wagoner
Hortense Calisher
Bernard Knox
Walker Percy

1968
John Malcolm Brinnin
Reuel Denny
John Frederick Nims
Richard G. Stern
Fred Chappell
Howard Moss
Julia Randall
Eleanor Ross Taylor

1969
John Ashbery
Allen Ginsberg
L. E. Sissman
George P. Elliott
Hugh Kenner

1970
Brewster Ghiselin
Richard Howard
Jerzy Kosinski
N. Scott Momaday
F. D. Reeve
Gordon S. Haight
Pauline Kael
James A. McPherson
Grace Paley
Kurt Vonnegut, Jr.

1971
Wendell Berry
Martin Duberman
Charles Gordone
Arthur Kopit
Leonard Nathan
Wilfrid Sheed
Stanley Burnshaw
Ronald Fair
Barbara Howes
Leonard Michaels
Reynolds Price

1972
Harry Crews
Paula Fox
Pauline Hanson
Israel Horovitz
Gilbert Rogin
Peter Davison
Penelope Gilliatt
Michael S. Harper
Walter Kerr
Ann Stanford

1973
Marius Bewley
Irving Feldman
Dorothy Hughes
Daniel P. Mannix
Jonathan Schell
Maeve Brennan
Frances FitzGerald
Philip Levine
Cynthia Ozick
Austin Warren

1974
Ann Cornelisen
Elizabeth Hardwick
Donald Justice
Charles Rosen
James Tate
Lanford Wilson
Stanley Elkin
Josephine Johnson
David Rabe
Sam Shepard
Henry Van Dyke

1975
William S. Burroughs
John Gardner
Terrence McNally
John Peck
Colin M. Turnbull
J. P. Donleavy
William H. Gass
Tillie Olsen
Mark Strand
Helen Hennessy Vendler

1976
Robert Coover
E. L. Doctorow
Kenneth Koch
John Simon
Susan Sontag
Robert Craft
Eugene D. Genovese
Charles Simic
Louis Simpson
Louis Zukofsky

1977
A. R. Ammons
Cynthia Macdonald
John McPhee
Paul Theroux
Robert Watson
Walter J. Bate
Joseph McElroy
James Schuyler
Anne Tyler
Charles Wright

1978
Renata Adler
William Arrowsmith
Lerone Bennett, Jr.
Terrence des Pres
Leslie Epstein
Michael Herr
Murray Kempton
Alison Lurie
Toni Morrison
Page Smith

1979
Arlene Croce
Barry Hannah
James McConkey
John N. Morris
Robert M. Pirsig
Richard Poirier
Philip Schultz
Dave Smith

1980
Ann Beattie
William Dickey
Paul Fussel
Maxine Kumin
George Oppen
Robert Pinsky
Lewis Thomas
Larry Woiwode

Hans Christian Andersen International Medal

INTERNATIONAL BOARD ON BOOKS FOR YOUNG PEOPLE
Leonhardsgraben 38A, CH-4051 Basel, Switzerland

The Hans Christian Andersen International Medal is given every two years to a living author and a living artist for an outstanding body of work that has made an important contribution to children's literature. An international jury appointed by the board's executive committee makes the selection.

1956 **Eleanor Farjeon,** (United Kingdom)
1958 **Astrid Lindgren,** (Sweden)
1960 **Erich Kastner,** (Germany)
1962 **Meindert DeJong,** (U.S.A.)
1964 **Rene Guillot,** (France)
1966 **Alois Carigiet,** (author) (Switzerland)
Tove Jansson, (illustrator) (Finland)
1968 **James Kriiss,** (author) (Germany)
Jose Maria Sanchez Silva, (author) (Spain)
Jiri Trnka, (illustrator) (Czechoslovakia)
1970 **Gianni Rodari,** (author) (Italy)
Maurice Sendak, (illustrator) (U.S.A.)
1972 **Scott O'Dell,** (author) (U.S.A.)
Ib Spang Olsen, (illustrator) (Denmark)
1974 **Maria Gripe,** (author) (Sweden)
Farshid Misghali, (illustrator) (Iran)
1976 **Cecil Bodker,** (author) (Denmark)
Tatjana Mawrina, (illustrator) (U.S.S.R.)
1978 **Paula Fox,** (Author) (U.S.A.)
.tto Svenic, (illustrator) (Denmark)
1980 **Bohumil Riha,** (author) (Czechoslovakia)
Suekichi Akaba, (illustrator) (Japan)

Anisfield-Wolf Award

ANISFIELD-WOLF AWARD COMMITTEE
321 Cherry Hill Rd., Princeton, N.J. 08540 (609/924-3756)

The Anisfield-Wolf Awards, with cash prizes of $1,500, are given annually for books published during the previous year that lead to improved intergroup relations in the judgment of an awards committee. Awards are given for scholarly books and for fiction, drama, poetry, biography, autobiography or any other form of creative writing. The award initially was sponsored by *The Saturday Review.*

1935 **Harold Gosnell,** *Negro Politicians: The Rise of Negro Politics in Chicago*
1936 **Julian Huxley and A. C. Haddon,** *We Europeans: A Survey of "Racial" Problems*
1937 **No award**
1938 **No award**
1939 **E. Franklin Frazier,** *The Negro Family in the United States*
1940 **No award**
1941 **Leopold Infeld,** *Quest*
James G. Leyburn, *The Haitian People*
1942 **Zora Neale Hurston,** *Dust Tracks on a Road*
Donald Pierson, *Negroes in Brazil*
1943 **Maurice Samuel,** *The World of Sholom Aleichem*
Roi Ottley, *New World A-Coming*
1944 **Gwethalyn Graham,** *Earth and High Heaven*
Gunnar Myrdal, *An American Dilemma*
1945 **Wallace Stegner and the editors of *Look*,** *One Nation*
St. Clair Drake and Horace Cayton, *Black Metropolis*
1946 **Sholem Asch,** *East River*
Pauline R. Kibbe, *Latin Americans in Texas*
1947 **Worth Tuttle Hedden,** *The Other Room*
John Collier, *The Indians of the Americas*
1948 **Alan Paton,** *Cry the Beloved Country*
J. C. Furnas, *Anatomy of Paradise*
1949 **S. Andhil Fineberg,** *Punishment Without Crime*
Shirley Graham, *Your Most Humble Servant*
1950 **John Hersey,** *The Wall*
Henry Gibbs, *Twilight in South Africa*
1951 **Laurens van der Post,** *Venture to the Interior*
Brewton Berry, *Race Relations*
1952 **Han Suyin,** *A Many-Splendored Thing*
Farley Mowat, *People of the Deer*
1953 **Vernon Bartlett,** *Struggle for Africa*
Langston Hughes, *Simple Takes a Wife*
1954 **Oden Meeker,** *Report on Africa*
Lyle Saunders, *Cultural Difference and Medical Care*
1955 **John P. Dean and Alex Rosen,** *A Manual of Intergroup Relations*
George W. Shepherd, Jr., *They Wait in Darkness*
1956 **Father Trevor Huddleston,** *Naught for Your Comfort*
Gilberto Freyre, *The Masters and the Slaves: A Study in the Development of Brazilian Civilization*
1957 **Jessie B. Sams,** *White Mother*
South African Institute of Race Relations, *Handbook on Race Relations*
1958 **Martin Luther King, Jr.,** *Stride Toward Freedom*
George Eaton Simpson and J. Milton Yinger, *Racial and Cultural Minorities*
1959 **John Haynes Holmes,** *I Speak for Myself*
Basil Davidson, *The Lost Cities of Africa*
1960 **E. R. Braithwaite,** *To Sir, With Love*
Louis E. Lomax, *The Reluctant African*
1961 **Dwight L. Dumond,** *Antislavery*
John Howard Griffin, *Black Like Me*
Gina Allen, *The Forbidden Man*
1962 **Theodosius Dobzhansky,** *Mankind Evolving*
1963 **Bernhard E. Olson,** *Faith and Prejudice*
Harold R. Isaacs, *The New World of Negro Americans*
Nathan Glazer and Daniel P. Moynihan, *Beyond the Melting Pot*
1964 **James W. Silver,** *Mississippi: The Closed Society*
Milton M. Gordon, *Assimilation in American Life*
James M. McPherson, *The Struggle for Equality: Abolitionists and the Negro in the Civil War and Reconstruction*
Abram L. Sachar, *A History of the Jews*
1965 **Amram Scheinfeld,** *Your Heredity and Environment*
Claude Brown, *Manchild in the Promised Land*
Malcolm X and Alex Haley, *Autobiography of Malcolm X*
H. C. Baldry, *Unity of Mankind in Greek Thought*
1966 **Oscar Lewis,** *La Vida*
David Brion Davis, *The Problem of Slavery in Western Culture*
1967 **Raul Hilberg,** *The Destruction of European Jews*
Norman Cohn, *Warrant for Genocide: The Myth of the Jewish World Conspiracy and The Protocols of the Elders of Zion*
Robert Coles, *Children of Crisis: A Study of Courage and Fear*
1968 **Gwendolyn Brooks,** *In the Mecca*
E. Earl Baughman and W. Grant Dahlstrom, *Negro and White Children*

Stuart Levine and Nancy O. Lurie, *The American Indian Today*
Leonard Dinnerstein, *The Leo Frank Case*
1969 **Florestan Fernandes,** *The Negro in Brazilian Society*
Vine Deloria, Jr., *Custer Died for Your Sins*
Dan T. Carter, *Scottsboro*
Audrie Girdner and Anne Loftis, *The Great Betrayal*
1972 **Lee Rainwater,** *Behind Ghetto Walls*
Betty Fladeland, *Men and Brothers*
Pat Conroy, *The Water is Wide*
1973 **Naboth Mokgatle,** *The Biography of an Unknown South American*
Michel Fabre, *The Unfinished Quest of Richard Wright*
Louis L. Snyder, *The Dreyfus Case*
Charles Duguid, *Doctor and the Aborigines*
Albie Sachs, *Justice in South Africa*
1974 **Leon Poliakov,** *The Aryan Myth*
Eugene D. Genovese, *Roll, Jordan, Roll*
1975 **Lucy S. Dawidowicz,** *The War Against the Jews, 1933-1945*
Raphael Patai and Jennifer P. Wing, *The Myth of the Jewish Race*
Thomas Kiernan, *The Arabs: Their History, Aims and Challenge to the Industrialized World*
1976 **Richard Kluger,** *Simple Justice*
Michi Weglyn, *Years of Infamy*
1977 **Maxine Hong Kingston,** *The Woman Warrior*
Allan Chase, *The Legacy of Malthus: The Social Costs of the New Scientific Racism*
1978 **Philip V. Tobias** (ed.), *The Bushmen: Sun Hunters and Herders of Southern Africa*
1979 **Urie Bronfenbrenner**, *The Ecology of Human Development*
Richard Borshay Lee, *The Ukung Sun: Men, Women and Work in a Foraging Society*
1980 **Not available at press time**

Art Publishing Award

ART LIBRARIES SOCIETY OF NORTH AMERICA
Box 3692, Glendale, Calif. 91201

The Art Publishing Award is given annually for the trade book(s) on art that display the best design, workmanship, illustrations and scholarly quality (indexes, bibliographies, etc.). The book, which must have been published in North America, is honored with a certificate.

1973 **Jonathan Green,** *Camera Work: A Critical Anthology* (Aperture)
Coy Ludwig, *Maxfield Parrish* (Watson-Guptil)
1974 **Lincoln Kirstein,** *Elle Nadelman* (Eakins Foundation Press)
Pierpont Morgan Library, *Major Acquisitions of the Pierpont Morgan Library, 1927-1974*
1975 **Dan Burne Jones,** *The Prints of Rockwell Kent* (University of Chicago Press)
1976 **Robert A Sobieszek and Odette M. Appel,** *The Spirit of Fact: Daguerrotypes of Southworth & Hawes, 1843-1862* (David R. Godine)
1977 **Detroit Institute of Arts and St. Louis Art Museum,** *Henri Matisse: Paper Cut-Outs*

Current status unknown

Athenaeum Literary Award

THE ATHENAEUM OF PHILADELPHIA
East Washington Sq., Philadelphia, Pa. 19106 (215/WA 5-2688)

The Athenaeum Literary Award medal is presented annually to authors residing within 30 miles of the Philadelphia City Hall at the time of writing an outstanding work of fiction or non-fiction and published during the previous year. A committee selects the winner of the bronze medal.

1949 **John L. LaMonte,** *The World of the Middle Ages*
1950 **Henry N. Paul,** *The Royal Play of MacBeth*
1951 **Arthur Hobson Quinn,** *The Literature of the American People*
1952 **Nicholas B. Wainwright,** *A Philadelphia Story*
1953 **Lawrence Henry Gipson,** *The British Empire Before the American Revolution,* Volume VIII
1954 **Davis Grubb,** *The Night of the Hunter*
1955 **Conyers Read,** *Mr. Secretary Cecil and Queen Elizabeth*
1956 **Samuel N. Kramer,** *From The Tablets of Sumer*
Livingston Biddle, Jr., *The Village Beyond*
1957 **Catherine D. Bowen,** *The Lion and the Throne*
Bettina Linn, *A Letter to Elizabeth*
1958 **Loren Eiseley,** *Darwin's Century*
L. Sprague DeCamp, *An Elephant for Aristole*
1959 **John Canaday,** *Mainstreams of Modern Art*
1960 **Edwin Wolf II,** *Rosenbach: A Biography*
David Taylor, *Storm the Last Rampart*
1961 **Lauren R. Stevens,** *The Double Axe*
Roy F. Nichols, *The Stakes of Power*
1962 **Curtis Bok,** *Maria*
Carleton S. Coon, *The Origins of Races*
Richard S. Dunn, *Puritans and Yankees*
1963 **Samuel N. Kramer,** *The Sumerians*
Daniel Hoffman, *The City of Satisfaction*
1964 **Dorothy S. White,** *Seeds of Discord*
Kristen Hunter, *God Bless the Child*
Elizabeth G. Vining, *Take Heed of Loving Me*
1965 **Laurence Lafore,** *The Long Fuse*
1966 **Edward S. Gifford,** *Father Against the Devil*
1967 **Edmund N. Bacon,** *Design of Cities*
Daniel P. Mannix, *The Fox and the Hound*
1968 **Robert C. Smith,** *Art of Portugal*
E. Earnest, *Expatriates and Patriots*
1969 **C. Henry Pitz,** *Brandywine Tradition*
Chaim Potok, *The Promise*
1970 **No award**
1971 **Loren Eiseley,** *The Night Country*
1972 **Jerre Mangione,** *The Dream and The Deal*
1973 **John Maass,** *The Glorious Enterprise*
1974 **John R. Coleman,** *Blue-Collar Journal*
1975 **Martin P. Snyder,** *City of Independence*
1976 **No award**
1977 **No award**
1978 **Anthony F.C. Wallace,** *Rockdale*
1979 **No award**
1980 **Not available at press time**

Atlantic "First" Award

THE ATLANTIC MONTHLY
8 Arlington St., Boston, Mass. 02116 (617/536-9500)

The Atlantic "First" Award was given as official recognition of the author of the most distinguished short story by a previously unpublished author to appear in

The Atlantic Monthly. The editors decided who received the awards, which consisted of a $750 and a $250 honorarium each year that the award was made. Winners of the $750 award, which has not been given since 1976, are listed here.

1972 **Wallace Knight,** *The Way We Went*
David Black, *Laud*
1973 **James Polk,** *The Phrenology of Love*
Tracy Kidder, *The Death of Major Great*
1974 **No award**
1975 **No award**
1976 **L. M. Rosenberg,** *Memory*

Bancroft Prize

COLUMBIA UNIVERSITY
202 Low Library, New York, N.Y. 10027 (212/280-1754)

The Bancroft Prize, which now carries a $4,000 honorarium, is awarded annually for one or more works on American history (including biography) and for one work on diplomacy published during the previous year. While the books may deal with North, Central or South America, they must be written in English. Books may be submitted for consideration by the Bancroft Prize jury.

1948 **Allan Nevins,** *Ordeal of the Union*
Bernard DeVoto, *Across the Wide Missouri*
1949 **Robert E. Sherwood,** *Roosevelt and Hopkins*
Samuel Eliot Morison, *The Rising Sun in the Pacific*
1950 **Lawrence H. Gipson,** *The Great War For the Empire,* Vol. III: *The Victorious Years, 1758-1760*
Herbert E. Bolton, *Coronado*
1951 **Arthur N. Holcombe,** *Our More Perfect Union*
Henry N. Smith, *Virgin Land*
1952 **Merlo J. Pusey,** *Charles Evans Hughes*
C. Vann Woodward, *Origins of the New South*
1953 **George Dangerfield,** *The Era of Good Feelings*
Eric F. Goldman, *Rendezvous With Destiny*
1954 **Clinton Rossiter,** *Seedtime of the Republic*
William L. Langer and S. Everett Gleason, *The Undeclared War*
1955 **Paul Horgan,** *Great River, The Rio Grande*
Leonard D. White, *The Jacksonians*
1956 **Elizabeth Stevenson,** *Henry Adams*
J.G. Randall and Richard N. Current, *Last Full Measure: Lincoln the President*
1957 **George F. Kennan,** *Russia Leaves the War*
Arthur S. Link, *The New Freedom*
1958 **Arthur M. Schlesinger, Jr.,** *The Crisis of the Old Order*
Frank Luther Mott, *A History of American Magazines,* Vol. IV
1959 **Ernest Samuels,** *Henry Adams, the Middle Years*
Daniel J. Boorstin, *The Americans, The Colonial Experience*
1960 **R.R. Palmer,** *The Age of the Democratic Revolution, A Political History of Europe and America, 1760-1800*
Margaret Leech, *In the Days of McKinley*
1961 **Merrill D. Peterson,** *The Jefferson Image in the American Mind*
Arthur S. Link, *The Struggle for Neutrality, 1914-1915*
1962 **Lawrence A. Cremin,** *The Transformation of the School*
Felix Gilbert, *To the Farewell Address: Ideas of Early American Foreign Policy*
Martin B. Duberman, *Charles Francis Adams, 1807-1866*
1963 **Page Smith,** *John Adams*
Roberta Wohlstetter, *Pearl Harbor: Warning and Decision*
John G. Stoessinger, *The Might of Nations: World Politics in Our Time*
1964 **William E. Leuchtenberg,** *Franklin D. Roosevelt and the New Deal, 1932-1940*
John L. Thomas, *The Liberator: William Lloyd Garrison*
Paul Seabury, *The Foreign Policy of the United States of America*
1965 **Bradford Perkins,** *Castlereagh and Adams: England and the United States, 1812-1823*
William B. Willcox, *Portrait of a General: Sir Henry Clinton in the War of Independence*
Dorothy Borg, *The United States and the Far Eastern Crisis of 1933-1938*
1966 **Richard B. Morris,** *The Peacemakers: The Great Powers and American Independence*
Theodore W. Friend III, *Between Two Empires: The Ordeal of the Philippines*
1967 **William W. Freehling,** *Prelude to Civil War: The Nullification Controversy in South Carolina, 1816-1836*
Charles Sellers, *James K. Polk, Continentalist, 1843-1846,* Vol. II
James Sterling Young, *The Washington Community, 1800-1828*
1968 **Henry Allen Bullock,** *The History of Negro Education in the South from 1619 to the Present*
Richard L. Bushman, *From Puritan to Yankee: Character and Social Order in Connecticut, 1690-1765*
Bernard Bailyn, *The Ideological Origins of the American Revolution*
1969 **Winthrop D. Jordon,** *White Over Black: American Attitudes Toward the Negro, 1550-1812*
N. Gordon Levin, Jr., *Woodrow Wilson and World Politics: America's Response to War and Revolution*
Rexford Guy Tugwell, *The Brain Trust*
1970 **Charles Coleman Sellers,** *Charles Willson Peale*
Gordon S. Wood, *The Creation of the American Republic, 1776-1787*
Dan T. Carter, *Scottsboro: A Tragedy of the American South*
1971 **Eric Barnouw,** *The Image Empire: A History of Broadcasting in the United States,* Vol. III
David M. Kennedy, *Birth Control in America: The Career of Margaret Sanger*
Joseph Frazier Wall, *Andrew Carnegie*
1972 **Carl N. Degler,** *Neither Black Nor White*
Robert Middlekauff, *The Mathers: Three Generations of Puritan Intellectuals, 1696-1728*
Samuel Eliot Morison, *The European Discovery of America: The Northern Voyages*
1973 **Frances FitzGerald,** *Fire in the Lake: The Vietnamese and the Americans in Vietnam*
John Lewis Gaddis, *The United States and the Origins of the Cold War*
Louis R. Harlan, *Booker T. Washington*
1974 **Ray Allen Billington,** *Frederick Jackson Turner: Historian, Scholar, Teacher*
Townsend Hoopes, *The Devil and John Foster Dulles*
Stephan Thernstrom, *The Other Bostonians: Poverty and Progress in the American Metropolis, 1880-1970*
1975 **Robert William Fogel and Stanley L. Engerman,** *Time on the Cross: The Economics of American Negro*

Slavery and *Time on the Cross: Evidence and Methods—A Supplement*
Alexander L. George and Richard Smoke, *Deterrence in American Foreign Policy: Theory and Practice*
Eugene Genovese, *Roll, Jordan, Roll*

1976 **David Brion Davis,** *The Problem of Slavery in the Age of Revolution, 1770-1823*
R.W.B. Lewis, *Edith Wharton: A Biography*

1977 **Alan Dawley,** *Class and Community: The Industrial Revolution in Lynn*
Robert A. Gross, *The Minutemen and Their World*
Barry W. Higman, *Slave Population and the Economy in Jamaica, 1807-1834*

1978 **Alfred D. Chandler, Jr.**, *The Visible Hand: The Managerial Revolution in American Business*
Morton J. Horwitz, *The Transformation of American Law*

1979 **Christopher Thorne**, *Allies of a Kind: The United States, Britain and the War Against Japan, 1941-1945*
Anthony F.C. Wallace, *Rockdale: The Growth of an American Foreign Policy, 1932-1945*

1980 **Robert Dallek**, *Franklin D. Roosevelt and American Foreign Policy, 1932-1945*
Thomas Dublin, *Women at Work: The Transformation of Work and Community in Lowell, Massachusetts, 1826-1860*
Donald Worster, *Dust Bowl: The Southern Plains in the 1930s*

Mildred L. Batchelder Award

AMERICAN LIBRARY ASSOCIATION
Children's Services Div., 50 E. Huron St., Chicago, Ill. 60611 (312/944-6780)

The Mildred L. Batchelder Award is given annually to the publisher of the children's book considered to be the most outstanding of those originally issued in a foreign language and subsequently published in the U.S. Until 1977, the award was made for a book published two years prior to the year in which it was honored. Now it is given for a book issued immediately preceding the year. A committee of the Division's members makes nominations and the membership of the Children's Services Division votes on the winner, who receives an engraved citation.

1968 **Alfred A. Knopf,** *The Little Man* by Erich Kastner
1969 **Scribner's,** *Don't Take Teddy* by Babbis-Friis Baastad
1970 **Holt, Rinehart & Winston,** *Wildcat Under Glass* by Eliki Zei
1971 **Pantheon,** *In the Land of Ur* by Hans Baumann
1972 **Holt, Rinehart & Winston,** *Friedrich* by Hans P. Richter
1973 **William Morrow,** *Pulga* by S.R. Van Herson
1974 **E.P. Dutton,** *Petros' War* by Eliki Zei
1975 **Crown Publishers,** *An Old Tale Carved Out of Stone* by A. Linevski
1976 **Henry Z. Walck,** *The Cat and the Mouse Who Lived in a House* by Ruth Hurlimann
1977 **Atheneum,** *The Leopard* by Cecil Bodker
1978 **No award**
1979 **Franklin Watts,** *Konrad* by Christine Nostlinger
Harcourt Brace Jovanovich, *Rabbit* by Jorge Steiner
1980 **E. P. Dutton,** *The Sound of the Dragon's Feet* by Aliki Zei

Curtis G. Benjamin Award for Creative Publishing

ASSOCIATION OF AMERICAN PUBLISHERS
One Park Ave., New York, N.Y. 10016 (212/689-8920)

The Curtis G. Benjamin Award for Creative Publishing is given annually for creative service to the industry from any area of publishing — editorial, marketing or general management. A nine-member committee and an AAP representative select the winner.

1976 **Charles Scribner**
1977 **William Kaufmann**
1978 **Chester Kerr**
1979 **C. Stewart Brewster**
1980 **Ursula Nordstrom**

Bennett Award

HUDSON REVIEW
65 E. 55th St., New York, N.Y. 10022 (212/755-9040)

The Bennett Award honors a writer of any nationality who is at a critical stage at which a substantial cash grant might be useful and who has not received full recognition for past work. The award totals $12,500 and is given every two years.

1976 **Jorge Gullen,** Spain
1978 **Andrei A. Sinyavsky,** France (born in U.S.S.R.)
1980 **V.S. Naipaul,** Trinidad

Benson Medal

ROYAL SOCIETY OF LITERATURE
1 Hyde Park Gardens, London W2, United Kingdom (Tel: 01-723-5104)

The Benson Medal, which is of silver, is presented at the discretion of the Society's council for distinguished work in belles lettres, biography, fiction, history or poetry.

1917 **Gabrielle d'Annunzio**
Benito Perez Galdos
Maurice Parres
1923 **Lytton Strachey**
1926 **Percy Lubbock**
Robert Lynd
Harold Nicolson
1928 **Gordon Bottomley**
George Santayana
1929 **F. A. Simpson**
Helen Waddell
1932 **Stella Benson**
1934 **Dame Edith Sitwell**
1938 **E. M. Forster**
G. M. Young
1939 **F. L. Lucas**
Andrew Young
1940 **John Galsworthy**
Christopher Hassall
1941 **Christopher La Farge**
1952 **Frederick S. Boas**
1966 **J. R. R. Tolkien**
Dame Rebecca West
1968 **E. V. Rieu**
1969 **C. Woodham-Smith**
1975 **Philip Larkin**

James Tait Black Memorial Prizes

UNIVERSITY OF EDINBURGH
Old College, Edinburgh, Scotland EH8 9YL, United Kingdom (031 664 1011)

The James Tait Black Memorial Prizes, which are among the largest in the United Kingdom and carry a £1,000 honorarium, go to the authors of the best novel and best biography published in Britain during the previous year. A professor of English at the University of Glasgow or a regis professor of English literature at the University of Edinburgh selects the winners.

FICTION

1920 **Hugh Walpole,** *The Secret City*
1921 **D. H. Lawrence,** *The Lost Girl*
1922 **Walter de la Mare,** *Memoirs of a Midget*
1923 **David Garnett,** *Lady into Fox*
1924 **Arnold Bennett,** *Riceyman Steps*
1925 **E. M. Forster,** *A Passage to India*
1926 **Liam O'Flaherty,** *The Informer*
1927 **Radclyffe Hall,** *Adam's Breed*
1928 **Francis Brett Young,** *Love Is Enough* (British Title: *Portrait of Clare)*
1929 **Siegfried Sassoon,** *Memoirs of a Fox-Hunting Man*
1930 **J. B. Priestley,** *The Good Companions*
1931 **E. H. Young,** *Miss Mole*
1932 **Kate O'Brien,** *Without My Cloak*
1933 **Helen Simpson,** *Boomerang*
1934 **A. G. Macdonell,** *England, Their England*
1935 **Robert Graves,** *I, Claudius* and *Claudius the God*
1936 **L. H. Myers,** *The Root and the Flower*
1937 **Winifred Holtby,** *South Riding*
1938 **Neil M. Gunn,** *Highland River*
1939 **C. S. Forester,** *A Ship of the Line* and *Flying Colours*
1940 **Aldous Huxley,** *After Many a Summer Dies the Swan*
1941 **Charles Morgan,** *The Voyage*
1942 **Joyce Cary,** *A House of Children*
1943 **Arthur Waley, trans.,** *Monkey* by Wu Ch'eng-en
1944 **Mary Lavin,** *Tales from Bective Bridge*
1945 **Forrest Reid,** *Young Tom*
1946 **L. A. G. Strong,** *Travellers*
1947 **Oliver Onions,** *Poor Man's Tapestry*
1948 **L. P. Hartley,** *Eustace and Hilda*
1949 **Graham Greene,** *The Heart of the Matter*
1950 **Emma Smith,** *The Far Cry*
1951 **Robert Henriques,** *Too Little Love* (British title: *Through the Valley)*
1952 **W. C. Chapman-Mortimer,** *Father Goose*
1953 **Evelyn Waugh,** *Men at Arms*
1954 **Margaret Kennedy,** *Troy Chimneys*
1955 **C. P. Snow,** *The New Men* and *The Masters*
1956 **Ivy Compton-Burnett,** *Mother and Son*
1957 **Rose Macaulay,** *The Towers of Trebizond*
1958 **Anthony Powell,** *At Lady Molly's*
1959 **Angus Wilson,** *The Middle Age of Mrs. Eliot*
1960 **Morris West,** *The Devil's Advocate*
1961 **Rex Warner,** *Imperial Caesar*
1962 **Jennifer Dawson,** *The Ha-Ha*
1963 **Ronald Hardy,** *Act of Destruction*
1964 **Gerda Charles,** *A Slanting Light*
1965 **Frank Tuohy,** *The Ice Saints*
1966 **Muriel Spark,** *The Mandelbaum Gate*
1967 **Christine Brooke-Rose,** *Such*
Aidan Higgins, *Langrishe, Go Down*
1968 **Margaret Drabble,** *Jerusalem the Golden*
1969 **Maggie Ross,** *The Gasteropod*
1970 **Elizabeth Bowen,** *Eva Trout*
1971 **Lily Powell,** *The Bird of Paradise*
1972 **Nadine Gordimer,** *A Guest of Honour*
1973 **John Berger,** *G*
1974 **Iris Murdoch,** *The Black Prince*
1975 **Lawrence Durrell,** *Monsieur, or The Prince of Darkness*
1976 **Brian Moore,** *The Great Victorian Collection*
1977 **John Le Carre,** *The Honourable Schoolboy*
1978 **Maurice Gee,** *Plumb*
1979 **William Golding,** *Darkness Visible*
1980 **Not available at press time**

BIOGRAPHY

1920 **H. Festing Jones,** *Samuel Butler*
1921 **G. M. Trevelyan,** *Lord Grey of the Reform Bill*
1922 **Lytton Strachey,** *Queen Victoria*
1923 **Percy Lubbock,** *Earlham*
1924 **Ronald Ross,** *Memoirs*
1925 **William Wilson,** *The House of Airlis*
1926 **Geoffrey Scott,** *The Portrait of Zelide*
1927 **H. B. Workman,** *John Wyclif*
1928 **H. A. L. Fisher,** *James Bryce*
1929 **John Buchan,** *Montrose*
1930 **Lord David Cecil,** *The Stricken Deer: or The Life of Cowper*
1931 **Francis Yeats-Brown,** *Lives of a Bengal Lancer*
1932 **J. Y. T. Greig,** *David Hume*
1933 **Stephen Gwynn,** *The Life of Mary Kingsley*
1934 **Violet Clifton,** *The Book of Talbot*
1935 **J. A. Neale,** *Queen Elizabeth*
1936 **R. W. Chambers,** *Thomas More*
1937 **E. Sackville-West,** *A Flame in Sunlight: The Life and Work of Thomas de Quincey*
1938 **Lord Eustace Percy,** *John Knox*
1939 **Sir Edmund Chambers,** *Samuel Taylor Coleridge*
1940 **David C. Douglas,** *English Scholars*
1941 **Hilda F. M. Prescott,** *Spanish Tudor*
1942 **John Gore,** *King George V*
1943 **Lord Ponsonby of Shulbrede,** *Henry Ponsonby: Queen Victoria's Private Secretary*
1944 **G. G. Coulton,** *Fourscore Years*
1945 **C. V. Wedgwood,** *William the Silent*
1946 **D. S. McColl,** *Philip Wilson Steer*
1947 **Richard Aldington,** *The Duke* (British title: *Wellington)*
1948 **Canon C. E. Raven,** *English Naturalists*
1949 **Percy A. Scholes,** *The Great Dr. Burney*
1950 **John Connell,** *W. E. Henley*
1951 **Mrs. Cecil Woodham-Smith,** *Florence Nightingale*
1952 **Noel G. Annan,** *Leslie Stephen*
1953 **G. M. Young,** *Stanley Baldwin*
1954 **Carola Oman,** *Sir John Moore*
1955 **Keith Feiling,** *Warren Hastings*
1956 **R. W. Ketton-Cremer,** *Thomas Gray*
1957 **St. John Ervine,** *George Bernard Shaw*
1958 **Maurice Cranston,** *John Locke*
1959 **Joyce Hemlow,** *History of Fanny Burney*
1960 **Christopher Hassall,** *Edward Marsh*
1961 **Canon Adam Fox,** *Dean Inge* (British title: *Life of Dean Inge)*
1962 **M. K. Ashby,** *Joseph Ashby of Tysoe*
1963 **Meriol Trevor,** *Newman, The Pillar and the Cloud, Vol. 1; Light in Winter, Vol. 2*
1964 **Georgina Battiscome,** *John Keble: A Study in Limitations*
1965 **Elizabeth Longford,** *Queen Victoria*

1966 **Mary Moorman,** *William Wordsworth: The Later Years 1803-1850*
1967 **Geoffrey Keynes,** *The Life of William Harvey*
1968 **Winifred Gerin,** *Charlotte Bronte*
1969 **Gordon S. Haight,** *George Eliot*
1970 **Lady Antonia Fraser,** *Mary Queen of Scots*
1971 **Jasper Ridley,** *Lord Palmerston*
1972 **Lady Julia Namier,** *Lewis Namier*
1973 **Quentin Bell,** *Virginia Woolf*
1974 **Robin Lane Fox,** *Alexander the Great*
1975 **John Wain,** *Samuel Johnson*
1976 **Karl Miller,** *Cockburn's Millennium*
1977 **John Branville,** *Doctor Copernicus*
1978 **Robert Gittings**, *The Older Hardy*
1979 **Brian Finney**, *Christopher Isherwood: A Critical Biography*
1980 **Not available at press time**

Critici in Erba Prize
Graphic Prize Fiera de Bologna

FIERA DEL LIBRO PER RAGAZZI
Ente Autonomo per le Fiere de Bólogna (Bologna Trade Fair Association), Piazza Constituzione 6, 40128 Bologna, Italy (Tel: 50-30-50)

The Critici in Erba Prize, which consists of a gold plate, is given annually for the best illustrated book presented at the International Bologna Children's Book Fair. A committee of nine children between six and nine years of age from the schools of Bologna selects the winner.

1966 **Xavier Saint-Justh,** *L'album de Bambi*
1967 **Franco Barberis,** *Ich schenk Dir einen Papagei*
1968 **Folco Quilici,** *Alla scoperta dell'Africa*
1969 **Jan Wahl,** *Pocahontas in London*
1970 **N.A.** *La Storia di Francesco e Chiara raccontata dai bimbi di Groce*
1971 **N.A.** *Alle meine blatter . . .*
1972 **N.A.** *Waltzing Matilda*
1973 **N.A.** *SnowWhite and the Seven Dwarfs*
1974 **N.A.** *A Year in the Woods*
1975 **N.A.** *Il Principe Felice*
1976 **Grere Janus Hertz,** *Das Gelbe Haus*
1977 **Jean de Brunhoff,** *Die Geschichte von Babar*
1978 **Mark Way**, *Nicholas and the Moon Eggs*
1979 **N.A.** *Ein Tag im Leben der Dorothea Wutz*
1980 **N.A.** *Das Buch vom Dorf*

The Graphic Prize Fiera de Bologna for Children and the Graphic Prize Fiera de Bologna for Youth, each of which is a gold plate, are given for works with outstanding graphic value based on graphic, artistic and technical criteria as judged by a committee of experts from the G.B. Bodoni Study Center in Parma. In the list below, "I" signifies works for young children while "Y" is for older children.

1966 **Emilio Radius,** *I/Y-Gesu oggi*
1967 **Hilde Heyduck,** *I-Drei Vogel*
Hilde Heyduck, *Y-Die Alte Linde Gondula*
1968 **Karin Brandt,** *I-Die Wichtelmanner*
Karin Brandt, *Y-Pribehy*
1969 **Samad Bahrang,** *I-The Little Black Fish*
Michel Ragon *Y-La cite de l'an 2000*
1970 **Eric Carle,** *I-1,2,3, Ein Zug Zum Zoo*
N.A. *Y-Vertel het uw kinderen*
1971 **Remy Charlip,** *I-Arm in Arm*
N.A. *Y-Tutto su Gerusalemme biblica*
1972 **Ruth Hurlimann,** *I-Stadtmaus und Landmaus*
N.A. *Y-Slavische Marchen*
1973 **N.A.** *I-Kopfblumen*
N.A. *Y-Hodina Nachove Ruze*
1974 **N.A.** *I-Rotkappchen*
N.A. *Y-The Last of the Mohicans*
1975 **N.A.** *I-Trois petit flocons*
N.A. *Y-Das Spraehbastelbuch*
1976 **Tsuguo Okuda,** *I-Magic for Sale*
Pushkin, *Y-Il cavallo di bronzo*
1977 **N.A.** *I-Schorschi Schrumpft*
N.A. *Y-Takeru*
1978 **Janusz Grabianski,** I-*Grabianski's Stadtmusikantan*
Mitumasa Anno, Y-*Anno's Unique World*
1979 **N.A.** I-*Histoire du petit Stephen Girard*
N.A. Y-*Aurora*
1980 **Mitumasa Anno,** I-*Anno's Song Book*
N.A. Y-*Himmelzelt und Schneckenhaus*

Booker McConnell Prize for Fiction

NATIONAL BOOK LEAGUE
Book House, 45 East Hill, London SW18 2QZB, United Kingdom

The Booker McConnell Prize for Fiction is given annually for the best English language novel published before November 23/24 of the year of presentation and written by a citizen of the Commonwealth, Eire, Pakistan or South Africa. The award, which was originally called the Booker Prize, now carries a £10,000 cash prize. A five-judge panel selects the winner.

1969 **P.H. Newby,** *Something To Answer For*
1970 **Bernice Rubens,** *The Elected Member*
1971 **V.S. Naipaul,** *In A Free State*
1972 **John Berger,** *G*
1973 **J.G. Farrell,** *The Seige Of Krishnapur*
1974 **Nadine Gordimer,** *The Conservationist*
Stanley Middleton, *Holiday*
1975 **Ruth Prawer Jhabvala,** *Heat And Dust*
1976 **David Storey,** *Saville*
1977 **Paul Scott,** *Staying On*
1978 **Iris Murdoch,** *The Sea, The Sea*
1979 **Penelope Fitzgerald,** *Offshore*
1980 **William Golding,** *Rites of Passage*

Boston Globe Horn Book Awards

BOSTON GLOBE/HORN BOOK, INC.
Boston Globe, 135 Morrissey Blvd., Boston, Mass. 02107 (617/288-8000); Horn Book, Inc., 31 St. James Ave., Boston, Mass. 02116 (617/482-5198)

The Boston Globe/Horn Book Awards, which carry $200 honoraria, go to the authors of non-fiction and fiction books and illustrators of books for children. Publishers may submit entries for consideration. A three-person committee selects the winners.

AUTHOR (FICTION)

1967 **Erik Christian Haugaard,** *The Little Fishes*
1968 **John Lawson,** *The Spring Rider*
1969 **Ursula K. LeGuin,** *The Wizard of Earthsea*
1970 **John Rowe Townsend,** *The Intruder*

1971 **Eleanor Cameron,** *A Room Made of Windows*
1972 **Rosemary Sutcliff,** *Tristan and Iseult*
1973 **Susan Cooper,** *The Dark is Rising*
1974 **Virginia Hamilton,** *M.C. Higgins, the Great*
1975 **T. Degens,** *Transport 7-41-R*
1976 **Jill Paton Walsh,** *Unleaving*
1977 **Laurence Yep,** *Child of the Owl*
1978 **Ellen Raskin,** *The Westing Game*
1979 **Sid Fleischman,** *Humbug Mountain*
1980 **Not available at press time**

ILLUSTRATOR

1967 **Peter Spier,** *London Bridge is Falling Down*
1968 **Blair Lent,** *Tikki, Tikki, Tembo*
1969 **John S. Goodall,** *The Adventures of Paddy Pork*
1970 **Ezra Jack Keats,** *Hi, Cat!*
1971 **Kazue Mizumura,** *If I Built A Village*
1972 **John Burningham,** *Mr. Grumpy's Outing*
1973 **Trina S. Hyman** *King Stork*
1974 **Tom Feelings,** *Jambo Means Hello: Swahili Alphabet Book*
1975 **Mitsumasa Anno,** *Anno's Alphabet*
1976 **Remy Charlip and Jerry Joyner,** *Thirteen*
1977 **Wallace Tripp,** *Grandfa' Grig Had a Pig, and Other Rhymes Without Reason from Mother Goose*
1978 **Mitsumasa Anno,** *Anno's Journey*
1979 **Raymond Briggs,** *The Snowman*
1980 **Not available at press time**

AUTHOR (NON-FICTION)

1976 **Alfred Tamarin and Shirley Glubok,** *Voyaging to Cathay: Americans in the China Trade*
1977 **Peter Dickinson,** *Chance, Luck and Destiny*
1978 **Ilse Koehn,** *Mischling, Second Degree: My Childhood in Nazi Germany*
1979 **David Kherdian,** *The Road from Home: The Story of An Armenian Girl*
1980 **Not available at press time**

Georg-Buchner Preis
Johann-Heinrich-Merck-Preis
Johann-Heinrich-Voss-Preis
Friedrich Gundolf-Preis

DEUTSCHE AKADEMIE FUR SPRACHE UND DICHTUNG
Alexandraweg 23, D-6100 Darmstadt, Federal Republic of Germany

The origin of the Georg-Buchner-Preis, or Georg Buchner Prize, was an honor given by the president of the State of Hesse to individuals for various cultural achievements. In its early years it was known as the Prize of the People's State of Hesse.

1923 **Arnold Mendelssohn**, composer
Adam Karillon, author
1924 **Paul Thesing**, painter
Alfred Bock, author
1925 **Wilhelm Michel**, author
Rudolph Koch, author
1926 **Wilhelm Petersen**, composer
Christian H. Kleukens, graphic artist
1927 **Johannes Bischoff**, chamber music singer
Kasimir Edschmid, author
1928 **Richard Hoelscher**, painter
Well Habicht, sculptor
1929 **Carl Zuckmayer**, author
Adam Antes, sculptor
1930 **Johannes Lippmann**, painter
Nickolaus Schwarzkopf, author
1931 **Alexander Posch**, painter
Hans Simon, composer and conductor
1932 **Adolf Bode**, painter
Albert H. Rausch, author
1933-44 **No awards**

After the Second World War the prizes were re-established by the city of Darmstadt and again given for cultural achievements

1945 **Hans Schiebelhuth**, author
1946 **Fritz Usinger**, author
1947 **Anna Seghers**, author
1948 **Hermann Heiss**, composer
1949 **Carl Gunschmann**, painter
1950 **Elisabeth Langasser**, author

In 1951 the Minister of Culture of Hesse, the Magistrate of the City of Darmstadt and the Academy for Language and Poetry agreed to change this honor into the Georg Buchner Preis and turn it into a literary award. The prize, which now carries an honorarium of 20,000 German marks is given to a writer whose works in German are particularly influential in present German culture.

1951 **Gottfried Benn**
1953 **Ernst Kreuder**
1954 **Martin Kessel**
1955 **Marie Luise Kaschnitz**
1956 **Karl Krolow**
1957 **Erich Kastner**
1958 **Max Frisch**
1959 **Gunter Eich**
1960 **Paul Celan**
1961 **Hans Erich Nossack**
1962 **Wolfgang Koeppen**
1963 **Hans Magnus Enzensberger**
1964 **Ingeborg Bachmann**
1965 **Gunter Grass**
1966 **Wolfgang Hildesheimer**
1967 **Heinrich Boll**
1968 **Golo Mann**
1969 **Helmut Heissenbuttel**
1970 **Thomas Bernhard**
1971 **Uwe Johnson**
1972 **Elias Canetti**
1973 **Peter Handke**
1974 **Hermann Kestes**
1975 **Manes Sperber**
1976 **Heinz Piontek**
1977 **Reiner Kunze**
1978 **Hermann Lenz**
1979 **Ernst Meister**
1980 **Christa Wolf**

The Johann-Heinrich-Merck-Preis, or Johann Heinrich Merck Prize, which now carries a 10,000 mark honorarium, is given annually for notable essays or criticism.

1964 **Gunter Blocker**
1965 **No award**
1966 **K. H. Ruppel**
1967 **Werner Weber**
1968 **Georg Hensel**
1969 **Erich Heller**
1970 **Joachim Kaiser**

1971 **Peter Huchel**
1972 **Horst Kruger**
1973 **H. H. Stuckenschmidt**
1974 **Joachim Gunther**
1975 **Walter Hollerer**
1976 **Peter Kuhmkorf**
1977 **Francois Bondy**
1978 **Karl Heinz Bohrer**
1979 **Werner Spies**
1980 **Sebastian Haffner**

The Sigmund-Freud-Preis, or Sigmund Freud Prize, which now carries a 10,000 mark honorarium, is given annually for scientific or scholarly prose.

1964 **Hugo Friedrich**
1965 **Adolf Portmann**
1966 **Emil Staiger**
1967 **Hannah Arendt**
1968 **Karl Barth**
1969 **Bruno Snell**
1970 **Werner Heisenberg**
1971 **Werner Krall**
1972 **Erik Wolf**
1973 **Karl Rahner**
1974 **Gunter Busch**
1975 **Ernst Bloch**
1976 **Jurgen Habermas**
1977 **Harald Weinrich**
1978 **Siegfried Melchinger**
1979 **Hans-Georg Gadamer**
1980 **Hans Blumentig**

The Johann-Heinrich-Voss-Preis for Ubersetzung, or Johann Heinrich Voss Translation Prize, which now carries a 10,000-mark honorarium, is given annually for outstanding achievements in translation, either a body of work or a single notable translation.

1958 **Edwin und Willa Muir**
1959 **Benno Geiger**
1960 **Frau Rahsin**
1961 **Jakob Hegner**
1962 **Rudolf Alexander Schroder**
1963 **Friedhelm Kemp**
1964 **Michael Hamburger**
1965 **Wolfgang Schadewaldt**
1966 **Eva Rechel-Mertens**
Philippe Jaccottet
1967 **Witold Wirpsza**
Karl Dedecius
1968 **Eva Hesse**
1969 **Hans Hennecke**
1970 **Janheinz Jahn**
1971 **Karl August Horst**
1972 **Elmar Tophoven**
1973 **Peter Gan (Richard Moering)**
1974 **Peter Urban**
1975 **Curt Meyer-Clason**
1976 **Hanns Grossel**
1977 **Edwin Maria Landau**
1978 **Thomas-von-Aquin-Ausgabe** translation team
1979 **Gerda und Helmut Scheffel**
1980 **Susanne Schimmel**

The Friedrich-Gundolf-Preis fur Germanistik im Ausland, or Friedrich Gundolf Prize for German Linguistics Abroad, which now carries a 10,000-mark honorarium, is given annually for outstanding achievements in German linguistics or language abroad.

1964 **Robert Minder**, Paris
1965 **Frederick Norman**, London
1966 **Victor Lange**, Princeton N.J.
1967 **Eudo C. Mason**, Edinburgh
1968 **Oskar Seidlin**, Columbus, Ohio
1969 **Eduard Goldsucker**, Prague
1970 **Erik Funding**, Aarhus
1971 **Zoran Konstantinovic**, Belgrade
1972 **Ladislao Mittner**, Venice
1973 **Gustav Korlen**, Stockholm
1974 **Herman Meyer**, Amsterdam
1975 **Elizabeth M. Wilkinson**, London
1976 **Marian Szyrocki**, Breslau
1977 **Franz H. Mautner**, Swarthmore, Pa.
1978 **Claude David**, Paris
1979 **Zenko Skreb**, Zagreb
1980 **Lew Kopelew**

Caldecott Medal

AMERICAN LIBRARY ASSOCIATION
Children's Services Div., 50 E. Huron St., Chicago, Ill. 60611 (312/944-6780)

The Caldecott Medal is given to the artist or illustrator of the most distinguished American picture book for children published in the preceding year. The artist must be a citizen or resident of the United States. While the text need not be the work of the artist, it must be worthy of the book. The medal is a reproduction of the work of the 19th-century British illustrator, Randolph Caldecott.

1938 **Dorothy Lathrop,** *Animals of the Bible.*
1939 **Thomas Handforth,** *Mei Li*
1940 **Ingri and Edgar d'Aulaire,** *Abraham Lincoln*
1941 **Robert Lawson,** *They Were Strong and Good*
1942 **Robert McCloskey** *Make Way for Ducklings*
1943 **Virginia Lee Burton,** *The Little House*
1944 **Louis Slobodkin,** *Many Moons,* by James Thurber
1945 **Elizabeth Orton Jones** *Prayer for a Child,* by Rachel Field
1946 **Maud and Miska Petersham,** *The Rooster Crows*
1947 **Leonard Weisgard,** *The Little Island,* by Golden MacDonald
1948 **Roger Duvoisin,** *White Snow, Bright Snow,* by Alvin Tresselt
1949 **Berta and Elmer Hader,** *The Big Snow*
1950 **Leo Politi,** *Song of the Swallows*
1951 **Katherine Milhous,** *The Egg Tree*
1952 **Nicolas Mordvinoff,** *Finders Keepers,* by Will Lipkind and Nicolas Mordvinoff
1953 **Lynd Ward,** *The Biggest Bear*
1954 **Ludwig Bemelmans,** *Madeline's Rescue*
1955 **Marcia Brown,** *Cinderella*
1956 **Feodor Rojankovsky,** *Frog Went A-Courtin,* by John Langstaff
1957 **Marc Simont,** *A Tree Is Nice,* by Janice May Udry
1958 **Robert McCloskey,** *Time of Wonder*
1959 **Barbara Cooney,** *Chanticleer and the Fox*
1960 **Marie Hall Ets,** *Nine Days to Christmas*
1961 **Nicolas Sidjakov,** *Baboushka and the Three Kings*
1962 **Marcia Brown,** *Once a Mouse*
1963 **Ezra Jack Keats,** *The Snowy Day*
1964 **Maurice Sendak,** *Where the Wild Things Are*
1965 **Beni Montresor,** *May I Bring a Friend?,* by Beatrice S. de Regniers
1966 **Nonny Hogrogian,** *Always Room for One More*
1967 **Evaline Ness,** *Sam, Bangs & Moonshine*
1968 **Ed Emberley,** *Drummer Hoff*

1969 **Uri Shulevitz,** *The Fool of the World and the Flying Ship,* by Arthur Ransome
1970 **William Steig,** *Sylvester and the Magic Pebble*
1971 **Gail E. Haley,** *A Story-A Story*
1972 **Nonny Hogrogian,** *One Fine Day*
1973 **Blair Lent,** *The Funny Little Woman,* retold by Arlene Mosel
1974 **Margot Zemach,** *Duffy and the Devil,* retold by Harvey Zemach
1975 **Gerald McDermott,** *Arrow to the Sun: A Pueblo Indian Tale*
1976 **Leo Dillon and Diane Dillon,** *Why Mosquitoes Buzz in People's Ears,* retold by Verna Aardema
1977 **Leo and Diane Dillon,** *Ashanti to Zulu: African Traditions,* retold by Margaret Musgrove
1978 **Peter Spier,** *Noah's Ark*
1979 **Paul Goble,** *The Girl Who Loved Wild Horses*
1980 **Barbara Cooney,** *Ox-Cart Man*

Campion Award

CATHOLIC BOOK CLUB
106 W. 56th St., New York, N.Y. 10019 (212/581-4640)

The Campion Award, which consists of a medallion, is awarded annually for long and distinguished service to Catholic letters. The club's editorial board selects the winner.

1955 **Jacques Maritain**
1956 **Helen C. White**
1957 **Paul Horgan**
1958 **James Brodrick, S.J.**
1959 **Sister Mary Madeleva**
1960 **Frank J. Sheed**
Maisie Ward
1961 **John La Farge, S.J.**
1962 **Harold C. Gardiner, S.J.**
1963 **T.S. Eliot**
1964 **Barbara Ward**
1965 **Msgr. John T. Ellis**
1966 **John Courtney Murray, S.J.**
1967 **Phyllis McGinley**
1968 **George N. Shuster**
1969 No award
1970 **G.B. Harrison**
1971 **Walter and Jean Kerr**
1972 No award
1973 No award
1974 **Karl Rahner, S.J.**
1975 No award
1976 **John Delaney**
1977 No award
1978 No award
1979 No award
1980 No award

Canada Belgium Literary Prize
Governor General's Literary Awards
Children's Literature Prizes
Translation Prize
Canada-Australia Literary Prize
Canada-Switzerland Literary Prize

CANADA COUNCIL
151 Sparks St., Box 1647, Ottawa, Ont. K1P 5V8, Canada (613/237-3400)

The Canada Belgium Literary Prize, which carries a $2,000 honorarium, is given alternately to a Canadian and a Belgian writing in the French language. The governments of the two countries administer the award, which is given for an author's complete works.

1971 **Geo Norge,** Belgian poet
1972 **Gaston Miron,** Canadian poet
1973 **Suzanne Lilar,** Belgian author
1974 **Rejean Ducharme,** Canadian novelist
1975 **Pierre Mertens,** Belgian writer
1976 **Marie-Claire Blais,** Canadian writer
1977 **Marcel Moreau,** Belgian novelist
1978 **Jacques Godbout,** Canadian writer
1979 **Hubert Juin,** Belgian writer
1980 **Not available at press time**

The Governor General's Literary Awards are $5,000 cash prizes now given annually to a maximum of six authors, three each for meritorious books in English and in French. An 18-member selection committee chooses a fiction, a non-fiction and a poetry/drama volume in each language.

1937 **Bertram Brooker,** *Think of the Earth*
T.B. Roberton, *T.B.R.—Newspaper Pieces*
1938 **Laura G. Salverson,** *The Dark Weaver*
E. J. Pratt, *The Fable of the Goats*
Stephen Leacock, *My Discovery of the West*
1939 **Gwethalyn Graham,** *Swiss Sonata*
Kenneth Leslie, *By Stubborn Stars*
John Murray Gibbon, *Canadian Mosaic*
1940 **Franklin D. McDowell,** *The Champlain Road*
Arthur S. Bourinot, *Under the Sun*
Laura G. Salverson, *Confessions of an Immigrant's Daughter*
1941 **Ringuet (pseudonym),** *Thirty Acres*
E. J. Pratt, *Brebeuf and His Brethren*
J. F. C. Wright, *Slava Bohu*
1942 **Alan Sullivan,** *Three Came to Ville Marie*
Anne Marriott, *Calling Adventurers*
Emily Carr, *Klee Wyck*
1943 **G. Herbert Sallans,** *Little Man*
Earle Birney, *David and Other Poems*
Bruce Hutchison, *The Unknown Country*
Edgar McInnis, *The Unguarded Frontier*
1944 **Thomas H. Raddall,** *The Pied Piper of Dipper Creek*
A. J. M. Smith, *News of the Phoenix*
John D. Robins, *The Incomplete Anglers*
E. K. Brown, *On Canadian Poetry*
1945 **Gwethalyn Graham,** *Earth and High Heaven*
Dorothy Livesay, *Day and Night*
Dorothy Duncan, *Partner in Three Worlds*
Edgar McInnis, *The War: Fourth Year*
1946 **Hugh MacLennan,** *Two Solitudes*
Earle Birney, *Now is Time*
Evelyn M. Richardson, *We Keep a Light*

Ross Munro, *Gauntlet to Overlord*
1947 **Winifred Bambrick,** *Continental Revue*
Robert Finch, *Poems*
Frederick Philip Grove, *In Search of Myself*
A. R. M. Lower, *Colony to Nation*
1948 **Gabrielle Roy,** *The Tin Flute*
Dorothy Livesay, *Poems for People*
William Sclater, *Haida*
R. MacGregor Dawson, *The Government of Canada*
1949 **Hugh MacLennan,** *The Precipice*
A. M. Klein, *The Rocking Chair and Other Poems*
Thomas H. Raddall, *Halifax, Warden of the North*
C. P. Stacey, *The Canadian Army, 1939-1945*
1950 **Philip Child,** *Mr. Ames Against Time*
James Reaney, *The Red Heart*
Hugh MacLennan, *Cross-country*
R. MacGregor Dawson, *Democratic Government in Canada*
R. S. Lambert, *Franklin of the Arctic*
1951 **Germaine Guevremont,** *The Outlander*
James Wreford Watson, *Of Time and the Lover*
Marjorie Wilkins Campbell, *The Saskatchewan*
W. L. Morton, *The Progressive Party in Canada*
Donalda Dickie, *The Great Adventure*
1952 **Morley Callaghan,** *The Loved and the Lost*
Charles Bruce, *The Mulgrave Road*
Josephine Phelan, *The Ardent Exile*
Frank MacKinnon, *The Government of Prince Edward Island*
John F. Hayes, *A Land Divided*
1953 **David Walker,** *The Pillar*
E. J. Pratt, *Towards the Last Spike*
Bruce Hutchison, *The Incredible Canadian*
Donald G. Creighton, *John A. Macdonald, The Young Politician*
Marie McPhedran, *Cargoes on the Great Lakes*
1954 **David Walker,** *Digby*
Douglas Le Pan, *The Net and the Sword*
N. J. Berrill, *Sex and the Nature of Things*
J. M. S. Careless, *Canada, A Story of Challenge*
John F. Hayes, *Rebels Ride at Night*
1955 **Igor Gouzenko,** *The Fall of a Titan*
P. K. Page, *The Metal and the Flower*
Hugh MacLennan, *Thirty and Three*
A. R. M. Lower, *The Most Famous Stream*
Marjorie Wilkins Campbell, *The Nor'westers*
1956 **Lionel Shapiro,** *The Sixth of June*
Wilfred Watson, *Friday's Child*
N. J. Berrill, *Man's Emerging Mind*
Donald G. Creighton, *John A. Macdonald, The Old Chieftain*
Kerry Wood, *The Map-Maker*
1957 **Adele Wiseman,** *The Sacrifice*
Robert A. D. Ford, *A Window on the North*
Pierre Berton, *The Mysterious North*
Joseph Lister Rutledge, *Century of Conflict*
Farley Mowat, *Lost in the Barrens*
1958 **Gabrielle Roy,** *Street of Riches*
Jay Macpherson, *The Boatman*
Bruce Hutchison, *Canada: Tomorrow's Giant*
Thomas H. Raddall, *The Path of Destiny*
Kerry Wood, *The Great Chief*
1959 **Colin McDougall,** *Execution*
James Reaney, *A Suit of Nettles*
Pierre Berton, *Klondike*
Joyce Hemlow, *The History of Fanny Burney*
Edith Lambert Sharp, *Nkwala*
1960 **Hugh MacLennan,** *The Watch That Ends the Night*
Irving Layton, *Red Carpet for the Sun*
Andre Giroux, *Malgre tout, la joie*
Felix Antoine Savard, *Le barachois*
1961 **Brian Moore,** *The Luck of Ginger Coffey*
Frank Underhill, *In Search of Canadian Liberalism*
Margaret Avison, *Winter Sun*
Paul Toupin, *Souvenirs pour demain*
Anne Hebert, *Poemes*
1962 **Malcolm Lowry,** *Hear Us O Lord from Heaven Thy Dwelling Place*
T. A. Goudge, *The Ascent of Life*
Robert Finch, *Acis in Oxford*
Yves Theriault, *Ashini*
Jean Le Moyne, *Convergences*
1963 **Kildare Dobbs,** *Running to Paradise*
Marshall McLuhan, *The Gutenberg Galaxy*
James Reaney, *Twelve Letters to a Small Town* and *The Killdeer and Other Plays*
Jacques Ferron, *Contes du pays incertain*
Gilles Marcotte, *Une litterature qui se fait*
Jacques Languirand, *Les insolites et les violons de l'automne*
1964 **Hugh Garner,** *Hugh Garner's Best Stories*
J. M. S. Careless, *Brown of the Globe*
Gatien Lapointe, *Ode au Saint-Laurent*
Gustave Lanctot, *Histoire du Canada*
1965 **Douglas Le Pan,** *The Deserter*
Phyllis Grosskurth, *John Addington Symonds*
Raymond Souster, *The Colour of the Times*
Jean-Paul Pinsonneault, *Les terres seches*
Rejean Robidoux, *Roger Martin du Gard et la religion*
Pierre Perrault, *Au coeur de la rose*
1966 **Alfred Purdy,** *The Cariboo Horses*
James Eayrs, *In Defence of Canada*
Gilles Vigneault, *Quand les bateaux s'en vont*
Gerard Bessette, *L'incubation*
Andre S. Vachon, *Le Temps et l'espace dans l'oeuvre de Paul Claudel*
1967 **Margaret Atwood,** *The Circle Game*
Rejean Ducharme, *L'avalee des avales*
Margaret Laurence, *A Jest of God*
Claire Martin, *La joue droite*
Marcel Trudel, *Le Comptoir, 1604-1627* (Vol. II of *Histoire de la Nouvelle France)*
George Woodcock, *The Crystal Spirit: A Study of George Orwell*
1968 **Jacques Godbout,** *Salut Galarneau*
Francoise Loranger, *Encore cinq minutes*
Eli Mandel, *An Idiot Joy*
Alden Nowlan, *Bread, Wine and Salt*
Robert-Lionel Seguin, *La Civilisation traditionnelle de l' "Habitant" aux XVIIe et XVIIIe siecles*
Norah Story, *The Oxford Companion to Canadian History and Literature*
1969 **Marie-Claire Blais,** *Manuscrits de Pauline Archange*
Fernand Dumont, *Le lieu de l'homme*
Alice Munro, *Dance of the Happy Shades*
Mordecai Richler, *Cocksure and Hunting Tigers Under Glass*
1970 **George Bowering,** *Rocky Mountain Foot* and *The Gangs of Kosmos*
Michel Brunet, *Les Canadiens apres la conquete*
Robert Kroetsch, *The Studhorse Man*
Gwendolyn MacEwen, *The Shadow-Maker*
Louise Maheux-Forcier, *Une foret pour Zoe*
Jean-Guy Pilon, *Comme eau retenue*
1971 **Monique Bosco,** *La femme de Loth*
Jacques Brault, *Quand nous serons heureux*
Dave Godfrey, *The New Ancestors*

bp Nichol, *Still Water, The True Eventual Story of Billy the Kid, Beach Head* and *The Cosmic Chef: An Evening of Concrete*
Michael Ondaatje, *The Collected Works of Billy the Kid*

1972 **Pierre Berton,** *The Last Spike*
Gerard Bessette, *Le cycle*
Gerald Fortin, *La fin d'un regne*
John Glassco, *Selected Poems*
Paul-Marie Lapointe, *Le reel absolu*
Mordecai Richler, *St. Urbain's Horseman*

1973 **Robertson Davies,** *The Manticore*
Dennis Lee, *Civil Elegies and Other Poems*
John Newlove, *Lies*
Jean Hamelin and Yves Roby, *Histoire economique du Quebec 1851-1896*
Gilles Henault, *Signaux pour les voyants*
Antoinine Maillet, *Don l'Orignal*

1974 **Ralph Gustafson,** *Fire on Stone*
Margaret Laurence, *The Diviners*
Charles Ritchie, *The Siren Years*
Victor-Levy Beaulieu, *Don Quichotte de la demanche*
Nicole Brossard, *Mecanique jongleuse suivi de Masculin grammaticale*
Louise Dechene, *Habitants et marchands de Montreal au XVIIe siecle*

1975 **Milton Acorn,** *The Island Means Minago*
Marion MacRae and Anthony Adamson, *Hallowed Walls*
Brian Moore, *The Great Victorian Collection*
Louis-Edmond Hamelin, *Nordicite canadienne*
Anne Hebert, *Les enfants du sabbat*
Pierre Perrault, *Chouennes*

1976 **Carl Berger,** *The Writing of Canadian History*
Marian Engel, *Bear*
Joe Rosenblatt, *Top Soil*
Andre Major, *Les rescapes*
Fernand Ouelett, *Les Bas Canada 1791-1840*
Alphonse Piche, *Poemes 1946-1968*

1977 **Timothy Findley,** *The Wars*
Gabrielle Roy, *Ces Enfants de Ma Vie*
Frank Scott, *Essays on the Constitution*
Denis Moniere, *Le Development des Ideologies au Quebec des Origines a Nos Jours*
O. G. Jones, *Under the Thunder, The Flowers Light Up the Earth*
Michel Garneau, *Les Celebrations (Adidou Adidouce)*

1978 **Roger Caron**, *Go Boy*
Alice Munro, *Who Do You Think You Are?*
Patrick Lane, *Poems New and Selected*
Francois-Marc Gagnon, *Paul-Emile Bordaus*
Jacques Poulin, *Les Grandes Marees*
Gilbert Langevin, *Mon refuge est un volcan*

1979 **Jacques Hodgins**, *The Resurrection of Joseph Bourne*
Marie-Claire Blaise, *Le sourd dans la ville*
Maria Tippett, *Emily Carr: A Biography*
Sheila McLeod Arnopolous, *Le fait anglais au Quebec*
Michael Ondaatje, *There's a Trick with a Knife I'm Learning to Do*
Robert Melancon, *Peinture aveugle*

1980 **Not available at press time**

The $5,000 Children's Literature Prizes are given annually to two Canadian writers, one who writes in English and one in French, for books for young people, whether or not these works were published in Canada. The Children's Literature Prize is occasionally shared by a writer and an illustrator of French or English Books.

1975 **Bill Freeman,** *Shantyman of Cache Lake*
Louise Aylwin, *Raminagradu*

1976 **Myra Paperny,** *The Wooden People*
Bernadette Renaud, *Emilie, la baignoire a pattes*

1977 **Jean Little,** *Listen for the Singing*
Denise Houle, *Lune de neige*
Claude La Fortune, *L'evangile en papier*

1978 **Kevin Major**, *Hold Fast*
Ann Blade (illustrator), *A Salmon for Simon*
Ginette Anfousse, *La varicelle* and *La chicane*

1979 **Barbara Classen Smucker**, *Days of Terror*
Laszlo Gal (illustrator), *The Twelve Dancing Princesses*
Gabrielle Roy, *Courte-Queue*
Roger Pare (illustrator), *Une fenetre dans ma tete*

1980 **Not available at press time**

The Translation Prize, which carries a $5,000 honorarium, is awarded annually for the best translation of a Canadian book. Now, one prize is given a year, alternately for an English-to-French and a French-to-English translation. Initially, two $2,500 prizes were given each year, one in each translation category. Textbooks and manuals are not considered for this award.

1974 **Sheila Fischman,** English translation of *Le deux-millieme etage* by Roch Carrier and *Le Loup* by Marie-Claire Blais under the titles *They Won't Demolish Me* and *The Wolf*
Michelle Tisseyre, French translation of *Such is My Beloved* and *Winter* by Morley Callaghan and *Seasons of the Eskimo* by Fred Bremmer under the titles *Telle est ma belle-aimee, L'hiver* and *L'Eskimo*

1975 **John Glassco,** English translation of the collected works of Saint-Denys Garneau under the title *Complete Poems of Saint-Denys Garneau*
Jean Simard, French translation of *Son of a Smaller Hero* by Mordecai Richler under the title *Mon pere, ce heros*

1976 **Joyce Marshall,** English translation of *Cet ete qui chantait* by Gabrielle Roy under the title *Enchanted Summer*

1977 **Frank Scott,** English translation of *Poems of French Canada* by Jean Pare, French translation of *L'homme de weekend (The Weekend Man)*

1978 **Michael Bullock**, English translation of *Contes pour buveurs attardes* by Michel Tremblay under the title *Stories for Late Night Drinkers*
Gilles Henault, French translation of *Without a Parachute* by David Fennario under the title *Sans parachute*

1979 **Allan Van Meer**, English translations of *La Celeste Greta* by Reynald Tremblay, *Une job* by Claude Roussin and *Encore un peu* by by Serge Mercier under the titles *Greta the Devine, Looking for a Job* and *A Little Bit Left*, all appearing in Vol. 5 of *A Collection of Canadian Plays*
Collette Tonge, French translation of *Dance of the Happy Shades* by Alice Munro under the title *La danse des ombres*

1980 **Not available at press time**

The annual $2,500 Canada-Australia Literary Prize alternately honors a Canadian and an Australian author writing in the English language. Each year an author from one country is chosen by a panel of judges from the other country on the basis of the writer's complete works.

1976 **John Romeril**, Australian playwright
1977 **Alice Munro**, Canadian author
1978 **Thomas Shapcott**, Australian poet
1979 **Michael Ondaatje**, Canadian poet
1980 **Not available at press time**

The $2,500 Canada-Switzerland Literary Prize honors alternately a Canadian or Swiss writer for a work published in French during the preceding eight years.

1980 **Alice Rivaz**, Swiss author, *Jette ton pain*

Canadian Young Adult Book Award

SASKATCHEWAN LIBRARY ASSOCIATION
c/o Saskatoon Public Library, 311 23rd St. E., Saskatoon, Sask. S7K 0J6, Canada

The Canadian Young Adult Book Award annually honors an English-language book for readers aged 13 to 18. Novels, plays and collections of poetry written by Canadian citizens or landed immigrants are eligible for consideration by a panel of judges.

1980 **Kevin Major**, *Far from Shore*

Carey-Thomas Award

PUBLISHERS' WEEKLY
1180 Ave. of the Americas, New York, N.Y. 10036
(212/764-5161)

The Carey-Thomas Award honors creative book publishing in its various aspects—editorial judgment, initiative, imagination, manufacture, promotion and marketing. The magazine's review staff makes nominations for selection by a three- to five-member jury of authors, critics, librarians and booksellers. The winner, usually a publishing company, receives a bronze plaque.

1942 **Farrar & Rinehart,** *Rivers of America* series
1943 **University of Chicago Press,** *A Dictionary of American English on Historical Principles*
1944 **E. P. Dutton & Co., Inc.,** *The World of Washington Irving,* by Van Wyck Brooks
1945 **Alfred A. Knopf, Inc.** *The American Language,* by H. L. Mencken
1946 **Duell, Sloan & Pearce, Inc.,** *The New World,* by Stefan Lorant
1947 **Oxford University Press,** *A Study of History,* by Arnold Toynbee
1948 **William Sloane Associates,** American Men of *Letters* series
1949 **Rand McNally & Co.,** *Cosmopolitan World Atlas*
1950 **Princeton University Press,** *The Papers of Thomas Jefferson,* edited by J. P. Boyd and others
1951 **Houghton Mifflin Co.,** *Life in America,* by Marshall B. Davidson
1952 **The Macmillan Co.,** *The Diary of George Templeton Strong, 1835-1875,* edited by Allan Nevins and Milton H. Thomas
1953 **Houghton Mifflin Co.,** *The Second World War,* by Sir Winston Churchill
1954 **Doubleday & Co.,** Anchor Books series
1955 **Belknap Press of Harvard University Press,** *The Poems of Emily Dickinson,* edited by T. H. Johnson
1956 **Doubleday & Co.,** Mainstream of America series
1957 **Frederick A. Praeger, Inc.,** *The New Class,* by Milovan Djilas
1958 **New York Graphic Society,** *Complete Letters,* by Vincent Van Gogh
1959 **Oxford University Press,** *James Joyce,* by Richard Ellmann
1960 **Simon & Schuster,** *The Rise and Fall of the Third Reich,* by William L. Shirer
1961 **Belknap Press of Harvard University Press,** *The Adams Papers: Diary and Autobiography of John Adams*
1962 **Shorewood Publishers,** *Great Drawings of All Time*
1963 **Wesleyan University Press,** *New York Landmarks,* edited by Alan Burnham
1964 **Sierra Club,** Sierra Club Exhibit Format series, edited by David Brower
1965 **Doubleday & Co.,** Anchor Bibles, edited by William Foxwell Albright and David Noel Freedman
1966 **George Braziller, Inc.,** *The Hours of Catherine of Cleves,* introduction by John Plummer
1967 **Holt, Rinehart & Winston,** *Wilderness Kingdom: The Journals and Paintings of Father Nicolas Point,* translated by Joseph P. Donnelly, S.J.
1968 **W. W. Norton & Co.,** *The Norton Facsimile: The First Folio of Shakespeare,* prepared by Charlton Hinman
1969 **Alfred A. Knopf, Inc.,** *Huey Long,* by T. Harry Williams
1970 **Random House with Maecenas Press and Chanticleer Press,** *Picasso 347*
1971 **Oxford University Press,** *The Compact Edition of the Oxford English Dictionary: Complete Text Micrographically Reproduced*
1972 **Yale University Press,** *The Children of Pride: A True Story of Georgia and the Civil War*
1973 **Princeton University Press,** The Bollingen Series
1974 **McGraw-Hill Book Company,** *Madrid Codices of Leonardo da Vinci* and *The Unknown Leonardo,* edited by Ladislao Reti
1975 **Pierpont Morgan Library of New York in association with David R. Godine,** *Early Children's Books and Their Illustration*
1976 **Basic Books,** *Berggasse 19,* by Edmund Engelman
1977 **Horizon Press,** *An Autobiography,* by Frank Lloyd Wright
1978 **Pushcart Press,** *Pushcart Prize, III: Best of the Small Presses,* edited by Bill Henderson
1979 **George Braziller**, exceptional publishing program
1980 **Not available at press time**

Carnegie Medal

THE LIBRARY ASSOCIATION
Ridgmount St., London WC1E 7AE, U.K. (01-636 7543)

The Carnegie Medal is awarded annually for an outstanding children's book published in the United Kingdom during the previous year. A committee selects the winner.

1936 **Arthur Ransome**, *Pigeon Poet*
1937 **Eve Garnett**, *The Family from One End Street*
1938 **Noel Steatfield**, *The Circus is Coming*
1939 **Eleanor Doorly**, *Radium Woman*
1940 **Kitty Barne**, *Visitors from London*
1941 **M. Treadgold**, *We Couldn't Leave Dinah*
1942 **D.J. Watkins-Pitchford**, *The Little Grey Men*
1943 **No award**
1944 **Eric Linklater**, *The Wind on the Moon*
1945 **No award**

1946 **Elizabeth Goudge**, *The Little White Horse*
1947 **Walter de la Mare**, *Collected Stories for Children 2*
1948 **R. Armstrong**, *Sea Change*
1949 **Agnes Allen**, *The Story of Your Home*
1950 **Elfrida Vipont Foulds**, *The Lark on the Wing*
1951 **Cynthia Harnett**, *The Woolpack*
1952 **Mary Norton**, *The Borrowers*
1953 **Edward Osmond**, *A Valley Grows Up*
1954 **Ronald Welch**, *Knight Crusader*
1955 **Eleanor Farjeon**, *The Little Bookroom*
1956 **C.S. Lewis**, *The Last Battle*
1957 **W. Mayne**, *A Grass Rope*
1958 **Ann Philippa Pearce**, *Tom's Midnight Garden*
1959 **Rosemary Sutcliff**, *The Lantern Bearers*
1960 **L.W. Cornwall**, *The Making of Man*
1961 **Lucy M. Boston**, *A Stranger at Green Knowe*
1962 **Pauline Clarke**, *The Twelve and the Genii*
1963 **Hester Burton**, *Time of Trial*
1964 **Sheena Porter**, *Nordy Bank*
1965 **Philip Turner**, *The Grange at High Force*
1966 **No award**
1967 **Alan Garner**, *The Owl Service*
1968 **Rosemary Harris**, *The Moon in the Cloud*
1969 **Kathleen Peyton**, *The Edge of the Cloud*
1970 **Leon Garfield** and **Edward Blishen**, *The God Beneath the Sea*
1971 **Ivan Southall**, *Josh*
1972 **Richard Adams**, *Watership Down*
1973 **Penelope Lively**, *The Ghost of Thomas Kempe*
1974 **Mollie Hunter**, *The Stronghold*
1975 **Robert Westall**, *The Machine Gunners*
1976 **Jan Mark**, *Thunder and Lightnings*
1977 **Gene Kemp**, *The Turbulent Term of Tyke Tiler*
1978 **David Rees**, *The Exeter Blitz*
1979 **Peter Dickinson**, *Tulku*
1980 **Not available at press time**

Children's Science Book Award

NEW YORK ACADEMY OF SCIENCES
2 E. 63rd St., New York, N.Y. 10021 (212/838-0230)

The academy anually honors meritorious books on science for young people. In addition to the first-place winners listed here, honorable mentions are made.

1971 **Robert Richardson**, *The Stars and Serendipity*

YOUNGER CATEGORY

1972 **Edward Gallob**, *City Leaves, City Trees*
1973 **Berniece Freschet**, *The Web in the Grass*
1974 **Roger Duvoisin**, *See What I Am*
1975 **Jean-Claude Deguine**, *Emperor Penguin*
1976 **Aliki**, *Corn is Maize*
1977 **Irene Brady**, *Wild Mouse*
1978 **Lucia Anderson** (author) and **Leigh Grant** (illus.), *The Smallest Life Around Us*
1979 **Karla Kuskin** (author) and **Marc Simont** (illus.), *A Space Story*
1980 **Vikki Cobb** and **Kathy Darling** (authors) and **Martha Weston** (illus.), *Bet You Can't!*

OLDER CATEGORY

1972 **Leonard Cortrell**, *Reading the Past*
1973 **Dorcas MacClintock** and **Ugo Mochi**, *A Natural History of Giraffes*
1974 **Ruth Kirk** and **Richard Daugherty**, *Hunters of the Whale*
1975 **Bruce Buchenholz**, *Doctor in the Zoo*
1976 **Bettyann Kevles**, *Watching the Wild Apes*
1977 **Elizabeth Burton Brown**, *Grains*
1978 **Herman Schneider** (author) and **Radu Vero** (illus.), *Laser Light*
1979 **Mario Salvadori** (author) and **Saralinda Hooker** and **Christopher Ragus** (illus.), *Building*
1980 **Jan Adkins**, *Moving Heavy Things*

Carr P. Collins Award

TEXAS INSTITUTE OF LETTERS
Box 3143, Dallas, Tex. 75275 (214/692-2000)

The Carr P. Collins Award, which carries a $1,000 honorarium, is given to honor a non-fiction book by a Texas author or on a Texas subject that, in the judges' opinion, is the most outstanding of the previous year.

1946 **Green Peyton,** *San Antonio in the Sun*
1947 **John A. Lomax,** *Adventures of a Ballad Hunter*
1948 **Herbert Gambrell,** *Anson Jones: The Last President of Texas*
1949 **Tom Lea,** *The Brave Bulls*
1950 **Roy Bedichek,** *Karankaway Country*
1951 **Joe B. Frantz,** *Gail Borden, Dairyman to a Nation*
1952 **J. Frank Dobie,** *The Mustangs*
1953 **Walter Prescott Webb,** *The Great Frontier*
1954 **Paul Horgan,** *Great River: The Rio Grande in American History*
1955 **John S. Spratt,** *The Road to Spindletop*
1956 **Roy Bedichek,** *Educational Competition: The Story of the University Interscholastic League*
1957 **Frank Vandiver,** *Mighty Stonewall*
1958 **Lon Tinkle,** *Thirteen Days to Glory*
1959 **Lewis Hanke,** *Aristotle and the American Indian*
1960 **John Graves,** *Goodbye to a River*
1961 **Frances S. Mossiker,** *The Queen's Necklace*
1962 **Rebecca Smith Lee,** *Mary Austin Holley*
1963 **Ellen Maury Slayden,** *Washington Wife*
1964 **Frances S. Mossiker,** *Napoleon and Josephine*
1965 **Henry D. and Frances T. McCallum,** *The Wire that Fenced the West*
1966 **William A. Owens,** *This Stubborn Soil*
1967 **Willie Morris,** *North Toward Home*
1968 **Tom Lea,** *A Picture Gallery*
1969 **C. C. White and Ada Morehead Holland,** *No Quittin' Sense*
1970 **Gene Schulze,** *The Third Face of War*
1971 **Charles W. Ferguson,** *Organizing to Beat the Devil: Methodists and the Making of America*
1972 **Joseph C. Goulden,** *The Superlawyers*
1973 **Lewis L. Gould,** *Progressives and Prohibitionists, Texas Democrats in the Wilson Era*
1974 **John Graves,** *Hard Scrabble*
1975 **Paul Horgan,** *Lamy of Santa Fe*
1976 **Thomas Thompson,** *Blood and Money*
1977 **William Humphrey,** *Farther off from Heaven*
1978 **J. Lon Tinkle,** *An American Original: The Life of J. Frank Dobie*
1979 **No award**
1980 **No award**

Companion of Literature

ROYAL SOCIETY OF LITERATURE
1 Hyde Park Gardens, London W2, United Kingdom (Tel. 01-723-5104)

The highest honor of the Royal Society of Literature is an invitation to become a Companion of Literature. This honor, which was initiated in 1961, is limited to 10 individuals at a time. The first seven names listed here were members in 1977, while the last three were invited to accept this honor in 1977.

Sir John Betjeman
Dame Rebecca West
Lord David Cecil
Angus Wilson
Lord Kenneth Clark
Arthur Koestler
Ruth Pittner
Philip Larkin
Stephen Spender
David Garnett

CIBC Award for Unpublished Writers

COUNCIL ON INTERRACIAL BOOKS FOR CHILDREN
1841 Broadway, New York, N.Y. 10023 (212/757-5339)

The Annual CIBC Award for Unpublished Writers is given to a U.S. writer from a racial minority whose manuscript best challenges stereotypes, supplies role models and/or portrays some distinctive aspect of their culture, as well as displays literary merit. The award has been suspended. Prize-winners in each of five ethnic categories received $500 each, and most of the winning manuscripts have ultimately been published.

BLACK

1969* **Walter D. Myers,** *Where Does the Day Go*
Kristin Hunter, *Soul Brothers and Sister Lou*
1970* **Virginia Cox,** *ABC: Story of the Alphabet*
Sharon Bell Mathis, *Sidewalk Story*
Margot S. Webb, *Letters from Uncle David: Underground Hero*
1971 **Ray Anthony Shepard,** *Sneakers*
1972 **Florenz Webb Marshall,** *The Rock Cried Out*
1973 **Mildred D. Taylor,** *Song of the Trees*
1974 **Aishah Abdullah,** *Midnight Simba Mweusi*
1975 **Emily R. Moore,** *Letters to a Friend on a Brown Paper Bag*

(* In the first years of the award, the only ethnic category was black, but winners were selected for books for different age groups.)

NATIVE AMERICAN

1971 **Virginia Driving and Hawk Sneve,** *Jimmy Yellowhawk*
1972 **No award**
1973 **Nanabah Chee Dodge,** *Morning Arrow*
Michele P. Robinson, *Grandfather's Bridge*

CHICANO

1971 **Juan Valenzuela,** *I Am Magic*
1972 **No award**
1973 **No award**
1974 **Abelardo Delgado,** *My Father Hijacked a Plane*

ASIAN-AMERICAN

1972 **Minfong Ho,** *Sing to the Dawn*
1973 **Dorothy Tomiye Okamoto,** *Eyak*

PUERTO RICAN

1972 **Theodor Languer-Franceschi,** *The Unusual Puerto Rican*
Cruz Martel, *Yagua Days* (Special Award)
1973 **Jack Agueros,** *El Pito de Plata de Pito*
1974 **Antonia Hernandez,** *Yari*
1975 **No award**
1976 **Lydia Milagros Gonzalez,** *El Mundo Maravilloso de Macu*

Bross Award

BROSS FOUNDATION
Lake Forest College, North Hall, Lake Forest, Ill. 60045 (312/234-3100)

The Foundation's $7,500 Bross Award, formerly known as the Decennial Prize, is now given every 10 years for a published book or a manuscript on a subject in the humanities, social sciences or any other branch of study as it relates to Christianity as interpreted by the Presbyterian Church or other American evangelical church. A committee of judges selected by the college chooses the winner.

1880 **Mark Hopkins,** *The Evidence of Christianity*
1903 **Marcus Dodds,** *The Bible, Its Origins and Nature*
1906 **Rev. James Orr,** *The Problem of the Old Testament*
1907 **J. Arthur Thomson,** *The Bible of Nature*
1908 **Frederick Bliss,** *Religions of Modern Syria and Palestine*
1911 **Josiah Royce,** *The Sources of Religious Insight*
1915 **Rev. Thomas J. Thoburn,** *The Mystical Interpretation of the Gospel*
Rev. John Neville Figgis, *The Will to Freedom*
1916 **Henry Wilkes Wright,** *Faith Justified by Progress*
1920 (Seveal authors; names unknown), *Christianity and Problems of Today*
1921 **Rev. John P. Peters,** *Bible and Spade*
1940 **Harris Franklin Rall,** *Christianity: An Inquiry Into Its Nature*
1950 **Amos Wilder,** *Modern Poetry and the Christian Traditions*
1960 **John A. Hutchinson,** *Language and Faith: An Essay in Sign, Symbol and Meaning*
1970 **Claude Welch,** *Protestant Thought in the Nineteenth Century,* Vol. I
1980 **James C. Livingston,** *Beyond the Burning Pain: A Study of Matthew Arnold's Religious Belief and Criticism*

Thomas Dehler Preis

BUNDESMINISTERIUM FUR INNERDEUTSCHE BEZIEHUNGEN
Godesberger Allee 140, 5300 Bonn 2, Federal Republic of Germany (02283061)

The 20,000-mark Thomas Dehler Prize is given by the Ministry for Intra-German Relations for a literary work on the division of Germany and its effect on the conditions of people in both German states. A jury selects the winner of this prize, which is now given no more often than every three years.

1968 **Ernst Richert**
Jochen Ziem
1969 **Alfred Kantorowicz**
1970 **Horst Kruger**
1973 **Joachim Fest**
1977 **Peter Weiss**

Emerson-Thoreau Medal

AMERICAN ACADEMY OF ARTS AND SCIENCES
Norton's Woods, 136 Irving St., Cambridge, Mass. 02138 (617/492-8800)

The Emerson-Thoreau Medal, which carries a $1,000 honorarium, recognizes distinguished achievement in literature and honors the overall body of an author's or poet's work. An academy committee selects the winner.

1959 **Robert Frost**
1960 **T. S. Eliot**
1961 **Henry Beston**
1962 **Samuel Eliot Morison**
1963 **Katherine Anne Porter**
1964 **Mark Van Doren**
1965 **Lewis Mumford**
1966 **Edmund Wilson**
1967 **Joseph Wood Krutch**
1968 **John Crowe Ransom**
1969 **Hannah Arendt**
1970 **Ivor Armstrong Richards**
1975 **Robert Penn Warren**
1977 **Saul Bellow**
1979 **James T. Farrell**

E-SU Book Award

ENGLISH-SPEAKING UNION
16 E. 69th St., New York, N.Y. 10021 (212/879-6800)

The English-Speaking Union Book Award, administered in conjuction with *Books Abroad*, is given annually to the author of a book published in English although his or her native language is not English. The award carries a $2,000 honorarium.

1973 **Kamala Markandaya,** *Two Virgins*
1974 **R.K. Narayan,** *My Days*
1975 **No award**
1976 **No award**
1977 **T. Obinkram Echewa,** *The Land's Lord*
1978 **No award**
1979 **No award**
1980 **Nuruddin Farah,** *Sweet and Sour Milk*

Esso Prize

LE CERCLE DU LIVRE DE FRANCE
8955 Blvd. Saint-Laurent, Montreal 435, Quebec, Canada (514/384-4131)

The Esso Prize is a $5,000 award given annually for an outstanding French-Canadian novel. Through 1975, the award was known as the Prix du Cercle du Livre de France (French Book Guild Prize) and carried a $1,000 honorarium. A jury of critics and authors from France and Canada selects the winner.

1949 **Francoise Loranger,** *Mathieu*
1950 **Bertrand Vac,** *Louise Genest*
1951 **Andre Langevin,** *Evade de la Nuit*
1952 **Bertrand Vac,** *Deux Portes, Une Adresse*
1953 **Andre Langevin,** *Poussiere sur la Ville (Dust over the City)*
1954 **Jean Vaillancourt,** *Les Canadiens Errants*
1955 **Jean Filiatrault,** *Chaines*
1956 **Eugene Cloutier,** *Les Inutiles*
Jean Simard, *Mon Fils Poutant Heureux*
Maurice Gagnon, *L'Echeance*
1957 **J. Marie Poirier,** *Le Prix du Souvenir*
1958 **Claire Martin,** *Avec ou sans Amour*
1959 **Pierre Gelinas,** *Les Vivants, les Morts et les Autres*
1960 **Claude Jasmin,** *La Corde au Cou*
1961 **Diane Giguere,** *Le Temps des Jeux*
1962 **No award**
1963 **Louise Maheux-Forcier,** *Amadou*
1964 **Georges Cartier,** *Le Poisson Peche*
1965 **Bertrand Vac,** *Histoires Galantes*
1966 **Andre Berthiaume,** *La Fugue*
1967 **Anne Bernard,** *Cancer*
1968 **Yvette Naubert,** *L'Ete de la Cigale*
1969 **Jovette Bernier,** *Non Monsieur*
1970 **No award**
1971 **Lise Parent,** *Les Iles Flottantes*
1972 **No award**
1973 **Huguette Legare,** *La Conversation entre Hommes*
1974 **Jean-Pierre Guay,** *Mise en Liberte*
1975 **Pierre Stewart,** *L'Amour d'Une Autre*
1976 **No award**
1977 **Simone Piuze,** *Les Cercles Concentriques*
1978 **Negovan Ragic,** *Les Hommes taupes*
1979 **Normand Rousseau,** *Les Jardins Secrets*
1980 **Francois Tessier,** *Le Salon Vert*

Christopher Ewart-Biggs Memorial Prize

NATIONAL BOOK LEAGUE
Book House, 45 East Hill, London SW18 2QZ, United Kingdom

The £1,300 Christopher Ewart-Biggs Memorial Prize is given annually to the author of a book which strengthens the links between the people of Ireland and Britain, promotes peace and understanding in Ireland and fosters closer cooperation between partners of the European community. An international panel of judges selects the winners.

1978 **Dervla Murphy,** *A Place Apart*
1979 **Stewart Parker,** *I'm a Dreamer, Montreal*
1980 **Not available at press time**

Geoffrey Faber Memorial Prize

FABER AND FABER LTD.
3 Queen Sq., London WCI N-3AU, United Kingdom (Tel: 01-278-6881)

The Geoffrey Faber Memorial Prize, which is now £500, is given yearly, alternately for fiction and poetry, to an author 40 years of age or under who is a citizen of the United Kingdom, any Commonwealth country, a British colony, Eire or the Republic of South Africa. Editors of publications which regularly run literary reviews select a three-judge panel, which chooses the winner.

1964 **Christopher Middleton,** *Torse Three*
George Macbeth, *The Broken Places*
1965 **Frank Tuohy,** *The Ice Saints*
1966 **Jon Silkin,** *Nature with Man*
1967 **William McIlvanney,** *Remedy is None*
John Noone, *The Man with the Chocolate Egg*
1968 **Seamus Heaney,** *Death of a Naturalist*
1969 **Piers Paul Read,** *The Junkers*
1970 **Geoffrey Hill,** *King Log*
1971 **J. G. Farrell,** *Troubles*
1972 **Tony Harrison,** *The Loiners*
1973 **David Storey,** *Pasmore*
1974 **John Fuller,** *Cannibals and Missionaries: Epistles to Several Persons*
1975 **Richard Wright,** *The Middle of a Life*
1976 **Douglas Dunn,** *Love or Nothing*
1977 **Carolyn Slaughter,** *The Story of the Weasel*
1978 **David Harsent,** *Dreams for the Dead*
Kit Wright, *The Bear Looked Over the Mountain*
1979 **Timothy Mo,** *The Monkey King*
1980 **George Sziertes,** *The Slant Door*
Hugo Williams, *Love Life*

E. M. Forster Award

AMERICAN ACADEMY AND INSTITUTE OF ARTS AND LETTERS
633 W. 155th St. New York, N.Y. 10032 (212/368-5900)

The E.M. Forster Award, based on a bequest of the American rights and royalties of the author's posthumous novel *Maurice,* is given as merited to a young English writer for a stay in the United States.

1972 **Frank Tuohy**
1973 **Margaret Drabble**
1974 **Paul Bailey**
1975 **Seamus Heaney**
1976 **Jon Stallworthy**
1977 **David Cook**
1978 **No award**
1979 **Bruce Chatwin**
1980 **No award**

International Publishers' Prize

FRANKFURT BOOK FAIR
Frankfurt, Federal Republic of Germany

The International Publishers' Prize, which carries an honorarium of about $5,000, is awarded annually for serious modern literature, often of a controversial political nature. The honor was instituted by a group of publishers from seven countries whose lists reflect interests in that type of literature. All members of this publishers' group plan publication of the winning author's work.

1977 **Erich Fried,** German poet

Current Status Unknown

A second award is also made, resulting in planned publication of the author's work by the seven publishers in the group.

1977 **Breyten Breytenbach,** South African poet

Current Status Unknown

Friends of American Writers Awards

FRIENDS OF AMERICAN WRITERS
c/o Mrs. William D. Wiener, 2650 Lakeview Ave., Chicago, Ill. 60614 (312/871-5143)

The Friends of American Writers Awards were established to encourage authors in the north-central and south-central states, either natives or current residents, or those who have written about the Midwestern region the previous calendar year. A $1,000 cash prize is given to the winner of adult book honors. In addition to the first-place award indicated here, a $300 runner-up prize is given. A 17-member committee evaluates books considered for the award and chooses the winner.

1938 **William Maxwell,** *They Came Like Swallows*
1939 **Herbert Krause,** *Wind without Rain*
1940 **Elgin Groseclose,** *Ararat*
1941 **Marcus Goodrich,** *Delilah*
1942 **Paul Engle,** *West of Midnight*
1943 **Kenneth S. Davis,** *In the Forests of the Night*
1944 **Paul Hughes,** *Retreat from Rostov*
1945 **Warren Beck,** *Final Score*
1946 **Dorothy Langley,** *Dark Medallion*
1947 **Walter Havighurst,** *Land of Promise*
1948 **A. B. Guthrie, Jr.,** *The Big Sky*
1949 **Michael De Capite,** *The Bennett Place*
1950 **Edward Nicholas,** *The Hours and the Ages*
1951 **Leon Statham,** *Welcome Darkness*
1952 **Vern Sneider,** *The Teahouse of the August Moon*
1953 **Leonard Dubkin,** *The White Lady*
1954 **Alma Routsong,** *A Gradual Joy*
1955 **Harriette Arnow,** *The Dollmaker*
1956 **Carol Brink,** *The Headland*
1957 **Thomas and Marva Belden,** *So Fell the Angels*
1958 **William F. Steuber, Jr.,** *The Landlooker*
1959 **Paul Darcy Boles,** *Parton's Island*
1960 **Otis Carney,** *Yesterday's Hero*
1961 **James McCague,** *Fiddle Hill*
1962 **A. E. Johnson (Annabel and Edgar Johnson),** *The Secret Gift*
1963 **Lois Phillips Hudson,** *The Bones of Plenty*
1964 **Harry Mark Petrakis,** *The Odyssey of Kostas Volakis*
1965 **William H. A. Carr,** *The Duponts of Delaware*
1966 **Jamie Lee Cooper,** *Shadow of a Star*
1967 **Frederick J. Lipp,** *Rulers of Darkness*
1968 **Allan W. Eckert,** *Wild Season* and *The Frontiersman*
1969 **Ellis K. Meacham,** *The East Indiaman*
1970 **Richard Marius,** *The Coming of Rain*
1971 **Edward Robb Ellis,** *A Nation in Torment*
1972 **Keyes Beech,** *Not Without the Americans*
1973 **Thomas Rogers,** *The Confession of a Child of the Century* by Samuel Heather
1974 **Robert Boston,** *A Thorn for the Flesh*
1975 **Wendell Berry,** *A Memory of Old Jack*
1976 **Margot Peters,** *Unquiet Soul*
1977 **William Brashler,** *City Dogs*
1978 **Jon Hassler,** *Staggerford*
1979 **Bette Howland,** *Blue in Chicago*
1980 **Nancy Price,** *An Accomplished Woman*

A $150-$250 honorarium is given to the author of a meritorious children's book based on the same criteria.

1960 **Clifford B. Hicks,** *First Boy on the Moon*
1961 **Dorothea J. Snow,** *Sequoyah, Young Cherokee Guide*
1962 **Mary Evans Andrews,** *Hostage to Alexander*
1963 **Nora Tully MacAlvay,** *Cathie and the Paddy Boy*
1964 **Ruth Painter Randall,** *I Jessie*
1965 **Rebecca Caudill,** *The Far-Off Land*
1966 **No award**
1967 **No award**
1968 **No award**
1969 **Charles Raymond,** *Jud*
1970 **Jean Maddern Pitrone,** *Trailblazer*
1971 **Anne E. Neimark,** *A Touch of Light*
1972 **Zibby Oneal,** *War Work*
1973 **Howard Knotts,** *The Winter Cat*
Peter Z. Cohen, *Foal Creek*
1974 **Betty Biesterveld,** *Six Days from Sunday*
1975 **Eric A. Kimmel,** *The Tartar's Sword*
1976 **Anne Snyder,** *First Step*
1977 **Robbie Branscum,** *Toby, Granny and George*
Robert V. Remini, *The Revolutionary Age of Andrew Jackson*
1978 **Audree Distal,** *The Dream Runner*
Carol Farley, *Loosen Your Ears*
1979 **Gloria Whelan,** *A Clearing in the Forest*
Jamie Gilson, *Harvey the Beer Can King*
1980 **Charlotte Towner Graeber,** *Grey Cloud*
Crystal Thrasher, *Between Dark and Daylight*

The writer-illustrator of a meritorious juvenile book is honored with a $150-$200 prize.

1979 **Carol Lerner,** *The Forest's Edge*
1980 **Brock Cole,** *The King at the Door*

Gavel Awards

AMERICAN BAR ASSOCIATION
1155 E. 60th St., Chicago, Ill. 60637 (312/974-4000)

The Gavel Awards are given annually to honor films, the media and books for their depiction of or reportage on the law and the legal profession. The Bar Association recognizes achievements which foster greater public understanding of the American legal and judicial system, disclose areas in need of improvement or correction and encourage efforts of all levels of government to update laws. Engraved gavels are given to the winners, and Certificates of Merit go to authors.

1964 **American Heritage Publishing Co.,** Series analyzing historic decisions of U.S. Supreme Court which helped shape American democracy
J.B. Lippincott Co., *The Man Who Rode the Tiger,* biography of Samuel Seabury, recounting his dedication and influence as a lawyer, judge and exposer of municipal corruption, by Herbert Mitgang
1965 **McGraw-Hill Co.,** *Justice on Trial,* history of the U.S. Senate fight in 1916 leading to the confirmation of Supreme Court Justice Louis D. Brandeis, by A.L. Todd
1966 **No award**
1967 **No award**
1968 **No award**
1969 **No award**
1970 **No award**
1971 **Macmillan Co.,** *The Self-Inflicted Wound,* which examines the due process and human rights revolution of the previous decade as a result of the Supreme Court's landmark cases
1972 **University of Michigan Press,** *The Assault on Privacy: Computers, Data Banks and Dossiers*
1973 **No award**
1974 **David McKay Co.,** *In His Own Image: The Supreme Court in Richard Nixon's America,* tracing the Court's philosophical transition under Chief Justice Warren Burger, by James F. Simon
1975 **Charles Scribner's Sons,** *The Appearance of Justice* on past judicial ethics, by John P. MacKenzie
1976 **Yale University Press,** *The Morality of Consent* outlining how democracy can survive, by Alexander M. Bickel
1977 **Oxford University Press,** *The Role of the Supreme Court in American Government,* by Archibald Cox
1978 **Harvard University Press,** *Government by Judiciary: The Transformation of the Fourteenth Amendment,* by **Raoul Berger**
1979 **Oxford University Press,** *In the Matter of Color: Race & The American Legal Process, The Colonial Period,* by **A. Leon Higginbotham**
1980 **Russel Sage Foundation,** *The Process Is the Punishment: Handling Cases in a Lower Criminal Court,* by **Malcolm M. Feeley**

Prix Goncourt

ACADEMIE GONCOURT
2 rue Mabillon, Paris 6, France

The Goncourt Prize is awarded annually, generally to a younger author, for a novel or other work of prose published during the previous year. It is given to encourage upcoming French writers. Although the 50-franc honorarium is not a significant sum, the prize is prestigious in France. A ten-member committee of literary experts selects the winner.

1903 **John-Antoine Nau,** *Force Ennemie*
1904 **Leon Frapie,** *La Maternelle*
1905 **Claude Farrere,** *Les Civilises*
1906 **Jerome and Jean Tharaud,** *Dingley, l'illustre ecrivain*
1907 **Emilie Moselly,** *Terres lorraines*
1908 **Francois de Miomandre,** *Ecrit sur de l'eau*
1909 **Martius and Ary Leblond,** *En France*
1910 **Louis Pergaud,** *De Goupil a Margot*
1911 **Alphonse de Chateaubriant,** *Monsieur de Lourines*
1912 **Andre Savignon,** *Filles de la pluie*
1913 **Marc Elder,** *Le Peuple de la mer*
1914 **Henri Barbusse,** *Le Feu*
1915 **Rene Benjamin,** *Gaspard*
1916 **Adrien Bertrand,** *L'Appel du sol*
1917 **Henri Malherbe,** *La Flamme au poing*
1918 **George Duhamel,** *Civilisation*
1919 **Marcel Proust,** *L'ombre des jeunes filles en fleur*
1920 **Ernest Perochon,** *Nene*
1921 **Rene Maran,** *Batouala*
1922 **Henri Beraud,** *La Marigre de l'obese*
1923 **Lucien Fabre,** *Rabevel*
1924 **Thierry Sandre,** *Le Chevrefeuilles*
1925 **Maurice Genevoix,** *Raboliot*
1926 **Henri Deberly,** *Le Supplice de Phedre*
1927 **Maurice Bedel,** *Jerome 60 ° latitude Nord*
1928 **Maurice Constantin-Weyer,** *Un homme se penche sur son passe*
1929 **Marcel Arland,** *L'Ordre*
1930 **Henri Fauconnier,** *Nalaisie*

1931 **Jean Fayard,** *Mai d'amour*
1932 **Guy Mazeline,** *Les Loups*
1933 **Andre Malraux,** *La Condition*
1934 **Roger Vercel,** *Capitaine Conan*
1935 **Joseph Peyre,** *Sang et Lumieres*
1936 **Maxence van der Meersch,** *L'Empreinte du Dieu*
1937 **Charles Plisnier,** *Faux Passeports*
1938 **Henri Troyat,** *L'Araigne*
1939 **Philippe Heriat,** *Les Enfants gates*
1940 **Francis Ambriere,** *Les Grandes Vacances*
1941 **Henri Pourrat,** *Vent de mars*
1942 **Marc Bernard,** *Pareils a des enfants*
1943 **Marius Grout,** *Passage de l'homme*
1944 **Elsa Triolet,** *Le Premier Accrucoute*
1945 **Jean-Louis Bory,** *Mon village a l'heure*
1946 **Jean-Jacques Gautier,** *Histoire d'un fait divers*
1947 **Jean-Louis Curtis,** *Les forets de la nuit*
1948 **Maurice Druon,** *Les Grands Familles*
1949 **Robert Merle,** *Week-end a Zuydcoote*
1950 **Paul Colin,** *Les Jeux sauvages*
1951 **Julien Gracq,** *Le Rivage des Syrtes* (prize declined)
1952 **Beatrix Beck,** *Leon Morin pretre*
1953 **Pierre Gascar,** *Le Temps des morts*
1954 **Simone de Beauvoir,** *Les Mandarins*
1955 **Roger Ikor,** *Les eaux melees*
1956 **Romain Gary,** *Les racines du ciel*
1957 **Roger Vailland,** *La Loi*
1958 **Francis Walder,** *St.-Germain ou la Negociation*
1959 **Andre Schwartz-Bart,** *Le Dernier des justes*
1960 **Vintila Horia,** *Dieu est ne en exil*
1961 **Jean Cau,** *La Pitie de Dieu*
1962 **Ann Langfus,** *Les Bagages de sable*
1963 **Armand Lanoux,** *Quand la mer se retire*
1964 **Georges Conchon,** *L'Etat sauvage*
1965 **Jacques Borel,** *L'Adoration*
1966 **Edmonde Charles-Roux,** *Oublier Palerme*
1967 **Andre Pieyre de Mandiargues,** *La Marge*
1968 **Bernard Clavel,** *Les fruits de l'hiver*
1969 **Felicien Marceau,** *Craezy*
1970 **Michel Tourier,** *Le Roi des auines*
1971 **Jacques Laurent,** *Les Betises*
1972 **Jean Carriere,** *L'Epervier de Maheux*
1973 **Jacques Chessex,** *L'Ogre*
1974 **Pascal Laine,** *La Dentelliere*
1975 **Emilie Ajar,** *La Vie devant soi*
1976 **Patrick Grainville,** *Les Flamboyants*
1977 **Didier Decoin,** *John l'Enfer*
1978 **Patrick Modiano,** *Rue des boutiques obscures*
1979 **Antoinette Maillet,** *Pelagie-La-Charette*
1980 **Yves Navarre,** *Le Jardin d'Acclimatation*

New Writers Award

GREAT LAKES COLLEGES ASSOCIATION
220 Collingwood, Ste. 240, Ann Arbor, Mich. 48103
(313/761-4833)

A panel of literature and writing professors from the Association's 12 member colleges annually selects a work of fiction and a work of poetry from books solicited from publishers of each writer's first work in any one particular field. The winners receive and are committed to accept an expense-paid speaking tour of member campuses, for which they receive $100 from each college.

1970 **Elizabeth Cullinan,** *House of Gold* (novel)
1971 **David Henderson,** *De Mayor of Harlem* (poetry)
James Park Sloan, *War Games* (novel)
1972 **Colette Inez,** *The Woman Who Loved Worms* (poetry)
Theodore Weener, *The Car Thief* (novel)
1973 **Daniel Halpern,** *Traveling on Credit* (poetry)
Inge Trachtenberg, *So Slow the Dawning* (novel)
Clark Blaise, *A North American Education* (short story)
1974 **Margaret Craven,** *I Heard an Owl Call My Name* (novel)
Alice Munro, *Dance of the Happy Shades* (short story)
1975 **Elisauitta Ritchie,** *Tightening the Circle Over Eel Country* (poetry)
Hilma Wolitzer, *Ending* (novel)
1976 **Betty Adcock,** *Walking Out* (poetry)
Rosellen Brown, *The Autobiography of My Mother* (novel)
1977 **David St. John** *Hush* (poetry)
Richard Ford, *A Piece of My Heart* (novel)
1978 **Eugene Ruggles,** *The Lifeguard in the Snow* (poetry)
Jonathan Penner, *Going Blind* (novel)
1979 **Leslie Ullman,** *Natural Histories* (poetry)
Caroline Richards, *Sweet Country* (novel)
1980 **Robert Bohm,** *In the Americas* (poetry)
Eve Shelnutt, *The Love Child* (novel)

Kate Greenaway Medal

THE LIBRARY ASSOCIATION
7 Ridgmount St., London WC1E 7AE, U.K. (01-636 7543)

The Kate Greenaway Medal is awarded annually for outstanding children's book illustration in a work published in the United Kingdom during the previous year. A committee selects the winner.

1956 **Edward Ardizzone,** *Tim All Alone*
1957 **V.H. Drummond,** *Mrs. Easter and the Storks*
1958 **No award**
1959 **Stobbs,** *W. Kashtanka* and *A Bundle of Ballads*
1960 **Gerald Rose,** *Old Winkle and the Seagulls*
1961 **Anthony Maitland,** *Mrs. Cockle's Cat*
1962 **Brian Wildsmith,** *ABC*
1963 **John Burningham** *Borka: The Adventures of a Goose with No Feathers*
1964 **C. Walter Hodges,** *Shakespeare's Theatre*
1965 **Victor Ambrus,** *The Three Poor Tailors*
1966 **Raymond Briggs,** *Mother Goose Treasury*
1967 **Charles Keeping,** *Charley, Charlotte and the Golden Canary*
1968 **Pauline Baynes,** *Dictionary of Chivalry*
1969 **Helen Oxenbury,** *The Quangle Wangle's Hat* and *The Dragon of an Ordinary Family*
1970 **John Burningham,** *Mr. Gumpy's Outing*
1971 **Jan Pienkowski,** *The Kingdom Under the Sea*
1972 **Krystyna Turska,** *The Woodcutter's Duck*
1973 **Raymond Briggs,** *Father Christmas*
1974 **Pat Hutchins,** *The Wind Blew*
1975 **Victor Ambrus,** *Horses in Battle* and *Mishka*
1976 **Gaile Haley,** *The Post Office Cat*
1977 **Shirley Hughes,** *Dogger*
1978 **Janet Ahlberg,** *Each Peach Pear Plum*
1979 **Jan Pienkowski,** *The Haunted House*
1980 **Not available at press time**

Sarah Josepha Hale Award

RICHARDS FREE LIBRARY
Newport, N.H. 03773 (603/863-3430)

The recipient of the Sarah Josepha Hale Award receives a medal in recognition of distinguished work in arts and letters reflecting New England atmosphere or influence. A committee of men and women in the book world selects the winner.

1956 **Robert Frost**
1957 **John P. Marquand**
1958 **Archibald MacLeish**
Dorothy Canfield Fisher
1959 **Mary Ellen Chase**
1960 **Mark Van Doren**
1961 **Catherine Drinker Bowen**
1962 **David McCord**
1963 **John Hersey**
1964 **Ogden Nash**
1965 **Louis Untermeyer**
Raymond Holden (Special Award)
1966 **Robert Lowell**
1967 **John Kenneth Galbraith**
1968 **Richard Wilbur**
1969 **Lawrance Thompson**
1970 **Elizabeth Yates**
1971 **Norman Cousins**
1972 **May Sarton**
1973 **Henry Steele Commager**
1974 **Nancy Hale**
1975 **Edwin Way Teale**
1976 **John Ciardi**
1977 **Roger Tory Peterson**
1978-79 **James MacGregor Burns**
1980 No award

Faculty Prize
Robert Troup Paine Prize

HARVARD UNIVERSITY PRESS
79 Garden St., Cambridge, Mass. 02138 (617/495-2600)

The $2,000 Faculty Prize is awarded annually to a member of the Harvard University teaching or research staff for a book-length manuscript in a scholarly field. A committee at the University Press selects the recipient. The award has been suspended.

1956 **Harry A. Wolfson,** *Faith, Trinity, Incarnation, The Philosophy of the Church Fathers,* Vol. 1
1957 **Mark DeWolfe Howe** *Justice Holmes: The Shaping Years, 1841-1870*
1958 **Franklin L. Ford,** *Strasbourg in Transition, 1648-1789*
1959 **Merle Fainsod,** *Smolensk Under Soviet Rule*
1960 **Renato Poggioli,** *The Poets of Russia, 1890-1930*
1961 **Sydney J. Freedberg,** *Painting of the High Renaissance in Rome and Florence, 1475-1521*
1962 **Herschel Baker,** *William Hazlitt*
1963 **Walter Kaiser,** *Praisers of Folly*
Barry Dean Karl, *Executive Reorganization and Reform*
1964 **Walter Jackson Bate,** *John Keats*
1965 **Bernard Bailyn,** *Pamphlets of the American Revolution,* Vol. 1
1966 **Don K. Price,** *The Scientific Estate*
1967 **Alfred B. Harbage,** *Conceptions of Shakespeare*
1968 **Giles Constable,** *The Letters of Peter the Venerable*
1969 No award
1970 **W. K. Jordan,** *Edward VI*
Simon Kuznets, *Economic Growth of Nations*
1971 **I. Bernard Cohen,** *Introduction to Newton's Principia*
John Rawls, *A Theory of Justice*
1972 No award
1973 **George M. A. Hanfmann,** *Letters from Sardis*
1974 **Stephan Thernstrom,** *The Other Bostonians: Poverty and Progress in the American Metropolis, 1880-1970*
1975 **Paul C. Mangelsdorf,** *Corn: Its Origin, Evolution and Improvement*

The Robert Troup Paine Prize is given every four years for an outstanding unpublished work on a subject specified by the Harvard University Press during the previous four years. The award consists of $3,000 over and above the royalties derived from publication by the Press.

1962 **Heiko A. Oberman,** *The Harvest of Medieval Theology*
1966 **Raymond A. M. DeRoover,** *The Rise and Decline of the Medici Bank, 1397-1494*
Alasdair I. MacBean, *Export Instability and Economic Development*
1970 **Ralph C. Croizier,** *Traditional Medicine in Modern China*
1974 **John Rawls,** *A Theory of Justice*
1978 No award

Heinemann Awards

ROYAL SOCIETY OF LITERATURE
1 Hyde Park Gardens, London W2 2LT, United Kingdom
(01-723-5104)

The Heinemann Awards, which each carry £ 200 cash prizes, are presented annually to individuals whose literary achievements have been in the less renumerative areas, such as poetry, biography and history. A committee selects the recipients on the basis of a work they have read.

1945 **Norman Nicholson,** *Five Rivers*
1946 **D. Colston-Baynes,** *In Search of Two Characters*
Andrew Young, *Prospect of Flowers*
1947 **Bertrand Russell,** *History of Western Philosophy*
V. Sackville-West, *The Garden*
1948 **J. Stuart Collis,** *Down to Earth*
Martyn Skinner, *Letters to Malaya*
1949 **John Betjeman,** *Selected Poems*
Frances Cornford, *Travelling Home*
1950 **John Guest,** *Broken Images*
Peter Quennell, *John Ruskin*
1951 **Patrick Leigh-Fermor,** *Travellers Tree*
Mervyn Peake, *Glassblowers and Gormanghast*
1952 **Nicholas Monsarrat,** *The Cruel Sea*
G. Winthrop Young, *Mountains with a Difference*
1953 **Edwin Muir,** *Collected Poems*
Reginald Pound, *Arnold Bennett*
1954 **Ruth Pitter,** *The Ermine*
L. P. Hartley, *The Go-Between*
1955 **Robert Gittings,** *John Keats: The Living Years*
R. S. Thomas, *Song at the Years Turning*
1956 **Vincent Cronin,** *Wise Man from the West*
R. W. Ketton-Cremer, *Thomas Gray*
1957 **Harold Acton,** *The Bourbons of Naples*
James Lees-Milne, *Roman Mornings*
1958 **Peter Green,** *Sword of Pleasure*
Gavin Maxwell, *A Reed Shaken by the Wind*

1959 **Hester Chapman,** *The Last Tudor King*
John Press, *The Chequer'd Shade*
1960 **C. A. Trypanis,** *The Cocks of Hades*
Morris West, *The Devil's Advocate*
1961 **James Morris,** *World of Venice* (English title: *Venice*)
Vernon Scannel, *The Masks of Love*
1962 **Christopher Fry,** *Curtmantle*
Christopher Hibbert, *The Destruction of Lord Raglan*
1963 **Alethea Hayter,** *Mrs. Browning*
1964 **Robert Rhodes James,** *Rosebery*
Alan Moorehead, *Cooper's Creek*
1965 **Harold Owen,** *Journey from Obscurity, II, Youth*
Wilfred Thesiger, *The Marsh Arabs*
1966 **Nigel Dennis,** *Jonathan Swift*
Derek Walcott, *The Castaway*
1967 **Jean Rhys,** *Wide Sargasso Sea*
Norman MacCaig, *Surroundings*
John Bayley, *Tolstoy and the Novel*
1968 **W. Gerin,** *Charlotte Bronte*
Michael Ayrton, *The Maze Maker*
1969 **Gordon S. Haight,** *George Eliot*
Jasmine Rose Innes, *Writing in the Dust*
V. S. Pritchett, *A Cab at the Door*
1970 **Ronald Blythe,** *Akenfield: Portrait of an English Village*
Brian Fothergill, *Sir William Hamilton*
Nicolas Wollaston, *Pharaoh's Chicken*
1971 **Corelli Barnett,** *Britain and Her Army*
R. W. Southern, *Medieval Humanism*
1972 **Dorothy Carrington,** *Granite Islands: Portrait of Corsica*
Geoffrey Hill, *Mercian Hymns*
Thomas Kilroy, *The Big Chapel*
1973 **William St. Clair,** *That Greece Might Still Be Free*
Thomas Keneally, *The Chant of Jimmy Blacksmith*
1974 **Robin Lane Fox,** *Alexander the Great*
Alastair MacLean, *From the Wilderness*
Barry Unsworth, *Mooncranker's Gift*
1975 **John Wain,** *Samuel Johnson*
Robin Furneaux, *William Wilberforce*
1976 **Malcolm Bradbury,** *The History Man*
William Trevor, *Angels at the Ritz*
1977 **Philip Ziegler,** *Melbourne*
Edward Crankshaw, *The Shadow of the Winter Palace*
1978 **Robert Gittings,** *The Older Hardy*
1979 **Frank Tuohy,** *Live Bait*
1980 **Not available at press time**

Ernest Hemingway Foundation Award

P.E.N. AMERICAN CENTER
156 Fifth Ave., New York, N.Y. 10010 (212/255-1977)

The $6,000 Ernest Hemingway Foundation Award is given to the best first novel or collection of short stories in the English language by an American author. Mysteries and westerns are ineligible unless their genre is secondary to their overall literary merit; children's books are not considered.

1976 **Loyd Little,** *Parthian Shot*
1977 **Renata Adler,** *Speedboat*
1978 **Darcy O'Brien,** *A Way of Life, Like Any Other*
1979 **Reuben Bercovitch,** *Hasen*
1980 **Alan Saperstein,** *Mom Kills Kids and Self*

David Higham Prize for Fiction

NATIONAL BOOK LEAGUE
Book House, 45 East Hill, London SW18 2QZ, United Kingdom (Tel: 01 870 9055)

The David Higham Prize for Fiction is given annually to a resident of Great Britain, the Commonwealth or Eire for a first novel or first book of short stories published in the year of presentation. A three-judge panel selects the recipient of the £500 award.

1975 **Jane Gardam,** *Black Faces, White Faces*
Matthew Vaughan, *Chalky*
1976 **Caroline Blackwood,** *The Stepdaughter*
1977 **Patricia Finney,** *A Shadow of Gulls*
1978 **Leslie Sliding,** *Sliding*
1979 **John Harvey,** *The Plate Shop*
1980 **Ted Harriott,** *Keep On Running*

Winifred Holtby Medal

ROYAL SOCIETY OF LITERATURE
1 Hyde Park Gardens, London W22LT, United Kingdom (Tel: 01-723-5104)

The Winifred Holtby Medal, which carries a £100 honorarium, is given annually for the best regional novel of the year.

1967 **David Bean,** *The Big Meeting*
1968 **Catherine Cookson,** *The Round Tower*
1969 **Ian MacDonald,** *The Humming Bird Tree*
1970 **Shiva Naipaul,** *Fireflies*
1971 **John Stewart,** *Last Cove Days*
1972 **No award**
1973 **No award**
1974 **Ronald Harwood,** *Articles of Faith*
Peter Tinniswood, *I Didn't Know You Cared*
1975 **Graham King,** *The Pandora Valley*
1976 **Eugene McCabe,** *Victims*
1977 **Not available**
1978 **Anita Desai,** *Fire on the Mountain*
1979 **Not available at press time**
1980 **Not available at press time**

Howells Medal

AMERICAN ACADEMY AND INSTITUTE OF ARTS AND LETTERS
633 W. 155th St., New York, N.Y. 10032 (212/368-5900)

The Howells Medal of the Academy is given every five years for the most distinguished American fiction of the period.

1925 **Mary E. Wilkins Freeman**
1930 **Willa Cather**
1935 **Pearl S. Buck**
1940 **Ellen Glasgow**
1945 **Booth Tarkington**
1950 **William Faulkner**
1955 **Eudora Welty**
1960 **James Gould Cozzens**
1965 **John Cheever**
1970 **William Styron**
1975 **Thomas Pynchon**
1980 **William Maxwell**

Hugo Awards

WORLD SCIENCE FICTION SOCIETY

c/o Howard DeVore, 4705 Weddel St., Dearborn Heights, Mich. 48125 (313/565-4157)

The Science Fiction Achievement Awards, known as the Hugo Awards, are given annually for the best science fiction works of various lengths and to individuals for contributions to science fiction writing, art and publishing. The winners are determined by a vote of the members who attend the World Science Fiction Convention. The award, informally named after Hugo Gernsback, an early science fiction publisher, is a rocket ship-shaped trophy, whose official name is the Science Fiction Achievement Award.

NOVEL

1953 **Alfred Bester,** *The Demolished Man*
1954 **No award**
1955 **Mark Clifton and Frank Riley,** *They'd Rather Be Right*
1956 **Robert A. Heinlein,** *Double Star*
1957 **No award**
1958 **Fritz Leiber,** *The Big Time*
1959 **James Blish,** *A Case of Conscience*
1960 **Robert A. Heinlein,** *Starship Troopers*
1961 **Walter M. Miller, Jr.,** *A Canticle for Leibowitz*
1962 **Robert A. Heinlein,** *Stranger in a Strange Land*
1963 **Philip K. Dick,** *The Man in the High Castle*
1964 **Clifford Simak,** *Way Station*
1965 **Fritz Leiber,** *The Wanderer*
1966 **Roger Zelazny,** *This Immortal*
Frank Herbert, *Dune*
1967 **Robert A. Heinlein,** *The Moon Is a Harsh Mistress*
1968 **Roger Zelazny,** *Lord of Light*
1969 **John Brunner,** *Stand on Zanzibar*
1970 **Ursula K. LeGuin,** *The Left Hand of Darkness*
1971 **Larry Niven,** *Ringworld*
1972 **Philip Jose Farmer,** *To Your Scattered Bodies Go*
1973 **Isaac Asimov,** *The Gods Themselves*
1974 **Arthur C. Clarke,** *Rendezvous with Rama*
1975 **Ursula K. LeGuin,** *The Dispossessed*
1976 **Joe Haldeman,** *The Forever War*
1977 **Kate Wilhelm,** *Where Late the Sweet Birds Sang*
1978 **Frederik Pohl,** *Gateway*
1979 **Vonda N. McIntyre,** *Dreamsnake*
1980 **Not available at press time**

NOVELLA

1968 **Philip Jose Farmer,** *Riders of the Purple Wage*
Anne McCaffrey, *Weyr Search*
1969 **Robert Silverberg,** *Nightwings*
1970 **Fritz Leiber,** *Ship of Shadows*
1971 **Fritz Leiber,** *Ill Met in Lankhmar*
1972 **Poul Anderson,** *The Queen of Air and Darkness*
1973 **Ursula K. LeGuin,** *The Word for World Is Forest*
1974 **James Tiptree, Jr.,** *The Girl Who Was Plugged In*
1975 **George R.R. Martin,** *A Song for Lya*
1976 **Roger Zelazny,** *Home Is the Hangman*
1977 **James Tiptree, Jr.,** *Houston, Houston, Do You Read?*
Spider Robinson, *By Any Other Name*
1978 **Jean and Spider Robinson,** *Stardance*
1979 **John Varley,** *The Persistence of Vision*
1980 **Not available at press time**

NOVELETTE/SHORT FICTION/SHORT STORY (SOMETIMES ONE AWARD; SOMETIMES SEPARATE)

1955 **Walter M. Miller, Jr.,** "The Darfsteller"*
Eric Frank Russell, "Allamagoosa"**
1956 **Murray Leinster,** "Exploration Team"*
Arthur C. Clarke, "The Star"**
1957 **No award**
1958 **Avram Davidson,** "Or All the Seas With Oysters"**
1959 **Clifford D. Simak,** "The Big Front Yard"*
Robert Bloch, "That Hell-Bound Train"**
1960 **Daniel Keyes,** "Flowers for Algernon"
1961 **Poul Anderson,** "The Longest Voyage"
1962 **Brian W. Aldiss,** "The Hothouse" Series
1963 **Jack Vance,** "The Dragon Masters"
1964 **Poul Anderson,** "No Truce With Kings"
1965 **Gordon R. Dickson,** "Soldier, Ask Not"
1966 **Harlan Ellison,** " 'Repent, Harlequin!' Said the Ticktockman"
1967 **Jack Vance,** "The Last Castle"*
Larry Niven, "Neutron Star"**
1968 **Fritz Leiber,** "Gonna Roll the Bones"*
Harlan Ellison, "I Have No Mouth, and I Must Scream"**
1969 **Poul Anderson,** "The Sharing of Flesh"*
Harlan Ellison, "The Beast That Shouted Love at the Heart of the World"**
1970 **Samuel R. Delany,** "Time Considered as a Helix of Semi-Precious Stones"**
1971 **Theodore Sturgeon,** "Slow Sculpture"**
1972 **Larry Niven,** "Inconstant Moon"**
1973 **Poul Anderson,** "Goat Song"*
R.A. Lafferty, "Eurema's Dam"**
Frederik Pohl and Cyril M. Kornbluth, "The Meeting"**
1974 **Harlan Ellison,** "The Deathbird"*
Ursula K. LeGuin, "The Ones Who Walk Away From Omelas"**
1975 **Harlan Ellison,** "Adrift Just Off the Islets of Langerhans: Latitude 38°54'N, 77°00'13 W"*
Larry Niven, "The Hole Man"**
1976 **Larry Niven,** "The Borderland of Sol"*
Fritz Leiber, "Catch That Zeppelin!"**
1977 **Isaac Asimov,** "The Bicentennial Man"*
Joe Haldeman, "Tricentennial"**
1978 **Joan D. Vinge,** "Eyes of Amber"*
Harlan Ellison, "Jefty is Five"**
1979 **Poul Anderson,** "Hunter's Moon"*
C.J. Cherryh, "Cassandra"**
1980 **Not available at press time**

*Novelette

**Short Story

All others: Short Fiction

PROFESSIONAL MAGAZINE

1953 ***Astounding***
Galaxy
1954 **No award**
1955 ***Astounding***
1956 ***Astounding***
1957 ***Astounding***
New Worlds (British)
1958 ***Fantasy and Science Fiction***
1959 ***Fantasy and Science Fiction***
1960 ***Fantasy and Science Fiction***
1961 ***Astounding/Analog****
1962 ***Analog***
1963 ***Fantasy and Science Fiction***
1964 ***Analog***
1965 ***Fantasy and Science Fiction***
1966 ***If***

1967 *If*
1968 *If*
1969 *Fantasy and Science Fiction*
1970 *Fantasy and Science Fiction*
1971 *Fantasy and Science Fiction*
1972 *Fantasy and Science Fiction*

*Name changed in mid-year

BEST PROFESSIONAL EDITOR

1973 Ben Bova
1974 Ben Bova
1975 Ben Bova
1976 Ben Bova
1977 Ben Bova
1978 George H. Scithers
1979 Ben Bova
1980 Not available at press time

BEST PROFESSIONAL ARTIST

1953 Virgil Finlay
Ed Emshwiller*
Hannes Bok*
1954 No award
1955 Frank Kelly Freas
1956 Frank Kelly Freas
1957 No award
1958 Frank Kelly Freas
1959 Frank Kelly Freas
1960 Ed Emshwiller
1961 Ed Emshwiller
1962 Ed Emshwiller
1963 Roy Krenkel
1964 Ed Emshwiller
1965 John Schoenherr
1966 Frank Frazetta
1967 Jack Gaughan
1968 Jack Gaughan
1969 Jack Gaughan
1970 Frank Kelly Freas
1971 Leo and Diane Dillon
1972 Frank Kelly Freas
1973 Frank Kelly Freas
1974 Frank Kelly Freas
1975 Frank Kelly Freas
1976 Frank Kelly Freas
1977 Rick Sternbach
1978 Rick Sternbach
1979 Vincent DiFate
1980 Not available at press time

*Best Cover Artists

BEST FANZINE, FAN MAGAZINE OR AMATEUR MAGAZINE (TITLES AND EDITORS)

1955 *Fantasy-Times,* James V. Taurasi Sr., and Ray Van Houten
1956 *Inside & Science Fiction Advertiser,* Ron Smith
1957 *Science-Fiction Times,* Taurasi, Van Houten and Prieto
1958 No award
1959 *Fanac,* Terry Carr and Ron Ellik
1960 *Cry of the Nameless,* F.M. and E. Busby, Toskey & Weber
1961 *Who Killed Science Fiction?,* Earl Kemp
1962 *Warhoon,* Richard Bergeron
1963 *Xero,* Pat and Dick Lupoff
1964 *Amra,* George Scithers
1965 *Yandro,* Robert and Juanita Coulson
1966 *ERB-dom,* Camille Cazedessus, Jr.
1967 *Niekas,* Edmund R. Meskys and Felice Rolfe
1968 *Amra,* George Scithers
1969 *Science Fiction Review,* Richard E. Geis
1970 *Science Fiction Review,* Richard E. Geis
1971 *Locus,* Charles and Dena Brown
1972 *Locus,* Charles and Dena Brown
1973 *Energumen,* Michael and Susan Wood Glicksohn
1974 *Algol,* Andy Porter
The Alien Critic, Richard E. Geis
1975 *The Alien Critic,* Richard E. Geis
1976 *Locus,* Charles and Dena Brown
1977 *Science Fiction Review,* Richard E. Geis
1978 *Science Fiction Review,* Richard E. Geis
1979 *Science Fiction Review,* Richard E. Geis
1980 Not available at press time

BEST FAN ARTIST

1967 Jack Gaughan
1968 George Barr
1969 Vaughn Bode
1970 Tim Kirk
1971 Alicia Austin
1972 Tim Kirk
1973 Tim Kirk
1974 Tim Kirk
1975 Bill Rotsler
1976 Tim Kirk
1977 Phil Foglio
1978 Phil Foglio
1979 Bill Rotsler
1980 Not available at press time

BEST FAN WRITER

1967 Alexei Panshin
1968 Ted White
1969 Harry Warner, Jr.
1970 Bob Tucker
1971 Richard E. Geis
1972 Harry Warner, Jr.
1973 Terry Carr
1974 Susan Wood
1975 Richard E. Geis
1976 Richard E. Geis
1977 Richard E. Geis
Susan Wood
1978 Richard E. Geis
1979 Bob Shaw
1980 Not available at press time

MISCELLANEOUS AWARDS (RECIPIENT AND ACHIEVEMENT)

1953 **Willy Ley,** Factual Articles
Philip Jose Farmer, Best New Science Fiction Author or Artist
Forrest J. Ackerman, Number 1 Fan Personality
1956 **Willy Ley,** Best Feature Writer
Damon Knight Best Book Reviewer
Robert Silverberg Most Promising New Author
1958 **Walter A. Willis,** Outstanding Actifan
1964 **Ace,** Best Science Fiction Book Publisher
1965 **Ballantine,** Best Publisher
1966 **"Foundation" series by Isaac Asimov,** Best All-time Series

SPECIAL HUGOS AND OTHER SPECIAL AWARDS

1955 Sam Moskowitz
1960 Hugo Gernsback
1962 Cele Goldsmith
Donald H. Tuck

Fritz Leiber and the Hoffman Electronic Corp.
1963 **P. Schuyler Miller**
Isaac Asimov
1967 **CBS Television** for *21st Century*
1968 **Harlan Ellison**
Gene Roddenberry
1969 **Neil Armstrong, Michael Collins** and **Edwin "Buzz" Aldrin**
1973 **Pierre Versins**
1974 **Chesley Bonestell**
1975 **Donald A. Wollheim**
Walt Lee
1976 **James Gunn**
1977 Club du Livre d'Anticipation
Harlan Ellison
Nueva Dimension

The World Science Fiction Convention also administers the voting for the following honors, which are not Hugo Awards.

JOHN W. CAMPBELL AWARD FOR BEST NEW WRITER

1973 **Jerry Pournelle**
1974 **Spider Robinson**
Lisa Tuttle
1975 **P.J. Plauger**
1976 **Tom Reamy**
1977 **C.J. Cherryh**
1978 **Gordon Scott Card**
1979 **Stephen R. Donaldson**
1980 **Not available at press time**

GANDALF AWARD FOR GRAND MASTER OF FANTASY

1974 **J.R.R. Tolkien**
1975 **Fritz Leiber**
1976 **L. Sprague de Camp**
1977 **Andre Norton**
1978 **Poul Anderson**
1979 **Ursula K. LeGuin**
1980 **Not available at press time**

GANDALPH AWARD FOR BEST BOOK-LENGTH FANTASY

1978 **J.R.R. Tolkien**, *The Simarillion*
1979 **Anne McCaffrey**, *The White Dragon*
1980 **Not available at press time**

Children's Book Award

INTERNATIONAL READING ASSOCIATION
800 Barksdale Rd., Newark, Del. 19711 (206/543-6636)

The Children's Book Award, which carries a $1,000 honorarium, is given annually for the first or second book of fiction or non-fiction by an author who shows unusual promise in the children's book field. A selection committee chooses the winners from entries submitted to the Association.

1975 **T. Degens**, *Transport T-41-R*
1976 **Laurence Yep**, *Dragonwings*
1977 **Nancy Bond**, *A String on the Harp*
1978 **Lois Lowry**, *A Summer to Die*
1979 **Alison Smith**, *Reserved for Mark Anthony Crowder*
1980 **Ouida Sebestyen**, *Words by Heart*

Award for Short Fiction

IOWA SCHOOL OF LETTERS
Dept. of English, University of Iowa, Iowa City, Iowa 52242 (IA 5-2242)

The $1,000 Award for Short Fiction is given annually to a writer who has not previously published a volume of prose fiction. Writers may submit new or revised manuscripts for preliminary screening by the Writers Workshop and final selection by a prominent writer or critic. In addition to the cash award, the winning manuscript is published by the University of Iowa Press.

1970 **Cyrus Colter**, *The Beach Umbrella*
1971 **Philip F. O'Connor**, *Old Morals, Small Continents*
1972 **Jack Cady**, *The Burning & Other Stories*
1973 **H.E. Francis**, *The Itinerary of Beggars*
1974 **Natalie L.M. Petesch**, *After the First Death, There is No Other*
1975 **Barry Targan**, *Harry Belten and the Mendelssohn Violin Concerto*
1976 **C.E. Poverman**, *The Black Velvet Girl*
1977 **Pat M. Carr**, Untitled
1978 **Lon Otto**, *A Nest of Hooks*
1979 **Mary Hedin**, *Fly Away Home*
1980 **James Felter**, *Impossible Appetites*

Jerusalem Prize

MUNICIPALITY OF JERUSALEM
Rehov Jaffa 22, Jerusalem, Israel (02/232251)

The Jerusalem Prize, which consists of $3,000 and a citation, is awarded biennially to a writer whose work expresses the idea of the freedom of the individual in society. A jury of Israeli intellectuals selects the recipient.

1963 **Bertrand Russell**
1965 **Max Frisch**
1967 **Andre Schwartz-Bart**
1969 **Ignazio Silone**
1971 **Jorge Luis Borges**
1973 **Eugene Ionesco**
1975 **Simone de Beauvoir**
1977 **Octavio Paz**
1979 **Sir Isaiah Berlin**

Jewish Heritage Award

B'NAI B'RITH
1640 Rhode Island Ave. NW, Washington, D.C. 20036 (202/857-6600)

The $1,000 Jewish Heritage Award is given annually for a body of literary work on Jewish life or Jewish thought. An awards committee selects the winner, who may be of any nationality and write originally in any language.

1966 **Elie Wiesel**
1967 **Maurice Samuel**
1968 **Saul Bellow**
1969 **Salo W. Baron**
1970 **Isaac Babel**
1971 **Abraham J. Heschel**
1972 **Jacob Glatstein**
1973 **Nahum N. Glatzer**

1974 **Gershom Scholem**
1975 **Eliezer Greenberg**
Irving Howe
1976 **Chaim Grade**
1977 **Bernard Malamud**
1978 **No award**
1979 **Abraham Sutzkever**
1980 **Jacob Katz**

Sue Kaufman Prize for First Fiction

AMERICAN ACADEMY AND INSTITUTE OF ARTS AND LETTERS
633 West 155th St., New York, N.Y. 10032 (212/368-5900)

The $1,000 Sue Kaufman Prize is awarded annually for a meritorious published first novel or collection of short stories during the previous year.

1980 **Jayne Anne Phillips,** *Black Tickets*

Coretta Scott King Award

CORETTA SCOTT KING AWARD COMMITTEE
1236 Oakcrest Dr. SW, Atlanta, Ga. 30311 (404/344-7265)

This award is given annually for an inspirational and educational work that promotes better understanding and appreciation of the culture and contribution of all peoples to the realization of the American dream, as symbolized by the life, works and dreams of the late Dr. Martin Luther King, Jr. The award consists of a $250 honorarium, a plaque and a set of the *Encyclopaedia Britannica.*

1970 **Lille Patterson,** *Dr. Martin Luther King, Jr.: Man of Peace*
1971 **Charlemae Rollins,** *Black Treasure: Langston Hughes*
1972 **Elton C. Fax,** *17 Black Artists*
1973 **Al Duckett,** *I Never Had It Made: The Autobiography of Jackie Robinson*
1974 **Sharon Bell Mathis,** *Ray Charles*
1975 **Dorothy Robinson,** *The Legend of Africania*
1976 **Pearl Bailey,** *Duey's Tale*
1977 **James Haskins,** *The Story of Stevie Wonder*

Current Status Unknown

Thomas-Mann-Preis

HANSASTADT LUBECK
Rathaus, 2400 Lubeck, Federal Republic of Germany (0451/12 24100)

The Thomas-Mann-Preis or Thomas Mann Prize, which carries a 10,000-mark honorarium, is awarded every three years by the Hanseatic city of Lubeck for distinguished literary or literary-scientific work with a sense of humanity as exemplified by the writings of Thomas Mann. A seven-person committee selects the winner.

1975 **Peter de Mendelssohn** (Munich), author and scientist for research on the works and life of Thomas Mann
1978 **Uwe Johnson** (Rostock, Berlin, New York, London), for such books as *Mutmassungen uber Jakob, Das Dritte Buch uber Achim* and *Jahrestage,* which deal with human problems caused by the division of Germany

Lucille J. Medwick Award

P.E.N. AMERICAN CENTER
47 Fifth Ave., New York, N.Y. 10003 (212/255-1977)

The $500 Lucille J. Medwick Memorial Award annually honors distinguished service to the literary community and a commitment to serve the young, the unrecognized and the unpopular authors.

1975 **Harry Smith**
1976 **Grace Schulman**
1977 **Alice S. Morris**
1978 **David R. Godine**
1979 **Ted Solotaroff**
1980 **Henry Robbins**

James Russell Lowell Prize
Howard R. Marraro Prize

MODERN LANGUAGE ASSOCIATION
62 Fifth Ave., New York, N.Y. 10011 (212/741-7854)

The $1,000 James Russell Lowell Prize is given annually to an MLA member for an outstanding linguistic or literary study, a critical edition or a critical biography. The five-member James Russell Lowell Prize Selection Committee gives the award to a person nominated by an individual or a publisher.

1969 **Helen Vendler,** *On Extended Wings*
1970 **Bruce A. Rosenberg,** *The Art of the American Folk Preacher*
1971 **Meyer H. Abrams,** *Natural Supernaturalism*
1972 **Theodore J. Ziolkowski,** *Fictional Transfigurations of Jesus*
1973 **Leslie A. Marchand,** *Byron's Letters and Journals*
1974 **Josephine Miles,** *Poetry and Change*
1975 **Jonathan Culler,** *Structuralist Poetics: Structuralism, Linguistics, and the Study of Literature*
1976 **Joseph Frank,** *Dostoevsky: The Seeds of Revolt, 1821-1849*
1977 **Stephen Booth,** *Shakespeare's Sonnets*
1978 **Andrew Welsh,** *Roots of Lyric: Primitive Poetry and Modern Poetics*
1979 **Barbara Kiefer Lewalski,** *Protestant Poetics and the Seventeenth-Century Religious Lyric*
1980 **Not available at press time**

The $750 Howard R. Marraro Prize has been given annually for outstanding achievement in Italian studies to an MLA member for scholarly study in Italian literature or comparative literature involving Italian. It is now a biennial honor. Members submit nominations which are voted on by the Howard R. Marraro Prize Selection Committee.

1973 **Bernard Weinberg,** *Trattati di poetica e retorica del Cinquecento*
1974 **Thomas G. Bergin,** Lifetime achievement
1975 **Beatrice Corrigan,** Lifetime achievement
1976 **Joseph G. Fucilla,** Lifetime achievement
1978 **Franco Fido,** *Guida a Goldoni: Teatro e societa nel Settecento*

1980 **Nicolas J. Parella,** *Midday in Italian Literature: Variations on an Archetypal Theme*

Medicis Prizes

c/o Francine Mallet, 25 Rue Dombasle, Paris 15, France (Tel: 828-76-90)

The Prix Medicis or Medicis Prize, which is accompanied by a cash honorarium, is awarded annually for avant-garde prose, which may be a novel or a collection of shorter works. It is given to a relatively unknown but talented French author. In 1970, a second award called the Prix Medicis Etranger was added for a notable non-French author.

FRENCH AUTHOR

1958 **Claude Ollier,** *La mise en scene*
1959 **Claude Mauriac,** *Le Diner en ville*
1960 **Henri Thomas,** *John Perkins*
1961 **Philippe Sollers,** *Le Parc*
1962 **Colette Audry,** *Derriere la baignoir*
1963 **Gerard Jarlot,** *Un chat qui aboie*
1964 **Monique Wittig,** *L'Opoponax*
1965 **Rene-Victor Pilnes,** *La Rhubarbe*
1966 **Marie-Claire Blais,** *Une saison dans la vie d'Emmanuel*
1967 **Claude Simon,** *Histoire*
1968 **Elie Wiesel,** *Le Mendiant de Jerusalem*
1969 **Helene Gixous,** *Dedans*
1970 **Camille Bourniquel,** *Seinonte ou la Chambre imperiale*
1971 **Pascal Laine,** *L'irrevolution*
1972 **Maurice Clavel,** *Le Tiers des etoiles*
1973 **Tony Duvert,** *Paysage de fantasie*
1974 **Dominique Fernandez,** *Porporino ou les Mysteres de Naples*
1975 **Jacques Almira,** *La voyage a Naucratis*
1976 **Marc Cholodenko,** *Les Etats du desert*
1977 **Michel Butel,** *L'Autre Amour*
1978 **Perec,** *La vie mode d'emploi*
1979 **Claude Durand,** *La nuit zoologique*
1980 **Jean Benoziglio,** *Cabinet portrait*
Jean La Hougue, *Compture des Height* (prize declined)

FOREIGN AUTHOR

1970 **Luigi Malerba,** *Saut de la Mort*
1971 **James Dickey,** *Deliverance*
1972 **Severo Sarduy,** *Cobra*
1973 **Milan Kundera,** *La vie est ailieurs*
1974 **Julio Cortazar,** *Livre de Manuel*
1975 **Steven Millhauser,** *La Vie trop breve d'Edwin Mulhouse*
1976 **Doris Lessing,** *The Golden Notebook*
1977 **Hector Bianciotti,** *Le traite des saisons*
1978 **Alexander Zino Yiev,** *L'avenir radieuse*
1979 **Alejo Carpentier,** *La harpe et l'ombre*
1980 **Andre Brink,** *Une saison blance et seche*

Samuel Eliot Morison Award

AMERICAN HERITAGE PUBLISHING CO.
10 Rockefeller Plaza, New York, N.Y. 10020 (212/399-8990)

The $5,000 Samuel Eliot Morison Award for the best book on American history by an American author that sustains the tradition of history as literature as well as scholarship has been suspended.

1977 **Joseph Lash,** *Roosevelt and Churchill; 1939-1941: The Partnership That Saved the West*
1978 **David McCullough,** *The Path Between the Seas: The Creation of the Panama Canal, 1870-1914*

Gold Medal

NATIONAL ARTS CLUB
15 Gramercy Park South, New York, N.Y. 10003 (212/475-3424)

As part of the club's honors program in the visual and performing arts and literature, a gold medal, also called the National Arts Club Literary Award, is presented annually. Other medalists are listed in the Music & Dance, Theatre and Visual Arts sections of this volume.

1968 **Louis Auchincloss**
1969 **W. H. Auden**
1970 **S.J. Perelman**
1971 **Ada Louise Huxtable**
1972 **Norman Cousins**
1973 **Anthony Burgess**
1974 **Eudora Welty**
1975 **Tennessee Williams**
1976 **Norman Mailer**
1977 **No award**
1978 **Saul Bellow**
1979 **Allen Ginsberg**
1980 **Isaac Bashevis Singer**

National Book Awards
American Book Awards

ASSOCIATION OF AMERICAN PUBLISHERS
One Park Ave., New York, N.Y. 10016 (212/689-8920)

The $1,000 National Book Awards were given annually for books by U.S. citizens "that have contributed most significantly to human awareness, to the vitality of our national culture and to the spirit of excellence." Panels of three judges selected the winners from works that were published during the previous calendar year. Until 1975, the National Book Committee administered the award. For the next two years, until the Association took it over, it was handled by the American Academy and Institute of Arts and Letters. The categories have changed over the years. Poetry awards will be found on p. 74.

FICTION

1950 **Nelson Algren,** *The Man with the Golden Arm*
1951 **William Faulkner,** *The Collected Stories of William Faulkner*
Brendan Gill, *The Trouble of One House*
1952 **James Jones,** *From Here to Eternity*
1953 **Ralph Ellison,** *Invisible Man*
1954 **Saul Bellow,** *The Adventures of Augie March*
1955 **William Faulkner,** *A Fable*
1956 **John O'Hara,** *Ten North Frederick*
1957 **Wright Morris,** *The Field of Vision*
1958 **John Cheever,** *The Wapshot Chronicle*
1959 **Bernard Malamud,** *The Magic Barrel*

1960 **Philip Roth,** *Goodbye, Columbus*
1961 **Conrad Richter,** *The Waters of Kronos*
1962 **Walker Percy,** *The Moviegoer*
1963 **J. F. Powers,** *Morte D'Urban*
1964 **John Updike,** *The Centaur*
1965 **Saul Bellow,** *Herzog*
1966 **Katherine Anne Porter,** *The Collected Stories of Katherine Anne Porter*
1967 **Bernard Malamud,** *The Fixer*
1968 **Thornton Wilder,** *The Eighth Day*
1969 **Jerzy Kosinski,** *Steps*
1970 **Joyce Carol Oates,** *Them*
1971 **Saul Bellow,** *Mr. Sammler's Planet*
1972 **Flannery O'Connor,** *Flannery O'Connor: The Complete Stories*
1973 **John Barth,** *Chimera*
John Williams, *Augustus*
1974 **Isaac Bashevis Singer,** *A Crown of Feathers and Other Stories*
Thomas Pynchon, *Gravity's Rainbow*
1975 **Robert Stone,** *Dog Soldiers*
Thomas Williams, *The Hair of Harold Roux*
1976 **William Gaddis,** *JR*
1977 **Wallace Stegner,** *The Spectator Bird*
1978 **Mary Lee Settle,** *Blood Tie*
1979 **Tim O'Brien,** *Going After Cacciato*

NON-FICTION

1950 **Ralph L. Rusk,** *Ralph Waldo Emerson*
1951 **Newton Arvin,** *Herman Melville*
1952 **Rachel L. Carson,** *The Sea Around Us*
1953 **Bernard De Voto,** *The Course of Empire*
1954 **Bruce Catton,** *A Stillness at Appomattox*
1955 **Joseph Wood Krutch,** *The Measure of Man*
1956 **Herbert Kubly,** *American in Italy*
1957 **George F. Kennan,** *Russia Leaves the War*
1958 **Catherine Drinker Bowen,** *The Lion and the Throne*
1959 **J. Christopher Herold,** *Mistress to an Age: A Life of Madame de Stael*
1960 **Richard Ellmann,** *James Joyce*
1961 **William L. Shirer,** *The Rise and Fall of the Third Reich*
1962 **Lewis Mumford,** *The City in History*
1963 **Leon Edel,** *Henry James: The Conquest of London* and *Henry James: The Middle Years*

ARTS AND LETTERS

1964 **Aileen Ward,** *John Keats: The Making of a Poet*
1965 **Eleanor Clark,** *The Oysters of Locmariaquer*
1966 **Janet Flanner (Genet),** *Paris Journal (1944-1965)*
1967 **Justin Kaplan,** *Mr. Clemens and Mark Twain*
1968 **William Troy,** *Selected Essays*
1969 **Norman Mailer,** *The Armies of the Night*
1970 **Lillian Hellman,** *An Unfinished Woman*
1971 **Francis Steegmuller,** *Cocteau*
1972 **Charles Rosen,** *The Classical Style: Haydn, Mozart, Beethoven*
1973 **Arthur M. Wilson,** *Diderot*
1974 **Pauline Kael,** *Deeper into the Movies*
1975 **Roger Shattuck,** *Marcel Proust*
Lewis Thomas, *The Lives of a Cell: Notes of a Biology Watcher*
1976 **Paul Fussell,** *The Great War and Modern Memory*

HISTORY AND BIOGRAPHY

1964 **William H. McNeill,** *The Rise of the West*
1965 **Louis Fischer,** *The Life of Lenin*
1966 **Arthur M. Schlesinger, Jr.,** *A Thousand Days*
1967 **Peter Gay,** *The Enlightenment*
1968 **George F. Kennan,** *Memoirs: 1925-1950*
1969 **Winthrop D. Jordan,** *White Over Black: American Attitudes Toward the Negro, 1550-1812*
1970 **T. Harry Williams,** *Huey Long*
1971 **James MacGregor Burns,** *Roosevelt: The Soldier of Freedom*

BIOGRAPHY

1972 **Joseph P. Lash,** *Eleanor and Franklin: The Story of Their Relationship Based on Eleanor Roosevelt's Private Papers*
1973 **James Thomas Flexner,** *George Washington: Anguish and Farewell (1793-1799)*
1974 **Douglas Day,** *Malcolm Lowry*
1975 **Richard Sewall,** *The Life of Emily Dickinson*

BIOGRAPHY AND AUTOBIOGRAPHY

1977 **W.A. Swanberg,** *Norman Thomas: The Last Idealist*
1978 **W. Jackson Bate,** *Samuel Johnson*
1979 **Robert M. Schlesinger, Jr.,** *Robert Kennedy and His Times*

HISTORY

1972 **Allan Nevins,** Ordeal of the Union series—Vol. 7, *The War for the Union: The Organized War, 1863-64;* Vol. 8, *The War for the Union: The Organized War to Victory, 1864-65*
1973 **Robert Manson Myers,** *The Children of Pride*
Isaiah Trunk, *Judenrat*
1974 **John Clive,** *Macauley: The Shaping of the Historian*
1975 **Bernard Bailyn,** *The Ordeal of Thomas Hutchinson*
1976 **David B. Davis,** *The Problem of Slavery in an Age of Revolution: 1770-1823*
1977 **Irving Howe,** *World of Our Fathers*
1978 **David McCullough,** *The Path Between the Seas: The Creation of the Panama Canal, 1870-1914*
1979 **Richard Beale Davis,** *Intellectual Life in the Colonial South, 1585-1763*

SCIENCE, PHILOSOPHY AND RELIGION

1964 **Christopher Tunnard and Boris Pushkarev,** *Man-Made America: Chaos or Control?*
1965 **Norbert Wiener,** *God and Golem, Inc.*
1966 **No award**
1967 **Oscar Lewis,** *La Vida*
1968 **Jonathan Kozol,** *Death at an Early Age*
1969 **R. J. Lifton,** *Death in Life: Survivors of Hiroshima*
1970 **Erik H. Erikson,** *Gandhi's Truth: On the Origins of Militant Nonviolence*

THE SCIENCES

1971 **Raymond Phineas Stearns,** *Science in the British Colonies of America*
1972 **George L. Small,** *The Blue Whale*
1973 **George B. Schaller,** *The Serengeti Lion: A Study of Predator-Prey Relations*
1974 **S. E. Luria,** *Life: The Unfinished Experiment*
1975 **Silvano Arieti,** *Interpretation of Schizophrenia*

PHILOSOPHY AND RELIGION

1972 **Martin E. Marty,** *Righteous Empire: The Protestant Experience in America*
1973 **Sydney E. Ahlstrom,** *A Religious History of the American People*
1974 **Maurice Natanson,** *Edmund Husserl: Philosopher of Infinite Tasks*
1975 **Robert Nozick,** *Anarchy, State and Utopia*

CONTEMPORARY AFFAIRS

1972 **Stewart Brand,** *The Last Whole Earth Catalog: Access to Tools*
1973 **Frances FitzGerald,** *Fire in the Lake: The Vietnamese and the Americans in Vietnam*
1974 **Murray Kempton,** *The Briar Patch: The People of the State of New York vs. Lumumba Shakur et al*
1975 **Theodore Rosengarten,** *All God's Dangers: The Life of Nate Shaw*
1976 **Michael J. Arlen,** *Passage to Ararat*

CONTEMPORARY THOUGHT

1977 **Bruno Bettelheim,** *The Uses of Enchantment: The Meaning and Importance of Fairy Tales*
1978 **Gloria Emerson,** *Winners & Losers: Battles, Retreats, Gains, Losses and Ruins from a Long War*
1979 **Peter Matthiessen,** *The Snow Leopard*

CHILDREN'S LITERATURE

1969 **Meindert DeJong,** *Journey from Peppermint Street*
1970 **Isaac Bashevis Singer,** *A Day of Pleasure: Stories of a Boy Growing Up in Warsaw*
1971 **Lloyd Alexander,** *The Marvelous Misadventurers of Sebastian*
1972 **Donald Barthelme,** *The Slightly Irregular Fire Engine or the Hithering Thithering Djinn*
1973 **Ursula K. LeGuin,** *The Farthest Shore*
1974 **Eleanor Cameron,** *The Court of the Stone Children*
1975 **Virginia Hamilton,** *M. C. Higgins the Great*
1976 **Walter D. Edmonds,** *Bert Breen's Barn*
1977 **Katherine Paterson,** *The Master Puppeteer*
1978 **Judith and Herbert Kohl,** *The View from the Oak: The Private World of Other Creatures*
1979 **Katherine Paterson,** *The Great Gilly Hopkins*

TRANSLATION

1967 **Willard Trask,** *History of My Life* by Casanova
Gregory Rabassa, *Hopscotch* by Julio Cortazar
1968 **Howard and Edna Hong,** *Soren Kierkegaard's Journals and Papers,* Vol. 1
1969 **William Weaver,** *Cosmicomics* by Italo Calvino
1970 **Ralph Manheim,** *Castle to Castle* by Louis-Ferdinand Celine
1971 **Frank Jones,** *Saint Joan of the Stockyards* by Bertolt Brecht
Edward G. Seidensticker, *The Sound of the Mountain* by Yasunari Kawabata
1972 **Austryn Wainhouse,** *Chance and Necessity: An Essay on the Natural Philosophy of Modern Biology* by Jacques Monad
1973 **Allen Mandelbaum,** *The Aeneid of Virgil*
1974 **Karen Brazell,** *The Confessions of Lady Nijo*
Helen Lane, *Alternating Currents* by Octavio Paz
Jackson Mathews, *Monsieur Teste* by Paul Valery
1975 **Anthony Kerrigan,** *The Agony of Christianity and Essays on Faith* by Miguel de Unamuno
1976 **No award**
1977 **Li-li Ch'en,** *Master Tung's Western Chamber Romance: A Chinese Chantefable*
1978 **Uwe George,** *In the Deserts of This Earth* by Richard and Clara Winston
1979 **Clayton Eshleman** and **Jose Rubia Barcia,** *The Complete Posthumous Poetry* by Cesar Vallejo

SPECIAL MERIT

1977 **Alex Haley,** *Roots.*

In 1979 the Association of American Publishers announced a plan to replace the National Book Awards with the American Book Awards, including a substantial change in and broadening of categories and an alteration in voting procedures. This controversial decision resulted in a boycott of the new honors by 50 prominent authors who objected to what they considered a commercialization of the awards. The categories below for which the first American Book Awards were given are scheduled to be changed yet again after 1980. The publishers' association again administers the program.

ART/ILLUSTRATED (Hardcover — collection)

1980 **Larry Rivers** with **Carol Brightman** and **Herman Strobach** (designer/art director), **Carol Southern** (editor) and **Michael Fragnito** (production), *Drawings and Digressions*

ART/ILLUSTRATED (Hardcover — original art)

1980 **Leonard Lubin** (illustrator) and **Barbara Hennessey** (art director), *The Birthday of the Infants*, by Oscar Wilde

ART/ILLUSTRATED (Paperback)

1980 **Emily Blair Chewning** and **Dana Levy** (designer) and **Frank Metz** (art director), *Anatomy Illustrated*

AUTOBIOGRAPHY (Hardcover)

1980 **Lauren Bacall,** *By Myself*

AUTOBIOGRAPHY (Paperback)

1980 **Malcolm Cowley,** *. . . And I Worked at the Writer's Trade: Chapters of a Literary History*

BIOGRAPHY (Hardcover)

1980 **Edmund Morris,** *The Rise of Theodore Roosevelt*

BIOGRAPHY (Paperback)

1980 **A. Scott Berg,** *Max Perkins: Editor of Genius*

CHILDREN'S BOOK (Hardcover)

1980 **Joan W. Blos,** *A Gathering of Days: A New England Girl's Journal, 1830-32*

CHILDREN'S BOOK (Paperback)

1980 **Madeline L'Engle,** *A Swiftly Tilting Planet*

CURRENT INTEREST (Hardcover)

1980 **Julia Child,** *Julia Child and More Company*

CURRENT INTEREST (Paperback)

1980 **Christopher Lasch,** *The Culture of Narcissism*

FIRST NOVEL

1980 **William Wharton,** *Birdy*

GENERAL FICTION (Hardcover)

1980 **William Styron,** *Sophie's Choice*

GENERAL FICTION (Paperback)

1980 **John Irving,** *The World According to Garp*

GENERAL NON-FICTION (Hardcover)

1980 **Tom Wolfe,** *The Right Stuff*

GENERAL NON-FICTION (Paperback)

1980 **Peter Matthiessen,** *The Snow Leopard*

GENERAL REFERENCE BOOK (Hardcover)

1980 **Elder Witt** (editor), *Congressional Quarterly's Guide to the U.S. Supreme Court*

GENERAL REFERENCE BOOK (Paperback)

1980 **Tim Brooks** and **Earle March**, *The Complete Directory to Prime Time Network TV Shows*

HISTORY (Hardcover)

1980 **Henry Kissinger**, *White House Years*

HISTORY (Paperback)

1980 **Barbara W. Tuchman**, *A Distant Mirror: The Calamitous 14th Century*

MYSTERY (Hardcover)

1980 **John D. MacDonald**, *The Green Ripper*

MYSTERY (Paperback)

1980 **William F. Buckley, Jr.**, *Stained Glass*

POETRY

1980 **Philip Levine**, *Ashes*

RELIGION/INSPIRATION (Hardcover)

1980 **Elaine Pagels**, *The Gnostic Gospels*

RELIGION/INSPIRATION (Paperback)

1980 **Sheldon Vanauken**, *A Severe Mercy*

SCIENCE (Hardcover)

1980 **Douglas Hofstadter**, *Godel, Escher, Bach: An Eternal Golden Braid*

SCIENCE (Paperback)

1980 **Gary Zukav**, *The Dancing Wu Li Masters: An Overview of the New Physics*

SCIENCE FICTION (Hardcover)

1980 **Frederik Pohl**, *Jem*

SCIENCE FICTION (Paperback)

1980 **Walter Wangerin, Jr.**, *The Book of the Dun Cow*

TRANSLATION

1980 **Jane Gary Harris** and **Constance Link**, *The Complete Critical Prose and Letters*, by Osip E. Mandelstam

WESTERN

1980 **Louis L'Amour**, *Bendigo Shafter*

The following Technical Achievements awards in publishing are also given.

BOOK DESIGN

1980 **Deborah Nevins** and **Robert A.M. Stern** (designers) and **R.D. Scudellari** (art director), *The Architect's Eye: American Architectural Drawings from 1799-1978*

COVER DESIGN

1980 **Joe Cottonwood** and **Ann Spinelli** (art director) and **David Myers** (designer), *Famous Potatoes*

JACKET DESIGN

1980 **Williams Wharton** and **Lidia Ferrara** (art director) and **Fred Marcellino** (designer), *Birdy*

National Book Critics Circle Award

NATIONAL BOOK CRITICS CIRCLE
4000 Tunlaw Rd. NW, Ste. 1019, Washington, D.C. 20007
(202/357-1547)

The National Book Critics Circle Award, a scroll, is presented annually to the authors of meritorious books in four categories. The organization, is made up of more than 200 book review editors and critics, 21 of whom comprise the board which nominates five books in each category and selects the winners.

FICTION

1975 **E.L. Doctorow**, *Ragtime*
1976 **John Gardner**, *October Light*
1977 **Toni Morrison**, *Song of Solomon*
1978 **John Cheever**, *The Stories of John Cheever*
1979 **Thomas Flanagan**, *The Year of the French*
1980 **Shirley Hazzard**, *The Transit of Venus*

POETRY

1975 **John Ashbery**, *Self Portrait in a Convex Mirror*
1976 **Elizabeth Bishop**, *Geography III*
1977 **Robert Lowell**, *Day by Day*
1978 **Peter Davison** (ed.), *Hellow Darkness: The Collected Poems of L.E. Sissman*
1979 **Philip Levine**, *Ashes* and *7 Years from Somewhere*
1980 **Frederick Seidel**, *Sunrise*

GENERAL NONFICTION

1975 **R.W.B. Lewis**, *Edith Wharton*
1976 **Maxine Hong Kingston**, *The Woman Warrior: Memoirs of a Girlhood Among Ghosts*
1977 **Walter Jackson Bate**, *Samuel Johnson*
1978 **Maureen Howard**, *Facts of Life*
Garry Wills, *Inventing America: Jefferson's Declaration of Independence*
1979 **Telford Taylor**, *Munich: The Price of Peace*
1980 **Ronald Steel**, *Walter Lippmann and the American Century*

CRITICISM

1975 **Paul Fussell**, *The Great War and Modern Memory*
1976 **Bruno Bettelheim**, *The Uses of Enchantment: The Meaning and Importance of Fairy Tales*
1977 **Susan Sontag**, *On Photography*
1978 **Meyer Schapiro**, *Modern Art: 19th & 20th Centuries, Selected Papers*
1979 **Elaine Pagels**, *The Gnostic Gospels*
1980 **Helen Vendler**, *Part of Nature, Part of Us: Modern American Poets*

BOARD AWARD

1979 **Flannery O'Connor**, Life's work, presented on the occasion of *The Habit of Being*, selected and edited by Sally Fitzgerald

Frank and Ethel S. Cohen Award
William and Janet Epstein Fiction Award
Rabbi Jacob Freedman Award
Leon Jolson Award
Morris J. Kaplun Memorial Award
Bernard H. Marks Award
Charles and Bertie G. Schwartz Award

NATIONAL JEWISH WELFARE BOARD
15 E. 26th St., New York, N.Y. 10010 (212/532-4949)

The $500 Frank and Ethel S. Cohen Award is given annually for the best work on Jewish thought written in English by an American or Canadian resident as determined by a committee of judges appointed by the board's Jewish Book Council.

1963 **Moses Ricshin,** *The Promised City*
1964 **Ben Zion Bokser,** *Judaism: Profile of a Faith*
1965 **Israel Efros,** *Ancient Jewish Philosophy*
1966 **David Polish,** *The Higher Freedom, A New Turning Point in Jewish History*
1967 **Nahum M. Sarna,** *Understanding Genesis: The Heritage of Biblical Israel*
1968 **Michael A. Mayer,** *Origins of the Modern Jew*
1969 **Emil L. Fackenheim,** *Quest for Past and Future: Essays in Jewish Theology*
1970 **Abraham Joshua Heschel,** *Israel: An Echo of Eternity*
1971 **Mordecai M. Kaplan,** *The Religion of Ethical Nationhood: Judaism's Contribution to World Peace*
1972 **Abraham E. Millgram,** *Jewish Worship*
1973 **Elie Wiesel,** *Souls on Fire*
Samuel Sandmel, *Two Living Traditions: Essays on Religion and the Bible*
1974 **Eugene B. Borowitz,** *The Mask Jews Wear, The Self-Deceptions of American Jewry*
1975 **Eliezer Berkovits,** *Major Themes in Modern Philosophies of Judaism*
1976 **Solomon B. Frehoff,** *Contemporary Reform Response*
1977 **David Hartman,** *Maimonodes: Torah and Philosophic Quest*
1978 **Raphael Patoi,** *The Jewish Mind*
1979 **Robert Gordis,** *Love and Sex: A Modern Jewish Perspective*
1980 **Gershom Scholem,** *Kabbalah and Counter History*

The $500 Bernard H. Marks Award annually honors a work which deals with some aspect of Jewish history written by a resident or citizen of the United States or Canada in English, Hebrew or Yiddish. Books on Israel or the Holocaust are not considered by the panel of judges appointed by the Jewish Book Council.

1973 **Arthur J. Zuckerman,** *A Jewish Princedom in Feudal France*
1974 **Bernard D. Weinryb,** *The Jews of Poland: A Social and Economic History of the Jewish Community in Poland from 1100 to 1800*
1975 **Solomon Seitlin,** Cumulative contribution to Jewish history
1976 **Rafael Patai and Jennifer Patai Wing,** *The Myth of the Jewish Race*
1977 **Irving Howe,** *World of Our Fathers*
1978 **Celia S. Heller,** *On the Edge of Destruction*
1979 **No award**

The Gerrard and Ella Berman Award on Jewish History is given annually.

1979 **Salo Baron,** Cumulative works
1980 **Todd M. Endelman,** *The Jews of Georgian England*

The $500 Morris J. Kaplun Memorial Award recognizes the most outstanding book on Israel published during the previous year in English, Hebrew or Yiddish by a resident of the United States or Canada. A panel of judges selects the winner.

1974 **Isaiah Friedman,** *The Question of Palestine, 1914-1918: British-Jewish-Arab Relations*
1975 **Arnold Kammer,** *The Forgotten Friendship: Israel and the Soviet Bloc, 1947-1953*
1976 **Melvin I. Urofsky,** *American Zionism from Herzl to the Holocaust*
1977 **Howard M. Sachar,** *A History of Israel: Israel from the Rise of Zionism to Our Time*
1978 **Hillel Halkin,** *Letters to an American Jewish Friend*
1979 **Ruth Gruber,** *Raquela: A Woman of Israel*
1980 **Emanuel Levy,** *The Habima—Israel's National Theater 1917-1977: A Study of Cultural Nationalism*

The $500 Leon Jolson Award for a book on the Nazi Holocaust honors the best non-fiction book about this period published during the three previous years, rotating annually for a book published in English, in Hebrew and in Yiddish. Works translated into either of these languages are eligible. The author must be a resident of the United States or Canada. A panel of judges selects the winner.

1966 **Zosa Szajkowski,** *Analytical Franco-Jewish Gazetteer, 1939-45*
1967 **Abraham Kin, Mordecai Kosover, and Isaiah Trunk, eds.,** *Algemeyne Entisklopedye: Yidn VII*
1968 **Jacob Robinson,** *And the Crooked Shall Be Made Straight*
1969 **Judah Pilch,** *The Jewish Catastrophe in Europe*
Nora Levin, *The Holocaust: The Destruction of European Jewry*
1970 **Zalman Zylbercweig,** *Lexicon of the Yiddish Theater: Martyrs Volume*
1971 **Rabbi Ephraim Oshry,** *Sheelot u-Teshuvot: Mi-Maamakim*
1972 **Henry L. Feingold,** *The Politics of Rescue: The Roosevelt Administration and the Holocaust, 1938-1945*
1973 **Aaron Zeitlin,** *Vaiterdike Lider fun Hurban un Lider fun Gloiben in Yanish Korshaks Letze Gang*
1974 **No award**
1975 **Isaiah Trunk,** *Judenrat: The Jewish Councils in Eastern Europe under Nazi Occupation*
1976 **Leyzer Ran,** *Yerushalayim de Lite: Jerusalem of Lithuania*
1977 **Rabbi Ephraim Oshry,** *Sefer Sheelot U'Teshuvot Mi-Maamakim,* Part IV
1978 **Terrence des Pres,** *The Survivor: An Anatomy of Life in a Death Camp*
1979 **Michael Seltzer,** *Deliverance Day*
1980 **Benjamin B. Ferencz,** *Less Than Slaves: Jewish Forced Labor and the Quest for Compensation*

The $500 William and Janet Epstein Fiction Award annually honors the previous year's best new fiction book by an American or Canadian citizen or resident on a Jewish theme and is sometimes given for an author's comulative body of work, as determined by a committee of judges appointed by the board's Jewish Book Council. Until 1972, this award was called the Harry and Ethel Daroff Memorial Fiction Award.

1949 **Howard Fast,** *My Glorious Brothers*
1950 **John Hersey,** *The Wall*
1951 **Soma Morgenstern,** *The Testament of the Lost Son*
1952 **Zelda Popkin,** *Quiet Street*
1953 **Michael Blankfort,** *The Juggler*
1954 **Charles Angoff,** *In the Morning Light*
1955 **Louis Zara,** *Blessed Is the Land*
1956 **Jo Sinclair,** *The Changelings*
1957 **Lion Feuchtwanger,** *Raquel: The Jewess of Toledo*
1958 **Bernard Malamud,** *The Assistant*
1959 **Leon Uris,** *Exodus*
1960 **Philip Roth,** *Goodbye, Columbus*
1961 **Edward L. Wallant,** *The Human Season*
1962 **Samuel Yellen,** *The Wedding Band*
1963 **Isaac Bashevis Singer,** *The Slave*
1964 **Joanne Greenberg,** *The King's Persons*
1965 **Elie Wiesel,** *The Town Beyond the Wall*
1966 **Meyer Levin,** *The Stronghold*
1967 **No award**
1968 **Chaim Grade,** *The Well*
1969 **Charles Angoff,** *Memory of Autumn*
1970 **Leo Litwak,** *Waiting for the News*
1971 **No award**
1972 **Cynthia Ozick,** *The Pagan Rabbi and Other Stories*
1973 **Robert Kotlowitz,** *Somewhere Else*
1974 **Francine Prose,** *Judah the Pious*
1975 **Jean Karsavina,** *White Eagle, Dark Skies*
1976 **Johanna Kaplan,** *Other People's Lives*
1977 **Cynthia Ozick,** *Bloodshed and Three Novellas*
1978 **Chaim Grade,** *The Yeshiva,* Vol. I and II
1979 **Gloria Goldreich,** *Leah's Journey*
1980 **Daniel Fuchs,** *The Apathetic Bookie Joint*

The $500 Rabbi Jacob Freedman Award is given annually to the translator of a book that is considered a Jewish classic for an English translation of literary merit. The book must have been translated into English during the previous two years by a citizen or resident of the United States or Canada from a work written before 1920 in any language. A panel of judges selects the winner.

1976 **Jewish Publication Society Committee of Translators of the Prophets (Max Arzt, Bernard J. Bamberger, Harry Freedman, H.L. Ginsberg, Solomon Grayzel and Harry Orlinsky),** *The Book of Isaiah*
1977 **Zvi L. Lampel,** *Maimonodes' Introduction to the Talmud*
1978 **No award**
1979 **William M. Brinner,** *Elegant Composition Concerning Relief After Adversity,* by Nissim ben Jacob Ibn Shahin
1980 **No award**

An award is now given for Yiddish literature

1980 **Peretz Miransky,** *Shmeichl un Trern*

The $500 Charles and Bertie G. Schwartz Award honors a Juvenile book on a Jewish theme that combines literary merit with an affirmative expression of Jewish thought. The book must be written by a United States or Canadian citizen or resident and have been published during the previous year. A panel of judges selects the winner. (The award has undergone several name changes.)

1952 **Sydney Taylor,** *All-of-a-Kind Family*
1953 **Lillian S. Freehof,** *Stories of King David; Star Light Stories*
1954 **Deborah Pessin,** *The Jewish People: Book Three*
1955 **Nora Benjamin Kubie,** *King Solomon's Navy*
1956 **Sadie Rose Weilerstein,** Cumulative contributions to Jewish juvenile literature
1957 **Elma Ehrlich Levinger,** Cumulative contributions to Jewish juvenile literature
1958 **Naomi Ben-Asher and Hayim Leaf,** *Junior Jewish Encyclopedia*
1959 **Lloyd Alexander,** *Border Hawk: August Bondi*
1960 **Sylvia Rothchild,** *Keys to a Magic Door: Isaac Leib Peretz*
1961 **Regina Tor,** *Discovering Israel*
1962 **Sadie Rose Weilerstein,** *Ten and a Kid*
1963 **Josephine Kamm,** *Return to Freedom*
1964 **Sulamith Ish-Kishor,** *A Boy of Old Prague*
1965 **Azriel Eisenberg and Dov Peretz Elkins,** *Worlds Lost and Found*
1966 **Betty Schechter,** *The Dreyfus Affair*
1967 **Meyer Levin,** *The Story of Israel*
1968 **No award**
1969 **No award**
1970 **Gerald Gottlieb,** *The Story of Masada by Yigael Yadin: Retold for Young Readers*
Charlie May Simon, *Martin Buber: Wisdom in Our Time*
1971 **Sonia Levitin,** *Journey to America*
1972 **Sulamith Ish-Kishor,** *The Master of Miracle: A New Novel of the Golem*
1973 **Johanna Reiss,** *The Upstairs Room*
1974 **Yuri Suhl,** *Uncle Misha's Partisans*
1975 **Bea Stadtler,** *The Holocaust: A History of Courage and Resistance*
1976 **Shirley Milgrim,** *Haym Salomon: Liberty's Son*
1977 **Chaya Burstein,** *Rifka Grows Up*
1978 **Milton Meltzer,** *Never to Forget: The Jews of the Holocaust*
1979 **Irina Narell,** *Joshua: Fighter for Bar Kochba*
1980 **Arnost Lustig,** *Dita Saxova*

National Medal for Literature

ASSOCIATION OF AMERICAN PUBLISHERS
One Park Ave., New York, N.Y. 10016 (212/689-8920)

The National Medal for Literature, which is of bronze and carries a $15,000 honorarium, is given annually to a living American writer for contributions to American letters. The award, which is endowed by the Guinzburg Fund, is now given in conjunction with the American Book Awards and was formerly presented in with the National Book Awards. A committee selects the winner.

1965 **Thornton Wilder**
1966 **Edmund Wilson**
1967 **W.H. Auden**
1968 **Marianne Moore**
1969 **Conrad Aiken**
1970 **Robert Penn Warren**
1971 **E.B. White**
1972 **Lewis Mumford**
1973 **Vladimir Nabokov**
1974 **No award**

1975 No award
1976 Allen Tate
1977 Robert Lowell
1978 Archibald MacLeish
1979 Eudora Welty
1980 No award

Nebula Awards

SCIENCE FICTION WRITERS OF AMERICA
68 Countryside Apts., Hackettstown, N.J. 07840
(201/852-8531)

The Nebula Awards, which consist of Lucite trophies designed by artist Judy Blish, are given annually for outstanding science fiction writing of various lengths. The membership nominates and votes on the winners, who themselves need not be members of the organization.

GRAND MASTER AWARD (GIVEN AS MERITED FOR LIFETIME ACHIEVEMENT)

1974 **Robert A. Heinlein**
1975 **Jack Williamson**
1976 **Clifford D. Simak**
1978 **L. Sprague de Camp**

NOVEL (40,000 words or more)

1965 **Frank Herbert,** *Dune*
1966 **Samuel R. Delany,** *Babel-17*
Daniel Keyes, *Flowers for Algernon*
1967 **Samuel R. Delany,** *The Einstein Intersection*
1968 **Alexei Panshin,** *Rite of Passage*
1969 **Ursula K. LeGuin,** *The Left Hand of Darkness*
1970 **Larry Niven,** *Ringworld*
1971 **Robert Silverberg,** *A Time of Changes*
1972 **Isaac Asimov,** *The Gods Themselves*
1973 **Arthur C. Clarke,** *Rendezvous with Rama*
1974 **Ursula K. LeGuin,** *The Dispossessed*
1975 **Joe Haldeman,** *The Forever War*
1976 **Frederik Pohl,** *Man Plus*
1977 **Frederik Pohl,** *Gateway*
1978 **Vonda N. McIntyre,** *Dreamsnake*
1979 **Arthur C. Clarke,** *The Fountains of Paradise*
1980 **Not available at press time**

NOVELLA (17,500-40,000 words)

1965 **Brian Aldiss,** "The Saliva Tree"
Roger Zelazny, "He Who Shapes"
1966 **Jack Vance,** "The Last Castle"
1967 **Michael Moorcock,** "Behold the Man"
1968 **Anne McCaffrey,** "Dragonrider"
1969 **Harlan Ellison,** "A Boy and His Dog"
1970 **Fritz Leiber,** "Ill Met in Lankhmar"
1971 **Katherine MacLean,** "The Missing Man"
1972 **Arthur C. Clarke,** "A Meeting with Medusa"
1973 **Gene Wolfe,** "The Death of Dr. Island"
1974 **Robert Silverberg,** "Born with the Dead"
1975 **Roger Zelazny,** "Home is the Hangman"
1976 **James Tiptree, Jr.,** "Houston, Houston, Do You Read?"
1977 **Spider and Jeanne Robinson,** "Stardance"
1978 **John Varley,** "The Persistence of Vision"
1979 **Barry B. Longyear,** "Enemy Mine"
1980 **Not available at press time**

NOVELETTE (7,500-17,500 words)

1965 **Roger Zelazny,** "The Doors of His Face, the Lamps of His Mouth"
1966 **Gordon R. Dickson,** "Call Him Lord"
1967 **Fritz Leiber,** "Gonna Roll The Bones"
1968 **Richard Wilson,** "Mother to the World"
1969 **Samuel R. Delany,** "Time Considered as a Helix of Semi-Precious Stones"
1970 **Theodore Sturgeon,** "Slow Sculpture"
1971 **Poul Anderson,** "The Queen of Air and Darkness"
1972 **Poul Anderson,** "Goat Song"
1973 **Vonda McIntyre,** "Of Mist, and Grass, and Sand"
1974 **Gregory Benford and Gordon Eklund,** "If the Stars Are Gods"
1975 **Tom Reamy,** "San Diego Lightfoot Sue"
1976 **Isaac Asimov,** "The Bicentennial Man"
1977 **Raccoona Sheldon,** "The Screwfly Solution"
1978 **Charles L. Grant,** "A Glow of Candles, A Unicorn's Eye"
1979 **George R.R. Martin,** "Sandkings"
1980 **Not available at press time**

SHORT STORY (under 7,500 words)

1965 **Harlan Ellison,** " 'Repent, Harlequin!', Said the Ticktockman"
1966 **Richard McKenna,** "The Secret Place"
1967 **Samuel R. Delany,** "Aye, and Gomorrah"
1968 **Kate Wilhelm,** "The Planners"
1969 **Robert Silverberg,** "Passengers"
1970 **No award**
1971 **Robert Silverberg,** "Good News from the Vatican"
1972 **Joanna Russ,** "When It Changed"
1973 **James Tiptree, Jr.,** "Love Is the Plan, the Plan Is Death"
1974 **Ursula K. LeGuin,** "The Day before the Revolution"
1975 **Fritz Leiber,** "Catch That Zeppelin"
1976 **Charles L. Grant,** "A Crowd of Shadows"
1977 **Harlan Ellison,** "Jeffty Is Five"
1978 **Edward Byrant,** "Stone"
1979 **Edward Byrant,** "giANTS"
1980 **Not available at press time**

State Prize for Literature (Hooft Prize)
State Prize for Children's and Youth's Literature
Prize of the Netherlands

NETHERLANDS MINISTRY OF CULTURE, RECREATION AND SOCIAL WELFARE
Steenvoordelaan 370, Rijwijk Z-H, Netherlands

The State Prize for Literature, known as the Hooft Prize, is given annually, alternately for important prose, poetry or essays written originally in Dutch. The prize now carries a cash award of 10,000 Guilders. A jury selects the winner.

1947 **A. van Schendel** and **A. van Haesolthe,** Prose
1948 **A.M. Hammacher,** Essay
1949 **G. Achterberg,** Poetry
1950 **S. Vestdijk,** Prose
1951 **E.J. Dijksterhuis,** Essay
1952 **J.C. Bloem,** Poetry
1953 **E. Bordewijk,** Prose
1954 **L.J. Rogier,** Essay
1955 **A. Roland Holst,** Poetry

1956 **A. Blaman**, Prose
1957 **P.C.A. Geyl**, Essay
1958 **P. Kemp**, Poetry
1959 **No award**
1960 **V.E. van Vriesland**, Essay
1961 **H.W.J.M. Keuls**, Poetry
1962 **Th. de Vries**, Prose
1963 **F. van der Meer**, Essay
1964 **L. Vroman**, Prose
1965 **No award**
1966 **W.J.M.A. Asselbergs,** Essay
1967 **L.J. Swaanswijk,** Poetry
1968 **G.K. van het Reve**, Prose
1969 **No award,** Essay
1970 **G. Kouwenaar,** Poetry
1971 **W.F. Hermans,** Prose (Prize declined)
1972 **A.J. Herzberg,** Essay
1973 **H. de Vries,** Poetry
1974 **S. Carmigglet,** Prose
1975 **Rudy Kousbroek**, Essay
1976 **Remco Campert**, Poetry
1977 **Harry Mulisch**, Prose
1978 **Cornelis Verhoeven**, Essay
1979 **Ida Gerhardt**, Poetry
1980 **Willem Brakman**, Prose

The State Prize for Children's and Youths' Literature (Staatsprijs voor Kinder- en Jeugdliteratuur) is given every three years for an author's complete body of work for young people. The prize now carries a cash award of 6,500 guilders. A jury selects the winner.

1964 **Annie M.G. Schmidt**
1967 **A. Rutgers van der Loeff**
1970 **Miep Diekman**
1973 **Paul Biegel**
1976 **Tonke Dragt**
1979 **Guus Kuijer**

The Prize of the Netherlands Literature (Prijs der Nederlands Lettern) is awarded every three years for an imortant literary work in the Dutch language or for a complete or partial literary work of an author from the Netherlands or Belgium. The prize now carries an award of 18,000 Guilders. The winner is selected by a Dutch-Belgian jury.

1956 **Herman Tierlinck,** Belgium
1959 **A. Roland Holst,** Netherlands
1962 **Stijn Streuvals,** Belgium
1965 **Jacques C. Bloem,** Netherlands
1968 **Gerard Walschap,** Belgium
1971 **Simon Vestdijk,** Netherlands
1974 **Marnix Gijsen,** Belgium
1977 **W. F. Hermans,** Netherlands
1980 **Maurice Giliams,** Belgium

Neustadt International Prize for Literature

WORLD LITERATURE TODAY
630 Parrington Oval, Room 110, Norman, Okla. 73019 (405/325-4531)

The Neustadt International Prize for Literature is awarded biennially for continuing artistic achievement in fiction, drama or poetry. An international committee of 12 judges nominates and selects the winner. Each of the dozen judges nominates one writer, and the jury as a whole votes for the winner. The award consists of a minimum of $10,000, a silver eagle feather trophy, a certificate and the dedication of one issue of *World Literature Today,* formerly *Books Abroad.*

1970 **Giuseppe Ungaretti,** Italy
1972 **Gabriel Garcia Marquez,** Colombia
1974 **Francis Ponge,** France
1976 **Elizabeth Bishop,** United States
1978 **Czeslaw Milosz,** Poland/United States
1980 **Josef Skvorecky**, Czechoslovakia/Canada

Newbery Medal

AMERICAN LIBRARY ASSOCIATION
CHILDREN'S SERVICES DIVISION
50 E. Huron St., Chicago, Ill. 60611 (312/944-6780)

The Newbery Medal is awarded annually for the most distinguished contribution to children's literature during the preceding year. The author must be a citizen or resident of the U.S., and the work must be original, or if traditional, must be the result of original research. A 23-member committee of the Children's Services Division selects the winner.

1922 **Hendrik Van Loon,** *The Story of Mankind*
1923 **Hugh Lofting,** *The Voyages of Doctor Doolittle*
1924 **Charles Boardman Hawes,** *The Dark Frigate*
1925 **Charles J. Finger,** *Tales from Silver Lands*
1926 **Arthur Bowie Chrisman,** *Shen of the Sea*
1927 **Will James,** *Smoky, the Cowhorse*
1928 **Dham Gopal Mukerji,** *Gay-Neck, the Story of a Pigeon*
1929 **Eric P. Kelly,** *The Trumpeter of Krakow, a Tale of the Fifteenth Century*
1930 **Rachel Field,** *Hitty, Her First Hundred Years*
1931 **Elizabeth Coatsworth,** *The Cat Who Went to Heaven*
1932 **Laura Adams Armer,** *Waterless Mountain*
1933 **Elizabeth Foreman Lewis,** *Young Fu of the Upper Yangtze*
1934 **Cornelia Meigs,** *Invincible Louisa*
1935 **Monica Shannon,** *Dobry*
1936 **Carol Ryrie Brink,** *Caddie Woodlawn*
1937 **Ruth Sawyer,** *Roller Skates*
1938 **Kate Seredy,** *The White Stag*
1939 **Elizabeth Enright,** *Thimble Summer*
1940 **James Daugherty,** *Daniel Boone*
1941 **Armstrong Sperry,** *Call it Courage*
1942 **Walter D. Edmonds,** *The Matchlock Gun*
1943 **Elizabeth Janet Gray,** *Adam of the Road*
1944 **Esther Forbes,** *Johnny Tremain: A Novel for Old and Young*
1945 **Robert Lawson,** *Rabbit Hill*
1946 **Lois Lenski,** *Strawberry Girl*
1947 **Carolyn Sherwin Bailey,** *Miss Hickory*
1948 **William Pene Du Bois,** *The Twenty-One Balloons*
1949 **Marguerite Henry,** *King of the Wind*
1950 **Marguerite De Angeli,** *The Door in the Wall*
1951 **Elizabeth Yates,** *Amos Fortune, Free Man*
1952 **Eleanor Estes,** *Ginger Pye*
1953 **Ann Nolan Clark,** *Secret of the Andes*
1954 **Joseph Krumgold,** *. . . And Now Miguel*
1955 **Meindert De Jong,** *The Wheel on the School*
1956 **Jean Lee Latham,** *Carry on, Mr. Bowditch*
1957 **Virginia Sorensen,** *Miracles on Maple Hill*
1958 **Harold Keith,** *Rifles for Watie*
1959 **Elizabeth George Speare,** *The Witch of Blackbird Pond*
1960 **Joseph Krumgold,** *Onion John*

1961 **Scott O'Dell,** *Island of the Blue Dolphins*
1962 **Elizabeth George Speare,** *The Bronze Bow*
1963 **Madeleine L'Engle,** *A Wrinkle in Time*
1964 **Emily Neville,** *It's Like This, Cat*
1965 **Maia Wojciechowska,** *Shadow of a Bull*
1966 **Elizabeth Borton de Trevino,** *I, Juan de Pareja*
1967 **Irene Hunt,** *Up a Road Slowly*
1968 **Elaine Konigsburg,** *From the Mixed-Up Files of Mrs. Basil E. Frankweiler*
1969 **Lloyd Alexander,** *The High King*
1970 **William H. Armstrong,** *Sounder*
1971 **Betsy Byars,** *Summer of the Swans*
1972 **Robert C. O'Brien,** *Mrs. Frisby and the Rats of NIMH*
1973 **Jean Craighead George,** *Julie of the Wolves*
1974 **Paula Fox,** *The Slave Dancer*
1975 **Virginia Hamilton,** *M. C. Higgins, the Great*
1976 **Susan Cooper,** *The Grey King*
1977 **Mildred D. Taylor,** *Roll of Thunder, Hear My Cry*
1978 **Katherine Paterson,** *Bridge to Terabithia*
1979 **Ellen Raskin,** *The Westing Game*
1980 **Joan W. Blos,** *A Gathering of Days*

Bourse Goncourt de la Nouvelle
Prix International de la Press
Grand Aigle d'Or de la Ville de Nice
Silver and Gold Eagles

FESTIVAL INTERNATIONAL DU LIVRE DE NICE
Palais des Expositions, 06300 Nice, France (Tel: 55-18-55); and 5, Rue Stanislas, 75006 Paris, France (Tel: 544-20-18)

The Bourse Goncourt de la Nouvelle, which carries an honorarium of 10,000 francs, was created to support the literary form of the novella. A 10-member jury selects the winner.

1978 **Henri Gougaud,** *Departements et Territoires d'Outre Mort*

Current status unknown

The Prix International de la Presse, which consists of a diploma and a medal, is given for a historical work or a document that appeared in its original language during the previous year. A seven-member jury of representatives from international news magazines, such as *Newsweek, The Observer, Le Nouvel Observateur,* selects the recipient.

1977 **Jurgen Fuchs,** *Gedachtnisprotokolle*

Current status unknown

The Grand Aigle d'Or de la Ville de Nice, which carries an honorarium of 30,000 francs, is given for the work of a great French author or foreign author whose work has been translated into French. A jury of French and non-French authors and editors of literary journals and representatives of the French press select the winner.

1969 **Giudo Piovene**
1970 **Ferreira de Castro**
1971 **Angus Wilson**
1972 **Per Olof Sundman**
1973 **Aldo Palazzecchi**
1975 **Nadine Gordimer**
1976 **Julio Cortazar**
1977 **Ernst Junger**

Current status unknown

Concepts and execution of books are honored with a Golden Eagle (overall honors) and Silver Eagles (specific categories) upon selection by a jury.

GOLDEN EAGLE

1977 ***La Route des Incas***, (Photographs by Hans Silvester; Editions du Chene; France)

Current status unknown

SILVER EAGLE (FINE ARTS)

1977 ***Hortes Antes: L'Oeuvre Gravee*** (Office du Livre Switzerland)

Current status unknown

SILVER EAGLE (REFERENCE WORKS)

1977 ***Le Livre de l'Outil*** (Edition Hier et Demain; France)

Current status unknown

SILVER EAGLE (CATALOGUES)

1977 ***Andy Warhol: Das Zeichnerische Werk 1949-75*** (Wurttembergisher Kunstverein; Federal Republic of Germany)

Current status unknown

SILVER EAGLE (PRACTICAL REFERENCE)

1977 ***Universal Atlas*** (George Phillips; Great Britain)

Current status unknown

SILVER EAGLE (HISTORICAL DOCUMENTS)

1977 ***Le Voix da la Liberte — Ici Londres*** (Editions Documentation Francias/Club Francais des Bibiliophiles; France)

Current status unknown

SILVER EAGLE (ILLUSTRATED BIOGRAPHY)

1977 ***Sigmund Freud*** (Suhnkamp Verlag: Federal Republic of Germany)

Current status unknown

SILVER EAGLE (YOUTH)

1977 ***The Pond Book*** (Penguin Books; Great Britain)

Current status unknown

SILVER EAGLE (EDUCATION)

1977 ***Slabikar*** (*Statni Pedagogicke Nakladatelstvi;* Czechoslovakia)

Current status unknown

SILVER EAGLE (SCIENCE)

1977 ***Atlas—SSO Technology, Medicine*** (SSO Atlas Switzerland)

Current status unknown

SILVER EAGLE (PAPERBACK)

1977 ***Alban Berg: Life and Work in Words and Pictures*** (Insel Verlag; Federal Republic of Germany)

Current status unknown

SILVER EAGLE (SPECIAL JURY AWARD)

1977 ***Die Panoramen*** (Editions Orell Fusseli; Switzerland)

Current status unknown

Niederdeutsche Preise

STIFTUNG F.V.S.

Georgsplatz 10, 2 Hamburg I, Federal Republic of Germany (Tel: 33-04-00 and 33-06-00)

Five prizes, cumulatively called the Niederdeutsche Preise, are awarded in annual rotation. A jury selects the recipient of the award, which carries a cash prize of 5,000 German marks.

HANS-BOTTCHER-PREIS (Broadcast play)

1960 **Heinrich Schmidt-Barrien,** Frankenburg
1962 **Konrad Hansen,** Bremen
1965 **Hinrich Kruse,** Braak bei Neumunster
1970 **Ernst-Otto Schlopke,** Bremen
1972 **Fritz Arend,** Uphusen bei Bremen
1974 **Wolfgang Sieg,** Offenau bei Elmshorn
1976 **No award**
1980 **Friedrich Karl Schaefer,** Ahrensburg

KLAUS-GROTH-PREIS (Lyrics)

1956 **Hermann Claudius Gronwohld**
1958 **Otto Tenne,** Hamburg
1960 **Carl Budich,** Lubeck
1963 **Norbert Johannimloh,** Munster/Westf.
1966 **Johann Diedrich Bellmann,** Hermannsburg
1968 **Hans Ehrke,** Kiel
1971 **Oswald Andrae,** Jever
1975 **Siegfried Kessemeier,** Munster/Westf.
1978 **Peter Kuhweide,** Bremen

RICHARD-OHNSORG-PREIS (Acting, production, direction and recitation)

1963 **Hans Mahler,** Hamburg
1966 **Hans Fleischer,** Hamburg
1969 **Walter A. Kreye,** Bremen
1973 **Ernst Waldau,** Bremen
1976 **Erwin Herzig,** Lubeck
1979 **Erika Rumsfeld,** Bremen

FRITZ-REUTER-PREIS (Narrative literature)

1955 **Heinrich Behnken,** Hamburg
1957 **Hans Henning Holm,** Hamburg
1959 **Moritz Jahn,** Gottingen
1962 **Rudolf Kinau,** Hamburg
1965 **Thora Thyselius,** Brake
1968 **Heinrich Schmidt-Barrien,** Frankenburg
1972 **Diederich Heinrich Schmidt,** Leer
1976 **Christian Holsten,** Bremen
1979 **Heinrich Kruse,** Braak

FRITZ-STAVENHAGEN-PREIS (Dramatic poetry)

1959 **Hans Ehrke,** Kiel
1961 **Hermann Otto,** Hamburg
1964 **Hans Heitmann,** Lubeck
1967 **Paul Jessen,** Hockensbull
1969 **Ivo Braak,** Kiel
1971 **Karl Bunje,** Oldenburg
1973 **Gunther Siegmund,** Hamburg
1975 **Konrad Hansen,** Bremen

Nobel Prize for Literature

NOBEL FOUNDATION

Nobel House, Sturegatan 14, 11436 Stockholm, Sweden

One of six Nobel Prizes given annually, the Nobel Prize for literature is generally recognized as the highest honor that can be bestowed upon an author for his or her total body of literary work. The award, which consists of a gold medal, diploma and large honorarium, is given at a ceremony on December 10 of each year at Stockholm's City Hall. The award itself is presented and administered by the Swedish Academy, which selects the recipient. The amount of cash fluctuates; in 1980, it was approximately $212,000.

1901 **Sully-Prudhomme (Rene Francois Armand Prudhomme),** France
1902 **C.M.T. Mommsen,** Germany
1903 **Bjornstjerne Bjornson,** Norway
1904 **Frederic Mistral,** France
Jose Echegaray, Spain
1905 **Henryk Sienkiewicz,** Poland
1906 **Giosue Carducci,** Italy
1907 **Rudyard Kipling,** Great Britain
1908 **Rudolf C. Eucken,** Germany
1909 **Selma Lagerlof,** Sweden
1910 **Paul J. L. Heyse,** Germany
1911 **Count Maurice Maeterlinck,** Belgium
1912 **Gerhart Hauptmann,** Germany
1913 **Rabindranath Tagore,** India
1914 **No award**
1915 **Romain Rolland,** France
1916 **Carl G. von Heidenstam,** Sweden
1917 **Karl A. Gjellerup,** Denmark
Henrik Pontoppidan, Denmark
1918 **No award**
1919 **Carl F. G. Spitteler,** Switzerland
1920 **Knut Hamsun,** Norway
1921 **Anatole France,** France
1922 **Jacinto Benavente,** Spain
1923 **William Butler Yeats,** Ireland
1924 **Wladyslaw S. Reymont,** Poland
1925 **George Bernard Shaw,** Great Britain (born in Ireland)
1926 **Grazia Deledda,** Italy
1927 **Henri Bergson,** France
1928 **Sigrid Undset,** Norway (born in Denmark)
1929 **Thomas Mann,** Germany
1930 **Sinclair Lewis,** U.S.A.
1931 **Erik A. Karlfeldt,** Sweden
1932 **John Galsworthy,** Great Britain
1933 **Ivan A. Bunin,** France (born in Russia)
1934 **Luigi Pirandello,** Italy
1935 **No award**
1936 **Eugene O'Neill,** U.S.A.
1937 **Roger Martin du Gard,** France
1938 **Pearl S. Buck,** U.S.A.
1939 **Frans E. Sillanpaa,** Finland
1940 **No award**
1941 **No award**
1942 **No award**
1943 **No award**

1944 **Johannes V. Jensen,** Denmark
1945 **Gabriela Mistral,** Chile
1946 **Hermann Hesse,** Switzerland (born in Germany)
1947 **Andre Gide,** France
1948 **T.S. Eliot,** Great Britain (born in U.S.A.)
1949 **William Faulkner,** U.S.A.
1950 **Bertrand Russell,** Great Britain
1951 **Par F. Lagerkvist,** Sweden
1952 **Francois Mauriac,** France
1953 **Sir Winston Churchill,** Great Britain
1954 **Ernest Hemingway,** U.S.A.
1955 **Halldor K. Laxness,** Iceland
1956 **Juan Ramon Jimenez,** Puerto Rico (born in Spain)
1957 **Albert Camus,** France
1958 **Boris L. Pasternak,** U.S.S.R. (Prize declined)
1959 **Salvatore Quasimodo,** Italy
1960 **Saint-John Perse,** France
1961 **Ivo Andric,** Yugoslavia
1962 **John Steinbeck,** U.S.A.
1963 **Giorgos Seferis,** Greece (born in Turkey)
1964 **Jean-Paul Sartre,** France (Prize declined)
1965 **Mikhail Sholokhov,** U.S.S.R.
1966 **Samuel Joseph Agnon,** Israel (born in Austria)
Nelly Sachs, Sweden (born in Germany)
1967 **Miguel Angel Asturias,** Guatemala
1968 **Yasunari Kawabata,** Japan
1969 **Samuel Beckett,** France (born in Ireland)
1970 **Aleksandr I. Solzhenitsyn,** U.S.S.R.
1971 **Pablo Neruda,** Chile
1972 **Heinrich Boll,** Germany
1973 **Patrick White,** Australia
1974 **Eyvind Johnson,** Sweden
Harry Edmund Martinson, Sweden
1975 **Eugenio Montale,** Italy
1976 **Saul Bellow,** U.S.A.
1977 **Vicente Aleixandre,** Spain
1978 **Isaac Bashevis Singer,** U.S.A. (born in Poland)
1979 **Odysseus Elytis,** Greece
1980 **Czeslaw Milosz,** U.S.A. (born in Poland)

Nordiska Radets Litteraturpris

THE NORDIC COUNCIL
Fack, S-103, 10 Stockholm, Sweden (Tel: 14-10-00 and 20-54-02)

The Nordiska Radets Litteraturpris is awarded to a literary work of high merit written in the language of one of the Nordic countries and published during the two previous years. The award carries an honorarium of 75,000 Danish crowns and is given annually. A committee of Nordic experts makes the selection from candidates nominated by delegates of the participating countries.

1962 **Eyvind Johnson** (Sweden), *Hans nades tid*
1963 **Vaino Linna** (Finland), *Soner av ett folk*
1964 **Tarjei Vesaas** (Norway), *Is-slottet*
1965 **William Heinesen** (Faeroe Islands), *Det gode Hab*
Olof Lagercrantz (Sweden), *Fran helvetet till paradiset*
1966 **Gunnar Ekelof** (Sweden), *Diwan over Fursten av Emgion*
1967 **Johan Borgen** (Norway), *Nye noveller*
1968 **Per Olof Sundman** (Sweden), *Ingenjor Andres luftfard*
1969 **Per-Olof Enquist** (Sweden), *Baltutlamningen*
1970 **Klaus Rifbjerg** (Denmark), *Anna, jeg, Anna*
1971 **Thorkild Hansen** (Denmark), *Slavernes oer*
1972 **Karl Vennberg** (Sweden), *Sju ord pa tunnelbanan*
1973 **Veijo Meri** (Finland), *Sergeantens pojke*
1974 **Villy Sorensen** (Denmark), *Uden Mal—og med*
1975 **Hannu Salama** (Finland), *Kommer upp i to*
1976 **Olafur Sigurdsson** (Iceland), *Du minns en brunn*
1977 **Bo Carpelan** (Finland), *I de morka rummen, i de ljusa*
1978 **Kjartan Flogstad**
1979 **Ivar Lo Johansson**
1980 **Sara Lidman**

William Riley Parker Prize

MODERN LANGUAGE ASSOCIATION
62 Fifth Ave., New York, N.Y. 10011 (212/741-7854)

The $500 William Riley Parker Prize is given to an MLA member for an outstanding article in *PMLA*, selected by the William Riley Parker Prize Selection Committee.

1964 **David DeLaura**
1965 **Rene Girard**
1966 **Elisabeth Schneider**
1967 **Donald Rackin**
1968 **Stanley B. Greenfield**
1969 **Rudolf P. Gottfried**
1970 **E.D. Lowry**
1971 **Frederic R. Jameson**
1972 **R.A. Yoder**
1973 **Elisabeth Schneider**
1974 **George T. Wright**
1975 **Walter J. Ong**
1976 **R.G. Peterson**
1977 **Evelyn N. Hinz**
1978 **Morris E. Eaves**
1979 **David H. Miles**
1980 **Roger W. Herzel**

Peace Prize of German Book Dealers

BORSENVEREIN DES DEUTSCHEN BUCHHANDELS
Grosser Hirschgraben 17-21, D-6000 Frankfurt-am-Main, Federal Republic of Germany

The Friedenspreis des Deutschen Buchhandels, or Peace Prize of German Book Dealers, is given annually for meritorious literary contribution to international understanding. The award carries 25,000-mark honorarium.

1950 **Max Tau**
1951 **Albert Schweitzer**
1952 **Romano Guardini**
1953 **Martin Buber**
1954 **Carl J. Burckhardt**
1955 **Hermann Hesse**
1956 **Reinhold Schneider**
1957 **Thornton Wilder**
1958 **Karl Jaspers**
1959 **Theodor Heuss**
1960 **Victor Gollancz**
1961 **Sarvepalli Radhakrishnan**
1962 **Paul Tillich**
1963 **Carl Friedrich von Weizsacker**
1964 **Gabriel Marcel**
1965 **Nelly Sachs**
1966 **Augustin Bea**

Willem A. Visser't Hooft
1967 Ernst Bloch
1968 Leopold Sedar Senghor
1969 Alexander Mitscherlich
1970 Gunnar and Alva Myrdal
1971 Marion Grafin Donhoff
1972 Janusz Korczak
1973 The Club of Rome
1974 The Frere Roger, Prior of Taize
1975 Alfred Grosser
1976 Max Frisch
1977 Leszek Kolakowski
1978 Astrid Lindgren
1979 Yehudi Menuhin
1980 Ernesto Cardenal

Henry M. Phillips Prize

AMERICAN PHILOSOPHICAL SOCIETY
104 S. Fifth St., Philadelphia, Pa. 19106 (215/627-0706)

The Henry M. Phillips Prize, which carries an honorarium of up to $2,000, is awarded as merited for an outstanding book or essay on the science and philosophy of jurisprudence.

1895 **George H. Smith,** "The Theory of State"
1900 **W.H. Hastings,** "The Development of Law as Illustrated by the Decisions Relating to the Police Power of the State"
1912 **Charles H. Burr,** "The Treaty-making Power of the United States and the Methods of Its Enforcement as Affecting the Police Powers of the States"
1921 **Quincy Wright,** "The Relative Rights, Duties, and Responsibilities of the President, of the Senate and the House, and the Judiciary in Theory and Practice"
1935 **Lon L. Fuller,** "American Legal Realism"
1942 **Edward S. Corwin,** *The President: Office and Powers* and articles on constitutional law
1950 **Philip C. Jessup,** *Modern Law of Nations*
1955 **Edmond Cahn,** *The Sense of Injustice* and his contribution to *Supreme Court and Supreme Law*
1957 **Catherine Drinker Bowen,** *The Lion and the Throne*
1960 **Roscoe Pound,** "Jurisprudence"
1962 **Karl Nickerson Llewellyn,** *The Common Law Tradition: Deciding Appeals*
1974 **John Rawls,** *A Theory of Justice*
1976 **Harry W. Jones,** *The Efficiency of Law* and "An Invitation to Jurisprudence," *Columbia Law Review*
Wolfgang Friedman, *Legal Theory* and *Law in a Changing Society*
1980 **Willard Hurst,** *Law and Social Order in the United States*

Lorne Pierce Medal

ROYAL SOCEITY OF CANADA
344 Wellington, Ottawa, Ont. K1A 0N4 (613/992-3468)

The Lorne Pierce Medal, which has been accompanied by a $1,000 honorarium since 1966, is now awarded every two years for an achievement of special significance in imaginative or critical literature, either in English or in French. Critical literature dealing with Canadian subjects has priority over non-Canadian subjects in the selection of the recipient by a Committee.

1948 Gabrielle Roy
1949 John Murray Gibbon
1950 Marius Barbeau
1951 E.K. Brown
1952 Hugh MacLennan
1953 Earle Birney
1954 Alain Grandbois
1955 William Bruce Hutchison
1956 Thomas H. Raddall
1957 A.M. Klein
1958 H. Northrop Frye
1959 Philippe Panneton
1960 Morley Callaghan
1961 Robertson Davies
1962 F.R. Scott
1963 Leo-Paul Desrosiers
1964 Ethel Wilson
1965 No award
1966 A.J.M. Smith
1968 R.D.C. Finch
1970 Roy Daniells
1972 Desmond Facey
1974 Rina Wasnier
1976 Douglas LePan
1978 Carl F. Klinck
1980 Antonine Maillet

Pilgrim Award

SCIENCE FICTION RESEARCH ASSOCIATION
c/o James Gunn, 2215 Orchard Lane, Lawrence, Kan.

A framed scroll is given to the winner of the Pilgrim Award, which annually honors an author of any nationality for scholarly contributions to science fiction and modern fantasy writing. The winner is selected by a committee.

1970 J.O. Bailey
1971 Marjorie Nicolson
1972 Julius Kagarlitski
1973 Jack Williamson
1974 I.F. Clarke
1975 Damon Knight
1976 James Gunn
1977 Thomas D. Clareson
1978 Brian W. Aldiss
1979 Darko Suvin
1980 Peter Nicholls

Playboy Writing Awards

PLAYBOY MAGAZINE
919 N. Michigan Ave., Chicago, Ill. 60611 (312/PL 1-8000)

Fiction and non-fiction writers are honored annually in the Playboy Writing Awards for the year's best contributions to the magazine, as determined by the editors. The exact composition of the awards has changed over the years, but has included both major works and short pieces and has recognized the best new contributors. In addition to the $1,000 first-place winners listed here, the magazine also honors runners-up in the polling.

MAJOR WORK: FICTION

1977 **John Le Carre,** *The Honourable Schoolboy*
1978 **William Hjortsberg** *Falling Angel*
1979 **Norman Mailer,** *The Executioner's Song*
1980 **John Le Carre,** *Smiley's People*

FICTION/SHORT STORY

1956 **Herbert Gold,** "The Right Kind of Pride"
1957 **George Langelaan,** "The Fly"
1958 **Richard Matheson,** "The Distributor"
1959 **John Wallace,** "I Love You, Miss Irvine"
1960 **Ken Purdy,** "The Book of Tony"
1961 **Harvey Jacobs,** "The Lion's Share"
1962 **James Jones,** "The Thin Red Line"
1963 **Bernard Malamud,** "The Naked Nude"
1964 **Romain Gary,** "A Bit of A Dreamer, A Bit of A Fool"
1965 **Roald Dahl,** "The Visitor"
1966 **Vladimir Nabokov,** "Despair"
1967 **Isaac Bashevis Singer,** "The Lecture"
1968 **John Cheever,** "The Yellow Room"
1969 **James Leigh,** "Yes, It's Me and I'm Late Again"
Vladimir Nabokov, "Ada"
1970 **Joyce Carol Oates,** "Saul Bird Says: Relate! Communicate! Liberate!"
Irwin Shaw, Three stories that became part of novel *Rich Man, Poor Man:* "Thomas in Elysium," "Rudolph in Money Land," "Rich Man's Weather"
1971 **George Axelrod,** "Where Am I Now That I Need Me?"
Sean O'Faolain, "Murder at Cobbler's Hulk"
1972 **Sean O'Faolain,** "Falling Rocks, Narrowing Road, Cul-de-Sac, Stop"
Dan Jenkins, "Semi-Tough"
1973 **Anthony Austin,** "Where the Americans Came"
George MacDonald Fraser, "Flashman at the Charge"
1974 **Saul Bellow,** "Humboldt's Gift"
John Updike, "Nevada"
1975 **George MacDonald Fraser,** "Flashman in the Great Game"
1976 **Norman Mailer,** "The Trial of the Warlock"
Kurt Vonnegut, "Slapstick or Lonesome No More"
Paul Theroux, "The Autumn Dog"
1977 **Paul Theroux,** "Adulterer's Luck"
1978 **John Updike,** "The Faint"
1979 **Paul Theroux,** "White Lies"
1980 **Asa Baber,** "Papageno"

FICTION: BEST NEW WRITER/CONTRIBUTOR

1966 **Tom Mayer,** "The Eastern Springs"
1967 **Rafael Steinberg,** "Day of Good Fortune"
1968 **Richard Duggin,** "Gamma, Gamma, Gamma"
1969 **Warner Law,** "The Thousand-Dollar Cup of Crazy German Coffee"
1970 **Hal Bennett,** "Dotson Gerber Resurrected"
1971 **William Hjorstberg,** "Gray Matters"
1972 **James Alan McPherson,** "The Silver Bullet"
1973 **Nadine Gordimer,** "The Conservationist"
1974 **Paul Reb,** "The Legend of Step-and-a-Half"
1975 **Larry McMurtry,** "Dunlap Crashes In"
1976 **Nicholas Meyer,** "The West End Horror"
1977 **Judith Johnson Sherwin,** "Voyages of a Mile-High Fille de Joie"
1978 **Trevanian,** "Switching"
1979 **Lynda Leidiger,** "Snake Head"
1980 **Philip K. Dick,** "Frozen Journey"

NON-FICTION/ARTICLE

1958 **John Keats,** "Eros and Unreason in Detroit"
1959 **Ralph Ginzburg,** "Cult of the Aged Leader"
1960 **Charles Beaumont,** "Chaplin"
1961 **Ken W. Purdy,** "Hypnosis"
1962 **Ken W. Purdy,** "Stirling Moss: A Nodding Acquaintance With Death"
1963 **William Iversen,** "Youth, Love, Death and the Hubby Image"
1964 **John Clellon Holmes,** "Revolution Below the Belt"
1965 **Kenneth Tynan,** "The Beatle in the Bull Ring"
1966 **Nat Hentoff,** "The Cold Society"
1967 **John Kenneth Galbraith,** "Resolving Our Vietnam Problem"
1968 **Alan Watts,** "Wealth Versus Money"
1969 **Eric Norden,** "The Paramilitary Right"
1970 **Alvin Toffler,** "Future Shock"
1971 **John McPhee,** "Centre Court"
1972 **Richard Rhodes,** "The Killing of the Everglades"
1973 **John Clellon Holmes,** "Gone in October"
1974 **Robert Woodward and Carl Bernstein,** "All the President's Men"
Ed McClanahan, "Little Enis Pursues His Muse"
1975 **Norman Mailer,** "The Fight"
1976 **Alex Haley,** "Roots"
1977 **Asa Baber,** "The Commodities Market"
1978 **Craig Vetter** "Pushed to the Edge"
1979 **Asa Baber,** "The Condominium Conspiracy"
1980 **David Black,** "Medicine and the Mind"

NON-FICTION: SATIRE/HUMOR

1964 **Dan Greenburg,** "How to be a Jewish Mother"
1965 **Jean Shepherd,** "Leopold Doppler and the Orpheum Gravy Boat Riot"
1966 **Jean Shepherd,** "Daphne Bigelow and the Spine-Chilling Saga of the Snail-Encrusted Tinfoil Noose"
1967 **Jean Shepherd,** "Return of the Smiling Wimpy Doll"
1968 **Marvin Kitman,** "How I Became a Renaissance Man in My Spare Time"
1969 **Woody Allen,** "Show White"
Jean Shepherd, "Wanda Hickey's Night of Golden Memories"
1970 **Marvin Kitman,** "George Washington's Expense Account"
Richard Curtis, "The Giant Chicken Eating Frog"
1971 **Bruce McCall and Brock Yates,** "Major Hody Bisby's Album of Forgotten Warbirds"
Robert Morley, "Morley Meets the Frogs"
1972 **G. Barry Golson,** "The People—Maybe!"
Dan Greenburg, "My First Orgy"
1973 **Wayne McLoughlin and Scott Morris,** "The Fallout Follies"
Bob Ottum and William Neely, as Stroker Ace, "I Lost it in the Second Turn"
1974 **Richard Curtis,** "Do Plants Have Orgasms?
Dick Tuck, "Watergate Wasn't All My Fault"
1975 **Robert S. Wieder,** "Clarke Ghent's School Days"
1976 **Dan Greenburg,** "Dominant Writer Seeks Submissive Miss"
1977 **Marshall Brickman,** "The Book of Coasts"
1978 **Buck Henry,** "My Night at Plato's Retreat"
1979 **Tony Hendra, Christopher Cerf** and **Peter Elbling,** "And That's The Way It Was 1980-1989"
1980 **Bruce Feirstein,** "Etiquette for the Eighties"

NON-FICTION: ESSAY

1969 **Martin Luther King,** "Testament of Hope"
1970 **David Halberstam,** "The Americanization of Vietnam"
1971 **John Clellon Holmes,** "Thanksgiving in Florence"
1972 **Herbert Gold,** "In the Community of Girls and the Commerce of Culture"
1973 **Germaine Greer,** "Seduction Is a Four-Letter Word"
1974 **Frederick Exley,** "Saint Gloria and the Troll"
1975 **No award**
1976 **Ron Kovic,** "Born on the Fourth of July"

1977 **D. Keith Mano,** "Rocky Mountain Hype"

NON-FICTION: BEST NEW WRITER/CONTRIBUTOR

1969 **Karl Hess,** "The Death of Politics"
1970 **Stanley Booth,** "Furry's Blues"
1971 **Arthur Hadley,** "Goodbye to the Blind Flash"
1972 **Ed McClanahan,** "Grateful Dead I Have Known"
1973 **Roger Rapoport,** "It's Enough to Make You Sick"
1974 **O'Connell Driscoll,** "Jerry Lewis, Birthday Boy"
1975 **Harry Crews,** "Going Down in Valdeez"
Jay Cronley, "Houston"
1976 **Jim Davidson,** "Punch Out the IRS"
1977 **Roy Blount, Jr.,** "Chairman Billy"
1978 No award
1979 **Richard Price,** "Bear Bryant's Miracles"
1980 **Nora Gallagher,** "The San Francisco Experience"

SPECIAL AWARD

1976 **Robert Scheer,** Jimmy Carter interview and accompanying article: "Jimmy, We Hardly Know Y'all"
1978 **Irwin Shaw,** One of *Playboy's* most prolific contributors since his first article appeared in 1955
1979 **Lawrence Grobel,** Interviews, specifically with "the elusive Marlon Brando" and with Al Pacino, "the reclusive actor"

Edgar Allen Poe Awards

MYSTERY WRITERS OF AMERICA
150 Fifth Ave., New York, N.Y. 10011 (212/255-7005)

The Edgar Allen Poe Awards, informally known as the Edgars, are given annually for outstanding achievement in mystery writing for the year. A scroll is awarded to the winner.

NOVEL

1954 **Charlotte Jay,** *Beat Not the Bones*
1955 **Raymond Chandler,** *The Long Goodbye*
1956 **Margaret Millar,** *Beast in View*
1957 **Charlotte Armstrong,** *A Dram of Poison*
1958 **Ed Lacy,** *Room to Swing*
1959 **Stanley Ellin,** *The Eighth Circle*
1960 **Celia Fremlin,** *The Hours Before Dawn*
1961 **Julian Symons,** *The Progress of a Crime*
1962 **J. J. Marric,** *Gideon's Fire*
1963 **Ellis Peters,** *Death and the Joyful Woman*
1964 **Eric Ambler,** *The Light of Day*
1965 **John Le Carre,** *The Spy Who Came in from the Cold*
1966 **Adam Hall,** *The Quiller Memorandum*
1967 **Donald Westlake,** *God Save the Mark*
1968 **Jeffrey Hudson,** *A Case of Need*
1969 **Dick Francis,** *Forfeit*
1970 **Maj Sjowall and Per Wahloo,** *The Laughing Policeman*
1971 **Frederick Forsyth,** *Day of the Jackal*
1972 **Warren Kiefer,** *The Lingala Code*
1973 **Tony Hillerman,** *The Dance of the Dead*
1974 **Jon Cleary,** *Peter's Pence*
1975 **Brian Garfield,** *Hopscotch*
1976 **Robert Parker,** *Promised Land*
1977 **William H. Hallahan,** *Catch Me, Kill Me*
1978 **Ken Follett,** *The Eye of the Needle*
1979 **Arthur Mailing,** *The Rheingold Route*
1980 **Not available at press time**

FIRST NOVEL

1946 **Julius Fast,** *Watchful at Night*
1947 **Helen Eustis,** *The Horizontal Man*
1948 **Frederic Brown,** *The Fabulous Clipjoint*
1949 **Mildred Davis,** *The Room Upstairs*
1950 **Alan Green,** *What a Body*
1951 **Thomas Walsh,** *Nightmare in Manhattan*
1952 **Mary McMullen,** *Strangle Hold*
1953 **William Campbell Gault,** *Don't Cry for Me*
1954 **Ira Levin,** *A Kiss before Dying*
1955 **Jean Potts,** *Go, Lovely Rose*
1956 **Lane Kauffmann,** *The Perfectionist*
1957 **Douglas McNutt Douglas,** *Rebecca's Pride*
1958 **William R. Weeks,** *Knock and Wait a While*
1959 **Richard Martin Stern,** *The Bright Road to Fear*
1960 **Henry Slesar,** *The Grey Flannel Shroud*
1961 **John Holbrooke Vance,** *The Man in the Cage*
1962 **Suzanne Blanc,** *The Green Stone*
1963 **Robert L. Fish,** *The Fugitive*
1964 **Cornelius Hirschberg,** *Florentine Finish*
1965 **Harry Kemelman,** *Friday the Rabbi Slept Late*
1966 **John Ball,** *In the Heat of the Night*
1967 **Ross Thomas,** *The Cold War Swap*
1968 **Michael Collins,** *Act of Fear*
1969 **Joe Gores,** *A Time of Predators*
1970 **Lawrence Sanders,** *The Anderson Tapes*
1971 **A. H. Z. Carr,** *Finding Maubee*
1972 **R. H. Shimer,** *Squaw Point*
1973 **Paul E. Erdman,** *The Billion Dollar Sure Thing*
1974 **Gregory MacDonald,** *Fletch*
1975 **Rex Burns,** *Alvarez Journal*
1976 **James Patterson,** *The Thomas Berryman Number*
1977 **Robert Ress,** *A French Friend*
1978 **William L. De Andrea,** *Killed in the Ratings*
1979 **Richard North Patterson,** *The Lasko Tangent*
1980 **Not available at press time**

FACT CRIME BOOK

1977 **George Jones** and **Barbara Amiel,** *By Persons Unknown*
1978 **Vincent Bugliosi** and **Ken Hurwitz,** *Till Death Us Do Part*
1979 **Robert Lindsay,** *The Falcon and the Snowman*
1980 **Not available at press time**

PAPERBACK

1977 **Mike John,** *The Quark Maneuver*
1978 **Frank Bandy,** *Deceit and Deadly Lies*
1979 **William L. De Andrea,** *The Hog Murders*
1980 **Not available at press time**

CRITICAL/BIOGRAPHICAL SKETCH

1977 **John McAleer,** *Rex Stout*
1978 **Gwen Robyns,** *The Mystery of Agatha Christie*
1979 **Ralph B. Hone,** *Dorothy L. Sayers, A Literary Biography*
1980 **Not available at press time**

Political Book Award

WASHINGTON MONTHLY
2712 Ontario Rd. NW, Washington, D.C. 20009
(202/462-0128)

The annual Political Book Award is given for the best book(s) of the preceding year on politics and government. The magazine features the winning book in a major review in the March issue. A panel of editors selects the winner.

1970 **Chester L. Cooper,** *The Lost Crusade*
George R. Reedy, *The Twilight of the Presidency*

1971 **Ronald J. Glasser,** *365 Days*
Julian K. Prescott, *A History of the Modern Age*
1972 **Daniel Ellsberg,** *Papers on the War*
Frances FitzGerald, *Fire in the Lake*
1973 **John Newhouse,** *Cold Dawn: The Story of SALT*
Ward Just, *The Congressman Who Loved Flaubert and Other Political Stories*
1974 **Robert A. Caro,** *The Power Broker: Robert Moses and the Fall of New York*
1975 **Martha Derthick,** *Uncontrollable Spending for Social Service Grants*
1976 **John Morton Blum,** *V Was for Victory*
John Dean, *Blind Ambition*
John Hollander, *Reflections on Espionage*
1977 **Simon Leys,** *Chinese Shadows*
Morris P. Fiorina, *Congress: Keystone of the Washington Establishment*
1978 **Theodore H. White,** *In Search of History*
1979 **Thomas Powers,** *The Man Who Kept the Secrets: Richard Helms and the CIA*
1980 **Ronald Steel,** *Walter Lippmann and the American Century*
Robert Woodward and **Scott Armstrong,** *The Brethren*

Poses Creative Arts Award

BRANDEIS UNIVERSITY
Brandeis University Commission Office, 12 E. 77th St., New York, N.Y. 10021 (212/472-1501)

One of a series of awards in the creative arts, The Jack I. and Lillian L. Poses Brandeis University Creative Arts Award is given annually to recognize talent in mid-career in literature. The award, which may not be applied for, carries an honorarium of $1,000 and a medal or citation. Professional juries chosen by the commission select the winners.

MEDAL AWARD

1957 **William C. Williams,** Poetry
1958 **John Crowe Ransom,** Poetry
1959 **"H.D." (Hilda Doolittle),** Poetry
1960 **Yvor Winters,** Poetry
1961 **Allen Tate,** Poetry
1962 **Louise Bogan,** Poetry
1963 **Marianne Moore,** Poetry
1964 **Vladimir Nabokov,** Fiction
1965 **Stanley Kunitz,** Poetry
1966 **Eudora Welty,** Fiction
1967 **Conrad Aiken,** Poetry
1968 **Lionel Trilling,** Non-fiction
1969 **Leonie Adams,** Poetry
1970 **Isaac Bashevis Singer,** Fiction
1971 **Richard Wilbur,** Poetry
1972 **Katherine Anne Porter,** Fiction
1973 **Alfred Kazin,** Non-fiction
1974 **Robert Francis,** Poetry
1975 **Christopher Isherwood,** Fiction
1976 **Irving Howe,** Non-fiction
1977 **Robert Lowell,** Poetry
1978 **Saul Bellow,** Fiction
1979 **Jeremy Bernstein,** Non-fiction
1980 **Edgar Bowers,** Poetry

CITATION

1957 **Katherine Hoskins,** Poetry
1958 **Barbara Howes,** Poetry
1959 **Hayden Carruth,** Poetry
1960 **John Berryman,** Poetry
1961 **Louis O. Coxe,** Poetry
1962 **Ben Belitt,** Poetry
1963 **Howard Nemerov,** Poetry
1964 **Richard Yates,** Fiction
1965 **Anthony Hecht,** Poetry
1966 **John Barth,** Fiction
1967 **May Swenson,** Poetry
1968 **Elizabeth M. Thomas,** Non-fiction
1969 **Galway Kinnell,** Poetry
1970 **Robert Coover,** Fiction
1971 **James Wright,** Poetry
1972 **Edward Hoagland,** Fiction
1973 **Theodore Solotaroff,** Non-fiction
1974 **John Frederick Nims,** Poetry
1975 **Harold Brodkey,** Fiction
1976 **Susan Sontag,** Non-fiction
1977 **Theodore Weiss,** Poetry
1978 **Grace Paley**
1979 **Peter Metthiessen**
1980 **No award**

Prix Litteraire Prince Pierre

FONDATION PRINCE PIERRE DE MONACO
Palais Princier, Principality of Monaco (30-19-21, Ext. 305)

The Prix Litteraire Prince Pierre, or Prince Pierre Literary Prize, is a 30,000-French-franc award given to a French writer or foreign writer in the French language for a body of work. A council selects the winner.

1951 **Julien Green**
1952 **Henri Troyat**
1953 **Jean Ciono**
1954 **Jules Roy**
1955 **Louise de Vilmorin**
1956 **Marcel Brion**
1957 **Herve Bazin**
1958 **Jacques Perret**
1959 **Joseph Kessel**
1960 **Alexis Curvers**
1961 **Jean Dutourd**
1962 **Gilbert Cesbron**
1963 **Denis de Rougemont**
1964 **Christian Murciaux**
1965 **Francoise Maillet-Joris**
1966 **Maurice Druon**
1967 **Jean Cassou**
1968 **Jean Cayrol**
1969 **Eugene Ionesco**
1970 **Jean-Jacques Gautier**
1971 **Antoine Blondin**
1972 **Marguerite Yourcenar**
1973 **Paul Guth**
1974 **Felicien Marceau**
1975 **Francois Nourissier**
1976 **Anne Hebert**
1977 **Leopold Sedar Senghor**
1978 **Pierre Gascar**
1979 **Daniel Boulanger**
1980 **Marcel Schneider**

Pulitzer Prize

COLUMBIA UNIVERSITY
Graduate School of Journalism, New York, N.Y. 10027 (212/280-3828) (Pulitzer Prizes: 212/280-3841)

Endowed by the will of Joseph Pulitzer, founder of the *St. Louis Post Dispatch* and administered by Columbia University, the annual Pulitzer Prizes include $1,000 awards in fiction, general nonfiction, history and biography, as well as journalism, drama, music and public service, found elsewhere in this volume. Four copies of each book nominated must be sent to the Advisory Committee on Pulitzer Prizes for consideration.

FICTION (CALLED NOVEL UNTIL 1947)

1917 No award
1918 **Ernest Poole,** *His Family*
1919 **Booth Tarkington,** *The Magnificent Ambersons*
1920 No award
1921 **Edith Wharton,** *The Age of Innocence*
1922 **Booth Tarkington,** *Alice Adams*
1923 **Willa Cather,** *One of Ours*
1924 **Margaret Wilson,** *The Able McLaughlins*
1925 **Edna Ferber,** *So Big*
1926 **Sinclair Lewis,** *Arrowsmith*
1927 **Louis Bromfield,** *Early Autumn*
1928 **Thornton Wilder,** *The Bridge of San Luis Rey*
1929 **Julia Peterkin,** *Scarlet Sister Mary*
1930 **Oliver LaFarge,** *Laughing Boy*
1931 **Margaret Ayer Barnes,** *Years of Grace*
1932 **Pearl S. Buck,** *The Good Earth*
1933 **T. S. Stribling,** *The Store*
1934 **Caroline Miller,** *Lamb in His Bosom*
1935 **Josephine Winslow Johnson,** *Now in November*
1936 **Harold L. Davis,** *Honey in the Horn*
1937 **Margaret Mitchell,** *Gone With the Wind*
1938 **John Phillips Marquand,** *The Late George Apley*
1939 **Marjorie Kinnan Rawlings,** *The Yearling*
1940 **John Steinbeck,** *The Grapes of Wrath*
1941 No award
1942 **Ellen Glasgow,** *In This Our Life*
1943 **Upton Sinclair,** *Dragon's Teeth*
1944 **Martin Flavin,** *Journey in the Dark*
1945 **John Hersey,** *A Bell for Adano*
1946 No award
1947 **Robert Penn Warren,** *All the King's Men*
1948 **James Michener,** *Tales of the South Pacific*
1949 **James Gould Cozzens,** *Guard of Honor*
1950 **A. B. Guthrie, Jr.,** *The Way West*
1951 **Conrad Richter,** *The Town*
1952 **Herman Wouk,** *The Caine Mutiny*
1953 **Ernest Hemingway,** *The Old Man and the Sea*
1954 No award
1955 **William Faulkner,** *A Fable*
1956 **MacKinlay Kantor,** *Andersonville*
1957 No award
1958 **James Agee,** *A Death in the Family*
1959 **Robert Lewis Taylor,** *The Travels of Jaimie McPheeters*
1960 **Allen Drury,** *Advise and Consent*
1961 **Harper Lee,** *To Kill a Mockingbird*
1962 **Edwin O'Connor,** *The Edge of Sadness*
1963 **William Faulkner,** *The Reivers*
1964 No award
1965 **Shirley Ann Grau,** *The Keepers of the House*
1966 **Katherine Anne Porter,** *The Collected Stories of Katherine Anne Porter*
1967 **Bernard Malamud,** *The Fixer*
1968 **William Styron,** *The Confessions of Nat Turner*
1969 **N. Scott Momaday,** *House Made of Dawn*
1970 **Jean Stafford,** *Collected Stories*
1971 No award
1972 **Wallace Stegner,** *Angle of Repose*
1973 **Eudora Welty,** *The Optimist's Daughter*
1974 No award
1975 **Michael Shaara,** *The Killer Angels*
1976 **Saul Bellow,** *Humboldt's Gift*
1977 No award
1978 **James Alan McPherson,** *Elbow Room*
1979 **John Cheever** *The Stories of John Cheever*
1980 **Norman Mailer,** *The Executioner's Song*

HISTORY

1917 **J. J. Jusserand,** *With Americans of Past and Present Days*
1918 **James Ford Rhodes,** *A History of the Civil War, 1861-65*
1919 No award
1920 **Justin H. Smith,** *The War with Mexico* (2 vols.)
1921 **William Sowden Sims and Burton J. Hendrick,** *The Victory at Sea*
1922 **James Truslow Adams,** *The Founding of New England*
1923 **Charles Warren,** *The Supreme Court in United States History*
1924 **Charles McIlwain,** *The American Revolution—A Constitutional Interpretation*
1925 **Frederic L. Paxson,** *A History of the American Frontier*
1926 **Edward Channing,** *The History of the United States*
1927 **Samual Flagg Bemis,** *Pinckney's Treaty*
1928 **Vernon Louis Parrington,** *Main Currents in American Thought* (2 vols.)
1929 **Fred Albert Shannon,** *The Organization and Administration of the Union Army, 1861-1865*
1930 **Claude H. Van Tyne,** *The War of Independence*
1931 **Bernadotte E. Schmitt,** *The Coming of the War: 1914*
1932 **John J. Pershing,** *My Experiences in the World War*
1933 **Frederick J. Turner,** *The Significance of Sections in American History*
1934 **Herbert Agar,** *The People's Choice*
1935 **Charles McLean Andrews,** *The Colonial Period of American History*
1936 **Andrew C. McLaughin,** *The Constitutional History of the United States*
1937 **Van Wyck Brooks,** *The Flowering of New England*
1938 **Paul Herman Buck,** *The Road to Reunion, 1865-1900*
1939 **Frank Luther Mott,** *A History of American Magazines*
1940 **Carl Sandburg,** *Abraham Lincoln: The War Years*
1941 **Marcus Lee Hansen,** *The Atlantic Migration, 1607-1860*
1942 **Margaret Leech,** *Reveille in Washington*
1943 **Esther Forbes,** *Paul Revere and the World He Lived In*
1944 **Merle Curti,** *The Growth of American Thought*
1945 **Stephen Bonsal,** *Unfinished Business*
1946 **Arthur M. Schlesinger Jr.,** *The Age of Jackson*
1947 **James Phinney Baxter III,** *Scientists Against Time*
1948 **Bernard DeVoto,** *Across the Wide Missouri*
1949 **Roy Franklin Nichols,** *The Disruption of American Democracy*
1950 **Oliver W. Larkin,** *Art and Life in America*
1951 **R. Carlyle Buley,** *The Old Northwest: Pioneer Period, 1815-1840*
1952 **Oscar Handlin,** *The Uprooted*
1953 **George Dangerfield,** *The Era of Good Feelings*
1954 **Bruce Catton,** *A Stillness at Appomattox*
1955 **Paul Horgan,** *Great River: The Rio Grande in North American History*
1956 **Richard Hofstadter,** *Age of Reform*
1957 **George F. Kennan,** *Russia Leaves the War: Soviet-American Relations, 1917-1920*

1958 **Bray Hammond,** *Banks and Politics in America—From the Revolution to the Civil War*
1959 **Leonard D. White, assisted by Jean Schneider,** *The Republican Era: 1869-1901*
1960 **Margaret Leech,** *In the Days of McKinley*
1961 **Herbert Feis,** *Between War and Peace: The Potsdam Conference*
1962 **Lawrence H. Gipson,** *The Triumphant Empire: Thunder-Clouds Gather in the West*
1963 **Constance McLaughlin Green,** *Washington: Village and Capital, 1800-1878*
1964 **Sumner Chilton Powell,** *Puritan Village: The Formation of a New England Town*
1965 **Irwin Unger,** *The Greenback Era*
1966 **Perry Miller,** *Life of the Mind in America: From the Revolution to the Civil War*
1967 **William H. Goetzmann,** *Exploration and Empire: The Explorer and Scientist in the Winning of the American West*
1968 **Bernard Bailyn,** *The Ideological Origins of the American Revolution*
1969 **Leonard Levy,** *Origins of the Fifth Amendment*
1970 **Dean G. Acheson,** *Present at the Creation: My Years in the State Department*
1971 **James MacGregor Burns,** *Roosevelt: The Soldier of Freedom, 1940-1945*
1972 **C. N. Degler,** *Neither Black Nor White*
1973 **Michael Kammen,** *People of Paradox: An Inquiry Concerning the Origin of American Civilization*
1974 **Daniel J. Boorstin,** *The Americans: The Democratic Experience*
1975 **Dumas Malone,** *Jefferson and His Time*
1976 **Paul Horgan,** *Lamy of Sante Fe*
1977 **David M. Potter,** *The Impending Crisis 1841-1846* (a posthumous publication; manuscript finished by Don E. Fehrenbacher)
1978 **Alfred D. Chandler, Jr.,** *The Visible Hand: The Managerial Revolution in American Business*
1979 **Don E. Fehrenbacher,** *The Dred Scott Case*
1980 **Leon F. Litwack,** *Been in the Storm So Long*

BIOGRAPHY OR AUTOBIOGRAPHY

1917 **Laura E. Richards, Maude Howe Elliot and Florence Howe Hall,** *Julia Ward Howe*
1918 **William Cabell Bruce,** *Benjamin Franklin, Self-Revealed*
1919 **Henry Adams,** *The Education of Henry Adams*
1920 **Albert J. Beveridge,** *The Life of John Marshall* (4 vols.)
1921 **Edward Bok,** *The Americanization of Edward Bok*
1922 **Hamlin Garland,** *A Daughter of the Middle Border*
1923 **Burton J. Hendrick,** *The Life and Letters of Walter H. Page*
1924 **Michael Idvorsky Pupin,** *From Immigrant to Inventor*
1925 **M. A. DeWolfe Howe,** *Barrett Wendell and His Letters*
1926 **Harvey Cushing,** *The Life of Sir William Osler* (2 vols.)
1927 **Emory Holloway,** *Whitman*
1928 **Charles Edward Russell,** *The American Orchestra and Theodore Thomas*
1929 **Burton J. Hendrick,** *The Training of an American: The Earlier Life and Letters of Walter H. Page*
1930 **Marquis James,** *The Raven*
1931 **Henry James,** *Charles W. Eliot*
1932 **Henry F. Pringle,** *Theodore Roosevelt*
1933 **Allan Nevins,** *Grover Cleveland*
1934 **Tyler Dennett,** *John Hay*
1935 **Douglas Southall Freeman,** *R. E. Lee*
1936 **Ralph Barton Perry,** *The Thought and Character of William James*
1937 **Allan Nevins,** *Hamilton Fish*
1938 **Odell Shepard,** *Pedlar's Progress*
Marquis James, *Andrew Jackson*
1939 **Carl Van Doren,** *Benjamin Franklin*
1940 **Ray Stannard Baker,** *Woodrow Wilson, Life and Letters,* Volumes VII and VIII
1941 **Ola E. Winslow,** *Jonathan Edwards*
1942 **Forrest Wilson,** *Crusader in Crinoline*
1943 **Samuel Eliot Morison,** *Admiral of the Ocean Sea*
1944 **Carleton Mabee,** *The American Leonardo: The Life of Samuel F. B. Morse*
1945 **Russell Blaine Nye,** *George Bancroft: Brahmin Rebel*
1946 **Linnie M. Wolfe,** *Son of the Wilderness*
1947 **William Allen White,** *The Autobiography of William Allen White*
1948 **Margaret Clapp,** *Forgotten First Citizen: John Bigelow*
1949 **Robert E. Sherwood,** *Roosevelt and Hopkins*
1950 **Samuel Bemis,** *John Quincy Adams and the Foundations of American Foreign Policy*
1951 **Margaret Louise Coit,** *John C. Calhoun: American Portrait*
1952 **Merlo J. Pusey,** *Charles Evans Hughes*
1953 **David J. Mays,** *Edmund Pendleton 1721-1803*
1954 **Charles A. Lindbergh,** *The Spirit of St. Louis*
1955 **William S. White,** *The Taft Story*
1956 **T. F. Hamlin,** *Benjamin Henry Latrobe*
1957 **John F. Kennedy,** *Profiles in Courage*
1958 **Douglas Southall Freeman;** *George Washington,* Volumes I-VI
Mary Ashworth and John Carroll, *George Washington,* Volume VII
1959 **Arthur Walworth,** *Woodrow Wilson, American Prophet*
1960 **Samuel Eliot Morison,** *John Paul Jones*
1961 **David Donald,** *Charles Sumner and the Coming of the Civil War*
1962 **No award**
1963 **Leon Edel,** *Henry James*
1964 **Walter Jackson Bate,** *John Keats*
1965 **Ernest Samuels,** *Henry Adams*
1966 **Arthur Schlesinger, Jr.,** *A Thousand Days*
1967 **Justin Kaplan,** *Mr. Clemens and Mark Twain*
1968 **George F. Kennan,** *Memoirs (1925-1950)*
1969 **Benjamin Reid,** *The Man from New York: George Quinn and His Friends*
1970 **T. Harry Williams,** *Huey Long*
1971 **Lawrance R. Thompson,** *Robert Frost: The Years of Triumph, 1915-1938*
1972 **J. P. Lash,** *Eleanor and Franklin*
1973 **W. A. Swanberg,** *Luce and His Empire*
1974 **Louis Sheaffer,** *O'Neill, Son, and Artist*
1975 **Robert A. Caro,** *The Power Broker: Robert Moses and the Fall of New York*
1976 **Richard Warrington Baldwin Lewis,** *Edith Wharton: A Biography*
1977 **John E. Mack,** *A Prince of Our Disorder: The Life of T. E. Lawrence*
1978 **Walter Jackson Bate,** *Samuel Johnson*
1979 **Leonard Baker,** *Days of Sorrow and Pain: Leo Baeck and the Berlin Jews*
1980 **Edmund Morris,** *The Rise of Theodore Roosevelt*

GENERAL NON-FICTION

1962 **Theodore H. White,** *The Making of the President 1960*
1963 **Barbara Tuchman,** *The Guns of August*

1964 **Richard Hofstadter,** *Anti-intellectualism in American Life*
1965 **Howard Mumford Jones,** *O Strange New World*
1966 **Edwin Way Teale,** *Wandering Through Winter*
1967 **David Brion Davis,** *The Problem of Slavery in Western Culture*
1968 **Will and Ariel Durant,** *Rousseau and Revolution*
1969 **Rene Dubos,** *So Human an Animal: How We Are Shaped by Surroundings and Events*
Norman Mailer, *The Armies of the Night*
1970 **Erik H. Erikson,** *Gandhi's Truth*
1971 **John Toland,** *The Rising Sun*
1972 **Barbara W. Tuchman,** *Stilwell and the American Experience in China, 1911-1945*
1973 **Frances FitzGerald,** *Fire in the Lake*
Robert Coles, *Children of Crisis*
1974 **Ernest Becker,** *The Denial of Death*
1975 **Annie Dillard,** *Pilgrim at Tinker Creek*
1976 **Robert N. Butler,** *Why Survive? Being Old in America*
1977 **William W. Warner,** *Beautiful Swimmers: Watermen, Crabs and the Chesapeake Bay*
1978 **Carl Sagan,** *The Dragons of Eden*
1979 **Edward O. Wilson,** *On Human Nature*
1980 **Douglas R. Hofstadter,** *Godel, Escher, Bach: An Eternal Golden Braid*

SPECIAL CITATIONS AND AWARDS

1957 **Kenneth Roberts,** Historical novels
1960 **Garrett Mattingly,** *The Armada*
1961 ***American Heritage Picture History of the Civil War***
1973 **James Thomas Flexner,** *George Washington,* Vol. I-IV
1977 **Alex Haley,** *Roots*
1978 **E. B. White,** Letters, essays and full body of work

Remembrance Award

BERGEN-BELSEN ASSOCIATIONS
Box 333, Lenox Hill Station, New York. N.Y. 10021

The Remembrance Award, which carried a $2,500 honorarium, recognized the author of a novel, drama, poetry, essay or memoir of high literary merit inspired by the Nazi Holocaust that uses the experiences to present a humanistic and enlightened vision of the contemporary world to the present and future generations. This award has been suspended.

1965 **Elie Wiesel** (United States), "Town Beyond the Wall" and writings
1966 **Manes Sperber** (France), *Than a Tear in the Sea*
1967 **Jean Cayrol** (France), collected poems
1968 **Jacob Presser** (Holland), *The Destruction of the Dutch Jews*
Yehoshua Vigodsky (Israel), *Collected Works*
1969 **Arthur Morse** (United States), *While the Six Million Died*
Chaim Grade (United States), *Seven Little Lanes*
Joshua Wygodski (Israel), *Collected Works*
1970 **The City of Jerusalem**
1971 **Abba Kovner** (Israel), *Little Sister of Mine*
1972 **Uri Zvi Greenberg** (Israel), *Poems from the Holocaust*
1973 **Jacob Robinson** (United States), Historical research
Itzhak Meras (Israel), *Stalemate With Death*
Daniel Stern (United States), *Who Shall Live and Who Shall Die*
Mendel Mann (France), *Holocaust Trilogy*
Leon Eitinger (Norway), *Psychological Studies of Survivors of the Holocaust*
Abraham Sutzkever (Israel), *Poems from the Sea of Death*
Leon Leneman (France), *The Tragedy of Russian Jewry*
Mordecai Tzanim (Israel), *Collected Works of Eastern European Jewry*
Michel Borwicz (France), *Jewish Resistance*
S. L. Schneiderman (United States), *When the Vistula Spoke Yiddish*
Leib Rochman (Israel), *In Your Blood You Shall Live*
1974 **George Steiner** (Great Britain), *In Bluebird's Castle*
1975 **Andre Ne'her** (France), *Collected Philosophical Works*

Renaudot Prize

THEOPHRASTE RENAUDOT SECRETARIAT
c/o Etienne Labou, 5 Villa Halle, Paris 14, France

The Theophraste Renaudot Prize annually honors the author of an original novel published during the preceeding year. While the 50-franc honorarium is an insignificant sum, the prize is important in the French literary world. A ten-member jury selects the winner.

1926 **Armand Lunel,** *Niccolo Peccavi*
1927 **Bernard Nabonne,** *Maitena*
1928 **Andre Obey,** *Le Joueur de triangle*
1929 **Marcel Ayme,** *La Table aux Creves*
1930 **Germaine Beaumont,** *Piege*
1931 **Philippe Heriat,** *L'innocent*
1932 **Louis-Ferdinand Celine,** *Voyage au bout de la nuit*
1933 **Charles Braibant,** *Le Roi dort*
1934 **Louis Francis,** *Blanc*
1935 **Francois de Roux,** *Jours sans gloire*
1936 **Louis Aragon,** *Les Beaux Quartiers*
1937 **Jean Rogissart,** *Mervale*
1938 **Pierre-Jean Launay,** *Leonie la bienheureuse*
1939 **Jean Malaquais,** *Les Javanais*
1940 **No award**
1941 **Paul Mousset,** *Quand le temps travaillait pour nous*
1942 **Robert Gaillard,** *Les Liens de chaine*
1943 **Andre Soubiran,** *J'etais medecin avec les chars*
1944 **Rogert Peyrefitte,** *Les Amities particulieres*
1945 **Henri Bosco,** *Le Mas Theotime*
1946 **Jules Roy,** *La Vallee heureuse*
David Rousset, *L'Univers Concentrationnaire*
1947 **Jean Cayrol,** *Je vivrai l'amour des autres*
1948 **Pierre Fisson,** *Voyage aux horizons*
1949 **Louis Guilloux,** *Le Jeu de patience*
1950 **Pierre Molaine,** *Les Orgues de l'enfer*
1951 **Robert Margerit,** *Le Dieu nu*
1952 **Jacques Perry,** *L'amour de rien*
1953 **Celia Bertin,** *La Derniere Innocence*
1954 **Jean Reverzy,** *Le Passage*
1955 **Georges Govy,** *Le Moissonneur d'epines*
1956 **Andre Perrin,** *La Pere*
1957 **Michel Butor,** *La Modification*
1958 **Edouard Glissant,** *La Lezarde*
1959 **Albert Palle,** *L'Experience*
1960 **Alfred Kern,** *Le Bonheur fragile*
1961 **Roger Bordier,** *Les Bles*
1962 **Simone Jacquemard,** *Le Veilleur de nuit*
1963 **Jean-Marie Le Clezio,** *Le Proces verbal*
1964 **Jean-Pierre Faye,** *L'Ecluse*
1965 **Georges Perec,** *Les Choses*

1966 **Jose Cabanis,** *La Bataille de Toulouse*
1967 **Salvat Etchart,** *Le Monde tel qu'il est*
1968 **Yambo Ouologuem,** *Le Devoir de violence*
1969 **Max Olivier-Lacamp,** *Les Feux de la Colere*
1970 **Jean Freustier,** *Isabelle ou l'Arriere-saison*
1971 **Pierre-Jean Remy,** *Le Sac du palais d'Ete*
1972 **Christopher Frank,** *La Nuit Americaine*
1973 **Suzanne Prou,** *La Terrasse des Bernardini*
1974 **Georges Borgeaud,** *Voyage a l'etranger*
1975 **Jean Joubert,** *L'homme de sable*
1976 **Michel Henry,** *L'amour les yeux fermes*
1977 **Alphonse Boudard,** *Les Combattants du Petit Bonheur*
1978 **Conrad Detrez,** *L'herbe a bruler*
1979 **Jean Marc Roberts,** *Affaire Etranger*
1980 **Daniel Sallenave,** *Les Portes de Gubbio*

John Llewelyn Rhys Memorial Prize

NATIONAL BOOK LEAGUE
Book House, 45 East Hill, London SW18 2QZB, United Kingdom (Tel: 01-870-9055)

The John Llewelyn Rhys Memorial Prize is given annually for a book by an author under 30 years who is a citizen of Great Britain or the Commonwealth. A panel of judges selects the winner of the £300 award.

1942 **Michael Richey,** *Sunk by a Mine*
1943 **Morwenna Donelly,** *Beauty for Ashes*
1944 **Alun Lewis,** *The Last Inspection*
1945 **James Aldridge,** *The Sea Eagle*
1946 **Oriel Malet,** *My Bird Sings*
1947 **Anne-Marie Walters,** *Moondrop to Gascony*
1948 **Richard Mason,** *The Wind Cannot Read*
1949 **Emma Smith,** *Maidens' Trip*
1950 **Kenneth Allsop,** *Adventure Lit Their Star*
1951 **E.J. Howard,** *The Beautiful Visit*
1952 **No award**
1953 **Rachel Trickett,** *The Return Home*
1954 **Tom Stacey,** *The Hostile Sun*
1955 **John Wiles,** *The Moon to Play With*
1956 **John Hearne,** *Voices under the Window*
1957 **Ruskin Bond,** *The Room on the Roof*
1958 **V. S. Naipaul,** *The Mystic Masseur*
1959 **Dan Jacobson,** *A Long Way from London*
1960 **David Caute,** *At Fever Pitch*
1961 **David Storey,** *Flight into Camden*
1962 **Robert Rhodes James,** *An Introduction to the House of Commons*
Edward Lucie-Smith, *A Tropical Childhood and Other Poems*
1963 **Peter Marshall,** *Two Lives*
1964 **Nell Dunn,** *Up the Junction*
1965 **Julian Mitchell,** *The White Father*
1966 **Margaret Drabble,** *The Millstone*
1967 **Anthony Masters,** *The Seahorse*
1968 **Angela Carter,** *The Magic Toyshop*
1969 **Melvyn Bragg,** *Without a City Wall*
1970 **Angus Calder,** *The People's War*
1971 **Shiva Naipaul,** *Fireflies*
1972 **Susan Hill,** *The Albatross*
1973 **Peter Smalley,** *A Warm Gun*
1974 **Hugh Fleetwood,** *The Girl Who Passed for Normal*
1975 **David Hare,** *Knuckle*
Tim Jeal, *Cushing's Crusade*
1976 **No award**
1977 **Richard Cork,** *Vorticism and Abstract Art in the First Machine Age,* Vol. I and II
1978 **Andrew N. Wilson,** *The Sweets of Pimlico*
1979 **Peter Boardman,** *The Shining Mountain*
1980 **Desmond Hogan,** *The Diamonds at the Bottom of the Sea*

Richard and Hinda Rosenthal Foundation Award for Fiction

AMERICAN ACADEMY AND INSTITUTE OF ARTS AND LETTERS
633 W. 155th St., New York, N.Y. 10032 (212/368-5900)

One of a pair of awards established under the same endowment (the other being for painting), the Richard and Hinda Rosenthal Foundation Award of $2,000 annually goes for a work of fiction published during the preceding 12 months which, although not a commercial success, was "a considerable literary achievement."

1957 **Elizabeth Spencer,** *The Voice At The Back Door*
1958 **Bernard Malamud,** *The Assistant*
1959 **Frederick Buechner,** *The Return Of Ansel Gibbs*
1960 **John Updike,** *The Poorhouse Fair*
1961 **John Knowles,** *A Separate Peace*
1962 **Paule Marshall,** *Soul Clap Hands And Sing*
1963 **William Melvin Kelley,** *A Different Drummer*
1964 **Ivan Gold,** *Nickel Miseries*
1965 **Thomas Berger,** *Little Big Man*
1966 **Tom Cole,** *An End To Chivalry*
1967 **Thomas Pynchon,** *The Crying Of Lot 49*
1968 **Joyce Carol Oates,** *A Garden Of Earthly Delights*
1969 **Frederick Exley,** *A Fan's Notes*
1970 **Jonathan Strong,** *Tike And Five Stories*
1971 **Christoper Brookhouse,** *Running Out*
1972 **Thomas McGuane,** *The Bushwhacked Piano*
1973 **Thomas Rogers,** *The Confession Of A Child Of The Century*
1974 **Alice Walker,** *In Love & Trouble*
1975 **Ishmael Reed,** *The Last Days Of Louisiana Red*
1976 **Richard Yates,** *Disturbing The Peace*
1977 **Spencer Holst,** *Spencer Holst Stories*
1978 **Douglas Day,** *Journal of the Wolf*
1979 **Diane Johnson,** *Lying Low*
1980 **Stanley Elkin,** *The Living End*

W. H. Smith Literary Award

W. H. SMITH & SON LTD.
Strand House, 10 New Fetter Lane, London EC4A 1AD, United Kingdom (Tel: 01-353-0277)

The W.H. Smith Literary Award, which now carries an honorarium of £2,500, is given annually to a Commonwealth author for an outstanding contribution to literature originally published during the previous year in the United Kingdom and written originally in English. A three-judge panel selects the winner.

1959 **Patrick White,** *Voss*
1960 **Laurie Lee,** *Cider With Rosie*
1961 **Nadine Gordimer,** *Friday's Footprint*
1962 **J.R. Ackerley,** *We Think the World of You*
1963 **Gabriel Fielding,** *The Birthday King*
1964 **E.H. Gombrich,** *Meditations On A Hobby Horse*
1965 **Leonard Woolf,** *Beginning Again*
1966 **R.C. Hutchinson,** *A Child Possessed*
1967 **Jean Rhys,** *Wild Sargasso Sea*
1968 **V.S. Naipaul,** *The Mimic Men*
1969 **Robert Gittings,** *John Keats*

1970 **John Fowles,** *The French Lieutenant's Woman*
1971 **Nan Fairbrother,** *New Lives, New Landscapes*
1972 **Kathleen Raine,** *The Lost Country*
1973 **Brian Moore,** *Catholics*
1974 **Anthony Powell,** *Temporary Kings*
1975 **Jon Stallworthy,** *Wilfred Owen: A Biography*
1976 **Seamus Heaney,** *North*
1977 **Ronald Lewin,** *Slim: The Standardbearer*
1978 **Patrick Leigh Fermor,** *A Time of Gifts*
1979 **Thom Gunn,** *Life in the English Country House*
1980 **Isabel Colgate,** *The Shooting Party*

Stephen Black Prize for Drama
Jochem van Bruggen-prys vir Prosa
Roy Campbell Prize for Poetry
G.W.F. Grosskopf-prys vir Drama
C. Louis Leipoldt-prys vir Poesie
Pauline Smith Prize for Prose

DEPT. OF NATIONAL EDUCATION
Private Bag X122, Pretoria 0001, Republic of South Africa (Tel: 269971)

A competition in such literary genres as drama, prose and poetry is held annually, with each category judged every three years by a panel appointed by the Minister of National Education. A top prize of 750 Rand is given for the best entry in English and Afrikaans. The author must be a South African citizen or resident for at least a year. There are no age or religious restrictions.

STEPHEN BLACK PRIZE FOR DRAMA

1965 **May Thomas,** *The Unrecorded Days*
1968 **J. Lodge,** *In a Man's Shadow*
1971 **J.A. Brown,** *Travels with a Collapsible Woman*
1974 **S.J. Curtis,** *Steadman's Folly*

Current Status Unknown

G.W.F. GROSSKOPF-PRYS VIR DRAMA

1968 **C. Seymore,** *Mag is n Vandaal*

Current Status Unknown

PAULINE SMITH PRIZE FOR PROSE

To date, this award has not been given.

Current Status Unknown

JOCHEM VAN BRUGGEN-PRYS VIR PROSA

1972 **P. Pistorius,** *n Spyker vir Slypsteenkop*

Current Status Unknown

ROY CAMPBELL PRIZE FOR POETRY

1959 **A. Delius,** *A Corner of the World*
A. Curry, *Of Africa and the East*
1963 **P.R.C. Adams,** *The Land at My Door*
1967 **R. Dederick,** *A Low Trajectory*

Current Status Unknown

C. LUIS LEIPOLDT-PRYS VIR POESIE

1973 **D. Sleigh,** *Bundel Gedigte*

Current Status Unknown

Literaturpreis des Landeshauptstadt Stuttgart

LANDESHAUPTSTADT STUTTGART
Postfach 161, 7000 Stuttgart 1, Federal Republic of Germany (0711-216-6703)

The Literatur preis der Landeshauptstadt Stuttgart, or Literature Prize of the State Capital of Stuttgart, is given every two years to two authors and one translator. Originally consisting of 5,000 marks to each awardee, the prize now consists of 10,000 for each of the three winners, who are selected by a jury.

1978 **Werner Durrson**, Author
Roland Lang, Author
Fritz Vogelsang, Translator
1980 **Irma Brender**, Author
Margarete Hannsmann, Author
Otto Bayer, Translator

Jesse H. Jones Award
Friends of the Dallas Public Library Award
Short Story Award
Steck Vaughn Award for Children's Fiction

TEXAS INSTITUTE OF LETTERS
Box 3143, Dallas, Tex. 75275 (214/692-2000)

The Jesse H. Jones Award, which carries a $1,000 honorarium, is given annually for the best fictional book about Texas or by a Texas author. Until 1959, when the Houston Endowment funded this award, it was known as the McMurray Bookshop Award.

1948 **David Westheimer,** *Summer on the Water*
1949 **Fred Gipson,** *Hound-Dog Man*
1950 **William Goyan,** *The House of Breath*
1951 **Dillon Anderson,** *I and Claudie*
1952 **George Williams,** *The Blind Bull*
1953 **Madison Cooper,** *Sironia, Texas*
1954 **William A. Owens,** *Walking on Borrowed Land*
1955 **Fred Gipson,** *Recollection Creek*
1956 **Curt Anders,** *The Price of Courage*
1957 **Sikes Johnson,** *The Hope of Refuge*
1958 **William Humphrey,** *Home from the Hill*
1959 **Hamilton "Tex" Maule,** *Jeremy Todd*
Walter Clemons, *The Poison Tree*
1960 **Bill Casey,** *A Shroud for a Journey*
1961 **Larry McMurtry,** *Horseman, Pass By*
1962 **Katherine Anne Porter,** *Ship of Fools*
1963 **J. Y. Bryan,** *Come to the Bower*
1964 **Tom Lea,** *The Hands of Cantu*
1965 **William Humphrey,** *The Ordways*
1966 **Larry McMurtry,** *The Last Picture Show*
Tom Pendleton, *The Iron Orchard*

1967 **Robert Flynn,** *North to Yesterday*
1968 **Marshall Terry,** *Tom Northway*
Tom Horn, *The Shallow Grass*
1969 **Willard Marsh,** *Beachhead in Bohemia*
1970 **Paul Horgan,** *Whitewater*
1971 **Nolan Porterfield,** *A Way of Knowing*
1972 **John Williams,** *Augustus*
1973 **Shelby Reed Hearon,** *The Second Dune*
Chester L. Sullivan, *Alligator Gar*
1974 **Charles W. Smith,** *Thin Men of Haddam*
1975 **Donald Barthelme,***The Dead Father*
1976 **Max Apple,** *The Oranging of America*
1977 **R. G. Vliet,** *Solitudes*
1978 **Shelby Hearon,** *A Prince of A Fellow*

Current Status Unknown

The Friends of the Dallas Public Library Award, which carries a $500 honorarium, is given annually for a book about Texas which contributes most to general knowledge about the state.

1959 **David L. Miller,** *Modern Science and Human Freedom*
1960 **Robert Vines,** *Trees, Shrubs, and Woody Vines*
1961 **W. W. Newcomb, Jr.,** *Indians of Texas*
1962 **Joseph Stephen Gallegly,** *Footlights on the Border*
1963 **Joseph Milton Nance,** *After San Jacinto*
1964 **Ramon Adams,** *Burrs under the Saddle*
1965 **Lois Wood Burkhalter,** *Gideon Lincecum*
1966 **William H. Goetzmann,** *Exploration and Empire*
1967 **W. W. Newcomb, Jr.,** *Rock Art of Texas Indians*
1968 **C. L. Sonnichsen,** *Pass of the North*
1969 **Bill C. Malone,** *Country Music, USA*
1970 **Richard B. Henderson,** *Maury Maverick*
1971 **Thomas Parke Hughes,** *Elmer Sperry, Inventor and Engineer*
1972 **A. C. Greene,** *The Last Captive*
1973 **Donald E. Green,** *Land of the Underground Rain, Irrigation on the Texas High Plains, 1910-1970*
1974 **Harry C. Oberholser,** *The Bird Life of Texas*
1975 **Elizabeth A. H. John,** *Storms Brewed in Other Men's Worlds*
1976 **Lawrence Goodwyn,** *Democratic Promise*
1977 **Frank E. Vandiver,** *Black Jack: The Life and Times of John J. Pershing*
1978 **Walt W. Rostow**, *The World Economy: History and Prospect*

Current status unknown

A $250 honorarium is given for the best short story.

1978 **Carolyn Osborn**, "The Accidental Trip to Jamaica"
Ellen Wier, "Cambell Oakley's Sun Shines on Roy Singing Grass"

Current status unknown

Alexander Gode Medal

AMERICAN TRANSLATORS ASSOCIATION
109 Croton Ave., Ossining, N.Y. 10562 (914/941-1500)

The Alexander Gode Medal is given annually on recommendations to the ATA Honors and Awards Committee for winners of the medallion, which honors distinguished service in the field.

1964 **Alexander Gode**
1965 **Kurt Gingold**
1966 **Richard and Clara Winston**
1967 **National Translation Center** (University of Texas)
1968 **Pierre-Francois Caille**
1969 **Henry Fischbach**
1970 **Carl V. Bertsche**
1971 **Lewis Bertrand**
1972 **Lewis Galantiere**
1973 **Jean-Paul Vinay**
1974 **Eliot F. Beach**
1975 **Frederick Ungar**
1976 **No award**
1977 **Eugene Nida**
1978 **Royal L. Tinsley**, Jr.,
1979 **No award**
1980 **Gregory Rabassa**

P.E.N. Translation Prizes

P.E.N. AMERICAN CENTER
47 Fifth Ave., New York, N.Y. 10003 (212/255-1977)

The $500 Goethe House-P.E.N. Translation Prize is given annually for the best book translated from German into English during the year.

1974 **Sophie Wilkins,** *The Lime Works,* by Thomas Bernhard
1975 **Peter Sander,** *Ice Age,* by Tancred Dorst
1976 **Ralph Manheim,** *A Sorrow Beyond Dreams,* by Peter Handke
1977 **Douglas Parmee,** *An Exemplary Life,* by Siegfried Lenz
1978 **Joachim Neugroschel**, *The Wonderful Years,* by Reiner Kunze
1979 **Leila Vennewitz**, works of Heinrich Boll
1980 **Joachim Neugroschel**, *The Tongue Set Free,* by Elias Canetti

The $1,000 P.E.N. Translation Prize, donated by the Book-of-the-Month Club, honors the best book-lengh translation from any language into English.

1963 **Archibald Colquhoun,** *The Viceroys* by Federico de Roberto
1964 **Ralph Manheim,** *The Tin Drum,* by Gunter Grass
1965 **Joseph Barnes,** *Story Of A Life,* by Konstantin Paustovsky
1966 **Geoffrey Skelton and Adrian Mitchell,** *Marat/Sade,* by Peter Weiss
1967 **Harriet de Onis,** *Sagarana,* by J. Guimaraes Rosa
1968 **Vladimir Markov and Merrill Sparks,** *Modern Russian Poetry*
1969 **W. S. Merwin,** *Selected Translations 1948-1968*
1970 **Sidney Alexander,** *The History Of Italy,* by Francesco Guicciardini
1971 **Max Hayward,** *Hope Against Hope,* by Nadezhda Mandelstam
1972 **Richard and Clara Winston,** *Letters of Thomas Mann*
1973 **J. P. McCulloch,** *Poems Of Sextus Propertius*
1974 **Hardie St. Martin and Leonard Mades,** *Obscene Bird Of Night,* by Jose Donoso
1975 **Helen R. Lane,** *Count Julian,* by Juan Goytisolo
1976 **Richard Howard,** *A Short History Of Decay,* by E. M. Cioran
1977 **Gregory Rabassa,** *The Autumn of the Patriarch,* by Gabriel Garcia Marquez
1978 **Adrienne Foulke**, *One Way or Another,* by Leonardo Sciascia
1979 **Charles Wright**, *The Storm & Other Poems,* by Eugenio Montale

1980 **Charles Simic,** *Homage to the Lame Wolf*, by Vasko Popa

Two $500 American-Scandinavian Foundation-P.E.N. Translation Prizes are given annually, one each for poetry and fiction for translations into English from Danish, Finnish, Icelandic, Norwegian or Swedish works by authors born after 1880.

POETRY

1980 **Anselm Hollo,** works by Pentti Saarikoski

FICTION

1980 **Jack Brondum,** *Complete Freedom*, by Tove Ditlevsen

The $500 Calouste Gulbenkian-P.E.N. Translation Prize is given biennially for translations from Portuguese into English.

1979 **Helen R. Lane,** *The Three Marias*

The Renato Poggioli Award of $3,000 is granted annually to promising young translators for projects at work.

1979 **Norman MacAfee**
1980 **Lawrence Venuti**

David D. Lloyd Prize

THE HARRY S. TRUMAN LIBRARY
Independence, Mo. 64050 (816/833-1400)

Award Correspondence: c/o Professor Thomas C. Blaisdell, Jr., Dept. of Political Science, 210 Barrows Hall, University of California, Berkeley, Calif. 94720

The $1,000 David D. Lloyd Prize is awarded biennially by the Harry S. Truman Library Institute for National and International Affairs for a book published during the preceding two years that deals primarily and substantially with some aspect of political, economic and social development in the United States, principally during the Truman presidency or with the public career of Harry S. Truman.

1967 **Earl Latham,** *The Communist Conspiracy in Washington from the New Deal to McCarthy*
1969 **Irwin Ross,** *The Loneliest Campaign: The Truman Victory of 1948*
1970 **Dean G. Acheson,** *Present at the Creation: My Years in the State Department*
Richard G. Hewlett, and Francis Duncan, *Atomic Shield, 1948-1952; My Years in the State Department*
1972 **Susan M. Hartmann,** *Truman and the 80th Congress*
1974 **Alonzo L. Hamby,** *Beyond the New Deal: Harry S. Truman and American Liberalism*
1976 **Lynn Estheridge Davis,** *The Cold War Begins: Soviet-American Conflict Over Eastern Europe*
1978 **David S. McLellan,** *Dean Acheson, The State Department Years*
1980 **John K. Emmerson,** *The Japanese Thread: A Life in the U.S. Foreign Service*

Ulisse Prize

RIVISTA ULISSE
Sezione Premio Cortina Ulisse, Via Po 11, 00198-Rome, Italy

The European Cortina *Ulisse* Prize, which carries a 1-million lire cash award, is given annually for a book which encourages that notion that "culture ought to be a common instrument of civilization and not the privilege of the few." The winner is selected by a jury, whose members are representatives of the Accademia Nazionale dei Lincei.

1949 **John Read,** (United Kingdom), *A Direct Entry to Organic Chemistry*
1950 **Carlo Morandi,** (Italy), *L'Idea dell'Unita Politica d'Europa nel XIX e XX secolo*
Pierre Belperron, (France), *La Guerre de Secession*
1951 **Lionello Venturi,** (Italy), *Come Si Comprende la Pittura*
1952 **Ernest Baldwin,** (United Kingdom), *Dynamic Aspects of Biochemistry*
1953 **No award**
1954 **Graham Hutton,** (United Kingdom), *We Too Can Prosper*
1955 **Edward Spranger,** (Germany), *Padagogische Perspektiven*
1956 **Luigi Preti,** (Italy), *Le Lotte Agrarie nella Valle Padana*
1957 **No award**
1958 **G. Lowenthal and J. Hausen,** (Germany), *Wir Werden durch Atome Leben*
1959 **George Elgozy,** (France), *La France devant le Marche Commun*
1960 **No award**
1961 **Felice Ippolito,** (Italy), *L'Italia e l'Energia Nucleare*
1962 **Werner Holzer,** (Germany), *Das Nackte Antlitz Africas*
1963 **No award**
1964 **Hans Herbert Goetz,** (Germany), *Weil Alle Besser Leben Wollen*
1965 **Ladislao Mittner,** (Italy), *Storia Della Letteratura Tedesca dal Pietismo al Romanticismo*
1966 **No award**
1967 **Giulio Carlo Argan,** (Italy), *Progetto e Destino*
1968 **Andre Martinet,** (France), *La Consideration Fonctionelle du Langage*
1969 **No award**
1970 **Edouard Bonnefous,** (France), *Le Monde Est-Il Surpeuple?*
1971 **Max Nicholson,** (United Kingdom), *The Environmental Revolution*
1972 **No award**
1973 **George Stainer,** (United Kingdom), *Language and Silence*
Ezio Raimondi, (Italy), *Tecniche delle Critica Letteraria*
1974 **Andrew Shonfield,** (United Kingdom), *Europe: Journey to an Unknown Destination*
1975 **No award**
1976 **Paul Bairoch,** (France), *Le Tiers-Monde dans l'impasse*
1977 **No awards**
1978 **Piero Angela** (Italy), *La zero a tre anni*
1979 **No award**
1980 **No award**

Harold D. Vursell Memorial Award

AMERICAN ACADEMY AND INSTITUTE OF ARTS AND LETTERS
633 w. 155th St., New York, N.Y. 10032 (212-368-5900)

The $5,000 Harold D. Vursell Memorial Award annually honors recent writing in book form that merits recognition for quality of its prose style.

1979 **Wallace Fowlie**
1980 **Tom Wolfe**

Wattie Book of the Year Award

BOOK PUBLISHERS ASSN. OF NEW ZEALAND
Box 78-071, Auckland 2, New Zealand (09-767-251)

The Wattie Book of the Year Award is funded by Wattie Industries and administered by the Book Publishers Assn. It is given to a citizen or permanent resident of New Zealand or its former Pacific territories for a work put out by a member publisher of the association. A panel of three independent judges selects the recipient. In addition to first place, currently carrying an NZ $4,000 honorarium listed here, second- and third-place authors also receive cash awards.

1968 **John Morton** and **M. Miller**, *The New Zealand Sea Shore*
1969 **A. Murray-Oliver**, *Augustus Earle in New Zealand*
1970 **John Dunmore**, *Fateful Voyage of the St. Jean Baptiste*
1971 **Rosemary Rolleston**, *William and Mary Rolleston*
1972 **Gil Docking**, *200 Years of New Zealand Painting*
1973 **Maurice Shadbolt**, *Strangers & Journeys*
1974 **Witi Ihimaera**, *Tangi*
1975 **Sir Edmund Hilary**, *Nothing Venture, Nothing Win*
1976 **Harry Morton**, *The Wind Commands*
1977 **James Bertram**, *Charles Brasch*
1978 **J.D. Raeside**, *Sovereign Chief: A Biography of Baron de Thierry*
1979 **Maurice Gee**, *Plumb*
1980 **Albert Wendt**, *Leaves of the Banyan Tree*

Western Heritage Award

NATIONAL COWBOY HALL OF FAME
1700 NE 63rd, Oklahoma City, Okla. 73111 (405/478-2252)

The Western Heritage Awards are presented annually to recognize the drama and heritage of the Old West in art, literature, music, film and theater which depict the history and legends of the American West. Winners, who are selected by the board of trustees which reviews entries, receive the Wrangler Trophy, a replica of Charles Russell's painting, *Night Herder*. Awards for films, television programs and music are listed elsewhere in this volume.

NON-FICTION BOOK

1962 **Alvin M. Josephy, Jr.** (Ed.), *The American Heritage Book of Indians*
1963 **John Rolph Burroughs**, *Where The West Stayed Young*
1964 **John Upton Terrell**, *Furs By Astor*
1965 **C. Gregory Crampton**, *Standing Up Country*
1966 **Alvin M. Josephy, Jr.** (Ed.), *The American Heritage History Of The Great West*
1967 **George W. Groh**, *Gold Fever*
1968 **John A. Hawgood**, *America's Western Frontier*
1969 **Robert Dykstra**, *The Cattle Town*
Laura Gilpin, *The Enduring Navajo*
1970 **Merrill J. Mattes**, *The Great Platte River Road*
1971 **Harry Sinclair Drago**, *The Great Range Wars*
1972 **Odie B. Faulk** and **Seymour V. Connor**, *North America Divided: The Mexican War*
1973 **Tom McHugh**, *The Time of the Buffalo*
Grace Dangberg, *Carson Valley*
S.L.A. Marshall, *Crimsoned Prairie*
1974 **George Ellis**, *Bell Ranch As I Knew It*
Richard Ketchum, *Will Rogers: The Man and His Times*
Mike Hanley and **Ellis Lucia**, *Owyhee Trails*
David Muench (photographs) and **N. Scott Momaday** (text), *Colorado Summer/Fall/Winter/Spring*
1975 **Benjamin Capps**, *The Warren Wagontrain Raid*
Robert O. Beatty, *Idaho—Pictorial Overview*
Roy P. Stewart, *Born Grown*
C. S. Sonnichsen, *Colonel Green and the Copper Skyrocket*
Margaret Sanborn, *American*
1976 **Jeff C. Dykes**, *Fifty Great Western Illustrators*
Don James, *Butte's Memory Book*
Turbese Lummis Fisk and Keith Lummis, *Charles F. Lummis: The Man and His West*
1977 **No award**
1978 **Angie Dobo**, *Geronimo: The Man, His Time, His Place*
Tim McCoy and **Ronald McCoy**, *Tim McCoy Remembers the West*
1979 **Nellie Snyder Yost**, *Buffalo Bill: His Family, Friends, Fame, Failures and Fortunes*
1980 **John D. Unruh, Jr.**, *The Plains Across*

NOVEL

1962 **James D. Horan**, *The Shadow Catcher*
1963 **Edward Abbey**, *Fire On The Mountain*
1964 **Robert Roripaugh**, *Honor Thy Father*
1965 **Thomas Berger**, *Little Big Man*
1966 **Vardis Fisher**, *Mountain Man*
1967 **Bill Gulick**, *They Came To A Valley*
1968 **Robert Flynn**, *North To Yesterday*
1969 **Fred Grove**, *The Buffalo Runners*
1970 **Benjamin Capps**, *The White Man's Road*
1971 **A. B. Guthrie**, *Arfive*
1972 **Frank Waters**, *Pike's Peak: A Family Saga*
1973 **Will Henry**, *Chiricahua*
1974 **Elmer Kelton**, *The Time It Never Rained*
1975 **James Michener**, *Centennial*
1976 **No award**
1977 **No award**
1978 **Dorothy M. Johnson**, *Buffalo Woman*
Bill Brett, *The Stolen Steers: A Tale of the Big Thicket*
1979 **Elmer Kelton**, *Good Old Boys*
1980 **Ruth Beebe Hill**, *Hanta Yo*

JUVENILE BOOK

1962 **Gene Caesar**, *King of the Mountain*
1963 **Charles Clifton**, *The Book of the West*
1964 **Betty Baker**, *Killer-of-Death*
1965 **Paul Wellman**, *The Greatest Cattle Drive*
1966 **Carl G. Hodges**, *Land Rush*
1967 **Marguerite Henry**, *Mustang: Wild Spirit of the West*

1968 **Eric Scott,** *Down the Rivers, Westward Ho!*
1969 **Weyman Jones,** *Edge of Two Worlds*
1970 **Jessie Hosford,** *An Awful Name To Live Up To*
1971 **Betty Baker,** *And One Was a Wooden Indian*
1972 **Richard Wormser,** *The Black Mustanger*
1973 **Bern Keating,** *Famous American Explorers*
1974 **No award**
1975 **Harold Keith,** *Susy's Scoundrel*
1976 **Natachee Scott Momaday,** *Owl in the Cedar Trees*
1977 **No award**
1978 **No award**
1979 **Harold Keith,** *The Obstinate Land*
1980 **Barbara M. Walker,** *The Little House Cookbook*

ART BOOK

1968 **E. Maurice Bloch,** *George Caleb Bingham: The Evolution of an Artist*
1969 **Ed Ainsworth,** *The Cowboy in Art*
1970 **William Reed,** *Olaf Wieghorst*
1971 **Robert F. Karolevitz,** *The Story of Harvey Dunn, Artist: Where Your Heart Is*
1972 **Paul E. Rossi and David Hunt,** *The Art of the Old West*
1973 **Walt Reed,** *Harold Von Schmidt Draws and Paints the Old West*
1974 **Frank Getlein,** *The Lure of the Great West*
1975 **Harold Davidson,** *Edward Borein Cowboy Artist*
1976 **Emmie D. Myghet and Roberta Cheney,** *Hans Kleiber: Artist of the Bighorn Mountains*
1977 **No award**
1978 **John K. Goodman,** *Ross Stefan: An Impressionistic Painter of the Contemporary Southwest*
1979 **Searles R. Boynton,** *The Painter Lady: Grace Carpenter Hudson*
Susan Peterson, *The Living Tradition of Maria Martinez*
1980 **Sandra Dallas,** *Sacred Paint: Ned Jacob*

MAGAZINE ARTICLES, SHORT STORIES OR POETRY

1961 **W. Bruce Bell,** "The Old Chisholm Trail," Article in *Kiwanis Magazine*
Steve Frazee, "All Legal and Proper," Short Story in *Ellery Queen Magazine*
1962 **Fred Grove,** "Comanche Son," Short Story in *Boy's Life*
Mari Sandoz, "The Look of the Last Frontier," Article in *American Heritage*
1963 **George Stewart,** "The Prairie Schooner Got Them There," Article in *American Heritage*
1964 **Herman Lehmann,** "Nine Years Among the Indians," Article in *Frontier Times*
1965 **J. Frank Dobie,** "Titans of Western Art," Article in *American Heritage*
1966 **Donald Jackson,** "How Lost Was Zebulon Pike," Article in *American Heritage*
1967 **Jack Guinn,** "The Red Man's Last Struggle," Article in *Empire Magazine*
1968 **Carolyn Woirhaye,** "The Snows of Rimrock Ridge," Article in *The Farm Quarterly*
1969 **Donnie D. Good,** "W. R. Leigh: The Artist's Studio Collection," Article in *The American Scene*
1970 **May Howell,** "Bennett Howell's Cow Country," Article in *Frontier Times*
1971 **James E. Serven,** "Cattle, Guns, and Cowboys," Article in *Arizona Highways Magazine*
1972 **David Humphreys,** "Echoes of the Little Bighorn," Article in *American Heritage*
1973 **James E. Serven,** "Horses of the West," Article in *Arizona Highways Magazine*
George Keithley, "The Donner Party," George Braziller, Inc.
1974 **Spike Van Cleve,** "40 Years Gathering," Article in *The Dude Rancher Magazine*
1975 **Jim Jennings,** "George Humphreys, Half Century With 6666," Article in *Quarter Horse Journal*
1976 **Patricia J. Broder,** "The Pioneer Woman: Image of Bronze," American Art Review

Whitbread Award

BOOKSELLERS' ASSOCIATION
154 Buckingham Palace Rd., London SW1W 9TZ, United Kingdom (Tel: 01-730-8214)

The £1,500 Whitbread Awards, which are administered by the Association and supported by Whitbread & Co., Ltd., the brewers, annually honor outstanding books in several categories published during the past year and written by authors who have lived in the United Kingdom for at least five years. A panel of judges chosen by the brewery and the Booksellers' Association of Great Britain and Northern Ireland selects the recipients.

NOVEL

1971 **Gerda Charles,** *The Destiny Waltz*
1972 **Susan Hill,** *The Bird of Night*
1973 **Shiva Naipaul,** *The Chip Chip Gatherers*
1974 **Iris Murdoch,** *The Sacred and Profane Love Machine*
1975 **William McIlvanney,** *Docherty*
1976 **William Trevor,** *The Children of Dynmouth*
1977 **Beryl Bainbridge,** *Injury Time*
1978 **Paul Theroux,** *Picture Palace*
1979 **Jennifer Johnson,** *The Old Jest*
1980 **David Lodge,** *How Far Can You Go?**

*Also named Book of the Year

FIRST BOOK

1974 **Claire Tomalin,** *The Life and Death of Mary Wollstonecraft*
1975 **Ruth Spalding,** *The Improbable Puritan: A Life of Bulstrode Whitelocke*

POETRY

1971 **Geoffrey Hill,** *Mercian Hymms*

CHILDREN'S BOOK

1972 **Rumer Godden,** *The Diddakoi*
1973 **Alan Aldridge and William Plomer,** *The Butterfly Ball and Grasshopper's Feast*
1974 **Russell Hoban and Quentin Blake,** *How Tom Beat Captain Najork and His Hired Sportsmen*
Jill Paton Walsh, *The Emperor's Winding Sheet*
1975 **No award**
1976 **Penelope Lively,** *A Stitch in Time*
1977 **Shelagh Macdonald,** *No End to Yesterday*
1978 **Phillipa Pearce,** *The Battle of Bubble and Squeak*
1979 **Peter Dickinson,** *Tulku*
1980 **Leon Garfield,** *John Diamond*

BIOGRAPHY

1971 **Michael Meyer,** *Henrik Ibsen*
1972 **James Pope-Hennessy,** *Trollope*

1973 **John Wilson,** *C.B.: The Life of Sir Henry Campbell-Bannerman*
1974 **Andrew Boyle,** *Poor Dear Brendan*
1975 **Helen Corke,** *In Our Infancy: An Autobiography, 1882-1912*
1976 **Winifred Gerin,** *Elizabeth Gaskell*
1977 **Nigel Nicolson,** *Mary Curzon*
1978 **John Grigg,** *Lloyd George: The People's Champion*
1979 **Penelope Mortimer,** *About Time*
1980 **David Newsome,** *On the Edge of Paradise: A.C. Benson the Diarist*

William Allen White Children's Book Award

WILLIAM ALLEN WHITE LIBRARY
State University, Emporia, Kan. 66801 (316/343-1200)

The William Allen White Children's Book Award, which consists of a bronze medal, is given annually for an outstanding children's book, as selected by a poll of Kansas youngsters from the fourth through the eighth grades from books chosen by representatives of educational and professional organizations in the state.

1953 **Elizabeth Yates,** *Amos Fortune: Free Man*
1954 **Doris Gates,** *Little Vic*
1955 **Jean Bailey,** *Cherokee Bill*
1956 **Marguerite Henry,** *Brighty of the Grand Canyon*
1957 **Phoebe Erickson,** *Daniel 'Coon*
1958 **Elliott Arnold,** *White Falcon*
1959 **Fred Gipson,** *Old Yeller*
1960 **William O. Steele,** *Flaming Arrows*
1961 **Keith Robertson,** *Henry Reed, Inc.*
1962 **Catherine O. Peare,** *The Helen Keller Story*
1963 **Scott O'Dell,** *Island of the Blue Dolphins*
1964 **Sheila Burnford,** *The Incredible Journey*
1965 **Zachary Ball,** *Bristle Face*
1966 **Sterling North,** *Rascal*
1967 **Annabel and Edgar Johnson,** *The Grizzly*
1968 **Beverly Cleary,** *The Mouse and the Motorcycle*
1969 **Keith Robertson,** *Henry Reed's Baby-Sitting Service*
1970 **Elaine L. Konigsburg,** *From the Mixed-Up Files of Mrs. Basil E. Frankweiler*
1971 **Walt Morey,** *Kavik, the Wolf Dog*
1972 **Barbara Corcoran,** *Sasha, My Friend*
1973 **E. B. White,** *The Trumpet of the Swan*
1974 **Robert O'Brien,** *Mrs. Frisby and the Rats of NIMH*
Zilpha K. Snyder, *The Headless Cupid*
1975 **William Steig,** *Dominic*
1976 **Beverly Cleary,** *Socks*
1977 **George Selden Thompson,** *Harry Cat's Pet Puppy*
1978 **Jean Van Leeuwen,** *The Great Christmas Kidnaping Caper*
1979 **Wilson Rawls,** *Summer of the Monkeys*
1980 **Betsy Byars,** *The Pinballs*

Laura Ingalls Wilder Medal

AMERICAN LIBRARY ASSOCIATION
Children's Services Division, 50 E. Huron St., Chicago, Ill. 60611 (312/944-6780)

The Laura Ingalls Wilder Medal is given every five years to an author or illustrator whose books, published in the U.S., have made a substantial and lasting contribution to children's literature. A committee of Children's Services Division members makes nominations, and the winner is selected by a mail vote of the membership.

1954 **Laura Ingalls Wilder**
1960 **Clara Ingram Judson**
1965 **Ruth Sawyer Durand**
1970 **E.B. White**
1975 **Beverly Cleary**
1980 **Theodor S. Geisel ("Dr. Seuss")**

Morton Dauwen Zabel Award

AMERICAN ACADEMY AND INSTITUTE OF ARTS AND LETTERS
633 W. 155th St., New York, N.Y. 10032 (212/368-5900)

The Morton Dauwen Zabel Award, which carries a $2,500 honorarium, is given each year to an American poet, writer of fiction or critic in rotation for "progressive, original and experimental tendencies rather than academic and conservative tendencies," as determined by a jury or by the institute's board of trustess.

1970 **George Steiner** (criticism)
1971 **Charles Reznikoff** (poetry)
1972 **Donald Barthelme** (fiction)
1973 **Marjorie Hope Nicolson** (criticism)
1974 **John Logan** (poetry)
1975 **Charles Newman** (fiction)
1976 **Harold Rosenberg** (criticism)
1977 **David Shapiro** (poetry)
1978 **Joan Didion** (fiction)
1979 **Richard Gilman** (criticism)
1980 **Donald Finkel** (poetry)

Fellowship of the Academy of American Poets
Copernicus Award
Lamont Poetry Selection
Harold Morton Landon Award
Edgar Allan Poe Award
Walt Whitman Award

ACADEMY OF AMERICAN POETS
177 E. 87th St., New York, N.Y. 10028 (212/427-5665)

The Fellowship of the Academy of American Poets "for distinguished poetic achievement," awarded annually to a living American poet, consists of a certificate and $10,000. At times, two awards are given. The Academy's twelve chancellors, who are themselves distinguished poets, nominate and elect the fellow. The fellowships may not be applied for, and chancellors may not be Academy fellows. Edwin Markham received the distinction in a special prefatory award.

1937 **Edwin Markham**
1946 **Edgar Lee Masters**
1947 **Ridgely Torrence**
1948 **Percy MacKaye**
1950 **e.e. cummings**
1952 **Padraic Colum**
1953 **Robert Frost**
1954 **Louise Townsend Nicholl**
1954 **Oliver St. George Gogarty**
1955 **Rolfe Humphries**

1956 **William Carlos Williams**
1957 **Conrad Aiken**
1958 **Robinson Jeffers**
1959 **Leonie Adams**
Louise Bogan
1960 **Jesse Stuart**
1961 **Horace Gregory**
1962 **John Crowe Ransom**
1963 **Ezra Pound**
1964 **Elizabeth Bishop**
1965 **Marianne Moore**
1966 **John Berryman**
Archibald MacLeish
1967 **Mark Van Doren**
1968 **Stanley Kunitz**
1969 **Richard Eberhart**
Anthony Hecht
1970 **Howard Nemerov**
1971 **James Wright**
1972 **W.D. Snodgrass**
1973 **W.S. Merwin**
1974 **Leonie Adams**
1975 **Robert Hayden**
1976 **J.V. Cunningham**
1977 **Louis Cox**
1978 **Josephine Miles**
1979 **Mark Strand**
May Swenson
1980 **Mona van Duyn**

The Copernicus Award, comprised of a certificate and $10,000, recognized a poet's "lifetime achievement and contribution to poetry as a cultural force." It was given annually to a living citizen of the United States over 45 years of age who preferably published a book of poems or about poetry during the two previous years. The award has been discontinued.

1974 **Robert Lowell**
1975 **Kenneth Rexroth**
1976 **Robert Penn Warren**
1977 **Muriel Rukeyser**

The Lamont Poetry Selection honors a living American poet's second book of poems. (Prior to 1975 the award was given for a poet's first book.) A three-poet panel judges manuscripts submitted by publishers. The Academy assures publication by purchasing from the publisher 1,000 copies of the winning book for distribution to contributors and friends.

1954 **Constance Carrier**, *The Middle Voice*
1955 **Donald Hall**, *Exiles and Marriages*
1956 **Philip Booth**, *Letter from a Distant Land*
1957 **Daniel Berrigan, S.J.**, *Time Without Number*
1958 **Ned O'Gorman**, *The Night of the Hammer*
1959 **Donald Justice**, *The Summer Anniversaries*
1960 **Robert Mezey**, *The Lovemaker*
1961 **X.J. Kennedy**, *Nude Descending a Staircase*
1962 **Edward Field**, *Stand Up, Friend, With Me*
1963 **No award**
1964 **Adrien Stoutenberg**, *Heroes Advise Us*
1965 **Henri Coulette**, *The War of the Secret Agents*
1966 **Kenneth O. Hanson**, *The Distance Anywhere*
1967 **James Scully**, *The Marches*
1968 **Jane Cooper**, *The Weather of Six Mornings*
1969 **Marvin Bell**, *A Probable Volume of Dreams*
1970 **William Harmon**, *Treasury Holiday*
1971 **Stephen Dobyns**, *Concurring Beasts*
1972 **Peter Everwine**, *Collecting the Animals*
1973 **Marilyn Hacker**, *Presentation Piece*
1974 **John Balaban**, *After Our War*
1975 **Lisel Mueller**, *The Private Life*
1976 **Larry Levis**, *The Afterlife*
1977 **Gerald Stern**, *Lucky Life*
1978 **Ai**, *Killing Floor*
1979 **Frederick Seidel**, *Sunrise*
1980 **Michael Van Walleghen**, *More Trouble With the Obvious*

The $1,000 Harold Morton Landon Award is given for a published translation of poetry from any language into English. One poet serves as judge, and winners must be living citizens of the United States. Beginning in 1978, the Landon Award became a biennial honor. Published books may be sent to the Academy for judging.

1976 **Robert Fitzgerald** for *The Iliad* of Homer
1977 **Galway Kinnell** for *The Poems of Francois Villon*
Howard Norman for *The Wishing Bone Cycle*
1978 **Galway Kimmell**, *The Poems of Francois Villon*
Howard Norman, *The Wishing Bone Cycle*
1980 **Edmunch Kelley**, *(Ritlor in Parenthesis)*

The Edgar Allan Poe Award comprised of a certificate and $5,000 was given annually to a living citizen of the United States under 45 years of age for the "continuing development of a younger poet's art on the occasion of a newly published book of poems." This award has been discontinued.

1974 **Mark Strand**, *The Story of Our lives*
1975 **Charles Simic**, *Return to a Place Lit by a Glass of Milk*
1976 **Charles Wright**, *Bloodlines*
1977 **Stan Rice**, *Whiteboy*

The Walt Whitman Award consisting of $1,000 and publication by a major publisher of a manuscript is given to a poet who has never published a book of poems, except in a small edition. The winner must be a living citizen of the United States, and the book-length poetry manuscript is selected from submitted works in open competition.

1975 **Reg Saner**, *Climbing into the Roots*, (Harper & Row)
1976 **Laura Gilpin**, *The Hocus-Pocus of the Universe*, (Doubleday)
1977 **Lauren Shakely**, *Guilty Bystander*, (Random House)
1978 **Karen Snow**, *Wonders* (Viking)
1979 **David Bottoms**, *Shooting Rats at the Bib County Dump* (Morrow)
1980 **Jared Carter**, *Work, for the Night is Coming* (Macmillan)

Bollingen Prize

YALE UNIVERSITY LIBRARY
New Haven, Conn. 06514 (203/436-2334)

The $5,000 Bollingen Prize is awarded biennially to an American citizen for a distinguished book of poetry published during the preceding two years, as selected by a jury, or in recognition of a poet's total achievements. This award was once given annually with a smaller monetary prize and was originally administered by the Library of Congress. Two poets occasionally share the prize.

1949 **Wallace Stevens**
1950 **John Crowe Ransom**
1951 **Marianne Moore,** *Collected Poems*
1952 **Archilbald MacLeish,** *Collected Poems: 1917-1952*
William Carlos Williams
1953 **W.H. Auden**
1954 **Leonie Adams,** *Poems: A Selection*
Louis Bogan, *Collected Poems: 1922-1953*
1955 **Conrad Aiken,** *A Letter from Li Po*
1956 **Allen Tate**
1957 **e.e. cummings**
1958 **Theodore Roethke,** *Words for the Wine*
1959 **Delmore Schwartz,** *Summer Knowledge*
1960 **Yvor Winters,** *Collected Poems*
1961 **John Hall Wheelock,** *The Gardener*
Richard Eberhart
1962 **Robert Frost,** *In the Clearing*
1964 **Horace Gregory,** *Collected Poems*
1966 **Robert Penn Warren,** *Selected Poems, New & Old, 1923-1966*
1968 **John Berryman,** *His Toy, His Dream, His Rest*
1970 **Mona Van Duyn,** *To See, To Take*
1972 **James Merrill,** *Braving the Elements*
1974 **A.R. Ammons,** *Sphere*
1976 **David Ignatow**
1978 **W.S. Merwin,** Body of published works
1980 **Howard Nemerov,** Body of published works
May Swenson, Body of published works

Witter Brynner Poetry Prize

AMERICAN ACADEMY AND INSTITUTE OF ARTS AND LETTERS
633 W. 155th St., New York, N.Y. 10032 (212/368-5900)

The Witter Brynner Poetry Prize, which carries a $1,350 honorarium, is given annually.

1980 **Pamela White Hadas**

Kovner Memorial Award

NATIONAL JEWISH WELFARE BOARD
15 E. 26th St., New York, N.Y. 10010 (212/532-4949)

The board's National Jewish Book Council now gives the $500 Harry and Florence Kovner Memorial Awards alternately to honor books of poetry in Yiddish, English or Hebrew written by citizens or residents of the United States or Canada. Volumes translated from another language into English are eligible if they are of Jewish interest. The book must have been published during the three previous years. Three judges' committees—one for each language—select the winners.

ENGLISH POETRY

1951 **Judah Stampfer,** *Jerusalem Has Many Faces*
1952 **A. M. Klein,** Cumulative contributions to English-Jewish poetry
1953 **Isidore Goldstick,** For translation of *Poems of Yehoash*
1954 **Harry H. Fein,** Cumulative contributions to English-Jewish poetry
1959 **Grace Goldin,** *Come Under the Wings: A Midrash on Ruth*
1960 **Amy K. Blank,** *The Spoken Choice*
1962 **Irving Feldman,** *Work and Days and Other Poems*
1963 **Charles Reznikoff,** *By the Waters of Manhattan*
1966 **Ruth Finer Mintz,** *The Darkening Green*
1969 **Ruth Whitman,** *The Marriage Wig and Other Poems*
1971 **Ruth Finer Mintz,** *Traveler through Time*
1974 **Harold Schimmel** (trans.), *Songs of Jerusalem and Myself* by Yehuda Amichai
1980 **Charles Reznikoff,** body of work

HEBREW POETRY

1951 **Aaron Zeitlin,** *Shirim U'Poemot*
1952 **Hillel Bavli,** Cumulative contributions to Hebrew poetry
1953 **A. S. Schwartz,** Cumulative contributions to Hebrew poetry
1954 **Ephraim E. Lisitzky,** *Be-Ohalei Kush (In Negro Tents)*
1955 **Gabriel Preil,** *Ner Mul Kochavin (Candle under the Stars)*
1956 **Hillel Bavli,** *Aderet Ha-Shanim (Mantle of Years)*
1957 **Moshe Feinstein,** *Avraham Abulafia*
1958 **Aaron Zeitlin,** *Bein Ha-Esh Veha-Yesha*
1959 **Moshe Ben Meir,** *Tzlil va Tzel*
1960 **Eisig Silberschlag,** *Kimron Yamai*
1961 **Ephraim E. Lisitzky,** *K'Mo Hayom Rad*
1962 **Gabriel Preil,** *Mapat Erev*
1963 **Arnold Band,** *Ha-Rei Boer ha-Esh*
1966 **Simon Halkin,** *Crossing the Jabbok*
1967 **Leonard D. Friedland,** *Shirim be-Sulam Minor*
1969 **Reuven Ben-Yosef,** *Derech Eretz*
1972 **Eisig Silberschlag,** *Igrotai El Dorot Aherim (Letters to Other Generations)*
1975 **Reuven Ben-Yosef,** *Metim ve-Ohavim*
1977 **T. Carmi,** *El Eretz Aheret*

YIDDISH POETRY

1951 **Ber Lapin,** *Der Fuller Krug (The Brimming Jug)*
1952 **Mordicai Jaffe,** Editing and translating *Anthology of Hebrew Poetry*
1953 **Mark Schwaid,** Collected poems
1954 **Eliezer Greenberg,** *Banachtiger Dialog (Night Dialogue)*
1955 **Alter Esselin,** *Lider fun a Midbarnik (Poems of a Hermit)*
1956 **Naphtali Gross,** Cumulative contributions to Yiddish poetry
1957 **Jacob Glatstein,** *Fun Mein Gantzer Mei*
1958 **I. J. Schwartz,** Cumulative contributions to Yiddish poetry
1959 **Benjamin Bialostotzky,** *Lid Tzu Lid*
1960 **Ephraim Auerbach,** *Gildene Shekiah*
1961 **Joseph Rubinstein,** *Megilath Russland*
1962 **Israel Emiot,** *In Nigun Eingehert*
1963 **Chaim Grade,** *Det Mentsh fun Fier*
1964 **Aaron Glanz-Leyeles,** *Amerika Un Ich*
1965 **Aleph Katz,** *Di Emesse Hasunah*
1966 **Kadia Molodowsky,** *Licht fun Dorenboim*
1967 **Jacob Glatstein,** *A Yid fun Lublin*
1968 **Aaron Zeitlin,** *Lider fun Hurban un Lider fun Gloiben*
1969 **Rachel H. Korn,** *Di Gnod fun Vort*
1970 **Eliezer Greenberg,** *Eibiker Dorsht (Eternal Thirst)*
1973 **Meir Sticker,** *Yidishe Landshaft*

1976 **M. Husid,** *A Shotn Tragt Main Kroin*
1979 **Moishe Steingart,** *In Droisen Fun Der Velt*

Juniper Prize

UNIVERSITY OF MASSACHUSETTS PRESS
Box 429, Amherst, Mass. 01004 (413/545-2217)

The Juniper Prize, which consists of $1,000 and publication of a manuscript, is given annually for an original, book-length manuscript of poetry in English.

1975 **Eleanor Lerman,** *Come the Sweet By and By*
1976 **David Dwyer,** *Ariana Olisvos: Her Last Works and Days*
1977 **Jane Shore,** *Eye Level*
1978 **William Dickey,** *The Rainbow Grocery*
1979 **Eleanor Wilner,** *maya*
1980 **Lucille Clifton,** *Two-Headed Woman*

Edwin Markham Poetry Prize

EUGENE V. DEBS FOUNDATION
Box 843, Terre Haute, Ind. 47808 (812/232-2163)

The $1,000 Edwin Markham Poetry Prize was to be given annually for an unpublished poem in the English language of 100 lines or less dealing with social protest or social justice. The award has been discontinued.

1976 **Dan Bogen,** "Lamento"

Lenore Marshall Poetry Prize

NEW HOPE FOUNDATION
430 Park Ave., New York, N.Y. 10022 (212/421-7200)

The Lenore Marshall Poetry Prize, which carries a $5,000 honorarium, is given annually to a living American author for the best book of poems published in the United States in the previous year, including new editions of selected and collected peoms. The winner is selected by one or more poets appointed as judges by the Foundation, which cosponsors the award with *The Saturday Review.*

1974 **Cid Corman,** *O*
I
1975 **Denise Levertov,** *The Freeing of the Dust*
1976 **Philip Levine,** *The Names of the Lost*
1977 **Allen Tate,** *Collected Poems, 1919-1976*
1978 **Hayden Carruth,** *Brothers, I Loved You All*
1979 **Stanley Kunitz,** *The Poems of Stanley Kunitz, 1928-1978*
1980 **Not available at press time**

National Book Award

ASSOCIATION OF AMERICAN PUBLISHERS
One Park Ave., New York, N.Y. 10016 (212/689-8920)

The $1,000 National Book Award in poetry is one of seven awarded annually for works by U.S. citizens "that have contributed most significantly to human awareness, to the vitality of our national culture and to the spirit of excellence." The other six awards are for prose and can be found on pp. The organizational and category changes which became effective when the National Book Awards were replaced by the American Book Awards, as well as the 1980 winner for poetry, can also be found on those pages.

1950 **William Carlos Williams,** *Paterson III and Selected Poems*
1951 **Wallace Stevens,** *The Auroras of Autumn*
1952 **Marianne Moore,** *Collected Poems*
1953 **Archibald MacLeish,** *Collected Poems: 1917-1952*
1954 **Conrad Aiken,** *Collected Poems*
1955 **Wallace Stevens,** *Collected Poems of Wallace Stevens*
e. e. cummings, *Poems: 1923-1954* (Special citation)
1956 **W. H. Auden,** *The Shield of Achilles*
1957 **Richard Wilbur,** *Things of This World*
1958 **Robert Penn Warren,** *Promises: Poems, 1954-1956*
1959 **Theodore Roethke,** *Words for the Wind*
1960 **Robert Lowell,** *Life Studies*
1961 **Randall Jarrell,** *The Woman at the Washington Zoo*
1962 **Alan Dugan,** *Poems*
1963 **William Stafford,** *Traveling Through the Dark*
1964 **John Crowe Ransom,** *Selected Poems*
1965 **Theodore Roethke,** *The Far Field*
1966 **James Dickey,** *Buckdancer's Choice*
1967 **James Merrill,** *Nights and Days*
1968 **Robert Bly,** *The Light Around the Body*
1969 **John Berryman,** *His Toy, His Dream, His Rest*
1970 **Elizabeth Bishop,** *The Complete Poems*
1971 **Mona Van Duyn,** *To See, To Take*
1972 **Howard Moss,** *Selected Poems*
Frank O'Hara, *The Collected Poems*
1973 **A. R. Ammons,** *Collected Poems: 1951-1971*
1974 **Allen Ginsberg,** *The Fall of America: Poems of These States, 1965-1971*
Adrienne Rich, *Diving into the Wreck*
1975 **Marilyn Hacker,** *Presentation Piece*
1976 **John Ashbery,** *Self-Portrait in a Convex Mirror*
1977 **Richard Eberhardt,** *Collected Poems: 1930-1976*
1978 **Howard Nemerov,** *The Collected Poems*
1979 **James Merrill,** *Mirabell*

Oscar Blumenthal Prize
Jacob Glatstein Memorial Prize
Bess Hokin Prize
Levinson Prize
Eunice Tietjens Memorial Award
English-Speaking Union Prize

POETRY MAGAZINE
601 S. Morgan St., Box 4348, Chicago, Ill. 60680 (312/996-7803)

The Oscar Blumenthal Prize, which until 1975 was known as the Oscar Blumenthal-Charles Leviton Prize, awards $200 for poetry published in the two previous volumes (one year) of the magazine. The editors select the winner.

1936 **Marion Strobel**
1937 **Thomas Hornsby Ferril**
1938 **Dylan Thomas**
1939 **Maxwell Bodenheim**
1940 **Muriel Rukeyser**
1941 **Stanley Kunitz**
1942 **E. L. Mayo**
1943 **John Ciardi**
1944 **P. K. Page**

1945 Yvor Winters
1946 George Moor
1947 James Merrill
1948 Weldon Kees
1949 Barbara Gibbs
1950 Richard Wilbur
1951 Randall Jarrell
1952 Roy Marz
1953 William Meredith
1954 Anne Ridler
1955 William Carlos Williams
1956 Sydney Goodsir Smith
1957 Ben Belitt
1958 Howard Nemerov
1959 Josephine Miles
1960 Charles Tomlinson
1961 Kathleen Raine
1962 e. e. cummings
1963 Karl Shapiro
1964 Robert Creeley
1965 Charles Olson
1966 Louis Zukofsky
1967 Guy Davenport
1968 James Wright
1969 Turner Cassity
1970 Jon Anderson
1971 Geoffrey Grigson
1972 Douglas Le Pan
1973 Brewster Ghiselin
1974 David Wagoner
1975 Sandra McPherson
1976 David Bromwich
1977 Alfred Corn
1978 Robert Pinsky
1979 Lynne Lawner
1980 Robert Beverley Ray

The Jacob Glatstein Memorial Prize, which carries a $100 honorarium, is given for poetry translations published in the the two previous volumes of the magazine. The editors select the winner.

1972 Rae Dalven
1973 Marya Zaturenska
1974 Raphael Rudnik
1975 Jayanta Mahapatra
1976 Martha Hollander
1977 Robert Siegel
1978 Daniel Weissbort
1979 Anne Winters
1980 Lisel Mueller

The Bess Hokin Prize, which carries a $100 honorarium, is given for poetry published in the two previous volumes of the magazine. The editors select the winner.

1948 William Abrahams
1949 Barbara Howes
1950 Lloyd Frankenberg
1951 M. B. Tolson
1952 L. E. Hudgins
1953 Ruth Stone
1954 Hayden Carruth
1955 Philip Booth
1956 Charles Tomlinson
1957 Sylvia Plath
1958 Alan Neame
1959 Jean Clower
1960 Denise Levertov
1961 X. J. Kennedy
1962 W. S. Merwin
1963 Adrienne Rich
1964 Gary Snyder
1965 Galway Kinnell
1966 Thomas Clark
1967 Wendell Berry
1968 Michael Benedikt
1969 Marvin Bell
1970 Charles Martin
1971 Erica Jong
1972 Sandra McPherson
1973 Jane Shore
1974 Margaret Atwood
1975 Charles O. Hartman
1976 Norman Dubie
1977 Bess Hokin
1978 Richard Kenney
1979 Robert Beverley Ray
1980 Gerald Stern

The Levinson Prize, which carries a $300 honorarium, is awarded for poetry published in the two previous volumes of the magazine. The editors select the winner.

1914 Carl Sandburg
1915 Vachel Lindsay
1916 Edgar Lee Masters
1917 Cloyd Head
1918 O. C. Underwood
1919 H. L. Davis
1920 Wallace Stevens
1921 Lew Sarett
1922 Robert Frost
1923 Edwin Arlington Robinson
1924 Amy Lowell
1925 Ralph Cheever Dunning
1926 Mark Turbyfill
1927 Maurice Lesemann
1928 Elinor Wylie
1929 Marjorie Seiffert
1930 Hart Crane
1931 Edna St. Vincent Millay
1932 No award
1933 Marianne Moore
1934 Horace Gregory
1935 Mary Barnard
1936 Robert Penn Warren
1937 Louise Bogan
1938 H. D.
1939 e. e. cummings
1940 Robinson Jeffers
1941 Archibald MacLeish
1942 Karl J. Shapiro
1943 John Malcolm Brinnin
1944 John Frederick Nims
1945 Dylan Thomas
1946 John Ciardi
1947 Muriel Rukeyser
1948 Randall Jarrell
1949 James Merrill
1950 John Berryman
1951 Theodore Roethke
1952 St.-John Perse
1953 Vernon Watkins
1954 William Carlos Williams
1955 Thom Gunn
1956 Stanley Kunitz

1957 Jay MacPherson
1958 Hayden Carruth
1959 Delmore Schwartz
1960 Robert Creeley
1961 David Jones
1962 Anne Sexton
1963 Robert Lowell
1964 Robert Duncan
1965 George Barker
1966 Basil Bunting
1967 Alan Dugan
1968 Gary Snyder
1969 A.D. Hope
1970 A.R. Ammons
1971 Turner Cassity
1972 Michael Hamburger
1973 Richard Howard
1974 John Hollander
1975 Howard Nemerov
1976 Judith Moffett
1977 John Ashbery
1978 Brewster Ghiselin
1979 Philip Levine
1980 Marilyn Hacker

The Eunice Tietjens Memorial Award, which carries a $200 honorarium, is given for poems published in the previous two volumes of the magazine. The editors select the winner.

1944 John Ciardi
1945 Marie Borroff
1946 Alfred Hayes
1947 Theodore Roethke
1948 Peter Viereck
1949 Gwendolyn Brooks
1950 Andrew Glaze
1951 Robinson Jeffers
1952 e. e. cummings
1953 Elder Olson
1954 Reuel Denney
1955 James Wright
1956 Mona Van Duyn
1957 Kenneth Rexroth
1958 James Merrill
1959 Barbara Howes
1960 Marie Ponsot
1961 Karl Shapiro
1962 Muriel Rukeyser
1963 Helen Singer
1964 Hayden Carruth
1965 Pauline Hanson
1966 Galway Kinnell
1967 Robert Duncan
1968 Adrienne Rich
1969 Charles Wright
1970 Jean Malley
1971 Louise Gluck
1972 Maxine Kumin
1973 Judith Moffett
1974 Judith Minty
1975 James McMichael
1976 Richard Kenney
1977 David Wagoner
1978 William Heyon
1979 Robert Morgan
1980 Sandra M. Gilbert

The $1,000 English-Speaking Union Prize honors poets for works published in the magazine

1979 John Ashbery
1980 David Wagoner

Bernice Ames Memorial Award
Witter Brynner Translation Prize
Gordon Barber Memorial Award
Melville Cane Award
Alice Fay di Castagnola Award
Gertrude R. Claytor Memorial Award
Gustav Davidson Memorial Award
Mary Carolyn Davies Memorial Award
Emily Dickinson Award
Consuelo Ford Memorial Award
Gold Medal
Cecil Hemley Award
Alfred Kreymborg Memorial Award
Elias Lieberman Student Poetry Award
John Masefield Memorial Award
Lucille Medwick Memorial Award
Christopher Morley Memorial Award
Poetry Society of America Awards
Shelley Memorial Award
Charles and Cecelia B. Wagner Award
William Carlos Williams Award

POETRY SOCIETY OF AMERICA
15 Gramercy Park, New York, N.Y. 10003 (212/254-9628)

The $100 Bernice Ames Memorial is given annually by vote of a jury.

1978 Phyllis Janowitz
1979 Alice McIntyre
1980 Patricia Hooper

The Witter Brynner Translation Prize for works of poetry translated into English carries a $1,000 honorarium.

1980 John and Bogdana Carpenter

The $200 Gordon Barber Memorial Award is given annually upon the vote of a jury.

1978 Thomas Heffernan
1979 Geraldine C. Little
1980 Myra Sklarew

The $500 Melville Cane Award annually honors the best book of poems by an American in odd-numbered years and the best book about poetry or a poet in even-numbered years. A jury selects the winner.

1962 **Richard Wilbur**
1963 **Clark Emory**
1964 **Joseph Langland**, Poems
1965 **Jean Hagstrum**, *William Blake, Poet and Painter*
1966 **James Dickey**, Poems
1967 **Lawrance Thompson**, *Robert Frost, The Early Years*
1968 **Jean Garrigue,** Poems
1969 **Ruth Miller,** *The Poetry of Emily Dickinson*
1970 **Rolfe Humphries,** Poems
1971 **Harold Bloom,** *Yeats*
1972 **James Wright,** Poems
1973 **Jerome J. McGann,** *Swinburne: An Experiment in Criticism*
1974 **William Stafford,** Poems
1975 **Richard B. Small,** *The Life of Emily Dickinson*
1976 **Charles Wright,** *Blood Lines*
1977 **Donald Howard,** *The Idea of the Canterbury Tales*
1978 **Michael Harper**, *Images of Kin*
1979 **Andrew Welsh**, *Roots of Lyrics*
1980 **Richard Hugo**, *Selected Poems*

The $2,000 Alice Fay di Castagnola Award is given annually for a work in progress, poetry or work about a poet or poetry by a member in the Poetry Society. A jury selects the winner.

1968 **Joseph Tusiani**
Ruth Whitman
1969 **Wade Van Dore,** A book on Robert Frost
1970 **Jenny Lind Porter**
Wallace Winchell
1971 **Cornel Lengyel**
Marcia Masters
1972 **Erica Jong**
Myra Sklarew
1973 **George Keithley**
Mary Oliver
1974 **Charles Eaton,** *The Man in the Green Chair: Poems*
1975 **Philip Appleman,** *In Mediterranean Air: Poems*
1976 **Ann Stanford,** *In Mediterranean Air: Poems*
1977 **Naomi Lazard**
Linda Pastan
1978 **Carol Muske**
1979 **No award**
1980 **Michael Heller**
Diana O'Hehir
Charles Simic

The $250 Gertrude R. Claytor Memorial Award is given annually to a member of the Poetry Society for a poem on an American scene or character. A jury selects the winner.

1975 **Charles A. Wagner**
1976 **Ulrich Troubetzkoy**
1977 **Gary Miranda**
1978 **Kathleen Spvack**
L.L. Zeiger
1979 **Isabel Nathaniel**
1980 **Marlene Rosen Fine**

The $500 Gustav Davidson Memorial Award is given annually to a member of the Poetry Society for a sonnet or sonnet sequence. A jury selects the winner.

1972 **Lisa Grenelle**
1973 **Sallie Nixon**
1974 **Sarah Singer**
1975 **Florence Jacobs**
1976 **Peter Meinke**
1977 **Ulrich Troubetzkoy**
1978 **Norma Farber**
1979 **Ulrich Troubetzkoy**
Richard Frost
1980 **William Barnstone**

The $250 Mary Carolyn Davies Memorial Award is given annually to a member of the Poetry Society for a lyric that can be set to music. A jury selects the winner.

1976 **Catherine Hayden Jacobs**
1977 **Diana Der Hovanessian**
1978 **Cheri Fein**
1979 **Ulrich Troubetzkoy**
1980 **Ralph Robin**

The $100 Emily Dickinson Award is given annually to a member of the Poetry Society for a poem "in the spirit of the New England poet." A jury selects the winner.

1971 **Olga Cabral**
Ree Dragonette
1972 **Harold Whitt**
1973 **Sandra McPherson**
1974 **No award**
1975 **Marjorie Hawksworth**
1976 **Floyd Skloot**
1977 **Siv Cedering Fox**
1978 **Phyllis Janowitz**
1979 **Mildred Nash**
1980 **Virginia Linton**

The $250 Consuelo Ford Memorial Award is given annually to a member of the Poetry Society for a lyric poem. A jury selects the winner.

1972 **Frances Minturn Howard**
1973 **Sarah Singer**
1974 **Mary Anne Coleman**
James Reiss
1975 **Ruth Whitman**
Florence Trefethen
1976 **Nina Nyhart**
Gary Miranda
1977 **Joan LaBombard**
1978 **Gary Miranda**
Grace Morton
1979 **Joan LaBombard**
1980 **Phyllis Janowitz**

The Society's Gold Medal is awarded as merited for distinguished overall contributions to and achievements in poetry.

1930 **Jessie Rittenhouse**
Clinton Scollard
George Edward Woodberry
Bliss Carman
1941 **Robert Frost**
1942 **Edgar Lee Masters**
1943 **Edna St. Vincent Millay**
1947 **Gustav Davidson**
1951 **Wallace Stevens**
1952 **Carl Sandburg**

1955 Leonora Speyer
1967 Marianne Moore
1974 John Hall Wheelock
1976 A. M. Sullivan

The $300 Cecil Hemley Award is given annually to a member of the Poetry Society for a poem based on a humanitarian theme. A jury selects the winner.

1969 Willis Barnstone
1970 Charles A. Brady
1971 Bernice Ames
1972 Ann Jonas
1973 Helen Sorrells
1974 Anne Marx
1975 Ruth Lisa Schechter
1976 No award
1977 Isabel Nathaniel
1978 Gary Miranda
1979 Geraldine Little
1980 L.L. Zeiger

The $100 Alfred Kreymborg Memorial Award is given annually to a member of the Poetry Society for "a poem worthy of the name." A jury selects the winner.

1975 Madeline Bass
1976 Colette Inez
1977 Geraldine C. Little
1978 Phyllis Janowitz
1979 Elizabeth Spires
1980 L.L. Zeiger

The Elias Lieberman Student Poetry Award is given annually for a poem by an American secondary school student. A jury selects the winner.

1971 Lyn Kelly
1972 Alan Farago
1973 Heidi Schmitt
1974 Jean Sherrard
1975 Psyche Anne Pascual
1976 Edward Gaillard
1977 Paul J. Davis
1978 Marilyn Plastric
1979 Catherine Talmadge
1980 Laura B. Margolis

The $500 John Masefield Memorial Award is given annually for a narrative poem. A jury selects the winner.

1969 Siv Cedering Fox
1970 Alvin K. Reiss
1971 Sallie W. Nixon
1972 Donald Junkins
1973 No award
1974 Penelope Schott Starkey
1975 Gail Trebbe
1976 Burt Blume, Ruth Whitman and Jack Zucker
1977 Lynn Sukenick and Fred Fierstein
1978 Dorothy Foltz-Gray
1979 G.N. Gebbard
1980 Ellery Akers

The $500 Lucille Medwick Memorial Award is given annually to a member of the Poetry Society for a poem on a humanitarian theme. A jury selects the winner.

1974 Joan LaBombard
1975 Violette Newton
1976 Olga Cabral
1977 Peter Klappert
1978 Willis Barnstone
1979 Gary Miranda
1980 Florence Grossman
Gary Miranda

The $500 Christopher Morley Memorial Award was given annually to a member of the Poetry Society for light verse. A jury selects the winner.

1969 David Ross
1970 Philip Appleman
1971 Sarah Lockwood
1972 R.F. Armknecht
Vinnie Marie D'Ambrosio
1973 Norma Farber
1974 Milton Kaplan and Gary Miranda
1975 Philip Appleman
1976 S. Gordden Link and Ralph Robin
1977 Darcy Gottlieb

The $200 and $300 Poetry Society of America Awards were given annually to recognize the best poetry of the year by members. The membership was balloted to select the winner.

1968 Charles A. Brady
Hyacinthe Hill
Mary Oliver
1969 Beren Van Slyke
Kinereth Gensler
Naomi Lazard
1970 Hamilton Warren
Hannah Kahn
Edsel Ford
1971 Charles A. Wagner
Dorothy Richardson
Carol Ann Pearce
1972 Frances Minturn Howard
William Childress
Ruth Feldman
1973 Larry Rubin
Margaret Rockwell
Helen Bryant
1974 Louise Gunn
Milton Kaplan
Gary Miranda
Harriet Blackwell
1975 Sarah Singer
Lawrence Spingarn
Elizavietta Ritchie
1976 Ryah Goodman
Colette Inez
1977 Helen Adam
Darrell Bartee

The Shelley Memorial Award which carries a $1750 honorarium, is given annually to a living American poet selected "with reference to his or her genius and need" upon a decision by a three-poet panel.

1929 Conrad Aiken
1930 Lizette Woodworth Reese

1931 Archibald MacLeish
1932 Stephen Vincent Benet
1933 Lola Ridge
Frances Frost
1934 Lola Ridge
Marya Zaturenska
1935 Josephine Miles
1936 Charlotte Wilder
Ben Belitt
1937 Lincoln Fitzell
1938 Robert Francis
Harry Brown
1939 Herbert Bruncken
Winfield T. Scott
1940 Marianne Moore
1941 Ridgely Torrence
1942 Robert Penn Warren
Percy MacKaye
1943 Edgar Lee Masters
1944 e.e. cummings
1945 Karl Shapiro
1946 Rolfe Humphries
1947 Janet Lewis
1948 John Berryman
1949 Louis Kent
1950 Jeremy Ingalls
1951 Richard Eberhart
1952 Elizabeth Bishop
1953 Kenneth Patchen
1954 Leonie Adams
1955 Robert Fitzgerald
1956 George Abbe
1957 Kenneth Rexroth
1958 Rose Garcia Villa
1959 Delmore Schwartz
1960 Robinson Jeffers
1961 Theodore Roethke
1962 Eric Barker
1963 William Stafford
1964 Ruth Stone
1965 David Ignatow
1966 Anne Sexton
1967 May Swenson
1968 Ann Stanford
1969 X.J. Kennedy
Mary Oliver
1971 Adrienne Rich
Louise Townsend Nicholl
1972 Galway Kinnell
1973 John Ashbery
Richard Wilbur
1974 W.S. Merwin
1975 Edward Field
1976 Gwendolyn Brooks
1977 Muriel Rukeyser
1978 Jane Cooper
William Everson
1979 Hayden Carruth
1980 Julia Randall

The Charles and Celia B. Wagner Award of $250 is given annually for a worthy poem.

1976 Sarah Singer
1977 Joan LaBombard
1978 Tony Weston
1979 Ona Siporin
1980 Phyllis Janowitz

The William Carlos William Award is given anually for a book of poetry published by a small press, non-profit press or university press. The Poetry Society agrees to purchase copies of the book at a trade discount for distribution to Society members when the publisher agrees to pay a royalty of at least 10 percent to the poet.

1979 **David Fischer**, *Teachings* (Back Roads Press)
1980 **David Ray**, *The Tramps Cup* (Chriton Press)

Pulitzer Prize

COLUMBIA UNIVERSITY
Graduate School of Journalism, New York, N.Y. 10027
(212/280-3828) (Pulitzer Prizes: 212/280-3841)

Endowed by the will of Joseph Pulitzer, founder of the *St. Louis Post Dispatch,* and administered by Columbia University, the annual Pulitzer Prizes include a $1,000 award for poetry. Four copies of each work must be submitted to the 15-member Advisory Committee on Pulitzer Prizes for consideration.

1918 **Sara Teasdale,** *Love Songs*
1919 **Carl Sandburg,** *Corn Huskers*
Margaret Widdemer, *Old Road to Paradise*
1920 No award
1921 No award
1922 **Edwin Arlington Robinson,** *Collected Poems*
1923 **Edna St. Vincent Millay,** *The Ballad of the Harp-Weaver; A Few Figs from Thistles;* eight sonnets in *American Poetry,* 1922, *A Miscellany*
1924 **Robert Frost,** *New Hampshire: A Poem with Notes and Grace Notes*
1925 **Edwin Arlington Robinson,** *The Man Who Died Twice*
1926 **Amy Lowell,** *What's O'Clock*
1927 **Leonora Speyer,** *Fiddler's Farewell*
1928 **Edwin Arlington Robinson,** *Tristram*
1929 **Stephen V. Benet,** *John Brown's Body*
1930 **Conrad Aiken,** *Selected Poems*
1931 **Robert Frost,** *Collected Poems*
1932 **George Dillon,** *The Flowering Stone*
1933 **Archibald MacLeish,** *Conquistador*
1934 **Robert Hillyer,** *Collected Verse*
1935 **Audrey Wurdemann,** *Bright Ambush*
1936 **R. P. Tristram Coffin,** *Strange Holiness*
1937 **Robert Frost,** *A Further Range*
1938 **Marya Zaturenska,** *Cold Morning Sky*
1939 **John Gould Fletcher,** *Selected Poems*
1940 **Mark Van Doren,** *Collected Poems*
1941 **Leonard Bacon,** *Sunderland Capture*
1942 **William Benet,** *The Dust Which Is God*
1943 **Robert Frost,** *A Witness Tree*
1944 **Stephen Vincent Benet,** *Western Star*
1945 **Karl Shapiro,** *V-Letter and Other Poems*
1946 No award
1947 **Robert Lowell,** *Lord Weary's Castle*
1948 **W. H. Auden,** *The Age of Anxiety*
1949 **Peter Viereck,** *Terror and Decorum*
1950 **Gwendolyn Brooks,** *Annie Allen*
1951 **Carl Sandburg,** *Complete Poems*
1952 **Marianne Moore,** *Collected Poems*
1953 **Archibald MacLeish,** *Collected Poems 1917-1952*
1954 **Theodore Roethke,** *The Waking*
1955 **Wallace Stevens,** *Collected Poems*
1956 **Elizabeth Bishop,** *Poems—North & South*
1957 **Richard Wilbur,** *Things of This World*
1958 **Robert Penn Warren,** *Promises: Poems 1954-56*
1959 **Stanley Kunitz,** *Selected Poems 1928-1958*

1960 **W. D. Snodgrass,** *Heart's Needle*
1961 **Phyllis McGinley,** *Times Three: Selected Verse from Three Decades*
1962 **Alan Dugan,** *Poems*
1963 **William Carlos Williams,** *Pictures from Breughel*
1964 **Louis Simpson,** *At the End of the Open Road*
1965 **John Berryman,** *77 Dream Songs*
1966 **Richard Eberhart,** *Selected Poems*
1967 **Anne Sexton,** *Live or Die*
1968 **Anthony Hecht,** *The Hard Hours*
1969 **George Oppen,** *Of Being Numerous*
1970 **Richard Howard,** *Untitled Subjects*
1971 **W. S. Merwin,** *The Carrier of Ladders*
1972 **James Wright,** *Collected Poems*
1973 **Maxine Winokur Kumin,** *Up Country*
1974 **Robert Lowell,** *The Dolphin*
1975 **Gary Snyder,** *Turtle Island*
1976 **John Ashbery,** *Self-Portrait in a Convex Mirror*
1977 **James Merrill,** *Divine Comedies*
1978 **Howard Nemerov,** *Collected Poems*
1979 **Robert Penn Warren,** *Now and Then*
1980 **Donald Justice,** *Selected Poems*

Carl Sandburg Award

INTERNATIONAL PLATFORM ASSN.
2564 Berkshire Rd., Cleveland Hgts., Ohio 44106

The Carl Sandburg Award is given for the individual judged to be the year's outstanding poet.

1978 **Rod McKuen**
1979 **William Meredith**
1980 **John Ciardi**

Voertman's Poetry Award

TEXAS INSTITUTE OF LETTERS
Box 3143, Dallas, Tex. 75275 (214/692-2000)

The Voertman's Poetry Award, which carries a $200 honorarium, is given annually for a volume of poetry by a Texan or on a Texas subject. (The award was known as the Daedalian Poetry Award until 1965.)

1945 **David Russell,** *Sing With Me Now*
1946 **Whitney Montgomery,** *Joseph's Coat*
1947 **Arthur M. Sampley,** *Of the Strong and the Fleet*
1948 **Vaida S. Montgomery,** *Hail for Rain*
1949 **Frances Alexander,** *Time at the Window*
1950 **Mary Poole,** *Being in Night*
1951 **Arthur M. Sampley,** *Furrow with Blackbirds*
1952 **William D. Barney,** *Kneel to the Stone*
1953 **Robert Lee Brothers,** *The Hidden Harp*
1954 **William Burford,** *Man Now*
1955 **William D. Barney,** *Permitted Proof*
1956 **Vassar Miller,** *Adam's Footprint*
1957 **Eloise Roach,** *Platero and I,* translated from the Spanish of Juan Ramon Jimenez
1958 **No award**
1959 **Ramsey Yelvington,** *A Cloud of Witnesses*
1960 **Vassar Miller,** *Wage War on Silence*
1961 **Walter E. Kidd,** *Time Turns West*
1962 **Frederick Will,** *A Wedge of Words*
1963 **Vassar Miller,** *My Bones Being Wiser*
1964 **Thomas Whitbread,** *Four Infinitives*
1965 **Roger Shattuck,** *Half Tame*
1966 **R. G. Vliet,** *Events and Celebrations*
1967 **Frederic Will,** *Planets*
1968 **Edgar Simmons,** *Driving to Biloxi*
1969 **No award**
1970 **R. G. Vliet,** *The Man with the Black Mouth*
1971 **Arthur M. Sampley,** *Selected Poems 1937-1971*
1972 **Gene Shuford,** *Selected Poems, 1933-1971*
1973 **Fania Kruger,** *Selected Poems*
1974 **Michael Ryan,** *Threats Instead of Trees*
1975 **Kurth Sprague,** *The Promise Kept*
1976 **Walt McDonald,** *Caliban in Blue*
1977 **Glenn Hardin,** *Giants*
Jack Myers, *The Family War*
1978 **Tess Gallagher,** *Under Stars*
Bin Ramke, *The Difference between Day and Night*

Current status unknown

Journalism

Contents

Related Awards

Fourth Estate Award

AMERICAN LEGION
700 N. Pennsylvania St., Indianapolis, Ind. 46206

The American Legion Fourth Estate Award is a bronze plaque given annually in appreciation of public relations efforts to the press, radio, television or other communications media or to owners or personnel of the media, for support of Legion policies or programs. The National Public Relations Commission is empowered by the National Executive Committee to make this award, which was originally known as the American Legion Mercury Award.

1958 **Jim Lucas**
1959 **Advertising Council, Inc.**
1959 ***Chicago Tribune***
1959 ***U.S. News & World Report***
1960 **Hearst Newspapers**
1961 **Scripps-Howard Newspapers**
1961 **Jack L. Warner,** Warner Brothers Pictures
1962 **Fulton Lewis, Jr.**
1963 **The Copley Press, Inc.**
1963 ***This Week*** **Magazine**
1964 ***Chicago Tribune***
1964 **Mississippi Publishers Corp.**
1965 **Clark Mollenhoff,** Cowles Publications
1965 **Paul Harvey,** American Broadcasting Co.
1965 **Golden West Broadcasters**
1966 **Mutual Broadcasting System**
1966 **The Booth Newspapers**
1966 ***Columbus Dispatch***
1967 ***St. Louis Globe-Democrat***
1968 **William S. White**
1969 **George W. Healy, Jr.**
1969 **Raymond J. McHugh**
1970 **James Geddes Stahlman,** *The Banner* (Nashville, Tenn.)
1970 **Jenkin Lloyd Jones,** *The Tribune* (Tulsa, Okla.)
1971 **Anheuser Busch, Inc.**
1971 **John Wayne**
1972 **Augustin Edwards,** *El Mercurio,* (Santiago, Chile)
1973 **Clare Boothe Luce**
1974 **James J. Kilpatrick, Jr.**
1975 **Jim Bishop**
1976 **Vic Cantone**
Thomas P. Chisman, Bicentennial Radio Network, Ltd.
1977 ***Columbus Dispatch***
Jess Gorkin, *Parade*
1978 **Mort Walker,** creator of "Beetle Bailey"
Milton Caniff, creator of "Steve Canyon"
1979 **Frank Mankiewiecz** and **National Public Radio**
1980 **Hy Rosen,** *Albany Times-Union* editorial cartoonist

Amos Award

NATIONAL NEWSPAPER ASSOCIATION
1627 K St. NW, Washington, D.C. 20006 (202/466-7200)

The Amos Award, which was created in 1938, recognizes distinguished service and/or contributions to the U.S. press in general and NNA programs in particular. An active newspaperman or -woman associated with a non-metropolitan paper in a community eith a population of 50,000 of less is eligible. Only the most recent recipients are listed here.

1976 **Ed Livermore**
1977 **William E. Branen**
1978 **Telford Work**
1979 **Walter W. Grunfeld**
1980 **Kenneth Robinson**

ASNE Award

AMERICAN SOCIETY OF NEWSPAPER EDITORS
556 Central Ave., St. Petersburg, Fla. 33701

The $1,000 ASNE Awards honor excellent in newspaper journalism and commentary. Entries are judged with an emphasis on quality of writing. In addition to the winners listed here, honorable mentions are made.

COMMENTARY

1979 **Everett S. Allen,** *New Bedford* (Mass.) *Standard-Times*
1980 **Ellen Goodman,** *Boston Globe*

NEWS

1979 **Richard Ben Cramer,** *Philadelphia Inquirer*
1980 **Carol McCabe,** *Providence Journal-Bulletin*

FEATURES

1979 **Thomas Oliphant,** *Boston Globe*
1980 **Cynthia Gorney,** *Washington Post*

SPORTS

1979 **Mary Ellen Corbett,** freelance in *Ft. Wayne* (Ind.) *News Sentinel*
1980 **No award**

AWA Writing Awards
Lauren D. Lyman Award
James J. Strebig Award
Robert S. Ball Memorial Award
Earl D. Osborn Award

AVIATION/SPACE WRITERS ASSOCIATION
Cliffwood Rd., Chester, N.J. 07930 (201/879-5635)

AWA Writing Awards are given for outstanding aviation and space writing and reporting in various categories of newspapers and magazines. A $100 honorarium and scroll are now given each year for aviation and space writing in six categories, for a total of twelve annual awards.

NEWSPAPERS OVER 50,000 CIRCULATION

1961 **Don Dwiggins**
1962 **Edwin G. Pipp**
1963 **Jack Foisie**
1964 **Howard Simons**
1965 **David H. Hoffman**
1966 **William Hines**
1967 **Howard S. Benedict**
1968 **Evert B. Clark**

NEWSPAPERS OVER 200,000 CIRCULATION

1969 **Howard Benedict**
1970 **Robert H. Lindsey** (Aviation)
Peter Reich (Space)
1971 **Charles L. Tracy** (Aviation)
Jim Maloney (Space)
1972 **Stephen M. Aug** (Aviation)
Edwin G. Pipp (Space)
1973 **Edwin G. Pipp** (Aviation)
Robert C. Cowen (Space)
1974 **John Finley** (Aviation)
Jim Maloney (Space)
1975 **Jerry Hulse** (Aviation)
Howard S. Benedict (Space)
1976 **Lawrence S. Kramer**, *San Francisco Examiner* (Aviation)
Joel J. Shurkin, *Philadelphia Inquirer* (Space)
1977 **Peter Reich**, *Chicago Tribune* (Aviation)
Edwin G. Pipp, *Detroit News* (Space)
1978 **Peter Reich**, *Chicago Tribune* (Space)
Jim Wright, *Dallas Morning News* (Aviation)
1979 **Robert Stickler** and **Kristen Kelch** (Aviation)
John Yemma (Space)
1980 **David C. Hackney** (Aviation)
Al Rossiter, Jr. (Space)

NEWSPAPERS UNDER 50,000 CIRCULATION

1962 **Tony Page**
1963 **James E. Cahill**
1964 **Dean Todd**
1965 **Dorothy M. Horzempa**
1966 **Harold Gold**
1967 **Sanders H. LaMont**
1968 **Sue Butler**

NEWSPAPERS UNDER 200,000 CIRCULATION

1969 **Sue Butler**
1970 **Arnold Lewis** (Aviation)
Sanders H. LaMont and Staff of *Today* (Space)
1971 **Jon R. Donnelly** (Aviation)
Everett Hosking (Space)
1972 **Jon R. Donnelly** (Aviation)
Ross Mackenzie (Space)
1973 **Eric Filson, Stacey J. Bridges, Linda Miklowitz, Skip Perez and Dave Reddick** (Aviation)
Sanders H. LaMont and staff of *Today* (Space)
1974 **Jon R. Donnelly** (Aviation)
Ed Arnone and Staff (Space)
1975 **Steve Sellers** (Aviation)
Sanders H. LaMont (Space)
1976 **Alan Goldsand,** *Journal of Commerce* (Aviation)
Robert B. Robinson, *Today*, Cocoa, Fla. (Space)
1977 **David Shugarts,** *Flight Line Times* (Aviation)
Grant Fjermedal, *Washington Daily News* (Space)
1978 **Larry Levy**, *Tulsa Daily Tribune* (Space)
Al L. Watts, *Seattle Post-Intelligencer* (Aviation)
1979 **Lew Townsend** (Aviation)
Dick Baumbach (Space)
1980 **Lew Townsend** (Aviation)
David Dooling (Space)

AVIATION/SPACE MAGAZINES

1961 **Claude Witze**
1962 **Don Downie**
1963 **Claude Witze**
1964 **William Leavitt**
1965 **David A. Anderton**
1966 **Claude Witze**
1967 **Jesse Samuel Butz, Jr.**
1968 **C. W. Borklund**
1969 **Capt. Robert P. Everett, USAF and Allan R. Scholin**
1970 **Edgar E. Ulsamer** (Aviation)
Michael Getler (Space)
1971 **John F. Judge** (Aviation)
Frank A. Burnham (Space
1972 **Stephen Wilkinson** (Aviation)
Edgar E. Ulsamer (Space)

GENERAL MAGAZINES

1961 **Devon Francis**
1962 **Kenneth F. Weaver**
1963 **Joseph A. Walker, USAF**
1964 **Albert Rosenfeld**
1965 **Arthur C. Clarke**
1966 **Keith Wheeler**
1967 **James H. Winchester**
1968 **Ray Bradbury**
1969 **Edwin Diamond, George Alexander, Evert Clark and Henry T. Simmons**
1970 **No award** (Aviation)
Kenneth F. Weaver (Space)
1971 **Clell Bryant** and **Jerry Hannifin** (Aviation)
Kenneth F. Weaver (Space)
1972 **David Butler** (Aviation)
C.V. Glines (Space)

MAGAZINES (one category only, not subdivided into Aviation/Space Magazines and General Magazines)

1973 **Dee Mosteller** (Aviation)
Henry S. F. Cooper, Jr. (Space)
1974 **James H. Winchester** (Aviation)
Peter Gwynne (Space)
1975 **Allan R. Scholin** (Aviation)
Thomas Y. Canby (Space)
1976 **Robert Hotz, Herb Coleman and Robert Ropelewski,** *Aviation Week and Space Technology* (Aviation)
Gene Bylinski, *Fortune* (Space)
1977 **C.A. Robinson and Staff,** *Aviation Week and Space Technology*
Willian Gregory and Staff, *Aviation Week and Space Technology*
David Alpern, *Newsweek*
James J. Haggerty, *Penthouse*
Peter Stoler, *Time*

MAGAZINES (General Interest)

1978 **Timothy Ferris,** *Rolling Stone* (Space)
Moira Johnston, *New West* (Aviation)
1979 **Jerry Hannifin** and **David Tinnin** (Aviation)
Frederic Golden, Leon Jaroff and **F. Sydnor Vanderschmidt** (Space)
1980 **Brent Welling** and **Anne Swardson** (Aviation)
Robert Jastrow (Space)

MAGZINES (special interest trade)

1978 **Jim Schefter,** *Popular Science* (Space)
Edward H. Kolcum and Staff, *Aviation Week & Space Technology*
1979 **G.V. Glines** (Aviation)
Clarence A. Robinson (Space)
1980 **Barbara Beyer, James D. Baumgarner, William V. Henzey, John Nammack** and **James P. Woolsey** (Aviation)
Trudy E. Bell (Space)

TELEVISION AND RADIO

1963 **Jules Bergman**

1964 **Jules Bergman**
1965 **Frank Hall**
1966 **John N. Davenport**
1967 **No award**
1968 **Jerome Kuehl, Chet Huntley and George Vicas**
1969 **Jim Kitchell and Frank McGee**
1970 **George H. Rhodes and WKYC-TV,** Cleveland (Aviation)
Robert Wussler and Walter Cronkite, CBS News, (Space)
1971 **Charles Spence** (Aviation)
Leonard Reiffel (Space)
1972 **Gary Robinson** (Aviation)
James Quigley (Space)
1973 **Brad Sherman** (Aviation)
Jules Bergman (Space)
1974 **Charles Spence and Fletcher Cox** (Aviation)
Mark Levinson (Space)
1975 **Steve Neuman** (Aviation)
John Lyons, Christine Lyons, Mark Knoller (Space)
1976 **Ed Turney and Paul Fine,** WMAL-TV, Washington, (Aviation)
Jules Bergman, ABC (Space)
1977 **Bill Neil,** KOCE-TV
Jules Bergman, ABC News
1978 **Jim Slade,** WMAL-AM, Washington, D.C. (Space)
Fred Casesar, Carl Stieneker and **Dick Ford,** KSD-TV, St. Louis (Aviation)
Dale Solly, WAVE-TV, Louisville, Ky. (Aviation)
1979 **Harry Muheim** (Aviation)
Larry Lee and **Joe Pennington** (Aviation)
1980 **Betty Wolden, Warren Corbett** and **Don Smith** (Space)

PHOTOJOURNALISM

1963 **James Yarnell**
1964 **Ralph Morse**
1965 **Howard Sochurek**
1966 **Charles Moore and Charles Bonnay**
1967 **Anthony E. Linck**
1968 **No award**
1969 **Col. Frank Borman, USAF, Capt. James A. Lovell, Jr., USN and Lt. Col. William Anders, USAF**
1970 **Charles E. Rotkin** (Aviation)
Jeff Bremer, NASA (Space)
1971 **Fred Hartman, Robert Murray, Joseph Sommers and Frank J. Delear** (Aviation)
Goddard Space Flight Center/National Oceanic and Atmospheric Administration (Space)
1972 **Lou Davis** (Aviation)
No award (Space)
1973 **Russell Munson and Stephan Wilkinson** (Aviation)
Tony Linck (Space)
1974 **James Gilbert** (Aviation)
1975 **Richard P. Benjamin** (Aviation)
James R. Blair (Space)
1976 **Robert Holt, Jr.,** *St. Louis Post Dispatch* (Aviation)
1977 **Robert B. Milnes**

PHOTOGRAPHY

1978 **Bruce Dale,** *National Geographic* (Aviation)
1979 **Roger Foley** (Aviation)
1980 **James A. Sugar** (Aviation)

BOOKS (non-fiction)

1961 **Martin Caidin**
1962 **Mel J. Hunter**
1963 **Maj. Gene Guerny, USAF**
1964 **Robert J. Serling**
1965 **Martin Caidin and Edward Hymoff**
1966 **James J. Haggerty, Jr. and H. G. Stever**
1967 **C. W. Borklund**
1968 **Don Dwiggins**
1969 **William R. Shelton**
1970 **Robert J. Serling** (Aviation)
John Noble Wilford (Space)
1971 **Joe Christy and Page Schamburger** (Aviation)
Davis Thomas (Space)
1972 **Ann Holtgren Pellegreno** (Aviation)
No award (Space)
1973 **James A. Arey** (Aviation)
Gene and Clare Gurney (Space)
1974 **Devon Francis** (Aviation)
No award (Space)
1975 **Robert J. Serling** (Aviation)
Philip J. Klass (Space)
1976 **Lloyd S. Jones,** *U.S. Fighters,* (Aviation)
1977 **David Anderton,** *Strategic Air Command*
William Wagner, *Rueben Fleet*
Lloyd S. Jones
1978 **Raymond F. Toliver** and **Trevor J. Constable**
1979 **Rosamond Young** (Aviation)
Robert M. Powers (Space)
1980 **Harry Combs** (Aviation)
Robert M. Powers (Space)

BOOKS (fiction)

1967 **Robert J. Serling**
1968 **Martin Caidin**

MANUALS

1964 **S. F. (Sandy) MacDonald**
1965 **Lt. Col. Gene Guerny, USAF and Capt. Joseph A. Skiera, USAF**
1966 **John Dohm**
1967 **John Smith**
1968 **Maj. James C. Elliott and Lt. Col. Gene Guerny**

BOOKS (technical)

1978 **Lloyd S. Jones**
1979 **David B. Thurston** (Aviation)
1980 **Rene J. Francillon** (Aviation)

VISUAL COMMUNICATIONS AWARD

1978 **Ferde Grofe, Jr.** *Sentimental Journey* and *Flying is Vari-Eze*
Cameron Graham, *Flight—The Passionate Affair Art School, Fantasy Flight*

COMPANY COMMUNICATIONS AWARD

1977 **Bernard Kovit** and **Burnham Lewis,** *Grumman Aerospace Horizons*
1978 **Bernard Kovit** and **Burnham Lewis,** *Grumann Aerospace Horizons*
1979 **Bernard Kovit** and **Burnham Lewis,** *Grumman Aerospace Horizons*
1980 **Pepe Labatina Thompson,** *TRW Systems & Energy* (Magazine)
Lee C. Bright, *Eastern Airlines Falcon* (Magazine)

The Lauren D. Lyman Award goes annually to an individual for a long and distinguished career in aviation writing and/or public relations, exemplifying integrity, accuracy and excellence in reporting and writing. The trophy is sponsored by United Technologies.

1973 **Wayne Parrish**
1974 **Robert Hotz**

1975 Willis Player
1976 Vern Haugland
1977 George E. Haddaway
1978 Devon Francis
1979 Jerry Hannifin
1980 Eric Bramley

The $500 James J. Strebig Award, sponsored by Teledyne Continental Motors Co., is given for outstanding aviation reporting or writing in any media.

1952 Arthur A. Riley
1953 Albert M. Skea
1954 Frank L. Harvey
1955 Frank Ellis and Marvin G. Miles
1956 Allan C. Fisher, Jr. and Marvin G. Miles
1957 James J. Haggerty, Jr. and Ansel E. Talbert
1958 Martin Caidin and Jean H. Pearson
1959 Marvin Miles and William G. Osmun
1960 George A. Carroll and Allan C. Fisher, Jr.
1961 Martin Caidin
1962 Tony Page
1963 Claude Witze
1964 Robert J. Serling
1965 David H. Hoffman
1966 Keith Wheeler
1967 James H. Winchester
1968 Warren R. Young
1969 John Saar and Ronald Bailey
1970 Edgar E. Ulsamer
1971 Charles L. Tracy
1972 Cecil Brownlow, Robert Hotz and Barry Miller
1973 Ronald A. Keith
1974 Dave McElhatton
1975 Donald S. Riggs
1976 Thomas G. Foxworth
1977 Peter Reich
1978 Staff of *Flying*
1979 Jerry Hannifin, *Time*
1980 Harry Combs

The $500 Robert S. Ball Memorial Award, sponsored by the Chrysler Corp., is given annually for outstanding space reporting or writing in any medium.

1962 Edwin G. Pipp
1963 Jesse Samuel Butz, Jr.
1964 William Leavitt
1965 Arthur C. Clarke
1966 William Hines
1967 Howard S. Benedict
1968 Ray Bradbury
1969 Howard S. Benedict
1970 Sanders H. LaMont and Staff of ***Today***
1971 Kenneth F. Weaver
1972 Cecil Brownlow, Robert Hotz and Barry Miller
1973 Henry S. F. Cooper, Jr.
1974 Kenneth F. Weaver
1975 Kenneth F. Weaver
1976 Jim Maloney
1977 William H. Gregory
1978 Timothy Ferris, *Rolling Stone*
1979 Frederic Golden, Leon Jaroff and F. Snydor Vanderschmidt
1980 Betty Wolden, Warren Corbett and Don Smith

The $500 Earl D. Osborn Award, sponsored by EDO Corp., is given annually for outstanding reporting or writing on general aviation in any medium.

1970 George H. Rhodes and WKYC-TV, Cleveland
1971 Charles Spence
1972 Stephan Wilkinson
1973 Lawrence W. Reithmaier
1974 Lew Townsend
1975 Richard L. Taylor
1976 Archie Trammel, Robert Stangarone and Gordon Gilbert
1977 Archie Trammell
1978 Richard L. Collins, *Flying Safety* (book)
1979 David B. Thurston
1980 Lew Townsend

Mike Berger Memorial Award

COLUMBIA UNIVERSITY
Graduate School of Journalism, Room 706, New York, N.Y. 10027 (212/280-3411)

The Mike Berger Memorial Award, presented in honor of Pulitzer Prize-winning reporter and feature writer Meyer (Mike) Berger, is open to all New York reporters and out-of-town reporters with New York assignments. Nominations are generally made by editors of the city's daily newspapers and New York bureaus of Associated Press and United Press International. Selection of the winners is by a panel of judges, who are journalists. The winners share a $1,500 prize, and each receives a certificate.

1961 Helen Dudar, *New York Post*
David Miller, *New York Herald Tribune*
McCandlish Phillips, *New York Times*
1962 Pete Hamill, *New York Post*
Lewis Lapham, *New York Herald Tribune*
1963 Newton H. Fullbright, *New York Herald Tribune*
Peter Kihss, *New York Times*
1964 Jimmy Breslin, *New York Herald Tribune*
Charles Grutzner, *New York Times*
1965 Homer Bigart, *New York Times*
Bernard Gavzer, Associated Press
1966 Robert Lipsyte, *New York Times*
William E. Blundell, *Wall Street Journal*
1967 Murray Schumach, *New York Times*
Leonard Victor, *Long Island Press*
1968 Felix Kessler, *Wall Street Journal*
J. Anthony Lukas, *New York Times*
1969 Robert Mayer, *Newsday*
Sy Safransky and Archie Waters, *Long Island Press*
1970 Art Sears, Jr. and Donald Moffitt, *Wall Street Journal*
1971 Robert Mayer, *Newsday*
1972 Frank Faso, Joseph Martin and Paul Meskil, *New York Daily News*
1973 John Hess, *New York Times*
Barry Cunningham, *New York Post*
1974 Penelope McMillan, *New York Sunday News*
N. (Sonny) Kleineld, *Wall Street Journal*
1975 Deirdre Carmody, *New York Times*
Peter Coutros, *Daily News*
1976 Israel Shenker, *New York Times*
Howard Blum, *Village Voice*
1977 Denis Hamill, *Village Voice*
Richard Severo, *New York Times*
1978 Ricki Fulman, *New York Daily News*
Carey Winfrey, *New York Times*
1979 Francis X. Clines, *New York Times*
Kenneth Gross, *Newsday*
1980 Joyce Wadler, *New York Daily News*
Laurie Johnston, *New York Times*

SPECIAL RECOGNITION

1970 **Richard Savero,** *New York Times*
Peter Coutros, *New York Daily News*
1971 **Jack Newfield,** *Village Voice*
Joseph Lelyveld, *New York Times*
1972 **Ray Kestenbaum,** *Newsday*
Diane Zimmerman, *New York Daily News*

Worth Bingham Prize

WORTH BINGHAM MEMORIAL FUND
1321 31st St. NW, Washington, D.C. 20007

The $1,000 Worth Bingham Prize honors newspaper or magazine reporting that investigates and analyzes situations of national significance in the Washington political community. A panel of judges selects the winner from entries.

1967 **William Lambert**, *Life*
1968 **Associated Press, Special Assignment Team**
1969 **Seymour Hersh**, *Dispatch News*
1970 **James Clayton**, *Washington Post*
1971 **Frank Wright**, *Minneapolis Tribune*
1972 **Carl Bernstein** and **Robert Woodward**, *Washington Post*
1973 **Jerry Landauer**, *Wall Street Journal*
1974 **Maxine Cheshire**, *Washington Post*
1975 **James Risser**, *Des Moines Register*
1976 **Morton Mintz**, *Washington Post*
1977 **Michael J. Sniffin** and **Richard E. Meyer**, Associated Press
1978 **David Hess**, *Akron Beacon Journal*
1979 **John Fialka**, *Washington Post*
1980 **Not available at press time**

Blakeslee Award

AMERICAN HEART ASSOCIATION
7320 Greenville Ave., Dallas, Tex. (214/750-5340)

The Blakeslee Award, which consists of a plaque and $500, is awarded annually for meritorious print and broadcast journalism in the field of medicine and health, specifically involving heart disease and treatment of heart disease. A committee selects the winner.

1953 **Wade Arnold**, NBC Radio
1954 **William A. Brams**, M.D., *Managing Your Coronary*
Howard Clive, *Woman's Home Companion*
Arthur Cornelius and **Cathy Covert**, *New York Herald Journal*
1955 **Frances Burns**, *Boston Daily Globe*
CBS Television Network
William Peters, *Cosmopolitan Magazine*
Jane Stafford, *Science Service*
1956 **Frank Carey**, Associated Press
Robert P. Goldman, *Parade Magazine*
Earl Hamner, NBC Radio Network
Nate Haseltine, *Washington Post* and *Washington Times Herald*
***Life* Science Department**
NBC Television Network
George Voutsas, NBC Radio Network
Paul Dudley White, Special award
Howard Whitman, NBC Television Network
1957 **Walter Bazar**, *New York Journal American*
Don Dunham, *Cleveland Press*
Leonard Engel, North American Newspaper Alliance
NBC Television Network
Steven Spencer, *The Saturday Evening Post*
1958 **CBS Television Network**
Lee Guist, *Business Week*
Eugene Taylor, *New York Times*
1959 **Ben Pearse**, *Saturday Evening Post*
WBBM-TV (Chicago)
1960 **Issac Asimov**, *The Living River*
Francis Bello, *Fortune*
H.M. Marvin, *Your Heart: A Handbook for Layman*
Barbara Milz, *Augusta* Georgia *Chronicle*
WCSH-TV (Portland)
1961 **James C.G. Coniff**, *Everywoman's Family Circle Magazine*
Douglas Ritchie, *Stroke*
Mildred Spencer, *New York Evening Times* (Buffalo)
WJXT-TV (Jacksonville, Fla.)
1962 **CBS Television Network**
Alexander Gifford, *Baltimore News-Post* and *Sunday American*
Robert A. Kuhn, *Everywoman's Family Circle Magazine*
Robert K. Plumb, *New York Times*
Bernard Seeman, *The River of Life*
1963 **Alton Blakeslee**, Associated Press
Matt Clark, *Newsweek*
Victor Cohn, *Minneapolis Tribune*
Thomas B. Morgan, *Look Magazine*
NBC Television Network
Harry Nelson, *Los Angeles Times*
WFIL-TV, (Philadelphia)
1964 **Jerry Bishop**, *Wall Street Journal*
Alton Blakeslee and **Jeremiah Stamler**, *Your Heart Has Nine Lives*
Charles Harbutt and the Editors of *Life Magazine*
Eric Hodgens, *Episode: Report on the Accident Inside My Skull*
Terry Morris, *Redbook*
WDSU-TV (New Orleans)
1965 **Matt Clark**, *Newsweek*
Francis D. Moore, *Give and Take: The Development of Tissue Transplanation*
Beverly Orndoff, *Richmond Times-Dispatch*
Charles Schaeffer, Newhouse National News Service
1966 **Dave Babitt**, WCFL Radio, Chicago
Barry Parrell, *Life*
Louis Hickman Lione, *Baltimore Sunday Sun*
NBC Television Network
Howard J. Sanders, *Chemical and Engineering News*
1967 ***Business Week***
Rou deGravelles, WJW-TV (Cleveland)
Jim Gordon, WINS Radio (New York)
Arthur J. Snider, *Chicago Daily News*
1968 **ABC Television Network**
CBS Radio
Matt Clark, *Newsweek*
David Cleary, *Philadelphia Bulletin*
Ronald Kotulak, *Chicago Tribune*
Lennart Nilsson, *Life*
WNBC-TV (New York)
1969 **Donald C. Drake**, *Philadelphia Inquirer*
C.P. Gilmore, *New York Times Magazine*
Cameron Hawley, *The Hurricane Years*
John W. Thorne, "Highway to Healty Hearts" (film)
WWJ-TV (Detroit)
1970 **Lou Adler**, WCBS Newsradio (New York)

National Educational Television
Bill Sidlinger, *Chicago Daily News*
WAGA-TV
Patrick Young, *The National Observer*
1971 **Mildred Alexander**, WTAR-TV (Norfolk, Va.)
Jane E. Brody, *New York Times*
Harold J. Eager, *Lancaster* (Pa.) *Sunday News*
Rachel Mackenzie, *The New Yorker*
WHDH-TV (Boston)
1972 **CBC Television Network**
KNXT-TV (Los Angeles)
Walter McQuade, *Fortune*
Howard J. Sanders, *Chemical and Engineering News*
WCCO-Radio (Minneapolis)
1973 **Audio Productions** (Rockford, Ill.)
Barbara Chapman, *The Sunday Register Star* and *The Register-Republic*
Edward Edelson, *Family Health Magazine*
David Hendin, *Enterprise Science News*
Jonathan Spivak, *Wall Street Journal*
1974 **Public Broadcasting Service**
Jack Slater, *Ebony*
WCBS Newsradio (New York)
WCVB-TV (Boston)
WTAR-TV (Norfolk)
1975 **Andy Guthrie**, WKYC-TV (Cleveland)
Joann Ellison Rodgers, *The Baltimore News American*
Joan Soloman, *Consumer Reports Magazine*
Jane Schoenberg and **JoAnn Stichman**, *How to Survive Your Husband's Heart Attack*
Tandem Production
1976 **Art Athens**, WCBS Newsradio (New York)
Donald C. Drake, *Philadelphia Inquirer*
Family Health Magazine
Daniel A. Koger, *Flint* Michigan *Journal*
Al Rossiter, Jr., United Press International
Tandem Productions
WEFI Newsradio (Boston)
1977 **CBS Television Network**
Gateway Communications, Inc.
Lawrence Hillock and **Irving Leibowitz**, *The Lorain* (Ohio) *Journal*
G. Timothy Johnson, *Harvard Magazine*
Richard A. Knox, *Boston Globe*
Gina Bari Kolata and **Jean L. Marx**, *Science Magazine*
William A. Nolen, *Surgeon Under the Knife*
Gary Schwitzer, WFAA-TV (Dallas)
Arthur Ulene, M.D., NBC Television Network
WBBM-TV (Chicago)
1978 **Gail Bronson**, *Wall Street Journal*
KFWB Radio (Los Angeles)
Joann Ellison Rodgers, *Woman's Day*
William H. Stuart, Jr., KMGH-TV (Denver)
WLS-TV (Chicago)
1979 **May W. Annexton**, Physicians Radio Network
Lewis Cope, *Minneapolis Tribune*
Steven Andrew Davis, KCBS Newsradio (San Francisco)
Lawrence Galton, *Family Circle*
Augusta Greenblatt and **I.J. Greenblatt**, *Your Genes and Your Destiny: A New Look at a Longer Life*
WBBM-TV (Chicago)
The Tomorrow Entertainment /Medcom Co.
William F. Turner, KCAU-TV (Sioux City, Iowa)
1980 **Gene Allen**, KPRC-TV (Houston)
Sheree L. Burger, *Gloucester County Times* (Woodbury, N.J.)
Edward D. Freis and **Gina Bari Kolata**, *The High Blood Pressure Book: A Guide For Patients and Their Families*
Elizabeth Gonzalez, *The Journal of the American Medical Association*
Gloria S. Hochman, *Philadelphia Inquirer*
Karl Idsvoog, KUTV-TV (Salt Lake City)
Jill Stein, KMOX Radio (St. Louis)

British Press Awards

BRITISH PRESS AWARDS
9 New Fetter Lane, Room 302, London EC4A 1AR, U.K.
(01 822 3504)

British Press Awards are presented annually to U.K. journalists in a variety of categories. Winners, who are selected by a panel of judges, receive commemorative paperweights and a sum of money, which is listed beside each award below. The honors were originally called the Hannen Swaffer Awards and from 1966 through 1973 were known as the International Publishing Corporation Awards.

REPORTER OF THE YEAR (£500)

1962 **Walter Terry**, *Daily Mail*

JOURNALIST OF THE YEAR (originally £500, now £1,000)

1963 **D.H. Hopkinson**, *Sheffield Telegraph*
1964 **Denis Hamilton**, *Sunday Times*
1965 **Michael Randall**, *Daily Mail*
1966 **Sir Gordon Newton**, *Financial Times*
1967 **John Pilger**, *Daily Mirror*
1968 **Victor Zorza**, *The Guardian*
1969 **Anthony Grey**, Reuters
1970 **Alastair Hetherington**, *The Guardian*
1971 **Simon Winchester**, *The Guardian*
1972 **Harold Evans**, *Sunday Times*
1973 **Adam Raphael**, *The Guardian*
1974 **Harry Longmuir**, *Daily Mail*
1975 **Jon Swain**, *Sunday Times*
1976 **No award**
1977 **Barry Askew**, editor; **Robert Satchwell**, assistant editor and **David Graham**, chief reporter, *Lancashire Evening Post*
1978 **Martin Bailey, Bernard Rivers** and **Peter Kellner**, *Sunday Times*
1979 **John Pilger**, *Daily Mirror*
1980 **Not available at press time**

INTERNATIONAL REPORTER (100 gns.)

1966 **Louis Heren**, *The Times*
1967 **Christopher Dobson**, *Daily Mail*
1968 **Walter Partington**, *Daily Express*
1969 **Murray Sayle**, *Sunday Times*
1970 **John Pilger**, *Daily Mirror*
1971 **Peter Hazelhurst**, *The Times*
Gavin Young, *The Observer*
1972 **John Fairhall**, *The Guardian*

INTERNATIONAL REPORTER OF THE YEAR (originally £100, now £250)

1973 **Peter Niesewand**, *The Guardian*
1974 **Colin Smith**, *The Observer*
1975 **Martin Wollacott**, *The Guardian*
1976 **Peter Niesewand**, *The Guardian*
1977 **Robin Smyth**, *The Observer*

1978 **Peter Lewis**, *Daily Mail*
1979 **Robert Fisk**, *The Times*
1980 **Not available at press time**

WOMAN JOURNALIST (100 gns.-£500)

1962 **Clare Hollingworth**, *The Guardian*
1963 **Anne Sharpley**, *Evening Standard*
1964 **Joan Seddon**, *Lancashire Evening Telegraph*
1965 **Wendy Cooper**, *Birmingham Post*
1966 **Barbara Buchanan**, *Bristol Evening Post*

WOMAN'S PAGE JOURNALIST

1967 **Christine Galpin**, Freelance "News of the World"
1968 **Marjorie Proops**, *Daily Mirror*
1969 **Felicity Green**, *Daily Mirror*
1970 **Elizabeth Prosser**, *The Sun*
1971 **Shirley Kaye**, *Halifax Evening Courier*
Jill Tweedie, *The Guardian*
1972 **Sue Hercombe**, *Newcastle Evening Chronicle*

DESCRIPTIVE WRITER

1962 **William Neil Connor**, *Daily Mirror*
1963 **Vincent Mulchrone**, *Daily Mail*
1964 **Anne Sharpley**, *Evening Standard*
1965 **James Cameron**, *Evening Standard*
1966 **John Pilger**, *Daily Mirror*
1967 **Donald Zec**, *Daily Mirror*
1968 **Angus McGill**, *Evening Standard*
1969 **Michael Frayn**, *The Observer*
1970 **Vincent Mulchrone**, *Daily Mail*
Keith Waterhouse, *Daily Mirror*
1971 **Geoffrey Goodman**, *Daily Mirror*

SPECIALIST WRITER OF THE YEAR (originally £100, now £250)

1972 **John Graham**, *Financial Times*
1973 **John Davis**, *The Observer*
1974 **Richard Milner**, *Sunday Times*
1975 **Andrew Alexander**, *Daily Mail*
1976 **Andrew Alexander**, *Daily Mail*
1977 **Oliver Gillie**, *Sunday Times*
1978 **John McCririck**, *The Sporting Life*
1979 **Angus MacPherson**, *Daily Mail*
1980 **Not available at press time**

NEWS REPORTER

1963 **Henry Brandon**, *Sunday Times*
1964 **Michael Gabbert**, *The People*
1965 **Anthony Carthew**, *Sun & Daily Mail*
1966 **Ken Gardner**, *The People*
1967 **David Farr**, *The People*
1968 **Harold Jackson**, *The Guardian*
1969 **Mary Holland**, *The Observer*
1970 **Monty Meth**, *Daily Mail*
1971 **John Clare**, *The Times*
1972 **Peter Harvey**, *The Guardian*

NEWS REPORTER OF THE YEAR (£100)

1973 **John Burns**, *Belfast Telegraph*
1974 **John Pilger**, *Daily Mirror*
1975 **John Edwards**, *Daily Mail*
1976 **Geraldine Norman**, *The Times*

REPORTER OF THE YEAR (£250)

1977 **Richard Stott**, *Daily Mail*
1978 **Roger Beam**, **Barry Wigmore**, **Frank Palmer** and **Kent Gavin**, *Daily Mail*
1979 **Melanie Phillips**, *The Guardian*
1980 **Not available at press time**

SPORTS WRITER (100 gns.)

1963 **J.L. Manning**, *Daily Mail*
1964 **George Whiting**, *Evening Standard*
1965 **Peter Wilson**, *Daily Mirror*
1966 **Hugh McIlvanney**, *The Observer*
1967 **Sam Leitch**, *Sunday Mirror*
1968 **Christopher Brasher**, *The Observer*
1969 **Hugh McIlvanney**, *The Observer*
1970 **Frank Butler**, *News of the World*
1971 **Ian Wooldridge**, *Daily Mail*
1972 **John Morgan**, *Daily Express*

SPORTS WRITER OF THE YEAR (£100)

1973 **Peter Batt**, *The Sun*
1974 **Ian Wooldridge**, *Daily Mail*
1975 **David Gray**, *The Guardian*

SPORTS JOURNALIST OF THE YEAR (£250)

1976 **Christopher Brasher**, *The Observer*
1977 **Hugh McIlvanney**, *The Observer*
1978 **Hugh McIlvanney**, *The Observer*
1979 **John Arlott**, *The Guardian*
1980 **Not available at press time**

CRITIC (100 gns.)

1963 **Alan Brien**, *Sunday Telegraph*
1964 **Philip Purser**, *Sunday Telegraph*
1965 **Michael Foot**, *Evening Standard*
1966 **Milton Shulman**, *Evening Standard*
1967 **Alan Brien**, *Sunday Telegraph*
1968 **Peter Black**, *Daily Mail*
1969 **Alexander Walker**, *Evening Standard*
1970 **George Melly**, *The Observer*
1971 **Derek Malcolm**, *The Guardian*
1972 **T.C. Worsley**, *Financial Times*

CRITIC OF THE YEAR (originally £100, now £250)

1973 **Alexander Walker**, *Evening Standard*
1974 **Michael Billington**, *The Guardian*
1975 **Paul Allen**, *Sheffield Morning Telegraph*
1976 **Chris Dunkley**, *Financial Times*
1977 **Clive James**, *The Observer*
1978 **Fay Maschler**, *Evening Standard*
1979 **Anthony Burgess**, *The Observer*
1980 **Not available at press time**

PROVINCIAL JOURNALIST (100 gns.)

1964 **Anthony Hancox**, *Sunday Mercury*
1965 **Frank Laws**, *Yorkshire Evening Post*
1966 **Peter Williams**, *Burnley Evening Star*
1967 **Ernest Moore**, *Lancashire Evening Post*
1968 **Len Doherty**, *Sheffield Star*
1969 **Eric Forster**, *Newcastle Evening Chronicle*
1970 **Alfred McCreary**, *Belfast Telegraph*
1971 **Barry Lloyd-Jones**, *Birmingham Post*
1972 **Chris Fuller**, *Birmingham Post*

PROVINCIAL JOURNALIST OF THE YEAR (originally £100, now £250)

1973 **Frank Brandston**, *Bedfordshire Times*
1974 **John Marquis**, *Watford Evening Echo*
1975 **Carol Roberton**, *Sunderland Echo*
1976 **Geoffrey Parkhouse**, *Glasgow Herald*
Alan Whitsitt, *Belfast News Letter*
1977 **Carol Roberton** and **John Bailey**, *Sunderland Echo*
1978 **Peter O'Reilly**, **Mike Attenborough**, **Janice Barker** and **Susan Pape**, *Oldham Evening Chronicle*
1979 **Peter Browne**, *Northampton Chronicle & Echo*
1980 **Not available at press time**

CAMPAIGNING JOURNALIST (originally 100 gns., later £100, now £250)

1965 **R. Stewart Campbell**, *The People*
1966 **Harold Evans**, *Northern Echo*
1967 **Colin McGlashan**, *The Observer*
1968 **Michael Leapman**, *The Sun*
Peter Harland, *Bradford Telegraph & Argus*
1969 **Ken Gardner**, *The People*
1970 **Colin Brannigan**, *Sheffield Star*
1971 **Barry Askew**, *Lancashire Evening Post*
1972 **Caren Meyer**, *Evening News*
1973 **Christopher Booker** and **Bennie Gray**, freelance
1974 **No award**
1975 **Mary Beith**, *Sunday People*
Angus King, *Yorkshire Post*
1976 **Douglas Thain**, **Alan Hurndall**, and **Graham Hind**, *Sheffield Star*
1977 **John Pilger**, *Daily Mirror*
1978 **Lyn May**, **Charles Nevin**, **John Toker** and **Vincent Kelly**, *Liverpool Echo*
1979 **John McCririck**, *The Sporting Life*
1980 **Not available at press time**

YOUNG JOURNALIST

1968 **Kevin Rafferty**, *The Sun*
1969 **Raymond Fitz-Walter**, *Bradford Telegraph & Argus*
1970 **Janice Cave**, *Southend Evening Echo*
1971 **Yvonne Roberts**, *Northampton Chronicle & Echo*
1972 **Andrew Kruyer**, *Southend Evening Echo*

YOUNG JOURNALIST OF THE YEAR (250)

1973 **Robert Beam**, *Lancashire Evening Post*
1974 **Gordon Ogilvie**, *Aberdeen Evening Express*
1975 **Melanie Phillips**, *Hemel Hempstead Evening Post-Echo*
1976 **Richard Woolveridge**, *South London Press*
1977 **Tina Brown**, *Telegraph Sunday Magazine*
Jad Adams, *South East London & Kentish Mercury*
1978 **Andrew Cooper**, *Walsall Observer*
1979 **Steven Latter**, *Buckinghamshire Advertiser*
1980 **Not available at press time**

COLUMNIST OF THE YEAR (originally £100, now £250)

1973 **Bernard Levin**, *The Times*
Keith Waterhouse, *Daily Mirror*
1974 **Bernard Levin**, *The Times*
1975 **Ian Wooldridge**, *Daily Mail*
1976 **Ian Wooldridge**, *Daily Mail*
1977 **Anthony Holden**, *Sunday Times*
1978 **Keith Waterhouse**, *Daily Mirror*
1979 **Sam White**, *Evening Standard*
1980 **Not available at press time**

PRESS PHOTOGRAPHER OF THE YEAR/PHOTOGRAPHER OF THE YEAR (£250)

1976 **David Cairns**, *Daily Express*
1977 **John Downing**, *Daily Express*
1978 **Mike Lloyd**, freelance
1979 **Graham Wood**, *Daily Mail*
1980 **Not available at press time**

NEWS PHOTOGRAPHER OF THE YEAR (£250)

1977 **J.A. Jedrej**, *Cambridge Evening News*
1978 **Reg Lancaster**, *Daily Express*
1979 **Kent Gavin**, *Daily Mirror*
1980 **Not available at press time**

DAVID HOLDEN AWARD (£250)

1978 **Altaf Gauhar** and **Ian Wright**, *The Guardian*

CHAIRMAN'S AWARD

1974 **Sidney Jacobson**, International Publishing Corp.
1977 **David Holden**, *Sunday Times*

SPECIAL AWARD

1966 **David Rhys Davies**, *Merthyr Express*
1967 **Peter Preston**, *The Guardian*
Suzanne Puddfoot, *The Times*
1968 **Henry Longhurst**, *Sunday Times*
1969 **Sir Neville Cardus**, *The Guardian*
1970 **Ken Gardner**, *The People*
1971 **William Rees-Mogg**, editor, *The Times*
Anthony Mascarenas, *Sunday Times*
1972 **Laurie Manifold**, *Sunday People*
David Williams, editor, *South End Evening Echo*
1973 **David English**, editor, *Daily Mail*
1974 **Brian Roberts**, editor, *Sunday Telegraph*
1976 **Stephen Fay** and **Hugo Young**, *Sunday Times*
1977 **Charles Raw**, *Sunday Times*
1978 **Stephen Fay** and **Hugo Young**, *Sunday Times*
1979 **David Leigh**, *The Guardian*

Heywood Broun Award

THE NEWSPAPER GUILD
1125 15th St. NW, Washington, D.C. 20005 (202/296-2990)

Outstanding journalistic achievement, "in the spirit of Heywood Broun," is honored annually with the $1,000 Heywood Broun Award. Employees of Newspaper Guild jurisdiction newspapers, news services, news magazines, radio stations and television stations in the United States, Puerto Rico and Canada are eligible. A panel of journalists selects the winner from material submitted by the creator or another individual on righting a wrong or showing concern for the underdog.

1941 **Tom O'Connor,** *PM* (Revealing hazardous mine conditions)
1942 **Dillard Stokes,** *Washington Post* (Uncovering Nazi propaganda network in the U.S.)
1943 **Milton J. Lapine, I.L Kenen, William M. Davy and E. George Green,** *Cleveland Union Leader* (Series of wartime ads)
1944 **Nathan Robertson,** *PM* (Distinguished Washington coverage)
1945 **Larry Guerin,** *New Orleans Item* (Local and state coverage)
1946 **James McGuire, Jack McPhaul and Karin Walsh,** *Chicago Times* (For helping free a prisoner unjustly accused of murder)
1947 **Bert Andrews,** *New York Herald Tribune* (Exposed disregard for civil rights in State Department security dismissals)
1948 **Elias A. McQuaid,** *Manchester (N.H.) News* (Uncovered fraud in state contracts awards)
1949 **Herbert L. Block,** *Washington Post* (Editorial cartoons)
Ted Poston, *New York Post* (Courageous coverage of Flordia rape trial)
1950 **Leonard Jackson,** *Bay City* (Mich.) *Times* (Exposed exploitation of migrant farm workers)
1951 **Jack Steele,** *New York Herald Tribune* (Exposed corruption in federal government bureaus)
1952 **Wallace Turner,** *Portland Oregonian* (Exposed fraud in sale of Indian timberlands)
1953 **Ralph S. O'Leary,** *Houston Post* (Expose of the Minute Women of Texas)

1954 **Anthony Lewis,** *Washington Daily News* (Helped reinstate federal employee wrongly fired as security risk)
1955 **Clark R. Mollenhoff,** Cowles Newspapers (Stories leading to reinstatement of security "risk" and new security rules)
1956 **Wallace Turner and William Lambert,** *Portland Oregonian* (Stories leading to racket indictments of union, police and city officials)
1957 **Aaron Epstein,** *Daytona Beach* (Fla.) *Journal News* (Stories leading to slum redevelopment)
Arthur W. Geiselman, Jr., *York* (Pa.) *Gazette & Daily* (Stories leading to community reforms)
1958 **George N. Allen,** *New York World-Telegram & Sun* (On-scene investigation of delinquencies in city schools)
1959 **William Haddad and Joseph Kahn,** *New York Post* (Exposed graft and mismanagement in slum clearance)
1960 **Harry Allen and Frank Drea,** *Toronto Telegram* (Exposed exploitation of Italian immigrant workers)
1961 **Michael Mok,** *New York World-Telegram & Sun* (Exposed conditions in mental hospital)
Dale Wright, *New York World-Telegram & Sun* (Disclosed exploitation of migrant workers)
1962 **Morton Mintz,** *Washington Post* (Report on thalidomide leading to protective legislation)
1963 **Arthur W. Geiselman, Jr.** *York* (Pa.) *Gazette & Daily* (Stories leading to prosecution of housing code violations)
Samuel Stafford, Washington Daily News (Expose of abuses in surplus food distribution)
1964 **Gene Goltz,** *Houston Post* (Stories leading to indictment of local officials for theft and conspiracy involving public funds)
1965 **John Frasca,** *Tampa Tribune* (Stories leading to release of innocent man convicted and imprisoned for robbery)
1966 **Gene Miller,** *Miami Herald* (Stories leading to release of two persons unjustly convicted of murder)
1967 **Robert Wyrick,** *Cocoa* (Fla.) *Today* (Stories exposing county government corruption, leading to indictments and conviction)
1968 **Mike Royko,** *Chicago Daily News* (Columns pleading the cause of the underdog, leading to redress for the abused)
1969 **William Lambert,** *Life* (Article resulting in Justice Abe Fortas's resignation and reexamination of ethics in public life)
1970 **Donald Singleton,** *New York Daily News* (Series spotlighting problems of crime in New York City)
1971 **Aaron Latham,** *Washington Post* (Examined failures of Junior Village, the capital's home for homeless children)
1972 **Carl Bernstein and Bob Woodward,** *Washington Post* (Series exposing political ramifications of the Watergate Affair)
1973 **Donald L. Barlett and James B. Steele,** *Philadelphia Inquirer* (Series exposing uneven sentencing and discrimination by judges and prosecutors)
1974 **Selwyn Raab,** *New York Times* (Revealed new evidence calling into question convictions of two men for triple murder)
1975 **Kent Pollock,** *Philadelphia Inquirer* (Documented spread of police brutality in Philadelphia)
1976 **Acel Moore and Wendell Rawls, Jr.,** *Philadelphia Inquirer* (Series exposing brutality, corruption and murder at Pennsylvania's Fairview State Hospital for the criminally insane)
1977 **Fredric N. Tulsky and David Phelps,** *Jackson* (Miss.) *Clarion Ledger* (Exposing police brutality and maladministration of justice by the city's police and court system)
1978 **Paul Magnusson and Susan Watson,** *Detroit Free Press* (Series exposing abusive treatment of retarded children in a state instutution)
1979 **Carl Hiaason, Patrick Malone, Gene Miller and William Montalbano,** *Miami Herald* (Expose of "dangerous doctors"—alcoholics, drug addicts, incompetents and psychopaths—practicing medicine in Florida)
1980 **Barb Brucker and Jim Underwood,** *Mansfield* (Ohio) *News Journal* (Series on police brutality toward prisoners resulting in at least one prisoner's death and the attendant cover-up by responsible authorities)

John Hancock Awards for Excellence

JOHN HANCOCK MUTUAL LIFE INSURANCE CO.
John Hancock Pl., Box 111, Boston, Mass. 02117
(617/421-6000)

The John Hancock Awards for Excellence are $1,000 annual prizes for writers judged to have contributed significantly to consumer understanding of business and finance. Writers may submit material in six categories for consideration by a panel of experts in business and business journalism.

1967 **Leonard Downie, Jr.,** *Washington Post*
Robert A. Foster, *Worcester* (Mass.) *Telegram*
Joseph L. Goodrich, *Providence Journal-Bulletin*
John K. Jessup, *Life*
David A. Jewell, *Washington Post*
J.A. Livingston, *Philadelphia Bulletin* and Publishers-Hall Syndicate
1968 **Thomas G. Hartley,** *Elmira* (N.Y.) *Star Gazette*
Edward S. Kerstein, *Milwaukee Journal*
J.A. Livingston, *Philadelphia Bulletin* and Publishers-Hall Syndicate
Carol J. Loomis, *Fortune*
Hobart Rowen, *Washington Post*
Max Shapiro, *Barron's Weekly*
1969 **Robert Metz,** *New York Times*
Theodore Levitt, *Harvard Business Review*
H. Erich Heinemann, *New York Times*
George H. Arris, *Providence Sunday Journal*
David L. Beal, *Binghamton Evening Press*
Charles E. Connelly, Jr., *Rapid City* (S.D.) *Guide*
1970 **John F. Lawrence and Paul E. Steiger,** *Los Angeles Times*
Richard A. Nenneman, *Christian Science Monitor*
George Church, *Time*
Fred Bleakley, *Institutional Investor*
Robert S. Rosefsky, Newsday Specials
John Hanchette, *Niagara Falls* (N.Y.) *Gazette*
1971 **Laurance F. Stuntz,** Associated Press
Frank Morgan, *Newsweek*
Frank Lalli, *Forbes*
Robert E. Dallos, *Los Angeles Times*
Harold Chucker, *Minneapolis Star*
George Chaplin, *Honolulu Advertiser*
1972 **John T. Cunniff,** Associated Press
George Church, *Time*
Philip B. Osborne, *Business Week*
Rudy Maxa, *Washington Post*
Al F. Ehrbar and Steve Petranek, *Rochester* (N.Y.) *Democrat and Chronicle*

Investigating Team, Sun Newspapers of Omaha (Neb.)
1973 **J.A. Livingston,** Publishers-Hall Syndicate
John Brooks, *The New Yorker*
Michael Demarest, Peter Swerdloff and William B. Mead, *Money*
Donald L. Barlett and James B. Steele, *Philadelphia Inquirer*
Richard A. Nenneman, *Christian Science Monitor*
George Chaplin, *Honolulu Advertiser*
1974 **Louise Cook,** Associated Press
Marshall Loeb, *Time*
Gordon L. Williams, *Business Week*
Donald L. Barlett and James B. Steele, *Philadelphia Inquirer*
Dick Youngblood, *Minneapolis Tribune*
Tom D. Miller, *Huntington* (W.Va.) *Herald-Advertiser*
1975 **Jane Bryant Quinn,** Washington Post Writers Group
William McWhirter, *Time*
Carol J. Loomis, *Fortune*
William S. Randall and Stephen D. Solomon, *Philadelphia Inquirer*
John Cranfill and Earl Golz, *Dallas Morning News*
Editorial Staff, *Eugene* (Ore.) *Register-Guard*
1976-77 **Lee Mitgang,** Associated Press
Steven Brill, *New York Magazine*
William Wolman and Philip B. Osborne, *Business Week*
Susan Trausch and Laurence Collins, *Boston Globe*
James Asher and Paul Schweizer, *Louisville Courier-Post*
Judd Cohen, *Yonkers* (N.Y.) *Herald-Statesman*
1978 **Brooks Jackson** and **Evans Witt**, Associated Press
William Tucker, *Harper's*
Chris Welles, *Institutional Investor*
Harry Nelson, **Paul Steiger**, **S.J. Diamond** and **Alexander Auerbach**, *Los Angeles Times*
Philip Moeller, **Larry Werner**, **Phil Norman, Ben Hershberg**, **Jim Thompson** and **Dan Kauffman**, *Louisville Courier-Journal*
Jeff Kosnett, *Charlestown* (W. Va.) *Daily Mail*
1979 **Louise Cook**, Associated Press
William C. Bryant and **Thomas H. Hughes**, *U.S. News and World Report*
Robert Henkel, *Business Week*
Richard Longworth and **Bill Neikirk**, *Chicago Tribune*
Ed Ryan, *Louisville Courier-Journal*
Polly Ross Hughes and **Bill Coats**, *Anderson* (S.C.) *Independent and Daily Mail*
1980 **John Hanchette**, **William Schmick** and **Carlton Sherwood**, Gannet News Service
Richard Longworth and **William Neikirk**, *Chicago Tribune*
Arnold Garson and **Larry Fruhling**, *Des Moines Register*
William Rosegen, *Billings* (Mont.) *Gazette*
Tom Bethell, *Harper's*
John Campbell and **William Wolman**, *Business Week*

Media Awards

AMOS TUCK SCHOOL OF BUSINESS ADMINISTRATION

Dartmouth College, Hanover, N.H. 03755 (603/643-5596)

The Media Awards for the Advancement of Economic Understanding, sponsored by Champion International Corporation and administered by the Tuck school, honor outstanding economic reporting and journalism in the general media. Original works published during the preceding year can be entered for consideration by a panel of judges. Top prizes of $5,000 are awarded. In addition to these first-place winners listed below, a $2,500 second prize is given in each category. Honors for television and radio journalism are elsewhere in this volume.

METRO NEWSPAPERS (250,000 and over circulation)

1977 **Fred McGunagle**, *Cleveland Press* ("Cleveland Going or Growing")
1978 **Robert W. Greene**, **Tom Morris**, **Michael Alexander**, **Stewart Diamond**, **Richard Galant**, **John Hildebrand**, **Daniel Kahn**, **Robert E. Kessler**, **Dick Kraus**, **Jerry Morgan**, **Susan Page**, **Jim Scovel** and **James Snider**, *Newsday*, Garden City, New York ("Long Island at the Crossroads")
N.R. Kleinfield, *New York Times* ("The Biggest Company on Earth")
1979 **Richard C. Longworth** and **William Neikirk**, *Chicago Tribune* ("The Changing American Worker")
1980 **Not available at press time**

NEWSPAPERS (50,000-100,000)

1977 **Selby McCash**, *Macon Telegraph* (Taxes . . . The Price You Pay")
1978 **Christopher C. Smith**, *Honolulu Advertiser* ("Sugar—Coping In a New World")
1979 **Garry Nielson**, **Geoff O'Connell**, **Linda Matys**, **Mary Young** and **Nick Grabbe**, *Valley Advocate* (Springfield, Massachusetts), ("The Pyramids in New England")

NEWSPAPERS (100,000-250,000)

1977 **David Bartel**, *Wichita Eagle and Beacon* ("Our Energy Search")
1978 **Lynda McDonnell**, *Minneapolis Tribune* ("Unemployment Admidst Prosperity")
1979 **Steve Johnson**, **David Morrison**, **Andrew Mollison**, **Sharon Bailey**, **Henry Eason**, **Frederick Allen**, **Andrew J. Glass**, **Bob Dart**, **Steven Hesse**, **Michael Pousner**, **Chester Goolrick**, **Angelo Lewis**, **Rebecca Linn**, **Roger Witherspoon**, **Joseph Albright**, **Leslie Henderson**, **Jay Bushinsky**, **Katharine Hatch**, **Joe Brown**, **Charlene P. Smith-Williams**, **Carole Ashkinaze**, **Peter Benesh**, **Rich Nichols**, **Jerry Ackerman**, **Lee Finley**, **Bob Burns**, **Don Muhm**, and **Margaret Studer**, *The Atlanta Constitution* ("Energy: A Consuming Problem")
1980 **Not available at press time**

NEWSPAPERS (10,000-50,000)

1977 **Alvin Gatch**, *Dubuque* (Iowa) *Telegraph Herald* ("Agriculture: Farm to Market")
1978 **Frank Clifford**, *The Santa Fe Reporter* ("The Promised Land")
1979 **Anthony Bianco**, *Willamette Week* (Portland, Ore.), ("Georgia-Pacific: The Untold Story")

1980 Not available at press time

NEWSPAPERS (under 10,000)

1977 **John Riley**, *Yarmouthport* (Mass.) *Register* ("Dealing in Land")
Seth Rolbein, *Yarmouthport* (Mass.) *Register* ("The Cape Nursing Home Industry")
1978 **Richard A. Fineberg**, *Alaska Advocate* (Anchorage), ("Alcan Pipeline: Who ARE Those Guys?")
1979 **Kathleen Stauder**, *Anderson* (S.C.) *Daily Mail* ("The Goose That Lays The Golden Egg")
1980 Not available at press time

SYNDICATES AND WIRE SERVICES

1977 **John Cunniff**, Associated Press ("Business Mirror")
J.A. Livingston, Field Newspaper Syndicate ("Great Britain in Adversity")
1978 **Louise Cook**, Associated Press, Consumer Reporting
1979 **J.A. Livingston**, *Philadelphia Inquirer,* and Field Newspaper Syndicate, "Insider America Columns on Inflation, Bonds, the Dollar, Oil, Recession and Living it Up"
1980 Not available at press time

MAGAZINES

1977 **Ken Auletta**, *New Yorker* ("A Reporter at Large: More or Less")
1978 **Robert J. Flaherty** and **Richard Greene**, *Forbes* ("Oxy vs. Mead: The Big One of '78")
1979 **Tom Bethell**, *Harper's Magazine*, ("The Gas Price Fixers")
1980 Not available at press time

By-Line Award

MARQUETTE UNIVERSITY COLLEGE OF JOURNALISM
1135 W. Wisconsin Ave., Milwaukee, Wisc. 53233
(414/224-7309)

The By-Line Award, which consists of a plaque, is given annually to an alumnus or alumna for competent journalism over the years and fulfillment of professional responsibility in newspaper or broadcast journalism, film, advertising, public relations or management. Alumni, students, faculty and others may make nominations for final selection by the journalism faculty and approval by the University Awards Committee.

1946 **Walter J. Abel,** *Catholic Herald Citizen*
Walter Belson, American Trucking Associations
Muriel Brechler, Ed Schuster & Co.
John Clifford, *Watertown* (Wisc.) *Times*
Maurice Early, *Indianapolis Star*
Joseph Helfert, *Beaver Dam* (Wisc.) *Citizen*
Don McNeill, *ABC Radio Breakfast Club*
Rev. D. F. Miller, *Liguorian Magazine* (Redemptorist Fathers)
Hugh A. Reading, J. Walter Thompson, Detroit
Aileen Ryan, *Milwaukee Journal*
John J. Shinners, *Hartford* (Wisc.) *Times-Press*
Alvin Steinkopf, Associated Press, Prague, Czechoslovakia
Raymond Welch, *National Geographic*
1947 **James Strebig,** Associated Press
1948 **Albert Schimberg,** *Catholic Herald Citizen* and author, *Story of Therese Neumann* and *The Larks of Umbria*
1949 **Walter Fitzmaurice,** *Newsweek* (formerly with International News Service, *Milwaukee Sentinel* and *Chicago Journal*)
1950 **L. Carroll Arimond,** Associated Press, Chicago
Marvin L. Tonkin, Associated Press, Chicago
1951 **Leo James Bormann,** WMT - Radio, Cedar Rapids, Iowa
1952 **Robert C. LaBlonde,** Foote, Cone and Belding International, New York
1953 **Donald E. Huth,** Associated Press, Manila, Philippines
1954 **Edward G. Gerbic,** Johnson and Johnson, New Brunswick, N.J.
1955 **Albert T. Rumbach,** *DuBois County Daily Herald* (Jasper, Ind.)
1956 **Athlyn Deshais Faulkner,** *Chicago Daily News*
Gordon R. Lewis, *South Milwaukee Voice-Journal*
William P. McCahill, President's Committee on Employment of the Physically Handicapped
Paul M. McMahon, *Milwaukee Journal*
Robert J. Riordan, *Milwaukee Sentinel*
1957 **Donald F. Daubel,** *Fremont* (Ohio) *News-Messenger*
1958 **Waldo E. McNaught,** Buick Motor Division, General Motors Corp.
1959 **Thomas E. Moore,** *Iron River* (Mich.) *Reporter*
1960 **Oliver E. Kuechle,** *Milwaukee Journal*
Gerald J. Liska, Associated Press, Chicago
Amos T. Thisted, *Milwaukee Sentinel*
1961 **Thomas P. Coleman,** Associated Press
John J. Ducas, Gaylor and Ducas, Inc.
Edward S. Kerstein, *Milwaukee Journal*
H. Leo Kissel, *Milwaukee Sentinel*
Joseph I. Pettit, International Harvester Co.
Eldon H. Roesler, Business Press & Editorial Service
Clarence M. Zens, *Catholic Standard* (Washington, D.C.)
1962 **Thaddeus L. Knap,** *Indianapolis Times*
John F. Loosbrock, *Air Force & Space Digest*
Joseph P. Wright, Prince & Co.
1963 **Loretta J. Fox,** Falk Corporation
1964 **Robert E. Gilka,** *National Geographic*
1965 **James E. Rasmusen,** *Gary* (Ind.) *Post-Tribune*
1966 **Marshall W. Berges,** Time-Life News Service, Los Angeles,
Edmund S. Carpenter, Marquette University
Charles H. Harbutt, Jr., Magnum Photos, Inc., New York
Newell G. Meyer, *Milwaukee Journal*
Leonard J. Scheller, *Milwaukee Journal*
1967 **George E. Lardner, Jr.,** *Washington Post*
1968 **Edwin A. Shanke,** Associated Press Scandinavian Services
1969 **J. Wallace Carroll,** *Winston-Salem* (N.C.) *Journal and Sentinel*
1970 **Daniel L. Satran and Robert L. Satran,** *Vilas County News-Review* and *Three Lakes News* (Eagle River, Wisc.)
1971 **John R. Springer,** John Springer Associates, Inc., New York, Los Angeles, Paris, London, Rome
1972 **David L. Bowen,** Associated Press
1973 **William R. Burleigh,** *Evansville* (Ind.) *Press*
1974 **Harold A. Schwartz,** *Milwaukee Journal and Sentinel*
1975 **Mary Lou Beatty,** *Washington Post*
1976 **James P. Gannon,** *Wall Street Journal,* Washington, D.C. Bureau
1977 **Paul Wilkes,** Freelance writer
1978 **Arthur Olszyk,** WTMJ-Radio and WTMF-TV
1979 **William M. Carley,** *Wall Street Journal*
1980 **Margo Huston,** *Milwaukee Journal*

Maria Moors Cabot Prize

COLUMBIA UNIVERSITY
Graduate School of Journalism, New York, N.Y. 10027
(212/280-3828)

The Maria Moors Cabot Prize is awarded by the trustees of the university on recommendation by the dean of the Graduate School of Journalism, assisted by an advisory committee of experts in inter-American affairs, for distinguished journalism by one United States and one Latin American journalist. In addition to the individual gold medal winners listed below, most of their and other notable newspapers are honored with a medal. Winners also share a $1,500 cash prize.

1939 **Jose Santos Gollan,** *La Prensa* (Buenos Aires, Argentina)
Luis Miro Quesada, *El Comercio* (Lima, Peru)
1940 **Augustin E. Edwards,** *El Mercurio* (Santiago, Chile)
Enrique Santos, *El Tiempo* (Bogota, Colombia)
Rafael Heliodoro Valle, Correspondent in Mexico City (Honduras)
James I. Miller, United Press Assns. (U.S.A.)
1941 **Paulo Bittencourt,** *Correio de Manha* (Rio de Janeiro, Brazil)
Silvia Bittencourt, *Correio de Manha* (Rio de Janeiro, Brazil)
Carlos Davila, Editors Press Service (Chile)
Jose Ignacio Rivero, *Diario de la Marina* (Havana, Cuba)
1942 **Luis Mitre,** *La Nacion* (Buenos Aires, Argentina)
Lorenzo Batlle Pacheo, *El Dia* (Montevideo, Uruguay)
1943 **Pedro Cue,** *El Mundo* (Havana, Cuba)
Rodrigo de Llano, *Excelsior* (Mexico City, Mexico)
Edward Tomlinson, National Broadcasting Co. (U.S.A.)
1944 **Carlos Mantilla Ortega,** *El Comercio* (Quito, Ecuador)
Jorge Pinto, *Diario Latino* (San Salvador, El Salvador)
Albert Victor McGeachy, *Star and Herald* (Panama City, Panama)
1945 **Francisco de Assis Chateaubriand,** *Diarios Associados* (Rio de Janeiro, Brazil)
Tom Wallace, *Louisville Times* (Louisville, Ky.)
Luis Teofilo Nunez, *El Universal* (Carcas, Venezuela)
1946 **Grant Dexter,** *Winnipeg Free Press* (Winnipeg, Man., Canada)
Miguel Lanz Duret, *El Universal* (Mexico City, Mexico)
Lee Hills, *Miami Herald* (Miami, Fla.)
1947 **Carlos Victor Aramayo,** *La Razon* (La Paz, Bolivia)
David Vela, *El Imparcial* (Guatemala City, Guatemala)
Alberto Lleras Camargo*, Pan American Union (Washington, D.C.)
1948 **Orlando Riberio Dantas,** *Diario da Noite* (Rio de Janeiro, Brazil)
Alfredo Silva-Carvallo, *La Union* (Valpariso, Chile)
Manuel Cisneros Sanchez, *La Cronica* (Lima, Peru)
Joseph L. Jones, United Press Assns. (U.S.A.)
1949 **Jose Santiago Castillo,** *El Telegraf* (Guayaquil, Ecuador)
Milton Bracker, *New York Times* (New York, N.Y.)
Eduardo Rodriguez Larretta, *El Pais* (Montevideo, Uruguay)
1950 **Maria Constanza Huergo,** *La Prensa* (Buenos Aires, Argentina)
John A. Brogan, King Features Syndicate (U.S.A.)
Joshua B. Powers, Editors Press Service, Inc. (New York, N.Y.)
Angel Ramos, *El Mundo* (San Juan, Puerto Rico)
Mons. Jesus Maria Pellin, *La Religion* (Caracas, Venezuela)
1951 **Elmano Cardim,** *Jornal Do Comercio* (Rio de Janeiro, Brazil)
Francisco Maria Nunez, *El Diario de Costa Rica* (San Jose, Costa Rica)
Julio Garzon, *La Prensa* (New York, N.Y.)
Ramon David Leon, *La Esfera* (Caracas, Venezuela)
1952 **Belarmino Austregesilo de Athayde,** *Diario da Noite* (Rio de Janeiro, Brazil)
Jorge Delano, *Topaze* (Santiago, Chile)
Juan B. Fernandez, *El Heraldo* (Barranquilla, Colombia)
Antonio Arias Bernal, *Hoy* (Mexico City, Mexico)
Jules Dubois, *Chicago Tribune* (Chicago, Ill.)
1953 **Carlos Lacerda,** *Tribuna da Imprensa* (Rio de Janeiro, Brazil)
Ismael Perez Castro, *El Universo* (Guayaquil, Ecuador)
Arturo Schaerer, *La Tribuno* (Ascuncion, Paraguay)
Crede H. Calhoun, *New York Times* (New York, N.Y.)
1954 **Danton Jobim,** *Diario Carioca* (Rio de Janeiro, Brazil)
Gabriel Cano, *El Espectador* (Bogota, Colombia)
Sidney Gerald Fletcher, *The Daily Gleaner* (Kingston, Jamaica)
Lloyd Stratton, Associated Press (New York, N.Y.)
Carlos Ramirez MacGregor, *Panorama* (Maracaibo, Venezuela)
1955 **Roberto Jorge Noble,** *Clarin* (Buenos Aires, Argentina)
Breno Caldas, *Correio do Povo* (Porto Alegre, Brazil)
Pedro G. Beltran, *La Prensa* (Lima, Peru)
John Oliver LaGorce, *National Geographic* (Washington, D.C.)
A.T. Steele, *New York Herald Tribune* (U.S.A.)
1956 **David Michel Torino,** *El Intransigente* (Salta, Argentina)
Roberto Garcia Pena, *El Tiempo* (Bogota, Colombia)
Jesus Alvarez del Castillo, *El Informador* (Guadalajara, Mexico)
Carl W. Ackerman, Graduate School of Journalism, Columbia University (New York, N.Y.)
Herbert L. Matthews, *New York Times* (New York, N.Y.)
1957 **Herbert Moses,** *O Globo* and president, Brazilian Press Assn. (Rio de Janeiro, Brazil)
Rene Silva Espejo, *El Mercurio* (Santiago, Chile)
Harry W. Frantz, United Press Assns. (U.S.A.)
1958 **Miguel Angel Quevedo** *Bohemia* (Havana, Cuba)
Emilio Azcarraga Vidaurreta, Cadena Radiodifusora Mexicana and Telesistema Mexicana (Mexico City, Mexico)
Eduardo Cardenas, *Selecciones del Reader's Digest* (Pleasantville, N.Y.)
Pbro. Jesus Hernandez Chapellin, *La Religion* (Caracas, Venezuela)
1959 **Hernane Tavares de Sa,** *Visao* (Sao Paulo, Brazil)
Ricardo Castro Beeche, *La Nacion* (San Jose, Costa Rica)
Clement David Hellyer, *San Diego Union* (San Diego, Calif.)
Tad Szulc, *New York Times* (New York, N.Y.)

1960 **Rudolfo N. Luque,** *La Prensa* (Buenos Aires, Argentina)
Jose Dutriz, Jr., *La Prensa Grafica* (San Salvador, El Salvador)
James B. Canel, Inter American Press Assn. (New York, N.Y.)
William M. Pepper, Jr., *Gainesville Daily Sun* (Gainesville, Fla.)

1961 **Fernando Gomez Martinez,** *El Colombiano* (Medellin, Colombia)
Alejandro Carrion, *El Universo* (Guayaquil, Ecuador)
Romulo O'Farrill, Sr., *Novedades* (Mexico City, Mexico)
Rev. Albert J. Nevins, M.M., *Maryknoll* magazine (Maryknoll, N.Y.)
John T. O'Rourke, *Washington Daily News* (Washington, D.C.)

1962 **Rudolfo Junco de la Vega,** *El Norte* and *El Sol* (Monterrey, Mexico)
John R. Herbert, *Patriot Ledger* (Quincy, Mass.)
John S. Knight, Knight Newspapers and *Miami Herald* (Miami, Fla.)
Raul Fontaina, *Radio Carve (Montevideo, Uruguay)*

1963 **Juan S. Valmaggia,** *La Nacion* (Buenos Aires, Argentina)
William Barlow, *Vision* magazine (U.S.A.)
Juan de Onis, *New York Times* (New York, N.Y.)
German Arciniegas*, Syndicated columnist, *Cuadernos* (Paris, France)
Jorge Fernandez*, Centro Internacional de Estudios Superiores de Periodismo para America Latina (Quito, Ecuador)

1964 **Enrique Nores Martinez,** *Los Principios* (Cordoba, Argentina)
Bertram B. Johansson, *Christian Science Monitor* (Boston, Mass.)
Virginia Prewett, *Washington Daily News* and North American Newspaper Alliance (U.S.A.)
Hugo Fernandez Artucio, *El Dia* (Montevideo, Uruguay)

1965 **Victoria Ocampo,** *Sur* (Buenos Aires, Argentina)
Roberto Marinho, *O Globo* (Rio de Janeiro, Brazil)
Gesford F. Fine, United Press International (U.S.A.)
Paul Sanders, Associated Press (U.S.A.)

1966 **Paul Kidd,** Southam News Service (Ottawa, Ont., Canada)
Augustin E. Edwards, *Empresa El Mercurio* (Santiago, Chile)
Alberto R. Cellario, *Life en Espanol* (New York, N.Y.)

1967 **M.F. do Nascimento Brito,** *Jornal do Brasil* (Rio de Janeiro, Brazil)
Peter Aldor, *El Tiempo* (Bogota, Colombia)
James S. Copley, Copley News Service (La Jolla, Calif.)
James Nelson Goodsell, *Christian Science Monitor* (Boston, Mass.)
Ramon Jose Velasquez Mujica, *El Nacional* (Caracas, Venezueala)

1968 **Alberto Gainza Paz,** *La Prensa* (Buenos Aires, Argentina)
Argentina S. Hills, *El Mundo* (San Juan, Puerto Rico)
Robert Berrellez, Associated Press (U.S.A.)
Guillermo Guierrez V-M*, Inter American Press Assn.

1969 **Alceu Amoroso Lima,** Author, essayist and literary critic (Rio de Janeiro, Brazil)
Luis Gabriel Cano, *El Espectador* (Bogota, Colombia)
Elsa Arana Freire, *7 Dias* (Lima, Peru)
Edward W. Barrett, Academy for Educational Development (New York, N.Y.)
George H. Beebe, *Miami Herald* (Miami, Fla.)

1970 **Alberto Dines,** *Jornal do Brasil* (Rio de Janeiro, Brazil)
John D. Harbron, *Toronto Telegram* (Toronto, Ont., Canada)
John Goshko, *Washington Post* (Washington, D.C.)

1971 **Landru (Juan Carlos Colombres),** Editorial cartoonist (Buenos Aires, Argentina)
Julio Scherer Garcia, *Excelsior* (Mexico City, Mexico)
Georgie Anne Geyer, *Chicago Daily News,* (Chicago., Ill.)

1972 **Tom Streithorst,** NBC News (U.S.A.)
Arturo Ulsar Pietri, *El Nacional* (Caracas, Venezuela)

1973 **David Belnap,** *Los Angeles Times* (Los Angeles, Calif.)
Rev. Donald J. Casey, M.M., World Horizon Films and *Maryknoll* magazine (Maryknoll, N.Y.)

1974 **Fernando Pedreira,** *O Estado de Sao Paulo* (Sao Paulo, Brazil)
Don Bohning, *Miami Herald* (Miami, Fla.)
William D. Montalbano, *Miami Herald* (Miami, Fla.)

1975 **Enrique Zileri Gibson,** *Caretas* (Lima, Peru)
Sam Sumerlin, Associated Press (U.S.A.)

1976 **Jorge S. Remonda-Ruibal,** *La Voz Del Interior* (Cordoba, Argentina)
Bernard Deiderich, Time-Life News Service (New York, N.Y.)

1977 **Pedro J. Chamorro,** *La Prensa* (Managua, Nicaragua)
Jonathan Kandell, *New York Times* (New York, N.Y.)
Anita von Kahler Gumpert,

1978 **Joseph Benham** and **Carl J. Migdail,** *U.S. News and World Report*
Carlos Castello Branco, *Jornal do Brasil*
Robert Cox, *Buenos Aires Herald*

1979 **Jeremiah O'Leary,** *Washington Star*
Juan Ferrer Zuleta, *El Colombiano*

1980 **Penny Lernoux,** Latin American correspondent (U.S.A.)
Alan Riding, *New York Times* Mexico City bureau chief
Guido Fernandez, *La Nacion* (San Jose, Costa Rica)

SPECIAL CITATION

1957 **Roberto Marinho,** *O Globo* (Brazil)
Paulo Bittencourt*
Miguel Lanz Duret*
Luis Franzini*
John S. Knight*
Carlos Mantilla*
Guillermo Martinez Marquez*
John T. O'Rourke*
James G. Stahlman*
Tom Wallace*

1959 **Juan Andres Ramirez,** *El Plata* (Uruguay)

1968 **Mons. Jose Joaquin Salcedo G.,** Accion Cultural Popular Bogota (Colombia)

1960 **Eduardo Santos,** *El Tiempo* (Colombia)

1972 **Pedro G. Beltran,** *La Prensa* (Peru)

1975 **David Kraiselburd,** *El Dia* (Argentina)
Norman A. Ingrey, *Buenos Aires Herald* and *Christian Science Monitor* (Argentina)

Walter Everett, American Press Institute (U.S.A.)
1976 **German E. Ornes,** *El Caribe* (Dominican Republic)
Robert U. Brown, *Editor & Publisher* (U.S.A.)
1977 **Anita von Kahler,** *Agence France-Presse* (France)
Joseph A. Taylor, Latin American Communication Program, University of Texas (U.S.A.)
1979 ***The Daily Gleaner*** (Jamaica)
Jerry Hannifin, *Time*
Andrew Heiskell, Time, Inc.
1980 **William Stewart** (ABC News)
Richard T. Baker, Cabot Advisory Board member and Professor of Journalism, Columbia University
*Honors for international scope

Reuben Award

NATIONAL CARTOONISTS SOCIETY
9 Ebony Court, Brooklyn, N.Y. 11229 (212/743-6510)

The Reuben Award, which consists of a statuette created by the late Rube Goldberg and named for him, is given to the outstanding cartoonist of the year. The winner is selected by a secret ballot of the society's members.

1946 **Milton Caniff,** *Steve Canyon*
1947 **Al Capp,** *Li'l Abner*
1948 **Chic Young,** *Blondie*
1949 **Alex Raymond,** *Rip Kirby*
1950 **Roy Crane,** *Buzz Sawyer*
1951 **Walt Kelly,** *Pogo*
1952 **Hank Ketcham,** *Dennis the Menace*
1953 **Mort Walker,** *Beetle Bailey*
1954 **Willard Mullin,** *Sports* cartoons
1955 **Charles Schulz,** *Peanuts*
1956 **Herblock,** Editorial cartoons
1957 **Hal Foster,** *Prince Valiant*
1958 **Frank King,** *Gasoline Alley*
1959 **Chester Gould,** *Dick Tracy*
1960 **Ronald Searle,** Illustrations
1961 **Bill Mauldin,** Editorial cartoons
1962 **Dik Browne,** *Hi & Lois*
1963 **Fred Lasswell,** *Barney Google and Snuffy Smith*
1964 **Charles Schulz,** Peanuts
1965 **Leonard Starr,** *On Stage*
1966 **Otto Soglow,** *The Little King*
1967 **Rube Goldberg,** *Humor in Sculpture*
1968 **John Hart,** *B.C.* and *Wizard of Id*
Pat Oliphant, Editorial cartoons
1969 **Walter Berndt,** *Smitty*
1970 **Alfred Andriola,** *Kerry Drake*
1971 **Milton Caniff,** *Steve Canyon*
1972 **Pat Oliphant,** Editorial cartoons
1973 **Dik Browne,** *Hagar the Horrible*
1974 **Dick Moores,** *Gasoline Alley*
1975 **Bob Dunn,** *They'll Do It Every Time*
1976 **Ernie Bushmiller,** *Nancy*
1977 **Chester Gould,**
1978 **Jeff MacNelly,** *Shoe*
Paul Szep, Editorial cartoons
1979 **Bud Blake,** *Tiger*
John Cullen Murphy, *Prince Valiant* (with **Hal Foster**)
Frank Johnson, *Hi & Lois* (with **Mort Walker** and **Dik Brown**)
1980 **Not available at press time**

SPECIAL T-SQUARE AWARD

1979 **Sylvan Byck,** for service to National Cartoonists' Society and contributions to profession as comics editor of King Features for 37 years

CIP Award

CATHOLIC INSTITUTE OF THE PRESS
1011 First Ave., Ste. 1920, New York, NY 10022; 212/371-6100

The CIP Award, a scroll awarded annually for service in the communications field that exemplified Catholic principles, has been discontinued.

1948 **Bob Considine**
1949 **Neil MacNeil**
1950 **Fulton Oursler**
1951 **Leo McCarey**
1952 **James M. O'Neill**
1953 **H.I. Phillips**
1954 **Martin Quigley**
1955 **Gene Lockhart**
1956 **Jim Bishop**
1957 **Arthur Daley**
"Red" Smith
1958 **Clare Booth Luce**
1959 **John La Farge, S.J.**
1960 **Phyllis McGinley**
1961 **Edwin O'Connor**
1962 **Barrett McGurn**
1963 **Paul Horgan**
1964 **Daniel Callahan**
1965 **NBC-TV and CBS-TV**
1966 **Gary MacEoin**

Columbia Journalism Award

COLUMBIA UNIVERSITY
Graduate School of Journalism, New York, N.Y. 10027 (212/280-3828)

The Columbia Journalism Award consists of a plaque given annually for distinguished service in the field of journalism to an individual selected by a faculty-student honors committee.

1970 **Walter Lippmann**
1971 **I.F. Stone**
1972 **Neil Sheehan**
1973 **Katharine Graham**
1974 **John H. Johnson**
1975 **William Shawn**
1976 **A.H. Raskin**
1977 **Journalists throughout the world who, through states' tyranny, have been denied their rights to free expression**
1978 **No award**
1979 **Theodore White**
1980 **Thomas (Tom) Wolfe**

Science Writers Award

AMERICAN DENTAL ASSOCIATION
211 E. Chicago Ave., Chicago, Ill. 60611 (312/440-2806)

The $1,000 Science Writers Award annually recognizes the best article in a magazine or newspaper on dental health and/or research. The Science Writers Award Committee selects the winner.

MAGAZINES

1966 **Norman A. Lobsenz and A. Norman Cranin,** *Redbook*
1967 **The Editors** of *Better Homes and Gardens*
1968 **Howard L. Lewis,** *Business Week*
1969 **Theodore Berland,** Freelance writer
1970 **Edward Edelson,** *Family Health*
1971 **Gerald M. Knox,** *Better Homes and Gardens*
1972 **Elizabeth Barley and William Glavin,** *Good Housekeeping*
1973 **Don Schanche,** *Today's Health*
1974 **Melba Rabinowitz,** *Children Today*
1975 **Jean Butler,** *Today's Health*
1976 **Constance Bille,** *Family Health*
1977 **Annette Stec,** *Exploring*
1978 **Ileen Fiddler,** Chicago, Ill.
1979 **Grace Weinstein,** Teaneck, N.J.
1980 **Howard J. Sanders,** *Chemical & Engineering News*

NEWSPAPERS

1966 **Ronald Kotulak,** *Chicago Tribune*
1967 **Alton Blakeslee,** Associated Press
1968 **Arthur J. Snider,** *Chicago Daily News*
1969 **Jean Latz Griffin,** *Joliet* (Ill.) *Herald News*
1970 **James G. Driscoll,** *National Observer*
1971 **Timothy D. Schellhardt,** *Wall Street Journal*
1972 **William Hager,** *Brandenton* (Fla.) *Herald*
1973 **Pat Atkinson,** *Tulsa Daily World*
1974 **Anita Buie Lamont,** *St. Louis Globe-Democrat*
1975 **Sarah Watke,** *Green Bay* (Wisc.) *Press Gazette*
1976 **Patricia McCormack,** United Press International
1977 **Lucy Eckberg,** *Winona* (Minn.) *Daily News*
1978 **Jane Brody,** *New York Times*
1979 **Sue Miller,** *Baltimore Sun*
1980 **Marge Hanley,** *Indianapolis News*

Eugene Cervi Award

INTERNATIONAL SOCIETY OF WEEKLY NEWSPAPER EDITORS
c/o Dept. of Journalism, Northern Illinois University, De Kalb, Ill. 60115 (815/753-1925)

The Eugene Cervi Award, a plaque, is given annually to an editor who has performed outstanding public service through community journalism and who has exhibited "the highest standards of the craft with deep reverence for the English language." The winner is chosen from submissions which are not listed by chronology and may, in fact, represent a career in community journalism.

1976 **Blair Macy,** *Keene Valley* (Colo.) *Sun*
1977 **Charles Russell,** and **Virginia Russell,** *Dewitt* (Ill.) *County Observer*
1978 **Tom Leathers,** *The Squire* (Missouri)
1979 **Houston Waring,** *Littleton* (Colo.) *Independent*
1980 **Robert Estabrook,** *Lakeville* (Conn.) *Journal*

CIBA-GEIGY Agricultural Writing Award
CIBA-GEIGY Farm Writers Award

CIBA-GEIGY
Box 11422, Greensboro, N.C. 27409 (919/292-7100)

The CIBA-GEIGY Agricultural Writing Award, which consists of a trophy and a trip to Switzerland where CIBA-GEIGY's home office is located, is given to a member of the American Agricultural Editors Association for an article, column or series about focusing on production, marketing, environment or other agricultural topics. In addition to the winner listed below, six $100 awards are made. A panel of judges selects the winner.

1970 **Syl Marking,** *The Farmer*
1971 **Al Bull,** *Wallaces Farmer*
1972 **Larry Graham,** *Prairie Farmer*
1973 **Richard Krumme,** *Successful Farming*
1974 **Milt Dunk,** *Poultry Tribune*
1975 **Dick Lehnert,** *Michigan Farmer*
1976 **Lee Searle,** *Successful Farming*
1977 **Bill Fleming,** *Beef Magazine*
1978 **Frank Lessiter,** *National Livestock Producer*
1979 **Bill Eftink,** *Successful Farming*
1980 **Bonnie Pollard,** *Michigan Farmer*

The CIBA-GEIGY Farm Writers Award, which consists of a trip to Switzerland and a trophy, is given annually for an article, column or series on production, marketing, environment or other agricultural topics. In addition to the winner listed below, six $100 awards are made. A panel of judges selects the winner, who must be a full-time writer reporting on agriculture for a daily newspaper or wire service.

1971 **James R. McGuire,** *Des Moines Register & Tribune*
1972 **B.J. Nobles,** *Portland Oregonian*
1973 **Don Muhm,** *Des Moines Register & Tribune*
1974 **Arlo Jacobson,** *Des Moines Register & Tribune*
1975 **Bob Buyer,** *Buffalo Evening News*
1976 **Mary Ognibene,** *Niagara Gazette*
1977 **Donald Diehl,** *Daily Democratic-News* (Marshall, Mo.)
1978 **Mick Cochran,** *State-Journal-Register* (Springfield, Ill.)
1979 **Gordon Billingsley,** *State-Journal-Register* (Springfield, Ill.)
1980 **Alan Gersten,** *Rocky Mountain News* (Denver)

Clarion Awards

WOMEN IN COMMUNICATIONS
Box 9561, Austin, Tex. 78766 (512/345-8922)

The Clarion Awards, which are plaques, are given annually in three divisions: human rights, the world we live in and the community we serve. In addition to the print journalism honors listed below, broadcast, journalism and public relations categories are honored and listed eleswhere in this volume. An entry fee is charged for submission of materials for consideration by a panel of communications professionals from across the country. In addition to the first-place-honors listed here, honorable mentions are made.

NEWSPAPER (articles or series in any division)

1973 **Margaret Beck Rex**, Sun Papers East (Cleveland Hgts., Ohio)
Pat Delo, *Springfield* (Mass.) *Daily News*
1974 **Laura White**, *Boston Herald American*
Christopher Cubbison and **Robert Hooker**, *St. Petersburg* (Fla.) *Times*
Margaret Moore Post, *Indianapolis News*
1975 **Jane Daugherty**, *St. Petersburg* (Fla.) *Times*
Margaret Moore Post, *Indianapolis News*
1976 **Michele Kamisher**, *Cambridge* (Mass.) *Real Paper*
Dorothy Storck, *Philadelphia Inquirer*
Gloria Anderson, *Charlotte* (N.C.) *Observer*
1977 **Acel Moore** and **Wendell Rawls, Jr.**, *Philadelphia Inquirer*
Amei Wallach, *Newsday* (Garden City, N.Y.)
Terry Malone, *National Catholic Reporter*
Muriel L. Cohen, *Boston Globe*
Charlotte Saikowski, *Christian Science Monitor*
1978 **Gail Marks Jarvis**, *National Catholic Reporter*
Linda M. Daniel, *Seattle Times*
Gloria Hochman, *Philadelphia Inquirer*
Andrew Feinberg, *Philadelphia Inquirer*
Carolyn Robbins-Chipkin, *Springfield* (Mass.) *Morning Union-Sunday Republican*
Carolyn Kortge, *Wichita Eagle and Beacon*
Cynthia Parsons, *Christian Science Monitor*
1979 **Patricia Fanning**, *Wall Street Journal*
Bruce Olds, *Bucks County Courier Times* (Levittown, Pa.)
Caryn Eve, *Middletown* (N.Y.) *Times-Herald*
Gary Thatcher, *Christian Science Monitor*
Lacy McCrary and **Bruce Keidan**, *Philadelphia Inquirer*
Jeanne Devlin, *Stillwater* (Okla.) *News-Press*
Carolyn Kortge, *Wichita Eagle and Beacon*
1980 **Ana Veciana**, *Miami News*
John J. Fried, *Long Beach* (Calif.) *Independent Press-Telegram*
Carol Stocker, *Boston Globe*
Gene Miller, **Carl Hiaasen** and **Patrick Malone**, *Miami Herald/ Charlotte* (N.C.) *Observer*
John Hanchette, **William F. Schmick** and **Carlton Sherwood**, Gannett News Service

MAGAZINE (articles or series in any division)

1973 **No award**
1974 **Letty Cottin Pogrebin**, *Ladies' Home Journal*
Trudy Dye Farrand, *Ranger Rick's Nature Magazine*
Gail R. Safian, *Focus*
1975 **Bess Myerson**, *Redbook*
Susan Edmiston, *Redbook*
1976 **Loretta Schwartz**, *Philadelphia Magazine*
Patricia Coleman, *Building Supply News*
Shana Alexander, *Redbook*
1977 **Loretta Schwartz**, *Philadelphia Magazine*
Dick Griffin, *Chicago Magazine*
Dan Rottenberg, *Chicago Magazine*
1978 **Jim Atkinson**, *D Magazine*
Frederic Golden, *Time*
Harry F. Waters, *Newsweek*
Loretta Schwartz and **Ann Northrop**, *Ms.*
John Mack Carter, *Good Housekeeping*
Judy Langford Carter and **Frances Ruffin**, *Redbook*
1979 **Peter Goldman** and **Dennis Williams**, *Newsweek*
Eileen Lynch, *Philadelphia Magazine*
Elizabeth Rodgers Dobell, *Redbook*
International Assn. of Business Communicators, San Francisco, Calif.
Tom Mathews, *Newsweek*
Kenneth L. Woodward, *Newsweek*
1980 **Gene Lyons**, *Texas Monthly*
Mike Vargo, **Pat Minarcin** and **Steve Fine**, *Pennsylvania Illustrated*
Mike Mallowe, *Philadelphia Magazine*
Susan Seliger, *Washingtonian*
Redbook
Gloria Steinem, **Ellen Sweet**, **Suzanne Levine**, and **Harriet Lyons**, *Ms.*

SPECIAL AWARD

1973 **Jo Hartley**, *Continuing Comment*, Claremont (Calif.) Colleges Div. of Continuing Education

Ben East Prize

MICHIGAN UNITED CONSERVATION CLUBS
Box 30235, Lansing, Mich. 48909 (517/371-1041)

The Ben East Prize, which consists of $1,000 and a plaque, is given annually for excellence in conservation journalism on a subject in Michigan. A five-judge panel selects the winner.

1977 **Kenneth L. Peterson**, newspaper series on land use and problems confronting the Natural Resources Agency
1978 **No award**
1979 **Glen Sheppard**, coverage of Indian fishing rights controversy
1980 **Eric Sharpe** and **Doug Hall**, series on toxic wastes dumping grounds

Higher Education Writer Award

AMERICAN ASSOCIATION OF UNIVERSITY PROFESSORS
One DuPont Cir., Ste. 500, Washington, D.C. 20036 (202/466-8050)

The Higher Education Writer Award, which consists of a plaque, is given annually to the individual selected by a panel of judges for having done outstanding interpretative reporting on issues in higher education.

1970 **Ronald Maselka**, *Buffalo Evening News*
1971 **John A. Crowl**, *Chronicle of Higher Education*
1972 **William Trombley**, *Los Angeles Times*
1973 **Edward R. Weidlein**, *Chronicle of Higher Education*
1974 **Philip Semas**, *Chronicle of Higher Education*
1975 **Eric Wentworth**, *Washington Post*
1976 **William Braden**, *Chicago Sun-Times*
Andrew Shaw, *Chicago Sun-Times*
1977 **Larry Van Dyne**, *Chronicle of Higher Education*
1978 **No award**
1979 **Cynthia Parsons**, *Christian Science Monitor*
1980 **Rosemary Frawley** and **Charles Reid**, *Tampa* (Fla.) *Tribune*

First Amendment Awards

AMERICAN JEWISH CONGRESS
15 East 84th St., New York, N.Y. 10028 (212/879-4500)

The American Jewish Congress honors individuals who have "upheld and expanded freedom of the press" with First Amendment Awards.

1978 **Shana Alexander**, magazine writer and editor and television commentator
Floyd Abrams, Yale Law School lecturer and, in private practice, specialist in First Amendment litigation
Thomas I. Emerson, emeritus law professor at Yale and writer on civil liberties
Tom Wicker, associate editor and columnist, *New York Times*
1979 **Jonathan Marshall**, *Scottsdale* (Ariz.) *Daily Progress*
1980 **Not available at press time**

Henry Johnson Fisher Award

MAGAZINE PUBLISHERS ASSOCIATION
575 Lexington Ave., New York, N.Y. 10022 (212/752-0055)

The Henry Johnson Fisher Award, which consists of a $1,000 honorarium to the recipient or to a charity, a Steuben crystal urn depicting "the arts" and a citation, is given annually to a notable individual or individuals in magazine publishing for contributions to the advancement of the industry. The Henry Johnson Fisher Award Committee selects the winner, approved by the board of directors of the association. In addition, the National Magazine Awards are given under a grant from the Magazine Publishers Assn. These will be found on pp.

1964 **DeWitt Wallace**
1965 **Henry R. Luce**
1966 **Richard E. Berlin**
1967 **Edward Weeks**
1968 **Arnold Gingrich**
1969 **A.L. Cole**
1970 **Roy E. Larsen and Maurice R. Robinson**
1971 **Gibson McCabe**
1972 **John H. Johnson**
1973 **Norman Cousins**
1974 **Laurence W. Lane, Jr., Melvin B. Lane and Mrs. Laurence W. Lane, Sr.**
1975 **Richard J. Babcock and Emory O. Cunningham**
1976 **Stephen E. Kelly**
1977 **No award**
1978 **Richard E. Deems**
1979 **Gerard Piel**
1980 **George H. Allen**

Forum Award

ATOMIC INDUSTRIAL FORUM
7101 Wisconsin Ave., Washington, D.C. 20014
(301/654-9260)

The $1,000 Forum Award is given annually for news-media contributions to the public understanding of nuclear energy. A panel of judges selects the winner. In addition to the print journalists listed here, the AIF also grants a Forum Award to the broadcast media, listed on p. 180.

1967 **William Hines**, *Washington Evening Star*
1968 **Frank Carey**, Associated Press
1969 **Joseph L. Myler**, United Press International
1970 **Harold Hughes** and **Wayne Thompson**, *Portland Oregonian*
1971 **Judith Fischer**, *Long Island* (N.Y.) *Press*
Charles H. Wickenberg, Jr., *The State* (Columbia, S.C.)
1972 **Ralph E. Lapp**, consultant, lecturer and author
1973 **Kenneth J. Anderberg**, *Manchester* (N.H.) *Union-Leader*
1974 **William J. Lanouette**, *National Observer*
Ray Pagel, *Green Bay* (Wis.) *Press-Gazette)*
1975 **John McPhee**, *The New Yorker*
David Perlman, *San Francisco Chronicle*
1976 **George Alexander**, *Los Angeles Times*
1977 **Jon Sawyer**, *St. Louis Post-Dispatch*
1978 **Robert Samuelson**, *National Journal*
Bruce Simons, *Brattleboro* (Vt.) *Reformer*
1979 **George J. Church**, *Time*
Kenneth F. Weaver *National Geographic*
1980 **Marilyn W. Thompson**, *Columbia* (S.C.) *Record*
William G. Reinhardt, *SciQuest*

Gavel Awards

AMERICAN BAR ASSOCIATION
1155 E. 60th St., Chicago, Ill. 60637 (312/947-4000)

The Gavel Awards are given annually to honor films, the media and books for their depiction of or reportage on the law and the legal profession. The Bar Association recognizes achievements which foster greater public understanding of the American legal and judicial system, disclose areas in need of improvement or correction and encourage efforts of all levels of government to update laws. Engraved gavels are given to executives of winning news organizations.

NEWSPAPERS

1958 ***Cleveland Plain Dealer*** (Editorials on court administration)
Richmond* (Va.) *News Leader (Weekly legal column)
St. Petersburg* (Fla.) *Times (Editorials and articles on law and the courts)
1959 ***St. Louis Post Dispatch*** (Series of articles on U.S. Supreme Court)
Moline* (Ill.) *Daily Dispatch (Editorials and articles on modernizing Illinois court system)
1960 ***Washington Post*** (Editorials on constitutional role of U.S. Supreme Court)
Pittsburgh Post Gazette (Editorials and articles explaining role of judges and lawyers)
The Oregonian, Portland, Ore. (Special Law Day USA magazine section)
Lindsay-Schaub Newspapers, Decatur, Ill. (Series on first National Conference of Judicial Selection and Court Administration)
1961 ***Hartford* (Conn.) *Times*** (Series on newly reorganized state court system)
Christian Science Monitor (Series documenting an alien's murder trial)
Chicago Tribune (Series analyzing Chicago court congestion problems)

1962 ***Christian Science Monitor*** (For journalistic enterprise in support of steps to strengthen probate court system in Massachusetts)
Washington Post (Articles interpreting Supreme Court decision on major constitutional issues)

1963 ***Washington Post*** (Distinguished interpretative reporting of Supreme Court decision of constitutional issues of great national significance)
Chicago Tribune (Series of distinguished editorials supporting adoption of Judicial Amendment of the Illinois Constitution to modernize Illinois courts)
Chicago Daily News (Articles and editorials supporting the organized bar campaign to modernize Illinois courts)

1964 ***Washington Star*** (Analytical reporting, under deadline pressure, of important Supreme Court decisions)
Oklahoma City Times (Series on significance of the rule by U.S. District Court reapportioning Oklahoma legislature)

1965 ***Kansas City Kansan*** (Eleven-part series analyzing public benefits of 1964 Code of Civil Procedures in the courts of Kansas)
Louisville* (Ky.) *Times (Series of twenty-four interpretative articles on the importance of Kentucky Court of Appeals decisions and supplementary coverage of new law)
The Blade, Toledo, Ohio (Comprehensive reporting and editorial interpretation of court decision, legislative enactments and organized bar efforts to improve the administration of justice)
Worcester* (Mass.) *Daily Telegram (Distinctive series of weekly articles interpreting developments and trends in judicial decisions and law enforcement)

1966 ***Christian Science Monitor*** (Distinguished ten-part series analyzing nature and impact of significant changes in the administration of criminal justice)
St. Petersburg* (Fla.) *Times (Comprehensive series of editorials urging modernization of Florida judicial system and nonpartisan selection of judges)

1967 ***Washington Post*** (Seven-part series by Leonard Downie, Jr., leading to reforms in Washington Court of General Session; also for articles by John P. MacKenzie interpreting Supreme Court decisions)
Daily Oklahoman and Times, Oklahoma City (Editorial leadership in initiative petition for statewide referendum on court reform; award based on editorial series by Clarke Thomas)
The Blade, Toledo, Ohio (Leadership in formulating voluntary code of fair practice in crime coverage news to guard rights of the accused)

1968 ***Christian Science Monitor*** ("Crisis in the Courts" series by Howard James examining strengths and weaknesses in state court systems and recommending improvements)
Los Angeles Times (Ronald J. Ostrow's distinguished series interpretating Supreme Court decisions and operations of U.S. Dept. of Justice)
St. Louis Post-Dispatch (Interpretative articles by James C. Millstone on decision-making processes of U.S. Supreme Court and related legal subjects.)
Louisville* (Ky.) *Courier-Journal (Voluntary adoption of code of fair practices to protect fair trial and free press in crime news reporting)
Philadelphia Inquirer Ten-part series by G. Warren Nutter contrasting legal, political and social institutions in the U.S. and Soviet Union)

1969 ***New York Times Magazine*** (Feature article by Herbert Mitgang on work of community lawyers for the disadvantaged)
Minneapolis Star (Austin Wehrwein's series of editorials and commentaries on developments in law and administration of justice)
Anchorage* (Alaska) *Daily News (Enterprising reportorial survey of administration of justice by lawyer-journalist C. Robert Zelnick)
Riverside* (Calif.) *Press-Enterprise (Distinguished series on crime and the courts)
Washington Post (For the book, *Ten Blocks from the White House,* a chronology of 1968 riots and resulting emergency measures of court administration)

1970 ***Kankakee* (Ill.) *Daily Journal*** (Initiating in-depth probe into conditions affecting administration of local justice)
Niagara Falls* (N.Y.) *Gazette (Series on quality of justice administration by lower courts and need for judicial reform)
Evansville* (Ind.) *Courier (Full publication of comprehensive study of local crime and law enforcement problems and editorial support of numerous recommendations of the study)
Washington Evening Star (Eleven-part series detailing serious problems besetting trial courts in Washington and suburbs)
Christian Science Monitor (Series of fifteen articles exposing brutal conditions in juvenile detention homes and offering 170 remedial suggestions)
Louisville* (Ky.) *Courier-Journal (Series describing archaic court conditions and urgent need for modernization)
New York Times (Series examining problems of free press, fair trial, self-incrimination, court challenges and law school enrollment practices)
Chicago Sun-Times (Series on legal subjects of public importance, including need for more Negro lawyers, new state income tax law and church-state relations)
***Parade* Sunday supplement** ("They Learn the Law—Before It's Too Late," explaining new law program for high school students)

1971 ***Record-Chronicle,* Denton, Texas** (Series explaining legal steps from time of arrest to trial of the accused)
Spartenburg* (S.C.) *Journal (Two-part series on how each court in the judicial process functions)
St. Petersburg* (Fla.) *Times (Series of more than fifty articles on prison conditions in Florida)
Valley News, Van Nuys, Calif. (Series on controversial decisions expanding individual rights)
Milwaukee Journal (Series of editorials supporting efforts to update Wisconsin's judicial system and Law Day USA supplement)
Minneapolis Star ("Judging the Law," weekly column)
National Observer (Series interpreting major Supreme Court decisions affecting all segments of society)

1972 ***Oregon Statesman,*** Salem, Ore. (Comprehensive explanation of key laws in Oregon's new Criminal Code)
Cincinnati Enquirer (Series about problems facing correctional institutional parole officers and parolees)
Christian Science Monitor (Best national reporting as represented by series of articles on American prisons)
Kansas City Star (Best local reporting as typified by series of editorials on problems of criminal justice and penal reform)
National Observer (Series interpreting major Supreme Court decisions affecting all segments of society)

1973 ***Illinois State Register*** (Comprehensive eighteen-part series on facets of American criminal justice system)

Tucson Daily Citizen (Four-part series on lax administration in Pima County probate system)
St. Louis Post-Dispatch (Five-part series on new forces and ideas in legal profession today)
St. Louis Globe Democrat (Series on corruption in Municipal Court)
Detroit Free Press (Eight-part series on conditions that are weakening the ability of the legal system to function properly)

1974 ***Poughkeepsie* (N.Y.) *Journal*** (Special section by Ed Baron and Joe Tinkleman providing study of New York State's new drug law)
Kansas City Star (Three-part series by Harry Jones, Jr., and J.J. Maloney on prison systems of Missouri and Kansas and federal institutions in those states)
Philadelphia Inquirer (Seven-part series by Donald L. Barlett and James B. Steele, revealing patterns of discrimination and bias, extreme disparity in sentencing and jailing of innocent persons by some judges)

1975 ***Sharon Herald***, Grove City, Pa. (Teresa Spatara's eighteen-part series on crime and criminal justice)
Albuquerque* (N.M.) *Journal (Scott Beaven's series on the way New Mexico handles the mentally ill and retarded)
Minneapolis Tribune (Frank Premack, Peter Vanderpoel and Doug Stone's comprehensive look at Hennepin County juvenile justice system)
Chicago Sun-Times (Roger Simon and Patrick Oster's in-depth investigation and report on Cook County criminal justice system)

1976 ***Shreveport* (La.) *Journal*** (Special edition entitled "Justice and Injustice")
Messenger-Inquirer, Owensboro, Ky. (Series of articles and editorials calling for adoption of constitutional amendment to modernize the state's court system)
Journal-Gazette, Fort Wayne, Ind. ("A Time for Appraisal," pinpointing strengths and weaknesses of new, unified Allen County Superior Court)

1976 ***Chicago Sun-Times*** (Series by Roger Simon on plea bargaining.)

1977 ***Lakeland Ledger (Fla)*** (John R. Harrison's editorial series directed toward youth and explaining the law as it applies to juveniles)
Oakland* (Mich.) *Press (James S. Granelli and Alan S. Lenhoff's series on day-to-day operations of local courts)
Philadelphia Inquirer (Jan Schaffer and Jonathan Neumann's series on the alleged mishandling by law enforcement officials of a racially motivated murder case)
Detroit Free Press ("Crime in Detroit: A Search for Solutions," eight-part series)

1978 ***Newport News*** (Va.) **Times-Herald**, Investigative report on jury trials by Gail Bronson, Bill Sizemore, Sigby Solomon and Carolyn Hines West
Camden (N.J.) **Courier=Post** (Dennis M. Culnan and Carl A. Winter's study of operations of New Jersey municipal courts)
Philadelphia Inquirer (Jonathan Neumann and William K. Marimow's four-part series, "The Homicide Files")
Chicago Sun-Times (Patrick Oster's 11-part series of news and features on law-related subjects)

1979 ***Philadelphia Inquirer*** (Philip R. Goldsmith's editorials, "The Supreme Disgrace" on Pennsylvania Supreme Court)
Chicago Sun-Times (Roger Simon's columns on law-related subjects)

NEWSPAPERS (50,000 circulation or less)

1980 ***Gloucester County Times*** (Woodbury, N.J.), (Three articles by Claire Brennan)

NEWSPAPERS (50,000-200,000 circulation)

1980 ***Jackson*** (Miss.) ***Clarion-Ledger*** (Stephanie Saul, Patrick Larkin, Laura Fistler and Tom Hayes's 24-page tabloid feature on jail conditions in Mississippi)
Village Voice (New York), (Nat Hentoff's series on civil rights and liberties abuse at correctional and mental institutions in New York, and analysis of secrecy provisions of Atomic Energy Act)

NEWSPAPERS (200,000-500,000 circulation)

1980 ***Philadelphia Inquirer*** (Jonathan Neumann and Marc Schogol's series on "public officials and mobsters joining hands to rob Pennsylvania taxpayers of $1-million a week through theft of cigarettes")
Miami Herald (Five-part series by six reporters on misuse of force by Dade County's two largest police agencies)

NEWSPAPER MAGAZINE SUPPLEMENTS

1979 **Westchester Rockland Newspapers** (N.Y.), (Tara Connell's feature on relevant laws dealing with insanity or impairment of mental faculties as a means for defense in criminal cases)
Chicago Tribune Magazine (Glen Elassner and Jack Fuller's feature on the inner workings of the U.S. Supreme Court)

1980 ***San Francisco Examiner's California Living Magazine*** (Norma B. Chatly's three-part series on employment discrimination as examined by the U.S. District Court in San Francisco)

MAGAZINES

1958 ***Life*** ("Crime in the U.S." series)
1959 ***Southern Telephone News*** (Series on law in American life)
Time (Coverage of Law Day USA)
1960 **No award**
1961 **No award**
1962 ***Fortune*** ("The Crisis in the Courts," a definitive article on court congestion)
Boys' Life (Series of illustrated articles on historical origins of our legal system)
1963 **No award**
1964 ***Look*** (Series on legal issues of current interest)
1965 ***Life*** ("Storm Center of Justice," distinguished assessment of record of U.S. Supreme Court in the previous decade)
1966 **Time** ("The Revolution in Criminal Justice," an essay, and for distinguished reporting of legal news in its law section)
Look (Account of reform in Chicago's police department and other discerning coverage of law news)
1967 ***Time*** ("Moving the Constitution Into the Police Station" on the impact of the 1964 Supreme Court decision in *Escobedo vs. Illinois* and its effect on police investigation)
Look ("The Lady Fights Back" by Julius Norwitz on a three-year court struggle by Negro attorney Cora Walker to obtain a certificate of occupancy for a renovated Harlem slum dwelling, and an article by Fletcher Knebel on jury system in U.S.)

1968 ***Newsweek*** ("The New Law Versus Tradition" by Peter Janssen on trends toward greater curriculum flexibility and increased social responsibilities in legal education)
Saturday Evening Post (Stewart Alsop's "The Supreme Court Asks A Question: Is It Fair?", an assessment of the Court and its members)
1969 **No award**
1970 ***Psychology Today*** (For contribution to original research in attitudes toward the law and courts, crime and punishment, the penal system rights and freedoms)
1971 ***Fortune*** (Article examining role of the Supreme Court over two decades)
Newsweek ("Prisons in Turmoil," on problems confronting penal systems)
U.S. News and World Report ("Interview with Chief Justice Warren E. Burger")
1972 ***Newsweek*** ("Justice on Trial," a comprehensive report on the police, courts and correctional facilities)
1973 ***Apartment Ideas*** (Three articles explaining legal aspects of common problems to apartment renters)
Harper's ("Your Phone Is A Party Line," detailing government's expanded bugging activities)
Reader's Digest (Three-article series on juvenile courts)
Time ("Up from Coverture" on discriminatory actions taken against women since the earliest days of civilization)
1974 ***Philadelphia*** ("The Last Whole Justice Catalog" by John Guinther, examining practices and procedures of Philadelphia courts)
The New Yorker ("Annals of Law: Boston Criminal Courts" by Richard Harris on how and whether justice is meted out in American courts)
1975 ***Philadelphia*** ("The Paint Job" by James N. Riggio on how a mayor was indicted on trumped-up charges; the investigative report was used in his defense)
The New Yorker ("A Scrap of Black Cloth." two-part article by Richard Harris on the ordeal of a New York teacher who wore an armband to express opposition to the Vietnam War)
Newsweek ("All About Impeachment" by David M. Alpern)
1976 ***Philadelphia*** ("A Child's Garden of Horrors" by John Guinther on injustices in Philadelphia's juvenile justice system)
U.S. News & World Report ("Big Change in Prisons — Punish Not Reform" by Patrick R. Oster and Donald P. Doane)
1977 ***Boston*** ("The Verdict" by Gwen Kincaid analyzing the effect the trial de novo system has upon the quality of justice in Massachusetts)
Newsweek (For Peter Axthelm and Anthony Marro's article on the de facto extradition process used by the U.S. Drug Enforcement Administration to obtain the release of suspected kingpins from foreign countries)
1978 ***The New Yorker*** ("Animals of Crime: A Prison and a Prisoner," three-part series on Green Haven prison life)
The New Yorker (Thomas Whiteside's two-part article, "Annals of Crime: Dead Souls in the Computer")
Newsweek ("The Furor Over Reverse Discrimination" by Jerrold K. Footlick and correspondents and "Too Much Law" by Jerrold K. Footlick)
1979 ***Congressional Quarterly*** (Four entries by Alan Berlow on various subjects relating to law and law-making)
Philadelphia (Paul Good and Emanuel Margolis's article on the civil liberties side of the question of obscenity)
Angolite (Angola, La.), (Wilbert Rideau's article, "Conversations With the Dead," on plight of prisoners)
Newsweek ("The Landmark Bakke Ruling") by Jerrold K. Footlick and correspondents)
1980 ***Angolite*** (Angola, La.), ("A Prison Tragedy" by Billy Sinclair on the killing of a prison inmate in 1973)
Washington Monthly (Two essays by Robert M. Kaus on the rise of congressional delegations of rule-making authority to administrative agencies)
New West (Ciji Ware's article, "Joint Custody: One Way to End the War")
Better Homes and Gardens (Five articles by Margarent V. Daily, Barbara Mantz and Barbara Humeston on various subjects)

WIRE SERVICES

1965 **Gannett News Service** ("Crime and the U.S. Supreme Court," six-article series analyzing landmark decisions broadening the rights of the accused in criminal cases)
1966 **No award**
1967 **No award**
1968 **Newhouse National News Service** (Series by Jack C. Landau on American system of military justice)
1969 **No award**
1970 **No award**
1971 **No award**
1972 **No award**
1973 ***Parade*** (Sunday supplement), (Article outlining problems facing the deaf in obtaining proper legal representation)
Birmingham News (Feature by Peggy Robertson on plea bargaining in "Dimension" supplement)
1974 **Public Insights Syndicate** (Series of weekly columns by Harry Humphreys, "Ideas, Issues and Insights")
1975 **McGraw-Hill World News** ("Your World Tomorrow" feature by Daniel B. Moskowitz on developments in consumer law)
1976 **No award**
1977 **Gannett News Service** (Robert L. King's four-part series on how closed adoption records cause tragic problems for adult adoptees)
1978 **Associated Press** (John Barbour's "Warehousing of Crime" and "Front Door to Crime," on plight of prisons today)
Gannett News Service (Two-part series by Carol Richards and Roger Hedges on governmental agency cheaters and welfare cheaters)
1980 **Associated Press** (Madison, Wis., Bureau for Timoghy Harper's weekly legal column, "Juris Prudent")

NEWS SYNDICATES

1978 ***Congressional Quarterly, Inc.*** ("Access to Justice" by Barry M. Haeger on role of courts in resolving conflicts and controversies)
1979 **No award**
1980 **No award**

Golden Hammer Award

NATIONAL ASSN. OF HOME BUILDERS
15th & M Sts. NW, Washington, D.C. 20005 (202/452-0200)

The Golden Hammer Award offering a $1,000 honorarium and a trophy in the form of a golden hammer is given annually for articles on housing issues in newspapers and magazines. In addition to the first-place honors listed here, second prizes are given and honorable mentions are made.

NEWSPAPERS

1979 **Don DeBat**, *Chicago Sun-Times*

NEWSPAPERS OVER 25,000 CIRCULATION

1980 **David R. Walker** and **Susan Kirvin**, *Daily News of Los Angeles*

NEWSPAPERS UNDER 25,000 CIRCULATION

1980 **Tim Miller**, *Morning Sun* (Mt. Pleasant, Mich.)

MAGAZINES

1979 **Susan Quinn**, *Boston Magazine*
1980 **Elise Vider**, *Connecticut*

Golden Pen of Freedom

INTERNATIONAL FEDERATION OF NEWSPAPER PUBLISHERS (F.I.E.J.)
6, rue Faubourg Poissonniere, 75101 Paris, France (Tel: 523 38 88).

The Golden Pen of Freedom is awarded annually to a person, group or institution for outstanding service to press freedom. The award consists of a gold pen and a plaque. The executive committee of F.I.E.J. selects the winner.

1961 **Ahmet Emin Yalman,** *Hur Vatan* (Istanbul, Turkey)
1962 **No award**
1963 **U Sein Win,** *The Guardian* (Rangoon, Burma)
1964 **Gabriel Makoso,** *Le Courreir d'Afrique* (Leopoldville, Congo)
1965 **Esmond Wickremesinghe,** Associated Newspapers of Ceylon (Colombo)
1966 **Jules Dubois,** Chicago Tribune Press Service (Chicago)
1967 **Mochtar Lubis,** *Indonesia Raya* (Djakarta)
1968 **Christos Lambrakis,** *Ta Vima* (Athens, Greece)
1969 **The Czech press striving for liberty**
1970 **Alberto Gainza Paz,** *La Prensa* (Buenos Aires, Argentina)
1971 **No award**
1972 **Hubert Beuve-Mery,** *Le Monde* (Paris, France)
1973 **Anton Betz,** *Rheinische Post* (Dusseldorf, Federal Republic of Germany)
1974 **Julio de Mesquita Neto,** *O Estado de Sao Paolo* (Brazil)
1975 **Sang-Man Kim,** *Dong-A Ilbo* (Seoul, South Korea)
1976 **Raul Rego,** *Republica* and *A Luta* (Lisbon, Portugal)
1977 **Robert Hugh Lilley,** *Belfast Telegraph* (United Kingdom)
1978 **Percy Qoboza** and **Donald Woods** (South Africa)
1979 **Claude Bellanger**, *Le Parisien Libre* (France)
1980 **Jacobo Timerman**, *La Opinion* (Buenos Aires), later *Maariv* (Tel Aviv)

Golden Quill

INTERNATIONAL SOCIETY OF WEEKLY NEWSPAPERS EDITORS
c/o Dept. of Journalism, Northern Illinois University, Dekalb, Ill. 60115 (815/753-1925)

The Golden Quill award annually honors the outstanding editorial writing in a weekly newspaper in the United States. A judge or panel of judges considers editorials submitted to ISWNE on the basis both of style and the "intestinal fortitude" of the writer. A plaque is given to the winner.

1961 **Hal De Cell, editor,** *Rolling Fork* (Miss.) *Deer Creek Pilot*
1962 **Don Pease, co-editor,** *Oberlin* (Ohio) *News Tribune*
1963 **Hazel Brannon Smith,** *Lexington* (Miss.) *Advertiser*
1964 **T.M.B. Hicks,** *Dallas* (Pa.) Post
1965 **Robert E. Fisher,** *Crosset* (Ark) *News Observer*
1966 **Owen J. McNamara, editor,** *Brookline* (Mass.) *Chronicle-Citizen*
1967 **Alvin J. Remmenga, editor,** *Cloverdale* (Calif.) *Reveille*
1968 **Henry H. Null IV,** *The Abington Journal,* (Clarks Summit, Pa.)
1969 **Dan Hicks, Jr.,** *Madisonville* (Tenn.) *Monroe County Democrat*
1970 **Richard Taylor,** *Kennett Square* (Pa.) *News and Advertiser*
1971 **Edward DeCourcy,** *Newport* (N.H.) *Argus Champion*
1972 **C. Peter Jorgensen,** *Arlington* (Mass.) *Advocate*
1973 **Robert Estabrook,** *Lakeville* (Conn.) *Journal*
1974 **Phil McLaughlin,** *Miami Republican,* (Paola, Kansas)
1975 **Betsy Cox,** *Madison County Newsweek* (Richmond, Ky.)
1976 **Peter Bodley,** *Coon Rapids Herald* (Anoka, Mont.)
1977 **Rodney A. Smith,** *Gretna* (Va.) *Gazette*
1978 **Robert Estabrook,** *Lakeville* (Conn.) *Journal*
1979 **R.W. van de Velde,** *Middlebury* (Vt.) *Valley Voice*
1980 **Garrett Ray,** *Littleton* (Colo.) *Independent*

Sidney Hillman Awards

SIDNEY HILLMAN FOUNDATION
15 Union Square, New York, N.Y. 10003 (212/242-0600)

Each year the foundation awards a series of $750 prizes to honor works that support the ideals of Sidney Hillman's life, including "the protection of individual civil liberties, improved race relations, a strengthened labor movement, the advancement of social welfare and economic security, greater world understanding and related problems." Contributions in print journalism and broadcast journalism awards may be submitted for consideration by a panel of judges.

DAILY PRESS

1950 **Murray Kempton,** *New York Post* (Labor in the South)
A.H. Raskin, *New York Times* (Labor relations)
1951 **Carl T. Rowan,** *Minneapolis Tribune* (Race relations in the South)
1952 **W. Horace Carter,** *Labor City* (N.C.) *Tribune* (Exposing the Ku Klux Klan)
Willard G. Cole, *Whiteville* (N.C.) *News & Reporter* (Exposing the Ku Klux Klan)

Jay Jenkins, *Raleigh* (N.C.) *News and Observer* (Exposing the Ku Klux Klan)
1953 **Ralph S. O'Leary,** *Houston Post* (Civil liberties)
1954 **Vic Reinemer,** *Charlotte* (N.C.) *News* (Civil liberties and civil rights)
Daniel R. Fitzpatrick, *St. Louis Post Dispatch* (Editorial cartoons)
1955 **Ben H. Badgikian,** *Providence Journal-Bulletin* (Civil liberties)
Murray Marder, *Washington Post* (Government security programs)
1956 **Robert H. Spiegel,** *Des Moines Tribune* (Segregation in Des Moines)
New York Times (Editorials on Middle East crisis)
1957 **Harry Ashmore,** *Arkansas Gazette* (Editorials on civil rights)
1958 **Harry L. and Gretchen Billings,** *The People's Voice,* Helena, Mont. (Editorials on civil liberties and public welfare)
Ralph McGill, *Atlanta Constitution* (Editorials defending public school system)
1959 **No award**
1960 **Sylvan Meyer,** *Gainesville* (Ga.) *Daily Times* (Editorials on race relations)
1961 **Patrick J. Owens,** *Pine Bluff* (Ark.) *Commercial* (Editorials on current issues)
1962 **Ira Harkey,** *Pascaluga* (Miss.) *Chronicle* (Editorials on the crisis at the University of Mississippi)
1963 **Horance C. Davis,** *Gainesville* (Fla.) *Daily Sun* (Editorials on civil rights)
1964 **J.O. Emmerich,** *Enterprise Journal,* McComb, Miss. (Editorials on civil rights crisis)
1965 **No award**
1966 **Robert Keveney and Douglas Walker,** *Dayton* (Ohio) *Daily News* (Articles on right wing groups)
Harrison Salisbury, *New York Times* (Reporting on North Vietnam)
1967 **Howard James,** *Christian Science Monitor* (Crisis in the courts)
1968 **James K. Batten and Dwayne Walls,** *Charlotte* (N.C.) *Observer* (For "The People Left Behind")
1969 **William J. Eaton,** *Chicago Daily News* (For The Appearance of Impropriety)
1970 **John Kifner,** *New York Times* (For reporting on the Kent State tragedy)
1971 **Alfred Friendly,** *Washington Post* (For "Victims of the Great American Red Hunt")
Neil Sheehan, *New York Times* (For "The Pentagon Papers")
1972 **Carl Bernstein and Robert Woodward,** *Washington Post* (Watergate investigation)
1973 **Donald L. Barlett and James B. Steele,** *Philadelphia Inquirer* (Investigative reporting)
1974 **Seymour M. Hersh,** *New York Times* (Reporting on the Central Intelligence Agency)
Boston Globe (Coverage of school integration crisis)
1975 **Willard S. Randall and Stephen D. Solomon,** *Philadelphia Inquirer* (For "54 Who Died")
1976 **John Seigenthaler,** *The Tennesseean,* Nashville (Courage in publishing)
1977 **Stan Swofford,** *Greensboro* (N.C.) *Daily News* (series on Wilmington 10 defendants)
1978 **Michael Flannery** and **Bruce Ingersoll**, *Chicago Sun-Times* (series on the working wounded)
1979 **Diedre Murphy**, *Rochester* (N.Y.) *Democrat & Chronicle* (series on poverty)
1980 **Not available at press time**

BOOKS

1950 **John Hersey,** *The Wall*
1951 **Alan Barth,** *The Loyalty of Free Men*
1952 **Herbert Block,** *The Herblock Book*
1953 **Theodore H. White,** *Fire in the Ashes*
1954 **Henry Steele Commager,** *Freedom, Loyalty and Dissent*
1955 **John Lord O'Brian,** *National Security and Individual Freedom*
1956 **Walter Gellhorn,** *Individual Freedom and Governmental Restraints*
1957 **Wilma Dykeman and James Stokely,** *Neither Black nor White*
1958 **John Kenneth Galbraith,** *The Affluent Society*
1959 **Harold M. Hyman,** *To Try Men's Souls*
1960 **Davis McEntire,** *Residence and Race*
William L. Shirer, *The Rise and Fall of the Third Reich*
1961 **Jane Jacobs,** *Death and Life of Great American Cities*
1962 **Michael Harrington,** *The Other America*
1963 **Richard Hofstadter,** *Anti-Intellectualism in American Life*
1964 **James W. Silver,** *Mississippi: The Closed Society*
Bernard D. Nossiter, *The Mythmakers*
1965 **Kenneth B. Clark,** *Dark Ghetto*
1966 **Joseph P. Lyford,** *The Airtight Cage*
1967 **Ronald Steel,** *Pax Americana*
Alan F. Westin, *Privacy and Freedom*
1968 **George R. Stewart,** *Not So Rich As You Think*
1969 **Rep. Richard McCarthy,** *The Ultimate Folly*
1970 **Ramsey Clark,** *Crime in America*
1971 **Morton Mintz and Jerry S. Cohen,** *America, Inc.*
1972 **Frances Fitz Gerald,** *Fire In The Lake*
1973 **Jervis Anderson,** *A. Philip Randolph: A Biographical Portrait*
Arthur M. Schlesinger, Jr., *The Imperial Presidency*
1974 **Richard J. Barnet and Ronald E. Muller,** *Global Reach*
Noel Mostert, *Super Ship*
1975 **E.J. Kahn, Jr.,** *The China Hands*
1976 **Richard Kluger,** *Simple Justice*
1977 **Philip Caputo,** *A Rumor of War*
1978 **Charles E. Silberman,** *Criminal Violence, Criminal Justice*
1979 **William Shawcross,** *Sideshow—Kissinger, Nixon and the Destruction of Cambodia*

SPECIAL AWARD

1973 **Alexandr Solzhenitsyn**

RADIO-TELEVISION

1953 **Edward R. Murrow,** *See It Now,* CBS Television (Civil liberties)
Gerald W. Johnson, WAAM, Baltimore (Civil liberties)
1954 **Eric Sevareid,** *American Week,* CBS Television (Civil rights issues)
1955 **No award**
1956 **No award**
1957 **Theodore Ayers** *Face the Nation,* CBS Television (Interview with Khrushchev)
George A. Vicas *Radio Beat,* CBS Radio (Debates between Soviet and American scientists)
1958 **Irving Gitlin,** CBS-TV unit supervision (Especially for *Who Killed Michael Farmer?* and *P.O.W.—A Study in Survival)*
1959 **Edward P. Morgan,** ABC Television News
WNTA-TV, New York (*Play of the Week*)
1960 **Walter Peters and Marshal Diskin,** ABC Television (*Cast the First Stone*)

1961 **Al Wasserman and Robert Young,** NBC Television White Paper (*Angola: Journey to a War*)
1962 **Warren Wallace,** WCBS-TV, New York (*Superfluous People*)
John Keats, George Dessart and David E. Wilson, WCAU-TV, Philadelphia (*Conformity*)
1963 **Millard Lampell,** CBS Television (*No Hiding Place*)
1964 **Joseph Wershba,** CBS Television (*Gideon's Trumpet: The Poor Man and The Law*)
1965 **No award**
1966 **William C. Jersey,** National Educational Television (*A Time for Burning*)
1967 **Jay L. McMullen,** CBS Television News, (*The Tenement*)
1968 **Bill Osterhous and Dick Hubert,** Westinghouse Broadcasting Co. (*One Nation Indivisible*)
1969 **Fred Freed,** NBC Television (*Who Killed Lake Erie?*)
1970 **Ronn Bonn and Walter Cronkite,** CBS Television News (*Can the World Be Saved?*)
1971 **Martin Carr,** NBC Television (*This Child is Rated X*)
1972 **Lucy Jarvis,** NBC Television (*What Price Health?*)
1973 **Paul Altmeyer,** Westinghouse Broadcasting Co. (*Freedom and Security: The Uncertain Balance*)
1974 **CBS Television Network** (*The Autobiography of Miss Jane Pittman*)
1975 **CBS Television** (*Fear on Trial*)
1976 **Paul Leaf,** NBC Television (*Judge Horton and the Scottsboro Boys*)
1977 **Bill Moyers,** CBS Television, (*The Fire Next Door*)
1978 **Abby Mann,** Abby Mann/Filmway/NBC (*King*)
1979 **Steve Singer** and **Tom Priestley,** ABC-TV News Closeup (*The Killing Ground*)
Carol Colman (WRFM-Radio, New York)
1980 **Not available at press time**

MAGAZINES

1950 **James H. Means,** *Atlantic Monthly* for "Doctors Lobby" and "England's Public Medicine: The Facts"
1951 **Arthur D. Mores,** *McCall's* for "Who's Trying to Ruin Our Schools?"
1952 **No award**
1953 **Joseph Wechsberg,** *The New Yorker* for "The Seventeenth of June"
1954 **Charlotte Knight,** *Collier's* for "What Price Security?"
1955 **Robert Engler,** *New Republic* for "Oil and Politics"
1956 **Robert Penn Warren,** *Life* for "Divided South Searches Its Soul"
John Fischer, *Harper's Magazine* for "The Harm Good People Do"
1957 **No award**
1958 **Giorgio De Santillana,** *The Reporter* for "Galileo and J. Robert Oppenheimer"
Harvey Swados, *The Nation* for "Myth of the Powerful Worker"
1959 **Harry W. Ernst and Charles H. Drake,** *The Nation* for "Poor, Proud and Primitive: The Lost Appalachians"
1960 **Fred J. Cook,** *The Nation* for "Gambling, Inc."
1961 **Lillian Smith,** *Redbook* for "The Ordeal of Southern Woman"
1962 **Margaret Parton,** *Ladies' Home Journal* for "Sometimes Life Just Happens"
1963 **Arnold Hano,** *Saga Magazine* for "The Burned Out Americans"
1964 **J. Robert Moskin,** *Look* for "Challenge to our Doctors"
1965 **Theodore Draper,** *Commentary* for "The Dominican Crisis—A Case Study in American Policy"
1966 **Richard Harris,** *The New Yorker* for "Medicare"
1967 **No award**
1968 **Charles and Bonnie Remsberg,** *Good Housekeeping* for "America's Hungry Families"
1969 **Daniel Lang,** *The New Yorker* for "Casualties of War"
1970 **Christopher H. Pyle,** *The Washington Monthly* for articles on army surveillance of political activity
1971 **Carolyn See, Kenneth Lasson, William Serrin, Robert Coles and Richard Todd,** *Atlantic Monthly* for "Work in America"
1972 **Frank J. Donner and Eugene Cerruti,** *The Nation* for "The Grand Jury Network"
1973 **Paul Broder,** *The New Yorker* for "Annals of Industry: Casualties of the Workplace"
Richard L. Strout, *New Republic* for columns signed "TRB"
1974 **No award**
1975 **Susan Sheehan,** *The New Yorker* for "A Welfare Mother"
1976 **Guy Neal Williams,** *Philadelphia Magazine* for "The Mushroom Pickers"
1977 **Eliot Marshall,** *New Republic* for series of higher health-care costs and inferior care
1978 **Tracy Kidder,** *Atlantic Monthly* for "Soldiers of Misfortune"
1979 **Michael H. Brown,** *Atlantic Monthly* for "Love Canal and the Poisoning of America"
1980 **Not available at press time**

SPECIAL AWARDS

1954 **The Progressive** (For special issue on Sen. Joseph McCarthy)
1954 **WNYC**, New York (For public service programming)
1973 **WNET**, New York (For outstanding programming)
1976 **Henry Steele Commager** (For lifetime contributions)
1977 **ABC Television Network** (*Roots*)
1978 **I.F. Stone**

Robert F. Kennedy Journalism Awards

ROBERT F. KENNEDY JOURNALISM AWARDS COMMITTEE
1035 30th St. NW, Washington, D.C. 20007 (202/338-7444)

The Robert F. Kennedy Journalism Award(s) for Outstanding Coverage of the Problems of the Disadvantaged are given annually for outstanding print, broadcast and photographic journalism. Cash prizes of $5,000 are available, $3,000 of which can go to the grand prize winner. A panel of professional journalists in all three fields selects the recipients. (Honorable mentions and citations are not listed here.)

1968 **CBS Television** (*Black History: Lost, Stolen or Strayed,* Andrew A. Rooney, producer)
WMCA-Radio, New York (Continuing special coverage of the problems of poverty and discrimination in New York City and New York State)
Nick Kotz, *Des Moines Register and Tribune* (Continuing coverage of poverty in America)
David Nevin, *Life* ("These Murdered Old Mountains")
1969 **ABC Television** (*Black Fiddler: Prejudice and the Negro,* Howard Enders, producer)

NBC Television (*Between Two Rivers* from the *First Tuesday* series; Tom Pettit, reporter; Anthony Potter, producer)
WRC-TV, Washington (*Perspective: New Set of Eyes,* Bill Leonard, producer)
WJR-Radio, Detroit (*I Am Not Alone,* Phil Jones, reporter)
Linda Rockey, *Chicago Sun-Times* (Series on the problems of hunger)
Dallas Kinney and Kent Polloc, *Palm Beach* (Fla.) *Post-Times* ("Migration to Misery" series)
Fred C. Shapiro, *The New Yorker* ("The Whitmore Confessions")

1970 **NBC Television** (*Migrant: An NBC White Paper,* Martin Carr, producer)
Westinghouse Broadcasting Co. (*When You Reach December*)
Ralph Looney, *Albuquerque Tribune* (Series on the Navajos)
Jerome Watson and Sam Washington, *Chicago Sun-Times* (Series on Illinois state schools for the mentally retarded)
Ruben Salazar, *Los Angeles Times* (Columns on culture and alienation of Chicanos)
The New Thing (Washington Arts Workshop*) (*This is the Home of Mrs. Levant Graham,* Topper Carew, producer)

1971 **Jon Nordheimer,** *New York Times* ("From Dakto to Detroit: Death of a Troubled Hero")
Patrick Zier and Joanne Wragg, *The Lakeland* (Fla.) *Ledger* ("The Battle for Dignity")
Newsweek ("Justice on Trial," by Edward Kosner, Peter Goldman and Don Holt)
Beekman Winthrop, New South ("Worms Turn People Off")
Group W (*The Suburban Wall,* Paul Altmeyer, producer)
Doug Fox, KTOK-Radio (*The Business of Being Black* series)

1972 **Jean Heller,** Associated Press ("The Tuskegee Syphilis Study")
WABC-TV, New York (*Willowbrook: The Last Great Disgrace,* written and reported by Geraldo Rivera)

1973 **John Guinther,** *Philadelphia Magazine* ("The Only Good Indian")
Bob Dotson, WKY-TV, Oklahoma City (*Through the Looking Glass Darkly*)
Dolores Katz and Jo Thomas, *Detroit Free Press* ("Psychosurgery—On Trial")

1974 **Mike Masterson,** *Hot Springs* (Ark.) *Sentinal Record* (Features, editorials and columns on poverty and discrimination)
Loretta Schwartz, *Philadelphia Magazine* ("Nothing to Eat")
Martin Berman, Peter Lance and Geraldo Rivera, WABC-TV, New York (*The Willowbrook Case: The People vs. the State of New York*)
Terence Gurley, WWVA-Radio, Wheeling, W. Va. (*Back to Bloody Harlan*)

1975 **Gene Miller,** *Miami Herald* (Coverage of the Pitts-Lee Case)
Michael O'Brien, *Miami News* ("John Madden: His Last Days," photojournalistic coverage)
Tom Pettit, NBC-TV News (*Feeding the Poor*)
Bob Cain and Cathleen Gurley, WWVA-Radio, Wheeling, W. Va. (*Care and Feeding of America*)
The Cavalier Daily, University of Virginia (*Benign Neglect*)

1976 **Acel Moore and Wendell Rawls,** *Philadelphia Inquirer* (Series on Farview State Hospital)
Evan White, KGO-TV, San Francisco ("Tenderloin Old Folks")

1977 **Bill Moyers, Tom Spain, Howard Stringer** and **Dan Lerner**, CBS-TV (*CBS Reports: The Fire Next Door*)
Jonathan Neumann and **William K. Marimow,** *Philadelphia Inquirer* (series on police violence)
Michael O'Brien, *Miami News* ("Culmer: The Tragic City")
Peter A. Silva, *Corpus Christi Caller* ("The Outsider")

1978 **Fredric Tulsky** with **Nancy Weaver** and **Don Hoffman**, *Mississippi Clarion-Ledger* ("Mississippi Justice")
Steven L. McVicker and **Jeanne Jones Riedmueller**, KPFT-Radio ("The Question of Accountability: A Look at the Houston Police Department")

1979 **Chester Goolrick** and **Paul Lieberman** with **Lee May, Charlene P. Smith-Williams** and **Steve Johnson**, *Atlanta Constitution* ("The Underpaid and the Underprotected")
Greg Barron and **David Carlton Felland,** KSJN/Minnesota Public Radio ("The Way to 8-A")
Howard Husock, WGBH-TV ("Community Disorder: Racial Violence in Boston")
Patrick Bernet, Prentice Cole, W.R. Everly III, E.W. Faircloth, Norman Y. Lono and **Denis F. O'Keefe**, *Philadelphia Daily News* ("A City Apart")

1980 **Not available at press time**

Liebling Award

MORE MAGAZINE

The A.J. Liebling Award was a plaque, given every year for career achievement in reporting or journalism over a long period. Until the demise of the publication, the editors of *More* selected the recipient.

1972 **I.F. Stone**
1973 **Homer Bigart,** *New York Times*
1974 **Morton Mintz,** *Washington Post*
1975 **Studs Terkel**
1976 ***60 Minutes,*** CBS
1977 **Murray Kempton**, *New York Post*

Lifeline Award

AMERICAN HEALTH FOUNDATION
320 East 43rd St., New York, N.Y. 10017 (212/953-1900)

The Lifeline Award, which consists of a plaque, honors the individual who is judged by a committee of the Public Health Action Group of the AHF to have contributed most to enhancing public awareness of the value of preventive medicine.

1977 **Jane Brody,** *New York Times*
Frank Field, NBC-TV
1978 **No award**
1979 **Mildred Scheel**, former First Lady of Germany and founder of *Deutsche Krebshilfe*, the German cancer research fund
1980 **Philip Abelson**, editor, *Science*

National Magazine Awards

AMERICAN SOCIETY OF MAGAZINE EDITORS
575 Lexington Ave., New York, N.Y. 10022 (212/752-0055)

The National Magazine Awards, which are sponsored by ASME and administered by Columbia University, consist of a silver plaque and a reproduction of an Alexander Calder stabile elephant. The awards annually honor editorial excellence and innovation in several categories. All regularly published magazines in the United States may enter upon payment of a $75 entry fee for consideration by a twenty-judge panel comprised of persons chosen by the university from the magazine industry and journalism educators.

NATIONAL MAGAZINE AWARD
(one award through 1969)

1966 *Look*
1967 *Life*
1968 *Newsweek*
1969 *American Machinist*

PUBLIC SERVICE

1970 *Life*
1971 *The Nation*
1972 *Philadelphia*
1973 No award
1974 *Scientific American*
1975 *Consumer Reports*
1976 *Business Week*
1977 *Philadelphia*
1978 *Mother Jones*
1979 *New West*
1980 *Texas Monthly*

GENERAL EXCELLENCE
(given once)

1973 *Business Week*

SPECIALIZED JOURNALISM

1970 *Philadelphia*
1971 *Rolling Stone*
1972 *Architectural Record*
1973 *Psychology Today*
1974 *Texas Monthly*
1975 *Medical Economics*
1976 *United Mine Workers' Journal*
1977 *Architectural Record*
1978 *Scientific American*
1979 *National Journal*
1980 *IEEE Spectrum*

VISUAL EXCELLENCE

1970 *Look*
1971 *Vogue*
1972 *Esquire*
1973 *Horizon*
1974 *Newsweek*
1975 *Country Journal*
National Lampoon
1976 *Horticulture*
1977 *Rolling Stone*
1978 *Architectural Digest*
1979 *Audubon*
1980 No award

FICTION, CRITICISM AND BELLES LETTRES

1970 *Redbook*
1971 *Esquire*
1972 *Mademoiselle*
1973 *Atlantic Monthly*
1974 *The New Yorker*
1975 *Redbook*
1976 *Essence*
1977 *Mother Jones*

ESSAYS AND CRITICISM

1978 *Esquire*
1979 *Life*
1980 *Natural History*

FICTION

1978 *The New Yorker*
1979 *The Atlantic Monthly*
1980 *Antaeus*

REPORTING EXCELLENCE

1970 *The New Yorker*
1971 *Atlantic Monthly*
1972 *Atlantic Monthly*
1973 *New York*
1974 *The New Yorker*
1975 *The New Yorker*
1976 *Audubon*
1977 *Audubon*
1978 *The New Yorker*
1979 *Texas Monthly*
1980 *Mother Jones*

SERVICE TO THE INDIVIDUAL

1974 *Sports Illustrated*
1975 *Esquire*
1976 *Modern Medicine*
1977 *Harper's*
1978 *Newsweek*
1979 *The American Journal of Nursing*
1980 *Saturday Review*

SINGLE-TOPIC ISSUE

1979 *Progressive Architecture*
1980 *Scientific American*

DESIGN

1980 *Geo*

AOA Journalism Awards

AMERICAN OSTEOPATHIC ASSOCIATION
212 E. Ohio St., Chicago, Ill. 60611 (312/944-2713)

The AOA Journalism Awards, which offer a total of $2,000 in prizes, are given each year for the best article or broadcast on osteopathic medicine to the scientific community and the general public. Entries may be submitted for consideration by a panel of professional journalists.

1963 **Theodore Berland,** Freelance
A.L. Schafer, Freelance
Don Walton, *Lincoln Star*
1964 **Dominic Crolla,** *Tucson Daily Citizen*
Jerry Flemmons, *Fort Worth Star-Telegram*
James Koethe, *Dallas Times-Herald*
1965 **John Langone,** *Boston Herald*

Herschel Fink, *Flint Journal*
Armand Gebert, *Detroit News*
1966 **No award**
1967 **Virginia Turner**, *El Paso Post*
Jean Pearson, *Detroit News*
Joe Western, *National Observer*
1968 **Jon McConal**, *Fort Worth Star-Telegram*
Warren Koon, Charleston (S.C.) Evening Post
1969 **Paula Gilliland**, *Newark Star Ledger*
Sue Ann Wood, *St. Louis Globe-Democrat*
Al Pagel, *Miami Herald*
1970 **Ruth Winter**, Freelance
Kenneth Levy, *Newark Star-Ledger*
1971 **Lew Larkin**, *Kansas City Star*
Frank Carey, Freelance
1972 **Judy Hamilton**, *Tampa Times*
Jeff Holladay, *Daily Oklahoman*
Kathleen Cochran, Freelance
1973 **Joan Osterhoudt**, *Newark Star-Ledger*
Marilyn Drago, *Tucson Star*
1974 **Podine Schoenberger**, *New Orleans Times- Picayune*
Patricia McCarron, *St. Louis Post-Dispatch*
Betty Walker, Freelance
1975 **Fraser Kent**, *Miami Herald*
Fabia Mahoney, *Camden Courier-Post*
Lee Linder, Associated Press
1976 **Elinor Benedict**, *Kettering Oakwood Times* (Ohio)
Herbert Deneberg, Freelance
Frank Dineen, Freelance
Carol Langston, *Daily Oklahoman*
1977 **Chuck Radis**, Freelance
Jon McConal, *Fort Worth Star-Telegram*
Michael McKeating, *Buffalo Evening News*
1978 **Carl Jon Denbow**, *Medical Dimensions*
Charles Remsberg, *Family Health*
Darrell Sifford, *Philadelphia Inquirer*
1979 **Millicent Lane**, *Lansing* (Mich.) *State Journal*
Mark Bloom, *Medical World News*
Nick Provenza, *Yakima* (Wash.) *Herald-Republic*
1980 **Lorrie Secrest**, WUBE-TV (Columbus, Ohio)
Mark Landsbaum, *Los Angeles Times*
Elaine Riccio, *Mesa Magazine*

International Editor of the Year

WORLD PRESS REVIEW
230 Park Ave., Ste. 1610, New York, N.Y. 10169
(212/697-6162)

The International Editor of the Year is honored for "courage, enterprise and leadership on an international level in advancing press freedom and responsibility, enhancing world understanding, defending human rights and fostering journalistic standards."

1975 **Harold Evans**, editor, *Sunday Times of London*
1976 **Andre Fontaine** editor in chief, *Le Monde* (Paris)
1977 **Julio Scherer Garcia**, editor in chief, *Proceso* (Mexico City)
1978 **S. Nihal Singh**, editor, *The Statesman* (Calcutta)
S. Mulgaokar, editor in chief, *Indian Express*
1979 **Rex Gibson**, editor, *Sunday Express* (Johannesburg)
Allister Sparks, *Rand Daily Mail* (Johannesberg)
1980 **Juan Luis Cebrian**, editor, *El Pais* (Madrid)

Gerald Loeb Awards

UCLA GRADUATE SCHOOL OF MANAGEMENT
405 Hilgard Ave., Los Angeles, Calif. 90024

The $1,000 Loeb Awards are given annually for distinguished business and financial writing. A committee of three judges consisting of two faculty members from the school and one person from the journalism community selects the winners from entries now generally representing small and large newspapers, magazines and editorial columns.

1958 **Werner Renberg**, *Business Week*
David Steinberg, *New York Herald Tribune*
1959 **Ernest Havemann**, *Life*
Nate White, *Christian Science Monitor*
1960 **John A. Conway**, *Newsweek*
Nate White, *Christian Science Monitor*
1961 **Leonard S. Silk**, *Business Week*
Wall Street Journal Staff Members
1962 **Robert E. Bedingfield**, *New York Times*
Richard Austin Smith, *Fortune*
1963 **Sandford Brown**, *Newsweek*
David R. Jones, *Wall Street Journal*
1964 **John Brooks**, *The New Yorker*
Robert E. Nichols, *Los Angeles Times*
Alfred P. Sloan, *Fortune*
1965 **Edwin L. Dale, Jr.**, *New York Times*
Leslie Gould, *New York Journal American*
Lee Silverman, *Harvard Business Review*
1966 **Marcus Gleisser**, *Cleveland Plain Dealer*
Ross M. Robertson, *Louisville Courier-Journal*
Charles E. Silberman, *Fortune*
1967 **David R. Francis**, *Christian Science Monitor*
Max Ways, *Fortune*
1968 **Michael Laurence**, *Playboy*
Nicholas Molodovsky, *Financial Analysts Journal*
Richard A. Nenneman, *Christian Science Monitor*
1969 **John Brooks**, *The New Yorker*
George J. W. Goodman ("Adam Smith"), Random House
Charles N. Stabler, *Wall Street Journal*
McGraw Hill Publications
1970 **Leland B. DuVall**, *Arkansas Gazette*
John F. Lyons, *Corporate Financing*
Philip B. Osborne, *Business Week*
Patricia Shontz, *Detroit News*
1971 **Philip Greer**, *Washington Post*
J. A. Livingston, *Philadelphia Evening Bulletin*
Chris Welles, *Institutional Investor*
1972 **Kenneth Auchincloss**, *Newsweek*
Robert E. Bedingfield, *New York Times*
Robert H. Metz, *New York Times*
James W. Michaels, *Forbes*
1973 **John Barbour**, Associated Press
Everett Mattlin, *Corporate Financing*
Clem Morgello, *Newsweek*
Louis Rukeyser, "Wall Street Week" Radio Program
1974 **John Brooks**, *The New Yorker*
Carol J. Loomis, *Fortune*
Paul E. Steiger, *The Los Angeles Times*
Livingston V. Taylor, *Louisville* (Ky.) *Courier-Journal*
Henry Wallich, *Newsweek*
1975 **Donald Barlett** and **James Steele**, *Philadelphia Inquirer*
Edwin Darby, *Chicago Sun-Times*
Marshall Loeb, *Time*
Tom Miller, *Los Angeles Herald Examiner*

Allan Sloan, *Detroit Free Press*
1976 **Willard Randall** and Stephen Solomon, *Philadelphia Inquirer*
David R. Francis, *Christian Science Monitor*
Gordon L. Wiliams, *Business Week*
J. A. Livingston, *Philadelphia Inquirer*
John Guinther, *Philadelphia*
1977 **Susan Trausch** and **Laurence Collins**, *Boston Globe*
Larry Kramer, *San Francisco Examiner*
Sally Jones and **Rosemary Shinohara**, *Anchorage Daily News*
David Warsh and **Lawrence Minard**, *Forbes*
Lee Mitgang, Associated Press
1978 **Paul E. Steiger, Robert Rosenblatt, Ronald Soble, Murray Seeger**, and **Sam Jameson**, *Los Angeles Times*
Harold Chucker, *Minneapolis Star*
Lewis Lapham, *Harper's*
Hobart Rowen, *Washington Post*
William Tucker, *Harper's*
1979 **R.C. Longworth** and **Bill Neikirk**, *Chicago Tribune*
N.R. Kleinfield, *New York Times*
Philip Moeller, *Louisville* (Ky.) *Courier-Journal*
William Tucker, *Harper's*
Robert L. Bartley, *Wall Street Journal*
Robert L. Heilbroner, *The New Yorker*
1980 **Gaylord Shaw, Tom Redburn, William C. Rempel, Cathleen Decker, William J. Eaton, Norman Kempster, Larry Pryor, Bill Stall** and **Penelope McMillan**, *Los Angeles Times*
Joe R. Cordero and **Tim W. Ferguson**, *Santa Ana* (Calif.) *Register*
Walter Guzzardi, Jr., *Fortune*
Alan Gersten, *Rocky Mountain News* (Denver)
Tom Bethell, *Harper's*

MEMORIAL AWARD

1974 **Joseph A. Livingston**, *Philadelphia Inquirer*
1975 **Vermont Royster**, *Wall Street Journal*
1976 **John McDonald**, *Fortune*
1977 **Leonard S. Silk**, *New York Times*
1978 **Hedley Donovan**, Time, Inc.

Ramon Magsaysay Award

RAMON MAGSAYSAY FOUNDATION
Box 3350, Manila, The Philippines (59-19-19)

The Ramon Magsaysay Award for Journalism, Literature and Creative Communication Arts is one of the five categories in which the annual awards of $20,000 each are given for achievements in Asia which reflect the ideals of the late Ramon Magsaysay. The foundation's board of trustees selects the recipient from nominations received. The funding for this honor, which until 1977 was $10,000, is from the Rockefeller Brothers Fund of New York.

1958 **Robert McCulloch Dick** (Philippines; born in Scotland)
Mochtar Lubis (Indonesia), "for the courageous and constructive contribution each has made in the profession of journalism as a power for the public good"
1959 **Tarzie Vittachi** (Ceylon), "for courageous reportage of abuses of power and social conflict"
Edward Michael Law Yone (Burma), "for consistent responsible editorship and courageous defense of human rights"
1960 **No award**
1961 **Amitabha Chowdhury** (India), "for scrupulous and probing investigative reporting in protection of individual rights and community interests"
1962 **Chang Chun-Ha** (Korea), "for editorial integrity in publication of a nonpartisan forum to encourage dynamic participation by intellectuals in national reconstruction"
1963 **No award**
1964 **Richard Garrett Wilson** (British), and **Kayser Sung** (British citizen; born in China), "for accuracy, impartiality and a continuing search for facts and insights in recording Asia's quest for economic advance"
1965 **Akira Kurosawa** (Japan), "for perceptive use of the film to probe the moral dilemma of man amidst the tumultuous remaking of his values and environment in the mid-20th century"
1966 **No award**
1967 **Satyajit Ray** (India), "for uncompromising use of the film as an art, drawing themes from his native Bengali literature to depict a true image of India"
1968 **Ton That Thien** (Vietnam), "for enduring commitment to free inquiry and debate"
1969 **Mitoji Nishimoto** (Japan), "for 44 years of discerning design of Japan's superior educational radio and television broadcasting system"
1970 **No award**
1971 **Prayoon Chanyavongs** (Thailand), "for use of pictorial satire and humor for over three decades in unswerving defense of the public interest"
1972 **Yasuji Hanamori** (Japan), "for cogent advocacy of the interests, rights, and well-being of the Japanese consumer, especially the hard-pressed housewives"
1973 **Michiko Ishimure** (Japan), "for being the 'voice of her people' in their struggle against the industrial pollution that has been distorting and destroying their lives"
1974 **Zacarias Sarian** (Philippines), "for standards of editing and publishing interesting, accurate and constructive farm news"
1975 **B. George Verghese** (India), "for superior developmental reporting of Indian society, balancing factual accounts of achievements, shortcomings and carefully-researched alternatives"
1976 **Sombhu Mitra** (India), "for creating a relevant theater movement in India by superb production, acting and writing"
1977 **Mahesh C. Regmi** (Nepal), "for enabling his people to discover their origins and delineating national options"
1978 **Yoon Suk-joong** (Korea), "for fostering through his poems and songs joyful, positive values among Korean children"
1979 **Not available at press time**
1980 **Not available at press time**

Overseas Press Club Annual Awards
Cartoon Award
Bache Award
Robert Capa Gold Medal
Bob Considine Award
Madeline Dane Ross Award

OVERSEAS PRESS CLUB
52 E. 41st St., New York, N.Y. 10017 (212/679-9650)

Annual awards in news reporting from abroad in print, broadcast and photographic journalism are based on selection by a panel of judges who are experts in the field. The awards originated as an almost spontaneous gesture to honor the work of journalists covering World War II.

DAILY NEWSPAPER OR WIRE SERVICE REPORTING FROM ABROAD (Hall Boyle Award)

1940 **Leland Stowe,** *Chicago Daily News* and *New York Post*
1941 **Cyrus L. Sulzberger,** *New York Times* (Europe)
Otto D. Tolichus, *New York Times* (Far East)
1942 **No award**
1943 **No award**
1944 **No award**
1945 **Drew Middleton,** *New York Times* (Berlin)
Frank Robertson, International News Service (Tokyo)
1947 **A.T. Steele,** *New York Herald Tribune*
1948 **Harold Callender,** *New York Times*
1949 **Joseph Newman,** *New York Herald Tribune*
1950 **Homer Bigart,** *New York Herald Tribune*
Hal Boyle, AP war reporting
1951 **Cyrus L. Sulzberger,** *New York Times*
1952 **Homer Bigart,** *New York Herald Tribune*
1953 **Joseph and Stewart Alsop,** *New York Herald Tribune*
1954 ***New York Times***
1955 **Clifton Daniel,** *New York Times*
1956 **Barrett McGurn,** *New York Herald Tribune*
1957 **Bob Considine, Frank Coniff and William Randolph Hearst, Jr.,** Hearst Newspapers
1958 **Bob Considine,** Hearst Newspapers
1959 **A.M. Rosenthal,** *New York Times*
1960 **Lynn Heinzerling,** Associated Press
1961 **Bob Considine,** Hearst Newspapers
1962 **Andrew C. Borowiec,** Associated Press
1963 **Malcolm Browne,** Associated Press
1964 **Saul Pett,** Associated Press
1965 **Richard Critchfield,** *Washington Star*
1966 **Hugh Mulligan,** Associated Press
1967 **Joe Alex Morris, Jr.,** *Los Angeles Times*
1968 **Peter Rehak,** Associated Press
1969 **William K. Tuohy,** *Los Angeles Times*
1970 **John Hughes,** *Christian Science Monitor*
1971 **Sydney Schanberg,** *New York Times*
1972 **Charlotte Saikowski,** *Christian Science Monitor*
1973 **Raymond R. Coffey,** *Chicago Daily News*
1974 **Robert Kaiser,** *Washington Post*
1975 **Sydney H. Schanberg,** *New York Times*
1976 **Edward Cody,** Associated Press
1977 **Robert C. Toth,** *Los Angeles Times*
1978 **Charles Krause,** *Washington Post*
1979 **Sajid Rizvi,** United Press International
1980 **Not available at press time**

PHOTOGRAPHS, DAILY NEWSPAPER OR WIRE SERVICE

1948 **Jack Birns,** *Life*
1949 **Henri Cartier-Bresson,** Magnum Photos
1950 **David Douglas Duncan,** *Life*
1951 **Frank Noel,** Associated Press
1952 **David Douglas Duncan,** *Life*
1953 **Michael Rougier,** *Life*
1954 ***Life***
1955 **Henri Cartier-Bresson,** Magnum Photos
1956 **John Sadovy,** *Life*
1957 **No award**
1958 **Andrew St. George,** Freelance in *Life*
1959 **Henri Cartier-Bresson,** *Life*
1960 **Yasushi Nagao,** United Press International
1961 **Peter Leibing,** Associated Press
1962 **Hector Rondon,** Associated Press
1963 **Henri Cartier-Bresson,** Magnum Photos
1964 **Akihiko Okamura,** *Life*
1965 **Kyoichi Sawada,** United Press International
1966 **Kyoichi Sawada,** United Press International
1967 **Peter Skingley,** United Press International
1968 **Edward T. Adams,** Associated Press
1969 **Horst Faas,** Associated Press
1970 **Dennis Cook,** United Press International
1971 ***New York Times***
1972 **Huynh Cong Ut,** Associated Press
1973 **Sydney Schanberg,** *New York Times*
1974 **Ovie Carter,** *Chicago Tribune*

BEST PHOTOGRAPHIC REPORTING FROM ABROAD

1976 **K. Kenneth Paik,** *Kansas City Times*
1977 **James Peter Blair,** *National Geographic*
1978 **Frank B. Johnston,** *Newsweek*
1979 **David Burnett,** Contact Press Images
1980 **Not available at press time**

PHOTOGRAPHS, IN A MAGAZINE OR BOOK

1966 **Marc Riboud,** Magnum
1967 **Lee Lockwood,** Black Star Publishing
1968 **David Robison** and **Priva Ramrahka,** *Life;*
Romano Cagnoni *Life*
1969 **Marc Riboud,** *Look*
1970 **Larry Burrows,** *Life*
1971 **Frank Fischbeck,** *Life*
1972 **Thomas J. Abercrombie,** *National Geographic*
1973 ***Life Special Report***
1974 **Eddie Adams,** *Time*
1975 **Eddie Adams,** *Time*
1976 **Robert W. Madden and W.E. Garrett,** *National Geographic*

OPC PRESIDENT'S AWARD

1956 **Endre Marton,** Associated Press
1968 **The newsmen of Czechoslovakia,** all media
1969 **Neil A. Armstrong**
1972 **International Committee to Free Journalists held in Southeast Asia**
1974 **Lowell Thomas**
1976 **Don Bolles**
1977 **Donald Woods**

The Overseas Press Club cash award honoring the best cartoon on foreign affairs was originally a $500 prize sponsored by three organizations. Currently, it has been dropped to $150, which is donated by the *New York Daily News.*

1968 **Don Wright,** *Miami News*
1969 **Paul F. Conrad,** Register and Tribune Syndicate
1970 **Tom Darcy,** *Newsday*
1971 **Don Wright,** *Miami News*
1972 **Tom Darcy,** *Newsday*
1973 **Warren King,** *New York Daily News*
1974 **Tony Auth,** *Philadelphia Inquirer*
1975 **Tony Auth,** *Philadelphia Inquirer*
1976 **Warren King,** *New York Daily News*
1977 **Ed Fisher,** *Omaha* (Neb.) *World Herald*
1978 **Jim Morin,** *Miami Herald*
1979 **Don Wright,** *Miami News*
1980 **Not available at press time**

A $500 award, called the E.W. Fairchild Award until 1969 and the Bache Award since 1970, is given each year for the best business reporting from abroad.

1959 **Peter Weaver,** McGraw-Hill World News
1960 **Edwin L. Dale, Jr.,** *New York Times*
1961 **Edwin L. Dale, Jr.,** *New York Times*
1962 **Joseph A. Livingston,** *Philadelphia Bulletin*
1963 **Ray Vicker,** *Wall Street Journal*
1964 **Don C. Winston,** *McGraw-Hill*
1965 **Bernard D. Nossiter,** *Washington Post*
1966 **Lawrence Malkin,** Associated Press
1967 **Ray Vicker,** *Wall Street Journal*
1968 **Clyde Farnsworth,** *New York Times*
1969 **Philip W. Whitcomb,** *Christian Science Monitor*
1970 **Leonard S. Silk,** *New York Times*
1971 **Clyde Farnsworth, Hy Maidenberg, Brendan Jones, Edward Cowan, Takashi Oka,** *New York Times*
1972 **Bob Wicker,** editor; **George Eberl, Ed Reavis, Ken Loomis, Jim Cole, Regis Bossu, Peter Jaeger,** *Stars and Stripes* (European Edition)
1973 **Ronald Koven and David B. Ottaway,** *Washington Post*
1974 **Philip W. Whitcomb,** *Christian Science Monitor*
1975 **J.A. Livingston,** McGraw Hill, *Business Week*
1976 **Alfred Zanker,** *U.S. News & World Report*
1977 **Carey Reich,** *Institutional Investor*
1978 **Andrew Nagorski,** *Newsweek International*
1979 **William Holstein,** United Press International
1980 **Not available at press time**

The Robert Capa Gold Medal, named after *Life* photographer, recognizes superlative photography requiring exceptional courage and enterprise abroad.

1955 **Howard Sochurek,** Magnum Photos, in *Life*
1956 **John Sadovy,** *Life*
1957 **No award**
1958 **Paul Bruck,** CBS
1959 **Mario Biasetti,** CBS
1960 **Yung Su Kwon,** NBC
1961 **No award**
1962 **Peter and Klaus, Dehmel,** NBC
1963 **Larry Burrows,** *Life*
1964 **Horst Faas,** AP
1965 **Larry Burrows,** *Life*
1966 **Henri Huet,** AP
1967 **David Douglas Duncan,** *Life* and ABC
1968 **John Olson,** *Life*
1969 **Anonymous Czech photographer**
1970 **Kyoichi Sawada,** UPI
1971 **Larry Burrows,** *Life*
1972 **Clive W. Limpkin,** London (book, *Battle of Bogside*, Penguin Books)
1973 **David Burnett, Raymond Depardon and Charles Gerretsen,** Gamma Presse Images
1974 **W. Eugene Smith,** *Camera 35*
1975 **Dick Halstead,** *Time*
1976 **Catherine Leroy,** Gamma, photos in *Time*
1977 **Eddie Adams,** Associated Press
1978 **Susan Meiselas,** *Time*
1979 **Kaveh Golestan,** *Time*
1980 **Not available at press time**

RADIO AND/OR TV

1941 **Cecil Brown,** MBS
1947 **Merrill Mueller,** NBC
1948 **Henry Cassidy,** NBC
1949 **William R. Downs,** CBS
1950 **Howard K. Smith,** CBS
1951 **Howard K. Smith,** CBS
1952 **Howard K. Smith,** CBS
1953 **Howard K. Smith,** CBS
1954 **Columbia Broadcasting System**
1955 **David Schoenbrun,** CBS
1956 **Irving R. Levine,** NBC
1957 **Frank Kearns and Yussef Masraff,** CBS
1958 **Winston Burdette,** CBS
1959 **Columbia Broadcasting System**

RADIO

1960 **Edwin Newman,** NBC
1961 **Marvin Kalb,** CBS
1962 **Sidney Lazard,** ABC
1963 **George Clay,** NBC
1964 **Dean Brelis,** NBC
1965 **Richard Valeriani,** NBC
1966 **Sam Jaffe,** ABC
1967 **Don North,** ABC
1968 **Bernard Redmont,** Group W Westinghouse
1969 **Steve Bell,** ABC
1970 **Lou Cioffi,** ABC; and **Emerson Stone,** director, with **Gerald Miller, John Laurence, Ike Pappas, William Plante, John Sheahan, Richard Threlkeld** and **Don Webster,** CBS team
1971 **Emerson Stone,** director, with **Thomas Fenton, John Laurence, William Plante, Bert Quint, Don Webster** and **Ernest Weatherall,** CBS team
1972 **Heywood Hale Broun, John Laurence, Dave Marash, Bruno Wessertheil, Bill McLaughlin, Mitchell Krauss,** CBS team
1973 **Gene Pell,** director, with **Jay Bushinsky, Koe Kamalick, Asher Wall, Bernard Redmont, Charles Bierbauer, Ed De Fontaine, Jim Anderson, Jerry Udwin,** Group W Westinghouse team
1974 **Sam Cioffi** and seventeen correspondents, ABC News team
1975 **Ed Bradley, Peter Collins, Bruce Dunning, Brian Ellis, Murray Fromson, Bill Plante, Bob Simon, Richard Threlked, Eric Cavaliero** and **Mike Snitowsky,** CBS team
1976 **William Blakemore, John Cooley, Charles Glass** and **Jerry King,** ABC team
Mike Lee and **Doug Tunnell,** CBS team

RADIO INTERPRETATION OF FOREIGN NEWS (Lowell Thomas Award)

1977 **Clark Tood,** NBC
1978 **Josh Darsa,** National Public Radio
1979 **CBS News team**
1980 **Not available at press time**

TELEVISION REPORTING/SPOT REPORTING

1949 **Ernest K. Lindley,** Dumont
1950 **Howard K. Smith,** CBS
1951 **Edward R. Murrow,** CBS
1952 **Edward R. Murrow,** CBS
1953 **Edward R. Murrow,** CBS
1955 ***See It Now,* CBS**
1955 **Edward R. Murrow,** CBS
1956 See above: Radio or TV
1957 See above: Radio or TV
1958 See above: Radio or TV
1959 See above: Radio or TV
1960 **Columbia Broadcasting System**
1961 **Helen Jean Rogers and William Hartigan,** ABC
1962 **NBC News**
1963 **Peter Kalischer,** CBS
1964 **Frank Bourgholtzer,** NBC
1965 **Morley Safer,** CBS
1966 **Morley Safer,** CBS
1967 **Ted Yates,** NBC
1968 **Liz Trotta,** NBC

1969 **Don Baker,** ABC
1970 **Kenley Jones,** NBC
1971 **Phil Brady,** NCB
1972 **Bob Simon,** correspondent, **Norman Lloyd,** cameramen, **Mai Van Duc,** camerman, CBS News team
1973 **John Laurence,** CBS
1974 **Lou Cioffi,** ABC
1975 **Bruce Dunning,** correspondent; **Mike Marriott,** camerman; **Mai Van Duc,** soundman, CBS team
1976 **Mike Lee,** CBS
1978 **Don Harris** and **Bob Brown,** NBC News
1979 **Bill Stewart** and **Jack Clark,** ABC News
1980 **Not available at press time**

BEST RADIO DOCUMENTARY ON FOREIGN AFFAIRS

1971 **John Rich,** NBC
1972 **Ramsey Clark,** ABC Radio News
1973 **Peter Wells, producer, Reid Collins,** correspondent, CBS News
1974 **Ted Koppel,** ABC News

BEST TV DOCUMENTARY ON FOREIGN AFFAIRS

1971 **George Watson and Ernest Pendrell,** ABC
1972 **Elmer Lower, Charles Murphy, John Sherman,** ABC team
1973 **Harry Reasoner,** ABC
1974 **Bill McLaughlin,** CBS News

BEST TV INTERPRETATION (Edward R. Murrow Award)

1977 **Barbara Walters,** ABC
1978 **ABC News Close Up,** "Terror in the Promised Land"
1979 **Ed Bradley, Andrew Lack, Howard Stringer, Greg Cooke** and **Ian Wilson,** CBS News
1980 **Not available at press time**

BEST MAGAZINE REPORTING FROM ABROAD

1955 **Theodore H. White,** *Collier's*
1956 **Flora Lewis,** *New York Times Magazine*
1957 **James Michener,** *Reader's Digest*
1958 **Joseph Kraft,** in *Saturday Evening Post*
1959 **George Bailey,** *The Reporter*
1960 ***The Reporter***
1961 **Charles J. V. Murphy,** *Fortune*
1962 **Robert Kaiser,** Time-Life News Service
1963 **Laura Bergquist,** *Look*
1964 ***Sports Illustrated***
1965 **Michael Mok and Paul Schutzer,** *Life*
1966 **Sybille Bedford,** *Saturday Evening Post*
1967 **Linda Grant Martin,** *New York Times Magazine*
1968 **J. Robert Moskin,** *Look*
1969 **Christopher Wren,** *Look*
1970 **Robert Shaplen,** *The New Yorker*
1971 **Arnaud de Borchgrave,** *Newsweek*
1972 **Joseph Kraft,** *The New Yorker*
1973 **Anthony Bailey,** *The New Yorker*
1974 **Frances FitzGerald,** *Harper's Magazine*
1975 **John J. Putnam,** *National Geographic*
1976 **Barry Came, Tony Clifton, Loren Jenkins and William Schmidt,** *Newsweek*

BEST MAGAZINE INTERPRETATION OF FOREIGN AFFAIRS

1977 **Joseph B. Treaster,** *Atlantic Monthly*
1978 **No award**
1979 **Sidney Zion** and **Uri Dan,** *New York Times Magazine*
1980 **Not available at press time**

MOTION PICTURES

1956 **Gerhard Schwartzkopff,** CBS
1957 See below: Still or Motion Pictures
1958 **Joseph Oexle,** NBC
1959 **Henry Toluzzi,** NBC
1960 **Yung Su Kwon,** NBC
1961 **Leonard Stark and Nobuo Hoshi,** NBC
1962 **NBC News**
1963 **Columbia Broadcasting System**

STILL OR MOTION PICTURES

1957 **Lisa Larsen,** Freelance, in *Life*

BEST REPORTING ORIGINATING IN U.S. OR U.N. ON WORLD AFFAIRS

1954 **James Reston,** *New York Times*
1955 **John Daly,** CBS

BEST REPORTING INVOLVING PERSONS, PLACES OR THINGS, BEYOND THE 48 STATES

1956 ***Sports Illustrated***

BEST INTERPRETATION OF FOREIGN AFFAIRS DAILY NEWSPAPER OR WIRE SERVICE

1947 **Anne O'Hare McCormick,** *New York Times*
1948 **James Reston,** *New York Times*
1949 **Joseph and Stewart Alsop,** *New York Herald Tribune*
1950 **James Reston,** *New York Times*
1951 **Joseph and Stewart Alsop,** *New York Herald Tribune*
1952 **James Reston,** *New York Times*
1953 **Walter Lippmann,** *New York Herald Tribune*
1954 ***New York Times***
1955 **Walter Lippmann,** *New York Herald Tribune*
1956 See below: All Media
1957 **Ernest K. Lindley** *Newsweek*
1958 **Graham Hovey,** *Minneapolis Star and Tribune*
1959 **Walter Lippmann,** *New York Herald Tribune*
1960 **Robert Hewett,** *Minneapolis Star and Tribune*
1961 **Phil Newsom,** United Press International
1962 **Flora Lewis,** *Washington Post*
1963 **Louis K. Rukeyser,** *Baltimore Sun*
1964 **Max Frankel,** *New York Times*
1965 **Jack Foisie,** *Los Angeles Times*
1966 **Robert S. Elegant,** *Los Angeles Times*
1967 **Michael R. McGrady,** *Newsday*
R. W. Apple. Jr., *New York Times*
1968 **Robert S. Elegant,** *Los Angeles Times*
Stanley Karnow, *Washington Post*
1969 **Max Frankel,** *New York Times*
1970 **Harrison E. Salisbury,** *New York Times*
1971 **Robert S. Elegant,** *Los Angeles Times*
1972 **William L. Ryan,** Associated Press
1973 **Al Burt,** *Miami Herald;*
William Montalbano, *Miami Herald*
1974 **Donald L. Barlett and James B. Steele,** *Philadelphia Inquirer*
1975 **Joseph C. Harsch,** *Christian Science Monitor*
1976 **Flora Lewis,** *New York Times*
1977 **Michael Robersteen,** *Minneapolis Tribune*

RADIO

1947 **Edward R. Murrow,** CBS
1948 **Elmer Davis,** ABC
1949 See below: Radio or TV
1950 **Edward R. Murrow,** CBS
1951 **Elmer Davis,** ABC
1952 **Elmer Davis,** ABC

1953 **Elmer Davis,** ABC
1954 **CBS World News Roundup**
1955 **Eric Sevareid.** CBS
1956 See below: All Media
1957-60 See below: Radio or TV
1961 **Howard K. Smith,** CBS
1962 **Alexander Kendrick,** CBS
1963 **Phil Clarke,** MBS
1964 **Bill Sheehan,** ABC
1965 **Edward P. Morgan,** ABC
1966 **NBC News**
1967 **Welles Hangen and James Robinson,** NBC
1968 **Elie Abel,** NBC
1969 **Alexander Kendrick,** CBS
1970 **Peter Burns, Kenley Jones, Bob Green, Phil Brady, Lou Davis, Robert Goralski,** NBC team
1971 **James Quigley,** producer; **Wilson Hall,** anchorman, NBC Team
1972 **John Chancellor,** NBC
1973 **Dan Rather, Marvin Kalb, Bob Schieffer,** CBS Team
1974 **John Chancellor,** NBC
1975 **Charles P. Arnot,** ABC Radio News; **Steve Bell,** ABC cameraman; **Lou Cioffi,** ABC: **John Grimes,** American Information Radio Network; **Peter Jennings,** ABC; **Ted Koppel,** ABC; **Mike Stein,** executive producer, and **George Watson,** ABC, on ABC News
Morton Dean, CBS News; correspondents **Murray Fromson, Bill Plante and Richard Threlkeld; Marvin Kalb; John Lawrence; Ike Pappas and Robert Pierpoint,** White House correspondent, CBS News
1976 **Charles Collingwood,** anchorman; **Jonathan Ward,** producer, **Frank Delecki and Norman Morris,** CBS News

BEST RADIO SPOT FROM ABROAD (Ben Grauer Award)

1977 **Reid Collins, Tom Fenton, Christopher Glen, Mike Lee, Bob McNamara, Burt Quint, John Sheehan, Bob Simon, Doug Tunnell and Bruno Wassertheil,** CBS Team
1978 **Tom Fenton,** Lou Wheaton and Hal Moore, Associated Press Radio Network

RADIO OR TELEVISION

1949 **Edward R. Murrow,** CBS
1950-55 See above: Radio
1956 See below: All Media
1957 **Chet Huntley,** NBC
1958 **Chet Huntley,** NBC
1959 **Quincy Howe,** ABC
1960 **Chet Huntley,** NBC

TELEVISION

1961 **David Schoenbrun,** CBS
1962 **Columbia Broadcasting System**
1963 **Fred Freed,** NBC
1964 **Marvin Kalb,** CBS
1965 **Fred Freed,** NBC
1966 **Howard K. Smith,** ABC
1967 **Eric Sevareid,** CBS
1968 **Charles Collingwood,** CBS
1969 **Elie Abel, Dean Brelis, Wilson Hall, George Murray,** NBC Team
1970 **Ted Koppel,** ABC
1971 **John Hart,** CBS
1973 **Helen Marmor,** producer; **Edwin Newman,** anchorman; and seventeen correspondents, NBC team
1974 **John Palmer, Tom Streithorst, Phil Brady, Liz Trotta,** NBC Nightly News Team
1975 **Bill Seamans and Howard K. Smith,** ABC
1976 **John Chancellor,** anchorman, and **Dan O'Connor,** producer, NBC News
1977 **Barbara Walters,** ABC News

ALL MEDIA

1956 **Cecil Brown,** NBC

MAGAZINE (Mary Hemingway Award)

1964 **Norman Cousins,** *Saturday Review*
1965 **A.M. Rosenthal,** *New York Times Magazine*
1966 **Erik Sevareid,** *Look*
1967 **Frances FitzGerald,** *Atlantic Monthly*
1968 **James C. Thomson, Jr.,** *Atlantic Monthly*
1969 **Carl Rowan,** *Reader's Digest*
Norman Cousins, *Saturday Review* and *Look*
1970 **Anthony Lewis,** *New York Times Magazine*
1971 **John L. Cobbs and Gordon L. Williams,** *Business Week*
1972 **James A. Michener,** *New York Times Magazine*
1973 **Edward R.F. Sheehan,** *New York Times Magazine*
1974 **Robert Shaplen,** *New Yorker*
1975 **Arnaud de Borchgarve,** *Newsweek*
1976 **Robert Shaplen,** *The New Yorker*
1977 **James Pringle, Elizabeth Peer, Arnaud de Bouchgarve and Kim Willenson,** *Newsweek*
1978 **Peter A. Iseman,** *Harper's*
1979 **Walter Isaacson** and **Donald Neff,** *Time*
1980 **Not available at press time**

BOOK (Cornelius Ryan Award)

1957 **David Schoenbrun,** *As France Goes*
1958 **John Gunther,** *Inside Russia Today*
1959 **Cornelius Ryan,** *The Longest Day*
1960 **William L. Shirer,** *The Rise and Fall of the Third Reich*
1961 **John Toland,** *But Not in Shame*
1962 **Seymour Freidin,** *The Forgotten People*
1963 **Dan Kurzman,** *Subversion of the Innocents*
1964 **Robert Trumbull,** *The Scrutable East*
1965 **Robert Shaplen,** *The Last Revolution*
1966 **Welles Hangen,** *The Muted Revolution*
1967 **George F. Kennan,** *Memoirs, 1925-1950*
1968 **George W. Ball,** *The Discipline of Power*
1969 **Townsend Hoopes,** *The Limits of Intervention*
1970 **John Toland,** *The Rising Sun*
1971 **Anthony Austin,** *The President's War*
1972 **David Halberstam,** *The Best and the Brightest*
1973 **C. L. Sulzberger,** *An Age of Mediocrity*
1974 **Cornelius Ryan,** *A Bridge Too Far*
1975 **Phillip Knightley,** *The First Casualty*
1976 **John Toland,** *Adolph Hitler*
1977 **David McCullough,** *The Path Between the Seas*
1978 **Tad Szulc,** *The Illusion of Peace: Foreign Policy in the Nixon Years*
1979 **Peter Wyden**
1980 **Not available at press time**

The Bob Considine Award, which carries a $1,000 stipend from King Features, is given for reporting from abroad in any medium that required exceptional courage and initiative.

1975 **Sydney Schanberg,** *New York Times*
1976 **Robin Wright,** *Christian Science Monitor*

1977 **Jim Hoagland,** *Washington Post*
1978 **Flora Lewis,** *New York Times*
1979 **Ray Vicker,** *Wall Street Journal*
1980 **Not available at press time**

SUPPLEMENTARY AWARDS

1940 **Halbert Abend,** *New York Times*
Edward R. Murrow, CBS

SPECIAL AWARDS

1961 **Robert Fuoss,** *Saturday Evening Post;* **John Denson,** *New York Herald Tribune,* for new and original concepts in the field of communication of ideas
1964 **John Scali,** ABC News, for outstanding journalistic achievement
Station KTLA-TV, Los Angeles, and **Baldwin Baker, Jr.** for outstanding journalistic achievement
1965 **David Sarnoff**
1966 **Henry R. Luce**

EDITORIAL

1979 **Paul Heath Hoeffel**
1980 **Not available at press time**

The $350 Madeline Dane Ross Award honors international reporting showing a concern for humanity.

1973 **Robert Northshield and Vo Huynh,** NBC
1974 **K. Kenneth Paik and Harry Jones, Jr.,** *Kansas City Times*
1975 **Mayo Moh,** *Time*
1976 **June Goodwin,** *Christian Science Monitor*
1977 **Reza Baraheni,** *Penthouse*
1978 **Alvaro Jose Brenes de Peralta** and **Jeannine Yeomans,** KRON-TV
1979 **Jean-Pierre LaFont,** Sygma Agency
1980 **Not available at press time**

First Prize

DREW PEARSON FOUNDATION

The $5,000 First Prize is awarded on a vote of the board of directors to recognize excellence in investigative journalism. The current status of the foundation and the award are unknown.

1971 **Neil Sheehan,** *New York Times* (Pentagon Papers)
1972 **Robert Woodward and Carl Bernstein,** *Washington Post* (Watergate)
1973 **Jerry Landauer,** *Wall Street Journal* (Vice President Spiro Agnew)
1974 **Richard E. Cady, William E. Anderson and Harley Bierce,** *Indianapolis News* (Police corruption)
1975 **No award**
1976 **Seymour Hersh,** *New York Times* (Central Intelligence Agency)

Current Status Unknown

Penney-Missouri Newspaper Awards
Penney-Missouri Magazine Awards

PENNEY-MISSOURI JOURNALISM AWARDS PROGRAM
University of Missouri, 213 Walter Williams Hall, Columbia, Mo. 65201 (314/882-7771)

The Penney-Missouri Newspaper Awards are given annually for excellence in reporting and editing stories on people and lifestyles in community, daily and weekly newspapers in the United States. The first-place winners, indicated below, receive a $1,000 cash award, a medallion and a certificate. Runnerup cash prizes are also given. A screening committee narrows down entries for an eight-judge committee, which makes the final selection.

METRO DAILIES

1973 **Ruth C. D'Arcy,** Detroit News
1974 **Richard Estrin,** *Newsday*
1975 **Richard Estrin,** *Newsday*
1976 **Martha Liebrum,** *Houston Post*
1977 **Janet Mandelstam,** *Detroit News*
1978 **Phyllis Singer,** *Newsday*
1979 **John Cashman,** *Newsday*
1980 **Frank Denton,** *Detroit Free Press*

CLASS I (Small circulation)

1960 **Carol Black and Ann DeLeo,** *Middleton* (N.Y.) *Daily Record*
1961 **Dorothy Clifford,** *Tallahassee* (Fla.) *Democrat*
1962 **Dorothy-Ann Flor,** *Pompano Beach* (Fla.) *Sun-Sentinel*
1963 **Anne Rowe,** *St. Petersburg* (Fla.) *Independent*
1964 **Florence Burge,** *Reno* (Nev.) *Evening Gazette*
1965 **Helen Cheney,** *Salisbury* (N.C.) *Post*
1966 **Marilyn Reynolds,** *Yakima* (Wash,) *Daily Republic*
1967 **Dorothy-Ann Flor,** *Lakeland* (Fla.) *Ledger*
1968 **Betty Danfield,** *The Paper,* (Oshkosh, Wisc.)
1969 **Betty Danfield,** *The Paper,* (Oshkosh, Wisc.)
1970 **Mary Bach,** *Scottsdale* (Ariz.) *Progress*
1971 **Betty Ann Raymond,** *Montana Standard* (Butte)
1972 **Lucille Kahn,** *Melbourne* (Fla.) *Times*
1973 **Lucille Kahn,** *Melbourne* (Fla.) *Times*
1974 **Pat Haley,** *Keene* (N.H.) *Sentinel*
1975 **Gloria Bledsoe,** *Salem* (Ore.) *Capitol Journal*
1976 **Joyce Gabriel,** Westchester-Rockland (N.Y.) Newspapers
1977 **Kathryn W. Foster,** *Greenville* (S.C.) *Piedmont*
1978 **Nancy Pate,** *Fayetteville (N.C.) Times*
1979 **Jennifer Thompson,** *Greenwich* (Conn.) *Time*
1980 **Glenna L. Neubert,** *Leesburg* (Fla.) *Commercial*

CLASS II (Medium circulation)

1960 **Margaret W. Claiborne,** *Charlotte* (N.C.) *News*
1961 **Margaret W. Claiborne,** *Charlotte* (N.C.) *News*
1962 **Edee Green,** *Fort Lauderdale* (Fla.) *News*
1963 **Marj Heyduck,** *Dayton* (Ohio) *Journal-Herald*
1964 **Marie Saulsbury,** *San Bernardino* (Calif.) *Daily Sun*
1965 **William Wundram,** *Davenport* (Iowa) *Times-Democrat*
1966 **Gloria Briggs,** *Today* (Cocoa, Fla.)
1967 **Arlene Alligood,** *Suffolk Sun* (Deer Park, N.Y.)
1968 **Kathryn Robinette,** *Palm Beach* (Fla.) *Post-Times*
1969 **Beryl Ann Brownell,** *Gary* (Ind.) *Post-Tribune*
1970 **Gloria Biggs,** *Today* (Cocoa, Fla.)
1971 **Betty Danfield,** *Riverside* (Calif.) *Press-Enterprise*

1972 **Jan Monahan,** *Pompano Beach* (Fla.) *Sentinel Sun*
1973 **Mary Ann Hill,** *Today* (Cocoa, Fla.)
1974 **Clara Trampe,** *Rockland County* (N.Y.) *Journal-News*
1975 **George M. Pica,** *Eugene* (Ore.) *Register-Guard*
1976 **George M. Pica,** *Eugene* (Ore.) *Register-Guard*
1977 **William Wundram,** *Quad-City Times* (Davenport, Iowa)
1978 **Myra T. Frosberg,** *Fort Myers* (Fla.) *News-Press*
1979 **Janet H. Woods,** *St. Petersburg* (Fla.) *Evening Independent*
1980 **Janet H. Woods,** *St. Petersburg* (Fla.) *Evening Independent*

CLASS III (Large circulation)

1960 **Marie Anderson,** *Miami Herald*
1961 **Marie Anderson,** *Miami Herald*
1962 **Nancy Taylor,** *Miami News*
1963 **Billie O'Day,** *Miami News*
1964 **Marie Anderson,** *Miami Herald*
1965 **Aileen Ryan,** *Milwaukee Journal*
1966 **Lou Schwartz,** *Newsday* (Garden City, N.Y.)
1967 **Madeleine McDermott,** *Houston Chronicle*
1968 **Marilyn Gardner,** *Milwaukee Journal*
1969 **Marie Anderson,** *Miami Herald*
1970 **Marie Anderson,** *Miami Herald*
1971 **Carol Sutton,** *Louisville Courier-Journal*
1972 **Marion Purcelli,** *Chicago Tribune*
1973 **Nan Trent,** *Christian Science Monitor*
1974 **Buddy Martin,** *St. Petersburg Times*
1975 **James McGuire,** *Des Moines Register*
1976 **Mary Mills,** *Fort Lauderdale* (Fla.) *News*
1977 **Joyce Gabriel,** *Akron* (Ohio) *Beacon-Journal*
1978 **J. Ford Huffman,** *Rochester* (N.Y.) *Times-Union*
1979 **Dorothy Smiljanich,** *St. Petersburg* (Fla.) *Times*
1980 **Melissa H. East,** *Fort Lauderdale News*

CLASS IV (weeklies)

1961 **Rosemary Madison,** *Dundee Sun* (Omaha, Neb).
1962 **Ethel Taylor,** *Van Nuys* (Calif.) *News*
1963 **Marianne Scott,** *Arlington Heights* (Ill.) *Herald*
1964 **Thelma Barrios,** *San Fernando Valley* (Calif.) *Sun*
1965 **Ethel Taylor,** *Van Nuys* (Calif.) *News*
1966 **Marianne Scott,** *Arlington Heights* (Ill.) *Herald*
1967 **Judy Flander,** *Coalinga* (Calif.) *Record*
1968 **Marianne Scott,** *Arlington Heights* (Ill.) *Herald*
1969 **Sandra Wesley,** *Boca Raton* (Fla.) *News*
1970 **Ann Clevenger,** *Encinitas* (Calif.) *Coast Dispatch*
1971 **Anita Richwine,** *Kettering-Oakwood* (Ohio) *Times*
1972 **Alice Snyder,** *Glenview Announcements* (Wilmette, Ill.)
1973 **Kristy Montee,** *Southfield* (Miss.) *Eccentric*
1974 **Jennifer Frosh,** *Montgomery County Sentinel* (Rockville, Md.)
1975 **Peter Cox,** *Maine Times*
1976 **Suzanne Ashmun,** *Gresham* (Ore) *Outlook*
1977 **Andy Zipser,** *Port Jefferson* (N.Y.) *Record*
1978 **Lori Varosh,** *Gresham* (Ore.) *Outlook*
1979 **Ande Zellman,** *Boston Phoenix*
1980 **Ande Zellman,** *Boston Phoenix*

FASHION AND CLOTHING REPORTING (no circulation limit)

1960 **Eleni Epstein,** *Washington Star*
1961 **Jean Cameron,** *Chicago American*
1962 **Graydon Heartsill,** *Dallas Times Herald*
1963 **Yvonne Petrie,** *Detroit News*
1964 **Ruth Wagner,** *Washington Post*
1965 **Anne Lee Singletary,** *Twin City Sentinel* (Winston-Salem, N.C.)
1966 **Marian Christy,** *Boston Globe*
1967 **Vivian Kawatzky,** *Milwaukee Sentinel*
1968 **Marian Christy,** *Boston Globe*
1969 **Marji Kunz,** *Detroit Free Press*
1970 **Marian Christy,** *Boston Globe*
1971 **Ruth Hawkins,** *Norfolk* (Va.) *Ledger-Star*
1972 **Jo Werne,** *Miami Herald*
1973 **Carol Sutton,** *Louisville* (Ky.) *Courier-Journal*
1974 **Judy Lunn,** *Houston Post*
1975 **Betty Ommerman,** *Newsday* (Garden City, N.Y.)
1976 **Marji Kunz,** *Detroit Free Press*
1977 **Eva Hodges,** *Denver Post*
1978 **Amy Griffith,** *Charleston* (W.Va.) *Daily Mail*
1979 **Nancy Webb Hatton,** *Miami News*
1980 **James McBride,** *Wilmington Evening Journal*

REPORTING-WRITING (no circulation limit)

1964 **Dorothy Brant Brazier,** *Seattle Times*
1965 **Lois Hagen Manly,** *Milwaukee Journal*
1966 **Pat Millard Hunter,** *Honolulu Advertiser*
1967 **Pat Millard Hunter,** *Honolulu Advertiser*
1968 **Bobbi McCallum,** *Seattle Post-Intelligencer*
1969 **Helen Fogel,** *Detroit Free Press*
1970 **Elaine Morrissey,** *Dayton* (Ohio) *Daily News*
1971 **Judith Anderson,** *San Francisco Chronicle*

PAUL MYHRE AWARD FOR EXCELLENCE IN REPORTING — SERIES

1972 **Bella Stumbo,** *Los Angeles Times*
1973 **Barbara Abel,** *Milwaukee Journal*
1974 **Sandy Flickner,** *Miami Herald*
1975 **Margo Huston,** *Milwaukee Journal*
1976 **Rosemary J. McClure,** *San Bernardino* (Calif.) *Sun-Telegram*
1977 **Margo Huston,** *Milwaukee Journal*
1978 **Mark Miller** and **Richard Whitmire,** *Binghamton* (N.Y.) *Sun Bulletin*
1979 **Kathy Satterfield** and **Carol Viescas,** *El Paso Times*
1980 **Richard Whitmire,** *Rochester* (N.Y.) *Times Union*

PAUL MYHRE AWARD FOR EXCELLENCE IN REPORTING — SINGLE STORY

1972 **Jan Grimley,** *Davenport* (Iowa) *Times-Democrat*
1973 **Ena Naunton,** *Miami Herald*
1974 **Judy Klemesrud,** *New York Times*
1975 **Andrew Malcolm,** *New York Times*
1976 **Frances Craig,** *Des Moines* (Iowa) *Register*
1977 **Richard Severo,** *New York Times*
1978 **Walter Bogdanich** and **Walter Johns, Jr.,** *Cleveland Plain Dealer*
1979 **Dan D. Morain,** *Longview* (Wash.) *Daily News*
1980 **Richard S. Vonier,** *Tucson Citizen*

PHOTOGRAPHY — PICTURE LAYOUT

1965 **George Skadding,** *Pompano Beach* (Fla.) *Sun-Sentinel*
1966 **Gary Settle,** *Wilmington* (Del.) *Journal*
1967 **James Johnson,** *Wichita* (Kans.) *Eagle Beacon*
1968 **Al McLaughlin,** *Daily Oklahoman* (Oklahoma City)
1969 **John Bowden,** *Washington Star*
1970 **Barry Edmonds,** *Flint* (Mich.) *Journal*
1971 **Nathan Benn,** *Palm Beach* (Fla.) *Post-Times*

PHOTOGRAPHY — STORY-TELLING PICTURE

1965 **Bob Eighmie,** *Fort Lauderdale* (Fla.) *News*
1966 **Gary Settle,** *Wilmington* (Del.) *Journal*

1967 **Anthony Lopez,** *Today* (Cocoa, Fla.)
1968 **Judd Gunderson,** *Los Angeles Times*
1969 **Cookie Snyder,** *Twin City Sentinel* (Winston-Salem, N.C.)
1970 **Gordon Alexander,** *New London* (Conn.) *Day*
1971 **Ken Wesley,** *San Bernardino* (Calif.) *Sun-Telegram*

PHOTOGRAPHY — PERSONALITY PORTRAIT

1965 **Don Martin,** *Charlotte* (N.C.) *News*
1966 **Donald Nussbaum,** *Milwaukee Journal*
1967 **Donn Gould,** *Pompano Beach* (Fla.) *Sun Sentinel*
1968 **Perry Riddle,** *Chicago Daily News*
1969 **Lee Romero,** *Providence* (R.I.) *Journal*
1970 **Ed Stein,** *Wisconsin State Journal* (Madison)
1971 **Fred Comegys,** *Wilmington* (Del.) *News-Journal*

WOMEN'S PAGE PHOTOGRAPHER OF THE YEAR

1965 **Mary Frampton,** *Los Angeles Times*
1966 **Al McLaughlin,** *Daily Oklahoman* and *Oklahoma City Times*
1967 **David Nance,** *Houston Chronicle*
1968 **James Johnson,** *Wichita* (Kans.) *Eagle and Beacon*
1969 **Gary Settle,** *Chicago Daily News*
1970 **Bill Luster,** *Louisville* (Ky.) *Courier-Journal* and *Times*
1971 **Bob Coyle,** *Dubuque* (Iowa) *Telegraph-Herald*

CONSUMER AFFAIRS REPORTING

1974 **Phil Weck,** *Bucks County Courier Times* (Levittown, Pa.)
1975 **Pat Ravenscraft,** *Akron* (Ohio) *Beacon-Journal*
1976 **Carolyn Nolte-Watts,** *St. Petersburg* (Fla.) *Times*
1977 **Jane E. Brody,** *New York Times*
1978 **Jim Sellers,** *Eugene* (Ore.) *Register-Guard*
1979 **Diane Clark** and **Don Carson,** *San Diego Union*
1980 **Linda Rockey** and **Carol Perkins,** *Seattle Post Intelligencer*

The Penney-Missouri Magazine Awards are given annually for excellent articles published the previous year on lifestyle in a magazine published in the United States, excluding company publications, fraternal magazines, alumnae publications and magazine supplements. Winners receive a $1,000 cash award and a Baccarat crystal obelisk. A screening committee narrows down entries for a four-judge panel which selects the winners.

HOME FURNISHINGS

1967 **Lois Whitcomb Bohling,** *House Beautiful*
1968 **Elizabeth Craster,** *Better Homes and Gardens*
1969 **Evan Frances,** *Ladies' Home Journal*
1970 **Dr. and Mrs. Edward Hall,** *House and Garden*
1971 **James A. Autry,** *Better Homes and Gardens*

HOUSEHOLD MANAGEMENT

1967 **Anna Fisher Rush,** *McCall's*
1968 **Peter Lindberg,** *Better Homes and Gardens*
1969 **Margaret Counsins,** *House Beautiful*
1970 **Selwyn Raab,** *McCall's*
1971 **Betty Furness,** *McCall's*

HEALTH

1967 **Matt Clark,** *Newsweek*
1968 **Gilbert Cant,** *Time*
1969 **Susanna McBee,** *Life*
1970 **Phyllis Starr,** *Glamour*
1971 **Matt Clark,** *Newsweek*
1972 **Walter McQuade,** *Fortune*
1973 **Paul J. Dolan,** *Family Health*
1974 **Charles and Bonnie Remsberg,** *Good Housekeeping*
1975 **Matt Clark,** *Newsweek*
1976 **Kathryn Livingston,** *Town and Country*
1977 **General Jonas,** *The New Yorker*
1978 **Berton Roueche,** *The New Yorker*
1979 **Janet Malvolm,** *The New Yorker*
1980 **Judson Gooding,** *Across the Board*

FASHION AND BEAUTY

1967 **Gloria Guiness,** *Harper's Bazaar*
1968 **Eleanor Carruth,** *Fortune*
1969 **Lawrence S. Martz, Jr.,** *Newsweek*
1970 **Mary Butler,** *Harper's Bazaar*
1971 **Harry F. Walters,** *Newsweek*

SPECIAL INTEREST

1967 **Ponchitta Pierce,** *Ebony*
1968 **Alex Poinsett,** *Ebony*
1969 **Sylvie Reice,** *McCall's*
1970 **Natalie Gittelson,** *Harper's Bazaar*
1971 **Kurt Vonnegut, Jr.,** *Vogue*

PHOTOGRAPHY

1968 **Otto Storch,** *McCall's*
1969 **Toni Frissell,** *Life*
1970 **Co Rentmeester,** *Life*
1971 **Co Rentmeester,** *Life*

SMALL CIRCULATION (under 400,000) MAGAZINES

1969 **Harriet Goslins,** *Pace*
1970 **Gloria Steinem,** *New York Magazine*
1971 **Jane O'Reilly,** *New York Magazine*
1972 **Peyton Bailey,** *Bride's Magazine*
1973 **Susan Edmiston,** *MS.*
1974 **Mimi Sheraton,** *New York Magazine*
1975 **Ann Geracimos,** *womenSports*
Barbara Baer and Glenna Matthews, *The Nation*
1976 **Prudence Mackintosh,** *Texas Monthly*
1977 **Sam Merrill,** *New Times*
Loretta Schwartz, *Philadelphia*
1978 **John Davidson,** *Texas Monthly*
Mavis Kennedy, *The Washingtonian*
1979 **Michael Ryan,** *Boston Magazine*
1980 **Vene Jackson,** *Chicago*

CONSUMERISM

1972 **Ralph Nader,** *Ladies' Home Journal*
1973 **Joseph N. Bell,** *Good Housekeeping*
1974 **Nora Ephron,** *Esquire*
1975 **William Mead,** *Money*
1976 **Maury Levy,** *Philadelphia*
1977 **Bil Gilbert,** *Sports Illustrated*
1978 **Mark Dowie,** *Mother Jones*
1979 **Susan Quinn,** *Boston Magazine*
1980 **George J. Church** and **Edward Magnuson,** *Time*

PERSONAL LIFESTYLE

1972 **Dorothy B. Seiberling,** *Life*
1973 **Betty Marker,** *Parents' Magazine*
1974 **Jean Stafford,** *Vogue*
1975 **Gail Sheehy,** *New York Magazine*
1976 **Dan Rottenberg,** *Philadelphia*
1977 **Judith Ramsey,** *Family Circle*
1978 **John McPhee,** *The New Yorker*

1979 **Malcolm Cowley,** *Life*
1980 **Nicholas Lemann,** *Texas Monthly*

EXPANDING OPPORTUNITIES

1972 **Richard Boeth, Elizabeth Peer, Ann Ray Martin and Lisa Whitman,** *Newsweek*
1973 **Gloria Emerson,** *Vogue*
1974 **Judith Viorst,** *Redbook*
1975 **Pete Axthelm,** *Newsweek*
1976 **Susan Edmiston,** *Redbook*
1977 **William Broyles,** *Texas Monthly*
1978 **Frank Graham, Jr.,** *Audubon*
Jack Star, *Chicago*
1979 **Elizabeth Pope Frank,** *Good Housekeeping*
1980 **Lawrence E. Maloney** and **George Jones,** *U.S. News and World Report*

CONTEMPORARY LIVING

1972 **George Bush,** *Better Homes and Gardens*
1973 **Fredelle Maynard,** *Woman's Day*
1974 **Stefan Kanfer,** *Time*
1975 **Michael Demarest,** *Time*
1976 **Loretta Schwartz,** *Philadelphia*
1977 **Susan Edmiston,** *Woman's Day*
1978 **Bil Gilbert,** *Sports Illustrated*
1979 **Bil Gilbert,** *Sports Illustrated*
1980 **Bonnie Ghazarbekian,** *Ms.*

Journalism Award

AMERICAN SOCIETY OF PLANNING OFFICIALS
1313 E. 60th St., Chicago, Ill. 60637 (312/947-2560)

The annual Journalism Award, which consists of a $50 prize and a certificate, honors efforts to support, improve or initiate planning programs, or to inform the public about issues, problems and choices that confront them in improving their communities. Any daily or weekly newspaper in the United States, its territories and possessions and Canada may submit articles for selection by a three- to five-member judges panel.

1960 ***Minneapolis Star and Tribune***
1961 ***Sacramento Bee***
1962 ***Worcester Evening Gazette***
1963 ***Gainesville Daily Times***
1964 ***Honolulu Star-Bulletin***
1965 **Lloyd Hollister Publications**
1966 ***Milwaukee Journal***
1967 ***Milwaukee Journal***
1968 ***Sandusky Register***
1969 ***Louisville Courier-Journal***
1970 ***Louisville Courier-Journal and Times***
1971 ***Miami Herald*** and reporter **Juanita Greene**
1972 ***Detroit News*** and reporter **Don Ball**
1973 ***Milwaukee Journal*** and urban affairs writers **Gary C. Rummler, Chris Lecos, James Parks, Michael Kirkhorn and Paul G. Hayes**
Honolulu Advertiser and environment writer **Harold Hostetler**
Chicago Today for series by **Michael Hirsley** and another by **Wesley Hartzell and Fred Orehek**
1974 ***Arizona Daily Star***
Hartford Times and editotial writer **Don O. Noel, Jr.**
1975 ***Las Cruces Sun News*** (N.M.) and reporter **Barbara Kerr Page**
Newsday (Garden City, N.Y.) and reporters **Tom Morris, Henry Pearson and Ed Lowe**
1976 ***Deseret News*** (Salt Lake City) and reporter **Nick Snow**
1977 ***Port Huron Times Herald*** (Mich.) and reporter **Linda Heyboer**
Quincy Patriot Ledger (Mass.) and reporter **Doris M. Melville**
Tulsa World and reporter **Ann Patton**
1978 ***Cleveland Press*** and reporter **Fred McGunagle**
Washington Post and reporter **Felicity Barringer**
Hagerstown (Md.) ***Morning Herald*** and reporter **Herb Perone**
Trenton (N.J.) ***Times*** and reporter **Mark Jaffe**
1979 ***Miami Herald*** and reporter **Frederic Tasker**
San Francisco Bay Guardian and editor **Bruce Brugman**
1980 ***Dayton*** (Ohio) ***Daily News***
Oregon Journal (Portland)
Edmonton Journal and reporter **Jim McNulty**
Wichita Beacon and reporter **Martin Donsky**
Lansdale (Pa.) ***Reporter*** and reporters **Craig R. McCoy and John McQuiggan**

McKinney Award

NATIONAL NEWSPAPER ASSN.
1627 K St. NW, Washington, D.C. 20006 (202/466-7200)

The McKinney Award, which was established in 1966, honors an active newspaperwoman closely associated with a non-metropolitan newspaper serving a community of 50,000 or fewer people. Only the most recent recipients are listed here.

1975 **Doris Thompson**
1976 **Mary Baily**
1977 **Carmela T. Martin**
1978 **Louise Eaton**
1979 **No award**
1980 **Charlotte Schexnayder**

George Polk Awards

LONG ISLAND UNIVERSITY
University Plaza, Brooklyn, N.Y. 11201 (212/834-6170)

The George Polk Awards recognize distinguished achievement in journalism. The recipients of the Polk plaque are recommended by a national panel of former award winners, deans of journalism schools and news executives in all media. The winners are now selected by a committee of university alumni and faculty. While neither the number of awards nor the categories are restricted, custom has directed recognition in certain fields of journalism plus special awards. Until 1975 the awards, then known as the George Polk Memorial Awards, were administered by the university's Department of Journalism, which selected the recipients.

FOREIGN REPORTING

1949 **Homer Bigart,** *New York Herald Tribune*
1950 **Six-member reporting team,** *New York Herald Tribune*
1951 **Homer Bigart,** *New York Herald Tribune*
1952 **Milton Bracker and Virginia Lee Warren,** *New York Times*

1953 **Marguerite Higgins,** *New York Herald Tribune*
1954 **Jim Lucas,** Scripps-Howard Newspapers
1955 **George Weller,** Chicago Daily News Syndicate
1956 **Barrett McGurn,** *New York Herald Tribune*
1957 **Hal Lehrman,**
1958 **Harrison E. Salisbury,** *New York Times*
1959 **Chet Huntley and Reuven Frank,** National Broadcasting Co.
1960 **A.M. Rosenthal,** *New York Times*
1960 **James Morris,** *The Guardian* (Manchester, England)
1962 **Morris H. Rubin,** *The Progressive*
1963 **Dana Adams Schmidt,** *New York Times*
1964 **David Halberstam,** *New York Times*
1965 **Malcome W. Browne,** Associated Press
1966 **Dan Kurzman,** *Washington Post*
1967 **Harrison E. Salisbury,** *New York Times*
1968 **R.W. Apple, Jr.,** *New York Times*
1969 **No award**
1970 **Henry Kamm,** *New York Times*
1971 **Gloria Emerson,** *New York Times*
1972 **Sydney H. Schanberg,** *New York Times*
1973 **Jean Thoravel and Jean Leclerc du Sablon,** Agence France-Presse
1974 **Henry S. Bradsher,** *Washington Star-News*
1975 **Donald Kirk,** *Chicago Tribune*
1976 **No award**
1977 **Robert C. Toth,** *Los Angeles Times*
1978 **John F. Burns, John Darnton and Michael T. Kaufman,** *New York Times*
1979 **John Kifner,** *New York Times*
1980 **Shirley Christian,** *Miami Herald*

INTERNATIONAL REPORTING

1955 **Thomas J. Hamilton,** *New York Times*
1956 **Thomas J. Hamilton,** *New York Times*
1969 **David Kraslow and Stuart H. Loory,** *Los Angeles Times*

METROPOLITAN REPORTING

1949 **Malcolm Johnson,** *New York Sun*
1950 **No award**
1951 **Fern Marja,** *New York Post*
1952 **Richard Carter,** *New York Compass*
1953 **Edward J. Mowry,** *New York World-Telegram and Sun*
1954 **William Longgood,** *New York World-Telegram and Sun*
1955 **James McGlincy and Sydney Mirkin,** *New York Daily News*
1956 **Fern Marja, Peter J. McElroy and William Dufty,** *New York Post*
1957 **Phil Santora,** *New York Daily News*
1958 **Mitchel Levitas,** *New York Post*
1959 **William Haddad,** *New York Post*
1960 **William Haddad and Joseph Kahn,** *New York Post*
1961 **William R. Clark and Alexander Milch,** *Newark News*
1962 **No award**
1963 **No award**
1964 **Norman C. Miller,** *Wall Street Journal*
1965 **A.M. Rosenthal,** *New York Times*
1966 **Barry Gottehrer,** *New York Herald Tribune*
1967 **Cal Olson,** *Fargo* (N.D.) *Forum*
1968 **J. Anthony Lukas,** *New York Times*
1969 **No award**
1970 **William Federici,** *New York Times*
1971 **Richard Oliver,** *New York News*
1972 **Donald L. Bartlett and James B. Steele,** *Philadelphia Inquirer*
1973 **Joseph Martin, Martin McLaughlin and James Ryan,** *New York News*
1974 **James Savage and Mike Baxter,** *Miami Herald*
Carol Talley and Joan Hayde, *Daily Advance* (Dover, N.J.)
1975 **Richard Severo,** *New York Times*
1976 **No award**
1977 **No award**
1978 **No award**
1979 **Walt Bogdanich** and **Walter Johns, Jr.,** *Cleveland Press*

LOCAL REPORTING

1977 **Len Ackland,** *Des Moines Register*
1978 ***Dallas Times-Herald***
1979 **Ed Petykicwicz,** *Saginaw* (Mich) *News*
1980 ***Miami Herald***

NATIONAL REPORTING

1950 **Ted Poston,** *New York Post*
1951 **Ira H. Freeman,** *New York Times*
1952 **Jay Nelson Tuck,** *New York Post*
1953 **A.H. Raskin,** *New York Times*
1954 **James Reston,** *New York Times*
1955 **Luther Huston,** *New York Times*
1956 **Milton Mayer,** *The Reporter*
1957 **Jack Lotto,** International News Service
1958 **Relman Morin,** Associated Press
1959 **Richard L. Strout,** *Christian Science Monitor*
1960 **Nathaniel Gerstenzang,** *New York Times*
1961 **John T. Cunniff,** Associated Press
1962 **Gerard Piel,** *Scientific American*
1963 **Mary McGrory,** *Washington Star*
1964 **American Broadcasting Co.**
Columbia Broadcasting System
National Broadcasting Co.
1965 **Paul Hope and John Barron,** *Washington Star*
1966 **No award**
1967 **Richard Harwood,** *Washington Post*
1968 **Clayton Fritchey,** *Newsday* Specials
1969 **Bernard D. Nossiter,** *Washington Post*
1970 **Walter Rugaber,** *New York Times*
1971 **The Knight Newspapers**
1972 ***New York Times***
1973 **Carl Bernstein and Robert Woodward,** *Washington Post*
1974 **Andrew H. Malcolm,** *New York Times*
1975 **Seymour M. Hersh,** *New York Times*
1976 **No award**
1977 **Walter Pincus,** *Washington Post*
1978 **Ronald Kessler,** *Washington Post*
1979 **Brian Donovan, Bob Wyrick** and **Stuart Diamond,** *Newsday*
1980 **Jonathan Meumann** and **Ted Gup,** *Washington Post*

SUBURBAN REPORTING

1949 **Larry Andrews,** *Nassau* (N.Y.) *Review Star*
1950 **Fred Hechinger,** *Bridgeport* (Conn.) *Herald*
1951 ***Long Island Daily Press***
1952 ***Yonkers Herald-Statesman***
1953 **No award**
1954 **No award**
1955 **Thomas Finnegan,** *Long Island Star-Journal*
1956 **Bob Greene,** *Newsday*
1957 **Mel Elfin,** *Long Island Press*

REGIONAL REPORTING

1969 **James K. Batten and Dwayne Walls,** *Charlotte Observer*

1978 ***Southern Exposure***
1979 **Jim Adams** and Jim Detjen, *Louisville* (Ky.) *Courier-Journal*
1980 ***Charlotte*** (N.C.) *Observer*

COMMUNITY SERVICE

1949 ***Brooklyn Eagle***
1950 ***Brooklyn Eagle***
1951 ***Newsday***
1952 ***New York World-Telegram and Sun***
1953 ***Brooklyn Eagle***
1954 ***Newsday***
1955 **WNYC**
1956 ***Redbook***
1957 **No award**
1958 **Edward Wakin,** *New York World-Telegram and Sun*
1959 ***Brooklyn Heights Press***
1960 **No award**
1961 ***The Village Voice***
1962 **Arnold Brophy and Joseph S. Glemis,** *Newsday*
1963 **No award**
1964 **No award**
1965 **Samuel F. Marshall,** *Cleveland Plain Dealer*
1966 **No award**
1967 **No award**
1968 ***Newsday***
1969 **David Burnham,** *New York Times*
1970 **No award**
1971 **Karl Grossman,** *Long Island Press*
1972 **No award**
1973 **Ronald Kessler,** *Washington Post*
1974 **William Sherman,** *New York Daily News*
1975 **William E. Anderson, Harley R. Bierce and Richard E. Cady,** *Indianapolis Star*

WIRE SERVICE REPORTING

1950 **Kingsbury Smith,** *International News Service*
1951 **Don Whitehead,** Associated Press
1955 **Alan J. Gould,** Associated Press (Team of **Don Whitehead, Saul Pett, Ben Price, Relman Morin and Jack Bell)**

EDUCATION REPORTING

1949 **Benjamin Fine,** *New York Times*
1950 **Lester Grant,** *New York Herald Tribune*
1951 **Fred Hechinger and Judith Christ,** *New York Herald Tribune*
1952 **Kalman Siegel,** *New York Times*
1953 **No award**
1954 **No award**
1955 **No award**
1956 **Gertrude Samuels,** *New York Times*
1972 **Joseph Lelyveld,** *New York Times*
1978 ***Chronicle of Higher Education***

SCIENCE REPORTING

1949 **Albert Deutsch,** *PM*
1950 **William Laurence,** *New York Times*
1951 **George Keaney,** *New York World-Telegram and Sun*
1952 **Alton Blakeslee,** Associated Press
1953-76 **No awards**
1977 ***New England Journal of Medicine***

CULTURAL REPORTING

1980 ***Artnews***

RADIO AND TELEVISION REPORTING (*Radio; **Television)

1955 **Eric Sevareid,** Columbia Broadcasting System
1956 **National Broadcasting Co.**
1957 **Columbia Broadcasting System**
1958 **Columbia Broadcasting System**
1959 **Jay McMullen,** Columbia Broadcasting System
1960 **Av Westin and Howard K. Smith,** Columbia Broadcasting System
1961 **Albert Wasserman and Robert Young,** National Broadcasting Co.
1962 **Robert Young and Charles Dorkins,** National Broadcasting Co.
1963 **WNDT-TV****
1964 **No award**
1965 **Edward P. Morgan*,** American Broadcasting Co.
Ted Yates,** National Broadcasting Co,
1966 **Morley Safer**,** Columbia Broadcasting Co.
1967 **No award**
1968 **No award**
1969 **NBC News, CBS News, ABC News****
1970 **Tom Pettit**,** National Broadcasting Co. (national reporting)
Lee Hanna, WCBS-TV (local reporting)
1971 **Alan M. Levin**,** National Educational Television
1972 **Phil Brady**,** NBC News
1973 **Jim McKay**,** American Broadcasting Co.
1974 **Public Broadcasting Service and National Public Affairs Center for Television****
1975 **No award**
1976 **No award**
1977 **Barry Lando**,** *60 Minutes,* CBS News
1978 **Don Harris** and **Bob Brown,** NBC-TV**

TELEVISION REPORTING FROM ABROAD

1979 **Ed Bradley,** CBS News
1980 **No award**

NATIONAL TELEVISION REPORTING

1979 **Bob Curri, Lea Thompson** and **Jack Cloherty,** WRC-TV4 (Washington, D.C.)
1980 **Charles Kuralt,** CBS News

LOCAL RADIO TELEVISION REPORTING

1977 **John Stossel,** WCBS-TV News, New York

LOCAL TELEVISION REPORTING

1980 **Stephen Talbot** and **Jonathan Dann,** KQED-TV (San Francisco)

NATIONAL RADIO REPORTING

1980 **National Public Radio**

LOCAL RADIO REPORTING

KMOX-Radio (St. Louis)

TELEVISION DOCUMENTARY/FILM DOCUMENTARY

1966 **Beryl Fox,** Canadian Broadcasting Corp.
1967 **No award**
1968 **ABC News**
1969 **No award**
1970 **No award**
1971 **No award**
1972 **Peter Davis, Perry Wolff and Roger Mudd,** CBS News
1973 ***60 Minutes,*** CBS News
First Tuesday, NBC News

1974 **Jeremy Isaacs,** *The World at War,* Thames Television (London)
1975 **NBC News**
1976 **No award**
1977 **No award**
1978 **Golden West Television Productions,** *Scared Straight*
1979 **Jack Willis** and **Saul Landau,** New Time Films
1980 **No award**

SPORTS REPORTING

1951 **Red Smith,** *New York Herald Tribune*
1952 **Ben Gould,** *Brooklyn Eagle*

RELIGIOUS REPORTING

1952 **Ann Elizabeth Price,** *New York Herald Tribune*

NEWS PHOTOGRAPHY

1953 **Bob Wendlinger,** *Brooklyn Eagle*
1954 **Peter Stackpole,** *Life*
1955 **Maureice Johnson,** International News Photos
1956 **William Sauro,** United Press Newspictures
1957 **Jack Young,** United Press Newspictures
1958 **Jack Jenkins,** United Press Newspictures
1959 **Paul Schutzer,** *Life*
1960 **Rangaswamy Satakopan,** Associated Press
1961 **Yasushi Nagao,** Mainichi Newspapers, Japan
1962 **Anonymous,** Associated Press
1963 **Hector Rondon,** *La Republica,* Caracas
1964 **Roger Asnong,** Associated Press
1965 **No award**
1966 **James A. Bourdier,** Associated Press
1967 **Horst Faas,** Associated Press
1968 **Catherine Leroy**
1969 **Edward T. Adams,** Associated Press
1970 **Stephen Dawson Starr,** Associated Press
1971 **John Darnell, John Filo and Howard Ruffner,** *Life*
1972 **Horst Faas and Michel Laurent,** Associated Press
1973 **Huynh Cong Ut,** Associated Press
1974 **George Brich,** Associated Press
1975 **Werner Baum** Deutsche Press-Agentur/United Press International
1976 **No award**
1977 **Eddie (Edward T.) Adams,** Associated Press
1978 **Eddie (Edward T.) Adams,** Associated Press
1979 **United Press International**
1980 **Oscar Sabetta,** United Press International

SPECIAL PAGE

1955 ***New York World-Telegram & Sun*** (School Page)

MAGAZINE REPORTING

1956 **William Attwood,** *Look*
1957 **No award**
1958 **Edmund Stevens and Phillip Harrington,** *Look*
1959 **Marya Mannes,** *The Reporter*
1960 ***The Times Literary Supplement*** (London)
1961 **No award**
1962 **No award**
1963 **James Baldwin,** *The New Yorker*
1964 **Gilbert A. Harrison,** *New Republic*
1965 **No award**
1966 **No award**
1967 ***Ramparts***
1968 ***Paris Review***
1969 **Norman Mailer,** *Harper's Magazine*
1970 **William Lambert,** *Life*
1971 ***The Washington Monthly***
1972 **Ross Terrill,** *Atlantic Monthly*
1973 **Frances FitzGerald** *The New Yorker*
1974 **John Osborne,** *New Republic*
1975 **Edward M. Brecher and Robert E. Harris,** *Consumer Reports*
1976 **No award**
1977 **Daniel Lang,** *The New Yorker*
1978 **No award**
1979 **No award**
1980 **No award**

CRITICISM

1964 ***New York Review of Books***
1965 **Robert Brustein,** *New Republic*
1966 **Susan Sontag**
1967 **Alfred Kazin**
1968 **Saul Maloff,** *Newsweek*
1969 **John Simon,** *New Leader*
1970 **No award**
1971 **Pauline Kael,** *The New Yorker*
1972 **Richard Harwood,** *Washington Post*
1973 **No award**
1974 **No award**
1975 **No award**
1976 **No award**
1977 **Peter S. Prescott,** *Newsweek*
1978 **No award**
1979 **No award**
1980 **No award**

CARICATURES

1966 **David Levine,** *The New York Review of Books*

EDITORIAL CARTOONS

1977 **Jeff MacNally,** *Richmond* (Va.) *News Leader*

SATIRIC DRAWINGS

1980 **Edward Sorel**

BOOKS

1967 **Wilson Follet,** *Modern American Usage*
1968 **Alan F. Westin,** *Privacy and Freedom*
1969 **Charles Rembar,** *The End of Obscenity*
1970 **Richard Ellmann,** Ed., *The Artist as Critic: The Critical Writings of Oscar Wilde*
1971 **Otto Friedrich,** *Decline and Fall*
1972 **Erik Barnouw,** *The History of Broadcasting in the United States*
1973 **Sanford J. Unger,** *The Papers & The Papers*
1974 **David Wise,** *The Politics of Lying: Government Deception, Secrecy and Power*
1975 **Mary Adelaide Mendelsohn,** *Tender Loving Greed*
1976 **No award**
1977 **No award**
1978 **No award**
1979 **William Shawcross,** *Sideshow: Kissinger, Nixon and the Destruction of Cambodia*

INVESTIGATIVE REPORTING

1973 **Jean Heller,** Associated Press
1974 **Seymour Hersh,** *New York Times*
1975 **No award**
1976 **No award**
1977 **No award**
1978 **No award**
1979 **No award**
1980 **No award**

COMMENTARY

1977 **Red Smith,** *New York Times*

1978 **Russell Baker**, *New York Times*
1979 ***The New Yorker***, for "Notes and Comments" section
1980 **Roger Angeil**, *The New Yorker*

EDITORIAL COMMENT

1966 **John B. Oakes** *New York Times*
1971 **James E. Clayton** *Washington Post*
1980 ***New York Times*** editorial board

INTERPRETIVE REPORTING

1966 **Bernard B. Fall**
1967 **Murray Kempton,** *New York Post*

SPECIAL INTEREST AWARD

1979 **Wilbert Rideau** and **Billy Sinclair**, *Angolite*

FREEDOM OF THE PRESS AWARD

1971 **Walter Cronkite,** *CBS Evening News*

PUBLIC SERVICE

1972 **Frances Cerra,** *Newsday*
1978 **Jane Shoemaker**, **Thomas Ferrick, Jr.**, and **William Encenbarger**, *Philadelphia Inquirer*

SPECIAL AWARDS

1951 ***New York Daily News*** **(Straw poll)**
1952 **Edward R. Murrow,** Columbia Broadcasting System
Sponsor Magazine
1953 **Jack Gould,** *New York Times*
The Reporter
Edward R. Murrow, Columbia Broadcasting System
New York Daily News
1954 **John Crosby,** *New York Herald Tribune*
Business Week
Leonard Engel
1955 **Dan Parker,** *New York Mirror*
Leo Rosten, *Look*
1956 **No award**
1957 **Emanuel R. Freedman,** *New York Times*
Endre Marton, Associated Press
Ilona Nyilas, United Press
1958 **Richard D. Heffner,** WRCA-TV
Edmund C. Arnold
1959 **Justice William O. Douglas**
Samuel G. Blackman, Associated Press
Walter Sullivan, *New York Times*
1960 **Wilbur Schramm,** Institute for Communication Research, Stanford University
1961 **Douglass Cater,** *The Reporter*
1962 **Jules Feiffer**
1963 **Michael Harrington,** *The Other America*
Morton Mintz, *Washington Post*
Theodore E. Kruglak
1964 **A.H. Raskin,** *New York Times*
WNEW-Radio
Peter Lyon
1965 **Oron J. Hale**
1966 **No award**
1967 **Arnold Gingrich,** *Esquire*
Time Essay, *Time*
1968 **No award**
1969 **No award**
1970 **Wes Gallagher,** Associated Press
Seymour M. Hersh
1971 **I.F. Stone**
1972 **No award**
1973 **Lesley Oelsner,** *New York Times*
1974 **Donald L. Barlett and James B. Steele,** *Philadelphia Inquirer*
1975 **No award**
1976 **No award**
1977 **Carey McWilliams,** *The Nation*
1978 **Richard S. Salant,** CBS News
1979 **Alden Whitman,** *New York Times*
1980 **No award**

George Polk Memorial Award

OVERSEAS PRESS CLUB
52 E. 41st St. New York, N.Y. 10017 (212/679-9650)

The OPC George Polk Memorial Award, with a $500 honorarium, was given until 1973 for the best reporting requiring exceptional courage and enterprise abroad. This award was, for a time, given concurrently with the George Polk Memorial Awards administered by the Long Island University Journalism Department.

1948 **Homer Bigart,** *New York Herald Tribune*
1949 **Wayne Richardson,** Associated Press
1950 **Marguerite Higgins,** *New York Herald Tribune*
1951 **William N. Oatis,** Associated Press
1952 **Homer Bigart,** *New York Herald Tribune*
1953 **No award**
1954 **Robert Capa,** *Life*
1955 **Gene Symonds,** United Press
1956 **Russell Jones,** United Press
1957 **Herbert Matthews,** *New York Times*
1958 **Joseph Taylor,** UPI
1959 **No award**
1960 **Henry N. Taylor,** Scripps-Howard Newspapers
Lionel Durant, *Newsweek*
1961 **Dickey Chapelle,** *Reader's Digest,* for magazine, book and photographic coverage
1962 **Dana Adams Schmidt,** *New York Times*
1963 **Richard Tregaskis,** for the book, *Vietnam Diary*
1964 **George Clay,** NBC
1965 **Morley Safer,** CBS
1966 **Ron Nessen, Vo Huynh and You Young Sang,** NBC
1967 **Eric Pace,** *New York Times*
1968 **Peter Rehak,** Associated Press
1969 **Horst Faas and Peter Barnett,** Associated Press
1970 **Rus Bensley, Ernest Leiser,** producers; crew, **John Lawrence, Keith Kay, James Clevenger,** CBS Team
1971 **Nicholas W. Stroh,** *Washington Star*
1972 **No award**
1973 **Leon Dash,** *Washington Post*

Pulitzer Prizes

COLUMBIA UNIVERSITY
Graduate School of Journalism, New York, N.Y. 10027
(212/280-3828) (Pulitzer Prizes: 212/280-3841)

The Pulitzer Prizes are the best-known American journalism prizes. Endowed by the will of Joseph Pulitzer, founder of the *St. Louis Post-Dispatch,* and administered under the trusteeship of Columbia University, each Pulitzer Prize in journalism carries a $1,000 cash award. Any individual may submit material published in an American daily, Sunday or weekly newspaper for consideration by university-appointed juries in each category. Each jury, based on collective and individual choice, must submit from three to six nominations per category for selection by the fifteen-member Advisory Board on Pulitzer Prizes.

REPORTING

1917 **Herbert Bayard Swope,** *The World* (New York, N.Y.)
1918 **Harold A. Littledale,** *New York Evening Post*
1919 **No award**
1920 **John J. Leary Jr.,** *The World* (New York)
1921 **Louis Seibold,** *The World* (New York)
1922 **Kirke L. Simpson,** Associated Press
1923 **Alva Johnston,** *New York Times*
1924 **Magner White,** *San Diego Sun*
1925 **James W. Mulroy and Alvin H. Goldstein,** *Chicago Daily News*
1926 **William B. Miller,** *Louisville Courier-Journal*
1927 **John T. Rogers,** *St. Louis Post-Dispatch*
1928 **No award**
1929 **Paul Y. Anderson,** *St. Louis Post-Dispatch*
1930 **Russell D. Owen,** *New York Times*
1931 **A. B. MacDonald,** *Kansas City Star*
1932 **W. C. Richards, D. D. Martin, J. S. Pooler, F. D. Webb and J. N. W. Sloan,** *Detroit Free Press*
1933 **Francis A. Jamieson,** Associated Press
1934 **Royce Brier,** *San Francisco Chronicle*
1935 **William H. Taylor,** *New York Herald Tribune*
1936 **Lauren D. Lyman,** *New York Times*
1937 **John J. O'Neill,** *New York Herald Tribune*
William L. Laurence, *New York Times;*
Howard W. Blakeslee, Associated Press
Gobind Behari Lal, Universal Service
David Dietz, Scripps-Howard newspapers
1938 **Raymond Sprigle,** *Pittsburgh Post-Gazette*
1939 **Thomas L. Stokes,** Scripps-Howard Newspaper Alliance
1940 **S. Burton Heath,** *New York World-Telegram*
1941 **Westbrook Pegler,** *New York World-Telegram*
1942 **Stanton Delaplane,** *San Francisco Chronicle*
1943 **George Weller,** *Chicago Daily News*
1944 **Paul Schoenstein and associates,** *New York Journal-American*
1945 **Jack S. McDowell,** *The Call-Bulletin* (San Francisco)
1946 **William L. Laurence,** *New York Times*
1947 **Frederick Woltman,** *New York World-Telegram*
1948 **George E. Goodwin,** *Atlanta Journal*
1949 **Malcolm Johnson,** *The Sun* (New York)
1950 **Meyer Berger,** *New York Times*
1951 **Edward S. Montgomery,** *San Francisco Examiner*
1952 **George de Carvalho,** *San Francisco Chronicle*

LOCAL INVESTIGATIVE REPORTING (Through 1963, this category was called "Reporting, No Edition Time")

1953 **Edward J. Mowery,** *New York World-Telegram & Sun*
1954 **Alvin S. McCoy,** *Kansas City Star*
1955 **Roland K. Towery,** *Cuero* (Tex.) *Record*
1956 **Arthur Daley,** *New York Times*
1957 **Wallace Turner and William Lambert,** *Portland Oregonian*
1958 **George Beveridge,** *Washington Evening Star*
1959 **John Harold Brialin,** *Scranton* (Pa.) *Tribune and Scrantonian*
1960 **Miriam Ottenberg,** *Washington Evening Star*
1961 **Edgar May,** *Buffalo Evening News*
1962 **George Bliss,** *Chicago Tribune*
1963 **Oscar O'Neal Griffin Jr.,** *Pecos* (Tex.) *Independent and Enterprise*
1964 **James V. Magee, Albert V. Gaudiosi and Frederick A. Meyer,** *Philadelphia Bulletin*
1965 **Gene Goltz,** *Houston Post*
1966 **John A. Frasca,** *Tampa* (Fla.) *Tribune*
1967 **Gene Miller,** *Miami Herald*
1968 **J. Anthony Lukas,** *New York Times*
1969 **Albert Delugach and Denny Walsh,** *St. Louis Globe-Democrat*
1970 **Harold E. Martin,** *Montgomery* (Ala.) *Advertiser*
1971 **William Hugh Jones,** *Chicago Tribune*
1972 **Ann DeSantis, S. A. Kurkjian, T. Leland, and G. M. O'Neill,** *Boston Globe*
1973 ***Sun*** **Newspapers,** (Omaha, Neb.)
1974 **William Sherman,** *New York Daily News*
1975 ***Indianapolis Star***
1976 **Staff of *Chicago Tribune***
1977 **Acel Moore and Wendell Rawls, Jr.,** *Philadelphia Inquirer*

LOCAL GENERAL REPORTING (Through 1963, this category was called "Reporting, Edition Time")

1953 ***Providence*** (R.I.) ***Journal and Evening Bulletin***
1954 ***Vicksburg*** (Miss.) ***Sunday Post-Herald***
1955 **Caro Brown,** *Alice* (Tex.) ***Daily Echo***
1956 **Lee Hills,** *Detroit Free Press*
1957 ***Salt Lake* (Utah) *Tribune***
1958 ***Fargo*** (N.D.) ***Forum***
1959 **Mary Lou Werner,** *Washington Evening Star*
1960 **Jack Nelson,** *Atlanta Constitution*
1961 **Sanche de Gramont,** *New York Herald Tribune*
1962 **Robert D. Mullins,** *Deseret News,* (Salt Lake City)
1963 **Sylvan Fox, Anthony Shannon and William Longgood,** *New York World-Telegram & Sun*
1964 **Norman C. Miller,** *The Wall Street Journal*
1965 **Melvin H. Ruder,** *Hungry Horse* (Mo.) *News*
1966 **Staff,** *Los Angeles Times*
1967 **Robert V. Cox,** *Chambersburg* (Pa.) *Public Opinion*
1968 ***Detroit*** (Mich.) ***Free Press***
1969 **John Fretterman,** *Louisville* (Ky.) *Courier-Journal*
1970 **Thomas Fitzpatrick,** *Chicago Sun-Times*
1971 ***Akron*** (Ohio) ***Beacon Journal***
1972 **R. I. Cooper and J. W. Machacek,** *Rochester* (N.Y.) *Times-Union*
1973 ***Chicago Tribune***
1974 **Arthur M. Petacque and Hugh F. Hough,** *Chicago Sun-Times*
1975 ***The Xenia*** (Ohio) ***Daily Gazette***
1976 **Gene Miller,** *Miami Herald*
1977 **Margo Huston,** *Milwaukee Journal*

GENERAL LOCAL REPORTING

1978 **Richard Whitt,** *Louisville* (Ky.) *Courier-Journal*
1979 ***San Diego*** (Calif.) ***Evening Tribune***
1980 ***Philadephia Inquirer***

SPECIAL LOCAL REPORTING

1978 **Anthony R. Dolan,** *Stamford* (Conn.) *Advocate*
1979 **Gilbert M. Gaul** and **Elliot G. Jaspin,** *Pottsville* (Pa.) *Republican*
1980 **Stephen A. Kurkjian, Alexander B. Hawes, Jr., Nils Bruzelius, Joan Vennochi** and **Robert M. Porterfield,** *Boston Globe*

CORRESPONDENCE (This category overlapped with "Telegraphic Reporting, National," and "Telegraphic Reporting, International," and all three were superseded in 1948 by the "National Reporting" and "International Reporting" categories)

1929 **Paul Scott Mowrer,** *Chicago Daily News*
1930 **Leland Stowe,** *New York Herald Tribune*

1931 **H.R. Knickerbocker,** *Philadelphia Public Ledger* and *New York Evening Post*
1932 **Walter Duranty,** *New York Times*
1933 **Charles G. Ross,** *St. Louis Post-Dispatch*
Edgar Ansel Mowrer, *Chicago Daily News*
1934 **Frederick R. Birchall,** *New York Times*
1935 **Arthur Krock,** *New York Times*
1936 **Wilfred C. Barber,** *Chicago Tribune*
1937 **Anne O'Hare McCormick,** *New York Times*
1938 **Arthur Krock,** *New York Times*
1939 **Louis P. Lochner,** Associated Press
1940 **Otto D. Tolichus,** *New York Times*
1941 **Group Award to news reporters** in the war zones of Europe, Africa and Asia from the beginning of the war
1942 **Carlos P. Romulo,** *Philippines Herald*
1943 **Hanson W. Baldwin,** *New York Times*
1944 **Ernest Taylor Pyle,** Scripps-Howard Newspaper Alliance
1945 **Harold V. "Hal" Boyle,** Associated Press
1946 **Arnaldo Cortesi,** *New York Times*
1947 **Brooks Atkinson,** *New York Times*

NATIONAL REPORTING (Through 1947, this category was called "Telegraphic Reporting (National)")

1942 **Louis Stark,** *New York Times*
1943 **No award**
1944 **Dewey L. Fleming,** *Baltimore Sun*
1945 **James B. Reston,** *New York Times*
1946 **Edward A. Harris,** *St. Louis Post-Dispatch*
1947 **Edward T. Folliard,** *Washington Post*
1948 **Bert Andrews,** *New York Herald Tribune*
Nat S. Finney, *Minneapolis Tribune*
1949 **Charles P. Trussell,** *New York Times*
1950 **Edwin O. Guthman,** *Seattle Times*
1951 **No award**
1952 **Anthony Leviero,** *New York Times*
1953 **Don Whitehead,** Associated Press
1954 **Richard Wilson,** Cowles Newspapers
1955 **Anthony Lewis,** *Washington Daily News*
1956 **Charles Bartlett,** *Chattanooga Times*
1957 **James Reston,** *New York Times*
1958 **Relman Morin,** Associated Press
1959 **Howard Van Smith,** *Miami News*
1960 **Vance Trimble,** Scripps-Howard
1961 **Edward R. Cony,** *Wall Street Journal*
1962 **Nathan G. Caldwell and Gene S. Graham,** *Nashville Tennessean*
1963 **Anthony Lewis,** *New York Times*
1964 **Merriman Smith,** United Press International
1965 **Louis Kohlmeier,** *Wall Street Journal*
1966 **Hayes Johnson,** *Washington Evening Star*
1967 **Monroe W. Karmin and Stanley W. Penn,** *Wall Street Journal*
1968 **Howard James,** *Christian Science Monitor*
Nathan Kotz, *Des Moines Register*
1969 **Robert Cahn,** *Christian Science Monitor*
1970 **William J. Seton,** *Chicago Daily News*
1971 **Lucinda Franks and Thomas Powers,** United Press International
1972 **Jack Anderson,** syndicated columnist
1973 **Robert Boyd and Clark Hoyt,** Knight Newspapers
1974 **James R. Polk,** *Washington Star-News*
Jack White, *Providence* (R.I.) *Journal-Bulletin*
1975 **Donald L. Barlett and James B. Steele,** *Philadelphia Inquirer*
1976 **James Risser,** *Des Moines Register*
1977 **Walter Mears,** Associated Press
1978 **Gaylord D. Shaw,** *Los Angeles Times*
1979 **James Risser,** *Des Moines Register*
1980 **Bette Swenson Orsini** and **Charles Stafford,** *St. Petersburg* (Fla.) *Times*

INTERNATIONAL REPORTING

1942 **Laurence E. Allen,** Associated Press
1943 **Ira Wolfert,** North American Newspaper Alliance
1944 **Daniel DeLuce,** Associated Press
1945 **Mark S. Watson,** *Baltimore Sun*
1946 **Homer W. Bigart,** *New York Herald Tribune*
1947 **Eddy Gilmore,** Associated Press
1948 **Paul W. Ward,** *Baltimore Sun*
1949 **Price Day,** *Baltimore Sun*
1950 **Edmund Stevens,** *Christian Science Monitor*
1951 **Keyes Beech and Fred Sparks,** *Chicago Daily News,* **Homer Bigart and Marguerite Higgins,** *New York Herald Tribune,*
Relman Morin and Don Whitehead, Associated Press
1952 **John M. Hightower,** Associated Press
1953 **Austin Wehrwein,** *Milwaukee Journal*
1954 **Jim G. Lucas,** Scripps-Howard Newspapers
1955 **Harrison Salisbury,** *New York Times*
1956 **William Randolph Hearst Jr., Kingsbury Smith and Frank Conniff,** International News Service
1957 **Russell Jones,** United Press
1958 ***New York Times***
1959 **Joseph Martin and Philip Santora,** *New York Daily News*
1960 **A. M. Rosenthal,** *New York Times*
1961 **Lynn Heinzerling,** Associated Press
1962 **Walter Lippmann,** New York Herald Tribune Syndicate
1963 **Hal Hendrix,** *Miami News*
1964 **Malcolm W. Browne,** Associated Press
David Halberstam, *New York Times*
1965 **J. A. Livingston,** *Philadelphia Bulletin*
1966 **Peter Arnett,** Associated Press
1967 **R. J. Hughes,** *Christian Science Monitor*
1968 **Alfred Friendly,** *Washington Post*
1969 **William Tuohy,** *Los Angeles Times*
1970 **Seymour M. Hersh,** Dispatch News Service
1971 **Jimmie Lee Hoagland,** *Washington Post*
1972 **Peter R. Kann,** *Wall Street Journal*
1973 **Max Frankel,** *New York Times*
1974 **Hedrick Smith,** *New York Times*
1975 **William Mullen and Ovie Carter,** *Chicago Tribune*
1976 **Sydney H. Schanberg,** *New York Times*
1977 **No award**
1978 **Henry Kamm,** *New York Times*
1979 **Richard Ben Cramer,** *Philadelphia Inquirer*
1980 **Joel Brinkley** and **Jay Mather,** *Louisville* (Ky.) *Courier-Journal*

EDITORIAL WRITING

1917 ***New York Tribune***
1918 ***Louisville Courier-Journal***
1919 **No award**
1920 **Harvey E. Newbranch,** *Omaha Evening World-Herald*
1921 **No award**
1922 **Frank M. O'Brien,** *New York Herald*
1923 **William Allen White,** *Emporia* (Kans.) *Gazette*
1924 ***Boston Herald***
1925 ***Charleston* (S.C.) *News and Courier***
1926 **Edward M. Kingsbury,** *New York Times*
1927 **F. L. Bullard,** *Boston Herald*
1928 **Grover Cleveland Hall,** *Montgomery* (Ala.) *Advertiser*
1929 **Louis I. Jaffe,** *Norfolk* (Va.) *Virginian-Pilot*
1930 **No award**

1931 **Charles S. Ryckman,** *Fremont* (Neb.) *Tribune*
1932 **No award**
1933 ***Kansas City Star***
1934 **E. P. Chase,** *Atlantic* (Iowa) *News-Telegraph*
1935 **No award**
1936 **Felix Morley,** *Washington Post*
George B. Parker, Scripps-Howard
1937 **John W. Owens,** *Baltimore Sun*
1938 **W. W. Waymack,** *Des Moines Register and Tribune*
1939 **Ronald G. Callvert,** *Portland Oregonian*
1940 **Bart Howard,** *St. Louis Post-Dispatch*
1941 **Reuben Maury,** *New York Daily News*
1942 **Geoffrey Parsons,** *New York Herald Tribune*
1943 **Forrest W. Seymour,** *Des Moines Register and Tribune*
1944 **Henry J. Haskell,** *Kansas City Star*
1945 **George W. Potter,** *Providence* (R.I.) *Journal-Bulletin*
1946 **Hodding Carter,** *Delta Democrat-Times* (Greenville, Miss.)
1947 **William Grimes,** *Wall Street Journal*
1948 **Virginius Dabney,** *Richmond Times-Dispatch*
1949 **John H. Crider,** *Boston Herald*
1950 **Carl M. Saunders,** *Jackson Citizen Patriot*
1951 **William Fitzpatrick,** *New Orleans States*
1952 **Louis LaCoss,** *St. Louis Globe-Democrat*
1953 **Vermont Royster,** *Wall Street Journal*
1954 **Don Murray,** *Boston Herald*
1955 **Royce Howes,** *Detroit Free Press*
1956 **Lauren K. Soth,** *Des Moines Register and Tribune*
1957 **Buford Boone,** *Tuscaloosa* (Ala.) *News*
1958 **Harry S. Ashmore,** *Arkansas Gazette* (Little Rock, Ark.)
1959 **Ralph McGill,** *Atlanta Constitution*
1960 **Lenoir Chambers,** *Norfolk Virginian-Pilot*
1961 **William J. Dorvillier,** *San Juan* (P.R.) *Star*
1962 **Thomas M. Storke,** *Santa Barbara* (Calif.) *News-Press*
1963 **Ira B. Harkey Jr.,** *Pascagoula* (Miss.) *Chronicle*
1964 **Hazel Smith,** *Lexington* (Miss.) *Advertiser*
1965 **John R. Harrison,** *Gainesville Sun*
1966 **Robert Lasch,** *St. Louis Post-Dispatch*
1967 **Eugene C. Patterson,** *Atlanta Constitution*
1968 **John S. Knight,** Knight Newspapers
1969 **Paul Greenberg,** *Pine Bluff* (Ark.) *Commercial*
1970 **Philip Geyelin,** *Washington Post*
1971 **Horance G. Davis Jr.,** *Gainesville* (Fla.) *Sun*
1972 **John Strohmeyer,** *Bethlehem* (Pa.) *Globe-Times*
1973 **Roger B. Linscott,** *The Berkshire Eagle* (Pittsfield, Mass.)
1974 **F. Gilman Spencer,** *The Trenton* (N.J.) *Trentonian*
1975 **John Daniell Maurice,** *The Charleston* (W. Va.) *Daily Mail*
1976 **Philip P. Kerby,** *Los Angeles Times*
1977 **Warren L. Lerude, Foster Church and Norman Cardoza,** *Reno Evening Gazette* and *Nevada State Journal*
1978 **Meg Greenfield,** *Washington Post*
1979 **Edwin M. Yoder, Jr.,** *Washington Star*
1980 **Robert L. Bartley,** *Wall Street Journal*

EDITORIAL CARTOONING /(UNTIL 1976 called "Cartoons")

1922 **Rollin Kirby,** *New York World*
1923 **No award**
1924 **Jay Norwood Darling,** *New York Tribune*
1925 **Rollin Kirby,** *New York World*
1926 **D. R. Fitzpatrick,** *St. Louis Post-Dispatch*
1927 **Nelson Harding,** *Brooklyn* (N.Y.) *Daily Eagle*
1928 **Nelson Harding,** *Brooklyn* (N.Y.) *Daily Eagle*
1929 **Rollin Kirby,** *New York World*
1930 **Charles R. Macauley,** *Brooklyn* (N.Y.) *Daily Eagle*
1931 **Edmund Duffy,** *Baltimore Sun*
1932 **John McCutcheon,** *Chicago Tribune*
1933 **Harold Morton Talburt,** *Washington Daily News*
1934 **Edmund Duffy,** *Baltimore Sun*
1935 **Ross A. Lewis,** *Milwaukee Journal*
1936 **No award**
1937 **Clarence Daniel Batchelor,** *New York Daily News*
1938 **Vaughn Shoemaker,** *Chicago Daily News*
1939 **Charles G. Werner,** *Daily Oklahoman,* (Oklahoma City)
1940 **Edmond Duffy,** *Baltimore Sun*
1941 **Jacob Burck,** *Chicago Times*
1942 **Herbert L. Block (Herblock),** Newspaper Enterprise Association Service
1943 **Jay Norwood Darling,** *New York Herald Tribune*
1944 **Clifford K. Berryman,** *Washington Evening Star*
1945 **William (Bill) Mauldin,** United Features Syndicate
1946 **Bruce Russell,** *Los Angeles Times*
1947 **V. Shoemaker,** *Chicago Daily News*
1948 **Reuben L. (Rube) Goldberg,** *New York Sun*
1949 **Lute Pease,** *Newark* (N.J.) *Evening News*
1950 **James T. Berryman,** *Washington Evening Star*
1951 **Reginald W. Manning,** *Arizona Republic* (Phoenix, Ariz.)
1952 **Fred L. Packer,** *New York Mirror*
1953 **Edward D. Kuekes,** *Cleveland Plain Dealer*
1954 **Herbert L. Block (Herblock),** *Washington Post & Times-Herald*
1955 **Daniel R. Fitzpatrick,** *St. Louis Post-Dispatch*
1956 **Robert York,** *Louisville* (Ky.) *Times*
1957 **Tom Little,** *Nashville Tennessean*
1958 **Bruce M. Shanks,** *Buffalo Evening News*
1959 **William (Bill) Mauldin,** *St. Louis Post-Dispatch*
1960 **No award**
1961 **Carey Orr,** *Chicago Tribune*
1962 **E. S. Valtman,** *Hartford* (Conn.) *Times*
1963 **Frank Miller,** *Des Moines* (Iowa) *Register*
1964 **Paul Conrad,** *Denver Post*
1965 **No award**
1966 **Don Wright,** *Miami News*
1967 **Patrick B. Oliphant,** *Denver Post*
1968 **E. G. Payne,** *Charlotte* (N.C.) *Observer*
1969 **John Fischetti,** *Chicago Daily News*
1970 **Thomas Darcy,** *Newsday* (Garden City, N.Y.)
1971 **Paul Conrad,** *Los Angeles Times*
1972 **J. K. MacNelly,** *Richmond* (Va.) *News Leader*
1973 **No award**
1974 **Paul Szep,** *The Boston Globe*
1975 **Garry Trudeau,** creator of "Doonesbury" comic strip
1976 **Tony Auth,** *Philadelphia Inquirer*
1977 **Paul Szep,** *Boston Globe*
1978 **Jeffery K. MacNelly,** *Richmond* (Va.) *News Leader*
1979 **Herbert L. Block,** *Washington Post*
1980 **Don Wright,** *Miami News*

PHOTOGRAPHY

1942 **Milton Brooks,** *Detroit News*
1943 **Frank Noel,** Associated Press
1944 **Frank Filan,** Associated Press
1945 **Joe Rosenthal,** Associated Press
1946 **No award**
1947 **Arnold Hardy,** Amateur photographer
1948 **Frank Cushing,** *Boston Traveler*
1949 **Nathaniel Fein,** *New York Herald Tribune*
1950 **Bill Crouch,** *Oakland* (Calif.) *Tribune*
1951 **Max Desfor,** Associated Press
1952 **John Robinson and Don Ultang,** *Des Moines Register and Tribune*

1953 **William M. Gallagher,** *Flint* (Mich.) *Journal*
1954 **Mrs. Walter M. Schau,** Photographer
1955 **John L. Gaunt Jr.,** *Los Angeles Times*
1956 ***New York Daily News***
1957 **Harry A. Trask,** *Boston Traveler*
1958 **William C. Beall,** *Washington Daily News*
1959 **William Seaman,** *Minneapolis Star*
1960 **Andrew Lopez,** United Press International
1961 **Yasushi Nagao,** Mainichi Newspapers, Tokyo, Japan
1962 **Paul Vathis,** Associated Press
1963 **Hector Rondon,** *La Republica* (Caracas, Venezuela)
1964 **Robert H. Jackson,** *Dallas Times Herald*
1965 **Horst Faas,** Associated Press
1966 **Kyoichi Sawada,** United Press International
1967 **Jack R. Thornell,** Associated Press

SPOT NEWS PHOTOGRAPHY

1968 **Rocco Morabito,** *Jacksonville* (Fla.) *Journal*
1969 **Edward T. Adams,** Associated Press
1970 **Steve Starr,** Associated Press
1971 **John Paul Filo,** Amateur photographer
1972 **H. Faas, M. Laurent,** Associated Press
1973 **Huynh Cong Ut,** Associated Press
1974 **Anthony K. Roberts,** Freelancer
1975 **Gerald H. Gay,** *Seattle Times*
1976 **Stanley Forman,** *Boston Herald-American*
1977 **Neal Ulevich,** Associated Press
Stanley Forman, *Boston Herald American*
1978 **John H. Blair,** United Press International
1979 **Thomas J. Kelly III,** *Pottstown* (Pa.) *Mercury*
1980 ***United Press International* photographer** (unnamed at press time for) coverage of firing squad in Iran

FEATURE PHOTOGRAPHY

1968 **Toshio Sakai,** United Press International
1969 **Moneta Sleet Jr.,** *Ebony* magazine
1970 **Dallas Kinney,** *Palm Beach Post*
1971 **Jack Dykinga,** *Chicago Sun-Times*
1972 **Dave Kennerly,** United Press International
1973 **B. Lanker,** *Topeka* (Kans.) *Capital-Journal*
1974 **Slava Veder,** Associated Press
1975 **Matthew Lewis,** *Washington Post*
1976 ***Louisville*** **(Ky.)** ***Courier-Journal and Times,*** staff photographers
1977 **Robin Hood,** *Chattanooga* (Tenn.) *Free Press*
1978 **J. Ross Baughman,** Associated Press
1979 ***Boston Herald American*** **Staff photographers**
1980 **Erwin H. Hagler,** *Dallas Times Herald*

CRITICISM

1970 **Ada Louise Huxtable,** *New York Times*
1971 **Harold C. Schonberg,** *New York Times*
1972 **Frank L. Peters Jr.,** *St. Louis Post-Dispatch*
1973 **Ronald Powers,** *Chicago Sun-Times*
1974 **Emily Genauer,** *Newsday* syndicate
1975 **Roger Ebert,** *Chicago Sun-Times*
1976 **Alan M. Kriegsman,** *Washington Post*
1977 **William McPherson,** *Washington Post*
1978 **Walter Kerr,** *New York Times*
1979 **Paul Gapp,** *Chicago Tribune*
1980 **William A. Henry III,** *Boston Globe*

COMMENTARY

1970 **Marquis Childs,** *St. Louis Post-Dispatch*
1971 **William A. Caldwell,** *The Record* (Hackensack, N.J.)
1972 **Mike Royko,** *Chicago Daily News*
1973 **David S. Broder,** *Washington Post*
1974 **Edwin A. Roberts Jr.,** *The National Observer*
1975 **Mary McGrory,** *Washington Star*
1976 **Walter W. (Red) Smith,** sports columnist, *New York Times*
1977 **George F. Will,** *Washington Post*
1978 **William Safire,** *New York Times*
1979 **Russell Baker,** *New York Times*
1980 **Ellen H. Goodman,** *Boston Globe*

FEATURE WRITING

1979 **Jon D. Franklin,** *Baltimore Evening Sun*
1980 **Madeleine Blais,** *Miami Herald*

NEWSPAPER HISTORY (given only once)

1918 **Minna Lewinson and Henry Beetle Hough,** History of services rendered to the public by the American press during 1917.

SPECIAL CITATIONS (Awarded as merited)

1924 **Frank I. Cobb,** *New York World*, special editorial writing award
1930 **William O. Dapping,** *Auburn* (N.Y.) *Citizen* for reportorial coverage of breakout at Auburn Prison.
1938 ***Edmonton Journal,*** For defending freedom of the press in Alberta, Canada
1941 ***New York Times,*** Public educational value of foreign news reporting
1944 **Mrs. William Allen White,** For interest in and service to the advisory board during previous seven years
Byron Price, Director, Office of Censorship, for creation of newspaper and radio codes
1945 **Cartographers of the American press,** For maps that increased public knowledge on progress of armies and navies in World War II
1947 **Columbia University and the Graduate School of Journalism,** For efforts to maintain and advance the high standards of the Pulitzer Prizes, given in Pulitzer Centennial Year
1948 **Dr. Frank Diehl Fackenthal,** A scroll recognizing interest and service over the years
1951 **Cyrus L. Sulzberger,** *New York Times,* for exclusive interview with Aloysius Stepinac, Roman Catholic Primate of Yugoslavia
1952 ***Kansas City Star,*** News coverage of 1951 regional flood
Max Case, *New York Journal-American,* for exposures of corruption in basketball
1953 ***New York Times,*** For its Review of the Week section
1958 **Walter Lippmann,** Nationally syndicated *New York Herald Tribune* columnist for wisdom, perception and high sense of responsibility in commenting on international and national news
1964 **Gannett Newspapers,** Rochester, N.Y., For "The Road to Integration," as an example of a newspaper group's resources to complement work of individual newspapers
1976 **John Hohenberg,** For twenty-two years of service as administrator of the Pulitzer Prizes
1978 **Richard Lee Strout,** For Washington commentary in *The Christian Science Monitor* and *The New Republic*

PUBLICE SERVICE AWARD

1917 **No award**
1918 ***New York Times***
1919 ***Milwaukee Journal***
1920 **No award**
1921 ***Boston Post***
1922 ***The World,*** **(New York)**
1923 ***Memphis Commercial Appeal***
1924 ***The World,*** **(New York)**

1925 No award

1926 *Enquirer Sun,* (Columbus, Ga.)

1927 *Canton* (Ohio) *Daily News*

1928 *Indianapolis Times*

1929 *Evening World* (New York)

1930 No award

1031 *Atlanta Constitution*

1932 *Indianapolis News*

1933 *New York World-Telegram*

1934 *Medford* (Ore.) *Mail Tribune*

1935 *Sacramento* (Calif.) *Bee*

1936 *Cedar Rapids* (Iowa) *Gazette*

1937 *St. Louis Post-Dispatch*

1938 *Bismarck* (N.D.) *Tribune*

1939 *Miami Daily News*

1940 *Waterbury* (Conn.) *Republican and American*

1941 *St. Louis Post-Dispatch*

1942 *Los Angeles Times*

1943 *World-Herald* (Omaha, Neb.)

1944 *New York Times*

1945 *Detroit Free Press*

1946 *Scranton* (Pa.) *Times*

1947 *Baltimore Sun*

1948 *St. Louis Post-Dispatch*

1949 *Nebraska State Journal*

1950 *Chicago Daily News*
St. Louis Post-Dispatch

1951 *Miami Herald*
Brooklyn (N.Y.) *Eagle*

1952 *St. Louis Post-Dispatch*

1953 *News Reporter,* (Whiteville, N.C.)
Tabor City (N.C.) *Tribune*

1954 *Newsday* (Garden City, N.Y.)

1955 *Columbus* (Ga.) *Ledger and Sunday Ledger-Enquirer*

1956 *Watsonville* (Calif.) *Register-Pajaronian*

1957 *Chicago Daily News*

1958 *Arkansas Gazette* (Little Rock, Ark.)

1959 *Utica* (N.Y.) *Observer-Dispatch*
Utica (N.Y.) *Daily Press*

1960 *Los Angeles Times*

1961 *Amarillo* (Tex.) *Globe-Times*

1962 *Panama City* (Fla.) *News-Herald*

1963 *Chicago Daily News*

1964 *St. Petersburg* (Fla.) *Times*

1965 *Hutchinson* (Kans.) *News*

1966 *Boston Globe*

1967 *Louisville* (Ky.) *Courier-Journal*
Milwaukee Journal

1968 *The Riverside* (Calif.) *Press*

1969 *Los Angeles Times*

1970 *Newsday* (Garden City, N.Y.)

1971 *Winston-Salem* (N.C.) *Journal and Sentinel*

1972 *New York Times*

1973 *Washington Post*

1974 *Newsday,* (Garden City, N.Y.)

1975 *Boston Globe*

1976 *Anchorage* (Alas.) *Daily News*

1977 *Lufkin* (Tex.) *News*

1978 *Philadephia Inquirer*

1979 *Point Reyes* (Calif.) *Light*

1980 Gannett News Service

Murray Kramer Scarlet Quill Award

BOSTON UNIVERSITY
285 Babcock St, Boston, Mass. 02215 (617/353-2872)

The Murray Kramer Scarlet Quill Award, which consists of a plaque, is given annually to honor outstanding coverage of intercollegiate sports by a journalist, columnist, broadcaster or cartoonist. A Hall of Fame Awards Committee selects the recipient from nominees.

1965 **Arthur Sampson,** *Boston Herald-Traveler*

1966 **Don Gillis,** WHDH-TV Boston

1967 **Murray Kramer,** *Boston Record-American*

1968 **Cliff Sundberg,** *Boston Herald-Traveler*

1969 **Roy Mumpton,** *Worcester Telegram & Gazette*

1970 **Jerry Nason,** *Boston Globe*

1971 **Dick Dew,** United Press International

1972 **Walter "Red" Smith,** Nationally syndicated columnist

1973 **Joe Concannon,** *Boston Globe*

1974 **Bob Monahan,** *Boston Globe*

1975 **Joe Giuliotti,** *Boston Herald-American*

1976 **Phil Bissell,** *Boston Herald-American*

1977 **Francis Rosa,** *Boston Globe*

1978 **Dave O'Hara,** Associated Press

1979 **Ernie Roberts,** *Boston Globe*

1980 **Frank O'Brien,** *Boston Globe*

Claude Bernard Science Journalism Awards

NATIONAL SOCIETY FOR MEDICAL RESEARCH
1000 Vermont Ave. NW, Ste. 1100, Washington, D.C. 20005 (202/347-9565)

The Claude Bernard Science Journalism Awards are given annually for science reporting that has contributed significantly to public understanding of basic research in the life sciences, including but not limited to experimental medicine. A $1,000 prize is given to winners in each category. Entries are judged by a panel of journalists and scientists on the basis of scientific accuracy, clarity, significance of the subject and public interest. Honorable mentions are also made. The awards were last given in 1978.

NEWSPAPER OVER 100,000 CIRCULATION

1967 **Irving S. Bengelsdorf,** *Los Angeles Times* ("Of Atoms and Men")

1968 **Ray Bruner,** *Toledo Blade* ("Has Life Been Created By Science: The Answer Depends on Definitions")

1969 **Judith Randal,** *Washington Evening Star* ("A Study in Immunity: Real Step Forward")

NEWSPAPER UNDER 100,000 CIRCULATION

1967 **Jerry Lochbaum,** *San Antonio Express* ("The Man Who Talks With Chimpanzees")

1968 **Marilyn Drago,** *Arizona Daily Star* ("Lowly Hamster Plays Key Role Into Birth Defects")

1969 **Jill Southworth,** *Columbia* (Mo.) *Daily Tribune* ("Mystromys: Diabetes Researcher")

1978 **Dave O'Hara,** Associated Press

1979 **Ernie Roberts,** *Boston Globe*

1980 **Frank O'Brien,** *Boston Globe*

1970 **Laurence H. Bush,** *Ann Arbor* (Mich.) *News* ("Lab Animals' Roles Important")

NEWSPAPER

1970 **Lawrence K. Altman,** *New York Times* ("Twelve Dogs Develop Lung Cancer in Group of 86 Taught to Smoke")
1971 **Ronald Kotulak,** *Chicago Tribune* ("Is a Cure for Cancer Around the Corner?")
1972 **William A. Rice,** *New York Times* ("Medicine Closes in on an Elusive Killer")
1973 **Arthur J. Snider,** *Chicago Daily News* ("Miracle of the Brain")
1974 **Lawrence K. Altman,** *New York Times* ("Baboon Experiment Shows Alcohol Damages Liver, Even With Good Diet")
1975 **Alton Blakeslee,** Associated Press ("The Stalled Diseases")
1976 **Cristine Russell,** *Washington Star* ("Just How Reliable Are the Tests on Animals?")
1977 **Donald C. Drake,** *Philadelphia Inquirer* ("The Breath of Life")
1978 **Bruce de Silva,** *Providence Sunday Journal* (Series on cancer research)

MAGAZINE

1967 **Judith Marcus and Gerald Cohen,** *Harper's* ("The Riddle of the Dangerous Bean")
1968 **C.P. Gilmore,** *New York Times Magazine* ("Instead of a Heart, a Man-Made Pump")
1969 **Robert Stock,** *New York Times Magazine* ("The Mouse State of the New Biology")
1970 **Morton Hunt,** *Playboy* ("Man and Beast")
1971 **Matt Clark,** *Newsweek* ("Probing the Brain")
1972 **Gene Bylinsky,** *Fortune* ("Upjohn Puts the Cell's Own Message to Work")
1973 **No award**
1974 **Gene Bylinsky,** *Fortune* ("What Science Can Do About Hereditary Disease")
1975 **Albert Rosenfeld et al.,** *Saturday Review* ("Inside the Brain: The Last Great Frontier")
1976 **No award**
1977 **Arthur Fisher,** Time-Life Nature/Science Annual ("Slow Viruses: Biological Time Bombs")
Joan Arehart-Treichel, *New York* ("Brain Proteins: Mind Over Matter")

Ernie Pyle Memorial Award
Edward J. Meeman Conservation Award
Edward Willis Scripps First Amendment Award
Walker Stone Editorial Award
Roy W. Howard Public Service Award

SCRIPPS-HOWARD FOUNDATION
1100 Central Trust Tower, Cincinnati, Ohio 45202

The Ernie Pyle Award, which consists of a medallion, a plaque and a $1,000 honorarium, is given annually to honor the newspaper writing that most nearly exemplifies the style and craft of the late Ernie Pyle. A panel of judges selects the winner. In addition to the first-place winner listed here, a runnerup receives a plaque and a $500 honorarium.

1953 **Jim G. Lucas,** Scripps-Howard Newspaper Alliance
1954 **Eldon Roark,** *Memphis Press-Scimitar*
1955 **Andrew F. Tully,** Scripps-Howard Newspaper Alliance
Kays Gary, *The Charlotte Observer*
1956 **Gordon S. Thompson,** *The Evansville* (Ind.) *Press*
Charles Kuralt, *The Charlotte News*
1957 **Walter Wingo,** *Washington Daily News*
Neil Morgan, *San Diego Tribune*
1958 **Don Dedera,** *Pheonix Republic*
1959 **Henry J. Taylor,** Scripps-Howard Newspaper Alliance
Dorothy R. Powers, *Spokane Spokesman-Review*
1960 **James O'Neill Jr.,** *Washington Daily News*
1961 **Guy Wright,** *San Francisco News-Call-Bulletin*
Al Burt, *Miami Herald*
1962 **Richard Starnes,** Scripps-Howard Newspaper Alliance
John A. Hamilton, *Lynchburg* (Va.) *News*
1963 **Jack Steele,** Scripps-Howard Newspaper Alliance
Bill Porterfield, *The Houston Chronicle*
1964 **Jim G. Lucas,** Scripps-Howard Newspaper Alliance
1965 **Tom Tiede,** Newspaper Enterprise Association
John Van Doorn, *Newsday*
1966 **Billy E. Bowles,** *The Charleston* (S.C.) *News and Courier*
1967 **Marty Gershen,** *Newark Star-Ledger*
William Thomas, *Memphis Commercial Appeal*
1968 **Jerry C. Bledsoe,** *Greensboro (N.C.) Daily News*
Don Tate, Scripps-Howard Newspaper Alliance
1969 **Kent Pollock,** *Palm Beach* (Fla.) *Post*
Nicholas Blatchford, *Washington Daily News*
1970 **Jerry Bledsoe,** *Greensboro* (N.C.) *Daily News*
1971 **Clettus Atkinson,** *Birmingham Post-Herald*
1972 **Bill Stokes,** *Milwaukee Journal*
1973 **Jim Wooten,** *Philadelphia Inquirer*
1974 **William D. Montalbano,** *Miami Herald*
1975 **Robert Hullihan,** *Des Moines Register*
1976 **Carol McCabe,** *Providence Journal-Bulletin*
1977 **Stephen Smith,** *Boston Globe*
1978 **Frank Rossi,** *Columbia* (Mo.) *Tribune*
1979 **Bob Morris,** *Ft. Myers* (Fla.) *News-Press*
1980 **Not available at press time**

The Edward J. Meeman Award, which carries a $2,500 and a bronze plaque, recognizes outstanding achievement toward better understanding and support of conservation efforts. A panel of judges selects the winner. In addition to the grand-prize winner listed here, two other substantial cash awards are made—one each to a journalist from a newspaper with a circulation of more than 100,000, and another to a journalist from a newspaper with a circulation of less than 100,000.

1967 **James Ryan,** *St. Petersburg* (Fla.) *Times*
1968 **Betty Klaric,** *Cleveland Press*
1969 **Tom Brown,** *Anchorage Daily News*
1970 **Gary Blonston, Ladd Neuman, Boyce Rensberger** and **Lee Winfrey,** *Detroit Free Press*
1971 **Gordon Bishop,** *Newark Star-Ledger*
1972 **Harry V. Martin,** *Napa* (Calif.) *Register*
1973 **George F. Neavoll,** *Fort Wayne* (Ind.) *Journal-Gazette*
1974 **David Johnston,** *Detroit Free Press*
1975 **Kenneth L. Robison,** *Idaho Statesman*
1976 **Tom Turner,** *Arizona Daily Star*
1977 **Bruce Ingersoll,** *Chicago Sun-Times*
1978 **John Hayes,** *Oregon Statesman*

1979 **Rod Nordland** and Josh Friedman, *Philadelphia Inquirer*
1980 **Not available at press time**

The Edward Willis Scripps Award consists of $2,500 which is given to the editor of the winning newspaper for distribution to the individual or individuals on the staff who contributed most significantly to the cause of the First Amendment guarantee of a free press. Newspapers may be cited for writing, reporting or public education in the fight against the threat of censorship, overcoming public unease with regard to press credibility, combating government secrecy and instilling public appreciation of the need to know. A bronze plaque is also given to the newspaper honored by the Edward Willis Scripps Award, upon the decision of a panel of judges from the high echelons of American publishing.

1976 ***Honolulu Advertiser***
1977 ***Sun Enterprise Newspapers*** (Monmouth, Ore.)
1978 ***Gannett Rochester Newspapers*** (N.Y.)
1979 ***Norfolk*** (Va.) ***Ledger-Star***
1980 **Not available at press time**

The $1,000 Walker Stone Prize is given for "graceful and vivid" editorial writing by a journalist who has won "wide recognition and admiration" in the profession. The criteria for judgment by a panel of distinugished journalists are general excellence.

1973 **Michael Pakenham**, *Philadelphia Inquirer*
1974 **John R. Harrison**, *The Lakeland* (Fla.) *Ledger*
1975 **David Bowes**, *Cincinnati Post*
1976 **John R. Harrison**, *Lakeland* (Fla.) *Ledger*
1977 **Michael Pakenham**, *Philadelphia Inquirer*
1978 **John R. Alexander**, *Greensboro* (N.C.) *Daily News*
1979 **Barbara Stanton**, *Detroit Free Press*
1980 **Not available at press time**

The Roy W. Howard Public Service Award, which consists of $2,500 and a bronze plaque, is given to recognize outstanding public service, which is defined as exposure or contribution toward the alleviation of corruption, crime, health or other problems. A panel of judges selects the winner. In addition to the first-place winner listed below, a runner-up prize of $1,000 is given. There is also a Roy W. Howard Public Service Award for broadcast, which will be found elsewhere in this volume.

1972 ***St. Louis Globe Democrat***
1973 ***Wall Street Journal***
1974 ***Milwaukee Journal***
1975 ***Louisville*** (Ky.) ***Courier-Journal***
1976 ***San Francisco Examiner***
1977 ***Philadelphia Inquirer***
1978 ***Philadelphia Inquirer***
1979 ***Deseret News*** (Salt Lake City)
1980 **Not available at press time**

AIP-USSF Science Writing Awards

AMERICAN INSTITUTE OF PHYSICS
335 E. 45th St., New York, N.Y. 10017 (212/661-9404)

The American Institute of Physics-United States Steel Foundation Science-Writing Award is given annually to a journalist for excellence in writing on physics or astronomy for the general public. The prize, which consists of a Moebius Strip and $1,500, is given to a citizen or permanent resident of the United States, Canada or Mexico, selected by a panel of judges.

1968 **William J. Perkinson,** *Baltimore Evening Sun* ("ABM Primer: Physics for Defense")
1969 **Walter Sullivan,** *New York Times* ("Flight of Apollo 8")
1970 **Clarence P. Gilmore,** Metromedia Television ("Can We Stop Earthquakes from Happening?")
1971 **Kenneth Weaver,** "Voyage to the Planets" (*National Geographic*)
1972 **Jerry E. Bishop,** "Celestial Clue" (*Wall Street Journal*)
1973 **Edward Edelson,** "The Mystery of Space" (*New York Daily News*)
1974 **Patrick Young,** "A Quake is Due at . . . " (*National Observer*)
1975 **Tom Alexander,** "Ominous Changes in the World's Weather" (*Fortune*)
1976 **Frederic Golden,** "Forecast: Earthquake" (*Time*)
1977 **William D. Metz,** "Fusion Research" (*Science Magazine*)
1978 **Timothy Ferris**, *The Red Limit: The Search for the End of the Universe* (book)
1979 **Robert Cowen**, "The New Astronomy" (*Christian Science Monitor*)
1980 **Dennis Overbye**, "The Wizard of Space and Time" (*Omni*)

A second AIP-USSF Science-Writing Award, also carrying a $1,500 cash prize and a Moebius Strip, is given for excellence in writing for the general public by a scientist. The selection is made from entrants who reside in or are citizens of the United States, Canada or Mexico by a panel of judges.

1969 **Kip S. Thorne,** California Institute of Technology ("The Death of a Star")
1970 **Jeremy Bernstein,** Stevens Institute of Technology ("The Elusive Neutrino")
1971 **Robert M. March,** University of Wisconsin ("Physics for Poets")
1972 **Dietrich Schroeer,** University of North Carolina/Chapel Hill ("Physics and Its Fifth Dimension: Society")
1973 **Banesh Hoffman,** Queens College, CUNY ("Albert Einstein: Creator and Rebel")
1974 **Robert D. Chapman,** NASA, Goddard Space Flight Center ("Comet Kohoutek")
1975 **Robert H. March,** University of Wisconsin ("The Quandary Over Quarks")
1976 **Jeremy Bernstein,** Stevens Institute of Technology ("Physicist I.I. Rabi")
1977 **Steven Weinberg,** Harvard University ("The First Three Minutes: A Modern View of the Origin of the Universe")
1978 **Edwin C. Krupp**, *In Search of Ancient Astronomies* (book)
1979 **Hans C. von Baeyer**, "The Wonder of Gravity"
1980 **William J. Kaufman III**, *Black Holes and Warped Spacetime* (book)

Sigma Delta Chi Awards

SOCIETY OF PROFESSIONAL JOURNALISTS/SIGMA DELTA CHI
840 N. Lake Shore Dr., Chicago, Ill. 60611 (312/664-4200)

Sigma Delta Chi Awards for Distinguished Service in Journalism annually honor noteworthy performance in print and broadcast journalism during the previous year. Bronze medallions and plaques are presented to the winners. Society chapters nominate individuals and media for final selection by a jury of distinguished veteran newsmen. (Broadcast journalism awards will be found on pp. 198-200.)

GENERAL REPORTING

1939 Meigs O. Frost
1940 Basil Brewer
1941 No award
1942 Jack Vincent
1943 Julius M. Klein
Ralph S. O'Leary
1944 Edward J. Doherty
1945 James P. McGuire
John J. McPhaul
1946 John M. McCullough
1947 George Goodwin
1948 Richard C. Looman
1949 Bob Considine
1950 Edward B. Simmons
1951 Victor Cohn
1952 Chalmers M. Roberts
1953 Carl T. Rowan
1954 Richard Hyer
William P. Walsh
1955 Victor Cohn
1956 Alfred Kuettner
1957 Pierre J. Huss
1958 Victor Cohn
1959 Saul Pett
1960 Robert Colby Nelson
1961 Joseph Newman
1962 Oscar Griffin
1963 Jimmy Breslin
1964 J. Harold Brislin
1965 Alton Blakeslee
1966 Stanley W. Penn
Monroe W. Karmin
1967 Charles Nicodemus
1968 Haynes Johnson
1969 Seymour M. Hersh
1970 *Washington Post* staff writers
1971 James B. Steele and Donald L. Barlett
1972 William F. Reed, Jr.
James M. Bolus
1973 James R. Polk
1974 Frank Sutherland
1975 William Mitchell, Billy Bowles, Kirk Cheyfitz, Julie Morris, Tom Hennessey, James Harper and Jim Neubacher, *Detroit Free Press*
1976 George Reasons and Mike Goodman, *Los Angeles Times*
1977 Fredric Tulsky and David Phelps, *Jackson* (Miss.) *Clarion-Ledger*
1978 Pamela Zekman
Zay N. Smith
James R. Frost
Eugene Pesek
1979 Gene Miller
Carl Hiaasen
Patrick Malone
William D. Montalbano
1980 Not available at press time

EDITORIAL WRITING

1939 W. W. Waymack
1940 Allen Drury
1941 No award
1942 Alexander Kendrick
1943 Milton Lehman
1944 Felix R. McKnight
1945 Francis P. Locke
1946 John W. Hillman
1947 Alan Barth
1948 Virginius Dabney
1949 John Crider
1950 Bradley L. Morison
1951 Robert M. White II
1952 Virginius Dabney
1953 John N. Reddin
1954 Robert Estabrook
1955 James Jackson Kilpatrick
1956 Sylvan Meyer
1957 Vermont Royster
1958 J. D. Maurice
1959 Cecil Prince
1960 Hodding Carter III
1961 James A. Clendinen
1962 Karl E. Meyer
1963 H. G. Davis, Jr.
1964 J. O. Emmerich
1965 Alfred G. Dickson
1966 Duane Croft
1967 Robert E. Fisher
1968 Robert M. White II
1969 Albert Cawood
1970 John R. Harrison
1972 Joanna Wragg
1972 John R. Harrison
1973 Frank W. Corrigan
1974 Michael Pakenham
1975 William Duncliffe
1976 George W. Wilson
1977 Desmond Stone
1978 Philip Goldsmith
1979 Rick Sinding
1980 Not available at press time

WASHINGTON CORRESPONDENCE

1942 Drew Pearson
Robert S. Allen
1943 Sam O'Neal
1944 Marquis W. Childs
1945 Peter Edson
1946 Wallace R. Deuel
1947 Bert Andrews
1948 W. McNeil Lowry
1949 Jack Steele
1950 William K Hutchinson
1951 John Hightower
1952 Clark R. Mollenhoff
1953 Richard L. Wilson
1954 Clark R. Mollenhoff
1955 Joseph and Stewart Alsop
1956 Bem Price
1957 Robert T. Hartmann
1958 James Reston
1959 Vance Trimble
1960 James Clayton
Julius Duscha
Murrey Marder
Bernard Nossiter
1961 James Marlow
1962 Jules Witcover
1963 Jerry Landauer
1964 Louis M. Kohlmeier
1965 Nick Kotz

1966 Richard Harwood
1967 Jack C. Landau
1968 Joe Western
1969 Ronald J. Ostrow
Robert Jackson
1970 Jared D. Stout
1971 Neil Sheehan
New York Times
1972 Carl Bernstein
Robert Woodward
1973 James M. Naughton
John M. Crewdson
Ben A. Franklin
Christopher Lydon
Agis Salpukas
1974 Seth Kantor
1975 James Risser
1976 Maxine Cheshire
Scott Armstrong
1977 Gaylord Shaw
1978 Joseph Albright
1979 Gordon Eliot White
1980 Not available at press time

FOREIGN CORRESPONDENCE

1939 Kenneth T. Downs
1940 Leland Stowe
1941 No award
1942 Keith Wheeler
1943 Frederick Kuh
1944 Frederick Kuh
1945 Arnaldo Cortesi
1946 Charles Gratke
1947 Daniel DeLuce
1948 Nat Barrows
1949 Kingsbury Smith
1950 Keyes Beech
Dan Whitehead
1951 Ferdinand Kuhn
1952 Ernest S. Pisko
1953 Alexander Campbell
1954 Carl T. Rowan
1955 Carl T. Rowan
1956 Russell Jones
1957 Harrison E. Salisbury
1958 John Strohm
1959 William H. Stringer
1960 Smith Hempstone, Jr.
1961 Gaston Coblentz
1962 William J. Woestendiek
1963 Malcolm W. Browne
1964 Henry Shapiro
1965 James Nelson Goodsell
1966 Robert S. Elegant
1967 Peter Arnett
1968 Clyde H. Farnesworth
Henry Kamm
Tad Szulc
1969 Anatole Shub
1970 Hugh Mulligan
1971 Peter Arnett
Bernard Gavzer
1972 Charlotte Saikowski
1973 Jacques Leslie
1974 Donald L. Barlett
James B. Steele
1975 Sydney H. Schanberg
1976 Joe Rigert
1977 Robert Toth
1978 Charles A. Krause
1979 Karen DeYoung
1980 Not available at press time

NEWS PHOTOGRAPHY

1946 Frank Q. Brown
1947 Paul Calvert
1948 Frank Jurkoski
1949 *Chicago Daily News*
1950 David Douglas Duncan
1951 Edward DeLuga
Roger Wrenn
1952 Robert I. Wendlinger
1953 Bill Wilson
1954 Leslie Dodds
1955 Richard B. Yager
1956 Dan Tompkins
1957 Eldred C. Reaney
1958 Andrew St. George
1959 Andrew Lopez
1960 J. Parke Randall
1961 Peter Leibing
1962 Cliff DeBear
1963 Bob Jackson
1964 Dom Ligato
1965 Henry Herr Gill
1966 Ray Mews
1967 Catherine Leroy
1968 Edward T. Adams
1969 Horst Faas
1970 John P. Filo
1971 Dong Jun Kim
1972 Huynh Cong "Nick" Ut
1973 Anthony K. Roberts
1974 Werner Baum
1975 Stanley J. Forman
1976 Bruce Fritz
1977 Eddie Adams
1978 Norman Y. Lono
1979 Eddie Adams
1980 Not available at press time

EDITORIAL CARTOONING

1942 Jacob Burck
1943 Charles Werner
1944 Henry Barrow
1945 Reuben L. Goldberg
1946 Dorman H. Smith
1947 Bruce Russell
1948 Herbert Block
1949 Herbert Block
1950 Bruce Russell
1952 Herbert Block
Bruce Russell
1952 Cecil Jensen
1953 John Fischetti
1954 Calvin Alley
1955 John Fischetti
1956 Herbert Block
1957 Scott Long
1958 Clifford H. Baldowski
1959 Charles Gordon Brooks
1960 Dan Dowling
1961 Frank Interlandi
1962 Paul F. Conrad
1963 William H. "Bill" Mauldin
1964 Charles O. Bissell
1965 Roy Justus
1966 Patrick B. Oliphant
1967 Eugene C. Payne
1968 Paul F. Conrad

1969 Bill Mauldin
1970 Paul Conrad
1971 Hugh Haynie
1972 Bill Mauldin
1973 Paul Szep
1974 Mike Peters
1975 Tony Auth
1976 Paul Szep
1977 Don Wright
1978 James Mark Borgman
1979 John P. Trever
1980 Not available at press time

PUBLIC SERVICE IN NEWSPAPER JOURNALISM

1949 *Star-Gazette* (Moose Lake, Minn.)
1950 *Atlanta* (Ga.) *Journal*
1951 *Chicago Sun-Times*
1952 *Wall Street Journal*
1953 *Chicago Daily News*
Houston Post
1954 *Cleveland Plain Dealer*
1955 *The Register-Pajaronian* (Watsonville, Calif.)
1956 *The Oregonian* (Portland, Ore.)
1957 *Des Moines Register* and *Tribune*
Minneapolis (Minn.) *Star* and *Tribune*
1958 *Tampa* (Fla.) *Tribune*
1959 *Atlanta* (Ga.) *Constitution*
1960 *The Daily Commercial,* (Leesburg, Fla.)
1961 *San Gabriel Valley Daily Tribune* (West Covina, Calif.)
1962 *Pascagoula* (Miss.) *Chronicle*
1963 *Chicago Daily News*
1964 *McComb* (Miss.) *Enterprise-Journal*
1965 *Miami Herald*
1966 *Los Angeles Times*
Long Island Press
1967 *Newsday* (Garden City, N.Y.)
1968 *St. Louis Globe-Democrat*
1969 *Chicago Daily News*
1970 *Newsday* (Garden City, N.Y.)
1971 *Boston Globe*
1972 Sun Newspapers, (Omaha, Neb.)
1973 *Newsday* (Garden City, N.Y.)
1974 *Indianapolis Star*
1975 *Louisville Courier-Journal*
1976 *Wall Street Journal*
1977 *Philadelphia Inquirer*
1978 *Chicago Sun-Times*
1979 *Miami Herald*
1980 Not available at press time

MAGAZINE REPORTING

1949 Lester Velie
1950 Gordon Schendel
1951 Bill Davidson
1952 Bill Davidson
1953 James P. O'Donnell
1954 Marshall MacDuffie
1955 Fletcher Knebel
1956 John Bartlow Martin
1957 Harold H. Martin
1958 John L. Cobbs
1959 John Robert Coughlan
1960 Hobart Rowen
1961 Joseph Morschauser
1962 Peter Goldman
1963 Theodore H. White
1964 Sam Castan
1965 Ben H. Bagdikian
1966 John G. Hubbell
1967 William Lambert
1968 Kristin Hunter
1969 William Lambert
1970 David L. Chandler
1971 Arthur Hadley
1972 Thomas Thompson
1973 Floyd Miller
1974 John Guinther
1975 Mike Mallowe
1976 Mary DuBois and Laurence Gonzales
1977 John Conroy
1978 Tony Green
1979 Michael W. Yargo
1980 Not available at press time

PUBLIC SERVICE IN MAGAZINE JOURNALISM

1949 *Collier's*
1950 *Collier's*
1951 *McCall's*
1952 *Look*
1953 *Look*
1954 *Saturday Evening Post*
1955 *Look*
1956 *Life*
1957 *The Reporter*
1958 *Life*
1959 *Saturday Evening Post*
1960 *Saturday Review*
1961 *Look*
1962 *Look*
1963 *Look*
1964 *Look*
1965 *Reader's Digest*
1966 *Life*
1967 *Philadelphia Magazine*
1968 *Life*
1969 *Philadelphia Magazine*
1970 *The Washingtonian Magazine*
1971 *New Orleans Magazine*
1972 *Philadelphia Magazine*
1973 *Philadelphia Magazine*
1974 *Philadelphia Magazine*
1975 *Philadelphia Magazine*
1976 *Philadelphia Magazine*
1977 *Mother Jones*
1978 *New West*
1979 *National Geographic*
1980 Not available at press time

RESEARCH ABOUT JOURNALISM

1935 Oscar W. Riegel
1936 Ralph O. Nafziger
1937 Alfred McClung Lee
1938 Frank Luther Mott
1939 Norval Neil Luxon
1940 Paul F. Lazarsfeld
1941 No award
1942 No award
1943 No award
1944 Earl English
1945 Frank Thayer
1946 Ralph D. Casey
Bruce Lannes Smith
Harold D. Lasswell
1947 James E. Pollard
1948 J. Edward Gerald
1949 Edwin Emery
1950 Robert S. Harper
1951 No award
1952 Curtis D. MacDougall

1953 **Harold L. Cross**
1954 **Edwin Emery**
Henry Ladd Smith
1956 **Theodore B. Peterson**
1957 **Frank Luther Mott**
1958 **L. John Martin**
1959 **Warren C. Price**
1960 **Leonard W. Levy**
1961 **Burton Paulu**
1962 **Theodore E. Kruglak**
1963 **David P. Forsyth**
1964 **John Hohenberg**
1965 **William L. Rivers**
1966 **Kenneth E. Olson**
1967 **John Hohenberg**
1968 **William A. Hachten**
1969 **Ronald T. Farrar**
1970 **William Small**
1971 **John C. Merrill**
Ralph L. Lowenstein
1972 **William Small**
1973 **Philip Meyer**
1974 **Loren Ghiglione**
1975 **Marvin Barrett**
1976 **No award**
1977 **Peter Braestrup**
1978 **John Hohenberg**
1979 **Lloyd Wendt**
1980 **Not available at press time**

SPECIAL AWARDS

1943 **Raymond Clapper**, William Allen White Memorial Award
1977 **Investigative Reporters and Editors, Inc., for Public Service**

The following award categories have been discontinued:

COURAGE IN JOURNALISM

1939 ***New Orleans*** (La.) ***States***
1942 ***Guthrie County Vedette***, Panora, Iowa
1943 ***Lowell*** (Mass.) ***Sunday Telegram***
1944 ***Milwaukee Journal***
1945 ***New Orleans*** (La.) ***States***
1946 ***Kansas City*** (Mo.) ***Star***
1947 ***Memphis Press-Scimiatar***
1948 ***Philadelphia Inquirer***

NEWSPAPER CARTOONING

1948 **Ed Dodd**
1950 **Milton Caniff**

WAR CORRESPONDENCE

1943 **Ernie Pyle**, Raymond Clapper Memorial Award
1944 **Ernie Pyle**, Human Interest
1945 **John Graham Dowling**

GOLD KEY AWARDS

1923-34 **Paul Scott Mowrer**
Philip Hale
Franklin P. Adams
Alexander Dana Noyes
Jay N. (Ding) Darling
Casper S. Yost

Silver Lady

KING FEATURES / THE BANSHEES
235 E. 45th St., New York, N.Y. 10017 (212/682-5600)

The Silver Lady, a statue given annually to honor excellence in journalism or cartooning and occasionally to a well-known entertainer, has been discontinued.

1946 **Milton Caniff**, Cartoonist, *Steve Canyon*
1947 **Walt Disney**, Cartoonist, *Mickey Mouse* and others
1948 **Chic Young**, Cartoonist, *Blondie*
1949 **Arthur "Bugs" Baer**, Humor columnist
1950 **Jimmy Hatlo**, Cartoonist, *They'll Do It Every Time*
1951 **George McManus**, Cartoonist, *Bringing Up Father*
1952 **Hal Foster**, Cartoonist, *Prince Valiant*
1953 **Bob Considine**, Columnist, "On the Line"
1954 **Westbrook Pegler**, Columnist
1955 **Mort Walker**, Cartoonist, *Beetle Bailey*
1956 **George Sokolsky**, Columnist, "These Days"
1957 **Burris Jenkins**, Editorial Cartoonist
1958 **Jim Bishop**, Columnist, "Jim Bishop: Reporter"
1959 **Rube Goldberg**, Cartoonist
1960 **Milton Caniff**, Cartoonist, *Steve Canyon*
1961 **Roy Crane**, Cartoonist, *Buz Sawyer*
1962 **Fred Lasswell**, Cartoonist, *Barney Google and Snuffy Smith*
1963 **Dik Browne**, Cartoonist, *Hi & Lois*
1964 **Heloise**, Columnist, "Hints From Heloise"
1965 **John Chamberlain**, Columnist, "These Days"
1966 **Bob Hope**, "American" (inscription)
1967 **William F. Buckley**, Columnist, "On The Right"
1968 **No award**
1969 **No award**
1970 **No award**
1971 **No award**
1972 **No award**
1973 **No award**
1974 **Jimmy Durante**, "The Greatest" (inscription)

Harold S. Hirsch Trophy

U.S. SKI WRITERS ASSOCIATION
7 Kensington Rd., Glens Falls, N.Y. 12801 (518/793-1201)

The Harold S. Hirsch Trophy, which consits of a silver-plated typewriter, is given to the ski writer who submits a portfolio of writing deemed to consist of major contributions and to be evidence of excellent reporting on the sport of skiing.

1963 **Bill Berry**, *Sacramento Bee*
1964 **Tom Place**, *Cleveland Plain Dealer*
1965 **Mike Beatrice**, *Boston Globe*
1966 **Bill Kattermann**, *Newark Star-Ledger*
1967 **Burt Sims**, *Los Angeles Herald-Examiner*
1968 **Luanne Pfeifer**, *Santa Monica* (Calif.) *Evening Outlook*
1969 **Dave Knickerbocker**, *Newsday* (Garden City, N.Y.)
1970 **Burt Sims**, *Los Angeles Herald Examiner*
1971 **L. Dana Gatlin**, *Christian Science Monitor*
1972 **Bill Hibbard**, *Milwaukee Journal*
1973 **Ralph Thornton**, *Minneapolis Star*
1974 **Joe Van Zandt**, *Skisport/Chicago*
1975 **Mike Madigan**, *Rocky Mountain News* (Denver, Colo.)
1976 **I. William Berry**, *Long Island* (N.Y.) *Press*
1977 **Charlie Meyers**, *Denver Post*

1978 **Charlie Meyers,** *Denver Post*
1979 **Alex Katz,** *Chicago Sun-Times*
1980 **Glenn Kramon,** *San Francisco Examiner*

Lincoln Steffens Award

INTERNATIONAL PLATFORM ASSOCIATION
2564 Berkshire Rd., Cleveland Hts., Ohio 44106
(216/932-0505)

The Lincoln Steffens Award, a bronze sculpture, went to the individual judged by the IPA Committee to be an outstanding investigative journalist for exercising great influence through newspapers. This award has been discontinued.

1975 **Jack Anderson**
1976 **Jack Anderson**

Stanley Walker Journalism Award

TEXAS INSTITUTE OF LETTERS
Box 3143, Dallas, Tex. 75275 (214/692-2000)

The Stanley Walker Journalism Award, which carries a $500 honorarium, is given annually for the best example of journalistic writing about the state in newspaper, magazine or book form.

1962 **Anita Brewer,** *Austin American-Statesman* ("Death Takes Noted Author")
1963 **A. C. Greene,** *Dallas Times-Herald* ("No Life is Lived without Influence")
Larry Grove, *Dallas Morning News* ("Rain, and a Day of Reflection")
1964 **Bill Porterfield,** *Houston Chronicle* ("The President's Homeland")
1965 **Paul Crume,** *Dallas Morning News* ("A Newsman Looks at the World's Week")
1966 **Jim Berry and Glen Castlebury,** *Austin American-Statesman* ("Sniper in U. T. Tower")
1967 **John Tackett,** *Fort Worth Star-Telegram* ("Time Stands Still")
1968 **Bill Porterfield,** *Houston Chronicle* ("The Archbishop and the Rebel Priests")
1969 **Greg Olds,** *The Texas Observer* (McCroklin Stories)
1970 **Elroy Bode,** *The Texas Observer* ("Requiem for a WASP School")
1971 **Charles Evans,** *Houston Chronicle* ("The Howard Hughes Series")
1972 **Larry L. King,** *Life* ("The Last Frontier")
1973 **Elroy Bode,** *The Texas Observer* ("The Making of a Legend")
1974 **Griffin Smith, Jr.,** *The Texas Monthly* ("Forgotten Places")
1975 **Archer Fullingim,** *Heidleberg Press* ("A Country Editor's View of Life")
1976 **Griffin Smith,** *The Texas Monthly* ("Why Does Dolph Briscoe Want to be Governor?")
1977 **Gary Cartwright,** *The Texas Monthly* ("The Endless Odyssey of Patrick Henry Polk")
1978 **Ronnie Dugger,** *Washington Post* ("To A Novelist Dying Young")

Current status unknown

Paul Tobenkin Memorial Award

COLUMBIA UNIVERSITY
Graduate School of Journalism, Room 706, New York, N.Y. 10027 (212/280-3411)

The Paul Tobenkin Memorial Award recognizes achievement in the field of newspaper writing "in the fight against racial and religious hatred, intolerance, discrimination and every form of bigotry, reflecting the spirit of Paul Tobenkin," who was for twenty-five years a reporter with the *New York Herald Tribune*. Nominations are generally made by editors. Winners, who share $250 and receive a certificate, are selected by a jury of educators and journalists

1961 **Bonnie Angelo,** *Newsday*
1962 **Dale Wright,** *World Telegram and Sun*
1963 **James K. Batten,** *Charlotte* (N.C.) *Observer*
1964 **Robert S. Bird,** *New York Herald Tribune*
1965 **No award**
1966 **No award**
1967 **Cal Olson,** *Fargo* (N.D.) *Forum*
1968 **Bill Burrus,** *New York Post*
1969 **Bernie Bookbinder and five colleagues,** *Newsday*
1970 **Kent Pollock,** *Palm Beach* (Fla.) *Post*
1971 **Richard Oliver,** *New York Post*
1972 **Jon Nordheimer** *New York Times*
1973 **Howard Kohn** *Detroit Free Press*
1974 **Tom Stundza,** *Gary* (Ind.) *Post-Tribune*
1975 **Mike Masterson,** *Hot Springs* (Ark.) *National Park Sentinel-Record*
1976 **Joe Stroud,** *Detroit Free Press*
1977 **Barry Siegel,** *Los Angeles Times*
1978 **Les Payne,** *Newsday*
1979 **Jim McGee,** *Fort Meyers* (Fla.) *News Press*
1980 **Leonard Yourist, George Cantor, James Kenyon, Cynthia Lee, John McAleenan** and **Hugh McCann,** *Detroit News*

Walter Haight Award

NATIONAL TURF WRITERS ASSOCIATION
6000 Executive Blvd., Ste. 317, Rockville, Md. 20852
(301/881-2266)

The Walter Haight Award is given annually for meritorious achievement in turf writing and the coverage of horse racing by a vote of the membership.

1972 **Jimmy Doyle,** *Cleveland Plain Dealer*
1973 **George Ryall,** *The New Yorker*
1974 **Raleigh Burroughs,** *Turf & Sport Digest*
1975 **Don Fair,** *Daily Racing Form*
1976 **Saul Rosen,** *Daily Racing Form*
1977 **Red Smith,** *New York Times*
1978 **Nelson Fisher,** San Diego
1979 **Barney Nagler,** *Daily Racing Form*
1980 **Joseph Nichols,** *New York Times*

Carr Van Anda Award

OHIO UNIVERSITY
School of Journalism, Athens, Ohio 45701 (614/594-5511)

The Carr Van Anda Award, which consists of a plaque and a citation, is given annually to honor enduring contributions to journalism. The faculty selects the winners.

1968 **Turner Catledge,** *New York Times*
Edward W. Barrett, Columbia University School of Journalism
Walter Cronkite, CBS News
1969 **Wes Gallagher,** Associated Press
Margaret Bourke-White, photojournalist
Osborne Elliott, *Newsweek*
1970 **John S. Knight,** Knight Newspapers
Gordon Parks, *Life*
Howard K. Smith, ABC News
1971 **James Reston,** *New York Times*
Norman Cousins, *Saturday Review*
1972 **Pauline Frederick,** NBC News
Richard Leonard, *Milwaukee Journal*
1973 **William Attwood,** *Newsday*
Harry Reasoner, ABC News
1974 **Otis Chandler,** *Los Angeles Times*
Shana Alexander, *Newsweek*
1975 **Katharine Graham,** *Washington Post*
Philip Meyer, Knight Newspapers
Eric Sevareid, CBS News
1976 **A. M. Rosenthal,** *New York Times*
Patricia Carbine, *Ms.*
1977 **Mike Wallace,** CBS-TV
Helen Thomas, United Press International
1978 **Paul Miller,** Gannett Company

Current status unknown

Gill Robb Wilson Award

AIR FORCE ASSOCIATION
1750 Pennsylvania Ave. NW, Washington, D.C. 20006
(202/637-3300)

The Gill Robb Wilson Award, until 1965 called the Arts and Letters Trophy, is presented annually for outstanding contributions to arts and letters. A committee selects the winner. Most of the individual winners have been journalists or authors of non-fiction books.

1948 **William Wilster Haines,** *Command Decision*
1949 **No award**
1950 **J.L. Cate** and **W.F. Craven,** *The Army Air Forces in World War II*
1951 **Maj. Alexander P. deSeversky,** *Air Power, Key to Survival*
1952 **Edward R. Murrow,** Columbia Broadcasting System
1953 **Milton Caniff,** King Features (*Steve Canyon* comic strip)
1954 **Charles J.V. Murphy,** *Fortune*
1955 **Vern Haugland,** Associated Press
1956 **Beirne Lay, Jr.,** Metro-Goldwyn-Mayer
1957 **Joseph Alsop** and **Stewart Alsop**
1958 **Air Photographic & Chartering Services, MATS**
1959 **Maj. James F. Sunderman,** USAF
1960 **Walter Lippman,** Columnist
1961 **Maj. Gen. Orvil A. Anderson,** USAF (Ret.)
Albert F. Simpson, Air Force Historical Foundation
1962 **Bob Considine,** Syndicated columnist
1963 **Lt. Col. George C. Bales,** USAF
1964 **Mark S. Watson,** *Baltimore Sun*
1965 **Elton C. Fay,** Associated Press
1966 **Society of Illustrators of New York City, Los Angeles, and San Francisco**
1967 **Robert E. Engel,** 1352d Photographic Group, MAC
1968 **Edward C. Walsh,** National Aeronautics & Space Council
1969 **No award**
1970 **Louis R. Stockstill,** *The Forgotten Americans of the Vietnam War*
1971 ***Airman*** Magazine
1972 **Hanson W. Baldwin,** military writer and analyst
1973 **Capt. Robert J. Hoag,** *USAF Fighter Weapons Review*
1974 **Capt. Tobias van Rossum Daum,** Chief, *Driver Magazine,*
1975 **Maxine McCaffrey,** Artist
1976 **Michael Collins,** Director, National Air and Space Museum, Washington, D.C.
1977 **Rowland Evans, Jr.** and **Robert D. Novak,** Columnists
1978 ***Wall Street Journal***
1979 **George Will,** Columnist
1980 **Charles Corddry,** *Baltimore Sun*

World Press Photo of the Year

STICHTING WORLD PRESS PHOTO HOLLAND
Box 51333, Weeperzijde 86, 1007 EH Amsterdam, The Netherlands (020-94-48-47)

The Press Photo of the Year honors go to the photographer who, in the opinion of a nine-member jury, has succeeded more than any other in portraying the essence of a news event, especially in a strikingly perceptive, honest and revealing way. In addition to the World Press Photo of the Year, which carries a Dfl. 5,000 cash award and which are listed here, published news photographs are eligible for smaller awards in eight more specific categories. The World Press Photo of the Year and category winners are exhibited and also appear in a yearbook.

1955 **M. von Haven** (Denmark), "Motor race"
1956 **H.R. Pirfath** (Federal Republic of Germany), "Spatheimkehrer"
1957 **D. Martin** (U.S.A.) "Little Rock"
1958 **No award**
1959 **S. Tereba** (Czechoslovakia), "Goalman and Water"
1960 **No award**
1961 **Y. Nagao** (Japan), "Attack on Japanese politician"
1962 **N. Rondon Lovera** (Venezuela), "Saved from Hell" (priest with wounded soldier)
1963 **N. Brown** (U.S.A.), "Burning monk"
1964 **D. McCullin** (England), "Crying woman on Cyprus"
1965 **N. Sawada** (Japan), "Escape to Freedom" (mother)
1966 **K. Sawada** (Japan), "Tank with dead body" ("Dusty Death")
1967 **C. Rentmeester** (U.S.A.), "Tank Commander"
1968 **E. Adams** (U.S.A.), "Execution of Vietcong soldier"
1969 **No award**
1970 **H.J. Anders** (Federal Republic of Germany), "We Want Peace" (Belfast)
1971 **No award**
1972 **W. Celler** (Federal Republic of Germany), "Arrest of Bankrobber"
1973 **N. Ut** (Vietnam), "Terror of War" (children escaping napalm)
1974 **Unknown photographer,** "Allende's last day"
1975 **O. Carter** (U.S.A.), "Suffer little children"
1976 **S. Forman** (U.S.A.), "Boston fire"
1977 **F. Demulder** (France), "Distress of Lebanon"
1978 **L. Hammond** (South Africa), "Tear gas terror"
1979 **S. Mikami** (Japan), "Narita Airport Demonstration"
1980 **D. Burnett** (U.S.A.), Mother and baby (Cambodia)

Award of Journalistic Merit

WILLIAM ALLEN WHITE FOUNDATION
105 Flint Hall, University of Kansas, Lawrence, Kan. 66045
(913/864-2700)

The Award of Journalistic Merit, which carries a $500 honorarium, is given annually for journalistic effort that exemplifies service both to the profession and to the community.

1950 **James B. Reston**
1951 **Ernest K. Lindley**
1952 **Erwin D. Canham**
1953 **Palmer Hoyt**
1954 **Grove Patterson**
1955 **Norman E. Isaacs**
1956 **Roy A. Roberts**
1957 **Irving Dilliard**
1958 **Jenkin Lloyd Jones**
1959 **Ben Hibbs**
1960 **Jules Dubios**
1961 **Hodding Carter**
1962 **Bernard Kilgore**
1963 **Paul Miller**
1964 **Clark R. Mollenhoff**
1965 **Earl J. Johnson**
1966 **Gardner Cowles**
1967 **Wes Gallagher**
1968 **Mark Ethridge**
1969 **Walter Cronkite**
1970 **Eugene Pulliam**
1971 **Vermont Royster**
1972 **John S. Knight**
1973 **Barry Bingham, Sr.**
1974 **Arthur O. Sulzberger**
1975 **Otis Chandler**
1976 **Peter Lisagor**
1977 **Sylvia Porter**
1978 **Sylvia Porter**
1979 **James Kilpatrick**
1980 **Eugene Patterson**

John Peter Zenger Award

UNIVERSITYOF ARIZONA
Dept. of Journalism, Tucson, Ariz. 85721 (602/884-2561)

The John Peter Zenger Award, which carries a $500 honorarium, annually honors distinguished service on behalf of freedom of the press and the public's right to know. Previous winners and the head of the Department of Journalism submit nominations, which appear on a ballot sent to approximately 400 newspapers for selection.

1954 **Palmer Hoyt,** *Denver Post*
1955 **Basil L. Walters,** *Chicago Daily News*
1956 **James S. Pope,** *Louisville* (Ky.) *Courier Journal*
1957 **James R. Wiggins,** *Washington Post* and *Times Herald*
1958 **John E. Moss,** Chairman, House Government Information Subcommittee
1959 **Herbert Brucker,** *Hartford Courant*
1960 **Virgil M. Newton, Jr.,** *Tampa* (Fla.) *Tribune*
1961 **Clark R. Mollenhoff,** Cowles Publications
1962 **John H. Colburn,** *Richmond* (Va.) *Times-Dispatch*
1963 **James B. Reston,** *New York Times*
1964 **John N. Heiskell,** *Arkansas Gazette*
1965 **Eugene C. Pulliam,** *Arizona Republic* and *Phoenix Gazette*
1966 **Arthur Krock,** *New York Times*
1967 **John S. Knight,** Knight Newspapers
1968 **Wes Gallagher,** Associated Press
1969 **J. Edward Murray,** *Arizona Republic* (Phoenix)
1970 **Erwin D. Canham,** *Christian Science Monitor*
1971 *New York Times*
1972 **Dan Hicks, Jr.,** *Monroe County Observer* (Madisonville, Tenn.)
1973 **Katharine M. Graham,** *Washington Post*
1974 **Thomas E. Gish,** *The Berkshire Eagle* (Pittsfield, Mass.)
1975 **Seymour M. Hersh,** *New York Times*
1976 **Donald F. Bolles,** *Arizona Republic* (Phoenix)
1977 **Robert W. Greene,** *Newsday* (Garden City, N.Y.)
1978 **Robert H. Estabrook,** *Lakeville* (Conn.) *Journal*
1979 **Jack C. Landau,** Reporters Committee for Freedom of the Press
1980 **Walter Cronkite,** "CBS Evening News"

Radio & Television

Contents

Related Awards

Armstrong Awards

ARMSTRONG MEMORIAL RESEARCH FOUNDATION
c/o Central Mailroom, 101 University Hall, Columbia University, New York, N.Y. 10027 (212/666-8786)

The Armstrong Awards, which are plaques, are presented annually to U.S. or Canadian radio stations for excellence and originality in broadcasting in several categories, which have changed slightly over the years. In addition to the first-place winners listed below, runners-up receive certificates of merit.

COMMUNITY SERVICE

1964 **WRVR-FM** (New York)
1965 **KPFK-FM** (N. Hollywood, Cal.)

COMMUNITY SERVICE/COMMERCIAL

1966 **WGEE** (Indianapolis)
1967 **WEFM-FM** (Chicago)
1968 **WFBM** (Indianapolis)
1969 **WOR-FM** (New York)
1970 **WEFM** (Chicago)
1971 **KAUM** (Houston)
1972 **WFMT** (Chicago)
1973 **WPST** (Trenton, N.J.)
1974 **WRFM** (New York)
1975 **KING-FM** (Seattle)

COMMUNITY SERVICE/NON-COMMERCIAL

1966 **KPFK** (N. Hollywood, Cal.)
1967 **WGBH-FM** (Boston)
1968 **WBUR** (Boston University, Boston)
1969 **WMUK** (University of Michigan, Kalamazoo)
1970 **WBST** (Ball State University, Muncie, Ind.)
1971 **WLVR** (Lehigh University, Bethelehem, Pa.)
1972 **WMUK** (Western Michigan University, Kalamazoo)
1973 **KPFA** (Berkeley, Cal.)
1974 **WBAI** (New York)
1975 **KSJN** (St. Paul)

COMMUNITY SERVICE

1976 **WRFM** (New York)
1977 **WILO-FM** (Frankfort, Ind.)
1978 **National Public Radio** (Washington)
1979 **WOR** (New York)
1980 **Not available at press time**

EDUCATION

1964 **WUHY-FM** (Philadelphia)
1965 **WRVR** (New York)

EDUCATIONAL/COMMERCIAL

1966 **No award**
1967 **WNCN** (New York)
1968 **CHUM** (Toronto)
1969 **KHFM** (Albuquerque)
1970 **KYTE** (Livermore, Cal.)
1971 **WFMT** (Chicago)
1972 **KHQ-FM** (Spokane)
1973 **WFMT** (Chicago)
1974 **Gamut Productions** (Barrington, Ill.)
1975 **WFMT** (Chicago)

EDUCATION/NON-COMMERCIAL

1966 **WBGO** (Newark)
1967 **WFCR** (Amherst, Mass.)
1968 **WAMU** (Washington)
1969 **WBUR** (Boston University, Boston)
1970 **CBC-FM** (Toronto)
1971 **WGUC** (University of Cincinnati, Cincinnati)
1972 **CBL-FM** (Toronto)
1973 **CBL-FM** (Toronto)
1974 **WOSU-FM** (Ohio State University, Columbus)
1975 **Earplay Productions** (Madison, Wis.)

EDUCATION

1976 **WBEN-FM** (Buffalo)
1977 **WGBH** (Boston)
1978 **CBC-FM** (Toronto)
1979 **WBEZ** (Chicago)
1980 **Not available at press time**

MUSIC

1964 **KHFI-FM** (Austin, Tex.)
1965 **KBCA** (Los Angeles)

MUSIC/COMMERCIAL

1966 **WPRB** (Princeton, N.J.)
1967 **KKHI** (San Francisco)
1968 **WNCN** (New York)
1969 **WFMT** (Chicago)
1970 **WEFM** (Chicago)
1971 **WFMT** (Chicago)
1972 **KSAN** (San Francisco)
1973 **WTIC-FM** (Hartford)
1974 **WCCO-FM** (Minneapolis)
1975 **WFMT** (Chicago)

MUSIC NON-COMMERCIAL

1966 **KPFK** (No. Hollywood, Cal.)
1967 **WAMU-FM** (Washington)
1968 **WUHY** (Philadelphia)
1969 **WFCR** (Amherst, Mass.)
1970 **WBAI** (New York)
1971 **KANU** (University of Kansas, Lawrence)
1972 **WITF-FM** (Hershey, Pa.)
1973 **WITF-FM** (Hershey, Pa.)
1974 **KANU** (University of Kansas, Lawrence)
1975 **WBAI** (New York)

MUSIC

1976 **WGMS-FM** (Rockville, Md.)
1977 **KNX-FM** (Los Angeles)
1978 **National Public Radio** (Washington)
1979 **CHFI** (Toronto)
1980 **Not available at press time**

NEWS

1964 **WFBE-FM** (Oak Grove Campus, Flint, Mich.)
1965 **WAMU-FM** (Washington)

NEWS/COMMERCIAL

1966 **KPEN** (San Francisco)
1967 **WTOA-FM** (Princeton, N.J.)
WFIL-FM (Philadelphia)
WNCN (New York)
1968 **CHUM** (Toronto)
1969 **WDAS** (Philadelphia)
1970 **CKFM** (Toronto)
1971 **KSAN** (San Francisco)
1972 **WBCN** (Boston)
1973 **WRVR** (New York)
1974 **WASH** (Washington)
1975 **WRFM** (New York)

NEWS/NON-COMMERCIAL

1966 **WBUR** (Boston University, Boston)
1967 **WBAI-FM** (New York)
KOAP-FM (Portland, Ore.)
1968 **WHA** (Madison, Wis.)
1969 **WTBS** (Cambridge, Mass.)
1970 **WBUR** (Boston University, Boston)
1971 **WBAI** (New York)
1972 **WBUR** (Boston University, Boston)
1973 **WOSU-FM** (Ohio State University, Columbus)
1974 **KSJN-FM** (St. Paul)
1975 **WBAI-FM** (New York)

NEWS

1976 **WXRT-FM** (Chicago)
1977 **WXRT-FM** (Chicago)
1978 **KSFO** (San Francisco)
1979 **WUHY-FM** (Philadelphia)
1980 **Not available at press time**

NEWS AND DOCUMENTARY

1976 **WBAI-FM** (New York)
1977 **WXRT-FM** (Chicago)
1978 **KPFA** (Pacifica Foundation, Berkeley, Cal.)
1979 **KYW** (Philadelphia)
1980 **Not available at press time**

CREATIVE USE OF THE MEDIUM

1976 **WFMT-FM** (Chicago)
1977 **Earplay** (Madison, Wis.)
1978 **National Public Radio** (Washington)
1979 **WGBH** (Boston)
1980 **Not available at press time**

SPECIAL AWARDS

1979 **WFMT** (Chicago), for technical achievement in broadcasting and innovative programming concept
Wayne Hetrich, National Public Radio (Washington), for technical achievement in broadcasting
Steve Ember, WETA-FM (Washington), for technical achievement in broadcasting

Robert Eunson Award

ASSOCIATED PRESS BROADCASTER SERVICES
50 Rockefeller Plaza, New York, N.Y. 10020 (212/262-6088)

The Robert Eunson Award, which consists of a plaque, is given annually on selection by the AP Broadcasters' board of directors to honor distinguished service to the broadcast industry.

1976 **Lawrence E. Spivak**
1977 **Robert Trout**
1978 **Elmer Lower**
1979 **Sen. Samuel J. Ervin, Jr.**
1980 **William S. Paley**

Prix Futura Berlin

SENDER FREIES BERLIN
Maurenallee 8-14, 1000 Berlin 19, Federal Republic of Germany (303-3100)

The International Radio and Television Competition, organized biennally by Sender Freies Berlin and Zweites Deutsches Fernsehen, is open to all broadcasting organizations authorized to provide broadcasting services. Four juries of five international radio and TV experts select the winners for outstanding productions. Each recipient of the Prix Futura Berlin gets 5,000 marks and a scroll.

TELEVISION

1969 **BBC**, U.K.
NHK, Japan
1971 **BBC**, U.K.
SRG, Switzerland
YLE, Finland
RTB, Belgium
1973 **BBC**, U.K.
SRG, Switzerland
ORTF, France
SR, Sweden
NHK, Japan
1975 **ARD**, Federal Republic of Germany
BBC, U.K.
ZDF, Federal Republic of Germany
NOS, Netherlands
JRT, Yugoslavia
BBC, U.K.
ARD, Federal Republic of Germany
1977 **BBC**, U.K.
FR 3, France
SR, Sweden
BRT, Belgium
1979 **NOS**, Netherlands
SR, Sweden

RADIO

1979 **BBC**, U.K.
CR, Denmark
SR, Sweden

Radio Programming Award Deejay of the Year Awards

Billboard
9000 Sunset Blvd., Los Angeles, Calif. 90069
(213/273-7040)

The Radio Programming Award, which consists of a plaque or scroll, annually honors outstanding achievements in programming, as based on votes of regional judges (in the case of deejay honors) and coupons in *Billboard* sent in by record and radio industry people.

1976 **Stan Monteiro** (Columbia), Vice-president in Charge of National Promotion
Bob Sherwood (Columbia), National Promotion Man
Mike Atkinson (Columbia, Los Angeles), Regional Promotion Man: West
Paul Ellis (Capricorn) Cincinnati), Regional Promotion Man: East
John Parker (Casablanca, Atlanta), Regional Promotion Man: South
Dick Lemke (Elektra/Asylum, Chicago), Regional Promotion Man: Midwest
Jerry Ross (Chrysalis, New York), Local Promotion Man: East
Barry Freeman (Atlantic, Los Angeles), Local Promotion Man: West
Lenny Zee (All South, New Orleans), Local Promotion Man: South

Dick Ware (Columbia, Kansas City), Local Promotion Man: Midwest
Paul Gallis, Independent Promotion Men
KFRC (San Francisco), Radio Station of the Year-Top 40 (Major Market)
WSGA (Savannah, Ga.), Radio Station of the Year-Top 40 (Small Market)
KEX (Portland, Ore.), Radio Station of the Year-MOR (Major Market)
WBT (Charlotte, N.C.), Radio Station of the Year-MOR (Small Market)
WHN (New York), Radio Station of the Year-Country (Major Market)
KCUB (Tucson, Ariz.), Radio Station of the Year-Country (Small Market)
KSAN (San Francisco), Radio Station of the Year-Progressive (Major Market)
KZEL (Eugene, Ore.), Radio Station of the Year-Progressive (Small Market)
WDIA (Memphis, Tenn.) Radio Station of the Year-R&B (Major Market)
WTMI (Miami), Radio Station of the Year-R&B (Small Market)
Bill Garcia (WRBQ, Tampa, Fla.), Program Director of the Year-Top 40 (Major Market)
Bill St. James (WBCQ, Roswell, N.M.), Program Director of the Year-Top 40 (Small Market)
Bob Hughes (WASH, Washington, D.C.), Program Director of the Year-MOR (Major Market)
Andy Bickel (WBT, Charlotte, N.C.), Program Director of the Year-MOR (Small Market)
Bill Robinson (WIRE, Indianapolis, Ind), Program Director of the Year-Country (Major Market)
Cyril Brennan (WBAM, Montgomery, Ala.), Program Director of the Year-Country (Small Market)
Rick Liebert (KGB, San Diego, Calif.), Program Director of the Year-Progressive (Major Market)
Stan Garrett (KZEL, Eugene, Ore.), Program Director of the Year-Progressive (Small Market)
Jim Maddox (KDIA, Oakland, Calif.), Program Director of the Year-R&B (Major Markets)
Shotgun Tom Kelly (KFMB, San Diego, Calif.), Air Personalities of the Year-Top 40 (Major Markets)
Terry Tyler (WIRK, W. Palm Beach, Fla.), Air Personalities of The Year-Top 40 (Small Markets)
Gene Klaven (WNEW, New York), Air Personalities of the Year-MOR (Major Markets)
Peter Hunn (WNLC, New London, Conn.), Air Personalities of the Year-MOR (Small Markets)
Alison Steele (WNEW-FM, New York), Air Personalities of the Year-Progressive (Major Markets)
Barry Grant (WPLR, New Haven, Conn.), Air Personalities of the Year-Progressive (Small Markets)
Deano Day (WDEE, Detroit), Air Personalities of the Year-Country (Major Markets)
Bob Barwick (WWVA, Wheeling, W.Va.), Air Personalities of the Year-Country (Small Markets)
J.J. Johnson (KDAY, Los Angeles), Air Personalities of the Year-R&B
TSgt. Bill Billingsley (TUSLOG Detachment 124, Incirlik CDI, Turkey), Military Air Personalities of the Year

1977 **Bill Robinson** (WIRE, Indianapolis, Ind.), Grand International Program Director of the Year
Gary Owens (KMPC, Los Angeles), Grand International Air Personality of the Year
Nat Stevens (KOY, Phoenix, Ariz.), Program Director of the Year-Adult Contemporary (Major Markets)
Bill Parris (WLPL, Baltimore), Program Director of the Year-Top 40 (Major Markets)
Bob Pittman (WKQX, Chicago), Program Director of the Year-Album Rock (Major Markets)
Bill Robinson (WIRE, Indianapolis, Ind.), Program Director of the Year-Country Music (Major Markets)
J.J. Johnson (KDAY, Los Angeles), Program Director of the Year-R&B (Major Markets)
Michael O'Shea (WFTL, Ft. Lauderdale, Fla.), Program Director of the Year-Adult Contemporary (Under a million population)
Dave Hamilton (WROK, Rockford, Ill.), Program Director of the Year-Country (Under a million population)
Tom Edwards (KEED, Eugene, Ore.), Program Director of the Year-Country (Under a million population)
Barry Grant (WPLR, New Haven, Conn.), Program Director of the Year-AlbumRock (Under a million population)
American Top 40 (Los Angeles), Best Regularly Scheduled Syndicated Program
The Evolution of Rock (CHUM, Toronto, Ont.), Syndicated Special of the Year
John Records Landecker (WLS, Chicago) and **Dan Ingram** (WABC, New York), Tie for Air Personality of the Year-Top 40 (Major Markets)
Lee Arnold (WHN, New York), Air Personality of the Year-Country (Major Markets)
Gary Owens (KMPC, Los Angeles), Air Personality of the Year-Adult Contemporary (Major Markets)
Ken Noble (KLOL, Houston), Air Personality of the Year-Album Rock (Major Markets)
Bobby Jay (WWRL, New York), Air Personality of the Year-Black Music (Major Markets)
Nick O'Neil (WGH, Norfolk, Va.), Air Personality of the Year-Top 40 (Under a million population)
Charlie Cook (WWVA, Wheeling, W.Va.), Air Personality of the Year-Country (Under a million population)
John Young (WSM, Nashville, Tenn.), Air Personality of the Year-Adult Contemporary (Under a million population)
Bernie Bernard (WBAB, Babylon, N.Y.), Air Personality of the Year-Album Rock (Under a million population)
Melvin Jones (WLOK, Memphis, Tenn.), Air Personality of the Year-Black Music (Under a million population)
Jose Mauro, (Radio TUPI, Rio de Janeiro, Brazil), International Program Director of the Year
Frank Jeffcoast (2ue, Sydney, Australia), International General Manager of the Year
WGR (Buffalo, N.Y.), Radio Station of the Year-Adult Contemporary (Major Markets)
KFRC (San Francisco), Radio Station of the Year-Top 40 (Major Markets)
KMET (Los Angeles), Radio Station of the Year-Album Rock (Major Markets)
WIRE (Indianapolis, Ind.), Radio Station of the Year-Country (Major Markets)
WDIA (Memphis, Tenn.), Radio Station of the Year-Black Music (Major Markets)
WFMT (Chicago), Radio Station of the Year- Classical Music (Major Markets)
WKZO (Kalamazoo, Mich.), Radio Station of the Year-Adult Contemporary (Under a million population)
WROK (Rockford, Ill.), Radio Station of the Year-Top 40 (Under a million population)
WPLR (New Haven, Conn.), Radio Station of the Year- Country (Under a million population)

KEED (Eugene, Ore.), Radio Station of the Year-Country (Under a million population)
John O'Day (WGAR, Cleveland), Newsperson of the Year (Major Markets)
Ray Carney (KPNW, Eugene, Ore.), Newsperson of the Year (Under a million population)
Bob Levy (AFNT, Taipei, Formosa), Best Military Personality of the Year
The Abby Drover Story (CFTR, Toronto, Ont.) Public Service Program Award
An Evening with Gordon Lightfoot (KNX-FM, Los Angeles), Entertainment Special of the Year
Car Tune (WHWH, Princeton, N.J.), Commercial of the Year
Water Safety (CFTR, Toronto, Ont.), Public Service Announcement of the Year
Ed Buterbaugh (CKLW, Detroit), Engineer of the Year
Bruce Wendell (Capitol Records), Chief Promotion Executive
Steve Meyer (Capitol Records), National Promotion Executive
Tim Kehr (20th Century Records), Regional Promotion Executive
Gene Denonovich (Columbia records), Local Promotion Executive
Doug Lee (Midwest Promotions, Minneapolis, Minn.), Independent Promotion Executive

Current status unknown

Poses Brandeis University Creative Arts Award

BRANDEIS UNIVERSITY
Brandeis University Commission Office, 12 E. 77th St., New York, N.Y. 10021 (212/472-1501)

One of a series of awards in the creative arts, the Jack I. and Lillian L. Poses Brandeis University Creative Arts Award is given annually to recognize talent in mid-career in theatre arts and film. The award, which may not be applied for, carries an honorarium of $1,000 and a medal or citation. Professional juries chosen by the commission select the winners.

MEDAL AWARD

1957 **Hallie Flanagan Davis** (Theatre arts)
1958 **Stark Young** (Theatre arts)
1959 **George Kelly** (Theatre arts)
1960 **Thornton Wilder** (Theatre arts)
1961 **Lillian Hellman** (Theatre arts)
1962 **Samuel N. Behrman** (Theatre arts)
1963 **Jo Mielziner** (Theatre arts)
1964 **Cheryl Crawford** (Theatre arts)
1965 **Tennessee Williams** (Theatre arts)
1966 **Eva Le Gallienne** (Theatre arts)
1967 **Jerome Robbins** (Theatre arts)
1968 **Richard Rodgers** (Theatre arts)
1969 **Boris Aronson** (Theatre arts)
1970 **Arthur Miller** (Theatre arts)
1971 **Charles Chaplin** (Film)
1972 **Alfred Lunt and Lynn Fontanne** (Theatre arts)
1973 **John Ford** (Film)
1974 **Helen Hayes** (Theatre arts)
1975 **King Vidor** (Film)
1976 **Harold Clurman** (Theatre arts)
1977 **Howard Hawks** (Film)
1978 **Jessica Tandy** and **Hume Cronyn** (Theatre arts)
1979 **George Cukor** (Film)
1980 **Lanford Wilson** (Theatre arts)

CITATION

1957 **The Shakespearewrights** (Theatre arts)
1958 **Paul Shyre** (Theatre arts)
1959 **Richard Hayes** (Theatre arts)
1960 **William Alfred** (Theatre arts)
1961 **Julian Beck and Judith Malina** (Theatre arts)
1962 **James P. Donleavy** (Theatre arts)
1963 **Joseph Papp** (Theatre arts)
1964 **Jack Richardson** (Theatre arts)
1965 **Michael Smith** (Theatre arts)
1966 **Alvin Epstein** (Theatre arts)
1967 **Ellen Stewart** (Theatre arts)
1968 **Tom O'Horgan** (Theatre arts)
1969 **The Negro Ensemble Company** (Theatre arts)
1970 **The Open Theater** (Theater arts)
1971 **Bruce Baillie** (Film)
1972 **The New Dramatists** (Theatre arts)
1973 **Stanley Brakhage** (Film)
1974 **Arena Stage** (Theatre arts)
1975 **Jordan Belson** (Film)
1976 **Sam Shepard** (Theatre arts)
1977 **John Hancock** (Film)
1978 **Long Wharf Theatre** (Theatre arts)
1979 **Bruce Conner** (Film)
1980 **No award**

Larry Boggs Award
Robert Beisswenger Memorial Award
Idell Kaitz Memorial Award

NATIONAL CABLE TELEVISION ASSOCIATION
916 16th St. NW, Washington, D.C. 20006 (202/457-6765)

The Larry Boggs Award is given annually to an active member of the cable-television industry on recommendation of association members and selection by an awards committee.

1965 **Bill Daniels**
1966 **Benjamin Conroy**
1967 **George Barco**
1968 **Fred Stevenson**
1969 **Martin Malarkey**
1970 **Irving B. Kahn**
1971 **Milton J. Shapp**
1972 **John Gwin**
1973 **E. Stratford Smith**
1974 **Frank Thompson**
1975 **Amos B. Hostetter, Jr.**
1976 **Alfred Stern**
1977 **Sam Haddock**
1978 **Ed Allen**
1979 **Burt I. Harris**
1980 **Robert Rosencrans**

The Robert Beisswenger Memorial Award goes annually to a member whose efforts on behalf of the association are judged as outstanding by the awards committee.

1975 **NCTA Associate Members**
1976 **Ray Schneider**
1977 **Richard Jackson**
1978 **Bruce Merrill**

1979 **Gerald W. Levin**
1980 **Sidney Topel**

The Idell Kaitz Memorial Award annually honors the significant contributions of a woman in the industry, as nominated from the membership and judged by an awards committee.

1973 **Yolanda Barco**
1974 **Polly Dunn**
1975 **Beverly Murphy**
1976 **Beverly Land**
1977 **No award**
1978 **Anna Marie Hutchinson**
1979 **Kay Koplovitz**
1980 **Gail Sermersheim**

John J. Gillin Jr. Award
H. Gordon Love News Trophy
Lloyd L. Moffat Award
Ted Rogers, Sr./Velma Rogers Graham Award
Colonel Keith S. Rogers Engineering Award

CANADIAN ASSOCIATION OF BROADCASTERS
85 Sparks St., Ste. 909, Ottawa, Ont. K1P 5S2, Canada
(613/233-4035)

The John J. Gillin Jr. Award is given to the AM Station of the Year for making the greatest public service or charitable contribution to its community. Stations may submit tape cassettes no longer than ten minutes for evaluation by a panel of judges. The winning station receives an engraved clock/barometer, and the winner's name is engraved on a permanent trophy.

1951 **CJOB** (Winnipeg)
1952 **CJOC** (Lethbridge, Alb.)
1953 **CKNW** (New Westminster, B.C.)
1954 **CJVI** (Victoria, B.C.)
1955 **CFAR** (Flin Flon, Man.)
1956 **CHAB** (Moose Jaw, Sask.)
1957 **CJVI** (Victoria, B.C.)
1958 **CJON** (St. John's, Nfld.)
1959 **CHAB** (Moose Jaw, Sask.)
1960 **Radio Nord** (Rouyn, Que.)
1961 **CHUM** (Toronto)
1962 **CKPR** (Thunder Bay [Fort William], Ont.)
1963 **CJBQ** (Belleville, Que.)
1964 **CHUM** (Toronto)
1965 **CFMB** (Montreal)
1966 **CKAC** (Montreal)
1967 **CJAD and CJMS** (Montreal)
1968 **No award**
1969 **CKLG** (Vancouver)
1970 **CHUM** (Toronto)
1971 **CKLG** (Vancouver)
1972 **CKXL** (Calgary)
1973 **CJCH** (Halifax)
1974 **CKDH** (Amherst, N.S.)
1975 **CHLN** (Trois-Rivieres, Que.)
1976 **CKBI** (Prince Albert, Sask.)
1977 **CHRC (Quebec City)**
CHML (Hamilton, Ont.)
1978 **CFAX** (Victoria, B.C.)
1979 **CFMB** (Montreal)
1980 **Not available at press time**

The H. Gordon Love News Trophy is awarded annually for a significant contribution to the improvement or increased availability of news material used by broadcasting stations in Canada and for making the public more conscious of the value of broadcast news. A committee of judges selects the winner, which receives a trophy that is a replica of an early microphone.

1968 **CFPL-TV** (London)
1969 **CJCH** (Halifax)
1970 **CJCH-TV** (Halifax)
1971 **CJCI** (Prince George)
1972 **CKLG** (Vancouver)
1973 **CKNW** (New Westminster)
1974 **CFRB** (Toronto)
1975 **CJCB** (Sydney)
1976 **CKY-TV** (Winnipeg)
1977 **CKY-TV** (Winnipeg)
1978 **BCTU** (Vancouver)
1979 **CFRB** (Toronto)
1980 **Not available at press time**

The Lloyd L. Moffat Award goes annually to the FM Station of the Year for making the greatest contribution to the community. Stations may submit tapes up to ten minutes long for evaluation by a panel of judges. The winner receives a trophy.

1968 **CJMS-FM (CKMF-FM)** (Montreal)
1969 **CHRC-FM** (Quebec)
1970 **CFPL-FM** (London)
1971 **CFPL-FM** (London)
1972 **CKLG-FM** (Vancouver)
1973 **CFMI-FM** (New Westminster, B.C.)
1974 **CFFM-FM** (Kamloops, B.C.)
1975 **CHSC-FM** (St. Catharines, Ont.)
1976 **CKFM-FM** (Toronto)
1977 **CHQM-FM** (Vancouver)
1978 **CJAY-FM** (Calgary)
1979 **CFMI-FM** (New Westminster, B.C.)
1980 **Not available at press time**

The Ted Rogers, Sr./Velma Rogers Graham Award honors an individual for significant single or continuing contributions to Canadian broadcasting or for exceptional community service. The award consists of an original oil painting. A committee of judges selects the winner.

1975 **A.A. Brunner,** Global TV
1976 **G.R.A. Rice,** CFRM-AM, -FM and -TV (Edmonton)
1977 **Alan F. Waters,** CHUM Ltd. (Toronto)
1978 **Conrad Lavigne**, Mid-Canada TV (Timmins, Ont.)
1979 **Ernie Rose**, BCTV (Vancouver, B.C.)
1980 **Not available at press time**

The Colonel Keith S. Rogers Engineering Award recognizes significant engineering accomplishments by a station or individual for the successful development of technical ideas, approaches or methods. A panel of judges selects the winner, who receives a trophy.

1950 **J. O. Blick, CJOB** (Winnipeg)
1951 **CJOB, CKRC and CKY** (Winnipeg)
1952 **George Chandler, CJOR** (Vancouver)
1953 **Glen Robitaille, CFPL** (London, Ont.)
1954 **William Forst, CKOM** (Saskatoon)
1955 **CFJB** Brampton and **CHUM** (Toronto)

1956 **No award**
1957 **CJON** (St. John's, Nfld.)
1958 **W.E. Jeynes, CHCH-TV** (Hamilton, Ont.)
1959 **No award**
1960 **No award**
1961 **Glen Robitaille, CFPL** (London, Ont.)
1962 **Clive Eastwood, CFRB** (Toronto)
1963 **W.B. Smith, Dept. of Transport** (Ottawa)
1964 **No award**
1965 **No award**
1966 **No award**
1967 **Ron Turnpenny, CHFI** (Toronto)
1968 **No award**
1969 **No award**
1970 **CFAM-CHSM** (Altona-Steinbach, Man.)
1971 **Conrad Lavigne, CFCL-TV** (Timmins, Ont.)
1972 **Western Broadcasting** (Vancouver)
1973 **Ernie Rose, CHAN-TV** (Vancouver)
1974 **No award**
1975 **CKXL** (Calgary)
1976 **No award**
1977 **Radiomutuel** (Montreal)
1978 **Mid-Canada Television** (Timmins, Ont.)
1979 **No award**
1980 **Not available at press time**

CIBA GEIGY/NAFB Award

CIBA-GEIGY
Box 11422, Greensboro, N.C. 27409 (919/292-7100)

The CIBA-GEIGY/NAFB Award is given annually to a member of the National Association of Farm Broadcasters. The recipient, who is chosen by a panel from agribusiness marketing, advertising and farming, is given a trophy and an expense-paid trip to Switzerland, where the donor's headquarters are located.

1970 **George Logan,** WIBW (Topeka, Kan.)
1971 **Barney Arnold,** WHAS (Louisville, Ky.)
1972 **Keith Kirkpatrick,** WHO (Des Moines, Iowa)
1973 **Russell Pierson,** WKY (Oklahoma City, Okla.)
1974 **Verne Strickland,** WRAL (Raleigh, N.C.)
1975 **Wey Simpson,** KHQ (Spokane, Wash.)
1976 **Ray Wilkinson,** WRAL (Raleigh, N.C.)
1977 **Royce Bodiford,** KGNC (Amarillo, Tex.)
1978 **Rich Hull,** WIBW (Topeka, Kan.)
1979 **Marvin Vines,** KAAY (Little Rock, Ark.)
1980 **Lee Kline,** WHO (Des Moines, Iowa)

Clarion Awards

WOMEN IN COMMUNICATIONS
Box 9561, Austin, Tex. 78766 (512/345-8922)

The Clarion Awards, which are plaques, are given annually in three divisions: human rights, the world we live in and the community we serve. In addition to the broadcast honors listed below, print journalism and public relations categories are honored and are listed elsewhere in this volume. Materials may be submitted for consideration by a panel of communications professionals from around the country. In addition to the first-place honors listed here, honorable mentions are made.

TELEVISION (in any division)

1973 **Marlene Sanders**, ABC News (New York)
Marilyn Salenger with **Jim Gordon**, WNAC-TV (Boston)
1974 **WKY-TV3** (Philadelphia)
ABC-TV (New York) for *Women's Place*
WTVF Montage (Miami)
KMGH-TV (Denver)
1975 **Vicki Monks**, KWTV (Oklahoma City)
Christine Lund, KABC-TV News (Los Angeles)
Herb Levy, KRON-TV (San Francisco)
1976 **ABC-TV** for *The American Woman: Portraits of Courage*
Marlene Sanders, ABC-TV
Gloria Penner and **Maureen Shiftan**, KPBS-TV (La Jolla, Calif.)
1977 **Patricia Lynch**, WNBC-TV (New York)
Sue Levit, KYW-TV
Erna Akuginow, WCAU-TV (Philadelphia)
1978 **ABC-TV** for *Roots*
Joan Konner, NBC News
Howard Stringer, **Tom Spain** and **Bill Moyers**, *CBS Reports*
Beverly Williams and **Cliff Abromats**, KYW-TV (Philadelphia)
Peter Miller Adato, WNET-13 (New York)
Susan Silk and **Garry Armstrong**, WNAC-TV (Boston)
1979 **CBS-TV** for *The Defection of Simas Kudirka*
CBS-TV for *The Body Human: The Red River*
Smithsonian Institution Office of Telecommunications (Washington)
Herbert Brodkin and **Robert Berger**, NBC-TV for *Holocaust*
Paula Woodward and **Sam Allen**, KBTV (Denver)
Dan Sitarski and **Erna Akuginow** WCAU-TV (Philadelphia)
Darrell Barton and **Ron Turner**, KTVY (Oklahoma City)
Patricia Lynch, *NBC-TV Nightly News*
1980 **Dennis Troute** and **John Gudjohnsen**, WFAA-TV (Dallas)
CBS-TV for *The Body Human: The Sexes*
Phillip Byrd and **Larry Lorenz**, WMVS-TV (Milwaukee)
Peter Karl and **Doug Longhini**, WLS-TV (Chicago)
Ted Koppel, **Mike von Fremd** and **Phil Bergman**, *ABC's World News Tonight*
NBC-TV for *Children's Public Service Composite*

RADIO (in any division)

1973 **No award**
1974 **WNYE-FM** (Brooklyn, N.Y.)
Miriam Bjerre, KNX-Radio
1975 **Gloria Gibson**, WWDC-AM/FM (Silver Spring, Md.)
Mike Sakillarides KGW (Portland, Ore.)
1976 **Joy Epps**, WMAL-Radio
Laura Wallace, KCBS-Radio
1977 **Barbara Esensten**, KFWB-Radio
Rachel Kranz, KCJN-FM Radio
Beverly Poppel, WRFM-Radio
1978 **Gale Cunningham**, KXL-AM/FM (Portland, Ore.)
Bill Cusack, WBZ-Radio (Boston)
Susan Stamberg, National Public Radio
1979 **Amy Sabrin** and **Patti Berman**, Associated Press Radio Network
Jack Miller and **Mark J. Weiner,** WCBS-FM (New York)
Beryl Pfizer and **Hank Miles**, NBC

John Merrow and **Barbara Reinhardt**, National Public Radio
David Ross, KIRO Newsradio 71 (Seattle)
Irene Cornell, WCBS Newsradio 88 (New York)
Robert Hyland, KMOX-Radio (St. Louis)

1980 **Danielle Karson**, Associated Press Radio Network
Nancy Fushan, KSJN/Minnesota Public Radio (St. Paul)
Ray Geraty, **Larry Kasoff** and **Alan Walden**, NBC
Mary Lou Johanek, KMOX-Radio (St. Louis)
Ira Flatow, National Public Radio (Washington)
Mary Gay Taylor, WCBS-Radio (New York)

ACT Achievement in Children's Television Award

ACTION FOR CHILDREN's TELEVISION
46 Austin St., Newtonville, Mass. 02160 (617/727-7870)

The ACT Achievement in Children's Television Award is presented annually to broadcasters who have made a significant achievement toward improving children's television. Individuals, stations, networks and companies or organizations that provide funding for exceptional programs or set meritorious advertising policies may be honored.

1972 **Post-Newsweek television stations** in Washington, D.C., and Florida for seeking quality programs and clustering commercials on such programs
Hallmark Cards, for sponsoring *The Snow Goose,* NBC
Health-tex, for institutional advertising on *Babar Comes to America,* NBC
Children's Television Workshop, for conceiving a creative unit devoted to producing children's shows and experimenting in television education for young children
Fred Rogers, for pioneering efforts to meet the emotional needs of young children through television
Robert Keeshan, for sixteen years of creative children's television on *Captain Kangaroo*
The Kids' Thing, WHDH-TV, Boston, for noncommercial school vacation week programs
Public broadcasting stations, for *Misterogers' Neighborhood, Sesame Street, Electric Company, Masquerade, ZOOM, Hodge Podge Lodge* and *What's New*

1973 **Sears-Roebuck Foundation,** for *Misterogers' Neighborhood*
Xerox Corp., for Spanish and Portuguese versions of *Sesame Street*
Mobil Oil Corp., for *Electric Company*
IBM, for *Sleeping Beauty* ballet, aired when many children were watching
Miles Laboratories, Sauter Labs/Hoffmann-La Roche and Bristol-Myers, for withdrawing vitamin pill advertising from children's programs
Avco and Meredith Broadcasting Corp., for combining resources to produce meaningful children's programs
ABC-TV, for *Afterschool Specials,* one hour monthly
CBS News, for *What's An Election All About* and *What's A Convention All About,* news specials for children
NBC-TV, for *Watch Your Child,* an attempt at a daily half-hour program with limited commercialism
Westinghouse Broadcasting, for continued commitment to science for children, specifically *Earth Lab*
WCVB-TV, Boston, for commitment to needs of community's children, specifically *Jabberwocky* and *Young Reporters*
WMAL-TV, Washington, for daily children's program with clustered commercials, *The Magic Door*
WPIX-TV, New York, for two local children's programs with clustered commercials, *Magic Garden* and *Joya's Fun School*
The 350,000 children who contributed creative material and ideas to *Zoom*
Forty-eight commercial stations who aired *Vision On,* the first children's program designed for both deaf and hearing children
Forty-four commercial stations, for airing *Sesame Street* without commercials

1974 **ABC-TV stations,** for *Over 7,* magazine format for family viewing
Alphaventure, for creating *Big Blue Marble* with ITT noncommercial backing and teacher materials to supplement the program
CBS-TV News, for *In the News,* brief Saturday morning reports
Chinese Committee for Affirmative Action, San Francisco, for *Yut, Yee, Sahm (Here We Come)*
Exxon USA Foundation, for supporting *Villa Alegre* on PBS
Prime Time School Television, Chicago, for developing and distributing educational materials for classroom use about televised prime-time specials and documentaries
WBZ-TV, Boston, for *Something Else,* featuring local children in a constructive alternative to Saturday morning viewing
WNET, New York, for two-week festival of quality daytime programming

1975 **CBS-TV,** for *The CBS Children's Film Festival*
CBS-TV News, for *Marshall Efron's Illustrated, Simplified and Painless Sunday School*
Children's Television Workshop, for *The Electric Company*
Robert Keeshan Associates, producers of *Captain Kangaroo*
KLRN-TV, Austin, Tex., for *Carrascolendas,* bilingual program
NBC-TV, for *GO-USA,* a series of historical dramas
Post-Newsweek stations, for *The Reading Show,* combining broadcast and published materials
Taft Broadcasting Co., for *Max B. Nimble*
Martin Tahse Productions, for bringing back *Kukla, Fran and Ollie*
Westinghouse Broadcasting Co., for *Call it Macaroni,* adventure series
WGBH, Boston, for *The Spider's Web,* daily radio storybook
WXYZ-TV, Detroit, for *Hot Fudge,* contributing to preventive medicine in mental health

1976 **ABC-TV,** for *ABC Afterschool Specials,* dramatic series
ABC-TV News, for *Animals Animals Animals*
Behrens Co., Miami, for *Kidsworld,* national news magazine for children with contributions for participating stations
Educational Development Center, Newton, Mass., for *Infinity Factory*
KETC-TV, St. Louis, for *Common Cents*
KOMO-TV, Seattle, for *Boomerang*
KRON-TV, San Francisco, for *Kidswatch*
NBC-TV, for *Muggsy*
NBC-TV, for *Special Treat*
WGBH-TV, Boston, for *Rebop*

WMAQ-TV, Chicago, for *Bubblegum Digest*
WQED-TV, Pittsburgh, for *Once Upon a Classic*
WSB-TV, Atlanta, for *Operation Education*
Sears Roebuck Foundation for *Misterogers' Neighborhood*

1977 **ABC,** for *Weekend Specials*
CBS, for *Fat Albert*
Corporation for Entertainment and Learning Inc.
Field Communications for *Snipets*
South Carolina ETV, for *Studio See*
Walt Disney Productions, for *The New* **Mickey Mouse Club**
WGBH, Boston, for *Captioned Zoom*
WIIC-TV, Pittsburgh, for *Catercousins*
WRC-TV, Washington, D.C., for *Beth and Bower Half Hour*
WSB-TB, Atlanta, for *Super 2*
WTTW-TV, Chicago, for *As *We* See* It*

1978 **Children's Television Workshop** on the 10th anniversary of *Sesame Street*
KHJ-TV, Los Angeles, for refusing to air commercials for highly sugared food products during its daily children's telecasts
CBS-TV News, for *30 Minutes*, a weekly series that comments on the current scene
KCET-TV, Los Angeles, for *Freestyle*, series of 13 programs that free children from the boundaries of ethnic and sex-role stereotyping
KING-TV, Seattle, for *I Like Myself* weekly series on nature
KRON-TV, San Francisco, for *Just Kidding*, weekly series on contemporary themes
KYW-TV, Philadelphia, for *Expressway,* daily program of music and movement for preschoolers
UA-Columbia Cablevision, for *Calliope*, weekly series of enchanting children's films for cable television
WBNG-TV, Binghamton, for *Action News for Kids*
WBZ-TV, Boston, for *The City Show*, a series of 15 programs on the excitement of the city
WGBH-Radio, Boston, for *The Spider's Web*, a daily program "that paints pictures in the mind"
WSOC-TV, Charlotte, for *Kidsworld*, weekly series that adds a regional flavor to a syndicated series
Workshop on Children's Awareness, American Institutes for Research, Cambridge, Mass., for *Feeling Free,* six-program series that "wages gentle combat with children's misconceptions and disabilities"

1979 **Agency for Instructional Television**, for *Think About,* "a series of astonished excellence that portrays with compassion the skills essential for learning"
KRON-TV, San Francisco, for "extra-special commitment to local programming for young audiences"
KING-TV, Seattle, for "extra-special commitment to local programming for young audiences"
Capital Cities Communications, Inc., for *Family Specials,* original dramas that "illuminate with candor and perception the problems of young adults"
KCOP-TV, Hollywood, for adding cultural and ethnic diversity to *Romper Room*
Warner Ames Satellite Entertainment Corp., for *Nickelodeon*, presenting daily uninterrupted programming for children
WAFB-TV, Baton Rouge, for *Storyland*, daily program for preschoolers —with helpful advice to parents
WBZ-TV, Boston, for *Get Off Your Block,* weekly series that explores the local scene
WCSH-TV, Portland, Me., for *Seesaw,* "a program that injects a new element of teenage analysis to a library of quality dramas"
WMAQ-TV, Chicago, for *Kidding Around,* a variety show highlighting the "talent and diversity of children"
WPLG-TV, Miami, for *Arthur and Company,* acknowledging its 10th year of "contributing gentle pleasures to very young audiences"
WPRI-TV, Providence, for *Allamaze,* a program "that brings life and liveliness" of art to children
WPVI-TV, Philadelphia, for *Captain Noah's Adventure,* dramatic portrayal of local history
WWLP-TV, Springfield, Mass., for *Odyssey,* a series "that sets the standards for responsibility to children and their families with special limits on advertising"

1980 **Not available at press time**

SPECIAL AWARDS

1975 **Agency for Instructional television** for informational and informative classroom programs
1976 **Public Broadcasting Service**
1977 **Westinghouse Broadcasting Co.**

OTHER AWARDS

1972 **Commendations** (for children's programming which were cited but did not meet ACT's criteria for limitation or absence of commercialism):
Earth Lab
Children's Film Festival
In the News
You Are There
Jackson Five
Curiosity Shop
Make A Wish
Take A Giant Step
Mr. Wizard

1973 **Special Mention:**
The Waltons
National Geographic Society Specials
Jacques Cousteau's specials

1978 **Citations for Continuing Excellence:**
ABC-TV, for *ABC Afterschool and Weekend Specials*
ABC News, for *Animals Animals Animals*
WGBH-TV, Boston, for *Rebop*
WQED-TV, Pittsburgh, for *Once Upon a Classic*
ACT Corporate Honor Roll Award:
McDonald's Corp., for support of PBS series, *Once Upon a Classic*

1979 **Citations for Continuing Excellence:**
ABC-TV, for *ABC Aftershool and Weekend Specials*
The Behrens Co., for *Kidsworld*
CBS-TV News, for *30 Minutes*
Multimedia, for *Young People's Specials*
WQED-TV, Pittsburgh, for *Once Upon a Classic*
ACT Corporate Honor Roll Award:
McDonald's Corp., for support of PBS series, *Once Upon a Classic*

1980 **Not available at press time**

Morgan Cox Award

WRITERS GUILD OF AMERICA, WEST
8955 Beverly Blvd., Los Angeles, Cal. 90048
(213/550-1000)

The Morgan Cox Award, which consists of a silver medallion, is a service award granted annually for perpetuation of the ideals represented by the life of Morgan Cox, including idealism, effort and personal sacrifice.

1970 **Barry Trivers**

1971 **Leonard Spigelgass**
1972 **Allen Rivkin**
1973 **David Harmon**
1974 **James R. Webb**
1975 **Edmund H. North**
1976 **William Ludwig**
1977 **Herbert Baker**
1978 **John Furia, Jr.**
1979 **George Seaton**
1980 **Fay Kanin**

DuPont-Columbia Awards

COLUMBIA UNIVERSITY
Graduate School of Journalism, New York, N.Y. 10027
(212/280-5047)

The Alfred I. DuPont-Columbia University Awards annually honor excellence in local and national broadcasting. The awards are based on research done in conjunction with the annual DuPont-Columbia Survey of Broadcast Journalism of news and public affairs broadcasting. Nominations may be made to the Survey and Awards Director for consideration by the jury. Until 1965 this award was known as the DuPont Award. No fixed categories exist.

1942 **KGEI Radio** (San Francisco)
Fulton Lewis, Jr.
1943 **WLW Radio** (Cincinnati)
WMAZ Radio (Macon, Ga.)
Raymond Gram Swing
1944 **WJR Radio** (Detroit)
WTAG Radio (Worcester, Mass.)
H.V. Kaltenborn
1945 **KDKA Radio** (Pittsburgh)
WNAX Radio (Yanktown, S.D.)
Lowell Thomas
1946 **WHO Radio** (Des Moines)
WKY Radio (Oklahoma City)
Elmer Davis
1947 **WBBM Radio** (Chicago)
WFIL Radio (Philadelphia)
Edward R. Murrow
1948 **WLS Radio** (Chicago)
KLZ Radio (Denver)
Henry J. Taylor
1949 **WNOX Radio** (Knoxville, Tenn.)
WWJ Radio (Detroit)
WPIX Television (New York)
American Broadcasting Co.
1950 **WFIL Television** (Philadelphia)
WAVZ Radio (New Haven, Conn.)
John Cameron Swayze
1951 **WCAU and WCAU-TV** (Philadelphia)
WEEI Radio (Boston)
Joseph C. Harsch
1952 **WBNS-TV** (Columbus, Ohio)
WMT-Radio (Cedar Rapids, Iowa)
Gerald W. Johnson
1953 **WBZ and WBZ-TV** (Boston)
WOI-TV (Ames, Iowa)
Pauline Frederick
1954 **WHAS Radio** (Louisville, Ky.)
KGAK Radio (Gallup, N.M.)
Eric Sevareid
1955 **WTIC Radio** (Hartford, Conn.)
WICC Radio (Bridgeport, Conn.)
Howard K. Smith
1956 **KNXT-TV** (Los Angeles)
WFMT Radio (Chicago)
Chet Huntley
1957 **KRON-TV** (San Francisco)
KARD Radio (Wichita, Kan.)
Clifton Utley
1958 **KLZ-TV** (Denver)
WSNY Radio (Schenectady, N.Y.)
David Brinkley
1959 **WNTA-TV** (Newark, N.J.)
KOLN-TV (Lincoln, Neb.)
David Schoenbrun
1960 **KDKA-TV** (Pittsburgh)
WAVZ Radio (New Haven, Conn.)
Edward P. Morgan
1961 **KING Radio** (Seattle)
KPFP Radio (Los Angeles)
Martin Agronsky
1962 **WFMT Radio** (Chicago)
KVOA-TV (Tucson, Ariz.)
Howard K. Smith
1963 **WFBM** (Indianapolis, Ind.)
WJZ-TV (Baltimore)
Louis M. Lyons
1964 **WFTV Radio** (Orlando, Fla.)
WRCV-TV (Philadelphia)
1965 **WBBM-TV** (Chicago)
KTWO-TV (Casper, Wyo.)
WCCO (Minneapolis)
WHCU (Ithaca, N.Y.)
WRVR (New York)
Cecil Brown
WFBM-TV (Indianapolis)
1966 **No awards**
1967 **No awards**
1968-69 **Everett Parker**
WRKL-Radio (Mount Ivy-New City, N.Y.)
KQED-TV (San Francisco)
NBC and *First Tuesday*, for "CBW—The Secrets of Secrecy"
Al Levin and Public Broadcast Library, for *Defense and Domestic Needs: The Contest for Tomorrow*
Don Widener and KNBC-TV (Los Angeles), for *The Slow Guillotine*
WSB-TV (Atlanta), for continuing coverage of organized crime in the community
1969-70 **Kenneth A. Cox, Frederick Wiseman and National Education Television,** for *Hospital*
John Laurence and *CBS Evening News* for "Charlie Company" series of reports
WCCO-TV (Minneapolis), for *Grunt's Little War*
Fred Freed and National Broadcasting Co., for *Pollution is a Matter of Choice*
WOOD-TV (Grand Rapids, Mich.) for *Our Poisoned World*
1970-71 **John Sharnik and CBS News,** for *Justice in America*
***First Tuesday* and NBC News,** for *The Man from Uncle (Sam)—the FBI*
Martin Carr and NBC News, for *This Child is Rated X—Migrant*
Susan Garfield and Group W, for *All the Kids Like That*
Geraldo Rivera and WABC-TV (New York), for *Drug Crisis in East Harlem*
Diane Orr and KUTV-TV (Salt Lake City, Utah), for *Warrior Without a Weapon*
1971-72 **Fred Freed and NBC News,** for *The Blue Collar Trap*

Robert Markowitz and CBS News, for *. . . but what if the dream comes true?*
Group W, for *The Search for Quality Education*
John Drimmer and WNJT (Trenton, N.J.), for *Towers of Frustration*
MTVJ (Miami) for A Seed of Hope and *The Swift Justice of Europe*
Tony Batten, *The 51st State,* WNET/13 (New York), for "Youth Gangs in the South Bronx"
Richard Thurston Watkins, *Like It Is* and WABC-TV (New York), for *Attica: The Unanswered Questions*
Mike Wallace, for outstanding reporting on *60 Minutes*
NPACT and KERA (Dallas, Tex.), for outstanding coverage of the 1972 political campaigns

1972-73 Arthur Holch and ABC News
Irv Drasnin and CBS News
Robert Northshield and NBC News
Dick Hubert and Group W
WBBM-TV, Chicago
WTIC-TV, Hartford, Conn.
KGW-TV, Portland, Ore.
Elizabeth Drew and NPACT

1973-74 Av Westin and ABC News, for *Close-Up*
Don Hewitt and CBS News, for *60 Minutes*
Fred Freed and NBC News, for *The Energy Crisis*
National Public Affairs Center for Television, for Watergate coverage
National Public Affairs Center for Television, for *Washington Week in Review*
KFWB Radio (Los Angeles), for *SLA 54th Street Shootout*
KNXT-TV (Los Angeles), for *Why Me?*
WKY-TV (Oklahoma City), for *Through the Looking Glass Darkly*
TVTV and WNET/13 (New York), for *The Lord of the Universe*
Frederick Wiseman and WNET/13 (New York), for *Juvenile Court*
WPVI-TV (Philadelphia), for *Public Bridges and Private Riches*

1974-75 National Public Radio, for *All Things Considered*
Tom Pettit and *NBC Nightly News,* for a series of reports on feeding the poor
Don Harris and KNBC-TV (Burbank, Calif.), for *Prison Gangs*
WBTV (Charlotte, N.C.), for news and documentary programming
WCCO-Radio (Minneapolis), for news and documentary programming
David Moore and WCCO-TV (Minneapolis), for *Moore on Sunday*
WGBH-TV (Boston), for *Arabs and Israelis*
Warren Doremus and WHEC-TV (Rochester, N.Y.), for *The Riots Plus 10 Years*
Clarence Jones and WPLG-TV (Miami), for crime reporting

1975-76 No awards

1976-77 Group W, for *Six American Families*
WBBM-TV (Chicago), for *Once A Priest*
WNET (New York) and **WEDA** (Washington), for *MacNeil/Lehrer Report*(PBS)
KCET-TV (Los Angeles), for *28 Tonight*
KGW-TV (Portland, Ore.), for *The Timber Farmers*
WSAA-TV (Dallas), for outstanding programming
WNBC News, for *Human Rights: A Soviet-American Debate* and *The Struggle for Freedom*
WNET (New York), for *The Police Tapes*
Walter Cronkite and **CBS** for *the CBS Evening News*

1977-78 KOOL-TV (Phoenix), for *Water: Arizona's Most Precious Resource*
KPIX-TV (San Francisco), for *Laser Con-Fusion*
WBBM-TV (Chicago), *Signs of Love* and *A Matter of Policy*
WFAA-TV (Dallas), for investigative reporting, TV for *Nova series and Chachaji: My Poor Relation*
WGBH-Radio (Boston), for *Banned in Chelsea*
WMHT-TV (Schenectady, N.Y.), for *Inside Albany*
WPLG-TV and **Clarence Jones**, for *Scandal at CETA: Poverty Profiteers*
Associated Press Radio and **J. Frederikse**, for *The New South: Shade Behind the Sunbelt*
WQED-TV (Pittsburgh) and **The National Geographic Society**, for *The Living Sands of Namib*
NBC-TV, for *NBC Reports: Africa's Defiant White Tribe*

1978-79 KCTS-TV (Seattle), *Do I Look Like I Want to Die?*
KDFW-TV (Dallas), reporting on aliens and children
KUTV (Salt Lake City), *Clouds of Doubt*
KXL Radio (Portland, Ore.), *The Air Space — How Safe?*
WGBH-TV (Boston), *World/Inside Europe: F-16 Sale of the Century*
WHA-TV (Madison, Wisc.), Catalyst Films and Wisconsin Educational Television Network, *An American Ism: Joe McCarthy*
ABC News, *Closeup: Arson, Fire for Hire!*
ABC News, *World News Tonight—Second to None*
CBS News, *CBS Reports—The Boat People*
CBS News, *60 Minutes*
Bill D. Moyers, outstanding reporting on CBS-TV and WNET-TV

1979-80 Walter Jacobson and **WBBM-TV** (Chicago), *Perspectives*
Mary Feldhaus-Weber, **Red Cloud Productions** and **WGBY-TV** (Springfield, Mass.), *Joan Robinson: One Woman's Story*
WLS-TV (Chicago) and ***Chicago Sun-Times***, *The Accident Swindlers*
Perry Miller Adato and **WNET**, *Picasso: A Painter's Diary*
Group W and **KYW-TV** (Philadelphia), **WBZ-TV** (Boston) and **WJZ-TV** (Baltimore), for I-team investigative reporting
Mississippi Center for Educational Television, *William Faulkner: A Life on Paper*
National Public Radio, *All Things Considered* and *Morning Edition*
ABC-TV, *The Iran Crisis: America Held Hostage*
Ed Bradley and **CBS-TV**, *CBS Reports: Blacks in America*
Roger Mudd and **CBS-TV**, *CBS Reports: Teddy*
Reuven Frank and **NBC-TV**, *NBC White Paper: If Japan Can . . . Why Can't We?*
Robert Riggs asnd **WAST-TV** (Albany), *Downhill Dollars*
WCCO-TV (Minneapolis), *The Moore Report*
WCVB-TV (Needham, Mass.), *Denise*
Robert Richter and **WGBH-TV** (Boston), *Nova: A Plague on Our Children*
Lorraine Gray and **WNET** (New York), *Independent Focus: With Babies and Banners*
Lea Thompson and **WRC-TV** (Washington), *Baby Formula: The Hidden Dangers*
Alan Griggs and **WSM-TV** (Nashville), *KKK: The Wizards at Odds*

Public Broadcasting Associates, *Odyssey: Seeking the First Americans*
ABC-TV, *Directions* and *Closeup: This Shattered Land*
CBS-TV, *Campaign '80* and *CBS Magazine*

A total of $20,000 is given to the individuals and/or organizations judged to have created the most meritorious independent production aired on television. The station first broadcasting the program shares the honors.

1979-80 **Carol Mon Pere** and **Sandra Nichols**, and **WTEH-TV** (San Jose, Cal.), *The Battle of the Westlands*

SPECIAL AWARD

1979 **Richard Salant**, president, CBS News

Emmy Awards

NATIONAL ACADEMY OF TELEVISION ARTS AND SCIENCES
110 W. 57th St., New York, N.Y. 10019 (212/586-8424)

The Emmy Award, which consists of a statuette, is presented annually for outstanding programs, performers and behind-the-scenes talent in television broadcasting, as well as for exceptional service or contributions to the industry. The first Emmys were given at a time when there were sixteen television stations and 190,000 sets across the country. Today, the award ceremony itself is an extravaganza telecast into tens of millions of homes. Winners are selected by "blue-ribbon panels" from nominees chosen by Academy members. Emmys are also given for daytime programming and for local programming in various cities. These are too numerous to list here. Because the categories in the national Emmy awards procedure change to a greater or lesser extent every year, national prime-time winners are listed year by year rather than by category.

1948 **Shirley Dinsdale and her puppet Judy Splinters,** Most Outstanding Television Personality
Pantomime Quiz Time, "Most Popular Television Program"
The Necklace, "Best Film Made for Television"
KTLA (Los Angeles), "Station Award for Outstanding Overall Achievement"
Charles Mesak, "Technical Award" (for the Phasefader)
Louis McManus, "Special Award" (for original design of the Emmy statuette)

1949 **Ed Wynn, KTTV,** "Best Live Show"
Texaco Star Theatre, "Best Kinescope Show"
Time for Beany, **"Best Children's Show"**
Ed Wynn, "Most Outstanding Live Personality"
Life of Riley, "Best Film Made for and Viewed on Television"
Milton Berle, "Most Outstanding Kinescoped Personality"
Crusade in Europe, "Best Public Service, Cultural or Educational Program"
Wrestling, "Best Sports Coverage"
KTLA (Los Angeles), "Station Achievement"
Lucky Strike/N.W. Ayer, "Best Commercial Made for Television"
Harold W. Jury, "Technical Award"

1950 **Alan Young,** "Best Actor"
Gertrude Berg, "Best Actress"
Groucho Marx, "Most Outstanding Personality"
City at Night, "Best Public Service"
Campus Chorus and Orchestra, "Best Cultural Show"
Departure of Marines for Korea, "Special Events"
Rams Football, "Best Sports Program"
The Alan Young Show, "Best Variety Show"
KFI-TV University, "Best Educational Show"
Time for Beany, "Best Children's Show"
Pulitzer Prize Playhouse, "Best Dramatic Show"
KTLA Newsreel, "Best News Program"
Truth or Consequences, "Best Game and Audience Participation Show"
KTLA (Los Angeles), "Station Achievement"
KNBH/NBC, "Technical Achievement for Orthogram TV"

1951 ***Studio One*** **(CBS),** "Best Dramatic Show"
Red Skelton Show (NBC), "Best Comedy Show"
Your Show of Shows (NBC), "Best Variety Show"
Sid Caesar, "Best Actor"
Imogene Coca, "Best Actress"
Red Skelton, "Best Comedian or Comedienne"
U.S. Sen. Estes Kefauver, "Special Achievement Award"

1952 ***Robert Montgomery Presents*** (NBC), "Best Dramatic Program"
Your Show of Shows (NBC), "Best Variety Program"
See It Now (CBS), "Best Public Affairs Program"
Dragnet (NBC), "Best Mystery, Action or Adventure Program"
I Love Lucy (CBS), "Best Situation Comedy"
What's My Line? (CBS), "Best Audience Participation, Quiz or Panel Program"
Time for Beany (KTLA), "Best Children's Program"
Thomas Mitchell, "Best Actor"
Helen Hayes, "Best Actress"
Jimmy Durante, "Best Comedian"
Lucille Ball, "Best Comedienne"
Bishop Fulton J. Sheen, "Most Outstanding Personality"

1953 ***U.S. Steel Hour*** (ABC), "Best Dramatic Show"
I Love Lucy (CBS), "Best Situation Comedy"
Omnibus (CBS), "Best Variety Program"
See It Now (CBS), "Best Program of News or Sports"
Victory at Sea (NBC), "Best Public Affairs Program"
Kukla, Fran and Ollie (NBC), "Best Children's Program"
Make Room for Daddy (ABC) and **U.S. Steel Hour** (ABC), "Best New Programs" (tie)
Donald O'Connor (*Colgate Comedy Hour,* NBC), "Best Male Star of Regular Series"
Eve Arden (*Our Miss Brooks,* CBS), "Best Female Star of Regular Series"
Art Carney (*The Jackie Gleason Show,* CBS), "Best Series Supporting Actor"
Vivian Vance (*I Love Lucy,* CBS), "Best Series Supporting Actress"
Dragnet (NBC), "Best Mystery, Action or Adventure Program"
This Is Your Life (NBC) and **What's My Line?** (CBS), "Best Audience Participation, Quiz or Panel Programs" (tie)
Edward R. Murrow (CBS), "Most Outstanding Personality"

1954 **George Gobel** (NBC), "Most Outstanding New Personality"
Omnibus (CBS), "Best Cultural, Religious or Educational Program"

Gillette Cavalcade of Sports (NBC), "Best Sports Program"
Lassie (CBS), "Best Children's Program"
Art Linkletter's House Party (CBS), "Best Daytime Program"
Stories of the Century (syndicated), "Best Western or Adventure Series"
John Daly (ABC), "Best News Reporter or Commentator"
This Is Your Life (NBC), "Best Audience, Guest Participation or Panel Program"
Robert Cummings (*Twelve Angry Men,* CBS), "Best Actor in a Single Performance"
Judith Anderson (*Macbeth,* on *Hallmark Hall of Fame,* NBC), "Best Actress in a Single Performance"
Perry Como (CBS), "Best Male Singer"
Dinah Shore (NBC), "Best Female Singer"
Art Carney (*The Jackie Gleason Show,* CBS), "Best Supporting Actor in a Regular Series"
Audrey Meadows (*The Jackie Gleason Show,* CBS), "Best Supporting Actress in a Regular Series"
Danny Thomas (*Make Room for Daddy,* ABC), "Best Actor Starring in a Regular Series"
Loretta Young (*The Loretta Young Show,* NBC), "Best Actress Starring in a Regular Series"
Dragnet (NBC), "Best Mystery or Intrigue Series"
Disneyland (ABC), "Best Variety Series Including Musical Varieties"
Make Room for Daddy *(ABC),* "Best Situation Comedy Series"
United States Steel Hour *(ABC),* "Best Dramatic Series"
Operation Undersea *(Disneyland,* ABC), "Best Individual Program of the Year"
Bob Markell (*Mallory's Tragedy on Mt. Everest,* CBS), "Best Art Direction of a Live Show"
Ralph Berger and Albert Pyke ("A Christmas Carol" on *Shower of Stars,* CBS) "Best Art Direction of a Filmed Show"
Lester Schorr ("I Climb the Stairs" on *Medic,* NBC), "Best Direction of Photography"
Reginald Rose (*Twelve Angry Men* on *Studio One,* NBC), "Best Written Dramatic Material"
James Allardice, Jack Douglas, Hal Kanter and Harry Winkler (*The George Gobel Show,* NBC), "Best Written Comedy Material"
Four Quadrant Screen (NBC for 1954 National Election Coverage/Robert Shelby), "Best Engineering Effects"
NBC and John West, "Best Technical Achievements for Color TV Policy"
George Nicholson (*Dragnet,* NBC), "Best Television Sound Editing"
Grant Smith and Lynn Harrison ("Operation Undersea" on *Disneyland,* ABC), "Best Television Film Editing"
Franklin Schaffner (*Twelve Angry Men* on *Studio One,* CBS), "Best Direction"
Walter Schumann (*Dragnet,* NBC), "Best Original Music Composed for TV"
Victor Young (*Diamond Jubilee of Lights,* four networks), "Best Scoring of a Dramatic or Variety Program"
June Taylor (*The Jackie Gleason Show,* CBS), "Best Choreographer"

1955 ***Lassie*** (CBS), "Best Children's Series"
Matinee Theatre, (NBC), "Best Contribution to Daytime Programming"
A-Bomb Coverage, (CBS), "Best Special Event or News Program"
Omnibus (CBS), "Best Documentary Program"
$64,000 Question (CBS), "Best Audience Participation Series"
Disneyland (ABC, especially for "Davy Crockett" series), "Best Action or Adventure Series"
Phil Silvers, *You'll Never Get Rich* (CBS), "Best Comedy Series"
***Ed Sullivan Show* (CBS),** "Best Variety Series"
Your Hit Parade (NBC), "Best Music Series"
Producers' Showcase (NBC), "Best Dramatic Series"
***Peter Pan* with Mary Martin** (*Producers' Showcase,* NBC), "Best Single Program of the Year"
Lloyd Nolan (*Caine Mutiny Court Martial* on *Ford Star Jubilee,* CBS), "Best Actor—Single Performance"
Mary Martin ("Peter Pan" on *Producers' Showcase,* NBC), "Best Actress—Single Performance"
Phil Silvers (*You'll Never Get Rich,* CBS), "Best Actor—Continuing Performance"
Lucille Ball (*I Love Lucy,* CBS), "Best Actress—Continuing Performance"
Art Carney, *The Honeymooners,* CBS), "Best Actor in a Supporting Role"
Nanette Fabray (*Caesar's Hour,* CBS), "Best Actress in a Supporting Role"
Phil Silvers (CBS), "Best Comedian"
Nanette Fabray (NBC), "Best Comedienne"
Perry Como (NBC), "Best Male Singer"
Dinah Shore, "Best Female Singer"
Perry Como (NBC), "Best M.C. or Program Host—Male or Female"
Edward R. Murrow (CBS), "Best News Commentator or Reporter"
Marcel Marceau (NBC), "Best Specialty Act—Single or Group"
Nat Hiken, Barry Blitser, Arnold Auerbach, Harvey Orkin, Vincent Bogert, Arnold Rosen, Coleman Jacoby, Tony Webster and Terry Ryan (*You'll Never Get Rich,* NBC), "Best Comedy Writing"
Rod Serling (*Kraft TV Theatre,* NBC), "Best Original Teleplay Writing"
Paul Gregory and Franklin Schaffner ("Caine Mutiny Court Martial" on *Ford Star Jubilee,* CBS), "Best Television Adaptation"
***Love and Marriage* from "Our Town"** (*Producers' Showcase,* NBC), "Best Musical Contribution"
Fred Coe (*Producers' Showcase,* NBC), "Best Producer—Live Series"
Walt Disney (*Disneyland,* ABC), "Best Producer—Film Series"
Franklin Schaffner ("Caine Mutiny Court Martial" on *Ford Star Jubilee,* CBS), "Best Director—Live Series"
Nat Hiken (*You'll Never Get Rich,* CBS), "Best Director—Film Series"
Otis Riggs ("Playwrights '56" and *Producers' Showcase,* NBC), "Best Art Direction—Live Series"
William Ferrari (*You Are There,* CBS) "Best Art Direction—Film Series"
William Scikner ("Black Friday" on *Medic,* NBC), "Best Cinematography for Television"
T. Miller (*Studio One,* CBS), "Best Camera Work—Live Show"
Edward Williams ("Breakdown" on *Alfred Hitchcock Presents,* CBS), "Best Editing of a Television Film"

Tony Charmoli ("Show Biz" on *Your Hit Parade,* NBC), "Best Choreographer"
RCA Tricolor Picture Tube, "Best Technical Achievement"
Ford, "Best Commercial Campaign"
President Dwight D. Eisenhower, "Governor's Award" (for his use and encouragement of television)

1956 **"Requiem for a Heavyweight"** (*Playhouse 90,* CBS), "Best Single Program of the Year"
Playhouse 90 (CBS), "Best New Program Series"
Phil Silvers Show (CBS), "Best Series—Half Hour or Less"
Caesar's Hour (NBC), "Best Series—One Hour or More"
See It Now (CBS), "Best Public Service Series"
Years of Crisis, year-end report with Edward R. Murrow and correspondents (CBS), "Best Coverage of a Newsworthy Event"
Robert Young (*Father Knows Best,* NBC), "Best Continuing Performance By an Actor in a Dramatic Series"
Loretta Young (*The Loretta Young Show,* NBC), "Best Continuing Performance By an Actress in a Dramatic Series"
Sid Caesar (*Caesar's Hour,* NBC), "Best Continuing Performance By a Comedian in a Series"
Nanette Fabray (*Caesar's Hour,* NBC), "Best Continuing Performance By a Commedienne in a Series"
Jack Palance ("Requiem for a Heavyweight" on *Playhouse 90,* CBS), "Best Single Performance by an Actor"
Claire Trevor ("Dodsworth" on *Producers' Showcase,* NBC), "Best Single Performance by an Actress"
Carl Reiner (*Caesar's Hour,* NBC), "Best Supporting Performance by an Actor"
Pat Carroll (*Caesar's Hour,* NBC), "Best Supporting Performance by an Actress"
Perry Como (NBC), "Best Male Personality—Continuing Performance"
Dinah Shore (NBC), "Best Female Personality—Continuing Performance"
Edward R. Murrow (CBS), "Best News Commentator"
James P. Cavanaugh ("Fog Closing In" on *Alfred Hitchcock Presents,* CBS), "Best Teleplay Writing—Half Hour or Less"
Rod Serling ("Requiem for a Heavyweight" on *Playhouse 90,* CBS), "Best Teleplay Writing—One Hour or More"
Nat Hiken, Billy Friedberg, Tony Webster, Leonard Stern, Arnold Rosen and Coleman Jacoby (*The Phil Silvers Show,* CBS), "Best Comedy Writing—Variety or Situation Comedy
Sheldon Leonard ("Danny's Comeback" on *The Danny Thomas Show,* ABC), "Best Direction—Half Hour or Less"
Ralph Nelson ("Requiem for a Heavyweight" on *Playhouse 90,* CBS), "Best Direction—One Hour or More"
Paul Barnes (*Your Hit Parade,* NBC), "Best Art Direction—Half Hour or Less"
Albert Heschong ("Requiem for a Heavyweight" on *Playhouse 90,* CBS), "Best Art Direction—One Hour or More"
Norbert Brodine ("The Pearl" on *The Loretta Young Show,* NBC), "Best Cinematography for Television
Frank Keller ("Our Mr. Sun" on *AT&T Science Series,* CBS), "Best Editing of a Film for Television"
Leonard Bernstein (composing and conducting for *Omnibus,* CBS), "Best Musical Contribution for Television"
"A Night to Remember" (*Kraft Television Theatre,* NBC), "Best Live Camera Work"
Development of videotape by Ampex and further development of practical applications by CBS, "Best Engineering or Technical Development"

1957 **"The Comedian"** (*Playhouse 90,* CBS), "Best Single Program of the Year"
Seven Lively Arts (CBS), "Best New Program Series of the Year"
Playhouse 90 (CBS), "Best Dramatic Anthology Series"
Gunsmoke (CBS), "Best Dramatic Series with Continuing Characters"
Phil Silvers Show (CBS), "Best Comedy Series"
Dinah Shore — Chevy Show (NBC), "Best Musical, Variety, Audience Participation or Quiz Series"
Omnibus (ABC and NBC), "Best Public Service Program or Series"
Coverage of Riker's Island (New York) **plane crash** on *World News Roundup* (CBS), "Best Coverage of an Unscheduled Newsworthy Event"
Robert Young (*Father Knows Best,* NBC), "Best Continuing Performance by an Actor in a Leading Role in a Dramatic or Comedy Series"
Jane Wyatt (*Father Knows Best,* NBC), "Best Continuing Performance by an Actress in a Leading Role in a Dramatic or Comedy Series"
Jack Benny (*The Jack Benny Show,* CBS), "Best Continuing Performance (Male) in a Series by a Comedian, Singer, Host, Dancer, M.C., Narrator, Panelist or Any Person Who Essentially Plays Himself"
Dinah Shore (*Dinah Shore — Chevy Show,* NBC), "Best Continuing Performance (Female) in a Series by a Comedienne, Singer, Hostess, Dancer, M.C., Narrator, Panelist or Any Person Who Essentially Plays Herself"
Peter Ustinov ("The Life of Samuel Johnson" on *Omnibus,* NBC), "Actor —Best Single Performance — Lead or Support"
Polly Bergen ("Helen Morgan Story" on *Playhouse 90,* CBS), "Actress —Best Single Performance —Lead or Support"
Carl Reiner (*Caesar's Hour,* NBC), "Best Continuing Support Performance by an Actor in a Dramatic or Comedy Series"
Ann B. Davis (*Bob Cummings Show,* CBS and NBC), "Best Continuing Support Performance by an Actress in a Dramatic or Comedy Series"
Edward R. Murrow (*See It Now,* CBS), "Best News Commentary"
Paul Monash ("The Lonely Wizard" on *Schlitz Playhouse of Stars,* CBS), "Best Teleplay Writing — Half Hour or Less"
Rod Serling ("The Comedian" on *Playhouse 90,* CBS), "Best Teleplay Writing — One Hour or More"
Nat Hiken, Billy Friedberg, Phil Sharp, Terry Ryan, Coleman Jacoby and Tony Webster (*The Phil Silvers Show,* CBS), "Best Comedy Writing"
Robert Stevens ("The Glass Eye" on *Alfred Hitchcock Presents,* CBS), "Best Direction — Half Hour or Less"
Bob Banner (*Dinah Shore — Chevy Show,* NBC), "Best Direction — One Hour or More"
Rouben ter-Arutunian (*Twelfth Night* on *Hallmark Hall of Fame,* NBC), "Best Art Direction"

Harold E. Wellman ("Hemo the Magnificent" on *Bell Telephone Science Series,* CBS), "Best Cinematography for Television"

Playhouse 90 (CBS), "Best Live Camera Work"

Mike Pozen ("How to Kill a Woman" on *Gunsmoke,* CBS), "Best Editing of a Film for Television"

Leonard Bernstein (Conducting and Analyzing Music of Johann Sebastian Bach on *Omnibus,* ABC), "Best Musical Contribution for Television"

Engineering and camera techniques (*Wide Wide World,* NBC), "Best Engineering or Technical Achievement"

Jack Benny "Trustees' Award"

1958-59 ***An Evening With Fred Astaire,*** (NBC), "Most Outstanding Single Program of the Year"

Playhouse 90 (CBS), "Best Dramatic Series — One Hour or Longer"

Alcoa-Goodyear Theatre (NBC), "Best Dramatic Series — Less Than One Hour"

Jack Benny Show (CBS), "Best Comedy Series"

Dinah Shore — Chevy Show (NBC), "Best Musical or Variety Series"

Maverick (ABC), "Best Western Series"

Omnibus (NBC), "Best Public Service Program or Series"

Huntley-Brinkley Report (NBC), "Best News Reporting Series"

What's My Line? (CBS), "Best Panel, Quiz or Audience Participation Series"

"Little Moon of Alban" (*Hallmark Hall of Fame,* NBC), "Best Dramatic Program — One Hour or Longer"

An Evening With Fred Astaire (NBC), "Best Special Musical or Variety Program — One Hour or Longer"

Face of Red China (CBS), "Best Special News Program"

Raymond Burr (*Perry Mason,* CBS), "Best Actor in a Leading Role in a Dramatic Series (Continuing Character)"

Loretta Young (*The Loretta Young Show,* NBC), "Best Actress in a Leading Role in a Dramatic Series (Continuing Character — Hostess)"

Jack Benny (*The Jack Benny Show,* CBS), "Best Actor in a Leading Role in a Comedy Series (Continuing Character)"

Jane Wyatt (*Father Knows Best,* CBS and NBC), "Best Actress in a Leading Role in a Comedy Series (Continuing Character)"

Dennis Weaver (*Gunsmoke,* CBS), "Best Supporting Actor in a Dramatic Series (Continuing Character)"

Barbara Hale (*Perry Mason,* CBS), "Best Supporting Actress in a Dramatic Series (Continuing Character)"

Tom Poston (*Steve Allen Show,* NBC), "Best Supporting Actor in a Comedy Series (Continuing Character)"

Ann B. Davis (*Bob Cummings Show,* NBC), "Best Supporting Actress in a Comedy Series (Continuing Character)"

Perry Como (*Perry Como Show,* CBS), "Best Performance by an Actor in a Musical or Variety Series (Continuing Character)"

Dinah Shore (*Dinah Shore — Chevy Show,* NBC), "Best Performance by an Actress in a Musical or Variety Series (Continuing Character)"

Fred Astaire (*An Evening With Fred Astaire,* NBC), "Best Single Performance by an Actor"

Julie Harris ("Little Moon of Alban" on *Hallmark Hall of Fame,* NBC), "Best Single Performance by an Actress"

Edward R. Murrow (CBS), "Best News Commentator or Analyst"

Jack Smight ("Eddie" on *Alcoa-Goodyear Theatre,* NBC), "Best Direction of a Single Program of a Dramatic Series — Less than One Hour"

George Schaefer ("Little Moon of Alban" on *Hallmark Hall of Fame,* NBC), "Best Direction of a Single Program of a Dramatic Series — One Hour or Longer"

Peter Tewksbury ("Medal for Margaret" on *Father Knows Best,* CBS), "Best Direction of a Single Program of a Comedy Series"

Bud Yorkin (*An Evening With Fred Astaire,* NBC), "Best Direction of a Single Musical or Variety Program"

Alfred Brenner and Ken Hughes ("Eddie" on *Alcoa—Goodyear Theatre,* NBC), "Best Writing of a Single Program of a Dramatic Series—Less Than an Hour"

James Costigan ("Little Moon of Alban" on *Hallmark Hall of Fame,* NBC), "Best Writing of a Single Dramatic Program—One Hour or Longer"

Sam Perrin, George Balzer, Hal Goldman and Al Gordon (*Jack Benny Show,* "With Ernie Kovacs," CBS), "Best Writing of a Single Program of a Comedy Series"

Ellis W. Carter ("Alphabet Conspiracy" on *Bell Telephone Special,* NBC), "Best Cinematography for Television"

An Evening With Fred Astaire (NBC), "Best Live Camera Work"

Claudio Guzman ("Bernadette" on *Westinghouse Desilu Playhouse,* CBS), "Best Art Direction in a Television Film"

Edward Stephenson (*An Evening With Fred Astaire* NBC), "Best Art Direction in a Live Television Program"

Silvio d'Alisera ("Meet Mr. Lincoln" on *Project 20,* NBC), "Best Editing of a Film for Television"

David Rose (Musical direction of *An Evening With Fred Astaire,* NBC), "Best Musical Contribution to a Television Program"

Hermes Pan (*An Evening With Fred Astaire,* NBC), "Best Choreography for Television"

Industry-wide improvement of editing of videotape as exemplified by ABC, CBS and NBC, "Best Engineering or Technical Achievement"

Cuban Revolution coverage by CBS,"Best On-the-Spot Coverage of a News Event — Any Length"

Bob Hope "for bringing the gift of laughter to all peoples, for selflessly entertaining American troops throughout the world for many years and for making television finer by these deeds and by the consistently high quality of his television programs," "Trustees' Award"

1959-60 ***Art Carney Special*** (NBC), "Outstanding Program Achievement in the Field of Humor"

Playhouse 90 (CBS), "Outstanding Program Achievement in the Field of Drama"

Fabulous Fifties (CBS), "Outstanding Program Achievement in the Field of Variety"

Huntley-Brinkley Report (NBC), "Outstanding Program Achievement in the Field of News"

Twentieth Century (CBS), "Outstanding Program Achievement in the Field of Public Affairs and Education"

Huckleberry Hound (syndicated), "Outstanding Achievement in the Field of Children's Programming"
Leonard Bernstein and the New York Philharmonic (CBS), "Outstanding Achievement in the Field of Music"
Laurence Olivier (*The Moon and Sixpence,* NBC), "Outstanding Single Performance by an Actor (Lead or Support)"
Ingrid Bergman (*The Turn of the Screw,* on *Ford Startime,* NBC), "Outstanding Single Performance by an Actress (Lead or Support)"
Robert Stack (*The Untouchables,* ABC), "Outstanding Performance by an Actor in a Series (Lead or Support)"
Jane Wyatt (*Father Knows Best,* CBS), "Outstanding Performance by an Actress in a Series (Lead or Support)"
Harry Belafonte ("Tonight With Belafonte," on *Revlon Revue,* CBS), "Outstanding Performance in a Variety or Musical Program Series"
Rod Serling (*Twilight Zone,* CBS), "Outstanding Writing Achievement in Drama"
Sam Perrin, George Balzer, Al Gordon and Hal Goldman (*Jack Benny Show,* CBS), "Outstanding Writing Achievement in Comedy"
Howard K. Smith and Av Westin (*The Population Explosion,* CBS), "Outstanding Writing Achievement in the Documentary Field"
Robert Mulligan (*The Moon and Sixpence,* NBC), "Outstanding Directorial Achievement in Drama"

Ralph Levy and Bud Yorkin (*Jack Benny Hour Specials,* CBS), "Outstanding Directorial Achievement in Comedy"
Ralph Berger and Frank Smith (*"Untouchables" on "Westinghouse Desilu Playhouse,"* CBS), "Outstanding Achievement in Art Direction and Scenic Design"
Charles Straumer ("Untouchables" on *Westinghouse Desilu Playhouse,* CBS), "Outstanding Achievement in Cinematography for Television"
Ben H. Ray and Robert L. Swanson (*"Untouchable"* CBS), "Outstanding Achievement in Film Editing for Television"
Winter Olympics (CBS), "Outstanding Achievement in Electronic Camera Work"
General Electric super-sensitive camera tube for colorcasting with no more light than is needed for black and white, "Best Engineering or Technical Achievement"
Frank Stanton (Columbia Broadcasting System), for advancing television as an arm of the free press), "Trustees' Award"
Ampex Corp., Radio Corp. of America, Michael R. Gargiulo and Richard Gillaspy (for capturing on videotape the Nixon-Khrushchev debate in Moscow), "Trustees' Citation"

1960-61 ***Jack Benny Show*** (CBS) "Outstanding Program Achievement in the Field of Humor"
Macbeth (*Hallmark Hall of Fame,* NBC), "Outstanding Program Achievement in the Field of Drama"
Astaire Time (NBC) "Outstanding Program Achievement in the Field of Variety"
Huntley-Brinkley Report (NBC), "Outstanding Program Achievement in the Field of News"
The Twentieth Century (CBS) "Outstanding Program Achievement in the Field of Public Affairs and Education"
Young People's Concert ("Aaron Copeland's Birthday Party," CBS), "Outstanding Achievement in the Field of Children's Programming"
Maurice Evans (*Macbeth* on *Hallmark Hall of Fame,* NBC), "Outstanding Single Performance by an Actor in a Leading Role"
Judith Anderson (*Macbeth* on *Hallmark Hall of Fame,* NBC), "Outstanding Single Performance by an Actress in a Leading Role"
Raymond Burr (*Perry Mason,* CBS), "Outstanding Performance by an Actor in a Series (Lead)"
Barbara Stanwyck (*Barbara Stanwyck Show,* NBC), "Outstanding Performance by an Actress in a Series (Lead)"
Roddy McDowall ("Not Without Honor" on *Equitable's American Heritage,* NBC), "Outstanding Performance by an Actor or an Actress in a Supporting Role"
Don Knotts (*Andy Griffith Show,* CBS), "Outstanding Performance in a Supporting Role by an Actor or Actress in a Series"
Fred Astaire (*Astaire Time,* NBC), "Outstanding Performance in a Variety or Musical Program or Series"
Macbeth (*Hallmark Hall of Fame,* NBC), "The Program of the Year"
Leonard Bernstein (*Leonard Bernstein and the Philharmonic,* CBS), "Outstanding Achievement in the Field of Music for Television"
Rod Serling (*Twilight Zone,* CBS), "Outstanding Writing Achievement in Drama"
Sherwood Schwartz, Dave O'Brien, Al Schwartz, Martin Ragaway and Red Skelton (*Red Skelton Show,* CBS), "Outstanding Writing Achievement in Comedy"
Victor Wolfson (*Winston Churchill, The Valiant Years,* ABC), "Outstanding Writing Achievement in the Documentary Field"
George Schaeffer (*Macbeth* on *Hallmark Hall of Fame,* NBC), "Outstanding Directorial Achievement in Drama"
Sheldon Leonard (*The Danny Thomas Show,* CBS), "Outstanding Directorial Achievement in Comedy"
John J. Lloyd (*Checkmate,* CBS), "Outstanding Achievement in Art Direction and Scenic Design"
George Clemens (*Twilight Zone,* CBS), "Outstanding Achievement in Cinematography for Television"
"Sounds of America" (*Bell Telephone Hour,* Red-eo-Tape mobile unit for NBC), "Outstanding Achievement in Electronic Camera Work"
Harry Coswick, Aaron Nibley and Milton Shifman (*Naked City,* ABC), "Outstanding Achievement in Film Editing for Television"
Radio Corp. of America and Marconi's Wireless Telegraph Co. (for independent development of 4½-in. image orthicon tube and cameras), "Outstanding Engineering or Technical Achievement"
National Educational Television and Radio Center and its affiliated stations, (for foresight and perseverence in developing educational television in the U.S.), "Trustees' Award"
Joyce C. Hall (Hallmark Cards), ("for his personal interest in uplifting the standards of television"), "Trustees' Award"

1961-62 ***Bob Newhart Show*** (NBC), "Outstanding Program Achievement in the Field of Humor"
The Defenders (CBS), "Outstanding Program Achievement in the Field of Drama"
Garry Moore Show (CBS), "Outstanding Program Achievement in the Fields of Variety or Music"

Leonard Bernstein and the New York Philharmonic in Japan (CBS), "Outstanding Program Achievement in the Field of Music"
Huntley-Brinkley Report (NBC), "Outstanding Program Achievement in the Field of News"
David Brinkley's Journal (NBC), "Outstanding Program Achievement in the Field of Education and Public Affairs"
New York Philharmonic Young People's Concerts with Leonard Bernstein (CBS), "Outstanding Achievement in the Field of Children's Programming"
Peter Falk ("The Price of Tomatoes" on *The Dick Powell Show,* NBC), "Outstanding Single Performance by an Actor in a Leading Role"
Julie Harris ("Victoria Regina" on *Hallmark Hall of Fame,* NBC), "Outstanding Single Performance by an Actress in a Leading Role"
E.G. Marshall (*The Defenders,* CBS), "Outstanding Performance by an Actor in a Series (Lead)"
Shirley Booth (*Hazel,* NBC), "Outstanding Performance by an Actress in a Series (Lead)"
Don Knotts (*Andy Griffith Show,* CBS), "Outstanding Performance in a Supporting Role by an Actor"
Pamela Brown ("Victoria Regina" on *Hallmark Hall of Fame,* NBC), "Outstanding Performance in a Supporting Role by an Actress"
Carol Burnett (*Garry Moore Show,* CBS), "Outstanding Performance in a Variety or Musical Program or Series"
Purex Specials for Women (NBC), "Outstanding Daytime Program (Program Specifically Created for Daytime Television)"
"Victoria Regina" (*Hallmark Hall of Fame,* NBC), "The Program of the Year"
Richard Rodgers (*Winston Churchill, the Valiant Years,* ABC), "Outstanding Achievement in Original Music Composed for Television"
Reginald Rose (*The Defenders,* CBS), "Outstanding Writing Achievement in Drama"
Carl Reiner (*Dick Van Dyke Show,* CBS), "Outstanding Writing Achievement in Comedy"
Lou Hazam ("Vincent Van Gogh: A Self-Portrait," NBC), "Outstanding Writing Achievement in the Documentary Field"
Franklin Schaffner (*The Defenders,* CBS), "Outstanding Directorial Achievement in Drama"
Nat Hiken (*Car 54, Where Are You?,* NBC), "Outstanding Directorial Achievement in Comedy"
Gary Smith (*Perry Como's Kraft Music Hall,* NBC), "Outstanding Achievement in Art Direction and Scenic Design"
John S. Priestley (*Naked City,* ABC), "Outstanding Achievement in Cinematography for Television"
Ernie Kovacs (*Ernie Kovacs Show,* ABC), "Outstanding Achievement in Electronic Camera Work"
Hugh Chaloupka, Aaron Nibley and Charles L. Freeman (*Naked City,* ABC), "Outstanding Achievement in Film Editing for Television"
ABC Videotape Expander (VTX), slow-motion tape developed under Albert Malang of Video Facilities, "Outstanding Engineering or Technical Achievement
CBS News, (for "A Tour of the White House" special) "Trustees' Award"
Jacqueline Kennedy, (for "A Tour of the White House" special) "Trustees' Award"
ABC, CBS and NBC News Department heads, "Trustees' Award" (for upholding country's policy of open reporting)
Brig. Gen. David Sarnoff, "Trustees' Award" (in recognition of his being "an illustrious statesman of our industry")

1962-63 ***The Tunnel*** (NBC) "Best Program of the Year"
The Dick Van Dyke Show (CBS), "Outstanding Program Achievement in the Field of Humor"
The Defenders (CBS), "Outstanding Program Achievement in the Field of Drama"
Julie and Carol at Carnegie Hall (CBS), "Outstanding Program Achievement in the Field of Music"
The Andy Williams Show (NBC), "Outstanding Program Achievement in the Field of Variety"
G-E College Bowl (CBS), "Outstanding Program Achievement in the Field of Panel, Quiz or Audience Participation"
Walt Disney's Wonderful World of Color (NBC), "Outstanding Achievement in the Field of Children's Programming"
The Tunnel (NBC), "Outstanding Achievement in the Field of Documentary Programs"
Huntley-Brinkley Report (NBC), "Outstanding Program Achievement in the Field of News"
David Brinkley's Journal (NBC), "Outstanding Program Achievement in the Field of News Commentary or Public Affairs"
Piers Anderton (NBC's Berlin correspondent for *The Tunnel*), "Outstanding Achievement in International Reporting or Commentary"
Trevor Howard in "The Invincible Mr. Disraeli" (*Hallmark Hall of Fame,* NBC), "Outstanding Single Performance by an Actor in a Leading Role"
Kim Stanley ("A Cardinal Act of Mercy" on *Ben Casey,* ABC), "Outstanding Single Performance by an Actress in a Leading Role"
E.G. Marshall (*The Defenders,* CBS), "Outstanding Continued Performance by an Actor in a Series (Lead)"
Shirley Booth (*Hazel,* NBC), "Outstanding Continued Performance by an Actress in a Series (Lead)"
Don Knotts (*The Andy Griffith Show,* CBS), "Outstanding Performance in a Supporting Role by an Actor"
Glenda Farrell ("A Cardinal Act of Mercy" on *Ben Casey,* ABC), "Outstanding Performance in a Supporting Role by an Actress"
Carol Burnett (*Julie and Carol at Carnegie Hall,* CBS), "Outstanding Performance in a variety or Musical Program or Series"
Robert Russell Bennett ("He is Risen" on *Project 20,* NBC), "Outstanding Achievement in Composing Original Music for Television"
Carroll Clark and Marvin Aubrey Davis (*Walt Disney's Wonderful World of Color,* NBC), "Outstanding Achievement in Art Direction and Scenic Design"
Robert Thom and Reginald Rose ("The Madman" on *The Defenders,* CBS), "Outstanding Writing Achievement in Drama"
Carl Reiner (*The Dick Van Dyke Show,* CBS), "Outstanding Writing Achievement in Comedy"
Stuart Rosenberg ("The Madman" on *The Defenders,* CBS), "Outstanding Directional Achievement in Drama"
John Rich (*The Dick Van Dyke Show,* CBS), "Outstanding Directorial Achievement in Comedy"
John S. Priestley (*Naked City,* ABC), "Outstanding Achievement in Cinematography for Television"
"The Invincible Mr. Disraeli" (on *Hallmark Hall of Fame,* (NBC), "Outstanding Achievement in Electronic Camera Work"

Sid Katz (*The Defenders,* CBS), "Outstanding Achievement in Film Editing for Television"
War and Peace (Granada TV Network of England), "The International Award"
Superfluous People (WCBS-TV, New York), "The Station Award"
American Telephone and Telegraph Co., "Trustees' Award"
Dick Powell, "Trustees' Award"
President John F. Kennedy, (for making news conferences available to television and for participating in the program, *Conversation with the President*), "Trustees' Citation"

1963-64 ***The Making of the President 1960*** (ABC), "Program of the Year"
The Dick Van Dyke Show *(CBS), "Outstanding Program Achievement in the Field of Comedy"*
The Defenders (CBS), "Outstanding Program Achievement in the Field of Drama"
Bell Telephone Hour (NBC), "Outstanding Program Achievement in the Field of Music"
The Danny Kaye Show (CBS), "Outstanding Program Achievement in the Field of Variety"
Discovery '63-'64 (ABC), "Outstanding Program Achievement in the Field of Children's Programming"
The Making of the President 1960 (ABC), "Outstanding Achievement in the Field of Documentary Programs"
Huntley-Brinkley Report (NBC), "Outstanding Program Achievement in the Field of News Reports"
Cuba Parts I & II—"The Bay of Pigs" and "The Missile Crisis" (NBC), "Outstanding Program Achievement in the Field of News Commentary or Public Affairs"
Jack Klugman ("Blacklist" on *The Defenders,* CBS), "Outstanding Single Performance by an Actor in a Leading Role"
Shelley Winters ("Two Is The Number" on *Bob Hope Presents the Chrysler Theatre,* NBC), "Outstanding Single Performance by an Actress in a Leading Role"
Dick Van Dyke (*The Dick Van Dyke Show,* CBS), "Outstanding Continued Performance by an Actor in a Series (Lead)"
Mary Tyler Moore (*The Dick Van Dyke Show,* CBS), "Outstanding Continued Performance by an Actress in a Series (Lead)"
Albert Paulsen ("One Day in the Life of Ivan Denisovich" on *Bob Hope Presents the Chrysler Theatre,* NBC), "Outstanding Performance by an Actor in A Supporting Role"
Ruth White ("Little Moon of Alban" on *Hallmark Hall of Fame,* NBC), "Outstanding Performance by an Actress in a Supporting Role"
Danny Kaye (*The Danny Kaye Show,* CBS), "Outstanding Performance in a Variety or Musical Program or Series"
Elmer Bernstein (*The Making of the President 1960,* ABC), "Outstanding Achievement in Composing Original Music for Television"
Warren Clymer (*Hallmark Hall of Fame,* NBC), "Outstanding Achievement in Art Direction and Scenic Design"
Rod Serling ("It's Mental Work" on *Bob Hope Presents The Chrysler Theatre,* NBC), "Outstanding Writing Achievement in Drama—Adaptation"
Ernest Kinoy ("Blacklist" on *The Defenders,* CBS), "Outstanding Writing Achievement in Drama—Original"
Carl Reiner, Sam Denoff and Bill Persky (*The Dick Van Dyke Show,* CBS), "Outstanding Writing Achievement in Comedy or Variety"
Tom Gries ("Who Do You Kill?" on *East Side/West Side,* CBS), "Outstanding Directorial Achievement in Drama"
Jerry Paris (*The Dick Van Dyke Show,* CBS), "Outstanding Directorial Achievement in Comedy"
Robert Scheerer (*The Danny Kaye Show,* CBS), "Outstanding Directorial Achievement in Variety or Music"
J. Baxter Peters (*The Kremlin,* NBC), "Outstanding Achievement in Cinemotography for Television"
The Danny Kaye Show (CBS), "Outstanding Achievement in Electronic Photography"
William T. Cartwright (*The Making of the President 1960,* ABC), "Outstanding Achievement in Film Editing for Television"
Les Raisins Verts" (Radiodiffusion Television Francais), "The International Award"
Operation Challenge — A Study in Hope (KPIX, San Francisco), "The Station Award"

1964-65 ***The Dick Van Dyke Show*** (CBS), "Outstanding Program Achievement in Entertainment"
"The Magnificent Yankee" (*Hallmark Hall of Fame,* NBC), "Outstanding Program Achievement in Entertainment"
My Name Is Barbra CBS), "Outstanding Program Achievement in Entertainment"
"What Is Sonata Form" (*New York Philharmonic Young People's Concerts With Leonard Bernstein,* CBS), "Outstanding Program Achievement in Entertainment"
Leonard Bernstein (*New York Philharmonic Young People's Concerts with Leonard Bernstein,* CBS), "Outstanding Individual Achievement in Entertainment: Actors and Performers"
Lynn Fontanne ("The Magnificent Yankee" on *Hallmark Hall of Fame,* NBC), "Outstanding Individual Achievement in Entertainment: Actors and Performers"
Alfred Lunt ("The Magnificent Yankee" on *Hallmark Hall of Fame,* NBC), "Outstanding Individual Achievement in Entertainment: Actors and Performers"
Barbra Streisand (*My Name Is Barbra,* CBS), "Outstanding Individual Achievement in Entertainment: Actors and Performers"
Dick Van Dyke (*The Dick Van Dyke Show,* CBS), "Outstanding Individual Achievement in Entertainment: Actors and Performers"
David Karp ("The 700 Year Old Gang" on *The Defenders,* CBS), "Outstanding Individual Achievement in Entertainment: Writer"
Paul Bogart ("The 700 Year Old Gang" on *The Defenders,* CBS), "Outstanding Individual Achievement in Entertainment: Director"
Joe Layton (*My Name Is Barbra,* CBS), "Outstanding Individual Achievement in Entertainment: Conception, Choreography and Staging"
Warren Clymer ("The Holy Terror" on *Hallmark Hall of Fame,* NBC), "Outstanding Individual Achievement in Entertainment: Art Directors and Set Decorators"
Noel Taylor ("The Magnificent Yankee" on *Hallmark Hall of Fame,* NBC), "Outstanding Individual Achievement in Entertainment: Costume Design"
Tom John (art) **and Bill Harp** (sets) (*My Name Is Barbra,* CBS), "Outstanding Individual Achievement in Entertainment: Art Directors and Set Decorators"

Robert O'Bradovich ("The Magnificent Yankee" on *Hallmark Hall of Fame,* NBC), "Outstanding Individual Achievement in Entertainment: Make-Up Artist"
Peter Matz (*My Name Is Barbra,* CBS), "Outstanding Individual Achievement in Entertainment: Musician"
William Spencer (*Twelve O'Clock High,* ABC), "Outstanding Individual Achievement in Entertainment: Cinematographer"
Henry Berman, Joseph Dervin and Will Glock, (*The Man from U.N.C.L.E.,* NBC), "Outstanding Individual Achievement in Entertainment: Lighting Direction"
Phil Hymes ("The Magnificent Yankee" on *Hallmark Hall of Fame,* NBC), "Outstanding Individual Achievement in Entertainment: Lighting Direction"
L.B. Abbott (*Voyage to the Bottom of the Sea,* ABC), "Outstanding Individual Achievement in Entertainment: Special Photographic Effects"
Production team (*Man From U.N.C.L.E.,* NBC), "Outstanding Individual Achievement in Entertainment: Special Effects"
Edward Ancona (*Bonanza,* NBC), "Outstanding Individual Achievement in Entertainment: Color Consultant"
Clair McCoy (*The Wonderful World of Burlesque,* NBC), "Outstanding Individual Achievement inEntertainment: Technical Director"
"I, Leonardo da Vinci" (*Saga of Western Man,* ABC), "Outstanding Program Achievement in News, Documentaries and Sports"
The Louvre (NBC), "Outstanding Program Achievement in News, Documentaries or Sports "
Richard Basehart (*Let My People Go,* syndicated), "Outstanding Individual Achievement in News, Documentary or Sports"
John J. Sughrue (*The Louvre,* NBC), "Outstanding Individual Achievement in News, Documentaries or Sports: Director"
Sidney Carroll (*The Louvre,* NBC), "Outstanding Individual Achievement in News, Documentaries or Sports: Writer"
Aram Boyajian (*The Louvre,* NBC), "Outstanding Individual Achievement in News, Documentaries or Sports: Film Editor"
Tom Priestley (*The Louvre,* NBC), "Outstanding Individual Achievement in News, Documentaries or Sports: Cinematographer"
Norman Dello Joio (*The Louvre,* NBC), "Outstanding Individual Achievement in News, Documentaries or Sports: Musician"
Le Barbier de Seville (Canadian Broadcasting Co.), "The International Award"
Ku Klux Klan (WDSU-TV, New Orleans), "The Station Award"

1965-66 ***The Dick Van Dyke Show*** (CBS), "Outstanding Comedy Series"
The Andy Williams Show (NBC), "Outstanding Variety Series"
Chrysler Presents the Bob Hope Christmas Special (NBC), "Outstanding Variety Special"
The Fugitive (ABC), "Outstanding Dramatic Series"
Ages of Man (CBS), "Outstanding Dramatic Program"
Frank Sinatra: A Man and His Music (NBC), "Outstanding Musical Program"
A Charlie Brown Christmas (CBS), "Outstanding Children's Program"
Cliff Robertson ("The Game" on *Bob Hope Presents the Chrysler Theatre,* NBC), "Outstanding Single Performance by an Actor in a Leading Role in a Drama"
Simone Signoret ("A Small Rebellion" on *Bob Hope Presents the Chrysler Theatre,* NBC), "Outstanding Single Performance by an Actress in a Leading Role in a Drama"
Bill Cosby (*I Spy,* NBC), "Outstanding Continued Performance by an Actor in a Leading Role in a Dramatic Series"
Barbara Stanwyck (*The Big Valley,* ABC), "Outstanding Continued Performance by an Actress in a Leading Role in a Dramatic Series"
Dick Van Dyke (*The Dick Van Dyke Show,* CBS), "Outstanding Continued Performance by an Actor in a Leading Role in a Comedy Series"
Mary Tyler Moore (*The Dick Van Dyke Show,* CBS), "Outstanding Continued Performance by an Actress in a Leading Role in a Comedy Series"
James Daly (Eagle in a Cage" on *Hallmark Hall of Fame,* NBC), "Outstanding Performance by an Actor in a Supporting Role in a Drama"
Lee Grant (*Peyton Place,* ABC), "Outstanding Performance by an Actress in a Supporting Role in a Drama"
Don Knotts (*The Andy Griffith Show,* CBS), "Outstanding Performance by an Actor in a Supporting Role in a Comedy"
Alice Pearce (*Bewitched,* ABC), "Outstanding Performance by an Actress in a Supporting Role in a Comedy"
Millard Lampell ("Eagle in a Cage" on *Hallmark Hall of Fame,* NBC), "Outstanding Writing Achievement in Drama"
Bill Persky and Sam Denoff ("Coast to Coast Big Mouth" on *The Dick Van Dyke Show,* CBS), "Outstanding Writing Achievement in Comedy"
Al Gordon, Hal Goodman and Sheldon Keller (*An Evening With Carol Channing,* CBS), "Outstanding Writing Achievement in Variety"
Sidney Pollack ("The Game" on *Bob Hope Presents the Chrysler Theatre,* NBC), "Outstanding Directorial Achievement in Drama"
William Asher (*Bewitched,* ABC), "Outstanding Directorial Achievement in Comedy"
Alan Handley (*The Julie Andrews Show,* NBC), "Outstanding Directorial Achievement in Variety or Music"
American White Paper: United States Foreign Policy (NBC), "Achievement in News and Documentaries: Programs"
KKK—The Invisible Empire, (CBS), "Achievement in News and Documentaries: Programs"
"Senate Hearings on Vietnam" (NBC), "Achievement in News and Documentaries: Programs"
Camera Three (CBS), "Achievement in Daytime Programming: Programs"
Mutual of Omaha's Wild Kingdom (NBC), "Achievement in Daytime Programming: Programs"
ABC Wide World of Sports (ABC), "Achievement in Sports: Programs"
CBS Golf Classic (CBS), "Achievement in Sports: Programs"
Shell's Wonderful World of Golf (NBC), "Achievement in Sports: Programs"
Julia Child (*The French Chef,* NET), "Achievements in Educational Television: Individual"
Laurence Rosenthal (*Michelangelo: The Last Giant,* NBC), "Individual Achievements in Music: Composition"

James Trittipo (*The Hollywood Palace,* ABC), "Individual Achievements in Art Direction"
Winston C. Hoch (*Voyage to the Bottom of the Sea,* ABC), "Individual Achievement in Cinematography"
L.B. Abbott and Howard Lydecker ("Voyage to the Bottom of the Sea," ABC), "Individual Achievement in Special Photographic Effects"
David Blewitt and William R. Cartwright (*The Making of the President 1964,* CBS), "Individual Achievement in Film Editing"
Marvin Coil, Everett Douglas and Ellsworth Hoagland (*Bonanza,* NBC), "Individual Achievement in Film Editing"
Laurence Schneider ("Seventh Annual Young Performers Program" on *The New York Philharmonic With Leonard Bernstein,* CBS), "Individual Achievement in Audio Engineering"
Craig Curtis and Art Schneider (*The Julie Andrews Show,* NBC), "Individual Achievement in Video Tape Editing"
Lon Stucky (*Frank Sinatra: A Man and His Music,* NBC), "Individual Achievement in Lighting"
O. Tamburri ("Inherit the Wind" on *The Hallmark Hall of Fame,* NBC), "Individual Achievement: Technical Director"
MVR Corporation and CBS for Stop Action Playback, "Individual Achievement in Engineering Development"
Hughes Aircraft Corporation and Communications Satellite Corporation for Early Bird Satellite, "Individual Achievement in Engineering Development"
Burr Tillstrom ("Berlin Wall" hand ballot on *That Was The Week That Was,* NBC), "Special Award for Engineering Development"
"Wyvern at War—No. 2," "Breakout" (Westward Television Ltd., Plymouth, England), "The International Award"
I See Chicago (WBBM, Chicago), "The Station Award"
Edward R. Murrow (for forty years in broadcasting and the journalistic standards he adhered to), "Trustees' Award"
Xerox Corporation (for being the rare sponsor who has subordinated its interest in television as an advertising medium to its capacity to inform, enlighten and entertain at its highest level), "Trustees' Award"

1966-67 ***The Monkees*** (NBC), "Outstanding Comedy Series"
The Andy Williams Show (NBC), "Outstanding Variety Series"
The Sid Caesar, Imogene Coca, Carl Reiner, Howard Morris Special (CBS), "Outstanding Variety Special"
Mission: Impossible (CBS), "Outstanding Dramatic Series"
"Death of a Salesman (CBS), "Outstanding Dramatic Program"
Brigadoon (ABC), "Outstanding Musical Program"
Jack and the Beanstalk, (NBC), "Outstanding Children's Program"
Peter Ustinov ("Barefoot in Athens" on *Hallmark Hall of Fame,* NBC), "Outstanding Single Performance by an Actor in a Leading Role in a Drama"
Geraldine Page ("A Christmas Memory" on *ABC Stage 67,* ABC), "Outstanding Single Performance by an Actress in a Leading Role in a Drama"
Bill Cosby (*I Spy,* NBC), "Outstanding Continued Performance by an Actor in a Dramatic Series"
Barbara Bain (*Mission: Impossible,* CBS), "Outstanding Continuing Performance by an Actress in a Dramatic Series"
Don Adams (*Get Smart,* NBC), "Outstanding Continued Performance by an Actor in a Comedy Series"
Lucille Ball (*The Lucy Show,* CBS), "Outstanding Continued Performance by an Actress in a Comedy Series"
Eli Wallach ("The Poppy Is Also a Flower" on *Xerox Special,* ABC), "Outstanding Performance by an Actor in a Supporting Role in a Drama"
Agnes Moorehead ("Night of the Vicious Valentine" on *Wild, Wild West,* CBS), "Outstanding Performance by an Actress in a Supporting Role in a Drama"
Don Knotts (*The Andy Griffith Show,* CBS), "Outstanding Performance by an Actor in a Supporting Role in a Comedy"
Frances Bavier (*The Andy Griffith Show,* CBS), "Outstanding Performance by an Actress in a Supporting Role in a Comedy"
Bruce Geller (*Mission: Impossible,* CBS), "Outstanding Writing Achievement in Drama"
Buck Henry and Leonard Stern ("Ship of Spies" on *Get Smart,* NBC), "Outstanding Writing Achievement in Comedy"
Mel Brooks, Sam Denoff, Bill Persky, Carl Reiner and Mel Tolkin (*The Sid Caesar, Imogene Coca, Carl Reiner, Howard Morris Special,* CBS), "Outstanding Writing Achievement in Variety"
Alex Segal (*Death of a Salesman,* CBS), "Outstanding Directorial Achievement in Drama"
James Frawley ("Royal Flush" on *The Monkees,* NBC), "Outstanding Directorial Achievement in Comedy"
Fielder Cook ("Brigadoon," ABC), "Outstanding Directorial Achievement in Variety or Music"
China: The Roots of Madness, (syndicated), "Achievement in News and Documentaries: Programs"
Hall of Kings (ABC), "Achievement in News and Documentaries: Programs"
The Italians (CBS), "Achievement in News and Documentaries: Programs"
Theodore H. White (*China: The Roots of Madness,* syndicated), "Achievement in News and Documentaries: Individual"
Ray Aghayan and Bob Mackie (*Alice Through the Looking Glass,* NBC), "Individual Achievement in Costume Design"
Dick Smith (*Mark Twain Tonight!,* CBS), "Individual Achievement in Make-Up"
L.B. Abbott (*The Time Tunnel,* ABC), "Individual Achievement in Photographic Special Effects"
Paul Krasny and Robert Watts (*Mission: Impossible,* CBS), "Individual Achievement in Film Editing"
Don Hall, Dick Legrand, Daniel Mandell and John Mills (*Voyage to the Bottom of the Sea,* ABC), "Individual Achievement in Sound Editing"
A.J. Cunningham (*Brigadoon,* ABC), "Individual Achievement in Electronic Production: Technical Director"
Leard Davis (*Brigadoon,* ABC), "Individual Achievement in Lighting Direction"
Bill Cole (*Frank Sinatra: A Man and His Music, Part II,* CBS), "Individual Achievement in Audio Engineering"
Robert Dunn, Gorm Erickson, Ben Wolf and Nick Demos (*Brigadoon,* ABC), "Individual Achievement in Electronic Production: Electronic Cameramen"

A.C. Philips Gloeilampenfabrieken for Plumbicon Tube, "Individual Achievement in Engineering Development"
Ampex Company for High-Band Video Tape Recorder, "Individual Achievement in Engineering Development"
Art Carney (*The Jackie Gleason Show,* CBS), "Special Award"
Truman Capote and Eleanor Perry (adaptation of "A Christmas Memory" on *ABC Stage 67,* ABC), "Special Award"
Arthur Miller (adaptation of "Death of a Salesman," CBS), "Special Award"
Mutual of Omaha's Wild Kingdom, (NBC), "Achievement in Daytime Programming: Program"
Mike Douglas (*The Mike Douglas Show,* syndicated), "Achievement in Daytime Programming: Individual"
ABC's Wide World of Sports (ABC), "Achievement in Sports: Program"
Big Deal at Gothenburg (Tyne Tees Television Ltd., Newcastle-upon-Tyne, England), "International Award"
The Road to Nowhere (KLZ-TV, Denver), "Station Award"
Sylvester L. "Pat" Weaver, Jr., "Trustees' Award" (for his constant conviction that the American public deserves better than it gets on the television screen, for introducing the "special" for providing us with the *Today* and *Tonight* shows, programs which have long demonstrated their validity and for imagination, courage, leadership and integrity for eighteen years in our medium")

1967-68 ***Crisis in the Cities*** (NET), "Achievement in News and Documentaries: Program"
John Laurence and Keith Kay (CBS News Correspondent and Cameraman for "1st Cavalry," "Con Thien" and other segments on *CBS Evening News With Walter Cronkite,* CBS), "Achievement in News and Documentaries: Individual"
Frank McGee (commentary on satellite coverage of Konrad Adenauer's funeral, NBC), "Outstanding Individual Achievement in Coverage of Special Events"
Africa (ABC), "Outstanding Program Achievement in News Documentaries"
Summer '67: What We Learned (NBC), "Outstanding Program Achievement in News Documentaries"
Harry Reasoner (writer of *CBS Reports* "What About Ronald Reagan?"), "Outstanding Individual Achievement in News and Documentaries"
Vo Huynh (Cameraman on "Same Mud, Same Blood," NBC), "Outstanding Individual Achievement in News and Documentaries"
"Eric Hoffer, The Passionate State of Mind" (*CBS News Special*), "Outstanding Program Achievement in Cultural Documentaries"
"Gauguin in Tahiti, The Search for Paradise" (*CBS News Special*), "Outstanding Program Achievement in Cultural Documentaries"
"John Steinbeck's America and Americans" (NBC), "Outstanding Program Achievement in Cultural Documentaries"
"Dylan Thomas: The World I Breathe" (NET), "Outstanding Program Achievement in Cultural Documentaries"
Nathaniel Dorsky (art photographer on "Gauguin in Tahiti, The Passionate State of Mind," CBS), "Outstanding Individual Achievement in Cultural Documentaries"
Harry Morgan (writer for the Wyeth phenomenon on "Who, What, When, Where, Why With Harry Reasoner," CBS), "Outstanding Individual Achievement in Cultural Documentaries"
Thomas A. Priestley and Robert Loweree (director of photography and film editor of *John Steinbeck's America and Americans,* NBC), "Outstanding Achievement in Cultural Documentaries"
The 21st Century (CBS), "Other News and Documentary Program Achievement"
Science and Religion: Who Will Play God? (CBS), "Other News and Documentary Program Achievement"
Georges Delerue (composer for *Our World,* Global Telecast, NET), "Other News and Documentary Individual Achievement"
Get Smart (NBC), "Outstanding Comedy Series"
Mission: Impossible (CBS), "Outstanding Dramatic Series"
"Elizabeth the Queen" (*Hallmark Hall of Fame,* NBC), "Outstanding Dramatic Program"
Rowan and Martin's Laugh-In (NBC), "Outstanding Musical or Variety Series"
Rowan and Martin's Laugh-In Special (NBC), "Outstanding Musical or Variety Program"
Melvyn Douglas ("Do Not Go Gentle Into That Good Night" on *CBS Playhouse,* CBS), "Outstanding Single Performance by an Actor in a Leading Role in a Drama"
Maureen Stapleton ("Among the Paths to Eden" on *Xerox Special,* ABC), "Outstanding Single Performance by an Actress in a Leading Role in a Drama"
Bill Cosby (*I Spy,* NBC), "Outstanding Continued Performance by an Actor in a Leading Role in a Dramatic Series"
Barbara Bain (*Mission: Impossible,* CBS), "Outstanding Continued Performance by an Actress in a Leading Role in a Dramatic Series"
Don Adams (*Get Smart,* NBC), "Outstanding Continued Performance by an Actor in a Leading Role in a Comedy Series"
Lucille Ball (*The Lucy Show,* CBS), "Outstanding Continued Performance by an Actress in a Leading Role in a Comedy Series"
Milburn Stone (*Gunsmoke,* CBS), "Outstanding Performance by an Actor in a Supporting Role in a Drama"
Barbara Anderson (*Ironside,* NBC), "Outstanding Performance by an Actress in a Supporting Role in a Drama"
Werner Klemperer (*Hogan's Heroes,* CBS), "Outstanding Performance by an Actor in a Supporting Role in a Comedy"
Marion Lorne (*Bewitched,* ABC), "Outstanding Performance by an Actress in a Supporting Role in a Comedy"
Loring Mandel ("Do Not Go Gentle Into that Good Night" on *CBS Playhouse,* CBS), "Outstanding Writing Achievement in Drama"
Allan Burns and Chris Hayward ("The Coming Out Party" on *He and She,* CBS), "Outstanding Writing Achievement in Comedy"
Chris Beard, Phil Hahn, Jack Hanrahan, Coslough Johnson, Paul Keyes, Marc London, Allan Mannings, David Panich, Hugh Wedlock and Digby Wolf (*Rowan and Martin's Laugh-In,* NBC), "Outstanding Writing Achievement in *Music* or Variety"
Paul Bogart ("Dear Friends" on *CBS Playhouse,* CBS), "Outstanding Directorial Achievement in Drama"

Bruce Bilson ("Maxwell Smart, Private Eye" on *Get Smart,* NBC), "Outstanding Directorial Achievement in Comedy"
Jack Haley, Jr. (*Movin' With Nancy,* NBC) "Outstanding Directorial Achievement in Music or Variety"
Earle Hagen ("Laya" on *I Spy,* NBC), "Outstanding Achievement in Musical Composition"
James W. Trittipo (*The Fred Astaire Show,* NBC), "Outstanding Achievement in Art Direction and Scenic Design"
Ralph Woolsey ("A Thief is a Thief" on *It Takes a Thief,* ABC), "Outstanding Achievement in Cinematography"
A.J. Cunningham (technical director) **and Edward Chaney, Robert Fonorow, Harry Tatarian and Ben Wolf** (cameramen), ("Do Not Go Gentle Into That Good Night" on *CBS Playhouse,* CBS), "Outstanding Achievement in Electronic Camerawork"
Peter Johnson ("The Sounds and Sights of Chicago" on *Bell Telephone Hour,* NBC), "Outstanding Achievement in Film Editing"
Today (NBC), "Outstanding Program Achievement in Day Time Programming"
ABC's Wide World of Sports (ABC), "Outstanding Program Achievement in Sports Programming"
Jim McKay (sports commentator on *ABC's Wide World of Sports,* ABC), "Outstanding Individual Achievement in Sports Programming"
Art Carney (*The Jackie Gleason Show,* CBS), "Special Classification of Individual Achievement"
Pat Paulsen (*The Smothers Brothers Comedy Hour,* CBS), "Special Classification of Individual Achievement"
Arthur Schneider (tape editor of *Rowan and Martin's Laugh-In Special,* NBC), "Outstanding Individual Achievement in Electronic Production"
Donald McGannon (President and Chairman of the Board, Westinghouse Broadcasting Company, Group W), "Trustees' Award" (for creative leadership of a dynamic radio and television group)
British Broadcasting Corporation, (for Electronic Field — Store Colour Television Standards Converter) "Outstanding Achievement in Engineering Development"
Now Is the Time (WCAU-TV, Philadelphia), "The Station Award"
The Other Side of the Shadow (WWL-TV, New Orleans), "Special Citation"
The Other Washington (WRC-TV, Washington), "Special Citation"
La Section Anderson (*The Anderson Platoon*) (Office de Radiodiffusion Television Francais, O.R.T.F., Paris), "The International Award (Documentary)"
"Call Me Daddy" (*Armchair Theatre* on ABC Television Ltd., Middlesex, G.B.), "The International Award (Entertainment)"

1968-69 **Coverage of Hunger in the United States** on *The Huntley-Brinkley Report* (NBC), "Outstanding Program Achievement Within Regularly Scheduled News Programs"
Charles Kuralt, James Wilson and Robert Funk (correspondent, cameraman and soundman), "On The Road" on *CBS Evening News* (CBS), "Outstanding Individual Achievement Within Regularly Scheduled Broadcasts"
CBS for coverage of Martin Luther King's assassination and its aftermath, "Outstanding Program Achievement in Coverage of Special Events"
CBS Reports: Hunger in America (CBS), "Outstanding News Documentary Program Achievement"
Law and Order (NET), "Outstanding News Documentary Program Achievement"
Perry Wolff and Andy Rooney (writers of "Black History: Lost, Stolen or Strayed — Of Black America," on *CBS News Hour,* CBS), "Outstanding News Documentary Individual Achievement"
"Don't Count the Candles" (*CBS News Hour,* CBS), "Outstanding Cultural Documentary and 'Magazine-Type' Program or Series Achievement (Program)"
"Justice Black and The Bill of Rights" (*CBS News Hour,* CBS), "Outstanding Cultural Documentary and 'Magazine-Type' Program or Series Achievement (Program)"
"Man Who Dances: Edward Villella" (*Bell Telephone Hour,* NBC) "Outstanding Cultural Documentary and 'Magazine-Type' Program or Series Achievement (Program)"
"The Great American Novel" (*CBS News Hour,* (CBS), "Outstanding Cultural Documentary and 'Magazine-Type' Program or Series Achievement (Program)"
Walter Dombrow and Jerry Sims (cinematographers of "The Great American Novel" on *CBS News Hour,* CBS), "Outstanding Cultural Documentary and 'Magazine-Type' Program or Series Achievement (Individual)"
Tom Pettit (producer of "CBW: The Secrets of Secrecy" on *First Tuesday,* NBC), "Outstanding Cultural Documentary and 'Magazine-Type' Program or Series Achievement (Individual)"
Lord Snowdon (cinematographer for "Don't Count the Candles" on *CBS News Hour,* NBC), "Outstanding Cultural Documentary and 'Magazine-Type' Program or Series Achievement (Individual)"
Get Smart (NBC), "Outstanding Comedy Series"
NET Playhouse (NET), "Outstanding Dramatic Series"
"Teacher, Teacher" on*Hallmark Hall of Fame*(NBC), "Outstanding Dramatic Program"
Rowan and Martin's Laugh-In, (NBC), "Outstanding Variety or Musical Series"
"The Bill Cosby Special" (NBC), "Outstanding Variety or Musical Program"
Paul Scofield ("Male of the Species" on *Prudential's On-Stage,* NBC), "Outstanding Single Performance by an Actor in a Leading Role"
Geraldine Page (*The Thanksgiving Visitor,* ABC), "Outstanding Single Performance by an Actress in a Leading Role"
Carl Betz (*Judd for the Defense,* ABC), "Outstanding Continued Performance by an Actor in a Leading Role in a Dramatic Series"
Barbara Bain (*Mission: Impossible,* CBS) "Outstanding Continued Performance by an Actress in a Leading Role in a Dramatic Series"
Don Adams (*Get Smart,* NBC), "Outstanding Continued Performance by an Actor in a Leading Role in a Comedy Series"
Hope Lange (*The Ghost and Mrs. Muir,* NBC), "Outstanding Continued Performance by an Actress in a Leading Role in a Comedy Series"
Anna Calder-Marshall ("The Male of the Species" on *Prudential's On-Stage,* NBC), "Outstanding Single Performance by an Actress in a Supporting Role"
Werner Klemperer (*Hogan's Heroes,* CBS) "Outstanding Continued Performance by an Actor in a Supporting Role"
Susan Saint James (*The Name of the Game,* NBC) "Outstanding Continued Performance by an Actress in a Supporting Role"

J.P. Miller ("The People Next Door" on *CBS Playhouse,* CBS), "Outstanding Writing Achievement in Drama"
Allan Blye, Bob Einstein, Murray Roman, Carl Gottlieb, Jerry Music, Steve Martin, Cecil Tuck, Paul Wayne, Cy Howard and Mason Williams (*The Smothers Brothers Comedy Hour,* CBS), "Outstanding Writing Achievement in Comedy"
David Green ("The People Next Door" on *CBS Playhouse,* CBS) "Outstanding Directorial Achievement in Drama"
John T. Williams (*Heidi,* NBC), "Outstanding Achievement in Musical Composition"
William P. Ross and Lou Hafley (art director and set decorator, "The Bunker" on *Mission: Impossible,* CBS), "Outstanding Achievement in Art Direction and Scenic Design"
George Folsey (*Here's Peggy Fleming,* NBC) "Outstanding Achievement in Cinematography"
A.J. Cunningham (technical director) **and Nick DeMos, Bob Fonarow, Fred Gough, Jack Jennings, Dick Nelson, Rick Tanzi and Ben Wolf** (cameramen), ("The People Next Door" on *CBS Playhouse,* CBS), Outstanding Achievement in Electronic Camerawork"
Bill Mosher ("An Elephant in a Cigarbox" on *Judd for the Defense,* ABC), "Outstanding Achievement in Film Editing"
The Dick Cavett Show (ABC), "Outstanding Program Achievement in Daytime Programming"
19th Summer Olympic Games (ABC), "Outstanding Program Achievement in Sports Programming"
Bill Bennington, Mike Freedman, Mac Memion, Robert Riger, Marv Schenkler, Andy Sidaris, Lou Volpicelli and Doug Wilson (*19th Summer Olympic Games,* ABC), "Outstanding Individual Achievement in Sports Programming"
Firing Line With William F. Buckley, Jr. (syndicated), "Special Classification Program Achievement"
Mutual of Omaha's Wild Kingdom (NBC), "Special Classification Program Achievement"
Arte Johnson (*Rowan and Martin's Laugh-In,* NBC), "Special Classification Individual Achievement (Variety Performances)"
Harvey Korman (*The Carol Burnett Show,* CBS), "Special Classification Individual Achievements (Variety Performances)"
Mort Lindsey (*Barbra Streisand: A Happening in Central Park,* CBS), "Outstanding Individual Achievement in Music"
Billy Schulman, "A Citation" (for extraordinary achievement for "Teacher, Teacher" on *The Hallmark Hall of Fame* for demonstrating a mentally retarded person can compete and accomplish as much or more than any youngsters of the same age)
William R. McAndrew, "Trustees' Award" (for his role in shaping television news as his permanent memorial)
Apollo VII, VIII, IX and X astronauts, "Trustees' Awards" (for sharing with the American public and the world the mysteries of outer space and the surface of the moon on live television)
Columbia Broadcasting System, "Citation" (for development of the Digital Control Technique used in the Mincam miniaturized color television cameras)
Pretty Soon Runs Out (WHA-TV, Madison, Wisc.), "The Station Award"
Assignment: The Young Greats (WFIL-TV, Philadelphia, PA.), "Special Citation"
The Last Campaign of Robert Kennedy (Swiss Broadcasting and Television, Zurich), "International Award (Documentary)"
A Scent of Flowers (Canadian Broadcasting Corporation, Ontario), "International Award (Entertainment)"

1969-70 **"An Investigation of Teenage Drug Addiction—Odyssey House"** on *The Huntley-Brinkley Report* (NBC), "Outstanding Program Achievements Within Regularly Scheduled News Programs"
"Can the World Be Saved?" on *CBS Evening News With Walter Cronkite* (CBS), "Outstanding Program Achievement Within Regularly Scheduled News Programs"
Apollo: A Journey to the Moon (Apollo X, XI and XII) (NBC), "Outstanding Program Achievement in Coverage of Special Events"
Solar Eclipse: A Darkness at Noon (NBC), "Outstanding Program Achievement in Coverage of Special Events"
Walter Cronkite (reporter for *Man On the Moon: The Epic Journey of Apollo XI,* CBS), "Outstanding Individual Achievement in Coverage of Special Events"
Hospital (NET), "Oustanding Program Achievement in News Documentary Programming"
Frederick Wiseman (director of *Hospital,* NET), "Outstanding Individual Achievement in News Documentary Programming"
Black Journal (NET), "Outstanding Program Achievement in Magazine-Type Programming"
Tom Pettit (reporter-writer for "Some Footnotes to 25 Nuclear Years" on *First Tuesday,* NBC), "Outstanding Individual Achievement in Magazine-Type Programming
"Arthur Rubinstein" (NBC), "Outstanding Program Achievement in Cultural Documentary Programming"
"Fathers and Sons" on *CBS News Hour* (CBS) "Outstanding Program Achievement in Cultural Documentary Programming"
"The Japanese" on *CBS News Hour* (CBS), "Outstanding Program Achievement in Cultural Documentary Programming"
Edwin O. Reischauer (commentator for "The Japanese" on *CBS News Hour,* CBS), "Outstanding Individual Achievement in Cultural Documentary Programming"
Arthur Rubinstein (*Arthur Rubinstein,* NBC) "Outstanding Individual Achievement in Cultural Documentary Programming"
My World and Welcome to It (NBC), "Outstanding Comedy Series"
Marcus Welby, M.D. (ABC), "Outstanding Dramatic Series"
"A Storm in Summer" on *Hallmark Hall of Fame* (NBC), "Oustanding Dramatic Program"
The David Frost Show (syndicated), "Oustanding Variety or Musical Series"
Annie, The Women in the Life of a Man (CBS), Outstanding Variety or Musical Program (Variety or Popular)"
Cinderella (National Ballet of Canada, NET), "Outstanding Variety or Musical Program (Classical)"
Room 222 (ABC), "Outstanding New Series"
Peter Ustinov ("A Storm in Summer" on *Hallmark Hall of Fame,* NBC), "Outstanding Single Performance by an Actor in a Leading Role"
Patty Duke ("My Sweet Charlie" on *World Premier,* NBC), "Outstanding Single Performance by an Actress in a Leading Role"

Robert Young (*Marcus Welby, M.D.*, ABC), "Outstanding Continued Performance by an Actor in a Leading Role in a Dramatic Series"
Susan Hampshire (*The Forsyte Saga*, NET), "Outstanding Continued Performance by an Actress in a Leading Role in a Dramatic Series"
William Windom (*My World and Welcome to It*, NBC), "Oustanding Continued Performance by an Actor in a Leading Role in a Comedy Series"
Hope Lange (*The Ghost and Mrs. Muir*, ABC), "Outstanding Continued Performance by an Actress in a Leading Role in a Comedy Series"
James Brolin (*Marcus Welby, M.D.*, ABC), "Outstanding Performance by an Actor in a Supporting Role in Drama"
Gail Fisher (*Mannix*, CBS), "Outstanding Performance by an Actress in a Supporting Role in Drama"
Michael Constantine (*Room 222*, ABC), "Outstanding Performance by an Actor in a Supporting Role in Comedy"
Karen Valentine (*Room 222*, ABC), "Outstanding Performance by an Actress in a Supporting Role in Comedy"
Richard Levinson and William Link ("My Sweet Charlie" on *World Premiere*, NBC), "Outstanding Writing Achievement in Drama"
Gary Belkin, Peter Bellwood, Herb Sargent, Thomas Meehan and Judith Viorst (*Annie, The Women in the Life of a Man*, CBS), "Outstanding Writing Achievement in Comedy, Variety or Music"
Paul Bogart ("Shadow Game" on **CBS Playhouse,** CBS), "Outstanding Directorial Achievement in Drama"
Dwight A. Hemion ("The Sound of Burt Bacharach," on *Kraft Music Hall*, NBC), "Outstanding Directorial Achievement in Comedy, Variety or Music"
Norman Maen (*This Is Tom Jones*,ABC), "Outstanding Achievement in Choreography"
Morton Stevens ("A Thousand Pardons, You're Dead" on *Hawaii Five-O*, CBS), "Outstanding Achievement in Music Composition (for a series in first year of use)"
Pete Rugolo ("The Challengers" on *CBS Friday Night Movies*, CBS), "Outstanding Achievement in Music Composition (for special program)"
Peter Matz ("The Sound of Burt Bacharach" on *Kraft Music Hall*, NBC), "Outstanding Achievement in Music Direction of a Variety, Musical or Dramatic Program"
Arnold Margolin and Charles Fox (*Love American Style*, ABC), "Outstanding Achievement in Music, Lyrics and Special Materials"
Jan Scott and Earl Carlson (art director and set decorator of "Shadow Game" on *CBS Playhouse*, CBS), "Outstanding Achievement in Art Direction or Scenic Design (dramatic program)"
E. Jay Krause (*Mitzi's 2nd Special*, NBC), "Outstanding Achievement in Art Direction or Scenic Design (musical or variety)"
Leard Davis and Ed Hill (video: Richard Scovel and Clive Bassett), ("Appalachian Autumn" on *CBS Playhouse*, CBS), "Outstanding Achievement in Lighting Direction"
Bob Mackie (*Diana Ross and The Supremes and the Temptations on Broadway*, NBC), "Outstanding Achievement in Costume Design"
Ray Sebastian and Louis A. Phillippi (*The Don Adams Special: Hooray for Hollywood*, CBS), "Outstanding Achievement in Make-Up"
Walter Strenge ("Hello, Goodbye, Hello" on *Marcus Welby, M.D.*, ABC), "Outstanding Achievement in Cinematography for Entertainment Programming (series or single program of a series)"
Lionel Lindon ("Ritual of Evil" on *NBC Monday Night Movies*, NBC), "Outstanding Achievement in Cinematography for Entertainment Programming (special or feature-length program made for television)"
Edward Winkle ("Model Hippie" on *The Huntley-Brinkley Report*, NBC), "Outstanding Achievement in Cinematography for News and Documentary Programming (regularly scheduled news programs and coverage of special events)"
Thomas B. Priestley ("Sahara: La Caravanne du Sel," NBC), "Outstanding Achievement in Cinematography for News and Documentary Programming (documentary, magazine-type or mini-documentary programs)"
Bill Mosher ("Sweet Smell of Failure" on *Bracken's Word*, NBC), "Outstanding Achievement in Film Editing for Entertainment Programming (series or single program of a series)"
Edward R. Abroms ("My Sweet Charlie" on *World Premiere*, NBC), "Outstanding Achievement in Film Editing for Entertainment Programming (special or feature-length program made for television)"
Michael C. Shugrue ("The High School Profile" on *The Huntley-Brinkley Report*, NBC), "Outstanding Achievement in Film Editing for News and Documentary Programming (series, single program, special program, program segment or elements within)"
John Soh ("The Desert Whales" on *The Undersea World of Jacques Cousteau*, ABC), "Outstanding Achievement in Film Editing for News and Documentary Programming (documentary, magazine-type or mini-documentary program)"
Douglas H. Grindstaff, Alex Bamattre, Michael Colgan, Bill Lee, Joe Kavigan and Josef von Stroheim ("The Immortal" on *Movie of the Week*, ABC), "Outstanding Achievement in Film/Sound Editing"
Richard E. Raderman and Norman Karlin ("Charlie Noon" on *Gunsmoke*, CBS), "Outstanding Achievement in Film/Sound Editing"
Gordon L. Day and Dominick Gaffney ("The Submarine" on *Mission: Impossible*, CBS), "Outstanding Achievement in Film/Sound Mixing"
Bill Cole and Dave Williams ("The Switched-On Symphony," NBC), "Outstanding Achievement in Live or Tape Sound Mixing"
John Shultis ("The Sound of Burt Bacharach" on *Kraft Music Hall*, NBC), "Outstanding Achievement in Video Tape Editing"
Heino Ripp (technical director) with **Al Camoin, Gene Martin, Donald Mulvaney and Cal Shadwell** (cameramen) ("The Sound of Burt Bacharach" on *Kraft Music Hall*, NBC), "Outstanding Achievement in Technical Direction and Electronic Camerawork"
Sesame Street (NET), "Outstanding Program Achievement in Children's Programming"
Joe Raposo and Jeffrey Moss (music and lyrics for *This Way to Sesame Street*, NBC), "Outstanding Individual Achievement in Children's Programming"
Jon Stone, Jeffrey Moss, Ray Sipherd, Jerry Juhl, Dan Wilcox, Dave Connell, Bruce Hart, Carole Hart and Virginia Schone ("Sally Sees Sesame Street" on *Sesame Street*, NET), "Outstanding Individual Achievement in Children's Programming"

Today (NBC), "Outstanding Program Achievement in Daytime Programming"
The NFL Games, (CBS), "Outstanding Program Achievement in Sports Programming"
ABC's Wide World of Sports (ABC), "Outstanding Program Achievement in Sports Programming"
Robert R. Forte (film editing for *Pre Game Program,* CBS), "Outstanding Individual Achievement in Sports Programming"
Mutual of Omaha's Wild Kingdom (NBC), "Special Classification of Outstanding Program Achievement"
Video Communications Division, NASA, and Westinghouse Corporation, "Outstanding Achievement in Engineering Development" for Apollo Color Television from Space
Ampex Corporation, "Citation" for HS-200 color television production system
The Slow Guillotine KNBC-TV, Los Angeles), "Station Award"
The Other Americans (WJZ-TV, Baltimore), "Special Citation"
The Presidents of the three network news divisions, NASA and the 3M Company, "The Trustees' Awards"

1970-71 Five-Part Investigation of Welfare (*NBC Nightly News,* NBC), "Outstanding Program Achievement Within Regularly Scheduled News Programs"
Bruce Morton (correspondent for "Reports From the Lt. Calley Trial" on *CBS Evening News With Walter Cronkite,* CBS), "Outstanding Individual Achievement Within Regularly Scheduled News Programs"
"CBS News Space Coverage for 1970-71" (CBS), "Outstanding Program Achievement in Coverage of Special Events"
Walter Cronkite (correspondent for "CBS News Space Coverage for 1970-71," CBS), "Outstanding Individual Achievement in Coverage of Special Events"
"The Selling of the Pentagon" (*CBS News,* CBS), "Outstanding Program Achievement in News Documentary Programming"
"The World of Charlie Company" (*CBS News,* CBS), "Outstanding Program Achievement in News Documentary Programming"
NBC White Paper: Pollution is a Matter of Choice (NBC), "Outstanding Program Achievement in News Documentary Programming"
John Laurence (correspondent for "The World of Charlie Company," CBS), "Outstanding Individual Achievement in News Documentary Programming"
Fred Freed (writer for *NBC White Paper: Pollution is a Matter of Choice,* NBC), "Outstanding Individual Achievement in News Documentary Programming"
Gulf of Tonkin segment on *60 Minutes* (CBS), "Outstanding Program Achievement in Magazine-Type Programming"
"The Great American Dream Machine" (PBS), "Outstanding Program Achievement in Magazine-Type Programming"
Mike Wallace (correspondent, *60 Minutes,* CBS), "Outstanding Individual Achievement in Magazine-Type Programming"
The Everglades (NBC), "Outstanding Program Achievement in Cultural Documentary Programming"
The Making of "Butch Cassidy & The Sundance Kid" (NBC), "Outstanding Program Achievement in Cultural Documentary Programming"
Arthur Penn 1922—Themes and Variants (PBS), "Outstanding Program Achievement in Cultural Documentary Programming"
Nana Mahomo (narrator for *A Black View of South Africa,* CBS), "Outstanding Individual Achievement in Cultural Documentary Programming"
Robert Guenette and Theodore H. Strauss (writers of *They've Killed President Lincoln,* NBC), "Outstanding Individual Achievement in Cultural Documentary Programming"
Robert Young (director of *The Eskimo: Fight for Life,* CBS), "Outstanding Individual Achievement in Cultural Documentary Programming"
All in the Family (CBS), "Outstanding Series—Comedy"
The Senator—The Bold Ones (NBC), "Outstanding Series—Drama"
The Andersonville Trial (PBS), "Outstanding Single Program—Drama or Comedy"
The Flip Wilson Show (NBC), "Outstanding Variety Series—Musical"
The David Frost Show (syndicated), "Outstanding Variety Series—Talk"
Singer presents Burt Bacharach (CBS), "Outstanding Single Program—Variety or Musical (variety and popular music)"
Leopold Stokowski (PBS), "Outstanding Single Program—Variety or Musical (classical)"
All in the Family (CBS), "Outstanding New Series"
George C. Scott ("The Price" on *Hallmark Hall of Fame,* NBC), "Outstanding Single Performance by an Actor in a Leading Role"
Lee Grant ("The Neon Ceiling" on *World Premiere NBC Monday Night at the Movies,* NBC), "Outstanding Single Performance by an Actress in a Leading Role"
Hal Holbrook (*The Senator—The Bold Ones,* NBC), "Outstanding Continued Performance by an Actor in a Leading Role in a Dramatic Series"
Susan Hampshire ("The First Churchills" on *Masterpiece Theatre,* PBS), "Outstanding Continued Performance by an Actress in a Leading Role in a Dramatic Series"
Jack Klugman (*The Odd Couple,* ABC), "Outstanding Continued Performance by an Actor in a Leading Role in a Comedy Series"
Jean Stapleton (*All in the Family,* CBS), "Outstanding Continued Performance by an Actress in a Leading Role in a Comedy Series"
David Burns ("The Price" on *Hallmark Hall of Fame,* NBC), "Outstanding Performance by an Actor in a Supporting Role in Drama"
Margaret Leighton ("Hamlet" on *Hallmark Hall of Fame,* NBC), "Outstanding Performance by an Actress in a Supporting Role in Drama"
Edward Asner (*The Mary Tyler Moore Show,* CBS), "Outstanding Performance by an Actor in a Supporting Role in Comedy"
Valerie Harper (*The Mary Tyler Moore Show,* CBS), "Outstanding Performance by an Actress in a Supporting Role in Comedy"
Daryl Duke ("The Day the Lion Died" on *The Bold Ones—The Senator,* NBC), "Outstanding Directorial Achievement in Drama (single program of a series)"
Fielder Cook ("The Price" on *Hallmark Hall of Fame,* NBC), "Outstanding Directorial Achievement in Drama (single program)"
Jay Sandrich ("Toulouse Lautrec is One of My Favorite Artists" on *The Mary Tyler Moore Show,* CBS), "Outstanding Directorial Achievement in Comedy (single program of a series)"

Mark Warren (*Rowan and Martin's Laugh-In,* NBC), "Outstanding Directorial Achievement in Variety or Music (single program of a series)"
Sterling Johnson (*Timex Presents Peggy Fleming at Sun Valley,* NBC) "Outstanding Directorial Achievement in Comedy, Variety or Music (special program)"
Ernest O. Flatt (*The Carol Burnett Show,* CBS) "Outstanding Achievement in Choreography"
Joel Oliansky ("To Taste of Death But Once" on *The Bold Ones—The Senator,* NBC), "Outstanding Writing Achievement in Drama (single program of a series)"
Tracy Keenan Wynn and Marvin Schwartz ("Tribes" on *Movie of the Week,* ABC), "Outstanding Writing Achievement in Drama, Original Teleplay"
Saul Levitt ("The Andersonville Trial" on *Hollywood Television Theatre,* PBS), "Outstanding Writing Achievement in Drama, Adaptation"
James L. Brooks and Allan Burns ("Support Your Local Mother" on *The Mary Tyler Moore Show,* CBS), "Outstanding Writing Achievement in Comedy (single program of a series)"
Herbert Baker, Hal Goodman, Larry Klein, Bob Weiskopf, Bob Schiller, Norman Steinberg and Flip Wilson (*The Flip Wilson Show,* NBC), "Outstanding Writing Achievement in Variety or Music (single program of a series)"
Bob Ellison and Marty Farrell (*Singer Presents Burt Bacharach,* CBS), "Outstanding Writing Achievement in Comedy, Variety or Music (special program)"
David Rose ("The Love Child" on *Bonanza,* NBC), "Outstanding Achievement in Music Composition (for a series in the first year of use)"
Walter Scharf ("The Tragedy of the Red Salmon" on *The Undersea World of Jacques Cousteau,* ABC), " Outstanding Achievement in Music Composition (special program)"
Dominic Frontiere ("Swing Out, Sweet Land," NBC), "Outstanding Achievement in Music Direction of a Variety, Musical or Dramatic Program"
Ray Charles (*The First Nine Months Are the Hardest,* NBC), "Outstanding Achievement in Music, Lyrics and Special Material"
Jack Marta ("Cynthia Is Alive and Living in Avalon" on *The Name of the Game,* NBC), "Outstanding Achievement in Cinematography for Entertainment Programming (series or single program of a series)"
Lionel Lindon ("Vanished," Parts I and II, on *Movie of the Week,* ABC), "Outstanding Achievement in Cinematography for Entertainment Program (special program)"
Bob Collins (*Timex Presents Peggy Fleming at Sun Valley,* NBC), "Outstanding Achievement in Cinematography for Entertainment Program (special program)"
Larry Travis ("Los Angeles—Earthquake" on *CBS Evening News With Walter Cronkite,* CBS), "Outstanding Achievement in Cinematography for News and Documentary Programming (regularly scheduled news and coverage of special events)"
Jacques Renoir ("The Tragedy of the Red Salmon" on *The Undersea World of Jacques Cousteau,* ABC), "Outstanding Achievement in Cinematography for News and Documentary Programming (documentary, mini-documentary or magazine-type programs)"
Peter Roden ("Hamlet" on *Hallmark Hall of Fame,* NBC), "Outstanding Achievement in Art Direction or Scenic Design (dramatic program or feature-length film)"
James W. Trittipo and George Gaines (*Robert Young and The Family,* CBS), "Outstanding Achievement in Art Direction or Scenic Design (musical or variety)"
Martin Baugh and David Walker ("Hamlet" on *Hallmark Hall of Fame,* NBC), "Outstanding Achievement in Costume Design"
Robert Dawn ("Catafalque" on *Mission: Impossible,* CBS), "Outstanding Achievement in Make-Up"
Michael Economou ("A Continual Roar of Musketry," Parts I and II, on *The Bold Ones—The Senator,* NBC), "Outstanding Achievement in Film Editing for Entertainment Programming (series or single program of a series)"
George J. Nicholson ("Longstreet" on *Movie of the Week,* ABC), "Outstanding Achievement in Film Editing for Entertainment Programming (special or feature-length program made for television)"
George L. Johnson ("Prisons," Parts I-IV, on *NBC Nightly News,* NBC), "Outstanding Achievement in Film Editing for News and Documentary Programming (series, single program of a series or segment)"
Robert B. Loweree and Henry J. Grennon (*Cry Help! An NBC White Paper On Mentally Disturbed Youth,*NBC), "Outstanding Achievement in Film Editing for News and Documentary Programming (documentary, magazine-type or mini-documentary program)"
Don Hall, Jack Jackson, Bob Weatherford and Dick Jensen ("Tribes" on *Movie of the Week,* ABC), "Outstanding Achievement in Film Sound Editing"
Theodore Sonderberg ("Tribes" on *Movie of the Week,* ABC), "Outstanding Achievement in Film Sound Mixing"
John Rook ("Hamlet" on *Hallmark Hall of Fame,* NBC), "Outstanding Achievement in Lighting Direction"
Henry Bird ("Hamlet" on *Hallmark Hall of Fame,* NBC), "Outstanding Achievement in Live or Tape Sound Mixing"
Marco Zappia (*Hee-Haw,* CBS), "Outstanding Achievement in Video Tape Editing"
Gordon Baird, Tom Ancell, Rick Bennewitz, Larry Bentley and Jack Reader ("The Andersonville Trial" on *Hollywood Television Theatre,* PBS), "Outstanding Achievement in Technical Direction and Electronic Camerawork"
Sesame Street (PBS), "Outstanding Program Achievement in Children's Programming"
Burr Tillstrom (performer on *Kukla, Fran and Ollie,* PBS), "Outstanding Individual Achievement in Children's Programming"
Today (NBC), "Outstanding Program Achievement in Daytime Programming"
ABC's Wide World of Sports (ABC), "Outstanding Program Achievement in Sports Programming"
Jim McKay (commentator on *ABC's Wide World of Sports*), "Outstanding Individual Achievement in Sports Programming"
Don Meredith (commentator on *NFL Monday Night Football,* ABC), "Outstanding Individual Achievement in Sports Programming"
Harvey Korman (*The Carol Burnett Show,* CBS), "Special Classification of Individual Achievement"
Lenwood B. Abbott and John C. Caldwell (photographic effects on "City Beneath the Sea" on *World Premiere NBC Monday Night at the Movies,* NBC), "Outstanding Achievement in Any Area of Creative Technical Crafts"

Gene Widhoff (courtroom sketches at the Manson trial on *The Huntley-Brinkley Report—NBC Nightly News*, NBC), " Outstanding Achievement in Any Area of Creative Technical Crafts"
Ed Sullivan, "Trustees' Award" (for serving as founder and first President of the Academy and for pioneering the variety format)
Columbia Broadcasting System, "Outstanding Achievement in Engineering Development" for the Color Corrector
American Broadcasting Co., "Outstanding Achievement in Engineering Development" for open-loop synchronizing system
General Electric, "Citation" for Portable Earth Station Transmitter
Stefan Kudelski, "Citation" for design of NAGRA IV Recorder
If You Turn On (KNXT, Los Angeles), "Station Award"

1971-72 **"Defeat of Dacca"** (*NBC Nightly News,* NBC), "Outstanding Program Achievement Within Regulary Scheduled News Programs"
Phil Brady (reporter on "Defeat of Dacca," on *NBC Nightly News,* NBC), "Outstanding Individual Achievement Within Regularly Scheduled News"
Bob Schieffer, Phil Jones, Don Webster and Bill Plante (correspondents covering "The Air War" on *CBS Evening News With Walter Cronkite,* CBS), "Outstanding Individual Achievement Within Regularly Scheduled News"
Chronolog (NBC), "Outstanding Program Achievement for Regularly Scheduled Magazine-Type Programs"
The Great American Dream Machine (PBS), "Outstanding Program Achievement for Regularly Scheduled Magazine-Type Programs"
Mike Wallace (correspondent on *60 Minutes,* CBS), "Outstanding Individual Achievement for Regularly Scheduled Magazine-Type Programming"
The China Trip (ABC), "Outstanding Program Achievement in Coverage of Special Events"
June 30, 1971, A Day for History: The Supreme Court and the Pentagon Papers (NBC), "Outstanding Program Achievement in Coverage of Special Events"
A Ride on the Moon: The Flight of Apollo 15 (CBS), "Outstanding Program Achievement in Coverage of Special Events"
"A Night in Jail, A Day in Court" (*CBS Reports*), "Outstanding Documentary Program Achievement (programs—current signficance)"
This Child is Rated X: An NBC News White Paper on Juvenile Justice (NBC), "Outstanding Documentary Program Achievement (programs—current signficance)"
"Hollywood: The Dream Factory" (*The Monday Night Special,* ABC), The "Outstanding Documentary Program Achievement (cultural)"
"A Sound of Dolphins" (*The Undersea World of Jacques Cousteau,* (ABC), "Outstanding Documentary Program Achievement (cultural)"
"The Unsinkable Sea Otter" (*The Undersea World of Jacques Cousteau,* ABC), " Outstanding Documentary Program Achievement (cultural)"
Louis J. Hazam (writer of *Venice Be Damned,* NBC), "Outstanding Documentary Program Achievement (individual)"
Robert Northshield (writer on *Suffer the Little Children—An NBC News White Paper on Northern Ireland,* NBC), "Outstanding Documentary Program Achievement (individual)"
All In the Family (CBS), "Outstanding Series—Comedy"
Elizabeth R (PBS), "Outstanding Series—Drama"
"Brian's Song" (*ABC's Movie of the Week,* ABC), "Outstanding Single Program—Drama or Comedy"
The Carol Burnett Show (CBS), "Outstanding Variety Series—Musical"
The Dick Cavett Show (ABC), "Outstanding Variety Series—Talk"
"Jack Lemmon in 'S Wonderful, 'S Mavelous, 'S Gershwin" (*Bell System Family Theatre,* NBC), "Outstanding Single Program — Variety or Musical (variety and popular music)"
Beethoven's Birthday: A Celebration in Vienna With Leonard Bernstein (CBS), "Outstanding Single Program — Variety or Musical (classical)"
Elizabeth R (PBS), "Outstanding New Series"
Keith Mitchell ("Catherine Howard" on *Six Wives of Henry VIII,* CBS), "Outstanding Single Performance by an Actor in a Leading Role (one-time appearance in a series or special program)"
Glenda Jackson ("Shadow In The Sun" on *Elizabeth R, Masterpiece Theatre,* PBS), "Outstanding Single Performance by an Actress in a Leading Role (one-time appearance in a series or special program)"
Peter Falk (*Columbo* on *NBC Mystery Movie,* NBC), "Outstanding Continued Performance by an Actor in a Leading Role in a Dramatic Series"
Glenda Jackson (*Elizabeth R* on *Masterpiece Theatre,* PBS), "Outstanding Continued Performance by an Actress in a Leading Role in a Dramatic Series"
Carroll O'Connor (*All in the Family,* CBS), "Outstanding Continued Performance by an Actor in a Leading Role in a Comedy Series"
Jean Stapleton (*All in the Family,* CBS), "Outstanding Continued Performance by an Actress in a Leading Role in a Comedy Series"
Jack Warden ("Brian's Song" on *Movie of the Week,* ABC), "Outstanding Performance by an Actor in a Supporting Role in Drama"
Jenny Agutter ("The Snow Goose" on *Hallmark Hall of Fame,* NBC), "Outstanding Performance by an Actress in Supporting Role in Drama"
Edward Asner (*The Mary Tyler Moore Show,* CBS), "Outstanding Performance by an Actor in a Supporting Role in Comedy"
Valerie Harper (*The Mary Tyler Moore Show,* CBS), "Outstanding Performance by an Actress in a Supporting Role in Comedy"
Sally Struthers (*All in the Family* CBS), "Outstanding Performance by an Actress in a Supporting Role in Comedy"
Harvey Korman (*The Carol Burnett Show,* CBS), "Outstanding Achievement by a Performer in Music or Variety"
Alexander Singer ("The Invasion of Kevin Ireland" on *The Bold Ones—The Lawyers,* NBC), "Outstanding Directorial Achievement in Drama (single program of a series)"
Tom Gries ("The Glass House" on *The New CBS Friday Night Movies,* CBS), "Outstanding Directorial Achievement in Drama (single program)"
John Rich ("Sammy's Visit" on *All In the Family,* CBS), "Outstanding Directorial Achievement in Comedy (series)"
Art Fisher (*The Sonny & Cher Comedy Hour,* CBS), "Outstanding Directorial Achievement in Variety or Music (series)"

Walter C. Miller and Marvin Charnin ("Jack Lemmon in 'S Wonderful, 'S Marvelous, 'S Gershwin" on *Bell System Family Theatre,* NBC), "Outstanding Directorial Achievement in Comedy, Variety or Music (special)"

Alan Johnson ("Jack Lemmon in 'S Wonderful, S' Marvelous, S' Gershwin," on *Bell System Family Theatre,* NBC), "Outstanding Achievement in Choreography"

Richard L. Levinson and William Link ("Death Lends a Hand" on *Columbo,* NBC), "Outstanding Writing Achievement in Drama (single program of a series)"

Allan Sloane (*To All My Friends on Shore,* CBS), "Outstanding Writing Achievement in Drama, Original Teleplay"

William Blinn ("Brian's Song" on *Movie of the Week,* ABC), "Outstanding Writing Achievement in Drama, Adaptation"

Burt Styler ("Edith's Problem" on *All in the Family,* CBS), "Outstanding Writing Achievement in Comedy"

Don Hinkley, Stan Hart, Larry Siegel, Woody Kling, Rober Beatty, Art Baer, Ben Joelson, Stan Burns, Mike Marmer and Arnie Rosen (*The Carol Burnett Show,* CBS), "Outstanding Writing Achievement in Variety or Music"

Anne Howard Bailey ("The Trial of Mary Lincoln" on *NET Opera Theatre,* PBS), "Outstanding Writing Achievement in Comedy, Variety or Music (special program)"

Peter Rugolo ("In Defense of Ellen McKay" on *The Bold Ones—The Lawyers,* NBC), "Outstanding Achievement in Music Composition (series or single program of a series)"

John T. Williams ("Jane Eyre" on *Bell System Family Theatre,* NBC), "Outstanding Achievement in Music Composition (special program)"

Elliot Lawrence ("Jack Lemmon in 'S Wonderful, 'S Marvelous, 'S Gershwin" on *Bell System Family Theatre,* NBC), "Outstanding Achievement in Music Direction of a Variety, Musical or Dramatic Program"

Ray Charles ("The Funny Side of Marriage," NBC), "Outstanding Achievement in Music, Lyrics and Special Material"

Jan Scott ("The Scarecrow" on *Hollywood Television Theatre,* PBS), "Outstanding Achievement in Art Direction or Scenic Design (dramatic program or feature-length film made for television)"

E. Jay Krause (*Diana!,* ABC), "Outstanding Achievement in Art Direction or Scenic Design (musical or variety program)"

Elizabeth Waller ("The Lion's Cub," *Elizabeth R* on *Masterpiece Theatre,* PBS), "Outstanding Achievement in Costume Design"

Frank Westmore ("Kung Fu" on *Movie of the Week,* ABC) "Outstanding Achievement in Make-Up"

Lloyd Ahern ("Blue Print for Murder" on *Columbo,* NBC), "Outstanding Achievement in Cinematography for Entertainment Programming (series or single program of a series)"

Joseph Biroc ("Brian's Song" on *Movie of the Week,* ABC) "Outstanding Achievement in Cinematography for Entertainment Programming (special or feature-length program made for television)"

Peter McIntyre and Lim Youn Choul ("Dacca" on *NBC Nightly News,* NBC), "Outstanding Achievement in Cinematography for News and Documentary Programming (regularly scheduled news programs and coverage of special events)"

Thomas Priestley (*Venice Be Damned,* NBC), "Outstanding Achievement in Cinematography for News and Documentary Programming (documentary, magazine-type of mini-documentary programs)"

Edward R. Abroms ("Death Lends a Hand" on *Columbo,* NBC), "Outstanding Achievement in Film Editing for Entertainment Programming (series or single program of a series)

Bud S. Isaacs ("Brian's Song" on *Movie of the Week,* ABC), "Outstanding Achievement in Film Editing for Entertainment Programming (special or feature-length program made for television)"

Darold Murray ("War Song" on *NBC Nightly News,* NBC), "Outstanding Achievement in Film Editing for News and Documentary Programming (regularly scheduled news programs and coverage of special events)"

Spencer David Saxon ("Monkeys, Apes and Man" on *National Geographic Society,* CBS), "Outstanding Achievement in Film Editing for News and Documentary Programming (documentary, magazine-type and mini-documentary programs)"

Jerry Christian, James Troutman, Ronald LaVine, Sidney Lubow, Richard Raderman, Dale Johnston, Sam Caylor, John Stacy and Jack Kirschner ("Duel" on *Movie of the Weekend,* ABC), "Outstanding Achievement in Film Sound Editing"

Theodore Soderberg and Richard Overton ("Fireball Forward" on *The ABC Sunday Night Movie,* ABC), "Outstanding Achievement in Film Sound Mixing"

Heino Ripp (technical director) and **Albert Camoin, Frank Gaeta, Gene Martin and Donald Mulvaney** (cameramen), ("Jack Lemmon in 'S Wonderful, 'S Marvelous, 'S Gershwin," NBC), "Outstanding Achievement in Technical Direction and Electronic Camerawork"

John Freschi ("Gideon" on *Hallmark Hall of Fame,* NBC), "Outstanding Achievement in Lighting Direction"

Pat McKenna ("Hogan's Goat" on *Special of the Week,* PBS), "Outstanding Achievement in Video Tape Editing"

Norman H. Dewes ("The Elevator Story" on *All in the Family,* CBS), "Outstanding Achievement in Live or Tape Sound Mixing"

"The Pentagon Papers" (*PBS Special*), "Special Classification of Outstanding Achievement—General Programming"

The Search for the Nile, Parts I-VI (NBC), "Special Classification of Outstanding Achievement—Docu-Drama Programming"

Michael Hastings and Derek Marlow (writers on *The Search for the Nile,* Parts I-VI, NBC), "Special Classfication of Outstanding Achievement—Individual"

ABC's Wide World of Sports (ABC), "Outstanding Program Achievement in Sports Programming"

William P. Kelley (technical director) and **Jim Culley, Jack Bennett, Buddy Joseph, Mario Ciarlo, Frank Manfredi, Corey Leible, Gene Martin, Cal Shadwell, Billy Barnes and Ron Charbonneau** (cameramen), (*AFC Championship Game,* NBC), "Outstanding Individual Achievement in Sports Programming"

Sesame Street (PBS), "Outstanding Program Achievement in Children's Programming"

The Doctors (NBC), "Outstanding Program Achievement in Daytime Drama"

Alfredo Antonini (music director of *And David Wept,* CBS), "Outstanding Individual Achievement in Religious Programming"
Lon Stucky (lighting director for *A City of the King,* syndicated), "Outstanding Individual Achievement in Religious Programming"
Pierre Goupil, Michael Deloire and Yves Omer (underwater cameramen for "Secrets of the Sunken Caves" on *The Undersea World of Jacques Cousteau,* ABC), "Outstanding Achievement in Any Area of Creative Technical Crafts"
Bill Lawrence, National Affairs Editor, ABC News, "Trustees' Award" for dedicating four decades of his life to reporting the news
Dr. Frank Stanton, President, CBS, "Trustees' Award" for selfless leadership and unwavering principle in defense of the industry
Lee Harrison, "Outstanding Achievement in Engineering Development" for Scanimate, electronic means of picture animation
Richard E. Hill and Electronic Engineering Company of California, "Citation" for time code and equipment to facilitate editing of magnetic video tape
National Broadcasting Company, "Citation" for Hum Bucker, practical means of correcting picture transmission defect common in remote pickups
Sickle Cell Disease: Paradox of Neglect (WZZM-TV, Grand Rapids, Mich.), "Station Award"

1972-73 ***All in the Family*** (CBS), "Outstanding Comedy Series"
The Waltons (CBS), "Outstanding Drama Series—Continuing"
Tom Brown's Schooldays, Parts I-V (PBS) "Outstanding Drama Series—Limited Episodes"
The Julie Andrews Hour (ABC), "Outstanding Variety Musical Series"
"A War of Children" on *The New CBS Tuesday Night Movies,* (CBS), "Outstanding Single Program—Drama or Comedy"
Singer Presents Liza With a 'Z' (NBC), "Outstanding Single Program—Variety or Popular Music"
The Sleeping Beauty (PBS), "Outstanding Single Program—Classical Music"
America (NBC), "Outstanding New Series"
The Edge of Night (CBS), "Outstanding Program Achievement in Daytime Drama"
Dinah's Place (NBC), "Outstanding Program Achievement in Daytime Programming"
Laurence Olivier (*Long Day's Journey Into Night,* ABC), "Outstanding Single Performance by an Actor in a Leading Role"
Cloris Leachman ("A Brand New Life" on *Tuesday Movie of the Week,* ABC), "Outstanding Single Performance by an Actress in a Leading Role"
Richard Thomas (*The Waltons,* CBS), "Outstanding Continued Performance by an Actor in a Leading Role (drama series—continuing)"
Anthony Murphy (*Tom Brown's Schooldays,* PBS), "Outstanding Continued Performance by an Actor in a Leading role (drama/comedy—limited episodes)"
Michael Learned (*The Waltons,* CBS), "Outstanding, Continued Performance by an Actress in a Leading Role (drama series-continuing)"
Susan Hampshire *(Vanity Fair,* Parts I-V, on *Masterpiece Theatre,* PBS) "Outstanding Continued Performance by an Actress in a Leading Role (drama/comedy—limited episodes)"
Jack Klugman (*The Odd Couple,* ABC), "Outstanding Continued Performance by an Actor in a Leading Role in a Comedy Series"
Mary Tyler Moore (*The Mary Tyler Moore Show,* CBS), "Outstanding Continued Performance by an Actress in a Leading Role in a Comedy Series"
Scott Jacoby ("That Certain Summer" on *Wednesday Night Movie of the Week,* ABC), "Outstanding Performance by an Actor in a Supporting Role in Drama"
Ellen Corby (*The Waltons,* CBS), "Outstanding Performance by an Actress in a Supporting Role in Drama"
Ted Knight (*The Mary Tyler Moore Show,* CBS), "Outstanding Performance by an Actor in a Supporting Role in Comedy"
Valerie Harper (*The Mary Tyler Moore Show,* CBS), "Outstanding Performance by an Actress in a Supporting Role in Comedy"
Tim Conway (*The Carol Burnett Show,* CBS), "Outstanding Achievement by a Supporting Performer in Music or Variety
Jerry Thorpe ("An Eye for an Eye" on *Kung Fu,* ABC), "Outstanding Directorial Achievement in Drama (single program of a series)"
Joseph Sargent ("The Marcus-Nelson Murders" on *The CBS Thursday Night Movies,* CBS), "Outstanding Directorial Achievement in Drama (single program)"
Jay Sandrich ("It's Whether You Win or Lose" on *The Mary Tyler Moore Show,* CBS), "Outstanding Directorial Achievement in Comedy (single program of a series)"
Bill Davis (*The Julie Andrews Hour,* ABC), "Outstanding Directorial Achievement in Variety or Music (single program of a series)"
Bob Fosse (*Singer Presents Liza With a "Z,"* NBC), "Outstanding Directorial Achievement in Comedy, Variety or Music (single program)"
Abby Mann ("The Marcus-Nelson Murders" on *The CBS Thursday Night Movies,* CBS), "Outstanding Writing Achievement in Drama, Original Teleplay"
Eleanor Perry (*The House Without a Christmas Tree,* CBS), "Outstanding Writing Achievement in Drama, Adaptation"
Michael Ross, Bernie West and Lee Kalcheim ("The Bunkers and The Swingers" on *All in the Family,* CBS), "Outstanding Writing Achievement in Comedy (single program of a series)"
Stan Hart, Larry Siegel, Gail Parent, Woody Kling, Roger Beatty, Tom Patchett, Jay Tarses, Robert Hilliard, Arnie Kogen, Bill Angelos and Buz Kohan (*The Carol Burnett Show,* CBS), "Outstanding Writing Achievement in Variety or Music (single program of a series)"
Renee Taylor and Joseph Bologna (*Acts of Love—And Other Comedies,* ABC), "Outstanding Writing Achievement in Comedy, Variety or Music (special program)"
Bob Fosse (*Singer Presents Liza With a "Z,"* NBC), "Outstanding Achievement in Choreography
Charles Fox (*Love, American Style,* ABC), "Outstanding Achievement in Music Composition (for a series or single program of a series in first year of use)"
Jerry Goldsmith ("The Red Pony" on *Bell System Family Theatre,* NBC), "Outstanding Achievement in Music Composition (special program)"
Peter Matz (*The Carol Burnett Show,* CBS), "Outstanding Achievement in Music Direction of a Variety, Musical or Dramatic Program"
Fred Ebb and John Kander (*Singer Presents Liza With a 'Z',* NBC), "Outstanding Achievement in Music, Lyrics and Special Material"

Tom John (*Much Ado About Nothing,* CBS), "Outstanding Achievement for Art Direction or Scenic Design (dramatic program or feature-length film made for television)"
Brian Bartholomew and Keaton S. Walker (*The Julie Andrews Hour,* ABC), "Outstanding Achievement in Art Direction or Scenic Design (musical or variety series or Special program)"
John Freschi and John Casagrande (*44th Oscar Awards,"* NBC), "Outstanding Achievement in Lighting Direction"
Truck Krone (*The Julie Andrews Hour Christmas Show,* ABC), "Outstanding Achievement in Lighting Direction"
Jack Bear (*The Julie Andrews Hour,* ABC) "Outstanding Achievement in Costume Design"
Del Armstrong, Ellis Burman and Stan Winston ("Jayoupes" on *New CBS Tuesday Night Movies,* CBS) "Outstanding Achievement in Make-up"
Jack Woolf ("Eye for an Eye" on *Kung Fu,* ABC), "Outstanding Achievement in Cinematography for Entertainment Programming (series or single program of a series)"
Howard Schwartz ("Night of Terror" on *Tuesday Movie of the Week,* ABC), "Outstanding Achievement in Cinematography for Entertainment Programming (special or feature-length film made for television)"
Gene Fowler, Jr., Marjorie Fowler and Anthony Wollner ("The Literary Man" on *The Waltons,* CBS), "Outstanding Achievement in Film Editing for Entertainment Programming (series or single program of a series)"
Peter C. Johnson and Ed Spiegel (*Surrender at Appomattox; Appointment With Destiny,* CBS), "Outstanding Achievement in Film Editing for Entertainment Programming (special or feature-length film made for television)"
Ross Taylor, Fred Brown and David Marshall ("The Red Pony" on *Bell System Family Theatre,* NBC), "Outstanding Achievement in Film Sound Editing"
Richard Wagner, George E. Porter, Eddie Nelson and Fred Leroy Granville (*Surrender at Appomatox; Appointment With Destiny,* CBS), "Outstanding Achievement in Film Sound Mixing"
Al Gramaglia and Mahlon Fox (*Much Ado About Nothing,* CBS), "Outstanding Achievement in Live or Tape Sound Mixing"
Nick Giordano and Arthur Schneider (*The Julie Andrews Hour,* ABC), "Outstanding Achievement in Video Tape Editing"
Ernie Buttelman (technical director) and **Robert A. Kemp, James Angel, James Balden and David Hilmer** (cameramen), (*The Julie Andrews Hour,* ABC), "Outstanding Achievement in Technical Direction and Electronic Camerawork"
Mary Fickett (performer in *All My Children,* ABC), "Outstanding Achievement by an Individual in Daytime Drama"
Sesame Street (PBS), "Outstanding Achievement in Children's Programming (entertainment/fictional)"
Zoom (PBS), "Outstanding Achievement in Children's Programming (entertainment/fictional)"
Tom Whedon, John Boni, Sara Compton, Tom Dunsmuir, Thad Mumford, Jeremy Stevens and Jim Thurman (writers on *The Electric Company,* PBS), "Outstanding Achievement in Children's Programming (entertainment/fictional)"
"Last of the Curlews" (*The ABC Afterschool Special,* ABC), "Outstanding Achievement in Children's Programming (informational/factual)"
Shari Lewis (performer on "A Picture of Us," on *NBC Children's Theatre,* NBC), "Outstanding Achievement in Children's Programming (informational/factual)"
ABC's Wide World of Sports (ABC), "Outstanding Achievement in Sports Programming"
1972 Summer Olympic Games (ABC), "Outstanding Achievement in Sports Programming
John Croak, Charles Gardner, Jakob Hierl, Conrad Kraus, Edward McCarthy, Nick Mazur, Alex Moskovic, James Parker, Louis Rende, Ross Skipper, Robert Steinback, John de Lisa, George Boettscher, Merrit Roesser, Leo Scharf, Randy Cohen, Vito Gerardi, Harold Byers, Winfield Gross, Paul Scoskie, Peter Fritz, Leo Stephan, Gerber McBeath, Louis Torino, Michael Wenig, Tom Wight and James Kelley (video tape editors on *1972 Summer Olympic Games,* (ABC), "Outstanding Achievement in Sports Programming"
Sony, "Outstanding Achievement in Engineering Development" for development of Trinitron picture tube
CMX Systems (CBS Memorex), "Outstanding Achievement in Engineering Development" for video tape editing system utilizing a computer
Take Des Moines . . . Please (KDIN-TV, Des Moines, Iowa), "National Award for Community Service"
"The U.S./Soviet Wheat Deal: Is There a Scandal?" (*CBS Evening News With Walter Cronkite,* CBS), "Outstanding Achievement Within Regularly Scheduled News Programs (award for program segments)"
Walter Cronkite, Dan Rather, Daniel Schorr and Joel Blocker, (correspondents on "The Watergate Affair," on *CBS Evening News With Walter Cronkite,* CBS), "Outstanding Achievement Within Regularly Scheduled News Programs (award to individuals contributing to program segments)"
David Dick, Dan Rather, Roger Mudd and Walter Cronkite, correspondents covering the shooting of Gov. George Wallace (*CBS Evening News With Walter Cronkite,* CBS), "Outstanding Achievement Within Regularly Scheduled News Programs (award to individuals contributing to program segments)"
Eric Sevareid, correspondent ("L.B.J. The Man and the President" on *CBS Evening News With Walter Cronkite,* CBS), "Outstanding Achievement Within Regularly Scheduled News Programs (award to individuals contributing to program segments)"
"The Poppy Fields of Turkey—The Heroin Labs of Marseilles—The N.Y. Connection" (*60 Minutes,* CBS), "Outstanding Achievement for Regularly Scheduled Magazine-Type Programs (award for programs or segments)"
"The Selling of Colonel Herbert" (*60 Minutes,* CBS), "Outstanding Achievement for Regularly Scheduled Magazine-Type Programs (award for programs or segments)"
60 Minutes (CBS), "Outstanding Achievement for Regularly Scheduled Magazine-Type Programs (award for programs or segments)"
Mike Wallace (correspondent on "The Selling of Colonel Herbert," on *60 Minutes,* CBS), "Outstanding Achievement for Regularly Scheduled Magazine-Type Programs (award to individuals contributing to program or segment)"

Mike Wallace (correspondent, *60 Minutes,* CBS), "Outstanding Achievement for Regularly Scheduled Magazine-Type Programs (award to individuals contributing to program or segment)"
ABC for coverage of the Munich Olympic tragedy, "Outstanding Achievement to the Coverage of Special Events (program achievement)"
Jim McKay (commentator on the Munich Olympic tragedy, ABC), "Outstanding Achievement to the Coverage of Special Events (program achievement)"
The Blue Collar Trap (*NBC News White Paper,* NBC), "Outstanding Documentary Program Achievement (for documentaries dealing with events or matters of current significance)"
"The Mexican Connection" (*CBS Reports,* CBS), "Outstanding Documentary Program Achievement (for documentaries dealing with events or matters of current significance)"
One Billion Dollar Weapon; And Now the War Is Over—, The American Military in the '70s (NBC), "Outstanding Documentary Program Achievement (for documentaries dealing with events or matters of current significance)"
America (NBC), "Outstanding Documentary Program Achievement (for programs dealing with artistic, historic or cultural subjects)"
Jane Goodall and the World of Animal Behavior (ABC), "Outstanding Documentary Program Achievement (for programs dealing with artistic, historic or cultural subjects)"
Alistair Cooke (narrator, *America,* NBC), "Outstanding Documentary Program Achievement (to individuals contributing to documentary programs)"
Alistair Cooke (writer, "A Fireball in the Night" on *America,* NBC), "Outstanding Documentary Program Achievement (to individuals contributing to documentary programs)"
Hugo van Lawick (director of *Jane Goodall and the World of Animal Behavior,* ABC), "Outstanding Documentary Program Achievement (to individuals contributing to documentary programs)"
The Advocates (PBS), "Special Classification of Outstanding Program and Individual Achievement"
VD Blues (PBS), "Special Classification of Outstanding Program and Individual Achievement"
Duty Bound (NBC), "Outstanding Achievement in Religious Programming"
Donald Feldstein, Robert Fontana and Joe Zuckerman (animation layout of Da Vinci's art for *Leonardo: To Know How to See,* NBC), "Outstanding Achievement in Any Area of Creative Technical Crafts"
Laurens Pierce (coverage of the shooting of Gov. George Wallace on *CBS Evening News With Walter Cronkite,* CBS), "Outstanding Achievement in Cinematography for News and Documentary Programming (regularly scheduled news programs and coverage of special events)"
Des and Jen Bartlett (*The Incredible Flight of the Snow Geese,* NBC), "Outstanding Achievement in Cinematography for News and Documentary Programming (documentary, mini-documentary or magazine-type programs)"
Patrick Minerva, Martin Sheppard, George Johnson, William J. Freeda, Miguel E. Portillo, Albert J. Helias, Irwin Graf, Jean Venable, Rick Hessel, Loren Berry, Nick Wilkins, Gerry Breese, Michael Shugrue, K. Su, Edwin Einarsen, Thomas Dunphy, Russell Moore and Albert Mole (*NBC Nightly News,* NBC), "Outstanding Achievement in Film Editing for News and Documentary Programming (regularly scheduled news or coverage of special events)"
Les Parry (*The Incredible Flight of the Snow Geese,* NBC) "Outstanding Achievement in Film Editing for News and Documentary Programming (documentary, magazine-type or mini-documentary programs"

1973-74 ***M*A*S*H*** (CBS), "Outstanding Comedy Series"
Upstairs, Downstairs (*Masterpiece Theatre,* PBS), "Outstanding Drama Series"
The Carol Burnett Show (CBS), "Outstanding Music/Variety Series"
Columbo (NBC), "Oustanding Limited Series"
The Autobiography of Miss Jane Pittman (CBS), "Oustanding Special—Comedy or Drama"
Lily (CBS), "Outstanding Comedy/Variety, Variety or Music Special"
Marlo Thomas and Friends in Free to Be . . . You and Me (ABC), "Oustanding Children's Special"
Alan Alda, (*M*A*S*H*,* CBS), "Best Lead Actor in Comedy Series"
Telly Savalas (*Kojak,* CBS), "Best Lead Actor in a Drama Series"
William Holden (*The Blue Knight,* NBC), "Best Lead Actor in a Limited Series"
Hal Holbrook ("Pueblo" on *ABC Theatre,* ABC), "Best Lead Actor in a Drama (special program or single appearance in a series)"
Alan Alda (*M*A*S*H*,* CBS) "Actor of the Year—Series"
Hal Holbrook ("Pueblo" on *ABC Theatre,* ABC), "Actor of the Year—Special"
Mary Tyler Moore (*The Mary Tyler Moore Show,* CBS) "Best Lead Actress in a Comedy Series"
Michael Learned (*The Waltons,* CBS), "Best Lead Actress in a Drama Series"
Mildred Natwick ("The Snoop Sisters" on *NBC Tuesday Night Mystery Movie,* NBC), "Best Lead Actress in a Limited Series"
Cicely Tyson (*The Autobiography of Miss Jane Pittman,* CBS), "Best Lead Actress in a Drama (special program or single appearance in a series)"
Mary Tyler Moore (*The Mary Tyler Moore Show,* CBS), "Actress of the Year—Series"
Cicely Tyson ("The Autobiography of Miss Jane Pittman," CBS), "Actress of the Year—Special"
Bob Reiner (*All in the Family,* CBS), "Best Supporting Actor in Comedy"
Michael Moriarty (*The Glass Menagerie,* ABC), "Best Supporting Actor in Drama"
Harvey Korman (*The Carol Burnett Show,* CBS), "Best Supporting Actor in Comedy-Variety, Variety or Music"
Michael Moriarty (*The Glass Menagerie,* ABC), "Supporting Actor of the Year"
Cloris Leachman ("The Lars Affair" on *The Mary Tyler Moore Show,* CBS), "Best Supporting Actress in Comedy"
Joanna Miles (*The Glass Menagerie,* ABC), "Best Supporting Actress in Drama"
Brenda Vaccaro (*The Shape of Things,* CBS), "Best Supporting Actress in Comedy-Variety, Variety or Music"
Joanna Miles (*The Glass Menagerie,* ABC), "Supporting Actress of the Year"
Robert Butler (*The Blue Knight,* Part III, NBC), "Best Directing in Drama (single program of a series)"
John Korty (*The Autobiography of Miss Jane Pittman,* CBS), "Best Directing in Drama (single program)"

Jackie Cooper ("Carry On, Hawkeye" on *M*A*S*H**, CBS), "Best Directing in Comedy"
Dave Powers ("The Australia Show" on *The Carol Burnett Show,* CBS), "Best Directing in Variety or Music (single program of a series)"
Dwight Hemion (*Barbra Streisand . . . and Other Musical Instruments,* CBS), "Best Directing in Comedy-Variety, Variety or Music (special program)"
Robert Butler (*The Blue Knight,* Part III, NBC), "Director of the Year—Series"
Dwight Hemion (*Barbra Streisand . . . and Other Musical Instruments,* CBS), "Director of the Year—Special"
Joanna Lee ("The Thanksgiving Story" on *The Waltons,* CBS), "Best Writing in Drama (single program of a series)"
Fay Kanin ("Tell Me Where It Hurts" on *GE Theater,* CBS), "Best Writing in Drama, Original Teleplay"
Tracy Keenan Wynn (*The Autobiography of Miss Jane Pittman,* CBS), "Best Writing in Drama, Adaptation"
Treva Silverman ("The Lou and Edie Story" on *The Mary Tyler Moore Show,* CBS), "Best Writing in Comedy (single program of a series)"
Ed Simmons, Gary Belkin, Roger Beatty, Arnie Kogen, Bill Richmond, Gene Perret, Rudy de Luca, Barry Levinson, Dick Clair, Jenna McMahon and Barry Harman (*The Carol Burnett Show,* CBS), "Best Writing in Variety or Music (single program of a series)"
Herb Sargent, Rosalyn Drexler, Lorne Michaels, Richard Pryor, Jim Rusk, James R. Stein, Robert Illes, Lily Tomlin, George Yanok, Jane Wagner, Rod Warren, Ann Elder and Karyl Geld (*Lily,* CBS), "Best Writing in Comedy-Variety, Variety or Music (special program)"
Treva Silverman (*The Mary Tyler Moore Show,* CBS), "Writer of the Year—Series"
Fay Kanin ("Tell Me Where It Hurts" on *GE Theater,* CBS), "Writer of the Year—Special"
Tony Charmoli (*Mitzi . . . A Tribute to the American Housewife,* CBS), "Outstanding Achievement in Choreography"
Morton Stevens ("Hookman" on *Hawaii Five-O,* CBS), "Best Music Composition (for a series in first year of use)"
Fred Karlin (*The Autobiography of Miss Jane Pittman,* CBS), "Best Music Composition (special program)"
Marty Paich and David Paich ("Light the Way" on *Ironside,* NBC), "Best Song or Theme"
Jack Parnell, Ken Welch and Mitzie Welch (*Barbra Streisand . . . and Other Musical Instruments,* CBS, "Best Music Direction of a Variety, Dramatic or Musical Program"
Gerry Bucci (technical director) and **Kenneth Tamburri, Dave Hilmer, Dave Smith, Jim Balden and Ron Brooks** (cameramen), "In Concert (With Cat Stevens)" on *ABC Wide World of Entertainment,* ABC), "Outstanding Achievement in Technical Direction and Electronic Camerawork"
William M. Klages ("The Lie" on *CBS Playhouse 90,* CBS), "Outstanding Achievement in Lighting Direction"
Charles M. Schulz (writer), *A Charlie Brown Thanksgiving* (CBS), "Outstanding Individual Achievement in Children's Programming"
William Zaharuk (art director) and **Peter Razmofski** (set decorator), ("The Borrowers" on *Hallmark Hall of Fame,* NBC), "Outstanding Individual Achievement in Children's Programming"
The Dick Cavett Show (ABC), "Special Classification of Outstanding Program and Individual Achievement"
Tom Snyder (*Tomorrow,* NBC), "Special Classification of Outstanding Program and Individual Achievement"
ABC's Wide World of Sports (ABC) "Outstanding Achievement in Sports Programming"
Jim McKay (host, *ABC's Wide World of Sports,* ABC), "Outstanding Achievement in Sports Programming"
Jack Parnell, Ken Welch and Mitzie Welch (*Barbra Streisand . . . and Other Musical Instruments,* CBS), "Musician of the Year"
Jan Scott (art director) and **Charles Kreiner** (set decorator), ("The Lie" (on *CBS Playhouse 90,* CBS), "Best Art Direction or Scenic Design (dramatic program or feature-length film made for television, single program of a series or special)"
Brian C. Bartholomew (*Barbra Streisand . . . and Other Musical Instruments,* CBS), "Best Art Direction or Scenic Design (musical or variety single program of a series or special)"
Jan Scott (art director) and **Charles Kreiner** (set decorator), ("The Lie" (on *CBS Playhouse 90,* CBS), "Art Director and Set Decorator of the Year"
Bruce Walkup and Sandy Stewart (*The Autobiography of Miss Jane Pittman,* CBS), "Outstanding Achievement in Costume Design"
Stan Winston and Rick Baker (*The Autobiography of Miss Jane Pittman,* CBS), "Outstanding Achievement in Make-Up"
Harry Wolf ("Any Old Port in a Storm" on *Columbo,* NBC), "Best Cinematography for Entertainment Programming (series or single program of a series)"
Ted Voigtlander ("It's Good to Be Alive" on *GE Theater,* CBS), "Best Cinematography for Entertainment Programming (special or feature-length program made for television)"
Ted Voigtlander ("It's Good to Be Alive" on *GE Theater,* CBS), "Cinematographer of the Year"
Gene Fowler, Jr., Marjorie Fowler and Samuel E. Beetley (*The Blue Knight,* NBC), "Best Film Editing for Entertainment Programming (series or single program of a series)"
Frank Morriss ("The Execution of Private Slovick" on *NBC Wednesday Night At The Movies,* NBC), "Best Film Editing for Entertainment Programming (special or feature-length program made for television)"
Frank Morriss ("The Execution of Private Slovick" on *NBC Wednesday Night At the Movies,* NBC), "Film Editor of the Year"
Bud Nolan ("Pueblo" on *ABC Theatre,* ABC), "Outstanding Achievement in Film Sound Editing"
Albert A. Gramaglia and Michael Shindler ("Pueb- lo" on *ABC Theatre,* ABC), "Outstanding Achievement in Film or Tape Sound Mixing"
Alfred Muller ("Pueblo" on *ABC Theatre,* ABC), "Outstanding Achievement in Video Tape Editing"
Lynda Gurasich (hairstylist on *The Autobiography of Miss Jane Pittman,* CBS), "Outstanding Achievement in Any Area of Creative Technical Crafts"
Consolidated Video Systems, Inc. "Outstanding Achievement in Engineering Development" for application of digital video control to Time Base Corrector for lighter, more portable video tape equipment

RCA, "Outstanding Achievement in Engineering Development" for quadraplex video tape cartridge equipment
Horizon: The Making of a Natural History Film, British Broadcasting Corp., London, "International Award—Non-fiction"
La Cabina, Television Espanola, Madrid, "International Award—Fiction"
Charles Curran, President, European Broadcasting Union, and Director General, British Broadcasting Corporation, "International Directorate Emmy Award"
Through the Looking Glass Darkly (WKY-TV, Oklahoma City), "National Award for Community Service"
The Doctors (NBC), "Outstanding Drama Series"
The Other Woman (ABC), "Outstanding Drama Special"
Password (ABC), "Outstanding Game Show"
The Merv Griffin Show (syndicated) "Outstanding Talk, Service or Variety Series"
Zoom (PBS), "Outstanding Entertainment Children's Series"
"Rookie of the Year" on *The ABC Afterschool Special* (ABC), "Outstanding Entertainment Children's Special"
Coverage of the October War from Israel's Northern Front (*CBS News With Walter Cronkite,* CBS), "Outstanding Achievement Within Regularly Scheduled News Programs (for program segments)"
The Agnew Resignation (*CBS Evening News With Walter Cronkite,* CBS), "Outstanding Achievement Within Regularly Scheduled News Programs (for program segments)"
The Key Biscayne Bank, Charter Struggle (*CBS Evening News With Walter Cronkite,* CBS), "Outstanding Achievement Within Regularly Scheduled News Programs (for program segments)"
Reports on World Hunger (*NBC Nightly News,* NBC), "Outstanding Achievement Within Regularly Scheduled News Programs (for program segments)"
"America's Nerve Gas Arsenal" (*First Tuesday,* NBC), "Outstanding Achievement for Regularly Scheduled Magazine-Type Programs"
"The Adversaries" (*Behind the Lines,* PBS), "Outstanding Achievement for Regularly Scheduled Magazine-Type Programs"
"A Question of Impeachment" (*Bill Moyers' Journal,* PBS), "Outstanding Achievement for Regularly Scheduled Magazine-Type Programs"
Watergate: The White House Transcripts (CBS), "Outstanding Achievement in Coverage of Special Events"
Watergate Coverage (PBS), "Outstanding Achievement in Coverage of Special Events"
"Fire!" (*ABC News Closeup,* ABC), "Outstanding Documentary Program Achievement (documentary programs dealing with events of current interest)
CBS News Special Report: The Senate and the Watergate Affair (CBS), "Outstanding Documentary Program Achievement (documentary programs dealing with events of current interest)"
"Journey to the Outer Limits," (*National Geographic Society,* ABC), "Outstanding Documentary Program Achievements (programs dealing with artistic, historical or cultural subjects)"
The World at War (syndicated), "Outstanding Documentary Program Achievements (programs dealing with artistic, historical or cultural subjects)"
CBS Reports: The Rockefellers, (CBS), "Outstanding Documentary Program Achievement (programs dealing with artistic, historical or cultural subjects)"
"Solzhenitsyn" (*CBS News Special,* CBS), "Outstanding Interview Program"
Henry Steele Commager (*Bill Moyers' Journal,* PBS), "Outstanding Interview Program"
Harry Reasoner (*ABC News,* ABC), "Outstanding Television News Broadcaster"
Bill Moyers ("Essay on Watergate," on *Bill Moyers' Journal,* PBS), "Outstanding Television News Broadcaster"
Ronald Baldwin (art director) and **Nat Mongioi** (set decorator), (*The Electric Company,* PBS), "Outstanding Individual Achievement in Children's Programming"
The Muppets (Jim Henson, Frank Oz, Carroll Spinney, Jerry Nelson, Richard Hunt and Fran Brill (performers on *Sesame Street,* PBS), "Outstanding Achievement in Children's Programming"
Jon Stone, Joseph A. Bailey, Jerry Juhl, Emily Perl, Kingsley, Jeffrey Moss, Ray Sipherd and Norman Stiles (writers on *Sesame Street,* PBS), "Outstanding Achievement in Children's Programming"
Kan Lamkin (technical director) and **Sam Drummy, Garry Stanton and Robert Hatfield** (cameramen), ("Gift of Tears" on *This Is The Life,* syndicated), "Outstanding Achievement in Religious Programming"
Pamela Hill ("Fire!", *ABC News Closeup,* ABC), "Outstanding Achievement in News and Documentary Directing"
Philippe Cousteau (Under ice photography in "Beneath the Frozen World" for *The Undersea World of Jacques Cousteau,* ABC), "Outstanding Achievement in Any Area of Creative Technical Crafts"
John Chambers and Tom Burman (make-up for "Struggle for Survival: Primal Man," ABC), "Outstanding Achievement in Any Area of Creative Technical Crafts"
Aggie Whelan (courtroom drawings for the Mitchell-Stans trial on *CBS Evening News With Walter Cronkite,* CBS), "Outstanding Achievement in Any Area of Creative Technical Crafts"
Make a Wish (ABC), "Outstanding Informational Children's Series"
The Runaways (ABC), "Outstanding Informational Children's Special"
Inside/Out (syndicated), "Outstanding Instructional Children's Programming"
Delos Hall ("Clanking Savannah Blacksmith" on "On the Road With Charles Kuralt," for *CBS Evening News With Walter Cronkite,* CBS), "Best Cinematography for News and Documentary Programming (regularly scheduled news program and coverage of special events)"
Walter Dumbrow ("Ballerina" on *60 Minutes,* CBS), "Best Cinematography for News and Documentary Programming (documentary, magazine-type or mini-documentary program)"
Walter Scharf ("Beneath the Frozen World" on *The Undersea World of Jacques Cousteau,* ABC), "Best Music Composition"
William Sunshine (*60 Minutes,* CBS), "Best Art Direction or Scenic Design"
William J. Freeda ("Profile of Poverty in Appalachia" on *NBC Nightly News,* NBC), "Best Film Editing for News and Documentary Programming (regularly scheduled news program)"

Ann Chegwidden ("The Baboons of Gombe" on *Jane Goodall and the World of Animal Behavior,* ABC), "Best Film Editing for News and Documentary Programming (documentary, magazine-type or mini-documentary program)"
Peter Pilafian, George R. Porter, Eddie J. Nelson and Robert L. Harman ("Journey to the Outer Limits" on *National Geographic Society,* ABC), "Best Film or Tape Sound Mixing"
Charles L. Campbell, Robert Cornett, Larry Caron, Larry Kaufman, Colin Moria, Don Warner and Frank R. White ("The Baboons of Gombe" on *Jane Goodall and the World of Animal Behavior,* ABC), "Best Film or Tape Sound Editing"
Gary Anderson (*Paramount Presents . . . ABC Wide World of Entertainment,* ABC), "Best Video Tape Editing"
Carl Schutzman (technical director) and **Joseph Schwartz and William Bell** (cameramen), (*60 Minutes,* CBS), "Best Technical Direction and Electronic Camerawork"

1974-75 ***The Mary Tyler Moore Show*** (CBS), "Outstanding Comedy Series"
Upstairs, Downstairs, (*Masterpiece Theatre,* PBS), "Outstanding Drama Series"
The Carol Burnett Show (CBS), "Outstanding Comedy/Variety or Music Series"
Benjamin Franklin (CBS), "Outstanding Limited Series"
"The Law" (*NBC World Premiere Movie,* NBC), "Outstanding Special—Drama or Comedy"
An Evening With John Denver (ABC), "Outstanding Special—Comedy/Variety or Music"
"Profile in Music: Beverly Sills" (PBS), "Outstanding Classical Music Program"
Tony Randall (*The Odd Couple,* ABC), "Outstanding Lead Actor in a Comedy Series"
Robert Blake (*Baretta,* ABC), "Outstanding Lead Actor in a Drama Series"
Peter Falk (*Columbo* on *NBC Saturday Night Mystery Movie,* NBC), "Outstanding Lead Actor in a Limited Series"
Laurence Olivier ("Love Among the Ruins" on *ABC Theatre,* ABC), "Outstanding Lead Actor in A Special Program—Drama or Comedy"
Valerie Harper (*Rhoda,* CBS), "Outstanding Lead Actress in a Comedy Series"
Jean Marsh (*Upstairs, Downstairs* on *Masterpiece Theatre,* PBS), "Outstanding Lead Actress in a Drama Series"
Jessica Walter (*Amy Prentiss* on *NBC Sunday Mystery Movie,* NBC), "Outstanding Lead Actress in a Limited Series"
Katharine Hepburn (*Love Among the Ruins* on *ABC Theatre,* ABC), "Outstanding Lead Actress in a Special Program—Drama or Comedy"
Ed Asner (*The Mary Tyler Moore Show,* CBS), "Outstanding Continued Performance by a Supporting Actor in a Drama Series"
Will Geer (*The Waltons,* CBS), "Outstanding Continuing Performance by a Supporting Actor in a Drama Series"
Jack Albertson (*Cher,* CBS), "Outstanding Continuing or Single Performance by a Supporting Actor in a Comedy or Drama Special"
Anthony Quayle (*QB VII,* Parts 1 and 2, *ABC Movie Special,* ABC), "Outstanding Single Performance by a Supporting Actor in a Comedy or Drama"
Patrick McGoohan ("By Dawn's Early Light" on *Columbo, NBC Sunday Mystery Movie,* NBC), "Outstanding Single Performance by a Supporting Actor in a Comedy or Drama Series"
Betty White (*The Mary Tyler Moore Show,* CBS), "Outstanding Continuing Performance by a Supporting Actress in a Comedy Series"
Ellen Corby (*The Waltons,* CBS), "Outstanding Continuing Performance by a Supporting Actress in a Drama Series"
Cloris Leachman (*Cher,* CBS), "Outstanding Continuing or Single Performance by a Supporting Actress in Variety or Music"
Juliet Mills (*QB VII,* Parts 1 & 2, *ABC Movie Special,* ABC), "Outstanding Single Performance by a Supporting Actress in a Comedy or Drama"
Cloris Leachman ("Phyllis Whips Inflation" on *The Mary Tyler Moore Show,* CBS), "Outstanding Single Performance by a Supporting Actress in a Comedy or Drama Series"
Zohra Lampert ("Queen of the Gypsies" on *Kojak,* CBS), "Outstanding Single Performance by a Supporting Actress in a Comedy or Drama Series"
Bill Bain (*Upstairs, Downstairs,* PBS), "Outstanding Directing in a Drama Series"
Gene Reynolds (*M*A*S*H*, CBS), "Outstanding Directing in a Comedy Series"
Dave Powers (*The Carol Burnett Show,* CBS), "Outstanding Directing in a Comedy/Variety or Music Series"
Bill Davis (*An Evening With John Denver,* ABC), "Outstanding Directing in a Comedy/Variety or Music Special"
George Cukor ("Love Among the Ruins" on *ABC Theatre,* ABC), "Outstanding Directing in a Special Program—Drama or Comedy"
Howard Fast ("The Ambassador" on *Benjamin Franklin,* CBS), "Outstanding Writing in a Drama Series"
Ed Weinberger and Stan Daniels ("Mary Richards Goes to Jail" on *The Mary Tyler Moore Show,* CBS), "Outstanding Writing in a Comedy Series"
Ed Simmons, Gary Belkin, Roger Beatty, Arnie Kogen, Bill Richmond, Gene Perret, Rudy De Luca, Barry Levinson, Dick Clair and Jenna McMahon (*The Carol Burnett Show,* CBS), "Outstanding Writing in a Comedy/Variety or Music Series"
Bob Wells, John Bradford and Cy Coleman (*Shirley MacLaine: If They Could See Me Now,* CBS), "Outstanding Writing in a Comedy/Variety or Music Special"
James Costigan ("Love Among the Ruins" on *ABC Theatre,* ABC), "Outstanding Writing in a Special Program—Drama or Comedy—Original Teleplay"
David W. Rintels (*IBM Presents Clarence Darrow,* NBC), "Outstanding Writing in a Special Program—Drama or Comedy—Adaptation"
Marge Champion (*Queen of the Stardust Ballroom,* CBS), "Outstanding Achievement in Choreography"
Billy Goldenberg ("The Rebel" on *Benjamin Franklin,* CBS), "Outstanding Achievement in Music Composition for a Series"
Jerry Goldsmith (*QB-VII,* Parts 1 and 2, on *ABC Movie Special,* ABC), "Outstanding Achievement in Music Composition for a Special"
Charles Lisanby (art director) and **Robert Checchi** (set Decorator), ("The Ambassador" on *Benjamin Franklin,* CBS), "Outstanding Achievement in Art Direction or Scenic Design (single episode of a comedy or drama series)"

Robert Kelly (art director) and **Robert Checchi** (set decorator), (*Cher,* CBS), "Outstanding Achievement in Art Direction or Scenic Design (single episode or comedy/variety or music series)"
Carmen Dillon (art director) and **Tess Davis** (set decorator) ("Love Among the Ruins" on *ABC Theatre,* ABC), "Outstanding Achievement in Art Direction or Scenic Design (dramatic special or feature-length program made for television)"
Phil Norman (*QB-VII,* Parts 1 and 2, on *ABC Movie Special,* ABC), "Outstanding Achievement in Graphic Design and Title Sequences"
Richard Glouner (*Columbo,* NBC), "Outstanding Achievement in Cinematography for Entertainment Programming for a Series"
David M. Walsh (*Queen of the Stardust Ballroom,* CBS), "Outstanding Achievement in Cinematography for Entertainment Programming for a Special"
Douglas Hines ("An Affair to Forget" on *The Mary Tyler Moore Show,* CBS), "Outstanding Film Editing for Entertainment Programming for a Series (comedy)"
Donald R. Rode ("Mirror, Mirror On the Wall" on *Petrocelli,* NBC), "Outstanding Film Editing for Entertainment Programming for a Series (drama)"
John A. Martinelli ("The Legend of Lizzie Borden" on *ABC Monday Night Movie,* ABC), "Outstanding Film Editing for Entertainment Programming for a Special"
Marvin I. Kosberg, Richard Burrow, Milton C. Burrow, Jack Milner, Ronald Ashcroft, James Ballas, Josef von Stroheim, Jerry Rosenthal, William Andrews, Edward Sandlin, David Horton, Alvin Kajita, Tony Garber and Jeremy Hoenack (*QB-VII,* Parts 1 and 2, on *ABC Movie Special,* ABC), "Outstanding Achievement in Film Sound Editing"
Marshall King (*The American Film Institute Salute to James Cagney,* CBS), "Outstanding Achievement in Film or Tape Sound Mixing"
Gary Anderson and Jim McElroy (*Judgment: The Court-Martial of Lt. William Calley,* ABC), "Outstanding Achievement in Video Tape Editing"
Ernie Buttelman (technical director) and **Jim Angel, Jim Balden, Ron Brooks and Art LaCombe** (cameramen), ("The Missiles of October" on *ABC Theatre,* ABC), "Outstanding Achievement in Technical Direction and Electronic Camerawork"
John Freschi (*The Perry Como Christmas Show,* CBS), "Outstanding Achievement in Lighting Direction"
Yes, Virginia, There Is a Santa Claus (ABC), "Outstanding Children's Special"
Jimmy Connors vs. Rod Laver Tennis Challenge (CBS), "Outstanding Sports Event"
Wide World of Sports (ABC), "Outstanding Sports Program"
Jim McKay (*Wide World of Sports,* ABC), "Outstanding Sports Broadcaster"
American Film Institute Salute to James Cagney (CBS), "Special Classification of Outstanding Program Achievement"
Alistair Cooke (*Masterpiece Theatre,* PBS), "Special Classification of Outstanding Individual Achievement"
Guy Verhille ("The Legend of Lizzie Borden" on *ABC Monday Night Movie,* ABC), "Outstanding Achievement in Costume Design"
Margaret Furse ("Love Among the Ruins" on *ABC Theatre,* ABC), "Outstanding Achievement in Costume Design"
Edie Panda (hairstylist), ("The Ambassador" on *Benjamin Franklin,* CBS), "Outstanding Achievement in Any Area of Creative Television Crafts"
Doug Nelson and Norm Schwartz, (double-system sound editing and synchronization for stereo broadcasting, *Wide World in Concert,* ABC), "Outstanding Achievement in Any Area of Creative Television Crafts"
Gene Schwarz (technical director), *1974 World Series,* NBC), "Outstanding Individual Achievement in Sports Programming"
Herb Altman (film editor), (*The Baseball World of Joe Garagiola,* NBC), "Outstanding Individual Achievement in Sports Programming"
Corey Leible, Len Basile, Jack Bennett, Lou Gerard and Ray Figelski (electronic cameramen), (*1974 Stanley Cup Playoffs,* NBC), "Outstanding Individual Achievement in Sports Programming"
John Pumo, Charles D'Onofrio, Frank Florio (technical directors) and **George Klimcsak, Robert Kania, Harold Hoffmann, Herman Lang, George Drago, Walt Deniear, Stan Gould, Al Diamond, Charles Armstrong, Al Brantley, Sig Meyers, Frank McSpedon, George F. Naeder, Gordon Sweeney, Jo Sidlo, William Hathaway, Gene Pescalek and Curly Fonorow** (cameramen), (*Masters Tournament,* CBS), "Outstanding Individual Achievement in Sports Programming"
Columbia Broadcasting System, "Outstanding Achievement in Engineering Development" for spearheading Electronic News Gathering System
Nippon Electric Company, "Outstanding Achievement in Engineering Development" for digital television frame synchronizers
Elmer Lower, American Broadcasting Company, "Trustees' Award"
Peter Goldmark, Goldmark Laboratories, "Trustees' Award"
The Willowbrook Case: The People vs. the State of New York, (WABC-TV, New York), "National Award for Community Service"
Mr. Axelford's Angel, Yorkshire Television Ltd., London, "International Award—fiction"
Aquarius: Hello Dali!, London Weekend Television, London, "International Award—non-fiction"
The Evacuees, British Broadcasting Corporation, London, "International Award—fiction"
Inside Story: Marek," British Broadcasting Corporation, London, "International Award—non-fiction"
Junzo Imamichi, Chairman of the Board, Tokyo Broadcasting System, "International Directorate Award"
Elinor Bunin (graphic design and title sequences for *Funshine Saturday & Sunday;* umbrella title animations, ABC), "Outstanding Individual Achievement in Children's Programming"

1975-76 ***The Mary Tyler Moore Show*** (CBS), "Outstanding Comedy Series"
Police Story (NBC), "Outstanding Drama Series"
NBC's Saturday Night (NBC), "Outstanding Comedy/Variety or Music Series"
Upstairs, Downstairs (*Masterpiece Theatre,* PBS), "Outstanding Limited Series"
"Eleanor and Franklin" (*ABC Theatre,* ABC), "Outstanding Special—Drama or Comedy"
Gypsy in My Soul (CBS), "Outstanding Special—Comedy-Variety or Music"
Bernstein and the New York Philharmonic (PBS), "Outstanding Classical Music Program"

Jack Albertson (*Chico and the Man,* NBC), "Outstanding Lead Actor in a Comedy Series"
Peter Falk (*Columbo,* NBC), "Outstanding Lead Actor in a Drama Series"
Hal Holbrook (*Sandburg's Lincoln,* NBC), "Outstanding Lead Actor in a Limited Series"
Anthony Hopkins ("The Lindbergh Kidnapping Case" on *NBC World Premiere Movie,* NBC), "Outstanding Lead Actor in a Drama or Comedy Special"
Edward Asner (*Rich Man, Poor Man,* ABC), "Outstanding Lead Actor for a Single Appearance in a Drama or Comedy Series"
Mary Tyler Moore (*The Mary Tyler Moore Show,* CBS), "Outstanding Lead Actress in a Comedy Series"
Michael Learned (*The Waltons,* CBS), "Outstanding Lead Actress in a Drama Series"
Rosemary Harris ("Notorious Woman" on *Masterpiece Theatre,* PBS), "Outstanding Lead Actress in a Limited Series"
Susan Clark (*Babe,* CBS), "Outstanding Lead Actress in a Drama or Comedy Special"
Kathryn Walker ("John Adams, Lawyer" on *The Adams Chronicles,* PBS), "Outstanding Lead Actress in a Single Appearance in a Drama or Comedy Series"
Ted Knight (*The Mary Tyler Moore Show,* CBS), "Outstanding Continued Performance by a Supporting Actor in a Comedy Series"
Anthony Zerbe (*Harry O,* ABC), "Outstanding Continued Performance by a Supporting Actor in a Drama Series"
Chevy Chase (*NBC's Saturday Night,* NBC), "Outstanding Continuing or Single Performance by a Supporting Actor in Variety or Music"
Ed Flanders (*A Moon for the Misbegotten,* ABC), "Outstanding Single Performance by a Supporting Actor in a Comedy or Drama Special"
Betty White (*The Mary Tyler Moore Show,* CBS), "Outstanding Continuing Performance by a Supporting Actress in a Comedy Series"
Ellen Corby (*The Waltons,* CBS), "Outstanding Continuing Performance by a Supporting Actress in a Drama Series"
Vicki Lawrence (*The Carol Burnett Show,* CBS), "Outstanding Continuing or Single Performance by a Supporting Actress in Variety or Music"
Rosemary Murphy ("Eleanor and Franklin" on *ABC Theatre,* ABC), "Outstanding Single Performance by a Supporting Actress in a Comedy or Drama Special"
Fionnuala Flanagan (*Rich Man, Poor Man,* ABC), "Outstanding Single Performance by a Supporting Actress in a Comedy or Drama Series"
David Greene (*Rich Man, Poor Man,* ABC), "Outstanding Directing in a Drama Series"
Gene Reynolds (*M*A*S*H*, CBS), "Outstanding Directing in a Comedy Series"
Dave Wilson (*NBC's Saturday Night,* NBC), "Outstanding Directing in a Comedy/Variety or Music Series"
Dwight Hemion (*Steve and Eydie: Our Love is Here to Stay,* CBS), "Outstanding Directing in a Comedy/Variety or Music Special"
Daniel Petrie ("Eleanor and Franklin" on *ABC Theatre,* ABC), "Outstanding Directing in a Special Program—Drama or Comedy"
Sherman Yellen (*The Adams Chronicles,* PBS), "Outstanding Writing in a Drama Series"
David Lloyd (*The Mary Tyler Moore Show,* CBS), "Outstanding Writing in a Comedy Series"
Anne Beatts, Chevy Chase, Al Franken, Tom Davis, Lorne Michaels, Suzanne Miller, Michael O'Donoghue, Herb Sargent, Tom Schiller, Rosie Schuster and Alan Zwiebel (*NBC's Saturday Night,* NBC), "Outstanding Writing in a Comedy/Variety or Music Series"
Jane Wagner, Lorne Michaels, Ann Elder, Christopher Guest, Earl Pomerantz, Jim Rusk, Lily Tomlin, Rod Warren and George Yanok (*Lily Tomlin,* ABC), "Outstanding Writing in a Comedy/Variety of Music Special"
James Costigan ("Eleanor and Franklin" on *ABC Theatre,* ABC), "Outstanding Writing in a Special Program—Drama or Comedy—Original Teleplay"
David W. Rintels (*Fear on Trial,* CBS), "Outstanding Writing in a Special Program—Drama or Comedy—Adaptation"
You're a Good Sport, Charlie Brown (CBS), "Outstanding Children's Special"
1975 World Series (NBC), "Outstanding Live Sports Special"
NFL Monday Night Football (ABC), "Outstanding Live Sports Series"
XII Winter Olympic Games *(ABC),* "Outstanding Edited Sports Special"
ABC's Wide World of Sports (ABC), "Outstanding Edited Sports Series"
Jim McKay (*ABC's Wide World of Sports,* ABC), "Outstanding Sports Personality"
Forgotten Children (WBBM-TV, Chicago), "National Award for Community Service"
Bicentennial Minutes (CBS), "Special Classification of Outstanding Program Achievement"
The Tonight Show Staring Johnny Carson (NBC), "Special Classification of Outstanding Program Achievement"
Ann Marcus, Jerry Adelman and Daniel Gregory Browne (writers), (*Mary Hartman, Mary Hartman,* syndicated), "Special Classification of Outstanding Program Achievement"
Andy Sidaris, Don Ohlmeyer, Roger Goodman, Larry Kamm, Ronnie Hawkins, and Ralph Mellanby (directors), (*XII Winter Olympic Games,* ABC), "Outstanding Individual Achievement in Sports Programming"
Tony Charmoli (*Gypsy in My Soul,* CBS), "Outstanding Achievement in Choreography"
Alex North (*Rich Man, Poor Man,* ABC), "Outstanding Achievement in Music Composition for a Series"
Jerry Goldsmith (*Babe, CBS), "Outstanding Achievement in Music Composition for a Special"*
Seiji Ozawa ("Central Park in the Dark/A Hero's Life" on *Evening at Symphony,* PBS), "Outstanding Achievement in Music Direction"
Tom John (art director) and **John Wendell and Wes Laws** (set decorators) for pilot of *Beacon Hill* (CBS), "Outstanding Achievement in Art Direction or Scenic Design (comedy or drama)"
Raymond Klausen (art director) and **Robert Checchi** (set decorator), (*Cher,* CBS), "Outstanding Achievement in Art Direction or Scenic Design (comedy-variety or music)"
Jan Scott (art director) and **Anthony Mondello** (set decorator), ("Eleanor and Franklin," ABC), "Outstanding Achievement in Art Direction or Scenic Design (dramatic special or feature-length film made for television)"
Norman Sunshine (*Addie and the King of Hearts,* CBS), "Outstanding Achievement in Graphic Design and Title Sequences"

Joe I. Tompkins ("Eleanor and Franklin," ABC), "Outstanding Achievement in Costume Design for a Drama Special"
Bob Mackie (*Mitzi . . . Roarin' In The '20s,* CBS), "Outstanding Achievement in Costume Design for Music and Variety"
Jane Robinson and Jill Silverside ("Recover," "Jenny" and "Lady Randolph Churchill" on *Great Performances,* PBS), "Outstanding Achievement in Costume Design for a Drama or Comedy Series"
Del Armstrong and Mike Westmore ("Eleanor and Franklin," ABC), "Outstanding Achievement in Make-up"
Harry L. Wolf ("Keep Your Eye on the Sparrow" on *Baretta,* ABC), "Outstanding Achievement in Cinematography for Entertainment Programming for a Series"
Paul Lohmann and Edward R. Brown ("Eleanor and Franklin," ABC), "Outstanding Achievement in Cinematography for Entertainment Programming for a Special"
Stanford Tischler and Fred W. Berger ("Welcome to Korea" on *M*A*S*H*,* CBS), "Outstanding Film Editing for Entertainment Programming for a Series (single episode of a comedy series)"
Samuel Beetley and Ken Zemke ("The Quality of Mercy" on *Medical Story,* NBC), "Outstanding Film Editing for Entertainment Programming for a Series (single spisode of a dramatic or limited series)"
Michael Kahn ("Eleanor and Franklin" on *ABC Theatre,* ABC), "Outstanding Film Editing for Entertainment Programming for a Special"
Douglas H. Grindstaff, Al Kajita, Marvin I. Kosberg, Hans Newman, Leon Selditz, Dick Friedman, Stan Gilbert, Hank Salerno, Larry Singer and William Andrews ("The Quality of Mercy" on *Medical Story,* NBC), "Outstanding Achievement in Film Sound Editing"
Don Bassman and Don Johnson ("Eleanor and Franklin" on *ABC Theatre,* ABC) "Outstanding Achievement in Film Sound Mixing"
Dave Williams (*Tonight Show Starring Johnny Carson,*anniversary show, NBC) "Outstanding Achievement in Tape Sound Mixing"
Grish Bhargava and Manfred Schorn, (*The Adams Chronicles,* PBS) "Outstanding Achievement in Video Tape Editing for a Series"
Nick V. Giordano ("Alice Cooper—The Nightmare" on "Wide World: In Concert, ABC) Outstanding Achievement in Video Tape Editing for a Special
Leonard Chumbley (technical director) and **Walter Edel, John Fehler and Steve Zink** (Cameramen), (*The Adams Chronicles,* PBS) "Outstanding Achievement in Technical Direction and Electronic Camerawork "
William Krages and Don Stuckey (*Mitzi and the Hundred Guys,* CBS) "Outstanding Achievement in Lighting Direction"
John Freschi (*Mitzi . . . Roarin' in the 20's,* CBS), "Outstanding Achievement in Lighting Direction"
Ken Welch, Mitzie Welch and Artie Malvin (*The Carol Burnett Show,* CBS) "Outstanding Achievement in Special Musical Material"
Jean Burt Reilly and Billie Laughridge (hairstylists), ("Eleanor and Franklin" on *ABC Theatre,* ABC), "Outstanding Achievement in Any Area of Creative Technical Crafts"
Donald Sahlin, Kermit Love, Caroly Wilcox, John Lovelady and Rollie Krewson (costumes and props for The Muppets), (*Sesame Street,* PBS), "Outstanding Achievement in Any Area of Creative Technical Crafts"
Rene Lagler (art director) and **Richard Harvey** (set decorator), (*Dinah!,* syndicated) "Outstanding Individual Achievement in Daytime Programming"
Jeff Cohan, Joe Aceti, John Delisa, Lou Frederick, Jack Gallivan, Jim Jennett, Carol Lehti, Howard Shapiro, Katsumi Aseada, John Fernandez, Peter Fritz, Eddie C. Joseph, Ken Klingbeil, Leo Stephan, Ted Summers, Michael Wenig, Ron Ackerman, Michael Bonifazio, Barbara Bowman, Charlie Burnham, John Croak, Charles Gardner, Marvin Gench, Victor Gonzales, Jakob Hierl, Nick Mazur, Ed McCarthy, Alex Moskovic, Arthur Nace, Lou Rende, Erskin Roberts, Merritt Roesser, Arthur Volk, Roger Haenelt, Curt Brand, Phil Mollica, George Boettcher and Herb Ohlandt (tape editors) *XII Winter Olympic Games,* ABC), "Outstanding Individual Achievement in Sports Programming"
Dick Roes, Jack Kelly, Bill Sandreuter, Frank Bailey and Jack Kestenbaum (tape sound mixers), (*XII Winter Olympic Games,* ABC), "Outstanding Individual Achievement in Sports Programming"
Joseph J.H. Vadala (cinematographer on *A Determining Force,* NBC), "Outstanding Achievement in Religious Programming"
Bud Nolan and Jim Cookman (film sound editors on *Sound for Freedom,* NBC), "Outstanding Individual Achievement in Children's Programming"
Sony Corporation, "Outstanding Achievement in Engineering Development" for U-matic video cassette concept
Eastman Kodak, "Outstanding Achievement in Engineering Development" for Eastman Ektachrome Video News Film
Another World (NBC), "Outstanding Daytime Drama Series"
First Ladies' Diaries: Edith Wilson (NBC), "Outstanding Daytime Drama Special"
The $20,000 Pyramid (ABC), "Outstanding Daytime Game or Audience Participation Show"
Dinah! (syndicated), "Outstanding Daytime Talk, Service or Variety Series"
Big Blue Marble (syndicated), "Outstanding Entertainment Children's Series"
"Danny Kaye's Look-In at the Metropolitan Opera" on *The CBS Festival of Lively Arts for Young People,* (CBS), "Outstanding Entertainment Children's Special"
Go (NBC), "Outstanding Informational Children's Series"
Happy Anniversary, Charlie Brown (CBS), "Outstanding Informational Children's Special"
Grammar Rock (ABC), "Outstanding Instructional Children's Programming—Series and Specials"
The Muppets (Jim Jensen, Jack Oz, Jerry Nelson, Carroll Spinney and Richard Hunt), (*Sesame Street,* PBS) "Outstanding Individual Achievement in Children's Programming"

1976-77 Gary Burghoff (*M*A*S*H*,* CBS), "Outstanding Continuing Performance by a Supporting Actor in a Comedy Series"
Mary Kay Place (*Mary Hartman, Mary Hartman,* syndicated), "Outstanding Continuing Performance by a Supporting Actress in a Comedy Series"
Gary Frank (*Family,* ABC), "Outstanding Continuing Performance by a Supporting Actor in a Drama Series"

Kristy McNichol (*Family,* ABC), "Outstanding Continuing Performance by a Supporting Actress in a Drama Series"
"Ballet Shoes," Parts I and II (*Piccadilly Circus,* PBS), "Outstanding Children's Special"
Allan Burns, James L. Brooks, Ed Weinberger, Stan Daniels, David Lloyd and Bob Ellison (*Mary Tyler Moore Show,* CBS), "Outstanding Writing in a Comedy Series"
Alan Alda (*M*A*S*H*,* CBS), "Outstanding Directing in a Comedy Series"
Louis Gossett, Jr. (*Roots,* Part 2, ABC), "Outstanding Lead Actor for a Single Appearance in a Drama or Comedy Series"
Beulah Bondi ("The Pony Cart" on *The Waltons,* CBS), "Outstanding Lead Actress for a Single Appearance in a Drama or Comedy Series"
Anne Beatts, Dan Aykroyd, Al Franken, Tom Davis, James Downey, Lorne Michaels, Marilyn Suzanne Miller, Michael O'Donoghue, Herb Sargent, Tom Schiller, Rosie Schuster, Alan Zweibel, John Belushi and Bill Murray (*NBC's Saturday Night,* NBC), "Outstanding Writing in a Comedy/Variety of Music Series"
Tim Conway (*The Carol Burnett Show,* CBS) "Outstanding Continuing or Single Performance by a Supporting Actor in Variety or Music"
Rita Moreno (*The Muppet Show,* syndicated), "Outstanding Continuing or Single Performance by a Supporting Actress in Variety or Music"
"American Ballet Theatre: Swan Lake" (*Live from Lincoln Center/Great Performances,* PBS), "Outstanding Classical Program in the Performing Arts"
Burgess Meredith ("Tail Gunner Joe" on *The Big Event,* NBC), "Outstanding Performance by a Supporting Actor in a Comedy or Drama Special"
Diana Hyland ("The Boy in the Plastic Bubble" on *The ABC Friday Night Movie,* ABC), "Outstanding Performance by a Supporting Actress in a Comedy or Drama Special"
Daniel Petrie ("Eleanor and Franklin: The White House Years" on *ABC Theatre,* ABC), "Outstanding Directing in a Special Program/Drama or Comedy"
Stewart Stern ("Sybil" on *The Big Event,* NBC), "Outstanding Writing in a Special Program/Drama or Comedy/Adaptation"
Lane Slate ("Tailgunner Joe" on *The Big Event,* NBC), "Outstanding Writing in a Special Program/Drama or Comedy/Original Teleplay"
Ed Flanders (*Harry S. Truman: Plain Speaking,* PBS), "Outstanding Lead Actor in a Drama or Comedy Special"
Sally Field ("Sybil" on *The Big Event,* NBC), "Outstanding Lead Actress in a Drama or Comedy Special"
Ernest Kinoy and William Blinn (*Roots,* Part 2, ABC), "Outstanding Writing in a Drama Series"
David Green (*Roots,* Part 1, ABC), "Outstanding Directing in a Drama Series"
Edward Asner (*Roots,* Part 1, ABC), "Outstanding Single Performance by a Supporting Actor in a Comedy or Drama Series"
Olivia Cole (*Roots,* Part 8, ABC), "Outstanding Single Performance by a Supporting Actress in a Comedy or Drama Series"
The Tonight Show Starring Johnny Carson (NBC), "Special Classification of Outstanding Program Achievement"
John C. Moffitt, (director *The 28th Annual Emmy Awards,* ABC), "Outstanding Individual Achievement in Coverage of Special Events"
Carroll O'Connor (*All in the Family,* CBS), "Outstanding Lead Actor in a Comedy Series"
Beatrice Arthur (*Maude,* CBS), "Outstanding Lead Actress in a Comedy Series"
The Mary Tyler Moore Show (CBS), "Outstanding Comedy Series"
Alan Buz Kohan and Ted Strauss (*America Salutes Richard Rodgers: The Sound of His Music,* CBS), "Outstanding Writing in a Comedy/Variety or Music Special"
Dwight Hemion (*American Salutes Richard Rodgers: The Sound of His Music,* CBS), "Outstanding Directing in a Comedy/Variety or Music Special"
The Barry Manilow Special (ABC), "Outstanding Special/Comedy/Variety or Music"
Dave Powers (*The Carol Burnett Show,* CBS), "Outstanding Directing in a Comedy/Variety or Music Series"
Dick Van Dyke and Company (NBC) "Outstanding Comedy/Variety or Music Series"
Christopher Plummer ("The Moneychangers" on *NBC World Premiere: The Big Event,* NBC), "Outstanding Lead Actor in a Limited Series"
Patty Duke Astin (*Captains and the Kings* on *NBC's Best Seller,* NBC), "Outstanding Lead Actress in a Limited Series"
Roots (ABC), "Outstanding Limited Series"
James Garner (*The Rockford Files,* NBC), "Outstanding Lead Actor in a Drama Series"
Lindsay Wagner (*The Bionic Woman,* ABC), "Outstanding Lead Actress in a Drama Series"
Upstairs, Downstairs (*Masterpiece Theatre,* PBS), "Outstanding Drama Series"
"Eleanor and Franklin: The White House Years" (*ABC Theatre,* ABC), "Outstanding Special/Drama or Comedy"
"Sybil" (*NBC World Premiere Movie: The Big Event,* NBC), "Outstanding Special/Drama or Comedy"
Quincy Jones and Gerald Fried (*Roots,* Part 1, ABC), "Outstanding Achievement in Music Composition for a Series (Dramatic Underscore)"
Leonard Rosenman, Alan Bergman and Marilyn Bergman ("Sybil" on *The Big Event,* NBC), "Outstanding Achievement in Music Composition for a Special (Dramatic Underscore)"
Ian Fraser (*America Salutes Richard Rodgers: The Sound and His Music,* CBS), "Outstanding Achievement in Music Direction"
Ric Waite (*Captains and the Kings,* Chapter 1, on *NBC's Best Seller,* NBC), "Outstanding Cinematography in Entertainment Programming for a Series"
William Butler ("Raid on Entebbe" on *The Big Event,* NBC), "Outstanding Cinematography in Entertainment Programming for a Special"
Douglas Hines (*The Mary Tyler Moore Show,* CBS), "Outstanding Film Editing in a Comedy Series"
Neil Travis (*Roots,* Part 1, ABC), "Outstanding Film Editing in a Drama Series"
Rita Roland and Michael S. McLean ("Eleanor and Franklin: The White House Years" on *ABC Theater,* ABC), "Outstanding Film Editing for a Special"
Larry Carow, Larry Neiman, Don Warner, Colin Mouat, George Fredrick, Dave Pettijohn and Paul Bruce Richardson (*Roots,* Part 2, ABC), "Outstanding Achievement in Film Sound Editing for a Series"
Bernard F. Pincus, Milton C. Burrow, Gene Eliot, Don Ernst, Tony Garber, Don V. Isaacs, Larry Kaufman, William L. Manger, A. David Marshall, Richard Oswald, Edward L. Sandlin and Russ Tinsley ("Raid on Entebbe" on *The Big Event,* NBC),

"Outstanding Achievement in Film Sound Editing for a Special"
Alan Bernard, George E. Porter, Eddie J. Nelson and Robert L. Harman ("The Savage Bees" on *NBC Monday Night at the Movies,* NBC), "Outstanding Achievement in Film Sound Mixing"
Thomas E. Azzari (art director), (*Fish,* ABC), "Outstanding Art Direction or Scenic Design for a Comedy Series"
Tim Harvey (scenic designer), (*The Pallisers,* Episode 1, PBS), "Outstanding Art Direction or Scenic Design for a Drama Series"
Romain Johnston (art director), (*The Mac Davis Show,* NBC), "Outstanding Art Direction or Scenic Design for a Comedy/Variety or Music Series"
Jan Scott (art director) and **Anne D. McCulley** (set decorator) ("Eleanor and Franklin: The White House Years," on *ABC Theatre,* ABC), "Outstanding Art Direction or Scenic Design for a Dramatic Special"
Robert Kelly (art director), (*America Salutes Richard Rodgers: The Sound of His Music,* CBS), "Outstanding Art Direction or Scenic Design for a Comedy/Variety or Music Special"
Eytan Keller and Stu Bernstein (*Bell Telephone Jubilee,* NBC), "Outstanding Achievement in Graphic Design and Title Sequences"
Joe I. Tompkins ("Eleanor and Franklin: The White House Years," on *ABC Theatre,* ABC), "Outstanding Achievement in Costume Design for a Drama Special"
Jan Skalicky ("The Barber of Seville" on *Live From Lincoln Center: Great Performances,* PBS), "Outstanding Achievement in Costume Design for Music/Variety"
Raymond Hughes (*The Pallisers,* Episode 1, PBS), "Outstanding Achievement in Costume Design for a Drama or Comedy Series"
Ken Chase (make-up design) and **Joe DiBella** (make-up artist), ("Eleanor and Franklin: The White House Years," on *ABC Theatre,* ABC) "Outstanding Achievement in Make-Up"
Ron Field (*America Salutes Richard Rodgers: The Sound of His Music,* CBS), "Outstanding Achievement in Choreography"
William M. Klages and Peter Edwards (*The Dorothy Hamill Special,* ABC), "Outstanding Achievement in Lighting Direction"
Doug Nelson (*John Denver and Friend,* ABC), "Outstanding Achievement in Tape Sound Mixing"
Roy Stewart ("The War Window" on *Visions,* PBS), "Outstanding Achievement in Video Tape Editing for a Series"
Gary H. Anderson (*American Bandstand's 25th Anniversary,* ABC), "Outstanding Achievement in Video Tape Editing for a Special"
Karl Messerschmidt (technical director) and **Jon Olson, Bruce Gray, John Gutierrez, Jim Dodge** and **Wayne McDonald** (cameramen), (*Doug Henning's World of Magic,* NBC), "Outstanding Achievement in Technical Direction and Electronic Camerawork"
Jean de Joux and **Elizabeth Savel** (videoanimation), **Bill Hargate** (costume design) and **Jerry Greene** (videotape editor) ("Peter Pan" on *Hallmark Hall of Fame: The Big Event,* NBC), "Outstanding Individual Achievement in Children's Programing"
Emma di Vittorio and Vivienne Walker (hairstylists), ("Eleanor and Franklin: The White House Years" on *ABC Theatre,* ABC), "Outstanding Achievement in Any Area of Creative Technical Crafts"
Allen Brewster, Bob Roethle, William Lorenz, Manuel Martinez, Ron Fleury, Mike Welch, Jerry Burling, Walter Balderson and Chuck Droege (videotape editing), ("The First Fifty Years" on *The Big Event,* NBC), "Special Classification of Outstanding Individual Achievement"
Brian C. Bartholomew and Keaton S. Walker (art directors) (*The 28th Annual Emmy Awards,* ABC), "Outstanding Individual Achievement in Coverage of Special Events"
American Broadcasting Company, "Special Award" for leadership in establishing Circularly Polarized Transmission to improve television reception
Varian Associates "Special Citation" for improving the efficiency of UHF Klystrons

1977-78 **Mort Lachman** (exec. prod.) and **Milt Josefsberg** (prod.), *All in the Family* (CBS), "Outstanding Comedy Series"
Meta Rosenberg (exec. prod.), **Stephen J. Cannell** (sup. prod.) and **David Chase** and **Charles Floyd Johnson** (prod's.) *The Rockford Files* (NBC), "Outstanding Drama Series"
David Lazer (exec. prod.), **Jim Henson** (prod.) and **Frank Oz, Jerry Nelson, Richard Hunt, Dave Goelz** and **Jim Henson** (The Muppets: Stars) *The Muppet Show* (synd.), "Outstanding Comedy, Variety or Music Series"
Herbert Brodkin (exec. prod.) and **Robert Berger** (prod.), *Holocaust* (NBC), "Outstanding Limited Series"
Joseph Barbera (exec. prod.) and **Harry R. Sherman** (prod.), *The Gathering* (ABC), "Outstanding Special—Drama or Comedy"
Aaron Russo (exec. prod.), **Gary Smith and Dwight Hemion** (prod's.) and **Bette Midler** (star), *Bette Midler— Ol' Red Hair Is Back* (NBC), "Outstanding Special—Comedy-Variety or Music"
John Goberman (prod.), *American Ballet Theatre's 'Giselle,' Live from Lincoln Center* (PBS), "Outstanding Classical Program in the Performing Arts"
David H. Dell and **Fritz Freleng** (exec. prod's.) and **Ted Geisel** (prod.), *Halloween is Grinch Night* (ABC), "Outstanding Children's Special"
Thomas W. Moore (exec. prod.) and **Alfred Kelman** (prod.), *The Body Human* (CBS), "Outstanding Informational Series"
Thomas Skinner and **Dennis B. Kane** (exec. prod's.) and **Nicolas Nixon** (prod.), *The Great Whales, National Geographic* (PBS), "Outstanding Informational Special"
Fred de Cordova (prod.) and **Johnny Carson** (star), *The Tonight Show Starring Johnny Carson* (NBC), "Special Classification of Outstanding Program Achievement"
Carroll O'Connor, *All In the Family* (CBS), "Outstanding Lead Actor in a Comedy Series"
Edward Asner, *Lou Grant* (CBS), "Outstanding Lead Actor in a Drama Series"
Michael Moriarty, *Holocaust* (NBC), "Outstanding Lead Actor in a Limited Series"
Fred Astaire, *A Family Upside Down* (NBC), "Outstanding Lead Actor in a Drama or Comedy Special"
Barnard Hughes, *Lou Grant* (CBS), "Outstanding Lead Actor for a Single Appearance in a Drama or Comedy Series"
Jean Stapleton, *All In the Family* (CBS), "Outstanding Lead Actress in a Comedy Series"
Sada Thompson, *Family* (ABC), "Outstanding Lead Actress in a Drama Series"

Meryl Streep, *Holocaust* (NBC), "Outstanding Lead Actress in a Limited Series"
Joanne Woodward, *See How She Runs* (CBS), "Outstanding Lead Actress in a Drama or Comedy Special"
Rita Moreno, *The Rockford Files* (NBC), "Outstanding Lead Actress for a Single Performance in a Drama or Comedy Series"
Rob Reiner, *All in the Family* (CBS), "Outstanding Continuing Performance by a Supporting Actor in a Comedy Series"
Robert Vaughn, *Washington: Behind Closed Doors* (ABC), "Outstanding Continuing Performance by a Supporting Actor in a Drama Series"
Tim Conway, *The Carol Burnett Show* (CBS), "Outstanding Continuing Performance by a Supporting Actor in Variety or Music"
Howard da Silva, *Verna: USO Girl* (PBS), "Outstanding Performance by a Supporting Actor in a Comedy or Drama Special"
Ricardo Montalban, *How the West Was Won Part II* (ABC), "Outstanding Single Performance by a Supporting Actor in a Comedy or Drama Series"
Julie Kavner, *Rhoda* (CBS), "Outstanding Continuing Performance by a Supporting Actress in a Comedy Series"
Nancy Marchand, *Lou Grant* (CBS), "Outstanding Continuing Performance by a Supporting Actress in a Drama Series"
Gilda Radner, *NBC's Saturday Night Live*, "Outstanding Continuing or Single Performance by a Supporting Actress in Variety or Music"
Eva Le Gallienne, *The Royal Family* (PBS), "Outstanding Performance by a Supporting Actress in a Drama or Comedy Special"
Blanche Baker, *Holocaust, Part I* (NBC), "Outstanding Single Performance by a Supporting Actress in a Comedy or Drama Series"
Bob Weiskopf and **Bob Schiller** (teleplay), and **Barry Harman** and **Harve Bosten** (story), "Cousin Liz" on *All in the Family* (CBS), "Outstanding Writing in a Comedy Series (Single Episode)"
Gerald Green, *Holocaust* (NBC), "Outstanding Writing in a Drama Series"
Ed Simmons, Roger Beatty, Rick Hawkins, Liz Sage, Robert Illes, James Stein, Franielle Silver, Larry Siegel, Tim Conway, Bill Richmond, Gene Perret, Dick Clair and **Jenna McMahon**, *The Carol Burnett Show* with **Steve Martin** (CBS), "Outstanding Writing in a Comedy-Variety or Music Series"
Lorne Michaels, Paul Simon, Chevy Chase, Tom Davis, Al Franken, Charles Grodin, Lily Tomlin and **Alan Sweibel**, *The Paul Simon Special* (NBC), "Outstanding Writing in a Comedy-Variety or Music Special"
George Rubino, *The Last Tenant* (ABC), "Outstanding Writing in a Special Program — Drama or Comedy — Original Teleplay"
Caryl Ledner, *Mary White* (ABC), "Outstanding Writing in a Special Program — Drama or Comedy — Adaptation"
Paul Bogart, "Edith's 50th Birthday" on *All in the Family* (CBS), "Outstanding Directing in a Comedy Series"
Marvin J. Chomsky, *Holocaust* (NBC), "Outstanding Directing in a Drama Series"
David Lowell Rich, *The Defection of Simas Kudirka* (CBS), "Outstanding Directing in a Special Program — Drama or Comedy"
Dave Powers, *The Carol Burnett Show* with Steve Martin (CBS), "Outstanding Directing in a Comedy-Variety or Music Series"
Dwight Hemion, *The Sentry Collection Presents Ben Vereen* (ABC), "Outstanding Directing in a Comedy-Variety or Music Special"

1978-79 **James L. Brooks, Stan Daniels, David Davis** and **Ed Weinberger** (exec. prod's.), and **Glen Charles** and **Les Charles** (prod's.), *Taxi* (ABC), "Outstanding Comedy Series"
Steve Lawrence and **Gary Smith** (exec. prod's.), **Gary Smith** and **Dwight Hemion** (prod's.) and **Steve Lawrence** and **Eydie Gorme** (stars), *Steve and Eydie Celebrate Irving Berlin* (NBC), "Outstanding Comedy-Variety or Music Program"
Gene Reynolds (exec. prod.) and **Seth Freeman** and **Gary David Goldberg**, (prod's.), *Lou Grant* (CBS), "Outstanding Drama Series"
David L. Wolper (exec. prod.) and **Sam Murgulies** (prod.), *Roots: The Next Generation* (ABC), "Outstanding Limited Series"
Martin Starger (exec. prod.), **Philip Barry** (prod.), and **Fay Kanin** (co-prod.), *Friendly Fire* (ABC), "Outstanding Drama or Comedy Special"
Arnold Shapiro (prod.), *Scared Straight* (synd.), "Outstanding Informational Program"
Jac Venza (exec. prod.), **Merrill Brockway** (series prod.), **Emile Ardolino** (series coord.) and **Judy Kinberg** (prod.), *Balanchine IV: Dance in America, Great Performances* (PBS), "Outstanding Classical Program in the Performing Arts"
David Connell (exec. prod.) and **Steve Melendez** (prod.), *The Lion, The Witch and The Wardrobe* (CBS), "Outstanding Animated Program"
Jon Stone (exec. prod.) and **Dulcy Singer** (prod.), *Christmas Eve on Sesame Street* (PBS), "Outstanding Children's Program"
Jack Haley, Jr. (prod.), *51st Annual Awards Presentation of the Academy of Motion Picture Arts and Sciences* (ABC), "Outstanding Program Achievement — Special Events"
Fred de Cordova (prod.) and **Johnny Carson** (star), *The Tonight Show Starring Johnny Carson* (NBC), "Outstanding Program Achievement — Special Class"
Thomas W. Moore and **Robert E. Fuisz** (exec. prod's.), **Alfred Kelman** (prod.) and **Geof Bartz** (co-prod.), *Lifeline* (NBC), "Outstanding Program Achievement — Special Class"
Sally Struthers, *All In the Family* (CBS), "Outstanding Supporting Actress in a Comedy or Comedy-Variety or Music Series"
Robert Guillaume, *Soap* (ABC), "Outstanding Supporting Actor in a Comedy or Comedy-Variety or Music Series"
Kristy McNichol, *Family* (ABC), "Outstanding Supporting Actress in a Drama Series"
Stuart Margolin, *The Rockford Files* (NBC), "Outstanding Supporting Actor in a Drama Series"
Esther Rolle, *Summer of my German Soldier* (NBC), "Outstanding Supporting Actress in a Limited Series or Special"
Marlon Brando, *Roots: The Next Generation* (ABC), "Outstanding Supporting Actor in a Limited Series or Special"
Ruth Gordon, *Taxi* (ABC), "Outstanding Lead Actress in a Comedy Series"
Carroll O'Connor, *All In the Family* (CBS), "Outstanding Lead Actor in a Comedy Series"
Mariette Hartley, *The Incredible Hulk* (CBS), "Outstanding Lead Actress in a Drama Series"

Ron Liebman, *Kaz* (CBS), "Outstanding Lead Actor in a Drama Series"
Bette Davis, *Strangers: The Story of a Mother and Daughter* (CBS), "Outstanding Lead Actress in a Limited Series or Special"
Peter Strauss, *The Jericho Mile* (ABC), "Outstanding Lead Actor in a Limited Series or Special"
Noam Pitlik, "The Harris Incident" on *Barney Miller* (ABC), "Outstanding Directing in a Comedy or Comedy-Variety or Music Series (Single Episode)
Jackie Cooper, *The White Shadow* (CBS), "Outstanding Directing in a Drama Series"
David Greene, *Friendly Fire* (ABC), "Outstanding Directing in a Limited Series or Special"
Alan Alda, "Inga" on *M*A*S*H* (CBS), "Outstanding Writing in a Comedy or Comedy-Variety or Music Series (Single Episode)"
Michele Gallery, "Dying" on *Lou Grant* (CBS), "Outstanding Writing in a Drama Series (Single Episode)"
Patrick Nolan and **Michael Mann**, *The Jericho Mile* (ABC), "Outstanding Writing in a Limited Series or Special"
Bill Melendez and **David Connell** (writers), *The Lion, The Witch and The Wardrobe* (CBS), "Outstanding Individual Achievement — Animation Program"
John Korty (dir.), *Who Are the Debolts —and Where Did They Get 19 Kids?* (ABC), "Outstanding Achievement — Informational Program"
Mikhail Baryshnikov, *Baryshnikov at the White House* (PBS), "Outstanding Individual Achievement — Special Events"
Milton Berle, Special Award
Walter Cronkite, ATAS Governor's Award
Don Harris, **Robert Brown** and **Bill Stewart**, Academy Tribute

1979-80 **James L. Brooks**, **Stan Daniels** and **Ed Weinberger** (exec. prod's.) and **Glen Charles** and **Les Charles** (prod's.), *Taxi* (ABC), "Outstanding Comedy Series"
Gene Reynolds (exec. prod.) and **Seth Freeman** (prod.), *Lou Grant* (CBS), "Outstanding Drama Series"
Andrew Brown (prod.), *Edward & Mrs. Simpson* (synd.), "Outstanding Limited Series"
Herman Krawitz (exec. prod.), **Gary Smith** and **Dwight Hemion** (prod's.) and **Mikhail Baryshnikov** (star), *IBM Presents Baryshnikov on Broadway* (ABC), "Outstanding Variety or Music Program"
Raymond Katz and **Sandy Gallin** (exec. prod's.) and **Fred Coe** (prod.), *The Miracle Worker* (NBC), "Outstanding Drama or Comedy Special"
Alvin Cooperman and **Judith De Paul** (prod's.), *Live from Studio 8H: A Tribute to Toscanini* (NBC), "Outstanding Classical Program in the Performing Arts"
Joe Camp (exec. prod.) and **Fielder Baker** (prod.), *Benji at Work* (ABC), "Outstanding Children's Program"
Lorenzo Music and **Barton Dean** (prod's.), *Carlton Your Doorman* (CBS), "Outstanding Animated Program"
Richard Mulligan, *Soap* (ABC), "Outstanding Lead Actor in a Comedy Series"
Ed Asner, *Lou Grant* (CBS), "Outstanding Lead Actor in a Drama Series"
Powers Boothe, *Guyana Tragedy: The Story of Jim Jones* (CBS), "Outstanding Lead Actor in a Limited Series or Special"
Cathryn Damon, *Soap* (ABC), "Outstanding Lead Actress in a Comedy Series"
Barbara Bel Geddes, *Dallas* (CBS), "Outstanding Lead Actress in a Drama Series"
Patty Duke Astin, *The Miracle Worker* (NBC), "Outstanding Lead Actress in a Limited Series or Special"
Harry Morgan, *M*A*S*H* (CBS), "Outstanding Supporting Actor in a Comedy or Variety or Music Series"
Stuart Margolin, *The Rockford Files* (NBC), "Outstanding Supporting Actor in a Drama Series"
George Grizzard, *The Oldest Living Graduate* (NBC), "Outstanding Supporting Actor in a Limited Series or Special"
Loretta Swit, *M*A*S*H* (CBS), "Outstanding Supporting Actress in a Comedy or Variety or Music Series"
Nancy Marchand, *Lou Grant* (CBS), "Outstanding Supporting Actress in a Drama Series"
Mare Winningham, *Amber Waves* (ABC), "Outstanding Supporting Actress in a Limited Series or Special"
James Burrows, "Louie and the Nice Girl" on *Taxi* (ABC), "Outstanding Directing in a Comedy Series (Single Episode)"
Roger Young, "Cop" on *Lou Grant* (CBS), "Outstanding Directing in a Drama Series (Single Episode)"
Dwight Hemion, *IBM Presents Baryshnikov on Broadway* (ABC), "Outstanding Directing in a Variety or Music Program"
Marvin J. Chomsky, *Attica* (ABC), "Outstanding Directing in a Limited Series or Special"
Alan Johnson, *Shirley MacLaine . . . "Every Little Movement"* (CBS), "Outstanding Achievement in Choreography
Bob Colleary, "Photographer" in *Barney Miller* (ABC), "Outstanding Writing in a Comedy Series (Single Episode)"
Seth Freeman, "Cop" on *Lou Grant* (CBS), "Outstanding Writing in a Drama Series (Single Episode)"
Buz Kohan, *Shirley MacLaine . . . 'Every Little Movement'* (CBS), "Outstanding Writing in a Variety or Music Program"
David Chase, on *Off the Minnesota Strip* (ABC), "Outstanding Writing in a Limited Series or Special"
Enzo A. Martinelli, 'Breakthrough" on *The Contender* (CBS), "Outstanding Cinematography for a Series (Single Episode)"
Gayne Rescher, *Moviola* (NBC), "Outstanding Cinematography for a Limited Series or Special"
James D. Bissel (art dir.) and **William Webb** (set dec.), "The Old Sister" on *Palmerstown, U.S.A.* (CBS), "Outstanding Art Direction for a Series (Single Episode)"
Wilfrid Shingleton (prod. des.), **Julian Sacks** (art dir.), **Jean Taillandier** (art dir.) and **Cheryal Kearney** and **Robert Christides** (set dec's.), *Gaugin The Savage* (CBS), "Outstanding Art Direction for a Limited Series or Special"
Charles Lisanby (art dir.) and **Dwight Jackson** (set dec.), *IBM Presents Baryshnikov on Broadway* (ABC), "Outstanding Art Direction for a Variety or Music Program"
Patrick Williams, *Lou Grant* (CBS), "Outstanding Music Composition for a Series (Dramatic Underscore)"
Jerry Fielding, *High Midnight* (CBS), "Outstanding Achievement in Music Composition in a Limited Series or Special (Dramatic Underscore")

Alan Fraser (music dir.), **Ralph Burns** and **Billy Byers** (arrangers), *IBM Presents Baryshnikov on Broadway* (ABC), "Outstanding Achievement in Music Direction"
Pete Menefee, *The Big Show* (NBC), "Outstanding Costume Design for a Series"
Travilla, *Moviola* (NBC), "Outstanding Costume Design for a Limited Sheries or Special"
Richard Blair, *Moviola* (NBC), "Outstanding Achievement in Makeup"
Larry Germaine and **Donna Gilbert**, *The Miracle Worker* (NBC), "Outstanding Achievement in Hairstyling"
Phill Norman, *The French Atlantic Affair* (ABC), "Outstanding Achievement in Graphic Design and Title Sequences"
M. Pam Blumenthal, *Taxi* (ABC), "Outstanding Achievement in Film Editing for a Series"
Bill Blunden and **Alan Pattillo**, *All Quiet on the Western Front* (CBS), "Outstanding Film Editing for a Limited Series or Special"
Don Crosby, **Mark Dennis**, **Tony Garber**, **Doug Grindstaff**, **Don V. Isaacs**, **Hank Salerno** and **Larry Singer**, *Power, Part I* (NBC), "Outstanding Achievement in Film Sound Editing"
Ray Barons, **David Campbell**, **Bob Pettis** and **John Reitz**, *The Ordeal of Dr. Mudd* (CBS), "Outstanding Achievement in Film Sound Mixing"
Bruce Burns and **Jerry Clemens**, *Sinatra, The First Forty Years* (NBC), "Outstanding Achievement in Tape Sound Mixing"
John Hawkins, *The Muppet Show* with **Liza Minnelli** (synd.), "Outstanding Video Tape Editing for a Series"
Danny White, *Olivia Newton-John—Hollywood Nights* (ABC), "Outstanding Video Tape Editing for a Limited Series or Special"
Wayne Parsons, **Tom Geren**, **Dean Hall**, **Bob Highton**, **William Landers** and **Ron Sheldon**, *The Oldest Living Graduate* (NBC), "Outstanding Achievement in Technical Direction and Electronic Camerawork"
Peter G. Edwards, **William Knight** and **Peter S. Passas**, *F.D.R., The Last Year* (NBC), "Outstanding Achievement in Lighting Direction (Electronic)"
Larry Grossman (music) and **Buz Kohan** (lyrics), *52nd Annual Awards Presentation of the Academy of Motion Picture Arts and Sciences* (ABC), "Outstanding Individual Achievement — Special Events"
Bryan Anderson, **Bob Elefstrom** and **Al Giddings**, (cinematographers), *Mysteries of the Sea* (ABC), "Outstanding Individual Achievement — Informational Program"
David C. Clark, **Joel Fein**, **Robert L. Harman** and **George E. Porter** (film sound mixers), *Dive to the Edge of Creation, National Geographic Special* (PBS), "Outstanding Individual Achievement — Informational Program"
Robert Eisenhardt, **Hank O'Karma** and **James Kurson** (film ed's.), *The Body Human: The Body Beautiful* (CBS), "Outstanding Indivudual Achievement — Informational Program"
Geof Bartz (film ed.), *Operation Lifeline* (NBC), "Outstanding Individual Achievement — Special Class"
Scott Schachter (live audio mixing), *Live From Studio 8H: A Tribute to Toscanini* (NBC), "Outstanding Individual Achievement — Creative Technical Crafts"
Mark Schubin, *Live From Lincoln Center: Luciano Pavarotti and the New York Philharmonic* (PBS), "Outstanding Individual Achievement — Creative Crafts"
Bob O'Bradovich (makeup), *The Halloween that Almost Wasn't* (ABC), "Outstanding Individual Achievement — Children's Program"

Forum Award

ATOMIC INDUSTRIAL FORUM
7101 Wisconsin Ave., Washington, D.C. 20014
(301/654-9260)

The $1,000 Forum Award is given annually for news-media contributions to the public understanding of nuclear energy. A panel of judges selects the winner. In addition to the broadcast journalists listed here, the AIF grants a Forum Award to the print media, listed on p. xx.

1974 **Greg Harney** and **"The Advocates" staff**, WGBH Educational Foundation
1975 **No award**
1976 **Fred Huff** and **Tom Sherlock**, KPHO-TV (Phoenix)
1977 **Richard N. Hughes**, WPIX-TV (New York)
1978 **Peter Cook**, "The Advocates," WGBH-TV (Boston)
Gerald Stone, Nine Network Australia
1979 **Robert MacNeil** and **James Lehrer**, "The MacNeil Lehrer Report"
1980 **Not available at press time**

Gavel Awards

AMERICAN BAR ASSOCIATION
1155 E. 60th St., Chicago, Ill. 60637 (312/974-4000)

The Gavel Awards are given annually to honor films, the media and books for their depiction of or reportage on the law and the legal profession. The Bar Association recognizes achievements which foster greater public understanding of the American legal and judicial system, disclose areas in need of improvement or correction and encourage efforts of all levels of government to update laws. Engraved gavels are presented to executives of the honored stations and networks.

RADIO

1960 **WRCV** (Philadelphia) for "Law in Action"
WHAS (Louisville, Ky.) for "It's the Law"
1961 **KMOX** (St. Louis) for "A Case In Point"
1962 **WRFB** (Tallahassee, Fla.) for "So Highly We Value"
1963 **WMAQ** (Chicago) for "A Look at the Law" and contributions to public understanding through this public service series
KYW (Cleveland) for "A Look at the Law," Lawyer/layman interview series
1964 **KMPC** (Los Angeles) for "Heritage" series
1965 **WIBG** (Philadelphia) for "Government of Man by Law"
1966 **KMPC** (Los Angeles) for "The Second Civil War" on causes of the Watts riots
WMAL (Washington) for "The Abused Witness"
1967 **Group W, Westinghouse Broadcasting Co.** for "Crime and Punishment in the 60's," twenty-one-part documentary series

1968 **WMAL** (Washington) for "Perspective D.C. Crime Report" on the import of the recommendations of the President's Crime Commission
WEEI (Boston) for "Benzaquin's Notepad," series of background reports on developments in the law, bar and courts
1969 **NBC Radio News** for "The Cop and the Court"
WJR (Detroit) for "The Rule of Law," scholarly educational series
KLAC (Los Angeles) for "Law for Laymen," educational series
1970 **KFWB** (Los Angeles) for "Ignorance and the Law," educational editorial series urging teaching of fundamental and basic statute law to children
1971 **NBC Radio Network-NBC News** for "The Prison System: Accomplice After the Fact"
WMAL (Washington) for "Streets of Fear," "Franklin Moyler and the Question of Bail" and "Congress and the Crime Bill," three-part documentary
KGO (San Francisco) for "Quality of Justice," editorial broadcasts
KEAR (San Francisco) for "Joe Bleakley," documentary
1972 **WNBC** (New York) for series of educational documentary programs explaining operations of New York City court system
KXYZ (Houston) for "Old Fashioned Citizenship," six-part series segment
KEEL (Shreveport, La.) for "Angola: The Crime of Louisiana Punishment," documentary on prison conditions
1973 **KTOK** (Oklahoma City) for "Poverty in the Courtroom" and "Behind the Walls of Big Mac"
WCCO (Minneapolis/St. Paul) for "You the Jury: Law Day 1972," presenting a factual court procedure and a jury composed of the station's audience
1974 **KNX Newsradio** (Los Angeles) for "Is Our Flag Still There?", documentary on Bill of Rights
WMAL (Washington) for "The Legend of Lenient Justice," testing the performance of the new District of Columbia Superior Court
National Public Radio for "All Things Considered" and "Every Tenth American: A New Look at our Public Mental Health System"
1975 **CBS News Radio** for "A Hearing for American Justice," thirty-part series
NBC News Radio for "Capital Punishment: Dead or Alive," documentary on "Second Sunday"
WWVA (Wheeling, W. Va.) for coverage by Jerry Kelanic of investigation, indictment and trial of United Mine Workers President Tony Boyle for the murder of Joseph Yablonski
WCBS/Newsradio (New York) for "Rape: The Law and You," a WCBS Progress Report, twenty-part series
WHLO (Akron, Ohio) for "Inside the Grand Jury," five-part series
American Forces Network (Europe) for "High Crimes and Misdemeanors," exploring two impeachment proceedings of the 19th century
1976 **KMOX** (St. Louis) for six programs calling upon community resources for a summit conference on crime
WRFM (New York) for crime in the streets exploration in thirty-two miniprograms
WBRU-FM (Providence R.I.) for "Brutality at the Children's Center"
KOB (Albuquerque N.M.) for six special investigative reports on misuse of authority in the Bernalillo County Sheriff's Department
1977 **WCBS** (New York) for "Criminal Justice System: A WCBS News Radio 88 Status Report," a thirty-part weekly series examining different aspects of the system
KFWB (Los Angeles) for "John Swaney's Report on the Law," three programs on integration, small claims court and reform of the tort system, and a special series on California property tax laws
WWVA (Wheeling, W.Va.) for "Don't Hit That Lady, She's Your Wife," examining the increase in family physical violence, expecially against wives
1978 **WCBS Radio** (New York), for "New Green Sneakers and Other Lessons of the Street" on juvenile crime and the juvenile justice system in New York
WIRE Radio (Indianapolis), for "The Tony Kiritsis Affair" on the arrest, indictment and trial of Kiritsis for kidnapping and the efforts to commit him to the department of mental health
KHVH Radio (Honolulu) for "The Law Report" on recent appellate cases in the U.S.
KSJN (St. Paul) for "The Role of the Courts in a Changing Society"
1979 **KMOX** (St. Louis) for 18-part documentary, "In the Common Good" on legal system and legal ethics
WRFM (New York), for "What Eric Learned in Jail Today" on prisons and jails of New York City and State
WNCI Radio (Columbus, Ohio) for "What Are They Doing to Our Children?", a six-part series on the Federal District Court and a class action desegragation suit
WCIR (Manchester, N.H.), for "A Night With the Manchester Police Department"
KHVH Radio (Honolulu), for "The Law Report," a daily report on recent appellate court decisions
National Public Radio (Washington, D.C.), for "The Supreme Court Reporting of Nine Totenberg"
Pacifica Radio/KPFA-FM (Berkeley, Calif.), for six documentaries analyzing complex and controversial civil liberties issues
1980 **CBS News** for "The Supreme Court on the Air: The Pentagon Papers Cases Revisited" anchored by news correspondent Fred Graham **WWVA** (Wheeling, W.Va.) and **WKTQ** Radio (Pittsburgh), for "Divorce in Pennsylvania: For Better, For Worse, For No-Fault"
WFAA-AM (Dallas), for "A Child to Love," a documentary on adoption
Mid America Media Wire Radio News (Indianapolis) for "Public Defenders: Justice for the Poor," on public defender system in Marion County, Ind.
WBUR (Boston) for "The Grand Jury"

TELEVISION

1958 **Columbia Broadcasting System** for *The Greeg Case* and *The Verdict is Yours*
National Broadcasting Company for *An Act of Law* and *American Trial by Jury*
1959 **American Broadcasting Company** for *Day in Court*
Columbia University Press for *The Constitution: Whose Interpretation?*
1960 **KPIX** (San Francisco) for *A Life in the Balance*
WRC-TV (Washington) for series on the role of juvenile court
Piasano Productions for *Perry Mason* series, dramatizing basic legal safeguards afforded the accused
Tulane University for "With Justice for All" from *Closeup*
1961 **Armstrong Circle Theatre** for dramatization of the work of the Legal Aid Society
University of Michigan Television Center for *Blessings of Liberty* series dramatizing constitutional rights

CBS Reports for "A Real Case of Murder," documentary

1962 **CBS Television Network,** for "Iron Man" segment, of *The Defenders*

1963 **National Broadcasting Company** for *The Judge,* as a contribution to public understanding of judicial role and ethical principles

Columbia Broadcasting System, for *CBS Reports'* two-part documentary, "Storm Over the Supreme Court"

1964 **Columbia Broadcasting System** for *CBS Reports* documentary, "The Crisis of Presidential Succession"

University of Michigan Television Center for *A Quest of Certainty,* twenty-part educational series

Plautus Producations, for "The Blacklist" segment of *The Defenders*

1965 **Columbia Broadcasting System** for *Gideon's Trumpet: The Poor Man and the Law,* documentary on the 1963 Supreme Court decision clarifying the right of the accused to legal counsel

National Broadcasting Company for *The Magnificent Yankee,* documentary of the thirty-year career of U.S. Supreme Court Justice Oliver Wendall Holmes

Robert Saudek Associates for *Profiles in Courage* drama of Charles Evans Hughes' struggle against ouster of New York state legistors accused of radicalism

1966 **Columbia Broadcasting System** for *Abortion and the Law* documentary

WCAU-TV (Philadelphia) for *Girard College: The Will and the Wall,* documentary on the law as adjudicator

1967 **National Broadcasting Company,** for *Meet the Press* documentary on the report of the President's Commission on Law Enforcement and *The Statesman,* historical drama on the efforts of a little-known minister for a Bill of Rights

WTVN-TV (Columbus, Ohio) for *View From the High Bench,* interview with Supreme Court Justice Potter Stewart

WNBC-TV (New York), Due Process for the Accused, for segments of ten-part series on arrest and search, eavesdropping and fair trials, etc.

1968 **National Broadcasting Company,** for *Justice For All?,* documentary on legal problems of the nation's poor

American Broadcasting Company for *A Case of Libel,* drama on fundamental principles of American justice through recreation of a famous trial

20th Century Fox, for "Commitment," segment of *Judd for the Defense*

1969 **Columbia Broadcasting System,** for *Justice Black and the Bill of Rights,* interview on role of Supreme Court

WMAQ-TV (Chicago), for "The Quality of Justice," documentary on Illinois reform program

1970 **National Broadcasting Company** for *Voices on the Inside* and *Between Two Rivers,* documentaries on prison conditions and plight of Indians

Universal City Studios for *The D.A.: Murder One,* on the role of the district attorney in prosecuting a murder case

American Broadcasting Company for *The Young Lawyers,* drama

National Educational Television for *The Warren Years,* documentary

WNED-TV (Buffalo) for *Are Campus Disorders Out of Hand?*

1971 **CBS News Division,** for *Bill of Rights,* survey and examination of public attitudes on constitutional rights

National Broadcasting Company for "A Continual Roar of Musketry," segment of *The Bold Ones*

WCAU-TV (Philadelphia), for *Case of Reform,* examining prisoner rehabilitation in Bucks County Prison

1972 **CBS News** for *CBS Reports'* documentary, "Justice in America, Part I," "Some are More Equal than Others"

NBC News, for *This Child is Rated X: An NBC White Paper on Juvenile Justice*

Midwestern Educational Television for "The Baseball Glove," produced by KTCA-TV for children on why rules and laws are necessary

WGBH-TV (Boston) and KCET-TV (Los Angeles) for "Jail with No Bail," from *The Advocates* series

1973 **NBC, BBC, Time-Life Films,** for "Inventing A Nation," from *America* series, examining opinions of leading members of the Constitutional Convention

NBC News for "Guilty By Reason of Race," on plight of 110,000 Japanese-Americans detained in camps throughout World War II

KNXT-TV (Los Angeles) for *Rape,* a news special

WKBF-TV (Cleveland) for *The Crime of Our Courts,* public service program

KING-TV (Seattle) for *Are Prisons for People?* on juvenile and adult incarceration methods

WMAR-TV (Baltimore) for *Bars to Progress,* on Maryland's correctional system and possible changes

New Hampshire Network/WENH-TV (Durham) for *Society's Child,* documentary on juvenile reformatory

1974 **ABC News** for *The First and Essential Freedom,* a three-part documentary

CBS News for four part series on Supreme Court decisions by Fred Graham on *CBS Evening News*

NBC News for *Watergate: The President Speaks* and *How Watergate Changed Government*

WRC-TV (Washington), for *News 4 Washington Probe: By Reason of Insanity* on discharge policies of potentially dangerous mental patients

KPIX-TV (San Francisco) for *A Case of Arson,* a children's educational program and primer on the judicial process

WMAR-TV (Baltimore) for *There Ought to be a Law,* documenting how a new law is enacted in Maryland

WTIC-TV (Hartford, Conn.), for *The Nine-Year-Old in Norfolk Prison,* documentary on trial and conviction of mentally retarded individual

KYTV (Springfield, Mo.) for *Start Inmates: Experimental Man,* documenting plight of inmates in the Medical Center for Federal Prisoners in Springfield, Mo.

WNET-TV (New York) for *Bill Moyers' Journal: An Essay on Watergate*

1975 **American television industry and ABC News Television,** for pool coverage and broadcast of the House Judiciary Committee impeachment proceedings

American television industry and CBS News, for broadcast of House Judiciary Committee impeachment proceedings

American television industry and NBC, for broadcast of House Judiciary Committee impeachment proceedings

American Television industry and Public Broadcasting Service, for broadcast of House Judiciary Committee impeachment proceedings

CBS News, for *What's It All About* explaining functions of Supreme Court, House of Representatives and processes of impeachment

National Broadcasting Company for *A Case of Rape*

WNBC-TV (New York) for *Legal Ethics: What's Happening?*
KATU-TV (Portland, Ore.) for *Is It Justice?*
WCCO-TV News (Minneapolis) for *The Time Machine,* documentary
WTTW-TV (Chicago) for *Criminal Court*
Indiana University Radio & Television Service for *The Role of the Lawyer*
Complete Channel TV (Madison, Wisc.), for *Halfway to Somewhere*

1976 **CBS News** for *The Case Against Milligan,* historical drama about suspension of habeas corpus during Civil War
WMAQ-TV (Chicago) for *"When Is Justice Coming,"* Part I on *The Overloaded Criminal Courts* and *Code 39*
WCVB-TV (Needham, Mass.) for *Crime: The War We're Losing*
WCCO-TV (Minneapolis) for *Home Sweet Prison*
WNET/13 (New York) for *OURSTORY—The Peach Gang,* the first of nine re-enactments of a 1638 trial
National Public Affairs Center for Television, WETA/26 (Washington), for *Levi and the Law: A Colloquy with th Attorney General*
WGBH-TV (Boston) for *Edelin Conviction,* dramatic re-enactment of the manslaughter trial of Dr. Kenneth Edelin

1977 **ABC News** for *Gun Control: Pro and Con,* documentary
WKYC-TV (Clevelnd) for *Both Sides of Busing* and *The Trouble With Kids*
WFAA-TV (Dallas) for *A Time To Die,* documentary on the death penalty
KPRC-TV (Houston), for *Inside the FBI* and *What is Your Citizenship, Please?*, documentaries on the agency's attempt to catch criminals and solve crimes and on illegal aliens in the Southwest
Maryland Center for Public Broadcasting, for *See You In Court,* about small claims courts
Hampton Roads Educational Telecommunications Association. (Norfolk, Va.) for *Rights and Responsibilities: Sign Here, 11-part series* on citizenship
International Media Laboratory, University of Wisconsin (Milwaukee), for *Civil Commitment Hearings,* dramatization of six involuntarily civil commitment hearings from Wisconsin court records

1978 **ABC News** for *ABC News Closeup* on the inequities of sentencing
KPIX-TV (San Francisco) for *The Choice—Between Life and Death,* a two-part program consisting of a 60-minute courtroom trial and a 90-minute viewer-participation program on the issue of life in prison or death
KENS-TV (San Antonio) for *. . . And Justice for All,* examining progress since the issuance of a report on the Mexican-American and the administration of justice in the Southwest
Maryland Center for Public Broadcasting, for *Consumer Survival Kit, Lawyers: Advise and Represent,* examining lawyers, legal fees and legal clinics and shows how to obtain competent legal counsel
Women In Communications, Inc., and **KERA-TV** (Dallas), for *Who Remembers Mama?*, on the emotional and financial problems of middle-aged women who have lost their roles as homemakers through divorce
Connecticut Public Television, for *Connecticut Law Day Quiz,* consisting of law quiz and viewers' telephoned legal questions

1979 **CBS News** for *The Politics of Abortion,* examining the organized movement to reverse the 1973 Supreme Court decision legalizing abortion
WBBM-TV (CBS; Chicago) for *The Public Guardian,* news report on the Cook County Public Guardian
KTLA/Golden West Broadcasters (Los Angeles) for *Scared Straight,* in which convicted murderers and rapists held encounter sessions with hardened juvenile offenders on realities of prison life
WDBO-TV (Orlando, Fla.) for *Cameras in the Courtroom,* examining year-long experiment permitting use of audio and electronic equipment in Florida state courts
WPBT (N. Miami, Fla.) for *TV on Trial,* focusing on the murder trial of 15-year-old **Ronney Zamora**

1980 **ABC News** for *ABC News Closeup—"The Shooting of Big Man: Anatomy of a Criminal Case"*
WMAQ-TV (NBC, Chicago) for *Strip and Search,* disclosing widespread practice by Chicago police of strip-searching women for minor traffic violations
KYW-TV (Philadelphia) for four entries from its *Meeting House* program
KAS-TV (Forth Worth) for its investigative reporting, *Legally Fixed,* detailing how a group of attorneys and non-lawyers were fixing traffic tickets
WTMJ (Milwaukee) for *Juvenile Crime: No Minor Problem* on juvenile crime and corrections in Wisconsin
WOWT (Omaha) for *Not Guilty by Reason of Insanity: A Case Study,* a documentary

Roy. W. Howard Public Service Award

SCRIPPS-HOWARD FOUNDATION
1100 Central Trust Tower, Cincinnati, Ohio 45202
(513/621-0130)

The Roy. W. Howard Public Service Award, which consists of $2,500 and a bronze plaque, is given annually to recognize outstanding public service, which is defined as exposure or contribution toward the alleviation of corruption, crime, health or other problems. A panel of judges selects the winner. In addition to the first-place winner, a runner-up prize of $1,000 is given. There is also a Roy W. Howard Public Service Award for newspapers, which will be found elsewhere in this volume.

1972 **WABC-TV** (New York)
1973 **KGW-TV** (Portland, Ore.)
1974 **WABC-TV** (New York)
1975 **KGW-TV** (Portland, Ore.)
1976 **KMOX-TV** (St. Louis)
1977 **KOY-Radio** (Phoenix)
1978 **WBBM-TV** (Chicago)
1979 **KOCO-TV** (Oklahoma City)
1980 **Not available at press time**

Humanitas prize

HUMAN FAMILY & CULTURAL INSTITUTE
Box 861, Pacific Palisades, Calif. 90272 (213/454-8769)

Humanitas Prizes, which consist of substantial cash awards listed below, are given for prime-time telecasts which demonstrate "human values." The award is endorsed by the Lilly Foundation. The Institute's trustees select the winners from three nominees in each category.

30-MINUTE BROADCASTS (Currently $10,000)

1975 **Charles Coehn**, "Angel of Doom" on *Sunshine*
1976 **Larry Gelbart**, "The Interview" on *M*A*S*H*
1977 **Earl Pomerantz**, "Ted's Change of Heart" on *The Mary Tyler Moore Show*
1978 **Larry Rhine** and **Mel Tolkin**, "The Brother" on *All in the Family*
1979 **Michael Leeson**, "Blind Date" on *Taxi*
1980 **Alan Alda** and **James Jay Rubinfier**, "Dreams" on *M*A*S*H*

60-MINUTE BROADCASTS (Currently $15,000)

1975 **Joel Oliansky**, "Complaint Amended" on *The Law*
1976 **Jay Presson Allen**, "Family" on *Family* pilot
1977 **James Lee** and **William Blinn**, *Roots*, Part 4
1978 **Carol Evan McKeand** and **David Jacobs**, "Annie Laurie" on *Family*
1979 **Leon Tokatyan**, "Vet" on *Lou Grant*
1980 **Sally Robinson**, "Thanksgiving on *Family*

90-MINUTES OR LONGER (Currently $25,000)

1975 **David Seltzer**, *Larry*
1976 **Jean Wkatsuki Houston**, **James D. Houston** and **John Kotty**, *Farewell to Mansana*
1977 **David Seltzer** and **Eugene Logan**, *Green Eyes*
1978 **John Sacret Young**, *Special Olympics*
1979 **Jane Howard-Hammerstein**, *Summer of My German Soldier*
1980 **Suzi Lyte Kaufman**, **Barry Neil Kaufman** and **Stephen Kandel**,m *Son-Rise—A Miracle of Love*

DOCUMENTARY (Non-monetary prize)

1977 **Tom Spain** (prod.) and **Bill Moyers** (corres.), *CBS Reports: The Fire Next Door*
1978 **Tom Spain** (prod.) and **Bill Moyers** (corres.), *CBS Reports: The Aliens*
1979 **John Jorty** and **Dan McCann** (prod.), *Who Are the Debolts?*
1980 **Bill McLaughlin** and **Anthony Potter**, *NBC White Paper: We're Moving Up[The Hispanic Migration*

Maggie Award

PLANNED PARENTHOOD FEDERATION OF AMERICA
810 Seventh Ave., New York, N.Y. 10019 (212/541-7800)

The Maggie Award honors outstanding treatments in the national broadcast media of issues of concern to the federation.

1978 **Tandem/Tat Production House, for episodes of *One Day At A Time, Good Times* and *All In the Family* which dealt with teenage pregnancy "in a realistic and responsible way"**
1979 **No award**
1980 **Michael Hirsh** and **WTTW-TV** Chicago, for *Guess Who's Pregnant? An Update*, which aired on Public Broadcasting System stations across the country

Ernst-Reuter-Preis Jakob-Keiser-Preis

BUNDESMINISTERIUM FUR INNERDEUTSCHE BEZIEHUNGEN
Godesberger Allee 140, 5300 Bonn 2, Federal Republic of Germany (02283061)

The 10,000-mark Ernst-Reuter-Preis is given by the Ministry for Intra-German Relations for the best radio play and documentary on the division of Germany and its effect on the conditions of people in both German states. A jury selects the winners.

1960 **Dieter Menschsner**, "Rikchen von Rreetz" (radio play)
1961 **Hans Georg Berthold** and **Tom Toelle**, "Aus 15 Jahren Berliner Geschichte" (documentary)
1962 **Alfred Berndt** with **Richard Kitschigin**, **Peter Krebs** and **Lea Rosh**, "Sie kamen aus Europa — Junge Redakteure aus 13 Landern beobachten das geteilte Berlin" (broadcast)
1963 **Ingeborg Orewitz**, "Das Layrinth" (play)
1964 **No award**

RADIO PLAY

1965 **Kay Hoff**, "Die Chance"
1966 **Hermann Rudolph**, "Horspiel von Hermann Rudolph"
1967 **Horst Monnich**, "Einreisegenemigung oder Ein Deutscher fahrt nach Deutschland"
1968 **No award**
1969 **No award**
1970 **Horst Monnich**, "Quarantane"
1971 **Richard Kitschigin**, **Detlev E. Otto**, **Hans-Gunter Goldbeck-Lowe** and **Claudio Isani**, "Stimmen der Jugend — Traume und Wirklichkeiten in einem geteilten Land"
1972 **No award**
1973 **No award**
1974 **Gerhard Zwerenz**, "Briefwechsel mit einem Kollegen"
1975 **Horst Kruger**, "Die Grenze"
1976 **Dieter Streipert**, **Hans-Gunter Goldbeck-Lowe** and **Jurgen Vietig**, "Ich nennte mich Jagger"
1977 **Olaf Leitner**, "Rock — Szene DDR"
Horst Varaseck, "Deutschland — Ein Wintermarchen"
1978 **Thomas Brasch**, "Robert, ich, Fastnacht und die anderen"
1979 **No award**
1980 **Not available at press time**

DOCUMENTARY

1965 **Andreas Fuchs**, educational broadcasts
1966 **Traute Hellberg**, "Die Entscheidung fallt morgen"
1967 **No award**
1968 **No award**
1969 **Lothar Wichert**, "Von der 'Kommode' zum Millionenschrank — Die neue Staatsbibliothek in Berlin, vorzeitig eroffnet"
Producers of 'Politik und Zeitgeschehn" for "Deutschland 1968" and "Moglichkeiten einer Politik zur Widervereinigung"
1970 **Rudolph Jacobs,** "Die Moderne Grenze — Beobachtungen an Der Demarkationslinie"
Werner Hill, "Volkseigene Rechtsprechung — Gesellschaftliche Gerichte, Schieds- und Konflictkommissionen in der DDR"

Carola Stern and **Ulrich Gembardt**, "Ulrichts Bilanz"
1971 **Erika Runge**, "Eine Reise nach Rostock"
Heinz Klunker, "Ist Entspannungspolitik konterrolutionar? "
1972 **No award**
1973 **Karl Wilhelm Fricke** and **Peter Dittmar**, "Gegan 99,8 Prozent"
Hans-Gunter Goldbeck-Lowe, "Beat — Sozialismus"
Manfred Rexin, "Die nationale Frage" and "Ein deutscher Aufstand"
1974 **Willi Knecht**, "Anatomie eines Tories — Deutsche Nachbetragung zur X. Fussballweltmeisterschaft"
Marianne Scheuerl, "Jugend in der DDR — Eine sozialistische Generation?"
1975 **Traute Hellberg**, "1000 Jahre Weimar"
Karl-Heinz Wenzel, three-part series on life in the German Democratic Republic
1976 **Bernt Richter**, "Ein Abstecher ins Ausserpreussische und ein Stuck Fontane hinterher Reiseeindruck aus der DDR"
Hans Jurgen Fink, **Sigrid Nebelung** and **Klaus Sauer**, "Die abgegrentzte Kultur"
1977 **Werner Hill**, reports on the Weinhold trial
Wolfgang Meisenkothen, "Berlin — eine geteilte Stadt"
1978 **Peter Wapnewski**, "Die gespaltene zunge — Die eine Sprache und die zwei Staaten"
1979 **No award**
1980 **Not available at press time**

The 10,000-mark Jakob-Kaiser-Preis is awarded on a similar basis for telecasts.

1960 **Gunter Lincke**, "Elbe — Grenzfluss oder Handelsweg"
1961 **Matthias Walden**, "Ich rufe Dresden"
1962 **Gunther Hahn** with **Lothar Kompatzki**, **Jurgen Reidl**, **Rosemarie Weber**, **Waltraud Lindner** and **Dietrich Schmidt**, "Die Mauer"

DOCUMENTARY

1963 **Eberhard Kruppa**, **Lars Griene** and **Jurgen Stahf**, "Kontakte"
1964 **No award**
1965 **No award**
1966 **No award**
1967 **Michael Blackwood**, "Menschen in Ostberlin"
1968 **Hanns Werner Schwarze**,"Druben"
Fritz Schenk, "Unerwunscht und abgeschoben — Wanderer zwischen Ost und West"
1969 **Thilo Koch**, "Menschen an der Grenze"
Wolfgang Weinert, "Musse fur die Musen?"
1970 **Dieter Wedel**, "Gedenktag"
1971 **Wolfgang Venohr**, "Die Erben der Barone" and "Halb Preussen/Halb Sachsen"
Rudinger Humpert and **Carlheinz Caspari**, "Aus dem Alltag in der DDR — Der dritte Versuch einer Rekonstruktion nach Berichten und Dialogen"
1972 **No award**
1973 **Lutz Lehmann**, "Ein Mittwoch im Juni"
1974 **No award**
1975 **No award**
1976 **Lutz Lehmann** and **Peter Schultze**, "Ein Sonntag im August"
Holger Oehrens, "Mit Hammer und Zirkel"
1977 **No award**
1978 **Lutz Lehmann** and **Fritz Pleitgen**, "Hoffnungslos zufrieden? — Notizen aus der DDR"
1979 **No award**
1980 **Peter Pechel**, East/West Magazine "Kontraste"

TV FILMS & DRAMAS

1963 **Helmut Reinhardt**, "Der Rennsteig"
1964 **Will Tremper** and **Rolf Hadrich**, "Verspatung in Marienborn"
1965 **No award**
1966 **Dieter Meichsner** and **Egon Monk**, "Preis der Freiheit"
1967 **Wolfgang Menge**, "Begrundung eines Urteiles"
1968 **Deiter Meichsner** and **Rolf Busch**, "Gerhard Langhammer und die Freiheit"
1969 **Wolfgang Menge** and **Eberhard Itzenplitz**, "Die Dubrow-Krise"
1970 **Helmut Krapp** and **Volker Vogeler**, "Varna"
1971 **No award**
1972 **No award**
1973 **No award**
1974 **No award**
1975 **No award**
1976 **Johannes Hendrich**, "Maria Morzeck"
1977 **No award**
1978 **Stefan Roth** and **Peter Schulz-Rohr**, "Mein Leben selber bestimmen"
1979 **No award**
1980 **Eberhard Fechner** and **Walter Kempowkis**, "Ein Kapitel fur sich"

Golden Globe Awards

HOLLYWOOD FOREIGN PRESS ASSOCIATION
8732 Sunset Blvd., Suite 210, Los Angeles, Calif. 90069
(213/657-1707 and 657-1731)

After more than two decades of honoring achievements in motion picture making (see pp. 226-232), the association in 1956 expanded its Golden Globe Awards to honor outstanding television productions of the previous year as well. Selection is by secret ballot of the membership.

BEST TELEVISION SHOWS (To individuals or for specific programs)

1956 **Dinah Shore**
Lucy & Desi
The American Comedy
Davy Crockett
1957 ***Cheyenne***
Mickey Mouse Club
Playhouse 90
Theatre Matinee
This Is Your Life
1958 **Eddie Fisher**
Alfred Hitchcock
Jack Benny
Mike Wallace
1959 **Paul Oates**
Ann Southern
Loretta Young
Red Skelton
Ed Sullivan
William Orr
1960 **David Susskind**
Chuck Connors
Pat Boone
77 Sunset Strip
Dinah Shore
Ed Sullivan

Edward R. Murrow
1961 *Hanna-Barbera Presents*
Perry Mason
Bell Telephone Hour
Hong Kong
Walter Cronkite
1962 *What's My Line?*
My Three Sons
1963 *The Dick Powell Show*
The Defenders
Mr. Ed
Telstar
1964 *The Richard Boone Show*
The Danny Kaye Show
The Dick Van Dyke Show
1965 *The Rogues*
Burke's Law
1966 *The Man from U.N.C.L.E.*
1967 *I Spy*
1968 *Mission Impossible*
1969 *Laugh-In*

BEST DRAMA SHOW

1970 *Marcus Welby M.D.*
1971 *Medical Center*
1972 *Mannix*
1973 *Columbo*
1974 *The Waltons*
1975 *Upstairs, Downstairs*
1976 *Kojak*
1977 *Rich Man Poor Man,* Book I
1978 *Sixty Minutes*
1979 *Lou Grant*
1980 *Shogun*

BEST MUSICAL OR COMEDY SHOW

1970 *The Governor and J.J.*
1971 *The Carol Burnett Show*
1972 *All in the Family*
1973 *All in the Family*
1974 *All in the Family*
1975 *Rhoda*
1976 *Barney Miller*
1977 *Barney Miller*
1978 *Taxi*
1979 *Alice*
Taxi
1980 *Taxi*

BEST MALE TELEVISION STAR (Dramatic only, after 1970)

1962 Bob Newhart
John Daly
1963 Richard Chamberlain
Rod Serling
1964 Mickey Rooney
1965 Gene Barry
1966 David Janssen
1967 Dean Martin
1968 Martin Landau
1969 Carl Betz, *Judd for the Defense*
1970 Mike Connors, *Mannix*
1971 Peter Graves, *Mission: Impossible*
1972 Robert Young, *Marcus Welby M.D.*
1973 Peter Falk, *Columbo*
1974 James Stewart *Hawkins*
1975 Telly Savalas Kojak
1976 Robert Blake, *Baretta*
Telly Savalas, *Kojak*
1977 Richard Jordan, *Captains and the Kings* A
1978 Michael Moriarty, *Holocaust*
1979 Ed Asner, *Lou Grant*
1980 Richard Chamberlain, *Shogun*

BEST FEMALE TELEVISION STAR (Dramatic only, after 1970)

1962 Pauline Fredericks
1963 Donna Reed
1964 Inger Stevens
1965 Mary Tyler Moore
1966 Anne Francis
1967 Marlo Thomas
1968 Carol Burnett
1969 Diahann Carroll, *Julia*
1970 Linda Cristal, *High Chaparral*
1971 Peggy Lipton, *Mod Squad*
1972 Patricia Neal, *The Homecoming*
1973 Gail Fisher, *Mannix*
1974 Lee Remick, *The Blue Knight*
1975 Angie Dickinson, *Police Woman*
1976 Lee Remick *Jennie*
1977 Susan Blakely, *Rich Man, Poor Man,* Book I
1978 Rosemary Harris, *Holocaust*
1979 Natalie Wood, *From Here to Eternity*
1980 Yoko Shimada, *Shogun*

BEST ACTOR (Musical or Comedy)

1970 Dan Dailey, *The Governor and J.J.*
1971 Flip Wilson
1972 Carroll O'Connor, *All in the Family*
1973 Redd Foxx, *Sanford and Son*
1974 Jack Klugman, *The Odd Couple*
1975 Alan Alda, *M.A.S.H.*
1976 Alan Alda, *M.A.S.H.*
1977 Henry Winkler, *Happy Days*
1978 Robin Williams, *Mork and Mindy*
1979 Alan Alda, *M*A*S*H*
1980 Alan Alda, *M*A*S*H*

BEST ACTRESS (Musical or Comedy)

1970 Carol Burnett
Julie Sommers
1971 Mary Tyler Moore
1972 Carol Burnett, *The Carol Burnett Show*
1973 Jean Stapleton, *All in the Family*
1974 Jean Stapleton, *All in the Family*
Cher Bono, *Sonny and Cher*
1975 Valerie Harper, *Rhoda*
1976 Cloris Leachman, *Phyllis*
1977 Carol Burnett, *The Carol Burnett Show*
1978 Linda Lavin, *Alice*
1979 Linda Lavin, *Alice*
1980 Katherine Helmond, *Soap*

BEST SUPPORTING ACTOR IN A TELEVISION SHOW

1972 Edward Asner, *The Mary Tyler Moore Show*
1973 James Brolin, *Marcus Welby M.D.*
1974 McLean Stevenson, *M.A.S.H.*
1975 Harvey Korman, *The Carol Burnett Show*
1976 Edward Asner, *The Mary Tyler Moore Show*
Tim Conway, *The Carol Burnett Show*
1977 Edward Asner, *Rich Man, Poor Man,* Book I
1978 Norman Fell, *Three's Company*
1979 Danny De Vito, *Taxi*
Vic Tayback, *Alice*
1980 Pat Harrington, *One Day at a Time*
Vic Tayback, *Alice*

BEST SUPPORTING ACTRESS IN A TELEVISION SHOW

1972 **Sue Ann Langdon,** *Arnie*
1973 **Ruth Buzzi,** *Laugh-In*
1974 **Ellen Corby** *The Waltons*
1975 **Betty Garrett,** *All in the Family*
1976 **Hermoine Baddeley,** *Maude*
1977 **Josette Banzet,** *Rich Man, Poor Man,* Book I
1978 **Polly Holliday,** *Alice*
1979 **Polly Holliday,** *Alice*
1980 **Valerie Bertinelli,** *One Day at a Time*
Diane Ladd, *Alice*

BEST MOVIE MADE FOR TELEVISION

1973 ***That Certain Summer***
1974 **No award**
1975 **No award**
1976 ***Babe***
1977 ***Eleanor and Franklin***
1978 ***A Family Upside Down***
1979 ***All Quiet on the Western Front***
1980 ***The Shadow Box***

Media Awards

AMOS TUCK SCHOOL OF BUSINESS ADMINISTRTION
Dartmouth College, Hanover, N.H. 03755 (603/646-2084)

The Media Awards for the Advancement of Economic Understanding, sponsored by Champion International Corporation and administered by the Tuck school, honor outstanding economic reporting and journalism in the general media. Original works broadcast or telecast during the preceding year can be entered for consideration by a panel of judges. Top prizes of $5,000 are awarded. In addition to these first-place winners listed below, a $2,500 second prize is given in each category. Honors for print journalism are elsewhere in this volume.

TELEVISION (Network and nationally distributed programs)

1977 **Asustin Hoyt, Elizabeth Deane, Gerald Lange, Bruce Shah, Janet Krause** and **Ben Wattenberg** WGBH-TV, Boston ("There's No Business Like Big Business")
1978 **No award**
1979 **Dan Gordtz, Bernard Cohen** and **Av Westin,** ABC-TV "1979: Stretching the Shrinking Dollar"
1980 **Not available at press time**

TELEVISION (Markets ranked 1 to 25)

1977 **Patrick Clawson,** KTVI-TV, St. Louis ("The Co-op Conspiracy: Pyramid of Shame")
1978 **Robert MacNeil, Al Vecchione, Jim Lehrer, Ken Witty** and **Lewis Silverman,** WNET/Thirteen (New York) and WETA (Washington, D.C.), "The New Wall Street"
1979 **Susan Horowitz, Susan Levit, Diane Berson,** KYW-TV (Philadelphia), "Inflation: How to Survive"
1980 **Not available at press time**

TELEVISION (Markets ranked 26 to 100)

1977 **Daniel Miller** and **John Leiendecker,** KDIN-TV, Des Moines ("Farm Digest: Ag Land Trust")
1978 **Judy Crouse** and **Gary Gottschalk,** WTOL-TV (Toledo, Ohio), "Tax Abatement: Catalyst or Coercion"
1979 **Daniel Miller, Richard Gray, John Leiendecker,** Iowa Public Broadcasting Network (Des Moines, Iowa), "Farm Digest: Meat Price Reporting"
1980 **Not available at press time**

TELEVISION (Markets ranked 101 and smaller)

1977 **Larry Makinson,** KAKM-TV, Anchorage ("Inside the Budget: A Taxpayer's Eye View")
1978 **Doug Carlson, Tom Howe, Jim Levy, Syndie McAfee, Alex Moscu, John Beck, Kevin Caffrey, George Osborn, Shar Osborn, Jim Randall, Ken Rieur, Rich Schudiske, Ken Slagel, Doug Stanley, Don Tremain,** and **Don Ward,** KUON-TV (University of Nebraska Television, Lincoln, Nebraska), "The Commodity Futures Industry"
1979 **Betsy Brenneman, Sheila Toomey** and **Robert Roark,** KTOO-TV (Juneau, Alas.), "Beaufort Basics"
1980 **Not available at press time**

RADIO

1978 **Fred Kennedy** and **Clark Todd,** NBC Radio News, "What Ever Happened to the Almighty Dollar?"

RADIO NETWORK

1979 **Dan Cordtz, Peter Flannery** and **Nancy Gabiner,** American Entertainment Radio Network — ABC News, "Corporate Profit Figures/Productivity — Dan Cordtz on the Economy"
1980 **Not available at press time**

RADIO TOP 50 MARKETS

1979 **Jay Lloyd, Ed Kasuba, Susan Weiner, Nelson Cohen** and **Elaine Weinstock,** KYW-Newsradio, Philadelphia, Pennsylvania, 'Biting the Budget"
1980 **available at press time**

RADIO MARKETS RANKED 51 AND SMALLER

1979 **Pete Fretwell,** KALS-FM (Kalispell, Mont.), "A Primer: Inflation & You"
1980 **Not available at press time**

Music City Award

MUSIC CITY NEWS
Box 22975, Nashville, Tenn. 37023 (615/244-5187)

In addition to a number of honors to entertainers and songwriters, which appear in the Music & Dance section of this volume, *Music City News* annually gives an award to the country television program selected in a poll of its readers. The award is made in a nationally televised ceremony from the Grand Ole Opry in Nashville.

1970 ***Hee Haw***
1971 ***Hee Haw***
1972 ***Hee Haw***
1973 ***Hee Haw***
1974 ***Hee Haw***
1975 ***Hee Haw***
1976 ***Hee Haw***
1977 ***Hee Haw***
1978 ***150 Years of Country Music***
1979 ***The Grand Ole Opry*** (PBS)
1980 ***PBS Live from the Grand Ole Opry***

Patsy Award

AMERICAN HUMANE ASSOCIATION
8480 Beverly Blvd., Los Angeles, Calif. 90048
(213/653-3394)

In 1958 the Patsy Award was extended to honor animals who were outstanding in television performances. For more details on this award, see the Patsy listing in the "Cinema" section. Beginning in 1978, animal performances were categorized by type of animal rather than by media. For convenience, these have also been grouped in the "Cinema" section.

1958 **Lassie** (collie), *Lassie*
Cleo (bassett hound), *The People's Choice*
Rin Tin Tin (German shepherd), *Rin Tin Tin*
1959 **Lassie** (collie), Lassie
Asta (dog), *The Thin Man*
Rin Tin Tin (German shepherd), *Rin Tin Tin*
1960 **Asta** (dog) *The Thin Man*
Lassie (collie), *Lassie*
Fury (horse), *Bachelor Father*
Jasper (N.A.), *Bachelor Father*
1961 **Tramp** (old English sheepdog), *My Three Sons*
Lassie (collie), *Lassie*
Fury (horse), *Bachelor Father*
1962 **Mister Ed** (horse), *Mister Ed*
Lassie (collie), *Lassie*
Tramp (old English sheepdog), *My Three Sons*
1963 **Mister Ed** (horse), *Mister Ed*
Lassie (collie), *Lassie*
Tramp (Old English sheepdog), *My Three Sons*
1964 **Lassie** (collie), *Lassie*
Mister Ed (horse), *Mister Ed*
Tramp (old English Sheepdog), *My Three Sons*
1965 **Flipper** (porpoise), *Flipper*
Lassie (collie), *Lassie*
Mister Ed (horse), *Mister Ed*
1966 **Flipper** (porpoise), *Flipper*
Lord Nelson (dog), *Please Don't Eat the Daisies*
Higgins (dog), *Petticoat Junction*
1967 **Judy** (chimpanzee), *Daktari*
Flipper (porpoise), *Flipper*
Arnold (pig), *Green Acres*
1968 **Arnold** (pig), *Green Acres*
Gentle Ben (bear), *Gentle Ben*
Judy (chimpanzee), *Daktari*
1969 **Arnold** (pig), *Green Acres* (series)
Timmy (chimpanzee), *Beverly Hillbillies* (single performance)
1970 **Scruffy** (dog), *The Ghost and Mrs. Muir* (series)
Algae (seal), *The Ghost and Mrs. Muir* (single performance)
1971 **Arnold** (pig) *Green Acres* (series)
Lassie's three puppies, *Lassie* (single performance)
Margie (elephant), *Wonderful World of Disney* (grand award)
1972 **Pax** (dog), *Longstreet* (series)
Ott (horse), *Lassie* (single performance)
1973 **Farouk** (German shepherd), *Ironside*
1974 **Midnight** (cat), *Mannix* and *Barnaby Jones* (series)
Caesar (Doberman Pinscher), *Trapped* (single performance)
1975 **Elsa** (lion), *Born Free* (series)
Ginger and cubs (coyotes), *The Indestructible Outcasts* (single performance)
1976 **Fred** (cockatoo), *Baretta* (series)
17 (cat), *Dr. Shrinker* (single performance)
JoJo (raven), *Duffy Moon* (single performance)
Sled team and Kodiak (dogs), *Call of the Wild* (single performance)
Bourbon (dog), *Call of the Wild* (single performance)
YoYo (horse), *Banjo Hackett* (single performance)
Neal (lion), *The Bionic Woman* (series)
Heller (cougar), *Shazam* (Series)

TELEVISION COMMERCIAL

1968 **Samba, Jr** (African lion), Dreyfus Fund
1969 **Chauncey** (cougar), Ford Motor Co.
1973 **Morris** (cat), Nine Lives (cat food)
1974 **Scruffy** (dog), Chuckwagon (dog food)
1975 **Lawrence** (red deer elk), Hartford Insurance
1976 **Lawrence** (red deer elk), Hartford Insurance
Unnamed horse, Top Dog

George Foster Peabody Broadcasting Award

HENRY W. GRADY SCHOOL OF JOURNALISM
University of Georgia, Athens, Ga. 30602 (404/542-3785)

The George Foster Peabody Broadcasting Award is given annually for outstanding service in broadcasting, either for programs broadcast during the calendar year for which the awards are made or to individuals for special achievements. Entries are screened by the university faculty committee, and the final selections are made by the Peabody Awards National Advisory Board. The awards categories have changed radically since the inception of the award in 1940, growing in complexity as television joined radio as a significant medium and as the Peabody organization chose to honor more types of programming and a greater number of stations and individuals. This listing, therefore, is chronological rather than by category. (In some years the awards were not assigned categories.)

1940 **CBS,** Network public service
WLW-Radio, (Cincinnati), Public service by a large station
WGAR-Radio, (Cleveland), Public service by a medium-sized station
KRFU, (Columbia, Mo.), Public service by a small station
Elmer Davis, News reporting
1941 **Cecil Brown,** (CBS), News reporting
Sandra Michael and John Gibbs, "Against the Storm," and **Norman Corwin,** "The Bill of Rights," Drama entertainment
Alfred Wallenstein, (Mutual), Music entertainment
Chicago Roundtable of the Air, (NBC), Educational program
The International Short Wave Broadcasters, Public service
1942 **Charles Collingwood** (CBS), News reporting
The Man Behind the Gun (CBS), Drama entertainment
"The Standard Symphony" (NBC Pacific Coast Network), Music entertainment
"Afield With Ranger Mac" (WHA-Radio, Madison, Wisc.), Educational program
"Our Hidden Enemy-Venereal Disease" (KOAC-Radio, Corvallis, Ore.), Public service by a local station
"The Home Front" (WCHS-Radio, Charleston, W.Va.), Public service by a regional station

1943 **"These Are Americans"** (KNX-Radio, Los Angeles), Public service by a regional station
"Calling Longshoremen" (KYA-Radio, San Francisco), Community service by a local station
Edward R. Murrow (CBS), News reporting
Lux Radio Theatre (CBS) and ***An Open Letter to the American People (CBS),***Drama entertainment
"Music and the Spoken Word" (KSL-Radio, Salt Lake City), Music entertainment
American Town Meeting (The Blue Network), Educational program
Let's Pretend (CBS), Children's program
Bob Hope, Special citation

1944 **Raymond Gram Swing** (Blue Network — ABC), News commentary
WLW (Cincinnati), News reporting
Cavalcade of America (NBC), Drama entertainment
Fred Allen (CBS), Special award for comedy
Telephone Hour (NBC), Entertainment in music
Human Adventure (Mutual), Educational program
Philharmonic Young Artists Series (KFI-Radio, Los Angeles), Program for youth
Col. Edward M. Kirby (War Dept. Radio Branch), Special award for adaptation of radio to the requirements of the armed forces and on the home front
Worcester and the World (WTAG-Radio, Worcester, Mass.), Public service by a regional station
WNYC-Radio and Mayor Fiorello LaGuardia, Public service by a local station Cross-Roads (WIBN-Radio, Utica, N.Y.), Public service by local stations
Song of the Columbia (KOIN-Radio, Portland, Ore.); ***Syracuse on Trial*** (WFBL-Radio, Syracuse, N.Y.); ***Southwest Forum,*** (KVOO-Radio, Tulsa, Okla.) and **St. Louis Speaks,** (KMOX-Radio, St. Louis), Regional awards

1945 **CBS and Paul White,** News reporting
KRNT-Radio (Des Moines, Iowa), News reporting, special citation
Edgar Bergen (NBC) and **Arch Oboler** (Mutual), Drama entertainment
The NBC Symphony of the Air and **Howard Hanson,** Eastman School of Music, and WHAM-Radio, (Rochester, N.Y.) Music entertainment
America's Town Meeting of the Air (ABC) and **George V. Denney, Jr.,** Educational program
We March With Faith (KUWH-Radio, Omaha, Neb.), Children's Program
Toward A Better World (KFWB-Radio, Hollywood, Calif.), Special citation, regional public service
Mr. Colombo Discovers America (WOV-Radio, New York) Regional public service and ***Arnold Hartley*** and **Wake Up Kentucky** (WHAS-Radio, Louisville, Ky.), Regional public service
Save A Life (KOMA-Radio, Oklahoma City), Local public service

1946 ***Operation Big Muddy*** (WOW-Radio, Omaha), Public service by a regional station
The Harbor We Seek (WSB-Radio, Atlanta), Special citation, regional public service
Our Town (WELL-Radio, Battle Creek, Mich.), Public service by local station
The Radio Edition of the Weekly Press (WHCU-Radio, Ithaca, N.Y.), Special citation, local public service
William L. Shirer (CBS), News reporting and interpretation
Meet the Press (Mutual), Special news citation
The Columbia Workshop, Drama entertainment
Henry Morgan (ABC) and ***Suspense*** (CBS), Special drama citations
Orchestras of the Nation (NBC), Music entertainment
Invitation to Music (CBS), Special citation, music entertainment
WMCA-Radio (New York), Education program
Hiroshima (Robert Saudek, ABC), Special education citation
Books Bring Adventure (Junior League of America), Special children's program citation
John Crosby (*The New York Herald Tribune*), Special award for contribution to radio through writing

1947 ***Report Uncensored*** (WBBM-Radio, Chicago), Public service by regional station
As the Twig Is Bent (WCCO-Radio, Minneapolis), Special citation, regional public service
"Disaster Broadcast From Cotton Valley" (KXAR-Radio, Hope, Ark.), Public service by local station
CBS Views the Press and **Elmer Davis** (ABC), News reporting and interpretation
The Boston Symphony Orchestra (ABC), Music entertainment
Theatre Guild on the Air (ABC), Drama entertainment
Studio One (CBS), Special drama citation
CBS Documentary Unit Series, Educational programs
The Children's Hour (WQQW, Washington, D.C.), Children's program
United Nations Today (United Nations Network), Special citation

1948 ***Forests Aflame*** (KNBC-Radio, San Francisco), Public service by regional station
You and Youth (WDAR-Radio, Savannah, Ga.), Public service by local station
Edward R. Murrow (CBS), News reporting and interpretation
The NBC University Theatre and ***The Groucho Marx Show*** (ABC), Drama entertainment
NBC for overall contributions of broadcasting good music, Music entertainment
Communism — U.S. Brand (ABC), Education program
Rocky Mountain Radio Council and **Lowell Institute Broadcasting Council,** Special education citations
Howdy Doody (NBC), Children's program
CBS for overall contributions, especially for Larry LeSeur's broadcasts, Promotion of international understanding
"Little Songs About U.N." (WNEW, New York), Special citation
Actor's Studio (ABC), Contribution to television art

RADIO

1949 **WWJ-Radio** (NBC, Detroit), Public service by regional station
KXLJ-Radio (NBC, Helena, Mont.), Public service by local station
Eric Sevareid (CBS), News reporting and interpretation
WMAZ-Radio (CBS, Macon, Ga.) and **Erwin Canham,** *The Monitor Views the News* (ABC), Special news citations
Jack Benny (CBS), Drama entertainment
The Greatest Story Ever Told (ABC), Special citation
WQXR (New York), Music entertainment

Author Meets the Critics (ABC), Educational program
Mind Your Manners (WTIC, NBC, Hartford, Conn.), Children's program
United Nations Project (NBC), Contribution to international understanding

TELEVISION

The Ed Wynn Show (CBS), Entertainment
Crusade in Europe (ABC), Education
United Nations in Action (CBS), News reporting and interpretation
Kukla, Fran and Ollie (NBC), Children's program

SPECIAL CITATIONS

H.T. Webster, cartoon, *Unseen Audience;* United Nations and American broadcasters generally, **Harold W. Ross,** *The New Yorker*

RADIO

1950 ***The Quiet Answer*** (WBBM, CBS, Chicago), Public service by regional station
WEPL-FM (Louisville Free Public Library, Ky.), Public service by local station
Elmer Davis (ABC), News reporting and interpretation
Hear It Now (CBS), Special news citation
Halls of Ivy (NBC), Drama entertainment
Metropolitan Opera (ABC), Music entertainment
Ira Hirschman (WABF-FM, New York), Special music citation
The Quick and the Dead (NBC), Education
Radio Free Europe, Contribution to international understanding
WNYC (New York) and **Pursuit of Peace** (Mutual and United Nations Radio), Special citations for contributions to international understanding

TELEVISION

Jimmy Durante (NBC), Entertainment
The Johns Hopkins Science Review (WAAM-TV, DuMont, Baltimore), Education
Zoo Parade (NBC) and ***Saturday at the Zoo*** (ABC), Children's programs

SPECIAL AWARDS

ABC, specifically to **President Robert E. Kitner** and his associates, **Robert Saudek and Joseph McDonald**
Providence Journal, specifically to editor **Sevellon Brown** and reporter **Ben Bagdikian**

1951 ***The Nation's Nightmare,*** (CBS), Radio educational program
The New York Times Youth Forums (WQXR, New York), Radio youth program
Bob and Ray (NBC), Nonmusical radio entertainment
Letter From America (Alistair Cooke, British Broadcasting Corporation), Radio's contribution to international understanding
What in the World (WCAU, CBS, Philadelphia), Television educational program
Amahl and the Night Visitors (NBC), Television musical entertainment
Celanese Theatre (ABC), Television nonmusical entertainment
Edward R. Murrow (*See It Now,* CBS), Television news and interpretation
Careers Unlimited (KPOJ, Mutual, Portland, Ore.), Local public service by radio
WSB (NBC, Atlanta), Regional public service by radio and television

1952 **Martin Agronsky** (ABC), Radio news
The New York Philharmonic Symphony Ochestra, (CBS), and ***The Standard Symphony*** (NBC), Radio music
The Johns Hopkins Science Review (WAAM-TV, DuMont, Baltimore), Television education
Meet the Press (NBC), Television news
Mister Peepers (NBC), and ***Your Hit Parade*** (NBC), Television entertainment
Ding Dong School (NBC), Youth and children's program
Victory at Sea (NBC), Television special award
WIS-Radio (NBC, Columbia, S.C.), Regional public service including promotion of international understanding
WEWS-TV (ABC) and **CSB** (Cleveland), Local public service

1953 **Chet Huntley** (KABC, ABC, Los Angeles), Radio news
Gerald W. Johnson (WAAM-TV, Baltimore), Television news
NBC Television Opera Theatre, Television music
Television Playhouse (NBC), and ***Imogene Coca*** (NBC), Television entertainment
Cavalcade of Books (KNXT, CBS, Los Angeles) and ***Camera Three*** (WCBS-TV, New York), Television education
Mr. Wizard (NBC), Television youth and children's program
Coverage of the Coronation (British Broadcasting Company), Promotion of international understanding through television
WSB-AM-FM-TV (NBC, Atlanta), Public service by regional radio-TV station
WBAW (Barnwell, S.C.), Public service by local station
Edward R. Murrow (CBS), Special award

1954 **John Daly** (ABC), Radio-television news
George Gobel (NBC), Television entertainment
Adventure (CBS), Television education
Omnibus (CBS) and ***The Search*** (CBS), Television special awards
Disneyland (ABC), Youth and children's programs
Industry on Parade (National Association of Manufacturers), Television national public service
"Hurricane Carol" (WJAR-TV, Providence), Television regional public service
Conversation (NBC), Radio entertainment
Man's Right to Knowledge (CBS), Radio education
"Pauline Frederick at the U.N." (NBC), Radio contribution to international understanding
The Navajo Hour (KGAK, Gallup, N.M.), Radio local public service
Boris Goldovsky, Metropolitan Opera (NBC), Radio music special citation

1955 **Douglas Edwards** (CBS), Television news
Perry Como (NBC) and **Jackie Gleason** (CBS), Television entertainment
Producers' Showcase (NBC), Television dramatic entertainment
Lassie (CBS), Television youth and children's program
Frank Baxter (KNXT, CBS), Television education
Omnibus and ***Adams Family Series*** (CBS), Special television education citation
Voice of Firestone (ABC), Radio-television music

Sylvester L. Weaver, Jr. (NBC) for pioneering programing concepts, Radio-television public service
Quincy Howe (ABC), Radio-television promotion of international understanding
Assignment: India (NBC-TV), Special citation for promotion of international understanding
Biographies in Sound (NBC), Radio education
KIRO (CBS, Seattle), Local radio public service
KFYO (CBS, Lubbock, Tex.), Special citation, radio public service
WMT-TV (CBS, Cedar Rapids, Iowa) and **KQED** (San Francisco), Special citations, local radio public service

1956 **John Charles Daly and associates** (ABC convention coverage), Television news
The Ed Sullivan Show (CBS), Television entertainment
You Are There (CBS), Television education
Youth Wants to Know (NBC), Television children's and/or youth program
World in Crisis (CBS), Television public service
The Secret Life of Danny Kaye (UNICEF), Television promotion of international understanding
Rod Serling, Television writing
Edward P. Morgan and the News (ABC), Radio news
Bob and Ray (Mutual and NBC), Radio entertainment
Books in Profile (WNYC, New York), Radio education
Little Orchestra Society Concerts (WNYC, New York), Radio youth and/or children's program
Regimented Raindrops, (WOW, Omaha, Neb.), Radio/television local-regional public service
United Nations Radio and Television, Special award for promotion of international understanding
Jack Gould, *The New York Times,* Special award for contributions to radio and television through writing

1957 **CBS NEWS** for depth and range, Radio and television news
John Charles Daly and associates, "Prologue '58" (ABC), Television news
Louis M. Lyons (WGBH, Boston), Local radio-television news
The Dinah Shore Chevy Show (NBC), Musical television entertainment
Hallmark Hall of Fame (NBC), Nonmusical television entertainment
The Heritage Series (WQED, Pittsburgh), Television education
You Are the Jury (WKAR, E. Lansing, Mich.), Local radio education
Captain Kangaroo (CBS), Television youth and children's program
Wunda, Wunda (KING-TV, ABC, Seattle), Local television youth and children's program
Panorama (KLZ-TV, CBS, Denver), Local television public service
The Last Word (CBS), Television public service
KPFA-FM (Berkeley, Calif.), Local radio public service
Bob Hope (NBC), Television contribution to international understanding
Education programs fed to educatial stations and "Know Your Schools," (NBC stations) and Westinghouse Broadcasting Co. Boston Conference, Special radio-television awards

1958 ***NBC News—The Huntley-Brinkley Report,*** Television news
Playhouse 90 (CBS), Television dramatic entertainment
Lincoln Presents Leonard Bernstein and the New York Philharmonic (CBS), Television musical entertainment
The Steve Allen Show (NBC), Television entertainment with humor
Continental Classroom (NBC), Television education
College News Conference (ABC), Television program for youth
The Blue Fairy (WGN, Chicago), Television program for children
M.D. International (NBC), Television contribution to international understanding
CBS-TV, Television public service
James Costigan, "Little Moon of Alban," on *Hallmark Hall of Fame* (NBC), Television writing
"An Evening With Fred Astaire" (NBC) and **Orson Welles,** "Fountain of Youth," (*Colgate Theatre,* NBC), Television special awards
WNEW (New York), Radio news
"The Hidden Revolution" (CBS), Radio public service
Standard School Broadcast (Standard Oil Company of California), Radio education
Easy as ABC (ABC-UNESCO), Radio contribution to international understanding

1959 **"Khrushchev Abroad"** (ABC), Television news
The Play of the Week (WNTA-TV, Newark, NJ.) and **David Susskind,** *The Moon and Sixpence* (NBC), Nonmusical television entertainment
The Bell Telephone Hour (NBC) and ***Great Music From Chicago*** (WGN-TV, Chicago), Television musical entertainment
The Population Explosion (CBS) and ***Decisions*** (WGBH, Boston and the World Affairs Council), Television education
The Ed Sullivan Show (CBS) and ***Small World*** (CBS), Television contribution to international understanding
WDSU-TV (New Orleans), Local television public service
Frank Stanton (CBS) and ***The Lost Class of '59*** (CBS), Television special awards
The World Tonight (CBS), Radio news
Family Living '59 (NBC), Radio public service
WCCO (Minneapolis), Local radio public service

1960 ***The Texaco Huntley-Brinkley Report*** (NBC), Television news
The Fabulous Fifties (CBS), Television entertainment
NBC White Paper Series, Television education
GE College Bowl (CBS), Television youth program
The Shari Lewis Show, (NBC), Television children's program
CBS 1960 Olympic coverage, Television contribution to international understanding
CBS Reports, Television public service
Musical Spectaculars (WQXR, New York), Radio entertainment
Ireene Wicker (WNYC, New York), Radio children's program
Texaco-Metropolitan Opera Network, Radio public service
Broadcasting and Film Commission, National Council of Churches of Christ in the U.S.A., for various programs on different networks and local stations, Radio-television education
WOOD and WOOD-TV (Grand Rapids, Mich.), **KPFK** (Los Angeles), **WCKT** (Miami) and

WCCO-TV (Minneapolis), Locally produced radio-television
Frank Stanton (CBS), Special award

1961 ***David Brinkley's Journal*** (NBC), Television news
The Bob Newhart Show (NBC), Television entertainment
An Age of Kings (BBC) and ***Vincent Van Gogh: A Self-Portrait*** (NBC), Television education
Expedition! (ABC), Television youth and children's program
Walter Lippmann and CBS, Television contribution to international understanding
Let Freedom Ring (KSL-TV, CBS, Salt Lake City), Television public service
Fine Arts Entertainment (WFMT, Chicago), Radio entertainment
The Reader's Almanac and ***Teen Age Book Talk*** (WNYC, New York), Radio education
WRUL (Worldwide Broadcasting), (New York) for coverage of U.N. General Assembly proceedings in English and Spanish, Radio contribution to international understanding
Fred Friendly (CBS), **Capital Cities Broadcasting Corporation,** "Verdict for Tomorrow: The Eichmann Trial on Television," and **Newton N. Minow,** Chiarman, Federal Communications Commission, Special awards

1962 **Walter Cronkite** (CBS), Television news
Du Pont Show of the Week (NBC) and **Carol Burnett** (CBS), Television entertainment
Biography (Official Films, Inc.), Television education
Exploring (NBC) and **Walt Disney** (NBC), Television youth and children's programming
Adlai Stevenson Reports (ABC), Television contribution to international understanding
A Tour of the White House With Mrs. John F. Kennedy (CBS), Television public service
Elliot Norton Reviews (WGBH-TV Boston), ***Books for Our Time*** (WNDT, New York) and ***San Francisco Pageant*** (KPIX-TV, WBC), Locally produced television
WQXR (New York), Radio news
Adventures in Good Music (WJR, Detroit), and ***The Eternal Light*** (NBC), Radio entertainment
Science Editor (KNX, CBS, Los Angeles), Radio education
Carnival of Books (WMAQ, NBC, Chicago), Radio youth and children's program
William R. MacAndrew and NBC News and NAB for study on television's effects on the young viewer, Special awards

1963 **Eric Sevareid** (CBS), Television news commentary
The Danny Kaye Show (CBS) and ***Mr. Novak*** (NBC), Television entertainment
American Revolution '63 (NBC) and ***The Saga of Western Man*** (ABC), Television education
The Dorothy Gordon Forum (WNBC-TV and Radio, New York), Television youth program
Treetop House (WGN, Chicago), Television children's program
Town Meeting of the World (CBS) and **Frank Stanton,** Television contribution to international understanding
CBS Reports: Storm Over the Supreme Court, Television public service
Sunday Night Monitor (NBC), Radio news
WLW (Cincinnatti), Radio education
Voice of America and Edward R. Murrow, Radio contribution to international understanding
KSTP (Minneapolis), Radio public service
Broadcasting industry of the U.S.A. for coverage of the assassination of President Kennedy and related events, Special award

1964 ***CBS Reports***
Profiles in Courage (NBC)
William H. (Bill) Lawrence (ABC)
Joyce Hall, *Hallmark Hall of Fame* (NBC)
Julia Child, *The French Chef* (WGBH-TV, Boston, and NET)
INTERTEL: International Television Federation
Off the Cuff (WBKB, ABC, Chicago)
Riverside Radio (WRVR-FM, New York)
The Louvre (NBC)
Burr Tillstrom
The networks and the broadcasting industry for confronting the American public with the realities of racial discontent

1965 **Frank McGhee** (NBC), **Morley Safer** (CBS) and **KTLA,** Television news
The Julie Andrews Show (NBC), ***My Name is Barbra*** (CBS), and ***Frank Sinatra — A Man and His Music*** (NBC), Television entertainment
National Educational Television, Television education
A Charlie Brown Christmas (CBS), Television youth and children's program
CBS Reports: KKK—The Invisible Empire, Television public service
The National Driver's Test (CBS), Television innovation
The Mystery of Stonehenge (CBS), Television's most inventive art documentary
A Visit to Washington with Mrs. Lyndon B. Johnson — On Behalf of a More Beautiful America (ABC), Television special award
Xerox Corporation Television contribution to international understanding
"Music 'til Dawn" (CBS), Radio entertainment
WCCO-Radio (Minneapolis), Radio public service

1966 **Harry Reasoner** (CBS), Television news
A Christmas Memory: ABC Stage 67, Television entertainment
National Geographic Specials (CBS) and ***American White Paper: Organized Crime in the United States*** (NBC), Television education
The World of Stuart Little (NBC), Television youth and children's program
The Wide World of Sports (ABC) and ***Siberia: A Day in Irkutsk*** (NBC), Television promotion of international understanding
Bell Telephone Hour (NBC), **Tom John** (CBS), **National Educational Television, and "CBS Reports: The Poisoned Air,"** Television special awards
"The Dorothy Gordon Youth Forum: Youth and Narcotics—Who Has the Answer? (WNBC-TV and WNBC-Radio), Television-radio public service
Kup's Show (WBKB-TV, Chicago), Television local news-entertainment
Artists' Showcase (WGN-TV, Chicago) and **"A Polish Millennium Concert"** (WTMJ-TV, Milwaukee), Television local music
Assignment Four (KRON-TV, San Francisco), Television local public service
Edwin Newman (NBC), Radio news
Elmo Ellis (WSB, Atlanta), Radio local public service
Community Opinion (WLIB, New York), Radio local education

1967 **Elie Abel,** *The World and Washington* (NBC), Radio news

The Eternal Light (NBC), Radio education
Eric Sevareid (CBS), Radio-television news analysis and commentary
CBS Playhouse and ***"An Evening at Tanglewood"*** (NBC), Television entertainment
The Children's Film Festival (CBS), and ***Mr. Knozit*** (WIS-TV), Television youth or children's program
"Africa" (ABC), Television promotion of international understanding
The Opportunity Line (WBBM-TV), Television public service
Meet the Press and **Bob Hope** (NBC), Radio-television special awards
The Ed Sullivan Show (CBS), Television special award
James H. Killiam, Jr., Chairman, Massachusetts Institute of Technology, Special broadcasting education award

1968 ***Second Sunday*** (NBC), Radio news
Leonard Reiffel, *The World Tomorrow* (WEEI, CBS, Boston), Radio education
Steinway Hall (WQXR, New York), Radio entertainment
Kaleidoscope (WJR, CBS, Detroit), Radio public service
Charles Kuralt, "On the Road" (CBS), Television news
Robert Cromie, *Book Beat* (WTTW, Chicago) and **ABC** for its creative 1968 documentaries, Television education
Playhouse (NET), Television entertainment
Misterogers' Neighborhood (NET), Television youth or children's program
1968 Olympic Games (ABC), Television promotion of international understanding
One Nation Indivisible (Westinghouse Broadcasting), Television public service
"CBS Reports: Hunger in America," Television special award

1969 **"When Will It End?"** (WRNG, Atlanta), Radio news
"On Trial: The Man in the Middle" (NBC, New York), Radio education
Voice of America (Washington), Radio promotion of international understanding
Higher Horizons (WLIB, New York), Radio public service
Newsroom (KQED, San Francisco) and **Frank Reynolds** (ABC-TV, New York), Television news
The Advocates (WGBH-TV, Boston) and **KCET** Los Angeles) and ***Who Killed Lake Erie?*** (NBC-TV), Television education
Experiment in Television (NBC) and **Curt Gowdy,** Television entertainment
Sesame Street (Children's Television Workshop, New York), Television youth or children's program
"The Japanese" (CBS), Television promotion of international understanding
Tom Pettit (Investigative reporting for NBC), Network television public service
The Negro in Indianapolis (WFBM-TV, Indianapolis), Local television public service
J.T. (CBS-TV), Special television writing award
Chet Huntley, Television special award
Bing Crosby, Special individual award

1970 **Douglas Kiker,** "Jordan Reports" (NBC), Radio news
"The Danger Within: A Study of Disunity in America" (NBC), Radio education
Voice of America and **Garry Moore,** Radio promotion of international understanding
Listening/4 (WFBE-FM, Flint, Mich.), Radio youth or children's programs
"Medical Viewpoint" and **"Pearl Harbor, Lest We Forget"** (WAHT, Lebanon, Pa.), Radio public service
60 Minutes (CBS) and **"Politithon '70"** (WPBT, Miami), Television news
Flip Wilson Show (NBC), ***Evening at Pops*** (PBS), and ***The Andersonville Trial*** (PBS and KCET, Los Angeles), Television entertainment
Eye of the Storm (ABC), Television education
The Dr. Seuss Programs (CBS) and ***Hot Dog*** (NBC-TV), Television youth and children's program
Civilisation (BBC) and ***This New Frontier*** (WWL-TV, New Orleans), Television promotion of international understanding
Peace . . . On Our Time and ***The Death of Rueben Salazar*** (KMEX-TV, Los Angeles) and ***Migrant: An NBC White Paper,*** Television public service
The Selling of the Pentagon (CBS), Television special award

1971 **John Rich** (NBC Radio and Television), Broadcast news
Wisconsin on the Move (WHA, Madison, Wisc.), Radio education
Junior Town Meeting of the Air (WWVA, Wheeling, W. Va.), Radio youth or children's program
Voice of America (Washington), Radio promotion of international understanding
Second Sunday (NBC), Radio public service
The Heart of the Matter (WCCO, Minneapolis), and **Arthur Godfrey** (CBS), Radio special awards
NBC-TV dramatic programing; *The American Revolution: 1770-1783, A Conversation with Lord North* (CBS) and ***Brian's Song*** (ABC), Television entertainment
Make A Wish (ABC-TV News), Television youth or children's program
"The Turned On Crisis" (WQED, Pittsburgh), Television education
Mississippi Authority for Educational Television, Special television education
United Nations Day Concert with Pablo Casals (United Nations Television, New York), Television promotion of international understanding
"This Child is Rated X" (NBC), Television public service
George Heinemann (NBC-TV), Special television award
Frank Stanton (CBS), Special award

RADIO

1972 ***NBC Monitor*** (NBC Radio Network)
"Conversations With Will Shakespeare and Certain of His Friends (KOAC, Corvallis, Ore.)
The Noise Show (Washington, D.C., Schools Radio Project)
Open Door (KGW, Portland, Ore.)
Broadcasting Foundation of America (New York)
Voice of America
Breakdown (Group W, New York)
No Fault Insurance—Right Road or Wrong? and *Second Sunday,* NBC and NBC owned and -operated stations)
All Things Considered (National Public Radio, Washington)

TELEVISION

Bill Monroe (*Today,* NBC) for news reporting
The Waltons (CBS-TV)
NBC/TV for three special programs devoted to twentieth century American music
WHRO-TV (Norfolk, Va.) for overall classroom programing
"The Search for the Nile" (BBC and NBC)
ABC Afterschool Specials (ABC-TV)
"The Restless Earth" (WNET, New York, and BBC)
Captain Kangaroo (CBS-TV)
"China '72: A Hole in the Bamboo Curtain" (WWL-TV, New Orleans)
"Pensions: The Broken Promise" (NBC)
"Willowbrook" The Last Great Disgrace" (WABC-TV, New York)
XX Olympiad (ABC)
Alistair Cooke

RADIO

1973 **Lowell Thomas,** News broadcast
Lyric Opera Live Broadcasts and ***Music in Chicago,*** **(WFMT, Chicago)** and ***"Project Experiment*** (NBC Radio, live concerts), Entertainment
(WFMT, Chicago) and "Project Experiment (NBC Radio, live concerts), Entertainment
Second Sunday (NBC Radio) and **"The American Past: Introduction"** (KANU-FM, Lawrence, Kans.), Education
"From 18th Street: Destination Peking" (WIND, Chicago), Promotion of international understanding
"Marijuana and the Law," (KNOW, Austin, Tex.), Public service

TELEVISION

Close-Up (ABC News), News
Peter Lisagor (Chicago Daily News), Special news award
"Myshkin" (WTIU, Bloomington, Ind.) and **"Red Pony"** (NBC), ***Pueblo***and ***The Glass Menagerie,*** (ABC) and ***The Catholics,*** (*CBS Playhouse 90*),Entertainment
The First and Essential Freedom (ABC), **Learning Can Be Fun,** and ***Dusty's Treehouse*** (KNXT, Los Angeles), Education
The Borrowers and ***Street of the Flower Boxes*** (NBC), Youth and children's program
Overture to Friendship: The Philadelphia Orchestra in China (WCAU), Promotion of international understanding
"Home Rule Campaign" (WRC, NBC), Public service
Pamela Ilott for *Lamp Unto My Feet* and *Look Up and Live* (CBS News), Personal public service award
"The Energy Crisis . . . An American White Paper" (NBC), Television special award
Joe Garagiola, *The Baseball World of Joe Garagiola* (NBC-TV), Special sports award

1974 **"The Hit and Run Players"** (KTW-Radio, Seattle)
The CBS Radio Mystery Theatre (CBS Radio Network)
The Second Sunday (NBC Radio Network)
Through the Looking Glass (KFAC-Radio, Los Angeles)
Conversations From Wingspread (The Johnson Foundation, Racine, Wisc.)
WSB-Radio (Atlanta), for public and community service
Battles Just Begun (WMAL-Radio, Washington)
Pledge A Job (WNBC-Radio, New York)
WCKT-TV (Miami), for investigative reporting
The Execution of Private Slovik,The Law, and ***IBM Presents Clarence Darrow*** (NBC Television Network)
Benjamin Franklin CBS Television Network
Theatre in America, (WNET and The Public Broadcasting Service)
Nova (WGBH-TV, Boston)
Free to Be . . . You and Me (ABC Television Network)
Go! (NBC Television Network)
How Come? (KING-TV, Seattle)
From Belfast With Love (WCCO-TV, Minneapolis)
Sadat: Action Biography (ABC Television Network)
"Tornado! 4:40 P.M., Xenia, Ohio" (NBC Television Network)
NPACT (National Public Affairs Center for Television), Washington
"The Right Man" (KPRC, Houston)
Carl Stern (NBC News)
Fred Graham (CBS News)
Marilyn Baker formerly of KQED-TV San Francisco)
Julian Goodman (Chairman, NBC)

RADIO

1975 **Jim Laurie** (NBC News)
"Sleeping Watchdogs," (KMOX-Radio, St. Louis)
The Collector's Shelf and ***200 Years of Music in America*** (WGMS, Bethesda, Md., WGMS-FM, Washington)
Standard School of Broadcast (San Francisco)
Music in Chicago: Stravinsky '75 (WFMT, Chicago)
"Land of Poetry" (WSOU-FM, S. Orange, N.J.)
"The Battle of Lexington" (Voice of America)
"A Life to Share" (WCBS-Radio, New York)
KDKB (Mesa, Ariz.) for community service
"Suffer the Little Children" and **"The Legend of the Bermuda Triangle"** (WMAL-Radio, Washington)

SPECIAL POSTHUMOUS AWARD

Paul Porter, member, Peabody Awards National Advisory Board

TELEVISION

"Harambee: For My People" and **"Everywoman: the Hidden World"** (WTOP, Washington)
WCKT-TV (Miami) for investigative reporting
Charles Kurault (CBS News) for "On the Road to '76"
"The Dale Car: A Dream or A Nightmare" (KABC-TV, Los Angeles)
M.A.S.H. (CBS-TV)
ABC Theatre: Love Among the Ruins (ABC-TV)
Weekend (NBC-TV)
WCVB-TV (Boston)
Call It Macaroni1 (Group W, New York)
The ABC Afterschool Specials (ABC-TV)
Snipets (Kaiser Broadcastong, San Francisco)
Big Blue Marble (Alphaventure, New York)
Mr. Rooney Goes to Washington (CBS News)
A Sunday Journal (WWL-TV, New Orleans)
The American Assassins (CBS News)
"Las Rosas Blancas," (WAPA-TV, San Juan, P.R.)

James Killian, Boston
1976 ***American Popular Song With Alec Wilder and Friends*** (South Carolina Educational Radio Network, Columbia, S.C.)
"Flashback 1976" (WGIR-AM-FM, Manchester, N.H.)
"The Garden Plot: Food As a Weapon" (Associated Press Radio, Washington)
"Power Politics in Mississippi" (WLBT-TV, Jackson, Miss.)
Primary Colors, An Artist on the Campaign Trail (Franklin McMahon, WBBM-TV, Chicago)
Charles Barthold (WHO-TV, Des Moines) for filming tornado
The CBS Morning News (Hughes Rudd and Bruce Morton)
***Weekend's* "Sawyer Brothers" segment** (NBC-TV, Sy Pearlman)
Visions (KCET/28, Los Angeles)
Sybil *(NBC-TV)*
Eleanor and Franklin (ABC-TV)
Animals Animals Animals (ABC News)
1976 Winter Olympic Games and 1976 Summer Olympic Games (ABC Sports)
Judge Horton and the Scottsboro Boys (Tomorrow Entertainment, Inc., New York)
In Performance at Wolf Trap (WETA-TV Washington)
Perry Comos Christmas in Austria (NBC-TV)
In the News (CBS News)
"A Thirst in the Garden" (KERA-TV, Dallas)
'76 Presidential Debates (Jim Karayn and The League of Women Voters)
The Adams Chronicles (WNET/13, New York)
In Celebration of US (CBS News)
Suddenly An Eagle (ABC News)
A Conversation With Jimmy Carter (WETA-TV, Washington and WNET/13, New York)
60 Minutes (CBS News)

RADIO

1977 **WXYZ Radio** (Detroit) for ***Winter's Fear: the Children, the Killer, the Search***, "for a competent investigative effort, presented in compelling fashion to enable listeners to distinguish fact from fancy"
Paul Hume, WGMS (Rockville, Md.) for **A Variable Feast**, in which "critic Hume shares with listeners his vast knowledge of composers and their compositions in a superb blend of creative elements"
WHA (Madison, Wis.) for ***Earplay***, "a high quality radio theater combining works of talented authors with top-flight dramatic talent"
KSJN (St. Paul, Minn.) for ***The Prairie Was Quiet*** "a magnificent portrait of the richness of life on the prairie"
KPFA (Berkeley, Cal.) for the ***Science Story*** series, which "removes science from the laboratory and places it in everyday life in such a way as to make it understandable to the average person"
National Public Radio (Washington, D.C.) for ***Crossroads: Sea Island Sketches***, "off the coast of Georgia and South Carolina are a reservoir for the most distinctive African-American culture left in the United States"
WHLN (Harlan, Ky.) for coverage of the floods in the area "in the finest tradition of local broadcasting."

TELEVISION

KABC-TV (Los Angeles) for ***Police Accountability*** a part of ***Eyewitness News***, "an example of a local TV station serving the public interest in the vital issue of access to information"
KCMO-TV (Kansas City, Mo.) for ***Where Have All the Flood Cars Gone?***, a part of ***Eyewitness News***, an investigative effort in which KCMO traced flood-damaged automobiles to the buyers, resulting in a major insurance company reclaiming the damaged cars and making proper settlement with purchasers
WNBC-TV, (New York) ***F.I.N.D. Investigative Reports*** "for an impressive use of resources of a great metropolitan television station to effect something for the common good"
WNET-TV (New York) and **WETA** (Arlington, Va.) for ***The MacNeil/Lehrer Report*** "consistently thorough and well-balanced views of timely and important issues"
WBTV (Charlotte, N.C.) for ***The Rowe String Quartet Plays on Your Imagination***, in which the quartet and the North Carolina Dance Theater combined to "act out" the fantasies of people attending a concert"
Lorimar Productions for the ***ABC Theater*** presentation of "Green Eyes", "a touching, moving treatment of the story of a young, black veteran of the Vietnam war who goes back to the scene of that conflict searching for the child he fathered but left behind"
David Wolper and **ABC-TV**, for ***Roots***, "dramatically exposing us to an aspect of our history that many of us never knew but all of us will never forget"
Norman Lear, for ***All In the Family***, "for giving us comedy with a social conscience"
London Weekend Television, (London, England) for ***Upstairs Downstairs***, "that superb British series which captured the hearts of Americans and added luster to the PBS stations that carried it"
MTM Enterprises for ***The Mary Tyler Moore Show***, "for a consistent standard of excellence—and for a sympathetic portrayal of a career woman in today's changing society"
Steve Allen, KCET (Los Angeles) ***Meeting of Minds*** , "for his ingenious recreation of the essence of historical personages who come alive in a theatrical form rich in philosophical fireworks and engaging wit"
NBC-TV (New York) ***Tut: The Boy King***, "for this exceptional accomplishment in bringing outstanding cultural treasures to a widespread public with dramatic force"
Metropolitan Opera Association (New York), ***Live from the Met*** as exemplified by performances of ***La Boheme*** and ***Rigoletto*** which "brought millions of music lovers into the Metropolitan Opera House"
WNET-TV (New York), for ***A Good Dissonance Like a Man*** "an affectionate look at the life of American composer Charles Ives"
Multimedia Program Productions, (Cincinnati), for ***Joshua's Confusion***, "the touching story of a young Amish boy as he deals with his eighteenth-century lifestyle in a twentieth-century world"
NBC-TV, Arthur Rankin and **Jules Bass** for ***The Hobbit***, "a vividly orginal and enchanting version of J.R.R. Tolkien's classic"
WCBS-TV (New York), for ***Camera Three***, for "the consistent high quality of this long-running series which explores th art world"
WPIX (New York), for ***The Lifer's Group—I Am My Brother's Keeper***, "a slice of prison life from the inside"
WNBC-TV (New York), ***Buyline: Betty Furness*** for "her in-depth reporting and her distinction as a public conscience"

WNET-TV (New York), for Police Tapes, "a documentary depicting the South Bronx from a squad car"

1978 **CBS News** (New York), for ***World News Roundup***, a daily roundup of top news stories reported in depth and with authority

National Radio Theatre (Chicago), for imaginative radio drama, classic to fantasy, done with style and flair

WMUK (Kalamazoo, Mich.) for exceptional live radio dramas presented as part of the city's Super Summer Arts Festival

WABE-FM (Atlanta), for ***The Eyewitness Who Wasn't*** an exceptional documentary about one of Georgia's most provacative murder mysteries.

NBC Radio (New York City), for the series ***Second Sunday***, which delved deeply into important current topics of national interest.

National Public Radio (Washington, D.C.) for ***Dialogues On a Tightrope: An Italian Mosaic***, which gave listeners a penetrating look at Italy following the murder of Premier Aldo Moro.

WOCB (W. Yarmouth, Mass.), for ***The Last Voyage of the Cap'n Bill***, a briskly done look at the last days of a famous fishing vessel and the people to whom it mattered most

Jewish Theological Seminary of America for ***The Eternal Light***, a consistently noteworthy religious program broadcast for 35 years on the NBC Radio Network

Bob Keeshan, (New York), who as "Captain Kangaroo" has provided superior entertainment for children and as Bob Keeshan has promoted quality television in all forms

Richard S. Salant (New York), for his staunch defense of the First Amendment guarantee of a free press, especially in the field of electronic journalism

"The Muppets", brain-children of **Jim Henson**, for gentle satire, clever characters, genuine good humor and for high standards for family viewing

Titus Productins, Inc., and **NBC-TV**, for ***Holocaust***, a truly distinguished series that has won international acclaim despite the controversial nature of its subject in some countries of the world

Baptist Radio and TV Commission (Fort Worth, Tex.) for ***A River to the Sea***, broadcast by CBS-TV, a fascinating look at English history from the Roman occupation of Britain to modern times

WDVM-TV (Washington, D.C.) for ***Your Health And Your Wallet***, an exceptional mini-seies focusing on rising medical costs

WENH-TV (Durham, N.H.) for ***Arts In New Hampshire*** which proves that news of the arts can indeed be news, particularly when enhanced by good photography and excellent editing

CBS News (New York), for ***The Battle For South Africa***, a first-rate, in-depth look by anchorman Bill Moyers at the terrorist war waged against the South African government

Tomorrow Entertainment/Medcom Company and the **CBS Television Network** for ***The Body Human: The Vital Connection***, a marvelous and absorbing excursion into the workings of the human brain, with particular focus on medical miracles used to correct brain-related illnesses

Survival Anglia Ltd./World Wildlife Fund and the **NBC Television Network** for ***Mysterious Castles of Clay***, which explored the functioning of termite societies within the huge earthen mounds they build to live in

KDGO-TV (San Francisco) for ***Old Age: Do Not Go Gentle,*** two years in preparation, which reveals with candor the poverty, neglect and fear in which many of our elderly citizens find themselves

WDVM-TV (Washington, D.C.) for ***Race War In Rhodesia***, a one-hour special report by columnist/commentator **Carl T. Rowan** which captured the essence of the conflict in that nation in a manner which enabled viewers to perceive the issues and the situation

KQED (San Francisco) for ***Over Easy***, with host **Hugh Downs** and an able staff who have come to grips with the rights, options and issues of concern to older Americans meaningful both to the old and the not-so-old.

Four D Productions/Trisene Corp. (Hollywood) and **ABC Television Network** for ***Barney Miller***, an example of excellence in scripting, the use of humor with a message and entertainment of value

Newsweek Broadcasting (New York) for ***Cartoon-a-torial***, which has successfully translated the editorial cartoon from the newspaper page to the television screen with humor, style and meaning

KHET (Honolulu) for ***Damien***, the story of the leper priest of Molokai, Joseph deVeuster, who battled bureaucracy, both lay and clerical, to become a legend in his own time

CBS News (New York) for ***30 Minutes***, the excellent television magazine for teen-agers which has effectively grappled with many of the major issues facing young people

M.T.M. Productions (Hollywood) and **CBS-TV** (New York) for ***Lou Grant***, the entertaining yet realistic look at the problems and issues which face those who are involved in the "Fourth Estate"

WAVE-TV (Louisville, Ky.) for ***Whose Child Is This***, a realistic documentary about child abuse from the perspective of the teacher, who is often instrumental in recognizing the problem

WQED (Pittsburgh) for ***A Connecticut Yankee In King Arthur's Court***, the first all-American production, part of the highly acclaimed ***Once Upon A Classic*** series.

Gertrude G. Broderick (Washington, D.C.) and **I. Keith Tyler**, (Columbus, Ohio) for their distinguished service on the Peabody Board

1979 **WCBS Radio** (New York) for ***Follow That Cab: The Great Taxi Rip-off***, which exposed the practice of some New York City cabbies taking advantage of unknowledgeable passengers

WGBH Radio (Boston) for ***Currer Bell, Esquire***, a ***Masterpiece Radio Theatre*** presentation, conceived by and starring Julie Harris in a one-woman performance on the life of Charlotte Bronte

Children's Radio Theatre (Washington, D.C.) for ***Henny Penny Playwrighting Contest***, in which original play scripts by children age 5-13 were performed professional actors exactly as written

Canadian Broadcasting Corp. for ***The Longest Journey***, a documentary of the longest and most traumatic journey of life, the nine months prior to birth

KSJN/Minnesota Public Radio (St. Paul) for ***The Way To 8-A***, a study of the legal process governing commitment to mental institutions in Minnesota

TELEVISION

KTVI (St. Louis, Mo.) for ***The Adventures Of Whistling Sam***, locally produced cartoon comments produced with great humor, sharp satire and sound common sense

WMAQ-TV (Chicago) for "Strip and Search," a ***Unit 5 Investigative Report*** which exposed the practice by Chicago police of routinely strip-searching women brought in on minor charges, including traffic violations

CBS News (New York) for ***CBS News Sunday Morning***, hosted by Charles Kuralt

Sylvia Fine Kaye (Beverly Hills, Cal.) for ***Musical Comedy Tonight***, an entertaining look at American musical comedy through four significant eras.

ABC-TV (New York) for ***Valentine*** a sensitive and sentimental love story of two people in their declining years

ABC-TV (New York) for ***Friendly Fire***, a powerful dramatization of the human tragedy of an American family's involvement in the Vietnam War

CBS-TV (New York) for ***Dummy***, the story of an illiterate black deaf youth, who suffered injustice after his arrest as a murder suspect because of his handicap

NBC-TV (New York) for ***When Hell Was In Session*** an ***NBC Theater*** presentation detailing the true story of Navy Cdr. Jeremiah Denton, a Vietnam prisoner of war for 7½ years

KOOL Television (Phoenix) for ***The Long Eyes Of Kitt Peak***, which gave viewers a look at what has been called "the largest and most complex astronomical research facility on earth"

NBC and the **BBC** for ***Treasures Of the British Crown***, an intriguing look at the priceless paintings and crown jewels of the Royal Collection in Britain, as described by members of the Royal Family

ABC-TV (New York) for ***A Special Gift***, an ***ABC Afterschool Special***, the story of a young boy with two talents: ballet and basketball, and how he comes to reconcile the problems brought on by his unique abilities

KRON-TV (San Francisco) for ***Politics Of Poison***, which exposed public health problems caused by herbicide sprayings in northern California

CBS News (New York) for ***The Boston Goes To China***, coverage of the Boston Symphony Orchestra's trip and the combined concert presented by the Symphony and Peking Philharmonic

Robert Trout, ABC News, for nearly 50 years of service as a thoroughly knowledgeable and articulate commentator on national and international affairs

1980 **NBC Radio** for ***The Hallelujah Caucus***, a Source Report, an incisive and revealing look at the emerging power of the religious "right"—their political action and influence

Minnesota Public Radio (St. Paul) for ***A Prairie Home Companion***, a delightful rendering of down-home music and humor in a conversational style

WNCN Radio (New York) for its overall station performance in broadcasting classical music as exemplified by ***Conversations With Horowitz***

National Public Radio (Washington, D.C.) for ***Jazz Alive***, an exeptional effort to bring jazz to disadvantaged areas of New York City

Canadian Broadcasting Corp. (Toronto) for ***The Wonderful World Of Science***, designed to spark interest and curiosity in young school-aged children

Canadian Broadcasting Corp. (Toronto) for ***Peniel***, from the ***Hornby Collection*** series, the sensitive account of a young woman minister's battle with cancer

San Francisco Opera for the opera radio broadcasts, with intermission features which complement and enhance the operatic experience

Studs Terkel, WFMT Radio (Chicago) for his radio interviews which highlight the essence of America: the working man

CBS News for ***Universe***, a science magazine series exploring the widest range of human curiosity

Mary Nissenson, WTVJ (Miami), for ***Poland: Changing Nation***, an in-depth and professional study of the labor crisis in Poland and its effect on all sectors of Polish society

CBS Entertainment for ***Gideon's Trumpet***, a compelling true story of a Florida convict who alters the course of legal history through a handwritten campaign directed at the United States Supreme Court

NBC and **Paramount Television** for ***Shogun***, a tasteful and exciting adaptation of James Clavell's novel concerning an English navigator who became Shogun of Japan

Sol Taishoff, a true broadcasting pioneer, "who in his 50 years of reporting and interpreting the news in radio and television—and more recently cable—has earned the respect and admiration of the industry he serves with such distinction

Public Broadcasting Service and **Robert Geller** (exec. prod.) for ***The American Short Story*** series, dramatizing the works of American writers

ABC-TV for ***IBM Presents Baryshnikov on Broadway***, a dazzling display of internationally famous ballet dancer Mikhail Baryshnikov's foray into Broadway musical dance classics

Elaine Green, WCPO/TV (Cincinnati) for her extreme poise and professionalism in conducting a searching personal interview with a captor who held her a gunpoint

ABC for ***Amber Waves***, a strong statement concerning the work ethic in America and how it influences and shapes our destinies

CBS Entertainment for ***Playing for Time***, the dramatic memoirs of an Auschwitz survivor who, as a member of an all-woman orchestra, lives through the horror, indignity and degradation of a Nazi concentration camp

British Broadcasting Corp. (London), for ***All Creatures Great and Small***, "which portrays the real happenings in the life of a small town veterinarian in England's Yorkshire countryside with warmth and charm"

Carroll O'Connor for ***Edith's Death***, an episode of ***Archie Bunker's Place***, "in which his sensitive reaction to the loss of his beloved Edith is so profound, so moving and so real that it becomes more than performance—it has all the agony of real grief"

KCET, Adrian Malone and **Carl Sagan** for ***Cosmos***, a visually beautiful adventure into the world of science, designed to appeal to all ages

Maryland Instructional Television, (Owings Mills.) for ***Terra: Our World***, a look at the world and its problems in a manner designed to stimulate young minds

WQED (Pittsburgh) and **National Geographic Society** for ***National Geographic Specials***, unsurpassed excellence in documentaries as exemplified by "Mysteries of the Mind", "The Supeliners: Twilight of an Era," and "The Invisible World"

KTEH, Carol Mon Pere and **Sandra Nichols** for ***The Battle Of Westlands***, a concise study of the struggle between agribusiness giants and small farmers, and its effect on the American consumer

Phil Donahue host of ***The Donahue Show***, for sensitive yet probing interviews on issues relevant to today's society

KQED-TV (San Francisco) for ***Broken Arrow: Can A Nuclear Weapons Accident Happen Here?***, a documentary which examines the history of nuclear weapons accidents and focuses on San Francisco in particular

KUED-TV and **WNET/13**, for ***The MX Debate***, a special edition of ***Bill Moyers' Journal***, a clear and complete statement of MX Missile system conflict, bringing to light important questions concerning the consequences of MX deployment

Walter Cronkite, CBS News, for his unsurpassed skills and integrity in reporting the news

Gold Medal Awards

PHOTOPLAY
205 E. 42nd St., New York, N.Y. 10017 (212/340-7500)

The Photoplay Gold Medal Awards are made annually for the most popular television program and performers. The most recent awards were based on ballots of more than 60,000 readers of the magazine.

TV SHOW

1966 ***The Big Valley***
1967 ***Star Trek***
1968 ***Mod Squad***
1969 ***Marcus Welby, M.D.***
1970 ***The Partridge Family***
1971 ***All In the Family***
1972 ***The Waltons***
1973 ***The Waltons***
1974 ***Rhoda***
1975 ***Starsky & Hutch*** (evening)
The Young and The Restless (daytime)
1976 ***Starsky & Hutch*** (evening)
Days of Our Lives (daytime)
I Love Lucy (all-time favorite)

Current Status Unknown

COMEDY STAR

1967 **Carol Burnett**
1968 **Carol Burnett**
1969 **Carol Burnett**
1970 **Carol Burnett**
1971 **Carol Burnett**
1972 **Paul Lynde**
1973 **No award**
1974 **Jack Oakie** (Award renamed the Joakie)
1975 **Henry Winkler**
1976 **Henry Winkler**

Current Status Unknown

VARIETY STAR

1973 **Sammy Davis**
1974 **Elvis Presley**
1975 **Elvis Presley**
1976 **Elvis Presley**

Current Status Unknown

FAVORITE MALE TV STAR

1976 **Michael Glasser,** *Starsky and Hutch*

Current Status Unknown

FAVORITE FEMALE TV STAR

1977 **Farrah Fawcett-Majors,** *Charlie's Angels*

Current Status Unknown

FAVORITE MALE DAYTIME TV STAR

1976 **Bill Hayes,** *Days of Our Lives*

Current Status Unknown

FAVORITE FEMALE DAYTIME TV STAR

1976 **Susan Seaforth Hayes,** *Days of Our Lives*

Current Status Unknown

FAVORITE YOUNG STAR

1976 **Kristy McNichol,** *Family*

Current Status Unknown

FAVORITE LIVE ANIMAL STAR

1976 **Fred** (cockatoo), *Baretta*

Current Status Unknown

Photoplay also gives awards for the most popular male and female newcomers, which include (in fact, in recent years have been dominated by) television personalities.

Sigma Delta Chi Awards

SOCIETY OF PROFESSIONAL JOURNALISTS/SIGMA DELTA CHI
840 N Lake Shore Dr., Chicago, Ill. 60611 (312/664-4200)

Sigma Delta Chi Awards for Distinguished Service in Journalism annually honor noteworthy performance in broadcast and print journalism. Bronze medallions and plaques are presented to the winners. Society chapters nominate individuals and stations for final selection. (See pp. 129-133 for winners of Sigma Delta Chi Awards in the print media).

RADIO REPORTING

1946 **Allen Stout**
1947 **James C. McNamara**
1948 **George J. O'Connor**
1949 **Sid Pletzsch**
1950 **Jack E. Krueger**
1951 **Jim Monroe**
1952 **Charles and Eugene Jones**
1953 **Gordon Gammack**
1954 **Richard Chapman**
1955 **John Chancellor**
1956 **Edward J. Green**
1957 **Dave Muhlstein**
1958 **Winston Burdett**
1959 **Donald H. Weston**
1960 **Frederick A. Goerner**
1961 **KDKA News Staff** (Pittsburgh, Pa.)
Wip Robinson and Frank O'Roark, WSVA (Harrisonburg, Va.)
1962 **WINS News Staff,** (New York)
1963 **WINS News Staff** (New York)
1964 **WNEW News** (New York)
1965 **WNEW News** (New York)
1966 **KTBC Radio News** (Austin, Tex.)

1967 **WJR News** (Detroit, Mich.)
1968 **KFWB News** (Los Angeles, Calif.)
1969 **Ed Joyce,** WCBS (New York)
1970 **Bob White,** KRLD (Dallas, Tex.)
1971 **John Rich,** NBC Radio
1972 **Val Hymes,** WTOP Radio (Washington)
1973 **Eric Engberg,** Group W/Westinghouse Broadcasting
1974 **Jim Mitchell, Gary Franklin, Herb Humphries, and Hank Allison,** KFWB Radio (Los Angeles)
1975 **WHBF AM-FM Radio News Team** (Rock Island, Ill.)
1976 **Mike Lee and Doug Tunnell** (CBS News)
1977 **Paul McGonigle** (KOY Radio, Phoenix)
1978 **WGST Newsradio** (Atlanta)
1979 **ABC Radio News**
1980 **Not available at press time**

PUBLIC SERVICE IN RADIO JOURNALISM

1949 **WTTS** (Bloomington, Ind.)
1950 **WAVZ** (New Haven, Conn.)
1951 **WMAQ** (Chicago)
1952 **WMT** (Cedar Rapids, Iowa)
1953 **CBS Radio Network**
1954 **CBS Radio Network**
1955 **WMAQ** (Chicago)
1956 **CBS Radio Network**
1957 **KNX** (Los Angeles)
1958 **CBS Radio Network**
1959 **WIP** (Philadelphia)
1960 **WBT** (Charlotte, N.C.)
1961 **KNUZ** (Houston Tex.)
1962 **WBZ** (Boston)
1963 **WSB** (Atlanta)
1964 **KSEN** (Shelby, Mont.)
1965 **WCCO** (Minneapolis-St. Paul)
1966 **WIBW** (Topeka, Kans.)
1967 **Westinghouse Broadcasting Co., Inc.**
1968 **WBZ** (Boston)
1969 **WHN** (New York)
1970 **WWDC** (Washington)
1971 **WBZ** (Boston)
1972 **WGAR** (Cleveland)
1973 **WMAL** (Washington)
1974 **WIND** (Chicago)
1975 **WRVA Radio** (Richmond, Va.)
1976 **WCAU-AM Radio News** (Philadelphia)
1977 **WSGN-AM** (Birmingham, Ala.)
1978 **KXL Radio** (Portland, Ore)
1979 **WJR Radio** (Detroit)
1980 **Not available at press time**

EDITORIALIZING ON RADIO

1963 **WRTA** (Altoona, Pa.)
1964 **WXYZ** (Detroit)
1965 **KDKA** (Pittsburgh)
1966 **W-A-I-T** (Chicago)
1967 **WSBA** (York-Lancaster-Harrisburg, Pa.)
1968 **Theodore Jones,** WCRB (Waltham, Mass.)
1969 **WWDC** (Washington)
1970 **WLPR** (Mobile, Ala.)
1971 **WSOC-AM** (Charlotte, N.C.)
1972 **Frank Reynolds,** ABC News (New York)
1973 **WGRC** (Pittsfield, Mass.)
1974 **Jim Branch,** WRFM (New York)
1975 **Charles B. Cleveland,** (WIND Chicago)
1976 **Ed Hinshaw,** WTMJ (Milwaukee)
1977 **Jay Lewis** Alabama Information Network
1978 **KWY Newsradio** (Philadelphia)
1979 **WTLC Radio** (Indianapolis)
1980 **Not available at press time**

TELEVISION REPORTING

1952 **Charles and Eugene Jones**
1953 **No award**
1954 **Spencer Allen**
1955 **Paul Alexander**
Gael Boden
1956 **Ernest Leiser**
Jerry Schwartzkopff
Julian B. Hoshal
Dick Hance
1957 **Jim Bennett**
1958 **WBBM-TV News** (Chicago)
1959 **WGN-TV News** (Chicago)
1960 **WTVJ-TV News** (Miami)
1961 **WKY-TV** (Oklahoma City,)
1962 **KWTV News** (Oklahoma City)
1963 **WBAP-TV** (Fort Worth, Tex.)
1964 **WFGA-TV** (Jacksonville, Fla.)
1965 **Morley Safer,** CBS News
1966 **WSB-TV News** (Atlanta)
1967 **John Laurence,** CBS News
1968 **Station KNXT** (Los Angeles)
1969 **WCCO** News (Minneapolis)
1970 **KBTV** (Denver)
1971 **Robert Schakne,** CBS News
1972 **Laurens Pierce,** CBS News
1973 **Steve Young and Roger Sims,** CBS News
1974 **Lee Louis,** KGTV10 (San Diego)
1975 **WHAS-TV News** (Louisville, Ky.)
1976 **KMJ-TV** (Fresno, Calif.)
1977 **KPIX-TV** Eyewitness News Team, (San Francisco)
1978 **Steve Howell** and **John Britton,** KCST-TV (San Diego)
1979 **ABC-TV News** and **Bob Dyk**
1980 **Not available at press time**

PUBLIC SERVICE IN TV JOURNALISM

1952 **WBNS-TV** (Columbus, Ohio)
1953 **WHAS-TV** (Louisville, Ky.)
1954 **Dumont Television Network**
American Broadcasting Co.
1955 **KAKE-TV** (Wichita, Kans.)
1956 **KPIX** (San Francisco)
1957 **WBZ-TV** (Boston)
1958 **KNXT** (Hollywood, Calif.)
1959 **WBZ-TV** (Boston)
1960 **NBC Television Network**
1961 **Station KHOU-TV** (Houston, Tex.)
1962 **KGW-TV** (Portland, Ore.)
1963 **KDKA-TV** (Pittsburgh)
National Broadcasting Co.
1964 **Columbia Broadcasting System**
1965 **WABC-TV** (New York)
1966 **KLZ-TV** (Denver)
1967 **National Broadcasting Co.**
1968 **WIBW-TV** (Topeka, Kans.)
1969 **WDSU-TV** (New Orleans)
1970 **KING-TV** (Seattle)
1971 **Columbia Broadcasting System**
1972 **WABC-TV** (New York)
1973 **WSOC-TV News** (Charlotte, N.C.)
1974 **ABC News**
1975 **WCKT-TV** (Miami)
1976 **KNXT-TV** (Los Angeles)
1977 **KOOL-TV** (Phoenix)
1978 **WCCO-TV** (Minneapolis)

1979 **KXAS** (Fort Worth-Dallas)
1980 **Not available at press time**

EDITORIALIZING ON TELEVISION

1963 **Tom Martin,** KFDA-TV (Amarillo, Tex.)
1964 **KDKA-TV** (Pittsburgh)
1965 **WTOP-TV** (Washington)
1966 **WFBM-TV** (Indianapolis, Ind.)
1967 **KWTV** (Oklahoma City)
1968 **WOOD-TV** (Grand Rapids, Mich.)
1969 **KCPX Television** (Salt Lake City)
1970 **WCCO-TV** (Minneapolis)
1971 **Robert Schulman,** WHAS-TV (Louisville, Ky.)
1972 **WCKT-TV** (Miami)
1973 **KRON-TV** (San Francisco)
1974 **Jay Lewis,** WSFA-TV (Montgomery, Ala.)
1975 **Don McGaffin and Charles Royer,** KING-TV (Seattle)
1976 **WCVB-TV** (Boston)
1977 **Rich Adams,** WTOP-TV (Washington, D.C.)
1978 **Peter Kahler,** WCBS-TV (New York)
1979 **KPIX-TV** (San Francisco)
1980 **Not available at press time**

RADIO OR TV COMMENTARY

1961 **KDKA-TV** (Pittsburgh)
1962 **Harold Keen, WFMB-TV** (San Diego, Calif.)

RADIO OR TV NEWSWRITING

1939 **Albert Warner**
1940 **Cecil Brown**
1942 **Fulton Lewis, Jr.**
1943 **No award**
1944 **No award**
1945 **No award**
1946 **Harry M. Cochran**
1947 **Alex Dreier**
1948 **Merrill Mueller**
1949 **Elmer Davis**
1950 **Leo O'Brien**
Howard Maschmeier
1951 **William E. Griffith, Jr.**
1952 **Clifton Utley**
1953 **Charles J. Chatfield**
1954 **Reuven Frank**
1955 **Charles Shaw**
1956 **Howard K. Smith**
1957 **Jerry Rosholt**
1958 **Harold R. Meier**
1959 **Gene Marine**
1960 **David Brinkley**

Lowell Thomas Award

International Platform Association
2564 Berkshire Rd., Cleveland Hts., Ohio 44106
(216/932-0505)

The Lowell Thomas Award, which consists of an engraved bowl, is given annually to the individual judged by the IPA Committee, Lowell Thomas and Dan T. Moore, to be the outstanding broadcast journalist of the year.

1974 **Lowell Thomas**
1975 **Eric Sevareid**
1976 **Howard K. Smith**
1977 **Barbara Walters**
1978 **Harry Reasoner**
1979 **Jim Lehrer**
1980 **Frank Reynolds**

Television-Radio Awards
Laurel Award for Television

WRITERS GUILD OF AMERICA, WEST
8955 Beverly Blvd., Los Angeles, Calif. 90048
(213/550-1000)

The annual Television-Radio Awards honor outstanding scripts, which are submitted to a three-judge panel for evaluation and selection. Awards are made in several categories. The early awards are listed by year. Later awards, when the categories became consistent, are listed by category and year.

1956 **Donald S. Sandforc** (teleplay) and **John Nesbitt,** ("The Golden Junkman" on *Telephone Time*), One-Half Hour TV Anthology Drama
Kenneth Kolb ("She Walks in Beauty" on *Medic*), One-Half Hour TV Episodic Drama
Leonard Stern and Sydney Zelinka ("The $99,000 Answer" on *The Jackie Gleason Show*), One-Half Hour TV Situation Comedy
Hal Kanter, Howard Leeds, Harry Winkler and Everett Greenbaum, (*The George Gobel Show*), Comedy-Variety Certificate of Excellence
Rod Serling ("Requiem for a Heavyweight" on *Playhouse 90*), One Hour or More TV Drama
J. Harvey Howells ("Goodbye, Grey Flannel" on *Robert Montgomery Presents*), One Hour TV Comedy
John Whedon and George Roy Hill ("A Night to Remember" on *Kraft TV Theatre*), TV Documentary
Thelma Robinson (teleplay) and **Warren Wilson** and **Claire Kennedy** (story) ("The Visitor" on *Lassie*), Children's Program
1957 **Joseph Mindel** ("Degree of Freedom"), One Half-Hour TV Anthology Drama
Everett DeBaun ("Pearls of Talimeco" on *Jim Bowie*), One-Half Hour TV Episodic Drama
Jerry McNeely ("The Staring Match" on *Studio One*), One Hour Anthology Drama
Gene Roddenberry ("Helen of Abajinian" on *Have Gun, Will Travel*), Television Western, Any Length
Kenneth Enochs ("Elmer the Rainmaker" on *Circus Boy*), Children's Program
Erick Moll ("The Fabulous Irishman" on *Playhouse 90*), Any Program More Than One Hour in Length
Sydney Zelinka and A.J. Russell ("Papa Bilko" on *The Phil Silvers Show*), One-Half Hour or Less TV Comedy and Sketches
Irwin Rosten ("The Human Explosion"), TV Documentary
Devery Freeman ("The Great American Hoax"), One Hour TV Comedy
1958 **Valentine Davies and Kurt Vonnegut, Jr.** ("Auf Wiedersehen" on *The GE Theatre*), Best Script, 30 Minutes or Less Program Length
Shimon Wincelberg ("The Sea is Boiling Hot" on *Kraft Television Theatre*), Best Script, 60 Minutes or Less, But More Than 30 Minutes Program Length
Rod Serling ("A Town Has Turned to Dust" on *Playhouse 90*), Best Script, More Than 60 Minutes Program Length
Steven Fleishman ("Face of Crime" on *20th Century*), TV Documentary-News Analysis or News in Depth
Sherwood Schwartz, Jesse Goldstein and Dave O'Brien ("Freddie's Thanksgiving" on *The Red Skel-*

ton Show), Best Comedy/Variety or Variety, Any Length

1959 **Christopher Knopf** ("Interrogation" on *Zane Grey Theater*), One-Half Hour TV Anthology Drama
Richard Matheson ("Yawkey" on *Lawman*), One-Half Hour TV Episodic Drama
Tony Webster ("Call Me Back" on *The Art Carney Show*), TV Anthology, More Than One-Half Hour
William Spier ("The Assassination of Cermak" on *The Untouchables*), Television Episodic, More Than One-Half Hour
Irving G. Nieman ("Child of Our Times" on *Playhouse 90*), Television Adaptation, Any Length
Dorothy Cooper ("Margaret's Old Flame" on *Father Knows Best*), TV Episodic Comedy, Any Length
Max Wilk and A.J. Russell ("The Fabulous Fifties"), TV Variety, Any Length
Richard Hanser ("Mark Twain's America" on *Project 20*), TV Documentary, Any Length
Earle Luby ("Down Range" on *20th Century*), TV Documentary, Any Length

ANTHOLOGY DRAMA, ANY LENGTH/TV ANTHOLOGY, ANY LENGTH/BEST ANTHOLOGY/BEST ORIGINAL ANTHOLOGY

1961 **Christopher Knopf** ("Death of the Temple Bay" on *The June Allyson Show*)
1962 **Richard Alan Simmons** ("The Price of Tomatoes" on *The Dick Powell Show*)
1963 **Richard Alan Simmons** ("The Last of the Big Spenders" on *The Dick Powell Show*)
1964 **Howard Rodman** ("The Game With Glass Pieces" on *Chrysler Theater*)
1965 **Harlan Ellison** ("Demon With a Glass Hand" on *Outer Limits*)
1966 **S. Lee Pogostin** ("The Game" on *Chrysler Theatre*)
1967 **S. Lee Pogostin** ("Crazier Than Cotton" on *Chrysler Theatre*)
1968 **Earl Hamner** ("Heidi")
1969 **George Bellak** ("Sadbird" on *CBS Playhouse*)
1970 **Tracy Keenan Wynn and Marvin Schwartz** ("Tribes" on *ABC Movie of the Week*)
1971 **Carol Sobieski and Howard Rodman** ("The Neon Ceiling" on *NBC World Premiere*)
1972 **Richard Levinson and William Link** ("That Certain Summer" on *ABC Movie of the Week*)
1973 **Abby Mann** ("The Marcus-Nelson Murders" on *CBS Movie of the Week*)
1974 **Joel Oliansky, story by William Sackhein and Joel Oliansky** ("The Law" on *NBC World Premiere*)
1975 **Jerome Kass** (*Queen of the Stardust Ballroom*)
1976 **Robert Collins** ("The Quality of Mercy" on *NBC Thursday Night Movie*)
1977 **Carol Sobieski** ("Christmas Sunshine" on *NBC World Premiere*)
1978 **Christopher Knopf**, "Scott Joplin — King of Ragtime" on *NBC World Premiere*
1979 **Millard Lampell** and **Dorothea Petrie**, "Orphan Train" on *CBS Motion Pictures*
1980 **David Chase**, *Off the Minnesota Strip*

EPISODIC DRAMA, ANY LENGTH/TV EPISODIC, ANY LENGTH/BEST DRAMATIC EPISODIC

1961 **Barry Trivers** ("The Fault in Our Stars" on *Naked City*)
1962 **Kenneth Rosen and Howard Rodman** ("Today the Man Who Kills the Ants is Coming" on *Naked City*)
1963 **Lawrence B. Marcus** ("Man Out of Time" on *Route 66*)
1964 **Arnold Perl** ("Who Do You Kill?" on *East Side/West Side*)
1965 **John D.F. Black** ("With a Hammer in His Hand, Lord, Lord!" on *Mr. Novak*)
1966 **David Ellis** ("No Justice for the Judge" on *Trials of O'Brien*)
1967 **Harlan Ellison** ("The City on the Edge of Forever" on *Star Trek*)
1968 **Robert Lewin** ("To Kill a Madman" on *Judd for the Defense*)
1969 **Robert Lewin** ("An Elephant in a Cigar Box" on *Judd for the Defense*)
1970 **David Rintels** ("A Continual Roar of Musketry" on *The Bold Ones*)
1971 **Thomas Y. Drake, Herb Bermann, Jerrold Freedman and Bo May** ("Par for the Course" on *The Psychiatrist*)
1972 **Herman Miller** ("King of the Mountain" on *Kung Fu*)
1973 **Harlan Ellison** ("Phoenix Without Ashes" on *The Starlost*)
1974 **Jim Byrnes** ("Thirty a Month and Found" on *Gunsmoke*)
1975 **Arthur Ross** (teleplay) and **Stephen Kandel** (story) ("Prior Consent" on *The Law*)
1976 **Loring Mandel** ("Crossing the River" on *Sandburg's Lincoln*)
1977 **Mark Rodgers** ("Pressure Point" on *Police Story*)
1978 **Seth Freeman**, "Prisoner" on *Lou Grant*
1979 **Leon Tokatyan**, "Vet" on *Lou Grant*
1980 **Stephen J. Cannell**, *Tenspeed and Brown Shoe* pilot

MULTI-PART LONG FORM SERIES

1978 **John Wilder**, "Only the Rocks Live Forever," Chapt. I of *Centennial*
1979 **Gwen Bagni** and **Paul Dubov**, *Backstairs at the White House*, Part I
1980 **Ernest Tidyman**, *Guyana Tragedy: The Story of Jim Jones*, Part I

TV COMEDY-VARIETY, ANY LENGTH

1962 **Gary Belkin and Nat Hiken** ("I Won't Go!" on *Car 54, Where Are You?*)
1963 **Everett Greenbaum and Jim Fritzell** ("Barney's First Car" on *The Andy Griffith Show*)

BEST COMEDY, EPISODIC

1964 **Bill Idelson and Sam Bobrick** ("The Shoplifters" on *The Andy Griffith Show*)
Martin Ragaway ("My Husband is the Best One" on *The Dick Van Dyke Show*)
1965 **Dale McRaven and Carl Kleinschmitt** ("Br-room Br-room" on *The Dick Van Dyke Show*)
1966 **Jack Winter** ("You Ought to Be in Pictures" on *The Dick Van Dyke Show*)
1967 **Marvin Marx, Walter Stone and Gordon Rod Parker** ("Movies Are Better Than Ever" on *The Jackie Gleason Show*)
1968 **Bill Idelson and Sam Bobrick** ("Viva Smart" on *Get Smart*)
1969 **Allan Burns** ("Funny Boy" on *Room 222*)
1970 **Richard DeRoy** ("The Valediction" on *Room 222*)
1971 **Martin Cohan** ("Thoroughly Unmilitant Milly" on *The Mary Tyler Moore Show*)
1972 **Larry Gelbart** ("Chief Surgeon Who" on *M*A*S*H*)
1973 **Bob Weiskopf and Bob Schiller** ("Walter's Problem," Part II, on *Maude*)

1974 **Larry Gelbart and Laurence Marks** ("O.R." on *M*A*S*H**)
1975 **Everett Greenbaum, Jim Fritzell and Larry Gelbart** ("Welcome to Korea" on *M*A*S*H**)
1976 **Alan Alda** ("Dear Sigmund" on *M*A*S*H**)
1977 **Larry Rhine and Mel Tolkin** ("Archie Gets the Business" on *All in the Family*)
1978 **Gary David Goldberg**, "Baby It's Cold Outside" on *M*A*S*H*
1979 **Thad Mumford** and **Dan Wilcox**, "Are You Now, Margaret?" on *M*A*S*H*
Ken Estin, "The Reluctant Fighter" on *Taxi*
1980 **Stan Daniels** and **Ed Weinberger**, "The Censors" on *The Associates*

COMEDY ANTHOLOGY, ORIGINAL OR ADAPTED

1980 **Carmen Culver**, *To Race the Wind*

BEST COMEDY VARIETY

1964 **Herbert Baker, Sheldon Keller, Saul Ilson, Ernest Chambers, Gary Belkin, Paul Mazursky, Larry Tucker and Mel Tolkin** (*The Danny Kaye Show*)
1965 **Sheldon Keller, Gary Belkin, Ernest Chambers, Larry Tucker, Paul Mazursky, Billy Barnes, Ron Friedman and Mel Tolkin** (*The Danny Kaye Show*)
1966 **Garry Marshall and Jerry Belson** ("The Road to Lebanon" on *The Danny Thomas Special*)

BEST COMEDY, NON-EPISODIC

1967 **Mel Brooks, Sam Denoff, Bill Persky, Carl Reiner and Mel Tolkin** (*The Sid Caesar, Imogene Coca, Carl Reiner, Howard Morris Special*)
1968 **Sam Bobrick, Ron Clark, Danny Simon, Marty Farrell and Martin Ragaway** (*Alan King's Wonderful World of Aggravation*)

BEST VARIETY

1969 **Herbert Baker and Treva Silverman** (*Norman Rockwell's America*)
1970 **Gary Belkin, Peter Bellwood, Thomas Meehan, Herb Sargent and Judith Viorst** (*Annie, the Women in the Life of a Man*)
1971 **Don Hinkley, Jack Mendelsohn, Stan Hart, Larry Siegel, Woody Kling, Roger Beatty, Arnie Rosen, Kenny Solms and Gail Parent (writing supervised by Arthur Julian)** (*The Carol Burnett Show*)
1972 **Neil Simon** (*The Trouble With People*)
1973 **Norman Barasch, Jack Burns, Avery Schreiber, Bob Ellison, Bob Garland, Carroll Moore and George Yanok** (*The Burns & Schreiber Comedy Hour*)
1974 **Ed Simons, Gary Belkin, Roger Beatty, Arnie Kogen, Bill Richmond, Gene Perret, Rudy DeLuca, Barry Levinson, Dick Clair and Jenna McMahon** (*The Carol Burnett Show*)
1975 **Sybil Adelman, Barbara Gallagher, Gloria Banta, Pat Nardo, Stuart Birnbaum, Matt Neuman, Lorne Michaels, Marilyn Miller, Earl Pomerantz, Rosie Ruthchild, Lily Tomlin and Jane Wagner** (*Lily*)
1976 **Anne Beatts, Chevy Chase, Al Franken, Tom Davis, Lorne Michaels, Marilyn Suzanne Miller, Michael O'Donoghue, Herb Sargent, Tom Schiller, Rosie Schuster and Alan Zweibel** (*NBC Saturday Night Live*)
1977 **Elon Packard, Fred S. Fox and Seaman Jacob** (*The George Burns One-Man Show*)
1978 **Jerry Juhl, Chris Langham, Jim Henson** and **Don Hinkley**, *The Muppet Show* with Marisa Berenson
1979 **Jerry Juhl, David Odell, Jim Henson** and **Don Hinkley**, *The Muppet Show* with **Liza Minelli**
Dan Ackroyd, Anne Beatts, James Downey, Brian Doyle-Murray, Al Franken, Tom Davis, Brian McConnachie, Lorne Michaels, Don Novello, Herb Sargent, Tom Schiller, Rose Shuster, Walter Williams and **Alan Zweibel**, *Saturday Night Live* with **Richard Benjamin**
1980 **Michael Elias, Jack Handey, Carmen Finestra, Robert Garland, Con Turner** and **Steve Martin**, *Comedy is Not Pretty*

BEST VARIETY SPECIAL

1974 **Norman Steinberg, Alan Uger, Howard Albrecht, Sol Weinstein, John Boni, Thad Mumford, Chevy Chase, Herb Sargent and Alan King** (*Alan King's Energy Crisis, Rising Prices and Assorted Vices Comedy Hour*)

ADAPTATION FROM MATERIAL NOT ORIGINALLY WRITTEN FOR TELEVISION /BEST ADAPTATION BEST ANTHOLOGY (ADAPTATION)

1961 **Bernard C. Schoenpeld** ("The Little Mermaid" on *The Shirley Temple Show*)
1962 **Gordon Russell** ("The Forgery" on *DuPont Show of the Month*)
1963 **Richard DeRoy and Iris Dornfeld** ("Jeeney Ray" on *Alcoa Premiere*)
1964 **Mark Rodgers, Russel Crouse and Clarence Greene** ("One Day in the Life of Ivan Denisovich" on *Chrysler Theatre*)
1965 **Robert Hartung** ("The Magnificent Yankee" on *Hallmark Hall of Fame*)
1966 **Robert Hartung** ("Lamp at Midnight" on *Hallmark Hall of Fame*)
1967 Category not voted on; included in "Best Anthology" above.
1968 Category not voted on; included in "Best Anthology" above.
1969 Category not voted on; included in "Best Anthology" above.
1970 Category not voted on; included in "Best Anthology" above.
1971 **William Blinn** ("Brian's Song" on *ABC Movie of the Week*)
1972 **Richard Matheson** ("The Night Stalker" on *ABC Movie of the Week*)
1973 **Carol Sobieski** ("Sunshine" on *CBS Movie of the Week*)
1974 **Tracy Keenan Wynn** ("The Autobiography of Miss Jane Pittman" on *CBS Movie of the Week*)
1975 **Fay Kanin** ("Hustling" on *ABC Movie of the Week*)
David W. Rintels ("Fear on Trial" on *CBS Movie of the Week*)
1976 **Stewart Stern** ("Sybil" on *NBC Movie*)
1977 **Steven Gethers** ("A Circle of Children" on *CBS Movie*)
1978 **Stewart Stern,** "A Christmas to Remember" on *CBS Movie Premiere*
Leonne Elder III, "A Woman Called Moses" on *NBC Movie Premiere*
1979 **Fay Kanin**, "Friendly Fire"
1980 **David Rintels**, *Gideon's Trumpet*

TV DOCUMENTARY (Any Length)

1961 **Philip H. Reisman, Jr.** ("The Real West" on *NBC Project 20*)
1962 **Arthur Holch** ("Walk in My Shoes" on *Bell & Howell Close-Up*)

1963 **Frank DeFelitta and Robert Northshield** ("Chosen Child")
1964 **Albert Waller** ("In the American Grain: William Carlos Williams" on *Eye on New York*)
1965 **Robert Rogers** ("Vietnam: It's a Mad War")
1966 **Andrew A. Rooney and Richard Ellison** ("The Great Love Affair")

BEST DOCUMENTARY (Features)/BEST DOCUMENTARY (Other Than Current Events)/BEST DOCUMENTARY FEATURE/BEST FEATURE DOCUMENTARY

1967 **Theodore Strauss and Terry Sanders** ("The Legend of Marilyn Monroe")
1968 **James Fleming, Blaine Littell and Richard F. Siemanowski** ("Africa")
Perry Wolff and Andrew Rooney ("Black History—Lost, Stolen or Strayed" on *Of Black America*)
1969 **David Davidson** ("The Ship That Wouldn't Die: U.S.S. Franklin")
Shimon Wincelberg ("Max Brod: Portrait of the Artist in His Own Right")
1970 **Marianna Norris** ("Gertrude Stein: A Biography")
1971 **Andrew A. Rooney** ("An Essay on War")
1972 **Robert Northshield** ("Guilty by Reason of Race")
1973 **Marc Siegel** ("Rendezvous With Freedom")
1974 **Marlene Sanders** ("The Right to Die")
1975 **Irv Drasnin** ("The Guns of Autumn")
1976 **Paul W. Greenberg** ("Friends, Romans, Communists")
1977 **George Crile, III** ("The CIA's Secret Army")
1978 **Robert R. Fuisz**, *The Body Human: The Vital Connection*
1979 **Robert B. Fuisz** and **Hank Whittemore**, *The Body Human: The Magic Sense*
1980 **Irwin Rosten**, *Mysteries of the Mind*

BEST DOCUMENTARY (Current Events)

1967 **Robert Rogers** ("The Battle for Asia," Part I, "Thailand, The New Front" on *NBC News*)
1967 **Peter Davis and Martin Carr** ("Hunger in America" on *CBS Reports*)
1969 **Harry E. Morgan** ("Fathers and Sons")
1970 **Craig B. Fisher** ("Survival on the Prairie")
1971 **Peter Davis** ("Vietnam Hindsight," Parts I and II)
1972 **Robert Northshield** ("Suffer the Little Children")
1973 **James Fleming** ("The First and Essential Freedom")
1974 **Howard Stringer** ("The Palestinians")
1975 **Andrew Rooney** ("Mr. Rooney Goes to Washington")
1976 **Andrew Rooney** ("Mr. Rooney Goes to Dinner")
1977 **Marc Siegel** ("The Panama Canal—A Test of Conscience")
1978 **Perry Wolff**, *CBS News Special, 1968*
1979 **William Peters**, *Death of a Family*
1980 **Michael Connor, Kathy Slobogin, Steve Singer** and **Peggy Brim**, *The Killing Ground — An Update*

BEST TV NEWSWRITING

1972 **Charles West, Rabun Matthews, Gary Gates and John Merriman** (*CBS Evening News with Walter Cronkite*)
Richard Cannon ("Land Fury" on *Six o'Clock Report*, WCBS-TV)
1973 **Charles West, Rabun Matthews and Carol Ross** (*CBS Evening News with Walter Cronkite*)
1974 **Charles West** ("Two Presidents: Transition in the White House")
1975 **Sandor Polster, William H. Moran and Carol Ross** (*CBS Evening News with Walter Cronkite*)
1976 **William Moran, Ray Gandolf and Charles L. West** ("In Celebration of US, July 4, 1976")
1977 **Lee Townsend, Sandor M. Polster, Charles West, Allison Owings and Mary Earle** (*CBS Evening News with Walter Cronkite*)
1978 **Hugh Heckman, John Mosedale** and **Sandor M. Polster**, *CBS Evening News* (Nov. 21, 1978)
1979 **John M. Mosedale, Gordon Joseloff, Charles West** and **Sandor M. Polster**, *CBS Evening News* (Mar. 20, 1979)
Mervin Block, a selection of anchor leadins at the political conventions
Raphael Rothstein, Obituary on the Shah of Iran

BEST DAYTIME SERIAL

1972 **Loring Mandel, Nancy Ford, Kim Louis Ringwald and Max McClellan** (*Love of Life*)
1973 **Ralph Ellis and Eugene Hunt with Bibi Wein and Jane Chambers** (*Search for Tomorrow*)
1974 **Ann Marcus, Joyce Perry, Pamela Wylie and Ray Goldstone** (*Search for Tomorrow*)
1975 **Claire Labine, Paul Mayer, Mary Munisteri and Allan Leicht** (*Ryan's Hope*)
1976 **Claire Labine, Paul Avila Mayer and Mary Munisteri** (*Ryan's Hope*)
1977 **Claire Labine, Paul Avila Mayer, Judith Pinsker and Mary Munisteri** (*Ryan's Hope*)
1978 **Claire Labine, Jeffrey Lane, Paul Avila Mayer, Mary Munisteri** and **Judith Pinkster**, *Ryan's Hope*
1979 **Jerome Dobson** and **Bridget Dobson, Chuck Dizenzo, Parri Dizenzo, Robert White** and **Phyllis White, Robert Soderberg** and **Jean Rouverol**, *Guiding Light*
1980 **Claire Labine, Paul Avila Mayer, Mary Munisteri** and **Jeffrey Lane**, *Ryan's Hope*

BEST CHILDREN'S SHOW SCRIPT

1975 **Yanna Brandt** (*The Superlative Horse*)
1976 **Arthur Barron** (*Blind Sunday*)
1977 **Art Wallace** (*Little Vic*)
1978 **Irma Reichert** and **Daryl Warner**, *Mom and Dad Can't Hear Me*
1979 **Edward Pomerantz**, *New York City Too Far From Tampa Blues*
1980 **Paul A. Golding**, *The Secret of Lost Valley*

RADIO DRAMA, ANY LENGTH

1956 **Allan Sloane** ("Bring On The Angela")
1957 **Thomas F. Hanley, Jr.** ("Misfire" on *Suspense*)

RADIO COMEDY, ANY LENGTH

1956 **Si Rose** (*The Edgar Bergen Show*)
1957 **Stan Freberg and Pete Barnum** ("Incident at Los Voraces" on *The Stan Freberg Show*)

RADIO SERIES OR SERIAL EPISODE, ANY LENGTH

1956 **Stanley Niss** (*The Penny*)

RADIO DOCUMENTARY

1956 **Robert S. Greene** ("Decision For Freedom")
1957 **Jules Maitland** ("Judgment")

BEST RADIO SCRIPT (Any Type, Any Length) /BEST RADIO/RADIO DOCUMENTARY

1959 **Jay McMullen** ("Who Killed Michael Farmer" on *Unit One Series*)
1960 **George E. Lord and Ivan R. Ladizinsky** ("One Deadly Drink")
1961 **Robert S. Greene** ("The Lincoln Story")

1962 **Joseph Mindel** ("The Hand of Esau" on *The Eternal Light*
1963 **Marlene Sanders** ("Battle of the Warsaw Ghetto")
1964 **Sol Panitz** ("The Long Silence")
1965 **Sol Panitz** ("The Profit of Change")
1966 **Sol Panitz** ("The Legend of LeMans")
1967 **Peter Woititz** ("A Deadly Mistake")
1968 **Susan A. Meyer** ("The Problem Children")
1969 **Robert Juhren** ("No Matter Where You Are")
1970 **Michael Hirsh** ("Guerilla Warfare in Cairo, Illinois: There Are Three Sides to Every Story")
1971 **Sol Panitz** ("A Walk With Two Shadows")
Edward Hanna ("America the Violent" on *Second Sunday*)
1972 **Sol Panitz** ("The Firebrand")
1973 **Norman S. Morris and Joan M. Burke** ("The American Woman")
1974 **Harvey Jacobs** ("Summer on a Mountain of Spices")
1975 **Norman Morris and Dale Minor** ("The American Inheritance")
1976 **Roberta Hollander and Phil Chin** ("Prologue to the Democratic Convention: Issues and Attitudes")
1977 **Martin Burke and Joseph Williams** ("The American Man")
1978 **Joan Martin Bruke, Frank Deleki, Jr., Norman S. Morris** and **Joyce Ozarchuk**, *Exploring '78*
1979 **Andrew Rooney**, *Happiness, The Elusive Pursuit*
1980 **Mel Granick**, *Report on Medicine: Alopecia*

BEST RADIO NEWS

1972 **Paul Glynn** ("Flashback, 1972")
Joe Cook ("The Reasoner Report: A Maddened Minority")
1973 **Alfred E. Downs** (Newscript for Harry Birrell)
1974 **Gil Longin** (*Voices in the Headlines*)
1975 **Hill Edell** (*Voices in the Headlines*)
1976 **Gil Longin** (*Voices in the Headlines*)
1977 **Gil Longin** (*Voices in the Headlines*)
1978 **Gil Longin**, *Voices in Headlines*
1979 **Philip Chin**, *Newsbreak*
Gil Longpin, *Voices in the Headlines*
1980 **Tom Ryan**, *15 Minute Iranian Special*

BEST RADIO DRAMATIC

1975 **Sam Dann** (*Goodbye, Karl Eric*)
1976 **Sam Dunn** (*The Midas Touch*)
1977 **Allan Sloane** (*A Very Special Place*)
1978 **Sol Panitz**, *The Ballad of Hairy Joe, ICA*
1979 **Andy Nance**, *A Short History of Bac Ha*
1980 **John A. Boyle**, *The Longest Walk*

SPECIAL AWARD

1966 **Shimon Wincelberg** (*The Long, Long Curfew*)

The Laurel Award for Television is given annually to a member of the Guild who, in the opinion of the board of directors, has advanced the literature of television or made outstanding contributions to the television writing profession.

1976 **Rod Serling**
1977 **Everett Greenbaum and James Fritzell**
1978 **Ernest Kinoy**
1979 **James Costigan**
1980 **Howard Rodman**

Cultural

ife & Entertainment

Contents

Related Awards

Award of Merit
Gold Medals
Award for Distinguished Service to the Arts
Marjorie Peabody Waite Award
Blashfield Foundation Address

AMERICAN ACADEMY AND INSTITUTE OF ARTS AND LETTERS
633 W. 155th St., New York, N. Y. 10032 (212/368-5900)

The Academy's Award of Merit, which consists of a medal and a $1,000, is given annually to an individual who is not a member of the academy for outstanding achievement in painting;, sculpture, fiction, poetry or drama. The academy has merged with the National Institute of Arts and Letters, and awards made for specific achievements in those individual fields will be found elsewhere in this volume.

1942 **Charles E. Burchfield**
1943 **Carl Milles**
1944 **Theodore Dreiser**
1945 **Wystan Hugh Auden**
1946 **John van Druten**
1947 **Andrew Wyeth**
1948 **Donal Hord**
1949 **Thomas Mann**
1950 **St. John Perse**
1951 **Sidney Kingsley**
1952 **Rico Lebrun**
1953 **Ivan Mestrovic**
1954 **Ernest Hemingway**
1955 **Jorge Guillen**
1956 **Enid Bagnold**
1957 **Raphael Soyer**
1958 **Jean de Marco**
1959 **Aldous Huxley**
1960 **Hilda Doolittle**
1961 **Clifford Odets**
1962 **Charles Sheeler**
1963 **Chaim Gross**
1964 **John O'Hara**
1965 **No award**
1966 **No award**
1967 **John Heliker**
1968 **Joseph Cornell**
1969 **Vladimir Nabokov**
1970 **Reed Whittemore**
1971 **No award**
1972 **Clyfford Still**
1973 **Reuben Nakian**
1974 **Nelson Algren**
1975 **Galway Kinnell**
1976 **No award**
1977 **No award**
1978 **Tony Smith**
1979 **William Gass**
1980 **Richard Howard**

In addition to these awards in the arts, generally, honors bestowed by the American Academy and Institute of Arts and Letters in specific arts will be found elsewhere in this volume.

Each year the institute awards two Gold Medals for distinguished achievement in various fields of the arts: words, music and fine arts rotating according to a complicated formula. The award, in all cases, is based on the recipient's entire body of work and consists of a medal designed by Adolph A. Weinman.

1909 **Augustus Saint-Gaudens**, Sculpture
1910 **James Ford Rhodes**, History
1911 **James Whitcomb Riley**, Poetry
1912 **W. Rutherford Mead**, Architecture
1913 **Augustus Thomas**, Drama
1914 **John Singer Sargent**, Painting
1915 **William D. Howells**, Fiction
1916 **John Burroughs**, Essays and belles-lettres
1917 **Daniel Chester French**, Sculpture
1918 **William R. Thayer**, History and biography
1919 **Charles M. Loeffler**, Music
1921 **Cass Gilbert**, Architecture
1922 **Eugene G. O'Neill**, Drama
1923 **Edwin H. Blashfield**, Painting
1924 **Edith Wharton**, Fiction
1925 **William C. Brownell**, Essays and belles-lettres
1926 **Herbert Adams**, Sculpture
1927 **William M. Sloane**, History and biography
1928 **George W. Chadwick**, Music
1929 **Edwin A. Robinson**, Poetry
1930 **Charles Adams Platt**, Architecture
1931 **William Gillette**, Drama
1932 **Gari Melchers**, Painting
1933 **Booth Tarkington**, Fiction
1935 **Agnes Repplier**, Essays and belles-lettres
1936 **George G. Barnard**, Sculpture
1937 **Charles M. Andrews**, History and biography
1938 **Walter Damrosch**, Music
1939 **Robert Frost**, Poetry
1940 **Williams Adams Delano**, Architecture
1941 **Robert E. Sherwood**, Drama
1942 **Cecilia Beaux**, Painting
1943 **Stephen Vincent Benet**, Literature
1944 **Willa Cather**, Fiction
1945 **Paul Manship**, Sculpture
1946 **Van Wyck Brooks**, Essays and criticism
1947 **John Alden Carpenter**, Music
1948 **Charles Austin Beard**, History and biography
1949 **Frederick Law Olmsted**, Architecture
1950 **John Sloan**, Painting
Henry L. Mencken, Essays and criticism
1951 **James Earle Fraser**, Sculpture
Igor Stravinsky, Music
1952 **Thornton Wilder**, Fiction
Carl Sandburg, History and biography
1953 **Marianne Craig Moore**, Poetry
Frank Lloyd Wright, Architecture
1954 **Maxwell Anderson**, Drama
Reginald Marsh, Graphic Art
1955 **Edward Hopper**, Painting
Edmund Wilson, Essays and Criticism
1956 **Ivan Mestrovic**, Sculpture
Aaron Copland, Music
1957 **John Dos Passos** Fiction
Allan Nevins, History and biography
1958 **Conrad Aiken**, Poetry
Henry R. Shepley, Architecture
1959 **Arthur Miller**, Drama
George Grosz, Graphic Art
1960 **Charles E. Burchfield**, Painting
E.B. White, Essays and criticism
1961 **William Zorach**, Sculpture
Roger Sessions, Music
1962 **William Faulkner**, Fiction
Samuel Eliot Morison, History and biography
1963 **William Carlos Williams**, Poetry
Ludwig Mies Van Der Rohe, Architecture

1964 **Lillian Hellman,** Drama
Ben Shahn, Graphic Art
1965 **Andrew Wyeth,** Painting
Walter Lippmann, Essays and criticism
1966 **Jacques Lipchitz,** Sculpture
Virgil Thomson, Music
1967 **Katherine Anne Porter,** Fiction
Arthur Schlesinger, Jr., History and Biography
1968 **R. Buckminster Fuller,** Architecture
Wystan Hugh Auden, Poetry
1969 **Tennessee Williams,** Drama
Leonard Baskin, Graphic Art
1970 **Lewis Mumford,** Belles-lettres
Georgia O'Keeffe, Painting
1971 **Elliott C. Carter,** Music
Alexander Calder, Sculpture
1972 **Eudora Welty,** Novels
Henry Steele Commager, History
1973 **Louis T. Kahn,** Architecture
John Crowe Ransom, Poetry
1974 **Saul Steinberg,** Graphic Art
1975 **Kenneth Burke,** Belles-lettres and criticism
Willem de Kooning, Painting
1976 **Leon Edel,** Biography
Samuel Barber, Music
1977 **Saul Bellow,** Novels
Isamu Noguchi, Sculpture
1978 **Barbara W. Tuchman,** History
Peter Taylor, Short story
1979 **I.M. Pei,** Architecture
Archibald MacLeish, Poetry
1980 **Edward Albee,** Drama
Peggy Bacon, Graphic art

The Award for Distinguished Service to the Arts is made as merited to an American citizen who is not a member of the Institute but to whom the world of the arts ows a special debt.

1941 **Robert Moses**
1944 **Samuel S. McClure**
1949 **Mrs. Edward MacDowell**
1952 **Mrs. Simon Guggenheim**
1954 **Sen. J. William Fulbright**
1955 **Henry Allen Moe**
1957 **Francis Henry Taylor**
1958 **Lincoln Kirstein**
1959 **Elizabeth Ames**
1962 **Paul Mellon**
1963 **Mrs. Hugh Bullock**
1965 **Frances Steloff**
1968 **Alfred H. Barr, Jr.**
1969 **Leopold Stokowski**
1970 **Martha Graham**
1973 **Felicia Geffen**
1974 **Walker Evans**
1975 **George Balanchine**
1977 **James Laughlin**
1978 **John Brademas**
1979 **Lloyd Goodrich**
1980 **No award**

The $1,500 Marjorie Peabody Waite Award is conferred annually on an older person for continuing achievement and integrity in his or her art and is given in rotation to an artist, a composer and a writer.

1956 **Fred Nagler**
1957 **Theodore Ward Chanler**
1958 **Dorothy Parker**
1959 **Leon Hartl**
1960 **Louise Talma**
1961 **Edward McSorley**
1962 **Abraham Walkowitz**
1963 **Richard Donovan**
1964 **Dawn Powell**
1965 **Paul Burlin**
1966 **Harry Partch**
1967 **Stringfellow Barr**
1968 **Abraham Harriton**
1969 **Herbert Elwell**
1970 **Ramon Guthrie**
1971 **Ben Benn**
1972 **Vittorio Rieti**
1973 **A. Hyatt Mayor**
1974 **Ray Prohaska**
1975 **Leo Ornstein**
1976 **Rene Wellek**
1977 **Kenzo Okada**
1978 **Dane Rudhyar**
1979 **James Still**
1980 **Sidney Laufman**

The Evangeline Wilbour Blashfield Foundation Address was established "to assist . . . in an effort in . . . both the preservation of the English language in its beauty and integrity, and its cautious enrichment by such terms as grown out of modern conditions." The income of the fund is devoted to an annual address on some aspect of the arts or letters by a distinguished speaker.

1917 **Paul Elmer More,** "English and Englistic"
William Milligan Sloane, "The American Academy and the English Language"
William Crary Brownell, "The Academy and the Language"
1918 **Brander Matthews,** "The English Language and the American Academy"
1919 **Bliss Perry,** "The Academy and the Language"
1920 **Paul Shorey,** "The American Language
1921 **No address**
1922 **Henry Van Dyke,** "The Fringe of Words"
1923 **William Crary Brownell,** "Style"
1924 **No address**
1925 **Robert Underwood Johnson,** "The Glory of Words"
1928 **Wilbur L. Cross,** "The Modern English Novel"
1929 **George Pierce Baker,** "Speech in Drama"
1930 **John H. Finley,** "Virgil's Two Thousand Years"
1931 **No address**
1932 **Irving Babbitt,** "The Problem of Style in a Democracy"
1933 **Chauncey Brewster Tinker,** "Stedman as a Poet"
1934 **William Lyon Phelps,** "Two American Novels"
1935 **No address**
1936 **No address**
1937 **Owen Wister,** "William Dean Howells"
1938 **Hamlin Garland,** "Literary Fashions Old and New"
1939 **No address**
1940 **Stephen Vincent Benet,** "The Power of the Written Word"
1941 **No address**
1942 **Lewis Mumford,** "The Salvation of Letters"
1943 **Van Wyck Brooks,** "Thomas Jefferson, Man of Letters"
1944 **Archibald MacLeish,** "The Power of the Spoken Word"
1945 **Walter Lippmann,** "American Destiny"
1946 **J. William Fulbright,** "Our Foreign Policy"
1947 **Helen Keller,** "Power of the Spoken Word"
1948 **Thornton Wilder,** "A Time of Troubles"
1949 **E.M. Forster,** "Art for Art's Sake"

1950 **Robert Frost,** "How Hard It Is to Keep from Being King When It's in You and in the Situation"
1951 **Mark Van Doren,** "The Artist in the Changing World"
1952 **Aaron Copland,** "Creativity in America"
1953 **Elizabeth Bowen,** "Subject and the Time"
1954 **Robert E. Sherwood,** "Benjamin Franklin's Country"
1955 **E.N. Van Kleffens,** "The Spoken Word"
1956 **Joseph Wood Krutch,** "Geometry and Morals"
1957 **Salvador de Madariaga,** "Meditations on Leonardo's St. Anne"
1958 **A. Whitney Griswold,** "Further Obsequies for the Grammarian"
1959 **Meyer Schapiro,** "On the Humanity of Abstract Painting"
1960 **Virgil Thomson,** "Music Now"
1961 **Robert Graves,** "The Word Baraka"
1962 **Aldous Leonard Huxley,** "Utopias, Positive and Negative"
1963 **Loren Eiseley,** "The Divine Animal"
1964 **Sir Kenneth Clark,** "Popular Art"
1965 **Julian Parks Boyd,** "Thomas Jefferson and the Republic of Letters"
1966 **Jacob Bronowski,** "The Reach of Imagination"
1967 **Sir Maurice Bowra,** "Useless Knowledge"
1968 **Kenneth Burke,** "I Just Don't Know: Thoughts on the Problem of Style"
1969 **Richard Hughes,** "Fiction as Truth"
1970 **Muriel Spark,** "The Desegregation of Art"
1971 **Kurt Vonnegut, Jr.,** "The Happiest Day in the Life of My Father"
1972 **Iris Murdoch,** "Salvation by Words"
1973 **Victoria Ocampo,** "The Nights of Ithaca"
1974 **Arthur Schlesinger, Jr.,** "Language and Politics"
1975 **Stephen Spender,** "Are We Decadent?"
1976 **Henry Steele Commager,** "Recreating the Community of Culture"
1977 **No address**
1978 **No address**
1979 **John Updike**
1980 **No address**

Harry Blackstone Award

INTERNATIONAL PLATFORM ASSOCIATION
2654 Berkshire Rd., Cleveland Hts., Ohio 44106 (216/932-0505)

The Harry Blackstone Award is given to the individual judged to present the best magic performance of the year.

1980 **Harry Blackstone, Jr.**

Edward MacDowell Medal

MACDOWELL COLONY
Peterborough, N.H. 03458 (603/924-3886)

The MacDowell medal is awarded annually for outstanding contributions to the arts and is given in rotation among visual artists, writers and composers. A committee in each of these fields selects the recipient.

1960 **Thornton Wilder**
1961 **Aaron Copland**
1962 **Robert Frost**
1963 **Alexander Calder**
1964 **Edmund Wilson**
1965 **Edgard Varese**
1966 **Edward Hopper**
1967 **Marianne Moore**
1968 **Roger Sessions**
1969 **Louise Nevelson**
1970 **Eudora Welty**
1971 **William Schuman**
1972 **Georgia O'Keeffe**
1973 **Norman Mailer**
1974 **Walter Piston**
1975 **Willem de Kooning**
1976 **Lillian Hellman**
1977 **Virgil Thomson**
1978 **Richard Diebenkorn**
1979 **John Cheever**
1980 **Samuel Barber**

SPECIAL AWARD

1974 **Martha Graham**

Poses Brandeis University Creative Arts Award

BRANDEIS UNIVERSITY
Brandeis University Commission Office, 12 E. 77th St., New York, N.Y. 10021 (212/472-1501)

One of a series of awards, the Jack I. and Lillian L. Poses Brandeis University Creative Arts Award is given annually to recognize notable achievement in the creative arts. A professional jury chosen by the commission selects the winner, who receives an honorarium of $1,000.

1964 **R. Buckminster Fuller**
1965 **Alfred H. Barr, Jr.**
1966 **Meyer Schapiro**
1967 **Kenneth Burke**
1968 **Martha Graham**
1969 **Lewis Mumford**
1970 **Lloyd Goodrich**
1971 **George Balanchine**
1972 **I. A. Richards**
1973 **Leonard Bernstein**
1974 **No award**
1975 **Aaron Copland**
1976 **Isaac Stern**
1977 **Alfred A. Knopf**
1978 **No award**
1979 **Edwin Denby**
1980 **No award**

Entertainer of the Year Awards

AMERICAN GUILD OF VARIETY ARTISTS
1540 Broadway, New York, N.Y. 10036 (212/765-0800)

The Entertainer of the Year Awards are given annually in a ceremony videotaped for broadcast from Caesar's Palace in Las Vegas for achievements in music, comedy and other fields of entertainment. The winners received statues of George M. Cohan, which are better known as Georgies. Selection is made by a mail vote of the membership of the American Guild of Variety Artists.

ENTERTAINER OF THE YEAR

1970 Bob Hope
1971 Bob Hope
1972 Liza Minnelli
1973 Sammy Davis, Jr.
1974 No award
1975 Ben Vereen
1976 Johnny Carson
1977 Totie Fields
1978 Steve Martin
1979 Robin Williams
1980 Not available at press time

MALE SINGING STAR OF THE YEAR/MALE VOCALIST OF THE YEAR

1970 Tom Jones
1971 Tom Jones
1972 Neil Diamond
1973 Sammy Davis, Jr.
1974 No award
1975 John Denver
1976 Barry Manilow
1977 Engelbert Humperdinck
1978 Barry Manilow
1979 Billy Joel
1980 Not available at press time

FEMALE SINGING STAR OF THE YEAR/FEMALE VOCALIST OF THE YEAR

1970 Barbra Streisand
1971 Barbra Streisand
1972 Vikki Carr
1973 Roberta Flack
1974 Helen Reddy
1975 Shirley Bassey
1976 Eydie Gorme
1977 Barbra Streisand
1978 Debby Boone
1979 Donna Summer
1980 Not available at press time

MALE COMEDY STAR OF THE YEAR

1970 Flip Wilson
1971 Flip Wilson
1972 Carroll O'Connor
1973 Redd Foxx
1974 Rich Little
1975 Paul Lynde
1976 David Brenner
1977 Steve Martin
1978 Steve Martin
1979 Robin Williams
1980 Not available at press time

FEMALE COMEDY STAR OF THE YEAR

1970 Carol Burnett
1971 Carol Burnett
1972 Carol Burnett
1973 Carol Burnett
1974 Carol Burnett
1975 Joan Rivers
1976 Nancy Walker
1977 Totie Fields
1978 Carol Burnett
1979 Gilda Radner
1980 Not available at press time

MUSICAL GROUP OF THE YEAR/MUSICAL ACT OF THE YEAR/VOCAL ACT OF THE YEAR/VOCAL GROUP OF THE YEAR

1970 Blood, Sweat and Tears
1971 Richard and Karen Carpenter
1972 Sonny and Cher
1973 No award
1974 Chicago
Gladys Knight and the Pips
1975 Tony Orlando and Dawn
1976 Captain and Tennille
1977 Donny and Marie
1978 Bee Gees
1979 Village People
1980 Not available at press time

INSTRUMENTAL ACT OF THE YEAR

1975 Liberace
1976 Lawrence Welk
1977 Chicago
1978 Chuck Mangione
1979 Doc Severinsen
1980 Not available at press time

RISING STAR OF THE YEAR/MOST PROMISING NEWCOMER OF THE YEAR

1970 Melba Moore
1971 Lily Tomlin
1972 Lorna Luft
1973 No award
1974 Olivia Newton-John
1975 Ben Vereen
1976 Natalie Cole
1977 Shields and Yarnell
1978 Andrea McArdle
1979 Gino Vannelli
1980 Not available at press time

OUTSTANDING ANIMAL OF THE YEAR/ANIMAL ACT OF THE YEAR

1970 Tanya the Elephant
1971 Tanya the Elephant
1972 No Award
1973 Tanya the Elephant
1974 Mr. Jiggs
1975 Tony the Wonder Horse
1976 Benji
1977 Fred the Bird
1978 Lassie
1979 Benji
1980 Not available at press time

COUNTRY AND WESTERN STAR OF THE YEAR/COUNTRY STAR OF THE YEAR

1972 Jimmy Dean
1973 Roy Clark
1974 Charlie Rich
1975 Linda Ronstadt
1976 John Denver
1977 Dolly Parton
1978 Dolly Parton
1979 Kenny Rogers
1980 Not available at press time

SONG AND DANCE STAR OF THE YEAR

1974 Joel Grey
1975 Ben Vereen
1976 Lola Falana
1977 Shirley MacLaine

1978 **Ann-Margret**
1979 **Mitzi Gaynor**
1980 **Not available at press time**

GOLDEN AWARD

1970 **Jimmy Durante**
1971 **Jack Benny**
1972 **Duke Ellington**
1973 **Kate Smith**
1974 **George Burns**
1975 **Lucille Ball**
1976 **Edgar Bergen**
1977 **Milton Berle**
1978 **Buddy Ebsen**
1979 **Red Skelton**
1980 **Not available at press time**

OTHER AWARDS

1970 **Radio City Music Hall,** Outstanding Production Number of the Year
Flying Alexanders, Novelty or Circus Act of the Year
1972 **Tanya the Elephant,** Circus Act of the Year
1973 **Gunther Gebel-Williams,** Circus Award
Thomas H. Scallen, Ice Follies, Special Award
1974 **Peggy Fleming,** Special Attractions Award
1975 **Cathy Rigby,** Special Attraction of the Year
1976 **Jim Hensen's Muppets,** Novelty Act and Special Attraction of the Year
1977 **Shields and Yarnell,** Novelty Act and Special Attraction of the Year
1978 **Doug Henning,** *The Magic Show*
1979 **Wayland Flowers and Madame**
1980 **Not available at press time**

Europe Prize for Folk Art
Hanseatic Goethe Prize
Gottfried von Herder Prizes
Shakespeare Prize
Henrik Steffens Prize
Joost van den Vondel Prize

STIFTUNG F.V.S.
Georgsplatz 10, 2 Hamburg 1, Federal Republic of Germany (Tel: 33 04 00 and 33 06 00)

The Europe Prize for Folk Art, which carries a 20,000-mark honorarium, recognizes accomplishments in folk art, music and dance.

1973 **Folk dance troupe of the Marie Curie Sklodowska University** (Lublin, Poland)
Popular Alsatian Art Group (Berstett, France)
Finkwarder Speeldeel (Hamburg, Germany)
1974 **France Marolt Folklore Academy** (Lubljana, Yugoslavia)
Folksong group (Plana, Bulgaria)
Leksands troupe (Leksand, Sweden)
Siamsa Tire, Irish Folk Theatre (Kerry, Ireland)
Alois Senti (Bern, Switzerland)
1975 **Bela Bartok Folkdance Ensemble** (Budapest, Hungary)
Calusul Folk Art Ensemble (Scornicesti-Olt, Rumania)
Renaat Veremanskoor (Bruges, Belgium)
Tarvon Troupe (Helsinki, Finland)
Alfred Cammann, education commissioner (Bremen, Germany)
1976 **Not available**
1977 **Not available**
1978 **Folkart Ensemble of Bistrica** (Sofia vicinity, Bulgaria)
Mooskirchner Alsteirermusik (Austria)
Traditional Abington Morris Dancers (Abington, U.K.)
1979 **Epotik Hajdu Tancegyuttese** (Debrecen, Hungary)
Pjoodansfelag Rekjavikur (Reykjavik, Iceland)
Lous Paloumayres (Hoosegor, France) and **Lous Cigalouns** (Morcenx, France)
1980 **Mara Ensemble from the Folk Culture House Sighetu Maramtiei (Maramures, Rumania)**
Aald Heilpen (Hindloopen, Netherlands)
Pontusgriechen in Athen (Athens, Greece)
Norwegian Folk Museum Dance Troupe, (Oslo)

The Hanseatic Goethe Prize, which carries a 31,000-mark cash award, is given biennually to honor intellectual and humanitarian works which transcend national boundaries, The cash consists of a 25,000-mark prize and a 6,000-mark stipend.

1950 **Carl Jacob Burckhardt** (Switzerland)
1951 **Martin Buber** (Israel)
1952 **Eduard Spranger** (Tubingen, Germany)
1953 **Bishop Eivind Berggrav** (Norway)
1954 **Thomas Stearns Eliot** (Great Britain)
1955 **Gabriel Marcel** (France)
1956 **Walter Gropius** (U.S.A.)
1957 **Alfred Weber** (Heidelberg, Germany)
1958 **Paul Tillich** (U.S.A.)
1959 **Theodor Heuss** (Bonn, Germany)
1961 **Benjamin Britten** (Great Britain)
1963 **Wilhelm Flitner** (Hamburg, Germany)
1965 **Hans Arp** (France)
1967 **Salvador de Madariaga** (Spain and Great Britain)
1969 **Robert Minder** (France)
1971 **Giorgio Strehler** (Italy)
1972 **Albin Lesky** (Austria)
1973 **Manes Sperber** (France)
1975 **Carlo Schmid** (Bonn, Germany)
1977 **Willem A. Vissert't Hooft** (Geneva, Switzerland)
1979 **Hans-Georg Wormit** (Berlin)

Current Status Unknown

The Gottfried von Herder Prizes, which carry 20,000-mark honoraria, are given annually to seven individuals for the preservation of cultural life in eastern and southeastern Europe. Art, city planning, conservation, folklore and philosophy are among the fields in which such achievement is recognized. A jury selects the winners of the prizes, which are administered by the University of Vienna.

1964 **Jan Kott** (Poland)
Stanislaw Lorentz (Poland)
Otto Bihalji-Merin (Yugoslavia)
Lucijan Maria Skerjanc (Yugoslavia)
1965 **Emanuel Hruska** (Czechoslovakia)
Hugo Rokyta (Czechoslovakia)
Zoltan Kodaly (Hungary)
Laszlo Nemeth (Hungary)
Tudor Arghezi (Rumania)
Christo Vakareski (Bulgaria)
Manolis Chatzidakis (Greece)
1966 **Aleksander Kobzdej** (Poland)
Jan Cikker (Czechoslovakia)
Zlatko Gorjan (Yugoslavia)
Niko Kuret (Yugoslavia)

Dezso Dercsenyi (Hungary)
Dimiter Statkow (Bulgaria)
Anton Kriesis (Greece)
1967 **Witold Lutoslawski** (Poland)
Vladimir Kompanek (Czechoslovakia)
Svetozar Radojcic (Yugoslavia)
Ivan Fenyo (Hungary)
Alexandru Philippide (Rumania)
Mihai Pop (Rumania)
Spyridon Marinatos (Greece)
1968 **Roman Ingarden** (Poland)
Ludvik Kunz (Czechoslovakia)
Miroslav Krleza (Yugoslavia)
Lajos Vayer (Hungary)
Constantin Daicoviciu (Rumania)
Pantscho Wladigeroff (Bulgaria)
Anastasios Orlandos (Greece)
1969 **Ksawery Piwocki** (Poland)
Albin Brunovsky (Czechoslovakia)
Bohuslav Fuchs (Czechoslovakia)
Marijan Matkovic (Yugoslavia)
France Stele (Yugoslavia)
Jolan Balogh (Hungary)
Mihail Jora (Rumania)
1970 **Jan Bialostocki** (Poland)
Jan Filip (Czechoslovakia)
Milovan Gavazzi (Yugoslavia)
Gyula Illyes (Hungary)
Zoltan Franyo (Rumania)
Zeko Torbov (Bulgaria)
Yannis A. Papaioannou (Greece)
1971 **Kazimierz Michalowski** (Bulgaria)
Jiri Kolar (Czechoslovakia)
Blaze Koneski (Yugoslavia)
Bence Szabolsci (Hungary)
Zaharia Stancu (Rumania)
Michael Sokolovski (Bulgaria)
Georgios A. Megas (Greece)
1972 **Henryk Stazewski** (Poland)
Jaroslav Pesina (Czechoslovakia)
Dragotin Cvetko (Yugoslavia)
Branko Maksimovic (Yugoslavia)
Gyula Ortutay (Hungary)
Virgil Vatasianu (Rumania)
Atanas Dalcev (Bulgaria)
1973 **Zbigniew Herbert** (Czechoslovakia)
Jan Racek (Czechoslovakia)
Peter Lubarda (Yugoslavia)
Janos Harmatta (Hungary)
Eugen Jebeleanu (Rumania)
Veselin Besevliev (Bulgaria)
Stylianos Charkianakis (Greece)
1974 **Wladyslaw Czerny** (Poland)
Jan Podolak (Czechoslovakia)
Ivo Franges (Yugoslavia)
Laszlo Gero (Hungary)
Zeno Vancea (Rumania)
Ivan Dujcev (Bulgaria)
Stylianos Pelekanidis (Greece)
1975 **Jozef Burszta** (Poland)
Stanislav Libensky (Czechoslovakia)
Stanojlo Rajicic (Yugoslavia)
Gabor Preisich (Hungary)
Maria A. Musicescu (Rumania)
Christo M. Danov (Bulgaria)
Pandelis Prevelakis (Greece)
1976 **Jagoda Buic** (Yugoslavia)
Marin Goleminov (Bulgaria)
Joannes Theoph (Greece)
Deszo Keresztury (Hungary)
Nichita Stanescu (Rumania)
Rudolf Turek (Czechoslovakia)
Kazimierz Wejchert (Poland)
1977 **Riko Debenjak** (Yugoslavia)
Emmanuel Kriaras (Greece)
Albert Kutal (Czechoslovakia)
Mate Major (Hungary)
Krzysztof Penderecki (Poland)
Anastas Petrov (Bulgaria)
Ion Vladutiu (Rumania)
1978 **Eugen Barbu** (Rumania), author
Djurdje Boskovic (Yugoslavia), archeologist
Kasimierz Dejmek (Poland), stage director
Stojan Djoudjeff (Bulgaria), music ethnologist
Bela Gunda (Hungary), ethnologist
Jiri Hruza (Czechoslovakia), architect
Jannis Spryropoulos (Greece), painter
1979 **Gordana Babic-Djordjevic** (Yugoslavia), art historian
Ivan Balassa (Hungary), ethnologist
Kamil Lhotak (Czechoslovakia), historian and cultural authority
Vera Petrova Mutafcieva (Bulgaria), author
Elexandru Rosetti (Rumania), author and linguist
Wiktor Zin (Poland), monument preservationist
1980 **Magdalena Abakanowicz** (Poland), artist
Ferenc Farkas (Hungary), composer
Zdenko Kolacio (Yugoslavia), architect
Atanas Natew (Bulgaria), scientist, literature, the arts
Andras Suto (Rumania), author
Pavel Trost (Czechoslovakia), linguist
Apostolos Vacalopoulos (Greece), historian

The Shakespeare Prize, which carries a 25,000-mark cash award and a 6,000-mark stipend, is given for accomplishments in the arts, architecture, archeology, folklore or music stemming from Europe's English-speaking countries. The award was given briefly in the 1930s, dropped, and has been renewed as an annual honor.

1937 **R.C. Williams,** Composer
1938 **John Masefield,** Poet
1967 **Peter Hall,** Producer and director
1968 **Graham Greene,** Author
1969 **Roy Pascal,** German professor
1970 **Harold Pinter,** Playwright, actor and producer
1971 **Janet Baker,** Singer
1972 **Paul Scofield,** Actor
1973 **Peter Brook,** Producer and director
1974 **Graham Sutherland,** Artist
1975 **John Pritchard,** Director
1976 **Philip A. Larkin,** Poet
1977 **No award**
1978 **John Dexter,** Producer
1979 **Tom Stoppard,** Playwright
1980 **Roy Colin Strong,** Director, Victoria and Albert Museum

The Henrik Steffens Prize, which carries a 25,000-mark cash award and a 6,000-mark stipend, is given annually for accomplishments in the arts, archeology, folklore or music stemming from Scandinavia. The award is administered by the University of Kiel.

1966 **Rolf Herman Nevanlinna** (Finland)
1967 **Johannes Edfelt** (Sweden)
1968 **Asbjorn E. Herteig** (Norway)
1969 **Carl-Henning Pederson** (Denmark)
1970 **Magnus Mar Larusson** (Iceland)

1971 **Arvi Kivimaa** (Finland)
1972 **Harry Martinson** (Sweden)
1973 **Rolf Nesch** (Norway)
1974 **Villy Sorenson** (Denmark)
1975 **Hannes Petursson** (Iceland)
1976 **Bjorn Landstrom** (Finland)
1977 **Not available**
1978 **Hans Peter L'Orange** (Oslo), archeologist
1979 **Knud Ejler Logstrup** (Denmark), theologian
1980 **Halgrimur Helgason** (Iceland), composer

The Joost van den Vondel Prize, which carries a 20,000 Swiss franc cash award, annually honors achievements in Low German, Flemish or Dutch culture. A jury selects the recipients of the prize, which is administered by Munster University.

1960 **Antoon Coolen** (Netherlands)
Max Lamberty (Belgium)
1961 **Rev. Christian Boeck** (Germany)
1962 **Frans Masereel** (Belgium, Flemish)
1963 **Albert van Balsum** (Netherlands)
1964 **Hermann Teuchert** (Germany)
1965 **Monsg. Honore von Waeyenbergh** (Belgium)
1966 **Jef Last** (Netherlands)
1967 **Hans M. Ruwoldt** (Germany)
1968 **Maurits de Meyer** (Belgium, Flemish)
1969 **Klaas Hanzen Heeroma** (Netherlands)
1970 **Franz Petri** (Germany)
1971 **Fernand Jozef Maria Collin** (Belgium, Flemish)
1972 **Horst Gerson** (Netherlands)
1973 **Peter Elster** (Germany)
1974 **Leo Cappuyns** (Belgium)
1975 **Hebe Kohlbrugge** (Netherlands)
1976 **Not available**
1977 **Not available**
1978 **Gerard Edward Langemeijer** (Netherlands), law philosopher
1979 **Torsten Dahlberg** (Sweden), philologist
1980 **Cyriel Paul Coupe** (Belgium), author and translator

Charles Lang Freer Medal

SMITHSONIAN INSTITUTION
1000 Jefferson Dr. SW, Washington, D.C. 20560
(202/357-1300)

The Charles Lang Freer Medal, which is of bronze, is awarded as merited for distinguished contribution to the knowledge and understanding of Oriental civilizations as reflected in their arts.

1956 **Osvald Siren** (Stockholm), Chinese art
1960 **Ernst Kuhnel,** Islamic art
1965 **Yukio Yashiro** (Osio, Japan) Japanese scholarship
1973 **Tanaka Ichimatsu,** Japanese painting
Laurence Sickman (Kansas City, Mo.), Chinese art
1974 **Roman Chirshman,** Iranian art

Golden Apple Trophy

CUE MAGAZINE
c/o New York Magazine, 755 Second Ave., New York, N.Y. 10017 (212/986-4600)

The Golden Apple Trophy is given annually for service to New York in the fields of entertainment or leisure. The editors selected the receipients of this honor in a changing series of categories until the trophy was discontinued when *Cue* merged with *New York Magazine.*

1976 **Abraham Beame,** Special award for contributions to New York City
All the President's Men, Best motion picture
Robert Redford, *All the President's Men,* Best motion picture performance by an actor
For Colored Girls Who Have Considered Suicide/When the End of the Rainbow is Enuf, Best play
Jack Weston, *California Suite,* Best performance by an actor in a play
Rita Moreno, *The Ritz,* Best motion picture performance by an actress
Preston Jones, *A Texas Trilogy,* Playwright award
Jane Oliver, Cabaret award
James Levine, Metropolitan Opera, Conducting award
Clamma Dale, Opera award
Martine van Hammel, American Ballet Theatre, Dance award
Rich Man, Poor Man, Television award
WNYC-FM, Radio award
George Benson, *Breezin',* Best record album
WNEW-TV, Community service programming
Thurman Munson, Sports award
Tavern on the Green, Best restaurant
1977 **Market Square, World Trade Center,** Best restaurant
Annie, Best Musical
The Gin Game, Best play
The Fantasticks, Special award
Al Pacino, *The Private War of Pavlo Hummel,* Best performance by an actor in a play
Estelle Parsons, *Miss Magerita's Way,* Best performance by an actress in a play
Mike Nichols, *The Gin Game,* Best director
Mike Ashford and Valerie Simpson, *Send It,* Best single
James Taylor, *J.T.,* Best album
Shirley MacLaine, Special award
Commissioner Arlene Wolf, Public service award
Annie Hall, Best movie
Richard Burton, *Equus,* Best motion picture performance by an actor
Jane Fonda, *Julia,* Best motion picture performance by an actress
Erich Leinsdorf, Conducting award
Alice Tully, Special award
New York Yankees, Sports award
Shirley Verrett, Opera award
Cy Coleman, *I Love My Wife,* Composing award
WNCN-Radio, Radio award
WNET/13, Television award

Handel Medallion

CITY OF NEW YORK
Office of the Mayor, City Hall, New York, N.Y. 10007
(212/566-1520)

The Handel Medallion is the City of New York's highest cultural award and is given as merited to outstanding figures in the arts who have contributed to the cultural life of the city. The Mayor's staff selects the recipients

1959 **John Celebre**
Hon. John M. Conway

Thea Dispeker
Hon. Ruggero Ferace di Villeforesta
Robert W. Dowling
John Effrat
Equitable Choral Club
Georg Federer
Virginia Innes-Brown
Newel Jenkins
Antoine T. Koppers
John E. McCarthy
John McKeen
James F. Oates
Charles Pappas
Richard C. Patterson, Jr.
James J. Rorimer
Rose M. Singer
Hon. Sir Hugh Stephenson
William Zeckendorf
1960 Elizabeth Barry
Sara Baum
Stuart Canin
Joan Davis
Malcolm Frager
Jaime Laredo
Isaac Stern
1961 No award
1962 No award
1963 Rudolf Bing
Leopold Stokowski
Earl Wrightson
1964 S. Arthur Keith-Swenson
Sidney Poitier
John D. Rockefeller III
George Seuffert
Paul Taubman
1965 Band of the Fiji Military Forces
Joseph B. Martinson
Henry Moore
Carlos Moseley
Julius Rudel
1966 Pablo Casals
Justino Diaz
Benny Goodman
Lionel Hampton
Jane Marsh
Jan Peerce
David Sarnoff
1967 Robert Russell Bennett
Marc Chagall
George T. Delacorte
Rebekah Harkness
Richard Rodgers
William Schuman
Richard Tucker
1968 Charles Beetz
Janet Schenck
1969 Milton Cross
Helen Hull
Claire Reis
Peter Wilhousky
1970 George Balanchine
Ben Chancy
Martha Graham
Hall Johnson
Robert Merrill
John L. Motley
Alice Tully
William Warfield
1971 Aaron Copland
Dorothy Kirsten
Joseph Papp
1972 Charles Chaplin
Dizzy Gillespie
Francis Robinson
Virgil Thomson
1973 Harold Arlen
Louis Armstrong
Duke Ellington
Geraldine Fitzgerald
Gary Graffman
Melissa Hayden
Sol Hurok
Louise Nevelson
Arthur Rubinstein
1974 Orotorio Society of New York
1975 Lucia Chase
Joshua Logan
The Metropolitan Opera
Oliver Smith
1976 George Abbott
Agnes de Mille
Dame Margot Fonteyn
Eva La Gallienne
Yehudi Menuhin
Jerome Robbins
1977 Leonard Bernstein
1978 Elliott Carter

Current Status Unknown

Man of the Year Award
Woman of the Year Award

HASTY PUDDING INSTITUTE OF 1770
12 Holyoke St., Cambridge, Mass. 02138 (617/495-5205)

The Woman of the Year Award is given annually, almost always to a woman in the theatre or entertainment world. The elaborate award presentation consists of a parade, banquet, presentation of gifts, plaques and other recognition as organized by the Harvard University students who belong to Hasty Pudding. The nomination and balloting procedure of members of Hasty Pudding Theatricals is secret.

1951 Gertrude Lawrence
1952 Barbara Bel Geddes
1953 Mamie Eisenhower
1954 Shirley Booth
1955 Debbie Reynolds
1956 Peggy Ann Garner
1957 Carroll Baker
1958 Katharine Hepburn
1959 Joanne Woodward
1960 Carol Lawrence
1961 Jane Fonda
1962 Piper Laurie
1963 Shirley MacLaine
1964 Rosalind Russell
1965 Lee Remick
1966 Ethel Merman
1967 Lauren Bacall
1968 Angela Lansbury
1970 Dionne Warwicke
1971 Carol Channing
1972 Ruby Keeler
1973 Liza Minnelli
1974 Faye Dunaway
1975 Valerie Harper

1976 **Bette Midler**
1977 **Elizabeth Taylor**
1978 **Beverly Sills**
1979 **Candice Bergen**
1980 **Meryl Streep**

More recently, a Man of the Year selection has also been added. The selection and awards procedure is similar but does not include a parade.

1967 **Bob Hope**
1968 **Paul Newman**
1969 **Bill Cosby**
1970 **Robert Redford**
1971 **James Stewart**
1972 **Dustin Hoffman**
1973 **Jack Lemmon**
1974 **Peter Falk**
1975 **Warren Beatty**
1976 **Robert Blake**
1977 **Johnny Carson**
1978 **Richard Dreyfuss**
1979 **Robert De Niro**
1980 **Alan Alda**

Kennedy Center Honors

JOHN F. KENNEDY CENTER FOR THE PERFORMING ARTS
Washington, D.C. 20566 (202/828-4000)

The Kennedy Center Honors are medals presented at a celebrity- filled, black-tie ceremony and performance gala, which is usually televised nationwide, at the John F. Kennedy Center for the Performing Arts. The awards, which were created as a national showcase for the arts, are given for lifetime contributions to the performing arts.

1978 **Marian Anderson**
Fred Astaire
George Balanchine
Richard Rodgers
Arthur Rubenstein
1979 **Aaron Copland**
Ella Fitzgerald
Henry Fonda
Martha Graham
Tennessee Williams
1980 **Leonard Bernstein**
James Cagney
Agnes de Mille
Lynn Fontanne
Leontyne Price

New York State Award

NEW YORK STATE COUNCIL ON THE ARTS
80 Center St., New York, N.Y. 10013 (212/488-3846)

The New York State Award, which consists of a sculpture, was given until 1975 to honor contributions to the cultural or artistic life of New York State. Individuals and groups were eligible for selection.

1966 **Binghamton Commission on Architecture and Urban Design**
Buffalo Festival of the Arts Today
Citizens Advisory Committee for the Town and Village of Cazenovia
Corning Community College
Judson Memorial Church, New York
New York State Racing Association, Jamaica
New York Shakespeare Festival, New York
St. James Community Center, New York
Stockade Association, Schenectady
Syracuse Savings Bank
Mrs. Albert D. Lasker
1967 **American Craftsmen's Council,** New York
Carborundum Co., Niagara Falls
First Unitarian Church of Rochester
Historic Pittsford, Inc.
The Jacob Riis Houses Plaza, New York
Jazzmobile, Inc., New York
Kleinhans Music Hall, Buffalo
Lake George Opera Festival, Glens Falls
New York City Department of Parks
Olana Preservation, Inc., Hudson
Saratoga Performing Arts Center, Saratoga Springs
Whitney Museum of American Art, New York
Ada Louise Huxtable
1968 **Albright-Knox Art Gallery,** Buffalo
Art on Tour, Scarsdale
Eastern Airlines, New York
Endo Laboratories Inc., Garden City
Ford Foundation, New York
Hudson Valley Philharmonic Society, Poughkeepsie
Lake George Park Commission, Ticonderoga
Paley Park, New York
Society for the Preservation of Landmarks in Western New York, Rochester
Waterford Historical Museum and Cultural Center
WBAI-FM, New York
Alfred H. Barr, Jr.
1969 **Air Preheater Company, Inc.,** Wellsville
American Museum of Natural History, New York
Brooklyn Academy of Music
Committee for a Library in the Jefferson Courthouse, New York
Everson Museum of Art, Syracuse
Geneva Historical Society
Lincoln Center for the Performing Arts, New York
New York University, New York
Albert A. Lasker Foundation, New York
92nd Street Young Men's and Young Women's Hebrew Association, New York
Rochester Museum and Science Center
State University Construction Fund, Albany
Xerox Corporation, Rochester
1970 **Adirondack Museum,** Blue Mountain Lake
Alice Tully Hall, New York
The Asia Society, New York
Bedford Lincoln Neighborhood Museum (MUSE), Brooklyn
Children's Television Workshop, New York
City Center of Music and Drama, New York
Erie County and the City of Buffalo
Metropolitan Museum of Art, New York
New York State Conservation Bill of Rights
Scriven Foundation and the Citizens of Cooperstown
Syracuse University Press
Youtheatre, Rochester
John B. Hightower
1971 **Abraham & Straus,** Brooklyn
Center of the Creative and Performing Arts in the State University of New York at Buffalo

James Prendergast Library Association, Jamestown
Lithopinion, New York
South Mall Riverfront Pumping Station, Albany
Temple Beth Zion, Buffalo
Valley Development Foundation, Binghamton
Carl Carmer
Henry Allen Moe

1972 **Hudson River Museum,** Yonkers
Madison County Historical Society, Oneida
New York City Landmarks Preservation Commission
New York State Bar Association, Albany
Six Nations Indian Museum, Onchiota
Three Village Reconstruction at Stony Brook, Setauket and Old Field, and Ward and Dorothy Melville
George Balanchine
Joseph Papp

1973 **Alvin Ailey City Center Dance Theater,** New York
County of Orange
Kenan Center, Lockport
La Mama Experimental Theatre Club, New York, **and Ellen Stewart**
New York Zoological Society (Bronx Zoo), New York
Theatre Development Fund, New York
Martha Graham

1974 **Chautauqua Institution**
City of Albany and Albany Board of Education
Dance Theatre of Harlem, New York, **and Arthur Mitchell**
International Arts Relations (INTAR), New York
Municipal Art Society of New York, New York
The New Yorker, New York, **and William Shawn**
Paper Bag Players, New York
F. & M. Schaefer Brewing Co., Brooklyn
Tri-Cities Opera, Binghamton
Nelson A. Rockefeller
Kenneth Dewey and Donald Harper

1975 **Cayuga County Homesite Development Corporation,** Auburn
Cooper Union for the Advancement of Science and Art, New York
Corning Glass Works Foundation
Cunningham Dance Foundation, New York
Gotham Book Mart, New York, **and Frances Steloff**
Negro Ensemble Company, New York
Rensselaer County Junior Museum, Troy
South Street Seaport Museum, New York
Young Filmaker's Foundation, New York
Aaron Copland
Sheldon and Caroline Keck
Seymour H. Knox, Special Citation

1976 **No award**
1977 **No award**

Current Status Unknown

Gold Medal Awards

PHOTOPLAY
205 E. 42nd St., New York, N.Y. 10017 (212/983-5600)

In addition to awards specifically in the fields of motion pictures, television and music, *Photoplay* annually gives a Gold Medal to the most popular newcomer entertainers of the year, as voted by readers of the publication.

MALE

1961 **Warren Beatty**
1962 **Gary Clarke**
1963 **Robert Walker**
1964 **Robert Goulet**
1965 **Chris Connelly**
1966 **Noel Harrison**
1967 **Henry Darrow**
1968 **Glen Campbell**
1969 **Jim Brolin**
1970 **David Cassidy**
1971 **Chris Mitchum**
1972 **David Birney**
1973 **Tony Musante**
1974 **Freddie Prinze**
1975 **Gabe Kaplan**
1976 **Gregg Henry**
1977 **Not announced at press time**

Current Status Unknown

FEMALE

1961 **Deborah Walley**
Paula Prentiss
1962 **Suzanne Pleshette**
1963 **Tippi Hedren**
1964 **Barbara Parkins**
1965 **Pat Morrow**
1966 **Marlo Thomas**
1967 **Tina Cole**
1968 **Peggy Lipton**
1969 **Karen Valentine**
1970 **Susan Dey**
1971 **Sandy Duncan**
1972 **Diana Ross**
1973 **Michelle Phillips**
1974 **Julie Kavner**
1975 **Pamela Hensley**
1976 **Jaclyn Smith**
1977 **Not announced at press time**

Current Status Unknown

Paul Robeson Award

ACTORS' EQUITY ASSOCIATION
165 W. 46th St., New York, N.Y. 10036 (212/869-0358)

The Paul Robeson Award, a citation, annually honors the entertainer whose life and career, in the opinion of the awards committee, fill the concepts and fit the example of Paul Robeson himself in terms of concern for his or her fellows, respect for the dignity of the individual, freedom of expression, universal brotherhood and his or her contributions to the performing arts. A plaque is presented to the winner.

1974 **Paul Robeson**
1975 **Ruby Dee and Ossie Davis**
1976 **Lillian Hellman**
1977 **Pete Seeger**
1978 **Sam Jaffee**
1979 **Harry Belafonte**
1980 **Alice Childress**

Theodore Roosevelt Award

INTERNATIONAL PLATFORM ASSOCIATION
2564 Berkshire Rd., Cleveland Hts., Ohio 44106
(216/932-0505)

The Theodore Roosevelt Award, which consists of an engraved bowl, is given annually for excellence in public service.

1973 **Henry Kissinger**
1974 **No award**
1975 **Gov. Reuben Askew**
1976 **No award**
1977 **James Schlesinger**
1978 **Sen. William Proxmire**
1979 **No award**
1980 **No award**

Ruby Award

AFTER DARK
10 Columbus Circle, New York, N.Y. 10019 (212/399-2400)

The Ruby Award named in honor of Ruby Keeler is given annually for outstanding achievements in entertainment and arts. A silver bowl is awarded by a decision of *After Daek* magazine's editors.

1971 **Ruby Keeler**
1972 **Dorothy Collins**
1973 **Bette Midler**
1974 **Lucille Ball**
1975 **Ann-Margret**
1976 **Barry Manilow**
1977 **Mae West**

Current Status Unknown

Schillerpreis der Stadt Mannheim

CITY OF MANNHEIM
Rathaus E-5, Mannheim, Federal Republic of Germany

The Schillerpreis der Stadt Mannheim, or Schiller Prize of the City of Mannheim, is now awarded every four years and carries a cash prize of 25,000 German marks. It is given to an individual who has contributed or promised to contribute to cultural evolution. Until 1974, the prize carried a 10,000-mark honorarium and was given every two years.

1954 **Mary Wigmann,** Dance
1956 **Jurgen Fehling,** Producer-director
1958 **Friedrich Durrenmatt,** Dramatist
1960 **Theodor Eschenburg,** Political science professor
1962 **Elisabeth Bergner,** Actress
1964 **Golo Mann,** Historian and publicist
1966 **Carl Wurster,** Member of the science council and the senate of the Max Planck Institute
1968 **Hartmut von Hentig,** University professor
1970 **Ida Ehre,** Director
1972 **Peter Handke,** Author
1974 **Horst Janssen,** Graphic artist
1978 **Peter Stein,** Producer-director

Mark Twain Award

INTERNATIONAL PLATFORM ASSOCIATION
2564 Berkshire Rd., Cleveland Hts., Ohio 44106
(216/932-0505)

The Mark Twain Award, which consists of an engraved bowl, is given annually to the individual judged by the IPA Committee as "Mark Twain's successor as America's most delightful entertainer, gentle depictor of the virtues and weaknesses of humanity with humor's paintbrush."

1970 **Hal Holbrook**
1971 **No award**
1972 **Bob Hope**
1973 **Erma Bombeck**
1974 **Victor Borge**
1975 **Art Buchwald**
1976 **Jean Shepherd**
1977 **Norman Lear**
1978 **Charles Jarvis**
1979 **Danny Kaye**
1980 **Mark Russell**

Theater

Contents

Related Awards

St. Clair Bayfield Award

ACTORS' EQUITY ASSOCIATION
1560 Broadway, New York, N.Y. 10036 (212/869-8530)

The St. Clair Bayfield Award, which consists of a changing cash prize and a scroll, is given annually to an unfeatured actor or actress in a Shakespearean production staged within fifty miles of New York during the previous season. The panel which selects the winner includes drama critics, Mrs. Bayfield and the President of Actors' Equity.

1973 **Barnard Hughes,** *Much Ado About Nothing* (Shakespeare in the Park and the Winter Garden Theatre)
1974 **Randall Duc Kim,** *The Tempest* (Mitzi Newhouse Theatre at Lincoln Center)
1975 **John Glover,** *The Winter's Tale* (American Shakespeare Festival, Stratford, Conn.)
1976 **Caroline McWilliams,** *Measure for Measure* (Shakespeare in the Park)
1977 **No award**
1978 **Carmen de Lavallade,** *Othello* (Roundabout Theatre)
1979 **Robert Christian,** *Coriolanus* (Shakespeare in the Park)
1980 **No award**

Clarence Derwent Awards

ACTORS' EQUITY ASSOCIATION
1500 Broadway, New York, N.Y. 10036 (212/869-8530)

The Clarence Derwent Awards, which each carry a $1,000 cash prize and an engraved crystal egg, annually honor the most promising male and female actors on the New York metropolitan scene. The award honors a meritorious performance in a supporting part in a Broadway or off-Broadway play. Stars and featured performers are ineligible for consideration by a committee of drama critics.

1945 **Frederick O'Neal,** *Anna Lacasta*
Judy Holliday, *Kiss Them for Me*
1946 **Paul Douglas,** *Born Yesterday*
Barbara Bel Geddes, *Deep are the Roots*
1947 **Tom Ewell,** *John Loves Mary*
Margaret Phillips, *Another Part of The Forest*
1948 **Lou Gilbert,** *Hope is a Thing With Feathers*
Catherine Ayers, *Moon of the Caribbean* and *Long Way From Home*
1949 **Ray Watson,** *Summer & Smoke*
Leora Dana, *Mad Woman of Chaillot*
1950 **Douglas Watson,** *Wisteria Trees*
Gloria Lane, *The Consul*
1951 **Logan Ramsey,** *High Ground*
Frederic Warriner, *Getting Married*
Phyllis Love, *Rose Tattoo*
1952 **Iggie Wolfington,** *Mrs. McThing*
Anne Meacham, *The Long Watch*
1953 **David J. Stewart,** *Camino Real*
Jenny Egan, *The Crucible*
1954 **David Lewis,** *King of Hearts*
Vilma Murer, *The Winner*
1955 **Fritz Weaver,** *The White Devil*
Vivian Nathan, *Anastasia*
1956 **Gerald Hiken,** *Uncle Vanya*
Frances Sternhagen, *The Admiral Bashville*
1957 **Ellis Rabb,** *The Misanthrope*
Joan Croydon, *The Potting Shed*
1958 **George C. Scott,** *Richard III*
Colin Wilcox, *The Day the Money Stopped*
1959 **David Hurst,** *Look After Lulu*
Lois Nettleton, *God & Kate Murphy*
1960 **Rochelle Oliver,** *Toys in the Attic*
William Daniels, *The Zoo Story*
1961 **Rosemary Murphy,** *Period of Adjustment*
Eric Christmas, *Little Moon of Alban*
1962 **Rebecca Darke,** *Who'll Save the Plowboy?*
Gene Wilder, *Complaisant Lover*
1963 **Jessica Walter,** *Photo Finish*
Gene Hackman, *Children From Their Games*
1964 **Joyce Ebert,** *The Trojan Women*
Richard McMurray, *A Case of Libel*
1965 **Elizabeth Hubbard,** *The Physicist*
Jame Sanchez, *Conerico Was Here to Stay*
1966 **Jean Hepple,** *Sgt. Musgrave's Dance*
Christopher Walken, *The Lion in Winter*
1967 **Reva Rose,** *You're A Good Man, Charlie Brown*
Austin Pendleton, *The Alchemist*
1968 **Catherine Burns,** *The Prime of Miss Jean Brodie*
David Birney, *Summertree*
1969 **Marlene Warfield,** *Great White Hope*
Ron O'Neal, *No Place to Be Somebody*
1970 **Pamela Payton-Wright,** *The Effect of Gamma Rays on Man in the Moon Marigolds*
Jeremiah Sullivan, *A Scent of Flower*
1971 **Katherine Helmond,** *The House of Blue Leaves*
James Woods, *Saved*
1972 **Pamela Bellwood,** *Buterflies are Free*
Richard Backus, *Promenade All*
1973 **Mari Gorman,** *Hot L Baltimore*
Christopher Murney, *Tricks*
1974 **Ann Reinking,** *Over Here*
Thom Christopher, *Noel Coward in 2 Keys*
1975 **Marybeth Hurt,** *Love For Love*
Reyno, *The First Breeze of Summer*
1976 **Nancy Snyder,** *Knock, Knock*
Peter Evans, *Streamers*
1977 **Rose Gregorio,** *The Shadow Box*
Barry Preston, *Bubbling Brown Sugar*
1978 **Margaret Hilton,** *Molly*
Morgan Freeman, *The Mighty Gents*
1979 **Laurie Kennedy,** *Man and Superman*
Richard Cox, *Dan Danger in Platinum*
1980 **Diane Wiest,** *The Art of Dining*
Eric Peterson, *Billy Bishop Goes to War*

SPECIAL CITATION:

1966 **Tom Ahearne,** *Hogan's Goat*
1967 **Philio Bosco,** *Hal Scrawdyke*

Actors' Fund Medal Award of Merit

ACTORS' FUND OF AMERICA
1501 Broadway, Suite 2600, New York, N.Y. 10036
(212/221-7300)

The Actors' Fund Medal With Citation is awarded as merited for service to the theatre. The medal was given once, retired and reactivated in 1958. The board of trustees selects the winners.

1910 **President William Howard Taft,** Opening of Actors' Fund Fair
1958 **Walter Vincent**
Charles Dow Clark
Helen Hayes

Actors' Equity Association
League of New York Theatres
J. J. Shubert
Fact Finding Committee of Entertainment Unions in New York City

1959 Council of Resident Stock Theatres
Council of Stock Theatres
Musical Arena Theatre Association
Stephen P. Kennedy
Ralph Bellamy
Mary Martin

1960 Music Fair Enterprise
Nanette Fabray
Sam Levene

1962 American Shakespeare Festival
Hon. Robert F. Wagner

1963 Newbold Morris
League of Off-Broadway Theatres
Lawrence Shubert Lawrence, Jr.

1964 Angus Duncan
Floyd W. Stoker
Zero Mostel

1966 Warren A. Schenck

1967 Ed Sullivan

1968 Angela Lansbury

1969 Hon. John V. Lindsay

1970 Katharine Hepburn
Brooks Atkinson
Ethel Merman

1971 Danny Kaye
Richard Rodgers
Warren P. Munsell

1972 Alfred Lunt and Lynn Fontanne
Harold Prince for *Fiddler On The Roof*
Neil Simon

1973 Clive Barnes
Harry Hershfield

1974 Debbie Reynolds
Jacob I. Goodstein

1975 Robert Preston
Vincent Sardi
Ellen Burstyn
Charles Grodin

1976 Louis A. Lotito

1977 Joseph Papp, New York Shakespeare Festival

1978 Gerald Schoenfeld
Bernard B. Jacobs

1979 Frances McCarthy

1980 Nedda Harrigan Logan

The Actors' Fund Award of Merit is given as warranted for service to the Actors' Fund both on and off the stage. The board of trustees selects the winners, of whom there have been too many to list—more than a thousand in the past twenty years.

Actors Studio Award

THE ACTORS STUDIO
432 W. 44th St., New York, N.Y. 10036 (212/757-0870)

The Actors Studio made "once-in-a-lifetime" Actors Studio Awards recognizing people who studied there for contributions to the theatre arts. The honorees had all previously been nominated for or won Oscar, Emmy or Tony awards. The Actors Studio Awards, bronze masks of actress Eleanor Duse, were presented at a gala dinner.

1980 Lee Allen
Lou Antonio
Beatrice Arthur
Barbara Bain
Carroll Baker
Martin Balsam
Anne Bancroft
Martine Bartlett
Barbara Baxley
Richard Boone
Marlon Brando
Roscoe Lee Brown
Ellen Burstyn
Zoe Caldwell
Pat Carroll
Jill Clayburgh
Gabriel Dell
Robert De Niro
Sandy Dennis
Bruce Dern
Bradford Dillman
Mildred Dunnock
Robert Duvall
Joan Ellis
Tom Ewell
Norman Fell
Sally Field
Gail Fisher
Jane Fonda
John Forsythe
Anthony Franciosa
Al Freeman, Jr.
George Furth
Vincent Gardenia
Ben Gazzara
Michael V. Gazzo
Carlin Glynn
Lee Grant
William Greaves
Barbara Harris
Julie Harris
June Havoc
Gerald Hiken
Dustin Hoffman
Celeste Holm
Kim Hunter
Early Hyman
Anne Jackson
Elia Kazan
Sally Kellerman
Shirley Knight
Diane Ladd
Martin Landau
Cloris Leachman
Ron Liebman
Viveca Lindfors
Barbara Loden
Sidney Lumet
Robert Lupone
Karl Malden
Nancy Marchand
E.G. Marshall
Nan Martin
Peter Masterson
Walter Matthau
Kevin McCarthy
Steve McQueen
Burgess Meredith
Joanna Miles
Sylvia Miles

Terry Moore
Michael Moriarty
Rosemary Murphy
Patricia Neal
Lois Nettleton
Paul Newman
Julie Newmar
Jack Nicholson
Kathleen Nolan
Carroll O'Connor
Al Pacino
Geraldine Page
Estelle Parsons
Albert Paulsen
Arthur Penn
Anthony Perkins
Eleanor Perry
Frank Perry
Sidney Poitier
Sydney Pollack
David Pressman
Gilbert Price
Robert Reed
Martin Ritt
Jerome Robbins
Cliff Robertson
Eva Marie Saint
Gene Saks
Alan Schneider
Kim Stanley
Maureen Stapleton
Rod Steiger
Jan Sterling
Beatrice Straight
Lee Strasberg
Susan Strasberg
Shepperd Strudwick
Inga Swenson
Vic Tayback
Rip Torn
Joan Van Ark
Jo Van Fleet
Ralph Waite
Robert Walden
Christopher Walken
Eli Wallach
Ray Walston
David Wayne
Dennis Weaver
Ann Wedgeworth
James Whitmore
Gene Wilder
Paul Winfield
Shelley Winters
Joanne Woodward

Richard Craven Award

AMERICAN HUMANE ASSOCIATION,
8480 Beverly Blvd., Los Angeles, Calif. 90048
(213/653-3394)

The Richard Craven Award, which consists of a trophy, is given annually (or as merited) for an outstanding feat performed by an animal before a live audience, either in theatre, rodeo or other entertainment. Animal performances for television and films are not eligible for this award. However, for details on the selection procedure, see the Patsy listing on p. 188 in the Cinema Section.

1951 **Tamba Tamba** (chimpanzee)
1952 **Smoky** (fighting stallion)
1953 **Brackett** (jumping horse)
1954 **Cocaine** (falling horse)
1955 **Flash** (falling and lying-down horse)
1956 **Flame** (German shepherd)
1957 **King Cotton** (white stallion)
1958 **Roy Rogers and Trigger** (25th anniversary in show business)
1959 **Baldy** (rearing horse)
1960 **Sharkey, Dempsey, Choctaw and Joker** (four-up horse team)
1961 **No award**
1962 **No Award**
1963 **Mickey O'Boyle** (fighting horse)
1964 **No award**
1965 **Little Buck** (falling and lying-down horse)
1966 **Smoky** (trick horse)
1967 **No award**
1968 **No award**
1969 **No award**
1970 **No award**
1971 **Kilroy** (falling horse)
1972 **Cocaine** (falling horse)
1973 **No award**
1974 **No award**
1975 **No award**
1976 **No award**
1977 **No award**
1978 **Sandy** (dog in *Annie*)
1979 **No award**
1980 **No award**

Delia Austrian Medal

DRAMA LEAGUE OF NEW YORK
c/o Julia Hansen, 555 Park Ave., New York, N.Y. 10021
(212/838-5859)

The Delia Austrian Medal, which is of bronze, is presented annually for the most outstanding performance of the season on the New York stage. It may be awarded to an actor or an actress, but performances in one-man shows are not considered. The winner is chosen by a vote of the membership.

1935 **Katharine Cornell,** *Romeo and Juliet*
1936 **Helen Hayes,** *Victoria Regina*
1937 **Maurice Evans,** *Richard III*
1938 **Cedric Hardwicke,** *Shadow and Substance*
1939 **Raymond Massey,** *Abe Lincoln in Illinois*
1940 **Paul Muni,** *Key Largo*
1941 **Paul Lukas,** *Watch on the Rhine*
1942 **Judith Evelyn,** *Angel Street*
1943 **Alfred Lunt and Lynn Fontanne,** *The Pirate*
1944 **Elisabeth Bergner,** *The Two Mrs. Carrolls*
1945 **Mady Christians,** *I Remember Mama*
1946 **Louis Calhern,** *The Magnificent Yankee*
1947 **Ingrid Bergman,** *Joan of Lorraine*
1948 **Judith Anderson,** *Medea*
1949 **Robert Morley,** *Edward My Son*
1950 **Grace George,** *The Velvet Glove*
1951 **Claude Rains,** *Darkness at Noon*
1952 **Julie Harris,** *I Am A Camera*
1953 **Shirley Booth,** *Time of the Cuckoo*
1954 **Josephine Hull,** *The Solid Gold Cadillac*
1955 **Viveca Lindfors,** *Anastasia*

1956 **David Wayne,** *The Ponder Heart*
1957 **Eli Wallach,** *Major Barbara*
1958 **Ralph Bellamy,** *Sunrise at Campobello*
1959 **Cyril Ritchard,** *The Pleasure of His Company*
1960 **Jessica Tandy,** *Five Finger Exercise*
1961 **Hume Cronyn,** *Big Fish, Little Fish*
1962 **Paul Scofield,** *A Man For All Seasons*
1963 **Charles Boyer,** *Lord Pengo*
1964 **Alec Guinness,** *Dylan*
1965 **John Gielgud,** *Tiny Alice*
1966 **Richard Kiley,** *Man of La Mancha*
1967 **Rosemary Harris,** *The Wild Duck*
1968 **Zoe Caldwell,** *The Prime of Miss Jean Brodie*
1969 **Alec McCowen,** *Hadrian The Seventh*
1970 **James Stewart,** *Harvey*
1971 **Anthony Quayle,** *Sleuth*
1972 **Eileen Atkins, Claire Bloom,** *Vivat! Vivat! Regina*
1973 **Alan Bates,** *Butley*
1974 **Christopher Plummer,** *The Good Doctor*
1975 **John Wood,** *Sherlock Holmes*
1976 **Eva Le Gallienne,** *The Royal Family*
1977 **Tom Courtney,** *Otherwise Engaged*
1978 **Frank Langella,** *Dracula*
1979 **Frances Sternhagen,** *On Golden Pond*
1980 **Roy Scheider,** *Betrayal*

SPECIAL AWARD

1980 **Circle Repertory Company,** Drama League Special Assistance Award to begin a program of assistance to playwrights.

Gold Medal

NATIONAL ARTS CLUB
15 Gramercy Park South, New York, N.Y. 10003
(212/475-3424)

As part of the club's honors program in the visual and performing arts and literature, a gold medal, also called the National Arts Club Drama Award, is presented annually for contributions to the theatre. Other medalists are listed in the Music and Dance, Visual Arts and Literature sections of this volume.

1973 **John Houseman**
1978 **Lauren Bacall**
1979 **Rex Harrison**
1980 **No award**

George Jean Nathan Award

GEORGE JEAN NATHAN TRUST
c/o Manufacturers Hanover Trust, 600 Fifth Ave., New York, N.Y. 10020 (212/350-4469)

The George Jean Nathan Award for Dramatic Criticism, which consists of $5,000, a citation and a silver medallion, is given annually for outstanding writings on the legitimate theater or drama criticism. Authors, critics and reviewers who are United States citizens and whose work is published in U.S. newspapers, magazines, books or other periodicals or is broadcast on television or radio programs originating in the U.S. are eligible. Authors or publishers may submit work published during the theatrical year for evaluation by the selection committee, which consists of the heads of the English Departments at Cornell, Princeton and Yale universities.

1959 **Harold Clurman,** Drama critic (*The Nation*) and author of reviews and essays ("Lies Like Truth")
1960 **C.L. Barber,** Amherst College, author (*Shakespeare's Festive Comedy*)
1961 **Jerry Tallmer,** drama critic (*The Village Voice*), for reviews, particularly of the off-Broadway theater
1962 **Robert Brustein,** theater critic (*The New Republic*) for articles and reviews
1963 **Walter Kerr,** drama critic (*New York Herald-Tribune*)
1964 **Elliot Norton,** drama critic (*Boston Record American* and *Sunday Advertiser*) for newspaper and television reviews
1965 **Gerald Weales,** University of Pennsylvania, for reviews in *Drama Survey*
1966 **Eric Russell Bentley,** Columbia University, for articles, two of which appeared in the *Tulane Drama Review*
1967 **Elizabeth Hardwick,** advisory editor (*New York Review of Books*) for reviews and discussions
1968 **Martin Gottfried,** drama critic (*Women's Wear Daily*) for book (*A Theater Divided: The Postwar American Stage*)
1969 **John Lahr,** drama critic (*Evergreen Review* and *The Village Voice*) and for essays
1970 **John Simon,** drama critic (*Hudson Review* and *New York Magazine*) for reviews
1971 **Richard Gilman,** Yale University, author (*Common and Uncommon Masks: Writings on Theatre, 1961-1970*)
1972 **Jay Carr,** theater and music critic (*Detroit News*) for selected drama reviews
1973 **Stanley Kauffmann,** film and theater critic (*New Republic*) for selected drama reviews
1974 **Albert Bermel,** City University of New York, for selected drama reviews
1976 **Michael Goldman,** Princeton University, author (*The Actor's Freedom: Toward a Theory of Drama*)
1977 **Bernard Knox,** Center for Hellenic Studies, Washington, D.C., review of *Agamemnon* published in The *New York Review of Books*
1978 **Mel Gussow,** for essay "A Rich Crop of Writing Talent Brings New Life to The American Theater" and for daily reporting of modern and classical drama in *The New York Times*
1979 **Jack Kroll,** for nine reviews and essays published in *Newsweek*
1980 **Not available at press time**

NETC Annual Award
NETC Community Theatre Drama Festival Award
NETC Special Award
John Gassner Memorial Playwriting Award
Moss Hart Memorial Award

NEW ENGLAND THEATRE CONFERENCE
50 Exchange St., Waltham, Mass. 02154 (617/893-3120)

The NETC Annual Award honors significant creative achievement by individuals, groups or organizations in the performing arts. A Revere bowl is awarded to the prize winner, who is selected by nominations from the

NETC membership, board of directors and advisory council and chosen by the board and council.

1957 **Jo Mielziner**
1958 **Joshua Logan**
1959 **Richard Rodgers and Oscar Hammerstein II**
1960 **Moss Hart**
1961 **Howard Lindsay and Russel Crouse**
1962 **Lawrence Langner**
1963 **Joseph Papp**
1964 **Repertory Theater of Lincoln Center (Harold Clurman, Elia Kazan and Robert Whitehead)**
1965 **Morris Carnovsky**
1966 **William Gibson**
1967 **David Hays**
1968 **David Merrick**
1969 **Arthur Miller**
1970 **Harold Prince**
1971 **The Open Theatre**
1972 **John Houseman**
1973 **Lillian Hellman**
1974 **Elliot Norton**
1975 **Eva Le Gallienne**
1976 **Adrian Hall**
1977 **Cheryl Crawford**
1978 **Harold Clurman**
1979 **Kitty Carlisle**
1980 **Uta Hagen**

The winner of the NETC Community Theatre Drama Festival Award receives a trophy honoring the best production of a New England community theatre production. A professional adjudicator sees all productions and offers a public critique of each to select the recipient.

1954 **Natick Footlighters** (Natick, Mass.), *Fumed Oak*
1955 **Quannapowitt Players** (Reading, Mass.), *The Old Lady Shows Her Medals*
1956 **Linden Players** (Needham, Mass.), *The Full House*
1957 **Civic League Players** (Framingham, Mass.), *Fumed Oak*
1958 **M.I.T. Community Players** (Cambridge, Mass.), *A Phoenix Too Frequent*
1959 **Concord Players** (Concord, Mass.), *A Trap Is a Small Place*
1960 **Norwood Curtain-Timers** (Norwood, Mass.), *Cat On a Hot Tin Roof*
1961 **Shrewsbury Players Guild** (Shrewsbury, Mass.), *No Exit*
1962 **Community Players** (Framingham, Mass.), *Waltz of the Toreadors*
1963 **Concord Players,** (Concord, Mass.), *The Browning Version*
1964 **Drama Workshop** (Worcester Community Center, Worcester, Mass.), *The Death of Bessie Smith*
1965 **Entr' Actors Guild** (Worcester, Mass.), *The Bald Soprano*
1966 **Hovey Players** (Waltham, Mass.), *Snowangel*
1967 **Concord Players** (Concord, Mass.), *A Taste of Honey*
1968 **Entr'Actors Guild** (Worcester, Mass.), *Chamber Music*
1969 **Winthrop Playmakers** (Winthrop, Mass.), *Crawling Arnold*
1970 **Entr'Actors Guild** (Worcester, Mass.), *Interview*
1971 **Center Players** (Springfield, Mass.), *The Lion in Winter*
1972 **Entr'Actors Guild** (Worcester, Mass.), *Brecht on Brecht*
1973 **Sudbury Players** (Sudbury, Mass.), *Schubert's Last Serenade*
1974 **Garrett Players** (Lawrence, Mass.), *Endgame*
1975 **Newton Country Players** (Newton, Mass.), *The Real Inspector Hound*
1976 **Garrett Players** (Lawrence, Mass.), *1776*
1977 **Marblehead Little Theatre** (Marblehead, Mass.), *The Love Course*
1978 **Shrewsbury** (Mass.) **Players Production Co.,** *Canterbury Tales*
1979 **Peninsula Players** (Nahant, Mass.), *Godspell*
1980 **Garrett Players** (Lawrence, Mass.), *Suicide in Bb*

The NETC Special Award annually recognizes national achievement, contribution or innovation in the interest, support and advancement of theatre on a national level. A plaque is awarded to the winner, who is nominated by the NETC membership, board of directors and advisory council and selected by the board and council.

1957 **Hill and Wang**
1958 **Norris Houghton**
1959 ***Playhouse 90***
1960 **David Susskind**
1961 **Grove Press and National Thespian Society**
1962 **The Living Theatre**
1963 **Frederick O'Neal**
1964 **Richard Boone, Jewish Theological Seminary of America and Raymond Sovey**
1965 **Alvin Ailey, Free Southern Theatre, John Gassner and Adrienne Kennedy**
1966 **American Place Theatre and Viola Spolin**
1967 **Horace Armistead, Theodore Fuchs, Earle Hyman and Stanley McCandless**
1968 **Orlin and Irene Corey, Lyn Ely and Tom O'Horgan**
1969 **Karl Malden, Julius L. Novick, The Playwrights' Unit and Budd Schulberg and the Watts Writers' Workshop and Edwin Sherin**
1970 **Boris Aronson, Michael Butler, Joe Layton and Peter Stone**
1971 **Merce Cunningham and The Chelsea Theater Center**
1972 **American Playwrights' Theatre and Harold Scott**
1973 **Alexander H. Cohen and Patricia Zipprodt**
1974 **Brooks Atkinson, Zelda Fichandler and Louis Sheaffer**
1975 **Theatre Development Fund and *The Village Voice***
1976 **Alois Nagler, *Theater in America* and Theatre Communications Group**
1977 **Lehman Engel and Manhattan Theatre Club**
1978 **Uta Hagen, Foundation for the Extension & Development of the American Professional Theatre**
1979 **Woodie King, Jr., Ming Cho Lee, Harvey Sabinson**
1980 **Jon Jory and the Actors Theatre of Louisville** (Ky.), **Gerald Bordman, Ellis Rabb**

Regional Citations annually honor accomplishments of New England regional theatre.

1957 **Community Players of Concord,** N.H., and **Massachusetts High School Drama Guild**
1958 **Herschel L. Bricker, F. Curtis Canfield, Harlan F. Grant and WGBH, Boston**
1959 **The Council for a TV Course in the Humanities in the Secondary School, Gregory Falls, Newton High School and Poet's Theatre**
1960 **Marston Balch, The Charles Playhouse, WBZ-TV and Barbara Wellington**
1961 **Boston Arts Festival, Boston Children's Theatre, Mrs. Howard J. Chidley, Elliot Norton and Edwin Burr Pettet**

1962 **Joseph D. Batcheller, *Boston Globe*, Harold L. Cail, Marie L. Phillips, Portland Children's Theatre, Provincetown Playhouse and Weston Community Club, Inc. and The Townspeople of Weston, Vt.**
1963 **Warner Bentley, Boston College, Premiere Performance Company and Elsi Rowland**
1964 **Lucy Barton, Sarah Caldwell, Ruth St. Denis and Ted Shawn**
1965 **The Boston Herald Traveler Corporation, Connecticut College, Edward Finnegan, Hartford Stage Company, Theatre by the Sea** (Portsmouth, N.H.) **and Trinity Square Repertory Company**
1966 **Boston University School of Fine and Applied Arts, Francis Grover Cleveland, Richard Eberhart, Long Wharf Theatre and Theatre Company of Boston**
1967 **Arlington Friends of the Drama, Edward C. Cole, Elma Lewis and Project TRY**
1968 **Boston Herald Traveler Corporation, Harvey Grossman, Robert J. Guest, Northeastern University and George C. White, Jr.**
1969 ***Boston After Dark*, Brandeis University Theatre Arts Department, Entr' Actors Guild, Looking Glass Theatre and Jack Stein**
1970 **Emerson College Musical Theatre Society,! Improvise!, *Maine Times*, The Proposition and James Spruill**
1971 **Maxine Klein, Stage I Drama Workshop, Theatre Workshop Boston, Inc., and Rhode Island Festival: Theatre '71 (Brown University, Providence College, Rhode Island College, Rhode Island Junior College, Rhode Island School of Design, Roger Williams College, the University of Rhode Island, and the Rhode Island State Council on the Arts)**
1972 **Sarah Minchin Baker, Fisherman's Players of Cape Cod/Richard Waters, Sen. Claiborne Pell, Summerthing and E. Virginia Williams**
1973 **Richard Kneeland, Metropolitan Cultural Alliance, William H. Rough and Theatre Association of Maine**
1974 **Tony Montanaro and the Celebration Mime Theatre, Eugene O'Neill Memorial Theater Center and Gerald Roberts**
1975 **Harvard Theatre Collection and Stage/West**
1976 **Bread and Puppet Theatre, Michael P. Price/Goodspeed Opera House, Ralf Coleman and Gustave Johnson**
1977 **Norman H. Leger, Evangeline Machlin and Pilobolus Dance Theatre**
1978 **Berkshire Theatre Festival** (Stockbridge, Mass.), **Champlain Shakespeare Festival** (Burlington, Vt.), **Donald Gramm** (Boston and New York)
1979 **George Hamlin, Loeb Drama Center** (Harvard University, Cambridge, Mass.), **Catharine S. Huntington,** Provincetown Playhouse (Boston), **The Next Move Theater** (Boston)
1980 **Errol G. Hill,** Dartmouth College (Hanover, N.H.), **George H. Quinby,** Bowdoin College (Brunswick, Me.), **Crane, Dreskin, Friedman** and **Kauffman** (student playwrights from Brandeis University, Waltham, Mass.)

The John Gassner Memorial Playwriting Award, which consists of a cash stipend of to $150 plus script-in-hand showcase performance with critique, is offered for the best new, original, one-act play by a U.S. playwright. The play must be commercially unpublished, unproduced and of a twenty-minute to one-hour duration. A screening committee reads all entered plays and selects about two dozen which are submitted to the judging committee, which chooses the winner. Run- nerup cash awards are also made.

1963 **George Hickenlooper,** *Caviar For the General*
Robert Lehan, *A Matter of Character*
Jack Murphy, *Benjamin*
Brice Weisman, *Beamlight With the Red Flasher*
1964 **Robert Lehan,** *The Waiting Room*
Jack Murphy, *Golden Days*
1965 **No award**
1966 **Gerald Kean,** *Immediate Occupancy*
1967 **Tim Kelly,** *The Natives Are Restless*
1968 **No award**
1969 **Eric Meredith Lord,** *Lions Four, Christians Nothing*
1970 **Craig Clinton,** *The Lunch Hours*
1971 **Burt French,** *Thank You, Mrs. Garrigan; It Was Nothing Mr. God*
1972 **Burt French,** *Chowder and Cherries*
1973 **L.E. Preston,** *It's Your Move*
1974 **Rome Kingson,** *Love in Little Wotting*
1975 **Richard Barron,** *National Pastime*
1976 **Robert Lehan,** *Lovesong*
1977 **John C. Cox,** *The Waverly Local*
1978 **Jess Gregg,** *The Organ Recital at the New Grand*
1979 **Louis Damelio,** *The Private Prop. of Roscoe Pointer*
1980 **William Wise,** *Traveler's Rest*

The Moss Hart Memorial Award is a trophy given annually for superior production of a play, demonstrating human courage and taking a positive attitude toward the human condition. The play must be full-length and produced in the previous year by a theatre company resident in New England.

1962 **Drama Club of the State College at Fitchburg,** Mass., *The Diary of Anne Frank*
1963 **Scitamard Players** (Providence, R.I.), *A Raisin in the Sun*
1964 **Community Players** (Concord, N.H.), *Inherit the Wind*
1965 **The People's Theater** (Cambridge, Mass.), *Noah*
1966 **Wheelock College Drama Club** (Boston, Mass.), *Jacobowsky and the Colonel*
1967 **Arlington Friends of the Drama** (Arlington, Mass.), *The Crucible*
1968 **Staples High School Players** (Westport, Conn.), *War and Pieces*
1969 **No award**
1970 **Staples High School Players** (Westport, Conn.), *Soldier, Soldier*
1971 **University of Hartford Players** (Hartford, Conn.), *The Ceremony of Innocence*
1972 **Arlington Friends of the Drama** (Arlington, Mass.), *Fiddler on the Roof*
1973 **Reagle Players,** Waltham Summer Theatre (Waltham, Mass.), *1776*
1974 **Harwich Winter Theatre** (W. Harwich, Mass.), *Uncle Vanya*
1975 **Concord Players** (Concord, Mass.), *A Flurry of Birds*
1976 **Roger Ludlowe High School,** (Fairfield, Conn.), *The Miracle Worker*
1977 **Dartmouth Players** (Dartmouth College, Hanover, N.H.), *Blood Wedding*
1978 **Hamden** (Conn.) **High School,** *The Crucible*
1979 **Concord** (Mass.) **Players,** *The Glass Menagerie*
1980 **Rhode Island College Theatre** (Providence), *To Kill A Mockingbird*

New York Drama Critics Circle Award

275 Central Park West, New York, N.Y. 10023
(212/741-4043)

Members of the Circle annually vote for the best play of the year, best American/foreign play and best musical. If the best play is by an American author, another award is frequently given to the author of the best foreign play. The top award carries a $1,000 cash prize, while scrolls are presented to other honored playwrights. New plays produced in New York during the season are eligible for these honors.

AMERICAN PLAY

1936 **Maxwell Anderson,** *Winterset*
1937 **Maxwell Andersen,** *High Tor*
1938 **John Steinbeck,** *Of Mice and Men*
1939 No award
1940 **William Saroyan,** *The Time of Your Life*
1941 **Lillian Hellman,** *The Watch on the Rhine*
1942 No award
1943 **Sidney Kingsley,** *The Patriots*
1944 No award
1945 **Tennessee Williams,** *The Glass Menagerie*
1946 No award
1947 **Arthur Miller,** *All My Sons*
1948 **Tennessee Williams,** *Streetcar Named Desire*
1949 **Arthur Miller,** *Death of a Salesman*
1950 **Carson McCullers,** *The Member of the Wedding*
1951 **Sidney Kingsley,** *Darkness at Noon*
1952 **John Van Druten,** *I Am a Camera*
1953 **William Inge,** *Picnic*
1954 **John Patrick,** *The Teahouse of the August Moon*
1955 **Tennessee Williams,** *Cat on a Hot Tin Roof*
1956 **Frances Goodrich and Albert Hackett,** *The Diary of Anne Frank*
1957 **Eugene O'Neill,** *Long Day's Journey into Night*
1958 **Ketti Frings,** *Look Homeward, Angel*
1959 **Lorraine Hansberry,** *A Raisin in the Sun*
1960 **Lillian Hellman,** *Toys in the Attic*
1961 **Tad Mosel,** *All the Way Home*
1962 **Tennessee Williams,** *The Night of the Iguana*
1963-68 No awards in this category
1969 **Paul Zindel,** *The Effect of Gamma Rays on Man-in-the-Moon Marigolds*
1970 No award
1971 **John Guare,** *The House of Blue Leaves*
1972 No award
1973 **Lanford Wilson,** *Hot L Baltimore*
1974 **Miguel Pinero,** *Short Eyes*
1975 **Ed Bullins,** *The Taking of Miss Janie*
1976 **David Rabe,** *Streamers*
1977 **David Mamet,** *American Buffalo*

FOREIGN PLAY

1938 **Paul Vincent Carroll,** *Shadow and Substance*
1939 **Paul Vincent Carroll,** *The White Steed*
1940 No award
1941 **Emlyn Williams,** *The Corn is Green*
1942 **Noel Coward,** *Blithe Spirit*
1943 No award
1944 **Franz Werfel and S. N. Behrman,** *Jacobowsky and the Colonel*
1945 No award
1946 No award
1947 **Jean-Paul Sartre,** *No Exit*
1948 **Terence Rattigan,** *The Winslow Boy*
1949 **Maurice Valency,** *The Madwoman of Chaillot*
1950 **T.S. Eliot,** *The Cocktail Party*
1951 **Christopher Fry,** *The Lady's Not for Burning*
1952 **Christopher Fry,** *Venus Observed*
1953 **Peter Ustinov,** *The Love of Four Colonels*
1954 **Maurice Valency,** *Ondine*
1955 **Agatha Christie,** *Witness for the Prosecution*
1956 **Christopher Fry,** *Tiger at the Gates*
1957 **Jean Anouilh,** *Waltz of the Toreadors*
1958 **John Osborne,** *Look Back in Anger*
1959 **Friederich Duerrenmatt,** *The Visit*
1960 **Peter Shaffer,** *Five Finger Exercise*
1961 **Shelagh Delaney,** *A Taste of Honey*
1962 **Robert Bolt,** *A Man for All Seasons*
1963-79 No awards
1980 **Harold Pinter,** *The Betrayal*

BEST PLAY

1963 **Edward Albee,** *Who's Afraid of Virginia Woolf?*
1964 **Frank Gilroy,** *The Subject Was Roses*
1965 **John Osborne,** *Luther*
1966 **Peter Weiss,** *Marat/Sade*
1967 **Harold Pinter,** *The Homecoming*
1968 **Tom Stoppard,** *Rosencrantz and Guildenstern Are Dead*
1969 **Howard Sackler,** *The Great White Hope*
1970 **Frank McMahon,** *Borstal Boy*
1971 **David Storey,** *Home*
1972 **Jason Miller,** *That Championship Season*
1973 **David Storey,** *The Changing Room*
1974 **David Storey,** *The Contractor*
1975 **Peter Shaffer,** *Equus*
1976 **Tom Stoppard,** *Travesties*
1977 **Simon Gray,** *Otherwise Engaged*
1978 **Hugh Leonard,** *Da*
1979 **Bernard Pomerance,** *The Elephant Man*
1980 **Lanford Wilson,** *Talley's Folly*

MUSICAL

1946 ***Carousel***
1947 ***Brigadoon***
1948 No award
1949 ***South Pacific***
1950 ***The Consul***
1951 ***Guys and Dolls***
1952 ***Pal Joey***
1953 ***Wonderful Town***
1954 **John Latouche and Jerome Moross,** *The Golden Apple*
1955 ***The Saint of Bleecker Street***
1956 **Alan Jay Lerner,** *My Fair Lady*
1957 ***The Most Happy Fella***
1958 **Meredith Wilson,** *The Music Man*
1959 ***La Plume de Ma Tante***
1960 **George Abbott, Jerome Weidman, Sheldon Harnick, and Jerry Bock,** *Fiorello!*
1961 **Michael Stewart and Bob Merrill,** *Carnival!*
1962 **Abe Burrows, Jack Weinstock, Willie Gilbert and Frank Loesser,** *How to Succeed in Business Without Really Trying*
1963 No award
1964 ***Hello, Dolly!***
1965 ***Fiddler on the Roof***
1966 **Dale Wasserman, Mitch Leigh and Joe Darion,** *Man of La Mancha*
1967 **F. Ebb et al.,** *Cabaret*
1968 ***Your Own Thing***
1969 **S. Edwards and P. Stone,** *1776*
1970 **Stephen Sondheim and George Furth,** *Company*
1971 **Stephen Sondheim and James Goldman,** *Follies*

1972 **Galt MacDermot and John Guare,** *Two Gentlemen of Verona*
1973 **Hugh Wheeler and Stephen Sondheim,** *A Little Night Music*
1974 ***Candide***
1975 **Michael Bennett** (choreographer and director), **James Kirkwood and Nicholas Dante** (book), **Marvin Hamlisch** (music), **Edward Kleban** (lyrics), ***A Chorus Line***
1976 **Stephen Sondheim** (music and lyrics), **John Weidman** (book), and **Hugh Wheeler** (additional material), *Pacific Overtures*
1977 **Charles Strous** (music), **Martin Charnin** (lyrics), **Thomas Meehan** (book), **Mike Nichols** (producer), *Annie*
1978 **Fats Waller's** music, *Ain't Misbehavin'*
1979 **Stephen Sondheim,** *Sweeney Todd*
1980 **Harold Prince** (producer), *Evita*

SPECIAL CITATION

1980 **Peter Brook,** Le Centre International de Creations Theatrale, for repertory season at La Mama, New York

Obie Award

VILLAGE VOICE
80 University Place, New York, N.Y. 10003 (212/741-0030)

The Obie Award, which consists of a plaque and sometimes a monetary prize as well, is given annually for excellence and creative achievement in off-Broadway theatre. A panel of expert judges in the field selects the winners from the season's productions. The names of the categories have been changed over the years.

SUSTAINED ACHIEVEMENT/LIFETIME ACHIEVEMENT

1978 **Peter Schumman**'s Bread & Puppet Theatre
1979 **Al Carmines**
1980 **No award**

BEST PLAY/BEST NEW AMERICAN PLAY

1956 ***Absalom*** (Lionel Abel)
1957 ***A House Remembered*** (Louis A. Lippe)
1958 ***Endgame*** (Samuel Beckett)
1959 ***The Quare Fellow*** (Brendan Behan)
1960 ***The Connection*** (Jack Gelber)
1961 ***The Blacks*** (Jean Genet)
1962 ***Who'll Save the Plowboy?*** (Frank D. Gilroy)
1963 **No award**
1964 ***Play*** (Samuel Beckett)
Dutchman (LeRoi Jones)
1965 ***The Old Glory*** (Robert Lowell)
1966 ***The Journey of the Fifth Horse*** (Ronald Ribman)
1967 **No award**
1968 **No award**
1969 **See separate 1969 Obie listing below**
1970 ***The Effect of Gamma Rays on Man-in-the-Moon Marigolds*** (Paul Zindel)
Approaching Simone (Megan Terry)
1971 ***House of Blue Leaves*** (John Guare)
1972 **No award**
1973 ***Hot L Baltimore*** (Lanford Wilson)
The River Niger (Joseph A. Walker)
1974 ***Short Eyes*** (Miguel Pinero)
1975 ***The First Breeze of Summer*** (Leslie Lee)
1976 **No award**
1977 ***Curse of the Starving Class*** (Sam Shepard)
1978 **Lee Breuer,** *Shaggy Dog Animation*
1979 **Michael McClure,** *Josephine*

BEST FOREIGN PLAY

1950 ***The Balcony*** (Jean Genet)
1962 ***Happy Days*** (Samuel Beckett)
1968 ***The Memorandum*** (Vaclav Havel)
1969 **See separate 1969 Obie listing below**
1970 ***What the Butler Saw*** (Joe Orton)
1974 ***The Contractor*** (David Storey)

BEST ADAPTATION

1958 ***The Brothers Karamazov*** (Boris Tumarin and Jack Sydow)

BEST REVIVAL

1958 ***The Crucible*** (Arthur Miller, directed by World Baker)

BEST COMEDY

1958 ***Comic Strip*** (George Panetta)

BEST ONE-ACT PLAY

1958 ***Guest of the Nation*** (Neil McKenzie)

BEST MUSICAL

1956 ***Three Penny Opera*** (Bertolt Brecht and Kurt Weill; adapted by Marc Blitzstein)
1959 ***A Party With Betty Comden and Adolph Green***
1962 ***Fly Blackbird*** (C. Jackson, James Hatch and Jerome Eskow)
1968 ***In Circles*** (Gertrude Stein and Al Carmines)
1969 **See separate 1969 Obie listing below**
1970 ***The Last Sweet Days of Isaac*** (Gretchen Cryer and Nancy Ford)
The Me Nobody Knows (Robert Livingston, Gary William Friedman and Will Holt)

BEST REVUE

1959 ***Diversions*** (Steven Vinaver)

BEST OFF-OFF-BROADWAY PRODUCTION

1961 ***The Premise*** (Produced and directed by Theodore Flicker)

DISTINGUISHED PLAYS

1960 ***Krapp's Last Tape*** (Samuel Beckett)
The Prodigal (Jack Richardson)
The Zoo Story (Edward Albee)
1964 ***Home Movies*** (Rosalyn Drexler)
Funny House of a Negro (Adrienne Kennedy)
1965 ***Promenade*** and ***The Successful Life of Three*** (Maria Irene Fornes)
1966 ***Good Day*** (Emmanuel Peluso)
Chicago, Icarus's Mother and ***Red Cross*** (Sam Shepard)
1967 ***Futz*** (Rochelle Owens)
La Turista (Sam Shepard)
1968 ***Muzeeka*** (John Guare)
The Indian Wants the Bronx (Israel Horovitz)
Melodrama Play (Sam Shepard)
1969 **See separate 1969 Obie listing below**
1970 ***The Deer Kill*** (Murray Mednick)
The Increased Difficulty of Concentration (Vaclav Havle)
1973 ***The Tooth of Crime*** (Sam Shepard)
Big Foot (Ronald Tavel)
What If I Had Turned Up Heads? (J.E. Gaines)
1974 ***Bad Habits*** (Terrence McNally)

When You Comin' Back, Red Ryder? (Mark Medoff)
The Great MacDaddy (Paul Carter Harrison)

DISTINGUISHED PLAYWRITING

1971 **Ed Bullins,** *The Fabulous Miss Marie* and *In New England Winter*
David Rabe, *Basic Training of Pavlo Hummel*
1979 **Rosalyn Drexler,** *The Writer's Opera*
Susan Miller, *Nasty Rumors and Final Remarks*
Richard Nelson, *Vienna Notes*
Bernard Pomerance, *The Elephant Man*
Sam Shepard, *Buried Child*
1980 **Lee Breuer,** *A Prelude to Death in Venice*
Christopher Durang, *Sister Mary Ignatius Explains It All for You*
Romulus Linney, *Tennessee*
Roland Muldoon, *Full Confessions of a Socialist*
Jeff Weiss, *That's How the Rent Gets Paid (Part Three)*

DISTINGUISHED FOREIGN PLAY

1971 ***Boesman and Lena*** (Athol Fugard)
AC/DC (Heathcote Williams)
Dream on Monkey Mountain (Derek Walcott)
1973 ***Not I*** (Samuel Beckett)
Kasper (Peter Handke)

BEST PRODUCTION

1956 ***Uncle Vanya*** (Fourth Street Theatre)
1957 No award
1958 No award
1959 ***Exiles*** (Renata Theatre)
1960 ***The Connection*** (Living Theatre)
1961 ***Hedda Gabler*** (Fourth Street Theatre)
1962 No award
1963 ***Six Characters in Search of an Author*** (Martinique Theatre)
The Boys From Syracuse (Theatre Four)
1964 ***The Brig*** (Living Theatre)
What Happened (Judson Poets Theatre)
1965 ***The Cradle Will Rock*** (Theatre Four)

DISTINGUISHED PRODUCTION

1971 ***The Trial of the Catonsville Nine***
1977 ***The Club***
For Colored Girls Who Have Considered Suicide/When the Rainbow is Enuf
Dressed Like an Egg

BEST THEATRE PIECE

1972 ***The Mutation Show*** (The Open Theatre)

BEST ACTRESS

1956 **Julie Bovasso,** *The Maids*
1957 **Colleen Dewhurst,** *The Taming of the Shrew, The Eagle Has Two Heads* and *Camille*
1958 **Anne Meacham,** *Suddenly Last Summer (Garden District)*
1959 **Kathleen Maguire,** *The Time of the Cuckoo*
1960 **Eileen Breenan,** *Little Mary Sunshine*
1961 **Anne Meacham,** *Hedda Gabler*
1962 **Barbara Harris,** *Oh Dad, Poor Dad, Momma's Hung You in the Closet and I'm Feelin' So Sad*
1963 **Colleen Dewhurst,** *Desire Under the Elms*
1964 No award
1965 **See Distinguished Performances below**
1966 **Jane White,** *Coriolanus* and *Love's Labours Lost*
1967 No award
1968 **Billie Dixon,** *The Beard*

BEST ACTOR

1956 **Jason Robards Jr.,** *The Iceman Cometh*
George Voskovec, *Uncle Vanya*
1957 No award
1958 **George C. Scott,** *Richard III, As You Like It* and *Children of Darkness*
1959 **Alfredo Ryder,** *I Rise in Flame, Cried the Phoenix*
1960 **Warren Finnerty,** *The Connection*
1961 **Khigh Dhiegh,** *In the Jungle of Cities*
1962 **James Earl Jones,** *Clandestine on the Morning Line, The Apple* and *Moon on a Rainbow Shawl*
1963 **George C. Scott,** *Desire Under the Elms*
1964 No award
1965 **See Distinguished Performances below**
1966 **Dustin Hoffman,** *The Journey of the Fifth Horse*
1967 **Seth Allen,** *Futz*
1968 **Al Pacino,** *The Indian Wants the Bronx*
1969 No award
1970 No award
1971 **Jack MacGowran,** *Beckett*

DISTINGUISHED PERFORMANCES (Male and Female)

1964 **Gloria Foster,** *In White America*
1965 **Roscoe Lee Browne, Frank Langella and Lester Rawlins,** *The Old Glory*
1970 **Sada Thompson,** *The Effect of Gamma Rays on Man-in-the-Moon Marigolds*
1974 **Barbara Barrie,** *The Killdeer*
Joseph Buloff, *Hard to Be a Jew*
Kevin Conway, *When You Comin' Back, Red Ryder?*
Conchata Ferrell, *The Sea Horse*
Loretta Greene, *The Sirens*
Barbara Montgomery, *My Sister, My Sister*
Zipora Spaizman, *Stepnyu*
Elizabeth Sturges, *When You Comin' Back, Red Ryder?*
1975 **Reyno,** *The First Breeze of Summer*
Moses Gunn, *The First Breeze of Summer*
Dick Latessa, *Philemon*
Kevin McCarthy, *Harry Outside*
Stephen D. Newman, *Polly*
Christopher Walken, *Kid Champion*
Ian Trigger, *The True History of Squire Jonathan*
Cara Duff-McCormick, *Craig's Wife*
Priscilla Smith, *Trilogy*
Tanya Berezin, *The Mound Builders*
Tovah Feldshuh, *Yentl the Yeshiva Boy*
1976 **Robert Christian,** *Blood Knot*
Pamela Payton-Wright, *Jesse and the Bandit Queen*
Priscilla Smith, *The Good Woman of Setzuan*
David Warrilow, *The Lost Ones*
June Gable, *Comedy of Errors*
Sammy Williams, *A Chorus Line*
Priscilla Lopez, *A Chorus Line*
Joyce Aaron, *Acrobatics*
Mike Kellin, *American Buffalo*
Roberts Blossom, *Ice Age*
Crystal Field, *Day Old Bread*
Tony LoBianco, *Yankees 3, Detroit 0*
T. Miratti, *The Shortchanged Revue*
Kate Manheim, *Rhoda In Potatoland*
1977 **Danny Aiello,** *Gemini*
Martin Balsam, *Cold Storage*
Lucinda Childs, *Einstein on the Beach*
James Coco, *The Transfiguration of Benno Blimpie*
Anne DeSalvo, *Gemini*
John Heard, *G. R. Point*

Jo Henderson, *Ladyhouse Blues*
William Hurt, *My Life*
Joseph Maher, *Savages*
Roberta Maxwell, *Ashes*
Brian Murray, *Ashes*
Lola Pashalinski, *Der Ring Gott Farblonjet*
Marian Seldes, *Isadora Duncan Sleeps with the Russian Navy*
Margaret Wright, *A Manoir*
1978 **Richard Bauer,** *Landscape of the Body* and *The Dybbuk*
Nell Carter, *Ain't Misbehavin'*
Alma Cuevo, *Uncommon Women*
Swoosie Kurtz, *Uncommon Women*
Kaiulani Lee, *Safe House*
Bruce Myers, *The Dybbuk*
Lee S. Wilkof, *The Present Tense*
1979 **Mary Alice,** *Nongogo* and *Julius Caesar*
Philip Anglim, *The Elephant Man*
Joseph Buloff, *The Price*
Constance Cummings, *Wings*
Fred Gwynne, *Grand Magic*
Judd Hirsch, *Talley's Folly*
Marcell Rosenblatt, *Vienna Notes*
Meryl Streep, *Taken in Marriage*
Elizabeth Wilson, *Taken in Marriage*
1980 **Michael Burrell,** *Hess*
Michael Cristofer, *Chinchilla*
Lindsay Crouse, *Reunion*
Elizabeth Franz, *Sister Mary Ignatius Will Explain It All for You*
Morgan Freeman, *Mother Courage* and *Coriolanus*
John Heard, *Othello* and *Split*
Michael Higgins, *Reunion*
Madelaine Le Roux, *La Justice*
Jon Polito, Dodger Theatre Company and BAM Theatre Company performances
Bill Raymond, *A Prelude to Death in Venice*
Diane Wiest, *The Art of Dining*
Hattie Winston, *Mother Courage* and *The Michigan*

DISTINGUISHED PERFORMANCES (Actresses)

1956 **Peggy McKay**
Shirlee Emmons
Frances Sternhagen
Nancy Wickwire
1957 **Marguerite Lenert**
Betty Miller
Jutta Wolf
1958 **Tammy Grimes**
Grania O'Malley
Nydia Westman
1959 **Rosina Fernhoff**
Anne Fielding
Nancy Wickwire
1960 **Patricia Falkenhain**
Alisa Loti
Nancy Marchand
1961 **Joan Hackett**
Gerry Jedd
Surya Kumari
1962 **Sudie Bond**
Vinnette Carrol
Rosemary Harris
Ruth White
1963 **Jacqueline Brooks**
Olympia Dukakis
Anne Jackson
Madeline Sherwood
1964 **Joyce Ebert**
Lee Grant
Estelle Parsons
Diana Sands
Marian Seldes
1965 **Margaret De Priest**
Rosemary Harris
Frances Sternhagen
Sada Thompson
1966 **Clarice Blackburn**
Marie-Claire Charba
Gloria Foster
Sharon Gains
Florence Tarlow
1967 **Bette Henritze**
1968 **Jean David**
Mari Gorman
Peggy Pope
1969 **See separate 1969 Obie listing below**
1970 **Rue McClanahan**
Roberta Maxwell
Fredericka Weber
Pamela Payton-Wright
1971 **Susan Batson**
Margaret Braidwood
Joan Macintosh
1972 **Salome Bey**
Marilyn Chris
Jeanne Hepple
Marilyn Sokol
Kathleen Widdoes
Elizabeth Wilson
1973 **Mari Gorman**
Lola Pashalinski
Alice Playten
Roxie Roker
Jessica Tandy
1974 **Barbara Barrie**
Conchata Ferrell
Loretta Greene
Barbara Montgomery
Zipora Spaizman
Elizabeth Sturges

DISTINGUISHED PERFORMANCES (Actors)

1956 **Gerald Hiken**
Alan Ansara
Roberts Blossom
Addison Powell
1957 **Thayer David**
Michael Kane
Arthur Maiet
1958 **Leonardo Cimino**
Jack Cannon
Robert Geiringer
Michael Higgins
1959 **Zero Mostel**
Lester Rawlins
Harold Scott
1960 **William Daniels**
Donald Davis
Vincent Gardenia
John Heffernan
Jack Linvingston
1961 **Godfrey M. Cambridge**
James Coco
Lester Rawlins
1962 **Clayton Corzatte**
Geoff Garland
Gerald O'Laughlin
Paul Roebling

1963 Joseph Chalkin
Michael O'Sullivan
James Patterson
Eli Wallach
1964 Philip Bruns
David Hurst
Taylor Mead
Hack Warden
Ronald Weyand
1965 Brian Bedford
Roberts Blossom
Dean Dittman
Robert Duvall
James Earl Jones
1966 Frank Langella
Michael Lipton
Kevin O'Connor
Jess Osuna
Douglas Turner
1967 Tom Aldredge
Robert Bonnard
Alvin Epstein
Neil Flanagan
Stacy Keach
Terry Kiser
Eddie McCarty
Robert Salvio
Rip Torn
1968 John Cazale
James Coco
Cliff Gorman
Moses Gunn
Roy R. Schneider
1969 See separate 1969 Obie listing below
1970 Beeson Carroll
Vincent Gardenia
Harold Gould
Anthony Holland
Lee Kissman
Ron Liebman
Austin Pendleton
1971 Hector Elizondo
Donald Ewer
Sonny Jimm
Stacy Keach
Harris Laskawy
William Schallert
James Woods
1972 Maurice Blanc
Alex Bradford
Ron Faber
Danny Sewall
Ed Zang
1973 Hume Cronyn
James Hilbrant
Stacy Keach
Christopher Lloyd
Charles Ludlam
Douglas Turner Ward
Sam Waterston
1974 Joseph Buloff
Kevin Conway

BEST DIRECTOR

1956 Jose Quintero, *The Iceman Cometh*
1957 Gene Frankel, *Volpone*
1958 Stuart Vaughan, New York Shakespeare Festival
1959 William Ball, *Ivanov* (foreign play)
Jack Ragotzy, Arthur Laurents cycle (American plays)
1960 Gene Frankel, *Machinal*
1961 Gerald A. Freedman, *The Taming of the Shrew*
1962 John Wulp, *Red Eye of Love*
1963 Alan Schneider, Pinter plays
1964 Judith Malina, *The Brig*
1965 Ulu Grosbard, *A View from the Bridge*
1966 No award
1967 Tom O'Horgan, *Futz*
1968 Michael A. Schultz, *Song for the Lusitanian Bogey*
1969 See separate 1969 Obie listing below

DISTINGUISHED DIRECTION

1964 Lawrence Kornfeld
1966 Remy Charlip
Jacques Levy
1968 John Hancock
Rip Torn
1969 See separate 1969 Obie listing below
1970 Alan Arkin
Melvin Bernhardt
Maxine Klein
Gilbert Moses
1971 John Berry
Jeff Bleckner
Gordon Davidson
John Hirsch
Larry Kornfeld
1972 Wilford Leach and John Braswell
Mel Shapiro
Michael Smith
Tom Sydorick
1973 Jack Gelber
William E. Lathan
Marshall W. Mason
1974 Marvin Felix Camillo
Robert Drivas
David Licht
John Pasquin
Harold Prince
1975 Lawrence Kornfeld, *Listen to Me*
Marshall W. Mason, *Battle of Angels* and *The Mound Builders*
Gilbert Moses, *The Taking of Miss Janie*
1976 Marshall W. Mason, *Knock Knock* and *Serenading Louie*
JoAnne Akalaitis, *Cascando*
1977 Melvin Bernhardt, *Children*
Gordon Davidson, *Savages*
1978 Robert Allan Ackerman, *Prayer for My Daughter*
Thomas Bullard, *Statements After an Arrest Under the Immorality Act*
Elizabeth Swados, *Runaways*
1979 Maria Irene Fornes, *Eyes on the Harem*
Jack Hofsiss, *The Elephant Man*
1980 A.J. Antoon, *The Art of Dining*
Edward Cornell, *Johnny on a Spot*
Elizabeth LaCompte, *Point Judith*

SETS, LIGHTING OR COSTUMES

1956 Klaus Holm
Alvin Colt
1957 No award
1958 David Hays
Will Steven Armstrong
Nikola Cernovich
1960 David Hays
1961 No award
1962 Norris Houghton
1963 No award
1964 Julian Beck

1965 Willa Kim
1966 Lindsey Decker
Ed Wittstein
1967 John Dodd
1968 Robert La Vigna
1969 See separate 1969 Obie listing below
1970 No award
1971 No award
1972 Video Free America (visual effects)
1973 No award
1974 Theoni Aldredge
Holmes Easley
Christopher Thomas

DISTINGUISHED SET DESIGN/DESIGN AND LIGHTING

1975 Robert U. Taylor, *Polly*
John Lee Beatty, *Down by the River . . .*, *Battle of Angels* and *The Mound Builders*
1976 Donald Brooks, *The Tempest*
1977 No award
1978 Garland Wright and John Arnone, *K*
Robert Yodice, *Museum*
1979 Theatre X, *A Fierce Longing*
Jennifer Tipton, Public Theatre
1980 Ruth Maleczech and Julie Archer, *Vanishing Pictures*
Sally Jacobs, *Conference of the Birds*
Beverly Emmons, distinguished lighting design
Laura Crow, costumes for *Mary Stuart*

MUSIC

1958 David Amram
1961 Teiji Ito
1964 Al Carmines
1972 Micki Grant
Liz Swados
1974 Bill Elliott
1976 Philip Glass

1969 AWARDS

An altered format resulted in awards for distinguished achievement rather than citations for specific categories of accomplishment. The winners:

The Living Theatre, *Frankenstein*
Jeff Weiss, *The International Wrestling Match*
Julie Bovasso, *Gloria and Esperanza*
Judith Malina and Julian Beck, *Antigone*
Israel Horvitz, *The Honest-to-Goodness Schnozzola*
Jules Feiffer, *Little Murders*
Ronald Tavel, *The Boy on the Straight Back Chair*
Nathan George and Ron O'Neal, *No Place to be Somebody*
Arlene Rothlein, *The Poor Little Match Girl*
Theatre Genesis, Sustained excellence
The Open Theatre, *The Serpent*
Om Theatre, *Riol*
The Performance Group, *Dionysus in '69*

SPECIAL CITATIONS AND AWARDS WHICH DO NOT FIT INTO OTHER CATEGORIES

1956 The Phoenix Theatre
The Shakespearean Workshop Theatre (later, The New York Shakespeare Festival)
The Tempo Playhouse
1957 Paul Shyre
1958 The Phoenix Theatre
The Theatre Club
Lucille Lortel
1959 Hal Holbrook
1960 Brooks Atkinson
1961 Bernard Frechtman
1962 Ellis Rabb for *The Hostage*
1963 Jean Erdman
The Second City
1964 Judson Memorial Church
1965 The Paper Bag Players
Caffe Cino and Cafe La Mama
1966 Joseph H. Dunn
H.M. Koutakas
Peter Schumann
Theatre for Ideas
Theatre in the Street
1967 La Mama Troupe
The Open Theatre
Tom Sankey
The Second Story Players
Jeff Weiss
1968 The Fortune Society
The Negro Ensemble Company
San Francisco Mime Troupe
El Teatro Campesino
1969 See separate 1969 Obie listing above
1970 Chelsea Theatre Center
Gardner Compton and Emile Ardolino for *Elephant Steps*
Andre Gregory
The Ridiculous Theatrical Company
Theatre of the Ridiculous
1971 *Orlando Furioso*
Kirk Kirksey
1972 Charles Stanley
Meredith Monk
Theatre of Latin America
Free the Army
1973 Richard Foreman
San Francisco Mime Troupe
City Center Acting Company
Workshop of the Player's Art
1974 Bread and Puppet Theatre
Brooklyn Academy of Music
CSC Repertory Company
Robert Wilson
1975 Andrei Serban for *Trilogy*
The Royal Shakespeare Company for *Summerfolk*
Charles Ludlam for *Professor Bedlam's Punch and Judy Show*
The Henry Street Settlement
Charles Pierce
Mabou Mines
Special 20-Year Obies to:
Judith Malina and Julian Beck
Ted Mannand the Circle in the Square
Joseph Papp
Ellen Stewart
The Fantasticks
1976 Richard Foreman, *Rhoda in Potatoland*
David Mamet, *American Buffalo* and *Sexual Perversity in Chicago*
Ralph Lee, *The Halloween Parade*
Morton Lichter and Gordon Rogoff, *Old-Timers' Sexual Symphony*
Santo Loquasto, sets and costumes of *Comedy of Errors*
Meredith Monk, *Quarry*
Edward Bond, *Bingo* at the Yale Repertory Theatre
Neil Flanagan for outstanding contribution to off-off-Broadway
Chile! Chile! (special documentary theatre award)

Creators of ***A Chorus Line***
1977 **Barbara Garson,** *The Dinosaur Door*
Manhattan Theatre Club for sustained excellence
New York Street Theatre Caravan for sustained excellence
Theatre for the New City for sustained excellence
Philip Glass, the music for *Einstein on the Beach*
Ping Chong, *Humboldt's Current*
The creators of *Night Club Cantata*
Charles Ludlam, the design of *Der Ring Gott Farblonjet*
Carole Oditz for costumes, **Douglas Schmidt** for set, and **Burl Hass** for lighting for *Crazy Locomotive*
Henry Millman for set and **Edward M. Greenberg** for lighting for *Domino Courts*
1978 ***Ain't Misbehavin'***
Eric Bentley
Joseph Dunn and Irja Koljonen, *Preface*
James Lapine, *Photograph*
Jerry Mayer, *Taud Show*
Stuart Sherman
Squat
Winston Tong
1979 **Gordon Chater, Richard Wherett and Steve J. Spears,** *The Elocution of Benjamin*
JoAnne Akalaitis, Ellen McElduff and David Warrilop, *Southern Exposure*
Tadeusz Kantor, *The Dead Class*
The Negro Ensemble Company for sustained excellence
New York University French Dept. for Samuel Beckett Festival
1980 **Flying Karamazov Brothers**
Le Centre Internal de Creations Theatrales actors for outstanding ensemble performances
Ellen Stewart and La Mamma E.T.C. for contributions to the American theater by the importation of foreign companies
David Jones and Richard Nelson for innovative programming at the B.A.M. Theatre Company
Ntozake Shange for adaption of *Mother Courage*

Antoinette Perry Award

AMERICAN THEATRE WING
681 Fifth Ave., New York, N.Y. 10022 (212/759-5001)

The Antoinette Perry Award, known as the Tony, honors distinguished achievement in American theatre. Occasionally, multiple awards in individual categories have been given. Now, some 450 theatre people vote for the recipients of Tonys in various categories from a publicized list of nominees. These categories have changed over the years. The award, which was designed by Herman Rosse, depicts the masks of comedy and tragedy on one side and the profile of actress Antoinette Perry on the other. The awards are presented annually on nationwide television for a production at one of forty one eligible Broadway theatres.

ACTOR (Dramatic)

1947 **Jose Ferrer,** *Cyrano de Bergerac*
Fredric March, *Years Ago*
1948 **Henry Fonda,** *Mister Roberts*
Paul Kelly, *Command Decision*
Basil Rathbone, *The Heiress*
1949 **Rex Harrison,** *Anne of the Thousand Days*
1950 **Sidney Blackmer,** *Come Back, Little Sheba*
1951 **Claude Rains,** *Darkness at Noon*
1952 **Jose Ferrer,** *The Shrike*
1953 **Tom Ewell,** *The Seven Year Itch*
1954 **David Wayne,** *The Teahouse of the August Moon*
1955 **Alfred Lunt,** *Quadrille*
1956 **Paul Muni,** *Inherit the Wind*
1957 **Fredric March,** *Long Day's Journey Into Night*
1958 **Ralph Bellamy,** *Sunrise at Campobello*
1959 **Jason Robards, Jr.,** *The Disenchanted*
1960 **Melvyn Douglas,** *The Best Man*
1961 **Zero Mostel,** *Rhinoceros*
1962 **Paul Scofield,** *A Man for All Seasons*
1963 **Arthur Hill,** *Who's Afraid of Virginia Woolf?*
1964 **Alec Guinness,** *Dylan*
1965 **Walter Matthau,** *The Odd Couple*
1966 **Hal Holbrook,** *Mark Twain Tonight*
1967 **Paul Rogers,** *The Homecoming*
1968 **Martin Balsam,** *You Know I Can't Hear You When the Water's Running*
1969 **James Earl Jones,** *The Great White Hope*
1970 **Fritz Weaver,** *Child's Play*
1971 **Brian Bedford,** *The School for Wives*
1972 **Cliff Gorman,** *Lenny*
1973 **Alan Bates,** *Butley*
1974 **Michael Moriarty,** *Find Your Way Home*
1975 **John Kani,** *Sizwe Banzi*
Winston Ntshona, *The Island*
1976 **John Wood,** *Travesties*
1977 **Al Pacino,** *The Basic Training of Pavlo Hummel*
1978 **Barnard Hughes,** *Da*
1979 **Tom Conti,** *Whose Life Is It Anyway?*
1980 **John Rubinstein,** *Children of a Lesser God*

ACTRESS (Dramatic)

1947 **Ingrid Bergman,** *Joan of Lorraine*
Helen Hayes, *Happy Birthday*
1948 **Judith Anderson,** *Medea*
Katharine Cornell, *Antony and Cleopatra*
Jessica Tandy, *A Streetcar Named Desire*
1949 **Martitia Hunt,** *The Madwoman of Chaillot*
1950 **Shirley Booth,** *Come Back, Little Sheba*
1951 **Uta Hagen,** *The Country Girl*
1952 **Julie Harris,** *I Am a Camera*
1953 **Shirley Booth,** *Time of the Cuckoo*
1954 **Audrey Hepburn,** *Ondine*
1955 **Nancy Kelly,** *The Bad Seed*
1956 **Julie Harris,** *The Lark*
1957 **Margaret Leighton,** *Separate Tables*
1958 **Helen Hayes,** *Time Remembered*
1959 **Gertrude Berg,** *A Majority of One*
1960 **Anne Bancroft,** *The Miracle Worker*
1961 **Joan Plowright,** *A Taste of Honey*
1962 **Margaret Leighton,** *Night of the Iguana*
1963 **Uta Hagen,** *Who's Afraid of Virginia Woolf?*
1964 **Sandy Dennis,** *Any Wednesday*
1965 **Irene Worth,** *Tiny Alice*
1966 **Rosemary Harris,** *The Lion in Winter*
1967 **Beryl Reid,** *The Killing of Sister George*
1968 **Zoe Caldwell,** *The Prime of Miss Jean Brodie*
1969 **Julie Harris,** *Forty Carats*
1970 **Tammy Grimes,** *Private Lives*
1971 **Maureen Stapleton,** *Gingerbread Lady*
1972 **Sada Thompson,** *Twigs*
1973 **Julie Harris,** *The Last of Mrs. Lincoln*
1974 **Colleen Dewhurst,** *A Moon for the Misbegotten*
1975 **Ellen Burstyn,** *Same Time, Next Year*
1976 **Irene Worth,** *Sweet Bird of Youth*
1977 **Julie Harris,** *The Belle of Amherst*
1978 **Jessica Tandy,** *The Gin Game*
1979 **Constance Cummings,** *Wings*

Carole Shelley, *The Elephant Man*
1980 **Phyllis Frelich,** *Children of a Lesser God*

ACTOR, SUPPORTING OR FEATURED (Dramatic)

1949 **Arthur Kennedy,** *Death of a Salesman*
1950 **No award**
1951 **Eli Wallach,** *The Rose Tattoo*
1952 **John Cromwell,** *Point of No Return*
1953 **John Williams,** *Dial M for Murder*
1954 **John Kerr,** *Tea and Sympathy*
1955 **Francis L. Sullivan,** *Witness for the Prosecution*
1956 **Ed Begley,** *Inherit the Wind*
1957 **Frank Conroy,** *The Potting Shed*
1958 **Henry Jones,** *Sunrise at Campobello*
1959 **Charlie Ruggles,** *The Pleasure of His Company*
1960 **Roddy McDowall,** *The Fighting Cock*
1961 **Martin Gabel,** *Big Fish, Little Fish*
1962 **Walter Matthau,** *A Shot in the Dark*
1963 **Alan Arkin,** *Enter Laughing*
1964 **Hume Cronyn,** *Hamlet*
1965 **Jack Albertson,** *The Subject Was Roses*
1966 **Patrick Magee,** *Marat/Sade*
1967 **Ian Holm,** *The Homecoming*
1968 **James Patterson,** *The Birthday Party*
1969 **Al Pacino,** *Does a Tiger Wear a Necktie?*
1970 **Ken Howard,** *Child's Play*
1971 **Paul Sand,** *Story Theatre*
1972 **Vincent Gardenia,** *The Prisoner of Second Avenue*
1973 **John Lithgow,** *The Changing Room*
1974 **Ed Flanders,** *A Moon for the Misbegotten*
1975 **Frank Langella,** *Seascape*
1976 **Edward Herrmann,** *Mrs. Warren's Profession*
1977 **Jonathan Price,** *Comedians*
1978 **Lester Rawlins,** *Da*
1979 **Michael Gough,** *Bedroom Farce*
1980 **David Rounds,** *Mornings at Seven*

ACTRESS, SUPPORTING OR FEATURED (Dramatic)

1947 **Patricia Neal,** *Another Part of the Forest*
1948 **No award**
1949 **Shirley Booth,** *Goodbye, My Fancy*
1950 **No award**
1951 **Maureen Stapleton,** *The Rose Tattoo*
1952 **Marian Winters,** *I Am a Camera*
1953 **Beatrice Straight,** *The Crucible*
1954 **Jo Van Fleet,** *The Trip to Bountiful*
1955 **Patricia Jessel,** *Witness for the Prosecution*
1956 **Una Merkel,** *The Ponder Heart*
1957 **Peggy Cass,** *Auntie Mame*
1958 **Anne Bancroft,** *Two For The Seasaw*
1959 **Julie Newmar,** *The Marriage-Go-Round*
1960 **Anne Revere,** *Toys in the Attic*
1961 **Colleen Dewhurst,** *All the Way Home*
1962 **Elizabeth Ashley,** *Take Her, She's Mine*
1963 **Sandy Dennis,** *A Thousand Clowns*
1964 **Barbara Loden,** *After the Fall*
1965 **Alice Ghostley,** *The Sign in Sidney Brustein's Window*
1966 **Zoe Caldwell,** *Slapstick Tragedy*
1967 **Marian Seldes,** *A Delicate Balance*
1968 **Zena Walker,** *Joe Egg*
1969 **Jane Alexander,** *The Great White Hope*
1970 **Blythe Danner,** *Butterflies Are Free*
1971 **Rae Allen,** *And Miss Reardon Drinks A Little*
1972 **Elizabeth Wilson,** *Sticks and Bones*
1973 **Leora Dana,** *The Last of Mrs. Lincoln*
1974 **Frances Sternhagen,** *The Good Doctor*
1975 **Rita Moreno,** *The Ritz*
1976 **Shirley Knight,** *Kennedy's Children*
1977 **Trazana Beverley,** *For Colored Girls Who Have Considered Suicide/When the Rainbow is Enuf*
1978 **Ann Wedgeworth,** *Chapter Two*
1979 **Joan Hickson,** *Bedroom Farce*
1980 **Dinah Manoff,** *I Ought To Be In Pictures*

ACTOR (Musical)

1948 **Paul Hartman,** *Angel in the Wings*
1949 **Ray Bolger,** *Where's Charley?*
1950 **Ezio Pinza,** *South Pacific*
1951 **Robert Alda,** *Guys and Dolls*
1952 **Phil Silvers,** *Top Banana*
1953 **Thomas Mitchell,** *Hazel Flagg*
1954 **Alfred Drake,** *Kismet*
1955 **Walter Slezak,** *Fanny*
1956 **Ray Walston,** *Damn Yankees*
1957 **Rex Harrison,** *My Fair Lady*
1958 **Robert Preston,** *The Music Man*
1959 **Richard Kiley,** *Redhead*
1960 **Jackie Gleason,** *Take Me Along*
1961 **Richard Burton,** *Camelot*
1962 **Robert Morse,** *How to Succeed in Business Without Really Trying*
1963 **Zero Mostel,** *A Funny Thing Happened on the Way to the Forum*
1964 **Burt Lahr,** *Foxy*
1965 **Zero Mostel,** *Fiddler on the Roof*
1966 **Richard Kiley,** *Man of La Mancha*
1967 **Robert Preston,** *I Do! I Do!*
1968 **Robert Goulet,** *The Happy Time*
1969 **Jerry Orbach,** *Promises, Promises*
1970 **Cleavon Little,** *Purlie*
1971 **Hal Linden,** *The Rothschilds*
1972 **Phil Silvers,** *A Funny Thing Happened on the Way to the Forum*
1973 **Ben Vereen,** *Pippin*
1974 **Christopher Plummer,** *Cyrano*
1975 **John Cullum,** *Shenandoah*
1976 **George Rose,** *My Fair Lady*
1977 **Barry Bostwick,** *The Robber Bridegroom*
1978 **John Cullum,** *On the Twentieth Century*
1979 **Len Cariou,** *Sweeney Todd*
1980 **Jim Dale,** *Barnum*

ACTRESS (Musical)

1948 **Grace Hartman,** *Angel With Wings*
1949 **Nanette Fabray,** *Love Life*
1950 **Mary Martin,** *South Pacific*
1951 **Ethel Merman,** *Call Me Madam*
1952 **Gertrude Lawrence,** *The King & I*
1953 **Rosalind Russell,** *Wonderful Town*
1954 **Dolores Gray,** *Carnival in Flanders*
1955 **Mary Martin,** *Peter Pan*
1956 **Gwen Verdon,** *Damn Yankees*
1957 **Judy Holliday,** *Bells Are Ringing*
1958 **Thelma Ritter,** *New Girl In Town*
Gwen Verdon, *New Girl In Town*
1959 **Gwen Verdon,** *Redhead*
1960 **Mary Martin,** *The Sound of Music*
1961 **Elizabeth Seal,** *Irma la Douce*
1962 **Anna Maria Alberghetti,** *Carnival*
Diahann Carroll, *No Strings*
1963 **Vivien Leigh,** *Tovarich*
1964 **Carol Channing,** *Hello, Dolly!*
1965 **Liza Minnelli,** *Flora, the Red Menace*
1966 **Angela Lansbury,** *Mame*
1967 **Barbara Harris,** *The Apple Tree*
1968 **Patricia Routledge,** *Darling of the Day*
Leslie Uggams, *Hallelujah, Baby!*
1969 **Angela Lansbury,** *Dear World*

1970 **Lauren Bacall,** *Applause*
1971 **Helen Gallagher,** *No, No, Nanette*
1972 **Alexis Smith,** *Follies*
1973 **Glynis Johns,** *A Little Night Music*
1974 **Virginia Capers,** *Raisin*
1975 **Angela Lansbury,** *Gypsy*
1976 **Donna McKechnie,** *A Chorus Line*
1977 **Dorothy Loudon,** *Annie*
1978 **Liza Minelli,** *The Act*
1979 **Angela Lansbury,** *Sweeney Todd*
1980 **Patti LuPone,** *Evita*

ACTOR SUPPORTING OR FEATURED (Musical)

1947 **David Wayne,** *Finian's Rainbow*
1948 **No award**
1949 **No award**
1950 **Myron McCormick,** *South Pacific*
1951 **Russell Nype,** *Call Me Madam*
1952 **Yul Brynner,** *The King & I*
1953 **Hiram Sherman,** *Two's Company*
1954 **Harry Belafonte,** *John Murray Anderson's Almanac*
1955 **Cyril Ritchard,** *Peter Pan*
1956 **Russ Brown,** *Damn Yankees*
1957 **Sydney Chaplin,** *Bells Are Ringing*
1958 **David Burns,** *The Music Man*
1959 **Russell Nype,** *Goldilocks*
Cast, *La Plume de Ma Tante*
1960 **Tom Bosley,** *Fiorello!*
1961 **Dick Van Dyke,** *Bye, Bye Birdie*
1962 **Charles Nelson Reilly,** *How to Succeed in Business Without Really Trying*
1963 **David Burns,** *A Funny Thing Happened on the Way to the Forum*
1964 **Jack Cassidy,** *She Loves Me*
1965 **Victor Spinetti,** *Oh, What A Lovely War*
1966 **Frankie Michaels,** *Mame*
1967 **Joel Grey,** *Cabaret*
1968 **Hiram Sherman,** *How Now, Dow Jones*
1969 **Ronald Holgate,** *1776*
1970 **Rene Auberjonois,** *Coco*
1971 **Keene Curtis,** *The Rothschilds*
1972 **Larry Blyden,** *A Funny Thing Happened on the Way to the Forum*
1973 **George S. Irving,** *Irene*
1974 **Tommy Tune,** *Seesaw*
1975 **Ted Rose,** *The Wiz*
1976 **Sammy Williams,** *A Chorus Line*
1977 **Lenny Baker,**pf 4I Love My Wife
1978 **Kevin Kline,** *On The Twentieth Century*
1979 **Henderson Forsythe,** *The Best Little Whorehouse in Texas*
1980 **Manny Patinkin,** *Evita*

ACTRESS, SUPPORTING OR FEATURED (Musical)

1950 **Juanita Hall,** *South Pacific*
1951 **Isabel Bigley,** *Guys and Dolls*
1952 **Helen Gallagher,** *Pal Joey*
1953 **Sheila Bond,** *Wish You Were Here*
1954 **Gwen Verdon,** *Can-Can*
1955 **Carol Haney,** *The Pajama Game*
1956 **Lotte Lenya,** *The Threepenny Opera*
1957 **Edith Adams,** *Li'l Abner*
1958 **Barbara Cook,** *The Music Man*
1959 **Pat Stanley,** *Goldilocks*
Cast, *La Plume de Ma Tante*
1960 **Patricia Neway,** *The Sound of Music*
1961 **Tammy Grimes,** *The Unsinkable Molly Brown*
1962 **Phyllis Newman,** *Subways Are for Sleeping*
1963 **Anna Quayle,** *Stop the World —I Want to Get Off*
1964 **Tessie O'Shea,** *The Girl Who Came to Supper*
1965 **Maria Karnilova,** *Fiddler on the Roof*
1966 **Beatrice Arthur,** *Mame*
1967 **Peg Murray,** *Cabaret*
1968 **Lillian Hayman,** *Hallelujah, Baby!*
1969 **Marian Mercer,** *Promises, Promises*
1970 **Melba Moore,** *Purlie*
1971 **Patsy Kelly,** *No, No Nanette*
1972 **Linda Hopkins,** *Inner City*
1973 **Patricia Elliot,** *A Little Night Music*
1974 **Janie Sell,** *Over Here!*
1975 **Dee Dee Bridgewater,** *The Wiz*
1976 **Carole Bishop,** *A Chorus Line*
1977 **Delores Hall,**Your Arms Too Short to Box with God
1978 **Nell Carter,** *Ain't Misbehavin'*
1979 **Carlin Glynn,** *The Best Little Whorehouse in Texas*
1980 **Priscilla Lopez,** *A Day in Hollywood/A Night in the Ukraine*

PLAY (and Playwright)

1948 ***Mister Roberts,*** Thomas Heggen and Joshua Logan based on novel by Thomas Heggen
1949 ***Death of a Salesman,*** Arthur Miller
1950 ***The Cocktail Party,*** T.S. Eliot
1951 ***The Rose Tattoo,*** Tennessee Williams
1952 ***The Fourposter,*** Jan de Hartog
1953 ***The Crucible,*** Arthur Miller
1954 ***The Teahouse of the August Moon,*** John Patrick
1955 ***The Desperate Hours,*** Joseph Hayes
1956 ***The Diary of Anne Frank,*** Frances Goodrich and Albert Hackett
1957 ***Long Day's Journey Into Night,*** Eugene O'Neill
1958 ***Sunrise at Campobello,*** Dore Schary
1959 ***J.B.,*** Archibald MacLeish
1960 ***The Miracle Worker,*** William Gibson
1961 ***Becket,*** Jean Anouilh, translated by Lucienne Hill
1962 ***A Man for All Seasons,*** Robert Bolt
1963 ***Who's Afraid of Virginia Woolf?,*** Edward Albee
1964 ***Luther,*** John Osborne
1965 ***The Subject Was Roses,*** Frank Gilroy
1966 ***Marat/Sade,*** Peter Weiss, English version by Geoffrey Skelton
1967 ***The Homecoming,*** Harold Pinter
1968 ***Rosencrantz and Guildenstern Are Dead,*** Tom Stoppard
1969 ***The Great White Hope,*** Howard Sackler
1970 ***Borstal Boy,*** Frank McMahon
1971 ***Sleuth,*** Anthony Shaffer
1972 ***Sticks and Bones,*** David Rabe
1973 ***The Championship Season,*** Jason Miller
1974 ***The River Niger,*** Joseph A. Walker
1975 ***Equus,*** Peter Shaffer
1976 ***Travesties,*** Tom Stoppard
1977 ***The Shadow Box,*** Michael Cristofer
1978 ***Da,*** Hugh Leonard
1979 ***The Elephant Man,*** Bernard Pomerance
1980 ***Children of a Lesser God***

AUTHOR (Dramatic)

1948 **Thomas Heggen and Joshua Logan,** *Mister Roberts*
1949 **Arthur Miller,** *Death of a Salesman*
1950 **T.S. Eliot,** *The Cocktail Party*
1951 **Tennessee Williams,** *The Rose Tattoo*
1952 **No award**
1953 **Arthur Miller,** *The Crucible*
1954 **John Patrick,** *The Teahouse of the August Moon*
1955 **Joseph Hayes,** *The Desperate Hours*
1956 **Frances Goodrich and Albert Hackett,** *The Diary of Anne Frank*
1957 **Eugene O'Neill,** *Long Day's Journey Into Night*
1958 **Dore Schary,** *Sunrise at Campobello*

1959 **Archibald MacLeish,** *J.B.*
1960 **William Gibson,** *The Miracle Worker*
1961 **Jean Anouihl,** *Becket*
1962 **Robert Bolt,** *A Man for All Seasons*
1963 **No award**
1964 **John Osborne,** *Luther*
1965 **Neil Simon,** *The Odd Couple*

PRODUCER (Dramatic)

1948 **Leland Hayward,** *Mister Roberts*
1949 **Kermit Bloomgarden and Walter Fried,** *Death of a Salesman*
1950 **Gilbert Miller,** *The Cocktail Party*
1951 **Cheryl Crawford,** *The Rose Tattoo*
1952 **No award**
1953 **Kermit Bloomgarden,** *The Crucible*
1954 **Maurice Evans and George Schaefer,** *The Teahouse of the August Moon*
1955 **Howard Erskine and Joseph Hayes,** *The Desperate Hours*
1956 **Kermit Bloomgarden,** *The Diary of Anne Frank*
1957 **Leigh Connell, Theodore Mann and Jose Quintero,** *Long Day's Journey Into Night*
1958 **Lawrence Langner, Theresa Helburn, Armina Marshall and Dore Schary,** *Sunrise at Campobello*
1959 **Alfred de Liagre, Jr.,** *J.B.*
1960 **Fred Coe,** *The Miracle Worker*
1961 **David Merrick,** *Becket*
1962 **Robert Whitehead and Roger L. Stevens,** *A Man for All Seasons*
1963 **Richard Barr and Clinton Wilder,** *Who's Afraid of Virginia Woolf?*
1964 **Herman Shumlin,** *The Deputy*
1965 **Claire Nichtern,** *Luv*
1966 **No award**
1967 **No award**
1968 **David Merrick Arts Foundation,** *Rosencrantz and Guildenstern Are Dead*
1969 **No award**
1970 **No award**
1971 **Helen Bonfils, Morton Gottlieb and Michael White,** *Sleuth*

DIRECTOR

1947 **Elia Kazan,** *All My Sons*
1948 **No award**
1949 **Elia Kazan,** *Death of a Salesman*
1950 **Joshua Logan,** *South Pacific*
1951 **George S. Kaufman,** *Guys and Dolls*
1952 **Jose Ferrer,** *The Shrike, The Fourposter* and *Stalag 17*
1953 **Joshua Logan,** *Picnic*
1954 **Alfred Lunt,** *Ondine*
1955 **Robert Montgomery,** *The Desperate Hours*
1956 **Tyrone Guthrie,** *The Matchmaker*
1957 **Moss Hart,** *My Fair Lady*
1958 **No award**
1959 **Elia Kazan,** *J.B.*

DIRECTOR (Dramatic)

1958 **Vincent J. Donehue,** *Sunrise at Campobello*
1959 **No award**
1960 **Arthur Penn,** *The Miracle Worker*
1961 **Sir John Gielgud,** *Big Fish, Little Fish*
1962 **Noel Willman,** *A Man for All Seasons*
1963 **Alan Schneider,** *Who's Afraid of Virginia Woolf?*
1964 **Mike Nichols,** *Barefoot in the Park*
1965 **Mike Nichols,** *Luv* and *The Odd Couple*
1966 **Peter Brook,** *Marat/Sade*
1967 **Peter Hall,** *The Homecoming*
1968 **Mike Nichols,** *Plaza Suite*
1969 **Peter Dews,** *Hadrian VII*
1970 **Joseph Hardy,** *Child's Play*
1971 **Peter Brook,** *Midsummer Night's Dream*
1972 **Mike Nichols,** *The Prisoner of Second Avenue*
1973 **A.J. Antoon,** *The Championship Season*
1974 **Jose Quintero,** *A Moon for the Misbegotten*
1975 **John Dexter,** *Equus*
1976 **Ellis Rabb,** *The Royal Family*
1977 **Gordon Davidson,** *The Shadow Box*
1978 **Melvin Bernhardt,** *Da*
1979 **Jack Hofsiss,** *The Elephant Man*
1980 **Vivian Matalon,** *Mornings at Seven*

MUSICAL (M-music; L-lyrics; B-book; P-produced)

1949 ***Kiss Me Kate*** (M&L by Cole Porter, B by Bella and Samuel Spewack)
1950 ***South Pacific*** (M by Richard Rodgers, L by Oscar Hammerstein II, B by Oscar Hammerstein II and Joshua Logan)
1951 ***Guys and Dolls*** (M&L by Frank Loesser, B by Jo Swerling and Abe Burrows)
1952 ***The King and I*** (B&L by Oscar Hammerstein II, M by Richard Rodgers)
1953 ***Wonderful Town*** (B by Joseph Fields and Jerome Chodorov, M by Leonard Bernstein, L by Betty Comden and Adolph Green)
1954 ***Kismet*** (B by Charles Lederer and Luther Davis, M by Alexander Borodin, adapted by and with L by Robert Wright and George Forrest)
1955 ***The Pajama Game*** (B by George Abbott and Richard Bissell, M&L by Richard Adler and Jerry Ross)
1956 ***Damn Yankees*** (B by George Abbott and Douglass Wallop, M by Richard Adler and Jerry Ross, P by Frederick Brisson, Robert Griffith, Harold S. Prince in assn. with Albert B. Taylor)
1957 ***My Fair Lady*** (B&L by Alan Jay Lerner, M by Frederick Loewe, P by Herman Levin)
1958 ***The Music Man*** (B by Meredith Willson and Franklin Lacey, M&L by Meredith Willson)
1959 ***Redhead*** (B by Herbert and Dorothy Fields, Sidney Sheldon and David Shaw, M by Albert Hague, L by Dorothy Fields)
1960 **Fiorello!** (B by Jerome Weidman and George Abbott, L by Sheldon Harnick, M by Jerry Bock, P by Robert E. Griffith and Harold S. Prince)
1961 **Bye, Bye Birdie** (B by Michael Stewart, M by Charles Strouse, L by Lee Adams, P by Edward Padula in assn. with L. Slade Brown)
1962 **How to Succeed in Business Without Really Trying** (B by Abe Burrows, Jack Weinstock and Willie Gilbert, M&L by Frank Loesser P by Cy Feuer and Ernest Martin)
1963 ***A Funny Thing Happened on the Way to the Forum*** (B by Burt Shrevrelove and Larry Gelbart, M&L by Stephen Sondheim, P by Harold Prince)
1964 ***Hello, Dolly!*** (B by Michael Stewart, M&L by Jerry Herman, P by David Merrick)
1965 ***Fiddler on the Roof*** (B by Joseph Stein, M by Jerry Bock, L by Sheldon Harnick, P by Harold Prince)
1966 ***Man of La Mancha*** (B by Dale Wasserman, M by Mitch Leigh, L by Joe Darion, P by Albert W. Selden and Hal James)
1967 ***Cabaret*** (B by Joseph Masteroff, M by John Kander, L by Fred Ebb, P by Harold Prince in assn. with Ruth Mitchell)
1968 ***Hallelujah, Baby!*** (B by Arthur Laurents, M by Jule Styne, L by Betty Comden and Adolph Green, P by Al-

bert W. Selden, Hal James, Jane C. Nussbaum and Harry Rigby)
1969 ***1776*** (B by Peter Stone, M&L by Sherman Edwards, P by Stuart Ostro)
1970 ***Applause*** (B by Betty Comden and Adolph Green, M by Charles Strouse, L by Lee Adams, P by Joseph Kipness and Lawrence Kasha)
1971 ***Company*** (P by Harold Prince)
1972 ***Two Gentlemen of Verona*** (P by the New York Shakespeare Festival, Joseph Papp)
1973 ***A Little Night Music*** (P by Harold Prince)
1974 ***Raisin*** (P by Robert Nemiroff)
1975 ***The Wiz*** (P by Ken Harper)
1976 ***A Chorus Line*** (P by Ken Harper)
1977 ***Annie,*** (P by Mike Nichols)
1978 ***Ain't Misbehavin'***
1979 ***Sweeney Todd***
1980 ***Evita***

AUTHOR (Musical)

1949 **Bella and Samuel Spewack,** *Kiss Me Kate*
1950 **Oscar Hammerstein II and Joshua Logan,** *South Pacific*
1951 **Jo Swerling and Abe Burrows,** *Guys and Dolls*
1952 **No award**
1953 **Joseph Fields and Jerome Chodorov,** *Wonderful Town*
1954 **Charles Lederer and Luther Davis,** *Kismet*
1955 **George Abbott and Richard Bissell,** *The Pajama Game*
1956 **George Abbott and Douglass Wallop,** *Damn Yankees*
1957 **Alan Jay Lerner,** *My Fair Lady*
1958 **Meredith Willson and Franklin Lacey,** *The Music Man*
1959 **Herbert and Dorothy Fields, Sidney Sheldon and David Shaw,** *Redhead*
1960 **Jerome Weidman and George Abbott,** *Fiorello!*
Howard Lindsay and Russel Crouse, *The Sound of Music*
1961 **Michael Stewart,** *Bye, Bye Birdie*
1962 **Abe Burrows, Jack Weinstock and Willie Gilbert,** *How to Succeed in Business Without Really Trying*
1963 **Burt Shrevelove and Larry Gelbart,** *A Funny Thing Happened on the Way to the Forum*
1964 **Michael Stewart,** *Hello, Dolly!*
1965 **Joseph Stein,** *Fiddler on the Roof*

PRODUCER (Musical)

1949 **Saint-Subber and Lemuel Ayers,** *Kiss Me Kate*
1950 **Richard Rodgers, Oscar Hammerstein II and Joshua Logan,** *South Pacific*
1951 **Cy Feuer and Ernest Martin,** *Guys and Dolls*
1952 **No award**
1953 **Robert Fryer,** *Wonderful Town*
1954 **Charles Lederer,** *Kismet*
1955 **Frederick Brisson, Robert Griffith and Harold S. Prince,** *The Pajama Game*
1956 **Frederick Brisson, Robert Griffith and Harold S. Prince in assn. with Albert B. Taylor,** *Damn Yankees*
1957 **Herman Levin,** *My Fair Lady*
1958 **Kermit Bloomgarden, Herbert Greene, Frank Productions,** *The Music Man*
1959 **Robert Fryer and Lawrence Carr,** *Redhead*
1960 **Leland Hayward and Richard Halliday,** *The Sound of Music*
Robert Griffith and Harold Prince, *Fiorello!*
1961 **Edward Padula,** *Bye, Bye Birdie*
1962 **Cy Feuer and Ernest Martin,** *How to Succeed in Business Without Really Trying*
1963 **Harold Prince,** *A Funny Thing Happened on the Way to the Forum*
1964 **David Merrick,** *Hello, Dolly!*
1965 **Harold Prince,** *Fiddler on the Roof*
1966 **No award**
1967 **No award**
1968 **Albert Selden, Hal James, Jane C. Nussbaum and Harry Rigby,** *Hallelujah, Baby!*
1969 **No award**
1970 **No award**
1971 **Harold Prince,** *Company*

DIRECTOR (Musical)

1960 **George Abbott,** *Fiorello!*
1961 **Gower Champion,** *Bye, Bye Birdie*
1962 **Abe Burrows,** *How to Succeed in Business Without Really Trying*
1963 **George Abbott,** *A Funny Thing Happened on the Way to the Forum*
1964 **Gower Champion,** *Hello, Dolly!*
1965 **Jerome Robbins,** *Fiddler on the Roof*
1966 **Albert Marre,** *Man of La Mancha*
1967 **Harold Prince,** *Cabaret*
1968 **Gower Champion,** *The Happy Time*
1969 **Peter Hunt,** *1776*
1970 **Ron Field,** *Applause*
1971 **Harold Prince,** *Company*
1972 **Harold Prince and Michael Bennett,** *Follies*
1973 **Bob Fosse,** *Pippin*
1974 **Harold Prince,** *Candide*
1975 **Geoffrey Holder,** *The Wiz*
1976 **Michael Bennett,** *A Chorus Line*
1977 **Gene Saks,** *I Love My Wife*
1978 **Richard Maltby, Jr.,** *Ain't Misbehavin'*
1979 **Harold Prince,** *Sweeney Todd*
1980 **Harold Prince,** *Evita*

COMPOSER & LYRICIST

1949 **Cole Porter,** *Kiss Me Kate*
1950 **Richard Rodgers (C),** *South Pacific*
1951 **Frank Loesser,** *Guys and Dolls*
1952 **No award**
1953 **Leonard Bernstein (C),** *Wonderful Town*
1954 **Alexander Borodin (C),** *Kismet*
1955 **Richard Adler and Jerry Ross** *The Pajama Game*
1956 **Richard Adler and Jerry Ross,** *Damn Yankees*
1957 **Frederick Loewe (C),** *My Fair Lady*
1958 **Meredith Willson,** *The Music Man*
1959 **Albert Hague (C),** *Redhead*
1960 **Jerry Bock (C),** *Fiorello!*
Richard Rodgers (C), *The Sound of Music*
1961 **No award**
1962 **Richard Rodgers,** *No Strings*
1963 **Lionel Bart,** *Oliver!*
1964 **Jerry Herman,** *Hello, Dolly!*
1965 **Jerry Bock and Sheldon Harnick,** *Fiddler on the Roof*
1966 **Mitch Leigh and Joe Darion,** *Man of La Mancha*
1967 **John Kander and Fred Ebb,** *Cabaret*
1968 **Jule Styne, Betty Comden and Adolph Green,** *Hallelujah, Baby!*
1969 **No award**
1970 **No award**
1971 **Stephen Sondheim,** *Company*
1972 **Stephen Sondheim,** *Follies*
1973 **Stephen Sondheim,** *A Little Night Music*
1974 **Frederick Loewe (C) and Alan Jay Lerner (L),** *Gigi*

1975 **Charlie Smalls,** *The Wiz*
1976 **Ed Kleban (L) and Marvin Hamlisch (C),** *A Chorus Line*
1977 **Charles Strouse and Martin Chernin,** *Annie*

BOOK (musical)

1978 ***On The Twentieth Century***
1979 ***Sweeney Todd***
1980 ***Evita***

SCORE

1978 ***On the Twentieth Century***
1979 ***Sweeney Todd***
1980 ***Evita***

CONDUCTOR AND MUSICAL DIRECTOR

1949 **Max Meth,** *As the Girls Go*
1950 **Maurice Abravanel,** *Regina*
1951 **Lehman Engel,** *The Consul*
1952 **Max Meth,** *Pal Joey*
1953 **Lehman Engel,** *Wonderful Town*
1954 **Louis Adrian,** *Kismet*
1955 **Thomas Schippers,** *The Saint of Bleeker Street*
1956 **Hal Hastings,** *Damn Yankees*
1957 **Franz Allers,** *My Fair Lady*
1958 **Herbert Greene,** *The Music Man*
1959 **Salvatore Dell'Isola,** *Flower Drum Song*
1960 **Frederick Dvonch,** *The Sound of Music*
1961 **Franz Allers,** *Camelot*
1962 **Elliot Lawrence,** *How to Succeed in Business Without Really Trying*
1963 **Donald Pippin,** *Oliver!*
1964 **Shepard Coleman,** *Hello, Dolly!*

SCENIC DESIGNER

1948 **Horace Armistead,** *The Medium*
1949 **Jo Mielziner,** *Sleepy Hollow, Summer and Smoke, Anne of the Thousand Days, Death of a Salesman* and *South Pacific*
1950 **Jo Mielziner,** *The Innocents*
1951 **Boris Aronson,** *The Rose Tattoo, The Country Girl* and *Season in the Sun*
1952 **Jo Mielziner,** *The King & I*
1953 **Raoul Pene du Bois,** *Wonderful Town*
1954 **Peter Larkin,** *Ondine* and *The Teahouse of the August Moon*
1955 **Oliver Messel,** *House of Flowers*
1956 **Peter Larkin,** *Inherit the Wind* and *No Time for Sergeants*
1957 **Oliver Smith,** *A Clearing in the Woods, Candide, Auntie Mame, My Fair Lady, Eugenia and A Visit to a Small Planet*
1958 **Oliver Smith,** *West Side Story*
1959 **Donald Oenslager,** *A Majority of One*
1960 **Oliver Smith,** *The Sound of Music*
Howard Bam, *Toys in the Attic*
1961 **Oliver Smith,** *Camelot* and *Becket*
1962 **Will Steven Armstrong,** *Carnival*
1963 **Sean Kenny,** *Oliver!*
1964 **Oliver Smith,** *Hello, Dolly!*
1965 **Oliver Smith,** *Baker Street*
1966 **Howard Bay,** *Man of La Mancha*
1967 **Boris Aronson,** *Cabaret*
1968 **Desmond Heeley,** *Rosencrantz and Guildenstern Are Dead*
1969 **Boris Aronson,** *Zorba*
1970 **Jo Mielziner,** *Child's Play*
1971 **Boris Aronson,** *Company*
1972 **Boris Aronson,** *Follies*
1973 **Tony Walton,** *Pippin*
1974 **Franne and Eugene Lee,** *Candide*
1975 **Carl Toms,** *Sherlock Holmes*
1976 **Boris Aronson,** *Pacific Overtures*
1977 **David Mitchell,** *Annie*
1978 **Robin Wagner,** *On The Twentieth Century*
1979 **Eugene Lee,** *Sweeney Todd*
1980 **John Lee Beattey,** *Talley's Folly*
David Mitchell, *Barnum*

COSTUME DESIGNER

1947 **Lucinda Ballard,** *Happy Birthday, Another Part of the Forest, Street Scene, John Loves Mary* and *The Chocolate Soldier*
David Ffolkes, *Henry VIII*
1948 **Mary Percy Schenck,** *The Heiress*
1949 **Lemuel Ayers,** *Kiss Me Kate*
1950 **Aline Bernstein,** *Regina*
1951 **Miles White,** *Bless You All*
1952 **Irene Sharaff,** *The King & I*
1953 **Miles White,** *Hazel Flagg*
1954 **Richard Whorf,** *Ondine*
1955 **Cecil Beaton,** *Quadrille*
1956 **Alvin Colt,** *Pipe Dream*
1957 **Cecil Beaton,** *My Fair Lady*
1958 **Motley,** *The First Gentleman*
1959 **Rouben Ter-Arutunian,** *Redhead*
1960 **Cecil Beaton,** *Saratoga*
1961 **Adrian, and Tony Duquette,** *Camelot*
1962 **Lucinda Ballard,** *The Gay Life*
1963 **Anthony Powell,** *The School for Scandal*
1964 **Freddy Wittop,** *Hello, Dolly!*
1965 **Patricia Zipprodt,** *Fiddler on the Roof*
1966 **Gunilla Palmstierna-Weiss,** *Marat/Sade*
1967 **Patricia Zipprodt,** *Cabaret*
1968 **Desmond Heeley,** *Rosencrantz and Guildenstern Are Dead*
1969 **Loudon Sainthill,** *Canterbury Tales*
1970 **Cecil Beaton,** *Coco*
1971 **Raoul Pene Du Bois,** *No, No Nanette*
1972 **Florence Klotz,** *Follies*
1973 **Florence Klotz,** *A Little Night Music*
1974 **Franne Lee,** *Candide*
1975 **Geoffrey Holder,** *The Wiz*
1976 **Florence Klotz,** *Pacific Overtures*
1977 **Theoni V. Aldredge,** *Annie*
Santo Loquasto, *The Cherry Orchard*
1978 **Edward Gorey,** *Dracula*
1979 **Franne Lee,** *Sweeney Todd*
1980 **Theoni V. Aldredge,** *Barnum*

CHOREOGRAPHER

1947 **Agnes de Mille,** *Brigadoon*
Michael Kidd, *Finian's Rainbow*
1948 **Jerome Robbins,** *High Button Shoes*
1949 **Gower Champion,** *Lend an Ear*
1950 **Helen Tamiris,** *Touch and Go*
1951 **Michael Kidd,** *Guys and Dolls*
1952 **Robert Alton,** *Pal Joey*
1953 **Donald Saddler,** *Wonderful Town*
1954 **Michael Kidd,** *Can-Can*
1955 **Bob Fosse,** *The Pajama Game*
1956 **Bob Fosse,** *Damn Yankees*
1957 **Michael Kidd,** *Li'l Abner*
1958 **Jerome Robbins,** *West Side Story*
1959 **Bob Fosse,** *Redhead*
1960 **Michael Kidd,** *Destry Rides Again*
1961 **Gower Champion,** *Bye, Bye Birdie*
1962 **Agnes de Mille,** *Kwamina*
Joe Layton, *No Strings*

1963 **Bob Fosse,** *Little Me*
1964 **Gower Champion,** *Hello, Dolly!*
1965 **Jerome Robbins,** *Fiddler on the Roof*
1966 **Bob Fosse,** *Sweet Charity*
1967 **Ronald Field,** *Cabaret*
1968 **Gower Champion,** *The Happy Time*
1969 **Joe Layton,** *George M*
1970 **Ron Field,** *Applause*
1971 **Donald Saddler,** *No, No Nanette*
1972 **Michael Bennett,** *Follies*
1973 **Bob Fosse,** *Pippin*
1974 **Michael Bennett,** *Seesaw*
1975 **George Faison,** *The Wiz*
1976 **Michael Bennett and Bob Avian,** *A Chorus Line*
1977 **Peter Gennaro,** *Annie*
1978 **Bob Fosse,** *Dancin'*
1979 **Michael Bennett and Bob Avian,** *Ballroom*
1980 **Tommy Tune and Thommie Walsh,** *A Day in Hollywood/A Night in the Ukraine*

LIGHTING DESIGNER

1970 **Jo Mielziner,** *Child's Play*
1971 **H.R. Poindexter,** *Story Theater*
1972 **Tharon Musser,** *Follies*
1973 **Jules Fisher,** *Pippin*
1974 **Jules Fisher,** *Ulysses in Nighttown*
1975 **Neil Patrick Jampolis,** *Sherlock Holmes*
1976 **Tharon Musser,** *A Chorus Line*
1977 **Jennifer Tipton,** *The Cherry Orchard*
1978 **Jules Fisher,** *Dancin'*
1979 **Roger Morgan,** *The Crucifer of Blood*
1980 **David Hersey,** *Evita*

MOST INNOVATIVE PRODUCTION OF A REVIVAL/REPRODUCTION (Play or Musical)

1978 ***Dracula***
1979 **No award**
1980 ***Mornings at Seven***

STAGE TECHNICIAN

1948 **George Gebhardt**
George Pierce
1949 **No award**
1950 **Joe Lynn,** *Miss Liberty*
1951 **Richard Raven,** *The Autumn Garden*
1952 **Peter Feller,** *Call Me Madam*
1953 **Abe Kurnit,** *Wish You Were Here*
1954 **John Davis,** *Picnic*
1955 **Richard Rodda,** *Peter Pan*
1956 **Harry Green,** *Middle of the Night* and *Damn Yankees*
1957 **Howard McDonald,** *Major Barbara*
1958 **Harry Romar,** *Time Remembered*
1959 **Sam Knapp,** *The Music Man*
1960 **John Walters,** *The Miracle Worker*
1961 **Teddy Van Bemmel,** *Becket*
1962 **Michael Burns,** *A Man for All Seasons*
1963 **Solly Pernick,** *Mr. President*
Milton Smith, *Beyond the Fringe*

SPECIAL AWARDS

1947 **Dora Chamberlain**
Mr. and Mrs. Ira Katzenberg
Jules Leventhal
Burns Mantle
P.A. MacDonald
Arthur Miller
Vincent Sardi, Sr.
Kurt Weill
1948 **Vera Allen**
Paul Beisman
Joe E. Brown
Robert Dowling
Experimental Theatre, Inc.
Rosamond Gilder
June Lockhart
Mary Martin
Robert Porterfield
James Whitmore
1949 **No award**
1950 **Maurice Evans**
Eleanor Roosevelt
1951 **Ruth Green**
1952 **Edward Kook**
Judy Garland
Charles Boyer
1953 **Beatrice Lillie**
Danny Kaye
Equity Community Theatre
1954 **No award**
1955 **Proscenium Productions**
1956 ***The Threepenny Opera***
The Theatre Collection of the New York Public Library
1957 **American Shakespeare Festival**
Jean-Louis Barrault, French Repertory
Robert Russell Bennett
William Hammerstein
Paul Shyre
1958 **New York Shakespeare Festival**
Mrs. Martin Beck
1959 **John Gielgud**
Howard Lindsay and Russel Crouse
1960 **John D. Rockefeller 3rd**
James Thurber and Burgess Meredith, *A Thurber Carnival*
1961 **David Merrick**
The Theatre Guild
1962 **Brooks Atkinson**
Franco Zeffirelli
Richard Rodgers
1963 **W. McNeil Lowry**
Irving Berlin
Alan Bennett
Peter Cook
Jonathan Miller
Dudley Moore
1964 **Eva Le Gallienne**
1965 **Gilbert Miller**
Oliver Smith
1966 **Helen Menken**
1967 **No award**
1968 **Audrey Hepburn**
Carol Channing
Pearl Bailey
David Merrick
Maurice Chevalier
APA-Phoenix Theatre
Marlene Dietrich
1969 **The National Theatre Company of Great Britain**
The Negro Ensemble Company
Rex Harrison
Leonard Bernstein
Carol Burnett
1970 **Noel Coward**
Alfred Lunt and Lynn Fontanne
New York Shakespeare Festival
Barbra Streisand
1971 **Elliot Norton**

Ingram Ash
Playbill
Roger L. Stevens
1972 **The Theatre Guild-American Theatre Society**
Richard Rodgers
Fiddler on the Roof
Ethel Merman
1973 **John Lindsay**
Actors' Fund of America
Shubert Organization
1974 **Liza Minnelli**
Bette Midler
Peter Cook and Dudley Moore, *Good Evening*
A Moon for the Misbegotten
Candide
Actors' Equity Assn.
Theatre Development Fund
John F. Wharton
Harold Friedlander
1975 **Neil Simon**
Al Hirschfield
1976 **Mathilde Pincus**
Circle in the Square
Thomas H. Fitzgerald
The Arena Stage
1977 **National Theatre for the Deaf**
Diana Ross
Lily Tomlin
Barry Manilow
Actors' Equity Theatre, New York
Mark Taper Forum Theatre, Los Angeles
1978 **Long Wharf Theatre**
1979 **Henry Fonda**
Walter F. Diehl
Eugene O'Neill Memorial Theater Center
American Conservatory Theater
1980 **Mary Tyler Moore**
Actors Theatre of Louisville
Goodspeed Opera House

Pulitzer Prize

COLUMBIA UNIVERSITY
Graduate School of Journalism, New York, N.Y. 10027; 212/280-3828 (Pulitzer Prizes: 212/280-3841)

Endowed by the will of Joseph Pulitzer, founder of the *St. Louis Post Dispatch*, and administered by Columbia University, the annual Pulitzer Prizes include a $1,000 award for drama. The award is made for a distinguished play by an American playwright, preferably dealing with American life and original in source. Entry must be made to the fifteen-member advisory board on Pulitzer Prizes while the work is being performed, together with copies of the manuscript.

1917 **No award**
1918 ***Why Marry?*** Jesse L. Williams
1919 **No award**
1920 ***Beyond the Horizon,*** Eugene O'Neill
1921 ***Miss Lulu Bett,*** Zona Gale
1922 ***Anna Christie,*** Eugene O'Neill
1923 ***Icebound,*** Owen Davis
1924 ***Hell-Bent for Heaven,*** Hatcher Hughes
1925 ***They Knew What They Wanted,*** Sidney Howard
1926 ***Craig's Wife,*** George Kelly
1927 ***In Abraham's Bosom,*** Paul Green
1928 ***Strange Interlude,*** Eugene O'Neill
1929 ***Street Scene,*** Elmer L. Rice
1930 ***The Green Pastures,*** Marc Connelly
1931 ***Alison's House,*** Susan Glaspell
1932 ***Of Thee I Sing,*** George S. Kaufman, Ira Gershwin and Morris Ryskind
1933 ***Both Your Houses,*** Maxwell Anderson
1934 ***Men in White,*** Sidney Kingsley
1935 ***The Old Maid,*** Zoe Akins
1936 ***Idiot's Delight,*** Robert E. Sherwood
1937 ***You Can't Take It With You,*** Moss Hart and George S. Kaufman
1938 ***Our Town,*** Thornton Wilder
1939 ***Abe Lincoln in Illinois,*** Robert E. Sherwood
1940 ***The Time of Your Life,*** William Saroyan
1941 ***There Shall Be No Night,*** Robert E. Sherwood
1942 **No award**
1943 ***The Skin of Our Teeth,*** Thornton Wilder
1944 **No award**
1945 ***Harvey,*** Mary Chase
1946 ***State of the Union,*** Russel Crouse and Howard Lindsay
1947 **No award**
1948 ***A Streetcar Named Desire,*** Tennessee Williams
1949 ***Death of a Salesman,*** Arthur Miller
1950 ***South Pacific,*** Richard Rodgers, Oscar Hammerstein II and Joshua Logan
1951 **No award**
1952 ***The Shrike,*** Joseph Kramm
1953 ***Picnic,*** William Inge
1954 ***The Teahouse of the August Moon,*** John Patrick
1955 ***Cat on a Hot Tin Roof,*** Tennessee Williams
1956 ***Diary of Anne Frank,*** Albert Hackett and Frances Goodrich
1957 ***Long Day's Journey Into Night,*** Eugene O'Neill
1958 ***Look Homeward, Angel,*** Ketti Frings
1959 ***J.B.,*** Archibald MacLeish
1960 ***Fiorello!,*** Jerome Weidman and George Abbott
1961 ***All the Way Home,*** Tad Mosel
1962 ***How to Succeed in Business Without Really Trying,*** Frank Loesser and Abe Burrows
1963 **No award**
1964 **No award**
1965 ***The Subject Was Roses,*** Frank Gilroy
1966 **No award**
1967 ***A Delicate Balance,*** Edward Albee
1968 **No award**
1969 ***The Great White Hope,*** Howard Sackler
1970 ***No Place to Be Somebody,*** Charles Gordone
1971 ***The Effect of Gamma Rays on Man-in-the-Moon Marigolds,*** Paul Zindel
1972 **No award**
1973 ***That Championship Season,*** Jason Miller
1974 **No award**
1975 ***Seascape,*** Edward Albee
1976 ***A Chorus Line,*** musical; conceived, choreographed and directed by Michael Bennett; book by James Kirkwood and Nicholas Dante; music by Marvin Hamlisch; lyrics by Edward Kleban
1977 ***The Shadow Box,*** Michael Cristofer
1978 ***The Gin Game,*** Donald L. Coburn
1979 ***Buried Child,*** Sam Shepard
1980 ***Talley's Folly,*** Lanford Wilson

SPECIAL AWARD

1944 **Richard Rodgers and Oscar Hammerstein II,** ***Oklahoma!***

Susan Smith Blackburn Prize

SUSAN SMITH BLACKBURN, INC.
911 Walker St., Ste. 1200, Houston, Tex. 77002

The Susan Smith Blackburn Prize, which carries a $2,000 honorarium, is awarded annually for a meritorious English language play written by a female playwright. A committee selects the winner.

1978 **Susan O'Malley,** *Once a Catholic*
1979 **Barbara Schneider,** *Details Without a Map*
1980 **Wendy Kesselman,** *My Sister in This House*

George Spelvin Award

THE MASQUERS
1765 N. Sycamore Ave., Hollywood, Calif. 90028
(213/874-0840)

The George Spelvin Award, which consits of a statuette, is given annually for outstanding dedication to the field of acting and devotion to theater and community. A committee selects the one or two annual winners.

1972 **Debbie Reynolds**
1973 **Edith Head**
1974 **Mae West**
1975 **Liza Minnelli**
Lee Strasberg
1976 **Groucho Marx**
Carroll O'Connor
1977 **Lois Nettleton**
J. Pasternak
1978 **Stan Davis**
Shirley Temple Black
1979 **Ginger Rogers**
1980 **Gene Autrey** and the California Angels
Lurene Tuttle

Other Spelvin Awards winners are as follows: Dorothy Malone, John Huston, Lucille Ball, Desi Arnaz, Humphrey Bogart, Ronald Reagan, Karl Malden. The years in which they (and others) were honored are not available.

Stanley Drama Award

WAGNER COLLEGE
Staten Island, N.Y. 10301 (212/390-3256)

The Stanley Drama Award, which carries a cash honorarium of $800, is given annually for playwriting. Any theatre professional (producer, director, playwright, actor, agent, etc.) may nominate a play that has not yet been produced commercially or published by a trade publisher. Preliminary readers select finalists, from which a winner is selected by a panel of judges.

1962 **Terrence McNally,** *This Side of the Door*
1963 **Adrienne Kennedy,** *Funnyhouse of a Negro* and *The Owl Answers*
1964 **Megan Terry,** *Hothouse*
Joseph Baldwin, *Thompson*
1965 **Lonne Elder III,** *Ceremonies in Dark Old Men*
1966 **Albert Zuckerman,** *To Become a Man*
1967 **William Parchman,** *The Prize in the Crackerjack Box*
1968 **Venable Herndon,** *Bag of Flies*
1969 **Bernard Sabath,** *A Happy New Year to the Whole World Except Alexander Graham Bell*
Yale Udoff, *The Club*
1970 **Richard Lortz,** *Three Sons (of Sons and Brothers)*
1971 **Ben Rosa,** *Obtuse Triangle*
1972 **Marvin Denicoff,** *Fortune Teller Man*
1973 **C. Richard Gillespie,** *Carnivori*
1974 **Gus Weill,** *Son of the Last Mule Dealer*
1975 **Alan Riefe and Robert Haymes,** *Jonathan (A Musical)*
1976 **Carol Mack,** *A Safe Place*
1977 **Jack Zeman,** *Past Tense*
1978 **Barry Knower,** *Cutting Away*
1979 **Robert Riche,** *Stag at Eve*
1980 **Norman Wexler,** *Private Opening*

John F. Wharton Theater Award

THEATER DEVELOPMENT FUND
1501 Broadway, New York, N.Y. 10036 (212/221-0885)

The John F. Wharton Theater Award, which carries a $5,000 cash prize, is given annually to an individual or group for creative contributions to the production of musicals or plays for either profit or not-for-profit theater. A committee selects the winner.

1980 **W. McNeil Lowry,** Ford Foundation Office of Policy and Div. of Humanities

Cinema

Contents

Related Awards

Academy Awards

ACADEMY OF MOTION PICTURE ARTS AND SCIENCES
8948 Wilshire Blvd., Beverly Hills, Calif. 90211
(213/278-8990)

The Academy Award, a statuette known as the Oscar, is given annually for excellence in some twenty categories of motion picture achievement for films released in Los Angeles during the calendar year, plus special honors for contributions to cinema, which are given as merited. Academy members in each field of endeavor may make nominees in their own category. Up to five nominees per category are submitted for secret ballot by the entire membership. Special honors for overall achievement are conferred by the Academy's board of governors. The presentation of the Academy Award has developed from a small dinner for 250 persons in 1928 to a gala spectacle telecast to an audience estimated at more than 150-million viewers. The Oscar is the motion picture industry's best known American honor, and one of the most coveted in the world.

BEST PICTURE

1928 ***Wings***
1929 ***The Broadway Melody***
1930 ***All Quiet on the Western Front***
1931 ***Cimarron***
1932 ***Grand Hotel***
1933 ***Cavalcade***
1934 ***It Happened One Night***
1935 ***Mutiny on the Bounty***
1936 ***The Great Ziegfeld***
1937 ***The Life of Emile Zola***
1938 ***You Can't Take It with You***
1939 ***Gone With the Wind***
1940 ***Rebecca***
1941 ***How Green Was My Valley***
1942 ***Mrs. Miniver***
1943 ***Casablanca***
1944 ***Going My Way***
1945 ***The Lost Weekend***
1946 ***The Best Years of Our Lives***
1947 ***Gentleman's Agreement***
1948 ***Hamlet***
1949 ***All the King's Men***
1950 ***All About Eve***
1951 ***An American in Paris***
1952 ***The Greatest Show on Earth***
1953 ***From Here to Eternity***
1954 ***On the Waterfront***
1955 ***Marty***
1956 ***Around the World in 80 Days***
1957 ***The Bridge on the River Kwai***
1958 ***Gigi***
1959 ***Ben-Hur***
1960 ***The Apartment***
1961 ***West Side Story***
1962 ***Lawrence of Arabia***
1963 ***Tom Jones***
1964 ***My Fair Lady***
1965 ***The Sound of Music***
1966 ***A Man for All Seasons***
1967 ***In the Heat of the Night***
1968 ***Oliver!***
1969 ***Midnight Cowboy***
1970 ***Patton***
1971 ***The French Connection***
1972 ***The Godfather***
1973 ***The Sting***
1974 ***The Godfather, Part II***
1975 ***One Flew Over the Cuckoo's Nest***
1976 ***Rocky***
1977 ***Annie Hall***
1978 ***The Deer Hunter***
1979 ***Kramer vs. Kramer***
1980 ***Ordinary People***

BEST ACTOR

1928 **Emil Jannings,** *The Way of All Flesh* and *The Last Command*
1929 **Warner Baxter,** *In Old Arizona*
1930 **George Arliss,** *Disraeli*
1931 **Lionel Barrymore,** *A Free Soul*
1932 **Fredric March,** *Dr. Jekyll and Mr. Hyde,*
Wallace Beery, *The Champ*
1933 **Charles Laughton,** *The Private Life of Henry VIII*
1934 **Clark Gable,** *It Happened One Night*
1935 **Victor McLaglen,** *The Informer*
1936 **Paul Muni,** *The Story of Louis Pasteur*
1937 **Spencer Tracy,** *Captains Courageous*
1938 **Spencer Tracy,** *Boys Town*
1939 **Robert Donat,** *Goodbye, Mr. Chips*
1940 **James Stewart,** *The Philadelphia Story*
1941 **Gary Cooper,** *Sergeant York*
1942 **James Cagney,** *Yankee Doodle Dandy*
1943 **Paul Lukas,** *Watch on the Rhine*
1944 **Bing Crosby,** *Going My Way*
1945 **Ray Milland,** *The Lost Weekend*
1946 **Fredric March,** *The Best Years of Our Lives*
1947 **Ronald Colman,** *A Double Life*
1948 **Laurence Olivier,** *Hamlet*
1949 **Broderick Crawford,** *All the King's Men*
1950 **Jose Ferrer,** *Cyrano de Bergerac*
1951 **Humphrey Bogart,** *The African Queen*
1952 **Gary Cooper,** *High Noon*
1953 **William Holden,** *Stalag 17*
1954 **Marlon Brando,** *On the Waterfront*
1955 **Ernest Borgnine,** *Marty*
1956 **Yul Brynner,** *The King and I*
1957 **Alec Guinness,** *The Bridge on the River Kwai*
1958 **David Niven,** *Separate Tables*
1959 **Charlton Heston,** *Ben-Hur*
1960 **Burt Lancaster,** *Elmer Gantry*
1961 **Maximilian Schell,** *Judgment at Nuremberg*
1962 **Gregory Peck,** *To Kill a Mockingbird*
1963 **Sidney Poitier,** *Lilies of the Field*
1964 **Rex Harrison,** *My Fair Lady*
1965 **Lee Marvin,** *Cat Ballou*
1966 **Paul Scofield,** *A Man for All Seasons*
1967 **Rod Steiger,** *In the Heat of the Night*
1968 **Cliff Robertson,** *Charly*
1969 **John Wayne,** *True Grit*
1970 **George C. Scott,** *Patton*
1971 **Gene Hackman,** *The French Connection*
1972 **Marlon Brando,** *The Godfather*
1973 **Jack Lemmon,** *Save the Tiger*
1974 **Art Carney,** *Harry and Tonto*
1975 **Jack Nicholson,** *One Flew Over the Cuckoo's Nest*
1976 **Peter Finch,** *Network*
1977 **Richard Dreyfuss,** *The Goodbye Girl*
1978 **John Voight,** *Coming Home*
1979 **Dustin Hoffman,** *Kramer vs. Kramer*
1980 **Robert Di Niro,** *Raging Bull*

BEST ACTRESS

1928 **Janet Gaynor,** *Seventh Heaven, Street Angel* and *Sunrise*
1929 **Mary Pickford,** *Coquette*
1930 **Norma Shearer,** *The Divorcee*
1931 **Marie Dressler,** *Min and Bill*
1932 **Helen Hayes,** *The Sin of Madelon Claudet*
1933 **Katharine Hepburn,** *Morning Glory*
1934 **Claudette Colbert,** *It Happened One Night*
1935 **Bette Davis,** *Dangerous*
1936 **Luise Rainer,** *The Great Ziegfeld*
1937 **Luise Rainer,** *The Good Earth*
1938 **Bette Davis,** *Jezebel*
1939 **Vivien Leigh,** *Gone With the Wind*
1940 **Ginger Rogers,** *Kitty Foyle*
1941 **Joan Fontaine,** *Suspicion*
1942 **Greer Garson,** *Mrs. Miniver*
1943 **Jennifer Jones,** *The Song of Bernadette*
1944 **Ingrid Bergman,** *Gaslight*
1945 **Joan Crawford,** *Mildred Pierce*
1946 **Olivia de Havilland,** *To Each His Own*
1947 **Loretta Young,** *The Farmer's Daughter*
1948 **Jane Wyman,** *Johnny Belinda*
1949 **Olivia de Havilland,** *The Heiress*
1950 **Judy Holliday,** *Born Yesterday*
1951 **Vivien Leigh,** *A Streetcar Named Desire*
1952 **Shirley Booth,** *Come Back Little Sheba*
1953 **Audrey Hepburn,** *Roman Holiday*
1954 **Grace Kelly,** *The Country Girl*
1955 **Anna Magnani,** *The Rose Tattoo*
1956 **Ingrid Bergman,** *Anastasia*
1957 **Joanne Woodward,** *The Three Faces of Eve*
1958 **Susan Hayward,** *I Want to Live!*
1959 **Simone Signoret,** *Room at the Top*
1960 **Elizabeth Taylor,** *Butterfield 8*
1961 **Sophia Loren,** *Two Women*
1962 **Anne Bancroft,** *The Miracle Worker*
1963 **Patricia Neal,** *Hud*
1964 **Julie Andrews,** *Mary Poppins*
1965 **Julie Christie,** *Darling*
1966 **Elizabeth Taylor,** *Who's Afraid of Virginia Woolf?*
1967 **Katharine Hepburn,** *Guess Who's Coming to Dinner*
1968 **Katharine Hepburn,** *The Lion in Winter*
Barbra Streisand, *Funny Girl*
1969 **Maggie Smith,** *The Prime of Miss Jean Brodie*
1970 **Glenda Jackson,** *Women in Love*
1971 **Jane Fonda,** *Klute*
1972 **Liza Minnelli,** *Cabaret*
1973 **Glenda Jackson,** *A Touch of Class*
1974 **Ellen Burstyn,** *Alice Doesn't Live Here Anymore*
1975 **Louise Fletcher,** *One Flew Over the Cuckoo's Nest*
1976 **Faye Dunaway,** *Network*
1977 **Diane Keaton,** *Annie Hall*
1978 **Jane Fonda,** *Coming Home*
1979 **Sally Field,** *Norma Rae*
1980 **Sissy Spacek,** *Coal Miner's Daughter*

BEST DIRECTOR

1928 **Frank Borzage,** *Seventh Heaven*
Lewis Mileston, *Two Arabian Nights*
1929 **Frank Lloyd,** *The Divine Lady*
1930 **Lewis Milestone,** *All Quiet on the Western Front*
1931 **Norman Taurog,** *Skippy*
1932 **Frank Borzage,** *Bad Girl*
1933 **Frank Lloyd,** *Cavalcade*
1934 **Frank Capra,** *It Happened One Night*
1935 **John Ford,** *The Informer*
1936 **Frank Capra,** *Mr. Deeds Goes to Town*
1937 **Leo McCarey,** *The Awful Truth*
1938 **Frank Capra,** *You Can't Take It with You*
1939 **Victor Fleming,** *Gone With the Wind*
1940 **John Ford,** *The Grapes of Wrath*
1941 **John Ford,** *How Green Was My Valley*
1942 **William Wyler,** *Mrs. Miniver*
1943 **Michael Curtiz,** *Casablanca*
1944 **Leo McCarey,** *Going My Way*
1945 **Billy Wilder,** *The Lost Weekend*
1946 **William Wyler,** *The Best Years of Our Lives*
1947 **Elia Kazan,** *Gentleman's Agreement*
1948 **John Huston,** *Treasure of Sierra Madre*
1949 **Joseph L. Mankiewicz,** *A Letter to Three Wives*
1950 **Joseph L. Mankiewicz,** *All About Eve*
1951 **George Stevens,** *A Place in the Sun*
1952 **John Ford,** *The Quiet Man*
1953 **Fred Zinnemann,** *From Here to Eternity*
1954 **Elia Kazan,** *On the Waterfront*
1955 **Delbert Mann,** *Marty*
1956 **George Stevens,** *Giant*
1957 **David Lean,** *The Bridge on the River Kwai*
1958 **Vincente Minnelli,** *Gigi*
1959 **William Wyler,** *Ben-Hur*
1960 **Billy Wilder,** *The Apartment*
1961 **Robert Wise and Jerome Robbins,** *West Side Story*
1962 **David Lean,** *Lawrence of Arabia*
1963 **Tony Richardson,** *Tom Jones*
1964 **George Cukor,** *My Fair Lady*
1965 **Robert Wise,** *The Sound of Music*
1966 **Fred Zinnemann,** *A Man for All Seasons*
1967 **Mike Nichols,** *The Graduate*
1968 **Sir Carol Reed,** *Oliver!*
1969 **John Schlesinger,** *Midnight Cowboy*
1970 **Franklin J. Schaffner,** *Patton*
1971 **William Friedkin,** *The French Connection*
1972 **Bob Fosse,** *Cabaret*
1973 **George Roy Hill,** *The Sting*
1974 **Francis Ford Coppola,** *The Godfather, Part II*
1975 **Milos Forman,** *One Flew Over the Cuckoo's Nest*
1976 **John G. Avildsen,** *Rocky*
1977 **Woody Allen,** *Annie Hall*
1978 **Michael Cimino,** *The Deer Hunter*
1979 **Robert Benton,** *Kramer vs. Kramer*
1980 **Robert Redford,** *Ordinary People*

BEST SUPPORTING ACTOR

1936 **Walter Brennan,** *Come and Get It*
1937 **Joseph Schildkraut,** *The Life of Emile Zola*
1938 **Walter Brennan,** *Kentucky*
1939 **Thomas Mitchell,** *Stagecoach*
1940 **Walter Brennan,** *The Westerner*
1941 **Donald Crisp,** *How Green Was My Valley*
1942 **Van Heflin,** *Johnny Eager*
1943 **Charles Coburn,** *The More the Merrier*
1944 **Barry Fitzgerald,** *Going My Way*
1945 **James Dunn,** *A Tree Grows in Brooklyn*
1946 **Harold Russell,** *The Best Years of Our Lives*
1947 **Edmund Gwenn,** *Miracle on 34th Street*
1948 **Walter Huston,** *Treasure of Sierra Madre*
1949 **Dean Jagger,** *Twelve O'Clock High*
1950 **George Sanders,** *All About Eve*
1951 **Karl Malden,** *A Streetcar Named Desire*
1952 **Anthony Quinn,** *Viva Zapata!*
1953 **Frank Sinatra,** *From Here to Eternity*
1954 **Edmond O'Brien,** *The Barefoot Contessa*
1955 **Jack Lemmon,** *Mister Roberts*
1956 **Anthony Quinn,** *Lust for Life*
1957 **Red Buttons,** *Sayonara*
1958 **Burl Ives,** *The Big Country*
1959 **Hugh Griffith,** *Ben-Hur*
1960 **Peter Ustinov,** *Spartacus*

1961 **George Chakiris,** *West Side Story*
1962 **Ed Begley,** *Sweet Bird of Youth*
1963 **Melvyn Douglas,** *Hud*
1964 **Peter Ustinov,** *Topkapi*
1965 **Martin Balsam,** *A Thousand Clowns*
1966 **Walter Matthau,** *The Fortune Cookie*
1967 **George Kennedy,** *Cool Hand Luke*
1968 **Jack Albertson,** *The Subject Was Roses*
1969 **Gig Young,** *They Shoot Horses, Don't They?*
1970 **John Mills,** *Ryan's Daughter*
1971 **Ben Johnson,** *The Last Picture Show*
1972 **Joel Grey,** *Cabaret*
1973 **John Houseman,** *The Paper Chase*
1974 **Robert De Niro,** *The Godfather, Part II*
1975 **George Burns,** *The Sunshine Boys*
1976 **Jason Robards,** *All The President's Men*
1977 **Jason Robards,** *Julia*
1978 **Christopher Walken,** *The Deer Hunter*
1979 **Melvyn Douglas,** *Being There*
1980 **Timothy Hutton,** *Ordinary People*

BEST SUPPORTING ACTRESS

1936 **Gale Sondergaard,** *Anthony Adverse*
1937 **Alice Brady,** *In Old Chicago*
1938 **Fay Bainter,** *Jezebel*
1939 **Hattie McDaniel,** *Gone With the Wind*
1940 **Jane Darwell,** *The Grapes of Wrath*
1941 **Mary Astor,** *The Great Lie*
1942 **Teresa Wright,** *Mrs. Miniver*
1943 **Katina Paxinou,** *For Whom the Bell Tolls*
1944 **Ethel Barrymore,** *None But the Lonely Heart*
1945 **Anne Revere,** *National Velvet*
1946 **Anne Baxter,** *The Razor's Edge*
1947 **Celeste Holm,** *Gentleman's Agreement*
1948 **Claire Trevor,** *Key Largo*
1949 **Mercedes McCambridge,** *All the King's Men*
1950 **Josephine Hull,** *Harvey*
1951 **Kim Hunter,** *A Streetcar Named Desire*
1952 **Gloria Grahame,** *The Bad and the Beautiful*
1953 **Donna Reed,** *From Here to Eternity*
1954 **Eva Marie Saint,** *On the Waterfront*
1955 **Jo Van Fleet,** *East of Eden*
1956 **Dorothy Malone,** *Written on the Wind*
1957 **Miyoshi Umeki,** *Sayonara*
1958 **Wendy Hiller,** *Separate Tables*
1959 **Shelley Winters,** *The Diary of Anne Frank*
1960 **Shirley Jones,** *Elmer Gantry*
1961 **Rita Moreno,** *West Side Story*
1962 **Patty Duke,** *The Miracle Worker*
1963 **Margaret Rutherford,** *The V.I.P.'s*
1964 **Lila Kedrova,** *Zorba the Greek*
1965 **Shelley Winters,** *A Patch of Blue*
1966 **Sandy Dennis,** *Who's Afraid of Virginia Woolf?*
1967 **Estelle Parsons,** *Bonnie and Clyde*
1968 **Ruth Gordon,** *Rosemary's Baby*
1969 **Goldie Hawn,** *Cactus Flower*
1970 **Helen Hayes,** *Airport*
1971 **Cloris Leachman,** *The Last Picture Show*
1972 **Eileen Heckart,** *Butterflies Are Free*
1973 **Tatum O'Neal,** *Paper Moon*
1974 **Ingrid Bergman,** *Murder on the Orient Express*
1975 **Lee Grant,** *Shampoo*
1976 **Beatrice Straight,** *Network*
1977 **Vanessa Redgrave,** *Julia*
1978 **Maggie Smith,** *California Suite*
1979 **Meryl Streep,** *Kramer vs. Kramer*
1980 **Mary Steenburgen,** *Melvin and Howard*

ART DIRECTION

1928 **William Menzies,** *The Dove* and *The Tempest*
1929 **Cedric Gibbons,** *The Bridge of San Luis Rey*
1930 **Herman Rosse,** *King of Jazz*
1931 **Max Ree,** *Cimarron*
1932 **Gordon Wiles,** *Transatlantic*
1933 **William S. Darling,** *Cavalcade*
1934 **Cedric Gibbons and Frederic Hope,** *The Merry Widow*
1935 **Richard Day,** *The Dark Angel*
1936 **Richard Day,** *Dodsworth*
1937 **Stephen Goosson,** *Lost Horizon*
1938 **Carl Weyl,** *The Adventures of Robin Hood*
1939 **Lyle Wheeler,** *Gone With The Wind*

ART DIRECTION/COLOR

1940 **Vincent Korda,** *The Thief of Bagdad*
1941 **Cedric Gibbons and Urie McCleary,** *Blossoms In the Dust*
1942 **Richard Day and Joseph Wright,** *My Gal Sal*
1943 **Alexander Golitzen and John B. Goodman,** *The Phantom of the Opera*
1944 **Wiard Ihnen,** *Wilson*
1945 **Hans Dreier and Ernst Fegte,** *Frenchman's Creek*
1946 **Cedric Gibbons and Paul Groesse,** *The Yearling*
1947 **Alfred Junge,** *Black Narcissus*
1948 **Hein Heckroth,** *The Red Shoes*
1949 **Cedric Gibbons and Paul Groesse,** *Little Women*
1950 **Hans Dreier and Walter Tyler,** *Samson and Delilah*
1951 **Cedric Gibbons and Preston Ames,** *An American in Paris*
1952 **Paul Sheriff,** *Moulin Rouge*
1953 **Lyle Wheeler and George W. Davis,** *The Robe*
1954 **John Meehan,** *20,000 Leagues Under the Sea*
1955 **William Flannery and Jo Mielziner,** *Picnic*
1956 **Lyle R. Wheeler and John de Cuir,** *The King and I*

ART DIRECTION/BLACK AND WHITE

1940 **Cedric Gibbons and Paul Groesse,** *Pride and Pejudice*
1941 **Richard Day and Nathan Juran,** *How Green Was My Valley*
1942 **Richard Day and Joseph Wright,** *This Above All*
1943 **James Basevi and William Darling,** *The Song of Bernadette*
1944 **Cedric Gibbons and William Ferrari,** *Gaslight*
1945 **Wiard Ihnen,** *Blood On the Sun*
1946 **Lyle Wheeler and William Darling,** *Anna and the King of Siam*
1947 **John Bryan,** *Great Expectations*
1948 **Roger K. Furse,** *Hamlet*
1949 **Harry Horner and John Meehan,** *The Heiress*
1950 **Hans Dreier and John Meehan,** *Sunset Boulevard*
1951 **Richard Day,** *A Streetcar Named Desire*
1952 **Cedric Gibbons and Edward Carfagno,** *The Bad And The Beautiful*
1953 **Cedric Gibbons and Edward Carfagno,** *Julius Caesar*
1954 **Richard Day,** *On the Waterfront*
1955 **Hal Pereira and Tambi Larsen,** *The Rose Tattoo*
1956 **Cedric Gibbons and Malcolm F. Brown,** *Somebody Up There Likes Me*

ART DIRECTION

1957 **Ted Haworth,** *Sayonara*
1958 **William A. Horning and Preston Ames,** *Gigi*

ART DIRECTION/COLOR

1959 **William A. Horning and Edward Carfagno,** *Ben-Hur*
1960 **Alexander Golitzen and Eric Orbom,** *Spartacus*

1961 **Boris Leven,** *West Side Story*
1962 **John Box and John Stoll,** *Lawrence of Arabia*
1963 **John De Cuir, Jack Martin Smith, Hilyard Brown, Herman Blumenthal, Elven Webb, Maurice Pelling and Boris Juraga,** *Cleopatra*
1964 **Gene Allen and Cecil Beaton,** *My Fair Lady*
1965 **John Box and Terry Marsh,** *Dr. Zhivago*
1966 **Jack Martin Smith and Dale Hennesy,** *Fantastic Voyage*

ART DIRECTION/BLACK AND WHITE

1959 **Lyle R. Wheeler and George W. Davis,** *The Diary of Anne Frank*
1960 **Alexander Trauner,** *The Apartment*
1961 **Harry Horner,** *The Hustler*
1962 **Alexander Goltizen and Henry Bumstead,** *To Kill A Mockingbird*
1963 **Gene Callahan,** *America, America*
1964 **Vassilis Fotopoulos,** *Zorba The Greek*
1965 **Robert Clatworthy,** *Ship of Fools*
1966 **Richard Sylbert,** *Who's Afraid of Virginia Woolf?*

ART DIRECTION

1967 **John Truscott and Edward Carrere,** *Camelot*
1968 **John Box and Terence Marsh,** *Oliver!*
1969 **John De Cuir, Jack Martin Smith and Herman Blumenthal,** *Hello, Dolly!*
1970 **Urie McCleary and Gil Parrondo,** *Patton*
1971 **John Box, Ernest Archer, Jack Maxsted and Gil Parrondo,** *Nicholas and Alexandra*
1972 **Rolf Zehetbauer and Jurgen Kiebach,** *Cabaret*
1973 **Henry Bumstead,** *The Sting*
1974 **Dean Tavoularis and Angelo Graham,** *The Godfather, Part II*
1975 **Ken Adam and Roy Walker,** *Barry Lyndon*
1976 **George Jenkins,** *All The President's Men*
1977 **John Barry, Norman Reynolds and Leslie Dilley,** *Star Wars*
1978 **Paul Sylbert** and **Edwin O'Donovan** (art direction) and **George Gaines** (set decoration), *Heaven Can Wait*
1979 **Philip Rosenberg** and **Tony Walton** (art decoration) and **Edward Stewart** and **Gary Brink** (set decoration), *All That Jazz*
1980 **Pierre Guffroy** and **Jack Stephens,** *Tess*

CINEMATOGRAPHY

1928 **Charles Rosher and Karl Struss,** *Sunrise*
1929 **Clyde De Vinna,** *White Shadows In The South Seas*
1930 **Joseph T. Rucker and Willard Van Der Veer,** *With Byrd At The South Pole*
1931 **Floyd Crosby,** *Tabu*
1932 **Lee Garmes,** *Shanghai Express*
1933 **Charles Bryant Lang, Jr.,** *A Farewell To Arms*
1934 **Victor Milner,** *Cleopatra*
1935 **Hal Mohr,** *A Midsummer Night's Dream*
1936 **Tony Gaudio,** *Anthony Adverse*
1937 **Karl Freund,** *The Good Earth*
1938 **Joseph Ruttenberg,** *The Great Waltz*

CINEMATOGRAPHY/COLOR

1939 **Ernest Haller and Ray Rennahan,** *Gone With the Wind*
1940 **George Perrinal,** *The Thief of Bagdad*
1941 **Ernest Palmer and Ray Rennahan,** *Blood And Sand*
1942 **Leon Shamroy,** *The Black Swan*
1943 **Hal Mohr and W. Howard Greene,** *The Phantom Of The Opera*
1944 **Leon Shamroy,** *Wilson*
1945 **Leon Shamroy,** *Leave Her To Heaven*
1946 **Charles Rosher, Leonard Smith and Arthur Arling,** *The Yearling*
1947 **Jack Cardiff,** *Black Narcissus*
1948 **Joseph Valentine, William V. Skall and Winton Hoch,** *Joan Of Arc*
1949 **Winton Hoch,** *She Wore A Yellow Ribbon*
1950 **Robert Surtees,** *King Solomon's Mines*
1951 **Alfred Gilks and John Alton,** *An American in Paris*
1952 **Winton C. Hoch and Archie Stout,** *The Quiet Man*
1953 **Loyal Griggs,** *Shane*
1954 **Milton Krasner,** *Three Coins In The Fountain*
1955 **Robert Burks,** *To Catch A Thief*
1956 **Lionel Lindon,** *Around The World In 80 Days*
1957 **Jack Hildyard,** *The Bridge On The River Kwai*
1958 **Joseph Ruttenberg,** *Gigi*
1959 **Robert L. Surtees,** *Ben-Hur*
1960 **Russell Metty,** *Spartacus*
1961 **Daniel L. Fapp,** *West Side Story*
1962 **Fred A. Young,** *Lawrence of Arabia*
1963 **Leon Shamroy,** *Cleopatra*
1964 **Harry Stradling,** *My Fair Lady*
1965 **Freddie Young,** *Dr. Zhivago*
1966 **Ted Moore,** *A Man For All Seasons*

CINEMATOGRAPHY/BLACK AND WHITE

1939 **Gregg Toland,** *Wuthering Heights*
1940 **George Barnes,** *Rebecca*
1941 **Arthur Miller,** *How Green Was My Valley*
1942 **Joseph Ruttenberg,** *Mrs. Miniver*
1943 **Arthur Miller,** *The Song of Bernadette*
1944 **Joseph LaShelle,** *Laura*
1945 **Harry Stradling,** *The Picture of Dorian Gray*
1946 **Arthur Miller,** *Anna And The King Of Siam*
1947 **Guy Green,** *Great Expectations*
1948 **William Daniels,** *The Naked City*
1949 **Paul C. Vogel,** *Battleground*
1950 **Robert Krasker,** *The Third Man*
1951 **William C. Mellor,** *A Place In The Sun*
1952 **Robert Surtees,** *The Bad And The Beautiful*
1953 **Burnett Guffey,** *From Here To Eternity*
1954 **Boris Kaufman,** *On The Waterfront*
1955 **James Wong Howe,** *The Rose Tattoo*
1956 **Joseph Ruttenberg,** *Somebody Up There Likes Me*
1957 **No award**
1958 **Sam Leavitt,** *The Defiant Ones*
1959 **William C. Mellor,** *The Diary Of Anne Frank*
1960 **Freddie Francis,** *Sons and Lovers*
1961 **Eugen Shuftan,** *The Hustler*
1962 **Jean Bourgoin and and Walter Wottitz,** *The Longest Day*
1963 **James Wong Howe,** *Hud*
1964 **Walter Lassally,** *Zorba The Greek*
1965 **Ernest Laszlo,** *Ship Of Fools*
1966 **Haskell Wexler,** *Who's Afraid of Virginia Woolf?*

CINEMATOGRAPHY

1967 **Burnett Guffey,** *Bonnie and Clyde*
1968 **Pasqualino De Santis,** *Romeo & Juliet*
1969 **Conrad Hall,** *Butch Cassidy and The Sundance Kid*
1970 **Freddie Young,** *Ryan's Daughter*
1971 **Oswald Morris,** *Fiddler On The Roof*
1972 **Geoffrey Unsworth,** *Cabaret*
1973 **Sven Nykvist,** *Cries and Whispers*
1974 **Fred Koenekamp and Joseph Biroc,** *The Towering Inferno*
1975 **John Alcott,** *Barry Lyndon*

1976 **Haskell Wexler,** *Bound for Glory*
1977 **Wilmos Zsigmond,** *Close Encounters of the Third Kind*
1980 **Geoffrey Unsworth** and **Ghislain Cloquet,** *Tess*

WRITING/ACHIEVEMENT

1929 **Hans Kraly,** *The Patriot*
1930 **Frances Marion,** *The Big House*

WRITING/ORIGINAL STORY

1928 **Ben Hecht,** *Underworld*
1929 **No award**
1930 **No award**
1931 **John Monk Saunders,** *The Dawn Patrol*
1932 **Frances Marion,** *The Champ*
1933 **Robert Lord,** *One Way Passage*
1934 **Arthur Caesar,** *Manhattan Melodrama*
1935 **Ben Hecht and Charles MacArthur,** *The Scoundrel*
1936 **Pierre Collings and Sheridan Gibney,** *The Story of Louis Pasteur*
1937 **Robert Carson and William A. Wellman,** *A Star Is Born*
1938 **Dore Schary and Eleanore Griffin,** *Boys Town*
1939 **Lewis R. Foster,** *Mr. Smith Goes to Washington*
1940 **Benjamin Glazer and John S. Toddy,** *Arise, My Love*
1941 **Harry Segall,** *Here Comes Mr. Jordan*
1942 **Emeric Pressburger,** *The Invaders*
1943 **William Saroyan,** *The Human Comedy*
1944 **Leo McCarey,** *Going My Way*
1945 **Charles G. Booth,** *The House on 92nd Street*
1946 **Clemence Dane,** *Vacation From Marriage*
1947 **Valentine Davies,** *Miracle on 34th Street*

WRITING/MOTION PICTURE STORY

1948 **Richard Schweizer and David Wechsler,** *The Search*
1949 **Douglas Marrow,** *The Stratton Story*
1950 **Edna Anhalt and Edward Anhalt,** *Panic in the Streets*
1951 **Paul Dehn and James Bernard,** *Seven Days to Noon*
1952 **Fredric M. Frank, Theodore St. John and Frank Cavett,** *The Greatest Show on Earth*
1953 **Ian McLellan Hunter,** *Roman Holiday*
1954 **Philip Yordan,** *Broken Lance*
1955 **Daniel Fuchs,** *Love Me or Leave Me*
1956 **Dalton Trumbo,** *The Brave One*

WRITING/TITLE

1928 **Joseph Farnham,** *The Fair Co-Ed, Laugh, Clown, Laugh* and *Telling The World*

WRITING/ADAPTATION

1928 **Benjamin Glazer,** *Seventh Heaven*
1929 **No award**
1930 **No award**
1930 **Howard Estabrook,** *Cimarron*
1932 **Edwin Burke,** *Bad Girl*
1933 **Sarah Y. Mason and Victor Heerman,** *Little Women*
1934 **Robert Riskin,** *It Happened One Night*
1935 **No award**
1936 **No award**
1937 **No award**
1938 **W.P. Lipscomb, Cecil Lewis and Ian Dalrymple,** *Pygmalion*

WRITING/BEST WRITTEN SCREENPLAY

1935 **Dudley Nichols,** *The Informer*
1936 **Pierre Collings and Sheridan Gibney,** *The Story of Louis Pasteur*
1937 **Norman Reilly Raine, Heinz Herald and Geza Herzceg,** *The Life of Emile Zola*
1938 **George Bernard Shaw,** *Pygmalion*
1939 **Sidney Howard,** *Gone With the Wind*
1940 **Donald Ogden Stewart,** *The Philadelphia Story*
1941 **Sidney Buchman and Seton I. Miller,** *Here Comes Mr. Jordan*
1942 **Arthur Wimperis, George Froeschell, James Hilton and Claudine West,** *Mrs. Miniver*
1943 **Julius J. Epstein, Philip C. Epstein and Howard Koch,** *Casablanca*
1944 **Frank Butler and Frank Cavett,** *Going My Way*
1945 **Charles Brackett and Billy Wilder,** *The Lost Weekend*
1946 **Robert E. Sherwood,** *The Best Years of Our Lives*
1947 **George Seaton,** *Miracle on 34th Street*
1948 **John Juston,** *Treasure of Sierre Madre*
1949 **Joseph L. Mankiewicz,** *A Letter to Three Wives*

WRITING/ORIGINAL SCREENPLAY

1940 **Preston Sturges,** *The Great McGinty*
1941 **Herman J. Mankiewicz and Orson Welles,** *Citizen Kane*
1942 **Ring Lardner, Jr., and Michael Kanin,** *Woman of the Year*
1943 **Norman Krasna,** *Princess O'Rourke*
1944 **Lamar Trotti,** *Wilson*
1945 **Richard Schweizer,** *Marie-Louise*
1946 **Muriel Box and Sidney Box,** *The Seventh Veil*
1947 **Sidney Sheldon,** *The Bachelor and the Bobbysoxer*

WRITING/STORY AND SCREENPLAY

1949 **Robert Pirosh,** *Battleground*
1950 **Charles Brackett, Billy Wilder and D.M. Marshman, Jr.,** *Sunset Boulevard*
1951 **Alan Jay Lerner,** *An American in Paris*
1952 **T.E.B. Clarke,** *The Lavender Hill Mob*
1953 **Charles Brackett, Walter Reisch and Richard Breen,** *Titanic*
1954 **Budd Schulberg,** *On The Waterfront*
1955 **William Ludwig and Sonya Levien,** *Interrupted Melody*
1956 **James Poe, John Farrow and S.J. Perelman,** *Around the World in 80 Days* (adapted)
Albert Lamorisse, *The Red Balloon* (original)
1957 **George Wells,** *Designing Woman*
1958 **Nathan E. Douglas and Harold Jacob Smith,** *The Defiant Ones*
1959 **Russell Rouse and Clarence Greene (story) and Stanley Shapiro and Maurice Richlin (screenplay),** *Pillow Talk*
1960 **Billy Wilder and I.A.L. Diamond,** *The Apartment*
1961 **William Inge,** *Splendor in the Grass*
1962 **Ennio de Concini, Alfredo Giannetti and Pietro Germi,** *Divorce—Italian Style*
1963 **James R. Webb,** *How the West Was Won*
1964 **S.H. Barnett (story) and Peter Stone and Frank Tarloff (screenplay),** *Father Goose*
1965 **Frederick Raphael,** *Darling*
1966 **Claude Lelouch (story) and Pierre Uytterhoeven and Claude Lelouch (screenplay),** *A Man and A Woman*
1967 **William Rose,** *Guess Who's Coming to Dinner*
1968 **Mel Brooks,** *The Producers*

1969 **William Goldman,** *Butch Cassidy and The Sundance Kid*
1970 **Francis Ford Coppola and Edmund H. North,** *Patton*
1971 **Paddy Chayefsky,** *The Hospital*
1972 **Jeremy Larner,** *The Candidate*
1973 **Davis S. Ward,** *The Sting*

WRITING/ORIGINAL SCREENPLAY

1974 **Robert Towne,** *Chinatown*
1975 **Frank Pierson,** *Dog Day Afternoon*
1976 **Paddy Chayefsky,** *Network*
1977 **Woody Allen and Marshall Brickman,** *Annie Hall*
1978 **Nancy Dowd** (story) and **Waldo Salt** and **Robert C. Jones** (screenplay), *Coming Home*
1979 **Steve Tesich,** *Breaking Away*
1980 **Bo Goldman,** *Melvin and Howard*

WRITING/SCREENPLAY BASED ON MATERIAL FROM ANOTHER MEDIUM

1957 **Pierre Boulle,** *The Bridge on the River Kwai*
1958 **Alan Jay Lerner,** *Gigi*
1959 **Neil Paterson,** *Room at the Top*
1960 **Richard Brooks,** *Elmer Gantry*
1961 **Abby Mann,** *Judgment at Nuremberg*
1962 **Horton Foote,** *To Kill a Mockingbird*
1963 **John Osborne,** *Tom Jones*
1964 **Edward Anhalt,** *Becket*
1965 **Robert Bolt,** *Dr. Zhivago*
1966 **Robert Bolt,** *A Man for All Seasons*
1967 **Stirling Silliphant,** *In the Heat of the Night*
1968 **James Goldman,** *The Lion in Winter*
1969 **Waldo Salt,** *Midnight Cowboy*
1970 **Ring Lardner, Jr.,** *M*A*S*H*
1971 **Ernest Tidyman,** *The French Connection*
1972 **Mario Puzo and Francis Ford Coppola,** *The Godfather*
1973 **William Peter Blatty,** *The Exocist*

WRITING/SCREENPLAY ADAPTED FROM OTHER MATERIAL

1974 **Francis Ford Coppola and Mario Puzo,** *The Godfather, Part II*
1975 **Lawrence Hauben and Bo Goldman,** *One Flew Over the Cuckoo's Nest*
1976 **William Goldman,** *All The President's Men*
1977 **Alvin Sargent,** *Julia*
1978 **Oliver Stone,** *Midnight Express*
1979 **Robert Benton,** *Kramer vs. Kramer*
1980 **Alvin Sargent,** *Ordinary People*

ASSISTANT DIRECTOR

1933 **William Tummel,** 20th Century Fox
Charles Dorian, Metro-Goldwyn-Mayer
Charles Barton, Paramount
Dowey Starkey, RKO Radio
Fred Fox, United Srtists
Scott Beal, Universal
Gordon Hollingshead, Warner Bros.
1934 **John Waters,** *Viva Villa*
1935 **Clen Beauchamp and Paul Wing,** *Lives of a Bengal Lancer*
1936 **Jack Sullivan,** *The Charge of the Light Brigade*
1937 **Robert Webb,** *In Old Chicago*

COSTUME DESIGN/BLACK AND WHITE

1948 **Roger K. Furse,** *Hamlet*
1949 **Edith Head and Gile Steele,** *The Heiress*
1950 **Edith Head and Charles Le Maire,** *All About Eve*
1951 **Edith Head,** *A Place in the Sun*
1952 **Helen Rose,** *The Bad and the Beautiful*
1953 **Edith Head,** *Roman Holiday*
1954 **Edith Head,** *Sabrina*
1955 **Helen Rose,** *I'll Cry Tomorrow*
1956 **Jean Louis,** *The Solid Gold Cadillac*
1957 **No award**
1958 **No award**
1959 **Orry-Kelly,** *Some Like It Hot*
1960 **Edith Head and Howard Stevenson,** *The Facts of Life*
1961 **Piero Gherardi,** *La Dolce Vita*
1962 **Norma Koch,** *Whatever Happened to Baby Jane?*
1963 **Piero Gherardi,** *Federico Fellini's 8½*
1964 **Dorothy Jeakins,** *The Night of the Iguana*
1965 **Julie Harris,** *Darling*
1966 **Irene Sharaff,** *Who's Afraid of Virginia Woolf?*

COSTUME DESIGN/COLOR

1948 **Dorothy Jeakins and Karinska,** *Joan of Arc*
1949 **Leah Rhodes, Travilla and Marjorie Best,** *Adventures of Don Juan*
1950 **Edith Head, Dorothy Jeakins, Elois Jenssen, Gile Steele and Gwen Wakeling,** *Samson and Delilah*
1951 **Orry-Kelly, Walter Plunkett and Irene Sharaff,** *An American in Paris*
1952 **Marcel Vertes,** *Moulin Rouge*
1953 **Charles Le Maire and Emile Santiago,** *The Robe*
1954 **Sanzo Wada,** *Gate of Hell*
1955 **Charles Le Maire,** *Love is a Many-Splendored Thing*
1956 **Irene Sharaff,** *The King and I*
1957 **Orry-Kelly,** *Les Girls*
1958 **Cecil Beaton,** *Gigi*
1959 **Elizabeth Haffenden,** *Ben-Hur*
1960 **Valles and Bill Thomas,** *Spartacus*
1961 **Irene Sharaff,** *West Side Story*
1962 **Mary Wills,** *The Wonderful World of the Brothers Grimm*
1963 **Irene Sharaff, Vittorio Nino Novarese and Renie,** *Cleopatra*
1964 **Cecil Beaton,** *My Fair Lady*
1965 **Phillis Dalton,** *Dr. Zhivago*
1966 **Elizabeth Haffenden and Joan Bridge,** *A Man For All Seasons*

COSTUME DESIGN

1967 **John Truscott,** *Camelot*
1968 **Danilo Donati,** *Romeo and Juliet*
1969 **Margaret Furse,** *Anne of the Thousand Days*
1970 **Nino Novarese,** *Cromwell*
1971 **Yvonne Blake and Antonio Castillo,** *Nicholas and Alexandra*
1972 **Anthony Powell,** *Travels with My Aunt*
1973 **Edith Head,** *The Sting*
1974 **Theoni V. Aldredge,** *The Great Gatsby*
1975 **Ulla-Britt Soderlund and Milena Cananero,** *Barry Lyndon*
1976 **Danilo Donati,** *Fellini's Casanova*
1977 **John Mollo,** *Star Wars*
1978 **Anthony Powell,** *Death on the Nile*
1979 **Albert Wolsky,** *All That Jazz*
1980 **Anthony Powell,** *Tess*

MUSIC/SCORE

1934 **Columbia Studio Music Dept.** (Louis Silvers, dept. head; thematic music by Victor Schertzinger and Gus Kahn), *One Night of Love*

1935 **RKO Studio Music Dept.** (Max Steiner, dept. head and composer of winning score), *The Informer*
1936 **Warner Bros. Studio Music Dept.** (Leo Forbstein, dept. head; Erich Wolfgang Korngold, composer), *Anthony Adverse*
1937 **Universal Studio Music Dept.** (Charles Previn, dept. head), *One Hundred Men and a Girl*
1938 **Alfred Newman,** *Alexander's Ragtime Band*

MUSIC/BEST SCORE

1939 **Richard Hageman, Franke Harling, John Leipold and Leo Shuken,** *Stagecoach*
1940 **Alfred Newman,** *Tin Pan Alley*

MUSIC/ORIGINAL SCORE

1939 **Herbert Sothart,** *The Wizard of Oz*
1940 **Leigh Harline, Paul J. Smith and Ned Washington,** *Pinocchio*

MUSIC/SCORE OF A MUSICAL PICTURE

1941 **Frank Churchill and Oliver Wallace,** *Dumbo*
1942 **Ray Heindorf and Heinz Roemheld,** *Yankee Doodle Dandy*
1943 **Ray Heindorf,** *This is the Army*
1944 **Morris Stoloff and Carmen Dragon,** *Cover Girl*
1945 **Georgie Stoll,** *Anchors Aweigh*
1946 **Morris Stoloff,** *The Jolson Story*
1947 **Alfred Newman,** *Mother Wore Tights*
1948 **Johnny Green and Roger Edens,** *Easter Parade*
1949 **Roger Edens and Lennie Hayton,** *On The Town*
1950 **Adolph Deutsch and Roger Edens,** *Annie Get Your Gun*
1951 **Johnny Green and Saul Chaplin,** *An American in Paris*
1952 **Alfred Newman,** *With a Song in My Heart*
1953 **Alfred Newman,** *Call Me Madam*
1954 **Adolph Deutsch and Saul Chaplin,** *Seven Brides for Seven Brothers*
1955 **Robert Russell Bennett, Jay Blackton and Adolph Deutsch,** *Oklahoma!*
1956 **Alfred Newman and Ken Darby,** *The King and I*
1957 **No award**
1958 **Andre Previn,** *Gigi*
1959 **Andre Previn and Ken Darby,** *Porgy and Bess*
1960 **Morris Stoloff and Harry Sukman,** *Song Without End*
1961 **Saul Chaplin, Johnny Green, Sid Ramin and Irwin Kostal,** *West Side Story*

MUSIC/SCORE OF A DRAMATIC OR COMEDY PICTURE

1941 **Bernard Herrmann,** *All That Money Can Buy*
1942 **Max Steiner,** *Now, Voyager*
1943 **Alfred Newman,** *The Song of Bernadette*
1944 **Max Steiner,** *Since You Went Away*
1945 **Miklos Rozsa,** *Spellbound*
1946 **Hugo Friedhofer,** *The Best Years of Our Lives*
1947 **Miklos Rozsa,** *A Double Life*
1948 **Brian Easdale,** *The Red Shoes*
1949 **Aaron Copland,** *The Heiress*
1950 **Franz Waxman,** *Sunset Boulevard*
1951 **Franz Waxman,** *A Place in the Sun*
1952 **Dimitri Tiomkin,** *High Noon*
1953 **Bronislau Kaper,** *Lili*
1954 **Dimitri Tiomkin,** *The High and The Mighty*
1955 **Alfred Newman,** *Love is a Many-Splendored Thing*
1956 **Victor Young,** *Around the World in 80 Days*
1957 **Malcolm Arnold,** *The Bridge on the River Kwai*
1958 **Dimitri Tiomkin,** *The Old Man and The Sea*
1959 **Miklos Rozsa,** *Ben-Hur*
1960 **Ernest Gold,** *Exodus*
1961 **Henry Mancini,** *Breakfast at Tiffany's*

MUSIC/SCORE SUBSTANTIALLY ORIGINAL/ORIGINAL MUSIC SCORE

1962 **Maurice Jarre,** *Lawrence of Arabia*
1963 **John Addison,** *Tom Jones*
1964 **Richard M. Sherman and Robert B. Sherman,** *Mary Poppins*
1965 **Maurice Jarre,** *Dr. Zhivago*
1966 **John Barry,** *Born Free*
1967 **Elmer Bernstein,** *Thoroughly Modern Millie*

MUSIC/ADAPTATION OR TREATMENT

1962 **Ray Heindorf,** *The Music Man*
1963 **Andre Previn,** *Irma La Douce*
1964 **Andre Previn,** *My Fair Lady*
1965 **Irwin Kostal** *The Sound of Music*
1966 **Ken Thorne,** *A Funny Thing Happened on the Way to the Forum*

1967 **Alfred Newman and Ken Darby,** *Camelot*

MUSIC/ORIGINAL SCORE FOR A MOTION PICTURE (NOT A MUSICAL)

1968 **John Barry,** *The Lion in Winter*
1969 **Burt Bacharach,** *Butch Cassidy and The Sundance Kid*
1970 **Francis Lai,** *Love Story*
1971 **Michael Legrand,** *Summer of '42*
1972 **Charles Chaplin, Raymond Rasch and Larry Russell,** *Limelight*
1973 **Marvin Hamlisch,** *The Way We Were*
1974 **Nino Rota and Carmine Coppola,** *The Godfather, Part II*
1975 **John Williams,** *Jaws*
1976 **Jerry Goldsmith,** *The Omen*
1977 **John Williams,** *Star Wars*
1978 **Giorgio Moroder,** *Midnight Express*
1979 **Georges Delerue,** *A Little Romance*
1980 **Michael Gore,** *Fame*

MUSIC/SCORE FOR A MUSICAL (ORIGINAL OR ADAPTATION)

1968 **John Green,** *Oliver*
1969 **Lenny Hayton and Lionel Newman,** *Hello, Dolly!*
1970 **The Beatles,** *Let It Be*
1971 **John Williams,** *Fiddler on the Roof*
1972 **Ralph Burns,** *Cabaret*

MUSIC/ORIGINAL SONG SCORE AND ADAPTATION SCORING: ADAPTATION

1973 **Marvin Hamlisch,** *The Sting*
1974 **Nelson Riddle,** *The Great Gatsby*
1975 **Leonard Rosenman,** *Barry Lyndon*
1976 **Leonard Rosenman,** *Bound for Glory*
1977 **Jonathan Tunick,** *A Little Night Music*
1978 **Joe Renzetti,** *The Buddy Holly Story*
1979 **Ralph Burns,** *All That Jazz*
1980 **No award**

MUSIC/BEST SONG

1934 **Con Conrad (music) and Herb Magidson (lyrics),** *Continental* from *The Gay Divorcee*
1935 **Harry Warren (music) and Al Dubin (lyrics),** *Lullaby of Broadway* from *Gold Diggers of 1935*
1936 **Jerome Kern (music) and Dorothy Fields (lyrics),** *The Way You Look Tonight* from *Swingtime*
1937 **Harry Owens,** *Sweet Leilani* from *Waikiki Wedding*

1938 **Ralph Raininger (music) and Leo Robin (lyrics),** *Thanks for the Memory* from *The Big Broadcast of 1938*
1939 **Harold Arlen (music) and E.Y. Harbug (lyrics),** *Over the Rainbow* from *The Wizard of Oz*
1940 **Leigh Harline (music) and Ned Washington (lyrics),** *When You Wish Upon a Star* from *Pinocchio*
1941 **Jerome Kern (music) and Oscar Hammerstein II (lyrics),** *The Last Time I Saw Paris* from Lady Be Good
1942 **Irving Berlin,** *White Christmas* from *Holiday Inn*
1943 **Harry Warren (music) and Mack Gordon (lyrics),** *You'll Never Know* from *Hello, Frisco, Hello*
1944 **James Van Heusen (music) and Johnny Burke (lyrics),** *Swinging on a Star* from *Going My Way*
1945 **Richard Rodgers (music) and Oscar Hammerstein II (lyrics),** *It Might As Well Be Spring* from *State Fair*
1946 **Harry Warren (music) and Johnny Mercer (lyrics),** *On The Atchison, Topeka and Santa Fe* from *The Harvey Girls*
1947 **Allie Wrubel (music) and Ray Gilbert (lyrics),** *Zip-A-Dee-Doo-Dah* from *Song of the South*
1948 **Jay Livingston and Ray Evans (music and lyrics),** *Buttons and Bows* from *The Paleface*
1949 **Frank Loesser,** *Baby It's Cold Outside,* from *Neptune's Daughter*
1950 **Ray Evans and Jay Livingston (music and lyrics),** *Mona Lisa* from *Captain Carey, USA*
1951 **Hoagy Carmichael (music) and Johnny Mercer (lyrics),** *In the Cool, Cool, Cool of the Evening* from *Here Comes the Groom*
1952 **Dimitri Tiomkin (music) and Ned Washington (lyrics),** *High Noon (Do Not Forsake Me, Oh My Darlin)* from *High Noon*
1953 **Sammy Fain (music) and Paul Francis Webster (lyrics),** *Secret Love* from *Calamity Jane*
1954 **Jule Styne (music) and Sammy Cahn (lyrics),** *Three Coins in the Fountain* from *Three Coins in the Fountain*
1955 **Sammy Fain (music) and Paul Francis Webster (lyrics),** *Love Is a Many-Splendored Thing* from *Love Is a Many-Splendored Thing*
1956 **Ray Evans and Jay Livingston (music and lyrics),** *Whatever Will Be, Will Be (Que Sera, Sera)* from *The Man Who Knew Too Much*
1957 **James Van Heusen (music) and Sammy Cahn (lyrics),** *All the Way* from *The Joker Is Wild*
1958 **Frederick Lowe (music) and Alan Jay Lerner (lyrics),** *Gigi* from *Gigi*
1959 **James Van Heusen (music) and Sammy Cahn (lyrics),** *High Hopes* from *A Hole in the Head*
1960 **Manos Hadjidakis,** *Never on Sunday* from *Never on Sunday*
1961 **Henry Mancini (music) and Johnny Mercer (lyrics),** *Moon River* from *Breakfast at Tiffany's*
1962 **Henry Mancini (music) and Johnny Mercer (lyrics),** *Days of Wine and Roses* from *Days of Wine and Roses*
1963 **James Van Heusen (music) and Sammy Cahn (lyrics),** *Call Me Irresponsible* from *Papa's Delicate Condition*
1964 **Richard M. Sherman and Robert B. Sherman (music and lyrics),** *Chim Chim Cher-ee* from *Mary Poppins*
1965 **Johnny Mandel (music) and Paul Francis Webster (lyrics),** *The Shadow of Your Smile* from *The Sandpiper*
1966 **John Barry (music) and Don Black (lyrics),** *Born Free* from *Born Free*
1967 **Leslie Bricusse,** *Talk to the Animals* from *Doctor Doolittle*
1968 **Michael Legrand (music) and Alan and Marilyn Bergman (lyrics),** *The Windmills of Your Mind* from *The Thomas Crown Affair*
1969 **Burt Bacharach (music) and Hal David (lyrics),** *Raindrops Keep Fallin' on My Head* from *Butch Cassidy and The Sundance Kid*
1970 **Fred Karlin (music) and Robb Royer and James Griffin a.k.a. Robb Wilson and Arthur James (lyrics),** *For All We Know* from *Lovers and Other Strangers*
1971 **Isaac Hayes,** Theme from *Shaft*
1972 **Al Kasha and Joel Hirschhorn (music and lyrics),** *The Morning After* from *The Poseidon Adventure*
1973 **Marvin Hamlisch (music) and Alan and Marilyn Bergman (lyrics),** *The Way We Were* from *The Way We Were*
1974 **Al Kasha and Joel Hirschhorn (music and lyrics),** *We May Never Love Like This Again* from *The Towering Inferno*
1975 **Keith Carradine,** *I'm Easy* from *Nashville*
1976 **Barbra Streisand (music) and Paul Williams (lyrics),** *Evergreen* from *A Star Is Born*
1977 **Joseph Brooks (music and lyrics),** *You Light Up My Life*
1978 **Paul Jabara,** *Last Dance* from *Thank God It's Friday*
1979 **David Shire** (music) and **Norman Gimbel** (lyrics), *It Goes Like It Goes* from *Norma Rae*
1980 **Michael Gore** (music) and **Dean Pitchford** (lyrics), *Fame* from *Fame*

DANCE DIRECTION

1935 **Dave Gould,** *I've Got a Feeling You're Fooling* from *Broadway Melody of 1936* and *Straw Hat* from *Folies Bergere*
1936 **Seymour Felix,** *A Pretty Girl Is Like a Melody* from *The Great Ziegfeld*
1937 **Hermes Pan,** *Fun House* from *Damsel in Distress*

SET DECORATION OR INTERIOR DECORATION BLACK AND WHITE

1941 **Thomas Little,** *How Green Was My Valley*
1942 **Thomas Little,** *This Above All*
1943 **Thomas Little,** *The Song of Bernadette*
1944 **Edwin B. Willis and Paul Huldschinsky,** *Gaslight*
1945 **A. Roland Fields,** *Blood on the Sun*
1946 **Thomas Little and Frank E. Hughes,** *Anna and the King of Siam*
1947 **Wilfred Shingleton,** *Great Expectations*
1948 **Carmen Dillon,** *Hamlet*
1949 **Emile Kuri,** *The Heiress*
1950 **Sam Comer and Ray Moyer,** *Sunset Boulevard*
1951 **George James Hopkins,** *A Streetcar Named Desire*
1952 **Edwin B. Willis and Keogh Gleason,** *The Bad and The Beautiful*
1953 **Edwin B. Willis and Hugh Hunt,** *Julius Caesar*
1954 **No award**
1955 **Sam Comer and Arthur Krams,** *The Rose Tattoo*
1956 **Edwin S. Willis and Keogh Gleason,** *Somebody Up There Likes Me*
1957 **No award**
1958 **No award**
1959 **Walter M. Scott and Stuart A. Reiss,** *The Diary of Anne Frank*
1960 **Edward G. Boyle,** *The Apartment*
1961 **Gene Callahan,** *The Hustler*
1962 **Oliver Emert,** *To Kill a Mockingbird*
1963 **No award**
1964 **No award**

1965 Joseph Kish, *Ship of fools*
1966 George James Hopkins, *Who's Afraid of Virginia Woolf?*

SET DIRECTION OR INTERIOR DECORATION/COLOR

1941 Edwin B. Willis, *Blossoms in the Dust*
1942 Thomas Little, *My Gal Sal*
1943 Russell A. Gausman and Ira S. Webb, *The Phantom of the Opera*
1944 Thomas Little, *Wilson*
1945 Sam Comer, *Frenchman's Creek*
1946 Edwin B. Willis, *The Yearling*
1947 Alfred Junge, *Black Narcissus*
1948 Arthur Lawson, *The Red Shoes*
1949 Edwin B. Willis and Jack D. Moore, *Little Women*
1950 Sam Comer and Ray Moyer, *Samson and Delilah*
1951 Edwin B. Willis and Keogh Gleason, *An American in Paris*
1952 Marcel Vertes, *Moulin Rouge*
1953 Walter M. Scott and Paul S. Fox, *The Robe*
1954 Emile Kuri, *20,000 Leagues Under the Sea*
1955 Robert Priestley, *Picnic*
1956 Walter M. Scott and Paul S. Fox, *The King and I*
1957 Robert Priestley, *Sayonara*
1958 Henry Grace and Keogh Gleason, *Gigi*
1959 Hugh Hunt, *Ben-Hur*
1960 Russell A. Gausman and Julia Heron, *Spartacus*
1961 Victor A. Gangelin, *West Side Story*
1962 Dario Simoni, *Lawrence of Arabia*
1963 Walter M. Scott, Paul S. Fox and Ray Moyer, *Cleopatra*
1964 George James Hopkins, *My Fair Lady*
1965 Dario Simoni, *Doctor Zhivago*
1966 Walter M. Scott and Stuart A. Reiss, *Fantastic Voyage*

SET DECORATION

1967 John W. Brown, *Camelot*
1968 Vernon Dixon and Ken Muggleston, *Oliver!*
1969 Walter M. Scott, George Hopkins and Raphael Bretton, *Hello, Dolly!*
1970 Antonio Mateos and Pierre-Louis Thevenet, *Patton*
1971 Vernon Dixon, *Nicholas and Alexandra*
1972 Herbert Strabel, *Carabet*
1973 James Payne, *The Sting*
1974 George R. Nelson, *The Godfather, Part II*
1975 Vernon Dixon, *Barry Lyndon*
1976 George Gaines, *All the President's Men*
1977 Roger Christian, *Star Wars*

SOUND RECORDING OR SOUND

1931 Paramount Studio Sound Dept.
1932 Paramount Studio Sound Dept.
1933 Paramount Studio Sound Dept. (Franklin Hansen, sound dir.), *A Farewell to Arms*
1934 Columbia Studio Sound Dept. (John Livadary, sound dir.), *One Night of Love*
1935 Metro-Goldwyn-Mayer Sound Dept. (Douglas Shearer, sound dir.), *Naughty Marietta*
1936 Metro-Goldwyn-Meyer Sound Dept. (Douglas Shearer, sound dir.), *San Francisco*
1937 Samuel Goldwyn Studio Sound Dept. (Thomas T. Moulton, sound dir.), *The Hurricane*
1938 Samuel Goldwyn Studio Sound Dept. (Thomas T. Moulton, sound dir.), *The Cowboy and the Lady*
1939 Universal Studio Sound Dept. (Bernard B. Brown, sound dir.), *When Tomorrow Comes*
1940 Metro-Goldwyn-Mayer Sound Dept. (Douglas Shearer, sound dir.), *Strike Up the Band*
1941 Alexander Korda, United Artists; General Service Studio Sound Dept. (Jack Whitney, sound dir.), *That Hamilton Woman*
1942 Warner Bros. Studio Sound Dept. (Nathan Levinson, sound dir.), *Yankee Doodle Dandy*
1943 RKO Radio Studio Sound Dept. (Stephen Dunn, sound dir.), *This Land is Mine*
1944 20th Century-Fox Studio Sound Dept. (E.H. Hansen, sound dir.), *Wilson*
1945 RKO Radio Studio Sound Dept. (Stephen Dunn, sound dir.), *The Bells of St. Mary's*
1946 Columbia Studio Sound Dept. (John Livadary, sound dir.), *The Jolson Story*
1947 Samuel Goldwyn Studio Sound Dept. (Gordon Sawyer, sound dir.), *The Bishop's Wife*
1948 20th Century-Fox Studio Sound Dept. (Thomas T. Moulton, sound dir.), *The Snake Pit*
1949 20th Century-Fox Studio Sound Dept. (Thomas T. Moulton, sound dir.), *Twelve O'Clock High*
1950 20th Century-Fox Studio Sound Dept. (Thomas T. Moulton, sound dir.), *All About Eve*
1951 Metro-Goldwyn-Mayer Studio Sound Dept. (Douglas Shearer, sound dir.), *The Great Caruso*
1952 London Films Studio Sound Dept., *Breaking the Sound Barrier*
1953 Columbia Studio Sound Dept. (John Livadary, sound dir.), *From Here to Eternity*
1954 Universal-International Studio Sound Dept. (Leslie I. Carey, sound dir.), *The Glenn Miller Story*
1955 Todd-AO Sound Dept. (Fred Hynes, sound dir.), *Oklahoma!*
1956 20th Century-Fox Studio Sound Dept. (Carl Faulkner, sound dir.), *The King and I*
1957 Warner Bros. Studio Sound Dept. (George R. Groves, sound dir.), *Sayonara*
1958 Todd-AO Sound Dept. (Fred Hynes, sound dir.), *South Pacific*
1959 Metro-Goldwyn-Mayer Studio Sound Dept. (Franklin E. Milton, sound dir.), *Ben-Hur*
1960 Samuel Goldwyn Studio Sound Dept. (Gordon E. Sawyer, sound dir.) and Todd-AO Sound Dept. (Fred Hynes, sound dir.), *The Alamo*
1961 Todd-AO Sound Dept. (Fred Hynes, sound dir.) and Samuel Goldwyn Studio Sound Dept. (Gordon E. Sawyer, sound dir.), *West Side Story*
1962 Shepperton Studio Sound Dept. (John Cox, sound dir.), *Lawrence of Arabia*
1963 Metro-Goldwyn-Mayer Studio Sound Dept. (Franklin E. Milton, sound dir.), *How the West Was Won*
1964 Warner Bros. Studio Sound Dept. (George E. Groves, sound dir.), *My Fair Lady*
1965 20th Century-Fox Studio Sound Dept. (James P. Corcoran, sound dir.) and Todd-AO Sound Dept. (Fred Hynes, sound dir.), *The Sound of Music*
1966 Metro-Goldwyn-Mayer Studio Sound Dept. (Franklin E. Milton, sound dir.), *Grand Prix*
1967 Samuel Goldwyn Studio Sound Dept., *In the Heat of the Night*
1968 Shepperton Studio Sound Dept., *Oliver!*
1969 Jack Solomon and Murray Sivack, Chenault Productions, 20th Century-Fox, *Hello Dolly!*
1970 Douglas Williams and Don Bassman, 20th Century-Fox, *Patton*
1971 Gordon McCallum and David Hildyard, Mirisch-Cartier Productions, United Artists, *Fiddler on the Roof*

1972 Robert Knudson and David Hildyard, ABC Pictures, Allied Artists, *Cabaret*
1973 Robert Knudson and Chris Newman, Hoya Productions, Warner Bros., *The Exorcist*
1974 Ronald Pierce and Melvin Metcalfe, Sr., Universal-Mark Robson-Filmakers Group Production, Universal, *Earthquake*
1975 Robert L. Hoyt, Roger Heman, Earl Madery and John Carter, Universal Zanuck/Brown Production, Universal, *Jaws*
1976 Arthur Piantadosi, Les Fresholtz, Dick Alexander and Jim Webb, Wildwood Enterprises Production, Warner Bros., *All the President's Men*
1977 Don MacDouglass, Ray West, Bob Minkler and Derek Ball, *Star Wars*
1978 Richard Portman, William McCaughey, Aaron Rochin and Darin Knight, *The Deer Hunter*
1979 Walter Murch, Mark Berger, Richard Beggs and Nat Boxer, *Apocalypse Now*
1980 Bill Varney, Steve Maslow, Greg Landaker and Peter Sutton, *The Empire Strikes Back*

ENGINEERING EFFECTS

1928 Roy Pomeroy, *Wings*

SPECIAL EFFECTS

1940 Lawrence Butler (photographic) and Jack Whitney (sound), *The Thief of Bagdad*
1941 Farciot Edouart and Gordon Jennings (photographic) and Louis Mesenkop (sound), *I Wanted Wings*
1942 Gordon Jennings, Farciot Edouart and William L. Pereira (photographic) and Louis Mesenkop (sound), *Reap the Wild Wind*
1943 Fred Sersen (photographic) and Roger Heman (sound), *Crash Dive*
1944 A. Arnold Gillespie, Donald Jahraus and Warren Newcombe (photographic) and Douglas Shearer (sound), *Thirty Seconds Over Tokyo*
1945 John Fulton (photographic) and Arthur W. Johns (sound), *Wonder Man*
1946 Thomas Howard (photographic), *Blithe Spirit*
1947 A. Arnold Gillespie and Warren Newcombe (visual) and Douglas Shearer and Michael Steinore (audible), *Green Dolphin Street*
1948 Paul Eagler, J. McMillan Johnson, Russell Shearman and Clarence Slifer (visual) and Charles Freeman and James G. Stewart (audible), *Portrait of Jennie*
1949 ARKO Productions, *Mighty Joe Young*
1950 George Pal (producer), *Destination Moon*
1951 No award
1952 No award
1953 No award
1954 Walt Disney Studios, *20,000 Leagues Under the Sea*
1955 Paramount Studio, *The Bridges at Toko-Ri*
1956 John Fulton, *The Ten Commandments*
1957 Walter Rossi (audible), *The Enemy Below*
1958 Tom Howard (visual), *tom thumb*
1959 A. Arnold Gillespie and Robert MacDonald (visual) and Milo Lory (audible), *Ben-Hur*
1960 Gene Warren and Tim Baar (visual), *The Time Machine*
1961 Bill Warrington (visual) and Vivian C. Greenham (audible), *The Guns of Navarone*
1962 Robert MacDonald (visual) and Jacques Maumont (audible), *The Longest Day*
1963 Emil Kosa, Jr., *Cleopatra*

SPECIAL VISUAL EFFECTS

1964 Peter Ellenshaw, Hamilton Luske and Eustace Lycett, *Mary Poppins*
1965 John Stears, *Thunderball*
1966 Art Cruickshank, *Fantastic Voyage*
1967 L.B. Abbott, *Doctor Doolittle*
1968 Stanley Kubrick, *2001: A Space Odyssey*
1969 Robbie Robertson, *Marooned*
1970 A.D. Flowers and L.B. Abbott, *Tora! Tora! Tora!*
1971 Alan Maley, Eustace Lycett and Danny Lee, *Bedknobs and Broomsticks*

BEST VISUAL EFFECTS

1977 John Stears, John Dykstra, Richard Edlund, Grant McCune and Robert Blalack, *Star Wars*
1978 No award
1979 H.R. Giger, Carlo Rambaldi, Brian Johnson, Nick Allder and Denys Ayling, *Alien*

FILM EDITING

1934 Conrad Nervig, *Eskimo*
1935 Ralph Dawson, *A Midsummer Night's Dream*
1936 Ralph Dawson, *Anthony Adverse*
1937 Gene Milford and Gene Havlick, *Lost Horizon*
1938 Ralph Dawson, *The Adventures of Robin Hood*
1939 Hal C. Kern and James E. Newcom, *Gone With the Wind*
1940 Anne Bauchens, *North West Mounted Police*
1941 William Holmes, *Sergeant York*
1942 Daniel Mandell, *The Pride of the Yankees*
1943 George Amy, *Air Force*
1944 Barbara McLean, *Wilson*
1945 Robert J. Kern, *National Velvet*
1946 Daniel Mandell, *The Best Years of Our Lives*
1947 Francis Lyon and Robert Parrish, *Body and Soul*
1948 Paul Weatherwax, *The Naked City*
1949 Harry Gerstad, *Champion*
1950 Ralph E. Winters and Conrad A. Nervig, *King Solomon's Mines*
1951 William Hornbeck, *A Place in the Sun*
1952 Elmo Williams and Harry Gerstad, *High Noon*
1953 William Lyon, *From Here to Eternity*
1954 Gene Milford, *On the Waterfront*
1955 Charles Nelson and William A. Lyon, *Picnic*
1956 Gene Ruggiero and Paul Weatherwax, *Around the World in 80 Days*
1957 Peter Taylor, *The Bridge on the River Kwai*
1958 Adrienne Fazan, *Gigi*
1959 Ralph E. Winters and John D. Dunning, *Ben-Hur*
1960 Daniel Mandell, *The Apartment*
1961 Thomas Stanford, *West Side Story*
1962 Anne Coates, *Lawrence of Arabia*
1963 Harold F. Kress, *How the West Was Won*
1964 Cotton Warburton, *Mary Poppins*
1965 William Reynolds, *The Sound of Music*
1966 Fredric Steinkamp, Henry Berman, Steward Linder and Frank Santillo, *Grand Prix*
1967 Hal Ashby, *In the Heat of the Night*
1968 Frank P. Keller, *Bullitt*
1969 Francoise Bonnot, *Z*
1970 Hugh S. Fowler, *Patton*
1971 Jerry Greenberg, *The French Connection*
1972 David Bretherton, *Cabaret*
1973 William Reynolds, *The Sting*
1974 Harold F. Kress and Carl Kress, *The Towering Inferno*
1975 Verna Fields, *Jaws*

1976 Richard Halsey and Scott Conrad, *Rocky*
1977 Paul Hirsch, Marcia Lucas and Ricard Chew, *Star Wars*
1978 Peter Zinner, *The Deer Hunter*
1979 Alan Heim, *All That Jazz*
1980 Thelma Schoonmaker, *Raging Bull*

FOREIGN LANGUAGE FILM

1956 *La Strada*
1957 *The Nights of Cabiria*
1958 *My Uncle*
1959 *Black Orpheus*
1960 *The Virgin Spring*
1961 *Through A Glass Darkly*
1962 *Sundays and Cybele*
1963 *Federico Fellini's 8½*
1964 *Yesterday, Today and Tomorrow*
1965 *The Shop on Main Street*
1966 *A Man and A Woman*
1967 *Closely Watched Trains*
1968 *War and Peace*
1969 *Z*
1970 *Investigation of a Citizen Above Suspicion*
1971 *The Garden of the Finzi-Continis*
1972 *The Discreet Charm of the Bourgeoisie*
1973 *Day for Night*
1974 *Amarcord*
1975 *Dersu Uzala*
1976 *Black and White in Color*
1977 *Madame Rosa*
1978 *Get Out Your Handkerchiefs*
1979 *The Tin Drum*
1980 *Moscow Does Not Believe in Tears*

DOCUMENTARY (feature)

1942 *Battle of Midway*
Kokoda Front Line
Moscow Strikes Back
Prelude to War
1943 *Desert Victory*
1944 *The Fighting Lady*
1945 *The True Glory*
1946 No award
1947 *Design for Death*
1948 *The Secret Land*
1949 *Daybreak in Udi*
1950 *The Titan: The Story of Michelangelo*
1951 *Kon-Tiki*
1952 *The Sea Around Us*
1953 *The Living Desert*
1954 *The Vanishing Prairie*
1955 *Helen Keller in Her Story*
1956 *The Silent World*
1957 *Albert Schweitzer*
1958 *White Wilderness*
1959 *Serengeti Shall Not Die*
1960 *The Horse With the Flying Tail*
1961 *Le Ciel et La Boue* (*Sky Above and Mud Beneath*)
1962 *Black Fox*
1963 *Robert Frost: A Lover's Quarrel with the World*
1964 *Jacques-Yves Cousteau's World Without Sun*
1965 *The Eleanor Roosevelt Story*
1966 *The War Game*
1967 *The Anderson Platoon*
1968 *Journey Into Self*
1969 *Arthur Rubinstein—The Love of Life*
1970 *Woodstock*
1971 *The Hellstrom Chronicle*
1972 *Marjoe*
1973 *The Great American Cowboy*
1974 *Hearts and Minds*
1975 *The Man Who Skied Down Everest*
1976 *Harlan County, U.S.A.*
1977 *Who Are the DeBolts? And Where Did They Get Nineteen Kids?*
1978 *Scared Straight!*
1979 *Best Boy*
1980 *From Mao to Mozart: Isaac Stern in China*

DOCUMENTARY (short subject)

1943 *December 7th*
1944 *With The Marines at Tarawa*
1945 *Hitler Lives?*
1946 *Seeds of Destiny*
1947 *First Steps*
1948 *Toward Independence*
1949 *A Chance to Live*
So Much for So Little
1950 *Why Korea?*
1951 *Benjy*
1952 *Neighbours*
1953 *The Alaskan Eskimo*
1954 *Thursday's Children*
1955 *Men Against the Arctic*
1956 *The True Story of the Civil War*
1957 No award
1958 *Ama Girls*
1959 *Glass*
1960 *Guiseppina*
1961 *Project Hope*
1962 *Dylan Thomas*
1963 *Chagall*
1964 *Nine from Little Rock*
1965 *To Be Alive!*
1966 *A Year Toward Tomorrow*
1967 *The Redwoods*
1968 *Why Man Creates*
1969 *Czechoslovakia 1968*
1970 *Interviews with My Lai Veterans*
1971 *Sentinels of Silence*
1972 *This Tiny World*
1973 *Princeton: A Search for Answers*
1974 *Don't*
1975 *The End of the Game*
1976 *Number Our Days*
1977 *Gravity Is My Enemy*
1978 *The Flight of the Gossamer Condor*
1979 *Paul Robeson: Tribute to an Artist*
1980 *Karl Hess: Toward Liberty*

SHORT SUBJECTS (cartoon)/ short films (animated)

1932 *Flowers and Trees*
1933 *Three Little Pigs*
1934 *The Tortoise and the Hare*
1935 *Three Orphan Kittens*
1936 *Country Cousin*
1937 *The Old Mill*
1938 *Ferdinand the Bull*
1939 *The Ugly Duckling*
1940 *Milky Way*
1941 *Lend a Paw*
1942 *Der Fuehrer's Face*
1943 *Yankee Doodle Mouse*
1944 *Mouse Trouble*
1945 *Quiet, Please*
1946 *The Cat Concerto*
1947 *Tweetie Pie*
1948 *The Little Orphans*
1949 *For Scent-Imental Reasons*
1950 *Gerald McBoing-Boing*

1951 *Two Mouseketeers*
1952 *Johann Mouse*
1953 *Toot, Whistle, Plunk and Boom*
1954 *When Magoo Flew*
1955 *Speedy Gonzales*
1956 *Mister Magoo's Puddle Jumper*
1957 *Birds Anonymous*
1958 *Knighty Knight Bugs*
1959 *Moonbird*
1960 *Munro*
1961 *Ersatz*
1962 *The Hole*
1963 *The Critic*
1964 *The Pink Phink*
1965 *The Dot and The Line*
1966 *Herb Alpert and the Tijuana Brass Double Feature*
1967 *A Place to Stand*
1968 *Winnie the Pooh and the Blustery Day*
1969 *It's Tough to Be a Bird*
1970 *Is It Always Right to Be Right?*
1971 *The Crunch Bird*
1972 *A Christmas Carol*
1973 *Frank Film*
1974 *Closed Mondays*
1975 *Great*
1976 *Leisure*
1977 *Sand Castle*
1978 *Special Delivery*
1979 *Every Child*
1980 *The Fly*

SHORT SUBJECTS (comedy)

1932 *The Music Box*
1933 *So This is Harris*
1934 *La Cucaracha*
1935 *How to Sleep*

SHORT SUBJECTS (novelty)

1932 *Wrestling Swordfish*
1933 *Krakatoa*
1934 *City of Wax*
1935 *Wings Over Mt. Everest*

SHORT SUBJECTS (color)

1935 *Give Me Liberty*
1937 *Penny Wisdom*

SHORT SUBJECTS (one reel)

1936 *Bored of Education*
1937 *Private Life of the Gannets*
1938 *That Mothers Might Live*
1939 *Busy Little Bears*
1940 *Quicker 'n a Wink*
1941 *Of Pups and Puzzles*
1942 *Speaking of Animals and Their Families*
1943 *Amphibious Fighters*
1944 *Who's Who in Animal Land*
1945 *Stairway to Light*
1946 *Facing Your Danger*
1947 *Goodbye, Miss Turlock*
1948 *Symphony of a City*
1949 *Aquatic House-Party*
1950 *Grandad of Races*
1951 *World of Kids*
1952 *Light in the Window*
1953 *The Merry Wives of Windsor Overture*
1954 *This Mechanical Age*
1955 *Survival City*
1956 *Crashing the Water Barrier*

SHORT SUBJECTS (two reel)

1936 *The Public Pays*
1937 *Torture Money*
1938 *Declaration of Independence*
1939 *Sons of Liberty*
1940 *Teddy, The Rough Rider*
1941 *Main Street on the March*
1942 *Beyond the Line of Duty*
1943 *Heavenly Music*
1944 *Won't Play*
1945 *Star in the Night*
1946 *A Boy and His Dog*
1947 *Climbing the Matterhorn*
1948 *Seal Island*
1949 *Van Gogh*
1950 *In Beaver Valley*
1951 *Nature's Half Acre*
1952 *Water Birds*
1953 *Bear Country*
1954 *A Time Out of War*
1955 *The Face of Lincoln*
1956 *The Bespoke Overcoat*

SHORT SUBJECTS (live action)/SHORT FILM (Live Action)

1957 *The Wetback Hound*
1958 *Grand Canyon*
1959 *The Golden Fish*
1960 *Day of the Painter*
1961 *Seawards the Great Ships*
1962 *Heureux Anniversaire*
1963 *An Occurrence at Owl Creek Bridge*
1964 *Casals Conducts: 1954*
1965 *The Chicken*
1966 *Wild Wings*
1967 *A Place to Stand*
1968 *Robert Kennedy Remembered*
1969 *The Magic Machines*
1970 *The Resurrection of Broncho Billy*
1971 *Sentinels of Silence*
1972 *Norman Rockwell's World . . . An American Dream*
1973 *The Bolero*
1974 *One-Eyed Men Are Kings*
1975 *Angel and Big Joe*
1976 *In the Region of Ice*
1977 *I'll Find A Way*
1978 *Teenage Father*
1979 *Board and Care*
1980 *The Dollar Bottom*

SCIENTIFIC OR TECHNICAL/CLASS I (ACADEMY STATUETTE)

1931 **Electrical Research Products, Inc., RCA-Photophone, Inc. and RKO Radio Pictures, Inc.,** For Noise-reduction recording equipment
DuPont Film Manufacturing Corp. and Eastman Kodak Co., For Supersensitive panchromatic film
1936 **Douglas Shearer and the Metro-Goldwyn-Mayer Studio Sound Dept.,** For developing practical two-way horn system and a biased Class A push-pull recording system
1937 **AGFA Ansco Corp.,** For AGFA Supreme and AGFA Ultra Speed pan motion picture negatives
1940 **20th Century-Fox Film Corp. and Daniel Clark, Grover Laube, Charles Miller and Robert W.**

Stevens, For design and construction of silenced camera
1949 **Eastman Kodak Co.,** For development and introduction of improved safety-base motion picture film
1952 **Eastman Kodak Co.,** For introduction of Eastman color negative and color print films
Ansco Div., General Aniline and Film Corp., For introduction of Ansco color negative and color print films
1953 **Henri Chretien and Earl Sponable, Sol Halprin, Lorin Grignon, Herbert Bragg and Carl Faulkner of 20th Century-Fox Studios,** For creating, developing and engineering the equipment, processes and techniques of Cinerama
Fred Waller, For designing and developing the multiple photographic and projection systems for Cinerama
1957 **Todd-AO Corp. and Westrex Corp.,** For developing method of producing and exhibiting wide-film motion pictures
Motion Picture Research Council, For design and development of high-efficiency projection screen for drive-in theatres
1964 **Petro Vlahos, Wadsworth E. Pohl and Ub Iwerks,** For conception and perfection of Color Traveling Matte Composition Cinematography
1968 **Philip V. Palmquist of Minnesota Mining and Mfg. Co., Herbert Meyer of Motion Picture and Television Research Center and Charles D. Staffell of Rank Organization,** For developing the successful embodiment of the reflex background projection system for composite cinematography
Eastman Kodak Co., For developing and introducing a color reversal intermediate film for motion pictures
1977 **Frank Warner,** for sound effects editing, *Star Wars*
Benjamin Burtt, J., for creation of alien creature and robot voices, *Star Wars*
Cinema Procucts, for development of Steadycam
1978 **Eastman Kodak Co.**, For Duplicating Color Film for Motion Pictures
Stephen Kudelski, Nagra Magnetic Records, For research and development of motion-picture sound recorder
Panavision, Inc., and engineering staff under Robert E. Gottschalk for concept, design and continuous development of Panaflex motion-picture camera system
1979 **Mark Serrurier**, For progressive development of the Moviola, which was invented in 1924 by his father, **Iwan r Serrurier**
1980 **Linwood G. Dunn** and **Cecil D. Love** and **Acme Tool and Manufacturing Co.**, For the concept, engineering and development of the Acme-Dunn Optical Printer for motion picture special effects

SCIENTIFIC OR TECHNICAL/CLASS II (CERTIFICATE UNTIL 1937; ACADEMY PLAQUE SINCE 1938)

1931 **Fox Film Corp.,** For effective use of synchro-projection composite photography
1932 **Technicolor Motion Picture Corp.,** For color cartoon process
1933 **Electrical Research Products, Inc.,** For their recording and reproducing equipment
RCA-Victor Co., For high-fidelity recording and reproducing system
1934 **Electrical Research Products, Inc.,** For development of vertical cut disco method of sound recording (hill and dale recording)
1935 **AGFA Ansco Corp.,** For AGFA infra-red film
Eastman Kodak Co., For Eastman Pola-Screen
1936 **E.C. Wente and Bell Telephone Laboratories,** For multi-cellular high-frequency horn and receiver
RCA Mfg. Co., For rotary stabilizer sound head
1937 **Walt Disney Productions, Inc.,** For design and application of multi-plane camera
Eastman Kodak Co., For two fine-grain duplicating film stocks
Farciot Edouart and Paramount Pictures, Inc., For dual screen transparency camera set-up
Douglas Shearer and Metro-Goldwyn-Mayer Studio Sound Dept., For a method of varying the scanning width of variable density sound tracks (squeeze tracks) to obtain increased noise reduction
1938 **No award**
1939 **No award**
1940 **No award**
1941 **Electrical Research Products Div., Western Electric Co.,** For development of the precision integrating sphere densitometer
RCA Mfg. Co., For design and development of MI-3043 uni-directional microphone
1942 **Carroll Clark, F. Thomas Thompson and RKO Studio Art and Miniature Depts.,** For design and construction of moving cloud and horizon machine
Daniel B. Clark and 20th Century-Fox Film Corp., For developing a lens calibration system and the application of this system to exposure control in cinematography
1943 **Farciot Edouart, Earle Morgan, Barton Thompson and Paramount Studio and Engineering Dept.,** For development and application of method of duplicating and enlarging natural color photographs, transferring the image emulsions to glass plates and projecting these slides by especially designed stereopticon equipment
Photo Products Dept., E.I. duPont de Nemours & Co., Inc., For development of fine-grain motion picture films
1944 **Stephen Dunn and RKO Radio Studio Sound Dept. and Radio Corp. of America,** For design and development of electronic compressor-limiter
1945 **No award**
1946 **No award**
1947 **C.C. Davis and Electrical Research Products Div., Western Electric Co.,** For development and application of improved film drive filter mechanism
C.R. Daily and Paramount Studio Film Laboratory, Still and Engineering Depts., For development and first practical application to motion picture and still photography of a method of increasing film speed as first suggested to the industry by du Pont
1948 **Victor Caccialanza, Maurice Ayers and Paramount Studio Set Construction Dept.,** For development and application of Paralite, new lightweight plaster process for set construction
Nick Kalten, Louis J. Witti and 20th Century-Fox Studio Mechanical Effects Dept., For process of preserving and flame-proofing foliage
1949 **No award**
1950 **James B. Gordon and 20th Century Fox Studio Camera Dept.,** For design and development of multiple image film viewer
John Paul Livadary, Floyd Campbell, L.W. Russell and Columbia Studio Sound Dept., For development of multi-track magnetic re-recording system
Loren L. Ryder and Paramount Studio Sound Dept., For studio-wide application of magnetic sound recording to motion picture production
1951 **Gordon Jennings, S.L. Stancliffe and Paramount Studio Special Photographic and Engineering Depts.,** For design, construction and application of servo-operated recording and repeating device

Olin L. Dupy of Metro-Goldwyn-Mayer Studio., For design, construction and application of motion picture reproducing system
Radio Corp. of America, Victor Div., For pioneering direct positive recording with anticipatory noise reduction

1952 **Technicolor Motion Picture Corp.,** For improved method of color photography under incandescent light

1953 **Reeves Soundcraft Co.,** For developing a process of applying stripes of magnetic oxide to motion picture film for sound recording and reproduction

1954 **No award**

1955 **Eastman Kodak Co.,** For Eastman Tri-X panchromatic negative film
Farciot Edouart, Hal Corl and Paramount Studio Transparency Dept., For engineering and developing double-frame, triple-head background projector

1956 **No award**

1957 **Societe d'Optiques et de Mecanique de Haute Precision,** For developing high-speed vari-focal photographic lens
Harlan L. Baumbach, Lorand Wargo, Howard M. Little and Unicorn Engineering Corp., For developing an automatic printer light selector

1958 **Don W. Prideaux, LeRoy G. Leighton and Lamp Div., General Electric Co.,** Development and production of improved 10-kilowatt lamp for set lighting
Panavision, Inc., For design and development of Auto Panatar anamorphic lens for 35mm CinemaScope photography

1959 **Douglas Shearer of Metro-Goldwyn-Mayer, Inc., and Robert E. Gottschalk and John R. Moore of Panavision, Inc.,** For developing a system of producing and exhibiting wide-film motion pictures known as Camera 65
Wadsworth E. Pohl, William Evans, Werner Hopf, S.E. Howse, Thomas P. Dixon, Stanford Research Institute and Technicolor Corp., For design and development of Technicolor electronic printing timer
Wadsworth E. Pohl, Jack Alford, Henry Imus, Joseph Schmit, Paul Fassnacht, Al Lofquist and Technicolor Corp., For development and application of equipment for wet printing
Howard S. Coleman, A. Francis Turner, Harold H. Schroeder, James R. Benford and Harold E. Rosenberger of Bausch and Lomb Optical Co., For developing the Bacold projection mirror
Robert P. Gutterman of General Kinetics, Inc., and Lipsner Smith Corp., For design and developing of the CF-2 Ultra-Sonic Film Cleaner

1960 **Ampex Professional Products Co.,** For producing a well-engineered, multi-purpose sound system combining high quality, convenience of control, dependability and simple emergency provisions

1961 **Sylvania Electric Products, Inc.,** For developing a hand-held high-power lighting unit known as the Sun Gun Professional
James Dale, S. Wilson, H.E. Rice, John Rude, Laurie Atkin, Wadsworth E. Pohl, H. Peasgood and Technicolor Corp., For automatic selective printing process
20th Century-Fox Research Dept. under E.I. Sponable and Herbert E. Bragg, De Luxe Laboratories, Inc., with the assistance of F.D. Leslie, R.D. Whitmore, A.A. Alden, Endel Pool and James B. Gordon, For system of decompressing and recomposing CinemaScope pictures for conventional aspect ratios

1962 **Ralph Chapman,** For design and development of advanced motion picture camera crane
Albert S. Pratt, James L. Wassell and Hans C. Wohlrab of Professional Div., Bell & Howell Co., For design and development of improved motion picture additive color printer
North American Philips, Inc., For developing Norelco 70/35mm projector
Charles E. Sutter, William Bryson Smith and Louis C. Kennell of Paramount Pictures Corp., For engineering and application of new system of electric power distribution

1963 **No award**

1964 **Sidney P. Solow, Edward H. Reichard, Carl W. Hauge and Job Sanderson of Consolidated Film Industries,** For design and development of versatile Automatic 35mm Composite Color Printer
Pierre Angenieux, For developing 10-to-1 zoom lens for cinematography

1965 **Arthur J. Hatch of Strong Electric Corp.,** For developing Air Blown Carbon Arc Projection Lamp
Stefan Kudelski, For developing the Nagra portable -in. tape recording system for sound recording

1966 **Mitchell Camera Corp.,** For Mitchell Mark II 35mm portable reflex camera
Arnold & Ritcher KG, For developing Arriflex portable 35mm reflex camera

1967 **No award**

1968 **Donald W. Norwood,** For development of Norwood Photographic Exposure Meter
Eastman Kodak Co. and Producers Service Co., For development of high-speed step-optical reduction printer
Edmund M. DiGiulio, Neils G. Petersen and Norman S. Hughes of Cinema Product Development Co., For design and application of a conversion which makes available reflex viewing system for motion picture cameras
Optical Coating Laboratory, Inc., For developing an improved anti-reflection coating for photographic and projection lens systems
Eastman Kodak Co., For introduction of high-speed motion picture color negative film
Panavision Inc., For conception, design and introduction of a 65mm hand-held motion picture camera
Todd-AO Co. and Mitchell Camera Co., For design and development of Todd-AO hand-held motion picture camera

1969 **Hazeltine Corp.,** For developing Hazeltine Color Film Analyzer
Fouad Said, For design and introduction of Cinemobile equipment trucks for location production
Juan de la Cierva and Dynasciences Corp., For development of Dynalens optical image motion compensator

1970 **Leonard Sokolow and Edward H. Reichard of Consolidated Film Industries,** For concept and engineering of Color Proofing Printer

1971 **John A. Wilkinson of Optical Radiation Corp.,** For development and engineering of a system of xenon arc lamphouses for motion picture production

1972 **Joseph E. Bluth,** For research and development in electronic photography and transfer of video tape to film
Edward E. Reichard and Howard T. La Zare of Consolidated Film Industries and Edward Efron of IBM, For engineering of a computerized light valve monitoring system for motion picture printing
Panavision Inc., For development and engineering of Panaflex camera

1973 **Joachim Gerb and Erich Kastner of Arnold & Richter Co.,** For developing and engineering Arriflex 35BL camera
Magna-Tech Electronic Co., For engineering and developing a high-speed re-recording system
William W. Valliant of PSC Technology, Inc., Howard F. Ott of Eastman Kodak Co. and Gerry Diebold of Richmark Camera Service, Inc., For developing liquid-gate system for motion picture printers
Harold A. Scheib, Clifford Ellis and Roger W. Banks of Research Products, Inc., For concept and engineering of Model 2101 optical printer for motion picture optical effects

1974 **Joseph E. Kelly of Glen Glenn Sound,** For new audio control consoles which advanced state of sound recording and re-recording
Burbank Studios Sound Dept., For new audio control consoles engineered and constructed by Quad-Eight Sound Corp.
Samuel Goldwyn Studios Sound Dept., For design of a new audio control console engineered and constructed by Quad-Eight Sound Corp.
Quad-Eight Sound Corp., For engineering and constructing new audio control consoles designed by the Burbank and Goldwyn Sound Depts.
Waldon O. Watson, Richard J. Stumpf, Robert J. Leonard and Universal City Studios Sound Dept., For developing and engineering Sensurround System for motion picture presentation

1975 **Chadwell O'Connor of O'Connor Engineering Laboratories,** For concept and engineering of fluid-damped camera head
William F. Miner of Universal City Studios and Westinghouse Electric Corp., For development of solid-state, 500-kilowatt direct-current static rectifier for motion picture lighting

1976 **Consolidated Film Industries and Barneby-Cheney Co.,** For development of system for recovery film-cleaning solvent vapors in a laboratory
William L. Graham, Manfred G. Michelson, Geoffrey F. Norman and Siegfried Seibert of Technicolor, For development and engineering of continuous, high-speed, color motion picture printing system

1977 **Glen Glenn Sound** for concept and development of post-production audio processing system
Panavision, Inc., for concept and engineering of an improvement incorporated in the Panaflex motion picture camera
N. Paul Kenworthy, Jr., and William R. Laterdy for invention and development of the Kenworth snorkel camera system
John. C. Dykstra for development of facility oriented toward visual-effects photography
Alva J. Miller and Jerry Jeffress for engineering of electronic motion control system
Eastman Kodak Co. for development and introduction of new duplicating film
Stefan Kudelski of Nagra Magnetic Recorders, Inc., for engineering of improvement incorporated in Nagra 4.2L sound recorder

1978 **Ray M. Dolby, Ioan B. Allen, David P. Robinson, Stephen M. Katz** and **Philip S.J. Boole, Dolby Laboratories,** For development and implementation of improved sound recording and reproducing systems

1979 **Neiman Tiller Associates,** For creative development, and **Mini-/Micro-Systems,** For design and engineering of automated, computer-controlled editing system (ACCESS) for motion-picture post-production

1980 **Jean-Marie Lavalou, Alain Masseron** and **David C. Samuelson, Samuelson Alga Cinema S.A.** and **Samuelson Film Service, Ltd.,** For the engineering and development of the Louma Camera Crane and remote control system for motion picture production
Edward B. Krause, Filmline Corp., For the engineering and manufacture of the micro-demand drive for continuous motion picture film processors
Ross Taylor, For the concept and development of a system of air guns for propelling objects used in special effects motion picture production
Bernhard Ruhl and **Werner Block, OSRAM GmbH,** For the progressive engineering and manufacture of the OSRAM HMI light source for motion picture color photography
David A. Grafton, For the optical design and engineering of a telecentric anamorphic lens for motion picture optical effects printers

SCIENTIFIC OR TECHNICAL/CLASS III (Certificate of Honorable Mention)

1931 **Electrical Research Products, Inc.,** For moving coil microphone transmission
RKO Radio Pictures, Inc., For reflex-type microphone concentrators
RCA-Photophone Pictures, Inc., For ribbon microphone transmitters

1932 **Eastman Kodak Co.,** For Type-II-B Sensitometer

1933 **Fox Film Corp., Fred Jackman and Warner Bros. Pictures, Inc., and Sidney Sanders of RKO Studios, Inc.,** For developing translucent cellulose screen for composite photography

1934 **Columbia Pictures Corp.,** For the application of the vertical-cut disc method of recording sound for motion pictures (hill and dale recording)
Bell & Howell Co., For developing fully automatic sound and picture printer

1935 **Metro-Goldwyn-Mayer Studio,** For anti-directional negative and positive development by jet turbulation and its application to all negative and print processing to the producing company's entire product
William A. Mueller of Warner Bros.-First National Studio Sound Dept., For method of dubbing, in which level of dialogue automatically controls level of accompanying music and sound effects
Mole-Richardson Co., For development of Solar-Spot lamps
Douglas Shearer and Metro-Goldwyn-Mayer Studio Sound Dept., For automatic control system for cameras and sound recording machines and auxiliary stage equipment
Electrical Research Products, Inc., For design and construction of Paramount transparency air turbine developing machine
Nathan Levinson of Warner Bros.-First National Studio, For method of intercutting variable-density and variable-area soundtracks to secure increased effective range of sound

1936 **RCA Mfg. Co., Inc.,** For method of recording and printing sound records utilizing restricted spectrum (ultra-violet light recording)
Electrical Research Products, Inc., For ERPI Type Q portable recording channel
RCA Mfg. Co., Inc., For practical design and specifications for non-slip printer
United Artists Studio Corp., For developing practical, efficient and quiet wind machine

1937 **John Arnold and Metro-Goldwyn-Mayer Studio Camera Dept.,** For improved semi-automatic focus device and its application to all studio's cameras

John Livadary of Columbia Pictures Corp., For application of bi-planar light valve to motion-picture sound recording

Thomas T. Moulton and the United Artists Studio Sound Dept., For application of volume indicator with peak reading response and linear db scales to motion picture sound recording

RCA Mfg., Co., Inc., For introduction of modulated high-frequency method of determining optimum photographic processing conditions for variable soundtracks

Joseph E. Robbins and Paramount Pictures, Inc., For exceptional application of acoustic principles to sound-proofing of gasoline generators and water pumps

Douglas Shearer and Metro-Goldwyn-Mayer Studio Sound Dept., For design of film-drive mechanism in ERPI 1010 reproducer

1938 **John Aalberg and RKO Radio Studio Sound Dept.** For application of compression to variable-area recording

Byron Haskin and Special Effects Dept. of Warner Bros. Studio, For pioneering triple-head background projector

1939 **George Anderson of Warner Bros. Studio,** For improved positive head for sun arcs

John Arnold of Metro-Goldwyn-Mayer Studio, For mobile camera crane

Thomas T. Moulton, Fred Albin and Sound Dept. of Samuel Goldwyn Studio, For origination and application of Delta db test to sound recording in motion pictures

Farciot Edouart, Joseph E. Robbins, William Rudolph and Paramount Pictures, Inc., For design and construction of quiet portable treadmill

Emery Huse and Ralph B. Atkinson of Eastman Kodak Co., For specifications for chemical analysis of photographic developers and fixing baths

Harold Nye of Warner Bros. Studio, For miniature incandescent spot lamp

A.J. Tondreau of Warner Bros. Studio, For improved soundtrack printer

Multiple Award for contributions to development of new improved process projection equipment:

F.R. Abbott, Haller Belt, Alan Cook and Bausch & Lomb Optical Co., For faster projection lens

Mitchell Camera Co., For new-type process projection head

Mole-Richardson Co., For new-type automatically controlled projection arc lamp

Charles Handley, David Joy and National Carbon Co., For improved and more stable high-intensity carbons

Winton Hoch and Technicolor Motion Picture Corp., For auxiliary optical system

Don Musgrave and Selznick International Pictures, Inc., For pioneering in the use of coordinated equipment in the production of *Gone With the Wind*

1940 **Warner Bros. Studio Art Dept. and Anton Grot,** For design and perfection of water ripple and wave illusion machine

1941 **Ray Wilkinson and Paramount Studio Laboratory,** For pioneering use of fine-grain positive stock

Charles Lootens and the Republic Studio Sound Dept., For pioneering use of Class-B push/pull variable-area recording

Wilbur Silvertooth and the Paramount Studio Engineering Dept., For the design and computation of a relay condenser system applicable to transparency process projection

Paramount Pictures, Inc., and 20th Century-Fox, Inc., For automatic scene-slating device

Douglas Shearer and Metro-Goldwyn-Mayer Studio Sound Dept. and Loren Ryder and Paramount Studio Sound Dept., For development of fine-grain emulsions for variable-density original sound recording in studio production

1942 **Robert Henderson and Paramount Studio Engineering and Transparency Depts.,** For design and construction of adjustable light bridges and frames for transparency process photography

Daniel J. Bloomberg and Republic Studio Sound Dept., For device for marking action negative for pre-selection purposes

1943 **Daniel J. Bloomberg and Republic Studio Sound Dept.,** For design and development of inexpensive conversion of Moviolas to Class B push-pull reproduction

Charles Galloway Clarke and 20th Century-Fox Studio Camera Dept., For development and application of device for composing artificial clouds into motion picture scenes during production photography

Farciot Edouart and Paramount Studio Transparency Dept., For automatic electric transparency cueing timer

Willard H. Turner and RKO Studio Sound Dept., For design and construction of phono-cue starter

1944 **Linwood Dunn, Cecil Love and Acme Tool Mfg.,** For Acme-Dunn Optical Printer

Grover Laube and 20th Century-Fox Studio Camera Dept., For continuous-loop projection device

Western Electric Co., For 1126A Limiting Amplifier for variable-density sound recording

Russell Brown, Ray Hinsdale and Joseph E. Robbins, For floating hydraulic boat rocker

Gordon Jennings, For nodal-point tripod

Radio Corp. of America and RKO Radio Studio Sound Dept., For reverberation chamber

Daniel J. Bloomberg and Republic Studio Sound Dept., for design and development of multi-interlock selector switch

Bernard B. Brown and John Livadary, For separate soloist and chorus recording room

Paul Zeff, S.J. Twining and George Seid of Columbia Studio Laboratory, For formula and application of simplified variable-area sound negative developer

Paul Lerpae, For traveling matte projection and photographing device

1945 **Loren L. Ryder, Charles R. Daily and Paramount Studio Sound Dept.,** For first dial-controlled, step-by-step sound channel line-up and test circuit

Michael S. Leshing, Benjamin Robinson, Arthur B. Chatelain and Robert C. Stevens of 20th Century-Fox Studio and John G. Capstaff of Eastman Kodak Co., For film-processing machine

1946 **Harlan L. Baumbach and Paramount West Coast Laboratory,** For improved method for quantitative determination of hydroquinone and metal in photographic development baths

Herbert E. Britt, For formulas and equipment for producing cloud and smoke effects

Burton F. Miller and Warner Bros. Studio Sound and Electrical Depts., For motion picture arc-lighting generator filter

Carl Faulkner of 20th Century-Fox Studio Sound Dept., For reversed bias method, including double bias method, for light value and galvonometer desnity recording

Mole-Richardson Co., For Type 450 super high-intensity carbon arc lamp
Arthur F. Blinn, Robert O. Cook, C.O. Slyfield and Walt Disney Studio Sound Dept., For audio finder and track viewer for checking and locating noise in soundtracks
Burton F. Miller and Warner Bros. Studio Sound Dept., For equalizer to eliminate relative spectral-energy distortion in electronic compressors
Marty Martin and Hal Adkins of RKO Radio Studio Miniature Dept., For equipment producing visual bullet effects
Harold Nye and Warner Bros. Studio Electric Dept., For electronically controlled fire and gaslight effect

1947 **Nathan Levinson and Warner Bros. Studio Sound Dept.,** For constant-speed sound editing machine
Farciot Edouart, C.R. Daily, Hal Corl, H.G. Cartwright and Paramount Studio Transparency and Engineering Depts., For first application of special anti-solarizing glass to high-intensity background and spot arc projections
Fred Ponedel of Warner Bros. Studio, For pioneering fabrication and application of large translucent photographic backgrounds
Kurt Singer and RCA-Victor Div., Radio Corp. of America, For continuously variable band elimination filter
James Gibbons of Warner Bros. Studio, For large dyed plastic filters

1948 **Marty Martin, Jack Lannon, Russell Shearman and RKO Radio Studio Special Effects Dept.,** For new method of simulating falling snow on motion picture sets
A.J. Moran and Warner Bros Studio Electrical Dept., For a method of remote control for shutters on arc lighting equipment

1949 **Loren L. Ryder, Bruce H. Denney, Robert Carr and Paramount Studio Sound Dept.,** For supersonic playback and public address system
M.B. Paul, For first successful large-area seamless translucent backgrounds
Herbert Britt, For formulas and equipment producing artificial snow and ice for motion picture sets
Andre Coutant and Jacques Mathot, For design of Eclair Camerette
Charles R. Daily, Steve Csillag and Paramount Studio Engineering Dept., For precision method of computing variable tempo-click tracks
International Projector Corp., For simplified, self-adjusting take-up device for projection machines
Alexander Velcoff, For application of infra-red photographic evaluator

1950 **No award**

1951 **Richard M. Haff, Frank P. Herrnfeld, Garland C. Misener and Ansco Div., General Aniline and Film Corp.,** For Ansco color scene tester
Fred Ponedel, Ralph Ayres and George Brown of Warner Bros. Studio, For air-driven water motor to provide flow, wake and white water for marine sequences
Glen Robinson and Metro-Goldwyn-Mayer Studio Construction Dept., For development of balsa falling snow

1952 **Carlos Rivas of Metro-Goldwyn-Mayer Studio,** For automatic magnetic film splicer
Projection, Still Photographic and Development Engigeering Depts. of Metro-Goldwyn-Mayer Studio, For improved method of projecting photographic backgrounds
John G. Frayne and R.R. Scoville and Westrex Corp., For method of measuring distortion in sound reproduction
Photo Research Corp., For creating Spectra color temperature meter
Gustav Jirouch, For Robot automatic film splicer
Carlos Rivas of Metro-Goldwyn-Mayer Studio, For sound reproducer for magnetic film

1953 **Westrex Corp.,** For new film editing machine

1954 **David S. Horsley and Universal International Studio Special Photographic Dept.,** For portable remote-control device for process projectors
Karl Freund and Frank Crandell of Photo Research Corp., For direct-reading brightness meter
Wesley C. Miller, J.W. Stafford, K.N. Frierson and Metro-Goldwyn-Mayer Studio Sound Dept., For electronic sound printing comparison device
John P. Livadary, Lloyd Russell and Columbia Studio Sound Dept., For improved limiting amplifier as applied to sound-level comparison devices
Carlos Rivas, G.M. Sprague and Metro-Goldwyn-Mayer Studio Sound Dept., For magnetic sound editing machine
Fred Wilson of Samuel Goldwyn Studio Sound Dept., For variable multiple-band equalizer
P.C. Young of Metro-Goldwyn-Mayer Studio Projection Dept., For practical application of variable focal length attachment to projection lenses
Fred Knoth and Orien Ernest of Universal-International Studio Technical Dept., For hand-portable, electric, dry oil-fog machine

1955 **20th Century-Fox Studio and Bausch & Lomb Co.,** For new combination lenses for CinemaScope photography
Walter Jolley, Maurice Larson and R.H. Spies of 20th Century-Fox Studio, For a spraying process creating simulated metal surfaces
Steve Krilanovich, For improved camera dolly incorporating multi-directional steering
Dave Anderson of 20th Century-Fox Studio, For improved spotlight capable of maintaining fixed circle of light at constant intensity over varied distances
Loren L. Ryder, Charles West, Henry Fracker and Paramount Studio, For projection film index to establish proper framing for various aspect ratios
Farciot Edouart, Hal Corl and Paramount Studio Transparency Dept., For improved dual stereopticon background projector

1956 **Richard Ranger of Rangertone, Inc.,** For synchronous recording and reproducing system for -in. magnetic tape
Ted Hirsch, Carl Hauge and Edward Reichard of Consolidated Film Industries, For automatic scene counter for laboratory projection rooms
Technical Depts. of Paramount Pictures Corp., For light-weight, horizontal-movement Vista-Vision cameras
Roy C. Stewart and Sons of Stewart-Trans Lux Corp., C.R. Daily and Transparency Dept. of Paramount Pictures Corp., For HiTrans and Para-HiTrans rear projection screens
Construction Dept. of Metro-Goldwyn-Mayer Studio, For new hand-portable fog machine
Daniel J. Bloomberg, John Pond, William Wade and Engineering and Camera Depts. of Republic Studio, For Naturama adpatation to the Mitchell camera

1957 **Charles E. Sutter, William B. Smith, Paramount Pictures Corp. and General Cable Corp.,** For application of aluminum light-weight electrical cable and connectors to studio use

1958 **Willy Borberg and General Precision Laboratory, Inc.,** For high-speed intermittent movement for 35mm theatre projection equipment

Fred Ponedel, George Brown and Conrad Boye of Warner Bros. Special Effects Dept., For new rapid-fire marble gun

1959 **Ub Iwerks of Walt Disney Productions,** For improved optical printer for special effects and matte shots

E.L. Stones, Glen Robinson, Winfield Hubbard and Luther Newman of Metro-Goldwyn-Mayer Construction Dept., For multiple cable remote-controlled winch

1960 **Arthur Holcomb, Petro Vlahos and Columbia Studio Camera Dept.,** For camera flicker-indicating device

Anthony Paglia and 20th Century-Fox Studio Mechanical Effects Dept., For miniature flak gun and ammunition

Carl Hauge, Robert Grubel and Edward Reichard of Consolidated Film Laboratories, For automatic developer-replenisher system

1961 **Hurletron, Inc., Electric Eye Equipment Div.,** For automatic light-changing system for printers

Wadsworth E. Pohl and Technicolor Corp., For integrated sound and picture transfer process

1962 **Electro-Voice, Inc.,** For highly directional dynamic line microphone

Louis G. MacKenzie, For selective sound effects repeater

1963 **Douglas A. Shearer and A. Arnold Gillespie of Metro-Goldwyn-Mayer Studios,** For improved Background Process Projection System

1964 **Milton Forman, Richard B. Glickman and Daniel J. Pearlman of ColorTran Industries,** For advances in lighting units using quartz iodine lamps

Stewart Filmscreen Corp., For seamless translucent Blue Screen for Traveling Matte Color Cinematography

Anthony Paglia and 20th Century-Fox Studio Mechanical Effects Dept., For improved method of processing explosion flash effects

Edward H. Reichard and Carl W. Hauge of Consolidated Film Industries, For Proximity Cue Detector and its application to motion picture printers

Edward H. Reichard, Leonard L. Sokolow and Carl W. Hauge of Consolidated Film Industries, For design and application of stroboscopic scene tester for color and black-and-white film

Nelson Tyler, For improved helicopter camera system

1965 **No award**

1966 **Panavision, Inc.,** For Panatron Power Inverter and its application to camera operation

Carroll Knudson, For production of composers' manual for motion picture music synchronization

Ruby Raksin, For production of composers' manual for motion picture music synchronization

1967 **Electro-Optical Div., Kollmorgen Corp.,** For series of projection lenses

Panavision, Inc., For variable-speed motor for cameras

Fred R. Wilson of Samuel Goldwyn Studio Sound Dept., For audio level clamper

Walden O. Watson and Universal City Studio Sound Dept., For new concepts in design of music scoring stage

1968 **Carl W. Hauge and Edward Reichard of Consolidated Film Laboratories and E. Michael Meahl and Roy J. Ridenour of Ramtronics,** For automatic exposure control for printing machine lamps

Eastman Kodak Co., and Consolidated Film Industries, For new direct positive film and for the application of this film to post-production work prints

1969 **Otto Popelka of Magna-Tech Electronics Co., Inc.,** For electronically controlled looping system

Fenton Hamilton of Metro-Goldwyn-Mayer Studios, For mobile battery-power unit for location lighting

Panavision, Inc., For Panaspeed motion picture camera motor

Robert M. Flynn and Russell Hessy of Universal City Studios, For machine-gun modification for motion picture photography

1970 **Sylvania Electric Products, Inc.,** For series of compact tungsten halogen lamps

B.J. Losmandy, For concept, design and application of micro-miniature solid-state amplifier modules in recording equipment

Eastman Kodak Co. and Photo Electronics Corp., For improved video color analyzer for laboratories

Electro-Sound, Inc., For Series 8000 sound system for theatres

1971 **Thomas Jefferson Hutchinson, James R. Rochester and Fenton Hamilton,** For Sunbrute system of xenon arc lamps for location lighting

Photo Research Div., Kollmorgen Corp., For film/lens-balanced three-color meter

Robert D. Auguste and Cinema Products Co., For new crystal-controlled lightweight motor for 35mm Arriflex cameras

Producers Service Corp. and Consolidated Film Industries, and Cinema Research Corp. and Research Products, Inc., For engineering and implementation of fully automatic blow-up printing systems

Cinema Products Co., For control motor to actuate zoom lenses on cameras

1972 **Photo Research Div. of Kollmorgen Corp., and PSC Technology, Inc., Acme Products Div.,** For Spectra Gate Photometer for printers

Carter Equipment Co. and Ramtronics, For light-valve photometer for printers

David Degenkolb, Harry Larson, Manfred Michelson and Fred Scobey of DeLuxe General Inc., For development of computerized printer and process control system

Jiro Mukai and Ryusho Hirose of Canon, Inc., and Wilton R. Holm of AMPTP Motion Picture and Television Research Center, For Canon Macro Zoom Lens

Philip V. Palmquist and Leonard L. Olson of 3M Co. and Frank P. Clark of AMPTP Motion Picture and Television Research Center, For Nextel simulated blood for color photography

E.H. Geissler and G.M. Berggren of Wil-Kin, Inc., For Ultra-Vision theatre projection system

1973 **Rosco Laboratories, Inc.,** For technical advances and development of complete system of light-control materials for photography

Richard H. Vetter of Todd-AO Corp., For improved anamorphic focusing system

1974 **Elemack Co.,** For Spyder camera dolly

Louis Ami of Universal City Studios, For reciprocating camera platform for special visual effects photography

1975 **Lawrence W. Butler and Roger Banks,** For concept of applying low-inertia and stepping electric motors to film transport systems and optical printers

David J. Degenkolb and Fred Scobey of DeLuxe General Inc., and John C. Dolan and Richard DuBois of Akwaklame Co., For technique of silver recovery from photographic wash waters by ion exchange
Joseph Westheimer, For a device to obtain shadowed titles on film
Carter Equipment Co. and RAMtronics, For computerized tape-punching system for programming laboratory printing machines
Hollywood Film Co., For computerized tape-punching system for programming laboratory printing machines
Bell & Howell Co., For computerized tape-punching system for programming laboratory printing machines
Fredrick Schlyter, For computerized tape-punching system for programming laboratory printing machines

1976 **Fred Bartscher of Kollmorgen Corp. and Glenn Berggren of Schneider Corp.,** For single-lens magnifier for projection lenses
Panavision, Inc., For super-speed lenses for photography
Hiroshi Suzukawa of Canon and Wilton R. Holm of AMPTP Motion Picture and Television Research Center, For super-speed lenses for photography
Carl Zeiss Co., For super-speed lenses for photography
Photo Research Div., Kollmorgen Corp., For Spectra Tri-Color Meter

1977 **Ernst Nettman of Astrovision Div., Continental Camera Systems, Inc.,** For engineering of periscope aerial camera system
Electronic Engineering Co. of California, For developing method of interlocking non-sprocketed film and tape media used in motion picture production
Bernhard Kuhl and Werner Block of OSRAM GmBH, For development of mercury-medium iodide, high-efficiency discharge lamp
Panavision, Inc., For design of Panalite, camera-mounted controllable light
Panavision, Inc., For engineering of Panahead gear head for motion picture cameras
Piclear, Inc., For developing a projector attachment to improve screen image quality

1978 **Karl Macher** and **Glenn M. Berggren, Isco Optische Werke,** For Cinelux-ULTRA lens for 35mm motion-picture photography
David J. Degenkolb, Arthur L. Ford and **Fred J. Scobey, DeLuxe General,** For method to recycle laboratory wash waters via ion exchange
Kiichi Sekiguchi, CINE-FI Intl., For CINE-FI sound system for drive-in theatres
Leonard Chapman, Leonard Equipment Co., For a small, mobile camera platform, the Chapman Hustler Dolly
James L. Fisher, J.L. Fisher, Inc., For a small, mobile camera platform, the Fisher Moden Ten dolly
Robert Stindt, Production Grip Equipment Co., For a small, mobile camera platform, the Stindt Dolly

1979 **Michael V. Chewey, Walter G. Eggers** and **Allen Hecht, M-G-M Laboratories,** For developing computer-controlled paper-tape programmer system and its applications in the laboratory
Irwin Young, Paul Kaufman and **Fredrik Schlyter, Du-Art Film Laboratories,** For computer-controlled paper-tape programmer system and its applications in the laboratory
James S. Stanfield and **Paul W. Trester,** for development and manufacture of a device to repair or protect sprocket holes in film
Zoran Perisic, Courier Films, For Zoptic special optical effects device
Kollmorgen Corp. Photo Research Div., For Spectra Series II Cine Special exposure meter
A.D. Flowers and **Logan R. Frazee,** For a device to control flight of miniature airplanes for photography
Bruce Lyon and **John Lamb,** For Video Animation System for testing motion-picture sequences
Ross Lowell, Lowel-Light Mfg., for compact lighting equipment

1980 **Carter Equipment Co.,** For developing of a continuous-contact, total-immersion, additive color motion picture printer
Hollywood Film Co., For the development of a continuous contact, total immersion, additive color motion picture printer
Andre DeBrie S.A., For the development of a continuous contact, total immersion, additive color motion picture printer
Charles Vaughn and **Eugene Nottingham, Cinetron Computer Systems,** For the development of a versatile general purpose computer system for animation and optical effects motion picture photography
John W. Lang, Walter Hrastnik and **Charles J. Watson, Bell and Howell Co.,** For the development and manufacture of a modular continuous contact motion picture film printer
Worth Baird, LaVezzi Machine Works, For the advanced design and manufacture of a film sprocket for motion picture projector
Peter A. Regla and **Dan Slater, Elicon,** For the development of a follow focus system for motion picture optical effects printers and animation stands

SOUND EFFECTS

1964 **Norman Wantsall,** *Goldfinger*
1965 **Tregoweth Brown,** *The Great Race*
1966 **Gordon Daniel,** *Grand Prix*
1967 **John Poyner,** *The Dirty Dozen*

SPECIAL ACHIEVEMENT AWARD FOR SOUND EDITING

1979 **Alan Splet,** *The Black Stallion*

SPECIAL EFFECTS

1951 ***When Worlds Collide***
1952 ***Plymouth Adventure***
1953 ***War of the Worlds***

SPECIAL ACHIEVEMENT AWARD FOR VISUAL EFFECTS

1972 ***The Poseidon Adventure***
1976 ***King Kong***
Logan's Run
1978 **Les Bowie, Colin Chilvers, Denys Coop, Roy Field, Derek Meddings** and **Zoran Perisic,** *Superman*
1980 **Brian Johanson, Richard Edlund, Denis Muren** and **Bruce Nicholson,** *The Empire Strikes Back*

JEAN HERSHOLT HUMANITARIAN AWARD

1956 **Y. Frank Freeman**
1957 **Samuel Goldwyn**
1958 **No award**
1959 **Bob Hope**
1960 **Sol Lesser**
1961 **George Seaton**
1962 **Steve Broidy**
1963 **No award**
1964 **No award**
1965 **Edmond L. DePatie**

1966 George Bagnall
1967 Gregory Peck
1968 Martha Raye
1969 George Jessel
1970 Frank Sinatra
1971 No award
1972 Rosalind Russell
1973 Lew Wasserman
1974 Arthur B. Krim
1975 Jules Stein
1976 No award
1977 Charlton Heston
1978 Leo Jaffe
1979 Robert Benjamin
1980 No award

IRVING G. THALBERG MEMORIAL AWARD

1937 Darryl F. Zanuck
1938 Hal B. Wallis
1939 David O. Selznick
1940 No award
1941 Walter E. Disney
1942 Sidney Franklin
1943 Hal B. Wallis
1944 Darryl F. Zanuck
1945 No award
1946 Samuel Goldwyn
1947 No award
1948 Jerry Wald
1949 No award
1950 Darryl F. Zanuck
1951 Arthur Freed
1952 Cecil B. DeMille
1953 George Stevens
1954 No award
1955 No award
1956 Buddy Adler
1957 No award
1958 Jack L. Warner
1959 No award
1960 No award
1961 Stanley Kramer
1962 No award
1963 Sam Spiegel
1964 No award
1965 William Wyler
1966 Robert Wise
1967 Alfred Hitchcock
1968 No award
1969 No award
1970 Ingmar Bergman
1971 No award
1972 No award
1973 Lawrence Weingarten
1974 No award
1975 Marvyn LeRoy
1976 Pandro S. Berman
1977 Walter Mirisch
1978 No award
1979 Ray Stark
1980 No award

HONORARY AWARDS

FOREIGN LANGUAGE FILM AWARD

1948 *Monsieur Vincent* (France)
1949 *The Bicycle Thief* (Italy)
1950 *The Walls of Malapaga* (France/Italy)
1951 *Rashomon* (Japan)
1952 *Forbidden Games* (France)
1953 No award
1954 *Gate of Hell* (Japan)
1955 *Samurai* (Japan)

SPECIAL AWARDS

1928 **Warner Bros.,** For producing *The Jazz Singer*
Charles Chaplin, For his versatility and genius in writing, acting, directing and producing *The Circus*

1932 **Walt Disney,** For creating Mickey Mouse

1934 **Shirley Temple,** In recognition of her outstanding contribution to screen entertainment during 1934

1935 **David Wark Griffith,** For distinguished creative achievements as director and producer and lasting contributions to the progress of the motion picture arts

1935 **The March of Time,** For its significance to motion pictures for revolutionizing an important branch of the industry, the newsreel

1936 **W. Howard Greene and Harold Rosen,** For color cinematography of *The Garden of Allah*

1937 **Mack Sennett,** For lasting contributions to comedy technique on the screen
Edgar Bergen, For creating Charlie McCarthy
Museum of Modern Art Film Library, For its significant work collecting films dating from 1895 and making study of them available to the public
W. Howard Greene, For color photography of *A Star Is Born*

1938 **Deanna Durbin and Mickey Rooney,** For significant contribution to bringing to the screen the spirit and personification of youth and setting a high standard of ability and achievement for juvenile players
Harry M. Warner, In recognition of patriotic service in the production of historical short subjects
Walt Disney, For *Snow White and The Seven Dwarfs,* a significant screen innovation and pioneering field for the motion picture cartoon
Oliver Marsh and Allen Davey, For color photography of *Sweethearts*
Gordon Jennings assisted by Jan Domela, Dev Jennings, Irmin Roberts and Art Smith (special effects), Farciot Edouart assisted by Loyal Griggs (transparencies) and Loren Ryder assisted by Harry Mills, Louis Mesenkop and Walter Oberst (sound effects), For outstanding special photographic and sound effects in *Spawn of the North*
J. Arthur Ball, For outstanding contributions to the advancement of color in motion picture photography
Douglas Fairbanks, A commemorative award for his unique contribution as the Academy's first president
Motion Picture Relief Fund and Jean Hersholt (president), Ralph Morgan (chairman, Executive Committee), Ralph Block (first vice president) and Conrad Nagel, For services to the industry and progressive leadership
Technicolor Co., For contributions for successfully bringing the three-color feature to the screen
Judy Garland, For outstanding performance as a screen juvenile during the previous year
William Cameron Menzies, For outstanding achievement in use of color for enhancement of the dramatic mood in *Gone With the Wind*

1940 **Bob Hope,** For his unselfish services to the motion picture industry
Col. Nathan Levinson, For outstanding service to the industry and the Army during the past nine years, making possible the efficient mobilization of the motion picture industry for the production of Army training films

1941 **Churchill's Island,** Canadian National Film Board, Citation for distinctive achievement in short documentary subjects
Rey Scott, For extraordinary achievement in producing *Kukan,* a film record of China's struggle, with a 16mm camera under the most difficult and dangerous conditions
British Ministry of Information, For vivid and dramatic presentation of the Royal Air Force in its documentary *Target for Tonight*
Walt Disney, William Garity, John N.A. Hawkins and RCA Mfg. Co., For outstanding contribution to advancement of sound in motion pictures through the production of *Fantasia*
Leopold Stokowski and associates, For unique achievement in creating a new form of visualized music in *Fantasia,* thereby widening the scope of the motion picture as entertainment and art form

1942 **Charles Boyer,** For progressive cultural achievement in establishing French Research Foundation in Los Angeles as a source of reference for the industry
Noel Coward, For outstanding production achievement for *In Which We Serve*
Metro-Goldwyn-Mayer Studio, For presenting the American way of life in the production of the Andy Hardy series of films

1943 **George Pal,** For developing novel methods and techniques in production of Puppetoons short subjects

1944 **Margaret O'Brien,** As the outstanding child actress of 1944
Bob Hope, For his many services to the Academy, a Life Membership

1945 **Walter Wanger,** For his six years as president of the Academy
Peggy Ann Garner, As the outstanding child actress of 1945
Fran Ross and Mervyn LeRoy (producers), Albert Maltz (screenplay) Earl Robinson and Lewis Allen (title song) and Frank Sinatra (star), For *The House I Live In,* a short subject promoting tolerance
Republic Studios, Daniel J. Bloomberg and the Republic Studio Sound Dept., For building an outstanding musical scoring auditorium

1946 **Laurence Olivier,** For outstanding achievement as actor, producer and director in bringing *Henry V* to the screen
Harold Russell, For bringing hope and courage to fellow veterans through his appearance in *The Best Years of Our Lives*
Ernst Lubitsch, For distinguished contributions to the art of the motion picture
Claude Jarman, Jr., As the outstanding child star of 1946

1947 ***Bill and Coo,*** A novel and entertaining use of the motion picture medium
Shoe-Shine, An Italian production of superlative quality made under adverse circumstances
Col. William N. Selig, Albert E. Smith, George K. Spoor and Thomas Armat, For their contributions as motion picture pioneers to the development of the film industry
James Baskett, For his characterization of Uncle Remus in *Song of the South*

1948 **Ivan Jandl,** For outstanding juvenile performance of 1948 in *The Search*
Sid Grauman, Master showman who raised the standard of exhibition of motion pictures
Adolph Zukor, For 40 years of service to the industry
Walter Wanger, For distinguished service to the industry in adding to its moral stature in the world community through the production of *Joan of Arc*

1949 **Bobby Driscoll,** As the outstanding juvenile actor of 1949
Fred Astaire, For unique artistry and contributions to musical motion pictures
Cecil B. DeMille, Distinguished pioneer for 37 years of brilliant showmanship
Jean Hersholt, For distinguished service to the industry

HONORARY AWARDS

1950 **George Murphy,** For services to the film industry and the country at large
Louis B. Mayer, For distinguished service to the industry

1951 **Gene Kelly,** In appreciation of his versatility as an actor, singer, director and dancer, and specifically for his brilliant achievements in film choreography

1952 **George Alfred Mitchell,** For the design and development of the camera which bears his name for his continued and dominant presence in cinematography
Joseph M. Schenck, For long and distinguished service to the industry
Merian C. Cooper, For many innovations and contributions to the art of motion pictures.
Harold Lloyd, Master comedian and good citizen
Bob Hope, For contributions to the laughter of the world, service to the industry and devotion to the American promise

1953 **Pete Smith,** For witty and pungent observations of the American scene in his series *Pete Smith Specialties*
20th Century-Fox Film Corp., In recognition of imagination, showmanship and foresight in introducing the revolutionary process, CinemaScope
Joseph I. Breen, For conscientious, open-minded and dignified management of the Motion Picture Production Code
Bell & Howell Co., For pioneering and basic achievements in the advancement of the industry

1954 **Bausch & Lomb Optical Co.,** For contributions to the advancement of the industry
Kemp R. Niver, For development of the Renovare Process, making possible the restoration of the Library of Congress Film Collection
Greta Garbo, For her unforgettable film performances
Danny Kaye, For his unique talents, service to the Academy, the industry and the American people
Jon Whitely, For outstanding juvenile performance in *The Little Kidnappers*
Vincent Winter, For outstanding juvenile performance in *The Little Kidnappers*

1956 **Eddie Cantor,** For distinguished service to the industry

1957 **Charles Brackett,** For distinguished service to the Academy
B.B. Kahane, For distinguished service to the industry
Gilbert M. "Broncho Billy" Anderson, For his contributions as a motion picture pioneer to the development of film as entertainment
Society of Motion Picture and Television Engineers, For contributions to the advancement of the industry

1958 **Maurice Chevalier,** For contributions to the world of entertainment for more than half a century

1959 **Lee de Forest,** For pioneering inventions that brought sound to motion pictures

Buster Keaton, For unique talents which brought immortal comedies to the screen

1960 **Gary Cooper,** For his many memorable screen performances and international recognition he gained for the industry

Stan Laurel, For creative pioneering in cinema comedy

Hayley Mills, For the most outstanding juvenile performance of 1960 in *Pollyanna*

1961 **William L. Hendricks,** For outstanding patriotic service in conception, writing and production of Marine Corps film, *A Force in Readiness*

Jerome Robbins, For brilliant achievements in choreography on film

Fred L. Metzler, For dedication and service to the Academy

1964 **William Tuttle,** For outstanding make-up achievement in *7 Faces of Dr. Lao*

1965 **Bob Hope,** For unique and distinguished service to the industry and Academy

1966 **Y. Frank Freeman,** For unusual and outstanding service to the Academy during 30 years in Hollywood

Yakima Cannutt, For achievements as a stunt man and for developing safety devices to protect stunt men everywhere

1967 **Arthur Freed,** For distinguished service to the Academy and the production of six awards telecasts

1968 **John Chambers,** For outstanding make-up achievement in *Planet of the Apes*

Onna White, For outstanding choreography in *Oliver!*

1969 **Cary Grant,** For unique mastery of the art of screen acting with the respect and affection of his colleagues

1970 **Lillian Gish,** For superlative artistry and distinguished contribution to motion picture progress

Orson Welles, For superlative artistry and versatility in the creation of motion pictures

1971 **Charles Chaplin,** For the incaculable effect he has had in making motion pictures the art form of this century

1972 **Charles S. Boren,** A leader for 38 years of the industry's enlightened labor relations and architect of its policy of non-discrimination, with respect and affection of all who work in films

Edward G. Robinson, As a great player, patron of the arts and dedicated citizen—"a Renaissance man"

1973 **Henri Langlois,** For his devotion to the art of film, massive contributions to preserving its past and unswerving faith in its future

Groucho Marx, In recognition of his brilliant creativity and the unequalled achievements of the Marx Brothers in the art of motion picture comedy

1974 **Howard Hawks,** Master American filmmaker, whose creative efforts hold a distinguished place in world cinema

Jean Renoir, A genius who with grace, responsibility and devotion through silent and sound film, documentary, feature film and television has won the world's admiration

1975 **Mary Pickford,** In recognition of her unique contributions to the industry and the development of film as an artistic medium

1977 **Maggie Booth,** In honor of years a film editor

1978 **Walter Lantz,** For bringing joy and laughter to the world through his unique animated motion pictures

Laurence Olivier, For the full body of his work, unique achievements of his entire career and lifetime contributions to the art of film

1979 **Henry Fonda,** For the consummate actor, in recognition of his brilliant accomplishments and enduring contribution to the art of motion pictures

King Vidor, For incomparable achievements as a cinematic creator and innovator

Museum of Modern Arts Dept. of Film (New York) For the contribution it has made to the public's perception of film as an art form

1980 **Hal Elias,** For his dedication and distinguished service to the Academy of Motion Picture Arts and Sciences

Alec Guiness, For advancing the art of screen acting through a host of memorable distinugished performances

MEDAL OF COMMENDATION

(For outstanding service and dedication in upholding the high standards of the Academy of Motion Picture Arts and Sciences)

1978 **Linwood G. Dunn**
Loren L. Ryder
Waldon O. Watson
1979 **John O. Aalberg**
Charles G. Clarke
John G. Frayne
1980 **Fred Hynes**

Life Achievement Award

AMERICAN FILM INSTITUTE

Kennedy Center, Washington, D.C. 20566 (202/828-4000)

The Life Achievement Award, which consists of a statuette presented annually at a nationally televised banquet, is given to an individual who "in a fundamental way contributed to the filmmaking art; whose accomplishments have been acknowledged by scholars, critics, professional peers and the general public; and whose work has stood the test of time." The institute's board of trustees selects the winner.

1973 **John Ford,** Director
1974 **James Cagney,** Actor
1975 **Orson Welles,** Actor and director
1976 **William Wyler,** Director
1977 **Bette Davis,** Actress
1978 **Henry Fonda,** Actor
1979 **Alfred Hitchcock,** Producer and director
1980 **James Stewart,** Actor

Golden Berlin Bear

BERLIN INTERNATIONAL FILM FESTIVAL

Budapesterstrasse 50, 1000 Berlin 30, Federal Republic of Germany (Tel: 030-263 41)

The Berlin International Film Festival is held each summer for films from all countries which have been released not more than one year prior to the festival year. A nine-member jury selects prize winners in various categories. The Grand Prize winner in each category receives a Golden Bear Statuette. Additionally, up to eight Silver Bears and several Bronze Bears are awarded for other film aspects, and Honorable or Special Mentions are frequently made. These are not listed here. Further, the Festival is the framework in which other special honors are made. Film titles not in their original language below are translated or transliterated into German.

FEATURE FILM—GRAND PRIZE—GOLDEN BERLIN BEAR

1951 ***Sans Laisser d'adresse,*** France
Justice Est Faite, France
Die Vier im Jeep, Switzerland
Cinderella, U.S.A.
1952 ***Hon Dansade en Sommar,*** Sweden
1953 **No award**
1954 ***Hobson's Choice,*** Great Britain
1955 ***Die Ratten,*** Federal Republic of Germany
1956 ***Vor Sonnenuntergang,*** Federal Republic of Germany
Invitation to the Dance, U.S.A.
1957 ***Twelve Angry Men,*** U.S.A.
1958 ***Smultronstallet (Wild Strawberries),*** Sweden
1959 ***Les Cousins,*** France
1960 ***El Lazarillo de Tormes,*** Spain
1961 ***La Notte,*** Italy
1962 ***A Kind of Loving,*** Great Britain
1963 ***La Diavolo,*** Italy
Bushino Zankoku Monogatari, Japan
1964 ***Susuz Yaz,*** Turkey
1965 ***Alphaville,*** France
1966 ***Cul-de-Sac,*** Great Britain
1967 ***Le Depart,*** Belgium
1968 ***Ole Dole Doff,*** Sweden
1969 ***Rani Radovi,*** Yugoslavia
1970 **No award**
1971 ***Il Giardino dei Finzi-Contini,*** Italy
1972 ***Canterbury Tales,*** Italy
1973 ***Ashani Sanket,*** India
1974 ***The Apprenticeship of Duddy Kravitz,*** Canada
1975 ***Orokbefogadas,*** Hungary
1976 ***Buffalo Bill and the Indians,*** U.S.A.
1977 ***Woschozdenie,*** U.S.S.R.
1978 **"Total Spanish contributions"**
1979 ***David,*** Federal Republic of Germany
1980 ***Heartland, U.S.A.*** (U.S.A.)
Palermo or Wolfsburg (Federal Republic of Germany)

SHORT FILM—GRAND PRIZE—GOLDEN BERLIN BEAR

1951 ***Der Film Entdeckte Kunstwerke Indianischer Vorzeit,*** Federal Republic of Germany
Kleine Nachtgespenster, Federal Republic of Germany
The Story of Time, Great Britain
1952 **No award**
1953 **No award**
1954 **No award**
1955 ***Zimmerleute des Waldes,*** Federal Republic of Germany
1956 ***Paris La Nuit,*** France
1957 ***Gente Lontana,*** Italy
1958 ***La Lunga Raccolta,*** Italy
1959 ***Prijs de Zee,*** Netherlands
1960 ***Le Songe des Chevaux Sauvages,*** France
1961 ***Gesicht von der Stange,*** Federal Republic of Germany
1962 ***De Werkelijkheid von Karel Appel,*** Netherlands
1963 ***Bouwspelment,*** Netherlands
1964 ***Kirdi,*** Austria
1965 ***Yeats Country,*** Ireland
1966 **KNUD,** Denmark
1967 ***Through the Eyes of a Painter,*** India
1968 ***Portrait Orson Welles,*** France
1969 ***To See or Not to See,*** Canada
1970 **No award**
1971 ***1501½ (The Apartment),*** U.S.A.
1972 ***Flyaway,*** Great Britain
1973 ***Colter's Hell,*** Great Britain
1974 ***The Convert,*** Great Britain
1975 **No award**
1976 **No award**
1977 ***Ortsfremd . . . Wohnhaft Vormals Mainzerlandstrasse,*** Federal Republic of Germany
1978 ***Lo Isone Udelali Slepicum*** Czechlosovakia
1979 ***Ubu,*** Great Britain
1980 ***History of the World in Three Minutes Flat,*** Canada

LONG DOCUMENTARY—GRAND PRIZE—GOLDEN BERLIN BEAR

1951 ***Beaver Valley,*** U.S.A.
1952 **No award**
1953 **No award**
1954 ***The Living Desert,*** U.S.A.
1955 ***The Vanishing Prairie,*** U.S.A.
1956 ***Kein Platz Fur Wilde Tiere,*** Federal Republic of Germany
1957 ***Man Against the Arctic,*** U.S.A.
Secrets of Life, U.S.A.
1958 ***Perri,*** U.S.A.
1959 ***White Wilderness,*** U.S.A.
1960 ***Faja Lobbi,*** Netherlands
1961 ***Description d'un Combat,*** Israel
1962 **No award**
1963 **No award**
1964 ***Alleman,*** Netherlands

Cannes Honors

FESTIVAL INTERNATIONAL DU FILM

71 Rue du Faubourg-Saint-Honore, 75008 Paris, France
(Tel: 266-92-20)

The Festival International du Film, known as the Cannes Film Festival, annually honors creativity on both sides of the motion-picture camera. The categories have changed over the years. A jury of international filmmakers selects the winners. The titles are given here as they appear in the festival—that is, normally in their original language or in French; some foreign names will have been translated or transliterated into French.

The first two years of the festival do not conform in format to any other and are therefore listed separately here.

The Grand Prize, the Gold Palm and other awards and mentions made to international filmmakers by a jury of international filmmakers has changed from year to year in the three decades of the festival now known as the Cannes Film Festival. Therefore, in a departure from the system used elsewhere in this volume, Cannes honors are listed year by year, with notations indicating the specific categories set up for that particular year and the winners. The film titles are given as they appear in the Festival; that is, normally in their original language or in French; some foreign names will have been transliterated into French.

GRAND PRIZE OF THE INTERNATIONAL FILM FESTIVAL

1946 **Czechoslovakia:** ***Les Hommes Sans Ailes,*** produced by M. Cap
Denmark: ***La Terre Sera Rouge,*** produced by Bodil Ipsen and L. Lauritzen

France: ***La Symphonie Pastorale,*** produced by Jean Delannoy
Great Britain: ***Brief Encounter,*** produced by David Lean
India: ***Neecha Nagar,*** produced by Chetan Anand
Italy: ***Roma Citta Aperta,*** produced by Roberto Rossellini
Mexico: ***Maria Candelaria,*** produced by Emilio Fernandez
Sweden: ***L'Epreuve,*** produced by Alf Sjoberg
Switzerland: ***La Derniere Chance,*** produced by Leopold Lindtberg
U.S.A.: ***The Lost Weekend,*** produced by Billy Wilder
U.S.S.R.: ***Le Tournant Decisif,*** produced by Frederic Ermler

PRIX DU JURY INTERNATIONAL (International Jury Prize)

Rene Clement, producer, *La Bataille du Rail* **(France)**

GRANDS PRIX INTERNATIONALS (International Grand Prizes)

Rene Clement, director, *La Bataille du Rail* (France)
Michele Morgan, actress, *La Symphonie Pastorale* (France)
Ray Milland, actor, *The Lost Weekend* (U.S.A.)

OTHER JURY PRIZES FOR SHORT FILMS

Tchirkov, screenplay, *Le Tournant Decisif* (U.S.S.R.)
Romm, producer, *Matricule 217* (U.S.S.R.)
Georges Auric, music, (France)
Figueroa, *Maria Candelaria* and *Les Trois Mousquetaires* (Mexico)
A. Ptouchko, color, *Fleur de Pierre* (U.S.S.R.) *Berlin* (U.S.S.R.)
Walt Disney, animation, *Make Mine Music* (U.S.A.)

PRIX INTERNATIONAL DE LA PAIX (International Peace Prize)

Leopold Lindtberg, producer, *La Derniere Chance* **(Switzerland)**

PRIX DU CIDALC (Prize of the International Committee for the Furtherance of Arts and Letters by Film)

Y. Cousteau, *Epaves* (France)

SHORT SUBJECTS: GRAND PRIX INTERNATIONAL

Documentary: *Ombres sur la Neige* (Sweden)
Scientific film: *La Cite des Abeilles* (U.S.S.R.)
Educational film: *Wieliczka* (Poland)
Newsfilm: *Jeanesse de Notre Pays* (U.S.S.R.)
Animated film: *Les Brigands et les Animaux* (Czechoslovakia)
Scenario: *Reve de Noel* (Czechoslovakia)
Peace prize: *Jeanesse de Notre Pays* (U.S.S.R.)

1947 **Psychology and love story:** *Antoine et Antoinette,* produced by Jacques Becker (France)
Adventure or police story: *Les Maudits,* produced by Rene Clement (France)
Sociological film: *Cross Fire,* produced by Edward Dmytryk (U.S.A.)
Musical comedy: *Ziegfeld Follies,* produced by Vincente Minnelli (U.S.A.)
Animation: *Dumbo,* produced by Walt Disney (U.S.A.)
Documentary: *Inondations en Pologne* (Poland)
Special Mention: *Mine Own Executioner,* produced by Anthony Kimmins (Great Britain)
Special Mention: *Skeep Tiel Induland,* produced by Ingmar Bergman (Sweden)

1948 **No festival**

FEATURE FILMS—GRAND PRIX DU FESTIVAL (Award to producer)

1949 **Carol Reed**, *The Third Man* (U.S.A.)
1950 **No festival**
1951 **Vittorio De Sica**, *Miracolo a Milano* (Italy)
Alf Sjoberg, *Froken Julie* (Sweden)
1952 **Renato Castellani**, *Due Soldi di Speranza* (Italy)
Orson Welles, *Othello* (Morocco)
1953 **Georges Clouzot**, *Le Salaire de la Peur* (France) with special mention for **Charles Vanel**, best male actor
1954 **Teinosuke Kinugasa**, *Jigoku-Mon* (Japan)

PALM D'OR DU FESTIVAL INTERNATIONAL DUE FILM

1955 **Paddy Chayefsky**, screenplay, **Delbert Mann**, director; and **Ernest Borgnine** and **Betsy Blair**, actors, *Marty* (U.S.A.)
1956 **Jacques Yves Cousteau** and **Louis Malle**, *Le Monde du Silence* (France)
1957 **William Wyler**, *Friendly Persuasion* (U.S.A.)
1958 **Michel Kalatozov**, *Letiat Jouravly* (U.S.S.R.) with special recognition for **Tatiana Samoilova**, actress
1959 **Marcel Camus**, *Orfeu Negro* (France)
1960 **Federico Fellini**, *La Dolce Vita* (Italy)
1961 **Luis Bunuel**, *Viridiana* (Spain)
Henri Caloi, *Une Aussi Longeur Absence* (France)
1962 **Anselmo Duarte**, *O Pagador de Promessas* (Brazil)
1963 **Luchino Visconti**, *Il Gattopardo* (Italy)
1964 **Jacques Demy**, *Les Parapluies de Cherbourg* (France)
1965 **Richard Lester**, *The Knack . . . and How to Get It* (Great Britain)

GRAND PRIX INTERNATIONAL DU FESTIVAL CANNES

1966 **Claude Lelouch**, *Un Homme et Une Femme* (France)
Pietro Germi, *Signore e Signori* (Italy)
1967 **Michelangelo Antonioni**, *Blow Up* (Great Britain)
1968 **Lindsay Anderson**, *If* (Great Britain)
1969 **No festival**
1970 **Robert Altman**, *M*A*S*H* (U.S.A.)
1971 **Joseph Losey**, *The Go-Between* (Great Britain)
1972 **Elio Petri**, *La Class Operaia Va in Paradiso* (Italy)
Francesco Rosi, *Il Caso Mettei* (Italy), with special recognition for **Gian-Maria Volonte** (actor)
1973 **Jerry Schtazberg** (producer) and **Al Pacino** and **Gene Hackman** (actors), *Scarecrow* (U.S.A.)
Alan Bridges (producer) and **Sarah Miles** , (actress), *The Hireling* (Great Britain)
1974 **Francis Ford Coppola**, *The Conversation* (U.A.A.)

PALM D'OR DU FESTIVAL INTERNATIONAL DU FILM CANNES

1975 **M. Lakhdar Hamina**, *Chronique des Annes de Braise* (Algeria)
1976 **Martin Scorcese**, *Taxi Driver* (U.S.A.)
1977 **Paolo Traviani** and **Vittorio Traviani**, *Padre Padrone* (Italy)
1978 **Ermanno Olmi**, *L'Albergo degli Zoccoli* (Italy)
1979 **Volker Schloendorff**, *Die Blechtrommel* (Federal Republic of Germany)
Francis Ford Coppola, *Apocolypse Now*, (U.S.A.)
1980 **Akira Kurosawa**, *Kagemusha* (Japan)
Bob Fosse, *All That Jazz* (U.S.A)

PRIX SPECIAL DU JURY (Special Jury Grand Prize)

1954 **Rene Clement**, *Knave of Hearts* (Great Britain)

1955 **Leonard Bonzi, Matio Craveri, Enrico Gras, F. Lavigno** and **G. Moser**, *Continente Perduto* (Italy), with special mention for poetic images and utilization of sound
1956 **Henri Georges Clouzot**, *Le Mystere Picasso* (France)
1957 **Andrejz Waljda**, *Kanal* (Poland)
Ingmar Bergman, *Det Sjunde Inseglet* (Sweden)
1958 **Jacques Tati**, *Mon Oncle* (France)
1959 **Konrad Wolf**, *Sterne* (Bulgaria)
1960 **No award**
1961 **Jerzy Kawalerowicz**, *Matka Joahna od Aniontow* (Poland)
1962 **Michelangelo Antonioni**, *L'Elisse* (Italy) and principal players **Katharine Hepburn, Ralph Richardson, Jason Robards, Jr.** and **Dean Stockwell**
Sidney Lumet, *Long Day's Journey Into Night* (U.S.A.)
Tony Richardson, *A Taste of Honey* (Great Britain) and principal players **Rita Tushingham** and **Murray Melvin**
1963 **Masaki Kobayashi**, *Seppuku* (Japan)
1964 **Hiroshi Teshigahara**, *Suna no Onna* (Japan)
1965 **Masaki Kobayashi**, *Kwaidan* (Japan)
1966 **Lewis Gilbert**, *Alfie* (Great Britain)
1974 ***Sugarland Express*** (U.S.A.) screenplay

GRAND SPECIAL PRIX DU JURY (Special Jury Grand Prize)

1967 **Joseph Losey**, *Accident* (Great Britain)
Aleksandr Petrovic, *Skulpjaci Perja* (Yugoslavia)
1968 **Bo Widerberg**, *Adalen 31* (Sweden)
1969 **No festival**
1970 **Elio Petri**, *Indagine su un Cittadino al di Sopra di Ogni Sospette* (Italy)
1971 **Milos Forman**, *Taking Off* (U.S.A.)
Dalton Trumbo, *Johnny Got His Gun* (U.S.A.)
1972 **Andrei Tarkovsky**, *Solaris* (U.S.S.R.)
1973 **Jean Eustache**, *La Maman et la Putain* (France)
1974 **Pier Paolo Pasolini**, *Il Fiore Mille e Une Notte* (Italy)
1975 **Werner Herzog**, *Jeder fur Sich und Gott Gegen Alle* (Federal Republic of Germany)
1976 **Carlos Saura**, *Cria Cuervos* (Spain)
Eric Rohmer, *Die Marquise von 'O'* (Germany)
1977 **No award**
1978 **Marco Ferreri**, *Ciao Maschio* (Italy)
Jerzy Skolimowski, *The Shout* (Great Britain)
1979 **Andrei Mikhalkov Kontchalovsky**, *Siberiada* (U.S.S.R.)
1980 **Alain Resnais**, *Mon Oncle d'Amerique* (France)

SPECIAL HONORS FOR FEATURE FILMS AND PRODUCERS

1954 **Fred Zinnemann**, *From Here to Eternity*
1957 **Grigori Tchoukhari**, (for original screenplay, human quality and romantic grandeur), *Sorok Pervyi* (U.S.S.R.)
1960 **Ingmar Bergman**, *Jungfrukallen* (Sweden)
Luis Bunuel, *The Young One* (Mexico)
1966 **Orson Welles**, the Grand Prix du XXeme Anniversaire du Festival du Film Cannes (Grand Prize of the 20th Anniversary of the Cannes Film Festival), for contributions to world cinema
1967 **Robert Bresson**, special honor for his works
1971 **Luchino Visconti**, for body of work and for one film, *Morte A Venezia* (Italy), the Prix du XXVeme Anniversaire du Festival International du Film (Prize of the 25th Anniversary of the International Film Festival)

1979 **Martin Ritt** (Grand Prize for Camera Technique), *Norma Rae* (U.S.A.)
John Hanson and **Rob Nilsson** (Golden Camera), *Northern Lights* (U.S.A.)
1980 **Gerald Calderon** (Grand Prize for Camera Technique), *The Risque de Vivre*
Jean-Pierre Denis (Golden Camera), *Histoire d'Adrien*

OTHER PRIZES FOR FEATURE FILMS/OTHER JURY PRIZES FOR FEATURE FILMS

1949 **Rene Clement** (director), *La Mura di Malapaga* (Italy)
Isa Miranda (actress), *La Mura di Malapaga* (Italy)
Edward G. Robinson (actor), *House of Strangers* (U.S.A.)
V. Shaler (screenplay), *Lost Boundaries* (U.S.A.)
Emilio Fernandez (music), *Pueblerina* (Mexico)
Claude Autan Lara (producer, award for sets), *Occupe-toi d'Amelie* (France)
A. Henning-Jensen (producer; award for subject), *Palle Seul au Monde* (Denmark)
Jean Mitry (producer; award for montage), *Pacific 231* (France)
William Novick (producer; award for color), *Images Medievales* (France)
Walt Disney (producer; award for newsfilm), *Seal Island* (U.S.A.)
1950 **No festival**
1951 **Joseph L. Mankiewicz** (producer; special prize), *All About Eve* (U.S.A.)
Luis Bunuel (director), *Los Olvidados* (Mexico)
Bette Davis (actress), *All About Eve* (U.S.A.)
Michael Redgrave (actor), *The Browning Version* (Great Britain)
Terence Rattigan (screenplay), *The Browning Version* (Great Britain)
Joseph Kosma (music), *Juliette ou La Clef des Songes* (France)
Luis-Maria Beltran (producer; award for photography), *La Caravelle Isabel Partira ce Soir* (Venezuela)
Souvorov A. Veksler (producer; award for sets), *Moussorgsky* (U.S.S.R.)
Michael Powell and **Emeric Pressburger** (producers; award for exceptional merit), *Les Contes d'Hoffman* (Great Britain)
Italy, a special diploma for having presented the best selection of entries
1952 **Andre Cayette** (producer; a special prize), *Nous Sommes Tous des Assassins* (France)
Gian Carlo Menotti (producer; award for lyrical film), *La Medium* (U.S.A.)
Christian-Jaque (director), *Fanfan la Tulip* (France)
Piero Fellini (screenplay), *Gendarmes et Voleurs* (Italy)
Lee Grant (actress), *Detective Story* (U.S.A.)
Marlon Brando (actor), *Viva Zapata* (U.S.A.)
Sven Skold (music), *Hon Dansade en Sommar* (Sweden)
Kohei Sugiyama (photography), *Genji Monogatari* (Japan)

PRIX INTERNATIONAUX (International Prizes)

1953 **L. Barreto** (producer; award for adventure film with special mention for music), *O Cangaciero* (Brazil)
Luis C. Berlanga, (producer; award for best humor film with special mention for screenplay), *Bienvenudo Mr. Marshall* (Spain)

Charles Walters (producer; award for best light film with special mention for charming interpretation), *Lili* (U.S.A.)
Daniel Mann (producer; award for best dramatic film) with special mention for **Shirley Booth** (best female actor), *Come Back, Little Sheba* (U.S.A.)
Erik Blomberg (producer; award for best legendary film), *Valkoinen Puera* (Finland)
Gian Gaspare Napolitano (producer; award for best exploration film with special mention for color), *Magia Verde* (Italy)
Emilio Fernandez (producer; award for best image), *La Red* (Mexico)
Edgar Neville (producer; special award), *Duende y Misterio del Flamenco* (Spain)

1954 **Helmut Kautner** (producer) with special mention for **Maria Schell** (actress), *Die Letzte Brucke* (Austria)
Walt Disney (producer) with special mention for the camermen, *The Living Dessert* (U.S.A.)
Andre Cayette and **Charles Spaak** (producers) with special mention for the cast, *Avant Le Deluge* (France)
Bimal Roy (producer), *Do Bighazamin (India)*
Ettore Giannini (producer), *Carosello Napoletano* (Italy)
Carlo Lizzani (producer), *Crinache di Peveri Amanti* (Italy)
Aleksandr Ford (producer) with special mention for direction, *Piatka z Ulicy Barskiej* (Poland)
Arne Sucksdorff (special mention), *Det Stora Aventyret* (Sweden)
Serge Youtkevitch (producer) with special mention for production work, *Veliky Voine Albany*, Scander-Beg (U.S.S.R.)

1955 **Serge Vassiliev** (direction), *Gueroite Na Chipka* (Bulgaria)
Jules Dassin, *Du Rififi chez les Hommes* (France)
Spencer Tracy (acting), *Bad Day at Black Rock* (U.S.A.)
Joseph Heifitz (producer) with honors for cast, *Bolchaia Semia* (U.S.S.R.)

1956 **Serge Youtkevitch** (producer), *Othello* (U.S.S.R.)
Susan Hayward (acting), *I'll Cry Tomorrow* (U.S.A.)
Ingmar Bergman (producer; award for poetic humor), *Sommernattens Leende* (Sweden)
Satyajit Ray (producer; award for human document), *Pather Panchali* (India)

1957 **No awards**

1958 **Ingmar Bergman** (direction), *Nara Livet* (Sweden)
P.P. Pasolini, **Massimo Franciosa** and **P. Festa Campanile** (screenplay) and **Maruo Bolinini** (producer), *Giovani Mariti* (Italy)
Bibi Anderson, **Eva Dahlbeck**, **Barbro Hiort-af-Ornas** and **Ingrid Thulin** (collective acting award; female), *Nara Livet* (Sweden)
Paul Newman (acting; male), *The Long Hot Summer* (U.S.A.)
Jacques Beratier (producer) and **Georges Schebade** (writer), (award for dialogue), *Goha* (Tunisia)
Bernard Taisant (award for veracity and authenticity and for the simple beauty of its images), *Visages de Bronze* (Switzerland)

OTHER PRIZES FOR FEATURE FILMS

1954 **Walt Disney** (producer; award for entertainment), *Toot-Whistle Plunk and Boom* (U.S.A.)
Bretislov Pojar (producer; award for marionettes), *O Sklenicku Vic* (Czechoslovakia)
Jerzy Bossack (producer; award for documentary with special mention for quality of the subject), *Stare Miasto* (Poland)
James Boughton (producer; award for poetic fantasy), *The Pleasure Garden* (Great Britain)
Mario Marret (producer; award for nature film), *Aptenodytes Foresteri* (France)
The Netherlands, special mention for the constant high quality of films
Rene Lucot (producer; award for dramatic film), *Leriche, Chirurgien de la Douleur* (France)

1955 **Elia Kazan** (producer; award for dramatic film), *East of Eden* (U.S.A.)
L. Arnchtam and **L. Lavrovsky** (producers; award for lyric film) with special mention for **Galiana Culanova** (dancer), *Romeo and Juliet* (U.S.S.R.)
"Baby" Naaz (special mention, children), *Boot Polish* (India)
Ladislo Vajda (producer), *Pan y Vino* (Spain)
Haya Hararit (producer; special mention), *Hill 24 Doesn't Answer* (Israel)

1956 **No awards**

1957 **Robert Bresson** (director), *Un Condamne a Morte s'est Echappe* (France)
Guilietta Masina (actress), *Le Notti de Cabiria* (Italy) with homage to **Federico Fellini**
John Kitzmiller (actor), *Dolina Miru* (Yugoslavia)
Sadao Imamura (producer; award for romantic documentary), *Shiroi Sammyaku* (Japan)
Erik Balling (producer), *Qivitoq* (Denmark)
Rajbans Khanna (producer; award for exceptional merit), *Gotoma the Buddha* (India)
Jules Dassin (producer; award for best selection), *Celui qui Doit Mourir* (France)
Robert Bresson (producer), *Un Condamne a Mort s'est Echappe* (France)
Edmond Sechan (producer), *Niok* (France)
Alain Resnais (producer), *Toute la Memoire du Monde* (France)

1958 **No awards**

1959 **Francois Truffaut** (director), *Les Quatre Cents Coups* (France)
Simone Signoret (actress), *Room at the Top* (Great Britain)
Dean Stockwell, **Bradford Dillman** and **Orson Welles** (actors), *Compulsion (U.S.A.)*
Mario Soldati (comedy award), *Policarpo dei Tappeti* (Italy)
Teinosuke Kinugasa (special mention), *Shirasagi* (Japan)
Grigori Tchoukhari (producer; award for best participation), *Ballada O Soldatie* (U.S.S.R.)
Michelangelo Antonioni (award for contributions to a new cinematic language), *L'Avventura* (Italy)
Kon Ichikawa (producer; award for courage of approach), *Kagi* (Japan)
Melina Mercouri (actress), *Jamais le Dimanche* e) (Greece)
Jeanne Moreau (actress), *Moderato Cantabile* (France)

1961 **Yultia Sontzeva** (director), *Povest Plamenykh Let* (U.S.S.R.)
Sophia Loren (actress), *La Ciociara* (Italy)
Anthony Perkins (actor), *Aimez-Vous Brahms?* (U.S.A.)
Daniel Petrie (producer; Gary Cooper Prize in Recognition of Humanity in Subject Treatment), *A Raisin in the Sun* (U.S.A.)

1962 **Michael Cacoyannis** (cinematography), *Electra* (Greece)

Pietro Germi (producer; award for best comedy), *Divorz all'Italiana* (Italy)

1963 **Marina Vlady** (actress), *Ape Regina* (Italy)
Richard Harris (actor), *This Sporting Life* (Great Britain)
S. Samsonov (producer; award for best evocation of a revolutionary theme), *Optimistitcheskaia Traguedia* (U.S.S.R.)
Henri Colpi (screenplay), *Condine* (Romania)
Robert Mulligan (Gary Cooper Prize), *To Kill A Mockingbird* (U.S.A.)

1964 **Anne Bancroft** (actress), *The Pumpkin Eater* (Great Britain)
Barbara Barrie (actress), *One Potato — Two Potato* (U.S.A.)
Antal Pager (actor), *Pacsirta* (Hungary)
Saro Urzi (actor), *Sedotta e Abbandonata* (Italy)
Andraej Munk (hommage for film left incomplete due to the death of its creator), *La Passager*
Jaromil Jires (special mention to young producer), *Le Premier Cri* (Czechoslovakia)
Georgui Danelia, *Romance a Moscou* (U.S.S.R.)
Manuel Summers, *La Jeune Fille en Deuil* (Spain)

1965 **Samantha Eggar** and **Terrence Stamp** (acting), *The Collector* (U.S.A.)
Liviu Ciulei (director), *Padurea Spinzuratilor* (Romania)
Sidney Lumet (screenplay), *The Hill* (Great Britain)
Pierre Schoendoerffer (screenplay), *317eme Section* (France)
Jozef Kroner (Czechoslovakia)
Ida Kaminska (Czechoslovakia)
Vera Kouznetsova (U.S.S.R.)

1966 **Vanessa Redgrave** (actress), *Morgan — A Suitable Case for Treatment* (Great Britain)
Per Oscarsson (actor), *Sult* (Denmark)
Toto (special mention)
Serge Youtkevitch (direction), *Lenine en Pologne* (U.S.S.R.)
Mircea Muresan (award for first work), *Rascoala* (Romania)

1967 **Pia Degermark** (actress), *Elvira Madigan* (Sweden)
Odded Kotler (actor), *Trois Jours et un Enfant* (Israel)
Ferenc Kosa (director), *Tizezer Nap* (Hungary)
Alain Jessua (screenplay), *Jeu de Massacre* (France)
Elio Petri and **Ugo Pierro**, *A Ciascuno Il Suo* (Italy)
Mohammed Lakhdar Hamina (award for first work), *Le Vent des Aures* (Algeria)

1968 **Vanessa Redgrave** (actress), *Isadora* (Great Britain)
Jean-Louis Trintignant (actor), *Z* (France)
Glauber Rocha (director), *Antonio-Das-Mortes* (Brazil)
Vojtech Jasny (director), *Vsichni Dobri Rodaci* (Czechoslovakia)
Dennis Hopper (award for first work), *Easy Rider* (U.S.A)

1969 **No festival**

1970 **Ottavia Piccolo** (actress), *Metello* (Italy)
Marcello Mastroianni (actor), *Dramma Della Gelosia . . . Tutti I Particolari in Cronaca* (Italy)
John Boorman (director), *Leo the Last* (Great Britain)
Istvan Gal (jury prize), *Magasiskola* (Hungary)
Stuart Hagman, *The Strawberry Statement* (U.S.A.)
Raoul Coutard (award for first work), *Hoa-Binh* (France)

1971 **Kitty Winn** (actress), *Panic in Needle Park* (U.S.A.)
Piccardo Cucciolla (actor), *Sacco and Vanzetti* (Italy)
Karoly Makk (producer) and **Lili Darvas** and **Mari Torocsik** (actresses; special jury prize), *Szerelem* (Hungary)
Nino Manfredi (award for first work), *Per Grazi Ricevuta* (Italy)

1972 **Susannah York** (actress), *Images* (Ireland)
Jean Yanne (actor), *Nous ne Vieillirons pas Ensemble* (France)
Miklos Jancso (director), *Meg Ker a Kep* (Hungary)
George Roy Hill (jury prize), *Slaughterhouse Five* (U.S.A.)

1973 **Joanne Woodward** (actress), *The Effect of Gamma Rays on Man-in-the-Moon Marigolds* (U.S.A.)
Actors in *Film d'Amore et 'Amarchia* (Italy)
Rene Lamous (special prize), *La Planet Sauvage* (France)
Wojciech Has (jury prize), *Sanitorium Pod Klepsydra* (Poland)
Claude Goretta, *L'Invitation* (Switzerland)
Arthur Barron (award for first work), *Jeremy* (U.S.A.)

1974 **Charles Boyer** (actor; special hommage), *Stavisky*
Marie-Jose Nat (actress), *Les Violons du Bal* (France)
Jack Nicholson (actor), *The Last Detail* (U.S.A.)

1975 **Valerie Perrine** (actress), *Lenny* (U.S.A.)
Vittorio Gassman (actor), *Profumo di Donna* (Italy)
Michel Brault (producer), *Les Ordres* (Canada)
Costa-Garvas (France), (special honor)
Delphine Seyrig (recognition)

1976 **Mari Torocsik** (actress), *Deryne Hol Van?* (Hungary)
Dominique Sanda, *L'eredita Ferramonti* (Italy)
Jose Luis Gomez (actor), *Pascal Duarte*
Ettore Scola (director), *Brutti, Sporchi, Cattivi* (Italy)

1977 **Shelley Duvall** (actress), *Three Women* (U.S.A.)
Monique Mercure, *J.A. Martin Photographe* (Canada)
Fernando Rey (actor), *Eliza, Vida Mia* (Spain)
Ridley Scott (award for first work), *The Duellists* (Great Britain)
Norman Whitfield (music), *Car Wash* (U.S.A.)

1978 **Jill Clayburgh** (actress), *An Unmarried Woman* (U.S.A.)
Isabelle Huppert (actress), *Violette Noziere* (France)
Jon Voight (actor), *Coming Home* (U.S.A.)
Nagisha Oshima (director), *Ai No Borei* (Japan)

1979 **Sally Field** (actress), *Norma Rae* (U.S.A.)
Jack Lemmon (actor), *China Syndrome* (U.S.A.)
Eva Mattes (best role interpretation by an actress), *Moyzeck* (Federal Republic of Germany)
Stefano Madio (best role interpretation by an actor), *Caro Papa* (Italy)
Terrence Malick (director), *Days of Heaven* (U.S.A.)
Miklos Jancso ("Hommage"), for total work (Hungary)
Jacques Doillon (Youth Prize), *La Drolesse* (France)

1980 **Anouk Aimee** (actress), *Salto nel Vuoto* (Italy)
Michel Piccoli (actor), *Salto nel Vuoto* (Italy)
Ettore Scola (writing), *La Terrazza* (Italy)
Krzysztif Zanussi, (director) *Constans* (Poland)
Carla Gravina (actress, supporting role), *La Terrazza* (Italy)
Milena Dravic (actress, supporting role), *Poseban Tretman*
Jack Thompson (actor, supporting role), *Breaker Morant*

SHORT FILMS — GRAND PRIX DU FESTIVAL (Award to producer)

1951 **Bert Haanstra**, *Mirrors de Hollande* (Netherlands)
1952 **Herman van der Horst**, *Het Schot is het Boord* (Netherlands)
1953 **Albert Lamorisse**, *Crin Blanc* (France)
1954 **No award**

PALM D'OR DU FESTIVAL INTERNATIONAL DU FILM

1955 **Norman McLaren**, *Blinkity Blank* (Canada)
1956 **Albert Lamorisse**, *La Ballon Rouge* (France)
1957 **Ion Pepesco Gopo**, *Courte Histoire* (Romania)
1958 **Joris Ivens**, *La Seine a Recontre Paris* (France)
Henri Gruel and **Jean Suyeux**, *La Joconde* (France)
1959 **Miro Bernat**, *Motyli Zde Neziji* (Czechoslovakia)
1960 **Serge Courgignon**, *Le Sourire* (France)
1961 **Carlos Villardebo**, *La Petite Cuillere* (France)
1962 **Robert Enrico**, *La Riviere du Hibou* (France)
1963 **Alex J. Seiler**, *A Fleur d'Eau* (Switzerland)
Edmond Sechan, *Le Haricot* (France)

GRAND PRIX DU FESTIVAL INTERNATIONAL DU FILME CANNES

1964 **Francois Reichenbach**, *La Douceur du Village* (France)
Nobulo Shibuya, *La Prix de la Victoire* (Japan)
1965 **Janos Vadusz**, *Nyitany* (Hungary)
1966 **Noel Black**, *Skater Dater* (U.S.A.)
1967 **John Ferno Fernhout**, *Ciels de Hollande* (Netherlands)
1968 **Mirel Iliesu**, *Cintecele Renasterii* (Romania)
1969 **No festival**
1970 **No award**
1971 **No award**
1972 **J. Chapot**, *Le Fusil a Lunette* (France)
1973 **Bretislav Pojar**, *Balablok* (Czechoslovakia)
1974 **V. Zuikov** and **E. Nazarov**, *Ostrov* (U.S.S.R.)

PALM D'OR DU FESTIVAL INTERNATIONAL DU FILM

1975 **Geoff Dunbar**, *Lautrec* (Great Britain)
1976 **Barry Greenwald**, *Metamorphosis*
1977 **Marcel Jankovics**, *Kuzdok* (Hungary)
1978 **Jean-Francois Laguionie**, *La Traversee de l'atlantique a la Rame* (France)
1979 **Raoul Servais**, *Harpye* (Belgium)
1980 **Oscar Grillo**, *Seaside Woman*

SPECIAL JURY PRIZES

1951 **Ki Gordon**, *La Voie est Ouest* (Poland)
1952 **Arne Sucksdorff**, *Indisk By* (Sweden)
1959 **Edmond Sechan** (award for poetic humor and rich inventiveness), *Histoire d'un Poisson Rouge* (France)
1962 **Witold Giersz** and **Ludwik Perski** (producers; award for originality poetry and impeccable technique of animation), *Oszekiwanie* (Poland)
Herman van der Horst (award for profound love of nature and qualities of visual and sound technique), *Pan* (Netherlands)
1963 **Zuonimir Berkovic,** *Moj Stan* (Yugoslavia)
Luigi Bazzoni, *Di Domenica* (Italy)
Istvan Szabo, *Toi* (Hungary)
1964 **Carson Davidson** (award for brilliant writing and experimental character accessible to all), *Help! My Snowman's Burning Down* (U.S.A.)
Serge Roullet (award for the authenticity which it suggests the secret affinities of countrymen), *Sillages* (France)
1965 **Jean Brismee**, *Monsieur Plateau* (Belgium)
Jan Svanmajer (award for research qualities), *Johann Sebastian Bach: Fantasie G Moll* (Czechoslovakia)
Alexandre Astruc (award for writing), *Evariste Gallois* (France)
1967 **Branko Natinovic and Zdenko Gasparovic**, *Jedan Plus Jedan Jeste Tri* (Yugoslavia)
Bernard Lemoine (special mention), *L'Emploi du Temps* (France)
1968 **Jean-Claude Carriere**, *La Prince a Ongles* (France)
1971 **Roger Flint**, *Star Spangled Banner* (U.S.A.)
De Jan Onk (mention), *Struiter* (Netherlands)
Carlos Vilardebo (mention), *Une Statuette* (France)
1972 **Raoul Servais**, *Operation X-70* (Belgium)
1973 **Sandor Riesenbuckler**, *1812* (Hungary)
1975 **Fedor Hitrouk**, *Dariou Tebe Zvezdou* (U.S.S.R.)
1977 **Glauber Rocha**, *Di Cavalcanti* (Brazil)
Peter Fouldes (Hommage for animation), (Canada)
1978 **Borge Ring**, *Oh My Darling* (Netherlands)
John Hubley and **Faith Hubley** and **Garry Trudeau**, *The Doonesbury Special* (U.S.A.)
1979 **Lluis Rancionero Grau**, *La Fiesta dels Bojos* (Spain)
Bretislav Pojar (animation), *Boom* (United Nations)
1980 **Zdenek Smetana**, *Krychle*
Norma Baily, *The Performer*

OTHER PRIZES FOR SHORT FILMS (category names change from year to year)

1951 **Domenico Baolella**, *L'Eruption de l'Etna* (Italy)
U.S.S.R. for *Ukraine en Fleurs* (M. Sloutzky, producer), *Lettonie sovietique* (F. Kissiliov, producer), *Esthonie Sovietique* (V. Tomber and I. Guidine, producers), and *Azerbaidjan Sovietique* (F. Kissiliov and M. Dadachev, producers)
1952 **Joan Foldes** and **Peter Foldes** (award for color), *Animated Genesis* (Great Britain)
Marcel Ichac (award for scientific or educational film), *Groenland* (France)
Italy, special diploma for having presented the best selection
Alexandre Astruc, young producer, for *Le Rideau Cramoisi* (France)
1953 **Herman van der Horst** (award for documentary), *Houen Zo* (Netherlands)
Wendy Toye (award for fiction), *The Stranger Left No Card* (Great Britain)
Olle Hellbom (for art film), *Doderhultarn (Sweden)*
Colin Low (for animated film), *Sports et Transports* (Canada)
1955 **V. Deseta**, *Isola di Fuoco* (Italy)
Henri Fabiani (award for newsfilm), *La Grande Peche* (France)
L. Atamanov, *Zolataia Antilopa* (U.S.S.R.)
1956 **Gian Luigi Polidori** (award for documentary), *La Corsa Delle Roche* (Italy)
Lucien Deroisy (award and documentary), *Lourdja Magdany* (Belgium)
Jiri Trnka (marionettes) and **Bruno Sefranek** (producer), (special mention), *Loutky Jiriho Trnky* (Czechoslovakia)
Lorenza Mazzetti (producer; award for research), *Together* (Great Britain)
Brassai, *Tant qu'il y Aura des Betes* (France)
1957 **Colin Low** and **Wolf Koenig** (producers; award for documentary) *Capitale d'Or* (Canada)
Heinz Sielmann (producer; award for nature film), *Wiesensommer* (Federal Republic of Germany)
S. Kogan (special mention), *Les Chasseurs des Mers du Sud* (U.S.S.R.)

Fritz Heydenreich (special prize for scientific interest and poetic vision of the world), C12H22O11 *Auf den Spuren des Lebens* (Federal Republic of Germany)
Jiri Brdecka (for ingenious use of photography and animation), *Nez Nam Narostla Kridla* (Czechoslovakia)

1959 **Francis Thompson**, *N.Y.-N.Y.* (U.S.A.)
Halina Bielinska and **Wodzimierz Haupe**, *Zmisna Warty* (Poland)
Serge Hanin (mention), *Le Petit Pecheur de la Mer de Chine* (Vietnam)
Jiri Trnka, *Sen Noci Svatojansku*; **Vojtech Jasny**, *Touha*; **Miro Bernat**, *Motylizde Neziji* (Czechoslovakia; best selection)

1960 **Pierre Prevert** (producer; award for plastic quality), *Paris La Belle* (France)
Jorgen Roos (producer; award for new form used in describing life in a city), *Une Ville Nommee Copenhague*) (Denmark)
Roman Kriotor (for perfection in exposing and illustrating a great scientific theme), *Notre Universe* (Canada)
Max de Haas (honorable mention), *Jours de Mes Annees* (Netherlands)
Edouard Luntz, *Enfants des Courants d'Air*; **Pierre Jallaud** and **Sylvie Jallaud**, *Le Journal de'un Certain David*; **Serge Bourguingon**, *Le Sourire* (France; best selection)

1961 **Gyula Maeskassy** (special prize for pleading with humor for peaceful use of the atom), *Parbaj* (Hungary)

1970 **Bob Curtis** (for poetic candor and joy), *Magic Machaines* (U.S.A.)
Jean-Pierre Richard (mention for emotional value from evocation of the past), *Et Salammbo?* (Tunisia)

Cindy Award

INFORMATION FILM PRODUCERS OF AMERICA
3518 Cahuenga Blvd. W., Suite 313, Hollywood, Calif. 90068 (213/874-2266)

The Cindy Award, which consists of a trophy and certificate, is given annually for excellence in film, videotape, filmstrip or slidefilm production in categories ranging from Government/Industry/Business to Environment and Ecology, plus special awards. Entries are judged by IFPA chapters throughout the U.S., and a Blue Ribbon Panel selects the winners from the finalists. In addition to the winners of gold Cindys indicated here, silver and bronze trophies are also given.

FILM AND VIDEOTAPE

1976 **Arthur H. Wolf,** *The American Phoenix*
Bruce McGee and Ron Phillips, *Prowler—the Lone Trailer Story*
Patricia Brose, *The Intrusion Conspiracy*
Bill Buffinger, *Trans-Alaska Pipeline—Fluor Report No. 2*
Bruce Cummings, *Team Kawasaki*
Yanna Kroyt Brandt, *The Superlative Horse*
John J. Hennessy, *Symbol B. Numbers*
The Creative Works, Inc. *The Legacy of Currier and Ives*
Chuck Braverman, *The Television Newsman*
Chuck Braverman, *Trader Vic*
Randall Hood, *A Walk in the Forest*
Potter, Orchard and Petrie, Inc., *Lonely Times—Happy Times*
The Filmakers, Inc., *Nosocomial Infections and Critical Care*
John P. Breeden, Jr., *Renaissance Center*
Mike Lubow, *Learn Not to Burn*
Julian Krainin, *To Communicate in the Beginning . . .*
Irwin Rosten, *The Incredible Machine*
Lawrence Winter, *Multiple Choice*
Ray Jewell, *Fire Solution*
Warren Miller, *Free Ride*
MPI Productions Ltd., *Come in from Away*
USC, Div. of Cinema, *The Preparatory*

1977 **Nick Bosutow, Dick Olson and Irv Millgate,** *I've Got a Woman Boss*
Los Angeles County Sheriff's Dept., *Officer Survival III*
Arthur H. Wolf, *A Day Under Sea*
Bob Crook, *Lunar Geology*
Richard A. Miner and H. Saunders, *Get It Together*
Dick Young, *Firewood—The Other Energy Crisis*
Louis Mucciolo, *Anta-Scanners*
Filmakers, Inc., *The March of 7Up*
Grania Gurievitch, *Speaking for Ourselves: The Challenge of Being Deaf*
Jamil D. Simon, *Help Yourself to Better Health*
Burson-Marstellar, *A Day at the Fair*
Gordon Films, *Lloyd Todd's Southern Ocean*
Paul Buck and Art Ciocco, *Equality*
Veriation Films, *Ocean Thermal Energy Conversion*
Jim Freeman and Greg MacGillivary, *The Magic Rolling Board*
Crawley Films and Film Counselors, *Indonesia—The Cahnging Face*
Tom Thayer, *Alcatraz*

Current Status Unknown

FILMSTRIP AND SLIDEFILM

1976 **Philip Werber,** *What Is Journalism?*
Sara Maxwell, *Adventures in Science: The Body*
Worris D. Wertenberger, *When I Get to Be 18*
Ed Schultz, *The Future*
Nahum Zilberberg, *The Secret is You*
Donald E. Miller, *Physical Assessment: Heart and Lungs*
Morris D. Wertenberger, *Fry Your Way to Fame and Fortune*
Universal Training Systems, *When It Leaves Your Hands*
Michael J. Enzer, *A Step Ahead: The Congoleum Theory*
Robert Intrater, ACI Media, Inc., *The Art—Composition and Light*

1977 **Lyceum Productions,** *Inscape: The Realm of Haiku*
Carole Coleman, *To Save a Living Sea*
M.D. Wertenberger, Jr., *You and Communication*
Cliff Braggins, *The Credit Squeeze*
Donna Lawrence, *A Newspaper Story*
M.D. Wertenberger, Jr., *Altec 1628 Microphone Mixer*

Current Status Unknown

SPECIAL ACHIEVEMENT AWARDS

1976 ***A Walk in the Forest,*** Best of Show
The Incredible Machine, Special Technical Achievement

The Preparatory, Best Direction
A Walk in the Forest, Best Writing
A Walk in the Forest, Best Photography
A Walk in the Forest, Best Editing
A Walking in the Forest, Best Music
The Owl Who Married a Goose, Best Animated Subject

1977 **Paul Buck and Art Ciocco,** *Equality,* Best of Show, Film and Videotape
Donna Lawrence, *The Newspaper Story,* Best of Show, Filmstrip and Slidefilm
Kingsmill on the James, Cinematography
Jim Freeman and Greg MacGillivary, *The Magic Rolling Board,* Special Photographic Achievement
Art Ciocco, *Equality,* Editing
Marshall Harvey, *A Sport Suite,* Editing
Frank Dobbs and Gary Carr, *A Thread of Hope,* Writing
Michael J. Seebeck, *Replere,* Special Achievement by a Student for Optical Effects

Current Status Unknown

Valentine Davies Award

WRITERS GUILD OF AMERICA, WEST
8955 Beverly Blvd., Los Angeles, Calif. 90048
(213/550-1000)

The Valentine Davies Award honors contributions to the motion picture community through the work and achievements of a professional writer. A silver medallion is presented to the winner.

1962 **Mary McCall, Jr.**
1963 **Allen Rivkin**
1964 **Morgan Cox**
1965 **James R. Webb**
1966 **Leonard Spigelgass**
1967 **Edmund H. North**
1968 **George Seaton**
1969 **Dore Schary**
1970 **Richard Murphy**
1971 **Daniel Taradash**
1972 **Michael Blankfort**
Norman Corwin
1973 **William Ludwig**
1974 **Ray Bradbury**
Philip Dunne
1975 **Fay Kanin**
1976 **Winston Miller**
1977 **Carl Foreman**
1978 **Norman Lear**
1979 **Melville Shavelson**
1980 **David Rintels**

Eddie Award

AMERICAN CINEMA EDITORS
422 S. Western Ave., Los Angeles, Calif. 90020
(213/386-1946)

The Eddie Award, which consists of a statue, is given annually by a vote of ACE membership for the best editing in four categories for films and television shows.

1962 **Philip W. Anderson,** *The Parent Trap*
1963 **Samuel E. Beetley,** *The Longest Day*
1964 **Harold Kress,** *How the West Was Won*
1965 **Cotton Warburton,** *Mary Poppins*
1966 **William Reynolds,** *The Sound of Music*
1967 **William B. Murphy,** *Fantastic Voyage*
1968 **Michael Luciano,** *The Dirty Dozen*
1969 **Frank Keller,** *Bullitt*
1970 **Warren Low,** *True Grit*
1971 **Hugh Fowler,** *Patton*
1972 **Folmar Blangsted,** *Summer of '42*
1973 **David Bretherton,** *Cabaret*
1974 **William Reynolds,** *The Sting*
1975 **Michael Luciano,** *The Longest Yard*
1976 **Verna Fields,** *Jaws*
1977 **Richard E. Halsey and Scott Conrad,** *Rocky*

Current status unknown

TELEVISION EPISODE

1962 **Desmond Marquette,** "Ricochet" segment, *The Dick Powell Show*
1963 **Desmond Marquette,** "The Court Marshall of Captain Wycliff' segment," *Dick Powell Theater*
1964 **Joseph Dervin,** "Four Feet in the Morning" segment, *Dr. Kildare*
1965 **Gene Fowler,** "No Dogs or Drovers" segment, *Rawhide*
1966 **Harry Coswick,** *A Slice of Sunday*
1967 **Jodie Copelan,** "The All-American" segment, *Twelve O'Clock High*
1968 **Desmond Marquette,** "The Disappearance" segment, *The Big Valley*
1969 **Norman Colbert,** *The Bob Hope Christmas Special*
1970 **Gene Palmer,** *Marcus Welby, M.D.* (pilot)
1971 **Richard Cahoon,** "Death Grip" segment, *Medical Center*
1972 **Richard Cahoon,** "The Imposter" segment, *Medical Center*
1973 **Fred W. Berger,** "Bananas, Crackers and Nuts" segment, *M*A*S*H**
1974 **Fred W. Berger and Stanford Tischler,** "The Trial of Henry Blake" segment, *M*A*S*H**
1975 **Red W. Berger and Stanford Tischler,** "A Full Rich Day" segment, *M*A*S*H**
1976 **Bob Bring,** "The Sky's The Limit," Parts I/II, *Wonderful World of Disney*
Howard Kunin, "Web of Lies" segment, *The Streets of San Francisco*
1977 **Howard Kunin,** "Dead or Alive" segment, *The Streets of San Francisco*

Current Status Unknown

TELEVISION SPECIAL

1973 **Ira Heymann,** "Visions," *Tuesday Night at the Movies*
1974 **Richard Wray,** *Portrait of a Man Whose Name Was John*
1975 **Frank E. Morriss,** *The Execution of Private Slovick*
1976 **Henry Berman,** *Babe*
1977 **Michael Kahn,** *Eleanor and Franklin*

Current Status Unknown

DOCUMENTARY

1973 **John Soh,** "Forgotten Mermaids," *Undersea World of Jacques Cousteau*
Axel Hubert, *The Bengal Tiger*
1974 **Leslie Parry,** *The Incredible Flight of the Snow Geese*
1975 **Bud Friedgen and David Blewitt,** *That's Entertainment*

1976 **David Saxon,** *Search for the Great Apes*
1977 **Robert K. Lambert and Peter Johnson,** *Life Goes to the Movies*

Current Status Unknown

SPECIAL AWARDS

1963 **Russell Tinsley,** *The Cadillac*
1964 **William T. Cartwright,** *The Making of the President,* A Wolper TV Special

John Grierson Award
Emily Trophy

EDUCATION FILM LIBRARY ASSOCIATION
43 W. 61st St., New York, N.Y. 10023 (212/246-4533)

The John Grierson Award, endowed by the National Film Board of Canada and Films Incorporated, is a plaque and a cash prize of $500 presented annually to a new filmmaker in the social documentary field. The winning film is selected by a special jury at the American Film Festival.

1973 **Martha Coolidge,** *David: Off and On*
1974 **Jerry Bruck, Jr.,** *I.F. Stone's Weekly*
Cinda Firestone, *Attica*
1975 **Howard Blatt, Steven Fischler** and **Joel Bucher,** Pacific Street Film Collective, *Frame-Up! The Imprisonment of Martin Sostre*
1976 **Richard Brick,** *Last Stand Farmer*
Daniel Keller, *Lovejoy's Nuclear War*
1977 **Barbara Kopple,** *Harlan County, U.S.A.*
1978 **Susan Wengraf,** *Love It Like a Fool*
1979 **Lorraine Gray,** *With Babies and Banners*
1980 **David Bradbury,** *Front Line*

Based on the ratings of two juries evaluating preliminary and final screenings of the American Film Festival, the Emily Trophy is presented annually to the non-theatrical film which receives the highest numerical rating. Blue Ribbons are awarded to films judged best in each of several categories The Emily listed here is a "best in show" award.

1969 ***Ski the Outer Limits***
1970 ***Pas de Deux***
1971 ***Sad Song of Yellow Skin***
1972 ***Rock-a-Bye Baby***
1973 ***The Three Robbers***
1974 ***I.F. Stone's Weekly***
1975 ***Antonia***
1976 ***The Gentleman Tramp***
1977 ***Harlan County, U.S.A.***
1978 ***Young Dr. Freud***
1979 ***With Babies and Banners***
1980 ***The Sky is Gray***

"Name Gala" Prize

FILM SOCIETY OF LINCOLN CENTER
140 West 65th St., New York, N.Y. 10023 (212/877-1800)

The society puts on a "name gala" to honor lifetime contributions of an individual to the cinematic art. Occasionally, a cinematic work is honored. These galas, which traditionally include a retrospective of the work of the honoree, are used as fundraisers for various film society programs and are televised.

1972 **Sir Charles Chaplin**
1973 **Fred Astaire**
1974 **Alfred Hitchcock**
1975 **Paul Newman** and **Joanne Woodward**
1976 ***That's Entertainment***
1977 ***New York, New York***
1978 **George Cukor**
1979 **Bob Hope**
1980 **John Huston**

Gavel Awards

AMERICAN BAR ASSOCIATION
1155 E. 60th St., Chicago, Ill. 60637 (312/974-4000)

The Gavel Awards are given annually to honor films, the media and books for their depiction of, or reportage on, the law and the legal profession. Films made for television release are included in the category listed below. The Bar Association recognizes achievements which foster greater public understanding of the American legal and judicial system, disclose areas in need of improvement or correction and encourage efforts of all levels of government to update laws. Engraved gavels are given to the winners.

1958 ***Twelve Angry Men,*** United Artists Corp.
1959 **No award**
1960 **No award**
1961 **No award**
1962 ***Judgment at Nuremburg,*** Stanley Kramer Corp.
1963 **No award**
1964 ***The Great Rights,*** Brandon Films
1965-71 **No awards**
1971 ***The D.A.: Conspiracy to Kill,*** Universal Television and Mark VII Ltd.
1972 Motion picture for television release which launched ***Owen Marshall, Counsellor at Law*** series on the ABC-TV Network, Groverton Production and Universal Television
1973 ***"Heat of Anger"*** **for** ***CBS Friday Night Movies,*** Berg-Metromedia Production
1974 **No award**
1975 **No award**
1976 ***Fear on Trial, the Life of John Henry Faulk,*** Aland Landsburg Productions
1977 ***Judge Horton and the Scottsboro Boys,*** Tomorrow Entertainment Films made for television release are included in the category listed below.
1978 **No award**
1979 ***A Death in Canaan,*** Warner Bros. Television
1980 ***Dummy,*** Warner Bros. Television

OTHER AWARDS

1975 **Dome Productions** (theatre), one-man play, *Clarence Darrow*

Golden Apple Awards
Louella O. Parsons Award

HOLLYWOOD WOMEN'S PRESS CLUB
9000 Sunset Blvd., Ste. 304, Hollywood, Calif.
(213/273-6579)

The Golden Apple Awards were originally established to "thank" the "most cooperative" stars at a time when the Hollywood Women's Press Association had a membership largely of correspondents and reporters. In 1967, when more press agents who might favor their own clients had joined the Association, the criteria changed to honor a "Star of the Year" and a "New Star of the Year." The former honors contributions to the motion picture industry, while the latter recognizes a new personality for his or her impact on the public during the year. A committee nominates and the membership votes on the recipients, who are given jewelry with a golden apple motif.

GOLDEN APPLE/MOST COOPERATIVE MALE STAR

1941 Bob Hope
1942 Cary Grant
1943 Bob Hope
1944 Alan Ladd
1945 Gregory Peck
1946 Dana Andrews
1947 Gregory Peck
1948 Glenn Ford
1949 Kirk Douglas
1950 Alan Ladd
1951 John Derek
William Holden
1952 Tony Curtis
1953 Roy Rogers
1954 Dean Martin and Jerry Lewis
1955 William Holden
1956 Charlton Heston
1957 Glenn Ford
1958 Tony Curtis
1959 David Niven
1960 Jack Lemmon
1961 No award
1962 Richard Chamberlain
1963 Dick Van Dyke
1964 Lorne Greene
1965 John Wayne
1966 Bill Cosby

GOLDEN APPLE/MALE STAR OF THE YEAR

1967 Sidney Poitier
1968 Fred Astaire
1969 Gregory Peck
1970 James Stewart
Robert Young
1971 Hal Holbrook
1972 Peter Falk
1973 Robert Redford
1974 Alan Alda
1975 George Burns
1976 John Wayne
1977 Frank Sinatra
1978 John Travolta
1979 Alan Alda
1980 Richard Chamberlain

GOLDEN APPLE/MOST COOPERATIVE FEMALE STAR

1941 Bette Davis
1942 Rosalind Russell
1943 Ann Sheridan
1944 Betty Hutton
1945 Joan Crawford
1946 Joan Crawford
1947 Joan Fontaine
1948 Dorothy Lamour
1949 June Haver
1950 Loretta Young
1951 Anne Baxter
1952 Janet Leigh
1953 Dale Evans
1954 Debbie Reynolds
1955 Jane Russell
1956 Deborah Kerr
1957 Kim Novak
1958 Dinah Shore
1959 Shirley MacLaine
1960 Nanette Fabray
Janet Leigh
1961 Barbara Stanwyck
1962 Connie Stevens
1963 Bette Davis
1964 Donna Reed
1965 Dorothy Malone
1966 Phyllis Diller

GOLDEN APPLE/FEMALE STAR OF THE YEAR

1967 Carol Channing
1968 Barbra Streisand
1969 Mae West
1970 Carol Burnett
1971 Mary Tyler Moore
1972 Liza Minnelli
1973 Lucille Ball
1974 Valerie Harper
1975 Katharine Hepburn
1976 Joanne Woodward
1977 Jane Fonda
1978 Jaqueline Bisset
1979 Jill Clayburgh
1980 Mary Tyler Moore

GOLDEN APPLE/NEW MALE STAR OF THE YEAR

1967 Tommy Steele
1968 Robert Brown Glen Campbell
1969 Elliott Gould
1970 Flip Wilson
1971 David Cassidy
1972 Richard Thomas
1973 John Davidson
1974 Freddie Prinze
1975 Jeff Bridges
1976 Nick Nolte
1977 John Denver
1978 Robin Williams
1979 Dudley Moore
1980 John Hurt

GOLDEN APPLE/NEW FEMALE STAR OF THE YEAR

1967 Faye Dunaway
1968 Diahann Carroll
1969 Goldie Hawn
1970 Carrie Snodgrass
1971 Sandy Duncan
1972 Diana Ross
1973 Tatum O'Neal

1974 Kate Jackson
1975 Susan Clark
1976 Susan Blakely
1977 Kathleen Quinlan
1978 Olivia Newton-John
1979 Mariette Hartley
1980 Yoko Shimada

The Louella O. Parsons Award is given annually to the person who, in the opinion of the membership, gives the best image of Hollywood to the world.

1970 Danny Thomas
1971 Gregory Peck
1972 Ross Hunter
1973 Rosalind Russell
1974 Jack Benny
1975 Bob Hope
1976 Shirley Temple Black
1977 Jack L. Warner
1978 James Stewart
1979 Carol Burnett
1980 George Burns

Golden Globe Awards

HOLLYWOOD FOREIGN PRESS ASSOCIATION
8732 Sunset Blvd., Ste. 210, Los Angeles, Calif. 90069
(213/657-1707 and 657-1731)

The Golden Globe Awards, which consist of statuettes, are awarded annually to motion pictures and television films of the previous calendar year that have been shown to the Association membership. Selection is by secret ballot of the membership. (For television awards see pp. 145-147.)

BEST MOTION PICTURE

1944 *The Song of Bernadette*
1945 *Going My Way*
1946 *Lost Weekend*
1947 *The Best Years of Our Lives*
1948 *Gentleman's Agreement*
1949 *Treasure of Sierra Madre*
Johnny Belinda
1950 *All the King's Men*
1951 *Sunset Boulevard*

BEST DRAMATIC MOTION PICTURE

1952 *A Place in the Sun*
1953 *The Greatest Show on Earth*
1954 *The Robe*
1955 *On the Waterfront*
1956 *East of Eden*
1957 *Around the World in 80 Days*
1958 *The Bridge on the River Kwai*
1959 *The Defiant Ones*
1960 *Ben Hur*
1961 *Spartacus*
1962 *The Guns of Navarone*
1963 *Lawrence of Arabia*
1964 *The Cardinal*
1965 *Becket*
1966 *Dr. Zhivago*
1967 *A Man for All Seasons*
1968 *In the Heat of the Night*
1969 *The Lion in Winter*
1970 *Anne of the Thousand Days*
1971 *Love Story*
1972 *The French Connection*
1973 *The Godfather*
1974 *The Exorcist*
1975 *Chinatown*
1976 *One Flew Over the Cuckoo's Nest*
1977 *Rocky*
1978 *Midnight Express*
1979 *Kramer vs. Kramer*
1980 *Ordinary People*

BEST MUSCIAL MOTION PICTURE

1952 *An American in Paris*
1953 *With A Song in My Heart*
1954 No award
1955 *Carmen Jones*
1956 *Guys & Dolls*
1957 *The King and I*
1958 *Les Girls*
1959 *Gigi*
1960 *Porgy and Bess*
1961 *Song Without End*
1962 *West Side Story*
1963 *The Music Man*
1964 No award
1965 *My Fair Lady*
1966 *The Sound of Music*
1967 No award
1968 No award
1969 *Oliver!*
1970 No award
1971 No award
1972 *Fiddler on the Roof*
1973 *Cabaret*
1974 No award
1975 No award
1976 No award
1977 *A Star Is Born*

BEST COMEDY MOTION PICTURE

1959 *Auntie Mame*
1960 *Some Like It Hot*
1961 *The Apartment*
1962 *A Majority of One*
1963 *That Touch of Mink*
1964 *Tom Jones*
1965 No award
1966 No award
1967 *The Russians Are Coming*
1968 *The Graduate*
1969 No award
1970 *The Secret of Santa Vittovia*
1971 *M*A*S*H*
1972 No award
1973 No award
1974 *American Graffiti*
1975 *The Longest Yard*
1976 *The Sunshine Boys*
1977 No award

BEST MUSICAL/COMEDY MOTION PICTURE

1978 *Heaven Can Wait*
1979 *Breaking Away*
1980 *Coal Miner's Daughter*

BEST FOREIGN FILM

In some years, separate awards were given for different language categories. In those years, films indicated by one asterisk (*) are English language films, while those indicated by two asterisks (**) are foreign language films. The countries are not always given, but most of the English language films were made in Great Britain. Films denoted by three asterisks (***) won the Silver Globe Award.

1950 ***The Bicycle Thief*** (Italy)
1951 No award
1952 No award
1953 No award
1954 No award
1955 ***Genevieve*** (Great Britain)
No Way Back (Germany)
Twenty-Four Eyes (Japan)
La Mujer de la Camelias (Argentina)
1956 ***Ordet*** (Denmark
Stella (Greece))
Eyes of Children (Japan)
Sons, Mothers and A General (Germany)
Dangerous Curves (Brazil)
1957 ***Richard III****
The White Reindeer* (Finland)
Before Sundown* (Germany)
The Girls in Black* (Greece)
Rose on the Arm* (Japan)
War & Peace* (Italy)
1958 ***Woman In A Dressing Gown****
The Confessions of Felix Krull* (Germany)
Yellow Crow* (Japan)
Tizok* (Mexico)
1959 ***Night to Remember****
The Road A Year Long* (Yugoslavia)
The Girl and the River* (France)
The Girl Rosemarie* (Germany)
1960 ***Black Orpheus*** (France)
Odd Obsession (Japan)
The Bridge (Germany)
Wild Strawberries (Sweden)
Aren't We Wonderful (Germany)
1961 ***The Man With the Green Carnation****
La Verite* (France)
Virgin Spring* (Sweden)
1962 ***Two Women*** (Italy)
Animas Trujano** (Mexico)
Good Soldier Schweik** (Germany)
1963 ***Divorce Italian Style*** (Italy)
Best of Enemies (Italy)
1964 ***Tom Jones****
Any Number Can Win**
1965 ***Marriage Italian Style**** (Italy)
Shallah* (Israel)
The Girl With the Green Eyes (England)
1966 ***Darling****
Giulietta of the Spirits* (Italy)
1967 ***Alfie****
A Man and a Woman* (France)
1968 ***The Fox**** (Canada)
Live for Life* (France)
1969 ***Romeo & Juliet****
War & Peace* (U.S.S.R.)
1970 ***Oh! What A Lovely War!****
Z* (Algeria)
1971 ***Women in Love****
Rider on the Rain**
1972 ***Sunday, Bloody Sunday****
The Policeman**
1973 ***Young Winston****
The Emigrants* (Part I)** and *The New Land* (Part II)* (Sweden)
1974 ***The Pedestrian***
1975 ***Scenes From a Marriage*** (Sweden)
1976 ***Lies My Father Told Me***
1977 ***Face to Face***
1978 ***Autumn Sonata***
1979 ***La Cage aux Folles***
1980 ***Tess***

BEST FILM PROMOTING INTERNATIONAL UNDERSTANDING

1947 ***The Last Change***
1948 **No award**
1949 ***The Search***
1950 ***The Hasty Heart***
1951 ***Broken Arrow***
1952 ***The Day the Earth Stood Still***
1953 ***Anything Can Happen***
1954 ***Little Boy Lost***
1955 ***Broken Lance***
1956 ***Love Is a Many-Splendored Thing***
1957 ***Battle Hymn***
1958 ***The Happy Road***
1959 ***Inn of the Sixth Happiness***
1960 ***Diary of Anne Frank***
1961 ***Hand In Hand***
1963 ***A Majority of One***
1964 ***To Kill A Mockingbird***
1965 ***Lilies of the Field***

BEST MOTION PICTURE ACTOR

1944 **Paul Lukas,** *Watch on the Rhine*
1945 **Alexander Knox,** *President Wilson*
1946 **Ray Milland,** *Lost Weekend*
1947 **Gregory Peck,** *The Yearling*
1948 **Ronald Coleman,** *Mourning Becomes Electra*
1949 **Laurence Olivier,** *Hamlet*
1950 **Broderick Crawford,** *All the King's Men*
1951 **Jose Ferrer,** *Cyrano de Bergerac*
1952 **Fredric March,** *Death of a Salesman*
1953 **Gary Cooper,** *High Noon*
1954 **Spencer Tracy,** *The Actress*
1955 **Marlon Brando,** *On The Waterfront*
1956 **Ernest Borgnine,** *Marty*
1957 **Kirk Douglas,** *Lust for Life*
1958 **Alec Guinness,** *The Bridge on the River Kwai*
1959 **David Niven,** *Separate Tables*
1960 **Anthony Franciosa,** *Career*
1961 **Burt Lancaster,** *Elmer Gantry*
1962 **Maximilian Schell,** *Judgment at Nuremberg*
1963 **Gregory Peck,** *To Kill A Mockingbird*
1964 **Sidney Poitier,** *Lilies of the Field*
1965 **Peter O'Toole,** *Becket*
1966 **Omar Sharif,** *Dr. Zhivago*
1967 **Paul Scofield,** *A Man for All Seasons*
1968 **Rod Steiger,** *In the Heat of the Night*
1969 **Peter O'Toole,** *The Lion in Winter*
1970 **John Wayne,** *True Grit*
1971 **George C. Scott,** *Patton*
1972 **Gene Hackman,** *The French Connection*
1973 **Marlon Brando,** *The Godfather*
1974 **Al Pacino,** *Serpico*
1975 **Jack Nicholson,** *Chinatown*
1976 **Jack Nicholson,** *One Flew Over the Cuckoo's Nest*
1977 **Peter Finch,** *Network*
1978 **Jon Voight,** *Coming Home*
1979 **Dustin Hoffman,** *Kramer vs. Kramer*
1980 **Robert De Niro,** *Raging Bull*

BEST ACTOR (Musical/Comedy)

1951 **Fred Astaire,** *Three Little Words*
1952 **Danny Kaye,** *On the Riviera*

1953 **Donald O'Connor,** *Singing in the Rain*
1954 **David Niven,** *The Moon is Blue*
1955 **James Mason,** *A Star is Born*
1956 **Tom Ewell,** *Seven-Year Itch*
1957 **Cantinflas,** *Around the World in 80 Days*
1958 **Frank Sinatra,** *Pal Joey*
1959 **Danny Kaye,** *Me and the Colonel*
1960 **Jack Lemmon,** *Some Like It Hot*
1961 **Jack Lemmon,** *The Apartment*
1962 **Glenn Ford,** *Pocket Full of Miracles*
1963 **Marcello Mastroianni,** *Divorce Italian Style*
1964 **Alberto Sordi,** *To Bed or Not to Bed*
1965 **Rex Harrison,** *My Fair Lady*
1966 **Lee Marvin,** *Cat Ballou*
1967 **Alan Arkin,** *The Russians Are Coming*
1968 **Richard Harris,** *Camelot*
1969 **Ron Moody,** *Oliver!*
1970 **Peter O'Toole,** *Goodbye, Mr. Chips*
1971 **Albert Finney,** *Scrooge*
1972 **Topol,** *Fiddler on the Roof*
1973 **Jack Lemmon,** *Avanti*
1974 **George Segal,** *A Touch of Class*
1975 **Art Carney,** *Harry and Tonto*
1976 **Walter Matthau,** *The Sunshine Boys*
1977 **Kris Kristofferson,** *A Star is Born*
1978 **Warren Beatty,** *Heaven Can Wait*
1979 **Peter Sellers,** *Being There*
1980 **Ray Sharkey,** *The Idolmaker*

BEST MOTION PICTURE ACTRESS

1944 **Jennifer Jones,** *The Song of Bernadette*
1945 **Ingrid Bergman,** *Bells of St. Mary*
1946 **Ingrid Bergman,** *Gaslight*
1947 **Rosalind Russell,** *Sister Kenny*
1948 **Rosalind Russell,** *Mourning Becomes Electra*
1949 **Jane Wyman,** *Johnny Belinda*
1950 **Olivia de Havilland,** *The Heiress*
1951 **Gloria Swanson,** *Sunset Boulevard*
1952 **Jane Wyman,** *The Blue Veil*
1953 **Shirley Booth,** *Come Back, Little Sheba*
1954 **Audrey Hepburn,** *Roman Holiday*
1955 **Grace Kelly,** *The Country Girl*
1956 **Anna Magnani,** *The Rose Tattoo*
1957 **Ingrid Bergman,** *Anastasia*
1958 **Joanne Woodward,** *Three Faces of Eve*
1959 **Susan Hayward,** *I Want to Live*
1960 **Elizabeth Taylor,** *Suddenly Last Summer*
1961 **Greer Garson,** *Sunrise at Campobello*
1962 **Geraldine Page,** *Summer & Smoke*
1963 **Geraldine Page,** *Sweet Bird of Youth*
1964 **Leslie Caron,** *The L-Shaped Room*
1965 **Anne Bancroft,** *The Pumpkin Eater*
1966 **Samantha Eggar,** *The Collector*
1967 **Anouk Aimee,** *A Man and a Woman*
1968 **Dame Edith Evans,** *The Whisperers*
1969 **Joanne Woodward,** *Rachel, Rachel*
1970 **Genevieve Bujold,** *Anne of the Thousand Days*
1971 **Ali MacGraw,** *Love Story*
1972 **Jane Fonda,** *Klute*
1973 **Liv Ullmann,** *The Emigrants*
1974 **Marsha Mason,** *Cinderella Liberty*
1975 **Gena Rowlands,** *A Woman Under the Influence*
1976 **Louise Fletcher,** *One Flew Over the Cuckoo's Nest*
1977 **Faye Dunaway,** *Network*
1978 **Jane Fonda,** *Coming Home*
1979 **Sally Field,** *Norma Rae*
1980 **Mary Tyler Moore,** *Ordinary People*

BEST ACTRESS (Comedy/Drama)

1951 **Judy Holliday,** *Born Yesterday*
1952 **June Allyson,** *Too Young to Kiss*
1953 **Susan Hayward,** *With a Song in My Heart*
1954 **Ethel Merman,** *Call Me Madam*
1955 **Judy Garland,** *A Star Is Born*
1956 **Jean Simmons,** *Guys & Dolls*
1957 **Deborah Kerr,** *The King & I*
1958 **Kay Kendall,** *Les Girls*
1959 **Rosalind Russell,** *Auntie Mame*
1960 **Marilyn Monroe,** *Some Like It Hot*
1961 **Shirley MacLaine,** *The Apartment*
1962 **Rosalind Russell,** *A Majority of One*
1963 **Rosalind Russell,** *Gypsy*
1964 **Shirley MacLaine,** *Irma La Douce*
1965 **Julie Andrews,** *Mary Poppins*
1966 **Julie Andrews,** *The Sound of Music*
1967 **Lynn Redgrave,** *Georgy Girl*
1968 **Anne Bancroft,** *The Graduate*
1969 **Barbra Steisand,** *Funny Girl*
1970 **Patty Duke,** *Me, Natalie*
1971 **Carrie Snodgrass,** *Dairy of a Mad Housewife*
1972 **Twiggy,** *The Boy Friend*
1973 **Liza Minnelli,** *Cabaret*
1974 **Glenda Jackson,** *A Touch of Class*
1975 **Racquel Welch,** *The Three Musketeers*
1976 **Ann-Margret,** *Tommy*
1977 **Barbra Streisand,** *A Star Is Born*
1978 **Ellen Burstyn,** *Same Time, Next Year*
Maggie Smith, *California Suite*
1979 **Bette Midler,** *The Rose*
1980 **Sissy Spacek,** *Coal Miner's Daughter*

BEST ACTOR IN SUPPORTING ROLE IN A MOTION PICTURE

1946 **J. Carrol Naish,** *Gaslight*
1947 **Clifton Webb,** *The Razor's Edge*
1948 **Edmund Gwenn,** *Miracle on 34th Street*
1949 **Walter Huston,** *Treasure of Sierra Madre*
1950 **James Whitmore,** *Battleground*
1951 **Edmund Gwenn,** *Mister 880*
1952 **Peter Ustinov,** *Quo Vadis*
1953 **Millard Mitchell,** *My Six Convicts*
1954 **Frank Sinatra,** *From Here to Eternity*
1955 **Edmond O'Brien,** *The Barefoot Contessa*
1956 **Arthur Kennedy,** *The Trial*
1957 **Earl Holliman,** *The Rainmaker*
1958 **Red Buttons,** *Sayonara*
1959 **Burl Ives,** *The Big Country*
1960 **Stephen Boyd,** *Ben Hur*
1961 **Sal Mineo,** *Exodus*
1962 **George Chakiris,** *West Side Story*
1963 **Omar Sharif,** *Lawrence of Arabia*
1964 **John Huston,** *The Cardinal*
1965 **Edmund O'Brien,** *Seven Days in May*
1966 **Oskar Werner,** *The Spy Who Came in From the Cold*
1967 **Richard Attenborough,** *The Sand Pebbles*
1968 **Richard Attenborough,** *Thoroughly Modern Millie*
1969 **Daniel Massey,** *Star*
1970 **Gig Young,** *They Shoot Horses, Don't They?*
1971 **John Mills,** *Ryan's Daughter*
1972 **Ben Johnson,** *The Last Picture Show*
1973 **Joel Gray,** *Cabaret*
1974 **John Houseman,** *Paper Chase*
1975 **Fred Astaire,** *The Towering Inferno*
1976 **Richard Benjamin,** *The Sunshine Boys*
1977 **Laurence Olivier,** *Marathon Man*
1978 **John Hurt,** *Midnight Express*
1979 **Melvyn Douglas,** *Being There*
Robert Duvall, *Apocolypse Now*
1980 **Timothy Hutton,** *Ordinary People*

BEST ACTRESS IN SUPPORTING ROLE IN A MOTION PICTURE

1946 Angela Lansbury, *Gaslight*
1947 Anne Baxter,*The Razor's Edge*
1948 Celeste Holm, *Gentleman's Agreement*
1949 Ellen Corby, *I Remember Mama*
1950 Mercedes McCambridge, *All the King's Men*
1951 Josephine Hull, *Harvey*
1952 Kim Hunter, *Streetcar Named Desire*
1953 Katy Jurado, *High Noon*
1954 Grace Kelly, *Mogambo*
1955 Jan Sterling, *The High and the Mighty*
1956 Marisa Pavan, *The Rose Tattoo*
1957 Eileen Heckart, *Bad Seed*
1958 Elsa Lancaster, *Witness for the Prosecution*
1959 Hermoine Gingold, *Gigi*
1960 Susan Kohner, *Imitation of Life*
1961 Janet Leigh, *Psycho*
1962 Rita Moreno, *West Side Story*
1963 Angela Lansburry, *The Manchurian Candidate*
1964 Margaret Rutherford, *VIP*
1965 Agnes Moorehead, *Hush, Hush Sweet Charlotte*
1966 Ruth Gordon, *Inside Daisy Clover*
1967 Jocelyn La Garde, *Hawaii*
1968 Carol Channing, *Thoroughly Modern Millie*
1969 Ruth Gordon, *Rosemary's Baby*
1970 Goldie Hawn, *Cactus Flower*
1971 Karen Black, *Five Easy Pieces*
Maureen Stapleton, *Airport*
1972 Ann-Margret, *Carnal Knowledge*
1973 Shelley Winters, *The Poseidon Adventure*
1974 Linda Blair, *The Exorcist*
1975 Karen Black, *The Great Gatsby*
1976 Brenda Vaccaro, *Once is Not Enough*
1977 Katharine Ross, *Voyage of the Damned*
1978 Dyan Cannon, *Heaven Can Wait*
1979 Meryl Streep, *Kramer vs. Kramer*
1980 Mary Steenaburgen, *Melvin and Howard*

MOST PROMISING NEWCOMERS /Male (Called "Best Acting Debut" since 1976)

1950 Richard Todd, *The Hasty Heart*
1951 Gene Nelson, *Tea for Two*
1952 Kevin McCarthy, *Death of a Salesman*
1953 Richard Burton, *My Cousin Rachel*
1954 Hugh O'Brian
Steve Forrest
Richard Egan
1955 Joe Adams
George Nader
Jeff Richards
1956 Ray Danton
Russ Tamblyn
1957 John Kerr
Paul Newman
Tony Perkins
Jacques Bergerac (foreign)
1958 James Garner
John Saxon
Pat Wayne
1959 Bradford Dillman
John Gavin
Efrem Zimbalist Jr.
1960 James Shigeta
Barry Coe
Troy Donahue
George Hamilton
1961 Michael Callan
Mark Damon
Brett Halsey
1962 Richard Beymer
Bobby Darin
Warren Beatty
1963 Keir Dullea
Omar Sharif
Terence Stamp
1964 Albert Finney
Robert Walker
Stathis Giallelis
1965 Harv Presnell
George Segal
Chaim Topol
1966 Robert Redford, *Inside Daisy Clover*
1967 James Farentino, *The Pad*
1968 Dustin Hoffman, *The Graduate*
1969 Leonard Whiting, *Romeo & Juliet*
1970 Jon Voight, *Midnight Cowboy*
1971 James Earl Jones, *The Great White Hope*
1972 Desi Arnaz, Jr., *Red Sky at Morning*
1973 Edward Albert, *Butterflies Are Free*
1974 Paul Le Mae, *American Graffiti*
1975 Joseph Bottoms, *The Dove*
1976 Brad Dourif, *One Flew Over the Cuckoo's Nest*
1977 Arnold Schwarzenegger, *Stay Hungry*
1978 Brad Davis, *Midnight Express*
1979 Ricky Schroeder, *The Champ*
1980 Timothy Hutton, *Ordinary People*

MOST PROMISING NEWCOMER /Female (Called Best Acting Debut Since 1976)

1950 Mercedes McCambridge, *All The King's Men*
1951 No award
1952 Pier Angeli, *Teresa*
1953 Collette Marchand, *Moulin Rouge*
1954 Pat Crowley
Bella Darvi
Barbara Rush
1955 Shirley MacLaine
Kim Novak
Karen Sharpe
1956 Anita Ekberg
Virginia Shaw
Dana Wynter
1957 Carroll Baker
Jayne Mansfield
Natalie Wood
Taina Elg (foreign)
1958 Sandra Dee
Carolyn Jones
Diana Varsi
1959 Linda Cristal
Susan Kohner
Tina Louise
1960 Tuesday Weld
Angie Dickinson
Janet Munro
Stella Stevens
1961 Ina Balin
Nancy Kwan
Hayley Mills
1962 Christine Kaufmann
Ann-Margret
Jane Fonda
1963 Patty Duke
Sue Lyon
Rita Tushingham
1964 Ursula Andress
Tippi Hedren
Elke Sommer
1965 Mia Farrow

Celia Kaye
Mary Ann Mobley
1966 **Elizabeth Hartman**, *A Patch of Blue*
1967 **Camilla Sparv**, *Dead Heat on a Merry Go Round*
1968 **Katharine Ross**, *The Graduate*
1969 **Olivia Hussey**, *Romeo & Juliet*
1970 **Ali MacGraw**, *Goodbye, Columbus*
1971 **Carrie Snodgrass**, *Diary of a Mad Housewife*
1972 **Twiggy**, *The Boy Friend*
1973 **Diana Ross**, *Lady Sings the Blues*
1974 **Tatum O'Neal**, *Paper Moon*
1975 **Susan Flannery**, *The Towering Inferno*
1976 **Marilyn Hassett**, *The Other Side of the Mountain*
1977 **Jessica Lange**, *King Kong*
1978 **Irene Miracle**, *Midnight Express*
1979 **Bette Midler**, *The Rose*
1980 **Natassia Kinsky**, *Tess*

BEST MOTION PICTURE DIRECTOR

1947 **Frank Capra**, *It's A Wonderful Life*
1948 **Elia Kazan**, *Gentleman's Agreement*
1949 **John Huston**, *Treasure of Sierra Madre*
1950 **Robert Rossen**, *All the King's Men*
1951 **Billy Wilder**, *Sunset Boulevard*
1952 **Laslo Benedek**, *Death of a Salesman*
1953 **Cecil B. DeMille**, *The Greatest Show on Earth*
1954 **Fred Zinnemann**, *From Here to Eternity*
1955 **Elia Kazan**, *On the Waterfront*
1956 **Joshua Logan**, *Picnic*
1957 **Elia Kazan**, *Baby Doll*
1958 **David Lean**, *Bridge On the River Kwai*
1959 **Vincente Minnelli**, *Gigi*
1960 **William Wyler**, *Ben Hur*
1961 **Jack Cardiff**, *Sons and Lovers*
1962 **Stanley Kramer**, *Judgment at Nuremberg*
1963 **David Lean**, *Lawrence of Arabia*
1964 **Elia Kazan**, *America, America*
1965 **George Cukor**, *My Fair Lady*
1966 **David Lean**, *Dr. Zhivago*
1967 **Fred Zinnemann**, *A Man for All Seasons*
1968 **Mike Nichols**, *The Graduate*
1969 **Paul Newman**, *Rachel, Rachel*
1970 **Charles Jarrott**, *Anne of the Thousand Days*
1971 **Arthur Hiller**, *Love Story*
1972 **William Friedkin**, *The French Connection*
1973 **Francis Ford Coppola**, *The Godfather*
1974 **William Friedkin**, *The Exorcist*
1975 **Roman Polanski**, *Chinatown*
1976 **Milos Forman**, *One Flew Over the Cuckoo's Nest*
1977 **Sidney Lumet**, *Network*
1978 **Michael Cimino**, *The Deer Hunter*
1979 **Francis Coppola**, *Apocolypse Now*
1980 **Robert Redford**, *Ordinary People*

BEST MOTION PICTURE SCREENPLAY

1948 **George Seaton**, *The Miracle on 34th Street*
1949 **Richard Schweizer**, *The Search*
1950 **Robert Pirosh**, *Battleground*
1951 **Joseph Mankiewicz**, *All About Eve*
1952 **Robert Buckner**, *Bright Victory*
1953 **Michael Wilson**, *Five Fingers*
1954 **Helen Deutsch**, *Lili*
1955 **Billy Wilder, Samuel Taylor and Ernest Lehman**, *Sabrina*
1956 No award
1957 No award
1958 No award
1959 No award
1960 No award
1961 No award
1962 No award
1963 No award
1964 No award
1965 No award
1966 **Robert Bolt**, *Dr. Zhivago*
1967 **Robert Bolt**, *A Man for All Seasons*
1968 **Sterling Silliphant**, *In the Heat of the Night*
1969 **Sterling Silliphant**, *Charly*
1970 **John Hale, Bridget Boland and Richard Sokolove**, *Anne of the Thousand Days*
1971 **Erich Segal**, *Love Story*
1972 **Paddy Chayefsky**, *The Hospital*
1973 **Francis Ford Coppola and Mario Puzo**, *The Godfather*
1974 **William Peter Blatty**, *The Exorcist*
1975 **Robert Towne**, *Chinatown*
1976 **Laurence Hauben and Bo Goldman**, *One Flew Over the Cuckoo's Nest*
1977 **Paddy Chayefsky**, *Network*
1978 **Oliver Stone**, *Midnight Express*
1979 **Robert Benton**, *Kramer vs. Kramer*
1980 **William Blatty**, *Twinkle, Twinkle and Killer Kane*

BEST ORIGINAL MOTION PICTURE SCORE

1948 **Max Steiner**, *Life With Father*
1949 **Brian Easdale**, *The Red Shoes*
1950 **Johnny Green**, *The Inspector General*
1951 **Franz Waxman**, *Sunset Boulevard*
1952 **Victor Young**, *September Affair*
1953 **Dmitri Tiomkin**, *High Noon*
1954 No award
1955 No award
1956 No award
1957 No award
1958 No award
1959 No award
1960 **Ernest Gold**, *On the Beach*
1961 **Dmitri Tiomkin**, *Alamo*
1962 **Dmitri Tiomkin**, *The Guns of Navarone*
1963 **Elmer Bernstein**, *To Kill A Mockingbird*
1964 No award
1965 **Dmitri Tiomkin**, *The Fall of the Roman Empire*
1966 **Maurice Jarre**, *Dr. Zhivago*
1967 **Elmer Bernstein**, *Hawaii*
1968 **Frederick Loewe**, *Camelot*
1969 **Alex North**, *The Shoes of the Fisherman*
1970 **Burt Bacharach**, *Butch Cassidy and the Sundance Kid*
1971 **Francis Lai**, *Love Story*
1972 **Isaac Hayes**, *Shaft*
1973 **Nino Rota**, *The Godfather*
1974 **Neil Diamond**, *Jonathan Livingston Seagull*
1975 **Alan Jay Lerner and Frederick Loewe**, *The Little Prince*
1976 **John Williams**, *Jaws*
1977 **Paul Williams and Kenny Ascher**, *A Star is Born*
1978 **Giorgio Moroder**, *Midnight Express*
1979 **Carmine Coppola and Francis Coppola**, *Apocolypse Now*
1980 **Dominic Frontiere**, *The Stunt Man*

BEST ORIGINAL SONG FROM A MOTION PICTURE

1962 **Dmitri Tiomkin and Ned Washington**, *Town Without Pity* title song
1963 No award
1964 No award
1965 **Dmitri Tiomkin and Ned Washington**, *Circus World*
1966 ***Forget Domani*** from *Yellow Rolls Royce*

1967 ***Strangers in the Night*** from *A Man Could Get Killed*
1968 ***If Ever I Should Leave You*** from *Camelot*
1969 ***The Windmills of Your Mind*** from *The Thomas Crown Affair*
1970 ***Jean*** from *The Prime of Miss Jean Brodie*
1971 ***Whistling Away the Dark*** from *Darling Lili*
1972 ***Life Is What You Make It*** from *Kotch*
1973 **Walter Scharf and Don Black,** *Ben* title song
1974 **Marvin Hamlisch and M. and A. Bergman,** *The Way We Were* title song
1975 **Euel and Betty Box,** *I Feel Love* from *Benji*
1976 **Keith Carradine,** *I'm Easy* from *Nashville*
1977 **Paul Williams and Kenny Ascher,** *Evergreen* from *A Star is Born*
1978 **N.A.,** *Last Dance* from *Thank God It's Friday*
1979 **N.A.,** *The Rose* from *The Rose*
1980 **Michael Gore** and **Dean Pitchford**, *Fame* from *Fame*

BEST CINEMATOGRAPHY

1948 **Jack Cardiff,** *Black Narcissus*
1949 **Gabriel Figueroa,** *The Pearl*
1950 **Frank Planer,** *Champion* (black and white)
Walt Disney Studios, *Ichabod and Mr. Toad* (color)
1951 **Frank Planer,** *Cyrano de Bergerac* (black and white)
Robert Surtees, *King Solomon's Mines* (color)
1952 **Frank Planer,** *Death of a Salesman* (black and white)
Robert Surtees and William V. Skall, *Quo Vadis* (color)
1953 **Floyd Crosby,** *High Noon* (black and white)
George Barnes and Peverell Marley, *The Greatest Show on Earth* (color)
1954 **No award**
1955 **Boris Kaufman,** *On the Waterfront* (black and white)
Joseph Ruttenberg, *Brigadoon* (color)
1963 ***The Longest Day*** (black and white)
Lawrence of Arabia (color)

CECIL B. DEMILLE AWARD

1952 **Cecil B. DeMille**
1953 **Walt Disney**
1954 **Darryl Zanuck**
1955 **Jean Hersholt**
1956 **Jack Warner**
1957 **Mervyn LeRoy**
1958 **Buddy Adler**
1959 **Maurice Chevalier**
1960 **Bing Crosby**
1961 **Fred Astaire**
1962 **Judy Garland**
1963 **Bob Hope**
1964 **Joseph E. Levine**
1965 **James Stewart**
1966 **John Wayne**
1967 **Charlton Heston**
1968 **Kirk Douglas**
1969 **Gregory Peck**
1970 **Joan Crawford**
1971 **Frank Sinatra**
1972 **Alfred Hitchcock**
1973 **Samuel Goldwyn**
1974 **Bette Davis**
1975 **Hal D. Wallis**
1976 **No award**
1977 **Walter Mirsch**
1978 **Lucille Ball**
1979 **Henry Fonda**
1980 **Gene Kelly**

WORLD FILM FAVORITE (Male)

1951 **Gregory Peck**
1952 **No award**
1953 **John Wayne**
1954 **Robert Taylor**
Alan Ladd
1955 **Gregory Peck**
1956 **Marlon Brando**
1957 **James Dean**
1958 **Tony Curtis**
1959 **Rock Hudson**
1960 **Rock Hudson**
1961 **Rock Hudson**
Tony Curtis
1962 **Charlton Heston**
1963 **Rock Hudson**
1964 **Paul Newman**
1965 **Marcello Mastroianni**
1966 **Paul Newman**
1967 **Steve McQueen**
1968 **Paul Newman**
1969 **Sidney Poitier**
1970 **Steve McQueen**
1971 **Clint Eastwood**
1972 **Charles Bronson**
Sean Connery
1973 **Marlon Brando**
1974 **Marlon Brando**
1975 **Robert Redford**
1976 **No award**
1977 **Robert Redford**
1978 **John Travolta**
1979 **Roger Moore**
1980 **No award**

WORLD FILM FAVORITE (female)

1951 **Jane Wyman**
1952 **No award**
1953 **Susan Hayward**
1954 **Marilyn Monroe**
1955 **Audrey Hepburn**
1956 **Grace Kelly**
1957 **Kim Novak**
1958 **Doris Day**
1959 **Deborah Kerr**
1960 **Doris Day**
1961 **Gina Lollobrigida**
1962 **Marilyn Monroe**
1963 **Doris Day**
1964 **Inger Stevens**
1965 **Sophia Loren**
1966 **Natalie Wood**
1967 **Julie Andrews**
1968 **Julie Andrews**
1969 **Sophia Loren**
1970 **Barbra Streisand**
1971 **Barbra Streisand**
1972 **Ali MacGraw**
1973 **Jane Fonda**
1974 **Elizabeth Taylor**
1975 **Barbra Streisand**
1976 **No award**
1977 **Sophia Loren**
1978 **Jane Fonda**
1979 **Jane Fonda**
1980 **No award**

In addition to the awards in consistent categories, the Association confers Special Awards, Merit Awards and other citations as warranted each year. By year, they are as follows:

1947 Award for Best Non-Professional Acting: **Harold Russell,** *The Best Years of Our Lives*

1948 Special Award to Best Juvenile Actor: **Dean Stockwell,** *Gentleman's Agreement*
Special Award for Furthering the Influence on the Screen: **Walt Disney**

1949 Special Award to Best Juvenile Actor: **Ivan Yandl,** *The Search*

1950 **No award**

1951 **No award**

1952 **No award**

1953 Special Award to Best Juvenile Actors: **Brandon de Wilde,** *Member of the Wedding*
Francis Kee Teller, *Navajo*

1954 Best Documentary of Historical Interest: **Walt Disney,** *Living Desert*
Best Western Star: **Guy Madison**
Honor Award: **Jack Cummings,** producer for 30 years at MGM

1955 Pioneer Award in the Motion Picture Industry: **John Ford**
Pioneer Award for Color on the Screen: **Herbert Kalmus**
Special Award for Creative Musical Contribution: **Dmitri Tiomkin**
Special Award for Experimental Film: ***Anywhere in Our Time***

1956 Hollywood Citizenship Award: **Esther Williams**
Best Outdoor Drama: ***Wichita***
Posthumous Award for Best Dramatic Actor: **James Dean**

1957 Recognition Award for Music in Motion Pictures: **Dmitri Tiomkin**
Special Award for Advancing Film Industry: **Edwin Schallert**
Hollywood Citizenship Award: **Ronald Reagan**
Award for Consistent Performance: **Elizabeth Taylor**

1958 Best Film Choreography: **Le Roy Prinz**
Best World Entertainment Through Musical Films: **George Sidney**
Special Award for Bettering the Standard of Motion Picture Music: **Hugo Friedhofer**
Most Versatile Actress: **Jean Simmons**
Most Glamorous Actress: **Zsa Zsa Gabor**
Ambassador of Good Will: **Bob Hope**

1959 Special Award to Best Juvenile: **David Ladd**
Special Award to Most Versatile Actress: **Shirley MacLaine**

1960 Special Award for Directing Chariot Race in Film *Ben Hur:* **Andrew Morton**
Outstanding Merit: ***The Nun's Story***
Journalistic Merit Awards: **Hedda Hopper** and **Louella H. Parsons**
Special Awards to Famous Silent Film Stars: **Francis X. Bushman** and **Ramon Navarro**

1961 Special Award for Comedy: **Cantinflas**
Special Award for Artistic Integrity: **Stanley Kramer**
Merit Award: ***The Sundowners***

1962 Special Merit Award: **Samuel Bronston,** *El Cid*
Special Journalistic Merit Awards: **Army Archerd** and **Mike Connolly**

1963 Special Award for International Contribution to Recording World: **Nat "King" Cole**
Samuel Goldwyn Award: ***Sunday and Cybele***

1964 Samuel Goldwyn Award: ***Yesterday, Today and Tomorrow***
International Contribution to the Recording World: **Connie Francis**

1965 **No award**

1966 **No award**

1967 **No award**

1968 **No award**

1969 **No award**

1970 **No award**

1971 **No award**

1972 **No award**

1973 Best Documentary Film: ***Elvis on Tour* and *Walls of Fire***

1974 Best Documentary Film: ***Visions of Eight***

1975 Best Documentary Film: ***Beautiful People***

1976 Best Documentary: ***Youthquake***

1977 Best Documentary: ***Altars of the World***

Hugo Award

WORLD SCIENCE FICTION SOCIETY
c/o Howard DeVore, 4705 Weddel St., Dearborn Heights, Mich. 48125 (313/565-4157)

The Hugo Award is given annually for an outstanding science fiction film or television program, as determined by a vote of the people who attend the Science Fiction Convention. The award is a rocket ship-shaped trophy, whose official name is the Science Fiction Achievement Award.

1960 ***Twilight Zone*** (Television)

1961 ***Twilight Zone*** (Television)

1962 ***Twilight Zone*** (Television)

1963 **No award**

1964 **No award**

1965 ***Dr. Strangelove*** (Film)

1966 **No award**

1967 **"The Menagerie" on *Star Trek*** (Television)

1968 **"City on the Edge of Forever" on *Star Trek*** (Television)

1969 ***2001: A Space Odyssey*** (Film)

1970 **Apollo XI coverage** (Television)

1971 **No award**

1972 ***A Clockwork Orange*** (Film)

1973 ***Slaughterhouse Five*** (Film)

1974 ***Sleeper*** (Film)

1975 ***Young Frankenstein*** (Film)

1976 ***A Boy and His Dog*** (N.A.)

1977 **No award**

1978 ***Star Wars,*** (Film)

1979 ***Superman,*** (Film)

1980 **Not available at press time**

Grand Prize of the City of Mannheim
Special Mayor's Prize
Josef von Sternberg Prize
Mannheim Film Ducats
Special Prize for TV Film

STADT MANNHEIM
Rathaus E5, Mannheim, Federal Republic of Germany
(0621 293 2202))

The Grand Prize of the City of Mannheim carries a cash honorarium of 10,000 marks. It is awarded to a fiction film selected by an international jury.

1962 **Henning Carlssen**, *Dilemma* (Denmark)
1963 **Vera Chytilova**, *Von etwas anderen* (Czechoslovakia)
1964 **Jan Nemec**, *Diamanten in der Nacht* a) (Czechoslovakia)
1965 **Hynek Bocan**, *Niemand wird lachen*) (Czechoslovakia)
1966 **Jiri Menzel**, *Scharf beobachtete Zuge* (Czechoslovakia)
1967 **Jim McBride**, *David Holzman's Dairy* (U.S.A.))
1968 **No award**
1969 **Dusan Hanak**, *322* (Czechoslovakia)
Haskell Wexler, *Medium Cool* (U.S.A.)
1970 **Jean-Pierre Lajournade**, *La Fin des Pyrenees* (France)
Georg Lehner, *Omnia Vincit Amor* (Federal Republic of Germany)
1971 **Gerardo Vallejo**, *El Camino hacia la muerte del Viejo Reales* (Argentina)
1972 **Miguel Bejo**, *La Famillia unida esperando la llegada de Hallewyn (Argentina)*
1973 **Yoichi Takabayahi**, *Gaki Zoshi* (Japan)
1974 **Gyula Maar**, *Vegul* (Hungary)
1975 **Krzysztof Kielowski**, *Personal* (Poland)
Istvan Darday, *Wer fahrt nach England* (Hungary)
1976 **Gabor Body**, *Amerikai Anzix* (Hungary)
1977 **German Lawrow** and **Stanislaw Lujbschin**, *Pozovi menja v dal svetluju* (U.S.S.R.)
Antonio Reis and **M.M. Cordeiro**, *Tras-os Montes* (Portugal)
1978 **Ahmed ef Maaouni**, *Alyam Alyam* (Morocco)
1979 **Bela Tarr**, *Caladi Tuzeszek* (Hungary)
Leon Ischaso and **Orland Jimenez-Leal**, *El Super* (U.S.A.)
1980 **Laszlo Vitezy** *Bekeido (Hungary)*

The Special Mayor's Prize, which is accompanied by 6,000 German marks, is awarded for a documentary no more than 45 minutes in length which is judged particularly distinguished in the area of sociopolitical commentary.

1973 **Affonso Beato**, *When the People Awake* (U.S.A.) xz
1974 **Anonymous, *Last Grave at Dimbaza* (Great Britain)**
1975 **Judit elek**, *Egyszeru Tortenet* (Hungary)
1976 **Richard Dindo and Niklaus Meienberg** *Die Erschiess-*
ung des Landesverraters Ernst S. (Switzerland)
1977 **Villi Hermann**, *San Gottardo* (Switzerland)
1978 **Kim Longinotto** and **Claire Pollak**, *Theatre Girls* (Great Britain)
1979 **Josh Hanig** and **David Davis**, *Song of the Canary* (U.S.A.)
1980 **Gertrud Pinkus**, *Das hochste gut der Frau ist ihr Schweigen* (Switzerland)

The Josef-von-Sternberg-Preis, or Josef von Sternberg Prize, carries a 3,500-mark honoarium for the film selected by the jury as the festival's most original.

1966 **Jan Svankmayer**, *Rakvickarna* (Czechoslovakia) z)
1967 **Juraj Jakusbisko**, *Kristove roky* (Czechoslovakia)
1968 **Adolf Winkeimann**, *Kassel 9.12.1967.11.45h, 31 Sprunge* and *Es spricht Ruth Schmidt* (Federal Republic of Germany)
1969 **Werner Schroeter**, *Eika Katappa* (Federal Republic of Germany)
1970 **Ed Emshwiller**, *Image, Flesh and Voice* (U.S.A.)
1971 **Shipsuke Ogawa**, *The Peasants of the Second Fortress* (Japan)
1972 **Zoltan Huszarik**, *Sinbad* (Hungary)
1973 **Gregorz Krolikiewicz**, *Ny Wylot* (Poland)
1974 **Richard Beymer**, *The Innerview* (U.S.A.)
1975 **Karen Arthur**, *Legacy* (U.S.A.)
1976 **Janos Veszi**, *Mundstock ur* (Hungary)
1977 **Ingemo Engstrom** and **Gerhard Theuring**, *Fluchtweg nach Marseille* (Federal Republic of Germany)
1978 **Johan van der Keuken**, *De platte Jungle* (Netherlands)
1979 **Ulrich Stein**, *Von Tag zu Tag* (Federal Republic of Germany)
Sandy Moore, *The Lives of Firecrackers* (U.S.A.)
1980 **Jim Jarmusch**, *Permanent Vacation* (U.S.A.)

Mannheim Film Ducats, made of gold and each accompanied by 1,500 German marks, annually honor five films deemed meritorious by a jury.

1958 **Jan Lenica** and **Walerian Borowczyk**, *Es war einmal* (Poland)
Alain Resnais, *Das Gedachtnis der Welt* (France)
Georges Franju, *Die erste Nacht* (France)
Albert Pierru, *Surprise Boogie* (France)
Stanislaw Konesz, *Das Doppelleben der Libelle* d) (Poland)
1959 **Jean Rouch**, *Moi, un noir* (France)
Francois Truffaut, *Les Mistons* (France)
H.R. Strobel and **H. Tichawsky**, *Der grosse Tag des Giovanni Farina* (Germany)
Theo von Haren Norman, *Niederlandische Passion* (Netherlands)
Paul Haeserts, *Sous le masque noir* (Belgium)
1960 **Robert Menegoz**, *La fin d'un desert* (France)
Ferdinand Khittl, *Das magische Band* (Germany)
Sidney Meyers, **Ben Maddow** and **Josef Strick**, *The Savage Eye* (U.S.A.)
1961 **Jean Rouch** and **Edgar Morin**, *Chronique d'un ete* (France)
Lucjan Jankowski, *Ziema i wegiel* (Poland)
Rene Laloux, *Les dents du singe* (France)
Kent Mackenzie, *The Exiles* (U.S.A.)
1962 **Ugo Gregoretti**, *I nuovi angeli* (Italy)
Susumu Hani, *Bad Boys* (Japan)
Frederic Rossif, *Le temps du ghetto (France)*
Jacques Rozier, *Adieu Philipine* (France)
1963 **Enzo Piagi**, *Italia proibita* (Italy)
Frederic Rossif, *Mourir a Madrid* (France)
Robert Menegoz, *Route sans sillage* (France)
Richard Ballentine and **Gordon Sheppard**, *The Most* (Canada)
Stan Vanderbeek, *Summit* (U.S.A.)
Chris Marker, *La jetee* (France)
1964 **Harold Mayer**, *The Inheritance* (U.S.A.)
Emile de Antonio and **Daniel Talbot** *Point of Order* (U.S.A.)

Bruno Iori, *Bagnola—Dorf zwischen schwarz und rot* (Germany)
N. Tikhonov, *Taini Minuvchevo* (U.S.S.R.)
Jan Svankmajer, *Posledni trik* (Czechoslovakia)
Joze Bevc, *Obcan Urban* (Yugoslavia)
1965 **Roland Klick**, *Zwei* (Germany)
Richard Beymer, *A Regular Bouquet* (U.S.A.)
Dragoslav Lazic, *Parnicenje* (Yugoslavia)
Gianni Amico, *Appunti per un film sul jazz* (Italy)
G.G. Kovasznai, *Doppelbildnis* (Hungary)
Ivan Passer, *Fadni odpoledne* (Czechoslovakia)
1966 **Peter Whitehead**, *Wholly Communion* (Great Britain)
Sheldon Rochlin, *Vali* (.S.A.)
Claude Otzenberger, *Demain la Chine* (France)
Vladimir Forgency, *Adolescence* (France)
Jan Svankmajer, *Rakviccarna* (Czechoslovakia)
Klaus Lemke, *Henker Tom* (Germany)
1967 **Richard Cohn-Vossen**, *Paul Dessau* (German Democratic Republic)
Bruce Torbert, *Super Artist Andy Warhol* (U.S.A.)
Frederick Wiseman, *Titicut Follies* (U.S.A.)
Walerian Borowcyk, *Le Theatre de Monsieur et Madame Kabal* (France)
Krzyztof Zanussi, *Smierc prowincjala* (Poland)
Peter Fleischmann, *Herbat der Gammler* (Germany)
1968 **Stan Vanderbeek**, *Super-Imposition* (U.S.A.)
J.J. Sedelmaier, *Because, That's Why* (U.S.A.)
Yves de Laurot, *Black Liberation* (Canada)
David Loeb Weiss, *No Vietnamese Ever Called Me Nigger* (U.S.A.)
1969 **David Maysles** and **Albert Maysles**, *Salesman* (U.S.A.)
Vlado Kristi, *Italiensches Capriccio* (Germany)
Rosa von Praunheim, *Schwestern der Revolution* (Germany)
Dusan Trancik, *Der Gaigen* (Czechoslovakia)
1970 **Judit Vas**, *Unbeendigt* (Hungary)
Kollektivarbeit, *Reinlichkeitserziehung* (Germany)
Ryszard Czekala, *Syn* (Poland)
Stephen Dwoskin, *Times For* (Great Britain)
Al Olney, *Manha Cincenta* (Brazil)
1971 **Raymundo Gleyzer**, *Mexico, la revolucion 2 congelada* (Argentina)
Lutz Eisholz, *Bruno — der Schwarze, eis blies ein Jager* (Federal Republic of Germany)
Paul Ronder, *Part of the Family* (U.S.A.)
Andrzej Brzozowski, *Ogien* (Poland)
Kollektiverbeit, *Akkordarbeiterin beim Os-ram-Kon-zern* (Federal Republic of Germany)
1972 **Jerome Hill**, *Film Portrait* (U.S.A.)
Daniel Schmid, *Heute Nacht oder nie* (Switzerland)
Tsuchimoto Noriaki, *Minamata* (Japan)
Saul Landau Nina Serrano and **Raul Ruiz**, *Que Hacer* (Chile/U.S.A.)
Marianne Ludcke and **Ingo Kratisch**, *Die Wollands* (Federal Republic of Germany)
1973 **Max D. Willutzki**, *Der lange Jammer* (Federal Republic of Germany)
Cinda Firestone, *Attica* (U.S.A.)
Atiat el Abnoudi, *Cheval de boue* (Egypt)
Richard Dindo, *Naive Maier in der Ostschweiz* (Switzerland)
Robert Cordier, *Injun Fender* (U.S.A.)
1974 **June Kovach**, *Wer einmal Jugt oder Viktor und die Erziehung* (Switzerland)
H. Blatt, J. Bucher and **S. Fischler**, *Frame-up: The Imprisonment of Martin Sostre* (U.S.A.)
Andrzei Trzos-Rastawiecki, *Zapis Zbrodni* (Poland)
Fernando Matos Silva, *O mal amado* (Portugal)
Awtar Krishen Kaul, *27 Down Bombay* (India)
1975 **Peter K. Smith**, *A Private Enterprise* (Great Britain
Daniel Wachsmann, *My Father* (Israel)
Richard Brick, *Last Stand Farmer* (U.S.A.)
Josh Hanig and **Will Roberts**, *Men's Lives* (U.S.A.)
Christian Schocher, *Die Kinder von Furna* (Switzerland)
1976 **Giles Foster**, *Devices and Desires* (Great Britai n)
Piotr Szulkin, *Dziewcze z Ciortem* (Poland)
Giovanni Doffini, *E Nojattri Apprendisti* (Switzerland)
Maja Borissova, *5 + 1* (Bulgaria)
Thomas Mauch, *Strafprotokoli aller und jeder* (Federal Republic of Germany)
1977 **Peter van Gunten**, *El Grito del pueblo* (Switzerland)
Goran Markovic, *Specijalno vaspitanje* (Bulgaria)
Martha Coolidge, *Le Soleil des Hyenes* (U.S.A.)
Barbara Margolis, *On the Line* (U.S.A.)
Martha Coolidge, *Not a Pretty Picture* (U.S.A.)
1978 **Girish Kasarvali**, *Ghatashraddha* (India)
Antony Thomas, *Six Days in Soweto* (Great Britain)
Luc Beraud, *La tortue sur le dos* (France)
Karen Gevorkian, *Zdec na etom perekrestke* (U.S.S.R.)
1979 **Marlies Graf**, *Behinderte Liebe* (Switzerland)
Alexander Reschwiaschwili, *Gruzinskaya Chronika* (U.S.S.R.)
Andre Blanchard, *L'hiver bleu* (Canada)
Selma Baccar, *Fatma 75* (Tunisia)
Paul Schneider, *People's Firehouse* (U.S.A.)
1980 **Ali Ozgenturk**, *Hazal* (Turkey)
Josh Waletzky, *Image Before my Eyes* (U.S.A.)
Issam B. Madissy, *Liars Dice* (U.S.A.)
Masihuddin Saker and **Sheikh Niamat Ali**, *Surja Dighal Bari* (Banghadesh)
Barbara Sass, *Bez Milosci* (Poland)

A Special Prize for the Best Television Film has been introduced at the Mannheim Film Week.

1980 **Mary Lampson**, *Until She Talks* (U.S.A.)

Dan T. Moore Award

INTERNATIONAL PLATFORM ASSOCIATION
2564 Berkshire Rd., Cleveland Hts., Ohio 44106
(216/932-0505)

The Dan T. Moore Award, which consists of an engraved gavel, is given annually on the decision of the IPA Committee, to the best film lecturer.

1975 **Dan Tyler Moore**
1976 **No award**
1977 **No award**

Current Status Unknown

NBRMP "Ten Best"
David Wark Griffith Awards

NATIONAL BOARD OF REVIEW OF MOTION PICTURES
Box 589, Lenox Hill Station, New York, N.Y. 10021
(212/535-2528)

The film board annually selects the "Ten Best" films and recognizes exceptional displays of talent by cast and crew. The board's review committee of about a hundred "public spirited men and women with an interest in the motion picture and a mature sense of social responsibility" votes on films recommended by the Board's committee on exceptional films. Though the Board started selecting and individuals the "Ten Best" in 1919, the present list of pictures and individuals begins with the first full year of sound motion pictures, and includes selections of top films cited by the Board in other specific categories. In 1979 the awards were renamed to honor David Wark Griffiths, the pioneering film-maker

AMERICAN

1930 ***All Quiet on the Western Front***
Holiday
Laughter
The Man from Blankley's
Men Without Women
Morocco
Outward Bound
Romance
The Street of Chance
Tol'able David

1931 ***Cimarron***
City Lights
City Streets
Dishonored
The Front Page
The Guardsman
Quick Millions
Rango
Surrender
Tabu

1932 ***I Am a Fugitive from a Chain Gang***
As You Desire Me
A Bill of Divorcement
A Farewell to Arms
Madame Racketeer
Payment Deferred
Scarface
Tarzan
Trouble in Paradise
Two Seconds

1933 ***Topaze***
Berkeley Square
Cavalcade
Little Women
Mama Loves Papa
The Piped Piper (cartoon)
She Done Him Wrong
State Fair
Three Cornered Moon
Zoo in Budapest

1934 ***It Happened One Night***
The Count of Monte Cristo
Crime Without Passion
Eskimo
The First World War
The Lost Patrol
Lost in Sodom (non-theatrical short)
No Greater Glory
The Thin Man
Viva Villa

1935 ***The Informer***
Alice Adams
Anna Karenina
David Copperfield
The Gilded Lily
Les Miserables
The Lives of the Bengal Lancers
Mutiny on the Bounty
Ruggles of Red Gap
Who Killed Cock Robin (cartoon)

1936 ***Mr. Deeds Goes to Town***
The Story of Louis Pasteur
Modern Times
Fury
Winterset
The Devil Is a Sissy
Ceiling Zero
Romeo and Juliet
The Prisoner of Shark Island
The Green Pastures

1937 ***Night Must Fall***
The Life of Emile Zola
Black Legion
Camille
Make Way for Tomorrow
The Good Earth
They Won't Forget
Captains Courageous
A Star Is Born
Stage Door

1938 ***The Citadel***
Snow White and the Seven Dwarfs
The Beachcomber
To the Victor
Sing You Singers
The Edge of the World
Of Human Hearts
Jezebel
South Riding
Three Comrades

1939 ***Confessions of a Nazi Spy***
Wuthering Heights
Stagecoach
Ninotchka
Young Mr. Lincoln
Crisis
Goodbye, Mr. Chips
Mr. Smith Goes to Washington
The Roaring Twenties
U-Boat 29

1940 ***The Grapes of Wrath***
The Great Dictator
Of Mice and Men
Our Town
Fantasia
The Long Voyage Home
Foreign Correspondent
The Biscuit Eater
Gone With the Wind
Rebecca

1941 ***Citizen Kane***
How Green Was My Valley
The Little Foxes
The Stars Look Down

Dumbo
High Sierra
Here Comes Mr. Jordan
Tom, Dick and Harry
The Road to Zanzibar
The Lady Eve
1942 *In Which We Serve*
One of Our Aircraft Is Missing
Mrs. Miniver
Journey for Margaret
Wake Island
The Male Animal
The Major and the Minor
Sullivan's Travels
The Moon and Sixpence
The Pied Piper
1943 *The Ox-Bow Incident*
Watch on the Rhine
Air Force
Holy Matrimony
The Hard Way
Casablanca
Lassie Come Home
Bataan
The Moon is Down
The Next of Kin
1944 *None But the Lonely Heart*
Going My Way
The Miracle of Morgan's Creek
Hail the Conquering Hero
The Song of Bernadette
Wilson
Meet Me in St. Louis
Thirty Seconds Over Tokyo
Thunder Rock
Lifeboat

FOREIGN

1930 *High Treason*
Old and New
Soil
Storm Over Asia
Zwei Herzen in 3/4 Takt
1931 *Die Dreigroschenoper*
Das Lied vom Leben
Le Million
Sous Les Toits de Paris
Vier von der Infantrie
1932 *A Nous la Liberte*
Der Andere
The Battle of Gallipoli
Golden Mountains
Kameradschaft
Madchen in Uniform
Der Raub der Mona Lisa
Reserved for Ladies
Road to Life
Zwei Menschen
1933 *Hertha's Erwachen*
Ivan
M
Morgenrot
Niemandsland (Hell on Earth)
Poil de Carotte
The Private Life of Henry VIII
Quatorze Juliette
Rome Express
Le Sang d'un Poete
1934 *Man of Aran*
The Blue Light
Catherine the Great
The Constant Nymph
Madame Bovary
1935 *Chapayev*
Crime et Chatiment
Le Dernier Milliardaire
The Man Who Knew Too Much
Marie Chapdelaine
La Maternelle
The New Gulliver
Peasants
Thunder in the East
The Youth of Maxim
1936 *Le Kermesse Heroique*
The New Earth
Rembrandt
The Ghost Goes West
Nine Days a Queen
We Are From Kronstadt
Son of Mongolia
The Yellow Cruise
Les Miserables
The Secret Agent
1937 *The Eternal Mask*
The Lower Depths
Baltic Deputy
Mayerling
The Spanish Earth
Golgotha
Elephant Boy
Rembrandt
Janosik
The Wedding of Palo
1938 *La Grande Illusion*
Ballerina
Un Carnet de Bal
Generals Without Buttons
Peter the First
1939 *Port of Shadows*
Harvest
Alexander Nevsky
The End of a Day
Robert Koch
1940 *The Baker's Wife*
1941 *Pepe Le Moko*
1942 No award
1943 No award
1944 No award

DOCUMENTARY

1940 *The Flight for Life*
1941 *Target for Tonight*
1942 *Moscow Strikes Back*
1943 *Desert Victory*
Battle of Russia
Prelude to War
Saludos Amigos
The Silent Village
1944 *The Memphis Belle*
Attack! (The Battle for New Britain)
With the Marines at Tarawa
Battle for the Marianas
Tunisian Victory

THE TEN BEST (Including documentaries)

1945 *The True Glory*
The Lost Weekend
The Southerner
The Story of G.I. Joe
The Last Chance

Colonel Blimp
A Tree Grows in Brooklyn
The Fighting Lady
The Way Ahead
The Clock
1946 *Henry V*
Open City
The Best Years of Our Lives
Brief Encounters
A Walk in the Sun
It Happened at the Inn
My Darling Clementine
The Diary of a Chambermaid
The Killers
Anna and the King of Siam
1947 *Monsieur Verdoux*
Great Expectations
Shoe-shine
Crossfire
Boomerang!
Odd Man Out
Gentleman's Agreement
To Live in Peace
It's a Wonderful Life
The Overlanders
1948 *Paisan*
Day of Wrath
The Search
Treasure of Sierra Madre
Louisiana Story
Hamlet
The Snake Pit
Johnny Belinda
Joan of Arc
The Red Shoes
1949 *The Bicycle Thief*
The Quiet One
Intruder in the Dust
The Heiress
Devil in the Flesh
Quartet
Germany, Year Zero
Home of the Brave
A Letter to Three Wives
The Fallen Idol

AMERICAN FILMS

1950 *Sunset Boulevard*
All About Eve
The Asphalt Jungle
The Men
Edge of Doom
Twelve O'Clock High
Panic in the Streets
Cyrano de Bergerac
No Way Out
Stage Fright
1951 *A Place in the Sun*
The Red Badge of Courage
An American In Paris
Death of a Salesman
Detective Story
A Streetcar Named Desire
Decision Before Dawn
Strangers On a Train
Quo Vadis
Fourteen Hours
1952 *The Quiet Man*
High Noon
Limelight
Five Fingers
The Snows of Kilimanjaro
The Thief
The Bad and the Beautiful
Singin' in the Rain
Above and Beyond
My Son John
1953 *Julius Caesar*
Shane
From Here to Eternity
Martin Luther
Lili
Roman Holiday
Stalag 17
Little Fugitive
Mogambo
The Robe
1954 *On the Waterfront*
Seven Brides for Seven Brothers
The Country Girl
A Star is Born
Executive Suite
The Vanishing Prairie
Sabrina
20,000 Leagues Under the Sea
The Unconquered
Beat the Devil
1955 *Marty*
East of Eden
Mister Roberts
Bad Day at Black Rock
Summertime
The Rose Tattoo
A Man Called Peter
Not As a Stranger
Picnic
The African Lion
1956 *Around the World in 80 Days*
Moby Dick
The King and I
Lust for Life
Friendly Persuasion
Somebody Up There Likes Me
The Catered Affair
Anastasia
The Man Who Never Was
Bus Stop
1957 *The Bridge on the River Kwai*
Twelve Angry Men
The Spirit of St. Louis
The Rising of the Moon
Albert Schweitzer
Funny Face
The Bachelor Party
The Enemy Below
A Hatful of Rain
A Farewell to Arms
1958 *The Old Man and the Sea*
Separate Tables
The Last Hurrah
The Long Hot Summer
Windjammer
Cat on a Hot Tin Roof
The Goddess
The Brothers Karamazov
Me and the Colonel
Gigi
1959 *The Nun's Story*
Ben-Hur
Anatomy of a Murder

The Diary of Anne Frank
Middle of the Night
The Man Who Understood Women
Some Like It Hot
Suddenly, Last Summer
On the Beach
North by Northwest

1960 *Sons and Lovers*
The Alamo
The Sundowners
Inherit the Wind
Sunrise at Campobello
Elmer Gantry
Home from the Hill
The Apartment
Wild River
The Dark at the Top of the Stairs

1961 *Question*
The Hustler
West Side Story
The Innocents
The Hoodlum Priest
Summer and Smoke
The Young Doctors
Judgment at Nuremberg
One, Two, Three
Fanny

1962 *The Longest Day*
Billy Budd
The Miracle Worker
Lawrence of Arabia
Long Day's Journey Into Night
Whistle Down the Wind
Requiem for a Heavyweight
A Taste of Honey
Birdman of Alcatraz
War Hunt

1963 *Tom Jones*
Lilies of the Field
All the Way Home
Hud
This Sporting Life
Lord of the Flies
The L-Shaped Room
The Great Escape
How the West Was Won
The Cardinal

1964 *Becket*
My Fair Lady
Girl With Green Eyes
The World of Henry Orient
Zorba the Greek
Topkapi
The Chalk Garden
The Finest Hours
Four Days in November
Seance on a Wet Afternoon

1965 *The Eleanor Roosevelt Story*
The Agony and the Ecstasy
Doctor Zhivago
Ship of Fools
The Spy Who Came in from the Cold
Darling
The Greatest Story Ever Told
A Thousand Clowns
The Sound of Music
The Train

1966 *A Man for All Seasons*
Born Free
Alfie
Who's Afraid of Virginia Woolf?
The Bible
Georgy Girl
Years of Lightning, Day of Drums
It Happened Here
The Russians Are Coming, The Russians Are Coming
Shakespeare Wallah

1967 *Far From the Madding Crowd*
The Whisperers
Ulysses
In Cold Blood
The Family Way
The Taming of the Shrew
Doctor Doolittle
The Graduate
The Comedians
Accident

1968 *The Shoes of the Fisherman*
Romeo and Juliet
The Yellow Submarine
Charly
Rachel, Rachel
The Subject Was Roses
The Lion in Winter
Planet of the Apes
Oliver!
2001: A Space Odyssey

1969 *They Shoot Horses, Don't They?*
Ring of Bright Water
Topaz
Goodbye, Mr. Chips
Battle of Britain
The Loves of Isadora
The Prime of Miss Jean Brodie
Support Your Local Sheriff
True Grit
Midnight Cowboy

1970 *Patton*
Kes
Women in Love
Five Easy Pieces
Ryan's Daughter
I Never Sang for my Father
Diary of a Mad Housewife
Love Story
The Virgin and the Gypsy
Tora, Tora, Tora

1971 *Macbeth*
The Boy Friend
One Day in the Life of Ivan Denisovich
The French Connection
The Last Picture Show
Nicholas and Alexandra
The Go-Between
King Lear
Peter Rabbit and Tales of Beatrix Potter
Death in Venice

1972 *Cabaret*
Man of La Mancha
The Godfather
Sounder
1776
The Effect of Gamma Rays on Man-in-the-Moon Marigolds
Deliverance
The Ruling Class
The Candidate
Frenzy

1973 *The Sting*

Paper Moon
The Homecoming
Bang the Drum Slowly
Serpico
O Lucky Man
The Last American Hero
The Hireling
The Day of the Dolphin
The Way We Were

1974 *The Converstion*
Murder on the Orient Express
Chinatown
The Last Detail
Harry and Tonto
A Woman Under the Influence
Thieves Like Us
Lenny
Daisy Miller
The Three Musketeers

1975 *Barry Lyndon/Nashville*
Conduct Unbecoming
One Flew Over the Cuckoo's Nest
Lies My Father Told Me
Dog Day Afternoon
Day of the Locust
The Passenger
Hearts of the West
Farewell, My Lovely
Alice Doesn't Live Here Anymore

1976 *All the President's Men*
Network
Rocky
The Last Tycoon
The Seven-Per-Cent Solution
The Front
The Shootist
Family Plot
Silent Movie
Obsession

1977 *The Turning Point*
Annie Hall
Star Wars
Julia
Close Encounters of the Third Kind
The Late Show
Saturday Night Fever
Equus
The Picture Show Man
Harlan County, U.S.A.

1978 *Days of Heaven*
Coming Home
Interiors
Superman
Movie, Movie
Midnight Express
An Unmarried Woman
Pretty Baby
Girlfriends
Comes A Horseman

1979 *Manhattan*
Yanks
The Europeans
The China Syndrome
Breaking Away
Apocalypse Now
Being There
Time After Time
North Dallas Forty
Kramer vs. Kramer

1980 Not available at press time

FOREIGN FILMS

1950 *The Titan*
Tight Little Island
The Third Man
Kind Hearts and Coronets
Paris 1900

1951 *Rashomon*
The River
Miracle in Milan
Kon Tiki
The Browning Version

1952 *Breaking the Sound Barrier*
The Man in the White Suit
Forbidden Games
Beauty and the Devil
Ivory Hunter

1953 *A Queen is Crowned*
Moulin Rouge
The Little World of Don Camillo
Strange Deception
Conquest of Everest

1954 *Romeo and Juliet*
The Heart of the Matter
Gate of Hell
The Diary of a Country Priest
The Little Kidnappers
Genevieve
Beauties of the Night
Mr. Hulot's Holiday
The Detective
Bread, Love and Dreams

1955 *The Prisoner*
The Great Adventure
The Divided Heart
Diabolique
The End of the Affair

1956 *The Silent World*
War and Peace
Richard III
La Strada
Rififi

1957 *Ordet*
Gervaise
Torero!
The Red Balloon
A Man Escaped

1958 *Pather Panchali*
Rouge et Noir
The Horse's Mouth
My Uncle
A Night to Remember

1959 *Wild Strawberries*
Room at the Top
Aparajito
The Roof
Look Back in Anger

1960 *The World of Apu*
General Della Rovere
The Angry Silence
I'm All Right, Jack
Hiroshima, Mon Amour

1961 *The Bridge*
La Dolce Vita
Two Women
Saturday Night and Sunday Morning
A Summer to Remember

1962 *Sundays and Cybele*
Barabbas
Divorce, Italian Style
The Island

Through a Glass Darkly
1963 *8½*
The Four Days of Naples
Winter Light
The Leopard
Any Number Can Win
1964 *World Without Sun*
The Organizer
Anatomy of a Marriage
Seduced and Abandoned
Yesterday, Today and Tomorrow
1965 *Juliet of the Spirits*
The Overcoat
La Boheme
La Tia Tula
Gertrud
1966 *The Sleeping Car Murder*
The Gospel According to St. Matthew
The Shameless Old Lady
A Man and a Woman
Hamlet
1967 *Elvira Madigan*
The Hunt
Africa Addio
Persona
The Great Train Robbery
1968 *War and Peace*
Hagbard and Signe ("The Red Mantle")
Hunger
The Two of Us
The Bride Wore Black
1969 *Shame*
Stolen Kisses
The Damned
La Femme Infidele
Adalen '31
1970 *The Wild Child*
My Night at Maud's
The Passion of Anna
The Confession
This Man Must Die
1971 *Claire's Knee*
Bed and Board
The Clowns
The Garden of the Finzi-Continis
The Conformist
1972 *The Sorrow and the Pity*
The Emigrants
The Discreet Charm of the Bourgeoisie
Chloe in the Afternoon
Uncle Vanya
1973 *Cries and Whispers*
Day for Night
The New Land
The Tall Blond Man with One Brown Shoe
Alfredo
Traffic
1974 *Amarcord*
Lacombe, Lucien
Scenes from a Marriage
The Phantom of Liberte
The Pedestrian
1975 *Story of Adele H*
Brief Vacation
Special Section
Stavisky
Swept Away
1976 *Marquise of O*
Face to Face
Small Change
Cousin Cousine
The Clockmaker
1977 *That Obscure Object of Desire*
The Man Who Loved Women
A Special Day
Cria
The American Friend
1978 *Autumn Sonata*
Dear Detective
Madame Rosa
A Slave of Love
Bread and Chocolate
1979 *La Cage aux Folles*
The Tree of Wooden Clogs
The Marriage of Maria Braun
Nosferatu, The Vampyre
Peppermint Soda
1980 **Not available at press time**

BEST ACTING

1937 **Harry Baur,** *The Golem*
Humphrey Bogart, *Black Legion*
Charles Boyer, *Conquest*
Nikolai Cherkassov, *Baltic Deputy*
Danielle Darrieux, *Mayerling*
Greta Garbo, *Camille*
Robert Montgomery, *Night Must Fall*
Maria Ouspenskaya, *Conquest*
Luise Rainer, *The Good Earth*
Joseph Schildkraut, *The Life of Emile Zola*
Mathias Wieman, *The Eternal Mask*
Dame May Whitty, *Night Must Fall*
1938 **Lew Ayres,** *Holiday*
Pierre Blanchar, *Un Carnet de Bal*
Harry Baur, *Un Carnet de Bal*
Louis Jouvet, *Un Carnet de Bal*
Raim, *Un Carnet de Bal*
James Cagney, *Angels With Dirty Faces*
Joseph Calleia, *Algiers*
Chico, *The Adventure of Chico*
Robert Donat, *The Citadel*
Will Fyffe, *To The Victor*
Pierre Fresnay, *La Grande Illusion*
Jean John, *La Grande Illusion*
Dita Parlo, *La Grande Illusion*
Eric Von Stroheim, *La Grande Illusion*
John Garfield, *Four Daughters*
Wendy Hiller, *Pygmalion*
Charles Laughton, *The Beachcomber*
Elsa Lanchester, *The Beachcomber*
Robert Morley, *Marie Antoinette*
Ralph Richardson, *South Riding* and *The Citadel*
Margaret Sullavan, *Three Comrades*
Spencer Tracy, *Boys Town*
1939 **James Cagney,** *Roaring Twenties*
Bette Davis, *Dark Victory* and *The Old Maid*
Geraldine Fitzgerald, *Wuthering Heights* and *Dark Victory*
Henry Fonda, *Young Mr. Lincoln*
Jean Gabin, *Port of Shadows*
Greta Garbo, *Ninotchka*
Francis Lederer, *Confessions of a Nazy Spy*
Paul Lukas, *Confessions of a Nazi Spy*
Thomas Mitchell, *Stagecoach*
Laurence Olivier, *Wuthering Heights*
Flora Robson, *We Are Not Alone*
Michel Simon, *Port of Shadows* and *End of Day*
1940 **Jane Bryan,** *We Are Not Alone*
Charles Chaplin, *The Great Dictator*
Jane Darwell, *The Grapes of Wrath*

Betty Field, *Of Mice and Men*
Henry Fonda, *The Grapes of Wrath* and *Return of Frank James*
Joan Fontaine, *Rebecca*
Greer Garson, *Pride and Prejudice*
William Holden, *Our Town*
Vivien Leigh, *Gone With the Wind* and *Waterloo Bridge*
Thomas Mitchell, *The Long Voyage Home*
Raimu, *The Baker's Wife*
Ralph Richardson, *The Fugitives*
Ginger Rogers, *The Primrose Path*
George Sanders, *Rebecca*
Martha Scott, *Our Town*
James Stewart, *The Shop Around the Corner*
Conrad Veidt, *Escape*

1941 **Sara Allgood,** *How Green Was My Valley*
Mary Astor, *The Great Lie* and *The Maltese Falcon*
Ingrid Bergman, *Rage in Heaven*
Humphrey Bogart, *High Sierra* and *The Maltese Falcon*
Gary Cooper, *Sergeant York*
Donald Crisp, *How Green Was My Valley*
Bing Crosby, *The Road to Zanzibar* and *Birth of the Blues*
George Coulouris, *Citizen Kane*
Patricia Collinge, *The Little Foxes*
Bette Davis, *The Little Foxes*
Isobel Elsom, *Ladies in Retirement*
Joan Fontaine, *Suspicion*
Greta Garbo, *Two-Faced Woman*
James Gleason, *Meet John Doe* and *Here Comes Mr. Jordan*
Walter Huston, *All That Money Can Buy*
Ida Lupino, *High Sierra* and *Ladies in Retirement*
Roddy McDowall, *How Green Was My Valley*
Robert Montgomery, *Rage in Heaven* and *Here Comes Mr. Jordan*
Ginger Rogers, *Kitty Foyle* and *Tom, Dick and Harry*
James Stephenson, *The Letter* and *Shining Victory*
Orson Welles, *Citizen Kane*

1942 **Ernest Anderson,** *In This Our Life*
Florence Bates, *The Moon and Sixpence*
James Cagney, *Yankee Doodle Dandy*
Charles Coburn, *H.M. Pulham, Esq., In This Our Life* and *Kings Row*
Jack Carson, *The Male Animal*
Greer Garson, *Mrs. Miniver* and *Random Harvest*
Sidney Greenstreet, *Across the Pacific*
William Holden, *The Remarkable Andrew*
Tim Holt, *The Magnificent Ambersons*
Glynis Johns, *The Invaders*
Gene Kelly, *For Me and My Gal*
Diana Lynn, *The Major and the Minor*
Ida Lupino, *Moontide*
Bernard Miles, *In Which We Serve*
John Mills, *In Which We Serve*
Agnes Moorehead, *The Magnificent Ambersons*
Hattie McDaniel, *In This Our Life*
Thomas Mitchell, *Moontide*
Margaret O'Brien, *Journey for Margaret*
Susan Peters, *Random Harvest*
Edward G. Robinson, *Tales of Manhattan*
Ginger Rogers, *Rosy Hart* and *The Major and the Minor*
George Sanders, *The Moon and Sixpence*
Ann Sheridan, *Kings Row*
William Severn, *Journey for Margaret*
Rudy Vallee, *The Palm Beach Story*
Anton Walbrook, *The Invaders*
Googie Withers, *One of Our Aircraft is Missing*
Monty Woolley, *The Pied Piper*
Teresa Wright, *Mrs. Miniver*
Robert Young, *H.M. Pulham, Esq., Joe Smith American* and *Journey for Margaret*

1943 **Gracie Fields,** *Holy Matrimony*
Katina Paxinou, *For Whom the Bell Tolls*
Teresa Wright, *Shadow of a Doubt*
Paul Lukas, *Watch on the Rhine*
Henry Morgan, *The Ox-Bow Incident* and *Happy Land*
Cedric Hardwicke, *The Moon is Down* and *The Cross of Lorraine*

1944 **Ethel Barrymore,** *None But the Lonely Heart*
Ingrid Bergman, *Gaslight*
Eddie Bracken, *Hail the Conquering Hero*
Humphrey Bogart, *To Have and Have Not*
Bing Crosby, *Going My Way*
June Duprez, *None But the Lonely Heart*
Barry Fitzgerald, *Going My Way*
Betty Hutton, *The Miracle of Morgan's Creek*
Jennifer Jones, *The Song of Bernadette*
Margaret O'Brien, *Meet Me in St. Louis*
Franklin Pangborn, *Hail the Conquering Hero*

BEST ACTRESS

1945 **Joan Crawford,** *Mildred Pierce*
1946 **Anna Magnani,** *Open City*
1947 **Celia Johnson,** *This Happy Breed*
1948 **Olivia de Havilland,** *The Snake Pit*
1949 **None cited**
1950 **Gloria Swanson,** *Sunset Boulevard*
1951 **Jan Sterling,** *The Big Carnival*
1952 **Shirley Booth,** *Come Back, Little Sheba*
1953 **Jean Simmons,** *Young Bess, The Robe* and *The Actress*
1954 **Grace Kelly,** *The Country Girl*
1955 **Anna Magnani,** *The Rose Tattoo*
1956 **Dorothy McGuire,** *Friendly Persuasion*
1957 **Joanne Woodward,** *The Three Faces of Eve* and *No Down Payment*
1958 **Ingrid Bergman,** *The Inn of the Sixth Happiness*
1959 **Simone Signoret,** *Room at the Top*
1960 **Greer Garson,** *Sunrise at Campobello*
1961 **Geraldine Page,** *Summer and Smoke*
1962 **Anne Bancroft,** *The Miracle Worker*
1963 **Patricia Neal,** *Hud*
1964 **Kim Stanley,** *Seance on a Wet Afternoon*
1965 **Julie Christie,** *Darling* and *Doctor Zhivago*
1966 **Elizabeth Taylor,** *Who's Afraid of Virginia Woolf?*
1967 **Edith Evans,** *The Whisperers*
1968 **Liv Ullmann,** *Hour of the Wolf* and *Shame*
1969 **Geraldine Page,** *Trilogy*
1970 **Glenda Jackson,** *Women in Love*
1971 **Irene Pappas,** *The Trojan Women*
1972 **Cicely Tyson,** *Sounder*
1973 **Liv Ullmann,** *The New Land*
1974 **Gena Rowlands,** *A Woman Under the Influence*
1975 **Isabelle Adjani,** *The Story of Adele H*
1976 **Liv Ullman,** *Face to Face*
1977 **Anne Bancroft,** *The Turning Point*
1978 **Ingrid Bergman,** *Autumn Sonata*
1979 **Sally Field,** *Norma Rae*
1980 **Not available at press time**

BEST ACTOR

1945 **Ray Milland,** *The Lost Weekend*
1946 **Laurence Olivier,** *Henry V*
1947 **Michael Redgrave,** *Mourning Becomes Elektra*

1948 **Walter Huston,** *The Treasure of the Sierra Madre*
1949 **Ralph Richardson,** *The Heiress* and *The Fallen Idol*
1950 **Alec Guinness,** *Kind Hearts and Coronets*
1951 **Richard Basehart,** *Fourteen Hours*
1952 **Ralph Richardson,** *Breaking the Sound Barrier*
1953 **James Mason,** *Face to Face, Desert Rats, The Man Between* and *Julius Caesar*
1954 **Bing Crosby,** *The Country Girl*
1955 **Ernest Borgnine,** *Marty*
1956 **Yul Brynner,** *The King and I, Anastasia* and *The Ten Commandments*
1957 **Alec Guinness,** *The Bridge on the River Kwai*
1958 **Spencer Tracy,** *The Old Man and the Sea* and *The Last Hurrah*
1959 **Victor Seastrom,** *Wild Strawberries*
1960 **Robert Mitchum,** *Home from the Hill* and *The Sundowners*
1961 **Albert Finney,** *Saturday Night and Sunday Morning*
1962 **Jason Robards, Jr.,** *Long Day's Journey Into Night*
1963 **Rex Harrison,** *Cleopatra*
1964 **Anthony Quinn,** *Zorba the Greek*
1965 **Lee Marvin,** *Cat Ballou* and *Ship of Fools*
1966 **Paul Scofield,** *A Man for All Seasons*
1967 **Peter Finch,** *Far From the Madding Crowd*
1968 **Cliff Robertson,** *Charly*
1969 **Peter O'Toole,** *Goodbye, Mr. Chips*
1970 **George C. Scott,** *Patton*
1971 **Gene Hackman,** *The French Connection*
1972 **Peter O'Toole,** *The Ruling Class* and *Man of La Mancha*
1973 **Al Pacino,** *Serpico*
Robert Ryan, *The Iceman Cometh*
1974 **Gene Hackman,** *The Conversation*
1975 **Jack Nicholson,** *One Flew Over the Cuckoo's Nest*
1976 **David Carradine,** *Bound For Glory*
1977 **John Travolta,** *Saturday Night Fever*
1978 **Jon Voight,** *Coming Home*
1979 **Laurence Olivier,** *The Boys from Brazil*
Peter Sellers, *Being There*
1980 **Not available at press time**

BEST SUPPORTING ACTRESS

1954 **Nina Foch,** *Executive Suite*
1955 **Marjorie Rambeau,** *A Man Called Peter* and *The View from Pompey's Head*
1956 **Debbie Reynolds,** *The Catered Affair*
1957 **Dame Sybil Thorndyke,** *The Prince and the Showgirl*
1958 **Kay Walsh,** *The Horse's Mouth*
1959 **Dame Edith Evans,** *The Nun's Story*
1960 **Shirley Jones,** *Elmer Gantry*
1961 **Ruby Dee,** *A Raisin in the Sun*
1962 **Angela Lansbury,** *The Manchurian Candidate* and *All Fall Down*
1963 **Margaret Rutherford,** *The V.I.P.s*
1964 **Dame Edith Evans,** *The Caulk Garden*
1965 **Joan Blondell,** *The Cincinnati Kid*
1966 **Vivien Merchant,** *Alfie*
1967 **Marjorie Rhondes,** *The Family Way*
1968 **Virginia Maskell,** *Interlude*
1969 **Pamela Franklin,** *The Prime of Miss Jean Brodie*
1970 **Karen Black,** *Five Easy Pieces*
1971 **Cloris Leachman,** *The Last Picture Show*
1972 **Marisa Berenson,** *Cabaret*
1973 **Sylvia Sidney,** *Summer Wishes, Winter Dreams*
1974 **Valerie Perrine,** *Lenny*
1975 **Ronee Blakely,** *Nashville*
1976 **Talia Shire,** *Rocky*
1977 **Diane Keaton,** *Annie Hall*
1978 **Angela Lansbury,** *Death on the Nile*
1979 **Meryl Streep,** *Manhattan, The Seduction of Joe Tynan* and *Kramer vs. Kramer*
1980 **Not available at press time**

BEST SUPPORTING ACTOR

1954 **John Williams,** *Sabrina* and *Dial M for Murder*
1955 **Charles Bickford,** *Not as a Stranger*
1956 **Richard Basehart,** *Moby Dick*
1957 **Sessue Hayakawa,** *The Bridge on the River Kwai*
1958 **Albert Salmi,** *The Brothers Karamazov* and *The Bravados*
1959 **Hugh Griffith,** *Ben-Hur*
1960 **George Peppard,** *Home from the Hill*
1961 **Jackie Gleason,** *The Hustler*
1962 **Burgess Meredith,** *Advise and Consent*
1963 **Melvyn Douglas,** *Hud*
1964 **Martin Balsam,** *The Carpetbaggers*
1965 **Harry Andrews,** *The Agony and the Ecstasy* and *The Hill*
1966 **Robert Shaw,** *A Man for All Seasons*
1967 **Paul Ford,** *The Comedians*
1968 **Leo McKern,** *The Shoes of the Fisherman*
1969 **Philippe Noiret,** *Topaz*
1970 **Frank Langella,** *Diary of a Mad Housewife* and *The Twelve Chairs*
1971 **Ben Johnson,** *The Last Picture Show*
1972 **Al Pacino,** *The Godfather*
Joel Grey, *Cabaret*
1973 **John Houseman,** *Paper Chase*
1974 **Holger Lowenadler,** *Lacombe, Lucien*
1975 **Charles Durning,** *Dog Day Afternoon*
1976 **Jason Robards,** *All the President's Men*
1977 **Tom Skerritt,** *The Turning Point*
1978 **Richard Farnsworth,** *Comes A Horseman*
1979 **Paul Dooley,** *Breaking Away*
1980 **Not available at press time**

BEST DIRECTION

1943 **William Wellman,** *The Ox-Bow Incident*
Tay Garnett, *Bataan* and *The Cross of Lorraine*
Michael Curtiz, *Casablanca* and *This Is the Army*
1944 **No award**
1945 **Jean Renoir,** *The Southerner*
1946 **William Wyler,** *The Best Years of Our Lives*
1947 **Elia Kazan,** *Boomerang!* and *Gentleman's Agreement*
1948 **Roberto Rossellini,** *Paisan*
1949 **Vittorio de Sica,** *The Bicycle Thief*
1950 **John Huston,** *The Asphalt Jungle*
1951 **Akira Kurosawa,** *Rashomon*
1952 **David Lean,** *Breaking the Sound Barrier*
1953 **George Stevens,** *Shane*
1954 **Renato Castellani,** *Romeo and Juliet*
1955 **William Wyler,** *The Desparate Hours*
1956 **John Huston,** *Moby Dick*
1957 **David Lean,** *The Bridge on the River Kwai*
1958 **John Ford,** *The Last Hurrah*
1959 **Fred Zinnemann,** *The Nun's Story*
1960 **Jack Cardiff,** *Sons and Lovers*
1961 **Jack Clayton,** *The Innocents*
1962 **David Lean,** *Lawrence of Arabia*
1963 **Tony Richardson,** *Tom Jones*
1964 **Desmond Davies,** *Girl With Green Eyes*
1965 **John Schlesinger,** *Darling*
1966 **Fred Zinnemann,** *A Man For All Seasons*
1967 **Richard Brooks,** *In Cold Blood*
1968 **Franco Zeffirelli,** *Romeo and Juliet*
1969 **Alfred Hitchcock,** *Topaz*
1970 **Francois Truffaut,** *The Wild Child*
1971 **Ken Russell,** *The Devils* and *The Boy Friend*
1972 **Bob Fosse,** *Cabaret*

1973 **Ingmar Bergman,** *Cries and Whispers*
1974 **Francis Ford Coppola,** *The Conversation*
1975 **Stanley Kubrick,** *Barry Lyndon*
Robert Altman, *Nashville*
1976 **Alan Pakula,** *All the President's Men*
1977 **Luis Bunuel,** *That Obscure Object of Desire*
1978 **Ingmar Bergman,** *Autumn Sonata*
1979 **John Schlesinger,** *Yanks*
1980 **Not available at press time**

BEST SCRIPT

1948 **John Huston,** *Treasure of Sierra Madre*
1949 **Graham Greene,** *The Fallen Idol*
1950 **None cited**
1951 **T.E.B. Clarke,** *The Lavender Hill Mob*

SPECIAL CITATIONS

1954 **Michael Kidd,** Choreography for *Seven Brides for Seven Brothers*
Machiko Kyo, Modernization of traditional acting in *Gate of Hell* and *Ugetsu*
Puppetry, *Hansel and Gretel*
1955 **Aerial Photography,** *Strategic Air Command*
1957 **Photographic innovations,** *Funny Face*
1958 **Robert Donat,** Valor of his last performance in *The Inn of the Sixth Happiness*
1959 **Ingmar Bergman,** Body of work
Andrew Marton and Yakima Canutt, Direction of the chariot race in *Ben-Hur*
1974 **Robert G. Youngson,** Pioneer work in compilation films, notably *The Golden Age of Comedy* and *When Comedy Was King*
Special effects department of 20th Century Fox and Warner Brothers, *The Towering Inferno*
Special effects department of Universal Pictures, *Earthquake*
Ray Harryhausen, For special effect in *The Golden Voyage of Sinbad*
1977 **Walt Disney Studios,** for animation, *The Rescuers*
Close Encounters of the Third Kind
1978 **Ira Wohl,** *Best Boy*

Interreligious Film Awards

NATIONAL COUNCIL OF THE CHURCHES OF CHRIST
475 Riverside Dr., New York, N.Y. 10027 (212/870-2567)

Until 1971, annual Interreligious Film Awards were made to honor meritorious films released to the public. The selections were made by the broadcasting and film commission of the Council, the Committee on Films of the Synagogue Council of America and the Division for Film and Broadcasting of the U.S. Catholic Conference. Although the Council has discontinued the awards, it issues a film newsletter citing noteworthy cinematic achievements.

1965 ***Darling***
The Eleanor Roosevelt Story
Juliet of the Spirits
Nobody Waved Goodbye
Nothing But A Man
A Patch of Blue
The Pawnbroker
The Sound of Music
World Without Sun
1966 ***And Now Miguel***
Born Free
Georgy Girl
The Gospel According to St. Matthew
A Man for All Seasons
The Russians Are Coming
The Sand Pebbles
The Shop on Main Street
Who's Afraid of Virginia Woolf?
1967 ***The Battle of Algiers***
Bonnie and Clyde
Elvira Madigan
In Cold Blood
In the Heat of the Night
Up the Down Staircase
The War Game
The Whisperers
1968 ***Faces***
The Heart Is A Lonely Hunter
Nazarin
Oliver
Rachel, Rachel
2001: A Space Odyssey
Yellow Submarine
1969 ***Oh! What A Lovely War***
The Reivers
Z
1970 ***I Never Sang for My Father***
Kes
My Night at Maud's
The Wild Child
1971 ***Fiddler on the Roof***
One Day in the Life of Ivan Denisovich
The Garden of the Finzi-Continis

SPECIAL AWARDS

1965 **Universal Pictures, Inc.**
1966 **Buena Vista Distributing Co., Inc.**
1969 **Robert Radnitz**
1970 **John Korty**
1971 **Corp. for Public Broadcasting**

Nebula Award

SCIENCE FICTION WRITERS OF AMERICA
68 Countryside Apts., Hackettstown, N.J. 07840
(201/852-8531)

In addition to Nebulas for science fiction writing, listed elsewhere in this volume, Nebula Awards are given as merited for films selected by the membership.

NEBULA FOR BEST DRAMATIC PRESENTATION

1973 ***Soylent Green***
1974 ***Sleeper***
1975 ***Young Frankenstein***
1976 **No award**
1977 **No award**
1978 **No award**
1979 **No award**
1980 **Not available at press time**

SPECIAL AWARD

1977 ***Star Wars***

New York Film Critics Circle Awards

NEW YORK FILM CRITICS CIRCLE
c/o Roger Greenspun, *Penthouse*, 909 Third Ave., New York, N.Y. (212/593-3301)

The New York Film Critics Circle Awards are presented annually for excellence in the creation and performance of films released commercially during the calendar year. Members of the Circle select the winners, who are presented with plaques.

BEST PICTURE

1935 ***The Informer***
1936 ***Mr. Deeds Goes to Town***
1937 ***The Life of Emile Zola***
1938 ***The Citadel***
1939 ***Wuthering Heights***
1940 ***The Grapes of Wrath***
1941 ***Citizen Kane***
1942 ***In Which We Serve***
1943 ***Watch on the Rhine***
1944 ***Going My Way***
1945 ***The Lost Weekend***
1946 ***The Best Years of Our Lives***
1947 ***Gentleman's Agreement***
1948 ***Treasure of Sierra Madre***
1949 ***All the King's Men***
1950 ***All About Eve***
1951 ***A Streetcar Named Desire***
1952 ***High Noon***
1953 ***From Here to Eternity***
1954 ***On the Waterfront***
1955 ***Marty***
1956 ***Around the World in 80 Days***
1957 ***The Bridge on the River Kwai***
1958 ***The Defiant Ones***
1959 ***Ben-Hur***
1960 ***The Apartment***
Sons and Lovers
1961 ***West Side Story***
1962 **No award**
1963 ***Tom Jones***
1964 ***My Fair Lady***
1965 ***Darling***
1966 ***A Man for All Seasons***
1967 ***In the Heat of the Night***
1968 ***The Lion in Winter***
1969 ***Z***
1970 ***Five Easy Pieces***
1971 ***A Clockwork Orange***
1972 ***Cries and Whispers***
1973 ***Day for Night***
1974 ***Amarcord***
1975 ***Nashville***
1976 ***All the President's Men***
1977 ***Annie Hall***
1978 ***The Deer Hunter***
1979 ***Kramer vs. Kramer***
1980 ***Ordinary People***

BEST ACTOR

1935 **Charles Laughton,** *Mutiny on the Bounty* and *Ruggles of Red Gap*
1936 **Walter Huston,** *Dodsworth*
1937 **Paul Muni,** *The Life of Emile Zola*
1938 **James Cagney,** *Angels With Dirty Faces*
1939 **James Stewart,** *Mr. Smith Goes to Washington*
1940 **Charles Chaplin,** *The Great Dictator*
1941 **Gary Cooper,** *Sergeant York*
1942 **James Cagney,** *Yankee Doodle Dandy*
1943 **Paul Lukas,** *Watch on the Rhine*
1944 **Barry Fitzgerald,** *Going My Way*
1945 **Ray Milland,** *The Lost Weekend*
1946 **Laurence Olivier,** *Henry V*
1947 **William Powell,** *Life with Father* and *The Senator was Indiscreet*
1948 **Laurence Olivier,** *Hamlet*
1949 **Broderick Crawford,** *All the King's Men*
1950 **Gregory Peck,** *Twelve O'Clock High*
1951 **Arthur Kennedy,** *Bright Victory*
1952 **Ralph Richardson,** *Breaking the Sound Barrier*
1953 **Burt Lancaster,** *From Here to Eternity*
1954 **Marlon Brando,** *On the Waterfront*
1955 **Ernest Borgnine,** *Marty*
1956 **Kirk Douglas,** *Lust for Life*
1957 **Alec Guinness,** *The Bridge on the River Kwai*
1958 **David Niven,** *Separate Tables*
1959 **James Stewart,** *Anatomy of a Murder*
1960 **Burt Lancaster,** *Elmer Gantry*
1961 **Maximilian Schell,** *Judgment at Nuremberg*
1962 **No award**
1963 **Albert Finney,** *Tom Jones*
1964 **Rex Harrison,** *My Fair Lady*
1965 **Oskar Werner,** *Ship of Fools*
1966 **Paul Scofield,** *A Man for All Seasons*
1967 **Rod Steiger,** *In the Heat of the Night*
1968 **Alan Arkin,** *The Heart is a Lonely Hunter*
1969 **Jon Voight,** *Midnight Cowboy*
1970 **George C. Scott,** *Patton*
1971 **Gene Hackman,** *French Connection*
1972 **Laurence Olivier,** *Sleuth*
1973 **Marlon Brando,** *The Godfather*
1974 **Jack Nicholson,** *Chinatown*
1975 **Jack Nicholson,** *One Flew Over the Cuckoo's Nest*
1976 **Robert De Niro,** *Taxi Driver*
1977 **Sir John Geilgud,** *Providence*
1978 **Jon Voight,** *Coming Home*
1979 **Dustin Hoffman,** *Kramer vs. Kramer*
1980 **Robert De Niro,** *Raging Bull*

BEST ACTRESS

1935 **Greta Garbo,** *Anna Karenina*
1936 **Luise Rainer,** *The Great Ziegfeld*
1937 **Greta Garbo,** *Camille*
1938 **Margaret Sullavan,** *Three Comrades*
1939 **Vivien Leigh,** *Gone With the Wind*
1940 **Katharine Hepburn,** *The Philadelphia Story*
1941 **Joan Fontaine,** *Suspicion*
1942 **Agnes Moorehead,** *The Magnificent Ambersons*
1943 **Ida Lupino,** *The Hard Way*
1944 **Tallulah Bankhead,** *Lifeboat*
1945 **Ingrid Bergman,** *Spellbound* and *The Bells of St. Mary's*
1946 **Celia Johnson,** *Brief Encounter*
1947 **Deborah Kerr,** *Black Narcissus* and *The Adventuress*
1948 **Olivia de Havilland,** *The Snake Pit*
1949 **Olivia de Havilland,** *The Heiress*
1950 **Bette Davis,** *All About Eve*
1951 **Vivien Leigh,** *A Streetcar Named Desire*
1952 **Shirley Booth,** *Come Back, Little Sheba*
1953 **Audrey Hepburn,** *Roman Holiday*
1954 **Grace Kelly,** *The Country Girl, Rear Window* and *Dial M for Murder*
1955 **Anna Magnani,** *The Rose Tattoo*
1956 **Ingrid Bergman,** *Anastasia*
1957 **Deborah Kerr,** *Heaven Knows, Mr. Allison*
1958 **Susan Hayward,** *I Want to Live!*
1959 **Audrey Hepburn,** *The Nun's Story*

1960 **Deborah Kerr,** *The Sundowners*
1961 **Sophia Loren,** *Two Women*
1962 No award
1963 **Patricia Neal,** *Hud*
1964 **Kim Stanley,** *Seance on a Wet Afternnon*
1965 **Julie Christie,** *Darling*
1966 **Elizabeth Taylor,** *Who's Afraid of Virginia Woolf?*
Lynn Redgrave, *Georgy Girl*
1967 **Dame Edith Evans,** *The Whisperers*
1968 **Joanne Woodward,** *Rachel, Rachel*
1969 **Jane Fonda,** *They Shoot Horses, Don't They?*
1970 **Glenda Jackson,** *Women in Love*
1971 **Jane Fonda,** *Klute*
1972 **Liv Ullmann,** *Cries and Whispers*
1973 **Joanne Woodward,** *Summer Wishes, Winter Dreams*
1974 **Liv Ullmann,** *Scenes from a Marriage*
1975 **Isabelle Adjani,** *The Story of Adele H*
1976 **Liv Ullmann,** *Face to Face*
1977 **Diane Keaton,** *Annie Hall*
1978 **Ingrid Bergman,** *Autumn Sonata*
1979 **Sally Field,** *Norma Rae*
1980 **Sissy Spacek,** *Coal Miner's Daughter*

BEST DIRECTION

1935 **John Ford,** *The Informer*
1936 **Rouben Mamoulian,** *The Gay Desperado*
1937 **Gregory La Cava,** *Stage Door*
1938 **Alfred Hitchcock,** *The Lady Vanishes*
1939 **John Ford,** *Stagecoach*
1940 **John Ford,** *The Grapes of Wrath* and *The Long Voyage Home*
1941 **John Ford,** *How Green Was My Valley*
1942 **John Farrow,** *Wake Island*
1943 **George Stevens,** *The More the Merrier*
1944 **Leo McCarey,** *Going My Way*
1945 **Billy Wilder,** *The Lost Weekend*
1946 **William Wyler,** *The Best Years of Our Lives*
1947 **Elia Kazan,** *Gentleman's Agreement* and *Boomerang*
1948 **John Huston,** *Treasure of Sierra Madre*
1949 **Carol Reed,** *The Fallen Idol*
1950 **Joseph L. Mankiewicz,** *All About Eve*
1951 **Elia Kazan,** *A Streetcar Named Desire*
1952 **Fred Zinnemann,** *High Noon*
1953 **Fred Zinnemann,** *From Here to Eternity*
1954 **Elia Kazan,** *On the Waterfront*
1955 **David Lean,** *Summertime*
1956 **John Huston,** *Moby Dick*
1957 **David Lean,** *The Bridge on the River Kwai*
1958 **Stanley Kramer,** *The Defiant Ones*
1959 **Fred Zinnemann,** *The Nun's Story*
1960 **Billy Wilder,** *The Apartment*
Jack Cardiff, *Sons and Lovers*
1961 **Robert Rossen,** *The Hustler*
1962 No award
1963 **Tony Richardson,** *Tom Jones*
1964 **Stanley Kubrick,** *Dr. Strangelove*
1965 **John Schlesinger,** *Darling*
1966 **Fred Zinnemann,** *A Man for All Seasons*
1967 **Mike Nichols,** *The Graduate*
1968 **Paul Newman,** *Rachel, Rachel*
1969 **Costa-Gavras,** *Z*
1970 **Bob Rafelson,** *Five Easy Pieces*
1971 **Stanley Kubrick,** *A Clockwork Orange*
1972 **Ingmar Bergman,** *Cries and Whispers*
1973 **Francois Truffaut,** *Day for Night*
1974 **Federico Fellini,** *Amarcord*
1975 **Robert Altman,** *Nashville*
1976 **Alan J. Pakula,** *All the President's Men*
1977 **Woody Allen,** *Annie Hall*
1978 **Terrence Malick,** *Days of Heaven*
1979 **Woody Allen,** *Manhattan*
1980 **Jonathan Demme,** *Melvin and Howard*

BEST FOREIGN-LANGUAGE FILM

1936 ***La Kermesse Heroique*** (French)
1937 ***Mayerling*** (French)
1938 ***Grande Illusion*** (French)
1939 ***Harvest*** (French)
1940 ***The Baker's Wife*** (French)
1941 No award
1946 ***Open City*** (Italian)
1947 ***To Live in Peace*** (Italian)
1948 ***Paisan*** (Italian)
1949 ***The Bicycle Thief*** (Italian)
1950 ***Ways of Love*** (Franco-Italian)
1951 ***Miracle in Milan*** (Italian)
1952 ***Forbidden Games*** (French)
1953 ***Justice Is Done*** (French)
1954 ***Gate of Hell*** (Japanese)
1955 ***Diabolique*** (French)
Umberto D. (Italian)
1956 ***La Strada*** (Italian)
1957 ***Gervaise*** (French)
1958 ***Mon Oncle*** (French)
1959 ***The 400 Blows*** (French)
1960 ***Hiroshima, Mon Amour*** (French)
1961 ***La Dolce Vita*** (Italian)
1962 No award
1963 ***8½*** (Italian)
1964 ***That Man From Rio*** (French)
1965 ***Juliet of the Spirits*** (Italian)
1966 ***The Shop on Main Street*** (Czech)
1967 ***La Guerre est Finie*** (French)
1968 ***War and Peace*** (Russian)
1979-77 Category suspended
1978 ***Bread and Chocolate*** (Italian)
1979 ***The Tree of Wooden Clogs*** (Italian)
1980 ***Mon Oncle D'Amerique*** (French)

SCREENPLAY WRITING

1958 **Nathan E. Douglas and Harold J. Smith,** *The Defiant Ones*
1959 **Wendell Mayes,** *Anatomy of a Murder*
1960 **Billy Wilder and I.A.L. Diamond,** *The Apartment*
1961 **Abby Mann,** *Judgment at Nuremberg*
1962 No award
1963 **Irving Ravetch and Harriet Frank, Jr.,** *Hud*
1964 **Harold Pinter,** *The Servant*
1965 No award
1966 **Robert Bolt,** *A Man for All Seasons*
1967 **David Newman and Robert Benton,** *Bonnie and Clyde*
1968 **Lorenzo Semple, Jr.,** *Pretty Poison*
1969 **Paul Mazursky and Larry Tucker,** *Bob & Carol & Ted & Alice*
1970 **Eric Rohmer,** *Ma Nuit Chez Maude*
1971 **Penelope Gilliatt,** *Sunday Bloody Sunday*
Larry McMurtry and Peter Bogdanovich, *The Last Picture Show*
1972 **Ingmar Bergman,** *Cries and Whispers*
1973 **George Lucas, Gloria Katz and Willard Huyck,** *American Graffiti*
1974 **Ingmar Bergman,** *Scenes from a Marriage*
1975 **Francois Truffaut, Jean Gruault and Suzanne Schiffman,** *The Story of Adele H*
1976 **Paddy Chayefsky,** *Network*
1977 **Woody Allen and Marshall Brickman,** *Annie Hall*
1978 **Paul Mazursky,** *An Unmarried Woman*
1979 **Steve Tesich,** *Breaking Away*

1980 **Bo Goldman**, *Melvin and Howard*

BEST SUPPORTING ACTOR

1972 **Robert Duvall,** *The Godfather*
1973 **Robert De Niro,** *Mean Streets*
1974 **Charles Boyer,** *Stavisky*
1975 **Alan Arkin,** *Hearts of the West*
1976 **Jason Robards,** *All the President's Men*
1977 **Maximilian Schell,** *Julia*
1978 **Christopher Walken,** *The Deer Hunter*
1979 **Melvyn Douglas,** *Being There*
1980 **Joe Pesci,** *Raging Bull*

BEST SUPPORTING ACTRESS

1972 **Jeannie Berlin,** *The Heartbreak Kid*
1973 **Valentina Cortese,** *Day for Night*
1974 **Valerie Perrine,** *Lenny*
1975 **Lily Tomlin,** *Nashville*
1976 **Talia Shire,** *Rocky*
1977 **Sissy Spacek,** *Three Women*
1978 **Maureen Stapleton,** *Interiors*
1979 **Meryl Streep,** *Kramer vs. Kramer* and *The Seduction of Joe Tynan*
1980 **Mary Steenburgen,** *Melvin and Howard*

CINEMATOGRAPHY

1980 **Ghislain Cloquet** and **Geoffrey Unsworth**, *Tess*

SPECIAL AWARDS

1964 ***To Be Alive,*** New York World's Fair (Johnson Wax pavilion)
1972 ***The Sorrow and the Pity*** (French documentary)
1980 **Ira Wohl,** *Best Boy* (Documentary)

Patsy Award

AMERICAN HUMANE ASSOCIATION
8480 Beverly Blvd., Los Angeles, Calif. 90048
(212/653-3394)

The Patsy Award, which consists of a trophy, is presented annually for outstanding film appearances by animals. The Humane Association receives nominations from producers and directors, its own field officers and animal trainers. A Patsy Committee narrows these to a field of nominees for selection by a blue-ribbon panel of prominent people. Beginning in 1978, awards were made by animal categories rather than media categories. (See pp. xx xx for television Patsy Awards.)

1951 **Francis** (talking mule), *Francis*
California (Palomino horse), *The Palomino*
Pierre (chimpanzee), *My Friend Irma Goes West*
1952 **Rhubarb** (cat), *Rhubarb*
Francis (talking mule), *Francis Goes to the Races*
Cheta (chimpanzee), *Tarzan's Peril*
1953 **Jackie** (African lion), *Fearless Fagin*
Bonzo (chimpanzee), *Bonzo Goes to College*
Trigger (horse), *Son of Paleface*
1954 **Laddie** (collie), *Hondo*
Francis (talking mule), *Francis Covers the Big Town*
Jackie (African lion), *Androcles and the Lion*
1955 **Gypsy** (black stallion), *Gypsy Colt*
Francis (talking mule), *Francis Joins the WACS*
Esmeralda (seal), *20,000 Leagues Under the Sea*
1956 **Wildfire** (bull terrier), *It's a Dog's Life*
Francis (talking mule), *Francis Joins the Navy*
Faro (dog), *The Kentuckian*
1957 **Samantha** (goose), *Friendly Persuasion*
War Winds (black stallion), *Giant*
Francis (talking mule), *Francis in the Haunted House*
1958 **Spike** (dog), *Old Yeller*
Beauty (horse), *Wild is the Wind*
Kelly (dog), *Kelly and Me*
1959 **Pyewacket** (cat), *Bell, Book and Candle*
Tonka (horse), *Tonka*
Harry (hare), *Geisha Boy*
1960 **Shaggy** (old English sheepdog), *The Shaggy Dog*
Herman (pigeon), *The Gazebo*
North Wind (horse), *The Sad Horse*
1961 **Cotton** (horse), *Pepe*
Spike (dog), *A Dog of Flanders*
Mr. Stubbs (chimpanzee), *Visit to a Small Planet*
Skip (N.A.), *Visit to a Small Planet*
1962 **Cat** (cat), *Breakfast at Tiffany's*
Pete (dog), *The Silent Call*
Flame (horse), *The Clown and the Kid*
1963 **Big Red** (dog), *Big Red*
Sydney (elephant), *Jumbo*
Zamba (Afican lion), *The Lion*
1964 **Tom Dooley** (dog), *Savage Sam*
Pluto (dog), *My Six Loves*
Raunchy (jaguar), *Rampage*
1965 **Patrina** (tiger), *A Tiger Walks*
Storm (dog), *Goodbye Charlie*
Junior (dog), *Island of the Blue Dolphins*
1966 **Syn** (Siamese cat), *That Darn Cat*
Clarence (African lion), *Clarence, the Cross-Eyed Lion*
Judy (chimpanzee), *The Monkey's Uncle*
1967 **Elsa** (African lioness), *Born Free*
Duke (dog), *The Ugly Dachshund*
Vindicator (bull), *The Rare Breed*
1968 **Gentle Ben** (bear), *Gentle Giant*
Sir Tom (mountain lion), *The Cat*
Sophie (sea lion), *Dr. Doolittle*
1969 **Albarado** (horse), *Horse in the Gray Flannel Suit*
1970 **Rascal** (raccoon), *Rascal*
1971 **Sancho** (wolf), *The Wild Country*
1972 **Ben** (rat), *Willard*
1973 **Ben** (rat), *Ben*
1974 **Alpha** (dolphin), *The Day of the Dolphin*
1975 **Tonto** (cat), *Harry and Tonto*
1976 **Valentine** (camel), *Hawmps*
Five dobermans (dogs), *The Amazing Dobermans*
Gus (dog), *Won Ton Ton, The Dog Who Saved Hollywood*
Gus (mule), *Gus*
Shoshone (horse), *Mustang Country*
Ollie (dog), *The Shaggy D.A.*
Bandit (raccoon), *Guardian of the Wilderness*
Bruno (bear), *Guardian of the Wilderness*

1977 **Not available**

CANINE

1978 **Sam** (golden Labrador), *Sam*
1979 **No award**
1980 **No award**

WILD ANIMAL

1978 **Farkas** (wolf), *Lucan*
1979 **No award**
1980 **No award**

EQUINE

1978 **Domengo** (horse), *Peter Lundy and the Medicine Hat Stallion*
1979 No award
1980 No award

SPECIAL CATEGORY

1978 **Amber** (cat), *The Cat from Outer Space*
1979 No award
1980 No award

SPECIAL SERVICE AWARD

1978 Betty White

Gold Medal Awards

PHOTOPLAY
205 E. 42nd St., New York, N.Y. 10017 (212/983-5600)

The *Photoplay* Gold Medal Awards are made for popular motion pictures, performers and occasionally for individuals' special achievements in the entertainment industry. The most recent awards were based on ballots of more than 60,000 readers of the magazine. The awards were halted after 1979. (*Photoplay* also gives other awards for popular entertainment personalities, which can be found on p. 217.)

FILMS

1920 *Humoresque*
1921 *Tol'Able David*
1922 *Robin Hood*
1923 *Covered Wagon*
1924 *Abraham Lincoln*
1925 *The Big Parade*
1926 *Beau Geste*
1927 *Seventh Heaven*
1928 *Four Sons*
1929 *Disraeli*
1930 *All Quiet On The Western Front*
1931 *Cimarron*
1932 *Smilin' Through*
1933 *Little Women*
1934 *Barretts of Wimpole Street*
1935 *Naughty Marietta*
1936 *San Francisco*
1937 *Captains Courageous*
1938 *Sweethearts*
1939 *Gone With the Wind*
1940 No award
1941 No award
1942 No award
1943 No award
1944 *Going My Way*
1945 *The Valley of Decision*
1946 *The Bells of St. Mary's*
1947 *The Jolson Story*
1948 *Sitting Pretty*
1949 *The Stratton Story*
1950 *Battleground*
1951 *Showboat*
1952 *With A Song In My Heart*
1953 *From Here to Eternity*
1954 *Magnificent Obsession*
1955 *Love Is A Many-Splendored Thing*
1956 *Giant*
1957 *An Affair to Remember*
1958 *Gigi*
1959 *Pillow Talk*
1960 No award
1961 *Splendor in the Grass*
1962 *The Miracle Worker*
1963 *How the West Was Won*
1964 *The Unsinkable Molly Brown*
1965 *The Sound of Music*
1966 *The Russians Are Coming, The Russians Are Coming*
1967 *The Dirty Dozen*
1968 *Rosemary's Baby*
1969 *True Grit*
1970 *Love Story*
1971 *Summer of '42*
1972 *The Godfather*
1973 *Walking Tall*
1974 *Towering Inferno*
1975 *Jaws*
1976 *A Star Is Born*

Current Status Unknown

ACTOR

1944 Bing Crosby
1945 Bing Crosby
1946 Bing Crosby
1947 Bing Crosby
1948 Bing Crosby
1949 James Stewart
1950 John Wayne
1951 Mario Lanza
1952 Gary Cooper
1953 Burt Lancaster
Frank Sinatra
1954 William Holden
1955 William Holden
1956 Rock Hudson
1957 Rock Hudson
1958 Tony Curtis
1959 Rock Hudson
1960 No award
1961 Troy Donahue
1962 Richard Chamberlain
1963 Richard Chamberlain
1964 Richard Chamberlain
1965 Robert Vaughn
1966 David Janssen
1967 Paul Newman
1968 Steve McQueen
1969 John Wayne
1970 Ryan O'Neal
1971 John Wayne
1972 Chad Everett
1973 Burt Reynolds
1974 Robert Redford
1975 Robert Redford
1976 John Wayne
1977 Not available at press time

ACTRESS

1944 Greer Garson
1945 Greer Garson
1946 Ingrid Bergman
1947 Ingrid Bergman
1948 Ingrid Bergman
1949 Jane Wyman
1950 Betty Hutton
1951 Doris Day
1952 Susan Hayward

1953 **Deborah Kerr**
1954 **June Allyson**
1955 **Jennifer Jones**
1956 **Kim Novak**
1957 **Deborah Kerr**
1958 **Debbie Reynolds**
1959 **Doris Day**
1960 **No award**
1961 **Connie Stevens**
1962 **Bette Davis**
1963 **Connie Stevens**
1964 **Ann-Margret**
1965 **Dorothy Malone**
1966 **Barbara Stanwyck**
1967 **Barbara Stanwyck**
1968 **Diahann Carroll**
1969 **Marlo Thomas**
1970 **Ali MacGraw**
1971 **Ann-Margret**
1972 **Ann-Margret**
1973 **Elizabeth Taylor**
1974 **Valerie Harper**
1975 **Angie Dickinson**
1976 **Barbra Streisand**

Current Status Unknown

ALL-TIME FAVORITES (voted in 1976)

1976 ***Gone With the Wind***—All-time favorite movie
John Wayne—All-stime favorite star

SPECIAL AWARD (Citation)

1952 **Marilyn Monroe,** For "her sensational rise to stardom"
Dean Martin and Jerry Lewis, "As a team whose pictures are constant winners at the box office"
William Goetz, Universal International, "For his efforts in the development of new talents in the fields of acting, writing and directing"
1954 **Y. Frank Freeman** (Paramount), "Magnificent contribution to motion pictures with the introduction . . . of Vistavision"
Otto Preminger, "For giving the film-going public a rare treat of translating the classic film of the opera *Carmen* into a distinguished American movie, *Carmen Jones*"
Van Johnson, Who "emerged during 1954 as an actor of real scope and force"
1955 **Columbia,** For "a delightful screen reflection of Americana in *Picnic*"
James Dean, "Outstanding dramatic appearances"
Glenn Ford and Eleanor Powell Ford, "For their magnificent contributions to the establishment of better relationships among boys and girls of their community"
Otto Preminger, "For his courage and great talent [in producing] *The Man With the Golden Arm*"
1956 **Cecil B. DeMille,** "For the creation of one of the screen's greatest emotional and religious experiences, *The Ten Commandments*"
Barbara Stanwyck, "For meeting with simplicity, honesty and superb craftsmanship the challenges of leading roles in 75 films"
Michael Todd, For the development of Todd-AO
1957 **No award**
1958 **Maurice Chevalier,** Year's Best Foreign Star
David Ladd, Youngest Hit

SPECIAL EDITOR'S AWARD

1964 **Bob Hope** (Public Service Award)
1965 **John Wayne**
1966 **Ginger Rogers**
1967 **Bob Hope**
Joey Bishop
Glenn Ford
1968 **James Stewart**
1969 **Danny Thomas**
1970 **Debbie Reynolds**
1971 **Johnny Carson**
1972 **Elvis Presley**
1973 **Andy Williams**
1977 **Alfred Hitchcock**
Joan Crawford (tribute)

San Remo Grand Prize

MOSTRA INTERNAZIONALE DEL FILM D'AUTORE
Rotonda dei Mille, 24100 Bergamo, Italy (Tel: 243.566 or 243.162)

The Grand Prize of the Mostra Internazionale del Film d'Autore (International Competition for Author Films) popularly known as the San Remo Film Festival is given annually to the author of the best 16mm or 35mm film prior to its release. A jury selects the winner on the basis of cultural and artistic considerations. The Grand Prize winner receives a cash award of 5,000,000 lire. The list below indicates the winners beginning with the Ninth Annual San Remo Film Festival; earlier winners are not available.

1966 ***Bariera,*** Poland (Jerzy Skolimowski, director)
1967 ***Sedmikrasky,*** Czechoslovakia (Vera Chytilova)
1968 ***O Slavnosti a Hostech,*** Czechoslovakia (Jan Nemec)
1969 **No award**
1970 ***Valerie a Tyden Divu,*** Czechoslovakia (Jaromil Jires)
1971 ***Sho o Suteyo, Machi e Deyo,*** Japan (Shuji Terayama)
Za Sciana, Poland (Kryzysztof Zanussi)
1972 ***Pilvilinna,*** Finland (Sakari Rimmiwen)
1973 ***Laukaus Tehtaalla,*** Finland (Erkko Kivikoski)
1974 ***Harmadik Nekifutas,*** Hungary (Peter Bacso)
Molba, U.S.S.R. (Tenghis Abuladse)
1975 ***Takiji Kobayashi,*** Japan (Tadashi Imai)
1976 ***Zofia,*** Poland (Ryszard Czekala)
1977 **No award**
1978 **Jack Gold,** *The Naked Civil Servant* (Great Britain)
Paul Ruiz, *La Vocation Suspendue* (France)
1979 **Lana Gogoberidze,** *Nrskolko Interwju Po Litschnym Woprosam* (U.S.S.R.)
Peter Vennerod, *Hvem Har Bestemt . . . ?* (Norway)
1980 **Vera Chytilova,** *Panel Story* (Czechoslovakia)
Ali Khamraev, *Triptich* (U.S.S.R.)

Screen Awards
Laurel Award for Screen

WRITERS GUILD OF AMERICA, WEST
8955 Beverly Blvd., Los Angeles, Calif. 90048
(213/550-1000)

The Screen Award, which consists of a bronze plaque, annually honorsexcellence in screenwriting by a Guild member in various motion picture categories.

COMEDY

1948 **F. Hugh Herbert,** *Sitting Pretty*
1949 **Joseph L. Mankiewicz,** *A Letter to Three Wives*
1950 **Joseph L. Mankiewicz,** *All About Eve*
1951 **Frances Goodrich and Albert Hackett,** *Father's Little Dividend*
1952 **Frank S. Nugent,** *The Quiet Man*
1953 **Ian McLellan Hunter and John Dighton,** *Roman Holiday*
1954 **Billy Wilder, Samuel Taylor and John Dighton,** *Sabrina*
1955 **Frank Nugent and Joshua Logan,** *Mr. Roberts*
1956 **James Poe, John Farrow and S.J. Perelman,** *Around the World in 80 Days*
1957 **Billy Wilder and I.A.L. Diamond,** *Love in the Afternoon*
1958 **S.N. Berhman and George Froeschel,** *Jacobowsky and the Colonel*
1959 **Billy Wilder and I.A.L. Diamond,** *Some Like It Hot*
1960 **Billy Wilder and I.A.L. Diamond,** *The Apartment*
1961 **George Axelrod,** *Breakfast at Tiffany's*
1962 **Stanley Shapiro and Nate Monaster,** *That Touch of Mink*
1963 **James Poe,** *Lilies of the Field*
1964 **Stanley Kubrick, Peter George and Terry Southern,** *Dr. Strangelove; Or How I Learned to Stop Worrying and Love the Bomb*
1965 **Herb Gardner,** *A Thousand Clowns*
1966 **William Rose,** *The Russians Are Coming, The Russians Are Coming*
1967 **Calder Willingham and Buck Henry,** *The Graduate*
1968 **Neil Simon,** *The Odd Couple*
1969 **Paul Mazursky and Larry Tucker,** *Bob & Carol & Ted & Alice*

BEST COMEDY WRITTEN DIRECTLY FOR THE SCREEN

1970 **Neil Simon,** *The Out-of-Towners*
1971 **Paddy Chayefsky,** *The Hospital*
1972 **Buck Henry, David Newman and Robert Benton,** *What's Up, Doc?*
1973 **Melvin Frank and Jack Rose,** *A Touch of Class*
1974 **Mel Brooks, Norman Steinberg, Andrew Bergman, Richard Pryor and Alan Uger,** *Blazing Saddles*
1975 **Robert Towne and Warren Beatty,** *Shampoo*
1976 **Bill Lancaster,** *The Bad News Bears*
1977 **Woody Allen and Marshall Brickman,** *Annie Hall*
1978 **Larry Gelbart** and **Sheldon Keller,** *Movie, Movie*
1979 **Steve Tesich,** *Breaking Away*
1980 **Not available at press time**

BEST COMEDY ADAPTED FROM ANOTHER MEDIUM

1969 **Arnold Schulman,** *Goodbye, Columbus*
1970 **Ring Lardner, Jr.,** *M*A*S*H*
1971 **John Paxton,** *Kotch*
1972 **Jay Presson Allen,** *Cabaret*
1973 **Alvin Sargent,** *Paper Moon*
1974 **Mordecai Richler,** *The Apprenticeship of Duddy Kravitz*
1975 **Neil Simon,** *Sunshine Boys*
1976 **Frank Waldman and Blake Edwards,** *The Pink Panther Strikes Again*
1977 **Larry Gelbart,** *Oh, God!*
1978 **Elaine May** and **Warren Beatty,** *Heaven Can Wait*
1979 **Jerzy Kozinski,** *Being There*
1980 **Not available at press time**

BEST DRAMA

1948 **Frank Partos and Millen Brand,** *The Snake Pit*
1949 **Robert Rossen,** *All the King's Men*
1950 **Charles Brackett, Billy Wilder and D.M. Marshman, Jr.,** *Sunset Boulevard*
1951 **Michael Wilson and Harry Brown,** *A Place in the Sun*
1952 **Carl Foreman,** *High Noon*
1953 **Daniel Taradash,** *From Here to Eternity*
1954 **Budd Schulberg,** *On the Waterfront*
1955 **Paddy Chayefsky,** *Marty*
1956 **Michael Wilson,** *Friendly Persuasion*
1957 **Reginald Rose,** *Twelve Angry Men*
1958 **Harold Jacob Smith and Nathan E. Douglas,** *The Defiant Ones*
1959 **Frances Goodrich and Albert Hackett,** *The Diary of Anne Frank*
1960 **Richard Brooks,** *Elmer Gantry*
1961 **Sidney Carroll and Robert Rossen,** *The Hustler*
1962 **Horton Foote,** *To Kill a Mockingbird*
1963 **Harriet Frank, Jr., and Irving Rovetch,** *Hud*
1964 **Edward Anhalt,** *Becket*
1965 **Morton Fine and David Friedkin,** *The Pawnbroker*
1966 **Ernest Lehman,** *Who's Afraid of Virginia Woolf?*
1967 **David Newman and Robert Benton,** *Bonnie and Clyde*
1968 **James Goldman,** *The Lion in Winter*

BEST DRAMA WRITTEN DIRECTLY FOR THE SCREEN

1969 **William Goldman,** *Butch Cassidy and The Sundance Kid*
1970 **Francis Ford Coppola and Edmund H. North,** *Patton*
1971 **Penelope Gilliatt,** *Sunday Bloody Sunday*
1972 **Jeremy Larner,** *The Candidate*
1973 **Steve Shagan,** *Save the Tiger*
1974 **Robert Towne,** *Chinatown*
1975 **Frank Pierson,** *Dog Day Afternoon*
1976 **Paddy Chayefsky,** *Network*
1977 **Arthur Laurents,** *The Turning Point*
1978 **Waldo Salt** and **Robert C. Jones,** *Coming Home*
1979 **Mike Gray, T.S. Cook** and **James Bridges,** *The China Syndrome*
1980 **Not available at press time**

BEST DRAMA ADAPTED FROM ANOTHER MEDIUM

1969 **Waldo Salt,** *Midnight Cowboy*
1970 **Robert Anderson,** *I Never Sang for My Father*
1971 **Ernest Tidyman,** *The French Connection*
1972 **Mario Puzo and Francis Ford Coppola,** *The Godfather*
1973 **Waldo Salt and Norman Wexler,** *Serpico*
1974 **Francis Ford Coppola and Mario Puzo,** *The Godfather, Part II*
1975 **Lawrence Hauben and Bo Goldman,** *One Flew Over the Cuckoo's Nest*
1976 **William Goldman,** *All the President's Men*
1977 **Alvin Sargent,** *Julia*
1978 **Oliver Stone,** *Midnight Express*
1979 **Robert Benton,** *Kramer vs. Kramer*
1980 **Not available at press time**

BEST MUSICAL

1948 **Sidney Sheldon, Frances Goodrich and Albert Hackett,** *Easter Parade*
1949 **Betty Comden and Adolph Green,** *On the Town*
1950 **Sidney Sheldon,** *Annie Get Your Gun*
1951 **Alan Jay Lerner,** *An American in Paris*
1952 **Betty Comden and Adolph Green,** *Singin' in the Rain*
1953 **Helen Deutsch,** *Lili*

1954 Albert Hackett, Frances Goodrich and Ernest Lehman, *Seven Brides for Seven Brothers*
1955 Daniel Fuchs and Isobel Lennart, *Love Me or Leave Me*
1956 Ernest Lehman, *The King and I*
1957 John Patrick, *Les Girls*
1958 Alan Jay Lerner, *Gigi*
1959 Melville Savelson and Jack Rose, *The Five Pennies*
1960 Betty Comden and Adolph Gren, *Bells Are Ringing*
1961 Ernest Lehman, *West Side Story*
1962 Marion Hargrove, *The Music Man*
1963 No Award
1964 Bill Walsh and Don Da Gradi, *Mary Poppins*
1965 Ernest Lehman, *The Sound of Music*

SCREENPLAY DEALING MOST ABLY WITH PROBLEMS OF THE AMERICAN SCENE (The Robert Meltzer Award)

1948 Frank Partos and Millen Brand, *The Snake Pit*
1949 Robert Rossen, *All the King's Men*
1950 Carl Foreman, *The Men*
1951 Robert Bruckner, *Bright Victory*

The Laurel Award for Screen which is represented by a silver medallion, annually recognizes contributions of note to the screenwriting profession. Only members of the Guild are eligible for this honor. A television award is also given, listed elsewhere in this volume.

1953 Sonya Levien
1954 Dudley Nichols
1955 Robert Riskin
1956 Julius and Philip Epstein
Albert Hackett
Frances Goodrich
1957 Charles Brackett
Billy Wilder
1958 John Lee Mahin
1959 Nunnally Johnson
1960 Norman Krasna
1961 George Seaton
1962 Philip Dunne
1963 Joseph L. Mankiewicz
1964 John Huston
1965 Sidney Buchman
1966 Isobel Lennart
1967 Richard Brooks
1968 Casey Robinson
1969 Carl Foreman
1970 Dalton Trumbo
1971 James Poe
1972 Ernest Lehman
1973 William Rose
1974 Paddy Chayefsky
1975 Preston Sturges
1976 Michael Wilson
1977 Samson Raphaelson
1978 Edward Anhalt
1979 Neil Simon
1980 Billy Wilder
I.A.L. Diamond

Music & Dance

Contents

Related Awards

AWAPA Statuette
Hall of Fame Induction

NATIONAL BAND ASSOCIATION
Box 6, Ada, Ohio 45810 (419/634-7600)

The nine-inch silver Academy of Wind and Percussion Arts statuette is awarded as merited to honor an individual for significant and outstanding contributions to bands and band music. A three-member commission appointed by the Academy's president selects the winner.

1961 **William Revelli,** Ann Arbor, Mich.
1962 **Karl L. King**
1963 **No award**
1964 **No award**
1965 **Harold D. Bachman**
Glenn Cliffe Bainum
1966 **No award**
1967 **No award**
1968 **Merle Evans,** Sarasota, Fla.
1969 **Harry Guggenheim**
Al G. Wright, W. Lafayette, Ind.
Paul V. Yoder, Fort Lauderdale, Fla.
1970 **Toshio Akiyama,** Tokyo, Japan
1971 **Richard Franko Goldman,** Baltimore, Md.
1972 **Richard M. Nixon,** Washington, D.C., and San Clemente, Calif.
John Paynter, Evanston, Ill.
1973 **Sir Vivian Dunn,** Sussex, U.K.
Traugott Rohner, Evanston, Ill.
1974 **Jan Molenaar,** Wormerveer, Netherlands
1975 **Frederick Fennell,** Miami, Fla.
1976 **George S. Howard,** San Antonio, Tex.
Harry Mortimer, London
1977 **Mark Hindsley,** Champaign-Urbana, Ill.
1978 **Vaclav Nelhybel,** Newton, Conn.
James Neilson, Kenosha, Wis.
1979 **Leonard Falcone,** E. Lansing, Mich.
Alfred Reed, Coral Gables, Fla.
1980 **Nilo Hovey,** Elkhart, Ind.
Arnold D. Gabriel, Washington, D.C.

The National Band Association has created a Hall of Fame for Distinguished Band Conductors. Nomination is open to all individuals who have reached the age of 65 and who have distinguished themselves as conductors in the band field. The Hall of Fame electors choose those to be inducted. The Hall of Fame is located on the campus of Troy State University, Troy, Ala.

G.H. Bainum
Col. Harold Bachman
Cdr. Charles Brendler
Capt. Howard Bronson
Herbert Clark
Patrick Conway
Henry Fillmore
Pat Gilmore
E.F. Goldman
A.A. Harding
Karl King
Col. Sam Loboda
A.R. McAllister
Arthur Pryor
Col. W.H. Santelman
Frank Simon
J.P. Sousa

Boston Ballet Award

BOSTON BALLET
553 Tremont St., Boston, Mass. 02116 (617/542-1323)

The Boston Ballet Award, which carries a $5,000 honorarium, highlights the annual International Choreographers Showcase. Choreographers who are citizens or residents of the United States are invited to submit applications, including a videotape or film and other supporting material, for a ballet which has not yet had a world premier before a paying audience and which requires 20 or fewer dancers and "minimal" costumes or scenery and which is performed to recorded music. The artistic staff of the Boston Ballet selects the finalists, whose works are performed by the Boston troupe before an opening night audience which includes three judges who select the winner.

1979 **Constantin Patsalas,** choreographer and soloist, National Ballet of Canada
1980 **Joel Schnee,** ballet director, Kassel Ballet (Germany)

Gran Premio Alfredo Casella
Daniela Napolitano Prize

ACCADEMIA MUSICALE NAPOLETANA
Via S. Pasquale 62, 80121 Naples, Italy (Tel. 415-292 and 397-708)

The Gran Premio Alfredo Casella is given to the winner of the biennial Alfredo Casella Piano Competition. Entrants between the ages of eighteen and thirty-two undergo a three-step elimination and judging process, the last being a public performance. The total cash award is 1.5-million lire, and a silver cup is given.

1952 **George Solchany,** Hungary
1954 **Esteban Sanchez Herrero,** Spain
Walter Blankentheim, Germany
1956 **Gabriel Tacchino,** "Italian-French"
1958 **Ivan Davis,** U.S.A.
1960 **Pierre Ives le Roux,** France
1962 **Richard Siracuse,** "Italian-American"
1964 **Sergio Varella Cid,** Portugal
1966 **Michele Campanella,** Italy
1968 **Franco Medori,** Italy (tied for second place; no first)
Ewa Anna Osinska, Poland (tied for second place; no first)
1970 **Alain Pierre Neveux,** France
1972 **Michel Krist,** Germany
1974 **Christian Blakschaw,** Great Britain
1976 **Sandro de Palma,** Italy
Gerald Oppitz, Germany

Current Status Unknown

The Daniela Napolitano Prize is given to the winner of the biennial Alfredo Casella Competition of Composition. An international jury selects the winner, who receives a gold medal and has his/her composition published.

1960 **Filip Pires,** Portugal
1962 **No award**
1964 **Carlo Cammarota,** Italy
Jose Soproni, Hungary
1966 **No award**
1968 **Mauro Bortolotti,** Italy
1970 **Teresa Procaccini,** Italy

1972 No award
1974 No award
1976 **David Saperstein,** U.S.A.

Current Status Unknown

American Dance Guild Award

AMERICAN DANCE GUILD
1133 Broadway, Room 1427, New York, N.Y. 10010 (212/691-7773)

The American Dance Guild Annual Award, which consists of a statuette and a plaque, is given annually for outstanding service to dance. The winner is selected by the awards committee, with approval of the board of directors.

1970 **Genevieve Oswald,** Established Dance Collection at Library of Performing Arts,
1971 **Marion Van Tuyl,** Educator at Mills College and editor of *Impulse*
1972 **Irmgard Bartenieff,** Pioneer in effort/shape and dance therapy
1973 **Ruth Lovell Murray,** Educator in dance in elementary education.
1974 **Martha Hill Davies,** Pioneer in college education
1975 **Katherine Dunham,** For work as a performer and in community-related work.
1976 **Selma Jeanne Cohen,** Dance scholar and historian
1977 **Antony Tudor,** Choreographer
1978 **Beate Gordon,** Asia Society Performing Arts Program
1979 **Merce Cunningham**
1980 **Anna Halprin**

American Music Conference Award

NATIONAL NEWSPAPER ASSOCIATION
1627 K St. NW, Ste. 400, Washington, D.C. 20006 (202/466-7200)

Plaques are awarded annually to the newspaper judged to do the most creative and effective job of reporting on the amateur musical scene in communities and local schools. Interviews, features and news stories are considered, but reviews are not. In addition to the first-place winners listed here awards are also given to second- and third-place newspapers. The winners of this award, which is sponsored by the American Music Conference and administered by the National Newspaper Association, receive plaques. A panel of newspaper editors and reporters selects the recipients.

OVER 4,000 CIRCULATION

1973 ***Meridien*** (Miss.) ***Towne Courier***
1974 ***North Platte*** (N.D.) ***Telegraph***

UNDER 4,000 CIRCULATION

1973 ***Orville*** (Ohio) ***Courier-Crescent***
1974 ***Monticello*** (Minn.) ***Times***
1975 ***Kettering-Oakwood*** (Ohio) ***Times***
Visalia (Calif.) ***Times-Delta***
Birmingham (Ala.) ***Shades Valley Sun***
1976 ***Fairbury*** (Ill.) ***Blade***
Selma (Calif.) ***Enterprise***
Birmingham (Ala.) ***Shades Valley Sun***
1977 ***Columbia*** (Md.) ***Flier***
Columbia (Mo.) ***News Sun***
Monticello (Minn.) ***Times***
1978 **Cardinal Free Press** (Carpenterville, Ill.)
1979 **Eugene** (Ore.) ***Register-Guard***
1980 **San Rafael** (Cal.) ***Independent-Journal***

ASCAP-Deems Taylor Awards

AMERICAN SOCIETY OF COMPOSERS, AUTHORS AND PUBLISHERS
1 Lincoln Plaza, New York, N.Y. 10023 (212/595-3050)

The ASCAP-Deems Taylor Awards, which consist of honorariums totaling $10,000 to writers and plaques to publishers, are given annually for the best nonfiction books and articles in magazines or newspapers published in the United States on the subject of music or its creators. Six ASCAP judges—three each in popular and symphonic music—select the winners. The awards, though annual, are not given out regularly. In the list below, the awards are assigned to the year in which most of the work under consideration was completed and published.

BOOKS

1968 **George T. Simon,** *The Big Bands* (Macmillan Co.)
Sidney Shemel and M. William Krasilovsky, *More About this Business of Music* (*Billboard*)
George Eells, *The Life That Late He Led* (G.P. Putnam's Sons)
1969 **Gunther Schuller,** *Early Jazz* (Oxford University Press)
Ravi Shankar, *My Music, My Life* (Simon & Schuster)
Otto Deri, *Exploring Twentieth-Century Music* (Holt, Rinehart and Winston)
1970 **Alan Rich,** *Music: Mirror of the Arts* (Praeger Publishers and Ridge Press)
Irving Kolodin, *The Continuity of Music* (Alfred A. Knopf)
Milton Goldin, *The Music Merchants* (Macmillan Co.)
1971 **Lee Elliot Berk,** *Legal Protection for the Creative Musician* (Berklee Press)
Ned Rorem, *Critical Affairs—A Composer's Journal* (George Braziller)
Aksel Schiotz, *The Singer and His Art* (Harper & Row)
1972 **Charles Rosen,** *The Classical Style: Haydn, Mozart, Beethoven* (Viking Press)
Eileen Southern, *The Music of Black Americans, A History* (W. W. Norton and Co.)
Tom Stoddard, *Pops Foster—The Autobiography of a New Orleans Jazzman* (University of California Press)
Martin Williams, *The Jazz Tradition* (Oxford University Press)
1973 **Lillian Libman,** *And Music At The Close: Stravinsky's Last Years* (W. W. Norton & Co.)
Alec Wilder, *American Popular Song—The Great Innovators, 1900-1950* (Oxford University Press)
Richard A. Peterson and R. Serge Denisoff, *Sounds of Social Change* (Rand McNally)
Boris Schwarz, *Music and Musical Life In Soviet Russia 1917-1970* (W. W. Norton & Co.)
Lehman Engel, *Words With Music* (Macmillan Co.)

1974 **Henry-Louis de La Grange,** *Mahler* (Doubleday & Co.)
Max Wilk, *They're Playing Our Song* (Atheneum)
Myra Friedman, *Buried Alive* (Wm. Morrow & Co.)
Duke Ellington, *Music Is My Mistress* (Doubleday & Co.)
Philip Hart and Claire Brook, *Orpheus In The New World* (W.W. Norton & Co.)

1975 **J. H. Kwabena Nketia,** *The Music Of Africa* (W. W. Norton & Co.)
Ned Rorem, *The Final Diary* (Holt, Rinehart and Winston)
Edward T. Cone, *The Composer's Voice* (University of California Press)
Howard Dietz, *Dancing In The Dark* (Quadrangle)
Hampton Hawes and Don Asher, *Raise Up Off Me* (Coward, McCann & Geoghegan)

1976 **Vera Brodsky Lawrence,** *Music for Patriots, Politicians, and Presidents* (Macmillan)
Philip S. Foner, *American Labor Songs of the Nineteenth Century* (University of Illinois Press)
Frank R. Rossiter, *Charles Ives & His America* (Liveright Publishing)
Leonard Stein, *Style and Idea* (St. Martin's Press)
Charles Rosen, *Arnold Schoenberg* (Viking Press)

1977 **Dan Morgenstern,** *Jazz People* (Harry N. Abrams)
Albert Murray, *Stomping The Blues* (McGraw Hill)
Larry Sandberg and Dick Weissman, *The Folk Music Sourcebook* (Alfred A. Knopf)
Geoffrey Stokes, *Starmaking Machinery* (Bobbs-Merrill Co.)
Leo Kraft, *Gradus* (W. W. Norton & Co.)

1978 **John Hammond**, *John Hammond on Record* (Ridge Press)
Edward Lowinsky, *Josquin de Prez* (Oxford University Press)
Howard E. Smither, *A History of the Oratorio* (University of North Carolina Press)
Maynard Solomon, *Bethoven* (Schirmer Books)
Jeff Todd Titon, *Early Downhome Blues* (University of Illinois Press)

1979 **H.C. Robbins Landon**, *Hayden: Chronicle and Works,* Vol. II (Indiana University Press)
Richard H. Hoppin, *Medieval Music* (W.W. Norton)
Paul F. Berliner, *The Soul of Moira* (University of California Press)
Warren Babb and **Paul V. Palisca**, *Hucbald, Guido & John on Music — Three Medieval Treatises* (Yale University Press)
Arnold Shaw, *Honkers and Shouters* (Macmillan)
James Haskins and **Kathleen Benson**, *Scott Joplin — The Man Who Made Ragtime* (Doubleday)

1980 **Samuel Lipman**, *Music After Modernism* (Basic Books)
Hans Moldenhsuer and **Rosaleen Moldenhauer**, *Anton von Webern* (Knopf)
Daniel W. Patterson, *The Shaker Spiritual* (Princeton University Press)
Isabel Pope and **Masakata Kanazawa**, *The Musical Manuscript —Montecasino 871* (Oxford University Press)
Roger Sessions, *Roger Sessions on Music* (Princeton University Press)
Solomon Velkov and **Antonia W. Bouis**, *Testimony — The Memoirs of Dmitri Shostakovich* (Harper & Row)
David Baskerville, *Music Business Handbook and Career Guide* (Sherwood)
Xavier M. Frascogna, Jr., and **H. Lee Hetherington**, *Successful Artist Management* (Billboard Books)
Nolan Porterfield, *The Life and Times of America's Blue Yodeler —Jimmie Rodgers* (University of Illinois Press)
William P. Gottlieb, *The Golden Age of Jazz* (Simon & Schuster)
Eric von Schmidt and **Jim Rooney**, *Baby, Let Me Follow You Down* (Anchor Books)

ARTICLES

1968 **James Ringo,** five reviews (*The American Record Guide*)
Arnold Shaw, articles (*Cavalier*)
Joan Peyser, article (*Columbia University Forum*)

1969 **Joan Peyser,** article (*New York Times*)
James Ringo, article (*American Record Guide*)
James Lyons, notes (*Boston Symphony Orchestra Program*)

1970 **Ralph J. Gleason,** article (*Lithopinion*)
Alan Rich, article (*New York Magazine*)
Issachar Miron, article (*New York Times*)

1971 **Boris E. Nelson,** 19 articles (*Toledo Blade*)
Paul Glass, "A Hiatus in American Music History" (*Afro-American Studies*)
Louis Carp, "Mozart: His Tragic Life and Controversial Death" (*Bulletin,* N.Y. Academy of Medicine)

1972 **Elliott W. Galkin,** articles (*Baltimore Sun*)
George Perle, "Webern's Twelve-Tone Sketches" (*The Musical Quarterly*)
Ralph J. Gleason, "God Bless Louis Armstrong" (*Rolling Stone*)
Irving Lowens, articles (*Washington Star*)

1973 **Martin Bernheimer,** article (*Los Angeles Times*)
Alan Rich, article (*New York Magazine*)
Robert Finn, article (*Cleveland Plain Dealer*)
Bruce Pollock, article (*Rock Magazine*)

1974 **Jack O'Brien,** syndicated columns
Hubert Saal, (*Newsweek*)
Ben Fong Torres, (*Rolling Stone*)
Alan Rich, (*New York Magazine*)

1975 **Richard Franko Goldman,** "American Music: 1918-1960" chapter in *The New Oxford History of Music* (Oxford University Press)
Ralph J. Gleason, "Farewell to the Duke" (*Rolling Stone*)
Elliott W. Galkin, articles (*Baltimore Sun*)
Andrew Porter, articles (*The New Yorker*)
David Hamilton, articles (*The New Yorker*)

1976 **Robert Commanday,** (*San Francisco Chroncile*)
Richard Dyer, (*Boston Globe*)
Jack O'Brien, syndicated columns (King Features Syndicate)
Gary Giddins, articles (*Village Voice*)

1977 **Paul Baratta,** (*Songwriter Magazine*)
Gary Giddins, (*Village Voice*)
Maureen Orth, (*Newsweek*)
Samuel Lipman, (Commentary)
Karen Monson, (*Chicago Daily News*)
Irving Lowens, (*Washington Star*)
Richard Dyer, (*Boston Globe*)
John Ardoin, (*Dallas Morning News*)

1978 **Martin Bernheimer,** (*Los Angeles Times*)
Andrew Porter (*The New Yorker*)
David Burge (*Contemporary Keyboard*)
George Perle (*International Alban Berg Society Newsletter*)
Gene Lees (*High Fidelity*)
Joe Klein (*Rolling Stone*)

1979 **David Burge** (*Contemporary Keyboard*)
Robert Finn (*Cleveland Plain Dealer*)
Bernard Hollander (*Pittsburgher*)
Leighton Kerner (*Village Voice*)
Michael Nelson (*Baltimore Magazine*)
Paul Nelson (*Rolling Stone*)
Jack O'Brian King Features
Tony Schwartz (*Newsweek*)
1980 **Margaret Mary Barela** (*College Music Symposium*)
Samuel Lipman (*Commentary*)
Walter Schenkman (*American Music Teacher*)
Lloyd Schwartz (*Boston Phoenix*)
Michael Walsh (*San Francisco Examiner and Chronicle*)
Witney Balliet (*The New Yorker*)
Michele Kort (*Songwriter*)
John Lahr (*Harper's*)
Diane Sward Rapaport (*Contemporary Keyboard*)

Bach International Award

AMERICAN BACH FOUNDATION
1211 Potomac St. NW, Washington, D.C. 20007
(202/338-1111)

The Johann Sebastian Bach International Competitions are held almost every year at Washington's George Washington University under the sponsorship of the Eugene and Agnes E. Meyer Foundation, organized by the American Bach Foundation. The winners receive a number of performance options plus various cash awards, now including the $500 H.E. Berndt von Staden Award presented by the Ambassador of the Federal Republic of Germany, the $1,000 Mr. and Mrs. David Lloyd Kreeger first prize for violinists and the $1,000 Youth Concerts Foundation Award for first place in the cello competition. Additionally, cash prizes are given to the second- and third-place winners. Starting in 1978, violinists and cellists between seventeen and thirty-five years of age may enter the competition, which is judged by a three-person panel. Previously, the contest was for pianists, who received prizes similar to those offered to string musicians in 1978.

PIANISTS

1960 **Zola Shaulis,** U.S.A.
1961 **Tasker Polk,** U.S.A.
1962 **Bonnie Boggle,** U.S.A.
1963 **No award**
1964 **Michele Levin,** U.S.A.
1965 **Pamela Le Nevez,** Australia
1966 **Paul Posnak,** U.S.A.
Sontraud Speidel, Germany
1967 **No award**
1968 **Mari-Elizabeth Morgen,** Canada
1969 **Marilyn Engle,** Canada
1970 **No award**
1971 **Peter Vinograde,** U.S.A.
1972 **No award**
1973 **Hans Carl Boepple,** U.S.A.
1974 **No award**
1975 **Bronislawa Kawalla,** Poland
1976 **Michael Landrum,** U.S.A.
1977 **No award**

PIANISTS AND STRING INSTRUMENTALISTS

1978 **Charles Curtis** (cellist)
Timothy Baker (violinist)
1979 **No award**
1980 **Pi'hsein Chen**

BMI Awards to Student Composers Commendation of Excellence

BROADCAST MUSIC INCORPORATED
320 W. 57th St., New York, N.Y. 10019 (212/586-2000)

The annual BMI Awards to Student Composers total $15,000 and now range from $500 to $2,500 per recipient, awarded at the discretion of a judges' panel, which selects winners from manuscripts or recorded works. Applicants must be citizens or permanent residents of a Western Hemisphere country, be under twenty-six years of age and be enrolled in an accredited secondary or postsecondary school or study music privately with established teachers. Only one original composition, created during the previous year, may be entered. In addition to the winners listed below, Honorable Mentions are occasionally made.

1952 **Elnora Case**
Eugene Cramer
Alvin L. Epstein
Robert Gauldin
Virginia Gittens
Barrie W. Heitkamp
Donald Jenni
Donald Martino
Earl K. Scott, Jr
Hale Smith, Jr.
Rodger D. Vaughan
Jean Winters
1953 **Dominick Argento**
William Bolcom
Ramiro Cortes
Higo H. Harada
Frederick Heutte
Michael Kassler
Teo Macero
Donald Martino
Donald Scavarda
David Ward-Steinman
1954 **Genevieve Chinn**
Ramiro Cortes
David M. Epstein
Edwin A. Freeman
Jack S. Gottlieb
John Harbison
Donald Jenni
Russell J. Peck
Arno Safran
Roland Trogan
David Ward-Steinman
1955 **Donald Jenni**
Michael Kassler
1956 **Bruce Archibald**
Jan Bach
Robert Bernat
Allen Brings
Richmond Browne
George H. Crumb
George C. Forest
Samuel Gale
Michael Kassler
Robert Lombardo
Leon Clayton Nedbalek

Michael Sahl
Jose Serenbrier
1957 Seymour Altucher
Richmond Browne
Frank Philip Campo
William Bayard Carlin
Ramiro Cortes
Paul Glass
Michael Kassler
Jack Normain Kimmel
Robert Lombardo
Donal R. Michalsky
Henry Onderdonk
1958 David S. Bates
Jed Curtis
Marjorie Greif
Michael M. Horvit
Gerald Humel
Alan Kemler
J. Theodore Prochazka
Thomas R. Putsche
William Wilder
1959 Mario Davidovsky
Philip M. Glass
Ellen Glickman
David Serrendero Proust
David Ward-Steinman
Charles Wuorinen
1960 Stephen J. Albert
Mark Bernard DeVoto
Stephen D. Fisher
William Hibbard
Arthur Murphy
Fredric Myrow
Robert Sheff
David Ward-Steinman
1961 William H. Albright
Michael Fink
Robert Fraser Glover
Arthur B. Hunkins
Marlos Nobre
David Saperstein
Robert Suderburg
Charles Wuorinen
1962 Conal Boyce
Charles M. Dodge
Alan Leichtling
William McKinley
Arthur Murphy
Richard Toensing
Charles Wuorinen
1963 Alvin S. Curran
Charles M. Dodge
Humphrey Evans III
Steve Gellman
Steven Gilbert
Peter F. Huse
Dennis K.M. Kam
Ellene S. Levenson
Fredric Myrow
John Earl Rogers
David Saperstein
Hal Tamblyn
Richard Toensing
Charles Wuorinen
1964 Luis Arias
Harley Gaber
John Heineman
Russell J. Peck
Phillip C. Rhodes
David Saperstein
1965 William Benjamin
Robert S.W. Buckley
Peter M. Dickey
Charles M. Dodge
Steven Gilbert
Robert Henderson
Roger O. Johnson
Judith Lang
Richard Manners
Frank L. McCarty
Joan Panetti
Phillip C. Rhodes
Joseph C. Schwantner
David N. Stewart
1966 William H. Albright
Charles M. Dodge
Humphrey Evans III
Daniel Foley
David Foley
Clare Franco
Steven Gilbert
Hugh Hartwell
Brian M. Israel
John M. Mills-Cockell
Lawrence Morton
Peter Ness
Joan Panetti
Russell J. Peck
Dennis D. Riley
Eric N. Robertson
Joseph C. Schwantner
Luis Maria Serra
Richard T. Trifan
Alice Webber
1967 Richard S. Ames
Stephen S. Dankner
Stephen Dickman
Primous Fountain III
Harley Gaber
Dennis K.M. Kam
Howard Lubin
William David Noon
Eugene O'Brien
Dennis D. Riley
Joseph C. Schwantner
Daria Semegen
Kathleen Solose
Greg A. Steinke
1968 Bruce M. Adolphe
William H. Albright
Kurt Carpenter
Stephen Dickman
Dennis J. Eberhard
Paul H. Epstein
David Foley
Clare Franco
Peter Griffith
John Hawkins
Brian M. Israel
Terrence T. Kincaid
Howard Lubin
Robert Morris
Russell J. Peck
John Rea
Walter B. Saul
Ryan L. Whitney
Hugh M. Wolff
1969 Robert Boury
Humphrey Evans III

Daniel Foley
Andrew Frank
Stephen Hartke
Jeffrey Jones
Daniel Kessner
Jeffrey Kresky
Gerald Levinson
Denis Lorrain
Howard Lubin
John M. Mann
Peter Salemi
Walter B. Saul
Daria Semegen
Donald A. Steven
Preston Trombly
Hugh M. Wolff

1970 John Adams
William Eric Benson
Mickey Cohen
Daniel Foley
Andrew Frank
Joan Harkness
Daniel Kessner
David Koblitz
Gerald Levinson
Philip Magnuson
Robert P. Mounsey
William David Noon
Eugene O'Brien
Steven Sandberg
Michael Seyfrit
Michael Udow
Hugh M. Wolff

1971 Kurt Carpenter
John A. Celona
John Stepehn Dydo
Guy Hallman
Stephen Hartke
Joel Hoffman
David Koblitz
Matthias Kriesberg
Michel Longtin
Stephen L. Mosko
John Sarracco
Ira Taxin
David Winkler

1972 Donald Crockett
Sydney Goodwin
Gary Hardie
Denis Lorrain
William Matthews
Christopher Rouse
Brian Schober
Charles Sepos
Philip Stoll
Bruce J. Taub
Wayne A. Walker
Mark E. Wilson

1973 W. Claude Baker, Jr.
Larry Bell
Ronald Braunstein
Stephen Chatman
Robert Dick
Eric Ewazen
David Koblitz
Rachel Kutten
Gerald Levinson
William Matthews
Stephen L. Mosko
Jay Reise
Christopher Rouse
Helge Skjeveland
Ira Taxin

1974 Stephen Chatman
Stephen Dembski
Richard Derby
Hal Freedman
Margaret Ann Griebling
Murray Gross
Stephen A. Jaffe
Carson Kievman
William Matthews
Jay Reise
Rodney I. Rogers
Christopher Roze

1975 Todd Brief
Alexander Cardona
Stephen Chatman
Theodore Dollarhide
Jonathan Drexler
Burton Goldstein
Dan Gutwin
Carson Kievman
Stephen Lano
William Maiben
Daniel Plante
Rodney I. Rogers
David Shuler
Jeffrey Wood
Lenard Yen

1976 Allen Anderson
Alexander Xavier Cardona
Thomas Crawford
William C. Heinrichs
Joseph A. Hudson
Ralph N. Jackson
Aaron Kernis
David Moser McKay
Cindy McTee
Rodney Rogers
Philip Rosenberg
Mark Howard Steidel
Randall Edgar Stokes

1977 Scott M. Fessler
Ralph N. Jackson
Michael H. Kurek
Mindy Lee
Tobias Picker
Edgardo J. Simone
David Snow
Lenard Yen

1978 Michael P. Arnowitt
Daniel Asia
Susan Blaustein
Michael Cherry
Jeffrey V. Cotton
Corey Field
Matthew L. Harris
Matthias Kriesberg
Anne LeBaron
Denise Ondishko
Matthew Rosenblaum
Monte Schwartzwalder
Keith A. Paulson Thorp
Jeffrey Wood

1979 Corey Field
Mark Gustavson
Kevin Hanion
Charles N. Mason
Priya Mayadas

William Neil
Larry Polansky
David Show
Jeffrey Wood
1980 **Donald R. Davis**
Corey Field
Mark Gustavson
Rebecca Hammann
Charles N. Mason
Priya Mayadas
William Neil
Larry Polansky
Thomas Sergey
Ray Shattenkirk
David Snow
Jeffrey Wood

The Commendation of Excellence is award for long and outstanding contribution to the world of concert music.

1979 **Joseph C. Schwantner**, 1979 Pulitzer Prize winner and three-time recipient of the BMI Student Composer Prize
1980 **William Schuman**, Pulitzer Prize winner and for 28 years chairman of the BMI Awards Judging Panel

Beethoven Piano Prize

HOCHSCHULE FUR MUSIK UND DARSTELLENDE KUNST
Lothringerstrasse 18, A-1037 Vienna, Austria (0222-56 16 85)

The quadrennial International Beethoven Piano Competiton carries a 60,000-schilling honorarium for the first-place winner, plus cash awards for the second- and third-place honorees. The competition is open to pianists aged 17 through 32.

1961 **Dieter Weber**, Austria (second prize; no first given)
1965 **Lois Carole Pachucki**, U.S.A.
1969 **Mitsuko Uchida**, Japan
1973 **John O'Connor**, Ireland
1977 **Natalia Pankova**, U.S.S.R.

Busoni Prize

CONCORSO BUSONI
Vicolo Gummer, 39100 Bolzano, Italy

The Busoni Prize is given in conjunction with the annual International Piano Competition run by the Savings Bank of the Province of Bolzano until 1980 and by the Municipality of Bolzano beginning in 1981. A jury hears applicants perform a twenty- to thirty-minute musical program, which conforms to a proscribed set of requirements. A million-lire contract for a concert and recital series is offered to the winner. In addition to the first-place winners listed here, second-, third- and fourth-place honors are given here. The Busoni Competition began in 1949, but the first prize was not awarded until 1952 and is frequently not granted.

1952 **Sergio Perticaroli,** Italy
1953 **Ella Goldstein,** U.S.A.
1954 **Aldo Mancinelli,** U.S.A.
1955 **No award**
1956 **Joerg Demus,** Austria
1957 **Martha Argerich,** Argentina
1958 **No award**
1959 **No award**
1960 **No award**
1961 **Jerome Rose,** U.S.A.
1962 **No award**
1963 **No award**
1964 **Michael Ponti,** U.S.A.
1965 **No award**
1966 **Garrick Ohlsson,** U.S.A.
1967 **No award**
1968 **Vladimir Selivochin,** U.S.S.R.
1969 **Ursula Oppens,** U.S.A.
1970 **No award**
1971 **No award**
1972 **Arnaldo Cohen,** Brazil
1973 **No award**
1974 **Robert Benz,** Germany
1975 **No award**
1976 **Roberto Cappello,** Italy
1977 **No award**
1978 **Boris Bloch,** U.S.A.
1979 **Catherine Vickers Steiert**, Canada
1980 **No award**

Buxtehude Preis

HANSASTADT LUBECK
Rathaus, 24000 Lubeck, Germany (0451/121)

The Buxtehude-Preis or Buxtehude Prize is given approximately every two years for outstanding work in the field of church music. The award, which carries a 5,000-mark honorarium, is given on nomination by the Lubeck board of Culture and ratification by the Council of the Hansastadt Lubeck.

1951 **Hugo Distler**, Composer
1952 **Johann Nepomuk David**, Composer
1953 **Ernst Pepping**, Composer
1957 **Eberhard Wenzel**, Composer and musician
1959 **No award**
1961 **No award**
1963 **Oskar Sohngen**, Music scientist
1965 **No award**
1967 **No award**
1969 **Bruno Grusnick**, Music scientist and musician
1972 **Soren Sorensen**, Music scientist
1975 **Marie-Claire Alain**, Organist
1978 **Georg Karstadt**, Music scientist

Capezio Dance Award

CAPEZIO FOUNDATION
755 Seventh Ave., New York, N.Y. 10019 (212/245-7740)

The Capezio Dance Award is given annually for a lifetime contribution to dance by artists and devotees of dance. An award committee selects the winner, who receives $1,000 and a plaque.

1952 **Zachary Solov**
1953 **Lincoln Kirstein**
1954 **Doris Humphrey**
1955 **Louis Horst**
1956 **Genevieve Oswald**
1957 **Ted Shawn**
1958 **Alexandra Danilova**
1959 **Sol Hurok**
1960 **Martha Graham**

1961 Ruth St. Denis
1962 Barbara Karinska
1963 Donald McKayle
1964 Jose Limon
1965 Maria Tallchief
1966 Agnes De Mille
1967 Paul Taylor
1968 Lucia Chase
1969 John Martin
1970 William Kolodney
1971 Arthur Mitchell
1972 Gladys and Reginald Laubin
La Meri
1973 Isadora Bennett
1974 Robert Joffrey
1975 Robert Irving
1976 Jerome Robbins
1977 Merce Cunningham
1978 Hanya Holm
1979 Alvin Ailey
1980 Walter Terry

Alessandro Casagrande Piano Prize

CONCORSO INTERNAZIONALE DE PIANO ISTICO ALLESANDRO CASAGRANDE
Comune di Terni, I-05100, Terni, Italy (40 11 73 -56 120)

The Concorso Internazaionale Pianistico Alessandro Casagrande is an annual piano competiton for musicians thirty-two years of age or younger. The jury selects the recipient of the first prize, which carries a 2,000,000-lire honorarium, plus two other cash awards.

1966 **Guiliano Silveri**, Italy
1967 **Fausto Di Cesare**, Italy
1968 No award
1969 **Bozidar Moev**, Bulgaria
1970 **Martha Dejanova**, Bulgaria
1971 **Luis Medalha**, Brazil
Laslo Simon, Hungary
1972 **Nine Lichman**, U.S.A.
1973 **Kathleen Solose**, Canada
1974 **Robert Groslot**, Belgium
1975 **Petrushansky Boris**, U.S.S.R.
1976 **Takeda Makiko**, Japan
1977 **Alexander Longrich**, Germany
1978 **Ivo Pogorelic**, Yugoslavia
1979 No award
1980 **Guher Pekinel** and **Suher Pekinel**, Turkey

Concert Artists Guild Awards

CONCERT ARTISTS GUILD
154 W. 57th St., New York, N.Y. 10019 (212/757-8344)

A maximum of 10 awards a year are available to instrumentalists thirty years old or younger, singers thirty-five or younger and ensembles averaging thirty or younger who have not made a formal New York debut. Awards, based on preliminary and final auditions, are made at the Carnegie Recital Hall. The Guild assumes the recital cost and gives a cash award of $250 for soloists and $500 for ensembles.

1951 Anita Katchen
Frank Martori
Robin Allardice
Richard Leshin
Ira Shur
Nathan Goldstein
Elizabeth Devlin
Barbara Berkman
Kenneth Chertok
Alan Grishman
Sandra Propp
Laurence Watson
Otis Wilensky
Sally Allen
Angela Pistelli
Thaddeus Brys
Ruth Brall
Roger Kamien
Yvette Rudin
Vincent Sperando
Rosalie Adagna
Pasquale Verduce
Thea Glussman
Mme. Simon Barere
Harriet Emerson
Helen Rice
Samuel Sanders
1952 Catalina Zandueta
Leah Mellman
Gabriel Banat
Esther Fernandez
Ara Charles Adrian
Eleanor Mandel
Olanda Drewery
Virginia-Gene Shankel
Shirley Bardin
Byron Goode
Helen Spina
Mary-Louise Brown
Robert Natkoff
Valerie Lamoree
Samuel Sanders
Militades Siadimas
Charlotte Bloecher
Harry Wimmer
Allen Rogers
Dina Soresi
Daniel Abrams
Louis F. Simon
Joseph Plon
Andrew Frierson
1953 Ellen Alexander
Paul Gurevich
David Wells
Robert Hearn
Leyna Gabriele
Leonor Umstead
Barbara Allen
Beverly Somach
Anita Katchen
Muriel Kirby
Oliver Colbentson
Ruth Lakeway
Allen Brown
Norma Ferris
Uzi Wiesel
William deValentine
Stephen Manes
Arabella Honig
Stanley Babin
Dorothy Phillips
Christina C. Cardillo
1954 Evelyn Lear

Isador Lateiner
Sheila Minzer
Gertrude Prinzi
Martin Canin
Nancy Cirillo
Thomas Stewart
Bruce Stegg
Martin Eshelman
Mara Shorr
Mitchell Andrews
Charles Dunn
Bernard Kreger
Shirley Givins
Sosio Manzo
Marvin Morgenstern
Eileen DiTullio
Donald Betts
Robert Menga
Emilia Cundari
1955 Betty Allen
Erick Friedman
Dorothy Happel
Andrew Heath
Ellen Pahl
Zelda Gilgore
Alexander Horvath
Sara Jane Fleming
Frances Bartley
Ramy Shevelov
Joan Marie Moynagh
Emilio Rosario
Elaine Bonazzi
John Browning
William Metcalf
Ralph Feinstein
Clifford Snyder
Audrey Kooper
Harry Wimmer
Donna Pegors
Eugenia Hyman
Lorraine Wollnik
John Pidgeon
1956 Charles Castleman
Daniel Pollack
Ada Pinchuk
Madelyn Vose
Nancy Hall
Manuel Maramba
Lynn Rasmussen
Harold Jones
Margarita Zambrana
Deanne Garcy
Denver Oldham
Sophia Steffan
Mary Freeman
Angelica Lozada
Morey Ritt
Thomas Carey
1957 Shirley Verrett
Reri Grist
Tana Bawden
Donn Alexander-Feder
Richard Syracuse
Eva Marie Wolff
Grant Williams
Clifton Matthews
Mary Hensley
Charles Engel
Annina Celli
Olegna Fuschi
Jeanette Scovotti
Joseph Schwartz
Hyman Bress
Sheila Henig
1958 Judith Raskin
Howard Aibel
Joy Pottle
Harold S. Johnson
Margaret Kalil
Victoria Markowski
Francesco Cedrone
Mayne Miller
Judith Basch
Hugh Matheny
Herbert Chatzky
Howard Lebow
Raymond Michalski
Ramon Gilbert
Lois Carole Pachucki
Georgia Davis
Agustin Anievas
Martina Arroyo
1959 Alexander Fiorello
Dan Marek
Richard Kuelling
Doris Allen
Helen Cox Raab
Marilyn Anne Laughlin
Rita Schoen
Andre De La Varre
Enid Dale
Beatrice Rippy
Lois Carole Pachucki
Deborah Reeder
Maris-Stella Bonell
Phyllis Frankel
Jack Dane Litten
1960 George Shirley
Michael Rogers
Joan Wall
Carol Wilder
Charles Haupt
Catherine Wallace
Arline Billings
Mark Bellfort Chalat
Dolores Holtz
Patricia MacDonald
Naomi Weiss
Joanne Cohen
Albertine Baumgartner
Charles Wendt
Ronald Rogers
Ilana Vered
Laurel Miller
Toby Saks
1961 Vera Graf
Thomas S. Vasiloff
Maria Luisa Lopez-Vito
Rama Jucker
Malka Silberberg
Miguel Pinto
Harriet Lawyer
Marcia Heller
Alpha Brawner
David Rosentsein
Kenneth Goldsmith
Jesse Levine
Edgar Fischer
Edward Zolas
Gene Boucher

1962 Daniel Domb
Bonnie Bogle
Ernest Chang
Madeline Stevenson
Donald Walker
Isabel Berg
Donna Precht
Sanford Margolis
Masako Fujii
Evangelin Marko
Alan Finell
Marilyn Dubow
David Kaiserman
Marie Traficante
James Stafford
Alexandra Hunt
Wanda Maximillian
1963 Edward Aldwell
Nina Kaleska
Lee Dougherty
David Yeomans
Jung-ja Kim
Nan Gullo
Glen Jacobson
Evelyn Watson
Neal O'Doan
Grace Di Battista
Verica Fassel
Helen Merritt
Jamesetta Holliman
William Steck
Leonidas Lipovetsky
Mary Beck
Janet Goodman
1964 Richard Syracuse
William Cheadle
Jean Kraft
Stephen Flamberg
Winifred Dettore
Takaho Nishizaki
Shirley Love
Constance C. Douglass
Fernando Illanes
Louis Nagel
William Greene
Matithahu Braun
Sheila Schonbrun
Findlay Cockrell
Nancy Wyner
1965 Robert Preston
Phyllis Mailing
Roe Van Boskirk
Joan Summers
Ruth Glasser
Judith Allen
Sheldon Shkolnik
Clyde Tipton
David Garlock
Ruth McCoy Gatto
James Stroud
Mertine Johns
Karen Shaw
Sylvia Chambless Patrick
John Large
Richard Allen
1966 Richard Anderson
Gisela Depkat
Richard Allen
Sheila Schonbrun
Grayson Hirst
Jerome Rosen
Eleanor Edwards
LaVergne Monette
Ellen Hassman
Virginia Marks
Almita Hyman-Vamos
Judith Davidoff
Lanoue Davenport
Bruce Prince-Joseph
Ronald Roseman
1967 Christine Edinger
Yehuda Hanani
Odette Noslier
John Cerminaro
Romauld Tecco
Peter Basquin
Sivia Serrlya
Jody Lasky
Arthur Ozolins
Masako Yanagita
Donald Green
1968 Jerome Bunke
Barbara Chenault
Daniel Epstein
Diane Walsh
Michael Haran
Carmen Alvarez
Nathan Brand
Judith Hubbell
Hidemitsu Hayashi
Shari Anderson
1969 Yolanda Roman
Paul Posnak
Ivan Oak
Sandra Darling
Edith Kraft
Li-Ping Hsieh
Noelle Rogers
Betty Jones
1970 Gabriel Chodos
Elaine Comparone
Larry Graham
Irene Gubrud
Alan Marks
Yoko Nozaki
Gerardo Ribeiro
Idith Zvi
Justin Blasdale
James Kreger
Marsha Heller
Interaction:
Yuval Waldman
Paul Posnak
Jonathan Abramowitz
Daniel Epstein
James Kreger
William Henry
1971 Annie Kavafian
Robert Christesen
David Stern
Marioara Trifan
Daniel Waitzman
Etsuko Tazaki
1972 Susan Davenny Wyner
Pawel Checinski
Donald Green
Richard Fredrickson
Paul Tobias
Pamela Mia Paul
Davi Oei

Carol Wincenc
Sung-Kil Kim
David Stern
1973 Harvey Pittel
Susan Salm
Andrew Rangell
Sandra Miller
Nancy Evers
Marian Hahn
Jane Hamborsky
David Shifrin
Amanza Trio:
 Ida Bieler
 Eugene Moye, Jr.
 Mary Louise Vetrano
1974 Manuel Barrueco
Emanuel Gruber
Karen Johnson
David Northington
Gary Steigerwalt
Robin McCabe
Alan Weiss
Arisos Woodwind Quintet:
 Nadine Asin
 Anne Leek
 Gary McGee
 Daniel Worley
 David Wakefield
1975 Peter Corey
Annette Parker
Laufman Duo
Nancy Green
Raphael Trio:
 Daniel Epstein
 Susan Salm
 Charles Castleman
1976 Eugene Drucker
Elizabethan Enterprise:
 Lucy Cross
 Mary Springfels
 Wendy Gillespie
 David Hart
 Peter Becker
William Grubb
Mary Elizabeth Stephenson
Jacob Krichaf
Stewart Newbold
Stephanie Jutt
Katherine Ciesinski
William Black
Pamela Guidetti
1977 Chang/Kogan Duo (Lynn Chang and Richard Kogan)
Lois Shapiro
Quintet di Legno:
 Eric Thomas
 Gail Gillespie
 Ronald Haroutunian
 Thomas Haunton
 Claudia Wann
Michael Thomopoulos
Karen Buranskas
Daisietta Kim
William Hoyt
Franck Avril
1978 Trio d'Accordo:
 Jorja Fleezanis
 Yizhak Schotten
 Karen Andric
Rita Kneusel
Beverly Morgan
James Miller
Sonos Chamber Ensemble:
 George Plasko
 Karen Cornelius
 David Deveau
Dieuwke Schreuder
Ralph Evans
Michael Boriskin
Gwendolyn Bradley
1979 David Jolley
Marie Laferriere
Tyra Gilb
Martha Hartman Whitmore
Regina Mushabac
Sioned Williams
Janus Ensemble
1980 Ingrid Jacoby
Rhona Rider
Ann Hart
John Feeney and Julius Berger
Laura Hunter
Christopher Green-Armytage
One Plus One

Country Music Award

COUNTRY MUSIC ASSOCIATION
Box 22299, Nashville, Tenn. 37202 (615/244-2840)

Nominations for the Country Music Award, which is a bullet-shaped trophy, are submitted by members of the Association and subjected to a vote. Winners are announced on a national television show.

ENTERTAINER OF THE YEAR

1967 Eddy Arnold
1968 Glen Campbell
1969 Johnny Cash
1970 Merle Haggard
1971 Charley Pride
1972 Loretta Lynn
1973 Roy Clark
1974 Charlie Rich
1975 John Denver
1976 Mel Tillis
1977 Ronnie Milsap
1978 Dolly Parton
1979 Willie Nelson
1980 Barbara Mandrell

SINGLE OF THE YEAR

1967 *There Goes My Everything,* Jack Greene, Decca
1968 *Harper Valley P.T.A.,* Jeannie C. Riley, Plantation
1969 *A Boy Named Sue,* Johnny Cash, Columbia
1970 *Okie From Muskogee,* Merle Haggard, Capitol
1971 *Help Me Make It Through The Night,* Sammi Smith, Mega
1972 *Happiest Girl In The Whole U.S.A.,* Donna Fargo, Dot
1973 *Behind Closed Doors,* Charlie Rich, Epic
1974 *Country Bumpkin,* Cal Smith, MCA
1975 *Before The Next Teardrop Falls,* Freddy Fender, ABC/Dot
1976 *Good Hearted Woman,* Waylon Jennings and Willie Nelson, RCA
1977 *Lucille,* Kenny Rogers, United Artists Records
1978 *Heaven's Just A Sin Away*, The Kendalls (Ovation)

1979 *The Devil Went Down To Georgia*, Charlie Daniels Band (Epic)
1980 *He Stopped Loving Her Today*, George Jones (Epic)

ALBUM OF THE YEAR

1967 *There Goes My Everything,* Jack Greene, Decca
1968 *Johnny Cash At Folsom Prison,* Johnny Cash, Columbia
1969 *Johnny Cash At San Quentin Prison,* Johnny Cash, Columbia
1970 *Okie From Muskogee,* Merle Haggard, Capitol
1971 *I Won't Mention It Again,* Ray Price, Columbia
1972 *Let Me Tell You About A Song,* Merle Haggard, Capitol
1973 *Behind Closed Doors,* Charlie Rich, Epic
1974 *A Very Special Love Song,* Charlie Rich, Epic
1975 *A Legend In My Time,* Ronnie Milsap, RCA
1976 *Wanted — The Outlaws,* Waylon Jennings, Jessi Colter, Tompall Glaser and Willie Nelson, RCA
1977 *Ronnie Milsap Live,* Ronnie Milsap, RCA
1978 *It Was Almost Like A Song*, Ronnie Milsap (RCA)
1979 *The Gambler*, Kenny Rogers (UA)
1980 *Coal Miner's Daughter*, Original Motion Picture Soundtrack (MCA)

SONG OF THE YEAR

1967 *There Goes My Everything,* Dallas Frazier
1968 *Honey,* Bobby Russell
1969 *Carroll County Accident,* Bob Ferguson
1970 *Sunday Morning Coming Down,* Kris Kristofferson
1971 *Easy Loving,* Freddie Hart
1972 *Easy Loving,* Freddie Hart
1973 *Behind Closed Doors,* Kenny O'Dell
1974 *Country Bumpkin,* Don Wayne
1975 *Back Home Again,* John Denver
1976 *Rhinestone Cowboy,* Larry Weiss
1977 *Lucille,* Roger Bowling and Hal Bymun
1978 *Don't It Make My Brown Eyes Blue*, **Richard Leigh**
1979 *The Gambler*, **Don Schlitz** (Writers Night Music)
1980 *He Stopped Loving Her Today*, **Bobby Braddock & Curly Putman** (Tree International)

FEMALE VOCALIST OF THE YEAR

1967 **Loretta Lynn**
1968 **Tammy Wynette**
1969 **Tammy Wynette**
1970 **Tammy Wynette**
1971 **Lynn Anderson**
1972 **Loretta Lynn**
1973 **Loretta Lynn**
1974 **Olivia Newton-John**
1975 **Dolly Parton**
1976 **Dolly Parton**
1977 **Crystal Gayle**
1978 **Crystal Gayle**
1979 **Barbara Mandrell**
1980 **Emmylou Harris**

MALE VOCALIST OF THE YEAR

1967 **Jack Greene**
1968 **Glen Campbell**
1969 **Johnny Cash**
1970 **Merle Haggard**
1971 **Charley Pride**
1972 **Charley Pride**
1973 **Charlie Rich**
1974 **Ronnie Milsap**
1975 **Waylon Jennings**
1976 **Ronnie Milsap**
1977 **Ronnie Milsap**
1978 **Don Williams**
1979 **Kenny Rogers**
1980 **George Jones**

VOCAL GROUP OF THE YEAR

1967 **The Stoneman Family**
1968 **Porter Wagoner and Dolly Parton**
1969 **Johnny Cash and June Carter**
1970 **The Glaser Brothers**
1971 **The Osborne Brothers**
1972 **The Statler Brothers**
1973 **The Statler Brothers**
1974 **The Statler Brothers**
1975 **The Statler Brothers**
1976 **The Statler Brothers**
1977 **The Statler Brothers**
1978 **The Oak Ridge Boys**
1979 **The Statler Brothers**
1980 **The Statler Brothers**

VOCAL DUO OF THE YEAR

1970 **Porter Wagoner and Dolly Parton**
1971 **Porter Wagoner and Dolly Parton**
1972 **Conway Twitty and Loretta Lynn**
1973 **Conway Twitty and Loretta Lynn**
1974 **Conway Twitty and Loretta Lynn**
1975 **Conway Twitty and Loretta Lynn**
1976 **Waylon Jennings and Willie Nelson**
1977 **Jim Ed Brown and Helen Cornelius**
1978 **Kenny Rogers** and **Dottie West**
1979 **Kenny Rogers** and **Dottie West**
1980 **Moe Bandy** and **Joe Stampley**

INSTRUMENTAL GROUP OR BAND OF THE YEAR

1967 **The Buckaroos**
1968 **The Buckaroos**
1969 **Danny Davis and the Nashville Brass**
1970 **Danny Davis and the Nashville Brass**
1971 **Danny Davis and the Nashville Brass**
1972 **Danny Davis and the Nashville Brass**
1973 **Danny Davis and the Nashville Brass**
1974 **Danny Davis and the Nashville Brass**
1975 **Roy Clark and Buck Trent**
1976 **Roy Clark and Buck Trent**
1977 **Original Playboys**
1978 **The Oak Ridge Boys Band**
1979 **The Charlie Daniels Band**
1980 **The Charlie Daniels Band**

INSTRUMENTALIST OF THE YEAR

1967 **Chet Atkins**
1968 **Chet Atkins**
1969 **Chet Atkins**
1970 **Jerry Reed**
1971 **Jerry Reed**
1972 **Charlie McCoy**
1973 **Charlie McCoy**
1974 **Don Rich**
1975 **Johnny Gimble**
1976 **Hargus "Pig" Robbins**
1977 **Roy Clark**
1978 **Roy Clark**
1979 **Charlie Daniels**
1980 **Roy Clark**

COMEDIAN OF THE YEAR

1967 Don Bowman
1968 Ben Colder
1969 Archie Campbell
1970 Roy Clark

HALL OF FAME

1977 Merle Travis

Dance Magazine Award

DANCE MAGAZINE
1180 Ave. of the Americas, New York, N.Y. 10036
(212/921-9300)

Dance Magazine annually gives the Dance Magazine Award, a plaque, for outstanding achievements and contributions to the dance world. Selections are made by the magazine's editorial staff.

1954 Max Liebman
Omnibus
Tony Charmoli
Adventure
1955 Moira Shearer
Jack Cole
Gene Nelson
1956 Martha Graham
Agnes de Mille
1957 Alicia Markova
Lucia Chase
Jerome Robbins
Jose Limon
1958 Doris Humphrey
Gene Kelly
Igor Youskevitch
Alicia Alonso
1959 Dorothy Alexander
Fred Astaire
George Balanchine
1960 Merce Cunningham
Igor Moiseyev
Maria Tallchief
1961 Melissa Hayden
Gwen Verdon
Anna Sokolow
1962 Margot Fonteyn
Bob Fosse
Isadora Bennett
1963 Gower Champion
Robert Joffrey
Pauline Koner
1964 Edward Villella
John Butler
Peter Gennaro
1965 Margaret H'Doubler
Edwin Denby
Maya Plisetskaya
1966 Sol Hurok
Carmen de Lavallade
Wesleyan University Press
1967 Alwin Nikolais
Violette Verdy
Eugene Loring
1968 Carla Fracci
Erik Bruhn
Katherine Dunham
1969 Sir Frederick Ashton
Carolyn Brown
Ted Shawn
1970 No award
1971 No award
1972 Judith Jamison
Anthony Dowell
1973 The Christensen Brothers (Lew, Harold, and William)
Rudolf Nureyev
1974 Gerald Arpino
Maurice Bejart
Antony Tudor
1975 Cynthia Gregory
Arthur Mitchell
Alvin Ailey
1976 Michael Bennett
Suzanne Farrell
E. Virginia Williams
1977 Peter Martins
Natalia Makarova
Murray Louis
1978 Mikhail Baryshnikov
Raoul Gilabert
Bella Lewitzky
1979 Aaron Copland
Jorge Donn
Erick Hawkins
1980 Patricia McBride
Ruth Page
Paul Taylor

SPECIAL AWARD

1980 **Herbert Ross** and **Nora Kaye**, for *Turning Point*

Dent Medal

ROYAL MUSICAL ASSOCIATION
British Library, Great Russell St., London WCI, U.K. (Tel: 01-636 1544)

The Dent Medal, which is of gold, is given annually for a specific work or group of works published in the field of musicology. Usually, the winner is forty years of age or older and is honored for works of the previous three to five years. The Directorium of the International Musicological Society submits a list of nominees to the council of the Royal Musical Assocation. The council then selects the winner from this list and from any other musicologists it adds to that list.

1961 **Gilbert Reany,** Great Britain
1962 **Solange Corbin,** France
1963 **Denes Bartha,** Hungary
1964 **Pierre Pidoux,** Switzerland
1965 **Barry S. Brook,** U.S.A.
1966 **Alberto Gallo,** Italy
1967 **William W. Austin,** U.S.A.
1968 **Heinrich Huschen,** Federal Republic of Germany
1969 **Willem Elders,** Holland
1970 **Daniel Heartz,** U.S.A.
1971 **Klaus Wolfgang Niemoller,** Federal Republic of Germany
1972 **Jozef Robijns,** Belgium
1973 **Max Lutolf,** Switzerland
1974 **Andrew McCredie,** Australia
1975 **Martin Stachelin,** Federal Republic of Germany
1976 **No award**
1977 **Reinhard Strohm,** Great Britain
1978 **Christoph Wolff,** U.S.A.
1979 **Margaret Bent,** U.S.A.

1980 **Craig M. Wright,** U.S.A.

Disco Forum Awards

Billboard
9000 Sunset Blvd., Los Angeles, Calif. 90069
(213/273-7040)

The Disco Forum Awards, which consist of plaques, are awarded for various achievements in the discotheque field, as determined by a vote by more than 2,000 disco disc jockeys and others in the field.

1975 ***The Hustle,*** Disco Record of the Year
KC and the Sunshine Band, TK Productions, Disco Album of the Year
Atlantic Records, Disco Company of the Year
Donna Summer, Casablanca Records, Most Promising New Artist of the Year
Casey & Finch, TK Productions, Producer of the Year
Labelle, Epic Records, Disco Artist of the Year
Salsoul Orchestra, Disco Orchestra of the Year
Richard Nader, Disco Concert Promoter of the Year
Disco Sound Associates, Specialist Company of the Year
Dimples, Consumer Publication of the Year
Michael O'Harro, Disco Consultant of the Year
2001 Clubs, Disco Franchise of the Year
Earl Young, The Trammps, Drummer of the Year
Johnny Walker, London's BBC Radio-1 Deejay, U.K. DJ of the Year

1976 **The Trammps,** Atlantic Records, Disco Artist of the Year
Disco Party, The Trammps, Atlantic Records, Disco Cut of the Year
That's Where The Happy People Go, The Trammps, Alantic Records, Disco Album of the Year
Van McCoy, H&L Records, Disco Arranger
Van McCoy, H&L Records, Disco Instrumentalist
Love Hangover, Diana Ross, Disco/Radio Single
Vicki Sue Robinson, RCA Records, Most Promising New Disco Artist
Jesse Green, Disco Single Award
Salsoul Orchestra, Disco Orchestra
Dave Crawford, Disco Composer
Casablanca Records, Tied for Disco Label of Year
Salsoul Records, Tied for Disco Label of the Year
Salsoul Records, Most Important New Disco Software Product
Salsoul Records, Innovative 12-inch Disco Disk for Consumers
Tom Sevarese, Tied for Disco Deejay of the Year
Bobby D.J., Tied for Disco Deejay of the Year
Burma East Music Tied for Disco Music Publisher
Bull Pen Music/Perren-Vibes Music, Tied for Disco Music Publisher
Michael O'Harro, Tramps Discotheque, Washington, D.C., Disco Consultant of the Year
Michael O'Harro, Tramps Discotheque, Washington, D.C., Disco Club Owner of the Year
Tom Moulton, Disco Mixing Award
Freddie Perren, Disco Producer
Norby Walters, Disco Concert Promoter of the Year
Sigma Sound, Philadelphia, Disco Recording Studio of the Year
2001 Clubs, Disco Franchiser of the Year
Dave Todd, RCA Records, Disco Promotion Person of the Year
Cerwin Vega's, "Earthquake" Speaker, Best New Disco Audio Product
Digital Lighting's 6×9 Modular Programmable dimming System, Best New Disco Lighting Product

DEEJAY OF THE YEAR—LOCAL

1977 **Jim Burgess,** Atlanta
John Luongo, Boston
Howard Metz, Dallas
Sam Meyer, Houston
Bob Vitteriti, Miami Area
Bobby DJ and Tom Sevarese, New York
Jim Weatherly, Phoenix
Wes Bradley, San Francisco
Bill Owens, Baltimore/Washington, D.C.
Mike Graber, Chicago
Joel Levin, Detroit
Paul Dougan, Los Angeles
Stu Neal, New Orleans
Kurt Borusiewicz, Philadelphia
Gary Larkin, Pittsburgh
John Bush, Seattle

DEEJAY OF THE YEAR (Individual and Disco)

1977 **Tom Sevarese;** The Sandpiper, New York
Paul Dougan; Studio One, Los Angeles
John Hedges; The City, San Francisco
Kurt Borusiewicz; D.C.A., Philadelphia
Marty Ross; Menjo's, Detroit
Artie Feldman; Sunday's, Chicago
Jim Stuard; 1270 Disco, Boston
Jim Burgess; The Casbah, Atlanta
Ram Rocha; Old Plantation, Houston
Bill Owens; Lost & Found, Washington, D.C. Baltimore/Washington
Gary Larkin; The Giraffe, Pittsburgh
Jack Wetherby; Maggie's Back Door Disco, Phoenix
Tom Neff; Sportspage, Denver
David Lowe; Windward Resort, Miami
Victor Ocasio; Puerto Rico
Paul Werth; Boren Street Disco, Seattle

DISCO FORUM AWARD

1977 ***Don't Leave Me This Way*** (Thelma Houston), Single of the Year (Heavy Disco/Heavy Radio Combined Play)
I Don't Wanna Lose Your Love (Emotions), Single of the Year (Heavy Disco/Light Radio Combined Play)
I Feel Love (Donna Summer), Disco Single/LP Cut of the Year
Disco Inferno (Trammps and Dr. Buzzards Original Savannah Band), Tie for Disco Album of the Year
Georgio Moroder and Peter Bellotti, Best Producers of a Disco Record
Donna Summer, Georgio Moroder and Peter Bellotti, Disco Composer of the Year
Donna Summer, Disco Artist of the Year
Grace Jones, Most Promising New Disco Artist of the Year
Elton Ahi, for *Uptown Festival,* Disco DJ Mix of the Year
Uptown Festival (Shalemar), Disco DJ's Favorite 12-inch disc
Casablanca and TK Records, Tie for Disco Record Label of the Year
Ray Caviano, Disco Record Promotion Person of the Year (in-house)
Marc Simon, Disco Record Promotion Person of the Year (independent)
Salsoul Orchestra, Disco Orchestra of the Year

GLI Mixer 3880, Best New Audio Product of the Year
Meteor Sonalight (Lighting controllers), Best New Disco Lighting Product of the Year
Norby Walters, Disco Concert Promoter
2001 Clubs, Disco Club Franchiser of the Year
Michael O'Harro, Disco Club Consultant of the Year
Ralph McDonald and Dennis Coffey, Tie for Disco Instrumentalist of the Year
Vince Montana, Disco Music Arranger of the Year
Bobby DJ and Tom Sevarese, Disco Deejay of the Year

Current status unknown

Alfred Einstein Award

AMERICAN MUSICOLOGICAL SOCIETY
201 S. 34th St., Philadelphia, Pa. 19104 (215/243-5000)

The annual Alfred Einstein Award, carrying a cash prize of $400, is awarded for a musicological article published by a young scholar during the previous year.

1967 **Richard L. Crocker,** "The Troping Hypothesis" (*Musical Quarterly*)
1968 **Ursula Kirkendale,** "The Ruspoli Documents on Handel" (*Journal of the American Musicological Society*)
1969 **Philip Gossett,** "Rossini in Naples: some major works recovered" (*Musical Quarterly*)
1970 **Lawrence Gushee,** "New Sources for the Biography of Johannes de Muris" (*Journal of the American Musicological Society*)
1971 **Lewis Lockwood,** "The Autograph of the first movement of Beethoven's Sonata for Violoncello and Pianforte, opus 69" (*Music Forum*)
1972 **Sarah Fuller,** "Hidden Polyphony—a Reappraisal" (*Journal of the American Musicological Socie- ty*)
1973 **Rebecca A. Baltzer,** "Thirteenth-Century Illuminated Miniatures and the date of the Florence Manuscript" (*Journal of the American Musicological Society*)
1974 **Lawrence F. Bernstein,** "La Courone et fleur des chansons a troys: A Mirror of the French Chanson in Italy in the Years between Ottaviano Petrucci and Antonio Gardano" (*Journal of the American Musicological Society*)
1975 **Eugene K. Wolf and Jean K. Wolf,** "A Newly Identified Complex of Manuscripts from Mannheim" (*Journal of the American Musicological Society*)
1976 **Craig Wright,** "Dufay at Cambrai: Discoveries and Revisions" (*Journal of the American Musicological Society*)
1977 **James Webster,** "Violoncello and Double Bass in the Chamber Music of Haydn and his Viennese Contemporaries, 1750-1780" (*Journal of the American Musicological Society*)
1978 **Charles Atkinson,** "The Earliest Agnus Dei Melody and Its Tropes" (*Journal of the American Musicological Society*)
1979 **Curtis A. Price,** N.A.
1980 **Richard Tariskin,** N.A.

Avery Fisher Awards
Avery Fisher Prize

LINCOLN CENTER FOR THE PERFORMING ARTS
Attn.: Avery Fisher Artist Program, New York, N.Y. 10023 (212/580-8700)

The Avery Fisher Artist Program began with one presentation of the Avery Fisher Awards, which went to two outstanding young instrumentalists who established major reputations and had already given proof of their abilities as solo performers. The Award consisted of a $5,000 honorarium and numerous performance engagements with the New York Philharmonic and other leading musical organizations.

1975 **Lynn Harrell,** Cellist
Murray Perahia, Pianist

Subsequently, the Avery Fisher Artists Program was restructured as the Avery Fisher Prize, which goes annually to exceptionally talented, younger American instrumentalists who have demonstrated to experts in the musical field that they deserve wider attention. This is not a playing competition but a system whereby nominations are made by a board of nationally known conductors, instrumentalists, educators and others for selection by an executive committee. Each winner receives a an honoarium that originally was $2,500 and, since only one winner has been named each year, is now $5,000, plus a debut engagement with the New York Philharmonic and engagements with several other musical organizations.

1976 **Ani Kavafavian,** Violinist
Heidi Lehwader, Harpist
Ursula Oppens, Pianist
Paul Schenly, Pianist
1977 **Andre-Michel Schub,** Pianist
Richard Stoltzman, Clarinetist
1978 **Yo-Yo Ma**, Cellist
1979 **Emmanuel Ax**, Pianist
1980 **Richard Goode**, Pianist

The Recital Award of the Avery Fisher Arts Program is a $2,500 cash award and a solo recital in Alice Tully Hall.

1980 **Sharon Robinson**, Cellist
Mona Golabek, Pianist

Gold Baton

AMERICAN SYMPHONY ORCHESTRA LEAGUE
Box 669, Vienna, Va. 22180 (703/281-1230)

The Gold Baton annually honors service by individuals, organizations or corporations to music in particular and the arts in general. Plaques are given to the winner(s), selected by the board of directors upon recommendation of a special awards committee.

1948 **Ernest La Prade,** *NBC Orchestras of the Nations*
1952 **John B. Ford,** President, Detroit Sympathy Orchestra
1956 **Marjorie Merriweather Post,** Vice President, Washington National Symphony
1958 **Samuel Rosenbaum, Henry B. Cabot, Dudley T. Easby, Jr., Charles Garside and Henry Allen Moe,** The Study Committee on Orchestra Legal Documents

1959 **Leonard Bernstein,** conductor, New York Philharmonic
1960 **Association of Junior Leagues of America**
Charles Farnsley, former Mayor, Louisville, Ky.
1961 **Arthur Judson,** former manager, New York Philharmonic
1962 **Women's Association of Symphony Orchestras**
1963 **John D. Rockefeller,** 3rd
Officers and directors of Lincoln Center for the Performing Arts
1964 **Richard Lert,** music director, Pasadena Symphony
Paul Mellon, A. W. Mellon Educational and Charitable Trusts, Richard King Mellon Charitable Trusts, Howard Heinz Endowment
1965 **American Federation of Musicians**
1966 **Ford Foundation**
1967 **American Telephone and Telegraph Co.**
1968 **Leopold Stokowski**
Jouett Shouse
1969 **New York State Council on the Arts**
1970 **Helen M. Thompson**
1971 **Martha Baird Rockefeller**
1972 **Amyas Ames**
1973 **Danny Kaye**
1974 **Nancy Hanks and National Council on the Arts**
1975 **John S. Edwards,** manager, Chicago Symphony
1976 **Arthur Fiedler**
1977 **Avery Fisher**
1978 **Aaron Copland**
1979 **Eugene Ormandy**
1980 **Beverly Sills**

CORPORATIONS AND ORGANIZATIONS

1977 **Alcoa Foundation**
1978 **Exxon Corp.**
1979 **Bell System**
1980 **Minnesota Five Percent Club**

Grammy Awards

NATIONAL ACADEMY OF RECORDING ARTS AND SCIENCES

4444 Riverside Dr., Ste. 202, Burbank, Calif. 91505
(213/843-8233)

The Grammy statuette, which depicts an early gramophone, is presented annually in nationally telecast ceremonies to honor oustanding creativity in artistic and technical areas of recording. Academy members and recording companies recommend recordings of merit released during the specified year. Special committees and the local governors and national trustees of the Academy select finalists (usually five) in each category for a second round of balloting, which determines the winners. Members are limited to voting in their area of expertise. Unless otherwise specified, singles and albums are considered for Grammys in the same categories.

RECORD OF THE YEAR

1958 ***Nel Blu Dipinto di Blu (Volare)*** Domenico Modugno
1959 ***Mack the Knife,*** Bobby Darin
1960 ***Theme from 'A Summer Place,'*** Percy Faith
1961 ***Moon River,*** Henry Mancini
1962 ***I Left My Heart in San Francisco,*** Tony Bennett
1963 ***The Days of Wine and Roses,*** Henry Mancini
1964 ***The Girl from Ipanema,*** Stan Getz and Astrud Gilberto
1965 ***A Taste of Honey,*** Herb Alpert & the Tijuana Brass (prod. by Herb Alpert and Jerry Moss)
1966 ***Strangers in the Night,*** Frank Sinatra (prod. by Jimmy Bowen)
1967 ***Up, Up and Away,*** 5th Dimension (prod. by Marc Gordon and Johnny Rivers)
1968 ***Mrs. Robinson,*** Simon & Garfunkel (prod. by Paul Simon, Art Garfunkel and Roy Halee)
1969 ***Aquarius, Let the Sunshine In,*** 5th Dimension (prod. by Bones Howe)
1970 ***Bridge Over Troubled Water,*** Simon & Garfunkel (prod. by Paul Simon, Art Garfunkel and Roy Halee)
1971 ***It's Too Late,*** Carole King (prod. by Lou Adler)
1972 ***The First Time Ever I Saw Your Face,*** Roberta Flack (prod. by Joel Dorn)
1973 ***Killing Me Softly With His Song,*** Roberta Flack (prod. by Joel Dorn)
1974 ***I Honestly Love You,*** Olivia Newton-John (prod. by John Farrar)
1975 ***Love Will Keep Us Together,*** Captain & Tenille (prod. by Daryl Dragon)
1976 ***This Masquerade,*** George Benson (prod. by Tommy Lipuma)
1977 ***Hotel California,*** The Eagles (prod. by Bill Szymczyk)
1978 ***Just the Way You Are,*** Billy Joel (prod. by Phil Ramone)
1979 ***What A Fool Believes,*** Doobie Brothers (prod. by Ted Templeman)
1980 **Christopher Cross,** *Sailing* (prod. by Michael Omartian)

ALBUM OF THE YEAR

1958 ***The Music From Peter Gunn,*** Henry Mancini
1959 ***Come Dance With Me,*** Frank Sinatra
1960 ***Button Down Mind,*** Bob Newhart
1961 ***Judy at Carnegie Hall,*** Judy Garland
1962 ***The First Family,*** Vaughn Meader
1963 ***The Barbra Streisand Album,*** Barbra Streisand
1964 ***Getz/Gilberto,*** Stan Getz and Joao Gilberto
1965 ***September of My Years,*** Frank Sinatra (prod. by Sonny Burke)
1966 ***Sinatra: A Man and His Music,*** Frank Sinatra (prod. by Sonny Burke)
1967 ***Sgt. Pepper's Lonely Hearts Club Band,*** The Beatles (prod. by George Martin)
1968 ***By the Time I Get to Phoenix,*** Glen Campbell (prod. by Al de Lory)
1969 ***Blood, Sweat & Tears,*** Blood, Sweat & Tears (prod. by James Guerico)
1970 ***Bridge Over Troubled Water,*** Simon & Garfunkel (prod. by Paul Simon, Art Garfunkel and Roy Halee)
1971 ***Tapestry,*** Carole King (prod. by Lou Adler)
1972 ***The Concert for Bangla Desh,*** George Harrison, Ravi Shankar, Bob Dylan, Leon Russell, Ringo Starr, Billy Preston, Eric Clapton and Klaus Voormann (prod. by George Harrison and Phil Spector)
1973 ***Innervisions,*** Stevie Wonder (prod. by Stevie Wonder)
1974 ***Fulfillingness' First Finale,*** Stevie Wonder (prod. by Stevie Wonder)
1975 ***Still Crazy After All these Years,*** Paul Simon (prod. by Paul Simon and Phil Ramone)
1976 ***Songs in the Key of Life,*** Stevie Wonder (prod. by Stevie Wonder
1977 ***Rumors,*** Fleetwood Mac (prod. by Richard Pashut and Ken Caillat)

1978 ***Saturday Night Fever***, Bee Gees, David Shire, Yvonne Elliman, Tavares Kool and The Gang, K.C. and The Sunshine Band, MFSB, Trammps, Walter Murphy and Ralph MacDonald (prod. by Bee Gees, Karl Richardson, Albhy Galuten, Freddie Perren, Bill Oakes, David Shire, Arif Mardin, Thomas J. Valentino, Ralph MacDonald, W. Salter, K.G. Productions, H.W. Casey, Richard Finch, Bobby Martin, Broadway Eddie and Ron Kersey)
1979 ***52nd Street***, Billy Joel (prod. by Phil Ramone)
1980 ***Christopher Cross***, Christopher Cross, (prod. by Michael Omartian)

SONG OF THE YEAR (Award to songwriter)

1958 **Domenico Modugno,** *Nel Blu Dipinto di Blu*
1959 **Jimmy Driftwood,** *The Battle of New Orleans*
1960 **Ernest Gold,** Theme from *Exodus*
1961 **Henry Mancini and Johnny Mercer,** *Moon River*
1962 **Leslie Bricusse and Anthony Newley,** *What Kind of Fool Am I*
1963 **Henry Mancini and Johnny Mercer,** *The Days of Wine and Roses*
1964 **Jerry Herman,** *Hello, Dolly!*
1965 **Paul Francis Webster and Johnny Mandel,** *The Shadow of Your Smile*
1966 **John Lennon and Paul McCartney,** *Michelle*
1967 **Jim Webb,** *Up, Up and Away*
1968 **Bobby Russell,** *Little Green Apples*
1969 **Joe South,** *Games People Play*
1970 **Paul Simon,** *Bridge Over Troubled Water*
1971 **Carole King,** *You've Got a Friend*
1972 **Ewan MacColl,** *The First Time Ever I Saw Your Face*
1973 **Norman Gimbel and Charles Fox,** *Killing Me Softly With His Song*
1974 **Marilyn and Alan Bergman and Marvin Hamlisch,** *The Way We Were*
1975 **Stephen Sondheim,** *Send in the Clowns*
1976 **Bruce Johnson,** *I Write the Songs*
1977 **Barbra Streisand and Paul Williams,** *Evergreen*
Joe Brooks, *You Light Up My Life*
1978 **Billy Joel,** *Just the Way You Are*
1979 **Kenny Loggins** and **Michael McDonald**, *What A Fool Believes*
1980 **Christopher Cross,** *Sailing*

BEST NEW ARTIST OF THE YEAR

1959 **Bobby Darin**
1960 **Bob Newhart**
1961 **Peter Nero**
1962 **Robert Goulet**
1963 **Swingle Singers**
1964 **The Beatles**
1965 **Tom Jones**
1966 **Category not voted on**
1967 **Bobbie Gentry**
1968 **Jose Feliciano**
1969 **Crosby, Stills and Nash**
1970 **The Carpenters**
1971 **Carly Simon**
1972 **America**
1973 **Bette Midler**
1974 **Marvin Hamlisch**
1975 **Natalie Cole**
1976 **Starland Vocal Band**
1977 **Debby Boone**
1978 **A Taste of Honey**
1979 **Rickie Lee Jones**
1980 **Christopher Cross**

BEST VOCAL PERFORMANCE/BEST SOLO VOCAL PERFORMANCE/BEST CONTEMPORARY POP VOCAL PERFORMANCE (Female)

1958 **Ella Fitzgerald,** *Ella Fitzgerald Sings the Irving Berlin Song Book*
1959 **Ella Fitzgerald,** *But Not for Me*
1960 **Ella Fitzgerald,** *Mack the Knife* (single)
Ella Fitzgerald, *Mack the Knife—Ella in Berlin* (album)
1961 **Judy Garland,** *Judy at Carnegie Hall* (album)
1962 **Ella Fitzgerald,** *Ella Swings Brightly With Nelson Riddle* (album)
1963 **Barbra Streisand,** *The Barbra Streisand Album* (album)
1964 **Barbra Streisand,** *People* (single)
1965 **Barbra Streisand,** *My Name Is Barbra* (album)
1966 **Eydie Gorme,** *If He Walked Into My Life* (single)
1967 **Bobbie Gentry,** *Ode to Billy Joe* (single
1968 **Dionne Warwicke,** *Do You Know the Way to San Jose?* (single)
1969 **Peggy Lee,** *Is That All There Is* (single)
1970 **Dionne Warwicke,** *I'll Never Fall in Love Again* (album)
1971 **Carole King,** *Tapestry* (album)
1972 **Helen Reddy,** *I Am Woman* (single)
1973 **Roberta Flack,** *Killing Me Softly With His Song* (single)
1974 **Olivia Newton-John,** *I Honestly Love You* (single)
1975 **Janis Ian,** *At Seventeen* (single)
1976 **Linda Ronstadt** *Hasten Down the Wind* (album)
1977 **Barbra Streisand** *Evergreen* (single)
1978 **Anne Murray,** *You Needed Me* (single)
1979 **Dionne Warwick,** *I'll Never Love This Way Again* (single)
1980 **Bette Midler,** *The Rose* (single)

BEST VOCAL PERFORMANCE/BEST SOLO VOCAL PERFORMANCE/BEST CONTEMPORARY POP VOCAL PERFORMANCE (Male)

1958 **Perry Como,** *Catch a Falling Star*
1959 **Frank Sinatra,** *Come Dance With Me*
1960 **Ray Charles,** *Georgia On My Mind* (single)
Ray Charles, *Genius of Ray Charles* (album)
1961 **Jack Jones,** *Lollipops and Roses* (single)
1962 **Tony Bennett,** *I Left My Heart in San Francisco* (album)
1963 **Jack Jones,** *Wives and Lovers* (single)
1964 **Louis Armstrong,** *Hello, Dolly!* (single)
1965 **Frank Sinatra,** *It Was a Very Good Year* (single)
1966 **Frank Sinatra,** *Strangers in the Night* (single)
1967 **Glen Campbell,** *By the Time I Get to Phoenix* (single)
1968 **Jose Feliciano,** *Light My Fire* (single)
1969 **Harry Nilsson,** *Everybody's Talkin*
1970 **Ray Stevens,** *Everything Is Beautiful* (single)
1971 **James Taylor,** *You've Got a Friend* (single)
1972 **Harry Nilsson,** *Without You* (single)
1973 **Stevie Wonder,** *You Are The Sunshine of My Life* (single)
1974 **Stevie Wonder,** *Fulfillingness' First Finale* (album)
1975 **Paul Simon,** *Still Crazy After All These Years* (album)
1976 **Stevie Wonder,** *Songs in the Key of Life* (album)
1977 **James Taylor,** *Handy Man* (album)
1978 **Barry Manilow,** *Copacabana* (single)
1979 **Billy Joel,** *52nd Street* (album)
1980 **Kenny Loggins,** *This Is It* (track)

BEST PERFORMANCE BY AN ORCHESTRA/BEST INSTRUMENTAL PERFORMANCE/POP INSTRUMENTAL PERFORMANCE

1958 **Billy May,** *Billy May's Big Fat Brass*
1959 **David Rose and his Orchestra with Andre Previn,** *Like Young*
1960 **Henry Mancini,** *Mr. Lucky*
1961 **Henry Mancini,** *Breakfast at Tiffany's*
1962 **Peter Nero,** *The Colorful Peter Nero*
1963 **Al Hirt,** *Java*
1964 **Henry Mancini,** *Pink Panther*
1965 **Herb Alpert & the Tijuana Brass,** *A Taste of Honey*
1966 **Herb Alpert & the Tijuana Brass,** *What Now My Love*
1967 **Chet Atkins,** *Chet Atkins Picks the Best*
1968 **Mason Williams,** *Classical Gas*
1969 **Blood, Sweat and Tears,** *Variations on a Theme by Eric Satie*
1970 **Henry Mancini,** *Theme from 'Z' and Other Film Music*
1971 **Quincy Jones,** *Smackwater Jack*
1972 **Billy Preston,** *Outa-Space*
Isaac Hayes, *Black Moses*
1973 **Eumir Deodato,** *Also Sprach Zarathustra* (theme from *2001: A Space Odyssey)*
1974 **Marvin Hamlisch,** *The Entertainer*
1975 **Van McCoy and the Soul City Symphony,** *The Hustle*
1976 **George Benson,** *Breezin'*
1977 **John Williams conducting the London Symphony Orchestra,** *Star Wars*
1978 **Chuck Mangione Group,** *Children of Sanchez*
1979 **Herb Alpert,** *Rise*
1980 **Bob James** and **Earl Klugh,** *One on One*

BEST PERFORMANCE BY A DANCE BAND/BEST PERFORMANCE OF A BAND FOR DANCING/BEST PERFORMANCE BY AN ORCHESTRA FOR DANCING

1958 **Count Basie,** *Basie*
1959 **Duke Ellington,** *Anatomy of a Murder*
1960 **Count Basie,** *Dance With Basie*
1961 **Si Zentner,** *Up a Lazy River*
1962 **Joe Harnell,** *Fly Me to the Moon Bossa Nova*
1963 **Count Basie,** *This Time by Basie! Hits of the 50s and 60s*

BEST ARRANGEMENT/BEST INSTRUMENTAL ARRANGEMENT (Award to arranger)

1958 **Henry Mancini,** *The Music from 'Peter Gunn'*
1959 **Billy May,** *Come Dance With Me*
1960 **Henry Mancini,** *Mr. Lucky*
1961 **Henry Mancini,** *Moon River*
1962 **Henry Mancini,** *Baby Elephant Walk*
1963 **Quincy Jones,** *I Can't Stop Loving You*
1964 **Henry Mancini,** *Pink Panther*
1965 **Herb Alpert,** *A Taste of Honey*
1966 **Herb Alpert,** *What Now My Love*
1967 **Burt Bacharach,** *Alfie*
1968 **Mike Post,** *Classical Gas*
1969 **Henry Mancini,** Love Theme from *Romeo and Juliet*
1970 **Henry Mancini,** Theme from *Z*
1971 **Isaac Hayes and Johnny Allen,** Theme from *Shaft*
1972 **Don Ellis,** Theme from *The French Connection*
1973 **Quincy Jones,** *Summer in the City*
1974 **Pat Williams,** *Threshold*
1975 **Mike Post and Pete Carpenter,** *The Rockford Files*
1976 **Chick Corea,** *Leprechaun's Dream*
1977 **Harry Betts, Perry Botkin, Jr., and Barry de Vorzan,** *Nadia's Theme*
1978 **Quincy Jones** and **Robert Freedman,** Main title/Overture Part I from *The Wiz Original Soundtrack*
1979 **Claus Ogerman,** *Soulful Strut*
1980 **Quincy Jones** and **Jerry Hey,** *Dinorah, Dinorah*

BEST INSTRUMENTAL THEME/BEST INSTRUMENTAL COMPOSITION (EXCLUDING JAZZ) (Award to Composer)

1961 **Galt McDermott,** *African Waltz*
1962 **Bobby Scott and Ric Marlow,** *A Taste of Honey*
1963 **Norman Newell, Nino Oliviero and Riz Ortolani,** *More* (theme from *Mondo Cane)*
1964 **Henry Mancini,** *The Pink Panther Theme*
1965 **Category not voted on**
1966 **Neal Hefti,** *Batman* theme
1967 **Lalo Shifrin,** *Mission: Impossible*
1968 **Mason Williams,** *Classical Gas*
1969 **John Barry,** *Midnight Cowboy*
1970 **Alfred Newman,** *Airport Love Theme*
1971 **Michel Legrand,** Theme from *Summer of '42*
1972 **Michal Legrand,** *Brian's Song*
1973 **Gato Barbieri,** *Last Tango in Paris*
1974 **Mike Oldfield,** *Tubular Bells* (from *The Exorcist)*
1975 **Michel Legrand,** *Images*
1976 **Chuck Mangione,** *Bellavia*
1977 **John Williams,** Main Title theme from *Star Wars*
1978 **John Williams,** Theme from *Close Encounters of the Third Kind*
1979 **John Williams,** Main title theme from *Superman*
1980 **John Williams,** *The Empire Strikes Back*

BEST BACKGROUND ARRANGEMENT/BEST ACCOMPANIMENT ARRANGEMENT FOR VOCALIST(S) OR INSTRUMENTALISTS/BEST ARRANGEMENT ACCOMPANYING VOCALISTS (Award to Arranger)

1962 **Marty Manning,** *I Left My Heart in San Francisco*
1963 **Henry Mancini,** *The Days of Wine and Roses*
1964 **Peter Matz,** *People*
1965 **Gordon Jenkins,** *It Was a Very Good Year*
1966 **Ernie Freeman,** *Strangers in the Night*
1967 **Jimmie Haskell,** *Ode to Billie Joe*
1968 **Jim Webb,** *MacArthur Park*
1969 **Fred Lipsius,** *Spinning Wheel*
1970 **Paul Simon, Art Garfunkel, Jimmie Haskell, Ernie Freeman and Larry Knechtel,** *Bridge Over Troubled Waters*
1971 **Paul McCartney,** *Uncle Albert/Admiral Halsey*
1972 **Michel Legrand,** *What Are You Doing the Rest of Your Life?*
1973 **George Martin,** *Live and Let Die*
1974 **Joni Mitchell and Tom Scott,** *Down to You*
1975 **Ray Stevens,** *Misty*
1976 **Jimmie Haskell and James William Guerico,** *If You Leave Me Now*
1977 **Ian Freebairn-Smith,** *Evergreen*
1978 **Maurice White,** *Got to Get You Into My Life*
1979 **Michael McDonald,** *What a Fool Believes*
1980 **Michael Omartian** and **Christopher Cross,** *Sailing*

BEST ARRANGEMENT FOR VOICES (Duo, Group or Chorus)

1976 **Starland Vocal Band,** *Afternoon Delight*
1977 **Eagles,** *New Kid in Town*
1978 **Bee Gees,** *Stayin' Alive*
1979 **No award**
1980 **Janis Siegel,** *Birdland*

BEST PERFORMANCE BY A VOCAL GROUP OR CHORUS

1958 **Louis Prima and Keely Smith,** *That Old Black Magic*

BEST PERFORMANCE BY A CHORUS/BEST CONTEMPORARY POP CHORUS PERFORMANCE

1959 **Mormon Tabernacle Choir (Richard Condie, conductor),** *Battle Hymn of the Republic*
1960 **Norman Luboff Choir,** *Songs of the Cowboy*
1961 **Johnny Mann Singers,** *Great Band with Great Voices*
1962 **New Christy Minstrels,** *Presenting the New Christy Minstrels*
1963 **Swingle Singers,** *Bach's Greatest Hits*
1964 **Swingle Singers,** *The Swingle Singers Going Baroque*
1965 **Swingle Singers,** *Anyone for Mozart?*
1966 **Ray Conniff & Singers,** *Somewhere My Love*
1967 **5th Dimension,** *Up, Up and Away*
1968 **Alan Copeland Singers,** *Mission Impossible/Norwegian Wood*
1969 **Percy Faith Orchestra & Chorus,** *Romeo and Juliet* love theme

BEST ROCK AND ROLL RECORDING

1961 **Chubby Checker,** *Let's Twist Again*
1962 **Bent Fabric,** *Alley Cat*
1963 **Nino Tempo and April Stevens,** *Deep Purple*
1964 **Petula Clark,** *Downtown*

BEST CONTEMPORARY R & R SINGLE

1965 **Roger Miller,** *King of the Road*
1966 **New Vaudeville Band,** *Winchester Cathedral*

BEST CONTEMPORARY SOLO VOCAL PERFORMANCE

1965 **Petula Clark** (female), *I Know A Place*
Roger Miller (male), *King of the Road*
1966 **Paul McCartney,** *Eleanor Rigby*

BEST CONTEMPORARY R&R PERFORMANCE GROUP

1965 **Statler Brothers,** *Flowers on the Wall*
1966 **Mamas & Papas,** *Monday, Monday*

BEST ROCK PERFORMANCE (Female)

1979 **Donna Summer,** *Hot Stuff*
1980 **Pat Benatar,** *Crimes of Passion*

BEST ROCK PERFORMANCE (Male)

1979 **Bob Dylan,** *Gotta Serve Somebody*
1980 **Billy Joel,** *Glass Houses*

BEST ROCK PERFORMANCE BY A DUO OR GROUP

1979 **Eagles,** *Heartache Tonight*
1980 **Bob Seger & The Silver Bullet Band,** *Against the Wind*

BEST ROCK INSTRUMENTAL PERFORMANCE

1979 **Wings,** *Rockestra Theme*
1980 **Police,** *Regatta de Blanc*

BEST DISCO RECORDING

1979 **Gloria Gaynor** (prod. by Freddie Perrene and Dino Fekaris), *I Will Survive*
1980 **No award**

BEST CONTEMPORARY SINGLE

1967 **5th Dimension** (prod. by Marc Gordon and Carlie Rivers), *Up, Up and Away*

BEST CONTEMPORARY SONG (Award to songwriter)

1969 **Joe South,** *Games People Play*
1970 **Paul Simon,** *Bridge Over Troubled Water*

BEST CONTEMPORARY ALBUM

1967 **The Beatles** (prod. by George Martin), *Sgt. Pepper's Lonely Hearts Club Band*

BEST PERFORMANCE BY A VOCAL GROUP/BEST CONTEMPORARY VOCAL DUO OR GROUP PERFORMANCE/BEST POP VOCAL PERFORMANCE BY A DUO, GROUP OR CHORUS

1960 **Steve Lawrence and Eydie Gorme,** *We Got Us*
1961 **Lambert, Hendricks and Ross,** *High Flying*
1962 **Peter, Paul and Mary,** *If I Had A Hammer*
1963 **Peter, Paul and Mary,** *Blowin' in the Wind*
1964 **The Beatles,** *A Hard Day's Night*
1965 **Anita Kerr Singers,** *We Dig Mancini*
1966 **Anita Kerr Singers,** *A Man and A Woman*
1967 **5th Dimension,** *Up, Up and Away*
1968 **Simon & Garfunkel,** *Mrs. Robinson*
1969 **5th Dimension,** *Aquarius/Let the Sunshine In*
1970 **Carpenters,** *Close to You*
1971 **Carpenters,** *Carpenters*
1972 **Roberta Flack and Donny Hathaway,** *Where Is the Love*
1973 **Gladys Knight & The Pips,** *Neither One of Us (Wants to Be the First to Say Goodbye)*
1974 **Paul McCartney & Wings,** *Band on the Run*
1975 **Eagles,** *Lyin' Eyes*
1976 **Chicago,** *If You Leave Me Now*
1977 **Bee Gees,** *How Deep is Your Love?*
1978 **Bee Gees,** *Saturday Night Fever*
1979 **Doobie Brothers,** *Minute by Minute*

BEST JAZZ PERFORMANCE/SOLO/SOLO OR SMALL GROUP/SMALL GROUP OR SOLOIST WITH (SMALL) GROUP

1958 **Ella Fitzgerald,** *Ella Sings the Duke Ellington Song Book*
1959 **Ella Fitzgerald,** *Ella Swings Lightly*
1960 **Andre Previn,** *West Side Story*
1961 **Andre Previn,** *Andre Previn Plays Harold Arlen*
1962 **Stan Getz,** *Desafinado*
1963 **Bill Evans,** *Conversations with Myself*
1964 **Stan Getz,** *Getz/Gilberto*
1965 **Ramsey Lewis Trio,** *The 'In' Crowd*
1966 **Wes Montgomery,** *Goin' Out of My Head*
1967 **Cannonball Adderly Quintet,** *Mercy, Mercy, Mercy*
1968 **Bill Evans Trio,** *Bill Evans Trio at the Montreux Jazz Festival*
1969 **Wes Montgomery,** *Willow Weep for Me*
1970 **Bill Evans,** *Alone*
1971 **Bill Evans,** *The Bill Evans Album*
1972 **Gary Burton,** *Alone at Last*

BEST JAZZ PERFORMANCE BY A SOLOIST

1973 **Art Tatum,** *God Is in the House*
1974 **Charlie Parker,** *First Recordings*
1975 **Dizzy Gillespie,** *Oscar Peterson and Dizzy Gillespie*

BEST JAZZ VOCAL PERFORMANCE, SOLOIST

1976 **Ella Fitzgerald,** *Ella & Pass . . . Again*
1977 **Al Jarreau,** *Look to the Rainbow*

1978 **All Jarreau**, *All Fly Home*
1979 **Ella Fitzgerald**, *Fine and Mellow*

BEST JAZZ PERFORMANCE (FEMALE)

1980 **Ella Fitzgerald**, *A Perfect Match: Ella and Basie*

BEST JAZZ PERFORMANCE (MALE)

1980 **George Benson**, *Moody's Mood*

BEST JAZZ INSTRUMENTAL PERFORMANCE, SOLOIST

1976 **Count Basie**, *Basie and Zoot*
1977 **Oscar Peterson**, *The Giants*
1978 **Oscar Peterson**, *Montreux '77*
1979 **Oscar Peterson**, *Jousts*
1980 **Bill Evans**, *I Will Say Goodbye*

BEST JAZZ PERFORMANCE, GROUP

1958 **Count Basie**, *Basie*
1959 **Jonah Jones**, *I Dig Chicks*

BEST JAZZ PERFORMANCE BY A LARGE GROUP/INSTRUMENTAL/LARGE GROUP OR SOLOIST WITH LARGE GROUP

1960 **Henry Mancini**, *Blues and the Beat*
1961 **Stan Kenton**, *West Side Story*
1962 **Stan Kenton**, *Adventures in Jazz*
1963 **Woody Herman Band**, *Encore Woody Herman, 1963*
1964 **Laurindo Almeida**, *Guitar from Ipanema*
1965 **Duke Ellington Orchestra**, *Ellington '66*
1966 **Category not voted on**
1967 **Duke Ellington**, *Far East Suite*
1968 **Duke Ellington**, *And His Mother Called Him Bill*
1969 **Quincy Jones**, *Walking in Space*
1970 **Miles Davis**, *Bitches Brew*

BEST JAZZ PERFORMANCE BY A GROUP

1971 **Bill Evans Trio**, *The Bill Evans Album*
1972 **Freddie Hubbard**, *First Light*
1973 **Supersax**, *Supersax Plays Bird*
1974 **Oscar Peterson, Joe Pass and Neils Pedersen**, *The Trio*
1975 **Chick Corea and Return to Favor**, *No Mystery*
1976 **Chick Corea**, *The Leprechaun*
1977 **Phil Woods**, *The Phil Woods Six, Live from the Showboat*

BEST JAZZ INSTRUMENTAL PERFORMANCE, GROUP

1978 **Chick Corea**, *Friends*
1979 **Gary Burton** and **Chick Corea**, *Duet*
1980 **Bill Evans**, *We Will Meet Again*

BEST JAZZ PERFORMANCE BY A BIG BAND

1971 **Duke Ellington**, *New Oreleans Suite*
1972 **Duke Ellington**, *Toga Brava Suite*
1973 **Woody Herman**, *Giant Steps*
1974 **Woody Herman**, *Thundering Herd*
1975 **Phil Woods with Michel Legrand and His Orchestra**, *Images*
1976 **Duke Ellington**, *The Ellington Suites*
1977 **Count Basie**, *Prime Time*
1978 **Thad Jones** and **Mel Lewis**, *Live in Munich*
1979 **Duke Ellington**, *At Fargo, 1940 Live*
1980 **Count Basie**, *On the Road*

BEST JAZZ FUSION PERFORMANCE, VOCAL OR INSTRUMENTAL

1979 **Weather Report**, *8:30*
1980 **Manhattan Transfer**, *Birdland*

BEST ORIGINAL JAZZ COMPOSITION

1961 **Galt MacDermott**, *African Waltz*
1962 **Vince Guaraldi**, *Cast Your Fate to the Winds*
1963 **Steve Allen and Ray Brown**, *Gravy Waltz*
1964 **Lalo Shifrin**, *The Cat*
1965 **Lalo Shifrin**, *Jazz Suite on the Mass Texts*
1966 **Duke Ellington**, *In the Beginning God*

BEST COMEDY PERFORMANCE

1958 **David Seville**, *The Chipmunk Song*
1959 **Shelley Berman**, *Inside Shelley Berman*
Homer and Jethro, *The Battle of Kookamonga*
1960 **Bob Newhart**, *Button Down Strikes Back*
Jonathan and Darlene Edwards, *Jonathan and Darlene Edwards in Paris*
1961 **Mike Nichols and Elaine May**, *An Evening With Mike Nichols and Elaine May*
1962 **Vaughn Meader**, *The First Family*
1963 **Allan Sherman**, *Hello Muddah, Hello Faddah*
1964 **Bill Cosby**, *I Started Out As a Child*
1965 **Bill Cosby**, *Why Is There Air?*
1966 **Bill Cosby**, *Wonderfulness*
1967 **Bill Cosby**, *Revenge*
1968 **Bill Cosby**, *To Russell, My Brother, Whom I Slept With*
1969 **Bill Cosby**, *Bill Cosby*
1970 **Flip Wilson**, *The Devil Made Me Buy This Dress*
1971 **Lily Tomlin**, *This Is a Recording*
1972 **George Carlin**, *FM & AM*
1973 **Cheech and Chong**, *Los Cochinos*
1974 **Richard Pryor**, *That Nigger's Crazy*
1975 **Richard Pryor**, *Is It Something I Said?*
1976 **Richard Pryor**, *Bicentennial Nigger*
1977 **Steve Martin**, *Let's Get Small*
1978 **Steve Martin**, *A Wild and Crazy Guy*
1979 **Robin Williams**, *Reality . . . What a Concept*
1980 **Rodney Dangerfield**, *No Respect*

BEST PERFORMANCE, FOLK/BEST FOLK PERFORMANCE

1959 **Kingston Trio**, *The Kingston Trio at Large*
1960 **Harry Belafonte**, *Swing Dat Hammer*
1961 **Belafonte Folk Singers**, *Belafonte Folksingers at Home and Abroad*
1962 **Peter, Paul and Mary**, *If I Had a Hammer*
1963 **Peter, Paul and Mary**, *Blowin' in the Wind*
1964 **Gale Garnett**, *We'll Sing in the Sunshine*
1965 **Harry Belafonte and Miriam Makeba**, *An Evening With Belafonte/Makeba*
1966 **Cortelia Clark**, *Blues in the Street*
1967 **John Hartford**, *Gentle on My Mind*
1968 **Judy Collins**, *Both Sides Now*
1969 **Joni Mitchell**, *Clouds*

BEST ETHNIC OR TRADITIONAL RECORDING

1970 **T-Bone Walker**, *Good Feelin'*
1971 **Muddy Waters**, *They Call Me Muddy Waters*
1972 **Muddy Waters**, *The London Muddy Waters Session*
1973 **Doc Watson**, *Then and Now*
1974 **Doc and Merle Watson**, *Two Days in November*
1975 **Muddy Waters**, *The Muddy Waters Woodstock Album*
1976 **John Hartford**, *Mark Twang*
1977 **Muddy Waters**, *Hard Again*
1978 **Muddy Waters**, *I'm Ready*
1979 **Muddy Waters**, *Muddy "Mississippi" Waters Live*
1980 **Isaiah Ross, Maxwell Street Jimmmy, Big Joe Williams, Son House, Rev. Robert Wilkins, Little**

Brother Montgomery and **Sunnyland Slim,** *Rare Blues*

BEST LATIN RECORDING

1975 **Eddie Palmieri,** *Sun of Latin Music*
1976 **Eddie Palmieri,** *Unfinished Masterpiece*
1977 **Mongo Santamaria,** *Dawn*
1978 **Tito Puente,** *Homanaje a Beny More*
1979 **Irakere,** *Irakere*
1980 **Cal Tjader,** *La Onda Va Bien*

BEST COUNTRY AND WESTERN PERFORMANCE/BEST COUNTRY AND WESTERN RECORDING

1958 **Kingston Trio,** *Tom Dooley*
1959 **Johnny Horton,** *Battle of New Orelans*
1960 **Marty Robbins,** *El Paso*
1961 **Jimmy Dean,** *Big Bad John*
1962 **Burl Ives,** *Funny Way of Laughin'*
1963 **Bobby Bare,** *Detroit City*
1964 **Roger Miller,** *Dang Me* (single)
Roger Miller, *Dang Me/Chug-a-Lug* (album)
1965 **Roger Miller,** *King of the Road* (single)
Roger Miller, *The Return of Roger Miller* (album)
1966 **David Houston,** *Almost Persuaded*
1967 **Glen Campbell** (produced by Al DeLory), *Gentle on My Mind*

BEST COUNTRY (and Western) VOCAL PERFORMANCE (Female)

1964 **Dottie West,** *Here Comes My Baby*
1965 **Jody Miller,** *Queen of the House*
1966 **Jeannie Seely,** *Harper Valley P.T.A.*
1967 **Tammy Wynette,** *I Don't Wanna Play House*
1968 **Jeannie C. Riley,** *Harper Valley P.T.A.*
1969 **Tammy Wynette,** *Stand By Your Man*
1970 **Lynn Anderson,** *Rose Garden*
1971 **Sammi Smith,** *Help Me Make It Through the Night*
1972 **Donna Fargo,** *Happiest Girl in the Whole USA*
1973 **Olivia Newton-John,** *Let Me Be There*
1974 **Anne Murray,** *Love Song*
1975 **Linda Ronstad,** *I Can't Help It (If I'm Still in Love with You)*
1976 **Emmylou Harris,** *Elite Hotel*
1977 **Crystal Gale,** *Don't It Make My Brown Eyes Blue*
1978 **Dolly Parton,** *Here You Come Again*
1979 **Emmylou Harris,** *Blue Kentucky Girl*
1980 **Anne Murray,** *Could I Have This Dance?*

BEST COUNTRY (and Western) VOCAL PERFORMANCE (Male)

1964 **Roger Miller,** *Dang Me*
1965 **Roger Miller,** *King of the Road*
1966 **David Houston,** *Almost Persuaded*
1967 **Glen Campbell,** *Gentle on My Mind*
1968 **Johnny Cash,** *Folsom Prison Blues*
1969 **Johnny Cash,** *A Boy Named Sue*
1970 **Ray Price,** *For the Good Times*
1971 **Jerry Reed,** *When You're Hot, You're Hot*
1972 **Charley Pride,** *Charley Pride Sings Heart Songs*
1973 **Charlie Rich,** *Behind Closed Doors*
1974 **Ronnie Milsap,** *Please Don't Tell Me How the Story Ends*
1975 **Willie Nelson,** *Blue Eyes Cryin' in the Rain*
1976 **Ronnie Milsap,** *(I'm a) Stand By My Woman Man*
1977 **Kenny Rogers,** *Lucille*
1978 **Willie Nelson,** *Georgia on My Mind*
1979 **Kenny Rogers,** *The Gambler*
1980 **George Jones,** *He Stopped Loving Her Today*

BEST COUNTRY AND WESTERN DUET, TRIO OR GROUP (Vocal or Instrumental)

1967 **Johnny Cash and June Carter,** *Jackson*
1968 **Flatt & Scruggs,** *Foggy Mountain Breakdown*

BEST COUNTRY PERFORMANCE BY A DUO OR GROUP/BEST COUNTRY VOCAL PERFORMANCE BY A DUO OR GROUP

1969 **Waylon Jennings and the Kimberlys,** *MacArthur Park*
1970 **Johnny Cash and June Carter,** *If I Were a Carpenter*
1971 **Conway Twitty and Loretta Lynn,** *After the Fire Is Gone*
1972 **Statler Brothers,** *Class of '57*
1973 **Kris Kristofferson and Rita Coolidge,** *From the Bottle to the Bottom*
1974 **Pointer Sisters,** *Fairytale*
1975 **Kris Kristofferson and Rita Coolidge,** *Lover Please*
1976 **Amazing Rhythm Aces,** *The End Is Not in Sight* (The Cowboy Tune)
1977 **The Kendalls,** *Heaven's Just a Sin Away*
1978 **Waylon Jennings** and **Willie Nelson,** *Mamas Don't Let Your Babies Grow Up to be Cowboys*
1979 **Charlie Daniels Band,** *The Devil Went Down to Georgia*
1980 **Roy Orbison** and **Emmylou Harris,** *That Lovin' You Feelin' Again*

BEST COUNTRY INSTRUMENTAL PERFORMANCE

1969 **Danny Davis and the Nashville Brass,** *The Nashville Brass Featuring Danny Davis Play More Nashville Sounds*
1970 **Chet Atkins and Jerry Reed,** *Me & Jerry*
1971 **Chet Atkins,** *Snowbird*
1972 **Charlie McCoy,** *Charlie McCoy/The Real McCoy*
1973 **Eric Weissberg and Steven Mandell,** *Dueling Banjos*
1974 **Chet Atkins and Merle Travis,** *The Atkins-Travis Traveling Show*
1975 **Chet Atkins,** *The Entertainer*
1976 **Chet Atkins and Les Paul,** *Chester & Lester*
1977 **Hargus "Pig" Robbins,** *Hargus 'Pig' Robbins*
1978 **Asleep at the Wheel,** *One O'Clock Jump*
1979 **Doc and Merle Watson,** *Big Sandy/Leather Britches*
1980 **Gilley's Urban Cowboy Band,** *Orange Blossom Special/Hoedown*

BEST COUNTRY (and Western) Song (Award to Songwriter)

1964 **Roger Miller,** *Dang Me*
1965 **Roger Miller,** *King of the Road*
1966 **Billy Sherrill and Glenn Sutton,** *Almost Persuaded*
1967 **John Hartford,** *Gentle on My Mind*
1968 **Bobby Russell,** *Little Green Apples*
1969 **Shel Silverstein,** *A Boy Named Sue*
1970 **Marty Robbins,** *My Woman, My Woman, My Wife*
1971 **Kris Kristofferson,** *Help Me Make It Through the Night*
1972 **Ben Peters,** *Kiss an Angel Good Morning*
1973 **Kenny O'Dell,** *Behind Closed Doors*
1974 **Norris Wilson and Billy Sherrill,** *A Very Special Love Song*
1975 **Chips Moman and Larry Butler,** *(Hey, Won't You Play) Another Somebody Done Somebody Wrong*
1976 **Larry Gatlin,** *Broken Lady*
1977 **Richard Leigh,** *Don't It Make My Brown Eyes Blue*
1978 **Don Schlitz,** *The Gambler*

1979 **Bob Morrison** and **Debbie Hupp**, *You Decorated My Life*
1980 **Willie Nelson**, *On the Road Again*

BEST RHYTHM AND BLUES PERFORMANCE

1958 **The Champs**, *Tequila*
1959 **Dinah Washington**, *What a Difference a Day Makes*
1960 **Ray Charles**, *Let the Good Times Roll*
1961 **Ray Charles**, *Hit the Road Jack*
1962 **Ray Charles**, *I Can't Stop Loving You*
1963 **Ray Charles**, *Busted*
1964 **Nancy Wilson**, *How Glad I Am*
1965 **James Brown**, *Papa's Got a Brand New Bag*
1966 **Ray Charles**, *Crying Time*

BEST RHYTHM AND BLUES RECORDING, SOLO VOCAL

1966 **Ray Charles**, *Crying Time*
1967 **Aretha Franklin**, *Respect (prod. by Jerry Wexler),*

BEST RHYTHM AND BLUES VOCAL PERFORMANCE

1967 **Aretha Franklin**, *Respect*
1968 **Aretha Franklin**, *Chain of Fools*
1969 **Aretha Franklin**, *Share Your Love With Me*
1970 **Aretha Franklin**, *Don't Play That Song*
1971 **Aretha Franklin**, *Bridge Over Troubled Water*
1972 **Aretha Franklin**, *Young, Gifted and Black*
1973 **Aretha Franklin**, *Master of Eyes*
1974 **Aretha Franklin**, *Ain't Nothing Like the Real Thing*
1975 **Natalie Cole**, *This Will Be*
1976 **Natalie Cole**, *Sophisticated Lady (She's a Different Lady)*
1977 **Thelma Houston**, *Don't Leave Me This Way*
1978 **Donna Summer**, *Last Dance*
1979 **Dionne Warwick**, *Deja Vu*
1980 **Stephanie Mills**, *Never Knew Love Like This Before*

BEST RHYTHM AND BLUES VOCAL PERFORMANCE

1967 **Lou Rawls**, *Dead End Street*
1968 **Otis Redding**, *(Sittin' on) The Dock of the Bay*
1969 **Joe Simon**, *The Chokin' Kind*
1970 **B.B. King**, *The Thrill Is Gone*
1971 **Lou Rawls**, *A Natural Man*
1972 **Billy Paul**, *Me and Mrs. Jones*
1973 **Stevie Wonder**, *Superstitition*
1974 **Stevie Wonder**, *Boogie on Raggae Woman*
1975 **Ray Charles**, *Living for the City*
1976 **Stevie Wonder**, *I Wish*
1977 **Lou Rawls**, *Unmistakably Lou*
1978 **George Benson**, *On Broadway*
1979 **Michael Jackson**, *Don't Stop 'til You Get Enough*
1980 **George Benson**, *Give Me the Night*

BEST RHYTHM AND BLUES GROUP PERFORMANCE

1966 **Ramsey Lewis**, *Hold It Right There*
1967 **Sam & Dave**, *Soul Man*
1968 **The Temptations**, *Cloud Nine*

BEST RHYTHM AND BLUES VOCAL PERFORMANCE BY A GROUP OR DUO/DUO, GROUP OR CHORUS

1969 **Isley Brothers**, *It's Your Thing*
1970 **The Delfonics**, *Didn't I (Blow Your Mind This Time)?*
1971 **Ike & Tina Turner**, *Proud Mary*
1972 **The Temptations**, *Papa Was A Rolling Stone*
1973 **Gladys Knight & The Pips**, *Midnight Train to Georgia*
1974 **Rufus**, *Tell Me Something Good*
1975 **Earth, Wind & Fire**, *Shining Star*
1976 **Marilyn McCoo and Billy Davis, Jr.**, *You Don't Have to be a Star (to Be in My Show)*
1977 **Emotions**, *Best of My Love*
1978 **Earth, Wind & Fire**, *All 'n All*
1979 **Earth Wind & Fire**, *After the Love Has Gone*
1980 **Manhattan**, *Shining Star*

BEST RHYTHM AND BLUES INSTRUMENTAL PERFORMANCE

1969 **King Curtis**, *Games People Play*
1970 **Category not voted on**
1971 **Category not voted on**
1972 **The Temptations** (Paul Riser, cond.), *Papa Was A Rolling Stone*
1973 **Ramsey Lewis**, *Hang On Sloopy*
1974 **MFSB**, *TSOP (The Sound of Philadelphia)*
1975 **Silver Convention**, *Fly, Robin, Fly*
1976 **George Benson**, *Theme from Good King Bad*
1977 **Brothers Johnson**, *Q*
1978 **Earth, Wind & Fire**, *Runnin'*
1979 **Earth, Wind & Fire**, *Boogie Wonderland*
1980 **George Benson**, *Off Broadway*

BEST RHYTHM AND BLUES SONG (Award to Songwriter)

1968 **Otis Redding and Steve Cropper**, *(Sittin' on) The Dock of the Bay*
1969 **Richard Spencer**, *Color Him Father*
1970 **Ronald Dunbar and General Johnson**, *Patches*
1971 **Bill Withers**, *Ain't No Sunshine*
1972 **Barrett Strong and Norman Whitfield**, *Papa Was a Rolling Stone*
1973 **Stevie Wonder**, *Superstitition*
1974 **Stevie Wonder**, *Living for the City*
1975 **Harry Wayne Casey, Richard Finch, Willie Clarke and Betty Wright**, *Where Is the Love?*
1976 **Boz Scaggs and David Paich**, *Lowdown*
1977 **Lou Sayer and Vini Poncia**, *You Make Me Feel Like Dancing*
1978 **Paul Jabara**, *Last Dance*
1979 **David Foster**, **Jay Craydon** and **Bill Champlain**, *After the Love Has Gone*
1980 **Reggie Lucas** and **James Mtume**, *Never Knew Love Like This Before*

BEST GOSPEL OR OTHER RELIGIOUS RECORDING

1961 **Mahalia Jackson** *Everytime I Feel the Spirit*
1962 **Mahalia Jackson** *Great Songs of Love and Faith*
1963 **Soeur Sourire**, *Dominique*
1964 **Tennessee Ernie Ford**, *Great Gospel Songs*
1965 **George Beverly Shea and the Anita Kerr Singers**, *Southland Favorites*

BEST INSPIRATIONAL PERFORMANCE

1977 **B.J. Thomas**, *Home Where I Belong*
1978 **B.J. Thomas**, *Happy Man*
1979 **B.J. Thomas**, *You Gave Me Love (When No One Gave Me a Prayer)*
1980 **Debby Boone**, *With My Song I Will Praise Him*

BEST SACRED RECORDING/BEST SACRED PERFORMANCE/BEST INSPIRATIONAL PERFORMANCE/BEST GOSPEL PERFORMANCE, CONTEMPORARY OR INSPIRATIONAL

1966 **Porter Wagoner and the Blackwood Brothers**, *Grand Old Gospel*
1967 **Elvis Presley**, *How Great Thou Art*
1968 **Jake Hess**, *Beautiful Isle of Somewhere*
1969 **Jake Hess**, *Ain't That Beautiful Singing*

1970 **Jake Hess,** *Everything Is Beautiful*
1971 **Charley Pride,** *Did You Think to Pray?*
1972 **Elvis Presley,** *He Touched Me*
1973 **Bill Gaither Trio,** *Let's Just Praise the Lord*
1974 **Elvis Presley,** *How Great Thou Art*
1975 **Bill Gaither Trio,** *Jesus, We Just Want to Thank You*
1976 **Gary S. Paxton,** *The Astonishing, Outrageous, Amazing, Incredible, Unbelievable, Different World of Gary S. Paxton*
1977 **Imperials,** *Sail On*
1978 **Larry Hart,** *What a Friend*
1979 **Imperials,** *Heed the Call*
1980 **Reba Rambo, Dony McGuire, B. J. Thomas, Andrae Crouch, The Archers, Walter & Tramaine Hawkins, Cynthia Clawson,** *The Lord's Prayer*

BEST SOUL GOSPEL PERFORMANCE

1968 **Dottie Rambo,** *The Soul of Me*
1969 **Edwin Hawkins Singers,** *Oh, Happy Day*
1970 **Edwin Hawkins Singers,** *Every Man Wants to Be Free*
1971 **Shirley Caesar,** *Put Your Hand in the Hand of the Man from Galilee*
1972 **Aretha Franklin,** *Amazing Grace*
1973 **Dixie Hummingbirds,** *Love Me Like a Rock*
1974 **James Cleveland and the Southern California Community Choir,** *In the Ghetto*
1975 **Andrae Crouch and the Disciples,** *Take Me Back*
1976 **Mahalia Jackson,** *How I Got Over*
1977 **James Cleveland,** *James Cleveland at Carnegie Hall*

BEST SOUL GOSPEL PERFORMANCE, CONTEMPORARY

1977 **Eddie Hawkins and the Eddie Hawkins Singers,** *Wonderful*
1978 **Andrea Crouch** and **the Disciples,** *Live in London*
1979 **Andrea Crouch,** *I'll Be Thinking of You*
1980 **Shirley Caesar,** *Rejoice*

BEST SOUL GOSPEL PERFORMANCE, TRADITIONAL

1978 **Mighty Clouds of Joy,** *Live and Direct*
1979 **Mighty Clouds of Joy,** *Changing Times*
1980 **James Cleveland** and the **Charles Fold Singers,** *Lord, Let Me Be an Instrument*

BEST GOSPEL PERFORMANCE (Other than Soul Gospel)/BEST GOSPEL PERFORMANCE, TRADITIONAL

1967 **Porter Wagoner and the Blackwood Brothers,** *More Grand Old Gospel*
1968 **Happy Goodman Family,** *The Happy Gospel of the Happy Goodmans*
1969 **Porter Wagoner and the Blackwood Brothers,** *In Gospel Country*
1970 **Oak Ridge Boys,** *Talk About the Good Times*
1971 **Charley Pride,** *Let Me Live*
1972 **Blackwood Brothers,** *Love*
1973 **Blackwood Brothers,** *Release Me (from My Sin)*
1974 **Oak Ridge Boys,** *The Baptism of Jesse Taylor*
1975 **Imperials,** *No Shortage*
1976 **Oak Ridge Boys,** *Where the Soul Never Dies*
1977 **Oak Ridge Boys,** *Just a Little Talk with Jesus*
1978 **Happy Goodman Family,** *Refreshing*
1979 **Blackwood Brothers,** *Lift Up the Name of Jesus*
1980 **Blackwood Brothers,** *We Come to Worship*

BEST ORIGINAL CAST ALBUM, BROADWAY OR TV

1958 **Meredith Wilson,** *The Music Man*

BEST BROADWAY SHOW ALBUM/BEST SHOW ALBUM

1959 **Ethel Merman,** *Gypsy*
Gwen Verdon, *Redhead*
1960 **Mary Martin** (composed by **Richard Rodgers** and **Oscar Hammerstein II**), *The Sound of Music*
1961 **Frank Loesser,** *How to Succeed in Business Without Really Trying*
1962 **Richard Rodgers,** *No Strings*
1963 **Jerry Block and Sheldon Harnick,** *She Loves Me*
1964 **Jule Styne and Bob Merrill,** *Funny Girl*
1965 **Alan Lerner and Burton Lane,** *On a Clear Day*
1966 **Jerry Herman,** *Mame*
1967 **Fred Ebb and John Kander (prod. by Goddard Lieberson),** *Cabaret*
1968 **Gerome Ragni, James Rado and Galt MacDermott** (prod. by **Andy Wiswell**), *Hair*
1969 **Burt Bacharach and Hal David** (prod. by **Henry Jerome** and **Phil Ramone**), *Promises, Promises*
1970 **Stephen Sondheim** (prod. by **Thomas Z. Shepard**), *Company*
1971 **Stephen Schwartz** (prod. by **Stephen Schwartz**), *Godspell*
1972 **Micki Grant** (prod. by **Jerry Ragnvoy**), *Don't Bother Me, I Can't Cope*
1973 **Stephen Sondheim** (prod. by **Goddard Lieberson**), *A Little Night Music*
1974 **Judd Woldin and John Brittan** (prod. by **Thomas Z. Shepard**), *Raisin*
1975 **Charlie Smalls** (prod. by **Jerry Wexler**), *The Wiz*
1976 **Hugo & Luigi** (prod.), *Bubbling Brown Sugar*
1977 **Charles Strase and Martin Chernin** (prod. by **Larry Morton** and **Charles Strase**), *Annie*
1978 **Thomas Z. Shepard,** (prod.) *Ain't Misbehavin'*
1979 **Stephen Sondheim** (prod. by **Thomas Z. Shepard**), *Sweeney Todd*
1980 **Andrew Lloyd Webber** and **Tim Rice** (prod. by **Andrew Lloyd Webber** and **Tim Rice**), *Evita*

BEST SOUNDTRACK ALBUM, DRAMATIC PICTURE SCORE OR ORIGINAL CAST

1958 **Andre Previn,** *Gigi*

BEST SOUNDTRACK ALBUM OR RECORDING OF MUSIC SCORE FROM MOTION PICTURE OR TELEVISION

1959 **Duke Ellington,** *Anatomy of A Murder*
1960 **Ernest Gold,** *Exodus*
1961 **Henry Mancini,** *Breakfast at Tiffany's*
1962 **Category not voted on**
1963 **John Addison,** *Tom Jones*
1964 **Richard M. and Roger B. Sherman,** *Mary Poppins*
1965 **Johnny Mandel,** *The Sandpiper*
1966 **Maurice Jarre,** *Dr. Zhivago*
1967 **Lalo Shifrin,** *Mission: Impossible*
1968 **Paul Simon** (additional music by **David Grusin**), *The Graduate*
1969 **Burt Bacharach,** *Butch Cassidy & The Sundance Kid*
1970 **John Lennon, Paul McCartney, George Harrison and Ringo Starr,** *Let It Be*
1971 **Isaac Hayes,** *Shaft*
1972 **Nino Rota,** *The Godfather*
1973 **Neil Diamond,** *Jonathan Livingston Seagull*
1974 **Marvin Hamlisch, Alan and Marilyn Bergman,** *The Way We Were*
1975 **John Williams,** *Jaws*
1976 **Norman Whitfield,** *Car Wash*
1977 **John Williams,** *Star Wars*
1978 **John Williams,** *Close Encounters of the Third Kind*
1979 **John Williams,** *Superman*

1980 **John Williams**, *The Empire Strikes Back*

BEST SOUNDTRACK ALBUM, ORIGNAL CAST, MOTION PICTURE OR TELEVISION

1959 **Andre Previn and Ken Darby,** *Porgy and Bess*
1960 **Cole Porter** (composer), *Can Can*
1961 **Johnny Green, Saul Chaplin, Sid Ramin and Irwin Kostal** (collaborators), *West Side Story*

BEST RECORDING FOR CHILDREN

1958 **David Seville,** *The Chipmunk Song*
1959 **Peter Ustinov** (narrator) and **Herbert von Karajan** (conductor), *Peter and the Wolf*
1960 **David Seville,** *Let's All Sing with the Chipmunks*
1961 **Leonard Bernstein conducting the New York Philharmonic,** *Peter and the Wolf*
1962 **Leonard Bernstein,** *Saint Saens: Carnival of the Animals/Britten: Young Person's Guide to the Orchestra*
1963 **Leonard Bernstein,** *Bernstein Conducts for Young People*
1964 **Julie Andrews and Dick Van Dyke,** *Mary Poppins*
1965 **Marvin Miller,** *Dr. Seuss Presents "Fox in Sox" and "Green Eggs and Ham"*
1966 **Marvin Miller,** *Dr. Seuss Presents "If I Ran the Zoo" and "Sleep Book"*
1967 **Boris Karloff,** *Dr. Seuss Presents "How the Grinch Stole Christmas"*
1968 **No award**
1969 **Peter, Paul and Mary,** *Peter Paul and Mary*
1970 **Joan Cooney** (producer), *Sesame Street*
1971 **Bill Cosby,** *Bill Cosby Talks to Kids About Drugs*
1972 **Christopher Cerf** (proj. dir.), **Lee Chamberlain, Bill Cosby, Rita Moreno and Joe Raposa** (producer), *The Electric Company*
1973 ***Sesame Street*** **cast and Joe Raposa** (producer), *Sesame Street Live*
1974 **Sebastian Cabot, Sterling Holloway and Paul Winchell,** *Winnie the Pooh & Tigger Too*
1975 **Richard Burton,** *The Little Prince*
1976 **Hermione Gingold and Karl Bohm,** *Prokofiev: Peter and the Wolf/Saint Saens: Carnival of the Animals*
1977 **Christopher Cerf and Jimmy Timmens,** *Aren't You Glad You're You*
1978 **Jim Henson**, *The Muppet Show*
1979 **Jim Henson** (creator) and **Paul Williams** (prod.), *The Muppet Movie*
1980 **The Doobie Brothers, James Taylor, Carly Simon, Bette Midler, Muppets, Al Jarreau, Linda Ronstadt, Wendy Waldman, Libby Titus & Dr. John, Livingston Taylor, George Benson & Pauline Wilson, Lucy Simon, Kate Taylor, & The Simon/Taylor Family,** *In Harmony/A Sesame Street Record*

BEST PERFORMANCE, DOCUMENTARY OR SPOKEN WORD/BEST SPOKEN WORD OR DRAMA RECORDING

1958 **Stan Freberg,** *The Best of the Stan Freberg Show*
1959 **Carl Sandburg,** *A Lincoln Portrait*
1960 **Robert Bailek** (producer), *F.D.R. Speaks*
1961 **Leonard Bernstein,** *Humor in Music*
1962 **Charles Laughton,** *The Story-Teller: A Session with Charles Laughton*
1963 **Edward Albee,** *Who's Afraid of Virginia Woolf?*
1964 ***That Was the Week That Was*** **cast,** *BBC Tribute to John F. Kennedy*
1965 **Goddard Lieberson** (producer), *John F. Kennedy—As We Remember Him*
1966 **Edward R. Murrow,** *Edward R. Murrow—A Reporter Remembers,* Vol. I, *The War Years*
1967 **Sen. Everett M. Dirksen,** *Gallant Men*
1968 **Rod McKuen,** *Lonesome Cities*
1969 **Art Linkletter and Diane,** *We Love You, Call Collect*
1970 **Martin Luther King, Jr.,** *Why I Oppose the War in Vietnam*
1971 **Les Crane,** *Desiderata*
1972 **Bruce Botnick** (producer), *Lenny*
1973 **Richard Harris,** *Jonathan Livingston Seagull*
1974 **Peter Cook and Dudley Moore,** *Good Evening*
1975 **James Whitmore,** *Give 'Em Hell, Harry*
1976 **Orson Welles, Henry Fonda, Helen Hayes and James Earl Jones,** *Great American Documents*
1977 **Julie Harris,** *The Belle of Amherst*
1978 **Orson Welles,** *Citizen Kane*
1979 **John Gielgud,** *Ages of Man (Readings from Shakespeare)*
1980 **Pat Carroll,** *Gertrude Stein, Gertrude Stein, Gertrude Stein*

BEST HISTORICAL REISSUE

1978 **Michael Brooks** (prod.) *Lester Young Story* Vol. 3
1979 **Jerry Korn** and **Michael Brooks** (prod.), *Billie Holiday (Giants of Jazz)*
1980 **Keith Hardwick** (prod.), *Segovia — The EMI Recordings 1927-39*

ALBUM OF THE YEAR, CLASSICAL (Awards to Artist and Producer)

1961 **Igor Stravinsky conducting the Columbia Symphony,** *Stravinsky Conducts, 1960: Le Sacre du Printemps; Petrouchka*
1962 **Vladimir Horowitz,** *Columbia Records Presents Vladimir Horowitz*
1963 **Benjamin Britten conducting the London Symphony Orchestra and Chorus,** *Britten: War Requiem*
1964 **Leonard Bernstein conducting the New York Philharmonic,** *Bernstein Symphony No. 3 (Kaddish)*
1965 **Vladimir Horowitz** (prod. by **Thomas Frost**), *Horowitz at Carnegie Hall (An Historic Return)*
1966 **Morton Gould conducting the Chicago Symphony** (prod. by **Howard Scott**), *Ives: Symphony No. 1 in D Minor*
1967 **Pierre Boulez and the Paris National Opera** (prod. by **Thomas Z. Shepard**), *Berg: Wozzeck*
Leonard Bernstein and the London Symphony Orchestra (prod. by **John McClure**), *Mahler: Symphony No. 8 in E Flat Major (Symphony of a Thousand)*
1968 **No award**
1969 **Walter Carlos** (prod. by **Rachel Elkind**), *Switched-on Bach*
1970 **Colin Davis and the Royal Opera House Orchestra** (prod. by **Erik Smith**), *Berlioz: Les Troyens*
1971 **Vladimir Horowitz** (prod. by **Richard Killough** and **Thomas Frost**), *Horowitz Plays Rachmaninoff*
1972 **Georg Solti conducting the Chicago Symphony Orchestra, Vienna Boys' Choir, Vienna State Opera Chorus and Vienna Sangerverein chorus and soloists** (prod. by **David Harvey**), *Mahler: Symphony No. 8*
1973 **Pierre Boulez conducting the New York Philharmonic** (prod. by **Thomas Z. Shepard**), *Bartok: Concerto for Orchestra*
1974 **Gerog Solti conducting the Chicago Symphony Orchestra** (prod. by **David Harvey**), *Berlioz: Symphonie Fantastique*

1975 **Sir Georg Solti conducting the Chicago Symphony Orchestra** (prod. by **Ray Minshull**), *Beethoven: Symphonies (9) Complete*
1976 **Artur Rubinstein and Daniel Barenboim conducting the London Philharmonic** (prod. by **Max Wilcox**), *Beethoven: The Five Piano Concertos*
1977 **Leonard Bernstein, Vladimir Horowitz, Isaac Stern, Mstislav Rostropovich, Dietrich Fischer-Dieskau, Yehudi Menuhin and Lyndon Woodside** (prod. by **Thomas Fronts**), *Concert of the Century*
1978 **Itzhak Perlman** with **Carlo Maria Guilini** and the **Chicago Symphony Orchestra** (prod. by **Christopher Bishop**), *Brahms: Concerto for Violin in D Major*
1979 **Sir Georg Solti** conducting the **Chicago Symphony Orchestra**, (prod. by **James Mallinson**), *Brahms: Symphonies Complete*
1980 **Pierre Boulez** conducting **Orchestre de l'Opera de Paris** (prod. by **Guenther Breest** and **Michael Horwath**) and **Teresa Stratas, Yvonne Minton, Franz Mazura** and **Toni Blankenheim**, *Berg: Lulu*

BEST CLASSICAL PERFORMANCE, ORCHESTRAL

1958 **Felix Slatkin and the Hollywood Bowl Symphony Orchestra,** *Gaite Parisienne*
1959 **Charles Munch conducting the Boston Symphony Orchestra,** *Debussy: Images for Orchestra*
1960 **Fritz Reiner conducting the Chicago Symphony Orchestra,** *Bartok: Music for Strings, Percussion and Celeste*
1961 **Charles Munch conducting the Boston Symphony Orchestra,** *Ravel: Daphnis and Chloe*
1962 **Igor Stravinsky conducting the Columbia Symphony,** *Stravinsky: The Firebird Ballet*
1963 **Erich Leinsdorf conducting the Boston Symphony Orchestra,** *Bartok: Concerto for Orchestra*
1964 **Erich Leinsdorf conducting the Boston Symphony Orchestra,** *Mahler: Symphony in C Sharp Minor/Berg: 'Wozzeck' Excerpts*
1965 **Leopold Stokowski conducting the American Symphony Orchestra,** *Ives: Symphony No. 4*
1966 **Erich Leinsdorf conducting the Boston Symphony Orchestra,** *Mahler: Symphony No. 6 in A Minor*
1967 **Igor Stravinsky conducting the Columbia Symphony,** *Stravinsky: Firebird & Petrouchka Suites*
1968 **Pierre Boulez conducting the New Philharmonic Orchestra,** *Boulez Conducts Debussy*
1969 **Pierre Boulez conducting the Cleveland Orchestra,** *Boulez Conducts Debussy,* Vol. 2, *Images Pour Orchestre*
1970 **Pierre Boulez conducting the Cleveland Orchestra,** *Stravinsky: Le Sacre du Printemps*
1971 **Carlo Maria Giulini conducting the Chicago Symphony Orchestra,** *Mahler: Symphony No. 1 in D Major*
1972 **Georg Solti conducting the Chicago Symphony Orchestra,** *Mahler: Symphony No. 7*
1973 **Pierre Boulez conducting the New York Philharmonic,** *Bartok: Concerto for Orchestra*
1974 **Georg Solti conducting the Chicago Symphony,** *Berlioz: Symphonie Fantastique*
1975 **Pierre Boulez conducting the New York Philharmonic,** *Ravel: Daphnis and Chloe*
1976 **Sir Georg Solti conducting the Chicago Symphony** (prod. by Ray Minshull), *Strauss: Also Sprach Zarathustra*
1977 **Carlo Maria Giulini conducting the Chicago Symphony Orchestra** (prod. by Gunther Breest), *Mahler: Symphony No. 9*
1978 **Herbert von Karajan** conducting the **Berlin Philharmonic** (prod. by **Michael Glotz**), *Beethoven: Symphonies*
1979 **Sir Georg Solti** conducting the **Chicago Symphony Orchestra** (prod. by **James Mallinson**), *Brahms: Symphonies Complete*
1980 **Sir Georg Solti** conducting the **Chicago Symphony Orchestra** (prod. by **Ray Minshull**, *Bruckner: Symphony No. 6 in A Major*

BEST CLASSICAL PERFORMANCE, INSTRUMENTAL, CONCERTO OR INSTRUMENTAL SOLOIST (Concerto Scale)

1958 **Van Cliburn, pianist, and Kiril Kondrashin and his Symphony Orchestra,** *Tchaikovsky: Concerto No. 1 in B Flat Minor, Op. 23*
1959 **Van Cliburn, pianist, and Kiril Kodrashin conducting the Symphony of the Air,** *Rachmaninoff: Piano Concerto No. 3*
1960 **Siavtoslav Ritcher with Eric Leinsdorf conducting the Chicago Symphony Orchestra,** *Brahms: Piano Concerto No. 2 in B Flat*
1961 **Isaac Stern, violinist, with Eugene Ormandy conducting the Philadelphia Orchestra,** *Bartok: Concerto No. 1 for Violin and Orchestra*
1962 **Isaac Stern with Igor Stravinsky conducting the Columbia Symphony,** *Stravinsky: Concerto in D for Violin*
1963 **Artur Rubinstein with Erich Leinsdorf conducting the Boston Symphony Orchestra,** *Tchaikovsky: Concerto No. 1 in B Flat Minor for Piano and Orchestra*
1964 **Isaac Stern with Eugene Ormandy conducting the Philadelphia Orchestra,** *Prokofieff: Concerto No. 1 in D Major for Violin*
1965 **Artur Rubinstein with Erich Leinsdorf conducting the Boston Symphony Orchestra,** *Beethoven: Concerto No. 4 in G Major for Piano and Orchestra*

BEST CLASSICAL PERFORMANCE, INSTRUMENTALIST

1958 **Andres Segovia,** *Segovia Golden Jubilee*

BEST CLASSICAL PERFORMANCE — INSTRUMENTAL SOLOIST (Other than Full Orchestral Accompaniment)

1959 **Artur Rubinstein,** *Beethoven: Sonata No. 21 in C, Op. 53; Sonata No. 18 in E Flat, Op. 31,* No. 3
1960 **Laurindo Almeida,** *The Spanish Guitars of Laurindo Almeida*

BEST PERFORMANCE — INSTRUMENTAL SOLOIST(S)

1966 **Julian Bream,** *Baroque Guitar*
1967 **Vladimir Horowitz,** *Horowitz in Concert*
1968 **Vladimir Horowitz,** *Horowitz on Television*
1969 **Walter Carlos,** *Switched-On Bach*
1970 **David Oistrakh and Mstislav Rostropovich,** *Brahms: Double Concerto (Concerto in A Minor for Violin and Cello)*

BEST CLASSICAL PERFORMANCE — INSTRUMENTAL SOLOIST OR DUO WITHOUT ORCHESTRA

1961 **Laurindo Almeida,** *Reverie for Spanish Guitars*
1962 **Vladimir Horowitz,** *Columbia Records Presents Vladimir Horowitz*
1963 **Vladimir Horowitz,** *The Sound of Horowitz*
1964 **Vladimir Horowitz,** *Vladimir Horowitz Plays Beethoven, Debussy, Chopin*

1965 Vladimir Horowitz, *Horowitz at Carnegie Hall —An Historic Return*

BEST INSTRUMENTAL SOLOIST PERFORMANCE

1971 Vladimir Horowitz, *Horowitz Plays Rachmaninoff*
1972 Vladimir Horowitz, *Horowitz Plays Chopin*
1973 Vladimir Horowitz, *Horowitz Plays Scriabin*
1974 Alicia de Larrocha, *Albeniz: Iberia*
1975 Nathan Milstein, *Bach: Sonatas and Partitas for Violin Unaccompanied*
1976 Vladimir Horowitz, *Horowitz Concerts 1975/76*
1977 Artur Rubinstein, *Beethoven: Sonata for Piano No. 18/Schumann: Fantasiestucke*
1978 Vladimir Horowitz, *The Horowitz Concerts 1977-78*
1979 Vladimir Horowitz, *The Horowitz Concerts 1978-79*
1980 No award

BEST INSTRUMENTAL SOLOIST PERFORMANCE (With Orchestra)

1971 Julian Bream, *Villa Lobos: Concerto for Guitar*
1972 Artur Rubinstein, *Brahms: Concerto No. 2*
1973 Vladimir Ashkenazy with Georg Solti conducting the Chicago Symphony Orchestra, *Beethoven: Concerti (5) for Piano and Orchestra*
1974 David Oistrakh, *Shostakovich: Violin Concerto No. 1*
1975 Alicia de Larrocha with De Burgos and Foster conducting the London Philaharmonic, *Ravel: Concerto for Left Hand and Concerto for Piano in G Major/Faure: Fantasie for Piano and Orchestra*
1976 Artur Rubinstein with Daniel Barenboim conducting the London Philharmonic, *Beethoven: The Five Piano Concertos*
1977 Itzhak Perlman with the London Philharmonic Orchestra, *Vivaldi: The Four Seasons*
1978 Vladimir Horowitz with the **Philadelphia Orchestra** conducted by **Eugene Ormandy,** *Rachmaninoff: Concerto No. 3 in D Minor for Piano (Horowitz Golden Jubilee)*
1979 Maurio Pollini with the **Chicago Symphony Orchestra** conducted by **Claudio Abbado,** *Bartok: Concertos for Piano Nos. 1 & 2*
1980 Itzhak Perlman with **Seiji Ozawa** conducting the **Boston Symphony Orchestra,** *Berg: Concerto for Violin & Orchestra* and *Stravinsky: Concerto in D Major for Violin & Orchestra*

BEST CLASSICAL PERFORMANCE, CHAMBER MUSIC/VOCAL OR INSTRUMENTAL CHAMBER MUSIC

1958 Hollywood String Quartet, *Beethoven Quartet 130*
1959 Artur Rubinstein, *Beethoven: Sonata No. 21 in C, Op. 53; Sonata No. 18 in E Flat, Op. 31, No. 3*
1960 Laurindo Almeida, *Conversations with the Guitar*
1961 Jascha Heifetz, Gregor Piatigorsky and William Primrose, *Beethoven: Serenade, Op. 8/Kodaly: Duo for Violin and Cello, Op. 7*
1962 Jascha Heifetz, Gregor Piatigorsky and William Primrose, *The Heifetz-Piatigorsky Concerts with Primrose, Pennario and Guests*
1963 Julian Bream Consort, *Evening of Elizabethan Music*
1964 Jascha Heifetz and Gregor Piatigorsky (with Jacob Lateiner, pianist), *Beethoven: Trio No. 1 in E Flat, Op. 1, No. 1*
New York Pro Musica, cond. by Noah Greenberg, *It Was A Lover and His Lass (Morley, Bird and Others)*
1965 Juilliard String Quartet, *Bartok: The Six String Quartets*
1966 Boston Symphony Chamber Players, *Boston Symphony Chamber Players*
1967 Ravi Shankar and Yehudi Menuhin, *West Meets East*
1968 E. Power Biggs with Edward Tarr Ensemble and Gabrieli Consort cond. by Victor Negri, *Gabrieli: Canzoni for Brass, Winds, Strings and Organ*
1969 Philadelphia, Cleveland and Chicago Brass Ensembles, *Gabrieli: Antiphonal Music of Gabriele (Canzoni for Brass Choirs)*
1970 Eugene Istomin, Isaac Stern and Leonard Rose, *Beethoven: The Complete Piano Trios*
1971 Juilliard Quartet, *Debussy: Quartet in G Minor/Ravel: Quartet in F Major*
1972 Julian Bream and John Williams, *Julian and John*
1973 Gunther Schuller and the New England Conservatory Ragtime Ensemble, *Joplin: The Red Back Book*
1974 Artur Rubinstein, Henryk Szeryng and Pierre Fournier, *Brahms and Schumann Trios*
1975 Artur Rubinstein, Henryk Szeryng and Pierre Fournier, *Schubert: Trios Nos. 1 in B Flat Major, Op. 99 and 2 in E Flat Major, Op. 100 (The Piano Trios)*
1976 David Munrow conducting Early Music Consort of London, *The Art of Courtly Love*
1977 Juilliard Quartet, *Schoenberg: Quartets for Strings*
1978 Itzhak Perlman and Vladimir Ashkenazy, *Beethoven: Sonatas for Violin and Piano*
1979 Dennis Russell Davies conducting the St. Paul Chamber Orchestra, *Copland: Appalachian Spring*
1980 Itzhak Perlman and Pinchas Zukerman, *Violins/Shostakovitch: Duets/Prokofiev: Sonata for Two Violins*

BEST CLASSICAL PERFORMANCE—VOCAL SOLOIST

1958 Renata Tebaldi, *Operatic Recital*
1959 Jussi Bjoerling, *Bjoerling in Opera*
1960 Leontyne Price, *A Program of Song*
1961 Joan Sutherland, *The Art of the Prima Donna*
1962 Eileen Farrell, *Wagner: Gotterdammerung —Brunnhilde's Immolation Scene/Wesendonck Songs*
1963 Leontyne Price, *Great Scenes from Gershwin's Porgy and Bess*
1964 Leontyne Price, *Berlioz: Nuits d'Ete (Song Cycle)/Falla: El Amor Brujo*
1965 Leontyne Price, *Strauss: Salome (Dance of the Seven Veils, Interlude, Final Scene); The Egyptian Helen (Awakening Scene)*
1966 Leontyne Price, *Prima Donna*
1967 Leontyne Price, *Prima Donna, Vol. 2*
1968 Montserrat Caballe, *Rossini Rarities*
1969 Leontyne Price, *Barber: Two Scenes from "Antony and Cleopatra"/Knoxville: Summer of 1915*
1970 Dietrich Fischer-Dieskau, *Schubert: Lieder*
1971 Leontyne Price, *Leontyne Price Sings Robert Schumann*
1972 Dietrich Fischer-Dieskau, *Brahms: Die Schone Magelone*
1973 Leontyne Price, *Puccini: Heroines (La Boheme, La Rondine, Tosca, Manon Lescault)*
1974 Leontyne Price, *Leontyne Sings Richard Strauss*
1975 Janet Baker, *Mahler: Kindertotenlieder*
1976 Beverly Sills, *Music of Victor Herbert*
1977 Janet Baker, *Bach Arias*
1978 Luciano Pavarotti, *Luciano Pavarotti — Hits from Lincoln Center*
1979 Luciano Pavarotti, *O Sole Mio*
1980 Leontyne Price, *Prima Donna, Vol. 5*

BEST CLASSICAL PERFORMANCE — OPERATIC OR CHORAL

1958 **Roger Wagner Chorale,** *Virtuoso*
1959 **Erich Leinsdorf conducting the Vienna Philharmonic Orchestra,** *Mozart: The Marriage of Figaro*

BEST CLASSICAL OPERA PRODUCTION/BEST OPERA RECORDING

1960 **Renata Tebaldi, Birgit Nilsson, Jussi Bjoerling and Giorgio Tozzi with Erich Leinsdorf conducting the Rome Opera House Chorus and Orchestra,** *Puccini: Turandot*
1961 **Gabriele Santini conducting the Rome Opera House Chorus and Orchestra,** *Puccini: Madama Butterfly*
1962 **Georg Solti conducting the Rome Opera House Chorus and Orchestra and Leontyne Price, Jon Vickers, Rita Gorr, Robert Merrill and Giorgio Tozzi,** *Verdi: Aida*
1963 **Erich Leinsdorf conducting the RCA Italiana Opera Orchestra with Leontyne Price, Richard Tucker and Rosalind Elias,** *Puccini: Madama Butterfly*
1964 **Herbert von Karajan conducting the Vienna Philharmonic Orchestra and Chorus with Leontyne Price, Franco Correlli, Robert Merrill and Mirella Freni,** *Bizet: Carmen*
1965 **Karl Bohm conducting the Orchestra of the German Opera with Dietrich Fischer-Dieskau, Evelyn Lear and Fritz Wunderlich,** *Berg: Wozzeck*
1966 **Georg Solti conducting the Vienna Philharmonic with Birgit Nilsson, Regine Crespin, Christa Ludwig, James King and Hans Hotter,** *Wagner: Die Walkure*
1967 **Pierre Boulez conducting the Paris National Opera with Walter Berry, Strauss, Fritz Uhl and Karl Doench,** *Berg: Wozzeck*
1968 **Erich Leinsdorf conducting the New Philharmonia Orchestra and Ambrosian Opera Chorus with Leontyne Price, Judith Raskin, Madelena Troyanos, Sherill Milnes, Shirley and Ezio Flagello,** *Mozart: Cosi Fan Tutti*
1969 **Herbert von Karajon conducting the Berlin Philharmonic with Jess Thomas, Thomas Stewart, Gerhard Stolze, Helga Dernesch, Zoltan Keleman, Oralia Dominguez, Catherine Goyer and Karl Ridderbusch,** *Wagner: Siegfried*
1970 **Colin Davis conducting the Royal Opera House Orchestra and Chorus with Jon Vickers, Josephine Veasey and Berret Lindholm,** *Berlioz: Les Troyens*
1971 **Erich Leinsdorf conducting the London Philharmonic with Leontyne Price, Placido Domingo, Sherrill Milnes, Grace Bumbry and Ruggerro Raimondi,** *Verdi: Aida*
1972 **Colin Davis conducting the BBC Symphony Orchestra and Chorus of Covent Garden,** *Berlioz: Benvenuto Cellini*
1973 **Leonard Bernstein conducting the Metropolitan Opera Orchestra and Manhattan Opera Chorus with Marilyn Horne, James McCracken, Adriana Maliponte and Tom Krause,** *Bizet: Carmen*
1974 **Georg Solti (conductor),** *Puccini: La Boheme*
1975 **Colin Davis conducting the Royal Opera House Orchestra with Montserrat Caballe, Janet Baker, Nicolai Gedda, Vladimiro Ganzarolli, Richard Van Allen and Ileana Cotrubas,** *Mozart: Cosi Fan Tutti*
1976 **Lorin Maazel conducting the Cleveland Orchestra and Chorus,** *Gershwin: Porgy and Bess*
1977 **John De Main conducting Sherwin M. Goldman/ Houston Grand Orchestra,** *Gershwin: Porgy and Bess*
1978 **Julius Rudel** conducting the New York City Opera and Chorus with **Beverly Sills** and **Titus,** *The Merry Widow*
1979 **Colin Davis** conducting the Orchestra and Chorus of the Royal Opera House, Covent Garden, with **John Vickers, Harper and Summers,** ***Britten: Peter Grimes***

BEST CLASSICAL PERFORMANCE, CHORAL (including Oratorio)/BEST CLASSICAL CHORAL PERFORMANCE

1960 **Sir Thomas Beecham conducting the Royal Philharmonic Orchestra and Chorus,** *Handel: The Messiah*
1961 **Robert Shaw Chorale,** *Bach: B Minor Mass*
1962 **Philharmonia Choir with William Pitz, choral dir., and Otto Klemperer conducting the Philharmonia Orchestra,** *Bach: St. Matthew Passion*
1963 **Bach Choir and Highgate School Choir dir. by Edward Chapman and Benjamin Britten conducting the London Symphony Orchestra,** *Britten: War Requiem*
1964 **Robert Shaw Chorale,** *Britten: A Ceremony of Carols*
1965 **Robert Shaw Chorale,** *Stravinsky: Symphony of Psalms/Poulenc: Gloria*
1966 **Robert Shaw Chorale,** *Handel: Messiah*
Gregg Smith conducting the Columbia Chamber Orchestra, Gregg Smith Singers and Ithaca College Concert Choir and George Bragg conducting the Texas Boys Choir, *Ives: Music for Chorus*
1967 **Leonard Bernstein conducting the London Symphony Orchestra,** *Mahler: Symphony in E Flat Major*
Robert Page conducting the Temple University Chorus and Eugene Ormandy conducting the Philadelphia Orchestra, *Orff: Catulli Carmina*
1968 **Vittorio Negri, conductor; Gregg Smith Singers, Texas Choir Boys, Edward Tarr Ensemble (George Bragg, dir.) and E. Power Biggs,** *The Glory of Gabrieli*
1969 **Swingle Singers and Luciano Berio conducting the New York Philharmonic,** *Berio: Sinfonia*
1970 **Gregg Smith Singers and Columbia Chamber Ensemble,** *(Ives) New Music of Charles Ives*
1971 **Colin Davis conducting the London Symphony Orchestra, Russell Burgess conducting the Wandsworth School Boys Choir and Arthur Oldham conducting the London Symphony Chorus,** *Berlioz: Requiem*
1972 **Georg Solti conducting Chicago Symphony Orchestra, Vienna Boys Choir, Vienna State Opera Chorus and Vienna Sangerverein chorus and soloists,** *Mahler: Symphony No. 8*
1973 **Andre Previn conducting the London Symphony Orchestra and Arthur Oldham conducting the London Symphony Orchestra Chorus,** *Walton: Belshazzar's Feast*
1974 **Colin Davis (conductor),** *Berlioz: The Damnation of Faust*
1975 **Robert Page directing the Cleveland Orchestra Chorus and Boys Choir and Michael Tilson Thomas conducting the Cleveland Orchestra,** *Orff: Carmina Burana*
1976 **Arthur Oldham (chorus master) of the London Symphony Chorus and Andre Previn conducting the London Symphony Orchestra,** *Rachmaninoff The Bells*

1977 **Margaret Hillis (choral dir.) and the Chicago Symphony Chorus with Sir Georg Solti conducting the Chicago Symphony Orchestra,** *Verdi; Requiem*
1978 **Margaret Hills** (choral dir.) and the **Chicago Symphony and Chorus** (**Sir Georg Solti**, cond.), *Beethoven: Missa Solemnis*
1979 **Marget Willis** (choral dir.) and the Chicago Symphony Orchestra and Chorus (**Sir Georg Solti**, cond.), *Brahms: A German Requiem*
1980 **Carlo Maria Giulini** (cond.) and **Norbert Balatsch** (chorus master) and **Philadelphia Orchestra** and Chorus, *Mozart: Requiem*

BEST COMPOSITION FIRST RECORDED AND RELEASED DURING YEAR/BEST CONTEMPORARY CLASSICAL COMPOSITION/BEST CLASSICAL COMPOSITION BY A CONTEMPORARY COMPOSER

1958 **Nelson Riddle,** *Cross Country Suite*
1959 **Duke Ellington,** *Anatomy of a Murder*
1960 **Aaron Copland,** *Orchestral Suite from Tender Land Suite*
1961 **Laurindo Almeida,** *Discantus*
Igor Stravinsky, *Movements for Piano and Orchestra*
1962 **Igor Stravinsky,** *The Flood*
1963 **Benjamin Britten,** *War Requiem*
1964 **Samuel Barber,** *Piano Concerto*
1965 **Charles Ives,** *Symphony No. 4*

BEST ENGINEERED RECORD, OTHER THAN CLASSICAL/BEST ENGINEERING CONTRIBUTION/BEST ENGINEERED RECORDING OTHER THAN CLASSICAL

1958 **Ted Keep,** *The Chipmunk Song*
1959 **Robert Simpson,** *Belafonte at Carnegie Hall*
1960 **Luis P. Valentin,** *Ella Fitzgerald Sings the George and Ira Gershwin Song Book*
1961 **Robert Arnold,** *Judy at Carnegie Hall*
1962 **Al Schmitt,** *Hatari!*
1963 **James Malloy,** *Charade*
1964 **Phil Ramone,** *Getz/Gilberto*
1965 **Larry Levine,** *A Taste of Honey*
1966 **Eddie Brackett and Lee Herschberg,** *Strangers in the Night*
1967 **Geoff Emerick,** *Sgt. Pepper's Lonely Hearts Club Band*
1968 **Joe Polito and Hugh Davies,** *Wichita Lineman*
1969 **Geoff Emerick and Phillip McDonald,** *Abbey Road*
1970 **Roy Halee,** *Bridge Over Troubled Water*
1971 **Dave Purple, Ron Capone and Henry Bush,** *Theme from Shaft*
1972 **Armin Steiner,** *Moods*
1973 **Robert Margouleff and Malcolm Cecil,** *Innervisions*
1974 **Geoff Emerick,** *Band on the Run*
1975 **Brooks Arthur, Larry Alexander and Russ Payne,** *Between the Lines*
1976 **Al Schmitt,** *Breezin'*
1977 **Roger Nichols, Elliot Scheiner, Bill Schnee and Al Schmitt,** *AJA*
1978 **Roger Nichols** and **Al Schmitt,** *FM (No Static At All)*
1979 **Peter Henderson,** *Breakfast in America*
1980 **James Guthrie,** *The Wall*

BEST ENGINEERING CONTRIBUTION, NOVELTY/NOVELTY OR SPECIAL EFFECTS

1959 **Ted Keep,** *Alvin's Harmonica*
1960 **John Kraus,** *The Old Payola Roll Blues*
1961 **John Kraus,** *Stan Freberg Presents the United States of America*
1962 **Robert Fine,** *The Civil War,* Vol. 1
1963 **Robert Fine,** *The Civil War,* Vol. 2
1964 **Dave Hassinger,** *The Chipmunks Sing the Beatles*

BEST ALBUM COVER/BEST ALBUM COVER, GRAPHIC ARTS/BEST ALBUM PACKAGE (Award to art director)

1959 **Robert M. Jones,** *Shostakovitch Symphony No. 5*
1960 **Marvin Schwartz,** *Latin a la Lee*
1961 **Jim Silke,** *Judy at Carnegie Hall*
1962 **Robert M. Jones,** *Lena . . . Lovely and Alive*
1963 **John Berg,** *The Barbra Streisand Album*
1964 **Robert Cato (art. dir.) and Don Bronstein (photographer),** *People*
1965 **See cover photography category below; no separate graphics category for non-classical**
1966 **Klaus Voormann,** *Revolver*
1967 **Peter Blake and Jann Haworth,** *Sgt. Pepper's Lonely Hearts Club Band*
1968 **John Berg and Richard Mantel (art dirs.) and Horn/Griner Studio (photography),** *Underground*
1969 **Evelyn J. Kelbish (painting) and David Stahlberg (graphics),** *America the Beautiful*
1970 **Robert Lochart (design) and Ivan Nagy (photography),** *Indianola Mississippi Seeds*
1971 **Dean O. Torrance (album design) and Gene Browell (art dir.),** *Pollution*
1972 **Acy Lehman (art dir.) and Harvey Dinerstein (artist),** *The Siegel Schwall Band*
1973 **Wilkes and Braun, Inc. (art dir.),** *Tommy*
1974 **Ed Thrasher and Christopher Whorf,** *Come & Gone*
1975 **Jim Ladwig,** *Honey*
1976 **John Berg,** *Chicago X*
1977 **Kosh,** *Simple Dreams*
1978 **Johnny Lee** and **Tony Lane** (art. dir.), *Boys in the Trees*
1979 **Mike Doud** and **Mick Haggerty** (art dir.), *Breakfast in America*
1980 **Ray Kohara** (art dir.), *Against the Wind*

BEST ALBUM COVER PHOTOGRAPHY

1965 **Robert Jones (art dir.) and Ken Whitmore (photographer),** *Jazz Suite on the Mass Texts*
1966 **Robert Jones (art dir.) and Les Leverette (photographer),** *Confessions of a Broken Man*
1967 **John Carto (art dir.) and Roland Scherman (photographer),** *Bob Dylan's Greatest Hits*

BEST ALBUM COVER, CLASSICAL

1961 **Marvin Schwartz,** *Puccini: Madama Butterfly*
1962 **Marvin Schwartz,** *The Intimate Bach*
1963 **Robert Jones,** *Puccini: Madama Butterfly*
1964 **Robert Jones (art dir.) and Jan Balet (graphic artist),** *Saint-Saens: Carnival of the Animals/Britten: Young Person's Guide to the Orchestra*
1965 **George Estes (art dir.) and James Alexander (graphic arts),** *Bartok: Concerto No. 2 for Violin/Stravinsky: Concerto for Violin*

BEST ALBUM NOTES (Award to annotator)

1963 **Stanley Dance and Leonard Feather,** *The Ellington Era*
1964 **Stanton Catlin and Carleton Beals,** *Mexico (Legacy Collection)*
1965 **Stan Cornyn,** *September of My Years*
1966 **Stan Cornyn,** *Sinatra at the Sands*
1967 **John D. Loudermilk,** *Suburban Attitudes in Country Verse*

1968 **Johnny Cash,** *Johnny Cash at Folsom Prison*
1969 **Johnny Cash,** *Nashville Skyline*
1970 **Chris Albertson,** *The World's Greatest Blues Singer*
1971 **Sam Samudio,** *Sam, Hard and Heavy*
1972 **Tom T. Hall,** *Tom T. Hall's Greatest Hitts*
1973 **Dan Morgenstern,** *God is in the House*
1974 **Charles R. Townsend,** *For the Last Time*
Dan Morgenstern, *The Hawk Flies*
1975 **Pete Hamill,** *Blood on the Tracks*
1976 **Dan Morgenstern,** *The Changing Face of Harlem*
1977 **George T. Simon,** *Bing Crosby: A Legendary Performer*
1978 **Michael Brooks,** *A Bing Crosby Collection,* Vols. I and II
1979 **Bob Porter** and **James Patrick,** *Charlie Parker: The Complete Savoy Sessions*
1980 **David McClintock,** *Segovia — The EMI Recordings 1927-39*

BEST ENGINEERED RECORD, CLASSICAL/BEST ENGINEERING CONTRIBUTION, CLASSICAL RECORDING/BEST ENGINEERED RECORDING, CLASSICAL

1958 **Sherwood Hall III,** *Duets with a Spanish Guitar*
1959 **Lewis W. Layton,** *Victory at Sea,* Vol. 1
1960 **Hugh Davies,** *Spanish Guitars of Laurindo Almeida*
1961 **Lewis W. Layton,** *Ravel: Daphnis and Chloe*
1962 **Lewis W. Layton,** *Strauss: Also Sprach Zarathustra, Op. 30*
1963 **Lewis W. Layton,** *Madama Butterfly*
1964 **Douglas Larter,** *Britten: Young Person's Guide to the Orchestra*
1965 **Fred Plaut,** *Horowitz at Carnegie Hall*
1966 **Anthony Salvatore,** *Wagner: Lohengrin*
1967 **Edward T. Graham,** *The Glorious Sound of Brass*
1968 **Gordon Parry,** *Mahler: Symphony No. 9 in D Major*
1969 **Walter Carlos,** *Switched-On Bach*
1970 **Fred Plaut, Ray Moore and Arthur Kendy,** *Stravinsky: Le Sacre du Printemps*
1971 **Vittorio Negri,** *Berlioz: Requiem*
1972 **Gordon Parry and Kenneth Wilkinson,** *Mahler: Symphony No. 8*
1973 **Edward T. Graham and Raymond Moore,** *Bartok: Concerto for Orchestra*
1974 **Kenneth Wilkinson,** *Berlioz: Symphonie Fantastique*
1975 **Edward T. "Bud" Graham, Ray Moore and Milton Cherin,** *Ravel: Daphnis and Chloe*
1976 **Edward T. Graham, Ray Moore and Milton Cherin,** *Gershwin: Rhapsody in Blue*
1977 **Kenneth Wilkinson** *Ravel: Bolero*
1978 **Bud Graham, Arthur Kendy** and **Ray Moore,** *Varese: Ameriques/Ionisation*
1979 **Anthony Salvatore,** *Sondheim: Sweeney Todd*
1980 **Karl-August Naegler,** *Berg: Lulu*

BEST PRODUCER OF THE YEAR

1974 **Thom Bell**
1975 **Arif Mardin**
1976 **Stevie Wonder,** *Songs in the Key of Life*
1977 **Peter Asher**
1978 **Bee Gees, Albhy Galuten** and **Karl Richardson**
1979 **Larry Butler**
1980 **Phil Ramone**

PRODUCER OF THE YEAR, CLASSICAL

1979 **James Mallinson**
1980 **Robert Woods**

BEST ALBUM NOTES, CLASSICAL (Award to annotator)

1972 **James Lyons,** *Vaughn Williams: Symphony No. 2*
1973 **Glenn Gould,** *Hindemith: Sonatas for Piano (Complete)*
1974 **Rory Guy,** *The Classic Erich Wolfgang Korngold*
1975 **Gunther Schuller,** *Footlifters*

SPECIAL NATIONAL TRUSTEES AWARDS FOR ARTISTS AND REPERTOIRE CONTRIBUTION

1959 **Bobby Darin (prod. by Ahmet Ertegun),** *Mack the Knife* (Record of the Year)
Frank Sinatra (prod. by Dave Cavanaugh), *Come Dance With Me* (Album of the Year)
1960 **Ernest Altschuler (producer),** *Theme from "A Summer Place"* (Record of the Year)
George Avakian (producer), *Button Down Mind* (Album of the Year)

SPECIAL TRUSTEES' AWARD

1967 **Greg Culshaw (producer) and Georg Solti (conductor),** *Wagner: Der Ring Des Niebelungen*
1968 **Krzysztof Penderecki (composer),** *The Passion According to St. Luke*
Billy Strayhorn and Duke Ellington, for overall contributions and for composing *The Far East Suite*
1970 **Robert Moog,** for the Moog Synthesizer
1971 **John Hammond and Chris Albertson (co-producers) and Larry Hiller (engineer),** *Bessie Smith Reissue Series*
Paul Weston, founding father and first national president of the Academy, for years of dedication
1972 **The Beatles,** for revolutionizing music and recordings with talent, originality and musical creativity

MISCELLANEOUS AWARDS

1959 **Nat "King" Cole,** *Midnight Flyer,* Best Performance by a "Top 40" Artist
1960 **Ray Charles,** *Georgia on My Mind,* Best Performance by a Pop Single Artist
Miles Davis and Gil Evans, *Sketches of Spain,* Best Jazz Composition of More Than Five Minutes Duration
1963 **Andre Watts,** Most Promising New Recording Artist
1964 **Marilyn Horne,** Most Promising New Recording Artist
Roger Miller, Best New Country and Western Artist of 1964
1965 **Peter Serkin,** Most Promising New Recording Artist
Statler Brothers, Best New Country and Western Artist

The Bing Crosby Award, which consists of a plaque rather than a Grammy statuette, is presented periodically to members of the industry for creative contributions of outstanding artistic or scientific significance of the field of phonograph records. The trustees select the winner.

1963 **Bing Crosby,** "Thirty years of making records of outstanding musicianship, uncompromising dignity and never-failing enthusiasm"
1965 **Frank Sinatra,** "Continuing dedication to the highest standards both as a performer and as a recording artist"
1966 **Duke Ellington,** "Tremendously high standards of musicianship and creativity through a career as a composer, pianist, arranger and conductor"
1967 **Ella Fitzgerald,** "Superb musicianship and consistent musical integrity"

1968 **Irving Berlin,** "More than half a century of composing so many songs, seemingly simple yet filled with warmth"
1971 **Elvis Presley,** "Artistic creativity and influence in the field of recorded music upon a generation of performers and listeners"
1972 **Mahalia Jackson,** "World's Greatest Gospel Singer, whose voice and lifelong commitment to God have epitomized the ennobling role of music"
1972 **Louis Armstrong,** "America's Good Will Ambassador, for outstanding contributions to music and for leading the way for millions of jazz musicians of all horns and colors, and for hundreds of brilliant recordings"

Hot 100 Awards

Billboard
9000 Sunset Blvd., Los Angeles, Calif. 90069
(213/273-7040)

The Hot 100 Award, which consists of a plaque, is given to the record that achieves the top position on the *Billboard* record chart.

1977 ***You Don't Have to be a Star,*** Marilyn McCoo/Billy Davis
You Make Me Feel Like Dancin', Leo Sayer
I Wish, Rose Royce
Car Wash, Rose Royce
Torn Between Two Lovers, Mary MacGregor
Blinded by the Light, Manfred Mann's Earth Band
New Kid in Town, Eagles
Love Theme from "A Star Is Born," Barbra Streisand
Rich Girl, Daryl Hall/John Oates
Dancing Queen, Abba
Don't Give up on Us, David Soul
Don't Leave Me This Way, Thelma Houston
Southern Nights, Glen Campbell
Hotel California, Eagles
When I Need You, Leo Sayer
Sir Duke, Stevie Wonder
I'm Your Boogie Man, K C & Sunshine Band
Dreams, Fleetwood Mac
Got to Give It Up, Marvin Gayle
Gonna Fly Now (Theme from "Rocky"), Bill Conti
Undercover Angel, Alan O'Day
Da Doo Ron Ron, Shaun Cassidy
Looks Like We Made It, Barry Manilow
I Just Want to be Your Everything, Andy Gibb
Best of My Love, Emotions
Star Wars Title Theme, Meco
You Light Up My Life, Debby Boone
How Deep Is Your Love, Bee Gees

Current Status Unknown

Jeunesses Musicales Prizes

INTERNATIONAL COMPETITION OF YOUNG MUSICIANS (JEUNESSES MUSICALES)
Terazije 26, 1100e-Belgrade, Yugoslavia (Tel: 326-485)

The competition is held annually to give young musicians at the start of their careers opportunities to win cash prizes and performance opportunities. A panel of judges selects winners from the instrumentalists and vocalists eligible in any given year. In 1978, for instance, the competition will be for cellists and string quartets. The individual first-place winner will receive 17,000 dinars, while the quartet will share 34,000 dinars. Second- and third-place winners also receive a monetary award. Solo musicians must be thirty years of age or under, while no member of a group may be older than thirty-five.

1971 **James Campbell** (Canada), Clarinette
Gotfried Schneider (Federal Republic of Germany), Violin
String quartet (U.S.S.R.)
1972 **Elena Kuznethova** (U.S.S.R.), Piano
Mosconcert Trio (U.S.S.R.)
1973 **Ivan Konsulov** (Bulgaria), Male voice
Jolanta Omiljanowitz (Poland), Female voice
Agneza Miteva and Philippe Pavlov (Bulgaria), Violin and piano duo
1974 **Irena Grafenauer** (Yugoslavia), Flute
Dusan Bogdanvic (Yugoslavia), Guitar
Paul Taffanel (France), Wind Quintet
1975 **Mineo Hayashi** (Japan), Cello
Academica (Rumania), String quartet
1976 **Kim Seung Ho** (Democratic Peoples' Republic of Korea), Violin
News Prague Trio (Czechoslovakia), Piano trio
1977 **Philippe Bianconi** (France), Piano
Camillo and Umberto Bertetti (Italy), Piano duo
1978 **Ina Joost** (Federal Republic of Germany), Cello
1979 **Michael Travlos** (Greece), Composition (orchestral work)
Jean-Claude Wolff (France), Composition (Concerto for Violin and Orchestra)
1980 **Alexis Galperine** (France), violin

International Singing Contest Medals

SOCIEDADE BRASILEIRA DE RALIZACNOES
Av. F. Roosevelt 23, S/310-Rio de Janeiro, Brazil (Tel: 3-920681)

Gold medals are awarded to the four young singers who win the International Singing Contest held every two years in Rio de Janeiro. In addition, $6,000 in prizes are given, as are silver medals, diplomas and recital bookings to runners-up.

1963 **Vera Soukupova** (Czechoslovakia)
Halina Slonicka (Poland)
Alfonz Bartha (Hungary)
1965 **Ludwig Spiess** (Rumania)
Teresa Tourne (Spain)
1967 **Irina Bogachova** (U.S.S.R.), Mezzo
Taru Valjjaka (Finland), Soprano
Rimma Volkova (U.S.S.R.), Soprano
1969 **Angela Beale** (Great Britain), Soprano
Helja Angervo (Finland), Mezzo
Marcos Bakker (Holland) Bass
1971 **Ana Toumowa** (Bulgaria), Soprano
Wolfgang Schone (Germany), Baritone
Lucien Marinescu (Rumania), Baritone
1973 **Kloos Kovacs** (Hungary), Bass
Christina Gorantcheva (Bulgaria), Coloratura soprano
Hariana Branisteanu (Rumania), Soprano
1975 **Ruth Falcon** (U.S.A.), Soprano
Olga Basistiuk (U.S.S.R.), Soprano

Anatole Ponomarenko (U.S.S.R.), Baritone
Istvan Gati (Hungary), Bass baritone
La Verne Williams (U.S.A.), Soprano
1977 **Akeshi Wakamoto** (Japan), Tenor
Ludmila Chemchouk (U.S.S.R.), Mezzo
Tatiana Novikova (U.S.S.R.), Soprano
Betty Lane (U.S.A.), Soprano
1979 **Ewa Maria Podles** (Poland), Mezzo
Francine Laurent (Belgium), Dramatic Soprano
Ismail Djialilov (U.S.S.R.), Tenor
Donna Robin (U.S.A.), Colorartura

International Voice Competition

CONCOURS INTERNATIONAL DE CHANT
Theatre du Capitole, 3100 Toulouse, France (Tel: 21-20-78 and 21-80-41)

The City of Toulouse awards the winners of the International Voice Competition 10,000 francs, diplomas and bookings to perform. The competition is open to male and female vocalists between the ages of eighteen and thirty-five of any nationality. A panel of judges selects the winners.

WOMEN

1954 **Francoise Ogeas,** France
1955 **Enriquetta Tarres-Rabassa,** Spain
1956 **Janine Panis,** France
1957 **Galina Olenitchenko,** U.S.S.R.
1958 **Dories Mayes,** U.S.A.
1959 **Nadyda Kniplova,** Czechoslovakia
1960 **Hanna Rumowska,** Poland
1961 **Julia Buciuceanu,** Rumania
1962 **Galina Kovalieva,** U.S.S.R.
1963 **Margaret Sun,** China
1964 **Viorica Cortez,** Rumania
1965 **Anna-Maria Higueras-Rodriguez,** Spain
1966 **Alexandrina Miltcheva,** Bulgaria
1967 **Zdzislawa Donat,** Poland
1968 **Stefka Popangelova,** Bulgaria
1969 **Magdalena Cononovici,** Rumania
1970 **Eugenia Moldoveanu,** Rumania
1971 **Nina Fomina,** U.S.S.R.
1972 **Nadaja Krasnaya,** U.S.S.R.
1973 **No competition**
1974 **Bozena Porznyska,** Poland
1975 **No award**
1976 **Betty Lane,** U.S.A.
1977 **Ludmila Chirina,** U.S.S.R.
1978 **Petranka Malakova,** Bulgaria
1979 **Marion V. Moore,** U.S.A.
1980 **No award**

MEN

1954 **Julien Haas,** Belgium
1955 **No award**
1956 **Krsta B. Krstic,** Yugoslavia
1957 **Ladislau Konya,** Rumania
1958 **Antonin Svorc,** Czechoslovakia
1959 **Remy Corazza,** France
1960 **Takao Okamura,** Japan
1961 **Jose van Damme,** Belgium
1962 **Ramon Calzadilla,** Cuba
1963 **No award**
1964 **Ludovico Spiess,** Rumania
1965 **Kazimierz Myrlak,** Poland
1966 **George Pappas,** Greece
1967 **Louis Hagen-William,** U.S.A.
1968 **No award**
1969 **Lucian Marinescu,** Rumania
1970 **William Parker,** U.S.A.
1971 **Vatslovas Daounoras,** U.S.S.R.
1972 **Robert Christensen,** U.S.A.
1973 **No competition**
1974 **Pietr Gluboky,** U.S.S.R.
1975 **No award**
1976 **No award**
1977 **Ion Tudoroiu,** Romania
1978 **Roberto Nalerio-Frachia,** Uruguay
1979 **No award**
1980 **James P. Doghan,** Great Britain

Koussevitzky International Recording Award

AMERICAN INTERNATIONAL MUSIC FUND
30 W. 60th St., New York N.Y. 10023 (212/CO 5-0277)

The Koussevitzky International Recording Award, which carries a $1,000 honorarium, is made annually to the living composer of an outstanding symphonic work or a chamber music work for a minimum of sixteen players released on commercial recordings during the previous year. A jury selects the winner.

1963 **Edgard Varese,** *Arcana,* CBS
1964 **Witold Lutoslawski,** *Trois Poemes d'Henri Michaux,* Polski Nagrania in connection with the Festival of Contemporary Music, Zagreb, 1963
1965 **Ingvar Lidholm,** *Poesies per Orchestra,* Columbia in cooperation with the Naumberg Foundation
1966 **Peter Maxwell Davies,** *Leopardi Fragments,* EMI as part of the Gulbenkian Foundation's Music Today series
1967 **Olivier Messiaen,** *Trios Petites Liturgies de la Presence Divine,* Erato (Music Guild in the U.S.A.)
1968 **Carlos Chavez,** *Six Symphonies,* Columbia
1969 **Roberto Gerhard,** *Concerto for Orchestra,* Argo
1970 **Stefan Wolpe,** *Chamber Piece No. 1,* Nonesuch
Seymour Shifrin, *Satires of Circumstance,* Nonesuch
1971 **George Crumb,** *Ancient Voices of Children,* Nonesuch
1972 **Seymour Shifrin,** *Three Pieces for Orchestra,* CRI
1974 **Roque Cordero,** *Concerto for Violin and Orchestra,* Columbia
1975 **No award**
1976 **Henri Dutilleux,** *Tout un Monde Lointain,* EMI

Current Status Unknown

Clara Haskil Competiton Prize

FESTIVAL DE MUSIQUE MONTREUX-VEVEY
Av. des Alpes 14, Case 124, CH-1820 Montreux, Switzerland (021 61 33 84)

The Clara Haskil Competiton is held every two years for pianists 32 years of age and younger. An international jury selects the winner, who receives a 10,000-Swiss-franc cash prize and several recital engagements. The competition began in 1963. Only the most recent winners are listed here.

1973 **Richard Good**
1975 **Michael Dalberto**

1976 **Eugeni Korolyov**
1979 **Cynthia Raim**

Kennedy Center Friedheim Award

JOHN F. KENNEDY CENTER FOR THE PERFORMING ARTS
Washington, D.C. 20566 (202/254-6838)

The Kennedy Center Friedheim Award is presented annually for meritorious compositions of orchestral or chamber music. Composers of instrumental orchestral works are honored in even-numbered years and composers of chamber orchestral works in odd-numbered years. In addition to the $5,000 first-place winners listed below, cash awards are given to second- and third-place composers and two more honorable mentions are made. Anyone including the composer may nominate selections for consideration by a jury of music experts.

1978 **Vincent Perischetti**, *Concerto for English Horn and String Orchestra*
1979 **George Rochberg**, *String Quartet No. 4*
1980 **John Harbison**, *Piano Concerto*

Laurel Leaf Award

AMERICAN COMPOSERS ALLIANCE
170 W. 74th St., New York, N.Y. 10023 (212/362-8900)

The Laurel Leaf Award is a parchment scroll given annually to an individual or organization for encouraging American music.

1951 **WGBH-Radio,** Boston
1952 **Maro and Anahid Ajemian**
1953 **Herman Neuman**, Green Bay (Wisc.) Symphonette
1955 **George Szell**
1956 **Robert Whitney**
1957 **Howard Hanson**
Juilliard String Quartet
1958 **Thor Johnson**
1959 **Martha Graham**
Jack Benny
1960 **Howard Mitchell**
Oliver Daniel
1961 **Helen Thompson**
William Stickland
1962 **Bethany Beardslee**
Hugh Ross
Samuel Rosenbaum
1963 **Clair Reis**
Carl Haverlin
1964 **Walter Hinrichsen**
Margaret L. Crofts
Max Pollikoff
1965 **Henry Cowell**
Avery Claflin
Elizabeth Ames
1966 **Henry A. Moe**
Lawrence Morton
1967 **WBAI-Radio,** New York
Fromm Foundation
Composers' Forum
1968 **Aaron Copland**
1969 **Group for Contemporary Music**
1970 **Otto Luening**
Harris Danziger
1971 **Alice M. Ditson Fund**
1972 **Leopold Stokowski**
1973 **MacDowell Colony**
1974 **Theresa Sterne**
1975 **Nelson Rockefeller**
1976 **Gunther Schuller**
1977 **Arthur Weisberg**
1978 **James Dixon**
1979 **Ralph Shappi**
Contemporary Chamber Players, University of Chicago
1980 **John Duffy**
Joseph Machlis

Leeds International Pianoforte Competition

UNIVERSITY OF LEEDS
Leeds LS2 9JT, U.K. (Tel: Bradford-0274 33321)

The winner of the Leeds International Pianoforte Competition receives a gold medal and 2,850 and more than fifty engagements. Eligible pianists may be of any nationality but must be under thirty years of age. An international panel selects the winner of this triennial award.

1963 **Michael Roll**
1966 **Raphael Orozco**
1969 **Radu Lupu**
1972 **Murray Perahia**
1975 **Dimitry Alexeev**
1978 **Michael Dalberto**

Musician of the Year

MUSICAL AMERICA
825 Seventh Ave., New York, N.Y. 10019 (212/265-8360)

A Musician of the Year is named annually by *Musical America,* a classical music publication, generally for contributions in vocal, instrumental or orchestral performances and recording

1960 **Leonard Bernstein**
1961 **Leontyne Price**
1962 **Igor Stravinsky**
1963 **Erich Leinsdorf**
1964 **Benjamin Britten**
1965 **Vladimir Horowitz**
1966 **Yehudi Menuhin**
1967 **Leopold Stokowski**
1968/9 **Birgit Nilsson**
1970 **Beverly Sills**
1971 **Michael Tilson Thomas**
1972 **Pierre Boulez**
1973 **George Balanchine**
1974 **Sarah Caldwell**
1975 **Eugene Ormandy**
1976 **Arthur Rubinstein**
1977 **Placido Domingo**
1978 **Alicia De Larrocha**
1979 **Rudolf Serkin**
1980 **Zubin Mehta**

Otto Kinkeldy Award

American Musicological Society
201 S. 34th St., Philadelphia, Pa. 19104 (215/243-5000)

The Otto Kinkeldy Award, which consists of $400 and a scroll, is given annually to an American or Canadian author for a notable full-length study in any branch of musicology. A special committe selects the recipient.

1967 **William W. Austin,** *Music in the Twentieth Century*
1968 **Rulan Chao Pian,** *Song Dynasty Musical Sources and their Interpretation*
1969 **Edward Lowinsky,** *The Medici Codex of 1518*
1970 **Nino Pirrotta,** *Li due Orfei, da Poliziano a Monteverdi*
1971 **Daniel Heartz,** *Pierre d'Attaignant, Royal Printer of Music*
Joseph Kerman, *Ludwig van Beethoven, Autograph Miscellany from ca. 1786 to 1799*
1972 **Albert Seay,** *Jacobus Arcadelt, Opera Omnia.*, Vol. II
1973 **H. Colin Slim,** *A Gift of Madrigals and Motets*
1974 **Robert L. Marshall,** *The Compositional Process of J.S. Bach*
1975 **Vivian Perlis,** *Charles Ives Remembered, an Oral History*
1976 **David P. McKay & Richard Crawford,** *William Billings of Boston: Eighteenth-Century Composer*
1977 **H. C. Robbins Landon, Hayden:** *Chronicle and Works, Vol. 3; Hayden in London 1791-1795*
1978 **Richard L. Crocker,** *The Early Medieval Sequence*
1979 **No award**
1980 **Leeman L. Perkins** and **Howard Garey,** *The Mellon Chansionier*, two vols.
Nicholas Temperley, *The Music of the English Parish Church, two vols.*

Arts and Letters Awards
Marc Blitzstein Award
Charles Ives Award
Ives Grant Award
Goddard H. Lieberson Fellowship

AMERICAN ACADEMY AND INSTITUTE OF ARTS AND LETTERS
633 W. 155th St., New York, N.Y. 10023 (212/368-6361)

To encourage qualified musicians and help them continue their creative work, the Institute annually gives cash awards currently $5,000 each to non-members. These Arts and Letters Awards may not be applied for. Similar awards in literature and art are found elsewhere in this volume.

1941 **Frederick Woltmann**
1942 **Bernard Hermann**
Edward Margetson
Robert McBride
1943 **Paul Creston**
William Schuman
1944 **Nicolai Berezowsky**
David Diamond
Burrill Phillips
1945 **William Bergsma**
Jerzy Fitelberg
Gian Carlo Menotti
1946 **Marc Blitzstein**
Norman Dello Joio
Otto Luening
Peter Mennin
Robert Palmer
Robert Ward
1947 **Alexei Haieff**
Ulysses Kay
Norman Lockwood
1948 **Henry Cowell**
Lou Harrison
Vincent Persichetti
1949 **John Cage**
Louis Mennini
Stefan Wolpe
1950 **Elliott C. Carter**
Andrew Imbrie
Ben Weber
1951 **Alan Hovhaness**
Leon Kirchner
Frank Wigglesworth
1952 **Robert Kurka**
John Lessard
Howard Swanson
1953 **Peggy Glanville-Hicks**
Roger Goeb
Nikolai Lopatnikoff
1954 **Ingolf Dahl**
Colin McPhee
Hugo Weisgall
1955 **Henry Brant**
Irving Fine
Adolph Weiss
1956 **Ross Lee Finney**
Robert Moevs
Jacques Louis Monod
1957 **Lukas Foss**
Lee Hoiby
Seymour Shifrin
1958 **Arnold Franchetti**
Hunter Johnson
Billy Jim Layton
1959 **Milton Babbitt**
John Bavicchi
Mark Bucci
Noel Lee
1960 **Arthur Berger**
Easley Blackwood
Salvatore Martirano
Gunther Schuller
1961 **Ramiro Cortes**
Halsey Stevens
Lester Trimble
Yehudi Wyner
1962 **Ernst Bacon**
John LaMontaine
George Rochberg
William Sydeman
1963 **Chou Wen-chung**
Mel Powell
Russell Smith
Vladimir Ussachevsky
1964 **Leslie Bassett**
Gordon Binkerd
Hall Overton
Julia Perry
1965 **Mario Davidovsky**
Gerald Humel
Earl Kim
Harvey Sollberger
1966 **Walter Aschaffenburg**
Richard Hoffman

John MacIvor Perkins
Ralph Shapey
1967 George H. Crumb
Donald Martino
Julian Orbon
Charles Wuorinen
1968 David Del Tredici
William Flanagan
Ned Rorem
Francis Thorne
1969 Michael Brozen
Jacob R. Druckman
Nicolas Roussakis
Claudio Spies
1970 William Albright
Arnold Elston
Morton Feldman
George Bach Wilson
1971 Sydney Hodkinson
Fred Lerdahl
Roger Reynolds
Loren Rush
1972 Earle Brown
John Eaton
John Harbison
William Overton Smith
1973 John C. Heiss
Betsy Jolas
Barbara Kolb
Curry Tison Street
1974 Richard Felciano
Raoul Pleskow
Phillip Rhodes
Olly W. Wilson
1975 Marc Antonio Consoli
Charles Dodge
Daniel Perlongo
Christian Wolff
1976 Dominick Argento
Robert Helps
Robert Hall Lewis
Richard Wernick
1977 Harold Blumenfeld
Paul Cooper
Paul Lansky
Geroge Perle
1978 Wallace Berry
Curtis O.B. Curtis-Smith
Elie Siegmeister
Richard Swift
1979 Paul Chihara
Vivian Fine
Robert Starer
Morton Subotnick
1980 Donald Grantham
Eugene O'Brien
Malcolm Peyton
Lawrence L. Widdoes

The $2,500 Marc Blitzstein Award for the Musical Theater is given periodically to encourage the creation of works of merit for the musical theatre by a composer, lyricist or librettist.

1965 William Bolcom
1968 Jack Beeson
1976 John Olon-Scrymgeour

The Charles Ives Award consists of $5,000 in scholarships to young composers for further study in composition.

1970 Joseph C. Schwantner
1971 Louis Smith Weingarden
1972 Thomas Janson
Robert J. Krupnick
Michael Seyfrit
1973 Philip Caldwell Carlsen
Robert Gerster
Peter Lieberson
1974 Paul Alan Levi
Allen Shearer
Ira Taxin
1975 Chester Biscardi
Stephen Chatman
David Koblitz
1976 Michael Eckert
Joseph A. Hudson
Tod Machover
Robert E. Martin
William Matthews
Bruce Saylor
1977 Gregory Ballard
Larry Thomas Bell
John Halvor Benson
Matthias Kriesberg
John Anthony Lennon
Maurice Wright
1978 Daniel Brewbaker
Justin Dello Joio
Lee Scott Goldstein
Arthur W. Gottschalk
Thomas Mountain
David Olan
1979 Robert Beaser
Susan Blaustein
Marilyn Bliss
Carl Brenner
David Goodman
Tobias Picker
1980 Thomas E. Barker
Laura Clayton
Lowell Limberman
William Maiben
Mario J. Felusi
George Tsontakis

The Ives Grant is awarded to further the publication and performances of the music of Charles E. Ives. The Institute is the beneficiary of the royalties of Ive's music, which are divided between scholarship awards and this grant. Recently the grant has carried an honorarium of more than $20,000.

1970 John Kirkpatrick
1971 Vivian Perlis
1972 Harold Farberman
1973 Charles E. Ives Society
1975 Yale University Music Library
1978 Charles E. Ives Society

The Goddard Lieberson Fellowship of $10,000 is given annually to one or more young composers judges to have extraordinary gifts.

1979 Gerald Levinson
Bruce MacCombie
1980 David Chaitkin
Robert Xavier Radriguez

Levintritt Prize

LEVINTRITT FOUNDATION
1 Passaic St., Woodridge, N.J. 07075 (201/777-3111)

The Levintritt Prize is given to the winner of the Leventritt International Competition, which was established to help young musicians of exceptional talent launch and develop their careers. The winner receives $10,000, an RCA recording contract, orchestral engagements with leading orchestras and a gold medal. In addition to the winners listed below, each competition honors several finalists, who receive $1,000 and a three-year management contract with appearances both in recital and as soloists with orchestras. A board of judges from the music world evaluates candidates over a prolonged period and in a variety of contexts. No major award was made in the years 1942, 1950, 1951, 1971 and 1973 although finalists were selected for those years. The competition was suspended several times, most recently the 1970-80 period. The next Leventritt Prize will be awarded in 1981.

1940 Sidney Foster
1941 Erno Valasek
1942 No award
1943 Eugene Istomin
1944 Jeanne Therrien
1945 Louise Meiszner
1946 David Nadien
1947 Alexis Weissenberg
1948 Jean Graham
1949 Gary Graffman
1950 No award
1951 No award
1952 No award
1953 No award
1954 Van Cliburn
1955 Betty Jean Hagan
John Browning
1956 No award
1957 Anton Kuerti
1958 Arnold Steinhardt
1959 Malcolm Prager
1960 No award
1961 No award
1962 Michel Block
1963 No award
1964 Itzhak Perlman
1965 Tong Il Han
1966 No award
1967 Kyung wha Chung
1968 No award
1969 Joseph Kalichstein
1970-80 No award

Music City Awards

MUSIC CITY NEWS
Box 22975, Nashville, Tenn. 27023 (615/244-5187)

The Music City News annually presents the Music City Awards to country entertainers and songwriters selected by a poll of its readers. The awards are presented in a nationally televised ceremony from the Grand Old Opry in Nashville.

NUMBER ONE MALE ARTST

1967 Merle Haggard
1968 Merle Haggard
1969 Charley Pride
1970 Charley Pride
1971 Charley Pride
1972 Charley Pride
1973 Charley Pride
1974 Conway Twitty
1975 Conway Twitty
1976 Conway Twitty
1977 Conway Twitty
1978 Larry Gatlin
1979 Kenny Rogers
1980 Marty Robbins

NUMBER ONE FEMALE ARTIST

1967 Loretta Lynn
1968 Loretta Lynn
1969 Loretta Lynn
1970 Loretta Lynn
1971 Loretta Lynn
1972 Loretta Lynn
1973 Loretta Lynn
1974 Loretta Lynn
1975 Loretta Lynn
1976 Loretta Lynn
1977 Loretta Lynn
1978 Loretta Lynn
1979 Barbara Mandrell
1980 Loretta Lynn

MOST PROMISING MALE ARTIST

1967 Tom. T. Hall
1968 Cal Smith
1969 Johnny Bush
1970 Tommy Cash
1971 Tommy Overstreet
1972 Billy "Crash" Craddock
1973 Johnny Rodriguez
1974 Johnny Rodriguez
1975 Ronnie Milsap
1976 Mickey Gilley
1977 Larry Gatlin
1978 Don Williams
1979 Rex Allen, Jr.
1980 Hank Williams, Jr.

MOST PROMISING FEMALE ARTIST

1967 Tammy Wynette
1968 Dolly Parton
1969 Peggy Sue
1970 Susan Raye
1971 Susan Raye
1972 Donna Fargo
1973 Tanya Tucker
1974 Olivia Newton-John
1975 Crystal Gayle
1976 Barbara Mandrell
1977 Helen Cornelius
1978 Debby Boone
1979 Janie Fricke
1980 Charly McClain

NUMBER ONE SONGWRITER

1967 Bill Anderson
1968 Bill Anderson
1969 Bill Anderson
1970 Merle Haggard

1971 Kris Kristofferson
1972 Kris Kristofferson
1973 Kris Kristofferson
1974 Bill Anderson
1975 Bill Anderson
1976 Bill Anderson
1977 Larry Gatlin
1978 Larry Gatlin
1979 Eddie Rabbit
1980 Marty Robbins

SINGLE OF THE YEAR

1967 *There Goes My Everything*
1968 No award
1969 *All I Have to Offer You*
1970 *Hello Darling*
1971 *Help Me Make It Through the Night*
1972 *Kiss An Angel*
1973 *Why Me, Lord?*
1974 *You've Never Been This Far Before*
1975 *Country Bumpkin*
1976 *Blue Eyes Crying in the Rain*
1977 *I Don't Want to Have to Marry You*
1978 *Heaven's Just a Sin Away*
1979 *The Gambler*
1980 *Coward of the Country*

NUMBER ONE BAND OF THE YEAR

1967 The Buckaroos
1968 The Buckaroos
1969 The Buckaroos
1970 The Buckaroos
1971 The Strangers
1972 The Strangers
1973 The Po' Boys
1974 The Buckaroos
1975 The Coalminers
1976 The Coalminers
1977 The Coalminers
1978 Larry Gatlin Band
1979 Oak Ridge Boys
1980 Charlie Daniels Band

NUMBER ONE VOCAL GROUP

1967 Tom Pall and The Glasers
1968 Tom Pall and the Glasers
1969 Tom Pall and the Glasers
1970 Tom Pall and the Glasers
1971 The Statler Brothers
1972 The Statler Brothers
1973 The Statler Brothers
1974 The Statler Brothers
1975 The Statler Brothers
1976 The Statler Brothers
1977 The Statler Brothers
1978 The Statler Brothers
1979 The Statler Brothers
1980 The Statler Brothers

NUMBER ONE DUET

1968 Dally Parton and Porter Wagoner
1969 Dolly Parton and Porter Wagoner
1970 Dolly Parton and Porter Wagoner
1971 Loretta Lynn and Conway Twitty
1972 Loretta Lynn and Conway Twitty
1973 Loretta Lynn and Conway Twitty
1974 Loretta Lynn and Conway Twitty
1975 Loretta Lynn and Conway Twitty
1976 Loretta Lynn and Conway Twitty
1977 Loretta Lynn and Conway Twitty
1978 Loretta Lynn and Conway Twitty
1979 Kenny Rogers and Dottie West
1980 Loretta Lynn and Conway Twitty

NUMBER ONE INSTRUMENTALIST

1969 Roy Clark
1970 Roy Clark
1971 Roy Clark
1972 Roy Clark
1973 Charlie McCoy
1974 Roy Clark
1975 Buck Trent
1976 Buck Trent
1977 Johnny Gimble
1978 Roy Clark
1979 Roy Clark
1980 Roy Clark

NUMBER ONE INSTRUMENTAL ENTERTAINER

1974 Charlie McCoy
1975 Roy Clark
1976 Roy Clark
1977 Roy Clark

COMEDY ACT

1971 Mel Tillis
1972 Archie Campbell
1973 Mel Tillis
1974 Mel Tillis
1975 Mel Tillis
1976 Mel Tillis
1977 Mel Tillis
1978 Mel Tillis
1979 Jerry Clower
1980 The Statler Brothers

BLUEGLASS GROUP

1971 The Osborne Brothers
1972 The Osborne Brothers
1973 The Osborne Brothers
1974 The Osborne Brothers
1975 The Osborne Brothers
1976 The Osborne Brothers
1977 The Osborne Brothers
1978 The Osborne Brothers
1979 The Osborne Brothers
1980 Bill Monroe

NUMBER ONE TOURING ROAD SHOW

1974 Loretta Lynn, The Coalminers and Kenny Starr

NUMBER ONE ALBUM

1976 Loretta Lynn, *When the Tingle Becomes a Chill*
1977 *I Don't Want to Have to Marry You*
1978 Felton Jarvis, *Moody Blue*
1979 Connie Smith, *Entertainers On and Off the Record*
1980 The Statler Brothers, *The Originals*

GOSPEL GROUP

1979 Connie Smith
1980 The Carter Family

FOUNDER AWARD

1977 Ralph Emery
1978 Ernest Tubb
1979 Pee Wee King
1980 Buck Owens

Johnny Mercer Award

NATIONAL ACADEMY OF POPULAR MUSIC
1 Times Sq., New York, N.Y. 10036 (212/221-1252)

The Johnny Mercer Award is given annually to an individual for contributions to popular music. The Academy's Board of Directors selects the winner.

1980 Frank Sinatra

Gold Medal

NATIONAL ARTS CLUB
15 Gramercy Park South, New York, N.Y. 10003
(212/475-3424)

As part of the club's honors program in the visual and performing arts and literature, a gold medal is awarded annually for outstanding contributions to music. Other medalists are listed in the Theatre, Literature and Visual Arts sections of this volume.

1957 Herman Neuman
1958 Julius Rudel
1959 Minnie Guggenheimer
1960 Thomas Scherman
1961 August Belmont
1962 Howard Hanson
1963 Olga Koussevitzky
Paul Creston
1964 William Schuman
1965 Stanley Adams
1966 Lytle Hull
Richard Korn
1967 Clifton Muir
Douglas S. Moore
1968 Leonard Bernstein
1969 Richard Rodgers
1970 Peter Mennin
1971 Jouett Shouse
George F. Seuffert
1972 Edward M. Cramer
1973 Rudolf Bing
1974 Van Cliburn
1975 Alice Tully
1976 Jack Beeson
1977 Arthur Fiedler
1978 Avery Fisher
1979 Robert Sherman
1980 Charles Wadsworth

National Music Awards

AMERICAN MUSIC CONFERENCE
1000 Skokie Blvd., Wilmette, Ill. 60091 (312/251-1600)

The National Music Awards were made as a Bicentennial gesture in 1976 to honor performers, lyricists and composers who have contributed significantly to music in America between 1776 and 1956. In order to eliminate fad music, only contributions twenty or more years in the past were considered. Living winners received a trophy, which depicts abstractly the continuation of music. Three panels of judges with expertise in classical, popular (including country and show) and jazz (including blues) selected the winners.

1976 Harold Arlen
Louis "Satchmo" Armstrong
Milton Babbitt
Samuel Barber
William "Count" Basie
Mrs. H. H. A. Beach
Leon Bismarck "Bix" Beiderbecker
Irving Berlin
Leonard Bernstein
Charles Edward Anderson "Chuck" Berry
William Billings
Jimmy Blanton
Clifford Brown
John Cage
Hoagland Howard "Hoagy" Carmichael
Benjamin Carr
Bennett Lester "Benny" Carter
Elliott Carter
George Whitefield Chadwick
Ray Charles (Ray Charles Robinson)
Charles "Charlie" Christian
George M. Cohan
Nat "King" Cole (Nathaniel Adams Coles)
Aaron Copland
Henry Cowell
Miles Davis, Jr.
Norman Dello Joio
B. G. "George Gard" "Buddy" DeSylva
Robert Nathaniel Dett
Warren "Baby" Dodds
Walter Donaldson
Thomas A. "Tommy" Dorsey
Paul Dresser
Edward Kennedy "Duke" Ellington
Daniel Decatur Emmett
Ian Ernest Gilmore Green "Gil" Evans
Arthur Farwell
Ella Fitzgerald
Stephen Collins Foster
William Henry Fry
George Gershwin
Ira Gershwin
Stanley "Stan" Getz
Henry Franklin Belknap Gilbert
John Birks "Dizzy" Gillespie
Benjamin David "Benny" Goodman
Louis Moreau Gottschalk
Charles Tomlinson Griffes
Woody Guthrie
Oscar Hammerstein II
William Christopher "W.C." Handy
Howard Harold Hanson
Roy Harris
Lorenz Hart
Coleman Hawkins
Anthony Philip Heinrich
Fletcher Henderson
Victor Herbert
Woodrow Charles "Woody" Herman
James Hewitt
John Hill Hewitt
Earl "Fatha" Hines
Billie Holiday
Francis Hopkinson
Charles Ives
Mahalia Jackson
Milton "Milt" Jackson
James "J.J." Johnson
James Price Johnson
Robert Johnson
Scott Joplin

Stanley Newcomb "Stan" Kenton
Jerome Kern
Leon Kirchner
Gene Krupa
Eddie Lang
James Melvin "Jimmie" Lunceford
James Lyon
Edward MacDowell
Daniel Gregory Mason
Lowell Mason
Gian-Carlo Menotti
John H. "Johnny" Mercer
Thelonius Monk
Douglas Stuart Moore
John Knowles Paine
Charles Christopher "Charlie Bird" or "Yardbird" Parker
Horatio Parker
Cole Porter
Earl "Bud" Powell
Chano Pozo (Luciano Pozo Gonzales)
Donald Matthew "Don" Redman
Alexander Reinagle
Wallingford Riegger
Maxwell "Max" Roach
James Charles "Jimmie" Rodgers
Richard Rodgers
George Frederick Root
George Russell
Henry Russell
William Howard Schuman
Roger Sessions
Bessie Smith
John Philip Sousa
Arthur "Art" Tatum
Deems Taylor
Weldon John "Jack" Teagarden
Virgil Thomson
Leonard Joseph "Lennie" Tristano
Edgard Varese
Sarah Vaughan
Giuseppe "Joe" Venuti
Harry Von Tilzer
Thomas "Fats" Waller
Harry Warren
Richard A. Whiting
Hank Williams
Bob Wills
Henry Clay Work
Vincent Youmans
Lester "Pres" Young

Naumburg Awards

WALTER W. NAUMBURG FOUNDATION
144 W. 66th St., New York, N.Y. 10023 (212/874-1150)

Begun as a way for young chamber musicians to gain performance experience and critical review, the Naumburg Foundation's annual awards program has been altered and expanded to honor other instrumentalists, vocalists, recording artists and composers. The awards, originally known as the Naumburg Auditions, have undergone many changes over the years. Now, four traditional categories of piano, woodwinds, strings and voice rotate. The piano competition is known as the William Kappel Award. The winners receive a cash award and several recital appearances, including ones at New York's Alice Tully Hall and now a recording by Musical Heritage.

1925 **Catherine Wade Smith,** violin
Adeline Masino, violin
Bernard Ocko, violin
1926 **Phyllis Kraeuter,** cello
Margaret Hamilton, piano
Sonia Skalka, piano
1927 **Dorothy Kendrick,** piano
William Sauber, piano
Sadah Stuchari, violin
Daniel Saidenberg, cello
Julian Kahn, cello
Sadie Schwartz, violin
1928 **Adele Marcus,** piano
Helen Berlin, violin
Louis Kaufman, violin
Olga Zundel, cello
George Rasely, tenor
August Werner, baritone
1929 **No winners**
1930 **Helen McGraw,** piano
Ruth Culbertson, piano
Mila Wellerson, cello
Louise Bernhardt, contralto
1931 **Lillian Rehberg Goodman,** cello
Marguerite Hawkins, soprano
Edwina Eustis, contralto
Kurtis Brownell, tenor
1932 **Milo Miloradovich,** soprano
Foster Miller, bass-baritone
Dalies Frantz, piano
Huddie Johnson, violin
Inez Lauritano, violin
1933 **Catherine Carver,** piano
Harry Katzman, violin
1934 **Joseph Knitzer,** violin
Ruby Mercer, soprano
1935 **Benjamin deLoache,** baritone
Judith Sidorsky, piano
Aniceta Shea, soprano
Harvey Shapiro, cello
Florence Vickland, soprano
Marshall Moss, violin
1936 **Frederick Buldrini,** violin
1937 **Jorge Bolet,** piano
Ida Krehm, piano
Pauline Pierce, mezzo-soprano
Maurice Bialkin, cello
1938 **Carroll Glenn,** violin
1939 **Mara Sebriansky,** violin
William Horne, tenor
Zadel Skolovsky, piano
Gertrude Gibson, soprano
1940 **Abbey Simon,** piano
Harry Cykman, violin
Thomas Richner, piano
1941 **William Kappell,** piano
Robert Mann, violin
Lura Stover, soprano
1942 **Jane Rogers,** contralto
Annette Elkanova, piano
David Sarser, violin
1943 **Dolores Miller,** violin
Constance Keene, piano
Ruth Geiger, piano
1944 **Jeanne Therrien,** piano
Jean Carlton, soprano
Carol Brice, contralto
1945 **Jane Boedeker,** mezzo-soprano

Paula Lenchner, soprano
1946 **Leonid Hambro**, piano
Jeanne Rosenblum, piano
Anahid Ajemian, violin
1947 **Berl Senofsky**, violin
Abba Bogin, piano
Jane Carlson, piano
1948 **Sidney Harth**, violin
Paul Olefsky, cello
Theodore Lettvin, piano
1949 **Lorne Munroe**, cello
1950 **Angelene Collins**, soprano
Esther Glazer, violinist
Betty Jean Hagen, violin
Margaret Barthel, piano
1951 **June Kovach**, piano
Laurel Hurley, soprano
Joyce Flissler, violin
1952 **Diana Steiner**, violin
Yoko Matsuo, violin
Lois Marshall, soprano
1953 **Gilda Muhlbauer**, violin
Lee Cass, bass-baritone
Georgia Laster, soprano
1954 **William Doppmann**, piano
Jean Wentworth, piano
Jules Eskin, cello
Martha Flowers, soprano
1955 **Ronald Leonard**, cello
Mary MacKenzie, contralto
Nancy Cirillo, violin
1956 **Donald McCall**, cello
Wayne Connor, tenor
George Katz, piano
1957 **Regina Sarfaty**, mezzo-soprano
Angelica Lozada, soprano
Michael Grebanier, cello
1958 **Joseph Schwartz**, piano
Shirley Verrett, mezzo-soprano
Elaine Lee, violin
1959 **Howard Aibel**, piano
Sophia Steffan, voice
Ralph Votapek, piano
1960 **Joseph Silverstein**, violin (Recording: Bach: Sonata in G Minor/Bartok: Violin Solo Sonata)
1961 **Werner Torkanowsky**, conductor (Recording: Rochberg: Chamber Concerto)
1964 **Elizabeth Mosher**, soprano
1968 **Jorge Mester**, conductor
1971 **Kun-Woo Paik**, piano
Zola Shaulis, piano (Recording: Barber: Excursions Gruenberg: Polychroma/Bloch: Sonata)
1972 **Robert Davidovici**, violin
1973 **Edmund LeRoy**, baritone
Barbara Hendricks, soprano
Susan Davenny Wyner, soprano
1974 **Andre-Michel Schub**, piano
Edith Kraft, piano
Richard Atamian, piano
1975 **Dickran Atamian**, piano
Elmar Oliveira, violin
Clamma Dale, soprano
Joy Simpson, soprano
1976 **No award**
1977 **Nathaniel Rosen**, cello
1978 **Carol Wincenc**, flute
1979 **Peter Orth**, piano
1980 **Lucy Shelton**, soprano
Irene Gubrud, soprano
Jan Opalach, bass-baritone
Faith Esham, soprano

The Naumburg Chamber Award consists of a recital at Alice Tully Hall and a specially commissioned work by a composer selected by the Naumburg Foundation. The foundation has now combined the Chamber Award with its Recording Award, and now the winner records the commissioned composition with Musical Heritage.

1965 **Beaux Arts String Quartet**
Leon Kirchner: *Quartet No. 3 for Strings and Electronic Tape* (composition)
1971 **The Contemporary Group** (University of Washington)
University of Michigan Contemporary Ensemble
1972 **Speculum Musicae**
Donald Martino: *Notturno* (composition)
Charles Wuorinen: *Speculum Speculi* (composition)
Concord String Quartet
George Rochberg: *String Quartet No. 3* (composition)
1973 **Cambridge Consort**
Seymour Shifrin (composition)
John Harbison (composition)
Da Capo Chamber Players
Milton Babbitt: *Arie da Capo* (composition)
Harvey Sollberger: *Riding the Wind* (composition)
1974 **American String Quartet**
Claus Adam (composition)
Francesco Trio
Earl Kim (composition)
1975 **New York Renaissance Band**
Alvin Brehm (composition)
1976 **Empire Brass Quintet**
Stanley Silverman (composition)
Sequoia String Quartet
Thomas McKinley (composition)
1977 **Jubal Trio**
Joseph Schwanter (composition)
Primavera String Quartet
Paul Chihara (composition)
1978 **Emerson String Quartet**
Aulos Wind Quintet
1979 **New World String Quartet**
1980 **Liederkreis Ensemble**
New Arts Trio

NAUMBURG RECORDING AWARDS

1949 **Roger Sessions:** *Symphony No. 2* (New York Philharmonic, Dimitri Mitropoulos, cond.)
1950 **William Schuman:** *Symphony No. 3* (Philadelphia Orchestra, Eugene Ormandy, cond.)
1951 **Wallingford Riegger:** *Symphony No. 3* (Eastman-Rochester Symphony Orchestra, Howard Hanson, cond.)
1952 **Peter Mennin:** *Symphony No. 3* (New York Philharmonic, Dimitri Mitropoulos, cond.)
1953 **Walter Piston:** *Symphony No. 4* (Philadelphia Orchestra, Eugene Ormandy, cond.)
1954 **Leon Kirchner, piano; Leon Kirchner:** *Concerto for Piano and Orchestra* (New York Philharmonic, Dimitri Mitropoulos, cond.)
Harold Shapero: *String Quartet No. 1* (Robert Koff, Paul Bellam, Walter Trampler, Charles McCracken)
1955 **Roy Harris:** *Symphony No. 7* (Philadelphia Orchestra, Eugene Ormandy, cond.)
1956 **Jacob Avshalomov:** *Sinfonietta* (Columbia Symphony Orchestra, Jacob Avshalomov, cond.)

Elliott Carter: *Sonata for Flute, Oboe, Violoncello, and Harpsichord* (Annabelle Brieff, Josef Marx, Loren Bernsohn, Robert Conant)

1957 **Lukas Foss:** *The Song of Songs* (Jennie Tourel, mezzo-soprano; New York Philharmonic, Leonard Bernstein, cond.)

1958 **Robert Helps:** *Symphony No. 1* (Columbia Symphony Orchestra, Zoltan Rozsnyai, cond.)

1959 **George Barati** *Chamber Concerto* (Members of the Philadelphia Orchestra, Eugene Ormandy, cond.)
Cecil Effinger: *Little Symphony No. 1* (Columbia Symphony Orchestra, Zoltan Rozsnyai, cond.)

1960 **Andrew Imbrie:** *Violin Concerto* (Carroll Glenn, violin; Columbia Symphony Orchestra, Zoltan Rozsnyai, cond.)

1961 **George Rochberg:** *Symphony No. 2* (New York Philharmonic, Werner Torkanowsky, cond.)

1962 **Richard Donovan:** *Music for Six; Five Elizabethan Lyrics* (Columbia Chamber Ensemble, Gunther Schuller, cond.; Adele Addison, soprano; Galimir String Quartet)

1963 **Carl Ruggles:** *Sun Treader* (Columbia Symphony Orchestra, Zoltan Rozsnyai, cond.)

1964 **Arthur Berger:** *Chamber Music for Thirteen Players; Three Pieces for Two Pianos* (Columbia Chamber Ensemble, Gunther Schuller, cond.; Paul Jacobs and Gilbert Kalish, pianos)

1966 **Ralph Shapey:** *Rituals for Symphony Orchestra; String Quartet No. 6* (London Sinfonietta, Ralph Shapey, cond.; Lexington Quartet of the Contemporary Chamber Players of the University of Chicago)

1967 **Henry Weinberg:** *String Quartet No. 2* (Composers Quartet)

1970 **Seymour Shifrin:** *Three Pieces for Orchestra* (London Sinfonietta, Jacques Monod, cond.)

1972 **David Diamond:** *String Quartet No. 9; Nonet* (Composers Quartet String Ensemble cond. by Charles Wuorinen)
David del Tredici: *I Hear an Army; Scherzo* (Phyllis Bryn-Julson, soprano; Composers Quartet; Robert Helps and David del Tredici, pianos)

1973 **Mario Davidovsky:** *Inflexions; Chacona* (Ensemble cond. by David Gilbert; Jeanne Benjamin, violin; Joel Krosnick, cello; Robert Miller, piano)
Tison Street: *String Quartet* (Concord String Quartet)
Richard Trythall: *Coincidences* (Richard Trythall, piano)

1974 **Donald Erb:** *Three Pieces for Brass Quintet and Piano* New York Brass Quintet; James Smolko, piano; Matthias Bamert, cond.)
Leslie Bassett: *Sextet for Piano and Strings* (Concord String Quartet; John Graham, viola; Gilbert Kalish, piano)
George Edwards: *Kreuz und Quer* (Boston Musica Viva, Richard Pittman, cond.)
Robert MacDougall: *Anacoluthon: A Confluence* (Contemporary Chamber Ensemble, Arthur Weisberg, cond.)

1975 **Walter Mays:** *Six Invocations to the Svara Mandala for Percussion Orchestra;*
Richard Wernick: *A Prayer for Jerusalem* (Jan DeGaetani, mezzo-soprano; Glenn Steele, percussion)

1976 **No award**

1977 **Edwin Dugger,** *Intermezzi* and *Abwesenheiten und wiedersehen*
Fred Lerdahl, *Eros*

Nordiska Radets Musikpris

THE NORDIC COUNCIL
Box 19506, 104-32 Stockholm 19, Sweden (Tel: 14 10 00 and 20 54 02)

The Nordiska Radets Musikpris, which carries a cash honorarium that is now 75,000 Danish crowns, is awarded biennially to a living composer for a recent composition which meets the highest artistic standards. A committee of Nordic experts makes the selection from candidates nominated by delegates of participating countries.

1965 **Karl Birger Blomdahl** (Sweden), *Aniara* (opera)
1968 **Joonas Kokkonen** (Finland), *Symfoni nr 3*
1970 **Lars Johan Werle** (Sweden), *Drommen om Therese* (opera)
1972 **Arne Nordheim** (Norway), *ECO*
1974 **Per Norgard** (Denmark), *Gilgamesh* (opera)
1976 **Atli Heimir Sveinsson** (Iceland), *Koncert for flojte og orkester*
1978 **Aulis Sallinen** (Finland), *Ratsumies*
1980 **Pelle Gudmundsen-Holmgren** (Denmark), *Synfoni/Antifoni*

No. 1 Awards

BILLBOARD
9000 Sunset Blvd., Los Angeles, Calif. 90069
(213/273-7040)

Billboard No. 1 Awards annually recognize top records, recording artists, producers and labels, based on a point-value structure of the publication's record charts of radio airplay and record sales. The winners of the No. 1 honors receive Lucite trophies. In addition to the top winner in each category listed here, *Billboard* annually publishes the runner-up places. The categories have changed over the years.

SINGLE OF THE YEAR-POP

1975 ***Love Will Keep Us Together,*** The Captain and Tennille
1976 ***Silly Love Songs,*** Wings
1977 ***Tonight's the Night,*** Rod Stewart

Current Status Unknown

ALBUM OF THE YEAR-POP

1975 ***Elton John's Greatest Hits,*** Elton John
1976 ***Frampton Comes Alive,*** Peter Frampton
1977 ***Rumors,*** Fleetwood Mac

Current Status Unknown

ARTISTS OF THE YEAR AND NO. 1 AWARDS (Pop unless indicated otherwise)

1975 **John Denver,** Singles Artist No. 1 Award
John Denver, Singles—Male Artist
Linda Ronstadt, Singles—Female Artist
America, Singles—Duos and Groups
Van McCoy and the Soul City Symphony, Singles—Instrumentalists
Elton John, Albums Artist No. 1 Award
Elton John, Albums—Male Artists
Olivia Newton-John, Albums—Female Artists
The Blackbyrds, Albums—Instrumentalists

Average White Band, Albums—Duos and Groups
1976 **Aerosmith,** Album Artists
Barry Manilow, Singles—Male Artist
Diana Ross, Singles—Female Artist
Rhythm Heritage, Singles—Instrumentalist Duos and Groups
Hagood Hardy, Singles—Instrumentalist
Bee Gees, Singles—Duos and Groups
John Denver, Albums—Male Artist
Diana Ross, Albums—Female Artists
Aerosmith, Albums—Duos and Groups
George Benson, Albums—Instrumentalist Duos and Groups
Salsoul Orchestra, Albums—Instrumentalist
1977 **Stevie Wonder,** Male Artist of the Year
Linda Ronstadt, Female Artist of the Year
Barbra Streisand, Easy Listening Artist of the Year
Fleetwood Mac, Group of the Year
Waylon Jennings, Country Artist of the Year
Stevie Wonder, Soul Artist of the Year
Foreigner, Pop New Artist of the Year
Rod Stewart, Pop Single of the Year—*Tonight's the Night (Gonna be Alright)*
Fleetwood Mac, Album of the Year—*Rumors*
Rod Stewart, Pop Singles—Male Artist
Barbra Streisand, Pop Singles—Female Artist
London Symphony Orchestra, Pop Singles—Instrumentalist Duos and Groups
Maynard Ferguson, Pop Singles—Instrumentalists
Steve Miller Band, Pop Singles—Duos and Groups
Stevie Wonder, Pop Albums—Male Artist
Linda Ronstadt, Pop Albums—Female Artist
Fleetwood Mac, Pop Albums—Duos and Groups
Salsoul Orchestra, Pop Albums—Instrumentalist Duos and Groups
Maynard Ferguson, Pop Albums—Instrumentalists

Current Status Unknown

SINGLES LABLES — POP

1975 **Capitol**
1976 **Capitol**
1977 **Warner Brothers**

Current Status Unknown

ALBUM LABELS — POP

1975 **Columbia**
1976 **Columbia**
1977 **Warner Brothers**

Current Status Unknown

PRODUCERS — POP

1975 **Gus Dudgeon**
1976 **Freddie Perren**
1977 **Richard Perry**

Current Status Unknown

PUBLISHERS

1975 **Jobete**
1976 **Jobete**
1977 **Jobete**

Current Status Unknown

HONOR ROLL OF NEW ARTISTS AND NO. 1 AWARDS

1975 **Pure Prairie League,** New Album Artist
Freddy Fender, Singles — New Male Artist
Jessi Colter, Singles — New Female Artist
Captain and Tennille, Singles — New Duos and Groups
Van McCoy and the Soul City Symphony, Singles — New Instrumentalists
Freddy Fender, Albums — New Male Artist
Gloria Gaynor, Albums — New Female artist
Pure Prairie League, Albums — New Duos and Groups
Van McCoy and the Soul City Symphony, Albums — New Instrumentalists
1976 **Rhythm Heritage,** New Singles Artists
Brass Construction, New Album Artists
Dorothy Moore, Singles — New Female Artist
Gary Wright, Singles — New Male Artist
Rhythm Heritage, Singles — New Instrumentalists
Wild Cherry, Singles — New Duos and Groups
Vicki Sue Robinson, Albums — New Female Artist
John Travolta, Albums — New Male Artist
Lee Oskar, Albums — New Intrumentalist
Brass Construction, Albums — New Duos and Groups
1977 **Foreigner,** New Pop Artist
Foreigner, New Pop Album Artist
Kenny Nolan, New Pop Singles Artist
Jennifer Warnes, New Pop Singles Female Artist
Kenny Nolan, New Pop Singles Male Artist
Cerrone, New Pop Singles Instrumentalists
Foreigner, New Pop Singles Duos and Groups
Mary MacGregor, New Pop Albums Female Artist
Teddy Pendergrass, New Pop Albums Male Artist
Lonnie Liston Smith, New Pop Albums Instrumentalists
Foreigner, New Pop Albums Duos and Groups

Current Status Unknown

COUNTRY SINGLES

1975 ***Rhinestone Cowboy,*** Glen Campbell
1976 ***Convoy,*** C.W. McCall
1977 ***Luckenbach, Texas,*** Waylon Jennings

Current Status Unknown

SINGLES ARTIST — COUNTRY

1975 **Joe Stampley**
1976 **Freddy Fender**
1977 **Waylon Jennings**

Current Status Unknown

COUNTRY ALBUM

1975 ***Back Home Again,*** John Denver
1976 ***The Sound in Your Mind,*** Willie Nelson
1977 ***Ol' Waylon,*** Waylon Jennings

Current Status Unknown

ALBUMS ARTIST — COUNTRY

1975 **Charlie Rich**
1976 **Willie Nelson**
1977 **Waylon Jennings**

Current Status Unknown

SINGLES NEW ARTIST — COUNTRY

1975 **Freddy Fender**
1976 **Dave and Sugar**

1977 Vern Gosdin

Current Status Unknown

SINGLES LABELS — POP

1975 Columbia
1976 RCA
1977 RCA

Current Status Unknown

ALBUMS LABELS — COUNTRY

1975 RCA
1976 RCA
1977 RCA

Current Status Unknown

PUBLISHERS — COUNTRY

1975 Acuff-Rose
1976 Tree
1977 Tree

Current Status Unknown

EASY LISTENING SINGLES

1975 ***Midnight Blue,*** Melissa Manchester
1976 ***Paloma Blanca,*** George Baker Selection
1977 ***Nobody Does It Better,*** Carly Simon

Current Status Unknown

SINGLES ARTIST — EASY LISTENING

1975 John Denver
1976 Olivia Newton-John
1977 Barbra Streisand

Current Status Unknown

LABELS — EASY LISTENING

1975 Columbia
1976 Columbia
1977 Columbia

Current Status Unknown

PUBLISHERS — EASY LISTENING

1975 Warner Brothers
1976 Warner Brothers
1977 Unart

Current Status Unknown

SOUL SINGLES

1975 ***Fight the Power,*** Isley Brothers
1976 ***Disco Lady,*** Johnny Taylor
1977 ***Float On,*** Floaters

Current Status Unknown

SINGLES ARTIST — SOUL

1975 Gladys Knight and the Pips
1976 Johnny Taylor
1977 Natalie Cole

Current Status Unknown

NEW ARTISTS — SOUL SINGLES

1975 Major Harris
1976 Brothers Johnson
1977 Floaters

Current Status Unknown

SINGLES LABELS — SOUL

1975 Atlantic
1976 Columbia
1977 ABC

Current Status Unknown

SOUL ALBUMS

1975 ***That's the Way of the World,*** Earth, Wind and Fire
1976 ***Rufus Featuring Chaka Khan,*** Rufus Featuring Chaka Kahn
1977 ***Songs in the Key of Life,*** Stevie Wonder

Current Status Unknown

ALBUMS ARTIST — SOUL

1975 Ohio Players
1976 Rufus Featuring Chaka Kahn
1977 Stevie Wonder

Current Status Unknown

ALBUMS LABELS — SOUL

1975 Atlantic
1976 Columbia
1977 Tamila

Current Status Unknown

PUBLISHERS — SOUL

1975 Mighty Three
1976 Mighty Three
1977 Jobete

Current Status Unknown

JAZZ ALBUMS

1975 ***Pieces of Dreams,*** Stanley Turrentine
1976 ***Breezin',*** George Benson
1977 ***In Flight,*** George Benson

Current Status Unknown

ALBUM ARTISTS — JAZZ

1975 Stanley Turrentine
1976 George Benson
1977 George Benson

Current Status Unknown

ALBUM LABELS — JAZZ

1975 Columbia
1976 Columbia
1977 Columbia

Current Status Unknown

CLASSICAL ALBUMS

1975 *Snowflakes Are Dancing: The Newest Sounds of Debussy,* Isao Tomita
1976 ***Pachelbel Canon,*** Stuttgart Chamber Orchestra
1977 ***The Great Pavarotti,*** Luciano Pavarotti

Current Status Unknown

ALBUM LABELS — CLASSICAL

1975 London
1976 London
1977 Columbia

Current Status Unknown

GOSPEL ALBUMS

1975 ***Live at Carnegie Hall,*** Andrae Crouch
1976 ***Jesus Is the Best Thing That Ever Happened to Me,*** James Cleveland and Charles Fold Singers
1977 ***Love Alive,*** Walter Hawkins and the Love Center Choir

Current Status Unknown

ALBUM LABELS — GOSPEL

1975 Savoy
1976 Savoy
1977 Savoy

Current Status Unknown

GOSPEL ARTISTS

1977 Andrae Crouch and the Disciples

Current Status Unknown

SOUNDTRACK

1975 *Tommy*
1976 *Barry Lyndon*
1977 *A Star Is Born*

Current Status Unknown

COMEDY SINGLE

1975 ***Mr. Jaws,*** Dickie Goodman
1976 ***Yes, Yes, Yes,*** Bill Cosby
1977 No award

Current Status Unknown

COMEDY ALBUM

1975 ***Wedding Album,*** Cheech and Chong
1976 ***Sleeping Beauty,*** Cheech and Chong
1977 No award

Current Status Unknown

COMEDY ALBUM ARTIST

1977 Richard Pryor

Current Status Unknown

DISCO — AUDIENCE RESPONSE

1976 ***That's Where the Happy People Go,*** Trammps
1977 ***Anyway You Like It/Don't Leave Me This Way,*** *Thelma Houston*

Current Status Unknown

DISCO ARTIST

1976 Donna Summer
1977 Donna Summer

Current Status Unknown

DISCO LABEL

1976 Motown
1977 Casablanca

Current Status Unknown

LATIN POP ARTIST

1977 Julio Iglesias

Current Status Unknown

LATIN SALSA ARTIST

1977 Celia, Johnny, Justo & Papo

Current Status Unknown

BOX OFFICE AWARDS:

1977 **Peter Frampton/Lynyrd Skynyrd/Santana/The Outlaws,** Oakland (Calif.) Stadium, (7/2-4/77)

Current Status Unknown

ARTIST

1976 Peter Frampton
1977 Peter Frampton

Current Status Unknown

PROMOTER

1976 Bill Graham
1977 Bill Graham

Current Status Unknown

FACILITY

1976 Oakland (Calif.) Stadium
1977 Oakland (Calif.) Stadium

Current Status Unknown

ARENAS (6-20,000)

1976 **Elton John,** Madison Sq. Garden, N.Y. (8/10-17/76)
1977 **Pink Floyd,** Madison Sq. Garden, N.Y., (7/1-4/77)

Current Status Unknown

ARTIST

1976 Elton John
1977 Elvis Presley

Current Status Unknown

PROMOTER

1976 Electric Factory Concerts
1977 Bill Graham

Current Status Unknown

FACILITIES

1976 Spectrum Theater, Philadelphia
1977 Spectrum Theater, Philadelphia

Current Status Unknown

AUDITORIUMS (under 6,000)

1976 **Ella Fitzgerald/Oscar Peterson/Count Basie Orchestra/Joe Pass,** Shubert Theater, Century City, Calif. (5/4-9/76)
1977 **Johnny Mathis,** Avery Fisher Hall, N.Y., (4/1-3/77)

Current Status Unknown

ARTIST

1976 **Lynyrd Skynyrd**
1977 **George Benson**

Current Status Unknown

PROMOTER

1976 **Bill Graham**
1977 **Electric Factory Concerts**

Current Status Unknown

FACILITIES

1976 **Civic Auditorium, Santa Monica, Calif.**
1977 **Tower Theater, Philadelphia**

Current Status Unknown

One-Act Opera Competition

NEW YORK CITY OPERA
Lincoln Center for the Performing Arts, New York, N.Y. 10023 (212/877-4700)

The first-place winner in the New York City Opera's one-time One-Act Opera Competition received a $10,000 cash prize and had his work produced by the City Opera. The contest was administered by the American Music Center and was judged by a selection panel.

1980 **Jan Bach**, *The Student from Salamanca*

N. Paganini International Violin Competition Prize

CITY OF GENOA
Palazzo Tursi, Via Garibaldi 9, Genoa, Italy (Tel: 010 2098)

The first-place winner of the N. Paganini International Violin Competition Prize is currently awarded 3 million lire. The three-round competition is open to musicians under thirty-five years of age. Judging is by a jury of six non-Italians and three Italians.

1956 **Gerard Poulet,** France
Gyorgy Pauk, Hungary
1957 **No award**
1958 **Salvatore Accordo,** Italy
1959 **Stuart Canin,** U.S.A.
1960 **No award**
1961 **Emil Kamilarow,** Bulgaria
1962 **Maryvonne Le Dizes,** France
1963 **Oleg Kryssa,** U.S.S.R.
1964 **Jean Jacques Kantorow,** France
1965 **Vittorio Pikaisen,** U.S.S.R.
1966 **No award**
1967 **Gregorio Gislin,** U.S.S.R.
1968 **Miriam Fries,** Israel
1969 **Ghidon Kremmer,** U.S.S.R.
1970 **No award**
1971 **Mose Secler,** U.S.S.R.
1972 **Eugene Fodor,** U.S.A.
1973 **Allesandro Kravarov,** U.S.S.R.
1974 **No award**
1975 **Yuri Korcinsky,** U.S.S.R.
1976 **Lenuta Ciulei,** Rumania
1977 **Ilja Groubert,** U.S.S.R.
1978 **Eugen Sarbu,** Rumania
1979 **Florin Paul,** Rumania
1980 **Tudor Nicolae,** Rumania

Paris International Voice Competition

CONCOURS INTERNATIONAL DE CHANT DE PARIS
14 bis, avenue du President Wilson, F-75016 Paris, France (Tel: 723 62 23)

The Paris International Voice Competition now offers three major prizes, a Grand Prize and first prizes for a man and a woman. In addition to cash awards, finalists and prize winners are offered concert and recital engagements. Singers up to the age of thirty-two years are eligible. The recipients are selected by a jury. Until now, the Competition has been held annually. After 1978, it will become a biennial event.

1967 **Anna Maria Miranda,** France
Sylvia Valet, France
1968 **Evelyn Brunner,** Switzerland
1969 **Zuinglio Faustini,** Argentina
Christiane Issartel, France
1970 **Robert Dume,** France
Gerda Hartmann, South Africa
1971 **William Parker,** U.S.A.
Esther Casas Coll, Spain
1972 **Pavlov Raptis,** Poland
Barbara Hendricks, U.S.A.
Edith Tremblay, Canada
1973 **Robert Currier Christensen,** U.S.A.
1974 **Lajos Miller,** Hungary
1975 **No award**
1976 **Serge Leiferkouss,** U.S.S.R.
1977 **John Aler,** U.S.A.
Christina Manolova, Bulgaria
1978 **Judith Nicosia,** U.S.A.

GRAND PRIZE

1977 **Katherine Ciesinski,** U.S.A.
1978 **Zehava Gal,** Israel
1980 **Jo Ann Pickens,** U.S.A.

FRENCH MELODY PRIZE

1978 **Catherine Robbin,** Canada

Gold Medal Awards

PHOTOPLAY
205 E. 42nd St., New York, N.Y. 10017 (212/983-5600)

The Photoplay Gold Medal Awards are made for popular music performers. The most recent awards were based on ballots of more than 60,000 readers of the magazine.

FAVORITE COUNTRY MUSIC STAR

1976 **Charley Pride**
1977 **Not available at press time**

Current Status Unknown

FAVORITE POP MUSIC STAR

1976 **Barry Manilow**
1977 **Not available at press time**

Current Status Unknown

Poses Brandeis University Creative Arts Award

BRANDEIS UNIVERSITY
Brandeis University Commission Office, 12 E. 77th St., New York, N.Y. 10021 (212/472-1501)

One of a series of awards in the creative arts, the Jack I. and Lillian L. Poses Brandeis University Creative Arts Award is given annually to recognize talent in mid-career in music or dance. All awards through 1973 were in the field of music; since then they have alternated between music and dance. Each year's medal and citation winners are from the same field. The award, which may not be applied for, carries an honorarium of $1,000 and a medal or citation. Professional juries chosen by the Commission select the winners.

1957 **William Schuman** (Medal), **Robert Kurka** (Citation), Music
1958 **Roger Sessions** (Medal), **Andrew Imbrie** (Citation), Music
1959 **Ernest Bloch** (Medal), **Seymour Shifrin** (Citation), Music
1960 **Aaron Copland** (Medal), **Gunther Schuller** (Citation), Music
1961 **Wallingford Riegger** (Medal), **Billy Jim Layton** (Citation), Music
1962 **Edgard Varese** (Medal), **Ralph Shapey** (Citation), Music
1963 **Walter Piston** (Medal), **Yehudi Wyner** (Citation), Music
1964 **Carl Ruggles** (Medal), **Donald Martino** (Citation), Music
1965 **Elliott Cook Carter** (Medal), **Salvatore Martirano** (Citation), Music
1966 **Stefan Wolpe** (Medal), **Mario Davidovsky** (Citation), Music
1967 **Ross Lee Finney** (Medal), **Claudio Spies** (Citation), Music
1968 **Virgil Thomson** (Medal), **Easley Blackwood** (Citation), Music
1969 **Ernst Krenek** (Medal), **Henry Weinberg** (Citation), Music
1970 **Milton Babbitt** (Medal), **Charles Wuorinen** (Citation), Music
1971 **Earl Kim** (Medal), **John Harbison** (Citation), Music
1972 **Merce Cunningham** (Medal), **Twyla Tharp** (Citation), Dance
1973 **Roy Harris** (Medal), **David Del Tredici** (Citation), Music
1974 **Anna Sokolow** (Medal), **William Dunas and Meredith Monk** (Citation), Dance
1975 **Vincent Perischetti** (Medal), **Jacob Druckman** (Citation), Music
1976 **Antony Tudor** (Medal), **Eliot Feld** (Citation), Dance
1977 **Leon Kirchner** (Medal), **Earle Brown** (Citation), Music
1978 **Paul Taylor** (Medal), **Pilobolaus Dance Theatre** (Citation), Dance
1979 **George Crumb** (Medal), **Tison Street** (Citation), Music
1980 **Not available at press time**

Pulitzer Prize

COLUMBIA UNIVERSITY
Graduate School of Journalism, New York, N.Y. 10027 (212/280-3828) (Pulitzer Prizes: 212/280-3841)

Endowed by the will of Joseph Pulitzer, founder of the *St. Louis Post Dispatch,* and administered by Columbia University, the annual Pulitzer Prizes include a $1,000 award for music. Entry must be made to the fifteen-member advisory board on Pulitzer Prizes in the form or scores or recordings.

1943 **William Schuman,** *Secular Cantata No. 2*
1944 **Howard Hanson,** *Symphony No. 4, opus 34*
1945 **Aaron Copland,** *Appalachian Spring*
1946 **Leo Sowerby,** *The Canticle of the Sun*
1947 **Charles Ives,** *Symphony No. 3*
1948 **Walter Piston,** *Symphony No. 3*
1949 **Virgil Thomson,** *Louisiana Story*
1950 **Gian-Carlo Menotti,** *The Consul*
1951 **Douglas S. Moore,** *Giants in the Earth*
1952 **Gail Kubik,** *Symphony Concertante*
1953 **No award**
1954 **Quincy Porter,** *Concerto for Two Pianos and Orchestra*
1955 **Gian-Carlo Menotti,** *The Saint of Bleecker Street*
1956 **Ernst Toch,** *Symphony No. 3*
1957 **Norman Dello Joio,** *Meditations on Ecclesiastes*
1958 **Samuel Barber,** The Score of *Vanessa*
1959 **John La Montaine,** *Concerto for Piano and Orchestra*
1960 **Elliott Cook Carter, Jr.,** *Second String Quartet*
1961 **Walter Piston,** *Symphony No. 7*
1962 **Robert Ward,** *The Crucible*
1963 **Samuel Barber,** *Piano Concerto No. 1*
1964 **No award**
1965 **No award**
1966 **Leslie Bassett,** *Variations for Orchestra*
1967 **Leon Kirchner,** *Quartet No. 3*
1968 **George Crumb,** *Echoes of Time and the River*
1969 **Karel Husa,** *String Quartet No. 3*
1970 **Charles W. Wuorinen,** *Time's Encomium*
1971 **Mario Davidovsky,** *Synchronisms No. 6*
1972 **Jacob Druckman,** *Windows*
1973 **Elliott Carter,** *String Quartet No. 3*
1974 **Donald Martino,** *Notturno*
1975 **Dominick Argento,** *From the Diary of Virginia Woolf*
1976 **Ned Rorem,** *Air Music,* 10 etudes for orchestra
1977 **Richard Wernick,** *Visions of Terror and Wonder*
1978 **Michael Coalgrass,** *Deja Vu for Percussion Quartet and Orchestra*
1979 **Joseph Schwantner,** *Aftertones of Infinity*
1980 **David Del Tredici,** *In Memory of a Summer Day*

SPECIAL AWARDS AND CITATIONS

1974 **Roger Sessions,** Life's work in compsition
1976 **Scott Joplin,** Bicentennial honor bestowed posthumously for contributions to American music

Recording Academy Hall of Fame

NATIONAL ACADEMY OF RECORDING ARTS AND SCIENCES

4444 Riverside Dr., Suite 202, Burbank, Calif. 91505
(213/843-8233)

Admission to the Recording Academy Hall of Fame honors outstanding historical, qualitative or lasting recordings. The honor includes permanent enshrinement in the Hall of Fame and inscribed certificates to all creative participants. A ninety-person committee of musicologists and experts in the field selects the recordings to be honored.

INDUCTED PRIOR TO 1974-77 (Date indicates when recording was made)

1907 **Enrico Caruso**, *Leoncavallo: Pagliacci, Vesti la Giubba*, Act 1
1927 **Paul Whiteman** and **George Gershwin**, *Gershwin: Rhapsody in Blue* (RCA Victor)
1927 **Frankie Trumbauer** and his Orchestra featuring **Bix Beiderbecke** on cornet, *Singin' the Blues* (Okeh)
1928 **Louis Armstrong**, *West End Blues* (Okeh)
1929 **Sergei Rachmaninoff** (piano) and the Philadelphia Orchestra with **Leopold Stowkowski** conducting, *Rachmaninoff: Piano Concerto No. 2 in C Minor* (Victor)
1930 **Duke Ellington**, *Mood Indigo* (Brunswick)
1937 **Bunny Berigan**, *I Can't Get Started* (Victor)
Arthur Schnabel, *Beethoven Piano Sonatas* (Beethoven Piano Society/RCA)
1939 **Coleman Hawkins**, *Body and Soul* (Bluebird)
1941 **Billie Holliday**, *God Bless the Child* (Okeh)
Duke Ellington and his Orchestra, *Take the A Train* (Victor)
1942 **Bing Crosby**, *White Christmas* (Decca)
1943 **Alfred Drake** and other members of original cast; **Jay Blackton** directing orchestra and chorus, *Oklahoma!* (Decca)
1949-54 **Wanda Landowska**, *Bach: The Well-Tempered Clavier* (RCA Victor)
1950 **Benny Goodman**, *Carnegie Hall Jazz Concert* (Columbia)
1950-53 **Arturo Toscanini** conducting the NBC Symphony Orchestra, *Beethoven: Nine Symphonies* (RCA Victor)
1951 **Lehmen Engel**, conductor, and original cast incl. **Lawrence, Winters, Cammella, Williams**, *Porgy and Bess* (Columbia)
1954 **Nat "King" Cole**, *Christmas Song* (Capitol)
1956 **Rex Harrison** and **Julie Andrews** (orig. cast), *My Fair Lady* (Columbia)

INDUCTED 1978

1927 **Leopold Stowkowski** conducting the Philadelphia Orchestra, *Bach-Stowkowski: Toccata and Fugue in D Minor* (Victrola)
1928 **Gene Austin**, *My Blue Heaven* (Victor)
1939 **Billie Holliday**, *Strange Fruit* (Commodore)
1948-60 **Edward R. Murrow**, *I Can Hear It Now*, Vols. 1-3 (Columbia)
1954-55 **Art Tatum**, *The Genius of Art Tatum*, Vols. 1-13 (Clef)

INDUCTED 1979

1935 **Sergei Rachmaninoff** (piano) and the Philadelphia Orchestra conducted by **Leopold Stowkowski**, *Rachmaninoff: Rhapsody on a Theme of Paganini* (RCA Victor)
1937 **Count Basie**, *One O'Clock Jump* (Decca)
1951 **Les Paul** and **Mary Ford**, *How High the Moon* (Capitol)

INDUCTED 1980

1927 **Bix Beiderbecke**, *In a Mist* (Okeh)
1940 **Paul Robeson**, *Ballad for Americans* (Victor)
1949-50 **Ferdinand "Jelly Roll" Morton**, *Jelly Roll Morton: The Saga of Mr. Jelly Lord*, 12 albums (Circle Sound)

Rock Music Awards

ROCK MUSIC ASSOCIATION

The Rock Music Awards have been given annually since 1975 in nationally telecast ceremonies for excellence in this area of popular music. Neither details of the selection process nor 1975-6 or recent winners are available.

ROCK PERSONALITY OF THE YEAR

1977 **Fleetwood Mac**

BEST FEMALE VOCALIST

1977 **Linda Ronstadt**

BEST MALE VOCALIST

1977 **Stevie Wonder**

BEST GROUP

1977 **Fleetwood Mac**

BEST NEW FEMALE VOCALIST

1977 **Yvonne Elliman**

BEST NEW MALE VOCALIST

1977 **Stephen Bishop**

BEST NEW GROUP

1977 **Boston**

BEST R&B SINGLE

1977 **Boz Scaggs,** *Low Down*

BEST R&B ALBUM

1977 **Stevie Wonder,** *Songs in the Key of Life*

BEST SINGLE

1977 **Boz Scaggs,** *Low Down*

BEST ALBUM

1977 **Fleetwood Mac,** *Rumors*

BEST SONG COMPOSER

1977 **Bruce Springsteen,** *Blinded by the Light*

BEST PRODUCER

1977 **Fleetwood Mac**

PUBLIC SERVICE AWARD

1977 **Joan Baez**
Bee Gees
Harry Chapin
Fleetwood Mac
Kansas
Spinners

ROCK MUSIC HALL OF FAME
1977 **Elvis Presley**
Current status unknown

Leopold Stowkowski Award

AMERICAN SYMPHONY ORCHESTRA
119 W. 57th St., New York, N.Y. 10019 (212/581-1365)

The Leopold Stowkowski Award is given annually to a young conductor of note and promise. The prize consists of a bronze medal and an opportunity to conduct the American Symphony Orchestra in concert.

1979 **Calvin Simmons**
1980 **David Ramadamoff**

International Jean Sibelius Violin Competition

SIBELIUS SOCIETY
P. Rautatiekatu 9, SF-00100 Helsinki, Finland (Tel: 90-492 223)

The International Jean Sibelius Violin Competition is held every five years for violinists between the ages of sixteen and thirty-three. A jury selects the winner, who is awarded a cash honorarium, currently $5,000. In addition to the first-place winners listed here, cash awards are given to the second- through eighth-place finishers.

1965 **Oleg Kagan,** U.S.S.R.
1970 **Liana Isakadze,** U.S.S.R.
Pavel Kogan, U.S.S.R.
1975 **Yuval Yaron,** Israel
1980 **Viktoria Mullova,** U.S.S.R.

Talent Forum Award

BILLBOARD
9000 Sunset Blvd., Los Angeles, Calif. 90069 (213/273-7040)

The Talent Forum Award, which consists of a plaque, honors achievement in the live-talent field as determined by a vote of Talent Forum registrants.

1976 **Bill Graham,** Concert promoter
Dee Anthony, Bandana Productions, Personal manager
Frank Barsalona, Premier, Independent booking agent
Tom Ross, ICM, Staff booking agent
Magid, Bijou, Philadelphia, Nightclub operator
Chuck Morris, Ebbets Field, Denver, Nightclub operator (small clubs)
Elmer Valentine, Roxy, Los Angeles, Nightclub operator in Los Angeles or New York
Claire Rothman, Los Angeles Forum, Facility manager
Mike Klenfner, Arista, Artists relations executive
Bob Levinson, Levinson Associates, Publicist
Stuart Allen, Aladdin, Las Vegas, Talent buyer (hotels)
Sonny Anderson, Disneyland, Top talent buyer (fairs and parks)
Joff Dubin, U. of Calif. at Berkeley, Talent buyer (colleges)
Eagles, Warner Bros., Talent Attraction of the Year
1977 **Dee Anthony,** Personal manager
Nat Weiss, Entertainment attorney
Ron Delsener, Concert promoter
Boston, Breakout artist
Barbara Skydell, Premier, Staff booking agent
Joe Cohen, Madison Sq. Garden, Facility manager
Frank Barsalona, Premier, Independent booking agent
Susan Blond, Publicist
Allan Pepper and Stanley, Sandowsky, Bottom Line, Nightclub operator
Suzanne Young, U. of Michigan, College talent buyer
Jonathan Coffino, Columbia, Artist relations Executive
James Tamer, Aladdin, Talent Buyer of the Year
Performing Arts Theatre, (hotels, fairs, parks)

Current status unknown

International Tchaikovsky Awards

INTERNATIONAL TCHAIKOVSKY COMPETITION
15 Neglinnaya St., Moscow, U.S.S.R. (Tel: 294-64-61; 223-13-87; 294-14-20)

The International Tchaikovsky Competition takes place every four years for pianists, violinists, cellists and solo singers of any nationality between the ages of sixteen and thirty. Two preliminary and one final round of competition before the public are held, and winners are expected to participate gratis in concerts that mark the closing of the competition. Six cash awards are made in each category, with the top prize consisting of 2,500 rubles and a gold medal.

PIANO
1958 **Van Cliburn** (U.S.A.)
1962 **John Andrew Howard Ogden** (Great Britain)
1964 **Grigory Sokolov** (U.S.S.R.)
1970 **Vladimir Krainev** (U.S.S.R.)
1974 **Andrei Gavrilov** (U.S.S.R.)
1978 **Andre Leplante** (Canada)

VIOLIN
1958 **Valery Klimov** (U.S.S.R.)
1962 **Boris Gutnikov** (U.S.S.R.)
1966 **Viktor Tretyakov** (U.S.S.R.)
1970 **Gideon Kramer** (U.S.S.R.)
1974 Tied for second place; no first-prize winner:
Ruben Agaronyan (U.S.S.R.)
Eugene Fodor (U.S.A.)
Rusudan Gvasaliya (U.S.S.R.)

CELLO
1962 **Natalya Shakhovskaya** (U.S.S.R.)
1966 **Karine Georgian** (U.S.S.R.)
1970 **David Geringas** (U.S.S.R.)
1974 **Boris Pergamentchikov** (U.S.S.R.)
1978 **Nathaniel Rosen** (U.S.A.)

VOICE (Male)
1966 **Vladimir Atlantov** (U.S.S.R.)
1970 **Evgeny Nesterenko** (U.S.S.R.)

1974 **Ivan Ponomorenko** (U.S.S.R.)

VOICE (Female)

1966 **Jane Marsh** (U.S.A.)
1970 **Elena Obratsova** (U.S.S.R.)
1974 Tied for second place; no first-prize winner:
Stefka Evstatieva (Bulgaria)
Sylvia Sass (Hungary)
Liudmila Sergienko (U.S.S.R.)

Trendsetter Award

Billboard
9000 Sunset Blvd., Los Angeles, Calif. 90069
(213/273-7040)

The Trendsetter Award, which consists of a Lucite statue, is given for outstanding achievement in the music field that represents a specific innovation or trend in the industry. The management, editors and sales staff of *Billboard* select the members of the industry who receive this annual honor.

1976 **David Infante,** Laser Physics, Opening disco and concert areas to laser light shows
Joe Cayre, Salsoul Records, Developing first 12-inch single for commercial sale
Don Biederman, ABC Records, Crusade to halt retailers from selling counterfeit and promotional albums
Lee Fisher, Aladdin Hotel, Las Vegas, Nev., Opened Las Vegas's first concert hall on the Strip
Tony Martell, CBS Records, Developing the country music prepack album program
Neil Bogart, Casablanca Records, Developing a program of limited edition LPS for major artists
Ernest Fleischman & the Los Angeles Philharmonic, Developing a formula with the American Federation of Musicians to allow orchestra to record without paying for a full complement of musicians.
George De Rado, TEAC, Expanding the market for semi-professional sound equipment
1977 **Creed Taylor,** Creating cross-over brand of jazz, appealing to pop and disco fans
Chris Blackwell and Denny Cordell, Introduction of Jamaican reggae music to U.S. market
John Denver, Musical style which draws adults into pop market
Freddy Fender and Huey Meaux, Established Tex-Mex music on national market
CBS Records and Vice President Bruce Lundvall and Jack Graigo, Promoting wide-margin price concept for catalogue LPs
Atlantic Records and Dickie Klein and Henry Allen, Series of 12-in. singles for discotheques
Andy Park, Devising adventurous programing of various sounds for Scotland's commercial station, Radio Clyde
Moffat Communications, Installing computer-assisted programing system at its Canadian radio stations
Willem van Kooten, Masterminding and guiding international impact of Dutch talent
Wonderama, Presenting top-name contemporary music acts to young children via Sunday morning TV
Exxon Corp., Leading corporate funding of classical concert music on radio, television and in concert

Current status unknown

Varna Prize

INTERNATIONAL BALLET COMPETITION
56 Alabin St., 1000-Sofia, Bulgaria (Tel. 880853)

The International Ballet Competition for men and women currently takes place biennially in Varna and comprises three stages of contemporary and classical dance programs. Male and female dancers are evaluated separately by juries, whether they enter as soloists or duos. Class A competition is for dancers nineteen years of age or over, while Class B is for young dancers between fourteen and nineteen years of age. The first-place Class A winners receive 2000 leva, a gold medal and a diploma, while the first-place Class B dancers receive 800 leva, a diploma and a medal. In addition to the first-place winners listed here, Class A prizes are awarded down to the fifth place and Class B prizes to the third place.

1964 **Vladimir Vassilev** (U.S.S.R.) Grand Prize
Ala Sizova (U.S.S.R.) First Prize
Ekaterina Maximova (U.S.S.R.) First Prize
Vera Kirova (Bulgaria) First Prize
Sergei Vikulov (U.S.S.R.) First Prize
Nikita Dolgushin (U.S.S.R.) First Prize
1965 **Mikhail Lavrovsky** (U.S.S.R.) First Prize
Loipa Araujo (Cuba) First Prize
Vladimir Tikhonov (U.S.S.R.) First Prize
Natalia Bessmertnova (U.S.S.R.) First Prize
1966 **Mikhail Baryshnikov** (U.S.S.R.) Junior First Prize
Martine van Hamel (Canada) Junior First Prize
Olga Vtorushina (U.S.S.R.) Junior First Prize
Marin Stanse (Romania) Junior First Prize
Yuriy Vladimirov (U.S.S.R.) Senior First Prize
Nina Sorekina (U.S.S.R.) Senior First Prize
Aurora Bosch (Cuba) Senior First Prize
Marta Drotnerova (Czechoslovakia) Senior First Prize
1968 **Jan Nuits** (Belgium) Junior First Prize
Bisser Beyanou (Bulgaria) Junior First Prize
Mirta Garcia (Cuba) Junior First Prize
Villen Gastian (U.S.S.R.) Senior First Prize
1970 **Rosario Suarez** (Cuba) Junior First Prize
Eva Evdokimova (U.S.A.) Senior First Prize
1972 **Hana Vlacilova** (Czechoslovakia) Junior First Prize
Gabor Kevehazy (Hungary) Junior First Prize
Lyubov Konakova (U.S.S.R.) Senior First Prize
Vladimir Fedyanin (U.S.S.R.) Senior First Prize
1974 **Yoko Morishita** (Japan)
Fernando Bujones (U.S.A.), Technical Award
Mihail Civin (U.S.S.R.)
Bisser Dejanov (Bulgaria)
Galina Tessjolkina (Special Award)
Soile Hainonen (Finland)
1976 (Tied for senior second prize; no first prize)
Hana Vlacilova (Czechoslovakia)
Larissa Mathiuhina (U.S.S.R.)
Marin Bojeru (Romania), Senior First Prize
Alla Mihalchenko (U.S.S.R.), Junior First Prize
Ben van Kauenberg (Belgium), Junior Second Prize; no First Prize awarded
1978 **Raissa Khilko** (U.S.S.R.)
Lubomir Rafka (Czechoslovakia), First Prize
Clotild Veie (France), Junior First Prize
Vladimir Derevyanks (U.S.S.R.), Special Award (Junior)
1980 **Not available at press time**

Verdi Medal of Achievement

METROPOLITAN OPERA NATIONAL COUNCIL
Metropolitan Opera, Lincoln Center for the Performing Arts, New York, N.Y. 10023 (212/799-3100)

The Verdi Medal of Achievement is awarded annually to the individual who has made the greatest contribution to opera in the previous year. The medal, which is of bronze, was sculpted by Betti Richard. A committee selects the winner.

1977 **Maria F. Rich,**
1978 **Osie Hawkins**
1979 **Albert F. Hubay**
1980 **Mrs. Charles F. Gimbel**

Wihuri-Sibelius Prize

JENNY AND ANTTI WIHURI FOUNDATION
Arkadiankatu 21 B 25, 00100-Helsinki 10, Finland (Tel: 444 145)

Among the prizes, honors and scholarships awarded by this foundation and its research institute is the Wihuri-Sibelius Prize, given as warranted for merit in music.

1953 **Jean Sibelius**
1955 **Paul Hindemith**
1958 **Dmitri Shostakovich**
1963 **Igor Stravinsky**
1965 **Benjamin Britten**
Erik Bergman
Usko Merilainen
Einojuhani Rautavaara
1971 **Olivier Messiaen**
1973 **Witold Lutoslawski**
Joonas Kokkonen

Grand Prix

YAMAHA MUSIC FOUNDATION
3-24-22, Shimoneguro, Meguro-ku, Tokyo 153, Japan (Tel: 03/719-3101)

The Grand Prix of the World Popular Music Festival, which consisists of $5,000 and a gold medallion, is given annually for the best original song unpublished —except under special circumstances —before the festival. A panel of international judges selects the winners. In addition to the Grand Prix, lesser cash awards are given for excellence in performance and composition.

1970 ***I Dream of Naomi,*** by David Krivoshi, performed by Hedva and David (Israel)
1971 ***The Song of Departure,*** by Hitoshi Komuro, performed by Kamijo and Rokumonsen (Japan)
Un Jour L'Amour, by Andre Popp, performed by Martine Clemenseau (France)
1972 ***Feeling,*** by Peter Yellowstone and Jane Schwarz, performed by Capricorn (United Kingdom)
Life Is Just For Livin', by Ernie Smith, performed by Ernie Smith (Jamaica)
1973 ***I Wish You Were Here With Me,*** by Akiko Kosaka, performed by Akiko Kosaka (Japan)
If All the Kings and Castles, by Shawn Phillips, performed by Shawn Phillips (U.S.A.)
Head Over Heels, by Zack Lawrence, performed by Keeley Ford (United Kingdom)
How Strange Paris is Sometimes, by Gino Mescoli and Alfred Ferrari, performed by Gilda Giuliani (Italy)
1974 ***Someday,*** by Yoshimi Hamada, performed by Yoshimi Hamada (Japan)
You Made Me Feel I Could Fly, by Kristian Lindeman, performed by Ellen Nikolaysen (Norway)
1975 ***Lucky Man,*** by Jorge Garcia-Castil, performed by Mr. Loco (Mexico)
Time Goes Around, by Miyuki Nakajima, performed by Miyaki Nakajima (Japan)
1976 ***Goodbye Morning,*** by Kaoru Nakajima, performed by Sandy (Japan)
My Love, by Gino Mescoli, performed by Franco and Regina (Italy)
1977 ***A Ballad for You,*** by Masanori Sera, performed by Masanori Sera and Twist (Japan)
Can't Hide My Love, by Richard Gillinson and David Hayes, performed by Rags (United Kingdom)
1978 ***Fly On All The Way***, composed and performed by **Hiroshi Makaoda** (Japan)
Love Rocks by **Biddu** and performed by **Tina Charles** (Great Britain)
1979 ***In the City of Strangers*** by **Michio Yamashita** and performed by **The Crystal King** (Japan)
Sitting on the Edge of the Ocean by **Ronnie Scott** and **Steve Wolfe** (composers) and performed by **Bonnie Tyler** (Great Britain)
1980 ***What's the Use*** by **Mary MacGregor**, **Marty Rodgers** and **David Bluefield** and performed by **Mary MacGregor** (U.S.A.)
Oh My Good-Bye Town by **Tetsuya Itami** and performed by **Tetsya Itami** and **Sided by Side** (Japan)

Visual Arts

Contents

Related Awards

ADDA Award

ART DEALERS ASSOCIATION OF AMERICA
575 Madison Ave., New York, N.Y. 10022 (212/940-8590)

The $5,000 ADDA Award accompanied by an Alexander Calder sculpture is given annually to an art historian for overall of lifetime contributions to art. A committee selects the winner.

1972 Alfred H. Barr, Jr.
1973 Meyer Schapiro
1974 Millard Meiss
1975 Wolfgang Stechow
1976 Jakob Rosenberg
1977 Lloyd Goodrich
1978 George Heard Hamilton
1979 Seymour Slive
1980 Julius S. Held

ASMP Awards

AMERICAN SOCIETY OF MAGAZINE PHOTOGRAPHERS
205 Lexington Ave., New York, N.Y. 10016 (212/889-9144)

The ASMP annually confers awards on individuals in the photographic world for contributions in the creative, technical or curatory aspects of the field. The Awards Committee chooses the recipients, who are presented with a certificate, in areas such as Photographer of the Year, Technical Achievement and others. Neither these areas of honor nor the number of winners is fixed. In addition, special awards, including an Honor Roll citation, are given as merited.

1953 Henri Cartier-Bresson
Roland S. Potter
Roy Stryker
1954 Ernst Haas
Alexey Brodovitch
1955 Robert Capa
Werner Bischof
John A. Leermakers
Wayne Miller
Edward Steichen
1956 Ylla
Roman Vishniac
1957 Richard Avedon
Will Connell
Allen F. Gifford
1958 Marty Forscher
Emil Schulthess
Wilson Hicks
1960 Gordon Parks
Edwin Land
Richard Simon
David Douglas Duncan
1961 Irving Penn
Japanese Camera Industry
John Simon Guggenheim Foundation
1962 Brian Brake
George Silk
Bill Brandt
1963 Gjon Mili
1964 Art Kane
Polaroid Corp.
Berenice Abbott
Charles Moore
1965 David Linton
Ralph Baum
Morris Gordon
Imogen Cunningham
Lennart Nilsson
Harold Edgerton
1966 Andreas Feininger
Victor Hasselblad
1967 Vietnam War photographers, living and dead
Charles Wycoff
Dennis Gabor
Emmett Leith
Juris Upatnieks
1968 David Douglas Duncan
Cornell Capa
Lisette Model
Homer Newell
Leopold Godowski
Leopold Manners
Alexander Smakula
Beaumont Newhall
Grace Mayer
1969 Hiro
Fritz Gruber
Ben Rose
Yoichi R. Okamoto
Romana Javits
Edwin L. Wisherd
James Van Derzee
Ott Schade
Oscar Bernack
1970 Bruce Davidson
Diane Arbus
Jerry Uelsmann
Jacob Deschin
Walter Clark
Peter C. Goldmark
1972 David B. Eisendrath
Lee D. Witkin
1975 Philippe Halsman
Arnold Newman
Donald McCullin
Alexander Liberman
Edwin Land
1976 No award
1977 No award
1978 Fritz Goro
Alfred Eisenstadt
Lawrence Fried
Barbara Ringer
Anna Farova
Jay Maisel
1979 No award
1980 Carl Mydans
Edward Thompson
Ilford
Eddie Adams
Irving Penn

FOUNDERS AWARD

1965 Allan Gould
Michael Elliot
Ewing Krainin
Ike Vern
Bradley Smith
John Adam Knight

HONOR ROLL

- **1961** Man Ray
- **1962** Roy Stryker
  Alexey Brodovitch
  Edward Steichen
  Will Connell
- **1963** Dorothea Lange
  Walker Evans
  Cecil Beaton
  Paul Strand
  George Hoyningen-Huene
- **1964** Margaret Bourke-White
- **1965** Andre Kertesz
- **1966** Ansel Adams
  Brassai
- **1967** Roman Vishniac
  Bill Brandt
- **1968** Beaumont Newhall
- **1969** Fritz Gruber
- **1970** W. Eugene Smith
- **1971** Ernst Haas
- **1972** Henri Cartier-Bresson
- **1975** Cornell Capa
- **1976** No award
- **1977** No award
- **1978** Barrett Gallagher
- **1979** No award
- **1980** Gjon Mili
  Ben Rose

Arts and Letters Awards
Richard & Hinda Rosenthal Award

AMERICAN ACADEMY AND INSTITUTE OF ARTS AND LETTERS
633 W. 155th St., New York, N.Y. 10032 (212/368-6361)

To encourage qualified artists, the Institute gives annual cash awards currently $5,000 each to non-members. These Arts and Letters Awards may not be applied for. Similar awards are given in music and literature and may be found on pp. 73 and 338 of this volume.

1941
Jon Corbino
Arthur Lee

1942
Peggy Bacon
Donal Hord
Cathal B. O'Toole

1943
Isabel Bishop
Hugh Ferris
Gertrude K. Lathrop
Bruce Moore

1944
Janet de Coux
Charles Locke
Berta Margoulies
Eleanor Platt
Charles Rudy
Esther Williams

1945
Peter Dalton
Donald De Lue
Vincent Glinsky
Edward Laning
Andree Ruellan
Raphael Soyer

1946
Richmond Barthe
Louis Gugliemi
Robert Gwathmey
Rosella Hartman
Jack Levine
Harry Rosin
Concetta Scaravaglione
Zoltan Sepeshy

1947
Peter Blume
Dorothea Greenbaum
Joseph Hirsch
Victoria Hutson Huntley
Mitchell Jamieson
Carl Schmitz

1948
Louis Bosa
Robert H. Cook, Jr.
Stephen Csoka
Philip Guston
Oronzio Maldarelli
John W. Taylor

1949
Federico Castellon
Carl Hall
Henry Kreis
John McCrady
William Pachner
Harry Wickey

1950
Jean de Marco
Lamar Dodd
Sue Fuller
Peter Hopkins
Bruno Mankowski
Sol Wilson

1951
Saul Baizerman
Lu Duble
Joseph Floch
Xavier Gonzalez
Peppino Mangravite
William Thon

1952
Clara Fasano
H.L. Kammerer
Edward Melcarth
Doris Rosenthal
Walter Stuempfig
Charles White

1953
Hyman Bloom
Albino Cavallito
Jacob Lawrence
William Palmer
Carl M. Schultheiss
Francis Speight

1954
Virginia Cuthbert
Koren Der Harootian
Edwin Dickinson
Hazard Durfee
Antonio Frasoni
David K. Rubins

1955
George Beattie
Hazel Janicki
Julian Levi
Zygmunt Menkes
Mitchell Siporin
Albert Stewart
Sahl Swarz

1956
Henry Di Spirito
Philip Evergood
Morris Graves
Chaim Gross
Barbara Lekberg
Theodoros Stamos

1957
John Heliker
Jonah Kinigstein
Kenzo Okada
Anne Poor
Hugo Robus
Polygnotos Vagis

1958
Charles H. Alston
David Aronson
Al Blaustein
Herbert Katzman
Seymour Lipton
Jack Zajac

1959
Jose de Rivera
Frank Duncan

Ruth Gikow
Minna Harkavy
James Kearns
John Guerin
Nathaniel Kaz

1960

Chen Chi
Eugene Ludins
George Tooker
Walter Williams
Marvin Cherney
Rhoda Sherbell
Harold Tovish

1961

Leonard Baskin
Kahlil Gibran
Walter Murch
Joseph Solman
Paul Cadmus
Philip Grausman
Gregorio Prestopino

1962

Robert M. Broderson
Richard Diebenkorn
Camilo Egas
Bernard Reder
Nicolai Cikovsky
Seymour Drumlevitch
Dimitri Hadzi

1963

Harold Altman
Elmer Bischoff
James McGarrell
Karl Zerbe
Wolfgang Behl
Jan Doubrava
Raymond Saunders

1964

Thomas B. Cornell
Reuben Kramer
Bernard Perlin
Charles Wells
Edward J. Hill
Michael Mazur
Sarai Sherman

1965

Sigmund Abeles
David V. Hayes
Elliott Offner
Thomas Stearns
Lee Gatch
Richard Mayhew
Joyce Reopel

1966

Romare Bearden
Carroll Cloar
Ezio Mantinelli
Richard Claude Ziemann
Lee Bontecou
Ray Johnson
Karl Schrag

1967

Byron Burford
Stephen Greene
Dennis Leon
Louis Tytell
Jared French
Leo Kenney
Hugh Townley

1968

Robert A. Birmelin
Leon Goldin
Vincent D. Smith
Charles Wilson
Kenneth Callahan
Joe Lasker
Elbert Weinberg

1969

Lennart Anderson
Frank Gallo
Red Grooms
Ben Kamihira
William Christopher
Leonel Gongora
Sidney J. Hurwitz
Alice Neel

1970

Leland Bell
Kenneth Campbell
Ralston Crawford
Charles F. Cajori
Giorgio Cavallon
Allan D'Arcangelo
Harvey Weiss

1971

Ilya Bolotowsky
Alfred Leslie
Ludwig Sander
Harold Tovish
Robert Goodnough
Norman Lewis
Hedda Sterne

1972

Richard Aakre
Lowry Burgess
Maud F. Gatewood
Anton Van Dalen
Varujan Boghosian
Mary Frank
Herman Rose

1973

Rudolf Baranik
Robert Grosvenor
Michio Ihara
Philip Pearlstein
Leon Golub
Raoul Hague
Clement Meadmore

1974

Perle Fine
Marilynn Gelfman-Pereira
Nancy Grossman
Charlotte Park
Richard Fleischner
George Griffin
Ibram Lassaw

1975

Calvin Albert
Barbara Falk
Leonid
William Talbot
Harry Bertoia
Claus Hoie
Seymour Pearlstein

1976

Judith Brown
William Kienbusch
Anthony Padovano
Joseph Wolins
Gregory Gillespie
Julio F. Larraz
Sidney Simon

1977

Nina Bohlen
Alex Markhoff
Fritz Scholder
Alan Gussow
Paul Resika
Susan Smyly

1978

Daniel Maloney
Richard McDermott Miller
Reuben Tam
Herman Maril
Sara Roszak
Ulfert Wilke

1979

Fletcher Benton
Anne Healy
Arthur Levine
Randall Deihl
Wolf Kahn

1980

Richard Anuszkiewicz
Marion Lerner Levine
Charmion von Wiegand
Edward Dugmore
Howard Newman

One of a pair of awards established under the same endowment (the other being for a work of fiction, see pp. 65), the Richard and Hinda Rosenthal Award in art is a $2,000 honorarium given to a young American painter of distinction who has not yet been accorded due recognition. This award may not be applied for.

1960 Ann Steinbrocker
1961 Zubel Kachadoorian
1962 Robert Andrew Parker
1963 Karen Arden

1964 **Gregory Gillespie**
1965 **Marcia Marcus**
1966 **Howard Hack**
1967 **Robert D'Arista**
1968 **Elizabeth Osborne**
1969 **Nicholas Sperakis**
1970 **George Schneeman**
1971 **Donald Perlis**
1972 **Barkley L. Hendricks**
1973 **Jim Sullivan**
1974 **Julie Curtis Reed**
1975 **Richard Merkin**
1976 **Carl Nicholas Titolo**
1977 **Sigrid Burton**
1978 **Clifford Ross**
1979 **Nicholas Issak**
1980 **Dolores Milmoe**

Poses Brandeis University Creative Arts Award

BRANDEIS UNIVERSITY
Brandeis University Commission Office, 12 E. 77th St., New York, N.Y. 10021 (212/472-1501)

One of a series of awards in the creative arts, the Jack I. and Lillian L. Poses Brandeis University Creative Arts Award is given annually to recognize talent in mid-career in the fine arts—painting, sculpture and architecture. The award, which may not be applied for, carries an honorarium of $1,000 and a medal or citation. Professional juries chosen by the Commission select the winner. (The other Poses Brandeis awards may be found on pp. 61, 143, 210 and 349.)

1957 **Stuart Davis** (Medal); **Jimmy Ernst** (citation); Painting
1958 **Jacques Lipchitz** (Medal); **Richard Lippold** (citation); Sculpture
1959 **Edwin Dickinson** (Medal); **Theodoros Stamos** (citation); Painting
1960 **Naum Gabo** (Medal); **James Rosati** (citation); Sculpture
1961 **Karl Knaths** (Medal); **George Mueller** (citation); Painting
1962 **Alexander Calder** (Medal); **Davis Slivka** (citation); Sculpture
1963 **Georgia O'Keeffe** (Medal); **Ellsworth Kelly** (citation); Painting
1964 **David Smith** (Medal); **Peter Agostini** (citation); Sculpture
1965 **Mark Rothko** (Medal); **Kenneth Noland** (citation); Painting
1966 **Isamu Noguchi** (Medal); **Richard Stankiewicz** (citation); Sculpture
1967 **Ludwig Mies van der Rohe** (Medal); **Kevin Roche** (citation); Architecture
1968 **Joseph Cornell** (Medal); **Frank Stella** (citation); Painting
1969 **Jose de Rivera** (Medal); **Mark di Suvero** (citation); Sculpture
1970 **Barnett Newman** (Medal); **Jasper Johns** (citation); Painting
1971 **Louise Nevelson** (Medal); **Claes Oldenburg** (citation); Sculpture
1972 **Louis I. Kahn** (Medal); **Ian McHarg** (citation); Architecture
1973 **Willem de Kooning** (Medal); **Joan Mitchell** (citation); Painting
1974 **Tony Smith** (Medal); **Robert Morris** (citation); Sculpture
1975 **Isabel Bishop** (Medal); **Robert Whitman** (citation); Painting & Visual Arts
1976 **Philip Johnson** (Medal); **Robert Venturi** (citation); Architecture
1977 **Rueben Nakiacio** (Medal); **Mary Frank**(citation); Sculpture
1978 **Robert Rauschenberg** (Medal); **Lester Johnson** (Citation); Painting
1979 **George Rickey** (Medal); **Jackie Winsor** (Citation)
1980 **Philip Guston** (Medal)

Mary Martin Award

AMERICAN NEEDLEPOINT GUILD
6342 Brolwood Rd., Charlotte, N.C. 28211 (704/366-5692)

The Mary Martin Award is given annually for excellence and creativity in needlepoint and especially for promotion of the craft. The winner, who receives a plaque, is selected by an advisory board.

1974 **Princess Grace of Monaco,** Needlepoint enthusiast
1975 **Pat Trexler,** Syndicated columnist
1976 **Erica Wilson,** Author
1977 **Maggie Lane,** Author

Current status unknown

Collector's Institute Award

TEXAS INSTITUTE OF LETTERS
Box 3143, Dallas, Tex. 75275

The $250 Collectors' Institute Award is given for the best book design relating to Texas.

1978 **William D. Wittliff,** *David Novros: Fresco Drawings*

Current Status Unknown

Gold Medal

AMERICAN ACADEMY OF NATURAL SCIENCES OF PHILADELPHIA
19th and The Parkway, Philadelphia, Pa. 19103 (212/299-1015)

The Gold Medal for Distinction in Natural History Art is given annually for photographs, paintings, drawings and other illustrations of the natural world.

1980 **Roger Tory Peterson**

Herbert Adams Memorial Medal
Mrs. Louis Bennett Prize
Council of American Artists' Societies' Award
C. Percival Dietsch Sculpture Prize
Gold, Silver & Bronze Medals
John Gregory Award
Henry Hering Memorial Medal
Dr. Maurice B. Hexter Prize
Walter Lantz Youth Award
Medal of Honor of the National Sculpture Society
Lindsay Morris Memorial Prize
Therese and Edwin H. Richard Memorial Prize
John Spring Art Founder Award
Tallix Foundry Prize

NATIONAL SCULPTURE SOCIETY
15 E. 26th St., New York, N.Y. 10010 (212/889-6960)

The Herbert Adams Memorial Medal, designed in 1946 by Thomas G. Lo Medico, is presented as the occasion arises for service to American sculpture or to a sculptor for outstanding achievement.

1947 Adeline Valentine Pond Adams
1953 Cecil Howard
1954 Robert G. Eberhard
Avard Fairbanks
Walker Hancock
Jean de Marco
Lee Lawrie
1955 Leo Friedlander
Leo Lentelli
1956 Sidney Waugh
1957 Ivan Mestrovic
1958 Albino Cavallito
1961 Adolph Block
1962 Paul Fjelde
Pietro Montana
Wheeler Williams
1963 No award
1964 Joseph Kiselewski
1965 Daniel Chester French Foundation
Saint-Gaudens Memorial
1966 Moissaye Marans
1967 Donald De Lue
1968 Eugene F. Kennedy, Jr.
1969 J. Kellum Smith, Jr.
1970 Karel Yasko
Irving Stone
1971 Thomas S. Carroll
1972 Bruno Mankowski
1973 Donald S. Nelson
1974 Alfred Easton Poor
Paul A. Thiry
1975 Harry N. Abrams
Patricia Janis Broder
1976 John Dole
EvAngelos Frudakis
Pennsylvania Academy of the Fine Arts
1977 Thomas Armstrong, Whitney Museum Hall of Fame for Great Americans
1978 Joseph Veach Noble
Coy Eklund
1979 Beatrice Proske
Fairmount Park Art Assoc.
Julius Lauth
A. Webb Roberts
1980 Edmond Amateis
Beatrice Fenton
Katherine Thayer Hobson
Michael Lantz

The Mrs. Louis Bennett Prize of $50 is given to a young bas-relief sculptor for a meritorious entry in the Society's annual exhibition.

1942 Albert W. Wein
1943 No award
1944 John Flanagan
1945 No award
1946 Donald De Lue
1947 Michael Lantz
1948 Jean De Marco
1949 Thomas G. Lo Medico
1950 No award
1951 John Amore
1952 Robert A. Weinman
1953 Bruno Mankowski
1954 Frank Eliscu
1955 Theodore Spicer-Simson
1956 Abram Belskie
1957 No award
1958 Ferenc Varga
1959 Dexter Jones
1960 Anthony Notaro
1961 Richard Frazier
1962 Karen Worth
1963 Laci De Gerenday
1964 Henry Berge
1965 Adlai S. Hardin
1966 Wheeler Williams
1967 Kristin C. Lothrop
1968 Donald Miller
1969 No award
1970 Frances Lamont
1971 Edward Grove
1972 Eleanor Platt
1973 George Gach
1974 Joel Rudnick
1975 Nina Winkel
1976 Theodore Barbarossa
1977 Gertrude K. Lathrop
1978 Elizabeth Jones
1979 Patricia Verani
1980 Gerd Hesness

The $100 Council of American Artists' Societies' Award is given for outstanding traditional work.

1966 Harriet Whitney Frishmuth
1967 Anthony Notaro
1968 Jean De Marco
1969 Richard Frazier
1970 Charles C. Parks
1971 Gaetano Cecere
1972 Marilyn Newmark
1973 Jane B. Armstrong
1974 Eric Parks
1975 Bunny Adelman
1976 Brian Rodden
1977 Laci de Gerenday

1978 **Spero Anargyros**
1979 **Isidore Margulies**
1980 **Jose Boscaglia**

The $200 C. Percival Dietsch Sculpture Prize is given for sculpture in the round.

1968 **Vincent Glinsky**
1969 **Frances Lamont**
1970 **Clark T. Bailey**
1971 **Adolph Block**
1972 **Christopher Parks**
1973 **Joan Bugbee**
1974 **George Gach**
1975 **Edward Widstrom**
1976 **Cleo Hartwig**
1977 **Marilyn Newmark**
1978 **John Cavanaugh**
1979 **Kent Ullberg**
1980 **Albert Wein**

The National Sculpture Society gold, silver and bronze medals designed by Hermon MacNeil are awarded annually.

1966 **Donald De Lue,** Gold
Charlotte Dunwiddie, Silver
Adlai S. Hardin, Bronze
1967 **Vincent Glinsky,** Gold
Adolph Block, Silver
Nina Winkel, Bronze
1968 **C. Paul Jennewein,** Gold
Arthur E. Lorenzani, Silver
Terry Iles, Bronze
1969 **Elizabeth B. Holbrook,** Gold
Cleo Hartwig, Silver
Kenneth R. Bunn, Bronze
1970 **George Gach,** Gold
Waylande Gregory, Silver
Stanley Bleifeld, Bronze
1971 **Charles Parks,** Gold
Harriet Frishmuth, Silver
Nina Winkel, Bronze
1972 **EvAngelos Frudakis,** Gold
Edward Widstrom, Silver
Vincent Glinsky, Bronze
1973 **Charles Rudy,** Gold
E.F. Hoffman, III, Silver
Richardson White, Bronze
1974 **No award,** Gold
Gary Leddy, Silver
Leonda Finke, Bronze
1975 **Karl Gruppe,** Gold
Margaret Boots, Silver
Grete Schuller, Bronze
1976 **Maurice B. Hexter,** Gold
Bruno Mankowski, Silver
Jane B. Armstrong, Bronze
1977 **Frank James Morgan,** Gold
Richard Kislov, Silver
Moissaye Marans, Bronze
1978 **Bruno Mankowski,** Gold
Beverly Seamans, Silver
Patrick Villiers Farrow, Bronze
1979 **maurice Aexter,** Gold
Agod Agopoff, Silver
Gerald G. Balcair, Bronze
1980 **Isidore Margulies,** Gold
Gregory B. Glasson, Silver
Norman Holen, Bronze

The $500 John Gregory Award is given to U.S. citizens under forty-five years of age showing originality and imagination.

1959 **William M. Philips**
Mary Tilden Strebeigh
1960 **Betti Richard**
1961 **Dexter Jones**
1962 **Tylden W. Street**
1963 **Neil Estern**
EvAngelos Frudakis
1964 **Stanley Bleifeld**
1965 **Kahlil Gibran**
Joseph Turkaly
1966 **No award**
1967 **Philip E. Fowler**
1968-73 **No awards**
1974 **Tom Yglesias**
1975 **Christopher Parks**
1976 **Michael Stelzer**
1977 **Norman Holen**
1978 **Don Gale**
1979 **Peter Cozzolino**
1980 **Jerry Luisi**

The Henry Hering Memorial Medal, designed by Albino Manca, is awarded for outstanding collaboration between architect, owner and sculptor in the distinguished use of sculpture on religious, monumental, institutional and commercial sites.

RELIGIOUS

1960 **Voorhees, Walker, Smith and Haines** (Architect)
Loyola Seminary, Shrub Oak, N.Y. (Site)
Society of Jesus (Owner)
Donald De Lue, Gleb Derujinsky, Henry Kreis, Joseph Kiselewski, Oronzio Maldarelli, Carl L. Schmitz (Sculptors)
1961 **Eugene F. Kennedy, Jr. of Maginnis, Walsh & Kennedy,** Boston, Mass. (Architect)
National Shrine of the Immaculate Conception, Washington, D.C. (Site)
The Catholic Clergy and Faithful of the United States, His Eminence Francis Cardinal Spellman representing (Owner)
John Angel, Ulysses A. Ricci, Adolph Block, Joseph C. Fleri, Lee Lawrie, Thomas G. Lo Medico, Ivan Mestrovic, Pietro Montana, George H. Snowden (Sculptors)
Eugene F. Kennedy Jr., Boston, Mass. (Architect)
Cathedral of Mary Our Queen, Baltimore, Md. (Site)
The Catholic Clergy and Faithful of the United States, His Excellence Most Reverend Francis P. Keough, DD, Archbishop of Baltimore (Owner)
Theodore C. Barbarossa, Arcangelo Cascieri, Joseph Coletti, Jean de Marco, Gleb Derujinsky, Adio di Biccari, Leo Friedlander, Michael Lantz, Ernest E. Morenon (Sculptors)
1962 **No award**
1963 **Maurice Reinholt Salo** (Architect)
The Community Church of New York, 40 East 35 St., New York City (Site)
The Community Church, Donald S. Harrington (Owner)
Moissaye Marans (Sculptor)
1964 **No award**
1965 **No award**
1966 **Eugene F. Kennedy,** Boston, Mass. (Architect)

Chapel of Our Mother Of Sorrow, National Shrine of the Immaculate Conception, Washington, D.C. (Site)
The Catholic Clergy and Faithful of the U.S., His Eminence Francis Cardinal Spellman (Owner)
Ernest E. Morenon (Sculptor)

1967 **No award**
1968 **Philip Frohmann** (Architect)
Cathedral Church of St. Peter & St. Paul, Washington, D.C. (Site)
Protestant Episcopal Cathedral Foundation, Richard T. Feller, Clerk of the Works of the Cathedral, (Owner)
Granville W. Carter (Sculptor)
1969 **No award**
1970 **No award**
1971 **No award**
1972 **Cyrus Silling,** West Virginia (Architect)
Many Faiths Chapel, University Hospital, W. Va. (Site)
West Virginia University, (Owner)
Milton Horn (Sculptor)
1973 **No award**
1974 **No award**
1975 **No award**
1976 **No award**
1977 **No award**

Current status unknown

MONUMENTAL

1960 **Harbeson, Hough, Livingston & Larson** (Architect)
St. Laurent Cemetery, France (Site)
American Battle Monuments Commission (Owner)
Donald De Lue (Sculptor)
1961 **Eric Gugler of Gugler, Kimball & Husted,** New York City (Architect)
Sicily-Rome American Memorial at Anzio-Nettuno, Italy (Site)
American Battle Monuments Commission (Owner)
Paul Manship (Sculptor)
1962 **No award**
1963 **Richard E. Collins** (Architect)
Virginia World War II & Korean War Memorial, Richmond, Va. (Site)
State of Virginia, Senator John J. Wicker, Jr. (Owner)
Leo Friedlander (Sculptor)
1964 **No award**
1965 **Clark & Beauttler,** San Francisco, Calif. (Architect)
West Coast World War II Memorial, San Francisco, Calif. (Site)
American Battle Monuments Commission (Owner)
Jean de Marco (Sculptor)
1966 **No award**
1967 **No award**
1968 **Ernest Weihe** (Architect)
Honolulu Memorial, National Cemetery of the Pacific, Honolulu (Site)
American Battle Monuments Commission (Owner)
Bruce Moore (Sculptor)
1969 **No award**
1972 **William Gehron, Gilbert Seltzer,** New York, N.Y, (Architect)
East Coast Memorial, New York City (Site)
American Battle Monuments Commission, (Owner)
Albino Manca (Sculptor)
1973-77 **No awards**

Current status unknown

COMMERCIAL

1960 **Emery Roth & Sons** (Architect) 160 Church Street and 529 Fifth Avenue, New York City (Site)
Erwin S. Wolfson (Owner)
Frank Eliscu (Sculptor)

INSTITUTIONAL

1972 **John Richards,** Ohio (Architect)
Union Building (Site)
Ohio State University, (Owner)
Marshall Fredericks (Sculptor)
1976 **Paul A. Thiry** (Architect)
Libby Dam Treaty Tower, Kootenai River, Mont. (Site)
Brig. Gen. Walter O. Bachus, U.S. Army Corps of Engineers (Owner)
Albert Wein (Sculptor)

The $500 Dr. Maurice B. Hexter Prize is given for creative sculpture in the round.

1972 **Roger Williams**
1973 **Donald De Lue**
1974 **Barbara Lekberg**
1975 **Christopher Parks**
1976 **Richardson White**
1977 **Theodore C. Barbarossa**
1978 **Gerald Balciar**
1979 **Edward Fenno Hoffman III**
1980 **Stanley Bleifeld**

The Walter Lantz Youth Award of $250 is given to a sculptor under forty-five years of age.

1973 **Jerry Luisi**
1974 **Lloyd Radell**
1975 **Don Gale**
1976 **Eric Parks**
1977 **Sherry St. Renz**
1978 **Anthony Fudakis**
1979 **Greg Wyatt**
1980 **Gerd Hesness**

The Medal of Honor of the National Sculpture Society is awarded to individuals for notable achievement in and for encouragement of American sculpture. The medal was designed by Laura Gardin Fraser.

1929 **Archer M. Huntington**
Adeline Adams
Daniel Chester French
1933 **Richard Welling**
1940 **Dwight James Baum**
Herbert Adams
1942 **Paul Manship**
1943 **A.F. Brinckerhoff**
1945 **Robert Moses**
1948 **Adolph Alexander Weinman**
1951 **Alfred Geiffert, Jr.**
James Earle Fraser
Leo Friedlander
1952 **George Lober**
1953 **Frederick H. Zurmuhlen**
1956 **John Gregory**
1958 **Clyde C. Trees**
1959 **Rudulph Evans**
1964 **Malvina Hoffman**
John F. Harbeson
1967 **C. Paul Jennewein**
1969 **Frances K. Trees**
1970 **Gilmore D. Clarke**
1971 **Francis Keally**
1974 **Donald De Lue**

1975-79 No awards
1980 Karl Gruppe

The $150 Lindsay Morris Memorial Prize is given for a meritorious bas-relief sculpture.

1933 Anthony De Francisci
1934 Carl L. Schmitz
1935 Gaetano Cecere
1936 Henry Kreis
1937 Erwin Springweiler
1938 Chester Beach
1939 Richard H. Recchia
1941 Walker Hancock
1942 Donald De Lue
1943 Janet De Coux
1944 Gertrude K. Lathrop
1945 Jean De Marco
1946 Albert W. Wein
1947 Edmond Amateis
1948 Edmondo Quattrocchi
1949 Theodore C. Barbarossa
1950 Michael Lantz
1951 Abram Belskie
1952 Thomas G. Lo Medico
1953 Paul Manship
1954 Gleb Derujinsky
1955 Laci De Gerenday
1956 Adlai S. Hardin
1957 Paul Fjelde
1958 Adolph Block
1959 Pietro Montana
1960 Katharine Lane Weems
1961 No award
1962 Bryant Baker
1963 Albert T. D'Andrea
1964 Agop Agopoff
1965 John Terken
1966 Granville W. Carter
1967 Edward R. Grove
1968 Karl Gruppe
1969 Margaret C. Grigor
1970 Leonda Finke
1971 Charlotte Dunwiddie
1972 Joseph Kiselewski
1973 Roger Williams
1974 Elizabeth Weistrop
1975 Albino Manca
1976 Frieda Rosenstein
1977 Marcel Jovine
1978 Bruno Mankowski
1979 Karen Worth
1980 Agop Agopoff

The Therese and Edwin H. Richard Memorial Prize of $300 is awarded for outstanding portrait sculpture in the round. The competition is open to all sculptors, and selection is made on the basis of photographs.

1965 Eleanor Platt
Bashka Paeff (Hon. Mention)
Maysie Stone (Mention)
1966 Edmondo Quattrochi
1967 Vernita Haynes
1968 Donald De Lue
1969 Jose de Creeft
Winifred Gordon (Hon. Mention)
1970 Philip Fowler
1971 Richard Frazier
1972 EvAngelos Frudakis
Moissaye Marans
1973 Dexter Jones
1974 John Cavanaugh
1975 Agop Agopoff
1976 Ruth Nickerson
1977 Karl Gruppe
1978 Joseph Kiselewski
1979 Neal Martz
1980 Granville Carter

The John Spring Art Founder Award consists of a life-size head cast in bronze by the Modern Art Foundry to a sculptor chosen at the National Sculpture Society's annual exhibition.

1973 Edward Widstrom
1974 Fritz Cleary
1975 Spero Anargyros
1976 Anthony Notaro
1977 Antonio Frudakis
1978 Richard Frazier
1979 Ruth Nickerson
1980 Domenico Facci

The Tallix Foundry Prize consists of casting a life-size head or sculpture of similar size and complexity by a woman sculptor under thirty-five years of age.

1974 Ruth Nickerson
1975 Marilyn Newmark
1976 Jean Donner Grove
1977 Leonda Finke
1978 Maryvonne Rose
1979 Elisabeth Gordon Chandler
1980 Donald R. Miller

Playboy Awards

PLAYBOY MAGAZINE
919 N. Michigan Ave., Chicago, Ill. 60611 (312/PL 1-8000)

As an adjunct to their long-standing Playboy Writers Awards, the editors of *Playboy* magazine have instituted similar honors for artists and photographers whose contributions have been published in the preceding year.

BEST NON-FICTION ILLUSTRATION

1977 **Alan Magee**, "Good Night, Sweet Prinze"
1978 **Herb Davison**, "Telly Loves Ya"
1979 **Marshall Arisman**, "The Executioner's Song"
1980 **Sandra Hendler**, "Silverfinger"

BEST FICTION ILLUSTRATION

1977 **Kathy Calderwood,** "Adulterer's Luck"
1978 **Frank Gallo**, "The Faint"
1979 **Roger Brown**, "Used in Evidence"
1980 **Mel Odom**, "Still Life with Woodpecker"

BEST SERVICE ILLUSTRATION

1979 **Martin Hoffman**, fashion illustrations

BEST PICTORIAL ESSAY

1977 **Pompeo Posar,** "Playmate of the Year"
1978 **Bill Arsenault**, "Close Encounters of the Fourth Kind"
1979 **Arny Freytag**, "Another Loving Look"
Richard Fegley, "Moonraker"
1980 **David Chan** and **Nicholas de Sciose**, "Girls of the Southwest Conference"

BEST SERVICE PICTORIAL

1977 **Mario Casilli,** "Shields and Yarnell"
1978 **Don Azuma**, "Christmas Gift Guide"
1979 **No award**
1980 **Richard Fegley**, "To Paris —with Love and the Concord"

BEST PLAYMATE PICTORIAL

1977 **Robert Scott Hooper,** September Playmate Debra Jo Fondren
1978 **Ken Marcus**, February Playmate Janis Schmitt
1979 **Mario Casilli**, February Playmate Lee Ann Michelle
1980 **Pompeo Posar** and **Ken Marcus**, September Playmate Lisa Welch

BEST BLACK-AND-WHITE PHOTOGRAPH

1977 **Norman Seeff**, of John Travolta

BEST PICTORIAL REPORTAGE

1978 **Robert Scott Hooper**, "Public-Sex Breakthrough"

BEST COMIC STRIP

1978 **Harvey Kurtzman** and **Will Elder**, October "Little Annie Fanny"

BEST CARTOON SERIES

1978 **B. Kliban**, "Tiny Footprints and Other Drawings"

BEST BLACK-AND-WHITE CARTOON

1978 **J.B. Handelsman**
1979 **No award**
1980 **Brian Savage**

BEST COLOR CARTOON

1978 **Eldon Dedini**
1979 **No award**
1980 **John Dempsey**

SPECIAL AWARD

1977 **Brad Holland,** "Ribald Classics" illustrations
1978 **Leroy Neiman**, contributions to *Playbody* illustrations beginning in 1954
Pompeo Posar, photographer or 39 *Playboy* covers
Mario Casilli, photographic contributions to *Playboy*
Gahan Wilson, cartoons in *Playboy* since 1957
1979 **David Chan**, photographic contributions to *Playboy*
Shel Silverstein, illustrations in *Playboy* contributed over more than 20 years
1980 **Pat Nagel**, *Playboy Advisor* graphics since 1975

RISD President's Fellows Award

RHODE ISLAND SCHOOL OF DESIGN
2 College St., Providence, R.I. 02903 (401/331-3511, Ext. 210)

The RISD President's Fellows Award, a bronze medal of "RISD Athena" designed by Merlin Szsoz, is presented annually for creative excellence in the visual arts and design. Recipients are asked to deliver lectures and participate in seminars to benefit students in the fine and applied arts.

1978 **Tatyana Grossman**, founder, Universal Limited Art Editions
Les Line, editor, *Audubon* magazine
Robert Rauschenberg, painter
1979 **Richard Avedon**, photographer
Mary McFadden, designer
Reuben Nakian, sculptor
I.M. Pei, architect
1980 **Roy Hamilton**, ceramist and textile designer
Ellsworth Kelly, painter
Warren Planter, architect and designer
Diana Vreeland, former editor-in-chief, *Vogue*, and special consultant, Metropolitan Museum of Art Costume Institute

Sanberg Prize for Israel Art
Enrique Kalvin Photography Prize
Sanberg Prize for Research and Development
Beatrice S. Kolliner Award
Joseph N. Hazen Art Essay Award

ISRAEL MUSEUM
Hakiryah, Jerusalem, Israel 91012 (636231-02)

The Sanberg Prize for Israel Art, which consists of a scroll and I£20,000, is given annually for achievements in Israeli art by a resident of the country. A jury selects the winner.

1976 **Aviva Uri**
Avigor Stematsky
1977 **Michael Gross**
1978 **Menashe Kadishman**
1979 **Pinhas Cohen-Gan**
1980 **Micha Ullman**

The Enrique Kalvin Photography Prize, which consists of a scroll and a cash grant, annually honors achievements in the field of photography by an Israeli resident. A jury selects the winner.

1976 **Dahlia Amotz-Weislib**, Jerusalem photographer
1977 **Joseph Coehn**, creative work in photography
1978 **S.J. Schweig**, pioneer archeological photograph
1979 **Bezalel Art School Dept.** of Photography
1980 **Nahum Tim Gidal**, photojournalist

The Sandberg Prize for Research and Development, which consists of a scroll and a cash honorarium, is given annually for achievements in research and development respective to the visual arts. A jury selects the winner.

1977 **S'sdya Mendel**
Eli Gross
1978 **Paul Konrad Hoenich**
1979 **Victor Frustig**
1980 **Ilan Molcho**

The Beatrice S. Kolliner Award, which carries an I£9,000 honorarium, is given annually to a young Israeli artist. A jury selects the winner.

1976 **Mordechai Mizrachi**
1977 **Efrat Natan**
Michel Haded
1978 **Dalia Meiri**
1979 **Larry Abramson**
1980 **Yehosua Borokowski**

The Joseph H. Hazen Art Essay Award, which consists of a scroll and a cash honorarium, is given annually to an Israeli for meritorious art scholarship. A jury selects the winner.

1978 **Gila Balas**
1979 **Ziva Amishai-Maisels**
1980 **Mira Friedman**

W. Eugene Smith Award for Humanistic Photography

W. EUGENE SMITH FOUNDATION
170 West End Ave., 15th floor, New York, N.Y. 10023

The $10,000 W. Eugene Smith Award for Humanistic Photography is given annually as a grant to a photographer who exemplifies the ideals of the photographic essayist after whom the award is named and whose estate funds it. The winner is chosen on the basis of work submitted to an awards panel.

1980 **Jane Evelyn Atwood**

Special Project: Sculpture Competition
Ziuta and Joseph James Akston Foundation Award
Owen H. Kenan Award
Atwater Kent Award

THE SOCIETY OF THE FOUR ARTS
Four Arts Plaza, Palm Beach, Fla. 33480 (305/655-7226)

The Society gives several awards, generally bearing cash honoraria, to artists whose work is shown in the Society's Annual Exhibition of Contemporary American Paintings, which in 1980 reaches its fortieth year. In addition, the Society sponsored in 1974 as a special project a major sculpture competition. The Society has supplied the names only of recent awards winners.

SPECIAL PROJECT (Sculpture competition made possible by a grant from the Ziuta and Joseph James Akston Foundation):

1974 **Robert Morris** ($25,000 sculpture project grant)
Isamu Noguchi ($10,000 sculpture project grant)
Richard Stankiewicz ($5,000 sculpture project grant)

ANNUAL EXHIBITION OF CONTEMPORARY AMERICAN PAINTINGS: Ziuta and Joseph James Akston Foundation Award

1974 **LaMonte Anderson** ($1,500)
1975 **Michael Klezmer** ($1,000)
1976 **Emilio Falero** ($1,500)
1977 **Jim Houser** ($1,500)
1978 **Linda Fernandez** ($2,000)
1979 **Jim Furr** ($2,000)
1980 **Don McKinney** ($2,000)

OWEN H. KENAN AWARD

1974 **Anne Minich** ($1,500)
1975 **Bruce L. Marsh** ($1,500)
1976 **Harriet Lefkowitz** ($750)
1976 **Walter Z. Prochownik** ($750)
1977 **Philip Carpenter** ($500)

ATWATER KENT AWARD

1974 **Judith Boodon** ($2,500)
1975 **Gary L. Matthews** ($2,000)
1976 **Jim Houser** ($2,000)
1977 **John H. Woodworth** ($2,000)
Elenora Chambers ($500)
Henry C. Ransom, Jr. ($500)

rchitecture & Design

Contents

Related Awards

AIA Medals
Architectural Firm Award
Gold Medal
Edward C. Kemper Award
Reynolds Aluminum Grand Prize
R.S. Reynolds Award
R.S. Reynolds Award for Community Architecture
Twenty-Five Year Award

AMERICAN INSTITUTE OF ARCHITECTS
1735 New York Ave. NW, Washington, D.C. 20006
(202/626-7300)

AIA Medals are now awarded in one group encompassing five areas of achievement related to architecture, the architectural profession and architectural projects. These are presented to artists or craftsmen; illustrators or recorders; individuals or organizations who have influenced the profession; individuals or organizations responsible for a specific project; and individuals or groups responsible for specific interdisciplinary accomplishments related to architecture. In 1976 AIA rules were changed to provide for the presentation of ten medals a year, no more than three in any of these categories. The five categories of awards and medals consolidate the dozen separate and narrower categories used before 1975.

ARCHITECTURE CRITICS' MEDAL

1968 **Lewis Mumford**
1969 **Ada Louise Huxtable**
1970 **Henry-Russell Hitchcock**
1971 **Sibyl Moholy-Magy**
1972 **Wolf Von Eckardt**
1973 **Robin Boyd**
1974 **Walter McQuade**
1975 **Peter Blake**

ARCHITECTURE CRITICS' CITATION

1968 **George McCue**
1969 **No award**
1970 **"Cosmopolis," documentary presented by American Broadcasting Companies, Inc.**
1971 ***Perspecta,*** The Yale Architectural Journal
1972 **Peter Collins**
1973 **Alan Dunn**
1974 **Regional Plan Association**
1975 **Jane Jacobs**

FINE ARTS MEDAL

1921 **Paul Manship,** Sculpture
1922 **No award**
1923 **Arthur F. Mathews,** Decorative Painting
1924 **No award**
1925 **John Singer Sargent,** Mural Painting
1926 **Leopold Stokowski,** Music
1927 **Lee Lawrie,** Sculpture
1928 **H. Siddons Mowbray,** Mural Painting
1929 **Diego Rivera,** Painting
1930 **Adolph Alexander Weinman,** Sculpture
1931 **Frederick Law Olmsted,** Landscape Architecture
1932 **No award**
1933 **No award**
1934 **James Henry Breasted,** Literature
1935 **No award**
1936 **Robert Edmond Jones,** Theatre Design
1937 **No award**
1938 **Carl Milles,** Sculpture
1939-44 **No awards**
1945 **John Taylor Arms,** Etching
1946 **No award**
1947 **Samuel Chamberlain,** Etching
1948 **John Marin,** Painting
1949 **Louis Conrad Rosenberg,** Etching
1950 **Edward Steichen,** Photography
1951 **Thomas Church,** Landscape Architecture
1952 **Marshall Fredericks,** Sculpture
1953 **Donal Hord,** Sculpture
1954 **Judan Hoke Harris,** Sculpture
1955 **Nan Mestrovic,** Sculpture
1956 **M. Hidreth Meiere,** Painting
1957 **Mark Tobey,** Painting
1958 **Viktor Schreckengost,** Sculpture
1959 **Kenneth Hedrich,** Photography
1960 **Thomas Hart Benton,** Painting and Murals
1961 **Alexander Calder,** Sculpture
1962 **Stuart Davis,** Painting
1963 **Isamu Noguchi,** Sculpture
1964 **Henry Moore,** Sculpture
1965 **Roberto Burle Marx,** Landscape Architecture, Painting
1966 **Ben Shahn,** Artist
1967 **Costantino Nivola,** Sculpture
1968 **Gyorgy Kepes,** Art
1969 **Jacques Lipchitz,** Sculpture
1970 **Richard Lippold,** Sculpture
1971 **Anthony Smith,** Sculpture
1972 **George Rickey,** Sculpture
1973 **Harry Bertoia,** Sculpture
1974 **Ruth Asawa Lanier,** Sculpture
1975 **Josef Albers,** Art

COLLABORATIVE ACHIEVEMENT IN ARCHITECTURE AWARD

1964 **The Seagram Building, its Plaza and the Four Seasons Restaurant,** New York
1965 **No award**
1966 **Ghirardeli Square,** San Francisco
1967 **No award**
1972 **Rochester Institute of Technology,** N.Y.
1973 **Bay Area Rapid Transit (BART),** San Francisco and environs
1974 **No award**
1975 **No award**

HENRY BACON MEDAL FOR MEMORIAL ARCHITECTURE

1966 **Gateway Arch,** St. Louis, Mo.
1967 **No award**
1968 **No award**
1969 **Fosse Ardeatine Caves,** Rome
1970-74 **No awards**
1975 **Le Memorial des Martyrs de la Deportation,** Paris

CRAFTSMANSHIP MEDAL

1920 **Samuel Yellin,** Iron Work
1921 **Henry C. Mercer,** Ceramics
1922 **No award**
1923 **Frederic W. Goudy,** Typography
1924 **No award**
1925 **Charles Jay Connick,** Stained Glass
1926 **V. F. Von Lossberg,** Metal Work

1927 **Frank J. Holmes,** Ceramics
1928 **William D. Gates,** Ceramics
1929 **Cheney Brothers,** Textiles
1930 **John Kirchmayer,** Wood Carving
1931 **Leon V. Solon,** Terra Cotta, Faience
1932 **No award**
1933 **No award**
1934 **Walter W. Kantack,** Metal and Glass
1935 **No award**
1936 **John J. Earley,** Masonry, Concrete
1937 **No award**
1938 **J. H. Dulles Allen,** Ceramics
1939 **No award**
1940-46 **No awards**
1947 **Dorothy Wright Liebes,** Textiles
Wilbur Herbert Burnham, Stained and Leaded Glass
1948 **No award**
1949 **No award**
1950 **Joseph Gardiner Reynolds, Jr.,** Stained Glass
1951 **No award**
1952 **George Nakashima,** Furniture
1953 **Emil Frei,** Stained Glass
1954 **Maria Montoya Martinez,** Pottery
1955 **John Howard Benson,** Calligraphy
1956 **Harry Bertoia,** Metal Design
1957 **Charles Eames,** Furniture
1958 **Francois Lorin,** Stained Glass
1959 **No award**
1960 **William L. DeMatteo,** Silversmith
1961 **Anni Albers,** Art of Weaving
1962 **Theodore Conrad,** Model Making
1963 **Paolo Soleri,** Ceramics
1964 **Jan de Swart,** Stained Glass
1965 **No award**
1966 **Harold Balazs,** Wood Sculpture
1967 **Sister Mary Remy Revor,** Fabric Design
1968 **Jack Lenor Larsen,** Fabric Design
1969 **Henry Easterwood,** Fabric Design
1970 **Trude Guermonprez,** Textiles
1971 **Wharton Esherick,** Wood Furniture
1972 **No award**
1973 **Helena Hemmarck,** Tapestries
1974 **Sheila Hicks,** Textile Sculpture
1975 **No award**

ARCHITECTURAL PHOTOGRAPHY MEDAL

1960 **Roger Sturtevant**
1961 **Ezra Stoller**
1962 **Ernst Haas**
1963 **G. E. Kidder Smith**
1964 **Balthazar Korab**
1965 **Robert Damora**
1966 **Moorley Baer**
1967 **William C. Hedrich**
1968 **Ernest Braun**
1969 **Julius Shulman**
1970 **George Cserna**
1971 **Alexandre Georges**
1972 **Robert C. Lautman**
1973 **No award**
1974 **David Hirsch**
1975 **Yukio Futagawa**

INDUSTRIAL ARTS MEDAL

1958 **Merle Armitage**
1959 **No award**
1960 **No award**
1961 **Florence Schust Knoll**
1962 **Sundberg-Ferar Inc.**
1963 **No award**
1964 **George Nelson**
1965 **Eliot Noyes**
1966 **Gideon Kramer**
1967 **Chermayeff & Geismar**
1968 **Paul Grotz**
1969 **Carl Koch**
1970 **Barbara Stauffacher Solomon**
1971 **Edith Heath**
1972 **Charles Eames**
1973 **Lella and Massimo Vignelli**
1974 **C. Olivetti & CSpA**
1975 **Gemini C.E.L.**

AIA MEDAL FOR RESEARCH

1972 **Christopher Alexander**
1973 **Harold B. Gores**
1974 **Ralph Knowles**
1975 **Environmental Research and Development Corp.**

ALLIED PROFESSIONS MEDAL

1958 **Fred N. Severud**
1959 **Robert Moses**
1960 **William Francis Gibbs,** Naval Architect
1961 **No award**
1962 **Othmar H. Ammann & Charles S. Whitney**
1963 **R. Buckminster Fuller**
1964 **Lawrence Halprin**
1965 **Leonardo Zeevaert**
1966 **Alexander Girard**
1967 **Richard Kelly**
1968 **Le Messurier Associates Inc.**
1969 **John Skilling**
1970 **Robert L. Van Nice**
1971 **Daniel U. Kiley**
1972 **Ian L. McHarg**
1973 **Hideo Sasaki**
1974 **Kevin Lynch**
1975 **Carl Sapers**

WHITNEY M. YOUNG JR. CITATION (Social Consciousness Award)

1972 **Robert J. Nash**
1973 **Architects Workshop of Philadelphia**
1974 **Stephan Cram**
1975 **Van B. Bruner, Jr.**

CITATION OF AN ORGANIZATION

1947 **Tennessee Valley Authority**
1948-50 **No awards**
1951 **Steuben Glass Inc.**
1952 **No award**
1953 **Reinhold Publishing Corp.,** Architectural Publishing
1954 **No award**
1955 **Kohler Foundation Inc.**
1956 **Society of Architectural Historians**
1957 **Office of Foreign Buildings, U.S. Dept. of State**
1958 **United States Steel Corp.**
1959 **General Services Administration**
1960 **Providence City Plan Commission**
General Motors Corp.
International Business Machines Corp.
1961 **Philadelphia City Planning Commission**
1962 **Museum of Modern Art, New York**
1963 **American Craftsmen's Council**
1964 **Educational Facilities Laboratories**
1965 **Architectural League of New York**
1966 **Museum of Modern Art,** New York
1967 **Boston Architectural Center**

1968 **The Graham Foundation,** Chicago
1969 **State University Construction Fund,** Albany, N.Y.
1970 **National Park Service, U.S. Dept. of Interior**
1971 **San Francisco Bay Commission**
1972 **New York State Dormitory Authority**
1973 **San Francisco Planning Commission**
1974 **New York State Urban Development Corp.**
1975 **Cummins Engine Foundation**

AIA MEDALS

1976 **Edmund N. Bacon**
Charles A. Blessing
Wendell J. Campbell
Gordon Cullen
Institute for Architecture and Urban Studies
Robert Le Ricolais
New York City Planning Commission and New York City Landmarks Preservation Commission
Saul Steinberg
James Marston Fitch
1977 **Claes Oldenburg**
Louise Nevelson
Arthur Drexler
Historic American Buildings Survey
G. Holmes Perkins
Barbara Ward Jackson
Walker Art Center
City of Boston
Pittsburgh History and Landmarks Foundation
Montreal Metro System

SPECIAL CITATIONS

1936 **Restoration of Colonial Williamsburg** (Perry, Shaw and Hepburn; John A. Shurcliff; John D. Rockefeller, Jr., and William A. R. Goodwin)

AWARD FOR OUTSTANDING SERVICE TO ARCHITECTURE (by Non-Architectural Group, Society, or Business)

1956 ***Fortune Magazine***

EXHIBITION MEDAL

1921 **Betram Goodhue and Lee Lawrie,** Ecclesiastical
Reginald Johnson, Domestic
Charles Z. Klauder, Institutional
Howard Dwight Smith, Public Buildings
George C. Nimmons and Co., Industrial Buildings
1925 **Charles D. Maginnis and Timothy Walsh,** Ecclesiastical
Edward L. Tilton and Alfred Morton Githens, Public Buildings
Sproatt and Rolph, Institutional Buildings
A. Stewart Walker and Leon N. Gillette, Domestic Buildings
Arthur Loomis Harmon, Commercial Buildings

ASC/AIA AWARD FOR EXCELLENCE IN ARCHITECTURAL EDUCATION

1976 **Jean Labatut,** Princeton University

CITATION OF HONOR

1956 **Pearl Chase**
Nathan Haris, President, Far Eastern Society of Architects
1957 **Milton Horn,** Sculptor
1958 **No award**
1959 **Kansas City Chapter,** AIA—Field of Planning
1960 **No award**
1961 **No award**
1962 **Lewis Mumford,** Author-Critic
John Fitzgerald Kennedy
1963 **No award**
1964 **Lister Hill**
Harold H. Burton
Marie C. McGuire
1965 **Lyndon Baines Johnson**
Stewart Lee Udall

In addition to the awards and medals listed here, the Institute recognizes exceptional architectural excellence in recently completed projects by presenting architects, engineers and other professionals with Honor Awards. These citations were initiated to encourage appreciation of excellence in architecture in the United States and by American architects working abroad.

1949 **Marsh, Smith and Powell Architects,** for Corona del Mar School, Corona del Mar, Calif.
Frederick J. Langhorst, for Dr. and Mrs. Alex J. Ker's residence, Marin County, Calif.
1950 **A. Quincy Jones, Jr.,** for H.C. Hvistendahl residence, San Diego, Calif.
Harold M. Heatley and Ketchum, Gina and Sharp, Assoc., for Davis-Paxton Company Store, Augusta, Ga.
1951 **Thorshov and Cerney,** for Clearwater County Memorial Hospital, Bagley, Mont.
Stone and Pitts, for Coca Cola bottling plant, Houston, Tex.
1952 **Skidmore, Owings and Merrill Assoc.,** for Lever House, New York
William S. Beckett, for William S. Beckett's office, Los Angeles
Young and Richards, Carleton and Detlie, for Gaffney's Lake Wilderness, Maple Valley, Wisc.
1953 **Saarinen, Saarinen & Assoc., and Smith, Hinchman and Grylls,** for Engineering Staff Bldgs., General Motors Technical Center, Warren, Mich.
Matthew Nowicki, William Henry Dietrick and Severud-Elstad-Kreuger, for North Carolina State Fair Pavilion, Raleigh N.C.
1954 **Richard P. Neutra and Dion Neutra,** for Moore residence, Ojai, Calif.
Vincent G. King, for Lankenau Hospital, Philadelphia
John P. Wiltshire and J. Herschel Fisher, for Fort Brown Memorial Civic Center, Brownsville, Tex.
Curtis and Davis, for Twomy Lafon School, New Orleans
Perkins and Will and Caudill, Rowlett, Scott Assoc., for Norman High School, Norman, Okla.
Marsh Smith and Powell, for Santa Monica City College, Calif.
1955 **Ralph Rapson and John van der Meulen,** for American Embassy, Stockholm, Sweden
Eero Saarinen and Assoc. and Smith, Hinchman & Grylls, for Central Restaurant Bldg., General Motors Technical Center, Warren, Mich.
Eero Saarinen and Assoc., for Women's Dormitories and Dining Hall, Drake University, Des Moines, Iowa.
Ernest J. Kump, for North Hillsborough Elementary School, Hillsborough, Calif.
Charles B. Genther of Pace Assoc., for General Telephone Co. of the Southwest, San Antonio, Tex.
1956 **John Lyon Reid & Partners,** for Hillsdale School, San Mateo, Calif.
Wurster, Bernardi & Emmons, for Center for Advanced Study in Behavioral Sciences, near Palo Alto, Calif.

Hellmuth, Yamasaki & Leinweber, for Lambert St. Louis Municipal Airport Terminal Bldg., St. Louis, Mo.
Skidmore, Owings & Merrill, for Manufacturers Trust Co., Fifth Ave. branch, New York, N.Y.
Philip C. Johnson, for Hodgson house, New Canaan, Conn.

1957 **Anderson, Beckwith and Haible,** for office building for Middlesex Mutual Building Trust, Waltham, Mass.
Warren H. Ashley, for Junior/Senior School, Greenburgh, N.Y.
Eliot Noyes, for house, New Cannan, Conn.
Caudill, Rowlett, Scott & Assoc., for Brazos County Court House and Jail, Brazos, Tex.
Antonin Raymond and L.L. Rado, for St. Anselm's Priory for the Benedictine Fathers, Tokyo, Japan
Anshen and Allen, for Chapel of the Holy Cross, Sedona, Ariz.

1958 **Skidmore, Owings & Merrill,** for home office building for Connecticut General Life Insurance Co., Bloomfield, Conn.
Edward D. Stone, for pharmaceutical headquarters for the Stuart Co., Pasadena, Calif.
Mario J. Ciampi, for elementary school, Sonoma, Calif.
Pereira and Luckman, for specialty shop, Robinson's, Palm Springs, Calif.

1959 **Colbert, Lowrey & Assoc.,** For Dias-Simon Pediatric Clinic, New Orleans, La.
Kenneth W. Brooks and Bruce W. Walker, for Central Service Facility, Spokane, Wash.
Minoru Yamasaki & Assoc., for McGregor Memorial Community Conference Center, Detroit, Mich.
Eero Saarinen & Assoc., for Concordia Senior College, Fort Wayne, Ind.
I.M. Pei & Assoc., for Zeckendorf Plaza Development, May D&F Dept. Store, Denver, Colo.

1960 **Sherwood, Mills and Smith,** for Mutual Insurance Co. of Hartford, Conn.
Robert L. Geddes, Melvin Brecher, Warren W. Cunningham, partners in Geddes Brecher, Qualls, for Moore School of Electrical Engineering, University of Pennsylvania, Philadelphia
Killingsworth, Brady and Smith, for Mr. and Mrs. Richard Opdahl's residence, Long Beach, Calif.
Corbett & Kman Kitchen and Hunt, for Blyth Arena, Squan Valley, Calif.
Eero Saarinen and Assoc., for U.S. Embassy Office Bldg., Oslo, Norway

1961 **Edward Durell Stone,** for United States Embassy, New Delhi, India
Mario J. Ciampi and Paul Reiter, for Fernando Rivera Elementary School, Daly City, Calif.
Philip Johnson, for Shrine, New Harmony, Ind.
Minoru Yamasaki, for Reynolds Metal Regional Sales Office Bldg., Detroit
Philip Johnson, for Nuclear reactor, Rehovot, Israel
Skidmore, Owings & Merrill, for Pepsi-Cola World Headquarters, New York
Birkerts & Straub, for Summer house, Northville, Mich.

1962 **Ernest J. Kump and Masten & Hurd,** for Foothill College, Los Altos, La.
Anshen and Allen, for Interational Bldg., San Francisco

1963 **Eero Saarinen & Assoc.,** for Stiles and Morse Colleges, Yale University New Haven, Conn.
Skidmore, Owings & Merrill, for Albright-Knox Art Gallery Addition, Buffalo, N.Y.
Ralph M. Parsons Co. and Minoru Yamasaki, for Dhahran International Air Terminal, Dharran, Saudi Arabia
Joseph Salerno, for United Church House of Worship, Rowayton, Conn.

1964 **Architects Collaborative,** for Phillips Academy Arts and Communications Center and Science Bldg., Andover, Mass.
Skidmore, Owings & Merrill, for Ehmart Mfg. Co. headquarters bldg., Bloomfield, Conn.
Paul Rudolph, for Yale University School of Art and Architecture, New Haven, Conn.
Skidmore, Owings and Merrill, for BMA Tower, Kansas City, Mo.

1965 **Reid & Tarics,** for Eleanor Connelly Erdman Memorial Chapel, Pebble Beach, Calif.
Sert, Jackson and Gourley, for Francis Greenwood Peabody Terrace, Cambridge, Mass.
Eero Saarinen and Assoc., for Deere & Co. Administrative Center, Moline, Ill.
I.M. Pei & Assoc., for School of Journalism, S.I Newhouse Communications Center, Syracuse University, Syracuse, N.Y.

1966 **Eero Saarinen and Assoc.,** for Columbia Broadcasting System Headquarters Bldg., New York, N.Y.
Eero Saarinen and Assoc., for Dulles International Airport Terminal Bldg., Chantilly, Va.
Keyes, Lethbridge & Condon, for Tiber Island, Washington, D.C.

1967 **Fred Bassetti & Co.,** for Ridgeway Men's Dormintories/Phase III, Western Washington State College, Bellingham, Wash.
Caudill, Rowlett, Scott, for Jesse H. Jones Hall for the Performing Arts, Houston, Tex.
Hammel Green & Abrahamson, for St. Bede's Priory, Eau Claire, Wisc.
Vincent G. Kling, for Municipal Services Bldg., Philadelphia, Pa.
Ian MacKinley, for Boreal Ridge, Truckee, Calif.
Moore, Lyndon, Turnbull, Whitaker, for Sea Ranch Condominium I, The Sea Ranch, Calif.
I.M. Pei & Partners, for University Plaza, New York University, New York
Skidmore Owings & Merrill, for National Headquarters Bldg., American Republic Insurance Co., Des Moines, Iowa
Pomerance & Breines, for amphitheatre and plaza, Jacob Riis Houses, New York
Skidmore Owings and Merrill, for Mauna Kea Beach Hotel, Kamuela, Ha.
Skidmore Owings and Merrill, for Banque Lambert, office building and residence, Brussels, Belgium
Skidmore Owings and Merrill, for Beinecke Rare Book and Manuscript Library, Yale Univ., New Haven, Conn.
Skidmore Owings and Merrill, for Vannevar Bush Center for Materials Science and Engineering, Massachusetts Institute of Technology, Cambridge, Mass.
Smith, Hinchman & Grylls, for First Federal Office Bldg., Detroit
Neill Smith and Assoc., for Redwood National Bank, Napa, Calif.
Stickney & Hull, for Los Gatos Civic Center, Los Gatos, Calif.
Edward Durell Stone, for Museo de Arte de Ponce, Ponce, Puerto Rico
Architects Collaborative, for Dormitory and Commons Bldg. Quadrangle, Clark University, Worcester, Mass.

Architects Collaborative and Campbell, Aldrich & Nulty, for C. Thurston Chase Learning Center, Eaglebrook School, Deerfield, Mass.
Toombs, Amisano & Wells, for John Knox Presbyterian Church, Marietta, Ga.

1968 **Fred Bassetti & Co.,** for East Pine Receiving Station, Seattle, Wash.
C.F. Murphy Assoc; Skidmore, Owings & Merrill, and Loebl, Schlossman, Bennett & Dart, for Chicago Civic Center, Chicago, Ill.
Crites and McConnell, for Covenant United Presbyterian Church, Danville, Ill.
William N. Breger, for Civic Center Synagogue, New York, N.Y.
Giorgio Cavaglieri, for Jefferson Market Branch Library, New York, N.Y.
Davis, Brody & Assoc. and Horowitz and Chun, for Humanities/Social Science Center, Long Island University, Brooklyn, N.Y.
Alfred De Vido, for Hale Matthews House, East Hampton, N.Y.
Joseph Esherick, for Adlai E. Stevenson College, University of California, Santa Cruz, Calif.
Stevenson Flemer, Eason Cross, Harry Adreon, for Washington & Lee High School Gymnasium, Montross, Va.
R. Buckminster Fuller/Fuller and Sadao Inc., Geometrics Inc, and Cambridge Seven Assoc., for U.S. Exhibition at Expo 67, Ilse Ste. Helene, Montreal, Que., Canada
Gruzen & Partners and Abraham W. Geller, for Suburban YM & YWHA, W. Orange, N.J.
Gwathmey & Henderson, for residence, Purchase, N.Y.
Hirshen/Van der Ryn, for Migrant Master Plan, Indio Camp, Indio, Calif.
Mackinley/Winnacker, for Syntex Interim Facilities, Stanford Industrial Park, Palo Alto, Calif.
MLTW/Moore Turnbull, for Sea Ranch Swim & Tennis, The Sea Ranch, Calif.
McCue Boone Tomsick, for Research Laboratory D, Richmond, Calif.
Office of Oberwarth Assoc., for classroom building, Kentucky State College, Frankfort, Ky.
Reid, Rockwell, Banwell & Taries, for Health & Sciences Instruction & Research, San Francisco Medical Center, University of California, San Francisco
Rogers, Taliaferro, Kostritsky, Lamb, for John Deere Co., Timonium, Md.
Benjamin Thompson & Assoc., for dormitories and fraternity, Colby College, Waterville, Me.

1969 **Desmond-Miremont-Birks,** for D.C. Reeves Elementary School, Ponchatonla, La.
Frank L. Hope Assoc., for San Diego Stadium, San Diego, Calif.
Hugh Newell Jacobsen, for Bolton Square, Baltimore, Md.
Kallman, McKinnell & Knowles and Campbell, Aldrich & Nulty, for Boston City Hall, Boston, Mass.
Vincent G. Kling & Assoc., for Monsanto Co. Cafeteria, St. Louis, Mo.
Ernest J. Kump Assoc. and the Office of Masten & Hurd, for DeAnza College, Cupertino, Calif.
Richard Meier, for Smith house, Darien, Conn.
Neill Smith & Assoc. and Dreyfuss & Blackford, for Collegetown, Phase I, Sacramento, Calif.
I.M. Pei & Partners, for Des Moines Art Center Addition, Des Moines, Iowa
I.M. Pei & Partners and Pederson, Hueber, Hares & Glavin, for Everson Museum of Art, Syracuse, N.Y.
John B. Rogers, for Girls' Dormitory, Putney School, Putney, Vt.
Skidmore, Owings & Merrill, for Tenneco Bldg., Houston, Tex.
Smotrich & Platt, for Exodus house, New York.
Walker/McGough, Foltz and Lyerla/Peden, for Convent of the Holy Names, Spokane, Wash.
Harry Weese & Assoc., Cromlie Taylor, for Auditorium Theatre Restoration, Chicago.
Wurster, Bernardi & Emmons, for Mill Valley Library, Mill Valley, Calif.

1970 **Gunnar Birkerts and Assoc.,** for Lincoln Elementary School, Columbus, Ind.
Marcel Breuer and Hamilton Smith, Michael H. Irving, for Whitney Museum of American Art, New York.
Cerny Associates, for pedestrian skyways, Minneapolis.
Joseph Esherick and Assoc., for The Cannery, San Francisco.
Faulkner, Stenhouse, Fryer & Faulkner, for National Collection of Fine Arts and National Portrait Gallery, Washington, D.C.
Ulrich Franzen & Assoc., for Bradfield and Emerson Halls, Cornell University, Ithaca, N.Y.
Hartman-Cox, for Phillips/Brewer residence, Chevy Chase, Md.

1971 **Davis, Brody & Assoc./Richard Dattner & Assoc.,** for Estee Lauder Laboratories, Melville, N.Y.
Davis, Brody, Chermayeff, Geismar, DeHarak Assoc. and Ohbayashi-Bumi Ltd., for U.S. Pavilion, Japan World Exposition 1970, Osaka, Japan
Ulrich Franzen, for Christensen Hall, University of New Hampshire, Durham, N.H.
Hartman-Cox, for Florence Hollis Hand Chapel, Mount Vernon College, Washington, D.C.
Richard Meier, for Westbeth Artists' Housing, New York, N.Y.
Pierce & Pierce, for Avco Everett Research Laboratory, Everett, Mass.
Quinn & Oda, for Church of Our Divine Savior, Chico, Calif.
The Architects Collaborative, for Children's Hospital Medical Center, Boston
Benjamin Thompson & Assoc., for Design Research Bldg., Cambridge, Mass.
Wolf Assoc., for North Carolina National Bank Branch, Charlotte, N.C.

1972 **Edward Larrabee Barnes,** for Walker Art Center, Minneapolis.
Marcel Breuer & Herbert Beckhard, for Koerfer House, Lago Maggiore, Switzerland
Ulrich Franzen, for Alley Theatre, Houston, Tex.
John M. Johansen, for Mummers Theater, Oklahoma City, Okla.
C.F. Murphy Assoc., for McCormick Place-On-The-Lake, Chicago
James Stewart Polshek & Assoc., for New York State Bar Center, Albany, N.Y.
Claude Samton & Assoc., for YM-YWHA Camp, Mt. Olive, N.J.
Skidmore Owings & Merrill, for Weyerhaeuser Headquarters, Tacoma, Wash.
Wurster, Bernardi and Emmos, for Ice Houses I & II, San Francisco.

1973 **John Anderws/Anderson/Baldwin,** for Harvard Graduate School of Design George Gund Hall, Cambridge, Mass.
Marcel Breuer and Herbert Beckhard, for St. Francis de Sales College, Muskegon, Mich.

Edward Cuetara, for Woolner Residence, Chilmark, Mass.
Esherick Homsey Dodge & Davis, for Julian McPhee College Union, California Polytechnic State University, San Luis Obispo, Calif.
Ronald Gourley and Carleton R. Richmond, Jr., for faculty housing, Radcliffe College, Cambridge, Mass.
William Kessler Assoc., for public housing for the elderly, Wayne, Mich.
Loebl Schlossman Bennett and Dart, for St. Procopius Abbey, Lisle, Ill.
McCue Boone Tomsick, for vacation residence, San Mate County, Calif.
MLTW/Moore Turnbull, for beach house, Santa Cruz County, Calif.
RTKL Inc., for Fountain Square, Cincinnati, Ohio
Skidmore Owings and Merrill, for American Can Co., Greenwich, Conn.
Harry Weese & Assoc., for Time & Life Bldg., Chicago

1974 **Daniel L. Dworsky & Assoc.,** for multi-purpose track and field stadium, University of California, Los Angeles
Holabird and Root, for 4A Equipment Bldg., Illinois Bell Telephone Co., Northbrook, Ill.
John Carl Warnecke and Assoc. and Hugh Newell Jacobsen, for Renwick Gallery, Washington, D.C.
Richard Meier & Assoc., for Twin Parks Northeast Housing, Bronx, N.Y.
Mitchell/Giurgola Assoc., for MDRT Foundation Hall, Adult Learning Research Laboratory, Bryn Mawr, Pa.
William Morgan Architects, for Morgan residence, Atlantic Beach, Fla.
I.M. Pei & Partners, for Paul Mellon Center for the Arts, Choate School, Wallingford, Conn.
Wolf Assoc., for North Carolina National Bank, Charlotte, N.C.

1975 **Louis I. Kahn,** for Kimbell Art Museum, Fort Worth, Tex.
Muchow Assoc., for Park Central, Denver, Colo.
I.M. Pei & Partners, for H.F. Johnson Museum, Ithaca, N.Y.
I.M. Pei & Partners, for 88 Pine Street, New York, N.Y.
Michael Graves, for Hanselmann residence, Fort Wayne, Ind.
Mitchell/Giurgola Assoc., for Columbus East H.S., Columbus, Ind.
Skidmore Owings & Merrill, for The Republic, Columbus, Ind.
Philip Johnson/John Burgee, for I.D.S. Center, Minneapolis, Minn.
Ralph Rapson & Assoc., for Cedar Square West, Minneapolis, Minn.

1976 **Anderson Notter Assoc.,** for Old Boston City Hall, Boston
Davis, Brody & Assoc., for Waterside, New York
Myron Goldfinger, for Marcus house, Bedford, N.Y.
Gwathmey Siegel Architects, for dormitory, dining and student union facility State University College, Purchase, N.Y.
Gwathmey Siegel Architects, for Whig Hall, Princeton University, Princeton, N.J.
Hardy Holzman Pfeiffer Assoc., for Columbus Occupational Health Center, Columbus, Ind.
William Kessler and Assoc., for Center for Creative Studies, Detroit
Richard Meier and Assoc., for Douglas house, Harbor Springs, Mich.
Miller Hanson Westerbeck Bell, for Butler Square, Minneapolis.
C.F. Murphy Assoc., for Crosby Kemper Memorial Arena, Kansas City, Mo.

1977 **No awards**

The annual Architectural Firm Award, which is the highest honor that can be bestowed on a firm, is given for continuing collaboration among individuals who have caused the organization to be the principal force in consistently producing distinguished architecture for at least ten years.

1962 **Skidmore, Owings & Merrill**
1963 **No award**
1964 **The Architects Collaborative**
1965 **Wurster, Bernardi & Emmons**
1966 **No award**
1967 **Hugh Stubbins & Associate**
1968 **I. M. Pei & Partners**
1969 **Jones and Emmons Architects**
1970 **Ernest J. Kump, Associates**
1971 **Albert Kahn Associates Inc.**
1972 **Caudill Rowlett Scott**
1973 **Shepley Bulfinch Richardson and Abbott**
1974 **Kevin Roche John Dinkeloo & Associates**
1975 **David, Brody and Associates**
1976 **Mitchell/Giurgola, Architects**
1977 **Sert, Jackson and Associates**

Current status unknown

The Gold Medal is awarded annually to an individual for distinguished service to the architectural profession or to the Institute. It is the Institute's highest honor.

1907 **Sir Aston Webb,** London
1908 **No award**
1909 **Charles Follen McKim,** New York
1910 **No award**
1911 **George B. Post,** New York
1912 **No award**
1913 **No award**
1914 **Jean Louis Pascal,** Paris
1915-21 **No awards**
1922 **Victor Laloux,** Paris
1923 **Henry Bacon,** New York
1924 **No award**
1925 **Sir Edwin Landseer Lutyens,** London
1925 **Bertram Grosvenor Goodhue,** New York
1926 **No award**
1927 **Howard Van Doren Shaw,** Chicago
1928 **No award**
1929 **Milton Bennett Medary,** Philadephia
1929-33 **No awards**
1934 **Ragnar Ostberg,** Stockholm
1935-37 **No awards**
1938 **Paul Philippe Cret,** Philadelphia
1939-45 **No awards**
1946 **Louis Henri Sullivan,** Chicago
1947 **Eliel Saarinen,** Bloomfield Hills, Mich.
1948 **Charles Donagh Maginnis,** Boston
1949 **Frank Lloyd Wright,** Spring Green, Wisc.
1950 **Sir Patrick Abercrombie,** London
1951 **Bernard Ralph Maybeck,** San Francisco
1952 **Auguste Perret,** Paris
1953 **William Adams Delano,** New York
1954 **No award**
1955 **Willem Marinus Dudok,** Hilversum, Netherlands
1956 **Clarence S. Stein,** New York
1957 **Ralph Walker,** New York (Centennial Medal of Honor)

1957 **Luis Skidmore,** New York
1958 **John Wellborn Root,** Chicago
1959 **Walter Gropius,** Cambridge, Mass.
1960 **Ludwig Mies van der Rohe,** Chicago
1961 **"Le Corbusier" (Charles Edouard Jeanneret-Gris),** Paris
1962 **Eero Saarinen,** Bloomfield Hills, Mich.
1963 **Alvar Aalto,** Helsinki
1964 **Pier Luigi Nervi,** Rome
1965 **No award**
1966 **Kenzo Tange,** Tokyo
1967 **Wallace K. Harrison,** New York
1968 **Marcel Breuer,** New York
1969 **William W. Wurster,** San Francisco
1970 **Richard Buckminster Fuller,** Carbondale, Ill.
1971 **Louis I. Kahn,** Philadelphia
1972 **Pietro Belluschi,** Boston
1973-76 **No awards**
1977 **Richard Joseph Neutra,** Los Angeles

Current status unknown

The Edward C. Kemper Award is given annually to an AIA member for significant contributions to the profession of architecture and to the Institute.

1950 **William Perkins**
1951 **Marshall Shaffer**
1952 **William Stanley Parker**
1953 **Gerrit J. De Gelleke**
1954 **Henry H. Saylor**
1955 **Turpin C. Bannister**
1956 **Theodore Irving Coe**
1957 **David C. Baer**
1958 **Edmund R. Purves**
1959 **Bradley P. Kidder**
1960 **Philip D. Creer**
1961 **Earl H. Reed**
1962 **Harry D. Payne**
1963 **Samuel E. Lunden**
1964 **Daniel Schwartzman**
1965 **Joseph Watterson**
1966 **William W. Eshbach**
1967 **Robert H. Levison**
1968 **E. James Gambaro**
1969 **Philip J. Meathe**
1970 **Ulysses Floyd Rible**
1971 **Gerald McCue**
1972 **David N. Yerkes**
1973 **Bernard B. Rothschild**
1974 **Jack D. Train**
1975 **F. Carter Williams**
1976 **Leo A. Daly**
1977 **Ronald A. Straka**

Current status unknown

The Reynolds Aluminum Grand Prize for architectural students honors original design for aluminum components in building. A $5,000 honorarium is divided between the student and the school.

1961 **John L. Dewey,** University of Cincinnati
1962 **Jon H. Starnes,** University of Texas
1963 **Manual A. Fernandez,** University of New Mexico
1964 **John F. Torti,** Notre Dame University
1965 **Douglas F. Trees,** Ohio State University
1966 **William R. Mitchell,** North Carolina State University
1967 **Kent C. Underwood,** Ohio State University
1968 **Charles R. Ansell, John W. Bradford,** Virginia Polytechnic Institute
1969 **Gerald Runkel,** Ohio State University
1970 **John Ahrendes, Joe Eng,** University of California, Berkeley
1971 **Hugh L. McMillan, Rick W. Redden,** University of Arkansas
1972 **L. Wayne Barcelon, Darlene S. Jang,** University of California, Berkeley
1973 **Raymond D. Snowden, Steven Lee Kinzler,** University of Arkansas
1974 **No award**
1975 **Joseph R. Barker, Laurance P. Dickie, Harold A. Ruck, Eric Stein, David R. Wilson,** University of Tennessee
1976 **Allen Koster,** University of Minnesota
1977 **Daniel T. Dolen,** Yale University

Current status unknown

The R.S. Reynolds Award, which carries a $25,000 honorarium and is accompanied by a sculpted emblem, recognizes the creators of a significant work of architecture in which aluminum has been used as an important contributing factor.

1957 **Cesar Oritz-Echague, Manual Barbero Rebolledo and Rafael de la Joya,** Madrid
1958 **T.F. Hoet-Segers, H. Montois, R. Courtois, J. Goossens-Bara, R. Moens de Hase and A. Lipski,** Brussels
1959 **Yuncken, Freeman Brothers, Griffiths and Simpson and Barry B. Patten,** Melbourne, Australia
1960 **Jean Tschumi,** Lausanne, Switzerland
1961 **Joseph D. Murphy and Eugene J. Mackey,** St. Louis, Mo.
1962 **Guy Lagneau, Michel Weill and Jean Dimitrijeuic,** Le Havre, France
1963 **Hans Maurer,** Munich
1964 **Skidmore, Owings and Merrill,** Chicago
1965 **James Stirling and James Gowan,** Leicester, England
1966 **Hans Hollein,** Vienna
1967 **Victor Christ-Janer,** New Cannaan, Conn.
1968 **Eijkelenboom & Middelhoek,** Holland, and **George F. Eber**, Canada
1969 **Boyd Auger,** London
1970 **Marcel Lods, Paul Depondt, Henri Beauclair,** France
1971 **Walter Custer, Fred Hochstrasser and Hans Bleiker,** Switzerland
1972 **Willi Walter,** Switzerland
1973 **Hannes Westermann,** Braunschweig, Federal Republic of Germany
1974 **no award**
1975 **Gustav Peiche,** Austria
1976 **Norman Foster,** London
1977 **Richard Maier,** New York

Current status unknown

The R.S. Reynolds Award for Community Architecture, which carries a $25,000 cash prize and an original aluminum sculpture, honors a community for using architectural design to solve problems of modern urban living. It is awarded approximately every three years.

1967 **Cumbemauld New Town,** Scotland, Architects and Planners of Cumbernauld
1969 **Beersheba,** Israel
1974 **Pedestrian Way,** Munich
1977 **Edmund N. Bacon,** City of Philadelphia

Current status unknown

The Twenty-Five Year Award honors architectural design of enduring significance to a project judged to have withstood the test of time.

1969 **Rockefeller Center**
1970 **No award**
1971 **Crow Island School**
1972 **Baldwin Hills Village**
1973 **Taliesin West**
1974 **Johnson's Wax Administration Bldg.**
1975 **Philip Johnson's residence**
1976 **860-880 North Lake Shore Drive Apartments**

Distinguished Service Award
Honor Award
Merit Award
Meritorious Program Award
Chapter Achievement Award
Diana Donald Award
Special Award
Special Fiftieth Anniversary Awards

AMERICAN PLANNING ASSOCIATION
1776 Massachusetts Ave. NW, Washington, D.C. 20036
(202/872-0611)

The Distinguished Service Award were given by the American Institute of Planners, a predecessor of the APA, to annually honor individuals active over a period of at least 15 years for contributions to local, regional, state or nationalplanning, in research or education, theory or philosophy, techniques and practices, implementation or administration or advancement of planning.

1953 **Frederick Bigger**
Russell Van Nest Black
Frederick Olmstead
1954 **Tracy D. Augur**
1955 **Frederick J. Adams**
Harland Bartholomew
Flavel Shurtleff
1956 **Charles B. Bennett**
1957 **Walter H. Blucher**
HaroldM. Lewis
Ladislas Segoe
Lawrence V. Sheridan
1958 **Harold S. Buttenheim**
Clarence S. Stein
1959 **Robert B. Mitchell**
Gordon Whitnall
1960 **S. R. DeBoer**
1961 **Charles W. Eliot**
Lawrence M. Orton
1962 **Henry S. Churchill**
Hugh R. Pomeroy
1963 **John T. Howard**
1964 **Francis A. Pitkin**
Warren J. Vinton
1965 **Dennis O'Harrow**
Max Wehrly
1966 **Howard Menhinick**
1967 **No award**
1968 **F. Stuart Chapin, Jr.**
1969 **Hans Blumenfeld**
1970 **Charles Abrams**
1971 **Edmund Bacon**
1972 **C. McKim Norton**
Coleman Woodbury
1973-76 **No awards**
1977 **Richard L. Steiner**

The AIP Honor Award was given as merited to communities or regional organizations for noteworthy planning efforts.

1962 **Fremont, Calif.**
1963 **Cincinnati, Ohio**
1964 **Rye, N.Y.,** (population under 50,000)
Pomona, Calif., (population 50,000 - 500,000)
Detroit, Mich., (population over 500,000)
1965 **Rockville, Md.,** (under 50,000)
New Haven, Conn., (50,000 - 500,000)
1966 **Camden, N.J.,** (50,000 - 500,000)
Capital Region, Conn., (over 500,000)
1968 **City and County of Denver, Colo.,** (over 500,000)

The AIP Merit Award honored significant works and programs in planning.

1968 ***Planning for Balanced Growth in Connecticut***
1969 **Bay Conservation and Development Commission Plan**
Goals for Dallas Program
Principles and Practice of Urban Planning
1971 **Education Program,** Philadelphia Regional Chapter
Goals for Texas Program, State of Texas

The AIP Meritorious Program Award continues to be given by the APA to recognize a significant work in the areas of professional education and training, community planning, regional and state planning, urban design or social responsibility.

1972 **Baltimore Metro Center, Md.**
Salt River Indian Community Planning Program, Ariz.
Twin Cities Area of Minneapolis-St. Paul and its Metropolitan Council
1973-76 **No awards**
1977 **Urban National Cultural Parks Plan,**
1978 **No award**
1979 **Kenneth Stratton** (dir.), Land Use Regulation Commission, Maine Dept. of Conservation
Lawrence M. Irvin (dir.), Minneapolis City Planning Dept.
George Crandall, Skidmore Owings & Merrill, Portland (Ore.) Conservation Project
1980 **Not available at press time**

The Chapter Achievement Award honors chapters for contributions to the planning profession and the organization through an outstanding chapter program, activities or efforts that have advanced planning policy, development or the chapter.

1972 ***Little Magazine,*** Minnesota Chapter
1973-76 **No awards**
1977 **National Capital Area Chapter**
1978 **No award**
1979 **Florida Chapter**
1980 **Not available at press time**

The Diana Donald Award, originally an AIP honor, continues to be given to an outstanding planner who has made substantial contributions to women's rights, as demonstrated by significant contributions to the profession, the holding of a responsible management position and the devotion of substantial effort to community service.

1977 **Margaret Lotspeich**
1978 **No award**
1979 **Ruth C. Crone**
1980 **Not available at press time**

Special Awards are given upon a decision by an awards jury to honor outstanding service to AIP.

1970 **Alan M. Voorhees**
Harold F. Wise
1971 **No award**
1972 **Flavel Shurtleff**
1972 **Frederick Aschman**
1973-76 **No awards**
1977 **Paul Opperman**

SPECIAL AIP FIFTIETH ANNIVERSARY AWARDS

American Society of Planning Officials, Citation for contribution to the public acceptance and technical effectiveness of planning as a part of the process of government in the United States

City of Philadelphia, Citation honoring a city, two of its distinguished mayors who brought it through some decisive years of change (Joseph S. Clark and Richardson Dilworth) and a planner inseparably identified with the transformation these years have wrought

National Resources Planning Board, Citation as the spiritual forerunner of contemporary planning in the United States

Regional Plan Association (New York, New Jersey and Connecticut Metropolitan Area), Citation for achievement and contribution in Metropolitan Planning

Tennessee Valley Authority, Citation for achievement in carrying through a pioneering philosophy of resource use; in recognition of an uninterrupted line of inspired leadership from its board of directors; to honor the contributions from its distinguished and innovative professionals

Frederick Johnstone Adams, Citation for achievement and contribution in planning education

Harland Bartholomew, Citation for achievement and contributionin planning practice

Alfred Bettman, Citation for achievement and contribution in planning law

Kevin Lynch, Citation for achievement and contribution in planning and design theory

Martin Meyerson, Citation for achievement and contribution in planning theory and research

Lewis Mumford, Citation for achievement and contribution in planning philosophy

Ladislas Segoe, Citation for achievement and contribution in planning practice

Clarence S. Stein, Citation for achievement and contribution in planning design principles

Catherine Bauer Wurster, Citation for achievement and contribution in planning criticism

Albert S. Bard Award

CITY CLUB OF NEW YORK
33 W. 42nd St., New York, N.Y. 10036 (212/921-9870)

The Albert S. Bard Award annually honors distinguished achievement in urban architecture in New York. An awards jury of prominent architects selects the winners from entries submitted by architects or owners or of their own choosing. Certificates are given in three categories.

FIRST HONOR AWARDS

1964 **Skidmore, Owings & Merrill,** for Pepsi-Cola Building

1965 **I.M. Pei & Associates and S.J. Kessler & Sons,** for Kips Bay Plaza
Warner, Burns, Toan, Lunde, for Warner Weaver Hall, New York University

1966 **Philip C. Johnson,** for Henry Moses Institute, Montefiore Hospital
Philip C. Johnson and Zion & Breen, for Sculpture Garden, Museum of Modern Art
Philip Johnson Associates; Eero Saarinen & Associates; Skidmore, Owings & Merrill; Pietro Belluschi, and Catalono & Westerman, with Dan Kiley, landscape consultant, for Lincoln Center Plaza North

1967 **I.M. Pei & Partners,** for University Plaza Apartments
Kelly & Gruzen, for Chatham Towers Apartments
Wallace, McHarg, Roberts & Todd and Alan M. Voorhees & Associates, for Lower Manhattan Plan

1968 **Kevin Roche, John Dinkeloo & Associates,** for Ford Foundation
Marcel Breuer, Hamilton Smith and Michael Irving, consulting architect, for Whitney Museum of American Art
Zion & Breen Associates and Albert Preston Moore, for Paley Park

1969 **Davis, Brody & Associates,** for Riverbend Houses
Edelman & Salzman, for 9-G Cooperative

1970 **Pietro Belluschi and Catalono & Westerman,** for Concert Halls, the Julliard School
Hardy Holzman Pfeiffer Associates, for Bedford Lincoln Community Center

1971 **No award**

1972 **I.M. Pei & Associates,** for National Airlines Terminal
Abraham W. Geller, for Henry Ittelson Center for Child Research

1973 **Gruzen & Partners,** for Bronx State Hospital Rehabilitation Center
Morris Lapidus Associates, for Bedford-Stuyvesant Community Pool
Davis, Brody & Associates, for East Midtown Plaza
Richard Meier & Associates, for Twin Parks Northeast
Prentice & Chan, Ohlhausen, for Twin Parks Northwest, Site 5 & 11

1974 **No award**

1975 **Caudill Rowlett Scott,** for Salanter-Akiba-Riverdale Academy

1976 **Holden/Yang/Raemsch/Terjesen,** for bus stop shelters
Prentice & Chan, Ohlhausen, for Arts for Living Center
Hodne/Stageberg Partners, for 1199 Plaza Cooperative Towers

1977 **Richard Meier & Associates,** for Bronx Developmental Center

1978 **Hugh Stebbins & Assoc.,** Citicorp Center
Mitchell/Giurgola, Sherman Fairchild Center for the Life Sciences
Alexander Kouzanoff & Asso., Avery Hall Extension, Graduate School of Architecture and Planning
Ulrich Franzen & Assoc., Harlem School of the Arts
James Stewart Polshek, Physical education building
Edward Larrabee Barnes, Conservatory restoration, New York Botanical Garden

1979 **Gruzen & Partners,** 265 E. 66th St. building
Johansen & Bahvani, Abraham Goodman House

Witthoft & Rudolph, pedestrian shelter, TWA Flight Center
Bernard Rothzeid, Turtle Bay Towers
1980 **No award**

AWARDS FOR MERIT

1964 **Marcel Breuer,** for Bergrisch Hall, New York University University Heights Campus
Mayer, Whittlesey & Glass, for Premier Apartment House
Abraham Geller and Ben Schlanger, for Cinema I and Cinema II
1965 **Harrison & Abramovitz,** for Terminal Building, LaGuardia Airport
1966 **No award**
1967 **Pomerance & Breines and M. Paul Friedberg & Associates,** for Riis Amphitheatre and Plaza
1968 **No award**
1969 **Smotrich & Platt,** for Exodus House
Morris Ketchum Jr. & Associates, for Exhibition Building for Nocturnal Animals, Bronx Zoo
1970 **Perkins & Will Partnership,** for Wagner College Student Union
Walker Hodgetts, Mangurian & Godard, for Creative Playthings
Bill Hoch, for Latinas
Ulrich Franzen, for Paraphernalia
Hans Hollein, for Richard Feigen Gallery
Paul K.Y. Chen and George Thiel, for Zum Zum Restaurants
Isabel Hebey and Justin Henshell, for Rive Gauche Boutique
1971 **Carl J. Petrilli,** for The Mall, Graduate Center, City University of New York
Marcel Breuer and Hamilton B. Smith, for Technology Building II, New York University
1972 **No award**
1973 **No award**
1974 **No award**
1975 **Mayers & Schiff,** for Times Square Theatre Center
Edelman and Salzman, for reclamation of the Graveyards, St. Marks Church-in-the-Bouwerie
Castro Blanco, Piscionieri & Feder, PC and Gruzen & Partners, for Arthur A. Schomburg Plaza Apartments
Richard D. Kaplan/Stevens, Bertin, O'Connell & Harvey, for Crown Gardens
Davis, Brody & Associates, for Waterside
Ciardullo/Ehmann, for Plaza Borinquen/Motthaven Infill Housing
1976 **No award**
1977 **Johnson/Burgee; Giorgio Cavaglieri; Johansen & Bhavnani; Sert, Jackson & Associates; Lev Zetlin Associates; Prentice & Chan, Ohlhausen; Kallmann & McKinnell; New York State Urban Development Corp. and Roosevelt Island Development Corp.,** for Roosevelt Island

SPECIAL AWARDS

1965 **Pomerance & Breines and M. Paul Friedberg,** for Carver Houses Plaza
Marquesa de Duevas, for 680 and 684 Park Avenue
1967 **Stewart L. Udall,** Secretary of the Interior
1968 **Giorgio Cavaglieri,** for Public Theatre Center, New York Shakespeare Festival; Old Astor Library rehab
1975 **Warren W. Gran & Associates,** for Clinton study
1976 **New York City Department of Highways,** for reconstruction of the Ave. of the Americas
1977 **William N. Breger Associates,** for C.A.B.S. Nursing Home
Gruzen & Partners, for U.S. Courthouse and Metropolitan Correctional Center
Gwathmey Siegel, for Shezan Restaurant
Kevin Roche/John Dinkeloo Associates, for Fifth Avenue Plaza and East Front, Metropolitan Museum of Art
Helmuth, Obata & Kassabaum, for Greenwich Savings Bank
Hardy Holman Pfeiffer Associates, for Smithsonian's Cooper-Hewitt National Museum of Design

CITATIONS

1978 **Paul K.Y. Chen**, Tavern on the Green
Macy's, New York, for The Cellar
Harry van Dyke, Addition to the Frick Collection

Paul-Bonatz-Preis

LANDESHAUPTSTADT STUTTGART
Postfach 161, 7000 Stuttgart 1, Federal Republic of Germany (0711-216-6703)

The Paul-Bonatz-Preis, or Paul Bonatz Prize, is awarded every four years for outstanding works of architecture, design, landscape design, sculpture, painting or related arts completed during the previous four years. A five-member jury selects the recipient.

1959 **Fritz Leonhardt**
1963 **Gunter Behnisch**
Rolf Gutbier
Hans Kammerer
Hans Volkart
1967 **Walter Belz**
Rolf Gutbrod
Hans Scharoum
1971 **Max Bacher**
Walter Belz
Rolf Gutbrod
1975 **Max Bacher**
Walter Belz
Egon Eiermann
1979 **Not available at press time**

Brevoort-Eickemeyer Prize

COLUMBIA UNIVERSITY
Office of the Secretary, New York, N.Y. 10027

The Brevoort-Eickmeyer Prize is given every five years to an individual who has made meritorious contributions to the field of design. The National Academy of Design recommends nominees to the trustees of the university.

1955 **Joseph Flock**, for painting, "On the Terrace"
1960 **Hobson Pittman**, for painting, "Interior with Flowers"
1965 **Edwin Dickinson**, for painting, "Self Portrait"
1970 **No award**
1975 **Jose de Creeft**, for work in sculpture
1980 **Eric Isenburger**, for distinguished work in painting and teaching

Arnold W. Brunner Prize

AMERICAN ACADEMY AND INSTITUTE OF ARTS AND LETTERS
633 W. 155th St., New York, N.Y. 10032 (212/368-6361)

The $1,000 Arnold W. Brunner Prize in Architecture is given annually to an architect who has contributed to the field as an art. A committee of Institute members who are architects selects the winner.

1955 **Gordon Bunshaft**
1956 **John Yeon**
1957 **John Carl Warnecke**
1958 **Paul Rudolph**
1959 **Edward Larrabee Barnes**
1960 **Louis I. Kahn**
1961 **Ieoh Ming Pei**
1962 **Ulrich Franzen**
1963 **Edward Charles Bassett**
1964 **Harry Weese**
1965 **Kevin Roche**
1966 **Romaldo Giurgola**
1968 **John M. Johansen**
1969 **Noel Michael McKinnell**
1970 **Charles Gwathmey**
Richard Henderson
1971 **John Andrews**
1972 **Richard Meier**
1973 **Robert Venturi**
1974 **Hugh Hardy with Norman Pfeiffer and Malcolm Holzman**
1975 **Lewis Davis and Samuel Brody**
1976 **James Frazer Stirling**
1977 **Henry N. Cobb**
1978 **Cesar Pelli**
1979 **Charles W. Moore**
1980 **Michael Graves**

Library Building Award

AMERICAN LIBRARY ASSOCIATION
Library Administration Div., 50 E. Huron St. Chicago, Ill. 60611 (312/944-6780)

The Library Building Award, cosponsored by the Association and the American Institute of Architects, is given biennially for excellence in architectural design and planning of libraries. A jury of four architects and three librarian/building experts selects the winners, which are honored with a plaque and certificate. New buildings, renovations and additions of all kinds of libraries in the U.S. and elsewhere are included.

HONOR AWARDS (PLAQUE AND CERTIFICATES)

1963 **Bennington** (Vt.) **College Library**
Undergraduate Library, University of South Carolina
Walnut Hills Branch of the Dallas (Tex.) **Public Library**
Skokie (Ill.) **Public Library**
Flossmoor (Ill.) **Public Library**
1964 **Beinecke Rare Book Room & Manuscript Library,** Yale University, New Haven, Conn.
Charles Patterson Van Pelt Library, University of Pennsylvania, Philadelphia, Pa.
Flora B. Tenzler Memorial Library, Pierce County, Tacoma, Wash.
1966 **Magnolia Branch Library,** Seattle (Wash.) **Public Library**
1968 **No award**
1970 **Bancroft Elementary Library,** Andover, Mass.
1972 **Providence College Library,** Providence, R.I.
Ohio Historical Center Library-Archives, Columbus, Ohio
1974 **Monroe C. Gutman Library,** Harvard Graduate School of Education, Cambridge, Mass.
North Branch Library, Omaha, Neb.
Southdale Hennepin Area Library, Edina, Minn.
1976 **Stephen B. Luce Library,** State University Maritime College, Fort Schulyer, Bronx, N.Y.
Lineberger Memorial Library, Lutheran Theological Southern Seminary, Columbia, S.C.
Joseph Mark Lauinger Memorial Library, Georgetown University, Washington, D.C.
Nathan Marsh Pusey Library, Harvard University, Cambridge, Mass.
Randall Memorial Library, Stow, Mass
Marin County Library, Novato, Calif.
Rockford Road Branch, Hennepin County Library, Crystal, Minn.
Corning Public Library and Southern Tier Library System, Corning, N.Y.
1978 **Sarah Lawrence College Library**, Bronxville, N.Y.
Michigan City (Ind.) **Public Library**
Houston (Tex.) **Central Library**

MERIT AWARD (CERTIFICATE)

1963 **Lourdes Library,** Gwynedd Mercy Junior College, Gwynedd Valley, Pa.
Grinnell College Burling Library, Grinnell, Iowa
Schulz Memorial Library, Concordia Theological Seminary, Springfield, Ill.
Foothill College Library, Los Altos Hills, Calif.
Douglass College Library, Rutgers University, New Brunswich, N.J.
Washington State Library, Olympia, Wash
Louisiana State Library Baton Rouge, La.
New Orleans (La.) **Public Library**
Santa Fe Springs (Calif.) **City Library**
Sequoyah Hills Branch, Knoxville (Tenn.) Public Library
Wellesley (Mass.) **Free Library**
West Bloomfield Township Library, Orchard Lake, Mich.
1964 **Archbishop Alemany Library,** Dominican College, San Rafael, Calif.
Leverett House Library, Harvard University, Cambridge, Mass.
Lafayette College Library, Easton, Pa.
Hollis F. Price Library, Le Moyne College, Memphis, Tonn.
Otto G. Richter Library, University of Miami, Coral Gables, Fla.
Southwest Branch, Seattle (Wash,) Public Library
Sprain Brook Branch, Yonkers (N.Y.) Public Library
Silas Bronson Library, Waterbury, Conn.
Detroit (Mich.) **Public Library**
Coconut Grove Branch, Miami (Fla.) Public Library
Willey Library, Seaside High School, Fort Ord, Calif.
Redwood High School Library, Larkspur, Calif.
Westtown School Library, Westtown, Chester County. Pa.
1966 **University Research Library,** University of California at Los Angeles
Swirbul Library, Adelphi University, Garden City, N.Y.

Countway Library of Medicine, Harvard University Medical School, Boston, Mass.
Wilmot Branch Library, Tucson (Ariz.) Public Library
South Branch of the Berkeley (Calif.) **Public Library**
New Jersey State Library, Trenton, N.J.
Casa View Branch, Dallas (Tex.) Public Library
W. Clarke Swanson Library, Omaha, Neb.
Salt Lake City (Utah) **Public Library**
McBean Library, Cate School, Carpinteria, Calif.

1968 **Library Institute for Advanced Education,** Princeton, N.J.
St. John's University Library, Collegeville, Minn.
Hofstra University Library, Hempstead, N.Y.
Mill Valley (Calif) **Public Library**
La Crosse (Wisc.) **Public Library**
Wichita (Kans.) **Public Library**
Mount Anthony Union High School Library, Bennington, Vt.

1970 **Adlai Stevenson College Library,** University of California at Santa Cruz
Robert Hutchings Goddard Library, Clark University, Worcester, Mass.
Anna E. Waden Branch Library, San Francisco, Calif.
Madden Hills Branch Library, Dayton, Ohio
Henry B. DuPont Library, Pomfret School, Pomfret, Conn.

1972 **Bailey Library,** Hendrix College, Conway, Ark.
Loomis Library, Loomis Institute, Windsor, Conn.
Joseph Regenstein Library, University of Chicago
Richardson (Tex.) **Public Library**
South County Library, Deale, Md.
Corte Madera Branch, Marin County Library, Corte Madera, Calif.
Tate Library of the Fieldston School, Riverdale, N.Y.

1974 **Loyola-Notre Dame Library,** Baltimore, Md.
Library of the Villa Angela Academy, Cleveland, Ohio.

1976 **Bates College,** Lewiston, Me.
Pekin Public Library and Everett McKinley Dirksen Congressional Leadership Research Center, Pekin, Ill.
Jefferson Market Branch Library, New York, N.Y.
Hapeville (Ga.) **Public Library**

1978 **Selby Public Library**, Sarasota, Fla.
Des Moines (Iowa) **Public Library**
Biloxi (Miss.) **Library and Cultural Center**
Troy-Miami County Public Library, Troy, Ohio
Tredyffrin Public Library, Stafford, Pa.
Scripps Institution of Oceanography Library, Carl Eckhart Bldg., **University of California**, La Jolla, Calif.
Long Island University Library/Learning Center, Brooklyn, N.Y.
Chula Vista (Calif.) **Public Library**

AWARD OF EXCELLENCE

1980 **University of Minnesota Law Library**, Minneapolis
Providence (R.I.) **Athenaeum**
New Rochelle (N.Y.) **Public Library**
Lyndon State College Library, Lindynville, Vt.
Morley Elementary School Library, W. Hartford, Conn.

Gold Medal

NATIONAL ARTS CLUB
15 Gramercy Park South, New York, N.Y. 10003
(212/475-3424)

As part of the art's honors program in the visual and performing arts and literature, a gold medal is awarded annually for constanding contributions to art exhibition. Other medalists are listed in the Music & Dance, Literature and Theatre sections of this volume.

1960 **Paul Manship**
1961 **Senator William Benton**
1962 **Malvina Hoffman**
1963 **John Koch**
1964 **Charles A. Aiken**
1965 **Salvador Dali**
1966 **Chen Chi**
1967 **Norman Kent**
Ogden Pleissner
1968 **Isabel Bishop**
1969 **Tore Asplund**
Frank Bensing
1970 **John Canaday**
1971 **Eric Larrabee**
1972 **J. Carter Brown**
1973 **Louise Nevelson**
1974 **Eric Sloane**
Thomas Hart Benton
1975 **Jose deCreeft**
1976 **R. Buckminster Fuller**
1977 **Stewart Klonis**
1978 **Xavier Gonzalez**
1979 **Raphael Soyer**
1980 **Clement Conger**

Pritzker Architecture Prize

PRITZKER FOUNDATION
2 First National Plaza, Chicago, Ill. 60603 (312/860-1234) or Attn.: Carleton Smith, 250 Park Ave., Ste. 915, New York, N.Y. 10017

The Pritzker Architecture Prize consists of $100,000 and a small Henry Moore sculpture. The prize is given for a body of architectural work of international importance. It is given for a combination of "talent, vision and commitment that has produced consistent and significant contributions to humanity and the environment."

1979 **Philip Johnson** (U.S.A.)
1980 **Luis Barragan** (Mexico)

Rechter's Award

ISRAELI INSTITUTE OF ARCHITECTS
200 Dizengoff Rd., Tel Aviv, Israel (03-240274)

Rechter's Award, which is accompanied by a plaque and an honorarium equivalent to about $550, is given biennially for architectural achievement and contributions to the advancement of Israeli architecture for a project built during the previous 10 years. A jury examines the plans and visits the site before chosing the prize-winner.

1962 **Nahum Zolotov**, Inn in Avdath, The Negev

1965 **David Reznik** and **Hans Rau**, Synagogue, Hebrew University, Givath Ram, Jerusalem
1967 **Ram Carmi**, Beduin Market, Beer Sheva
1969 **Ahsa** and **Daniel Havkin**, Dormitories, Technion City, Haifa
1971 **Abraham Yaski**, Hospital for Chronic Patients, Gedera
1973 **J. Yashar** and **Dan Eitan**, Tel Aviv Museum
1975 **Drexler**, **Sofer**, **Bixon**, **Kolodni**, **Schwartz** and **Dobrovski**, Housing neighborhood, Ramot, Jerusalem
1977 **Arie Saron** and **Eldar Saron**, Museum Yad Mordechai
1979 **Al Manfeld**, Residential unit, Stella, Maris, Haifa

The Roscoe

RESOURCES COUNCIL
979 Third Ave., New York, N.Y. 10022 (212/752-9040)

The Roscoe, a crystal trophy designed by Tiffany, annually honors excellence and innovation in design and technology of household furnishings and fixtures. Entries are accepted at $75 each. A judges' panel narrows the field down from hundreds of entries for a vote by attendees at a Council designers' market, which in 1977 was a four-day event. Until the introduction of the trophy in 1977, certificates were awarded to winners in a variety of categories and by different voting procedures. Award winners are listed here, but honorable mentions are not.

1971 **Wolf Bauer,** "Wheels & Yves," printed textiles
Francisca Reichardt, "Omahar," printed textiles
Gretl and Leo Wollner, "Sling," printed textiles
Ulrike Rhomberg, "Slant," printed textiles
Al Marsh, "Interplay," wallcovering
James Hill, "Kaleidoscope," wool rug
Lee Rosen, "Prismatic," ceramic wall design
Fritz Haller, Haller Program, collection of office furniture
William Sklaroff and Thomas H. Janicz, Uniplane desk and credenza
1972 **Frank O. Gehry,** Edgeboard contour rocker
William C. Andrus, "Soft Seating Group"
Jack Lenor Larsen, "The Great Colour of China," textile collection
James Seeman Studios, "Kaleidoscope," collection of murals and super-graphics
Roger McDonald and Paul W. V'Soske, "Northern Lights" and "Strata," wool rugs
Magee Design Studios, "Glen Eagle" and "Empire Stripe," wool carpets
Herbert Bright, "Polka Dots," "Gingham" and "Houndstooth," vinyl flooring collection
Richard Ludwig, "Sang-de-Boeuf," hand-thrown stoneware lamps
Nando Vigo, "Golden Gate," arc floor lamp
Achille Castiglioni, "Parenthesis," lighting fixture
1973 **Kibrel Steele Terry,** Marble and steel dining table
William H.P. Tacke, "Ergo," secretarial chair
Ken Millette, "Expresso-X," indoor/outdoor folding chair
Theodore R. Meyer, "Galaxy," plexiglass desk
Margaret D. Nelson, "Botanical," crewel embroidery fabric
Schule-McCarville, "Harriet," fabric
Dorothy A. Christie, "Star and Block," upholstery fabric
Robert O. Webb, Woven aluminum window shade
Anthony W. V'Soske, "Gridola," wool rug
Allied Chemical Design Studio, "Kinder Karpet"
Monogram Design Studio, "Bandana," wool area rug
Herbert Bright, "Ultrabronze," and stainless steel flooring
Dan Hawkins, "All-Most," hand-screened wallpaper
Helen Watkins, "Xanadu," wallpaper mural
Michael Babbitts, "Berberwool," wool wallcovering
William M. Groff, "Mono-Facade," ceramic wall tile
Eric Mulvany, "Quadri," Plexiglas lamp
Brent J. Bennett, Stoneware hanging lantern
Lenox Design Dept., "Dewdrops," Temperware china
Marie Creamer, "International Set," towel and rug collection
William Sklaroff Design Associates, "Radius One," desk accessories
Don Doman Associates, "Birthday Bath," bath tub
1974 **Henry A. Olko,** Rattan and reed daybed in the Oriental manner
William Sklaroff, Sled-base, contour-back armchair
Linda Sparrow, "Sampler," upholstery fabric
Joseph Grusczak, "Knits for Windows and Walls," fabric
Levolor Lorentzen Design Studio, "Gingham," Riviera blinds
Monogram Design Studio, "Mountain Mist," area rug
Hamdi and Brunhild El Attar, "Country House," sisal carpet tile
Herbert Bright, "Country Plaid," vinyl floor tile
Francois Benjamin, "Roxy," handscreened wallpaper
Jack Lenor Larsen, "Muralto," wall-surfacing textile
Eric Mulvany, "Trio," table lamp
Ben Mayer Design Studio, "Envelite," illuminated ceiling system
Ena de Silva, Batik bedspread
John W. Ledford, "The Spiral," staircase
Gino Valle and Herbert Ohl, "Metrix," dining/conference table
Suzanne Hugeunin, "Sequoia," upholstery fabric
Stanley J. V'Soske, Jr., "Avenues," area rug
David Nordahl, "Clouds," lithographic wall mural
1975 **Eve Frankl,** "Multi," series "Z" table
Roger Kenneth Leib, Modular lounge seating
Lawrence Peabody, Bronze and Haitian Sea Grass dining chair
Albert Zellers, "Carnations," fabric
Louis M. Bromante, "King Tut," quilted fabric
V'Soske Studios, "Puntilla," wool and silk area rug
Jack Lenor Larsen, "Happiness," carpet
Henry Torreggiani, "Geometric," ceramic tile
Arthur Athas, Barry Crooks and F. Galacar, "The Jaffrey Room," wallpaper
Cindi Mufson, "Hardrock," wallcovering
Adam Tihany/Joey Mancini, Unigram, Inc., "Triangolo," lamp series
Leon Conn, Innervisions bronze mirror lighting fixture
F.V. Herr and C.A. Tucker, "Eclipse," desk accessories
Fabio Lenci, "2001," shower in the round
C.J. Corona, "Superstone," synthetic fossilized stone
1976 **O.B. Solie and R.G. Sonnenleiter,** "Parabola," dining table
Ray Wilkes, Modular sofa group
William Stumpf, "Ergon," chair
Everett Brown Associates, "Sweet Potata," fabric
Jack Lindsay, "Djakarta," fabric
Kirk-Brummel Studios, "Lorelei," fabric

Larsen Design Studio, "Pastorale-Sheer," fabric
Levolor Design Dept., Riviera Tiltone duo-colored blind
Nadia Stark, Rumanian Kilim rug
Walter Dorwin Teague Associates and Anthony V'Soske, "Zap," area rug
Alan Meiselman, "Quadro," Berber broadloom
Nadia Stark, "Pande," broadloom carpet
Sylvia Gold Spellos, "Barnside," vinyl flooring
Laura Ashley, "A Fine & Private Place," wallpaper
Antonio Rodbechia, "Rodbechia," ceramic wall tile
Eric Mulvany, "Capricorn," table lamp
Habitat Design Team, Habitat Designers' Fluorescent
Paul Mayen, Desk-top accessory unit
Fabio Lenci, Bath and shower in the round
Maya, Tie-dyed floor canvas

1977 **Jay S. Goldsamt,** Chinese altar table
Doug Bickle, Dining/conference table
Ray Wilkes, Shelf Life Unlimited
George Nelson, Daniel Lewis and David Schowalter, Office furniture system
Henry Olko, Rattan Manau chair
Craig and Saul Goldman, "Quiltessence," fabric
Kirk-Brummel Studios, "Staccato Weave," fabric
Connaissance Studio, "Grand Prix," jacquard fabric
Marella Agnelli, "Sorbiers," fabric
Federico Forquet and Gustav Zumsteg, "Tahiti," fabric
Joel Berman, Mecho-Shade for windows
Lee Rosen, Grid relief pattern ceramic floor tile
Arthur Athas, Frederic Galacar and Barry Crooks, "Birds of Paradise," wallcovering
Andre Matenciot Design Studio, "Patches," wallcovering
Eric Mulvany, "Emerald," acryclic lamp
Barbara Roth, Egyptian lamp
Rolando T. Curtis, "Mirra Dome," lighting
Enzo Mari, Bowl, Danese Ceramic Collection
William Sklaroff, Covered face clock
Yolanda Quitman, Plexiglas medicine cabinet
Maya Romanoff, "Red Sienna Rain," Palangi-dyed leather and suede
Shirley Mellinger, "Ferocious Lion," rug
Joseph Freitag, "Botanica," stencils on sisal rug
John and Steven Stark, "Agadir," Berber broadloom carpet

Current status unknown

Fritz Schumacher Foundation Award

STIFTUNG F.V.S.
Georgsplatz 10, 2 Hamburg 1, Federal Republic of Germany (Tel: 33 04 00 and 33 06 00)

The Fritz Schumacher Foundation Award honors achievements in city- and land-planning, architecture, environmentalism and historic preservation in Europe. Two cash prizes of 20,000 German marks each are offered. The Technical University of Hanover administers the award.

1960 **Wolfgang Bangert** (Kassel, Germany
Alwin Seifert (Munich, Germany)
1961 **C. van Traa** (Rotterdam, Netherlands)
Fritz Leonhardt (Stuttgart, Germany)
1962 **Heinrich Wiepking** (Munster, Germany)
Horst Linde (Stuttgart, Germany)
1963 **Arne Jacobsen** (Copenhagen, Denmark)
Gunther Grundmann (Hamburg, Germany)
1964 **Adolf Ciborowski** (Warsaw, Poland)
Konstanty Gutschow (Hamburg, Germany)
1965 **Francisco Caldeira Cabral** (Lisbon, Portugal)
Josef Umlauf (Stuttgart, Germany)
1966 **Friedrich Tamms** (Dusseldorf, Germany)
Gerhard Ziegler (Stuttgart, Germany)
1967 **Cornelis van Leeuwen** (Bloemdedaal, Netherlands)
Arie C. Krijn (Bussum, Netherlands)
Jan H. van Loenen (Beverwijk, Netherlands)
Rudolf Wurzer (Vienna, Austria)
1968 **Robert Will** (Strasbourg, France)
Fernand Guri (Strasbourg, France)
Javier Carvajal (Madrid, Spain)
Ricardo Bofill (Barcelona, Spain)
1969 **Wilhelm Wortmann** (Hanover, Germany)
Renato Bazzoni (Milan, Italy)
1970 **Sir Hubert Bennett** (London, England)
Heikki von Hertzen (Tapiola, Finland)
1971 **Colin Douglas Buchanan** (London, England)
Walter Rossow (Berlin, Germany)
1972 **Elisabeth Pfeil** (Hamburg, Germany)
Harald Clauss (Nuremberg, Germany)
Heinz Schmeissner (Nuremberg, Germany)
1973 **M. Robert Vassas** (Paris, France)
Friedrich Cordes (Kiel, Germany)
1974 **Herman Hertzberger** (N.A.)
Frank van Klingeren (Amsterdam, Netherlands)
Erich Kuhn (Aachen, Germany)
1975 **Pier Luigi Cervellati** (Bologna, Italy)
Armando Sarti (Bologna, Italy)
Hubert Kath (Celle, Germany)
Fritz Schmidt (Celle, Germany)
Fred Angerer (Lochham bei Munchen, Germany)
Eberhard Haller (Lindau, Germany)
Horst Heidhardt (Oldenburg, Germany)
Friedrich Hasskamp (Oldenburg, Germany)
Hans Petzholdt (Trier, Germany)
1977 **Jon de Ranitz** (Rotterdam, Netherlands)
Helmut Gebhard (Munich, Germany)
Gerd Ruile (Regensburg, Germany)
1978 **Bertrand Monnet** (Paris, France)
John Darbourne (London, Great Britain)
Geoffrey Dark (London, Great Britain)
1979 **Hans Paul Bahrt** (Gottingen, Germany)
Dieter Desterlen (Hanover, Germany)
1980 **Louis Arretche** (Paris, France)
Hans Luz (Stuttgart, Germany)

UNESCO Prize for Architecture

UNITED NATIONS EDUCATIONAL, SCIENTIFIC AND CULTURAL ORGANIZATION
7 Place du Fontenoy, 75700 Paris, France (Tel: 577 16 10, Ext. 4004)

The UNESCO Prize for Architecture, which carries a $4,000 honorarium, is given every three years to a student or faculty member in architecture in UNESCO member states for a meritorious architectural project. The International Union of Architects conducts an international competition, from which the winner is selected.

1969 **Mitsuo Morozumi** (Japan), Social housing scheme
1972 **Vladimir Kirpitshev** (U.S.S.R.), Collective recreational facilities

1975 **Alka Shah and Vidyadhar Chavda** (India), Emergency habitat

1978 **Ana Sigrid Keiko Hartung Ashida, Carmen Esther Ortiz Marin, Carlos Enrique Ashida Cueto, Victor Manuel Perez Sandi y de Alba, Jose Rafael Ignacio Gutierrez Hermosillo de la Pena, Salvador de Alba Martinez** and **Gaspar Alarcon Orendain** (Mexico), Students at the Institute of Tecnologico de Estudios Superiores de Occidente, Guadalajara

Librarianship &

Information Sciences

Contents

Related Awards

Armed Forces Librarians Achievement Citation

AMERICAN LIBRARY ASSOCIATION
Armed Forces Librarians Section, 50 E. Huron St., Chicago, Ill. 60611 (312/944-6780)

The Armed Forces Librarians Achievement Citation is given annually for significant contributions to the development of armed forces library services and to organizations that encourage interest in libraries and reading. The AFLS Awards Committee selects the recipient.

1965 **Helen E. Fry**
1966 **Harry F. Cook**
1967 **Ruth Sheahan Howard**
1968 **Agnes Crawford**
1969 **Mary J. Carter**
1970 **Frances M. O'Halloran**
1971 **Dorothy Fayne**
1972 **Lucia Gordon**
1973 No award
1974 **Josephine Neil**
Robert W. Severance
1975 No award
1976 **Mariana J. Thurber**
1977 No award

Current status unknown

Besterman Medal

THE LIBRARY ASSN.
7 Ridgemount St., London WC1E 7AE, U.K. (01-636 7543)

The Besterman Medal annually honors an outstanding bibliography or guide to literature first published in the United Kingdom during the preceding year. Members of the association are eligible for selection by a panel of judges.

1970 **J.E. Arnott** and **J.W. Robinson**, *English Theatrical Literature*
1971 **Brenda White**, Sourcebook of planning information
1972 **G.H. Martin** and **Sylvia McIntyre**, *A Bibliography of British and Irish Municipal History*
1973 No award
1974 **E.A.R. Bush**, *Agriculture: A Bibliographical Guide*
1975 **Ralph Hyde**, *Printed Maps of Victorian London*
1976 **Central Statistical Office**, *Guide to Official Statistics No. 1*
1977 **E.W. Padwick**, *A Bibliography of Cricket*
1978 No award
1979 **Grainne Morby**, *Knowhow*, a guide to information, training and campaigning materials
J.D. Pearson, *South Asian Bibliography*
1980 Not available at press time

John Cotton Dana Library Public Relations Award

AMERICAN LIBRARY ASSOCIATION.
Library Administration and Management Div., 50 E. Huron, Chicago, Ill. 60611 (312/944-6780)

The John Cotton Dana Library Public Relations Award, cosponsored by the Association and the H.W. Wilson Co., recognizes effective public relations programs or projects, as documented by scrapbooks and non-print materials submitted for evaluation. A panel of library experts selects the recipients of the Dana Certificate.

1974 **Orlando, Fla., Public Library**
San Mateo, Calif., Public Library
Glendale, Calif., Public Library
Pomona, Calif., Public Library
Cortez, Colo., Public Library
Denver, Colo., Public Library
Indianapolis-Marion County, Ind., Public Library
Northwestern Regional Library, Elkin N.C.
Tulsa City-County Library, Okla.
Houston, Tex., Public Library
Vancouver Island Regional Library, Nanaimo, B.C., Canada
Metropolitan Toronto, Ont., Central Library, Canada
Connecticut State Library, Hartford, Conn.
University of Colorado Libraries, Boulder, Colo.
University of Texas at Austin Graduate School of Library Science
Oak Park and River Forest High School Library, Ill.
Whetstone High School Library, Columbus, Ohio
Elizabeth Redd Primary School Library, Richmond, Va.
Floyd E. Kellam High School Library, Virginia Beach, Va.
Clark AFB Library, Philippines
Scott AFB Library, Ill.
Fort Monmouth Post Library, N.J.
Minot AFB Library, N.D.
Lackland AFB Library, Tex.
Randolph AFB Library, Tex.
1975 **Greenville, S.C., County Library**
Glendale, Calif., Public Library
Vancouver Island Regional Library, Nanaimo, B.C., Canada
George S. Houston Memorial Library, Dothan, Ala.
Mono County Free Library, Bridgeport, Calif.
Pomona, Calif., Public Library
San Francisco, Calif., Public Library
Cortez, Colo., Public Library
Denver, Colo., Public Library
Hartford, Conn., Public Library
Broward County Library, Ft. Lauderdale, Fla.
Paducah, Ky. Public Library
Washington County Library System, Greenville, Miss.
East Meadow, N.Y., Public Library
Farmingdale, N.Y., Public Library
Troy-Miami County Public Library, Troy, Ohio
Salt Lake County Library System, Salt Lake City, Utah
Timberland Regional Library, Lacey, Wash.
Laramie County Library System, Cheyenne, Wyo.
York Regional Library, Fredricton, N.B., Canada
West Virginia Library Commission, Wheeling, W. Va.
South Carolina State Library, Charleston, S.C.

State University of New York at Buffalo
Alaska Library Assn.
U.S. Military Academy Library, West Point, N.Y.
Toledo, Ohio, Public Schools
Wheeler AFB Library, Ha.
Chanute AFB Library, Ill.
Clark AFB Library, Philippines
Randolph AFB Library, Tex.
Webb AFB Library, Tex.
Fletcher Library, U.S. Navy, Adak, Alas.

1976 **Pomona, Calif., Public Library**
Sacramento, Calif., Public Library
Cortez, Colo., Public Library
Pueblo Regional Library District, Pueblo, Colo.
Perry County Public Library, Hazard, Ky.
Clark County Library District, Las Vegas, Nev.
Buffalo & Erie County Public Library, Buffalo, N.Y.
Public Library of Charlotte and Mecklenburg County, N.C.
Beaver County Federated Library System, Monaca, Pa.
Salt Lake County Library System, Salt Lake City, Utah
Long Beach, Calif., Public Library
Los Angeles, Calif., Public Library
Santiago Library System, Orange, Calif.
S. Pasadena, Calif., Public Library
Evergreen, Colo., Regional Library
Danbury, Conn., Public Library
Broward County Library System, Ft. Lauderdale, Fla.
Orlando, Fla., Public Library
Atlanta, Ga., Public Library
Scott Candler Library, Decatur, Ga.
Iberville Parish Library, Plaquemine, La.
Cambridge, Mass., Public Library
Concord, Mass., Free Public Library
Watertown, Mass., Free Public Library
Detroit, Mich., Public Library
Mideastern Michigan Library Cooperative, Flint, Mich.
Pike-Amite Library System, McComb, Miss.
Madison, N.J., Public Library
Public Library of Youngstown and Mahoning County, Ohio
Pioneer Multi-County Library, Norman, Okla.
Fulton County Library Project, McConnellsburg, Pa.
Montgomery County-Norristown Public Library, Pa.
Greenville, S.C., County Library
Fairfax County Public Library, Springfield, Va.
Timberland Regional Library, Lacy, Wash.
Brown County Library, Green Bay, Wisc.
Madison, Wisc., Public Library
Bankstown, Australia, Municipal Library
Dartmouth Regional Library, N.S., Canada
West Virginia Library Commission, Wheeling, W. Va.
State Prison of Southern Michigan, Jackson, Mich.
Orange County Law Library, Santa Ana, Calif.
Maryland State Dept. of Education, Div. of Instructional Television
Seneca County Library Council, Tiffin, Ohio.
West Point Academy Library, N.Y.
Salem State College Library, Mass.
University of Denver Library, Colo.
Allegany Community College Library, Cumberland, Md.
Hampshire College Library Center, Amherst, Mass.
University of Wisconsin-Parkside Library, Kenosha, Wisc.
Greenwich, Conn., Public Schools
Monroe Junior High School Library, Columbus, Ohio
Azalea Middle School, St. Petersburg, Fla.
Board of Education of Baltimore County, Towson, Md.
Rocky Hill Library, Knoxville, Tenn.
Yongsan Library, U.S. Army Recreation Services Agency, Korea
Barksdale AFB Library, La.
Travis AFB Library, Calif.
K.I. Sawyer AFB Library, Mich.
Columbus AFB Library, Miss.
Minot AFB Library, N.D.

1977 **Public Library of Columbus and Franklin County,** Columbus, Ohio
Cherokee Regional Talking Book Center, La Fayette, Ga.
University of Texas Library at Austin
Travis AFB Library, Calif.
Birmingham, Ala., Public Library
Mobile, Ala., Public Library
Altadena, Calif., Library District
Sacramento, Calif., Public Library
Orlando, Fla., Public Library
Ewa Beach Community-School Library, Haw.
Makiki Library, Honolulu, Haw.
Ames, Iowa, Public Library
Watertown, Mass., Public Library
Bad Axe, Mich., Public Library
Clark County Library District, Las Vegas, Nev.
Buffalo and Erie County Public Library, N.Y.
Public Library of Charlotte and Mecklenburg County, Charlotte, N.C.
Public Library of Cincinnati and Hamilton County, Cincinnati, Ohio
El Paso, Tex., Public Library
Metropolitan Toronto Library, Ont., Canada
State Library of North Carolina
West Virginia Library Commission
Pennsylvania Library Assn.
Metropolitan Library Service Agency, St. Paul, Minn.
Mid-Bergen Federation of Libraries, N.J.
Hickam AFB Library, Haw.
K.I. Sawyer AFB Library, Mich.
Minot AFB Library, N.D.

1978 **Houston** (Tex.) **Public Library**
Milwaukee (Wisc.) **Public Library**
Timberland Regional Library, Olympia, Wash.
Broward County Library, Fort Lauderdale, Fla.
Bryant Library, Roslyn, N.Y.
Concord (Mass.) **Free Public Library**

Memorial Hall Library, Andover, Mass.
Mobile (Ala.) **Public Library**
Public Library of Columbus and **Franklin County**, Ohio
Seattle (Wash.) **Public Library**
Tacoma (Wash.) **Public Library**
Metropolitan Library Service Agency, St. Paul, Minn.
Mid-Hudson Library System, Poughkeepsie, N.Y.
National Library Service for the Blind and Physically Handicapped, Washington, D.C.
Florida Library Assn.
Lutheran Library Assn., Minneapolis, Minn.
Texas Library Assn.
Folke Bernadotte Memorial Library, Gustavus Adolphus College, St. Peter, Minn.
Biblioteca Artigas-Washington, Montivideo, Uruguay

1979 **Tacoma** (Wash.) **Public Library**
Tri-County Libraries, Portland, Ore.
U.S. Air Force Base Library, RAF Upper Heyford, U.K.
Mobile (Ala.) **Public Library**
Atlanta (Ga.) **Public Library**
Lincoln Library, Springfield, Ill.
Robbins Library, Arlington, Mass.
Bad Axe (Mich.) **Public Library**
Fiske Free Library, Claremont, N.H.
Somers (N.Y.) **Public Library**
Peoples Library, New Kensington, Pa.
Albany County Public Library, Laramie, Wyo.
Mideastern Michigan Library Cooperative, Flint, Mich.
Onondaga County Public Library, Syracuse, N.Y.
King County Library, Seattle, Wash.
Brown County Library, Green Bay, Wisc.
Lakeland Library Region, N. Battleford, Sask., Canada
Lutheran Church Library Assn., Minneapolis, Minn.
University of Oklahoma Health Sciences Center Library
Westfield (N.J.) **High School Library**
Travis AFB Library, Calif.
Nellis AFB Library, Nev.
U.S. Air Force Base Library, RAF Lakenheath, U.K.

1980 **Not available at press time**

Dartmouth Medal

AMERICAN LIBRARY ASSOCIATION
Reference and Adult Services Div., 50 E. Huron St., Chicago, Ill. 60611 (312/944-6780)

The Dartmouth Medal, which is of bronze designed by Rudolph Ruzicka, annually recognizes the creation of reference works judged as outstanding and significant. The work involved may be writing, compilation, editing or publishing books or other reference materials during the preceding year. A Dartmouth Medal Awards Committee selects the winner.

1975 **New England Board of Higher Education,** Northeast Academic Science Information Center Wellsley, Mass

1976 **No award**
1977 **Lester J. Cappon,** *Atlas of Early American History: The Revolutionary Era 1760-1790*
1978 **Benjamin B. Wolman,** Editor-in-Chief, *International Encyclopedia of Psychiatry, Psychology and Neurology*
1979 **Warren T. Reich,** Editor, *Encyclopedia of Bioethics*
1980 **No award**

Hammond Inc. Library Award

AMERICAN LIBRARY ASSOCIATION
50 E. Huron St., Chicago, Ill. 60611 (312/944-6780)

The $500 Hammond Inc. Library Award was awarded annually to a librarian or a library in a community or school in recognition of an unusual contribution of lasting value for effective use or increased interest in maps, atlases and globes by children and young people. The award is no longer given.

1963 **Clara E. LeGear**
1964 **No award**
1965 **James M. Day**
1966 **No award**
1967 **No award**
1968 **Ellen Freeman**
1969 **No award**
1970 **No award**
1971 **University of Chicago Laboratory Schools High School Library**
1972 **Patterson Library,** Westfield, N.Y.
1973 **Betty Ryder,** Pasadena Public Library, Calif.
1974 **No award**
1975 **No award**
1976 **Gail Borden Library District,** Elgin, Ill., for their work with the LaSalle Expedition II
1977 **Upper Hudson Library Federation,** Albany, N.Y.

Melvil Dewey Award

AMERICAN LIBRARY ASSOCIATION
50 E. Huron, St., Chicago, Ill. 60611 (312/944-6780)

The Melvil Dewey Award, which consists of a medal and citation, is given annually for recent professional creative achievement in such fields as library management, training, cataloging and classification. A five-person jury appointed by the ALA Awards Committee chairperson selects the winner.

1953 **Ralph R. Shaw**
1954 **Herman H. Fussler**
1955 **Maurice F. Tauber**
1956 **Norah Albanell MacColl**
1957 **Wyllis E. Wright**
1958 **Janet S. Dickson**
1959 **Benjamin A. Custer**
1960 **Harriet E. Howe**
1961 **Julia C. Pressey**
1962 **Leon Carnovsky**
1963 **Frank B. Rogers**
1964 **John W. Cronin**
1965 **Bertha Margaret Frick**
1966 **Lucile Morsch**
1967 **Walter Herbert Kaiser**
1968 **Jesse H. Shera**
1969 **William S. Dix**

1970 **Joseph Treyz**
1971 **William J. Welsh**
1972 **Jerrold Orne**
1973 **Virginia Lacy Jones**
1974 **Robert B. Downs**
1975 **No award**
1976 **Louis Round Wilson**
1977 **Seymour Lubetsky**
1978 **Frederick C. Kilgour**
1979 **Russell E. Bidlack**
1980 **Robert D. Stueart**

Robert B. Downs Award

UNIVERSITY OF ILLINOIS GRADUATE SCHOOL OF LIBRARY SCIENCE
410 David Kinley Hall, 1407 W. Gregory St., Urbana, Ill. 61801 (217/333-3280)

The Robert B. Downs Award is given for outstanding contributions to the cause of intellectual freedom in libraries by vote of the school's faculty. The award is given annually and consists of $500 and a certificate.

1969 **LeRoy Charles Merritt,** Dean, School of Librarianship, University of Oregon (Eugene)
1970 **Orrin Dow,** Public Library, Farmingdale, N.Y.
1971 **President's Commission on Obscenity & Pornography**
1972 **John T. Carey,** St. Mary's College (St. Mary's City, Md.)
1973 **Alex P. Allain,** Attorney, Jeannerette, La.
1974 **Everett T. Moore,** University of California at Los Angeles
1975 **No award**
1976 **Eli Oboler,** Idaho State University (Pocatello)
1977 **Irene Turin,** Island Trees High School (Levittown, N.Y.)
1978 **Judith F. Krug**, Freedom to Read Foundatin
1979 **Ralph E. McCoy**, publications documenting freedom of the press
1980 **Jeanne Layton**, for courageous fight in a censorship battle in Davis County, Utah

Facts on File Award

AMERICAN LIBRARY ASSOCIATION
Reference and Adult Services Div., 50 E. Huron St., Chicago, Ill. 60611 (312/944-6780)

The Facts on File Award annually honors a librarian for efforts to make current affairs more meaningful to an adult audience in an informal setting. A five-member committee selects the winner.

1980 **Harva Sheeler**, Automated Legislative Information Service, Fairfax County, Va.

Grolier Foundation Award

AMERICAN LIBRARY ASSOCIATION
50 E. Huron St., Chicago, Ill. 60611 (312/944-6780)

The $1,000 Grolier Foundation Award is given annually to a community or school librarian for unusual contributions to the stimulation and guidance of reading by children and young people. A five-person jury appointed by the ALA Awards Committee chairperson selects the winner from nominations received.

1954 **Siddie Joe Johnson**
1955 **Charlemae Rollins**
1956 **Georgia Sealoff**
1957 **Margaret Alexander Edwards**
1958 **Mary Peacock Douglas**
1959 **Evelyn Sickels**
1960 **Margaret Scoggin**
1961 **Della Louise McGregor**
1962 **Alice McGuire**
1963 **Caroline W. Field**
1964 **Inger Boye**
1965 **Sarah Lewis Jones**
1966 **Mildred L. Batchelder**
1967 **Lura E. Crawford**
1968 **Augusta Baker**
1969 **Anne R. Izard**
1970 **Julia Losinski**
1971 **Sara Siebert**
1972 **Ronald W. McCracken**
1973 **Eleanor Kidder**
1974 **Regina U. Minudri**
1975 **Jane B. Wilson**
1976 **Virginia Haviland**
1977 **Elizabeth Fast**
1978 **Dorothy C. McKenzie**
1979 **Anne Pellowski**
1980 **Mable Williams**

Grolier National Library Week Grant

AMERICAN LIBRARY ASSOCIATION
National Library Week Committee, 50 E. Huron, St., Chicago, Ill. 60611 (312/944-6780)

The Grolier National Library Week Grant of $1,000 is presented annually to the state library association submitting the best proposal to promote library services. The ALA National Library Week Committee selects the winner during the Association's mid-winter conference.

1975 **West Virginia Library Assn.,** "Information Power" (public relations program)
1976 **Illinois Library Assn.,** "Librarians to the People" (speaker's bureau project)
1977 **New Jersey Library Assn.,** "Influencing City Hall" (public relations program)
1978 **Mississippi Library Assn.**
1979 **Utah Library Assn.**
1980 **South Carolina Library Assn.**

Library Research Round Table Award

AMERICAN LIBRARY ASSOCIATION
Library Research Round Table, 50 E. Huron St., Chicago, Ill. 60611 (312/944-6780)

The $400 Library Research Round Table award is given annually for a piece of completed research in the area of library and information science, based on the decision of a selection committee which judges papers submitted to it.

1975 **Robert L. Burr,** "Toward a General Theory of Circulation"

Maurice P. Marchant, "University Libraries as Economic Systems" and "Patterns of Staff Involvement in University Library Management"
1976 **James D. Baughman,** "Toward a Structural Approach to Collection Development"
Ruth Wender, Esther Fruehauf, Marilyn Vent and Connie Wilson, "The Determination of Clinician Continuing Education Needs from a Literature Study Search"
1977 **Herbert S. White and Karen Hasenjager,** "Some Measurements of the Impact of the Rapid Growth of Library Doctoral Programs'
Robert W. Burns, Jr., "Library Performance Measures as Seen in the Descriptive Statistics Generated by a Computer Managed Circulation System"
1978 **Wayne A. Wiegand,** "Scholarly research in American Library History: Herbert Putnam's Appointment as Librarian of Congress as a Test Case"
1979 **Charles R. McClure,** "Preceived Values of Information Sources Library Decision-Making"
Pauline Wilson, "Librarians and their Stereotype"
1980 **George D'Elia,** "The Development and Testing of a Conceptual Model of Public Library User Behavior"

Joseph W. Lippincott Award

AMERICAN LIBRARY ASSOCIATION
50 E. Huron St., Chicago, Ill. 60611 (312/944-6780)

The Joseph W. Lippincott Award, consisting of $1,000, a medal and a citation, is given annual to a librarian for outstanding participation in the activities of professional associations, notable professional writings and other significant activities. A jury appointed by the ALA chairperson selects the recipients from nominations received.

1938 **Mary U. Rothrock**
1939 **Herbert Putnam**
1940 **No awards**
1948 **Carl H. Milam**
1949 **Harry M. Lydenberg**
1950 **Halsey W. Wilson**
1951 **Helen Haines**
1952 **Carl Vitz**
1953 **Marian C. Manley**
1954 **Jack Dalton**
1955 **Emerson Greenaway**
1956 **Ralph A. Ulveling**
1957 **Flora Belle Ludington**
1958 **Carleton B. Joeckel**
1959 **Essae Martha Culver**
1960 **Verner W. Clapp**
1961 **Joseph L. Wheeler**
1962 **David H. Clift**
1963 **Frances W. Henne**
1964 **Robert B. Downs**
1965 **Frances Clarke Sayers**
1966 **Keyes DeWitt Metcalf**
1967 **Edmon Low**
1968 **Lucile Nix**
1969 **Germaine Krettek**
1970 **Paul Howard**
1971 **William S. Dix**
1972 **Guy Lyle**
1973 **Jesse H. Shera**
1974 **Jerrold Orne**
1975 **Leon Carnovsky**
1976 **Lester Asheim**
1977 **Virginia Lacy Jones**
1978 **Henry T. Drennan**
1979 **Helen H. Lyman**
1980 **E.J. Josey**

Margaret Mann Citation

AMERICAN LIBRARY ASSOCIATION
Resources and Technical Services Division,

50 E. Huron St., Chicago, Ill. 60611 (312/944-6780, Ext. 228)

The Margaret Mann Citation is awarded annually for outstanding achievement in cataloging and/or classification. A jury selects the winner.

1951 **Lucile M. Morsch,** "Rules for Descriptive Cataloging"
1952 **Marie Louise Prevost,** Promotion and establishment of the *Journal of Cataloging and Classification*
1953 **Maurice F. Tauber,** Planning, organizing, conducting and reporting on subject analysis of library materials
1954 **Pauline A. Seely,** Outstanding participation in national, regional and local activities
1955 **Seymour Lubetzky,** Scholarly analysis and critiques that stimulated and influenced revision of cataloging rules
1956 **Susan G. Akers,** Author, teacher, leader of cataloging activities in Southeast and throughout U.S.
1957 **David J. Haykin,** Subject cataloging and classification
1958 **Esther J. Piercy,** Editor, *Journal of Cataloguing and Classification,* and its successor, *Library Resources & Technical Services*
1959 **Andrew D. Osborn,** Contributions to cataloging
1960 **M. Ruth MacDonald,** Distinguished service to field
1961 **John W. Cronin,** Centralized cataloging and bibliographic services
1962 **Wyllis E. Wright,** Leadership in securing wide acceptance here and abroad of cataloging principles
1963 **Arthur H. Chaplin,** "Draft Statement of Principles," basis for international agreement
1964 **Catherine MacQuarrie,** Contributions to development of mechanicially produced catalog in book form
1965 **Laura C. Colvin,** *Cataloging Sampler*
1966 **F. Bernice Field,** Scholarly and practical leadership in descriptive cataloging
1967 **C. Sumner Spalding,** *Anglo-American Cataloging Rules*
1968 **Paul S. Dunkin,** Contributions to philosophy and techniques of organizing recorded human knowledge
1969 **Katharine L. Ball,** International activities in cataloging, teaching, publication and participation in professional associations
1970 **S.R. Ranganathan,** Colon classification
1971 **Henriette D. Avram,** Contributions to promotion of standard format for bibliographic records in machine-readable form
1972 **Edmond L. Applebaum,** Contribution to National Program for Acquisitions and Cataloging
1973 **Doralyn J. Hickey,** Contributions to all aspects of cataloging and classification
1974 **Frederick G. Kilgour,** Organizing and putting into operation the first practical centralized computer bibliographic center
1975 **Margaret W. Ayrault,** Leadership in cataloging and classification
1976 **Eva Verona,** *Corporate Headings*

1977 **Phyllis A. Richmond,** Teaching of cataloging and classification, scholarly publication and contributions to professional associations

Current status unknown

McColvin Medal

THE LIBRARY ASSOCIATION
7 Ridgmount St., London WC1E, 7AE, U.K. (01-636 7543)

The McColvin Medal is given annually for the most outstanding reference book published during the preceding year. A committee selects the winner.

1970 **I.G. Anderson**, *Councils, Committees and Boards: A Handbook of Advisory, Consultative, Executive and Similar Bodies in British Public Life*
1971 **Walter Shepherd**, *Shepherd's Glossary of Graphic Signs and Symbols*
1972 **Arthur Jacobs**, *Music Yearbook 1972/73*
1973 **No award**
1974 **W.F. Maunder**, *Reviews of United Kingdom Statistical Sources*
1975 **Peter Kennedy**, *Folksongs of Britain and Ireland*
1976 **C.G. Allen**, *A Manual of European Languages for Librarians*
1977 **No award**
1978 **No award**
1979 **No award**

Isidore Gilbert Mudge Citation

AMERICAN LIBRARY ASSOCIATION
Reference and Adult Services Div., 50 E. Huron St., Chicago, Ill. 60611 (312/944-6780)

The Isidore Gilbert Mudge Citation is awarded annually to an individual for distinguished contribution to reference librarianship, as evidenced by an imaginative and constructive program in a particular library, the writing of a significant book or articles in the reference field, active participation in professional associations, teaching or any other noteworthy accomplish- ment. The Isidore Gilbert Mudge Citation Committee selects the winner.

1959 **Mary Neill Barton**
1960 **Constance Mabel Winchell**
1961 **Edith M. Coulter**
1962 **Frances Neel Cheney**
1963 **Mable Conat**
1964 **Ruth Walling**
1965 **Katharine G. Harris**
1966 **Frances B. Jenkins**
1967 **Louis Shores**
1968 **Thomas S. Shaw**
1969 **No award**
1970 **Theodore Besterman**
1971 **James Bennet Childs**
1972 **Thomas J. Galvin**
1973 **William A. Katz**
1974 **Florence E. Blakely**
1975 **Jean L. Connor**
1976 **John Neal Waddell**
1977 **Bohdan S. Wynar**
1978 **G. Edward Wall**
1979 **Henry J. Dubester**
1980 **Hylda Kamisar**

Eunice Rockwell Oberly Memorial Award

ASSOIATION OF COLLEGE AND RESEARCH LIBRARIES
50 E. Huron St., Chicago, Ill 60611 (312/944-6780)

The Eunice Rockwell Oberly Memorial Award is given biennially for a research source.

1979 **James B. Beard**, **Harriet J. Beard** and **David P. Martin**, *Turfgrass: Bibliography from 1672-1972*

Esther J. Piercy Award

AMERICAN LIBRARY ASSOCIATION
Resources and Technical Services Div., 50 E. Huron St., Chicago, Ill. 60611 (312/944-6780, Ext. 228)

The Esther J. Piercy Award is given for outstanding promise in the field of technical services by a librarian with no more than 10 years of professional experience. A jury annually selects the recipient of the citation which signifies this honor.

1969 **Richard M. Dougherty,** Research, teaching and administrative leadership
1970 **John B. Corbin,** Promise as an organizer, supervisor, consultant, author and editor
1971 **John Phillip Immroth,** Research, writing and teaching leadership
1972 **Carol A. Nemeyer,** *Scholarly Reprint Publishing in the United States*
1973 **Glen A. Zimmerman,** Library of Congress Cataloging in Publication (CIP) program
1974 **No award**
1975 **John D. Byrum, Jr.,** Talent for understanding and developing cataloging rules
1976 **Ruth L. Tighe,** Leadership, innovation and expedition in bibliographic exchange
1977 **No award**
1978 **S. Michael Malinconico,** Work in library automation
1979 **Pamela Darling,** Work in preservation of library materials
1980 **Nancy Olson,** Work in organization and cataloging of audio-visual materials

Prize for Bibliography

INTERNATIONAL LEAGUE OF ANTIQUARIAN BOOKSELLERS
c/o Dr. Frieder Kocher-Benzing, Rathenaustrasse 21, D-7000, Stuttgart, Federal Republic of Germany

The Prize for Bibliography, which carries a $1,000 honorarium, is awarded triennially for a learned bibliographical work or research into the history of books or typography. The work must be published in a language "which is universally used." A six-person panel selects the winner.

1962 **I.C. Koeman**, *Atlantes Neerlandici*
1966 **J. Peeters-Fontainas**, *Bibliographie des Impressions espagnoles des Pays-Bas meridionaux*
1968 **Wutze** and **Lotte Hellinga**, *The Fifteenth Century Printing Types of the Low Countries*
1971 **Claus Nissen**, *Die Zoologische Buchillustration*
1974 **C. William C. Miller**, *Benjamin Franklin's Philadelphia Printing*

1977 **Blanche Henrey,** *British Botanical and Horticultural Literature Before 1800*
1980 **Not available at press time**

Herbert Putnam Honor Fund Award

AMERICAN LIBRARY ASSOCIATION
50 E. Huron St., Chicago, Ill. 60611 (312/944-6780)

The $500 Herbert Putnam Honor Fund Award is given approximately every five years to an American librarian as a grant-in-aid for travel, writing or other use that might improve his or her service to the library profession. The ALA Awards Committee selects the winner from nominations received.

1949 **Carleton B. Joeckel**
1954 **Louis Round Wilson**
1963 **Mary V. Gaver**
1972 **Michael H. Harris**
1975 **Wayne A. Weigand**
1978 **Isabel Schon**

Robinson Medal

THE LIBRARY ASSOCIATION
7 Ridgemont St., London WC1E 7AE, U.K. (01-636-7543)

The Robinson Medal is given biennially for originality and inventiveness by librarians and others in devising new and improved methods in library technology or administration. A selection panel chooses the winner, who may be an individual or company or company and must be an association member.

1968 **Mansell Information/Publishing Ltd.**, Development of automatic abstracting camera for producing book catalogues from library cards or other sequential material
1970 **Frank Gurney**, Automatic Library Systems Ltd. Computer book-charging
1972 **University of Lancaster Library Research**, Development of simulation games in education for library management
1974 **No award**
1976 **No award**
1978 **No award**

Current status unknown

Ralph R. Shaw Award

AMERICAN LIBRARY ASSOCIATION
50 E. Huron St., Chicago, Ill. 60611 (312/944-6780)

The $500 Ralph R. Shaw Award for Library Literature is given to an American librarian for library literature published during the preceding three years. A jury of five appointed by the chairperson of the ALA Awards Committee makes the selection from nominations received.

1960 **Marjorie Fiske Lowenthal,** *Book Selection and Censorship*
1961 **No award**
1962 **Sarah K. Vann,** *Training for Librarianship Before 1923*
1963 **Joseph L. Wheeler and Herbert Goldhor,** *Practical Administration of Public Libraries*
1964 **Edward G. Holley,** *Charles Evans, American Bibliographer*
1965 **Roberta Bowler,** *Local Public Library Administration*
1966 **Keyes DeWitt Metcalf,** *Planning Academic and Research Library Buildings*
1967 **No award**
1968 **Lester Asheim,** *Librarianship in the Developing Countries*
1969 **Ralph McCoy,** *Freedom of the Press: An Annotated Bibliography*
1970 **Lowell Martin,** *Library Response to Urban Change*
1971 **Irene Braden Hoadley,** *The Undergraduate Library*
1972 **No award**
1973 **No award**
1974 **Jesse H. Shera,** *Foundations of Education for Librarianship*
1975 **No award**
1976 **Herman Fussler,** *Research Libraries and Technology*
1977 **Kathleen Molz,** *Federal Policy and Library Support*
1978 **Frederick W. Lancaster**
1979 **Joan K. Marshall**
1980 **Rhea J. Rubin,** *Using Bibliotherapy* and *Bibliotherapy Sourcebook*

Resources Scholarship Award

American Library Association
Resources and Technical Services Division, 50 E. Huron St., Chicago, Ill. 60611 (312/944-6780, Ext. 228)

The Resources Scholarship Award, which carries a $1,000 honorarium, is given for a monograph, published article or original paper on acquisitions pertaining to college and university libraries. A jury selects the winner.

1976 **Hendrik Edelman, Carol Nemeyer and Sandra Paul,** "The Library Market: A Special Publisher's Weekly Survey"
1977 **Herbert White,** "Publishers, Libraries and Costs of Journal Subscriptions in Times of Funding Retrenchment"

Current status unknown

Trustee Citation

AMERICAN LIBRARY TRUSTEE ASSOCIATION
50 E. Huron St., Chicago, Ill. 60611 (312/944-6780)

The American Library Trustee Association administers the Trustee Citation, which is given annually by the ALA for distinguished service to library development on any level and involving libraries of any size. A five-member jury selects recipients from nominations by library boards, individual library trustees, station library extensions or various other organizations in the field.

1941 **Rush Barton**
William Elder Marcus
1942 **James Oliver Modisette**
Charles Whedbee
1943 **Marian Doren Tomlinson**
Ora L. Wildermuth
1944 **Lenore W. Smith**

B. F. Coen
1945 M. M. Harris
Lucy Wilson Errett
1946 James J. Weadock
Mrs. James E. Price
1947 Mary E. Frayser
Thomas J. McKaig
1948 Emma V. Baldwin
Thomas J. Porro
1949 Julia Brown Asplund
Robert B. Tunstall
1950 Hasel M. Wills
Anthony Joseph Cerrato
1951 Charles B. Farnsley
Milton G. Farris
1952 A. J. Quigley
Harold J. Bailey
1953 Jacob M. Lashley
Frank A. Smith
1954 Mrs. Merlin M. Moore
Joseph B. Fleming
1955 Mrs. George Rodney Wallace
Ralph D. Remley
1956 Mrs. Otis G. Wilson
Eugene A. Burdick
1957 J. N. Heiskell
Stephen M. Pronko
1958 Mrs. J. Henry Mohr
Cecil U. Edmonds
1959 Francis Bergan
Alan Neil Schneider
1960 Mrs. Emil G. Bloedow
Thomas Dreier
1961 Paul D. Brown
Walter Varner, Jr.
1962 S. L. Townsend
Mrs. Raymond A. Young
1963 Kenneth U. Blass
John E. Fogarty
1964 Mrs. Weldon Lynch
Mrs. Samuel Berg
1965 Mrs. Henry Steffens
Jacob A. Meckstroth
1966 Mrs. Bruce "C'Ceal" Coombs
Charles E. Reid
1967 Mrs. J. R. Sweasy
James L. Love
1968 Raymond Holden
John Bennett Shaw
1969 Rachel Gross
Alex P. Allain
1970 George W. Coen
John Veblen
1971 Jacqueline Enochs
Jean Smith
1972 Story Birdseye
Mrs. V. Kelsey Carlson
1973 Alice Ihrig
Carroll K. Shakelford
1974 Eldred C. Wolzien
R. A. Cox
1975 Marie Cole
Dorothy E. Rosen
1976 Elizabeth F. Ruffner
James A. Hess
1977 C. E. Campbell Beall
Daniel W. Casey

SPECIAL CITATION:

1977 President Jimmy Carter

Current Status Unknown

Wheatley Medal

THE LIBRARY ASSOCIATION
7 Ridgemont St., London WC1E 7AE, U.K. (01-636 7543)

The Wheatley Medal is presented annually for an outstanding index first published in the United Kingdom during the previous three years. Members of the Library Association, the Society of Indexers, publishers and others are eligible for selection by a panel.

1962 **Michael Maclagan**, *Clemency Canning*
1963 **J.M. Dickie**, *How to Catch Trout*
1964 **Guy Parsloe**, *The Warden's Accounts of the Worshipful Company of Founders of the City of London*
1965 **Alison Quinn**, *The Principal Navigations of Voyages and Discoveries of the English Nation*
1966 **No award**
1967 **G. Norman Knight**, *Winston S. Churchill Vol 2*
1968 **Doreen Blake** and **Ruth Bowden**, *Journal of Anatomy, First 100 Years, 1866-1966*
1969 **James Thornton**, *The Letters of Charles Dickens*, Vol. 2
1970 **E.L.C. Mullins**, *A Guide to the Historical and Archaelogical Publications of Societies in England and Wales, 1901-1933*
1971 **No award**
1972 **No award**
1973 **K. Boodson**, *Index to Non-Ferrous Metals*
1974 **C.C. Banwell**, *Encyclopaedia of Forms and Precedents*
1975 **M.D. Anderson**, *Copy-Editing*
1976 **John A. Vickers**, *The Works of John Wesley: The Appeals to Men of Reason and Religion and Certain Related Open Letters, Vol. 11*
1977 **T. Rowland Pavel** *Archaeologia Cambrensis 1901-60*
1978 **No award**
1979 **Pitman Medical**, *Circulation of the Blood*

H.W. Wilson Co. Library Periodical Award

AMERICAN LIBRARY ASSOCIATION
50 E. Huron St., Chicago, Ill. 60611 (312/944-6780)

The $250 H.W. Wilson Co. Library Periodical Award is given annually to a periodical published by a local, state or regional library group in the U.S. or Canada which has made an outstanding contribution to librarianship. A jury selected by the chairperson of the ALA Awards Committee chooses the winner.

1961 ***The California Librarian,*** California Library Association, William R. Eshelman, Editor
1962 ***North Country Libraries,*** New Hampshire State Library and the Vermont Free Public Library Commission, Louise Hazelton, Editor
1963 ***Bay State Librarian,*** Massachusetts Library Association, John Berry, Editor
1964 ***The California Librarian,*** California Library Association, Miller Madden, Editor
1965 ***PNLA Quarterly,*** Pacific Northwest Library Association, Eli M. Oboler, Editor

1966 ***Ohio Library Association Bulletin,*** Gerald Shields, Editor

1967 ***British Columbia Library Quarterly,*** Alan Woodland, Editor

1968 ***The California Librarian,*** California Library Association, Richard D. Johnson, Editor

1969 ***Missouri Library Association Quarterly,*** Missouri Library Association, John Gordon Burke, Editor

1970 ***Synergy,*** sponsored by Bay Area Reference Center, San Francisco Public Library, Celeste West, Editor

1971 ***Texas Library Journal,*** Texas Library Association, Mary Pound, Editor

1972 ***Synergy,*** sponsored by Bay Area Reference Center, San Francisco Public Library, Celeste West, Editor

1973 ***Illinois Libraries,*** Illinois State Library, Springfield, Irma Bostian, Editor

1974 ***Ohio Library Association Bulletin,*** Robert F. Cayton, Editor

1975 ***PNLA Quarterly,*** Pacific Northwest Library Association, Richard Moore, Editor

1976 ***Hennepin County Library Cataloging Bulletin,*** Edina, Minn., Sanford Berman, Editor

1977 ***Utah Libraries,*** Blaine H. Hall, Editor

1978 ***Documentation et Bibliotheques***, Quebec, Canada

1979 ***Southeastern Librarian***, Southeastern Library Association, Leland Park, Editor

1980 ***PLA Bulletin***, Pennsylvania Library Association, Mary Stillman, Editor

Humani

ties & Social Sciences

Contents

Related Awards

European Essay Prize

FONDATION CHARLES VEILLON
Route de Crissier, 1030 Bussigny-pres-Lausanne, Switzerland (021-89-29-11)

Te European Essay Prize, which is accompanied by a 10,000-Swiss-franc honorarium, annually honors a published essay on the culture of Europe, including criticism or commentary on contemporary societies, their way of living and their ideologies. A jury selects the winner.

1975 **Jacques Ellul**, *Trahison de I'Occident*
1976 **Ernst F. Schumacher**, *Small is Beautiful*
1977 **Alexandre Zinoviev**, *Les Hauteurs Beantes*
1078 **Roger Caillois**, *Le Fleuve Alphee*
1979 **Manes Sperber**, *Churban, oder die unfassbare Gewissheit*
1980 **Leszek Kolakowski**, body of work

Hegel-Preis

LANDESHAUPTSTADT STUTTGART
Postfach 161, 7000 Stuttgart 1, Federal Republic of Germany (0711-216-6703)

The Hegel-Preis, named for philosopher George Wilhelm Friedrich Hegel, is awarded triennially for outstanding contributions to the humanities, alternately to a philosopher and to a general scholar in the humanities. Originally worth 10,000 marks, the honorarium of this award was raised to 20,000 marks beginning with the next honor, to be given in 1982. A committee selects the winner.

1970 **Bruno Snell**, Ancient philology
1973 **Jurgen Habermas**, Philosophy and sociology
1976 **Sir Ernest Gombar**, Art history and director, Warburg Institute (London)
1979 **Hans-Georg Gadamer**, Philosophy

Jefferson Lecture

NATIONAL ENDOWMENT FOR THE HUMANITIES
805 15th St. NW, Washington, D.C. 20506 (202/724-0256)

The Fefferson Lecture is the highest award given by the federal government outside of the world of science. The honor is bestowed annually to an individual for distinguished intellectual achievement and carries a $1,000 honorarium.

1972 **Lionel Trilling**
1973 **Erik Eriksen**
1974 **Robert Penn Warren**
1975 **Paul Freund**
1976 **John Hope Franklin**
1977 **Saul Bellow**
1978 **C. Vann Woodward**
1979 **Edward Shils**
1980 **No award**

Huxley Memorial Lecture and Medal
Curl Lecture
Henry Myers Lecture
Rivers Memorial Medal

ROYAL ANTHROPOLOGICAL INSTITUTE OF GREAT BRITAIN AND IRELAND
56 Queen Anne St., London W1M 9LA, United Kingdom (01-486-6832)

The Huxley Memorial Lecture and Medal is the Institute's highest honor in the field. A special council selects the recipient of the annual medal. Part of the award is publication of the lecture.

1960 **S. Lothrop**
1961 **A.E. Mourant**
1962 **A.D. Garrod**
1963 **E.E. Evans-Pritchard**
1964 **G.H.R. Von Konigswald**
1965 **C. Levi-Strauss**
1966 **J.E.S. Thompson**
1967 **S.L. Washburn**
1968 **G.H. Riviere**
1969 **I. Schapera**
1970 **C.D. Forde**
1971 **G.P. Murdock**
1972 **L.L. Cavilli-Sforza**
1973 **K. Wachsmann**
1974 **J.D. Clark**
1975 **G. Reichel-Dolmatoff**
1976 **M.N. Srinivas**
1977 **M. Fortes**
1978 **J.S. Weiner**
1979 **Gordon Willey**
1980 **Sir Edmund Leach**

The Curl Lecture consists of a fifty-guinea honorarium plus publication of the lecture, which is preferably in the fields of physical anthropology, archeology, material culture or linguistics by an anthropologist under 40 years of age. A council selects the winner of this biennial honor.

1963 **D.F.B. Roberts**
1965 **Anthony Forge**
1967 **G. Ainsworth Harrison**
1969 **Peter Ucko**
1971 **Warwick Bray**
1973 **Caroline Humphrey**
1975 **A.J. Boyce**
1977 **Richard E. Leakey**
1978 **No award**
1979 **David Parkin**
1980 **John Baines**

The Henry Myers Lecture honors a noteworthy lecture on some aspect of the role of religion in society with publication. A council selects the winner of this biennial honor.

1945 **A.R. Radcliffe-Brown**
1948 **Raymond Firth**
1950 **E.O. James**
1952 **E.D. Smith**
1954 **E.E. Evans-Pritchard**
1956 **Dorothy Emmett**
1958 **Isaac Schapera**
1960 **Meyer Fortes**
1962 **Claude Levi-Strauss**
1964 **Joseph Needham**

1966 Edmund Leach
1968 Audrey Richards
1970 Louis Dumont
1972 Mary Douglas
1974 C. von Furer-Haimendorf
1976 Jean La Fontaine
1978 No award
1980 Rodney Needham

The Rivers Memorial Medal is awarded annually for a recent body of published work on social, physical or cultural anthropology or archeology. A council selects the winner.

1924 A.C. Haddon
1925 C.G. Seligman
1926 Edward Westermarck
1927 Sir W. Baldwin Spencer
1928 Sidney H. Ray
1929 John Henry Hutton
1930 Bronislaw Malinowski
1931 E.W. Smith
1932 Melville William Seligman
1933 Brenda Zara Seligman
1934 Gertrude Caton-Thompson
1935 A.M. Hocart
1936 Peter H. Buck
1937 Edward Evan Evans-Pritchard
1938 Dorothy Ann Elizabeth Garrod
1939 Isaac Schapera
1940 Raymond Firth
1941 Diamond Jenness
1942 James Philip Mills
1943 Beatrice Mary Blackwood
1944 James Hornell
1945 J. Eric Thompson
1946 Ian J. Hogbin
1947 Meyer Fortes
1948 Verrier Elwin
1949 C. von Furer-Haimendorf
1950 S.F. Nadel
1951 R.F. Fortune
1952 L.S.B. Leakey
1953 Donald F. Thomson
1954 Max Gluckman
1955 M.N. Srinivas
1956 Daryll Forde
1957 Phyllis M. Kaberry
1958 E.R. Leach
1959 J.A. Barnes
1960 J.C. Mitchell
1961 Hilda Kuper
1962 H. Lehman
1963 Derek Stenning
1964 Adrian Mayer
1965 V. Turner
1966 Philip Gulliver
1967 Philip Mayer and N.A. Barnicot
1968 Eric Higgs and Mary Douglas
1969 J.S. Weiner
1970 Rodney Needham
1971 No award
1972 J. Waechter
1973 S.J. Tambiah
1974 D.F. Pocock
1975 J.R. Goody
1976 A. Strathern and M. Strathern
1977 Peter Ucko
1978 Phillip J. Robins
1979 Colin Renfrew
1980 Abner Cohen

Gold Medal
Olivia James Traveling Fellowship
Harriet Pomerance Fellowship

ARCHAEOLOGICAL INSTITUTE OF AMERICA
53 Park Place, New York, N.Y. 10007 (212/732-6677)

The Gold Medal for Distinguished Archaeological Achievement is presented annually to a member of the Institute for field work, teaching, publication or a combination of these.

1965 **Carl William Blegen,** Professor Emeritus of Classical Archaeology, University of Cincinnati and excavator of Troy and the Palace of Nestor at Pylos
1965 **Hetty Goldman,** Professor Emeritus, Institute for Advanced Study in Princeton and pioneer woman excavator in Greece and Near East
1967 **William Foxwell Albright,** Professor Emeritus of Near Eastern Studies (Semantic Languages), Johns Hopkins University
1968 **Gisela Marie Augusta Richter,** scholar and curator
1969 **Oscar Theodore Broncer,** discoverer of the site of the Isthmian Games and the Sanctuary Poseidon at the Isthmus of Corinth
Rhys Carpenter, Professor Emeritus of Clasical Archaeology, Bryn Mawr College
William Bell Dinsmoor, author and past president of the Archaeological Institute of America
1970 **George Emmanuel Mylonas,** Washington University, director of archaeological excavation at Aghios, Kosmos, Eleusis and Mycenae
1971 **Robert John Braidwood,** archaeologist, anthropologist and author in Near Eastern prehistorical studies
1972 **Homer Armstrong Thompson,** expert on the topography and monuments of ancient Athens
1973 **Gordon Randolph Wiley,** New World archaeologist
1974 **Margaret Bieber,** authority on the archaeology of the Greek and Roman theater, ancient dress and the sculpture of the Hellenistic Age
1975 **Eugene Vanderpool,** American School of Classical Studies at Athens, authority on the antiquities and the topography of Greece
1976 **Lucy Shoe Merritt,** scholar, editor and teacher
1977 **Edith Porada,** Columbia University
1978 **George M.A. Hanfmann,** Harvard University
1979 **Dows Dunham,** Curator Emeritus of Egyptian Art, Museum of Fine Arts, Boston
1980 **John L. Caskey,** University of Cincinnati

The Olivia James Traveling Fellowship, carrying a maximum stipend of $7,000, is given each academic year for a proposed project or plan of study in Greece, the Aegean Islands, Sicily, southern Italy or Asia Minor for studies in classics, sculpture, architecture, archeology or history.

1975 Eric Hostetter
1976 Michal Eisman
Trudy S. Kawami
1977 Patricia M. Bikai
Ira S. Mark
1978 Irene F. Bald
Susan I. Rotroff
1979 Margaret Miles
1980 Sarah P. Morris
Helayna I. Thickpenny
Donald R. Keller

The Harriet Pomerance Fellowship, carrying a $1,750 stipend, is given to a resident of the U.S. or Canada for an individual scholarly project relating to the Aegean Bronze Age archeology, preferably for travel to the Mediterranean to pursue the project.

1975 **Livingston V. Watrous**
Robert R. Stieglitz
1976 **Kenneth C. Gutwein**
Jeffrey S. Soles
1977 **Halford W. Haskell**
Paul Yule
1978 **Faith C.D. Hentschel**
1979 **Thomas G. Palaima**
1980 **David S. Reese**

Percia Schimmel Award

ISRAEL MUSEUM
Hakiryah, Jerusalem, Israel 91012 (636231-02)

The Percia Schimmel Award, which consists of a medal and a scroll, is given annually to an Israeli resident for achievements in the archeological research of Eretz Yisrael and the lands of the Bible.

1979 **Richard Barnett**
Nahman Avigad
1980 **Benjamin Mazar**
Frank Moore Cross

Fellow of the Athenaeum

THE ATHENAEUM OF PHILADELPHIA
East Washington Sq., Philadelphia, Pa. 19106 (215/WA 5-2688)

The Fellow of the Athenaeum honor is bestowed annually for outstanding contribution to 19th-century studies. It consists of a scroll and lifetime membership in the Athenaeum.

1977 **Henry Russell Hitchcock,**
Nathaniel Burt,
1978 **Brendan J. Gill**
Charles E. Peterson
1979 **George B. Tatum**
William J. Murtagh
1980 **Not available at press time**

Distinguished Service Award

AMERICAN ASSOCIATION OF CRIMINOLOGY
Box 1115, N. Marshfield, Mass. 02059 (617/837-0052)

The Distinguished Service Award is given annually according to a vote of the Committee on Credentials for outstanding contribution to the advancement in criminology, psychology and sociology.

1965 **Chief Raymond G. Dehn,** Law enforcement
1966 **Jan S. Olbrycht,** Forensic medicine
1970 **Commissioner George Puig,** Criminal identification
1971 **Patrick B. Kelly,** Criminal law
1972 **J.H. Drose,** Criminal sociology
1973 **Edward Podolsky,** Forensic medicine
1974 **Bruce Harrison,** Criminology
1975 **Yvan Van Garsse,** Criminalistics
1976 **Harold L. Gluck,** Criminal jurisprudence
1977 **Judge Robert L. Pruett, Sr.,** Criminal jurisprudence

Current Status Unknown

Edwin H. Sutherland Award
August Vollmer Award

AMERICAN SOCIETY OF CRIMINOLOGY
1314 Kinnear Rd., Ste. 212, Columbus, Ohio 43212 (614/422-9207)

The Edwin H. Sutherland Award, which consists of a silver plaque, is given annually to recognize outstanding contributions to research or theoretical work in criminology. The award may be for a single book or for a body of work on criminal or deviant behavior, the criminal justice system, corrections, law or justice.

1960 **Thorsten Sellin,** University of Pennsylvania
1961 **Orlando Wilson,** Chicago Police Superintendent; Professor Emeritus, University of California
1962 **Negley Teeters,** Temple University
1963 **Herbert Wechsler,** Columbia University Law School
Walter Reckless, Ohio State University
1964 **Hon J.C. McRuer,** Chairman Royal Commission on Civil Rights; former Chief Justice of Ontario
1965 **No award**
1966 **George Vold,** University of Minnesota
1967 **Donald R. Cressey,** University of California/Santa Barbara
1968 **Denis Szabo,** University of Montreal
1969 **Lloyd Ohlin,** Harvard University Law School
1970 **Alfred Lindesmith,** University of Indiana
1971 **Marshall Clinard,** University of Wisconsin
1972 **Leslie Wilkins,** State University of New York at Albany
1973 **Edwin Lemert,** University of California
1974 **Simon Dinitz,** Ohio State University
1975 **C. Ray Jeffery,** Florida State
1976 **Daniel Glaster,** University of Southern California
1977 **Solomon Kobrin,** University of California/Los Angeles
1978 **Seymour Halleck,** University of North Carolina
1979 **James Short,** Washington State University
1980 **Gresham M. Sykes,** Wniversity of Virginia

The August Vollmer Award, which consists of a silver plaque, recognizes contributions to justice or to the control, treatment or prevention of criminal or deviant behavior. The award may be made for a single contribution or a series of contributions.

1960 **Marvin Wolfgang,** University of Pennsylvania
Paul Bohannon, Northwestern University
1961 **Sheldon and Eleanor Glueck,** Harvard University Law School
1962 **James Bennett,** Director, U.S. Bureau of Prisons
1963 **Austin MacCormick,** Executive Director, The Osborne Assn.
1964 **Hon J. Adrien Robert,** Director, Montreal Police Department; Chief, Quebec Provincial Police
1965 **No award**
1966 **Judge George Edwards,** former Justice, Supreme Court of Michigan; Police Commissioner of Detroit; Justice U.S. Circuit Court of Appeals
1967 **Howard Leary,** Police Commissioner of New York
1968 **Myrl Alexander,** Director, U.S. Bureau of Prisons
1969 **Hon, Joseph Tydings,** U.S. Senator, Maryland
1970 **Milton Rector,** Executive Director of the National Council on Crime and Delinquency
1971 **No award**
1972 **Jerome Skolnick,** University of California/Berkeley
1973 **E. Preston Sharpe,** General Secretary, American Correctional Assn.
1974 **Patrick Murphy,** President, Police Foundation

Sol Rubin, Counsel Emeritus, National Council on Crime and Delinquency
1975 **No award**
1976 **Patricia M. Wald,** Litigation Director, Mental Health Law Project, Washington, D.C.
1977 **Richard A. McGee,** President, American Justice Institute, Sacramento, Calif.
1978 **Judge David Bazelon**, U.S. District Court of Appeals, Washington, D.C.
1979 **Norval Morris**, University of Chicago Law School
1980 **Gerhard O.W. Mueller**, United Nations

John Bates Clark Medal
Francis A. Walker Medal

AMERICAN ECONOMIC ASSOCIATION.
1313 21st Ave. S., Nashville, Tenn. 37212 (615/322-2595)

The John Bates Clark Medal, which is of bronze, is given every two years to an American economist 40 years of age or under who is a member of the Association for significant contributions to economic thought and knowledge.

1947 **Paul A. Samuelson**
1949 **Kenneth E. Boulding**
1951 **Milton Friedman**
1953 **No award**
1955 **James Tobin**
1957 **Kenneth J. Arrow**
1959 **Lawrence R. Klein**
1961 **Robert M. Solow**
1963 **Hendrik S. Houthakker**
1965 **Zvi Griliches**
1967 **Gary S. Becker**
1969 **Marc Leon Nerlove**
1971 **Dale W. Jorgenson**
1973 **Franklin M. Fisher**
1975 **Daniel McFadden**
1977 **Martin Feldstein**
1979 **Joseph Stieglitz**

The Francis A. Walker Medal, which is of silver, is awarded every five years for great contributions made to economics in the career of a living American member of the Association.

1947 **Wesley C. Mitchell**
1952 **John Maurice Clark**
1957 **Frank H. Knight**
1962 **Jacob Viner**
1967 **Alvin H. Hansen**
1972 **Theodore W. Schultz**
1977 **Simon Kuznets**

Nobel Prize for Economics

NOBEL FOUNDATION
Nobel House, Sturegatan 14, 11436-Stockholm, Sweden

One of six Nobel Prizes given annually, the Nobel Prize for Economics is generally recognized as the highest honor which can be bestowed on an economist. The award, which consists of a gold medal, diploma and large honorarium, is given at a ceremony on December 10 of each year at Stockholm's City Hall. The award itself is presented and administered by the Royal Swedish Academy of Sciences. The amount of the honorarium fluctuates; in 1980, it was approximately $212,000.

1969 **Ragnar Frisch** (Norway), Developed mathematical models for analyzing economic activity.
Jan Tinbergen (Netherlands), Developed mathematical models for analyzing economic activity.
1970 **Paul A. Samuelson** (U.S.A.), Raised the level of scientific analysis in economic theory.
1971 **Simon Kuznets** (U.S.A.), Worked out methods to determine a country's gross national product.
1972 **Kenneth J. Arrow** (U.S.A.), Pioneered theory of general economic equilibrium.
Sir John R. Hicks (Great Britain), Pioneered theory of general economic equilibrium.
1973 **Wassily Leontif** (U.S.A.; born in Russia), Developed the "input-output" method of economic analysis used by most industrial nations.
1974 **Gunnar Myrdal** (Sweden), Pioneered the theory of money and economic fluctuations.
Friedrich A. von Hayek (Austria), Pioneered the theory of money and economic fluctuations.
1975 **Leonid V. Kantorovich** (Russian), Contributed to the theory of the optimum allocation of resources.
Tjalling C. Koopmans (U.S.A., born in the Netherlands),Contributed to the theory of the optimum allocation of resources.
1976 **Milton Friedman** (U.S.A.), Work in consumption analysis, monetary history and theory, and demonstration of the complexity of stabilization policy.
1977 **Bertil Ohlin** (Sweden) and **James E. Meade** (Great Britain), Contributed to theory of international trade and capital movement
1978 **Herbert A. Simon**, (U.S.A.), Research on decision-making processes within economic organizations
1979 **Sir Arthur Lewis** (U.S.A., British subject born in the West Indies) and **Theodore W. Schultz** (U.S.A.), Work on economic problems of developing nations
1980 **Lawrence R. Klein** (U.S.A.), Development of models for forecasting economic trends and designing policies to deal with them

Herbert Baxter Adams Prize
George Louis Beer Prize
Albert J. Beveridge Award
Albert B. Corey Prize
John H. Dunning Prize
John K. Fairbank Prize
Leo Gershoy Award
Clarence H. Haring Prize
Howard R. Marraro Prize
Robert Livingston Schuyler Prize
Watumull Prize
J. Franklin Jameson Prize

AMERICAN HISTORICAL ASSOCIATION
400 A St. SE, Washington, D.C. 20003 (202/544-2422)

The $300 Herbert Baxter Adams Prize, a prestigious award despite the modest honorarium, now annually honors an American citizen's book on European history. The prize rotates on a two-year cycle between the pre- and post-1600 period. The winners of this and all other American Historical Association prizes are selected by expert committees in the field.

1938 **Arthur McCandless Wilson,** *French Foreign Policy During the Administration of Cardinal Fleury, 1726-1743*
1940 **John Shelton Curtiss,** *Church and State in Russia, 1900-1917*
1942 **E. Harris Harbison,** *Rival Ambassadors at the Court of Queen Mary*
1944 **R. H. Fisher,** *The Russian Fur Trade, 1550-1700*
1946 **A. W. Salomone,** *Italian Democracy in the Making*
1948 **Raymond de Roover,** *The Medici Bank: Its Organization, Management, Operations, and Decline*
1950 **Hans W. Gatzke,** *Germany's Drive to the West*
1952 **Arthur J. May,** *The Hapsburg Monarchy, 1867-1914*
1954 **W. C. Richardson,** *Tudor Chamber Administration, 1485-1547*
1956 **Gordon Craig,** *Politics of the Prussian Army, 1640-1945*
1958 **Arthur Wilson,** *Diderot: The Testing Years*
1960 **Caroline Robbins,** *The Eighteenth Century Commonwealthman*
1962 **Jerome Blum,** *Lord and Peasant in Russia*
1964 **Archibald S. Foord,** *His Majesty's Opposition, 1714-1830*
1966 **Gabriel Jackson,** *The Spanish Republic and the Civil War, 1931-39*
1968 **Arno J. Mayer,** *Politics and Diplomacy of Peacemaking: Containment and Counter-Revolution at Versailles 1918-1919*
1970 **John P. McKay,** *Pioneers for Profit: Foreign Entrepreneurship and Russian Industrialization, 1885-1913*
1971 **Edward E. Malefakis,** *Agrarian Reform and Peasant Revolution in Spain, Origins of the Civil War*
1972 **Richard Hellie,** *Enserfment and Military Change in Moscovy*
1973 **Martin Jay,** *The Dialectical Imagination: A History of the Frankfurt School and the Institute for Social Research, 1923-1950*
1974 **Joan Wallach Scott,** *The Glassworkers of Carmaux: French Craftsmen and Political Action in a Nineteenth-Century City*
1975 **James S. Donnelly, Jr.,** *The Land and the People of Nineteenth-Century Cork*
1976 **Frederick H. Russell,** *The Just War in the Middle Ages*
1977 **Charles S. Maier,** *Recasting Bourgeois Europe: Stabilization in France, Germany and Italy in the Decade After World War 1*
1978 **A.N. Galpern,** *The Religions of the People in Sixteenth Century Champagne*
1979 **Kendall E. Bailes,** *Technology Under Lenin and Stalin: Origins of the Soviet Technical Intelligensia, 1917-1941*
1980 **William E. Kapelle,** *The Norman Conquest of the North: The Region and Its Transformation 1000-1135*

The $300 George Louis Beer Prize annually honors the best book by an American on European international history since 1895.

1930 **Bernadotte Everly Schmitt,** *The Coming of the War*
1931 **Oran James Hale,** *Germany and the Diplomatic Revolution: A Study in Diplomacy and the Press, 1904-1906*
1932 **Oswald H. Wedel,** *Austro-German Diplomatic Relations, 1908-1914*
1933 **Robert Thomas Pollard,** *China's Foreign Relations, 1917-1931*
1934 **Ross J. S. Hoffman,** *Great Britain and the German Trade Rivalry, 1875-1914*
1935 **No award**
1936 **No award**
1937 **Charles Wesley Porter,** *The Career of Theophile Declasse*
1938 **Rene Albrecht-Carrie,** *Italy at the Paris Peace Conference*
1939 **Pauline Relyea Anderson,** *Background of Anti-English Feeling in Germany, 1890-1902*
1940 **Richard Heathcote Heindel,** *The American Impact on Great Britain, 1898-1914*
1941 **Arthur J. Marder,** *The Anatomy of British Sea Power*
1942 **No award**
1943 **Arthur Norton Cook,** *British Enterprise in Nigeria*
1944-51 **No awards**
1952 **Robert H. Ferrell,** *Peace in Their Time: The Origins of the Kellogg-Briand Pact*
1953 **Russell Fifield,** *Woodrow Wilson and the Far East*
1954 **Wayne S. Vucinich,** *Serbia Between East and West: The Events of 1903-1908*
1955 **Richard Pipes,** *The Formation of the Soviet Union*
1956 **Henry Cord Meyer,** *Mitteleuropa in German Thought and Action, 1815-1945*
1957 **Alexander Dallin,** *German Rule in Russia, 1941-1945*
1958 **Vincent Marmety,** *The United States and East Central Europe*
1959 **Ernest R. May,** *The World War and American Isolation 1914-17*
1960 **Rudolph Binion,** *Defeated Leaders: The Political Fate of Caillaux, Jouvenel and Tardieu*
1961 **Charles F. Delzell,** *Mussolini's Enemies: The Italian Anti-Fascist Resistance*
1962 **Piotr S. Wandycz,** *France and Her Eastern Allies, 1919-1925*
1963 **Edward W. Bennett,** *Germany and the Diplomacy of the Financial Crisis, 1931*
Hans A. Schmitt, *The Path to European Union*
1964 **Ivo J. Lederer,** *Yugoslavia at the Paris Peace Conference*
Harold I. Nelson, *Land and Power: British and Allied Policy on Germany's Frontiers, 1916-1919*
1965 **Paul Spencer Guinn, Jr.,** *British Strategy and Politics 1914 to 1918*
1966 **No award**
1967 **George A. Brinkley,** *The Volunteer Army and the Revolution in South Russia*
Robert Wohl, *French Communism in the Making*
1968 **No award**
1969 **Richard H. Ullman,** *Britain and the Russian Civil War, November 1918-February 1920*
1970 **Samuel R. Williamson, Jr.,** *The Politics of Grand Strategy: Britain and France Prepare for War, 1904-1914*
1971 **Gerhard L. Weinberg,** *The Foreign Policy of Hitler's Germany, Diplomatic Revolution in Europe, 1933-36*
1972 **Jon Jacobson,** *Locarno Diplomacy: Germany and the West*
1973 **No award**
1974 **No award**
1975 **No award**
1976 **Charles S. Maier,** *Recasting Bourgeois Europe: Stabilization in France, Germany and Italy in the Decade after World War I*
1977 **Stephen A. Schuker,** *The End of French Predominance in Europe: The Financial Crisis of 1924 and the Adoption of the Dawes Plan*
1978 **No award**

1979 **Edward W. Bennett,** *German Rearmament and the West, 1932-1933*
1980 **No award**

The $1,000 Albert J. Beveridge Award is given annually for the best book in English on the history of the Western Hemisphere from 1492 to the present.

1939 **John T. Horton,** *James Kent: A Study in Conservatism*
1941 **Charles A. Barker,** *The Background of the Revolution in Maryland*
1943 **Harold Whitman Bradley,** *The American Frontier in Hawaii: The Pioneers, 1789-1843*
1945 **John Richard Alden,** *John Stuart and the Southern Colonial Frontier*
1946 **Arthur E. Bestor,** *Backwoods Utopias: The Sectarian and Owenite Phases of Communitarian Socialism in America, 1663-1829*
1947 **Lewis Hanke,** *The Struggle for Justice in the Spanish Conquest of America*
1948 **Donald Fleming,** *John William Draper and the Religion of Science*
1949 **Reynold M. Wik,** *Steam Power on the American Farm: A Chapter in Agricultural History, 1850-1920*
1950 **Glyndon G. Van Deusen,** *Horace Greeley: Nineteenth Century Crusader*
1951 **Robert Twymann,** *History of Marshall Field and Co., 1852-1906*
1952 **Clarence Versteeg,** *Robert Morris, Revolutionary Financier*
1953 **George R. Bentley,** *A History of the Freedman's Bureau*
1954 **Arthur M. Johnson,** *The Development of American Petroleum Pipelines: A Study in Enterprise and Public Policy*
1955 **Ian C. C. Graham,** *Colonists from Scotland: Emigration to North America, 1707-1783*
1956 **Paul Schroeder,** *The Axis Alliance and Japanese-American Relations, 1941*
1957 **David Fletcher,** *Rails, Mines, and Progress: Seven American Promoters in Mexico*
1958 **Paul Conkin,** *Tomorrow a New World: The New Deal Community Program*
1959 **Arnold M. Paul,** *Free Conservative Crisis and the Rule of Law: Attitudes of Bar and Bench, 1887-1895*
1960 **C. Clarence Clendenen,** *The United States and Pancho Villa*
Nathan Miller, *The Enterprise of A Free People: Canals and the Canal Fund in the New York Economy, 1792-1838*
1961 **Calvin DeArmond Davis,** *The United States and the First Hague Peace Conference*
1962 **Walter LaFeber,** *The New Empire: An Interpretation of American Expansion, 1860-1898*
1963 **No award**
1964 **Linda Grant De Pauw,** *The Eleventh Pillar: New York State and the Federal Constitution*
1965 **Daniel M. Fox,** *The Discovery of Abundance*
1966 **Herman Belz,** *Reconstructing the Union: Conflict of Theory and Policy during the Civil War*
1967 **No award**
1968 **Michael Paul Rogin,** *The Intellectuals and McCarthy: The Radical Specter*
1969 **Sam Bass Warner, Jr.,** *The Private City: Philadelphia in Three Periods of Its Growth*
1970 **Sheldon Hackney,** *Populism to Progressivism in Alabama*
Leonard L. Richards, *Gentlemen of Property and Standing: Anti-Abolition Mobs in Jacksonian America*
1971 **Carl N. Degler,** *Neither Black nor White: Slavery and Race Relations in Brazil and the United States*
David J. Rothman, *The Discovery of the Asylum: Social Order and Disorder in the New Republic*
1972 **James T. Lemon,** *The Best Poor Man's Country*
1973 **Richard L. Slotkin,** *Regeneration through Violence: The Mythology of the American Frontier, 1600-1850*
1974 **Peter H. Wood,** *Black Majority*
1975 **David Brion Davis,** *The Problem of Slavery in the Age of Revolution, 1700-1823*
1976 **Edmund S. Morgan,** *American Slavery-American Freedom: The Ordeal of Colonial Virginia*
1977 **Henry F. May,** *The Enlightenment in America*
1978 **Lohn Leddy Phelan,** *The People and the King: The Comunero Revolution in Colombia, 1781*
1979 **Calvin Martin,** *Keepers of the Game: Indian-Animal Relationships and the Fur Trade*
1980 **John W. Reps,** *Cities of the American West: A History of Frontier Urban Planning*

The $1,000 Albert B. Corey Prize in Canadian-American Relations, awarded jointly by the American and Canadian Historical Associations, biennially recognizes the best book on the history of Canadian-American relations or the history of the two countries.

1967 **Gustave Lanctot,** *Canada and the American Revolution*
1969 **Kenneth Bourne,** *Britain and the Balance of Power in North America, 1815-1908*
1971 **No award**
1972 **Charles P. Stacey,** *Arms, Men and Governments: The War Policies of Canada 1939-45*
1974 **Lester B. Pearson,** *Mike, The Memoirs of the Right Honourable Lester B. Pearson*
1976 **No award**
1978 **Michael B. Katz,** *The People of Hamilton, Canada West: Family and Class in a Mid-Nineteenth Century City*
1980 **No award**

The $300 John H. Dunning Prize is given biennially for the best book on American history.

1929 **Haywood J. Pearce, Jr.,** *Benjamin H. Hill: Secession and Reconstruction*
1931 **Francis B. Simkins and R. H. Woody,** *South Carolina During Reconstruction*
1933 **Amos A. Ettinger,** *The Mission to Spain of Pierre Soule*
1935 **Angie Debo,** *The Rise and Fall of the Choctaw Republic*
1937 **No award**
1938 **Robert A. East,** *Business Enterprise in the American Revolutionary Era*
1940 **Richard W. Leopold,** *Robert Dale Owen*
1942 **Oscar Handlin,** *Boston's Immigrants*
1944 **Elting E. Morison,** *Admiral Sims and the Modern American Navy*
1946 **David Ellis,** *Landlords and Farmers in the Hudson Mohawk Region*
1948 **William E. Livezey,** *Mahan and Seapower*
1950 **Henry Nash Smith,** *Virgin Land: The American West as Symbol and Myth*
1952 **Louis C. and Beatrice J. Hunter,** *Steamboats on the Western Rivers: An Economic and Technological History*
1954 **Gerald Carson,** *The Old Country Store*
1956 **John Higham,** *Strangers in the Land: Patterns of American Nativitism*
1958 **Marvin Meyers,** *The Jacksonian Persuasion*

1960 **Eric McKitrick,** *Andrew Johnson and Reconstruction*
1962 **E. James Ferguson,** *The Power of the Purse: A History of American Public Finance, 1776-1790*
1964 **John H. and LaWanda Cox,** *Politics, Principle, and Prejudice, 1865-1866*
1966 **John Willard Shy,** *Toward Lexington: The Role of the British Army in the American Revolution*
1968 **Robert L. Beisner,** *Twelve Against Empire: The Anti-Imperialists, 1898-1900*
1970 **Gordon S. Wood,** *The Creation of the American Republic, 1776-1787*
1972 **John P. Diggins,** *Mussolini and Fascism: The View from America*
1974 **Paul Boyer and Stephen Nissenbaum,** *Salem Possessed: The Social Origins of Witchcraft*
1976 **Thomas S. Hines,** *Burnham of Chicago: Architect and Planner*
1978 **J. Mills Thornton III,** *Politics and Power in a Slave Society: Alabama, 1800-1860*
1980 **John D. Unruh Jr.,** *The Plains Across: The Overland Emigrants and the Trans-Mississippi West, 1940-1860*

The $500 John K. Fairbank Prize in East Asian History is awarded every two years for a noteworthy book on the history of China, Chinese Central Asia, Japan, Korea, Manchuria, Mongolia or Vietnam from 1800 to the present.

1969 **Tetsuo Najita,** *Hara Kei in the Politics of Compromise, 1905-1915*
Harold Schiffrin, *Sun Yat-sen and the Origins of the Chinese Revolution*
1971 **Jerome B. Greider,** *Hu Shih and the Chinese Renaissance: Liberalism in the Chinese Revolution, 1917-1937*
1973 **W. G. Beasley,** *The Meiji Restoration*
1975 **Jen Yu-wen,** *The Taiping Revolutionary Movement*
1977 **Gail Lee Bernstein,** *Japanese Marxist: A Portrait of Kawakami Hajine, 1879-1946*
1979 **Guy S. Alitto,** *The Last Confucian: Liang Shu-Ming and the Chinese Dilemma of Modernity*

The $1,000 Leo Gershoy Award is given every two years for an outstanding book on 17th- and 18th-century European history published in English.

1977 **Simon Chama,** *Patriots and Liberators: Revolution in the Netherlands, 1790-1813*
1979 **Robert Darnton,** *The Business of Enlightenment: A Publishing History of the Encylopedie*

The $500 Clarence H. Haring Prize is given every five years for the best book on Latin American history written during the previous half-decade.

1966 **Daniel Cosio Villegas,** *Historia Moderna de Mexico*
1971 **Luis Gonzalez,** *Pueblo en vilo*
1976 **Tulio Halperin-Donghi,** *Politics, Economics and Society in Argentina in the Revolutionary Period*

The $500 Howard R. Marraro Prize is awarded annually for the best book or article on Italian cultural history or American-Italian relations written by a resident of the United States or Canada.

1973 **Edward R. Tannenbaum,** *The Fascist Experience: Italian Society and Culture, 1922-1945*
1974 **Benjamin F. Brown,** *The Complete Works of Sidney Sonnino*
1975 **Robert Brentano,** *Rome before Avignon: A Social History of Thirteenth Century Rome*
1976 **Richard A. Webster,** *Industrial Imperialism in Italy, 1908-1915*
1977 **Gene A. Brucker,** *The Civic World of Early Renaissance Florence*
1978 **Virginia Yans-McLaughlin,** *Family and Community: Italian Immigrants in Buffalo, 1880-1930*
1979 **John W. O'Malley,** *Praise and Blame in the Reanissance: Rhetoric, Doctrine and Reform in the Sacred Orators of the Papal Court, c. 1450-1521*
1980 **No award**

The $500 Robert Livingston Schuyler Prize is given every five years for the most outstanding book on British history (modern, Commonwealth or Imperial) written by an American citizen. This award may be applied for.

1951 **Howard Robinson,** *Britain's Post Office*
1956 **David Harris Willson,** *King James VI and I*
1961 **Mark H. Curtis,** *Oxford and Cambridge in Transition, 1558-1642*
1966 **Philip D. Curtin,** *The Image of Africa: British Ideas and Action, 1780-1850*
1971 **W. K. Jordan,** *Edward VI: The Young King* and *The Threshold of Power,* 2 vols.
1976 **John Clive,** *Macaulay: The Shaping of the Historian*

The $1,000 Watumull Prize is awarded every two years for the best work(s) on the history of India published in the United States.

1945 **Ernest J. H. Mackay,** *Chanhu-Daro Excavations, 1935-36*
1947 **No award**
1949 **Gertrude Emerson Sen,** *The Pageant of India History*
Holden Furber, *John Company at Work*
1951 **T. Walter Wallbank,** *India in the New Era*
Louis Fischer, *The Life of Mahatma Gandhi*
1954 **D. Mackenzie Brown,** *The White Umbrella: Indian Political Thought from Manu to Gandhi*
W. Norman Brown, *The United States and India and Pakistan*
1956 **No award**
1958 **William de Bary, ed.,** *Sources of the Indian Tradition*
1960 **Michael Brecher,** *Nehru: A Political Biography*
1962 **George D. Bearce,** *British Attitudes Toward India, 1784-1858*
Stanley A. Wolpert, *Tilak and Gokhale: Revolution and Reform in the Making of Modern India*
1964 **Charles A. Drekmeier,** *Kingship and Community in Early India*
Charles H. Heimsath, *Indian Nationalism and Hindu Social Reform*
1966 **B. R. Nayar,** *Minority Politics in the Punjab*
Thomas R. Metcalf, *The Aftermath of Revolt: India, 1857-1870*
1968 **John Broomfield,** *Elite Conflict in a Plural Society: Twentieth Century Bengal*
Myron Weiner, *Party Building in a New Nation*
1970 **Stephen N. Hay,** *Asian Ideas of East and West: Tagore and His Critics in Japan, China, and India*
David Kopt, *British Orientalism and the Bengal Renaissance: The Dynamics of Indian Modernization, 1773-1835*
Eugene F. Irschick, *Politics and Social Conflict in South India: The Non-Brahman Movement and Tamil Separatism, 1916-1929*
1972 **Elizabeth Whitcombe,** *Agrarian Conditions in Northern India, Vol. 1: The United Provinces Under British Rule, 1860-1900*

1974 **Leonard A. Gordon,** *Bengal: The Nationalist Movement, 1876-1940*
1976 **Michael Pearson,** *Merchants and Rulers in Gujarat: The Response to the Portuguese in the Sixteenth Century*
1978 **John R. McLane,** *Indian Nationalism and the Early Congress*
1980 **Joseph E. Schwartzberg,** *A Historical Atlas of the South*

The J. Franklin Jameson Prize is awarded for outstanding editing of historical sources.

1980 **Harold C. Syrett,** *The Papers of Alexander Hamilton,* Vols. 21-25 (Columbia University Press)

1974 **Gary May** (University of California/Los Angeles), "The China Service of John Carter Vincent, 1924-1953"
1975 **Robert Davidoff** (Cornell University), "The Education of Edmund Randolph"
1976 **John McCardell** (Harvard University), "The Idea of a Southern Nation," published as *Southern Nationalists and Southern Nationalism, 1830-1860*
1977 **Mark Schwehn,** (Stanford University), "The Making of a Modern Consciousness: A Study of Henry Adams and William James"
1978 **John Ettling** (Harvard University), *The Germ of Laziness: The Rockefeller Sanitary Commission in the Southern States, 1909-1914.*
1979 **Steven Hahn** (Yale University), "The Roots of Southern Populism: Yeoman Farmers and the Transformation of Georgia's Upper Piedmont, 1850-1890."
1980 **Not available at press time**

Allan Nevins Award
Francis Parkman Award

SOCIETY OF AMERICAN HISTORIANS
610 Fayerweather Hall, Columbia University, New York, N.Y. 10027 (212/280-2555)

The $1,000 Allan Nevins Award goes annually for the best doctoral dissertation completed during the previous year in American history, which exhibits scholarly distinction and literary grace. The winner is selected by a panel of judges from entries submitted by college and university history departments.

1960 **Waldo H. Heinrichs, Jr.** (Harvard University), "American Ambassador: Joseph C. Grew and the Development of the United States Diplomatic Tradition"
1961 **John L. Thomas** (Brown University), "The Liberator: William Lloyd Garrison"
1962 **Willie Lee Rose** (Johns Hopkins University), "Rehearsal for Reconstruction: The Port Royal Experiment"
1963 **Joanne L. Neel** (Bryn Mawr College), "Phineas Bond: A Study in Anglo-American Relations, 1786-1812"
1964 **William W. Freehling** (University of California/Berkeley), "Prelude to Conflict: The Nullification Controversy in South Carolina, 1816-1836"
1965 **Robert L. Beisner** (University of Chicago), "Twelve Against the Empire: The Anti-Imperialists, 1898-1900"
1966 **Alan Lawson** (University of Michigan), "The Failure of Independent Liberalism"
1967 **Jerome Sternstein** (Brown University), "Nelson Aldrich: The Early Years"
1968 **Steven A. Channing** (University of North Carolina), "Crisis of Fear"
1969 **Mary Beth Norton** (Harvard University), "The British-Americans"
1970 **Edward H. McKinley** (University of Wisconsin), "The Lure of Africa: The American Interest in Tropical Africa, 1919-1939"
1971 **Heath Twitchell, Jr.** (American University), "The Biography of General Henry T. Allen"
1972 **George Bernard Forgie** (Stanford University), "Father Past and Child Nation: The Romantic Imagination and the Origins of the American Civil War," published as *Patricide in the House Divided: A Psychological Interpretation of Lincoln and His Age*
1973 **James L. Roark** (Stanford University), "Masters Without Slaves: Southern Planters in the Civil War and Reconstruction"

The $500 Francis Parkman Award is given annually for the book published in American history which best exhibits scholarly merit and literary grace. A panel of judges selects the winner, who also receives a bronze medal.

1956 **George F. Kennan,** *Russia Leaves the War*
1957 **Arthur M. Schlesinger, Jr.,** *The Crisis of the Old Order, 1919-1933*
1958 **Ernest Samuels,** *Henry Adams: The Middle Years, 1877-1891*
1959 **Matthew Josephson,** *Edison: A Biography*
1960 **Elting E. Morison,** *Turmoil and Tradition: A Study in the Life and Times of Henry L. Stimson*
1961 **Leon Wolff,** *Little Brown Brother: How the United States Purchased and Pacified the Philippine Islands at the Century's Turn*
1962 **James Thomas Flexner,** *The Wilder Image: The Painting of America's Native School from Thomas Cole to Winslow Homer*
1963 **William E. Leuchtenberg,** *Franklin D. Roosevelt and the New Deal, 1932-1940*
1964 **Willie Lee Rose,** *Rehearsal for Reconstruction: The Port Royal Experiment*
1965 **Daniel J. Boorstin,** *The Americans: The National Experience*
1966 **William H. Goetzmann,** *Exploration and Empire*
1967 **No award**
1968 **Winthrop D. Jordan,** *White Over Black: American Attitudes Toward the Negro, 1550-1812*
1969 **Theodore A. Wilson,** *The First Summit: Roosevelt and Churchill at Placentia Bay, 1941*
1970 **James MacGregor Burns,** *Roosevelt: The Soldier of Freedom, 1940-1945*
1971 **Joseph P. Lash,** *Eleanor and Franklin*
1972 **Kenneth S. Davis,** *F.D.R.: The Beckoning of Destiny, 1882-1928*
1973 **Robert W. Johannsen,** *Stephen A. Douglas*
1974 **Robert A. Caro,** *The Power Broker: Robert Moses and the Fall of New York*
1975 **Edmund S. Morgan,** *American Slavery, American Freedom*
1976 **Irving Howe,** *World of Our Fathers*
1977 **David McCullough,** *The Path Between the Seas*
1978 **R. David Edmunds,** *The Potawatomis*
1979 **Leon F. Litwack,** *Been In the Storm So Long*
1980 **Not available at press time**

Frank S. and Elizabeth D. Brewer Prize
Philip Schaff Award

AMERICAN SOCIETY OF CHURCH HISTORY
305 E. Country Club La., Wallingford, Pa. 19086
(215/566-7126)

The Frank S. and Elizabeth D. Brewer Prize, which carries a $2,000 honorarium to assist in the publication of a meritorious manuscript, is awarded to the author of a book-length manuscript on church history.

1980 **James David Essig**, *"Break Every Yoke: American Evangelicals Against Slavery, 1770-1808*

The $1,000 Philip Schaff Prize honors the best book published in English in the North American scholarly community and presenting original research or interpretation in the history of Christianity or any period thereof.

1980 **Thomas N. Tentler**, *Sin and Confession on the Eve of the Reformation*

Ray A. Billington Award
Binkley-Stephenson Award
Charles Thomson Prize
Frederick Jackson Turner Award
Louis Pelzer Memorial Award
Merle Curti Award

ORGANIZATION OF AMERICAN HISTORIANS
112 N. Bryan St., Bloomington, Ind. 47401 (812/337-7311)

The Ray A. Billington Award, which consists of $500 and a medal, is given annually for a book written during the previous year on American frontier history. A committee chooses the winner.

1980 **John D. Unruh**, *The Plains Across*

The $500 Binkley-Stephenson Award annually recognizes the best scholarly article published in the *Journal of American History* during the previous year.

1973 **Richard H. Kohn**, "The Washington Administration's Decision to Crush the Whiskey Rebellion"
1974 **Caroll Smith-Rosenberg** and **Charles Rosenberg**, "The Female Animal: Medical and Biological Views of Woman and Her Role in Nineteenth-Century America"
1975 **Albro Martin**, "The Troubled Subject of Railroad Regulation in the Gilded Age — A Reappraisal"
1976 **Richard Allen Gerber**, "The Liberal Republican"
1977 **Brian A. Villa**, "The U.S. Army, Unconditional Surrender and the Potsdam Proclamation"
1978 **Burton I. Kaufman**, "Mideast Multinational Oil, U.S. Foreign Policy and Antitrust, the 1950s"
1979 **Athan Theoharis**, "The Truman Administration and the Decline of Civil Liberties"
1980 **Karen Ordahl Kupperman**, "Apathy and Death in Early Jamestown"
David Alan Rosenburg, "American Atomic Strategy"

The $500 Charles Thomson Prize annually honors an article whose subject was researched in the National Archives, regional archives or one of the presidential libraries. The winner also receives the publication *Prologue: The Journal of the National Archives*. A committee selects the recipient of the award.

1980 **Donald Sweig**, "Reassessing the Human Dimension of the Interstate Slave Trade"

The Frederick Jackson Turner Award annually honors a book-length study of American history submitted by a university press. The author receives $500 and certificate, and the university press receives $3,000. A committee selects the winner.

1973 **Mary O. Furner**, N.A.
1974 **Thomas H. Bender**, N.A.
1975 **No award**
1976 **No award**
1977 **Merritt Roe Smith**, N.A.
1978 **Daniel T. Rodgers**, *Work Ethic in Industrial America, 1850-1920*
1979 **Charles F. Fanning, Jr.**, *Peter Finley and Mr. Dolley: The Chicago Years*
1980 **John Mack Farragher**, *Women & Men on the Overland Trail*

The Louis Pelzer Memorial Award, which consists of $500 and a medal, annually honors the graduate-student author of the best essay in the *Journal of American History*. A committee selects the winner.

1973 **Kenneth L. Kusmer**
1974 **Charles W. McCurdy**
1975 **No award**
1976 **Deborah L. Haines**
1977 **David A. Corgin**
1978 **John R. Nelson, Jr.**
1979 **Ellen Nore**
1980 **Cindy S. Aron**

The Merle Curti Award consists of $500, a medal and a certificate presented annually to the author of the best book on social and intellectual history published by a university or commercial press during the previous year. A committee chooses the recipient.

1977 **Henry F. May**, *The Enlightenment of America*
1978 **No Award**
1979 **Garry Wills**, *Inventing America: Jefferson's Declaration of Independence*
1980 **Paul E. Johnson**, *A Shopkeeper's Millenium: Society and Revivals in Rochester, New York, 1815-1860*
Thomas Dublin, *Women at Work: The Transformation of Work and Community in Lowell, Massachusetts, 1826-1860*

Stuart Bernath Book Prize
Stuart Bernath Article Prize
Stuart Bernath Lecture Prize

SOCIETY FOR HISTORIANS OF AMERICAN FOREIGN RELATIONS
c/o University of Akron, Dept. of History, Akron, Ohio 44325 (216/375-7008)

The Stuart Bernath Book Prize, which carries a $500 honorarium, is awarded annually for an author's first or second book published on an aspect of American foreign relations. Copies of books entered are submitted to a special committee for review and selection

1972 **Joan Hoff Wilson**, *American Business and Foreign Policy, 1920-1933*

1972 **Kenneth E. Shewmaker,** *American and Chinese Communists, 1927-1945.*
1973 **John Gaddis,** *The United States and the Origins of the Cold War, 1941-1947*
1974 **Michael H. Hunt,** *Frontier Defense and the Open Door: Manchuria and Chinese-American Relations, 1895-1911*
1975 **Frank D. McCann, Jr.,** *The Brazilian-American Alliance, 1937-1945*
1975 **Stephen E. Pelz,** *Race to Pearl Harbor: The Failure of the Second London Naval Conference and the Onset of World War II*
1976 **Martin Sherwin,** *A World Destroyed: The Atomic Bomb and the Grand Alliance*
1977 **Roger V. Dingman,** *Power in the Pacific: The Origins of Naval Arms Limitations, 1914-1922*
1978 **James R. Leutze** (University of North Carolina)
1979 **Phillip J. Baram** (Program Manager, Boston)
1980 **Michael Schaller** (University of Arizona)

The $200 Stuart L. Bernath Article Prize is awarded annually for a published article, one of the author's first seven published scholarly works, on a topic in American foreign relations. A special committee of the Society selects the winner.

1977 **John Stagg** (University of Auckland, New Zealand), "James Madison and the 'Malcontents': The Political Origins of the War of 1812"
1978 **Michael Hunt** (University of North Carolina)
1979 **Brian L. Villa** (University of Ottawa)
1980 **James I. Matray** (University of Texas, Arlington)
David Rosenberg (University of Chicago)

The Stuart L. Bernath Lecture Prize, which carries a $300 honorarium, recognizes scholars under 45 years of age for excellence in teaching and research. A special committee of the Society selects the winner.

1977 **Joan Hoff Wilson,** "Foreign Policy Trends Since the 1920s"
1978 **David Patterson** (U.S. Department of State)
1979 **Marilyn Young** (University of Michigan)
1980 **John Caddis** (Ohio University)

Clarence E. Holte Prize

TWENTY-FIRST CENTURY FOUNDATION
112 W. 120th St., New York, N.Y. 10027 (212/666-0345)

The Clarence E. Holte Prize, which carries a $5,000 honorarium, is awarded bienially for significant contributions to black heritage, the cultural heritage of Africa and the African diaspora.

1980 **Chancellor Williams,** professor of African history at Howard University and author of *A Destruction of Black Civilization*

Tyrrell Medal

ROYAL SOCIETY OF CANADA
344 Wellington, Ottawa, Ont. K1A ON4 (613/992-3468)

The Tyrrell Medal, which has been accompanied by a $1,000 honorarium since 1966, is awarded not more frequently than every two years for outstanding work in the history of Canada. A selection committee chooses the recipient.

1947 **A.R.M. Lower**
1948 **L. Groulx**
1949 **Reginald G. Trotter**
1950 **John Bartlet Brebner**
1951 **Jean Bruchesi**
D.G. Creighton
1952 **C.B. Sissons**
1953 **Seraphin Marion**
1954 **G.P. de T. Glazebrook**
1955 **C.P. Stacey**
1956 **Olivier Maurault**
1957 **George F.G. Stanley**
1958 **W.L. Morton**
1959 **Arthur Maheux**
1960 **S.D. Clark**
1961 **Guy Pregault**
1962 **J.M.S. Careless**
1963 **F.H. Underhill**
1964 **Marcel Trudel**
1965 **W. Kaye Lamb**
1966 **Edgar McInnis**
1968 **G.W.L. Nicholson**
1970 **Fernand Ouellet**
1972 **Jean Hamelin**
1975 **Ramsay Cook**
1979 **F.W. Eccles**

John Gilmary Shea Prize

AMERICAN CATHOLIC HISTORICAL ASSOCIATION
The Catholic University of America, Mullen Library, Washington, D.C. 20064 (202/635-5656)

The John Gilmary Shea Prize, which carries a $300 honorarium, is given annually to honor an outstanding book on Catholic history written by an American or Canadian citizen or resident. Books may be entered for consideration by a jury, which consists of Association officials plus three historians specializing in different fields of history.

1946 **Carlton J. H. Hayes,** *Wartime Mission in Spain*
1947 **No award**
1948 **No award**
1949 **No award**
1950 **John H. Kennedy,** *Jesuit and Savage in New France*
1951 **George Pare,** *The Catholic Church in Detroit, 1701-1888*
1952 **No award**
1953 **No award**
1954 **Philip Hughes,** *The Reformation in England*
1955 **Annabelle M. Melville,** *John Carroll of Baltimore*
1956 **John Tracy Ellis,** *American Catholicism*
1957 **Thomas T. McAvoy, C.S.C.,** *The Great Crisis in American Catholic History, 1895-1900*
1958 **John M. Daley, S.J.,** *Georgetown University: Origin and Early Years*
1959 **Robert A. Graham, S.J.,** *Vatican Diplomacy: A Study of Church and State on the International Plane*
1960 **Maynard J. Geiger, O.F.M.,** *The Life and Times of Junipero Serra*
1961 **John Courtney Murray, S.J.,** *We Hold These Truths: Catholic Reflections on the American Proposition*
1962 **Francis Dvornik,** *The Slavs in European History and Civilization*
1963 **Oscar Halecki,** *The Millennium of Europe*
1964 **Helen C. White,** *Tudor Books of Saints and Martyrs*

1965 **John T. Noonan, Jr.,** *Contraception: A History of Its Treatment by the Catholic Theologians and Canonists*
1966 **Robert Ignatius Burns, S.J.,** *The Jesuits and the Indian Wars of the Northwest*
1967 **Robert Ignatius Burns, S.J.,** *The Crusader Kingdom of Valencia: Reconstruction on a Thirteenth-Century Frontier*
1968 **Edward Surtz, S.J.,** *The Works and Days of John Fisher, 1469-1535, Bishop of Rochester, in the English Renaissance and the Reformation*
1969 **Robert Brentano,** *Two Churches: England and Italy in the Thirteenth Century*
1970 **David M. Kennedy,** *Birth Control in America: The Career of Margaret Sanger*
1971 **Jaroslav Pelikan,** *The Emergence of the Catholic Tradition (100-600)*
1972 **John T. Noonan, Jr.,** *Power to Dissolve: Lawyers and Marriages in the Courts of the Roman Curia*
1973 **Robert E. Quirk,** *The Mexican Revolution and the Catholic Church, 1910-1929*
1974 **Thomas W. Spalding,** *Martin John Spalding, American Churchman*
1975 **Jay P. Dolan,** *The Immigrant Church: New York's Irish and German Catholics, 1815-1865*
1976 **Emmett Larkin,** *The Roman Catholic Church and the Creation of of Modern Irish State," 1978-1886*
1977 **Timothy Tackett,** *Priest and Parish in 18th Century France*
1978 **Charles W. Jones,** *Saint Nicholas of Myra, Bari and Manhattan: Biography of a Legend*
1979 **Kenneth Meyer Setton,** *The Papacy and the Levant, 1204-1571*
1980 **Not available at press time**

Lee Max Friedman Award

AMERICAN JEWISH HISTORICAL SOCIETY
2 Thornton Rd., Waltham, Mass. 02154 (617/891-8110)

The Lee Max Friedman Award Medal, which is of gold, annually honors distinguished service and contributions to the field of American Jewish history. A committee comprised of previous medal recipients and the executive committee of the Society selects the winner.

1960 **Isidore Solomon Meyer**
1961 **Jacob Rader Marcus**
1962 **David de Sola Pool**
1963 **Salo Wittmayer Baron**
1964 **Betram Wallace Korn**
1966 **Maurice Jacobs**
1967 **Abram Kanof**
1968 **Leon Jacob Obermayer**
1970 **Philip David Sang**
1974 **Abram Vossen Goodman**
1975 **Oscar I. Janowsky**
1976 **Abraham Joseph Karp**
1977 **Moshe Davis**
1978 **Abram Leon Sachar**
1979 **Malcolm Henry Stern**
1980 **David R. Pokross**

Howard R. Marraro Prize

MODERN LANGUAGE ASSOCIATION
62 Fifth Ave., New York, N.Y. 10011 (212/741-7854)

The $750 Howard R. Marraro Prize is given for outstanding achievement in Italian studies to an MLA member for scholarly study in Italian Literature or comparative literature involving Italian. It had been an annual honor through 1976, but it is now given every two years. Members submit nominations which are voted on by the Howard R. Marraro Prize Selection Committee.

1973 **Bernard Weinberg,** *Trattati di poetica e retorica del Cinquecento*
1974 **Thomas G. Bergin,** Lifetime achievement
1975 **Beatrice Corrigan,** Lifetime achievement
1976 **Joseph G. Fucilla,** Lifetime achievement
1978 **Franco Fido,** *Guida a Goldoni: Teatro e soecieta nel Settecento*
1980 **Nicolas J. Perella,** *Midday in Italian Literature: Variations on an Archetypal Theme*

Ossian Prize

STIFTUNG F.V.S.
Georgsplatz 10, C-2000 Hamburg 1, Federal Republic of Germany (33-04-00)

The Ossian Prize, which consists of 20,000 marks, a bronze medal and a certificate, annually honors a creative individual or association for outstanding services to the preservation and promotion of smaller languages and cultural communities. An international jury selects the winner.

1974 **Derick Thomson,** Glasgow, Scotland
1975 **Societa Retorumantscha,** Chur, Switzerland
1976 **Robert Lafont,** Nimes, France
1977 **Mirtin O'Direain,** Dublin, Ireland
1978 **Francesc de B. Moll,** Palma de Mallorca, Spain
1979 **Jelle Hendriks Brouwer,** Leeuwarden, Netherlands
1980 **Societat Filologjche Furlane G.I. Ascoli,** Udine, Italy

Pitirim A. Sorokin Award
MacIver Award
Dubois-Johnson-Frazier Award
General Award
Stouffer Award

AMERICAN SOCIOLOGICAL ASSOCIATION
1722 N St. NW, Washington, D.C. 20036 (202/833-3410)

The $500 Pitirim A. Sorokin Award was given annually to an Association member to recognize a published piece which contributed "to an outstanding degree" to progress in sociology. The award has been discontinued.

1968 **Peter Blau, Otis D. Duncan and Andrea Tyree,** *The American Occupational Structure*
1969 **William A. Gamson,** *Power and Discontent*
1970 **Arthur L. Stinchcombe,** *Constructing Social Theories*
1971 **Robert W. Friedrichs,** *A Sociology of Sociology*

Harrison C. White, *Chains of Opportunity: Systems Models of Mobility in Organization*
1972 **Eliot Friedson,** *Profession of Medicine: A Study of the Sociology of Applied Knowledge*
1973 **No award**
1974 **Clifford Geerts,** *The Interpretation of Cultures*
Christopher Jenks, *Inequality*
1975 **Immanuel Wallerstein,** *The Modern World System*
1976 **Robert Bellah,** *The Broken Covenant: American Civil Religion in Time of Trial*
Jeffrey Paige, *Agrarian Revolution: Social Movements and Export Agriculture in the Underdeveloped World*
1977 **Kai T. Erikson,** *Everything in Its Path*
Perry Anderson, *Considerations on Western Marxism*
1978 **No award**
1979 **Helen Fein,** *Accounting for Genocide*

The MacIver Award, honoring publications prior to the establishment of the Sorokin Award, is no longer given.

1956 **E. Franklin Frazier,** *The Black Bourgeoisie*
1958 **Reinhard Bendix,** *Work and Authority in Industry*
1959 **August B. Hollingshead and Frederick C. Redlich,** *Social Class and Mental Illness: A Community Study*
1960 **No award**
1961 **Erving Goffman,** *The Presentation of Self in Everyday Life*
1962 **Seymour Martin Lipset,** *Political Man: The Social Bases of Politics*
1963 **Wilbert E. Moore,** *The Conduct of the Corporation*
1964 **Shmuel N. Eisenstadt,** *The Political Systems of Empires*
1965 **William J. Goode,** *World Revolution and Family Patterns*
1966 **John Porter,** *The Vertical Mosaic: An Analysis of Social Class and Power in Canada*
1967 **Kai T. Erikson,** *Wayward Puritan*
1968 **Barrington Moore, Jr.,** *Social Origins of Dictatorship and Democracy*

The Dubois-Johnson-Frazier Award, which carries a $500 cash prize, biennially honors a member of the Association for development of scholarly efforts. When the award is made to an institution, a commemorative plaque is also given. The Dubois-Johnson-Frazier Award Committee selects the recipient.

1971 **Oliver Cromwell Cox**
1973 **St. Clair Drake**
1976 **Hylan Garnett Lewis**
1978 **Ira de Augustine Reid**
1980 **Joseph S. Himes**

In 1980 the American Sociological Association established general awards in three areas to replace honors which had been discontinued. A selection committee chooses the winners.

ASA AWARD FOR A CAREER OF DISTINGUISHED SCHOLARSHIP

1980 **Robert K. Merton**

ASA AWARD FOR A DISTINGUISHED CONTRIBUTION TO SCHOLARSHIP

1980 **Peter Blau**
Theda Skocpol

ASA AWARD FOR CONTRIBUTIONS TO TEACHING

1980 **Everett K. Wilson**

The Stouffer Award, which carries a $500 honorarium, was given annually for a work or a series of works published during the previous five years which notably advanced the methodology of sociological research. The award has been discontinued.

1973 **Hubert M. Blalock, Jr.**
1974 **O.C. Duncan**
Leo A. Goodman
1975 **James S. Coleman**
Harrison C. White
1976 **No award**
1977 **Otis Dudley Duncan**

Special Award

1973 **Paul F. Lazarsfeld**

Louis I. Dublin Award

AMERICAN ASSOCIATION OF SUICIDOLOGY
Box 3264, Houston, Tex. 77001 (713/644-7911)

The recipient of the Louis I. Dublin Award receives a plaque in recognition of contributions to the field of suicidology and suicide prevention.

1971 **Karl Menninger**
1972 **Edwin Shneidman**
1973 **Norman Farberow**
1974 **Reverend Chad Varah**
1975 **Robert Felix**
1976 **Theodore Curphey**
1977 **Avery Weisman**

Current Status Unknown

Socio-Psychological Prize

AMERICAN ASSOCIATION FOR THE ADVANCEMENT OF SCIENCE
1515 Massachusetts Ave. NW, Washington, D.C. 20005 (202/467-4400)

The $1,000 AAAS Socio-Psychological Prize is given annually for a meritorious paper that furthers the understanding of human psychological-social-cultural behavior and "fosters liberation from philosophic-academic conventions and from dogmatic boundaries between different disciplines." The winner is selected by a panel.

1952 **Arnold M. Rose**, "A Theory of Social Organization and Disorganization"
1953 **No award**
1954 **No award**
1955 **Yehudi A. Cohen**, "Food and Its Vicissitudes: A Cross-cultural Study of Sharing and Nonsharing in 60 Folk Societies"
1956 **Herbert C. Kelman**, "Compliance, Identification, and Internationalization: A Theoretical and Experimental Approach to the Study of Social Influence"
1957 **Irving A. Taylor**, "Similarities in the Structure of Extreme Social Attitudes"
1958 **No award**
1959 **Stanley Schachter**, "The Psychology of Affiliation"
1960 **Robert Rosenthal** and **Kemit Fode**, "Three Experiments in Experimenter Bias"
1961 **Morton Deutsch** and **Robert M. Krauss**, "Experimental Studies of Interpersonal Bargaining"

1962 **William A. Gamson**, "A Theory of Coalition Formation"
1963 **William J. McGuire**, "Immunization against Persuasion"
Morris Rosenberg, "Society and the Adolescent Self-Image"
1964 **Stanley Milgram**, "Some Conditions of Obedience and Disobedience to Authority"
1965 **No award**
1966 **Ivo K. Feierabend** and **Rosalind L. Feierabend**, "Systemic Conditions of Political Aggression: An Application of Frustration-Aggression Theory"
1967 **Irving Janis**, "Effects of Fear Arousal on Attitude Change: Recent Developments in Theory and Experimental Research"
1968 **Bibb Latane** and **John M. Darley**, "The Unresponsive Bystander: Why Doesn't He Help?"
1969 **Zick Rubin**, "The Social Psychology of Romantic Love"
1970 **Elliot Aronson**, "Some Antecedents of Interpersonal Attraction"
1971 **David C. Glass** and **Jerome E. Singer**, "The Urban Condition: Its Stress and Adaptation"
1972 **Norman H. Anderson**, "Information Integration Theory: A Brief Survey"
1973 **Lenora Greenbaum**, "Socio-Cultural Influences on Decision Making: An Illustrative Investigation of Possession-Trance in Sub-Saharan Africa"
1974 **William E. McAuliffe** and **Robert A. Gordon**, "A Test of Lindesmith's Theory of Addiction: The Frequency of Euphoria among Long-Term Addicts"
1975 **R.B. Zajong** and **Gregory B. Markus**, "Intellectual Environment and Intelligence"
1976 **No award**
1977 **Jonathan Kelley** and **Herbert S. Klein**, "Revolution and the Rebirth of Inequality: The Bolivian National Revolution"
1978 **Murray Melbin**, "Night as Frontier"
1979 **Ronald S. Wilson**, "Synchronies in Mental Development: An Epigenetic Perspective"
1980 **Bibb Latane**, **Stephen Harkins** and **Kipling Williams**, "Many Hands Make Light the Work: Causes and Consequences of Social Loafing"

Chauveau Medal

ROYAL SOCIETY OF CANADA
344 Wellington, Ottawa, Ont. K1A ON4 (613/992-3468)

The Chauveau Medal, which is of silver and carries a $1,000 honorarium, is awarded every two years for distinguished contributions and knowledge in the humanities in fields other than Canadian Literature or history. A selection committee chooses the winner.

1952 **Pierre Daviault**
1953 **B.K. Sandwell**
1954 **Gererd Morisset**
1955 **Jean-Marie Gauvreau**
1956 **Victor Morin**
1957 **Claude Melancon**
1959 **Harry Bernard**
1960 **F.C.A. Jeanneret**
1961 **Gerard Malchelosse**
1962 **Maurice Lebel**
1963 **Arthur Maheux**
1964 **Rosaire Dion-Levesque**
1965 **Robert Charbonneau**
1966 **Louis-Philippe Audet**
1968 **B. Wilkinson**
1970 **Northrop Frye**
1972 **Louis-Edmond Hamelin**
1974 **Wilfred Cantwell Smith**
1976 **Edward Togo Salmon**
1979 **Kathleen Coburn**

Innis-Gerin Medal

ROYAL SOCIETY OF CANADA
344 Wellington, Ottawa, Ont. K1A ON4 (613/992-3468)

The Innis-Gerin Medal, which is of bronze and is accompanied by a $1,000 cash prize, is awarded every two years for distinquished and sustained contributions to the literature of the social sciences, including human geography and social psychology. A selection committee chooses the recipient.

1967 **W.A. Mackintosh**
1968 **Esdras Minville**
1969 **Alexander Brady**
1971 **Jacques Henripin**
1973 **Jean-Charles Falardeau**
1975 **Noel Mailloux**
1977 **H.G. Johnson**
1979 **Marc-Adelard Tremblay**

King Abdul Aziz Award in Historical Research

KING ABDUL AZIZ RESEARCH CENTRE
Daret King Abdul Aziz, Box 2945, Riyadh, Saudi Arabia (Tel. 4038646)

The King Abdul Aziz Research Award, which carries a 20,000-riyal first prize as well as runnerup honorariums, is awarded as merited for the best research paper on the history, literature or geography of Saudi Arabia, the Arabian Peninsula or the Islamic world generally.

1977 **Abdul Fattah Abu Alia**

Education

Contents

Related Awards

Agronomic Education Award

AMERICAN SOCIETY OF AGRONOMY
677 S. Segoe Rd., Madison, Wisc. 53711 (608/274-1212)

The $200 Agronomic Education Award annually recognizes educational innovations developed and used successfully, with a focus on educational contributions of classroom teachers, extension agronomists, industrial agronomists and others whose primary concern is teaching of the science. A Selection Committee picks the recipient from a list of nominees.

1957 **T.H. Goodding**
1958 **D.F. Metcalfe**
1959 **H.D. Foth**
1960 **J.K. Patterson**
1961 **A.R. Hilst**
1962 **A.A. Johnson**
1963 **H.W. Smith**
1964 **A.W. Burger**
1965 **S.R. Aldrich**
1966 **M.D. Dawson**
1967 **B.A. Krantz**
1968 **W.H. Scholtus**
1969 **W.L. Colville**
1970 **L.H. Smith**
1971 **W.F. Keim**
1972 **D.P. McGill**
1973 **W.O. Scott**
1974 **S.L. Ahlrichs**
1975 **E.A. Emery**
1976 **D.A. Miller**
1977 **K.L. Larson**

AGRONOMIC RESIDENT EDUCATION AWARD

1978 **M.H. Milford**
1979 **D.F. Post**
1980 **D.E. Green**

AGRONOMIC EXTENSION EDUCATION AWARD

1978 **E.L. Knake**
1979 **D.A. Rohweder**
1980 **J.E. Baylor**

Western Electric Fund Award
Dow Jones Award

AMERICAN ASSEMBLY OF COLLEGIATE SCHOOLS OF BUSINESS
11500 Olive Blvd., Suite 142, St. Louis, Mo. 63141
(314/872-8481)

The Western Electric Fund Award honors institutions and individuals for innovations in undergraduate education in business administration. Deans or heads of business schools that are AACSB members may nominate faculty members for unique classroom programs. A selection committee choses the winner. The individual receives $1,000 and the sponsoring university or college receives $5,000.

1970 **University of Oregon and John R. Wish,** "Beachhead College"

1971 **Indiana University and William G. Panschar,** "Four-Course Integrative Core"

1972 **Massachusetts Institute of Technology Sloan School of Management and John F. Rockart,** "An Integrated Use of Available Resource (Student, Professor, and Technology) in the Learning Process"

1973 **Washington State University and Mark Hammer and C. Obert Henderson,** "A Program for Improving Large Class Instruction"

1974 **University of Hawaii and Bruce M. Hass,** "Time-Compressed Speech"

1975 **Southern Illinois University, Edwardsville and David J. Werner,** "Management Problem Laboratory Program"

1976 **Carnegie Mellon University and Gerald L. Thompson,** "Self-Managed Learning of Mathematics—Operations Research"

1977 **Miami University and John P. Maggard,** "Laws, Hall and Associates"

1978 **Brigham Young Unaiversity** and **E. Doyle Robinson,** "The Skaggs Institute of Retail Management"

1979 **California State University** (San Bernardino) and **Margaret King Gibbs,** "Training Women in Administration in Videotape"

1980 **University of Pennsylvania** and **Howard Kunruther,** "Decision Sciences Applied to University Problems"

The Dow Jones Award, which carries a $7,500 cash grant donated to the college or university of the winner's choice, honors individuals for contributions to business education. The Assembly considers nominess irrespective of an association with the organization.

1974 **Walter Hoving, Tiffany & Co.,** donated to The Wharton School, University of Pennsylvania

1975 **E.G. Bach, Frank E. Buck Professor of Economics and Public Policy, Stanford University,** donated to Stanford University and Carnegie-Mellon University

1976 **Paul Garner, Dean Emeritus, College of Commerce, University of Atlanta,** donated to University of Alabama and University of Texas

1977 **Charles J. Dirksen, Dean of the Graduate School, University of Santa Clara,** donated to University of Santa Clara

1978 **McKee Fisk,** Dean Emeritus, School of Business and Administration Sciences, California State University (Fresno), donated to California State University (Fresno)

1979 **Milton Wilson,** Dean, School of Business and Public Administration, Howard University, donated to Howard University

1980 **William F. Sharpe,** Professor, Stanford University, donated to Stanford University

Exxon Award

AMERICAN ASSEMBLY OF COLLEGIATE SCHOOLS OF BUSINESS
1150 Olive Blvd., Ste. 142, St. Louis, Mo. 63141
(314/872-8481)

The $10,000 Exxon Award annually awards innovation and contributions in graduate education for business administration and management. A selection committee chooses the winner from nominations submitted by deans of heads of business administration units of AACAB-accredited institutions offering masters degrees.

1979 **Richard A. Johnson** and **William T. Newell** (University of Washington), for development of concentrated, one-quarter packages of basic management concepts, theories and techniques offered to graduate student in the university's departments and colleges other than business

1980 **Ray Miles** (University of California, Berkeley), for program in which student teams participate on top policy-making aboards and committees of the Kaiser Aluminum and Chemical Corp.

Union Carbide Award for Chemical Education
Polysar Award

CHEMICAL INSTITUTE OF CANADA
151 Slater St., Ste. 906, Ottawa, Canada K1P 5H3
(613/233-5623)

The Union Carbide Award for Chemical Education, formerly called the Chemical Education Award, is a $750 honor given for outstanding contributions in Canada at any level or education in chemistry or chemical engineering. A committee selects the winner from nominations received.

1961 **R.P. Graham**, "Too Much and Not Enough"
1962 **R.B. Sandin**, "Put the Spotlight on the Student—not on Yourself"
1963 **G.B. Frost**, "Chemical Education — The Future Perspective"
1964 **C. Sivertz**, "Problems of Science Education in the New Age"
1965 **J.B. Phillips**, "Trends in Chemical Engineering Education in Canada"
1966 **L.H. Cragg**, "The Central Purpose of Chemical Education"
1967 **W.A.E. McBryde**, "The Case for Iroquois College"
1968 **A.B. Van Cleave**, "Science Education Policy? That's Not Our business. We're Scientists"
1969 **C. Ouellet**, "L'Humanite sera-t-elle toujours a l'ecole?"
1970 **C.A. Winkler**, "Education— for Craft and Commerce, or Comprehension?"
1971 **A.N. Campbell**, "Forty Years in Chemistry"
1972 **R.L. McIntosh**, "Maunderings on the Usual Themes"
1973 **J.M. Holmes** "Whither Chemical Education"
1974 **K.J. Laidler**, "Too Much to Know"
1975 **W.E. Harris**, "Analyzing Teaching"
1976 **R.J. Gillespie**, "Chemistry — Fact or Fiction?"
1977 **B.T. Newbold**, "Chemical Education — The Current Challenging Scene."
1978 **R.J. Thibert**, "Formal Training Programs in Clinical Chemistry"
1979 **R.H. Tomlinson**, "Trends and Opinions Related to Chemical Education"
1980 **Not available at press time**

The Polysar Award, which carries a $250 honorarium, is made annually for excellence in teaching chemistry at a community or technical college level in Canada. A committee selects two winners a year from nominations received.

1977 **R.A. DiMenna**
S. Jalil
1978 **A.H. Allman**
B.J. Hutchinson
1979 **W.A. Mohun**
M.A. Ryant
1980 **Not available at press time**

Lamme Award
George Westinghouse Award
Senior Research Award
Curtis W. McGraw Research Award
James H. McGraw Award
Chester F. Carlson Award
Bendix Minorities in Engineering Award
Clement J. Freuch Award
William Elgin Wickenden Award
Professional and Technical Division Awards
Western Electric Fund Award
Dow Outstanding Young Facility Award
Outstanding Zone Campus Activity/Committee Award

AMERICAN SOCIETY FOR ENGINEERING EDUCATION
One DuPont Cir., Ste. 400, Washington, D.C. 20036
(202/293-7080)

The Lamme Award is given to an outstanding engineering educator for excellence in teaching and for contributions to teaching, research and technical literature. The winner receives a gold medal and a certificate. An award committee selects the honoree.

1928 **George F. Swain**
1929 **Irving P. Church**
1930 **Charles F. Scott**
1931 **Dugald C. Jackson**
1932 **Arthur N. Talbot**
1933 **Dexter S. Kimball**
1934 **Edward R. Mauer**
1935 **William E. Wickenden**
1936 **Herman Schneider**
1937 **Frederick E. Turneaure**
1938 **Robert L. Sackett**
1939 **Stephen P. Timoshenko**
1940 **Andrey A. Potter**
1941 **Anson Marston**
1942 **Roy A. Seaton**
1943 **Thomas E. French**
1944 **Hardy Cross**
1945 **Harry P. Hammond**
1946 **Robert E. Doherty**
1947 **Warren K. Lewis**
1948 **Alexander G. Christie**
1949 **Karl T. Compton**
1950 **Fred B. Seely**
1951 **Allan R. Cullimore**
1952 **Solomon C. Hollister**
1953 **Harry S. Rogers**
1954 **Thorndike Saville**
1955 **Vannevar Bush**
1956 **Llewellyn M.K. Boelter**
1957 **William L. Everitt**
1958 **Linton E. Grinter**
1959 **Gordon S. Brown**
1960 **Theodore Von Karman**

1961 Olaf A. Hougen
1962 Harold L. Hazen
1963 B. Richard Teare, Jr.
1964 Frederick E. Terman
1965 Eric A. Walker
1966 Frederick C. Lindvall
1967 Daniel C. Drucker
1968 Morrough P. O'Brien
1969 Joseph C. Elgin
1970 Jacob P. Den Hartog
1971 Richard G. Folsom
1972 Glenn Murphy
1973 Max S. Peters
1974 George W. Hawkins
1975 John R. Whinnery
1976 John J. McKetta
1977 Ascher H. Shapiro
1978 Mac Elwyn Van Valkenburg
1979 William H. Corcoran
1980 John C. Hancock

The George Westinghouse Award is given annually to an educator 45 years of age or younger whose past accomplishments give the award committee reason to believe that the recipient will continue to be an excellent and innovative teacher of engineering. The winner receives $1,500 and his academic department is given $500.

1946 James N. Goodier
1947 B. Richard Teare, Jr.
1948 Hunter Rouse
1949 Joseph Marin
1950 Rolf Eliassen
1951 Glenn Murphy
1952 Gordon S. Brown
1953 Edward F. Obert
1954 Thomas J. Higgins
1955 Robert R. White
1956 Milton C. Shaw
1957 Robert E. Treybal
1958 Willis W. Harman
1959 Max S. Peters
1960 R. Byron Bird
1961 David C. White
1962 Paul M. Naghdi
1963 Mac E. Van Valkenburg
1964 Cedomir M. Sliepcevich
1965 John G. Truxal
1966 Ali B. Cambel
1967 Charles L. Miller
1968 Klaus D. Timmerhaus
1969 Arthur E. Byrson, Jr.
1970 Ali A. Seireg
1971 Charles E. Wales
1972 Jack P. Holman
1973 Martin D. Bradshaw
1974 Joseph Bordogna
1975 Donald G. Childers
1976 Jerome B. Cohen
1977 Roger A. Schmitz
1978 C. Judson King
1979 J. Michael Duncan
1980 William B. Krantz

The Senior Research Award, a gold medal, annually honors the member of a college of engineering faculty or staff for significant contributions to engineering research. A committee selects the winner.

1979 Thomas J. Hanratty
1980 August J. Durelli

The $1,000 Curtis W. McGraw Research Award annually recognizes an individual 40 years of age or younger for achievements in college research. A committee selects the winner.

1957 George Gerard
1958 Cedomir M. Sliepcevich
1959 R. Byron Bird
1960 Ali B. Cambel
1961 William A. Nash
1962 Michael Boudart
1963 Thomas J. Hanratty
1964 Joseph E. Rowe
1965 Frank S. Barnes
1966 Gareth Thomas
1967 John P. Hirth
1968 Eric Baer
1969 Robert G. Jahn
1970 George I. Haddad
1971 George S. Ansell
1972 Jose B. Cruz, Jr.
1973 Stephen E. Harris
1974 Julian Szekely
1975 Jan D. Achenbach
1976 John H. Seinfeld
1977 Dan Luss
1978 Gerald L. Kulcinski
1979 Thomas K. Gaylord
1980 Clark K. Colton

The James H. McGraw Award, which carries a $1,000 honorarium, is awarded annually for outstanding service to engineering education. A committee chooses the recipient.

1950 Harry P. Hammond
1951 Robert H. Spahr
1952 Arthur L. Williston
1953 Charles W. Beese
1954 Arthur C. Harper
1955 Frederick E. Dobbs
1956 Charles S. Jones
1957 Arthur L. Townsend
1958 Karl O. Werwath
1959 Henry P. Adams
1960 Kenneth L. Holderman
1961 H. Russell Beatty
1962 Eugene H. Rietzke
1963 Lawrence V. Johnson
1964 A. Ray Sims
1965 Clyde L. Foster
1966 Walter M. Hartung
1967 Cecil C. Tyrrell
1968 William N. Fenninger
1969 Winston D. Purvine
1970 Hugh E. McCallick
1971 Melvin R. Lohmann
1972 Richard J. Ungrodt
1973 G. Ross Henninger
1974 Merritt A. Williamson
1975 Louis J. Dunham, Jr.
1976 Eugene Wood Smith
1977 Donald C. Metz
1978 Joseph J. Gershon
1979 Robert J. Wear
1980 Lyman L. Francis

The $1,000 Chester F. Carlson Award annually honors an innovator in engineering or engineering technology education for contributions to the field specifically in response to the influence of a changing sociological and technological environment. A committee selects the recipient.

1973 George C. Beakley
1973 Kenneth A. McCollom
1974 Henry O. Fuchs
Robert Steidel, Jr.
1975 Robert W. Dunlap
Gordon H. Lewis
1976 James E. Shamblin
1977 Hugh E. McCallick
1978 Robert P. Morgan
1979 William R. Grogan
1980 Billy V. Koen

The Vincent Bendix Award was given until 1978 for contributions to engineering education. It has been replaced by the more specific William Bendix Minorities in Engineering Award.

1956 Clifford C. Furnas
1957 Theodore Von Karman
1958 Hunter Rouse
1959 Robert F. Mehl
1960 Maurice J. Zucrow
1961 Nathan M. Newmark
1962 Roy Bainer
1963 Arthur T. Ippen
1964 John Bardeen
1965 William R. Sears
1966 Charles S. Draper
1967 George W. Housner
1968 Harry G. Drickamer
1969 Earl R. Parker
1970 Neal R. Amundson
1971 Egon Orowan
1972 Ernst R.G. Eckert
1973 John R. Low, Jr.
1974 James W. Westwater
1975 Aldert van der Ziel
1976 Harry Bolton Seed
1977 Ven Te Chow
1978 Robert A. Huggins

The Vincent Bendix Minorities in Engineering Award, which carries a $1,000 honorarium and a $500 travel stipend, is given annually to an engineering educator for motivating minority and/or female candidates to enter and continue engineering studies. A committee selects the winner.

1978 F. William Schutz, Jr.
1979 Howard L. Wakeland

The $1,000 Clement J. Freund Award annually honors an individual in business, industry, government or education for a significant positive impact on cooperative education programs in engineering or engineering technology. An award committee chooses the recipient.

1979 Clement J. Freund
1980 Cornelius Wandmacher

The William Elgin Wickenden Award, which consists of $1,000 and a plaque, annually recognizes the author of the best paper published in *Engineering Education*, as chosen by an award committee.

1978 A.W. Engin and A.F. Engin
1979 Lawrence P. Grayson
1980 William R. Grogan

Honorary Membership is conferred to members and nonmembers of the ASEE for eminent and distinguished service in engineering and engineering education or allied fields. To be selected, a nominee must receive three-fourths approval of the Board of Directors.

1953 Harry P. Hammond
1953 Andrey A. Potter
1958 Dwight D. Eisenhower
1959 Nathan W. Dougherty
1960 James S. Thompson
1960 Henry T. Heald
1961 Vannevar Bush
1961 Solomon C. Hollister
1962 Linton E. Grinter
1962 Roy A. Seaton
1963 James R. Killian, Jr.
1964 Thorndike Saville
1964 Maynard M. Borning
1965 Huber O. Croft
Erik A. Walker
1966 Llewellyn M.K. Boelter
1966 Frederick E. Terman
1967 Frederick C. Lindvall
1967 Stephen Timoshenko
1968 William L. Everitt
1968 B. Richard Teare, Jr.
1969 Richard G. Folsom
1969 Morrough P. O'Brien
1970 Kurt F. Wendt
1970 Glenn Murphy
1971 W. Leighton Collins
1971 George D. Lobingier
1972 George A. Hawkins
1972 Ernst Weber
1973 Carl C. Chambers
1973 Elmer C. Easton
1974 Archie Higdon
1974 Robert H. Roy
1975 Melvin R. Lohmann
1975 Merritt A. Williamson
1976 Harold A. Rolz
1976 Joseph M. Pettit
1977 Ralph E. Fadum
1977 Robert W. Van Houten
1978 George Burnet
1978 John C. Calhoun
1979 Cornelius Wandmacher
1979 Walter M. Hartung
1980 Lee Harrisberger
1980 Ricard Ungrodt

The Distinguished and Unusual Service Award is the highest award for service to engineering and engineering technology education and allied fields. To be selected, an individual must be chosen by the Member Recognition Committee, subject to ratification by a three-fourths vote of the Board of Directors.

1971 W. Leighton Collins
1972 L. E. Grinter
1974 Leslie B. Williams
1978 M.R. Lohmann
1979 Joseph M. Pettit
1980 William Everitt

The Distinguished Service Citation annually honors a member, who may be an individual or an organization, for long, continous and distinguished service to engineering and engineering technology education. The Member Recognition Committee selects the winner, subject to a three-fourths vote of approval by the Board of Directors.

1975 Frank D. Hansing

1976 Western Electric Company
1977 Joseph M. Biedenbach
1977 Lawrence P. Grayson
1977 Junior Engineering Technical Society
1978 Student Competion in Relevant Engineering (SCORE)
1979 Archie Higdon
1980 Fred N. Peebles
1980 International Association for the Exchange of Students for Technical Experience/U.S. (IAESTE/US)

The ASEE gives a variety of Professional and Technical Division Awards for excellent in specific fields of engineering and engineering technology. Some carry cash prizes. An awards committee selects the recipients.

UNIQUE AND MERITORIOUS SERVICE TO ENGINEERING EDUCATION AWARD, AEROSPACE DIVISION

1974 Ben M. Pollard

EDUCATIONAL ACHIEVEMENT AWARD, AEROSPACE DIVISION/AIAA

1975 Jack E. Fairchild
1976 Barnes W. McCormick
1977 Stanley H. Lowy
1978 Robert F. Brodsky
1979 Donnell W. Dutton
1980 Thomas J. Mueller

LECTURESHIP AWARD, CHEMICAL ENGINEERING DIVISION

1963 Arthur B. Metzner
1964 Charles R. Wilke
1965 Leon Lapidus
1966 Octave Levenspiel
1967 Andraes Acrivos
1968 L. Edward Scriven
1969 Cornelius J. Pings
1970 Joe M. Smith
1971 William R. Schowalter
1972 Dale F. Rudd
1973 Rutherford Aris
1974 Elmer L. Gaden, Jr.
1975 John M. Prausnitz
1976 Abraham E. Dukler
1977 Robert C. Reid
1978 Theodore Vermeulen
1979 Daniel D. Perlmutter
1980 Klaus D. Timmerhaus

EUGENE L. GRANT AWARD, ENGINEERING ECONOMY DIVISION

1966 J. Morley English
1967 Richard L. Norgaard
1968 Laurence C. Rosenberg
1969 Gerald W. Smith
1970 Robert F. Kleusner
1971 James C. T. Mao
John F. Brewster
1972 Raymond P. Lutz
Harold A. Cowles
1973 William Rudko, Jr.
Richard J. Tersine
1974 Lynn E. Bussey
G.T. Stevens, Jr.
1975 J. Morley English
1976 Nabil A. El-Ramley
Richard E. Peterson
K.K. Seo
1977 Gerald J. Theusen
1978 Peter G. Sassone
1979 James R. Buck
Glen H. Sullivan
Phillip E. Nelson
1980 John Freidenfeld
Michael D. Kennedy

DISTINGUISHED SERVICE AWARD, ENGINEERING DESIGN GRAPHICS DIVISION

1950 Frederic G. Higbee
1951 Frederick E. Giesecke
1952 George J. Hood
1953 Carl L. Svenson
1954 Randolph P. Hoelscher
1955 Justus Rising
1956 Ralph S. Paffenbarger
1957 Frank A. Heacock
1958 H. Cecil Spencer
1959 C. Elmer Rowe
1960 Clifford H. Springer
1961 William E. Street
1962 Jasper Gerardi
1963 Theodore T. Aakhus
1964 Warren J. Luzadder
1965 Ralph T. Northrup
1966 James S. Rising
1967 Ivan L. Hill
1968 B. Leighton Wellman
1969 Edward M. Griswold
1970 J. Howard Porsch
1971 Matthew McNeary
1972 Paul M. Reinhard
1973 Edward W. Jacunski
1974 Irwin Wladaver
1975 Robert H. Hammond
1976 Eugene G. Pare
1977 Percy H. Hill
1978 Charles G. Sanders
1979 William B. Rogers
1980 Mary F. Blade

OPPENHEIMER AWARD, ENGINEERING DESIGN GRAPHICS DIVISION

1979 John T. Demel, Alan D. Kent
1980 Arvid E. Eide

G. EDWIN BURKS AWARD, MECHANICAL ENGINEERING DIVISION

1970 Jesse S. Doolittle
1971 Edward F. Obert
1972 William C. Reynolds
1973 Reginald I. Vachon
1974 Warren H. Giedt

RALPH COATS ROE AWARD, MECHANICAL ENGINEERING DIVISION

1976 John R. Dixon
1977 Stothe P. Kezios
1978 Ephraim M. Sparrow
1979 Robert H. Page
1980 Wilbert F. Stoecker

OUTSTANDING TEACHER AWARD, MECHANICAL ENGINEERING DIVISION

1975 Bei Tse Chao

DISTINGUISHED SERVICE AWARD, CONTINUING PROFESSIONAL DEVELOPMENT DIVISION

1976 Joseph M. Biedenbach
1976 John P. Klus
1977 Monroe W. Kriegel
1978 Donald B. Miller, Howard R. Shelton
1979 Lionel V. Baldwin
1980 Lindon E. Saline

FREDERICK EMMONS TERMAN AWARD, ELECTRICAL ENGINEERING DIVISION

1969 Michael Athans
1970 Andrew P. Sage
1971 Joseph W. Goodman
1972 Taylor L. Booth
1973 Sanjit Kumar Mitra
1974 Leon O. Chua
1975 Michael L. Dertouzos
1976 Stephen W. Director
1977 J. Leon Shohet
1978 Ronald A. Rohrer
1979 Martha E. Sloan
1980 V. Thomas

GEORGE O. HAYS AWARD

1969 Douglas C. Williams
1970 Warren W. Wood
1971 Burton J. Gleason

ARTHUR L. WILLISTON AWARD

1964 G. Ross Henninger
1965 Maurice R. Grancy
1966 James L. McGraw
1967 Karl O. Werwath, Robert W. Hays
1968 Harold A. Foecke
1969 H. Walter Shaw
1970 Jerry S. Dobrovbolny
1973 Jesse J. Defore

JOHN A. CURTIS LECTURE AWARD, COMPUTERS IN EDUCATION DIVISION

1978 C. Norman Kerr
1979 Dean K. Frederick, Gary L. Waag

DISTINGUISHED EDUCATOR AWARD, MECHANICS DIVISION

1977 Archie Higdon
1978 James L. Meriam
1979 Egor P. Popov
1980 Ferdinand P. Beer

GLENN MURPHY AWARD, NUCLEAR ENGINEERING DIVISION

1976 Raymond L. Murray
1977 Edward H. Klevans
1978 Thomas W. Kerlin, Jr.
1979 Glenn F. Knoll
1980 Allen F. Henry

EMINENT LECTURESHIP AWARD, EDUCATIONAL RESEARCH AND METHODS DIVISION

1969 Harold E. Mitzel
1970 Robert M. Gagne
1971 Lewis B. Meyhew

DISTINGUISHED LECTURER

1966 **Ralph W. Tyler**, Director, Center for Advanced Study in the Behavioral Sciences, Stanford, Calif.
1967 **Robben W. Fleming**, Chancellor, University of Wisconsin, Madison, Wis.
1968 **Lee A. DuBridge**, President, California Institute of Technology
1969 **James A. Perkins**, President, Cornell University.

ALVAH K. BORMAN MERITORIOUS SERVICE AWARD, COOPERATIVE EDUCATION

1979 Alvah K. Borman, Stewart B. Collins, Henry G. Hutton
1980 John L. Campbell

The Dow Outstanding Young Faculty Awards are given annually to 12 ASEE members, all under 36 years of age, to attend the association's annual conference. The award consists of a certificate and travel expenses. A committee in each of the ASEE's 12 regional sections choses one recipient each year.

1969 T.L. Anderson, T. Bonnema, G.A. Cushman, T.A. Haliburton, J.L. Herrington, D.E. Kirk, J.P. Klus, J.T. Pfeffer, W.D. Seider, B.A. Tschantz, G.Z. Watters, R.M. Zimmerman
1970 J.M. Able, E.M. Bailey, M.O. Breitmeyer, F.E. Burris, A.M. Despain, R.A. Ellson, J.S. Gooding, C.A. Killgore, M.H. Richman, C.H. Sprague, G.T. Taoka, P.K. Turnquist
1971 V.K. Feiste, W.M. Phillips, J.W. Willhide, J.T. Sears, J. Counts, N.C. Kerr, J.R. Hopper, L.D. Goss, W. Petsch, A.A. Torvi, R.E. Lave, W.B. Krantz
1972 R.A. Peura, L.S. Fletcher, R.D. Findlay, W.G. Wyatt, H.A. Siebesta, T.C. Owens, G.W. Neudeck, H.S. Fogler, O.N. Garcia, C.E. Cartmill, K.D. Linstedt, T.G. Stoebe
1973 F.L. Bennett, W.L. Carson, W.L. Dickson, J.T. Emanuel, L.L. Hench, J.S. Hirschhorn, T.H. Houlihan, R.G. Jeffers, C.M. Lovas, G.W. May, Lee Rosenthal, R.A. Shaw
1974 W.R. Adrion, R.M. Anderson, Jr., J.S. Boland, III, A.R. Eide, R.C. Pare, O.A. Peku, W.R. Ramirez, R.P. Rhoten, C.A. Rosselli, T.E. Shoup, W.C. Van Buskirk, W.S. Venable
1975 W.D. Carroll, D.S. Frederick, R.M. Haralick, H.Y. Ko, R.B. Landis, G.W. Lowery, J.J. McDonough, R.W. Mortimer, S.L. Rice, M.A. Sloan, D.R. Utela, D.N. Weiman
1976 G.T. Craig, T.P. Cullinane, W.T. Darby, L.J. Griffiths, R.B. Hayter, R.G. Hoelzeman, L.L. Northrop, M.E. Parten, H.S. Peavy, W.W. Recker, W.T. Rhodes, J. M. Samuels, Jr..
1977 W.S. Reed, D.L. Cohn, J.A. Kirk, J.A. Alic, J.W. Cipolla, Jr., J.T. Cain, R.J. Niederjohn, R.Y. Itani, M.M. Cirovic, K.P. Chong, C.E. Halford, R.W. Mayne.
1978 C.J. Waugaman, R.O. Buckius, R.J. Craig, J.E. Fagan, M. Kupferman, R.D. Gilson, J.P. Sadler, P.P. Fasang, P.F. Pfaelzer, M. Criswell, R. Garcia-Pacheco, D.G. Ullman
1979 R.N. Andrews, D. Apelian, T.J. Boehm, H.J. Freeman, M.F. Hein, M. Jolles, I. Kaneko, M.E. Ryan, R.J. Scranton, E.D. Sloan, G.H. Sutherland, L.N. Walker
1980 J. Collura, R.C. Eck, T.B. Edil, R.D. Flack, J.W. Haslett, V.K. Kinra, T.W. Lester, C.D. Pegden, H.B. Puttgen, S.W. Stafford, R.S. Subramanian, P.C. Wankat

The $1,000 Western Electric Fund Awards are given annually to meritorious teachers of any subject in the engineering or engineering technology curriculum of a four-year institution granting engineering degrees. The subject matter need not be limited to scientific or technical courses. A committee in each of the ASEE's 12 regional sections chooses the winners. There is one award in each section with fewer than 1,000 members and two winners in sections with more than 1,000 members.

1965 A.G. Bose, A.D. Brickman, L.B. Cherry, J.S. Doolittle, E.R.G. Eckert, R.S. Hartenberg, D.S. Hoffman, W.H. Huggins, E.J. Lindahl, K.A. Newhouse, W.D. Nix, R.K. Osborn, G.R. Siegmon, M.A. Tuttle, B. Webb, Jr., R.H. Zimmerman

1966 W.A. Bradley, E.F. Cross, J.H. Dittfach, R.C. Dove, R. Edse, F.J. Maher, C.H. Mulligan, A.T. Murphy, A.V. Pohm, R.R. Rothfus, M.F. Rubenstein, A.R. Spalding, J.N. Warfield

1967 S.W. Angrist, C.M. Angulo, C.L. Barker, R.E. Beckett, H.D. Bowen, M.H. Cobble, E.W. Harris, H.C. Hesse, W.C. Johnson, C.A. Keyser, E.H. Kopp, R.C.McMaster, A.L. Ruoff, J.O. Smith, E.E. Stansbury, C.M. Thatcher, J.W. Willard, J.C. Wolford

1968 K.E. Brown, L.N. Canjar, W.S. Chalk, R.A. Chipman, J.G. Clarke, F.M. Gryna, Jr., L.A. Hill, Jr., F.G. Hochgraf, R.D. Kelly, R.A. Kliphardt, E.M. Lonsdale, W.J. Luebbert, R.H. Page, D.H. Pletta, H.B. Voelcker, Jr., D.H. Young, A. van der Ziel, C.F. Zorowski

1969 M.D. Bradshaw, A.B. Butler, M.G. Fontana, V.D Frechette, W.H. Giedt, R.D. Guyton, B. Hazeltine, J.J. Jonsson, E.R. Johnston, Jr., J.C. Liebman, P.W. Likins, A.B. Macnee, M.I. Mantell, L.J. McCeady, G.K. Mesmer, H.A. Moench, F.E. Raven, C.E. Work

1970 J.J. Blum, W.H. Corcoran, R.F. Crank, R.W. Day, A.E. Durling, M.M. El-Wakil, W.C. Hahn, Jr., M. Liu, J.A.M. Lyon, J.R. Melcher, H. Menand, Jr., Z.A. Munir, W.F. Stoecker, H.C. Van Ness, D.H. Vliet, C.E. Wales, E.R. Whitehead, J.C. Williams, III

1971 E.H. Gaylord, E J. Freise, H.A. Estrin, B. Johnson, F.M. White, R.E. Stickney, E.M. Williams, R.W. Little, P.C. Cribbins, S.F. Adams, G.P. Francis, C.R. Nichols, C.H. Sprague, M.A. Larson, W.R. Tovey, N.J. Castellan, R.D. Strum, W.R. Tovey, N.J. Castellan, R.D. Strum, W.L. Fletcher

1972 V.L. Pass, J.C. Whitwell, E.T. Misiaszek, H.A. Haus, I.B. Thomas, J.W. Bayne, D.T. Wasan, H.B. Kendall, D.G. Childers, M.N. Ozisik, J. Coates, G.H. Duffrey, K.N. Reid, Jr., A.S. Levens, J.F. Gibbons, R.C. Smith, D.A. Firmage

1973 D.E. Alexander, B.T. Chao, E.R. Chenette, V.E. Denny, D.L. Dietmeyer, E.T.B. Gross, L.D. Harris, W.H. Hayt, Jr., J.L. Melsa, A.W. Pense, E.L. Saxer, K.E. Scott, J.E. Shamblin, R.F. Steidel, Jr., R.I. Vachon, A.S. Weinstein, P.F. Wiggins, J.W. Willhide

1974 F.P. Beer, G. Boothroyd, J. Brodogna, C.M. Butler, A.B. Carlson, V.T. Chow, H. D'Angelo, G.H. Flammer, N.N. Cunaji, H.A. Hassan, W.E. Kastenberg, A.P. Marino, L. Padulo, G.W. Powell, J.T. Sears, B.L. Smith, B.S. Swanson, T.T. Williams

1975 C.M. Bacon, L.D. Feisel, H.S. Haas, J.R. Hauser, J.F. Lestingi, H.R. Martens, J.L. Massey, W.G. McLean, G.W. Neudeck, E.R. Parker, H.L. Plants, R. Seagrave, J.R. Smith, W.A. Sowa, J.E. Stephens, F.F. Videon, C.R. Viswanathan, F.L. Worley, Jr.

1976 G.E. Anner, A.J. Brainard, L.S. Caretto, M.ER. Council, J. Estrin, C.T.A. Johnk, J.M. Kendall, J.R. Kittrell, R.E. Peck, A.J. Perna, R.A. Peura, B.C. Ringo, R.H. Seacat, Jr., F.H. Shair, F.G. Stremier, G.E. Whitehouse, D.J. Wood, P. Zia

1977 Mo-Shing Chen, G.H. Miley, B.J. Pelan, H.H. West, N. Dean Eckhoff, R.R. Hagglund, J.K. Roberge, J.F. McDonough, D.T. Worrell, J.D. Stevens, T.G. Stoebe, G.C. Beakley, Jr., E.P. Popov, F.M. Long, J.S. Boland, III, H.F. Keedy, H.J. McQueen

1978 D.L. Vines, R.G. Squires, R. Bhattacharyya, B.R. Maxwell, W.C. Turner, W.R. Bennett, Jr., E.O. Doebelin, G.T. Hankins, V. Favelic, L.T. Bruton, R.S. Elliott, D.F. Tuttle, Jr., J.K.C. Cheng, W.F. Babcock, M.A. Littlejohn, G.R. Youngquist

1979 S. Ahmed, O.A. Arnas, T. Au, R.M. Brach , M.M. Douglass, W.C. Flowers, R.J. Mattauch, W.F. Phillips, F.N. Rad, L.C. Redekopp, R.P. Santoro, C.L. Sayre. Jr., A.C. Scordelis, J.K. Shultis, J.G. Webster, J.J. Wert

1980 M.M. Abbott, R.G. Boggs, K.E. Case, C.T. Crowe, R.M. Koerner, N. Levan, J.K. Mitchell, F.D. Hart, N.A. Peppas, W.M. Portnoy, W.F. Ramirez, Jr., C.G. Salmon, D.S. Shupe, R.K. Toner, B.A. Tschantz, D.T. Tuma

The Outstanding Zone Campus Activity/Committee Award, which consists of a plaque or certificate, is awarded annually for excellent service as the ASEE's representative on a campus and contributions for staunch support of the society. Committees in four zones select the recipients.

1980 J.P. Burgess, D.R. Huffman, L.B. Greenfield, R.D. Noble

Butler Medal in Gold

COLUMBIA UNIVERSITY
Office of the Secretary, New York, N.Y. 10027

The Butler Medal in Gold is awarded every five years for distinguished contributions to philosophy or to educational theory, practice or administration anywhere in the world.

1915 Bertrand Russell
1920 Benedetto Croce
1925 Edward Lee Thorndike
1930 Alfred North Whitehead
1935 John Dewey
1940 Henri Bergson
1945 George Santayana
1950 Clarence Irving Lewis
1955 George E. Moore
1960 Charlie Dunbar Broad
1965 Rudolf Carnap
1970 Willard van Orman Quine
1975 Jean Paul Sartre
1980 Ernest Nagel

James Bryant Conant Award

AMERICAN CHEMICAL SOCIETY
1155 Sixteenth St. NW, Washington, D.C. 20036
(202/872-4481)

The James Bryant Conant Award in High School Chemistry Teaching is sponsored by the Ethyl Corp. to recognize, encourage and stimulate outstanding chemistry teaching in American high schools. The award, which currently carries a $2,000 honorarium, has been under the sponsorship of various bodies since its establishment. In addition to the national award winners listed here, local and regional honors are made. The awards from 1967 through 1972 were granted to individuals from six districts and were, at the time, the highest level on which the award was made.

1967 **Raymond T. Byrne**
Elaine M. Kilbourne
Harry C. Taylor
Theodore E. Molitor
Elaine W. Ledbetter
Harold E. Alexander
1968 **Daniel P. Corr**
Harold W. Ferguson
Robert M. Sims
Charles F. McClary
Marion Nottingham
George T. Bazzetta
1969 **Elizabeth V. Lamphere**
Joseph S. Schmuckler
Lee R. Summerlin
Ben O. Propeck
Frank S. Quiring
W. Keith MacNab
1970 **Dorothy W. Gifford**
James V. DeRose
William B. Robertson
Newell Smeby
Charles D. Mickey
George Birrell
1971 **Elizabeth W. Sawyer**
Audrey J. Cheek
Bernard Toan
Leo J. Klosterman
Clara Weisser
Nellie G. Fletcher
1972 **Frank J. Tuzzolino**
Albert J. Judge
Anne A. Wiseman
Henrietta A. Parker
Harold I. Pearson
Irma Griesel
1973 **Melvin Greenstadt**
1974 **Wallace J. Gleekman**
1975 **George W. Stapleton**
1976 **Dorothea H. Hoffman**
1977 **Sidney P. Harris**
1978 **Samuel H. Perlmutter**
1979 **Shirley E. Richardson**
1980 **Evelyn R. Bank**

Friend of Education Award

NATIONAL EDUCATION ASSOCIATION
Government Relations Office, 1201 16th St. NW, Washington, D.C. 20036 (202/833-5412)

The Friend of Education Award is an annual award by the Board of Directors to a single individual who has made a significant national contribution to the betterment of American education.

1972 **Lyndon B. Johnson**
1973 **Sen. Abraham Ribicoff**
1974 **Rep. Carl Perkins**
1975 **Terry Sanford**, Duke University
1976 **Roy Wilkins**, NAACP
1977 **Hubert H. Humphrey**
1978 **Joan Ganz Cooney**, Children's Television Workshop
1979 **Thurgood Marshall**, Justice, U.S. Supreme Court
1980 **Jimmy Carter**

Distinguished Service Award

COUNCIL OF CHIEF STATE SCHOOL OFFICERS
379 Hall of the States, 400 N. Capitol St. NW, Washington, D.C. 20001 (202/624-7702)

The Distinguished Service Award, an engraved certificate, is presented annually to an individual for outstanding leadership in the cause of education. Council members nominate candidates for selection by the board of directors.

1955 **Worth McClure**
1956 **Mrs. Newton P. Leonard**
1957 **No award**
1958 **No award**
1959 **Finis E. Englman**
Rep. John E. Fogarty
1960 **Lawrence G. Derthick**
Maurice R. Robinson
1961 **No award**
1962 **Fred F. Beach**
1963 **W. Earl Armstrong**
1964 **No award**
1965 **Francis Keppel**
1966 **No award**
1967 **Wayne O. Reed**
1968 **Sen. Wayne L. Morse**
Jim Jerry Pearson
Rep. Carl D. Perkins
1970 **Terrel H. Bell**
Don M. Dafoe
1971 **Carl. H. Pforzheimer, Jr.**
1972 **Sindey P. Marland, Jr.**
1973 **Edgar L. Morphet**
1974 **W. Willard Wirtz**
Stephen K. Bailey
1975 **Rep. John Brademas**
1976 **Rep. Albert H. Quie**
1977 **Sen. Hubert H. Humphrey**
1978 **Rev. Jesse L. Jackson**
1979 **Fred M. Hechinger**
1980 **Pres. Lyndon B. Johnson**
Harold How II

Konrad Duden Preis der Stadt Mannheim

CITY OF MANNHEIM
Rathaus E-5, Mannheim, Federal Republic of Germany

The Konrad-Duden der Stadt Mannheim, or Konrad Duden Prize of the City of Mannheim, is awarded every two years by the City of Mannheim and the Bibliographisches Institut Mannheim (Bibliographic Institute of Mannheim) for meritorious contributions to the German language. The award consisted of 5,000 marks through 1979, but the 1980 prize-winner will receive 15,000 marks.

1960 **Leo Weisgerber**
1961 **Hans Glinz**
1963 **Hugo Moser**

1965 **Louis L. Hammerich**
1966 **Gerhard Storz**
1967 **Jost Trier**
Gustav Korlen
1969 **Johannes Erben**
1971 **Hans Eggers**
1973 **Jean Fourquet**
1975 **Ludwik Zabrocki**
1977 **Heinz Rupp**
1979 **Peter von Polenz**

C. Albert Koob Award

NATIONAL CATHOLIC EDUCATIONAL ASSN.
One Dupont Cir. NW, Ste. 350, Washington, D.C. 20036 (202/293-5954)

The C. Albert Koob Award is given as merited, usually annually, to any individual who has made an outstanding contribution to Catholic education in America. An award committee appointed by the chairman of the board reviews nominees and submits their names to board members for a vote.

1968 **Most Rev. Ernest J. Primeau**
1969 **Msgr. Carl J. Ryan**
Msgr. Frank M. Schneider
William F. Conley
Msgr. Sylvester J. Hobel
Msgr. James E. Hoflich
Msgr. Felix N. Pitt
1970 **Most Rev. William E. McManus**
Msgr. John T. Foudy
Sister Mary Emil Penet, IHM
William B. Ball
David J. Young
Msgr. O'Neil C. D'Amour
Sister M. Rufina Lutz, OSF
1971 **Brother Anthony Wallace**, FSC
Rev. Theodore M. Hesburgh, CSC
1972 **Msgr. Eugene J. Molloy**
Sister M. Sheila Haskett, OSF
1973 **No award**
1974 **Rev. C. W. Friedman**
Rev. C. Albert Koob
1975 **Most Rev. Raymond J. Gallagher**
1976 **J. Lloyd Trump**
Sister M. Lillian McCormack, SSND
Most Rev. William E. McManus
1977 **Rev. Theodore M. Hesburgh**, CSC
Sister Kathleen Short, OP
Rev. Andrew Greeley
1978 **Most Rev. Cletus O'Donnell**
Msgr. Elmer H. Berhmann
Hon. Carl Perkins
1979 **Sister Maria de la Cruz Aymes**
1980 **Msgr. Wilfrid Paradis**

Warren K. Lewis Award

AMERICAN INSTITUTE OF CHEMICAL ENGINEERS
345 E. 47th St., New York, N.Y. 10017 (212/644-8025)

The Warren K. Lewis Award, which is sponsored jointly by Exxon International, Inc., and the Exxon Research and Engineering Co., annually honors distinguished contributions to chemical engineering education. The award consists of $2,000 and a scroll and is made according to the decision of a committee.

1963 **Barnett F. Dodge**
1964 **Olaf A. Hougen**
1965 **Edwin F. Gilliland**
1966 **Richard H. Wilhelm**
1967 **Donald L. Katz**
1968 **Joseph H. Koffolt**
1969 **John J. McKetta, Jr.**
1970 **Robert L. Pigford**
1971 **Neal R. Amundson**
1972 **Thomas K. Sherwood**
1973 **W.L. McCabe**
1974 **R. Byron Bird**
1975 **Joseph C. Elgin**
1976 **Robert C. Reid**
1977 **Arthur B. Metzner**
1978 **Stuart W. Churchill**
1979 **Max S. Peters**
1980 **Not available at press time**

Maracay Inter-American Prize

ORGANIZATION OF AMERICAN STATES
Dept. of Educational Affairs, 1889 F. St. NW, 5th Floor, Washington, D.C. 20006 (202/789-3319)

The $30,000 Maracay Inter-American Prize in Education annually honors a person, persons or institution for outstanding achievements in education. A five-member panel of international judges selects the winner from nominees presented by ministries of education, universities or bodies of professional educators of an OAS member state.

1979 **Juan Gomez Millas**, Chile
Luis Beltran Prieto, Venezuela
1980 **Emilio Uzcategui**, Ecuador

AERA/ACT Award
American Educational Research Association Award

AMERICAN EDUCATIONAL RESEARCH ASSOCIATION
1230 17th St. NW, Washington, D.C. 20036 (202/223-9485)

The AERA/ACT (American College Testing) Award, which consists of $1,500 and a scroll, is given annually for a work of outstanding research dealing with college student growth and development. The award was instituted to encourage sophisticated work in the field and is awarded to a recipient selected by a joint committee of the two organizations.

1972 **Wilbert J. McKeachie**
1973 **Theodore M. Newcomb**
1974 **Ralph Tyler**
1975 **William Sewell**
1976 **Ralph F. Berdie**
1977 **T. R. McConnell**
1978 **Roger Hayns**
1979 **Burton Clark**
1980 **Paul Dressel**

The American Educational Research Association Award for Distinguished Contributions to Research in

Education, which consists of $1,000 and a scroll, is awarded for meritorious achievements in and distinguished contributions to the field. It honors the overall contributions of a scholar who is selected by the Awards Committee.

1964 **Arthur I. Gates**
1965 **Ralph W. Tyler**
1966 **T. R. McConnell**
1967 **E. F. Lindquist**
1968 **Jean Piaget and Barbel Inhelder**
1969 **Lawrence A. Cremin**
1970 **Benjamin S. Bloom**
1971 **Patrick Suppes**
1972 **Robert M. Gagne**
1973 **Robert J. Havighurst**
1974 **James S. Coleman**
1975 **Urie Bronfenbrenner**
1976 **Robert Glaser**
1977 **Lee J. Cronbach**
1978 **B.F. Skinner**
1979 **John B. Carroll**
1980 **Julian Stanley**

Ruth Strang Research Award

NATIONAL ASSOCIATION FOR WOMEN DEANS, ADMINISTRATORS AND COUNSELORS
1028 Connecticut Ave. NW, Suite 922, Washington, D.C. 20036 (202/659-9330)

The $500 Ruth Strang Research Award is given annually for excellence in research among individuals early in their careers in a historical, philosophical, evaluative or descriptive field deemed of timely and professional importance to NAWDAC members. Original manuscripts up to 50 pages long may be submitted to the Ruth Strang Research Award Committee for consideration.

1974 **Dolores Muhich,** title unknown
1975 **Barbara S. Knox,** "Trends in Counseling Women in Higher Education, 1957-1973"
1976 **Elizabeth A. Ashburn,** "Motivation, Personality and Work-Related Characteristics of Women in Male-Dominated Professions"
1977 **Katherine Van Wessem Goerss,** "Women Administrators in Education: A Review of Research 1960-1976"

Current status unknown

National Teacher of the Year Award

COUNCIL OF STATE SCHOOL OFFICERS
400 N. Capitol St. NW, Washington, D.C. 20001 (202/624-7715)

The National Teacher of the Year award is given annually by the President or the First Lady at a White House ceremony and honors a full-time career public-classroom teacher. The award consists of a tie clasp or brooch, a certificate and a Presidential appointment to the Commission on Presidential Scholars. The award was established by the Council in cooperation with the *Encyclopaedia Britannica, The Ladies' Home Journal* and *Look* magazine to focus on America's best teachers and to encourage all teachers.

1952 **Geraldine Jones,** First grade; Hope Public School, Santa Barbara, Calif.
1953 **Dorothy Hamilton,** Social studies; Milford High School, Milford, Conn.
1954 **Willard Widerberg,** Seventh grade; DeKalb Junior High School, DeKalb, Ill.
1955 **Margaret Perry,** Fourth grade; Monmouth Elementary, Monmouth, Ore.
1956 **Richard Nelson,** Science; Flathead County High School, Kalispell, Mont.
1957 **Eugene G. Bizzell,** Speech, English, and debate; A. N. McCallum High School, Austin, Tex
Mary F. Schartz, Third grade; Bristol Elementary, Kansas City, Mo.
1958 **Jean Listebarger Humphrey,** Second grade; Edwards Elementary, Ames, Iowa
1959 **Edna Donley,** Mathematics and speech; Alva High School, Alva, Okla.
1960 **Hazel B. Davenport,** First grade; Central Elementary, Beckley, W. Va.
1961 **Helen Adams,** Kindergarten, Cumberland Public School, Cumberland, Wisc.
1962 **Marjorie French,** Mathematics, Topeka High School, Topeka, Kans.
1963 **Elmon Ousley,** Speech, American government and world problems; Bellevue Senior High School, Bellevue, Wash.
1964 **Lawana Trout,** English; Charles Page High School, Sand Springs, Okla.
1965 **Richard E. Klinck,** Sixth grade; Reed Street Elementary, Wheat Ridge, Colo.
1966 **Mona Dayton,** First grade; Walter Douglas Elementary, Tucson, Ariz.
1967 **Roger Tenney,** Music; Owatonna Jr.-Sr. High, Owatonna, Minn.
1968 **David E. Graf,** Vocational education and industrial arts; Sandwich Community High School, Sandwich, Ill.
1969 **Barbara Goleman,** Language arts; Miami Jackson High School, Miami, Fla.
1970 **Johnnie T. Dennis,** Physics and math analysis; Walla Walla High School, Walla Walla, Wash.
1971 **Martha M. Stringfellow,** First grade; Lewisville Elementary, Chester County, S.C.
1972 **James M. Rogers,** American history and black studies; Durham High School, Durham, N.C.
1973 **John A. Ensworth,** Sixth grade; Kenwood School, Bend, Ore.
1974 **Vivian Tom,** Social studies; Lincoln High School, Yonkers, N.Y.
1975 **Robert G. Heyer,** Science; Johanna Junior High School, St. Paul, Minn.
1976 **Ruby Murchison,** Social studies; Washington Drive Junior High School, Fayetteville, N.C.
1977 **Myrra Lee,** Social living; Helix High School, La Mesa, Calif.
1978 **Elaine Barbour**, Sixth grade: Cole Creek Elementary Schol, Montrose, Colo.
1979 **Marilyn W. Black**, Elementary art; Bernice A. Ray School, Hanover, N.H.
1980 **Beverly J. Bimes**, English; Hazelwood East High School, St. Louis, Mo.

Mohammed Reza Pahlavi Prize
Nadezhda K. Krupskaya Prize
International Reading Association Literacy Award
Noma Prize

UNITED NATIONS EDUCATIONAL, SCIENTIFIC AND CULTURAL ORGANIZATION
7 Place du Fontenoy, 75700 Paris, France (Tel: 577 16 10, Ext. 3420)

The Mohammed Reza Pahlavi Prize annually awarded $5,000 to institutions, organizations or individuals for outstanding work in combatting illiteracy. After the deposition of the Shah, the award was discontinued. In addition to the winners listed below, honorable mentions were made each year.

1967 **Girls attending the secondary school in Tabora,** Tanzania
1968 **Basic Education Movement,** Brazil
1969 **Royal National Committee for Literacy,** Cambodia
1970 **Popular-action Radio School of Sutatenza,** Colombia
1971 **General Literacy Supervisory and Coordinating Committe,** Burma
1972 **Gram Shikshan Mohim,** India
1973 **Emma Espina, Sergio Arevalo and Arnulfo Reubilar,** authors of "Suggestions for Literacy," Chile
1974 **All-Pakistan Women's Association,** Pakistan
1975 **Paulo Freire,** Brazil
1976 **Pasteur Jacques Kofi Adzomada,** Togo
1977 **No award**
1978 **Mwanza Functional Literacy Project,** Tanzania

The Nadezhda K. Krupskaya Prize, founded by the government of the U.S.S.R., carries an honorarium of 5,000 rubles and is awarded annually for outstanding work in combatting illiteracy. The governments of United Nations member states, in consultation with their UNESCO National Commissions, and non-governmental international educational organizations having consultant status with UNESCO nominate candidates for selection by the Director General. In addition to the winners listed below, honorable mentions are made each year.

1970 **Institute of Language and Literature and the Academy of Sciences,** People's Republic of Mongolia
1971 **Program for adult literacy,** Zambia
1972 **Armee du Savoir,** (Army of Knowledge), Iran
1973 **Literacy project in the Western Lake region,** Tanzania
1974 **Cercle for the Development of the Shyorongi Commune (CEDECOS),** Rwanda
1975 **Abdirizak Mohamoud Abukar,** Somalia
1976 **Department of Literacy of the Ministry of Education and Culture,** Syria
1977 **No award**
1978 **Commune of Cambinh,** Pilot Literacy and Complementary Education Unit, Vietnam
1979 **Supreme Council of the National Campaign for Compulsory Literacy of Iraq**
Popular Union of Peruvian Woman
1980 **Nicaraguan Literacy Campaign**

The International Reading Association Literacy Award is given annually under similar conditions to the Krupskaya Prize.

1979 **Papua-New Guinean Branch of the Summer Institute of Linguistics**
1980 **No award**

The Noma Prize is awarded annually under similar conditions to the Krupskaya Prize.

1980 **National Directorate of Functional Literacy and Applied Linguistics of Mali**

Hoyt S. Vandenburg Award

AIR FORCE ASSOCIATION
1750 Pennsylvania Ave. NW. Washington, D.C. 20008 (202/637-3300)

The Hoyt S. Vandenburg Award is presented annually for outstanding contributions to aerospace education. A committee selects the winner from nomination submitted by individuals and organizations with deep interest in aerospace activities.

1948 **Jacqueline Cochran**, Aviatrix
1949 **Capt. James Gallagher** and the men behind the flight of "Lucky Lady II"
1950 **D.W. Rentzel**, Administrator, CAA
1951 **Gen. Carl A. Spaatz**, First Chief of Staff, USAF
1952 **Gen. Hoyt S. Vandenberg**, Chief of Staff, USAF
1953 **Lt. Gen. James H. Doolittle,** USAF (Ret.) pilot, soldier-scientist
1954 **Gill Robb Wilson**, Air Force Association
1955 **Maj. Gen. Lucas V. Beau**, Civil Air Patrol
1956 **Arthur Godfrey**, Columbia Broadcasting System
1957 **Gen. George C. Kenney**, USAF (Ret.)
1958 **Ralph J. Cordiner**, Chairman, Military Pay Study Commission
1959 **Frank E. Sorensen**, University of Nebraska
1960 **Wayne O. Reed**, Deputy Commissioner, U.S. Office of Education
1961 **Charles H. Boehm**, Supt. of Public Instruction, Pennsylvania
1962 **Lindley J. Stiles**, Dean, School of Education, University of Wisconsin
1963 **Brig. Gen. Robert F. McDermott**, Dean of Faculty, USAF Academy
1964 **Air University Aerospace Presentations Team**
1965 **Brig. Gen. William C. Lindley**, Commandant, Air Force ROTC
1966 **Dr. B.F. Skinner**, Harvard University
1967 **No award**
1968 **Marion B. Folson**, Former Secretary, HEW
1969 **No award**
1970 **Lt. Gen. Solmon W. Wells**, Inspector General, USAF
1971 **F. Edward Hebert**, House of Representatives
1972 **Maj. Richard L. Craft**, Hq. Tactical Air Command
1973 **Community College of the Air Force**
1974 **Lt. Col. Gregory J. Butler**
1975 **Aerospace Audiovisual Service**, Norton AFB, Calif.
1976 **David P. Taylor**, Assistant Secretary of Defense
1977 **USAF School of Aerospace Medicine**, Brooks AFB, Tex.
1978 **Air Force Orientation Group**, Wright-Patterson AFB, Ohio
1979 **USAF Special Operations School**, Hurlburt Field, Fla.
1980 **Air force Institute of Technology**, Wright-Patterson AFB, Ohio

S

Contents

cience & Technology

COMPUTER SCIENCE

ENGINEERING

Related Awards

Niels Bohr Gold Medal

DANSK INGENIORFORENING
Vester Farimagsgade 29-31, DK-1606 Copenhagen V, Denmark (01-15 65 65)

The Niels Bohr Gold Medal is awarded every three years by the Danish Society of Chemical, Civil, Electrical and Mechanical Engineers for contributions to the peaceful use of nuclear science. A committee selects the winner.

1955 **Niels Bohr**
1958 **John Cockcroft**
1961 **George de Hevesy**
1964 **P.L. Kapitza**
1967 **Isidor Isaac Rabi**
1970 **Werner Karl Heisenberg**
1973 **Richard P. Feynman**
1976 **Hans A. Bethe**
1979 **Charles H. Townes**

Burnet Lecture
Matthew Flinders Lecture

AUSTRALIAN ACADEMY OF SCIENCE
Box 783, Canberra, ACT 2601, Australia (062-48 6011)

The Burnet Lecture is given biennially by "a scientist of the highest standing." A selection committee chooses the laureate, who is presented with a bronze plaque.

1971 **J.F.A.P. Miller**
1973 **E.J. Underwood**
1975 **R.N. Robertson**
1977 **W. Hayes**
1979 **G.J.V. Nossal**

The Matthew Flinders Lecture is given bienially by "a scientist of the highest standing." A selection committee chooses the winner, who receives a bronze plaque and $Aust. 200.

1957 **J.L. Pawsey**
1959 **F.M. Burnet**
1961 **M.L. Oliphant**
1963 **J.C. Eccles**
1965 **J.S. Anderson**
1967 **F.J. Fenner**
1969 **K.E. Bullen**
1972 **A.J. Birch**
1974 **J.P. Wild**
1976 **C.H.B. Priestley**
1978 **A.E. Ringwood**
1980 **A. Walsh**

Davis Research Award

STEVENS INSTITUTE OF TECHNOLOGY
Castle Point, Hoboken, N.J. 07030 (201/792-2700)

The $1,000 Davis Research Award goes annually to honor research published during the previous calendar year in pure or applied science. A faculty committee selects the winner.

1961 **George Schmidt,** Theoretical plasma physics
1962 **Everett R. Johnson,** Radiation chemistry
1963 **Earl L. Koller and Snowden Taylor,** High energy physics
1964 **Stephen J. Lukasik and Chester E. Grosch,** Wave-induced seabed pressures
1965 **Robert F. McAlevy III,** Combustion mechanisms
1965 **Daniel Savitsky,** Performance of planning hulls
1966 **Franklin Pollock,** Vortex motions in ideal fluids
1966 **John P. Breslin and Stavros Tsakonas,** Propeller induced vibrations
1967 **Winnifred Jacobs,** Stability of ships
1968 **Salvatore Stivala,** Heparin extraction techniques
1969 **Ajay K. Bose and Maghar S. Manhas,** Total synthesis of penicillin
1970 **Rodney D. Andrews Jr. and Edward A. Friedman,** Inelastic light scattering in polymers
1971 **John G. Daunt and Eugenio Lerner,** Low temperature absorption
1972 **Milton Ohring,** Electro-migration in thin films
1973 **Winston H. Bostick, Vittorio Nardi and William Prior,** Experimental plasma physics
1974 **Haruzo Eda,** Ship controllability
1974 **Hans Meissner and Robert Peters,** Low temperature physics
1975 **Gerald M. Rothberg,** Mossbauer effect studies
1976 **Cheung H. Kim,** Ship motions
1977 **No award**
1978 **Robert F. McAlevy III,** Evaluation of electric vehicle performance and use in energy policy analysis
1979 **James L. Anderson,** approximation methods in general relativity
1980 **Not available at press time**

Eadie Medal

ROYAL SOCIETY OF CANADA
344 Wellingtron, Ottawa, Ont. K1A 0N4 (613/992-3468)

The Thomas W. Eadie Medal, which is of silver and is accompanied by $1,000 from Bell Canada, annually honors an individual for major contributions is applied science as it relates to the standard of living in Canada. A committee chooses the winner.

1975 **Marshall Kulka**
1976 **John W. Hilborn**
1977 **Alec Sehon**
1978 **Armand Frappier**
1980 **Bernard Etkin**

Richard Hopper Day Memorial Medal

ACADEMY OF NATURAL SCIENCES OF PHILADELPHIA
19th and The Parkway, Philadelphia, Pa. 19103 (215/299-1015)

The Richard Hopper Day Memorial Medal, which is of bronze, is awarded at the discretion of the donor and the director of the Academy to honor outstanding exploration and discovery in natural sciences.

1960 **Jacques Piccard**
Lt. Lawrence A. Shumaker, USN
Andreas B. Rechnitzer
Lt. Don Walsh, USN
1964 **L.S.B. Leakey**
1966 **H. Bradford Washburn**
1967 **Charles A. Berry**
1969 **Ruth Patrick**

1973 Harrison H. Schmitt
1980 Crawford H. Greenwalt

Francqui Prize

FRANCQUI FOUNDATION
11 Egmont St., 1050 Brussels, Belgium (Tel: 02/511 81 00)

The Francqui Prize, which carries an honorarium of one million Belgian francs, is given annually to a Belgian scientists under the age of 50 for distinguished research. An international jury selects the recipient.

1933 Henri Pirenne
1934 Georges Lemaitre
1935 No award
1936 Franz Cumont
1937 No award
1938 Jacques Errera
1939 No award
1940 Pierre Nolf
1940-45 No awards
1946 Marcel Florkin
Francois-L. Ganshof
Frans-H. van den Dungen
1947 No award
1948 Zenon-Marcel Bacq
Jean Brachet
Marc de Hemptinne
Leon-H. Dupriez
Pol Swings
1949 Leon Rosenfeld
1950 Paul Harsin
1951 Henri Koch
1952 Florent-Joseph Bureau
1953 Etienne Lamotte
Claire Preaux
1954 Raymond Jeener
1955 Ilya Prigogine
1956 Louis Remacle
1957 Lucien Massart
1958 Leon Van Hove
1959 Gerard Garitte
1960 Christian de Duve
1961 Jules Duchesne
Adolphe Van Tiggelen
1962 Chaim Perelman
1963 Hubert Chantrenne
1964 Paul Ledoux
1965 Roland Mortier
1966 Henri Hers
1967 Jose Fripiat
1968 Jules Horrent
1969 Isidoor Leusen
1970 Radu Balescu
1971 Georges Thines
1972 Jean-Edouard Desmedt
1973 Pierre Macq
1974 Raoul van Caenegem
1975 Rene Thomas
1976 Walter Fiers
1977 Jacques Taminiaux
1978 Jacques Nihoul
1979 Jozef Schell
1980 Jozef Ijsewijn

Prix Poncelet
Prix Cuvier
Prix Fonde par l'Etat
Prix Le Conte
Prix Marie-Guido Triossi
Prix Alexandre Joannides
Prix Lamb

ACADEMIE DES SCIENCES
Institut de France, 23, Quai de Conti, Paris VIe, France

The Academy of Sciences of the French Institute awards several prizes for scientific achievement.

PRIX PONCELET

1963 Pierre Brousse
1966 Andre Neron
1969 Jean Vaillant
1972 Michel Lazard
1975 Jean Cea
1978 M. Henri Skoda

PRIX CUVIER

1964 Jean Roger
1967 Thomas Szabo
1970 Robert Barone
1973 Jean-Claude Gall
1976 Evelyne Lopex

PRIX FONDE PAR L'ETAT

1973 Pierre Souzou
1974 Andre Martin
1975 Marcel Bessis
1976 Jacques Tits
1977 Helene Charniaux-Cotton
1978 Noel Filici

PRIX LE CONTE

1963 Henri V. Valois
1966 Jean Teillac
1969 Daniel Laurent
1972 Antoine Craya
1975 Pierre Buser
1978 Marcel Berger

PRIX MARIE-GUIDO TRIOSSI

1959 Pierre Lepine
1963 Jean Mandel
1967 Pierre Sloninski
1971 Louis Michel
1975 Noel Rist

PRIX ALEXANDRE JOANNIDES

1973 Jean Hamburger
1974 Jean Robieux
1975 Henri Duranton with Remy Peter, Dominique Stehelin and Daniel Collot
1976 Daniel Cribier
1977 Jean-Pierre Changeux
1978 Bernard Cagnac

PRIX LAMB

1968 Michel Garnier
1970 Pierre Carriere, Andre Chesne and Pierre Faugeras
1972 Jacques Dorey

Micheline Matrot Calis
1974 Robert Dautray
1976 Emilie J. Stauff
Henri Labrunie
1978 R. Marguet
L. Lemanach

Otto Hahn Prize

GERMAN PHYSICAL SOCIETY
Hauptstrasse 5, D-5340 Bad Honnef, Federal Republic of Germany (02224-71061)

The Otto Hahn Prize for Chemistry and Physics, awarded jointly by the German Physical Society and the German Central Board for Chemistry, is given as merited for outstanding scientific achievement by a German chemist. The award consists of 50,000 marks, a gold medal and a citation. A committee selects the winner.

1955 Lise Meitner
Heinrich Weiland
1959 Hans Meerwein
1962 Manfred Eigen
1965 Erich Huckel
1967 Georg Wittig
1974 Friedrich Hund
1979 Rolf Huisgen

Dannie Heineman Prize

AKADEMIE DER WISSENSCHAFT IN GOTTINGEN
Theaterstrasse 7, D-3400 Gottingen, Federal Republic of Germany (Tel: 0551/41298)

The Dannie Heineman Prize is given every two years for an outstanding work, usually in the field of natural sciences. A 30,000-mark honorarium accompanies the prize. The winner is selected by members of the Academy.

1962 James Franck, (University of North Carolina, Durham), Photosynthesis
1963 Edmund Hlawka, (University of Vienna), Mathematics
1965 Georg Wittig, (University of Heidelberg), Chemistry
1967 Martin Schwarzschild, (Princeton University), Astronomy
H. Gobind Khorana, (University of Wisconsin), Molecular Biology
1969 Alfred Brian Pippard, (Cambridge University), Physics
1971 Neil Bartlett, (University of California, Berkeley), Chemistry
1973 Igor R. Schafarevitsch, (University of Moscow), Mathematics
1975 Philip W. Anderson, (Bell Telephone Laboratories), Physics
1977 Albert Eschenmoser (Eidgenossische Technische Hochschule, Zurich,) Organic Chemistry
1979 Phillip Griffiths (Cambridge, Mass.), Transcending algebraic geometry

Gilles Holst Medal

ROYAL NETHERLANDS ACADEMY OF ARTS AND SCIENCES
Kloveniersburgwal 29, Amsterdam, The Netherlands (Tel: 020 22 29 02)

The Gilles Holst Medal, which is of gold, is given approximately every four years for research inthe field of applied physics or applied chemistry. A selection committee chooses the winner, who must be of Dutch nationality.

1963 W.G. Burgers, Rijswijk
1967 M.C. Teves, Amsterdam
1971 J.D. Fast, Einhoven
1976 P.M. de Wolff, Delft

Bernardo A. Houssay Award

ORGANIZATION OF AMERICAN STATES
17th St. and Constitution Ave. NW, Washington, D.C. 20006 (202/789-3369)

The Bernardo A. Houssay Award, which carries a $30,000 honorarium, is awarded annually for notable contributions in scientific research in the biological sciences, pure sciences, agricultural sciences or technical research by an individual from a Latin American country. A jury selects the winner.

1972 Alberto Hurtado (Peru), High-altitude biology
1973 Venancio Denlofeu (Argentina), Achievements in the sciences and teaching accomplishments
1974 Arturo Burkart (Argentina), Research agricultural sciences and animal husbandry
1975 Jose Gandolfo (Argentina), Technical research hydraulic engine
1976 Roberto Caldeyro Barcia, (Uruguay), Biological sciences (gynecology and obstetrics)
1977 Cesar Lattes (Brazil), Exact sciences (nuclear physics)
1978 Johanna Dobereiner (Brazil), Agricultural sciences (research)
1979 Oreste Moretto (Argentina), Technical research (engineering)
1980 Not available at press time

Sarah Zinder Leedy Memorial Award

WEIZMANN INSTITUTE OF SCIENCE
Box 26, Rehovot, Israel (Tel: 054-82111)

The Sarah Zinder Leedy Memorial Award alternates each year between biological sciences and physical-mathematical sciences.

1962 A. Balugrund, Nuclear physics
Haim Ginsburg, Genetics
1964 Arnon Dar, Nuclear physics
1965 Israel Shechter, Chemical immunology
1966 Haim Harari, Nuclear physics
1967 Jonathan Gressel, Plant genetics, specifically for work on photo-induction and RNA synthetics involving the mechanism of spore formation in a fungus
1968 Gabriel Veneziano, Physics, specifically for work on the properties of elementary particles
1969 No award

1970 **Max Herzberg,** Biological ultrastructure, specifically for contributions to the elucidation of the structural basis of the production of proteins
Adam Schwimmer, Nuclear physics, specifically for contributions to the description of the duality properties of strong interactions and the hadron spectrum
1971 **No award**
1972 **Richard Hornreich,** Electronics, for contribution in the field of magnetoelastic effect
Zelig Rabinowitz, Genetics, for work on the reversion of transformed cells by non-viral carcinogenesis
1973 **Abraham Nimrod,** Biodynamics, specifically for work on the biosynthesis of estrogenic hormones and metabolism of progesterone in the rat ovary in relation to ovum implantation
1974 **Dorit Carmeli,** For work on mathematical modeling and quantitative inheritance
1975 **No award**
1976 **Abraham Amsterdam,** Hormone research specifically for work on cell membrane cytoskeleton in information transfer between and within cells
1977 **David Mukamel,** Accomplishments in phase transition, critical and multi-critical behavior
1978 **David Mukamel**, Electronics
1979 **No award**
1980 **Joseph Schlessinger**, Chemical immunology

Leeuwenhoek Medal

ROYAL NETHERLANDS ACADEMY OF ARTS AND SCIENCES
Kloveniersburgwal 29, Amsterdam, The Netherlands (Tel: 020 22 29 02)

The Leeuwenhoek Medal, which is of gold, is given every 10 years for outstanding research in the field of microscopical organisms. A selection committee chooses the winner of this international honor.

1875 **C.G. Ehrenberg,** Berlin, Germany
1885 **Ferdinand Cohn,** Breslau, Germany
1895 **Louis Pasteur,** Paris, France
1905 **M.W. Beijerinck,** Delft, The Netherlands
1915 **Sir David Bruce,** London, England
1925 **Felix d'Herelle,** Alexandria, Egypt
1935 **Sergei Nikolaevitch Winogradsky,** Brie/Comte-Robert, France
1950 **Selman A. Waksman,** New Brunswick, N.J.
1960 **Andre Lwoff,** Paris, France
1970 **C.B. van Niel,** Pacific Grove, Calif.
1980 **R.Y. Stanier,** Paris, France

Thomas Rankin Lyle Medal

AUSTRALIAN ACADEMY OF SCIENCE
Box 783, Caberra, ACT 2601 Australia (062-48 6011)

The Thomas Ranken Lyle Medal, which is of bronze, is awarded biennially for research in methematics or physics by a resident of Australia. A committee chooses the winner.

1957 **B.Y. Mills**
1959 **E.S. Barnes**
1961 **H.O. Lancaster**
1963 **G.R.A. Ellis**
P.A.P. Moran
1966 **S.T. Butler**
1968 **G. Szekeres**
1970 **R. Hanbury Brown**
1972 **H.A. Buchdahl**
1975 **J.P. Wild**
1977 **K. Mahler**
1979 **E.J. Hannan**

Joseph Leidy Award

ACADEMY OF NATURAL SCIENCES OF PHILADELPHIA
19th and The Parkway, Philadelphia, Pa. 19103 (215/299-1015)

The Joseph Leidy Award, which consists of a bronze medal and a $100 honorarium, is given every three years for the best publication, exploration, discovery or research in the natural sciences, as judged by a committee of Academy and non-Academy scientists.

1925 **Herbert Spencer Jennings**
1928 **Henry A. Pilsbry**
1931 **William Morton Wheeler**
1934 **Gerrit Smith Miller, Jr.**
1937 **Edwin Linton**
1940 **Merritt Lyndon Fernald**
1943 **Chancey Juday**
1946 **Ernst Mayr**
1949 **Warren P. Spencer**
1952 **G. Evelyn Hutchinson**
1955 **Herbert Friedmann**
1958 **H.B. Hungerford**
1961 **Robert Evans Snodgrass**
1964 **Carl L. Hubbs**
1967 **Donn Eric Rosen**
1970 **Arthur Cronquist**
1975 **James Bond**
1979 **Edward O. Wilson**

Lomonosov Medal

ACADEMY OF SCIENCES
Leninsky Prospekt 14, Moscow 117901, USSR (Tel: 232-29-10)

The Lomonosov Medal, which is of gold, is the Soviet Union's highest scientific award. Initially, one medal was awarded each year, but since 1967 one Soviet and one foreign scholar annually receive a Lomonosov Medal to honor outstanding work in the natural or social sciences.

1959 **Pyotr L. Kapista (USSR),** Physics
1960 **No award**
1961 **No award**
1962 **A.N. Nesmeyanov (USSR),** Chemistry
1963 **No award**
1964 **S. Tomanaga (Japan),** Physics
1965 **G. Florie (Great Britain),** Medicine
N.V. Belov (USSR), Crystallography
1966 **No award**
1967 **I.E. Tamm (USSR),** Theoretical physics
S.F. Powell (Great Britain), Elementary-particle physics
1968 **V.A. Engelhardt (USSR),** Biochemistry and molecular biology
Istvan Rusnak (Hungary), Medicine
1969 **N.N. Semyonov (USSR),** Chemical physics
Giulio Natta (Italy), Polymer chemistry
1970 **I.M. Vinogradov (USSR),** Mathematics

Arnaud Danjoie (France), Mathematics

1971 **V.A. Ambartsumyan (USSR),** Astronomy and astrophysics
Hans Alven (Sweden), Plasma physics and astrophysics

1972 **N.I. Muskhelishvili, (USSR),** Mathematics and mechanics
Max Steinbeck (German Democratic Republic), Plasma physics

1973 **A.P. Vinogradov (USSR),** Geochemistry
Vladimir Zoubek (Czechoslovakia), Geology

1974 **A.I. Tselikov (USSR),** Geology
Angel Balevsky (Bulgaria), Metal technology

1975 **M.V. Keldysh (USSR),** Mathematics, mechanics and cosmic research
Maurice Rouault (France), Mechanics and applied mechanics

1976 **S.I. Wolfkovich (USSR),** Chemistry and phosphorous technology; development of scientific bases for USSR agricultural chemistry
Herman Klary (German Democratic Republic), Chemistry

1977 **M.A. Lavrentiev (USSR),** Mathematics and mechanics
Linus Pauling (U.S.A.), Chemistry and biochemistry

Lubell Memorial Award

WEIZMANN INSTUTUTE OF SCIENCE
Box 26, Rehovot, Israel (951721)

The Jeanette and Samuel L. Lubell Memorial Award is given every second year for achievement in any field of research by a Weizmann Institute scientist 40 years of age or under holding the grade of senior scientist or below.

1971 **Ada Zamir,** Biochemistry, for contribution to the study of the nature and mode of action of ribosomes
1973 **Adam Schwimmer,** Nuclear physics, specifically for contribution to understanding high energy scattering processes of elementary particles
1975 **Ruth Sperling and Michael Bustin,** Chemical physics, for work on the assembly and structure of chromosomes of higher organisms
1977 **Ada Zamir,** Biochemistry
1979 **Yoram Groner,** Virology

National Academy of Sciences Award in Aeronautical Engineering
Alexander Agassiz Gold Medal
NAS Award in Applied Mathematics and Numerical Analysis
Arctowski Medal
John J. Carty Medal
Comstock Prize
Arthur Day Prize
Henry Draper Medal
Daniel Giraud Elliot Medal
NAS Award for Environmental Quality
Gibbs Brothers Medal
Benjamin Apthorp Gould Fund
NAS Public Welfare Medal
Robertson Memorial Lecture
J. Lawrence Smith Medal
U.S. Steel Foundation Award in Molecular Biology
Mary Clark Thompson Medal
Selman A. Waksman Award in Microbiology
Charles Doolittle Walcott Medal
G. K. Warren Prize
James Craig Watson Medal
NAS Award for Distinguished Service

NATIONAL ACADEMY OF SCIENCES
2101 Constitution Ave. NW, Washington, D.C. 20418
(202/389-6134)

The Hunsaker Fund has endowed the $4,000 National Academy of Sciences Award in Aeronautical Engineering given every five years.

1968 **Leroy Randle Grumman**
1973 **Donald Wills Douglas, Sr.**
1980 **James S. McDonnell**

The Murray Fund awards the Alexander Agassiz Gold Medal, which carries a $1,000 honorarium, approximately every three years for original contributions to oceanography. A four-member committee selects the winner.

1913 **Johan Hjort**
1918 **Albert I, Prince of Monaco**
1920 **Charles Dwight Sigsbee**
1924 **Otto Sven Pettersson**
1926 **Wilhelm Bjerknes**
1927 **Max Weber**
1928 **Walfrid Vagn Ekman**
1929 **Stanley J. Gardiner**
1930 **Johannes Schmidt**
1931 **Henry Bryant Bigelow**

1932 Albert Defant
1933 Bjorn Helland-Hansen
1934 Haakon Hasberg Gran
1935 Wayland T. Vaughan
1936 Martin Knudsen
1937 Edgar Allen Johnson
1938 Ulrik Harald Sverdrup
1939 Frank Rattray Lillie
1942 Columbus Iselin II
1946 Joseph Proudman
1947 Felix Andries Vening Meinesz
1948 Thomas Gordon Thompson
1951 Harry A. Marmer
1952 H. W. Harvey
1954 Maurice Ewing
1955 Alfred Clarence Redfield
1959 Martin Wiggo Johnson
1960 Anton Frederik Bruun
1962 George Edward Raven Deacon
1963 Roger R. Revelle
1965 Sir Edward Bullard
1966 Carl Eckart
1969 Frederick C. Fuglister
1972 Seiya Uyeda
1973 John H. Steele
1976 Walter Heinrich Munk
1979 Henry M. Stommel

The NAS Award in Applied Mathematics and Numerical Analysis, which carries a $5,000 prize, is awarded irregularly. A four-member committee selects the winner.

1972 Kurt Otto Friedrichs
1973 Samuel Karlin
1976 Chia-Chiao Lin
1980 George F. Carrier

The Henryk Arctowski Medal carries a $5,000 prize and is awarded approximately every three years for studies of short- or long-duration solar activity changes and their effects on the ionosphere and the terrestrial atmosphere. A four-member committee selects the winner.

1969 Eugene Norman Parker
Paul J. Wild
1972 Francis Severin Johnson
1975 Jacques M. Beckers
1978 John R. Winckler

The John J. Carty Medal and Award for the Advancement of Science, now consisting of a gold medal and $5,000 honorarium, is awarded approximately every three years for noteworthy and distinguished achievement in any field of science within the scope of the Academy. A four-member committee selects the winner.

1932 John J. Carty
1936 Edmund Beecher Wilson
1939 Sir William Bragg
1943 Edwin Grant Conklin
1945 William Frederick Durand
1947 Ross Granville Harrison
1950 Irving Langmuir
1953 Vannevar Bush
1961 Charles Hard Townes
1963 Maurice Ewing
1965 Alfred Henry Sturtevant
1968 Murray Gell-Mann
1971 James Dewey Watson
1975 J. Tuzo Wilson
1978 John N. Mather

The Cyrus B. Comstock Prize, which now carries a cash award of $5,000, is given every five years for the most important discovery or investigation in electricity, magnetism or radiant energy.

1913 Robert A. Millikan
1918 Samuel J. Barnett
1923 William Duane
1928 C. J. Davisson
1933 Percy W. Bridgman
1938 Ernest O. Lawrence
1943 Donald W. Kerst
1948 Merle A. Tuve
1953 William Shockley
1958 Charles Hard Townes
1963 Chien-Shiung Wu
1968 Leon N. Cooper
J. Robert Schrieffer
1973 Robert H. Dicke
1978 Raymond Davis, Jr.

The Arthur Day Fund established the Arthur L. Day Prize and Lectureship to advance the study of the physics of the Earth. The recipient of the Day Award, which carries a $10,000 honorarium, is chosen by a four-member committee.

1972 Hatten S. Yoder
1975 Drummond H. Matthews
Fred J. Vine
1978 John Verhoogen

The Henry Draper Medal, which is of gold and carries a $1,000 honorarium, is awarded not more often than every two years for investigations in astronomical physics.

1886 Samuel P. Langley
1888 E. C. Pickering
1890 H. A. Rowland
1893 H. K. Vogel
1899 J. E. Keeler
1901 Sir William Huggins
1904 George E. Hale
1906 W. W. Campbell
1910 C. G. Abbot
1913 H. Deslandres
1915 Joel Stebbins
1916 A. A. Michelson
1918 W. S. Adams
1919 Charles Fabry
1920 Alfred Fowler
1921 Pieter Zeeman
1922 Henry Norris Russell
1924 Sir Arthur Stanley Eddington
1926 Harlow Shapley
1928 William Hammond Wright
1931 Annie Jump Cannon
1932 V. M. Slipher
1934 John Stanley Plaskett
1936 C. E. Kenneth Mees
1940 Robert Williams Wood
1942 Ira Sprague Bowen
1945 Paul W. Merrill
1947 Hans Albrecht Bethe
1949 Otto Struve
1951 Bernard Lyot
1955 Hendrik C. van de Hulst
1957 Horace W. Babcock
1960 Martin Schwarzschild

1963 Richard Tousey
1965 Martin Ryle
1968 Bengt Edlen
1971 Subrahmanyan Chandrasekhar
1974 Lyman Spitzer Jr.
1977 Arno Penzias and Robert W. Wilson

The Daniel Giraud Elliot Medal, which carries a $1,000 honorarium, is awarded for the most meritorious work in zoology or paleontology published in a three- to five-year period. A four-member committee selects the winner.

1917 F. M. Chapman
1918 William Beebe
1919 Robert Ridgway
1920 Othenio Abel
1921 Bashford Dean
1922 William Morton Wheeler
1923 Ferdinand Canu
1924 Henri Breuil
1925 Edmund B. Wilson
1927 Erik A. Stensio, Jr.
1928 Ernest Thompson Seton
1929 Henry Fairfield Osborn
1930 George Ellett Coghill
1931 Davidson Black
1932 James P. Chapin
1933 Richard Swann Lull
1934 Theophilus Shickel Painter
1935 Edwin H. Colbert
1936 Robert Cushman Murphy
1937 George Howard Parker
1938 Malcolm Robert Irwin
1939 John Howard Northrop
1940 William Berryman Scott
1941 Theodosius Dobzhansky
1942 Sir D'Arcy W. Thompson
1943 Karl Spencer Lashley
1944 George Gaylord Simpson
1945 Sewall Green Wright
1946 Robert Broom
1947 John Thomas Patterson
1948 Henry B. Bigelow
1949 Arthur Cleveland Bent
1950 Raymond Carrol Osburn
1951 Libbie Henrietta Hyman
1952 Archie Fairly Carr
1953 Sven P. Ekman
1955 Herbert Friedmann
1956 Alfred Sherwood Rober
1957 Philip J. Darlington Jr.
1958 Donald Redfield Griffin
1965 George Gaylord Simpson
1967 Ernst Mayr
1971 Richard Alexander
1976 Howard Ensign Davis
1979 G. Arthur Cooper
Richard E. Grant

The $5,000 NAS Award for Environmental Quality, which may be awarded annually, was given for outstanding scientific or technological contributions to improve the quality of the environment or to control its pollution. The award has been discontinued.

1972 Arie Jan Haagen-Smit
1973 W. Thomas Edmonson
1974 G. Evelyn Hutchinson
1975 John T. Middleton
1976 David M. Evans
1977 Miron L. Heinselman
1978 No award
1979 Alexander Hollander
1980 Gilbert F. White

The $1,000 Gibbs Brothers Medal is awarded not more often than every two years for outstanding contributions in naval engineering or marine architecture. A four-member committee selects the winner.

1965 Frederick Henry Todd
1967 Alfred Adolph Heinrich Kiel
1971 Henry A. Schade
1974 Phillip Eisenberg
1976 John Charles Niedermaier
1979 Matthew Galbraith Forrest

The $5,000 Benjamin Apthorp Gould Fund is given every two or three years for outstanding contributions in astronomy, the mechanics of orbits of asteroids or problems of local galactic structure. A four-member committee selects the winner.

1971 Elizabeth Roemer
1973 Kenneth I. Kellermann
1975 Lodewijk Woltjer
1979 Irwin I. Shapiro

The NAS Public Welfare Medal is awarded as merited for distinguished contributions in the application of science to the public welfare. A committee comprising the Council Committee on National Science Policy selects the winner.

1914 G. W. Goethals
W. C. Gorgas
1916 Cleveland Abbe
Gifford Pinchot
1917 S. W. Stratton
1920 Herbert Hoover
1921 C. W. Stiles
1928 Charles V. Chapin
1930 Stephen Tyng Mather
1931 Wickliffe Rose
1932 William Hallock Park
1933 David Fairchild
1934 August Vollmer
1935 F. F. Russel
Hugh S. Cumming
1937 Willis Rodney Whitney
1939 John Edgar Hoover
1943 John D. Rockefeller, Jr.
1945 Vannevar Bush
1947 Karl Taylor Compton
1948 George Harrison Shull
1951 David E. Lilienthal
1956 James R. Killian, Jr.
1957 Warren Weaver
1958 Henry Allen Moe
1959 James H. Doolittle
1960 Alan T. Waterman
1962 James A. Shannon
1963 J. George Harrar
1964 Detlev Wulf Bronk
1966 John W. Gardner
1969 Lister Hill
1972 Leonard Carmichael
1976 Emilio Q. Daddorio
1977 Leona Baumgartner
1978 Donald Ainslie Henderson
1979 Cecil Green and Ida M. Green
1980 Walter Sullivan

The Howard P. Robertson Memorial Lecture Fund provides a $2,500 stipend and invites distinguished scientists from anywhere in the world to present the Robertson Memorial Lecture to the Academy. A four-member committee selects the recipient approximately every three years.

1967 **John A. Wheeler**
1971 **Paul Doty**
1975 **Martin Rees**
1978 **Sir George Porter**

The J. Lawrence Smith Medal, which is of gold and is accompanied by a $2,000 prize, is awarded approximately every three years for investigations in meteoric bodies. A four-member committee selects the winner.

1888 **H. A. Newton**
1922 **George P. Merrill**
1945 **Stuart Hoffman Perry**
1949 **Fred Lawrence Whipple**
1954 **Peter Mackenzie Millman**
1957 **Mark G. Inghram**
1960 **Ernst J. Opik**
1962 **Harold Clayton Urey**
1967 **John Hamilton Reynolds**
1970 **Edward Porter Henderson**
1971 **Edward Anders**
1973 **Clair Cameron Patterson**
1976 **John Armstead Wood**

The $5,000 U.S. Steel Foundation Award in Molecular Biology may be presented annually for a recent notable discovery in molecular biology by a young scientist. A four-member committee selects the winner.

1962 **Marshall W. Nirenberg**
1953 **Matthew S. Meselson**
1964 **Charles Yanofsky**
1965 **Robert Stuart Edgar**
1966 **Norton D. Zinder**
1967 **Robert W. Holley**
1968 **Walter Gilbert**
1969 **William Barry Wood III**
1970 **Armin Dale Kaiser**
1917 **Masayasu Nomura**
1972 **Howard Martin Temin**
1973 **Donald David Brown**
1974 **David Baltimore**
1975 **Bruce M. Alberts**
1976 **Daniel Nathans**
1977 **Aaron J. Shatkin**
1978 **Gunter Blobel**
1979 **Mark Ptashne**
1980 **Phillip A. Sharp**

The Mary Clark Thompson Medal, which carries a $1,000 prize, is given not more often than every three years for the most important contributions to geology or paleontology. A four-member committee selects the winner.

1921 **Charles Doolittle Walcott**
1923 **Emmanuel de Margerie**
1925 **John Mason Clarke**
1928 **James Perrin Smith**
1930 **William Berryman Scott**
Edward Oscar Ulrich
1931 **David White**
1932 **Francis Authur Bather**
1934 **Charles Schuchert**
1936 **Amadeus William Grabua**
1941 **David Meredith Seares Watson**
1942 **Sir Arthur Smith Woodward**
Edward Wilber Berry
1943 **George Gaylord Simpson**
1944 **William Joscelyn Arkell**
1945 **T. Wayland Vaughan**
1946 **John Bernard Reeside, Jr.**
1948 **Frank McLearn**
1949 **Lauge Koch**
1952 **Lloyd William Stephenson**
1954 **Alfred Sherwood Romer**
1957 **Gustav Arthur Cooper**
1958 **Roman Kozlowski**
1961 **Norman Dennis Newell**
1964 **Milton Nunn Bramlette**
1967 **Wendell Phillips Woodring**
1970 **Raymond Cecil Moore**
1973 **Hollis Dow Hedberg**
1976 **James Morton Schopf**

The $5,000 Selman A. Waksman Award in Microbiology of the Foundation for Microbiology is awarded annually or biennially for contributions in the field. A four-member committee selects the winner.

1968 **Jack L. Strominger**
1970 **Earl Reece Stadtman**
1972 **Charles Yanofsky**
1974 **Renato Dulbecco**
1976 **Wallace Prescott Rowe**
1978 **Howard Green**
1980 **Julius Adler**

The Charles Doolittle Walcott Medal, which is of bronze and carries a $1,000 prize, is awarded not more often than every five years to stimulate research in pre-Cambrian or Cambrian life. A four-member committee selects the winner.

1934 **David White**
1939 **A. H. Westergaard**
1947 **Alexander G. Vologdin**
1952 **Franco Rasetti**
1957 **Pierre Hupe**
1962 **Armin Alexander Opik**
1967 **Allison Ralph Palmer**
1972 **Elso Sterrenberg Barghoorn**
1977 **Preston Cloud**

The $1,000 G.K. Warren Prize is awarded approximately every four years for accomplishment in any field of science within the scope of the Academy charter, with a preference for fluviatile geology. A two-member committee selects the winner.

1969 **R.A. Bagnold**
1973 **Luna Bergere Leopold**
1976 **Walter B. Langbein**

The James Craig Watson Medal, which is of gold and carries a $5,000 honorarium, is awarded approximately every three years for contributions to astronomy and to support astronomical research. A four-member committee selects the winner.

1887 **Benjamin A. Gould**
1889 **Ed. Schoenfeld**
1891 **Arthur Auwers**
1894 **S. C. Chandler**
1899 **Sir David Gill**
1913 **J. C. Kapteyn**
1916 **A. O. Leuschner**
1924 **C. V. L. Charlier**
1929 **Willem de Sitter**

1936 **Ernest William Brown**
1948 **Samuel A. Mitchell**
1951 **Herbert R. Morgan**
1955 **Chester B. Watts**
1957 **George Van Biesbroeck**
1960 **Yusuke Hagihara**
1961 **Otto Heckmann**
1964 **Willem Jacob Luyten**
1965 **Paul Herget**
1966 **Wallace J. Eckert**
1969 **Jurgen Kurt Moser**
1972 **Andre Deprit**
1975 **G. M. Clemence**
1979 **Charles T. Kowal**

J. Robert Oppenheimer Memorial Prize

CENTER FOR THEORETICAL STUDIES
University of Miami, Box 249055, Coral Gables, Fla. 33124
(305/284-4455)

The J. Robert Oppenheimer Memorial Prize, which consists of a medal, certificate and a $1,000 honorarium, is awarded annually for outstanding contributions to the theoretical natural sciences (physics, chemistry, biology), mathematics and the philosophy of science. A committee selects the recipient from nominations submitted by heads and members of recognized institutions of higher learning and research. The work for which the individual is cited must have been done during the preceding decade, and the intention is to honor an individual still young enough to continue to pursue their inquiries and "perhaps to exceed the contribution for which they are rewarded."

1969 **P.A.M. Dirac**
1970 **Freeman Dyson**
1971 **Abdus Salam**
1972 **Robert Serber**
1973 **Steven Weinberg**
1974 **Edwin E. Salpeter**
1975 **Nicholas Kemmer**
1976 **Yoichiro Nambu**
1977 **Feza Gursey**
Sheldon Glashow
1978 **Jocelyn Bell Burnell**
1979 **Abraham Pais**
1980 **Richard H. Dalitz**

National Medals of Science
Alan T. Waterman Award

NATIONAL SCIENCE FOUNDATION
1800 G St. NW, Washington, D.C. 20550 (202/632-4050)

The National Medals of Science presented annually by the President of the United States honor outstanding contributions to knowledge in the physical, biological, mathematical or engineering sciences.

1962 **Theodore von Karman,** Professor of Aeronautical Engineering, Emeritus, California Institute of Technology

1963 **Luis Walter Alvarez,** Professor of Physics, University of California, Berkeley

Vannevar Bush, Administrator; Electrical engineer; former President, Carnegie Institution of Washington; Honorary Chairman, MIT Corp.

John Robinson Pierce, Executive Director, Communications Division Systems, Bell Telephone Laboratories

Cornelis B. van Niel, Professor of Microbiology, Stanford University

Norbert Wiener, Professor of Mathematics, Massachusetts Institute of Technology

1964 **Roger Adams,** Professor of Chemistry, Emeritus, University of Illinois

Othmar H. Ammann, Consulting Engineer, Ammann and Whitney, Rye, N.Y.

Theodosius Dobzhansky, Member, The Rockefeller Institute

Charles Stark Draper, Head, Dept. of Aeronautics and Astronautics, Massachusetts Institute of Technology

Solomon Leftschetz, Professor of Mathematics, Emeritus, Princeton University

Neal Elgar Miller, Professor of Psychology, Yale University

Harold Marston Morse, Professor of Mathematics, Institute for Advanced Studies

Marshall Warren Nirenberg, Chief, Section of Biochemical Genetics, National Institutes of Health

Julian Schwinger, Professor of Physics, Harvard University

Harold Clayton Urey, Professor of Chemistry, University of California, Berkeley

Robert Burns Woodward, Professor of Chemistry, Harvard University

1965 **John Bardeen,** Professor of Electrical Engineering and Physics, University of Illinois

Peter J.W. Debye, Professor of Chemistry, Emeritus, Cornell University

Hugh L. Dryden, Former Deputy Administrator, National Aeronautics and Space Administration

Clarence Leonard Johnson, Vice President for Advanced Development Projects, Lockheed Aircraft Corp.

Leon M. Lederman, Professor of Physics, Columbia University

Warren Kendall Lewis, Professor of Chemical Engineering, Emeritus, Massachusetts Institute of Technology

Francis Peyton Rous, Member, Emeritus, The Rockefeller Institute

William Walden Rubey, Professor of Geology and Geophysics, University of California, Los Angeles

George Gaylord Simpson, Professor of Vertebrate Paleontology, Harvard University

Donald D. Van Slyke, Research Chemist, Brookhaven National Laboratories

Oscar Zariski, Professor of Mathematics, Harvard University

1966 **Jacob Bjerknes,** Professor of Meteorology, University of California, Los Angeles

Subrahmanyan Chandrasekhar, Professor of Theoretical Astrophysics, University of Chicago

Henry Eyring, Dean, Graduate School, University of Utah

E.F. Knipling, Director, Entomology Research Div., U.S. Dept of Agriculture

Fritz A. Lipman, Professor of Biochemistry, Rockefeller University

John W. Milnor, Professor of Mathematics, Princeton University

William C. Rose, Professor of Chemistry, Emeritus, University of Illinois
Claude E. Shannon, Donner Professor of Science, Massachusetts Institute of Technology
J.H. Van Vleck, Professor of Physics, Harvard University
Sewall Wright, Professor of Genetics, Emeritus, University of Wisconsin
Vladimir Kosma Zworykin, Radio Corp. of America

1967 **J.W. Beams,** Professor of Physics, University of Virginia
A. Francis Birch, Professor of Geological Sciences, Harvard University
Gregory Breit, Professor of Physics, Yale University
Paul J. Cohen, Professor of Mathematics, Stanford University
Kenneth S. Cole, Senior Research Biophysicist, National Institutes of Health
Louis Plack Hammett, Professor of Chemistry, Columbia University
Harry F. Harlow, Professor of Psychology, University of Wisconsin
Michael Heidelberger, Professor of Immunochemistry, New York University
G.B. Kistiakowsky, Professor of Chemistry, Harvard University
Edwin Herbert Land, President, Polaroid Corp.
Igor I. Sikorsky, Former Engineering Manager, Sikorsky Aircraft Div. of United Aircraft Corp.
Alfred Henry Sturtevant, Professor of Biology, Emeritus, California Institute of Techonology

1968 **Horace Albert Baker,** Professor of Biochemistry, University of California, Berkeley
Paul D. Bartlett, Professor of Chemistry, Harvard University
Bernard B. Brodie, Chief, Laboratory of Chemical Pharmacology, National Institutes of Health
Detlev W. Bronk, President Emeritus, Rockefeller University
J. Presper Eckert, Vice President, Remington Rand Univac Div., Sperry Rand Corp.
Herbert Friedman, Superintendent, Atmosphere and Astrophysics Div., Naval Research Laboratory
Jay L. Lush, Professor of Animal Breeding, Iowa State University
N.M. Newmark, Professor of Civil Engineering, University of Illinois
Jerzy Neyman, Professor of Mathematics, University of California, Berkeley
Lars Onsager, Professor of Chemistry, Yale University
Eugene P. Wigner, Professor of Mathematical Physics, Princeton University

1969 **Herbert C. Brown,** Professor of Chemistry, Purdue University
William Feller, Professor of Mathematics, Princeton University
Robert Joseph Huebner, Chief, Viral Carcinogenesis Branch, National Cancer Institute, National Institutes of Health
Jack S.C. Kilby, Manager, Customer Requirements Dept., Texas Instruments
Ernst Mayr, Director and Professor, Museum of Comparative Zoology, Harvard University
W.K.H. Panofsky, Director, Stanford Linear Accelerator Center, Stanford University

1970 **Richard D. Brauer,** Professor of Mathematics, Harvard University
Robert H. Dicke, Cyrus Fogg Brackett Professor of Physics, Princeton University
Barbara McClintock, Distinguished Service Member, Carnegie Institute of Washington
George E. Mueller, Senior Vice President, General Dynamics Corp.
Albert B. Sabin, President, Weizmann Institute of Science, Rehovot, Israel
Allan R. Sandage, Staff Member, Hale Observatories, Carnegie Institute of Washington; California Institute of Technology
John C. Slater, Professor of Physics and Chemistry, University of Florida
John Archibald Wheeler, Joseph Henry Professor of Physics, Princeton University
Saul Winstein, Professor of Chemistry, University of California, Los Angeles

1971 **No award**

1972 **No award**

1973 **Daniel I. Amon,** Professor and Chairman, Dept. of Cell Physiology and Biochemist in the Agricultural Experiment Station, University of California, Berkeley
Carl Djerassi, Professor of Chemistry, Stanford University
Harold E. Edgerton, Professor Emeritus, Massachusetts Institute of Technology
William Maurice Ewing, Distinguished Professor, Electrical Engineering, Marine Institute, University of Texas, Galveston
Arie J. Haagen-Smit, Professor of Biochemistry, Emeritus, California Institute of Technology
Vladimir Haensel, Vice President for Research and Development, Universal Oil Products Corp.
Frederick Seitz, President, Rockefeller University
Earl W. Sutherland, Jr., Professor of Biochemistry, University of Miami
John W. Tukey, Professor of Statistics, Princeton University
Richard Travis Whitcomb, Aeronautical engineer, Langley Research Center
Robert R. Wilson, Director, Fermi National Accelator Laboratory, Weston, Ill.

1974 **Nicolaas Bloembergen,** Professor of Applied Physics, Harvard University
Britton Chance, Director, Johnson Research Foundation; Chairman Dept. of Physics, University of Pennsylvania
Erwin Chargaff, Professor of Biochemistry, Columbia University
Paul John Flory, Jackson Wood Professor of Chemistry, Stanford University
William A. Fowler, Professor of Physics, California Institute of Technology
Kurt Godel, Professor of Mathematics, Institute for Advanced Study
Rudolf Kompfner, Professor of Applied Physics, Stanford University
James V. Neel, Lee R. Dice Professor of Human Genetics, University of Michigan Medical School
Linus Pauling, Professor of Chemistry, Stanford University
Ralph Brazelton Peck, Consultant; Foundation Engineer; Professor Emeritus, University of Illinois
K.S. Pitzer, Professor of Chemistry, University of California, Berkeley
James A. Shannon, Special Adviser to the President; Rockefeller University
Abel Wolman, Professor Emeritus, Sanitary Engineering, Johns Hopkins University

1975 **John Backus,** IBM staff member, San Jose Research Laboratory, Calif.

Manson Benedict, Institute Professor Emeritus, Massachusetts Institute of Technology
Hans A. Bethe, Emeritus John Wendell Anderson Professor of Physics, Cornell University
Shiing-shen Chern, Professor of Mathematics, University of California, Berkeley
George Bernard Dantzig, Professor of Operations Research and Computer Science, Stanford University
Hallowell Davis, Director Emeritus of Research, Central Institute for the Deaf; Emeritus Professor of Otolaryngology, Washington University
Paul Gyorgy, Professor Emeritus of Pediatrics, University of Pennsylvania Medical School; Consultant, Philadelphia General Hospital
Sterling B. Hendricks, Formerly Chief Chemist, Beltsville Plant Industry Station, U.S. Dept of Agriculture
Joseph Oakland Hirschfelder, Homer Adkins Professor of Theoretical Chemistry, University of Wisconson, Madison
William H. Pickering, Director, Jet Propulsion Laboratory, California Institute of Technology
Lewis Hastings Sarett, President, Merck, Sharp and Dohme Research Laboratories
Frederick Emmons Terman, Provost Emeritus, Stanford University
Orville Alvin Vogel, Professor Emeritus, Dept. of Agronomy and Soils, Washington State University
E. Bright Wilson, Theodore William Richards Professor of Chemistry, Harvard University
Chien-Shiung Wu, Michael I. Pupin Professor of Chemistry, Columbia University

1976 **Morris Cohen**, Institute Professor, Dept. of Metallurgy & Materials Science, Massachusetts Institute of Technology
Kurt Otto Friedrichs, Courant Institute of Mathematical Sciences, New York University
Peter C. Goldmark, President, Goldmark Communications Corp., Stamford, Conn.
Samuel A. Goudsmit, Dept. of Physics, University of Nevada
Roger C.L. Guillemin, Dept. of Neuroendocrinology, Salk Institute, San Diego
Herbert S. Gutowsky, Dept. of Chemistry, University of Illinois
Erwin W. Mueller, Dept. of Physics, Pennsylvania State University
Keith R. Porter, Dept. of Molecular, Cellular & Developmental Biology, University of Colordao
Efraim Racker, Section of Biochemistry, Molecular & Cell Biology, Cornell University, Ithaca, N.Y.
Frederick D. Rossini, Dept. of Chemistry, Rice University, Houston
Verner E. Suomi, Professor of Meteorology & Environmental Studies and Director of Space Sciences & Engineering Center, University of Wisconsin
Henry Taube, Dept. of Chemistry, Stanford University
George E. Uhlenbeck, Professor of Physics, Rockefeller University
Hassler Whitney, Institute for Advanced Studies, Princeton, N.J.
Edward O. Wilson, Museum of Comparative Zoology Laboratories, Harvard University

1977 **No award**

1978 **No award**

1979 **Robert H. Burris**, W.H. Peterson Professor of Biochemistry, University of Wisconsin
Elizabeth C. Crosby, Professor Emeritus of Anatomy, University of Michigan
Joseph L. Doob, Department of Mathematics, University of Illinois
Richard P. Feynman, Theoretical Physics, California Institute of Technology
Donald E. Knuth, Fletcher Jones Professor Department of Computer Science, Stanford University
Arthur Kornberg, Professor & Executive Head Department of Biochemistry, Stanford University School of Medicine
Emmett N. Leith, Professor of Electrical Engineering, University of Michigan
Herman F. Mark, Dean (Emeritus) of the Faculty, Polytechnic Institute of Brooklyn
Raymond D. Mindlin, Professor Emeritus of Civil Engineering, Columbia University
Robert N. Noyce, Chairman, Intel Corp.
Severo Ochoa, Professor of Biochemistry, New York University
Earl R. Parker, Professor of Metallurgy, University of California, Berkeley
Edward M. Purcell, Professor of Physics, Harvard University
Simon Ramo, Vice Chairman of the Board, Thompson, Ramo, Wooldridge Inc.
John H. Sinfelt, Scientific Adviser, EXXON Corporate Research Labs, ESSO Research & Engineering Co.
Lyman Spitzer, Jr., Professor of Astronomy, Princeton University
Earl R. Stadtman, Head, Laboratory of Biochemistry, National Heart & Lung Institute, National Institutes of Health
G. Ledyard Stebbins, Assistant Professor, Dept. of Genetics, University of California, Davis
Paul A. Weiss, Emeritus Member, Rockefeller University
Victor F. Weisskopf, Professor & Chairman, Dept. of Physics, Massachusetts Institute of Technology

1980 **No award**

The Alan T. Waterman Award, which consists of a maximum-$50,000 grant for up to three years, is given annually to an outstanding American scientist under 35 years of age in mathematical, biological, engineering, social or other science. A selection committee choses the winner.

1976 **Charles L. Fefferman,** Dept. of Mathematics, Princeton; "Research in Fourier analysis, partial differential equations and several complex variables which have contributed signally to the advancement of modern mathematical analysis"

1977 **J. William Schopf,** Dept. of Geology, University of California, Los Angeles; "For outstanding geochemical and micropaleontological analyses of pre-Cambrian organic matter, pioneering study of delicate and ancient micro-organisms and development of techniques for their examination and identification"

1978 **Richard A. Muller**, Lawrence Berkeley Laboratory and Space Sciences Laboratory, University of California, Berkeley, "For highly original and innovative research, which has led to important discoveries and inventions in diverse areas of physics, including astrophysics, radioisotope dating and optics"

1979 **William P. Thurston**, Professor of Mathematics, Princeton University; "In recognition of his achievements in introducing revolutionary new geometrical methods in the theory of foliations, function theory and topology"

1980 **Roy F. Schwitters**, Professor of Physics, Harvard University; "for his contributions to the understanding of the basic structure of matter through experiments that discovered and explored an entirely new collection of subatomic particles. The experiments led to the interpretation of the new particles as being composed of simpler constituents, possessing a new property of matter."

Pfizer Award

HISTORY OF SCIENCE SOCIETY
c/o Prof. Sally Kohlstedt, Department of History, 311 Maxwell Hall, Syracuse University, Syracuse, N.Y. 13210 (315/423-3307)

The Pfizer Award, which carries a $1,000 cash prize and a citation, is given annually for an outstanding monograph appearing on science in an American or Canadian publication, as judged by a committee.

1959 **Marie Boas Hall**
1960 **Marshall Clagett**
1961 **Cyril Stanley Smith**
1962 **Henry Guerlac**
1963 **Lynn T. White**
1964 **Robert E. Schofield**
1965 **C.D. O'Malley**
1966 **L. Pearce Williams**
1967 **Howard B. Adelmann**
1968 **Edwin Rosen**
1969 **Margaret T. May**
1970 **Michael Ghiselin**
1971 **David Joravsky**
1972 **Richard S. Westfall**
1973 **Joseph S. Fruton**
1974 **Susan Schlee**
1975 **Frederic L. Holmes**
1976 **Otto Neugebauer**
1977 **Stephen Brush**
1978 **Allen G. Debus** and **Merritt Roe Smith**
1979 **Susan F. Cannon**
1980 **Frank J. Sulloway**

Ernst Richert Preis

BUNDESMINISTERIUM FUR INNERDEUTSCHE BEZIEHUNGEN
Godesberger Allee 140, 5300 Bonn 2, Federal Republic of Germany (02283061)

The 20,000-mark Ernst-Richert-Preis is given by the Ministry for Intra-German Relations for scientific achievements concering the German Democratic Republic in comparative advance in the Federal Republic. A jury selects the recipient.

1980 **Gunther Heydemann**, Scientific history of divided Germany

Royal Medal
Copley Medal

THE ROYAL SOCIETY
6 Carlton House Terr., London, United Kingdom SW1Y 5AG (01-839 5561)

The Copley Medal, which is of silver gilt and is accompanied by a £1,000 honorarium, annually honors "such philosophical research as may appear to be deserving of the honor." The Copley Medal was established in 1731, but only the most recent winners are listed here.

1978 **Robert Burns Woodward**, Contributions to the synthesis of complex natural products and discovery of the importance of orbital symmetry
1979 **Max Ferdinand Perutz**, Contributions to molecular biology through studies on the structure and biological activity of hemoglobin and leadership in the development of the subject
1980 **Sir Derek Barton**, Contributions to a wide range of problems in structural and synthetic organic chemistry and, in particular, introduction of conformational analysis into sterochemistry

Three Royal Medals are presented annually to distinguished scientific achievement. Two are given for the contributions deemed most important to the advancement of natural knowledge and the third for contributions in the applied scienes. The medals, which are of gold, are given by Her Majesty the Queen upon the recommendation of the council of the Royal Society. While the medals were established in 1825 and 1965, respectively, only the most recent winners are given here.

1978 **Abdus Salam**, physics of elementary particles with special reference to the unification of the electromagnetic and weak interactions
Roderic Alfred Gregory, studies of the biological activity of peptide hormones in relation to their structure
Tom Kilburn development of computer hardware in the U.K. over the last thirty years
1979 **Sir Charles Frank**, theory of crystal growth, dislocations, phase transformations and polymers with wide applications in physics, chemistry and geology
Hans Walter Kisterlitz, work on narcotics leading to the discovery of the enkephalins
Vernon Ellis Cosslett, design and development of the X-ray microscope, the scanning electron microprobe analyser, the high-voltage and ultrahigh-resolution (0.25 nm) electron microscopes and their applications in many disciplines
1980 **Sir Denys Wilkinson**, original research in nuclear physics—giant resonances, radiative widths, second-class beta decay and the fundamental symmetries of nuclear interactions and on instrumentation
Henry Harris, development of cell fusion for the study of somatic cell genetics and differentiation, including the genetic control of malignancy
J.P. Wild, conception of the basic principles of the Interscan aircraft instrument landing system and the guidance of its development

Rumford Medal

AMERICAN ACADEMY OF ARTS AND SCIENCES
Norton's Woods, 136 Irving St., Cambridge, Mass. 02138 (617/492-8800)

The Rumford Medal, which is accompanied by an honorarium, is presented periodically for work with or discovery in the field of heat and light that is beneficial to mankind. The Rumford Committee selects the winner.

1839 **Robert Hare,** Philadelphia, Invented compound or oxyhydrogen blowpipe
1862 **John Ericsson,** New York, Improvements in heat management, particularly the caloric engine

1865 **Daniel Treadwell,** Cambridge, Mass., Improvements in heat management, especially involving construction of large-caliber cannons
1866 **Alvan Clark,** Cambridge, Mass., Improved manufacture of refracting telescopes
1869 **George Henry Corliss,** Providence, R.I., Improved steam engine
1871 **Joseph Harrison, Jr.,** Philadelphia, Improved steam-boiler safety through construction method
1873 **Lewis Morris Rutherford,** New York, Improved astronomical photography
1875 **John William Draper,** New York, Research on radiant energy
1880 **Josiah Willard Gibbs,** New Haven, Conn., Research on thermodynamics
1883 **Henry Augustus Rowland,** Baltimore, Research on light and heat
1886 **Samuel Pierpont Langley,** Allegheny, Pa., Research on radiant energy
1888 **Albert Abraham Michelson,** Cleveland, Determination of velocity of light, research on motion of luminferous ether and work on absolute determination of wave-lengths of light
1891 **Edward Charles Pickering,** Cambridge, Mass., Work on photometry of stars and on stellar spectra
1895 **Thomas Alva Edison,** Orange, N.J., Investigations in electric lighting
1898 **James Edward Keeler,** Allegheny, Pa., Application of spectroscope to astronomical problems, especially investigations of proper motions of nebulae and physical constitution of Saturn's rings by use of that instrument
1899 **Charles Francis Brush,** Cleveland, Practical development of electric arc lighting
1900 **Carl Barus,** Providence, R.I., Research on heat
1901 **Elihu Thomson,** Lynn, Mass., Inventions in electric welding and lighting
1902 **George Ellery Hale,** Chicago, Investigations in solar and stellar physics, especially invention and perfection of spectro-heliograph
1904 **Ernest Fox Nichols,** New York, Research on radiation, especially pressure due to radiation, star heat and infra-red spectrum
1907 **Edward Goodrich Acheson,** Niagara Falls, N.Y., Application of heat in electric furnaces to industrial production of carborundum, graphite and other substances
1909 **Robert Williams Wood,** Baltimore, Discoveries in light, especially optical properties of sodium and other metallic vapors
1910 **Charles Gordon Curtins,** New York, Improved utilization of heat as work in the steam turbine
1911 **James Mason Crafts,** Boston, Research in high-temperature thermometry and determination of new fixed points on the thermometric scale
1912 **Frederic Eugene Ives,** Woodcliff-on-Hudson, N.Y., Optical inventions, especially in color photography and photo-engraving
1913 **Joel Stebbins,** Urbana, Ill., Developed selenium photometer for application to astronomical problems
1914 **William David Coolidge,** Schenectady, N.Y., Invented ductile tungsten for application to production of radiation
1915 **Charles Greeley Abbot,** Washington, D.C., Research on solar radiation
1917 **Percy Williams Bridgman,** Cambridge, Mass., Thermodynamical research of extremely high pressure
1918 **Theodore Lyman,** Cambridge, Mass., Research on light of very short wave length
1920 **Irving Langmuir,** Schenectady, N.Y., Research in thermionic and allied phenomena
1925 **Henry Norris Russell,** Princeton, N.J., Research in stellar radiation
1926 **Arthur Holly Compton,** Chicago, Research in Rontgen rays
1928 **Edward Leamington Nichols,** Ithaca, N.Y., Research in spectrophotometry
1930 **John Stanley Plaskett,** Victoria, B.C., Canada, Stellar spectrographic research
1931 **Karl Taylor Compton,** Cambridge, Mass., Research in thermionics and spectroscopy
1933 **Harlow Shapley,** Cambridge, Mass., Research on luminosity of stars and galaxies
1937 **William Weber Coblentz,** Washington, D.C., Pioneer in technology and measurement of heat and light
1939 **George Russell Harrison,** Boston, Improved spectroscopic technique
1941 **Vladimir Kosma Zworykin,** Princeton, N.J., Invented iconoscope and other television devices
1943 **Charles Edward Mees,** Rochester, N.Y., Contributions to science of photography
1945 **Edwin Herbert Land,** Cambridge, Mass., New applications in polarized light and photography
1947 **Edmund Newton Harvey,** Princeton, N.J., Investigations into nature of bioluminescence
1949 **Ira Sprague Bowen,** Pasadena, Calif., Solution of the mystery of nebulium and other work in spectroscopy
1951 **Herbert E. Ives,** Montclair, N.J., Contributions to optics
1953 **Enrico Fermi,** Chicago, Ill., Studies of radiation theory and nuclear energy
Willis E. Lamb, Jr., Stanford, Calif., Studies of atomic hydrogen spectrum
Lars Onsager, New Haven, Conn., Contributions to thermodynamics of transport processes
1955 **James Franck,** Chicago, Ill., Fundamental studies on photosynthesis
1957 **Subrahmanyan Chandrasekhar,** Williams Bay, Wisc., Work on radiative transfer of energy in interior of stars
1959 **George Wald,** Cambridge, Mass., Studies in biochemical basis of vision
1961 **Charles Hard Townes,** New York, for Development of the maser
1963 **Hans Albrecht Bethe,** Ithaca, N.Y., Theoretical studies of energy production in stars
1965 **Samuel Cornette Collins,** Cambridge, Mass., Invented Collins Helium Cryostat and pioneered low-temperature research
William David McElroy, Baltimore, Work on molecular basis of bioluminescence
1967 **Robert Henry Dicke,** Princeton, N.J., Contributions to microwave radiometry and to understanding of atomic structure
Cornelis B. Van Niel, Stanford, Calif., Contributions to understanding of photosynthesis
1968 **Maarten Schmidt,** Pasadena, Calif., Discoveries in spectra of quasi-stellar objects
1971 **M.I.T. Group,** Cambridge, Mass. **(John A. Ball, Alan H. Barrett, Bernard F. Burke, Joseph C. Carter, Patricia P. Crowther, James M. Moran, Jr., and Alan E. Rogers), Canadian Group (Norman W. Broten, R.M. Chisholm, John A. Galt, Herbert P. Gush, Thomas H. Legg, Jack L. Locke, Charles W. McLeish, Roger S. Richards and Jui Lin Yen) and NRAO-Cornell Group (C.C. Bare, Barry G. Clark, Marshall H. Cohen, David L. Jauncey and Kenneth I. Kellermann),** Work in long-baseline interferometry

1973 **E. Bridge Wilson,** Cambridge, Mass., Early recognition of importance of symmetry properties in polyatomic molecules and pioneering development of microwave spectroscopy
1976 **Bruno Rossi,** Cambridge, Mass., Discoveries in nature and origins of cosmic radiations
1980 **Chen Ning Yang**, Stony Brook, N.Y., and **Robert L. Mills**, Columbus, Ohio, Development of a generalized gauge invariant field theory
Gregorio Weber, Urbana, Ill., Work on the theory and application of fluorescence

Rutherford Memorial Medals

ROYAL SOCIETY OF CANADA
344 Wellington, Ottawa, Ont. K1A 0N4 (613/992-3468)

The Rutherford Medals, which carry $1,000 cash prizes, are awarded annually to two scientists preferably under 40 years of age, one for outstanding research in chemistry and one for physics. Two selection committees, one in each branch of science, choose the winners.

CHEMISTRY

1980 **G. Michael Bancroft**

PHYSICS

1980 **Malcolm J. Stott**

Glenn Seaborg Award

INTERNATIONAL PLATFORM ASSOCIATION
2564 Berkshire Rd., Cleveland Heights, Ohio 44106

The Glenn Seaborg Award is made annually to honor the individual judges to have done the most to encourage and stimulate public interest in science.

1979 **Isaac Asimov**
1980 **Walter S. Sullivan, Jr.**

Henry Marshall Tory Medal

ROYAL SOCIETY OF CANADA
344 Wellington, Ottawa, Ont. K1A 0N4 (613/992-3468)

The Henry Marshall Tory Medal, which has been accompanied by a $1,000 cash prize since 1966, is now given every two years for outstanding research in astronomy, chemistry, mathematics, physics or an applied science carried out primarily during the preceding eight years. A selection committee chooses the recipient.

1943 **John L. Synge**
1944 **Frank Allen**
1945 **Otto Maass**
1946 **John F. Foster**
1947 **E.F Burton**
1949 **N.M.S. Coxeter**
1951 **T. Thorvaldson**
1953 **G. Herzberg**
1955 **E.W.R. Steacie**
1957 **C.S. Beale**
1959 **H.G. Thode**
1961 **R.M. Petrie**
1963 **H.L. Welsh**
1965 **H.E. Duckworth**
1967 **I. Halperin**
1969 **W.G. Schneider**
1971 **H.E. Johns**
1973 **B.N. Brockhouse**
1975 **W.T. Tutte**
1977 **J.N. Polanyi**
1979 **N.S. Mendelsohn**

Kalinga Prize for the Popularization of Science
UNESCO Science Prize
Carlos J. Finlay Prize

UNITED NATIONS EDUCATIONAL, SCIENTIFIC AND CULTURAL ORGANIZATION
Place de Fontenoy, 75700 Paris (Tel: 577 16 10, Ext. 3206, 3207)

The Kalinga Prize for the Popularization of Science, funded by the Kalinga Trust Foundation of India, annually honors individuals for popularizing science with a cash award of 1,000 British pounds and a trip to India. Nominations are submitted through UNESCO National Commissions, which forward them to Paris for selection by a jury and approval by the director general of UNESCO.

1952 **Prince Louis de Broglie** (France)
1953 **Sir Julian Huxley** (Great Britain)
1954 **Waldemar Kaempffert** (U.S.A.)
1955 **Augusto Pi Suner** (Venezuela)
1956 **George Gamow** (U.S.A.)
1957 **Bertrand Russell** (Great Britain)
1958 **K. von Frisch** (Federal Republic of Germany)
1959 **Jean Rostand** (France)
1960 **Ritchie Calder,** C.B.E. (Great Britain)
1961 **Arthur C. Clarke** (Great Britain)
1962 **Gerard Piel** (U.S.A.)
1963 **Jagjit Singh** (India)
1964 **Warren Weaver** (U.S.A.)
1965 **Eugene Rabinowitch** (U.S.A.)
1966 **Paul Couderc** (France)
1967 **Fred Hoyle** (Great Britain)
1968 **Sir Gavin de Beer** (Great Britain)
1969 **Konrad Lorenz** (Austria)
1970 **Margaret Mead** (U.S.A.)
1971 **Pierre Auger** (France)
1972 **Philip H. Abelson** (U.S.A.)
Nigel Calder (Great Britain)
1973 **No award**
1974 **Jose Reis** (Brazil)
Luis Estrada (Mexico)
1975 **No award**
1976 **Sir George Porter** (Great Britain)
1977 **A.I. Oparin** (U.S.S.R.)
Fernand Seguin (Canada)
1978 **Heimar von Ditfurth** (Federal Republic of Germany)
1979 **Not available at press time**
1980 **Not available at press time**

The biennial UNESCO Science Prize, which carries a $3,000 honorarium, honors outstanding contributions to the development of any United Nations member state or region through the application of science and technology. Nominations may be submitted by any individual or group through National Commissions for

UNESCO, which forward them to Paris for selection by a jury and approval by the director general of UNESCO.

1968 **Robert Simpson** (Great Britain), Discovery of a process for the demineralalization of sea water
1970 **International Maize and Wheat Improvement Center** (Mexico), Improvement strains of cereals
International Rice Research Institute (Philippines), Improved strains of cereals
1972 **Viktor A. Kovda** (U.S.S.R.), Theory on hydromorphic origin of soils of the great plains of Asia, Africa, America and Europe
Nine Austrian research workers (Austria), Development of L-D steel production process to help small developed country compete economically and effectively with large, highly industrialized nations
1976 **Alfred Champagnat** (France), For findings on low-cost mass production of new proteins from petroleum
1978 **Seven researchers from the Lawes Agricultural Trust, Rothamsted Experimental Station** (London, Great Britain), Synthetic insecticides related to natural pyrethrum
1980 **J.G. Belton, M.L. Conalty, J.F.D. Sullivan** and **D. Twomey** (Ireland), Synthesis of antileprosy agent "b.633"

The Carlos J. Finlay Prize, donated by the government of Cuba, is given every two years for meritorious work in microbiology. The $5,000 prize follows the nomination and selection procedures above.

1980 **Roger Y. Stanier**

Theodore von Karman Award

AIR FORCE ASSOCIATION
1750 Pennsylvania Ave. NW, Washington, D.C. 20006 (202/637-3300)

The Theodore von Karman Award, which was originally known as the Science Trophy, is given annually for outstanding contributions to science and engineering as it relates to aerospace applications. The awards committee selects the winners from nominations from individuals and organizations with interest in aerospace activity.

1948 **John Stack**, NACA Designer
1949 **R.C. Sebold, R.H. Widmer** and **Ray O. Ryan**, contributors to the development of the B-36
1950 **Theodore von Karman**, Chairman, Scientific Advisory Board, U.S. Air Force
1951 **George E. Valley**, Department of Physics, MIT
1952 **Edward Teller**, Radiation Laboratory, University of California
1953 **Melvin J. Kelly**, Bell Telephone Laboratories
1954 **Lt. Col. John Paul Stapp**, U.S. Air Force
1955 **John F. von Neumann** Atomic Energy Commission
1956 **Chalmers W. Sherwin**, University of Illinois
1957 **Charles Stark Draper**, MIT
1958 **H. Julian Allen**, Ames Aeronautical Laboratory
1959 **W. Randolph Lovelace, II**, and **Brig. Gen. Don D. Flickinger**, U.S. Air Force
1960 **Louis N. Ridenour, Jr.**, Lockheed Aircraft Corp.
1961 **Allen F. Donovan**, Aerospace Corporation
1962 **Charles H. Townes**, Provost, MIT
1963 **Clarence L. "Kelly" Johnson**, Lockheed Aircraft Corp.
1964 **Clarence L. "Kelly" Johnson**, Lockheed Aircraft Corp.
1965 **Capt. Robert M. Silva**, U.S. Air Force
1966 **6555th Aerospace Test Wing, AFSC**
1967 **Col. Alterio Gallerani**, Aerospace Audio Visual Service
1968 **Lt. Col. Harry F. Rizzo**, U.S. Air Force
1969 **No award**
1970 **Maj. Gen. Kenneth F. Schultz**, Deputy for Minutemen, SAMSO
1971 **Fred D. Orazio, Sr.**, Scientific Director, Aeronautical Systems Div.
1972 **Lt. Col. Donald G. Carpenter**, U.S. Air Force, for advancing the US space defense capability
1973 **Lt. Col. Roy Robinette, Jr.**, U.S. Air Force (Ret.)
1974 **USAF's Space and Missile Systems Organization**
1975 **Maj. Gen. Kendall Russell, Brig. Gen. Lawrence A. Skantze** and **Mark K. Miller**, Boeing Aerospace Co., representing U.S. Air Force/industry team
1976 **James S. Martin, Jr.**, NASA, and **Thomas G. Pownall**, Martin Marietta Corp., representing NASA/industry team
1977 **John B. Walsh**, Deputy Director, Strategic Space Systems ODDR&E
1978 **Brig. Gen. Donald L. Lamberson**, Deputy for Development and Acquisition, Armament Development and Test Center
1979 **Gen. Alton D. Slay**, U.S. Air Force, Commander, Air Force Systems Command
1980 **Capt. Randal L. Richey**, U.S. Air Force

Bradford Washburn Award
Walker Prize

MUSEUM OF SCIENCE
Science Park, Boston, Mass. 02114 (617/723-2500)

The Bradford Washburn Award, which consists of a gold medal and a $5,000 honorarium, recognizes outstanding contributions toward public understanding of science and "appreciation of the vital role it plays in all our lives."

1964 **Melville Bell Grosvenor,** Contributing to great interest in science through *The National Geographic*
1965 **Jacques-Yves Cousteau,** Undersea explorer; film-maker
1966 **Gerard Piel,** Publisher, *Scientific American*
1967 **Donald B. MacMillan,** Arctic explorer; leader; teacher
1968 **George Wald,** Biologist and teacher
1969 **Sir George Taylor,** Director, Royal Botanic Gardens, United Kingdom
1970-71 **Walter Cronkite,** Senior CBS news correspondent, for reporting on U.S. space program
1972 **Walter Sullivan,** Science editor, *New York Times*
1973 **Rene Dubos,** Micro-biologist; author; lecturer
1974 **Jane Goodall and Hugo van Lawick,** Writer; student of primates; and photographer and film-maker
1975 **Jean Mayer,** Nutritionist; writer; lecturer
1976 **Loren Eiseley,** Anthropologist; writer
1977 **Arthur C. Clarke,** Science fiction and science writer
1978 **Carl Sagan**
1979 **Isaac Asimov**
1980 **Mary D. Leakey**
Kenneth F. Weaver

The Walker Prize, which carries a $5,000 honorarium, is given as merited for worthy published scientific investigation and discovery. When the prize was started in the 19th century, it was divided into several small cash awards. The winners below have been selected by the Committee of Trustees since the consolidation of the smaller prizes into one award carrying a significant amount of money.

1967 **Martin H. Moynihan,** Naturalist of the Tropics
1968 **Howard E. Evans,** Studies of the wasp
1969 **Robert K. Selander,** Ornithologist
1970 **Irven DeVore,** Studies of baboons and Bushmen
1971 **Ernst Mayr,** Contributions to understanding process of evolution
1973 **Alfred C. Redfield,** Oceanographer
1976 **Richard M. Eakin,** Zoologist
1978 **Sherwood L. Washburn**

Shmuel Yaroslavsky Memorial Award

WEIZMANN INSTITUTE OF SCIENCE
Box 26, Rehovot, Israel (Tel: 054-82111)

The Shmuel Yaroslavsky Memorial Award is given for biological and physical research with potential for industrial applications.

1968 **Mati Fridkin,** Use of polymers as reagents in organic synthesis
Sara Ehrlich-Rogozinsky, Special award for completing Dr. Yaroslavsky's research and preparing his last results for publication
1969 **Haim Rosen,** Polymer research, specifically for work on dimerization and cross-dimerization of acrylic monomers
1970 **Michael Martan,** Plastics, specifically for work on oxidation in liquid phase of hydronaphthalenes
1972 **David Gabison,** Biophysics, specifically for rennin for manufacture of cheese
1974 **Stephen Daren,** Work on the industrial synthesis of bromostyrene
1976 **Moshe Shapiro,** Chemical physics, specifically for work on a theoretical study of photodissociation and exothermic chemical reactions with possible applications to photodissociation lasers and chemical lasers
1978 **Hadassah Degani,** Developed use of magnetics resonance spectroscopic to determine mechanism and kinetics of ion transport processes in the membrane system
1980 **Stephen Weiner,** Isotope research

CIBA-GEIGY American Society of Agronomy Award
CIBA-GEIGY American Phytopathological Society Award
CIBA-GEIGY Entomological Society of America Award
CIBA-GEIGY Agricultural Award
CIBA-GEIGY Weed Science Society of America Award

CIBA-GEIGY Box 11422, Greensboro, N.C. 27409 (919/292-7100)

CIBA-GEIGY, a chemical firm, annually funds a series of awards in agriculture, agronomy and related fields. Awards concists of a trophy and a trip to Switzerland, where the firm is headquartered. The associations each select the winners of the awards.

CIBA-GEIGY AMERICAN SOCIETY OF AGRONOMY AWARD

1970 **H.A.L. Greer**
1971 **R.E. Doersch**
1972 **J.G. Clapp, Jr.**
1973 **L.S. Murphy**
1974 **H.E. White**
1975 **G.A. Peterson**
1976 **D.W. Nelson**
1977 **C.G. Messersmith**
1978 **V.L. Lechtenberg**
1979 **R.G. Hoeft**
1980 **A.R. Martin**

CIBA-GEIGY AMERICAN PHYTOPATHOLOGICAL SOCIETY AWARD

1976 **D.J. Hagedorn**
A.L. Shigo
1977 **W.W. Hare**
1978 **G.S. Abawi**
1979 **A.L. Jones**
1980 **A.A. MacNab**

CIBA-GEIGY ENTOMOLOGICAL SOCIETY OF AMERICA AWARD

1970 **L.D. Newsom**
1971 **O.H. Graham**
1972 **Richard L. Ridgway**
1973 **Stanley C. Hoyt**
1974 **Robert L. Rabb**
1975 **Tommy L. Harvey**
1976 **Carlo Maramorosch**
1977 **Robert L. Metcalf**
1978 **Harold F. Madsen**
1979 **Henry V. Morton**
1980 **J. Alexander Hair**

CIBA-GEIGY NACAA* AGRICULTURAL AWARD

1970 **H.H. Hecht**
1971 **Olaiver Hamrick, Jr.**
1972 **Herbert Crown**
1973 **Robert A. Lamar**
1974 **Lloyd C. Baron**
1975 **John Andrews**
1976 **Dennis Ikehara**
1977 **James Read**

1978 Luther Fitch
1979 John Shearer
1980 Arnold Rieckman

*National Association of County Agricultural Agents

CIBA-GEIGY WEED SOCIETY OF AMERICA AWARD

1971 **A.P. Appleby**, Teacher
1972 **E.L. Knake**, Extension worker
1973 **D.E. Moreland,** Research
1974 **J.D. Nalewaja**, Teacher
1975 **L.E. Anderson**, Extension worker
1976 **J.L. Hilton**, Research
1977 **G.F. Warren**, Teacher
1978 **L.W. Mitich**, Extension worker
1979 **O.C. Burnside**, Research
1980 **R.E. Frans**, Teacher

Eunice Rockwell Oberly Memorial Award

AMERICAN LIBRARY ASSOCIATION
Association of College Research Libraries, 50 E. Huron St., Chicago, Ill. 60611 (312/944-6780)

The Eunice Rockwell Oberly Memorial Award, which consists of a citation and an honorarium, is awarded biennially by the Association's Agriculture and Biological Services Section for the best bibliography in the field of agriculture or related sciences. An awards committee selects the winner from nominations previously received.

1925 **Max Meisel**
1927 **Mary G. Lacy, Annie M. Hannay and Emily E. Day**
1929 **Annie M. Hannay**
1931 **Everett E. Edwards**
1933 **Louise O. Bercaw and Esther Marie Colvin**
1935 **Louise O. Bercaw, Annie M. Hannay and Esther Marie Colvin**
1937 **Victor A. Schaefer**
1939 **Louise O. Bercaw and Annie M. Hannay**
1941 **Elmer D. Merrill and Egbert H. Walker**
1943 **No award**
1945 **S.F. Blake and Alice Atwood J.C. Cunningham**
1947 **Burch Hart Schneider**
1949 **Ina L. Hawes and Rose Eisenberg**
1951 **Richard Weibe and Janina Nowakowska**
1953 **Dorothy B. Skau, Ralph W. Planck and Frank C. Pack**
1955 **Arthur Rose and Elizabeth Rose**
1957 **Ira J. Condit and Julius Enderud**
1959 **J. Richard Blanchard and Harald Ostvold**
1961 **Egbert H. Walker**
1963 **Allan Stevenson**
1965 **Ida Kaplan Langman**
1967 **George Neville Jones**
1969 **No award**
1971 **John T. Schlebecker**
1973 **Olga Landvay**
1975 **Ann E. Kerker and Henry T. Murphy**
1977 **Helen Purdy Beale**
1979 **James B. Beard, Harriet J. Beard and David P. Martin**

Agronomic Research Award
Edward Browning Award for Improvement of Food Sources
International Service in Agronomy Award
Soil Science Award

AMERICAN SOCIETY OF AGRONOMY AND SOIL SCIENCE SOCIETY OF AMERICA
677 S. Segoe Rd., Madison, Wisc. 53711 (608/274-1212)

The SSSA's $200 Agronomic Research Award recognizes discoveries, techniques, inventions or materials that increase crop yields, improve crop quality, food products, land and water development, environmental quality or conservation. A selection committee picks the recipient from a list of nominees.

1975 **A.J. Ohlrogge**
1976 **T.M. McCalla**
1977 **George Stanford**
1978 **Lewis H. Stolzy**
1979 **Richard L. Bernard**
1980 **Frank J. Stevenson**

The ASA's $5,000 Edward Browning Award for Improvement of Food Sources, which consists of a bronze medal and a certificate, is given annually to an individual who has made outstanding improvement of food sources anywhere in the world within the previous 10 years. Each nominee must be sponsored by a recognized professional association and society, and the recipient is chosen by a selection committee.

1971 **J.G. Harrar**
1972 **O.A. Gobel**
1973 **E.R. Burmester**
1974 **E.G. Mertz and O.E. Nelson**
1975 **G.W. Burton**
1976 **E.A. Black**
1977 **E.O. Heady**
1978 **Robert H. Burris**
1979 **Richard Bradfield**
1980 **Douglas Ensminger**

The $200 International Service in Agronomy Award recognizes influence on the growth and development of agronomy outside the United States, with a focus on creative efforts, relevance and effectiveness of the recipient's international agronomic activities. An ASA selection committee picks the winner from a list of nominees.

1968 **N. E. Borlaug**
1969 **E.J. Wellhausen**
1970 **R.W. Cummings**
1971 **R.A. Olson**
1972 **R.F. Chandler**
1973 **Richard Bradfield**
1974 **Matthew Drosdoff**
1975 **Sterling Worthman**
1976 **J.R. Harlan**
1977 **H.W. Ream**
1978 **Bertil A. Krantz**
1979 **Ernest W. Sprague**
1980 **Te-Tzu Chang**

The SSA's Soil Science Award is a $200 prize which honors demonstrated creativity, reasoning and/or technical skill or research contributions to basic or applied soil science. A selection committee picks the winner from a list of nominees.

1975 **Dale Swartzendruber**
1976 **Max Mortland**
1977 **Edwin L. Schmidt**
1978 **Champ B. Tanner**
1979 **James P. Martin**
1980 **Willard L. Lindsay**

Justus von Liebig Prizes

STIFTUNG F.V.S.
Georgesplatz 10, 2 Hamburg 1, Federal Republic of Germany (Tel: 33 04 00 and 33 06 00)

The Justus von Liebig Prizes, which each carry a 20,000-mark cash award, are given annually for the advancement of agriculture in Europe. The award is administered by the University of Kiel.

1949/50 **Theodor Roemer,** Halle, Germany
Carl Heinz Dencker, Bonn, Germany
1951 **Emil Alfred,** Neckarelz, Wurttemberg, Germany
1952 **Walter Laube,** Gottingen, Germany
1953 **August Block,** Rittergut Banteln, Germany
Richard von Flemming, Uelzen, Germany
1954 **Walter Kubiena,** Vienna, Austria
1955 **Peter Rasmussen,** Apenrade, Denmark
1956 **Ernst Klapp,** Bonn, Germany
1957 **Wilhelm Ries,** Michelstadt, Germany
1958 **Walter Wittich,** Hann.-Munden, Germany
1959 **Hans Lembke,** Rostock, Germany
Otto Bolten Rothenstein/Kreis Eckernforde, Germany
1960 **Arthur Hanau,** Gottingen, Germany
Roderich Plate, Stuttgart-Hohenheim, Germany
1961 **Hans-Ulrich von Oertzen,** Bad Godesberg, Germany
1962 **P.B. de Boers,** Stiens, Holland,
Count Ian D. Hamilton, Barseback, Sweden
1963 **Bernard Poullain,** La Queue-les-Yvelines, France
Bernhard Rademacher, Stuttgart-Hohenheim, Germany
1964 **Walter Mader,** Bruck a.d. Leitha, Austria
Fritz Schilke, Hambourg
1965 **Giovanni Haussmann,** Lodi, Italy
Constantin von Dietze, Freiburg i. Br., Germany
1966 **Paul Nicolai,** Gorsem, Belgium
Anton Freiherr von Herzogenberg, Salem/Baden, Germany
1967 **Kutzenhausen Community,** France
Dietz Freiherr von Thungen, Thungen, Unterfranken, Germany
1968 **Sir Richard Trehane,** Wimborne, Dorset, United Kingdom
Paul Rintelen, Munich, Germany
1969 **Karl Brandt,** Palo Alto, Calif.
Hans Rabe Jr., Sonke-Nissen-Koog, Germany
1970 **Hjalmar Clausen,** Copenhagen, Denmark,
Georg Blohm, Kiel, Germany
1971 **Charles Kiss,** La Menitre, France
Hermann Strehle, Reichertsweilerhof bei Donauworth, Germany
1972 **Harald Skjervold** Vollebekk, Norway,
Klauss Kleeberg, Eisbergen b. Minden, Germany
1973 **Luigi Cavazza,** Bologna, Italy
Count Heinrich Finck von Finckenstein, Winterburen/Hessen, Germany
1974 **Lucijan Krivec,** Ljubljana, Yugoslavia
Ulrich Dieckmann, Schaumburg, Germany
1975 **Ingvar Ekesbo,** Skara, Sweden
Joachim von Wulfing, Swisttal-Heimerzheim, Germany
1976 **Leopold Wiklicky,** Tulln, Austria
Philipp Kuhne, Gottingen, Germany
1977 **Per Henrick Sumelius,** Helsinki, Finland
1978 **Gerhard Fischbeck**, Munich
Francois Ravier and **Edouard Robotton**, Morestel, France
1979 **Albert Huber**, Aue-Dusseldorf
San Antonio Abad Cooperative, Milagros, Spain
1980 **A. van Arendonk**, Bavel, Netherlands
Werner Koch, Stuttgart

Wolf Prize in Agriculture

WOLF FOUNDATION
Box 398, Herzliah-Bet, Israel

The $100,000 Wolf Prize in Agriculture honors an outstanding achievement in agricultural research, as determined by a committee of internationally known judges. The award is part of a $500,000 annual prize distribution for exceptional achievement in five fields of science.

1978 **George F. Sprague** (University of Illinois), Research on the genetic ameliorization of maize for human welfare
John C. Walker (University of Wisconsin), Research in plant pathology, developing of disease-resistant varieties of major food plants
1979 **Jay L. Lush** (Iowa State University), Pioneering contributions to the application of genetics to livestock improvement
Sir Kenneth Blaxter (Rowett Research Institute, Aberdeen, Scotland), Fundamental contributions to science and practice of ruminant nutrition and livestock production
1980 **Karl Maramorosch** (Rutgers University), Pioneering studies on interactions between insects and disease agents in plants

Annie J. Cannon Award in Astronomy
Helen B. Warner Prize for Astronomy
Newton Lacey Pierce Prize in Astronomy
Henry Norris Russell Lectureship

AMERICAN ASTRONOMICAL SOCIETY
1816 Jefferson Pl. NW, Washington, D.C. 20036 (609/452-3819)

The Annie J. Cannon Award in Astronomy is a grant given not more often than every two years to a woman under 35 years of age in support of astronomy research. The American Association of University Women makes the award to an applicant who normally has already earned her doctorate. The AAUW, assisted by the American Astronomical Society, selects the recipient.

1934 **C. Payne-Gaposchkin** (Harvard College Observatory), Stellar spectroscopy

1937 **C. M. Sitterly** (Princeton University Observatory), Atomic and solar spectra
1940 **J. M. Vinter-Hansen** (Royal Observatory, Copenhagen), Minor planets and comets
1943 **A. C. Maury** (Harvard College Observatory), Stellar spectra, Beta Lyrae
1946 **E. W. Vyssotsky** (Leander McCormick Observatory), Color indices, stellar spectra
1949 **H. S. Hogg** (David Dunlap Observatory), Globular star clusters
1952 **I. Barney** (Yale University Observatory), Fundamental star catalogues
1955 **H. D. Prince** (McMath-Hulbert Observatory), Solar investigations
1958 **M. W. Mayall** (AAVSO), Variable stars
1962 **M. Harwood** (Maria Mitchell Observatory), Variable stars
1965 **E. Bohm-Vitense** (Institut fur Theoretische Physik, Kiel, Germany), Theoretical astrophysics
1968 **H. H. Swope** (Hale Observatories), Stellar statistics
1976 **Catherine Garmany** (Unaffiliated), Stellar dynamics
1978 **Paula Szkody**
1980 **Lee Ann Willson**

The Helen B. Warner Prize for Astronomy, which carries a $1,000 honorarium, is awarded annually for significant contributions to astronomy during the five years preceding the award. Any member of the Society may nominate candidates who are North American residents and who are under 35 years of age for consideration by the Warner Prize Committee.

1954 **A. B. Meinel,** Infrared
1955 **G. H. Herbig,** Stellar spectroscopy
1956 **H. Johnson,** Photometry
1957 **A. R. Sandage,** Extraglactic
1958 **M. F. Walker,** Photometry
E. M. and G. Burbidge, Neucleosynthesis
1960 **H. C. Arp,** Extragalactic
1961 **J. W. Chamberlain,** Aurora
1962 **R. P. Kraft,** Stellar spectroscopy
1963 **B. F. Burke,** Radio observation
1964 **M. Schmidt,** Quasars
1965 **G. W. Preston,** Stellar atmospheres
1966 **R. Giacconi,** X-rays
1967 **P. Demarque,** Stellar interiors
1968 **F. J. Low,** Infrared observations
1969 **W. L. W. Sargent,** Extraglactic
1970 **J. C. Bahcall,** Neutrinos
1971 **K. I. Kellermann,** Radio interferometry
1972 **J. P. Ostriker,** Degenerate stars
1973 **G. R. Carruthers,** Instrumentation
1974 **D. Mihalas,** Stellar atmospheres
1975 **B. Zuckerman and B. Palmer,** Interstellar molecules
1976 **S. Strom,** Stellar structure
1977 **F. Shu,** Stellar dynamics
1978 **David N. Shramm**
1979 **Arthur Davidsen**
1980 **Paul C. Joss**

The Newton Lacey Pierce Prize in Astronomy, which consists of an honorarium and a certificate or other token determined by the Council, is awarded annually to an astronomer under 35 years of age for outstanding achievement over the previous five years in observational research based on measurements of radiation coming from any kind of astronomical object. Any member of the Society may nominate a candidate who is a resident of North America for consideration.

1973 **E. Kellogg,** X-ray instrumentation
1974 **E. Becklin,** Infrared instrumentation
1975 **No award**
1976 **R. Angel,** Polarization instrumentation
1977 **D.N.B. Hall,** Interferometry
1978 **James M. Moran**
1979 **D.A. Harper**
1980 **Jack Baldwin**

The Henry Norris Russell Lectureship, which carries an honorarium of $500, is given annually for eminence in astronomical research. The candidate is selected by the Russell Lecture Committee with the approval of the Council.

1946 **H. N. Russell,** Structure
1947 **W. S. Adams,** Spectroscopy
1948 **No award**
1949 **S. Chandrasekhar,** Structure
1950 **H. Shapley,** Galactic structure
1951 **J. H. Oort,** Galactic structure
1952 **No award**
1953 **E. Fermi,** Neutrino theory
L. Spitzer, Jr., Plasma theory
1954 **No award**
1955 **P. W. Merrill,** Spectroscopy
1956 **J. Stebbins,** Photometry
1957 **O. Struve,** Spectroscopy
1958 **W. Baade,** Galaxies
1959 **G. P. Kuiper,** Planetary
1960 **M. Schwarzschild,** Atmospheres
1961 **W. W. Morgan,** Classification
1962 **G. Reber,** Radio observation
1963 **W. A. Fowler,** Neucleosynthesis
1964 **I. S. Bowen,** Atomic theory
1965 **B. G. Stromgren,** Photometry
1966 **R. Tousey,** Rocket observation
1967 **O. Neugebauer,** Infrared
1968 **J. G. Bolton,** Radio observation
1969 **E. N. Parker,** X-ray theory
1970 **J. Greenstein,** Degenerate stars
1971 **F. Hoyle,** Cosmology
1972 **A. R. Sandage,** Cosmology
1972 **L. Goldberg,** Solar physics
1974 **E. Salpeter,** Stellar structure
1975 **G. Herbig,** Interstellar
1976 **C. P. Gaposchkin,** Variable stars
1977 **O. C. Wilson,** Spectroscopy
1978 **Maarten Schmidt**
1979 **Peter Goldreich**
1980 **Jeremiah P. Ostriker**

Astronomical League Award Presidential Citation

ASTRONOMICAL LEAGUE
Box 3332, Papillion, Neb. 68046 (402/592-1196)

The Astronomical League Award plaque is given upon nomination and vote by the incumbent and two past presidents of the League for outstanding work in amateur astronomical societies or general astronomy.

1951 **Albert L. Ingalis,** "Father of Amateur Astronomy," author and telescope maker
1952 **Walter H. Haas,** Director, Assn. of Lunar and Planetary Observation
1953 **Charles A. Federer, Jr.,** Charter member of League; editor-in-chief, *Sky & Telescope Magazine*
1954 **H. Percy Wilkins,** English professional astronomer; author

Armand Spitz, Lecturer; general benefactor of amateur astronomy; initiator, Moon Watch program
1955 **Carl P. Richards,** Pioneer League member; author of League history
1956 **Harlow Shapley,** Author; lecturer; head, Harvard School of Science
Charlie M. Noble, Teacher; benefactor; involved with junior amateur astronomers
1957 **No award**
1958 **Clarence E. Johnson,** Publisher, monthly newsletter for junior astronomers; League junior chairman
1959 **Grace Scholz Spitz,** Charter member, executive secretary and president of the League; benefactor
1960 **No award**
1961 **No award**
1962 **Robert Cox,** Master telescope maker; *Sky & Telescope* columnist
1963 **Wilma A. Cherup,** League executive secretary for 23 years
1964 **Margaret W. Mayall,** Director, American Assn. of Variable Star Observers
1965 **G.R. (Bob) Wright,** League charter member
1966 **No award**
1967 **Norman Edmund,** Publisher, League Newsletter
1968 **Leslie Peltier,** Author; observer
1969 **Leonard G. Pardue,** League treasurer for 11 years
1970 **Russell C. Maag,** League officer; editor, League observer manual
1971 **Ralph K. Dakin,** League president; lecturer
1972 **Edward Halbach,** First elected League president
1973 **No award**
1974 **Walter Scott Houston,** Observer with own observatory; *Sky & Telescope* columnist
1975 **No award**
1976 **No award**
1977 **William and Cathryn DuVall** Contributions to the League
1978 **No award**
1979 **No award**
1980 **No award**

PRESIDENTIAL CITATION

1977 **Wilma A. Cherup**

Barnard Medal

COLUMBIA UNIVERSITY
Office of the Secretary, New York, N.Y. 10027

The Barnard Medal is given every five years for a discovery in physical or astronomical science or for a novel application of science beneficial to the human race made during the previous five years. The National Academy of Sciences selects the winner.

1895 **Lord Raleigh** and **Sir William Ramsey**
1900 **Wilhelm Conrad von Rontgen**
1905 **M. Henri Becquerel**
1910 **Ernest Rutherford**
1915 **Sir William H. Bragg** and **William L. Bragg**
1920 **Albert Einstein**
1925 **Neils Bohr**
1930 **Werner Heisenberg**
1935 **Edwin Powell Hubble**
1940 **No award**
1945 **Frederic Joliot** and **Irene Curie-Joliot**
1950 **Enrico Fermi**
1955 **Merle Antony Tuve**
1960 **I.I. Rabi**
1965 **William A. Fowler**
1970 **No award**
1975 **Louis P. Hammett**
1980 **Andre Weil**

Flavelle Medal

ROYAL SOCIETY OF CANADA
344 Wellington, Ottawa, Ont. K1A 0N4 (613/992-3468)

The Flavelle Medal, which since 1966 has carried a $1,000 honorarium, is now awarded every two years for outstanding contributions to biological science over the previous decade or for significant additions to a previous outstanding contribution. A selection committee chooses the recipient.

1942 **J.H. Craigie**
1943 **B.P. Babkin**
1944 **V.E. Henderson**
1945 **R.B. Thomson**
1946 **William Rowan**
1947 **G.B. Reed**
1948 **Margaret Newton**
1949 **W.P. Thompson**
1950 **C.H. Best**
1951 **Wilder G. Penfield**
1952 **A.G. Huntsman**
1953 **E.G.D. Murray**
1954 **D.A. Scott**
1955 **C.S. Hanes**
1956 **George Lyman Duff**
1957 **T.W.M. Cameron**
1958 **A.G. Lochhead**
1959 **Murray L. Barr**
1960 **E.M. Walker**
1961 **C.P. Leblond**
1962 **F.E.J. Fry**
1963 **R.J. Rossiter**
1964 **G. Krotkov**
1965 **W.S. Hoar**
1966 **Erich Baer**
1968 **Jacques Genest**
1970 **W.E. Ricker**
1972 **D. Harold Copp**
1974 **J.H. Quastel**
1976 **Michael Shaw**
1978 **Louis Siminovitch**
1980 **Gordon H. Dixon**

Gottschalk Medal

AUSTRALIAN ACADEMY OF SCIENCE
Box 783, Canberra, ACT 2601 Australia (062-48 6011)

The Gottschalk Medal, which is of bronze and is accompanied by an honorarium of $Aust. 100, annually honors research in biological or medical science by an individual under 36 years of age. A selection committee chooses the winner.

1979 **G.R. Parish**
1980 **Marilyn B. Renfree**

Harrison Prize

ROYAL SOCIETY OF CANADA
344 Wellington, Ottawa, Ont. K1A 0N4 (613/992-3468)

The Harrison Award, which consists of $150 and a scroll, is usually given every three years for fundamental work in bacteriology, excluding work done for direct clinical application. A selection committee chooses the recipient.

1960 R.A. McLeod
1963 P.C. Fitz-James
1966 J.J. Miller
1969 J.J.R. Campbell
1972 L.C. Vining
1975 H.J. Jennings
1978 Andre Hurst

Horowitz Prize

COLUMBIA UNIVERSITY
Office of the Secretary, New York, N.Y. 10027

The Horowitz Prize is awarded annually to a scientist for outstanding contributions in basic research in the fields of biology and biochemistry.

1966 Luis F. Leloir
1967 No award
1968 Har Gobind Khoranda
Marshall Warren Nirenberg
1969 Max Delbruck
Salvador Edward Luria
1970 Albert Claud
George Palade
Keither Porter
1971 H.E. Huxley
1972 Stephen W. Kuffler
1973 Renato Dulbecco
Harry Eagle
Theodore Puck
1974 Boris Ephrussi
1975 K. Sune
D. Bergstrom
Bengt Samuelsson
1976 Seymour Benzer
Charles Yanofsky
1977 Michael Heidelberger
Elvin A. Kabat
Henry Kunkel
1978 David H. Hubel
Vernon B. Mountcastle
Torsten N. Wiesel
1979 Walter Gilbert
Frederick Sanger
1980 Cesar Milstein

Waterford Bio-Medical Science Award

SCRIPPS CLINIC & RESEARCH FOUNDATION
10666 N. Torrey Pines Rd., La Jolla, Calif. 92037
(714/455-9100)

The $7,500 Waterford Bio-Medical Science Award was initiated to honor significant achievements in biomedical research. Waterford Crystal supports the award, which is administered by the Scripps Foundation. A crystal trophy accompanies the honor. The recipient, who may be of any nationality, is selected by a scientists' committee.

1977 **Maclyn McCarty,** Rockefeller University
1978 **Neils Kaj Jerne,** Basel Institute, Switzerland
1979 **Keith Roberts Porter,** University of Colorado
1980 **Baruj Benacerraf,** Harvard Medical School
Henry J. Kunkel, Rockefeller University

Botanical Society of America Merit Awards
Darbaker Prize

BOTANICAL SOCIETY OF AMERICA
School of Biological Science, University of Kentucky, Lexington, Ky. 40506 (606/258-8770)

Three Botanical Society of America Merit Award certificates are given generally now each year for outstanding contributions in botanical science as selected by the president of the society.

1956 Harry Ardell Allard
Edgar Anderson
Dixon Lloyd Bailey
Irving Widmer Bailey
Harley Harris Bartlett
George Wells Beadle
Ernst Athearn Bessey
Sidney Fay Blake
Emma Lucy Braun
Stanley Adair Cain
Ralph Works Chaney
Agnes Chase
Jens Christian Clausen
Ralph Erskine Cleland
Henry Shoemaker Conard
William Skinner Cooper
John Nathaniel Couch
Bernard Ogilvie Dodge
Benjamin Minge Duggar
Arthur Johnson Eames
Katherine Esau
Alexander William Evans
Henry Allan Gleason
Thomas H. Kearney
George Wannamaker Keitt
Paul Jackson Kramer
Louis Otto Kunkel
Daniel Trembly MacDougal
George Willard Martin
Maximino Martinez
Frederick Wilson Popenoe
William Jacob Robbins
Andrew Denney Rodgers III
Jacques Rousseau
Karl Sax
Paul Bigelow Sears
Homer Leroy Shantz
Edmund Ware Sinnott
Folke Karl Skoog
Gilbert Morgan Smith
Elvin Charles Stakman
George Ledyard Stebbins, Jr.
John Albert Stevenson
Kenneth Vivian Thimann
Edgar Nelson Transeau
Cornelius Bernardus Van Niel

John Ernst Weaver
Fritz Warnolt Went
Ralph Harley Wetmore
Truman George Yuncker
1957 Donald F. Jones
Paul Mangelsdorf
Barbara McClintock
William H. Weston
1958 Harry James Fuller
Philip Alexander Munz
Lester Whyland Sharp
1959 James Bonner
Lincoln Constance
Adriance S. Foster
Bernard S. Meyer
Loren C. Petry
1960 James P. Bennett
William Dwight Billings
Walter Conrad Muenscher
Kenneth B. Raper
Reed Clark Rollins
1961 F. C. Steward
William Randolph Taylor
1962 David R. Goddard
Marcus M. Rhoades
1963 Harry A. Borthwick
Vernon I. Cheadle
John C. Walker
1964 Ralph Emerson
Sterling Hendricks
Ira Wiggins
1965 Daniel I. Arnon
Harold C. Bold
1966 Henry N. Andrews, Jr.
R. H. Burris
George F. Papenfuss R. H. Burris
1967 C. J. Alexopoulos
William M. Miesey
1968 Elso S. Barghoorn
F. K. Sparrow
1969 Armin C. Braun
John R. Raper
Jacob R. Schram
Alex H. Smith
1970 Charles Drechsler
Arthur Galston
James M. Schopf
Albert C. Smith
1971 Murray F. Buell
Verne Grant
Ruth Patrick
A. Earling Porsild
1972 Charles B. Heiser, Jr.
Frank Harlan Lewis
Aaron J. Sharp
1973 Charles Stacy French
Mildred Esther Mathias
Richard Cawthon Starr
1974 Chester A. Arnold
Arthur Cronquist
Gerald W. Prescott
1975 Harlan P. Banks
F. Herbert Bormann
William C. Steere
1976 Charles M. Rick
Paul Weatherwax
Thomas W. Whitaker
1977 Sherwin Carlquist
Rogers McVaugh
Peter Raven
1978 Lyman D. Benson
Theodore Delevoryas
Warren H. Wagner, Jr.
W. Gordon Whaley
1979 David W. Bierhorst
Margaret H. Fulford
Anton Lang
Samel Postelthwait
1980 Herbert G. Baker
Oswaldo Tippo
Carol L. Wilson

One Darbaker Prize of $400 is given each year to a resident of North America for meritorious work in the study of microscopical algae. Selection is made by a Botanical Society committee selected by the president.

1955 R. C. Starr
1956 R. W. Krauss
1957 No award
1958 R. A. Lewin
P. C. Silva
1959 J. Myers
1960 J. Stein
1961 Paul Green
1962 Mary B. Allen
1963 Y. Dawson
1964 R. Scagel
1965 F. R. Trainor
1966 R. D. Wood
1967 J. Lewin
1968 R. Guillard and J. S. Craigie
1969 Isabella A. Abbott
Norma J. Lang
1970 Bruce C. Parker
1971 Richard W. Eppley
Michael J. Wynne
1972 Michael Neushul
1973 John West
1974 Jeremy David Pickett-Heaps
1975 Sarah P. Gibbs
Larry R. Hoffman
1976 Kenneth Stewart
Karl Mattox
1977 Alfred Loeblich III
1978 Patricia L. Walne
R. Malcolm, Jr.
1979 G. Benjamin Bouck
1980 C. Peter Wolk

Mary Soper Pope Award

CRANBROOK INSTITUTE OF SCIENCE
500 Lone Pine Rd., Box 807, Bloomfield Hills, Mich. 48013
(313/645-3200)

The Mary Soper Pope Award, which consists of a medal designed by Marshall M. Fredericks, is given as warranted for accomplishment in education or research in the botanical sciences. A six-member awards committee selects the recipient.

1947 Frans Verdoorn
1948 William Vogt
1949 Charles Deam
1950 Jens C. Clausen, David D. Keck, and William M. Hiesey
1951 Martin Cardenas
1952 E. Lucy Braun
1954 Irving W. Bailey

1959 **Kenneth W. Neatby**
1962 **Edmund H. Fulling**
1964 **Edgar T. Wherry**
1966 **Karl and Hally Jolivette Sax**
1969 **Stanley Adair Cain**
1970 **William Campbell Steere**

Nobel Prize in Chemistry

NOBEL FOUNDATION
Nobel House, Sturegatan 14, 11436-Stockholm, Sweden

The Nobel Prize in Chemistry is generally recognized as the highest honor which can be bestowed upon a chemist for an exceptionally noteworthy discovery in this scientific field. The award, which consists of a gold medal, diploma and a large honorarium, is given in a ceremony on December 10 of each year at Stockholm's City Hall. The awards are presented and administered by the Royal Swedish Academy of Sciences. The amount of the honorarium fluctuates. In 1980, it was approximately $212,000.

1901 **Jacobus H. van't Hoff** (Netherlands), Discovered chemical-dynamics laws and osmotic pressure in solutions

1902 **Hermann E. Fisher** (Germany), Research on sugar and purine syntheses

1903 **Svante E. Arrhenius** (Sweden), Electrolytic theory of dissociation

1904 **Sir William Ramsey** (Great Britain), Discovered inert gaseous elements in air and determined their place in the periodic system

1905 **Johann von Baeyer** (Germany), Work on organic dyes and hydroaromatic compounds

1906 **Henri Moissan** (France), Study and isolation of fluorine; development of an electric furnace

1907 **Eduard Buchner** (Germany), Biochemical research on cell-free fermentatation

1908 **Ernest Rutherford** (Great Britain), Work on disintegration of elements and chemistry of radioactive substances

1909 **Wilhelm Ostwald** (Germany), Research on catalysis and basic principles of chemical equilibria and rates of reaction

1910 **Otto Wallach** (Germany), Pioneering work in alicyclic compounds

1911 **Marie Curie** (France, born in Poland), Discovered radium and polonium, isolated radium and studied its nature

1912 **Victor Grignard** (France), Discovered Grignard reagent
Paul Sabatier (France), Hydrogenated organic compounds in the presence of disintegrated metals

1913 **Alfred Werner** (Switzerland, born in Germany), Linked atoms in molecules

1914 **Theodore W. Richards** (U.S.A.), Determination of atomic weight of many elements

1915 **Richard M. Willstatter** (Germany), Research on plant pigments, particularly chlorophyll

1916 **No award**

1917 **No award**

1918 **Fritz Haber** (Germany), Synthesized ammonia

1919 **No award**

1920 **Walter H. Nernst** (Germany), Research in thermochemistry

1921 **Frederick Soddy** (Great Britain), Studied radioactive substances and investigated the origin and nature of isotopes

1922 **Francis W. Alston** (Great Britain), Discovered isotopes in many non-radioactive materials

1923 **Fritz Pregl** (Austria), Invented method of microanalyzing organic substances

1924 **No award**

1925 **Richard A. Zsigmondy** (Germany), Demonstrated hetrogeneous nature of colloid solutions

1926 **Theodor Svedberg** (Sweden), Dispersion-system research

1927 **Heinrich O. Wieland** (Germany), Studied bile acids and related substances

1928 **Adolf O.R. Windaus** (Germany), Research on sterols and their relation to vitamins

1929 **Arthur Harden** (Great Britain), Research on fermentation of sugar and fermentative enzymes
Hans von Euler-Chelpin (Sweden), Research on fermentation of sugar and fermentative enzymes

1930 **Hans Fischer** (Germany), Work on haemin and chlorophyll

1931 **Friedrich Bergius** (Germany), Developed chemical high-pressure methods

1932 **Irving Langmuir** (U.S.A.), Surface-chemistry research

1933 **No award**

1934 **Harold C. Urey** (U.S.A.), Discovered heavy hydrogen

1935 **Frederic Joliot-Curie and Irene Joliot-Curie** (France), Synthesized new radioactive elements

1936 **Peter J.W. Debye** (Netherlands), Work on molecular structure via studies of dipole moments and diffraction of X-rays and electrons in gases

1937 **Walter N. Haworth** (Great Britain), Work on carbohydrates and vitamin C
Paul Karrer (Switzerland, born in Russia), Work on carotenoids, flavin and vitamins A and B2

1938 **Richard Kuhn** (Germany), Work on vitamins

1939 **Adolf F. J. Butenandt** (Germany), Work on sex hormones
Leopold Ruzicka (Switzerland), Research on polymethylenes and higher terpenes

1940 **No award**

1941 **No award**

1942 **No award**

1943 **Georg de Hevesy** (Hungary), Use of isotopes as chemical tracers

1944 **Otto Hahn** (Germany), Heavy-nuclei fission

1945 **Artturi I. Virtanen** (Finland), Agricultural and nutrition chemistry

1946 **James B. Summer** (U.S.A.), Crystallization of enzymes
John H. Northrup and Wendell M. Stanley (U.S.A.), Prepared pure form of enzymes

1947 **Sir Robert Robinson** (Great Britain), Investigated biologically important plant products

1948 **Arne W.K. Tiselius** (Sweden), Work on electrophoresis and adsorption analysis

1949 **William F. Giauque** (U.S.A.), Chemical thermodynamic research, especially on the behavior of substances at extremely low temperatures

1950 **Kurt Adler and Otto P.H. Diels** (Germany), Discovered and developed diene synthesis

1951 **Edwin M. McMillan and Glenn T. Seaborg** (U.S.A.), Research on transuranium elements

1952 **Archer J.P. Martin and Richard L.M. Synge** (Great Britain), Invented partition chromatography to analyze mixtures

1953 **Hermann Staudinger** (Germany), Macromolecular chemistry research

1954 **Linus C. Pauling** (U.S.A.), Research on nature of chemical bond and its application to the elucidation of complex substance structure

1955 **Vincent du Vigneaud** (U.S.A.), Research of biochemically significiant compounds, particularly the synthesis of a polypeptide hormone
1956 **Sir Cyril N. Hinshelwood** (Great Britain) **and Nikolai N. Semenov** (U.S.S.R.) Research on chemical-reaction mechanisms
1957 **Sir Alexander R. Todd** (Great Britain), Research on nucleotides and nucleotide coenzymes
1958 **Frederick Sanger** (Great Britain), Work on protein structure, especially of insulin
1959 **Jaroslav Heyrovsky** (Czechoslovakia), Discovered and developed polarographic methods of analysis
1960 **Willard F. Libby** (U.S.A.), Used carbon 14 dating for age determination in archeology, geology, geophysics, etc.
1961 **Melvin Calvin** (U.S.A.), Research on assimilation of carbon dioxide in plants
1962 **John C. Kendrew** (Great Britain) **and Max F. Perutz** (Great Britain, born in Austria), Research on structures of globular proteins
1963 **Guilio Natta** (Italy) **and Karl Ziegler** (Germany), Research of chemistry and technology of high polymers
1964 **Dorothy Crowfoot Hodgkin** (Great Britain), Discovered structure of significant biochemical substances by X-ray
1965 **Robert B. Woodward** (U.S.A.), Synthesized complicated organic compounds
1966 **Robert S. Mulliken** (U.S.A.), Basic work on chemical bonds and electronic structure of molecules by the modular orbital method
1967 **Manfred Eigen** (Germany), **Ronald G.W. Norrish** (Great Britain) **and George Porter** (Great Britain), Work on extremely rapid chemical reactions accomplished by disturbing the equilibrium with short pulses of energy
1968 **Lars Onsager** (U.S.A., born in Norway), Discovered reciprocal relations fundamental to thermodynamics of irreversible processes
1969 **Derek H.R. Barton** (Great Britain) **and Odd Hassel** (Norway), Development and application of conformation in chemistry
1970 **Luis F. Leloir** (Argentina), Discovered sugar nucleotides
1971 **Gerhard Herzberg** (Canada, born in Germany), Research in electronic structure and geometry of molecules
1972 **Christian B. Anfinsen, Stanford Moore and William H. Stein** (U.S.A.), Work on chemical structure and biological reactions of protein, especially ribonuclease
1973 **Ernst Otto Fischer** (Germany) **and Geoffry Wilkinson** (Great Britain), Merged organic and metallic compounds as part of auto-pollution control research
1974 **Paul J. Flory** (U.S.A.), Analytical methodology for studying longchain molecules for development of synthetics
1975 **John Warcus Cornforth** (Great Britain), **and Vladimir Prelog** (Switzerland, born in Yugoslavia), Stereochemistry research involving how properties of chemical compounds are influenced by arrangement of their atoms
1976 **William N. Lipscomb** (U.S.A.), Research on structure and bonding of boranes and nature of chemical bonding
1977 **Ilya Prigogine** (U.S.A. and Belgium, born in Russia), Contributions to nonequilibrium thermodynamics, especially theory of dissipative structures
1978 **Peter Mitchell** (Great Britain), Contribution to the understanding of biological energy transfer through the formulation of the chemiosmotic theory
1979 **Herbert C. Brown** (U.S.A.) and **Georg Wittig** (Federal Republic of Germany), Developing a group of substances to facilitate very difficult chemical reactions
1980 **Paul Berg** (U.S.A.), considered "the father of genetic engineering for manipulation of gene structures, and **Walter Gilbert** (U.S.A.) and **Frederick Sanger** (United Kingdom), for reading the fine details of the structure of DNA

Roger Adams Award in Organic Chemistry
ACS Creative Invention Award
ACS Award for Creative Work in Synthetic Organic Chemistry
ACS Award in Chemical Education
ACS Award for Distinguished Service in the Advancement of Inorganic Chemistry
ACS Award in Colloid or Surface Chemistry
ACS Award in Nuclear Applications in Chemistry
ACS Award in Analytical Chemistry
ACS Award in Chromatography
ACS Award in Inorganic Chemistry
ACS Award in Petroleum Chemistry
ACS Award in Polymer Chemistry
ACS Award in Pure Chemistry
ACS Award in the Chemistry of Plastics and Coatings
Alfred Burger Award
Arthur C. Cope Award
Peter Debye Award
Garvan Medal
James R. Grady Award
Ernest Guenther Award
Ipatieff Prize
Frederick Stanley Kipping Award
Irving Langmuir Award
E. V. Murphree Award
Nobel Laureate Signature Award
James Flack Norris Award
Charles Lathrop Parsons Award
Priestley Medal

AMERICAN CHEMICAL SOCIETY
1155 Sixteenth St. NW, Washington, D.C. 20036
(202/872-4481)

American Chemical Society Awards are made through nomination by Society members and selection by a committee of experts in each field. Recipients must appear at the ACS annual meeting; each award includes a travel stipend in addition to the honorarium indicated, as well as a medal, scroll or citation.

The $10,000 Roger Adams Award in Organic Chemistry, accompanied by a gold medal and a silver replica, sponsored by Organic Reactions, Inc., is presented biennially for research defined in its broadest sense. The recipient must deliver a lecture at the Biennial National Organic Chemistry Symposium.

1959 D.H.R. Barton
1961 Robert B. Woodward
1963 Paul D. Bartlett
1965 Arthur C. Cope
1967 John D. Roberts
1969 Vladimir Prelog
1971 Herbert C. Brown
1973 Georg Wittig
1975 Rolf Huisgen
1977 William S. Johnson
1979 Melvin S. Newman

The $2,000 ACS Creative Invention Award, sponsored by the Society's corporation associates, honors an individual residing in the United States or Canada for successful applications of research in chemistry and/or chemical engineering that contributes "to the material prosperity or happiness of people." The recipient also gets a gold medal and a bronze replica.

1968 William G. Pfann
1969 J. Paul Hogan
1970 Gordon K. Teal
1971 S. Donald Stookey
1972 H. Tracy Hall
1973 Carl Djerassi
1974 Charles C. Price
1975 James D. Idol, Jr.
1976 Manuel M. Baizer
1977 Herman A. Bruson
1978 LeGrand G. Van Uitert
1979 Leo H. Sternbach
1980 Stephanie L. Kwoleck

The $2,000 ACS Award for Creative Work in Synthetic Organic Chemistry, sponsored by Aldrich Chemical Co., recognizes outstanding creative work in synthetic organic chemistry published by an American journal during the five preceeding years.

1957 Robert B. Woodward
1958 William S. Johnson
1959 John C. Sheehan
1960 Herbert C. Brown
1961 Melvin S. Newman
1962 Charles R. Hauser
1963 Nelson J. Leonard
1964 Lewis H. Sarett
1965 Donald J. Cram
1966 William von E. Doering
1967 Gilbert J. Stork
1968 Theodore L. Cairns
1969 H. Gobind Khorana
1970 Eugene E. van Tamelen
1971 Elias J. Corey
1972 Bruce Merrifield
1973 George Buchi
1974 Edward C. Taylor
1975 Herbert O. House
1976 Franz Sondheimer
1977 No award
1978 Storu Masamune
1979 George A. Olah
1980 Yoshito Kishi

The $2,000 ACS Award in Chemical Education, sponsored by Union Carbide Corp., recognizes contributions to chemical education in its broadest meaning, including the training of professional chemists, dissemination of reliable information about the field and the integration of chemistry into our educational system. The recipient's activities may lie in teaching any level, organization or administration. Preference is given to American citizens.

1952 Joel H. Hildebrand
1953 Howard J. Lucas
1954 Raymond E. Kirk
1955 Gerrit Van Zyl
1956 Otto M. Smith
1957 Norris W. Rakestraw
1958 Frank E. Brown
1959 Harry F. Lewis
1960 Arthur F. Scott
1961 John C. Bailar, Jr.
1962 William G. Young
1963 Edward L. Haenisch
1964 Alfred B. Garrett
1965 Theodore A. Ashford
1966 W. Conway Pierce
1967 Louis F. Fieser
1968 William F. Kieffer
1969 L. Caroll King
1970 Hubert N. Alyea
1971 Laurence E. Strong
1972 J. Arthur Campbell
1973 Robert C. Brasted
1974 George S. Hammond
1975 William T. Lippincott
1976 Leallyn B. Clapp
1977 Robert W. Parry
1978 Lloyd N. Ferguson
1979 Gilbert P. Haight, Jr.
1980 Henry A. Bent

The $2,000 ACS Award to a Society member for Distinguished Service in the Advancement of Inorganic Chemistry, sponsored by Mallinckrodt, Inc., honors extensive contributions in the field, such as teaching, writing, research and administration.

1965 Robert W. Parry
1966 George H. Cady
1967 Henry Taube
1968 William N. Lipscomb, Jr.
1969 Anton B. Burg
1970 Ralph G. Pearson
1971 Joseph Chatt
1972 John C. Bailar, Jr.
1973 Ronald J. Gillespie
1974 F. Albert Cotton
1975 Fred Basolo
1976 Daryle H. Busch
1977 James L. Hoard
1978 Harry J. Emeleus
1979 Carl L. Muetterties
1980 Arthur F. Martell

The $2,000 ACS Award in Colloid or Surface Chemistry, sponsored by The Kendall Co., honors the achievements of a resident of the U.S. or Canada in colloid or surface chemistry.

1954 Harry N. Holmes
1955 John W. Williams
1956 Victor K. La Mer
1957 Peter J. W. Debye
1958 Paul H. Emmett
1959 Floyd E. Bartell
1960 John D. Ferry
1961 Stephen Brunauer
1962 George Scatchard
1963 William Albert Zisman
1964 Karol J. Mysels
1965 George D. Halsey, Jr.
1966 Robert S. Hansen
1967 Stanley G. Mason
1968 Albert C. Zettlemoyer
1969 Terrell L. Hill
1970 Jerome Vinograd
1971 Milton Kerker
1972 Egon Matijevic
1973 Robert L. Burwell, Jr.
1974 W. Keith Hall
1975 Robert Gomer
1976 Robert J. Good
1977 Michel Boudart
1978 Harold A. Scheraga
1979 Arthur W. Adamson
1980 Howard Reiss

The $2,000 ACS Award in Nuclear Applications in Chemistry, sponsored by G.D. Searle & Co., was given in recognition for contributions to nuclear isotopic applications in the field of chemistry.

1955 Henry Taube
1956 Willard F. Libby
1957 Melvin Calvin
1958 Jacob Bigeleisen
1959 John E. Willard
1960 Charles D. Coryell
1961 Joseph J. Katz
1962 Truman P. Kohman
1963 Martin D. Kamen
1964 Isadore Perlman
1965 Stanley G. Thompson
1966 Arthur C. Wahl
1967 Gerhart Friedlander
1968 Richard L. Wolfgang
1969 George E. Boyd
1970 Paul R. Fields
1971 Alfred P. Wolf
1972 Anthony Turkevich
1973 Albert Ghiorso
1974 Lawrence E. Glendenin
1975 John R. Huizenga
1976 John O. Rasmussen
1977 Glen E. Gordon
1978 Paul D. Kuroda
1979 Raymond Davis, Jr.

The $3,000 ACS Award for nuclear Chemistry replaces the ACS Award in Nuclear Applications. In even-numbered years, it is sponsored by EG&G ORTEC and in odd-numbered years by an anonymous donor.

1980 Arthur M. Poskanzer

The $2,000 ACS Award in Analytical Chemistry, sponsored by the Fisher Scientific Co., honors a resident of the U.S. or Canada for contributions in the field, with special consideration given to independence of thought and originality shown, or to the importance of the work when applied to public welfare, economics or the needs and desires of humanity.

1948 N. Howell Furman
1949 G.E.F. Lundell
1950 Isaac M. Kolthoff
1951 H. H. Willard
1952 Melvin G. Mellon
1953 Donald D. Van Slyke
1954 G. Frederick Smith
1955 Ernest H. Swift
1956 Harvey Diehl
1957 John H. Yoe
1958 James J. Lingane
1959 James I. Hoffman
1960 Philip J. Elving
1961 Herbert A. Laitinen
1962 H. A. Liebhafsky
1963 David N. Hume
1964 John Mitchell, Jr.
1965 Charles N. Reilley
1966 Lyman C. Craig
1967 Lawrence T. Hallett
1968 Lockhart B. Rogers
1969 Roger G. Bates
1970 Charles V. Banks
1971 George H. Morrison
1972 W. Wayne Meinke
1973 James D. Winefordner
1974 Philip W. West
1975 Sidney Siggia
1976 Howard V. Malmstadt
1977 George G. Guilbault
1978 Henry Freiser
1979 Velmer A. Fassel
1980 J. Calvin Giddings

The $3,000 ACS Award in Chromatography, sponsored by SUPELCO, Inc., is given for contributions to chromography, with particular considerations to new methods.

1961 Harold H. Strain
1962 L. Zechmeister
1963 Waldo E. Cohn
1964 Stanford Moore and William H. Stein
1965 Stephen Dal Nogare
1966 Kurt A. Kraus
1967 J. Calvin Giddings
1968 Lewis G. Longsworth
1969 Morton Beroza
1970 Julian F. Johnson
1971 No award
1972 J.J. Kirkland
1973 Albert Zlatkis
1974 Lockhart B. Rogers
1975 Egon Stahl
1976 James S. Fritz
1977 Raymond P.W. Scott
1978 A.J.P. Martin
1979 Evan C. Horning
1980 James E. Lovelock

The $2,000 ACS Award in Inorganic Chemistry, sponsored by the Monsanto Co., honors accomplishments in the preparation, properties, reactions or structure of inorganic substances. Texas Instruments, Inc., sponsored the award until 1976.

1962 F. Albert Cotton
1963 Daryle H. Busch
1964 Fred Basolo
1965 Earl L. Muetterties

1966 Geoffrey Wilkinson
1967 John L. Margrave
1968 Jack Halpern
1969 Russell S. Drago
1970 Neil Bartlett
1971 Jack Lewis
1972 Theodore L. Brown
1973 M. F. Hawthorne
1974 Lawrence F. Dahl
1975 James P. Collman
1976 Richard H. Holm
1977 No award
1978 Harry B. Gray
1979 James A. Ibers
1980 Alan M. Sargeson

The $5,000 ACS Award in Petroleum Chemistry, sponsored by the Lubrizol Corp., is given to a resident of the U.S. or Canada for outstanding research in the chemistry of petroleum or fundamental research that contributes directly and materially to the knowledge of petroleum and its products. Special consideration is given for independence of thought and originality. The award was sponsored by Precision Scientific Co. through 1973.

1949 Bruce H. Sage
1950 Kenneth S. Pitzer
1951 Louis Schmerling
1952 Vladimir Haensel
1953 Robert W. Schiessler
1954 Arthur P. Lien
1955 Frank Ciapetta
1956 Milburn J. O'Neal, Jr.
1957 C. Gardner Swain
1958 Robert P. Eischens
1959 George C. Pimentel
1960 Robert W. Taft, Jr.
1961 George S. Hammond
1962 Harold Hart
1963 John P. McCullough
1964 George A. Olah
1965 Glen A. Russell
1966 James Wei
1967 Andrew Streitwieser, Jr.
1968 Keith U. Ingold
1969 Alan Schriesheim
1970 Lloyd R. Snyder
1971 Gerasimos J. Karabatsos
1972 Paul G. Gassman
1973 Joe W. Hightower
1974 No award
1975 No award
1976 John H. Sinfelt
1977 Sidney W. Benson
1978 Ellis K. Fields
1979 Robert L. Banks
1980 William A. Prior

The $2,000 ACS Award in Polymer Chemistry, sponsored by Witco Chemical Corp. Foundation, recognizes achievements in the field.

1964 Carl S. Marvel
1965 Herman F. Mark
1966 Walter H. Stockmayer
1967 Frank R. Mayo
1968 Charles G. Overberger
1969 Frank A. Bovey
1970 Michael M. Szwarc
1971 Georges J. Smets
1972 Arthur V. Tobolsky
1973 Turner Alfrey, Jr.
1974 John D. Ferry
1975 Leo Mandelkern
1976 Paul W. Morgan
1977 William J. Bailey
1978 Junji Furukawa
1979 Henri Benoit
1980 George B. Butler

The $2,000 ACS Award in Pure Chemistry, sponsored by the Alpha Chi Sigma Fraternity is given to an individual under 36 years of age "on the threshold of his career" for research of unusual merit, with special consideration for originality of research which must have been done in North America and for independence of thought.

1931 Linus Pauling
1932 Oscar K. Rice
1933 Frank H. Spedding
1934 C. Frederick Koelsch
1935 Raymond M. Fuoss
1936 John Gamble Kirkwood
1937 E. Bright Wilson, Jr.
1938 Paul D. Bartlett
1939 No award
1940 Lawrence O. Brockway
1941 Karl A. Folkers
1942 John Lawrence Oncley
1943 Kenneth S. Pitzer
1944 Arthur C. Cope
1945 Frederick T. Wall
1946 Charles C. Price, III
1947 Glenn T. Seaborg
1948 Saul Winstein
1949 Richard T. Arnold
1950 Verner Schomaker
1951 John C. Sheehan
1952 Harrison S. Brown
1953 William von E. Doering
1954 John D. Roberts
1955 Paul Delahay
1956 Paul M. Doty
1957 Gilbert J. Stork
1958 Carl Djerassi
1959 Ernest M. Grunwald
1960 Elias J. Corey
1961 Eugene E. van Tamelen
1962 Harden M. McConnell
1963 Stuart A. Rice
1964 Marshall Fixman
1965 Dudley Herschbach
1966 Ronald Breslow
1967 John D. Baldeschwieler
1968 Orville L. Chapman
1969 Roald Hoffmann
1970 Harry B. Gray
1971 R. Bruce King
1972 Roy G. Gordon
1973 John I. Brauman
1974 Nicholas J. Turro
1975 George M. Whitesides
1976 Karl F. Freed
1977 Barry M. Trost
1978 Jesse Beauchamp
1979 Henry F. Schaefer III
1980 John E. Bercew

The $2,000 ACS Award in the Chemistry of Plastics and Coatings, sponsored by the Borden Foundation, is given to a resident of the U.S. or Canada under 46 years of age for achievements in the chemistry and application of plastics and coatings to adhesives, printing and thermoplastic polymers.

1968 Harry Burrell
1969 Sylvan O. Greenlee
1970 Raymond F. Boyer
1971 Raymond R. Myers
1972 Richard S. Stein
1973 Carl S. Marvel
1974 Vivian T. Stannett
1975 Maurice L. Huggins
1976 Herman F. Mark
1977 William A. Zisman
1978 John K. Gillham
1979 Roger S. Porter
1980 John W. Vanderhoff

The $2,000 ACS Award for Creative Advances in Environmental Science and Technology, sponsored by Air Products and Chemicals, Inc., is given for research and technology or methods of analysis to provide scientific bases for environmental control decisions or for practical technologies that reduce health risk.

1980 James J. Morgan

The $3,000 Alfred Burger Award in Medicinal Chemistry, sponsored by SmithKline Corp., biennially honors outstanding contributions in the field.

1980 T.Y. Shen

The $10,000 Arthur C. Cope Award recognizes outstanding achievement in organic chemistry, whose significance has become apparent within the previous five years. A gold medal and bronze replica are also awarded in this biennial honor. In addition, an unrestricted grant-in-aid of $10,000 for research in organic chemistry under the direction of the Cope Award recipient may be made to a university or non-profit institution selected by the recipient

1973 Robert B. Woodward and Roald Hoffmann
1974 Donald J. Cram
1976 Elias J. Corey
1978 Orville L. Chapman
1980 Gilbert Stork

The $2,000 Peter Debye Award in Physical Chemistry, sponsored by E.I. du Pont de Nemours & Co., annually honors outstanding research in the field. The award was established by Humble Oil and Refining Co., and sponsored until 1976 by Exxon Chemical Co. The du Pont sponsorship becomes effective with the 1981 award.

1962 E. Bright Wilson, Jr.
1963 Robert S. Mulliken
1964 Henry Eyring
1965 Lars Onsager
1966 Joseph O. Hirschfelder
1967 Joseph E. Mayer
1968 George B. Kistiakowsky
1969 Paul J. Flory
1970 Oscar K. Rice
1971 Norman Davidson
1972 Clyde Hutchison, Jr.
1973 William N. Lipscomb, Jr.
1974 Walter H. Stockmayer
1975 H. S. Gutowsky
1976 Robert W. Zwanzig
1977-80 No awards

The $2,000 Garvan Medal, which is of gold and has been sponsored by W.R. Grace & Co., since 1979, recognizes distinguished service by a woman chemist who is a citizen of the United States.

1937 Emma P. Carr
1940 Mary E. Pennington
1942 Florence B. Seibert
1946 Icie G. Macy-Hoobler
1947 Mary Laura Sherrill
1948 Gerty T. Cori
1949 Agnes Fay Morgan
1950 Pauline Beery Mack
1951 Katherine B. Blodgett
1952 Gladys A. Emerson
1953 Leonora N. Bilger
1954 Betty Sullivan
1955 Grace Medes
1956 Allene R. Jeans
1957 Lucy W. Pickett
1958 Arda A. Green
1959 Dorothy V. Nightingale
1960 Mary L. Caldwell
1961 Sarah Ratner
1962 Helen M. Dyer
1963 Mildred Cohn
1964 Birgit Vennesland
1965 Gertrude E. Perlmann
1966 Mary L. Peterman
1967 Marjorie J. Vold
1968 Gertrude B. Elion
1969 Sofia Simmonds
1970 Ruth R. Benerito
1971 Mary Fieser
1972 Jean'ne M. Shreeve
1973 Mary L. Good
1974 Joyce J. Kaufman
1975 Marjorie C. Caserio
1976 Isabella L. Karle
1977 Marjorie C. Horning
1978 Madeleine M. Joullie
1979 Jenny P. Glusker
1980 Helen M. Free

The $2,000 James R. Grady Award for Interpreting Chemistry for the Public honors noteworthy presentations through a public-communication medium to increase the American public's understanding of chemistry and chemical progress.

1957 David H. Killeffer
1958 William L. Laurence
1959 Alton L. Blakeslee
1960 Watson Davis
1961 David Dietz
1962 John F. Baxter
1963 Lawrence Lessing
1964 Nate Haseltine
1965 Isaac Asimov
1966 Frank E. Carey
1967 Irving S. Bengelsdorf
1968 Raymond A. Bruner
1969 Walter Sullivan
1970 Robert C. Cowen
1971 Victor Cohn
1972 Dan Q. Posin
1973 O. A. Battista
1974 Ronald Kotulak
1975 Jon Franklin
1976 Gene Bylinsky

1977 Patrick Young
1978 Michael Woods
1979 Peter Gwynne
1980 Edward Edelson

The $2,000 Ernest Guenther Award in the Chemistry of Essential Oils and Related Products, sponsored by Fritzsche Dodge & Olcott, Inc., honors work in analysis, structure elucidation, chemical synthesis of essential oils, flavors and related substances, with special consideration for independence of thought and originality.

1949 John L. Simonsen
1950 A. J. Haagen-Smit
1951 Edgar Lederer
1952 Yves-Rene Naves
1953 Max Stoll
1954 A. R. Penfold
1955 Hans Schinz
1956 Herman Pines
1957 D.H.R. Barton
1958 George H. Buchi
1959 Frantisek Sorm
1960 Carl Djerassi
1961 C.F. Seidel
1962 E.R.H. Jones
1063 Arthur J. Birch
1964 Oscar Jeger
1965 Konrad E. Bloch
1966 Albert J. Eschenmoser
1967 George A. Sim
1968 Elias J. Corey
1969 John W. Cornforth
1970 Duilio Arigoni
1971 Ernest Wenkert
1972 Guy Ourisson
1973 William G. Dauben
1974 Gunther Ohloff
1975 S. Morris Kupchan
1976 Alastair I. Scott
1977 Robert E. Ireland
1978 Koji Nakanishi
1979 James A. Marshall
1980 Sukh Dev

The $3,000 Ipatieff Prize is awarded every three years to an individual under 40 years of age for outstanding chemical experimental work in the field of catalysis or high pressure. While preference is given to American chemists, the work may have been carried out in any country or by scientists of any nationality. Special consideration is given for independence or thought and originality.

1947 Louis Schmerling
1950 Herman E. Ries
1953 Robert B. Anderson
1956 Harry G. Drickamer
1959 Cedomir M. Sliepcevich
1962 Charles Kemball
1965 Robert H. Wentorf, Jr.
1968 Charles R. Adams
1971 Paul B. Venuto
1974 George A. Samara
1977 Charles A. Eckert
1980 Denis Foster

The $5,000 Frederick Stanley Kipping Award in Organosilicon Chemistry, sponsored by the Dow Corning Corp., honors achievement in the field over the previous 10 years. The measure of this achievement is the winner's significant publications and may also include contributions in a related field. Beginning in 1976, the award became a biennial rather than an annual honor.

1962 Henry Gilman
1963 Leo H. Sommer
1964 Colin Eaborn
1965 Eugene G. Rochow
1966 Gerhard Fritz
1967 Makoto Kumada
1968 Ulrich Wannagat
1969 Robert A. Benkeser
1970 Robert West
1971 Alan G. MacDiarmid
1972 Dietmar Seyferth
1973 Adrian G. Brook
1974 Hubert Schmidbaur
1975 Hans Bock
1976 Michael F. Lappert
1978 Hideki Sakurai
1980 E.A.V. Ebsworth

The $5,000 Irving Langmuir Award in Chemical Physics, sponsored by the General Electric Foundation, honors a resident of the United States for achievement during the previous 10 years in chemical physics or physical chemistry. The honorarium must be used in the United States. The selection and presentation are alternately made by the ACS and the Division of Chemical Physics of the American Physical Society.

1965 John H. Van Vleck
1966 H. S. Gutowsky
1967 John C. Slater
1968 Henry Eyring
1969 Charles P. Slichter
1970 John A. Pople
1971 Michael E. Fisher
1972 Harden M. McConnell
1973 Peter M. Rentzepis
1974 Harry G. Drickamer
1975 Robert H. Cole
1976 John S. Waugh
1977 Aneesur Rahman
1978 Rudolph A. Marcus
1979 Donald S. McClure
1980 William Klemperer

The $2,000 E.V. Murphree Award in Industrial and Engineering Chemistry, sponsored by Exxon Research and Engineering Co., honors research of a theoretical or experimental nature in industrial chemistry or chemical engineering.

1957 Warren K. Lewis
1958 duBois Eastman
1959 Edwin R. Gilliland
1960 Neal R. Amundson
1961 Olaf A. Hougen
1962 Eugene J. Houdry
1963 Manson Benedict
1964 Bruce H. Sage
1965 Vladimir Haensel
1966 Richard H. Wilhelm
1967 Alfred Clark
1968 Melvin A. Cook
1969 Alex G. Oblad
1970 Peter V. Danckwerts
1971 Heinz Heinemann
1972 Paul B. Weisz

1973 Thomas K. Sherwood
1974 Herman S. Bloch
1975 Donald L. Katz
1976 James F. Roth
1977 Alexis Voorhies, Jr.
1978 Donald F. Othmer
1979 John M. Prausnitz
1980 Milton Orchin

The Nobel Laureate Signature Award for Graduate Education in Chemistry, which is sponsored by the J.T. Baker Chemical Co., consists of $2,000 and a plaque containing the signatures of Nobel Prize laureates. The award honors an outstanding graduate student in chemistry. In addition to the student, his or her preceptor also receives $2,000 and a plaque.

1980 **Wayne L. Gladfelter,** Pennsylvania State University

The $2,000 James Flack Norris Award in Inorganic Chemistry, sponsored by the Northeastern Section ACS, honors contributions in physical inorganic chemistry.

1965 Christopher K. Ingold
1966 Louis P. Hammett
1967 Saul Winstein
1968 George S. Hammond
1969 Paul D. Bartlett
1970 Frank H. Westheimer
1971 Cheves Walling
1972 Stanley J. Cristol
1973 Kenneth B. Wiberg
1974 Gerhard L. Closs
1975 Kurt M. Mislow
1976 Howard E. Zimmerman
1977 Edward M. Arnett
1978 Jerome A. Berson
1979 John D. Roberts
1980 Ronald Breslow

The $2,000 Charles Lathrop Parsons Award is generally given at intervals of two years or greater to an American citizen and ACS member for outstanding public service as part of or outside the individual's field.

1952 Charles L. Parsons
1955 James B. Conant
1958 Roger Adams
1961 George B. Kistiakowsky
1964 Glenn T. Seaborg
1967 Donald F. Hornig
1970 W. Albert Noyes, Jr.
1973 Charles C. Price
1974 Russell W. Peterson
1976 William O. Baker
1978 Charles G. Overberger

The Priestley Medal, which is of gold, annually honors an individual's services to chemistry.

1923 Ira Remsen
1926 Edgar F. Smith
1929 Francis P. Garvan
1932 Charles L. Parsons
1935 William A. Noyes
1938 Marston T. Bogert
1941 Thomas Midgley, Jr.
1944 James B. Conant
1945 Ian Heilbron
1946 Roger Adams
1947 Warren K. Lewis
1948 Edward R. Weidlein
1949 Arthur B. Lamb
1950 Charles A. Kraus
1951 E.J. Crane
1952 Samuel C. Lind
1953 Robert Robinson
1954 W. Albert Noyes, Jr.
1955 Charles A. Thomas
1956 Carl S. Marvel
1957 Farrington Daniels
1958 Ernest H. Volwiler
1959 H.I. Schlesinger
1960 Wallace R. Brode
1961 Louis P. Hammett
1962 Joel H. Hildebrand
1963 Peter J. W. Debye
1964 John C. Bailar, Jr.
1965 William J. Sparks
1966 William O. Baker
1967 Ralph Connor
1968 William G. Young
1969 Kenneth S. Pitzer
1970 Max Tishler
1971 Frederick D. Rossini
1972 George B. Kistiakowsky
1973 Harold C. Urey
1974 Paul J. Flory
1975 Henry Eyring
1976 George S. Hammond
1977 Henry Gilman
1978 Melvin Calvin
1979 Glenn T. Seaborg
1980 Milton Harris

Chemical Pioneers Scroll
Presidential Citation
Gold Medal

AMERICAN INSTITUTE OF CHEMISTS
7315 Wisconsin Ave., Washington, D.C. 20014
(301/652-2447)

The Chemical Pioneers Scroll is awarded annually to chemists whose research ideas have benefited mankind and expanded the frontiers of knowledge and technology.

1966 **Carl E. Barnes,** Applied chemistry
Herman A. Bruson (Olin Mathieson Corp.), Organic chemistry
C.H. Fisher (U.S. Dept. of Agriculture), Rubber chemistry
Robert M. Joyce, Inorganic chemistry
Charles C. Price (University of Notre Dame), Polymer chemistry
Eugene G. Rochow, Inorganic chemistry

1967 **Vladimir Haensel,** Petrochemistry
William E. Hanford (Olin Mathieson Corp.), Industrial chemistry
Henry B. Hass (Pullman Kellogg Corp.), Gas chromotopography
Carl S. Marvel (Wright Patterson AFB), Polymer chemistry
Benjamin Phillips (Union Carbine Corp.), Polymer chemistry
David W. Young (Sinclair Oil Corp.), Petrochemistry

1968 **Ralph A. Connor** (Rohm and Haas Co.), Industrial chemistry
James D. Idol, Jr. (Standard Oil Co. of Ohio), Petrochemistry

Percy L. Julian, Medicinal chemistry
Glenn T. Seaborg (University of California), Nuclear energy
Max Tishler (Merck and Co.), Nutrition and drug research

1969 **O.A. Battista** (FMC Corp.), Colloidal chemistry
Irving E. Levine, Industrial applications
Roy J. Plunkett (E.I. du Pont de Nemours), Industrial chemistry, "Teflon"
William G. Toland, Industrial chemistry
Harold C. Urey (Columbia University), Nuclear research
Harvey H. Voge (Shell Chemical Co.), Catalysis theory

1970 **Gerald C. Cox** (University of Pittsburgh), Fluoride research
H. Tracy Hall (General Electric Research), Diamond synthesis
Foster D. Snell, Surface chemistry, aerosols
William J. Sparks, Rubber chemistry

1971 **C. Kenneth Banks** (American Can Corp.), Molecular chemistry, "Promacetin"
Oliver W. Burke, Jr., Synthetic rubber
Sterling B. Hendricks (U.S. Dept. of Agriculture), Photoperiodism
Everett C. Hughes (Standard Oil Co. of Ohio), Petrochemistry
Joseph H. Simons, Fluorocarbons

1972 **J. Paul Hogan** (Phillips Petroleum Co.), Polymer chemistry
Herman F. Mark (Polytechnic Institute of N.Y.), Polymer chemistry
Alex G. Oblad, Petrochemistry
E. Emmet Reid, Organic chemistry
Lewis Sarett (Merck Sharp and Dohme), Medicinal chemistry, "Decadron"

1973 **Melvin A. Cook,** Explosives
Carl Djerassi (Syntex S.A.), Medicinal chemistry
Paul J. Flory, Polymer chemistry
Percival C. Keith, Atomic energy
Bartholomeus van't Riet (Medical College of Virginia), Medicinal chemistry

1974 **C.C. Hobbs** (Celanese Chemical Co.), Hydrocarbon research
Samuel E. Horne, Jr. (B.F. Goodrich Co.), Rubber chemistry
Charles J. Plank (Mobil Oil Corp.), Petrochemistry
Paul B. Weisz (Mobil Research and Development Corp.), Petrochemistry

1975 **Herbert C. Brown** (Purdue University), Borane chemistry
Rachel Brown (N.Y. State Dept. of Health), Antibiotic chemistry
Elizabeth Hazen, Medicinal chemistry, "Nystatin"
Linus C. Pauling, Body of thought
Christian Van Dijk (M.W. Kellogg Co.), Chlorine Research

1976 **Rowland C. Hansford** (Union Oil Co. of Calif.), Petrochemistry
Edwin T. Mertz (Purdue University), Nutrition research
Wilson C. Reeves, Fabric treatment
Jerome S. Spevack (Deuterium Corp.), Rubber chemistry

1977 **John Bjorksten** (Bjorksten Research Institute), Biochemistry
John Kollar (Redox Technologies), Petrochemistry
Henry McGrath (TRW), Chemical engineering
Donald Othmer (Polytechnic Institute of N.Y.), Chemical engineering

1978 **George E.F. Brewer**
Karl Klager
Lewis G. MacDowell
John Patton

1979 **Karl P. Cohen**
Paul Hartech
Barnett Rosenberg
Leo H. Sternbach

1980 **Paul H. Emmett**
Denis Forster
Stephanie Kwolek
Robert Milton

A Presidential Citation of Merit is awarded as warranted to honor innovation and creativity in addressing the problems facing the individual chemist or chemical engineer or the professional environmewnt in which they work.

1979 **Ernest R. Gilmont**
1980 **O.A. Battista**

The Gold Medal is given annually to stimulate and recognize service to the science of chemistry or to the professions of chemist and chemical engineer.

1926 **William Blum**
1927 **Lafayette B. Mendel**
1929 **Mr. and Mrs. Francis P. Garvan**
1930 **George Eastman**
1931 **Andrew W. and Richard B. Mellon**
1932 **Charles H. Herty**
1933 **Henry C. Sherman**
1934 **James Bryant Conant**
1936 **Marston Taylor Bogert**
1937 **James F. Norris**
1938 **Frederick G. Cottrell**
1940 **Gustav Egloff**
1941 **Henry G. Knight**
1942 **William Lloyd Evans**
1943 **Walter S. Landis**
1944 **Willard H. Dow**
1945 **John W. Thomas**
1946 **Robert Price Russell**
1947 **Moses Leverock Crossley**
1948 **Charles Allen Thomas**
1949 **Warren K. Lewis**
1950 **Walter J. Murphy**
1951 **Harry N. Holmes**
1952 **Fred J. Emmerich**
1953 **J.C. Warner**
1954 **William J. Sparks**
1955 **Carl S. Marvel**
1956 **Raymond Stevens**
1957 **Roy C. Newton**
1958 **Lawrence Flett**
1959 **Crawford H. Greenewalt**
1960 **Ernest H. Volwiler**
1961 **Alden H. Emery**
1962 **W. George Parks**
1963 **Ralph Connor**
1964 **Roger Adams**
1965 **Brig. Gen. Edwin Cox**
1966 **John H. Nair**
1967 **Wayne E. Kuhn**
1968 **Orville E. May**
1969 **Henry B. Hass**
1970 **Willard F. Libby**
1971 **Emmett B. Carmichael**
1972 **Harold C. Urey**
1973 **Glenn T. Seaborg**
1974 **W. E. (Butch) Hanford**

1975 William O. Baker
1976 Kenneth S. Pitzer
1977 Max Tishler
1978 Norman Hackerman
1979 Melvin Calvin
1980 Arthur M. Bueche

AOCS Award in Lipid Chemistry

AMERICAN OIL CHEMISTS SOCIETY
508 S. Sixth St., Champaign, Ill. 61820 (217/359-2344)

The American Oil Chemists Society Award in Lipid Chemistry, which consists of $2,500 granted by the Applied Science Labs Div. of Milton Roy, Inc., and a plaque, is awarded annually for original research in the field as presented in a meritorious technical paper. A committee selects the winner.

1964 Erich Baer
1965 Ernest Klenk
1966 H.E. Carter
1967 Sune Bergstrom
1968 Daniel Swern
1969 H.J. Dutton
1970 E.P. Kennedy
1971 E.S. Lutton
1972 A.T. James
1973 F.D. Gunstone
1974 P.K. Stumpf
1975 W.O. Lundberg
1976 No award
1977 George Popjack
1978 Ralph Holman
1979 Stephen S. Chang
1980 James F. Mead

Netherlands Fund for Chemistry Prize

ROYAL NETHERLANDS ACADEMY OF ARTS AND SCIENCES
Kloveniersburgwal 29, Amsterdam, the Netherlands (Tel: 020 22 29 02)

The Netherlands Fund for Chemistry Prize, which carries an honorarium, is given approximately every five years for research in chemistry. A Selection Committee chooses the winner, who must be of Dutch nationality.

1959 **J.F. Arens,** Groningen
1964 **H.J. den Hartog,** Wageningen
1969 **G.J.M. van der Kerk,** Utrecht
1975 **Th.J. de Boer,** Amsterdam
1980 **M. S. de Groot,** Bussum

Chemical Institute of Canada Medal
Merck Sharp & Dohme Lecture Award
Montreal Medal
R.S. Jane Memorial Lecture Award
Union Carbide Award
Noranda Lecture Award
Fischer Scientific Lecture Award
ERCO Award
Canada Society for Chemical Engineering Award
Dunlop Lecture Award
Catalyst Award
John Labatt Ltd. Award
Alcan Lecture Award
Protective Coatings Award
Norman and Marion Bright Memorial Award
Chemical Institute of Canada Environmental Improvement Award

CHEMICAL INSTITUTE OF CANADA
151 Slater St., Ste. 906, Ottawa, Canada K1P 5H3 (613/233-5623)

The Chemical Institute of Canada Medal is awarded annually for outstanding contributions to chemistry or chemical engineering in Canada. Nominations must be made by at least three professional members of the institute and ratified by a committee.

1951 **Thorbergur Thorvaldson**, "The Training of Chemists for Industry"
1952 **Otto Maass**, "Some Underlying Factors Involving the Process of Wood Pulp Production"
1953 **E.W.R. Steacie**, "Present Status of Radical Mechanisms for Organic Decompositions"
1954 **R.K. Stratford**, "Thirty-years in Petroleum Research"
1955 **A.R. Gordon**, "Current Problems in the Field of the Electrolytes"
1956 **Leo Marion**, "The Biogenesis of Alkaloids"
1957 **H.G. Thode**, "The Geochemistry of the Sulphur Isotopes"
1958 **C.A. Winkler**, "Active Nitrogen"
1959 **R.H. Manske**, "Fifty Years with Alkaloids"
1960 **C.B. Purves**, "Locating Substituents in Cellulose — A Review"
1961 **W.G. Schneider**, "Probing q Electrons"
1962 **Erich Baer**, "Natural Phospholipids—Synthesis and Structure"
1963 **Karel Wiesner**, "Ten Years of Studies on Basic Terpenes at the University of New Brunswick"
1964 **R.U. Lemieux**, "The Chemical Synthesis of Glycosides"
1965 **P.A. Giguere**, "Thirty Years of Peroxide Chemistry"
1966 **W.H. Gauvin**, "High Temperature Research"
1967 **H.E. Gunning**, "Sulphur Atom Chemistry"
1968 **J.A. Morrison**, "The Unexpected Behavior of Solid Methane at Very Low Temperatures"
1969 **C.A. McDowell**, "Photoelectron Spectroscopy"

1970 **D.J. LeRoy**, "The Kinetics of the Simplest Chemical Reactions"
1971 **K.J. Laidler**, "Adventures in Chemical Kinetics"
1972 **G. Herzberg**, "Spectra of Simple Free Radicals"
1973 **S.G. Mason**, "The Micro-Rheology of Disperse Systems"
1974 **H.J. Bernstein**, "Resonance Raman Spectroscopy"
1975 **B.E. Conway**, "Electrochemical Studies in Surface Sciences"
1976 **J.C. Polanyi**, "Molecular Motions in Chemical Reactions"
1977 **R.J. Gillespie**, "Structural Chemistry of the Main Group Elements"
1978 **R.J. Cvetanovic** "Some Current Trends in Chemical Kinetics"
1979 **B. Belleau**, "The Curse of Opium: Requital through Medicinal organic chemistry"
1980 **Not available at press time**

The Merck Sharp & Dohme Lecture Award, which carries a $1,000 honorarium, is made for distinguished contributions in organic chemistry or biochemistry in Canada. A committee selects the recipient from nominations made by members.

1955 **S. Kirkwood**, "The Thyroid Gland as Viewed Through the Eyes of a Chemist"
1956 **R.U. Lemieux**, "The Significance of the Half-Chair Conformation in Carbohydrate Chemistry"
1957 **A.C. Neish**, "The Biosynthesis of Carbohydrates in Plants"
1958 **H.C. Khorana**, "Recent Progress in the Synthesis an Structural Analysis of Polynucleotides"
1959 **J.F. Morgan**, "Tissue Culture as a Tool in Biochemical Research"
1960 **O.E. Edwards**, "Some Perspectives in Natural Products Research"
1961 **A.S. Perlin**, "The Chemistry of Oligosaccharides"
1962 **B. Belleau**, "Some Recent Developments in the Chemistry of Enzyme — Subtrate and Enzyme — Inhibitor Complexes"
1963 **P. Yates**, Studies on Gamboge
1964 **G.M. Tener**, "Studies on Soluble Ribonucleic Acid"
1965 **L.C. Vining**, "Antibiotics, Mould Metabolites and their Biosynthesis"
1966 **P. de Mayo**, "Photochemical Cycloaddition and Synthesis"
1967 **Z. Valenta**, "Synthetic Study of Ormosia Alkaloids"
1968 **J.P. Kutney**, "Recent Studies in Natural Products"
1969 **E.W. Warnhoff**, "Mechanistic Variations in the Favorskii Reaction"
1970 **W.A. Ayer**, "Recent Studies in Alkaloid Chemistry"
1971 **J.B. Stothers**, "Organic Applications of ^{13}C NMR Spectroscopy"
1972 **S. Wolfe**, "Sulphur-free Penicillin Derivatives"
1973 **J.W. ApSimon**, "Terpenoid Meanderings"
1974 **S. Hannessian**, "New Synthetic Methods: From Carbohydrates to Antibiotics and Beyond"
1975 **L.D. Hall**, "A Fourth Dimension for NMR Spectroscopy"
1976 **J.F. King**, "The Middle Word on Sulfenes"
P. Deslongchamps, "Synthentic Studies Toward Ryanodine"
1977 **B.O. Fraser-Reid**, "Some Mistakes We Would Gladly Make Again"
1978 **I.C.P. Smith**, "Molecular Details of Complex Biological Systems as Seen by Magnetic Resonance"
1979 **E. Piers**, "Recent Studies in Organic Synthesis"
1980 **Not available at press time**

The Montreal Medal of the Chemical Institute of Canada honors a resident of Canada for significant leadership in or outstanding contribution to chemistry or chemical engineerings. A committee selects the recipient, who must have received the nomination of at least five professional members of the society.

1956 **R.R. Mclaughlin**, "Industry Must Help to Prepare to Train Them"
1957 **Leon Lortie**, "Professional Responsibilities of Canadian Chemists"
1958 **T.W. Smith**, "Legislative Handicaps to the Development of Canadian Secondary Industry"
1959 **Thorbergur Thorvaldson**, "The Role of Basic Scientific Research"
1960 **J.W. Bain**, "Recollections of Early Days in the CIC"
1961 **H.B. Marshall**, "Why Join the CIC"
1962 **J.R. Donald**, "Chemical Engineering Reminescences"
1963 **C.J. Mackenzie**, "The New Scientific Technology — Canada's Obligations and Opportunities"
1964 **E.A.G. Colls**, "The Chemical Engineer Today"
1965 **L.H. Cragg**, "Educating Tomorrow's Professional Chemists and Chemical Engineers"
1966 **W.N. Hall**, "What Can The Chemical Institute Do For Canada?"
1967 **J.A. Davis**, "Who's in Charge Here?"
1968 **E. Lozinski**, "The View from Without"
1969 **L. Marion**, "Chemistry in the Science Turmoil"
1970 **L.J. Rubin**, "Canadian Science — The Age of Aquarius"
1971 **I.E. Puddington**, "Technological Timing"
1972 **H.S. Sutherland**, "It Depends on the Approach"
1973 **W.G. Schneider**, "Science in Transition"
1974 **R. Gaudry**, 'Chemistry for What?"
1975 **B.B. Migicovsky**, "Contributions of Chemistry to Food Production"
1976 **A.N. Bourns**, "A Scientific Generation Neglected is a Generation Lost"
1977 **J.W.T. Spinks**, "Science and Social Change"
1978 **J.W. Hodgins**, "Where has all the Laughter Gone?"
1979 **L. Yaffe**, "The Health Hazards of Not Going Nuclear"
1980 **Not available at press time**

The Robert Stephen Jane Memorial Lecture Award, which consists of $300 and a scroll, annually honors exceptional achievement in chemistry of chemical engineering in Canada. A committee selects the recipient upon nomination by at least five professional members of the society.

1960 **E.R. Rowzee**, "Rubber, Research and Human Resources"
1961 **K.G. Blaikie**, "Thirty-seven Years of Research at Shawinigan Chemicals Ltd."
1962 **F.A. Forward**, "Chemical Metallurgy as a Component of the Chemical Industry"
1963 **W.H. Gauvin**, "Chemical Engineering Research in Canada; Progress or Stagnation"
1964 **G.W. Govier**, "Developments in the Understanding of the Vertical Flow of Two Flooding Phases"
1965 **W.H. Rapson**, "From Laboratory Curiosity to Heavy Chemical"
1966 **P.E. Gishler**, "Operation of an Industrial Research Laboratory"
1967 **V.N. Mackiw**, "Current Trends in Chemical Metallurgy"
1968 **L.S. Renzoni**, "Extractive Metallurgy at International Nickel — a Half Century of Progress"
1969 **M. Katz**, "Photochemical Reactions of Atmospheric Pollutants"

1970 **N.I. Battista**, "The Chemical Engineer and the Viscose Rayon Industry"
1971 **H. Freeman**, "Chemical and Physical Properties of Gold, and its Economic Significance"
1972 **N.S. Grace**, "Three C's for Accomplishment — Creativity, Communication and Cooperation"
1973 **O.C.W. Allenby**, "Down with the 'Cargo Cults' "
1974 **A. Cholette**, N.A.
1975 **I.E. Puddington**, "Technology and the Good Life"
1976 **R.H. Wright**, "Odorous Comparisons"
1977 **J.B. Hyne**, "Sulphur — From Bottom Hole to End Use"
1978 **H.K. Rae**, "The Changing Face of Nuclear R&D"
1979 **D.S. Montgomery**, N.A.
1980 **Not available at press time**

The Noranda Lecture Award, which carries a $1,000 honorarium, annually honors a distinguished contribution to physical chemistry in Canada. A committee selects the winner.

1963 **N.C. Bartlett**, "Some Unusual Oxidation States of the Noble Elements"
1964 **B.E. Conway**, "Electrochemical Catalysis"
1965 **J.A. Davies**, "Electrochemistry as a Tool of Nuclear Science and Vice Versa"
1966 **R.J. Gillespie**, "Acids - Old and New"
1967 **J.C. Polanyi**, "Energy Distribution Among Reaction Products"
1968 **H.C. Clark**, "Synthetic Studies in Organometallic Chemistry"
1969 **L.W. Reeves**, "The Future of Nuclear Magnetic Resonance as a Tool in Chemistry"
1970 **W.A.G. Graham**, "Metal Carbonyl Derivatives, including Silicon, Germanium and Tin"
1971 **A.G. Harrison**, "Bimolecular Reactions of Gaesous Ions"
1972 **J. Trotter**, "X-Ray Diffraction Studies in Inorganic Structural Chemistry"
1973 **T.P. Schaeffer**, "Reminiscences of an Old-fashioned NMR Spectrosopist"
1974 **W.R. Cullen**, "Unnatural Products"
1975 **B.R. James**, "Rhodium — Expensive, but Rich in Chemistry"
1976 **J.R. Bolton**, "Photochemical Storage of Solar Energy"
1977 **C.E. Brion**, "Spectroscopy in the Dark"
1978 **B. Bosnich**, "Asymetric Synthesis. The Ultimate Synthetic Method"
1979 **A. Vijh**, "Electrochemistry and Energy Science"
1980 **Not available at press time**

The Fisher Scientific Lecture Award, which carries a $1,000 honorarium, is made annually for distinguished contributions to analytical chemistry in Canada. A committee selects the recipient upon nomination by at least three institute members.

1968 **F.E. Beamish**, "Analytical Chemistry and the University"
1969 **W.E. Harris**, "Gas Chromatography — Developments in Temperature Programming and Prolysis G.C."
1970 **R.P. Graham**, "Analytical Chemistry — Some Prospects and Retrospects"
1971 **R.N. Jones**, "Data Banking for Science and Technology"
1972 **D.E. Ryan**, "Trace Analysis by Solution Spectroscopy"
1973 **W.A.E. McBryde**, "Solution Chemistry — An Analyst's Playground"
1974 **G.C.B. Cave**, "Solvates and Aggregates of Solvent-Extraction Systems"
1975 **S. Barabas**, "Water Quality — A Global Problem of Many Common Denominators"
1976 **I. Hoffman**, "Environmental Cause/Effect Data — Some Preliminary Conclusions"
1977 **J. Lloyd Monkman**, "Is Chemistry Necessary Today?"
1978 **R.E. Jervis**, "Neutrons on the Trail of those Trace Elements — an Analytical Pursuit"
1979 **D.S. Russell**, "Some Features in Inorganic Trace Analysis — Much Ado About Nothing"
1980 **Not available at press time**

The ERCO Award of the Canadian Society of Chemical Engineers is a $500 award accompanied by a silver medallion made annually for distinguished contributions to chemical engineering in Canada. A committee selects the winner.

1970 **T.W. Hoffman**, "Translating Fundamentals to Practise"
1971 **N.J. Themelis**, "Development of a New Process: a Case History"
1972 **I.S. Pasternak**, "I Think I Can — I Knew I Could (The Technology Challenge)"
1973 **M. Moo-Young**, "Food Production from Unconventional Sources"
1974 **A.E. Hamieler**, "Polymer Reaction Engineering — An Overview"
1975 **C.E. Capes**, "Basic Studies in Particle Technology and Some Novel Applications"
1976 **M.E. Charles**, 'Fluid Mechanics and Resource Development"
1977 **B.B. Pruden**, "Ten Per Cent More Oil"
1978 **E. Rhodes**, "Can Anybody Find a Use for Technology Developed in Canadian Universities?"
1979 **A.P. Watkinson**, N.A.
1980 **Not available at press time**

The Canadian Society of Chemical Engineering Award in Industrial Practice is awarded annually for distinguished contributions to the application of chemical engineering or industrial chemistry to the industrial sphere. The award, which consists of a plaque and $300, is given to an individual selected by a committee which judges nominations received.

1977 **J.F. Gilbert**
1978 **R.F. Routledge**
1979 **J. Pugi**
1980 **Not available at press time**

The Dunlop Lecture Award for Macromolecular Science, formerly called the Dunlop Lecture Award, is given biennally for distinguished contributions to macromolecular science of technology in Canada. The award consists of $1,000 and a scroll, and the winner is selected by a committee from nominations received.

1971 **G.S. Whitby**, "Reflections on the Early Days of Canadian Polymer Chemistry"
1973 **S. Bywater**, "Recent Advances in Ionic Polymerization"
1975 **S.G. Mason**, "Some New Aspects of Wetting Solids by Liquids"
1977 **H.L. Williams**, "Dynamic Properties of Polymers"
1979 **J.E. Guillet**, "Some Light on Plastic Molecules"

The Catalysis Award/Prix de Catalyse is given biennially for contributions in the field of catalysis made while working in Canada. The winner, who receives a medal, is chosen by a committee from nominations received.

1977 **R.J. Cvetanovic**, and **Y. Amenomiya**, "Development of a Technique for Catalyst Studies"
1979 **R.B. Anderson**, "Some Catalysts I Have Known"

The Alcan Lecture Award, which carries a $1,000 honorarium accompanied by a scroll, is given annually for distinguished contributions to inorganic chemistry or electrochemistry in Canada. A committee selects the winner from nominations received.

1979 **R.G. Cavell**, "Excursions in Phosphorous Chemistry"
1980 **Not available at press time**

The John Labatt Ltd. Award, which is accompanied by a $1,000 honorarium and a scroll, is given annually for achievement in biochemical or organic chemical research, with particular emphasis on biological systems, when possible for work pertinent to food or beverage supply, manufacture, quality or nutritional value. A committee selects the winner from nominations received.

1977 **J.E. Zajic**, "Perspective Horizons in Biochemical Engineering"
1978 **C.P. Lentz**, "Interaction Between Engineers and Biochemists in Research"
1979 **No award**
1980 **Not available at press time**

The Protective Coatings Award, which carries a $1,000 honorarium, is awarded annually for outstanding contributions to the field of coatings or to outstanding practitioners in the industry in Canada. A committee chooses the winner from papers submitted.

1977 **H.P. Schreiber**, "Physical Interactions in Coatings: Coping with the Problem"
1978 **A.E. Hamielec**, "Liquid Exclusion Chromatography"
1979 **J.W. Tomecko**, N.A.
1980 **Not available at press time**

The Chemical Institute of Canada Environmental Improvement Award, which consists of "an artifact" for the organization and certificates for any individuals cited, annually honors significant contributions to environmental improvement in Canada. A selection chooses the recipient from nominations.

1975 **B & W Heat Treating Ltd.** and **University of Waterloo**
1976 **DuPont of Canada Ltd.**
1977 **Dow Chemical & Diversy (Canada) Ltd.**
1978 **St. Lawrence Cement Co.**
1979 **Shell Canada Resources Ltd.**
1980 **Not available at press time**

Colwyn Medal
Hancock Medal
Prince Philip Award
Swinburne Award

PLASTICS AND RUBBER INSTITUTE
11 Hobart Place, London Sw1W OHL, United Kingdom
(01-245 9555)

The Colwyn Medal annually honors outstanding service to the plastics and rubber industry of a scientific, technical or engineering nature. A committee selects the winner.

1928 **G. Stafford Whitby**
1929 **W.H. Stevens**
1930 **No award**
1931 **No award**
1932 **No award**
1933 **W.H. Paull**
1934 **O. de Vries**
1935 **D.F. Twiss**
1936 **C.J. Beaver**
1937 **No award**
1938 **B.D. Porritt**
1939 **S.S. Pickles**
1940 **P. Schidrowitz**
H.P. Stevens
1941 **B.J. Eaton**, OBE
1942 **No award**
1943 **A. Healey**
1944 **S.A. Brazier**, OBE
1945 **W.J.S. Naunton**
1946 **George Martin**
1947 **R.P. Dinsmore**
1948 **J.R. Scott**
1949 **E.A. Murphy**
1950 **A. van Rossem**
1951 **C.E.T. Mann**
1952 **G. Gee**, FRS
1953 **D. Parkinson**
1954 **P.J. Flory**
1955 **H.N. Ridley**, CMG, FRS
C. Falconer Flint
1956 **W.B. Wiegand**
1957 **H.W. Melville**, FRS
1958 **J. Le Bras**
1960 **Erich Conrad**
1961 **L.R. G. Treloar**
1962 **L.C. Bateman**, CMG, FRS
1963 **E.W. Madge**
1964 **G.E. Bloomfield**
1965 **W.C. Wake**
1966 **L. Mullins**
1967 **V.E. Gough**
1968 **W.F. Watson**, CBE
1969 **B.C. Sekhar**
1970 **A. Schallamach**
1971 **J.D. Ferry**
1972 **A.R. Payne**
1973 **C.E.H. Bawn**, CBE, FRS
1974 **J.I. Cuneen**
1975 **J. Furukawa**
1976 **J.M. Massoubre**
1977 **A.N. Gent**
1978 **A.G. Thomas**
1979 **M. Morton**
1980 **Not available at press time**

The Hancock Medal annually honors outstanding service to the institute in such fields as industrial safety, education, organization and management. A committee selects the winner.

1951 **R.W. Lunn**
1952 **T.J. Drakeley**, CBE
1953 **H. Rogers**
1954 **R. Ascoli**, CIE
1955 **J.M. Wright**
1956 **S.D. Sutton**
1957 **F.M. Panzetta**, MBE
1958 **H. Wilshaw**, OBE
1959 **J.H. Carrington**
1960 **C.B. Copeman**
1961 **M.M. Heywood**
1962 **C.H. Birkitt**

1963 **F.H. Cotton**
1964 **D. Banerjee**
1965 **G.A. Shires**
1966 **L.L. Roe**
1967 **H.C. Baker**
J.A. Smithson
1968 **L.R. Mernagh**
1969 **G.E.M. Godfrey**, MBE
1970 **J.M. Buist**
1971 **E.R. Gardner**
1972 **C.M. Blow**
1973 **M.J. Jordan**
1974 **D. Bulgin**
R.C.W. Moakes
1975 **M.A. Birkin**
1976 **H.M. Collier**
1977 **H. Jackson**
H.G. Parkes
1978 **L.G. Harrison**, OBE
1979 **D.M. Turner**
1980 **Not available at press time**

The Prince Philip Medal, which is of gold, is awarded not more frequently than every two years and honors contributions of "plastics in the service of man." These can be in the area of conservation of resources, applications to extend the use of essential and/or scarce materials, preservation of nature, food processing, medical science, engineering or other applications. The Prince Philip Award Committee chooses the winner.

1976 **Sir John Charnley**, Plastic hip joint
1978 **F.D. Mercer**, OBE, Netlon
1980 **BXL Plastics Ltd.**, Plastazote, cross-linked polyethylene form

The Swinburne Award, which consists of an honorarium, a gold medal and a scroll, is awarded not more frequently than every two years and not less than one every five years for outstanding contributions to polymer science and technology. The Swinburne Award Committee chooses the recipient.

1960 **R. Gee**
1962 **J.C. Swallow**
1963 **K. Ziegler**
1964 **C.E.H. Bawn**
1968 **H.F. Mark**
1970 **L.R.G. Treloar**
1972 **R.F. Boyer**
1974 **A. Keller**
1976 **H. Schnell**
1978 **P.W. Morgan**
1980 **Not available at press time**

Somach Sachs Memorial Award

WEIZMANN INSTITUTE OF SCIENCE
Box 26, Rehovot, Israel (Tel: 054-82111 and 83111)

The Somach Sachs Memorial Award honors outstanding work in chemistry by a scientist under 35 years of age at the Weizmann Institute. It is given every second year.

1961 **Z. Luz**, Nuclear magnetic resonance
B. Silver, Isotope research
1964 **Raphael Mechoulam**, Organic chemistry, specifically the isolation and elucidation of the structure of the active constituent of hashish
1966 **Harry Friedmann**, Nuclear physics, specifically for "The Rotation-Translation Coupling Spectrum of Matrix-Isolated Molecules"
1968 **Rachel Goldman**, Biophysics, specifically for work on membranes having enzymatic activity
1970 **Michael Revel**, Biochemistry, specifically for the elucidation of the basic processes in the production of the protein molecule in the living cell
1972 **Michael Inbar**, Genetics, specifically for his work in the use of carbohydrate-binding protein concanavalin to measure the location of certain carbohydrate-containing sites on the surface of membrane cells
1974 **Ada Yonath**, Structural chemistry, specifically for work on the structure of biological molecules
1976 **Victor Yakhot**, Structural chemistry and chemical physics, specifically for work on geometric distortions in excited states
1978 **Moshe Shapiro**, Chemical physics
1980 **Shimon Vega**, Isotope research

Wolf Prize in Chemistry

WOLF FOUNDATION
Box 398, Herzliah-Bet, Israel

The $100,000 Wolf Prize in Chemistry honors an outstanding body of work in chemistry, as determined by a committee of international known judges. The award is part of a $500,000 annual prize distribution for exceptional achievement in five fields of science.

1978 **Carl Djerassi** (Stanford University), Work in bio-organic chemistry, application of new spectroscopic techniques and support of international cooperation
1979 **Herman F. Mark** (Polytechnic Institute of New York), Contributions to the understanding of the structure and behavior of natural and synthetic polymers
1980 **Henry Eyring** (University of Utah), Development of the absolute rate theory and its imaginative applications to chemical and physical processes

Henry Goode Memorial Award Distinguished Information Sciences Award

AMERICAN FEDERATION OF INFORMATION PROCESSING SOCIETIES
505 Busse Hwy., Park Ridge, Ill. 60068 (312/825-8124)

The Henry Goode Memorial Award annually honors individuals for pioneering contributions to the furtherance of computer science and information processing. An awards committee selects the recipient of the bronze medal.

1964 **Howard Hathaway Aiken**, Digital computers
1965 **George Robert Stibitz and Konrad Zuse**, Automatic computing
1966 **J. Presper Eckert, John** and **William Mauchly**, ENIAC/BINAC/UNIVAC computers
1967 **Samuel Nathan Alexander**, Computers in the federal government
1968 **Maurice Vincent Wilkes**, Computer engineering and software
1969 **Alston Scott Householder**, Numerical intelligence/programming
1970 **Grace Murray Hopper**, Computer software

1971 **Allen Newell,** Artificial intelligence/programming
1972 **Seymour R. Cray,** Digital computers and multiprocessing systems
1974 **Edsger W. Dijkstra,** Computer programming/ALGOL
1975 **Kenneth E. Iverson,** Computer programming/APL
1976 **Lawrence G. Roberts,** Computer-communication systems
1977 **Jay W. Forrester,** Core storage; Whirlwind 1; computer modeling and simulation; system dynamics
1978 **Gordon E. Moore,** N.A.
Robert M. Noyce, N.A.
1979 **Herman H. Goldstine,** N.A.
1980 **Fernando J. Corbato,** Time-shared computer systems; Multics operating system

The DPMA Distinguished Information Sciences Award annually honors outstanding contributions in the field of data processing.

1978 **Irwin J. Sirkin,** Aetna Life & Casualty, Hartford, Conn.
1979 **Ruth M. Davis,** U.S. Dept. of Energy, Washington, D.C.
1980 **John Diebold,** Diebold Group, New York

Harry Levine Prize in Computer Sciences

Weizmann Institute of Science
Box 26, Rehovot, Israel (Tel: 054-82111 and 83111)

The Harry Levine Prize in Computer Sciences is awarded every second year for outstanding work in the field.

1976 **Amiram Caspi and Zvi Lapidot**
1978 **No award**
1980 **No award**

Cyrus Hall McCormick Medal
John Deere Medal
Metal Building Manufacturers Award
Massey-Ferguson Medal
Hancor Soil and Water Engineering Award
George W. Kable Electrification Award
Kishida International Award
DFISA-ASAE Food Engineering Award
Engineering Achievement Award
Doerfer Engineering Concept of the Year Award
John G. Sutton Memorial Award
G.R. Gunlogson Countryside Engineering Award
Allis-Chalmers National Student Design Award

AMERICAN SOCIETY OF AGRICULTURAL ENGINEERS
420 Main St., Box 410, St. Joseph, Mo. 49085
(616/429-0300)

The Cyrus Hall McCormick Medal, which is of gold, is annually awarded for exceptional engineering achievement in agriculture. A jury selects the winner.

1932 **Oscar V.P. Stout**
1933 **J. Bornwlee Davidson**
1934 **Mark L. Nichols**
1935 **Theo Brown**
1936 **Elwood Mead**
1937 **Chester O. Reed**
1938 **Edward A. Johnston**
1939 **Philip S. Rose**
1940 **Oliver B. Zimmerman**
1941 **Harry C. Merritt**
1942 **William D. James**
1943 **Bert R. Benjamin**
1944 **Leonard J. Fletcher**
1945 **Charles A. Bennett**
1946 **William G. Kaiser**
1947 **Henry Giese**
1948 **Roy Bainer**
1949 **Eugene G. McKibben**
1950 **Arnold P. Yerkes**
1951 **Charles E. Seitz**
1952 **Charles J. Scranton**
1953 **Andrey A. Potter**
1954 **W.H. Worthington**
1955 **Robert P. Messenger**
1956 **Martin Ronning**
Harris P. Smith
1957 **Rudolph H. Driftmier**
1958 **Dent Parrett**
Thomas Caroll
1959 **Floyd W. Duffee**
1960 **Fred A. Brooks**
Walter H. Silver
1961 **John R. Orelind**

1962 Chauncey W. Smith
1963 Clarence F. Kelly
1964 Robert M. Merrill
1965 Walter M. Carleton
1966 Merlin Hansen
1967 Truman E. Hienton
1968 Howard F. McColly
1969 Edgar L. Barger
1970 Carlton L. Zink
1971 Henry J. Barre
1972 Stanley A. Witzel
1973 Jerome W. Sorenson, Jr.
1974 Karl H. Norris
1975 Orval C. French
1976 Lester F. Larsen
1977 Clarence B. Richey
1978 Russell R. Poynor
1979 Glen E. Vanden Berg
1980 Not available at press time

The John Deere Medal, which is of gold, is presented annually for distinugished achievement in the application of science to the soil. A jury selects the winner.

1938 Samuel H. McCrory
1939 Harry B. Walker
1940 Walter W. McLaughlin
1941 Robert W. Trullinger
1942 David P. Davies
1943 William Boss
1944 Charles E. Ramser
1945 C. Harold White
1946 Edgar V. Collins
1947 Frank Adams
1948 Dalton G. Miller
1949 Hugh H. Bennett
1950 Roy R. Gray
1951 Charles N. Stone
1952 Ivan D. Wood
1953 Orson W. Israelson
1954 Raymond Olney
1955 Walter W. Weir
1956 Arthur W. Clyde
1957 Archie A. Stone
1958 Wallace Ashby
1959 Fred R. Jones
1960 William V. Hukill
1961 Virgil Overholt
1962 Samuel P. Lyle
1963 Edwin W. Tanquary
1964 Mortimer R. Lewis
1965 Emil W. Lehmann
1966 Harry F. Blaney
1967 Ernest F. Blackwelder
1968 Dwight D. Smith
1969 Arthur W. Cooper
1970 Wayne D. Criddle
1971 G. Wallace Giles
1972 John T. Phillips, Jr.
1973 John W. Borden
1974 Lawrence H. Skromme
1975 John H. Zich
1976 John C. Stephens
1977 Jan van Schilfgaarde
1978 Lloyd L. Harrold
1979 Fiepko Coolman
1980 Not available at press time

The Metal Building Manufacturers Association Award annually honors an ASAE member for distinguished work in the farm structures field.

1959 Theodore E. Bond
1960 Gordon L. Nelson
1961 James S. Boyd
1962 Alvin C. Dale
1963 Franklyn H. Theakston
1964 Sherwood S. DeForest
1965 Norman C. Teter
1966 Merle L. Esmay
1967 James O. Curtis
1968 Donald W. Richter
1969 Landis L. Boyd
1970 Howard K. Johnson
1971 Thamon E. Hazen
1972 Robert R. Rowe
1973 Bruce A. McKenzie
1974 John N. Walker
1975 Warren L. Roller
1976 G. LeRoy Hahn
1977 Frank Wiersma
1978 George L. Pratt
1979 James A. DeShazer
1980 Not available at press time

The Massey-Ferguson Medal annually honors advancement of agricultural knowledge and practice by a teacher in the field. A jury selects the recipient.

1965 Rudolph H. Driftmier
1966 Mack M. Jones
1967 Price Hobgood
1968 Frederick C. Fenton
1969 Ervin W. Schroeder
1970 No award
1971 Arthur W. Farrall
1972 G. Edwin Henderson
1973 Dennis L. Moe
1974 Frank B. Lanham
1975 Frank W. Peikert
1976 Carl W. Hall
1977 S. Milton Henderson
1978 William E. Splinter
1980 Not available at press time

The Hancor Soil and Water Engineering Award annually honors contributions to the advancement of soil and water engineering in teaching, research, planning, design, construction, management or methods and materials. A jury selects the winner.

1966 William W. Donnan
1967 Philip W. Manson
1968 Glenn O. Schwab
1969 James N. Luthin
1970 John R. Carreker
1971 Robert P. Beasley
1972 Ernest H. Kidder
1973 E. Paul Jacobsen
1974 Marvin E. Jensen
1975 Elmer W. Gain
1976 Neil P. Woodruff
1977 Benjamin A. Jones, Jr.
1978 Howard P. Johnson
1979 Melville L. Palmer
1980 Not available at press time

The George W. Kable Electrification Award annually honors an agricultural engineer for outstanding personal and professional contributions in applying electrical energy to the advancement of agriculture. A jury selects the winner.

1969 Everette C. Easter
1970 H. Seymour Pringle

1971 **Morris H. Lloyd**
1972 **Nolan Mitchell**
1973 **William E. McCune**
1974 **Kenneth L. McFate**
1975 **Frank W. Andrew**
1976 **Olin W. Glinn**
1977 **Clesson N. Turner**
1978 **Dean Searls**
1979 **Richard L. Witz**
1980 **Not available at press time**

The $1,000 Kishida International Award annually honors outstanding contributions to engineering, mechanization and technological programs of education, research, development, consultation or technology that have resulted in significant improvements outside the United States.

1978 **Ralph C. Hay**
1979 **Bruce H. Anderson**
1980 **Not available at press time**

The DFISA-ASAE Food Engineering Award, which consists of $2,000, a gold medal and a certificate, is given biennially for original contributions in research, development, design or management of food-processing equipment or techniques of significant economic value to the food industry and the consumer. A jury selects the winner.

1972 **Arthur W. Farrell**
1974 **Robert P. Graham**
1976 **Walter M. Urbain**
1978 **Marcus Karel**
1980 **Not available at press time**

Engineering Achievement Awards are presented annually to ASAE members 40 years of age or younger for outstanding contributions to the profession and to stimulate further professional achievements. Plaques are presented to the winners, who are selected by a committee.

FMC CORPORATION YOUNG DESIGNER AWARD

1972 **James L. Fouss, Jr.**
1973 **Douglas L. Bosworth**
1974 **John E. Morrison, Jr.**
1975 **Ronald T. Noyes**
1976 **Roger W. Curry**
1977 **Richard W. Hook**
1978 **John C. Knobloch**
1979 **Gustaaf M.L. Persoons**
1980 **Not available at press time**

A.W. FARRELL YOUNG EDUCATOR AWARD

1972 **Paul K. Turnquist**
1973 **Donald M. Edwards**
1974 **E. Paul Taiganides**
1975 **Bobby L. Clary**
1976 **Larry J. Segerlind**
1977 **No award**
1978 **David B. McWhorter**
1979 **Thomas L. Thompson**
1980 **Not available at press time**

FIEI YOUNG RESEARCHER AWARD

1972 **Robert B. Fridley**
1973 **Roscoe L. Pershing**
1974 **Dennis R. Heldman**
1975 **Charles T. Haan**
1976 **C. Gene Haugh**
1977 **Edward A. Hiler**
1978 **Billy J. Barfield**
1979 **Louis D. Albright**
1980 **Not available at press time**

AEROVENT YOUNG EXTENSION MAN AWARD

1973 **Byron H. Nolte**
1974 **Myron D. Paine**
1975 **L. Bynum Driggers**
1976 **Peter D. Bloome**
1977 **William Mayfield**
1978 **George A. Duncan**
1979 **Donald R. Price**
1980 **Not available at press time**

The Doefer Engineering Concept of the Year Award is presented annually to an engineer for the contribution deemed the most outstanding development or achievement concept. A jury chooses the winner, who receives a plaque.

1974 **Herbert N. Stapleton**
1975 **John G. Alphin**
1976 **Robert B. Fridley**
1977 **Donald L. Peterson**
1978 **Dale E. Marshall**
1979 **Lambert H. Wilkes**
1980 **Not available at press time**

The John G. Sutton Memorial Award annually honors an outstanding junior student in an agricultural engineering department of a U.S. institution of learning

1969 **Richard Stroshine**, Ohio State University
1970 **Thomas L. Hamby**, University of Georgia
1971 **Alan W. Johnson**, Kansas State University
1972 **Ronald Elliott**, University of Illinois
1973 **Donald G. Colliver**, University of Kentucky
1974 **Ronnie G. Morgan**, Oklahoma State University
1975 **Jerry D. Walker**, Texas A&M University
1976 **Carol Cassel**, Oklahoma State University
1977 **Thomas E. Glenn**, University of Illinois
1978 **Betty L. Brockett**, Pennsylvania State University
1979 **Michael Bret Thurmond**, University of Georgia
1980 **Not available at press time**

The G.B. Gunlogson Countryside Engineering Award annually honors outstanding engineering contributions to the "healthy climate of the American countryside and to a viable economy for its small towns."

1975 **Junius L. Kendrick**
1976 **Robert C. Ward**
1977 **No award**
1978 **Frank J. Humenick**
1979 **E.A. Olson**
1980 **Not available at press time**

The ASAE Student Paper Award is given annually for a meritorious paper by an agricultural engineering student.

1952 **Merle L. Esmay**, University of Missouri,
1953 **G.E. Williams,** University of Nebraska
Robert Palmer, Oklahoma State University
1954 **E.E. Nelson**, Ohio State University
1955 **Gerald Zachariah**, Kansas State University
1956 **Daniel Van Duyne**, Pennsylvania State University
1957 **Irvin Eickmeyer**, University of Illinois
1958 **Robert Mensch**, Iowa State University
1959 **Roland Gehman**, Pennsylvania State University
1960 **George Merva**, Ohio State University
1961 **John Cannon**, Utah State University

1962 **James Smith**, University of Illinois
1963 **Neil Webster**, University of Maine
1964 **John Hummel**, University of Maryland
1965 **James Burkholder**, Virginia Polytechnic Institute and State University
1966 **David Thompson**, Purdue University
1967 **Will Hamilton**, Oklahoma State University
1968 **Larry Kluesner**, University of Missouri
1969 **James Steichen**, Oklahoma State University
1970 **R.A. Ridout**, Virginia Polytechnic Institute and State University
1971 **Thomas Hudson**, West Virginia University
1972 **Larry Billen**, Oklahoma State University
1973 **Ronnie Morgan**, Oklahoma State University
1974 **Jacob LaRue**, North Dakota State University
1975 **Ronnie Morgan**, Oklahoma State University
1976 **Dirk Peterson**, University of Nebraska
1977 **Rick Marshall**, Cornell University
1978 **Mark A. Clark**, Washington State University
1979 **Charles W. Binder**, Colorado State University
1980 **Not available at press time**

The Allis-Chalmers National Student Design Award is given to the winner of a competition that stresses the use of basic sciences, mathematics and engineering skills to achieve optimum conversion of resources to meet the objectives of the project entry.

1977 **Joe A. Haffener, George A. Johnson, David L. Malm, Steven L. Phillips, Michael D. Schwarz, David Skinner**, and **Dennis J. Stucky**, Kansas State University, for post poker
1978 **Bryan W. Coover, Lance O. Leebrick, James Leiszler, Donald A. Suderman** and **Frederick L. Yarrow**, Kansas State University, for combine power unplugger
1979 **Brady G. Bauer, Kenneth G. Meill, Patrick P. Parke, Wayne L. Thompson**, and **Tom J. Voeje**, Kansas State University for chip chucker
1980 **Not available at press time**

Norman Medal
J. James R. Cross Medal
Arthur M. Wellington Prize
ASCE State-of-the-Art Award
A.P. Greensfelder Construction Prize
Thomas Fitch Rowland Prize
Construction Management Award
Theodore von Karman Medal
Nathan M. Newmark Medal
Alfred M. Freudenthal Medal
Rudolph Hering Medal
Samuel Arnold Greeley Award
Wesley W. Horner Award
Simon W. Freese Environmental Engineering Award
Thomas A. Middlebrooks Award
Karl Terzaghi Award
Karl Terzaghi Lecture
Martin S. Kapp Foundation Award
Karl Emil Hilgard Hydraulic Prize
J.C. Stevens Award
Royce J. Tipton Award
Stephen Bechtel Pipeline Engineering Award
Rickey Medal
Moisseiff Award
T.Y. Lin Award
Raymond Reese Research Prize
Surveying and Mapping Award
Harland Batholomew Award
Frank M. Masters Transportation Engineering Award
Julian Hinds Award
John G. Moffat-Frank E. Nichol Award
Maurico Porraz Award
Collingwood Prize
James Laurie Prize
Daniel W. Mead Prizes
Walter Huber Oil Engineering Prize
Ernest E. Howard Award
Edmund Friedman Award
Civil Government Award
Civil Engineering History Award
National Historic Civil Engineering Landmark
Can-Am Civil Engineering Amity

Award
Edmund Friedman Young Engineer Award
ASCE President's Award
Parcel-Sverdrup Civil Engineering Management Award

AMERICAN SOCIETY OF CIVIL ENGINEERS
345 E. 47th St., New York, N.Y. 10017 (212/644-7496)

The Norman Medal, which is of gold and is accompanied by a bronze replica and a certificate, annually honors the author(s) of an original paper presented to the ASCE by a member or members. A committee selects the winner.

1874 J. James R. Croes
1875 Theodore G. Ellis
1877 William W. MacLay
Julius H. Striedonger*
1879 Edward P. North
Max E. Schmidt*
1880 Theodore Cooper
1881 L.L. Buck
1882 A. Fteley and F.P. Stearns
1883 William P. Shinn
1884 James Christie
1885 Eliot C. Clarke
1886 Edward Bates Dorsey
1887 Desmaond Fitzgerald
1888 E.E. Russel Tratman
1889 Theodore Cooper
1890 John R. Freeman
1891 John R. Freeman
1892 William Starling
1893 Desmond Fitzgerald
1894 Alfred E. Hunt
1895 William Ham. Hall
1896 John E. Greiner
1897 Julius Baier
1898 B.F. Thomas
1899 E. Herbert Stone
1900 James A. Seddon
1901 No award
1902 Gardener S. Williams, Clarence W. Hubbell and George H. Henkell
1904 Emile Low
1905 C.C. Schneider
1906 John S. Sewell
1907 Leonard M. Cox
1908 C.C. Schneider
1909 J.A.L. Waddell
1910 C.E. Grunsky
1911 George Gibbs
1912 Wilson Sherman Kinnear
1913 J.V. Davies
1914 Caleb Mills Saville
1915 Allen Hazen
1916 J.A.L. Waddell
1917 Benjamin F. Groat
1918 L.R. Jorgensen
1919 William Barclay Parsons
1920 J.A.L. Waddell
1921 No award
1922 Charles H. Paul
1923 D.B. Steinman
1924 B.F. Jakobsen
1925 Harrison P. Eddy
1926 Julian Hinds
1927 B.F. Jakobsen
1928 Charles E. Sudler
1929 G.T. Rude
1930 Karl Terzaghi
1931 Floyd A. Nagler and Albion Davis
1933 Hardy Cross
1934 Leon S. Moisseiff
1935 O.C. Henny
1936 Daniel W. Mead
1937 J.C. Stevens
1938 Hunter Rouse
1939 Charles H. Lee
1940 Shortridge Hardesty and Harold E. Wessman
1941 J.A. Van den Broek
1942 Karl Terzaghi
1943 Thomas E. Stanton
1944 Ralph B. Peck
1945 Merrill Bernard
1946 Karl Terzaghi
1947 Boris A. Bakhmeteff and William Allan
1948 Alfred M. Freudenthal
1949 Gerard H. Matthes
1950 Frederich Bleich
1951 D.B. Steinman
1952 No award
1953 Frederich Bleich and L.W. Teller
1954 Robert H. Sherlock
1955 Karl Terzaghi
1956 Carl E. Kindsvater and Rolland W. Carter
1957 Alfred W. Freudenthal
1958 Anestis S. Veletsos and Nathan M. Newmark
1959 Willard J. Turnbull and Charles R. Foster
1960 Carl E. Kindsvater and Rolland W. Carter
1961 Lorenz G. Straub and Alvin G. Anderson
1962 William McGuire and Gordon P. Fisher
1963 Bruno Thurlimann
1964 T. William Lambe
1965 Gerald A. Leonards and Jagdish Narain
1966 Charles H. Lawrence
1967 Daniel Dicker
1968 H. Bolton Seed and Kenneth L. Lee
1969 Basil W. Wilson
1970 Cyril J. Galvin, Jr.
1971 John H. Schmertmann
1972 Nicholas C. Costes, W. David Carrier, III, James K. Mitchell and Ronald F. Scott
1973 Bobby O. Hardin and Vincent P. Drenevich
1974 James R. Coffer
1975 Roy E. Olson, and David E. Daniel, Jr., Thomas K. Liu
1976 Charles C. Ladd and Roger Foott
1977 H. Bolton Seed, Kenneth L. Lee, Izzat M. Idriss, and Faiz I. Makdisi
1978 Richard D. Barksdale
1979 Anil K. Chopra
1980 John L. Cleasby and James C. Lorence

***Book award**

The James R. Cross Medal, which is of gold and is accompanied by a bronze replica and a certificate, is awarded annually to the author(s) of a paper "next in order of merit to the paper for which the Norman Medal is awarded." A committee selects the recipient.

1913 B.F. Cresson, Jr.
1914 J.B. Lippincott
1915 Richard R. Lyman
1916 C.E. Smith

1917 Henry S. Prichard
1918 Israel V. Werbin
1919 D.B. Steinman
1920 B.A. Smith
1921 Fred A. Noetzli
1922 William Cain
1923 James F. Sanborn
1924 Joel D. Justin
1925 Charles S. Whitney
1926 Clarence S. Jarvis
1927 Henry Clay Ripley
1930 H. de B. Parsons
1931 John R. Freeman
1932 David L. Yarnell and Floyd A. Nagler
1933 Earl I. Brown
1934 H.M. Westergaard
1935 A.T. Larned and W.S. Merrill
1936 Wilbur M. Wilson
1937 Inge Lyse and Bruce G. Johnston
1938 F.C. Hartmann
1939 C.A. Mockmore
1940 Edward J. Rutter, Quintin B. Graves, and Franklin F. Snyder
1941 Earl I. Brown
1942 Charles F. Ruff
1943 C.H. Gronquist
1944 N.M. Newmark
1945 G.H. Hickox
1946 Gail A. Hathaway
1947 Thomas R. Camp
1948 Karl DeVries
1949 F.H. Kellogg
1950 L.F. Harza
1951 M.E. von Seggern
1952 No award
1953 Paul Rogers
1954 Fu-Kuei Chang and Bruce G. Johnston
1955 John S. McNown
1956 Jack W. Carter, Kenneth H. Lenzen and Lawrence T. Wyly
1957 William E. Wagner
1958 William J. Oswald and Harold B. Gotaas
1959 Charles I. Mansur and Robert I. Kaufman
1960 H. Bolton Seed and Clarence K. Chan
1961 George Winter
1962 H. Bolton Seed and C.K. Chan
1963 Melvin L. Baron, Hans Bleich and Paul Wiedlinger
1964 Daryl B. Simons and Maurice L. Albertson
1965 jack G. Bouwkamp
1966 John W. Clark and Richard L. Rolf
1967 Carl H. Plumlee
1968 William R. Hudson and Hudson Matlock
1969 Hugo B. Fischer
1970 John M. Henderson
1971 Erich J. Plate and John H. Nath
1972 H. Bolton Seed and Izzat M. Idriss
1973 David J. D'Appolonia, Harry G. Poulos, and Charles C. Ladd
1974 Subrata K. Chakrabarti
1975 G.E. Blight
1976 Frank H. Pearson and Archie J. McDonnell
1977 John A. Peplogle
1978 Gregory N. Richardson, Daniel Feger, Arthur Fong, and Kenneth L. Lee
1979 Charles W. Roeder and Egor P. Popov
1980 Roger G. Bea, Jean M.E. Audibert, and M. Kadwan Akky

The Arthur M. Wellington Prize, which consists of a plaque and a certificate, annually honors the author(s) of a meritorious paper on transport on land, water or air or closely related to such subjects. A committee selects the winner.

1923 J.P. Newell
1924 Rufus W. Putnam
1925 William M. Black
1926 Charles W. Kutz
1927 John A. Miller, Jr.
1928 Roy G. Finch
1929 F.C. Carstarphen
1930 George Gibbs
1931 G.F. Schlesinger
1932 Fred Lavis
1933 D.J. Kerr
1934 J.C. Evans
1935 Hawley S. Simpson
1936 No award
1937 E.C. Harwood
1938 Charles M. Noble
1939 Rufus W. Putnam
1941 Fred Lavis
1942 William J. Wilgus
1943 Milton Harris
1946 James H. Stratton
1947 No award
1948 Joseph Barnett
1949 Arthur Casagrande
1950 A.A. Anderson
1951 Alexander Hrennikof
1952 Basil Wrigley Wilson
1953 L.A. Nees
1954 Claude H. Chorpening
1955 R.J. Ivy, T.Y. Lin, Stewart Mitchell, N.R. Rabb, V.J. Richey, and C.F. Scheffey
1956 John Hugh Jones and Robert Horonjeff
1957 Wesley G. Holtz and Harold J. Gibbs
1958 Hamilton Gray
1959 Frank H. Newnam, Jr.
1960 John M. Biggs, Herbert S. Suer and Jacobus M. Louw
1961 T. William J. Lambe
1962 James D. Parsons
1963 F.E. Richart, Jr.
1964 H.W. Reeves
1965 Ralph B. Peck and Tonis Raamaot
1966 William J. Oswald, Clarence G. Golueke, and Donald O. Horning
1967 Leopold H. Just, Ira J. Levy and Vladimir F. Obrician
1968 H. Bolton Seed and Stanley D. Wilson
1969 Melvin L. Baron, Hans H. Bleich, and Joseph P. Wright
1970 Edwin W. Eden, Jr.
1971 Jean J. Janin and Guy F. LeSciellour
1972 Daniel Dicker
1973 James L. Sherard, Rey S. Decker, and Norman L. Ryker
1974 William K. MacKay
1975 Eli Robinsky, Keith E. Bespflug, and Joel P. Leisch
1976 Rodney E. Engelen
1977 Eugene L. Marquis and Graeme D. Weaver
1978 Srikanth Rao, Thomas D. Larson and Theodore H. Poister
1979 Charles G. Schilling and Karl H. Klippstein
1980 A. James Birkmyer

The ASCE State-of-the-Art Civil Engineering Award, a plaque and a certificate, annually honors the author(s) of a paper reviewing and interpreting the state-of-the-art of the benefit of colleagues in the field. A committee selects the winner.

1968 **Boris Bresler** and **James G. MacGregor**
1969 **Ali Sabzevari** and **Robert H. Scanlan**
1970 **William S. Pollard, Jr.**, and **Daniel W. Moore**
1971 **Bramlette McClelland**, **John A. Focht, Jr.**, and **William J. Emrich**
1972 **Flory J. Tamanini**
1973 **The Task Committee on Structural Safety of the Structural Division's Administrative Committee on Analysis and design**, and **Alfredo H.S. Ang** (chairman)
1974 **Joint ASCE-ACI Task Committee 426 on Shear and Diagonal Tension of the Committee on Masonry and Reinforced Concrete of the Structural Division**, and **James G. MacGregor** (chairman)
1975 **Committee on Atmospheric Pollution of the Environmental Engineering Division**
1976 **Richard Field** and **John A. Lager**
1977 **John H. Schmertmann**
1978 **Carl L. Monismith** and **Fred N. Finn**
1979 **John A. Focht, Jr.** and **Leland M. Kraft, Jr.**
1980 **Paul Kruger** and the **Task Committee on Nuclear Effects**

The A.P. Greensfelder Construction Prize, which consists of $150, a plaque and a certificate, annually honors the author(s) of the best original scientific or educational article on construction published in *Civil Engineering*. The executive committee of the construction division selects the winner.

1939 **Howard L. King**
1940 **Russell G. Cone**
1941 **E. Leland Durkee**
1942 **Frederic R. Harris**
1943 **Carl B. Jansen**
1944 **Fred W. Stiefel**
1945 **C. Glenn Cappel**
1946 **George K. Leonard**
1947 **No award**
1948 **C. Glenn Cappel**
1950 **W.C. Mason**
1951 **James G. Tripp**
1952 **John N. Newell**
1953 **Ben C. Gerwick, Jr.**
1954 **Samuel D. Sturgis, Jr.**
1955 **John A. Dominy**, **Charles C. Zellman** and **Henon Pearce**
1956 **Arve S. Wikstrom**
1957 **John N. Newell**
1958 **Myers van Buren**
1959 **Edward E. White**
1960 **Joseph Peraino**
1961 **Gail Knight**
1962 **John W. Fowler**
1963 **Bertold E. Weinberg**
1964 **Robert E. White**
1965 **Gabriel A. Reti**
1966 **Ernest Graves, Jr.**
1967 **Louis W. Riggs, Jr.**
1968 **J.A. Sterner**
1969 **W.W. Wolcott** and **J. Birkmyer**
1970 **Martin S. Kapp**
1971 **Paul J. Varello**
1972 **Carlton T. Wise** and **D.D. Ghelespi**
1973 **Edward Peterson** and **Peter Frobenius**
1974 **Ernest C. Harris** and **John A. Talbott**
1975 **No award**
1976 **A.P. Bezzone**
1977 **Harold G. Arthur**
1978 **Thomas W. Taylor**
1979 **Lawrence W. Gubbe**
1980 **F.B. Couch** and **A.L. Ressi di Cerria**

The Thomas Fitch Rowland Prize, which consists of a certificate and a plaque, is awarded annually for a paper describing accomplished works of construction, including costs and, if applicable, errors in design or execution. The Construction Division's executive committee suggests the winner for ratification by the society's board of directors.

1883 **G. Lindenthal**
1884 **Hamilton Smith, Jr.**
1885 **A.M. Wellington**
1886 **Charles C. Schneider**
1887 **William Metcalf**
1888 **Clemens Herschel**
1889 **James D. Schuyler**
1890 **O. Chanute**, **John F. Wallace** and **William H. Breithaupt**
1891 **William H. Burr**
1892 **Samuel M. Rowe**, **Stillman W. Robinson**, and **Henry H. Quimby**
1893 **William Murray Black**
1894 **David L. Barnes**
1895 **William R. Hill**
1896 **H. St. L. Coppee**
1897 **Arthur L. Adams**
1898 **Henry Goldmark**
1899 **R.S. Buck**
1900 **Allen Hazen**
1901 **L.G. Montony**
1902 **William W. Harts**
1903 **George W. Fuller**
1904 **George Cecil Kenyon**
1905 **Charles L. Harrison** and **Silas H. Woodward**
1906 **George B. Francis** and **W.F. Dennis**
1907 **James D. Schuyler**
1908 **Edward E. Wall**
1909 **William J. Wilgus**
1910 **John H. Gregory**
1911 **B.H.M. Hewitt** and **W.L. Brown**
1912 **Eugene Klapp** and **W.J. Douglas**
1913 **Burgis G. Coy**
1914 **H. T. Cory**
1915 **Charles W. Staniford**
1916 **E.L. Sayers** and **A.C. Polk**
1917 **John Vipond Davies**
1918 **F.W. Scheidenhelm**
1919 **O.H. Ammann**
1920 **Charles Evan Fowler**
1921 **Ernest E. Howard**
1922 **Gustav Lindenthal**
1923 **F.W. Peek, Jr.**
1924 **No award**
1925 **H. de B. Parsons**
1926 **Nicholas S. Hill Jr.**
1927 **L.S. Stiles**
1928 **Roderick B. Young**
1929 **D.B. Steinman** and **William G. Grove**
1930 **R. McC. Beanfield**
1931 **Samuel A. Greeley** and **William D. Hatfield**
1932 **Clifford Allen Betts**
1933 **J.C. Baxter**
1934 **Miles J. Killmer**
1935 **W.H. Kirkbride**

1936 A.V. Karpov and R.L. Templin
1937 Eugene A. Hardin
1938-40 No awards
1940 J.D. Galloway
1941 O.J. Todd and S. Eliassen
1942 Shortridge Hardesty and Alfred Hedefine
1943 Paul Baumann
1944 Eugene L. Grant
1945 Donald N. Becker
1946 James B. Hays
1947 R.F. Blanks and H.S. Meissner
1948 M.M. Fitzhugh, J.S. Miller, and Karl Terzaghi
1949 H.M. Westergaard
1950 R.N. Bergendoff and Josef Sorkin
1951 William K. Boyd and Charles R. Foster
1952 Clarence E. Keefer
1953 E. Montford Fucik
1954 A. Warren Simonds
1955 Maurice N. Quade
1956 Jonathan Jones
1957 Harry N. Hill, Ernest C. Hartmann, and John Wood Clark
1958 Charles I. Mansur and Robert I. Kaufman
1959 J. George Thon and Gordon L. Coltrin
1960 Jack W. Hilf
1961 H. Bolton Seed, Robert I. McNeill, and Jacques de Guenin
1962 James D. Parsons
1963 Marvin J. Kudroff
1964 Francis E. Mullen
1965 Kent S. Ehrman
1966 L. Earl Tabler, Jr.
1967 John W. Kinney, Herman Rothman and Frank Stahl
1968 C. Y. Lin
1969 James Douglas
1970 Norman L. Liver
1971 Richard E. Whitaker
1972 Hans Sacrison
1973 John V. Bartlett, Tadeusz M. Noskiewicz, and James A. Ramsay
1974 Russell C. Borden and Carl E. Selander
1975 No award
1976 Daniel J. Smith, Jr.
1977 Thor L. Anderson and Melvin C. Williams
1978 Charles H. Thornton and Paul A. Gossen
1979 Marcello H. Soto
1980 Laurent Hamel and David M. Nixon

The Construction Management Award, which consists of a plaque and a certificate, is awarded annually to a society member for a contribution to construction management in general and the application of theoretical aspects of engineering in particular. The executive commjittee of the Construction Division selects the recipient.

1974 Joseph C. Kellogg
1975 James Douglas
1976 James J. O'Brien
1977 John W. Fondahl
1978 Louis R. Shaffer
1979 Robert L. Peurifoy
1980 Rolland Melvin Wilkening

The Theodore von Karman Medal annually recognizes distinguished achievement in engineering, mechanics in any branch of civil engineering. A committee selects the winner.

1960 William Prager
1961 R.D. Mindlin
1962 Nathan M. Newmark
1963 Hunter Rouse
1964 Eric Reissner
1965 Warner T. Koiter
1966 Daniel C. Drucker
1967 Maurice A. Biot
1968 Lloyd H. Donnell
1969 Sir Geoffrey Ingram Taylor
1970 Wilhelm Flugge
1971 Alfred M. Freudenthal
1972 Nicholas J. Hoff
1973 Hans H. Bleich
1974 George W. Housner
1975 John H. Argyris
1976 Yuan-Chang B. Fung
1977 George Francis Carrier
1978 Rodney Hill
1979 Henry L. Langhaar
1980 George Herrmann

The Nathan M. Newmark Medal, which is of gold and is accompanied by a certificate, annually goes to a society member for substantially strengthening the scientific base of structural engineering. A committee selects the winner.

1976 John E. Goldberg
1977 Melvin Baron
1978 Anestis S. Veletsos
1979 Ray W. Clough
1980 Olgierd C. Zienkiewicz

The Alfred M. Freudenthal Medal biennially honors distinguished achievement in safety and reliability studies applicable to civil engineering. A committee chooses the recipient.

1976 Emilio Rosenbleuth
1978 Masanobu Shinozuka
1980 Jack R. Benjamin

The Rudolph Hering Medal is now given annually to the author(s) of a paper on water works, sewerage works, drainage, refuse collection and disposal or environmental engineering. A three-member committee of the Environmental Engineering Division selects the winner.

1927 Harrison P. Eddy
1931 Samuel A. Greeley and W.D. Hatfield
1935 John H. Gregory, R.H. Simpson, Orris Bonney, and Robert A. Allton
1937 W.W. Horner and F.L. Flynt
1939 A.J. Schafmayer and B.E. Grant
1940 J.W. Ellms
1941 Thomas H. Wiggin
1942 Robert T. Regester
1943 George J. Schroepfer
1945 Langdon Pearse
1947 A.L. Genter
1948 C.E. Jacob
1953 Ralph Stone and William F. Garber
1954 Harold A. Thomas, Jr. and Ralph S. Archibald
1955 W.F. Langelier, Harvey F. Ludwig, and Russell G. Ludwig
1956 Thomas R. Camp
1957 Alfred C. Ingersoll, Jack E. McKee, and Norman H. Brooks
1958 William I. Oswald and Harold B. Gotaas
1959 Donald J. O'Connor and William E. Dobbins
1960 Charles G. Gunnerson
1961 A.L. Tholin and Clint J. Keifer

1962 **A.M. Rawn**, **F.R. Bowermann**, and **Norman H. Brooks**
1963 **Peter A. Krenkel** and **Gerald T. Orlob**
1964 **Ross E. McKinney**
1965 **William E. Dobbins**
1966 **Donald J. O'Connor**
1967 **Charles G. Gunnerson**
1968 **Robert L. Johnson** and **John L. Cleasby**
1969 **Raymond C. Loehr** and **Robert W. Agnew**
1970 **Kou-Ying Hsung** and **John L. Cleasby**
1971 **Committee on Environmental Quality Management of the Sanitary Engineering Division**
1972 **Harvey F. Collins**, **Robert E. Selleck**, and **George C. White**
1973 **John D. Parkhurst** and **Richard D. Pomeroy**
1974 **Kenneth S. Price** and **Richard A. Conway**
1975 **W.C. Boyle**, **P.M. Berthouex**, and **T.C. Rooney**
1976 **C.F. Guarino**, **M.D. Nelson** and **A.B. Edwards**
1977 **William F. Garber**, **George T. Ohara**, and **Sagar K. Raksit**
1978 **David Di Gregorio** and **Gerald L. Shell**
1979 **John T. Novak**, **Harry Becker** and **Andrew Zurrow**
1980 **John C. Crittenden** and **Walter J. Weber**

The Samuel Arnold Greeley Award, a plaque, is awarded as merited to the author(s) of a paper, making the most valuable contribution to environmental engineering.

1969 **Thomas R. Camp** and **S. David Graber**
1970 **Roy E. Ramseier**
1971 **Robert C. Moore**
1972 **No award**
1973 **Ralph G. Berk**
1974 **James A. Mueller**, **Thomas J. Mulligan**, and **Dominic M. DiToro**
1975 **No award**
1976 **Ralph Stone**
1977 **David L. Eisenhauer**, **Ronald B. Sieger**, and **Denny S. Parker**
1978 **No award**
1979 **No award**
1980 **Otto Brody**

The Wesley W. Horner Award, a plaque and a certificate, annually recognizes the author(s) of a meritorious paper on hydrology, urban drainage or sewerage. A committee of the Environmental Engineering Division selects a nominee.

1969 **David M. Greer** and **Douglas C. Moorhouse**
1970 **Joseph A. Cotteral, Jr.** and **Dan P. Norris**
1971 **Raymond M. Bremner**
1972 **No award**
1973 **No award**
1974 **Charles V. Gibbs**, **Stuart M. Alexander**, and **Curtis F. Leiser**
1975 **C.G. Gunnerson**
1976 **W.R. Giessner**, **R.T. Cockburn**, **F.H. Moss** and **M.E. Noonan**
1977 **Naresh K. Rohatgi** and **Kenneth Y. Chen**
1978 **Lars-Eric Janson**, **Stein Bendixen** and **Anders Harlaut**
1979 **Thomas K. Jewell**, **Thomas J. Nunno**, and **Donald D. Adrian**
1980 **Dominic M. Di Toro** and **Mitchell J. Small**

The $1,000 Simon W. Freese Environmental Engineering Award & Lecture, endowed by Freese & Nichols, is awarded annually for a distinguished person to prepare a lecture for the Environmental Engineering Division.

1977 **Daniel A. Okun**
1978 **Russel E. Train**
1979 **Perry J. McCarthy**
1980 **Carmen Guarino**

The Thomas A. Middlebrooks Award, which carries an honorarium determined annually by the executive committee of the Geotechnical Engineering Division, annually honors the author(s) of a paper contributing to geotechnical engineering. Young engineers are given preference by the division's executive committee, which selects the winner.

1956 **Allen J. Curtis** and **Frank E. Richart, Jr.**
1957 **Charles I. Mansure** and **John A. Focht, Jr.**
1958 **H. Bolton Seed** and **Lymon C. Reese**
1959 **Frank E. Richart, Jr.**
1960 **Frank E. Richart, Jr.**
1961 **I.C. Steele** and **J. Barry Cooke**
1962 **James K. Mitchell**
1963 **W.F. Swiger**
1964 **H. Bolton Seed**, **Richard J. Woodward, Jr.**, and **Raymond Lundgren**
1965 **Robert D. Darragh, Jr.**
1966 **Iraj Noorany** and **H. Boltn Seed**
1967 **John Lysmer** and **Frank E. Richart, Jr.**
1968 **Raul J. Marshal** and **Luis Ramirez de Arellano**
1969 **David D'Appolonia**, **Elio D'Appolonia**, and **Richard F. Brissette**
1970 **James K. Mitchell**, **Awtar Singh**, and **Richard Campanella**
1971 **H. Bolton Seed**, **Kenneth L. Lee**, and **I.M. Idriss**
1972 **Clyde N. Baker, Jr.** and **Fazlur Khan**
1973 **James K. Mitchell** and **William S. Gardner**
1974 **Aleksandar S. Vesic**
1975 **Kenneth L. Lee**, **Bobby Dean Adams**, and **Jean-Marie J. Vagneron**
1976 **Kenneth L. Lee**, and **John A. Focht, Jr.**
1977 **George F. Sowers**
1978 **James D. Parsons**
1979 **Bobby O. Hardin**
1980 **James M. Duncan**

The Karl Terzaghi Award, which consists of a $1,000 and a plaque, is usually given biennially to the author(s) of outstanding material on soil mechanics, subsurface or earthwork engineering and subsurface and earthwork construction. The executive committee of the Geotechnical Division selects the winner.

1963 **Arthur Casagrande**
1965 **M. Juul Hvorslev**
1968 **Willard J. Turnbull**
1969 **Ralph B. Peck**
1971 **Laurits Bjerrum**
1973 **H. Bolton Seed**
1975 **T. William Lambe**
1977 **Stanley D. Wilson**
1979 **Gregory P. Tschebotarioff**
1980 **F.E. Richart, Jr.**

The Karl Terzaghi Lectureship honors a distinguished engineer with an invitation to deliver the Terzaghi Lecture to an appropriate meeting of the society. The lecturer, who is selected by the executive committee of the division, receives $300 and a plaque.

1963 **Ralph B. Peck**
1964 **Arthur Casagrande**
1966 **Laurits Bjerrum**
1967 **H. Bolton Seed**
1968 **Philip C. Rutledge**

1969 Stanley D. Wilson
1970 T. William Lambe
1971 John Lowe, III
1972 Bramlette McClelland
1974 F.E. Richart, Jr.
1975 G.G. Meyerhof
1976 Lymon C. Reese
1977 Robert F. Legget
1978 Nathan M. Newmark
1979 George F. Sowers
1980 G.A. Leonards

The Martin S. Kapp Foundation Engineering Award, which consists of a plaque and a certificate, is awarded as merited for the most innovative design or construction of foundations, earthworks, underground construction or retaining structures. The executive committee of the Geotechnical Division nominates the winner.

1974 Anthony J. Tozzoli
1975 Ben C. Gerwick, Jr.
1976 No award
1977 Robert E. White
1978 Henri Vidal
1979 No award
1980 No award

The Karl Emil Hilgard Hydraulic Prize, consisting of a plaque and a certificate, now annually honors the author(s) of a meritorious theoretical or practical paper on a problem of flowing water. The executive committee of the Hydraulics Division selects the recipient.

1941 Thomas R. Camp
1943 Harold A. Thomas and Emil P. Schuleen
1945 L. Standish Hall
1947 A.A. Kalinske
1949 Vito A. Vanoni
1951 Maurice L. Albertson, Y.B. Dai, Randolph A. Jensen, and Hunter Rouse
1953 Arthur T. Ippen
1955 James M. Robertson and Donald Ross
1957 Donald Ross
1959 Emmett M. Laursen
1961 Hunter Rouse, Tien To Siao, and S. Nagaratna m Nagaratnam
1963 Gerald T. Orlob
1965 Francis F. Escoffier and Marden B. Boyd
1967 Hubert J. Tracy
1968 Samuel O. Russel and James W. Ball
1969 Donald Van Sickle
1970 Norman H. Brooks and Robert C. Y. Koh
1971 Edward R. Holley, Donald R. F. Harleman, and Hugo B. Fischer
1972 Robert W. Zeller, John A. Hoopes and Gerard A. Rohlich
1973 Wayne C. Huber, Donald R.F. Harleman, and Patrick J. Ryan
1974 George D. Ashton and John F. Kennedy
1975 Eduard Naudascher and Frederick A. Locher
1976 Task Committee for the Preparation of the Manual on Sedimentation of the Sedimentation Committee of the Hydraulics Division
1977 Poothrikka P. Paily and Enzo O. Macagno
1978 Mehmet S. Uzuner and John F. Kennedy
1979 Victor M. Ponce and Daryl B. Simons
1980 Y.H. Tsai and E.R. Holley

The J.C. Stevens Award, which consists of books usually worth about $50, annually honors the author(s) of a paper on hydraulics, including fluid mechanics and hydrology. The executive committee of the Hydraulics Division selects the winner.

1944 Boris A. Bakhmeteff and Nicholas V. Feodoroff
1945 Thomas R. Camp
1946 John S. McNown
1947 Maurice L. Albertson
1948 Preston T. Bennett
1949 Donald E. Blotcky
1950 William Allan
1951 James S. Holdhusen
1952 Harold R. Henry
1953 No award
1954 W. Douglas Baines
1955 Marion R. Carstens
1956 Serge Leliavsky
1957 Neal E. Minshall
1958 Frederick L. Hotes
1959 Norman H. Brooks
1960 Hans A. Einstein
1961 Daryl B. Simons and Everett V. Richardson
1962 R. Hugh Taylor and John F. Kennedy
1963 Thomas Maddock, Jr. and W.B. Langbein
1964 Herman J. Koloseus
1965 Alvin G. Anderson
1966 John L. French
1967 Richard R. Brock
1968 Ronald W. Jeppson
1969 Fred W. Blaisdell
1970 William W. Sayre
1971 Helmut Kobus
1972 Thomas R. Camp and S. David Graber
1973 Keith D. Stolzenbach and Donald R.F. Harleman
1974 Charles R. Neill
1975 A.R. Thomas
1976 D.L. Fread
1977 C. Samuel Martin and David C. Wigger
1978 Brent D. Taylor and Vito A. Vanoni
1979 George D. Ashton
1980 Charles C. S. Song and Chih Ted Tang

The Royce Tipton Award, a plaque and a certificate, annually honors a society member for a contribution to the advancement of irrigation and drainage engineering. The executive committee of the Irrigation and Draining Division selects the winner.

1966 Harry F. Blaney, Sr.
1967 Sidney T. Harding
1968 Dean F. Peterson, Jr.
1969 Harvey O. Banks
1970 Ellis L. Armstrong
1971 William F. Donnan
1972 George D. Clyde
1973 William R. Gianelli
1974 Arthur D. Soderberg
1975 Charles R. Maierhofer
1976 Jerald E. Christiansen
1977 Arthur F. Pillsbury
1978 Elmer W. Gain
1979 John L. Merriam
1980 Clyde E. Houston

The Stephen D. Bechtel Pipeline Engineering Award, consisting of a plaque and certificate, annually recognizes contributions to pipeline engineering. Each section, branch and technical division may enter the name of a nominee for selection by the executive committee of the Pipeline Division.

1971 Joseph B. Spangler
1972 Nathaniel Clapp

1973 **Eldon V. Hunt**
1974 **Maynard M. Anderson**
1975 **Joe E. Thompson**
1976 **Kenneth E. Britain**
1977 **Robert V. Phillips**
1978 **William A. Hunt**
1979 **Frederick E. Culvern**
1980 **Roland Triay**

The Rickey Medal, which is of gold and is accompanied by a bronze replica and a certificate, is awarded to the author(s) of a paper on hydroelectric engineering. When the medal is not awarded in any particular year, an equivalent cash honorarium may be added to the following year's award. The executive committee of the Power Division selects the winner.

1949 **Fred W. Blaisdell**
1950 **Robert E. Turner**
1952 **Donald J. Bleifuss**
1954 **Julian Hinds**
1955 **Edgar S. Harrison** and **Carl E. Kindsvater**
1956 **Adolf A. Meyer**
1957 **Carlo Semenza** and **Claudio Marcello**
1958 **William F. Uhl**
1959 **James P. Growdon**
1960 **J. Barry Cooke**
1961 **Torald Mundal**
1962 **Calvin V. Davis**
1963 **J. Edgar Revelle** and **John N. Pirok**
1964 **I. Cleveland Steele**
1965 **Ivor L. Pinkerton** and **Eric J. Gibson**
1966 **Ralph W. Spencer**, **Bruce R. Laverty** and **Dean A. Barber**
1967 **Andrew Eberhardt**
1968 **George R. Rich**
1969 **Alfred L. Parme**
1970 **Paul H. Gilbert**
1971 **J. George Thon**, **John W. O'Hara**, and **Clarence H. Whalin**
1972 **Committee on Hydro Power Project Planning and Design of the Power Division**
1974 **Wallace L. Chadwick**
1976 **Edward Loane** and **Franklyn Rogers**
1978 **George P. Palo**
1979 **E. Montford Fucik**
1980 **Wendell E. Johnson**

The Moisseiff Award, which consists of $300, a bronze medal and a certificate, annually recognizes an important paper in the field of structural design, including applied mechanics, theoretical analysis, constructive improvement or related areas. The executive committee of the Structural Division chooses the recipient.

1948 **George Winter**
1949 **Alexander Hrennikoff**
1950 **Nathan M. Newmark**
1951 **Frances R. Shanley**
1952 **Mario G. Salvadori**
1953 **Arthur W. Anderson**, **John A. Blume**, **Henry J. Degenkolb**, **Harold B. Hammill**, **Edward M. Knapik**, **Henry I. Marchand**, **Henry C. Powers**, **John E. Rinne**, **George A. Sedgwick**, and **Harold Q. Shoberg**
1954 **Jerome M. Raphael**
1955 **John M. Biggs**
1956 **George S. Vincent**
1957 **David J. Peery**
1958 **Walter J. Austin**, **Shahen Yegian**, and **Tie P. Tung**
1959 **Alfred L. Parme**
1960 **Frank Baron** and **Harold S. Davis**
1961 **John A. Blume**
1962 **Frank Baron** and **Anthony G. Arioto**
1963 **George S. Vincent**
1964 **Konrad Basler** and **Bruno Thurlimann**
1965 **John H. Wiggins, Jr.**
1966 **Emilio Rosenblueth**
1967 **Le Wu Lu**
1968 **Maxwell G. Lay** and **Theodore V. Galambos**
1969 **John A. Blume**
1970 **Harry H. West** and **Arthur R. Robinson**
1971 **Fred Moses** and **John D. Stevenson**
1972 **Toskikazu Takeda**, **Mete A. Sozen**, and **N. Norby Nielsen**
1973 **Leroy Z. Emkin** and **William A. Litle**
1974 **E. Alfred Picardi**, **Kanu S. Patel**, **Robert D. Logcher**, **Thomas G. Harmon**, **Robert J. Hansen**, **Jose M. Roessett**, and **R. Elangwe Efimba**
1975 **Paul Weidlinger**
1976 **C.S. Lin** and **A. Scordelis**
1977 **C. Allin Cornell** and **Hans A. Merz**
1978 **Robert Park** and **Shafiqui Islam**
1979 **Steven E. Ramberg** and **Owen M. Griffin**
1980 **Arthur A. Huckelbridge** and **Ray W. Clough**

The T.Y. Lin Award which consists of a $500 honorarium, a plaque and a certificate, annually goes to the author(s) of a meritorious paper written by members of the society or a student chapter dealing with prestressed concrete. The committee which recommends the winner to the board of directors gives preference to a younger author.

1969 **Robert F. Mast**
1970 **Howard W. Wahl** and **Richard J. Kosiba**
1971 **Arthur R. Anderson** and **Saad E. Moustafa**
1972 **Stanley L. Paul**
1973 **Robert F. Mast** and **Charles W. Dolan**
1974 **Raouf Sinno** and **Howard L. Furr**
1975 **Paul Zia** and **W.D. McGee**
1976 **Maher K. Tadros**, **Amin Ghali**, and **Walter H. Dilger**
1977 **Zdenek P. Bazant**, **Domingo J. Carriera**, and **Adolf Walser**
1978 **S.E. Moustafa**
1979 **George B. Barney**, **W. Gene Corley**, **John M. Hanson** and **Richard A. Parmlee**
1980 **A.F. Naaman** and **A. Siriaksorn**

The Raymond C. Reese Research Prize, consisting of a plaque and a certificate, annually honors a notable achievement in research related to structural engineering and its application. The Structural Division selects a nominee for ratifiation by the board of directors.

1970 **James O. Jirsa**, **Meta A. Sozen** and **Chester P. Siess**
1971 **John F. Wiss** and **Otto E. Curth**
1972 **Munther J. Haddadin**, **Sheu Tien Hong** and **Alan H. Mattock**
1973 **Richard A. Parmelee** and **John H. Wronkiewicz**
1974 **Peter W. Chen** and **Leslie E. Robertson**
1975 **R.J. Hansen**, **J.W. Reed**, and **E.H. Vanmarcke**
1976 **Joint ASCE-ACI Task Committee 426 on Shear and Diagonal Tension of the Committee on Masonry and Reinforced Concrete of the Structural Division.**
1977 **Ingvar H.E. Nilsson** and **Anders Losberg**
1978 **Hotten A. Elleby**, **Wallace W. Sanders, Jr.**, **F. Wayne Klaiber** and **M. Douglas Reeves**
1979 **James G. MacGregor** and **Sven E. Hage**

1980 **Lawrence F. Kahn** and **Robert D. Hanson**

The Surveying and Mapping Award, a plaque and certificate, is awarded annually to a society member for a contribution to the advancement of surveying and mapping. The executive committee of the Surveying and Mapping division recommends the recipient to the board of directors.

1970 **B. Austin Barry**
1971 **Curtis M. Brown**
1972 **William A. Radlinski**
1973 **Philip Kissam**
1974 **George D. Whitmore**
1975 **No award**
1976 **Kenneth S. Curtis**
1977 **Morris M. Thompson**
1978 **Robert H. Lyddan**
1979 **Eldon C. Wagner**
1980 **Ira Alexander**

The Julian Hinds Award, which carries a $1,000 cash prize plus a plaque certificate, annually recognizes a paper which makes a meritorious contribution to the field of water resources development. A committee of the Water Resources Planning and Management Division selects the winner.

1975 **Victor A. Koelzer**
1976 **Harry O. Banks**
1977 **Eugene W. Weber**
1978 **Ray K. Linsley**
1979 **Carl E. Kindsvater**
1980 **Dean F. Peterson**

The John G. Moffat-Frank A. Nichol Harbor and Coastal Engineering Award consisting of an honorarium and a certificate annually goes to a member for contributions to harbor and coastal engineering. A committee annually selects the winner and re-establishes the amount of the cash award every three years.

1978 **Robert L. Wiegel**
1979 **Thorndike Saville, Jr.**
1980 **Omar J. Lillievang**

The Collingwood Prize, which is comprised of a plaque and a certificate, annually goes to the author(s) of a paper describing engineering work with which they have been directly connected, recording investigations of engineering knowledge and containing a rational digest of the results. Both technical factors and style are considered by the judges in selecting the winner, who must be a society associate member.

1895 **Morton L. Byers**
1896 **Herbert Waldo York**
1897 **No award**
1898 **No award**
1899 **Julius Kahn**
1900 **Robert P. Woods**
1901 **F.A. Kummer**
1902 **No award**
1903 **Isaac Harby**
1904 **Herbert J. Wild**
1905 **E.P. Goodrich**
1906 **No award**
1907 **No award**
1908 **D.W. Krellwitz**
1909 **H.L. Wiley**
1910 **No award**
1911 **A. Kempkey, Jr.**
1912 **W.W. Clifford**
1913 **No award**
1914 **J.S. Longwell**
1915 **George Schobinger**
1916 **Harold Perrine** and **George E. Strehan**
1917 **Clement E. Chase**
1918 **James B. Hays**
1919 **Floyd A. Nagler**
1920 **Floyd A. Nagler**
1921 **L. Standish Hall**
1923 **Jacob Feld**
1924 **No award**
1925 **No award**
1926 **Cecil Vivian Von Abo**
1927 **William Breuer**
1928 **Franklin Hudson, Jr.**
1929 **William J. Cox**
1930 **No award**
1931 **No award**
1932 **A.R.C. Markl**
1933 **Bernard L. Weiner**
1934 **G.H. Hickox** and **G.O. Wessenauer**
1935 **C. Maxwell Stanley**
1936 **Clinton Morse**
1937 **Victor L. Streeter**
1938 **Douglas M. Stewart**
1939 **B.K. Hough, Jr.**
1940 **Kenneth D. Nichols**
1941 **Elmer Rock**
1942 **John F. Curtin**
1943 **Roy K. Linsley, Jr.** and **William C. Ackermann**
1944 **Walter L. Moore**
1945 **Carl E. Lindsvater**
1946 **C.O. Clark**
1947 **F.L. Ehasz**
1948 **John K. Yennard**
1949 **Alfred Machis**
1950 **Charles A. Lee** and **Charles E. Bowers**
1951 **John W. Forster** and **A. Skrinde**
1952 **T. William Lambe**
1953 **Kuang-Han Chu**
1954 **Vaughn E. Hansen**
1955 **William J. Bauer**
1956 **John H. Schmertmann**
1957 **George E. MacDonald**
1958 **Turgut Sarpkaya**
1959 **Norman H. Brooks**
1960 **Ralph L. Barnett**
1961 **Sidney A. Guralnick**
1962 **Ronald T. McLaughlin**
1963 **Robert L. Kondner**
1964 **Melvin T. Davisson** and **Henry L. Gill**
1965 **George G. Goble**
1966 **Russel C. Jones** and **John A. Hribar**
1967 **Richard N. White** and **Pen Jeng Fang**
1968 **Maurice L. Sharp**
1969 **Richard D. Woods**
1970 **Kenneth L. Lee** and **C.K. Shen**
1971 **P. Aarne Vesilind**
1972 **James M. Duncan** and **G. Wayne Clough**
1973 **Thomas M. Lee**
1974 **James C. Anderson** and **Raj P. Gupta**
1975 **Yuet Tsui** and **G. Wayne Clough**
1976 **John F. Novak** and **Gail E. Montgomery**
1977 **Ronald S. Steiner**
1978 **Nolan L. Johnson, Jr.**
1979 **Jean M. E. Audibert** and **Kenneth J. Nyman**
1980 **Phillip J.W. Roberts**

The James Laurie Prize, consisting of a plaque and a certificate, annually honors a member of the society for contributions to transportation engineering. Each section, branch and technical division may enter the name of a nominee for selection by the board of directors.

1913 M.M. O'Shaughnessy
1914 Samuel Tobias Wagner
1915 J.E. Greiner
1916 William G. Grove and Henry Taylor
1917 H.R. Stanford
1918 Charles W. Staniford
1919 F.W. Gardiner and S. Johannesson
1920 Dabney H. Maury
1921 W.C. Curd
1922 Arthur T. Safford and Edward Pierce Hamilton
1923 R.W. Gausmann and C.M. Madden
1924 C.M. Allen and I.A. Winter
1925 William Kelly
1926 Lewis A. Perry
1927 John R. Baylis
1928 James F. Case
1929 R.H. Keays
1930 John H. Gregory, C.B. Hoover, and C.B. Cornell
1931 No award
1932 Earl I. Brown
1933 W.W. Saunders
1934 E.W. Bowden and H.R. Seely
1935 Wilson T. Ballard
1936 Paul Baumann
1937 Boris A. Bakhmeteff and Arthur E. Matzke
1938 Leon S. Moissieff
1939 Stanley M. Dore
1940 A.M. Rawn, A. Perry Banta, and Richard Pomeroy
1941 Samuel A. Greeley
1942 W. Watters Pagon
1943 T.A. Middlebrooks
1944 Gordon R. Williams
1945 Ole Singstad
1946 L.A. Schmidt, Jr.
1947 Ross M. Riegel
1948 Hyde Forbes
1949 G.H. Hickox, A.J. Peterka, and R.A. Elder
1950 Harris G. Epstein
1951 Hans M. Bleich
1952 John M. Kyle
1953 Harold N. Fisk
1954 Thomas A. Middlebrooks
1955 Joseph N. Bradley
1956 Samuel I. Zack
1957 Walter L. Dickey and Glenn B. Woodruff
1958 Chesley J. Posey
1959 Bramlette McClelland and John A. Focht, Jr.
1960 Ernest F. Masur
1961 J. Barry Cooke
1962 Marvin Gates
1963 Norman J. Magneson
1964 Jean J. Martin
1965 Gail B. Knight
1966 Kenneth B. Woods
1967 Harmer E. Davis
1968 Robert Horonjeff
1969 Walter S. Douglas
1970 Charles E. Shumate
1971 Francis C. Turner
1972 Donald S. Berry
1973 Robert W. Brannan
1974 William A. Bugge
1975 Thomas M. Sullivan
1976 John Veerling
1977 Milton Pikarsky
1978 Willard F. Babcock
1979 Raymond Hodge
1980 Ronald W. Pulling

The Daniel W. Mead Prize is awarded annually to an associate member and a student for a meritorious paper on professional ethics. The award is a certificate. Associate members' submissions are judged by the Committee on Younger Members and those of students are judges by the Committee on Student Chapters.

ASSOCIATE MEMBERS

1940 Allen Jones, Jr.
1941 Don. P. Reynolds
1942-48 No awards
1949 S.L. McFarland
1950 Roy G. Cappel
1951 Edgar G. Baugh
1952 Howard L. Payne
1953 Charles William Griffin, Jr.
1954 Alfred E. Waters, II
1955 Merle H. Banta
1956 Robert A. Schaack
1957 Robert S. Braden
1958 No award
1959 Morgan I. Doyne
1960 James M. Abernathy
1961 Donald B. Baldwin
1962 James I. Taylor
1963 T.A. Faulhaber
1964 Francis Pandullo
1965 Paul M. Wright
1966 L. Douglas James
1967 Donald R. Buettner
1968 Francis A. Paul
1969 Theodore Fellinger
1970 Chester Lee Allen
1971 Charles G. Sudduth
1972 Charles R. Shrader
1973 No award
1974 John E. Spitko, Jr.
1975 Allen W. Hatheway
1976 Glenn R. Koepp
1977 Victor A. Perry, III
1978 A. Colin Lauchlan
1979 David T. Biggs
1980 Thomas A. McCrate

STUDENTS

1940 Harry A. Balmer
1941 Edward Wesp, Jr.
1942 Alfred C. Ingersoll
1943-46 No awards
1947 Lonnie G. Lamon
1948 Frank J. Kersnar
1949 William H. Blair
1950 Gordon L. Laverty
1951 Marion K. Harris
1952 Charles E. Negus, Jr.
1953 Carl Alan Rambow
1954 William H. Blackmer
1955 Jeremiah E. Abbott
1956 James Moser Anderson
1957 Robert Frowein
1958 William G. Benko
1959 L.G. McLaren
1960 Jack Keiser
1961 Robert A. Creed
1962 James R. Wright
1963 David H. Adams
1964 Dabney S. Cradock, III

1965 George E. Hunter
1966 Jerome W. Sargent
1967 Harald G. Biedermann
1968 Charles R. Schrader
1969 Theodore Fellinger
1970 Chester Lee Allen
1971 David Mann
1972 No award
1973 Harold H. Wagle
1974 Terry L. Turnock
1975 Thomas J. McCollough
1976 James P. Kiser
1977 Keith Strickland
1978 John S. Bruce
1979 Alice A. Tulloch
1980 Karen Kirk

The Walter L. Huber Civil Engineering Research Prize, consisting of $100 and a certificate, goes annually to no more than five members of the society, generally under 40 years of age, to recognize notable achievements in research and to encourage continued efforts. The Committee on Research reviews nominations submitted by divisions of the society.

1949 John S. McNown
1950-54 No awards
1955 Lynn S. Beedle
Eivind Hognestad
Philip F. Morgan
1956 Vinton Walker Bacon
Fred Burggraf
Chester Paul Siess
1957 Mikael Juul Hvorslev
Bruce G. Johnston
Lorenz G. Straub
1958 John Wood Clark
Hans A. Einstein
Warren J. Kaufman
Raymond D. Mindlin
Ivan M. Viest
1959 Charles L. Bretschneider
Norman H. Brooks
Arthur Casagrande
George S. Vincent
Daniel Frederick
1960 Ray W. Clough
Phil M. Ferguson
Donald R.F. Harleman
Bruno Thurlimann
David K. Todd
1961 Emmett M. Laursen
William H. Munse
H. Bolton Seed
Anestis Veletsos
Stanley D. Wilson
1962 Ven Te Chow
William Joel Hall
Alan Hanson Mattock
Robert V. Whitman
Robert L. Wiegel
1963 Peter S. Eagleson
Robert M. Haythornthwaite
Houssam M. Karara
Thorndike Saville, Jr.
Mete A. Sozen
1964 Steven J. Fenves
Theodore V. Galambos
John F. Kennedy
Perry L. McCarthy
Emilio Rosenblueth
1965 Herman Bouwer
James K. Mitchell
Joseph Penzien
Gordon G. Robeck
Rudolph P. Savage
1966 Melvin L. Baron
Louis R. Shaffer
George C. Driscoll
William W. Sayre
Paul W. Shuldiner
1967 Jack G. Pouwkamp
George Bugliarello
Donald L. Dean
T. Cameron Kenney
James M. Symons
1968 Alfredo H.S. Ang
Bobby O. Hardin
Marvin E. Jensen
Eduard Naudascher
Jimmie E. Quon
1969 John W. Fisher
Cyril J. Galvin
Charles C. Ladd
Arthur R. Robinson
Ronald F. Scott
1970 Kenneth L. Lee
Daniel P. Loucks
Lucien A. Schmit
Marshall R. Thompson
Jan Van Schilfgaarde
1971 Carl A. Cornell
Marvin Gates
Raymond J. Krizek
Norbert R. Morgenstern
Kam Wu Wong
1972 John A. Hoopes
William B. Ledbetter
Roy E. Olson
Masanobu Shinozuka
Robert L. Street
1973 Charles G. Culver
James M. Duncan
Lee E. King
John T. Oden
Chih Ted Yang
1974 Asit K. Biswas
Hugo B. Fischer
Alfred J. Hendron, Jr.
Thaomas T.C. Hsu
Paul C. Jennings
1975 Anil K. Chopra
Izzat M. Idriss
Ignacio Rodriguez-Iturbe
Larry A. Roesner
Don James Wood
1976 Zdenek F. Bazant
Danny L. Fread
Lester A. Hoel
Paul H. King
John Lysmer
1977 Ted B. Belytschko
G. Wayne Clough
David H. Marks
James P. Tullis
Harry G. Wenzel
1978 John D. Borcherding
Thomas J.R. Hughes
Tin-Kan Hung
James O. Jirsa
Phillip L.-F. Liu

1979 **Daniel W. Halpin**
Ju-Chang Huang
Hon-Yim Ko
Ruh-Ming Li
Keith D. Stolzenbach
1980 **Robert M. Clark**
Vincent P. Drnevich
Clive L. Dym
Bruce R. Ellingwood
Boyd C. Paulson, Jr.

The Ernest E. Howard Award, consisting of $300, a gold medal and a bronze replica, annually honors a member for contributions to structural engineering. A committee nominates the recipient for ratification by the Board of Directors.

1956 **Ralph E. Boeck**
1957 **William E. Dean, Jr.**
1958 **Nathan M. Newmark**
1959 **David B. Steinman**
1960 **Othmar H. Ammann**
1961 **Herschel H. Allen**
1962 **John A. Blume**
1963 **Lynn S. Beedle** and **Theodore R. Higgins**
1964 **Fred N. Severud**
1965 **Henry J. Brunnier**
1966 **T.Y. Lin**
1967 **Henry J. Degenkolb**
1968 **Chester P. Siess**
1969 **Thomas C. Kavanagh**
1970 **Ray W. Clough**
1971 **Stephenson B. Barnes**
1972 **George S. Richardson**
1973 **C. Martin Duke**
1974 **Bruce G. Johnston**
1975 **George E. Brandow**
1976 **Egor P. Popov**
1977 **Fazlur R. Khan**
1978 **Arsham Amirikian**
1979 **John W. Fisher**
1980 **Gerard Fox**

The Edmund Friedman Professional Recognition Award, a plaque, medal and certificate, annually honors a member judged to have contributed substantially to the profession by exemplary professional conduct, lasting achievement, an established reputation for professional service, significant contributions to the profession and other evidence of having advanced the society's objectives. A committee selects the winner.

1960 **E. Lawrence Chandler**
1961 **Finley B. Laverty**
1962 **Lloyd D. Knapp**
1963 **Donald H. Mattern**
1964 **Thomas R. Camp**
1965 **Harold T. Larsen**
1966 **Edwin C. Franzen**
1967 **Lawrence A. Elsener**
1968 **Walter E. Jessup**
1969 **Alfred C. Ingersoll**
1970 **Orley O. Phillips**
1971 **Elmer K. Timby**
1972 **Leo W. Ruth, Jr.**
1973 **Fred J. Benson**
1974 **Billy T. Sumner**
1975 **John W. Frazier**
1976 **Jack E. McKee**
1977 **Herbert A. Goetsch**
1978 **Willa W. Mylroie**
1979 **Myron D. Calkins**
1980 **Edward Wilson**

The Civil Government Award is made annually for meritorious achievements made by a society member by public service in an elective or appointive position in civil government. A committee selects the recipient of the plaque and certificate.

1964 **James K. Carr**
1965 **George D. Clyde**
1966 **Robert B. Pease**
1967 **Vinton W. Bacon**
1968 **No award**
1969 **William J. Hedley**
1970 **W. Scott McDonald**
1971 **Ben E. Nutter**
1972 **Kenneth A. Gibson**
1973 **Milton Pikarsky**
1974 **John W. Frazier**
1975 **Raymond J. Smit**
1976 **Floyd D. Peterson**
1977 **Martin Lang**
1978 **Leroy F. Greene**
1979 **John C. Kohl**
1980 **No award**

The Civil Engineering History and Heritage Award, a plaque and a certificate, annually honors contributions toward better knowledge or appreciation of the history of the professional. A committee selects the winner.

1966 **James K. Finch**
1968 **Ulysses S. Grant, III**
1969 **Gail A. Hathaway**
1970 **Stanley B. Hamilton**
1971 **Carl W. Condit**
1972 **Charles J. Merdinger**
1973 **Sara Ruth Watson**
1974 **No award**
1975 **Clifford A. Betts**
1976 **Neal Fitzsimons**
1977 **Joseph J. Rady**
1978 **David McCullough**
1979 **Robert M. Vogel**
1980 **Hunter Rouse**

The National Historic Civil Engineering Landmark Award annually honors nationally significant engineering projects which are designated as National Historic Civil Engineering Landmarks. A bronze plaque denoting this designation is supplied for a presentation ceremony.

1966 **Bollman Truss Bridge** (Savage, Md.)
1967 **Erie Canal** (Rome, N.Y.)
Middlesex Canal (Billerica, Mass.)
1968 **Central Pacific Railroad** (Sacramento, Calif.)
Durango Silverton Branch of the Denver & Rio Grande Western Railroad (Durango, Colo.)
Acequias of San Antonio (San Antonio, Texas)
Canal and Locks of the Potowmack Canal (Great Falls, Va.)
Joining of the Rails of the Transcontinental Railroad (Promontory Point, Utah)
Wheeling Suspension Bridge (Wheeling, W. Va.)
Ellicott's Stone (Mobile County, Ala.)
1969 **Charleston Hamburg Railroad** (Charleston to Hamburg, S.C.)
Alvord Lake Bridge (Golden Gate State Park, San Francisco, Calif.)
1970 **Cornish-Windsor Covered Bridge** (Windsor, Vt.)

Bridgeport Covered Bridge (Nevada County, Calif.)
Ascutney Mill Dam (Windsor, Vt.)
Frankford Avenue Bridge (Philadelphia, Pa.)
Union Canal Tunnel (Lebanon, Pa.)
Theodore Roosevelt Dam and Salt River Project (Near Phoenix, Ariz.)

1971 **The Mormon Tabernacle** (Salt Lake City, Utah)
Druid Lake Dam (Baltimore, Md.)
Old Bethlehem Waterworks (Bethlehem, Pa.)
First Owen's River Los Angeles Aqueduct (Inyo, Calif.; Kern & Los Angeles Counties, Calif.)
Eads Bridge (St. Louis, Mo.)

1972 **Miami Conservancy District** (Dayton, Ohio)
Gunnison Tunnel (Montrose, Colo.)
Roebling's Delaware Aqueduct (Lakawaxen, Pa.)
Chesborough's Chicago Water Supply System (Chicago, Ill.)
Cabin John Aqueduct (Cabin John, Md.)
Brooklyn Bridge (Brooklyn, N.Y.)

1973 **Buffalo Bill Dam** (Cody, Wyo.)
Pelton Impulse Water Wheel (Camptonville, Calif.)
Starrucca Viaduct (Lanesboro, Pa.)
Cheesman Dam (Denver, Colo.)
Ingalls Building (Cincinnati, Ohio)
Embudo, New Mexico Stream Gaging Station (Embudo, N.M.)

1974 **Milwaukee, Wisconsin, Metropolitan Sewage Treatment Plant**
Kansas City, Missouri, Park and Boulevard System
Philadelphia (Pennsylvania), Municipal Water Supply System
Stone Arch Bridge of the Burlington Northern Railroad at Minneapolis, Minnesota

1975 **Folsom Hydroelectric Power System** (Folsom, Calif.)
Lawrence Experiment Station (Lawrence, Mass.)
Marlette Lake Water System (Virginia and Gold Hill Water Company, Virginia City, Nev.)
Croton Water Supply Station (New York, N.Y.)
Hoosac Tunnel (Florida, Mass.)
Castillo De San Marcos (St. Augustine, Fla.)
Granite Railway (Quincy, Mass.)
Smithfield Street Bridge (Pittsburgh, Pa.)
Mount Washington Cog Railway (Mt. Washington, N.H.)
Tunkhannock Viaduc (Nicholson, Pa.)

1976 **The National Road** (Near Zanesville, Ohio)
King's Road (New Smyrna, Fla. to Georgia)
The First Concrete Pavement (Bellfontain, Ohio)
Elephant Butte Dam (Truth or Consequences, New Mexico)
Cumbres and Toltec Scenic Railway (Chama, New Mexico to Antonio, Colo.)
International Boundary Marker #1 (Between the United States and Mexico)
The Crozet's Blue Ridge Tunnel (Rockfish Gap, Afton, Va.)

1977 **First New York City Subway** (New York, N.Y.)
Ward House (Rye, N.Y.)
Minot's Ledge Lighthouse (Cohasset, Mass.)
Vulcan Street Plant (Appleton, Wisc.)
Great Falls Raceway and Power System (Paterson, N.J.)
Reversal of the Chicago River (Ill.)
Mullan Road (Pacific Northwest between Missouri River Basin and Columbia River Basin)
Mason-Dixon Line (Surveying dilenating the boundaries of several states)
Naval Drydocks (Boston, Mass. and Norfolk, Va.)

1978 **The Hudson and Manhattan Railroad Tunnei** (New York, N.Y.-Hoboken, N.J.)
The Boston Subway (Boston, Mass.)
Newark Airport (Newark, N.J.)
United States Military Academy (West Point, N.Y.)
Dunlap's Creek Bridge (Fayette County, Penn.)

1979 **Fink Deck Truss Bridge** (Lynchburg, Va.)
Cleveland Hopkins Airport (Ohio)
Fink Through Truss Bridge (Hamden, N.J.)
Rockville Stone Arch Bridge (Rockville, Penn.)
Moffat Tunnel (west of Denver, Colo)

1980 **Goodyear Airdock** (Akron, Ohio)
Morris Canal Hydraulic Powered Plane System (Northern New Jersey)

The Can-Am Civil Engineering Amity Award, consisting of a plaque and a certificate, annually honors a society member for either a specific instance that has had continuing benefit in understanding and goodwill or a career of professional activity that has contributed to the amity of the U.S. and Canada. A committee selects the winner.

1973 **L. Austin Wright**
1974 **Eugene Weber**
1975 **John B. Stirling**
1976 **John R. Kiely**
1977 **Alan G. Davenport**
1978 **Charles B. Molineaux**
1979 **James G. MacGregor**
1980 **No award**

The Edmund Friedman Young Engineer Award for Professional Achievement, a certificate, annually honors a society member younger than 32 years of age for significant professional achievement, service to the advancement of the profession, evidence of technical competence, high character and integrity, leadership and public service outside the profession. A committee chooses the winner.

1973 **D. Joseph Hagerty**
Gary Parks
J. Lawrence Von Thun

1974 **Eldon A. Cotton**
Fred H. Kulhawy
Bruce F. McCollom
Howard Schirmer, Jr.
Robert P. Wadell

1975 **Norman L. Buehring**
Donn E. Hancher
David B. Neptune
Bruce R. Scott
Edward W. Sizemore

1976 **Dean M. Golden**
Robert E. Heightchew, Jr.
Richard J. Scranton

1977 **Damodar S. Airan**
Joseph P. Klein, III

1978 **James H. Pope**
Daniel P. Sheer

1979 **Benjamin Morris, Jr.**
Robert Yourzak

1980 **Thomas McKenna**

The ASCE President's Award, a plaque bearing the likeness of George Washington, is awarded annually for distinguished service to the country by a society member. The award was created during the Bicentennial

Year in honor of the first President, himself a civil engineer.

1976 Lucius D. Clay
1977 Ben Moreell
1978 George R. Brown
1979 Herbert D. Vogel
1980 Lyman D. Wilbur

The John I. Parcel-Lief J. Sverdrup Civil Engineering Management Award is given annually to a society member for contributions to civil engineering management. The Committee on Engineering Management selects the winner, subject to the Board of Directors ratification.

1977 John Morris
1978 James A. Caywood
1979 Stephen D. Bechtel, Jr.
1980 Frank J. Moolin, Jr.

William H. Walker Award
Allan B. Colburn Award
Professional Progress Award
Founders Award
Alpha Chi Sigma Award
R.H. Wilhelm Award
Award for Service to Society
Award in Chemical Engineering Practice
F.J. Van Antwerpen Award
Institute Lecture

AMERICAN INSTITUTE OF CHEMICAL ENGINEERS
345 E. 47th St., New York, N.Y. 10019 (212/644-8025)

The William H. Walker Award, sponsored by the Monsanto Co., consists of $1,000, a plaque and a certificate and is given annually for an outstanding contribution to the literature of chemical engineering in the form of books, articles or other professional writing. A committee selects the winner.

1936 Allan P. Colburn
1937 Thomas Bradford Drew
1938 Warren L. McCabe
1939 George Granger Brown
1940 Walter L. Badger
1941 Thomas K. Sherwood
1942 E. Clifford Williams
1943 H.F. Johnstone
1944 O.A. Hougen
1945 Hoyt C. Hottel
1946 John H. Walthall and Philip Miller
1947 Manson Benedict and L.C. Rubin
1948 Kenneth M. Watson
1949 W.H. McAdams
1950 Barnett F. Dodge
1951 Richard H. Wilhelm
1952 John Henry Rushton
1953 W.R. Marshall
1954 E.R. Gilliland
1955 Edgar L. Piret
1956 Edward W. Comings
1957 Joseph Clifton Elgin
1958 Robert I. Pigford
1959 Bruce H. Sage
1960 Joe Mauk Smith
1961 Neal R. Amundson
1962 Robert Byron Bird
1963 Robert F. Heybal
1964 Thomas J. Hanratty
1965 Charles R. Wilke
1966 James W. Westwater
1967 John M. Drausnitz
1968 Donald L. Katz
1969 Stuart W. Churchill
1970 Arthur B. Metzner
1971 Theodore Vermeulen
1972 Harry G. Drickamer
1973 J.R. Fair
1974 Leon Lapidus
1975 Edwin N. Lightfoot, Jr.
1976 C. Judson King
1977 L.E. Scriven
1978 Cedomir Sliepcevich
1979 Sheldon K. Friedlander
1980 Not available at press time

The Allan P. Colburn Award, which is sponsored by E.I. du Pont de Nemours, consists of $1,000, a plaque and a certificate and honors meritorious publication in chemical engineering by an Institute member 35 years of age or younger. A committee selects the winner.

1945 Clyde McKinley and Robert R. White
1946 Charles E. Lapple
1947 Harry G. Drickamer
1948 J. Edward Vivian and Roy P. Whitney
1949 E.G. Scheibel
1950 F.M. Tiller
1951 Charles R. Wilke
1952 Thomas Baron and Lloyd G. Alexander
1953 LeRoy Alton Bromley
1954 Harold P. Grace
1955 William E. Ranz
1956 Theodore Weaver
1957 Thomas Joseph Hanratty
1958 Arthur B. Metzner Robert D. Vaughn and George L. Houghton
1959 S.K. Friedlander
1960 L.E. Scriven and Charles V. Sternling
1961 George R. Moore
1962 John M. Prausnitz
1963 Andreas Acrivos
1964 Herbert L. Toor
1965 Byron C. Sakiadis
1966 John A. Quinn
1967 Earl B. Adams and John C. Whitehead
1968 John B. Butt
1969 Edward F. Leonard
1970 Ronald B. Root and Roger A. Schmitz
1971 Dale F. Rudd
1972 Dan Luss
1973 C.A. Eckert
1974 William J. Ward, III
1975 Edward L. Cussler
1976 John H. Seinfeld
1977 Clark Kenneth Colton
1978 L. Gary Leal
1979 James E. Bailey
1980 Not available at press time

The Professional Progress Award in Chemical Engineering, which is sponsored by the Celanese Corp., annually recognizes a significant contribution to the science of chemical engineering made by an individual under 45 years of age. The winner, who receives $1,000 and a certificate, is honored for a theoretical discovery or development of a new principle, development of a new process or product, invention or development of new equipment or distinguished service to the field or to the Institute. A committee selects the recipient.

1948 Allan P. Colburn
1949 Mott Souders, Jr.
1950 Edwin R. Gilliland
1951 Chalmer G. Kirkbride
1952 Richard H. Wilhelm
1953 George E. Holbrook
1954 John Ridgway Bowman
1955 Robert L. Pigford
1956 Robert Roy White
1957 Vladimir Haensel
1958 W. Kenneth Davis
1959 W.R. Marshall, Jr.
1960 William Gardener Pfann
1961 Thomas Baron
1962 Jack A. Gerster
1963 George E.P. Box
1964 Stuart W. Churchill
1965 Robert Byron Bird
1966 Leon Lapidus
1967 Thomas J. Hanratty
1968 Andreas Acrivos
1969 Cornelius J. Pings
1970 James Wei
1971 John S. Bonner
1972 Arthur E. Humphrey
1973 P.L.T. Brian
1974 Julien Szekely
1975 John H. Sinfelt
1976 Kenneth B. Bischoff
1977 Morton M. Denn
1978 John B. Butt
1979 Dan Luss
1980 Not available at press time

The Founders Award, which consists of a certificate and a pin, annually honors members of the Institute who have had a profound effect on chemical engineering and whose achievements have advanced the profession. The Council of the Institute selects the winners.

1958 T.H. Chilton
J.V.N. Dorr
O.A. Hougen
S.D. Kirkpatrick
W.K. Lewis
1959 W.H. McAdams
F.J. Curtis
1960 Walter G. Whitman
Milton C. Whitaker
1961 George E. Holbrook
Warren L. McCabe
1962 Barnett F. Dodge
Joseph H. Koffolt
J. Henry Rushton
1963 John J. Healy, Jr.
Raymond P. Dinsmore
Raymond P. Generaux
Thomas K. Sherwood
1964 Donald L. Katz
Mott Souders, Jr.
1965 Francis C. Frary
Carl F. Prutton
1966 Manson Benedict
Ernest W. Thiele
Edward R. Weidlein
1967 William R. Collings
Hoyt C. Hottel
Chalmer G. Kirkbride
1968 William B. Franklin
William N. Lacey
1969 No award
1970 Jerry McAfee
William A. Cunningham
Walter E. Lobo
Donald B. Keyes
1971 Edwin R. Gilliland
John J. McKetta, Jr.
Paul D.V. Manning
1972 Joseph C. Elgin
Donald A. Dahlstrom
1973 T.A. Burtis
W.R. Marshall
J.J. Martin
R.L. Pigford
1974 W.H. Corcoran
H.D. Guthrie
M.S. Peters
1975 T.W. Tomkowit
Theodore Weaver
1976 Lawrence K. Cecil
Arthur L. Conn
James R. Fair, Jr.
Irving Leibson
1977 Kenneth E. Coulter
Harold S. Kemp
James G. Knudsen
F.J. Van Antwerpen
1978 Ernest B. Christiansen
Klaus D. Timmerhaus
1979 A. Sumner West
1980 Not available at press time

The Alpha Chi Sigma Award in Chemical Engineering Research, which carries a $1,000 honorarium and is accompanied by a certificate, annually honors outstanding achievements in fundamental or applied research carried out during the preceding 10 years. A committee selects the winner.

1966 H.G. Drickamer
1967 Donald B. Broughton
1968 Klaus D. Timmerhaus
1969 Rutherford Aris
1970 A.E. Dukler
1971 John H. Sinfelt
1972 Charles D. Prater
1973 C.J. Pings
1974 Sheldon K. Friedlander
1975 Arnold A. Bondi
1976 Howard Brenner
1977 Eli Ruckenstein
1978 John A. Quinn
1979 Reuel Shinnar
1980 Not available at press time

The R.H. Wilhelm Award in Chemical Reaction Engineering, which is sponsored by the Mobil Oil Corp., consists of $1,000 and a certificate given annually for significant new contributions in the field. A committee selects the winner.

1973 Neal R. Amundson
1974 Michel Boudart
1975 Rutherford Aris
1976 James J. Carberry

1977 Joe Mauk Smith
1978 Paul B. Weisz
1979 Octave Levenspiel
1980 Not available at press time

The $1,000 Award for Service to Society, sponsored by the Fluor Corp., is given annually for outstanding contributions to community service and the solution of socially oriented problems by a chemical engineer. A committee selects the winner, who must be a member of the Institute.

1973 I.K. Cecil
1974 Gerald A. Lessells
1975 John J. McKetta, Jr.
1976 Robert T. Jaske
1977 Frank W. Dittman
1978 Don E. Cox
1979 Gerald L. Decker
1980 Not available at press time

The Award in Chemical Engineering Practice, which carries a $1,000 honorarium and is sponsored by the Bechtel Corp., annually recognizes outstanding contributions by a chemical engineer in the industrial practice of the profession. A committee selects the winner.

1974 Robert G. Heitz
1975 James R. Fair, Jr.
1976 Jacob M. Geist
1977 David Brown
1978 John W. Scott
1979 No award
1980 Not available at press time

The $1,000 F.J. Van Antwerpen Award, which is sponsored by Dow Chemical, is awarded annually to an Institute member for outstanding contributions to the organization. The Council of the Institute selects the winner.

1978 F.J. Van Antwerpen
1979 J. Henry Rushton
1980 Not available at press time

The Institute Lecture is given annually by a member who presents a comprehensive and authoritative review of a field of specialization of the science of chemical engineering.

1949 W.L. McAdams, Massachusetts Institute of Technology
1950 Olaf A. Hougen, University of Wisconsin
1951 T.B. Drew, Columbia University
1952 W.R. Marshall, Jr., University of Wisconsin
1953 G.G. Brow, University of Michigan
1954 Manson Benedict, Massachusetts Institute of Technology
1955 John G. Roberts, E.I. du Pont de Nemours & Co.
1956 W.K. Lewis, Massachusetts Institute of Technology
1957 C.R. Wilke, University of California (Berkeley)
1958 Neal R. Amundson, University of Minnesota
1959 Thomas H. Chilton, University of California (Berkeley)
1960 Joel O. Hougen, Monsanto Chemical Co.
1961 Michael Boudart, University of California (Berkeley)
1962 Hugh M. Hulburt, American Cynamid
1963 Mott Souders, Piedmont, Calif.
1964 J.W. Westwater, University of Illinois
1965 Charles V. Sternling, Shell Development Co.
1966 R.L. Pigford, University of California (Berkeley)
1967 Robert C. Reid, Massachusetts Institute of Technology
1968 James Wei, Mobil Oil Corp.
1969 W.W. Akers, Rice Institute
1970 Henry Rushton, Purdue University
1971 Judson S. Swearingen, Roto Flow Corp.
1972 Aaron J. Teller, Teller Environmental Systems
1973 C.J. King, University of California (Berkeley)
1974 H.C. Hottel, Massachusetts Institute of Technology
1975 Alan S. Michaels, ALZA Research
1976 Arthur E. Humphrey, University of Pennsylvania
1977 Arthur M. Squires, Virginia Polytechnic Institute
1978 Vern W. Weekman, Mobil Research and Development Corp.
1979 James R. Fair, University of Texas
1980 Not available at press time

ASME Engineers Medal
Ralph Coats Roe Medal
Edwin F. Church Medal
Holley Medal
Charles Russ Richards Memorial Award
Gustus L. Larson Memorial Award
Spirit of St. Louis Medal
George Westinghouse Medal
Timoshenko Medal
Machine Design Award
Mayo D. Hersey Award
J. Hall Taylor Medal
Diesel and Gas Engine Power Award
Rufus Oldenburger Medal
R. Tom Sawyer Award
Melville Medal
Worcester Reed Warner Medal
Alfred Noble Prize
Henry Hess Award
Melville Medal
Arthur L. Williston Medal
Charles T. Main Award
"Old Guard" Prize
Blackall Machine Tool and Gauge Award
Prime Movers Committee Award
Gas Turbine Award
Rail Transportation Award
Freeman Scholar Award
Nadai Award
Heat Transfer Memorial Award
Burt L. Newkirk Tribology Award
Codes and Standards Medal
Bernard F. Langer Award
James N. Landis Medal
Harry James Potter Gold Medal
Pressure Vessel and Piping Award
Henry R. Worthington Award

AMERICAN SOCIETY OF MECHANICAL ENGINEERS
345 E. 47th St., New York, N.Y. 10017 (212/644-7722)

The ASME Engineers Medal, which is of gold and carries a $1,000 honorarium, is awarded annually for "eminently distinguished engineering achievement."

1921 Hjalmar G. Carlson
1922 Frederick A. Halsey
1923 John R. Freeman
1924-25 No awards
1926 R. A. Millikan
1927 Wilfred Lewis
1928 Julian Kennedy
1929 No award
1930 W. L. R. Emmet
1931 Albert Kingsbury
1932 No award
1933 Ambrose Swasey
1934 Willis H. Carrier
1935 Charles T. Main
1936 Edward Bausch
1937 Edward P. Bullard
1938 Stephen J. Pigott
1939 James E. Gleason
1940 Charles F. Kettering
1941 Theodore von Karman
1942 Ervin G. Bailey
1943 Lewis K. Sillcox
1944 Edward G. Budd
1945 William F. Durand
1946 Morris E. Leeds
1947 Paul W. Kiefer
1948 Frederick G. Keys
1949 Fred L. Dornbrook
1950 Harvey C. Knowles
1951 Glenn B. Warren
1952 Nevin E. Funk
1953 Crosby Field
1954 E. Burnley Powell
1955 Granville M. Read
1956 Harry F. Vickers
1957 L. M. K. Boelter
1958 Wilbur H. Armacost
1959 Martin Frisch
1960 C. Richard Soderberg
1961 No award
1962 Philip Sporn
1963 Igor I. Sikorsky
1964 Alan Howard
1965 Johnannes M. Burgers
1966 No award
1967 Mayo D. Hersey
1968 Samuel C. Collins
1969 Lloyd H. Donnell
1970 Robert Rowe Gilruth
1971 Horace Smart Beattie
1972 Waloddi Weibull
1973 Christopher C. Kraft, Jr.
1974 Nicholas J. Hoff
1975 Maxime A. Faget
1976 Raymond D. Mindlin
1977 Robert W. Mann
1978 No award
1979 Jacob P. Den Hartog
1980 No award

The Ralph Coats Roe Medal, a bronze medal endowed by Burns & Roe, Inc., is presented annually with a $1,000 honorarium to honor contributions to public understanding of the engineering profession's worth to contemporary society.

1974 Emilio Q. Daddario
1975 Walter Sullivan
1976 No award
1977 Robert C. Seamans, Jr.
1978 David Perlman
1979 William D. Carey
1980 Melvin Kranzberg

The Edwin F. Church Medal, which carries a $1,000 honorarium, annually honors mechanical engineering excellence in its broadest sense, including eminent service in increasing the value, importance and attractiveness of the mechanical engineering education, including in-house, continuing or other training programs as well as programs at universities and technical institutes.

1973 Wilbur Richard Leopold
1974 Hobart A. Weaver
1975 Harry Conn
1976 Frank W. Von Flue
1977 No award
1978 No award
1979 Kenneth A. Roe
1980 Dennis K. Bushnell

The Holley Medal, which is of gold, honors "some great and unique act of genius of an engineering nature which has accomplished a great and timely public benefit."

1924 Hjalmar G. Carlson
1928 Elmer A. Sperry
1930 Baron C. Shiba
1934 Irving Langmuir
1936 Henry Ford
1937 Frederick G. Cottrell
1938 Francis Hodgkinson
1939 Carl E. Johansson
1940 Edwin H. Armstrong
1941 John C. Garand
1942 Ernest O. Lawrence
1943 Vannevar Bush
1944 Carl L. Norden
1945 Sanford A. Moss
1946 Norman Gibson
1947 Raymond D. Johnson
1948 Edwin H. Land
1950 Charles G. Curtis
1951 George R. Fink
1952 Sanford L. Cluett
1953 Philip M. McKenna
1954 Walter A. Shewhart
1955 George J. Hood
1957 Charles S. Draper
1959 Col. Maurice J. Fletcher
1961 Thomas Elmer Moon
1963 William Shockley
1968 Chester F. Carlson
1969 Willis J. Whitfield
1973 Harold E. Edgerton
Kenneth J. Germeshausen
1975 George M. Grover
1976 Emmett N. Leith
Juris Upatnieks
1977 J. David Margerum
1978 No award
j1979 David G. Collipp
Douwe de Vries
1980 Solchiro Honda

The Charles Russ Richards Memorial Award, which is now supported by the Pi Tau Sigma Honorary Mechanical Engineering Fraternity, carries a $1,000 honorarium and recognizes outstanding mid-career mechanical engineering achievement. The recipient must have graduated from a recognized college or university engineering course not more than 25 nor less than 20 years prior to the year in which the award is given.

1947 Jacob P. Den Hartog
1948 No award
1949 Arthur M. Wahl
1950 Burgess H. Jennings
1951 J. Kenneth Salisbury
1952 Jess H. Davis
1953 Thomas M. Lumly
1954 Robert H. Hughes
1955 Sylan Cromer
1956 Everett M. Barber
1957 Wayne C. Edmister
1958 Donald C. Burnham
1959 M. Eugene Merchant
1960 Ascher H. Shapiro
1961 Harrison A. Storm, Jr.
1962 Dudley D. Fuller
1963 George F. Carrier
1964 Simon Ostrach
1965 Leonard J. Koch
1966 J. Lowen Shearer
1967 T. Cyril Noon
1968 Bernard W. Shaffer
1969 Robert E. Uhrig
1970 Ralph G. Nevins
1971 Howard L. Harrison
1972 Charles E. Jones
1973 Ali A. Seireg
1974 Richard J. Grosh
1975 Carl F. Zorowski
1976 Ali Suphi Argon
1977 Hassan A. Hassan
1978 John C. Chato
1979 John H. Lienhard
1980 Albert I. King

The Gustus L. Larson Memorial Award, funded by Pi Tau Sigma, carries a $1,000 honorarium and recognizes outstanding early-career achievement. The recipient must have graduated from a recognized college or university engineering course not more than 20 nor less than 10 years prior to the year in which the award is given.

1975 Chang-Lin Tien
1976 John G. Bollinger
1977 Nam P. Suh
1978 Philip H. Francis
1979 Gerald R. Seemann
1980 Arthur G. Erdman

The Pi Tau Sigma Gold Medal honors a young engineering graduate within 10 years of graduating from a recognized college or university engineering course.

1938 Wilfred E. Johnson
1939 John Yellot, Jr.
1940 George A. Hawkins
1941 R. Hosmer Norris
1942 John T. Rettaliata
1943-46 No awards
1947 David Cochrane
1948 Walter G. Vincenti
1949 Philip S. Meyers
1950 Arthur P. Adamson
1951 Warren M. Rohsenow
1952 Robert L. O'Brien
1953 Merle Baker
1954 Emmett E. Day
1955 Robert C. Dean, Jr.
1956 John A. Clark
1957 Patrick McDonald, Jr.
1958 Allison E. Simons

1959 Donald F. Hays
1960 George Hatsopoulos
1961 Ernest T. Selig
1962 E. Bruce Lee
1963 Herbert Richardson
1964 Richard L. Peskin
1965 John Bollinger
1966 Jason R. Lemon
1967 William O'Donnell
1968 Randall F. Barron
1969 Henry K. Newhall
1970 Richard Elwood Barrett
1971 James R. Rice
1972 John F. Stephens, III
1973 Christian Ernst
Georg Przirembel
1974 Jace W. Nunziato
1975 Ted B. Belytschko
1976 John S. Walker
1977 Richard E. Lovejoy
1978 David A. Peters
1979 No award
1980 Doyle D. Knight

The Spirit of St. Louis Medal, which is of gold, is awarded for meritorious service in the advancement of aeronautics and astronautics

1929 Daniel Guggenheim
1932 Paul Litchfield
1935 Will Rogers
1938 James H. Doolittle
1941 John E. Younger
1944 George W. Lewis
1947 John E. Northrup
1950 Helmut P. Kroon
1954 Arthur E. Raymond
1955 Ralph S. Damon
1958 George S. Schairer
1961 Samuel K. Hoffman
1962 Robert H. Widmer
1963 Frederick C. Crawford
1964 Robert R. Gilruth
1965 William H. Pickering
1966 Christopher C. Kraft
1967 Ira G. Hedrick
1968 George S. Moore
1969 G. Merritt Preston
1970 Clarence L. Johnson
1971 Ralph L. Creel
1972 Neil A. Armstrong
1973 John F. Yardley
1974 Abe Silverstein
1975 No award
1976 No award
1977 George D. McLean
1978 Paul B. MacCready
1979 Sir Freddie Laker
1980 Michael Collins

The George Westinghouse Medal, which is of gold, honors distinguished achievement of service in the power field of mechanical engineering. A second Westinghouse Medal, which is of silver, has been established to honor achievement in the field by an engineer 40 years of age or younger.

GOLD MEDAL

1953 Alexander G. Christie
1954 Walker L. Cisler
1955 Hyman G. Rickover
1956 Perry W. Pratt
1957 Alfred Iddles
1958 Frederick P. Fairchild
1960 Ernest C. Gaston
1961 Gerald V. Williamson
1962 Edwin Holmes Kreig
1963 Abbott L. Penniman, Jr.
1964 Frederick W. Argue
1965 Robert A. Bowman
1966 Robert C. Allen
1967 Robert A. Baker, Sr.
1968 Roland A. Budenholzer
1969 Ralph C. Roe
1970 Charles Aloysius Meyer
Robert C. Spencer, Jr.
1971 Wilfred McGregor Hall
1972 William States Lee
1973 Bernard F. Langer
1974 Charles W. Elston
1975 No award
1976 John W. Simpson
1977 No award
1978 Peter Fortescue
1979 William R. Gould
1980 Fred J. Moody

SILVER MEDAL

1972 William Eugene Rice
1973 Michael A. Ambrose
1974 Shelby L. Owens
1975 No award
1976 Richard V. Shanklin III
1977 James C. Corman
1978 Romano Salvatori
1979 Edward W. Stenby
1980 Robert L. Gamble

The Timoshenko Medal, which is of bronze, recognizes contributions to applied mechanics without restrictions on nationality or profession.

1957 Stephen P. Timoshenko
1958 Arpad L. Nadai
Sir Geoffrey Taylor
Theodore von Karman
1959 Sir Richard Southwell
1960 Cornelius B. Biezano
Richard Grammel
1961 James Norman Goodier
1962 Maurice Anthony Biot
1963 Michael James Lighthill
1964 Raymond D. Mindlin
1965 Sydney Goldstein
1966 William Prager
1967 Hillel Poritsky
1968 Warner T. Koiter
1969 Jakob Ackeret
1970 James Johnston Stoker
1971 Howard Wilson Emmons
1972 Jacob Pieter Den Hartog
1973 Eric Reissner
1974 Albert E. Green
1975 Chia-Chiao Lin
1976 Erastus Henry Lee
1977 John D. Eshelby
1978 George F. Carrier
1979 Jerald L. Ericksen
1980 Paul M. Naghdi

The Machine Design Award, which consists of a bronze plaque, is awarded to honor achievement or service in the field of machine design, including application, research, development or teaching of machine design.

1959 Charles E. Crede
1960 Rudolph E. Peterson
1961 Robert G. LeTourneau
1962 J. F. Downie Smith
1963 Colin Carmichael
1964 Rufus Oldenburger
1965 A. M. Wahl
1966 Beno Sternlicht
1967 Ernest Wildhaber
1968 C. Walton Musser
1969 Eugene L. Radzimovsky
1970 Reynold Benjamin Johnson
1971 Walter L. Starkey
1972 Ferdinand Freudenstein
1974 Allen S. Hall, Jr.
1975 No award
1976 Charles W. Radcliffe
1977 Mathew M. Kuts
1978 Ali A. Seireg
1979 Robert R. Slaymaker
1980 Merhyle F. Spotts

The Mayo D. Hersey Award, which consists of a bronze plaque, recognizes distinguished contributions over a substantial period of time to the advancement of lubrication engineering and science of a pure or applied nature.

1965 Mayo D. Hersey
1966 Harmen Blok
1967 Milton C. Shaw
1968 Ragnar Holm
1969 William A. Zisman
1970 Merrell Robert Fenske
1971 Dudley Dean Fuller
1972 Sydney J. Needs
1973 Donald F. Wilcock
1974 David Tabor
1975 Arthur F. Underwood
1976 John Boyd
1977 Robert L. Johnson
1978 Edward A. Saibel
1979 Duncan Dowson
1980 Nicolae Tipei

The J. Hall Taylor Medal, which is of bronze, recognizes distinction in the field of codes and services in the broad areas of piping and pressure vessels. Preference is given to Society members.

1966 Frank S.G. Williams
1967 David B. Wesstrom
1968 Max B. Higgins
1969 Everett O. Waters
1970 Bernard F. Langer
1971 James M. Guy
1972 William Rolfe Gall
1973 John Dalton Mattimore
1974 Jean L. Lattan
1975 Frederick A. Hough
Walter H. Davidson
Joseph J. King
Burton T. Mast
Andrew J. Shoup
1976 No award
1977 James S. Clarke
Raymond R. Maccary
1978 Adolph O. Schaefer
1979 John F. Harvey
1980 Paul M. Brister

The Diesel and Gas Engine Power Award, which consists of a bronze plaque, recognizes achievement over a substantial period of time in research, innovation or education in advancing the art of engineering in the field of internal combustion engines, or in directing the efforts of individuals so involved.

1967 Frederick P. Porter
1969 Leo T. Brinson, Jr.
1971 Melvin J. Helmich
1972 R. Rex Robinson
1973 Warren A. Rhoades
1974 Warren J. Severin
1975 William Speicher
1976 No award
1977 No award
1978 No award
1979 Helmuth G. Braendel
1980 No award

The Rufus Oldenburger Medal, which is of bronze, recognizes contributions and achievements in automatic control, including education, research, development, innovation and service. There are no restrictions of profession, nationality or Society membership for this honor.

1968 Rufus Oldenburger
1969 Nathaniel B. Nichols
1970 John R. Ragazzini
1971 Charles Stark Draper
1972 Albert J. Williams, Jr.
1973 Clesson E. Mason
1974 Herbert W. Ziebolz
1975 Hendrick W. Bode
Harry Nyquist
1976 Rudolph Emil Kalman
1977 Gordon S. Brown
Harold L. Hazen
1978 Yasundo Takahashi
1979 Henry M. Paynter
1980 Arthur E. Bryson, Jr.

The R. Tom Sawyer Award, which consists of a bronze plaque, honors contributions to the gas turbine industry and to the Gas Turbine Division of ASME.

1972 R. Tom Sawyer
1973 John W. Sawyer
1974 Waheeb Rizk
1975 Bruce O. Buckland
1976 Curt Keller
1977 Alexander L. London
1978 Sir Frank Whittle
1979 Sam B. Williams
1980 Ralph L. Boyer

The Worcester Reed Warner Medal, which is of gold and carries a $1,000 honorarium, is given for outstanding contributions to the permanent literature of engineering, which may be a single paper, treatise, book or series of papers dealing with progressive ideas on engineering, scientific and industrial research associated with mechnical engineering, design and operation of mechanical and association equipment, industrial engineering or management and other related subjects. The paper or treatise must be not less than five years old and may have been prepared by a member or non-member.

1933 Dexter S. Kimball
1934 Ralph E. Flanders

1935 Stephen P. Timoshenko
1936 Charles M. Allen
1937 Clarence Hirshfeld
1938 Lawford H. Fry
1939 Rupen Eksergian
1940 William Gregory
1941 Richard Southwell
1942 Fred H. Colvin
1943 Igor I. Sikorsky
1944 Earle Buckingham
1945 Joseph M. Juran
1946 No award
1947 Arpad L. Nadai
1948 Edward S. Cole
1949 Fred B. Seely
1950 Orlan W. Boston
1951 Jacob P. Den Hartog
1952 Max Jakob
1953 William McAdams
1954 Joseph Keenan
1955 Howard S. Bean
1956 J. Keith Louden
1957 William Prager
1958 Harold J. Rose
1959 Daniel Glasstone
1960 Lloyd H. Donnell
1961 C. L. W. Trinks
1962 Virgil M. Faires
1963 Frederick Morse
1964 Oscar J. Horger
1965 Ascher H. Shapiro
1966 Eric A. Farber
1967 Nicholas J. Hoff
1968 Merhyle F. Spotts
1969 Hans W. Liepmann
1970 Wilhelm Flugge
1971 Stephen H. Crandall
1972 Burgess H. Jennings
1973 Max Mark Frocht
1974 Victor L. Streeter
1975 Philip G. Hodge, Jr.
1976 Dennis C. Shepherd
1977 Joseph E. Shigley
1978 James H. Potter
1979 Darle W. Dudley
1980 Olgierd C. Zienkiewicz

The Alfred Noble Prize, which carries a variable cash honorarium, is awarded to a member of ASME or one of several other engineering associations for a technical paper of exceptional excellence accepted for publication by any of the cooperating societies. The author must be thirty years of age or younger and the award is for papers published in the year of the award by an individual author (no joint authorship).

1969 Ronald Gibala (AIME)
1970 Peter W. Marshall (ASCE)
1971 Ben G. Burke (ASCE)
1972 C. L. Magee (ASCE)
1974 Viney K. Gupta (ASME)
1975 William L. Smith (ASCE)
1976 S.N. Singh (AIME)
1977 J.E. Killough (SPE)
1978 No award
1979 No award
1980 No award

The Henry Hess Award, which carries a $250 honorarium, is given for an original technical paper by an author or authors thirty years of age or younger.

1915 Ernest Hickstein
1916 L.B. McMillan
1917 No award
1918 No award
1919 E.D. Whalen
1920 No award
1921 S. Logan Kerr
1922 R.H. Heilman and F.L. Kallam
1923 S.S. Sanford and S. Crocker
1924 R.H. Heilman
1925 Gilbert Schaller
1926 No award
1927 William M. Frame
1928 M.D. Aisenstein
1929 Arthur M. Wahl
1930 Ed S. Smith, Jr.
1931 Montrose Dewry
1932 Edmund M. Wagner
1933 Townsend Tinker
1934 John Yellott, Jr.
1935 Stanley Mikawa
1936 H.F. Mullikin, Jr.
1937 Leslie J. Hooper
1938 Arthur C. Stern
1939 No award
1940 Robert E. Newton
1941 John Rettaliata
1942 Winston M. Dudley
1943 Troels Warming
1944 No award
1945 Bruce Del Mar
1946 Martin Goland
1947 Gilbert T. Rowe
1948 Hunt Davis
1949 Gerhard Nothmann
1950 No award
1951 John D. Stantz
1952 Warren Rohsenow
1953 No award
1954 No award
1955 F. Freudenstein
1956 No award
1957 No award
1958 No award
1959 Victor Salesmann
1960 Gunnar Heskestad
Duane Olberts
1961 J. E. Fleckenstein
1962 Miklos Sajben
1963 A. Thiruvengadam
1964 R. J. McGrattan
1965 J. F. Booker
1966 Jerry R. Johanson
1967 Richard Barett
1968 No award
1969 James R. Rice
1970 T. L. Geers
1971 No award
1972 D. C. Gakenheimer
1973 Hazem A. Ezzat
Steve M. Rohde
1974 Lambert B. Freund
1975 No award
1976 G. D. Gupta
1977 R. J. Hannemann
1978 Maria Comninou
1979 Krishna C. Gupta
1980 Bharat Bhushan

The Melville Medal, which is of bronze and carries a $1,000 honorarium, is given for the best original paper presented before the Society during the previous calendar year, or published or approved for publication by the Society. The author or authors must hold ASME membership.

1927 Leon P. Alford
1928 No award
1929 Joseph W. Roe
1930 Herman Diederichs
William Pomeroy
1931 Arthur Grunert
1932 Alexey Stepanoff
1933 William Caldwell
1934 No award
1935 Oscar R. Wikander
1936 H. A. S. Howarth
1937 Alfred J. Buchi
1938 Alphonse Lipetz
1939 Lester Goldsmith
1940 Carl A. W. Brandt
1941 Roger V. Terry
1942 Kenneth Salisbury
1943 No award
1944 Ernest Robinson
1945 William J. King
1946 Troels Warming
1947 Raymond Martinelli
1948 Reginald Gillmor
1949 Harold B. Maynard
1950 Samuel J. Loring
1952 Neil P. Bailey
1953 Jefferson Falkner
1954 Edmund Sylvester
1955 Robert T. Knapp
1956 No award
1957 No award
1958 Thomas P. Goodman
1959 Stephen J. Kline
1960 William G. Steltz
1961 Otto Erich Balje
1962 T. P. Goodman
1963 J. S. Ausman
1964 J. K. Jakobsen
1965 W. Van Der Sluys
1966 No award
1967 Bernard Roth
1968 Yian-Nian Chen
1969 Leon R. Glicksman
1970 J. William Holl
A. L. Kornhauser
1971 Thomas Slot
1972 H. W. O'Connor
A. S. Weinstein
1973 No award
1974 V. H. Arakeri
Allan J. Acosta
1975 V. Turchina
David M. Sanborn
Ward O. Winer
1976 Bernard J. Hamrock
Duncan Dowson
1977 E.F. Fichter
K. H. Hunt
1978 D.E. Negrelli
J.R. Lloyd
J.L. Novotny
1979 Thomas J.R. Hughes
W.K. Liu
1980 Ravi Chandran
John C. Chen
Fred W. Staub

The Arthur L. Williston Medal, which is of bronze and carries a $500 honorarium, is given for the best paper submitted in the Williston-Main Awards Contest on a subject that challenges the engineering abilities of students and involves the supporting influence of engineering faculties.

1956 John A. Welsh
1957 Walter P. Logeman
1958 No award
1959 Rowe A. Giardinin
1960 Marc Fishbein
1961 James R. Stewart
1962 Charles H. Recht
1963 No award
1964 Kenneth E. Gawronski
1965 LaRoux K. Gillespie
1966 Eddie R. Howe
1967 L. Thomas Cooper III
1968 Frank A. Ralbovsky
1969 Arlo Fossum
1970 Steven H. Carlson
1971 James A. Willms
1972 Dennis L. Sandberg
1973 Frank H. Roubleau, Jr.
1974 James J. Calls
1975 No award
1976 Ehud David Laska
1977 Harry W. Groot
1978 Jitendra S. Goela
1979 Steven E. Stephens
1980 Charles S. Macaulay

The Charles T. Main Award, which now carries a $1,000 honorarium, supplements the Williston Award on a student level by honoring achievements in public service.

1925 **Clement R. Brown,** Catholic University of America
1926 **W. C. Taylor,** John Hopkins University
1927 **No award**
1928 **Robert M. Meyer,** Newark College of Engineering
1929 **No award**
1930 **Jules Podnosoff,** Polytechnic Institute of Brooklyn
1931 **Robert E. Klise,** University of Michigan
1931 **Marshall Anderson,** University of Michigan
1932 **No award**
1933 **George D. Wilkinson, Jr.,** Newark College of Engineering
1934 **Philip P. Self,** Colorado State College
1935 **G. Lowell Williams,** Lafayette College
1936 **No award**
1937 **Allan P. Stern,** Case School of Applied Science
1938 **Edward W. Connelly,** University of Detroit
1939 **James H. Bright,** Lehigh University
1940 **Frank de Pould,** Case School of Applied Science
1941 **John J. Balun,** University of Detroit
1942 **Bernard J. Isabella,** Case School of Applied Science
1943 **Mitchell C. Kazen,** University of Detroit
1944 **Fred M. Piaskowski,** University of Detroit
1945 **Jack Drandell,** Southern Methodist University
1946 **Victor S. Rykwalder,** University of Detroit
1947 **Alvaro R. Boera,** Stevens Institute of Technology
1948 **Earle Duane Stewart,** University of Pittsburgh
1949 **Stanley M. Kuvacheff,** University of Detroit
1950 **Richard T. Johnson,** University of Detroit
1951 **No award**
1952 **Israel E. Rubin,** Cooper Union School of Engineering

1953 **Peter Ashurkoff,** Princeton University
1954 **John B. Pendergrass, Jr.,** Carnegie Institute of Technology
1955 **Richard J. Slember,** Cooper Union School of Engineering
1956 **Marion J. Balcerzak,** University of Detroit
1957 **Joseph P. Hunter,** University of Detroit
1958 **Frank D. Sams,** Clemson Agricultural College
1959 **James L. Benson,** University of Vermont
1960 **John W. McDaniel,** Rice Institute
1961 **Lester W. Wurm,** Kansas State University
1962 **David W. Wieting,** Lamar State College of Technology
1963 **Robert Lafayette Ash,** Kansas State University
1964 **No award**
1965 **No award**
1966 **No award**
1967 **Muzzamil Niazi,** Wichita State University
1968 **Terry Dean Schmidt,** University of Washington
1969 **No award**
1970 **Steve H. Woodard,** Arizona State University
1971 **James M. Singleton,** University of Alabama
1972 **Harold Chapin Lowe,** University of Kansas
1973 **Gary Patrick Pezall,** University of Wisconsin, Madison
1974 **Adrian P. Villa,** Clarkson College of Technology
1975 **No award**
1976 **Scott Elliott Baker**
1977 **Charles S. Tamarin**
1978 **Emily Earle,** Auburn University
1979 **Richard A. Ferraro,** State University of New York at Buffalo
1980 **Russell S. Colvin,** Louisiana Tech University

The "Old Guard" Prize for ASME Student Members, which now consists of $500, is given for the best presentation of a technical paper by a student member. The "Old Guard" of members, who have reached 65 years of age and are exempt from ASME dues, supports this prize for the younger members.

1956 **Joseph W. Jacobson,** University of Texas
1957 **George M. Reynolds,** Northwestern University
1958 **Harry Hollinghaus,** University of Utah
1959 **James S. Kishi,** University of Texas
1960 **Joseph W. Lindsey,** University of Utah
1961 **Joseph J. Marino,** University of Connecticut
1962 **Jay S. Fein,** Rutgers University
1963 **Walter Clark Dean II,** Lehigh University
1964 **Robert J. Arnzen,** Washington University of St. Louis
1965 **Joseph P. Collins,** University of Wisconsin
1966 **John A. Leo, III,** Auburn University
1967 **William E. Hughes,** Brigham Young University
1968 **Maurice H. Bunn,** Arizona State University
1969 **Walter H. Peters, III,** Auburn University
1970 **Joseph R. Titone,** Cornell University
1971 **J. L. Lee,** Auburn University
1972 **Stanley W. Blossom,** Oklahoma State University
1973 **Steven H. Blossom,** Oklahoma State University
E. J. Strande, University of Washington
1974 **Gary L. Smith,** Oklahoma State University
1975 **Steven R. Bussolari,** Union College
1976 **Paul E. Hollis,** University of Washington
1977 **Pauline B. Cramer,** University of Washington
1978 **Jan A. Dozier,** Auburn University
1979 **Zoe D. Krececioglu,** University of Arizona
1980 **No award**

The Blackall Machine Tool and Gauge Award, which consists of $100 and a bronze plaque, honors the best paper or papers on the design and application of machine tools, gauges or dimensional measuring instruments submitted to the ASME for presentation and publication.

1965 **Carl J. Osford, Jr. and John Cook**
1966 **Orlan W. Boston and William W. Gilbert**
1967 **Bei T. Chao and Kenneth J. Trigger**
1968 **S.A. Tobias and Wilfred Fishwick**
1960 **B. Popper and David W. Pessen**
1961 **Joseph R. Roubik**
1962 **W.A. Mohn**
1963 **E.G. Thomsen, A.G. MacDonald and Shiro Kobayashi**
1964 **No award**
1965 **Robert S. Hahn**
1966 **No award**
1967 **J. Hopenfeld and R.R. Cole**
1968 **Kuo-King Wang, Shien-Ming Wu and Kazuaki Iwata**
1972 **No award**
1973 **No award**
1974 **S.P. Loutrel and N.H. Cook**
1975 **Sindre Holyen** and **Clayton D. Mote, Jr.**
1976 **No award**
1977 **No award**
1978 **No award**
1979 **No award**
1980 **Robert A. Thompson, Subbiah Ramalingam** and **John D. Watson**

The Prime Movers Committee Award consists of a certificate honoring outstanding contributions to the literature of thermal electric station practice or equipment through public presentation or publication.

1955 **Louis Elliott**
Walter F. Friend
Edward C. Duffy
Gustaf A. Gaffert
Fred W. Argue
Bernhardt G. A. Skrotski
1956 **Robert B. Donworth**
Walter J. Lyman
T. Harry Mandil
Nunzio J. Palladino
Milton Shaw
John W. Simpson
1957 **Heinrich Hegetschweller**
Robert L. Bartlett
1958 **Vivian F. Estcourt**
1959 **J. Kenneth Salisbury**
1960 **Sigmund N. Fiala**
James H. Harlow
1961 **Charles Strohmeyer, Jr.**
1962 **No award**
1963 **E.F. Walsh, R.L. Jackson, Walter Sinton and R.E. Warner**
1964 **Everett P. Partridge**
1965 **A.E. Weller, and W.T. Reid**
1966 **F.J. Hanzalek and P.G. Ipson**
1967 **Homer F. Hatfield and Mark G. Pfeiffer**
1968 **G.N. Stone and A.J. Clarke**
1969 **Paul Goldstein and Charles L. Burton**
1970 **Paul Leung and Raymond E. Moore**
1971 **Paul Leung and Raymond E. Moore**
1972 **G. S. Liao and Paul Leung**
1973 **G.S. Rahoi, R.C. Scarberry, J.R. Crum and P.E. Morris**
1974 **B. Bornstein and Paul Leung**
1975 **Karl A. Gulbrand and Paul Leung**
1976 **Wolfgang Mattick, Hans-Guenter Haddenhorst, Otto Weber and Z. Stanley Stys**

1977 **H. Haneda, M. Araoka, K. Setoguchi, J.D. Fox and W.F. Siddall**
1978 **No award**
1979 **Henry E. Lokay, D.G. Ramey** and **W.R Brose**
1980 **Heinz E. Termuehlen**

The Gas Turbine Award, which consists of a turbine wheel with bronze insert, recognizes outstanding contribution to the literature of combustion gas turbines or gas turbines combined thermally with nuclear or steam power plants or any aspect of this field. Papers published anywhere in the world are eligible.

1964 **A.L. London**
1965 **J.S. Alford**
1966 **No award**
1967 **F.O. Carta**
1968 **Arthur D. Bernstein, William H. Heiser and Charles M. Hevenor**
1969 **O.E. Balje**
1970 **Carlyle Reid**
1971 **H.A. Harmon, A.A. Mikolajczak and D. Marchant**
1972 **F.B. Metzger and D.B. Hanson**
1973 **John Moore**
1974 **G.L. Commerford and Lynn E. Snyder**
1975 **Edward M. Greitzer**
1976 **J.P. Gostelow**
1977 **Ivor J. Day, Nicholas M. Cumptsy** and **Edward M. Greitzer**
1978 **Frank J. Wiesner**
1979 **No award**
1980 **No award**

The Rail Transportation Award is a certificate given annually for an original paper on railroad mechnical engineering describing a new and basic technical discovery, or exhibiting original thinking on railway mechanical engineering beyond the routine, or describing such work in practice. The paper must have been presented during the calendar year prior to that of the award, although non-members are also eligible.

1966 **W.P. Manos**
J. C. Shang
1967 **F. E. King**
R. W. Radford
1968 **Thomas Schur**
1969 **Richard T. Gray**
Samuel Levy
James A. Bain
Estelle J. Playdon
1970 **H. C. Meacham**
R. D. Ahlbeck
1972 **L. A. Peterson**
W. H. Freeman
J. M. Wandrisco
1973 **G. E. Novak**
B. J. Eck
1974 **J. N. Siddall**
M. A. Dokainish
W. Elmaraghy
1975 **W. Terry Hawthorne**
1976 **M.R. Johnson, R. Edward Welch and K.S. Yeung**
1977 **No award**
1978 **R.W. Radford**
1979 **No award**
1980 **Bruce W. Shute**
Eric C. Wright
Charles K. Taft
William N. Banister

The Freeman Scholar Award consists of a $3,000 honorarium given every two years for fluids engineering. The recipient with wide experience in the field is expected to review a coherent topic in the specialty including a comprehensive statement of "the state of the art" and suggestions for key future research needs.

1971 **Jack W. Hoyt and Ronald F. Probstein**
1974 **Jack E. Cermak**
1976 **William J. McCroskey**
1978 **Benjamin Gebhart**
1980 **Edward M. Greitzer**

The Heat Transfer Memorial Award is given annually for meritorious contributions through teaching, research, design or publications. The award consists of a memorial booklet and a plaque.

1975 **Simon Ostrach**
Peter Griffith
1976 **Warren H. Giedt**
Raymond Viskanta
1977 **Robert D. Cess**
Rolf H. Sabersky
1978 **Richard J. Goldstein** and **John A. Clark**
1979 **Arthur E. Bergles** and **Yih-Yun Hsu**
1980 **John H. Leinhard**

The Burt L. Newkirk Tribology Award is presented annually for a notable contribution to tribology by a person thirty-five years of age or younger. The award consists of a certificate and publication of suitable articles in the *ASME Journal of Tribology.*

1976 **Francis E. Kennedy, Jr.**
1977 **Steve M. Rohde**
1978 **Pradeep Gupta**
1979 **Thomas A. Dow**
1980 **Stuart H. Lowenthal**

The Nadai Award, a plaque etched in the form of a certificate, is given annually for work in materials research and applications development.

1975 **George M. Sinclair**
1976 **Evan Albert Davis**
1977 **George R. Irwin**
1978 **Frank A. McClintock**
1979 **Louis F. Coffin**
1980 **Michael J. Manjoine**

The Codes and Standards Medal, which is of bronze and is accompanied by a certificate, is given annually for contributions to codes and standards.

1977 **William G. McLean**
1978 **Leonard P. Zick**
1979 **Joseph F. Sebald**
1980 **George F. Habach**

The Bernard F. Langer Nuclear Codes and Standards Award, a bronze plaque and certificate, is given annually to an individual who has contributed to the nuclear powerplant industry through development of ASME nuclear codes and standards.

1978 **William E. Cooper**
1979 **Wiliam R. Smith, Sr.**
1980 **Wendell P. Johnson**

The James N. Landis Medal, which is of bronze and is accompanied by a $1,000 honorarium and a certificate, annually recognizes outstanding personal performance in designing, constructing or managing a major steam-powered electric station using either fossil fuels of nuclear power.

1977 James N. Landis
1978 William E. Hopkins
1979 No award
1980 Harvey F. Brush

The James Harry Potter Gold Medal, recognizes eminent achievement or distinguished service in thermodynamics in mechanical engineering. The award can be for teaching or applications.

1980 Alexander L. London

The Pressure Vessel and Piping Award is given annually for contributions in research, development, teaching or significant advances in pressure vessel and piping technology.

1980 Dana Young

The Henry R. Worthington Award, which consists of a bronze medal, a certificate and $1,000, is awarded annually for development, design, management, education or literature pertaining to pumping machinery.

1980 Igor J. Karassik

IEEE Medal of Honor
Alexander Graham Bell Medal
Edison Medal
Founders Medal
Lamme Medal
IEEE Education Medal
Harry Diamond Memorial Award
William M. Habirshaw Award
Hernand and Sostheses Behn Award in International Communication
Morris E. Leeds Award
Morris N. Liebmann Memorial Award
Jack A. Morton Award
Frederik Philips Award
Emanuel R. Piore Award
David Sarnoff Award
Nikola Tesla Award
Vladimir K. Zworykin Award
W.R.G. Baker Prize
Browder J. Thompson Memorial Prize Award
Cleo Brunetti Award
Charles Proteus Steinmetz Award
Haraden Pratt Award

INSTITUTE OF ELECTRICAL AND ELECTRONICS ENGINEERS
345 E. 47th St., New York, N.Y. 10017 (212/644-7882)

The IEEE Medal of Honor, which consists of a gold medal, bronze replica and $10,000, is awarded as warranted for an exceptional addition to science and technology of concern to the Institute. Nominations are reviewed by a special committee and approved by the board of directors.

1917 E. H. Armstrong
1918 No award
1919 E. F. W. Alexanderson
1920 Guglielmo Marconi
1921 R. A. Fessenden
1922 Lee deForest
1923 John Stone-Stone
1924 M. I. Pupin
1925 No award
1926 G. W. Pickard
1927 L. W. Austin
1928 Jonathan Zenneck
1929 G. W. Pierce
1930 P. O. Pedersen
1931 G. A. Ferrie
1932 A. E. Kennelly
1933 J. A. Fleming
1934 S. C. Hooper
1935 Balth. van der Pol
1936 G. A. Campbell
1937 Melville Eastham
1938 J. H. Dellinger
1939 A. G. Lee
1940 Lloyd Espenschied
1941 A. N. Goldsmith
1942 A. H. Taylor
1943 William Wilson
1944 Haraden Pratt
1945 H. H. Beverage
1946 R. V. L. Hartley
1947 No award
1948 L. C. F. Horle
1949 Ralph Bown
1950 F. E. Terman
1951 V. K. Zworykin
1952 W. R. G. Baker
1953 J. M. Miller
1954 W. L. Everitt
1955 H. T. Friis
1956 J. V. L. Hogan
1957 J. A. Stratton
1958 A. W. Hull
1959 E. L. Chaffee
1960 Harry Nyquist
1961 Ernst A. Guillemin
1962 Edward V. Appleton
1963 John H. Hammond, Jr.
George C. Southworth
1964 Harold A. Wheeler
1965 No award
1966 Claude E. Shannon
1967 Charles H. Townes
1968 Gordon K. Teal
1969 Edward L. Ginzton
1970 Dennis Gabor
1971 John Bardeen
1972 Jay W. Forrester
1973 Rudolf Kompfner
1974 Rudolf E. Kalman
1975 John R. Pierce
1976 No award
1977 H. Earle Vauhan
1978 Robert N. Noyce
1979 Richard Bellman
1980 William Shockley

The Alexander Graham Bell Medal, which consists of a gold medal, bronze replica and $10,000, honors exceptional contributions to the advancement of telecommunications. A committee review nominations and the Board of Directors gives final approval.

1976 **Amos E. Joel, Jr.**
William Keister
Raymond W. Ketchledge
1977 **Eberhart Rechtin**
1978 **M. Robert Aaron**
John S. Mayo
Eric E. Sumner
1979 **Christian Jacobaeus**
1980 **Richard R. Hough**

The Edison Medal, which consists of a gold medal, small gold replica, certificate and $10,000, honors a career of meritorious achievement in electrical science, electrical engineering or the electrical arts. A committee reviews nominations and the board of directors gives final approval.

1909 **Elihu Thomson**
1910 **Frank J. Sprague**
1911 **George Westinghouse**
1912 **William Stanley**
1913 **Charles F. Brush**
1914 **Alexander Graham Bell**
1915 **No award**
1916 **Nikola Tesla**
1917 **John J. Carty**
1918 **Benjamin G. Lamme**
1919 **W. L. R. Emmet**
1920 **Michael I. Pupin**
1921 **Cummings C. Chesney**
1922 **Robert A. Millikan**
1923 **John W. Lieb**
1924 **John W. Howell**
1925 **Harris J. Ryan**
1926 **No award**
1927 **William D. Coolidge**
1928 **Frank B. Jewett**
1929 **Charles F. Scott**
1930 **Frank Conrad**
1931 **E. W. Rice, Jr.**
1932 **Bancroft Gherardi**
1933 **Arthur E. Kennelly**
1934 **Willis R. Whitney**
1935 **Lewis B. Stillwell**
1936 **Alex Dow**
1937 **Gano Dunn**
1938 **Dugald C. Jackson**
1939 **Philip Torchio**
1940 **George A. Campbell**
1941 **John B. Whitehead**
1942 **Edwin H. Armstrong**
1943 **Vannevar Bush**
1944 **E. F. W. Alexanderson**
1945 **Philip Sporn**
1946 **Lee deForest**
1947 **Joseph Slepian**
1948 **Morris E. Leeds**
1949 **Karl B. McEachron**
1950 **Otto B. Blackwell**
1951 **Charles F. Wagner**
1952 **Vladimir K. Zworykin**
1953 **John F. Peters**
1954 **Oliver E. Buckley**
1955 **Leonid A. Umansky**
1956 **Comfort A. Adams**
1957 **John K. Hodnette**
1958 **Charles F. Kettering**
1959 **James F. Fairman**
1960 **Harold S. Osborne**
1961 **William B. Kouwenhoven**
1962 **Alexander C. Monteith**
1963 **John R. Pierce**
1964 **No award; schedule revised**
1965 **Walker L. Cisler**
1966 **Wilmer L. Barrow**
1967 **George H. Brown**
1968 **Charles F. Avila**
1969 **Hendrik W. Bode**
1970 **Howard H. Aiken**
1971 **John W. Simpson**
1972 **William H. Pickering**
1973 **B. D. H. Tellegen**
1974 **Jan A. Rajchman**
1975 **Sidney Darlington**
1976 **Murray Joslin**
1977 **Henri G. Busignies**
1978 **Daniel E. Noble**
1979 **Albert Rose**
1980 **Robert Adler**

The Founders Medal, which consists of a cash award, a gold medal and bronze replica, is given periodically for major contributions in the leadership, planning and administration of "affairs of great value to the electrical and electronics engineering profession." A special committee reviews nominations, which are approved by the board of directors.

1953 **David Sarnoff**
1954 **Alfred N. Goldsmith**
1955 **No award**
1956 **No award**
1957 **Raymond A. Heising**
1958 **W. R. G. Baker**
1959 **No award**
1960 **Haraden Pratt**
1961 **Ralph Bown**
1962 **No award**
1963 **Frederick E. Terman**
1964 **Andrew G. L. McNaughton**
1965 **No award**
1966 **Elmer W. Engstrom**
1967 **Harvey Fletcher**
1968 **Patrick E. Haggerty**
1969 **E. Finley Carter**
1970 **Morris D. Hooven**
1971 **Ernst Weber**
1972 **Masaru Ibuka**
1973 **William R. Hewlett**
David Packard
1974 **Lawrence A. Hyland**
1975 **John G. Brainerd**
1976 **Edward W. Herold**
1977 **Jerome B. Wiesner**
1978 **Donald G. Fink**
1979 **Hanzo Omi**
1980 **Simon Ramo**

The Lamme Medal, which consists of a gold medal, bronze replica and certificate, is awarded for meritorious achievement in the development of electrical or electronic apparatus or systems.

1928 **Allan Bertram Field**
1929 **Rudolf E. Hellmund**
1930 **William J. Foster**
1931 **Giuseppe Faccioli**

1932 Edward Weston
1933 Lewis B. Stillwell
1934 Henry E. Warren
1935 Vannevar Bush
1936 Frank Conrad
1937 Robert E. Doherty
1938 Marion A. Savage
1939 Norman W. Storer
1940 Comfort A. Adams
1941 Forrest E. Ricketts
1942 Joseph Slepian
1943 A. H. Kehoe
1944 S. H. Mortensen
1945 David C. Prince
1946 J. B. MacNeill
1947 A. M. MacCutcheon
1948 Vladimir K. Zworykin
1949 C. M. Laffoon
1950 Donald I. Bohn
1951 Arthur E. Silver
1952 I. F. Kinnard
1953 F. A. Cowan
1954 A. M. deBellis
1955 C. R. Hanna
1956 H. H. Beverage
1957 H. S. Black
1958 P. L. Alger
S. Beckwith
1959 L. A. Kilgore
1960 John G. Trump
1961 Charles Concordia
1962 E. L. Harder
1963 Loyal V. Bewley
1964 No award; schedule revised
1965 A. Uno Lamm
1966 Rene Andre Baudry
1967 Warren P. Mason
1968 Nathan Cohn
1969 James D. Cobine
1970 Harry F. Olson
1971 Winthrop M. Leeds
1972 Yu H. Ku
Robert H. Park
1973 Charles S. Draper
1974 Seymour B. Cohn
1975 Harold B. Law
1976 C. Kumar N. Patel
1977 Bernard M. Oliver
1978 Harry W. Mergler
1979 James M. Lafferty
1980 Eugene C. Starr

The IEEE Education Medal, which consists of a gold medal, bronze replica and certificate, honors excellence in teaching and the ability to inspire students, and leadership in electrical engineering education through writings and publication.

1956 F. E. Terman
1957 W. L. Everitt
1958 J. F. Calvert
1959 G. S. Brown
1960 Ernst Weber
1961 George F. Corcoran
1962 Ernst A. Guillemin
1963 William G. Dow
1964 B. R. Teare, Jr.
1965 Hugh H. Skilling
1966 William H. Huggins
1967 John R. Whinnery
1968 Edward C. Jordan
1969 Donald O. Pederson
1970 Jacob Millman
1971 Franz Ollendorff
1972 M. E. Van Valkenburg
1973 Lotfi A. Zadeh
1974 John G. Truxal
1975 Charles A. Desoer
1976 John G. Linvill
1977 Robert M. Fanow
1978 Harold A. Peterson
1979 John R. Ragazzini
1980 Aldert van der Ziel

The Harry Diamond Memorial Award, which consists of a certificate and $2,000, honors technical contributions in government service in any country, as evidenced by publication in professional journals. A special committee reviews nominations, which are approved by the board of directors.

1950 A. V. Haeff
1951 M. J. E. Golay
1952 Newbern Smith
1953 R. M. Page
1954 Harold Zahl
1955 Bernard Salzberg
1956 W. S. Hinman, Jr.
1957 Georg Goubau
1958 E. W. Allen, Jr.
1959 J. W. Herbstreit
1960 K. A. Norton
1961 H. L. Brueckmann
1962 William Culshaw
1963 Allen H. Schooley
1964 James R. Wait
1965 George J. Thaler
1966 John J. Egli
1967 Rudolf A. Stampfl
1968 Harry I. Davis
1969 Maurice Apstein
1970 Allen V. Astin
1971 Arthur H. Guenther
1972 William B. McLean
1973 Harold Jacobs
1974 Chester H. Page
1975 Louis Costrell
1976 Maxime A. Faget
1977 Jacob Rabinow
1978 David M. Kerns
1979 Henry P. Kalmus
1980 Martin Greenspan

The William M. Habirshaw Award, which consists of a bronze medal and $1,000, recognizes contributions in the field of the transmission and distribution of power. A committee nominates and the board of directors approves the recipient.

1959 William A. Del Mar
1960 Selden B. Crary
1961 Samuel B. Griscom
1962 Herman Halperin
1963 L. M. Robertson
1964 C. S. Schifreen
1965 Wilfred F. Skeats
1966 I. Birger Johnson
1967 Robert J. Wiseman
1968 Eugene C. Starr
1969 James A. Rawls
1970 Fred J. Vogel
1971 Gunnar Jancke
1972 J. J. Archambault

Lionel Cahill
1973 Eugene W. Boehne
1974 Herbert R. Stewart
1975 Everett J. Harrington
1976 Francis J. Lane
1977 No award; schedule revised
1978 Martin H.McGrath
1979 Howard C. Barnes
Theodore J. Nagel
1980 Edward W. Kimbark

The Hernand and Sostheses Behn Award in International Communication, which consists of a plaque, certificate and $1,000, honors outstanding contributions in the field. A committee nominates and the board of directors approves the recipient.

1966 E. Maurice Deloraine
1967 Leonard Jaffe
1968 Edward W. Allen
1969 Henri Busignies
1970 Herre Rinia
1971 Eugene F. O'Neill
1972 Frank deJager
Johannes A. Greefkes
1973 Vladimir A. Kotelnikov
1974 Leslie H. Bedford
1975 John G. Puente
1976 Sidney Metzger
1977 No award; schedule revised
1978 F. Louis H.M. Stumpers
1979 A. Nejat Ince
1980 Armig B. Kandoian

The Morris E. Leeds Award, which consists of a certificate and $1,000, honors contributions in electrical measurement, with special consideration given to an engineer under 36 years of age. A special committee nominates the candidate, who is approved by the board of directors.

1959 Herbert B. Brooks
1960 Perry A. Borden
1961 Theodore A. Rich
1962 Bernard E. Lenehan
1963 Francis B. Silsbee
1964 John G. Ferguson
1965 Harold E. Edgerton
1966 William W. Mumford
1967 Henry R. Chope
1968 Albert J. Williams, Jr.
1969 Harry W. Houck
1970 Harold I. Ewen
1971 Martin E. Packard
1972 Forest K. Harris
1973 C. Howard Vollum
1974 Norbert L. Kusters
1976 Francis L. Hermach
1977 Arthur M. Thompson
1978 Thomas M. Dauphinee
1979 Robert D. Cutkosky
1980 Wallace H. Coulter

The Morris N. Liebmann Memorial Award, which consists of a certificate and $2,000, recognizes important contributions to emerging technologies during the three preceding calendar years. A special committee reviews nominations, which are approved by the board of directors.

1919 L. F. Fuller
1920 R. A. Weagant
1921 R. A. Heising
1922 C. S. Franklin
1923 H. H. Beverage
1924 J.R. Carson
1925 Frank Conrad
1926 Ralph Bown
1927 A. H. Taylor
1928 W. G. Cady
1929 E. V. Appleton
1930 A. W. Hull
1931 Stuart Ballantine
1932 Edmond Bruce
1933 Heinrich Barkhausen
1934 V. K. Zworykin
1935 F. B. Llewellyn
1936 B. J. Thompson
1937 W. H. Doherty
1938 G. C. Southworth
1939 H. T. Friis
1940 H. A. Wheeler
1941 P. T. Farnsworth
1942 S. A. Schelkunoff
1943 W. L. Barrow
1944 W. W. Hansen
1945 P. C. Goldmark
1946 Albert Rose
1947 J. R. Pierce
1948 S. W. Seeley
1949 C. E. Shannon
1950 O. H. Schade
1951 R. B. Dome
1952 William Shockley
1953 J. A. Pierce
1954 R. R. Warnecke
1955 A. V.-Loughren
1956 Kenneth Bullington
1957 O. G. Villard, Jr.
1958 E. L. Ginzton
1959 Nicolaas Bloembergen
C. H. Townes
1960 J. A. Rajchman
1961 Leo Esaki
1962 Victor H. Rumsey
1963 Ian Munro Ross
1964 Arthur L. Schawlow
1965 William R. Bennett, Jr.
1966 Paul K. Weimer
1967 No award
1968 Emmett N. Leith
1969 John B. Gunn
1970 John A. Copeland
1971 Martin Ryle
1972 Stewart E. Miller
1973 Nick Holonyak, Jr.
1974 Willard S. Boyle
George E. Smith
1975 A. H. Bobeck
P. C. Michaelis
H. E. D. Scovil
1976 Herbert J. Shaw
Horst H. Berger
1977 Siegfried K. Wiedmann
1978 Kuen C. Kao
Robert D. Maurer
John B. MacChesney
1979 Ping King Tien
1980 A.J. DeMaria

The Jack A. Morton Award, consisting of a bronze medal and $2,000, honors contributions in the field of solid state devices. The recipient is nominated by a special committee and approved by the board of directors.

1976 Robert N. Hall
1977 Morgan Sparks
1978 Juri Matisoo
1979 Martin P. Lepselter
1980 James F. Gibbons

The Frederik Philips Award, which consists of a gold medal, certificate and $2,000, recognizes accomplishments in research and development resulting in effective innovation in the electrical and electronics industry. The recipient is nominated by a special committee and approved by the board of directors.

1971 Frederik J. Philips
1972 William O. Baker
1973 John H. Dessauer
1974 Chauncey Guy Suits
1975 C. Lester Hogan
1976 Koji Kobayashi
1977 No award; schedule revised
1978 William E. Shoupp
1979 Gordon E. Moore
1980 William M. Webster

The Emanuel R. Piore Award, which consists of a bronze medal, a certificate, $2,000 and a $2,500 international travel grant, honors achievements in information processing related to computer science. The recipient is nominated by a special committee and approved by the board of directors.

1977 George R. Stibitz
1978 J. Presper Eckert
John W. Mauchly
1979 Richard W. Hamming
1980 Lawrence R. Rabiner
Ronald W. Schafer

The David Sarnoff Award, which consists of a gold medal, bronze replica, certificate and $1,000, honors an outstanding contribution in electronics. The recipient is nominated by a special committee and approved by the board of directors.

1959 David Sarnoff
1960 Rudolf Kompfner
1961 Charles H. Townes
1962 Harry B. Smith
1963 Robert N. Hall
1964 Henri G. Busignies
1965 Jack A. Morton
1966 Jack S. Kilby
1967 James Hillier
1968 Walter P. Dyke
1969 Robert H. Rediker
1970 John B. Johnson
1971 Alan L. McWhorter
1972 Edward G. Ramberg
1973 Max V. Mathews
1974 F. L. J. Sangster
1975 Bernard C. De Loach, Jr.
1976 George H. Heilmeier
1977 Jack M. Manley
Harrison E. Rowe
1978 Stephen E. Harris
1979 A. Gardner Fox
Tingye Li
1980 Marshall I. Nathan

The Nikola Tesla Award, which consists of a plaque and $1,000, honors achievements in the field of electric power. The recipient is nominated by a special committee and approved by the board of directors.

1976 Leon T. Rosenberg
1977 Cyril G. Vienott
1978 Charles H. Holley
1979 John W. Batchelor
1980 Philip H. Trickey

The Vladimir K. Zworykin Award, which consists of a certificate and $1,000, honors contributions in the field of electronic television. A special committee nominates and the board of directors approves the recipient.

1952 B. D. Loughlin
1953 Frank Gray
1954 A. V. Bedford
1955 H. B. Law
1956 F. J. Bingley
1957 Donald Richman
1958 C. P. Ginsburg
1959 P. K. Weimer
1960 No award
1961 P. C. Goldmark
1962 G. A. Morton
1963 P. J. Rice, Jr.
W. E. Evans, Jr.
1964 No award
1965 Norman F. Fyler
1966 Ray D. Kell
1967 Keiji Suzuki
1968 Kurt Schlesinger
1969 Otto H. Schade
1970 Charles H. Coleman
1971 Alfred C. Schroeder
1972 Robin E. Davies
1973 Albert Macovski
1974 Senri Miyaoka
1975 Eugene I. Gordon
Ralph E. Simon
1976 No award
1977 Dalton H. Pritchard
1978 Sam H. Kaplan
1979 Albert M. Morrell
1980 Walter Bruch

The W.R.G. Baker Prize, which consists of a certificate and $1,000, honors an outstanding paper in any of the *IEEE Transactions, Journals* or *Proceedings.* A special committee review authors' papers, and the board of directors approves the selection.

1957 D. R. Fewer
R. J. Kircher
R. L. Trent
1958 R. L. Kyhl
H. F. Webster
1959 R. D. Thornton
1960 E. J. Nalos
1961 Manfred Clynes
1962 Marvin Chodorow
Tore Wessel-Berg
1963 Leonard Lewin
1964 Donald L. White
1965 D. C. Youla
1966 Robert G. Gallager
1967 Dean E. McCumber
Alan G. Chynoweth
1968 J. Andersen
H. B. Lee

1969 Tosiro Koga
1970 George J. Friedman
Cornelius T. Leondes
1971 Andrew H. Bobeck
Robert F. Fischer
Anthony J. Perneski
J. P. Remeika
L. G. Van Uitert
1972 Dirk J. Kuizenga
Anthony E. Siegman
1973 Leon O. Chua
1974 David B. Large
Lawrence Ball
Arnold J. Farstad
1975 Stewart E. Miller
Enrique A. J. Marcatili
Tingye Li
1976 Robert W. Keyes
1977 Manfred Schroeder
1978 Eugene C. Sakshaug
James S. Kresge
Stanley A. Miske, Jr.
1979 Stephen W. Director
Gary D. Hachtel
1980 Gordon M. Jacobs
David J. Allstot
Robert W. Brodersen
Paul S. Gray

The Browder J. Thompson Memorial Prize Award, which consists of a certificate and $1,000, recognizes an outstanding paper by an author under 30 years of age in any IEEE publication. A special committee reviews the papers, and the board of directors approves the selection.

1946 G. M. Lee
1947 C. L. Dolph
1948 W. H. Huggins
1949 R. V. Pound
1950 J. F. Hull
A. W. Randals
1951 A. B. Macnee
1952 H. W. Welch, Jr.
1953 R. C. Booton, Jr.
1954 R. L. Petritz
1955 B. D. Smith, Jr.
1956 J. E. Bridges
1957 D. A. Buck
1958 Arthur Karp
1959 F. H. Blecher
1960 J. W. Gewartowski
1961 Eiichi Goto
1962 Henri B. Smets
1963 Chi-Tang Sah
1964 Harry B. Lee
1965 S. R. Hofstein
F. P. Heiman
1966 Kenneth M. Johnson
1967 Leon O. Chua
R. A. Rohrer
1968 Michael L. Dertouzos
1969 Malvin C. Teich
1970 J. David Rhodes
1971 L. J. Griffiths
1972 G. David Forney, Jr.
1973 Jerry Mar
1974 Jorn Justesen
1975 Nuggehally S. Jayant
1976 Russell M. Mersereau
Dan E. Dudgeon
1977 Michael R. Portnoff
1978 David A. Hounshell
1979 Marvin B. Lieberman
1980 Alan S. Willsky

The $10,000 Cledo Brunetti Award annually honors outstanding contributions in the field of miniaturization in the electronic arts.

1978 Jack S. Kilby
Robert N. Noyce
1979 Geoffrey W.A. Drummer
Philip J. Franklin
1980 Marcian E. Hoff, Jr.

The $1,000 Charles Proteus Steinmetz Award annually honors major contributions to the development of standards in the field of electrical and electronic engineering.

1980 Leon Podolsky

The Haraden Pratt Award, a certificate, annually honors outstanding service to the IEEE.

1972 Alfred N. Goldsmith
1973 Elgin B. Robertson, Jr.
1974 James H. Muligan, Sr.
1975 Walter J. Barrett
1976 Clarence H. Linder
1977 No award; schedule revised
1978 Ivan S. Coggeshall
1979 John D. Ryder
1980 Raymond W. Sears

MacRobert Award

MacROBERT TRUSTS
Balmuir, Tarland, Aboyne, Aberdenshire, Scotland (Tel. 0333981-444)

The MacRobert Award, which consists of £25,000 and a gold medal, is awarded annually to individuals or teams for an outstanding and innovative contribution in engineering or other physical technologies or in the application of physical sciences. Consideration is given for achievements which enhance the national prestige and prosperity of the United Kingdom. The Fellowship of Engineering in conjunction with the MacRobert Trust select the winner.

1969 **Freeman, Fox and Partners** five-member team, for the "novel superstructure of the Severn Bridge"
Rolls-Royce five-member team, for the Pegasus engine used in the Hawker Harrier trijet
1970 **British Petroleum** team of three geophysicists, for directing Alaskan North Slope oil field exploration
1971 **Gas Council** five-member team, for several processes for the manufacture of gas
1972 **Godfrey Hounsfield and EMI Ltd.**, for new X-ray techniques as the basis of a computerized system for diagnosing brain disease
1973 **Dunlop Ltd.** team, for Denovo tire and wheel system
1974 **ICI Ltd. Agricultural Division**, for development and manufacture of high-activity catalysts and their application to methanol synthesis and other processes
1975 **British Railways Board** five-member team, for developments in railway wheel suspensions
Westland Helicopters, for semi-rigid rotor system and conformal gearing for Lynx helicopter
1976 **No award**

1977 **Pilkington Brothers Ltd.,** for Ten-Twenty laminated windshield by Triplex Safety Glass Ltd. for automobiles and passenger aircraft
1977 **Royal Signal and Radar Establishment** and **Malvern Instruments Ltd.** for Malvern Correlator, electro-optical instrument to measure movement of particles or molecules
1979 **Sam Fedida** and **Post Office Telecommunications,** for Prestel, a viewdata software system
1980 **Johnson Matthey Group** five-member team, for contribution to catalytic systems to control emissions from motor vehicle exhausts

Founders Award

NATIONAL ACADEMY OF ENGINEERING
2101 Constitution Ave. NW, Washington, D.C. 20418 (202/389-6438)

The annual Founders Award is presented to an engineer (excluding founding members of the Academy) for "outstanding engineering accomplishments over a long period of time and of benefit to the people of the United States." The award, consisting of a gold-plated medal, bronze medal and citation, is given to a winner selected by a special awards committee appointed by the president and confirmed by the council.

1966 **Vannevar Bush**
1967 **James Smith McDonnell**
1968 **Vladimir K. Zworykin**
1969 **Harry Nyquist**
1970 **Charles S. Draper**
1971 **Clarence L. Johnson**
1972 **Edwin H. Land**
1973 **Warren K. Lewis**
1974 **J. Erik Jonsson**
1975 **James B. Fisk**
1976 **Manson Benedict**
1977 **John R. Pierce**
1978 **George M. Low**
1979 **David Packard**
1980 **Hoyt C. Hottel**

INDUCTION

INVENTORS HALL OF FAME
No address (Information phone: 414/273-3700)

Induction into the Inventors Hall of Fame gives public recognition to the inventor. Selection is by nomination from the general public and balloting by an independent Selection Committee.

1973 **Thomas A. Edison,** Lightbulb and other inventions
1974 **Alexander Graham Bell,** Telephone
Eli Whitney, Cotton gin
John Bardeen, Electronics innovations
Walter H. Brattain and William Shockley, Transistor
1975 **Wilbur and Orville Wright,** Airplane
Guglielmo Marconi, Radio telegraphy
Nikola Tesla, Induction motors
Samuel F. B. Morse, Telegraph
William D. Coolidge, Tungsten lamp filament and the X-ray tube
1976 **Cyrus H. McCormick,** Reaper
Charles M. Hall, Process for mfg. aluminum
Charles Goodyear, Vulcanized rubber
Enrico Fermi, Neutronic reactor
Rudolf Diesel, Internal combustion engine
Charles H. Townes, Maser and, from that, the laser
1977 **George Eastman,** Kodak camera and processes
Lee DeForest, Device for amplifying feeble electrical currents (Vacuum Tube)
Edwin H. Land, Polaroid camera
Charles P. Steinmetz, System of distribution by alternating currents
Vladimir K. Zworykin, Cathode ray tube

Current Status Unknown

Axel Axoson Johnson Lecture

ROYAL SWEDISH ACADEMY OF ENGINEERING SCIENCES
Box 5073, S-102 42 Stockholm, Sweden

The Axel Axoson Johnson Lecture is an international honor conferred every five or six years upon prominent engineering scientists in the fields of energy or power. The lecturer is selected by the Academy based on nominations from a three-member committee. A plaque is given as a tribute to the lecturer.

1955 **Pierre Ailleret,** Elektricite de France, France
1957 **Sir Christopher Hinton,** Atomic Energy Authority, Great Britain
1962 **Arthur Davenport,** New Zealand Electricity Dept., Wellington, N.Z.
1966 **Monroe E. Spaght,** Royal Dutch/Shell Group Companies, U.S.A.
1971 **A.M. Petrosyants,** Soviet Union State Committee for Atomic Energy, U.S.S.R.
1974 **Dixy Lee Ray,** Atomic Energy Commission, U.S.A.

Karl Jordan Medal

THE LEPIDOPTERISTS' SOCIETY
Dept of Entomology, Los Angeles County Museum of Natural History, 900 Exposition Blvd., Los Angeles, Calif. 90007 (213/746-0410)

The Karl Jordan Medal, which carries a $1,000 honorarium, is a silver medal given annually for an outstanding original contribution in lepidopterology, especially in morphology, zoogeography and natural history. An awards committee unanimously selects the winner from nominees.

1973 **Henri Stempfer,**
1974 **Frederick W. Stehr,**
1975 **No award**
1976 **No award**
1977 **Don R. Davis,**
1978 **Pierre E.L. Viette**
1979 **J.F. Gates Clark**
1980 **Keith S. Brown, Jr.**

Award of Excellence

AMERICAN FISHERIES SOCIETY
5410 Grosvenor La., Bethesda, Md. 20014 (301/897-8616)

The annual Award of Excellence, consisting of $1,000, a medal and a certificate, honors scientists in the fields of fisheries and aquatic biology. A committee selects the winner by substantial or unanimous agreement.

1969 **William E. Ricker** (British Columbia, Canada)
1970 **Stanislas Snieszko** (West Virginia)
1971 **F.E.J. Fry** (Ontario, Canada)
1972 **Ralph Hile** (Michigan)
1973 **Carl Hubbs** (California)
1974 **Clarence Tarzwell** (Rhode Island)
1975 **Robert Rush Miller** (Michigan)
1976 **A.W.H. Needler** (New Brunswick, Canada)
1977 **Arthur D. Hoster** (Wisconsin)

Current status unknown

Cullum Geographical Medal
Charles B. Daly Medal
David Livingstone Centenary Medal
Samuel Finley Breese Morse Medal
George Davidson Medal
O. M. Miller Cartographic Medal
Van Cleef Memorial Medal
Honorary Fellowship in the American Geographical Society

AMERICAN GEOGRAPHICAL SOCIETY
Broadway at 156th St., New York, N.Y. 10032
(212/234-8100)

The Cullum Geographical Medal, which is of gold, is awarded as merited for distinguished contributions to the science of geography or for outstanding geographical discoveries made by individuals or exploration parties of any nation.

1896 **Robert E. Peary**
1897 **Fridtjof Nansen**
1899 **Sir John Murray**
1901 **Thomas C. Mendenhall**
1902 **A. Donaldson Smith**
1903 **Duke of the Abruzzi**
1904 **Georg von Neumayer**
Sven Hedin
1906 **Robert Falcon Scott**
Robert Bell
1908 **William Morris Davis**
1909 **Francisco P. Moreno**
Sir Ernest Shackleton
1910 **Hermann Wagner**
1911 **Jean B. E. A. Charcot**
1914 **Ellen Churchill Semple**
John Scott Keltie
1917 **George W. Goethals**
1918 **Frederick Haynes Newell**
1919 **Emmanuel de Margerie**
Henry Fairfield Osborn
1921 **Albert I, Prince of Monaco**
1922 **Edward A. Reeves**
1924 **Jovan Cvijic**
1925 **Pedro C. Sanchez**
Lucien Gallois
Harvey C. Hayes
1929 **Hugh Robert Mill**
Jean Brunhes
Alfred Hettner
Jules de Schokalsky
1930 **Curtis F. Marbut**
1931 **Mark Jefferson**
1932 **Bertram Thomas**
1935 **Douglas Johnson**
1938 **Louise Arner Boyd**
1939 **Emmanuel de Martonne**
1940 **Robert Cushman Murphy**
1943 **Arthur Robert Hinks**
1948 **Hugh Hammond Bennett**
1950 **Hans W:son Ahlmann**
1952 **Roberto Almagia**
1954 **British Everest Expedition**
1956 **J. Russell Smith**
1958 **Charles Warren Thornthwaite**
1959 **Albert Paddock Crary**
1963 **Rachel Louise Carson**
1964 **John Leighly**
1965 **Kirtley Fletcher Mather**
1967 **Peter Haggett**
1968 **Luna B. Leopold**
1969 **Neil A. Armstrong**
Edwin E. Aldrin, Jr.
Michael Collins
1973 **Bruce Heezen**
1975 **Rene Dubos**

The Charles B. Daly Medal, which is of gold, honors distinguished service to geography.

1902 **Robert E. Peary**
1906 **Thorvald Thoroddsen**
1908 **George Davidson**
1909 **William W. Rockhill**
Charles Chaille-Long
1910 **Grove Karl Gilbert**
Roald Amundsen
1913 **Alfred H. Brooks**
1914 **Albrecht Penck**
1915 **Paul Vidal de la Blache**
1917 **George G. Chisholm**
1918 **Vilhjalmur Stefansson**
1920 **George Otis Smith**
1922 **Sir Francis Younghusband**
Adolphus W. Greely
Ernest de K. Leffingwell
1924 **Claude H. Birdseye**
Knud Rasmussen
1925 **Robert A. Bartlett**
David L. Brainard
1927 **Alois Musil**
1929 **Filippo De Filippi**
Emile Feliz Gautier
1930 **Joseph B. Tyrrell**
Nelson H. Darton
Lauge Koch
1931 **Gunnar Isachsen**
1935 **Roy Chapman Andrews**
1938 **Alexander Forbes**
1939 **Herbert John Fleure**
1940 **Carl Ortwin Sauer**
1941 **Julio Garzon Nieto**
1943 **Sir Halford J. Mackinder**
1948 **Henri Baulig**
1950 **Laurence Dudley Stamp**
1952 **J. M. Wordie**
1954 **John K. Wright**
1956 **Raoul Blanchard**
1959 **Richard Hartshorne**
1961 **Theodore Monod**
1962 **Osborn Maitland Miller**
1963 **Henry Clifford Darby**

1964 Jean Gottmann
1965 William Skinner Cooper
1966 Torsten Hagerstrand
1967 Marston Bates
1968 O.H.K. Spate
1969 Paul B. Sears
William O. Field
1971 Gilbert F. White
1973 Walter Sullivan
1974 Walter Wood
1978 Roman Drazniowsky

The David Livingstone Centenary Medal, which may be of gold, silver or bronze, is awarded as merited for scientific achievements in the geography of the Southern Hemisphere.

1916 Sir Douglas Mawson
1917 Theodore Roosevelt
Manuel Vincente Ballivian
1918 Candido Rondon
1920 William Speirs Bruce
Alexander Hamilton Rice
1923 Griffith Taylor
1924 Frank Wild
1925 Luis Riso Patron
1926 Erich von Drygalski
1929 Richard E. Byrd
1930 Jose M. Sobral
Laurence M. Gould
1931 Hjalmar Riiser-Larsen
1935 Lars Christensen
1936 Lincoln Ellsworth
1939 John R. Rymill
1945 Isaiah Bowman
1948 Frank Debenham
1950 Robert L. Pendleton
1952 Carlos Delgado de Carvalho
1956 George McCutchen McBride
1958 Paul Allman Siple
1959 William Edward Rudolph
1965 Bassett McGuire
1966 Preston E. James
1968 William H. Phelps, Jr.
1972 Akin L. Mabogunje

The Samuel Finley Breese Morse Medal, which is of gold, is awarded as merited for the encouragement of geographical research.

1928 Sir George Hubert Wilkins
1945 Archer M. Huntington
1952 Gilbert Grosvenor
1966 Charles B. Hitchcock
1968 Wilma B. Fairchild

The George Davidson Medal, which is of gold, is given as merited for outstanding research or exploration of the Pacific Ocean or of the land masses bordering the Pacific.

1952 George B. Cressey
1972 F. Raymond Fosberg
1974 Joseph Spencer
1975 Shinzo Kiuchi

The O. M. Miller Cartographic Medal, which is of gold, honors noteworthy contributions to cartography or geodesy.

1968 Richard Edes Harrison

The Van Cleef Memorial Medal, which is of gold, honors contributions of note to applied urban geography.

1970 John R. Bochert
1974 Harold Rose

Honorary Fellowship in the American Geographical Society is conferred upon explorers and scientists for meritorious contributions to the field.

1918 E. C. Andrews
Robert A. Bartlett
Pierre Denis
William Curtis Farabee
Emmanuel de Margerie
Emmanuel de Martonne
Marion E. Newbigin
Paul Walle
1919 Morton P. Porsild
Knud Rasmussen
1922 Gunnar Andersson
Charles Raymond Beazley
Jose J. Bravo
James Henry Breasted
Jean Brunhes
Henry Chandler Cowles
Baron Gerard De Geer
Albert Demangeon
Lucien Gallois
Guillaume Grandidier
Adolphus Washington Greely
David George Hogarth
Sir Thomas Holdich
Mark Jefferson
Curtis Fletcher Marbut
Olinto Marinelli
John Linton Myers
Charles Rabot
Sir Aurel Stein
Jean Tilho
Frederick Jackson Turner
Robert De Courcy Ward
1923 E. Deville
1924 Andre Allix
Edwin R. Heath
Lauge Koch
Paul Le Cointe
Count Byron Kuhn de Prorock
Homer Leroy Shantz
1930 Roberto Almagia
Henry Bryant Bigelow
Baron Sten De Geer
Carl Ben Eielson
Vernor Clifford Finch
Herbert John Fleure
Julio Garzon Nieto
Alfredo Jahn
William B. Mayo
Henri Francois Pittier
Sir Napier Shaw
Hussein Sirri Bey
Harald U. Sverdrup
1931 Louise Arner Boyd
1932 Field Marshall Lord Allenby
Harry Clifton Heaton
1935 Rafael Aguilar y Santillan
Hans Ahlmann
Charles Carlyle Colby
Osbert Guy Stanhope Crawford
Carlos M. Delgado de Carvalho
Charles Bungay Fawcett
Nevin M. Fenneman
Alexander Forbes
William Archibald Mackintosh

Lawrence Martin
Carl Ortwin Sauer
Camille Vallaux
1939 Ernst Antevs
Henri Baulig
Giotto Danielli
Sir Wilfred Grenfell
Ludwig Leonhard Mecking
William E. Rudolph
Paul Gerhard Schott
Laurence Dudley Stamp
1942 Albert Berthold Hoen
1943 Christovam Leite de Castro
Manuel Medina
1948 Charles H. Behre, Jr.
Owen Lattimore
John Leighly
George McCutchen McBride
Robert Larimore Pendleton
George H. H. Tate
Charles Warren Thornthwaite
1949 Wofford Benjamin Camp
1952 John Foster Dulles
1956 Jean Gottmann
Stephen B. Jones
Rafael Pico
1958 Felix Cardona Puig
1961 Clarence Fielden Jones
John Ewing Orchard
Robert H. Randall
H. Bradford Washburn
1962 F. Kenneth Hare
Samuel Van Valkenburg
1963 John Quincy Stewart
Gilbert Fowler White
Georg Wust
1964 Kenneth C. Cumberland
Arch C. Gerlach
S. V. Kalesnik
1965 Maxwell J. Dunbar
Peveril Meigs
1966 Waldo R. Tobler
1967 William A. Hance
1968 S. P. Chatterjee
Clara Egli Le Gear
Lionel A. Walford
J. Russell Whitaker
1969 Hans Boesch
Marvin Mikesell
1970 Charles W. M. Swithinbank
Alexander Melamid
1971 Louis O. Quam
Hans Kinzl
1972 Konstantin A. Salishchev
Richard L. Morrill
David Lowenthal
1973 Meredith F. Burrill
Sir A. Grenfell Price
1974 Marton Pecsi
Evelyn L. Pruitt
1975 Sir Laurence P. Kirwan
Andrew H. Clark

Hubbard Medal
Gold Medal
Grosvenor Medal
John Oliver La Gorce Medal
Jane McGrew Smith Award
Franklin L. Burr Prize for Science
Alexander Graham Bell Medal

NATIONAL GEOGRAPHIC SOCIETY
17th and M Sts. NW, Washington, D.C. 20036
(202/857-7000)

The Hubbard Medal, named for Gardiner Greene Hubbard, the first president of the Society, is given as warranted for distinction in exploration, discovery and research.

1906 **Cdr. Robert E, Peary,** Arctic explorations; farthest north 87°06

1907 **Capt. Roald Amundsen,** First traverse of Northwest Passage in a vessel; location of North Magnetic Pole

1909 **Capt. Robert A. Bartlett,** Attaining farthest north, 87°48, with Peary's 1909 expedition
Grove Karl Gilbert, Thirty years' investigations and achievements in physiographic research

1910 **Sir Ernest H. Shackleton,** Explorations in Antarctic; farthest south 88°23

1919 **Vilhjalmur Stefansson,** Discoveries in Canadian Arctic

1926 **Lt. Cdr. Richard E. Byrd, Jr.,** First to reach North Pole by airplane

1927 **Col. Charles A. Lindbergh,** Solo flight from New York to Paris

1931 **Roy Chapman Andrews,** Geographic discoveries in central Asia

1934 **Anne Morrow Lindbergh,** Notable flights as co-pilot on Charles A. Lindbergh aerial surveys

1935 **Capts. Albert W. Stevens and Orvil A. Anderson,** Research achieved while gaining world altitude record of 72,395 feet in Explorer II, National Geographic Society-U.S. Army Air Corps Stratosphere Expedition

1936 **Lincoln Ellsworth,** Heroic, extraordinary achievements in Arctic and Antarctic exploration

1945 **Gen. H.H. Arnold,** Contributions to the science of aviation

1953 **Comdr. Donald B. MacMillan,** Arctic explorations, 1908-52

1954 **Sir John Hunt** (leader), **Sir Edmund Hillary** and **Tenzing Norgay**, British Everest Expedition, Conquest of Earth's highest mountain

1958 **Paul A. Siple,** Scientific leadership of first group to winter at the South Pole; 30 years of Antarctic explorations

1959 **Secretary of the Navy Thomas S. Gates, Jr., Adm. Arleigh A. Burke** and **Rear Adm. George Dufek**, U.S. Navy Antarctic Expeditions, Exploring South Polar regions; establishing stations for International Geophysical Year
Sir Vivian Fuchs, Leadership of British Trans-Arctic Expedition; contribution to geographic knowledge

1962 **Louis S.B. Leakey and Mary Leakey,** Unearthing fossil bones of earliest man and giant animals in East Africa
Lt. Col. John H. Glenn, Jr., Extraordinary contributions to scientific knowledge of the world and beyond as a pioneer in exploring the ocean of space

1963 **Norman G. Dyhrenfurth,** Leader American Mount Everest Expedition, Contributions to geography through high-altitude research; conquest of Earth's highest peak; pioneering a West Ridge route and making the first summit traverse

1967 **Juan T. Trippe,** Extraordinary contributions to geography and exploration through the development of new air routes across continents and oceans, and a lifetime of service to the art and science of aviation

1969 **Col. Frank Borman, Capt. James A. Lovell, Jr.,** and **Lt. Col. William F. Anders,** Apollo 8 astronauts, Unique contributions to science and the exploration of space; first to break the bonds of earth and soar in orbit around the moon

1970 **Neil A. Armstrong, Col. Edwin E. Aldrin, Jr., and Lt. Col. Michael Collins,** Apollo 11 astronauts, Unique contributions to science and the exploration of space; first to land on the mysterious moon, set up scientific instruments and begin its exploration

1975 **Alexander Wetmore,** Outstanding contributions to geography through pioneering explorations and biological studies in the jungles of South and Central America, islands of the central Pacific Ocean and worldwide advancement of the science of ornithology

1978 **Marie Tharp** and **Bruce C. Heezen,** Geologist-cartographers with the Lamont-Doherty Geological Observatory for pioneering work in charting and interpeting the oceans

1979 **James E. Webb,** As administrator of the National Aeronautic and Space Administration, a key leader in the effort to put six teams of American astronauts on the moon and make the national a space-faring power

The Society's Special Gold Medal is given as merited for extraordinary geographic achievement.

1909 **Comdr. Robert E. Peary,** Discovery of the North Pole

1913 **Capt. Roald Amundsen,** Discovery of the South Pole

1914 **Col. George W. Goethals,** Directing completion of the Panama Canal

1926 **Floyd Bennett, USN,** Flight to North Pole with Byrd

1930 **Hugo Eckener,** First global navigation of an airship
Rear Adm. Richard E. Byrd, Jr., Adding to the knowledge of Antarctica; first attainment of the South Pole by air

1932 **Amelia Earhart,** First solo Atlantic flight by a woman

1937 **Thomas C. Poulter,** Achievements, Byrd Antarctic Expedition

1955 **Mrs. Robert E. Peary,** Contributions to Adm. Peary's expeditions to Greenland and Canadian Arctic

1957 **Prince Philip, Duke of Edinburgh,** Promoting science and better understanding among the world's people

1961 **Capt. Jacques-Yves Cousteau,** Giving earthbound man the key to undersea exploration

The Grosvenor Medal is awarded as merited for outstanding service to geography.

1949 **Gilbert Grosvenor,** Outstanding service as editor of *The National Geographic,* 1899-1949

1955 **John Oliver La Gorce,** Outstanding service to the increase and diffusion of geographic knowledge

1974 **Melville Bell Grosvenor,** Outstanding service to the increase and diffusion of geographic knowledge

1980 **Thomas W. McKnew,** Advisory Chairman of the Board of The National Geographic Society, for 48 years of service to the society

The John Oliver La Gorce Medal is awarded as merited for accomplishment in geographic exploration, or in the sciences, or for public service that advances international understanding.

1967 **American Antarctic Mountaineering Expedition,** For contributions to science and exploration through the first ascent of Antarctica's highest mountain to Nicholas B. Clinch (leader)

1968 **Harold E. Edgerton,** For contributions to science and exploration through invention and development of electronic photographic and geophysical equipment
Philip Van Horn Weems, Pioneering achievements in marine, air and space navigation

1979 **John J. Craighead** and **Frank C. Craighead, Jr.,** Twin brothers who have studied wildlife for more than 40 years, including pioneering work using biotelemetry and UHF radio location to keep track of animals and the behavior of entire wildlife populations

The Jane McGrew Smith Award medal was usually given annually from 1917 to 1964 to individuals for their contributions to scientific work, much of which was documented in *National Geographic* articles.

1917 **Hiram Bingham,** Historian, explorer
Alfred H. Brooks, Geologist
George Kennan, Authority on Russia
Henry Pittier, Agriculturist

1919 **Frank G. Carpenter,** Journalist
O.F. Cook, Plant explorer
William H. Dall, Naturalist
Robert F. Griggs, Botanist
William H. Holmes, Art curator
Stephen T. Mather, Park Service director
Edward W. Nelson, Biologist
Joseph T. Strauss, Rear Admiral, USN
Walter T. Swingle, Plant explorer

1921 **Frank M. Chapman,** Ornithologist
Herbert E. Gregory, Geologist
Lt. Donald B. Macmillan, USNR, Explorer
R.G. McConnell, Canadian explorer
J.B. Tyrell, Canadian explorer

1925 **Robert A. Bartlett,** Far north explorer
William Brooks Cabot, Author, engineer
Neil M. Judd, Archeologist
Joseph F. Rock, Agricultural explorer
Charles Sheldon, Alaska explorer
Philip Sidney Smith, Geologist

1926 **Knud Rasmussen,** Greenland explorer

1927 **Charles A. Lindbergh,** Transatlantic flight pioneer

1929 **Andrew E. Douglass,** Astronomer, dendrochronologist
Cornelius A. Pugsley, Banker, conservationist
Herbert Putnam, Librarian of Congress
Curtis D. Wilbur, Secretary of the Navy, ret.

1930 **Sir Wilfred Grenfell,** Surgeon, missionary, author

1931 **Andre Citroen,** Industrialist
Laurence M. Gould, Biologist
Douglas W. Johnson, Physiographer
Capt. Ashley C. McKinley, USA, Aerial photographer
Capt. Albert W. Stevens, USA, Aerial photographer

1933 **William H. Hobbs,** Geologist

1934 **Vernon Bailey,** Field naturalist
Clifford K. Berryman, Political cartoonist
Eugene Edward Buck, President, A.S.C.A.P.
Charles F. Marvin, Meteorologist
W. Coleman Nevils, S.J., President, Georgetown University
James. P. Thompson, Royal Geographical Society of Australia

1935 **Joseph P. Connelly,** Geologist, college president
Col. William R. Pope, U.S. Army
Leonhard Stejneger, Biologist

1936 **H.L. Baldwin,** U.S. Geological Survey, ret.

Rogers Birnie, U.S. Army, ret.
Lawrence W. Burpee, Canadian commissioner
Samuel S. Gannett, Geographer
Herbert Hollick-Kenyon, Pilot, Canadian Airways
His Majesty King Leopold, Belgium
Robert Muldrow, U.S. Geological Survey, ret.
A.E. Murlin, U.S. Geological Survey, ret.
W.J. Peters, U.S. Geological Survey, ret.
Capt. Randolph P. Williams, U.S. Army Air Corps

1937 **Web Hill,** Merchant
Prince Iyesato Tokugawa, Japan

1938 **Franklin Adams,** Authority on Latin America
Stephen R. Capps, Geologist

1940 **Maj. George W. Goddard, U.S.A.A.F.,** Aerial photographer

1941 **J. Fred Essary,** Journalist

1942 **Charles Henry Deetz,** Cartographer

1943 **Samuel Whittemore Boggs,** Geographer
Harry Warner Frantz, Journalist
Maj. Gen. Eli Helmick, U.S. Army, ret.
Mrs. William G. Paden, Author
Maj. Gen. Alexander M. Patch, U.S. Army
Edmund W. Starling, U.S. Secret Service

1944 **Christova Leite de Castro,** Geographer

1945 **Frank B. Jewett,** President, National Academy of Sciences
Frank Mace MacFarland, President, California Academy of Sciences
S.S. Visher, Geographer

1946 **Salvador Massip,** Geographer
Fleet Adm. Chester W. Nimitz, USN, Chief of Naval Operations

1947 **Maurice Ewing,** Geologist
Geoffrey T. Hellman, Essayist
Malcolm J. Proudfoot, Geographer

1948 **Nicholas H. Darton,** Geologist
Benjamin R. Hoffman, Geographical Society of Philadelphia

1949 **George J. Miller,** Editor, *Journal of Geography*
John O'Keefe, U.S. Army Map Service
Earl B. Shaw, President, Council of Geography Teachers

1950 **Mrs. Albert W. Stevens,** Smith life member widow
Mrs. Henry H. Arnold, Smith life member widow

1951 **Hugh L. Dryden,** Director, National Advisory Committee for Aeronautics
Herbert Friedmann, Curator of Birds, U.S. National Museum
Albert E. Giesecke, Government adviser, Peru
Mrs. J.R. Hildebrand, Widow of assistant editor, *National Geographic*
Ruth B. Shipley, Passport Office, U.S. Department of State

1952 **Gen. Andrew George Latta McNaughton,** Canadian Army, ret.

1953 **Robert M. Anderson,** Secretary of the Navy
Mrs. Franklin L. Fisher, Widow of illustrations editor, *National Geographic*
Col. Kenneth H. Gibson, U.S. Air Force
Maynard Owen Williams, Chief of foreign staff, *National Geographic*

1955 **Ira S. Bowen,** Astronomer
Ardito Desio, K-2 Expedition leader

1956 **Charles P. Mountford,** Anthropologist

1959 **Sir Vivian Fuchs,** Geologist, explorer
Sir Bruce Ingram, Editor, *London Illustrated News*
Edwin A. Link, Inventor, undersea pioneer
Albert A. Stanley, U.S. Coast and Geodetic Survey
Capt. P.V.H. Weems, USN, ret.

1960 **Adm. Arleigh A. Burke, USN,** Chief of Naval Operations

1962 **Lyndon B. Johnson,** Vice President of the United States

1964 **Calvin H. Plimpton,** President, Amherst College

The Franklin L. Burr Prize for Science is a cash award, which has ranged from $500 to $5,000 per recipient, that is given as merited to leaders in the Society's expeditions and researches for exceptionally meritorious work.

1933 **Capt. Albert W. Stevens,** Aerial phography

1936 **Capt. Albert W. Stevens,** Commanding "Explorer II" stratosphere flight, Nov. 11, 1935
Capt. Orvil A. Anderson, Piloting "Explorer II" stratosphere flight, Nov. 11, 1935
Capt. Randolph P. Williams, Ground officer and alternate pilot, "Explorer II" stratosphere flight, Nov. 11, 1935

1938 **Dr. and Mrs. William M. Mann,** Expedition to collect wild animals, 1937

1939 **Bradford Washburn,** Explorations in the Mount St. Elias region
Matthew W. Stirling, Archeological work in Veracruz State, Mexico, including discovery of world's oldest dated work

1941 **Matthew W. Stirling,** Discoveries of colossal basalt heads and carved jade, Veracruz State, Mexico
Mrs. Matthew W. Stirling, Field secretary of her husband's 1940-41 expeditions to southern Mexico

1944 **Alexander Wetmore,** Initiating, directing and participating in *National Geographic*-Smithsonian Institution's expeditions to southern Mexico

1945 **Thomas A. Jaggar,** Developing "Honukai" (Sea Turtle, forerunner of World War II amphibious Dukw [Duck])
Lyman J. Briggs, Outstanding direction of *National Geographic*-Army Air Corps stratosphere expeditions, 1934-36

1947 **George Van Biesbroeck,** Service to eclipse expedition to Brazil, 1947

1948 **Edward A. Halbach, Francis J. Heyden, Carl W. Miller, Charles H. Smiley and George Van Biesbroeck,** Achievement as participants to Society's solar eclipse expedition in Asia (Burma, China, Siam and Korea)
Arthur A. Allen, Locating and photographing Alaskan nesting place of bristle-thighed curlew

1950 **Charles P. Mountford,** Leader of expedition to Arnhem Land, northern Australia
Frank M. Setzler, Deputy leader of Arnhem Land expedition

1952 **Harold E. Edgerton,** Invention and development of high-speed photographic flash lighting equipment

1953 **George Van Biesbroeck,** Solar eclipse research in Khartoum, Sudan, with a bearing on Einstein's theory of relativity

1954 **Lyman J. Briggs,** Contributions to many fields of science and 20 years as chairman of the Committee for Research and Exploration, National Geographic Society

1955 **Neil M. Judd,** Pueblo Bonito research and monograph
Mrs. Robert E. Peary, For her notable part in her husband's early Arctic expeditions: 1891, 1893, 1897, 1900 and 1902
Marie Peary Stafford, Co-leader of 1932 expedition which built a memorial to her father at Kap York, Greenland

1956 **Robert F. Griggs,** Leader, Mount Katmai, Alaska expeditions, 1915-30

Matthew W. Stirling, Contributions to knowledge of New World pre-history as leader of 13 *National Geographic*-Smithsonian Institution expeditions

1959 **Carl F. Miller,** Leader of archeological investigation of Russell Cave, Ala.

1961 **Louis S.B. Leakey and Mary D. Leakey,** Outstanding paleontological revelations at Olduvai Gorge, Tanganyika

1962 **Jane Goodall,** Research on chimpanzees, East Africa
Lyman J. Briggs, Scientific achievement as chairman of Society's Committee for Research and Exploration for 28 years

1963 **Rear Adm. Donald B. Macmillan, USN,** Contributions from many explorations into the Arctic
Neil M. Judd, Archeological investigations at Pueblo Bonito, N.M., and series of monographs and related tree-ring studies
Barry C. Bishop, Mountaineering and scientific achievements in conquest of Mount Everest by the American Mount Everest Expedition, 1963

1964 **Jane van Lawick-Goodall,** Outstanding contributions to science through her studies of wild chimpanzees in Tanzania, unique technical achievements and dedicated and courageous pursuit of this research
Helge Ingstad and Anne Stine Ingstad, Outstanding contributions to archeological research through explorations of L'Anse aux Meadows, Newfoundland, which resulted in finding first authenticated pre-Columbian Viking settlement in North America

1965 **Richard E. Leakey,** Co-leader of Lake Natron expeditions, Kenya and Tanzania
Bradford Washburn, Contributions to geography through discovery of Mount Kennedy, Yukon Territory, Canada, 1935, and detailed mapping of the area, 1965
Norman G. Dyhrenfurth, Leader and organizer of American Mount Everest Expedition, 1963

1967 **Maynard M. Miller,** Outstanding contributions through leadership of four Alaskan Commemorative Glacier Projects and service as deputy leader of Mount Kennedy Survey Expedition 1965, and glaciologist on American Mount Everest Expedition, 1963

1973 **Dian J. Fossey,** Courageous and diligent field work in some of the most inaccessible forests of Africa and authority on behavior of the mountain gorilla
Richard E. Leakey, Studies of new, large, fossil-bearing area of East Africa and following in the footsteps of his distinguished parents
Kenan T. Erim, Classical archeologist for discoveries of world-recognized importance regarding structures and life of Aphrodiasias, once a city in what is now Turkey

The Alexander Graham Bell Medal for Research and Geography is given for outstanding achievement in the field.

1980 **Bradford Washburn** and **Barbara Washburn,** "for unique and notable contributions to the science of geography through exploration and discovery over more than four decades and culminating in the first large scale map of the Grand Canyon and the Colorado River"

Bancroft Award

ROYAL SOCIETY OF CANADA
344 Wellington, Ottawa, Ont. K1A 0N4 (613/992-3468)

The Bancroft Award, which consists of $1,000 and a scroll, is usually awarded every two years for publication, instruction or research in geology that has contributed to public understanding and appreciation of the subject. A selection committee chooses the recipient.

1968 **J. Tuzo Wilson**
1970 **D.M. Baird**
1975 **E.R.W. Neale**
1976 **Roger Blais**
1978 **F.K. North**
1980 **W.W. Hutchinson**

Gilbert H. Cady Award
Kirk Bryan Award
E.B. Burwell, Jr. Award
O.E. Meinzer Award
Penrose Medal
Arthur L. Day Medal

GEOLOGICAL SOCIETY OF AMERICA
3300 Penrose Place, Boulder, Colo. 80301 (303/447-2020)

The Gilbert H. Cady Award, which carries a monetary prize, is awarded biennially for contributions to the field of coal geology, generally in North America. The winner's name is submitted by the Coal Geology Division to the Geological Society Society council for approval.

1973 **James M. Schopf**
1975 **Jack A. Simon**
1977 **William Spackman, Jr.**
1979 **Peter A. Hacquebard**

The Kirk Bryan Award is given annually by the Society's Quarternary Geology Geomorphology Division to the author(s) of a published paper of distinction that advances the field or a related field. The Quarternary Geology and Geomorphology Division selects the winner for the approval of the council. The award consists of a certificate and a $500 honorarium.

1958 **Luna B. Leopold**
Thomas J. Maddock, Jr.
1959 **Jack L. Hough**
1960 **John F. Nye**
1961 **John T. Hack**
1962 **Anders Rapp**
1963 **Arthur H. Lachenbruch**
1964 **Robert P. Sharp**
1965 **Gerald M. Richmond**
1966 **Charles S. Denny**
1967 **Clyde A. Wahrhaftig**
1968 **David M. Hopkins**
1969 **Ronald L. Shreve**
1970 **Harold E. Malde**
1971 **A. Lincoln Washburn**
1972 **Dwight R. Crandell**
1973 **John T. Andrews**
1974 **Robert V. Ruhe**
1975 **James B. Benedict**

1976 Geoffrey S. Boulton
1977 Michael Church
1978 Richard L. Hay
1979 Stanley A. Schumm
1980 James A. Clark
William Elliston Farrell
W.R. Peltier

The E.B. Burwell, Jr. Award, which carries a monetary prize, is given annually for a published paper which advances knowledge about engineering geology, soil or rock mechanics or related areas. The Engineering Geology Division selects the winner with the approval of the council.

1969 Lloyd B. Underwood
1970 Glenn R. Scott
David J. Varnes
1971 Edwin B. Eckel
1972 R.J. Proctor
1973 J.E. Hackett
Murray R. McComas
1974 Robert F. Legget
1975 Erhard M. Winkler
1976 David J. Varnes
1977 Richard E. Goodman
1978 Nicholas R. Barton
1979 John W. Bray
Evert Hoek
1980 Kerry Edward Sieh

The O.E. Meinzer Award, which consists of a silver bowl and a certificate, annually honors a distinguished paper published in hydrogeology or a related field. The Hydrogeology Divison selects the winner with the approval of the council.

1965 Jozsef Toth
1966 Charles L. McGuinness
1967 Robert W. Stallman
1968 Mahdi S. Hantush
1969 Hilton H. Cooper, Jr.
1970 Victor T. Stringfield
1971 George B. Maxey
1972 Joseph F. Poland
George H. Davis
1973 William Back
Bruce B. Hanshaw
1974 R. Allan Freeze
1975 John D. Bredehoeft
George F. Pinder
1976 Shlomo P. Neuman
Paul A. Witherspoon
1977 Jacob Rubin
Ronald V. James
1978 R. William Nelson
1979 Patrick A. Domenico
John M. Sharp, Jr.
1980 Richard Lewis Cooley

The Penrose Medal, which is of gold, recognizes outstanding, original contributions or achievements which mark a "decided advance" in the science of geology. The medal is given as merited by the council of the Society.

1927 Thomas Chrowder Chamberlin
1928 Jakob Johannes Sederholm
1929 No award
1930 Francois Alfred Antoine Lacroix
1931 William Morris Davis
1932 Edward Oscar Ulrich
1933 Waldemar Lindgren
1934 Charles Schuchert
1935 Reginald Aldworth Daly
1936 Arthur Philemon Coleman
1937 No award
1938 Andrew Cowper Lawson
1939 William Berryman Scott
1940 Nelson Horatio Darton
1941 Norman Levi Bowen
1942 Charles Kenneth Leith
1943 No award
1944 Bailey Willis
1945 Felix Andries Vening-Meinesz
1946 T. Wayland Vaughan
1947 Arthur Louis Day
1948 Hans Cloos
1949 Wendell P. Woodring
1950 Morley Evans Wilson
1951 Pentti Eskola
1952 George Gaylord Simpson
1953 Esper S. Larsen, Jr.
1954 Arthur Francis Buddington
1955 Maurice Gignoux
1956 Arthur Holmes
1957 Bruno Sander
1958 James Gilluly
1959 Adolph Knopf
1960 Walter Herman Bucher
1961 Philip Henry Kuenen
1962 Alfred Sherwood Romer
1963 William Walden Rubey
1964 Donnel Foster Hewett
1965 Philip Burke King
1966 Harry H. Hess
1967 Herbert Harold Read
1968 J. Tuzo Wilson
1969 Francis Birch
1970 Ralph Alger Bagnold
1971 Marshall Kay
1972 Wilmot H. Bradley
1973 M. King Hubbert
1974 William Maurice Ewing
1975 Francis J. Pettijohn
1976 Preston Cloud
1977 Robert P. Sharp
1978 Robert M. Garrels
1979 J. Harlen Bretz
1980 Hollis Dow Hedberg

The Arthur L. Day Medal, which is of gold, honors distinctive contributions to geologic knowledge through the application of physics and chemistry to the solution of geologic problems. Except in unusual situations, the candidates considered by the council are North Americans. The honor carries with it honorary fellowship in the Society.

1948 George W. Morey
1949 William Maurice Ewing
1950 Francis Birch
1951 Martin J. Buerger
1952 Sterling Hendricks
1953 John F. Schairer
1954 Marion King Hubbert
1955 Earl Ingerson
1956 Alfred O. C. Nier
1957 Hugo Benioff
1958 John Verhoogen
1959 Sir Edward C. Bullard
1960 Konrad B. Krauskopf
1961 Willard F. Libby

1962 Hatten Schuyler Yoder
1963 Keith Edward Bullen
1964 James Burleigh Thompson, Jr.
1965 Walter H. Munk
1966 Robert M. Garrels
1967 O. Frank Tuttle
1968 Frederick J. Vine
1969 Harold C. Urey
1970 Gerald J. Wasserburg
1971 Hans P. Eugster
1972 Frank Press
1973 David T. Griggs
1974 A.E. Ringwood
1975 Allan Cox
1976 Hans Ramberg
1977 Akiho Miyashiro
1978 Samuel Epstein
1979 Walter M. Elasser
1980 Henry G. Thode

Hayden Memorial Geological Award

ACADEMY OF NATURAL SCIENCES OF PHILADELPHIA
19th and The Parkway, Philadelphia, Pa. 19103
(215/299-1015)

The Hayden Memorial Geological Award, which consists of a bronze medal and $300, was given every three years for the best publication, exploration, discovery or research in geology and paleontology as judged by a committee. After a lapse of several years, this award was re-established in 1979 as a biennial honor.

1890 James Hall
1891 Edward D. Cope
1892 Edward Suess
1893 Thomas H. Huxley
1894 Gabriel Augusto Daubree
1895 Karl A. von Zittel
1896 Giovanni Capellini
1897 A. Karpinski
1898 Otto Torell
1899 Gilles Joseph Gustave Dowalque
1902 Archibald Geikie
1905 Charles Doolittle Walcott
1908 John Mason Clarke
1911 John C. Branner
1914 Henry Fairfield Osborn
1917 William Morris Davis
1920 Thomas Chrowder Chamberlin
1923 Alfred Lacroix
1926 William B. Scott
1929 Charles Schuchert
1932 Reginald A. Daly
1935 Andrew C. Lawson
1938 Sir Arthur Smith Woodward
1941 Amadeus W. Grabau
1944 Joseph A. Cushman
1947 Paul Niggli
1950 George Gaylord Simpson
1953 Norman L. Bowen
1956 Raymond C. Moore
1959 Carl O. Dunbar
1962 Alfred S. Remer
1965 Normal D. Newell
1968 Elso S. Barghoorn
1971 Wilmot H. Bradley
1979 Daniel I. Axelrod

Vetlesen Prize

COLUMBIA UNIVERSITY LAMONT-DOHERTY GEOLOGICAL OBSERVATORY
Palisades, N.Y. 10964 (914/359-2900)

The Vetlesen Prize, which consists of $50,000 and a gold medal, is awarded every two years for outstanding scientific achievement resulting in a clearer understanding of the Earth, its history and its relationship to the rest of the Universe. The winner is selected by a committee named by the Lamont-Doherty Observatory and the Georg Unger Vetlesen Foundation.

1960 Maurice Ewing
1962 Sir Harold Jeffreys
Felix Andries Vening Meinesz
1964 Pentti Eelis Eskola
Arthur Holmes
1966 Jan Hendrik Oort
1968 Sir Edward Bullard
Francis Birch
1970 S. Keith Runcorn
Allan V. Cox
Richard D. Dolle
1972 William A. Fowler
1974 Chaim Lieb Pekaris
1977 J. Tuzo Wilson

Willet G. Miller Medal

ROYAL SOCIETY OF CANADA
344 Wellington, Ottawa, Ont. K1A 0N4 (613/992-3468)

The Willet G. Miller Medal, which carries a $1,000 cash prize, is awarded every two years for outstanding research in any branch of earth science. A selection committee chooses the recipient.

1943 Norman Levi Bowen
1945 Morley E. Wilson
1947 F.H. McLearn
1949 H.V. Ellsworth
1951 J.E Hawley
1953 C.H. Stockwell
1955 J. Tuzo Wilson
1957 J.E. Gill
1959 L.S. Russell
1961 W.H. White
1963 L.G. Berry
1965 R.J.W. Douglas
1967 R.E. Folinsbee
1969 R.A. Jeletzky
1971 R.W. Boyle
1973 R. Thorsteinsson
1975 J.R. Mackay
1977 A.M. Goodwin
1979 E.T. Tozer

William Bowie Medal
James B. Macelwane Award
Walter H. Bucher Medal
John Adam Fleming Medal
Robert E. Horton Medal
Maurice Ewing Award

AMERICAN GEOPHYSICAL UNION
1909 King St. NW, Washington, D.C. 20006 (202/231-0370)

The William Bowie Medal is given annually for outstanding contributions to fundamental geophysics and for unselfish cooperation in research.

1939 William Bowie
1940 Arthur Louis Day
1941 John Adam Fleming
1942 Nicholas Hunter Heck
1943 Oscar Edward Meinzer
1944 Henry Bryant Bigelow
1945 Jacob Aall Bonnevie Bjerknes
1946 Reginald Alsworth Daly
1947 Felix Andries Vening Meinesz
1948 James Bernard Macelwane
1949 Walter Davis Lambert
1950 Leason Heberling Adams
1951 Harald Ulrik Sverdrup
1952 Harold Jeffreys
1953 Beno Gutenberg
1954 Richard Montgomery Field
1955 Walter Hermann Bucher
1956 Weikko Aleksanteri Heiskanen
1957 William Maurice Ewing
1958 Johannes Theodoor Thijsse
1959 Walter M. Elsasser
1960 Francis Birch
1961 Keith Edward Bullen
1962 Sydney Chapman
1963 Merle Antony Tuve
1964 Julius Bartels
1965 Hugo Benioff
1966 Louis B. Slichter
1967 Lloyd V. Berkner
1968 Roger Revelle
1969 Walter B. Langbein
1970 Bernhard Haurwitz
1971 Inge Lehmann
1972 Carl Eckhart
1973 George P. Woollard
1974 A. E. Ringwood
1975 Edward Bullard
1976 Jules G. Charney
1977 James A. Van Allen
1978 Helmut E. Landesburg
1979 Frank Press
1980 Charles A. Whitten

The James B. Macelwane Award recognizes significant contributions by a physicist less than 36 years of age. A plaque is given to the winner(s).

1962 James N. Brune
1963 Alexander J. Dessler
1964 Klaus F. Hasselmann
1965 Gordon J. K. MacDonald
1966 Don L. Anderson
1967 Manik Talwani
1968 Michael B. McElroy
1969 Richard S. Lindzen
1970 Lynn R. Sykes
1971 Carl I. Wunsch
1972 John Michael Wallace
1973 R. Allan Freeze
1974 Amos M. Nur
1975 Dan McKenzie
V. Ytenis M. Vasyliunas
Gerald Schubert
1976 John S. Lewis
Kurt Lambeck
Robert L. Parker
1977 Paul G. Richards
Ignacio Rodrigues-Iturbe
Christopher T. Russell
1978 John M. Edmond
Thomas E. Holzer
1979 Ralph J. Cicerone
Michael C. Kelley
1980 Lawrence Grossman
Thomas Westfall Hill
Norman H. Sleep

The Walter H. Bucher Medal is now given every two years for original contributions to knowledge of the Earth's crust.

1968 J. Tuzo Wilson
1969 James Gilluly
1970 David. T. Griggs
1971 Robert S. Dietz
1972 William Jason Morgan
1974 Maurice Ewing
1975 Lynn Sykes
1977 Bruce C. Heezen
1979 Edward Irving

The John Adam Fleming Medal is given every two years for original research and technical leadership in geomagnetism, atmospheric electricity, aeronomy and related sciences.

1962 Lloyd V. Berkner
1963 James A. Van Allen
1964 Edward O. Hulburt
1965 Norman F. Ness
1966 Scott E. Forbush
1967 Ernest Harry Vestine
1968 Eugene N. Parker
1969 Allan Verne Cox
1970 Joseph Kaplan
1971 Walter M. Elsasser
1972 William Ian Axford
1973 Victor Vaquier
1975 Carl E. McIlwain
1977 Francis S. Johnson
1979 Syun-Ichi Akasofu

The Robert E. Horton Medal is awarded for outstanding contributions to the geophysical aspects of hydrology.

1976 Walter B. Langbein
1978 Harold A. Thomas, Jr.
1980 William C. Ackerman

The annual Maurice Ewing Award is given jointly by the AGU and the U.S. Navy for contributions for understanding physical, geophysical and geological process in the ocean, to engineering, technology and instrumentation and/or service to marine sciences.

1976 Walter H. Munk
1977 Henry Stommell
1978 Edward Bullard

1979 **Wallace Smith Broecker**
1980 **J. Tuzo Wilson**

Bocher Memorial Prize
Frank Nelson Cole Prizes in Algebra and Number Theory
Oswald Veblen Prize in Geometry
George David Birkhoff Prize in Applied Mathematics
Norbert Wiener Prize in Applied Mathematics
LeRoy P. Steele Prizes

AMERICAN MATHEMATICAL SOCIETY
201 Charles St., Box 6248, Providence, R.I. 02940
(401/272-9500)

The Bocher Memorial Prize is given every five years for "a notable research memoir in analysis" which appeared in the previous five years. The $1,450 prize goes to a Society member or to a contributor to a recognized North American journal.

1923 **G.D. Birkhoff,** "Dynamical Systems with Two Degrees of Freedom"
1924 **E.T. Bell,** "Arithmetical Paraphrases"
1928 **J.W. Alexander,** "Combinatorial Analysis Situs"
1933 **Marston Morse,** "The Foundations of a Theory of the Calculus of Variations in the Large M-Space"
1938 **John von Neumann,** "Almost Periodic Functions and Groups"
1943 **Jesse Douglas,** "Green's Function and the Problem of Plateau"
1948 **A.C. Schaeffer and D.C. Spencer,** "Coefficients of Schicht Functions"
1953 **Norman Levinson,** Contributions to the theory of linear, non-linear, ordinary and partial differential equation in various papers.
1959 **Louis Nirenberg,** Work in partial differential equations
1964 **Paul J. Cohen,** "On a Conjecture of Littlewood and Idempotent Measures"
1969 **I.M. Singer,** Work on the index problem.
1974 **Donald S. Ornstein,** "Bernoulli Shifts with the Same Entropy are Isomorphic"
1979 **Alberto P. Calderon,** Work on the theory of singular integrals and partial differential equations, specifically "Cauchy Integrals on Lipschitz Curves and Related Operators"

The Frank Nelson Cole Prize in Algebra and the Frank Nelson Cole Prize in Number Theory are each awarded at five-year intervals for contributions to algebra and the theory of numbers, under restrictions similar to those of the Bocher Prize. The present honorarium is $2,250.

1928 **L.E. Dickson,** "Algebren und Ihre Zahlentheorie"
1931 **H.S. Vandiver,** Papers on Fermat's last theorem
1939 **A. Adrian Albert,** Papers on the construction of Riemann matrices
1944 **Oscar Zariski,** Papers on algebraic varieties
1946 **H.B. Mann,** "A Proof of the Fundamental Theorem of the Density of Sums of Sets of Positive Integers"
1949 **Richard Bauer,** "On Artin's L-Series with General Group Characters"
1951 **Paul Erdos,** Papers on the theory of numbers
1954 **Harish-Chandra,** Papers on representations of semi-simple Lie algebras and groups
1956 **John T. Tate,** "The Higher Dimensional Cohomology Groups of Class Field Theory"
1960 **Serge Lang,** "Unramified Class Field Theory over Function Fields in Several Variables"
Maxwell E. Rosenlicht, "Generalized Jacobian Varieties"
1962 **Kenkichi Iwasawa,** "Gamma Extensions of Number Fields"
Bernard M. Dwork, "On the Rationality on the Zeta Function of an Algebraic Variety"
1965 **Walter Feit and John G. Thompson,** "Solvability of Groups of Odd Order"
1967 **James B. Ax and Simon B. Kochen,** "Diophantine Problems over Local Fields"
1970 **John R. Stallings,** "On Torsion-free Groups with Infinitely Many Ends"
Robert G. Swan, "Groups of Cohomological Dimension One"
1972 **Wolfgang M. Schmidt,** "On Simultaneous Approximations of Two Algebraic Numbers by Rationals" and other papers
1975 **Hyman Bass,** "Unitary Algebraic K-Theory"
Donald G. Quillen, "Higher Algebraic K-Theories"
1977 **Goro Shimura,** "Class Fields Over Real Quadratic Fields and Heche Operators" and "On Modular Forms of Half Integral Weight"
1980 **Melvin Hochester,** "Topics in the Homological Theory of Commutative Rings"
Michael Aschbacher, "A Characterization of Chevalley Groups Over Fields of Odd Order"

The Oswald Veblen Prize in Geometry is a $2,000 award, ordinarily made every five years under conditions similar to those of the Bocher Prize.

1964 **C.D. Papakyriakopoulos,** "On Solid Tori" and "On Dehn's Lemma and the Asphercity of Knots"
Raoul Bott, "The Space of Loops of a Lie Group" and "The Stable Homotopy of the Classical Groups"
1966 **Stephen Smale,** Contributions to differential topology
Morton Brown and Barry Mazur, Work on the generalized Schoenflies theorem
1971 **Robion C. Kirby,** "Stable Homeomorphisms and the Annulus Conjecture"
Dennis P. Sullivan, "On the Hauptvermutung for Manifolds"
1976 **William P. Thurston,** For work on foilations
James Simons, For work on minimal varieties and characteristic forms

The George David Birkhoff Prize in Applied Mathematics of $2,066 is normally awarded every five years jointly by the American Mathematical Society and the Society for Industrial and Applied Mathematics to a member of one of these societies who is a resident of the United States, Canada or Mexico.

1968 **Jurgen K. Moser,** Contributions to the theory of Hamiltonian dynamical systems
1973 **Fritz John,** Work in partial differential equations in numerical analysis
James B. Serrin, Fundamental contributions to the theory of non-linear partial differential equations
1978 **Garrett Birkhoff,** Bringing the methods of algebra and the highest standards of mathematics to scientific applications
Mark Kac, Contributions to statistical mechanics and to probability theory and its applications

Clifford Truesdell, Contributions to the understanding of rational mechanics and nonlinear materials, efforts to give precise mathematical formulations to classical subjects and contributions to applied mathematics in several areas of specialization

The $2,000 Norbert Wiener Prize in Applied Mathematics is made jointly by the American Mathematicl Society and the Society for Industrial and Applied Mathematics under conditions similar to the Birkhoff Prize. It is awarded every five years.

1970 **Richard E. Bellman,** Work in dynamic programming and for related work

1975 **Peter D. Lax,** Work on numerical and theoretical aspects of partial differential equations and on scattering theory

The LeRoy P. Steele Prizes, endowed by a $143,000 bequest, are awarded for outstanding published mathematical research. One or more prizes may be given as often as each year.

1970 **Solomon Lefschetz,** "A Page of Mathematical Autobiography"

1971 **James B. Carrell,** "Invariant Theory, Old and New," written with Jean A. Dieudonne
Jean A. Dieudonne, "Algebraic Geometry"
Phillip A. Griffiths, "Periods of Integrals on Algebraic Manifolds"

1972 **Edward B. Curtis,** "Simplical Homotopy Theory"
William J. Ellison, "Waring's Problem"
Lawrence F. Payne, "Isoperimetric Inequalities and Their Applications"
Dana S. Scott, "A Proof of the Independence of the Continuum Hypothesis"

1975 **Lipman Bers,** "Uniformization Moduli, and Kleinian Groups"
Martin D. Davis, "Hilbert's Tenth Problem is Unsolvable"
Joseph L. Taylor, "Measure Algebras"
H. Blaine Lawson, "Foliations"
George W. Mackey, "Ergodic Theory and Its Significance for Statistical Mechanics and Probability Theory"

1979 **Salomon Bochner**, Cumulative influence on fields of probability theory, Fournier analysis, several complex variables and differential geometry
Hans Lewy, For three fundamental papers published 1956-60
Antoni Zygmund, Cumulative influence on theory of Fournier series, real variables and related areas of analysis
Robin Hartshorne, "Equivalence Relations on Algebraic Cycles and Subvarieties of Small Codimension"
Joseph J. Kohn, "Harmonic Integrals on Strongly Convex Domains"

Wolf Prize in Mathematics

WOLF FOUNDATION
Box 398, Herzliah-Bet, Israel

The $100,000 Wolf Prize in Mathematics honors an outstanding body of work in mathematics, as determined by a committee of internationally known judges. The award is part of a $500,000 annual prize distribution for exceptional achievement in five fields of science.

1978 **I.M. Gelfand** (Moscow State University), Work on functional analysis, group representation and seminal contributions to many areas of mathematics and its applications
Carl L. Siegel (University of Gottingen), Contributions to the theory of numbers, theory of several complex variables and celestial mechanics

1979 **Jean Leray** (College de France, Paris), Pioneering work on the development and application of topological methods to the study of differential equations
Andre Weil (Institute for Advanced Study, Princeton, N.J.), Introduction of algebra-geometry methods to the theory of numbers

1980 **Henri Cartan** (University of Paris), Pioneering work in algebraic topology, complex variables and homological algebra and leadership of a generation of mathematicians
Andrei Kolmogrov (Moscow state University), Deep and original discoveries in Fournier analysis, probability theory, ergodic theory and dynamical studies

Acta Metallurgica Gold Medal

ACTA METALLURGICA, INC.
c/o R.L. Fullman, General Electric Research & Development Co., Box 8, Schenectady, N.Y. 12301 (518/385-8071)

The Acta Metallurgica Gold Medal, accompanied by a certificate is given annually for ability and leadership in materials research. Selections are made by an international panel of judges from nominations submitted by sponsoring or cooperating societies of Acta Metallurgica, Inc.

1974 **Bruce Chalmers**
1975 **W.G. Burgers**
1976 **Sir Alan Cottrell**
1977 **John Cahn**
1978 **Mats Hillert**
1979 **David Turnbull**
1980 **Johannes Weertman**

IMO Prize

INTERNATIONAL METEOROLOGICAL ORGANIZATION
Case postale 5, CH-1211 Geneva 20, Switzerland, (Tel. 022-34-64-00)

The IMO Prize, which consists of a gold medal, $1,200 and a parchment scroll, is given annually for outstanding work in meteorology or related fields for research or applications. Members of the World Meteorological Association may make nominations for selection by the executive committee.

1956 **Th. Hesselberg** (Norway)
1957 **C.G. Rossby** (Sweden and U.S.A.)
1958 **E. Gold** (United Kingdom)
1959 **J. Bjerknes** (Norway and U.S.A.)
1960 **J. Van Mieghem** (Belgium)
1961 **K.R. Ramanthan** (India)
1962 **A. Angstrom** (Sweden)
1963 **R.C. Sutcliffe** (United Kingdom)
1964 **F.W. Reichendorf** (U.S.A.)
1965 **S. Petterssen** (Norway and U.S.A.)
1966 **T. Bergeron** (Sweden)

1967 K. Ya. Kondratyev (U.S.S.R.)
1968 Sir Graham Sutton (United Kingdom)
1969 E.L. Palmen (Finland)
1970 R. Th. A. Sherhag (Federal Republic of Germany)
1971 J.G. Charney (U.S.A.)
1972 V.A. Bugaev (U.S.S.R.)
1973 C.H.B. Priestley (Australia)
J.S. Sawyer (United Kingdom)
1974 J. Smagorinsky (USA)
1975 W.L. Godson (Canada)
1976 E.K. Fedorov (U.S.S.R.)
1977 G.P. Cressman
1978 A. Nyberg (Sweden)
1979 H.E. Landsberg
1980 R.M. White (USA)

Carl-Gustaf Rossby Research Medal
Second Half Century Award
Charles Franklin Brooks Award
Cleveland Abbe Award for Distinguished Service to Atmospheric Sciences
Sverdrup Gold Medal
Clarence Leroy Meisinger Award
Award for Outstanding Service by a Weather Forecaster
Award for the Advancement of Applied Meteorology
Award for Outstanding Achievement in Bioclimatology
Award for Outstanding Services to Meteorology by a Corporation
Award for Outstanding Service by a Broadcast Meteorologist
Robert E. Horton Lecture
Editor's Award
Banner I. Miller Award
Father James W. Macelwane Awards in Meteorology
Special Awards

AMERICAN METEOROLOGICAL SOCIETY
45 Beacon St., Boston, Mass. 02108 (617/227-2425)

The Carl-Gustaf Rossby Research Medal, which is of gold, honors contributions to the understanding of the structure or behavior of the atmosphere. It is the Society's highest honor and is presented to an individual selected by the awards committee.

1951 Hurd Curtis Willett
1952 No award
1953 Carl-Gustaf Arvid Rossby
1954 No award
1955 Jerome Namias
1956 John von Neumann
1957 No award
1958 No award
1959 No award
1960 J. Bjerknes and Erik Palmen
1961 Victor P. Starr
1962 Bernhard Haurwitz
1963 Harry Wexler
1964 Jule G. Charney
1965 Arnt Elaissen
1966 Zdenek Sekera
1967 Dave Fultz
1968 Verner E. Suomi
1969 Edward N. Lorenz
1970 Hsiao-Lan Kuo
1971 Norman A. Phillips
1972 Joseph Smagorinsky
1973 Christian E. Junge
1974 Heinz H. Lettau
1975 Charles H.B. Priestley
1976 Hans A. Panofsky
1977 Akio Arakawa
1978 James W. Deardorff
1979 Herbert Riehl
1980 Sean A. Twomey

The Second Half Century Award, which consists of a medallion, honors a Society member for contributions to geofluid sciences. No more than three awards are given annually. They are generally made to individuals about 50 years of age at the time of presentation. The honor was instituted for the Society's 50th anniversery year.

1970 Rudolph Nael
Don T. Hilleary
Lewis D. Kaplan
David Q. Wark
1971 No award
1972 Richard J. Reed
1973 Douglas K. Lilly
1974 James W. Deardorff
Tiruvalam N. Krishnamurti
1975 Louis J. Battan
1976 Roger M. Lehrmitte
1977 Syukuro Manabe
1978 Joost A. Businger
1979 J. Murray Mitchell, Jr.
1980 Andre J. Robert and Frederick G. Shuman

The Charles Franklin Brooks Award is given as merited to an individual for service to the Society, usually over a period of years.

1951 Henry Southworth Shaw
1953 Harry Guggenheim
1955 Charles Franklin Brooks
1956 Robert Granville Stone
1957 Carl-Gustaf Arvid Rossby
1958 Henry Garrett Houghton
1960 Horace Robert Byers
1961 Howard T. Orville
1962 Sverre Petterssen
1963 David M. Ludlum
1964 Thomas F. Malone
1965 Patrick D. McTaggart-Cowan
1966 John C. Beckman
1967 Phil E. Church
1968 Kenneth C. Spengler
1969 Alfred K. Blackadar
1970 Robert Dawson Fletcher
1971 Louis J. Batton
1972 Helmut E. Landsberg
1973 Glenn R. Hilst
1974 David F. Landrigan

1975 Werner A. Baum
1976 Earl G. Droessler
1977 Eugene Bollay
1978 No award
1979 Robert M. White
1980 Verner E. Suomi

The Cleveland Abbe Award for Distinguished Service to Atmospheric Sciences, which consists of a certificate, is awarded as merited to an individual for progress in atmospheric science or its application to general social, economic or humanitarian welfare.

1963 Lloyd V. Berkner
1964 Francis W. Reichelderfer
1965 Sverre Petterssen
1966 Alan T. Waterman
1967 Arthur F. Merewether
1968 Thomas F. Malone
1969 Robert M. White
1970 Walter Orr Roberts
1971 Robert G. Fleagle
1972 Homer E. Newell
1973 Fred D. White
1974 Lester Machta
1975 George P. Cressman
1976 Patrick D. McTaggart-Cowan
1977 Richard M. Goody
1978 Horace R. Byers
1979 No award
1980 Jule E. Charney

The Sverdrup Gold Medal honors important research in the scientific knowledge of interactions between oceans and atmosphere. This medal is awarded as merited by the President of the Society upon the advice of an international committee in consultation with representatives of leading marine research facilities.

1964 Henry Stommel
1966 Walter H. Munk
1970 Kirk Bryan
1971 Klaus Hasselmann
1972 Vladimir Kamenkovich
1975 Owen M. Phillips
1976 Robert W. Stewart
1977 Raymond B. Montgomery
1978 John C. Swallow
1979 No award
1980 Hakon Mosby

The Clarence Leroy Meisinger Award annually recognizes research achievement that is, at least in part, aerological in nature. The award consists of an honorarium and a certificate. Preference is given to scientists 35 years of age or younger.

1938 Jerome Namias
1939 No award
1940 No award
1941 Joseph J. George
1942 No award
1943 No award
1944 No award
1945 No award
1946 Morris Neiburger
1947 Herbert Riehl
1948 James E. Miller
1949 Jule G. Charney and Arnt Eliassen
1950 John Freeman, Jr., and Morris Tepper
1951 Dave Fultz
1952 No award
1953 No award
1954 No award
1955 No award
1956 Ernest J. Fawbush and Robert C. Miller
1957 David Atlas
1959 Robert G. Fleagle
1960 Philip D. Thompson and Norman A. Phillips
1961 Verner E. Suomi
1962 Louis J. Battan
Joanne Starr Malkus
1963 Edward N. Lorenz
1964 Richard J. Reed
1965 Hans A. Panofsky
1966 George W. Platzman
1967 Tetsuya Fujita, Joseph Smargorinsky, Syukuro Manabe, Yale Mintz, Akio Arakawa and Cecil E. Leith
1968 Katsuyuki Ooyama
1969 Richard S. Lindzen
1970 William L. Smith
1971 Joseph Pedlosky
1972 Francis P. Bretherton
1973 Robert E. Dickinson
James R. Holton
1974 Keith A. Browning
1975 John M. Wallace
1976 Thomas W. Flattery
1977 Roger A. Pielke
1978 Alan K. Betts
1979 John C. Wyngaard
1980 Richard A. Anthes

The annual Award for Outstanding Service by a Weather Forecaster honors the Society member who has provided distinguished service that is a credit to the profession, especially involving public safety and well-being. A committee selects the winner.

1967 Charles L. Mitchell
1968 Gordon E. Dunn
1969 Lee George Dickinson
1970 Harlan K. Saylor
1971 Leonard W. Snellman
1972 Robert E. Clark
1973 Hilmer Crumrine
1974 W. Clyde Conner
Raymond H. Craft
1975 Robert C. Miller
1976 James F. Andrews
James F. O'Connor
1977 Capt. Charles R. Holliday, USAF
1978 Elbert C. Hill, Jr.
1979 Burnash Gustafson and Arthur F. Gustafson
1980 Vernon G. Bohl

The Award for the Advancement of Applied Meteorology annually honors an individual for contributions to direct application of the science to climatological knowledge toward the fulfillment of industrial or agricultural needs or to the development of scientific knowledge which ultimately can meet those needs.

1956 Joseph J. George
1957 William J. Schaefer
1958 No award
1959 Carl-Gustaf Arvid Rossby
1960 Henry T. Harrison
1961 Robert D. Elliott
1962 Alfred H. Glenn
1963 Herbert C.S. Thom
1964 No award
1965 Loren W. Crow

1966 **Eugene Bollay**
1967 **Charles Pennypacker Smith**
1968 **Wallace E. Howell**
1969 **E. Wendell Hewson**
1970 **Arthur F. Merewether**
1971 **George P. Cressman**
1972 **Vincent J. Oliver**
Howard B. Kaster
1973 **Harold A. Bedient**
Robert E. Munn
1974 **Robert A. McCormick**
1975 **William H. Klein**
1976 **Don G. Friedman**
Bernard Vonnegut
1977 **John E. Wallace**
1978 **No award**
1979 **No award**
1980 **Allan H. Murphy**

The Award for Outstanding Achievement in Bioclimatology is a certificate given as merited for outstanding contributions in the field. A Committee on Biometeorology submits a list of nominees to the Awards Committee for selection.

1960 **Frederick Sargent II**
1963 **Konrad J.K. Buettner**
1964 **Helmut E. Landsberg**
1966 **Frederick A. Brooks**
1967 **Paul E. Waggoner**
1969 **William G. Wellington**
1971 **David M. Gates**
1972 **Igho J. Kornblueh**
1973 **Harold D. Johnson**
1976 **G. LeRoy Hahn**
1977 **No award**
1978 **Norman J. Rosenberg**
1979 **No award**
1980 **Champ B. Tanner**

The annual Award for Outstanding Services to Meteorology by a Corporation honors advancement of the science or its application with a certificate.

1951 ***House Beautiful*** **magazine**
1952 **No award**
1953 **Munitalp Foundation**
1954 **National Broadcasting Co.**
1955 **Science Service, Inc.**
1956 ***New York Times***
1957 **Travelers Insurance Co.**
1958 **No award**
1959 **General Electric Co.**
1960 **American Airlines**
Eastern Airlines
Pan American World Airways
Trans World Airlines
United Air Lines
1961 **Pacific Gas and Electric Co.**
1962 **No award**
1963 **Radio Corp. of America**
1965 ***Christian Science Monitor***
1966 **Industrial Laboratories of the International Telephone and Telegraph Corp.**
1967 **Atlantic Research Corp.**
1968 **Hughes Aircraft Co.**
Santa Barbara Research Center
1969 **Science Associates, Inc.**
1970 **A.H. Glenn and Assoc.**
Murray and Trettel, Inc.
North American Weather Consultants
Northeast Weather Service
Weather Corp. of America
1971 ***Scientific American***
1973 **WTVT Television Service, Tampa, Fla.**
1974 **Barnes Engineering Co.**
1975 **National Geographic Society**
1976 **Franklin Institute**
1977 **University Corp. for Atmospheric Research**
1978 **Massachusetts Institute of Technology**
1979 **Environmental Research and Technology, Inc.**
1980 **Helen Dwight Reid Educational Foundation**

The Award for Outstanding Service by a Broadcast Meteorologist is given annually to honor a radio or television weather forecaster.

1980 **Donald E. Kent**

The Robert E. Horton Lecturer in Hydrology is selected in recognition of an individual's eminence as a scientist or for outstanding research on topics of interest to both hydrologists and meteorologists. The lecturer receives a certificate and an honorarium.

1980 **Eugene L. Peck**

The annual Editor's Award, which consists of a certificate, recognizes a manuscript of outstanding merit submitted to one of the Society's publications.

1969 **Norman A. Phillips**
1970 **Charles W. Newton**
1971 **Peter V. Hobbs**
1972 **James W. Deardorff**
1973 **George W. Platzman**
1974 **Norihiko Fukuta**
1975 **Gabriel T. Csanady**
1976 **Stanley L. Barnes**
Robert E. Dickinson
1977 **No award**
1978 **Jerry D. Mahlman**
1979 **John M. Wallace**
1980 **Kenneth H. Bergman**

The Banner I. Miller Award, which carries a $300 honorarium, is given for contributions to the science of the hurricane and tropical weather forecasting published during the preceding 24 months in a journal with international circulation.

1979 **Lloyd Shapiro**
1980 **No award**

The Father James W. Macelwane Awards in Meteorology, which carry cash prizes, annually honor the winners in a student paper contest, whose purpose it is to stimulate interest in the atmospheric sciences. Undergraduate students may enter the competition. The first prize, whose winners are listed here, is $200. Two other cash awards are given.

1960 **William E. Shenk,** Pennsylvania State University
1961 **No award**
1962 **No award**
1963 **John B. Armstrong,** University of British Columbia
1964 **Charles B. Pyke,** University of California/Los Angeles
1965 **William L. Woodley,** University of California/Los Angeles
1966 **Edward E. Hindman II,** Colorado State University
1967 **No award**
1968 **Peter H. Hildebrand,** University of Chicago
1969 **I.R. Graham,** University of Toronto

1970 **Andres J. Heymsfield,** State University of New York/Fredonia
1971 **Dean G. Duffy,** Case Institute of Technology
1972 **Robert M. Friedman,** New York University
1973 **Louis W. Uccelini,** University of Wisconsin
1974 **Robert M. Thompson, Jr.,** Florida State University
1975 **Paul W. Greiman,**Florida State University
1976 **Stephen J. Culucci,** State University of New York/Albany
1977 **David Schachterle,** University of Colorado
1978 **Paul E. Ciesielski**
1979 **John E. Lanzante**
1980 **Kevin A. Mundell**

Special awards and citations are made as merited to individuals or organizations whose accomplishments are noteworthy but which do not fit within the framework of the Society's regular awards program.

1957 **KSOK Radio,** Arkansas City, Kans.
WKY-TV, Oklahoma City, Okla.
Joseph Bartatto
Stuart Grazier Bigler
1959 **Maurice Levy**
Jean Felix Piccard
1960 **U.S. Forest Service**
Charles B. Moore
Malcolm D. Ross
Lee Lewis
Walter Rue
Nicholas Brango
1961 **William W. Kellogg**
Stanley M. Greenfield
John C. Freeman
Archie M. Kahan
1962 **Werner A. Baum**
1964 **Dean Blake**
Rev. Adelhelm Hess, O.S.B.
1965 **Gordon D. Cartwright**
Morton J. Rubin
1966 **Gertrude M. Woods**
1969 ***Fortune* magazine**
Lawrence Lessing
KCID, Spencer, Iowa
1970 **Hydrologic Services of the ESSA Weather Bureau**
Ferdinand C. Bates
Howard H. Hanks, Jr.
WMAQ-TV, Chicago
1971 **George L. Hammond**
Robert E. Cardinal
National Broadcasting Co.
WKY Television Systems, Inc., Oklahoma City, Okla.
Raymond E. Falconer
Raymond A. Wrightson
1972 **Robert Jastrow**
Francis W. Reichelderfer
Malcolm Rigby
1973 **Agricultural (Fruit Frost) Weather Forecasters, Ariz. and Calif.**
William H. Best, Jr.
James W. Reid
1974 **Illinois State Water Survey**
1975 **Robert O. Reid**
1974 **National Weather Service Office,** Huntsville, Ala. Det. 15, 15th Wea. Sq. 5th Wea. Wg., **Air Weather Service,** Wright-Patterson AFB, Ohio
1976 **Albert W. Duckworth**
1977 **John F. Henz**
Vincent R. Scheetz
Viking Meterology Flight Team
KCOL radio, Fort Collins, Colo.
Alan K. Betts
Stephen K. Cox
Edward J. Zipser
1978 **Morris Tepper**
7th Weather Wing, Detachment 4, Air Weather Service, Altus AFB, Okla.
1979 **Robert B. Rice**
Guy H. Gray, Jr., Benjamin Brown, William C. Henry, John E. Michener and **Leon Schirn**
1980 No award

Losey Atmospheric Sciences Award

AMERICAN INSTITUTE OF AERONAUTICS AND ASTRONAUTICS
1290 Ave. of the Americas, New York, N.Y. 10019
(212/581-4300)

The Losey Atmospheric Sciences Award, which through 1975 was called the Robert M. Losey Award, recognizes contributions to meteorology as applied to aeronautics. The award consists of a medal and certificate, and is made upon a decision of the honors and awards committee.

1940 **Henry G. Houghton, Jr.**
1941 **Horace R. Byers**
1942 **F.W. Riechelderfer**
1943 **Joseph J. George**
1944 **John C. Bellamy**
1945 **Harry Wexler**
1946 **Carl G. Rossby**
1947 **Benjamin G. Holzman**
1948 **Paul A. Humphrey**
1949 **William Lewis**
1950 **Roscoe R. Braham**
1951 **Ivan R. Tannehill**
1952 **Vincent J. Schaefer**
1953 **Henry T. Harrison, Jr.**
1954 **Hermann B. Wobus**
1955 **Robert C. Bundgaard**
1956 **Ross Gunn**
1957 **Jule G. Charney**
1958 **P.D. McTaggard-Cowan**
1959 **Herbert Riehl**
1960 **Thomas F. Malone**
1961 **Arthur F. Merewether**
1962 **Jacob A.B. Bjerknes**
1964 **Robert C. Miller**
1965 **George P. Cressman**
1966 **David Atlas**
1967 **Elmar R. Reiter**
1969 **Robert D. Fletcher**
1970 **Newton A. Lieurance**
1971 **Verner E. Suomi**
1972 **David Q. Wark**
1973 **George H. Fichtl**
1974 **Norman Sissenwine**
1975 **Paul W. Kadlec**
1976 **No award**
1977 **Robert Knollenberg**
1978 **Robert A. McClatchey**
1979 **Allan B. Bailey**
1980 **William W. Vaughan**

Buys Ballot Medal

Royal Netherlands Academy of Arts and Sciences
Kloveniersburgwal 29, Amsterdam, Holland (020 22 29 02)

The Buys Ballot Medal, which is of gold, is awarded every 10 years for research in meteorology. A selection committee chooses the winner of this international honor.

1893 **Julius Hann** (Austria)
1903 **R. Assmann and A. Berson** (Germany)
1913 **H. Hergesell** (France)
1923 **Sir Napier Shaw** (United Kingdom)
1933 **V. Bjerknes** (Norway)
1948 **S. Petterssen** (Norway)
1953 **G.J.H. Swoboda** (Switzerland)
1963 **E.H. Palmen** (Finland)
1973 **J. Smagorinsky** (U.S.A.)

Matthew Fontaine Maury Medal

SMITHSONIAN INSTITUTION
1000 Jefferson Dr. SW, Washington, D.C. 20560 (202/628-4422)

The Matthew Fontaine Maury Medal, which is of gold, honors distinguished contributions in underwater ocean science. It is awarded as merited.

1971 **Edwin A. Link and J. Seward Johnson,** Conception and development of Johnson-Sea-Link, the first in a class of submersible research vehicles
1976 **Robert M. White,** For distinguished service as first administrator of the National Oceanic and Atmospheric Administration and efforts in fostering research on a national level

Grand Prix de Physique Jean Ricard
Prix Robin
Prix Ancel
Prix Aime Cotton
Prix Lengvin
Prix Joliot-Curie
Prix Alain Berlot

SOCIETE FRANCAIS DE PHYSIQUE
33, rue Croulebarbe, 75013, Paris, France (1-707.32.98 and 1-331.00.11)

The Grand Prix Physique Jean Ricard, which consists of a plaque and an honorarium, is awarded annually upon a decision by the society's council for meritorious contributions to physics. It is the society's highest honor and is given to a French citizen.

1974 **J. Winter**
1975 **P. Musset**
1976 **G. Slodzian**
1977 **R. Balian**
1978 **M. Henon**
1979 **A. Libchabert**
1980 **M. Kleman**

The Prix Robin, which consists of a plaque and an honorarium, is awarded annually for the body of scientific work of a physician who is a citizen of france. The society's council selects the recipient.

1974 **M.P. Aigrain**
1975 **M.L. Michel**
1976 **J. Prentki**
1977 **B. Cagnac**
1978 **H. Benoit**
1979 **J.L. Steinberg**
1980 **J. Jacrot**

The Prix Ancel, consisting of a plaque and an honorarium, annually recognizes distinguished work in the physics of consensed matter. The society's council selects the winner.

1974 **P. Berge**
1975 **Ch. Caroli**
1976 **G. Jannink**
1977 **Ph. Monod**
1978 **M.X. Duval** and **M.A. Thomy**
1979 **G. Frossati**
1980 **P. Atten**

The Prix Aime Cotton, comprised of a plaque and an honorarium, is awarded annually for meritorious work in molecular or atomic physics. The council of the society chooses the recipient.

1974 **Ph. Cahuzac**
1975 **J. Romestain**
1976 **M. Gaillard**
1977 **G. Grynberg**
1978 **C. Camy-Peyret** and **J.M. Flaud**
1979 **M. Ledourneuf**
1980 **H. Dubost**

The Prix Langevin, consisting of a plaque and an honorarium, is given annually for work in theoretical physics. The society's council chooses the winner.

1974 **E. Brezin**
1975 **D. Vautherin**
1976 **G. Toulouse**
1977 **J. Zinn Justin**
1978 **J. Iliopoulos**
1979 **R. Schaeffer**
1980 **J. Magnen** and **R. Seneor**

The Prix Joliot-Curie, which is comprised of an honorarium and a plaque, is given annually for work in nuclear or particulate physics. The society's council selects the recipient

1974 **C. Detraz**
1975 **J.P. Vialle**
1976 **J. Galin**
1977 **M. Della Negra**
1978 **J. Delorme**
1979 **A. Diamant-Berger**
1980 **M.C. Mallet-Lemaire**

The Prix Alain Brelot, consisting of an honorarium and a plaque, is given each year to the author of a doctoral thesis in physics of condensed matter produced during the two previous years. The society's council selects the winner.

1975 **J.B. Theeten**
1976 **J.P. Farges**
1977 **C. Pariset**
1978 **S. Balibar**
1979 **J. Desseaux**
1980 **J. Rabier**

Nobel Prize in Physics

NOBEL FOUNDATION
Nobel House, Sturegatan 14, 11436-Stockholm, Sweden

The Nobel Prize in Physics is generally recognized as the highest honor which can be bestowed upon a physicist for an exceptionally noteworthy discovery in this scientific field. The award, which consists of a gold medal, diploma and a large honorarium, is given in a ceremony on December 10 of each year at Stockholm's City Hall. The awards are presented and administered by the Royal Swedish Academy of Sciences. The amount of the honorarium fluctuates. In 1980 it was approximately $212,000.

1901 **Wilhelm C. Roentgen** (Germany), Discovery of X-rays

1902 **Hendrik A. Lorentz and Pieter Zeeman** (Netherlands), Work on magnetic influences on radiation phenomena

1903 **Antoine Henri Becquerel** (France), Discovered spontaneous radioactivity
Marie Curie and Pierre Curie (France), Research on radiation phenomena discovered by Becquerel

1904 **Lord Rayliegh (John W. Strutt)** (Great Britain), Investigated densitites of important gases and discovered argon

1905 **Philipp E. von Lenard** (Germany, born in Hungary), Work on cathode rays

1906 **Sir Joseph J. Thomson** (Great Britain), Experimented and developed theories on conduction of electricity by gases

1907 **Albert A. Micheison** (U.S.A., born in Germany), Precision instruments for spectroscopic and meteorological studies

1908 **Gabriel Lippmann** (France), Reproduced colors photographically

1909 **Guglielmo Marconi** (Italy), Developed radio

1910 **Johannes D. van der Waals** (Netherlands), Research on equation of state for liquids and gases

1911 **Wilhelm Wien** (Germany), Work on laws of heat radiation

1912 **Nils G. Dalen** (Sweden), Invented automatic regulators for gas accumulators for lighthouse and buoy illumination

1913 **Heike Kamerlingh-Onnes** (Netherlands), Investigated properties of matters at low temperatures, leading to production of liquid helium

1914 **Max von Laue** (Germany), Discovered X-ray diffusion by crystals

1915 **Sir William H. Bragg and William L. Bragg** (Great Britain), Analyzed crystal structure by X-ray

1916 **No award**

1917 **Charles G. Barkla** (Great Britain), Discovered characteristic Roentgen radiation of elements

1918 **Max K.E.L. Planck** (Germany), Discovered energy quanta

1919 **Johannes Stark** (Germany), Discovered Doppler effect in canal rays and splitting of spectral lines in electric fields

1920 **Charles E. Guillaume** (France, born in Switzerland), Discovered anomalies in nickel-steel alloys

1921 **Albert Einstein** (U.S.A., born in Germany), Studies in theoretical physics, especially the law of photo-electric effect

1922 **Niels Bohr** (Denmark), Work on atomic structure and radiation

1923 **Robert A. Millikan** (U.S.A.), Research on elementary electric charge and photoelectric effect

1924 **Karl M.G. Siegbahn** (Sweden), Work on X-ray spectroscopy

1925 **James Franck and Gustav Hertz** (Germany), Discovered laws of impact of an electron on an atom

1926 **Jean B. Perrin** (France), Research on discontinuous structure of matter, particularly discovery of sedimentation equilibrium

1927 **Arthur H. Compton** (U.S.A.), Discovered Compton effect concerning increased wave length of X-rays and gamma rays scattered by electrons

1928 **Owen W. Richardson** (Great Britain), Thermionic research on phenomena of emission of electrically charged particles in a heated body and discovered of Richardson's Law

1929 **Prince Louis-Victor de Broglie** (France), Discovered wave nature of electrons

1930 **Sir Chandrasekhara V. Raman** (India), Research of light scattering and discovery of Raman effect

1931 **No award**

1932 **Werner Heisenberg** (Germany), Created quantium mechanics leading to discovery of allotrophic forms of hydrogen

1933 **Paul A.M. Dirac** (Great Britain) and **Erwin Schrodinger** (Austria), Extensions of atomic theory

1934 **No award**

1935 **James Chadwick** (Great Britain), Discovered neutrons

1936 **Carl D. Anderson** (U.S.A.), Discovered positron
Victor F. Hess (Austria), Discovered cosmic radiation

1937 **Clinton J. Davisson** (U.S.A.) and **George P. Thomson** (Great Britain), Research on diffraction of electrons by crystals

1938 **Enrico Fermi** (U.S.A., born in Italy), Used irradiation to demonstrate existence of new radioactive elements and discovered nuclear reactions caused by slow neutrons

1939 **Ernest O. Lawrence** (U.S.A.), Developed cyclotron to investigate artificial radioactive elements

1940 **No award**

1941 **No award**

1942 **No award**

1943 **Otto Stern** (U.S.A., born in Germany), Work on molecular ray method and discovered magnetic moment of proton

1944 **Isidor Isaac Rabi** (U.S.A.), Recorded magnetism of atomic nuclei via resonance method

1945 **Wolfgang Pauli** (U.S.A.), Discovered Pauli Principle, exclusion principle in quantum mechanics

1946 **Percy Williams Bridgman** (U.S.A.), Invented device to produce extremely high pressures, resulting in discoveries in high-pressure physics

1947 **Sir Edward V. Appleton** (Great Britain), Work on physics of upper atmosphere and discovery of Appleton layer of ionosphere

1948 **Patrick M.S. Blackett** (Great Britain), Developed Wilson cloud chamber method for research in nuclear physics and cosmic radiation

1949 **Hideki Yukawa** (Japan), Theoretical prediction of existences of mesons

1950 **Cecil F. Powell** (Great Britain), Developed photographic method for research on nuclear processes leading to discovery of mesons

1951 **Sir John D. Cockroft** (Great Britain) and **Ernest T.W. Walton** (Ireland), Work on atomic-nucleus transmutation by artificially accelerated atomic particles

1952 **Felix Bloch** (U.S.A., born in Switzerland), Developed methods of precisely measuring nuclear magnetism and related discoveries

1953 **Fritz Zernike** (Netherlands), Demonstrated phase-control method and invented phase-contrast microscope
1954 **Max Born** (Great Britain, born in Germany), Fundamental work in quantum mechanics
Walter Bothe (Germany), Coincidence method of counting
1955 **Polykarp Kusch** (U.S.A., born in Germany), Determined precisely the magnetic moment of the electron
Willis E. Lamb (U.S.A.), Discoveries in fine structure of the hydrogen spectrum
1956 **John Bardeen, Walter H. Brattain and William Shockley** (U.S.A.), Research on semi-conductors and invention of the transistor
1957 **Tsung-Dao Lee and Chen Ning Yang** (U.S.A., born in China), Investigations of parity laws, especially regarding elementary particles and resulting discoveries
1958 **Paval A. Cherenkov, Ilya M. Frank and Igor J. Tamm** (U.S.S.R.), Discovery and interpretation of the Cherenkov effect
1959 **Owen Chamberlain and Emilio G. Segre** (U.S.A.), Discovered the antiproton
1960 **Donald A. Glaser** (U.S.A.), Invented bubble chamber
1961 **Robert Hofstadter** (U.S.A.), Research on electron scattering and discoveries on nucleon structure
Rudolf L. Mossbauer (Germany), Studied resonance absorption of gamma radition and Mossbauer effect
1962 **Lev D. Landau** (U.S.S.R.), Theories on condensed matter, particularly liquid helium
1963 **Maria Goeppert-Mayer** (U.S.A.) and **J. Hans D. Jensen** (Germany), Discoveries on nuclear cell structures
Eugene P. Wigner (U.S.A.), Theories on atomic nucleus and elementary particles
1964 **Nikolai G. Basov** (U.S.S.R.), **Aleksandr M. Prochorov** (U.S.S.R.) and **Charles H. Townes** (U.S.A.), Basic research in quantum electronics and subsequent construction of maser-laser oscillators and amplifiers
1965 **Richard P. Feynman** (U.S.A.), **Julian S. Schwinger** (U.S.A.) and **Shinichiro Tomanaga** (Japan), Work in quantum electrodynamics, especially regarding elementary particles in high-energy physics
1966 **Alfred Kastler** (France), Developed optical methods for Herzian resonance atom study
1967 **Hans A. Bethe** (U.S.A., born in Germany), Nuclear-reaction theories, especially on energy production of stars
1968 **Luis W. Alvarez** (U.S.A.), Work of physics of subatomic particles, especially regarding many resonance states
1969 **Murray Gell-Mann** (U.S.A.), Discoveries about the classifications of elementary particles and their interactions
1970 **Hannes O.G. Alfven** (Sweden), Work in magnetohydrodynamics and its application in plasma physics
Louis E.F. Neel (France), Ferromagnetism and anti-ferromagnetism work with applications in solid state physics
1971 **Dennis Gabor** (Great Britain, born in Hungary), Invented holography
1972 **John Bardeen, Leon N. Cooper and John F. Schrieffer** (U.S.A.), Developed superconductivity theory for various metals at very low temperatures
1973 **Ivar Giaever and Leo Esaki** (U.S.A., born in Norway), Work in miniature electronic semiconductors and superconductors
1974 **Anthony Hewish and Martin Ryle** (Great Britain), Radiotelescopic study of the universe and discovery of pulsars
1975 **L. James Rainwater** (U.S.A.), **Aage Bohn** (Denmark) and **Ben Roy Mottelson** (Denmark, born in U.S.A.), Work on nuclei of atoms resulting in discovery that not all are spherical due to connection between collective motion and particle motion in the nucleus
1976 **Burton Richter and Samuel C.C. Ting** (U.S.A.), Discovered Psi or J particle, thought to be smallest building block of matter
1977 **Philip Anderson** (U.S.A.), **John Van Vleck** (U.S.A.) and **Nevill Mott** (Great Britain), Research in solid-state physics
1978 **Peter Leonidovitch Kapitsa** (U.S.S.R.), Basic inventions and discoveries in low-temperature physics
Arno A. Penzias and **Robert W. Wilson** (U.S.A.), Discovery of cosmic microwave background radiation
1979 **Steven Weinberg** (U.S.A.), **Sheldon L. Glashow** (U.S.A.) and **Abdus Salam** (Great Britain, born in Pakistan), Fundamental research toward the goal of finding a unifying thread binding four natural forces: gravitation, electromagneticism, strong interaction and weak interaction
1980 **James Cronin** and **Val Fitch** (U.S.A.), Discoveries concerning the physics of sub-atomic particles

Max Born Prize
Physics Prize
Max Planck Medal
Robert Wichard Pohl Prize
Karl Scheel Prize
Walte Shottky Prize

GERMAN PHYSICAL SOCIETY
Hauptstrasse 5, D-5340 Bad Honnef, Federal Republic of Germany (tel. 02224-71061)

The Max Born Prize, which consists of £150, a silver medal and a citation, is awarded jointly by ther German Physical Society and The Institute of Physics to an outstanding German or British physicist. The prize winners are listed on page 515 with other Institute of Physics laureates.

The Physics Prize, which consists of 5,000 marks and a certificate, annually honors achievements of young physicists.

1942 **Albert Kochendorfer** and **Wilhelm Walcher**
1943-60 **No awards**
1961 **Ekkehard Kroner**
1962 **Gernot Graff** and **Siegfried Wilking**
1963 **Ernest Feldtkeller, Ekkehard Fuchs, Joachim Heintze** and **Volker Soergel**
1964 **Josef Zahringer**
1965 **Ulrich Bonse** and **Heinrich Deichsel**
1966 **Erwin Reichert**
1967 **Wolfgang Pechhold**
1968 **Helmut Kronmuller**
1969 **Georg Alefeld** and **Max Maier**
1970 **Heinz Burfeindt, Gerd Buschhorn, Christoph Geweniger, Peter Heide, Ulrich Kotz, Rainer Kotthaus, Raymond A. Lewis, Peter Schmuser, Hans-Jurgen Skronn, Heinrich Wahl** and **Konrad Wegener, DESY Group F 35**
1971 **Werner Schmidt**
1972 **Rainer Haerten** and **Gerold Muller**
1973 **Albert H. Walenta**
1974 **Dirk Offermann** and **Albert Steyerl**

1975 Deiter Haidt
1976 Werner Lauterborn
1977 Detlev Buchholz and Gert-Rudiger Strobl
1978 Deitrich Habs and Volker Metag
1979 Helmuth Mohwald and Hans Reithler
1980 Paul Leiderer

The Max Planck Medal, which is of gold and is accompanied by a citation, annually honors outstanding achievements in the field of theoretical physics. A committee selects the winner.

1929 Max Planck and Albert Einstein
1930 Niels Bohr and Arnold Sommerfeld
1931 No award
1932 Max von Laue
1933 Werner Heisenberg
1934-36 No awards
1937 Erwin Schrodinger
1938 Louis de Broglie
1939-41 No awards
1942 Pasqual Jordan
1943 Friedrich Hund
1944 Walter Kossel
1945-47 No awards
1948 Max Born
1949 Otto Hahn and Lise Meitner
1950 Peter Debye
1951 James Franck and Gustav Hertz
1952 Paul A.M. Dirac
1953 Walther Bothe
1954 Enrico Fermi
1955 Hans Bethe
1956 Viktor F. Weisskopf
1957 Carl-Friedrich von Weizsacker
1958 Wolfgang Pauli
1959 Oskar Klein
1960 Lew D. Landau
1961 Eugene P. Wigener
1962 Ralph Kronig
1963 Rudolf Ernst Peierls
1964 Samuel Goudsmit and George E. Uhlenbeck
1965 No award
1966 Gerhart Luders
1967 Harry Lehmann
1968 Walter Heitler
1969 Freeman J. Dyson
1970 Rudolf Haag
1971 No award
1972 Herbert Frohlich
1973 Nikolai N. Bogolubov
1974 Leon C.P. van Hove
1975 Gregor Wentzel
1976 Ernst C.G. Stueckelberg
1977 Walter E. Thirring
1978 Paul P. Ewald
1979 Markus Fierz
1980 No award

The Robert Wichard Pohl Prize, which consists of 5,000 marks and a certificate, annually honors achievements in physics education. A committee chooses the recipient.

1980 Roman Sexl

The Karl Scheel Prize, which is given by the Berlin chapter of the Society, annually honors the achievements of a young Berlin physicist with a prize consisting of 5,000 marks, a bronze medal and a certificate. A committee selects the winner.

1958 Gerhard Hildebrandt
1959 Hans-Joachim Hamisch and Arthur Tausend
1960 Herbert Schirmer
1961 Gerhard Simonsohn
1962 Wolfgang-Dieter Riecke
1963 Klaus Grohmann
1964 Gunter Sauerbrey
1965 Gerd Koppelmann
1966 Jurgen Geiger, Klaus Mobius, Reinhrd Nink and Werner Stickel
1967 Dieter Hofmann and Fredrich Thon
1968 Gerd Herziger and Horst Weber
1969 Peter Rohner and Burkhard Wende
1970 Dietrich Neubert and Reinhart Radebold
1971 Jurgen Andra and Burkhard Lischke
1972 Heinrich Homeyer and Klaus-Eric Kirschfeld
1973 No award
1974 Faramarz Mahdjuri and Nikolaus Stolterfoht
1975 Gerhard Muller
1976 Walter Ekhardt and Berndt Kuhlow
1977 Heinz Deuling and Dietmar Theis
1978 Werner Rodewald
1979 Michael Steiner
1980 Klaus Grutzmacher and Joachim Seidel

The Walter Schottky Prize for Solid State Physics is awarded annually for achievements in the field by a young physicist. The award, which consists of 5,000 marks, and a certificate, is made on the decision of a committee.

1973 Peter Ehrhart
1974 Andreas Otto
1975 Karl-Heinz Zschauer
1976 Franz Wegner
1977 Siegfried Hunklinger
1978 Bernhard Authier and Horst Fischer
1979 Heiner Muller-Krumbhaar
1980 Klaus Funke

Thomas Young Medal and Prize
Rutherford Medal and Prize
Simon Memorial Prize
Max Born Medal and Prize
Maxwell Medal and Prize
Holweck Medal and Prize
Guthrie Medal and Prize
Duddell Medal and Prize
Glazebrook Medal and Prize
Charles Chree Medal and Prize
Charles Vernon Boys Prize
Bragg Medal and Prize

THE INSTITUTE OF PHYSICS
47 Belgrave Sq., London SW1X 8QX, United Kingdom (Tel. 01-235 6111)

The Thomas Young Medal and Prize, originally known as The Thomas Young Oration, is awarded in odd-numbered years for an outstanding work on optics. The prize consists of £150 and a bronze medal.

ORATORS

1907 Marius Hans Erik Tscherning
1910 Robert Williams Wood

1915 James Crichton-Browne
1921 Charles Sheard
1923 Moritz von Rohr
1928 G. W. Ritchey
1931 John H Parsons
1933 Herbert E. Ives
1935 Charles Fabry
1937 Richard James Lythgoe
1939 M. N. MacLeod
1941 Harold Spencer Jones
1943 Frederick Charles Bartlett
1945 Ragnar Granit
1947 F. Zernike
1949 Thomas Smith
1951 William David Wright
1953 No award
1955 Walter Stanley Stiles
1957 John Guild
1959 Robert William Ditchburn
1961 Harold Horace Hopkins

MEDALISTS

1963 Charles Hard Townes and Arthur Leonard Schawlow
1965 Andre Marechal
1967 Dennis Gabor
1969 Giuliano Toraldo di Francia
1971 Charles Gorrie Wynne
1973 Walter Thompson Welford
1975 Daniel Joseph Bradley
1977 Robert Clark Jones
1979 Claude Coehn-Tannoudji

The Rutherford Medal and Prize, initially known as The Rutherford Memorial Lecture, is made in even-numbered years for contributions to nuclear physics, elementary particle physics or nuclear technology. The prize consists of £150 and a bronze medal.

LECTURERS

1942 Harold Roper Robinson
1944 John D. Cockcroft
1946 Marcus Laurence Elwin Oliphant
1948 Ernest Marsden
1950 Alexander Smith Russell
1952 Rudolf Ernst Peierls
1954 Patrick Maynard Stuart Blackett
1956 Philip I. Dee
1958 Niels Bohr
1960 Cecil Frank Powell
1962 Denys Haigh Wilkinson
1964 Peter H. Fowler

MEDALISTS

1966 Peter Kapitza
1968 Brian Hilton Flowers
1970 Samuel Devons
1972 Aage Bohr
1973 James MacDonald Cassels
1974 Albert Edward Litherland
1976 Roger John Blin-Stoyle and Joan Maie Freeman
1978 Paul Taunton Matthews
1980 Paul Gayleard Murphy and John James Thresher

The Simon Memorial Prize of £ 300 and a certificate is awarded approximately every three years by the Low Temperature Group of the Society for a distinguished work in experimental or theoretical low temperature physics.

1959 H. London
1961 I. M. Lifschitz
1963 Henry Edgar Hall and William Frank Vinen
1965 John Charles Wheatley
1968 Kurt Alfred Georg Mendelssohn
1970 Walther Meissner
1973 Peter Kapitza
1976 David Morris Lee, Douglas Dean Osheroff and Robert Coleman Richardson

The Max Born Medal and Prize is awarded alternately by the councils of the Institute and the German Physical Society to a physicist selected from a list of nominees submitted by the other. The award, which consists of £150 and a silver medal, is given for outstanding contributions in the field.

1973 Roger Arthur Cowley
1974 Walter Greiner
1975 Trevor Simpson Moss
1976 Hermann Haaken
1977 Walter Eric Spear
1978 Herbert Walther
1979 John Brian Taylor
1980 Helmut Faissner

The Maxwell Medal and Prize recognizes outstanding contributions in theoretical physics over a 10-year period to physicists 35 years of age or less. The prize consists of £150 and a bronze medal.

1962 Abdus Salam
1964 Walter Charles Marshall
1966 Richard Henry Dalitz
1968 Roger James Elliott and Kenneth William Harry Stevens
1970 Richard John Eden
1971 John Bryan Taylor
1972 Volker Heine
1973 David James Thouless
1974 Samuel Frederick Edwards
1975 Anthony James Leggett
1976 Stephen William Hawking
1977 Eric Jakeman
1978 Michael Victor Berry
1979 Christopher Hubert Llewellyn Smith
1980 David James Wallace

The Holweck Medal and Prize, instituted jointly by the French and British Physical Societies, is made for distinguished work in experimental physics or theoretical physics if closely related to experimental work, which is either still in progress or has been carried out during the preceding 10 years. The £150 award and gold medal now goes to a French physicist in odd-numbered years and a British physicist in even-numbered years.

1946 Charles Sadron
1947 Edward Neville da Costa Andrade
1948 Yves Rocard
1949 Leslie Fleetwood Bates
1950 Pierre Jacquinot
1951 Thomas Ralph Merton
1952 Louis Neel
1953 John Ashworth Ratcliffe
1954 Alfred Kastler
1955 Nicholas Kurti
1956 Jean Paul Mathieu
1957 Denys Haigh Wilkinson
1958 Anatole Abragam

1959 Robert Hanbury Brown
1960 Jean Brossel
1961 Alfred Brian Pippard
1962 Jean-Francois Denisse
1963 Frederick Charles Frank
1964 Jacques Friedel
1965 Martin Ryle
1966 Raymond Castaing
1967 Heinrich Gerhard Kuhn
1968 Pierre-Gilles de Gennes
1969 Alan Howard Cottrell
1970 Pierre Connes
1971 Dennis Gabor
1972 Ionel Solomon
1973 Brian David Josephson
1974 Philippe Nozieres
Antony Hewish
1975 Evry Schatzman
1976 Harry Elliot
1977 Maurice Goldman
1978 William Frank Vinen
1979 Andre Blandin

The Guthrie Medal and Prize, originally established as a lecture, consists of £250 and a silver gilt medal and is given annually to a physicist of international reputation for exceptional contributions.

LECTURERS

1914 Robert Williams Wood
1916 William B. Hardy
1917 Paul Langevin
1918 John C. McLennan
1919 No award
1920 Charles Edouarde Guillaume
1921 Albert Abraham Michelson
1922 Niels Bohr
1923 James H. Jeans
1924 Maurice le Duc de Broglie
1925 Wilhelm Wien
1926 Charles Fabry
1927 Lord Rutherford of Nelson
1928 Joseph J. Thomson
1929 Percy Williams Bridgman
1930 Peter Debye
1931 Richard T. Glazebrook
1932 Max Planck
1933 Karl Manne Georg Siegbahn
1934 Charles V. Boys
1935 Arthur Holly Compton
1936 Lord Cherwell of Oxford
1937 Clifford C. Paterson
1938 Archibald Vivian Hill
1940 Patrick Maynard Stuart Blackett
1941 Edward Neville da Costa Andrade
1942 Edward V. Appleton
1943 Edmund T. Whittaker
1944 Joel H. Hildebrand
1945 Arturo Duperier
1946 Max Jakob
1947 John Desmond Bernal
1948 George P. Thomson
1949 Alexander Oliver Rankine
1950 George Ingle Finch
1951 Nevill Francis Mott
1952 W. Lawrence Bragg
1953 Max Born
1954 Geoffrey Taylor
1955 Edmund Clifton Stoner
1956 Francis Simon
1957 Harold C. Urey
1958 Willis Eugene Lamb
1959 Harrie Stewart Wilson Massey
1960 Fred Hoyle
1961 David Shoenberg
1962 Alfred Charles Bernard Lovell
1963 Leslie Fleetwood Bates
1964 Martin Ryle
1965 John Bertram Adams

MEDALISTS

1966 William Cochran
1967 James Chadwick
1968 Rudolf Ernst Peierls
1969 Cecil Frank Powell
1970 Alfred Brian Pippard
1971 John Ashworth Ratcliffe
1972 Brian David Josephson
1973 Hermann Bondi
1974 Rudolf Ludwig Mossbauer
1975 David Tabor
1976 Abdus Salam
1977 Sir Alan Cottrell
1978 Philip Warren Anderson
1979 Donald Hill Perkins
1980 Michael Ellis Fisher

The Duddell Medal and Prize is made annually to an individual who has contributed to the advancement of knowledge by the invention or design of scientific instruments or by the discovery of materials used in their construction or has made outstanding contributions to the application of physics. The prize is £150 and a bronze medal.

1923 Hugh Longbourne Callendar
1924 Charles V. Boys
1925 Albert Campbell
1926 Frank Twyman
1927 Frank E. Smith
1928 Charles Edouarde Guillaume
1929 Albert Abraham Michelson
1930 J. Ambrose Fleming
1931 Charles Thomson Rees Wilson
1932 Wolfgang Gaede
1933 Harold Dennis Taylor
1934 W. Ewart Williams
1935 Charles Vickery Drysdale
1936 Walter Guyton Cady
1937 Hans Geiger
1938 Robert William Paul
1940 Ernest Orlando Lawrence
1941 William David Collidge
1942 Cecil Reginald Burch
1943 John Guild
1944 Francis William Aston
1945 John Turton Randall
1946 Karl Weissenberg
1947 Robert Jemison Van de Graaff
1948 Karl Manne Georg Siegbahn
1949 Edwin Herbert Land
1950 Donald William Fry
1951 Albert Beaumont Wood
1952 Cecil Waller
1953 William Sucksmith
1954 Alfred Charles Bernard Lovell
1955 Rudolf Kompfner
1956 John Gilbert Daunt
1957 Charles Eryl Wynn-Williams
1958 Leonard Charles Jackson

1959 George William Hutchison and Gordon George Scarrott
1960 Reginald Victor Jones
1961 John Bertram Adams
1963 Bertram Neville Brockhouse
1965 Hugh Alastair Gebbie
1967 Keith Davy Froome and Robert Howard Bradsell
1969 Charles William Oatley
1971 Vernon Ellis Cosslett and Kenneth Charles Arthur Smith
1973 Albert Franks
1975 Ernst Ruska
1976 Godfrey Newbold Hounsfield
1977 Ronald Ferguson Pearson
1978 Edward George Sydney Paige
1979 John Riddle Sandercock
1980 Albert Victor Crewe

The Glazebrook Medal and Prize is made annually for outstanding contributions in the organization, utilization or application of science. The prize is £250 and a silver gilt medal.

1966 Christopher Hinton
1967 Charles Sykes
1968 Frank Philip Bowden
1969 William George Penney
1970 Eric Eastwood
1971 Francis Edgar Jones
1972 Gordon Brims Black McIvor Sutherland
1973 Kurt Hoselitz
1974 Basil John Mason
1975 Walter Charles Marshall
1976 Sir Montague Finniston
1977 Sir James Menter
1978 George Gray Macfarlane
1979 Thomas Gerald Pickavance
1980 Michael Crowley Crowley-Milling

The Charles Chree Medal and Prize is made every two years for distinguished research in terrestrial magnestism, atmospheric electricity and other aspects of geophysics. The prize is 150 pounds and a silver medal.

1941 Sydney Chapman
1943 Basil Ferdinand Jamieson Schonland
1945 John Adam Fleming
1947 Edward V. Appleton
1949 Gordon Miller Bourne Dobson
1951 George C. Simpson
1953 Julius Bartels
1955 David Forbes Martyn
1957 Edward C. Bullard
1959 Reginald Cockcroft Sutcliffe
1961 Scott Ellsworth Forbush
1963 Maurice Neville Hill
1965 Basil John Mason
1967 John Herbert Chapman
1969 Stanley Keith Runcorn
1971 Desmond George King-Hele
1973 David Robert Bates
1975 Raymond Hide
1977 Drummond Hoyle Matthews and Frederick John Vine
1978 John Theodore Houghton

The Charles Vernon Boys Prize is made annually to a physicist 35 years of age or less for distinguished research in experimental physics which is still in progress or which has been carried out in the previous 10 years. The prize is £ 150.

1945 Athelstan Hylas Stoughton Holbourn
1946 Robert William Sutton
1947 Cecil Frank Powell
1948 Samuel Tolansky
1949 Andre Jean Guinier
1950 Guiseppe Paolo Stanislao Occhialini
1951 James Howard Eagle Griffiths
1952 Brebis Bleaney
1953 Frederick Calland Williams
1954 Jeofry Stuart Courtney-Pratt
1955 John Wesley Mitchell
1956 George Dixon Rochester and Clifford Charles Butler
1957 Louis Essen
1958 Donald A. Glaser
1959 David West
1960 Frank Llewellyn Jones
1961 Alexander Walter Merrison
1962 Peter Bernhard Hirsch
1963 Keith Davy Froome
1964 Andrew Richard Lang
1965 Archibald Howie and Michael John Whelan
1966 Peter Duncumb
1967 Alan Hugh Cook
1968 John Owen
1969 Harold Percy Rooksby
1970 Anthony Hewish
1971 Michael Hart
1972 Michael Warwick Thompson
1973 John William Charles Gates
1974 Patrick George Henry Sanders
1975 Richard Anthony Stradling
1976 Stanley Desmond Smith
1977 John Clarke
1978 Robert Alan Sherlock and Adrian Frederick George Wyatt
1979 Derek Charles Robinson
1980 Alan Edward Costley

The Bragg Medal and Prize is given every two years for distinguished contributions to the teaching of physics. The prize is £150 and a bronze medal.

1967 Donald McGill
1969 John Logan Lewis
1971 George Robert Noakes
1973 Jon Michael Ogborn and Paul Joseph Black
1975 William Albert Coates
1977 Edward John Wenham
1979 Margaret Maureen Hurst

Bakhuis-Rooseboom Medal
Lorentz Medal

Royal Netherlands Academy of Arts and Sciences
Kloveniersburgwal 29, Amsterdam, The Netherlands (Tel: 020 22 29 02)

The Bakhuis-Rooseboom Medal, which is of gold, is awarded approximately every eight years for research in the field of phase theory. Prior to 1960, the medal was given every four or five years. A selection committee chooses the winner of this international honor.

1916 **F.A.H. Schreinemakers,** Leiden, Netherlands
1923 **Gustav Tammann,** Gottingen, Germany
1929 **J.J. van Laar,** Tavel sur Clarens
1933 **P.W. Bridgman,** Cambridge, U. K.
1939 **Arthur L. Day,** Maryland, U.S.A.

1950 **W. Hume-Rothery,** Oxford, U. K.
1954 **Norman L. Bowen,** Washington, D.C.
1960 **J.L. Meijering,** Eindhoven, Netherlands
1969 **F.P. Bundy,** Schenectady, N.Y.
1978 **M. H. Hillert,** Stockholm

The Lorentz Medal, which is of gold, is given about every four years for research in the field of pure physics. A selection committee chooses the winner of this international honor.

1927 **M. Planck,** Berlin
1931 **W. Pauli,** Zurich
1935 **P. Debije,** Leipzig
1939 **A. Sommerfeld,** Munich
1947 **H.A. Kramers,** Leiden, Netherlands
1953 **F. London,** Durham, N.C.
1958 **Lars Onsager,** New Haven, Conn.
1962 **R.E. Peierls,** Birmingham, U. K.
1966 **Freeman J. Dyson,** Princeton, N.J.
1970 **G.E. Uhlenbeck,** New York
1974 **J.H. van Vleck,** Cambridge, Mass.
1978 **N. Bloemberger,** Cambridge, Mass.

Pawsey Medal

AUSTRALIAN ACADEMY OF SCIENCE
Box 783, Canberra, ACT 2601, Australia (062-48 6011)

The Pawsey Medal, a silver plaque, is awarded annually to a scientist 35 years of age or younger who resides in Australia for research in experimental physics. A selection committee chooses the winner.

1967 **R.M. May**
1968 **No award**
1969 **K.G. McCracken**
1970 **R.A. Challinor**
1971 **B.W. Ninham**
1972 **K.C. Freeman**
1973 **B.H.J. McKellar**
1974 **D.B. Melrose**
1975 **R.J. Baxter**
1976 **W.M. Goss**
1977 **J.N. Israelachvili**
1978 **R.N. Manchester**
1979 **G.J. Clark**
1980 **J.E. Norris**

Wolf Prize in Physics

WOLF FOUNDATION
Box 398, Herzliah-Bet, Israel

The $100,000 Wolf Prize in Physics honors an outstanding body of work in physics, as determined by a committee of internationally known judges. The award is part of a $500,000 annual prize distribution for exceptional achievement in five fields of science.

1978 **Chien Shiung Wu** (Columbia University), Nuclear physics, especially experiments dealing with rays emitting from a spinning atom
1979 **George Uhlenbeck** (Rockefeller University), Discovery jointly with the late S.A. Goudsmit of the electron spin
Giuseppe Occhialini (University of Milan), Contributions to discovery of electron pair production and of the charged ion.
1980 **Michael E. Fisher** (Cornell University), **Leo P. Kadanoff** (University of Chicago) and **Kenneth G. Wilson** (Cornell University), Pathbreaking developments culminating in the general theory of the critical behavior at transitions between different thermodynamic phases of matter

Honorary Membership in the Society Outstanding Service Award

NATIONAL SPELEOLOGICAL SOCIETY
Cave Ave., Huntsville, Ala. 35810 (312/331-0011)

Honorary membership in the Society honors outstanding accomplishment in cave-oriented science, leadership or exploration. Memberships are conferred annually on recommendation of the awards committee and selection by the board of governors.

1941 **Vernon O. Bailey**
1942 **Roy J. Holden**
1943 **Ralph W. Stone**
1944 **Allyn Coats Swinnerton**
1945 **Alexander Wetmore**
1946 **Robert deJoly**
1947 **Don Bloch**
1948 **William J. Stephenson**
1949 **Robert Broom**
1950 **Mark R. Harrington**
1951 **Emil W. Haury**
1952 **Rene G. Jeannel**
1953 **Charles E. Mohr**
1954 **J. Harlen Bretz**
1955 **Abbe Henri Breuil**
1956 **Norbert Casteret**
1957 **Carl F. Miller**
1958 **Donald R. Griffin**
1959 **John S. Petrie**
1960 **William E. Davies**
1961 **No award; change in award year designation**
1962 **Julia L. Staniland Day**
1963 **Thomas C. Barr, Jr.**
1964 **A. Vandel**
1965 **William R. Halliday**
1966 **Brig. E. Aubrey Glennie**
1967 **Russell H. Gurnee**
1968 **G. Nicholas Sullivan**
1969 **Walter B. Jones**
1970 **Donald N. Cournoyer**
1971 **John A. Stellmack**
1972 **Jack Herschend**
1973 **Rodger Brucker**
1974 **Don Sawyer**
1975 **Derek C. Ford**
1976 **Marjorie M. Sweeting**
1977 **Herb and Jan Conn**

Current status unknown

The Outstanding Service Award recognizes outstanding service to the Society, leadership, science and/or exploration.

1973 **John Cooper**
1974 **Charles Larson**
1975 **William B. White**
1976 **William F. Cuddington III**
1977 **Roy A. Davis**

Current status unknown

M. W. Biejerinck-Virologie Medal

ROYAL NETHERLANDS ACADEMY OF ARTS AND SCIENCES
Kloveniersburgwal 29, Amsterdam, The Netherlands (Tel: 020 22 29 02)

The M.W. Biejerinck-Virologie Medal, which is of gold, is given every three years to a scientist, preferably of Dutch nationality, for research in virology, including biochemistry and biophysics. A selection committee chooses the recipient.

1966 **E. van Slogteren,** Bennebroek
1969 **R.L. Sinsheimer,** University of California/Pasadena
1972 **W. Berends,** Delft
1975 **E.M.J. Jaspars,** Leiden
A. van Kammen, Wageningen
1978 **A. J. van der Eb,** Leiden

Medicine & Health

Contents

Related Awards

Robert Bing Prize

SWISS ACADEMY OF MEDICAL SCIENCES
Petersplatz 13, CH-4051 Basel, Switzerland (061-25 49 77)

The Robert Bing Prize, which consists of an honorarium and a scroll, is awarded approximately every two years to a citizen of Switzerland, France, Holland or the U.S. for outstanding work in the recognition, treatment and cure of neurological diseases. A 10-member commission selects the winner.

1958 **D. Wildi** (Geneva)
1960 **Pierre Buser** (Paris)
Konrad Akert (Madison, Wisc.)
1962 **Pierre Gloor** (Montreal)
Heinrich Kaeser (Basel)
1964 **Peter W. Hunsperger** (Zurich)
Rene Tissot (Geneva)
1966 **Michel Jouvet** (Lyon)
Mario Wiesendanger (Zurich)
1968 **Peter Huber** (Bern)
Jean Lapresle (Paris)
1971 **Mahmud Gazi Yasargil** (Zurich)
Peter B.C. Matthews (Oxford, U.K.)
Walter Lichtensteiger (Zurich)
1973 **Leonhard Hosli** (Basel)
Michael Cuenod (Zurich)
1975 **Hans Rudolf Muller** (Basel)
Gilbert Assal (Lausanne)
Colin Brian Blakemore (Cambridge, U.K.)
1977 **Francois de Ribaupierre** (Lausanne)
Richard H.T. Edwards (London)
Bernard Fulpius (Geneva)
1979 **Ulrich Niklaus Wiesmann** (Bern)
M.A. Schwab (Boston)
Peter Streit (New York)

Bristol-Myers Award

BRISTOL-MYERS CO.
345 Park Ave., New York, N.Y. 10154 (212/644-4526 and 212/644-3894)

The $25,000 Bristol-Myers Award for Distinguished Achievement in Cancer Research is given annually to a scientist for an outstanding contribution to the progress of cancer research. A six-member committee of experts in the field selects the recipient from nominations which may be submitted by an officer of a medical school, hospital or cancer research center.

1978 **Elizabeth Miller** and **James Miller** (University of Wisconsin)
1979 **Gertrude Henle** and **Werner Henle** (Children's Hospital of Philadelphia and University of Pennsylvania Medical School)
1980 **Howard Earle Skipper** (Southern Research Institute and Kettering-Meyer Laboratory)

Dautrebande Prize

FONDATION PROFESSEUR LUCIEN DAUTREBAND
35 Chaussee de Liege, 5200 Huy, Belgium (085-21 12 80)

The Dautreband Prize is awarded every three years to the author of a work on human or animal clinical physiopathology, preferably involving therapeutic implications. The international award, which carries an honorarium of 1,500,000 Belgian francs, is designed to allow the recipient to continue investigative work. The selection is made from nominees submitted by members of national academies, university professors or previous winners of the award.

1973 **Professor Durrer** (Amsterdam), Cardiac physiology
1976 **Professor Gajdusek** (Bethesda, Md.), Slow viruses
1979 **Professor Desmedt** (Brussels), Electroencephalography

Distinguished Service Award
Joseph B. Goldberger Award
Dr. Benjamin Rush Award
Arnold and Marie Schwartz Award
Scientific Achievement Award
Dr. Rodman E. Sheen and Thomas G. Sheen Award

AMERICAN MEDICAL ASSOCIATION
535 N. Dearborn St., Chicago, Ill. 60610 (312/751-6000)

The Distinguished Service Award, consisting of a gold medal and citation, honors a member of the association for meritorious service in the sciences and art of medicine. The membership nominates and the Board of Trustees selects the recipient of this annual honor. (All the award winners are M.D.s unless otherwise indicated.)

1938 **Rudolph Matas,** New Orleans
1939 **James B. Herrick,** Chicago
1940 **Chevalier Jackson,** Philadelphia
1941 **James Ewing,** New York
1942 **Ludvig Hektoen,** Chicago
1943 **Elliott P. Joslin,** Boston
1944 **George Dock,** Pasadena
1945 **George R. Minot,** Boston
1946 **Anton J. Carlson,** Ph. D., Chicago
1947 **Henry A. Christian,** Boston
1948 **Isaac A. Abt,** Chicago
1949 **Seale Harris,** Birmingham, Ala.
1950 **Evarts A. Graham,** St. Louis
1951 **Allen C. Whipple,** New York
1952 **Paul Dudley White,** Boston
1953 **Alfred Blalock,** Baltimore
1954 **W. Wayne Babcock,** Philadelphia
1955 **Donald C. Balfour,** Rochester, Minn.
1956 **Walter L. Bierring,** Des Moines, Iowa
1957 **Tom Douglas Spies,** Birmingham, Ala.
1958 **Frank H. Krusen,** Rochester, Minn.
1959 **Michael E. De Bakey,** Houston
1960 **Charles Doan,** Columbus, Ohio
1961 **Walter H. Judd,** Washington, D.C., and Minneapolis
1962 **Russell L. Cecil,** New York
1963 **Lester R. Dragstedt,** Gainesville, Fla.
1964 **Irvine H. Page,** Cleveland
1965 **Tinsley R. Harrison,** Birmingham, Ala.
1966 **Warren H. Cole,** Chicago
1967 **E. W. Alton Ochsner,** New Orleans
1968 **Owen H. Wangensteen,** Minneapolis
1969 **Jay Arnold Bargen,** Temple, Tex.
1970 **Henry L. Bockus,** Philadelphia
1971 **George R. Herrmann,** Galveston
1972 **Milton Helpern,** New York
1973 **George Hoyt Whipple,** Rochester, N.Y.

1974 **William Fouts House,** Los Angeles
1975 **William R. Willard,** Moundville, Ala.
1976 **Claude E. Welch,** Boston, Mass.
1977 **Franz J. Ingelfinger,** Boston, Mass.
1978 **William P. Longmire, Jr.,** Los Angeles
1979 **William A. Sodeman, Sr.,** Toledo
1980 **Frank H. Mayfield,** Cincinnati

The $1,000 Joseph B. Goldberger Award and commemorative plaque honors medical investigation in public and private health and physicians who have made important contributions in the knowledge of nutrition.

1949 **Randolph West,** New York
1951 **Fuller Albright,** Boston
1952 **W. Henry Sebrell, Jr.,** New York
1953 **James S. McLester,** Birmingham, Ala.
1954 **Russell M. Wilder,** Rochester, Minn.
1957 **Paul Gyorgy,** Philadelphia
1958 **Virgil P. Sydenstricker,** Augusta, Ga.
1959 **Carl V. Moore,** St. Louis
1960 **Richard W. Vilter,** Cincinnati
1961 **Fredrick J. Stare,** Boston
1962 **Edwards A. Park,** Baltimore
1963 **John B. Youmans,** New York
1964 **William J. Darby,** Nashville
1965 **Grace A. Goldsmith,** New Orleans
1966 **William B. Castle,** Boston
1967 **Cicely D. Williams,** London, U.K.
1968 **L. Emmett Holt, Jr.,** New York
1969 **Nevin S. Scrimshaw,** Cambridge, Mass.
1970 **Jonathan E. Rhoads and Stanley J. Dudrick,** Philadelphia
1971 **John E. Canham,** Iowa City, Robert E. Hodges Denver
1972 **George G. Graham,** Baltimore
1973 **Clement A. Finch,** Seattle
1974 **Robert E. Olson,** St. Louis
1975 **Ananda S. Prasad,** Detroit
1976 **Charles E. Butterworth, Jr.,** Birmingham
1977 **George F. Cahill, Jr.Boston**
1978 **Lloyd J. Filer, Jr.,** Iowa City
1979 **Robert W. Wissler,** Chicago
1980 **Russell B. Scobie,** Newburgh, N.Y.

The $5,000 Dr. Benjamin Rush Award honors a physician for his professional achievements and as a patriot, social reformer and citizen. It is specifically given for contributions to the community above and beyond the call of duty as a practicing physician. The AMA Committee on Awards selects the recipient.

1973 **Otis R. Bowen,** Governor of Indiana
1974 **Charles E. Robert Parker,** Montgomery, Ala.
1975 **Francis E. West,** San Diego, Calif.
1976 **Mario E. Ramirez,** Rio Grande City, Tex.
1977 **Luis Martin Perez,** Sanford, Fla.
1978 **Hon. Tim Lee Carter,** Congressman from Kentucky
1979 **No award**
1980 **Robert E. Rice,** Greenville, Mich.

The Dr. William Beaumont Award, consisting of $2,500 and a plaque, encourages physicians 50 years of age or younger who are U.S. citizens toward further contributions in medical research, teaching or clinical practice. The honor was formerly called the Arnold and Marie Schwartz Award.

1973 **Lawrence L. Weed,** Vt.
1974 **Thomas E. Starzl,** Colo.
1975 **Stanley J. Dudrick,** Tex.
1976 **Alton I. Sutnick,** Pa.
1977 **Theodore Cooper,** D.C.
1978 **H. Belton P. Meyer,** Ariz.
1979 **H. William Strauss,** Mass.
1980 **John B. McCraw,** Va.

On recommendation of the Council of Scientific Assembly and approval by the board of trustees, the Scientific Achievement Award gold medal is given for achievement by a physician or non-physician.

1962 **Donald D. Van Slyke,** Ph. D., Upton, N.Y.
1963 **John F. Enders,** Ph. D., Boston, Mass.
1964 **Rene J. Dubos,** Ph. D., New York
1965 **Edward C. Kendall,** Ph. D., Princeton, N.J.
1966 **Wendell M. Stanley,** Ph. D., Berkeley, Calif.
1967 **Gregory Pincus,** Sc. D., Shrewsbury, Mass.
1968 **Arthur Kornberg,** M. D., Palo Alto, Calif.
1969 **Philip Handler,** Ph. D., Durham, N.C.
1970 **Choh Hao Li,** Ph. D., Berkeley, Calif.
1971 **Robert B. Woodward,** Cambridge, Mass.
1972 **William Bennett Kouwenhoven,** Dr. Ing., Baltimore
1973 **Edith Hinkley Quimby,** Sc. D., Palo Alto, Calif.
1974 **Philip Abelson,** Ph. D., Washington, D.C.
1975 **Rosalyn Yalow,** Ph. D., and **Solomon A. Berson,** M.D., Bronx, N.Y.
1976 **Harry Goldblatt,** M. D., Cleveland
1977 **Helen B. Taussig,** M. D., Baltimore
1978 **F. Mason Sones,** M.D., Cleveland
1979 **Orvan W. Hess,** M.D., New Haven, Conn.
1980 **Harold E. Kleinert,** M.D., Louisville, Ky.

The Dr. Rodman E. Sheen and Thomas G. Sheen Award, consisting of a $10,000 stipend and a plaque, honors the scientific accomplishment of a U.S. physician. The Awards Committee of the AMA Board of Trustees makes the selection.

1968 **Irvine E. Page,** Ohio
1969 **Robert E. Gross,** Mass.
1970 **Charles B. Huggins,** Ill.
1971 **Maxwell Finland,** Mass.
1972 **Paul Dudley White,** Mass.
1973 **William Bosworth Castle,** Mass.
1974 **R. Lee Clark,** Tex.
1975 **Rudolph H. Kampmeier,** Tenn.
1976 **Howard A. Rusk,** N.Y.
1977 **Robert M. Zollinger,** Ohio
1978 **Karl A. Menninger,** Kans.
1979 **Charles A. Berry,** Tex.
1980 **Jonathan E. Rhoads,** Pa.

The Citation of Layman for Distinguished Service is given annually to a person not of the medical profession who has contributed to the ideals of American medicine. The award is presented to the individual selected by the AMA's House of Delegates.

1948 **Rev. Alphonse M. Schwitalla,** S.J.
1952 **Howard W. Blakeslee**
1957 **Henry Viscardi**
1958 **Gobind Behari Lal**
Charles W. Sewell
1963 **M. Lowell Edwards**
1966 **Danny Thomas**
1969 **John D. Rockefeller, III**
1970 **John S. Millis**
1971 **J. Raymond Knighton**
Malcolm P. Aldrich
1972 **Mac F. Cahal**
1973 **Leslie Townes (Bob) Hope**
1974 **Nathan Stark**
1975 **Harry Schwartz**
1975 **Charles Lindbergh** (Special Award)

1976 **Hon. Paul Rogers**
1977 **Rev. Edward J. Moffett,** M.M.
1978 **J. Ed McConnell**
John Alexander McMahon
1979 **Ann Landers**
1980 **Howard Hassard**

Ammy Award

AMERICAN MEDICAL WRITERS ASSOCIATION
5272 River Rd., Suite 370, Bethesda, Md. 20016
(301/986-9119)

The Ammy, a commemorative cube, annually honors the creators of outstanding books and films in the field. Entries are reviewed by a panel of judges, which select the winners (listed below) plus numerous honorable mentions. It should be noted that information on the book awards prior to 1973 is not available. The book categories change almost annually. For convenience, these are grouped here into books for professional and lay audiences, plus others awarded periodically.

BOOK FOR PROFESSIONAL READERSHIP/ PHYSICIAN READERSHIP

1973 **Silvio Aladjem,** *Risks in the Practice of Modern Obstetrics*
Howard F. Conn, *Current Therapy*
1974 **Keith L. Moore,** *The Developing Human*
James F. Holland and Emil Frei III, *Cancer Medicine*
1975 **Sanford L. Palay and Victoria Chan-Palay,** *Cerebellar Cortex, Cytology and Organization*
David G. Nathan and Frank A. Oski, *Hematology in Infancy and Childhood*
Gilles R.G. Monif, *Infectious Diseases in Obstetrics and Gynecology*
1976 **Abraham I. Braude,** *Antimicrobial Drug Therapy*
David Malikin and Herbert Rusalem, *Contemporary Vocational Rehabilitation*
1977 **Alfred S. Evans,** *Viral Infections of Humans*
Irene Mortenson Burnside, *Nursing and the Aged*
1978 **Ancel Blaustein** *Pathology of the Female Genital Tract*
1979 **Richard H. Egdahl** (series ed.), **W. Scott McDougal, C. Lawrence Slade** and **Basil A. Pruitt, Jr.,** *Manual of Burns,* Vol. 2
1980 **Donald W. Thibeault** and **George A. Gregory,** *Neonatal Pulmonary Care*

BEST BOOK(S) FOR LAY READERSHIP/ TRADE BOOK

1973 **Shirley M. Linde,** *A Complete Guide to Prevention and Treatment*
Edward M. Brecher and the Editors of *Consumer Reports*, *Licit and Illicit Drugs*
1974 **David R. Zimmerman,** *Rh*
Meyer Friedman and Ray H. Rosenman, *Type 'A' Behavior and Your Heart*
1975 **Robert Massie and Suzanne Massie,** *Journey*
Spyros Andreopoulos, *Primary Care: Where Medicine Fails*
1976 **Alfred W. Crosby, Jr.,** *Epidemic and Peace 1918*
1977 **David Hendin,** *Life Givers*
1978 **David Werner,** *Where There is No Doctor*
1979 **William Bronston,** *Way to Go*
1980 **William Stockton,** *Altered Destinies*

ALLIED HEALTH

1980 **W. Grant Thompson,** *The Irritable Gut*

MEDICAL HISTORY BOOK

1975 **Guido Majno,** *The Healing Hand: Man and Wound in the Ancient World*

SEX EDUCATION BOOK

1976 **David S. Delvin,** *The Book of Love*

FILM

1974 **Noel Nosseck,** *First Aid Quiz 1: Saving a Life*
1975 **Cinemakers, Inc./American Cancer Society,** *Nursing Management of Children With Cancer*
1976 **Wexler Film Productions,** *Minilaparatomy Technique*
1977 **No award**
1978 **F.M.S. Productions,** *Get It Together*

FILM FOR MEDICAL AUDIENCE

1974 **U.S.C. School of Medicine/Ortho Pharmaceutical Corp.,** *Teaching Breast Self Examination*
1975 **Wright Mfg. Co.,** *Smith Total Ankle*

INSTRUCTIONAL FILM FOR MEDICAL AUDIENCES

1976 **University of Michigan School of Medicine,** *The Combined Collis-Belsey Operation*
Synthesis Communications, *Sex and the Heart Patient*
1977 **No award**
1978 **Medi-Cline Productions,** *Trauma Patient*
Wexler Film Productions, *Choice With Understanding*
University of Kansas Medical Care, *A Different Kind of Hurt*
University of San Francisco and **V.A. Hospital,** San Francisco, *Microsurgical Viterectomy and Lensectomy Instrumentation in Anterior Chamber Reconstruction*
1979 **The Filmakers,** *The Enablers and the Intervention*
1980 **Comtact,** *Surgical Techniques: Incisions and Closures*

PROMOTIONAL FILM FOR MEDICAL AUDIENCES

1976 **Teletronics Intl./American Academy of Pediatrics,** *You're Not Listening*
1977 **No award**
1978 **Peter Vogt & Assoc.** and **Pierce Atkins Productions for Johns Hopkins,** *Radiological Reporting: A New Aproach*
James B. Maas, Cornell University for CIBA-GEIGY, *Keep Us Awake*
1979 **Amram Howak Assoc.,** *Caring*
1980 **Edmund Levy, Inc.,** *A Crippler Still at Large*

INSTRUCTIONAL FILM FOR LAY AUDIENCES

1974 **Noel Nosseck,** *First Aid Quiz 1: Saving a Life*
1975 **Paramount Productions,** *How to Save a Choking Victim: The Heimlich Maneuver*
1976 **Professional Research, Inc.,** *Vasectomy*
1977 **American Society of Therapeutic Radiologist,** *Radiation: the Cancer Fighter*
1978 **Behavioral Sciences Media Lab,** UCLA, *Tourette Syndrome: The Sudden Intruder*
Wexler Film Productions, *A Family Talks About Sex*
R.S. Milbauer for American Podiatry Assn., *As Young As Your Feet*

Pyramid Films, *New Breath of Life*
1979 No award
1980 **American Chiropractic Assn.,** *What Is Chiropractic?*

INFORMATIONAL FILM FOR LAY AUDIENCES
1974 **Lawren Productions/Coppertone Corp.,** *Sun and Your Skin*
1975 **American Dental Assn.,** *The Haunted Mouth*

PROMOTIONAL FILM FOR LAY AUDIENCES
1977 **Richard S. Milbauer/American Podiatry Assn.,** *Feet: A Key to Keeping Fit*
1978 **A-V Services Corp.** for NASA, *Mobile Biological Isolation System*
1979 **Tapper Productions,** *The Tom Harper Story*

DOCUMENTARY FOR LAY AUDIENCES
1974 **Macmillan Films/ABC News,** *The Right to Die*
1975 **CBS News/KNXT-TV, Los Angeles,** *Why Me?*
1976 **John Cosgrove,** *A Gift of Life*
1977 **Case Western Reserve University,** *Mild Retardation: A Family Profile*
1978 **Tapper Productions,** *Ray of Hope*
Dave Bell Assoc., *Feminine Mistake*
1979 **Tom Spain** for CBS News, *Anyplace But Here*
1980 **Irwin Rosten,** National Geographic, *Mysteries of the Mind*

TELEVISION NEWS OR EDITORIAL PRODUCTION
1979 **Film Australia,** *Hospitals Don't Burn Down*
1980 **CRM Productions,** *Managing Stress*

FILM OR TELEVISION PRODUCTION, DRAMATIC
1979 **The Company** for American Assn. of Blood Banks, *Life Song*
1980 **Ron Ellis** and **Sarah Pillsbury,** *Board and Care*

BEST DIRECTION
1976 **Sy Wexler,** *The Human Brain*

BEST SCRIPT
1976 **Mark Orringer,** *The Combined Collis-Belsey Operation*
1977 **Lester T. Hibbard,** *Minilaparatomy Technique*

BEST EDITING
1976 **David Shapiro,** *Making A Good Impression*
1977 **Eric Johnson and Audrey Evans,** *Minilaparatomy Technique*

BEST CINEMATOGRAPHY
1976 **Edgar L. Sherman,** *The Combined Collis-Belsey Operation*

BEST TECHNICAL DEMONSTRATION
1976 **Gregor and David Rempel,** *The Human Brain*

SPECIAL RECOGNITION/MERIT/AWARD
1974 **Doctors Hospital (Tucker, Ga.)/Emory University/American Podiatry Assn.,** *An Arthoplastic Technique for Repair of the First Metatarsophalangeal Joint*
1975 No award
1977 **Richard C. Schneider,** *First Aid for Neck Injuries in Football*
1976 **James Hodge,** *The Use of Hypnosis in Psychotherapy*
American Occupational Therapy Assn., *Hand in Hand*
University of Kansas College of Health Sciences and Hospital, *Colostomy and Ileostomy: Module II: What to Expect Before, During and After Surgery*

Lita Annenberg Hazen Award

LITA ANNENBERG HAZEN AWARD COMMITTEE
Mount Sinai School of Medicine, Office of the Dean, 1 Gustav L. Levy Pl., New York, N.Y. 10029 (212/650-6976)

The $100,000 Lita Annenberg Hazen Award is given annually for outstanding clinical research achievements. The award is given in two parts: $50,000 goes to the honoree, who then selects a junior researcher to work with him/her supported by an additional $50,000 in the form of a fellowship. Applications are considered by a 14-member committee of prominent medical researchers to select the winner.

1979 **Jesse Roth** (National Institute of Arthritis, Metabolism and Digestive Diseases, National Institutes of Health, Bethesda, Md.), clinical research in the biology of insulin action and **James L. Rosenzweig,** fellow
1980 **Henry C. Kunkel** (Rockefeller University, New York), research in immunopathology, and **Mark David Grebenau,** fellow

Albert Lasker Awards

ALBERT AND MARY LASKER FOUNDATION
870 United Nations Plaza, New York, N.Y. 10017 (212/673-0920 and 212/533-7988)

The Albert Lasker Award which, carries a $15,000 honorarium, is given annually for medical research of a pioneering nature. Individuals and groups who have made significant contributions in basic or clinical research in the diseases which are the main causes of death and disability are considered for the honor by a 22-person committee. A symbolic statuette of the Winged Victory is also presented.

BASIC RESEARCH
1962 **Chou H. Li,** Pituitary-hormone chemistry
1963 **Lyman C. Craig,** Countercurrent distribution technique to separate biologically significant compounds, and isolation and structure studies of antibiotics
1964 **Renato Dulbecco and Harry Rubin,** Added to knowledge of relationship between cancer and cancer-producing DNA and RNA viruses
1965 **Robert W. Holley,** Determined chemical structure of an amino acid transfer RNA
1966 **George E. Palade,** Electron microscopy of biological materials
1967 **Bernard B. Brodie,** Biochemical pharmacology
1968 **Marshall W. Nierenberg,** Contributions toward deciphering the genetic code
H. Gobind Khorana, Contributions toward deciphering the genetic code
William F. Windle, Basic discoveries in developmental biology
1969 **Bruce Merrifield,** New synthesis of polypeptides and proteins

1970 **Earl W. Sutherland,** Discovery of cyclic AMP, and provision of comprehension of how this key chemical mechanism regulates hormonal action

1971 **Seymour Benzer,** Molecular genetics
Sydney Brenner, Molecular genetics
Charles Yanofsky, Molecular genetics

1972 **Ludwick Gross,** Discovered leukemia- and cancer-causing viruses in mammals and elucidated their biology and epidemology
Howard E. Skipper, Contributions to groundwork for the chemotherapy of cancer
Sol Spiegelman, Molecular biology, including molecular hybridization and synthesis of an infectious nucleic acid
Howard M. Temin, Biology of RNA-containing cancer viruses and elucidation of the mode of action of viral genes

1975 **Roger C.L. Guillemin,** Added to knowledge of interplay between the hypothalmus and endocrine system
Andrew V. Schally, Added to knowledge of interplay between hypothalmus and endocrine system
Frank J. Dixon, Contributed to creation of new medical discipline: immunopathology
Henry G. Kunkel, Contributed to creation of new medical discipline: immunopathology

1976 **Rosalyn S. Yalow,** Discovered and developed technique of radioimmunoassay

1977 **K. Sune D. Bergstrom,** Isolated prostaglandins and elucidated chemical structures of two types
Bengt Samuelsson, Elucidated mechanism of biosynthesis of prostaglandins and developed method for their measurement
John R. Vane, Discovered prostaglandin X (prostacyclin) which prevents formation of blood clots leading to heart attack and stroke

1978 **Solomon H. Snyder** and **Hans W. Kosterlitz,** discovery that the brain makes its own opiates and that there are receptor molecules in brain cells that account for the action of both natural and man-made opiates

1979 **Roger Wolcott Sperry,** Findings which shed new light on the development and functions of the brain, ultimately leading to a better understanding of the underlying causes of mental and psychosomatic illness
Walter Gilbert and **Frederick Sanger,** Independently arrived at methods for the rapid sequencing of DNA, a laboratory tool which helps unravel the secrets of the gene and ultimately expedite the work of researchers seeking cures for diseases of genetic origin

1980 **Paul Berg, Stanley N. Cohen, A. Dale Kaiser** and **Herbert W. Boyer,** Work with recombinent DNA, the genetic material in cells of all living things that has helped inaugurate a new, promising age of biomedical achievements

CLINICAL RESEARCH

1962 **Joseph Smadel,** Added to understanding, diagnosis and treatment of virus and rickettsial diseases

1963 **Michael E. DeBakey,** Leadership and accomplishments in cardiovascular surgery
Charles Huggins, Incitor and catalyst to modern endocrine studies of tumor control

1964 **Nathan S. Kline,** Introduced iproniazid to treat severe depression

1965 **Albert B. Sabin,** Development of live, oral polio- virus vaccine

1966 **Sidney Farber,** Use of Aminopterin and methotrexate to control acute childhood leukemia and constant search for chemical agents against cancer

1967 **Robert Alan Phillips**(Capt. MC, USN Ret.), Contributions to conquest of cholera

1968 **John H. Gibbon, Jr.,** Designed and developed heart-lung machine

1969 **George C. Cotzias,** Demonstrated effectiveness of L-DOPA to treat Parkinson's Disease

1970 **Robert A. Good,** Added to understanding of mechanism of immunity

1971 **Edward D. Freis,** Demonstrated effectiveness of drugs in treatment of hypertension

1972 **Min Chiu Li,** Contribution to chemotherapeutic treatment of gestational choriocarcinoma
Roy Hertz, Contribution to the successful chemotherapeutic treatment of gestational choriocarcinoma
Denis Burkitt, Identified Burkitt's tumor
Joseph H. Burchenal, Recognized importance of Burkitt's tumor as a unique model
V. Anomah Ngu, Expanded successful chemotherapeutic treatment of Burkitt's tumor
John L. Ziegler, Contribution in increasing the cure rate of Burkitt's tumor by chemotherapy
Edmund Klein, Treatment of premalignant and malignant cancers of the skin
Emil Frei III, Applied concept of combination chemotherapy to lymphoma and acute adult leukemia
Emil J. Freireich, Contributions in combination chemotherapy, and in supportive care of patients receiving combination chemotherapy for acute leukemia
James F. Holland, Contribution to the concept and application of combination therapy in the treatment of acute leukemia in children
Donald Pinkel, Advances in the concept of combination therapy in the treatment of acute leukemia in children
Paul P. Carbone, Contribution to the concept of combination therapy in the treatment of Hodgkin's disease
Vincent T. De Vita, Jr., Contribution to the concept of combination therapy in the treatment of Hodgkin's disease
Eugene J. Van Scott, Contribution to the concept of topical chemotherapy in the treatment of mycosis fungoides
Isaac Djerassi, Contribution in the supportive care, by platelet transfusion, for patients receiving intensive chemotherapy
C. Gordon Zubrod, Special Award for Leadership in expanding the frontiers of cancer chemotherapy

1973 **Paul M. Zoll,** Developed closed-chest defibrillator and pacemaker
William B. Kouwenhoven, Development of open- and closed-chest defibrillators and originated external cardiac massage technique

1974 **John Charnley,** Developed total hip-joint replacement

1975 **Godfrey N. Hounsfield,** Revolutionized diagnostic radiology
William Oldendorf, Envisaged revolution in diagnostic radiology through his work

1976 **Raymond P. Ahlquist,** Developed propranolol to treat heart disease
J.W. Black, Developed propranolol to treat heart disease

1977 **Inge G. Edler,** Pioneered clinical application of ultrasound to diagnosis of abnormalities of the heart
C. Helmuth Hertz, Pioneered ultrasound technology in medicine

1978 **Robert Austrian,** Developed a vaccine against pneumococcal pneumonia
Emil C. Gotschlich, Developed a vaccine against meningitis
Michael Heidelberger, Isolated chemicals from the cell wall of bacteria that can be used in vaccines

1979 No award
1980 **Vincent J. Freda, John Gorman** and **William Pollack,** and **Sir Cyril A. Clarke** and **Ronald Finn,** Two groups of researchers who independently arrived at utilizing immunological principles to create a vaccine for preventing Rh disease in the newborn

The Foundation also presents a series of other honors as merited to individuals and organizations for their work in and contributions to public health and disease control and cure.The honors carry a $15,000 honorarium.

SPECIAL PUBLIC SERVICE AWARDS

1963 **Melvin R. Laird,** U.S. House of Representatives, Recognition of new needs and challenges to legislative leadership in health
Oren Harris,U.S. House of Representatives, Dedication to congressional committee with jurisdiction over public health and safety legislation
1966 **Eunice Kennedy Shriver,** Encouraged national legislation to improve care of mentally retarded
President Lyndon Baines Johnson, Outstanding contributions to health of the people of the U.S.
1967 **Claude Pepper,** U.S. House of Representatives, Dedication to medical legislation
1968 **Lister Hill,**. Senate, Leadership in guiding passage of over 80 major pieces of health legislation
1973 **Warren Magnuson,**. Senate, Leadership and support of medical research
1975 **Jules Stein,** Contributions to preservation of vision and restoration of sight
1976 **World Health Organization,** Historic achievement in imminent and practical eradication of smallpox
1978 **Elliot L. Richardson,** As U.S. Secretary of Health, Education and Welfare, started the National High Blood Pressure Education Program
Theodore Cooper, As director of the National Heart Institute, played a pivotal role in organizing the National High Blood Pressure Education Program
1979 **Sir John Wilson,** Although himself blinded at age 12, was re-educated in Braille and went on to become one of the greatest moving forces in the world in the fight against blindness, especially in Third World countries

SPECIAL PUBLIC HEALTH AWARD

1975 **Karl H. Beyer, Jr., James M. Sprague, John E. Baer and Frederick C. Novello,**(Research Team of Merck Sharp and Dohme Research Laboratories). Creation of new spectrum of medications to control high blood pressure
1980 **Robert I. Levy** and the **Heart, Lung and Blood Institute** (National Institutes of Health), Creation of a landmark hypertension detection and follow up program derived from a monumental five-year study of 10,940 men and women with high blood pressure

ALBERT LASKER AWARDS GIVEN THROUGH THE INTERNATIONAL SOCIETY FOR THE REHABILITATION OF THE DISABLED

1954 **Henry H. Kessler,** Leadership in stimulating and improving services for the disabled
Juan Farill, Vision and leadership in developing international cooperation on behalf of the world's disabled
Viscount Nuffield, Services in international development of rehabilitation programs
1957 **Howard A. Rusk,** Eloquent spokesman and distinguished rehabilitation mentor
Fabian W.G. Langenskiold, Surgeon, educator and administrator
World Veterans Foundation, Leadership, technical assistance and support in advancing rehabilitation services
1960 **Mary E. Switzer,** Leadership in improving services for the world's handicapped
Gudmund Harlem, Physician, administrator and consultant for rehabilitation services in Norway
Paul W. Brand, Treatment and rehabilitation of persons disabled from leprosy
1963 **Renato Da Costa Bonfim,** Advanced rehabilitation services in Latin America
Kurt Jansson, Extended rehabilitation services through United Nations and World Veterans' Federation
Leonard W. Mayo, Global champion of rights of handicapped children, teacher and administrator
1966 **Poul Stochholm,** Brought rehabilitation trainees from all over the world to Denmark
Wiktor Dega, Advanced rehabilitation techniques in Poland
Eugene J. Taylor, Planned rehabilitation facilities for training programs and wrote on concepts and methods
1969 **G. Gringras,** Medical Director, Montreal Institute of Rehabilitation, who brought trainees from Latin America and Asia
Dr. and Mrs. Raden Soeharso, Founders and Directors, National Rehabilitation Center in Solo, Indonesia
Andre Trannoy, Himself a paraplegic, he founded coordination body for rehabilitation services in France
International Labour Union, Promoted vocational rehabilitation of the disabled for 50 years
1972 **James F. Garrett,** Assistant Administrator-Research, Development and Training, Social and Rehabilitation Service of U.S. Dept. of Health, Education and Welfare
Kamala V. Nimbkar, Editor and Founder, *Journal of Rehabilitation in Asia*
Jean Regniers, Businessman and philanthropist; Director of Belgian Assn. for Handicapped Children

The Lasker Awards were initially given by various medical and health organizations in appropriate fields rather than through the foundation which funds them.

ALBERT LASKER AWARDS GIVEN THROUGH THE AMERICAN PUBLIC HEALTH ASSN.—BASIC RESEARCH AWARDS

BASIC RESEARCH AWARDS

1946 **Carl Ferdinand Cori,** Work in carbohydrate metabolism, clarifying action of insulin in diabetes
1947 **Oswald T. Avery,** Studies on the chemical construction of bacteria
Thomas Francis, Jr., Influenza and development of vaccine against Types A and B
Homer Smith, Cardiovascular and renal physiology research
1948 **Vincent Du Vigneaud,** Basic studies of transmethylation and contributions to structure and synthesis of biotin and penicillin
Selman Waksman and Rene J. Dubos, Jointly for studies of antibiotic properties of soil bacteria; Dr. Waksman was also cited for discovery of streptomycin
1949 **Andre Cournand,** Work on physiology of circulation and diagnosis and treatment of heart disease
William S. Tillett and L.S. Christensen, Discovery and purification of streptokinase and streptodornase enzymes

1950 **George Wells Beadle,** Contributions to understanding of genetic control of metabolic processes
1951 **Karl F. Meyer,** Bacteriological research in parasitology
1952 **Sir F. MacFarlane Burnet,** Fundamentally modified knowledge of virus and inheritance of characteristics by viruses
1953 **Hans A. Krebs,** Discovered urea and citric acid cycles, basic to understanding of how body converts food into energy
Michael Heidelberger, Developed new subscience, the precise measuring tool of immunochemistry.
George Wald, Explained physiology of vision in man
1954 **Edwin B. Astwood,** Research on endocrine function, leading to control of hyperthyroidism
John Enders, Cultivation of viruses of poliomylitis, mumps and measles
1955 **Karl Paul Link,** Work on mechanism of blood clotting and development of methods of treatment for thromboembolic conditions
1956 **Karl Meyer and Francis O. Schmitt,** Pioneering studies of biochemical components of connective tissues, contributing to understanding of arthritis and rheumatic diseases
1957 **No award**
1958 **Peyton Rous,** Work on causes of cancers, the source of antibodies and mechanism of blood cell generation and destruction
Theodore Puck, Developed original methods for pure culture of living mammalian cells as basis for new research on nutrition, growth, genetics and mutation
Alfred D. Hershey, Gerhard Schramm and Heinz Fraenkel-Conrat, Jointly for Discoveries of fundamental role of nucleic acid in reproduction of viruses and transmission of inherited characterisitcs
1959 **Albert Coons,** Work in immunology, specifically development of fluorescent method of labeling proteins
Jules Freund, Discoveries in immunology and allergy, strengthening immunization procedures against tuberculosis, malaria, rabies and poliomylitis
1960 **M.H.F. Wilkins, F.H.C. Crick and James D. Watson,** Revealed structure of DNA molecule
James V. Neel and L.S. Penrose, Laid foundations for development of research in genetics, specifically to Dr. Neel for work on thalassemia and sickle cell anemia
Ernest Ruska and James Hillier, Contributed to design, construction, development and perfection of electron microscope

CLINICAL RESEARCH AWARDS

1946 **John Friend Mahoney,** Pioneer in treatment of syphilis with penicillin
1947 **No award**
1948 **No award**
1949 **Max Theiler,** Experiments leading to production of two effective vaccines against yellow fever
1950 **No award**
1951 **Elise L'Esperance and Catherine McFarlane,** Developed cancer detection clinics for discovery of early cancer or precancerous lesions
William G. Lennox and Fredric A. Gibbs, Research on epilepsy
1952 **Conrad A. Elvehjem,** Contributions to biochemical and nutrition research
Frederick S. McKay and H. Trendley Dean, Development of community-wide fluoridation programs
1953 **No award**
1954 **Alfred Blalock, Helen B. Taussig and Robert Gross,** Contributions to cardiovascular surgery and knowledge
1955 **C. Walton Lillehei, Morley Cohen, Herbert Warden and Richard L. Varco,** Advances in cardiac surgery, making possible more direct and safer approaches to the heart
Edward H. Robitzek, Irving Selikoff, Walsh McDermott and **Carl Muschenheim,** (Hoffman-LaRoche Research Laboratories, Squib Institute for Medical Research), Establishment of efficacy of isoniazid drugs to treat tuberculosis, meningitis and generalized miliary tuberculosis
1956 **Jonas E. Salk,** Developed safe and effective vaccine against poliomyelitis
V. Everett Kinsey and Arnall Patz, Discovered that excessive oxygen administration causes retrolental fibroplasia (blinding) in premature babies
1957 **Rustom Jal Vakil,** Systematic studies on Rauwolfia in hypertension
Nathan Kline, Demonstrated value of Rauwolfia derivatives, especially reserpine, in treatment of mental and nervous disorders
Robert Noce, Studies of reserpine treatment of mentally ill and mental defectives
Henri Laborit, Studies of surgical shock and post-operative illness resulting in use of chlorpromazine as therapeutic agent
Pierre Deniker, Introduction of chlorpromazine into psychiatry and demonstrating that a medication can influence the clinical course fo major psychosis
Heinz E. Lehmann, Demonstrated clinical uses of chlorpomazine in treatment of mental and nervous disorders
1958 **Robert W. Wilkins,** Work on control of heart and blood vessel diseases through investigations in causes, diagnosis and treatment of hypertension
1959 **John Holmes Dingle,** Work on knowledge of and ability to control acute respiratory diseases
Gilbert Dalldorf, Demonstrated ability of one virus to modify course of infection by another and discovered Coxsackie virus by a unique and broadly applicable technique

BASIC AND CLINICAL RESEARCH AWARDS

1946 **Karl Landsteiner, Alexander Wiener and Philip Levine,** Discovery of RH factor in blood and its significance both as a cause of sickness and death of infants before the afterbirth and in blood transfusions
1947 **No award**
1948 **No award**
1949 **Edward C. Kendall and Philip S. Hench,** Chemical, physiological and clinical studies of adrenal hormones culminating in the use of cortisone in rheumatic disease therapy
1950 **George Papincolaou,** Early diagnosis of cancer through cytological methods
1951-56 **No awards**
1957 **Richard E. Shope,** Better understanding of infectious diseases in animals and humans, and discovery of new microbiological principles

SPECIAL AWARDS

1947 **Thomas Parran,** Leadership in public health administration as Surgeon General of U.S., President of International Health Conference and contributions to control of venereal diseases
1949 **Haven Emerson,** Developed national program of rural community health services
1952 **Charles-Edward Amory Winslow,** More than a half century of inspiring and inspired leadership as teacher and exponent of public health

1956 **Alan Gregg,** Vice President, Rockefeller University, and leader in public health, medical education and research

1959 **Lister Hill,** U.S. Senate, and **John E. Fogarty,** U.S. House of Representatives, Contributions to public health and research through leadership in Congress

PUBLIC SERVICE AWARDS

1946 **Alfred Newton Richards,** Organization and Administration of Committee on Medical Research of the Office of Scientific Research and Development; supervised wartime mass production of penicillin and search for antimalarial drug and preparation of blood plasma
Fred L. Soper, Administrative achievement in control of yellow fever and malaria through eradication of insect carriers

1947 **Alice Hamilton,** Leader in toxology and contribution to prevention of occupational diseases and betterment of workers' health

1948 **R.E. Dyer,** Microbiological research and service as Director of National Institutes of Health during war and postwar years
Martha M. Eliot, Organization and operation of Emergency Maternal and Infant Care Program of the Children's Bureau

1949 **Marion W. Sheahan,** Leadership in nursing and public health

1950 **Eugene Lindsay Bishop,** Original accomplismments in public health administration

1951 **Florence R. Sabin,** Accomplishments in public health administration as chairman of the Health Committee of the Governor of Colorado's Post-War Planning Committee

1952 **Brock Chisholm,** First director of World Health Organization, for leadership in organization of this vast public health concept
Howard A. Rusk, Work in service of physically disabled and distinguished rehabilitation mentor to the world

1953 **Felix J. Underwood,** Demonstrated how long-sustained, sound and expanding health services benefits a people
Earle B. Phelps, Lifetime of pioneering leadership in public health and sanitary sciences

1954 **Leona Baumgartner,** Public health administration leadership and strengthening of community health

1955 **Robert Defries,** Development of preventive medicine and public health in Canada
Menninger Foundation and Karl and William Menninger, Sustained and highly productive attack against mental diseases
Lucile Petry Leone, Pearl McIver and Margaret G. Arnstein (Nursing Services of U.S Public Health Services), Distinguished contributions to advancement and well-being of the nation through public health nursing

1956 **William P. Shepard,** Pioneering as industrial health physician, educator and government advisor

1957 **Frank G. Boudreau,** Work with Milbank Memorial Fund to promote better mental health, good nutrition and healthful housing
C.J. Van Slyke, Laid foundations of national program of medical research and training
Reginald M. Atwater, Guided American Public Health Assn. to position of leadership in western world

1958 **Basil O'Connor,** Extraordinary administrative leadership on eradication of poliomyelitis through development of effective vaccine (March of Dimes)

1959 **Maurice Pate,** Service to world's children and skilled development of United Nation's Children's Fund program of improving maternal and child health

1960 **John B. Grant,** International statesman on public health, authority on problems of preventive medicine and medical care
Abel Wolman, Leader of lay and professional health groups, corporate consultant, engineer and organizer

GROUP AWARD CITATIONS

1946 **National Institutes of Health,** Contributions to prevention and control of diseases
Northern Regional Research Laboratory, U.S. Dept of Agriculture, Development of powerful penicillin-producing molds
Board for the Coordination of Malarial Studies, Comprehensive studies of anti-malarial agents
Bureau of Entomology and Plant Quarantine, U.S. Dept. of Agriculture, Solution to problems involving health and comfort of the Armed Forces, specifically regarding insect-borne diseases and the use of DDT
Army Epidemological Board, Research on influenza, mapping of its epidemiology and a vaccine

1947 **British Ministers of Food and Health,** Maintenance and even improvement of public health in Great Britain in spite of war
U.S. Committee on Joint Causes of Death, International statistical classification of diseases, injuries and causes of death

1948 **Veterans Administration,** Efficient program of medical care for millions of veterans

1949 **American Academy of Pediatrics,** Studies of personnel services and facilities for the protection of child health
Life Insurance Medical Research Fund, Initiation and support of research on main cause of cardiovascular disease

1950 **International Health Div., Rockefeller Foundation,** Control of infectious diseases and education of health personnel throughout the world

1951 **Health Insurance Plan of Greater New York,** Pioneering a combination of group medical practice and prepayments to provide comprehensive, high-quality care
Alcoholics Anonymous, Unique and highly successful approach to a public-health and social problem

1952 **No award**

1953 **Div. of Research Grants, National Institutes of Health,** Outstanding administration of research-grants program
University Laboratory of Physical Chemistry Related to Medicine, Harvard University, Basic protein studies leading to fundamental achievements in blood separation and gamma globulin preparation

1954 **Streptococcal Disease Laboratory, Armed Forces Epidemiological Board: Frances E. Warren AFB, Charles H. Rammelkamp, Jr., Dir.,** Contributions to knowledge of streptococcal diseases

1955 **No award**

1956 **Food and Drug Administration,** Half-century of public service safeguarding American people against contaminated or misrepresented products
Medical Care Program, Welfare and Retirement Fund, United Mine Workers of America, Model program of health services for a million and a half workers and their families

1957 **No award**

1958 **No award**

1959 **No award**

1960 **Crippled Children's Program of the Children's Bureau, Dept. of Health, Education and Welfare,** Stimulated comprehensive services for physically handicapped children
Chronic Disease Program, California State Dept. of Public Health, Making prevention and control of heart disease a matter of public concern

ALBERT LASKER AWARDS GIVEN THROUGH THE PLANNED PARENTHOOD—WORLD POPULATION

1945 **John McLeod,** Research on metabolism of mobility of human sperm cells
1946 **Robert Latou Dickinson,** Work on human fertility and its control, as gynecologist, anatomist, educator, scholar and artist
Irl Cephas Reggin, Making planned parenthood available as part of Virginia's state public health program
1947 **Alan F. Guttmacher,** Leadership in marriage counseling
Abraham Stone, Leadership in marriage counseling
1948 **John Rock,** Treatment of childless couples and help to parents in planning their families
Richard N. Pierson, Mobilized medical profession in behalf of family planning
1949 **George M. Cooper,** Services in maternal and child health
Carl G. Hartman, Physiology of human reproduction work
1950 **Margaret Sanger,** Singular role in founding the birth control movement
Bessie L. Moses, Enlisted concern and talents of physicians and nurses in family planning
1951 **Guy Irving Burch,** Interpretation to lay public of world population trends and problems
William Vogt, Presentation to a world audience of the critical relationship between dwindling resources and expanding population
1952 **William Roy Norton,** Leadership in making birth control an integral part of North Carolina public health services
Herbert Thomas, Developed techniques of natural child bearing; medical leadership in marriage counseling
Eleanor Bellows Pillsbury, Led Planned Parenthood to position of national and international force
1953 **Harry Emerson Fosdick,** Contribution to safeguarding the rights of motherhood in the pattern of constructive family life
Elise Ottesen-Jensen, Leadership in developing healthy and ethical sex education program in Swedish schools
1954 **Lady Dhanvanthi Rama Rau,** Contributions to family planning in India and the world
M.C. Chang, Research on physiologic fertility control
Howard C. Taylor, Furthered knowledge of human fertility
1955 **Warren O. Nelson,** Studies of the biology of spermatogenesis
Robert Carter Cook, Unique role with Population Reference Bureau in interpretation of the world population dilemma.
1956 **No award**
1957 **No award**
1958 **Harrison S. Brown,** Increased awareness that conservation of resources must be coupled with world-wide family planning
1959 **Sir Julian Huxley,** Helped achieve world recognition of population crisis and necessity of confronting it
1960 **Gregory Pincus,** Developed first oral contraceptive pill
1961 **John D. Rockefeller III,** Leadership in enlisting support of governments in attacking global population problems
1963 **Cass Canfield,** Leadership in world recognition of global population problems
1965 **C. Lee Buxton and Estelle T. Griswold,** Advancement of cause of voluntary parenthood in Connecticut and throughout the U.S.

ALBERT LASKER AWARDS GIVEN THROUGH THE NATIONAL COMMITTEE AGAINST MENTAL ILLNESS

1944 **Col. William C. Menninger,** Advancement of mental health in the field of war psychiatry
1945 **Maj. Gen. G. Brock Chisholm,** Advancement of mental health in rehabilitation
Brig. Gen. John Rawlings Rees, Advancement of mental health in rehabilitation
1946 **W. Horsley Gantt,** Experimental modification and analysis of behavior
Jules H. Masserman, Investigations into neurotic behavior
Walter Lerch and D.P. Sharpe, Aroused people of Ohio to start major improvements in hospital care of mental patients
1947 **Lawrence K. Frank,** Contributions through adult education, particularly through parent-child relationships and child-development programs
Catherine MacKenzie, Reporter and columnist who provided campaign of education on care and emotional development of children
1948 **C. Anderson Aldrich,** Educated physicians in psychological aspects of pediatrics
Mike Gorman, Reporter whose contributions resulted in new mental health legislation and increased appropriations in the field
Al Ostrow, Reporter who helped give public and legislative support for programs of care for the mentally ill in California
1949 **Mildred C. Scoville,** Integration of mental health concepts in medical education and practice
Albert Deutsch, Advancement of mental health through books, magazine and newspaper articles

ALBERT LASKER AWARDS GIVEN THROUGH THE AMERICAN HEART ASSN.—BASIC RESEARCH

1954 **Albert Szent-Gyorgyi,** Research in cardiovascular diseases, including the discovery of actomyosin, the essential contractible element of muscle
1955 **Carl J. Wiggers,** Contributions to understanding of cardiovascular physiology
1956 **No award**
1957 **Isaac Starr,** Work in heart and circulation research and development of first practical ballistocardiograph
1958 **Irvine H. Page,** Contributions to knowledge of basic mechanisms of hypertension

ALBERT LASKER AWARDS GIVEN THROUGH THE AMERICAN HEART ASSN.—CLINICAL RESEARCH

1953 **Paul Dudley White,** Distinguished achievement in pathology, diagnosis and treatment of heart diseases
1954 **No award**
1955 **No award**
1956 **No award**
1957 **No award**
1958 **No award**
1959 **Robert E. Gross,** Performed first successful operation on an inborn cardiovascular defect

ALBERT LASKER AWARDS GIVEN THROUGH THE AMERICAN HEART ASSN.—BASIC AND CLINICAL RESEARCH

1956 **Louis N. Katz,** Contributions in cardiovascular research and advancement of thesis that experimental atherosclerosis is a preventable and reversible metabolic disease
1957 **No award**
1958 **No award**
1959 **No award**
1960 **Karl Paul Link, Irving S. Wright and Edgar V. Allen,** Pioneering development and use of anticoagulant drugs

Gairdner Foundation International Award
Award of Merit
Wightman Award

GAIRDNER FOUNDATION
255 Yorkland Blvd., Ste. 220, Willowdale, Ont. M2J 1S3
(416/493-3101)

The Gairdner Foundation International Awards, which each carry a $15,000 honorarium, are given annually to individuals who have made outstanding discoveries or contributions in the conquest of disease and relief of human suffering. The foundation selects the winners.

1959 **Charles Ragan** and **Harry M. Rose** (New York), Contributions to knowledge of rheumatology and introduction of agglutination test to differentiate rheumatoid arthritis from other rheumatic diseases
W.D.M. Paton and **Eleanor J. Zaimis** (London, U.K.), Contributions to pharmacology, especially introduction of methonium compounds which are valuable in treating hypertension
W.G. Bigelow (Toronto), Contribution to cardiology, especially for development the hypothermia method of open-heart surgery
1960 **Joshua Harold Burn** (Oxford, U.K.), Contributions to pharmacology, cardiac-physiology and vaso-neurology, especially elucidating the role of various drugs, noradrenaline and the sympathetic nervous system in the excitation and control of cardio-vascular disease
John Heysham Gibbon, Jr. (Philadelphia), Contributions to cardiology, especially development and use of heart-lung machine
William Ferguson Hamilton (Augusta, Ga.), Contributions to cardiac physiology, especially developing the dye dilution technique to determine cardiac output
John McMichael (London, U.K.), Contributions to cardiology and clinical physiology, especially in early application of cardiac catheterization technique to measure cardiac pressure and output
Karl Meyer (New York), Contributions to pathology and immunology, especially for demonstrating the role of hypersensitivity in production of certain tissue lesions including in rheumatic and other diseases
Arthur Rice Rich (Baltimore), Contributions to pathology and immunology, especially demonstrating the role of hypersensitivity in the production of certain tissue lesions
1961 **Lord Brock** (London, U.K.), Contributions to the functional pathology, investigation and surgery of congenital rheumatic heart diseases and especially elucidation of factors which may obstruct blood flow from the heart into the main arteries of the lungs and body
Allan C. Burton (London, Ont.), Contributions to cardiovascular physiology, especially applying the basic laws of physics to the peripheral and pulminary circulations, bringing about an improved understanding of the behavior of blood vessels in health and disease
Alexander B. Gutman (New York), Contributions to rheumatology and biochemistry, especially in elucidating the metabolic defects present in gout, and demonstrating the action of certain drugs which increase the excretion of uric acid, leading to control over attacks of acute gout and prevention of gouty arthritis
Jonas H. Kellgren (Manchester, U.K.), Many contributions to knowledge of rheumatology and epidemiology, especially for leadership in devising and executing studies of rheumatoid arthritis
U.S. von Euler (Stockholm), Contributions to knowledge of substances released at the nerve endings of the sympathetic nervous system, especially for recognizing that noradrenaline was the most important of those substances present in a significant amount in all body organs, especially the heart
1962 **Albert H. Coons** (Boston), Contributions to pathology and immunology, especially development of fluorescent anti-body technique casting new light on hypersensitivity reactions
Clarence Crafoord (Stockholm), Contributions to cardiology and leadership in cardiac surgery
Henry G. Kunkel (New York), Contributions to knowledge of medicine, especially serological, immunological and metabolic studies of protein molecules
Stanley Sarnoff (Bethesda, Md.), Contributions to cardiac physiology, especially demonstrating the interrelated roles of the nervous system, hormones and heart size in the control of cardiac performance
1963 **Jacques Genest** (Montreal), Contributions to knowledge of vascular physiology, particularly studies of the mechanism of hypertension
Irvine H. Page (Cleveland), Contributions to cardiac and vascular physiology, pharmacology and endocrinology, including discoveries of the existence and the synthesis of angiotensin and existence of serotonin
Pierre Grabar (Paris), Contributions to biochemistry, particularly immunohisto-chemistry including development of immuno-electrophoretic technique, enabling specific identification of many bodily proteins
C. Walton Lillehie (Minneapolis), Contributions to cardiac surgery and cardiac physiology, particularly pioneering contributions to open-heart surgery
E.G.L. Bywaters (London, U.K.), Contributions to knowledge of rheumatology and pediatrics, particularly delineations of the natural history of juvenile rheumatoid arthritis and other rheumatic syndromes
1964 **Karl H. Leyer** (West Point, Penn.), Contributions to pharmacology and renal physiology, particularly research, observations and scientific leadership resulting in the discovery of uricosuric and improved diruetic drugs
Deborah Doniach and **Ian M. Roitt** (London, U.K.), Contributions to immunology, particularly demonstration of the presence of thryoglobulin antibodies in serum of patients with Hashimoto's disease and stimulation their research has given to the concept of disease of auto-immunity and studies in use of oral medications to control diabetes
Gordon F. Murray (Toronto), Contributions to cardiac physiology and pathology and development of important techniques in cardiac surgery

Keith R. Potter (Boston), Contributions to cellular biology, particularly development and application of electron microscopy techniques resulting in early demonstration of important features in cell structure

1965 **Jerome W. Conn** (Ann Arbor, Mich.), Contributions to endocrinology, particularly investigations establishing clinical significance of aldosterone, a hormone of the adrenal cortex, in various types of hypertension and edema

R.R.A. Coombs (Cambridge, U.K.), Contributions to development of serological techniques, particularly introduction of the test to detect presence of Rh antibodies on red blood cells, fundamental to advances in blood transfusions

Charles E. Dent (London, U.K.), Contributions to human metabolism and role as the first to apply the technique of paper chromatography to the isolation and identification of substances in the blood and body fluids of patients, revolutionizing investigation of a number of genetic disorders involving amino acids and other substances

Charles P. Leblond (Montreal), Contributions to cellular biology, developing technique of autoradiography to study thyroid gland function and cell growth rate and renewal

Daniel J. McCarty (Philadelphia), Contributions to rheumatology, particularly demonstration that crystals of uric acid and calcium in the fluids in and about the joints are ingested by leukocytes, releasing a substance which causes an inflammatory reaction, a discovery which bore on the mechanism of acute attacks of gout and possibly rheumatoid arthritis

Sir F. Horace Smirk (Dunedin, N.Z.), Contributions to understanding of causes and treatment of hypertension, particularly for clinical evaluation of nerve-blocking drugs in treating high blood pressure

1966 **Geoffrey S. Dawes** (Oxford, U.K.), Contributions to understanding physiological behavior and biochemical changes occuring to the fetus *in utero*, particularly clarification of adjustments at birth to extra-uterine life

Charles Huggins (Chicago), Pioneering work in treatment of cancer with hormonal substances and use of chemical means to monitor response in carcinoma of the prostate

W.J. Kolff (Cleveland), Early work in development of artificial kidney and continuing effort to develop other artificial organs

Luis Federico Leloir (Buenos Aires), Contributions to carbohydrate chemistry and metabolism, particularly discovery of sugar nucleotides and their fundamental reactions in the biosynthesis of di-saccharides and poly-saccharides

J.F.A.P. Miller (Melbourne, Australia), Fundamental contributions to understanding the role of the thymus in the development of normal immunological mechanisms in early life and their maintenance in adult life

Jan Waldenstrom (Malmo, Sweden), Contributions to knowledge of certain metabolic disorders, particularly clarification of serum protein abnormalities in multiple myeloma and in essential macroglobulinamia, contributing materially to better understanding of certain high molecular weight antibodies, structure of gamma globulins and cell types which give rise to them

1967 **Julius Axelrod** and **Sidney Udenfriend** (Bethesda, Md.), Wide-ranging and fundamental discoveries in the chemistry, biosynthesis, metabolism and pharmacology of biogenic amines, specially catecholamines, influencing fields of hypertension and pyschopharmacology

D. Harold Copp (Vancouver, B.C.), Contributions to problems of calcium homeostasis, particularly demonstration of existence e of new hormone calcitonin, which alters blood calcium levels, and confirmation of the ultimobranchial glands as source of this hormone; and

Iain MacIntyre (London, U.K.), Contributions in mineral metabolism, particularly studies of the physiology of calcitonin

Peter J. Moloney (Toronto), Many important contributions to immunology and diabetes, including introduction of toxoids for immunization against diphtheria and tetanus, demonstration of antibodies against insulin and development of sulphated insulin

J. Fraser Mustard (Hamilton, Ont.), Contributions in fields of thrombosis and atherosclerosis, particularly investigation of platelet economy, function and metabolism and for classical experimental flow model demonstrating sites of thrombus accumulation, demonstration of platelet phagocytosis and elucidation of factors affecting platelet aggregation

1968 **James Learmonth Gowans** (Oxford, U.K.), Contributions to understanding fate of lymphocyte and its function in immune reaction

George H. Hitchings (Tuckahoe, N.Y.), Leadership in development of metabolic inhibitors by systematic chemical modification of biologically important compounds to develop agents valuable in treating a variety of disorders

Jacques Oudin (Paris), Contribution to immunochemistry through analysis of antigen-antibody reactions and discovery and elucidation of genetic variables in the structure of immunoglobulins

J. Edwin Seegmiller (Bethesda, Md.), Elucidation of a number of inborn errors of metabolism, particularly discovery of an enzyme defect (phosphoribosyltransferase deficiency) in a neurological disease characterized by mental retardation, behavioral disturbances and over-production of uric acid

1969 **Frank J. Dixon** (La Jolla, Calif.), Contributions to immunology and immunopathology, particularly investigations of pathogenesis of serum sickness and of experimental and human glomerulonephritis

John P. Merrill (Boston), Contribution to nephrology, particularly pioneering work in kidney transplantation

Belding H. Scribner (Seattle), Concept of chronic intermittent hemodialysis, arteriovenous cannulas making it possible, development of "home" dialysis and continued basic and clinical investigations

Robert B. Salter (Toronto), Scientific contributions to the understanding of cartilage degeneration, epiphyseal necrosis, torsional deformation of bone and dysplasia of joints relating to numerous musculoskeletal disorders, especially congenital dislocation of the hip

Earl W. Sutherland (Nashville), Contributions to understanding central role of adenyl cyclase system in mediating many effects of hormones and the metabolic process

F. Mason Sones (Cleveland), Contributions to investigation and treatment of coronary artery disease, particularly introduction of selective arteriography technique, leading to precise localization of sites of obstructions

E.A. McCullough and **J.E. Till** (Toronto), Development of spleen colony technique for measuring capacity of primitive normal and neoplastic cells to multiply and differentiate in the body, a technique applied to research in normal and leukemic blood cell functions

1970 **Vincent P. Dole** (New York), Pioneering contributions to understanding of metabolism of free fatty acid and adipose tissue and also significant work in treating narcotic addiction with methadone
W. Richard S. Doll (Oxford, U.K.), Contributions to methodology of medical research and clarification of complex epidemiological problems, particularly in establishing the association between tobacco smoking and cancer of the lung and association between ionizing radiation and leukemia
Robert A. Good (Minneapolis), Contributions to understanding of host defense mechanisms and elucidation of an array of immunological deficiency syndromes in infants and children
Niels K. Jerne (Basel, Switz.), Contribution to knowledge of cellular basis of the immune response, formulation of the natural selection theory providing the first comprehensive model and discovery of rapid, quantitative method for enumerating antibody-producing cells via a new approach to experimental studies of cellular events during immunization
Robert Bruce Merrifield (New York), Work on solid phase method for synthesis of polypeptides and application of this method in the first synthesis of an enzyme
1971 **Charles H. Best** (Toronto), Participation in the discovery and development of insulin and many other contributions to medical research as a teacher, mentor and scientist
Rachmiel Levine (Duarte, Calif.), Contributions to the study of diabetes mellitus, especially pioneering work on the site of action of insulin
Frederick Sanger (Cambridge, U.K.), Contributions to the study of the structure of complex biochemical substances, particularly determining the precise composition of insulin
Donald F. Steiner (Chicago), Recognition that insulin is derived from a larger precursor molecule called pro-insulin
Solomon A. Berson and **Rosalyn S. Yalow** (New York), Development of a reliable, specific and sensitive method for the assay of plasma insulin and application of the same principles in measuring other polypeptide substances
1972 **Karl Sune Detlof Bergstrom** (Stockholm), Contributions to identification and chemical characterization of prostaglandins
Britton Chance (Philadelphia), Devising biophysical techniques for observation of molecular events in living tissues, cells and organelles and unique imaginativeness in applying these techniques to bridge the gap between knowledge of isolated enzymes and phenomena of physiology and pharmacology
Oleh Hornykiewicz (Toronto), Elucidation of the biochemical lesion in Parkinson's disease and other contributions to knowledge of the physiology of the brain
Robert Russell Race and **Ruth Sanger** (London, U.K.), Many contributions to knowledge of human blood groups and application of this knowledge to problems im immunology, genetics and clinical medicine
1973 **Roscoe O. Brady** (Bethesda, Md.), Work on enzymology of complex lipids and contribution to the management of lipid storage diseases
Denis P. Burkitt (London, U.K.), Recognition, clinical description and brilliant epidemiological study of the unusual lymphoma in Africa which now bears his name
John Charnley (Manchester, U.K.), Scholarly contributions to biomechanics and lubrication of joints, particularly development of a practical, low-friction arthoplasty for arthritis of the hip
Kimishige Ishizaka and **Teruko Ishizaka** (Baltimore), Identification and characterization of the new immunoglobulin class IgE, leading to increased understanding of allergic mechanisms
Harold E. Johns (Toronto), Pioneering work in developing cobalt and high-energy radiotherapy and many contributions to education and research in clinical physics and biophysics
1974 **David Baltimore** (Cambridge, Mass) and **Howard M. Temin** (Madison, Wis.), Research on mechanism of action of viruses in relation to tumor production
Hector F. DeLuca (Madison, Wis.), Elucidation of metabolism of Vitamin D
Roger Guillemin (San Diego) and **Andrew V. Schally** (New Orleans), Work on identification, synthesis and clinical application of hypothalamic releasing hormones
Hans J. Muller-Eberhard (La Jolla, Calif.), Contributions to understanding the molecular basis of the complement system in humans
Judah H. Quastel (Vancouver), Many contributions in biochemical research
1975 **Ernest Beutler** (Duarte, Calif.), Elucidation of the biochemical and genetic basis of the hemolytic anemias related to glucose-6-phosphate dehydrogenase deficiency and other studies on human erythrocytes
Baruch S. Blumberg (Philadelphia), Discovery of the Australian antigen and its association with hepatitis, enhancing knowledge of viral hepatitis type B and its prevention
Henri G. Hers (Brussels), Fundamental discoveries related to glycogen metabolism and its disorders, disorders of fructose metabolism and the lysosomal basis of several inborn errors of metabolism
Hugh E. Huxley (Cambridge, U.K.), Outstanding contributions to understanding the molecular basis of muscle contraction
John D. Keith (Toronto), Many important contributions to understanding the natural history of congenital heart disease, forming the basis for modern treatment of such malformations
William T. Mustard (Toronto), Contributions in cardiovascular surgery, particularly achievement of operation for the transposition of the great vessels which now bears his name
1976 **Thomas R. Dawber** (Boston) and **William B. Kannel** (Framingham, Mass.), Careful epidemiological studies, revealing risk factors in cardiovascular diseases with important implications for prevention of these disorders
Eugene P. Kennedy (Boston), Elucidation of biochemical pathways involved in triglyceride and phospholipid synthesis
George Klein (Stockholm), Contributions to understanding of the biology of neoplastic cells and distinguished work in tumor immunology
George D. Snell (Bar Harbor, Me.), Identification of major histocompatibility complex in mice and establishment of methods of study fundamental to immunogenetics
1977 **K. Frank Austen** (Boston), Contributions to understanding factors involved in initiation, amplification and control of the imflammatory response
Sir Cyril A. Clarke (Liverpool, U.K.), Original contribution to prevention of hemolytic disease of the newborn

Jean Dausset (Paris), Recognition of effects of histocompatibility antigens in humans and continuing leadership in application of this knowledge to transplantation, immunology and study of genetically determined diseases
Henry G. Friesen (Winnipeg), Contributions to understanding the biochemistry, physiology and pathophysiology of lactogenic hormones, particularly for the identification of human prolactin
Victor A. McKusick (Baltimore), Many contributions to development of clinical genetics and role in placing this field in the mainstream of clinical medicine
1978 **Sydney Brenner** (Cambridge, U.K.), Highly original and conceptual contributions to molecular biology and the understanding of how genetic information is read and translated
Jean-Pierre Changeux (Paris), Pioneering work in purifying and elucidating mechanisms of the cholinergic receptor
Donald S. Fredrickson (Bethesda, Md.), Contributions to understanding genetic, biochemical and clinical aspects of hyperlipoproteinemias
Samuel O. Freedman and **Phil Gold** (Montreal), Discovery of carcinoembryonic antigen and studies elucidating its biological and clinical significance
Edwin G. Krebs (Seattle), Elucidation of fundamental biochemical mechanisms related to glycogen breakdown, pioneering work that has enhanced knowledge of hormone action
Elizabeth C. Miller and **James A. Miller** (Madison, Wis.), Many contributions to understanding of how environmental chemicals, natural and man-made, induce cancer
Lars Terenius (Uppsala, Sweden), Development of radioreceptor methods, their application to opiates and the detection of an endogenous opiate-like substance in the nervous system
1979 **James W. Black** (Kent, U.K.), Role in identification of amine receptors and development of receptor-blocking drugs, Propranolol and Cimetidine
George F. Cahill, Jr. (Boston), Contributions to understanding of interrelationships of hormones and body fuels in differing nutritional states of humans
Walter Gilbert (Cambridge, Mass.), Contributions to understanding of gene replication and regulation and of development of methods for sequencing DNA and their application to studies of gene organization
Elwood V. Jensen (Chicago), Discovery of steriod receptors, leading to elucidation of the action of steriod hormones and to the development of tests guiding endocrine treatment for cancer of the breast
Frederick Sanger (Cambridge, U.K.), Development of methods for sequencing of DNA and contributions to the new concepts of gene structure
Charles R. Scriver (Montreal), Contribution to understanding genetic disease, particularly detection of genetically determined disease in large population groups and development of treatment programs for these disorders
1980 **Paul Berg** (Stanford, Calif.), Contributions to understanding the mechanisms of protein synthesis and interplay of viral and cellular genes in regulating growth and division
Irving B. Fritz (Toronto), Discovery of the role of carnitine in the regulation of fatty acid metabolism
H. Gobind Khorana (Cambridge, Mass.), Chemical synthesis of a functional gene
Efraim Racker (Ithaca, N.Y.), Contribution to knowledge of energy metabolism in cells and of transport in biological membranes
Jesse Roth (Bethesda, Md.), Elucidation of mechanisms through which insulin and other peptide hormones interact with cells and the ways in which these are altered in disease states
Michael Sela (Rehovot, Israel), Fundamental contribution to understanding the molecular basis of immunogenicity

The Gairdner Award of Merit, which is accompanied by a $25,000 honorarium, is made periodically for a discovery deemed to be the most outstanding consistency with the foundation's purposes.

1959 **Alfred Blalock** and **Helen B. Taussig** (Baltimore), Contribution to the knowledge of medicine, especially the outstanding achievement in developing an operation for the treatment of congenital heart lesions, introducing a new era in cardiac surgery
1962 **Francis H.C. Crick** (Cambridge, U.K.), Contribution to the knowledge of molecular biology and genetics, including inspiring investigations of nucleic acids showing how genetic information can be impressed and stores in germ cells of parents and transmitted to succeeding generations, studies of molecular structure of collagen and especially the brilliant development of the "coding" theory to explain the way information is carried in the genes
1963 **Murray L. Barr** (London, Ont.), Outstanding contributions to microanatomy and human cytogenetics, particularly discovery of a new technique for specific identification of male and female cells, opening vast areas for research into normal and abnormal development of body structures, leading to improved understanding of several congenital anomalies and some forms of mental retardation
Seymour Benzer (Lafayette, Ind.), Outstanding contributions to genetics and molecular biology, particularly elucidation of the fine structure of genes, making it possible to extend the limits of genetic resolution by relating genetic changes to chemical alterations
1966 **R.R. Porter** (London, U.K.), Outstanding achievements in immunochemistry, including application of the tools of the protein chemist to the problem of antibody structure
1967 **Christian DeDuve** (New York and Louvain, Belgium), Discovery of lysosomes, which are membrane-bound subcellular particles containing hydrolytic enzymes and other biologically active substances, leading to a better understanding of many disease processes and opening innumerable new avenues of research
Marshall W. Nirenberg (Bethesda, Md.), Contributions to understanding mechanisms of protein synthesis, leading eventually to a complete understanding of the chemical basis of the genetic code
George E. Palade (New York), Many contributions to developing methods of preparing cells and tissues so that subcellular components could be preserved and visualized in the electron microscope
1968 **Bruce Chown** (Winnipeg), Valuable contributions to knowledge of human blood groups, particularly for work on diagnosis, treatment and prevention of hemolytic disease of the newborn and for leadership in clinical immunohematology
1976 **Godfrey N. Hounsfield** (Middlesex, U.K.), Outstanding contribution to care of patients by pioneering development of computerized tomography

The $25,000 Gairdner Foundation Wightman Award is awarded periodically to a Canadian who has demonstrated outstanding leadership in medicine and medical science consistent with the purposes of the foundation.

1976 **Keith J. R. Wightman** (Toronto), Outstanding contributions to Canadian medicine as an educator, physician and leader of the profession

1979 **Claude Fortier** (Quebec City), Contributions to Canadian medicine as a scientist, teacher and scientific advisor to governments

Jason A. Hannah Medal

ROYAL SOCIETY OF CANADA
344 Wellington, Ottawa, Ont. K1A ON4 (613/992-3468)

The Jason A. Hannah Medal, which is of bronze and carries a $1,000 honorarium from Associated Medical Servies Inc., is awarded annually for an important publication in the history of medicine. It is normally given for work over the previous decade by a Canadian citizen or resident or about Canadian medicine. A selection committee chooses the recipient.

1978 **Henri Ellenberger**
1979 **John Farley**
1980 **Malcolm G. Taylor**

Jessie Stevenson Kovalenko Medal

National Academy of Sciences
2101 Constitution Ave. NW, Washington, D.C. 20418 (202/393-8100)

The Jessie Stevenson Kovalenko Medal, which is of gold and carries a $2,000 honorarium, is awarded approximately every three years for contributions to medical science. A four-member committee selects the winner.

1952 **Alfred Newton Richard**
1955 **Peyton Rous**
1958 **Ernest W. Goodpasture**
1959 **Eugene Lindsay Opie**
1961 **Karl Fredrich Meyer**
1962 **George Hoyt Whipple**
1966 **Rufus Cole**
1967 **Karl Paul Link**
1970 **Thomas Francis Jr.**
1973 **Seymour Solomon Kety**
1976 **Julius Hiram Comroe, Jr.**
1979 **Henry G. Kunkel**

Kettering Prize
Mott Prize
Sloan Prize

GENERAL MOTORS CANCER RESEARCH FOUNDATION
767 Fifth Ave., New York, N.Y. 10022 (212/486-2300)

Three General Motors Cancer Research Prizes, each consisting of $100,000 and a gold medal, are awarded annually for hallmark accomplishments of basic and clinical scientists in cancer research. An Awards Assembly of scientists expert in the three specific areas of the prizes selects the winners, who are invited to deliver a lecture on the subjects for which the prizes are awarded.

CHARLES F. KETTERING MEDAL (For the most outstanding recent contribution to the diagnosis or treatment of cancer)

1979 **Henry S. Kaplan** (Stanford University), For developing a therapeutic program which changed Hodgkin's Disease from an almost invariably fatal illness to a highly curable one

1980 **Elwood V. Jensen** (University of Chicago), For studies providing evidence linking human breast cancer to estrogen

CHARLES S. MOTT MEDAL (For the most outstanding recent contribution to the prevention of cancer, including environmental influences)

1979 **Richard Doll** (Oxford University, United Kingdom), For leadership in developing knowledge concerning the environmental causes of cancer in humans

1980 **James A. Miller** and **Elizabeth C. Miller** (University of Wisconsin), For contributions to the knowledge of the metabolism and action of chemical carcinogens

ALFRED P. SLOAN, JR., MEDAL (For the most outstanding recent contribution in basic science to cancer, particularly in the areas of etiology and pathogenesis)

1979 **George Klein** (Karolinska Institute, Sweden), For pioneering work on the interrelation of cancer and the immune system in mammalian species, including humans

1980 **Isaac Berenblum** (Weizmann Institute of Science, Israel), For discovering that the induction of cancer by chemicals is a stepwise process, a phenomenon central to carcinogenesis and the understanding of the process

McLaughlin Medal

ROYAL SOCIETY OF CANADA
344 Wellington, Ottawa, Ont. K1A ON4 (613/992-3468)

The McLaughlin Medal, which is accompanied by a $1,000 honorarium, was established by the R. Samuel McLaughlin Foundation to recognize distinguished achievement in medical science in Canada. It is awarded annually for sustained excellence in any branch of medical science. A selection committee chooses the recipient.

1979 **Bernard Belleau**
1980 **William Robert Bruce**

Nobel Prize for Medicine or Physiology

NOBEL FOUNDATION
Nobel House, Sturegatan 14, 11436-Stockholm, Sweden

One of six Nobel Prizes given annually, the Nobel Prize for Medicine or Physiology is generally recognized as the highest honor which can be bestowed upon a physician or scientist for an exceptionally significant contribution in medicine or physiology. The award, which consists of a gold medal, diploma and large honorarium, is given at a ceremony on December 10 of each year in Stockholm's City Hall. The award itself is presented and administered by the Caroline Institute in Stockholm, which selects the winner. The amount of the cash honorarium fluctuates. In 1980 it was approximately $212,000.

1901 **Emil A. von Behring** (Germany), Serum therapy, specifically for diphtheria
1902 **Sir Ronald Ross** (Great Britain), Investigation on how malaria parasites enter the body
1903 **Niels R. Finsen** (Denmark), Treatment of tubercular skin diseases, such as lupus vulgaris, with concentrated light radiation
1904 **Ivan P. Pavlov** (Russia), Physiological studies on digestion
1905 **Robert Koch** (Germany), Research on tuberculosis
1906 **Camillo Golgi** (Italy) and **Santiago Roman y Cajal** (Spain), Studied structure of the nervous system
1907 **Charles L. A. Laveran** (France), Research on role protozoa play in cause of disease
1908 **Paul Ehrlich** (Germany) and **Elie Metchnikoff** (France, born in Russia), Immunity research
1909 **Emil T. Kocher** (Switzerland), Study of thyroid, including pathology, physiology and surgery
1910 **Albrecht Kossel** (Germany), Research in proteins, specifically in the area of cell chemistry
1911 **Allvar Gullstrand** (Sweden), Research on eye dioptics
1912 **Alexis Carrel** (U.S.A., born in France), Transplantation and suture of blood vessels and organs
1913 **Charles R. Richet** (France), Research on allergies and anaphylaxis
1914 **Robert Barany** (Hungary), Physiology and pathology of inner ear
1915 **No award**
1916 **No award**
1917 **No award**
1918 **No award**
1919 **Jules Bordet** (Belgium), Immunity research
1920 **Schack A.S. Krogh** (Denmark), Discovered the motor-regulation mechanism of capallaries
1921 **No award**
1922 **Archibald V. Hill** (Great Britain), Work on production of heat in muscles
Otto F. Meyerhof (Germany), Discovered relationship between oxygen use and lactic-acid metabolism in muscle
1923 **Frederick G. Banting and John J.R. MacLeod,** (Canada), Discovered insulin
1924 **Willem Einthoven** (Netherlands), Discovered electrocardiogram mechanism
1925 **No award**
1926 **Johannes A.G. Fibiger** (Denmark), Experiments on producing cancer-like growths in rats
1927 **Julius Wagner-Jauregg** (Austria), Used inoculations against malaria to treat paralysis and mental deterioration from syphilis
1928 **Charles J.H. Nicolle** (France), Typhus research
1929 **Christiaan Eijkman** (Netherlands), Discovered effects of vitamin B deficiency
Sir Frederick G. Hopkins (Great Britain), Research on growth-stimulating vitamins
1930 **Kurt Landsteiner** (U.S.A., born in Austria), Discovered blood groups of humans
1931 **Otto H. Warburg** (Germany), Work in behavior of respiratory enzyme
1932 **Edgar D. Adrian and Sir Charles S. Sherrington** (Great Britain), Discoveries about nerve-cell functioning
1933 **Thomas H. Morgan** (U.S.A.), Research on role of chromosomes in heredity
1934 **George R. Minot, William P. Murphy and George H. Whipple** (U.S.A.), Research on liver therapy for anemia
1935 **Hans Spemann** (Germany), Discovered "organizer effect" of development of embryo
1936 **Otto Loewi** (U.S.A., born in Germany), (Great Britain), and **Sir Henry H. Dale** Research on chemical transmission of nerve impulses
1937 **Albert Szent-Gyorgyi von Nagyrapolt** (U.S.A., born in Hungary), Work in body metabolism, especially regarding vitamin C and fumaric acid
1938 **Corneille J.F. Heymans** (Belgium), Discovered role of sinus and aortic mechanisms in regulation of respiration
1939 **Gerhard Domagk** (Germany), Work on anti-bacterial properties of prontosil
1940 **No award**
1941 **No award**
1942 **No award**
1943 **Henrik C.P. Dam** (Denmark), Discovered vitamin K
Edward A. Doisy (U.S.A.), Work in chemistry of vitamin K
1944 **Joseph Erlanger** (U.S.A.), and **Herbert S. Gasser** (U.S.A.), Discoveries on differentiated functions of single nerve fibers
1945 **Sir Alexander Fleming Ernst B. Chain** and **Sir Howard W. Florey** (Great Britain), Discovered penicillin and its effect on curing certain infectious diseases
1946 **Hermann J. Muller** (U.S.A.), Discovered mutations by X-ray use
1947 **Carl F. Cori** (U.S.A.) and **Gerty T. Cori** (U.S.A., born in Czechoslovakia), Research on catalytic conversion of glycogen
Bernardo A. Houssay (Argentina), Work in role of anterior pituitary lobe hormone in metabolizing sugar
1948 **Paul H. Muller** (Switzerland), Discovered DDT as efficient insecticide
1949 **Walter R. Hess** (Switzerland), Discovered role of interbrain as a "coordinator" of internal organ activity
Antonio Moniz (Portugal), Work on treatment of some psychoses by prefrontal lobotomy
1950 **Philip S. Hench** (U.S.A.), **Edward C. Kendall** (U.S.A.) and **Tadeus Reichstein** (Switzerland, born in Poland), Work on adrenal cortex hormones, including their structural and biological effects
1951 **Max Theiler** (U.S.A., born in South Africa), Work combatting yellow fever
1952 **Selman A. Waksman** (U.S.A., born in Russia), Discovered streptomycin for tuberculosis treatment
1953 **Sir Hans A. Krebs** (Great Britain, born in Germany), Discovered cycle of citric acid
Fritz A. Lipmann (U.S.A., born in Germany), Discovered coenzyme A and its effect on intermediary metabolism
1954 **John F. Enders, Frederick C. Robbins** and **Thomas H. Weller** (U.S.A.), Discovered how poliomyelitis viruses grow in various tissue cultures
1955 **Alex H.T. Theorell** (Sweden), Work on oxidation enzymes
1956 **Andre F. Cournand** (U.S.A., born in France), **Werner Forssmann** (Germany) and **Dickinson W. Richards, Jr.** (U.S.A.), Work on heart catherization and changes in circulatory system
1957 **Daniel Bovet** (Italy, born in Switzerland), Work on synthetic compounds that curtail action of some body substances
1958 **George W. Beadle** and **Edward L. Tatum** (U.S.A.), Discovered that genes regulate certain chemical events

Joshua Lederberg (U.S.A.), Work in genetic recombination and organization of genetic material in bacteria

1959 **Arthur Kornberg** (U.S.A.) and **Severo Ochoa** (U.S.A., born in Spain), Discovered biological synthesis of RNA and DNA

1960 **Sir F. Macfarlane Burnet** (Australia) and **Sir Peter B. Medawar** (Great Britain, born in Brazil), Work in acquired immunological tolerance

1961 **Georg von Bekesy** (U.S.A., born in Hungary), Discovered physical mechanism of stimulation of the cochlea of the inner ear

1962 **Francis H.C. Crick** (Great Britain), **James D. Watson** (U.S.A.) and **Maurice H.F. Wilkins** (Great Britain), Research on molecular structure of nuclear acids and its importance in information transfer in living material

1963 **Sir John C. Eccles** (Australia), **Sir Alan L. Hodgkin** and **Sir Andrew F. Huxley** (Great Britain), Work on nerve cell membrane

1964 **Konrad Bloch** (U.S.A.) and **Feodor Lynen** (Germany), Work on mechanism and regulation of cholesterol and metabolism of fatty acid

1965 **Francois Jacob, Andre Lwoff** and **Jacques Monod** (France), Discovered regulatory processes of body cells contributing to genetic control of enzymes and virus synthesis

1966 **Charles B. Huggins** (U.S.A.), Work on hormonal treatment of prostrate gland cancer
Francis Peyton Rous (U.S.A.), Discovered tumor-inducing viruses in chickens

1967 **Ragnar Granit** (Sweden, born in Finland), **Haldan Keffer Hartline** (U.S.A.) and **George Wald** (U.S.A.) Work on primary chemical and physiological processes in the eye

1968 **Robert W. Holley** (U.S.A.), **Har Gobind Khorana** (U.S.A., born in India) and **Marshall W. Nirenberg** (U.S.A), Described genetic code that determines cell functions

1969 **Max Delbruck** (U.S.A., born in Germany), **Alfred D. Hershey** (U.S.A.) and **Salvador E. Luria** (U.S.A., born in Italy), Work on reproduction and genetic structure of viruses

1970 **Julius Axelrod** (U.S.A.), **Ulf von Euler** (Sweden) and **Sir Bernard Katz** (Great Britain), Basic research in nerve-transmission chemistry

1971 **Earl W. Sutherland, Jr.** (U.S.A.), Work on mechanisms of hormonal actions

1972 **Gerald M. Edelman** (U.S.A.) and **Rodney Porter** (Great Britain), Determined nature of an antibody

1973 **Karl von Frisch** (Austria), **Konrad Lorenz** (Austria) and **Nikolaas Tinbergen** (Great Britain, born in the Netherlands), Work on individual and social behavior patterns of birds and bees, specifically related to selection and survival of the species

1974 **Albert Claude** (U.S.A., born in Luxembourg), **Christian Rene De Duve** (Belgium) and **George Emil Palade** (U.S.A., born in Rumania), Founded cell-biology science, pioneered use of electron microscope to study living cells and discovered certain cell parts

1975 **David Baltimore** (U.S.A.), **Howard Martin Temin** (U.S.A.) and **Renato Dulbecco** (U.S.A., born in Italy), Research on tumor viruses and the genetic material of the living cell

1976 **Baruch S. Blumberg** (U.S.A.), Research on the hepatitis virus in donated blood and on a hepatitis vaccine
D. Carelton Gajdusek (U.S.A.), Discovered kuru disease virus among cannibals

1977 **Rosalyn Yalow** (U.S.A.), **Roger C. L. Guillemin** (U.S.A.) and **Andrew V. Schally** (U.S.A.), Research in hormones in human body

1978 **Werner Arber** (Switzerland), **Daniel Nathans** (U.S.A.) and **Hamilton O. Smith** (U.S.A.), Discovered restriction enzymes and their application to problems of molecular genetics

1980 **Allan McLeod Cormack** (U.S.A., born in South Africa), and **Godfrey Newbold Hounsfield** (Great Britain), Developing revolutionary X-ray scan technique, computerized axial tomography (CAT scan), which gives doctors a clear look inside the living human body

1980 **Baruj Benacerraf** (U.S.A., born in Venezuela), **George Snell** (U.S.A.) and **Jean Dausset** (France), Studies of antigens, the protein-carbohydrate complexes found on every cell membrane of the body, leading to the development of rules for the transplantability of human organs, explanations of the body's immunology system and development of transplant immunology

Passano Foundation Award

PASSANO FOUNDATION
c/o Williams & Wilkens Press, 428 E. Preston St.,
Baltimore, Md. 21202 (301/528-4000)

The Passano Foundation Award annually honors distinguished work done in the United States in medical research, especially work with a clinical application. Originally, one award was endowed. Now there are two each year, a Senior Award with at least a $20,000 cash prize and a Junior Award which varies from $5,000 to $10,000. The Board of Medical Directors of the foundation selects the recipients.

1945 **Edwin Joseph Cohn,** Harvard Medical School, Cambridge, Mass.

1946 **Ernest William Goodpasture,** Vanderbilt University, Nashville, Tenn.

1947 **Selman A. Waksman,** New Jersey Agricultural Experiment Station, Princeton, N.J.

1948 **Alfred Blalock,** Johns Hopkins, University School of Medicine, Baltimore
Helen Brooke Taussig, Johns Hopkins University School of Medicine, Baltimore

1949 **Oswald Theodore Avery,** Rockefeller Institute for Medical Research, New York

1950 **Edward Calvin Kendall,** Mayo Clinic, Rochester, Minn.
Philip Showalter Hench, Mayo Clinic, Rochester, Minn

1951 **Philip Levine,** Ortho Research Foundation, Raritan, N.J.
Alexander S. Wiener, Jewish Hospital, Brooklyn, N.Y.

1952 **Herbert McLean Evans,** University of California

1953 **John Franklin Enders,** Harvard Medical School and Children's Hospital, Boston, Mass.

1954 **Homer William Smith,** New York University College of Medicine

1955 **Vincent du Vigneaud,** Cornell University Medical College, New York

1956 **George Nicholas Papanicolaou,** Cornell University Medical College, New York

1957 **William Mansfield Clark,** Johns Hopkins University, Baltimore

1958 **George Washington Corner,** American Philosophical Society

1959 **Stanhope Bayne-Jones,** Office of the Surgeon General
1960 **Rene J. Dubos,** Rockefeller University, New York
1961 **Owen H. Wangensteen,** University of Minnesota Medical School
1962 **Albert H. Coons,** Harvard Medical School, Boston
1963 **Horace W. Magoun,** University of California School of Medicine, Los Angeles
1964 **Keith R. Porter,** Harvard University, Cambridge, Mass.
George E. Palade, Rockefeller University, New York
1965 **Charles B. Huggins,** Ben May Laboratory for Cancer Research, Chicago
1966 **John T. Edsall,** Harvard University, Cambridge, Mass.
1967 **Irvine H. Page,** Cleveland Clinic Foundation
1968 **John Eager Howard,** Johns Hopkins University School of Medicine, Baltimore
1969 **George Herbert Hitchings,** vice president in charge of research, Burroughs Wellcome & Company
1970 **Paul Charles Zamecnik,** Massachusetts General Hospital, Boston
1971 **Stephen W. Kuffler,** Harvard Medical School, Cambridge, Mass.
1972 **Kimishige Ishizaka,** Johns Hopkins University School of Medicine, Baltimore
Teruko Ishizaka, Johns Hopkins University School of Medicine, Baltimore
1973 **Roger W. Sperry,** California Institute of Technology, Pasadena

SENIOR AWARD

1974 **Seymour S. Cohen,** University of Colorado School of Medicine, Denver
1975 **Henry G. Kunkel,** Rockefeller University, New York
1976 **Roger Guillemin,** Salk Institute, San Diego, Calif.
1977 **Curt P. Richter,** Johns Hopkins University School of Medicine, Baltimore
1978 **Michael S. Brown** and **Joseph L. Goldstein,** University of Texas Health Center, Dallas
1979 **Donald F. Steiner,** University of Chicago
1980 **Seymour Solomon Kelly,** Harvard University

JUNIOR AWARD

1974 **Baruch S. Blumberg,** Institute for Cancer Research, Fox Chase, Philadelphia
1975 **Joan Argetsinger Steitz,** Yale University, New Haven, Conn.
1976 **Robert A. Bradshaw,** University of Washington School of Medicine, Seattle
1977 **Eric A. Jaffe,** Cornell University Medical College, New York
1978 **Robert J. Lefkowitz,** Duke University
1979 **Richard Axel,** Columbia University, New York
1980 **No award**

Georg Michael Pfaff Medal

GEORG MICHAEL PFAFF GEDACHTNISSTIFTUNG
Eisenbahnstrasse 28-30, D-6750 Kaiserslautern, Federal Republic of Germany (Tel: 0631/64265)

The Georg Michael Pfaff Medal is given approximately every two years, on a judgment by the foundation's board of trustees, for contributions in the health field.

1971 **Artbeitskreis Gesundheitskunde,** Healthy food for children
1973 **Gottfried Gulicher and Dieter Menninger,** Televised health education
1976 **Fritz Strempfer, Emma Stoll and Hans-Gunther Schumacher,** Contributions in health education
1978 **No award**

Lewis S. Rosenstiel Award

ROSENSTEIL BASIC MEDICAL SCIENCES RESEARCH CENTER
Brandeis University, 415 South St., Waltham, Mass. 02254 (617/647-2431)

The Lewis S. Rosenstiel Award for Distinguished Medical Research, which consists of $5,000 and a bronze medal, is awarded annually for an outstanding accomplishment in the development of basic science as it applies to medicine. An anonymous committee of scientists from institutions in the greater Boston area selects the winner from nominees.

1972 **David H. Hubel**
Torstein N. Wiesel
1973 **Boris Ephrussi**
1974 **H. Ronald Kaback**
Saul Roseman
1975 **Arthur B. Pardee**
H. Edwin Umbarger
1976 **Bruce N. Ames**
Elizabeth C. Miller
James A Miller
1977 **Peter D. Mitchell**
1978 **Barbara McClintock**
1979 **Caesar Milstein**
1980 **Howard Green**
Beatrice Mintz

T. Duckett Jones Memorial Award

HELEN HAY WHITNEY FOUNDATION
450 E. 63rd St., New York, N.Y. 10021 (212/751-8228)

The T. Duckett Jones Memorial Award, which included an honorarium, was presented annually for scientific achievement in biomedical research. The award is no longer given.

1958 **Luis F. LeLoir,** Instituto de Investigaciones Bioquimicas Fundacion Compomar, Buenos Aires, Isolation of uridine diphosphoglucose and other derivatives
1959 **Karl Meyer,** Columbia College of Physicians and Surgeons, New York, Pioneering work in mucopolysaccharides
1960 **Rebecca C. Lancefield,** Rockefeller University, New York, Biology of hemolytic streptococci
1961 **William T. Astbury,** University of Leeds, United Kingdom, Pioneering studies on molecular structure of variety of fibrous proteins and, in particular, collagen
1962 **Albert H. Coons,** Harvard Medical College, Boston, Work on labeling of antibodies with fluorescent dyes, enhancing our knowledge of immune reactions
1963 **Francis O. Schmitt,** Massachusetts Institute of Technology, Cambridge, Mass., Contributions to knowledge of the fine structure of properties of tissue components, particularly collagen, nerve and muscle
1964 **Michael Heidelberger,** Rutgers University Institute of Microbiology, News Brunswick, N.J., Pioneer work in quantitative immunochemistry

1965 **Eugene L. Opie,** Rockefeller Institute, New York, Contributions in experimental pathology over a period of many decades
1966 **George E. Palade,** Rockefeller University, New York Contributions to knowledge of cellular structure and function
1967 **George Wald,** Harvard University, Cambridge, Mass., Contributions to biology of vision and leadership in stimulating broad interest in the biological sciences
1968 **No award**
1969 **No award**
1970 **Karl A. Piez,** National Institute of Dental Research (National Institutes of Health), Bethesda, Md., Contributions to knowledge of chemical structure of collagen
1971 **Hans J. Muller-Eberhard,** Scripps Clinic and Research Foundation, La Jolla, Calif., Chemistry and biology of complement system
1972 **Jerome Vinograd,** California Institute of Technology, Pasadena, Conceptual and technical contributions to molecular biology
1973 **Saul Roseman,** Johns Hopkins University, Baltimore, Biochemistry of carbohydrates and their biological role
1974 **Henry G. Kunkel,** Rockefeller University, New York, Studies on immunological mechanisms of disease
1975 **Seymour Benzer,** California Institute of Technology, Pasadena, Microbial genetics and molecular and genetic approach to behavior
1976 **Baruj Benacerraf,** Harvard Medical School, Boston, Work on the immune response
1977 **Daniel E. Koshland, Jr.,** University of California/Berkeley, Pioneering work on enzyme function and structure and investigations of cell functions

Louis H. Bauer Founders Award
Walter M. Boothby Award
Howard K. Edwards Award
Mary T. Klinker Award
Eric Liljencrantz Award
Theodore C. Lyster Award
Harry G. Moseley Award
John A. Tamisea Award
Arnold D. Tuttle Award
Raymond F. Longacre Award
Julian E. Ward Memorial Award
Environmental Science Award

AEROSPACE MEDICAL ASSOCIATION
Washington National Airport, Washington, D.C. 20001
(202/892-2240)

The $500 Louis H. Bauer Founders Award, sponsored by Eaton Labroatories, annually honors the most significant contribution to the field of space medicine.

1961 **Lt. Col. Stanley C. White, USAF, MC**
1962 **Don Flickinger, M.D.**
1963 **Col. Paul A. Campbell, USAF, MC**
1964 **Col. William K. Douglas, USAF, MC**
1965 **Hubertus Strughold, M.D.**
1966 **Charles A. Berry, M.D.**
1967 **R/Adm Frank B. Voris, USN, MC**
1968 **James N. Waggoner, M.D.**
1969 **Maj. Gen. Otis O. Benson, Jr., USAF (Ret.)**
1970 **Walton L. Jones, M.D.**
1971 **Maj. Gen. James W. Humphreys, USAF (Ret.)**
1972 **Capt. Ralph L. Christy, MC, USN**
1973 **Karl H. Houghton, M.D.**
1974 **Willard R. Hawkins, M.D.**
1975 **Col. John Pickering, USAF (Ret.)**
1976 **Lawrence F. Dietlein, M.D., Ph.D.**
1977 **Rufus R. Hessberg, M.D.**
1978 **Oleg G. Gazenko,** M.D.
1979 **Carolyn S. Leach Huntoon,** Ph.D.
1980 **Arnauld E. T. Nicogossian,** M.D.

The Walter M. Boothby Award, which consists of a plaque and $1,000, sponsored by the Aviation Insurance Agency, is now given biennially and recognizes outstanding research in the prevention of disease and the promotion of health among airline pilots.

1961 **John E. Smith**
1962 **Ross A. McFarland**
1963 **Jan H. Tillisch**
1964 **Louis R. Krasno**
1965 **Earl T. Carter**
1966 **Stanley R. Mohler**
1967 **G. Earle Wight**
1968 **Charles R. Harper**
1969 **John S. Howitt**
1970 **Michael T. Lategola**
1971 **Kenneth G. Bergin**
1972 **George F. Catlett**
1973 **Charles E. Billings**
1975 **Karl E. Klein**
1977 **Wg/Cdr. Anthony N. Nicholson, RAF, MC**
1979 **Frank S. Preston**

The Howard K. Edwards Award, which carries a $1,000 honorarium and a plaque, sponsored by the Aviation Insurance Agency is now awarded biennially alternately with the Walter M. Boothby Award for the outstanding practice of clinical medicine pertaining to airline pilots.

1961 **George J. Kidera**
1962 **Otis B. Schreuder**
1963 **Ludwig G. Lederer**
1964 **Andre Allard**
1965 **John E. Smith**
1966 **Charles C. Gullett**
1967 **George F. Catlett**
1968 **Peter V. Siegel**
1969 **M. Frederick Leeds**
1970 **Joseph G. Constantino**
1971 **Heinrich Gartmann**
1972 **John K. Cullen**
1973 **Birger Hannisdahl**
1974 **Ian Anderson**
1976 **Eugene Lafontaine**
1978 **Jean Lavernhe**
1980 **C. Richard Harper**

The Mary T. Klinker Award, which is sponsored by the Douglas Aircraft Co. and consists of $500, a plaque and a watch, is given annually to the Flight Nurse of the Year for outstanding contributions to or achievement in service, education, research, aerospace nursing or aerospace evacuation.

1968 **Maj. Virginia M. Alena, USAF, NC**
1969 **Maj. Helen Kopczynski, USAF, NC**
1970 **Lt. Col. Pearl E. Tucker, USAF, NC**
1971 **Capt. Gertrude M. Campbell, USAF, NC**
1972 **Capt. Anne R. Spurlin, USAFR, NC**

1973 **Capt. Mary K. Littlejohn, USAF, NC**
1974 **Capt. LaDonn B. Cramer, USAF, NC**
1975 **Lt. Col. Patricia A. Farrell, USAF, NC**
1976 **Lt. Col. Dorothy R. Novotny, USAF, NC**
1977 **Lt. Col. Mary M. Thomas, USAF, NC**
1978 **Brig. Gen. Claire M. Garrecht,** USAF, NC
1979 **Lt. Col. Phyllis N. Goins,** USAF, NC
1980 **Lt. Col. Margaret M. Korach,** USAF, NC

The $500 Eric Liljencrantz Award, sponsored by Smith Kline and French Laboratories, is presented for basic research into the problems of acceleration and altitude as they affect the body.

1957 **Col. John P. Stapp, USAF, MC**
1958 **Brig. Gen. Victor A. Byrnes, USAF (Ret.)**
1959 **Capt. Edward L. Beckman, MC, USN**
1960 **James D. Hardy**
1961 **Capt. Ashton Graybiel, MC, USN**
1962 **Wilbur R. Franks**
1963 **Earl H. Wood**
1964 **Capt. Ralph L. Christy, MC, USN**
1965 **David M. Clark**
1966 **Henning von Gierke**
1967 **Charles F. Gell**
1968 **Edward J. Baldes**
1969 **Capt. Roger G. Ireland, MC, USN**
1970 **Sidney D. Leverett, Jr.**
1971 **Otto H. Gauer**
1972 **Capt. Marvin D. Courtney, MC, USN**
1973 **Adolf P. Gagge**
1974 **Cdr Donald J. Sass, MC, USN**
1975 **Wg./Cdr. John Ernsting, RAF, MC**
1976 **Ulrich C. Luft**
1977 **Channing L. Ewing**
1978 **Gp. Capt. Peter Howard,** RAF, MC
1979 **Leon Kazarian,** Dr., Eng.
1980 **Harold Sandler,** M.D.

The annual Theodore C. Lyster Award, which is sponsored by Purdue Fredrick Co.'s Keith Loring Gentilcore Memorial Fund and consists of a plaque and $500, is given for outstanding achievement in the general field of aerospace medicine.

1947 **Louis H. Bauer**
1948 **Wilbur R. Franks**
1949 **Maj. Gen. Harry G. Armstrong, USAF, MC**
1950 **Capt. Ashton Graybiel, MC, USN**
1951 **R/Adm. B. Groesbeck, Jr., MC, USN**
1952 **Kenneth A. Evelyn**
1953 **Capt. Wilbur E. Kellum, MC, USN**
1954 **W. R. Stovall**
1955 **Brig. Gen. Otis O. Benson, Jr., USAF, MC**
1956 **Brig. Gen. Don Flickinger, USAF, MC**
1957 **Capt. Charles F. Gell, MC, USN**
1958 **Hurbertus Strughold**
1959 **Capt. Clifford P. Phoebus, MC, USN**
1960 **Air Cdr. A. A. G. Corbet, RCAF**
1961 **Air Cdr. William K. Stewart, RAF**
1962 **Robert J. Benford**
1963 **Maj. Gen. M. Samuel White, USAF, MC**
1964 **William Randolph Lovelace, II**
1965 **William J. Kennard**
1966 **Brig. Gen. Eugen G. Reinartz, USAF, MC**
1967 **Brig. Gen. John M. Talbot, USAF, MC**
1968 **Jan H. Tillisch**
1969 **Ludwig G. Lederer**
1970 **George J. Kidera**
1971 **John P. Marbarger**
1972 **Joseph P. Pollard**
1973 **Andre Allard**
1974 **Col. Stanley C. White, USAF, MC**
1975 **Merrill H. Goodwin**
1976 **Maj. Gen. Heinz S. Fuchs, GAF, MC**
1977 **Maj. Gen. Spurgeon H. Neel, MC, USA**
1978 **J. Robert Dille,** M.D.
1979 **Col. Thomas J. Tredici,** USAF, MC
1980 **Capt. Robert E. Mitchell,** MC, USN

The Harry G. Moseley Award plaque, sponsored by the Lockheed Aircraft Corp. annually honors the year's most outstanding contribution to flight safety.

1961 **Capt. Carl E. Wilbur, MC, USN**
1962 **Col. F. M. Townsend, USAF, MC**
1963 **Brig. Gen. Kenneth E. Pletcher, USAF, MC**
1964 **Capt. W. Harley Davidson, USAF, MC**
1965 **Capt. Richard E. Luehrs, MC, USN**
1966 **Capt. Roland A. Bosee, MSC, USN**
1967 **Maj. Richard M. Chubb, USAF, MC**
1968 **John J. Swearingen**
1969 **W/C David I. Fryer, M.D., OBE, RAF**
1970 **Ernest B. McFadden**
1971 **William J. Reals**
1972 **A. Howard Hasbrook**
1973 **Capt. Frank H. Austin, Jr., MC, USN**
1974 **Stanley R. Mohler**
1975 **Richard G. Snyder**
1976 **Harry W. Orlady**
1977 **Homer L. Reighard**
1978 **J.D. Garner**
1979 **Anchard F. Zeller**
1980 **Kenneth M. Beers**

The $100 John A. Tamisea Award annually honors contributions to aviation medicine in general and its application to the aviation field.

1963 **Herbert F. Fenwick**
1964 **Delazon S. Bostwick**
1965 **Neil E. Baxter**
1966 **George B. McNeely**
1967 **Howard Allen Dishongh**
1968 **J. Harold Brown**
1969 **Thomas A. Coates**
1970 **H. D. Vickers**
1971 **William Gillespie**
1972 **James Y. Bradfield**
1973 **Harold N. Brown**
1974 **Luis A. Amezcua G.**
1975 **Robert L. Wick, Jr.**
1976 **Harry L. Gibbons**
1977 **Harold V. Ellingson**
1978 **Silvio Finkelstein**
1979 **Audie W. Davis, Jr.**
1980 **Charles E. Billings**

The Arnold D. Tuttle Award, which is sponsored by United Airlines and consists of a plaque and $500, recognizes the most significant contribution toward the solution of a challenging problem in aerospace medicine.

1952 **Edward H. Lambert**
1953 **James. P. Henry**
1954 **John P. Marbarger**
1955 **Fred A. Hitchcock**
1956 **W. H. Johnson**
1957 **Maj. David G. Simons, USAF, MC**
1958 **Siegfried J. Gerathewohl**
1959 **Lawrence E. Lamb**
1960 **Hermann J. Schaefer**
1961 **Lt. Col. Charles A. Berry, USAF, MC**
1962 **Clayton S. White**

1963 Charles I. Barron
1964 Vincent M. Downey
1965 Capt. Ashton Graybiel, MC, USN
1966 Lt. Col. James F. Culver, USAF, MC
1967 Billy E. Welch
1968 Dietrich E. Beischer
1969 Randall M. Chambers
1970 Christian J. Lambertsen
1971 G. Melvill Jones
1972 Harold J. von Beckh
1973 Surg/Capt John S. P. Rawlins, RN
1974 Henning E. von Gierke
1975 Col. Malcolm C. Lancaster, USAF, MC
1976 Russell R. Burton
1977 Kent K. Gillingham
1978 G. Donald Whedon
1979 Carlton E. Melton, Jr.
1980 Sarah A. Nunneley

The $500 Raymond F. Longacre Award annually honors outstanding contributions to the psychological or psychiatric aspects of aerospace medicine.

1947 Ross A. McFarland
1948 Detlev W. Bronk
1949 Sir Charles P. Symonds
1950 Donald W. Hastings
1951 Col. Neeley C. Mashburn, USAF (Ret.)
1952 Sir Frederick Bartlett
1953 Walter F. Grether
1954 John C. Flanagan
1955 Roy R. Grinker
1956 Saul B. Sells
1957 Brig. Gen. Eugen G. Reinartz, USAF, MC
1958 Col. Harry G. Moseley, USAF, MC
1959 Capt. George E. Ruff, USAF, MC
1960 Brant Clark
1961 Capt. Philip B. Phillips, MC, USN
1962 George T. Hauty
1963 Henry A. Imus
1964 Frederick H. Rohles
1965 Anchard F. Zeller
1966 Richard Trumbull
1967 Col. Don E. Flinn, USAF, MC
1968 Frederick E. Guedry, Jr.
1969 Bryce O. Hartman
1970 Capt. Roger F. Reinhardt, MC, USN
1971 William E. Collins
1972 Rosalie K. Ambler
1973 Claude J. Blanc
1974 Herbert C. Haynes
1975 Alan J. Benson
1976 W. Dean Chiles
1977 Capt. Joseph A. Pursch, MC, USN
1978 Col. Carlos J.G. Perry, USAF, MC
1979 Gloria Twine Chisum
1980 Barton Pakull

The $200 Julian E. Ward Memorial Award is given for outstanding achievement in aerospace medicine during medical residency training.

1963 Cdr. Frank H. Austin, Jr., USN, MC
1964 Maj. Samuel J. Brewer, USAF, MC
1965 Capt. Ronald E. Costin, USAF, MC
1966 Maj. Calvin Chapman, USAF, MC
1967 Capt. Kenneth W. Curtis, Jr., USAF, MC
1968 Maj. Charles R. O'Briant, USAF, MC
1969 George W. Hoffler
1970 Cdr. William W. Simmons, USN, MC
1971 Sarah Ann Nunneley
1972 Maj. William E. Barry, USAF, MC
1973 Maj. Frederic M. Brown, USAF, MC
1974 Cdr. Robert P. Caudill, USN, MC
1975 Maj. Hubert F. Bonfili, USAF, MC
1976 Maj. George K. Anderson, USAF, MC
1977 Joseph J. C. Degioanni
1978 Lt. Col. James R. Hickman, Jr., USAF, MC
1979 Micharl A. Perry
1980 Capt. Aaron Y. Barson, Jr., USAF, MC

The Environmental Science Award, sponsored by the McDonnell Douglas Corp., is presented annually for the best paper on environmental health published in *Aviation, Space and Environmental Medicine.*

1978 Ralph R. Bollinger
1979 Christian J. Lambertsen
1980 Russell R. Burton

Jeffries Medical Research Award

AMERICAN INSTITUTE OF AERONAUTICS AND ASTRONAUTICS
1290 Ave. of the Americas, New York, N.Y. 10019
(212/581-4300)

The Jeffries Medical Research Award, through 1975 the John Jeffries Award, honors outstanding contributions to aerospace medical research. The award consists of a medal and citation and is given by decision of an honors and awards committee.

1940 Louis H. Bauer
1941 Harry G. Armstrong
1942 Edward C. Schneider
1943 Eugen G. Reinartz
1944 Harold E. Wittingham
1945 John C. Adams
1946 Malcolm C. Grow
1947 J. Winifred Tice
1948 W. Randolph Lovelace, II
1949 A.D. Tuttle
1950 Otis O. Bensen, Jr.
1951 John R. Poppen
1952 John Stapp
1953 Charles F. Gell
1954 James P. Henry
1955 Wilbur E. Kellum
1956 Ross A. McFarland
1957 David C. Simons
1958 Hubertus Strughold
1959 Don Flickinger
1960 Joseph W. Kittinger
1961 Ashton Graybiel
1962 James L. Goddard
1964 Eugene Konecci
1965 William K. Douglas
1966 Charles A. Berry
1967 Charles I. Barron
1968 Loren D. Carlson
1969 Frank B. Voris
1970 Walton L. Jones
1971 Richard St. Johnston
1972 Roger G. Ireland
1973 Karl H. Houghton
1974 Malcolm Clayton Lancaster
1975 Lawrence F. Dietlein
1977 Harold von Beckh
1978 Heinz Fuchs
1979 William L. Smith
1980 Stephen L. Kimzey

Heart-of-the-Year Award

AMERICAN HEART ASSOCIATION
7320 Greenville Ave., Dallas, Tex. 75231 (214/750-5300)

The Heart-of-the-Year Award is presented annually to a distinguished American to show that cardiovascular disease is not a barrier to productivity and achievement. Winners are generally well-known public figures, and the award has been presented in White House ceremonies by Presidents of the United States from Dwight D. Eisenhower on—as well as to several Presidents and former Presidents.

1959 **Lyndon Baines Johnson,** Then Senate Majority Leader
1960 **Mrs. Dwight D. Eisenhower,** First Lady
1961 **Arthur Hays Sulzberger,** Editor and Publisher, *The New York Times*
1962 **Clarence B. Randall,** Retired Chairman of the Board, Inland Steel Co.
1963 **Gen. Lauris Norstad,** Former Supreme Allied Commander in Europe
1964 **Vice Adm. H.G. Rickover,** "Father of the Atomic Navy"
1965 **George Tebbets,** Manager, Cleveland Indians
1966 **John E. Fogarty,** U.S. Congressman
1967 **Dwight D. Eisenhower,** Former President
1968 **Patricia Neal,** Actress
1969 **Irvine H. Page,** Cleveland physician
1970 **Owen R. Cheatham,** Founder, Georgia-Pacific Corp.
1971 **Carl Albert,** Speaker, U.S. House of Representatives
1972 **Pearl Bailey,** Entertainer
1973 **Richard M. Nixon,** President of the United States
1974 **No award**
1975 **No award**
1976 **Donald Slayton,** Astronaut
1977 **Walter Matthau,** Actor
1978 **John Wayne,** Actor
1979 **John Hartman,** Newscaster and former actor
1980 **Not available at press time**

Distinguished Service Award

AMERICAN COLLEGE OF CARDIOLOGY
9111 Old Georgetown Rd., Bethesda, Md. 20014 (301/897-5400)

The Distinguished Service Award is given annually to a physician, scientist or layperson for contributions to medicine and/or the delivery of health care.

1967 **Pres. Lyndon Baines Johnson**
1968 **Sen. Lister Hill**
Mrs. Albert D. (Mary) Lasker
1969 **No award**
1970 **No award**
1971 **William B. Walsh**
1972 **Warren G. Magnuson**
1973 **Paul G. Rogers**
1974 **Professor Zednek Fejfar**
1975 **Theodore Cooper**
1976 **Rep. Daniel J. Flood**
1977 **No award**
1978 **Martin M. Cummings**
1979 **Richard E. Hurley**
1980 **Frank H. Netter**

Certificates of Meritorious Achievement

AMERICAN DENTAL ASSOCIATION
211 E. Chicago Ave., Chicago, Ill. 60611 (312/440-2803)

Two Certificates of Meritorious Achievement, each accompanied by $100 for scientific equipment, are given annually for high school science projects that are finalists at the International Science and Engineering Fair with application to dental health and oral research. A judging team of dental researchers and educators selects the winners.

1973 **Daniel Gallagher,** Michigan City, Ind.
Michael Marks, Florence, Ala.
1974 **Jewel Jurovich,** Metairie, La.
Keith Zych, Bayside, Wisc.
1975 **Joan Gartrell,** Reno, Nev.
Glenda Dale Knox, Vicksburg, Miss.
1976 **Stephen Budak,** Michigan City, Ind.
Deborah Malone, Grants, N.M.
1977 **Janice M. Russell,** Harrisville, R.I.
Deanna L. Sieren, Thornburg, Iowa

Current status unknown

McAlpine Medal

MENTAL HEALTH ASSOCIATION
1800 N. Kent St., Arlington, Va. 22209 (703/820-3351)

The Mental Health Assn. Research Achievement Award, known as the McAlpine Medal, is given annually for outstanding research in the causes and prevention of mental illness. The award consists of a plaque and $10,000 which may given to an individual or research team, providing the winner(s) are United States citizens. Nominations are made by professional organizations, MHA members and others, and the winner is selected by the Research Committee and National Board of the association.

1972 **Seymour Kety,** Biochemical research in schizophrenia
1973 **Robert Coles**
1974 **Erik H. Erikson,** Psychoanalysis and human development
1975 **Alexander Leighton,** Social psychiatry
1976 **William E. Bunney,** Biochemistry of depression
1977 **Lyman Winn and Margaret Singer,** Work on schizophrenia
1978 **Neal E. Miller**
1979 **Daniel X. Freedman**
1980 **Floyd E. Bloom**

Isaac Ray Award

AMERICAN PSYCHIATRIC ASSOCIATION
1700 18th St. NW, Washington, D.C. 20009 (202/797-4900)

The Isaac Ray Award, which carries a $1,500 cash prize, is given annually to a psychiatrist, attorney or judge for noteworthy contributions to psychiatry and the law and to close understanding between experts in the two fields. The recipient gives a series of lectures on the subject during the year.

1952 **Winfred Overholser,** St. Elizabeth's Hospital, Washington, D.C.
1953 **Gregory Zilboorg,** Professor of Psychiatry, New York State University Medical College, New York
1954 **Hon. John Biggs, Jr.,** Chief Judge of U.S. Court of Appeals for the Third Judicial Circuit, Wilmington, Del.
1955 **Henry Weihofen,** Professor of Law, University of New Mexico, Albuquerque
1956 **Philip Roche,** Associate in Psychiatry, University of Pennsylvania Medical School, Philadelphia
1957 **Manfred Guttmacher,** psychiatrist and Chief Medical Officer of the Supreme Bench of Baltimore
1958 **Alistair William McLeod,** Assistant Professor of Psychiatry, McGill University, Montreal, Canada
1959 **Maxwell Jones,** Director, Social Rehabilitation Unit, Belmont Hospital, Sutton, Surrey, U.K.
1960 **Judge David L. Bazelon,** U.S. Court of Appeals in Washington, D.C.
1961 **Sheldon Glueck,** Roscoe Pound Professor of Law, Harvard University, Cambridge, Mass
1962 **Karl A. Menninger,** Menninger Foundation, Topeka, Kans.
1963 **Judge Morris Ploscowe,** Associate Professor of Law, New York University, New York
1964 **Judge Justine Wise Polier,** New York
1965 **Georg K. Sturup,** Hellerup, Denmark
1966-67 **No awards**
1968 **Bernard Diamond,** University of California, Berkeley, Calif.
1969-74 **No awards**
1975 **Jay Katz,** Professor Adjunct of Law and Psychiatry, Yale University, New Haven, Conn.
1976 **Jonas Robitscher,** Henry R. Luce Professor of Law and Behavioral Sciences, Emory University School of Law, Atlanta, Ga.
1977 **Bruno Conier,** Professor, Dept. of Psychiatry, McGill University, Montreal, Canada
1978 **No award**
1979 **No award**
1980 **Seymour L. Halleck,** M.D.

Florence Nightingale Award

INTERNATIONAL COMMITTEE OF THE RED CROSS
17 Avenue de la Paix, CH-1211 Geneva, Switzerland (Tel: 34.60.01/283)

The Florence Nightingale Award, which consists of a gold medal and a diploma, is given every two years to not more than 36 nurses and voluntary aides, honoring exceptional devotion to the sick and wounded in difficult and perilous situations, such as those which often prevail in times of war, epidemics or natural disaster. National Red Cross organizations send nominees to the International Committee, which sets up a special commission to select the recipients. The first 41 recipients were honored specifically for their actions during World War I; 1947 awards recognize individuals for their World War II devotion.

1920 **Martha Paula Heller,** Austria
Maria Adamcycyk, Austria
Astley Campbell, Belgium (British citizen)
Kate Schandeleer, Belgium
Magdalene Tidemand, France
Helene Scott Hay, U.S.A.
Florence Merriam Johnson, U.S.A.
Martha M. Russel, U.S.A.
Linda K. Meirs, U.S.A.
Alma E. Foerster, U.S.A.
Mary E. Gladwin, U.S.A.
Marie Balli Panas, France
Louise Leclere Hugues, France
Germaine St.-Girons Legrix, France
Christine de Chevron de Villette, France
The Marquise de Clappiers (nee de Foresta), France
Marguerite Voisin, France
Renee Aline Flourens, France
Marie Elisabeth Lajusan, France
Alice Lockhart Lambert, Great Britain
Beatrice Isabel Jones, Great Britain
Gladys Laura White, Great Britain
Kate Maxey, Great Britain
Gertrude Mary Wilton Smith, Great Britain
Lucy Minchin, Great Britain
Hester MacLean, Great Britain (New Zealand)
E.R. Creagh, Great Britain (South Africa)
Helene Vassilopoulo, Greece
Baroness Gizella Apor, Hungary
Ilona Durgo, Hungary
S.A.R. Elena di Francia, Duchess of Aosta, Italy
Ina Battistella, Italy
Maria Concetta Clhudzinska, Italy
Maria Andina, Italy
Maria Natonietta Clerici, Italy
Take Hagiwara, Japan
Ya-o Yomamoto, Japan
Ume U-asa, Japan
Elonore Mihailescu, Rumania
Irene Metejickova, Czechoslavakia
Sylva Macharova, Czechoslovakia
Countess Alexandrine von Uexhall, Germany
Anni Roth, Germany
Dora Rothe, Germany
Elsbeth von Keudell, Germany
Agnes von Frankenberg und Proschlitz, Germany
Annemarie Wenzel, Germany
Christina Vateva, Bulgaria
Margaret Clotilde MacDonald, Canada
Marie Theresa Viotti, Italy
Delfia Jovanitch, Serbia
1923 **Maria Douglas,** Germany
Elza Haeckx, Belgium
Clara D. Noyes, U.S.A.
Laurence Pidiere des Prinveaux, France
Maud Emma McCarthy, Great Britain
Josephine Todorffy Viczian, Hungary
Rhoda de Bellegarde, Italy
Yuki Inada, Japan
Countess Marie Tarnowka (nee Princess Czetwertynska), Poland
Anka Durovic, Serbia
Alma Charlotte Brunskog, Sweden
Safie Hussein Bey (nee Ahmed Pacha), Turkey
1925 **Anna von Zimmermann,** Germany
Berta Hermine Schwarzott, Austria
Juliette Parmentier, Belgium
Maria del Carmen Angolotti y Mesa, Spain
Lucy Minnigerode, U.S.A.
Baroness Sophie Mannerheim, Finland
Helene Moulin, France
Marta Celmin, Latvia
Louise Sternlieb, Poland
Ljoubitza Loukovitsch, Rumania
Jindra Tilsova, Czechoslovakia
1927 **Marie Viehauser (Sister Silveria),** Germany

Eugenie Henry, Belgium
Idalia de Araujo Porte-Alegre, Brazil
Alice Fitzgerald, U.S.A.
Alice Krug, France
Dame Sidney Brown, Great Britain
Angelique Phikiori, Greece
Alice Abranyi, Hungary
Marquise Irene di Targiani Giunti, Italy
Tamaki-Ei, Japan
Anne Techbeltye, Lithuania
Josephine Dudajek, Poland
1929 **Countess Mathilde von Horn,** Germany
Jenny Lutterloh, Germany
Dame Sarah Swift, Great Britain
Sister Marie Gabrielle, Countess Lodron, Austria
Sister Josefa Weidinger, Austria
Grace Margaret Wilson, Australia
Jeanne Hellemans, Belgium
Sister Stoyanka Alexandrova, Bulgaria
Sister Anastassia Kirinkova, Bulgaria
Anne Hartley, Canada
Major Julia C. Stimson, U.S.A.
Carrie M. Hall, U.S.A.
Therese-Marie-Leonie Freminet, France
Marie-Leonie Genin, France
Alice Pezet Aubry, France
Sophie L. Deligeorges, Greece
Pauline Nahalka, Hungary
Anne Novadovsky Gasci, Hungary
Melanie Elaine Tippetts, India
Norah Beresford, India
Duchess Elisabetta Cita di Torrescuso (nee di Sambuy), Italy
Midori Kagawa, Japan
Kei Mizuno, Japan
Elza Grivans, Latvia
Rosalie Jachimovicz, Poland
Helene Nagorska, Poland
Emma Novakova, Czechoslovakia
1931 **Henny Dyckerhoff,** Germany
Sister Minna Weiss, Germany
Sister Leokadia Ammann, Austria
Cecile Mechelynck, Belgium
Sister Helena Radoikova, Bulgaria
Vivien Adlard Tremaine, Canada
Elizabeth Gordon Fox, U.S.A.
Henriette de Grancey de Bertier de Sauvigny, France
Marie-Eugenie Lapere, France
Dame Ann Beadsmore Smith, Great Britain
Julie Andreades, Greece
Helene Tricoupis, Greece
Baroness Marie de Fiath, Hungary
Suzanne Ferencz, Hungary
Antoinette Heyl, Hungary
Alice Rosina Lowe, India
Minnie Eda MacLean, India
Suye Otsuka, Japan
Shighe Homma, Japan
Justine Kushke, Latvia
Sister Karethe Johnsen, Norway
Stephanie Potocka-Ziembinska, Poland
Wanda Idzikowska, Poland
Marie Modrezewska, Poland
Constantza Ionescu Tarasof, Rumania
Zoe V. Iorga Georgescu, Rumania
Bossa Svet Rankovitch, Yugoslavia
1933 **Pia Bauer,** Germany
Juliane Husstedt, Germany
Charlotte Miller Heilman, U.S.A.
Edith Cornwell, Austrialia
Hermine Wadowska, Austria
Sister Rosa Jogna, Austria
Gabrielle Kaeckenbeck, Belgium
Sister Elena Pope Bojkova, Bulgaria
Felicie Marie Angele Dauch, France
Marguerite Charlotte Legros, France
Lloyd Still, Great Britain
Caroline Revay Mero, Hungary
Helene Hankiss Nyary, Hungary
Agatha Mary Phillips, India
W.E. Walters, India
E. MacFarlane, India
Sita Meyer Camperio, Italy
Yori Ono, Japan
Tomo Fujii, Japan
Elza Nulle-Siecenieks, Latvia
Rosalie Tomosiunaite, Lithuania
Ona Brazyte, Lithuania
Edwige Suffczynska, Poland
Hedwige Gronczynska, Poland
Micheline Mieleszkiewicz, Poland
Marie Benesova, Czechoslovakia
Sofia Igrochanatz, Yugoslavia
Sister Stefania Papailiolulos, Yugoslavia
1935 **Elisabeth Tomitius,** Germany
Elsbeth Hosig Vaughan, U.S.A.
Elsie Clare Pidgeon, Australia
Frederike Zehetner, Austria
Louise Guinotte-van der Stichelen, Belgium
Anna Sagaroska, Bulgaria
Jean Isabel Gunn, Canada
Leonie Chaptal de Chanteloup, France
Dame Ethel Hope Becher, Great Britain
Marie Negroponte, Greece
Paula Halper, Hungary
The Hon. Florence Mary MacNaughton, India
Countess Carolina Monroy di Ranchibile, Italy
Shika Morimoto, Japan
Sister Ailke Westerhof, Netherlands
Rev. Mother Sister Rosa, Peru
Sophie Szlenkierowna, Poland
Bertha Wellin, Sweden
Elisabeth von Bergen, Sweden
Josefa Andelova, Czechoslovakia
Roujitsa Helih, Yugoslavia
1937 **Erna Marie Auguste Anne Wittich,** Germany
Adelaide Maud Kellett, Australia
Berthe Marie Crutzen-de Vos, Belgium
Ida F. Butler, U.S.A.
Gertrude Marcelle Muzeau, France
Mrs. Maynard Linden Carter, Great Britain
Helene Paraskevopoula, Greece
Margit de Daniel, Hungary
Lorna Ellice MacKenzie, India
Mose Ono, Japan
Masayo Tabutchi, Japan
Maria Bellavita Pellizzari, Italy
Marie Elisabeth Joys, Norway
Adriana Elisabeth Schipper, Netherlands
Vera Schleimer, Yugoslavia
1939 **Gerda von Freyold,** Germany
Stella Mathews, U.S.A.
H.M. Queen Elisabeth of Belgium, Belgium
Agatha Mary Phillips, Great Britain
Jean Elizabeth Browne, Canada
Victoria Bianchi y Bianchi, Chile
Anette Massov, Estonia
Jeanne-Marie-Emilie-Leonie Le Pescheux Duhautbourg, France

Rennee-Anne-Berthe Blanc, France
Athena Messolora, Greece
Marie Bosnyak Gebhardt, Hungary
Dora Chadwick, India
Katherine Anne Duncan, India
Vincenza Campari, Italy
Miyo Akoyama, Japan
Tsune Numamoto, Japan
Helene Karoline Larsen, Norway
Marie Skorupska, Poland
Constance Cantacuzene, Rumania
Anna Mankova, Czechoslovakia
Zenie Berengovitch, Yugoslavia
1941 **No awards**
1943 **No awards**
1945 **No awards**
1947 **Lt. Col. Ida W. Danielson,** U.S.A.
Mrs. Walter Lippmann, U.S.A.
Col. Annie Moriah Sage, Australia
Capt. Vivian Bullwinkel, Australia
Cdr. Barbara Moriarty, Australia
Germaine Dewandre Van Hoegaerden, Belgium
Jeanne Rahier, Belgium
Jeanne Van Lier, Belgium
Zoe Helene Spilliaert, Belgium
Yvonne Cardon de Lichtbuer, Belgium
Dame Emily Mathieson Blair, Great Britain
Lyyli Ingrid Hagan, Finland
Venny Snellman, Finland
Martta Siitonen, Finland
Alice Soulange-Bodin, France
Mathilde-Marie Bernardine de Cleron D'Haussonville, France
Marcelle Barry, France
Marie-Therese Desse, France
Arriete Lambrinoudis Degleris, Greece
Marriete Velissariou, Greece
Sophie Marschalko, Hungary
Marie Radnay, Hungary
Marthe Mauks, Hungary
Etelka Endrey, Hungary
Irma Balazs, Hungary
Marie Kasics Vilmos Varnay, Hungary
Phyllis Widger, India
Winifred Grace McKenzie, India
Mercy John, India
Margaret Neal, India
S.A.I. Princess Achraf Pahlavi, Iran
Elisa Carini, Italy
Sofia Novellis di Coarazze, Italy
Antonietta Pedace, Italy
Constanza Bruno, Italy
Ermelinda Ducler, Italy
Elda Malagu, Italy
Emma Mazzolari, Italy
Etsu Kuno, Japan
Akie Higashiyama, Japan
Ai Fukui, Japan
Yoshio Tomura, Japan
Maria Adriana Anna Bloem, Netherlands
Leintje Jacoba Jobse, Netherlands
Regina M. Esser, Netherlands
Rev. Sister Stephania O.P. Netherlands
Helena Maria Verheul, Netherlands
Irene Flora Campbell, New Zealand
Wladyslawa Dyczakowska, Poland
Bronislawa Karpowicz, Poland
Wanda Peszke, Poland
Jadwiga Romanowska, Poland
Janina Tyszynska, Poland
Halina Swiatecka, Poland
Alice Wierzbicka, Poland
Maria Babicka-Zachertowa, Poland
Zofia Bittenek, Poland
Marguerite Zmudzka, Poland
Elisabet Lind, Sweden
Kerstin Nordendahl, Sweden
Sister Elsbeth Kasser, Switzerland
Zofie Lehocka, Czechoslovakia
Bozena Mandokova, Czechoslovakia
Ruzena Struzkova, Czechoslovakia
Anna Rypackova, Czechoslavakia
Bedriska Bohacova, Czechoslovakia
Anna Kralova, Czechoslovakia
Nan Mary Harper, South Africa
Margaret Ellen Stoney, South Africa
Elizabeth Jane Waugh, South Africa
Rose Millicent Vandecar, South Africa
1949 **Alta Elizabeth Dines,** U.S.A.
Mary M. Roberts, U.S.A.
Ruby Evelyn Storey, Australia
Maj. Alice Rose Appleford, Australia
Ingeborg Ellison-Nidlef, Austria
Maria Ultschning, Austria
Marie-Madeleine Bihet, Belgium
Irene Cotegipe de Miranda, Brazil
Dame Katherine Watt, Great Britain
Edith Kathleen Russell, Canada
Maria Fernandez Le Cappelain de Tinocco, Costa Rica
Eli Magnussen, Denmark
Rachel Edgren, Finland
Kyllikki Pohkola, Finland
Louise Bader-Gruber, France
Alice Le Sergen d'Hendecourt, France
Jeanne de Joannis, France
Thalie Lecou, Greece
Clea Vassilopoulos, Greece
Dorothy Grace Howard, India
Mariamma Thomas, India
Alice Reeves, Ireland
Sigridur Eriksdottir Thorvaldsson, Iceland
Paolo Menada, Italy
Sjoukje Hoyting, Netherlands
Eike Flikkema, Netherlands
Helen Iris Crooke, New Zealand
Bertha Helgestad, Norway
Bergljot Larsson, Norway
Gladys Ada Penhearow, Pakistan
Anna Rydel, Poland
Marie Wilkonska, Poland
Sanguanwan Fuang-Bejara, Siam
Marianne Edwaline Pfeiffer, South Africa
Elisabet Dillner, Sweden
1951 **Florence A. Blanchfield,** U.S.A.
Sophie C. Nelson, U.S.A.
Maria Josefina Ghiglione, Argentina
Rita Malcolm, Australia
Olive Pascke, Australia
Gretrud Finze, Austria
Anna Pia Goldschmid, Austria
Suzanne Lippens-Orban, Belgium
Rev. Mother Marie-Therese (nee Germaine Provoyeur), Belgium
Dame Doris Beale, Great Britain
Signe Jansen, Denmark
Tyyne Maria Luoma, Finland
Sister Agnes (nee Helene Hennart), France
Helly Chatzilazarou Adossides, Greece
Colliope Ghioulounda, Greece

Ethel Ellen Hutchings, India
Dorothy Davis, India
Amy Katharine Bullock, India
Linda MacWhinney, Ireland
Antonietta Colotti, Italy
Conchita Scotti Guerra, Italy
Maria Senni, Italy
Carmela Vidacovi, Italy
Yuki Ono, Japan
Myo Mizutani, Japan
Jasue Kunibe, Japan
Ritsu Sugiyama, Japan
Edna Jean House, New Zealand
Ingeborg Kolrud, Norway
Agnes Rimestad, Norway
Iris Murray, Pakistan
Mary Greta Borcherds, South Africa
Maria Amparo Larrosa Irizarry, Venezuela
Vera Lipovscak, Yugoslavia
1953 **Ethel Jessie Bowe**, Australia
Edith Johnson, Australia
Sarah Charlotte MacDonald, Australia
Florence H.M. Emory, Canada
Blanca Marti de David Almeida, Colombia
Beatrix Restrepo Herrera, Colombia
Ellen Marie Christensen, Denmark
Annabelle Peterson, U.S.A.
Jeanne Berlie, France
Madeleine Castan, France
Anne Chipon, France
Elisabeth Duval, France
Yvonne Foltz, France
Makie Fujimoto, Japan
Kin Kato, Japan
To Yameda, Japan
Nasra Aboudi, Jordan
Renee Araman, Lebanon
Rosa Maria Acosta Gonzalex, Mexico
Sister Karen Elise Moe, Norway
Gul Mehernosh Darrah, Pakistan
Gabriele Fries, Federal Republic of Germany
Maria Lerchl, Federal Republic of Germany
Else Weecks, Federal Republic of Germany
Beate Welschof, Federal Repulic of Germany
Daisy Caroline Bridges, United Kingdom
Gerda Hojer, Sweden
Karin Elfverson, Sweden
1955 **Blanca Julia Clermont**, Argentina
Sen. Sister Lucy Thelma Marshall, Australia
Sen. Sister Hermine Hansgirg, Austria
Sen. Sister Hertha Groller, Austria
Amelia Balmaceda Lazcano, Chile
Maja Edel Foget, Denmark
Ruby G. Bradley, U.S.A.
Isabel Maitland Stewart, U.S.A.
Genevieve de Galard-Terraube, France
Genevieve Ponsot, France
Jeanne Gavouyere, France
Despina Chouroglou, Greece
Nina Carakiozides, Greece
Margaretta Craig, India
Florence Taylor, India
Takeno Tanimoto, Japan
Haya Ishibashi, Japan
Ingrid Wyller, Norway
Anna Holthe, Norway
Begum Ismat Khanum Shah, Pakistan
Sister Sofie Kienzle, Federal Republic of Germany
Sister Marie Schickinger, Federal Republic of Germany
Gerda Dreiser, Federal Republic of Germnay
Sister Ella Priscilla Jorden, United Kingdom
Eva-Ulrika Beck-Friis, Sweden
Verna Hagman, Sweden
Sister Julie Fanny Lina Hofmann, Switzerland
Sister Jane McLarty, Union of South Africa
1957 **Joan Abbott**, Australia
Ana Maria Cermak, Bolivia
Helen G. McArthur, Canada
Maria Luisa Torres de la Cruz, Chile
Sister Eva Lyngby, Denmark
Zelna Mollerup, Denmark
Sigrid Eleonora Larsson, Finland
Anne Valette, France
Jeanne Le Camus, France
Regine Kohler, Federal Republic of Germany
Clare Port, Federal Republic of Germany
Sigridur Bachmann, Iceland
Tehmina K. Adranvala, India
Ellen Lund, India
Rosetta Sheridan, India
Mimy Rigat Macchi, Italy
Bice Enriques, Italy
Hisako Nagashima, Japan
Chiyo Mikami, Japan
Nabiha Salameh Wirr, Jordan
Sister Kuk Sin-bok, North Korea
Sister Li Myong-oo, North Korea
Hyo Chung Lee, South Korea
Marcelle Hochar, Lebanon
Eva Helou Serhal, Lebanon
Catherine Lynette Wells, New Zealand
Sister Martha Palm, Norway
Gladys Maure Hodgson, Pakistan
Dame Elizabeth Cockayne, United Kingdom
Elizabeth K. Porter, U.S.A.
Marion W. Sheahan, U.S.A.
1959 **Phyllis Mary Daymon**, Australia
Patricia Downes Chomley, Australia
Amanda Brieba de Lorca, Chile
Signe Henriette Vest, Denmark
Dorothea Frederikke Bengtzen, Denmark
Maria Elvira Yoder, Ecuador
Helene Rouvier, France
Emma Ruidavetz, France
Marguerite Patrimonio, France
Luise von Oertzen, Federal Republic of Germany
Louise Sophie Knigge, Federal Republic of Germany
Mary Edith McKay Buchanan, India
Aki Oku, Japan
Koto Imaru, Japan
Oshie Kinutani, Japan
Milica Zelovic, Yugoslavia
Frances Lee Whang, South Korea
A.E.W. Chr. Engelberts, Netherlands
Flora Jean Cameron, New Zealand
Borghild Kessel, Norway
Karin Louise Naess, Norway
Salma Tarin, Pakistan
Patricia E. Intenga, Philippines
Catalina Evangelista, Philippines
Effie J. Taylor, U.S.A.
Lucile Petry Leone, U.S.A.
Ruth Sleeper, U.S.A.
1961 **Margaret Jean Moloney**, Australia
Jean Evelyn Headberry, Australia
Paulina Perelman de Wilhelm, Chile
Blanca Luarte de Cavieres, Chile
Ellen Johanne Broe, Denmark
Anne Marie Krohn, Finland

Sen. Sister Benigna Niggl, Federal Republic of Germany
Marianne Petersen, Federal Republic of Germany
Maliese von Bechtolsheim, Federal Republic of Germany
Sister Olive Laura Colquhoun, Great Britain
Marjorie Eadon Craven, Great Britain
Mariam Korah, India
Sister Stella Diana, Italy
Sister Carolina Cresto Calvo, Italy
Sister Carolina Salvati Accolti Gil, Italy
Haru Shinozaki, Japan
Hideko Yamazaki, Japan
Yae Ibuka, Japan
Young-Jin Kim, South Korea
Sin-Eun Choi, South Korea
Doris Ogilvy Ramsay, New Zealand
Edith Mary Rudd, New Zealand
Sister Annie Margareth Skau, Norway
Amy Sajjad, Pakistan
Julita V. Sotejo, Philippines
Maria Stencel, Poland
Wanda Lorenczuk, Poland
Emma Dagmar Stenbeck, Sweden
Constance Anne Nothard, Union of South Africa
Irina Nikolaievna Levtchenko, U.S.S.R.
Lydia Philippovna Savtchenko, U.S.S.R.
Pearl McIver, U.S.A.
Sister Charles Marie (Frank), U.S.A.
Cecilia H. Haugues, U.S.A.

1963 **Rose Zelma Huppatz,** Australia
Maria Hafner, Austria
Sister Khin Ohn Mya, Burma
Mona Gordon Wilson, Canada
Elena Velasco de Castillo, Chile
Annemarie M.A. Van Bockhoven, Finland
Anne de Cadoudal, France
Germaine Tanguy, France
Yoland Bonnet de Paillerets, France
Sister Emmy Dorfet, German Democratic Republic
Sister Claudine Rohnisch, German Democratic Republic
Margaret Gerhardt, Federal Republic of Germany
Berta Veeck, Federal Repbulic of Germany
Sister Ernestine Thren, Federal Republic of Germany
Janet Patience Adams, Great Britain
Edith H. Paull, India
Rev. Mother Mary Martin, Ireland
Virginia Benussi, Italy
Eleonora Masini Lucceti, Italy
Yae Abe, Japan
Mitsu Yoshino, Japan
Kiyo Kawashima, Japan
Jeannette L. King, Liberia
Mary Ann Gidall, New Zealand
Maj. Margaret Caroline Bearcroft, Pakistan
Florita Loberiza Legayada, Philippines
Capt. Angelina R. Castro, Philippines
Irene M. Abelgas, Philippines
Rosario Andaya, Philippines
Ri-Kil Won, Republic of Korea (South)
Ioana Cruceanu, Rumania
Elena Zeleniuc, Rumania
Iris Irene Marwick, Union of South Africa
Ann K. Magnussen, U.S.A.
Nan L. Dorsey, U.S.A.
R. Louise McManus, U.S.A.

1963 **Special Posthumous Award: Nicole Vroonen,** Belgium

1965 **Lucy Wise MacIntosh,** Australia
Mary Dorothy Edis, Australia
Ines Yuraszeck Cantin de Schmidt, Chile
Anna Knapcokova, Czechoslovakia
Lilia de Vendeuvre, France
Gertrud Baltzer, Federal Republic of Germany
Sister Irene von Scheel, Federal Republic of Germany
Mary Sheelagh Patterson McConnel Folke, Great Britain
Irene Komarik, Hungary
Lt. Col. Florence St. Claire Watkins, India
Kikuyo Uchiyama, Japan
Kiyo Ushioda, Japan
Kise Makita, Japan
Chung-Sun Kim, South Korea
Bo-Shin Lo, South Korea
Muriel Jessie Jackson, New Zealand
Maj. Honorata P. Seraspi, Philippines
Basilia Hernando, Philippines
Maria Menez Concepcion, Philippines
Wladystawa Steffen, Poland
Luba Blum-Bielicka, Poland
Victoria May Freeman, South Africa
Maria Savelievna Chkarletova, U.S.S.R.
Marie Dmitrievna Serdiouk, U.S.S.R.
Agnia Ivanovna Khablova, U.S.S.R.
Faina Khoussainovna Tchanycheva, U.S.S.R.
Zenaida Mikhailovna Toussnolobova-Martchenko, U.S.S.R.

1967 **Betty Constance Lawson,** Australia
Gabrielle Revelard, Belgium
Alice M. Girard, Canada
Joanquina Escarpenter de Segeur, Chile
Marta Anna Sindlerova, Czechoslovakia
Aino Jenny Durchman, Finland
Lucie Roques, France
Marie Loprestis, France
Toni Stemmler, Germany Democratic Republic
Henni Thiessen, Federal Republic of Germany
Jula Muller, Federal Republic of Germany
Sister Anna Kellner, Federal Republic of Geramny
Elaine Hills-Young, Great Britain
Maria D. Eleftheriou, Greece
Elizabeth Kenny, Ireland
Shizu Kaneko, Japan
Iwano Niki, Japan
Moyo Suzuki, Japan
Ahn Kuy-Boon Kim, South Korea
Eul-Ran Kim, South Korea
Socorro Salamanca Dias, Philippines
Helen Nussbaum, Switzerland
Tawinwantg Dutiyabodhi, Thailand
Eugenie Maximovna Chevtschko, U.S.S.R.
Anna Romanovna Kousnetzova, U.S.S.R.
Irene Ivanova Klykova, U.S.S.R.
Claude Vassilievna Boutova, U.S.S.R.

1969 **Col. Edna Nell Doig,** Australia
Jean Elsie Ferguson, Australia
Sister Kathleen Tweedy, Australia
Elisa Ripamonti de Bulnes, Chile
Helena Misurdovna, Czechoslovakia
Elisabeth H. Larsen, Denmark
Irja Pohjala, Finland
Jeanne Euverte, France
Lucile Cantan, France
Johanna Held, Federal Repbulic of Germany
Eva G. Lancaster, Great Britain
Sarolta Deme, Hungary
Ilona Laborczi Smideliusz, Hungary

R. Murtasiah Soepomo, Indonesia
Anna Maria Platter, Italy
Shizv Koyama, Japan
Sei Tozawa, Japan
Sato Takahashi, Japan
Kwon Sok-Hei Kim, South Korea
Soon-Han New, South Korea
Nabila Saab Drooby, Lebanon
Danzangin Therma, Mongolia
Lidwina M. Ch. W. Verlinden, Netherlands
Sister Moya Clare McTamney, New Zealand
Mumtaz Painda Khan, Pakistan
Elisa R. Ochoa, Philippines
Felipa T. Javalera, Philippines
Zofia Muszka, Poland
Maria Hadera, Poland
Florentyna Wronska Kaczmarska, Poland
Charlotte Searle, South Africa
Agnes Wilson Simpson, South Africa
Dean Frances Reiter, U.S.A.

1971 **Gr. Off. Betty Bristow Docker,** Australia
Constance Amy Fall, Australia
Evelyn Agnes Pepper, Canada
Marie Hajkova, Czechoslovakia
Sister Luz Isabel Cueva Santana, El Salvador
Rita Birgitta Berggren, Finland
Marta Strasser, Democratic Republic of Germany
Gwyneth Ceris Jones, Great Britain
Marjorie Houghton, Great Britain
Aristea Papadatou, Greece
Olinga Fikiori, Greece
Otome Mori, Japan
Matsue Kobayashi, Japan
Soyo Kurimoto, Japan
Oak Soon Hong, South Korea
Shin Young Hong, South Korea
Dolores Campos de Estrada, Mexico
Batin Dulma, Mongolia
Dambin Norovdava, Mongolia
Helga Dagsland, Norway
Elsa Caroline Semmelmann, Norway
Safdari Beg, T.Q.A., Pakistan
Annie Sand, Philippines
A. Rabina Teodorica, Philippines
Doreen Henrietta Radloff, South Africa
Majsa Andrell, Sweden
Maria Zakharovna Chtcherbatchenko, U.S.S.R.
Zinaida Ivanovna Smirnova, U.S.S.R.
Matliuba Ichankhojaeva, U.S.S.R.
Dobrila Petronijevic, Yugoslavia
Darinka Nestorovic, Yugoslavia
Joveva Ivanka Karakjozova, Yugoslavia
Milesa Stanojlovic, Yugoslavia
Razija Ajanovic, Yugolsavia
Slavijanka Vlahceva, Yugoslavia

1973 **Maria de Jesus Tovar Bermeo,** Colombia
Maria Bizikova, Czechoslovakia
Ilona Ryskova, Czechoslovakia
Baroness Jacqueline Mallet, France
Beatrice de Foucaud, France
Yvonne Deschamps, France
Margarete Hildebrandt, German Democratic Republic
Ilse von Troschke, Federal Republic of Germany
Sister Mathilde Verhall, Federal Republic of Germany
Virginia Zanna, Greece
Sagy Ferencne, Hungary
Schonfeld Ferencne, Hungary
Lt. Col. Yeddu Vijayamma, India
Marina Caruana, Italy
Shima Yano, Japan
Ryu Saga, Japan
Masae Yukinaga, Japan
Keum Bong Lee, South Korea
Kwi Hyang Lee, South Korea
Soon Bong Kim, South Korea
Kofoworola Abeni Pratt, Nigeria
Angelita F. Corpus, Philippines
Helena Dabrowska, Poland
Elzbieta-Klementyna Krzywicka-Kowalik, Poland
Helen Joyce Cholmeley, United Kingdom
Sonia Denie Stromwall, United Kingdom
Maria Juana Marchesi de Podesta, Uruguay
Vera Sergueevna Kachtcheeva, U.S.S.R.
Matrena Semienovna Netchiportchukova, U.S.S.R.
Maria Petrovna Smirnova, U.S.S.R.
Djulietta Vartanovna Bagdasaryan, U.S.S.R.
Salipa Koublanova, U.S.S.R.
Sister Dina Urbancic, Yugoslavia
Sister Sita Lovrencic-Bole, Yugoslavia
Sister Jugoslava Polk-Bregant, Yugoslavia
Sister Ruza Stojanova, Yugoslavia

1975 **Jeanette Ouelett,** Canada
Karla Petrovicova, Czechoslovakia
Anna Benesova, Czechoslovakia
Anne Marie Beauchais, France
Christiane Sery, France
Sister Ilse Giese, German Democratic Republic
Sister Isa, Duchess von der Goltz, Federal Republic of Germany
Catherine Megapanou, Greece
Roza Almassy, Hungary
Zofia Maroskozi, Hungary
Marianne Tuapattinaya-Lohonauman, Indonesia
Fumiko Hosokawa, Japan
Matsuko Takase, Japan
Toyo Oka, Japan
Margaret Kattan, Jordan
Sung Soon Yew, South Korea
Bok Eum Kim, South Korea
Catherina M. MacKenzie, South Korea
Tourin Badamlynkhur, Mongolia
Sister Ngaire Kirkpatrick Simpson, New Zealand
Mumtaz Salma Lodhi, Pakistan
Irene F. Francia, Philippines
Maria Aleksandrowicz, Poland
Irena Weiman, Poland
Krystyna Stankowska, Poland
Julia Nenko, Poland
Remone Susan Quinn, United Kingdom
Vera Ivanovna Ivanova, U.S.S.R.
Ludmila Antonovna Rodiniova, U.S.S.R.
Nadeja Andreevna Boyko, U.S.S.R.
Sophia Vassilievna Goloukhova, U.S.S.R.
Razia Chakenovna Iskakova, U.S.S.R.
Evdokia Pavlovna Vartzaba, U.S.S.R.
Ekaterina Efimovna Sirenko, U.S.S.R.

1977 **Patricia G. Deal,** Australia
Bartz Schultz, Australia
Dorothy M. Percy, Canada
Maria Artigas Valls, Chile
Sister Anna Sipova, Czechoslovakia
Angela Zacharova, Czechoslovakia
Ruth Saynajarvi, Finland
Sister Senta Herdam, German Democratic Republic
Hanna Stoltenhoff, Federal Republic of Germany
Cleopatre Avayianou, Greece

Gabriella Majoros, Hungary
Erzsebet Karpati, Hungary
Bjarney Samuelsdottir, Iceland
Elisabetta Tufarelli Galati, Italy
Shizu Nagashio, Japan
Hana Koga, Japan
Masu Yumaki, Japan
Fumiko Watanabe, Japan
Young Nok Lee, South Korea
Marie Lysnes, Norway
Begum Mumtaz Chughtai, Pakistan
Lt. Col. Saula R. Magdaraog, Philippines
Juana Bactat, Philippines
Halina Szczudlowska, Poland
Janina Glinowicz, Poland
Wanda Wozniak, Poland
Maria Zakrzewska, Poland
Maria Elizabeth Venter, South Africa
Concepcion Bermejo Ruiz, Spain
Yvonne Hentsch, Switzerland
Somrak Hutinda, Thailand
Helen C. Fraser, United Kingdom
Patricia M. Ash, United Kingdom
Neza Jarnovic, Yugoslavia
Sasa Javorina, Yugoslavia
Mihaela Terzic, Yugoslavia

1979 **Edith Elizabeth Harler,** Australia
Jenny Elizabeth Leak, Australia
Edna Elizabeth Rossiter, Canada
Elena Quesada Saborio, Costa Rica
Evidia Alvarez Gonzales, Cuba
Juana Puentes Camachos, Cuba
Adele Laithier, France
Yvonne Le Bailly, France
Francoise Marminia, France
Jane Martin, France
Estela Ortega Pena, Guatemala
Erzsebet Alexander, Hungary
Agnes Bone, Hungary
Anna Kresz, Hungary
Zsofia Nitsch, Hungary
Marianna Roth, Hungary
Anna Sarospataky, Hungary
Gertrude A. Ram, India
Suzu Iizuka, Japan
Kiyoko Kobayashi, Japan
Elsje Adele van den Berg, Netherlands
Wanda Janina Batkowska, Poland
Josefa Juszczak, Poland
Irena Kowalska, Poland
Stanislawa Krol, Poland
Elzbieta Lohman, Poland
Am Nyo Kim, Republic of Korea
Diana Mary Elvidge, United Kingdom
Eileen Gilbert, United Kingdom
Daisy Saraphina Easmon-Delanay, Sierra Leone
Bozena Lackova, Czechoslovakia
Rabiab Panthupeng, Thailand
Ekaterina Diomina, U.S.S.R.
Saria Talychkhanova, U.S.S.R.
Arfenia Enguibarova, U.S.S.R.
Rikshi Mouminova, U.S.S.R.

Anna Fillmore Award
Lucille Petry Leone Award
NLN Distinguished Service Award
Mary Adelaide Nutting Award
Linda Richards Award

NATIONAL LEAGUE FOR NURSING
10 Columbus Circle, New York, N.Y. 10019 (212/582-1022)

The Anna Fillmore Award, which consists of a plaque, recognizes contributions in development and administration of community health services on a local, state or national level.

1977 **Eva M. Reese**
1979 **Virgina Coker Phillips**

The Lucile Petry Leone Award, which carries a $500 honorarium, is given every two years to an outstanding nurse-teacher with no more than seven years of teaching experience in the last 10 years.

1967 **Martha Clyde Davis**
1969 **Kathryn E. Barnard**
1971 **Ada Sue Hinshaw**
1973 **Rhoda B. Epstein**
1975 **Lillian Gatlin Stokes**
1977 **Gail Elaine Wiscarz Stuart**
1979 **Christine A. Tanner**

The NLN Distinguished Service Award honors an individual, groups or team with presentation of a Steuben crystal item for outstanding leadership and service in the development or implementation of one or more of the League's goals.

1967 **Mildred Gaynor**
Marion Sheahan
1969 **Alma B. Gault**
Frances Reiter
1971 **Mary C. Rockefeller**
Albama League for Nursing
1973 **Ruth Sleeper**
1975 **Anna M. Fillmore**
1977 **Lulu Wolf Hassenplug**
1979 **Lillian S. Brunner**

The Mary Adelaide Nutting Award, which consists of a silver medal, is given every two years to honor outstanding leadership and achievement in nursing education or nursing service.

1944 **Mary Adelaide Nutting**
1947 **International Council of Nurses**
Isabel Maitland Stewart
1949 **Annie Warburton Goodrich**
Mary M. Roberts
1951 **Frances Payne Bolton**
Maternity Center Association of New York
1955 **Stella Goostray**
1957 **Nell V. Beeby**
1959 **Effie J. Taylor**
1961 **Mary Breckenridge**
1963 **R. Louise MacManus**
1965 **Lulu Wolf Hassenplug**
1967 **Helen Nahm**
Ruth B. Freeman
1969 **Helen Bunge**
Mildred E. Newton
1971 **Jessie M. Scott**
W.K. Kellogg Foundation
1973 **Lucile Petry Leone**

Esther Lucile Brown
1975 Jo Eleanor Elliott
Mary Kelly Mullane
1977 Virginia Henderson
1979 Rena E. Boyle

The Linda Richards Award, which is a pin bearing the likeness of Linda Richards mounted on a maltese cross, honors an individual actively engaged in nursing whose contribution is unique, of a pioneering nature or of such excellence as to merit national recognition.

1963 Mildred L. Montag
1967 Signe S. Cooper
1969 Billie B. Larch
1971 No award
1973 Hildegard Peplau
Mabel Keaton Staupers
1975 Rosemary Wood
1977 M. Lucille Kinlein
1979 Loretta C. Ford

Ebert Prize
Kilmer Prize
APhA Foundation-Academy of Pharmaceutical Sciences Research Achievement Awards
Hugo H. Schaefer Award
Daniel B. Smith Award
Pharmacy Literary Award
Kolthoff Gold Medal
Remington Honor Medal

AMERICAN PHARMACEUTICAL ASSOCIATION
2215 Constitution Ave. NW, Washington, D.C. 20037
(202/628-4410)

The Ebert Prize, which consists of a medal and certificate, is given annually for the best original paper published during the preceding year in the *Journal of Pharmaceutical Sciences.*

1874 Charles Mitchell
1875 No award
1876 No award
1877 Frederick B. Power
1882 John Uri Lloyd
1883-85 No awards
1886 Emlen Painter
1887 Edward Kremers
1888 Joseph Geisler
1890 William T. Wenzell
1891 John Uri Lloyd
1892-96 No awards
1897 James W. T. Knox with Albert B. Prescott
1898 Virgil Coblentz
1899 Henry Kraemer
1900 Edward Kremers with Oswald Schreiner
1901 No award
1902 J. O. Schlotterbeck with H. C. Watkins
1903 Frederick B. Power
1904 No award
1905 Ernest Schmidt
1906 J. O. Schlotterbeck with H. C. Watkins
1907 Frederick B. Power with Frank Tutin
1908 A. B. Stevens with L. E. Warren
1909 Henry Kraemer
1910 Harry M. Gordin
1911 W. A. Puckner with L. E. Warren
1915 E. N. Gathercoal
1916 John Uri Lloyd
1917 No award
1918 No award
1919 Arno Viehover with C. O. Ewing and J. F. Clevenger
1920 George D. Beal
1921 Albert Schneider
1922 W. L. Scoville
1923 Paul S. Pittenger
1924 H. V. Arny and Abraham Taub
1925 H. W. Youngken
1926 J. A. Handy with L. F. Hoyt
1927 L. W. Rowe
1928 E. E. Swanson
1929 John C. Krantz Jr.
1930 M. R. Thompson
1931 H. W. Youngken
1932 Zdenek F. Klan
1933 Ewin Gillis with H. A. Langenhan
1934 No award
1935 Marvin J. Andrews
1936 Glenn L. Jenkins with Charles F. Bruening
1938 Frederick F. Johnson
1939 B. V. Christensen with L. G. Gramling
1940 Lloyd C. Miller
1941 William J. Husa
1942 Ole Gisvold
1943 No award
1944 No award
1945 Paul Jannke with Howard Jensen
1946 Lloyd W. Hazleton with Kathleen D. Talbert
1947 Walter H. Hartung
1948 Harry W. Hind with Frank M. Goyan
1949 Robertson Pratt with Jean Dufrenoy, P. T. Sah and Louis A. Strait
1950 Rudolph H. Blythe with Harlan H. Tuthill and John J. Gulesich
1951 Louis W. Busse with Takeru Higuchi
1952 Lloyd M. Parks with Arnold J. Hennig and Takeru Higuchi
1953 Ole Gisvold with Arnold J. Hennig, G. G. Krishnamurtz, W. F. White and Raymond E. Hopponen
1954 Takeru Higuchi with A. Narshima Rao and D. A. Zuck
1955 Fred W. Schueler
1956 Martin Barr with Martin Katz
1957 John E. Christian
1958 Joseph V. Swintosky with Manford J. Robinson
1959 Sidney Riegelman with W. J. Crowell
1960 S. Morris Kupchan
1961 John G. Wagner with Stuart Long and William Veldcamp
1962 Einar Brochmann-Hanssen
1963 Edward R. Garrett
1964 Bernard Randall Baker
1965 Howard J. Schaeffer
1966 Alfred N. Martin with John L. Colaizzi and Adelbert M. Knevel
1967 Gordon H. Svoboda with Gerald A. Poore
1968 William I. Higuchi
1969 Gerhard Levy
1970 William I. Higuchi with A. H. Ghanem and Anthony P. Simonelli

1971 Thomas J. Bardos with C. K. Nevada and Z. F. Chmielewicz
1972 Kenneth B. Bischoff with Robert L. Dedrick, Daniel S. Zaharko and James A. Longstreth
1973 Gordon L. Flynn with Samuel Yalkowsky
1974 Jacob L. Varsano with Seymour G. Gilbert
1975 Gordon L. Amidon with Samuel H. Yalkowsky
1976 J. T. Carstensen with Pakdee Pothisiri
1977 Michael J. Pikal, Lee Floyd Ellis and Anita L. Lukes
1978 Everett N. Hiestand with J.E. Wells, C. B. Post, and J.F. Ochs
1979 William Y. Chen with J.D. Andrade, A.R. Temple and D.L. Coleman
1980 Cheng-Der Yu with Jeffrey L. Fox, Norman F.H. Ho and William I. Higuchi

The Kilmer Prize, which consists of a medal and a $200 honorarium, goes to a member of a graduating class in pharmacology for a meritorious work in pharmacognosy documented in a paper on the subject.

1937 Milton Kahn
1939 Guilford G. Gross
1940 Barbara Jacobs
1941 Richard O. Vycital
1942 Charles Wendt
1946 Elaine Friedberg
1947 David Breenberg
1948 Charles R. Chase Jr.
1951 W. J. Kelleher
1952 Lionel Ward
1953 John E. Gardner
1954 Dolores Ann Strittmater
1955 Berton E. Ballard
1956 Fenna Lee Fisher
1957 Lee C. Schramm
1958 Phillip Catalfomo
1959 Edward E. Gonzalez
1960 Edward Caldwell
1961 Roger Bruce McPhail
1962 Thomas F. Burks
1963 Donna J. Drinkard
1964 Gregory T. Sinner
1965 Judy Taeko Miyata
1966 Marilyn L. Montfort
1967 Robert D. Imholte
1969 Bruce H. Mock
1970 Garre E. Blair
1971 James C. Cloyd
1972 Steven R. Adams
1973 Patrick J. Davis
1974 John DiGiovanni
1975 Gaetana Forte
1976 Christopher J. Linden
1978 No award
1979 Cathy C. Collins
1980 No award

The APhA Foundation-Academy of Pharmaceutical Sciences Research Achievement Awards annually honor outstanding individual achievements in specific areas of pharmacy. The awards consists of cash grants from various pharmaceutical firms and a certificate. Not all awards are given each year.

DRUG STANDARDS AND ASSAY (Justin L. Powers Award) changed to **PHARMACEUTICAL ANALYSIS** by 1973 and to **JUSTIN L. POWERS RESEARCH ACHIEVEMENT AWARD** IN 1977; Sponsored by Abbott Laboratories.

1962 John E. Christian
1963 Einar Brochmann-Hansen
1964 Takeru Higuchi
1965 Lloyd C. Miller
1966 William J. Mader
1967 Frank H. Wiley
1968 Morris E. Auerbach
1969 Albert Q. Butler
1970 Edward R. Garrett
1973 Klaus Biemann
1974 No award
1975 Ernest G. Wollish
1976 No award
1977 No award
1978 Daniel Banes
1979 No award
1980 Kenneth A. Connors

ADVANCEMENT OF PHARMACY; Discontinued

1962 Troy C. Daniels
1963 Linwood F. Tice
1964 No award
1965 Louis C. Zopf
1966 Lloyd M. Parks
1967 Louis W. Busse
1968 George P. Hager

PHARMACODYNAMICS changed to **PHARMACOLOGY** in 1972; sponsored by Eli Lilly and Co.

1962 E. Leong Way
1963 Lawrence C. Weaver
1964 Tom S. Miya
1965 Ewart A. Swinyard
1966 Joseph P. Buckley
1967 Karl H. Beyer Jr.
1968 Allan H. Conney
1969 David H. Tedeschi
1970 Sidney Riegelman
1971 No award
1972 Lewis S. Schanker
1973 No award
1974 No award
1975 Erminio Costa
1976 No award
1977 Louis S. Harris
1978 No award
1979 Wayne M. Levin
1980 No award

PHYSICAL PHARMACY: changed to **PHARMACEUTICS** in 1974; sponsored by Parke, Davis and Co. until 1970 and since then by Syntex Corp.

1962 Takeru Higuchi
1963 Edward R. Garrett
1964 Joseph V. Swintosky
1965 Dale E. Wurster
1966 Eino Nelson
1967 Alfred N. Martin
1968 Sidney Riegelman
1969 Gerhard Levy
1970 William I. Higuchi
1971 No award
1972 No award
1973 Arnold Beckett

1975 John L. Lach
1976 No award
1977 Jens T. Carstensen
1978 No award
1979 Leon O. Lachman
1980 No award

NATURAL PRODUCTS: Sponsored by Merck Sharp and Dohme until 1970, and since then by FMC Corp., Avicel Dept.

1962 Ole Gisvold
1963 Gordon H. Svoboda
1964 Taito O. Soine
1965 S. Morris Kupchan
1966 Varro E. Tyler, Jr.
1967 John C. Craig
1968 William I. Taylor
1969 Egil Ramstad
1970 Monroe Wall
1971 No award
1972 No award
1973 No award
1974 Norman R. Farnsworth
1975 No award
1976 Heinz G. Floss
1977 No award
1978 No award
1979 No award
1980 Lester A. Mitscher

STIMULATION OF RESEARCH: sponsored by Smith Kline and French Foundation

1962 Glenn L. Jenkins
1963 Rudolph H. Blythe
1964 Arthur E. Schwarting
1965 Arthur H. Uhl
1966 W. Lewis Nobles
1967 Takru Higuchi
1968 Daniel H. Murray
1969 Walter Fred Enz
1970 No award
1971 No award
1972 Bernard B. Brodie
1973 No award
1974 No award
1975 No award
1976 Milo Gibaldi
1977 No award

PHARMACEUTICAL AND MEDICINAL CHEMISTRY

1962 Joseph H. Burckhalter
1963 Bernard R. Baker
1964 James M. Sprague
1965 Edward E. Smissman
1966 John H. Biel
1967 Alfred Burger
1968 Joseph Sam
1969 Corwin H. Hansch
1970 William O. Foye
1972 Henry Rapoport
1973 No award
1974 Karl Folkers
1976 Everett May
1977 No award
1978 Eugene C. Jorgensen
1979 No award
1980 Philip J. Portoghese

ECONOMIC SOCIAL AND ADMINISTRATIVE SCIENCES

1978 Robert W. Hammel
1979 No award
1980 Mickey C. Smith

The Hugo H. Schaefer Award honors contributions to the profession of pharmacy and especially to the American Pharmaceutical Assn.

1964 Hugo H. Schaefer
1965 Hubert H. Humphrey
1966 William S. Apple
1967 Wallace Werble
1969 E. Claiborne Robins
1970 No award
1971 Harry C. Shirkey
1972 No award
1973 Willard B. Simmons
1974 Gaylord A. Nelson
1975 No award
1976 Philip R. Lee
1977 No award
1978 Arthur G. Zupko
1979 Grover C. Bowles
1980 Jere E. Goyan

The Daniel B. Smith Award honors achievements in community pharmacy by a practitioner distinguished by outstanding personal and professional performance. The award is a bronze medallion.

1965 Eugene V. White
1966 Raymond L. Dunn
1967 James W. Moore
1968 Arnold Snyder
1969 David J. Krigstein
1970 William F. Appel
1971 Wallace S. Klein
1972 Paul W. Lofholm
1973 Martin Rein
1974 Kenneth E. Tiemann
1975 Morris Boynoff
1976 Donald J. Wernik
1977 William R. Bacon
1978 Emil W. Baker
1979 Howard L. Dell
1980 Joseph A. Mosso

The Section on Pharmacy Literary Award, a plaque, recognized the best contribution to pharmacy literature made by an association member during the preceeding year dealing with the practice of pharmacy in which factual knowledge is incorporated into patient-related service or management, or of scientific or research nature. This award has been discontinued.

1965 Lt. Cdr. Theodore W. Tober
1966 Lowell R. Pfau
1967 Jules M. Meisler
1968 Joseph F. Gallelli
1969 Capt. William J. Briner
1970 Lt. Lloyd A. Fox
1971 Capt. Glidden N. Libby
1972 Douglas G. Christian
1973 Clarence L. Fortner
1974 William A. Cornelis with Clarence L. Fortner and Douglas Christian

The Kolthoff Gold Medal, which carries a $1,000 honorarium, is awarded every two years to a scientist who has contributed significantly to the advancement of pharmaceutical analysis. The nominee is selected by the Award Committee of the Academy's Section on Pharmaceutical Analysis and Control.

1967 I. M. Kolthoff
1969 A. J. P. Martin
1971 Lyman C. Craig
1973 Egon Stahl
1975 Sidney Siggia
1977 No award
1979 Charles N. Reilly

The Remington Honor Medal is given each year to the individual who has done the most for American pharmacy during the year of whose contributions to the advancement of pharmacy over a period of years have been outstanding.

1919 James Hartley Beal
1920 John Uri Lloud
1922 Henry Vincome Arny
1923 Henry Hurd Rusby
1924 George Mahlon Beringer
1925 Henry Milton Whelpley
1926 Henry A. B. Dunning
1928 Charles H. LaWall
1929 Wilbur Lincoln Scoville
1930 Edward Kremers
1931 Ernest Fullerton Cook
1932 Eugene G. Eberle
1933 Evander F. Kelly
1934 Sir Henry S. Wellcome
1935 Samuel Louis Hilton
1936 Edmund Norris Gathercoal
1937 J. Leon Lascoff
1938 Henry C. Christensen
1940 Robert L. Swain
1941 George D. Beal
1942 Josiah K. Lilly
1943 Robert P. Fischelis
1944 H. Evert Kendig
1945 Joseph Rosin
1947 Rufus Ashley Lyman
1948 Andrew Grover DuMez
1949 Ernest Little
1950 Edwin Leigh Newcomb
1951 Hugo H Schaefer
1952 Patrick Henry Costello
1953 Hugh C. Muldoon
1955 Roy Bird Cook
1956 Frank W. Moudry
1957 W. Paul Briggs
1958 Eli Lilly
1959 Justin L. Powers
1960 Ivor Griffith
1962 Harry J. Anslinger
1963 Glenn L. Jenkins
1964 Robert A. Hardt
1965 K. K. Chen
1967 William S. Apple
1969 George F. Archambault
1970 Donald E. Francke
1971 Linwood F. Tice
1972 Glenn Sonnedecker
1973 Grover C. Bowles
1974 Lloyd M. Parks
1975 Albert Doerr
1976 Melvin W. Green
1977 No award
1978 Eugene V. White
1979 No award
1980 Joseph D. Williams

Award for Excellence
International Award for Excellence
Edward W. Browning Achievement Award
Sedgwick Memorial Award
Matthew Rosenhaus Lecture

AMERICAN PUBLIC HEALTH ASSOCIATION
1015 Eighteenth St. NW, Washington, D.C. 20036
(202/467-5450)

The annual Award for Excellence, which consisted of $5,000 and a Steuben Glass gift,was given for a recognized contribution to an individual at a point in his/her career where further contributions can be expected in the field of public health. The award has been discontinued.

1973 H. Jack Geiger
1974 John D. Rockefeller III
1975 Kurt W. Deuschle
1976 June Jackson Christmas
1977 Sam Shapiro

The annual International Award for Excellence, consisting of $5,000 and a Steuben Glass gift, was given on the same criteria and has also been discontinued.

1973 James Westland Wright
1974 Nevin Stewart Scrimshaw
1975 Donald A. Henderson
1976 David J. Sencer
1977 Milton I. Roemer

The Edward W. Browning Achievement Award, which carries on honorarium of $5,000 and a medal, is given for outstanding contribution to the prevention of disease. A special Awards Committee selects the recipient.

1971 B. Russell Franklin
1972 E. Cuyler Hammond
1973 Hildrus A. Poindexter
1974 Harriet L. Hardy
1975 C. Henry Kempe
1976 John W. Knutson
1977 John C. Hume
1978 Bailus Walker, Jr.
1979 Daniel Horn
1980 Mary Calderone

The Sedgwick Memorial Medal is given annual for distinguished service and the advancement of public health knowledge and practice.

1929 Charles V. Chapin
1930 Theobald Smith
1931 George W. McCoy
1932 William H. Park
1933 Milton J. Rosenau
1934 Edwin O. Jordan
1935 Haven Emerson
1936 Frederick F. Russell
1938 Wade H. Frost
1939 Thomas Parran
1940 Hans Zinsser
1941 Charles Armstrong
1942 C.E.A. Winslow
1943 James S. Simmons
1944 Ernest W. Goodpasture
1946 Karl F. Meyer
1947 Reginald M. Atwater

1948 **Abel Wolman**
1949 **Henry V. Baughan**
1950 **Rolla Eugene Dyer**
1951 **Edward S. Godfrey, Jr.**
1952 **Kenneth F. Maxcy**
1953 **Carl E. Buck**
1954 **Willson G. Smillie**
1955 **Albert J. Chesley**
1956 **Frederick W. Jackson**
1957 **Lowell J. Reed**
1958 **Martha M. Eliot**
1959 **Louis I. Dublin**
1960 **Fred T. Foard**
1961 **Frank G. Boudreau**
1962 **Ira V. Hiscock**
1963 **Gaylord V. Anderson**
1964 **Leona Baumgartner**
1965 **Willimina R. Walsh**
1966 **Fred L. Soper**
1967 **George Baehr**
1968 **Herman E. Hilleboe**
1969 **Marion W. Sheahan**
1970 **Hugh R. Leavell**
1971 **Margaret G. Arnstein**
1972 **Paul B. Cornely**
1973 **Isidore S. Falk**
1974 **Myron E. Wegman**
1975 **Leroy E. Burney**
1976 **Malcolm H. Merrill**
1977 **Lester Breslow**
1978 **M. Allen Pond**
1979 **Doris E. Roberts**
1980 **Lorin E. Kerr**

The Matthew B. Rosenhaus Lecture, now discontinued, was an annual honor bestowed on an individual who shared his/her views on a topic of importance and timeliness in public health. The lecturer received a $2,000 honorarium.

1973 **Gov. Raymond P. Shaefer**
1974 **James Haughton**
1975 **John Higginson**
1976 **Mark Lalonde**
1977 **Sen. Edward M. Kennedy**

Francis Amory Prize

AMERICAN ACADEMY OF ARTS AND SCIENCES
Norton's Woods, 136 Irving St., Cambridge, Mass. 02138 (617/492-8800)

The Francis Amory Prize, which carries an honorarium was initially awarded every seven years for research or discoveries in human reproductive-organ diseases, particularly those of males, with several awards presented at the end of each septennium. After the 1968 awards, the requirement of a seven-year interval was removed.

1940 **Ernest Laquer,** Amsterdam
Joseph Francis McCarthy, New York
Carl Richard Moore, Chicago
Hugh Hampton Young, Baltimore
1947 **Alexander Benjamin Gutman,** New York
Charles Brenton Huggins, Chicago
Willem Johan Kolff, Kampen, Netherlands
Guy Frederic Marrian, Edinburgh, Scotland
George Nicholas Papanicolaou, New York
Selman Abraham Waksman, New Brunswick, N.J.
1954 **Frederic E.B. Foley,** St. Paul, Minn.
Choh Hao Li, Berkeley, Calif.
Thaddeus R.R. Mann, Cambridge, U.K.
Terence J. Millin, London
Warren O. Nelson, Iowa City, Iowa
Frederick J. Wallace, New York
Lawson Wilkins, Baltimore
1961 **J. Hartwell Harrison, David M. Hume and Joseph E. Murray,** Boston
John P. Merrill, Banjamin F. Miller and George W. Thorn, Boston
Harry Goldblatt and Eugene Poutasse, Cleveland
Eugene M. Bricker and Justin J. Cordonnier, St. Louis
1968 **Geoffrey Wingfield Harris,** Oxford, U.K.
Hans Henriksen Ussing, Copenhagen
1975 **Karl Sune Detlof Bergstrom,** Stockholm
Min-Chueh Chang, Worcester, Mass.
Howard Guy Williams-Ashman, Chicago
1977 **Mary Frances Lyon,** Harwell, U.K.
Jean D. Wilson, Dallas
Elwood Vernon Jensen, Chicago

Weicker Memorial Award

AMERICAN SOCIETY FOR PHARMACOLOGY AND EXPERIMENTAL THERAPEUTICS
9650 Rockville Pike, Bethesda, Md. 20014 (301/530-7060)

The Theodore Weicker Memorial Award, which carries a $10,000 honorarium accompanied by a certificate, is given annually to an active investigator for an outstanding research achievement in pharmacology, including the use of drugs, drug therapy and decreased toxicity of drugs. A selection committee chooses the winner, generally an individual whose achievements have not previously been honored with another major award.

1978 **Ernest Bueding,** Johns Hopkins University Medical School
1979 **Thomas H. Marin,** University of Florida College of Medicine
1980 **No award**

Wolf Prize in Medicine

WOLF FOUNDATION
Box 398, Herliah-Bet, Israel

The $100,000 Wolf Prize in Medicine honors an outstanding body of work in medical research, as determined by a committee of internationally known judges. The award is part of a $500,000 annual prize distribution for exceptional achievement in five fields of science.

1978 **George D. Snell** (Jackson Laboratory, Bar Harbor, Me.), Discovery of H-2 antigens, which code for major transplantation antigens and the onset of the immune response
Jean Dausset (Saint-Louis Hospital, Paris), Discovery of HL-A system, the major histocompatibility complex in humans and its primordial role in organ transplantation
Jon J. van Rood (University of Leiden), Contributions to the understanding of the complexity of the

HL-A system in humans and its implications in transplantation and in disease

1979 **Roger W. Sperry** (California Institute of Technology), Studies in the functional differentiation of the right and left hemispheres of the brain

Arvid Carlsson (Gothenburg University), Work establishing the role of dopamine as a neurotransmitter

Oleh Hornkiewicz (University of Vienna), New approach in the control of Parkinson's disease by L-Dopa

1980 **Cesar Milstein** (Medical Research Council, Laboratory of Molecular Biology, Cambridge, U.K.), **Leo Sachs** (Weizmann Institute of Science, Rehovot, Israel) and **James L. Cowans** (Medical Research Council, London), Contributions to the knowledge of the function and disfunction of the body cells through their studies on the immunological role of lymphocytes, development of specific antibodies and elucidation of mechanisms governing the control and differentiation of normal and cancer cells

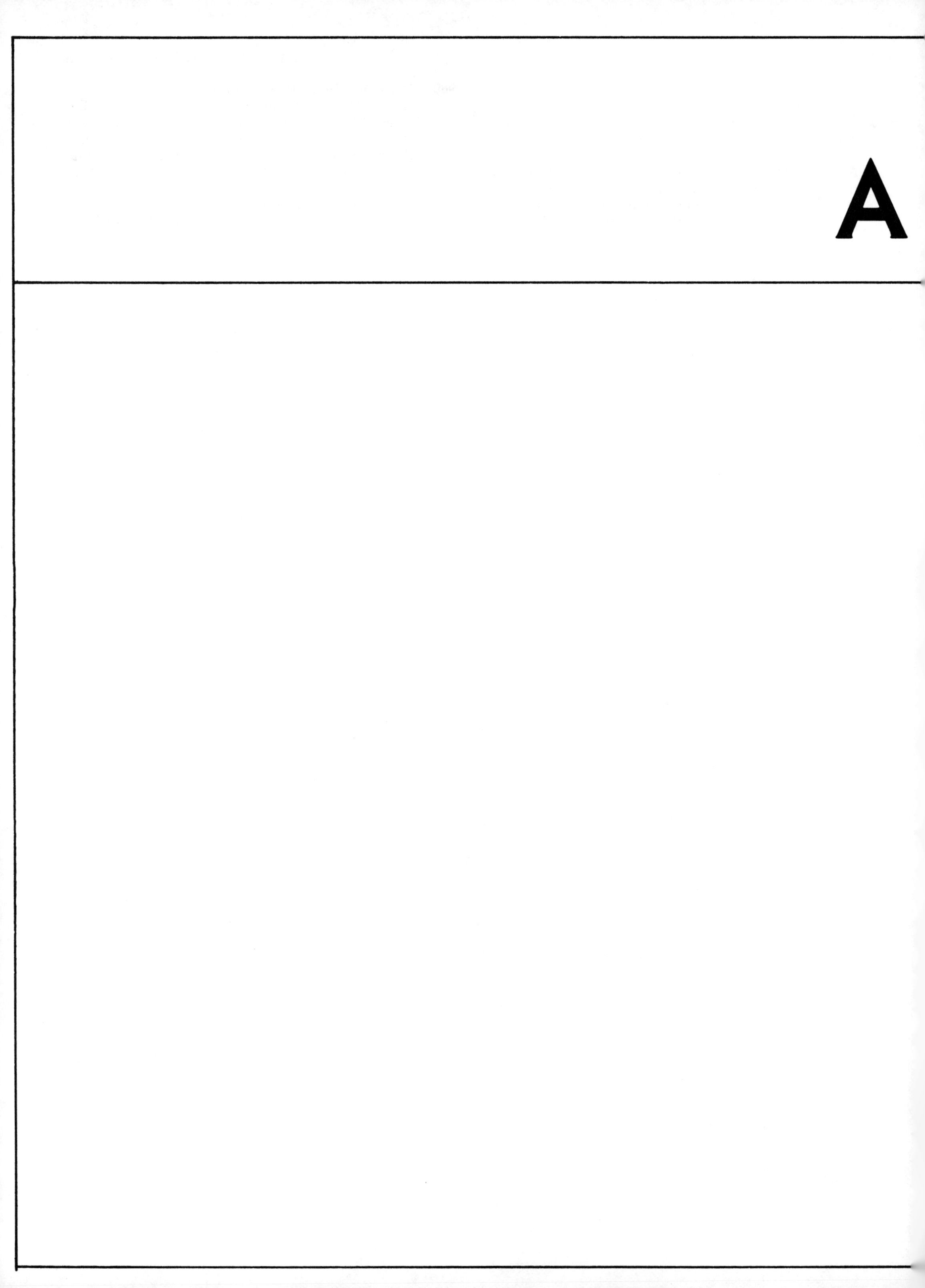

A

viation & Aeronautics

Contents

Related Awards

H. H. Arnold Award

AIR FORCE ASSOCIATION
1750 Pennsylvania Ave. NW, Washington, D.C. 20006
(202/637-3300)

The H.H. Arnold Award is given annually to an individual or group to honor outstanding contributions to aerospace. The award, which consists of a plaque, is in effect a "Man of the Year" award and is the association's highest honor. The recipient is selected by a committee.

1948 **W. Stuart Symington,** Secretary of the Air Force
1949 **Maj. Gen. William H. Turner and the men of the Berlin Airlift**
1950 **Airmen of the United Nations in the Far East**
1951 **Lt. Gen. Curtis E. LeMay and the personnel of Strategic Air Command**
1952 **Lyndon B. Johnson,** U.S. Senator
Joseph C. O'Mahoney, U.S. Senator
1953 **Gen. Hoyt S. Vandenberg,** former Chief of Staff, U.S. Air Force
1956 **W. Stuart Symington,** U.S. Senator
1957 **Edward P. Curtis,** Special Assistant to the President
1958 **Maj. Gen. Bernard A. Schriever,** Commander, Ballistic Missile Division, ARDC
1959 **Gen. Thomas S. Power,** Commander in Chief, Strategic Air Command
1960 **Gen. Thomas D. White,** Chief of Staff, U.S. Air Force
1961 **Lyle S. Garlock,** Assistant Secretary of the Air Force
1962 **A. C. Dickieson,** Bell Telephone Laboratories
John R. Pierce, Bell Telephone Laboratories
1963 **363d Tactical Reconnaissance Wing,** TAC, 4080th Strategic Wing, Strategic Air Command
1964 **Gen. Curtis E. LeMay,** chief of staff, U.S. Air Force
1965 **Second Air Division, PACAF,** U.S. Air Force
1966 **8th, 12th, 355th, 366th, and 388th Tactical Fighter Wings 432d and 460th Tactical Reconnaissance Wings**
1967 **Gen. William W. Momyer,** Commander, 7th Air Force, PACAF
1968 **Col. Frank Borman, Capt. James Lovell, Lt. Col. William Anders,** Apollo 8 Crew
1969 **No award**
1970 **J.L. Atwood, Lt. Gen. Samuel C. Phillips, Neil Armstrong, Col. Edwin E. Aldrin, Jr. and Col. Michael Collins,** Apollo 11 Team
1971 **John S. Foster, Jr.,** Director of Defense Research and Engineering
1972 **Air Units of the Allied Forces in Southeast Asia (U.S. Air Force, Navy, Army and Marine Corps, and Vietnamese Air Force)**
1973 **Gen. John D. Ryan,** U.S. Air Force
1974 **Gen. George S. Brown,** Chairman, Joint Chiefs of Staff
1975 **James R. Schlesinger,** Secretary of Defense
1976 **Barry M. Goldwater,** U.S. Senator
1977 **Howard W. Cannon,** U.S. Senator
1978 **Gen. Alexander M. Haig, Jr.,** U.S. Army, Supreme Allied Commander, Europe
1979 **John C. Stennis,** U.S. Senator
1980 **Gen. Richard H. Ellis,** U.S. Air Force, Commander in Chief, Strategic Air Command

Aeroacoustics Award
Aerodynamic Deceleration Systems and Balloon Technology Award
Aerospace Communications Award
Aerospasce Contribution to Society Award
Air Breathing Propulsion Award
Aircraft Design Award
AIAA Educational Achievement Award
Chanute Flight Award
De Florenz Training Award
Distinguished Service Award
Dryden Lectureship in Research
Fluid and Plasmadynamics Award
Goddard Astronautics Award
Daniel Guggenheim Medal Award
Haley Space Flight Award
History Manuscript Award
Information Systems Award
William Littlewood Memorial Lecture Award
Mechanics and Control of Flight Award
Pendray Aerospace Literature Award
Reed Aeronautics Award
Research Award in Structural Mechanics
Simulation and Ground Testing Award
Space Science Award
Space Systems Award
Lawrence Sperry Award
Structures, Structural Dynamics and Materials Award
Support Systems Award
System Effectiveness and Safety Award
Thermophysics Award
Von Karman Lectureship in Astronautics
Wright Brothers Lectureship in Aeronautics
Wyld Propulsion Award
Certificate of Merit

AMERICAN INSTITUTE OF AERONAUTICS AND

ASTRONAUTICS
1290 Ave. of the Americas, New York, N.Y. 10019
(212/581-4300)

The Aeroacoustics Award, which consists of a medal and certificate, is presented annually for achievement in aircraft community noise reduction upon a decision by an honors and awards committee.

1975 Michael J. Lighthill
1976 Herbert Ribner
1977 John E. Ffowes Williams
1978 No award
1979 Harvey H. Hubbard
1980 Alan Powell

The Aerodynamic Deceleration Systems and Balloon Technology Award, consisting of a medal and a certificate, is awarded biennially to a winner selected by an honors and awards committee.

1979 Helmut H. Heinrich

The Aerospace Communications Award, which consists of a medal and certificate, honors the achievement in the broad field of aerospace communications and is presented biennially on a decision by an honor and awards committee.

1968 Donald D. Williams
Harold A. Rosen
1969 Eberhardt Rechtin
1970 Edmund J. Habib
1971 Siegfried H. Reiger
1972 Wilbur Pritchard
1974 Arthur C. Clark
1976 Robert F. Garbarini
1978 Leonard Jaffe
1980 Not available at press time

The Aerospace Contribution to Society Award annually honors contributions by an individual selected by an honors and awards committee.

1978 Elmer P. Wheaton
1979 Richard S. Johnstone
1980 Seymour N. Stein

The Air Breathing Propulsion Award, which consists of a medal and certificate, honors air breathing populsion advances, including those in turbo-machinery or any other approach dependent on atmospheric air. An honors and awards committee selects the winner.

1976 Frederick T. Rall, Jr.
1977 Edward Woll
1978 William J. Blatz
1979 Arthur J. Wennerstom
1980 Melvin J. Hartmann

The Aircraft Design Award, which consists of a medal and certificate, recognizes advancement in aircraft design or design technology. An honors and awards committee selects the winner.

1969 Harold W. Adams
1970 Harrison A. Storms
1971 Joseph F. Sutter
1972 Ben R. Rich
1973 Herman D. Barkey
1974 Richard T. Whitcomb
1975 Walter E. Fellers
1976 Kendall Perkins
1977 Howard A. Evans
1978 John K. Wimpress
1979 Harold Raiklen
1980 Not available at press time

The AIAA Educational Achievement Award, presented jointly with the ASEE Aerospace Division, consists of an honorarium in recognition of improvements of lasting influence to aerospace engineering education.

1976 Barnes W. McCormick, Jr.
1977 No award
1978 Stanley H. Lowy
1979 Robert F. Brodsky
1980 Donnell W. Dutton

The Chanute Flight Award, originally called the Octavio Chanute Award, is a medal and certificate given to a pilot or test personnel for contributions to aeronautics.

OCTAVIO CHANUTE AWARD

1939 Edmund T. Allen
1940 Howard Hughes
1941 Melvin N. Gough
1942 A.L. MacClain
1943 William H. McAvoy
1944 Benjamin S. Kelsey
1945 Robert T. Lamson
Elliott Merrill
1946 Ernest A. Cutrell
1947 Lawrence A. Clousing
1948 Herbert H. Hoover
1949 Frederick M. Trapnell
1950 Donald B. MacDiarmid
1951 Marion E. Carl
1952 John C. Seal
1953 W.T. Bridgeman
1954 George E. Cooper
1955 Albert Boyd
1956 A.M. Johnston
1957 Frank K. Everest
1958 A. Scott Crossfield
1959 John P. Reeder
1960 Joseph J. Tymczyszyn
1961 Joseph A. Walker
1962 Neil Armstrong
1963 E.J. Bechtold
1964 Fred J. Drinkwater, III
Robert C. Innis
1965 Alvin S. White
1966 Donald F. McKusker
John L. Swigert, Jr.
1967 Milton O. Thompson
1968 William J. Knight
1969 William C. Park
1970 Jerauld P. Gentry
1971 William M. Magruder
1972 Donald R. Segner
1973 Cecil W. Powell
1974 Charles A. Sewell
1975 Alan L. Bean
Owen K. Garriott
Jack R. Lousma
1976 Thomas Stafford

CHANUTE FLIGHT AWARD

1977 No award
1978 No award
1979 Austin Bailey
1980 Carl B. Shelley

The De Florenz Training Award, which consists of a medal and certificate, is given annually for improvements in aerospace training. An honors and awards committee selects the winner.

1965 Lloyd L. Kelly
1966 Warren J. North
1967 Edwin H. Link
1968 Joseph La Russa
1969 Gifford Bull
1970 Harold G. Miller
1971 Walter P. Moran
1972 James W. Campbell
1973 Carroll H. Woodling
1974 Hugh Harrison Hurt, Jr.
1975 John C. Dusterberry
1976 No award
1977 John E. Duberg
1978 William Hagin
1979 James Burke
1980 Not available at press time

The Distinguished Service Award, which consists of a certificate, recognizes contributions by an AIAA member to the institute over a period of years, based on selection by the president, president-elect and vice presidents.

1968 Harvey M. Cook, Jr.
1969 Peter C. Johnson
1970 H. Dana Moran
1971 Frederick H. Roever
1972 William F. Chana
1973 H. Norman Abramson
1974 Charles Appleman
1975 Warren Curry
1977 Kenneth Randle
1978 Ann Dickson
1979 Charles W. Eyres
1980 N. A. "Tony" Armstrong

The Dryden Lectureship in Research, succeeding the Dryden Research Lecture, which was originally called the Research Award, recognizes achievement in basic research in the advancement of aeronautics and astronautics. The award consists of a medal and citation, and is made upon decision of an honors and awards committee with the approval of the board of directors.

RESEARCH AWARD

1961 James A. Van Allen
1962 A. Theodore Forrester
1964 Henry M. Shuey
1965 Wallace D. Hayes
1966 Shao-Chi Lin
1967 Edward W. Price

DRYDEN RESEARCH LECTURE

1968 Hans W. Liepmann
1969 Gerald P. Kuiper
1970 Bernard Budiansky
1971 Coleman D. Donaldson
1972 John C. Houbolt
1973 Herbert Friedman
1974 Herbert F. Hardrath
1975 Antonio Ferri
1976 Anatol Roshko

DRYDEN LECTURESHIP IN RESEARCH

1977 Abraham Hertzberg
1978 Gerald A. Soffen
1979 Dean R. Chapman
1980 Jack Kerrebrock

The Fluid and Plasmadynamics Award, which consists of a medal and certificate, recognizes contributions to the understanding of the behavior of liquids and gases in motion or of the physical properties and dynamical behavior of matter in the plasma state as related to aeronautics and astronautics. An honors and awards committee selects the winner.

1976 Mark Morkovin
1977 Harvard Lomax
1978 Charles E. Treanor
1979 Charles H. Kruger
1980 Not available at press time

The Goddard Astronautics Award has been broadened from the engineering science of propulsion to include the entire field of astronautics. The award consists of a medal and citation, and is given upon a decision by an honors and awards committee with the approval of the board of directors. Now the Institute's highest honor, it combines the ARS Goddard Memorial Award and Louis W. Hill Space Transportation Award.

ARS GODDARD MEMORIAL AWARD

1948 John Shesta
1949 Calvin M. Bolster
1950 Lovell Lawrence, Jr.
1951 Robert C. Traux
1952 Richard W. Porter
1953 David A. Young
1954 A.M.O. Smith
1955 E.N. Hall
1956 Chandler C. Ross
1957 Thomas F. Dixon
1958 Richard B. Canright
1959 Samuel K. Hoffman
1960 Theodore von Karman
1961 Wernher von Braun
1962 Robert R. Gilruth

GODDARD AWARD

1965 Frank Whittle
1966 Hans J.P. von Ohain
A.W. Blackman
George D. Lewis
1967 Robert O. Bullock
Irving A. Johnson
Seymour Lieblein
1968 Donald C. Berkey
Ernest C. Simpson
James E. Worsham
1969 Perry W. Pratt
Stanley G. Hooker
1970 Gerhard Neumann
1972 Howard E. Schumacher
Brian Brimelow
Gary Plourde
1973 Edward S. Taylor
1974 Paul D. Castenholz
Richard Mulready
John Sloop
1975 George Rosen
Gordon Holbrook

1976 Edward Price

LOUIS W. HILL SPACE TRANSPORTATION AWARD

1958 Robert H. Goddard
1959 James A. Van Allen
1960 S.K. Hoffman
Thomas F. Dixon
1961 Robert R. Gilruth
1962 C. Stark Draper
1963 Robert J. Parks
Jack M. James
1964 Hugh L. Dryden
1965 Wernher von Braun
1966 W. Randolph Lovelace, II
1967 Abe Silverstein
1968 W.H. Pickering
1969 George M. Low
1970 Christopher C. Kraft, Jr.
1971 Hubertus Strughold
1972 David G. Hoag
Richard H. Battin
1973 Kurt H. Debus
1974 Rocco A. Petrone
1975 Glenn Lunney

GODDARD ASTRONAUTICS AWARD

1977 James S. Martin, Jr.
1978 Joseph V. Charyk
1979 Maxime A. Faget
1980 Robert J. Parks

The Daniel Guggenheim Medal Award honors notable achievement in the advancement of aeronautics and is presented jointly by AIAA, American Society of Mechinical Engineers and Society of Automotive Engineers. The award consists of a medal and certificate.

1929 Orville Wright
1930 Ludwig Prandtl
1931 Frederick W. Lanchester
1932 Juan de la Cierva
1933 Jerome C. Unsaker
1934 William E. Boeing
1935 William F. Durand
1936 George W. Lewis
1937 Hugh Eckener
1938 Alfred H.R. Fedden
1939 Donald W. Douglas
1940 Glenn L. Martin
1941 Juan T. Trippe
1942 James H. Doolittle
1943 Edmund Turney Allen
1944 Lawrence D. Bell
1945 Theodore P. Wright
1946 Frank Whittle
1947 Lester Durand Gardner
1948 Leroy Randle Grumman
1949 Edward Pearson Warner
1950 Hugh Latimer Dryden
1951 Igor Ivan Sikorsky
1952 Sir Geoffrey De Havilland
1953 Charles A. Lindberg
1954 Clarence Decatur Howe
1955 Theodore von Karman
1956 Frederick B. Rentschler
1957 Arthur Emmons Raymond
1958 William Littlewood
1959 Sir George R. Edwards
1960 Grover Loening
1961 Jerome Lederer
1962 James H. Kindelberger
1963 James S. McDonnell, Jr.
1964 Robert H. Goddard
1965 Sir Sydney Camm
1966 Charles Stark Draper
1967 George Schairer
1968 H.M. Horner
1969 H. Julian Allen
1970 Jakob Ackeret
1971 Sir Archibald E. Russell
1972 William C. Mentzer
1973 William McPherson Allen
1974 Floyd L. Thompson
1975 Duane Wallace
1976 Marcel Dassault
1977 Cyrus R. Smith
1978 Edward Heinemann
1979 Gerhard Neumann
1980 Edward C. Wells

The Haley Space Flight Award, originally called the Astronautics Award, is now given every two years for outstanding contribution by an astronaut or flight test personnel. The award goes to the winner selected by an honors and awards committee, and consists of a medal and citation.

ASTRONAUTICS AWARD

1954 Theodore von Karman
1955 Wernher von Braun
1956 Joseph Kaplan
1957 Krafft Ehricke
1958 Ivan C. Kincheloe, Jr.
1959 Walter R. Dornberger
1960 A. Scott Crossfield
1961 Alan Shepard
1962 John H. Glenn, Jr.
1963 Walter M. Schirra, Jr.
Gordon Cooper
1964 Walter C. Williams
1965 Joseph S. Bleymaier

HALEY ASTRONAUTICS AWARD

1966 Neil A. Armstrong
David R. Scott
1967 Edward H. White, II
1968 Virgil I. Grissom
1969 Donn F. Eisele
R. Walter Cunningham
Walter M. Schirra, Jr.
1970 Frank Borman
James A. Lovell, Jr.
William Anders
1971 John Swigert
Fred W. Haise, Jr
James A. Lovell, Jr.
1972 David Worden
David Scott
James Irwin
1973 John Young
Thomas Mattingly, II
Charles Duke, Jr.
1974 Paul J. Weitz
Charles Conrad, Jr.
Joseph P. Kerwin
1975 Gerald Carr
William Pogue
Edward Gibson

1976 William H. Dana

HALEY SPACE FLIGHT AWARD

1979 Roger Winblade

The History Manuscript Award, which consists of a medal and certificate, honors the winner of an annual competition for the best historical manuscript on science, technology and/or the impact of aeronautics and astronautics on society. A technical committee is responsible for selecting the winner.

1969 Milton Lomask
Constance McLaughlin Green
1971 Richard C. Lukas
1972 Richard K. Smith
1973 William M. Leary, Jr.
1975 Richard P. Hallion
1977 Thomas Crouch
1978 Edward C. Ezell
Linda N. Ezell
1979 Roger Bilstein
1980 Not available at press time

The Information Systems Award, which consists of a medal and certificate, is presented biennially for contributions to technical and/or management contributions to space and aeronautics computer-sensing aspects of information technology. An honors and awards committee selects the winner.

1977 Albert Hopkins, Jr.
1979 Barry W. Boehm
Algirdas Avizienis

The William Littlewood Memorial Lecture Award, which consists of an honorarium to be decided by a committee and a certificate, is given jointly by the AIAA and the Society of Automotive Engineers.

1971 Peter G. Masefield
1972 John Borger
1973 Richard Jackson
1974 Edward Wells
1975 Gerhard Neumann
1976 Raymond Kelly
Franklin Kolk
1977 No award
1978 No award
1979 Willis Hawkins
1980 Norman Parment

The Mechanics and Control of Flight Award, which consists of a medal and certificate, honors outstanding recent technical or scientific contribution to the mechanics, guidance or control of flight. An honors and award committee selects the winner.

1967 Derek F. Lawden
1968 Robert V. Knox
1969 John P. Mayer
1970 Irving L. Ashkenas
Duane T. McRuer
1971 George W. Cherry
Kenneth J. Cox
William S. Widnall
1972 John V. Breakwell
1973 Henry J. Kelley
1974 Harold Roy Vaughn
1975 Bernard Etkin
1976 Charles Murphy
1977 Joseph R. Chambers
William P. Gilbert
1978 Richard H. Battin
1979 Morris Ostgaard
1980 Not available at press time

The Pendray Aerospace Literature Award, formerly called the G. Edward Pendray Award, honors outstanding contributions to recent aeronautical and astronautical literature, preferably within the previous three years. High quality and the influence of the work are valued more highly than the underlying technological contributions The award consists of a medal and certificate and is the responsibility of a technical committee.

G. EDWARD PENDRAY AWARD

1951 George P. Sutton
1952 M.J. Zucrow
1953 M.S. Tsien
1954 Martin Summerfield
1955 Walter Dornberger
1956 Herman Oberth
1957 Grayson Merrill
1958 Homer E. Newell
1959 Ali B. Cambell
1960 Luigi Crocco
1961 Krafft Ehricke
1962 Howard E. Seifert
1964 Andrew G. Haley
1965 Dinsmore Alter
1966 A.K. Oppenheim
1967 Robert A. Gross
1968 Arthur E. Bryson, Jr.
1970 Wilmot N. Hess
1971 Nicholas J. Hoff
1972 Edward W. Price
1973 Marcus F. Heidmann
Richard Priem
1974 Frederick Ordway
1975 William R. Sears
1976 Stanford S. Penner

PENDRAY AEROSPACE LITERATURE AWARD

1977 George Leitmann
1978 Arnold M. Kuethe
1979 Henry J. Kelley
1980 Fred E. C. Culick

The Reed Aeronautics Award, formerly the Sylvanus Albert Reed Award, honors the most notable achievement in aeronautical science and engineering. The award consists of a medal and citation, and is given upon a decision by an honors and awards committee with the approval of the board of directors. It is one of the AIAA's two highest honors.

SYLVANUS ALBERT REED AWARD

1934 C.G. Rossby
H.G. Willett
1935 Frank W. Caldwell
1936 Edward S. Taylor
1937 Eastman N. Jacobs
1938 Alfred Victor de Forest
1939 George J. Mead
1940 Hugh L. Dryden
1941 Theodore von Karman
1942 Igor I. Sikorsky
1943 Sanford A. Moss
1944 Fred E. Weick

1945 Charles S. Draper
1946 Robert T. Jones
1947 Galen B. Schubauer
Harold K. Skramstad
1848 George W. Brady
1949 George S. Schairer
1950 Robert R. Gilruth
1951 E.H. Heinemann
1952 John Stack
1953 Ernest G. Stout
1954 Clark B. Millikan
1955 H. Julian Allen
1956 Clarence L. Johnson
1957 R.L. Bisplinghoff
1958 Victor E. Carbonera
1959 Karel J. Bossart
1960 John W. Becker
1961 Alfred J. Eggers, Jr.
1962 Walter C. Williams
1964 Abe Silverstein
1965 Arthur E. Raymond
1966 Clarence L. Johnson
1967 Adloph Busemann
1968 William H. Cook
1969 Rene H. Miller
1970 Richard T. Whitcomb
1971 Ira Grant Hedrick
1972 Max Munk
1973 I.E. Garrick
1974 Willis Hawkins
1975 Antonio Ferri
1976 George Spangenberg

REED AERONAUTICS AWARD

1977 William C. Dietz
1978 James T. Stewart
1979 Paul B. MacCready
1980 Donald Malvern

The Research Award in Structural Mechanics, given jointly by the AIAA and the Office of Naval Research, consists of a medal, certificate and full-time support at the winner's current income level, usually for one year, to honor and encourage research related closely to naval structural mechanics problems. Individuals may apply for this award. A screening committee of the AIAA reviews the applicants for final selection by the ONR.

1970 Stanley B. Dong
1971 Lawrence H.N. Lee
1972 Robert E. Nickell
1973 Robert M. Jones
1974 Dave Bushnell
1975 Edward Stanton
1976 No award
1977 Jack R. Vinson
1978 No award
1979 William N. Findley
1980 Not available at press time

The Simulation and Ground Testing Award, which consists of a medal and a certificate, recognizes achievement in the development or utilization of technology procedures, facilities or model techniques for ground testing associated with astronautics or aeronautics. An honors and awards committee selects the winner.

1976 Bernhard H. Goethart
1977 No award
1978 Arthur B. Doty
1979 Jack D. Whitfield
1980 Frank L. Wattendorf

The Space Science Award, which consists of a medal and certificate, honors studies of the physics or atmosphere of celestial bodies or other related processes occurring in space or experienced by space vehicles. An honors and awards committee selects the winner.

1962 John R. Winkler
1963 No award
1964 Herbert Friedman
1965 Eugene N. Parker
1966 Francis S. Johnson
1967 Robert B. Leighton
1968 Kinsey A. Anderson
1969 Charles P. Sonnett
1970 Carl E. McIlwain
1971 William Ian Axford
1972 Norman F. Ness
1973 Paul W. Gast
1974 John H. Wolfe
1975 Murray Dryer
1976 Riccardo Giacconi
1977 Bruce Murray
1978 Laurence E. Peterson
1979 James B. Pollack
1980 Donald M. Hunten

The Space Systems Award, originally the Spacecraft Design Award, honors achievement in systems analysis, design and implementation in spacecraft and launch vehicle technology. The award consists of a medal and certificate and is presented upon a decision of an honors and awards committee.

SPACECRAFT DESIGN AWARD

1969 Otto E. Bartoe, Jr.
1970 Maxime A. Faget
1971 Anthony J. Iorillo
1972 Thomas J. Kelly
1973 Harold A. Rosen
1974 Harold Lassen
1975 Caldwell C. Johnson, Jr.

SPACE SYSTEM AWARD

1977 Walter O. Lowrie
1978 Wernher von Braun
1979 John R. Casani
1980 Charles F. Hall

The Lawrence Sperry Award, which consists of a medal and certificate, honors a notable contribution by an individual 35 years of age or younger to the advancement of aeronautics or astronautics. An honors and awards committee selects the winner.

1936 William C. Rockefeller
1937 Clarence L. Johnson
1938 Russell C. Newhouse
1939 Charles M. Kearns, Jr.
1940 William B. Oswald
1941 E.G. Stout
1942 E.C. Wells
1943 William B. Bergen
1944 William H. Phillips
1945 Richard Hutton
1946 Peter R. Murray
1947 N.A.N. Gaylor
1948 Allen E. Puckett

1949 Alexander H. Flax
1950 Frank N. Piasecki
1951 R.C. Seamans, Jr.
1952 Dean R. Chapman
1953 Donald Coles
1954 A. Scott Crossfield
1955 Giles J. Strickroth
1956 George F. Jude
1957 Clarence A. Syvertson
1958 Robert G. Loewy
1959 James E. McCune
1960 Robert B. Howell
1961 Douglas G. Harvey
1962 Robert O. Pilland
1964 Daniel M. Tellep
1965 Rodney C. Wingrove
1966 Joe H. Engle
1967 Eugene F. Kranz
1968 Roy V. Harris
1969 Edgar C. Lineberry, Jr.
1970 Glenn S. Lunney
1971 Ronald L. Berry
1972 Sheila E. Widnall
1973 Dino A. Lorenzini
1974 Jan Rusby Tulinius
1975 David Bushnell
1976 No award
1977 Joseph L. Weingarten
1978 Paul Kutler
1979 David A. Caughey
1980 William F. Ballhaus

The Structures, Structural Dynamics and Materials Award, which consists of a medal and certificate, honors scientific or technical contributions in aerospace structures, structural dynamics or materials. An honors and awards committee selects the winner.

1968 John C. Houbolt
1969 Holt Ashley
1970 Joseph D. Van Dyke, Jr.
1971 Nicholas J. Hoff
1972 M. Jonathan Turner
1973 Robert T. Schwartz
George P. Peterson
1974 William D. Cowie
1975 Theodore H.H. Pian
1976 Charles Tiffany
1977 Walter J. Mykytow
1978 Warren A. Staufer
1979 Lucien A. Schmit
1980 Not available at press time

The Support Systems Award, which consists of a medal and certificate, recognizes contributions to the over-all effectiveness of aeronautical or aerospace systems technology through improved support systems. An honors and awards committee selects the winner.

1976 Gene A. Petry
1977 Thomas A. Ellison
1978 No award
1979 Joseph J. O'Rourke
1980 Not available at press time

The System Effectiveness and Safety Award, which consists of a medal and certificate, recognizes contributions to system effectiveness or safety or related disciplines. An honors and awards committee selects the winner.

1977 Thomas D. Matteson
F. Stanley Nowland
1978 No award
1979 Willis Willoughby, Jr.
1980 I. Irving Pinkel

The Thermophysics Award, which consists of a medal and certificate, honors recent technical or scientific contribution to thermophysics as related to thermal energy transfer and especially to the study of environmental effects of radiation. An honors and awards committee selects the winner.

1976 Donald K. Edwards
1977 Chang-Lin Tien
1978 Allie M. Smith
1979 Raymond Viskanta
1980 Not available at press time

The Von Karman Lectureship in Astronautics, formerly the Von Karman Lecture, honors notable performance and technical distinction in astronautics. The award consists of a medal and citation, and is given upon a decision of an honors and awards committee with the approval of the board of directors.

VON KARMAN LECTURE

1962 Hugh L. Dryden
1964 Arthur Kantrowitz
1965 R.L. Bisplinghoff
1966 Nicholas J. Hoff
1967 Lester Lees
1968 William R. Sears
1979 Courtland D. Perkins
1970 Erik L. Mollo-Christensen
1971 Irmgard Flugge-Lotz
1972 Eugene Love
1973 Alan M. Lovelace
1974 Harrison Schurmeier
1975 I.E. Garrick

VON KARMAN LECTURESHIP IN ASTRONAUTICS

1977 Joseph V. Charyk
1978 Robert Fuhrman
1979 Christopher C. Kraft, Jr.
1980 Daniel J. Fink

The Wright Brothers Lectureship in Aeronautics, formerly the Wright Brothers Lecture, recognizes leadership in aeronautics. The award consists of a medal and citation, and is given upon a decision by an honors and awards committee with the approval of the Board of Directors.

WRIGHT BROTHERS LECTURE

1937 B. Melville Jones
1938 Hugh L. Dryden
1939 Clark B. Millikan
1940 Sverte Pettersen
1941 Richard V. Southwell
1942 Edmund T. Allen
1943 W. S. Farren
1944 John Stack
1945 H. Roxbee Cox
1946 Theodore von Karman
1947 Sydney S. Goldstein
1948 Abe Silverstein
1949 A.E. Russell
1950 William Bollay
1951 P.B. Walker
1952 William Littlewood

1953 Glenn L. Martin
1954 Bo K.O. Lundberg
1955 R.L. Bisplinghoff
1956 Arnold Hall
1957 H. Julian Allen
1958 Maurice Roy
1959 Alexander H. Flax
1960 A.W. Quick
1961 Robert Jastrow
1962 M. James Lighthill
1964 George S. Schairer
1965 Gordon N. Patterson
1966 C. Stark Draper
1967 P. Poisson-Quinton
1968 Charles W. Harper
1969 Pierre Satre
1970 F.A. Cleveland
1971 Robert L. Lickley
1972 Franklin Kolk
1973 H. Schlichting
1974 A.M.O. Smith
1975 Henri Ziegler

WRIGHT BROTHERS LECTURESHIP IN AERONAUTICS

1976 J.L. Atwood
1977 Gero Madelung
1978 George B. Litchford
1979 Jack Nielsen
1980 Bernard Etkin

The Wyld Propulsion Award, which consists of a medal and certificate, combines the former James H.Wyld Memorial Award and the Propulsion Award to honor achievement in the development or application of rocket propulsion systems. An honors and awards committee selects the winner.

PROPULSION AWARD

1948 Frank Malina
1949 James A. Van Allen
1950 Leslie Skinner
1951 William Avery
1952 A.L. Antonio
1953 Charles E. Bartley
1954 Harold W. Ritchey
1955 D.S. Miller
1956 Bruce H. Sage
1957 Levering Smith
1958 Barnet R. Adelman
1959 Ernest Roberts
1960 Ernst Stuhlinger
1961 Robert B. Young
1962 Samuel K. Hoffman
1964 David Altman

JAMES H. WYLD MEMORIAL AWARD

1954 Milton W. Rosen
1955 John P. Stapp
1956 Louis G. Dunn
1957 William H. Pickering
1958 Holger N. Toftoy
1959 K.J. Bossard
1960 Robert L. Johnson
1961 Harrison A. Storms
1962 William F. Raborn
1964 Joseph S. Bleymaier

JAMES H. WYLD PROPULSION AWARD

1965 Werner R. Kirchner
1966 Maurice J. Zucrow
1967 Adelbert O. Tischler
1968 Harold B. Finger
1969 Harold R. Kaufman
1970 Hans G. Paul
Joseph G. Thibodaux, Jr.
1971 Luigi M. Crocco
1972 Karl Klager
1973 Gerard W. Elverum, Jr.
Norman C. Reuel
1974 Clarence W. Schnare
1975 James Lazar
Rodrick Spence

WYLD PROPULSION AWARD

1976 Howard Seifert
1977 Martin Summerfield
1978 William C. Rice
1979 Derald A. Stuart
1980 Howard W. Douglass

Certificates of Merit are given as merited for technical and scientific excellence. The awards, which may be given in connection with a nationally sponsored AIAA activity, do not duplicate or interfere with the other technical awards given by the organization.

AIR BREATHING PROPULSION

1977 C.M. Willard
F.J. Capone
M. Komarski
H.L. Stevens
1979 Paul L. Russell
Gerry Brant
Richard Ernst
Francis N. Underwood, Jr.

STRUCTURES DESIGN

1979 Richard N. Hadcock

ATMOSPHERIC FLIGHT MECHANICS

1979 Kenneth W. Illif
Richard E. Maine

PROPELLANT

1980 James J. Pelough, Jr.

AIRCRAFT DESIGN

1980 Frederick Rall

Distinguished Public Service Award
Harry Lever Award
Special Citations
Monsanto Aviation Safety Award
Public Information Officer Awards
Public Relations Award

AVIATION/SPACE WRITERS ASSOCIATION
Cliffwood Rd., Chester N.J. 07930(201/879-5667)

AWA's Distinguished Public Service Award is a trophy presented annually to an individual who has "used the products of aviation and/or space technology to make exemplary contributions to the welfare and quality of life of fellow citizens."

1972 Frank Sinatra
1973 William G. Magruder
1974 Sen. Barry M. Goldwater
1975 Robert F. Six
1976 Arnold Palmer
1977 Michael Collins
Paul E. Garber

The Harry Lever Award annually recognizes outstanding service to AWA.

1958 LeRoy Whitman
1959 James J. Haggerty, Jr.
1960 M. L. (Bo) McLaughlin
1961 William A. Lookadoo
1962 Herbert O. Fisher
1963 Leon Shloss
1964 M. L. (Bo) McLaughlin
1965 William S. Beller
1966 E. H. Pickering
1967 Gerald J. McAllister
1968 Ronald S. Gall
1969 Lt. Col. Kenneth E. Grine, USAF
1970 Grover D. Nobles, Jr.
1971 Warren W. Kenn
1972 William F. Kaiser
1973 Warren H. Goodman Kenneth S. Fletcher
1974 Robert G. Button C. M. Plattner
1975 William J. McGinty
1976 H.F. (Jim) Roth
James L. Street
1977 No award
1978 Marvin G. Klemow
1979 William G. Browning
1980 James R. Greenwood

The AWA annually honors individuals and organizations with special citations.

1965 Vern Haugland
National Geographic Magazine
1967 Robert J. Serling
Ronald S. Gall
1968 Ansel E. Talbert
1969 Wayne W. Parrish
Maj. W. F. Gabella, USA
Col. Mark A. Gilman, USAF
1970 Grumman Aircraft
North American Rockwell
Eric Burgess
Frank J. Delear
Louis R. Stockstill
Jules Bergman
Frank McGee
Robert J. Sterling
Robert Burkhardt
1971 Edward G. Uhl Fairchild Industries
Edgar E. Ulsamer
Paul H. and Eleanore Wilkinson
Grover Loening
1972 Brig. Gen. Thomas P. Coleman, USAF
1973 Richard L. Taylor
Ansel E. Talbert
Howard Benedict
Philip J. Klass
Dave Swaim
Kenneth F. Weaver
Laurence L. Doty
Steven C. Paton
1974 James Street
Edwin G. Pipp
Joel N. Shurkin
Karl Kristofferson
Stephan Wikinson
Richard B. Weeghman
John T. Lyons
Kenneth S. Fletcher
Kenneth Hudson
Larry Levy
William D. Conner
Carroll V. Glines
Jerome Fanciulli
1975 Richard P. Benjamin
Duane Cole
David Crain
Vern Haugland
Ross MacKenzie
John B. Meyer
Marvin G. Miles
Barry Schiff
L.B. Taylor
Charles L. Tracy
Paul A. Turk
John J. Nopper
Steven C. Paton
Julian R. Levine
1976 Jon L. Allen
E.B. Berlinrut
Katherine Boyd
Jerry J. Boyer
E.J. Burke
Duncan Campbell
Janice Castro
William T. Coleman
J.L. DeCelles
John R. Donnelly
Jack Elliott
Jon Ellis
Lori Evans and staff
Frederick Golden
William Goodwin
Jim Hannah
Jerry Hannifin
Robin Higham and staff
David Lee
Christine Lyons
Chuck Lyons
John Lyons
Glenn McClure
Jay N. Miller
Robert Parke and staff
Phillip J. Parker
George Pica
Davis A. Shugarts
Glenn Singer
J.E. O'Brien
Thomas O'Toole
Jack Truluck
David Wallin
Kenneth F. Weaver
Patrick Young
1977 Glen B. Bavousett
Don Fairchilds
James R. Greenwood
Gladys E. Wise
1978 H.F. (Jim) Roth
1979 Maximilian Garavito
1980 Richard L. Collins
Charles Conrad, Jr.
Thomas D. Crouch
L.A. Dahlquest
Richard Drury

R. Eric Falk
Richard P. Hallion
Jim Hartz
R.W. Haskell
Vern Haugland
D.I. McGinnes
Richard Quinette
William A. Schoneberger
Tech. Sgt. Wayne Specht
W.R. Travers

The Monsanto Aviation Safety Award, administered by the Flight Safety Foundation, was awarded annually until 1969.

1958 Jerome Lederer
1959 Maj. Gen Joseph D. Caldara, USAF
1960 E. R. Quesada
1961 E. S. Calvert
1962 Otto E. Kirchner. Sr.
1963 William Littlewood
1964 Bo K. O. Lundbert
1965 Najeeb Halaby
1966 W. A. Patterson
1967 David D. Thomas
1968 Frank E. Christofferson
1969 Edwin A. Link

Public Information Officer Awards honor high standards in public information and effort performed by commissioned officers, enlisted personnel or civilian employees in the interest of aviation and space arms of the military and other branches of the federal government. The recipient of the award, which is sponsored by Grumman Corporation, is given a scroll and a silver tray. The various awards were restructured in 1972 into just one award.

ORVILLE WRIGHT AWARDS

1963 Maj Philip Salk, USAF
1964 Lt. Col. Stratton M. Appleman, USAF and
Maj. Harold A. Susskind, USAF
1965 Maj. James C. Elliott, USAF
1966 Col. William J. McGinty, USAF
1967 Maj. Sydney Lester, USAF
1968 Lt. Col. Lawrence J. Tacker, USAF
1969 Maj. Carroll Shershun, USAF
Lt. Col. Irving Neuwirth, USAF
1970 Capt. Robert E. Neely, USAF
1971 Maj. Peter L. Sloan, USAF
1972 Harold M. Helfman

WILBUR WRIGHT AWARD

1963 Col. William V. Schmitt, USA
1964 Col. Ben W. Legare, USA
1965 Capt. Mel R. Jones, USA
1966 Lt. Col. Thomas E. Thompson, USA
1967 Col. George R. Creel, USA
1968 Col. Roger R. Bankson, USA
1969 Brig. Gen. Winant Sidle, USA
1970 Lt. Col. Phillip H. Stevens, USA
1971 Maj. William F. Gabella, USA
1972 Maj. Joseph E. Burlas, USA

GLENN H. CURTISS AWARD

1963 Cdr. Kenneth W. Wade, USN
1964 Cdr. H. Harold Bishop, USN
1965 Capt. James S. Dowdell, USN
Cdr. Louis DiGiusto. Jr., USNR
1966 Rear Adm. William P. Mack, USN
Gy. Sgt. Clifton V. Stallings, USMC
1967 Col. Thomas M. Fields, USMC
1968 Capt. Pickett Lumpkin, USN
1969 Lt. Col. Arvid W. Realson, USMC
Capt. Kenneth Wade, USN
1970 Lt. Dan L. Davidson, USN
1971 No award
1972 Cdr. Williams S. Graves, USN

CHARLES L. LAWRENCE AWARD

1968 Edward E. Slattery, Jr.
1969 Volta Torrey
1970 John W. King
1971 Gene Kropf
1972 No award

PUBLIC INFORMATION OFFICER AWARD

1973 Capt. Arthur C. Forster, Jr., USAF
1974 Col. H. J. Dalton, Jr., USAF
1975 R/Adm. William Thompson, USN
1976 Col. Robert Hermann, USAF
1977 Lt. Col. William F. Gabella, USAF
Gladys E. Wise
1978 David W. Garrett, All-Service Award
Col. Richard K. King, USAF
Capt. Edward T. Wilbur, USN
1979 Capt. Douglas A. Kennett, USAF, All-Service Award
Lt. Col. Rallin J. Aars, USAF
Lt. Cdr. Kendell M. Pease, Jr., USN
James F. Lynch, Government
1980 Lt. Col. Leo M. Terrill, USAF
Col. James J. Breeh, USA
Albert W. Frascella, USN
William J. O'Donnell

The Public Relations Award is presented annually to an Associate Member of AWA in recognition of outstanding contributions in publicizing, promotion or otherwise bringing aviation and/or space activities to the public's attention.

1956 Walter T. Bonney and Information Staff of NACA
1957 Air Force Assn.
1958 Willis Player and Public Relations Staff of the Air Transport Assn.
1959 No award
1960 Peggy G. Hereford and James C. Fuller
1961 Lt. Col. Kenneth E. Grine, USAF
Lt. Col. Sid F. Spear, USAF
1962 Richard Larrick
1963 James R. Greenwood
1964 Gordon S. Williams
1965 Carl W. Dahlem
1966 Fred McClement
1967 Larry M. Hayes
1968 William G. Robinson
1969 Earl Blount
1970 No award
1971 Marvin G. Klemow
1972 Don Fairchilds
1973 Hubert K. Gagos
1974 Thomas H. Rhone
1975 Charles Gablehouse
1976 Robert V. Christian
1977 Richard J. Ferris
1978 William D. Perrault
1979 Joseph A. Daley
1980 Karen S. Coyle

PUBLIC RELATIONS CITATION
1977 **Don Fairchild**

Robert J. Collier Trophy

NATIONAL AERONAUTIC ASSOCIATION
821 15th St. NW, Washington, D.C. 20005 (202/347-2808)

The Robert J. Collier Trophy is given annually to an individual or a group of individuals for contributions to "improving the performance, efficiency or safety of air or space vehicles, the value of which has been thoroughly demonstrated by actual use during the preceding year." The winner is selected by the Collier Trophy Committee, appointed by the president of the association, and the presentation of the elaborate trophy which symbolizes flight is frequently made by the President of the United States in a White House ceremony.

1911 **Glenn H. Curtiss,** Hydro-aeroplane
1912 **Glenn H. Curtiss,** Flying boat
1913 **Orville Wright,** Automatic stabilizer
1914 **Elmer A. Sperry,** Gyroscopic control
1915 **W. Sterling Burgess,** Burgess-Dunner Hydro-aeroplane
1916 **Elmer A. Sperry,** Drift indicator
1917 **No award**
1918 **No award**
1919 **No award**
1920 **No award**
1921 **Grover Loening,** Aerial yacht
1922 **Personnel of the U.S. Air Mail Service**
1923 **Personnel of the U.S. Air Mail Service**
1924 **U.S. Army**
1925 **S. Albert Reed,** Metal propeller
1926 **Maj. E.L. Hoffman,** Practical parachute
1927 **Charles L. Lawrence,** Radial air-cooled engine
1928 **Aeronautics Branch, U.S. Dept. of Commerce,** Airways and air-navigation facilities
1929 **National Advisory Committee for Aeronautics,** NACA cowling
1930 **Harold Pitcairn and staff,** Autogiro
1931 **Packard Motor Car Co.,** Aircraft diesel engine
1932 **Glenn L. Martin,** Bi-engine, high-speed, weight-carrying airplane
1933 **Hamilton Standard Propeller Co. and chief engineer Frank W. Caldwell,** Controllable-pitch propeller
1934 **Maj. Albert F. Hegenberger,** Blind-landing experimentation
1935 **Donald Douglas and staff,** DC-2
1936 **Pan American Airways,** Trans-Pacific and over-water operations
1937 **Army Air Corps,** Sub-stratosphere airplane
1938 **Howard Hughes and crew,** Round-the-world flight
1939 **Airlines of the United States,** Record of air-travel safety
1940 **Sanford Moss and the Army Air Corps,** Turbo-supercharger
1941 **Air Forces and airlines,** Worldwide operations typified by Air Transport Command
1942 **General H.H. Arnold,** Organization and leadership of the "mightiest air force in the world"
1943 **Capt. Luis de Florez, USNR,** Synthetic training devices for flyers
1944 **Gen. Carl A. Spaatz,** Demonstrated air power concept through use of American aviation in war against Germany
1945 **Louis W. Alvarez,** Ground-controlled approach radar landing system
1946 **Lewis A. Robert,** Thermal ice-prevention system
1947 **John Stack, Lawrence Bell and Capt. Charles E. Yaeger,** Supersonic flight
1948 **Radio Technical Commission for Aeronatics,** System of air-traffic control to permit safe and unlimited operations under all weather conditions
1949 **William P. Lear,** Lear F-5 automatic pilot and automatic control coupler system
1950 **Helicopter industry, military services and Coast Guard,** Rotary-wing aircraft for air-rescue operations
1951 **John Stack and associates at Langley Aeronautical Laboratory,** Practical application of transonic wind-tunnel throat
1952 **Leonard S. Hobbs of United Aircraft Corp.,** J-57 jet engine
1953 **James H. Kindelberger and Edward H. Heinemann,** Supersonic airplanes in service
1954 **Richard T. Whitcomb,** Verification of area rule, yielding higher speed and range with same air power
1955 **William M. Allen and Boeing Co., and Gen. Nathan F. Twining and U.S. Air Force,** Operational use of B-52
1956 **Charles J. McCarthy and associates of Chance-Vought Aircraft, Inc., and V. Adm. James S. Russell and associates of U.S. Navy Bureau of Aeronautics,** F-8U Crusader
1957 **Edward P. Curtis,** Report, *Aviation Facilities Planning*
1958 **U.S. Air Force and industry team,** F-104 interceptor
Clarence L. Johnson of Lockheed Aircraft Corp., for F-104 airframe
Neil Burgess and Gerhard Neumann of General Electric Co., for F-104 J-79 turbojet engines
Maj. Howard C. Johnson, USAF, for F-104 world landplane altitude record
Capt. Walter W. Irwin USAF, for F-104 world straightaway speed record
1959 **U.S. Air Force, Convair Div. of General Dynamics and Space Technology Laboratories, Inc.,** Atlas, American's first intercontinental ballistic missile
1960 **V. Adm. William F. Raborn,** Polaris, Operational Fleet Balistic Missile Weapon System
1961 **Maj. Robert M. White, Joseph A. Walker, A. Scott Crossfield and Cdr. Forrest Petersen,** Test pilots of the X-15
1962 **Lt. Cdr. M. Scott Carpenter, USN; Maj. L. Gordon Cooper, USAF; Lt. Col. John H. Glenn, USMC; Maj. Virgil I. Grissom, USAF; Cdr. Walter M. Schirra, Jr., USN; Cdr. Alan B. Shepard, Jr., USN, and Maj. Donald K. Slayton, USAF,** Pioneering manned space flight in the United States
1963 **Clarence L. "Kelly" Johnson,** A-11 Mach 3 aircraft
1964 **Gen. Curtis E. LeMay,** Great achievements toward air vehicles and national defense
1965 **James E. Webb and Hugh L. Dryden,** Gemini program team representatives, for contributions to human experience in space flight
1966 **James S. McDonnell,** F-4 Phantom aircraft and Gemini space vehicles
1967 **Lawrence A. Hyland,** Surveyor Program Team that "put the eyes and hands of the United States on the Moon"
1968 **Col. Frank Borman, USAF; Capt. James A. Lovell, Jr., USN, and Lt. Col. William A. Anders, USAF,** Crew of Apollo 8, first manned lunar orbit expedition
1969 **Neil A. Armstrong, Col. Edwin E. Aldrin, Jr., USAF and Col. Michael Collins, USAF,** "Epic flight of

Apollo 11" and first landing of man on the surface of the Moon

1970 **Boeing Co.,** (with special recognition to **Pratt & Whitney and Pan American World Airways),** Commercial introduction of 747

1971 **Col. David R. Scott, USAF; Col. James B. Irwin, USAF; and Lt. Col. Alfred M. Worden, USAF and Robert R. Gilruth,** Apollo 15, "man's most prolonged and scientifically productive lunar mission"

1972 **Adm. Thomas H. Moorer, USN,** Representing 7th and 8th Air Forces of U.S. Air Force and Task Force 77 of U.S. Navy for Operation Linebacker II

1973 **Skylab Program,** with special recognition to **William C. Schneider**, program director, and three **Skylab crews,** "Proving beyond question the value of man in future explorations of space and production of data of benefit to all the people on Earth"

1974 **John F. Clark,** NASA and **Daniel J. Fink,** General Electric Co., with special recognition to **Hughes Aircraft Co.** and **RCA,** NASA/industry team responsible for LANDSAT, Earth Resources Technology Satellite Program

1975 **David S. Lewis, General Dynamics Corp., and F-16 Air Force-industry team,** Fighter-aircraft technology and innovations

1976 **Gen. David C. Jones, USAF, and Robert Anderson, Rockwell International,** Air Force-industry team responsible for B-1 strategic aircraft system

1977 **Gen. Robert V. Dixon, USAF (Ret.), and Air Force Tactical Air Command,** Red Flag, combat simulation flight-training program

1978 **Sam B. Williams,** Williams Research Corp., Conceiving and developing the world's smallest, high-efficiency turbofan engine which was selected to power U.S. cruise missiles

1979 **Paul B. MacCready,** Aerovironment, Inc., Design and construction of the "Gossamer Albatross," with which the first human-powered flight across the English Channel was accomplished, with Special Recognition to pilot **Bryan Allen**

1980 **Not available at press time**

Johann-Maria-Boykow-Preis
Wilhelm-Hoff-Preis
Ernst-Mach-Preis
Erich-Trefftz-Preis
Hugo-Junkers-Preis
Erich-Regener-Preis
Otto-Mader-Preis

DEUTSCHE FORSCHUNGS- UND VERSUCHSANSTALT FUR LUFT- UND RAUMFAHRT
Linder Hoehe, 5000 Cologne 90, Federal Republic of Germany

The German Institute for Development and Testing for Air and Space Travel biennially gives a series of honors for papers describing developments in these areas. Each award, consisting of a citation and an honorarium, is given to individuals chosen from nominees submitted by universities, industry and research laboratories.

JOHANN-MARIA-BOYKOW-PREIS

1964 **Ph. Hartl**
H. Porsche
L. Schmieder
1966 **W. Duffek**
W. Buschulte
K. Schadow
1968 **R. Brockhaus**
R. Fischer
1970 **J. Ackermann**
E. Lubeck
1972 **W. Kortum**
K.-H. Post
1974 **G. Graf**
G. Hirzinger
1976 **H. K. Gruner**
W. Goebel
1978 **D. Rahlfs**
1980 **N. Stuckenberg**

WILHELM-HOFF-PREIS

1964 **E. A. Bockemuller**
1966 **W. Bollermann**
1968 **E. D. Dickmanns**
1970 **E. D. Dickmanns**
1972 **H. Fuchs**
K.-L. Chao
1974 **M. Ch. Eckstein**
1976 **B. Krag**
H. Subke
G. Hoffmann
1978 **G. Kreisselmeier**
1980 **D. Hanke**
F. Henschel
H.-H. Lange

ERNST-MACH-PREIS

1964 **F. Bartlma**
D. Hummel
1966 **W. Schneider**
1968 **W. Lorenz-Meyer**
M. Fiebig
1970 **W. Korner**
R. Stuff
1972 **P.-A. Mackrodt**
M. Becker
1974 **H. Korner**
W. Geissler
1976 **W. Neise**
A. W. Neuberger
1978 **C. Weiland**
1980 **F. Lehthaus**

ERICH-TREFFTZ-PREIS

1964 **E. Berger**
A. Timme
D. Rues
1966 **P. Colak-Antic**
P. Freymuth
A. Michalke
1968 **K. Kirchgassner**
1970 **E. Wedemeyer**
T. Just
S. Stepanek
1972 **H. Sobieczky**
E. H. Hirschel
1974 **W. L. Bohn**
P. Hoffmann
H. Eberius

1976 **R. Schodl**
1978 **A. Schrott**
V. Stein
1980 **C.-H. Chun**

HUGO-JUNKERS-PREIS

1964 **G. Fischer**
O. Heise
1966 **H.-W. Forsching**
K. Schiffner
1968 **G. Jacoby**
H. Oette
1970 **H. Meyer-Piening**
1972 **B. Geier**
K. Rohwer
H. Nowack
1974 **G. Lutjering**
E. Breitbach
1976 **V. Carstens**
D. Munz
1978 **R. Kochendorfer**
1980 **R. Freymann**

ERICH-REGENER-PREIS

1968 **E. A. Bockemuller**
1970 **W. Stricker**
H. Meinel
1972 **E. E. Triendl**
D. Paffrath
1974 **B. Dorsch**
1976 **P. Haberacker**
M. Lehner
1978 **F. Bartlma**
1980 **E. Luneburg**
J. Hagenauer

OTTO-MADER-PREIS

1964 **N. Schmidt**
H. Selzer
1966 **F. Suttrop**
G. Winterfeld
1968 **W. Peschka**
F. Engeln
H. E. Hugel
G. Krulle
1970 **R. Lo**
K. Schadow
1972 **P. Roth**
H. J. Sternfeld
1974 **J. Nitsch**
H. Weyer
D. Eckardt
1976 **F. Maisenhalder**
R. Jacobson
1978 **No award**
1980 **P. Frank**

Thomas P. Gerrity Award

AIR FORCE ASSOCIATION
1750 Pennsylvania Ave. NW, Washington D.C. 20006
(202/637-3300)

The Thomas P. Gerrity Award is presented annually for outstanding achievements in systems and logistics as applied to aerospace. A committee selects the winner from nominations submitted by individuals and organizations with deep interest in aerospace activity.

1968 **Maj. Gen. Charles G. Chandler, Jr.,** Deputy Chief of Staff for Material Pacific Air Forces
1969 **MaJ. Gen. Frederick E. Morris, Jr.,** Director of Data Automation, Comptroller of the Air Force
1970 **Col. Levin P. Tull,** Deputy Director of Supply & Services, Air Force Deputy Chief of Staff, Systems & Logistics
1971 **Col. Shirl M. Nelson,** Director of Supply & Services, Hq. Tactical Air Command
1972 **Col. Owen J. McGonnell,** Asst. Deputy Chief of Staff/Logistics, Hq. Aerospace Defense Command
1973 **Col. Allen R. Rodgers,** Hq. 8th Air Force, D.C.S./ Logistics
1974 **Brig. Gen. Jack W. Waters,** P.A.C.A.F.
1975 **Lt. Gen. Charles E. Buckingham,** Comptroller of the Air Force
1976 **Col. James A. MacDouglas,** Deputy Commander for Maintenace, Air Defense Weapons Center, A.D.C.O.M.
1977 **Maj. Richard E. Ford,** Chief, Logistics Initiative Branch, Hq. Pacific Air Forces
1978 **Col. James K. Lowman,** Director, Resources Management, Hq. AFLC
1979 **Col. Thorne W. Longsworth,** U.S.A.F. (Ret.)
1980 **Col. William P. Bowden,** Oklahoma City Air Logistics Center, Tinker A.F.B., Okla.

De La Vaulx Medal
Yuri A. Gagarin Gold Medal
Gold Air Medal
Gold Space Medal
Nile Gold Medal
Bronze Medal

FEDERATION AERONAUTIQUE INTERNATIONALE
6 Rue Galilee, Paris 75782, France (Tel: 723-72-52 and 720-93-20)

The De La Vaulx Medal annually honors holders of recognized absolute world records of the previous year.

1969 **Janko Lutovac** (Yugoslavia)
1970 **Pierre Lard** (France)
1971 **Nadezhda Pryakhina** (U.S.S.R.)
1972 **No award**
1973 **Pierre Lemoigne** (France)
1974 **Steven Snyder** (U.S.A.)
1975 **Gerald P. Carr** (U.S.A.)
Edward G. Gibson (U.S.A.)
William R. Pogue (U.S.A.)
1976 **T. P. Stafford** (U.S.A.)
V. Brand (U.S.A.)
D. Slayton (U.S.A.)
A. A. Leonov (U.S.S.R.)
V. N. Koubasov (U.S.S.R.)
1977 **Capt. Eldon W. Joersz** (U.S.A.)
Maj. Adolphus H. Bledsoe, Jr. (U.S.A.)
Capt. Robert C. Helt (U.S.A.)
1978 **Alexandre Fedotov** (U.S.S.R.)
Ben L. Abruzzo (U.S.A.)
Maxie Anderson (U.S.A.)
Y. V. Romanenko (U.S.S.R.)
G. M. Grechko (U.S.S.R.)
V. V. Kovalyonok (U.S.S.R.)
A. Ivanchenkov (U.S.S.R.)
1979 **Vladimir Liakhov** (U.S.S.R.)
Valery Ryumin (U.S.S.R.)

1980 Not available at press time

The Yuri A. Gagarin Gold Medal is given in memory of the first astronaut and honors the space pilot who has accomplished the highest achievement in the conquest of space. The membership nominates candidates for a secret ballot by the federation's council.

1968 Georgy Timofeevitch Beregovoi (U.S.S.R.)
1969 Charles Conrad, Jr. (U.S.A.)
1970 A.G. Nikolayev (U.S.S.R.)
V.I. Sevastinov, (U.S.S.R.)
1971 V.A. Chatalov (U.S.S.R.)
A.S. Eliseev (U.S.S.R.)
1972 John W. Young (U.S.A.)
1973 Alan L. Bean (U.S.A.)
1974 Edward G. Gibson (U.S.A.)
1975 D.K. Slayton (U.S.A.)
V.D. Brand (U.S.A.)
V.N. Koubasov (U.S.S.R.)
1976 No award
1977 No award
1978 Vladimir Kovalyonok (U.S.S.R.)
1979 Valery Ryumin (U.S.S.R.)
1980 Not available at press time

The Gold Air Medal is awarded annually on a secret ballot of the Federation's Council from nominees by the membership for outstanding achievements in the development of aeronautics by activities, work, achievements, initiative or devotion to aviation.

1925 Gen. Francesco de Pinedo, Italy
1926 Sir Alan J. Cobham, Great Britain
1927 Charles A. Lindbergh, U.S.A.
1928 Bert Hinkler, Great Britain
1929 Capt. D. Costes, France
1930 Gen. Italo Balbo, Italy
1931 Dr. Eckener, Germany
1932 Don Juan La Cierva, Spain
1933 Wiley Post, U.S.A.
1934 C.W.A. Scott, Great Britain
1935 No award
1936 Jean Mermoz, France
1937 Jean Batten, Great Britain
1938-45 No awards
1946 Igor Sikorsky, U.S.A.
1947 No award
1948 Igor Sikorsky, U.S.A.
1947 No award
1948 Capt. Charles E. Yeager, U.S.A.
1949 No award
1950 Air Commodore Sir Frank Whittle, Great Britain
1951 Ed. P. Warner, U.S.A.
1952 No award
1953 Jacqueline Cochran, U.S.A.
1954 James H. Doolittle, U.S.A.
1955 Maurice Hurel, France
1956 L.P. Twiss, Great Britain
1957 Maj. David G. Simons, U.S.A.
1958 Andrey Mickolaevich Tupolev, U.S.S.R.
1959 Pierre Satre, France
1960 No award
1961 Yuri Gagarin, U.S.S.R.
1962 Sir Geoffrey de Havilland, Great Britain
1963 No award
1964 Jacqueline Auriol, France
1965 V. Kokkinaki, U.S.S.R.
1966 Col. Robert L. Stephens, U.S.A.
1967 Alexander S. Yakovlev, U.S.S.R.
1968 Joseph A. Walker, U.S.A.
1969 S.V. Iliouchine, U.S.S.R.
1970 Jose Luis Aresti, Spain
1970 M.H.T. "Dick" Merrill, U.S.A.
1971 Elgen M. Long, U.S.A.
1972 Marina L. Popovitch, U.S.S.R.
1973 Sir Donald Anderson, Australia
1974 Alexander Fedotov, U.S.S.R.
1975 Curtis H. Pitts, U.S.A.
1976 Sholto Hamilton Georgeson, New Zealand
1977 No award
1978 Hans Werner Grosse (Federal Republic of Germany)
Ben Abruzzo (U.S.A.)
Maxie Anderson (U.S.A.)
1979 Paul MacCready (U.S.A.)
1980 Not available at press time

The Gold Space Medal, which is of equal standing with the Gold Air Medal, annually honors an astronaut who has achieved outstanding performance in space. The membership nominates candidates for a secret ballot by the Federation's Council.

1963 A. Nikolaev, U.S.S.R.
P. Popovitch, U.S.S.R.
1964 Valentina Teretchkova, U.S.S.R.
1965 V. Komarov, U.S.S.R.
K. Feotistov, U.S.S.R.
B. Egorov, U.S.S.R.
1966 A.A. Leonov, U.S.S.R.
1967 James A. Lovell, Jr., U.S.A.
1968 Frank Borman, U.S.A.
1969 Neil A. Armstrong, U.S.A.
1970 James A. Lovell, Jr., U.S.A.
1971 David R. Scott, U.S.A.
1972 Eugene A. Cernan, U.S.A.
1973 Charles Conrad, Jr., U.S.A.
1974 Gerald P. Carr, U.S.A.
1975 Thomas P. Stafford, U.S.A.
Alexei Arkhipovitch Leonov, U.S.S.R.
1976 Michael Collins, U.S.A.
1977 Georgui Beregovoi, U.S.S.R.
1978 Yuri Romanenko, U.S.S.R.
Guerogui Grechko, U.S.S.R.
1979 Vladimir Liakhov, U.S.S.R.
1980 Not available at press time

The Nile Gold Medal is presented annually to the individual, group or organization for distinguished work in aerospace education, especially during the preceding year. Any active member of the federation can propose one candidate each year for selection by the International Aerospace Education Committee.

1972 Aer Lingus Training Section, Ireland
1973 Olavi M. Lumes, Finland
1974 Wayne R. Matson, U.S.A.
1975 General A.A. Rafat, Iran
1976 Vyatcheslav Bashkirov, U.S.S.R.
1977 George A. C. Cox, Great Britain
1978 La Ligue des Cadets de l'Air du Canada
1979 Michael Collins, U.S.A.
1980 Not available at press time

The Federation Aeronatuique Internationale annually awards a Bronze Medal for distinguished achievements.

1962 Jose Luis Aresti Aguirre, Spain
L. Hotteghem, France
1963 Gilbert Salomon, France
1964 Joseph K. Gaisbacher, Austria
1965 No award
1966 Henry J. Nicholls, Great Britain
1967 A. Gehriger, Switzerland

1968 **Jean Bleriot,** France
1969 **Maj. Jozef R. Fozo,** Austria
1970 **Ann Welch,** Great Britain
1971 **Odette Rousseau Balesi,** France
1972 **Ronald G. Moulton,** Great Britain
1973 **Col. Robert Genty,** France
1974 **Antal Reti,** Hungary
1975 **Werner Garitz,** German Democratic Republic
1976 **Fred Konz,** Luxembourg
1977 **Uwe Beckmann,** Federal Republic of Germany
1978 **G. A. (Peter) Lloyd,** Australia
1979 **Not available at press time**
1980 **Not available at press time**

Edward Warner Award

INTERNATIONAL CIVIL AVIATION ORGANIZATION
1000 Sherbrooke St. NW, Montreal, Quebec, H3A 2R4, Canada (514/285-8219)

The Edward Warner Award is given by ICAO on behalf of its 138 member states to an individual or institution for outstanding contributions towards the furthering of civil aviation. A nominations committee recommends the recipient of the gold medal for the approval of the ICAO council.

1959 **Albert Plesman** (Netherlands), Founder and President of KLM Royal Dutch Airlines
1961 **International Aeronautical Federation** (Est. 1905, Paris), Worldwide organization of national aero clubs
1963 **Max Hymans** (France), Secretary General for civil aviation in France; President of Air France
1965 **William Hildred** (Great Britain), Director General of Civil Aviation in the United Kingdom; Director General of the International Air Transport Assn.
1968 **Henri Bouche** (France), Founder of the Air Transport Institute, Paris; represented France on the ICAO Council
1971 **Ruben Martin Berta** (Brazil), Former President of Varig Airlines
1972 **Agence pour la Securite de la Navigation Aerienne en Afrique et a Madagascar,** Organization of 15 French-speaking states to ensure safety and regularity of civil air service in Africa
1973 **Shizuma Matsuo** (Japan), President and Chairman of the Board of Japan Air Lines; 23 years in government civil aviation posts including Director General of Aeronautics Safety Board and Director General of Japan Aeronautics Agency
1974 **Alex Meyer** (Federal Republic of Germany), Academician, jurist and aviator; established and directed Institute of Air Law and Space Law at Cologne University
1975 **Charles A. Lindbergh** (U.S.A.), Aviation pioneer, who through his 1927 solo flight across the Atlantic unveiled the potential of international air transport; lifetime dedication to aviation
1976 **Corporacion Centroamericana de Servicios de Navegacion Aerea** (Est. 1960), Provides efficient, coordinated air service for navigation and communications in Central American region
1977 **Mohammed Soliman El Hakim** (Egypt), former Director General of Civil Aviation who played a prominent role in the economic and technical development of civil air transport in the Arab countries.
1978 **Sir Donald Anderson,** C.B.E., (Australia), former Director General of Civil Aviation
1979 **Agnar Kofoed-Hansen** (Iceland), Director General of Civil Aviation, Iceland, for valuable contribution to international civil aviation and, in particular, for the prominent role he played in the development of air navigation services over the North Atlantic
1980 **Indalecio Regio Fernandez** (Spain), pilot, jurist and educator, he has dedicated himself with outstanding energy to the development of international civil aviation

Langley Medal

SMITHSONIAN INSTITUTION
1000 Jefferson Dr. SW, Washington, D.C. 20560 (202/6284422)

The Langley Medal, which is of gold, is awarded as merited for especially significant investigations connected with the sciences of aeronautics and astronautics.

1909 **Wilbur and Orville Wright**
1913 **Glenn H. Curtis**
Gustave Eiffel
1927 **Charles A. Lindbergh**
1929 **Charles Matthews Manly**
Richard E. Byrd
1935 **Joseph S. Ames**
1955 **Jerome C. Hunsaker**
1960 **Robert H. Goddard**
1962 **Hugh Latimer Dryden**
1964 **Alan B. Shepard, Jr.**
1967 **Wernher von Braun**
1971 **Samuel Phillips**
1976 **James Webb**
Grover Loening
1980 **R.T. Jones**
Charles Stark Draper

David C. Schilling Award

AIR FORCE ASSOCIATION
1750 Pennsylvania Ave. NW, Washington D.C. 20006 (202/637-3300)

The David C. Schilling Award, until 1956 called the Flight Trophy, is presented annually for the most outstanding contribution to the field of flight. A committee selects the winner from nominations received from organizations and individuals with an interest in aerospace activity.

1948 **Herbert H. Hoover,** N.A.C.A. Test Pilot
1949 **Bill Odom,** private pilot
1950 **Capt. James Jabara,** world's first jet ace
1951 **Brig. Gen. Albert Boyd,** Commanding General, Edwards A.F.B.
1952 **Col. David C. Schilling,** U.S.A.F.
1953 **Third Air Rescue Group,** MATS
1954 **Maj. Charles E. Yeager,** U.S.A.F.
1955 **Maj. Stuart Childs,** USAF
George Welch
1956 **Lt. Col. Frank K. Everest,** U.S.A.F.
1957 **Col. Patrick D. Fleming,** U.S.A.F.
1958 **Capt. Iven C. Kincheloe,** U.S.A.F.
1959 **Tactical Air Command**
1960 **Lt. Gen. Elwood R. Quesada,** F.A.A. Administrator

1961 **Maj. Robert M. White,** U.S.A.F., **A. Scott Crossfield,** North American Aviation, Inc., and **Joseph A. Walker,** N.A.S.A. —X-15 Project
1962 **Maj. Robert M. White,** U.S.A.F., America's "first winged astronaut"
1963 **Maj. L. Gordon Cooper, Jr.,** Mercury astronaut
1964 **Major Sidney J. Kubesch,** B-58 pilot
1965 **Col. Frank Borman,** Gemini 7 command pilot
1966 **Maj. Hallett P. Marston,** 15th Tactical Reconnaissance Photo Squadron
1967 **Col. Robin Olds,** U.S.A.F.
1968 **Capt. Albert R. Kaiser,** U.S.A.F.
1969 **No award**
1970 **Maj. James M. Rhodes, Jr.,** U.S.A.F.
1971 **Col. David R. Scott, Col. James B. Irwin, Lt. Col. Alfred M. Worden** —Apollo 15 crew
1972 **1st Strategic Reconnaissance Squadron,** SAC
1973 **17th Air Division,** 8th AF (SAC)
1974 **Military Airlift Command**
1975 **Maj. George B. Stokes,** 41st Recon Weather Rescue Wing, McClellan AFB, Calif.
1976 **Capt. Donald R. Backlund, 1551st Flying Training Squadron, Kirtland A.F.B., and Capt. Roland W. Purser,** Hq., Aerospace
1977 **4440th Tactical Fighter Group,** Nellis A.F.B., Nevada
1978 **Col. Joe H. Engle,** U.S.A.F., **Col. C. Gordon Fullerton,** U.S.A.F., **Fred Haise, Jr.,** and **Cmdr. Richard Truly,** U.S.N., astronauts
1979 **Maj. Dennis R. Mangum,** TAC
1980 **Not available at press time**

Distinguished Achievement Award

WINGS CLUB
The Biltmore, Madison Ave. and 43rd St., New York, N.Y. 10017 (212/867-1770)

The Distinguished Achievement Award is given annually for outstanding public service "of enduring value to aviation." A four-foot aluminum and rosewood sculpture designed by Toshiko Sakow on permanent display at the Wings Club bears the names of the recipients, who are presented with a citation. Members are invited to submit nominations for selection by an awards committee.

1975 **Gen. James A. Doolittle**
1976 **Neil Armstrong**
1977 **Laurance S. Rockefeller**
1978 **Willaim A. Patterson**
Robert F. Six
Cyrus R. Smith
Juan T. Trippe
1979 **William M. Allen**
Donald W. Douglas
Hall L. Hibbard
1980 **Sir Frank Whittle**
Hans von Ohain
Sir Stanley Hooker
Jack S. Parker
Arthur E. Smith

Wright Brothers Trophy

NATIONAL AERONAUTIC ASSOCIATION
821 15th St. NW, Washington, D.C. 20005 (202/347-2808)

The Wright Brothers Trophy, a replica of the Wright brothers' aircraft, is given annually to an American who, as a civilian, has rendered personal and direct service to American aviation. A seven-member jury appointed by the president of the association selects the winner.

1948 **William F. Durand**
1949 **Charles A. Lindbergh**
1950 **Grover Loening**
1951 **Jerome C. Hunsaker**
1952 **Lt. Gen. James A. Doolittle, USAF**
1953 **Carl Hinshaw,** U.S. Representative
1954 **Theodore von Karman**
1955 **Hugh L. Dryden**
1956 **Edward P. Warner**
1957 **Stuart Symington,** U.S. Senator
1958 **John Frederick Victory**
1959 **William P. McCracken, Jr**
1960 **Frederick C. Crawford**
1961 **A.S. "Mike" Monroney,** U.S. Representative and Senator
1962 **John Stack**
1963 **Donald W. Douglas, Sr.**
1964 **Harry F. Guggenheim**
1965 **Jerome Lederer**
1966 **Juan Terry Trippe**
1967 **Igor I. Sikorsky**
1968 **Warren G. Magnuson,** U.S. Senator
1969 **William M. Allen**
1970 **C.R. Smith**
1971 **Howard W. Cannon,** U.S. Senator
1972 **John H. Shaffer,**
1973 **Barry M. Goldwater,** U.S. Senator
1974 **Richard T. Whitcomb**
1975 **Clarence L. "Kelly" Johnson**
1976 **William Allan Patterson**
1977 **Ira C. Aker**
1978 **Jennings Randolph,** U.S. Senator
1979 **T. A. Wilson**
1980 **Olive Ann Beech**

Conserv

ation & Environment

Contents

Related Awards

Frank A. Chambers Award
S. Smith Griswold Award
Richard Beatty Mellon Award

AIR POLLUTION CONTROL ASSOCIATION
Box 2861, Pittsburgh, Pa. 15230 (412/621-1090)

The Frank A. Chambers Award recognizes major achievement in the science and art of air pollution control on a technical level. The winner receives a plaque.

1955 Moyer D. Thomas
1956 Ward F. Davidson
1957 Walter A. Schmidt
1958 Arie Jan Haagen-Smit
1959 Robert E. Swain
1960 No award
1961 Philip A. Leighton
1962 Bert L. Richards
1963 No award
1964 Charles W. Gruber
1965 Morris A. Katz
1966 Louis C. McCabe
1967 No award
1968 Sir Oliver Graham Sutton
1969 W. C. L. Hemeon
1970 A. Paul Altshuller
1971 Harry J. White
1972 No award
1973 W. L. Faith
1974 James P. Lodge
1975 E. R. Hendrickson
1976 Richard B. Engdahl
1977 Irving A. Singer
1978 Gaylord W. Penney
1979 No award
1980 Hiromi Niki

The S. Smith Griswold Award honors accomplishment in the prevention and control of air pollution by an individual who is a past or present governmental agency staff member. The winner receives a plaque.

1972 Robert L. Chass
1973 William H. Megonnell
1974 John A. Maga
1975 William A. Munroe
1976 Charles M. Copley, Jr.
1977 Morton Sterling
1978 Don R. Goodwin
1979 Charles R. Barden
1980 Alexander Rihm

The Richard Beatty Mellon Award goes to an individual whose contributions of a civic nature have aided the abatement of air pollution. The winner receives a plaque.

1956 Edward R. Weidlein, Sr.
1957 Raymond R. Tucker
1958 No award
1959 John F. Barkley
1960 Robert A. Kehoe
1961 No award
1962 Richard K. Mellon
1963 R. L. Ireland
1964 No award
1965 Edmund S. Muskie
1966 Leslie Silverman
1967 Arnold Marsh
1968 No award
1969 Vernon G. Mackenzie
1970 Arthur C. Stern
1971 Allen D. Brandt
1972 John T. Middleton
1973 No award
1974 W. Brad Drowley
1975 Maurice F. Strong
1976 No award
1977 Bernard J. Steigerwald
1978 No award
1979 No award
1980 Harold J. Paulus

Audubon Medal

NATIONAL AUDUBON SOCIETY
950 Third Ave., New York, N.Y. 10022 (212/832-3200)

The Audubon Medal, which is of gold, annually honors an individual who has served the cause of conservation.

1947 Hugh Bennett
1948 No award
1949 Ira N. Gabrielson
1950 John D. Rockefeller, Jr.
1951 No award
1952 Louis Bromfield
1953 No award
1954 No award
1955 Walt Disney
1956 Ludlow Griscom
1957 No award
1958 No award
1959 Olaus J. Murie
1960 Jay N. Darling
1961 Clarence Cottam
1962 William O. Douglas
1963 Rachel Carson
1964 Laurance S. Rockefeller
1965 No award
1966 A. Starker Leopold
1967 Stewart L. Udall
1968 Fairfield Osborn
1969 Horace M. Albright
1970 No award
1971 No award
1972 Roger Tory Peterson
1973 Barbara Ward
1974 Governor Tom McCall
1975 Maurice Strong
1976 John Oakes
1977 Russell Peterson

Burroughs Medal

JOHN BURROUGHS MEMORIAL ASSOCIATION
15 W. 77th St., New York, N.Y. 10024 (212/873-1300)

The Burroughs Medal honors a literary naturalist for a book published in English within the previous two years which combines literary merit and scientific worth. A five-person jury selects the winner of the bronze medal.

1926 William Beebe, *Pheasants of the World*
1927 Ernest Thompson Seton, *Lives of Game Animals*
1928 John Russell McCarthy, *Nature Poems*
1929 Frank M. Chapman, *Handbook of North American Birds*

1930 **Archibald Rutledge,** *Peace in the Heart*
1931 **No award**
1932 **Frederick S. Dellenbaugh,** *A Canyon Voyage*
1933 **Oliver Perry Medsgar,** *Spring; Summer; Fall; Winter*
1934 **W.W. Christman,** *Wild Pasture Pine*
1935 **No award**
1936 **Charles Crawford Ghorst,** *Recordings of Bird Calls*
1937 **No award**
1938 **Robert Cushman Murphy,** *Oceanic Birds of South America*
1939 **T. Gilbert Pearson,** *Adventures in Bird Protection*
1940 **Arthur Cleveland Bent,** *Life Histories of North American Birds*
1941 **Louis J. Halle, Jr.,** *Birds Against Man*
1942 **Edward Armstrong,** *Birds of the Grey Wind*
1943 **Edwin Way Teale,** *Near Horizons*
1944 **No award**
1945 **Rutherford Platt,** *This Green World*
1946 **Mr. and Mrs. Lee Jaques,** *Snowshoe Country*
1947 **No award**
1948 **Theodora Stanwell-Fletcher,** *Driftwood Valley*
1949 **Mr. & Mrs. Allan Cruickshank,** *Flight into Sunshine*
1950 **Roger Tory Peterson,** *Birds over America*
1951 **No award**
1952 **Rachel Carson,** *The Sea Around Us*
1953 **Gilbert Klingel,** *The Bay*
1954 **Joseph Wood Krutch,** *The Desert Year*
1955 **Wallace B. Grange,** *Those of the Forest*
1956 **Guy Murchie,** *Song of the Sky*
1957 **Archie Carr,** *The Windward Road*
1958 **Robert Porter Allen,** *On the Trail of Vanishing Birds*
1959 **No award**
1960 **John Kieran,** *Natural History of New York City*
1961 **Loren C. Eiseley,** *The Firmament of Time*
1962 **George Miksch Sutton,** *Iceland Summer*
1963 **Adolph Murie,** *A Naturalist in Alaska*
1964 **John Hay,** *The Great Beach*
1965 **Paul Brooks,** *Roadless Area*
1966 **Louis Darling,** *The Gull's Way*
1967 **Charlton Ogburn,** *The Winter Beach*
1968 **Hal Borland,** *Hill Country Harvest*
1969 **Louis deKiriline Lawrence,** *The Lovely and The Wild*
1970 **Victor B. Scheffer,** *The Year of The Whale*
1971 **John K. Terres,** *From Laurel Hill to Siler's Bog*
1972 **Robert Arbib,** *The Lord's Woods*
1973 **Elizabeth Barlow,** *The Forests and Wetlands of New York City*
1974 **Sigurd F. Olson,** *Wilderness Days*
1975 **No award**
1976 **Ann Haymond Zwinger,** *Run, River, Run*
1977 **Aldo Leopold,** *Sand County Almanac Illustrated*
1978 **Ruth Kirk,** *Desert, The American Southwest*
1979 **Barry H. Lopez,** *Of Wolves and Men*
1980 **Not available at press time**

Eminent Ecologist Award

ECOLOGICAL SOCIETY OF AMERICA
c/o Paul Risser, Chief, Illinois Natural History Survey, 172 Natural Resources Bldg., 607 Peabody, Champaign, Ill. 61820 (217/333-6830)

The Eminent Ecologist Award annually honors outstanding contributions to the field either in teaching or research.

1954 **H. S. Conrad,** botany, Grinnell
1955 **A. H. Wright,** zoology, Cornell
1956 **G. B. Rigg,** botany, University of Washington
1957 **D. P. Schmidt,** herpetology, Chicago
1958 **A. W. Sampson,** forestry, University of California
1959 **H. A. Gleason,** botany, New York Botanical Garden
1960 **W. P. Cottam,** botany, University of Utah
1961 **Charles Elton,** animal ecology, Oxford University
1962 **G. E. Hutchinson,** limnology, Yale
1963 **W. Cooper,** botany, Minnesota
1964 **S. R. Dice,** zoology, Michigan
1965 **Paul B. Sears,** botany, retired
1966 **A. Redfield,** marine biology, retired
1967 **A. E. Emerson,** zoology, retired
1968 **Victor Shelford,** zoology, retired
1969 **Stanley Cain,** botany, University of Michigan
1970 **Murray F. Buell,** botany, Rutgers
1971 **Thomas Park,** zoology, University of Chicago
1972 **Ruth Patrick,** limnology, Academy of Natural Sciences
1973 **No award**
1974 **Eugene P. Odum,** ecosystem ecology, University of Georgia
1975 **C. H. Muller,** ecology-community-allelopathy, University of California, Santa Barbara
1976 **Alton Lindsey,** plant ecologist, Purdue University
1977 **W. B. McDougall,** plant ecology, Northern Arizona Museum
1978 **S. Charles Kendeigh,** animal ecology, University of Illinois
1979 **Rexford F. Danbenmire,** plant ecology, Washington State University
1980 **Don W. Tinkle,** animal ecology, University of Michigan

Energy Achievement Award

NATIONAL ENERGY FOUNDATION
366 Madison Ave., Ste 705, New York, N.Y. 10017
(212/697-2920 and 212/697-6975)

The Energy Achievement Award is given annually for meritorious efforts in the conservation of energy.

1977 **Public Broadcasting Service**
American Association for the Advancement of Science
1978 **Maurice F. Granville,** Texaco Inc.
1979 **J. Stanford Smith,** International Paper Co.
1980 **Charles L. Brown,** American Telephone and Telegraph Co.
Thornton F. Bradshaw, Atlantic Richfield Co.

Award for Environmental Quality

NATIONAL ACADEMY OF SCIENCES
2101 Constitution Ave., Washington, D.C. 20418
(202/389-6134)

The Academy's annual Award for Environmental Quality is given to honor significant contributions to environmental quality or in the control of pollution. The award, established in honor of long-time Academy member Frederick Gardner Correll, is not currently given

1972 **Arie Jan Haagen-Smit**
1973 **W. Thomas Edmondson**
1974 **G. Evelyn Hutchinson**

1975 **John T. Middleton**
1976 **David M. Evans**
1977 **Miron Heinselman**

Europa Nostra Awards

EUROPA NOSTRA
86 Vincent Sq., London SW1P 2PG, United Kingdom
(01-834-5886)

The Europa Nostra Awards, which are medals and diplomas sponsored by the Franklin Mint, annually honor projects completed within the preceding 10 years that contribute to the conservation of Europe's architectural and natural heritage. Entries may be submitted by a governmental authority at any level, conservation society, owner, occupant, architect or designer. An international committee selects the winners.

MEDAL

1978 **Bremen** (Germany), For restoration and reanimation of the Schnoor District
Building Design Partnership (United Kingdom), For construction of a modern commercial center in Durham which harmonizes with the medieval character of its surroundings
Heusden (Netherlands), For superb restoration of the old town and its fortifications
Werdenberg (Switzerland), For comprehensive renovation of the small village and adaption of medieval houses to present requirements

1979 **Krems** (Austria), For excellent and comprehensive restoration of the town's historic quarters
Schwabach (Germany), For creation of fine pedestrian area and underground parking lot in the market square
Amsterdam (Netherlands), For admirable restoration and modernization of a continung series of old buildings
San Lorenzo de el Escorial (Spain), For the restoration of the Real Coliseo de Carlos III, an ancient theatre
Judburgh (United Kingdom), For rehabilitation of the town center and adaption of old buildings to new uses

1980 **Hornu** (Belgium), For restoration of early 19th-century industrial complex and its conversion into a cultural center
Osnabruck (Germany), For restoration of a 14th- and 16th-century house and its adaption as the city music library
Monemvassia (Greece), For extensive restoration and reconstruction of numerous old buildings in the ancient town
Paradores (Spain), Comprehensive restoration of historic castles and other old buildings and their conversion into *paradore* hotels
Covent Garden (United Kingdom), For the successful conversion of the former central market building into a high-grade shopping center

DIPLOMA

1978 **Salzburg** (Austria), For creating a superb panorama by floodlighting historic buildings
Selskabet for Bygnings- og Landskabkultur and Dansmarks Turistad (Copenhagen, Denmark), For converting a grain warehouse into a modern hotel
Selskabet til Bevarelse af Gamle Bygninger I Helsingor (Denmark), For restoration of a fine old house
Madame de Lacretelle (France), For fine restoration of the Chateau d'O in Normandy
Hameln (Germany), For restoration and conversion of old timbered house into a youth cultural center
Rotherburg ob der Tauber (Germany), For restoration and conversion of an old building for use as a cultural center
Monastery of Firogion (Greece), Restoration on the island of Sifnos
T. Zervas and **V. Zerva-Bozineki** (Greece), Architects of the restoration of abandoned buildings and their conversion into a resort in Koutsounari, Crete
Knappogue Castle (Ireland), Restoration
Deventer (Netherlands), Restoration of the old Berkwartier quarter
Stavanger (Norway), Conversion of warehouses into restaurant
Santander (Spain), Restoration and conversion of a castle into a museum
Covarrubias (Spain), Restoration of a 16th-century building
Skokloster Palace (Sweden), For restoration of palace near Stockholm and conversion into a museum
Washington Development Corp. (United Kingdom), For conversion of old buildings into the Biddick Farms Arts Centre
Portsmouth (United Kingdom), For restoration of Southsea Castle and adaptation as a museum
Culzean Country Park (United Kingdom), For conversion of an old building into a reception center
Essex County Council (United Kingdom), For restoration of 15-th century guildhall in Thaxted
Liverpool City Council (United Kingdom), For Inner City Conservation and Rehabilitation Programme

1979 **Graz** (Austria), For comprehensive restoration and revitalization of city center and creation of pedestrian areas
Bad Muhllacken (Austria), For design of new hotel in the countryside which respects its rural surroundings
Bruges (Belgium), For comprehensive restoration and revitalization of the historic city center
Namur (Belgium), For restoration of buildings in an ancient quarter and their adaptation to new uses
Avignon (France), For rehabilitation of the Palace of the Popes and the creation of a congress center with an underground parking lot
Troyes (France), For the restoration of the St.-Jean quarter and the creation of a pedestrian area
Bad Reichenhall (Germany), For extensive diversion of traffic from the city center and the creation of a garden area
Dusseldorf (Germany), For comprehensive reconstruction of the Rheinhalle as a fine concert hall
Eichstatt (Germany), For completion of the first of eight sectors of the old town which are being restored and renovated
Kirberg (Germany), For restoration of a notable 16th-century building and adaptation to present requirements
Winterbach (Germany), For restoration of the ancient town center and conversion of buildings to civic uses
Island of Santorini (Greece), For rehabilitation of the old village of Oia as a tourist area which preserved its existing character
Dublin (Ireland), For construction of a group of modern houses which harmonize with their older neighbors

Sterzing (Italy), For restorztion of the town hall and creation of a pedestrian area
Valletta (Malta), For restoration of the Sacred Infirmary of the Knights of St. John of Jerusalem and adaptation as a Mediterranean Conference Center
Vorden (Netherlands), For restoration of an old castle and conversion into the town hall
Willemstad (Netherlands), For restoration of a 16th-century building and its conversion into a town hall
Malmo (Sweden), For restoration of buildings and courtyards in the ancient quarter of St. Gertrud for leisuretime activities
Stockholm (Sweden), For the restoration of Fersen Palace and conversion into a bank
Sion (Switzerland), For restoration of the old town and creation of pedestrian areas
St. Gallen (Switzerland), For restoration of old buildings in the town center and the conversion of the Convent of St. Katherine into a library
Istanbul (Turkey), For restoration of the Malta Pavilion and its adaptation for public receptions and conferences
Ashby de la Zouch (United Kingdom), For restoration of 18th-century buildings and adaptation for use as shops
Isle of Barra (United Kingdom), For design of a new hotel which harmonizes with the rugged coastline and countryside
Fraserburgh (United Kingdom), For comprehensive redevelopment of town center in harmony with character, scale and texture of existing buildings
Leeds (United Kingdom), For restoration of a notable Victorian building in the city center and adaptation into offices
White Horse Hill (United Kingdom), For creation of discreetly sited visitors' parking lot

1980 **Styria** (Austria), For restoration of Rothelstein Castle and adaptation into a youth hostel
Klagenfurt (Austria), For comprehensive renovation of Cathedral Square and enlargement of the pedestrian area
Helmstedt (Germany), For restoration, repainting and floodlighting of a 16th-century university building and adaptation as a concert hall
Alsfeld (Germany), For restoration of two 17th-century townhouses and conversion to new uses
Luneburg (Germany), For external and internal restoration of a merchant's house
Wurzburg (Germany), For construction of a department store on a derelict site in the city center which harmonizes with its older neighbors
Heidelberg (Germany), For creation of attractive pedestrian area in the old city
Landshut (Germany), For reconstruction after a serious fire of Trausnitz Castle and conversion into a municipal cultural center
County Clare (Ireland), For design of an entrance building to Aillwee Cave
Brielle (Netherlands), For comprehensive restoration of old buildings and ramparts
Bergen (Norway), For rehabilitation of an 18th-century wooden building
Zaragoza (Spain), For restoration of the Palacio de los Pardo and adaptation into a museum
Lugo (Spain), For restoration of the Roman Wall and removal of numerous later buildings erected around it
Stockholm/Sibyllegatan (Sweden), For restoration of the 17th-century Crown Bakery and adaptation as a music museum and concert hall
Stockholm/Royal Palace (Sweden), For restoration of the basement and adaptation as the Royal Armory and Museum for Crown Treasures
Solothurn (Switzerland), For creation of attractive pedestrian area
Edinburgh (United Kingdom), For removal of unsightly shopfront extensions on early 19th-century buildings and restoration of original facades
Kenilworth (United Kingdom), For comprehensive restoration of a 16th-century hamlet
Wallingford (United Kingdom), For extensive revitalization of historic market town
Esher (United Kingdom), For large-scale restoration of Claremont Landscape Garden and provision of discreetly designed visitor's facilities
Kingston-upon-Hull (United Kingdom), For conversion of waterfront warehouse into a restaurant and hotel

J. Paul Getty Wildlife Conservation Prize

WORLD WILDLIFE FUND
1601 Connecticut Ave. NW, Washington, D.C.

The World Wildlife Fund administers the J. Paul Getty Wildlife Conservation Prize, which is accompanied by an honorarium, presented annually for outstanding achievement in wildlife and habitat conservation of international significance.

1978 **Maj. Ian R. Grimwood,** Kenya
1979 **Boonsong Lekagul,** Thailand
1980 **Harold J. Coolidge,** U.S.A.

Hodgkins Medal and Prize

SMITHSONIAN INSTITUTION
1000 Jefferson Dr. SW, Washington, D.C. 20560
(202/628-4422)

The Hodgkins Medal and Prize, which consists of a gold medal and a cash award, is given as merited to encourage and/or honor noteworthy contributions to environmental studies both from a scientific and a social standpoint. It is generally awarded annually or biennially after a lapse of several decades from the initial presentations.

1899 **James Dewar,** Great Britain
1902 **J.J. Thompson,** Great Britain
1965 **Sydney Chapman,** United States
Joseph Kaplan, United States
Marcel Nicolet, Belgium
1967 **John Grahame Douglas Clark,** Great Britain
Fritz W. Went, United States
1969 **Jule Gregory Charney,** United States
Arie Haagen-Smit, United States
1971 **Lewis Mumford,** Great Britain; Italy
1973 **Walter Orr Roberts,** United States
1976 **E. Cuyler Hammond,** United States
1978 **Alexander Delgarno,**United States

Alexander von Humboldt Medal

STIFTUNG F.V.S.

Georgsplatz 10, 2 Hamburg 1, Federal Republic of Germany (Tel: 33 04 00 and 33 06 00)

The Alexander von Humboldt Medal, which is of gold, is given annually for achievements in conservation and nature-park work in Europe.

1961 **Theodor Sonnemann,** Limperich bei Bonn, Germany
1962 **Hubert Schmitt-Degenhardt,** Aachen, Germany
1963 **Karl Asal,** Freiburg, Germany
1964 **Renzo Videsott,** Turin, Italy
1965 **Arthur Uehlinger,** Schaffhausen, Switzerland
1966 **Justus Danckwerts,** Hannover, Germany
Egon Selchow, Hamburg, Germany
1967 **Ludwig Seiterich,** Konstanz, Germany
1968 **Jean-Paul Harroy,** Brussels
1969 **Emil Meynen,** Bad Godesberg, Germany
Herbert Offner, Bonn, Germany
1970 **Sir Peter Smithers,** Vico Morcote, Switzerland
Helmut Schaefer, Hoffnungsthal, Germany
1971 **Tassilo Troscher,** Wiesbaden, Germany
1972 **Paul Hochstrasser,** Richterswil, Switzerland
Nikolaus Freiherr von und zu Bodman, Moggingen/Bodensee, Germany
1973 **Wolfgang Engelhardt,** Munich
1974 **Jean Servat,** Paris
1975 **H.R.H. Prince Bernhard of the Netherlands**
1976 **Reinhold Tuxen,** Todenmann uber Rinteln, Germany
1977 **Hermann Kerl,** Clausthal-Zellerfeld, Germany
1978 **Ernest Preiswig,** Hanover, Germany
1979 **Jean Sernet,** Toulouse, France
Gerhard Olsckowy, Bonn, Germany
1980 **No award**

Award for Distinguished Service in Environmental Planning

INDUSTRIAL DEVELOPMENT RESEARCH COUNCIL

1954 Airport Rd., Peachtree Air Terminal, Atlanta, Ga. 30341 (404/458-6026)

The Council and Conway Publications, Inc., annually present the Award for Distinguished Service in Environmental Planning for the harmonizing of new industrial facilities with the environment. A selection committee of council members and Conway personnel chooses the winner.

1972 **James B. Coulter,** Secretary, Maryland Dept. of Natural Resources
Charles Davis, Interstate Paper Co., Riceland, Ga.
L. Jack Davis, Gulf Coast Waste Disposal Authority, Houston, Tex.
James K. Keefe, Commissioner, Maine Dept. of Commerce and Industry
Jack Lacy, Spirit of '76, Junction City, Kans.
O.G. Linde, South Pacific Land Co., San Francisco
David F. McElroy, Northern States Power Co.
Calvin Rampton, Governor, State of Utah
Nelson Rockefeller, Governor, State of New York
Walt Disney World Co.
1973 **Jay D. Aldridge,** Penn's Southwest Assn., Pittsburgh
Max Brewer, Commissioner, Alaska Dept. of Environmental Conservation
Charles Dougherty, Union Electric Co., St. Louis
Paul A. Duke, Duke Enterprises, Norcross, Ga.
John J. Gilligan, Governor, State of Ohio
Harold Jensen, Real Estate IC Industries, Chicago
Howard T. Odum, Dept. of Environmental Engineering, University of Florida
Roger M. Scott, City Manager, Virginia Beach, Va.
Robert J. Worden, Executive Director, Arizona Dept. of Planning and Economic Development
1974 **Thomas W. Carmody,** SHARE, Ponce, P.R.
Charles Fraser, Palmas del Mar Co., Palmas del Mar, P.R.
Damon Harrison, Kentucky Commissioner of Commerce
Wendell J. Kelly, Illinois Power Co.
J. Andrew McAlister, Georgia Kraft Co., Rome and Macon, Ga.
Muskegon County (Mich.) Planning Commission
1975 **AT&T Bedminster and Basking Ridge (N.J.) facilities**
Joseph Baxter, City Councilman, Franklin, Ohio
Pierre Gousseland, AMAX, Inc., Fort Madison, Iowa
Donald Hall, Hallmark Cards, Kansas City, Mo.
John P. Moran, Vice President for Facilities, Princeton University, N.J.
Grant G. Simmons, Jr., Simmons Co., Norcross, Ga.
Raymond L. Watson, The Irvine Co., Irvine, Calif.
1976 **August A. Busch III,** Anheuser-Busch, Inc., Williamsburg, Va.
Robert F. Denig, Deere and Co., Davenport, Iowa
Wayne S. Doran, Ford Motor Land Development Co., Detroit
David L. Duensing, Armour & Co., Scottsdale, Ariz.
Stanley D. Fisher, F.I.P. Corp., Farmington, Conn.
Armand Hammer, Occidental Petroleum Corp., El Cajon, Calif.
Charles T. Keenan, Western Environmental Trade Assn.
1977 **C.H. Barre,** Marathon Oil Co.
Dwight F. Barger, Louisiana Refining Div., Marathon Oil Co.
Ernest H. Bennett, Textile Fibers Co., Du Pont Co., Charleston, S.C.
D. Scott Hudgens, Shenandoah Development Co., Inc.
Park Central, Dallas
William F. May, American Can Co., Milwaukee, Wisc.
Harry T. Morley, St. Louis Regional Commerce and Growth Assn.
Earl Wantland, Tektronix, Inc., Wilsonville, Ore.
Robert K. Zimmerman, Kansas City Power & Light Co.
1978 **G. Peter McColough,** Xerox Corp's International Center for Training and Management Development, Leesburg, Va.
Richard W. Morrow, Standard Oil Co.'s Amoco Chemical Cooper River Plant, S.C.
Chester Shepperly, Johns-Mannville Corp. headquarters and new town, Denver
Richard H. Sterling, Radnor Corp. Center, Radnor Township, Pa.
1979 **Louis C. Gilde,** Campbell Soup Co. wastewater purification application at various locations
William W. Eggleston, IBM Laboratory, Tucson
1980 **Roy W. James,** C.F. Industries and Wabash Valley Environmental Assn., Vigo County, Ind.
Monte C. Throdahl, Monsanto Co. Environmental Health Laboratory, Mo.

Wilhelm Leopold Pfeil Prize

STIFTUNG F.V.S.
Georgsplatz 10, 2 Hamburg 1, Federal Republic of Germany (Tel. 33 04 00 and 33 06 00)

The Wilhelm Leopold Pfeil Prize, which carries a cash award of 16,000 German marks, is awarded annually for modern, futuristic forestry in Europe. The University of Freiburg administers the award.

1963 **Victor Dieterich,** Stuttgart-Vaihingen, Germany
1964 **Gustav Kraub,** Germany
1965 **Ulrich Rodenwaldt,** Villingen, Germany
1966 **Kjeld Ladefoged,** Arhus, Netherlands
1967 **Gerben Hellinga,** Wageningen, Germany
Johannes Louis Frederic Overbeek, Zwolle, Germany
1968 **Wilhelm Hassenteufel,** Absam bei Innsbruck, Austria
Lukas Leiber, Freiburg i. Br., Germany
1969 **Hans Leibundgut,** Zurich, Switzerland
Hans Siebenbaum, Kitzeberg bei Kiel, Germany
1970 **Jon Popescu-Zeletin,** Bucharest, Rumania
1971 **Hermann Junack,** Gartow/Elbe, Germany
1972 **Jean Parde,** Nancy, France
Kurt Ruppert, Frankfurt am Main, Germany
1973 **Muharrem Miraboglu,** Ankara/Istanbul, Turkey
1974 **Gerhard Petsch,** Essen, Germany
1975 **Stanislaw Kasprzyk,** Warsaw, Poland
Josef Nikolaus Kostler, Ramsau, Germany
1976 **No award**
1977 **Carl Olof, Tamm,** Stockholm, Sweden
1978 **Ernst Jobst,** Munich, Federal Republic of Germany
1979 **Alessandro de Plilippio,** Florence, Italy
Gerhard Schlenker, Stuttgart, Federal Republic of Germany
1980 **Walter Kremser,** Hanover, Federal Republic of Germany

Charles A. Lindbergh Award

LINDBERGH MEMORIAL FUND
99 Park Ave., New York, N.Y. 10016 (212/688-3451)

The Charles A. Lindbergh Award is presented annually for careerlong achievements that balance the world of technology and nature. The award is a framed, enlarged replica of the $25,000 check awarded to Charles A. Lindbergh for his pioneering transatlantic flight.

1978 **Robert O. Anderson,** chairman, Atlantic Richfield Co. and environmentalist and humanist
1979 **Aurelio Teccei,** founder and president, Club of Rome
1980 **Edwin A. Link,** inventor of the Link pilot trainer and other devices for aviation and underwater applications

Louise du Pont Crowninshield Award
David E. Finley Award
Gordon Gray Award
President's Award

NATIONAL TRUST FOR HISTORIC PRESERVATION
1001 Connecticut Ave. NW, Washington D.C. (202/673-4000) Mailing address: 740-748 Jackson Pl. NW, Washington, D.C. 20006

The Louise du Pont Crowninshield Award is given for superlative achievement in the preservation and interpretation of sites, buildings, architecture, districts and objects of national significance. The award, which consists of a trophy and a stipend, may be made to a salaried worker, volunteer, organization, individual or several entities jointly. Nominations may be submitted for this award.

1960 **Mount Vernon Ladies Association of the Union,** Va.
1961 **Henry Francis du Pont,** Winterthur, Del.
1962 **Katherine Prentis Murphy,** N.Y. and Conn.
1963 **Mrs. Robert G. Robinson,** New Orleans, La.
1964 **Mr. and Mrs. Betram K. Little,** Brookline, Mass
1965 **Charles E. Peterson,** Philadelphia, Pa.
1966 **Ima Hogg,** Houston, Tex.
Mrs. John A. Kellenberger, N.C.
1967 **No award**
1968 **Mrs. J. M. P. Wright,** Annapolis, Md.
1969 **Mr. and Mrs. Henry N. Flynt,** Greenwich, Conn.
1970 **Frank L. Horton,** Winston-Salem, N.C.
1971 **Frances Edmunds,** Charleston, S.C.
1972 **Alice Winchester,** New York
1973 **Ricardo E. Alegria,** San Juan, P. R.
1974 **Mr. and Mrs. Jacob Morrison,** New Orleans, La.
1975 **No award**
1976 **Mrs. George Henry Warren** and **The Preservation Society of Newport County,** R.I.
1977 **San Antonio Conservation Society,** San Antonio, Tex.
1978 **Helen Duprey Bullock**
1979 **Old Post Office Landmark Committee,** St. Louis, Mo.
1980 **Ernest A. Connelly**
William J. Murtagh

The David E. Finley Award, formerly a citation that was renamed for the founder and first chairman of the Trust, is given for outstanding achievement in the preservation, restoration and interpretation of sites, buildings, architecture, districts and objects significant on a regional level. The award, which consists of a scroll, a trophy or both, may be given to a salaried worker, volunteer, organization, individual or several entities jointly. Nominations may be submitted for this award.

1971 **Foundation for Historic Christ Church, Inc.,** Irvington, Va.
James L. Cogar, President, Shakertown at Pleasant Hill, Ky.
Lydia Chichester Laird, New Castle, Del.
Society for the Preservation of Weeksville and Bedford-Stuyvesant History of Brooklyn, N.Y.
1972 **Pittsburgh History and Landmarks Foundation of Pittsburgh,** Pa.

Old Santa Fe Association, of Santa Fe, N.M.
Citizens to Preserve Overton Park of Memphis, Tenn.
1973 **Bishop Hill Heritage Association,** Bishop Hill, Ill.
Mrs. Malcolm G. Chace, Jr., Providence, R.I.
Pearl Chase, Santa Barbara, Calif.
Mrs. Lawrence K. (Amy Bess Williams) Miller, president, Shaker Community, Inc., Hancock Shaker Village, Hancock, Mass.
1974 **Wilbert Hasbrouck,** Chicago
Myra Ellen Jenkins, Santa Fe, N.M.
H. Merrill Roenke, Jr., Geneva, N.Y.
Mrs. Charles F. Loewer, Little Rock, Ark.
1975 **Harold Brooks,** Marshall, Mich.
The Community Design Commission, Medina, Ohio
Mrs. William Fluty, Wheeling, W.Va.
Mrs. Albert H. Powers, Oregon City, Ore.
Utah Heritage Foundation, Willard, Utah
1976 **Georgia Ray DeCoster and Elizabeth Musser,** St. Paul, Minn.
Anna F. Hesse and Historic Hermann, Hermann, Mo.
Junior League of Louisville, Ky.
New Mexico and Colorado Railroad Authority, Santa Fe, N.M.
1977 **Mark Twain Memorial,** Hartford, Conn.
Frank Fetch, and the German Village Society, Inc., Columbus, Ohio
Georgetown Society, Inc., Georgetown, Colo.
Pennsylvania Academy of Fine Arts, Philadelphia
1978 **Garden Club of Virginia,** Norfolk
John L. Cotter, Philadelphia
Historic Green Springs, Louisa Co., Va.
Mystic Seaport, Inc., Mystic, Conn.
Roosevelt University, Chicago, Ill.
Mrs. John V. Spachner, Chicago, Ill.
1979 **Christopher S. Bond,** Kansas City, Mo.
Camden District Heritage Foundation and Historic Camden, Inc., Camden, S.C.
Lloyd Thomas Smith, President, S/V Tool Co., Newton, Kan.
The Vizcayans, Miami, Fla.
1980 **No award**

The Gordon Gray Award, formerly a Special Award renamed in 1977 to honor the second chairman of the National Trust, recognizes outstanding achievement in special areas in support of historic preservation, though not necessarily in the field of preservation itself, such as banking, business, industry, communications media, scholarship, restoration architecture, traditional crafts, adaptive use of historical structures, public agencies or legislation. The award, which consists of a scroll, trophy or both, may go to an organization, individual or several entities jointly and may be applied for.

1971 **Ada Louise Huxtable,** *New York Times*
Nancy Carson Shirk, Boston, Mass.
Nancy Schultz, Washington D.C.
1972 **Samuel Chamberlain,** Mass.
Senator William S. James, Md.
1973 **Virginia Daiker,** Library of Congress, Washington, D.C.
George McCue, Arts and Urban Design Critic, *St. Louis Post Dispatch*
A. Edwin Kendrew, Williamsburg, Va.
1974 **Peter Pastreich,** Exec. Dir., The St. Louis Symphony Orchestra
James Marston Fitch, New York
William M. Roth, San Francisco
1975 **College of Charleston,** Charleston, S.C.
Frederick C. Williamson, Providence, R.I.
1976 **Childs Bertman Tseckares Associates, Inc.,** Boston, Mass.
Muriel Dinsmore, Eureka, Calif.
Sigma Phi Fraternity, University of Wisconsin Chapter, Madison, Wisc.
1977 **Lucille Basler,** Ste. Genevieve, Mo.
Senator and Mrs. Robert Edington, Mobile, Ala.
William Marlin, New York
1978 **Avenue Bank and Trust Company, First Bank of Oak Park, Oak Park Trust and Savings Bank,** and **Suburban Trust and Savings Bank,** Oak Park, Ill.
Gray D. Boone, Tuscaloosa, Ala.
City of Cambridge, Mass., and the Cambridge Historical Commission,
Nellie L. Longsworth, Washington, D.C.
1979 **Colonial Dames of America,** Chapter III, and **National Park Service,** Washington, D.C.
Corning Glass Works, Corning, N.Y.
City of Oakland (Cal.) Planning Department,
The Old House Journal, Brooklyn, N.Y.
Franco Scalamandre, Scalamandre Silks, Long Island City, N.Y.
Stewart Title Co., Houston, Tex.
1980 **No award**

The National Trust President's Award is given in recognition of an achievement in historic preservation of community significance. The award, which consists of a scroll may be given to an individual, organization or several entities jointly. The award may be applied for.

1977 **City Fathers of Bath, Sagadahoc Preservation Inc., Bath Area Chamber of Commerce, and Bath Maritime Museum;** Bath, Me.
Franklin Savings Association, Austin, Tex.
Kahuku Sugar Mill Restoration, Hawaii
1978 **Town of Alderson,** W. Va.
Cleveland Trust Company, Cleveland, Ohio
Rosemary Stroub Davison, Florissant, Mo.
Union Commerce Bank, Cleveland, Ohio
Whatcom County Park and Recreation Board, Bellingham, Wash.
1979 **Delaware Trust Co.,** Wilmington, Del.
Junior League of Corpus Christi, Tex.
Rose Josephine Boylan, East St. Louis, Ill.
Maritime Museum Association of San Diego, Calif.
1980 **No award**

Dr. John C. Phillips Medal

INTERNATIONAL UNION FOR THE CONSERVATION OF NATURE AND NATURAL RESOURCES
CH-1110 Morges, Switzerland (021-714401)

The Dr. John C. Phillips Medal is given every three years for distinguished service in international conservation. The medal is cast from a design by sculptor Ralph J. Menconi.

1963 **E.M. Nicholson,** Great Britain
1966 **E. Beltran,** Mexico
1969 **Salim Ali,** India
1972 **H.R.H. Prince Bernhard of the Netherlands**
1975 **Sir Frank Fraser Darling,** Great Britain
1978 **Harold J. Coolidge,** U.S.A.

Van Tienhoven Prize

STIFTUNG F.V.S.
Georgsplatz 10, 2 Hamburg 1, Federal Republic of Germany (Tel: 33 04 00 and 33 06 00)

The Van Tienhoven Prize, which carries a cash award of 10,000 German marks, is given annually for the furthering of nature parks in Europe. The University of Bonn administers the award.

1957 **Hermann Kunanz,** Konradsdorf, Germany
1958 **Walery Groetel,** Cracow, Poland
1959 **Rudi Ronge,** Hannover-Munden, Germany
Johannes Wiegand, Mainz, Germany
1960 **Sir Herbert Griffin,** London, U.K.
1961 **Otto Kraus,** Munich, Germany
1962 **Marinus van der Goes van Naters,** Wassenaar, Netherlands
1963 **Hans Krieg,** Wolfratshausen, Germany
1964 **Georges Wagner,** Clerf, Luxemburg
Konrad Schubach, Trier, Germany
1965 **Ernst Schlensker,** Arnsberg/Westphalia, Germany
1966 **Edgard Pisani,** Paris, France
1967 **Angela Piskernik,** Ljubljana, Yugoslavia
1968 **Ekkehard Lommel,** Heppenheim, Germany
1969 **Jaroslav Vesely,** Prague, Czechoslovakia
1970 **Meester Hans Paul Gorter,** Amsterdam, Netherlands
1971 **Jakob Bachtold,** Berne, Switzerland
1972 **Adalbert Mullmann,** Brilon/Westphalia, Germany
1973 **Norges Naturvernforbund,** Oslo, Norway
1974 **Erwin Stein,** Annerod/Gieben, Germany
Per Olof Swanberg, Skara, Sweden
1975 **Alexander von Mielecki,** Wolfhagen, Germany
1976 **Marcelin Melges** Ojcow, Poland
1977 **Victor Westhoff,** Groesbeek, Netherlands
1978 **Herman Delannois,** Antwerp, Belgium
Karl-Herman Reecius, Kessen, Germany
1979 **No award**
1980 **Robert Arville Boote,** London
Helmut Sauer, Eschwegel, Germany

Tyler Ecology Award

PEPPERDINE UNIVERSITY
Malibu, Calif. 90265 (213/456-2358)

Until its suspension in 1978, the Pepperdine University Tyler Ecology Award was given "to the individual or team of individuals working on a common project whose accomplishment has been recognized as conferring the greatest benefit on mankind in the fields of ecology and environment ." The recipients of the $150,000 tax-free award were selected from nominations reviewed by a selection committee composed of representatives of nine universi- ties.

1973 **Arie J. Haagen-Smit,** professor emeritus, California Institute of Technology, who discovered photochemical smog
F. Evelyn Hutchinson, professor emeritus, Yale University, for work in the chemistry of the atmosphere
Maurice F. Strong, Former executive director of the United Nations Environment Program for communications and environmental programs
1974 **Ruth Patrick,** Chairman of the Board, Academy of Natural Science (Philadelphia) for limnology and water pollution work
1975 **Charles Elton,** professor emeritus, Oxford University (England), for animal ecology
Rene Jules Dubos, professor emeritus, Rockefeller University (New York), for experiments in pathology
Abel Wolman, professor emeritus, Johns Hopkins University (Baltimore), for sanitation and water engineering
1976 **Eugene P. Odum,** professor, University of Georgia (Athens), for zoology and practical approach of ecology
1977 **Russel Train** (World Wildlife Fund), for services to conservation and wildlife protection

Pahlevi Environmental Prize

UNITED NATIONS
First Ave. & 42nd St., New York, N.Y. 10017
(212/754-1234)

The Pahlevi Environmental Prize, which carries a $50,000 honorarium, was awarded annually for exceptional contributions to world environmental protection and ecology. With the overthrow of the Shah of Iran, donor of the award, the prize was suspended.

1976 **Maurice Strong,** Founding Director of the U.N. Environmental Program
1977 **Jacques-Yves Cousteau,** Oceanographer and underwater film-maker
Sir Peter Scott, Founder, World Wildlife Fund
1978 **Thor Heyerdahl,** explorer and ethnologist
Mohamed El-Kassas, plant ecologist

"54" Founders Award

IZAAK WALTON LEAGUE OF AMERICA
1800 N. Kent St., Suite 806, Arlington, Va. 22209
(703/528-1818)

The "54" Founders Award, which consists of a plaque and citation, is presented annually to an individual, group or institution judged to have made an outstanding contribution to conservation of America's renewable natural resources during the previous year. The bronze plaque was designed by Louis Paul Jones.

1959 **Seth Gordon**
1960 **Maytag Co.**
1961 **No award**
1962 **Laurance S. Rockefeller**
1963 **Rachel Carson**
1964 **Stewart L. Udall**
1965 **Congressman Wayne N. Aspinall**
1966 **Mrs. Lyndon B. Johnson**
1967 **Paul H. Douglas**
1968 **Vinton W. Bacon**
1969 **Sigurd F. Olson**
1970 **Congressman John P. Saylor**
1971 **Raymond A. Haik**
1972 **Joseph W. Penfold**
1973 **Frank B. Hubachek**
1974 **Thomas E. Dustin**
1975 **Malcolm King**
1976 **No award**
1977 **No award**
1978 **No award**
1979 **M. L. "Bud" Heinselman**
Donald Fraser
1980 **Earl Sandvig**

National At-Large Conservation Awards
Special Conservation Award
Resources Defense Award
International Achievement Award

NATIONAL WILDLIFE FEDERATION
1412 16th St. NW, Washington, D.C. 20036 (202/797-6800)

The National At-Large Conservation Awards, consisting of Whooping Crane statuettes, recognize significant national achievement in four categories, plus special awards in fields outside these categories. The NWF Awards Committee selects winners from nominees submitted by board members, staff and affiliate officers.

CONSERVATIONIST OF THE YEAR (general achievement)

1965 Lady Bird Johnson
1966 Dorothy A. Buell
Paul H. Douglas
1967 Alan Bible
Thomas H. Kuchel
1968 Orville L. Freeman
1969 Victor J. Yannacone, Jr.
1970 H. James Morrison, Jr.
1971 Russell W. Peterson
1972 Jack C. Watson
1973 Tom McCall
1974 Russell E. Train
1975 Warren G. Magnuson
1976 William E. Towell
1977 Butler Derrick
1978 President Jimmy Carter
1979 No award
1980 Cecil Andrus

COMMUNICATIONS

1965 Outdoor Writers Assn. of America
1966 National Assn. of Broadcasters
1967 NBC News
1968 *Christian Science Monitor*
1969 Bill Mauldin
Pat Oliphant
1970 Jacques Cousteau
Patrick R. Cullen
1972 Lupi Saldana
Providence Journal-Bulletin
1974 Ernest B. Furguson
1975 *Detroit News*
1976 Brian Kelley, *Washington Star*
1977 *Arkansas Gazette* and George Fisher, cartoonist
1978 *Boston Globe*
1979 No award
1980 Walter Cronkite, CBS News

ORGANIZATION

1965 General Electric Co.
1966 Ford Motor Co.
1968 League of Women Voters
1969 Save Our Bay Action Committee
1970 Douglas MacArthur High School Anti-Pollution Committee
1972 The Scouting Movement of America
1973 The United States Jaycees Environmental Improvement Program
1974 Society for the Protection of New Hampshire Forests
1975 Gulf States Paper Corporation
1976 Rachel Carson Trust for the Living Environment
1977 Wildlife Management Institute
1978 Environmental Study Conference
1979 Izaak Walton League of America
1980 American Fisheries Society

LEGISLATIVE

1965 Frank Church
1966 Edmund S. Muskie
1967 John D. Dingell
1968 Gaylord Nelson
1969 Henry M. Jackson
1970 Philip A. Hart
1971 Henry S. Reuss
1972 Clinton P. Anderson
1973 Morris K. Udall
1974 Ernest F. Hollings
1975 Warren G. Magnuson
1976 Richard L. Ottinger
1977 Gary Hart
1978 Phillip Burton
1979 No award
1980 Edwin B. Forsythe

The Special Conservation Award honors the contributions of individuals and organizations which might otherwise be overlooked by allowing nominations to be made by persons outside the normal nomination structure for the At-Large Awards.

1965 Nelson A. Rockefeller
1968 George A. Selke
1969 Joseph W. Penfold
1972 Ralph A. MacMullan
1973 John S. Gottschalk
1974 Roger Tory Peterson
E. Budd Marter, III
Mrs. Lewis E. Smoot
1975 Richard H. Stroud
William A. Butler
Lily Peter
Arthur R. Marshall
Joseph M. Long
Carl N. Crouse
1976 Barbara Blum
Lewis E. Carpenter
Henry E. Clipper
William Hargis, Jr.
1977 Steve Galizioli
Seth Gordon
Henry Herrmann
Laurence Pringle
John E. Murphy

The Resources Defense Award honors special achievement in the protection of natural resources. It is given as merited or annually, and is an area the Federation especially wishes to encourage.

1976 J. Gus Speth
1977 Michael Osborne
1978 James Goetz
William Madden
1979 Bruce C. Anderson
1980 Joseph L. Sax

The International Achievement Award, which consists of a peregrine falcon, honors individuals for special achievement in international conservation. It is given as merited or annually, and is an area the federation especially wishes to encourage.

1972 **Maurice F. Strong**
1973 **No award**
1974 **No award**
1975 **No award**
1976 **Peter Markham Scott**
Robert M. White
1977 **Ruth C. Clusen**

Conservation Education Award
Group Achievement Award
Aldo Leopold Memorial Award
Wildlife Publication Award

WILDLIFE SOCIETY
7101 Wisconsin Ave. NW, Ste. 611, Washington, D.C. 20014 (202/986-8700)

The Conservation Education Award, a plaque, annually honors an individual's conservation efforts that influence public opinion in a constructive manner. The award is given on a three-year rotation for writing, audio-visual works and programs. A committee selects the winner from nominations received from wildlife professionals.

1954 **Charles Schwartz** and **Jack Sanford** (Missouri Conservation Commission), *Bobwhite Through the Year* (motion picture) and "Whirring Wings" (booklet)
1955 **Ted S. Pettit** (Boy Scouts), Conservation Good Turn Program
1956 **Ralph A. MacMullan** and **Oscar Warbach** (Michigan Dept. of Conservation), *The Life and Times of Michigan Pheasants*
Benjamin Draper and **Earl S. Hearld**, *Science in Action* (televison program)
1957 **Michael Huboda**, "Report from Washington" in *Sports Afield* and New York Sportmen's Conservation Workshop
1958 **David A. Arnold** and **Oscar Warbach** (Michigan Dept. of Conservation), *Red Foxes of Michigan*
1959 **Fred J. Schmeeckle** (Wisconsin State College), for model conservation program
1960 **Richard W. Westwood** (Intl. Union for the Protection of Nature), for work of the nature-study society and as editor of *Nature Magazine*
1961 **Byron S. Asbaugh** and **Muriel Beuschlein** (Conservation Education Assn. in cooperation with American Nature Assn., sponsor), *Things to Do in Science and Conservation*
1962 **Ray Dale Sanders** (Minnesota Foundation), *Land of the Prairie Duck* (film)
1963 **Rachel Carson**, *Silent Spring* (book)
1964 **Joseph P. Linduska** and **Remington Farms**, For publications and demonstration areas
1965 **Robert W. Hines**, "Ducks at a Distance" (booklet)
Douglas L. Gilbert, *Public Relations in Natural Resources Management* (book)
1966 **Ernest H. Linford**, Conservation newspaper editorials
1967 **Robert Scott Ellarson** (Wisconsin)
1968 **New Mexico Dept. of Game and Fish**, "New Mexico Wildlife Management"
1969 **Raymond F. Dassmann**, *Environmental Conservation* and *A Different Kind of Country*
1970 **David A. Munro**, *A Place for Everything*
1971 **Glenn D. Chambers**, *The Return of the Wild Turkey* (film)
1972 **Bruce E. Cowgill**, Nebraskaland Acres for Wildlife program
1973 **No award**
1974 **Missouri Dept. of Conservation**, *Wild Chorus* (film)
1975 **California Dept. of Fish and Game**, Public education programs
University of Maine Chapt. of Wildlife Society, Environmental-education community programs
1976 **James A. Trefethen**, *An American Crusade for Wildlife* (book)
1977 **Karl Maslowski** and **Stephen Maslowski** (Ohio Dept. of National Resources), *Ohio's Wild Places* (film)
1978 **William R. Hernbrode** (Arizona Game and Fish Dept.), Teacher education and volunteer conservation instructor programs
1979 **Oscar "Ozz" Warbach** (Michigan Dept. of Natural Resources), *Mother Nature's Michigan* (book)
1980 **Parks Canada** (Dept. of the Environment, Ottawa), *Bears and Man* (film)

The Group Achievement Award, a plaque, annually honors an organization's outstanding wildlife achievement during the preceding three years. A committee selects the winner from nominations submitted by wildlife professionals.

1973 **Tall Timbers Research Society**, Contributions to wildlife habitat management
1974 **National Audubon Society**, Successful worldwide efforts in natural resources conservation and public education
1975 **Wildlife Management Institute**, Outstanding involvement, inspiration, assistance and leadership in management of the nation's wildlife resources
1976 **Rob and Bessie Wilder Wildlife Foundation**, Public education in wildlife conservation through leadership, research and publication
1977 **Delta Waterfowl Research Station** (Portage La Prairie, Manitoba), Decades of support, research and management of North America's waterfowl
1978 **Ducks Unlimited, Inc.**, and **Ducks Unlimited (Canada)**, Four decades of dedicated efforts to perpetuate continental waterfowl resources
1979 **International Assn. of Fish and Wildlife Agencies**, Rational management of fish and wildlife and coordination of work of conservation agencies in North America
1980 **Arizona Desert Bighorn Sheep Society**, Design and execution of positive, measurable improvements for bighorn sheep habitat

The Aldo Leopold Memorial Award, a medal, is presented annually for distinguished service to wildlife conservation. The award is presented for individual long-term effort that has national or international significance. A committee selects the the winner from nominations submitted by wildlife professionals.

1950 **J. N. "Ding" Darling**
1951 **Mrs. Aldo Leopold**
Carl D. Shoemaker
1952 **Olaus J. Murie**
1953 **Ira N. Gabrielson**
1954 **Harold Titus**
1955 **Clarence Cottam**
1956 **Hoyes Lloyd**
1957 **C.R. Gutermuth**
1958 **E.R. Kalmbach**
1959 **Ernest F. Swift**

1960 **Enrique Beltran**
1961 **Walter P. Taylor**
1962 **Paul L. Errington**
1963 **Clarence M. Tarzwell**
1964 **Harry D. Ruhl**
1965 **A. Starker Leopold**
1966 **Homer S. Swingle**
1967 **Seth Gordon**
1968 **Stewart L. Udall**
1969 **Durward L. Allen**
1970 **Ian McTaggart Cowan**
1971 **Stanley A. Cain**
1972 **Joseph J. Hickey**
1973 **Gustav A. Swanson**
1974 **Lucille F. Stickel**
1975 **Russell E. Train**
1976 **John S. Gottschalk**
1977 **C. H. D. Clarke**
1978 **Henry S. Mosby**
1979 **Raymond F. Dasmann**
1980 **H. Albert Hochbaum**

The Wildlife Protection Award, a plaque, is presented annually for outstanding publication in wildlife science, specifically in the form of books, monographs or articles. Nominations received from wildlife professionals must appear in standard outlets available to the scientific community. A committee selects the winners, now three each year.

1940 **Paul L. Errington, Frances Hamerstrom** and **F.N. Hamerstrom, Jr.,** *The Great Horned Owl and Its Prey in the North Central U.S.*
1941 **No award**
1942 **Adolph Murie**, "Ecology of the Coyote in the Yellowstone" and "Fauna of the National Parks of the United States," *Conservation Bulletin of the U.S. Dept. of the Interior*
1943 **No award**
1944 **Henry S. Mosby** and **Charles O. Handley**, *The Wild Turkey in Virginia: Its Status, Life History and Management*
Richard Gerstell, *The Pace of Winter Feeding in Practical Wildlife Management*
1945 **H. Albert Hochbaum,** *The Canvasback on a Prairie Marsh*
Durward L. Allen, *Michigan Fox Squirrel Management*
1946 **W.L. McAtee** (ed.), *The Ring-Necked Pheasant and Its Management in North America*
1947 **Paul L. Errington,** *Predation and Vertabrate Populations*
1948 **Gardiner Bump, Robert W. Darrow, Frank C. Edminster** and **Walter F. Grissey,** *The Ruffed Grouse —Its Life History, Propogation, Management*
1949 **Arthur S. Einarson,** *The Pronghorn Antelope and Its Management*
1950 **No award**
1951 **Charles W. Schwartz** and **Elizabeth Reeder Schwartz,** *The Game Birds in Hawaii*
1952 **Olaus J. Murie,** *The Elk of North America*
1953 **Robert L. Patterson,** *The Sage Grouse of Wyoming*
1954 **Carol B. Koford,** *The California Condor*
1955 **Allen W. Stokes,** *Population Studies of Ring-Necked Pheasants on Pelee Island, Ontario*
1956 **Lyle K. Sowls,** *Prairie Ducks: A Study of Their Behavior, Ecology and Management*
1957 **H. Albert Hochbaum,** *Travels and Traditions of Waterfowl*
1958 **G.A. Ammann,** *The Prairie Grouse of Michigan*
F.N. Hamerstrom, Jr., Oswald E. Mattson and **Frances Hamerstrom,** *A Guide to Prairie Chicken Management*
1959 **Howard L. Mendall,** *The Ring-Necked Duck in the Northeast*
1960 **A. Starker Leopold,** *Wildlife of Mexico*
1961 **Halmut K. Buechner,** *The Bighorn Sheep of the United States*
Robert S. Dorney and **Cyril Kabat,** *Relation of Weather, Parasitic Diseases and Hunting to Wisconsin Ruffed Grouse Populations*
1962 **Leslie M. Tuck,** "The Murries — Their Distribution, Populations and Biology" (monograph)
1963 **No award**
1964 **Lee M. Talbot** and **Martha H. Talbot,** "The Wildeest in Western Masailand, East Africa" (monograph)
1965 **Charles J. Krebs,** "The Lemming Cycle at Baker Lane, Northwest Territories, During 1959-1962" (paper)
1966 **Cyril Kabat** and **Donald R. Thompson,** "Wisconsin Quail 1834-1962: Population Dynamics and Habitat Management"
George B. Schaller, *The Mountain Gorilla: Ecology and Behavior*
1967 **Harold C. Hanson,** *The Giant Canada Goose*
1968 **Reed H. Wagner, C.D. Besadny** and **Cyril Kabat,** *Population Ecology and Management of Wisconsin Pheasants*
1969 **John P. Kelsall,** *Migratory Barren-Ground Caribou of Canada*
1970 **Walter Rosene, Jr.,** *The Bobwhite Quail: Its Life and Management*
1971 **Karl W. Kenyon,** *The Sea Otter in the Eastern Pacific Ocean*
1972 **Valerius Geist,** *Mountain Sheep: A Study in Behavior and Evolution*
L. David Mech, *The Wolf: Ecology and Behavior of an Endangered Species*
1973 **Leslie M. Tuck,** "The Snipes: A Study of the Genus Capella" (monograph)

MONOGRAPH

1974 **Helmuth Strangaard** "The Roe Deer *(Capreolus capreolus)"*
1975 **Robert R. Dumke** and **Charles M. Pils,** "Mortality of Radio-Tagged Pheasants on the Waterloo Wildlife Area"
1976 **John M. Gates** and **James B. Hale,** "Seasonal Movement, Winter Habitat Use and Population Distribution of an East Central Wisconsin Pheasant Population"
1977 **Arthur M. Pearson,** "The Northern Interior Grizzly Bear *Ursus arctus L*"
1978 **Gerald L. Strom, Ronald D. Andres, Richard A. Bishop, Robert L. Phillips, Donald B. Sinoff** and **John R. Tester,** "Morphology, Reproduction, Dispersal and Mortality of Midwestern Red Fox Populations"
1979 **W. Leslie Robinette, Norman V. Hancock** and **Dale A. Jones,** "The Oak Creek Mule Deer Herd in Utah"
1980 **Rolf O. Peterson,** "Wolf Ecology and Prey Relations on Isle Royale, 1977"

BOOK

1974 **Carl H. Ernst** and **Roger W. Barbour,** *Turtles of the United States*
1975 **No award**
1976 **Iaian and Oria Douglas-Hamilton,** *Among the Elephants*
1977 **Frank C. Bellrose,** *Ducks, Geese and Swans of North America*

1978 **Graeme Caughley,** *Analysis of Vertebrate Population*
1979 **Harold C. Hanson** and **Robert L. Jones,** *The Biochemistry of Blue Snow and Ross Geese*
1980 **A. Starker Leopold,** *The California Quail*

ARTICLE

1975 **W. Leslie Robinette, Charles M. Levelese** and **Dale A. Jones**, "Field Tests of Strip Census Methods" in *Journal of Wildlife Management*
1976 **Charles M. Nixon, Milford W. McClain** and **Robert W. Donohoe**, "Effects of Hunting and Mast Grops on a Squirrel Population" in *Journal of Wildlife Management*
1977 **No award**
1978 **James E. Scarff,** "The International Management of Whales, Dolphins and Porpoises: An Interdiscinplinary Assessment" in *Ecology Law Quarterly*
1979 **Lester L. Eberhardt,** "Appraising Variability in Population Studies" in *Journal of Wildlife Management*
1980 **John L. Roseberry,** "Bobwhite Population Responses to Exploitation: Real and Simulated" in *Journal of Wildlife Management*

Business, M

anagement & Labor

Contents

Related Awards

Horatio Alger Award

HORATIO ALGER AWARDS COMMITTEE
1 Rockefeller Plaza, Suite 1609, New York, N.Y. 10020
(212/581-6433)

The Horatio Alger Award annually honors individuals who rose to success in America from humble beginnings. The award, which was conceived of by the American Schools and Colleges Association, is designed to encourage young people to realize that success in this country can be achieved by working in the free enterprise system, which the Horatio Alger Awards Committee supports. Recipients of the award are frequently in business, although public servants, educators and entertainers are also honored.

1947 **I. J. Fox**
Walter S. Mack, President, C & C Super Corporation
Grover A. Whalen, New York greeter and businessman
Charles E. Wilson, President, General Electric
Robert R. Young, Chairman, New York Central Railroad

1948 **Bernard Baruch,** Financier
Earl Bunting, Director, National Assn. of Manufacturers
George A. Hamid, Owner, Atlantic City Steel Pier
Charles Luckman, Pereira & Luckman
Dorothy Shaver, President, Lord & Taylor

1949 **Allen B. Dumont,** President, Allen Dumont Laboratories
Earl William Muntz, President, Muntz T.V., Inc.
Lee E. Nadeau, President, The Nestle-Le Muir Co.
Vincent Riggio, Chairman, American Tobacco Co.
Anna Rosenberg, Assistant Secretary of Defense

1950 **Thomas E. Courtney,** President, Northern Illinois Corp.
Alexander Harris, President, Ronson Corporation
C. N. Hilton, President, Hilton Hotels, Inc.
Alexander Milton Lewyt, Inventor, Lewyt Vacuum Cleaner
Charles Revson, Chairman and President, Revlon Corp.

1951 **Frank Bailey,** President, Title Guarantee & Trust Co.
James L. Kraft, Chairman, Kraft-Phoenix Cheese Corp.
Finn H. Magnus, President, The Magnus Harmonica Corp.
James J. Nance, Chairman, First Union Real Estate Investments
F. C. Russell, President, The F. C. Russell Company
Brig. Gen. David Sarnoff, Chairman, Radio Corporation of America
Harold E. Stassen, Special Assistant to the President and former Governor of Minnesota
Arthur Wiesenberger, President, Arthur Wiesenberger, Inc.

1952 **Ralph Johnson Bunche,** Nobel Prize winner and United Nations Delegate
Milton S. Eisenhower, President, Pennsylvania State University
James J. Kerrigan, Chairman Executive Committee, Merck & Company
Charles F. Kettering, Research Consultant, General Motors Corp.
Thomas E. Millsop, President, National Steel Corporation
Norman Vincent Peale, Minister, Marble Collegiate Church, and author
William A. Roberts, President Allis-Chalmers Manufacturing Company

1953 **Gen. Sandy Beaver,** Chairman and President, Riverside Military Academy, Calif.
Col. Henry Crown, President, Empire State Building and Materials Service Corp.
Walter D. Fuller, President and Chairman, Curtis Publishing Co.
Byron Alfred Gray, Chairman, International Shoe Co.
Paul Gray Hoffman, Chairman, Studebaker-Packard Corp.
Herbert Hoover, former President of the United States
John Jay Hopkins, Chairman and President, General Dynamics Corp.
J. C. Penney, Chairman, J. C. Penney Company
Harold Schaffer, President, Gold Seal Company
Thomas John Watson, Chairman, International Business Machines
Adolph Zukor, Chairman, Paramount Pictures Corporation

1954 **Michael Baker, Jr.,** President Michael Baker, Jr. Engineering Co.
Donald R. Brann, President, Easi-Bild Pattern Corporation
John Allan Bush, Chairman, Brown Shoe Company
Clifford F. Hood, President, United States Steel Corp.
Fred A. Lawson, President, E. L. Patch Company
William P. Lear, Chairman, Lear, Inc.
Daniel A. Poling, Editor, *Christian Herald*
Andrew R. Shea, President, Pan American Grace Airlines
Harold V. Smith, President, Home Insurance Co.
Joseph Sunnen, President, Sunnen Products Co.

1955 **Roger Ward Babson,** President, Babson's Statistical Service
Hugh Roy Cullen, President, Quintana Petroleum Corp.
Percy J. Ebbott, Vice Chairman, Chase Manhattan Bank of New York
William E. Levis, Chairman, Owens-Illinois Glass Company
James W. McAfee, President, Union Electric Company
Frank B. Rackley, President, Jessop Steel Co.
Arthur Rubloff, Chairman, Arthur Rubloff & Co.
James C. Self, President, Greenwood Mills
Carl J. Sharp, Chairman, Acme Steel Co.
Donald S. Smith, President, Perfection Stove Co.

1956 **Lester W. Carter,** President, American Hotel Assn.
Armando Conti, President, Trenton Beverage Co.
G. S. Eyssell, President, Rockefeller Center, Inc.
Allen Gellman, President, Elgin-American Company
Roy T. Hurley, President, Curtiss-Wright Company
John M. Joyce, President, Seven-Up Bottling Co.
William Cords Snyder, Jr., President, Blaw-Knox Manufacturing Co.
Edward Vernon Rickenbacker, Chairman and President, Eastern Air Lines

1957 **Charles C. Bales,** Head of C. C. Bales Agency
John Bentia, President, Alliance Manufacturing Co.
Thomas Carvel, President, The Carvel Company
Alwin F. Franz, President and Chairman, Colorado Fuel and Iron Corp.
Joyce C. Hall, President, Hallmark Greeting Card Co.
Gwilym A. Price, President and Chairman, Westinghouse Electric Corp.
John J. Sheinin, President, Chicago Medical School
Harry Sugar, President, Alsco, Inc.

John H. Ware, Chairman, American Water Works Co.
Adam Young, President, Young Television Corporation
Louis Zahn, President, Zahn Drug Company

1958 **J. H. Carmichael,** Chairman, Capital Airlines
Paul Dawson Eddy, President, Adelphi College (citation)
Benjamin F. Fairless, President, American Iron & Steel Institute
Milton G. Hulme, President, Hulme, Applegate & Humphrey, Inc.
Howard K. Moore, Headmaster, Peekskill Military Academy (citation)
William Thomas Payne, President, Big Chief Drilling Company
T. Claude Ryan, President, Ryan Aeronautical Company
Raymond E. Salvati, President, Island Creek Coal Co.
William B. Tabler, Architect
Peter Volid, Chairman, King Korn Trading Stamp Co.

1959 **Albert J. Berdis,** President, Great Lakes Steel Corp.
John F. Ernsthausen, President and Founder, Norwalk Truck Lines, Inc.
Alfred C. Fuller, "The Original Fuller Brush Man"
Alfred L. Hammell, President, Railway Express Agency, Inc.
Walter L. Jacobs, President, The Hertz Corporation
James P. Mitchell, U.S. Secretary of Labor
Charles F. Noyes, President, Charles F. Noyes Co., Inc.
Eric A. Walker, President, Pennsylvania State University
Benjamin H. Wooten, President, First National Bank in Dallas

1960 **Frank Armour, Jr.,** President, H. J. Heinz Company
John W. Galbreath, Realtor and owner, John W. Galbreath & Co.
Carl S. Hallauer, President and Board Chairman, Bausch & Lomb Optical Co.
Garvice D. Kincaid, Financier, Bankers & Securities, Inc.
Ed C. Leach, President, Jack Tar Hotels chain
James A. Ryder, President, Ryder System, Inc
John H. Slater, Owner and President, Slater Food Service Management
Robert S. Solinsky, President and Board Chairman, National Can Corp.
Vernon C. Beebe, Co-Founder, Beebe Advertising Agency, Inc. (citation)

1961 **John A. Barr,** Chairman, Montgomery Ward & Company
Dwight David Eisenhower, Former President of the United States
Richard Prentice Ettinger, Chairman, Prentice-Hall, Inc.
Warren G. Grimes, Board Chairman, Grimes Manufacturing Co.
William G. Karnes, President, Beatrice Foods Company
Merl C. Kelce, President, Peabody Coal Company
John D. MacArthur, President, Bankers Life & Casualty Co.
C. R. Smith, President, American Airlines
Walter J. Tuohy, President, Chesapeake & Ohio Railway
James W. Walter, President, Jim Walter Corporation

1962 **Charles W. Anderson,** President, Ametek, Inc.
Frank G. Atkinson, President, Joseph Dixon Crucible Co.
James R. Caldwell, Chairman, Rubbermaid, Inc.
James M. Hill, Hill Enterprises
J. Patrick Lannan, Chairman, Susquehanna Corp.
James J. Ling, President, Ling-Temco Vought, Inc.
Allen Ludden, Senior Executive, CBS, and *College Bowl* moderator
Clarence R. Moll, President, Pennsylvania Military College
E. J. Thomas, Chairman and Chief Executive, Goodyear Tire & Rubber Co.
Edward A. White, President, Bowmar Instrument Corporation

1963 **Charles R. Anthony,** President and Chairman, C. R. Anthony Co.
John Bowles, President, The Rexall Drug Company
Bernard Castro, President, Castro Convertible Corp.
Albert Dorne, Artist, Illustrator and President, Famous Artists Schools
Titus Haffa, Chairman of the Board, Webcor, Inc.
Wayne A. Johnston, President, Illinois Central Railroad
Abner Vernon McCall, President, Baylor University
George O. Nodyne, President, East River Savings Bank of New York
John W. Rollins, President, Rollins Leasing Corporation
R. Perry Shorts, Chairman, Second Nat'l Bank of Saginaw, Mich.
W. Clement Stone, President, Combined Insurance Company of America

1964 **Gene Autry,** Actor, producer and businessman
Charles Bates Thornton, Chairman, Litton Industries
Pearl Buck, Author
Carr P. Collins, Chairman, Fidelity Union Life Ins. Co.
T. Jack Foster, Building and Land Development
E. Ellis Johnson, President, Chicago, Rock Island & Pacific Railroad
Nathaniel Leverone, Chairman, Automatic Canteen Co. of America
J. C. Warner, President, Carnegie Institute of Technology
Herbert J. Watt, President, Peabody Institute
Minoru Yamasaki, Architect

1965 **Elmer Bobst,** Chairman, Warner-Lambert Pharmaceutical Co.
Paul Carnahan, Chairman, National Steel Corp.
R. Carl Chandler, Chairman, Standard Packaging Co.
Rev. Billy Graham, Evangelist, author and educator
Joseph E. Maddy, National Music Corporation
William A. Patterson, President, United Air Lines
Jeno F. Paulucci, President and Chairman, Chun King Corp.
Col. Harland Sanders, Founder, Kentucky Fried Chicken Corp.
George D. Sax, Chairman, Exchange National Bank
Louis S. Vosburgh, Chairman, Lincoln Extension Institute
Harry Winokur, Chairman, Mr. Donut of America, Inc.

1966 **Roy L. Ash,** President, Litton Industries
Walter Brennan, Actor
Chester Carlson, Inventor (Xerox Corporation)
William Forrest Foster, President, Merit Clothing Co.
William E. Grace, President and Chief Executive Officer, Fruehauf Corp.

Robert W. Hawkinson, President, Belden Manufacturing Co.
George W. Jenkins, President, Publix Super Markets, Inc.
John H. Johnson, President and Editor, Johnson Publishing Co., Inc.
Samuel H. Levinson, President, Railweight, Inc.
Elmer F. Pierson, President and Chairman, The Vendo Co.
Harold Toppel, Chairman, H. C. Bohack Co., Inc.
Leslie B. Worthington, President, U.S. Steel Corp.

1967 **Carl E. Anderson,** Chairman and President, E. W. Bliss Co.
Max Coffman, President, Mammoth Mart, Inc.
Davre J. Davidson, Chairman, Automatic Retailers of America
Michael E. Debakey, Chairman of Surgery, Baylor University, Tex.
John A. Howard, President, Rockford College
Ewing Marion Kauffman, President, Marion Laboratories, Inc.
Robert F. McCune, President, Robert F. McCune Associates, Inc.
Lewis Phillips, President, Nedick's Stores
Lawrence Welk, Musical conductor
Elmer L. Winter, President, Manpower, Inc.

1968 **Walter D. Behlen,** Chairman, Behlen Manufacturing Co.
Marvin Chandler, Chairman & President, Northern Illinois Gas Co.
Arthur J. Goldberg, Permanent Representitive of the U.S. to United Nations
George S. Halas, Owner and Coach, Chicago Bears football club
Bob Hope, Entertainer
Wallace E. Johnson, President, Holiday Inns of America, Inc.
Kenneth J. King, Sr., President, Kenny King's Family Restaurants
Charles W. Lubin, Chairman, Kitchens of Sara Lee
Thomas W. Moore, Group Vice President, American Broadcasting Co., Inc.
W. Dewey Presley, President, First National Bank in Dallas
Margaret Durham Robey, President, Southern Seminary & Jr. College
Joseph Timan, President, Horizon Land Corporation

1969 **Ragnar Benson,** Chairman, Ragnar Benson, Inc.
Winston A. Burnett, President and Chairman, Winston A. Burnett Co.
Emmett J. Culligan, Founder, Culligan, Inc.
Charles Deaton, Architect
Erik Jonsson, Mayor, Dallas, Tex.
Herman W. Lay, Chairman, PepsiCo, Inc.
Thurgood Marshall, Justice of the U.S. Supreme Court
Gerald C. O'Brien, President and Chairman, North American Development Corp.
Michael L. Rachunis, Eye, ear, nose and throat physician
Ronald Reagan, Governor, State of California
Meshulam Riklis, Chairman, Rapid-American, McCrory, Glen Alden Corp

1970 **Harry F. Chaddick,** President, Chicago Industrial District, Inc.
Sam M. Fleming, President, Third National Bank & NLT Corp.
Hiram L. Fong, U. S. Senator from Hawaii
Luther H. Hodges, Chairman, Research Triangle Foundation
Harold J. Richards, Chairman, Fidelity Corporation
Riley V. Sims, Chairman, Burnup & Sims, Inc.
Carl B. Stokes, Mayor, Cleveland, Ohio
Jackie Williams, Chairman and Chief Executive Officer, AAA Enterprises, Inc.
Kemmons Wilson, Chairman, Holiday Inns, Inc.
Sam Wyly, Chairman, University Computing Co.

1971 **Robert H. Abplanalp,** President and Chairman, Precision Valve Corp.
Lawrence A. Appley, Chairman, American Management Assn.
Adron Doran, President, Morehead State University
Robert S. Fogarty, Jr., Founder and President, Habitation Resources, Inc.
Alexander G. Hardy, Chairman, The AVEMCO Group
Leon W. "Pete" Harman, President, Harman-Managers Investment, Inc.
Charles Stewart Mott, Director, General Motors and founder, The Mott Foundation
Howard A. Rusk, Director, Institute of Rehabilitation Medicine
Edward Durell Stone, Architect
Lowell Thomas, Commentator and author

1972 **William G. Bailey,** Chairman, Bestline Products, Inc.
Lee S. Bickmore, Chairman, Nabisco, Inc.
Lt. Gen. James H. Doolittle, Awarded Congressional Medal of Honor
Walter J. Hickel, Governor, **of** Alaska
Ray A. Kroc, Chairman, McDonald's Corporation
Floyd Odlum, Financier
Patrick L. O'Malley, President, Canteen Corp.
H. Ross Perot, Chairman, Electronic Data Systems Corp.
James R. Price, Chairman, National Homes Corp.
James B. Reston, Vice-President, *The New York Times*
Henry G. Walter, Honorary Trustee, Illinois Masonic Medical Center

1973 **No awards**

1974 **Andrew F. Brimmer,** Board of Governors, Federal Reserve System
George P. Cullum, Sr., Founder and Chairman, Cullum Construction Co.
Robert Beverley Evans, Detroit Industrialist and Director, American Motors Corp.
Zenon C. R. Hansen, President and Chairman, Mack Trucks
Herbert C. Johnson, Chairman, Consolidated Natural Gas Co.
Clare Boothe Luce, Playwright, actress, Congress-woman, ambassador and lecturer
J. Willard Marriott, Founder and Chairman, Marriott Corp.
Arthur H. "Red" Motley, Chairman, *Parade* magazine
Harold G. Scheie, Director, Scheie Eye Institute
Norman H. Stone, Chairman and Chief Executive Officer, Stone Container Corp.
Frederic Whitaker, Founder, Audubon Artists

1975 **Helen F. Boehm,** Chairman, Edward Marshall Boehm, Inc.
Edward E. Carlson, Chairman of the Board, UAL, Inc.
R. J. Foresman, President and Chief Operating Officer, Michigan General Corp.
Dean W. Jeffers, General Chairman, Nationwide Insurance Companies
Ronald V. Markham, Co-Founder, Anvil Mining Corp.

Vincent G. Marotta, President, North American Systems, Inc.
Allen H. Neuharth, President and Chief Executive, Gannett Co.
Robert L. Rice, Founder and Chairman, Health Industries, Inc.
William G. Salatich, President, Gillette North America
George Shinn, President, George Shinn & Associates
Herbert J. Stiefel, President Stiefel/Raymond Advertising, Inc.

1976 **Carlos J. Arboleya,** President, Barnett Banks of Miami
Loren M. Berry, Founder, L.M. Berry & Company
Roy J. Carver, Founder and Chairman, Bandag, Inc.
William E. Dearden, Vice Chairman and Chief Executive Officer, Hershey Foods Corp.
Robert E. Farrell, President, Farrell's Ice Cream Parlour Restaurants
J. M. Haggar, Sr., Founder and Honorary Chairman, Haggar Company
Joseph H. Hirshhorn, Joseph H. Hirshhorn Museum & Sculpture Garden
Gen. Daniel James, Jr., Commander-in-Chief, North American Air Defense Command
Art Linkletter, Television and radio star, and chairman, Linkletter Enterprises
George M. Mardikian, Food consultant and owner, Omar Khayyam's Restaurant
Rod McKuen, Poet, pop composer, author, singer and classical composer
John Milano, President, Byer-Rolnick Company
Francine I. Neff, Treasurer of the United States
Ernest L. Wilkinson, President-Emeritus, Brigham Young University

1977 **Johnny Cash,** Entertainer
Robert P. Gerholz, President, Gerholz Community Homes, Inc.
J. Ira Harris, General Partner, Salomon Brothers
George J. Kneeland, Chairman, Executive Committee, St. Regis Paper Co.
David J. Mahoney, Chairman and President, Norton Simon, Inc.
Ruth Stafford Peale, Author, lecturer and publisher
Ann Person, Founder and President, Stretch & Sew, Inc.
Roger Tory Peterson, Artist, ornithologist and author
Rose Cook Small, Founder and Vice President, Bluebird, Inc.
L. Homer Surbeck, Partner, Hughes, Hubbard & Reed
Sarkes Tarzian, Founder and President, Sarkes Tarzian, Inc.
Jessie L. Ternberg, Director, Surgery, Pediatric Division, St. Louis Children's Hospital
Danny Thomas, Entertainer

1978 **Hank Aaron,** Baseball great
Mary Kay Ash, Chairman of the Board, Mary Kay Cosmetics, Inc.
Anthony Athanas, President and Chief Executive Officer, Anthony's Pier Four
Wofford B. Camp, Founder, W.B. Camp & Sons, Inc.
Mary C. Crowley, Founder and President, Home Interiors and Gifts, Inc.
Gilbert R. Ellis, Chairman of the Board, Household Finance Corp.
Clarence C. Finley, Corporate Group Vice President, Burlington Industries, Inc.
Michel T. Halbouty, Consulting geologist and petroleum engineer; independent producer and operator
Louis W. Menk, Chairman and Chief Executive Officer, Burlington Northern, Inc.
Wallace N. Rasmussen, Chairman and Chief Executive Officer, Beatrice Foods Co.
Samuel Rosen, Emeritus Clinical Professor of Otolaryngology, Mt. Sinai School of Medicine
George Shearing, Pianist, arranger and composer
William L. Shoemaker, World's "winningest" jockey
Joseph Solomon, Attorney and Senior Partner, Lehman, Rohrlich & Solomon

1979 **Karl D. Bays,** Chairman and Chief Executive Officer, American Hospital Supply Corp.
Michael Bongiovanni, President, U.S. Pharmaceutical Co. of E.R. Squibb & Sons, Inc.
Curtis L. Carlson, President and Chairman, Carlson Companies, Inc.
Catherine Taft Clark, Chairman of the Board of Directors, Brownberry Ovens, Inc.
David C. Collier, Group Vice President — Finance, General Motors Corp.
Lee Francis Flaherty, Founder and President, Flair Merchandising Agency, Inc.
Joseph B. Kirsner, Louis Block Distinguished Service Professor of Medicine, University of Chicago Hospitals and Clinics
Azie Taylor Morton, Treasurer of the United States; National Director, U.S. Savings Bonds Div.
Frank C. Nicholas, Chairman and President, Beech-Nut Foods Corp.
R. David Thomas, Founder and Chairman, Wendy's International, Inc.
Harold Warp, Founder, Flex-O-Glass, Inc.
Shepard Broad, Chairman of the Board, American Savings & Loan Assn.
Nick A. Caporella, President and Chief Executive Officer, Burnup & Sims, Inc.
E. Y. "Yip" Harburg, Lyricist, writer, lecturer and TV personality
Carl N. Karchner, Chairman and Chief Executive Officer, Carl Karchner Enterprises, Inc.
Jack Lalanne, President and owner, The Jack Lalanne Co.
Abraham Lincoln Marovitz, Senior U.S. District Court Judge, Northern District of Illinois
Joseph Robbie, President and owner, Miami Dolphins

1980 **W. Michael Blumenthal,** Vice Chairman, Burroughs Corp.
Joe Bruno, Chairman of the Board, Bruno's Food Stores
Woodrow W. Clements, Chairman and Chief Executive Officer, Dr. Pepper Co.
Thomas S. Haggai, President and Chief Executive Officer, Tom Haggai & Associates
Morris L. Hite, Chairman and President, Tracy-Locke Co., Inc.
Richard L. Lesher, President, Chamber of Commerce of the United States
Harry A. Merlo, Chairman and President, Louisiana Pacific Corp.
Gilbert F. Richards, Chairman and Chief Executive Officer, The Budd Co.
Robert G. Sampson, Vice President-Property and Special Assistant to the Chairman, United Airlines
Beurt R. SerVaas, Chairman of the Board, Curtis Publishing Co.
Lee R. Sollenbarger, Chairman of the Board, Transcon Lines

Jackson T. Stephens, President, Stephens, Inc.

Beyer Medal
President's Award
Junior Achievement Treasurer of the Year

National Association of Accountants
919 Third Ave., New York, N.Y. 10022 (212/754-9764)

The Beyer Medal, which is of gold, is given for the highest scores in a three-day examination for the Certificate in Management Accounting.

1972 **Robert F. Garland**
1973 **Scott G. Thompson**
1974 **Amit M. Nanavati**
1975 **Michael Duffy**
1976 **Bhaskar Bhave**
1977 **Kay A. Scheible**
Andrew D. Bailey, Jr.,
1978 **Kent R. Turner**
Lane K. Anderson
1979 **John J. Anderson**
James R. Fountain, Jr.,
1980 **Not available at press time**

The President's Award, which consists of a trophy, honors consistent performance over a five-year period as determined by year-end standing in annual incentive competitions among the 300 local chapters of the NAA.

1975 **Eugene, Ore.**
1976 **Piedmont Winston-Salem, N.C.**
1977 **Akron, Ohio**
1978 **Olean-Bradford Area,** N.Y.
1979 **Piedmont Winston-Salem,** N.C.
1980 **Piedmont Winston-Salem,** N.C.

The Junior Achievement Treasurer of the Year honors a high-school junior achiever who is judged the best treasurer of a Junior Achievement company. Judging is done first on a local level, then on a regional level and finally nationally. The winner receives $750 and a plaque.

1967 **Douglas Moore**
1968 **Charles Golay**
1969 **Michael Oslon**
1970 **Marie E. Cox**
1971 **Dennis Keenan**
1972 **Deborah Tierney**
1973 **Kay Boeskool**
1974 **Craig R. Choun**
1975 **Williams S. Simpkins**
1976 **Greg Maislin**
1977 **Kenneth Parrish**
1978 **David Esmail**
1979 **Sally Sackett**
1980 **William Herp**

Clarion Awards

WOMEN IN COMMUNICATIONS
Box 9561, Austin, Tex. 78766 (512/345-8922)

The Clarion Awards, which are plaques, are given annually in three divisions: Human rights, the world we live in and the community we serve. In addition to the public-relations and advertising honors listed below, print and broadcast journalism categories are honored and are listed elsewhere in this volume. Submitted material is considered by a panel of communications professionals from around the country. In addition to the first-place honors listed here, honorable mentions are made.

PUBLIC RELATIONS (in any divisions)

1973 **Nick Van Gelder, Jeanette Murphy, Candy Young, Veronica Allen, Carole Howard, Jim Kern,** and **Tal Jones,** Pacific Northwest Bell (Seattle)
Gerrie R. Shaffer, Philadelphia Electric Co.
Ruth Kassewitz, Communications Office, Metropolitan Dade County, (Fla.)
Pat Polakowski, Naval Electronics Laboratory, (San Diego)
1974 **Teddy Weigloss,** Pennsylvania Horticultural Society, and **Sheryl Bronkesh,** Sumers/Rosen
1975 **Shirley Bonnem** (Philadelphia)
1976 **Anne Lewis,** St. Paul Companies (Minn.)
1977 **Beverly Elam** (San Antonio)
Patricia Donovan (Chicago)
Kay Stepp, (Portland, Ore.)
1978 **David Crosson,** Ohio Dept. of Natural Resources (Columbus)
Greta DeBofsky and **Lou Williams,** Ruder & Finn of Mid-America (Chicago)
1979 **Jon Conlon,** Mitchell Energy & Development Corp. (Houston)
Ann E. Corwell, Pontiac Motor Div. General Motors (Pontiac, Mich.)
Mary Hopper, Public Library of Charlotte and Mecklenburg County (N.C.)
1980 **California Judges Assn.** (San Francisco)
Terrence E. Leedom, Sheila A. Castellarin and **Carolyn J. Reed,** Columbia Gas of Ohio
Shirley Bonnem, Children's Hospital of Philadelphia
Marlys Taege and **Kristen Dollase,** Bethesda Lutheran Home (Watertown, Wis.)

ADVERTISING (in any division)

1977 **Robert A. Mullen** (Phoenix)
1978 **Candance E. Medd** and **Amy Parker,** Minneapolis YWCA
1979 **No award**
1980 **No award**

Clio Awards

CLIO AWARDS
30 E. 60th St., New York., N.Y. 10022 (212/593-1900)

The Clio Award is a statue given annually to honor excellence in advertising, worldwide in all media. Entries are judged in product and campaign categories by advertising creative executives and groups of technical specialists. Judges, who must abstain from voting on their own work, comprise a panel of 450 members who represent 16 cities in 10 countries from five continents.

UNITED STATES

1974 **Old Home Bakeries, "Bread City", "Coffee Rolls", "Nice Buns"** (Campaign), Bozell & Jacobs/Visual Presentations

Thom McAn Shoes, "Standing On My Foot" (Apparel), Carole Langer/Horn-Griner
Johnson & Johnson Baby Powder, "Roommates" (Bath Products), Young & Rubican/Ampersand
Malt Duck, "It Certainly is . . ." (Beers and wines), W.B. Doner/Sedelmaier
M & M Candies, "Goddess" (Confections/snacks), Ted Bates/EUE
General Electric, "Absent Mother" (Corporate/institutional), BBDO/Gomes-Loew
Eau de Love, "Oh Da Flowers" (Cosmetics/toiletries-women), Wells, Rich, Greene/Wylde
Ocean Spray Cranapple Juice, "Sweet Tart" (Dairy products), Ted Bates/Chance III
Kodak Film, "Memories" (Gift items), J. Walter Thompson/EUE/Screen Gems
Frigidaire Range, "Tech Center" (Home furnishings), Needham, Harper, Steers/Wheiner-Berman
Slurp, "The Slurp" (Household items), The Project Group/Wylde
Metropolitan Life, "Ring" (Insurance) Young & Rubicam/Wylde
Pippin Show, "Dance" (Media promotion/entertainment), Blaine-Thompson/Pucci-Stone
Purina Meow Mix, "Singing Cats" (Pet products), Della Femina, Travisano/David Langley
Scope Mouthwash, "A Day in the Life" (Pharmaceuticals/dentifrices), Benton & Bowles/Jenkins- Covington
Muscular Dystrophy Assn., "Ezzard Charles" (Public service), Benton & Bowles/EUE
Titleist Golf Balls, "Snorkel" (Recreation equipment), Humphrey Browning MacDougall/Petersen
Benihana of Tokyo, "Graduation" (Retail food stores/restaurants), Kracauer & Marvin/Rick Levine
Barney's, "1923" (Retail stores/services), Scali, McCabe, Sloves/Ampersand
Tonka Toys, "Excuses" (Toys and games), Carl Ally
United Airlines, "Friends" (Travel), Leo Burnett/Opus III
AT&T Long Distance, "Friends" (Utilities), N.W. Ayer/Jenkins Covington
Dr. Pepper, "Pepperettes" (Soft drinks), Young & Rubicam/Ampersand

1975 **Southern Airways, "Orgy", "Party", "Bum"** (Campaign, Humor, Travel), McDonald Little/Sedelmaier
American Motors Pacer, "Shell" (Automotive), Cunningham & Walsh/Stone
No More Tangles, "Damaged" (Bath products), Compton/Gottlieb
Shaefer Beer, "Kites" (Beers/wines), BBDO/Garrett
Tic Tac Mints, "Bang Out of Life" (Confection/snacks), Chalek & Dreyer/Wylde, Sunlight
General Electric, "Bull in the Lexan Shop" (Corporate), BBDO/May Day
Pure Magic Lipstick, "Lips" (Cosmetics/toiletries-women), Rosenfeld, Sirowitz, Lawson/Lacy
Ultra-Bright, "Laura Baugh-Love Life" (Dentifrice), William Esty/Filmco
Kodak Film, "First Time Ever I Saw Your Face" (Gift items), J. Walter Thompson/MPO
Duracell Batteries, "Rabbits" (Home maintenance), Dancer Fitzgerald Sample/Lobell
M.O.N.Y., "Cabins" (Insurance), Marschalk/Horn
Mobil Oil, "Masterpiece Theatre" (Media promotion/entertainment), Varied Directions
Delmonte Catsup, "Catsup Moon" (Packaged foods), McCann-Erickson/Harris
Nat'l Alliance of Businessmen, "Toy Soldiers" (Public service), Grey/Ampersand
Kawasaki Motorcycles, "Garage" (Recreation equipment), Cunningham & Walsh/Pytka, Sandler
Big Ten Ford Dealers, "Hubcaps" (Retail auto), Mike Sloan/A&R
Barney's, "You're Big Enough" (Retail department stores), Scali, McCabe, Sloves/Horn
Pepsi Cola, "Pied Piper" (Soft Drinks), BBDO/Garrett
Diet Pepsi Cola, "Zipper" (Soft Drinks), BBDO/Michlin & Hill
Tonka Toys, "Elephant" (Demonstration toys/games) Carl Ally/Horn-Griner
Illinois Bell, "Teenager" (Utilities), N.W. Ayer ABH/Hil Covington

1976 **Exxon,** "Mark Twain", "Anne Sullivan" (Introduction Campaign)
Chevrolet, "Baseball, Hotdogs '76" (Automotive)
BF Goodrich, "Joan Rivers" (Auto Accessories)
Texaco, "Tortoise & Hare" (Gasolines/lubricants)
Diet Rite, "Hava" (Soft drinks)
Schmidts, "Tell a Coors" (Beers/wines)
Salada, "Saleman" (Coffee/tea)
Nair, "Sport Shorts" (Bath products)
Colgate, "Braces" (Dentifrice)
Pampers, "It's a Girl" (Household items)
Tic Tac, "Ballerina Bang" (Confections/snacks)
Old Home Bread, "Bread Bash" (Foods)
Straw Hat Pizza, "Time Lapse" (Retail food)
Sony Cassette, "Restaurant" (Gifts/personal items)
Celotex, "I'm a Roof" (Home maintenance)
Elmers Glue-All, "Bulldozer" (Product demo)
Tonka, "Factory" (Toys/games)
National Geographic, "Incredible Machine" (Media promotion)
Barney's, "English Room" (Retail specialty)
British Airways, "Horseman" (Travel transportation)
Xerox 9200, "Monks" (Office equipment)
Anti Defamation League, "The Prejudice Test" (Copywriting)
Kodak Trimline, "Scrooge" (Costuming/set design)
Exxon, "Dizzy Dean" (Cinematography)
Pepsi Cola, "Samantha" (Direction)
Boston Red Sox, "Keep Your Sox On" (Editing)
Levis, "Threads" (Animation)
East LA Health Task Force, "Drunk Driving" (Local low budget)
Peugeot, "Test Track" (Musical scoring)
Kodak Film, "In Session" (Music/lyrics)

1977 **Kodak Film,** "This Old House", "Time to Sow", (Introduction Campaign)
Fiat, "Over the Years", (Automotive)
Life Savers, "Karen", (Confections/snacks)
Breakstone Cottage Cheese, "Store", (Dairy products/Fruit drinks)
Mueller's Egg Noodles, "Dr. Joyce Brothers' Mother", (Packaged foods)
Sure Anti-Perspirant, "Take Off Your Coat America", (Bath products)
Faberge Babe, "Restaurant", (Women's products)
Downy Fabric Softener, "The Feeling's Fine", (Household items)
Purina Meow Mix, "Letters", (Pet products)
Pace CB Radios, "Girl", (Recreation equipment)
Hallmark Cards, "Moving Day", (Corporate)
Paine Webber Brokerage, "Antique Cars", (Banks/financial)
Illinois Bell Telephone/Disabled, "Alexander Graham Bell", (Utilities)

American Cancer Society, "Money Talks", (Public service)
Dayton's Warehouse Sale, "Mr. Shirley", (Retail specialty/department store)
Pan Am, "Millions of Americans", (Travel/transportation)
N.Y. Shakespeare Festival, "3 Penny Opera", (Media promotion)
General Electric, "Steinmetz", (Copy and male performance)
Farmland Industries, "History", (Cinematography)
National Beer, "Softball", (Editing)
Dean Witter Stocks/Bonds, "Omnibus", (Animation)
ITT, "Fiber Optics", (Film effects)
Wamsutta Sheets, "Designer Sheets", (Musical scoring)
Sugar Free Dr. Pepper, "Pinball", (Set design)
St. Regis, "Bridge", (Product demonstration)
Yamaha Motorcycles, "Police Chief", (Humor)

1978 **Pioneer Sound System,** "Drummer," "Sonny Rollins" (Overall Campaign)
Ford Trucks, "Four Generations" (Automotive)
Mobil Gas, "Long Line" (Gasoline/Lubricants)
Miller Lite Beer, "Bubba Smith" (Beers/Wines)
Dr. Pepper, "Pied Pepper — Cross Country" (Soft Drinks)
Right Guard Deodorant, "Jury" (Bath Products)
Trouble After Shave, "Max" (Men's Products)
Jontue Fragrance, "Boat" (Women's Products)
Kretschmer Wheat Germ, "Ballet" (Cereals)
California Strawberry Advisory Board, "Did You Forget?" (Foods)
Progresso Seafoods, "Waiter" (Oils/Dressings/ Condiments)
Pioneer Stereo Systems, "Tuthill" (Home Furnishings/ Appliances)
Rubbermaid Refuse Containers, "Ruthless" (Home Maintenance)
Meow Mix Cat Food, "Quiz Show" (Pet Products)
WLS-TV Eyewitness News, "Block Party" (Media Promotion)
New York Empire State Lottery, "Shortcut" (Entertainment/Promotion)
Hangman Game, "Bank" (Toys/Games)
Samsonite Luggage, "Samsonite vs. Steelers" (Personal/Gift Items)
American Cancer Society, "Church" (Public Service)
Manufacturers Hanover Trust, "Conway/Auto Loan" (Banks/Financial and U.S. Male Performance)
National Blue Cross/Blue Shield, "Family Dinner" (Insurance)
Illinois Bell Telephone, "Broken Phone" (Utilities)
U.S. Army Recruiting, "12 Months To Say Goodbye" (Recruitment)
Carousal Porsche-Audi-Renault Dealer, "Stop Pretending" (Retail Auto Dealers)
Fischer Office Furniture, "Low Overhead" (Office Equipment)
Illinois Bell Telephone, "History of Dialing" (Production Design)
Scripto Roller Pen, "Steve" (Costume Design)
Coca-Cola, "Street Song" (Direction)
Chevron Gas, "Staff of Life" (Animation)
Levi's, "Brand Name" (Film Effects)
A & W Root Beer, "Housewife," Baillee Gersten (Female Performance)
New York State Tourism, "I Love New York" (Music with Lyrics)

1979 **McDonald's Restaurant,** "Mary Ryan," "Hot Stuff" (Overall Campaign)
Fiat, "Waterfall" (Automotive)
Motorola Car Stereo System, "Best Stereo" (Auto Accessories)
Mobil "One" Oil, "Cold Weather" (Gasoline/Lubricants & Product Demonstration)
Manufacturers Hanover Trust, "Carwash" (Banking/ Financial)
Prudential Insurance Company of America, "Chase" (Insurance)
Cracked Wheat Crunch Cereal, "Sisters Revised" (Cereals)
Pepsi-Cola, "New Baby" (Soft Drinks)
Snowy Liquid Bleach, "Dirtball" (Household Items)
Meow Mix, "Famous Cats" (Pet Products)
Xerox Copier, "Hannigan Flannigan" (Office Equipment)
Federal Express, "Promise Them Anything" (Transportation-Cargo)
New York State Tourism, "Broadway-I Love New York" (Travel)
U.S. Army, "Feelin' Good" (Recruitment)
The Church of Jesus Christ of Latter-Day Saints/Marriage Colidarity, "Try Again" (Public Service & Direction and Editing)
Catholic Church of Maryland, "You Only Live Once" (Copywriting)
Blitz Weinhard Beer, "Rancher" (Cinematography)
3M Corporation, "Ivory Tower" (Set Design)
Jovan Man/Woman Cologne, "In The Beginning" (Film Effects)
Chemical Bank, "Neighborhoods" (Original Music Scoring)
Pan Am, "Theme" (Original Music With Lyrics)
Kentucky Fried Chicken, "America" (New Arrangement of Commercial Themes)

1980 **Kodak Colorburst,** "Two Families," "Circus" (Campaign)
Wembley Ties, "Tie Fetish" (Apparel)
Fiat Strada, "Cruising" (Automobiles)
Anco Wiper Blades, "Piano Movers" (Auto Accessories)
Frito Brand Corn Chips, "Baseball Baby" (Confection/ Snacks)
Texaco, "Taxi" (Corporate)
Borden Ice Cream, "Playground" (Dairy Products)
Mobil 1 Oil, "Gas Savings" (Gasolines)
Northern Electric Blanket, "Patent Office" (Home Furnishings/Appliance)
Dow Saran Wrap, "Ice Cubes" (Household Items)
Independent Life, "More Excuses" (Insurance)
Kodak Colorburst, "First Day in School" (Personal/ Gift Items/Direction and Editing)
Tuffy's Dog Food, "Look Alikes" (Pet Products)
Yamaha Motorcycles, "Beauty Or the Beast" (Recreation Equipment)
McDonald's Breakfast, "Morning Glory" (Retail Foods)
Coca Cola, "Mean Joe Greene" (Soft Drinks and Male Performance)
AT&T Long Lines, "Vignettes" (Utilities)
Church of Jesus Christ of Latter Day Saints, "Walking" (Eastman Kodak Award for U.S. Cinematography)
Jello Gelatin, "Cousins Reunion" (Music Openings, Tags or Donuts)
Wrigley's Doublemint Gum, "Single Most Favorite" (Music with Lyrics)

St. Regis Paper, "Ski Jump" (Product Demonstration)

INTERNATIONAL

1974 **7 Up, "Hippies" (Holland)** (Animation), Prad/ Anglo-Dutch Group
Ford F-100 Pickup, "You Don't Run Out of Pickup" (Argentina) (Demonstration), J. Walter Thompson/Casares
Pepsi Cola, "Stadium" (Brazil) (Music), Mauro Salles/Filmcenter
Toyota Corona, "Developing the New Corona" (Japan) (Auto), Dentsu/Nippon Recruit Center
Jun-Rope, "Jean" (Japan) (Apparel), Directors Circle
Rambo Hole Sealer (Holland) (Home maintenance), KVH/Forum
Rank Xerox, "Underground to Moscow" (England) (Office Equipment), Young & Rubicam
Nippon Voluntary Insurance, "The Egg" (Japan) (Services), Dentsu/Tokyo Publicity Center
Toronto Energy Conservation (Canada) (Public service), Vickers & Benson/Projections
Coca-Cola, "Surfing" (Australia) (Soft drinks), Hansen Rubensohn-McCann-Erickson/Telemark
Hypermarche Stores, "The Higher We Pile 'Em" (Canada) (Retail), W.B. Doner/Mayday
Cadbury Whole Nut Candy, "Director" (Ireland) (Confections), Peter Owens/GPA Films
Uncle Sam Deodorant, "Uncle Sam" (Australia) (Bath products), Hansen Rubensohn-McCann-Erickson/ Eric Porter
Benson & Hedges Special Panatellas, "Hat" (England) (Tobacco), Collett, Dickenson, Pearce/Alan Parker
Ize Electricity, "Helps to Live" (Germany) (Corporate), Die Werbe Euro/Franck Film
Hovis Bread, "Bike Ride" (England) (Foods/photography/direction), Collett, Dickenson, Pearce/RSA
Walls Ice Cream, "Walls Follies" (England) (Production design), Lintas/Illustra
Cockburns Special Reserve, "Shipwrecked" (England) (Beers and wines), Collett, Dickenson, Pearce/Alan Porter
Barclays Bank, "Hands" (England) (Editing), Charles Barker/Michael Warhurst/Studio Lambert
Ricore Cafe, "The Hunt" (France) (Coffee/tea), Publicis Conseil/Hamster
Vicks Vaporob, "Breathing Jar" (England) (Pharmaceuticals), Benton & Bowles/Gillie Potter
Sunday Times, "Wine" (England) (Media promotion), HSL
Gillette Foamy, "Split Screen" (England) (Men's toiletries), J. Walter Thompson/Streich Perkins
La Bonne Vie Cheese, "Monk's Lunch" (England) (Dairy products), Leo Burnett/HSL
Kodak Pocket Instamatic, "Handplay" (England) (Personal/gift items), J. Walter Thompson/Streich Perkins
Cie Railways, "The Super Train" (Ireland) (Travel), Arks/Scope
Swish Curtain Rack, "Bathroom", "Honey-mooners", "Speech" (England) (Home furnishings/overall campaign), Cogent Elliott/Alan Parker

1975 **Ford F-100, "Air Drop" (Argentina)** (Automotive demonstration), J. Walter Thompson/Casares
Cadbury, "Mona Lisa" (Canada) (Confections/ snacks), Doyle Dane Bernbach/Rabko
Crespi, "Pollution" (Argentina) (Corporate), Portillo Olson
Fuji Waste Disposal, "Recycling" (Japan) (Corporate), Hakuhodo/Tohoku Shin Sha
Walls Ice Cream, "Fizz Bang" (United Kingdom) (Dairy products), Lintas/Ridley Scott
Listerine, "Lifeboat Deck" (United Kingdom) (Dentrifrice/pharmaceuticals), J. Walter Thompson/GPA
Moulinex, "Electric Knife" (Switzerland) (Home furnishings/appliances), Walther & Leuenberger/Condor
Desk Top Lamps, "Dancing Lamps" (Japan) (Home furnishings/appliances), Hakunodo/O.T.V. Film
Decora, "Stains" (Brazil) (Home maintenance), Casabranca/Robert Bakker
Panasonic Batteries, "Robot" (Japan) (Home maintenance), Dentsu/Dentsu Motion Picture
Marlboro, "Wild Horses" (Australia) (Tobacco), USP Needham/Film House
KLM, "Surprising Amsterdam" (Holland) (Travel/ transportation), Vaz/Dies/Producers
Coca-Cola, "Waves" (Australia) (Cinematography), Hansen Rubenson/Telemark
Count Pushkin Vodka, "Transiberian Express" (South Africa) (Animation/graphics), ARL Services/Richard Williams
Country Pale, "Aqua Ballet" (France) (Production design), Dupuy/Compton/ID
Speedy Muffler, "Golfer" (Canada) (Humor), Goodis, Goldberg, Soren/Rabko

1976 **Eaton's, "Number One", "Timothy E" (Canada)**, (Campaign)
Levis, "The First Jean" (Argentina), (Apparel)
Wool Superwash, "Label" (Holland), (Apparel)
Tropical Tires, "Highways" (Brazil), (Auto Accessories)
Master Charge, "Dominoes" (Canada), (Services)
Lion Lager, "Barbeque" (South Africa), (Cinematography)
Coca-Cola, "Real You" (Australia), (Soft drinks)
Tetley Tea Bags, "Folk Dance" (United Kingdom), (Coffee/tea)
Ontario Milk Marketing Board, "Hats/Moustache" (Canada), (Dairy products)
Mazola Oil, "Growing Seed" (Germany), (Foods)
National Lamp, "Mosquito" (Japan), (Home furnishings)
Corco Plasticine, "Plasticine" (Puerto Rico), (Corporate)
Rapid Cement, "Balloon" (Japan) (Household items)
Optrex Eye Dew, "Mirror, Mirror" (United Kingdom), (Animation)
Uncle Sam Tooth Paste, "Need All" (Australia) (Dentifrice)
Chipmonks Potato Chips, "Chipmonks" (Canada), (Confections/snacks)
Solo, "More Real Than Brown" (Norway), (Humor)

1977 **Overseas Telecommunications,** "Greece", "Italy", Australia (Campaign)
Peugeot 104, "Slalom", France (Automotive)
Gilbey's Gin, "Phrase Book-Small", "Talk" World Wide (Beers/wines)
Evergood Coffee, "Evergood", Norway (Coffee/tea)
Johnson's Cotonetes, "Bored Baby", Brazil (Dentifrice/pharmaceuticals)
H.J. Heinz Canned Salad, "Ingredients", England (Packaged foods)

Taubmans Gaylon Paint, "Army", New Zealand (Household items)
The London Sunday Times, "Ageing", England (Media promotion)
Xerox 3103 Copier, "Great Performance", Japan (Office equipment)
Samsonite, "The Elephants", France/Germany/Holland (Gifts/personal items)
Sugar Free 7-Up, "Evolution", Canada (Soft drinks)
Singha Beer, "Monsoon", Thailand (Cinematography)
Martini Bianco, "Because You Know It's Right", England (Editing)
Aron-Alpha Instant Adhesive, "Sticking Power", Japan (Product demonstration)
4711 Eau de Cologne, "Young Generation", Germany (Music/lyrics)
Chrysler Avenger, "Avenger File '77", Ireland (Musical scoring)
Cadbury's Crunchie Bar, "Gold Rush", New Zealand (Confections/snacks and set design)

1978 **Toohey's Draught Beer,** "Sailing," "Football" (Overall Campaign) England
Dunlop Tires, "Russian Roulette" (Auto Accessories) England
Guiness Stout, "Island" (Beers) Ireland
Coca-Cola, "Summer, Water & Coke" (Soft Drinks) Australia
Nescafe Coffee, "Breakfast" (Coffee/Tea/Cocoa Mix) Spain
Rich Osborne Biscuits, "Perfect Dunking" (Confections/ Snacks) England
Campos Verdes Soap, "One Day" (Bath Products) Argentina
Shiseido Aquair Eye Make-Up, "Aquair in Water" (Women's Products) Japan
Urgo Bandages, "The Pick Up" (Dentrifrice/ Pharmaceuticals) France
Waterman Pens, "Love Story" (Personal/Gift Items) France
Sony Trinitron TV, "Tuning People In" (Home Appliances) England
Epeda Mattress, "The Hiccup" (Home Furnishings and Humor) France
Bamerindus Bank, "Absolute Silence" (Corporate) Brazil
Electricity Council, "Football" (Services) England
Danka Hardrock Adhesive, "Mid-Air Dump Truck" (Product Demonstration) Japan
Egg Authority Board, "Can Can" (Editing) England
Sharp Stereo Equipment, "Colors & Sounds of Our Land" (Animation) Brazil
Air Canada, "Canadians" (Music with Lyrics) Canada
Lemon & Paeroa, "Land Cruiser" (Music Scoring) New Zealand
Lord Extra Cigarettes, "Southward" (Cinematrography) Germany

1979 ***Sunday Times***, "Levin," "Business Man" (Overall Campaign) London
Lois Jeans "The West" (Apparel) Amsterdam
Leyland Automobiles, "Mad Dogs & Englishmen" (Automotive) Frankfurt
Hanky Panky, "Park Bench" (Confections/Snacks) London
Schlitz Malt Liquor, "Foxhole" (Beers) London
Cinzano Bianco, "Bianco" (Wines) London
Visir, "A Yearly Dose" (Public Service) Stockholm
Savlon "All Over the House" (Household Items) London
Rawlings Indian Tonic Water, "Trade Secret" (Soft Drinks) London
Singha Beer, "Melting" (Cinematography) Bangkok
Seiko UTI, "The Wedding" (Direction) Paris
Godewind, "Mona Lisa" (Animation) Hamburg
Benson & Hedges, "Battle For the Ashes" (Film Effects) Sydney
Department of Social Security, "Care for Kids" (Music with Lyrics) Sydney
Samsonite Luggage, "Man in a Suitcase" (Product Demonstration) Paris
Barclays Bank Limited, "Taxi" (Services) London
Accurist Watches, "Knightsbridge" (Humor) London
EMI Disco Album, "Don't Walk Boogie" (Personal/ Gift Items) England
Marsushita Cassette Tape, "Cassette Tape" (Production Design) Tokyo

1980 **St. Ive! Cream,** "Winning," "Childhood." "Apple Pie" (Campaign) England
Naturalizer Shoes, "The Assistant" (Apparel) England
Super Movil Oil, "Trip Inside the Motor" (Auto Accessories) Argentina
Ali Strax Freeze Dried, "Vikings" (Coffee/Tea) Norway
Hospital Benefits Association, "Punch & Judy" (Corporate) Australia
Bang & Olufsen Sound Equipment, "Strubelmeyer" (Home Appliance) South Africa
Aerofon Insecticide, "Funeral March" (Household Item) Brazil
Daily Mail, "Betty Ford" (Media Promotion) England
National Bicycle, "Training" (Media Promotion) England
Barclaycard, "Record Shop" (Services) England
Radio Pilot Cars, "Remote Control" (Toys/Games) France
Hamlet Cigars, "Edge of the World" (Tobacco Products) England
Cinzano Bianco, "Airliner" (Wine/Humor) England
Supersoft Hairspray, "Farmer Brooks" (Women's Products) England
Coruba Rum, "Island" (Animation) New Zealand
Fiat Strada, "Figaro" (Eastman Kodak Award for International Cinematography) England
Irish Defence Forces, "Go Places" (Editing) Ireland
Life Savers, "Tunnel" (Graphics) Canada
BASF Cassette Tapes, "Dear John" (Personal/Gift Items and Direction) New Zealand

TECHNIQUE

1974 **Sunbeam Lady Shavers, "Tricky Pair"** (Animation), N.W. Ayer/Kurtz & Friends
Nat'l Institute on Alcohol Abuse, "Typical Alcoholic" (Copy), Grey-North/James Garrett
Arrow Shirts, "Garden Party" (Costume design), Young & Rubicam/Ampersand
Eastern Air Lines, "Vacation Islands" (Editing), Young & Rubicam/Summit/Murffitt
U.S. Travel Bureau, "Ice Block" (Film effects), Young & Rubicam/Candian Cinegraph
First Nat'l Bank of Miami, "Robber" (Humor), Mike Sloan/Tulchin
Hush Puppies, "Hush Puppies Are Dumb" (Music with lyrics), Wells, Rich, Greene/Steve Karmen
Benihana of Tokyo, "Rookie" (Performance—Male), Kracauer & Marvin/Rick Levine

Alka Seltzer, "Wrestling Match" (Performance—female), Wells, Rich, Green/Gomes-Loew
Activ Panty Hose, "Activ City" (Set design), Young & Rubicam/Horn-Griner

1975 **Eastern Airlines, "Winter Wonderland"** (Animation), Young & Rubicam/Ovation
AT&T, "Maine" (Cinematography), N.W. Ayer ABH/Lear Levin
Burlington, "The Burlington Look" (Costuming), Doyle Dane Bernbach/Garrett
AAA of Michigan, "Travels of Charlie' (Direction), Stockwell-Marcuse/May Day
Gimbels, "Image" (Editing), Wyse/Editors Gas
Seven-Up, "Bubbles" (Film effects), J. Walter Thompson/EUE, Abel
Dr. Pepper, "Board Room" (Male performance) and (Set design), Young & Rubicam/Rick Levine
Colt 45 Malt Liquor, "Hotel" (Set design), W.B. Donner/Movie House

Advertising Hall of Fame

AMERICAN ADVERTISING FEDERATION
1225 Connecticut Ave. NW, Washington, D.C. 20036
(202/659-1800)

Election to the Advertising Hall of Fame recognizes individuals who have contributed to American advertising by the advancement of social and economic values of advertising and who have applied their expertise to some form of public service. A council of judges reviews nominations and selects new members of the Hall of Fame each year.

1949
Rollin C. Ayres
Alfred W. Erickson
Lewis B. Jones
Edwin T. Meredith
Walter A. Strong
Cyrus H. K. Curtis
William H. Johns
Theodore F. MacManus
John Irving Romer
John Wanamaker

1950
F. Wayland Ayer
Benjamin Franklin
Merle Sidener
Stanley Clague
James H. McGraw

1951
William Cheever D'Arcy
E. St. Elmo Lewis

1952
Erma Perham Proetz
J. Earle Pearson

1953
Samuel C. Dobbs
James O'Shaughnessy
Charles Coolidge Parlin

1954
Frank Presbrey
John E. Powers

1955
Henry T. Ewald
George Burton Hotchkiss

1956
No inductees

1957
Herbert S. Houston
Claude Clarence Hopkins

1958
Orlando Clinton Harn
Albert D. Lasker

1959
Merlin Hall Aylesworth
Kerwin Holmes Fulton

1960
Allen Loren Billingsly
James Randolph Adams

1961
Barney Link
Harley Procter

1962
Mac Martin
Donald W. Davis

1963
Gilbert T. Hodges
Paul B. West

1964
Homer J. Buckley
Jesse H. Neal
Edgar Kobak

1965
Robert M. Feemster
Harrison King McCann
Samuel C. Gale

1966
Lee Hastings Bristol
Walter Dill Scott

1967
Ernest Elmo Calkins
Mrs. Stanley B. Resor
Stanley B. Resor
George P. Rowell

1968
Russell T. Gray
Alex F. Osborn
Charles W. Mears

1969
Bruce Barton
Thomas D'Arcy Brophy

1970
Don Belding
Graham C. Patterson
Laurence W. Lane

1971
No inductees

1972
Leo Burnett
Philip Livingston Thomson
Ralph Starr Butler

1973
John P. Cunningham
Bernard C. Duffy

1974
James Webb Young
Raymond Rubicam

1975
Fairfax M. Cone
Artemas Ward
G. D. Crain, Jr.

1976
William Bernbach — David Ogilvy
Victor Elting, Jr.

1977
George Gallup — John Capels

1978
John H. Crichton — Barton A. Cummings
William A. Marsteller — J. Walter Thompson

1979
Atherton Wells Hobler — Neil Hosler McElroy

1980
Tom Dillon — Roy E. Larsen
Shirley Polykoff

Gold Medal

CIOS—WORLD COUNCIL OF MANAGEMENT
1, rue de Varembe, Case postale 20, CH-1211 Geneva 20, Switzerland (Tel: 34-14-30)

The CIOS Gold Medal is awarded every three years at the CIOS World Congress for literary or practical achievements in scientific management. CIOS members nominate and a medal selection committee chooses the recipient from six final nominees.

1929 Henri Le Chatelier, France
1932 Charles Adamiecki, Poland
1934 Masaryk Academy of Labor, Czechoslovakia
1935 Edmond Landauer, Great Britain
1938 Harry Arthur Hopf, U.S.A.
1947 Harlow S. Person, U.S.A.
1951 Lyndall F. Urwick, United Kingdom
1954 Lillian M. Gilbreth, U.S.A.
1960 John Ryan, United Kingdom
1963 Erwin H. Schell, U.S.A.
1966 Sir Walter Scott, Australia
1969 No award
1972 Peter F. Drucker, U.S.A.

Current Status Unknown

Distinguished Service Award
Grace Murray Hooper Award
A. M. Turing Award
Outstanding Contribution Award
Programming Systems and Languages Paper Award
Eckert-Mauchly Award

ASSOCIATION FOR COMPUTING MACHINERY
1133 Ave. of the Americas, New York, N.Y. 10036
(212/265-6300)

The Distinguished Service Award, which consists of a gift and a certificate, is given on the basis of the value and degree of an individual's services to the computer community, as judged by the awards committee.

1970 Franz L. Alt
1971 Don Madden
1972 George Forsythe
1973 William Atchison
1974 Saul Gorn
1975 John W. Carr III
1976 Richard G. Canning
1977 Thomas B. Steel, Jr.
1978 Eric A. Weiss
1979 Carl Hammer
1980 Bernard A. Galler

The $1,000 Grace Murray Hopper Award is given to an outstanding computer professional 30 years of age or under to honor a single recent technical or service contribution. An awards committee selects the winner.

1971 Donald E. Knuth
1972 Paul H. Dirkson
Paul H. Cress
1973 Lawrence Breed
Richard Lathwell
Roger Moore
1974 George N. Baird
1975 Allen L. Scherr
1976 Edward A. Shortliffe
1977 No award
1978 Raymon Kurzweil
1979 Stephen Wozniak
1980 Robert M. Metcalfe

The A.M. Turing Award, which now carries a $2,000 honorarium, is a technical award given annually to an individual for lasting and major contributions to the computer field. An awards committee selects the winner.

1966 A.J. Perlis
1967 Maurice Wilkes
1968 Richard W. Hamming
1969 Marvin Minsky
1970 J.H. Wilkinson
1971 John McCarthy
1972 E.W. Dijkstra
1973 Charles Bachman
1976 Donald Knuth
1975 Allen Newell
Herbert A. Simon
1976 Michael O. Rabin
Dana s. Scott
1977 John Backus
1978 Robert W. Floyd
1979 Kenneth E. Iverson
1980 Charles Antony Richard Hoare

The $1,000 Eckert-Mauchly Award is given annually to an individual for technical contributions to computer and digital systems architecture, encompassing combined hardware/software design and analysis of computing and of digital systems.

1978 Robert S. Barton
1979 Maurice V. Wilkes
1980 No award

The Outstanding Contribution Award, a certificate, annually honors up to three individuals for service to the association.

1976 Bruce W. Van Atta
1977 W. Smith Dorsey
1978 Kathleen A. Wagner
1979 M. Stuart Lynn
1980 No award

The $500 Programming and Language Paper Award is presented for the best paper on programming systems and languages published during the preceding 18 months in English.

1967 **Peter Lucas** and **Kurt Walk**
1968 **Peter J. Denning**
1969 **E. W. Dijkstra**
1970 **John C. Reynolds**
1971 **Donald R. Slutz, Richard L. Mattson, Irving L. Traiger,** and **Jan Gecsei**
1972 **C. A. R. Hoare**
1973 **Zohar Manna, Stephen Ness** and **Jean Vuillemin**
1974 **Daniel Bobrow** and **Ben Wegbreit**
1975 **Dennis M. Ritchie** and **Kenneth L. Thompson**
1976 **Frances E. Allen** and **John Cocke**
1977 **Susan Owicki** and **David Gries**
1978 **Niklaus Wirth**
1979 **David Parnas**
1980 **No award**

Stark Award

COLLECTIVE BARGAINING INSTITUTE
49 E. 68th St., New York, N.Y. 10021 (212/628-1010)

The $1,000 Stark Award is given periodically for excellence in reporting on collective bargaining and labor relations. The board of directors selects the winner.There was one winner prior to the 1977 honoree, but that name is not available.

1977 **A.H. Raskin,** *New York Times*

Distinguished Information Sciences Award

DATA PROCESSING MANAGEMENT ASSOCIATION
505 Busse Hwy., Park Ridge, Ill. 60068 (312/825-8124)

The Distinguished Information Sciences Award, which until 1978 was called the Computer Sciences Man-of-the-Year Award, is based on nominations from individual chapters and from the executive council, with the selection based on an executive council vote, for outstanding contributions and distinguished service in computer sciences and information processing.

1969 **Commander Grace Murray Hopper,** U.S. Navy
1970 **Frederick Phillips Brooks, Jr.,** University of North Carolina
1971 **No award**
1972 **Robert C. Cheek,** Westinghouse Tele-Computer Systems Corp.
1973 **Carl Hammer,** UNIVAC Div., Sperry Rand Corp.
1974 **Edward L. Glaser,** Case Western Reserve University
1975 **Willis H. Ware,** The Rand Corp.
Donald L. Bitzer, University of Illionois
1976 **Gene M. Amdahl,** Amdahl Corp.
1977 **J. Daniel Cougar,** Professor, University of Colorado
1978 **Irwin J. Sitkin,** Etna Life & Casualty Co.
1979 **Ruth M. Davis,** Deputy Undersecretary of Defense for Research and Advance Technology
1980 **John Diebold,** Diebold Group

Best Managed Companies List

DUN'S REVIEW
666 Fifth Ave., New York, N.Y. 10019 (212/489-2200)

In each year's December issue, the editors of *Dun's Review* cite the five companies they view as the best-managed, based on their observations of the American business scene. Corporations honored with designation also receive a silver plaque.

1972 **Mobil Oil**
Du Pont
Pfizer
Eastman Kodak
Xerox
1973 **Citibank**
Monsanto
J.C. Penney
Exxon
Weyerhaueser
1974 **Southern Railway**
American Telephone and Telegraph
R.J. Reynolds
Keer-McGee
Merck
1975 **Dow Chemical**
Hewlitt-Packard
S.S. Kresge
Merrill Lynch
Procter & Gamble
1976 **Haliburton**
Ralston-Purina
Bendix
Bank of America
Philip Morris
1977 **Beatrice Foods**
Delta Air Lines
Emerson Electric
McDonald's
General Motors
1978 **Boeing**
Caterpillar Tractor
Continental Illinois
General Electric
Schlumberger
1979 **American Broadcasting**
Digital Equipment
Raytheon
Revlon
Union Pacific
1980 **American Standard**
Gannett
Intel
Perkin-Elmer
Standard Oil (Indiana)

Eaton Award

INTERNATIONAL PLATFORM ASSOCIATION
2564 Berkshire Rd., Cleveland Heights, Ohio 44106 (216/932-0505)

The Eaton Award, which consists of an engraved bowl, is given annually to the individual judged by a committee of the International Platform Assn. and the Eaton Corp. to be the best business speaker of the year.

1976 **Charles E. Spahr**
1977 **Fletcher Byrom**

1978 Justin Dart
1979 Malcolm S. Forbes
1980 No award

Executive of the Year Award

NATIONAL MANAGEMENT ASSOCIATION
2210 Arbor Blvd., Dayton, Ohio 45439 (513/294-0421)

The Executive of the Year Award, which consists of a plaque, honors "outstanding contribution towards the preservation and advancement of the Free Enterprise System." Companies sponsoring membership in the association may make nominations for consideration by the Public Relations Committee and the executive board for ranking. A panel of judges selects the winner from the three finalists.

1915 R.W. Litchfield
1916 C.M. White
1917 A.A. Nicholson
1918 W.J. Cameron
1919 H.D. Bennett
1920 J.S. Thomas
1921 T.G. Graham
1922 B.D. Kunkle
1923 Louis Ruthenburg
1924 J.A. Voss
1925 W.C. Wright
1926 J.S. Strobel
1927 J.G. Jones
1928 A.A. Stockdale
1929 W.H. Hisey
1930 W.D. Henderson
1931 G.C.A. Hantleman
1932 C.C. Smith
1933 H.W. Barclay
1934 F.D. Slutz
1935 C.L. Proctor
1936 Frank H. Adams
1937 A.M. Degner
1938 C.C. Kendrick
1939 H.H. Woodhead
1940 George Spatta
1941 No award
1942 C.E. Wilson
1943 J.A. Robertshaw
1944 S.C. Allyn
1946 C.R. Hook
1947 J.H. Kindelberger and Robert E. Gross
1948 Fred Maytag II
1949 W.D. Robinson and George R. Fink
1950 Frank H. Irelan
1951 Robert F. Loetscher
1952 Mason M. Roberts
1953 Ralph S. Damon
1954 John T. Beatty
1955 Alva W. Phelps
1956 Gen. J.T. McNarney
1957 Gen. H.F. Safford
1958 Thomas E. Millsop
1959 George Romney
1960 Thomas W. Martin
1962 Frank J. Schaeffer
1961 John Mihalic
1963 Albrecht M. Lederer
1964 Floyd Dewey Gottwald
1965 Charles C. Gates, Jr.
1966 Daniel J. Haughton
1967 Russell DeYoung
1968 Lynn A. Townsend
1969 Donald C. Burnham
1970 Robert G. Dunlop
1971 George H. Weyerhaeuser
1972 Frederick G. Jaicks
1973 Melvin C. Holm
1974 W. Michael Blumenthal
1976 Willard F. Rockwell, Jr.
1976 William Plummer Drake
1977 Ray W. Macdonald
1978 Kenneth R. Danial
1979 Robert Dickey
1980 Robert Anderson

Captain Robert Dollar Memorial Award

NATIONAL FOREIGN TRADE COUNCIL
10 Rockefeller Plaza, New York, N.Y. 10020 (212/581-6420)

The Captain Robert Dollar Memorial Award is given annually for distinguished contribution to the advancement of American foreign trade and investments. An Annual Award Committee makes the nominations for approval by the board of directors. The recipient is honored with a plaque.

1938 Cordell Hull
1939 James A. Farrell
1940 Thomas J. Watson
1941 Eugene P. Thomas
1942 Sumner Welles
1943 Juan T. Trippe
1944 Eric A. Johnston
1945 Fred I. Kent
1946 William L. Clayton
1947 John Abbink
1948 Robert F. Loree
1949 Christian A. Herter
1950 Paul G. Hoffman
1951 James A. Farley
1952 Edward Riley
1953 Eugene Holman
1954 Clarence B. Randall
1955 George W. Wolf
1956 William S. Swingle
1957 Howard C. Sheperd
1958 W. Rogers Herod
1959 Samuel C. Waugh
1960 Henry W. Balgooyen
1961 J. Peter Grace
1962 William E. Knox
1963 James A. Farrell, Jr.
1964 David Rockefeller
1965 Thomas J. Watson, Jr.
1966 George S. Moore
1967 William Blackie
1968 Harold F. Linder
1969 Elis S. Hoglund
1970 Rudolph A. Peterson
1971 Henry Kearns
1972 Robert J. Dixson
1973 Walter B. Wriston
1974 George P. Shultz
1975 Stephen D. Bechtel
1976 Reginald H. Jones
1977 Irving S. Shapiro
1978 J. Paul Austin

1979 J. Robert Fluor
1980 T. A. Wilson

Fragrance Foundation Awards

THE FRAGRANCE FOUNDATION
116 E. 19th St., New York, N.Y. 10003 (212/673-5580)

An abstract column in crystal is annually awarded for various outstanding contributions in the fragrance industry, as voted by industry members. In additon to the individuals whose honors are listed here, the foundation grants awards to fragrance firms, retailers and publications for outstanding promotion of the sale and use of fragrances.

HALL OF FAME

1974 **Estee Lauder,** Estee Lauder
1975 **Charles Revson,** Revlon
1976 **H. Gregory Thomas,** Chanel
1977 **Jean Despres,** Coty
1978 **Richard Salomon,** Charles of the Ritz
1979 **Oscar Krolin,** Helena Rubinstein
1980 **Walter Lander,** Evyan

YEAR'S OUTSTANDING PERSON

1976 **Leonard Lauder,** Estee Lauder
1977 **Diane von Furstenberg**

PRESIDENT'S AWARD

1977 **Ernest Shifton,** Worldwide Perfumery, International Flavors and Fragrances
1978 **Van Venneri,** I. Magnin

Rodrigo Gomez Prize

CENTRE FOR LATIN AMERICAN MONETARY SYSTEMS
Durango 54, Mexico 7, D.F., Mexico (533-03-00)

The $5,000 Rodrigo Gomez Prize is presented annually for the best research paper or book on a topic of interest to Latin American central banks written by a citizen of a Latin American or Caribbean country. In addition to the first-place winner here, honor awards are given to the second- and third-place winners. Honor awards are sometimes made even when no first-place winner has been selected. The winning papers are also published. A jury composed of the presidents of five Latin American central banks selects the winner.

1972 **Aldo A. Arnaudo** (Argentina), *Economia Monetaria (Monetary Economics)*
1973 **Luis R. Sciffert** (Mexico), *Analisis del Mercado de Eurodolares: origen, desarrollo y consecuencias (Analysis of the Eurodollar market: origin, development and consequences*
1974 **No award**
1975 **No award**
1976 **Mario A. Blejer** (Argentina), *Dinero, Precios y la Balanza de Pagos: la experiencia de Mexico 1950-1973 (Money, Prices and the Balance of Payments: Mexico's experience 1950-1973)*
1977 **Julio Alfredo Genel** (Mexico), *La Estrategia del Estado en el Desarrollo Financiero (On the State's Strategy of Financial Development)*
1978 **Guillermo Ortiz Martinez** (Mexico), *Acumulacion de Capital y Crecimiento Economico (Captial Accumulation and Economic Growth)*
1979 **No award**
1980 **No award**

John Robert Gregg Award

McGRAW-HILL BOOK COMPANY
1221 Ave. of the Americas, New York, N.Y. 10020 (212/997-1221)

The $500 John Robert Gregg Award annually honors outstanding achievements in business education made during the two previous calendar years or for a series of achievements culminating in one evidenced during the two previous years.

1953 **Frederick G. Nichols**
1954 **Paul S. Lomax**
1955 **David D. Lessenberry**
1956 **Elvin S. Eyster**
1957 **Hamden L. Forkner**
1958 **Jessie Graham**
1959 **Ann Brewington**
1960 **Lloyd V. Douglas**
1961 **Paul A. Carlson**
1962 **Herbert A. Tonne**
1963 **Paul F. Muse**
1964 **Gladys Bahr**
1965 **Ray G. Price**
1966 **Russell J. Hosler**
1967 **Samuel J. Wanous**
1968 **McKee Fisk**
1969 **Bernard A. Shilt**
1970 **Alton B. Parker Liles**
1971 **Ruth I. Anderson**
1972 **J. Marshall Hanna**
1973 **Warren G. Meyer**
1974 **Lawrence W. Erickson**
1975 **Estelle L. Popham**
1976 **John L. Rowe**
1977 **F. Kendrick Bangs**
1978 **Louis C. Nanassy**
1979 **T. James Crawford**
1980 **Doris H. Crank**
Floyd D. Crank

James A. Hamilton Hospital Administrators' Book Award

AMERICAN COLLEGE OF HOSPITAL ADMINISTRATORS
840 N. Lake Shore Dr., Chicago, Ill. 60611 (312/943-0544)

The James A. Hamilton Hospital Administrators' Book Award is given in cooperation with the Alumni Assn. of the Graduate Program in Hospital and Health Care Administration of the University of Minnesota for a management book judged outstanding by a special committee. The award, which consists of $500, a bronze medallion and a certificate, honors a work published in the preceding two years.

1958 **Herbert A. Simon,** *Administrative Behavior*
1959 **Chris Argyris,** *Personality and Organization*
1960 **Harold Leavitt,** *Managerial Psychology*
1961 **Melville Dalton,** *Men Who Manage*

1962 **Douglas McGregor,** *The Human Side of Enterprise*
1963 **Rensis Likert,** *New Patterns of Management*
1964 **Basil S. Georgopoulos and Floyd C. Mann,** *The Community General Hospital*
1965 **Richard A. Johnson, Fremont E. Kast and James E. Rosenzweig,** *The Theory and Management of Systems*
1966 **Alfred P. Sloan, Jr.,** *My Years With General Motors*
1967 **Robert Golembiewski,** *Men, Management and Morality: Toward a New Organizational Ethic*
1968 **Daniel Katz and Robert Kahn,** *The Social Psychology of Organizations*
1969 **Paul R. Lawrence and Jay W. Lorsch,** *Organization and Environment*
1970 **Harry Levinson,** *The Exceptional Executive*
1971 **Clarence C. Walton,** *Ethos and the Executive Values in Managerial Decision Making*
1972 **John P. Campbell, Marvin D. Dunnette, Edward E. Lawler and Karl E. Weick,** *Managerial Behavior, Performance and Effectiveness*
1973 **Anne Ramsay Somers,** *Health Care in Transition: Directions for the Future*
1974 **Basil S. Georgopoulos,** *Organization Research on Health Institutions*
1975 **Peter F. Drucker,** *Management: Tasks, Responsibilities, Practices*
1976 **William Christopher,** *The Achieving Enterprise*
1977 **Robert N. Anthony and Regina E. Herzlinger,** *Management Control and Nonprofit Organizations*
1978 **Frederick I. Herberg,** *The Managerial Choice: To Be Efficient or to Be Human*
1979 **George A. Steiner** and **John B. Miner,** *Management Policy and Strategy*
1980 **Robert Blake** and **Jane Mouton**, *The New Managerial Grid*

Marketer of the Year Award

AMERICAN MARKETING ASSOCIATION/CHICAGO CHAPTER
222 S. Riverside Pl., Chicago, Ill. 60606 (312/726-0666)

The Association's Chicago Chapter, the nation's second largest, annually gives the Marketer of the Year Award to an outstanding professional in the Chicago area. Business, civic and academic leaders are asked for nominees, and the winner is selected by the board of directors on the basis of the company's innovative and successful marketing efforts as well as for the individual's social, civic and philanthropic involvement.

1958 **Floyd K. Thayer,** Abbott Latoratories
1959 **Leonard C. Truesdell,** Zenith Sales Corp.
1960 **Judson B. Branch,** Allstate Insurance Co.
1961 **B. Edward Bensinger,** Brunswick Corp.
1962 **Franklin J. Lunding,** Jewel Tea Co.
1963 **No award**
1964 **William Wood-Prince,** Armour & Co.
1965 **David M. Kennedy,** Continental Illinois National Bank
1966 **Leo Burnett,** Leo Burnett, Inc.
1967 **George E. Keck,** United Air Lines
1968 **Harold F. Werhane,** Culligan, Inc.
1969 **Robert D. Stuart, Jr.,** Quaker Oats Co.
1970 **Arthur C. Neilsen,** A.C. Neilsen Co.
1971 **James W. Button,** Sears, Roebuck & Co.
1972 **Ray A. Kroc,** McDonald's Corp.
1973 **Donald S. Perkins,** Jewel Co.
1974 **William O. Beers,** Kraftco Corp.
1975 **Edward E. Carlson,** United Air Lines and UAL, Inc.
1976 **William G. Karnes,** Beatrice Foods, Inc.
1977 **William B. Graham,** Baxter Travenol Laboratories
1978 **William Yivasker,** Gould, Inc.
1979 **Edward Ledder, Jr.,** Abbott Laboratories
1980 **William Watchman,** Swift, Inc.

Marketer of the Year

AMERICAN MARKETING ASSOCIATION/NEW YORK CHAPTER
420 Lexington Ave., New York, N.Y. 10017 (212/687-3280)

The Marketer of the Year is named annually for marketing excellence and community service. The winner, who receives a trophy, is selected by nominations from the New York Chapter's membership, recommendation by a committee and a final vote by the board of directors. The award had been given previously, was stopped for a number of years and was reinstituted in 1976.

1976 **Frank Braynar,** Operation Sail
1977 **John H. Iselin,** WNET Channel 13
1978 **Ed Finelstein,** R.C. Macy's

Current Status Unknown

McKinsey Award

McKINSEY FOUNDATION FOR MANAGEMENT RESEARCH
Harvard Business Review, Soldiers Field, Boston, Mass. 02163 (617/495-6175)

The McKinsey Foundation annually sponsors the $1,000 McKinsey Award, which is announced in the January-February issue of the *Harvard Business Review,* for the best article of the preceding year. Every year the editors choose a board of judges who make the selection based on the following criteria: helpfulness to executives in solving major internal management problems and/or in making strategic adjustments of the business to the environment and to competition; contribution to knowledge—innovation or originality of approach; depth of analysis and soundness of reasoning; provocativeness in challenging existing notions and present practices; readability—clarity and simplicity of style and interest of wording. A $500 second-place award is also given annually.

1970 **George Cabot Lodge,** "Top Priority: Renovating Our Ideology," September-October
1971 **J. Sterling Livingston,** "Myth of the Well-Educated Manager," January-February
1972 **Theodore Levitt,** "Production-Line Approach to Service," September-October
1973 **C. Jackson Grayson, Jr.,** "Let's Get Back to the Competitive Market System," November-December
1974 **George Cabot Lodge,** "Business and the Changing Society," March-April
1975 **Henry Mintzberg,** "The Manager's Job: Folklore and Fact," July-August
1976 **David C. McClelland and David H. Burnham,** "Power is the Great Motivator," March-April
1977 **Abraham Zaleznik,** "Managers and Leaders: Are They Different?", May-June

1978 **Alfred C. Neal,** "Immolation of Business Capital"
Richard Tanner Pascale, "Zen and the Art of Management"
1979 **Michael E. Porter,** "How Competitive Forces Shape Strategy"
1980 **Robert H. Hayes** and **William J. Abernathy,** N.A.

Domestic Car of the Year

MOTOR TREND
8490 Sunset Blvd., Los Angeles, Calif. 90069
(213/657-5100)

Motor Trend magazine annually selects vehicles of the year in various categories. The list below reflects the choices for the annual Domestic Car of the Year honors.

1949 **Cadillac**
1950 **No award**
1951 **Chrysler**
1952 **Cadillac**
1953 **No award**
1954 **No award**
1955 **No award**
1956 **Ford Motor Co.**
1957 **Chrysler Corp.**
1958 **Ford Thunderbird**
1959 **Pontiac Division**
1960 **Chevrolet Corvair**
1961 **Pontiac Tempest**
1962 **Buick Special**
1963 **AMC Rambler**
1964 **Ford Division**
1965 **Pontiac Division**
1966 **Oldsmobile Toronado**
1967 **Mercury Cougar**
1968 **Pontiac GTO**
1969 **Plymouth Road Runner**
1970 **Ford Torino**
1971 **Chevrolet Vega**
1972 **Citroen SM**
1973 **Chevrolet Monte Carlo**
1974 **Ford Mustang II**
1975 **Chevrolet Monza 2+2 V8**
1976 **Chrysler Corp.: Dodge Aspen and Plymouth Volare**
1977 **Chevrolet Caprice**
1978 **Chrysler Corp.,** Plymouth Horizon and Dodge Omni
1979 **Buick Riviera**
1980 **Chevrolet Citation**

Thomas Newcomen Award

NEWCOMEN SOCIETY IN NORTH AMERICA
Downington, Pa. 19335 (215/363-6600)

The $1,000 Thomas Newcomen Award, which is given every three years in conjunction with the Harvard Graduate School of Business, honors the author of an outstanding work on business history in the United States and Canada. The book may be about an individual firm, interactions between businesses, analysis of business philosophy or behavior or studies of business adjustments to changes in society. A committee representing the two organizations selects the winner.

1964 **Alfred D. Chandler, Jr.,** *Strategy and Structure: Chapters in the History of the Industrial Enterprise*
1967 **Sidney Pollard,** *The Genesis of Modern Management: A Study of the Industrial Revolution in Great Britain*
1970 **Robert W. Ozanne,** *A Century of Labor-Management Relations at McCormick and International Harvester and Wages in Practice and Theory: McCormick and International Harvester, 1860-1960*
1973 **Thomas C. Cochran,** *Business in American Life: A History*
1976 **Irvine H. Anderson, Jr.,** *The Standard Vacuum-Oil Company and United States East Asian Policy, 1933-1941*
1979 **Alfred D. Chandler, Jr.,** *The Visible Hand: The Managerial Revolution in American Business*

The $300 Thomas Newcomen Award in Business History, presented in cooperation with *Business History Review,* honors the year's best article appearing in that publication.

1979 **H. Thomas Johnson**
1980 **David S. Landes**

A second Thomas Newcomen Award in Business History, designated as a Special Award and accompanied by a $150 cash prize, is given to an author under 35 years of age who has not previously had a book published.

1979 **Joseph A. Pratt**
1980 **Elaine Glovka Spencer**

Louis Brownlow Book Award

NATIONAL ACADEMY OF PUBLIC ADMINISTRATION
1225 Connecticut Ave. NW, Washington, D.C. 20036
(202/659-9165)

The Louis Brownlow Book Award, consisting of a plaque and special recognition at the annual meeting, is given for new insights, fresh analysis and original ideas in public administration as expressed in a work published during the specified time period. A selection committee reviews works submitted by publishers.

1969 **Frederick C. Mosher,** *Democracy and the Public Service*
1970 **Emmette S. Redford,** *Democracy in the Administrative State*
James L. Sundquist, *Making Federalism Work*
1975 **Harlan Cleveland,** *The Future Executive*
Rufus E. Miles, Jr., *The Department of H.E.W.*
1976 **Louis Fisher,** *Presidential Spending Power*
1978 **Martha Derthick,** *Policymaking for Social Security*
1979 **Charles E. Linblom,** *Politics and Markets*
1980 **H. Hugh Heclo,** *A Government of Strangers*

Railroad Man of the Year
Golden Freight Car Award

MODERN RAILROADS MAGAZINE
5 S. Wabash Av., Chicago, Ill. 60603 (312/372-6880)

The Railroad Man of the Year is honored by the editors of *Modern Railroads* with a bronze bust of himself to reocognize outstanding contributions to railroading. The award was originally based on a readers' poll.

1964 **D. W. Brosnan,** Southern Railway System
1965 **Stuart T. Saunders,** Pennsylvania Railroad Co.
1966 **Stuart T. Saunders,** Pennsylvania Railroad Co.
1967 **Louis W. Menk,** Northern Pacific Railway
1968 **William B. Johnson,** Illinois Central Railroad
1969 **John W. Barriger,** Missouri-Kansas-Texas Railroad
1970 **John S. Reed,** Atchison, Topeka & Santa Fe Railway Co.
1971 **Jervis Langdon, Jr.,** Penn Central Transportation Co.
1972 **Charles Luna,** United Transportation Union
1973 **James W. Germany,** Southern Pacific Transportation Co.
1974 **L. Stanley Crane,** Southern Railway System
1975 **Frank E. Barnett,** Union Pacific Railroad
1976 **William J. Harris, Jr.,** Assn. of American Railroads
1977 **Edward G. Jordan,** Conrail

Current Status Unknown

The Golden Freight Car Award, which consists of a replica of a railroad freight car, is given annually to the railroad which, in the judgment of the magazine's editors, has made strides in the rail transport of freight.

1973 **Penn Central Transportation Co.**
1974 **Western Pacific**
1975 **Illinois Central Gulf**
1976 **No award**
1977 **Family Lines System**
1978 **Illinois Central Gulf**

Current Status Unknown

Robert E. Slaughter Research Award

McGRAW-HILL BOOK COMPANY
1221 Ave. of the Americas, New York, N.Y. 10020
(212/997-1221)

The $1,000 Robert E. Slaughter Research Award recognizes outstanding contributions to business and office education by up to three individuals in any given year, at least one of which must be for research in the teaching of Gregg shorthand. Studies may be scholarly, institutional or independent but must have been completed during the preceding 12 months,

1975 **Gary N. McLean,** University of Minnesota
L. Eugene Jones, Northeastern Louisiana University
1976 **M. Christine Gilmore,** Bishop College
Thomas O. Stanley, Missouri Southern College
Boyd G. Worthington, Brigham Young University
1977 **Thomas B. Duff,** University of Minnesota
Rita C. Kutie, Lakeland Community College
1978 **Norma Jean Olson,** North Hennepin Community College
1979 **Melvin J. Unger,** Bernard M. Baruch College of the City, University of New York
1980 **George F. Claffey,** Central Connecticut State College

Elmer A. Sperry Award

AMERICAN INSTITUTE OF AERONAUTICS AND ASTRONAUTICS
1290 Ave. of the Americas, New York, N.Y. 10019
(212/581-4300)

The Elmer A. Sperry Award, which consists of a bronze medal and certificate, is given jointly be the AIEE, the Institute of Electrical and Electronic Engineers, the Society of Automotive Engineers, the American Society of Mechnical Engineers and the SNAME in recognition of contributions to transportation engineering.

1965 **William H. Cook**
Richard L. Loesch, Jr.
Commercial Airplane Div., Boeing Co. (citation)
1966 **Hideo Shima**
Matsuataro Fujii
Shigenari Oishi
Japanese National Railways (citation)
1967 **Edward R. Dye**
Hugh DeHaven
Robert A. Wolf
Research Engineers, Cornell Aero. Lab., Cornell University Medical College (citation)
1968 **Christopher S. Cockerell**
Richard Stanton-Jones
British Hovercraft Corp. (citation)
1969 **Douglas C. MacMillan**
M. Nielsen
Edward L. Teale, Jr.
Wilbert C. Gumprich (citation)
George G. Sharp (citation)
Babock and Wilcox Co. (citation)
New York Shipbuilding Corp. (citation)
1970 **Charles Stark Draper**
1971 **Sedwig N. Wight**
George W. Baughman
William D. Hailes (citation)
Lloyd V. Lewis (citation)
Clarence S. Snavely (citation)
Herbert A. Wallace (citation)
Employees of General Railways Signal Co. (Signal and Communications Div.), Westinghouse Air Brake Co.
1972 **Perry W. Pratt**
Leonard S. Hobb
Pratt & Whitney (citation)
1973 **No award**
1974 **No award**
1975 **Jerome L. Goldman**
Frank A. Nemec
James J. Henry
Naval Architects & Marine Engineers of Friede & Goldman Inc. (citation)
Alfred H. Schwendtner (citation)
1976 **No award**
1977 **No award**
1978 **No award**
1979 **No award**
1980 **No award**

Elisabeth Cutter Morrow Award Salute to Women in Business

YWCA OF GREATER NEW YORK
610 Lexington Ave., New York, N.Y. 10022 (212/755-2700)

The initial Salute to Women in Business resulting during a reorganization in 1978 in induction into the YWCA's Academy of Women Achievers honored business achievements and public service by women selected by a committee of prominent individuals. The award consisted of a commemorative cube from Tiffany & Co.

1976 **Marion S. Adams,** Blythe Eastman Dillon & Co., Inc.
Rena R. Bartos, J. Walter Thompson Co.
Caroline Beebe, Bloomingdale's
Meg Bianco, Xerox Corp.
Barbara C. Blake, Chase Manhattan Bank N.A.
Mari Ann Blatch, Reader's Digest Assn., Inc.
Roberta Paula Books, Morgan Stanley & Co.
Joan-Ann Bostic, Pfizer, Inc.
Frankie Cadwell, Compton Advertising
Eleanor E. Campbell, Johnson & Higgins
Emilie Caravasios, American Stock Exchange
Frimet Celnik, New York Telephone
Paula Cholomondeley, International Paper Co.
Jeanne R. Corbett, Metropolitan Life Insurance Co.
Zoe Coulson, Good Housekeeping Institute
Gloria B. Deragon, Lever Brothers
Margaret B. Devlin, General Motors Corp.
Edith Drucker, B. Altman & Co.
Virginia A. Dwyer, American Telephone and Telegraph Co.
Rhoda Erickson, Sullivan & Cromwell
Sophie A. Fiattarone, First Boston Corp.
Josephine Foxworth, Jo Foxworth, Inc.
Dorothy L. Furness, J.C. Penney Co., Inc.
Elaine Garzarelli, Becker Securities Corp.
Dorothy Gregg, Celanese Corp.
Ruth Haase, Blue Cross & Blue Shield of Greater New York
Marjorie L. Hart, Exxon Corp.
Louise S. Hazeltine, Cornell University-New York Hospital School of Nursing
Peggy Healy, Young & Rubicam International, Inc.
Eleanor G. Hirsch, Holt Rinehart & Winston, CBS Educational Publishing
Charlotte Schiff Jones, Manhattan Cable Television, Inc.
Johanna Kaiser, YWCA of Greater New York
Jean D. Keaveny, International Telephone and Telegraph Corp.
Maryann N. Keller, Kidder, Peabody & Co., Inc.
Marion S. Kellogg, General Electric Co.
Moira Kelly, W.R. Grace & Co.
Dagnija D. Lacis, Burroughs Corp.
Natalie S. Lang, Booz, Allen & Hamilton, Inc.
Joy Levien, Singer Co.
Anna Maria Malachi, Port Authority of New York and New Jersey
Theresa A. Marmo, Bulova Watch Co., Inc.
Kay B. Maunsbach, Manhattan Life Insurance Co.
M. Jacqueline McCurdy, Joseph E. Seagram & Sons, Inc.
Sallie C. Melvin, Chemical Bank
Heidi Merrill, *Working Woman* magazine
Anne M. Meschino, Citibank N.A.
Birgit E. Morris, RCA Corp.
Dolores J. Morrissey, Bowery Savings Bank
Patricia Neighbors, Avon Products Inc.
Catherine A. Rein, Continental Group, Inc.
Ann Robb, Sperry and Hutchinson Co.
Marlene Sanders, American Broadcasting Co., Inc.
Eleanor J. Shehane, AT&T Long Lines Dept.
Judith G. Shepard, Goldman, Sachs & Co.
Doris H. Skutch, Burlington Industries, Inc.
Gail A. Wallace, Kennecott Copper Corp.
Dorothy Wayner, Byrde, Richard & Pound
Corrine Williams, Tiffany & Co.
Marjorie Worme, Parkchester Management Corp.
Kristina Wrba, Helena Rubinstein, Inc.
Mary Anne Wrenn, Merrill Lynch Pierce Fenner & Smith, Inc.
Ruth Ziff, Doyle Dane Bernbach, Inc.

Subsequently, Anne Morrow Lindbergh endowed the award, which was renamed in honor of her mother, Elizabeth Cutter Morrow. The award was redesigned in the form of an apple and was limited to 14 women a year, selected by a panel of judges.

1977 **Ruth S. Block,** Equitable Life Assurance Society of the U.S.
Elizabeth R. Clark, Bowery Savings Bank
Gail Erickson, W.R. Grace & Co.
Marilyn E. LaMarche, Citibank N.A.
Beverly C. Lannquist, Morgan Stanley & Co., Inc.
Helen Meyer, Dell Publishing Co., Inc.
Geraldine E. Rhoads, *Woman's Day* magazine
Mala Rubinstein, Helena Rubinstein
Sheila M. Smythe, Blue Cross & Blue Shield of Greater New York
Patricia Carry Stewart, Edna McConnell Clark Foundation
Carol C. Tatkon, Exxon Corp.
Carol C. Tucker, Avon Products, Inc.
Marilyn S. Watts, RCA Corp.
Shirley Wilkins, Roper Organization, Inc.

Restructured once again, the Elizabeth Cutter Morrow is now given to three women a year who have "made a difference in the quality of out lives in New York and, by their leadership and example, elevate the status of all women."

1978 **Carol Bellamy,** City Council President
Ada Louise Huxtable, *New York Times*
Jacqueline Wexler, Hunter College
1979 **Rep. Elizabeth Holzman**
Sylvia Porter, author
Joan Ganz Cooney, Children's Television Workshop
1980 **Mary Wells Lawrence,** Wells, Rich, Green
Louise Nevelson, Sculptor

Other prominent women in business, finance and communications were subsequently inducted into the YWCA Academy of Women Achievers, supplementing the honorees in the 1976 Salute to Women in Business.

1978 **Margaret Adams,** *Good Housekeeping*
Susan B. Bassin, ITT
Ann Berk, NBC-TV
Delores J. Bowens, Goldman, Sachs & Co.
Ruth Clay Bowman, Bowery Savings Bank
Marianne Burge, Price Waterhouse & Co.
Patricia Cassidy, New York Telephone
Sylvia L. Chambers, Xerox Corp.
Barbara J. Coe, New York University Graduate School of Business Administration
Betty Cott, Ruder & Finn
Judith L. Cromwell, Johnson & Higgins
Carole L. Cushmore, Baker & Taylor

Jacqueline Delafuente, F.W. Woolworth Co.
Doris Duenwald, Grosset & Dunlap
Ann Marie Flynn, Kidder, Peabody & Co.
Anita Gallo, B. Altman & Co.
Charlotte Gold, American Arbitration Assn.
Arlene Gordon, New York Assn. for the Blind
Veronica Hackett, Chemical Bank
Joyce Hergenhan, Consolidated Edison
Margaret Hofbeck, Bloomingdale's
Janet E. Hunt, Irving Trust Co.
Anne E. Impellizzeri, Metropolitan Life
Madie Ivy, Peat, Marwick, Mitchell
Sandra S. Jaffee, Citibank
Helen R. Jester, Equitable Life Insurance
Diane Michals Kissell, Lever Brothers
Kate Rand Lloyd, *Working Woman*
Amelia Lobsenz, Lobsenz-Stevens
Jane R. Lockshin, Singer Co.
Rita F. Mackey, Marine Midland Bank
Sandra Meyer, American Express
Susan E. Meyer, Billboard Publications
Therese M. Molloy, Ray Dirks Research/John Muir & Co.
Marie M. Olsen, European American Bank
Barbara Pesin, Avon Products
Audrey N. Pierce, 3M Co.
Marion Preston, J. Walter Thompson
R. Cynthia Pruett, IBM
Lena B. Purcell, Mutual of New York
Tina Santi, Colgate-Palmolive
Rose Ann Scamardella, WABC-TV
Joan Showalter, CBS Inc.
Eva Atkinson Trombley, Tobe-Coburn School
Patricia Wakefield, Celanese Fibers Marketing Co.
Connie Wiener, Seagram Distillers
Keven Wilder, Manhattan Cable TV
Marian Williams, Burlington Industries

1979 **No inductees**

1980 **Mary Hardiman Adams,** George B. Buck Consulting Actuaries
Marta Z. Amieva, Republic National Bank of New York
Dorothy Astarita, AMF Inc.
Joan Black Bakos, *Restaurant Business* magazine
Seemah Kim Bander, United States Life Insurance Co.
Adele M. Barrett, Kidder, Peabody, & Co., Inc.
Janet H. Beattie, Touche Ross & Co.
Ann Arthur Beck, Manhattan Cable Television
Ardith Berrettini, Revlon, Inc. (Princess Marcella Borghese Division)
Eleanor Lebenthal Bissinger, Lebenthal & Co., Inc.
Kay S. Breakstone, Kennecott Corp.
Jetta Brenner, Sheraton-Russell Hotel
Cynthia M. Burr, Connecticut General Insurance Corp.
Elizabeth M. Butson, Philip Morris International
Patricia Carbine, *Ms. Magazine*
Carolyn Chin, AT & T
Annette Choolfaian, Blue Cross/Blue Shield of Greater N.Y.
Dorothy Collins, Burson-Marsteller
Mary E. Cunningham, Bendix Corp.
Phyllis B. Davis, Avon Products, Incorporated
Judith DeMouth, Home Insurance Co.
Ann Atsaves Dessylas, St. Joe Minerals Corp.
Rita Farrelly, Mutual of New York
Margaret Filan, Xerox Corp./Northeast Region
Pamela Fiori, *Travel & Leisure*
Grace J. Fippinger, New York Telephone Co.
Pamela Potter Flaherty, Citibank
Janet Garlough, Trans World Airlines
Jeanne Golly, American Standard, Inc.
Patricia Greenwald, D'Arcy-MacManus & Masius/de Garmo
Helen B. Greenway, University Microfilms International
Joan Hafey, Young & Rubicam, Inc.
Guin Hall, New York Telephone Co.
E. Noel Harwerth, Kennecott Corp.
Winifred C. Heavey, C.B.S., Inc.
Ruth Hirschberg, Kayser Roth Intimate Apparel Co., Inc.
Ming Hsu, RCA Corp.
Dorothy E. Hull, Pfizer International
Teresa C. Infantino, Combe Inc.
Barbara Armstrong Jones, Hartford Fire Insurance Group
Marsha A. Kaminsky, WOR-TV
Patricia K. Kearney, International Business Machines Corp.
Winifred M. Kelly, F.W. Woolworth
Mary Joyce Kern, Equitable Life Assurance Society of the U.S.
Marion A. Klein, Bristol-Myers Co.
Patricia R. Krever, Turnkey Sales & Leasing, Inc.
Peggy E. Leak, The Atlantic Companies
Carol Ledda, Shiseido Cosmetics
Helen M. Lewis-Wistner, W.R. Grace & Co.
Kay M. Lindstrom, Price Waterhouse & Co.
Melina Lloyd, Sperry and Hutchinson Co.
Judith P. Lotas, SSC&B, Inc., Advertising
Catherine Lucht, Ward Howell International, Inc.
A. Kay Lund, United Airlines
Jane C. Mack, Alliance Capital Management Corp.
Harriet I. Matysko, United Business Publications Division
Mary A. McCravey, Georgia-Pacific Corp.
Marilyn I. Montgomery, Allied Chemical Corp., Fibers & Plastics Co.
Jo Moring, National Broadcasting Co.
Marianne Parrs, Internaitonal Paper Co.
Mary Jane Raphael, American Broadcasting Companies, Inc.
Patricia Rogoski, ITT Consumer Financial Corp.
Marilyn Romans, Western Electric, Corporate Product Planning
Rosemary Scanlon, Port Authority of N.Y. & N.J.
Ellen M. Shong, AMAX, Inc.
Laura Sinclair, Sterling Drug Inc.
Sally A. Stowe, Keefe, Bruyette & Woods, Inc.
Lynda Sussman, ITT Defense Communications Division
Betty Sutton, *Amsterdam News*
Carol A. Taber, *Working Woman* magazine
P. Jane Tanquary, Sears, Roebuck & Co.
Caroline F. Themm, Johnson & Higgins
Myra L. Tobin, Marsh and McLennan, Inc.
Lois B. Underhill, Cadwell Davis Savage/Advertising
Mary F. Voce, Breed, Abbott & Morgan
Beverley B. Wadsworth, Continental Corp.
Eleanor Wells, ITT United States Telephone & Telegraph, Inc.
Kay Wight, American Women in Radio & TV
Carolyn Williamson, Polariod Corp.
Lourdes Yabor de Diaz, ITT
Angela Zizzi-Dailey, Drexel Burnham Lambert Inc.

International Relati

ons & Understanding

Contents

Related Awards

Aspen Institute Award

ASPEN INSTITUTE FOR HUMANISTIC STUDIES
717 Fifth Ave., New York, N.Y. 10022 (212/759-1053)

The $5,000 Statesman-Humanist Award of the Aspen Institute periodically honors individuals for a commitment to human freedom and continued contribution to international peace and understanding.

1971 **Jean Monnet** (France)
1973 **Willy Brandt** (Germany)
1977 **John J. McCloy** (U.S.A.)
1978 **Alberto Lleras Camargo** (Colombia)

Adolphe Betinck Prize

ADOLPHE BETINCK PRIZE COMMITTEE
33 rue Poissoniere, 75002 Paris, France

The Adolphe Betinck Prize, which is now 20,000 francs, is given annually for a book contributing to European unity, the cause of peace or the struggle against fanatacism. A committee selects the winner from works submitted by publishers.

1976 **Jean Monnet**
1977 **Raymond Aron,** *Plaidoyer pour l'Europe Decadente*
1978 **Roy Jenkins**
1979 **Peter Hull,** *Europe 2000*
1980 **Emmanuele Gazzo**

Charlemagne Prize

GESELLSCHAFT FUR DIE VERLEIHUNG DES INTERNATIONALEN KARLSPREIS DER STADT AACHEN
Markt 39/41, D-5100, Aachen, Federal Republic of Germany (472341)

The International Prize of the City of Aachen, known as the Karlspreis or Charlemagne Prize, is awarded annually to people of merit for the promotion of Western unity by political, literary or economic endeavors. The prize consists of 5,000 German marks and a medallion. A jury selects the winner.

1950 **Graf Richard Coudenhove-Kalergi,** Creator of the Pan-European movement
1951 **Hendrik Brugmans,** Rector of the European College, Bruges
1952 **Alcide de Gasperi,** Italian Prime Minister
1953 **Jean Monnet,** President of the European Coal and Steel Community, Luxembourg
1954 **Konrad Adenauer,** Chancellor of the Federal Republic of Germany
1955 **Sir Winston S. Churchill,** Former Prime Minister of Great Britain
1956 **No award**
1957 **Paul Henri Spaak,** Secretary General of North Atlantic Treaty Organization
1958 **Robert Schuman,** President of European Parliament
1959 **George C. Marshall,** Former U.S. Secretary of State
1960 **Joseph Bech,** Honorary Minister of State —President of the Chamber of Deputies, Luxembourg
1961 **Walter Hallstein,** President of the Commission of the European Economic Community
1962 **No award**
1963 **Edward Heath,** Lord Privy Seal of Britain
1964 **Antonio Segni,** President of the Italian Republic
1966 **Jens Otto Krag,** Prime Minister of Denmark
1967 **Joseph Luns,** Minister of Foreign Affairs of the Royal Netherlands Government
1968 **No award**
1969 **The Commission of the European Communities**
1970 **Francois Seydoux de Clausonne,** Former French Ambassador to the Federal Republic of Germany
1971 **No award**
1972 **Roy Jenkins, M.P.**
1973 **Don Salvador de Madariaga**
1974 **No award**
1975 **No award**
1976 **Leo Tindemans,** Belgian Prime Minister
1977 **Walter Scheel,** President of the Federal Republic of Germany
1978 **Konstantin Karamanlis,** Prime Minister of the Greek Republic
1979 **Emilio Colombo,** President of European Parliament
1980 **Not available at press time**

Eisenhower Medallion

PEOPLE-TO-PEOPLE INTERNATIONAL
3 Crown Center, 2440 Pershing Rd., Suite G-30, Kansas City, Mo. 64108 (816/421-6343)

The Eisenhower Medallion is awarded to one or two individuals for exceptional contributions to world peace and understanding over a period of at least five years. Nominees must receive a unanimous vote of the executive committee of the board of trustees to be honored.

1968 **Mrs. Carter Collins**
Mrs. Renzo Sawada
Mrs. Guido Panteleoni
Louise Kim
Arnold Palmer
James A. McCain
1969 **Neil Armstrong, Edwin Aldrin, Jr. and Michael Collins**
George Venable Allen
Frank H. Krusen
1970 **Melville Bell Grosvenor**
1971 **Joyce C. Hall**
1972 **Albert Pick, Jr.**
1973 **Donald J. Hall**
1974 **No award**
1975 **No award**
1976 **Magnus von Braun**
1977 **No award**
1978 **No award**
1979 **No award**
1980 **Catharine Menninger**

Martin Luther King, Jr., Nonviolent Peace Prize

MARTIN LUTHER KING, JR., CENTER FOR NONVIOLENT SOCIAL CHANGE
503 Auburn Ave. NE, Atlanta, Ga. 30312 (404/524-1956)

The Martin Luther King, Jr., Nonviolent Peace Prize, which consists of $1,000 and a medallion of Dr. King, is presented annually for distinguished contributions to nonviolent social change in the United States or occasionally abroad. A committee of previous winners chooses the recipient.

1973 **Andrew Young**
1974 **Caezar Chavez**
1975 **John Lewis**
1976 **Randolph Blackwell**
1977 **Benjamin Mays**
1978 **Stanley Levison**
1979 **Jimmy Carter**
1980 **Rosa Parks**

SPECIAL AWARD

1978 **Kenneth Kaunda,** President of Zambia

International Lenin Prize for the Promotion of Peace Among the Nations

INTERNATIONAL LENIN PRIZE COMMITTEE
The Kremlin, Moscow, U.S.S.R. (Tel: 224-75-35)

The International Lenin Prize, often called the Lenin Peace Prize, is awarded annually to about five individuals of any nationality for outstanding activities in the promotion of peace, or for scientific achievements, works of literature or art or achievements in any area that contributes to the cause of peace among nations. The recipients are presented with a gold medal bearing a likeness of I.V. Lenin, a certificate and 25,000 rubles. The winners are selected by a committee which considers documentation of candidates' suitability for the honor from nominees suggested to the committee's Secretariat by organizations of all types. These awards, which parallel the Lenin Prizes given to Soviet citizens, were begun in 1950, but the names of early winners are not available

1968-69 **Ludvic Svoboda** (Czechoslovakia), Statesman and public figure
Linus Pauling (U.S.A.), Scientist and public figure
Shafi Ahmed al Cheih (Sudan), Public figure
Jaroslav Ivaschkevitch (Poland), Writer and public figure
Akira Ivai (Japan), Public figure
Bertil Svanstrem (Sweden), Journalist and public figure
Haled Mohi ad Deem (Egypt), Journalist and public figure

1970-71 **A.H.S. Burop** (United Kingdom), Scientist and President of the World Scientist Foundation
Renato Guttozo (Italy), Artist and public figure
Tsola Dragoicheva (Bulgaria), Political and public figure
Camal Djumblat (Lebanon), Political and public figure
Ernst Bush (German Democratic Republic), Artist
Alfredo Varela (Argentina), Writer and public figure

1972 **L.I. Brezhnev** (U.S.S.R.), General Secretary of the Central Committee of the Communist Part of the Soviet Union
James Aldridge (United Kingdom), Writer
Louis Carvalan (Chile), Senator and Secretary General of the Communist Party of Chile
Janne Marten Sisse (Guinea), Political and public figure
Raimon Goor (Belgium), Canon and public figure

1975-76 **Janosh Kadar** (Hungary), First Secretary of the Central Committee of the Hungarian Socialist Workers Party
Agostinho Neto (Angola), President of Angola
Samora M. Machel (Mozambique), President of Mozambique
Hortenzia Bussi de Allende (Chile), Public figure and honorable vice president of the International Democratic Women's Federation
Sean McBride (Ireland), Political and public figure
Pierre Poyade (France), Public figure
Yannis Ritsos (Greece), Poet and public figure

1977 **Gus Hall** (U.S.A.), Leader of the Communist Party in the United States
Other winners not available

1978 **Kurt Bakhman** (Federal Republic of Germany)
Freda Brown (Australia)
Angela Davis (U.S.A.)
Halina Skibnewska (Poland)
S. Kumar P.S. Menon (India)
Vilma Espin (Cuba)

1979 **Urho Kokkonen** (Finland)
Le Duan (Vietnam)
Miguel Otero (Venezuela)
Herve Bazin (France)
A. al-Hamisy (Egypt)

1980 **No award**

Ramon Magsaysay Award

RAMON MAGSAYSAY FOUNDATION
Box 3350, Manila, Philippines (59-19-59)

The Ramon Magsaysay Award for International Understanding is one of five $20,000 awards made annually for achievements in Asia reflecting the ideals of the late Ramon Magsaysay. The foundation's board of trustees selects the recipient from nominations received. The funding for this honor, which until 1977 was $10,000, is from the Rockefeller Brothers Fund of New York.

1958 **Operation Brotherhood** (Philippines), in acknowledgement of the spirit of service to other people in a time of need with which this group effort was conceived and has been carried forward and of the international amity it has fostered

1959 **No award**

1960 **Y. C. James Yen** (China), "for sharing his experience and creative leadership in rural reconstruction and bringing to the East and West an awareness of the urgency for meeting the aspirations of the Asian farmer for a fuller life"

1961 **Genevieve Caulfield** (American citizen), "for international citizenship and guidance to full and useful lives those in other lands afflicted like herself by blindness"

1962 **Mother Teresa** (India; born in Yugoslavia), "for merciful cognizance of the abject poor of a foreign land in whose services she has led a new congregation"

1963 **U.S. Peace Corps in Asia** (U.S.A.), "for voluntary service to the cause of peace and humanity in a direct and personal way"

1964 **Welthy Honsinger Fisher** (American citizen), "for unstinting personal commitment to the cause of literacy in India and other Asian countries whose teachers have sought her guidance"

1965 **Bayanihan Folk Arts Center and Its Supporting Entities** (Philippines), "for projection of a warm and artistic portrayal of the Filipino people to audiences on five continents"

1966 **Committee For Cordination of Investigation of The Lower Mekong Basin and Cooperating Entities** (Cambodian, Lao, Thai and Vietnamese members, international staff), "for purposeful progress toward harnessing one of Asia's greatest river systems, setting aside divisive national interests in deference to regional opportunities"

1967 **Shiroshi Nasu** (Japan), "for practical humanitarianism enhancing cooperation in agriculture by learning through multinational experience"

1968 **Cooperative for American Relief Everywhere** (U.S.A.), "for CARE's constructive humanitarianism fostering dignity among the needy in Asia and on three other continents for over 22 years"

1969 **International Rice Research Institute** (American-Philippine; international staff), "for seven years of innovative interdisciplinary teamwork by Asian and Western scientists, unprecedented in scope, that is achieving radical, rapid advances in rice culture"

1970 **No award**

1971 **Saburo Okita** (Japan), "for sustained and forceful advocacy of genuine Japanese partnership in the economic progress of her Asian neighbors"

1972 **No award**

1973 **Summer Institute of Linguistics** (U.S.A.), "for inspired outreach to nonliterate tribespeople, recording and teaching them to read their own languages and enhancing their participation in the larger community of man"

1974 **William F. Masterson** (born in U.S.A.), "for multinational education and inspiration of rural leaders prompting their return to and love of the land"

1975 **Patrick J. McGlinchey** (born in Ireland), "for mobilizing international support and foreign volunteers to modernize livestock farming in his adopted country"

1976 **Henning Holck-Larsen** (born in Denmark), "for his signal contribution towards India's technical modernization, complementing industrialization with human concern"

1977 **College of Agriculture** University of the Philippines at Los Banos (Philippines), "for its quality of teaching and research, fostering a sharing of knowledge in modernizing Southeast Asian agriculture"

1978 **Soedjatmoko** (Indonesia), "for persuasive presentation of the case for developing Asia's basic needs in the councils of world decision making"

1979 **Not available at press time**

1980 **Not available at press time**

Jawaharlal Nehru Award for International Understanding

INDIAN COUNCIL FOR CULTURAL RELATIONS
Azad Bhavan, I.P. Estate, New Delhi, India (Tel: 272114)

The Jawaharlal Nehru Award for International Understanding, which carries an honorarium of 100,000 rupees and a citation, is given annually for contributions to the promotion of international understanding, goodwill and friendship among the world's people. Nominations in writing may be made by former members of the selection jury, past recipients of the award, members of the Parliament of India, Nobel laureates, the secretary general of the United Nations and leaders of other international organizations whose objectives are the promotion of world peace, presidents or vice chancellors of universities, academicians, professors of social or natural sciences, heads of Indian missions abroad, heads of learned societies or research institutions or anyone else invited by the jury to submit a nomination. A seven-member jury appointed by the government of India selects the recipient.

1965 **U Thant,** Former secretary general of the United Nations

1966 **Martin Luther King,** Fighter against racial discrimination

1967 **Abdul Ghaffar Khan,** Freedom fighter

1968 **Yehudi Menuhin,** Violinist

1969 **Mother Teresa,** Missionary

1970 **Kenneth D. Kaunda,** President of Zambia

1971 **Josip Broz Tito,** President of Yugoslavia

1972 **Andre Malraux,** Writer and former French minister of Culture

1973 **Julius K. Nyerere,** President of Tanzania

1974 **Raul Prebisch,** Economist

1975 **Jonas Salk,** Biochemist

1976 **Giuseppe Tucci,** Indologist

Current Status Unknown

Nobel Peace Prize

NOBEL FOUNDATION
Nobel House, Sturegatan 14, 11436 Stockholm, Sweden

Of the six Nobel Prizes given annually, the Nobel Peace Prize is generally recognized as the highest honor which can be bestowed upon an individual or organization for furthering fraternity among nations and all humanity, reduction of standing armies and promotion of peace conferences. Although the other Nobel Prizes are awarded on the decision of Swedish juries at ceremonies in Sweden, the Nobel Peace Prize is administered and presented by the Nobel Peace Prize Selection Committee comprised of the Norwegian Parliament and the Norwegian Nobel Institute (address: 19 Dramensveien, Oslo, Norway). The award is presented concurrently with ceremonies in Stockholm on December 10; they take place in the presence of His Majesty, the King of Norway, in the Great Hall of Oslo University. The amount of the honorarium fluctuates. In 1980, it was approximately $212,000.

1901 **Jean H. Dunant,** Switzerland
Frederick Passy, France

1902 **Elie Ducommun,** Switzerland
Charles A. Gobat, Switzerland

1903 **Sir William R. Cremer,** Great Britain

1904 **Institute of International Law**

1905 **Baroness Bertha von Suttner,** Austria

1906 **Theodore Roosevelt,** U.S.A.

1907 **Ernesto T. Moneta,** Italy
Louis Renault, France

1908 **Klas P. Arnoldson,** Sweden
Fredrik Bajer, Denmark

1909 **Auguste M.F. Beernaert,** Belgium
Paul H.B.B. d'Estournelles de Constant, France

1910 **Permanent International Peace Bureau**

1911 **Tobias M.C. Asser,** Netherlands
Alfred H. Fried, Austria

1912 **Elihu Root,** U.S.A.

1913 **Henri La Fontaine,** Belgium

1914 **No award**

1915 **No award**

1916 **No award**
1917 **International Committee of the Red Cross**
1918 **No award**
1919 **Woodrow Wilson,** U.S.A.
1920 **Leon V. A. Bourgeois,** France
1921 **Karl H. Branting,** Sweden
Christian L. Lange, Norway
1922 **Fridtjof Nansen,** Norway
1923 **No award**
1924 **No award**
1925 **Sir J. Austen Chamberlain,** Great Britain
Charles G. Dawes, U.S.A.
1926 **Aristide Briand,** France
Gustav Stresemann, Germany
1927 **Ferdinand E. Buisson,** France
Ludwig Quidde, Germany
1928 **No award**
1929 **Frank B. Kellogg,** U.S.A.
1930 **Lars O.N. Soderblom,** Sweden
1931 **Jane Addams,** U.S.A.
Nicholas Murray Butler, U.S.A.
1932 **No award**
1933 **Sir Norman Angell,** Great Britain
1934 **Arthur Henderson,** Great Britain
1935 **Carl von Ossietzky,** Germany
1936 **Carlos de Saavedra Lamas,** Argentina
1937 **Viscount Cecil of Chelwood,** (Lord Edgar Algernon Robert Gascoyne Cecil) Great Britain
1938 **International Office for Refugees**
1939 **No award**
1940 **No award**
1941 **No award**
1942 **No award**
1943 **No award**
1944 **International Committee of the Red Cross**
1945 **Cordell Hull,** U.S.A.
1946 **Emily G. Balch,** U.S.A.
John R. Mott, U.S.A.
1947 **Friends Service Council,** Great Britain
American Friends Service Committee
1948 **No award**
1949 **Lord John Boyd Orr of Brechin,** Great Britain
1950 **Ralph J. Bunche,** U.S.A.
1951 **Leon Jouhaux,** France
1952 **Albert Schweitzer,** France (German-born)
1953 **George C. Marshall,** U.S.A.
1954 **Office of U.N. High Commissioner for Refugees**
1955 **No award**
1956 **No award**
1957 **Lester B. Pearson,** Canada
1958 **Georges Pire,** Belgium
1959 **Philip J. Noel-Baker,** Great Britain
1960 **Albert J. Lutuli,** South Africa
1961 **Dag Hammarskjold,** Sweden (posthumous)
1962 **Linus C. Pauling,** U.S.A.
1963 **International Committee of the Red Cross**
Red Cross Societies League
1964 **Martin Luther King, Jr.,** U.S.A.
1965 **United Nations Children's Fund (UNICEF)**
1966 **No award**
1967 **No award**
1968 **Rene Cassin,** France
1969 **International Labor Organization (ILO)**
1970 **Norman E. Borlaug,** U.S.A.
1971 **Willy Brandt,** Germany
1972 **No award**
1973 **Henry A. Kissinger,** U.S.A. (German-born) and **Le Duc Tho,** North Vietnam (prize declined)
1974 **Eisaku Sato,** Japan
Sean MacBride, Ireland
1975 **Andrei D. Sakharov,** U.S.S.R.
1976 **Betty Williams and Mairead Corrigan,** United Kingdom (Northern Ireland)
1977 **Amnesty International**
1978 **Muhammed Anwar al-Sadat** (Egypt) and **Menachem Begin** (Israel, born in Poland)
1979 **Mother Teresa** (India, born in Yugoslavia)
1980 **Not available at press time**

Robert Schuman Prize
Robert Schuman Medal

STIFTUNG F.V.S.
Georgsplatz 10, 2 Hamburg 1, Federal Republic of Germany (Tel: 33 04 00 and 33 06 00)

The Robert Schuman Prize, which carries a cash award of 30,000 marks, is given annually in recognition of the furtherance of European unity. The University of Bonn administers the award.

1966 **Jean Monnet,** France
1967 **Joseph Bech** Luxemburg
1968 **Sicco L. Mansholt,** Belgium
1969 **Walter Hallstein,** Federal Republic of Germany
1970 **Denis de Rougemont,** Switzerland
1971 **Alain Poher,** France
Silvius Magnago, Italy
1972 **Roy Jenkins,** Great Britain
1973 **Jens Otto Krag,** Denmark
1974 **Altiero Spinelli,** Belgium
1975 **Pierre Pflimlin,** France
1976 **Sir Christopher Soames,** Great Britain
1977 **Gaston Thorn,** Luxembourg
1978 **Louis Leprince-Briquet,** France
1979 **Kai-Uwe von Hassel,** Federal Republic of Germany
1980 **Leo Tindemans,** Belgium

The Robert Schuman Medal, which is of gold, is given annually for contributions to Franco-German understanding or European unity. The award is administered by the Society of the the Friends of Robert Schuman in Montigny-les-Metz.

1966 **Konrad Adenauer**
1967 **Rene Mayer**
Walter Hallstein
1968 **Emilio Colombo**
1969 **Paul-Henri Spaak**
1970 **Louis Armand**
1971 **Pierre Werner**
1972 **Hendrik Brugmans**
1973 **John Lynch**
1974 **Olivier Reverdin**
1975 **Francois-Xavier Ortoli**
1976 **No award**
1977 **Otto von Habsburg**
1978 **Louise Weiss**
1979 **Konstantinios Karamanlis**
1980 **Pierre Harmel**

James Brown Scott Prizes

INSTITUT DE DROIT INTERNATIONAL
82, Ave. du Castel, B-1200, Brussels, Belgium

The James Brown Scott Prizes are 13 honors which go according to pre-set criteria to authors of the best memoirs on the question of international public law.

The awards are made every two years for works at least 150 but not more than 500 pages, submitted by anyone but members and former members of the Institute. A jury selects the winner of the James Brown Scott Prize, which carries a cash honorarium, which since 1964 has been 2,000 Swiss francs.

1933 **John Westlake Prize: Anton Roth** (Germany)
1935 **Andres Bello Prize:** No award
1937 **Carlos Calvo Prize: A. Balasko** (France)
1950 **Grotius Prize: Martinus Willem Mouton** (Netherlands)
1952 **Francis Lieber Prize: Hedwig Maier** (Germany)
1954 **Frederic de Martins Prize: Theodor Schneid** (Germany)
1956 **Mancini Prize:** No award
1958 **Pufendorf Prize: Chava Schachor-Landau** (Israel)
1960 **Louis Renault Prize:** No award
1962 **G. Rolin-Jaequemyns Prize:** No award
1964 **Emer de Vattel Prize:** No award
1966 **Vitoria Prize:** No award
1968 **JohnWestlake Prize: Hugh W.A. Thirlway** (Great Britain)
1970 **Henri Wheaton Prize:** No award
1972 **Andres Bellow Prize:** No award
1974 **Carlos Calvo Prize:** No award

Current Status Unknown

United Nations Prizes

UNITED NATIONS
G.C. Box 20, New York, N.Y. 10017 (Tel. Geneva, Switzerland 34-60-11, Ext. 2723)

The United Nations Prizes are given every five years for outstanding contributions to the promotion and protection of human rights and fundamental freedoms embodied in the Universal Declaration of Human Rights. The establishment of this plaque honoring notable individuals was made under General Assembly Resolution 2217 (XXI).

1968 **Manuel Bianchi**
Rene Cassin
Albert Luthuli
Mehranguiz Manoutchehrian
P.E. Nedbaila
Eleanor Roosevelt
1973 **Taha Hussein**
Wildred Jenks
Maria Lavalle-Urbina
Bishop Abel Muzorewa
Sir Seewoosagur Ramgoolam
U Thant
1978 **International Committee of the Red Cross**
Vicaria de la Solidaridad
Amnesty International
Union des Femmes Tunisiennes
Begum Ra'Ana Liaquat Ali Khan
Helen Suzman
Martin Luther King, Jr.,
Price Sadruddin Aga Khan

U.N. Children's Fund Award

UNITED NATIONS
First Ave. and 42nd St., New York, N.Y. 10017
(212/754-8029)

The United Nations Children's Fund Award for Distinguished Service at the international level is presented periodically for efforts on behalf of and for contributions to the United Nations International Children's Emergency Fund.

1976 **Danny Kaye**
Robert Debre, France, Founder of UNICEF
1977 **Peter Ustinov**

Wateler Peace Prize

CARNEGIE FOUNDATION
Peace Palace, Carnegieplein 2, KJ-2517 The Hague, Netherlands (070-469 680)

The Wateler Peace Prize, which is now 40,000 guilders, is awarded annually to an individual or organization for rendering valuable service in the cause of peace or contributing to finding a means for combating war. The award is made alternately to a Dutch and to a foreign person or institution. The foundation's board of directors selects the winner.

1931 **Union Internationale des Associations pour la Societe des Nations**
1932 **Vereeniging voor Volkenbond en Vrede te 's-Gravenhage**
1933 **Arthur Henderson**
1934 **Afdeeling Nederland van den Wereldbond voor Internationale Vriendschap**
1935 **Radio Omroepdienst van den Volkenbond** (Geneva)
1936 **Haagsche Academie voor Internationaal Recht**
1937 **Lord Baden-Powell**
1938 **Nederlandsche Jeugd-Herberg Centrale**
Oecumenische Vereeniging in Nederland
Schenkingsrecht voldaan door de begiftigden
1939 **American Friends' Service Committee** (Philadelphia)
Friends' Service Council (London)
1940-46 **No award**
1947 **H. Ch. G. J. van der Mandere** (Wassenaar)
1948 **World Council of Churches** (Geneva)
1949 **Haagse Academie voor Internatinaal Recht**
1950 **Institut des Hautes Etudes Internationales a Geneve**
1951 **D. U. Stikkel**
1952 **Jean Monnet**
1953 **Nederlandse Raad der Europese Bewging 's-Gravenhage**
1954 **Sir Anthony Eden**
1955 **G. J. van Heuven Goedhart**
1956 **United Nations Children's Fund** (UNICEF)
1957 **A. Pelt**
1958 **Moens de Fernig**
1959 **Stichting Opbouwfonds Jeudherbergen**
1960 **W.A. Visser't Hooft**
1961 **Marguerite Nobs**
1962 **Dag Hammarskjold**
1963 **Jongeren Vriwilligers Programma**
1964 **Wereld Federatie van Vereigingen voor de Verenigde Naties** (WFUNA), (Geneva)
1965 **Eduard van Beinum Stichting** (Breukelen)

1966 **La Communaute de Taize** (France)
1967 **Interkerkelijk Overleg in Radio Aangelegenheden** (IKOR)
1968 **Coretta Scott King**
1969 **Nederlandse Vereniging voor Internationaal Recht**
1970 **International Social Service Headquarters** (Geneva)
1971 **B.V.A. Roling**
1972 **Alva Myrdal**
1973 **A.H. Boerma**
1974 **Henry A. Kissinger**
1975 **M. Kohnstamm**
1976 **Manfred Lachs**
1977 **Salvation Army in the Netherlands**
1978-80 **Not available**

Public Service, Human

Contents

Related Awards

itarianism & Heroism

Advertising Council Award for Public Service

THE ADVERTISING COUNCIL
825 Third Ave., New York, N.Y. 10022 (212/758-0400)
478 478

The Advertising Council Award for Public Service is a Sterling silver Paul Revere bowl given annually to an American business leader for notable contributions in public service to the welfare of the country and its citizens. The Council's board of directors selects the winner.

1954 Charles E. Wilson
1955 Clarence Francis
1956 Paul G. Hoffman
1957 Sidney J. Weinberg
1958 George M. Humphrey
1959 Roy E. Larsen
1960 Neil McElroy
1961 Henry Ford II
1962 Lucius D. Clay
1963 John J. McCloy
1964 Charles G. Mortimer
1965 David Sarnoff
1966 John A. McCone
1967 John T. Connor
1968 Robert S. McNamara
1969 Frank Stanton
1970 James M. Roche
1971 David Rockefeller
1972 Thomas J. Watson, Jr.
1973 Howard J. Morgens
1974 Katharine Graham
1975 J. Paul Austin
1976 Arthur M. Wood
1977 William F. May
1978 John D. de Butts
1979 Thomas A. Murphy
1980 Andrew Heiskell

Murray-Green-Meany Award

AFL-CIO
815 16th St. NW, Washington, D.C. 20006 (202/637-5000, Ext. 5189)

The Murray-Green-Meany Award, which carries a $5,000 grant and a medallion, is given annually to recognize outstanding contributions to the health, welfare and recreation of people everywhere, to stimulate leadership in the field of social welfare and to honor the memory of two American labor leaders, Philip Murray and William Green, whose lives exemplified the tradition of service. Any AFL-CIO affiliate or member may submit nominations for selection by the organization's Community Services Committee. Until 1956, the honor was known as the Philip Murray Award, and in 1979 it was again renamed following the death of labor leader and AFL-CIO President George Meany.

1947 Gen. Omar N. Bradley
1948 Sen. Robert F. Wagner
1949 No award
1950 No award
1951 Sen. James E. Murray
1952 No award
1953 Oscar R. Ewing
Robert H. MacRae
Wilbur F. Maxwell
United Nations Children's Emergency Fund
1954 Menninger Foundation
1955 Eleanor Roosevelt
1956 Herbert H. Lehman
1957 Jonas E. Salk
1958 Bob Hope
1959 President Harry S. Truman
1960 Agnes E. Meyer
1961 No award
1962 Gov. Louis Munoz Marin
1963 Gen. Alfred M. Gruenther
1964 Sen. Estes Kefauver
1965 Henry J. Kaiser
1966 Mr. and Mrs. Sargent Shriver
1967 Albert B. Sabin
1968 Wilbur J. Cohen
1969 Sen. Paul A. Douglas
1970 John W. Gardner
1971 Jerry Lewis
1972 A. Philip Randolph
1973 President Lyndon B. Johnson
1974 Sen. Hubert H. Humphrey
1975 Joseph Beirne
1976 Golda Meir
1977 Vice President Walter Mondale
1978 Danny Kaye
1979 Marvella Bayh
Irving J. Selikoff
1980 Bayard Rustin

National Law and Social Justice Award

AFRO-AMERICAN PATROLMEN'S LEAGUE
7126 S. Jeffrey Blvd., Chicago, Ill. 60649 (312/667-7384)

The National Law and Social Justice Award, which consists of a plaque, is given each year on decision by the board of directors, for outstanding work in the field of law or social justice.

1971 **Ramsey Clark,** U.S. Attorney General
1972 **Father Theodore Hesburgh,** President, Notre Dame University
1973 **Robert B. Blackwell,** Mayor, Highland Park, Mich.
Theodore M. Berry, Mayor, Cincinnati, Ohio
Thomas Bradley, Mayor, Los Angeles, Calif.
A.J. Cooper, Mayor, Prichard, Ala.
Doris Davis, Mayor, Compton, Calif.
Lelia Foley, Mayor, Taft, Okla.
Kenneth Gibson, Mayor, Newark, N.J.
William S. Hart, Mayor, East Orange, N.J.
Richard G. Hatcher, Mayor, Gary, Ind.
Charles F. Joseph, Mayor, Benton Harbor, Mich.
James H. McGee, Mayor, Dayton, Ohio
James Williams, Mayor, East St. Louis, Mo.
Maynard Jackson, Mayoral candidate, Atlanta, Ga.
1974 **No award**
1975 **Kirkland, Ellis & Rowe,** Law firm, Washington, D.C.
James Johnstone, Kirkland Ellis & Rowe
Douglas Serdehely, Kirkland, Ellis & Rowe
Ilana Rovner, Deputy Director of Public Protection, U.S. Attorney's Office
Donald Pailen, Justice Department, Washington, D.C.

Francis Cronin, Justice Department, Washington, D.C.
Arthur Jefferson, Center of National Policy Review, Washington, D.C.
Judith S. Bernstein, Lawyers' Committee for Civil Rights Under Law, Washington, D.C.
Harold Himmelman, Lawyers' Committee for Civil Rights Under Law, Washington, D.C.
Kermit B. Coleman, General Counsel, Afro-American Patrolmen's League
Eric Graham, General Counsel, Afro-American Patrolmen's League
William H. Brown, Chairman, Equal Opportunity Employment Commission
Leon M. Depres, Alderman, Fifth Ward, Chicago

1976 No award
1977 No award

Current Status Unknown

Agronomic Service Award

AMERICAN SOCIETY OF AGRONOMY
677 S. Segoe Rd., Madison, Wisc. 53711 (608/274-1212)

The $200 Agronomic Service Award annually recognizes development of service programs, practices and products and their acceptance by the public. This includes effective public relations programs designed to promote the understanding and use of agronomic science and technology by the public, government and others.

1961 M.H. McVickar
1962 J. Fieldings Reed
1963 D.E. Western
1964 W.L. Nelson
1965 W.H. Garman
1966 R.M. Love
1967 J.W. Neely
1968 H.H. Tucker
1969 H.D. Loden
1970 I.J. Johnson
1971 L.C. Meade
1972 S.L. Tisdale
1973 W.H. Daniel
1974 W.K. Griffith
1975 T.F. Pratt
1976 R.D. Munson
1977 J.R. Watson, Jr.

Current Status Unknown

American Bar Association Medal

AMERICAN BAR ASSOCIATION
77 S. Wacker Dr., Chicago, Ill. 60606 (312/621-9230)

The American Bar Association Medal honors "conspicuous service" to American jurisprudence by a lawyer, judge or law professor. While the award is not thus limited, it has frequently honored past presidents of the ABA. The board of governors makes recommendations for the recipient of the annual honor.

1929 Samuel Williston
1930 Elihu Root
1931 Oliver Wendell Holmes
1932 John Henry Wigmore
1933 No award
1934 George Woodward Wickersham
1935 No award
1936 No award
1937 No award
1938 Herbert Harley
1939 Edgar Bronson Tolman
1940 Roscoe Pound
1941 George Wharton Pepper
1942 Charles Evans Hughes
1943 John J. Parker
1944 Hatton W. Sumners
1945 No award
1946 Carl McFarland
1947 William L. Ransom
1948 Arthur T. Vanderbilt
1949 No award
1950 Orie L. Phillips
1951 Reginald Heber Smith
1952 Harrison Tweed
1953 Frank E. Holman
1954 George M. Morris
1955 No award
1956 Robert G. Storey
1957 William Clarke Mason
1958 E. Smythe Gambrell
1959 Greenville Clark
1960 William A. Schnader
1961 Jacob Mark Lashly
1962 Tom C. Clark
1963 Felix Frankfurter
1964 Henry S. Drinker
1965 Edmund M. Morgan
1966 Charles S. Rhyne
1967 Roger J. Traynor
1968 J. Edward Lumbard
1969 Walter V. Schaefer
1970 Frank C. Haymond
1971 Whitney North Seymour
1972 Harold J. Gallagher
1973 William J. Jameson
1974 Ross L. Malone
1975 Leon Jaworski
1976 Bernard D. Segal
1977 Edward L. Wright
1978 Erwin N. Griswold
1979 Lewis F. Powell, Jr.
1980 No award

Gold Distinguished Service Medal
National Certificate of Honor
International Amity Award
Canadian Friendship Award

AMERICAN LEGION
700 N. Pennyslvania, Indianapolis, Ind. 46204
(317/635-8411)

The Gold Distinguished Service Medal is awarded to no more than one recipient annually on a vote by the national committee for outstanding service to the nation and to the program of the Legion.

1921 **Marshall Foch,** France
Adm. Beatty, Great Britain
Gen. Baron Jacques, Belgium
Gen. Diaz, Italy
Charles Bertrand, France

1922 **Gen. John J. Pershing,** U.S.A.
1923 **Adm. R. E. Coontz,** U.S.A.
Gen. Josef Haller, Poland
1924 **No award**
1925 **No award**
1926 **Ignace Jan Paderewski,** Poland
1927 **Comte Francois Marie Robert DeJean,** France
1928 **Lord Allenby,** Great Britain
1929 **Judge Kenesaw M. Landis,** U.S.A.
1930 **Adm. William S. Sims,** U.S.A.
1931-41 **No awards**
1942 **Gen. Douglas MacArthur,** U.S.A.
1943 **Adm. Ernest J. King,** U.S.A.
Gen. George C. Marshall, U.S.A.
1944 **Gen. H. H. Arnold,** U.S.A.
Henry Ford, U.S.A.
Frank Knox, U.S.A.
1945 **Franklin D. Roosevelt,** U.S.A.
Henry L. Stimson, U.S.A.
Ernest Taylor "Ernie" Pyle, U.S.A.
Adm. Chester Nimitz, U.S.A.
Brig. Gen. Theodore Roosevelt, U.S.A.
Gen. Dwight D. Eisenhower, U.S.A.
1946 **William Randolph Hearst,** U.S.A.
Bob Hope, U.S.A.
Maj. Gen. Lewis B. Hershey, U.S.A.
J. Edgar Hoover, U.S.A.
Cordell Hull, U.S.A.
1947 **Fred M. Vinson,** U.S.A.
Edward Martin, U.S.A.
William S. Knudsen, U.S.A.
1948 **No award**
1949 **President Harry S. Truman,** U.S.A.
George Herman "Babe" Ruth, U.S.A.
Gen. Frank Parker, U.S.A.
1950 **Congresswoman Edith Nourse Rogers,** U.S.A.
Maj. Gen. Milton A. Reckord, U.S.A.
Charles F. Johnson, Jr., U.S.A.
1951 **Maj. Gen. Charles P. Summerall,** U.S.A.
1952 **No award**
1953 **Royal C. Johnson,** U.S.A.
1954 **Maj. Gen. George A. White,** U.S.A.
1955 **Jonas E. Salk,** U.S.A.
Maj. Gen. Ellard A. Walsh, U.S.A.
1956 **V. Adm. Joel T. Boone,** U.S.A.
Charles Stewart Mott, U.S.A.
1957 **Bishop Fulton J. Sheen,** U.S.A.
Gen. Mark. W. Clark, U.S.A.
1958 **Bernard M. Baruch,** U.S.A.
1959 **Sen. Robert S. Kerr,** U.S.A.
1961 **John F. Kennedy,** U.S.A.
1962 **Gen. Lucius D. Clay,** U.S.A.
Thomas A. Dooley, U.S.A.
1963 **Francis Cardinal Spellman,** Archbishop of New York, U.S.A.
1964 **Charles W. Mayo,** U.S.A.
1965 **James F. Byrnes,** U.S.A.
Herbert Clark Hoover, U.S.A.
1966 **Capt. Roger H.D. Donlon,** U.S.A.
1967 **Tom C. Clark,** U.S.A.
1968 **Lyndon B. Johnson,** U.S.A.
Gen. William C. Westmoreland, U.S.A.
1969 **Richard M. Nixon,** U.S.A.
1970 **Congressman Olin E. Teague,** U.S.A.
1971 **Hon. Richard Brevard Russell,** U.S.A.
Hon. L. Mendel Rivers, U.S.A.
1972 **DeWitt Wallace,** U.S.A.
Sen. John C. Stennis, U.S.A.
1973 **No award**
1974 **Henry F. Kissinger,** U.S.A.
Congressman F. Edward Hebert, U.S.A.
1975 **Harry Colmery,** U.S.A.
1976 **Pat O'Brien,** U.S.A.
1977 **Howard A. Rusk,** U.S.A.
1978 **Bowie K. Kuhn**
1979 **Thomas A. Murphy**
1980 **Gerald R. Ford**

The National Certificate of Honor is presented as merited to a legionnaire for exceptionally meritorious or distinguished service beyond that arising from membership in the organization. The committee on trophies and awards recommends the awarding of this certificate following a resolution of the Legion's departmental convention.

1927 **Wayne B. Davis**
1934 **Maj. Gen. P.C. Harris**
1951 **R. H. Levy**

The International Amity Award is a citation given annually to war veterans of any war-time ally of the United States from nominations by any American Legion member and selection by the National Trophies, Awards and Ceremonials Committee for contributions to international good will and service in veterans' affairs.

1962 **Raymond Triboulet,** France
Jean Louis Bonet-Maury, France
Robert A. Vivien, France
Maj.-Gen. Sir Richard Howard-Vyse, Great Britain
Gen. Sir Roy Bucher, Great Britain
P. N. Ferstenberg, Belgium
S. L. Woodcock, Canada
Donald Johnston, Canada
Jack Pothecary, Canada
Hugh J. McGivern, Canada
J. P. Nevins, Canada
A. J. Wickens, Canada
L. G. Howard, Canada
James Dickson, Canada
Don H. Thompson, Canada
I. C. Lundberg, Canada
G. R. Lang, Canada
J. D. Baxter, Canada
W. J. Maddison, Canada
C. A. Young, Canada
1963 **Antoine Ginee,** Belgium
Gen. Wladyslaw Anders, Poland
Jean Sainteny, France
Donald S. McTavish, Canada
Maj. Gen. Lucien Truyers, Belgium
1964 **Gen. Rueben Peralta y Alarcon,** Mexico
Gen. Roberto Fierro, Mexico
A. J. Carfrae, Canada
Gordon Thomson, Canada
Alex Shirra, Canada
Brig. James L. Melville, Canada
F. F. Bailey, Canada
John Ewasew, Canada
Lt. Gen. Augustin Olachea Avilez, Secretary of Defense, Mexico
1965 **Maj. Gen. Julien Bouhon,** Belgium
General of the Armies Martial Valin, France
Gen. Jacques P. L. DeGrancey, France
Henry J. Harvey, Canada
Fred T. O'Brecht, Canada
Ian Beresford, Canada
1966 **Byron Wilson,** Canada
W. Lorne Manchester, Canada

E. K. Carter, Canada
Gen. Piere Koenig, France
Meir Bar-Rav-Hay, Israel (United Kingdom)
A. J. Lee, Australia
Rev. H. Berry, Canada
Harold Berry, Canada
John Hall, Canada
George Waters, Canada
T. L. Fraser, Canada

1967 **Hamilton Mitchell,** New Zealand
The Right Honorable Lord Carew, Ireland (United Kingdom)
Thomas D. Bailey, Canada
Leonard Hall Turner, Canada
Montague Herbert Hurst, Canada

1968 **Gen. Henri Zeller,** France
Pierre Weber, France
Simeon C. Medalla, Philippines
Pham Xuan Chieu, Republic of Vietnam
R. N. Johnson, Canada
J. Albert Walker, Canada
Frank H. Farley, Canada
Albert Bianchini, Canada
Michael Popowich, Canada
L. J. Murphy, Canada
George Smith, Canada

1969 **Arthur Wallace,** Canada
James Hall, Canada
Edouard Emond Leon Dejean, Belgium

1970 **No award**

1971 **Jae Sung Kim,** Republic of South Korea
Stanislas Szewalski, Poland (France)

1972 **Jacques Medecin,** France

1973 **Leon DeCleyre,** Belgium
Tsu-Yu Chao, Republic of China (Taiwan)
Victor C.J. Chai, Republic of China (Taiwan)

1974 **No award**

1975 **Adelina Geurin-Beau,** France
William H. Craydon, United Kingdom

1976 **Alfonzo Cuellar Ponce de Leon,** Mexico
Claude-Lucien Ferrer, France

1977 **Yen Hsaio-Chang,** Republic of China (Taiwan)
Alejo S. Santos, Philippines
Andre Rigoine de Fougerolles, France
Glenn Grose, Canada

1978 **Pierre Taillacoit,** France
Maeng Kee Lee, Republic of Korea

1979 **Clementine Pletsier-Degrott,** Belgium
Pierre Leopold Henry Portier, France
Aime S. Leocard, France
Ferdinand Edralin Marcos, Philippines

1980 **Brig. Gen. Agustin Marking,** Philippines
Hon. Henry Brown, United Kingdom
Guy Cudell, Belgium

The Canadian Friendship Award, consisting of a citation and medal, is given annually to a Canadian veteran for outstanding service in the field of veterans' affairs and the perpetuation of good will and friendship between the United States and Canada and the veterans' organizations of the two countries. Any Legion member may make a nomination for selection by the National Trophies, Awards and Ceremonials Committee.

1970

Frank Washbrook
W. B. Morden
E. J. Potter
Russell Ward
S. Slater
Mel Rogers
Hugh Gillis

1971

Alexander Donald Grant
Mary C. Driscoll
Berrien Eaton
Robert Kohaly
William Albert Johns

1972

Andrew Hutton Black
J. C. McArthur
J. Hamilton
T. Holland
Jessie Iron
W. J. Ford
P. Fedosen
Stan Stiwell
John Redmond Roche
George Campbell
Richard Rigby
George Kemp
J. Stewart
R. Dunne
W. Talbot
A. G. Winnmill

1973

Rev. E. G. B. Foote
F. Gordon Wright
Francis W. Chaplin
Harry Paul

1974

Joseph J. Savage
Robert Murray Whipple
Fred Hake
Ben Miller
Irwin McNeeley
K. "Chuck" Karasin
R. G. Burns
W. G. Smith
J. J. Maurice Theoret
Jean E. A. J. Lamy
Keith Corrigan
J. M. Stewart
Charles M. Thompson
A. J. Hoyes
W. J. "Bill" Dobson
C. Cunningham
Gordon Westman
W. Pike

1975

Robert McChesney
Edward Doyle Dinsdale
Howard Goldrup
Sgt. William A. Lorette
Oliver Hrynchuk
Alex Cairns

1976

Allan S. Morrison
Walter Homes
Thomas Goddard
Reginald Swindlehurst
Rennie Crawford
Sam C. Isaacs
Ronald D. Jones
George Mabee
Stewart Robinson
Wilmont G. Wallace
William Whitehouse
Lionel Gagne
Ralph L. Smith
Brian Patrick O'Callaghan
Alfred G. Bull
Murray Edmunds
Joseph William Johnson
William E. Lamb
Harold V. McKenzie
George Rowntree
William S. White

1977

Nelson Leonard Wromell
Armand Daigle
Donald Lester Jensen
Douglas McDonald
Gerard Kit Belanger
George Wakeford
Archibald McKenzie

1978

Donald C. Armstrong
William A.R. Simmons
William Barteaux, Jr.
Alexandria Wallner
Clifford Boutilier
Frank Jull
William M. Graham
Frank E. Rice
Leopold Sylvain
J.S. Redfern
O. George Martin
William Walden Rewcastle
Edward Hodgert
Theodore E. Shaman
William Barteaux, Sr.
John P. Cole
James G. Alcorn
Ronald Murphy
M.J. Barnett
William Cook
Cyril T. Smith
William Kieswetter
Orville M. Grasley
Harry J. Tait
William Allen
Tom Reynolds

1979

Dennis Joseph
Tom Graham
Rupert V. McCabe
Patrick Phillips
Joseph Lacasse

1980

Frank Culver
A.D. Cox
Harper B. Brisbin
James Callon
Eliot N. Spear
Clive Morris
Veronica Whiting
Kenneth B. Dean
Alex Paul
George A. Todd
Ella Lewis
Marge Nelson
Joseph T. McConnachie
George Carviel
Jack Hainstock
John L. Williams
Charles A. Bockus
Leo P. Brown
John Betournay
Earl Fenwick
Les H. Sherlow

John Phillip Immroth Award for Intellectual Freedom

AMERICAN LIBRARY ASSOCIATION
50 E. Huron St., Chicago, Ill. 60611 (312/944-6780)

The John Phillip Immroth Award for Intellectual Freedom is given annually by the Association's Intellectual Freedom Roundtable for outstanding contributions to the cause. The Immroth Award Committee selects the winner, who receives a plaque and a $500 cash honorarium.

1976 **I.F. Stone,** Lifelong contributions
1977 **Irene Turin,** Librarian, Island Trees (N.Y.) High School
1978 **Sonja Coleman,** Librarian, Chelsea (Mass.) High School
1979 **Alex P. Allain,** Library Trustee, St. Mary Parish, La.
1980 **Elizabeth A. Phillips,** Vergennes (Vt.) Union High School Library

America's Democratic Legacy Award

ANTI-DEFAMATION LEAGUE OF B'NAI B'RITH
315 Lexington Ave., New York, N.Y. 10016 (212/689-7400)

The Democratic Legacy Award, which consists of a silver medallion, annually honors individuals or organizations for contributions to the enrichment of America's democratic traditions.

1948 **Eleanor Roosevelt**
Darryl Zanuck, Producer
Dore Schary, Writer-producer
Barney Balaban, President, Paramount Pictures
Charles E. Wilson, Chairman, President's Committee on Civil Rights
1949 **President Harry S. Truman**
1950 **J. Howard McGrath,** U.S. Attorney General
1951 **Henry Ford II,** Industrialist
1952 **Herbert H. Lehman,** U.S. Senator
1953 **President Dwight D. Eisenhower**
1954-55 **Carnegie Corporation**
Ford Foundation
Rockefeller Foundation
1956 **Herbert H. Lehman,** U. S. Senator
James P. Mitchell, U. S. Secretary of Labor
Charles P. Taft, Mayor of Cincinnati
1957 **85th Congress of the United States**
1958 **Columbia Broadcasting System**
***Look* magazine**
The *New York Times*
1959 **Actors' Equity Association**
Dramatists Guild
League of New York Theatres
Society of Stage Directors and Choreographers
1960 **Harvard University**
University of Notre Dame
Brandeis University
1961 **Adlai E. Stevenson,** U.S. Ambassador to the United Nations
1962 **President John F. Kennedy**
1963 **Eugene Carson Blake,** United Presbyterian Church
A. Philip Randolph, Brotherhood of Sleeping Car Porters
Walter Reuther, United Auto Workers
Roy Wilkins, NAACP
1964 **President Lyndon B. Johnson**
1965 **Arthur J. Goldberg,** U.S. Ambassador to the United Nations
1966 **Nicholas deB. Katzenbach,** Under Secretary of State
1967 **John W. Gardner,** National Urban Coalition
1968 **No award**
1969 **Earl Warren,** Former Chief Justice, U.S. Supreme Court
1970 **No award**
1971 **Abraham Joshua Heschel,** Jewish Theological Seminary of America
1972 **No award**
1973 **Jacob K. Javits,** U. S. Senator
Abraham A. Ribicoff, U. S. Senator
1974 **No award**
1975 **No award**
1976 **Saul Bellow,** Author
1977 **Arthur F. Burns,** Chairman, Federal Reserve Board
1978 **Benjamin R. Epstein**
1979 **Arnold Forster**
1980 **Henry A. Kissinger**

AVCA/AWA Helicopter Heroism Award

AVIATION/SPACE WRITERS ASSOCIATION
Cliffwood Rd., Chester, N.J. 07930

The AVCA/AWA Helicopter Heroism Award recognizes outstanding heroism of a pilot, crew member or other individual involving the use of a helicopter. There is a $500 honorarium with this award which is sponsored jointly with AVCO Corp.

1967 **Maj. Bruce P. Crandall**
1968 **Maj. Steven Pless, USMC.**
1969 **Sgt. Steve Northern,** USAF, Para-rescueman
1970 **Capt. Daniel A. Nicholson, USAF**
1971 **Warrant Officer I Mark M. Feinberg,** USA, combat
Lt. Cdr. James E. Rylee, USN, Non-combat
1972 **Maj. Kenneth E. Ernest,** USAF, Combat
Charles Allred, Non-combat
1973 **Capt. Billy H. Causey,** USA, Combat
Albert Carriger and John Lockwood, Non-combat
1974 **Flight Lieutenant Bernard Braithwaite and Master Air Electronics Operator Alister More,** Royal Air Force, Great Britain
1975 **Lt. Patrick W. Gregory and Crewman Terry E. Richardson,** U.S. Coast Guard

1976 **Siegfried Strangier and Beat Perren,** Swiss Air-Rescue
1977 **Cameron Bangs**
1978 **Capt. George Bain, Capt. Alaisdair Campbell, Capt. Campbell Bosanquet** and **Brian Johnstone,** British Airways Helicopters
1979 **1/Lt. Steven A. Stich,** USAF
1980 **Arthur S. Fantroy**

Bellarmine Medal

BELLARMINE COLLEGE
2001 Newburg Rd., Louisville, Ky. 40205 (502/452-8011)

The silver Bellarmine Medal is awarded annually to an individual, group or organization exemplifying the characterisitics of St. Robert Bellarmine and exhibiting justice, charity or temperateness when dealing with difficult or controversial subjects. A selection committee chooses the recipient.

1955 **Jefferson Caffrey**
1956 **Gen. Carlos Romulo**
1957 **John W. McCormack,** U.S. Representative
1958 **Frank M. Folsom**
1959 **Robert D. Murphy**
1960 **James P. Mitchell**
1961 **Frederick H. Boland**
1962 **Gen. Alfred M. Gruenther**
1963 **Henry Cabot Lodge**
1964 **R. Sargent Shriver**
1965 **Irene Dunne**
1966 **Everett M. Dirksen,** U.S. Senator
1967 **Nicholas Katzenbach**
1968 **Danny Thomas**
1969 **J. Irwin Miller**
1970 **Theodore M. Hesburgh,** C.S.C.
1971 **John Sherman Cooper,** U.S. Senator
1972 **No award**
1973 **William B. Walsh**
1974 **No award**
1975 **Rev. Fulton J. Sheen,** D.D.
1976 **No award**
1977 **William F. Buckley, Jr.**
1978 **No award**
1979 **Rev. Jesse L. Jackson**
1980 **No award**

Silver Buffalo Distinguished Eagle Scout Award

BOY SCOUTS OF AMERICA NATIONAL COURT OF HONOR
1325 Walnut Hill La., Irving, Tex. 75061 (214/659-2048)

The Silver Buffalo is the highest of the Boy Scouts of America's four service awards, the others being either of a more localized nature or dependent on a direct, long-term association with scouting. The Silver Buffalo is bestowed by the National Court of Honor upon the recommendation of the National Executive Board for distinguished service to youth. It is the only award made by the Boy Scouts of America that has no specific course of action, tests to be met or training as a requirement; rather, it honors committed service to young people.

1926 **Sir Robert S. S. Baden-Powell,** Gilwell Park, Great Britain, Chief Scout of the World
The Unknown Scout, Boy Scout
William D. Boyce, Chicago, Ill., Publisher; incorporator of Boy Scouts of America
Colin H. Livingstone, Washington, D.C., Financier
James J. Storrow, Boston, Mass., Banker; President, Boy Scouts of America
Daniel Carter Beard, Suffern, N.Y., National Scout Commissioner
Ernest Thompson Seton, New York, N.Y., Chief Scout
Edgar M. Robinson, Washington, D.C., Coorganizer of the Boy Scouts of America
Lee F. Hanmer, New York, N.Y., Coorganizer of the Boy Scouts of America
George W. Wingate, New York, N.Y., Advocate of organized outdoor recreation
Joseph Lee, Boston, Mass., Advocate of playground and outdoor recreation
Howard S. Braucher, New York, N.Y., Chairman, Committee on Organization, Boy Scouts of America
Mortimer L. Schiff, New York, N.Y., Philanthropist; President, Boy Scouts of America
Milton A. McRae, Detroit, Mich., Publisher; President, Boy Scouts of America
Frank Presbrey, New York, N.Y., Advertising man; developer of *Boys' Life*
George D. Pratt, New York, N.Y., Treasurer, Boy Scouts of America
John Sherman Hoyt, Darien, Conn., Manufacturer; Chairman, Finance Committee, Boy Scouts of America
Jeremiah W. Jenks, New York, N.Y., Educator; formulator of Scout Oath and Law
William D. Murray, Plainfield, N.J., Lawyer; Chairman, Editorial Board, Boy Scouts of America
G. Barrett Rich, New York, N.Y., Chairman, National Committee of Badges, Awards, and Scout Requirements
James E. West, New York, N.Y., Lawyer; Chief Scout Executive
George J. Fisher, New York, N.Y., Physician, Deputy Chief Scout Executive
1927 **William Howard Taft,** Washington, D.C., Chief Justice of the United States; First Honorary President, Boy Scouts of America
Hubert S. Martin, C.B.E., London, Great Britain, Director, Boy Scouts International Bureau
William Adams Welch, Washington, D.C., National and State Parks Commissioner
Stuart W. French, Pasadena, Calif., Business executive; organizer of Region 12
Bolton Smith, Memphis, Tenn., Banker; promoter of interracial understanding
Walter W. Head, Omaha, Neb., Banker; President, Boy Scouts of America
Brother Barnabas, F.S.C., New York, N.Y., Educator; Director, Catholic Bureau, Boy Scouts of America
1928 **The Unknown Soldier,** Patriot
Charles A. Lindbergh, Hopewell, N.J., Aviator; transatlantic pioneer
W. de Bonstetten, Kandersteg, Switzerland, President, Swiss Federation of Boy Scouts
Arthur N. Cotton, Buffalo, N.Y., Promoter of High-Y Clubs
Clarence H. Howard, St. Louis, Mo., Philanthropist; founder of Junior Chamber of Commerce
Charles D. Velie, Minneapolis, Minn., Philanthropist; promoter of scouting for rural boys

William H. Cowles, Spokane, Wash., Publisher, first Chairman, Region 11 Committee

1929 **Calvin Coolidge,** Plymouth, Vt., President, United States of America

Richard E. Byrd, Winchester, Va., Commander, U.S. Navy, Antarctic explorer

Wilbert E. Longfellow, Washington, D.C., Water safety promoter, American Red Cross

John H. Finley, New York, N.Y., Educator; founder of Junior American Red Cross

Howard F. Gillette, Chicago, Ill., Banker; promoter of sea scouting

Charles D. Hart, Philadelphia, Pa., Physician; promoter of troop camping

H.R.H. The Prince of Wales, Scouting enthusiast

1930 **Herbert Clark Hoover,** West Branch, Iowa, President, United States of America

James Earl Russell, New York, N.Y., Educator, scouter

Franklin D. Roosevelt, Hyde Park, N.Y., Governor, State of New York; advocate of scouting

James Austin Wilder, New York, N.Y., Developed and organized the Sea Scouts program

Charles L. Sommers, Minneapolis, Minn., Business executive; Chairman, Region 10

Charles C. Moore, San Francisco, Calif., Engineer, scouter

Lewis Warrington Baldwin, St. Louis, Mo., Railroad president; regional chairman

1931 **Lord Hampton, D.S.O.,** London, Great Britain, Distinguished British scouter

Griffith Ogden Ellis, Detroit, Mich., Editor and publisher, *American Boy* Magazine

Lewis Gawtry, New York, N.Y., Banker; philanthropist

George Welch Olmsted, Warren, Pa., Utilities executive; world scouter

Victor F. Ridder, New York, N.Y., Newspaper publisher; Catholic scouter

Robert P. Sniffen, Yonkers, N.Y., Merchandising consultant; Chairman, Committee on Supply Service

Mell R. Wilkinson, Atlanta, Ga., Manufacturer; National Executive Board Member

1932 **Dwight Filley Davis,** St. Louis, Mo., Public servant; advocate of athletics

William Edwin Hall, Greenwich, Conn., Lawyer; President, Boys' Clubs of America

Alfred W. Dater, Stamford, Conn., Utilities executive; first Chairman, Sea Scout Committee

Barron Collier, New York, N.Y., Philanthropist; promoter of scouting

Frank A. Bean, Minneapolis, Minn., Business executive, advocate of rural scouting

Hermann W. Merkel, New York, N.Y., Creative administrator of parks and camps

1933 **Vincent Massey,** Toronto, Canada, Canadian diplomat; philanthropist

Martin H. Carmody, New York, N.Y., Supreme Knight, Knights of Columbus

John P. Wallace, Des Moines, Iowa, Publisher; advocate of rural scouting

Cyrus Adler, Philadelphia, Pa., Educator; Chairman, Jewish Committee on Scouting

Reginald H. Parsons, Seattle, Wash., Developer of scouting in Pacific Northwest

John A. McGregor, San Francisco, Calif., Region 12 scouter; friend to youth

1934 **Newton D. Baker,** Cleveland, Ohio, Statesman; humanitarian

Paul Percy Harris, Chicago, Ill., Lawyer; founder of Rotary Club Movement

John M. Phillips, Pittsburgh, Pa., Conservationist, recipient of Silver Wolf award

Theodore Roosevelt, Jr., Oyster Bay, N.Y., Public servant; explorer

Charles E. Cotting, Boston, Mass., Philanthropist, promoter of New England scouting

Frederic Kernochan, New York, N.Y., Jurist; pioneer scouter; Urban League Executive

George Albert Smith, Salt Lake City, Utah, Business executive; religious leader; scouter

1935 **Booth Tarkington,** Indianapolis, Ind., Author; immortalizer of youth

Amos Alonzo Stagg, Stockton, Calif., Educator; dean of American coaches

Daniel A. Tobin, New York, N.Y., Banker; scouter; cofounder, Columbian Squires

Fielding Harris Yost, Ann Arbor, Mich., Scout Commissioner; exponent of clean sports

Calvin Derrick, Jamesburg, N.J., Educator; penologist; innovator

R. Tait McKenzie, Philadelphia, Pa., Educator; sculptor of Boy Scout statue

1936 **Frederick Russell Burnham,** Three Rivers, Calif., American-British adventurer

Hugh S. Cumming, Washington, D.C., United States Surgeon General

Lawrence Locke Doggett, Springfield, Mass., Educator; Pioneer for training for boys' work

Charles Horace Mayo, Rochester, Minn., Surgeon; health authority; pioneer scouter

George Edgar Vincent, Greenwich, Conn., Educator; adviser to scouting for health and safety

John Skinner Wilson, Gilwell Park, Great Britain, Gilwell Camp Chief; world scouter

1937 **No award**

1938 **Thomas E. Wilson,** Chicago, Ill., Promoter for rural youth and 4-H Clubs

William T. Hornaday, Stamford, Conn., Zoologist and conservationist; pioneer, scouter

George A. Allen, Washington, D.C., Presidential Representative to first National Jamboree

Frank Cody, Detroit, Mich., Educator; innovator with schools and scouting

Frank G. Hoover, Canton, Ohio, Longtime scouter; friend to youth

Cornelius "Connie Mack" McGillicuddy, Philadelphia, Pa., Advocate of good sportsmanship

C. B. Smith, Washington, D.C., Public servant; physician; worker for rural scouting

John A. Stiles, Ottawa, Canada, Canadian scouting official; recipient of Silver Wolf award

1939 **William Chalmers Covert,** Pittsburgh, Pa., Clergyman; scouter

Marshall Field, New York, N.Y., Business Executive; philanthropist; scouter

Elbert K. Fretwell, New York, N.Y., Educator; scouter; training innovator

Heber J. Grant, Salt Lake City, Utah, Industrialist; Mormon church official

Francis C. Kelley, Tulsa, Okla., Bishop of Oklahoma City and Tulsa; scouter

John R. Mott, New York, N.Y., Missionary; statesman, world youth leader

Norman Rockwell, Arlington, Vt., Artist; prime creator of scouting's image

1940 **Edward Roberts Moore,** New York, N.Y., Catholic clergyman; youth worker; scouter

George W. Truett, Dallas, Tex., Clergyman; world youth leader; scouter
Eugene D. Nims, St. Louis, Mo., Philanthropist; longtime scouter

1941 **C. Ward Crampton,** New York, N.Y., Scientist; author; physical fitness advocate
Homer Folks, New York, N.Y., Social welfare statesman
Edgar Rickard, Darien, Conn., Mining engineer; humanitarian; friend to scouting
J. E. H. Stevenot, Manila, Philippines, Creator of modern Philippine Scout Organization
Daniel A. Poling, Philadelphia, Pa., Clergyman; editor; scouter

1942 **Frank O. Lowden,** Oregon, Ill., Farmer; lawyer; statesman; philanthropist; scouter
Ragnvald Anderson Nestos, Minot, N.D., Lawyer; statesman; churchman; pioneer in rural scouting
Frank Phillips, Bartlesville, Okla., Banker; philanthropist; enthusiast for scouting
Bernard J. Sheil, Chicago, Il., Auxiliary Bishop of Chicago; founder of CYO; scouter
William Clay Smoot, Bartlesville, Okla., Banker; outdoorsman; worker for rural youth

1943 **J. Edgar Hoover,** Washington, D.C., Lawyer; criminologist; director of the FBI
Harry C. Knight, New Haven, Conn., Business executive; philanthropist; scouter
John Mortimer Schiff, New York, N.Y., Banker; philanthropist; president, Boy Scouts of America
William L. Smith, Louisville, Ky., Surgeon; public servant; author; scouter
Frank W. Wozencraft, Dallas, Tex., Businessman; lawyer; statesman; scouter

1944 **Oscar H. Benson,** Seven Stars, Pa., Educator; founder of the 4-H Clubs
Charles Evans Hughes, Glens Falls, N.Y., Jurist; statesman; diplomat; champion of youth
Elbridge W. Palmer, Kingsport, Tenn., Publisher; worker for crippled youth, racial harmony, and scouting
William C. Menninger, Topeka, Kans., Neuropsychiatrist; enthusiastic scouter
Philip L. Reed, Chicago, Ill., Business executive; scouter; member, advisory council
Edward Vernon Rickenbacker, New York, N.Y., Aviation pioneer; executive; wartime ace of aces; scouter
Arthur Herbert Tennyson Somers-Cocks, 6th Baron Somers, London, Great Britain, Chief Scout of the British Empire
Thomas J. Watson, New York, N.Y., Business executive; philanthropist; educator; scouter

1945 **Francis W. Hatch,** Boston, Mass., Publicist; scouter; chairman, *Boys' Life* committee
Amory Houghton, Corning, N.Y., Manufacturer; philanthropist; vice-president, Boy Scouts of America
Paul W. Litchfield, Akron, Ohio, Industrialist; developed First Air Scout Squadron
Earl C. Sams, New York, N.Y., Merchant; philanthropist; chairman, business division committee

1946 **John M. Bierer,** Wellesley Hills, Mass., Business executive; longtime scouter
William J. Campbell, Chicago, Ill., Jurist; promoter of scouting for Catholic boys
Walter E. Disney, Beverly Hills, Calif., Cinema executive; creator of Mickey Mouse
Dwight D. Eisenhower, Denison, Tex., General of the Army, Supreme Commander of Allied Expeditionary Forces in Europe
Raymond F. Low, Omaha, Neb., Business executive; scouter; Sea Scouting enthusiast
Wheeler McMillen, Trenton, N.J., Journalist; editor; advocate for rural scouting
Chester William Nimitz, Fredericksburg, Tex., Chief of Naval Operations; U.S. signator to Japanese surrender treaty
Vilhjalmur Stefansson, New York, N.Y., Arctic explorer; author; scouter
Frank L. Weil, New York, N.Y., Lawyer; scouter; cofounder, United Service Organizations

1947 **Bernard M. Baruch,** Camden, S.C., Economist; philanthropist; patriot
Manuel Camus, Manila, Philippines, Statesman; jurist; president, Boy Scouts of the Philippines
Cleveland E. Dodge, New York, N.Y., Financier; philanthropist; chairman, International Board of the Y.M.C.A.
Perrin C. Galpin, New York, N.Y., Educator; Scouter; child-health advocate
William H. Pouch, New York, N.Y., Industrialist; longtime scouter; civic leader
Paul A. Siple, Arlington, Pa., Geographer; explorer; author; member, first Byrd Antarctic expedition
Francis Cardinal Spellman, New York, N.Y., Archbishop of New York; author; patriot
R. Douglas Stuart, Chicago, Ill., Manufacturer; pioneer scouter; friend to youth

1948 **Irving Berlin,** New York, N.Y., Composer of "God Bless America"
Belmore Browne, Ross, Calif., Artist; explorer; cold-weather camping expert
Cherry Logan Emerson, Atlanta, Ga., Engineer; educator; servant of youth
Reuben Brooks Hale, San Francisco, Calif., Merchant; civic leader; advocate of Senior Scouting
Robert F. Payne, New York, N.Y., Educator; author; longtime scouter
Lord Rowallan, Ayrshire, Scotland, Chief Scout of British Commonwealth and Empire
Wade Warren Thayer, Honolulu, Hawaii, Attorney; author; exponent of Hawaiian scouting

1949 **David W. Armstrong,** New York, N.Y., Executive director, Boys' Clubs of America
Sheldon Clark, Chicago, Ill., Business executive; national Sea Scout commodore
Richard J. Cushing, Boston, Mass., Archbishop of Boston; lecturer; author; civic leader; head of all youth work of Catholic Chruch in U.S.A.
W. V. M. Fawcett, Boston, Mass., Business executive; civic leader; scouter
Charles R. Hook, Middletown, Ohio, Industrialist; advocate of Junior Achievement; scouter
Luther A. Weigle, New Haven, Conn., Educator; dean; Bible scholar; pioneer scouter

1950 **Harry Messiter Addinsell,** New York, N.Y., Financier; churchman; treasurer, Boy Scouts of America
Kenneth K. Bechtel, San Francisco, Calif., Business executive; vice-president, Boy Scouts of America
Charles Franklin Kettering, Dayton, Ohio, Engineer; manufacturer; philanthropist; innovator
Irving Langmuir, Schenectady, N.Y., Nobel Prize scientist; pioneer scouter
Byrnes MacDonald, New York, N.Y., Business executive; worker ofr underprivileged youth
Owen J. Roberts, Philadelphia, Pa., Jurist; public servant; longtime scouter
Arthur A. Schuck, New Brunswick, N.J., Chief Scout Executive, Boy Scouts of America

Lowell Thomas, Pawling, N.Y., Explorer; author; news commentator; scouter
Harry S. Truman, Independence, Mo., President, United States of America
Milburn Lincoln Wilson, Washington, D.C., National director, 4-H Clubs; scouter

1951 **Ralph J. Bunche,** Jamaica, N.Y., Educator; Nobel Peace Prize winner; scouter
James Lippitt Clark, New York, N.Y., Explorer; author; sculptor; conservationist; scouter
Edgar Albert Guest, Detroit, Mich., Writer; poet; Boys' Club official; friend of youth
Raymond W. Miller, Washington, D.C., Publicist; scouter; advocate of rural scouting
D. C. Spry, Ottawa, Canada, Chief Executive Commissioner, Canadian General Council of the Boy Scouts Association
James H. Douglas, Jr., Chicago, Ill., Attorney; public servant; longtime scouter
Henry Smith Richardson, Greensboro, N.C., Manufacturing chemist; longtime scouter
Jack P. Whitaker, Kansas City, Mo., Manufacturer; scouter; president, American Humanics Foundation

1952 **Julius Ochs Adler,** New York, N.Y., Journalist; patriot; veteran scouter
Roy Chapman Andrews, New York, N.Y., Explorer; zoologist; museum director; author
Frank Learoyd Boyden, Deerfield, Mass., Teacher; headmaster; friend to youth
Harmar D. Denny, Pittsburgh, Pa., Attorney; congressman; longtime scouter
Gale F. Johnston, St. Louis, Mo., Banker; civic leader; philanthropist; scouter
Carlos P. Romulo, Washington, D.C., Author; soldier; diplomat; cofounder, Boy Scouts of the Philippines
Louis John Taber, Columbus, Ohio, Farmer; granger; exponent of rural scouting; scouter

1953 **Alton Fletcher Baker,** Eugene, Ore., Journalist; publisher; civic leader; scouter
Henry B. Grandin, San Marino, Calif., Business executive; scouter; host to 3d National Jamboree
Ross L. Leffler, Pittsburgh, Pa., Business executive; civic leader; veteran scouter
Charles Francis McCahill, Cleveland, Ohio, Newspaper executive; philanthropist; scouter
David O. McKay, Salt Lake City, Utah, President, Church of Jesus Christ of Latter-day Saints

1954 **William H. Albers,** Cincinnati, Ohio, Business executive; philanthropist; scouter
Ellsworth Hunt Augustus, Cleveland, Ohio, Banker; civic leader; scouter
Ezra Taft Benson, Salt Lake City, Utah, Secretary of agriculture; church leader; scouter
Philip David Bookstaber, Harrisburg, Pa., Rabbi; scholar; exponent of scouting for Jewish boys
Norton Clapp, Seattle, Wash., Business executive; civic leader; veteran scouter
J. M. T. Finney, Jr., Baltimore, Md., Surgeon; churchman; civic leader; veteran scouter
Richard Oliver Gerow, Natchez, Miss., Bishop of Natchez, Miss.; longtime scouter
Edward Urner Goodman, Bondville, Vt., Church executive; pioneer scouter; founder, Order of the Arrow
George Lloyd Murphy, Beverly Hills, Calif., Producer; actor; publicist; scouter
Nathan Marvin Ohrbach, New York, N.Y., Business executive; philanthropist; scouter
Dewitt Wallace, Pleasantville, N.Y., Magazine founder; editor; publisher; philanthropist

1955 **Charles Dana Bennett,** Addison, Vt., Author; rural consulant; publicist; scouter
Rex Ivan Brown, Jackson, Miss., Utility executive; civic leader; veteran scouter
William Durant Campbell, New York, N.Y., Naturalist; world traveler; Eagle Scout; scouter
Francis John Chesterman, Philadelphia, Pa., Utilities executive; civic leader; scouter
Leonard Kimball Firestone, Los Angeles, Calif., Industrialist; churchman; civic leader; scouter
Charles William Froessel, Jamaica, N.Y., Jurist; churchman; civic leader; scouter
Robert Tyre Jones, Jr., Atlanta, Ga., Attorney; business executive; sportsman; champion athlete
Lewis Edward Phillips, Eau Claire, Wisc., Manufacturer; philanthropist; scouter
Frank Chambless Rand, Jr., Sante Fe, N.M., Business executive; publisher; civic leader; scouter
Thomas John Watson, Jr., New York, N.Y., Business executive; civic leader, philanthropist; scouter

1956 **Ivan Allen, Jr.,** Atlanta, Ga., Executive; banker; engineer; civic leader; scouter
Gerald F. Beal, New York, N.Y., Banker; financier; cultural and civic leader; scouter
Daniel W. Bell, Washington, D.C., Banker; public servant; community leader; scouter
Hugh Moss Comer, Sylacauga, Ala., Textile manufacturer; philanthropist; scouter
Walter Francis Dillingham, Honolulu, Hawaii, Executive; builder; philanthropist; statesman; scouter
Whitney Haskins Eastman, Minneapolis, Minn., Business executive; engineer; scientist; scouter
William Harrison Fetridge, Chicago, Ill. Editor; publisher; executive; community leader; scouter
William Jansen, New York, N.Y., Educator; author; churchman; administrator; scouter
Guy Lee Noble, Chicago, Ill., National 4-H Club executive; humanitarian
Harry Lloyd Schaeffer, St. Louis, Mo., Railroad executive; scouter
Henry Frederick Schricker, Knox, Ind., Statesman; banker; editor; pioneer scouter
Harold Edward Stassen, St. Paul, Minn., Educator; humanitarian; statesman; author; scouter
Edwin Joel Thomas, Akron, Ohio, Industrialist; civic leader; humanitarian; scouter

1957 **Harold Roe Bartle,** Kansas City, Mo., Attorney; civic leader; humanitarian; scouter
Brooks Hays, Washington D.C., Congressman; lawyer; humanitarian; scouter
Walter David Heller, San Francisco, Calif., Business executive; civic leader; philanthropist; scouter
Henry Cabot Lodge, Beverly, Mass., Journalist; national and international statesman
Abram Leon Sachar, Waltham, Mass., Educator; author; historian; university president
Herman Lee Turner, Atlanta, Ga., Clergyman; humanitarian; civic leader; scouter
Kenneth Dale Wells, Valley Forge, Pa., Economist; educator; president, Freedoms Foundation at Valley Forge

1958 **Robert Bernerd Anderson,** Washington, D.C., Secretary of the Treasury; lawyer; educator; scouter
John Hopkinson Baker, New York, N.Y., Conservation executive; governmental adviser
Hubert Hardison Coffield, Rockdale, Tex., Industrialist; rancher; churchman; humanitarian; scouter
Nathan Dauby, Cleveland, Ohio, Business Executive; civic leader; philanthropist; scouter

Jackson Dodds, Montreal, Canada, Banker; scouter; recipient of Silver Wolf and Bronze Wolf

John Randolph Donnell, Findlay, Ohio, Business executive; civic leader; scouter

Robert Newcomb Gibson, East Lansing, Mich., Business executive; lumberman; scouter

Frank Brittain Kennedy, Cohasset, Mass., Investment dealer; churchman; executive; scouter

Edward Leroy Kohnle, Dayton, Ohio, Business executive; churchman; cultural leader; scouter

Sol George Levy, Seattle, Wash., Import-export business executive; community leader; scouter

John Norton Lord, Detroit, Mich., Business executive; community leader; scouter

James Maitland Stewart, Beverly Hills, Calif., Actor; combat aviator; scouter

1959 **Milo William Bekins,** Los Angeles, Calif., Business executive; community leader; scouter

George Michael Dowd, Franklin, Mass., Clergyman; domestic prelate; youth leader; scout chaplain

Irving Jonas Feist, Newark, N.J., Business executive; community leader; scouter

Roger Stanley Firestone, Bryn Mawr, Pa., Manufacturing executive; humanitarian; scouter

Bob Hope, Beverly Hills, Calif., Cinema, radio, and television comedian; humanitarian

Jeffrey Louis Lazarus, Cincinnati, Ohio, Business executive; community leader; scouter

Walter Lee Lingle, Jr., Cincinnati, Ohio, Business executive; community leader; scouter

George Magar Mardikian, San Francisco, Calif., Restaurateur; author; philanthropist; scouter

Pliny Hunnicut Powers, New Brunswick, N.J., Educator; deputy chief scout executive, Boy Scouts of America

Charles Dudley Pratt, Honolulu, Hawaii, Attorney; civic leader; pioneer scouter

Joseph Frederic Wiese, Coatesville, Pa., Industrial executive; community leader; veteran scouter

1960 **Joe C. Carrington,** Austin, Tex., Insurance executive; rancher; churchman; youth worker; scouter

Thomas Campbell Clark, Washington, D.C., Associate Justice of the United States Supreme Court; humanitarian; veteran scouter

James Thomas Griffin, Cleveland, Ohio, Business executive; humanitarian; churchman; scouter

Alfred M. Gruenther, Washington, D.C., President, American National Red Cross; Supreme Allied Commander in Europe 1953-56; scouter

Roy Edward Larson, New York, N.Y., Publishing executive; civic leader; humanitarian

Robert John Lloyd, Tacoma, Wash., Business executive; community leader; scouter

Alexander White Moffat, Beverly Farms, Mass., Business executive; yachtsman; author; scouter

Clifford A. Randall, Milwaukee, Wisc., Lawyer; executive; humanitarian; Past President, Rotary International

Norman Salit, Lawrence, N.Y., Rabbi; attorney; humanitarian; veteran scouter

1961 **Wyeth Allen,** Ann Arbor, Mich., Educator; community leader; longtime scouter

Carl Otto Janus, Indianapolis, Ind., Business executive; civic leader; veteran scouter

Richard E. McArdle, Washington, D.C., Educator; public servant; conservationist; scouter

Charles B. McCabe, Jr., New York, N.Y., Publisher; broadcasting executive; veteran scouter

Lauris Norstad, Minneapolis, Minn., Supreme Allied Commander, Europe (SHAPE); promulgator of scouting

William T. Spanton, Washington, D.C., Cofounder, Future Farmers of America; scouter

Delbert Leon Stapley, Phoenix, Ariz., Business executive; church leader; veteran scouter

Charles M. White, Cleveland, Ohio, Industrialist; civic leader; youth worker; scouter

Robert E. Wood, Chicago, Ill., Retired army general; business executive; philanthropist; veteran scouter

1962 **Bruce Cooper Clarke,** Adams, N.Y., Commander in Chief, United States Army, Europe; veteran scouter

Zenon Clayton Raymond Hansen, Lansing, Mich., Business executive; civic leader Eagle Scout; scouter

Carl Hayden, Phoenix, Arix., Member, United States Senate; veteran scouter

Wayne Andrew Johnston, Chicago, Ill., Railroad executive; humanitarian; longtime scouter

Thomas J. Keane, Forest Hills, N.Y., Naval officer in two World Wars; veteran scouter

John Cook Parish, St. Paul, Minn., Business executive; civic leader; scouter

John Thurman, Gilwell Park, Great Britain, Camp chief of Gilwell Park; recipient of Silver Wolf and Bronze Wolf

Carl Vinson, Milledgeville, Ga., Member, House of Representatives; friend of scouting

Clarence E. Williams, Woodward, Okla., Physician; surgeon; Jamboree medical officer; scouter

1963 **Erwin Dain Canham,** Boston, Mass., Editor; author; broadcasting commentator; humanitarian

L. Osmond Crosby, Picayune, Miss., Industrialist; community leader; scouter

Herold C. Hunt, Cambridge, Mass., Educator; author; consultant; scouter

Walter H. Judd, Washington, D.C., Statesman; missionary; civic leader; veteran scouter

John T. Kimball, New York, N.Y., Utilities executive; civic leader; scouter

Harold B. Lee, Salt Lake City, Utah, Business executive; educator; church official; scouter

Douglas MacArthur, New York, N.Y., Corporation Chairman; General of the Army; recipient of Congressional Medal of Honor

Jack C. Vowell. El Paso, Tex., Business executive; engineer; civic leader; veteran scouter

Frederick M. Warburg, New York, N.Y., Banker; philanthropist; worker for youth; scouter

1964 **A. Frank Bray,** Martinez, Calif., Jurist; civic leader; friend to youth; scouter

Albert L. Cole, Greenwich, Conn., Publisher; president, Boys' Clubs of America; philanthropist

Lyndon B. Johnson, Johnson City, Tex., President, United States of America

Ralph W. McCreary, Indiana, Pa., Industrialist; civic leader; veteran scouter

Robert Moses, New York, N.Y., Public servant; builder; friend to youth; scouter

Ephraim Laurence Palmer, Ithaca, N.Y., Educator; author; conservationist; veteran scouter

Thomas F. Patton, Cleveland, Ohio, International industrialist; civic leader; scouter

Gilbert R. Pirrung, Bainbridge, Ga., Agriculturist; churchman; world scouter

Howard Tellepsen, Houston, Tex., Business leader; churchman; scouter

1965 **Irving Ben Cooper,** New York, N.Y., Jurist; humanitarian; friend to youth

Austin T. Cushman, Chicago, Ill, Merchandising executive; community leader; scouter
Harry J. Delaney, New York, N.Y., Business leader; churchman; scouter
Royal Firman, Jr., Cleveland, Ohio, Business, cultural, community and church leader; scouter
John H. Glenn, Jr., Houston, Tex., Colonel, Marine Corps (ret.); astronaut; scouter
Harry J. Johnson, New York, N.Y., Physician; educator; administrator; scouter
Harry G. McGavran, Quincy, Ill., Surgeon; community leader; humanitarian; scouter
David Sarnoff, New York, N.Y., Industrialist; communications expert; veteran scouter
Jo. S. Stong, Keosauqua, Iowa, Community leader; scouting enthusiast
Gustavo J. Vollmer, Caracas, Venezuela, Engineer; Venezuelan and world scouter

1966 **Richard W. Darrow,** Scarsdale, N.Y., Publicist; civic leader; Eagle Scout; scouter
John Henry Fischer, New York, N.Y., Educator; civic leader; Eagle Scout; scouter
Charles Zachary Hardwick, Findlay, Ohio, Business executive; humanitarian; scouter
Lewis Blaine Hershey, Washington, D.C., Lieutenant general, United States Army; director, Selective Service; scouter
Basil O'Connor, New York, N.Y., Lawyer; public servant; humanitarian; friend to youth
Philip Henry Powers, Greensburg, Pa., Engineer; educator; pioneer scouter

1967 **Paul G. Benedum,** Pittsburgh, Pa., Business executive; community leader; scouter
Sterling B. Doughty, Sacramento, Calif., Financial and management consultant; world scouter
Harold Keith Johnson, Washington, D.C., Chief of staff, United States Army; educator; scouter
Otto Kerner, Springfield, Ill., Governor of Illinois; scouter
Clarence "Biggie" Munn Lansing, Minn., Athletic director; coach; friend of youth; scouter
Crawford Rainwater, Pensacola, Fla., Business executive; community leader; scouter
Vittz-James Ramsdell, Portland, Ore., Business executive; community leader; scouter
Howard A. Rusk, New York, N.Y., Physician; educator; innovator; humanitarian
Dwight J. Thomson, Cincinnati, Ohio, Business leader; veteran scouter; world scouter
William C. Westmoreland, Washington, D.C., Commander, U.S. Military Assistance Command, Vietnam; CG, U.S. Army, Vietman; Eagle Scout; scouter

1968 **John Cardinal Cody,** Chicago, Ill., Archbiship of Chicago; recipient of the Silver Beaver; energetic scouter
John G. Detwiler, Williamsport, Pa., Industrialist; churchman; recipient of the Silver Beaver and Silver Antelope; National Executive Board Member
Robert T. Gray, Prospect, Ohio, Physician; Eagle Scout; medical officer at many national and world jamborees
Arthur Z. Hirsch, Santa Barbara, Calif., Veteran scouter; recipient of the Silver Beaver and Silver Antelope
John F. Lott, Lubbock, Tex., Rancher; world scouter; recipient of the Silver Beaver and Silver Antelope
William L. Schloss, Indianapolis, Ind., Banker; community leader; recipient of the Silver Beaver
James E. Webb, Washington, D.C., Lawyer; businessman; diplomat; educator; administrator, National Aeronautics and Space Administration

1969 **John M. Budd,** St. Paul, Minn., Executive . . . , champion of youth, dedicated scouter
Arleigh Burke, Washington D.C., Military leader, patriot, distinguished scouter
James F. Burshears, La Junta, Col., Imaginative scouter
M. Scott Carpenter, Houston, Tex., Aquanaut, astronaut, friend of scouting
Vincent T. Lombardi, Washington, D.C., Professional football general manager, friend of youth
John W. H. Miner, Quebec, Canada, Manufacturer, community leader, world scouter
James E. Patrick, Phoenix, Ariz., Banker, community leader, devoted scouter
Robert W. Reneker, Chicago, Ill., Executive, humanitarian, devoted scouter
John W. Starr, Kansas City, Mo., Executive, faithful scouter
N. Eldon Tanner, Salt Lake City, Utah, Churchman, executive, veteran scouter

1970 **Neil A. Armstrong,** El Lago, Tex., Astronaut, first man to walk on the Moon
Francisco Bueso, San Juan, P.R., Chamber of Commerce director, champion of scouting
Antonio C. Delgado, Manila, Philippines, Business executive, world scouter
Laurence C. Jones, Piney Woods, Miss., Educator, author, servant of youth
Aryeh Lev, New York, N.Y., Rabbi, chaplain, dedicated scouter
Leo Perlis, Washington, D.C., Organized labor official, humanitarian, friend of scouting
Bryan S. Reid, Jr., Chicago, Ill., Investment banker, community leader, devoted scouter
William H. Spurgeon III, Santa Ana, Calif., Children's hospital executive, "father" of special-interest exploring

1971 **William G. Connare,** Greensburg, Pa., Bishop, scouter, and champion of scouting
Elbert R. Curtis, Salt Lake City, Utah, Executive, community and church leader, veteran scouter
Thomas Stephens Haggai, High Point, N.C., Gifted public speaker, ordained minister, patriot, scouter
August F. Hook, Indianapolis, Ind., Business executive, community leader, dedicated scouter
William R. Jackson, Sewickley, Pa., Executive, devoted scouter, friend of youth
Fred C. Mills, Aptos, Calif., Outstanding scouter; retired director, Health and Safety Service, Boy Scouts of America
Arch Monson, Jr., San Francisco, Calif., Patron of the arts, humanitarian, executive
Richard Milhous Nixon, Washington, D.C., President, United States of America
Leon Howard Sullivan, Philadelphia, Pa., Humanitarian, peoples' champion

1972 **Louis R. Bruce, Jr.,** Washington, D.C., U.S. commissioner of Indian Affairs, champion of scouting
Harvey C. Christen, Burbank, Calif., Aircraft company executive, civic leader, devoted scouter
Louis G. Feil, Chipita Park, Colo., Consulting engineer, promoter of camping and Order of the Arrow
Edwin H. Gott, Pittsburgh, Pa., Corporate executive, community leader, vigorous promoter of Exploring
Donald P. Hammond, Monticello, N.Y., Business executive, civic leader, scouting enthusiast
Albert M. Jongeneel, Rio Vista, Calif., Retired rancher, dedicated scouter
Arthur L. Jung, Jr., New Orleans, La., Business executive, servant of youth, international scouter

Prime F. Osborn III, Jacksonville, Fla., Company president, friend of youth, advocate of scouting
George W. Pirtle, Tyler, Tex., Consulting geologist and independent oil producer, philanthropist, benefactor of scouting
Penn W. Zeigler, Cincinnati, Ohio, Business executive, humanitarian, veteran scouter

1973 **Ernest Banks,** Chicago, Ill., Baseball great, inspiration for boys, faithful scouter
Joseph A. Brunton, Jr., Matawan, N.J., Servant of youth, former chief scout executive
Victor T. Ehre, Utica, N.Y., Company president, community leader, dedicated scouter
Donald H. Flanders, Fort Smith, Ariz., Company founder and president, distinguished scouter
E. K. Jamison, Atlanta, Ga., Company president, devoted scouter
Max I. Silber, Nashua, N.H., Company president, loyal scouter, benefactor of students
Osborne K. Taylor, Montclair, N.J., Retired corporate executive, veteran scoutmaster, champion of scouting
J. Kimball Whitney, Wayzata, Minn., Company president, friend of youth, veteran scouter

1974 **Stephen A. Derby,** Honolulu, Hawaii, Retired banker, civic leader, faithful scouter
James E. Johnson, Los Angeles, Calif., Corporate board chairman, former assistant secretary of the Navy, distinguished scouter
Allen W. Mathis, Jr., Montgomery, Ala., Company Board Chairman, civic leader, dedicated scouter
James R. Neidhoefer, Menomonee Falls, Wisc., Company president, distinguished scouter, veteran scoutmaster
Melvin B. Neisner, Rochester, N.Y., Company president, community leader, devoted scouter
William H. Quasha, Manila, Philippines, Attorney, international scouter and scoutmaster
John K. Sloan, Los Angeles, Calif., Attorney, advocate of youth loyal scouter
Herman Stern, Valley City, N.D., Merchant, humanitarian, veteran scouter
Leif J. Sverdrup, St. Louis, Mo., Industrialist and engineer, zealous scouter
Wallace E. Wilson, Detroit, Mich., Corporate vice-president, friend of youth, dedicated scouter

1975 **Gerald R. Ford,** Washington, D.C., President, United States of America; symbol of integrity, example for youth

1976 **John T. Acree, Jr.,** Louisville, Ky., Company board chairman, civic leader, dedicated scouter
Perry R. Bass, Fort Worth, Tex., Corporate chairman and president, community benefactor, distinguished scouter
Milton Caniff, Palm Springs, Calif., Cartoonist, humanitarian, friend of scouting
Arthur H. Cromb, Mission Hills, Kans., Company president, inspirational scouter, university alumni leader
Thomas F. Hawkins, River Forest, Ill., University vice-president, scouter extraordinary
Elizabeth G. Knight, Waite Hill, Ohio, Philanthropist, benefactor of scouting
Joseph W. Marshall, Twin Falls, Ida., Retired physician and surgeon, churchman, faithful scouter
Louis W. Menk, South St. Paul, Minn., Company board chairman, transportation industry leader, loyal scouter
Max S. Norris, Indianapolis, Ind., Physician, businessman, devoted scouter
LaVern Watts Parmley, Salt Lake City, Ut., Churchwoman, benefactor of children, Cub Scouting advocate
Simon Rositzky, St. Joseph, Mo., Company president, conservationist, American Humanics chairman
Lester R. Steig, San Francisco, Calif., Educator, author, proponent of scouting

1978 **L. Jadwin Asfeld,** W. St. Paul, Minn., Company president, Red Cross leader, distinguished scouter
Jimmy Carter, Washington, D.C., 39th President, defender of human rights, friend of youth
Alec Chesser, Houston, Tex., Corporate leader, man of stature, devoted scouter
Dorothy Feist, New York, N.Y., Humanitarian, philanthropist, scouting "first lady"
Roy W. Johnson, St. Louis, Mo., Civil leader, good citizen, scouting stalwart
Richard W. Kiefer, Baltimore, Md., Attorney, versatile scouter, churchman
Katsumi Kometani, Honolulu, Haw., Dentist, dedicated scouter, advocate of youth
Thomas S. Monson, Salt Lake City, Utah, Church leader, noted speaker, scouter
John D. Murchison, Dallas, Tex., Partner, Murchison Brothers; civic leader, scouting proponent
John D. Schapiro, Baltimore, Md., International sportsman, businessman, faithful scouter
Forrest N. Shumway, Los Angeles, Cal., Corporate executive, friend of youth, veteran scouter
Bland W. Worley, Charlotte, N.C., Corporate executive, civic servant, greater scouter

1979 **No award**

1980 **Charles T. Clayton,** Birmingham, Ala., Executive, civic leader, dedicated scouter
William P. Clement, Jr., Dallas, Tex., Governor of Texas, executive, distinguished scouter
Frank William Gay, Encino, Calif., Business executive, churchman, devoted scouter
Thomas F. Gilbane, Providence, R.I., Business leader, dedicated scouter
Milton H. Gray, Chicago, Ill., Lawyer, civic leader, veteran scouter
William Hillcourt, Manlius, N.Y., "Green Bar Bill," the voice of scouting
Downing B. Jenks, St. Louis, Mo., Corporate executive, railroader, Boy Scouts of America president
Reuben R. Jensen, Detroit, Mich., Engineer, corporate executive, distinguished scouter
Sonia S. Maguire, Stamford, Conn., Humanitarian, benefactor of scouting
I. Willard Marriott, Washington, D.C., Corporation founder, churchman, benefactor of scouting
Archibald McClure, Chicago, Ill., Executive, community servant, loyal scouter
Henry J. Nave, Pinehurst, N.C., Corporate executive, sportsman, faithful scouter
Gene H. Sternberg, Sr., Granite City, Ill., Executive, civic leader, loyal scouter
Harry Thorsen, Jr., Sarasota, Fla., Scouts on Stamps Coecity Intl., executive

The Distinguished Eagle Scout Award was established in 1969 to honor men who were Eagle Scouts at least 25 years before and who subsequently distinguished themselves in business, one of the professions or in service to their country. The National Court of Honor selects the recipients of this award from nominees made by the Committee of Distinguished Eagle Scouts. The following is an alphabetical listing of the recipients of this honor through 1977 and the years in which they originally earned their Eagles; the years in which they were made Distinguished Eagle Scouts are not available. The list of Distinguished Eagle Scouts from 1978 on follows; see page 636.

Paul Haynes Abel, 1929
Frederick W. Ackroyd, 1944
Clyde Spears Alexander, 1933
E. Ross Allen, 1927
Thomas L. Allen, 1940
Paul Richard Allyn, Jr., 1928
Maj. Gen. E.H. Almquist, USA, 1933
Bryon Lesley Anderson, 1942
George W. Anderson, 1938
Carlos D. Arguelles, 1932
Neil Alden Armstrong, 1947
Louis C. Bailey, 1937
Alden G. Barber, 1933
Walter Carlyle Barnes, Jr., 1939
J.V. Bauknight, 1930
Louis H. Beechnau, 1942
John M. Belk, 1947
William H. Bell, 1926
Charles E. Bennett, 1925
Maj. Gen. John Charles Bennett, USA, 1938
Lloyd M. Bentsen, Jr., 1938
Louis P. Bergna, 1938
Maj. Gen. Sidney B. Berry, 1940
Morris R. Beschloss, 1948
Frank Blair, 1930
John A. Blatnik, 1926
Gen. Charles H. Bonesteel III, USA, 1925
Marvin Borman, 1937
Max Leo Bramer, 1927
Jack H. Braucht, 1936
James H. Brian, Sr., 1932
John C. Brizendine, 1940
Howell Harris Brooks, 1922
Newton Duncan Brookshire, Jr., 1937
Clarence J. Brown, 1943
Gen. George Scratchley Brown, USAF 1935
J. Royston Brown, 1942
Allen E. Brubaker, 1928
William K. Brumbach, 1929
Joseph A. Brunton, Jr., 1918
Rear Adm. Ross P. Bullard, 1930
M. Caldwell Butler, 1941
John Tyler Caldwell, 1926
William D. Campbell, 1922
Lester F. Canham, Jr., 1946
Milton Caniff, 1923
George Howard Capps, 1930
Gerald P. Carr, 1947
Jack Caskey, 1945
Henry Carroll Chambers, 1943
Hugh McMaster Chapman, 1946
Laurence Dreher Chapman, 1942
Walter E. Chapman, 1943
Paul R. Christen, 1943
Donald N. Clark, 1923
Harold R. Clark, 1939
Thomas Campbell Clark, 1914
Charles T. Clayton, 1924
Hugh C. Clayton, 1937
William P. Clements, Jr., 1930
Conrad P. Cleveland, Jr., 1937
Stephen H. Clink, 1928
Murray L. Cole, 1937
James D. Collins, Jr., 1933
Ralph J. Comstock, Jr., 1933
Lyman C. Conger, 1930
Lt. Gen. Albert O. Connor, 1928
David C. Cook III, 1928
William B. Crawford, 1940
Lon Worth Crow, Jr., 1926
William R. Cumerford, 1933
William J. Cure, 1935
Chester H. Curtis, 1926
Thomas B. Curtis, 1925
Loren S. Dahl, 1937
Richard W. Darrow, 1933
Joseph W. Davis, 1938
Philip Sheridan Davy, 1932
Antonio C. Delgado, 1933
Russell DeYoung, 1927
John E. Dolibois, 1934
Rulon W. Doman, 1923
Maj. Gen. Edwin I. Donley, 1932
Hedley Donovan, 1929
John D. Driggs, 1941
William T. Duboc, 1940
Everett H. Dudley, 1920
Gov. Michael S. Dukakis, 1949
Charles M. Duke, 1946
William W. Duke, 1949
William E. Dukes, Jr., 1946
Oscar Carroll Dunn, 1937
Grover B. Eaker, 1947
Ernest C. Ebrite, 1944
Lt. Gen. James V. Edmundson, 1929
Wallace W. Edwards, 1937
James Erwin Egger, 1937
Victor T. Ehre, 1927
Charles R. Ehrhardt, 1938
Arthur R. Eldred, 1912
Eugene E. Ellis, Jr., 1930
Charles Emmett Engel, 1922
Jacob R. Esser, 1935
Col. Bernhard Ettenson, USA, 1931
Daniel J. Evans, 1941
Bernhard I. Everson, 1929
William Harrison Fetridge, 1924
John L. Feudner, Jr., 1932
Edward Ridley Finch, Jr., 1936
Robert H. Finch, 1940
John H. Fischer, 1931
Donald H. Flanders, 1941
Jerome F. Foley, Jr., 1933
Gerald R. Ford, Jr., 1927
C. Richard Ford, Jr., 1938
Neal Randolph Fosseen, Sr., 1923
Dulany Foster, 1931
Edward M. Friend, 1925
Thomas Teasley Galt, 1942
Theodore R. Gamble, 1940
James F. Gary, 1937
Thomas F. Gilbane, 1928
William J. Gilbane, 1928
Hyde Gillette, 1921
Norman B. Gillis, Jr., 1940
Stanley J. Glaser, 1921
M. Thomas Goedeke, 1935
Robert H. Goldman, 1931
W. Richard Goodwin, 1940
Lawrence W. Gougler, 1936
John Underwood Graham, 1933
Milton H. Gray, 1926
Anthony S. Greene, 1941
Richard Putnam Gripe, 1935
Robert Charles Gunness, 1928
Gen. Ralph E. Haines, Jr., USA, 1928
Ezra A. Hale, 1924

Durward Gorham Hall, 1923
Brig. Gen. Ralph J. Hallenbeck, 1934
Robert D. Hammer, 1928
Gaines Wardlaw Hammond, Sr., 1929
Richardson Miles Hanckel, 1942
Raymond T. Hander, 1929
Zenon C.R. Hansen, 1926
Bernold M. Hanson, 1943
John K. Hanson, 1929
Samuel Elvis Hanvey, 1940
John M. Harbert III, 1937
John P. Harbin, 1931
Jack D. Harby, 1930
William Benjamin Harrell, Jr., 1925
Benjamin L. Harris, 1938
George A. Harris, 1924
James T. Harrison, 1929
Walter Kenneth Hartford, 1935
Robert T. Hartmann, 1933
Allan E. Hassinger, 1936
Thomas F. Hawkins, 1932
Jack A. Hayes, 1938
David Warrington Hedrick, 1932
Paul M. Herring, 1934
Robert R. Herring, 1941
Paul B. Heuston, 1936
Robert G. Hibbard, 1926
Lynn P. Himmelman, 1928
Lawrence L. Hirsch, 1941
Philip Bernhard Hofmann, 1925
Alex A. Hogan, 1930
Billie Holder, 1932
Gen. Joseph R. Holzapple, USAF, 1929
August F. Hook, 1922
Harold Swanson Hook, 1945
Ernest B. Hueter, 1936
James R. Hughes, Jr., 1921
A.D. Hulings, 1929
Robert N. Hunter, 1936
Don Hutson, 1927
Harry T. Ice, 1921
William L. Jeffords, 1944
Reuben R. Jenson, 1936
Bryan Johnson, 1929
George Dean Johnson, 1924
Ted Lincoln Johnson, 1941
William Kenneth Johnson, 1941
Edward Carey Joullian III, 1944
John J. Kamerick, 1935
O. Frank Kattwinkel, 1940
Ewing M. Kauffman, 1931
Brig. Gen. Paul A. Kauttu, USAF, 1947
Lewis Kayton, 1917
William P. Kemp, Jr., 1937
Ernest C. Keppler, 1935
Richard W. Kiefer, 1930
Norman Victor Kinsey, 1934
Robert E. Kirby, 1933
Rufus W. Kiser, 1928
Philip Monroe Klauber, 1930
Louis A. Klewer, 1917
John A. Kley, 1936
Joseph William Koch, 1924
Edward J. Kuntz, 1936
Louis Charles LaCour, Sr., 1943
John W. Lander, Jr., 1943
Carl T. Langford, 1934
John S. Langford, Jr., 1947
Louis A. Langie, Jr., 1945
Walter Philip Leber, 1932
Stanley Levingston, 1940
Lee M. Liberman, 1938
Walter Rearick Lohman, 1931
Thomas D. Long, 1941
Cook O.P. Lougheed, 1938
James A. Lovell, 1943
Richard G. Lugar, 1946
Paul H. Lyle, 1926
William C. MacDonald, Jr., 1921
Bruce G. MacMillan, 1936
Leander A. Malone, 1932
Robert A. Manchester II, 1920
Darrell F. Manley, 1940
William Donald Manly, 1939
H. Edward Manville, Jr., 1919
Robert S. Mars, Jr., 1940
John Otho Marsh, Jr., 1941
Allen W. Mathis, Jr., 1939
Joseph L. Matthews, 1931
Russell G. Mawby, 1944
William J. Maxion, 1934
C. Robert McBrier, 1931
Joseph J. McClelland, 1931
James A. McClure, 1933
James J. McClure, Jr., 1934
William Frazer McColl, Jr., 1944
James R. McConnell, 1934
Harold James McCurry, Jr., 1935
Robert Owen McCurry, 1935
Gen. John A. McDavid, USA, 1930
James Henry McGregor, 1939
Rear Adm. Robert W. McNitt, USN, 1931
Ferdinand Mendenhall, 1924
Ronald Clifford Metevier, 1941
Martin Michael, 1943
Donald P. Miller, 1922
George Fuller Miller, 1921
Morris F. Miller, 1934
Wallace T. Miller, 1937
James Selden Miner, 1928
Frank Warren Mogensen, 1940
O. William Moody, 1931
Lt. Gen. Joseph H. Moore, USAF, 1929
James A. Moreau, 1929
Graham J. Morgan, 1933
Howard J. Morgens, 1924
Charles Shoemaker Morris, Jr., 1933
Josh R. Morriss, Jr., 1939
Jerome Moskow, 1938
Franklin David Murphy, 1931
William Paul Murray, Jr., 1934
James R. Neidhoefer, 1941
Oswald George Nelson, 1920
Maj. Gen. Franklin A. Nichols, USAF, 1933
Max S. Norris, 1941
Edgar A. Oglesby, 1936
H. Ted Olson, 1949
John Roberts Opel, 1940
Jack W. Osborn, 1931
Nathaniel A. Owings, 1922
George M. Pardee, Jr., 1932
John C. Parish, 1926
James E. Patrick, 1923
Robert W. Paul, 1934
William G. Payne, 1931
H. Ross Perot, 1943
Edward Patterson Perrin, 1942
G. Freeland Phillips, 1950
John Temple Phillips, Jr., 1932
Samuel R. Pierce, Jr., 1936

Lt. Gen. Bryce Poe II, USAF, 1940
William Poole, 1923
Boone Powell, 1928
C. Dudley Pratt, 1942
G. Merritt Preston, 1931
Kenneth G. Pringle, 1930
William Howard Quasha, 1931
Paul W. Radichel, 1935
Vittz-James Ramsdell, 1936
Julian R. Rashkind, 1935
L. Edmund Rast, 1931
Fred A. Ratcliffe, 1921
Rulon W. Rawson, 1923
R.P. Reinemer, Jr., 1934
Paul Hansen Reistrup, 1948
Robert Field Ritchie, 1931
C.M.A. Rogers III, 1947
Philip S. Rogers, 1923
Gen. William Rosson, USA, 1933
Gabriel Rouquie, 1930
Herbert J. Rowe, 1944
Donald H. Rumsfeld, 1949
Ray L. Russell, 1946
Paul Salerno, 1930
Harrison Salisbury, 1924
James Terry Sanford, 1932
Thomas D. Sayles, Jr., 1948
Philip H. Schaff, Jr., 1934
John D. Schapiro, 1931
Ralph G. Schimmele, 1940
David G. Schmidt, 1924
Ernest F. Schmidt, 1926
Don B. Scott, 1942
Donald R. Seawell, 1929
Raymond P. Shafer, 1931
Robert H. Shaffer, 1930
Edgar Finley Shannon, Jr., 1932
Louis W. Shelburne, 1928
James Gilbert Shirley, 1932
Thomas M. Shive, 1938
Edward H. Sibley, 1928
Max I. Silber, 1936
Fred W. Sington, 1924
John K. Sloan, 1938
J. Harold Smith, 1927
Lloyd E. Smith, 1925
Marvin Hugh Smith, 1934
Robert L. Smith, 1931
Maj. Gen. Lawrence W. Snowden, 1937
William Layton Spruell, 1943
Frank Stanton, 1926
Jack J. Stark, 1929
Tom Steed, 1921
Richard C. Steele, 1930
Lester R. Steig, 1930
Lloyd M. Steward, 1924
Richard Stoner, 1935
Walter Franklin Story, Jr., 1935
Edmund D. Strang, 1932
Percy E. Sutton, 1936
Maj. Gen. Orwin Clark Talbott, USA, 1936
Thomas L. Tatham, 1927
George Brown Taylor, 1941
Harry D. Thorsen, Jr., 1929
Maj. Gen. William Gay Thrash, USMC, 1931
Bertram William Tremayne, Jr., 1934
Frederick C. Tucker, Jr., 1935
James McClure Turner, 1927
William Keener Ulerich, 1924
Victor Vincent Veysey, 1929
Rev. Frans A. Victorson, 1935
Benjamin Stuart Vincent, 1945
Jack C. Vowell, Jr., 1942
Laurence C. Walker 1938
W.E. Walker, Jr., 1943
J. Richard Walton, 1945
Carl Erwin Wasmuth, 1938
Elmer H. Wavering, 1922
Grady Webb, Jr., 1930
Adm. Maurice Franklin Weisner, USN, 1933
Louie Welch, 1933
Harold L. Wenaas, 1946
Fred W. Wenzel, 1930
Gen. William Childs Westmoreland, USA, 1930
Walter R. Whidden, 1922
Stephen White, 1925
Harold E. Wibberley, Jr., 1936
Harry G. Wiles, 1932
Joseph W. Wilkus, 1940
Charles S. Williams, Jr., 1937
Joseph W. Williams, Jr., 1930
Lyman Perry Williams, 1924
James McCrorry Willson, Jr., 1938
Delmer H. Wilson, 1927
Douglas E. Wilson, 1932
James Robert Gavin Wilson, 1930
R. Baxter Wilson, 1920
Richard Samuel Wilson, 1934
Wallace E. Wilson, 1925
John William Witt, 1949
Halbert O. Woodward, 1932
Earle W. Wright, 1915
Lt. Gen. John M. Wright, Jr., USA, 1929
Walter B. Wriston, 1934
Robert H. Young, Jr., 1937
Adm. Elmo Russell Zumwalt, Jr., USN, 1937

1978 **Elliott M. Estes**
Robert Stephen Wise
Robert V. Roosa
Ome Daiber
Ellis C. Littmann
Armand Edward Brodeur
Edmund R. Knauf
Don Shoemaker
William Snow Frates
Thomas Milton Orth
Curt J. Gronner
John J. Costa
Edgar A. Sherman
Frederick H. Lawson
E. Roy Stone, Jr.
Douglas B. Littlewood
Bernard Andrew Monaghan, Jr.
Clark Brower George
Jirah Delano Cole
Donald A. Boyd
Carl F. Pozzani
David H. Rariden
Barry E. Pidgeon
John E. Corbally
Claire Elwood Hutchin, Jr.
Champney A. McNair
John Conway Harrison
Harold A. Lenicheck
Edward L. Spellman
Robert Phillip Sharp
Henry H. Lowery
Wilson P. Cannon, Jr.

1979 **Albert M. Myers**
Edwin Joseph McWilliams

Raoul A. "Ray" Garrabrandt
Spurgeon Gaskins
David S. Hartig, Sr.
Roosevelt Gilliam
William B. Randall
Charles S. Daley
Kelly Waller
Robert F. Weinberg
Frank M. Hutchins
Alan W. Koppes
Harry P. Seward, Jr.
Frank F. Chuman
James Walker Ralph
Claude Shuford Abernethy, Sr.
James Francis Burshears
Donald C. Lutken
Rodney Clark Hermes
John R. Greenwood
Samuel Augustus Nunn, Jr.
William P. McCahill
Bruce W. Cunningham
Meyer M. Ueoka
Carrington Mason
Frederic W. Schermerhorn
William E. Slesnick
John H. Ware III
William Wesley Carroll
Thomas C. MacAvoy
Manning E. Case
Joseph L. Hogan
Harry J. Hutchens
Albert E. Cunliff
Frank C. DeGuire
Joseph R. Barnett
Clarence G. Beers
1980 James S. Black
Robert Beverley Evans
David Owen Johnson
Louis J. Kienzler
Constantine A. Karaberis
William Denby Hanna
Maurice F. Granville
Charles M. Pigott
Kenneth L. Robinson
John B. Stokes, Jr.
James Lee Tarr
Harold Thomas Walsh
John N. Dalton
Charles Marshall
Richard H. Eisenhart
James Acra Hackney, Jr.
James A. Hachney III
Grant Herman
Chauncey J. Medberry III
Philip B. Schnering
Robert W. Scott
Robert L. Seidner
S. Shepherd Tate
Robert H. Brummal
Russell J. Hart
Frank H. Heckrodt
Sheldon S. Baker
Francis H. Herndon
C. Ray Leininger, Jr.
William J. Rushton, Jr.
William J. Rushton III
C. Mercer Sloan

James J. and Jane Hoey Award for Interracial Justice
John Lafarge Memorial Award for Interracial Justice

CATHOLIC INTERRACIAL COUNCIL OF NEW YORK
225 E. 52nd St., New York, N.Y. 10022 (212/751-9445)

The James J. and Jane Hoey Award for Interracial Justice, which consists of a silver medal, is given annually to honor a black and a white Catholic for efforts to combat bigotry and promote interracial justice

1942 Frank A. Hall
Edward La Salle
1943 Philip Murray
Ralph H. Metcalfe
1944 Mrs. Edward V. Morrell
John L. Yancey
1945 Paul D. Williams
Richard Barthe
1946 Richard Reid
Charles L. Rawlings
1947 Julian J. Reiss
Clarence T. Hunter
1948 Anna McGarry
Ferdinand L. Rousseve
1949 John O'Connor
M.C. Clarke
1950 J. Howard McGrath
Lou Montgomery
1951 Mrs. Roger L. Putnam
Francis M. Hammond
1952 Charles F. Vatterot, Jr.
Joseph H. Yancey
1953 Joseph J. Morrow
John B. King
1954 Gladys D. Woods
Collins J. Seitz
1955 Millard F. Everett
James W. Hose
1956 Frank M. Folsom
Paul G. King
1957 George Meany
James W. Dorsey
1958 James T. Harris
Robert Sargent Shriver, Jr.
1959 Percy H. Steele, Jr.
John P. Nelson
1960 William Duffy, Jr.
George A. Moore
1961 Ralph Fenton
Osma Spurlock
1962 Benjamin Muse
Eugene T. Reed
1963 James T. Carey
Percy H. Williams
1964 Arthur J. Holland
Frederick O'Neal
1965 Gerard E. Sherry
James R. Dumpson
1966 Jane M. Hoey
Mrs. Roy Wilkins
1967 Frank Horne
Lt. Gov. Malcolm Wilson
1968 E.H. Molisani
John Strachan
1969 Harold E. McGannon

Hulan E. Jack
1970 George P. McManus
Alfred Del Bello
Maceo A. Thomas
Cleo Joseph L. Froix
1971 Rev. Francis J. Mugavero
Rev. Harold R. Perry
1972 Joseph F. Crangle
Alen E. Pinado
1973 Meade H. Esposito
Robert B. Boyd
1974 Harold A. Stevens
Thomas Van Arsdale
1975 N.A.
1976 N.A.
1977 N.A.
1978 J. Peter Grace
Hon. Basil A. Paterson
1979 Helen Hayes
Felisa Rincon de Gautier
Cecil E. Ward
1980 Maureen O'Sullivan
Peter J. Ottley
Jack John Olivero

The John LaFarge Memorial Award for Interracial Justice, which consists of a scroll, annually honors outstanding contributions to justice for all races.

1965 Francis Cardinal Spellman
1966 Sen. Jacob K. Javits
1967 Gov. Nelson A. Rockefeller
1968 George F. Meany
1969 Whitney M. Young, Jr.
1970 Harry Van Arsdale, Jr.
1971 John V. Lindsay
1972 Earl W. Brydges
1973 Louis K. Lefkowitz
1974 Arthur Levitt
1975 Robert J. Wagner
1976 N.A.
1977 N.A.
1978 E. Howard Molisani
1979 Hon. Hugh L. Carey
1980 Sen Daniel Patrick Moynihan
Hazel N. Dukes

Humanitarian Awards

UNITED CEREBRAL PALSY OF NEW YORK
122 E. 23rd St., New York, N.Y. 10010 (212/677-7400)

The United Cerebral Palsy Humanitarian Awards are now given annually for service to victims of the disease. An awards committee selects the winner, who receives a Tiffany crystal and silver obelisk. Prior to 1971, the award was given irregularly and exact dates of the honors ceremony are not available.

EARLIER RECIPIENTS:

Thomas E. Dewey
Peter Grimm
Stanley C. Hope
Joseph A. Martino
Roger S. Firestone
Jinx Falkenberg McCrary
William Clay Ford
Jane Pickens Langley
Gen. Dwight D. Eisenhower

1971 **Gov. and Mrs. Nelson A. Rockefeller,** New York
1972 **William S. Renchard,** Chairman of the Board, Chemical Bank
Richard E. Berlin, President, Hearst Corp.
1973 **T. Vincent Learson,** Chairman of the Board, IBM Corp.
John F. McGillicuddy, President, Manufacturers Hanover Trust Co.
1974 **Donald C. Platten,** Chairman of the Board, Chemical Bank
Edward R. Rowley, Chairman of the Board, NL Industries, Inc.
1975 **Bob Hope,** Honorary National UCP Chairman
Emil J. Pattberg, Jr., Chairman of the Board, First Boston Corp.
1976 **Mrs. Albert D. Lasker,** President, UCP Research & Educational Foundation
Willard C. Butcher, President, Chase Manhattan Bank N. A.
1977 **Gov. Hugh L. Carey,** New York
1978 Edgar M. Bronfman
John R. Miller
1979 Paul Anka
Donald C. Cook
1980 Ray C. Adam
Norborne Berkeley, Jr.

Richard S. Childs Lectureship

CITY CLUB OF NEW YORK
33 W. 42nd St., New York, N.Y. 10036 (212/921-9870)

The Richard S. Childs Lectureship is given annually to an expert in the field of municipal administration. It is one of the City Club's New York honors.

1978 Raymond Horton
1979 E. S. Sonas
1980 Richard P. Nathan

Premio Ciardi

FONDAZIONE PROFESSORE GIUSEPPE CIARDI
Gruppo Italiano della Societa Internazionale di Dritto Penale Militare, Viale delle Milizie 5C, 00192 Rome, Italy

The 500,000 lire Premio Ciardi, or Ciardi Prize, is presented triennially to an individual for a meritorious study of military law or related subjects. The study must be written in French, English, Dutch, German, Spanish or Italian.

1970 M.F. Jiemenez y Jiemenez
1973 F. Kalshoven
1976 Pietro Verri
Michael Bothe
1979 Klaus P. Fiedler

CBC Medal

CITIZENS BUDGET COMMISSION
110 E. 42nd St, New York, N.Y. 10017 (212/687-0711)

The CBC Medal, which is of bronze, annually honors distinguished civic service to New York City. An awards committee selects the recipient.

1953 Joseph M. Proskauer
1954 Devereux C. Josephs
1955 Stanley M. Isaacs
1956 David Rockefeller
Bernard F. Gimbel
1957 Herbert H. Lehman
1958 Harrison Tweed
1959 James Felt
1960 Samuel D. Leidesdorf
1961 John D. Rockefeller, 3rd
James Felt
1962 David M. Heyman
Emma Alden Rothblatt
1963 Austin J. Tobin
Mrs. Charles S. Payson
1964 Percy Uris
1965 Othmar Hermann Ammann
1966 Earl B. Schwulst
1967 Thomas P. F. Hoving
1968 McGeorge Bundy
1969 Robert W. Dowling
1970 Walter Cronkite
1971 Jacob K. Javits
1972 Arthur Levitt
1973 William J. Ronan
George Champion
1974 Abraham Beame
1975 J. Peter Grace
1976 Richard R. Shinn
1977 Hugh Carey
1978 Arthur F. Burns
1979 Donald C. Platten
1980 Felix G. Rohatyn

Winston Churchill Award

INTERNATIONAL PLATFORM ASSOCIATION
2564 Berkshire Rd., Cleveland Hgts., Ohio 44106
(216/932-0505)

The Winston Churchill Award, a silver bowl, is annually presented to the individual judged to have made statements from the platform which most affect the future of American citizens.

1978 Joseph A. Califano, Jr.
1979 Adm. Hyman Rickover
1980 No award

Secretary of Defense Award for Outstanding Public Service

DEPARTMENT OF DEFENSE
The Pentagon, OSD Incentive Awards Board, Washington, D.C. 20301 (202/697-3305)

The Secretary of Defense Award for Outstanding Public Service is given for civilian contributions to the nation's defense. Traditionally, the honor is presented most frequently by an outgoing Secretary of Defense to his people. While the award has been in existence for a number of years, winners prior to 1977 are not available.

1977

Ann P. Ulrey
Rodney C. Loehr
Fount L. Robison
J. Kevin Murphy
Robert C. Lewis
Thurston Hassell
Lotte Duker
John P. Stenbit
Solomon J. Buchsbaum
J. Robinson West
Kenneth L. Adelman
Maynard W. Glitman
Morton S. Abramowitz
Harry E. Bergold, Jr.
Will Hill Tankersley
Julian R. Levine
Daniel L. Mausser
R. W. Henderson
Edward B. Hudson
James B. Foley
Henry E. Glass
John Dunworth
Richard C. Steadman
Robert N. Smith
William W. Wisman
David O. Cooke
James S. Brady
Tod R. Hullin
John T. Hughes
Ferderick P. Hitz
Laurence J. Legere
Harold Meyer
James A. Messer
James E. Frank (USAR-Ret.)
Fount L. Robison

1978

Robert Strausz-Hupe
Norman R. Augustine
James W. Plummer
Seymour Weiss
U. Alexis Johnson
Albert Wohlstetter
Robert A. Goldwin
Stephen E. Herbits
William W. Kaufmann
Paul H. Nitze
Joseph L. Kirkland
Frank C. Carlucci
Thomas K. Latimer
Stanley R. Resor
Andrew W. Marshall
Alan Woods
William K. Brehm
Charles S. Minter
Richard H. Shriver
Fred P. Wacker
Richard A. Wiley
Frank A. Shrontz
Edward C. Aldridge, Jr.
James P. Wade, Jr.
Thomas C. Reed
J. William Middendorf II
Martin R. Hoffmann
Eugene U. McAuliffe
Brent Scowcroft
David R. MacDonald
Max L. Friedersdorf
William P. Clements, Jr.
Donald R. Cotter
John Slezak
Frau Hildegard Gohrum
Ernest C. Brace

1979 Sara E. Lister
William B. Bader
Hugh McCullough
1980 No award

Distinguished New Yorker Award

CITY CLUB OF NEW YORK
33 W. 42nd St., New York, N.Y. 10036 (212/921-9870)

The Distinguished New Yorker Award, which consists of a bronze medallion and a certificate, is given annually to individuals deemed to "act positively for New York and to have devoted energy, skill and talent to the improvement of the quality of New York life." The club's board of trustees makes the selection.

1967 **George Baehr,** President, Academy of Medicine
Roger Baldwin, Founder, American Civil Liberties Union
Detlev W. Bronk, Chairman, National Research Council; President, Johns Hopkins University; President, The Rockefeller University
Gordon Bunshaft, Partner, Skidmore, Owings & Merrill
Cass Canfield, Senior Editor, Harper and Brothers; leader, Planned Parenthood
Richard S. Childs, Past President, City Club; former Chairman, Citizens Union; Chairman, Municipal League; member, New York State Board of Regents
Kenneth B. Clark, President, Marc Corp.; Distinguished Professor of Psychology, City University of New York; member, New York State Board of Regents

Lou Crandall, Chairman of the Board, George A. Fuller Co.
Duke Ellington, Musician, whose 1927 Cotton Club orchestra gained acceptance for jazz as a musical form
Martha Graham, Creator of new dance form
Alvin Johnson, Founder, New School, University in Exile
Robert Moses, "Prime achiever among a forest of non-achievers"
David Sarnoff, For a career spanning the entire history of electronics and electronic communication
Earl B. Schwulst, Chairman, Bowery Savings Bank; Temporary Commission on City Finances
Whitney North Seymour, Partner, Simpson, Thacher & Bartlett; U.S. Attorney, Southern District, New York State
Arthur Hays Sulzberger, Publisher, *New York Times*
Austin J. Tobin, Former Chairman, Port Authority

1968 No award
1969 **Jacob S. Potofsky,** President, Amalgamated Clothing Workers of America
1970 **Mary Lasker,** Contributor to health and medicine fields; the Lasker Awards; beautification of New York City
1971 No award
1972 **Andrew Heiskell,** Former Chairman of the Board, Time Inc.
1973 **George Champion,** Former Chairman of the Board, Chase Manhattan Bank; Chairman and President, Economic Development Council of New York
John Chancellor, Former Director, Voice of America; anchorman and principal reporter, NBC nightly news
Walter Cronkite, Veteran journalist; space expert; anchorman and principal reporter, CBS Evening News
George T. Delacorte, Jr., Founder, Make New York Beautiful; publisher
Paul Foley, President, Inter-Public Group of Companies
Lloyd Goodrich, Author of distinguished works on American Art; former Director, Whitney Museum
Ada Louise Huxtable, Architecture critic, *New York Times*
Winfield H. James, President, publisher, *New York News*
Whitman Knapp, U.S. Judge, Southern District, New York State; Chairman Knapp Commission
Willie E. Mays, Baseball star
John P. McGrath, Chairman of the Board, East New York Savings Bank; lawyer; former Corporation Counsel of the City of New York
Arthur Mitchell, Former premier danseur, New York City Ballet; Director, Dance Theatre of Harlem
Bess Myerson, Former Commissioner, Department of Consumer Affairs; distinguished reporter, commentator
John B. Oakes, Editor of Editorial Page, *New York Times*; supervisor, "Op-Ed"; author, numerous articles on public affairs and conservation
Joseph Papp, Founder and producer, New York Shakespeare Festival; Public Theatre
Basil A. Paterson, Lawyer; member, board of editors, *New York Law Journal*; President, Institute for Mediation and Conflict Resolution
I.M. Pei, Architect, academician
Lewis Rudin, Executive Vice President, Rudin Management Co.; Chairman, Assn. for a Better New York
Dorothy Shiff, Editor-in-Chief, publisher, *New York Post,* oldest daily newspaper in continuous publication in the U.S.
Neil Simon, Playwright
Franklin A. Thomas, President, Bedford-Stuyvesant Restoration Corp.; former Deputy Police Commissioner
Preston R. Tisch, President, New York City Convention and Visitors Bureau; Chairman of the Board, Convention-Exhibition Center Corp.; builder
Lila Acheson Wallace, Co-chairman, *Reader's Digest*
1974 **George Agrell,** President, Addo Machine Co.; Trustee, Scandinavian-American Foundation
Cecelia Benattar, President, British Commercial Group; originator of financial arrangements for and supervision of construction of General Motors complex
Giovanni Buitoni, Founder, Buitoni Foods Corp.
Antonio Carillo-Flores, Director General, Committee on Population of the United Nations
Ramon Castroviejo, Innovator and leader, corneal surgery
Maurice Galy, President, Lycee Francais de New York
Rod Gilbert, New York Rangers
Soichi Kawazoe, Executive Vice President, Nissan Motor Corp. U.S.A., sponsor of "Plant a Tree" and "Send a Kid to Camp" test drives
Oivind Lorentzen, Jr., President, Flagship Cruises
Raymond J. Picard, Chairman, Rhodia, Inc.
Erwin A. Single, Publisher, *New York Staats-Zeitung und Herold*
Yoshio Teresawa, President, Nomura Securities International, Inc.
Leo Van Munching, President, Van Munching & Co.
1975 **Charles G. Bluhdorn,** Chairman of the Board, Gulf & Western Industries, Inc.
1976 No award
1977 **Donald T. Regan,** Chairman of the Board, Merrill, Lynch & Co.
1978 **Preston Robert Tisch,** President, Loews Corp.
1979 No award
1980 **George Weissman,** Chairman of the Board, Philip Morris, Inc.

Hall of Honor
Silver Medal of Valor
Distinguished Service Award

CIVIL AIR PATROL
Maxwell Air Force Base, Ala. 36112 (205/293-1190)

Of the many honors conferred by the Civil Air Patrol, an auxiliary of the U.S. Air Force, induction into the Hall of Honor is the highest overall honor.

1972 **Gill Robb Wilson**
Gen. Carl A. Spaatz, USAF (Ret)
Brig. Gen. D. Harold Byrd, CAP
Brig. Gen. William C. Whelen, CAP
Brig. Gen. Paul W. Turner, CAP
Brig. Gen. Lyle W. Castle, CAP
Brig. Gen. F. Ward Reilly, CAP
Col. Clara E. Livingston, CAP
Col. Joseph S. Bergin, CAP
Col. Allan C. Perkinson, CAP
1973 **Maj. Gen. Lucas V. Beau,** USAF (Ret)
Col. Edwin Lyons, CAP
1974 **Col. James E. Carter,** CAP
Brig. Gen. S. H. duPont, Jr., CAP
Brig. Gen. Earl L. Johnson
1975 No inductees
1976 **Col. Zack T. Mosley,** CAP

Brig. Gen. William M. Patterson, CAP
1977 No inductees

Current Status Unknown

The Silver Medal of Valor is the highest award for bravery. It is given as merited.

1962 Cdt. Ronald Baecher
1965 Lt. Leonard A. Gilliland
1968 Capt. Paul B. Crawford
Cdt. David R. Jaffe
Lt. Col. Robert C. Owen
1969 Lt. Eugene E. Dombrowski
Maj. John L. Elliott
Cdt. Scott Lyons
Capt. Herbert F. Santos
1970 Maj. Adelbert C. Cross
Cdt. David L. White
1971 No award
1972 Lt. Harold P. Parsons
1973 Lt. Raymond E. Bruen
1974 Capt. Bernard Berger
1975 Cdt. Charles T. Hughes
Cdt. Thomas R. Peoples
1976 Maj. Charles M. Brown
Capt. James V. Hotsinger
Lt. Michael J. Martin
Cdt. Robert J. Scott
1977 Lt. Col. Frank L. Hendrix
Lt. Col. James T. Higgins
Sm. Dorothy A. Kelly
Lt. James R. Pallariot
Maj. Paul E. Routhier

Current Status Unknown

The Distinguished Service Award is the Civil Air Patrol's highest award for service.

1960

Lt. Col. Virginia C. Capps
Capt. C.M. Kelley, Jr.
Lt. Col. Benjamin F. Miller
Col. Vee L. Phillips
Col. James E. Carter
Lt. Col. Leon N. Leboire
Maj. William C. Ooley

1961

Col. Marcus R. Barnes
Col. J Reed Capps
Col. Charles F. Howard
Col. James H. Laidlaw
Col. James J. Mitchell
Col. James J. O'Connor
Maj. Agnes M. Richards
Sm. Thomas M. Smith
Lt. Col. Louise M. Thaden
Col. James L. Camp
Col. Charles R. Chick
Maj. Margaret L. Howard
Lt. Col. Edwin T. Lovelace
Lt. Col. Alfred C. Nowitsky
Lt. Col. Richard L. Oliver
Col. Raymond A. Smith
Col. Herbert H. Stahnke

1962

Lt. Col. Sarah E. Adams
Col. Marcus R. Barnes
Lt. Col. Luther C. Bogard
Lt. Col. Vir N. James
Col. James J. O'Connor
Col. George J. Race
Col. Herbert H. Stahnke
Col. John D. Swarts
Maj. Elwood R. Angstadt
Col. Joseph S. Bergin
Col. Paul E. Burbank
Col. James H. Laidlaw
Lt. Col. Joseph M. O'Malley
Lt. Col. Lawrence Reibscheid
Reibscheid

1963

Maj. Ted Bagan
Col. Homer L. Bigelow, Jr.
Col. James E. Carter
Capt. Donald T. Mageen
Lt. Col. Charles W. Matthis, Jr.
Col. Joseph F. Moody
Col. Joseph J. Princen
Col. Paul W. Turner
Col. Harlon W. Bement
Col. Paul E. Burbank
Col. Robert H. Herweh
Col. Maurice A. Marrs
Col. Murray C. McComas
Col. Malcolm McDermid
Lt. Col. Doris M. Olson
Col. Richard W. Reynard
Col. James A. Wellons

1964

Col. Paul C. Ashworth
Col. Lyle W. Castle
Col. John E. Page
Col. Ward F. Reilly
Col. John R. Taylor
Col. Francis A. Blevins
Col. James E. O'Connell
Col. William M. Patterson
Col. Ralph M. Shangraw
Lt. Col. John N. Weaver

1965

Lt. Col. Sarah E. Adams
Capt. Robert L. Camina
Col. S.H. duPont, Jr.
Lt. Col. Vir N. James
Col. Stanhope Lineberry
Lt. Col. Joseph M. O'Malley
Lt. Col. Lawrence Reibscheid
Col. Herbert H. Stahnke
Maj. Theodore H. Walter
Col. Joseph S. Bergin
Lt. Col. James E. Carlton
Lt. Col. Francis G. Gomes
Lt. Col. Kenneth E. Jones
Capt. Andrew E. Mild
Lt. Col. Frank S. Patterson
Lt. Col. Amel Shultz
Lt. Col. Kenna T. Trout

1966

Col. Charles R. Chick
Lt. Col. Sarah E. Duke
Col. Daniel E. Evans
Lt. Col. Robert W. Hemphill
Col. Frank D. Landes
Col. Edwin Lyons
Capt. John L. O'Connor
Lt. Col. Albert Plotkin
Col. Robert M. shaw
Col. John R. Taylor
Maj. James R. Williams
Lt. Col. Louis Dellamonica
Col. S.H. duPont, Jr.
Col. George S. Hastings
Lt. Col. Gilbert O. Keeton
Col. Clara E. Livingston
Col. Louisa S. Morse
Col. Neil Pansey
Col. Ward F. Reilly (two DSAs in one year)
Maj. Theodore W. Walter
Maj. Louis D. Wolff

1967

Lt. Col. Warren D. Anderson
Col. Donald H. Denton
Lt. Col. Robert L. Forche
Maj. J. David Jones
Capt. Maurice G. Lambert
Lt. Col. Joseph M. O'Malley
Cdt. Alex H. Rocha
Lt. Col. A.H. Saunders
Lt. Col. John P. St. Clair
Col. Jess Strauss
Lt. Col. Edward C. Beauvais
Beauvais
Col. Roger A. Guilmett
Lt. Col. Reuben M. Katz
Lt. Col. Rupert M. Much
Lt. Col. Howard N. Pratt
Sm. Carl E. Sanders
Col. Wayne E. Smith
Col. Peter J. Stavneak

1968

Col. J.F.H. Bottom
Col. Julius Goldman
Lt. Col. Mildred C. Hicks
Lt. Col. Ira L. Kessler
Maj. D. Jean Maire
Col. Richard T. Murphy
Col. James E. O'Connell
Col. Walter M. Sanford
Lt. Col. Lewis H. Freeman
Lt. Col. Douglas E. Hicks
Lt. Col. Jonathan H. Hill
Lt. Col. William D. Madsen
Col. Ben S. McGlashan
Lt. Col. Gerard K. Nash
Lt. Col. Milton N. Popp
Col. Herbert H. Stahnke

1969

Col. Joseph S. Bergin
Lt. Col. James H. Cheek, Jr.
Col. Houston H. Doyle
Lt. Col. Kenneth Dunlap
Lt. Col. George W. Gentner
Lt. Col. William R. Brady
Capt. Bernard P. Dickerson
Col. Raymond H. Gaver
Lt. Col. William E.B. Hall

Lt. Col. Raymond L. Kraemer
Maj. George Loertscher
Col. Edwin Lyons
Capt. O.J. Marlborough
Lt. Col. Benjamin F. Miller
1st Lt. Maurita Nail
Col. William M. Patterson
C.W.O. James D. Rogers
Lt. Col. Ephraim W. Walton
Col. Stanhope Lineberry
Lt. Col. Harland B. Little, Jr.
Lt. Col. Lester G. Maddox
Lt. Col. John J. McNabb
Maj. Robert P. Miller
1st. Lt. Lawrence F. Parker
Col. Arthur F. Putz
Maj. Herbert W. Urry
S/Sgt. Lemmie F. Young

1970

Col. William R. Bass
Col. Howard L. Brookfield
Brig. Gen. Lyle W. Castle
Col. Obed A. Donaldson
1st Lt. James A. Flynt
Col. Donald E. Hale
Col. Robert H. Herweh
Col. Kenneth Lebo
Cdt. Julius A. Mink
Col. William M. Patterson
Capt. E.M. Rea
Col. Wayne E. Smith
Brig. Gen. Paul W. Turner
Col. Luther C. Bogard
Col. Thomas C. Casaday
Col. Claude L. Chambers
Lt. Col. Sarah E. Duke
Lt. Col. Willard E. Geiger, Jr.
Lt. Col. Raymond J. Johnson
Col. Edwin Lyons
Col. Richard T. Murphy
Col. F. Ward Reilly
Lt. Col. Wilson W. Ronda
1st. Lt. Walter L. Tribble

1971

Col. Arlie G. Andrews
Col. Marvin S. Donnaud
Col. David R. Ellsworth
Col. Charles W. Klann
Col. Theodore H. Limmer, Jr.
Col. Walter M. Markey
Lt. Col. Harold M. Mitchell
Col. Alvin S. Rousse
Col. Peter J. Stavneak
Lt. Col. Charles R. Thulin
Col. P.W. Burgmeestre
Col. Richard R. Dooley
Col. Ernest M. Green
Col. Frank D. Landes
Col. Clinton G. Litchfield
Col. Stephen E. Mills
Col. William H. Ramsey
Col. Arthur P. Schneider
Col. John R. Taylor

1972

Col. Luther C. Bogard
Col. James E. Carter
Col. Clarence M. Fountain
Col. Jonathan H. Hill
Col. Richard D. Law
Col. Edwin Lyons
Col. Gerald M. Quilling
Col. Roderick V. Riek
Col. Richard A. Salsman (two DSAs in one year)
Col. Frank L. Swaim (two DSAs in one year)
Lt. Col. Noel E. Bullock
Col. Donald D. Dixon
Col. Julius Goldman
Col. Thomas C. Jackson
Col. Clara E. Livingston
Col. William M. Patterson
Col. William H. Ramsey
Maj. Frank H. Rockwell
Col. Jess Strauss
Lt. Col. Norman Strauss
Maj. Robert S. Vankeuren

1973

Col. Leonard A. Brodsky
Col. Raymond A. Gaver
Capt. James L. Hile
Col. Eugene A. Kerwin
Col. Raymond S. Mabrey
Col. Barry N. Thompson
Lt. Col. Charles L. Wood
Brig. Gen S.H. duPont, Jr.
Col. Willard D. Gilbert
Lt. Col. Bernice R. Hill
Col. Palmer S. Kickland
Col. John M. Piane, Jr.
Col. Earl T. Van Stavern

1974

Maj. Harold W. Bowden
Col. Richard R. Dooley
Col. Jack Ferman
Col. Zenon C.R. Hansen
Col. Robert C. Owen
Col. Thomas C. Casaday
Lt. Col. Edward C. Feilinger
Col. Stanley F. Moyer, Jr.
Col. Edward L. Palka
Brig. Gen. William M. Patterson
Maj. John C. Samuel
Maj. Alvin J. Stewart
Col. John A. Vozzo
Col. Carl J. Platter
Col. Joseph F. Roemisch
Col. Lee F. Smith
Brig. Gen. Paul W. Turner

1975

Lt. Col. Robert E. Benoit
Col. Howard L. Brookfield
Col. William B. Cass
Col. Ivey M. Cook, Jr.
Col. Richard Damerow
Col. Julius Goldman
Col. Jonathan H. Hill
Col. Clark Johnston
Col. David P. Mohr
Col. William H. Ramsey (two DSAs in one year
Col. Luther C. Bogard
Col. James V. Brown, Jr.
Brig. Gen. Lyle W. Castle
Col. James E. Connor, Jr.
Brig. Gen. S.H. duPont, Jr.
Maj. Albert E. Henfy
Col. Bob E. James
Col. Roy G. Loughary
Col. E. Lee Morgan
Col. Frank L. Swaim
dsCol. John R. Taylor

1976

Col. Marcus R. Barnes
Lt. Col. Robert C. Bess
Col. Johnnie Boyd
Col. Richard T. Davis
Col. Obed A. Donaldson
Lt. Col. Lucille V. Evans
Lt. Col. David Floyd
Dr. James P. Gilligan
Col. Mary C. Harris
Col. Jonathan H. Hill
Col. Eugene G. Isaak
Col. Oscar J. Jolley
Col. Albert D. Lamb
Col. Larry D. Miller
Maj. Barbara Morris
Col. Thomas G. Patton
Col. Lindsey V. Rice
Col. Kermit K. Schaver
Col. Charles X. Suraci
Col. Gordon T. Weir
Col. Robert H. Wilson
Col. Frederick S. Bell
Maj. Joan C. Birns
Col. Thomas C. Casaday
Lt. Col. Iris T. Donaldson
Col. A. Sidney Evans
Col. Thomas S. Evans
Col. Clarence M. Fountain
Col. Robert E. Gobel
Col. Robert H. Herweh
Col. Harry J. Howes
Col. John T. Johnson
Col. Kenneth Kershner
Gen. Carl S. Miller
Col. Louisa S. Morse
Col. Ceclia A. Patterson
Col. John F. Price
Col. Randolph C. Ritter
Maj. Mark Shirk
Col. John A. (two DSAs in one year)
Col. William T. Winkert

1977

Col. Edgar M. Bailey
Col. William H. Cahill
Col. Henri P. Casenov
Col. William H. Everett
Col. Oscar K. Jolley
Col. Angelo A. Milano
Col. William H. Ramsey
Col. Lester W. Snyder
Lt. Col. Lucille E. Branscomb
Brig. Gen. S.H. duPont, Jr.
Col. Julius Goldman
Lt. Col. Betty W. McNabb
Col. Rolf H. Mitchel
Col. Leroy S. Riley
Col. Joseph B. Witkin

Current Status Unknown

President's Award for Distinguished Federal Civilian Service

U.S. CIVIL SERVICE COMMISSION
Office of Personnel Management, Incentive Awards Branch, Washington, D. C. 20415 (202/632-4596)

The President's Award for Distinguished Federal Civilian Service is presented annually for outstanding performance of duties and execution of office by federal career employees. The award is made in White House ceremonies by the President or Vice President, to individuals selected now by the chairman of the Civil Service Commission. Previously, a special board chose the recipients.

1958 **Loy W. Henderson,** Deputy Under Secretary of State for Administration
Sterling B. Hendricks, Chief Chemist, Department of Agriculture Pioneering Research Laboratory for Mineral Nutrition of Plants
John Edgar Hoover, Director, Federal Bureau of Investigation
Roger W. Jones, Assistant Director for Legislative Reference, Bureau of the Budget**William B. McLean,** Technical Director, U.S. Naval Ordnance Test Station (China Lake, Calif.)

1959 **James Bennett,** Director, Bureau of Prisons, Department of Justice
Robert D. Murphy, Deputy Undersecretary of State for Political Affairs, Department of State
Doyle L. Northrup, Technical Director, Special Weapons Squadron, Department of the Air Force
Hazel K. Stiebeling, Director, Institute of Home Economics, Department of Agriculture
Wernher Von Braun, Director, Development Operations Division, Army Ballistic Missile Agency

1960 **Andrew Barr,** Chief Accountant, Securities and Exchange Commission
Hugh L. Dryden, Deputy Administrator, National Aeronautics and Space Administration
William J. Hopkins, Executive Clerk, White House Office
Winfred Overholser, Superintendent, Saint Elizabeth's Hospital
Robert M. Page, Director of Research, Naval Research Laboratory

1961 **Bert B. Barnes,** Assistant Postmaster General, Bureau of Operations, Post Office Department
Wilbur S. Hinman, Jr., Technical Director, Diamond Ordinance Fuze Laboratories, Department of the Army
Frederick J. Lawton, Commissioner, U.S. Civil Service Commission
Richard E. McArdle, Chief, Forest Service, Department of Agriculture
William McCauley, Director, Bureau of Employee's Compensation, Department of Labor

1962 **J. Stanley Baughman,** President, Federal National Mortgage Association, Housing and Home Finance Agency
Robert R. Gilruth, Director, Manned Spacecraft Center, National Aeronautics and Space Administration (Houston, Tex.)
Donald E. Gregg, Chief, Department of Cardiorespiratory Diseases, Walter Reed Army Institute of Research
Waldo K. Lyon, head, Submarine and Arctic Research Branch, U.S. Navy Electronics Laboratory (San Diego, Calif.)
Llewellyn E. Thompson, Jr., Ambassador to the Union of Soviet Socialist Republics, Department of State

1963 **Winthrop G. Brown,** career minister, Department of State
Alain C. Enthoven, Deputy Comptroller for Systems Analysis, Office of the Secretary of Defense
Sherman E. Johnson, Deputy Administrator, Foreign Economics, Economic Research Service Department of Agriculture
David D. Thomas, Director, Air Traffic Service, Federal Aviation Agency
Fred L. Whipple, director, Smithsonian Institution Astrophysical Observatory

1964 **John Doar,** First Assistant to the Assistant Attorney General, Civil Rights Division, Department of Justice
Herbert Friedman, Superintendent, Atmosphere and Astrophysics Division, U.S. Naval Research Laboratory, Department of the Navy
Lyman B. Kirkpatrick, Jr., Executive Director-Comptroller, Central Intelligence Agency
Bromley K. Smith, Executive Secretary, National Security Council

1965 **Howard C. Grieves,** Assistant Director of the Bureau of the Census, Department of Commerce
William F. McCandless, Assistant Director for Budget Review, Bureau of the Budget
Homer E. Newell, Associate Administrator for Space Science and Applications, National Aeronautics and Space Administration
Frank B. Rowlett, Special Assistant to the Director, National Security Agency, Department of Defense
Clyde A. Tolson, Associate Director of Federal Bureau of Investigation, Department of Justice
Philip H. Trezise, Deputy Assistant Secretary for Economic Affairs, Department of State

1966 **Elson B. Helwig,** Pathologist, Armed Forces Institute of Pathology
Robert E. Hollingsworth
H. Rex Lee, Administrator, American Samoa
Thomas C. Mann
James A. Shannon, scientific administrator

1967 **Myrl E. Alexander,** director, Federal Bureau of Prisons, Department of Justice
Arthur E. Hess, Deputy Commissioner, Social Security Administration, Department of Health, Education, and Welfare
Sherman Kent, Director, National Estimates and Chairman of the Board, National Estimates, Central Intelligence Agency
C. Payne Lucas, Deputy Director, Africa Region, Peace Corps
William J. Porter, Ambassador to the Republic of South Korea, Department of State
Carl F. Romney, Seismologist, Department of the Air Force

1968 **James J. Rowley**

1969 **No award**

1970 **No award**

1971 **Samuel M. Cohn,** Assistant Director for Budget Review, Office of Management and Budget
U. Alexis Johnson, career ambassador, Under Secretary for Political Affairs, Department of State
Edward F. Knipling, Director, Entomology Research Division, Agricultural Research Service, Department of Agriculture
Fred Leonard, Scientific Director, Army Medical Biomechanical Research Laboratory, Walter Reed Army Medical Center, Department of the Army
George H. Willis, Deputy to the Assistant Secretary for International affairs, Department of the Treasury

1972-75 **No awards**

1976 **Ernest Ambler,** Acting Director, National Bureau of Standards, Department of Commerce
Lawrence S. Eagleburger, Deputy Under Secretary of State for Management and Executive Assistant to the Secretary, Department of State
Alfred J. Eggers, Jr., Assistant Director for Research Applications, National Science Foundation
E. Henry Knoche, Deputy Director of Central Intelligence, Central Intelligence Agency
Dale R. McOmber, Assistant Director for Budget Review, Office of Management and Budget

Barbara Ringer, Register of Copyrights, Library of Congress
1977 **Ellsworth Bunker,** Ambassador at Large, Department of State
Philip C. Habib, Under Secretary of State for Political Affairs, Department of State
John R. McGuire, Chief, Forest Service, Department of Agriculture
William H. Phillips, Chief, Flight Dynamics and Control Division, National Aeronautics and Space Administration
Stanley Sporkin, Director, Division of Enforcement, Securities and Exchange Commission
Rosalyn S. Yalow, Senior Medical Investigator, Veterans Administration
1978 **Alfred A. Atherton**
Thomas S. Austin
Sidney N. Graybeal
Leonard Niederlehner
Harold H. Saunders
Dorothy L. Starbuck
1979 **Mary de la Torre Pinkard,** Department of Housing and Urban Development Fair Housing and Equal Opportunities Program
Alonza H. Cotten, Authority on logistics and material management
John T. Hughes, Authority on reconnaissance intelligence and technology
Robert T. Jones, Authority on aeronautical engineering
Glenn W. Burton, Authority on crop breeding
Morton I. Abramowitz, Diplomat and guiding force in saving thousands of Cambodian lives
William H. Oldendorf, Veterans Administration clinician and researcher, specializing in diagnostic radiology
1980 **Not available at press time**

Grenville Clark Prize

THE GRENVILLE CLARK FUND AT DARTMOUTH COLLEGE
2501 Holmes St., Kansas City, Mo. 64108 (816/421-5058)

The Grenville Clark Prize, which carries an honorarium of $15,000, will be given every three years until the end of the 20th Century for a scholarly work or activity which, in the opinion of the Board of Directors of the Fund, exemplifies Grenville Clark's objectives in civil liberties, academic freedom, civic rights, world peace and good government.

1975 **Jean Monnet,** France
1978 **Sydney Kentridge,** South Africa
Theodore Hesburgh, U.S.A.
Jack Greenberg, U.S.A.

Eugene V. Debs Award

EUGENE V. DEBS FOUNDATION
Box 843, Terre Haute, Ind. 47808 (812/232-2163)

The Eugene V. Debs Award annually honors an individual for contributions in public service, labor or education. The plaque is given to an individual nominated by foundation members and selected by the executive board.

1965 **John L. Lewis**
1966 **Norman Thomas**
1967 **A. Philip Randolph**
1968 **Walter Reuther**
1969 **H.E. Gilbert**
1970 **Patrick E. Gorman**
1971 **No award**
1972 **Dorothy Day**
1973 **Michael Harrington**
1974 **Arthur Schlesinger, Jr.**
1975 **Ruben Levin**
1976 **Martin Miller**
1977 **Frank P. Zeidler**
1978 **Jesse Jackson**
1979 **Pete Seeger**
1980 **William N. Winspisinger**

Splendid American Award

THOMAS A. DOOLEY FOUNDATION
442 Post St., San Francisco, Calif. 94102 (415/397-0244)

The Splendid American Award, an engraved Steuben glass dish, has been given annually to honor personal accomplishments that have reflected well "the meaning and purpose of the United States to the world community." The board of directors of the foundation selects the American citizen(s) to receive the award.

1964 **Henry Cabot Lodge**
1965 **Bob Hope**
Dean Rusk
1966 **Danny Kaye**
Edwin O. Reischauer
1967 **Kirk Douglas**
Daniel K. Inouye
1968 **Eugene R. Black**
John H. Glenn, Jr.
1969 **Duke Ellington**
Samuel F. Pryor
1970 **No award**
1971 **Perle Mesta**
Lowell Thomas
1972 **Spiro T. Agnew**
Frank Sinatra

Current Status Unknown

Erasmus Prize

ERASMUS PRIZE FOUNDATION (Stichting Praemium Erasmianum)
5, Jan van Goyenkade, HN-1075 Amsterdam, Netherlands (Tel. 760222)

The Praemium Erasmianum or Erasmus Prize is given annually to honor individuals or institutions whose work is considered of outstanding merit for the spiritual and cultural values of Europe. The amount of the prize is 100,000 guilders for an individual winner or 150,000 guilders if it is to be shared, which is spent partially for cultural, social or socio-scientific projects. The winner is selected by the foundation's board of governors in consultation with Dutch and international experts and an international committee.

1958 **People of Austria,** Determination to preserve their European culture and character "under difficult circumstances"
1959 **Karl Jaspers (Germany) and Robert Schuman (France),** Living symbols of the unity of Europe on philosophical and political planes
1960 **Marc Chagall and Oskar Kokoschka,** Contributions to European painting
1961 **No award**
1962 **Romano Guardini,** "For his many-sided contribution toward to cultivation and intensification of European spiritual life"
1963 **Martin Buber,** For serving "the cause of European culture for more than 50 years in many domains"
1964 **Union Academique Internationale,** For initiating and encouraged "many ventures of learning which maintained and enhanced the high standing of the humanities in Europe"
1965 **Charles S. Chaplin and Ingmar Bergman,** Outstanding merits in cinematographic art
1966 **Sir Hubert Read and Rene Huyghe,** For deepening the receptivity of their contemporaries to the artist's message through their writings
1967 **Jan Timbergen,** For pioneering work in the new science of econometrics and important contributions to economic planning policies of developing countries
1968 **Henry Moore,** For vital contributions to the rebirth of European sculpture
1969 **Gabriel Marcel and Carl Frierich von Weizsacker,** Philosophical contributions to European intellectual life
1970 **Hans Scharoun,** For the expression his work has given to spatial architecture
1971 **Olivier Messiaen,** For enriching European music
1972 **Jean Piaget,** Discoveries in the theory of knowledge and the thinking of children
1973 **Claude Levi-Strauss,** Original research into the constants of human nature in primitive and developed societies
1974 **Dame Ninette de Valois and Maurice Bejart,** Development of the art of ballet
1975 **Sir Ernst Gombrich and Willem Sandberg,** For contributions to art
1976 **Rene David,** For work in comparative law **Amnesty International,** Activities in human rights.
1977 **Werner Keagi,** Swiss historian
Jean Monnet, French statesman
1978 **La Marionettistica Fratelli Napoli Catani,** Entertainment
Teatrul Tandarica, Entertainment
Ensemble Yves Joly, Entertainment
Peter Schumann and **Bread and Puppet Theater,** Entertainment
1979 ***Die Zeit*,** Journalism
***Neue Zurcher Zeitung*,** Journalism
1980 **Gustav Leonhardt,** Music
Nikolaus Harnoncourt, Music

Ethical Humanist Award

NEW YORK SOCIETY FOR ETHICAL CULTURE
2 W. 64th St., New York, N.Y. 10023 (212/977-4800)

The Ethical Humanist Award, which consists of a $500 donation in the name of the recipient to the cause of his or her choice and a plaque, is given annually by committee selection to "an individual who has performed an extraordinary act of moral courage, fully aware of the potential cost to his own or her life, career or reputation, and without the general sanction of his or her peers or of society, but with broad humanizing implications."

1970 **Michael A. Bernhardt,** Refusal to participate in My Lai Massacre
1971 **George M. Michaels,** Cast the deciding vote for passage of New York State's Abortion Law
1972 **Howard Levy,** Refusal to train Green Berets for ultimately brutal missions
1973 **Joseph A. Yablonski** (Posthumously), Fight against corruption in United Mine Workers
1974 **No award**
1975 **Judge Bruce McM. Wright,** For moral courage in the vigorous application of Constitutional principles in pursuit of equal justice under law
1976 **No award**
1977 **Orlando Letelier** (Posthumously), For undaunted pursuit of fundamental, personal and democratic freedoms for all people, which cost him his life.
1978 **Percy Qoboza,** For fighting for justice and human rights for the oppressed of South Africa
1979 **Dorothy Day,** For pursuit of social justice for the poor, and for work for religious and political ecumenicism
1980 **No award**

Henry N. Wilwers Fire Buff of the Year Award

INTERNATIONAL FIRE BUFF ASSOCIATES
2125 Eastern Ave., Baltimore, Md. 21231 (301/327-8323)

The Henry N. Wilwers Fire Buff of the Year Award, which consists of a plaque, is given for contributions to fire service or as a fire buff. Nominees are submitted by members to a committee which selects the recipient.

1967 **Henry N. Wilwers,** Chicago, Ill.
1968 **William H. Perkins,** Boston, Mass.
1969 **Edward R. Damaschke,** Ferndale, Mich.
1970 **William A. Brennan,** Trenton, N.J.
1971 **Albert J. Burch,** Detroit, Mich.
1972 **Charles C. Price,** Baltimore, Md.
1973 **Keith F. Franz,** Milwaukee, Wisc.
1974 **John I. Hruska,** Linthicum, Md.
1975 **Arthur D. Devlin,** Newark, N.J.
1976 **James H. Blomley,** Boston, Mass.
1977 **Henry G. Nathan,** Baltimore, Md.
1978 **Roman A. Kaminski,** Baltimore, Md.
1979 **Walter M.P. McCall,** Windsor, Ont.
1980 **Edward A. Massmann,** Orange, N.J.

Gold Medal Distinguished American Award

NATIONAL FOOTBALL FOUNDATION
201 E. 42nd St., Suite 1506, New York, N.Y. 10017 (212/682-0255)

The foundation's Gold Medal, its highest honor, is awarded for significant contributions by an individual in a career that "embodies the highest ideals for which the game of football stands." The recipient must have been associated with college football as a player, manager, coach or be a business, political or educational leader who played college football. The recipient must be an American citizen, most of whose business life has been spent in the U.S., and who has a reputation for notable and dedicated public service carrying out the basic values of amateur sport.

1958 Dwight D. Eisenhower
1959 Douglas A. MacArthur
1960 Herbert C. Hoover
Amos Alonzo Stagg
1961 John F. Kennedy
1962 Byron R. White
1963 Roger M. Blough
1964 Donald B. Lourie
1965 Juan T. Trippe
1966 Earl H. Blaik
1967 Frederick L. Hovde
1968 Chester J. LaRoche
1969 Richard M. Nixon
1970 Thomas J. Hamilton
1971 Ronald W. Reagan
1972 Gerald R. Ford
1973 John Wayne
1974 Gerald B. Zornow
1975 David Packard
1976 Edgar B. Speer
1977 Gen. Louis H. Wilson
1978 Vincent dePaul Draddy
1979 Rear Adm. Porter Lawrence
1980 Walter J. Zable

The Distinguished American Award, which is a gold medal, is given as merited to men of national or international stature who, through an involvement with college football, have demonstrated that the best qualities of the game can be applied to society.

1966 Capt. William Carpenter
1967 No award
1968 No award
1969 Archibald MacLeish
1970 Vincent Lombardi
1971 Frank Boyden
1972 Jerome H. Holland
1973 No award
1974 Bob Hope
1975 Rev. Theodore Hesburgh
1976 Gen. James A. Van Fleet
1977 Rev. Edmund P. Joyce
1978 No award
1979 John Kenneth Galbraith
1980 Fred Russell

George Washington Award
American Statesman Medal
National Service Medal
American Friendship Medal
American Patriots Medal
American Exemplar Medal
Private Enterprise Exemplar Medal
Freedom Leadership Foreign Award
National Recognition Award
Freedom Leadership Medal
Special Awards

FREEDOMS FOUNDATION
Valley Forge, Pa. 19481 (215/933-8825)

The Freedoms Foundation at Valley Forge annually honors hundreds of Americans in public and private life for "significant contributions toward making this nation a better country for all of us." The recipients are selected by a jury, which includes Supreme Court justices, officers of major national veterans' organizations, service organizations and patriotic groups. Each award consists of a medal, plaque or other memento. The following are the major honors given to recipients in public life. The dates in parentheses indicate the inception of the award; a complete list of winners is not available.

GEORGE WASHINGTON AWARD (1949)

1956 J. Edgar Hoover
1957 Herbert Hoover
1958 Arthur A. Schuck
1959 John L. McClellan
1960 No award
1961 J. Edgar Hoover
1962 Walt Disney
1963 Lt. Col. John Herschel Glenn, Jr., USMC
1964 DeWitt and Lila Wallace
1965 Civic Action Program
1966 PFC Hiram D. Strickland, USA (Posthumous)
1967 Frank J. Mrkva
1968 Gen. Harold K. Johnson, USA (Ret.)
1969 Michael Levesque
1970 Bill Pierson
1971 Gen. of the Army Omar N. Bradley
1972 Donald W. Hurrelbrink
1973 John Wayne
1974 No award
1975 No award
1976 No award
1977 Lowell Thomas
1978 No award
1979 Alton Ochsner
1980 No award

AMERICAN STATESMAN MEDAL (1949)

1959 John Foster Dulles
1968 James F. Byrnes
1969 Ellsworth Bunker
1969 Henry Cabot Lodge
1971 Clare Boothe Luce

NATIONAL SERVICE MEDAL (1949)

1966 Bob Hope
1967 Martha Raye

1968 Lawrence Welk
1969 Red Skelton
1970 John Wayne

AMERICAN FRIENDSHIP MEDAL (1949)

1965 Fritz Hans Harnisch
1973 Gordon Sinclair, Canada
1975 Alexander Solzhenitsyn, Switzerland
1976 Axel Springer, Federal Republic of Germany

AMERICAN PATRIOTS MEDAL (1949)

1961 Gen. of the Army Dwight D. Eisenhower
1965 Joseph A. Brunton, Jr.
1969 Maj. James N. Rowe, USA
1970 John W. McCormack
Victor Riesel
1971 No award
1972 Sol Freinstone
1973 William A. Smith
1975 Sr. M. Virgina Geiger
1976 Gene Autry
1977 Clay Smothers
1978 Joseph "Max" Cleland
Capt. Eugene B. McDaniel, USN
1979 No award
1980 No award

AMERICAN EXEMPLAR MEDAL (1960)

1968 Leon H. Sullivan
1969 Rev. Ralph W. Beiting
1970 Maj. Wesley V. Geary, USA
1971 Henry Viscardi, Jr.
1972 Rev. Melvin Floyd
1973 Earl Hamner, Jr.
1974 Frank E. Harris
1975 Randy Steffen
1976 Arthur Fiedler
1977 Helen Hayes
Dixy Lee Ray
1978 Mamie Doud Eisenhower
1979 Shirley Temple Black

PRIVATE ENTERPRISE EXEMPLAR MEDAL (1965)

1965 Alfred P. Sloan, Jr.
1968 J. Howard Wood
1969 Zenon C. R. Hansen
1970 Asa T. Spaulding
1971 W. Clement Slone
1972 James W. Walter
1974 Kenneth McFarland
1976 Phillips Petroleum Co.
1977 Milton Friedman
1978 J. Willard Marriott, Jr.
1979 Carl N. Karcher

FREEDOM LEADERSHIP FOREIGN AWARD

1955 Carlos Castillo Armas (Supreme Achievement Medal)
Ramon Magsaysay
Ernst Reuter
1957 Carlos P. Romulo
Konrad Adenauer
Ngo Dinh Diem
Syngman Rhee
Winston Churchill
1958 Chiang Kai-Shek

NATIONAL RECOGNITION AWARD

1963 Margaret Long Arnold
Virgil Miller Newton, Jr.
Russell Potter Reeder, Jr.
Sharon Sue Rountree
Elfrieda Freeman Tice
1964 Gen. Thomas S. Power, USAF (Ret)
Rev. James H. Smythe
Tournament of Roses Association
1965 Mattie Coney
Marie Davis Hunt
Mail Call—Vietnam
Maj. Gen. H. Nickerson, Jr., USMC
1966 Raymond Burr
Harold C. "Chad" McClellan
Joseph O'Malley
1967 Ernest Crain
Sheriff Donald S. Genung
Lt. Col. Samuel R. Loboda, USA
Ken and Jeanadele Magner
1968 George E. Foreman
Luke Greene
Mrs. Chester H. Lehman
Margaret Moore
George Putnam
Alice Widener
1969 Charles L. Gould
Art Linkletter
Eugene Ormandy
Kate Smith
Wernher von Braun
DeWitt Wallace
1970 Frank L. Rizzo
Sgt. Joseph J. Pfister, ANGUS
James E. Self
1971 Denise Evers
Walter Trohan
1972 George Mardikian
1973 Joy Eilers
Thomas Lakan
Mark Bute
1974 George S. Benson
Martin DeVries
1975 Vickie L. Jones
LeRoy Foster, Jr.
Mary Mullen
Caroline C. Myers
1977 Robert Moses
1978 Hon. Barbara Jordan

FREEDOM LEADERSHIP MEDAL (1949)

1954 William Robertson Coe
Charles Edward Merrill
Columbia University
1955 David Lawrence
1957 Gen. Curtis LeMay
Charles S. Mott
Gen. Lewis B. Hershey
1959 Wilber M. Brucker
Cdr. William R. Anderson
Ward Bond
Lt. Cdr. Donald M. Hanson
Armand Penha
Bob Hope
Ann Hawkes Hutton
Hon. Elwood Fouts
Ian Stuart
1960 Frank M. Tait
Dave Garroway
David Taylor
James McC. Willson
Cdr. Paul A. Terry

Arthur Godfrey
1962 Arch N. Booth
Perry E. Gresham
Walter Kerr
Christian Sanderson
George Todt
1963 Gen. Lauris Norstad, USAF (Ret.)
1964 Gene E. Bradley
Irving R. Melbo
Eric Sloane
1965 Capt. Roger H. C. Donlon, USA
James W. Turpin
1966 Milton Caniff
William H. Spurgeon III
1967 Walter and Cordelia Knott
Kenneth McFarland
William B. Walsh
1968 Stan Musial
1969 Anita Bryant
Eric Hoffer
Paul Harvey
Jenkin Lloyd Jones
1970 H. Ross Perot
1971 George C. Roche III
Alfred J. Barran
Albert M. Ettinger
1972 Armistead Maupin, Jr.
1973 George Foreman
1974 Hugh O'Brian
1975 Rev. Donald E. Mowery
1976 American Freedom Train Foundation, Inc.
1977 Douglas L. Brandow

SPECIAL AWARDS

1952 American Broadcasting Co.
American Legion
Columbia Broadcasting System
National Broadcasting Co.
National Committee for a Free Europe
U.S. Military Academy
Armed Forces I & E
1953 Boy Scouts of America
News Magazine of the Screen *Reader's Digest*
1954 Billy Graham
St. John's University
1955 E. I. duPont
Kiwanis International
Daughters of the American Revolution
Armed Forces I & E
1956 Disneyland
Gen. Federation of Women's Clubs
Lawrence C. Lockley
Col. John H. Shenkel
Helen Lynch
Warner Bros. Pictures, Inc.
1957 John Coleman
S/Sgt Herbert P. Weet
1969 National Aeronautics and Space Administration

Henrietta Szold Award

HADASSAH, THE WOMEN'S ZIONIST ORGANIZATION OF AMERICA
50 W. 58th St., New York, N.Y. 10019 (212/355-7900)

The Henrietta Szold Award and Citation, which carries a cash prize of $1,000, is given annually based on an awards committee recommendation to an individual of any age or nationality, organization, committee or nation to perpetuate the name of Henrietta Szold, the founder of Hadassah.

1949 Eleanor Roosevelt
1950 Selman A. Waksman
1951 President Harry S. Truman
1952 Herbert H. Lehman
1953 William O. Douglas, U.S. Supreme Court Justice
1954 Monnett B. Davis
1955 Mordecai M. Kaplan
1956 Isadore I. Rabi
1957 Louis Lipsky
1958 David Ben Gurion
1959 Rahel Yanait Ben Zvi
1960 Golda Meir, Public Service Centennial Award
Leonard W. Mayo, Youth Welfare Centennial Award
Mary Woodward Lasker, Medicine Centennial Award
Nahum Goldmann, Zionism Centennial Award
Martin Buber, Education Centennial Award
1961 No award
1962 No award
1963 Albert B. Sabin
1964 Moshe Sharett
Queen Mother Elizabeth of Belgium
1965 Hubert H. Humphrey
1966 No award
1967 Michael E. DeBakey
1968 Arthur Goldbert
Mrs. Heinie Heiman-Elkind on behalf of Hadassah Nurses
Mrs. James de Rothschild on behalf of Rothschild Family
1969 Christiaan Barnaard
Youth Aliyah
1970 Marvin Feldman
1971 Zalman Shazar
1972 Soviet Jewry
1973 The People of the Netherlands
1974 Teddy Kolleck
1975 No award
1976 Sir Harold Wilson
1977 No award
1978 Kalman J. Mann, Hadassah Medical Organization
1979 Simon Wiesenthal, for bringing Nazi war criminals to justice
1980 Jacobo Timmerman, for accepting imprisonment in defense of human rights in Argentina

Distinguished Public Service Award

U.S. DEPARTMENT OF HEALTH, EDUCATION AND WELFARE
330 Independence Ave. SW, Washington, D.C. 20201
(202/245-7456)

The Distinguished Public Service Award, originally a plaque, is given as merited for contributions by an individual, or institution, outside of the department to its growth and development. In 1978, the criteria changed to include recipients from inside the department as well and the award itself was changed to consist of a gold medal and a certificate. HEW no longer exists as a single government department.

1968 Lister Hill
Carl Elliott
1969 No award
1970 No award

1971 **Alfred Gilman**
William Middleton
Maurice Warsaw
1972 **WRC-TV,** Washington, D.C.
1973 **No award**
1974 **Elizabeth M. Boggs**
1975 **No award**
1976 **No award**
1977 **No award**
1978 **Arthur S. Flemming**
1979 **Mary Goodwin**
1980 **Leonard Shaeffer**

Stillman Award

AMERICAN HUMANE ASSOCIATION
5400 S. Syracuse St., Englewood, Col. 80111
(303/779-1400)

The Stillman Award, named for Dr. William O. Stillman by a bequest of Mrs. Morris H. Vandegrift, is presented annually to humans showing courage in the face of personal danger to rescue animals or animals who have saved human life. Gold, silver and bronze medals or certificates are awarded to people and animals for such heroism. The award has been given since 1928, but only the most recent recipients are listed here.

1965 **Fuzzy,** Dayton, Ohio
Comet, collie, Vineland, N.J.
Rocket Bruno, collie, Vineland, N.J.
King, border sheepdog, Austin, Tex.
Laddie, labrador, Helena, Mont.
Randy, poodle, Phoenix, Ariz.
King, German shepherd, Colorado Springs, Colo.
Fox Glen Zipper, terrier, Sharon, Pa.
Duke, German shepherd, Fillmore, Calif.
Pooch, mutt, Pittsburg, Kans.
Randy Simons, Tucson, Ariz
Tiger, terrier, Albany, N.Y.
Prince, chihuahua, Palm Beach, Fla.
Pamela and Jackie Carrico, Elkhart, Ind.
Scott Ray and Gilbert Larochelle, Auburn, Me.
Jerome Renhack, Oconomowoc, Wisc.
James L. Adams, Oregon City, Ore
Donald Serres, Oregon City, Ore.
Dave Stewart, Crescent City, Calif.
Gene Remington, John McDonald and Laurence Seckley, Tacoma, Wash.
Libby (posthumous), great dane, Kent, Wash.
Casey, mutt, Brookline, Mass.
Laddie, collie, Akron, Ohio
Jackie, german shepherd, Myrtle Beach, S.C.
Lady, dalmatian, Inkster, Miss.
Sultan, german shepherd, Hillsboro, Ore.
Midge, mutt, Greenville, Ohio
Spookie, cocker spaniel, Pompano, Fla.
Lassie, collie, Canajoharie, N.Y.
Fox Glen Bustling Buckaroo, terrier, Sharon, Pa.
Shep, collie, Freeport, N.Y.
James "Bucky" Welch, Louisville, Ky.
Rev. Russell Raker, Russell Raker III and Wendy, dog, Allentown, Pa.
1966 **Nancee Bickelhaupt,** Birmingham, Ala.
Mickey Mouse, Pittsburg, Kans.
Lassie, collie, Osceola, Fla.
Sir Scott and Donar, German shepherds, St. Louis, Mo.
Patrick Delp Colorado Springs, Colo.
Edward Lansberry, Cleveland, Ohio
Earl Boatman and Brownie, Knoxville, Tenn.
Elmer Zellner, Delafield City, Wisc.
Scooter, german shepherd, Waukesha, Wisc.
Misty and Catt Avery, cats, Augusta, Ga.
J.W. Doane and Charlie F. Weaver, Knoxville, Tenn.
Jake Orishan, Troy, N.Y.
James O'Beirne, Jr., Rochester, N.Y.
Charlie, Long Island, N.Y.
Gyp, Labrador, Princeton, Minn.
Bill Radix, Oconomowoc, Wisc.
Mrs. Ernest LeClair, Nassau, N.Y.
Stephen Rasputni and Stanley Odziemiec, Niagara Falls, N.Y.
Timmy Danley, James and Scott Decker and Stephen and Mark Littlewood, Alexandria, Va.
June Kickleiter, St. Petersburg, Fla.
Steris Sturquell, Amarillo, Tex.
David Lee Hess, Lancaster, Pa.
Willie Smith and Greg Williams, Easton, Md.
George Rebar and Charles Opitz, Sarasota, Fla.
April, Gallup, N.M.
Foxy, Kingsport, Tenn.
Sheriff Jorgen and Dwight
Booth, Pewaukee, Wisc.
Bodidly, Cleveland, Ohio
Tashka, Afghan hound, Vacaville, Calif.
Duchess, mutt, DeLand, Fla.
Jasper County Emergency Rescue Unit, Webb City, Mo.
Chester O. Young, Ronald Sauls, Russell Logan, Jr. and Tony Logan, Tuscumbia, Ala.
Volunteer Rescue Squad and Nosey, chihuahua, Knoxville, Tenn.
Ken Johnson, Menominee Falls, Wisc.
Donald Moore, Jackson Summit, N.Y.
Bounce, mutt, Florence, Ala.
Douglas Censiba, Palm Beach, Fla.
Mike Hall, Ironton, Ohio
Runt (posthumous), dog, Chesterton, Ind.
Richard Nicholson, Lansing, Mich.
Precious, cat, Wilmington, Del.
Roy J. Hamman, New Orleans, La.
Carbon and Shambie, Malibu, Calif.
Benjamin J. Parker and Randall E. Dotto, Springfield, Ohio
Stripey, cat, St. Paul, Minn.
Wallie, collie, Albuquerque, N.M.
Chuck Parsons, Greg Ballard, Ronnie Kayrouz, Scott Ballard and Marie C. Wiegand, Louisville, Ky.
Cindy, cocker spaniel, **and Bill Morgan,** Stockton, Calif.
Cliff McAdams and Teddy (posthumous), dog, Covina, Calif.
Lee N. Centell, Porterville, Calif,
Thomas J. Cervini, Vineland, N.J.
Roger Burggraf, Anchorage, Alas.
1968 **Butchie,** mutt, Terre Haute, Ind.
Kenneth Wright, Frankfort, Ind.
Rudolph (posthumous), Norwegian elkhound, Tacoma, Wash.
Thunder, collie, Asheville, N.C.
Sam, boxer, Utica, Mich.
Squeakie, mutt, Montgomery, Ala.
Tuffy, poodle, Medford, Ore.
Leigh Larson, Menominee Falls, Wisc.

Crew of the Rio Grande California Zephyr, Denver, Colo.
Soho Solange, cocker spaniel, Phoenix, Ariz.
Tinker, Australian terrier, Littleton, Colo.
Pepe, mutt, Cleveland, Ohio
Ernest T. Toth and Rodney Miller, Allentown, Pa.
Lassie, collie, **and Our Pup,** collie, Hamilton, Ala.
Taffy, poodle, Fresno, Calif.
Gretchen Rattweiler, Robert Rambo, George Fowler and Robert, Stockton, Calif.
Tweed, scottie, Detroit, Mich.
Big Boy, dog, Wilmington, N.C.
Gary J. Kunz (posthumous), St. Paul, Minn.
Edward Blotzner, Forest Hills, Pa.
Monroe Lerman, Hollywood, Fla.
Pierre, poodle, Cedarburg, Wisc.

1969 **Woodrow W. Smith, Joseph H. Armstrong, C. Warren Newbill, William B. Schultz and John Lockwood,** Portsmouth, Va.
Little Bit and Kansas, terriers, Spokane, Wash.
Scottie, mutt, Hagerstown, Md.
Elry Tice and Michael W. Becker, Saginaw, Mich.
Frisky Dan, Dalmatian, Richland, Wash.
Ruth, Sharon and Diana Haynes, Claremont, N.H.
Dick Yates, Springfield, Ore.
Harry Peterson, R. A. Linsley and Albert O'Neil, Barstow, Calif.
Don R. Griffin, Montgomery, Ala.
Bernie Ross, John Gustofson and Bill Richardson, Wheat Ridge, Colo.
Ladybird, Australian terrier, Oak Run, Calif.
Ricky, dog, Sacramento, Calif.
Rusty, Doberman pinscher, Salem, Mass.
Pokey (posthumous), terrier, Jacksonville, Fla.

1970 **Allen Bobb, Jr.,** Port Jervis, N.Y.
Tinkerbelle, Pekingese, Alexandria, Va.
Natalie Korniloff, Woodridge, N.Y.
Gene Fehlman and Jay Crockett, Logan, Utah
Christopher Hewells, Manakin, Va.
Raymond Pertinaci and John Hardy, W. Mifflin, Ohio
Amos, Persian cat, Centralia, Ill.
Suzanne Marie Smith, Minneapolis, Minn.
King E. Jordan, Savannah, Ga.
Ginger (posthumous), dog, Kenosha, Wisc.
Don Smetana, N.A.
Richard "Buster" Campbell, Missouri
Maybelle Neuguth (posthumous), Pennsylvania
Boris (posthumous), Michigan
John E. Ward, Georgia
Thomas Thelan, Wisconsin
Nallannna Chetty Venugopal, Madras, India
Samuel Lopez, California
Curly (posthumous), Pennsylvania
Heidi, boxer, Ohio

1971 **Ruby Katheryn,** mutt, Herrin, Ill.
Norman Blake, Denver, Colo.
James Turner, New Berlin, Wisc.
Gerald Slemmer, Philadelphia, Pa.
John J. Mahoney, Beverly, Mass.
Sheila, German shepherd, Braddock, Pa.
Jim Hawes, Boston, Mass.
Duchess and Polly, mutts, Tacoma, Wash.
Hooligan, St. Bernard, Clinton, Ill.
Cheryl Haugen, Aurora, Colo.
Shadow, German shepherd, Westfall, N.Y.
Boy Scout Troop # 413, Richmond, Va.
Anthony Zito and Alfred Mueller, Melrose Park, Ill.
Tim, Labrador, Marsh Hill, N.H.
Gigi, poodle, Ford City, Pa.
R.D. Hayes and L.I. Slife, Dayton, Ohio
Brandy, Chesapeake Bay retriever, Pelican, Minn
John D. MacArthur, Palm Beach Gardens, Fla.
Fraulein, German shepherd, Oak Brook, Ill
Tony Kelley, Kingston N.C.
Linda and Roger, collies, Vienna, Mich.

1972 **Tony,** mutt, Greenville, S.C.
Thomas Gonia, Point Place, Ohio
Brownie (posthumous), German shorthair, Milwaukee, Wisc.
Misty, collie, Minneapolis, Minn.
Hercules (posthumous), Maine coon cat, Arvada, Colo.
William Whelan, Peoria, Ill.
Lynn Parker (posthumous), Missoula, Mont.
Leon Norris, Robert Defresne and Louis Pennetti, Auburn, Me.
Tink, Labrador, Lafayette, La.
Thumper, German shepherd, Rapid City, S.D.
Lester Beard and Wayne Jet, Birmingham, Ala.
Fred, mutt, S. Williamsport, Pa.
Budweiser, St. Bernard, John's Island, S.C.

1973 **Cinders,** spaniel mixed, Minneapolis, Minn.
Homer Ellett, Castro Valley, Calif.
Baylor Horvath, Portsmouth, N.H.
King, Boston, Mass.
Patrick, German shepherd, Portland, Me.
Huntington Fire Companies 4 and 8, Huntington, W. Va.
Tony Rodriguez and Steve Chayka, Michigan
Dingaling, German shepherd, Indiana
Joe Matty, New Hampshire
Maurice, Florida
Frostie, terrier mixed, Missouri
Tom Anderson and John Grishaber, Wisconsin
Gary Hamilton (posthumous), Oregon
Fraulein, German shepherd, Oak Brook, Ill.
Ed Bottorff, Indiana
Fawnee, chihuahua, Pennsylvania
J. Marshall Hughes, Kentucky
Steve Epps, California
Ace of Spades, great Dane, Alabama
Queenie, Doberman pinscher, N.A.
Peanuts, poodle, South Carolina
Mort, cat, Indiana
William Wakeland, Illinois

1974 **Teddy,** German shepherd, Pennsylvania
Ladybug, mutt, North Carolina
Glen, Craig, Bobbi and Terry Wood, Washington
James H. Dula, North Carolina
Romie Bryant, Delaware
Tippy (posthumous), chihuahua, Wyoming
Kurt Gorbutt, Michigan
Tinny (posthumous), beagle, California
Duke, Labrador, Oregon
Gidget, Michigan
James Stremeckus (posthumous), Massachusetts
Taiwan, Siamese cat, Colorado
Smokey, Hawaii
Heidi, dachshund, Booth Bay Harbor, Maine
Martin Senna, Roland O'Neil and Clarence O'Neil, Barstow, California
Charlie, Mutt, South Carolina
Thomas Gherardi, Mt. Vernon, N.Y.
David Douglas Johnson (posthumous), Oregon

1975 **Barbara Sandblom, Ruth Colby, Fritz Haubner and Douglas Cole,** North Eastham, Mass.
Muffin, peekapoo, Birmingham, Ala.
Baron, dachshund, Rock Island Ill
Creek, Labrador, Charlottesville, Va.

Skipper (posthumous), pomeranian, Billings, Mont.
Buster, mutt, Salem, Oregon
Laddie, cocker/poodle, Lahaska, Pa.
Michael Walsh, Clear Lake, Ida.
Heidi, mutt, Medford, Ore.
Whitey, dog, Kingsport, Tenn.
Citizens of Ranier, Ranier, Minn.
Arnold Rose, Milwaukee, Wisc.
Chang Lo, s'hih-tzu, Dallas, Tex.
Jenny, cat, Peabody, Mass
Poochie, mutt, Westfield, N.J.
Moon, Afghan hound, Birmingham, Ala.
Barbetta Sherrer, Montgomery, Ala.
Bill Tabor and John Strodi, Terre Haute, Ind.
Roy Harvey, Toledo, Ohio
John Szczepanick (posthumous) **and Dennis J. Scheffer,** Newark, N.J.
Charles Southworth, Jackson, Mid.
Baron, golden retriever, St. Paul, Minn.
Bootsie, schnauzer, Rock Island, Ill.
Warren Sims, Milwaukee, Wisc.

1976 **Thomas V. Di Puma** (posthumous), Bronx, N.Y.
Sampson, German shepherd, Hartwell, Ohio
James Blake, Marine City, Mich.
Zorro, German shepherd, Oakland, Calif.
Snap, mutt, Natchez, Miss.
Kenneth Encarnacao, Dartmouth, Mass
St. Paul Fire Department Ladder Company #7 and Rescue Squad #1, St. Paul, Minn.
Red, Irish setter, St. Louis, Mo.
Samantha, Burmese cat, Vallejo, Calif.
Misty, poodle, Benton, Ark.
Sissy (posthumous), poodle, Brainard, Mass.
Tina, Shiloh and Midnight (posthumous), chihuahuas, N.A.

1977 **Jerry Morland and Dennis Jacobs,** Columbus, Ind.
Toby Krominga, St. Paul, Minn.
Snowball, Cocoa, Fla.
Bridgette, Clark Lake, Mich.
Mr. and Mrs. Donald White, Douglas and Brian Pardee, and Ernest Labidueur, Niagara Falls, N.Y.
Mark Bairel (posthumous), Wisconsin Rapids, Wisc.
Corky, Detroit, Mich.
Duke Sudell and Bruce Roed, Grand Forks, N.D.
Chipper, El Dorado, Ark.
George Hesse, Newark, N.J.
John Elmer Smith, Columbia, Pa.
Javier Garcia Chavez, Mexico
Ebony, Ohio
Soul, Ohio
Zachary, Michigan
Clyde Haggerty, Michigan
Meatball, New Jersey
William Dana Fish, California
Meatball, Alabama
Candy, South Carolina
Charles Ross (posthumous), Michigan

1978 **Lady,** dog, N.A.

1979 **Angel,** dog, N.A.

1980 **Mitzi,** dog, N.A.

Man of the Year

SOCIETY OF PROFESSIONAL INVESTIGATORS
Box 1197, Church Street Station, New York, N.Y. 10008

The plaque given annually to the Man of the Year commemorates outstanding service in law enforcement and the combat against crime, rackets and corruption.

1957 **Robert F. Kennedy,** Chief Counsel, U.S. Senate Select Committee on Improper Activities in the Labor or Management Field

1958 **Edgar D. Croswell,** State Police sergeant who uncovered the organized crime meeting at Apalachin, N.Y.

1959 **Detective Division,** New York City Police Department

1960 **Arthur H. Christy,** Chief of the Criminal Division, U.S. Attorney's Office, Southern District, New York

1961 **Urbanus Edmund Baughman,** Chief, U.S. Secret Service

1962 **Charles "Pat" Ward,** Agent-in-Charge, New York office, Federal Bureau of Narcotics

1963 **Joseph Kaitz,** New York Commissioner, Waterfront Commission of New York Harbor

1964 **Michael J. Murphy,** Police Commissioner, New York

1965 **William A. O'Connor,** Superintendent, Port of New York Authority Police Department

1966 **Alfred J. Scotti,** Chief Assistant, District Attorney's Office, New York County

1967 **Sanford D. Garelik,** Chief Inspector, New York City Police Department

1968 **John F. Malone,** Assistant Director, Federal Bureau of Investigation

1969 **Albert E. Whitaker,** Agent-in-Charge, U.S. Secret Service, New York

1970 **John L. Barry,** Police Commissioner, Suffolk County (N.Y.) Police Department

1971 **Louis J. Lefkowitz,** Attorney General, State of New York

1972 **Myles J. Ambrose,** Special Assistant Attorney General for Drug Abuse Law Enforcement

1973 **Clarence M. Kelley,** Director, Federal Bureau of Investigation

1974 **Michael J. Codd,** Police Commissioner, New York

1975 **William C. Connelie,** Superintendent, New York State Police

1976 **Mario Merola,** District Attorney of Bronx County, New York

Current Status Unknown

Jefferson Award

AMERICAN INSTITUTE FOR PUBLIC SERVICE
815 15th St. NW, Washington, D.C. 20005 (202/638-3000)

The Jefferson Award, which consists of an honorarium and a gold-on-silver medallion, is given each year for distinguished public service in five categories. The national winners receive $5,000 and each of the five local winners $1,000. Anyone may submit nominations, which are voted on by a large and distinguished board of selectors.

THE AWARD FOR THE GREATEST PUBLIC SERVICE PERFORMED BY AN ELECTED OR APPOINTED OFFICIAL:

1973 **Henry A. Kissinger,** Assistant to the President for National Security Affairs, "for his efforts to strengthen world peace by opening doors to China and by initiating closer economic and social ties with Russia."

1974 **Elliot L. Richardson,** Attorney General, "for upholding the principle that no man can stand above the law and for sacrificing private position for the good of the country."

1975 **Peter W. Rodino,** U.S. House of Representatives, "for his fair and bipartisan leadership as Chairman of the House Judiciary Committee."

1976 **Arthur F. Burns,** Chairman, Federal Reserve Board, **Alan Greenspan,** Chairman, President's Council of Economic Advisers, **William E. Simon,** Secretary of the Treasury, "for their joint efforts as chief architects of our national economic policy, and for their combined courage and conviction in cutting government spending to stop inflation and to stimulate economic recovery."

1977 **Michael J. Mansfied,** U.S. Ambassador to Japan

1978 **Hubert H. Humphrey,** Senator and former Vice President of the United States

1979 **Kenneth Gibson,** Mayor of Newark
William Donald Schaefer, Mayor of Baltimore
Coleman A. Young, Mayor of Detroit

1980 **Cyrus R. Vance,** former Secretary of State

THE AWARD FOR THE GREATEST PUBLIC SERVICE PERFORMED BY A PRIVATE CITIZEN:

1973 **John W. Gardner,** Chairman, Common Cause, "for the zeal and imagination which he has brought to the creation of an effective national citizens' lobby."

1974 **Ralph Nader,** consumer advocate, "for being champion and protector of the rights of the American consumer."

1975 **Katharine Graham,** Chairman of the Board, Washington Post Co., "for her relentless pursuit of the truth, and for her courage in using the media to uphold the principle of the people's right to know."

1976 **John D. Rockefeller III,** Honorary Chairman, Rockefeller Foundation, "for a lifetime of dedication to public service and for his effective dramatization of the need to control national and world population growth."

1977 **Art Buchwald,** essayist

1978 **Paul Mellon,** president, National Gallery of Art

1979 **Howard Jarvis,** Proposition 13 creator and proponent

1980 **Norman Borlaug,** for his work in developing high-yield cereals as head of the Wheat Research and Production Project, International Maize and Wheat Improvement Center

THE AWARD FOR THE GREATEST PUBLIC SERVICE BENEFITING THE DISADVANTAGED:

1973 **Cesar Chavez,** President, United Farm Workers, "for his efforts in protecting the rights of migrant workers."

1974 **Thomas Szasz,** Professor of Psychiatry, State University of New York, "for his campaign to defend the civil rights of the mentally retarded."

1975 **Rev. Leon Sullivan,** Founder, Opportunities Industrialization Centers, "for his special leadership in founding the IOCs across the country to offer job training to unskilled, low-income people."

1976 **Rev. Theodore M. Hesburgh,** President, Notre Dame University, "for his unwavering, long-term commitment to protect and expand the civil rights of the nation's minorities."

1977 **Howard Rusk,** director, New York University Rehabilitation center

1978 **Jerry Lewis,** national chairman, Muscular Dystrophy Foundation

1979 **Jesse Jackson,** for Operation PUSH

1980 **Allard K. Lowenstein,** lawyer and former U.S. Representative

THE AWARD FOR THE GREATEST PUBLIC SERVICE PERFORMED BY AN INDIVIDUAL THIRTY-FIVE YEARS OR UNDER:

1973 **Joseph A. Yablonski,** General Counsel, United Mine Workers, "for his courageous campaign to restore integrity to unionism."

1974 **Maynard Jackson,** Mayor, Atlanta, Ga., "as the first black mayor of a major Southern city since Reconstruction."

1975 **R. Emmett Tyrrell, Jr.,** Editor, *The Alternative,* "for his work as founder and editor of *The Alternative* magazine for offering an alternative and conservative viewpoint to college students in America."

1976 **Vilma S. Martinez,** President, Mexican-American Legal Defense and Educational Fund, "for her substantial accomplishments in expanded bilingual education and voting rights for Mexican-Americans and women through legal processes."

1977 **Max Cleland,** administrator, U.S. Veterans' Administration

1978 **Bernard Powell,** Kansas City community organizer

1979 **Denis Hayes,** organizer of Sun Day and advocate of solar energy

1980 **U.S. Olympic Hockey Team,** which achieved the "impossible dream" by winning a gold medal at the 1980 Winter Olympics

THE AWARD FOR THE GREATEST PUBLIC SERVICE BENEFITING LOCAL COMMUITIES:

1974 **Robert T. Bates,** interior designer, "for his efforts to save a small Midwestern town, Albia, Iowa, by building industry and job opportunities."
James Ellis, lawyer, "for his leadership in the battle against the pollution of Lake Washington."
James Masten, former sociology instructor, California State University, "for his varied contributions to improving the lives of retired people in Fresno, Calif.
Ellen S. Straus, founder, Call for Action, "for origination the program that now functions as an ombudsman in 50 cities."
Peter Wilson, Mayor, San Diego, Calif., "for his attack on the problems of urban growth."

1975 **No award**

1976 **Felix G. Rohatyn,** Chairman, Municipal Assistance Corp., "for utilizing his special skills and toughness to restore fiscal integrity to New York City, averting default and a potential national economic crisis."

1977 **Rev. Alfred Boddeker,** founder, St. Anthony's Dining Room, San Francisco
Jean Chaudhuri, founder, Traditional Indian Alliance, Tucson, Ariz.
Leonard Cobb, director of cardiology, Harborview Medical Center, Seattle, Wash.
Olga Mele, family counselor, Community Renewal Team, Hartford, Conn.
Marjory Taylor, founder, First Marlboro-Westboro Mental Health, Association, Southboro, Mass.

1978 **Thomas Cannon,** postal clerk from Richmond, Va., for sending unsolicited checks totaling $33,000 to needy people he read about in newspapers
Sister Mary Kathleen Clark, founder of a home for battered children in Tucson, Ariz., which is credited with rescuing 2,700 infants
J.O. Asbjornson, retired rancher from Winifred, Mont., for helping residents of that isolated community
Robert J. Levy, a Houstonian who founded Taping for the Blind, a volunteer organization that was a prototype for the Library of Congress Talking Books program

Elizabeth C. Maier, for improving the quality of life for elderly patients in Philadelphia area nursing homes

1979 **Cornelius D. Banks,** for working with underprivileged children in St. Louis

Ann Hines, established Hannah Hoc Children's Clinic in Danbury, Conn., and for offering her medical service free to underprivileged families

Joyce Hunter, for setting up center for abused women in Millilani, Haw.

Father Bruce Ritter, for establishing Covenant House and working with runaways and sexually abused children in New York

Clarence H. Snyder, one of original founders of Alcoholics Anonymous

1980 **John Carpenter,** developer of the Heaven on Earth Ranch for the handicapped in California

Elaine Briebenow, a nurse from Minneapolis who volunteered to work with Cambodian refugees in Thailand

Tilda Kemplen, director, Mountain Communities Child Care Development Centers (Campbell County, Tenn.), day care for families in Appalachia

Lee Klein, director, Deed Club Children's Cancer Clinic, University of Miami, for 24 years of service to underprivileged, retarded and terminally ill children

Louis Mantucci, founder of The Bridge at Fox Chase, a Philadelphia residential community for young drug users

Freedom Award

INTERNATIONAL RESCUE COMMITTEE
386 Park Ave. S., New York, N.Y. 10016 (212/OR 9-0010)

The Freedom Award is given as merited for contributions to the cause of refugees and human freedom. The board of directors chooses the winner, who is given a plaque. The Committee maintains no records as to the year in which the following individuals received the Freedom Award, which has not been given since 1977.

Winston Churchill
Adm. Richard E. Byrd
David Dubinsky
Gen. W.J. "Wild Bill" Donovan
Willy Brandt
George Meany
David Sarnoff
Gen. Lucius D. Clay
Jacob K. Javits
Leo Cherne
Bruno Kreisky

Lyndon Baines Johnson Foundation Award

LYNDON BAINES JOHNSON FOUNDATION
2313 Red River, Austin, Tex. 78705 (512/478-7829)

The Lyndon Baines Johnson Foundation Award, which carries a $25,000 honorarium, was given annually to an American citizen for outstanding contributions to the national well-being in fields such as civil rights, urban affairs and solar energy. An award committee of prominent Americans selected the recipient. The award has been suspended.

1973 **Roy Wilkins,** Civil rights
1974 **Ivan Allen and Franklin Thomas,** Urban affairs
1975 **No award**
1976 **George O.G. Lof,** Solar energy.
1977 **Sidney R. Garfield,** Medical care

Helen Keller International Award

HELEN KELLER INTERNATIONAL
22 W. 17th St., New York, N.Y. 10011 (212/924-0420)

The Helen Keller International Award is presented to recognize outstanding contributions in the field of blindness. The award, which consists of a trophy, is given as merited. The recipient is selected from nominees from various sources by the executive director with the approval of the board of directors.

1960 **Col. Edwin A. Baker,** founder and managing director, Canadian National Institute for the Blind
1968 **Georges L. Raverat,** (France), European office director, American Foundation for the Overseas Blind
1970 **Sir John F. Wilson,** (United Kingdom), director and chief executive officer, Royal Commonwealth Society for the Blind
1971 **Lord Fraser of Lonsdale,** (United Kingdom), chairman, St. Dunstan's, London
1973 **James S. Adams,** (U.S.A.), industrialist, investment banker and president, Research to Prevent Blindness
1976 **John Feree,** (U.S.A.), director, National Society for the Prevention of Blindness, and member, American Foundation for Overseas Blind Advisory Committee on Blindness Prevention
1977 **Henry Labouisse,** director, United Nations Children's Emergency Fund (UNICEF)
1978 **Eric T. Boulter,** C.B.E. (United Kingdom), for outstanding leadership in International Source to the blind
1979 **International Association of Lions Clubs,** for 50 years of assistance to the blind throughout the world
1980 **Agency for International Development,** for support of projects to prevent and alleviate blindness in developing countries

Philip Arnow Award
Service Awards

U.S. DEPARTMENT OF LABOR
200 Constitution Ave. NW, NDOL Bldg., Frances Perkins Bldg., Room N4427, Washington, D.C. 20210 (202/523-7700)

The $1,000 Philip Arnow Award is given annually in recognition of consistently outstanding performance and service to the department over a 15-year period. The Secretary's Honors Awards Committee selects the winners.

1973 **Alfred G. Albert**
1974 **William B. Hewitt**
1975 **Beatrice J. Dvorak**
1976 **No award**
1977 **Alfred M. Zuck**
1978 **Robert B. Zagather**
1979 **Janet Norwood**
1980 **Howard Rosen**

The Secretary of Labor's Service Awards recognize outstanding career employees by underwriting a year's training in an academic institution or government agency other than the Labor group. It is given annually to employees who have demonstrated ability, achievement and growth potential on the recommendation of the Secretary's Honors awards committee.

1966 **Robert M. Guttman**
Denis Foster Johnston
1967 **No award**
1968 **No award**
1969 **No award**
1970 **No award**
1971 **Paul A. Heise**
Henry Rose
1972 **Irving I. Kramer**
Lauriston Hardin Long
1973 **Donald J. McNulty**
Gresham C. Smith
1974 **No award**
1975 **Alfred G. Albert**
Elaine Louise Sealock
1976 **No award**
1977 **Paul M. Ryscavage**
1978 **No award**
1979 **Dominic Sorrentino**
1980 **Earl D. Veath**

Fiorello LaGuardia Award

NEW SCHOOL FOR SOCIAL RESEARCH
66 W. 12th St., New York, N.Y. 10011 (212/741-5667)

The Fiorello LaGuardia Award, which consists of a bronze statue of New York City's former mayor, is given annually for outstanding public service.

1973

Amyas Ames
Gustave L. Levy
Kenneth B. Clark
Ellen Stewart

1974

WNET, Channel 13
David Rose
Roy Wilkins
Mrs. John L. Loeb
Francisco Trilla

1975

James Reed Ellis
Ada Louise Huxtable
Patrick Vincent Murphy
Leon Howard Sullivan
Kenneth A. Gibson
Richard Green Lugar
Pete Seeger

1976

William M. Ellinghaus
Felix G. Rohatyn
Richard Ravitch

1977

J. Richardson Dilworth
Preston Robert Tisch
Emil Mosbacher, Jr.

1978

Bess Myerson

1979

Victor Gotbaum

1980

No award

Ramon Magsaysay Awards

RAMON MAGSAYSAY FOUNDATION
Box 3350, Manila, Philippines (59-19-59)

The Ramon Magsaysay Awards for Government Service, Public Service and Community Leadership represent three of the five categories in which the annual awards of $20,000 each are given for achievements in Asia reflecting the ideals of the late Ramon Magsaysay. The foundation's board of trustees selects the recipients from nominations received. The funding for this honor, which until 1977 was $10,00, is from the Rockefeller Brothers Fund of New York.

GOVERNMENT SERVICE

1958 **Chiang Mon-Ling** (China), Rural reconstruction
1959 **Chintaman Dwarkanath Deshmukh** (India) **and Jose Vasquez Aquilar** (Philippines), Exemplary service
1960 **No award**
1961 **Raden Kodijat** (Indonesia), Directed yaws campaign
1962 **Francisca Reyes Aquino** (Philippines), Research to preserve national folk heritage
1963 **Akhter Hameed Khan** (Pakistan), Rural reform in East Pakistan
1964 **Yukiharu Miki** (Japan), Community-wide modernization
1965 **Puey Ungphakorn** (Thailand), Management of public finance
1966 **Phon Sangsingkeo** (Thailand), Mental Health services
1967 **Keo Viphakone** (Laos), Public services for villagers
1968 **Li Kwoh-Ting** (China), Economics
1969 **Hsu Shih-Chu** (China), Rural health, sanitation and family planning
1970 **No award**
1971 **Ali Sadikin** (Indonesia), Modern administration
1972 **Goh Keng Swee** (Singapore), Industrialization of Singapore
1973 **Balachandra Chakkingal Sekhar** (Malaysia), Scientific and technical developments in rubber
1974 **Hiroshi Kuroki** (Japan), Administrative modernization of a Prefecture
1975 **Tun Mohamed Suffian bin Hashim** (Malaysia), Adaptation of Western legal forms to own Asian society
1976 **Elsie Elliot** (Hong Kong), leader of crusade to make government more responsive to the poor
1977 **Benjamin Galstaun** (Indonesia), "for guiding a new generation of Indonesians toward understanding and valuing animals and nature in Asia's moist tropics."
1978 **Shahrum Bin Yuib** (Malaysia), "for making a living museum an enlightening experience for all ages."
1979 **Not available at press time**
1980 **Not available at press time**

PUBLIC SERVICE

1958 **Mary Rutnam** (Ceylon), Dedicated service as private citizen
1959 **Father Joaquin Vilallonga** (Spaniard) **and Daw Tee Tee Luce** (Burma),For compassionate service to others
1960 **Sir Henry Holland** (Pakistan) **and Ronald Holland** (British), For selfless dedication of surgical skills
1961 **Nilawan Pintong** (Thailand), Leadership of effective civil action
1962 **Lawrence and Horace Kadoorie** (British), Practical philanthropy to promote rural welfare

1963 **Helen Kim** (Korea), Leadership in emancipation of Korean women
1964 **Father Nguyen Lac Hoa** (Vietnam), Extraordinary valor in defence of freedom
1965 **Jayaprakash Narayan** (India), Constructive articulation of public conscience
1966 **Kim Yong-Ki** (Korea), Improvement of rural life through application of Christian principles
1967 **M.C. Sithiporn Kridakara** (Thailand), Pioneering experiments and education in agriculture
1968 **Seiichi Tobata** (Japan), Modernization of agriculture
1969 **Kim Hyung Seo** (Korea), Leadership of refugees in reclaiming new agricultural lands
1970 **No award**
1971 **Pedro T. Orata** (Philippines), Creative work in education, especially of rural youth
1972 **Cecile R. Guidote and Gilopez Kabayao** (Philippines), Leadership in the performing arts
1973 **Msgr. Antonia Y. Fortich and Benjamin C. Gaston** (Philippines), Rural development
1974 **M.S. Subbulakshmi** (India), For devotional song and support of numerous public causes
1975 **Phra Chamroon Parnichand** (Thailand), Curing drug addicts with herbal and spiritual treatments
1976 **Hermenegild Joseph** (Sri Lanka), missionary schoolteacher devoted to helping youth
1977 **Lela R. Blatt** (India), "for making a reality of the Ghandian principles of truth and non-violent self-help among the most depressed work force of self-employed women"
1978 **Pratheep Ungsongtham** (Thailand), "for bringing learning, better health and hope to children in the slums of Klong Toey"
1979 **Not available at press time**
1980 **Not available at press time**

COMMUNITY LEADERSHIP

1958 **Vinoba Bhave** (India), Inspiration and help to "the man on the land"
1959 **The Dalai Lama** (Tibet), For defense of his people's right to live and worship in their own way
1960 **Tunku Abdul Rahman Putra** (Malaysia), For guiding a multi-racial socity toward communal alliance and national solidarity
1961 **Gus Borgeest** (British/Hong Kong), For human concern and courage on "Sunshine Island"
1962 **Harley Koesna Poeradiredja** (Indonesia) **and Palayil Pathazapurayil Narayanan** (Malayasia), For their championship of the workers' cause through responsible unionism
1963 **Dara N. Khorody, Tribhuvandas K. Patel and Verghese Kurien** (India), For coordination of government and private efforts in improving the supply of essential food and sanitation in a major city, and living standards in villages
1964 **Pablo Torres Tapia** (Philippines), For mobilizing the savings of a community for its productive needs
1965 **Lim Kim San** (Singapore), Decent, moderately priced housing
1966 **Kamaladevi Chattopadhyay** (India), Creativity in handicrafts, cooperatives, politics, art and theatre
1967 **Tun Abdul Razak bin Hussein** (Malaysia), Administration
1968 **Silvino and Rosario Encarnacion** (Philippines), Management of a credit cooperative
1969 **Ahangamage T. Ariyaratne** (Ceylon), Services to villages
1970 **No award**
1971 **Moncompu Sambasiva Swaminathan** (India), Scientist, educator and administrator
1972 **Hans Westenberg** (Indonesia), Practical propagation of new crops and better methods among small farmers
1973 **Krasae Chanawongse** (Thailand), Establishment of medical services
1974 **Fusaye Ichikawa** (Japan), Advancement of her countrywomen's public and personal freedom
1975 **Lee Tai-Young** (Korea), For the cause of equal juridical rights for the liberation of Korean women
1976 **Toshikazu Wakatsuki** (Japan), "for bringing to his country's most depressed citizens the highest type of technically competent and humanely inspired health care, thus creating a model for rural medicine"
1977 **Ela R. Bhatt** (India), "for making a reality of the Gandhian principles of truth and nonviolent self-help among the most depressed work force of self-employed women"
1978 **Tahrunnessa A. Abdullah** (Bangladesh), "for leading rural Bangladeshi Muslim women from the constraints of *purdah* toward more equal citizenship and fuller family responsibility"
1979 **No award**
1980 **No award**

Distinguished Service Award

MILITARY ORDER OF THE WORLD WARS
1100 17th St. NW, Suite 1000, Washington, D.C. 20036
(202/296-3923)

The Distinguished Service Award annually honors an American citizen for notable contributions to national defense and the preservation of American constitutional liberties. A selection committee studies the records of accomplishment and selects the winner of the gold medallion and scroll.

1963 **Sen. Barry Goldwater**
1964 **Sen. J. Strom Thurmond**
1965 **Commander Copley**, Copley Press
1966 **Gen. Lewis B. Hershey**
1967 **Francis Cardinal Spellman**
1968 **Sen. John Stennis**
1969 **Gen. William C. Westmoreland**
1970 **Gen. Lyman L. Lemnitzer**
1971 **Adm. Thomas H. Moorer**
1972 **F. Edward Hebert**,Congressman
1973 **Richard M. Nixon**
1974 **Gen. Harold K. Johnson**
1975 **Gen. George S. Brown**
1976 **James R. Schlesinger**, Dept. of Energy
1977 **Willard F. Rockwell, Jr.**, Chairman, Rockwell International
1978 **Lt. Gen. Ira C. Eaker**, USAF,-Ret
1979 **Gen. Alexander M. Haig, Jr.**, USA-Ret
1980 **Gen. Lewis W. Walt**, USMC-Ret

All-America City Awards

NATIONAL MUNICIPAL LEAGUE
47 E. 68th., New York, N.Y. 10021 (212/535-5700)

The All-America City Awards are given annually to cities for community improvement through citizen action. Cities submit entry forms describing community projects, which are reviewed by staff and by two impartial panels of experts in citizen organization and community development. The winners are awarded citations plus special recognition in the media.

1949

Bayonne, N.J.
Cincinnati, Ohio
Des Moines, Iowa
Philadelphia, Pa.
Poughkeepsie, N.Y.
Worcester, Mass.
Boston, Mass.
Cleveland, Ohio
Grand Rapids, Mich.
Pittsburgh, Pa.
San Antonio, Tex.

1950

Cincinnati, Ohio
Kansas City, Mo.
Montgomery County, Md.
Phoenix, Ariz.
Richmond, Va.
Youngstown, Ohio
Hartford, Conn.
Montclair, N.J.
New Orleans, La.
Portland, Me.
Toledo, Ohio

1951

Atlanta, Ga.
Boston, Mass.
Dayton, Ohio
Kansas City, Mo.
Pawtucket, R.I.
San Antonio, Tex.
Asheville-Buncombe Co., N.C.
Columbia, S.C.
Kalamazoo, Mich.
Mount Vernon, Ill.
Philadelphia, Pa.

1952

Torrance, Calif.
Worcester, Mass.
Setauket, N.Y.
Pawtucket, R.I.
Houston, Tex.
Richmond, Va.
Daytona Beach, Fla.
Kansas City, Mo.
Wilkes-Barre, Pa.
Columbia, S.C.
San Antonio, Tex.

1953

Richmond, Calif.
Park Forest, Ill.
Shreveport, La.
De Soto, Mo.
Scranton, Pa.
Port Angeles, Wash.
Daytona Beach, Fla.
Peoria, Ill.
Flint, Mich.
Canton, Ohio
Petersburg, Va.

1954

Maricopa County, Ariz.
Modesto, Calif.
Chicago, Ill.
Rockville, Md.
Mexico, Mo.
Warren, Ohio
Decatur, Ark.
Pueblo, Colo.
Rock Island, Ill.
Richfield, Minn.
Newark, N.J.

1955

Phenix City, Ala.
Savannah, Ga.
Joliet, Ill.
Port Huron, Mich.
Cambridge, Ohio
Bellevue, Wash.
Riverside, Calif.
Bloomington, Ill.
St. Paul, Minn.
Grand Island, Neb.
Reading, Pa.

1956

Anchorage, Alas.
Torrance, Calif.
St. Louis, Mo.
Laurinburg, N.C.
Altus, Okla.
Tacoma, Wash.
Oakland, Calif.
Elgin, Ill.
Springfield, Mo.
Zanesville, Ohio
Brattleboro, Vt.

1957

Albuquerque, N.M.
Galesburg, Ill.
Clarksburg, W.Va.
Ketchikan, Alas.
Miami-Dade County, Fla.
Neosho, Mo.
Philadelphia, Pa.
Yankton, S.D.
Middletown, Ohio
Omaha, Neb.
Vancouver, Wash.

1958

Bloomington, Ind.
Granite City, Ill.
Highland Park, Ill.
Leadville, Colo.
Phoenix, Ariz.
Westport, Conn.
Columbus, Ohio
Hayden, Ariz.
Huntington, W.Va.
New Haven, Conn.
Sheridan, Wyo.

1959

Alton, Ill.
East St. Louis, Ill.
Lamar, Colo.
San Juan, P.R.
Seattle, Wash.
Winston-Salem, N.C.
De Soto, Mo.
Fargo, N.D.
Norfolk, Va.
Santa Fe Springs, Calif.
Vallejo, Calif.

1960

Bloomington, Minn.
East Providence, R.I.
Town of Las Vegas, N.M.
Radford, Va.
Salem, Ore.
Worcester, Mass.
Decatur, Ill.
Grand Rapids, Mich.
Marin County, Calif.
Richland, Wash.
San Jose, Calif.

1961

Anacortes, Wash.
Galveston, Tex.
Independence, Mo.
Milton-Freewater, Ore.
Salisbury, N.C.
Wichita, Kans.
Falls Church, Va.
Hartford, Conn.
Lynwood, Calif.
Rockville, Md.
Sioux City, Iowa

1962

Allentown, Pa.
Boston, Mass.
Dade County, Fla.
Grand Junction, Colo.
Knoxville, Tenn.
San Diego, Calif.
Bartlesville, Okla.
Chattanooga, Tenn.
Grafton, W.Va.
High Point, N.C.
Quincy, Ill.

1963

Alexandria, Va.
Gastonia, N.C.
Minneapolis, Minn.
Roseville, Calif.
Sidney, Ohio
Woodstock, Ill.
Aztec, N.M.
Louisville, Ky.
Oil City, Pa.
Seward, Alas.
Woodbridge, N.J.

1964

Bluefield, W.Va.
Fort Worth, Tex.
Hazleton, Pa.
Keene, N.H.
South Portland, Me.
Winston-Salem, N.C.
Columbia, S.C.
Green Bay, Wisc.
Hopkinsville, Ky.
Niles, Ill.
White Bear Lake, Minn.

1965

Anchorage, Alas.
Florence, S.C.
Michigan City, Ind.
Ogallala, Neb.
Seward, Alaska
Valdez, Alaska
Flat River, Mo.
La Crosse, Wisc.
Mount Vernon, Ohio
Pikeville, Ky.
Trenton, N.J.
Wilmington, N.C.

Worcester, Mass.

1966

Ann Arbor, Mich.
Cohoes, N.Y.
Greensboro, N.C.
Peoria, Ill.
Presque Isle, Me.
Seattle, Wash.
Clearfield, Pa.
Detroit, Mich.
Malden, Mass.
Pinellas Co., Fla.
Richmond, Va.

1967

Auburn, Me.
Fresno, Calif.
Hickory, N.C.
Leavenworth, Wash.
South Bend, Ind.
Wheaton, Ill.
Cape Girardeau, Mo.
Grand Island, Neb.
Laurinburg, N.C.
Royal Oak, Mich.
Tupelo, Miss.

1968

Charlotte, N.C.
Danville, Ky.
Fairbanks, Alas.
New Albany, Ind.
San Diego, Calif.
Snyder, Tex.
Cottage Grove, Ore.
Edinburg, Tex.
Jacksonville, Fla.
Saginaw, Mich.
Savannah, Ga.

1969

Asheville, N.C.
Cuero, Tex.
Eugene, Ore.
Martinsville, Va.
Rock Hill, S.C.
Springfield, Ill.
Borger, Tex.
El Paso, Tex.
Kalamazoo, Mich.
Maryville, Mo.
Rocky Mount, N.C.

1970

Ardmore, Okla.
Bloomfield, Conn.
Enfield, Conn.
Gainesville, Fla.
Lakeland, Fla.
Shelby, N.C.
Birmingham, Ala.
Dallas, Tex.
Fitchburg, Mass.
Indianapolis, Ind.
Lumberton, N.C.

1971

Beloit, Wisc.
Chickasha, Okla.
Lowell, Mass.
Placentia, Calif.
Twin Cities, Minn.
Carbondale, Ill.
Jamaica, N.Y.
North Branford, Conn.
Santa Fe Springs, Calif.

1972

Chewelah, Wash.
Hampton, Va.
Modesto, Calif.
St. Petersburg, Fla.
Verdigre, Neb.
Wilson, N.C.
Erie, Pa.
Johnstown, Pa.
Poplar Bluff, Mo.
Somerville, Mass.
Wilmington, Del.

1973

Albion, Mich.
LaHabra, Calif.
Lexington, Neb.
North Adams, Mass.
St. Cloud, Minn.
Jameston, N.Y.
Lewistown, Pa.
Macon, Mo.
Port Arthur, Tex.
Tulsa, Okla.

1974

Allentown, Pa.
Fall River, Mass.
Grand Prairie, Tex.
Pontiac, Mich.
South El Monte, Calif.
Spokane, Wash.
Excelsior Springs, Mo.
Gardner, Mass.
Norfolk, Neb.
Raleigh, N.C.
Spencer, W.Va.
Wooster, Ohio

1975

Cleveland Heights, Ohio
Harbor Springs, Mich.
Montebello, Calif.
Plainfield, N.J.
San Pablo, Calif.
Frederick, Md.
Marshall, Tex.
Oak Park, Ill.
Portsmouth, Va.
Toccoa, Ga.

1976

Anderson, Ind.
Danville, Va.
Newton, Mass.
Rockville, Md.
Tarboro, N.C.
Baltimore, Md.
Des Moines, Iowa
Park Forest, Ill.
San Bernardino, Calif.
Union, N.J.

1977

Anniston, Ala.
Cleveland Heights, Ohio
Dennis, Mass.
Lincoln, Neb.
Mankato, Minn.
Ottumwa, Iowa
Charleston, S.C.
Dayton, Ohio
Duluth, Minn.
Madison, Wisc.
Oklahoma City, Okla.
Ravenna, Neb.

1978

Anniston, Ala
Cleveland Heights, Ohio
Dennis, Mass.
Lincoln, Neb.
Mankato, Minn.
Ottumwa, Iowa
Charleston, S.C.
Dayton, Ohio
Duluth, Minn.
Madison, Wisc.
Oklahoma City, Okla.
Revenna, Neb.

1979

Charlottesville, Va.
La Moure, N.D.
Roanoke Valley, Va.
Roswell, N.M.
Southfield, Mich.
Winona, Minn.
Haverhill, Mass.
Mesa, Ariz.
Rockville, Md.
Southbridge, Mass.
Vincennes, Ind.

1980

Bellingham, Wash.
Phoenix, Ariz.
Portsmouth, Ohio
Seminole, Okla.
Shreveport, La.
Gardena, Calif.
Portland, Ore.
Rockingham, N.C.
Sherman, Tex.

James Kilpatrick Award

INTERNATIONAL PLATFORM ASSOCIATION
2564 Berkshire Rd., Cleveland Hgts., Ohio 44106
(216/932-0505)

The James Kilpatrick Award, a silver bowl is presented annually to the individual judged to be the nation's "most effective conservative voice."

1978 William E. Simon
1979 Sen. Jesse Helms
1980 Reed Larson

Award of Valor

NATIONAL COLLEGIATE ATHLETIC ASSOCIATION
Box 1906, Shawnee Mission, Kans. 66222 (913/384-3220)

The Award of Valor, which consists of a medal, is awarded as merited to any current or former intercollegiate varsity letterman from an NCAA school who has averted or minimized potential disaster by courageous action in a non-military situation.

1973 **Ursinus College Basketball Team—Robert E. Cattell, William J. Downy, Warren Fry,** (head coach), **Robert Handwerk,** (assistant coach), **George P. Kinek, Jack S. Messenger, Norman Reichenback,** (trainer), **Randy D. Stubits, Thomas E. Sturgeon, and Michael C. Weston**
Charles C. Driesell, University of Maryland
William Jeffrey Miller, University of Texas, Arlington
1974-76 **No awards**
1977 **Dwayne A. Wright,** St. Mary's of California
1978-80 **No awards**

Charles Evans Hughes Medallion

NATIONAL CONFERENCE OF CHRISTIANS AND JEWS
43 W. 57th St., New York, N.Y. 10019 (212/688-7530)

The Charles Evans Hughes Medallion, accompanied by a hand-lettered scroll, is presented annually for "courageous leadership in governmental, civic and humanitarian affairs." The conference executive board selects the recipient.

1965 **Gov. Edmund (Pat) G. Brown,** California
Gov. Leroy Collins, Florida
Gov. Nelson A. Rockefeller, New York
Gov. George Romney, Michigan
1966 **General of the Army Dwight D. Eisenhower**
1967 **Harry S. Truman**
Sen. Edward W. Brooke
Paul H. Douglas
1968 **Adm. Lewis L. Strauss,** (Ret.)
John W. Gardner
Mayor Ivan Allen, Jr.
1969 **Chief Justice Earl Warren,** (Ret.)
1970 **Constance Baker Motley**
Rev. Theodore M. Hesburgh
1971 **Gen. Lucius D. Clay,** (Ret.)
Associate Justice Tom C. Clark, (Ret.)
Walter E. Washington
1972 **Ambassador Jerome H. Holland**
1973 **Secretary of State Henry A. Kissinger**
1974 **David Rockefeller**
1975 **Brooks Hays**
Linwood Holton
Ambassador Robert D. Murphy
1976 **John D. deButts**
1977 **Betty Ford**
Gerald R. Ford
1978 **No award**
1979 **Bob Hope**
1980 **Gen. Alexander M. Haig, Jr.**

James Forrestal Memorial Award

NATIONAL SECURITY INDUSTRIAL ASSOCIATION
1015 15th St. NW, Washington, D.C. 20005 (202/393-3620)

The James Forrestal Memorial Award, consisting of a gold medal and citation, is "given annually to the individual who most effectively applied the concept of a continuing close-working partnership between industry and government in the interest of national security." The Forrestal Award Selection Committee chooses the winner from nominations by member companies of the organization.

1954 **Dwight David Eisenhower,** President of the United States
1955 **Gen. David Sarnoff,** Chairman of the Board, Radio Corp. of America
1956 **Gen. Alfred M. Gruenther,** Supreme Allied Commander, Europe
1957 **Arthur W. Radford,** Chairman, Joint Chiefs of Staff
1958 **Mervin J. Kelley,** President, Bell Telephone Laboratories
1959 **Wilfred J. McNeil,** Assistant Secretary of Defense
Donald A. Quarles, Deputy Secretary of Defense
1960 **Gen. N.F. Twining,** Chairman Joint Chiefs of Staff
1961 **Adm. Arleigh A. Burke,** Chief of Naval Operations
1962 **Gen. Lauris Norstad,** Supreme Allied Commander, Europe
1963 **Robert S. McNamara,** Secretary of Defense
1964 **Gen. Curtis E. LeMay,** Chief of Staff, U.S. Air Force
1965 **Vice Adm. William F. Raborn, Jr.,** Director, Polaris Project
1966 **H. Mansfield Horner,** Chairman of the Board, United Aircraft Corp.
1967 **William M. Allen,** Chairman of the Board, The Boeing Co.
1968 **Richard B. Russell,** U.S. Senator from Georgia
1969 **John S. Foster, Jr.,** Director, Defense Research and Engineering
1970 **L. Mendel Rivers,** Chairman, Committee on Armed Services, U.S. House of Representatives
1971 **David Packard,** Deputy Secretary of Defense
1972 **James S. McDonnell,** Chairman of the Board, McDonnell Douglas Corp.
1973 **Adm. Thomas H. Moorer,** Chairman, Joint Chiefs of Staff
1974 **John C. Stennis,** Chairman, Armed Services Committee, U.S. Senate
1975 **T.A. Wilson,** Chairman and Chief Executive Officer, The Boeing Co.
1976 **George A. Mahon,** Chairman, Appropriations Committee, U.S. House of Representatives
1977 **Vice Adm. Levering Smith,** Office, U.S. Navy Director, Strategic Systems Project
1978 **Gen. Alexander M. Haig, Jr.,** Supreme Allied Commander, Europe
1979 **Bob Wilson,** U.S. Representative from California
1980 **Sen. Barry Goldwater** from Arizona

Museum Medal

NETHERLANDS GOVERNMENT
The Hague, The Netherlands

The Museum Medal (Museummedaille) is given as merited to those who have benefited art and scientific collections open to the public. Gold, silver and bronze medals are awarded as tokens of recognition upon recommendation and consultation with the State Committee for Museums. All awards are not given every year.

GOLD MEDAL

1891 W.G.A.C. Christan
1900 F. Uldall
1901 Sir Henry Howard
1908 Mohamed Siranoedin
1911 Ch. L.J. Palmer v.d. Broek
1913 A. Mauritz
1916 The London family
1920 A.J. Gooszen
C.P.D. Pape
1922 J.P. van der Schilden
1923 M.L. Drucker-Fraser
F.G. Waller
1925 de Wed. de Basel-Oorschot
1926 Ir. C. Hofstede de Groot
J.H. Holwerda
A.J.E.A. Bik
J.Th. de Visser
1930 Eduina van Heek-Erving
1931 Princess de Croy, nee Countess de l'Espine
1932 D.G. van Beuningen
W.J.M. d'Ablaing
1933 E. Heldring
1934 J.G. de Bruyn-Van der Leeuw
1935 Edwin van Rath
H.E.L.J. Kroller-Muller
H.E. van Gelder
1937 P. Boendermaker
1938 W. van de Verm
Kaichiro Netsu
1939 H.E. ten Cate
1940 E.A. van Beresteyn
H.K. Westendorp
1946 J.K. van der Haagen
P.A. Regnault
1947 J.C. Bierens de Haan
W. Martin
I.S. Scholton
1953 J.H. van Heek
Henry v.d. Velde
1954 Fritz Lugt
N. Ottema
1957 J. Lugt-Klever
1960 P. Sybrandy
1964 R.M.A. Willemsen-Widdershoven
1966 Joh. G. Wertheim
1970 Ir. V.W. van Gogh
1972 C.H. van der Leeuw
L.R.J. Ridder van Rappard
1974 Frank D. Robson
F.J.E. van Lennep
1975 J.G. van Gelder
D.W.F. Langelaan
1976 Netherlands Museum Society

Current Status Unknown

SILVER MEDAL

1906 J.N.A. Panken
1914 P. van Hulstijn
1915 W. Zweerts de Jongh
1919 J.A. Saurel
J.L. Cadet-Kempers
P.F.T. Van Veen
1920 C.W. Bruinvis
N.J.A.P.H. van Es
F.J.G. ten Raa
H.A. le Bron de Vexela
A.E. Brinckmann
P. Muller Heymer
1921 H.M. Werner
J.S. Goekoop de Jongh
1922 J. Hoynck van Papendrecht
1923 G.M. Kam
T.A. Boeree
1924 W. Spijer
A. Baron van Aerssen Beyeren van Voshol
1925 R. Magnee de Horn
J.J.H. Sieben
1926 H.J. Voskuil
H.J.S. Terstappen
1927 Pangeran Hario Hadiwidjojo
1928 J. Valckenier Suringar
J.G. Kist
1929 D.S. van Zuiden
1931 J.A.H. Alexander
H. van Oort van Lauwenrecht
1933 W. van Rijn
A. Averkamp
1935 P.G. van Tienhoven
1936 L.A. Springer
Eugene Stiels
Pangeran Ario Poerbonagoro
1937 Kaspar Freiherr von Furstenberg-Kortling-L4hausen
L.C.F. Engelen
1938 J.M. Somer
D.L. Warsinck
1947 M.P.T. van Mastenbroek-Wellsted
C.A. van Woelderen
1948 E.L.L. Colin
C.A. Crommelin
C.J. van der Klaauw
1949 A. Preston Pearce
1950 J.J. Vost tot Nederveen Cappel
1952 J.B. Bernik
K. Tinholt
1953 H. Muller
J.R. Schuiling
C.F. Venema
1954 J.J.H.H. Asselberghs
W.F. Bax
M.J. van Sambeek
1955 C. Eisneo
1956 D.H. Huygen
1957 H.K. Remmers
1958 H.A. Fonteyn-Kuypers
H. van Hoogdalen
H.M.A.F. Six
1959 C. Franssen
D.J. Kamminga
1960 R. Wartena
P.J. Yperlaan
1961 C.B. Nicolas
H.S. Christoffelsz
1962 J.M. de Nooyer
B.W. Schot
1963 J.W.G.H.M. Huysmans
Ir. J. Struik Dalm
A.M. Sustring
1965 D. Barneveld
1968 D. Fledderus
1969 E.D. van Wijngaarden
F. G. de Wilde

1970 **General Hoefer Military Museum,** Leyden
H.J. Feyfer
F.E. Feyfer-Teutelink
1971 **C.E. Smit-Dyserinck**
Pater J.B. van Croonenburg
1972 **J.J.A. Jongenelen**
H. Offerhaus
A. Komter
E.J. Nieuwenhuijs
1975 **J. Zibrandtsen**
1976 **W. Stroman**
P.C. van den Berg
Current Status Unknown

BRONZE MEDAL

1930 **H. de Jongh**
1931 **F. Bloemen**
C.J. Kortenbach
1953 **A. Hollander**
1955 **S.B. Slipjer**
1960 **H. Boon**
J.G.C.C. Hendriks
O. Koster
Current Status Unknown

ASPO Medal
Planner of the Year Award

AMERICAN SOCIETY OF PLANNING OFFICIALS
1313 E. 60th St., Chicago, Ill. 60637 (312/947-2560)

The ASPO Medal is awarded annually for continual leadership and outstanding contribution in the field, with special consideration for non-professionals and professionals in other fields. The silver medal was designed by sculptor John Amore. A three-member committee nominates the winner for approval by the board of directors.

1949 **Harold Buttenheim,** In tribute of 40th anniversary as editor of *The American City*
1950 **No award**
1951 **No award**
1952 **Lawson Purdy,** Lawyer, for developing zoning principles and techniques
Frank B. Williams, Lawyer, for major contributions in drafting New York Zoning Resolution of 1916, the nation's first comprehensive zoning ordinance
1953 **Edward H. Bennett,** Architect and city planner, pioneer planner (e.g., 1905 San Francisco plan and 1906 Chicago plan)
Louis Brownlow, Public administrator on various national committees and contributor to planning and zoning literature
1954 **Elizabeth Herlihy,** Planner, for 40-year career in Massachusetts
Harlean James, Executive Secretary of American Planning and Civic Assn.
Katherine McNamara, Librarian, for 40 years' service to planning and landscape architecture library at Harvard University and lecturer in city planning department
1955 **Clarence Stein,** Architect, author and civic designer
1956 **No award**
1957 **Benjamin Kizer,** Lawyer, influential citizen, for service to planning boards in the Northwest
1958 **John Ihlder,** Planner, especially in the field of good housing
1959 **Walter H. Blucher,** Planner, ASPO Executive Director and consultant for 25 years
1960 **Sir Frederic Osborn,** Planner, for advocacy of greenbelts and new towns
1961 **Francis A. Pitkin,** Planner, for outstanding role in state planning
1962 **Harold Osborne,** Engineer and municipal official, for pioneering contributions in telephone communications and second career in municipal and regional planning
1963 **L. Perry Cookingham,** City planner, for imaginative planning and leadership
Hugh R. Pomeroy, Planner, for 37-year career in planning, zoning, housing and government
1964 **Harland Bartholomew,** Planner, in tribute of his unparalleled career as head of a planning agency, consulting firm, chairman of the National Capitol Planning Commission and professor
1965 **Lewis Mumford,** Author and critic, for illuminations of potentials and problems of cities
Catherine Bauer Wurster, Planner, for contributions to national policy for housing and planning
1966 **Ernest J. Bohn,** Legislator, administrator, planning commissioner and presidential advisor, for pioneering policy in law of housing and slum clearance
Sears-Roebuck Foundation, In tribute to leadership in initiating a large-scale program of financial assistance for education of planners and other projects
1967 **Tracy Augur,** Planner, for urban, regional, national and international planning as public official, private consultant and author
Rexford Guy Tugwell, Planner, public official, educator and author
1968 **Dennis O'Harrow,** "The Conscience of the Profession" for contributions to literature and techniques of planning
1969 **Fairfield Osborn and The Conservation Foundation,** For pioneering and continued influence to expand the concept of conservation
1970 **Charles Abrams,** Planner, author, lawyer and public servant
1971 **Charles McKim Norton,** For major influence on New York region and on the concepts and laws of regional planning during 31 years as leader in the Regional Plan Assn. of New York
1972 **Rene Dubos,** Scientist and humanist, in tribute to his writings on effects of environment on human life
Charles W. Eliot II, Planner, for bridging gap between early landscape architecture and later city and regional planning
Ladislas Segoe, Planner, for rare quality of his products during 50 years of practice, including directing the National Resources Committee landmark report on American cities
1973 **No award**
1974 **Robert E. Simon,** For value and objectives embodied in plan of Reston, Va., a symbol of aspiration for the contemporary new town
William L.C. Wheaton, Planner and teacher
1975 **Hans Blumenfeld,** Planner, for contributions to planning analysis
T.J. Kent, Jr., Planner, for work on the general urban plan, political and planning practice, and planning education
John T. Howard, Planner, for work on the general urban plan, political and planning practice, and planning education
John R. Parker, For leadership in planning education and teaching

1976 No award
1977 No award

Current Status Unknown

The Planner of the Year Award is given annually to honor specific achievements in advancing the field of planning, as recognized and evaluated by the groups affected. A three- to five-member committee of professionals and citizen representatives selects the recipient of the certificate from nominations made by ASPO members. Winners may be ASPO members or non-members, individuals or groups.

1974 **Frank G. Colley,** Citizen-planner of Meeker, Colo., for vision and leadership in public awareness in region threatened by oil-shale development
Ralph D. Smith, Citizen-planner of Boston for leading and validating a neighborhood voice, initiating plans and implementing techniques to upgrade inner-city development
1975 **Anthony H. Mason,** Planning commissioner of Phoenix for inspiring the confidence upon which an independent planning commission depends
1976 No award
1977 No award

Current Status Unknown

Orwell Award

NATIONAL COUNCIL OF TEACHERS OF ENGLISH
1111 Kenyon Rd., Urbana, Ill. 61801 (217/328-3870)

The Orwell Award is presented annually for a work which is an outstanding contribution to the critical analysis of public discourse. A committee selects the recipient.

1978 **Sissela Bok,** *Lying: A Moral Choice in Public and Private Life*
1979 **Erving Goffman,** *Gender Advertisements*
1980 **Sheila Harty,** *Hucksters in the Classroom: A Review of Industry Proaganda in Schools*

Providence Human Relations Commission National Award

PROVIDENCE HUMAN RELATIONS COMMISSION
40 Fountain St., Providence, R.I. 02903 (401/421-3708)

The Providence Human Relations Commission National Award is presented annually to an individual who has promoted human rights in America. The commission selects the winner.

1979 **Ramsay Clark,** former United States Attorney General
1980 **Robert Drinian,** House of Representatives

Daniel Webster Award

INTERNATIONAL PLATFORM ASSOCIATION
2564 Berkshire Rd., Cleveland Heights, Ohio 44106 (216/932-0505)

The Daniel Webster Award, which consists of an engraved bowl, is given annually for the speech judged to deal with the most important problem facing the United States and its citizens.

1976 **Glenn Seaborg**
1977 **Kenneth H. Cooper**
1978 **Howard Jarvis**
1979 **Arthur B. Laffer**
1980 No award

Margaret Sanger Award

PLANNED PARENTHOOD FEDERATION OF AMERICA
810 Seventh Ave., New York, N.Y. 10019 (212/541-7800)

The $1,000 Margaret Sanger Award is presented annually for service to the cause of family planning and population control. The award includes a statue and a citation. The Margaret Sanger Awards Committee selects the winner.

1966 **Gen. William H. Draper**
Carl G. Hartman
Lyndon B. Johnson
Rev. Martin Luther King, Jr.
1967 **John D. Rockefeller III**
1968 **Ernest Gruening**
1969 **Lord Caradon**
1970 **Joseph D. Tydings**
1971 **Louis M. Hellman**
1972 **Alan F. Guttmacher**
1973 **Sarah Lewit**
Christopher Tietze
1974 **Harriet F. Pilpel**
1975 **Cass Canfield**
1976 **John Rock**
1977 **Bernard Berelson**
1978 **Julia Henderson**
Frederick Jaffe
Edris Rice-Wray
1979 **Alfred Moran**
Sen. Robert Packwood
1980 **Mary Calderone**
Sarah Weddington

Servant of Justice Award

LEGAL AID SOCIETY
15 Park Row, New York, N.Y. 10007 (212/577-3300)

The Servant of Justice Award is given annually to a lawyer or non-lawyer for contributions to the status of the legal profession.

1978 **John J. McCloy**
1979 **Whitney North Seymour, Sr.**
1980 **Walter Cronkite**

Henry Medal

SMITHSONIAN INSTITUTION
1000 Jefferson Dr. SW, Washington, D.C. 20560
(202/628-4422)

The Henry Medal, which is of gold, is given as merited with an honorarium for distinguished service, achievement or contributions to the prestige and growth of the Smithsonian Institution. The board of regents bestows this honor.

1967 **David E. Finley,** First director, National Gallery of Art
1968 **Frank A. Taylor,** Smithsonian's Director General of Museums and Director, United States National Museum
1970 **Charles G. Abbott,** For 16 years, Secretary of the Smithsonian, and prior to that, Director of the Smithsonian Astrophysical Observatory and founder and Director of the Radiation Biology Laboratory
1973 **Fred L. Whipple,** Director, Smithsonian Astrophysical Observatory
Edward K. Thompson, Editor, *Smithsonian* magazine
1975 **John Nicholas Brown,** Citizen regent of the Smithsonian for 18 years
1976 **T. Dale Stewart,** Smithsonian Anthropologist Emeritus
Martin H. Moynihan, Founder and former director, Smithsonian Tropical Research Institute
1977 **Hubert H. Humphrey,** U.S. Senator, and former Vice President and Smithsonian regent

Gold Medal

NATIONAL INSTITUTE OF SOCIAL SCIENCES
150 Amsterdam Ave., New York, N.Y. 10023
(212/787-1000)

The Institute's Gold Medal is given annually to distinguished individuals—usually Americans—who have served their country and humanity in an outstanding capacity. The medals committee selects and the president and board of trustees approve the winners.

1913
Archer M. Huntington
William H. Taft
Samuel L. Parrish

1914
Charles W. Eliot
Abraham Jacobi
Gen. George W. Goethals
Henry Fairfield Osborn

1915
Luther Burbank
Andrew Carnegie

1916
Robert Bacon
Adolph Lewisohn
Mrs. H. Hartley Jenkins

1917
George W. Crile
John Purroy Mitchell
Michael Idvorsky Pupin
Surgeon-Gen. William Gorgas

1918
Henry P. Davison
Herbert C. Hoover
William J. Mayo

1919
Samuel Gompers
William Henry Welch

1920
Alexis Carrel
Sir Wilfred T. Grenfell
H. Holbrook Curtis
Harry Pratt Judson

1921
Charles Frederick Chandler
Marie Curie
Calvin Coolidge
Cleveland H. Dodge

1923
Charles B. Davenport
Emory R. Johnson
John D. Rockefeller, Sr.
Sir Auckland Geddes
Jules J. Jusserand

1924
Walter Hampden
Mrs. C. Lorillard Spencer
Charles E. Hughes

1925
Mrs. E.H. Harriman
Elihu Root
William H. Park

1926
S. Parkes Cadman
Stephen Tying Mather
Mary Schenck Woolman
Clarence Hungerford Mackay

1927
George Pierce Baker
Harry Emerson Fosdick
Walter Damrosch
Adolph S. Ochs

1928
Liberty Hyde Bailey
Willis R. Whitney
Robert W. deForest

1929
Valeria Langeloth
John D. Rockefeller, Jr.
Daniel Willard
Rose Livingston
James T. Shotwell

1930
Anna Billings Gallup
William Lyon Phelps
George R. Minot
Nathan Straus

1931
Grace Abbott
Grace Goodhue Coolidge
Richard Clarke Cabot
Frank B. Kellogg

1932
Edward E. Allen
William C. Redfield
James Howell Post
Gerard Swope

1933
Newton D. Baker
Evangeline Booth
Clifford W. Beers

1934
Eleanor Robson Belmont
Samuel Seabury
Walter B. Cannon

1935
Cornelius N. Bliss
Carter Glass
Harvey Cushing
George E. Vincent

1936
Nicholas Murray Butler
William Edwin Hall
Mrs. Harrison Eustis
J. Pierpont Morgan

1937
James Rowland Angell
J. Edgar Hoover
Mrs. Edward W. Bok
Wesley Clair Mitchell

1938
John W. Davis
Dorothy Thompson
Walter S. Gifford

1939
Martha Berry
George Wharton Pepper
William Church Osborn

1940
Carrie Chapman Catt
Wendell L. Willkie
James E. West

1941
Norman H. Davis
Alfred E. Smith
Mrs. J. Borden Harriman

1942
Rufus B. von KleinSmid
Donald M. Nelson
Anne O'Hare McCormick

1943
Madame Chiang Kai-shek
Cdr. Mildred H. McAffee, USNR
Edwin Grant Conklin
Juan Terry Trippe

1944
Bernard M. Baruch
James G.K. McClure
Mrs. Henry Pomeroy Davison

1945
Vannevar Bush
William Mather Lewis
Mrs. John Henry Hammond

1946
Virginia C. Gildersleeve
Edwin R. Stettinius. Jr.
Robert Moses

1947
Katharine F. Lenroot
Thomas J. Watson, Sr.
Edward Johnson

1948
Georgiana Farr Sibley
Warren R. Austin
Basil O'Connor

1949
Lillian M. Gilbreth
Alfred P. Sloan. Jr.
General of the Army George Catlett Marshall

1950
Henry Bruere
Gen. Carlos P. Romulo
Sarah Gibson Blanding

1951
Bayard Foster Pope
John Foster Dulles
Paul G. Hoffman
Lewis W. Douglas
General of the Army Douglas MacArthur

1952
Harold Raymond Medina
John Jay McCloy
Helen Adams Keller
Robert Abercrombie Lovett

1953
E. Roland Harriman
Charles F. Kettering
Oveta Culp Hobby

1954
Howard A. Rusk
Gen. Walter Bedell Smith
Mrs. Lytle Hull

1955
Samuel D. Leidesdorf
Henry Cabot Lodge, Jr.
Elizabeth Luce Moore

1956
Clarence G. Michalis
Henry T. Heald
Mary Pillsbury Lord

1957
William F. Graham, Jr.
Gen. Alfred M. Gruenther
Clare Boothe Luce

1958
Marion Anderson
Robert Bernard Anderson
James R. Killian, Jr.
Herbert Hoover

1959
Helen Hayes
Jonas E. Salk
Laurance S. Rockefeller

1960
Sir Rudolf Bing
Millicent C. McIntosh
Gilbert Darlington
Grayson L. Kirk

1961
Marie L. Bullock
William C. Menninger
Karl Menninger
Edward Durell Stone

1962
Mary I. Bunting
John W. Gardner
Ralph J. Bunche
Gen. Lucius D. Clay

1963
Arthur H. Dean
Nathan M. Pusey
Katharine E. McBride
Frank Stanton

1964
Margaret Chase Smith
Frederick R. Kappel
Dean Rusk
Bob Hope

1965
Dorothy Buffam Chandler
James A. Perkins
Gen. Maxwell D. Taylor

1966
Lady Bird Johnson
David Sarnoff
Danny Kaye
Francis Cardinal Spellman
Keith Funston

1967
John D. Rockefeller, 3rd
Laurance S. Rockefeller
David Rockefeller
Nelson A. Rockefeller
Winthrop Rockefeller
The Rockefeller Family

1968
Anne Morrow Lindbergh
Eugene R. Black
Ralph W. Sockman
Charles A. Lindbergh

1969
Lady Jackson
Rev. Theodore M. Hesburgh
Col. Frank Borman
Lester B. Pearson

1970
Katharine Graham
Eric Sevareid
Gen. Lauris Norstad
William P. Rogers. Jr.

1971
Joan Ganz Cooney
Arthur K. Watson
Charles H. Malik
Thomas J. Watson, Jr.

1972
George Bush
Mrs. Laurance Rockefeller
Henry A. Kissinger
Rev. Fulton J. Sheen

1973
Brig. Gen. John T. Flynn
Rev. Paul Moore, Jr.
Jean Kerr
Elliott L. Richardson

1974
Col. Peter M. Dawkins
George P. Schultz
Golda Meir
Roy Wilkins

1975
Nancy Hanks
Donald K. Slayton
Lowell Thomas, Jr.
William E. Simon
Lowell Thomas

1976
Barry M. Goldwater
John J. McCloy
Peter J. Peterson
Norman Vincent Peale
Barbara Walters

1977
Anne Armstrong
Mr. and Mrs. Clifford William Rockefeller Robertson (Dina Merrill)
William B. Walsh
Sir Edwin Leather, Bermuda

1978
Hernrik Beer
Julia Child
Arthur F. Burns
James R. Dumpson

1979
McGeorge Bundy
Jane Pickens Hoving
C. Douglas Dillon
Linus Pauling

1980
Gen. Alexander M. Haig
William J. McGill
Henry Labouisse
William McChesney Martin
Iphigene Ochs Sulzberger

Secretary's Award
Award for Heroism
Award for Valor

U.S. DEPARTMENT OF STATE
Office of Performance Evaluation, Room 2803,
Washington, D.C. 20520 (202/632-3412)

The Secretary's Award, which consists of a plaque, is given annually to individuals in government service abroad who have performed official duties at the sacrifice of personal health or life. The Department Awards Committee selects the recipients. (* Posthumous)

1968-70 **Robert D. Handy***, Vietnam
Don Mitrione*, Vietnam
Donald M. Sladkin, Vietnam
1970-72 **Joseph A. Smith***, Vietnam
1972-73 **Thomas M. Gompertz***, Vietnam
Robert R. Little*, Vietnam
Jeffrey S. Lundstedt*, Vietnam
George Curtis Moore*, Khartoum, Sudan
Cleo A. Noel, Jr.*, Khartoum, Sudan
Thomas W. Ragsdale*, Vietnam
1973-74 **Steven A. Haukness**, Vietnam
Roger P. Davies*, Nicosia, Cyprus
John P. Egan*, Cordoba, Spain
Alfred A. Laun III, Cordoba, Spain
Antoinette M. Varnava*, Nicosia, Cyprus
1974-75 **Francis E. Meloy, Jr.***, Beirut, Lebanon
Robert O. Waring*, Beirut, Lebanon
Zohair Moghrabi*, Beirut, Lebanon
1976 **No award**
1977 **No award**

Current Status Unknown

The Award for Heroism, which consists of a plaque, is given annually to individuals in government service abroad for performance of an act of heroism without regard for personal safety, related to his or her official duties or not. The Department Awards Committee selects the recipients. (* Posthumous)

1968-70 **Hugh G. Appling**, Vietnam
Paul E. Barbian, Vietnam
David L. Buckles, Vietnam
Francis B. Corry, Vietnam
Thomas W. Culbertson, Vietnam
Curtis C. Cutter, Porto Alegre, Brazil
Frederick D. Elfers, Vietnam
Peter F. Hurst, Vietnam
Terry L. Lambacher, Vietnam
Thomas D. Maher, Vietnam
Kenneth R. Mahony, Vietnam
Edward L. Merseth, Vietnam
Hawthorne Q. Mills, Vietnam
John S. Powley, Vietnam
Thomas J. Rice, Frankfurt, Federal Republic of Germany
Stephen H. Rimmer, Vietnam
Robert E. Runyon, Vietnam
William H. Saunders, Vietnam
Edward W. Schaefer, Mogadishu, Somalia
Samuel L. Turner, Vietnam
Loring A. Waggoner, Vietnam
John C. Ziegler, Vietnam
1970-72 **Eugenia Antonescu**, Bucharest, Rumania
William A. Levis, Vientiane, Laos
Sanda Pansitescu, Bucharest, Rumania
Charles E. Sothan, Vietnam

Angela Voicu, Bucharest, Rumania
1972-73 No award
1973-74 No award
1974-75 Barbara A. Hutchinson, Santo Domingo, Dominican Republic
Ronald A. Webb*, Cambridge, England
1975-76 No award
1976-77 Bernard A. Johnson, New York
George R. Mitchell, New York

Current Status Unknown

The Award for Valor, which consists of a plaque, is given annually to individuals in government service abroad for performance under dangerous circumstances that required personal bravery and perseverance to complete an assignment. The Department Awards Committee selects the recipients. (* Posthumous)

1968-70 Group Award to the staff of 43 of the American Embassy in Amman, Jordan
1970-72 Thomas O. Brennan, Vietnam
Martin S. Christie, Vietnam
John Hollingsworth, Jordan
William P. Hovis, La Paz, Bolivia
Desaix B. Myers, Dacca, Bangladesh
Richard B. Peterson, Vietnam
Thomas Polgar, Buenos Aires, Argentina
David A. Reinhardt, Vietnam
Herbert W. Timrud, Vietnam
1972-73 Susan A. Beauvais, Vietnam
Michael D. Benge, Vietnam
Norman J. Brookens, Vietnam
William A. Cole, Addis Ababa, Ethiopia
Philip W. Manhard, Vietnam
Douglas K. Ramsay, Vietnam
Edward W. Sprague, Vietnam
Richard W. Utrecht, Vietnam
Charles E. Willis, Vietnam
1973-74 Thomas J. Barnes, Vietnam
Henry B. Cushing, Vietnam
1974-75 Mark E. Mulvey, Nicosia, Cyprus
Frixos Yerolemou, Nicosia Cyprus
Group Award to American Embassy Staff, Nicosia, Cyprus
1975-76 Rached Mohamed Bahi, Tunis, Tunisia
Ted D. Morse, Addis Ababa, Ethiopia
Paul A. Struharik, Vietnam
Reinaldo Vieira-Ribeiro, Hong Kong
Group Award to Political Section (Consulate General), Asmara, Saudi Arabia
1976-77 Philip R. Cook, Jr., Nha Trang, Vietnam
Julio Correia, Luanda, Angola
William Dykes*, Beirut, Lebanon
Charles Gallagher, Beirut, Lebanon
Nicholas MacNeil, Beirut, Lebanon
Brunson McKinley, Da Nang, Vietnam
Horace H. Mitchell, Philadelphia
Dough Van Nghia, Danang, Vietnam
Kenneth N. Rogers, Angola
Sidney T. Telford, Beirut, Lebanon

Current Status Unknown

Distinguished Service Award

U.S. DEPARTMENT OF THE TREASURY
15th St. and Pennsylvania Ave., Washington, D.C. 20220
(202/376-0282)

The Distinguished Service Award is given annually for outstanding service to the Department of the Treasury by an individual or individuals not employed by the Department. The Secretary of the Treasury approves of the winners from nominees submitted. A gold medal and a certificate are presented to the recipient of the award.

1964
J. Vaughan Gary
Robert G. Rouse

1965
Frank R. Milliken

1966
William C. Decker

1967
No award

1968
Francis M. Bator
Edward M. Bernstein
Harold Boeschenstein
Bert S. Cross
Frederic G. Donner
G. Keith Funston
Kermit Gordon
Robert M. McKinney
Andre Mayer
Frank R. Milliken
Reno Odlin
David Rockefeller
Sidney J. Weinberg
Henry S. Wingate
Eugene N. Beesley
Roger M. Blough
Charles A. Coombs
Paul L. Davies
Edward R. Fried
Thomas S. Gates, Jr.
Walter W. Heller
William McChesney Martin, Jr.
Albert L. Nickerson
David Packard
Robert V. Roosa
Frazer B. Wilde

1969
Alfred Hayes
J. L. Robertson

1970
No award

1971
James M. Roche

1972-75
No awards

1976
James S. Fish

1977
Arthur M. Burns

1978
No award

1979
No award

1980
New York City Police Dept. Detective Bureau, Operation Sweep Lester E. Edmond
Donald E. Syvrud
Sam Y. Cross
Colbert I. King

USO Woman of the Year

UNITED SERVICE ORGANIZATIONS
110 E. 42nd St., New York, N.Y. 10017 (212/697-3840)

The United Service Organization annually honors a Woman of the Year at a luncheon designed as a fund-raising activity for USO projects. The recipient of the award, who is presented with jewelry, is a woman who has benefited the military, either by entertaining service personnel or in another capacity. A committee, consisting of representatives of the board of directors and the USO's Women's Division, selects the Woman of the Year.

1961 Mary Martin
1962-64 No awards
1965 Joan Crawford
1966 No award
1967 Martha Raye
1968 Pearl Bailey
1969 Gypsy Rose Lee
1970 No award
1971 No award
1972 Mrs. Dwight D. (Mamie) Eisenhower
1973 Mrs. Douglas MacArthur
1974 Helen Hayes
1975 Kitty Carlisle
1976 Mrs. Bob Hope
1977 Mrs. Gerald R. (Betty) Ford
1978 Lillian Gish
1979 Lady Bird Johnson
1980 Jane Pickens Hoving

Veterans Administration Employee of the Year

AIR FORCE ASSOCIATION
1750 Pennsylvania Ave. NW, Washington, D.C. 20006 (202/637-3300)

The Veterans Administration Employee of the Year Award is presented annually for the most outstanding performance of duty as determined by a committee from names put in nomination by individuals and organizations.

1978 **Rosalyn S. Yalow,** Senior Medical Investigator, VA Hospital, Bronx, N.Y.
Andrew V. Schally, Senior Medical Investigator, VA Hospital, New Orleans, La.
1979 **Donald Morton,** Veterans Services Division, Training Coordinator
Lydia Wilson, Veterans Benefits Counselor, VA Regional Office
1980 **Dorothy L. Starbuck,** Chief Benefits Director, Washington, D.C.

Freiherr von Stein Prize

STIFTUNG F.V.S.
Georgplatz 10, 2 Hamburg 1, Federal Republic of Germany (Tel: 33 04 00 and 33 06 00)

The Freiherr von Stein Prize, which carries a cash award of 25,000 German marks, is now given every two years to honor public service in the Federal Republic of Germany. A jury selects the winner.

1954 Klaus von Bismarck
1955 Alfred Flender
1956 Otto A. Friedrich
1957 August Schmidt
1958 Fritz Freiherr von Babo
Heinrich Blum
Friedrich Greiff
1960 Alexander Rustow
1962 Kurt Hahn
1964 Gen. Johann Adolf Graf von Kielmannsegg
Lt. Gen. Wolf Graf Baudissin
Lt. Gen. Ulrich de Maiziere
1966 Wilhelm Kaisen
1968 President Kurt Baurichter
1970 Franz Bohm
1972 Etta Grafin Waldersee
1973 Herbert Weichmann
1974 Ludwig Erhard
Alfred Muller-Armack
1976 Ludwig Raiser
1978 Werner Bahlsen
1980 Heinz Maier-Leibnitz

Federal Woman's Award

FEDERAL WOMAN'S AWARD BOARD OF TRUSTEES
c/o V. Oldham, Veterans Administration, 810 Vermont Ave. NW, Washington, D.C. 20420 (202/389-2530)

The Federal Woman's Award, which consisted of a medallion, a pendant and a certificate, was given annually to a female employee of the federal government for outstanding contributions to the efficiency and quality of government career service. Federal agencies, including the District of Columbia government, made nominations to the Board of Trustees of the Federal Woman's Award, the independent organization which selected six recipients for the honor. The Federal Woman's Award has been suspended.

1961 **Beatrice Aitchison,** Director, Transportation Research, Post Office Dept.
Ruth Elizabeth Bacon, Charge D'Affairs, American Embassy, New Zealand
Nina Kinsella, Warden, Federal Reformatory for Women
Charlotte Moore Sitterly, Physicist, Department of Commerce
Aryness Joy Wickens, Economic Adviser, Department of Labor
Rosalyn S. Yalow, Physicist and Principal Scientist, Veterans Administration Hospital, Bronx, N.Y.
1962 **Katherine W. Bracken,** Director, Office of Central American and Panamanian Affairs, Department of State
Margaret H. Brass, Chief, General Litigation Section, Department of Justice

Thelma B. Dunn, Head, Cancer Induction and Pathogenesis Section, Department of Health, Education and Welfare
Evelyn Harrison, Deputy Director, Bureau of Programs and Standards, U.S. Civil Service Commission
Allene R. Jeanes, Research Chemist, Department of Agriculture
Nancy Grace Roman, Chief of Astronomy and Solar Physics, National Aeronautics and Space Administration

1963 **Eleanor L. Makel,** Supervisory Medical Officer, Department of Health, Education and Welfare
Bessie Margolin, Associate Solicitor, Department of Labor
Katherine Mather, Chief, Petrography Section, Department of the Army
Verna C. Mohagen, Director of Personnel, Soil Conservation Service, Department of Agriculture
Blanche W. Hoyes, Air Marketing Specialist, Federal Aviation Agency
Eleanor C. Pressly, Head, Vehicles Section, National Aeronautics and Space Administration

1964 **Evelyn Anderson,** Research Scientist, Ames Research Center, National Aeronautics and Space Administration
Gertrude Blanch, Air Force Scientist, Wright-Patterson Air Force Base
Selene Gifford, Assistant Commissioner, Bureau of Indian Affairs
Elizabeth F. Messer, Assistant to the Deputy Director, Bureau of Retirement and Insurance, U.S. Civil Service Commission
Margaret Wolman Schwartz, Director, Office of Foreign Assets Control, Department of the Treasury
Patricia G. van Delden, Deputy Public Affairs Officer, Attache, American Embassy, U.S. Information Agency, Germany

1965 **Ann Z. Caracristi,** Senior Intelligence Research Analyst, National Security Agency
Elizabeth B. Drewry, Director, Franklin D. Roosevelt Library
Dorothy Morrow Gilford, Director, Mathematical Sciences Division, Department of the Navy
Carol C. Laise, Deputy Director, Office of South Asian Affairs, Department of State
Sarah E. Stewart, Head, Human Virus Studies Section, Department of Health, Education and Welfare
Penelope Hartland Thunberg, Deputy Chief, International Division, Central Intelligence Agency

1966 **Fannie M. Boyls,** Hearing Examiner, National Labor Relations Board
Stella E. Davis, Desk Officer for East and South Africa, U.S. Information Agency
Jocelyn R. Gill, Program Chief, National Aeronautics and Space Administration
Ida Craven Merriam, Assistant Commissioner for Research and Statistics, Department of Health, Education and Welfare
Irene Parsons, Assistant Administrator and Director of Personnel, Veterans Administration
Ruth G. Van Cleve, Director, Office of Territories, Department of the Interior

1967 **Elizabeth Ann Brown,** Director of the Office of the United Nations, Department of State
Barbara Moulton, Medical Officer, Federal Trade Commission
Anne Mason Roberts, Deputy Regional Administrator, New York Region, Department of Housing and Urban Development
Kathryn Grove Shipp, Research Chemist, Department of the Navy
Wilma Louise Victor, Superintendent, Intermountain Indian School, Department of the Interior
Marjorie J. Williams, Director, Pathology and Allied Sciences Service, Veterans Administration

1968 **Ruth Rogan Benerito,** Research Chemist and Investigations Leader, Department of Agriculture
Mabel Kunce Gibby, Clinical Psychologist and Coordinator of Counseling Psychology, Veterans Administration Hospital, Coral Gables, Fla.
Frances M. James, Chief Statistician, Council of Economic Advisors, Executive Office of the President
Ruby Grant Martin, Director, Operations Division, Office for Civil Rights, Department of Health, Education and Welfare
Lucille Farrier Stickel, Wildlife Research Biologist, Department of the Interior
Rogene L. Thompson, Supervisory Air Traffic Control Specialist and Crew Leader, Department of Transportation
Nina Bencich Woodside, Chief, Bureau of Chronic Disease Control, District of Columbia Department of Public Health

1969 **Mary Hughes Budenbach,** Senior Cryptologist and Deputy Group Chief, National Security Agency
Edith N. Cook, Associate Solicitor, Department of Labor
Eileen R. Donovan, Assistant Director, Office of Caribbean Affairs, Department of State
Jo Ann Smith Kinney, Supervisory Psychologist, Vision Branch, Submarine Medical Research Laboratory, Department of the Navy
Esther Christian Lawton, Assistant Director of Personnel, Department of the Treasury
Dorothy L. Starbuck, Area Field Director, Veterans Administration

1970 **Jean Apgar,** Research Chemist, Department of Agriculture
Sarah B. Glindmeyer, Chief, Bureau of Nursing, District of Columbia Department of Public Health
Margaret Pittman, Chief, Laboratory of Bacterial Products, Department of Health, Education and Welfare
Valerija B. Raulinaitis, Chief of Staff, Veterans Administration Hospital, Downey, Ill.
Naomi R. Sweeney, Assistant Director, Office of Legislative Reference, Bureau of the Budget
Margaret Joy Tibbetts, Deputy Assistant Secretary for European Affairs, Department of State

1971 **Jeanne Wilson Davis,** Staff Secretary, National Security Council
Florence Johnson Hicks, Special Assistant to the Director of Public Health, District of Columbia Dept. of Human Resources
Juanita Morris Moody, Chief, Information and Reporting Element, National Security Agency
Essie Davis Morgan, Chief, Socio-economic Rehabilitation and Staff Development, Veterans Administration
Rita M. Rapp, Subsystems Manager for Apollo Food and Personal Hygiene Items, National Aeronautics and Space Administration
Joan Raup Rosenblatt, Chief, Statistical Engineering Laboratory, Department of Commerce

1972 **Lois Albro Chatham,** Chief, Narcotics Addict Rehabilitation Branch, Department of Health, Education and Welfare
Phyllis Dixon Clemmons, Director, Suicide Prevention and Emergency Mental Health Consultation Ser-

vice, District of Columbia Department of Human Resources

Ruth M. Davis, Director, Center for Computer Sciences and Technology, Department of Commerce

Mary Harrover Ferguson, Comptroller, Office of Naval Research and Special Assistant to the Assistant Secretary for Research and Development, Department of the Navy

Ruth Mandeville Leverton, Science Advisor, Department of Agriculture

Patricia Ann McCreedy, Public Health Physician, Vientiane, Laos (Agency for International Development)

1973 **Bernice L. Bernstein,** Director, Region II, Department of Health, Education and Welfare

Marguerite S. Chang, Research Chemist, Naval Ordnance Systems Command, Department of the Navy

Janet Hart, Assistant Director, Division of Supervision and Regulations, Board of Governors of the Federal Reserve System

Marilyn E. Jacox, Research Chemist, National Bureau of Standards

Isabella L. Karle, Research Physicist, Office of Naval Research, Department of the Navy

Marjorie R. Townsend, Project Manager, Small Astronomy Satellite, Goddard Space Flight Center, National Aeronautics and Space Administration

1974 **Henriette D. Avram,** Library of Congress

Edna A. Boorady, Agency for International Development

Roselyn Payne Epps, Physician, District of Columbia Government

Brigid Gray Leventhal, Physician, National Cancer Institute

Gladys P. Rogers, Department of State

Madge Skelly, Veterans Administration

1975 **Anita F. Alpern,** Assistant Commissioner, Internal Revenue Service

Beatrice J. Dvorak, Supervisory Personel Research Psychologist, Employment and Training Administration, Department of Labor

Evans Hayward, Nuclear Physicist, National Bureau of Standards, Department of Commerce

Wilda H. Martinez, Research Chemist, Department of Agriculture

Marie U. Nylen, Chief, Laboratory of Biological Structure, National Institutes of Health

Marguerite M. Rogers, Assistant Technical Director for Systems and Head, Systems Development Department, Naval Weapons Center, China Lake, Calif.

1976 **I. Blanche Bourne,** Deputy Director of Public Health, District of Columbia Department of Human Resources

Carin Ann Clauss, Associate Solicitor for Fair Labor Standards, Department of Labor

Dorothy I. Fennell, Microbiologist, Dept. of Agriculture, North Regional Research Center, Peoria, Ill.

Marion J. Finkel, Associate Director for New Drug Evaluation, Food and Drug Administration

M. Patricia Murray, Chief, Kinesiology Research Laboratory, Veterans Administration Center, Wood, Wisc.

Joyce J. Walker, Deputy Associate Director for Economics and Government, Office of Management and Budget

Contents

Sports

Public Recreation Award
Public Relations Award
James E. Sullivan Memorial Award
Arthur Callins Toner, Jr. Memorial Award
Barron Silver Bowl Award

AMATEUR ATHLETIC UNION OF THE UNITED STATES
3400 W. 86th St., Indianapolis, Ind. 46268 (317/297-2900)

The Public Recreation Award was established to honor the outstanding leaders, generally one man and one woman, in the field of public recreation during the year.

1963 **Eugene Fuller,** Florida Association
Beryl Kelly, Central Association
1964 **Ben York,** Florida Gold Coast Association
Dorothy Boyce, Central Association
1965 **Nathan Mallison,** Florida Association
Elizabeth Falbisaner, Central Association
Hertha Goedde, New Jersey Association
1966 **Eugene Fuller,** South Carolina Association
Dorothy Boyce, Central Association
1967 **Ray Kisiah,** North Carolina Association
Lucille Wilson, Central Association
1968 **George Cron,** New Jersey Association
Arlene Illsman, Central Association
1969 **Herman Riese,** Central California Association
Ethel Stevens, Central Association
1970 **Ralph Hileman,** Missouri Valley Association
John A. Bauer, Central Association
1971 **David Scheuermann,** Southern Association
Erna Wachtel, Central Association
1972 **John Lawson,** Missouri Valley Association
1973 **George R. Hoagland,** New Jersey Association
Jane Dickens, Central Association
1974 **Dalby Shirley,** Southern Nevada Association
Betty Baldwin, Lake Erie Association
1975 **Bret McGinnis,** Ohio Association
Betty Baldwin, Lake Erie Association
1976 **Joseph B. Sharpless,** Potomac Valley Association
1977 **Morris Weissbrot,** Queens, N.Y.
1978 **Jane Devine Sims**
Marion Diehl, North Carolina Association
1979 **Grace Thuis**
William W. Cowan III
1980 **Larry E. Pressler**
No Women's Award

The Public Relations Award is awarded annually by the Public Relations Committee for outstanding public relations contribution on behalf of amateur athletes.

1966 **June Fergusson**
1967 **George Thornber**
1968 **George Thornber**
1969 **No award**
1970 **No award**
1971 **Denny Hawkins**
1972 **John B. Kelly, Jr.**
1973 **Jane Dickens**
1974 **No award**
1975 **No award**
1976 **Marvin Thomas**
1977 **"Buck" Johnson**
1978 **No award**
1979 **No award**
1980 **No award**

The AAU Media Man of the Year honors journalistic achievement and accurate presentation of AAU goals and programs.

1976 **Buck Johnson,** *Chattanooga Times*
1977 **Don Hurlburt,** *Arizona Republic* (Phoenix)
1978 **No award**
1979 **Don Criqui,** Broadcaster
Don Krone, Print journalist
1980 **Not available at press time**

The James E. Sullivan Memorial Award, which is considered the highest honor in American amateur sports, consists of a trophy given annually to the outstanding amateur athlete in the United States, based on a ballot of the media and the AAU's board of governors from nominees selected at the organization's annual convention.

1930 **Bobby Jones,** Golf
1931 **Bernard Berlinger,** Track and field
1932 **James Bausch,** Track and field
1933 **Glenn Cunningham,** Track and field
1934 **Bill Bonthron,** Track and field
1935 **Lawson Little,** Golf
1936 **Glenn Morris,** Track and field
1937 **Don Budge,** Tennis
1938 **Don Lash,** Track and field
1939 **Joseph Burk,** Crew
1940 **Greg Rice,** Track and field
1941 **Leslie McMitchell,** Track and field
1942 **Cornelius Warmerdam,** Track and field
1943 **Gil Dodds,** Track and field
1944 **Ann Curtis,** Swimming
1945 **Felix Blanchard,** Football
1946 **Arnold Tucker,** Football
1947 **Jack Kelly,** Crew
1948 **Bob Mathias,** Track and field
1949 **Dick Button,** Figure skating
1950 **Fred Wilt,** Track and field
1951 **Bob Richards,** Track and field
1952 **Horace Ashenfelter,** Track and field
1953 **Sammy Lee,** Diving
1954 **Mal Whitfield,** Track and field
1955 **Harrison Dillard,** Track and field
1956 **Patricia McCormick,** Diving
1957 **Bobby Morrow,** Track and field
1958 **Glenn Davis,** Track and field
1959 **Parry O'Brien,** Track and field
1960 **Rafer Johnson,** Track and field
1961 **Wilma Rudolph,** Track and field
1962 **James Beatty,** Track and field
1963 **John Pennel,** Track and field
1964 **Don Schollander,** Swimming
1965 **Bill Bradley,** Basketball
1966 **Jim Ryun,** Track and field
1967 **Randy Matson,** Track and field
1968 **Debbie Meyer,** Swimming
1969 **Bill Toomey,** Track and field
1970 **John Kinsella,** Swimming
1971 **Mark Spitz,** Swimming
1972 **Frank Shorter,** Track and field
1973 **Bill Walton,** Basketball
1974 **Rich Wohlhuter,** Track and field
1975 **Tim Shaw,** Swimming
1976 **Bruce Jenner,** Track and field
1977 **John Naber,** Swimming
1978 **Tracy Caulkins,** Swimming
1979 **Kurt Thomas,** Gymnastics
1980 **Eric Heiden,** Speed skating

The Arthur Callins Toner, Jr. Memorial Award annually honors distinguished registration service to the Amateur Athletic Union of the United States.

1974 **Warren Emery**
1975 **Harold W. Heller**
1976 **Charles O. Roeser**
1977 **Pincus Sober**
1978 **Ray Weakley**
1979 **Richard Harkins**
1980 **John Nagy**
Frances Kazuleski

The Barron Silver Bowl Award is annually presented to any individual who has served the Amateur Athletic Union at the national level for 50 years and has attained the age of 80.

1970 **Daniel J. Ferris**
Avery Brundage
Emil Breitkreutz
1971 **Fred Schmertz**
Al Sandell
1972 **Mrs. E. Fullard-Leo**
1973 **Edward Rosenblum**
1974 **No award**
1975 **Paul Staff**
1976 **Beth Kaufman**
1977 **Harry Hainsworth**
Ray Moore
Mrs. Charles Ornstein
1978 **Douglas F. Roby**
Robert Hoffman
Carl Hansen
1979 **Robert Grueninger**
Billy Mitchell
Ollie Downs
1980 **John Glattfelder**
Al Zahorsky
Clifford H. Buck

Masters Athlete of the Year (for active competitors in Masters Class)

1977 **Herb Anderson**

Athlete of the Year

ASSOCIATED PRESS

50 Rockefeller Plaza, New York, N.Y. 10020 (212/262-4000)

Sports editors of Associated Press member newspapers annually select the male and female Athlete of the Year from both professional and amateur ranks.

MEN

1931 **Pepper Martin,** Baseball
1932 **Gene Sarazen,** Golf
1933 **Carl Hubbell,** Baseball
1934 **Dizzy Dean,** Baseball
1935 **Joe Louis,** Boxing
1936 **Jesse Owens,** Track and field
1937 **Don Budge,** Tennis
1938 **Don Budge,** Tennis
1939 **Nile Kinnick,** Football
1940 **Tommy Harmon,** Football
1941 **Joe DiMaggio,** Baseball
1942 **Frank Sinkwich,** Football
1943 **Gunder Haegg,** Track and field
1944 **Byron Nelson,** Golf
1945 **Byron Nelson,** Golf
1946 **Glenn Davis,** Football
1947 **Johnny Lujack,** Football
1948 **Lou Boudreau,** Baseball
1949 **Leon Hart,** Football
1950 **Jim Konstanty,** Baseball
1951 **Dick Kazmaier,** Football
1952 **Bob Mathias,** Track and field, Football
1953 **Ben Hogan,** Golf
1954 **Willie Mays,** Baseball
1955 **"Hopalong" Cassady,** Football
1956 **Mickey Mantle,** Baseball
1957 **Ted Williams,** Baseball
1958 **Herb Elliott,** Track and field
1959 **Ingemar Johansson,** Boxing
1960 **Rafer Johnson,** Track and field
1961 **Roger Maris,** Baseball
1962 **Maury Wills,** Baseball
1963 **Sandy Koufax,** Baseball
1964 **Don Schollander,** Swimming
1965 **Sandy Koufax,** Baseball
1966 **Frank Robinson,** Baseball
1967 **Carl Yastrzemski,** Baseball
1968 **Denny McLain,** Baseball
1969 **Tom Seaver,** Baseball
1970 **George Blanda,** Football
1971 **Lee Trevino,** Golf
1972 **Mark Spitz,** Swimming
1973 **O.J. Simpson,** Football
1974 **Muhammad Ali,** Boxing
1975 **Fred Lynn,** Baseball
1976 **Bruce Jenner,** Track and field
1977 **Steve Cauthen,** Horse Racing
1978 **Ron Guidry,** Baseball
1979 **Willie Stargell,** Baseball
1980 **U.S. Olympic Hockey Team**

WOMEN

1931 **Helene Madison,** Swimming
1932 **Babe Didrikson,** Track and field
1933 **Helen Jacobs,** Tennis
1934 **Virginia Van Wie,** Golf
1935 **Helen Wills Moody,** Tennis
1936 **Helen Stephens,** Track and field
1937 **Katherine Rawls,** Swimming
1938 **Patty Berg,** Golf
1939 **Alice Marble,** Tennis
1940 **Alice Marble,** Tennis
1941 **Betty Hicks Newell,** Golf
1942 **Gloria Callen,** Swimming
1943 **Patty Berg,** Golf
1944 **Ann Curtis,** Swimming
1945 **Babe Didrikson Zaharias,** Golf
1946 **Babe Didrikson Zaharias,** Golf
1947 **Babe Didrikson Zaharias,** Golf
1948 **Fanny Blankers-Koen,** Track and field
1949 **Marlene Bauer,** Golf
1950 **Babe Didrikson Zaharias,** Golf
1951 **Maureen Connolly,** Tennis
1952 **Maureen Connolly,** Tennis
1953 **Maureen Connolly,** Tennis
1954 **Babe Didrikson Zaharias,** Golf
1955 **Patty Berg,** Golf
1956 **Pat McCormick,** Diving
1957 **Althea Gibson,** Tennis
1958 **Althea Gibson,** Tennis
1959 **Maria Bueno,** Tennis
1960 **Wilma Rudolph,** Track and field
1961 **Wilma Rudolph,** Track and field
1962 **Dawn Fraser,** Swimming
1963 **Mickey Wright,** Golf

1964 **Mickey Wright,** Golf
1965 **Kathy Whitworth,** Golf
1966 **Kathy Whitworth,** Golf
1967 **Billie Jean King,** Tennis
1968 **Peggy Fleming,** Figure skating
1969 **Debbie Meyer,** Swimming
1970 **Chi Cheng,** Track and field
1971 **Evonne Goolagong,** Tennis
1972 **Olga Korbut,** Gymnastics
1973 **Billie Jean King,** Tennis
1974 **Chris Evert,** Tennis
1975 **Chris Evert,** Tennis
1976 **Nadia Comaneci,** Gymnastics
1977 **Chris Evert,** Tennis
1978 **Nancy Lopez,** Golf
1979 **Tracy Austin,** Tennis
1980 **Chris Evert Lloyd,** Tennis

Honorary Membership

THE ATHLETIC INSTITUTE
200 Castlewood Dr., N. Palm Beach, Fla. 33408
(305/842-3600)

Honorary membership in the Athletic Institute and a bowl are awarded annually to those who distinguish themselves in service to athletics, physical education and recreation in the opinion of the Institute's executive committee.

1974 **G. Marvin Shutt,** Executive Director, National Sporting Goods Assn.
1975 **Carl Benkert,** President, Athletic Institute
1976 **C.C. Johnson Spink,** Editor, *The Sporting Goods Dealer*
1977 **H.W. Colburn,** President, Athletic Institute
1978-80 **No awards**

Air Canada Amateur Sports Award

AIR CANADA
1 Place Ville Marie, Montreal H3B 3P7, Que., Canada
(514/874-4390)

The Air Canada Amateur Sports Awards are made annually to honor dedication to amateur sports and consist of air transportation for participation in the winning executive's, coach's and official's sport. A selection committee chooses the recipients, who must be Canadian citizens who receive no renumeration for participation in their sports.

EXECUTIVE

1966 **Paul Hauch**, Swimming
1967 **William Tinsdale**, Skiing
1968 **William Lumsden**, Curling
1969 **Ray Getliffe**, Golf
1970 **Craig Swayze**, Rowing
1971 **Vaughan L. Baird**, Diving
1972 **Joe Kryczka**, Hockey
1973 **Lorne Flower**, Water skiing
1974 **W. Stuart Maddin**, Swimming
1975 **Norman Gloag**, Basketball
1976 **Bruce M. Taylor**, Gymnastics
1977 **Lawrence F. Strong**, Lawn tennis
1978 **G.L. Moffitt**, Squash racquets
1979 **D. Asuma**, Women's field hockey
1980 **Peter J. King**, Rowing

COACH

1973 **Lionel Pugh**, Track & field
1974 **Gordon Russell**, Boxing
1975 **Gordon Currie**, Football
1976 **Mac Hickox**, Canoeing
1977 **Andre Simard**, Gymnastics
1978 **Adrian Lavigne**, Softball
1979 **Rudy Wieler**, Rowing
1980 **Jacques Blais**, Speed skating

OFFICIAL

1977 **Thomas D. Lord**, Track & field
1978 **C.A. Letheren**, Gymnastics
1979 **M.E. Eurchuk**, Wrestling
1980 **Eugene Orschyn**, Gymnastics

Induction

CANADA'S SPORTS HALL OF FAME
Exhibition Place, Toronto, Ont. M6K 3C3, Canada
(416/575-1046)

Athletes selected annually are awarded a Lucite mounted crest and a permanent citation displayed in Canada's Sports Hall of Fame for excellence nationally and internationally in sport or for significant contributions to the development of sports.

1955 **Frank Amyot,** Paddling
Norman Baker, Basketball
Norris Bowden, Figure skating
Lou Brouillard, Boxing
Tommy (Noah Brusso) Burns, Boxing
The Bluenose, Schooner
Ethel Catherwood, High jumping
Lionel Conacher, All-round athlete
Johnny Coulon, Boxing
Louis Cyr, Weightlifting
Francis Dafoe, Figure skating
Jack Delaney, Boxing
Etienne Desmarteau, Hammer throwing
George Dixon, Boxing
Jack Guest, Sr., Sculling
George Genereux, Trap shooting
George Goulding, Walking
Charles Gorman, Speed skating
Horace "Lefty" Gwynne, Boxing
Ned Hanlan, Sculling
Doug Hepburn, Weightlifting
1956 **Albert "Frenchy" Belanger,** Boxing
Cal Bricker, Broad jumping
Eugene Brosseau, Boxing
George Brown, Sculling
Cyril Coafee, Sprints
Gerard Cote, Marathon running
Jake Gaudaur, Sculling
Robert Fulton, Samuel Hutton, George Price, Elija Ross, The Paris Crew, Rowing
Emile St. Godard, Dogsled racing
George Woolf, Jockey
1957 **Gerry Ouellette,** Rifle shooting
Robert Paul, Figure skating
Barbara Wagner, Figure skating
Donald Arnold, Walter d'Hondt, Lorne Loomer, Archie McKinnon, University of British Columbia Crew, Rowing
1958 **Marilyn Bell,** Marathon swimming

Gilmour S. Boa, Rifle shooting
Walter Ewing, Trap shooting
George "Mooney" Gibson, Baseball
Johnny Longden, Jockey
Lucille Wheeler, Skiing
1959 James A. Ball, Running
Frank S McGill, Swimming/Football
Edward "Ted" Reeve, Lacrosse/Football
George Hodgson, Swimming
Sam Langford, Boxing
Edouard "Newsy" Lalonde, Lacrosse
Tom Longboat, Marathon running
George S. Lyon, Golf
Ada Mackenzie, Golf
Howie Morenz, Hockey
Jimmy McLarnin, Boxing
Duncan McNaughton, High jumping
James Naismith, Basketball
J. Percy Page, Basketball
William "Torchy" Peden, Cycling
Bobbie Rosenfeld, Myrtle Cook, Florence Bell, Ethel Smith, Sprint relay team
Bobbie Rosenfeld, All-round athlete
William J. Roue, *Bluenose* designer
Louis Rubenstein, Marathon running
Bert Schneider, Boxing
Lou F. Scholes, Sculling
Barbara Ann Scott, Figure skating
Bill Sherring, Marathon running
Sandy Somerville, Golf
David Turner, Soccer
Captain Angus Walters, *Bluenose* Skipper
Jean Wilson, Speed skating
Jack Wright, Tennis
Joe Wright, Sr., Rowing
Joe Wright, Jr., Sculling
Percy Williams, Sprints
George Young, Swimming
Bobby Kerr, Sprints
Walter Knox, All-round athlete
Jack Purcell, Badminton
Earl Thompson, Hurdles
1960 Robert Hayward, Speedboat racing
Anne Heggtveit, Skiing
Jack Laviolette, Lacrosse
Jack McCulloch, Speed skating
Miss Supertest III, Speedboat
James Thompson, Speedboat designing
James Trifunov, Wrestling
1961 William Fitzgerald, Lacrosse
Daniel A. MacKinnon, Harness racing
Dorothy Walton, Badminton/Tennis
1962 George Herrick Duggan, Yachting
Donald Jackson, Figure skating
Maria Jelinek, Figure skating
Otto Jelinek, Figure skating
Wilbert Martel, Candlepin bowling
Marlene Stewart Streit, Golf
1963 Norval Baptie, Speed skating
R.S. McLaughlin, Horse racing
Donald McPherson, Figure skating
Gus Ryder, Swimming
1964 Douglas Anakin, Bobsledding
John Emery, Bobsledding
Victor Emery, Bobsledding
Edouard Fabre, Marathon running
George Hungerford, Rowing
Roger Jackson, Rowing
Peter Kirby, Bobsledding
Stanley Leonard, Golf
Alvin Ritchie, Hockey/Football
1965 Petra Burka, Figure skating
Patrick Joseph Lally, Lacrosse
Northern Dancer, Horse racing
Joseph Cyril O'Brien, Harness racing
Gerald Presley, Bobsledding
Michael Young, Bobsledding
1966 John O'Neil, Rowing
Peggy Seller, Synchronized swimming
R. James Speers, Horse racing
1967 Gary Cowan, Golf
Nancy Greene, Skiing
Earl McCready, Wrestling
Johnny Miles, Marathon running
1968 James Day, Equestrian team
James Elder, Equestrian team
Elmer Ferguson, Sports writing
Tom Gayford, Equestrian team
Bruce Kidd, Marathon running
Arnold Richardson, Ernie Richardson, Garnet Richardson, Wes Richardson, Curling
1969 Al Balding, Golf
Jackie Callura, Boxing
George Duthie, Administration
Herve Filion, Harness racing
George Knudson, Golf
R. A. "Bob" Porter, All-round athlete
Ken Watson, Curling
1970 Betsy Clifford, Skiing
Ron Northcott, Curling
Harry L. Price, Administration
Marjory Shedd, Badminton
1971 Donald H. "Dan" Bain, All-round athlete
George Chenier, Snooker pool
Eric Coy, Track and field
William Crothers, Track and field
Phyllis Dewar, Swimming
Harry Jerome, Sprints
Charles Mayer, Administration
Noel MacDonald, Basketball
Graydon "Blondie" Robinson, Bowling
Fred J. Robson, Speed skating
Thomas F. Ryan, Bowling
William Simpson, Soccer
Elaine Tanner, Swimming
Nick Weslock, Golf
1972 Lela Brooks, Speed skating
Desmond Burke, Marksmanship
J.W. "Jack" Hamilton, Builder
Richard "Kid" Howard, Boxing
Msgr. Athol Murray, Builder
Hilda Strike, Sprints
Walter Windeyer, Sailing
1973 George Anderson, Soccer builder
Matt Baldwin, Curling
David Bauer, Hockey builder
Victor Delamarre, Weightlifting
George Gray, Shotput
Karen Magnussen, Figure skating
Ray Mitchell, Bowling
Levi "Shorty" Rodgers, Rowing
Keith Waples, Harness racing
1974 George Athans, Jr., Waterskiing
Conrad S. Riley, Builder
Frank Stack, Speed skating
Edward P. Taylor, Builder
Frank J. Shaughnessy, Jr., Builder
1975 Yvon Durelle, Boxing
Pat Fletcher, Golf
H.R. "Bobby" Pearce, Sculls

Jack Dennett, Builder
H.A. Wilson, Speedboat racing

The following hockey players were admitted in 1975:

Jack Adams
Jean Beliveau
Hector "Toe" Blake
Frank Boucher
C.S. Campbell
Francis Clancy
Charlie Conacher
Bill Cook
Syl Apps, Sr.
Aubrey "Dit" Clapper
Charlie Gardiner
Eddie Gerard
Doug Harvey
Foster Hewitt
Gordon Howe
Dick Irvin
Leonard "Red" Kelly
Aurel Joliat
Edouard "Newsy" Lalonde
Joe Malone
Frank Nighbor
Lester Patrick
Maurice Richard
Frank Patrick
Joe Primeau
Art Ross
Terry Sawchuk
Milt Schmidt
Frank J. Selke
Eddie Shore
Joe Simpson
Conn Smythe
Nels Stewart
Fred "Cyclone" Taylor
Harvey Jackson

The following football players were admitted in 1975:

Harry Batstone
Ab Box
Joseph M. Breen
Wes Cutler
Ernest Cox
Ross Brown Craig
John DeGruchy
Eddie Emerson
A.H. "Cap" Fear
Hugh Gall
Tony Golab
Harry Griffith
G. Sydney Halter
Robert Isbister, Sr.
Russ Jackson
Eddie "Dynamite" James
Joe Krol
Normie Kwong
Smirle Lawson
Frank R. "Pep" Leadley
Percy Molson
Ted Morris
Gordon Perry
Norman Perry
S.P. "Silver" Quilty
Jeff Russel
Paul Rowe
Joseph B. Ryan
David Sprague
Hugh Stirling
Brian Timmis
Joe Tubman
Benjamin L. Simpson
Hawley "Huck" Welch

1976 **Bob Abate,** Builder
Kathy Kreiner, Skiing
Cliff Lumsdon, Swimming
Hartland MacDougall, All-round athlete
Phil Marchildon, Baseball
Lloyd Percival, Builder
W. Harold Rea, Builder
Andy Tommy, Football

1977 **Arnie Boldt,** High jump
Sylvia Burka, Speed skating
Toller Cranston, Figure skating
Sylvie Fortier, Synchronized swimming
Ralph Hutton, Swimming
Lucille Lessard, Archery
Dorothy Lidstone, Archery
Susan Nattrass, Shooting
George Orton, Track and field
The Outer Cove Crew, Rowing
John Primrose, Trapshooting
Bruce Robertson, Swimming
Doug Rogers, Judo
Cathy Townnsend, Bowling
Howard Wood, Curling

1978 **No inductees**

1979 **No inductees**

1980 **Ron Turcott,** Horse racing
Barney Hartman, Skeet shooting
Andy O'Brien, Sports writing
Sheldon Galbraith, Coaching
Ken Murray, Administration

World Trophy
Athletes of the Year
College Basketball National Championship Team
College Basketball Player of the Year
College Football Championship Team of the Year
College Football Player of the Year

CITIZENS SAVINGS ATHLETIC FOUNDATION
9800 S. Sepulveda Blvd., Los Angeles, Calif. 90045
(213/670-7550)

The World Trophy is presented each year to the foremost amateur athlete from each of the six continents, as selected by the Citizens Savings Hall board. Although the awards were not instituted until 1948, selections were dated back to 1896 for Australasia, Europe and North America and to 1920 for Africa, Asia and South-America/Caribbean, following several years of research and contacts with amateur sports authorities throughout the world.

AFRICA

1920 **Bevil Rudd (South Africa),** Track and field
1921 **B. I. C. Norton (South Africa),** Tennis
1922 **Herbert Taylor (South Africa),** Cricket

1923 **Louis Raymomd (South Africa),** Tennis
1924 **William Smith (South Africa),** Boxing
1925 **Arthur Newton (South Africa),** Distance running
1926 **Pierre Albertjin (South Africa),** Rugby
1927 **Sydney Atkinson (South Africa),** Track and field
1928 **Mohamed El Ouafi (Algeria),** Marathon
1929 **E. L. Heine (South Africa),** Tennis
1930 **Benjamin Osler (South Africa),** Rugby
1931 **Daniel J. Joubert (South Africa),** Track and field
1932 **David E. Carstens (South Africa),** Boxing
1933 **William Zeller (South Africa),** Rugby
1934 **Harry B. Hart (South Africa),** Track and field
1935 **Arthur B. Locke (South Africa),** Golf
1936 **Khadr El Touni (Egypt),** Weightlifting
1937 **Hardy R. Ballington (South Africa),** Distance running
1938 **Thomas P. Lavery (South Africa),** Track and field
1939 **Ibrahim Shams (Egypt),** Weightlifting
1940 **No selections**
1941 **No selections**
1942 **No selections**
1943 **No selections**
1944 **No selections**
1945 **Denis Shore (South Africa),** Track and field
1946 **Aaron Geffin (South Africa),** Rugby
1947 **Bruce Mitchell (South Africa),** Cricket
1948 **George Hunter (South Africa),** Boxing
1949 **Eric Sturgess (South Africa),** Tennis
1950 **Thiam Papa Gallo (French W. Africa),** Track and field
1951 **Wally Hayward (South Africa),** Distance running
1952 **Joan Harrison (South Africa),** Swimming
1953 **John Cheetham (South Africa),** Cricket
1954 **Emmanuel Ifeajuna (Nigeria),** Track and field
1955 **Jan Barnard (South Africa),** Distance running
1956 **Julius Chigbolu (Nigeria),** Track and field
1957 **Gerhardus Potgieter (South Africa),** Track and field
1958 **Grant Webster (South Africa),** Boxing
1959 **Sandra Reynolds (South Africa),** Tennis
1960 **Abebe Bikila (Ethiopia),** Marathon
1961 **Abdul Amu (Nigeria),** Track and field
1962 **Seraphino Antao (Kenya),** Track and field
1963 **George Hazle (South Africa),** Track and field
1964 **Mohamed Gammoudi (Tunisia),** Track and field
1965 **Kipchoge Keino (Kenya),** Track and field
1966 **Karen Muir (South Africa),** Swimming
1967 **Naftali Temu (Kenya),** Track and field
1968 **Mamo Wolde (Ethiopia),** Marathon
1969 **Charles Asati (Kenya),** Track and field
1970 **Philip Waruinge (Kenya),** Boxing
1971 **Eric Broberg (South Africa),** Track and field
1972 **John Akii-Bua (Uganda),** Track and field
1973 **Benjamin Jipcho (Kenya),** Track and field
1974 **Filbert Bayi (Tanzania),** Track and field
1975 **Mike Boit (Kenya),** Track and field
1976 **Jonty Skinner (South Africa),** Track and field
1977 **Miruts Yifter (Ethiopia),** Track and field
1978 **Henry Rono (Kenya),** Track and field
1979 **Suleiman Nyambui (Tanzania),** Track and field
1980 **Eshetu Tura (Ethiopia),** Track and field

ASIA

1920 **Ichiya Kumagae (Japan),** Tennis
1921 **J.K. Taduran (Philippines),** Decathlon
1922 **Zenzo Shimizu (Japan),** Tennis
1923 **Masonosuke Fukuda (Japan),** Tennis
1924 **Katsuo Takaishi (Japan),** Swimming
1925 **Takeichi Harada (Japan),** Tennis
1926 **Sekio Tawara (Japan),** Tennis
1927 **Mikio Oda (Japan),** Track and field
1928 **Yoshiyuki Tsuruta (Japan),** Swimming
1929 **Kinuye Hitomi (Japan),** Track and field
1930 **Simeon Toribio (Philippines),** Track and field
1931 **Chuhei Nambu (Japan),** Track and field
1932 **Kusuo Kitamura (Japan),** Swimming
1933 **Jiro Satoh (Japan),** Tennis
1934 **Masao Harada (Japan),** Track and field
1935 **Shozo Makino (Japan),** Swimming
1936 **Kee Chung Sohn (Japan),** Marathon
1937 **Sueo Oe (Japan),** Track and field
1938 **Tomikatsu Amano (Japan),** Swimming
1939 **Hiroshi Tanaka (Japan),** Track and field
1940 **Chengkong Kin (Japan),** Track and field
1941 **No selections**
1942 **No selections**
1943 **No selections**
1944 **No selections**
1945 **No selections**
1946 **No selections**
1947 **Yun Bok Suh (Korea),** Distance running
1948 **Duncan White (Ceylon),** Track and field
1949 **Hironoshin Furuhashi (Japan),** Swimming
1950 **Kee Yong Ham (South Korea),** Distance running
1951 **Shigeki Tanaka (Japan),** Distance running
1952 **K. D. "Babu" Singh (India),** Field hockey
1953 **Keizo Yamada (Japan),** Marathon
1954 **Shazo Sasahara (Japan),** Wrestling
1955 **Hideo Hamamura (Japan),** Marathon
1956 **Masura Furukawa (Japan),** Swimming
1957 **Takashi Ishimoto (Japan),** Swimming
1958 **Chuan-Kwang Yang (Formosa),** Track and field
1959 **Milkha Singh (India),** Track and field
1960 **Naseer Ahmad (Pakistan),** Field hockey
1961 **Tsuyoshi Yamanaka (Japan),** Swimming
1962 **Satoko Tanaka (Japan),** Swimming
1963 **Takeo Sugahara (Japan),** Track and field
1964 **Yukio Endo (Japan),** Gymnastics
1965 **Morio Shigematsu (Japan),** Marathon
1966 **Ramanathan Krishran (India),** Tennis
1967 **Kenji Kimihara (Japan),** Marathon
1968 **Sawao Katoh (Japan),** Gymnastics
1969 **Chi Cheng (Formosa),** Track and field
1970 **Ni Chih-Chin (China),** Track and field
1971 **Shigenobu Murofushi (Japan),** Track and field
1972 **Yukio Kasaya (Japan),** Skiing
1973 **Mohammed Nassiri (Iran),** Weightlifting
1974 **Shigeru Kasamatsu (Japan),** Gymnastics
1975 **Shozo Fujii (Japan),** Judo
1976 **Mitsuo Tsukahara (Japan),** Gymnastics
1977 **Yuji Takada (Japan),** Wrestling
1978 **Shigeru Sou (Japan),** Track and field
1979 **Toshihiko Seko (Japan),** N.A.
1980 **Nobuyuki Kajitani (Japan),** Gymnastics

AUSTRALIA

1896 **Edwin H. Flack (Australia),** Track and field
1897 **A. B. Sloan (Australia),** Rowing
1898 **Victor Trumper (Australia),** Cricket
1899 **Stanley R. Rowley (Australia),** Track and field
1900 **Frederick C. V. Lane (Australia),** Swimming
1901 **G. A. Moir (Australia),** Track and field
1902 **James Donald (Australia),** Rowing
1903 **Richmond Cavill (Australia),** Swimming
1904 **H. H. Hunter (Australia),** Track and field
1905 **Barney B. Kieran (Australia),** Swimming
1906 **Nigel C. Barker (Australia),** Track and field
1907 **Norman E. Brookes (Australia),** Tennis
1908 **Reginald L. Baker (Australia),** All-around
1909 **Anthony Wilding (New Zealand),** Tennis

1910 **Frank E. Beaurepaire (Australia),** Swimming
1911 **Harold Hardwick (Australia),** Swimming
1912 **Cecil Healy (Australia),** Swimming
1913 **Cecil McVilly (Australia),** Rowing
1914 **William Longworth (Australia),** Swimming
1915 **Fanny Durack (Australia),** Swimming
1916 **No selections**
1917 **No selections**
1918 **No selections**
1919 **H. C. Disher (Australia),** Rowing
1920 **Ivo H. Whitton (Australia),** Golf
1921 **Edward W. Carr (Australia),** Track and field
1922 **Gerald L. Patterson (Australia),** Tennis
1923 **Anthony Winter (Australia),** Track and field
1924 **Andrew M. Charlton (Australia),** Swimming
1925 **Victor S. Richardson (Australia),** All-around
1926 **R. Rose (New Zealand),** Track and field
1927 **Stanley Lay (New Zealand),** Track and field
1928 **H. Robert Pearce (Australia),** Rowing
1929 **James A. Carlton (Australia),** Track and field
1930 **Donald G. Bradman (Australia),** Cricket
1931 **Noel P. Ryan (Australia),** Swimming
1932 **Edgar L. Gray (Australia),** Cycling
1933 **John B. Crawford (Australia),** Tennis
1934 **John P. Metcalfe (Australia),** Track and field
1935 **Cecil H. Matthews (New Zealand),** Distance running
1936 **John E. Lovelock (New Zealand),** Track and field
1937 **Robin Biddulph (Australia),** Swimming
1938 **James B. Ferrier (Australia),** Golf
1939 **D. Brian Dunn (Australia),** Track and field
1940 **No selections**
1941 **No selections**
1942 **No selections**
1943 **No selections**
1944 **No selections**
1945 **No selections**
1946 **John Treloar (Australia),** Track and field
1947 **John A. Winter (Australia),** Track and field
1948 **Mervyn T. Wood (Australia),** Rowing
1949 **Syd Patterson (Australia),** Cycling
1950 **John B. Marshall (Australia),** Swimming
1951 **Frank A. Sedgman (Australia),** Tennis
1952 **Marjorie Jackson (Australia),** Track and field
1953 **John Landy (Australia),** Track and field
1954 **Jon Henricks (Australia),** Swimming
1955 **Shirley S. de la Hunty (Australia),** Track and field
1956 **Lorraine Crapp (Australia),** Swimming
1957 **Stuart MacKenzie (Australia),** Rowing
1958 **Herbert Elliott (Australia),** Track and field
1959 **Jon Konrads (Australia),** Swimming
1960 **Peter Snell (New Zealand),** Track and field
1961 **Dawn Fraser (Australia),** Swimming
1962 **Murray Rose (Australia),** Swimming
1963 **Tony Sneazwell (Australia),** Track and field
1964 **Betty Cuthbert (Australia),** Track and field
1965 **Ron Clarke (Australia),** Track and field
1966 **Fred Stolle (Australia),** Tennis
1967 **Judy Pollock (Australia),** Track and field
1968 **Michael Wenden (Australia),** Swimming
1969 **Pamela Kilborn (Australia),** Track and field
1970 **Kerry O'Brien (Australia),** Track and field
1971 **Shane Gould (Australia),** Swimming
1972 **Gail Neall (Australia),** Swimming
1973 **Stephan Holland (Australia),** Swimming
1974 **Jenny Turrall (Australia),** Swimming
1975 **John Walker (New Zealand),** Track and field
1976 **Dick Quax (New Zealand),** Track and field
1977 **Edward Palubinskas (Australia),** Basketball
1978 **Tracey Wickham (Australia),** Swimming
1979 **Rod Dixon (New Zealand),** N.A.
1980 **Michelle Ford (Australia),** Swimming

EUROPE

1896 **Spiridon Luis (Greece),** Marathon
1897 **William G. Grace (England),** Cricket
1898 **Reginald F. Doherty (England),** Tennis
1899 **John Ball (England),** Golf
1900 **Michel Theato (France),** Marathon
1901 **Peter J. O'Connor (Ireland),** Track and field
1902 **Joseph Binks (England),** Track and field
1903 **Hugh L. Doherty (England),** Tennis
1904 **Alfred Shrubb (England),** Track and field
1905 **Frederick S. Kelly (England),** Rowing
1906 **H. Jalmar Mellander (Sweden),** Pentathlon
1907 **Con Leahy (Ireland),** Track and field
1908 **Henry Taylor (England),** Swimming
1909 **A. W. Gore (England),** Tennis
1910 **Hannes Kolehmainen (Finland),** Distance running
1911 **Harold H. Hilton (England),** Golf
1912 **Erik V. Lemning (Sweden),** Track and field
1913 **Jean Bouin (France),** Distance running
1914 **Mrs. Lambert Chambers (England),** Golf
1915 **No selections**
1916 **No selections**
1917 **No selections**
1918 **No selections**
1919 **Jean Vermeulen (France),** Distance running
1920 **Helge Lovland (Norway),** Decathlon
1921 **Cecil Leitch (England),** Golf
1922 **Paavo Nurmi (Finland),** Distance running
1923 **Suzanne Lenglen (France),** Tennis
1924 **Willie Ritola (Finland),** Distance running
1925 **Joyce Wethered (England),** Golf
1926 **Jack Beresford, Jr. (England),** Rowing
1927 **Rene Lacoste (France),** Tennis
1928 **Paavo Yrjola (Finland),** Decathlon
1929 **Henri Cochet (France),** Tennis
1930 **Jules Ladoumegue (France),** Track and field
1931 **Klas Thunberg (Finland),** Speed skating
1932 **Jean Borotra (France),** Tennis
1933 **Matti Jarvinen (Finland),** Track and field
1934 **Hans H. Sievert (Germany),** Decathlon
1935 **Frederick J. Perry (England),** Tennis
1936 **Sonja Henie (Norway),** Figure skating
1937 **Sidney C. Wooderson (England),** Distance running
1938 **Ragnhild Hveger (Denmark),** Swimming
1939 **Taisto Maki (Finland),** Distance running
1940 **Rudolf Harbig (Germany),** Track and field
1941 **Mario Lanzi (Italy),** Track and field
1942 **Gunder Haegg (Sweden),** Distance running
1943 **Arne Andersson (Sweden),** Distance running
1944 **Verner Hardmo (Sweden),** Walking
1945 **Viljo Heino (Finland),** Distance running
1946 **Rune Gustafson (Sweden),** Distance running
1947 **Lennart Strand (Sweden),** Distance running
1948 **Fanny Blankers-Koen (Netherlands),** Track and field
1949 **Emil Zatopek (Czechoslovakia),** Distance running
1950 **Ignace Heinrich (France),** Decathlon
1951 **Adolfo Consolini (Italy),** Track and field
1952 **Joseph Barthel (Luxemburg),** Track and field
1953 **Gordon Pirie (England),** Track and field
1954 **Roger Bannister (England),** Track and field
1955 **Sandor Iharos (Hungary),** Track and field
1956 **Vladimir Kuts (USSR),** Track and field
1957 **Ron Delany (Ireland),** Track and field
1958 **Vasiliy Kuznyetsov (USSR),** Track and field
1959 **Karl Martin Lauer (Germany),** Track and field
1960 **Livio Berruti (Italy),** Track and field

1961 **Valeriy Brumel (USSR),** Track and field
1962 **Vyacheslav Ivanov (USSR),** Rowing
1963 **Tamara Press (USSR),** Track and field
1964 **Gaston Roelants (Belgium),** Track and field
1965 **Michel Jazy (France),** Track and field
1966 **Manolo Santana (Spain),** Tennis
1967 **Liesel Westermann (W. Germany),** Track and field
1968 **Jean-Claude Killy (France),** Skiing
1969 **Liese Prokop (Austria),** Track and field
1970 **Chris Papanicolaou (Greece),** Track and field
1971 **Walter Schmidt (W. Germany),** Track and field
1972 **Lasse Viren (Finland),** Track and field
1973 **Klaus Wolfermann (W. Germany),** Track and field
1974 **Irena Szewinska (Poland),** Track and field
1975 **Ludmila Turischeva (USSR),** Gymnastics
1976 **Nadia Comaneci (Rumania),** Gymnastics
Kornelia Ender (E. Germany), Swimming
1977 **Ulrike Tauber (E. Germany),** Swimming
1978 **Vladimir Yashchenko (U.S.S.R.),** Track and field
1979 **Sebastian Coe (G. Britain),** Track and field
1980 **Pietro Mennea (Italy),** Track and field

NORTH AMERICA (All U.S.A. except as noted)

1896 **Robert Garrett,** Track and field
1897 **Robert D. Wrenn,** Tennis
1898 **Juliette P. Atkinson,** Tennis
1899 **T. Truxton Hare,** Football
1900 **Alvin C. Kraenzlein,** Track and field
1901 **Charles Daly,** Football
1902 **William A. Larned,** Tennis
1903 **Walter J. Travis,** Golf
1904 **James Lightbody,** Track and field
1905 **May Sutton,** Tennis
1906 **Walter Eckersall,** Football
1907 **Martin J. Sheridan,** Track and field
1908 **Melvin Sheppard,** Track and field
1909 **Charles M. Daniels,** Swimming
1910 **Fred C. Thomson,** Track and field
1911 **Hazel Hotchkiss,** Tennis
1912 **James Thorpe,** Football, track and field
1913 **Maurice McLoughlin,** Tennis
1914 **Francis Ouimet,** Golf
1915 **Jerome D. Travers,** Golf
1916 **J. E. "Ted" Meredith,** Track and field
1917 **Molla Bjurstedt,** Tennis
1918 **Avery Brundage,** Track and field
1919 **William Johnston,** Tennis
1920 **Charles W. Paddock,** Track and field
1921 **William T. Tilden II,** Tennis
1922 **Thomas Hitchcock, Jr.,** Polo
1923 **John Weissmuller,** Swimming
1924 **Harold "Red" Grange,** Football
1925 **Ernest Nevers,** Football
1926 **Robert T. Jones,** Golf
1927 **Benjamin Oosterbaan,** Football, basketball
1928 **Percy Williams (Canada),** Track and field
1929 **Helen Wills,** Tennis
1930 **Glenna Collett,** Golf
1931 **Helene Madison,** Swimming
1932 **H. Ellsworth Vines,** Tennis
1933 **Glenn Cunningham,** Track and field
1934 **W. Lawson Little,** Golf
1935 **Jesse Owens,** Track and field
1936 **Glenn Morris,** Track and field
1937 **J. Donald Budge,** Tennis
1938 **Angelo Luisetti,** Basketball
1939 **Alice Marble,** Tennis
1940 **J. Gregory Rice,** Track and field
1941 **Robert L. Riggs,** Tennis
1942 **Cornelius Warmerdam,** Track and field
1943 **Gilbert Dodds,** Track and field
1944 **Ann Curtis,** Swimming
1945 **Glenn Davis,** Football
1946 **Pauline Betz,** Tennis
1947 **John A. Kramer,** Tennis
1948 **Robert Mathias,** Track and field
1949 **Melvin Patton,** Track and field
1950 **Richard Attlesey,** Track and field
1951 **Robert Richards,** Track and field
1952 **Horace Ashenfelter,** Track and field
1953 **Malvin Whitfield,** Track and field
1954 **Wes Santee,** Track and field
1955 **Patricia McCormick,** Diving
1956 **Parry O'Brien,** Track and field
1957 **Robert Gutowski,** Track and field
1958 **Rafer Johnson,** Track and field
1959 **Ray Norton,** Track and field
1960 **Wilma Rudolph,** Track and field
1961 **Ralph Boston,** Track and field
1962 **Terry Baker,** Football
1963 **Brian Sternberg,** Track and field
1964 **Alfred Oerter,** Track and field
1965 **Michael Garrett,** Football
1966 **James Ryun,** Track and field
1967 **J. Randel Matson,** Track and field
1968 **Robert Beamon,** Track and field
1969 **William Toomey,** Track and field
1970 **Gary Hall,** Swimming
1971 **Pat Matzdorf,** Track and field
1972 **Mark Spitz,** Swimming
1973 **Keena Rothhammer,** Swimming
1974 **Tim Shaw,** Swimming
1975 **Shirley Babashoff,** Swimming
1976 **John Naber,** Swimming
1977 **Edwin Moses,** Track and field
1978 **Rick Leach,** Football, baseball
1979 **Renaldo Nehemiah,** Track and field
1980 **Eric Heiden,** Speed skating

SOUTH AMERICA/CARIBBEAN

1920 **Juan Jorquera (Chile),** Distance running
1921 **Lewis L. Lacey (Argentina),** Polo
1922 **John B. Miles (Argentina),** Polo
1923 **J. A. E. Traill (Argentina),** Polo
1924 **Luis Brunetto (Argentina),** Track and field
1925 **Jack D. Nelson (Argentina),** Polo
1926 **Miguel Plaza (Chile),** Distance running
1927 **Erwin Gevert (Chile),** Decathlon
1928 **Alberto Zorilla (Argentina),** Swimming
1929 **Pedro J. C. Velarde (Peru),** Track and field
1930 **Arturo Kenny (Argentina),** Polo
1931 **Juan C. Zabala (Argentina),** Marathon
1932 **Santiago Lovell (Argentina),** Boxing
1933 **Lucio A. P. Castro (Brazil),** Track and field
1934 **Manuel Andrada (Argentina),** Polo
1935 **Jose Ribas (Argentina),** Distance running
1936 **Oscar Cassanovas (Argentina),** Boxing
1937 **Anita Lizana (Chile),** Tennis
1938 **Oscar Bringas (Peru),** Track and field
1939 **S. de M. Padilha (Brazil),** Track and field
1940 **Jose B. de Assis (Brazil),** Track and field
1941 **Raul Ibarra (Argentina),** Distance running
1942 **Maria Lenk (Brazil),** Swimming
1943 **Francisco Segura (Ecuador),** Tennis
1944 **Mario Gonzales (Argentina),** Golf
1945 **Elisabeth Muller (Brazil),** Track and field
1946 **Mario Recordion (Chile),** Track and field
1947 **Unrique Kistenmacher (Argentina),** Track and field
1948 **Delfo Cabrera (Argentina),** Marathon

1949 **Roberto Cavanaugh (Argentina),** Polo
1950 **Oscar Furlong (Argentina),** Basketball
1951 **Adhemar Da Silva (Brazil),** Track and field
1952 **Reinaldo Gorno (Argentina),** Distance running
1953 **Pedro Galvao (Argentina),** Swimming
1954 **Jose I. de Conceicao (Brazil),** Track and field
1955 **Oswaldo Suarez (Argentina),** Track and field
1956 **Miguel Agostini (Trinidad),** Track and field
1957 **Luis Ayala (Chile),** Tennis
1958 **Alejandro Olmedo (Peru),** Tennis
1959 **Maria Bueno (Brazil),** Tennis
1960 **Manoel Dos Santos (Brazil),** Swimming
1961 **Wlamir Marques (Brazil),** Basketball
1962 **Luis Nicolao (Argentina),** Swimming
1963 **Juan C. Dyrzka (Argentina),** Track and field
1964 **Wendell Mottley (Trinidad),** Track and field
1965 **Edwin Roberts (Trinidad),** Track and field
1966 **Alvaro Mejia (Colombia),** Track and field
1967 **Jose Fiolo (Brazil),** Swimming
1968 **Nelson Prudencio (Brazil),** Track and field
1969 **Juan Bello (Peru), Swimming**
1970 **F. A. Brito-Rodriguez (Venezuela),** Boxing
Olga de Angulo (Colombia), Swimming
1971 **Alberto Dimiddi (Argentina),** Rowing
1972 **Teofilo Stevenson (Cuba),** Boxing
1973 **Donald Quarrie (Jamaica),** Track and field
1974 **Silvio Leonard (Cuba),** Track and field
1975 **Joao Carlos de Oliveira (Brazil),** Track and field
1976 **Alberto Juantorena (Cuba),** Track and field
1977 **Alejandro Cadanas (Cuba),** Track and field
1978 **Jesse Vassallo (Puerto Rico),** Swimming
1979 **Djan Madruga (Brazil),** N.A.
1980 **Luis Delis (Cuba),** Track and field

In addition to an Athlete of the Month honor (not listed here), which involves display in the Circle of Champions in the Hall of the Athletic Foundation, Athletes of the Year are chosen for Northern and Southern California, resulting in permanent enshrinement in the Hall. The Southern California Awards were instituted in 1939 and dated back to 1900, while the Northern California awards were established in 1973 and dated back to 1890. The individuals honored receive medals.

SOUTHERN CALIFORNIA

1900 **James J. Jeffries,** Boxing
1901 **Dean Cromwell,** Football, basketball, track and field
1902 **Ralph Noble,** Football and other sports
1903 **Charles Bazata,** Football, basketball and other sports
1904 **Eustace Newton,** Baseball
John Hagerman, Track and field and other sports
1905 **May Sutton,** Tennis
1906 **Charles Parsons,** Track and field
1907 **Stanislaus Burek,** Football, baseball
1908 **Frank "Cap" Dillon,** Baseball
1909 **William Tozer,** Baseball
1910 **Fred Thompson,** Track and field, football
1911 **Walter Carlisle,** Baseball
1912 **Fred Kelly,** Track and field
1913 **Harry Kirkpatrick,** Football and other sports
1914 **Mary K. Browne,** Tennis
Sidney Foster, Football and other sports
1915 **Sam McClung,** Football and other sports
1916 **Olen Finch,** Football and other sports
1917 **Earl Cooper,** Auto racing
1918 **Bruce Kirkpatrick,** Football and other sports
1919 **Charles Paddock,** Track and field
1920 **Roy Evans,** Football and other sports
1921 **Samuel Thomson,** Track and field
1922 **Jakie May,** Baseball
1923 **Jack Dempsey,** Boxing
1924 **Clarence "Bud" Houser,** Track and field,
1925 **Morton Kaer,** Football and other sports
1926 **Arnold Statz,** Baseball
George Von Elm, Golf
1927 **Morley Drury,** Football and other sports
1928 **Jesse Mortensen,** Football, track and field, basketball
1929 **Harlow Rothert,** Football, track and field, basketball
1930 **Eric Pedley,** Polo
1931 **Frank Wykoff,** Track and field
1932 **H. Ellsworth Vines,** Tennis
1933 **Harry Hinkel,** Walking
1934 **Olin Dutra,** Golf
1935 **Floyd Vaughn,** Baseball
1936 **Louis Meyer,** Auto racing
1937 **Earle Meadows,** Track and field
William Sefton, Track and field
1938 **Henry Armstrong,** Boxing
1939 **Kenneth Washington,** Football, baseball
1940 **Alice Marble,** Tennis
1941 **Frank Albert,** Football
1942 **Frederick Schroeder,** Tennis
1943 **Manuel Ortiz,** Boxing
1944 **James Hardy,** Football, baseball
1945 **Glenn Davis,** Football and other sports
1946 **Jack Kramer,** Tennis
1947 **Ralph Kiner,** Baseball
1948 **Victoria Draves,** Diving
1949 **Melvin Patton,** Track and field
1950 **Richard Attlesey,** Track and field
1951 **Florence Chadwick,** Swimming
1952 **Malvin Whitfield,** Track and field
Cy Young, Track and field
1953 **Maureen Connolly,** Tennis
1954 **Parry O'Brien,** Track and field
1955 **Edwin "Duke" Snider,** Baseball
1956 **Patricia McCormick,** Diving
1957 **Sam Hanks,** Auto racing
1958 **Greta Andersen,** Swimming
1959 **Wally Moon,** Baseball
Larry Sherry, Baseball
1960 **Rafer Johnson,** Track and field, basketball
1961 **Jerry Barber,** Golf
1962 **Jim Beatty,** Track and field
1963 **Sandy Koufax,** Baseball
1964 **Michael Larrabee,** Track and field
1965 **Michael Garrett,** football
1966 **John Longden,** Horse racing
1967 **Gary Beban,** Football
O.J. Simpson, Football
1968 **David Jones,** Football
1969 **William Toomey,** Track and field
1970 **William Shoemaker,** Horse racing
1971 **Frank Heckl,** Swimming
1972 **Sandra Nielson,** Swimming
Merlin Olsen, Football
1973 **Nolan Ryan,** Baseball
1974 **Steve Garvey,** Baseball
1975 **Randy Jones,** Baseball
1976 **John Naber,** Swimming
1977 **Carlos Palomino,** Boxing
1978 **Darrell McHargue,** Horce racing
Jerry Robinson, Football
1979 **Charles White,** Football
1980 **Earvin Johnson,** Basketball

NORTHERN CALIFORNIA

1890 **Joe Choynski,** Boxing
1891 **Young Mitchell,** Boxing
1892 **James Corbett,** Boxing
1893 **Harry Walton,** Football, baseball
1894 **Guy Cochran,** Football
1895 **William Lange,** Baseball
1896 **Charles Fickert,** Football, track and field
1897 **Solly Smith,** Boxing
1898 **Lawrence Kaarsberg,** Football, baseball
1899 **James Hughes,** Baseball
1900 **Alfred Plaw,** Track and field
1901 **Orval Overall,** Football, baseball
1902 **James Britt,** Boxing
1903 **Francis Neil,** Boxing
1904 **Sam Berger,** Boxing
1905 **Michael Donlin,** Baseball
1906 **Harold Chase,** Baseball
1907 **Theodore Vandervoort,** Rugby, track and field
1908 **Ralph Rose,** Track and field
1909 **Harry Krause,** Baseball
1910 **Frank Bodie,** Baseball
1911 **Hazel Hotchkiss,** Tennis
1912 **Willie Ritchie,** Boxing
1913 **Maurice McLoughlin,** Tennis
1914 **William James,** Baseball
1915 **William Johnston,** Tennis
1916 **Fred Murray,** Track and field
1917 **Norman Ross,** Swimming
1918 **R. Lindley Murray,** Track and field
1919 **Harry Liversedge,** Track and field
Robert Templeton, Football, track and field
1920 **Walter Mails,** Baseball
1921 **Harold Muller,** Football, track and field
1922 **William Kamm,** Baseball
1923 **Harry Heilmann,** Baseball
1924 **Helen Wills,** Tennis
1925 **Ernest Nevers,** Football, baseball
1926 **Albert White,** Diving
1927 **Lawrence Bettencourt,** Football, baseball
1928 **Robert King,** Track and field
1929 **Frank O'Doul,** Baseball
Lewis Fonseca, Baseball
1930 **Joe Cronin,** Baseball
1931 **Alfred Banuet,** Handball
Charles Hafey, Baseball
1932 **Benjamin Eastman,** Track and field
1933 **Helen Jacobs,** Tennis
Max Baer, Boxing
1934 **W. Lawson Little,** Golf
Vernon Gomez, Baseball
1935 **Robert Clark,** Track and field
Oscar Eckhardt, Baseball
1936 **Archie Williams,** Track and field
1937 **J. Donald Budge,** Tennis
1938 **Angelo Luisetti,** Basketball
Ernest Lombardi, Baseball
1939 **Joe DiMaggio,** Baseball
1940 **Alice Marble,** Tennis
1941 **Grover Klemmer,** Track and field
1942 **Cornelius Warmerdam,** Track and field
1943 **Harold Davis,** Track and field
1944 **Ann Curtis,** Swimming
1945 **Helen Crlenkovitch,** Diving
1946 **Zoe Ann Olsen,** Diving
1947 **Margaret Osborne,** Tennis
1948 **Jack Jensen,** Football, baseball
1949 **Joe Perry,** Football
1950 **Arthur Larsen,** Tennis
1951 **William McColl,** Football
1952 **Robert Mathias,** Football, track and field
1953 **Carl Olson,** Boxing
1954 **Billy Vukovitch,** Auto racing
1955 **Harvie Ward,** Golf
1956 **Bill Russell,** Basketball
1957 **Don Bowden,** Track and field
1958 **Willie Mays,** Baseball
1959 **Ray Norton,** Track and field
1960 **Darrall Imhoff,** Basketball
1961 **Orlando Cepeda,** Baseball
1962 **Jack Sanford,** Baseball
1963 **Juan Marichal,** Baseball
1964 **Don Schollander,** Swimming
1965 **John Brodie,** Football
Tony Lema, Golf
1966 **Rick Barry,** Basketball
Gaylord Perry, Baseball
1967 **Claudia Kolb,** Swimming
Daryle Lamonica, Football
1968 **Deborah Meyer,** Swimming
1969 **Willie McCovey,** Baseball
1970 **George Blanda,** Football
Jim Plunkett, Football
1971 **Vida Blue,** Baseball
1972 **Mark Spitz,** Swimming
1973 **Johnny Miller,** Golf
1974 **Joe Rudi,** Baseball
1975 **Chuck Muncie,** Football
1976 **Bruce Jenner,** Track and field
1977 **John Lofton,** Track and field
1978 **Linda Jezek,** Swimming
1979 **Ken Margerum,** Football, track & field
1980 **Michael Norris,** Baseball

The Citizens Savings Athletic Foundation names the College Basketball National Championship Team by compiling the records to determine which team scored to the greatest degree for an over-all season, with consideration also given for postseason play in the selection. The coach's name appears with the team.

1901 **Yale,** No coach
1902 **Minnesota,** Louis Cooke
1903 **Yale,** No coach
1904 **Columbia,** No coach
1905 **Columbia,** No coach
1906 **Dartmouth,** No coach
1907 **Chicago,** Joseph Raycroft
1908 **Chicago,** Joseph Raycroft
1909 **Chicago,** Joseph Raycroft
1910 **Columbia,** Harry A. Fisher
1911 **St. John's (Brooklyn),** Claude B. Allen
1912 **Wisconsin,** Walter Meanwell
1913 **U.S. Naval Academy,** Louis P. Wenzell
1914 **Wisconsin,** Walter Meanwell
1915 **Illinois,** Ralph R. Jones
1916 **Wisconsin,** Walter Meanwell
1917 **Washington State,** J. Fred Bohler
1918 **Syracuse,** Edmund A. Dollard
1919 **Minnesota,** Louis Cooke
1920 **Pennsylvania,** Lon W. Jourdet
1921 **Pennsylvania,** Edward McNichol
1922 **Kansas,** Forrest C. Allen
1923 **Kansas,** Forrest C. Allen
1924 **North Carolina,** Norman Shepard
1925 **Princeton,** Albert Wittmer
1926 **Syracuse,** Lewis P. Andreas
1927 **Notre Dame,** George E. Keogan
1928 **Pittsburgh,** Clifford Carlson
1929 **Montana State,** Schubert Dyche
1930 **Pittsburgh,** Clifford Carlson

1931 **Northwestern,** Arthur Lonborg
1932 **Purdue,** Ward Lambert
1933 **Kentucky,** Adolph Rupp
1934 **Wyoming,** Willard Witte
1935 **New York University,** Howard Cann
1936 **Notre Dame,** George Keogan
1937 **Stanford,** John W. Bunn
1938 **Temple,** James Usilton
1939 **Long Island,** Clair F. Bee
1940 **Southern California,** Justin M. Barry
1941 **Wisconsin,** Harold E. Foster
1942 **Stanford,** Everett S. Dean
1943 **Wyoming,** Everett Shelton
1944 **U.S. Military Academy,** Edward Kelleher
1945 **Oklahoma State,** Henry P. Iba
1946 **Oklahoma State,** Henry P. Iba
1947 **Holy Cross,** Alvin F. Julian
1948 **Kentucky,** Adolph Rupp
1949 **Kentucky,** Adolph Rupp
1950 **City College of New York,** Nat Holman
1951 **Kentucky,** Adolph Rupp
1952 **Kansas,** Forrest C. Allen
1953 **Indiana,** Branch McCracken
1954 **Kentucky,** Adolph Rupp
1955 **San Francisco,** Phil Woolpert
1956 **San Francisco,** Phil Woolpert
1957 **North Carolina,** Frank McGuire
1958 **Kentucky,** Adolph Rupp
1959 **California,** Pete Newell
1960 **Ohio State,** Fred Taylor
1961 **Cincinnati,** Ed Jucker
1962 **Cincinnati,** Ed Jucker
1963 **Loyola (Chicago),** George Ireland
1964 **UCLA,** John Wooden
1965 **UCLA,** John Wooden
1966 **Texas Western,** Don Haskins
1967 **UCLA,** John Wooden
1968 **UCLA,** John Wooden
1969 **UCLA,** John Wooden
1970 **UCLA,** John Wooden
1971 **UCLA,** John Wooden
1972 **UCLA,** John Wooden
1973 **UCLA,** John Wooden
1974 **North Carolina State,** Norman Sloan
1975 **UCLA,** John Wooden
1976 **Indiana,** Bob Knight
1977 **Marquette,** Al McGuire
1978 **Kentucky,** Joe B. Hall
1979 **Michigan State,** Jud Heathcote
1980 **Louisville,** Denny Crum

COLLEGE BASKETBALL PLAYER OF THE YEAR

1905 **Chris Steinmetz,** Wisconsin
1906 **George Grebenstein,** Dartmouth
1907 **Gilmore Kinney,** Yale
1908 **Charles Keinath,** Pennsylvania
1909 **John Schommer,** Chicago
1910 **Harlan "Pat" Page,** Chicago
1911 **Theodore Kiendl,** Columbia
1912 **Otto Stangel,** Wisconsin
1913 **Eddie Calder,** St. Lawrence
1914 **Gil Halstead,** Cornell
1915 **Ernest Houghton,** Union
1916 **George Levis,** Wisconsin
1917 **Ray Woods,** Illinois
1918 **William Chandler,** Wisconsin
1919 **Erling Platou,** Minnesota
1920 **Howard Cann,** New York
1921 **George Williams,** Missouri
1922 **Charles Carney,** Illinois
1923 **Paul Endacott,** Kansas
1924 **Charles Black,** Kansas
1925 **Earl Mueller,** Colorado College
1926 **John Cobb,** North Carolina
1927 **Victor Hanson,** Syracuse
1928 **Victor Holt,** Oklahoma
1929 **John A. Thompson,** Montana State
1930 **Charles Hyatt,** Pittsburgh
1931 **Bart Carlton,** East Central Oklahoma
1932 **John Wooden,** Purdue
1933 **Forest Sale,** Kentucky
1934 **Wesley Bennett,** Westminster (Pa.)
1935 **Leroy Edwards,** Kentucky
1936 **John Moir,** Notre Dame
1937 **Angelo Luisetti,** Stanford
1938 **Angelo Luisetti,** Stanford
1939 **Chester Jaworski,** Rhode Island
1940 **George Glamack,** North Carolina
1941 **George Glamack,** North Carolina
1942 **Stan Modzelewski,** Rhode Island
1943 **George Senesky,** St. Joseph's
1944 **George Mikan,** De Paul
1945 **George Mikan,** De Paul
1946 **Robert Kurland,** Oklahoma State
1947 **Gerald Tucker,** Oklahoma
1948 **Ed Macauley,** St. Louis
1949 **Anthony Lavelli,** Yale
1950 **Paul Arizin,** Villanova
1951 **Richard Groat,** Duke
1952 **Clyde Lovellette,** Kansas
1953 **Robert Houbregs,** Washington
1954 **Tom Gola,** La Salle
1955 **Bill Russell,** San Francisco
1956 **Bill Russell,** San Francisco
1957 **Leonard Rosenbluth,** North Carolina
1958 **Elgin Baylor,** Seattle
1959 **Oscar Robertson,** Cincinnati
1960 **Oscar Robertson,** Cincinnati
1961 **Jerry Lucas,** Ohio State
1962 **Paul Hogue,** Cincinnati
1963 **Arthur Heyman,** Duke
1964 **Walter Hazzard,** U.C.L.A.
1965 **Bill Bradley,** Princeton
Gail Goodrich, U.C.L.A.
1966 **Cazzie Russell,** Michigan
1967 **Lew Alcindor,** U.C.L.A.
1968 **Lew Alcindor,** U.C.L.A.
1969 **Lew Alcindor,** U.C.L.A.
1970 **Pete Maravich,** Louisiana State
Sidney Wicks, U.C.L.A.
1971 **Sidney Wicks,** U.C.L.A.
Austin Carr, Notre Dame
1972 **Bill Walton,** U.C.L.A.
1973 **Bill Walton,** U.C.L.A.
1974 **David Thompson,** N.Caro. St.
Bill Walton, U.C.L.A.
1975 **Kevin Grevey,** Kentucky
David Meyers, U.C.L.A.
1976 **Kent Benson,** Indiana
Scott May, Indiana
1977 **Marques Johnson,** U.C.L.A.
1978 **Jack Givens,** Kentucky
1979 **Larry Bird,** Indiana State
1980 **Darrell Griffith,** Louisville

The Citizens Savings Athletic Foundation names the College Football Championship Team of the Year, based primarily on season-long play but also considering postseason play and other honors accorded to players on the team. The coach's name appears with the team, unless otherwise designated.

1883 **Yale,** Ray Tompkins, captain
1884 **Yale,** Eugene Richards, captain
1885 **Princeton,** C.M. DeCamp, captain
1886 **Yale,** Robert Corwin, captain
1887 **Yale,** Harry Beecher, captain
1888 **Yale,** Walter Camp
1889 **Princeton,** Edgar A. Poe, captain
1890 **Harvard,** George A. Stewart
George C. Adams
1891 **Yale,** Walter Camp
1892 **Yale,** Walter Camp
1893 **Princeton,** Alex Moffatt
1894 **Yale,** William C. Rhodes
1895 **Pennsylvania,** George W. Woodruff
1896 **Princeton,** Langdon Lea
1897 **Pennsylvania,** George W. Woodruff
1898 **Harvard,** W. Cameron Forbes
1899 **Harvard,** Benjamin H. Dibblee
1900 **Yale,** Malcolm L. McBride
1901 **Michigan,** Fielding H. Yost
1902 **Michigan,** Fielding H. Yost
1903 **Princeton,** A.R.T. Hillebrand
1904 **Pennsylvania,** Carl S. Williams
1905 **Chicago,** Amos Alonzo Stagg
1906 **Princeton,** William W. Roper
1907 **Yale,** William Knox
1908 **Pennsylvania,** Sol Metzger
1909 **Yale,** Howard H. Jones
1910 **Harvard,** Percy D. Haughton
1911 **Princeton,** William W. Roper
1912 **Harvard,** Percy D. Haughton
1913 **Harvard,** Percy D. Haughton
1914 **U.S. Military Academy,** Charles Daly
1915 **Cornell,** Albert H. Sharpe
1916 **Pittsburgh,** Glenn S. Warner
1917 **Georgia Tech,** John W. Heisman
1918 **Pittsburgh,** Glenn S. Warner
1919 **Harvard,** Robert Fisher
1920 **California,** Andrew L. Smith
1921 **Cornell,** Gilmour Dobie
1922 **Cornell,** Gilmour Dobie
1923 **Illinois,** Robert Zuppke
1924 **Notre Dame,** Knute K. Rockne
1925 **Alabama,** W. Wallace Wade
1926 **Alabama,** W. Wallace Wade
Stanford, Glenn S. Warner
1927 **Illinois,** Robert Zuppke
1928 **Georgia Tech,** William A. Alexander
1929 **Notre Dame,** Knute K. Rockne
1930 **Notre Dame,** Knute K. Rockne
1931 **Southern California,** Howard H. Jones
1932 **Southern California,** Howard H. Jones
1933 **Michigan,** Harry Kipke
1934 **Minnesota,** Bernard W. Bierman
1935 **Minnesota,** Bernard W. Bierman
1936 **Minnesota,** Bernard W. Bierman
1937 **California,** Leonard B. Allison
1938 **Texas Christian,** Leo R. Meyer
1939 **Texas A & M,** Homer H. Norton
1940 **Stanford,** Clark Shaughnessy
1941 **Minnesota,** Bernard W. Bierman
1942 **Wisconsin,** Harry Stuhldreher
1943 **Notre Dame,** Frank W. Leahy
1944 **U.S. Military Academy,** Earl H. Blaik
1945 **U.S. Military Academy,** Earl H. Blaik
1946 **U.S. Military Academy,** Earl H. Blaik
Notre Dame, Frank W. Leahy
1947 **Notre Dame,** Frank W. Leahy
Michigan, Herbert O. Crisler
1948 **Michigan,** Benjamin G. Oosterbaan
1949 **Notre Dame,** Frank W. Leahy
1950 **Oklahoma,** Charles Wilkinson
1951 **Michigan State,** Clarence Munn
1952 **Michigan State,** Clarence Munn
1953 **Notre Dame,** Frank W. Leahy
1954 **U.C.L.A.,** Henry R. Sanders
Ohio State, W. Woodrow Hayes
1955 **Oklahoma,** Charles Wilkinson
1956 **Oklahoma,** Charles Wilkinson
1957 **Auburn,** Ralph Jordan
1958 **Louisiana State,** Paul F. Dietzel
1959 **Syracuse,** Floyd Schwartzwalder
1960 **Washington,** James Owens
1961 **Alabama,** Paul W. Bryant
1962 **Southern California,** John McKay
1963 **Texas,** Darrell Royal
1964 **Arkansas,** Frank Broyles
1965 **Michigan State,** Hugh Daugherty
1966 **Notre Dame,** Ara Parseghian
Michigan State, Hugh Daugherty
1967 **Southern California,** John McKay
1968 **Ohio State,** W. Woodrow Hayes
1969 **Texas,** Darrell Royal
1970 **Nebraska,** Robert S. Davaney
1971 **Nebraska,** Robert S. Devaney
1972 **Southern California,** John McKay
1973 **Notre Dame,** Ara Parseghian
1974 **Oklahoma,** Barry Switzer
Southern California, John McKay
1975 **Ohio State,** W. Woodrow Hayes
Oklahoma, Barry Switzer
1976 **Pittsburgh,** John Majors
1977 **Pittsburgh,** John Majors
1978 **Alabama,** Paul "Bear" Bryant
Oklahoma, Barry Switzer
Southern California, John Robinson
1979 **Alabama,** Paul "Bear" Bryant
1980 **Georgia,** Vince Dooley

COLLEGE FOOTBALL PLAYER OF THE YEAR (B-Back, C-Center, E-End, G-Guard, T-Tackle)

1900 **Truxton Hare,** University of Pennsylvania (G)
1901 **Charles Daly,** U.S. Military Academy (B)
1902 **James Hogan,** Yale (T)
1903 **John DeWitt,** Princeton (G)
1904 **William Heston,** University of Michigan (B)
1905 **Thomas Shevlin,** Yale (E)
1906 **Walter Eckersall,** Chicago (B)
1907 **Adolph Schulz,** Michigan (C)
1908 **Walter Steffen,** Chicago (B)
1909 **Edward Coy,** Yale (B)
1910 **John Kilpatrick,** Yale (E)
1911 **Sanford White,** Princeton (E)
1912 **James Thorpe,** Carlisle (B)
1913 **Charles Brickley,** Harvard (B)
1914 **H. Hardwick,** Harvard (E)
1915 **Edward Mahan,** Harvard (B)
1916 **Elmer Oliphant,** U.S. Military Academy (B)
1917 **Wilbur Henry,** Washington-Jefferson (T)
1918 **Paul Robeson,** Rutgers (E)
1919 **Alvin McMillin,** Centre (B)
1920 **George Gipp,** Notre Dame (B)
1921 **Harold Muller,** California (E)
1922 **Harry Kipke,** Michigan (B)
1923 **George Pfann,** Cornell (B)
1924 **Harold "Red" Grange,** Illinois (B)
1925 **Ernest Nevers,** Stanford (B)
1926 **Ben Oosterbaan,** Michigan (E)

1927 **Morley Drury,** So. Calif. (B)
1928 **Christian Cagle,** U.S. Military Academy (B)
1929 **Jack Cannon,** Notre Dame (G)
1930 **Frank Carideo,** Notre Dame (B)
1931 **John Baker,** Southern California (G)
1932 **Harry Newman,** Michigan (B)
1933 **Beattie Feathers,** Tennessee (B)
1934 **Millard Howell,** Alabama (B)
1935 **Jay Berwanger,** Chicago (B)
1936 **Sammy Baugh,** Texas Christian (B)
1937 **Byron White,** Colorado (B)
1938 **Davey O'Brien,** Texas Christian (B)
1939 **Tom Harmon,** Michigan (B)
1940 **Frank Albert,** Stanford (B)
1941 **Bruce Smith,** Minnesota (B)
1942 **Frank Sinkwich,** Georgia (B)
1943 **Angelo Bertelli,** Notre Dame (B)
1944 **Glenn Davis,** U.S. Military Academy (B)
1945 **Felix Blanchard,** U.S. Military Academy (B)
1946 **Glenn Davis,** U.S. Military Academy (B)
1947 **Charles Conerly,** Mississippi (B)
1948 **Charles Bednarik,** Pennsylvania University (C)
1949 **Leon Hart,** Notre Dame (E)
1950 **Francis Bagnell,** Pennsylvania University (B)
1951 **William McColl,** Stanford (E)
1952 **Steve Meilinger,** Kentucky (E)
1953 **John Lattner,** Notre Dame (B)
1954 **Kurt Burris,** Oklahoma (C)
1955 **Howard Cassady,** Ohio St. (B)
1956 **Paul Hornung,** Notre Dame (B)
1957 **John Crow,** Texas A & M (B)
1958 **Randy Duncan,** Iowa (B)
1959 **Billy Cannon,** Louisiana State (B)
1960 **Joseph Bellino,** U.S. Naval Academy (B)
1961 **Bobby Bell,** Minnesota (T)
1962 **Terry Baker,** Oregon State (B)
1963 **Roger Staubach,** U.S. Naval Academy (B)
1964 **John Huarte,** Notre Dame (B)
1965 **Michael Garrett,** University of Southern California (B)
1966 **Steve Spurrier,** Florida (B)
1967 **Gary Beban,** U.C.L.A. (B)
1968 **O.J. Simpson,** University of Southern California (B)
1969 **Steve Owens,** Oklahoma (B)
1970 **Jim Plunkett,** Stanford (B)
1971 **Jerry Tagge,** Nebraska (B)
1972 **Johnny Rodgers,** Nebraska (B)
1973 **John Cappelletti,** Penn State (B)
1974 **Archie Griffin,** Ohio State (B)
1975 **Archie Griffin,** Ohio State (B)
1976 **Tony Dorsett,** Pittsburgh (B)
1977 **Earl Campbell,** Texas (B)
1978 **Billy Sims,** Oklahoma (B)
1979 **Charles White,** USC (B)
1980 **George Rogers,** South Carolina (B)

The Rose Bowl Football Player of the Game is selected by the Citizens Savings Hall Board and is presented with the award immediately after the annual Rose Bowl game on New Year's Day in Pasadena.

1902 **Neil Snow** (F), Michigan
1916 **Carl Deitz** (F), Washington State
1917 **John Beckett** (T), Oregon
1918 **Hollis Huntingdon** (F), Mare Island
1919 **George Halas** (E), Great Lakes
1920 **Edward Casey** (HB), Harvard
1921 **Harold Muller** (E), California
1922 **Russell Stein** (T), Washington & Jefferson
1923 **Leo Calland** (G), Southern California
1924 **Ira McKee** (Q), Navy
1925 **Elmer Layden** (F), Notre Dame
Ernest Nevers (F), Stanford
1926 **John Mack Brown** (HB), Alabama
George Wilson (HB), Washington
1927 **Fred Pickhard** (T), Alabama
1928 **Clifford Hoffman** (F), Stanford
1929 **Benjamin Lom** (HB), California
1930 **Russell Saunders** (Q), Southern California
1931 **John Campbell** (Q), Alabama
1932 **Erny Pinckert** (HB), Southern California
1933 **Homer Griffith** (Q), Southern California
1934 **Cliff Montgomery,** (Q), Columbia
1935 **Millard Howell** (HB), Alabama
1936 **James Moscrip** (E), Stanford
Keith Topping (E), Stanford
1937 **William Daddio** (E), Pittsburgh
1938 **Victor Bottari** (HB), California
1939 **Doyle Nave** (Q), Southern California
Alvin Krueger (E), Southern California
1940 **Ambrose Schindler** (Q), Southern California
1941 **Peter Kmetovic** (HB), Stanford
1942 **Donald Durdan** (HB), Oregon State
1943 **Charles Trippi** (HB), Georgia
1944 **Norman Verry** (G), Southern California
1945 **James Hardy** (Q), Southern California
1946 **Harry Gilmer** (HB), Alabama
1947 **Claude Young** (HB), Illinois
Julius Rykovich (HB), Illinois
1948 **Robert Chappius** (HB), Michigan
1949 **Frank Aschenbrenner** (HB), Northwestern
1950 **Fred Morrison** (F), Ohio State
1951 **Donald Dufek** (F), Michigan
1952 **William Tate** (HB), Illinois
1953 **Rudy Bukich** (HB), Southern California
1954 **Billy Wells** (HB), Michigan State
1955 **Dave Leggett** (Q), Ohio State
1956 **Walter Kowalczvk** (HB), Michigan State
1957 **Kenneth Ploen** (Q), Iowa
1958 **Jack Crabtree** (Q), Oregon
1959 **Bob Jeter** (HB), Iowa
1960 **Bob Schloredt** (Q), Washington
George Fleming (HB), Washaington
1961 **Bob Schloredt** (Q), Washington
1962 **Sandy Stephens** (Q), Minnesota
1963 **Pete Beathard** (Q), Southern California
Ron VanderKelen (Q), Wisconsin
1964 **Jim Grabowski** (F), Illinois
1965 **Mel Anthony** (F), Michigan
1966 **Bob Stiles** (DB), UCLA
1967 **John Charles** (DB), Purdue
1968 **O.J. Simpson** (HB), Southern California
1969 **Rex Kern** (Q), Ohio State
1970 **Bob Chandler** (FL), Southern California
1971 **Jim Plunkett** (Q), Stanford
1972 **Don Bunce** (Q), Stanford
1973 **Sam Cunningham** (F), Southern California
1974 **Cornelius Greene** (Q), Ohio State
1975 **Pat Haden** (Q), Southern California
John McKay (E), Southern California
1976 **John Sciarra** (Q), UCLA
1977 **Vince Evans** (Q), Southern California
1978 **Warren Moon** (Q), Washington
1979 **Rich Leach** (Q), Michigan
Charles White (B), Southern California
1980 **Charles White** (B), Southern California

Theodore Roosevelt Award
Silver Anniversary Top Five
Today's Top Five

NATIONAL COLLEGIATE ATHLETIC ASSOCIATION
Box 1906, Shawnee Mission, Kans. 66222 (913/384-3220)

The Theodore Roosevelt Award, the NCAA's highest honor, recognizes an individual whose distinguished career has been influenced by competitive collegiate athletics. A trophy and medal are presented to the winner.

1967 **Dwight D. Eisenhower,** General of the Army and former President of the United States
1968 **Leverett Saltonstall,** former Unites States Senator and Governor of Massachusetts
1969 **Byron R. White,** United States Supreme Court Justice
1970 **Frederick L. Hovde,** president, Purdue University
1971 **Christopher C. Kraft, Jr.,** National Aeronautics and Space Administration
1972 **Jerome H. Holland,** U.S. Ambassador to Sweden
1973 **Omar N. Bradley,** General of the Army
1974 **Jesse Owens,** Jesse Owens, Inc.
1975 **Gerald R. Ford,** President of the United States and former House Minority Leader
1976 **Thomas J. Hamilton,** Rear Admiral, U.S. Navy
1977 **Tom Bradley,** Mayor of Los Angeles
1978 **Gerald B. Zornow**
1979 **Otis Chandler**
1980 **Denton A. Cooley**

The Silver Anniversary Top Five Awards honor five former collegiate athletes 25 years after their graduation from college, based both on their collegiate years and career achievement since graduation. A medal is presented to the winners.

1973 **Ray R. Evans** (University of Kansas), bank president
John Feraro (University of Southern California), city councilman
John D. Hopper (Dickinson College), insurance consultant
Donald G. Mulder (Hope College), surgeon
Stewart L. Udall (University of Arizona), lawyer and former Cabinet Secretary
1974 **Howard H. Callaway** (United States Military Academy), Secretary of the Army
Robert S. Dorsey (Ohio State University), jet engine expert
Robert B. McCurry, Jr. (Michigan State University), vice-president Chrysler Corp.
Robert J. Robinson (Baylor University), minister
Eugene T. Rossides (Columbia University), lawyer
1975 **Robert S. Folsom** (Southern Methodist University), investor
Billy M. Jones (Vanderbilt University), president, Memphis State University
William J. Keating (University of Cincinnati), president, *Cincinnati Enquirer*
Ralph E. O'Brien (Butler University), insurance
Philip J. Ryan (U.S. Naval Academy), commander, U.S. Navy
1976 **Napolean A. Bell** (Mount Union College), attorney
Ernest Jackson Curtis (Vanderbilt University), corporate marketing
H. Samuel Greenawalt (University of Pennsylvania), banking
Ross J. Pritchard (University of Arkansas), president, Arkansas State University
Wade Roger Stinson (University of Kansas), banking
1977 **Donald E. Coleman** (Michigan State University), minority programs director, College of Osteopathic Medicine, Michigan State University
Richard W. Kazmaier (Princeton University), president, L & R Industries, Inc., and Eastern Sports Sales, Inc.
Vincent George Rhoden (Morgan State University), podiatrist and surgeon
William J. Wade (Vanderbilt University), assistant vice-president, Third National Bank
Frederick A. Yonkman (Hope College), executive vice president and general counsel, American Express Company
1978 **W. Thane Baker**
Andrew J. Kozar
Rev. Donn D. Moomaw
Lowell W. Perry
Cecil J. Silas
1979 **Charles B. Barcelona**
Paul A. Ebert
Robert L. Pettit, Jr.
Hamilton F. Richardson
Richard A. Rosenthal
1980 **Alan D. Ameche**
Richard J. Boushka
Thomas J. Gola
Larry C. Morris
John K. Twyman

The Today's Top Five Awards are presented annually to the five seniors judged to be the most outstanding, based on academic achievement and character as well as on sports accomplishments. Medals are presented to the winners.

1973 **Robert Wesley Ash** (Cornell College), football
Bruce Patrick Bannon (Pennsylvania State University), football
Blake Lynn Ferguson (Drexel University), lacrosse
Jerry Alan Heidenreich (Southern Methodist University), swimming
Sidney Allen Sink (Bowling Green State University), track and field
1974 **David A. Bladino** (University of Pittsburgh), football
Paul Douglas Collins (Illinois State), basketball
David D. Gallagher (University of Michigan), football
Gary W. Hall (Indiana University), swimming
David J. Wottle (Bowling Green State University), track and field
1975 **John R. Baiorunos** (Pennsylvania State University), football
Patrick C. Haden (University of Southern California), football
Randy L. Hall (University of Alabama), football
Jarrett T. Hubbard (University of Michigan), wrestling
Tony G. Waldrop (University of North Carolina), track and field
1976 **Marvin Lawrence Cobb** (University of Southern California), baseball and football
Archie Griffin (Ohio State University), football
Bruce Alan Hamming (Augustana College), basketball
Patrick Timothy Moore (Ohio State University), diving
John Michael Sciarra (UCLA), football
1977 **Jeffrey Dankworth** (UCLA), football

Randolph Dean (Northwestern University), football
Steven Furniss (University of Southern California), swimming
John Hencken (Stanford University), swimming
Gerald Huesken (Susquehanna University), football

1978 **Michael J. Boudreau**
Daniel R. Mackesey
John P. Naber
S. Gifford Nielsen

1979 **William Augustus Banks III**
Robert Wayne Dugas
Stephen Ray Fuller
Daniel Lee Harrigan
James Joseph Kovach

1980 **Gregory Kelser**
Paul B. McDonald
R. Scott Neilson
Steadman S. Shealy
Marc D. Wilson

Hickok Belt

HICKOK MANUFACTURING COMPANY
845 Ave. G East, Arlington, Tex. 76011 (817/640-1800)

The Hickok Belt, a trophy of gold, diamonds and other jewels last worth about $35,000, was awarded annually to the leading professional athlete of the year. A poll of 270 leading newspaper sports editors in the U.S. determined the recipient. The award has been discontinued.

1950 **Phil Rizzuto,** Baseball
1951 **Allie Reynolds,** Baseball
1952 **Rocky Marciano,** Boxing
1953 **Ben Hogan,** Golf
1954 **Willie Mays,** Baseball
1955 **Otto Graham,** Football
1956 **Mickey Mantle,** Baseball
1957 **Carmen Basilio,** Boxing
1958 **Bob Turley,** Baseball
1959 **Ingemar Johansson,** Boxing
1960 **Arnold Palmer,** Golf
1961 **Roger Maris,** Baseball
1962 **Maury Wills,** Baseball
1963 **Sandy Koufax,** Baseball
1964 **Jim Brown,** Football
1965 **Sandy Koufax,** Baseball
1966 **Frank Robinson,** Baseball
1967 **Carl Yastrzemski,** Baseball
1968 **Joe Namath,** Football
1969 **Tom Seaver,** Baseball
1970 **Brooks Robinson,** Baseball
1971 **Lee Trevino,** Golf
1972 **Steve Carlton,** Baseball
1973 **O.J. Simpson,** Football
1974 **Muhammad Ali,** Boxing
1975 **Pete Rose,** Baseball
1976 **Kenny Stabler,** Football

National Sports Award

UNITED STATES OF MEXICO, UNDER-SECRETARIAT OF YOUTH RECREATION AND SPORTS
Argentina #28, Mexico, D.F., Mexico (Tel: 512.55.93)

The Mexican National Sports Award is given annually for distinguished performance in or contributions to sports by individuals or teams. Individuals must be under 25 years of age. The winner is nominated by Mexican sports federations, organizations and similar institutions and selected by a panel of judges. The award is a gold medal and a diploma signed by the president of the Republic.

1975 **Carlos Giron,** Diving
1976 **Daniel Bautista,** 20,000-meter walk

Current Status Unknown

Seven Crowns of Sports Awards

JOSEPH E. SEAGRAM & SONS, INC.
375 Park Ave., New York, N.Y. 10022 (212/572-7000)

The $10,000 Seagram's Seven Crowns of Sports Award honors excellence in a season's competition in each of seven major professional spectator sports. A complex mathematical formula has been established to determine the top performers in both team and individual sports. In team sports, the individual player's performance is evaluated in light of to what degree it contributes to the team's accomplishment, while in individual sports, the evaluation is made on the basis of head-to-head competition with other athletes.

FOOTBALL

1975 **Otis Armstrong**
1976 **O.J. Simpson**
1977 **Walter Payton**
1978 **Earl Campbell**
1979 **Earl Campbell**
1980 **Not available at press time**

FOOTBALL—OFFENSIVE LINEMAN

1975 **Dan Dierdorf**
1976 **George Kunz**
1977 **George Kunz**
1978 **John Hannah**
1979 **Leon Gray**
1980 **Not available at press time**

FOOTBALL—DEFENSIVE PLAYER

1975 **Alan Page**
1976 **Jack Lambert**
1977 **Harvey Martin**
1978 **Randy White**
1979 **Lee Roy Selmon**
1980 **Not available at press time**

BASEBALL

1975 **Joe Morgan**
1976 **Joe Morgan**
1977 **Rod Carew**
1978 **Ron Guidry**
1979 **Fred Lynn**
1980 **Not available at press time**

TENNIS—MEN
1975 Manuel Orantes
1976 Jimmy Connors
1977 Bjorn Borg
1978 Bjorn Borg
1979 Bjorn Borg
1980 Not available at press time

TENNIS—WOMEN
1975 Chris Evert
1976 Chris Evert
1977 Chris Evert
1978 Martina Navratilova
1979 Martina Navratilova
1980 Not available at press time

GOLF—MEN
1975 Jack Nicklaus
1976 Jack Nicklaus
1977 Jack Nicklaus
1978 Tom Watson
1979 Tom Watson
1980 Not available at press time

GOLF—WOMEN
1975 Sandra Palmer
1976 JoAnne Carner
1977 Judy Rankin
1978 Nancy Lopez
1979 Nancy Lopez
1980 Not available at press time

BASKETBALL
1975 Bob McAdoo
1976 Kareem Abdul-Jabbar
1977 Bobby Jones
1978 George Gervin
1979 George Gervin
1980 Not available at press time

HOCKEY
1975 Bernie Parent
1976 Guy Lafleur
1977 Marcel Dionne
1978 Ken Dryden
1979 Guy Lafleur
1980 Not available at press time

HORSERACING
1975 Bill Shoemaker
1976 Jorge Tejeira
1977 Steve Cauthen
1978 Carrel McHargue
1979 Laffit Pincay
1980 Not available at press time

Most Valuable Player

SPORT MAGAZINE
641 Lexington Ave., New York, N.Y. 10022 (212/872-8000)

The editors of *Sport* magazine annually select the Most Valuable Player in the championship tournaments of various professional sports. The award consists of a trophy and a new car.

BASEBALL (World Series)
1955 **Johnny Podres,** Brooklyn Dodgers
1956 **Don Larsen,** New York Yankees
1957 **Lew Burdette,** Milwaukee Braves
1958 **Bob Turley,** New York Yankees
1959 **Larry Sherry,** Los Angeles Dodgers
1960 **Bobby Richardson,** New York Yankees
1961 **Whitey Ford,** New York Yankees
1962 **Ralph Terry,** New York Yankees
1963 **Sandy Koufax,** Los Angeles Dodgers
1964 **Bob Gibson,** St. Louis Cardinals
1965 **Sandy Koufax,** Los Angeles Dodgers
1966 **Frank Robinson,** Baltimore Orioles
1967 **Bob Gibson,** St. Louis Cardinals
1968 **Mickey Lolich,** Detroit Tigers
1969 **Donn Clendenon,** New York Mets
1970 **Brooks Robinson,** Baltimore Orioles
1971 **Roberto Clemente,** Pittsburgh Pirates
1972 **Gene Tenace,** Oakland A's
1973 **Reggie Jackson,** Oakland A's
1974 **Rollie Fingers,** Oakland A's
1975 **Pete Rose,** Cincinnati Reds
1976 **Johnny Bench,** Cincinnati Reds
1977 **Reggie Jackson,** New York Yankees
1978 **Bucky Dent,** New York Yankees
1979 **Willie Stargell,** Pittsburgh Pirates
1980 **Willie Stargell,** Pittsburgh Pirates

BASKETBALL (National Basketball Association Playoffs)
1969 **Jerry West,** Los Angeles Lakers
1970 **Willis Reed,** New York Knicks
1971 **Kareem Abdul-Jabbar,** Milwaukee Bucks
1972 **Wilt Chamberlain,** Los Angeles Lakers
1973 **Willis Reed,** New York Knicks
1974 **John Havlicek,** Boston Celtics
1975 **Rick Barry,** Golden State Warriors
1976 **Jojo White,** Boston Celtics
1977 **Bill Walton,** Portland Trailblazers
1978 **Wes Unseld,** Washington Bullets
1979 **Dennis Johnson,** Seattle Supersonics
1980 **Earvin "Magic" Johnson,** Los Angeles Lakers

BASKETBALL (American Basketball Association Playoffs)
1973 **George McGinnis,** Indiana Pacers
1974 **Julius Erving,** New York Nets
1975 **Artis Gilmore,** Kentucky Colonels
1976 **Julius Erving,** New York Nets

BASKETBALL (College Basketball Player of the Year)
1977 **Marques Johnson,** UCLA

FOOTBALL (National Football Association Championship Games)
1958 **Johnny Unitas,** Baltimore Colts
1959 **Johnny Unitas,** Baltimore Colts
1960 **Norm Van Brocklin,** Philadelphia Eagles
1961 **Paul Hornung,** Green Bay Packers
1962 **Ray Nitschke,** Green Bay Packers
1963 **Larry Morris,** Chicago Bears
1964 **Gary Collins,** Cleveland Browns
1965 **Jim Taylor,** Green Bay Packers

FOOTBALL (Super Bowl)
1967 **Bart Starr,** Green Bay Packers
1968 **Bart Starr,** Green Bay Packers
1969 **Joe Namath,** New York Jets
1970 **Len Dawson,** Kansas City Chiefs
1971 **Chuck Howley,** Dallas Cowboys

1972 **Roger Staubach,** Dallas Cowboys
1973 **Jake Scott,** Miami Dolphins
1974 **Larry Csonka,** Miami Dolphins
1975 **Franco Harris,** Pittsburgh Steelers
1976 **Lynn Swann,** Pittsburgh Steelers
1977 **Fred Biletnikoff,** Oakland Raiders
1978 **Randy White** and **Harvey Martin**, Dallas Cowboys
1979 **Terry Bradshaw**, Pittsburgh Steelers
1980 **Terry Bradshaw**, Pittsburgh Steelers

HOCKEY (Stanley Cup)

1971 **Ken Dryden,** Montreal Canadiens
1972 **Bobby Orr,** Boston Bruins
1973 **Yvan Cournoyer,** Montreal Canadiens
1974 **Bernie Parent,** Philadelphia Flyers
1975 **Bernie Parent,** Philadelphia Flyers
1976 **Larry Robinson,** Montreal Canadiens
1977 **Guy Lafleur,** Montreal Canadiens
1978 **Larry Robinson,** Montreal Canadiens
1979 **Bob Gainey**, Montreal Canadiens
1980 **Bryan Trottier**, New York Islanders

Man of the Year

SPORTING NEWS
1212 N. Lindbergh Blvd., St. Louis, Mo. 63132
(314/997-7111)

The editors of *The Sporting News* annually select outstanding athletes and teams in various sports as well as the Man of the Year. That latter honor, whose recipients are listed here, is given for the greatest sports accomplishment during the calendar year. A trophy is presented to the athlete selected.

1968 **Denny McLain,** Baseball
1969 **Tom Seaver,** Baseball
1970 **John Wooden,** College basketball
1971 **Lee Trevino,** Golf
1972 **Charles O. Finley,** Baseball
1973 **O.J. Simpson,** Professional football
1974 **Lou Brock,** Baseball
1975 **Archie Griffith,** College football
1976 **Lawrence O'Brien,** National Basketball Association
1977 **Steve Cauthen,** Horse racing
1978 **Ron Guidry**, Baseball
1979 **Willie Stargell**, Baseball
1980 **George Brett**, Baseball

Sportsman of the Year

SPORTS ILLUSTRATED
Time & Life Bldg., 1271 Ave. of the Americas, New York, N.Y. 10020 (212/586-1212)

The editors of *Sports Illustrated* annually select a male or female amateur or professional athlete as Sportsman of the Year, based on excellence in sport, either over an extended period or for a single, outstanding victory. The honor, therefore, is for *arete*—pure excellence. The trophy is a reproduction of a Greek amphora, or vase, with a sport motif dated at least 510 B.C.

1954 **Roger Bannister,** Track and field
1955 **Johnny Podres,** Baseball
1956 **Bobby Morrow,** Football
1957 **Stan Musial,** Baseball
1958 **Rafer Johnson,** Track and field
1959 **Ingemar Johansson,** Boxing
1960 **Arnold Palmer,** Golf
1961 **Jerry Lucas,** Basketball
1962 **Terry Baker,** Football
1963 **Pete Rozelle,** Football
1964 **Ken Venturi,** Golf
1965 **Sandy Koufax,** Baseball
1966 **Jim Ryun,** Track and field
1967 **Carl Yastrzemski,** Baseball
1968 **Bill Russell,** Basketball
1969 **Tom Seaver,** Baseball
1970 **Bobby Orr,** Hockey
1971 **Lee Trevino,** Golf
1972 **John Wooden,** Basketball coach
Billie Jean King, Tennis
1973 **Jackie Stewart,** Auto racing
1974 **Muhammad Ali,** Boxing
1975 **Pete Rose,** Baseball
1976 **Chris Evert,** Tennis
1977 **Steve Cauthen,** Horse racing
1978 **Jack Nicklaus**, Golf
1979 **Terry Bradshaw**, Football
Willie Stargell, Baseball
1980 **U.S. Olympic Hockey Team**

Pierre de Coubertin International Fair Play Trophy

UNITED NATIONS EDUCATIONAL, SCIENTIFIC AND CULTURAL ORGANIZATION
7 Place de Fontenoy, 75007 Paris, France (Tel: 976 22 54)

The Pierre de Coubertin International Fair Play Trophy, given by the International Committee for Fair Play (Comite International pour le Fair-Play, Frascati 4,00-483, Warsaw, Poland), annually recognizes the highest standards of sports spirit. The committee selects the winner, who receives a medallion/sculpture and a certificate, on the recommendation of national Olympic committees. The ceremony takes place at the UNESCO house in Paris.

1964 **Eugenio Monti** (Italy), Bobsled
1965 **Willye White** (U.S.A.), Long Jump
West Ham United (England), Soccer
Munich 60 (Federal Republic of Germany), Soccer
Isztvan Zsolt (Hungary), Soccer
1966 **Stevan Horvat** (Yugoslavia), Wrestling
1967 **Istvan Gulyas** (Hungary), Tennis
1968 **Japanese Soccer National Team** (Japan), Soccer
1969 **Pedro Zaballa** (Spain), Soccer
Francisco Buscato (Spain), Basketball
1970 **Ryszard Szurkowski** (Poland), Cycling
1971 **Meta Antenen** (Switzerland), Long Jump
1972 **Stan Smith** (U.S.A.), Tennis
Emiliano Rodriguez (Spain), Basketball
1973 **Yan Hallam, Will Moore, Mick Bennettand, Rick Evans** (England), Cycling
Bobby Charlton (England), Soccer
1974 **Claude Rovonel** (Switzerland), Karate
Lia Manoliu (Rumania), Discus
1975 **Victor Niederhoffer** (U.S.A.), Squash racquets
Bob Mathias (U.S.A.), Decathlon
Emil Zatopek (Czechoslovakia), Marathon
1976 **Jeno Kamuti** (Hungary), Fencing
1977 **Gustav Killian** (Federal Republic of Germany), Cycling

John Naber (U.S.A.), Swimming
Japanese spectators at the Volleyball World Cup (Japan), Volleyball

1978 **Gareth Edwards** (Great Britain), Rugby
Tamas Wichmann (Hungary), Canoeing

1979 **Sven Thofelt** (Sweden), Modern pentathlon
Philippe Roux (Switzerland), Motoring

1980 **Giacinto Pacchetti** (Italy), Soccer
Stanley Rous (Great Britain), Soccer

Hall of Fame Award
Today's Sportswoman Award
Contribution to Women's Sports Award

WOMEN'S SPORTS FOUNDATION
195 Moulton, San Francisco, Cal. 94123 (415/563-6266)

Induction into the Women's Sports Hall of Fame is the highest honor bestowed on sportswomen for athletic performance and continuing commitment to the development of women's sports. A unanimous vote of the nominating committee is required for induction of pioneering women who performed prior to 1960. A majority vote is required for for those who competed after 1960, and only one person from a sport is nominated annually.

HALL OF FAME PIONEER (prior to 1960)

1980 **Patty Berg**, Golf
Amelia Earhart, Aviation
Gertrud Ederle, Swimming
Althea Gibson, Tennis
Babe Didrickson Zaharias, Track and field, and golf
Eleanor Holm Whalen, Swimming

HALL OF FAME NOMINEE (since 1960)

1980 **Janet Guthrie**, Auto racing
Billie Jean King, Tennis
Wilma Rudolph, Track and field

The Today's Sportswoman Award honors outstanding amateur and professional athletes whose performance over the preceding 12 months has been exceptional. New records, new precedents, breakthroughs and/or new styles in sports are the criteria. A selection committee chooses one athlete per sport and a nominating committee chooses three professional and three amateur athletes annually.

PROFESSIONAL

1980 **Donna Adamek**, Bowling
Tracy Austin, Tennis
Nancy Lopez Melton, Golf

AMATEUR

1980 **Mary Decker**, Track and field
Nancy Lieberman, Basketball
Cynthia "Sippy" Woodhead, Swimming

The Contribution to Women's Sports Award is made to non-athletes for significant contributions to the development of women's sports. Individuals and organizations are eligible for the honor. A nominating committee selects three candidates for this honor.

1980 **Association for Intercollegiate Athletics for Women**, for leadership role in enforcing the Title IX amendment of the Equal Education Act
Bonne Bell Co., for long-time support of women's sports programs, including bicycling, long-distance running, skiing and tennis for women
Dorothy Harris, for major research projects which have dispelled myths relating for women in sports and for organizing the first National Research Congress on Women's Sports

Joe Cronin Award

AMERICAN LEAGUE OF PROFESSIONAL BASEBALL CLUBS
280 Park Ave., New York, N.Y. 10017 (212/682-7000)

The Joe Cronin Award, which consists of a trophy and two special watches, is given annually for significant achievement in baseball during the season or through a career. Member clubs nominate players for a vote by League executives.

1973 **Nolan Ryan** (California Angels), Record 383 strikeouts in season

1974 **Al Kaline** (Detroit Tigers), 3,000 hits in 22-year career

1975 **Rod Carew** (Minnesota Twins), Fourth consecutive batting championship

1976 **Jim Palmer** (Baltimore Orioles), Winner of 20 or more games in six of previous seven years; three-time Cy Young Award winner

1977 **Brooks Robinson** (Baltimore Orioles), 23-year career in which he recorded the highest field average of all third basemen (.971), played on 18 consecutive American League All-Star Teams and won 16 consecutive Golden Glove Awards for the best fielding in the League, among other honors

1978 **Jim Rice** (Boston Red Sox)
Ron Guidry (New York Yankees)

1979 **Carl Yastrzemski** (Boston Red Sox)

1980 **George Brett** (Kansas City Royals)

Induction

NATIONAL BASEBALL HALL OF FAME
Cooperstown, N.Y. 13326 (607/547-9988)

The Baseball Writers' Association of America annually elects new members of the National Baseball Hall of Fame from the ranks of retired players who were active in the Major Leagues during a period beginning 20 years before and ending five years prior to the election. Playing ability, integrity, sportsmanship, character and contributions to their teams and to the sport are considered, first by a screening committee and then by active members of the BWAA. The Committee on Veterans selects inductees active more than 25 years before. Baseball managers and executives are eligible for election, but no member of the Baseball Hall of Fame Committee may be considered while he is serving on the committee.

1936

Tyrus R. Cobb
Walter P. Johnson
Christopher Mathewson
George H. "Babe" Ruth
John P. "Honus" Wagner

1937

Morgan G. Bulkeley
Napoleon "Larry" Lajoie
Connie Mack
George Wright
Byron B. "Ban" Johnson
John J. McGraw
Tristram E. Speaker
Denton T. "Cy" Young

1938

Grover C. Alexander
Alexander J. Cartwright, Jr.
Henry Chadwick

1939

Adrian C. "Cap" Anson
Charles A. Comiskey
William B. "Buck" Ewing
William H. "Willie" Keeler
George H. Sisler
Albert G. Spalding
Edward T. Collins
William A. "Candy" Cummings
H. Louis Gehrig
Charles G. Radbourne

1942

Rogers Hornsby

1944

Kenesaw M. Landis

1945

Roger P. Bresnahan
Frederick C. Clarke
Edward J. Delahanty
Hugh A. Jennings
James H. O'Rourke
Dennis "Dan" Brouthers
James J. Collins
Hugh Duffy
Michael J. "King" Kelly
Wilbert Robinson

1946

Jesse C. Burkett
John D. Chesbro
Clark C. Griffith
Joseph J. McGinnity
Joseph B. Tinker
Edward A. Walsh
Frank L. Chance
John J. Evers
Thomas F. McCarthy
Edward S. Plank
George E. "Rube" Waddell

1947

Gordon S. "Mickey" Cochrane
Robert M. "Lefty" Grove
Frank F. Frisch
Carl O. Hubbell

1948

Herbert J. Pennock
Harold J. "Pie" Traynor

1949

Mordecai P. Brown
Charles A. "Kid" Nichols
Charles L. Gehringer

1951

James E. Foxx
Melvin T. Ott

1952

Harry E. Heilmann
Paul G. Waner

1953

Edward G. Barrow
Thomas H. Connolly
William J. Klem
Roderick J. J. "Bobby" Wallace
Charles A. "Chief" Bender
Jay H. "Dizzy" Dean
Aloyius H. Simmons
William H. "Harry" Wright

1954

William M. Dickey
William H. Terry
Walter J. "Rabbit" Maranville

1955

J. Franklin Baker
Charles L. "Gabby" Hartnett
Raymond W. Schalk
Joseph P. DiMaggio
Theodore A. Lyons
Arthur C. "Dazzy" Vance

1956

Joseph E. Cronin
Henry B. Greenberg

1957

Samuel E. Crawford
Joseph V. McCarthy

1959

Zachariah D. Wheat

1960

No inductees

1961

Max G. Carey
William R. Hamilton

1962

Robert W.A. Feller
Jack R. Robinson
William B. McKechnie
Edd J. Roush

1963

John G. Clarkson
Edgar C. "Sam" Rice
Elmer H. Flick
Eppa Rixey

1964

Lucius B. "Luke" Appling
Burleigh A. Grimes
Timothy J. Keefe
John M. Ward
Urban C. "Red" Faber
Miller J. Huggins
Henry E. "Heinie" Manush

1965

James F. "Pud" Galvin

1966

Charles D. "Casey" Stengel
Theodore S. Williams

1967

W. Branch Rickey
Lloyd J. Waner
Charles H. "Red" Ruffing

1968

Hazen S. "Kiki" Cuyler
Joseph M. Medwick
Leon A. "Goose" Goslin

1969

Roy Campanella
Waite C. Hoyt
Stanley A. Coveleski
Stanley F. Musial

1970

Louis Boudreau
Ford C. Frick
Earle B. Combs
Jesse J. "Pop" Haines

1971

David J. Bancroft
Charles J. "Chick" Hafey
Joseph J. Kelley
Leroy R. "Satchel" Paige
George M. Weiss
Jacob P. Beckley
Harry B. Hooper
Richard W. "Rube"

1972
Lawrence P. "Yogi" Berra
Vernon L. "Lefty" Gomez
Sanford Koufax
Early Wynn
Ross M. Youngs
Joshua Gibson
William Harridge
Walter F. "Buck"

1973
Roberto W. Clemente
Monford "Monte" Irvin
Warren E. Spahn
William G. Evans
George L. Kelly
Michael F. Welch

1974
James T. "Cool Papa" Bell
John B. "Jocko" Conlan
Mickey C. Mantle
James L. Bottomley
Edward C. "Whitey" Ford
Samuel L. Thompson

1975
H. Earl Averill
William J. Herman
William J. "Judy" Johnson
Stanley R. "Bucky" Harris
Ralph M. Kiner

1976
Oscar M. Charleston
R. Cal Hubbard
Frederick C. Lindstrom
Roger Connor
Robert G. Lemon
Robin E. Roberts

1977
Ernest Banks
John H. Lloyd
Amos W. Rusie
Martin Dihigo
Alfonso R. Lopez
Joseph W. Sewell

1978
Adrian Joss
Edwin L. Mathews
Leland S. "Larry" MacPhail

1979
Warren C. Giles
Lewis Wilson
Willy H. Mayes

1980
Albert W. Kaline
Edwin D. "Duke" Snider
Charles H. Klein
Thomas A. Yawkey

Major League Player of the Year

THE SPORTING NEWS
1212 N. Lindbergh, St. Louis, Mo. 63132 (314/997-7171)

The editors of *The Sporting News* annually select the outstanding baseball player of the season as the Major League Player of the Year. An engraved watch is presented to the winner.

1936 **Carl Hubbell,** New York (National League)
1937 **Johnny Allen,** Cleveland (American League)
1938 **Johnny Vander Meer,** Cincinnati (National League)
1939 **Joe DiMaggio,** New York (American League)
1940 **Bob Feller,** Cleveland (American League)
1941 **Ted Williams,** Boston (American League)
1942 **Ted Williams,** Boston (American League)
1943 **"Spud" Chandler,** New York (American League)
1944 **Marty Marion,** St. Louis (National League)
1945 **Hal Newhouser,** Detroit (American League)
1946 **Stan Musial,** St. Louis (National League)
1947 **Ted Williams,** Boston (American League)
1948 **Lou Boudreau,** Cleveland (American League)
1949 **Ted Williams,** Boston (American League)
1950 **Phil Rizzuto,** New York (American League)
1951 **Stan Musial,** St. Louis (National League)
1952 **Robin Roberts,** Philadelphia (National League)
1953 **Al Rosen,** Cleveland (American League)
1954 **Willie Mays,** New York (National League)
1955 **Duke Snider,** Brooklyn (National League)
1956 **Mickey Mantle,** New York (American League)
1957 **Ted Williams,** Boston (American League)
1958 **Bob Turley,** New York (American League)
1959 **Early Wynn,** Chicago (American League)
1960 **Bill Mazeroski,** Pittsburgh (National League)
1961 **Roger Maris,** New York (American League)
1962 **Maury Wills,** Los Angeles (National League)
Don Drysdale, Los Angeles (National League)
1963 **Sandy Koufax,** Los Angeles (National League)
1964 **Ken Boyer,** St. Louis (National League)
1965 **Sandy Koufax,** Los Angeles (National League)
1966 **Frank Robinson,** Baltimore (American League)
1967 **Carl Yastrzemski,** Boston (American League)
1968 **Denny McLain,** Detroit (American League)
1969 **Willie McCovey,** San Francisco (National League)
1970 **Johnny Bench,** Cincinnati (National League)
1971 **Joe Torre,** St. Louis (National League)
1972 **Billy Williams,** Chicago (National League)
1973 **Reggie Jackson,** Oakland (American League)
1974 **Lou Brock,** St. Louis (National League)
1975 **Joe Morgan,** Cincinnati (National League)
1976 **Joe Morgan,** Cincinnati (National League)
1977 **Rod Carew,** Minnesota (American League)
1978 **Ron Guidry,** New York (American League)
1979 **Willie Stargell,** Pittsburgh (National League)
1980 **George Brett,** Kansas City (American League)

Relief Man Award

WARNER-LAMBERT COMPANY
201 Tabor Rd., Morris Plains, N.J. 07950 (201/540-2000)

Recognizing the growing importance of the relief pitcher (or "fireman") in major league baseball, Rolaids present the Relief Man Award to the most outstanding relief pitchers in the American and National Leagues each season, based on wins and saves versus losses. The winners receive trophies.

AMERICAN LEAGUE

1976 **Bill Campbell,** Minnesota Twins
1977 **Bill Campbell,** Minnesota Twins
1978 **Rich Gossage,** New York Yankees
1979 **Jim Kern,** Texas Rangers
1980 **Don Quisenberry,** Kansas City Royals

NATIONAL LEAGUE

1976 **Rawly Eastwick,** Cincinnati Reds
1977 **Rollie Fingers,** San Diego Padres
1978 **Rollie Fingers,** San Diego Padres
1979 **Bruce Sutter,** Chicago Cubs
1980 **Rollie Fingers,** San Diego Padres

Most Valuable Player
Rookie of the Year
Cy Young Award

BASEBALL WRITERS ASSOCIATION OF AMERICA
36 Brookfield Rd., Ft. Salonga, N.Y. 11768

The association votes for the American League and National League Most Valuable Player for the baseball season. This is officially—though infrequently—called the Kenesaw M. Landis Award.

AMERICAN LEAGUE

1931 **Robert M. Grove** (Philadelphia), Pitcher
1932 **James E. Foxx** (Philadelphia), First baseman
1933 **James E. Foxx** (Philadelphia), First baseman
1934 **Gordon Cochrane** (Detroit), Catcher
1935 **Henry B. Greenburg** (Detroit), First baseman
1936 **Henry L. Gehrig** (New York), First baseman
1937 **Charles L. Gehringer** (Detroit), Second baseman
1938 **James E. Foxx** (Boston), First baseman
1939 **Joseph P. DiMaggio** (New York), Outfielder
1940 **Henry B. Greenburg** (Detroit), Outfielder
1941 **Joseph P. DiMaggio** (New York), Outfielder
1942 **Joseph L. Gordon** (New York), Second baseman
1943 **Spurgeon F. Chandler** (New York), Pitcher
1944 **Harold Newhouser** (Detroit), Pitcher
1945 **Harold Newhouser** (Detroit), Pitcher
1946 **Theodore S. Williams** (Boston), Outfielder
1947 **Joseph P. DiMaggio** (New York), Outfielder
1948 **Louis Boudreau** (Cleveland), Shortstop
1949 **Theodore S. Williams** (Boston), Outfielder
1950 **Philip F. Rizzuto** (New York), Shortstop
1951 **Lawrence P. "Yogi" Berra** (New York), Catcher
1952 **Robert C. Schantz** (Philadelphia), Pitcher
1953 **Albert C. Rosen** (Cleveland), Third baseman
1954 **Lawrence P. "Yogi" Berra** (New York), Catcher
1955 **Lawrence P. "Yogi" Berra** (New York), Catcher
1956 **Mickey C. Mantle** (New York), Outfielder
1957 **Mickey C. Mantle** (New York), Outfielder
1958 **Jack E. Jensen** (Boston), Outfielder
1959 **J. Nelson Fox** (Chicago), Second baseman
1960 **Roger E. Maris** (New York), Outfielder
1961 **Roger E. Maris** (New York), Outfielder
1962 **Mickey C. Mantle** (New York), Outfielder
1963 **Elston G. Howard** (New York), Catcher
1964 **Brooks C. Robinson** (Baltimore), Third baseman
1965 **Zoilo C. Versalles** (Minnesota), Shortstop
1966 **Frank Robinson** (Baltimore), Outfielder
1967 **Carl M. Yastrzemski** (Boston), Outfielder
1968 **Dennis D. McLain** (Detroit), Pitcher
1969 **Harmon C. Killebrew** (Minnesota), Third baseman
1970 **John W. Powell** (Baltimore), First baseman
1971 **Vida Blue** (Oakland), Pitcher
1972 **Richard A. Allen** (Chicago), Third baseman
1973 **Reggie Jackson** (Oakland), Outfielder
1974 **Jeff Burroughs** (Texas), Outfielder
1975 **Fred Lynn** (Boston), Outfielder
1976 **Thurman Munson** (New York), Catcher
1977 **Rod Carew** (Minnesota), Second baseman
1978 **Jim Rice** (Boston), Outfielder
1979 **Don Baylor** (California), First baseman
1980 **George Brett** (Kansas City), Third baseman

NATIONAL LEAGUE

1931 **Frank Frisch** (St. Louis), Second baseman
1932 **Charles H. Klein** (Philadelphia) Outfielder
1933 **Carl O. Hubbell** (New York), Pitcher
1934 **Jerome H. Dean** (St. Louis), Pitcher
1935 **Charles L. Hartnett** (Chicago), Catcher
1936 **Carl O. Hubbell** (New York), Pitcher
1937 **Joseph M. Medwick** (St. Louis), Outfielder
1938 **Ernest N. Lombardi** (Cincinnati), Catcher
1939 **William H. Walters** (Cincinnati), Pitcher
1940 **Frank A. McCormick** (Cincinnati), First baseman
1941 **Adolph L. Camilli** (Brooklyn), First baseman
1942 **Morton C. Cooper** (St. Louis), Pitcher
1943 **Stanley F. Musial** (St. Louis), Outfielder
1944 **Martin W. Marion** (St. Louis), Shortstop
1945 **Philip J. Cavarretta** (Chicago), First baseman
1946 **Stanley F. Musial** (St. Louis), First baseman
1947 **Robert I. Elliott** (Boston), Third baseman
1948 **Stanley F. Musial** (St. Louis), Outfielder
1949 **Jack R. Robinson** (Brooklyn), Second baseman
1950 **C. James Konstanty** (Philadelphia), Pitcher
1951 **Roy Campanella** (Brooklyn) Catcher
1952 **Henry J. Sauer** (Chicago), Outfield
1953 **Roy Campanella** (Brooklyn), Catcher
1954 **Willie H. Mays** (New York), Outfielder
1955 **Roy Campanella** (Brooklyn), Catcher
1956 **Donald Newcombe** (Brooklyn), Pitcher
1957 **Henry L. Aaron** (Milwaukee), Outfielder
1958 **Ernest Banks** (Chicago), Shortstop
1959 **Ernest Banks** (Chicago), Shortstop
1960 **Richard M. Groat** (Pittsburgh), Shortstop
1961 **Frank Robinson** (Cincinnati), Outfielder
1962 **Maurice M. Wills** (Los Angeles), Shortstop
1963 **Sanford Koufax** (Los Angeles), Pitcher
1964 **Kenton L. Boyer** (St. Louis), Third baseman
1965 **Willie H. Mays** (San Francisco), Outfielder
1966 **Roberto W. Clemente** (Pittsburgh), Outfielder
1967 **Orlando M. Cepeda** (St. Louis), First baseman
1968 **Robert Gibson** (St. Louis), Pitcher
1969 **Willie L. McCovey** (San Francisco), First baseman
1970 **Johnny L. Bench** (Cincinnati), Catcher
1971 **Joseph P. Torre** (St. Louis), Third baseman
1972 **Johnny L. Bench** (Cincinnati), Catcher
1973 **Pete Rose** (Cincinnati), Outfielder
1974 **Steve Garvey** (Los Angeles), First baseman
1975 **Joe Morgan** (Cincinnati), Second baseman
1976 **Joe Morgan** (Cincinnati), Second baseman
1977 **George Foster** (Cincinnati), Outfielder
1978 **Dave Parker** (Pittsburgh), Outfielder
1979 **Willie Stargell** (Pittsburgh), First baseman
1980 **Mike Schmidt, Keith Hernandez**, (St. Louis), First baseman

The Rookie of the Year selection honors one American League and one National League player as the best during the first year of major league play.

AMERICAN LEAGUE

1947 **Only one selection; see National League listing**
1948 **Only one selection; see National League listing**
1949 **Roy E. Sievers** (St. Louis), Outfielder
1950 **Walter O. Dropo** (Boston), First baseman
1951 **Gilbert J. McDougald** (New York), Third baseman
1952 **Harry G. Byrd** (Philadelphia), Pitcher
1953 **Harvey E. Kuenn** (Detroit), Shortstop
1954 **Robert A. Grim** (New York), Pitcher
1955 **Herbert J. Score** (Cleveland), Pitcher
1956 **Louis E. Aparicio** (Chicago), Shortstop
1957 **Anthony Kubek** (New York), Outfielder
1958 **Albert Pearson** (Washington), Outfielder
1959 **W. Robert Allison** (Washington), Outfielder
1960 **Ronald L. Hansen** (Baltimore), Shortstop
1961 **Donald B. Schwall** (Boston), Pitcher
1962 **Thomas M. Tresh** (New York), Shortstop

1963 **Gary C. Peters** (Chicago), Pitcher
1964 **A. Pedro Oliva** (Minnesota), Outfielder
1965 **Curtis L. Blefary** (Baltimore), Outfielder
1966 **Tommie L. Agee** (Chicago), Outfielder
1967 **Rodney C. Carew** (Minnesota), Second baseman
1968 **Stanley R. Bahnsen** (New York), Pitcher
1969 **Louis V. Piniella** (Kansas City), Outfielder
1970 **Thurman L. Munson** (New York), Catcher
1971 **C. Christopher Chambliss** (Cleveland), First baseman
1972 **Carlton E. Fisk** (Boston), Catcher
1973 **Al Bumbry** (Baltimore), Outfielder
1974 **Mike Hargrove** (Texas), First baseman
1975 **Fred Lynn** (Boston), Outfielder
1976 **Mark Fidrych** (Detroit), Pitcher
1977 **Eddie Murray** (Baltimore), Designated hitter
1978 **Lou Whitaker** (Detroit), Infielder
1979 **John Castino** (Minnesota), Infielder
1980 **Alfred Griffin** (Toronot), Infielder

NATIONAL LEAGUE

1947 **Jack R. Robinson** (Brooklyn), First baseman
1948 **Alvin R. Dark** (Boston), Shortstop
1949 **Donald Newcombe** (Brooklyn), Pitcher
1950 **Samuel Jethroe** (Boston), Outfielder
1951 **Willie H. Mays** (New York), Outfielder
1952 **Joseph Black** (Brooklyn), Pitcher
1953 **James W. Gilliam** (Brooklyn), Second baseman
1954 **Wallace W. Moon** (St. Louis), Outfielder
1955 **William C. Virdon** (St. Louis), Outfielder
1956 **Frank Robinson** (Cincinnati), Outfielder
1957 **John S. Sanford** (Philadelphia), Pitcher
1958 **Orlando M. Cepeda** (San Francisco), First baseman
1959 **Willie L. McCovey** (SanFrancisco), First baseman
1960 **Frank O. Howard** (Los Angeles), Outfielder
1961 **Billy L. Williams** (Chicago), Outfielder
1962 **Kenneth D. Hubbs** (Chicago), Second baseman
1963 **Peter E. Rose** (Cincinnati), Second baseman
1964 **Richard A. Allen** (Philadelphia), Third baseman
1965 **James K. Lefebvre** (Los Angeles), Second baseman
1966 **Tommy V. Helms** (Cincinnati), Third baseman
1967 **G. Thomas Seaver** (New York), Pitcher
1968 **Johnny L. Bench** (Cincinnati), Catcher
1969 **Ted C. Sizemore** (Los Angeles), Second baseman
1970 **Carl W. Morton** (Montreal), Pitcher
1971 **Earl C. Williams** (Atlanta), Catcher
1972 **Jonathan T. Matlack** (New York), Pitcher
1973 **Gary Matthews** (San Francisco), Outfielder
1974 **Bake McBride** (St. Louis), Outfielder
1975 **John Montefusco** (San Francisco), Pitcher
1976 **Pat Zachry** (Cincinnati), Pitcher
Butch Metzger (San Diego), Pitcher
1977 **Andre Dawson** (Montreal), Outfielder
1978 **Bob Horner** (Atlanta), Infielder
1979 **Rick Sutcliffe** (Los Angeles), Pitcher
1980 **Steve Howe** (Los Angeles), Pitcher

The Cy Young Award is awarded annually to the best pitcher in each league. Through 1966, only one award was made for both leagues

1956 **Donald Newcomb** (National League), Brooklyn
1957 **Warren E. Spahn** (National League), Milwaukee
1958 **Robert Turley** (American League), New York
1959 **Early Wynn** (American League), Chicago
1960 **Vernon Law** (National League), Pittsburgh
1961 **Edward C. Ford** (American League), New York
1962 **Donald S. Drysdale** (National League), Los Angeles
1963 **Sanford Koufax** (National League), Los Angeles
1964 **W. Dean Chance** (American League), Los Angeles
1965 **Sanford Koufax** (National League), Los Angeles
1966 **Sanford Koufax** (National League), Los Angeles

AMERICAN LEAGUE

1967 **James R. Lonborg,** Boston
1968 **Dennis D. McLain,** Detroit
1969 **Miguel A. Cuellar,** Baltimore
Dennis D. McLain, Detroit
1970 **James E. Perry,** Minnesota
1971 **Vida Blue,** Oakland
1972 **Gaylord J. Perry,** Cleveland
1973 **James Palmer,** Baltimore
1974 **James Hunter,** Oakland
1975 **James Palmer,** Baltimore
1976 **James Palmer,** Baltimore
1977 **Sparky Lyle,** New York
1978 **Ron Guidry,** New York
1979 **Mike Flanagan,** Baltimore
1980 **Steve Stone,** Baltimore

NATIONAL LEAGUE

1967 **Michael F. McCormick,** San Francisco
1968 **Robert Gibson,** St. Louis
1969 **G. Thomas Seaver,** New York
1970 **Robert Gibson,** St. Louis
1971 **Ferguson A. Jenkins,** Chicago
1972 **Steven N. Carlton,** Philadelphia
1973 **G. Thomas Seaver,** New York
1974 **Michael Marshall,** Los Angeles
1975 **G. Thomas Seaver,** New York
1976 **Randy Jones,** San Diego
1977 **Steven N. Carlton,** Philadelphia
1978 **Gaylord Perry,** San Diego
1979 **Bruce Sutter,** Chicago
1980 **Steve Carlton,** Philadelphia

Colonel Harry D. Henshel Award
Louis G. Wilke Memorial Award

AMATEUR ATHLETIC UNION OF THE UNITED STATES
3400 W. 86th St., Indianapolis, Ind. 46268 (317/297-2900)

The Colonel Harry D. Henshel Award is a trophy presented annually to the winning team in the Men's AAU National Basketball Championship.

1963 **Phillips 66**
1964 **Goodyear Wingfoots**
1965 **Armed Forces All-Stars**
1966 **Ford Mustangs**
1967 **Akron Goodyear**
1968 **Armed Forces All-Stars**
1969 **Armed Forces All-Stars**
1970 **Armed Forces All-Stars**
1971 **Armed Forces All-Stars**
1972 **Armed Forces All-Stars**
1973 **Marathon Oil**
1974 **Jacksonville, Fla., AAU**
1975 **Capitol Insulation,** Los Angeles, Calif.
1976 **Athletes in Action,** Tustin, Calif.
1977 **Armed Forces All-Stars**
1978 **Christian Youth Center,** Joliet, Ill.
1979 **Christian Youth Center,** Joliet, Ill.
1980 **Iowa City Airliners,** Iowa City, Iowa

In 1962, the Louis G. Wilke Memorial Award, was set up as the official trophy for the Most Valuable Player of the National AAU Basketball Tournament.

1954 **George Macuga,** U.S. Army

1955 **George Bales,** U.S. Marine Corps
1956 **Jim Bond,** Pasadena Mirror Glaze
1957 **Tom Meschery,** San Francisco Olympic Club
1958 **Harvey Schmidt,** D-C Truckers
1959 **Dick Boushka,** Wichita Vickers
1960 **Bob Boozer,** Peoria Cats
1961 **Horace Walker,** D-C Truckers
1962 **Gary Thompson,** Phillips "66"
1963 **Don Kojis,** Phillips "66"
1964 **Larry Brown,** Goodyear Wingfoots
1965 **Verne Benson,** Armed Forces All-Stars
1966 **Cazzie Russell,** Ford Mustangs
1967 **Harold Sergent,** Phillips "66"
1968 **Mike Barrett,** Armed Forces All-Stars
1969 **Garfield Smith,** Armed Forces All-Stars
1970 **Michael Silliman,** Armed Forces All-Stars
1971 **Darnell Hillman,** Armed Forces All-Stars
1972 **Richard Harris,** Marion-Kay
1973 **George Bryant,** Marathon Oil
1974 **Rick Coleman,** Jacksonville, Fla. AAU
1975 **Larry Hollifield,** Capitol Insulation
1976 **Irvin Kiffin,** Athletes in Action
1977 **Jyrona Ralston,** Armed Forces All-Stars
1978 **Tim Bryant,** Christian Youth Center
1979 **Allen Hardy,** Christian Youth Center
1980 **William Mayfield,** Iowa City Airliners

John W. Bunn Award
Frances P. Naismith Hall of Fame Award
Joe Lapchick Award
James A. Naismith Trophy
Induction

NAISMITH MEMORIAL BASKETBALL HALL OF FAME
Box 175, Highland Station, Springfield, Mass. 01109
(413/781-6500)

The John W. Bunn Award is given annually for outstanding contributions to basketball in particular and sports in general. The Hall of Fame board of trustees select the recipient of the silver bowl.

1973 **John W. Bunn,** Coach, author, prime mover in founding the Hall of Fame
1974 **John Wooden,** "The most successful coach ever in the history of collegiate basketball"; first at Indiana State and then at UCLA
1975 **J. Walter Kennedy,** National Basketball Assn. Commissioner
1976 **Henry P. Iba,** Collegiate coach at University of Colorado State and Oklahoma State Universities; three-time U.S. Olympic basketball coach
1977 **Clifford B. Fagan,** President of the Basketball Hall of Fame, Secretary of the National Basketball Committee of the United States and Canada, Board of Directors of the U.S. Olympic Committee, President of the Basketball Federation of the U.S.A., President of the Amateur Basketball Assn. of the U.S.A. and official of other basketball and sports organizations
1978 **Curt Gowdy,** television sportscaster
1979 **Eddie Gottlieb,** devoted entire life to basketball; founder and coach Philadelphia Shas; president, gen. mgr. Philadelphia Warriors
1980 **Arnold "Red" Auerbach,** former coach, now president and general manager of Boston Celtics

The Frances P. Naismith Hall of Fame Award honors exceptional all-round basketball ability and special qualities of character, leadership and loyalty as demonstrated by a national college senior player under six feet tall. Collegiate coaches nominate players, and the recipient is selected by a committee of basketball writers and members of the Hall of Fame board of trustees.

1969 **William C. Keller,** Purdue University
1970 **John Rinka,** Kenyon College
1971 **Charlie Johnson,** University of California at Berkeley
1972 **Scott Martin,** University of Oklahoma
1973 **Cadet Robert Sherwin,** U.S. Military Academy
1974 **Mike Robinson,** Michigan State University
1975 **Monte Towe,** North Carolina State University
1976 **Frank Alagia, Jr.,** St. John's University (Queens, N.Y.)
1977 **Jeff Jonas,** University of Utah
1978 **Mike Scheib,** Susquehanna University
1979 **Alton Byrd,** Columbia University
1980 **James D. Sweeney,** Boston College

The Joe Lapchick Award, sponsored by St. John's University of New York, is presented annually to the top senior collegiate basketball player in the country. A committee selects the winner.

1971 **Sidney Wicks,** UCLA
1972 **Travis Grant,** Kentucky State
1973 **Ernie DiGregorio,** Providence College
1974 **Bill Walton,** UCLA
1975 **David Thompson,** North Carolina State
1976 **Scott May,** Indiana
1977 **Jeff Jonas,** University of Utah
1978 **Butch Lee,** Marquette
1979 **Larry Bird,** Indiana State
1980 **Darrell Griffith,** Louisville

The James A. Naismith Trophy, sponsored by the Tip-Off Club of Atlanta, Ga., is awarded annually to the most outstanding college basketball player.

1969 **Lou Alcindor,** UCLA
1970 **Peter Mavarich,** LSU
1971 **Austin Carr,** Notre Dame
1972 **Bill Walton,** UCLA
1973 **Bill Walton,** UCLA
1974 **Bill Walton,** UCLA
1975 **David Thompson,** North Carolina State
1976 **Scott May,** Indiana
1977 **Marques Johnson,** UCLA
1978 **Butch Lee,** Marquette
1979 **Larry Bird,** Indiana State
1980 **Mark Aquirre, DePaul**

Induction into the Naismith Basketball Hall of Fame is an honor given to individuals in four categories: players retired for at least five years, coaches with at least 25 years of service, referees retired for at least five years and contributors for outstanding contributions to the sport. Nominations are screened by a committee and submitted to a 16-member honors committee. Selection is based on a 75% vote of that committee.

1959 **James Naismith,** contributor
Oswald Tower, contributor
Ralph Morgan, contributor
John J. Schommer, college player
Forrest Clare "Phog" Allen, contributor
Henry C. Carlson, coach
Luther H. Gulick, contributor
Edward J. Hickox, contributor

Charles D. Hyatt, college player
Matthew P. Kennedy, referee
Angelo Luisetti, college player
Walter E. Meanwell, coach
George L. Mikan, college player
Harold G. Olsen, contributor
Amos Alonzo Stagg, contributor
First Team, 1891
Original Celtics, team
1960 **Ernest A. Blood**, coach
Victor A. Hanson, college player
George T. Hepbron, referee
Frank W. Keaney, coach
Edward C. Macauley, college player
Branch McCracken, college player
Charles C. Murphy, college player
Henry V. Porter, contributor
John R. Wooden, player
Ward L. Lambert, coach
1961 **Forrest S. DeBernardi**, AAU player
George H. Hoyt, referee
George E. Keogan, coach
Robert A. Kurland, college player
Ernest C. Quigley, referee
John S. Roosma, college player
Leonard D. Sachs, coach
Arthur A. Schabinger, contributor
Christian Steinmetz, college player
David Tobey, contributor
Arthur L. Trester, contributor
Edward A. Wachter, pro player
David H. Walsh, referee
Bernhard Borgmann, pro player
John J. O'Brien, contributor
Andy Phillip, college player
Buffalo Germans, team
1962 **Jack McCracken**, AAU player
Frank Morgenweck, contributor
Harlan O. Page, college player
Barney Sedran, pro player
Lynn St. John, contributor
John A. Thompson, college player
1963 **Robert F. Gruenig**, AAU player
William A. Reid, contributor
New York Renaissance, team
1964 **John W. Bunn**, contributor
Harold E. Foster, college player
Nat Holman, pro player
Edward S. Irish, contributor
R. William Jones, contributor
Kenneth D. Loeffler, coach
John D. Russell, pro player
1965 **Walter A. Brown**, contributor
Paul D. Hinkle, contributor
Howard A. Hobson, coach
William G. Mokray, contributor
1966 **Everett S. Dean**, coach
Joe Lapchick, pro player
1967 **Clair F. Bee**, contributor
Howard G. Cann, coach
Amory T. Gill, coach
Alvin F. Julian, coach
1968 **Arnold J. Auerbach**, coach
Henry G. Dehnert, player
Henry P. Iba, coach
Adolph F. Rupp, coach
Charles H. Taylor, contributor
1969 **Bernard L. Carnevale**, coach
Robert E. Davies, player
1970 **Robert J. Cousy**, player
Robert L. Pettit, player
Abraham M. Saperstein, contributor
1971 **Edgar A. Diddle**, coach
Robert L. Douglas, contributor
Paul Endacott, player
Max Friedman, player
Edward Gottlieb, contributor
W.R. Clifford Wells, contributor
1972 **John Beckman**, player
Bruce Drake, coach
Arthur C. Lonborg, coach
Elmer H. Ripley, contributor
Adolph Schayes, player
John R. Wooden, coach
1973 **Harry A. Fisher**, contributor
Maurice Podoloff, contributor
Ernest J. Schmidt, player
1974 **Joseph R. Brennan**, player
Emil S. Liston, contributor
William F. Russell, player
Robert P. Vandivier, player
1975 **Thomas J. Gola**, player
Edward W. Krause, player
Harry Litwack, coach
William W. Sharman, player
1976 **Elgin Baylor**, player
Charles T. Cooper, player
Lauren Gale, player
William C. Johnson, player
Frank J. McGuire, coach
1977 **Paul J. Arizin**, player
Joseph E. Fulks, player
Clifford O. Hagen, player
John P. Nucatola, referee
James C. Pollard, player
1978 **Justin M. "Sam" Barry**, coach
Wilton N. Chamberlain, player
James E. Enright, referee
Edgar S. Hickey, coach
John B. McLendon, Jr., contributor
Raymond J. Meyer, coach
Peter F. Newell, contributor
1979 **Lester Harrison**, contributor
Jerry R. Lucas, player
Oscar P. Robertson, player
Everett F. Shelton, coach
J. Dallas Shirley, referee
Jerry A. West, player

Eastman Award

NATIONAL ASSOCIATION OF BASKETBALL COACHES
Box 175, Highland Station, Springfield, Mass. 01109
(413/781-6500)

The Eastman Award, a trophy sponsored by the Eastman Kodak Co., annually honors an outstanding college basketball player for playing ability, display of sportsmanship, significant contribution to team play, display of excellent citizenship and a maintenance of scholastic average. The association selects the winner, who becomes a member of the All-America first team.

1975 **David Thompson**, North Carolina State University
1976 **Scott May**, Indian University
1977 **Marques Johnson**, UCLA
1978 **Phil Ford**, University of North Carolina
1979 **Larry Bird**, Indian State University

1980 **Michael Brooks,** LaSalle College

Most Valuable Player Podoloff Cup
Rookie of the Year
Coach of the Year
All-Time Team

NATIONAL BASKETBALL ASSOCIATION
645 Fifth Ave., New York, N.Y. 10022 (212/826-7000)

The Podoloff Cup, named after former league Commissioner Maurice Podoloff, is given annually to the Most Valuable Player of the season, based on a vote of players on National Basketball Association teams.

1956 **Bob Pettit,** St. Louis
1957 **Bob Cousy,** Boston
1958 **Bill Russell,** Boston
1959 **Bob Pettit,** St. Louis
1960 **Wilt Chamberlain,** Philadelphia
1961 **Bill Russell,** Boston
1962 **Bill Russell,** Boston
1963 **Bill Russell,** Boston
1964 **Oscar Robertson,** Cincinnati
1965 **Bill Russell,** Boston
1966 **Wilt Chamberlain,** Philadelphia
1967 **Wilt Chamberlain,** Philadelphia
1968 **Wilt Chamberlain,** Philadelphia
1969 **Wes Unseld,** Baltimore
1970 **Willis Reed,** New York
1971 **Lew Alcindor,** Milwaukee
1972 **Kareem Abdul-Jabbar,** Milwaukee
1973 **Dave Cowens,** Boston
1974 **Kareem Abdul-Jabbar,** Milwaukee
1975 **Bob McAdoo,** Buffalo
1976 **Kareem Abdul-Jabbar,** Los Angeles
1977 **Kareem Abdul-Jabbar,** Los Angeles
1978 **Bill Walton,** Portland
1979 **Moses Malone,** Houston
1980 **Kareem Abdul-Jabbar,** Los Angeles

The writers and broadcasters who cover basketball annually vote for the Rookie of the Year for outstanding performance in the first season of NBA play. The winner receives a trophy.

1953 **Don Meineke,** Ft. Wayne
1954 **Ray Felix,** Baltimore
1955 **Bob Pettit,** Milwaukee
1956 **Maurice Stokes,** Rochester
1957 **Tom Heinsohn,** Boston
1958 **Woody Sauldsberry,** Philadelphia
1959 **Elgin Baylor,** Minneapolis
1960 **Wilt Chamberlain,** Philadelphia
1961 **Oscar Robertson,** Cincinnati
1962 **Walt Bellamy,** Chicago
1963 **Terry Dischinger,** Chicago
1964 **Jerry Lucas,** Cincinnati
1965 **Willis Reed,** New York
1966 **Rick Barry,** San Francisco
1967 **Dave Bing,** Detroit
1968 **Earl Monroe,** Baltimore
1969 **Wes Unseld,** Baltimore
1970 **Lew Alcindor,** Milwaukee
1971 **Dave Cowens,** Boston
Geoff Petrie, Portland
1972 **Sidney Wicks,** Portland
1973 **Bob McAdoo,** Buffalo
1974 **Ernie DiGregorio,** Buffalo
1975 **Keith Wilkes,** Golden State
1976 **Alvan Adams,** Phoenix
1977 **Adrian Dantley,** Buffalo
1978 **Walter Davis,** Phoenix
1979 **Phil Ford,** Kansas City
1980 **Larry Bird,** Boston

The writers and broadcasters who cover basketball annually select the Coach of the Year. The winner receives a clock.

1963 **Harry Gallatin,** St. Louis
1964 **Alex Hannum,** San Francisco
1965 **Red Auerbach,** Boston
1966 **Dolph Schayes,** Philadelphia
1967 **Johnny Kerr,** Chicago
1968 **Richie Guerin,** St. Louis
1969 **Gene Shue,** Baltimore
1970 **Red Holzman,** New York
1971 **Dick Motta,** Chicago
1972 **Bill Sharman,** Los Angeles
1973 **Tom Heinsohn,** Boston
1974 **Ray Scott,** Detroit
1975 **Phil Johnson,** K.C.-Omaha
1976 **Bill Fitch,** Cleveland
1977 **Tom Nissalke,** Houston
1978 **Hubie Brown,** Atlanta
1979 **Cotton Fitzsimmons,** Kansas City
1980 **Bill Fitch,** Boston

Until the merger of the American Basketball Association into the National Basketball Association, comparable awards were made in that league as well.

MOST VALUABLE PLAYER

1968 **Connie Hawkins,** Pittsburgh
1969 **Mel Daniels,** Indiana
1970 **Spencer Haywood,** Denver
1971 **Mel Daniels,** Indiana
1972 **Artis Gilmore,** Kentucky
1973 **Billy Cunningham,** Carolina
1974 **Julius Erving,** New York
1975 **George McGinnis,** Indiana
Julius Erving, New York
1976 **Julius Erving,** New York

ROOKIE OF THE YEAR

1968 **Mel Daniels,** Minnesota
1969 **Warren Armstrong,** Oakland
1970 **Spencer Haywood,** Denver
1971 **Charlie Scott,** Virginia
Dan Issel, Kentucky
1972 **Artis Gilmore,** Kentucky
1973 **Brian Taylor,** New York
1974 **Swen Nater,** San Antonio
1975 **Marvin Barnes,** St. Louis
1976 **David Thompson,** Denver

COACH OF THE YEAR

1968 **Vince Cazetta,** Pittsburgh
1969 **Alex Hannum,** Oakland
1970 **Bill Sharman,** Los Angeles
Joe Belmont, Denver
1971 **Al Bianchi,** Virginia
1972 **Tom Nissalke,** Dallas
1973 **Larry Brown,** Carolina
1974 **Babe McCarthy,** Kentucky
Joe Mullaney, Utah
1975 **Larry Brown,** Denver
1976 **Larry Brown,** Denver

To celebrate its 35th anniversary, the NBA named an All-Time Team of exceptional professional players selected by a poll of the Professional Basketball Writers of America.

1980 **Bill Russell**
John Havlicek
Oscar Robertson
Bob Pettit
Wilt Chamberlain
Bob Cousy
Jerry West
Elgin Baylor
George Mikan
Kareem Abdul-Jabbar
Julius Irving

Margaret Wade Trophy Coach of the Year

STAYFREE WOMEN IN SPORTS PROGRAM
Box 228, Mountainhome, Pa. 13342

The Margaret Wade Trophy annually goes to the top women's collegiate basketball player. A nationwide committee of coaches, sports information directors and journalists nominate three candidates from each of 10 regions for selection by the Assn. for Intercollegiate Athletics for Women.

1978 **Carol Blazejowski**, Montclair State College
1979 **Nancy Lieberman**, Old Dominion University
1980 **Nancy Lieberman**, Old Dominion University

A Coach of the Year Award is presented annually to each of three women's collegiate basketball coaches representing large colleges, small colleges and junior or community colleges. A committee selects the winner.

LARGE COLLEGE

1978 **Billie Moore**, UCLA
1979 **Marianne Stanley**, Old Dominion University
1980 **Jody Contradt**, University of Texas

SMALL COLLEGE

1978 **Betty Norman**, Biola College
1979 **Wanda Briley**, High Point College
1980 **Maryalyce Jeremiah**, University of Dayton

COMMUNITY/JUNIOR COLLEGE

1978 **Frances Garmon**, Temple Junior College
1979 **Rose Marie Battaglia**, Bergen Community College
1980 **Betty Jo Crumm**, Weatherford College

Baton Twirling Achievement Award

AMATEUR ATHLETIC UNION OF THE UNITED STATES
3400 W. 86th St., Indianapolis, Ind. 46268 (317/297-2900)

No additional information is available on this award or the method of selecting the winners.

BATON TWIRLING ACHIEVEMENT AWARD

1973 **Edith Pratt**
Kathy Stewart
1974 **No award**
1975 **Peter Villerea**
1976 **Ernestine Mignone**
Niagara Association AAU
1977 **Vikki Vallone**
Chuck Medve
1978 **Kathy Clapper**
Louise Miller
1979 **No award**
1980 **Not available at press time**

Bowler of the Year

BOWLING WRITERS ASSOCIATION OF AMERICA
c/o Jim Fitzgerald, Chicago Tribune, 435 N. Michigan Ave., Chicago, Ill. 60611 (312/222-3232)

The Bowler of the Year, named by the bowling writers, receives a large trophy to recognize year-long excellence in professional bowling competition.

MEN

1942 **Johnny Crimmins,** Detroit, Mich.
1943 **Ned Day,** Milwaukee, Wisc.
1944 **Ned Day,** Milwaukee, Wisc.
1945 **Buddy Bomar,** Chicago, Ill.
1946 **Joe Wilman,** Chicago, Ill.
1947 **Buddy Bomar,** Chicago, Ill.
1948 **Andy Varipapa,** Brooklyn, N.Y.
1949 **Connie Schwoegler,** Madison, Wisc.
1950 **Junie McMahon,** Fairlawn, N.J.
1951 **Lee Jouglard,** Detroit, Mich.
1952 **Steve Nagy,** Cleveland, Ohio
1953 **Don Carter,** St. Louis, Mo.
1954 **Don Carter,** St. Louis, Mo
1955 **Steve Nagy,** Cleveland, Ohio
1956 **Bill Lilliard,** Chicago, Ill
1957 **Don Carter,** St. Louis, Mo
1958 **Don Carter,** St. Louis, Mo.
1959 **Ed Lubanski,** Detroit, Mich.
1960 **Don Carter,** St. Louis, Mo.
1961 **Dick Weber,** St. Louis, Mo.
1962 **Don Carter,** St. Louis, Mo.
1963 **Dick Weber,** St. Louis, Mo.
1964 **Billy Hardwick,** Louisville, Ky.
1965 **Dick Weber,** St. Louis, Mo
1966 **Wayne Zahn,** Atlanta, Ga.
1967 **Dave Davis,** Phoenix, Ariz.
1968 **Jim Stefanich,** Joliet, Ill.
1969 **Billy Hardwick,** Louisville, Ky.
1970 **Nelson Burton Jr.,** St. Louis, Mo.
1971 **Don Johnson,** Akron, Ohio
1972 **Don Johnson,** Akron, Ohio
1973 **Don McCune,** Munster, Ind.
1974 **Earl Anthony,** Tacoma, Wash.
1975 **Earl Anthony,** Tacoma, Wash.
1976 **Earl Anthony,** Tacoma, Wash.
1977 **Mark Roth,** Staten Island, N.Y.

Current Status Unknown

WOMEN

1948 **Val Mikiel,** Detroit, Mich.
1949 **Val Mikiel,** Detroit, Mich.
1950 **Marion Ladewig,** Grand Rapids, Mich.
1951 **Marion Ladewig,** Grand Rapids, Mich.
1952 **Marion Ladewig,** Grand Rapids, Mich.
1953 **Marion Ladewig,** Grand Rapids, Mich.

1954 **Marion Ladewig,** Grand Rapids, Mich.
1955 **Sylvia Martin,** Philadelphia, Pa.
1956 **Anita Cantaline,** Detroit, Mich.
1957 **Marion Ladewig,** Grand Rapids, Mich.
1958 **Marion Ladewig,** Grand Rapids, Mich.
1959 **Marion Ladewig,** Grand Rapids, Mich.
1960 **Sylvia Martin,** Philadelphia, Pa.
1961 **Shirley Garms,** Chicago, Ill.
1962 **Shirley Garms,** Chicago, Ill.
1963 **Marion Ladewig,** Grand Rapids, Mich.
1964 **LaVerne Carter,** St. Louis, Mo.
1965 **Betty Kuczynski,** Chicago, Ill.
1966 **Joy Able,** Chicago, Ill.
1967 **Millie Martorella,** Rochester, N.Y.
1968 **Dotty Fothergill,** North Attleboro, Mass.
1969 **Dotty Fothergill,** North Attleboro, Mass.
1970 **Mary Baker,** Central Islip, N.Y.
1971 **Paula Sperber,** Miami, Fla.
1972 **Patty Costello,** New Carollton, Md.
1973 **Judy Cook,** Grandview, Mo.
1974 **Betty Morris,** Stockton, Calif.
1975 **Judy Soutar,** Kansas City, Mo.
1976 **Patty Costello,** Scranton, Pa.
1977 **Berry Morris,** Stockton, Calif.

Current Status Unknown

Boxer of the Year Award
Boxing Hall of Fame Award
Boxing Sportsman of the Year Award
Arthur Morse Boxing Coach of the Year

AMATEUR ATHLETIC UNION OF THE UNITED STATES
3400 W. 86th St., Indianapolis, Ind. 46268 (317/297-2900)

The Boxing Hall of Fame Award is a plaque presented annually to an individual for outstanding services to amateur boxing. It is donated by the *San Francisco Examiner*.

1967 **John J. "Tam" Sheehan**
Al Sandell
1968 **F. X. "Pat" Duffy**
1969 **Paul Staff**
1970 **Ben Becker**
1971 **Leo Salakin**
1972 **Roland Schwartz**
1973 **Bill Downey**
1974 **Ollie Downs**
1975 **Robert J. Surkein**
Clyde Quisenberry
1976 **Vern Woodward**
1977 **Matthew Cusak**
1978 **Tony Mange**
1979 **Loring Baker**
1980 **J.B. Davis**

BOXER OF THE YEAR

1973 **Mike Hess**
1974-79 **No awards**
1980 **Jackie Beard**

COACH OF THE YEAR

1980 **Rayford Collins**

SPORTSMAN OF THE YEAR (BOXING)

1976 **Marvin Sugarman**
1977-80 **No awards**

The Arthur Morse Boxing Coach of the Year Award is a plaque presented by the *New York Daily News,* to an outstanding boxing coach.

1969 **Pat Nappi**
1970 **Arrington B. Klice**
1971 **Tom Johnson**
1972 **Joe Clough**
1973 **William Cummings, Jr.**
1974 **No award**
1975 **William Cummings, Jr.**
1976 **Joe Clough**
1977 **Joe Clough**
1978 **Fred Ortogero**
1979 **Pat Nappi**
1980 **Not available at press time**

Cat of the Year

CATS MAGAZINE
Box 37, Port Orange, Fla. 32109 (904/788-2770)

Cats Magazine's Cat of the Year selections are based on point evaluations of various breeds of cats accumulated through the cat show season. The winning cat receives a ribbon and a certificate. In addition to the Cat of the Year honors listed here, the Best Longhair and Shorthair are also cited.

1947 **Wimauma Masterpiece of Chalsu,** Blue Persian male
1948 **Dixi-Land's Pearl Harbor Yank,** Blue Persian male
1949 **Dixi-Land's Felice of Nor-Mont,** Blue Persian male
1950 **Lavender Liberty Beau,** Blue Persian male
1951 **Pied Piper of Barbe Bleue,** Black Persian male
1952 **Great Lakes Timothy of Rosemont,** Blue Persian male
1953 **Arlington's Sensation II,** Chinchilla Persian female
1954 **Kerry Lu Ramon of Casa Contenta,** Chinchilla Persian male
1955 **Kerry Lu Ramon of Casa Contenta**
1956 **Tempura Yours Truly,** Bluepoint Siamese male
1957 **Dixi-Land's Sir Gai of Nor-Mont,** Blue Persian male
1958 **Rosemont Golden Boy,** Cream Persian male
1959 **Vel-Vene's Voodoo,** Black Persian male
1960 **Shawnee Moonflight,** Copper-eyed white Persian male
1961 **Shawnee Moonflight,** Copper-eyed white Persian male
1962 **Chez Moumette Cal of Nor-Mont,** Cream Persian male
1963 **Azulita Paleface of Casa Cielo,** Copper-eyed White Persian male
1964 **Shawnee Moonflight,** Copper-eyed White Persian male
1965 **Shawnee Trademark,** Silver Tabby American male
1966 **Pharoh Ramses II,** Ruddy Abyssinian male
1967 **Mizpah's Ferdnand of Brierwood,** Sable Burmese male
1968 **Burm-Si's Sir Henry,** Sable Burmese male
1969 **Conalan's Miss Prettee of Walhall,** Black Persian female
1970 **Walhall's Isolde,** Black Persian female
1971 **Lowland's Zeus of Lin-Lea,** Cream Persian male
1972 **Joelwyn Columbyan,** Silver Tabby American male

1973 **Joelwyn The Wild One III of Nile,** Ruddy Abyssinian male
1974 **Kalico's Mary Poppins of Marvonack,** Blue British Shorthair female
1975 **Hawthorne Nite Liter of Lee,** Black Persian male
1976 **Thaibok Tyrone,** Sealpoint Siamese male
1977 **Kalico's Lolly of Welcome,** British Blue shorthair male
1978 **Jesilieu's Pong To Ko of Solna,** Korat male
1979 **Ky-Ro's Pharoh,** Black Persian male
1980 **Surfside Sadi of Rog-Mar,** Copper-Eyed White Persian Female

Best in Show

WESTMINSTER KENNEL CLUB
51 E. 42nd St., Room 1611, New York, N.Y. 10017
(212/682-6852)

The annual Westminster Kennel Club Show is generally regarded as the most prestigious dog show in the United States. One hundred twenty-two breeds are recognized by the American Kennel Club. Champions of record and dogs credited with championship points from among these breeds may be entered in the Westminster show, which takes place in New York. Judges select the winners in various categories, the most significant of which is the Best in Show citation. The list below includes the name of the dog, the breed and the owner's name.

1907 **Ch. Warren Remedy,** Fox terrier (smooth), Winthrop Rutherfurd
1908 **Ch. Warren Remedy,** Fox terrier (smooth), Winthrop Rutherfurd
1909 **Ch. Warren Remedy,** Fox terrier (smooth), Winthrop Rutherfurd
1910 **Ch. Sabine Rarebit,** Fox terrier (smooth), Sabine Kennels
1911 **Ch. Tickle Em Jock,** Scottish terrier, A. Albright, Jr.
1912 **Ch. Kenmare Sorceress,** Airedale terrier, William P. Wolcott
1913 **Ch. Strathtay Prince Albert,** Bulldog, Alex H. Stewart
1914 **Ch. Slumber,** Old English sheepdog, Mrs. Tylor Morse
1915 **Ch. Matford Vic,** Fox terrier (wire), George W. Quintard
1916 **Ch. Matford Vic,** Fox terrier (wire), George W. Quintard
1917 **Ch. Conejo Wycollar Boy,** Fox terrier (wire), Mrs. Roy A. Rainey
1918 **Ch. Haymarket Fruitless,** Bull terrier, R. H. Elliott
1919 **Ch. Briergate Bright Beauty,** Airedale terrier, G. L. L. Davis
1920 **Ch. Conejo Wycollar Boy,** Fox terrier (wire), Mrs. Roy A. Rainey
1921 **Ch. Midkiff Seductive,** Cocker spaniel, William T. Payne
1922 **Ch. Boxwood Barkentine,** Airedale terrier, Frederic C. Hood
1923 **No Best in Show award.**
1924 **Ch. Barberyhill Bootlegger,** Sealyham terrier, Bayard Warren
1925 **Ch. Governor Moscow,** Pointer, Robert F. Maloney
1926 **Ch. Signal Circuit of Halleston,** Fox Terrier (wire), Halleston Kennels
1927 **Ch. Pinegrade Perfection,** Sealyham terrier, Frederic C. Brown
1928 **Ch. Talavera Margaret,** Fox terrier (wire), R. M. Lewis
1929 **Laund Loyalty of Bellhaven,** Collie, Florence B. Ilch
1930 **Ch. Pendley Calling of Blarney,** Fox terrier (wire) John G. Bates
1931 **Ch. Pendley Calling of Blarney,** Fox terrier (wire) John G. Bates
1932 **Ch. Nancolleth Markable,** Pointer, Giralda Farms
1933 **Ch. Warland Protector of Shelterock,** Airedale terrier, S. M. Stewart
1934 **Ch. Flornell Spicy Bit of Halleston,** Fox terrier (wire), Halleston Kennels
1935 **Ch. Nunsoe Duc de la Terrace of Blackeen,** Standard poodle, Blakeen Kennels
1936 **Ch. St. Margaret Magnificent of Clairedale,** Sealyham terrier, Clairedale Kennels
1937 **Ch. Flornell Spicy Piece of Halleston,** Fox terrier (wire), Halleston Kennels
1938 **Ch. Daro of Maridor,** English setter, Maridor Kennels
1939 **Ch. Ferry v. Rauhfelsen of Giralda,** Doberman pinscher, Giralda Farms
1940 **Ch. My Own Brucie,** Cocker spaniel, H. E. Mellenthin
1941 **Ch. My Own Brucie,** Cocker spaniel, H. E. Mellenthin
1942 **Ch. Wolvey Pattern of Edgerstoune,** West Highland white terrier, Mrs. J. G. Winant
1943 **Ch. Pitter Patter of Piperscroft,** Miniature poodle, Mrs. P. H. B. Frelinghuysen
1944 **Ch. Flornell Rare-Bit of Twin Ponds,** Welsh terrier, Mrs. Edward P. Alker
1945 **Ch. Shieling's Signature,** Scottish terrier, Mr. and Mrs. T. H. Snethen
1946 **Ch. Hetherington Model Rhythm,** Fox terrier (wire), Mr. and Mrs. T. H. Carruthers, III
1947 **Ch. Warlord of Mezelaine,** Boxer, Mr. and Mrs. Richard C. Kettles, Jr.
1948 **Ch. Rock Ridge Night Rocket,** Bedlington terrier, Mr. and Mrs. William A. Rockefeller
1949 **Ch. Mezelaine Zazarac Brandy,** Boxer, Mr. and Mrs. John Phelps Wagner
1950 **Ch. Walsing Winning Trick of Edgerstoune,** Scottish terrier, Mrs. J. G. Winant
1951 **Ch. Bang Away of Sirrah Crest,** Boxer, Dr. and Mrs. R. C. Harris
1952 **Ch. Rancho Dobe's Storm,** Doberman pinscher, Mr. and Mrs. Len Carey
1953 **Ch. Rancho Dobe's Storm,** Doberman pinscher, Mr. and Mrs. Len Carey
1954 **Ch. Carmor's Rise and Shine,** Cocker spaniel, Mrs. Carl E. Morgan
1955 **Ch. Kippax Fearnought,** Bulldog, John A. Saylor
1956 **Ch. Wilber White Swan,** Toy poodle, Bertha Smith
1957 **Ch. Shirkhan of Grandeur,** Afghan hound, Sunny Shay and Dorothy Chenade
1958 **Ch. Puttencove Promise,** Standard poodle, Puttencove Kennels
1959 **Ch. Fontclair Festoon,** Miniature poodle, Dunwalke Kennels
1960 **Ch. Chik T'Sun of Caversham,** Pekingese, Mr. and Mrs. C. C. Venable
1961 **Ch. Cappoquin Little Sister,** Toy poodle, Florence Michelson
1962 **Ch. Elfinbrook Simon,** West Highland white terrier, Wishing Well Kennels
1963 **Ch. Wakefield's Black Knight,** English springer spaniel, Mrs. W. J. S. Borie
1964 **Ch. Courtenay Fleetfoot of Pennyworth,** Whippet Pennyworth Kennels
1965 **Ch. Carmichael's Fanfare,** Scottish terrier, Mr. and Mrs. Charles C. Stalter

1966 **Ch. Zeloy Moormaide's Magic,** Fox terrier (wire), Marion G. Bunker
1967 **Ch. Bardene Bingo,** Scottish terrier, E. H. Stuart
1968 **Ch. Stingray of Derryabah,** Lakeland terrier, Mr. and Mrs. James A. Farrell, Jr.
1969 **Ch. Glamoor Good News,** Skye terrier, Walter F. and Adele F. Goodman
1970 **Ch. Arriba's Prima Donna,** Boxer, Dr. and Mrs. P. J. Pagano and Dr. Theodore S. Fickes
1971 **Ch. Chinoe's Adamant James,** English springer spaniel, Milton E. Prickett
1972 **Ch. Chinoe's Adamant James,** English springer spaniel, Milton E. Prickett
1973 **Ch. Acadia Command Performance,** Standard poodle, E. B. Jenner and J. Sering
1974 **Ch. Gretchenhof Columbia River,** German shorthaired pointer, Richard P. Smith
1975 **Ch. Sir Lancelot of Barvan,** Old English sheepdog, Mr. and Mrs. R. Vanword
1976 **Ch. Jo Ni's Red Baron of Crofton,** Lakeland terrier, Virginia K. Dickson
1977 **Ch. Dersade Bobby's Girl,** Sealyham terrier, Pool Forge Kennels
1978 **Ch. Cede Higgins**, Yorkshire terrier, Barbarb and **Charles Switzer**
1979 **Ch. Oak Trees Irishtocrat**, Irish water spaniel, **Anne E. Snelling**
1980 **Ch. Innisfree's Sierra**, Siberian husky, Col. and Mrs. **Norbert Kanyler**

Coach of the Year
Tuss McLaughery Award
Amos Alonzo Stagg Award

AMERICAN FOOTBALL COACHES ASSOCIATION
Box 8705, Durham, N.C. 27707 (919/489-8160)

The Coach of the Year is elected by a vote of active members of the association and is honored at a presentation dinner. Beginning in 1960, two awards have been given annually—one to a large university and one to a college.

1935 **Lynn Waldorf,** Northwestern
1936 **Dick Harlow,** Harvard
1937 **Hooks Mylin,** Lafayette
1938 **Bill Kern,** Carnegie Tech
1939 **Eddie Anderson,** Iowa
1940 **Clark Shaughnessy,** Stanford
1941 **Frank Leahy,** Notre Dame
1942 **Bill Alexander,** Georgia Tech
1943 **Amos Alonzo Stagg,** College of Pacific
1944 **Carroll Widdoes,** Ohio State
1945 **Bo McMillin,** Indiana
1946 **Red Blaik,** Army
1947 **Fritz Crisler,** Michigan
1948 **Benny Oosterbaan,** Michigan
1949 **Bud Wilkinson,** Oklahoma
1950 **Charley Caldwell,** Princeton
1951 **Chuck Taylor,** Stanford
1952 **Biggie Munn,** Michigan State
1953 **Jim Tatum,** Maryland
1954 **Red Sanders,** U.C.L.A.
1955 **Duffy Daugherty,** Michigan State
1956 **Bowden Wyatt,** Tennessee
1957 **Woody Hayes,** Ohio State
1958 **Paul Dietzel,** Louisiana State
1959 **Floyd Schwartzwalder,** Syracuse
1960 **Murray Warmath,** Minnesota
Warren Woodson, New Mexico State
1961 **Paul W. Bryant,** Alabama
Alonzo S. Gaither, Florida A&M
1962 **John McKay,** Southern California
William M. Edwards, Wittenberg
1963 **Darrell Royal,** Texas
William M. Edwards, Wittenberg
1964 **Frank Broyles,** Arkansas
Ara Parseghian, Notre Dame
Clarence Stasavich, East Carolina College
1965 **Tommy Prothro,** U.C.L.A.
Jack Curtice, Univ. of Cal. at Santa Barbara
1966 **Tom Cahill,** U.S. Military Academy
Dan Jessee, Trinity College
1967 **John Pont,** Indiana
A. C. "Scrappy" Moore, Chattanooga
1968 **Joe Paterno,** Penn State
Jim Root, New Hampshire
1969 **Bo Schembechler,** Michigan
Larry Naviaux, Boston University
1970 **Darrell Royal,** Texas
Charles McClendon, Louisiana State
Bennie Ellender, Arkansas State
1971 **Paul Bryant,** Alabama
Harold Raymond, Delaware
1972 **John McKay,** Southern California
Harold Raymond, Delaware
1973 **Paul Bryant,** Alabama
Dave Maurer, Wittenberg
1974 **Grant Teaff,** Baylor
Roy Kramer, Central Michigan
1975 **Frank Kush,** Arizona State
Dave Maurer, Wittenberg
1976 **John Majors,** Pittsburgh
Jim Dennison, Akron
1977 **Don James,** University of Washington
Bill Manlove, Widener College
1978 **Joe Paterno,** Penn State
Lee Tressel, Baldwin-Wallace
1979 **Earle Bruce,** Ohio State
Bill Narduzzi, Youngstown State
1980 **Vince Dooley,** Georgia
Rick Carter, Dayton

The Tuss McLaughery Award is given annually to a distinguished American to honor service to others.

1964 **Gen. Douglas MacArthur**
1965 **Bob Hope**
1966 **Lyndon B. Johnson**
1967 **Dwight D. Eisenhower**
1968 **J. Edgar Hoover**
1969 **Rev. Billy Graham**
1970 **Richard M. Nixon**
1971 **Neil Armstrong, Michael Collins and Edwin Aldrin**
1972 **No award**
1973 **John Wayne**
1974 **Gerald R. Ford**
1975 **No award**
1976 **No award**
1977 **Gen. James A. Van Fleet**
1978 **No award**
1979 **Jimmy Stewart**
1980 **Lt. Gen. Jimmy Doolittle**

The Amos Alonzo Stagg Award is given annually to the individual, group or institution whose services have advanced the best interests of football.

1940 **Donald G. Herring, Jr., and family**
1941 **William H. Crowell**
1946 **Grantland Rice**
1947 **William Alexander**
1948 **Gilmour Dobie**
Glenn S. "Pop" Warner
Robert C. Zuppke
1949 **Richard C. Harlow**
1950 **No award**
1951 **DeOrmond McLaughrey**
1952 **A.N. "Bo" McMillin**
1953 **Lou Little**
1954 **Dana X. Bible**
1955 **Joseph J. Tomlin**
1956 **No award**
1957 **Robert R. Neyland**
1958 **Bernard Bierman**
1959 **John W. Wilce**
1960 **Harvey J. Harman**
1961 **Ray Elior**
1962 **E.E. "Tad" Wieman**
1963 **Andrew Kerr**
1964 **Don Faurot**
1965 **Harry Stuhldreher**
1966 **Bernie Moore**
1967 **Jess Neeley**
1968 **Abe Martin**
1969 **Rip Engle**
1970 **Lynn Waldorf**
1971 **Bill Murray**
1972 **Jack Curtice**
1973 **Lloyd Jordan**
1974 **A.S. "Jake" Gaither**
1975 **Gerald B. Zornow**
1976 **No award**
1977 **Floyd "Ben" Schawartzalder**
1978 **Tom Hamilton**
1979 **H.O. "Fritz" Crisler**
1980 **No award**

Heisman Trophy

DOWNTOWN ATHLETIC CLUB
19 West St., New York, N.Y. 10004 (212/425-7000)

The Heisman Trophy is awarded annually to the individual voted by the members as the best college football player of the year. The trophy is a bronze statue of a running back. (RB=running back; HB=halfback; QB=quarter back; FB=Fullback; E=end; TB=tailback)

1935 **Jay Berwanger,** Chicago, HB
1936 **Larry Kelley,** Yale, E
1937 **Clint Frank,** Yale, HB
1938 **Davey O'Brien,** T.C.U., QB
1939 **Nile Kinnick,** Iowa, HB
1940 **Tom Harmon,** Michigan, HB
1941 **Bruce Smith,** Minnesota, HB
1942 **Frank Sinkwich,** Georgia, HB
1943 **Angelo Bertelli,** Notre Dame, QB
1944 **Les Horvath,** Ohio State, QB
1945 **Doc Blanchard,** U.S. Military Academy, FB
1946 **Glenn Davis,** U.S. Military Academy, HB
1947 **John Lujack,** Notre Dame, QB
1948 **Doak Walker,** S.M.U., HB
1949 **Leon Hart,** Notre Dame, E
1950 **Vic Janowicz,** Ohio State, HB
1951 **Dick Kazmaier,** Princeton, HB
1952 **Billy Vessels,** Oklahoma, HB
1953 **John Lattner,** Notre Dame, HB
1954 **Alan Ameche,** Wisconsin, FB
1955 **Howard Cassady,** Ohio State, HB
1956 **Paul Hornung,** Notre Dame, QB
1957 **John Crow,** Texas A & M, HB
1958 **Pete Dawkins,** U.S. Military Academy, HB
1959 **Billy Cannon,** L.S.U., HB
1960 **Joe Bellino,** U.S. Naval Academy, HB
1961 **Ernie Davis,** Syracuse, HB
1962 **Terry Baker,** Oregon State, QB
1963 **Roger Staubach,** U.S. Naval Academy, QB
1964 **John Huarte,** Notre Dame, QB
1965 **Mike Garrett,** Southern California, HB
1966 **Steve Spurrier,** Florida, QB
1967 **Gary Beban,** U.C.L.A., QB
1968 **O. J. Simpson,** Southern California, TB
1969 **Steve Owens,** Oklahoma, HB
1970 **Jim Plunkett,** Stanford, QB
1971 **Pat Sullivan,** Auburn, QB
1972 **Johnny Rodgers,** Nebraska, RB
1973 **John Cappelletti,** Penn State, TB
1974 **Archie Griffin,** Ohio State, TB
1975 **Archie Griffin,** Ohio State, TB
1976 **Tony Dorsett,** Pittsburgh, TB
1977 **Earl Campbell,** Texas, RB
1978 **Billy Sims,** Oklahoma
1979 **Charles White,** Southern California
1980 **George Rogers,** South Carolina

Grantland Rice Trophy
Outland Trophy
Coach of the Year
Bert McGrane Award

FOOTBALL WRITERS ASSOCIATION OF AMERICA
Box 1022, Edmond, Okla. 73034 (405/341-4731)

A five-man committee of football writers annually votes for the best collegiate football team of the season to receive the Grantland Rice Trophy, which is a bronze football mounted on a base.

1954 **U.C.L.A.**
1955 **Oklahoma**
1956 **Oklahoma**
1957 **Ohio State**
1958 **Iowa**
1959 **Syracuse**
1960 **Mississippi**
1961 **Ohio State**
1962 **Southern California**
1963 **Texas**
1964 **Arkansas**
1965 **Michigan State**
Alabama
1966 **Notre Dame**
1967 **Southern California**
1968 **Ohio State**
1969 **Texas**
1970 **Nebraska**
1971 **Nebraska**
1972 **Southern California**
1973 **Notre Dame**
1974 **Southern California**

1975 **Oklahoma**
1976 **Pittsburgh**
1977 **Notre Dame**
1978 **Alabama**
1979 **Alabama**
1980 **Not available at press time**

The Outland Trophy, which consists of a plaque, is given to the outstanding interior lineman of the year on a vote by the membership of the assocation, subject to confirmation by the FWAA All-America Committee.

1946 **George Connor,** Notre Dame
1947 **Joe Steffy,** U.S. Military Academy
1948 **Bill Fischer,** Notre Dame
1949 **Ed Bagdon,** Michigan State
1950 **Bob Gain,** Kentucky
1951 **Jim Weatherall,** Oklahoma
1952 **Dick Modzelewski,** Maryland
1953 **J.D. Roberts,** Oklahoma
1954 **William (Bud) Brooks,** Arkansas
1955 **Calvin Jones,** Iowa
1956 **Jim Parker,** Ohio State
1957 **Alex Karras,** Iowa
1958 **Zeke Smith,** Auburn
1959 **Mike McGee,** Duke
1960 **Tom Brown,** Minnesota
1961 **Merlin Olson,** Utah State
1962 **Bobby Bell,** Minnesota
1963 **Gordon Scott, Appleton,** Texas
1964 **Steve DeLong,** Tennessee
1965 **Tommy Nobis,** Texas
1966 **Lloyd Phillips,** Arkansas
1967 **Ron Yary,** Southern California
1968 **Bill Stanfill,** Georgia
1969 **Mike Reid,** Penn State
1970 **Jim Stillwagon,** Ohio State
1971 **Larry Jacobson,** Nebraska
1972 **Rich Glover,** Nebraska
1973 **John Hicks,** Ohio State
1974 **Randy White,** Maryland
1975 **Leroy Selmon,** Oklahoma
1976 **Ross Browner,** Notre Dame
1977 **Brad Shearer,** University of Texas
1978 **Greg Roberts,** Oklahoma
1979 **Jim Richter,** North Carolina State
1980 **Mark May,** Pittsburgh

The full membership of the FWAA votes on the Coach of the Year for the individual doing the most outstanding coaching job in college football. A plaque is given to the winner.

1957 **Woody Hayes,** Ohio State
1958 **Paul Dietzel,** Louisiana State
1959 **Ben Schwartzwalder,** Syracuse
1960 **Murray Warmath,** Minnesota
1961 **Darrell Royal,** Texas
1962 **John McKay,** Southern California
1963 **Darrell Royal,** Texas
1964 **Ara Parseghian,** Notre Dame
1965 **Duffy Daugherty,** Michigan State
1966 **Tom Cahill,** U.S. Military Academy
1967 **John Pont,** Indiana
1968 **Woody Hayes,** Ohio State
1969 **Bo Schembechler,** Michigan
1970 **Alex Agase,** Northwestern
1971 **Bob Devaney,** Nebraska
1972 **John McKay,** Southern California
1973 **Johnny Majors,** Pittsburgh
1974 **Grant Teaff,** Baylor
1975 **Woody Hayes,** Ohio State
1976 **Johnny Majors,** Pittsburgh
1977 **Lou Holtz,** Arkansas
1978 **Joe Paterno,** Penn State
1979 **Earle Bruce,** Ohio State
1980 **Not available at press time**

The Bert McGrane Award, which consists of a plaque, is given annually on committee decision to a member of FWAA for meritorious service to the association.

1974 **Charley Johnson,** *Minneapolis Star*
1975 **Wilfrid Smith,** *Chicago Tribune*
1976 **Paul Zimmerman,** *Los Angeles Times*
1977 **Dick Cullum,** *Minneapolis Tribune*
1978 **Wilbur Evans,** Cotton Bowl
1979 **Tom Siler,** *Knoxville (Tenn.) News-Sentinel*
1980 **Maury White,** *Des Moines Register*

Scholar Athlete Award MacArthur Bowl

NATIONAL FOOTBALL FOUNDATION
201 E. 42nd St., Suite 1506, New York, N.Y. 10017
(212/682-0255)

The Scholar Athlete Award, which consists of a silver bowl and $1,000, is given annually to college seniors who have demonstrated academic application and performance as well as outstanding football ability and performance and school leadership. College athletic directors nominate candidates who are voted on by the foundation's award committee and approved by the executive committee.

1959 **Paul Choquette,** Brown
Gerhard Schwedes, Syracuse
Neyle Solle, Univ. of Tennessee
Philip Ross, Ohio Wesleyan
Harry Tolly, Univ. of Nebraska
Maurice Doke, Univ. of Texas
Pat Smyth, Univ. of Wyoming
Donald Patrick Newell, Univ. of California
1960 **Alan Rozycki,** Dartmouth
Paul Benke, Rutgers
Edmund Dyas, Auburn
John Easterbrook, Illinois
Frederick Brossart, Missouri
Jerry Mays, Southern Methodist
Bruce Henry, Colorado School of Mines
Barry Bullard, Washington
1961 **Davey Thompson,** Tufts
Alex Kroll, Rutgers
Wade Butcher, Vanderbilt
Albert Iosue, Western Reserve
Joseph Romig, Colorado
Bob E. Johnson, Rice
Merlin Olsen, Utah State
Mike Kline, Oregon State
1962 **Al Snyder,** Holy Cross
Tim Callard, Princeton
Gary Cuozzo, Virginia
Robert Heckman, Dayton
Rex Russell, Oklahoma State
John Pat Culpepper, Texas
Ron Joseph Manno, Utah
Terry Wayne Baker, Oregon State
1963 **Kenneth Ancell,** Colorado School of Mines
Mike Briggs, Washington
Richard Deller, Illinois
Frank Drigotas, Bowdoin

David Gill, Missouri
Algis Grigaliunas, Pittsburgh
Joe Ince, U.S. Naval Academy
Don Trull, Baylor
Russell Walls, Davidson
1964 **Cosmo Iacavazzi,** Princeton
Arnold Chonko, Ohio State
Bill Zadel, U.S. Military Academy
Bob Timberlake, Michigan
Archie Roberts, Columbia
Ron Oelshlager, Kansas
Jimmy Bell, Clemson
Kenneth Gousens, Amherst
Mel Carpenter, Utah
Horst Paul, Houston
Bill Douglas, Washington
1965 **Charles Arrobio,** Southern California
Sam Champi, U.S. Military Academy
John Cochran, Auburn
David Fronek, Wisconsin
Stephen Juday, Michigan State
Dan Jones, Texas Christian
Allen Roodhouse, U.S. Naval Academy
Williard Sander, Ohio State
1966 **Thomas Allen,** Bowdoin
Robert Etter, Georgia
Stanley Juk, South Carolina
James R. Lynch, Notre Dame
Charles Peters, Princeton
William Powell, Missouri
John Richards, Texas Christian
Michael Ryan, Washington
1967 **Gary Beban,** UCLA
Alan Douglas Bersin, Harvard
William P. Eastman, Georgia Tech
Barry Furst, Ohio Wesleyan
Robert Johnson, Tennessee
Thomas W. Lawhorne, Georgia
John R. McCarthy, Yale
Keith Miles, Trinity
Bohdan Neswiacheny, U.S. Military Academy
John Pierson Root, Stanford
John Scovell, Texas Tech
Steve F. Warren, North Carolina State
Robert Weber, Princeton
1968 **Allen Brenner,** Michigan State
David Foley, Ohio State
John Hendricks, Iowa
Stephen Hindman, Mississippi
George Kunz, Notre Dame
William Moody, Arizona
William Payne, Georgia
Michael Perrin, Texas
David Rea, Amherst
Richard Sandler, Princeton
Robert Stein, Minnesota
1969 **Tim Callaway,** Georgia
John Cramer, Harvard
Harry Gonso, Indiana
George Joseph, Penn
Harry Khasigian, Southern California
Charles Longenecker, U.S. Air Force Academy
Mike Oriard, Notre Dame
Daniel Pike, U.S. Naval Academy
Theodore Shahid, U.S. Military Academy
Terry Stewart, Arkansas
1970 **William Bogan,** Dartmouth
James Cooch, Colorado
Don Denbo, Tennessee
Leo Dillon, Dayton
Larry DiNardo, Notre Dame
Dennis Dummit, U.C.L.A.
David Elmendorf, Texas A&M
Rex Kern, Ohio State
Thomas Lyons, Georgia
Thomas Neville, Yale
Robert Parker, U.S. Air Force Academy
John Sande III, Stanford
Willie Frank Zapalac, Texas
1971 **William Brafford,** North Carolina
Dennis Ferguson, Utah State
Thomas Gatewood, Jr., Notre Dame
Darryl Owen Hass, U.S. Air Force Academy
David M. Joyner, Penn State
John Sefcik, Columbia
William Thomson, Indiana
Michael McCoy, Kansas
Larry Mildren, Jr., Oklahoma
John Musso, Alabama
Thomas Nach, Jr., Georgia
1972 **Bruce Bannon,** Penn State
William Cahill, Washington
Frank Dowsing, Mississippi State
Floyd Harvey, Grambling
Richard Homburg, U.S. Air Force Academy
Richard Jauron, Yale
Greg Marx, Notre Dame
Timothy Quinn, Dayton
Fred Radke, Dartmouth
Charles Whitener, Southern Methodist
Joe Wylie, Oklahoma
1973 **Forrest Anderson,** Nebraska
Richard Len Bland, Colorado
David Arthur Blandino, Pittsburgh
David John Casper, Notre Dame
David Dillon Gallagher, Michigan
Randolph C. Gradishar, Ohio State
Thomas Mark Harmon, U.C.L.A.
James H. Jennings, Rutgers
Patrick Michael Kelly, Texas
Mark Markovich, Penn State
Norris Lee Weese, Mississippi
1974 **John R. Baiorunos,** Penn State
David Lynn Chambers, Colorado
William R. Cregar, South Carolina
Peter K. Demmerle, Notre Dame
Patrick C. Haden, Southern California
Randall L. Hall, Alabama
Timothy S. Harden, U.S. Naval Academy
J. Randy Hughes, Oklahoma
Douglas H. Martin, Vanderbilt
Patrick J. McInally, Harvard
Todd W. Toerper, Pittsburgh
1975 **Brian Dale Baschnagel,** Ohio State
Robert Joseph Elliott, Univ. of Iowa
Scott Dale Gillogly, U.S. Military Academy
Thomas Heiser, Univ. of Nebraska
Darryl W. Jackson, North Carolina State
Ralph Abraham Jackson, New Mexico State
Richard T. Lawrence, U.C.L.A.
Kirk John Lewis, Michigan
John M. Sciarra, Univ. of California
LeRoy Selmon, Univ. of Oklahoma
Randall J. Stockham, Utah State
1976 **John R. Bushy,** Univ. of Arkansas
Jeffrey A. Dankworth, U.C.L.A.
Randolph H. Dean, Northwestern
Vince A. Ferragamo, Univ. of Nebraska
Kevin R. Fox, Princeton
Gerry Huesken, Susquehanna

Michael G. Mauck, Univ. of Tennessee
Duncan McColl, Stanford
Stephen D. Miller, Brigham Young
Stone S. Phillips, Yale
Patrick M. Sullivan, Dartmouth

1977 **Gary Wayne Bethel,** U.C.L.A.
Jonathan E. Claiborne, Univ. of Maryland
Morgan Lee Copeland, Jr., Univ. of Texas
Curtis J. Downs, U.S. Military Academy
Tom Robert Fitch, Univ. of Kansas
Joseph E. Holland, Cornell
Jeffrey Young Lewis, Univ. of Georgia
Kevin Monk, Texas A&M
Richard Scudellari, Boston College
David Williams Vinson, Notre Dame
Mark Wichman, Bowling Green State Univ.

1978 **Robert Bookmiller**, Virginia Military Institute
Charles A. Correal, Penn State
William C. Crowley, Yale
Jeffrey John Delaney, University of Pittsburgh
Robert W. Dugas, Louisiana State
Thomas R. Foertsch, U.S. Air Force Academy
Stephen Ray Fuller, Clemson
Christopher Garlich, University of Missouri
Christopher Mott, Arizona State
Joseph William Restic, University of Notre Dame
William Bradford Shoup, University of Arkansas

1979 **Angelo Colosimo**, Colgate
Bruce Filarsky, University of the Pacific
Richard Jones, Virginia Military Institute
Edward Kloboves, Cincinnati
James Laughlin, Ohio State
Kenneth Loushin, Purdue
Paul McDonald, Southern California
Leon Shadowen, Kentucky
Steadman Shealy, Alabama
Thomas Strauss, Wisconsin
James O. Tubbs, U.S. Air Force Academy

1980 **Robert R. Burger**, Notre Dame
Kevin R. Czinger, Yale
William F. Donnalley, North Carolina
Theodore F. Dumbauld, U.S. Naval Academy
Sheldon Fox, Georgia Tech
Milt McColl, Stanford
Jay D. McKim, Oklahoma
Stanley R. March, U.S. Military Academy
Rand Lee Schleusener, Nebraska
Kevin Speer, Indiana
John W. Walsh, Penn State

The MacArthur Bowl, named after Gen. Douglas MacArthur, is awarded annually to the season's outstanding college football team. It is made of silver, fashioned in the form of a football stadium, and was created by Tiffany.

1959 **Syracuse University**
1960 **Univ. of Minnesota**
1961 **Univ. of Alabama**
1962 **Univ. of Southern California**
1963 **Univ. of Texas**
1964 **Univ. of Notre Dame**
1965 **Michigan State**
1966 **Michigan State**
Univ. of Notre Dame
1967 **Ohio State Univ.**
1968 **Ohio State Univ.**
1969 **Univ. of Texas**
1970 **Ohio State Univ.**
Univ. of Texas
1971 **Univ. of Nebraska**
1972 **Univ. of Southern California**
1973 **Univ. of Notre Dame**
1974 **Univ. of Southern California**
1975 **Univ. of Oklahoma**
1976 **Univ. of Pittsburgh**
1977 **Univ. of Notre Dame**
1978 **University of Alabama**
1979 **University of Alabama**
1980 **University of Georgia**

Jim Thorpe Trophy
Joe F. Carr Trophy
George Halas Trophy
Player of the Year
National Football Conference Player of the Year Award
Bert Bell Trophy

NEWSPAPER ENTERPRISE ASSOCIATION
200 Park Ave., New York, N.Y. 10017 (212/557-5840)

The Jim Thorpe Trophy is awarded annually to the most valuable National Football League player as determined by a poll conducted by the Newspaper Enterprise Association of the players on the 26 league teams.

1955 **Narlon Hill,** N.A.
1956 **Frank Gifford,** New York Giants
1957 **John Unitas,** Baltimore Colts
1958 **Jim Brown,** Cleveland Browns
1959 **Charley Conerly,** New York Giants
1960 **Norm Van Brocklin,** Philadelphia Eagles
1961 **Y.A. Tittle,** New York Giants
1962 **Jim Taylor,** Green Bay Packers
1963 **Jim Brown,** Cleveland Browns
Y.A. Tittle, New York Giants
1964 **Lenny Moore,** Baltimore Colts
1965 **Jim Brown,** Cleveland Browns
1966 **Bart Starr,** Green Bay Packers
1967 **John Unitas,** Baltimore Colts
1968 **Earl Morrall,** Baltimore Colts
1969 **Roman Gabriel,** Los Angeles Rams
1970 **John Brodie,** San Francisco 49ers
1971 **Bob Griese,** Miami Dolphins
1972 **Larry Brown,** Washington Redskins
1973 **O.J. Simpson,** Buffalo Bills
1974 **Ken Stabler,** Oakland Raiders
1975 **Fran Tarkenton,** Minnesota Vikings
1976 **Bert Jones,** Baltimore Colts
1977 **Walter Payton,** Chicago Bears
1978 **Earl Campbell,** Houston Oilers
1979 **Earl Campbell,** Houston Oilers
1980 **Earl Campbell,** Houston Oilers

The Joe F. Carr Trophy was an award given until 1946 to the league's Most Valuable Player.

1938 **Mel Hein,** New York Giants
1939 **Parker Hall,** Cleveland Rams
1940 **Ace Parker,** Brooklyn Dodgers
1941 **Don Hutson,** Green Bay Packers
1942 **Don Hutson,** Green Bay Packers
1943 **Sid Luckman,** Chicago Bears
1944 **Frank Sinkwich,** Detroit Lions
1945 **Bob Waterfield,** Los Angeles Rams
1946 **Bill Dudley,** Pittsburgh Steelers

The George Halas Trophy is given annually to the year's outstanding defensive player, based on a vote by news service sports editors.

1966 **Larry Wilson,** St. Louis Cardinals
1967 **Deacon Jones,** Los Angeles Rams
1968 **Deacon Jones,** Los Angeles Rams
1969 **Dick Butkus,** Chicago Bears
1970 **Dick Butkus,** Chicago Bears
1971 **Alan Page,** Minnesota Vikings
Carl Eller, Minnesota Vikings
1972 **Joe Greene,** Pittsburgh Steelers
1973 **Dick Anderson,** Miami Dolphins
Alan Page, Minnesota Vikings
1974 **Joe Greene,** Pittsburgh Steelers
1975 **Mel Blount,** Dallas Cowboys
Curley Culp, Kansas City Chiefs
Jack Youngblood, Los Angeles Rams
1976 **Wally Chambers,** Chicago Bears
Jack Lambert, Pittsburgh Steelers
Jerry Sherk, Cleveland Browns
1977 **Harvey Martin,** Dallas Cowboys
1978 **No award**
1979 **No award**
1980 **Lester Hayes**

The American Football League was merged with the National Football League in 1969, becoming the American Football Conference. News service sports editors annually select a Player of the Year from the teams in this group.

1960 **Abner Haynes,** Dallas Texans
1961 **George Blanda,** Houston Oilers
1962 **Len Dawson,** Kansas City Chiefs
1963 **Clem Daniels,** Oakland Raiders
1964 **Gino Cappelletti,** Boston Patriots
1965 **Paul Lowe,** San Diego Chargers
1966 **Jim Nance,** Boston Patriots
1967 **Daryle Lamonica,** Oakland Raiders
1968 **George Blanda,** Oakland Raiders
1971 **Bob Griese,** Miami Dolphins
Otis Taylor, Kansas City Chiefs
1972 **Earl Morrall,** Miami Dolphins
O.J. Simpson, Buffalo Bills
1973 **O.J. Simpson,** Buffalo Bills
1974 **Ken Stabler,** Oakland Raiders
1975 **O.J. Simpson,** Buffalo Bills
1976 **Bert Jones,** Baltimore Colts

The National Football League's own Player of the Year Award became the National Football Conference Player of the Year Award after the merger of the two leagues in 1969. News service sports editors select the winner.

1953 **Otto Graham,** Cleveland Browns
1954 **Joe Perry,** San Francisco 49ers
1955 **Otto Graham,** Cleveland Browns
1956 **Frank Gifford,** New York Giants
1957 **Y.A. Tittle,** San Francisco 49ers
1958 **Jim Brown,** Cleveland Browns
1959 **John Unitas,** Baltimore Colts
1960 **Norm Van Brocklin,** Philadelphia Eagles
1961 **Paul Hornung,** Green Bay Packers
1962 **Y.A. Tittle,** New York Giants
1963 **Jim Brown,** Celeveland Browns
1964 **John Unitas,** Baltimore Colts
1965 **Jim Brown,** Cleveland Browns
1966 **Bart Starr,** Green Bay Packers
1967 **John Unitas,** Baltimore Colts
1968 **Earl Morrall,** Baltimore Colts
1969 **Roman Gabriel,** Los Angeles Rams
1970 **John Brodie,** San Francisco 49ers
1971 **Alan Page,** Minnesota Vikings
1972 **Larry Brown,** Washington Redskins
1973 **John Hadl,** Los Angeles Rams
1974 **Jim Hart,** St. Louis Cardinals
1975 **Fran Tarkenton,** Minnesota Vikings
1976 **Chuck Foreman,** Minnesota Vikings

The Bert Bell Trophy is given to the first-year player selected as the Rookie of the Year by news service sports editors. The award honors the player deemed to be the most outstanding from the group playing their first year of professional football.

1958 **Bobby Mitchell,** Cleveland Browns
1959 **Nick Pietrosante,** Detroit Lions
1960 **Gail Cogdill,** Detroit Lions (NFL)
Abner Haynes, Dallas Texans (AFL)
1961 **Mike Ditka,** Chicago Bears (NFL)
Earl Faison, San Diego Chargers (AFL)
1962 **Ronnie Bull,** Chicago Bears (NFL)
Curtis McClinton, Kansas City Chiefs (AFL)
1963 **Paul Flatley,** Minnesota Vikings (NFL)
Billy Joe, Denver Broncos (AFL)
1964 **Charlie Taylor,** Washington Redskins (NFL)
Matt Snell, New York Jets (AFL)
1965 **Gale Sayers,** Chicago Bears (NFL)
Joe Namath, New York Jets (AFL)
1966 **John Roland,** St. Louis Cardinals (NFL)
Bobby Burnett, Buffalo Bills (AFL)
1967 **Mel Farr,** Detroit Lions (NFL)
George Webster, Houston Oilers (AFL)
1968 **Earl McCullouch,** Detroit Lions (NFL)
Paul Robinson, Cincinnati Bengals (AFL)
1969 **Calvin Hill,** Dallas Cowboys (NFL)
Carl Garrett, Boston Patriots (AFL)
1970 **Dennis Shaw,** Buffalo Bills (AFC)
Bruce Taylor, San Francisco 49ers (NFC)
Ray Chester, Oakland Raiders (AFC)
1971 **John Brockington,** Green Bay Packers (NFC)
Jim Plunkett, New England Patriots (AFC)
Isaiah Robertson, Los Angeles Rams (NFC)
1972 **Franco Harris,** Pittsburgh Steelers (AFC)
Willie Buchanan, Green Bay Packers (NFC)
Chester Marcol, Green Bay Packers (NFC)
1973 **Chuck Foreman,** Minnesota Vikings (NFC)
Bobby Clark, Cincinnati Bengals (AFC)
Wally Chambers, Chicago Bears (NFC)
Charles Young, Philadelphia Eagles (NFC)
1974 **Don Woods,** San Diego Chargers (AFC)
Jack Lambert, Pittsburgh Steelers (AFC)
1975 **Mike Thomas,** Washington Redskins (NFC)
Robert Brazile, Houston Oilers (AFC)
1976 **Mike Haynes,** New England Patriots (AFC)
Sammy White, Minnesota Vikings (NFC)
1977 **Tony Dorsett,** Dallas Cowboys
1978 **Earl Campbell,** Houston Oilers
1979 **O.J. Anderson,** St. Louis
1980 **Billy Sims,** Detroit Lions

Induction

PRO FOOTBALL HALL OF FAME

2121 Harrison Ave, NW, Canton, Ohio 44708
(216/456-8207)

Induction in the Pro Football Hall of Fame honors any professional football player, owner or coach who has been retired for at least five years for an outstanding career. Anyone may nominate candidates for consideration by a board of selection, which consists of a football writer or broadcaster from each city with a professional football team and one officer from the Pro Football Writers Association. At least 80 per cent of the the selectors must be in favor of the candidate for permanent enshrinement in the Hall of Fame. The years below are the years of induction into the Hall of Fame.

1963 **Sammy Baugh**, Washington Redskins
Bert Bell, commissioner, National Football League; founder Philadelphia Eagles
Joe Carr, co-organizer, American Professional Football Assn.
Earl "Dutch" Clark, Detroit Lions
Harold "Red" Grange, Chicago Bears, New York Yankees
George Halas, co-organizer, American Professional Football Assn.; Chicago Staleys, Chicago Bears
Mel Hein, New York Giants
Wilbur "Pete" Henry, New York Giants
Robert "Cal" Hubbard, New York Giants, Green Bay Packers
Don Hutson, Green Bay Packers
Earl "Curly" Lambeau, Green Bay Packers
Tim Mara, New York Giants
George Preston Marshall, Boston Braves (later Redskins)
John "Blood" McNally, Green Bay Packers, Pittsburgh Pirates
Bronko Nagurski, Chicago Bears
Ernie Nevers, Chicago Cardinals
Jim Thorpe, New York Giants, Chicago Cardinals; president, American Professional Football Assn.

1964 **Jimmy Conzelman**, Detroit Panthers, Providence Steamroller
Ed Healey, Chicago Bears
Clarke Hinkle, Green Bay Packers
William Roy "Link" Lyman, Chicago Bears
August "Mike" Michalski, New York Yankees, Green Bay Packers
Art Rooney, Pittsburgh Pirates, Pittsburgh Steelers
George Trafton, Chicago Bears

1965 **Guy Chamberlin**, Chicago Cardinals
John "Paddy" Driscoll, Chicago Cardinals, Chicago Bears
Danial J. Fortmann, Chicago Bears
Otto Graham, Cleveland Browns
Sid Luckman, Chicago Bears
Steve Van Buren, Philadelphia Eagles
Bob Waterfield, Cleveland Rams, Los Angeles Rams

1966 **Bill Dudley**, Pittsburgh Steelers, Detroit Lions
Joe Guyon, Kansas City Cowboys, New York Giants
Arnie Herber, Green Bay Packers, New York Giants
Walt Kiesling, Chicago Cardinals, Chicago Bears, Green Bay Packers, Pittsburgh Pirates
George McAfeem, Chicago Bears
Steven Owen, Kansas City Cowboys, New York Giants
Hugh "Shorty" Ray, technical advisor and supervisor of officials, National Football League
Clyde "Bulldog" Turner, Chicago Bears

1967 **Chuck Bednarik**, Philadelphia Eagles
Charles W. Biddwill, Sr., owner, Chicago Cardinals
Paul E. Brown, head coach and general manager, Cleveland Browns
Bobby Layne, Detroit Lions, Pittsburgh Steelers
Dan Reeves, Cleveland Rams, Los Angeles Rams
Ken Stron, New York Giants, New York Yanks
Joe Stydahar, Chicao Bears
Emlen Tunnell, New York Giants, Green Bay Packers

1968 **Cliff Battles**, Boston Braves, Boston Redskins, Washington Redskins
Art Donovan, Baltimore Colts, New York Yanks, Dallas Texans
Elroy "Crazylegs" Hirsch, Los Angeles Rams
Wayne Millner, Boston Redskins, Washington Redskins
Marion Motley, Cleveland Browns, Pittsburgh Steelers
Charley Trippi, New York Giants, Green Bay Packers
Alex Wojciechowicz, Detroit Lions, Philadelphia Eagles

1969 **Albert Glen "Turk" Edwards**, Boston Braves (later Redskins), Washington Redskins
Early "Greasy" Neale, head coach, Philadelphia Eagles
Leo Nomellini, San Francisco 49ers
Fletcher "Joe" Perry, San Francisco 49ers, Baltimore Colts
Ernie Stautner, Pittsburgh Steelers

1970 **Jack Christiansen**, Detroit Lions
Tom Fears, Los Angeles Rams
Hugh McElhenny, San Francisco 49ers, Minnesota Vikings
Pete Pihos, Philadelphia Eagles

1971 **Jim Brown**, Cleveland Browns
Bill Hewitt, Chicago Bears, Philadelphia Eagles
Frank "Bruiser" Kinard, Brooklyn Dodgers, New York Yanks
Vince Lombardi, head coach, Green Bay Packers, Washington Redskins
Andy Robustelli, Los Angeles Rams, New York Giants
Y.A. Tittle, Baltimore Colts, San Francisco 49ers, New York Giants

1972 **Lamar Hunt**, founder, American Football League; owner, Dallas Texans, Kansas City Chiefs
Gino Marchetti, San Francisco 49ers
Ollie Matson, Chicago Cardinals, Los Angeles Rams, Detroit Lions, Philadelphia Eagles
Clarence "Ace" Parker, Brooklyn Dodgers, Boston Yanks, New York Yankees

1973 **Raymond Berry**, Baltimore Colts
Jim Parker, Baltimore Colts
Joe Schmidt, Detroit Lions

1974 **Tony Canadeo**, Green Bay Packers
Bill George, Chicago Bears, Los Angeles Rams
Lou Groza, Cleveland Browns
Richard "Night Train" Lane, Los Angeles Rams, Chicago Cardinals, Detroit Lions

1975 **Roosevelt Brown**, New York Giants
George Connor, Chicago Bears
Dante Lavelli, Cleveland Browns
Leonard "Lenny" Moore, Baltimore Colts

1976 **Ray Flaherty**, Boston Redskins, Washington Redskins, New York Yankees, Chicago Hornets
Leonard "Len" Ford, Los Angeles Dons, Cleveland Browns, Green Bay Packers
Jim Taylor, Green Bay Packers, New Orleans Saints

1977 **Frank Gifford**, New York Giants
Forrest Gregg, Green Bay Packers, Dallas Cowboys
Gale Sayers, Chicago Bears
Bart Starr, Green Bay Packers
Bill Willis, Cleveland Browns

1978 **Lance Alworth**, San Diego Chargers, Dallas Cowboys
Weeb Ewbank, head coach, Baltimore Colts; head coach and general manager, New York Jets
Alphonse "Tuffy" Leemans, New York Giants
Ray Nitschke, Green Bay Packers

Larry Wilson, St. Louis Cardinals
1979 **Dick Butkus**, Chicago Bears
Yale Lary, Detroit Lions
Ron Mix, Los Angeles Chargers, San Diego Chargers
Johnny Unitas, Baltimore Colts
1980 **Herb Adderley**, Green Bay Packers
David "Deacon" Jones, Los Angeles Rams, San Diego Chargers, Washington Redskins
Bob Lilly, Dallas Cowboys
Jim Otto, Oakland Raiders

Lombardi Award

ROTARY CLUB OF HOUSTON FOUNDATION
Shamrock Hilton Hotel, 6900 S. Main, Houston, Tex. 77030
(713/228-1327)

The Lombardi Award, a trophy, is presented annually to the nation's best lineman in college football during the previous season.

1971 **Jim Stillwagon,** Ohio State
1972 **Walt Patulski,** Notre Dame
1973 **Rich Glover,** Nebraska
1974 **John Hicks,** Ohio State
1975 **Randy White,** Maryland
1976 **LeRoy Selmon,** Oklahoma
1977 **Wilson Whitley,** Houston
1978 **Ross Browner**, Notre Dame
1979 **Bruce Clark**, Penn State
1980 **Brad Budde**, USC

Most Improved Golfer
Rookie of the Year
Mickey Wright Award
Byron Nelson Award

GOLF DIGEST
495 Westport Ave., Norwalk, Conn. 06856 (203/847-5811)

Golf Digest magazine keeps tabs on performances of top golfers and cites a number of outstanding accomplishments in the sport. The editors select the winners on the basis of performance during the previous year.

MOST IMPROVED (men)

1953 **Doug Ford**
1954 **Bob Toski**
1955 **Mike Souchak**
1956 **Dow Finsterwald**
1957 **Paul Harney**
1958 **Ernie Vossler**
1959 **Don Whitt**
1960 **Don January**
1961 **Gary Player**
1962 **Bobby Nichols**
1963 **Tony Lema**
1964 **Ken Venturi**
1965 **Randy Glover**
1966 **Gay Brewer**
1967 **Dave Stockton**
1968 **Bob Lunn**
1969 **Dave Hill**
1970 **Dick Lotz**
1971 **Jerry Heard**
1972 **Jim Jamieson**
1973 **Tom Weiskopf**
1974 **Tom Watson**
1975 **Pat Fitzsimons**
1976 **Ben Crenshaw**
1977 **Bruce Litzke**
1978 **Gil Morgan**
1979 **Larry Nelson**
1980 **Curtis Strange**

MOST IMPROVED (women)

1954 **Beverly Hanson**
1955 **Fay Crocker**
1956 **Marlene Hagge**
1957 **Mickey Wright**
1958 **Bonnie Randolph**
1959 **Murle MacKenzie**
1960 **Kathy Whitworth**
1961 **Mary Lena Faulk**
1962 **Kathy Whitworth**
1963 **Marilynn Smith**
1964 **Judy Torluemke**
1965 **Carol Mann**
1966 **Gloria Ehret**
1967 **Susie Maxwell**
1968 **Gerda Whalen**
1969 **Donna Caponi**
1970 **Jane Blalock**
1971 **Jane Blalock**
1972 **Betty Burfeindt**
1973 **Mary Mills**
1974 **JoAnne Carner**
1975 **JoAnn Washam**
1976 **Pat Bradley**
1977 **Debbie Austin**
1978 **Nancy Lopez**
1979 **Jerilyn Britz**
1980 **Beth Daniel**

ROOKIE OF THE YEAR (men)

1957 **Ken Venturi**
1958 **Bob Goalby**
1959 **Joe Campbell**
1960 **Mason Rudolph**
1961 **Jacky Cupit**
1962 **Jack Nicklaus**
1963 **Raymond Floyd**
1964 **R. H. Sikes**
1965 **Homero Blancas**
1966 **John Schlee**
1967 **Lee Trevino**
1968 **Bob Murphy**
1969 **Grier Jones**
1970 **Ted Hayes, Jr.**
1971 **Hubert Green**
1972 **Lanny Wadkins**
1973 **Tom Kite**
1974 **Ben Crenshaw**
1975 **Roger Maltbie**
1976 **Jerry Pate**
1977 **Graham Marsh**
1978 **Pat McGowan**
1979 **John Fought**
1980 **Gary Hallberg**

ROOKIE OF THE YEAR (women)

1962 **Mary Mills**
1963 **Clifford Ann Creed**
1964 **Susie Maxwell**
1965 **Margie Masters**

1966 **Jan Ferraris**
1967 **Sharron Moran**
1968 **Sandra Post**
1969 **Jane Blalock**
1970 **JoAnne Carner**
1971 **Sally Little**
1972 **Jocelyne Bourassa**
1973 **Laura Baugh**
1974 **Jan Stephenson**
1975 **Amy Alcott**
1976 **Tu Ai-Yu**
1977 **Nancy Lopez**
1978 **Janet Anderson**
1979 **Beth Daniel**
1980 **Myra Van Hoose**

MICKEY WRIGHT AWARD FOR TOURNAMENT VICTORIES (wins in parentheses)

1955 **Patty Berg,** (6)
1956 **Marlene Hagge,** (8)
1957 **Patty Berg,** (5)
1958 **Mickey Wright,** (5)
1959 **Betsy Rawls,** (10)
1960 **Mickey Wright,** (6)
1961 **Mickey Wright,** (10)
1962 **Mickey Wright,** (10)
1963 **Mickey Wright,** (13)
1964 **Mickey Wright,** (11)
1965 **Kathy Whitworth,** (8)
1966 **Kathy Whitworth,** (9)
1967 **Kathy Whitworth,** (8)
1968 **Kathy Whitworth,** (10)
1969 **Carol Mann,** (8)
1970 **Shirley Englehorn,** (4)
1971 **Kathy Whitworth,** (4)
1972 **Kathy Whitworth,** (5)
1973 **Kathy Whitworth,** (7)
1974 **JoAnne Carner,** (6)
1975 **Sandra Haynie,** (4)
1976 **Judy Rankin,** (6)
1977 **Judy Rankin,** (N.A.)
1978 **Nancy Lopez** (N.A.)
1979 **Nancy Lopez-Melton** (N.A.)
1980 **Donna Caponi Young** (N.A.)

BYRON NELSON AWARD FOR TOURNAMENT VICTORIES (wins in parentheses)

1955 **Cary Middlecoff,** (5)
1956 **Ted Kroll,** (3)
1957 **Arnold Palmer,** (4)
1958 **Ken Venturi,** (4)
1959 **Gene Littler,** (5)
1960 **Arnold Palmer,** (8)
1961 **Arnold Palmer,** (5)
1962 **Arnold Palmer,** (7)
1963 **Arnold Palmer,** (7)
1964 **Jack Nicklaus,** (4)
1965 **Jack Nicklaus,** (5)
1966 **Billy Casper,** (4)
1967 **Jack Nicklaus,** (5)
1968 **Billy Casper,** (6)
1969 **Dave Hill,** (3)
1970 **Billy Casper,** (4)
1971 **Lee Trevino,** (5)
1972 **Jack Nicklaus,** (7)
1973 **Jack Nicklaus,** (7)
1974 **Johnny Miller,** (8)
1975 **Jack Nicklaus,** (5)
1976 **Ben Crenshaw,** (3)
1977 **Tom Watson,** (N.A.)
1978 **Tom Watson** (N.A.)
1979 **Tom Watson** (N.A.)
1980 **Tom Watson** (N.A.)

The Comeback of the Year Award is given annually to the professional golfer whose performance has returned after a slump or setback.

1978 **John Mahaffey**
1979 **Lou Graham**
1980 **Jack Nicklaus**

Charlie Bartlett Award
Ben Hogan Award
Richardson Award
Player of the Year

GOLF WRITERS ASSOCIATION OF AMERICA
1720 Section Rd., Suite 210, Cincinnati, Ohio 45237
(513/631-4400)

The Charlie Bartlett Award annually honors a playing professional for unselfish contributions to the betterment of society. A special committee selects the winner of this award, which has not been given recently.

1971 **Billy Casper**
1972 **Lee Trevino**
1973 **Gary Player**
1974 **Chi Chi Rodriguez**
1975 **Gene Littler**
1976 **Arnold Palmer**
1977 **Lee Elder**

The Ben Hogan Award, which consists of a trophy, recognizes the achievements of an individual who has continued to be active in golf in spite of a physical handicap.

1954 **Babe Didrikson Zaharias**
1955 **Ed Furgol**
1956 **President Dwight D. Eisenhower**
1957 **Clint Russell**
1958 **Dale Bourisseau**
1959 **Charlie Boswell**
1960 **Skip Alexander**
1961 **Horton Smith**
1962 **Jimmy Nichols**
1963 **Bobby Nichols**
1964 **Bob Morgan**
1965 **Ernest Jones**
1966 **Ken Venturi**
1967 **Warren Pease**
1968 **Shirley Englehorn**
1969 **Curtis Person**
1970 **Joe Lazaro**
1971 **Larry Hinson**
1972 **Ruth Jessen**
1973 **Gene Littler**
1974 **Gay Brewer**
1975 **Patty Berg**
1976 **Paul Hahn**
1977 **Des Sullivan**
1978 **Dennis Walters**
1979 **John Mahaffey**
1980 **Kathy Linney**

The Richardson Award, which consists of a plaque, is presented annually to the individual who has consistently made outstanding contributions to golf. It is the GWAA's highest honor.

1948 Robert A. Hudson
1949 Scotty Fessenden
1950 Bing Crosby
1951 Richard Tufts
1952 Chick Evans
1953 Bob Hope
1954 Babe Didrikson Zaharias
1955 President Dwight D. Eisenhower
1956 George S. May
1957 Francis Ouimet
1958 Bob Jones
1959 Patty Berg
1960 Fred Corcoran
1961 Joseph C. Dey
1962 Walter Hagen
1963 Joe and Herb Graffis
1964 Cliff Roberts
1965 Gene Sarazen
1966 Robert E. Harlow
1967 Max Elbin
1968 Charles Bartlett
1969 Arnold Palmer
1970 Roberto de Vicenzo
1971 Lincoln Werden
1972 Leo Fraser
1973 Ben Hogan
1974 Byron Nelson
1975 Gary Player
1976 Herbert W. Wind
1977 Mark Cox
1978 Jack Nickalus
1979 Jim Gaquin
1980 Robert Trent Jones

The Golf Writers Association of America annually selects a man and a woman active in golf competition as Player of the Year.

1968 Billy Casper
1969 Orville Moody
1970 Billy Casper
1971 Lee Trevino
1972 Jack Nicklaus
Kathy Whitworth
1973 Tom Weiskopf
Kathy Whitworth
1974 Johnny Miller
JoAnne Carner
1975 Jack Nicklaus
Sandra Palmer
1976 Jack Nicklaus and Jerry Pate
Judy Rankin
1977 Tom Watson
Judy Rankin
1978 Tom Watson
Nancy Lopez
1979 Tom Watson
Nancy Lopez
1980 Tom Watson
Beth Daniel

Player of the Year
Rookie of the Year
Vare Trophy
Teacher of the Year
Hall of Fame

LADIES' PROFESSIONAL GOLF ASSOCIATION
919 Third Ave., New York, N.Y. 10022 (212/751-8181)

The Player of Year selection is based on the most consistent and outstanding record in LPGA-sponsored events during the tournament year.

1966 Kathy Whitworth
1967 Kathy Whitworth
1968 Kathy Whitworth
1969 Kathy Whitworth
1970 Sandra Haynie
1971 Kathy Whitworth
1972 Kathy Whitworth
1973 Kathy Whitworth
1974 JoAnne Carner
1975 Sandra Palmer
1976 Judy T. Rankin
1977 Judy T. Rankin
1978 Nancy Lopez
1979 Nancy Lopez
1980 Beth Daniel

The Rookie of the Year title honors the most outstanding tournament performance during the first year of professional play.

1962 Mary Mills
1963 Clifford Ann Creed
1964 Susie Maxwell Berning
1965 Margie Masters
1966 Jan Ferraris
1967 Sharron Moran
1968 Sandra Post
1969 Jane Blalock
1970 JoAnne Gunderson Carner
1971 Sally Little
1972 Jocelyne Bourassa
1973 Laura Baugh
1974 Jan Stephenson
1975 Amy Alcott
1976 Bonnie Lauer
1977 Debbie Massey
1978 Nancy Lopez
1979 Beth Daniel
1980 Myra Van Hoose

The Vare Trophy honors the LPGA player for consistency in professional competition as shown in low strokes-per-round during tournament play.

1953 Patty Berg
1954 Babe Didrikson Zaharias
1955 Patty Berg
1956 Patty Berg
1957 Louise Suggs
1958 Beverly Hanson
1959 Betsy Rawls
1960 Mickey Wright
1961 Mickey Wright
1962 Mickey Wright
1963 Mickey Wright
1964 Mickey Wright
1965 Kathy Whitworth
1966 Kathy Whitworth

1967 Kathy Whitworth
1968 Carol Mann
1969 Kathy Whitworth
1970 Kathy Whitworth
1971 Kathy Whitworth
1972 Kathy Whitworth
1973 Judy Rankin
1974 JoAnne Carner
1975 JoAnne Carner
1976 Judy T. Rankin
1977 Judy T. Rankin
1978 Nancy Lopez
1979 Nancy Lopez
1980 Amy Alcott

The Teacher of the Year Award recognizes an LPGA Teaching Division Class A member for dedication, leadership and promotion of the sport of golf. Teaching Division members nominate candidates for selection by a vote of the membership.

1958 Helen Dettweiler
1959 Shirley Spork
1960 Barbara Rotvig
1961 Peggy Kirk Bell
1962 Ellen Griffin
1963 Vonnie Colby
1964 Sally Doyle
1965 Goldie Bateson
1966 Ann Casey Johnstone
1967 Jackie Pung
1968 Gloria Fecht
1969 JoAnne Winter
1970 Gloria Armstrong
1971 Jeannette Rector
1972 Lee Spencer
1973 Penny Zavichas
1974 Mary Dagraedt
1975 Carol Johnson
1976 Marge Burns
1977 DeDe Owens
1978 Shirley Englehorn
1979 Bobbie Ripley
1980 No award

Induction into the LPGA Hall of Fame honors a woman's professional golf career. She must be an association member for at least 10 consecutive years and the winner of at least 30 tour events with two championships, 40 events with one championship or 40 events. The Hall of Fame is a wing of the World Golf Hall of Fame in Pinehurst, Ga. Induction is as merited.

1951 Patty Berg
Betty Jameson
Louise Suggs
Babe Didrikson Zaharias
1960 Betsy Rawls
1964 Mickey Wright
1975 Kathy Whitworth
1977 Sandra Haynie
Carol Mann
1978-80 No inductees

Player of the Year
Professional of the Year
Vardon Trophy
Ed Dudley Award
Horton Smith Award

PROFESSIONAL GOLFERS' ASSOCIATION OF AMERICA
Box 12458, Lake Park, Fla. 33403 (305/844-5000)

The Player of the Year is selected by a poll of the PGA Executive Committee as the most outstanding competitor in professional golf. The winner receives a plaque.

1948 Ben Hogan
1949 Sam Snead
1950 Ben Hogan
1951 Ben Hogan
1952 Julius Boros
1953 Ben Hogan
1954 Ed Furgol
1955 Doug Ford
1956 Jack Burke, Jr.
1957 Dick Mayer
1958 Dow Finsterwald
1959 Art Wall
1960 Arnold Palmer
1961 Jerry Barber
1962 Arnold Palmer
1963 Julius Boros
1964 Ken Venturi
1965 Dave Marr
1966 Billy Casper
1967 Jack Nicklaus
1968 No award
1969 Orville Moody
1970 Billy Casper
1971 Lee Trevino
1972 Jack Nicklaus
1973 Jack Nicklaus
1974 Johnny Miller
1975 Jack Nicklaus
1976 Jack Nicklaus
1977 Tom Watson
1978 Tom Watson
1979 Tom Watson
1980 Tom Watson

A plaque is presented to the working club professional chosen as Professional of the Year based on service to golf in general and the association, to the club and to promotion of the sport of golf. The winner must be a PGA member for a minimum of 10 years.

1955 **Bill Gordon,** Tam O'Shanter C.C., Chicago, Ill.
1956 **Harry Shepard,** Mark Twain Community G.C., Elmira, N.Y.
1957 **Dugan Aycock,** Lexington C.C., Lexington, N.C.
1958 **Harry Pezzullo,** Mission Hills G.C., Northbrook, Ill.
1959 **Eddie Duino,** San Jose C.C., San Jose, Calif.
1960 **Warren Orlick,** Tam O'Shanter C.C., Orchard Lake, Mich.
1961 **Don Padgett,** Green Hills C.C., Selma, Ind.
1962 **Tom Lo Presti,** Haggin Oaks G.C., Sacramento, Calif.
1963 **Bruce Herd,** Flossmoor C.C., Flossmoor, Ill.
1964 **Lyle Wehrman,** Merced G.&C.C., Merced, Calif.
1965 **Hubby Habjan,** Onwentsia Club, Lake Forest, Ill.
1966 **Bill Strausbaugh Jr.,** Turf Valley C.C., Ellicott City, Md.

1967 **Ernie Vossler,** Quail Creek C.C., Oklahoma City, Okla.
1968 **Hardy Loudermilk,** Oak Hills, C.C., San Antonio, Tex.
1969 **A. Hubert Smith,** Arnold Center C.C., Tullahoma, Tenn.
Wally Mund, Midland Hills C.C., St. Paul, Minn.
1970 **Grady Shumate,** Tanglewood G.C., Clemmons, N.C.
1971 **Ross Collins,** Dallas A. C. C. C., Dallas, Tex.
1972 **Howard Morrette,** Twin Lakes C.C., Kent, Ohio
1973 **Warren Smith,** Cherry-Hills C.C., Englewood, Colo.
1974 **Paul Harney,** Paul Harney's G.C., Hatchville, Mass.
1975 **Walker Inman, Jr.,** Scioto C.C., Columbus, Ohio
1976 **Ron Letellier,** Cold Spring Harbor C.C., N.Y.
1977 **Don Soper,** Royal Oak, Mich.
1978 **Walter Lowell**, N.A.
1979 **Gary Ellis**, N.A.
1980 **Stan Thirsk**, N.A.

The Vardon Trophy honors consistency in professional competition as shown in low strokes-per-round during tournament play.

1937 **Harry Cooper**
1938 **Sam Snead**
1939 **Byron Nelson**
1940 **Ben Hogan**
1941 **Ben Hogan**
1942-46 **No awards**
1947 **Jimmy Demaret**
1948 **Ben Hogan**
1949 **Sam Snead**
1950 **Sam Snead**
1951 **Lloyd Mangrum**
1952 **Jackie Burke**
1953 **Lloyd Mangrum**
1954 **Dutch Harrison**
1955 **Sam Snead**
1956 **Cary Middlecoff**
1957 **Dow Finsterwald**
1958 **Bob Rosburg**
1959 **Art Wall**
1960 **Billy Casper**
1961 **Arnold Palmer**
1962 **Arnold Palmer**
1963 **Billy Casper**
1964 **Arnold Palmer**
1965 **Billy Casper**
1966 **Billy Casper**
1967 **Arnold Palmer**
1968 **Billy Casper**
1969 **Dave Hill**
1970 **Lee Trevino**
1971 **Lee Trevino**
1972 **Lee Trevino**
1973 **Bruce Crampton**
1974 **Lee Trevino**
1975 **Bruce Crampton**
1976 **Don January**
1977 **Tom Watson**
1978 **Tom Watson**
1979 **Tom Watson**
1980 **Lee Trevino**

The Ed Dudley Award was given first once and then twice annually to the low-qualifying player in the PGA Players' Division qualification tournament. It has been discontinued.

1965 **John Schlee,** (144 holes)
1966 **Harry Toscano,** (144 holes)
1967 **Bobby Cole,** (144 holes)
1968 (Spring) **Bob Dickson,** (144 holes)
(Fall) **Grier Jones,** (144 holes)
Martin Roesink, (144 holes)
1969 (Spring) **Bobby Eastwood,** (72 holes)
(Fall) **Doug Olson,** (72 holes)
1970 **Bob Barbarossa,** (72 holes)
1971 **Bob Zender,** (108 holes)
1972 **Larry Stubblefield,** (108 holes)
1973 **Ben Crenshaw,** (144 holes)
1974 **Fuzzy Zoeller,** (144 holes)
1975 (Spring) **Joey Dills,** (108 holes)
(Fall) **Jerry Pate,** (108 holes)
1976 (Spring) **Woody Blackburn,** (108 holes)
(Fall) **Keith Fergus,** (108 holes)
1977 (Spring) **Phil Hancock,** (108 holes)
(Fall) **Ed Fiori** N.A.

The Horton Smith Trophy honors the professional who is judged to have made the greatest contributions to professional golf education.

1965 **Emil Beck,** Black River C.C., Port Huron, Mich.
1966 **Gene C. Mason,** Columbia-Edgewater C.C., Portland, Ore.
1967 **Donald E. Fischesser,** Evansville C.C., Evansville, Ind.
1968 **R. William Clarke,** Hillendale C.C., Phoenix, Md.
1969 **Paul Hahn,** Miami, Fla.
1970 **Joe Walser,** Oklahoma City C.C., Oklahoma City, Okla.
1971 **Irving Schloss,** Dunedin, Fla.
1972 **John Budd,** New Port Richey, Fla.
1973 **George Aulbach,** Pecan Valley C.C., San Antonio, Tex.
1974 **Bill Hardy,** Chevy Chase Club, Chevy Chase, Md.
1975 **John P. Henrich,** Elma Meadows G.C., Elma, N.Y.
1976 **Jim Bailey,** Adams Park Golf Course, Brighton, Colo.
1977 **Paul Runyan,** Green Gables C.C., Denver, Colo.
1978 **Andy Nusbaum**, N.A.
1979 **Howard Smith**, N.A.
1980 **Dale Mead**, N.A.

Bob Jones Award
Green Section Award

U.S. GOLF ASSOCIATION
Golf House, Far Hills, N.J. 07931 (201/234-2300)

The Bob Jones Award is given annually to honor individuals whose personal qualities exemplify those which are esteemed in sports, such as generosity of spirit, manner of playing or behaving so as to show respect for the game and the people in it, unselfishness, self-control and fair play.

1955 **Michael Bonallack**
1956 **Francis D. Ouimet**
1957 **William C. Campbell**
1958 **Mildred "Babe" Didrikson Zaharias**
1959 **Margaret Curtis**
1960 **Findlay S. Douglas**
1961 **Charles Evans, Jr.**
1962 **Joseph B. Carr**
1963 **Horton Smith**
1964 **Patty Berg**
1965 **Charles R. Coe**
1966 **Mrs. Edwin H. Vare, Jr.**
1967 **Gary Player**
1968 **Richard S. Tufts**
1969 **Robert B. Dickson**

1970 Gerald H. Micklem
1971 Roberto DeVicenzo
1972 Arnold Palmer
1973 Gene Littler
1974 Byron Nelson
1975 Jack Nicklaus
1976 Ben Hogan
1977 Joseph C. Dey, Jr.
1978 Bing Crosby
Bob Hope
1979 Tom Kite, Jr.
1980 Charles R. Yates

The Green Section Award recognizes service to golf through work with turfgrass. Nominees may be involved with research, extension, superintendence, maintenance or any other direct work.

1961 John Monteith
1962 Lawrence S. Dickinson
1963 O.J. Noer
1964 Joseph Valentine
1965 Glenn W. Burton
1966 H. Burton Musser
1967 Elmer J. Michael
1968 James L. Haines
1969 Fred V. Grau
1970 Eberhardt R. Steiniger
1971 Thomas Mascaro
1972 Herb and Joe Graffis
1973 Marvin Ferguson
1974 Howard B. Sprague
1975 Fannie Fern Davis
1976 James R. Watson
1977 Edward J. Casey
1978 Jesse de France
1979 Arthur A. Snyder
1980 C. Reed Funk

Milton B. Davis Trampoline Coach of the Year Rotating Trophy Award
Roy E. Moore Award
James A. Rozanas Memorial Tumbling Coach of the Year

AMATEUR ATHLETIC UNION OF THE UNITED STATES
3400 W. 86th St., Indianapolis, Ind. 46268 (317/297-2900)

The Milton B. Davis Trampoline Coach of the Year Rotating Trophy Award is given to the coach for outstanding dedication to faith and morals, athletics, the betterment of the sport and the principles of competition and sportsmanship.

1976 David Coons
1977 Donald Waters
1978 Paul Swafford
1979 Bil Copp
1980 Not available at press time

SERVICE AWARD

1977 Robert Thurston

The Roy E. Moore Award is awarded annually to the team winning the Men's Senior National Gymnastic Championship.

1957 Los Angeles Turners
1958 Los Angeles Turners
1959 Los Angeles Turners
1960 Pennsylvania State University
1961 Southern Illinois University
1962 Los Angeles Turners
1963 Los Angeles Turners
1964 Los Angeles Turners
1965 Southern Connecticut Gymnastics Club
1966 Southern Connecticut Gymnastics Club
1967 Northwestern Louisiana State College
1968 Husky Gymnastics Club (Seattle, Wash.)
1969 Husky Gymnastics Club (Seattle, Wash.)
1970 New York Athletic Club
1971 New York Athletic Club
1972 New York Athletic Club
1973 New York Athletic Club
1974 New York Athletic Club
1975 New York Athletic Club
1976 National Gymnastics Center (Woodward, Pa.)
1977 New York Athletic Club
1978 New York Athletic Club
1979 New York Athletic Club
1980 Athletes in Action (Fountain Valley, Col.)

The James A. Ronzanas Memorial Tumbling Coach of the Year award is given for outstanding dedication, commitment, enthusiasm and tireless efforts in teaching not only the skills but also the morals and discipline of good sportsmanship in furthering the sport of tumbling.

1976 Dave Green
Roger Brown
1977 Pat Henderson
1978 Clark Gangwish
1979 Cindy Kwiek Morano
1980 Not available at press time

Prince of Wales Trophy
Clarence S. Campbell Bowl
Hart Memorial Trophy
Calder Memorial Trophy
James Norris Memorial Trophy
Art Ross Trophy
Vezina Trophy
Lady Byng Memorial Trophy
Lester Patrick Trophy
Conn Smythe Memorial Trophy
Bill Masterton Memorial Trophy

NATIONAL HOCKEY LEAGUE
920 Sun Life Bldg., Montreal H3B 2W2, Canada (514/871-9220)

The Prince of Wales Trophy, originally donated by His Royal Highness and given until 1974 for team excellence in league division performance in regular-season play, is now awarded to the winner of the Prince of Wales Conference at the end of the regular championship season.

1925 Montreal Canadiens
1926 Montreal Maroons
1927 Ottawa Senators
1928 Boston Bruins

1929 **Boston Bruins**
1930 **Boston Bruins**
1931 **Boston Bruins**
1932 **New York Rangers**
1933 **Boston Bruins**
1934 **Detroit Red Wings**
1935 **Boston Bruins**
1936 **Detroit Red Wings**
1937 **Detroit Red Wings**
1938 **Boston Bruins**
1939 **Boston Bruins**
1940 **Boston Bruins**
1941 **Boston Bruins**
1942 **New York Rangers**
1943 **Detroit Red Wings**
1944 **Montreal Canadiens**
1945 **Montreal Canadiens**
1946 **Montreal Canadiens**
1947 **Montreal Canadiens**
1948 **Toronto Maple Leafs**
1949 **Detroit Red Wings**
1950 **Detroit Red Wings**
1951 **Detroit Red Wings**
1952 **Detroit Red Wings**
1953 **Detroit Red Wings**
1954 **Detroit Red Wings**
1955 **Detroit Red Wings**
1956 **Montreal Canadiens**
1957 **Detroit Red Wings**
1958 **Montreal Canadiens**
1959 **Montreal Canadiens**
1960 **Montreal Canadiens**
1961 **Montreal Canadiens**
1962 **Montreal Canadiens**
1963 **Toronto Maple Leafs**
1964 **Montreal Canadiens**
1965 **Detroit Red Wings**
1966 **Montreal Canadiens**
1967 **Chicago Black Hawks**
1968 **Montreal Canadiens**
1969 **Montreal Canadiens**
1970 **Chicago Black Hawks**
1971 **Boston Bruins**
1972 **Boston Bruins**
1973 **Montreal Canadiens**
1974 **Boston Bruins**
1975 **Buffalo Sabres**
1976 **Montreal Canadiens**
1977 **Montreal Canadiens**
1978 **Montreal Canadiens**
1979 **Montreal Canadiens**
1980 **Buffalo Sabres**

The Clarence S. Campbell Bowl is presented annually to the team finishing with the most points in the Clarence S. Campbell Conference.

1968 **Philadelphia Flyers**
1969 **St. Louis Blues**
1970 **St. Louis Blues**
1971 **Chicago Black Hawks**
1972 **Chicago Black Hawks**
1973 **Chicago Black Hawks**
1974 **Philadelphia Flyers**
1975 **Philadelphia Flyers**
1976 **Philadelphia Flyers**
1977 **Philadelphia Flyers**
1978 **New York Islanders**
1979 **New York Islanders**
1980 **Philadelphia Flyers**

The Hart Memorial Trophy, which carries a cash award of $1,500, is awarded annually to the player judged to be the most valuable to his team by a poll of the Professional Hockey Writers' Association.

1924 **Frank Nighbor,** Ottawa Senators
1925 **Billy Burch,** Hamilton
1926 **Nels Stewart,** Montreal Maroons
1927 **Herb Gardiner,** Montreal Canadiens
1928 **Howie Morenz,** Montreal Canadiens
1929 **Ray Worters,** New York Americans
1930 **Nels Stewart,** Montreal Maroons
1931 **Howie Morenz,** Montreal Canadiens
1932 **Howie Morenz,** Montreal Canadiens
1933 **Eddie Shore,** Boston Bruins
1934 **Aurel Joliat,** Montreal Canadiens
1935 **Eddie Shore,** Boston Bruins
1936 **Eddie Shore,** Boston Bruins
1937 **"Babe" Siebert,** Montreal Canadiens
1938 **Eddie Shore,** Boston Bruins
1939 **Toe Blake,** Montreal Canadiens
1940 **Ebbie Goodfellow,** Detroit Redwings
1941 **Bill Cowley,** Boston Bruins
1942 **Tommy Anderson,** New York Americans
1943 **Bill Cowley,** Boston Bruins
1944 **"Babe" Pratt,** Toronto Maple Leafs
1945 **Elmer Lach,** Montreal Canadiens
1946 **Max Bentley,** Chicago Black Hawks
1947 **Maurice Richard,** Montreal Canadiens
1948 **Buddy O'Connor,** New York Rangers
1949 **Sid Abel,** Detroit Red Wings
1950 **Chuck Rayner,** New York Rangers
1951 **Milt Schmidt,** Boston Bruins
1952 **Gordie Howe,** Detroit Red Wings
1953 **Gordie Howe,** Detroit Red Wings
1954 **Al Rollins,** Chicago Black Hawks
1955 **Ted Kennedy,** Toronto Maple Leafs
1956 **Jean Beliveau,** Montreal Canadiens
1957 **Gordie Howe,** Detroit Red Wings
1958 **Gordie Howe,** Detroit Red Wings
1959 **Andy Bathgate,** New York Rangers
1960 **Gordie Howe,** Detroit Red Wings
1961 **Bernie Geoffrion,** Montreal Canadiens
1962 **Jacques Plante,** Montreal Canadiens
1963 **Gordie Howe,** Detroit Red Wings
1964 **Jean Beliveau,** Montreal Canadiens
1965 **Bobby Hull,** Chicago Black Hawks
1966 **Bobby Hull,** Chicago Black Hawks
1967 **Stan Mikita,** Chicago Black Hawks
1968 **Stan Mikita,** Chicago Black Hawks
1969 **Phil Esposito,** Boston Bruins
1970 **Bobby Orr,** Boston Bruins
1971 **Bobby Orr,** Boston Bruins
1972 **Bobby Orr,** Boston Bruins
1973 **Bobby Clarke,** Philadelphia Flyers
1974 **Phil Esposito,** Boston Bruins
1975 **Bobby Clarke,** Philadelphia Flyers
1976 **Bobby Clarke,** Philadelphia Flyers
1977 **Guy Lafleur,** Montreal Canadiens
1978 **Guy Lafleur,** Montreal Canadiens
1979 **Bryan Trottier,** New York Islanders
1980 **Wayne Gretzky,** Edmonton Oilers

The Calder Memorial Trophy, which carries a cash award of $1,500, is awarded annually to the player selected as the most proficient in his first year of competition in the National Hockey League in a poll by the Professional Hockey Writers' Association.

1952 **Bernie Geoffrion,** Montreal Canadiens
1953 **Gump Worsley,** New York Rangers

1954 **Camille Henry,** New York Rangers
1955 **Ed Litzenberger,** Chicago Black Hawks
1956 **Glenn Hall,** Detroit Red Wings
1957 **Larry Regan,** Boston Bruins
1958 **Frank Mahovlich,** Toronto Maple Leafs
1959 **Ralph Backstrom,** Montreal Canadiens
1960 **Bill Hay,** Chicago Black Hawks
1961 **Dave Keon,** Toronto Maple Leafs
1962 **Bobby Rousseau,** Montreal Canadiens
1963 **Kent Douglas,** Toronto Maple Leafs
1964 **Jacques Laperriere,** Montreal Canadiens
1965 **Roger Crozier,** Detroit Reg Wings
1966 **Brit Selby,** Toronto Maple Leafs
1967 **Bobby Orr,** Boston Bruins
1968 **Derek Sanderson,** Boston Bruins
1969 **Danny Grant,** Minnesota North Stars
1970 **Tony Esposito,** Chicago Black Hawks
1971 **Gilbert Perreault,** Buffalo Sabres
1972 **Ken Dryden,** Montreal Canadiens
1973 **Steve Vickers,** New York Rangers
1974 **Denis Potvin,** New York Islanders
1975 **Eric Vail,** Atlanta Flames
1976 **Bryan Trottier,** New York Islanders
1977 **Willi Plett,** Atlanta Flames
1978 **Mike Bossy,** New York Islanders
1979 **Bobby Smith,** Minnesota North Stars
1980 **Ray Bourque,** Boston Bruins

The James Norris Memorial Trophy, which carries a cash award of $1,500, is awarded annually to the defensive player in the National Hockey League who demonstrates the greatest season-long ability, as selected in a poll of the Professional Hockey Writers' Association.

1954 **Red Kelly,** Detroit Red Wings
1955 **Doug Harvey,** Montreal Canadiens
1956 **Doug Harvey,** Montreal Canadiens
1957 **Doug Harvey,** Montreal Canadiens
1958 **Doug Harvey,** Montreal Canadiens
1959 **Tom Johnson,** Montreal Canadiens
1960 **Doug Harvey,** Montreal Canadiens
1961 **Doug Harvey,** Montreal Canadiens
1962 **Doug Harvey,** New York Rangers
1963 **Pierre Pilote,** Chicago Black Hawks
1964 **Pierre Pilote,** Chicago Black Hawks
1965 **Pierre Pilote,** Chicago Black Hawks
1966 **Jacques Laperriere,** Montreal Canadiens
1967 **Harry Howell,** New York Rangers
1968 **Bobby Orr,** Boston Bruins
1969 **Bobby Orr,** Boston Bruins
1970 **Bobby Orr,** Boston Bruins
1971 **Bobby Orr,** Boston Bruins
1972 **Bobby Orr,** Boston Bruins
1973 **Bobby Orr,** Boston Bruins
1974 **Bobby Orr,** Boston Bruins
1975 **Bobby Orr,** Boston Bruins
1976 **Denis Potvin,** New York Islanders
1977 **Larry Robinson,** Montreal Canadiens
1978 **Denis Potvin,** New York Islanders
1979 **Denis Potvin,** New York Islanders
1980 **Larry Robinson,** Montreal Canadiens

The Art Ross Trophy, which carries a cash award of $1,000, is given annually to the league player who leads in scoring during the regular season.

1952 **Gordie Howe,** Detroit Red Wings
1953 **Gordie Howe,** Detroit Red Wings
1954 **Gordie Howe,** Detroit Red Wings
1955 **Bernie Geoffrion,** Montreal Canadien
1956 **Jean Beliveau,** Montreal Canadiens
1957 **Gordie Howe,** Detroit Red Wings
1958 **Dickie Moore,** Montreal Canadiens
1959 **Dickie Moore,** Montreal Canadiens
1960 **Bobby Hull,** Chicago Black Hawks
1961 **Bernie Geoffrion,** Montreal Canadiens
1962 **Bobby Hull,** Chicago Black Hawks
1963 **Gordie Howe,** Detroit Red Wings
1964 **Stan Mikita,** Chicago Black Hawks
1965 **Stan Mikita,** Chicago Black Hawks
1966 **Bobby Hull,** Chicago Black Hawks
1967 **Stan Mikita,** Chicago Black Hawks
1968 **Stan Mikita,** Chicago Black Hawks
1969 **Phil Esposito,** Boston Bruins
1970 **Bobby Orr,** Boston Bruins
1971 **Phil Esposito,** Boston Bruins
1972 **Phil Esposito,** Boston Bruins
1973 **Phil Esposito,** Boston Bruins
1974 **Phil Esposito,** Boston Bruins
1975 **Bobby Orr,** Boston Bruins
1976 **Guy Lafleur,** Montreal Canadiens
1977 **Guy Lafleur,** Montreal Canadiens
1978 **Guy Lafleur,** Montreal Canadiens
1979 **Bryan Trottier,** New York Islanders
1980 **Marcel Dionne,** Los Angeles Kings

The Vezina Trophy, which carries a cash award of $1,500, is given annually to the goalkeeper(s) playing at least 25 games for the team with the fewest goals scored against it.

1952 **Terry Sawchuk,** Detroit Red Wings
1953 **Terry Sawchuk,** Detroit Red Wings
1954 **Harry Lumley,** Toronto Maple Leafs
1955 **Terry Sawchuk,** Detroit Red Wings
1956 **Jacques Plante,** Montreal Canadiens
1957 **Jacques Plante,** Montreal Canadiens
1958 **Jacques Plante,** Montreal Canadiens
1959 **Jacques Plante,** Montreal Canadiens
1960 **Jacques Plante,** Montreal Canadiens
1961 **Johnny Bower,** Toronto Maple Leafs
1962 **Jacques Plante,** Montreal Canadiens
1963 **Glenn Hall,** Chicago Black Hawks
1964 **Charlie Hodge,** Montreal Canadiens
1965 **Terry Sawchuk,** Toronto Maple Leafs
Johnny Bower, Toronto Maple Leafs
1966 **Gump Worsley,** Montreal Canadiens
Charlie Hodge, Montreal Canadiens
1967 **Glenn Hall,** Chicago Black Hawks
Denis DeJordy, Chicago Black Hawks
1968 **Gump Worsley,** Montreal Canadiens
Rogatien Vachon, Montreal Canadiens
1969 **Jacques Plante,** St. Louis Blues
Glenn Hall, St. Louis Blues
1970 **Tony Esposito,** Chicago Black Hawks
1971 **Ed Giacomin,** New York Rangers
Gilles Villemure, New York Rangers
1972 **Tony Esposito,** Chicago Black Hawks
Gary Smith, Chicago Black Hawks
1973 **Ken Dryden,** Montreal Canadiens
1974 **Bernie Parent,** Philadelphia Flyers
Tony Esposito, Chicago Black Hawks
1975 **Bernie Parent,** Philadelphia Flyers
1976 **Ken Dryden,** Montreal Canadiens
1977 **Ken Dryden,** Montreal Canadiens
Michel Larocque, Montreal Canadiens
1978 **Key Dryden,** Montreal Canadiens
Michel Larocque, Montreal Canadiens
1979 **Ken Dryden,** Montreal Canadiens
Michel Larocque, Montreal Canadiens
1980 **Bob Sauve,** Buffalo Sabres
Don Edwards, Buffalo Sabres

The Lady Byng Memorial Trophy, which carries a cash award of $1,500, is given annually to the player judged to have "exhibited the best type of sportsmanship and gentlemanly conduct combined with a high standard of playing ability" during the previous playing season, as selected by a poll of the Professional Hockey Writers' Association.

1925 **Frank Nighbor,** Ottawa Senators
1926 **Frank Nighbor,** Ottawa Senators
1927 **Billy Burch,** New York Americans
1928 **Frank Boucher,** New York Rangers
1929 **Frank Boucher,** New York Rangers
1930 **Frank Boucher,** New York Rangers
1931 **Frank Boucher,** New York Rangers
1932 **Joe Primeau,** Toronto Maple Leafs
1933 **Frank Boucher,** New York Rangers
1934 **Frank Boucher,** New York Rangers
1935 **Frank Boucher,** New York Rangers
1936 **Doc Romney,** Chicago Black Hawks
1937 **Marty Barry,** Detroit Red Wings
1938 **Gordie Drillon,** Toronto Maple Leafs
1939 **Clint Smith,** New York Rangers
1940 **Bobby Baver,** Boston Bruins
1941 **Bobby Baver,** Boston Bruins
1942 **Phil Apps,** Toronto Maple Leafs
1943 **Max Bentley,** Chicago Black Hawks
1944 **Clint Smith,** Chicago Black Hawks
1945 **Bill Mosienko,**Chicago Black Hawks
1946 **"Toe" Black,** Montreal Canadiens
1947 **Bobby Baver,** Boston Bruins
1948 **Buddy O'Connor,** New York Rangers
1949 **Bill Quackenbush,** Detroit Red Wings
1950 **Edgar Laprade,** New York Rangers
1951 **Red Kelly,** Detroit Red Wings
1952 **Sid Smith,** Toronto Maple Leafs
1953 **Red Kelly,** Detroit Red Wings
1954 **Red Kelly,** Detroit Red Wings
1955 **Sid Smith,** Toronto Maple Leafs
1956 **Earl Reibel,** Detroit Red Wings
1957 **Andy Hebenton,** New York Rangers
1958 **Camille Henry,** New York Rangers
1959 **Alex Delvecchio,** Detroit Red Wings
1960 **Don McKenney,** Boston Bruins
1961 **Red Kelly,** Toronto Maple Leafs
1962 **Dave Keon,** Toronto Maple Leafs
1963 **Dave Keon,** Toronto Maple Leafs
1964 **Ken Wharram,** Chicago Black Hawks
1965 **Bobby Hull,** Chicago Black Hawks
1966 **Alex Delvecchio,** Detroit Red Wings
1967 **Stan Mikita,** Chicago Black Hawks
1968 **Stan Mikita,** Chicago Black Hawks
1969 **Alex Delvecchio,** Detroit Red Wings
1970 **Phil Goyette,** St. Louis Blues
1971 **Johnny Bucyk,** Boston Bruins
1972 **Jean Ratelle,** New York Rangers
1973 **Gilbert Perreault,** Buffalo Sabres
1974 **Johnny Bucyk,** Boston Bruins
1975 **Marcel Dionne,** Detroit Red Wings
1976 **Jean Ratelle,** New York Rangers and Boston Bruins
1977 **Marcel Dionne,** Los Angeles Kings
1978 **Butch Goring,** Los Angeles Kings
1979 **Bob MacMillan,** Atlanta Flames
1980 **Wayne Gretzky,** Edmonton Oilers

The Lester Patrick Trophy is awarded annually to the players, officials, coaches and referees judged to have given the most outstanding service to hockey in the United States. The winner is selected by an award committee consisting of the NHL president, NHL governor, a hockey writer for a U.S. national news service, a nationally syndicated sports columnist, an ex-player in the Hockey Hall of Fame and a sports director of a national broadcast network.

1966 **Jack Adams**
1967 **Gordie Howe**
Charles F. Adams
James Norris, Sr.
1968 **Thomas F. Lockhart**
Walter Brown
Gen. John R. Kilpatrick
1969 **Bobby Hull**
Edward Jeremiah
1970 **Eddie Shore**
James Hendy
1971 **William M. Jennings**
John B. Sollenberger
Terry Sawchuk
1972 **Clarence S. Campbell**
John Kelley
Cooney Weiland
1973 **Walter L. Bush, Jr.**
1974 **Alex Delvecchio**
Murray Murdoch
Weston W. Adams, Sr.
Charles L. Crovat
1975 **Donald M. Clark**
William L. Chadwick
Thomas N. Ivan
1976 **Stan Mikita**
George A. Leader
Bruce A. Norris
1977 **John Bucyk**
Murray Armstrong
John Mariucci
1978 **Phil Esposito**
Tom Fitzgerald
William T. Tutt
William W. Wirtz
1979 **Bobby Orr**
1980 **Bobby Clarke**
Ed Snider
Fred Shero
1980 U.S. Olympic Hockey Team

The Conn Smythe Memorial Trophy is given to the individual deemed the most valuable player in the league play-offs.

1965 **Jean Beliveau,** Montreal Canadiens
1966 **Roger Crozier,** Detroit Red Wings
1967 **Dave Keon,** Toronto Maple Leafs
1968 **Glenn Hall,** St. Louis Blues
1969 **Serge Savard,** Montreal Canadiens
1970 **Bobby Orr,** Boston Bruins
1971 **Ken Dryden,** Montreal Canadiens
1972 **Bobby Orr,** Boston Bruins
1973 **Yvan Cournoyer,** Montreal Canadiens
1974 **Bernie Parent,** Philadelphia Flyers
1975 **Bernie Parent,** Philadelphia Flyers
1976 **Reggie Leach,** Philadelphia Flyers
1977 **Guy Lafleur,** Montreal Canadiens
1978 **Larry Robinson,** Montreal Canadiens
1979 **Bob Gainey,** Montreal Canadiens
1980 **Bryan Trottier,** New York Islanders

The Bill Masterton Memorial Trophy honors perseverence, sportsmanship and dedication to professional hockey.

1968 **Claude Provost,** Montreal Canadiens
1969 **Ted Hampson,** Oakland

1970 **Pit Martin,** Chicago Black Hawks
1971 **Jean Ratelle,** New York Rangers
1972 **Bobby Clarke,** Philadelphia Flyers
1973 **Lowell MacDonald,** Pittsburgh Penguins
1974 **Henri Richard,** Montreal Canadiens
1975 **Don Luce,** Buffalo Sabres
1976 **Rod Gilbert,** New York Rangers
1977 **Ed Westfall,** New York Islanders
1978 **Butch Goring,** Los Angeles Kings
1979 **Serge Savard,** Montreal Canadiens
1980 **Al MacAdam,** Minnesota North Stars

Avco World Trophy
Gordie Howe Trophy
W.D. "Bill" Hunter Trophy

WORLD HOCKEY ASSOCIATION
c/o National Hockey League, 920 Sun Life Bldg., Montreal H3B 2W2, Canada (514/871-9220)

The World Hockey Association no longer exists, but the awards listed below were presented while it functioned as a league of professional hockey teams. Some of these teams are now in the NHL, while others no long- er exist.

The Avco World Trophy was awarded to the WHA championship team.

1973 **New England Whalers**
1974 **Houston Aeros**
1975 **Houston Aeros**
1976 **Winnipeg Jets**
1977 **Quebec Nordiques**

The Gordie Howe Trophy honored the Most Valuable Player in the league, selected by a vote of the media people covering WHA teams.

1973 **Bobby Hull,** Winnipeg Jets
1974 **Gordie Howe,** Houston Aeros
1975 **Bobby Hull,** Winnipeg Jets
1976 **Marc Tardif,** Quebec Nordiques
1977 **Robbie Ftorek,** Phoenix Roadrunners

The W.D. "Bill" Hunter Trophy was given to the league scoring leader.

1973 **Andre Lacroix,** Philadelphia Blazers
1974 **Mike Walton,** Minnesota Fighting Saints
1975 **Andre Lacroix,** San Diego Mariners
1976 **Marc Tardif,** Quebec Nordiques
1977 **Real Cloutier,** Quebec Nordiques

Horseman of the Year

HORSEMAN AND FAIR WORLD PUBLISHING CO.
Box 11688, Lexington, Ky. 40511 (606/254-4026)

The subscribers to *Horseman and Fair World* annually vote on the individual to be honored as the Horseman of the Year on the basis of contributions to harness racing. The winner receives a set of silver mint julep cups on a silver tray and is the subject of a feature in the magazine.

1956 **Delvin Miller**
1957 **John Simpson, Sr.**
1958 **William Haughton**
1959 **Joe O'Brien**
1960 **Clint Hodgins**
1961 **Frank Ervin**
1962 **Stanley Dancer**
1963 **Ralph Baldwin**
1964 **Frank Ervin**
1965 **Frank Ervin**
1966 **Robert Farrington**
1967 **William Haughton**
1968 **Stanley Dancer**
1969 **Mr. and Mrs. Frederick Van Lennep**
1970 **Stanley F. Bergstein**
1971 **William R. Hayes II**
1972 **Mr. and Mrs. H. Willis Nichols**
1973 **E. Roland Harriman**
1974 **Elgin Armstrong**
1975 **Henry C. Thomson**
1976 **Norman Woolworth and David Johnston**
1977 **Lloyd Arnold**
1978 **Charles Hill**
1979 **C.F. Gaines**
1980 **Not available at press time**

Eclipse Awards

THOROUGHBRED RACING ASSOCIATION
3000 Marcus Ave., Suite 2W4, Lake Success, N,Y. 11042 (516/328-2660)

The Eclipse Awards, which are statuettes, are given annually to various individuals and horses for contributions to and achievements in thoroughbred horseracing. A vote of three groups representing North American racing secretaries, turf writers and *The Daily Racing Form* determines the recipients.

HORSE OF THE YEAR

1971 **Ack Ack**
1972 **Secretariat**
1973 **Secretariat**
1974 **Forego**
1975 **Forego**
1976 **Forego**
1977 **Seattle Slew**
1978 **Affirmed**
1979 **Affirmed**
1980 **Spectacular Bid**

OLDER COLT, HORSE OR GELDING

1971 **Ack Ack**
1972 **Autobiography**
1973 **Riva Ridge**
1974 **Forego**
1975 **Forego**
1976 **Forego**
1977 **Forego**
1978 **Seattle Slew**
1979 **Affirmed**
1980 **Spectacular Bid**

OLDER FILLY OR MARE

1971 **Shuvee**
1972 **Typecast**
1973 **Susan's Girl**
1974 **Desert Vixen**
1975 **Susan's Girl**
1976 **Proud Delta**
1977 **Cascapedia**

1978 Late Bloomer
1979 Waya
1980 Glorious Song

THREE-YEAR-OLD COLT

1971 Canonero II
1972 Key to the Mint
1973 Secretariat
1974 Little Current
1975 Wajima
1976 Bold Forbes
1977 Seattle Slew
1978 Affirmed
1979 Spectacular Bid
1980 Temperence Hill

THREE-YEAR-OLD FILLY

1971 Turkish Trousers
1972 Susan's Girl
1973 Desert Vixen
1974 Chris Evert
1975 Ruffian
1976 Revidere
1977 Our Mims
1978 Tempest Queen
1979 Davona Dale
1980 Genuine Risk

TWO-YEAR-OLD COLT

1971 Riva Ridge
1972 Secretariat
1973 Protagonist
1974 Foolish Pleasure
1975 Honest Pleasure
1976 Seattle Slew
1977 Affirmed
1978 Spectacular Bid
1979 Rockhill Native
1980 Lord Avie

TWO-YEAR-OLD FILLY

1971 Numbered Account
1972 La Prevolante
1973 Talking Picture
1974 Ruffian
1975 Dearly Precious
1976 Sensational
1977 Lakeville Miss
1978 Candy Eclair
It's in the Air
1979 Smart Angle
1980 Heavenly Cause

TURF HORSE

1971 Run the Gantlet
1972 Cougar II
1973 Secretariat
1974 Dahlia
1975 Snow Knight
1976 Youth
1977 Johnny D
1978 Mac Diarmida

BEST GRASS HORSE — MALE

1978 Bowl Game
1980 John Henry

BEST GRASS HORSE — FEMALE

1979 Trillion
1980 Just A Game II

SPRINTER

1971 Ack Ack
1972 Chou Croute
1973 Shecky Greene
1974 Forego
1975 Gallant Bob
1976 My Juliet
1977 What a Summer
1978 Dr. Patches
J.O. Tobin
1979 Star de Naskra
1980 Plugged Nickle

STEEPLECHASE OR HURDLE HORSE

1971 Shadowbrook
1972 Soothsayer
1973 Athenian Idol
1974 Gran Kan
1975 Life's Illusion
1976 Straight and True
1977 Cafe Prince
1978 Cafe Prince
1979 Martie's Anger
1980 Zaccio

MAN OF THE YEAR

1972 John W. Galbreath
1973 Edward Plunket Taylor
1974 William L. McKnight
1975 John A. Morris

AWARD OF MERIT

1976 Jack J. Dreyfus
1977 Steve Cauthen
1978 Ogden Mills "Dinny" Phipps
1979 Frank E. "Jimmy" Kilroe
1980 John D. Schapiro

OUTSTANDING BREEDER

1974 John W. Galbreath
1975 Fred W. Hooper
1976 Nelson Bunker Hunt
1977 Edward Plunket Taylor
1978 Harbor View Farm
1979 Claiborne Farm
1980 Mrs. Henry D. Paxson

OUTSTANDING OWNER

1971 Mr. and Mrs. E. E. Fogelson
1974 Dan Lasater
1975 Dan Lasater
1976 Dan Lasater
1977 Maxwell Gluck
1978 Harbor View Farm
1979 Harbor View Farm
1980 Mr. and Mrs. Bertram Firestone

OUTSTANDING OWNER-BREEDER

1971 Paul Mellon
1972 Meadow Stable/Meadow Stud (C. T. Chenery)
1973 Meadow Stable/Meadow Stud (C. T. Chenery)

OUTSTANDING TRAINER

1971 Charles Whittingham

1972 Lucien Laurin
1973 H. Allen Jerkens
1974 Sherrill Ward
1975 Steve DiMauro
1976 Lazaro Barrera
1977 Lazaro Barrera
1978 Lazaro Barrera
1979 Lazaro Barrera
1980 Bud Delp

OUTSTANDING JOCKEY

1971 Laffit Pincay, Jr.
1972 Braulio Baeza
1973 Laffit Pincay, Jr.
1974 Laffit Pincay, Jr.
1975 Braulio Baeza
1976 Sandford D. Hawley
1977 Steve Cauthen
1978 Darrel McHargue
1979 Laffit Pincay, Jr.
1980 Chris McCarron

OUTSTANDING APPRENTICE JOCKEY

1971 Gene St. Leon
1972 Thomas Wallis
1973 Steve Valdez
1974 Chris McCarron
1975 Jimmy Edwards
1976 George Martens
1977 Steve Cauthen
1978 Ron Franklin
1979 Cash Asmussen
1980 Frank Lovato, Jr.

SPECIAL AWARD

1971 Robert J. Kleberg
1974 Charles Hatton
1976 Bill Shoemaker
1980 John T. Landry
Pierre E. "Peb" Bellocq

OUTSTANDING ACHIEVEMENT AWARD

1971 Charles Engelhard
1972 Arthur B. Hancock, Jr.

Meritorious Service Award

HORSEMEN'S BENEVOLENT & PROTECTIVE ASSOCIATION
6000 Executive Blvd., Suite 317, Rockville, Md. 20852 (301/881-7191)

The Association annually honors an individual for meritorious service to racing. A selection committee chooses the person to be honored. Unofficially, the recipient of this award is usually referred to as the Man of the Year. A trophy is presented to the winner.

1953 George Widener
1954 Marshall Cassidy
1955 Lou Smith
1956 Charles H. Strub
1957 Benjamin Lindheimer
1958 Leo O'Donnell
1959 J. Samuel Perlman
1960 J. J. "Jake" Isaacson
1961 James D. Stewart
1962 Irving Gushen
1963 Wathen Knebelkamp
1964 Neil J. Curry
1965 Edward P. Taylor
1966 Raymond R. Guest
1967 William H. May
1968 Thomas J. Brogan
1969 No award
1970 Harry Farnham
1971 Herve Racivitch
1972 Eugene Bierhaus
1973 Burt Bacharach
Bill Shoemaker
1974 William McKnight
1975 Ray H. Freeark
1976 American Horse Council
1977 David A. "Sonny" Werblin
1978 Hon. Jack Kemp
1979 Frank E. "Jimmy" Kilroe
1980 No award

Racehorse of the Year Award
National Hunt Champion Award

RACECOURSE ASSOCIATION
42 Portman Sq., London W1H 0JE, U.K. (Tel: 01-486 4571)

The Racehorse of the Year Award, a bronze statuette of a horse and jockey, is given annually for outstanding achievements by a horse racing on the flat. A committee of racing writers votes on the winner, which must have raced on a British course during the season for which the award is made.

1965 Sea Bird II
1966 Charlottown
1967 Busted
1968 Sir Ivor
1969 Park Top
1970 Nijinsky
1971 Mill Reef
1972 Brigadier Gerard
1973 Dahlia
1974 Dahlia
1975 Grundy
1976 Pawneese
1977 The Minstrel
1978 Shirley Heights
1979 Troy
1980 Moorestyle

The National Hunt Champion Award, a bronze statuette of a horse and jockey, is given annually to the outstanding horse that has competed in a British steeplechase or hurdle course during the previous season. A committee of racing writers selects the winner.

1966 **Arkle,** Steeplechaser
1967 **Mill House,** Steeplechaser
1968 **Persian War,** Hurdler
1969 **Persian War,** Hurdler
1970 **Persian War,** Hurdler
1971 **Bula,** Hurdler
1972 **Bula,** Hurdler
1973 **Pendil,** Steeplechaser
1974 **Red Rum,** Steeplechaser
1975 **Comedy of Errors,** Hurdler
1976 **Night Nurse,** Hurdler
1977 Midnight Court
1978 Midnight Court
1979 Sea Pigeon

1980 Not available at press time

Induction

RACING HALL OF FAME

Union Ave., Saratoga Springs, N.Y. 12866 (518/584-0400)

The Hall of Fame honors trainers, jockeys and horses (thoroughbred male and female horses, flat runners and steeplechasers). A nominating committee of three or more members appointed by the executive committee of the National Museum of Racing proposes candidates in all three categories for selection by a 100-member voting committee comprised of sportswriters and radio and television racing announcers. To be eligible, a horse must have been retired from racing, and a person must have retired or served as a jockey or trainer for more than 20 years in the United States.

TRAINERS

1955 William P. Burch
Thomas J. Healey
Sam Hildreth
Andrew J. Joyner
John W. Rogers
James Rowe, Sr.
1956 William Duke
John J. Hyland
Henry McDaniel
1957 No new inductees
1958 Sunny Jim Fitzsimmons
Hirsch Jacobs
Ben Jones
1959 Max Hirsch
H.A. "Jimmy" Jones
1960 William Molter, Jr.
1961 No new inductees
1962 No new inductees
1963 Preston M. Burch
1964 Louis Feustel
1965 No new inductees
1966 John M. Gaver
1967 J. Dallett "Dolly" Byers
Burt Mulholland
1968 Frank Childs
1969 J. Howard Lewis
Herbert J. Thompson
1970 Marion H. Van Berg
R.W. Walden
1971 Harvey Guy Bedwell
William C. Winfrey
1972 John Nerud
1973 Fred Burlew
Thomas Hitchcock, Sr.
Hollie Hughes
1974 Alfred P. Smithwick
Charlie Whittingham
1975 D. Michael Smithwick
1976 Robert A. "Whistling Bob" Smith
W.C. "Woody" Stephens
1977 Lucien Lauren
Sylvester Veitch
1978 Sherrill Ward
Frank Whitley
1979 Lazaro Barrera
1980 J. Elliott Burch
Horation Luro

JOCKEYS

1955 Laverne Fator
Edward R. Garrison
Daniel Mahrer
James McLaughlin
Walter Miller
Isaac Murphy
George M. Odom
Earl Sande
Tod Sloan
Fred Taral
Nash Turner
George Woolf
1956 Henry Griffin
Linus McAtee
Winnie O'Connor
Frank O'Neill
John Reiff
1957 Ted Atkinson
1958 Eddie Arcaro
John Longden
William Lee "Willie" Shoemaker
1959 William John Hartack John Loftus
1960 Ralph Reeves
1961 No inductees
1962
Lavelle "Buddy" Ensor
1963 Steve Brooks
Joseph A. "Joe" Notter
1964 No inductees
1965 John Adams
1966 No inductees
1967 Charles F. Kurtsinger
1968 Rigan McKinney
Jimmy Stout
1969 George H. Bostwick
Mack Garner
Willie Knapp
1970 Frank David Adams
Frank Coltiletti
Gilbert Patrick
Samuel Purdy
Carroll Shilling
1971 Albert Johnson
1972 Carroll K. Bassett
Eric Guerin
Clarence Kummer
1973 Sam Boulmetis
Robert H. Crawford
Bayard Tuckermen, Jr.
Raymond Workman
1974 Conn McCreary
1975 Laffit Pincay, Jr.
1976 Braulio Baeza
1977 Willie Simms
Manuel Ycaza
1978 Joseph Aitcheson, Jr.
Ivan Park
1979 Ron Turcotte
1980 Robert Ussery

HORSES

1955 Ben Brush
Boston
Domino
Hanover
Hindoo
Kingston
Lexington
Luke Blackburn

Salvator
Sir Archy
1956 Artful
Beldame
Broomstick
Colin
Commando
Fair Play
Good and Plenty
Peter Pan
Roseben
Sysonby
1957 Blue Larkspur
Equipoise
Exterminator
Gallant Fox
Grey Lag
Man O'War
Regret
Sarazen
Sir Barton
Twenty Grand
1958 Seabiscuit
War Admiral
1959 Citation
Whirlaway
1960 Tom Fool
1961 No inductees
1962 Count Fleet
1963 Armed
Gallorette
Native Dancer
Twilight Tear
1964 Assault
Busher
1965 Imp
Jolly Roger
Nashua
Omaha
1966 Elkridge
Neji
Swaps
Top Flight
1967 Bushranger
Cicada
Kelso
Miss Woodford
1968 Old Rosebud
1969 Battleship
Discovery
1970 American Eclipse
Buckpasser
1971 Dr. Fager
Jay Trump
Longfellow
1972 Pan Zareta
Round Table
1973 Bold Ruler
1974 Damascus
Dark Mirage
Secretariat
1975 Carry Back
Ruthless
Shuvee
Stymie
1976 Alsab
Bed O'Roses
L'Escargot
1977 No inductees
1978 Reigh Count
Native Diver
Oedipus
Searching
Silver Spoon
1979 Desert Vixen
Forego
Myrtlewood
Whisk Broom II
1980 Affirmed
Devil Diver
Fashion
Gamely

Joe Palmer Award

NATIONAL TURF WRITERS ASSOCIATION
6000 Executive Blvd., Suite 317, Rockville, Md. 20852
(301/881-2266)

The Joe Palmer Award is given annually for meritorious service to racing. A plaque is presented to the winner of a balloting of the association membership.

1964 Wathen Knebelkamp
1965 John D. Schapiro
1966 Marshall Cassidy
1967 John Longden
1968 Marion Van Berg
1969 Raymond Guest
1970 Warner L. Jones
1971 Bill Shoemaker
1972 Paul Mellon
1973 John Galbreath
1974 Secretariat
1975 I. J. Collins
1976 Fred W. Hooper
1977 Nelson Bunker Hunt
1978 Steve Cauthen
1979 Lazaro Barrera
1980 Not available at press time

Karate Award
Henry Stone Award
David G. Rivenes Award
Jujitsu Award

AMATEUR ATHLETIC UNION OF THE UNITED STATES
3400 W. 86th St., Indianapolis, Ind. 46268 (317/297-2900)

An Outstanding Service Award is presented annually for contributions to the development of karate.

1976 Jerry Thomson
1977 John Evans
1978 Anne Small
1979 Noel Smith
1980 Not available at press time

The Henry Stone Award is a plaque given annually to an individual for sustained contributions to the development of sport of judo.

1968 E. K. Koiwai
1969 Joseph Fitzsimmons
1970 Yosh Uchido
1971 Thomas Dalton
1972 Tom Nagamatsu
1973 Shag Okada

1974 **Frank Fullerton**
1975 **Wey Seng Kim**
James Takemori
1976 **James Colgan**
1977 **Mel Appelbaum**
1978 **Faye Allen**
1979 **Major Paul Maruyama**
1980 **Frank Fullerton**

The David G. Rivenes Award is presented annually for contributions to the development of *tae kwan do.*

1976 **Ken Min**
1977 **Dong Ja Yang**
1978 **Hwa Chong**
1979 **Kyong Won Ahn**
1980 **Not available at press time**

The Jujitsu Pioneer Award goes annually to an individual for promotion the sport.

1980 **Bud Estes**

The Jutjitsu Service Award is presented annually for overall contributions to the sport.

1980 **Ken Regennitter**

Craig Sweeney Award

U.S.A. RUGBY FOOTBALL UNION
27 E. State St., Sherburn, N.Y. 13460 (607/674-5381)

The Craig Sweeney Award is presented annually for outstanding leadership of a player who exemplifies the qualities of character and sportsmanship.

1979 **Mickey Ording**
1980 **Tom Selfridge**

Competitor of the Year Awards

SKI RACING
Box 79, Fair Haven, Vt. 05743 (802/468-5666)

Ski Racing's editors annually select the top skiers — amateur and professional, Alpine and Nordic — as the most outstanding performers in their specialties during the previous year.

COMPETITOR OF THE YEAR

1975 **Gustavo Thoeni,** Italy
1976 **Rosi Mittermaier,** Federal Republic of Germany
1977 **Ingemar Stenmark,** Sweden
1978 **Annemarie Moser-Proell,** Austria
1979 **Oddvar Braa,** Norway
1980 **Hanni Wenzel,** Liechenstein

WORLD CUP COMPETITOR OF THE YEAR - MALE

1975 **Gustavo Thoeni,** Italy
1976 **Ingemar Stenmark,** Sweden
1977 **Ingemar Stenmark,** Sweden
1978 **Ingemar Stenmark,** Sweden
1979 **Ingemar Stenmark,** Sweden
1980 **Ingemar Stenmark,** Sweden

WORLD CUP COMPETITOR OF THE YEAR - FEMALE

1975 **Annemarie Moser-Proell,** Austria
1976 **Rosi Mittermaier,** Federal Republic of Germany
1977 **Lise-Marie Morerod,** Switzerland
1978 **Annemarie Moser-Proell,** Austria
1979 **Annemarie Moser-Proell,** Austria
1980 **Hanni Wenzel,** Liechenstein

PRO RACER OF THE YEAR-MALE

1975 **Hank Kashiwa**
1976 **Henri Duvillard**
1977 **Henri Duvillard**
1978 **Andre Arnold**
1979 **Andre Arnold**
1980 **Andre Arnold**

PRO RACER OF THE YEAR-FEMALE

1978 **Toril Forland**
1979 **Toril Forland**
1980 **Toril Forland**

U.S. ALPINE RACER OF THE YEAR - MALE

1975 **Greg Jones,** Tahoe City, Calif.
1976 **Phil Mahre,** White Pass, Wash.
1977 **Phil Mahre,** White Pass, Wash.
1978 **Phil Mahre,** White Pass, Wash.
1979 **Phil Mahre,** White Pass, Wash.
1980 **Phil Mahre,** White Pass, Wash.

U.S. ALPINE RACER OF THE YEAR - FEMALE

1975 **Cindy Nelson,** Lutsen, Minn.
1976 **Cindy Nelson,** Lutsen, Minn.
1977 **Abbi Fisher,** South Conway, N.H.
1978 **Cindy Nelson,** Lutsen, Minn.
1979 **Cindy Nelson,** Lutsen, Minn.
1980 **Christen Cooper**

INTERNATIONAL NORDIC COMPETITOR OF THE YEAR - MALE

1975 **Oddvar Braa,** Norway
1976 **Anton Innauer,** Austria
1977 **Walter Steiner,** Switzerland
1978 **Sven Ake Lundback,** Sweden
1979 **Oddvar Braa,** Norway
1980 **Nikokuy Zimyatov,** U.S.S.R.

INTERNATIONAL NORDIC COMPETITOR OF THE YEAR - FEMALE

1975 **Galina Kulakova,** U.S.S.R.
1976 **Raisa Smetanina,** U.S.S.R.
1977 **Galina Kulakova,** U.S.S.R.
1978 **Hilkka Riihivori,** Finland
1979 **Gulina Kulakova,** U.S.S.R.
1980 **Hilkka Riihivoari,** Finland

U.S. NORDIC COMPETITOR OF THE YEAR - MALE

1975 **Bill Koch,** Putney, Vt.
1976 **Bill Koch,** Putney, Vt.
1977 **Jim Denney,** Duluth, Minn.
1978 **Stan Dunklee**
1979 **Bill Koch**
1980 **Bill Koch**

U.S. NORDIC COMPETITOR OF THE YEAR - FEMALE

1975 **Martha Rockwell,** West Lebanon, N.H.
1976 **Martha Rockwell,** West Lebanon, N.H.
1977 **Alison Owen Spencer,** Anchorage, Alas.
1978 **Alison Owen**
1979 **Alison Owen**
1980 **Alison Owen**

FREESTYLE COMPETITOR OF THE YEAR - MALE

1975 **Mark Stiegemeier,** Boise, Idaho

1976 **Scott Brooksbank,** Stillwater, Minn.
1977 **John Eaves,** Montreal, Que., Canada
1978 **John Eaves,** Montreal, Que., Canada
1979 **John Eaves,** Montreal, Que., Canada
1980 **Greg Athans,** Vancouver, B.C., Canada

FREESTYLE COMPETITOR OF THE YEAR - FEMALE

1975 **Genia Fuller,** Framingham, Mass.
1976 **Marion Post,** Averill Park, N.Y.
1977 **Marion Post,** Averill Park, N.Y.
1978 **Genia Fuller,** Park West Utah
1979 **Stephanie Sloan,** Toronto, Ont., Canada
1980 **Stephanie Sloan,** Toronto, Ont., Canada

Golden Quill
Outstanding Competitor Award

U.S. SKI WRITERS ASSOCIATION
7 Kensington Rd., Glens Falls, N.Y. 12801 (518/793-1201)

The Golden Quill, which is depicted as a sculpture, is awarded annually upon nomination by the Golden Quill Committee and ratification by the board of directors for outstanding contributions to skiing.

1968 **Merritt H. Stiles,** U.S. Ski Association
1969 **Ralph "Doc" Des Roches,** Ski Industries America
1970 **Robert P. Beattie,** International Ski Racers Association
1971 **Harold S. Hirsch,** White Stag, Inc.
1972 **Dorice Taylor,** Sun Valley resort, Idaho
1973 **Willy Schaeffler,** U.S. Ski Association
1974 **Fred Pabst, Jr.,** Bromley Mt., Vt.
1975 **Robert Parker,** Vail Associates, Colo.
1976 **Rudi Mattesich,** Ski Touring Council
1977 **Lowell Thomas,** Skier, broadcaster, author
1978 **Dave McCoy,** Mammoth Mountain, Cal.
1979 **Tony Wise,** Mt. Telemark, Wisc.
1980 **Clif Taylor,** Ski instructor and developer of short-ski teaching approach

The Outstanding Competitor Award is given annually to the ski racer, Alpine or Nordic, amateur or professional, who has contributed most to American skiing.

1967 **Jimmy Heuga**
1968 **John Bower**
1969 **No award**
1970 **Billy Kidd**
1971 **Cochran family**
1972 **Barbara Ann Cochran**
1973 **Jean-Claude Killy**
1974 **Martha Rockwell**
1975 **Hank Kashiwa**
1976 **Bill Koch**
1977 **Phil Mahre**
1978 **No award**
1979 **Phil Mahre**
1980 **Phil Mahre**

College Soccer Award

INTERCOLLEGIATE SOCCER ASSOCIATION OF AMERICA
c/o Robert Reasso, Rutgers University, New Brunswick, N.J. 08930 (201/932-4206)

A plaque is awarded annually for an outstanding contribution to college soccer in the previous year to a recipient nominated by the membership and selected by a committee.

1972 **Wayne Sunderland,** National rating system
1973 **Dettmar Cramer,** National Coaching School
1974 **John McKeon,** National Soccer Bowl
1975 **No award**
1976 **Don Yonker,** Editor, *National Soccer Coaches' Association Journal*
1977 **Frank Longo,** Quincy (Ill.) College

Current Status Unknown

Most Valuable Player
Rookie of the Year
Lead Goalkeeper
Coach of the Year
Hermann Trophy

NORTH AMERICAN SOCCER LEAGUE
1133 Ave. of the Americas, New York, N.Y. 10036 (212/575-0066)

The Most Valuable Player is selected annually by a poll of players on North American Soccer League teams conducted by *The Sporting News* The winner currently receives a Toyota automobile.

1967 **Ruben Navarro** (Philadelphia Spartans)
1968 **John Kowalik** (Chicago Mustangs)
1969 **Cirilio Fernandez** (Kansas City Spurs)
1970 **Carlos Metidieri** (Rochester Lancers)
1971 **Carlos Metidieri** (Rochester Lancers)
1972 **Randy Horton** (New York Cosmos)
1973 **Warren Archibald** (Miami Toros)
1974 **Peter Silvester** (Baltimore Comets)
1975 **Steven David** (Miami Toros)
1976 **Pele** (New York Cosmos)
1977 **Franz Beckenbauer** (New York Cosmos)
1978 **Mike Flanagan** (New England Tea Men)
1979 **Johan Cruyff** (Los Angeles Aztecs)
1980 **Roger Davies** (Seattle Sounders)

The Rookie of the Year is selected annually by a poll of players on North American Soccer League teams conducted by *The Sporting News.*

1967 **Willie Roy** (Chicago Spurs)
1968 **Kaizer Motaung** (Atlanta Chiefs)
1969 **Siegfried Stritzi** (Baltimore Bays)
1970 **Jim Leeker** (St. Louis Stars)
1971 **Randy Horton** (New York Cosmos)
1972 **Mike Winter** (St. Louis Stars)
1973 **Kyle Rote, Jr.** (Dallas Tornado)
1974 **Douglas McMillan** (Los Angeles Aztecs)
1975 **Chris Bahr** (Philadelphia Atoms)
1976 **Steve Pecher** (Dallas Tornado)
1977 **Jim McAlister** (Seattle Sounders)
1978 **Gary Etherington** (New York Cosmos)
1979 **Larry Hulcer** (Los Angeles Aztecs)
1980 **Jeff Durgan** (New York Cosmos)

Lead Goalkeeper honors go annually to the athlete with the most saves in the season's North American Soccer League play.

1967 **Mirko Stojanovic** (Oakland Clippers)
1968 **Ataulfo Sanchez** (San Diego Toros)
1969 **Manfred Kammerer** (Atlanta Chiefs)
1970 **Lincoln Phillips** (Washington Darts)

1971 **Mirko Stojanovic** (Dallas Tornado)
1972 **Ken Cooper** (Dallas Tornado)
1973 **Bob Rigby** (Philadelphia Atoms)
1974 **Barry Watling** (Seattle Sounders)
1975 **Shep Messing** (Boston Minutemen)
1976 **Tony Chursky** (Seattle Sounders)
1977 **Ken Cooper** (Dallas Tornado)
1978 **Phil Parkes** (Vancouver Whitecaps)
1979 **Phil Parkes** (Vancouver Whitecaps)
1980 **Jack Brand** (Seattle Sounders)

Coaches and general managers of North American Soccer League teams annually select an individual as Coach of the Year.

1968 **Phil Woosnam** (Atlanta Chiefs)
1969 **No information available**
1970 **No information available**
1971 **No information available**
1972 **Casey Frankiewicz** (St. Louis Stars)
1973 **Al Miller** (Philadelphia Atoms)
1974 **John Young** (Miami Toros)
1975 **John Sewell** (St. Louis Stars)
1976 **Eddie Firmani** (Tampa Bay Rowdies)
1977 **Ron Newman** (Fort Lauderdale Strikers)
1978 **Tony Walters** (Vancouver Whitecaps)
1979 **Timo Liekoski** (Houston Hurricane)
1980 **Alan Hinton** (Seattle Sounders)

The Hermann Trophy is given annually to the individual chosen as the leading college soccer player of the year, based on a poll conducted by *The Sporting News* of college soccer coaches.

1967 **Dov Markus** (Long Island University, N.Y.)
1968 **Mani Hernandez** (San Jose State, Calif.)
1969 **Al Trost** (St. Louis University, Mo.)
1970 **Al Trost** (St. Louis University, Mo.)
1971 **Mike Seerey** (St. Louis University, Mo.)
1972 **Mike Seerey** (St. Louis University, Mo.)
1973 **Dan Counce** (St. Louis University, Mo.)
1974 **Farrukh Quraishi** (Oneonta State, N.Y.)
1975 **Steve Ralbovsky** (Brown University, R.I.)
1976 **Glenn Myernick** (Hartwick College, N.Y.)
1977 **Bill Gazonas** (Hartwick College, N.Y.)
1978 **Angelo Dibernardo** (Indiana University)
1979 **Jim Stamatis** (Penn State)
1980 **Joe Morrone** (University of Connecticut)

Duke Kahanamoku Trophy

AMERICAN SURFING ASSOCIATION
Box 1315, Beverly Hills, Cal. 90213 (213/246-7603)

A bronze bust of the late Duke Kahanamoku is awarded as the Duke Kahanamoku Trophy for the highest individual contribution to the sport.

1977 **James Nystrom,** coach, Marina High School, Huntington Beach, Calif.
1978 **Verne Kelsey,** outstanding surfing coach
1979 **John K. Kerwin, Jr.,** 50 years of surfing leadership
1980 **Paul Hastings Freebairn,** expanded amateur competition from Maine to Hawaii

Lawrence J. Johnson Award
United States Aquatic Sports Award
Robert J.H. Kiphuth Award
American Swimming Coaches Appreciation Award
Pettigrew Award
Lillian McKeller Award

UNITED STATES SWIMMING
3400 W. 86th St., Indianapolis, Ind. 46268 (317/872-2900)

The Lawrence J. Johnson Award is an aquatics award, presented annually in rotation to an outstanding male swimmer, female swimmer, male diver, female diver, synchronized swimmer and water polo player.

1964 **Don Schollander**
1965 **Cathy Ferguson**
1966 **Bernie Wrightson**
1967 **Leslie Bush**
1968 **Margo McGrath**
1969 **Gary P. Sheerer**
1970 **Michael J. Burton**
1971 **Susie Atwood**
1972 **Dick Rydze**
1973 **Cynthia Potter**
1974 **Gail Johnson**
1975 **Bruce Bradley**
1976 **John Naber**
1977 **Wendy Boglioli**
1978 **Phil Boggs**
1979 **Janet Ely Thorborn**
1980 **Linda Shelley**

The United States Aquatic Sports Award, formerly the the AAU Swimming Award, is a bronze replica of a life-size statue located in the Payne Whitney Gymnasium at Yale University that is awarded annually to an individual or organization for outstanding contributions to the advancement of swimming.

1954 **Federation Internationale De Natation Amateur**
1955 **Amateur Swimming Federation of Japan**
1956 **Beth Kaufman,** Chairman, National AAU Age Group Committee
1957 **Amateur Swimming Union of Australia**
1958 **Lawrence J. Johnson,** ASUA
Robert J.H. Kiphuth, Yale University
R. Max Ritter, FINA
1959 **Carl O. Bauer,** Missouri Athletic Club
1960 **F. Jeffery Farrell,** New Haven Swim Club
1961 **Mary Freeman Kelly,** Vesper Boat Club
1962 **I. Murray Rose,** Los Angeles Athletic Club ASU of Australia
1963 **James Counsilman,** Indiana University
1964 **Harold W. Henning,** Chairman, National AAU Men's Swimming Committee
1965 **George F. Haines,** Santa Clara Swim Club
1966 **College Swimming Coaches Association of America**
Harry Hainsworth, AAU Aquatics Administrator
1967 **Albert Schoenfield,** Swimming World
1968 **Deborah Meyer,** Arden Hills Swim Club
1969 **Federacion Mexicana de Natacion**
1970 **Michael J. Burton**
Charles McCaffree, Jr.
1971 **A. R. "Red" Barr**
1972 **Mark Spitz**
Kenneth Treadway

1973 **Edwin Olson**
1974 **John Bogert**
1975 **Peter Daland**
1976 **John Naber**
1977 **Phillips Petroleum Co.,** Bartlesville, Okla.
1978 **Sherman Chavoor**
1979 **William A. Lippman, Jr.**
1980 **Soichi Sakamoto**

The Robert J. H. Kiphuth Award is awarded to the male and female high point scorers in the Short Course and Long Course Swimming Championships.

1968 **Charles Hickcox,** Short Course
Deborah Meyer, Short Course
Mark Spitz, Long Course
Sue Pedersen, Long Course
1969 **Mike Burton,** Short Course
Susie Atwood, Short Course
Gary Hall, Long Course
Sue Pedersen, Long Course
1970 **Gary Hall,** Short Course
Susie Atwood, Short Course
Gary Hall, Long Course
Susie Atwood, Long Course
1971 **Frank Heckl,** Short Course
Susie Atwood, Short Course
Mark Spitz, Long Course
Susie Atwood, Long Course
1972 **Mark Spitz,** Short Course
Susie Atwood, Short Course
No championship held, Long Course
1973 **Shane Gould,** Short Course
Rick Colella, Short Course
Lynn Colella, Long Course
Keena Rothhammer, Long Course
Rick Colella, Long Course
1974 **Shirley Babashoff,** Short Course
Rick Colella, Short Course
Shirley Babashoff, Long Course
Bruce Furniss, Long Course
1975 **Shirley Babashoff,** Short Course
John Naber, Short Course
Shirley Babashoff, Long Course
Bruce Furniss, Long Course
1976 **John Naber,** Indoor Long Course
Shirley Babashoff, Indoor Long Course
John Naber, Long Course
Donnalee Wennerstrom, Long Course
1977 **Scott Spann,** Short Course
Tracy Caulkins, Short Course
Brian Goodell, Long Course
Tracy Caulkins, Long Course
1978 **Scott Spann,** Short Course
Tracy Caulkins, Short Course
Jesse Vassallo, Long Course
Tracy Caulkins, Long Course
1979 **Brian Goodell,** Short Course
Tracy Caulkins, Short Course
Jesse Vassallo, Long Course
Tracy Caulkins, Long Course
1980 **Mike Bruner,** Indoors
Tracy Caulkins, Indoors
Mike Bruner, Outdoors
Tracy Caulkins, Outdoors

AMERICAN SWIMMING COACHES ASSOCIATION APPRECIATION AWARD

1972 **John B. Kelly, Jr.**
1973 **Bob Miller**
1974 **George Breen**
1975 **Mark Schubert**
1976 **Mark Schubert**
1977 **Paul Bergen**

Current Status Unknown

The Pettigrew Award is given by Central Swimming, Inc., in recognition of outstanding service by an official.

1977 **Ken Pettigrew**
1978 **Paul Bay, Richard Close**
1979 **Stanley Brown**
1980 **Kay Meyer**

The Lillian MacKeller Award goes to an individual who has given unselfishly of herself for synchronized swimming without thought of personal gain, and with a particular emphasis on working for the benefit of the athlete.

1971 **Lillian MacKellar**
1972 **Joy Cushman**
1973 **Dawn Ben**
1974 **No award**
1975 **Kay Vilen**
1976 **No award**
1977 **Theresa Anderson**
1978 **Don Kane**
1979 **Re Calcaterra**
1980 **Dorothy Sowers**

SPECIAL AWARD

1977 **Harold Henning,** for the advancement of synchronized swimming

Age Group Diving Coach of the Year
Mike Malone Memorial Diving Award

UNITED STATES DIVING
3400 W. 86th St., Indianapolis, Ind. 46268 (317/872-2900)

The Age Group Diving Coach of the Year Award is presented annually by the Pennsylvania Diving Association.

1969 **Bernie Wrightson**
1970 **Lesley Bush**
1971 **Jim Blickenstaff**
1972 **Paul Flack**
1973 **Don Gartiez**
1974 **Charles Casuto**
1975 **Richard Kimball**
1976 **Glen McCormick**
1977 **Dave Glander**
1978 **Van Austin**
1979 **Bob Rydze, Jr.**
1980 **Steve McFarland**

The Mike Malone Memorial Diving Award is presented annually for outstanding contributions to diving.

1969 **Al White**
1970 **R. Jackson Smith**
1971 **Stan Kistler**
1972 **Richard Kimball**
1973 **Hobie Billingsley**
1974 **Ron O'Brien**
1975 **Mike Peppe**
1976 **Robert A. Rydze**
1977 **Betty Perkins**
1978 **Aaron S. Weinstein**
1979 **Raymond F. Hain**

1980 Dick Smith

Induction

INTERNATIONAL SWIMMING HALL OF FAME

1 Hall of Fame Dr., Ft. Lauderdale, Fla. 33316
(305/462-6536)

Induction in the Hall of Fame honors an outstanding swimmer, diver, coach or contributor. Any aquatic personality in the world is eligible for nomination and a vote by 1,700 aquatic coaches and other swimming authorities. Those honored are permanently recognized with an alcove displaying his or her achievements in the sport.

1965 Buster Crabbe
C. M. "Charlie" Daniels
Gertrude Ederle
Dawn Fraser
Beulah Gundling
Jamison Handy
Duke Kahanamoku
Adolph Kiefer
Robert J. H. Kiphuth
Kusuo Kitamura
Commodore Longfellow
Pat McCormick
Matt Mann II
Pam Morris
R. Max Ritter
Murray Rose
Don Schollander
Matthew Webb
Johnny Weissmuller
Al White
Katherine Rawls

1966 Dave Armbruster
Bill Bachrach
Arne Borg
Ernst Brandsten
Steve Clark
Georgia Coleman
Ann Curtis
Pete Desjardins
Alan Ford
Alfred Hajos
Eleanor Holm
Ragnhild Hveger
Edward T. Kennedy
Helene Madison
Shelly Mann
Jack Medica
Wally O'Connor
Mike Peppe
Clarence Pinkston
Wally Ris
Soichi Sakamoto
Bill Smith
Joe Verdeur
Chris Von Saltza
Esther Williams

1967 Miller Anderson
Carl Bauer
Sybil Bauer
Sir Frank Beaurepaire
Ethelda Bleibtrey
"Ma" Braun
Teddy Cann
Jacques Yves Cousteau
Fanny Durack
Hironoshin Furuhashi
L. deB. Handley
Beth Kaufman
Al Neuschaefer
Martha Norelius
Betty Becker Pinkston
Paul Radmilovic
Aileen Riggin
Norman Ross
The Spence Brothers

1968 Jeff Farrell
Benjamin Franklin
Zolten de Halmay
Harry Hebner
George Hodgson
John Jarvis
Warren Kealoha
George Kojac
Sammy Lee
Hendrika Mastenbroek
Emil Rausch
E. Carroll Schaeffer
Dorothy Poynton
David Theile
Yoshiyuki Tsuruta

1969 Greta Andersen
Fred Cady
Donna deVarona
Vickie Draves
Stephen Hunyadfi
Barney Kieran
Ethel Lackie
Freddie Lane
Michael McDermott
James Nemeth
Al Patnik
Henry Taylor

1970 Walter Bathe
Cavill Family
Florence Chadwick
Jack Cody
Willy den Ouden
Olga Dorfner
Claire Galligan
Richard R. Hough
Jimmy McLane
Henri Padou
Charlie Sava
Robert Webster

1971 George Corsan, Sr.
Ray Daughters
Dick Degener
Jennie Fletcher
Budd Goodwin
John Higgins
Martin Homonnay
Cor Kint
Konrads Kids
Helen Meany
Mike Troy
Bill Yorzyk

1972 Stan Brauninger
Andrew M. "Boy" Charlton
Earl Clark
Lorraine Crapp
Ford Konno
Mario Majoni
Erich Rademacher

Sharon Stouder
Helen Wainwright
1973 Greta Brandsten
Bruce Harlan
John Henricks
Walter Laufer
John Marshall
Eva and Ilona Novak
Yoshi Oyakawa
Jan Stender
Nell Van Vliet
1974 Capt. Bert Cummins
Charlotte Epstein
Harold Fern
Ellen Fullard-Leo
William Henry
Annette Kellerman
Fred Luehring
John Trudgeon
Alick Wickham
1975 George Breen
David "Skippy" Browning
Karen Harup
Claudia Kolb
Ingrid Kramer
Frank McKinney
Keo Nakama
Tom Robinson
Mina Wylie
1976 Catie Ball
Joaquin Capilla
Forbes Carlile
James Counsilman
Marjorie Gestring
Dezso Gyarmati
Charles Hickcox
Ada Kok
Charles McCaffree
Carl Robie
Sylvia Ruuska
Roy Saari
Charles Silvia
Eva Szekely
Alberto Zorrilla
1977 Mike Burton
Sherm Chavoor
Peter Daland
Shane Gould
George Haines
Alex Jany
Chet Jastremski
Debbie Meyer
Galina Prozumenshikova
Mickey and Johnny Riley
Mark Spitz
1978 Istvan Barany
Lynn Burke
Cathy Ferguson
Peter Fick
Ralpah Flanagan
Valerie Gyenge
Oliver Halassy
Micki King
Seiji Kiyowaka
Walt Schlueter
Gary Tobian
Kay Vilen
1979 Kay Curtis
John Devitt
Kaye Hall
Jan Henne
Harold Henning
Gunnar Larsson
Hideko Maehata
Paul Jean Myers Pope
Dick Smith
Harold "Dutch" Smith
Allen Stack
Don Talbot
Michael Wenden
1980 Kevin Berry
Marie Braun
Robert Clotworthy
Thomas K. Cureton
Juno Stover Irwin
Mary Kok
Lance Larson
Hakan Malmrot
Alban Minville
Phil Moriarty
Karen Muir
Heidi O'Rourke
Clarke Scholes
Elaine Tanner
George Wilkinson

Rookie of the Year
Most Improved Player

TENNIS MAGAZINE
495 Westport Ave., Norwalk, Conn. 06856 (203/847-5811)

The editors of this publication spotlight noteworthy achievements among professional tennis players.

ROOKIE OF THE YEAR (male)

1972 Jimmy Connors
1973 Brian Gottfried
1974 Paul Ramirez
1975 Sandy Mayer
1976 Billy Martin
1977 John McEnroe
1978 Jose-Luis Clerc
1979 Ivan Lendl
1980 Mel Purcell

ROOKIE OF THE YEAR (female)

1974 Martina Navratilova
1975 Greer Stevens
1976 Natasha Chmyreva
1977 Tracy Austin
1978 Pam Shriver
1979 Kathy Jordan
1980 Andrea Jaeger

MOST IMPROVED PLAYER (male)

1976 Wojtek Fibak
1977 Brian Gottfried
1978 John McEnroe
1979 Victor Pecci
1980 Ivan Lendl

MOST IMPROVED PLAYER (female)

1976 Sue Barker
1977 Wendy Turnbull
1978 Virgina Ruzici
1979 Tracy Austin

1980 Hana Mandlikova

COMEBACK PLAYER OF THE YEAR

1978 Arthur Ashe
1979 Bille Jean King
1980 Bob Lutz

DiBenedetto Award
Colonel Charles J. Dieges Award
Scott Hamilton Award for Leadership in Road Running
J.B. "Cap" Haralson Award
Long Distance Running Merit Award
Mobil Cup
Joseph Robichaux Award
C. C. Jackson Award
WomenSports Team Championship Award
WomenSports Foundation Female Long Distance Runner of the Year

THE ATHLETICS CONGRESS/USA
Box 120, Indianapolis, Ind. 46206 (317/638-9155)

The Lawrence DiBeneditto Award is a trophy awarded annually for the outstanding individual track and field performance of the year.

1959 Parry O'Brien
1960 Ralph Boston
1961 Ralph Boston
1962 James Beatty
1963 John Pennel
1964 Lt. Billy Mills
1965 Randy Matson
1966 James Ryun
1967 James Ryun
1968 Bob Beamon
1969 George Young
1970 Ralph Mann
1971 Patrick Matzdorf
1972 Rodney Milburn, Jr.
1973 Rodney Milburn, Jr.
1974 Rick Wohlhuter
1975 William Rodgers
1976 Edwin Moses
1977 Edwin Moses
1978 Mike Tully
1979 Renaldo Nehemiah
1980 Edwin Moses

The Colonel Charles J. Dieges Award is presented to the outstanding performer at the National Men's Indoor and Outdoor AAU Track and Field Championships. For a time, women were also honored.

INDOOR

1954 Parry O'Brien
1955 Arnie Sowell
1956 Parry O'Brien
1957 Phil Reavis
1958 Ron Delaney
1959 John Thomas
1960 Allan Lawrence
1961 Ralph Boston
1962 Jim Beatty
1963 Jim Beatty
1964 Ron Clarke
1965 Billy Mills
1966 Bob Seagren
Edith McGuire
1967 Tracy Smith
Madeline Manning
1968 Eleanor Montgomery
Pat Van Wolvelaere
1969 George Young
1970 Martin McGrady
1971 Frank Shorter
1972 Kjell Isaksson
1973 Tracy Smith
1974 Richard Wohlhuter
1975 Miruts Yifter
1976 Filbert Bayi
1977 Filbert Bayi
1978 Houston McTear
1979 Eamonn Coghlan
1980 Jeff Woodard

OUTDOOR

1954 Arthur Bragg
1955 Arnie Sowell
1956 No award
1957 Reggie Pearman
1958 No award
1959 Ray Norton
1960 No award
1961 No award
1962 No award
1963 Bob Hayes
1964 No award
1965 No award
1966 Jim Ryun
1967 No award
1968 No award
1969 No award
1970 Frank Shorter
1971 Rod Milburn
1972 No award
1973 No award
1974 Richard Wohlhuter
1975 Donald Quarrie
1976 Mac Wilkins
1977 Edwin Moses
1978 Clancy Edwards
1979 Carl Lewis
1980 La Monte King

SCOTT HAMILTON AWARD FOR LEADERSHIP IN ROAD RUNNING

1976 Harold DeMoss
Fred Brown
1977 Vincent Fandetti
1978 Bill Rodgers
1979 George Kleeman
1980 Edward Kozloff

The J. B. "Cap" Haralson Award is a plaque awarded annually for outstanding service as an AAU Track and Field official.

1967 Robert Giegengack
1968 S. B. "Si" Tyler
1969 Albert Post
1970 Daniel J. Ferris

1971 Lawrence E. Houston
1972 Pincus Sober
1973 George Wilson
1974 Hilmer Lodge
1975 John Oelkers
1977 Ted Haydon
1977 Ralph Colson
1978 Joseph Yancey
1979 Andy Bakjian
1980 Payton Jordan

LONG DISTANCE RUNNING MERIT AWARD

1969 H. Browning Ross
1970 Robert S. Campbell
1971 Ted Corbitt
1972 Frank Shorter
1973 Robert E. DeCelle
1974 Aldo M. Scandurra
1975 Harold Canfield
1976 John Brennand
1977 Joseph Kleinman
1978 Anthony Diamond
1979 Stanley Stafford
1980 Norm Brand

The Mobil Cup formerly the *Redbook* Award and briefly the Fleischmann's Cup is presented to the outstanding female athlete at both the National Women's Indoor and Outdoor Track and Field Championships.

1973 Mable Fergerson
1974 No award
1975 Madeline Manning Jackson
1976 Jan Merrill
1977 Francie Larrieu
Evelyn Ashford
1978 Deby La Plante
Jodi Anderson
1979 Evelyn Ashford
1980 Cindy Bremser
Madeline Manning

The Joseph Robichaux Award is given annually to one who has made an outstanding contribution to the women's track and field program in the United States.

1972 Edward Temple
1973 C. C. Jackson
1974 Juner Bellew
1975 Conrad Ford
1976 Roxanne Andersen
1977 Harmon Brown
1978 Ken Foreman
1979 Eileen Goodnight
1980 Neil Jackson

The C. C. Jackson Award, formerly the Saettel Award, is given annually to the female track and field competitors who exhibit the most outstanding performances for the year.

SAETTEL AWARD

1965 Wyomia Tyus
1966 Charlotte Cook
1967 Doris Brown
1968 Madeline Manning
1969 Elinor Montgomery
1970 Willye White
1971 Iris Davis
1972 Kathy Hammond
1973 Martha Watson
1974 Francie Larrieu
1975 No award
1976 Joni Huntley
Jane Frederick
1977 Kathy McMillan

TRACK

1978 Jan Merrill
1979 Evelyn Ashford
1980 Mary Decker

FIELD

1978 Judi Anderson
1979 Maren Seidler
1980 Karin Smith

Originated by *WomenSports* magazine, the Female Long Distance Runner of the Year and Team Championship Awards are now continued by the publication's successor, the WomenSports Foundation, and honor excellence in women's athletics

WOMENSPORTS TEAM CHAMPIONSHIP AWARD

1974 Atoms Track Club
1975 Sports International Track Club
1976 Atoms Track Club
1977 Los Angeles Mercurettes Track Club
1978 Tennessee State Univ. Track Club
1979 Los Angeles Naturite Track Club
1980 Los Angeles Naturite Track Club

WOMENSPORTS FOUNDATION FEMALE LONG DISTANCE RUNNER OF THE YEAR

1977 Miki Gorman
1978 Nina Kuscsik
1979 Doris Heritage
1980 Joan Ullyot

Induction

NATIONAL TRACK AND FIELD HALL OF FAME

1524 Kanawha Blvd. E., Charleston, W.Va. 25311
(304/345-0087)

Induction in the National Track and Field Hall of Fame honors American athletes whose accomplishments, in the judgment of the board of governors, has been exemplary.

1974

Ralph H. Boston
Lee Q. Calhoun
Glenn Cunningham
Harold Davis
Harrison Dillard
Ray Ewry
Brutus Hamilton
Alvin Kraenzlein
Michael C. Murphy
Parry O'Brien
Harold M. Osborn
Wilma Rudolph
Lester Steers
Malvin G. Whitfield
Avery Brundage
Dean B. Cromwell
Glenn Davis
Mildred "Babe" Didrikson Zaharias
Daniel J. Ferris
Rafer Johnson
Robert B. Mathias
Lawrence Myers
Al Oerter
Jesse Owens
Robert I. Simpson
Cornelius "Dutch" Warmerdam

1975

Horace Ashenfelter III
M.E. "Bill" Easton
Edward M. "Ted" Haydon
Ralph Metcalfe
Rob Richards
James Francis Thrope
Stella Walsh
Alice Coachman Davis
John J. Flanagan
Edward P. Hurt
Bobby Joe Morrow
Helen Stephens
William A. Toomey

1976

Dee Boeckmann
Robert L. Hayes
Billy Mills
Steve Prefontaine
Mae Faggs Star
J. Kenneth Doherty
Hayes Wendell Jones
Charles Paddock
Joie Ray
Forrest Towns

1977

Bob Beamon
Thomas Jones
Jackson V. Scholz
Andy Stanfield
James E. Sullivan
Frank Wykoff
Wilbur Hutsell
Greg Rice
Elizabeth Robinson Schwartz
Earl Thompson

1978

Thomas W. Courtney
Tommie C. Smith
Larry N. Snyder
Robert F. Geigengack
Glenn F. Hardin
John Y. Woodruff

1979

James Bausch
Fortune E. Gordien
Ward Haylett
Clarence "Bud" Houser
Edith McGuire DuValle
William B. Curtis
John Griffith
James Hines
DeHart W. Hubbard

1980

Dave Albritton
John Kelley
Wyomia Tyus
Bruce Jenner
Jim Ryun

Emil Breitkreutz Leadership Award

AMATEUR ATHLETIC UNION OF THE UNITED STATES
3400 W. 86th St., Indianapolis, Ind. 46268 (317/297-2900)

Established by the National A.A.U. Volleyball Committee, the Emil Breitkreutz Leadership Award honors contributions to volleyball.

1970 Emil Breitkreutz
1971 Dorothy Boyce
1972 Joe Sharpless
1973 No award
1974 Ethel Stevens
1975 Dorothy Boyce
1976 James J. Fox
1977 Jack Shatz
1978 John Eaton
1979 Jack Schatz
1980 Not available at press time

TAC-USA Racewalking Awards

THE ATHLETIC CONGRESS/USA
Box 120, Indianapolis, Ind. 46206 (317/638-9155)

Achievements in and contributions to racewalking are recognized by a series of annual awards, which were originally given by the Amateur Athletic Union and are now presented by The Athletic Congress/USA.

RON ZINN MEMORIAL ATHLETE AWARD (to the oustanding U.S. racewalker)

1975 Larry Young
1976 Ron Laird
1977 Neil Pyke
1978 Marco Evoniuk
1979 Dan O'Connor
1980 Marco Evoniuk (20 kilometers)
Carl Schueler (50 kilometers)

RON ZINN RACE WALKING ASSOCIATION AWARD (to an association)

1975 New Jersey Association
1976 Missouri Valley Association
1977 Wisconsin Association
1978 Potomac Valley Association
1979 Niagara Association
1980 Michigan Association

RON ZINN RACE WALKING INDIVIDUAL AWARD (to an individual)

1975 Bruce MacDonald
1976 Jack Mortland
1977 Charlie Silcock
1978 Larry Larson
1979 Joseph Tigerman
1980 Dean Ingram

SPECIAL AWARD

1977 Joseph Tigerman, for meritorious service

John J. Curren Award
James W. Lee Award

AMATEUR ATHLETIC UNION OF THE UNITED STATES
3400 W. 86th St., Indianapolis, Ind. 46268 (317/297-2900)

The John J. Curren Award is given annually by the New York Athletic Club to the outstanding player in the National AAU Men's Indoor Water Polo Championships.

1962 William Kooistra
1963 Charles Bittick
1964 Edward Jaworski
1965 Charles Harris
1966 Dean Willeford
1967 Sam Kooistra
1968 Irwin Okumura
1969 Patrick McClellan
1970 Jerry Christy
1971 Gary Sheerer
1972 No award
1973 William Harris
1974 No award
1975 Charles Harris
1976 No award

1977 William Harris

Current Status Unknown

The James W. Lee Award is given annually to the outstanding player in the National AAU Men's Outdoor Water Polo Championship.

1963 Stan Sprague
1964 George Stransky
Chuck Bittick
1965 Dave Ashleigh
1966 Gary Sheerer
1967 Dean Willeford
1968 Tony Van Dorp
1969 Steve Barnett
1970 Gary Sheerer
1971 Thomas Walsh
1972 Doug Arth
1973 Eric Ferguson
1974 Eric Lindroth
1975 Peter Asch
1956 Steve Hamann
1977 Gary Figueroa

Current Status Unknown

Exemplary Wrestling Award
Sustained Superior Performance Award
Wrestling Man of the Year
Nicki Edington Award

AMATEUR ATHLETIC UNION OF THE UNITED STATES
3400 W. 86th St., Indianapolis, Ind. 46268 (317/297-2900)

EXEMPLARY WRESTLING AWARD

1972 Fendley Collins
1973 Ivan Olsen
1974 No award
1975 No award
1976 Newt Copple
1977 No award
1978 Billy Vandiver
1979 John Schendel
1980 No award

WRESTLING COACH OF THE YEAR

1980 Dan Gable

WRESTLING OFFICIAL OF THE YEAR

1980 Rick Tucci

WRESTLING'S OUTSTANDING CONTRIBUTOR OF THE YEAR

1980 John Willey

The Sustained Superior Performance Award is a plaque given annually to an individual who "at the grass roots level" has made an outstanding contribution to wrestling for a number of years. The award is sponsored by the U.S. Wrestling Foundation.

1967 Bill Schriver
1968 Maurice E. "Pat" McGill
1969 John K. Eareckson
1970 Steere Noda
1971 George Myerson
1972 Fendley Collins
1973 Ivan Olsen
1974 Billy Martin
1975 Cy Mitchell
1976 Roy Moore
1977 Andrew Kovacz
1978 Pepi King
1979 Larry Warren
Jim Herold
1980 Capt. Stephen Archer

AAU WRESTLING MAN OF THE YEAR AWARD

1978 Joseph Scalzo
1979 Guenther Kruss
1980 Don Murray

The Nicki Edington Award is presented annually to recognize contributions of women to the sport of wrestling.

1980 Nicki Edington

Beauty & Fashion

Contents

Related Awards

Miss America

MISS AMERICA PAGEANT
1325 Boardwalk, Boardwalk and Tennessee Ave., Atlantic City, N.J. 08401 (609/345-7571)

Miss America is chosen annually from contestants from the 50 states, the District of Columbia and U.S. territories by a panel of celebrity judges on the basis of beauty, talent, poise and charm. The winner, who is crowned on a national telecast, receives a year's appearance contract and various prizes, including a $20,000 scholarship. In addition to the scholarship awarded to Miss America, 10 runnersup and several non-finalists are given scholarships as well. The winner for any given year is selected at the Atlantic City pageant the previous September.

1921 **Margaret Gorman,** Washington, D.C.
1922 **Mary Campbell,**Columbus, Ohio
1923 **No pageant** Columbus, Ohio
1924 **Ruth Malcolmson,** Philadelphia, Pa.
1925 **Fay Lanphier,** Oakland, Calif.
1926 **Norma Smallwood,** Tulsa, Okla.
1927 **Lois Delaner,** Joliet, Ill.
1928-32 **No pageants**
1933 **Marion Bergeron,** West Haven, Conn.
1934 **No pageant**
1935 **Henrietta Leaver,** Pittsburgh, Pa.
1936 **Rose Coyle,** Philadelphia, Pa.
1937 **Bette Cooper,** Bertrand Island, N.J.
1938 **Marilyn Meseke,** Marion, Ohio
1939 **Patricia Donnelly,** Detroit, Mich.
1940 **Frances Marie Burke,** Philadelphia, Pa.
1941 **Rosemary LaPlanche,** Los Angeles, Calif.
1942 **Jo-Carroll Dennison,** Tyler, Tex.
1943 **Jean Bartel,** Los Angeles, Calif.
1944 **Venus Ramey,** Washington D.C.
1945 **Bess Myerson,** New York, N.Y.
1946 **Marilyn Buferd,** Los Angeles, Calif.
1947 **Barbara Walker,** Memphis, Tenn.
1948 **BeBe Shopp,** Hopkins, Minn.
1939 **Jacque Mercer,** Litchfield, Ariz.
1950 **No pageant**
1951 **Yolande Betbeze,** Mobile, Ala.
1952 **Coreen Kay Hutchins,** Salt Lake City, Utah
1953 **Neva Jane Langley,** Macon, Ga.
1954 **Evelyn Margaret Ay,** Ephrata, Pa.
1955 **Lee Meriwether,** San Francisco, Calif.
1956 **Sharon Ritchie,** Denver, Colo.
1957 **Marian McKnight,** Manning, S.C.
1958 **Marilyn Van Derbur,** Denver, Colo.
1959 **Mary Ann Mobley,** Brandon, Miss.
1960 **Lynda Lee Mead,** Natchez, Miss.
1961 **Nancy Fleming,** Montague, Mich.
1962 **Maria Fletcher,** Asheville, N.C.
1963 **Jacquelyn Mayer,** Sandusky, Ohio
1964 **Donna Axum,** El Dorado, Ark.
1965 **Vonda Kay Van Dyke,** Phoenix, Ariz.
1966 **Deborah Irene Bryant,** Overland Park, Kans.
1967 **Jane Anne Jayroe,** Laverne, Okla.
1968 **Debra Dene Barnes,** Moran, Kans.
1969 **Judith Anne Ford,** Belvidere, Ill.
1970 **Pamela Anne Eldred,** Birmingham, Mich.
1971 **Phyllis Ann George,** Denton, Tex.
1972 **Laurie Lea Schaefer,** Columbus, Ohio
1973 **Terre Anne Meeuwsen,** DePere, Wisc.
1974 **Rebecca Ann King,** Denver Colo.
1975 **Shirley Cothran,** Fort Worth, Tex.
1976 **Tawny Elaine Godin,** Yonkers, N.Y.
1977 **Dorothy Kathleen Benham,** Edina, Minn.
1978 **Susan Perkins,** Columbus, Ohio
1979 **Kylene Barker,** Roanoke, Va.
1980 **Cheryl Prewitt,** Ackerman, Miss.

Miss Black America

J. MORRIS ANDERSON PRODUCTIONS, INC.
24 W. Chilton Ave., Philadelphia, Pa. 19144 (215/VI 4-8872)

Miss Black America is selected on a national telecast pageant by a panel of judges based on beauty, talent and personality criteria after competitions on local and state levels. The winner receives cash, merchandise and trips, currently including $10,000, screen tests and performance contracts and a variety of other prizes.

1968 **Sandy Williams,** Pennsylvania
1969 **"G.O." Smith,** New York
1970 **Stephanie Clark,** Washington, D.C.
1971 **Joyce Warner,** Florida
1972 **Linda Barney,** New Jersey
1973 **Arnice Russell,** New York
1974 **VonGretchen Sheppard,** California
1975 **Helen Ford,** Mississippi
1976 **Twanna Kilgore,** Washington, D.C.
1977 **Claire Ford,** Tennessee
1978 **Lydia Jackson**
1979 **Veretta Shankle**
1980 **Sharon Wright**

Most Beautiful American Women

HARPER'S BAZAAR
717 Fifth Ave., New York, N. Y. 10022 (212/935-5900)

The editors of *Harper's Bazaar* compiled a list of the 10 Most Beautiful Women in America and highlighted their selections in the magazine.

1978 **Candice Bergen**
Diahann Carroll
Faye Dunaway
Princess Grace of Monaco
Lena Horne
Lauren Hutton
Farrah Fawcett-Majors
Ali MacGraw
Elizabeth Taylor
Cheryl Tiegs

Playmate of the Year

PLAYBOY MAGAZINE
919 N. Michigan Ave., Chicago, Ill. 60611 (312/PL 1-8000)

The editors of *Playboy* annually vote for the Playmate of the Year from among the previous year's Playmates of the Month. In addition to the original modeling fee, the Playmate of the Year receives $10,000 and a variety of merchandise prizes.

1960 **Ellen Stratton**
1961 **Linda Gamble**
1962 **Christa Speck**
1963 **June Cochran**
1964 **Donna Michelle**

1965 **Jo Collins**
1966 **Allison Parks**
1967 **Lisa Baker**
1968 **Angela Dorian**
1969 **Connie Kreski**
1970 **Claudia Jennings**
1971 **Sharon Clark**
1972 **Liv Lindeland**
1973 **Marilyn Cole**
1974 **Cyndi Wood**
1975 **Marilyn Lange**
1976 **Lillian Muller**
1977 **Patti McGuire**
1978 **Debra Jo Fondren**
1979 **Monique St. Pierre**
1980 **Dorothy Stratten**

Miss U.S.A.
Miss Universe

MISS UNIVERSE, INC.
640 Fifth Ave., New York, N.Y. 10019 (212/757-9396)

In nationally televised pageants each year, a panel of celebrity judges selects the winner of the annual Miss U.S.A. and Miss Universe titles. Miss U.S.A. is chosen from among contestants in franchised pageants in the various states and the District of Columbia, while Miss Universe is selected from international contestants. The winner of the Miss U.S.A. contest receives an $11,000 cash award, a cash scholarship, a year-long $10,000 personal appearance contract and various prizes, principally clothing, a fur coat and a car. Miss Universe receives a $10,000 cash award, a $3,500 scholarship, a one-year contract with Paramount Pictures with a guarantee of at least $15,000, a $10,000 year-long personal-appearance contract and various prizes, principally clothing, a fur coat and a car.

MISS U.S.A.

1952 **Jackie Loughery,** New York
1953 **Myrna Hansen,** Illinois
1954 **Miriam Stevenson,** South Carolina
1955 **Carlene King Johnson,** Vermont
1956 **Carol Morris,** Iowa
1957 **Charlotte Sheffield,** Utah
1958 **Arlene Howell,** Louisiana
1959 **Terry Lynn Huntington,** California
1960 **Linda Bement,** Utah
1961 **Sharon Brown,** Louisiana
1962 **Macel Wilson,** Hawaii
1963 **Marite Ozers,** Illinois
1964 **Bobbie Johnson,** District of Columbia
1965 **Sue Downey,** Ohio
1966 **Maria Remenyi,** California
1967 **Cheryl-Ann Patton,** Florida
1968 **Didi Anstett,** Washington
1969 **Wendy Dascomb,** Virginia
1970 **Debbie Shelton,** Virginia
1971 **Michele McDonald,** Pennsylvania
1972 **Tanya Wilson,** Hawaii
1973 **Amanda Jones,** Illinois
1974 **Karen Morrison,** Illinois
1975 **Summer Bartholomew,** California
1976 **Barbara Peterson,** Minnesota
1977 **Kimberly Louise Tomes,** Texas
1978 **Judi Andersen,** Hawaii
1979 **Mary Therese Friel,** New York
1980 **Janeane Marie Ford,** Arizona

MISS UNIVERSE

1952 **Armi Kuusela,** Finland
1953 **Christiane Martel,** France
1954 **Miriam Stevenson,** U.S.A.
1955 **Hellevi Rombin,** Sweden
1956 **Carol Morris,** U.S.A.
1957 **Gladys Zender,** Peru
1958 **Luz Marina Zuluaga,** Colombia
1959 **Akiko Kojima,** Japan
1960 **Linda Bement,** U.S.A.
1961 **Marlene Schmidt,** Federal Republic of Germany
1962 **Norma Nolan,** Argentina
1963 **Ieda Maria Vargas,** Brazil
1964 **Corinna Tsopei,** Greece
1965 **Apasra Hongsakula,** Thailand
1966 **Margareta Arvidsson,** Sweden
1967 **Sylvia Hitchcock,** U.S.A.
1968 **Martha Vasconellos,** Brazil
1969 **Gloria Diaz,** Philippines
1970 **Marisol Malaret,** Puerto Rico
1971 **Georgina Risk,** Lebanon
1972 **Kerry Anne Wells,** Australia
1973 **Margarita Moran,** Philippines
1974 **Amparo Munoz,** Spain
1975 **Anne Marie Pohtamo,** Finland
1976 **Rina Messinger,** Israel
1977 **Janelle Commissiong,** Trinidad & Tobago
1978 **Margaret Gardiner,** South Africa
1979 **Maritza Sayalero,** Venezuela
1980 **Shawn Nichols,** U.S.A.

Best Dressed Women
Best Dressed Men
Hall of Fame Entrants

NEW YORK COUTURE GROUP
1633 Broadway, New York, N.Y. 10019 (212/887-8274)

Qualified experts and observers in the fields of women's and men's fashions vote by ballot for the Best Dressed Women and Men and Hall of Fame entrants each year. The ballots are tabulated by a committee of fashion editors. The criteria for these honors are "distinguished application of fashion to contemporary living, without extravagance or ostentation." Individuals named to the Best Dressed List do not receive anything but publicity. The Best Dressed List has at times been compiled according to relative voting strength of the individuals named to the list; at other times, it has appeared alphabetically. The lists have refered to married women in different ways in different years, using their own first names or their husband's. In each case, we have reproduced each year's list as we received it from the coordinator.

BEST-DRESSED WOMEN

1940 **Mrs. Harrison Williams**
Mrs. Ronald Balcom (Millicent Rogers)
Mrs. Thomas Shevlin
Mrs. Byron Foy
Countess Haugwitz Reventlow (Barbara Hutton)
Mrs. William Paley
Mrs. Howard Linn

Gladys Swarthout
Ina Claire
Mrs. Gilbert Miller
Mrs. Lawrence Tibbett
Lynn Fontanne
Mrs. S. Kent Legare
Mrs. Harold Talbott
Mrs. William Rhinelander Stewart
1941 The Duchess of Windsor
Mrs. Stanley Mortimer
Mrs. Byron Foy
Mrs. Harrison Williams
Mrs. Rodman Arturo de Heeren
Mrs. Thomas Shevlin
Mme. Felipe A. Espil
Mrs. Robert W. Miller
Mrs. Robert Sherwood
Rosalind Russell
1942 No list
1943 Clare Boothe Luce
The Duchess of Windsor
Mrs. Byron Foy
Mrs. Walter Hoving
Mrs. Harrison Williams
Mrs. Andre Embiricos
Mme. Chiang Kai-Shek
Lily Pons
Mrs. Harold Talbott
Mrs. Lawrence Tibbett
Rosalind Russell
1944 Mrs. Stanley Mortimer
Mrs. Byron Foy
Mrs. William Rhinelander Stewart
Mrs. S. Kent Legare
The Hon. Clare Boothe Luce
Mrs. William Paley
Mrs. Andre Embiricos
Mrs. Michael Phipps
Mrs. Howard Hawks
The Duchess of Windsor
1945 Mrs. Stanley Mortimer
Mrs. Byron Foy
Mrs. Millicent Rogers
Mrs. Lawrence Tibbett
The Duchess of Windsor
Mrs. George Schlee (Valentina)
Mrs. Harry Hopkins
Rosalind Russell
Mrs. Robert Sarnoff
The Hon. Clare Boothe Luce
1946 Mrs. Howard Hawks
The Duchess of Windsor
Mrs. Cushing Mortimer
Mrs. Byron Foy
Mrs. Thomas Shevlin
Mrs. Millicent Rogers
Mrs. Harrison Williams
Mrs. William Rhinelander Stewart
Mrs. William Paley
The Hon. Clare Boothe Luce
1947 The Duchess of Windsor
Mrs. William Paley
Mrs. Harrison Williams
Mrs. William Rhinelander Stewart
Mrs. Byron Foy
Mrs. John C. Wilson
Mrs. Millicent Rogers
Mrs. Howard Hawks
Mrs. Geoffrey Gates
Mrs. William Wallace (Ina Claire)
1948 Mrs. William Paley
Mrs. Millicent Rogers
The Duchess of Windsor
Mrs. Andre Embiricos
Mrs. Alfred Gwynne Vanderbilt
Mrs. William Randolph Hearst, Jr.
Mrs. Harrison Williams
The Duchess of Kent
Mme. Louis Arpels
Mrs. Howard Hawks
1949 Mrs. William Paley
The Duchess of Windsor
Mrs. Harrison Williams
The Duchess of Kent
Mrs. Leland Hayward
Mrs. William Randolph Hearst, Jr.
Mary Martin
Mrs. Byron Foy
Mme. Louis Arpels
Mrs. Kingman Douglass (Adele Astaire)
1950 The Duchess of Windsor
Mrs. William Paley
Mrs. Byron Foy
Mrs. William O'Dwyer (Sloane Simpson)
Mrs. William Randolph Hearst, Jr.
Faye Emerson
Gloria Swanson
Mme. Louis Arpels
Mrs. Andre Embiricos
Mrs. Leland Hayward
1951 The Duchess of Windsor
Mrs. William Paley
Mme. Louis Arpels
Mrs. Byron Foy
Irene Dunne
Mrs. William Randolph Hearst, Jr.
Marlene Dietrich
The Duchess of Kent
Mrs. Alfred Gwynne Vanderbilt
Mrs. Douglas MacArthur
Mrs. George McGhee
Mrs. Henry Ford II
Princess Margaret Rose
Countess Uberto Corti
1952 The Duchess of Windsor
Mrs. William Paley
The Duchess of Kent
Mrs. Byron Foy
Mme. Louis Arpels
Marlene Dietrich
Mrs. William Randolph Hearst, Jr.
Mrs. Winston Guest
Countess Rodolfo Crespi
Mme. Henri Bonnet
Mrs. Dwight D. Eisenhower
Mrs. Oveta Culp Hobby
1953 Mrs. William Paley
Mrs. Winston Guest
Mrs. Byron Foy
Mme. Henri Bonnet
Mrs. William Randolph Hearst, Jr.
Ovetta Culp Hobby
Mme. Louis Arpels
Princess Margaret Rose
Mrs. Henry Ford II
Mrs. Alfred G. Vanderbilt
The Duchess of Windsor
Mary Martin
1954 Mrs. William Paley
The Duchess of Windsor

Mrs. Byron Foy
Princess Margaret Rose
Mme. Henri Bonnet
Mme. Louis Arpels
Mrs. Alfred Gwynne Vanderbilt
Ambassador Clare Boothe Luce
Mme. Arturo Lopez-Willshaw
Mrs. William Randolph Hearst, Jr.
Mrs. Harold E. Talbott
Queen Frederica

1955 Mrs. William Paley
Grace Kelly
The Duchess of Windsor
Princess Margaret Rose
Mrs. Byron Foy
Countess Rodolfo Crespi
Mrs. Winston Guest
Mrs. William Randolph Hearst, Jr.
Mme. Jacques Balsan
Mrs. Alfred Gwynne Vanderbilt
Mrs. Henry Ford II
Mme. Arturo Lopez-Willshaw
The Countess of Quintanilla
Mrs. Oveta Culp Hobby

1956 Mrs. William Paley
The Duchess of Windsor
Princess Grace of Monaco
Mrs. Winston Guest
Audrey Hepburn
Marlene Dietrich
Mrs. William Randolph Hearst, Jr.
Countess Consuelo Crespi
Rosalind Russell
The Duchess of Kent
Princess Margaret Rose
Countess of Quintanilla
Mrs. Henry Ford II
Countess Mona von Bismarck

1957 Mrs. William Paley
The Duchess of Windsor
Mrs. Winston Guest
Countess Consuelo Crespi
Queen Elizabeth II
Audrey Hepburn
Mrs. Henry Ford II
Vicomtesse Jacqueline de Ribes
Claudette Colbert
Mrs. William R. Hearst, Jr.
The Countess of Quintanilla
Countess Mona Von Bismarck
Mrs. Norman K. Winston
Mrs. Thomas Bancroft, Jr.

1958 Mrs. Winston Guest
Countess Rodolfo Crespi
Mrs. Henry Ford II
Princess Margaret Rose
Countess of Quintanilla
Mme. Arturo Lopez-Willshaw
Mrs. William Randolph Hearst, Jr.
Kay Kendall
Mrs. Thomas Bancroft
Mrs. Norman K. Winston
Audrey Hepburn
Dina Merrill
Mrs. David K. Bruce
Merle Oberon

1959 Donna Marella Agnelli
HRH Princess Alexandra of Kent
Mme. Herve Alphand
Mrs. Thomas Bancroft, Jr.
Mrs. Walther de Moreira Salles
Vicomtesse Jacqueline de Ribes
Princess Grace of Monaco
Mrs. Loel Guinness
Audrey Hepburn
Mrs. Bruno Pagliai
Mrs. John Barry Ryan III
Mrs. Norman K. Winston

1960 Mrs. John F. Kennedy
Vicomtesse Jacqueline de Ribes
Audrey Hepburn
Mrs. Norman K. Winston
Donna Marella Agnelli
Mrs. Loel Guinness
Mrs. Patrick Guinness
Princess Alexandra of Kent
Mrs. John Barry Ryan III
Mrs. David K. Bruce
Mrs. Stavros Niarchos
Queen Sirikit of Thailand

1961 Mrs. John F. Kennedy
Mrs. Loel Guinness
Princess Stanislas Radziwill
Queen Sirikit of Thailand
Signora Gianni Agnelli
Vicomtesse Jacqueline de Ribes
Mrs. David Bruce
Mme. Herve Alphand
Princess Alexandra of Kent
Mrs. Charles Wrightsman
Mrs. John Barry Ryan III
Signora Uberto Agnelli

1962 Mrs. John F. Kennedy
Mrs. Loel Guinness
Princess Lee Radziwill
Mrs. Gianni Agnelli
Mme. Herve Alphand
Mrs. David Bruce
Mrs. Gloria Vanderbilt Lumet
Mrs. Walther Moreire-Salles
Mrs. John Barry Ryan III
Mrs. Charles Wrightsman
Mrs. Frederick Eberstadt
Baroness Henry Thyssen-Bornemisza

1963 Mrs. Loel Guinness
Princess Lee Radziwill
Dina Merrill
Gloria Vanderbilt (Mrs. Wyatt Cooper)
Baroness Henry Thyssen-Bornemisza
Mrs. Walther Moreira-Salles
Mrs. David Bruce
Queen Farah Pahlavi
Mrs. Charles Wrightsman
Princess Alexandra of Kent
Mrs. T. Charlton Henry
Mrs. Alfred G. Vanderbilt

1964 Queen Sirikit of Thailand
Mrs. John F. Kennedy
Mrs. Joseph P. Kennedy
Mrs. Charles Wrightsman
Princess Lee Radziwill
Dina Merrill (Mrs. Stanley Rumbough, Jr.)
Mrs. Wyatt Cooper
Mrs. Alfred Gwynne Vanderbilt
Mrs. William McCormick Blair, Jr.
Mrs. Paul Mellon
Mrs. Alfred Bloomingdale
The Misses Anne and Charlotte Ford

1965 Mrs. Carter Burden
Mrs. Alfred Gwynne Vanderbilt

Mrs. Wyatt Cooper (Gloria Vanderbilt)
Anne and Charlotte Ford (Mrs. Giancarlo Uzielli and Mme. Stavros Niarchos)
Mrs. Joseph P. Kennedy
Mrs. Kirk Douglas
Mrs. Angus Ogilvy (Princess Alexandra of Kent)
Barbra Streisand
Mrs. Charles Engelhard
Mrs. William McCormick Blair
Princess Luciana Pignatelli
Princess Paola of Belgium

1966 **Princess Lee Radziwill**
Mrs. S. Carter Burden
Lauren Bacall
Mrs. Wyatt Cooper (Gloria Vanderbilt)
Mrs. Lyndon B. Johnson
Mrs. Alfred Gwynne Vanderbilt
Mrs. Patrick Guinness
Mrs. Charlotte Niarchos
Sophia Loren
Mrs. Angier Biddle Duke
Mrs. Henry Ford II
Mrs. Harilaos Theodoracopulos

1967 **Mrs. Wyatt Emory Cooper** (Gloria Vanderbilt)
Mrs. Carter A. Burden,
Mrs. Charlotte Ford Niarchos
Mrs. Harilaos Theodoracopulos
Mrs. Angier Biddle Duke
Princess Lee Radziwill
Lauren Bacall
Mrs. Henry Ford II
Mrs. Charles Spittal Robb (Lynda Bird Johnson)
Mrs. Ronald Reagan
Princess Alexandra of Kent (Mrs. Angus Ogilvy)
Faye Dunaway

1968 **Mrs. Alfred Bloomingdale**
Mrs. Chalres Revson
Mrs. Graham Mattison
Mrs. Charles Engelhard, Jr.
Princess Ira Furstenberg
Mrs. Gianni Uzielli (Anne Ford)
Mrs. Harilos Theodoracopulos
Marquesa Carol de Portago
Mrs. Liberman Savitt
Mrs. Vincente Minnelli
The Duchess de Cadaval
Mme. Ahmed Benhima

most imaginative dressers

Barbra Streisand (Mrs. Elliott Gould)
Baroness Philippe de Rothschild
Miss Marisa Berenson
Mrs. Thomas Kempner
Mrs. Wyatt Cooper (Gloria Vanderbilt)
Mrs. Renny Saltzman
Mrs. Ahmet Ertegun
Mrs. William Rayner
Diahann Carroll
Mrs. Robin Butler
Mme. Maya Plisetskaya
Marisol (Escobar)

1969 **Mrs. William McCormick Blair, Jr.**
Mrs. Wyatt Cooper (Gloria Vanderbilt)
Mrs. Kirk Douglas
Mrs. Ahmet Ertegun
Mrs. Robert Evans (Ali McGraw)
Mrs. Patrick Guinness
Her Highness Princess Salima wife of the Aga Kahn (Lady Sarah Chrichton-Stuart)
Mrs. Graham Mattison
Mrs. Charlotte Niarchos (Charlotte Ford)
Mrs. Robert Sakowitz
Mrs. Harilaos Theodoracopulos

1970 **H.R.H. The Begum Aga Kahn** (Lady Sarah Crichton-Stuart)
Mme. Ahmed Benhima
Diahann Carroll
Catherine Deneuve
Sophia Loren
Mrs. Denise Minnelli
Mme. George Pompidou
Mrs. Richard Pistell (Marquesa Carol de Portago)
Mrs. Ronald Reagan
Mrs. Samuel P. Reed
Mrs. Charles Revson
Mrs. Harilaos Theodoracopulos

1971 **H.R.H. The Begum Aga Khan** (Lady Sarah Crichton-Stuart)
Mrs. Ronald Reagan
Mrs. Richard Pistell
Mme Francios Catroux (Betsy Saint)
Mrs. Frederick Melhado (Louise Savitt)
Mrs. Sidney Brody
Miss Liza Minnelli
Mme. Pierre Schlumberger
Mrs. Reinaldo Herrera, Jr.
Cher Bono
Twiggy (Leslie Hornby)
Kitty Hawks
Jan Weymouth

1972 **Marisa Berenson**
Baroness Thierry van Zuylen
H.R.H. Princess Salima Kahn (Lady Sarah Crichton-Stuart)
Mrs. Henry Ford II
Mrs. Reinaldo Herrera
Mrs. Ronald Reagan
Mrs. Frederick Melhado
Signora Gianluigi Gabetti
Mrs. Mick Jagger
Mrs. William Buckley, Jr.
Mrs. William Clay Ford

1973 **Marisa Berenson**
Countess Brando Brandolini
Mrs. Sidney Brody
Mme. Bernard Camu
Duchess de Cadaval
Duchess de Cadiz (Carmencita Martinez-Bordiu y Franco)
Mme. Francois Catroux
Baroness Arnaud de Rosnay (Isabelle Goldsmith)
Senora Reinaldo Herrera, Jr.
Mrs. Harding Lawrence (Mary Wells)
Baroness Thierry van Zuylen
Mrs. Oscar Wyatt, Jr.

1974 **Mrs. William F. Buckley, Jr.**
Mme. Bernard Camu
Princess Caroline of Monaco
Mme. Francois Catroux
Baroness Arnaud de Rosnay (Isabelle Goldsmith)
Senora Gabriel Echevarria (Pilar Crespi)
Mrs. Gerald Ford
Kay Graham
Mrs. Henry Kissinger
Mrs. Harding Lawrence (Mary Wells)
Mrs. Frederick Melhado
Mrs. Jan (Lally) Weymouth

1975 **Marisa Berenson**
Mme. Francois Catroux
Kitty Hawks
Mrs. Reinaldo Herrera, Jr.

Mrs. Irving Lazar
H.R.H. Princess Edouard de Lobkowicz
Silvana Mangano (Sra. Dino de Laurentiis)
Mme. Manuel Machado-Macedo
Mrs. Frederick Melhado
Mrs. Paul Peralta-Ramos
Mrs. Charles Percy
Mrs. Oscar Wyatt, Jr.
1976 Louise Nevelson
Baronne David (Olympia) de Rothschild
H.H. Farah Diba Empress of Iran
Mary Tyler Moore
Sra. Reinaldo (Carolina) Herrera, Jr.
Sra. Manuel (Jacqueline) Machado-Macedo
Mrs. Oscar (Lynn) Wyatt, Jr.
Mrs. Irving (Mary) Lazar
H.R.H. Princesse Francoise de Bourbon-Parme
Mrs. William Averill Harriman
Mrs. Thomas (Olive) Watson, Jr.
Lady Antonia Fraser
1977 Diane Keaton
Mrs. Smith Begley
Olive Behrendt
Sra. Manuela Macado de Macedo
Countess Hubert d'Orano
Mrs. Gordon Getty
Sra. Reinaldo Herrera, Jr.
Mrs. Irving Lazar
Sra. Antonio A. Mayrank-Veiga
Lacey Newhouse
Mrs. T. Suffern Tailer
Baronne Thierry van Zuylen
1978-79 Timothee n'gutta Ahoua
Candace Bergen
Olive Behrendt
Her Majesty Queen Noor alla Hussein
Mrs. J. Gordon Getty
Mrs. Reinaldo Herrera, Jr.
Countess of Iveigh
Mrs. Irving Lazar
Paloma Picasso
Diana Ross
Mrs. T. Suffern Tailer
Sra. Antonio Mayrank-Veiga
1980 Paloma Picasso
Diana Ross
Duchess of Kent
Vittoria de Nora
Olympia Rothschild
Mrs. Francis Kellogg
Constance Mellon
Irithe Landau
Mrs. Geoffrey Holder
Mrs. Christian de Giognon
Estee Lauder
Grace, Countess of Dudley

BEST DRESSED MEN

1968 Prince Philip Duke of Edinburgh
Wyatt Cooper
Bill Blass
Patrick Earl of Litchfield
George Hamilton
Baron Alexis de Rede
George W. Widener
Cecil Beaton
Jean-Claude Killy
Bernard Lanvin
Count Rudolfo Crespi
Hubert de Givenchy
1969 Gianni Agnelli
Adolphus Andrews
Harry Belafonte
Gianni Bulgari
Michael Butler
James Coburn
Wyatt Cooper
Frank Gifford
George Hamilton
Jean-Claude Killy
Baron Eric de Rothschild
David Susskind
1970 Frederic Byers III
Yul Brynner
Hernando Courtwright
John Galliher
Hon. Angus Ogilvy
Armando Orsini
Giorgio Pavone
Baron Alexis de Rede
Thomas Shevlin
Bobby Short
Lord Snowdon (Antony Armstrong-Jones)
Hon. Sargent Shriver
1971 Baron Alexis de Rede
Gianni Bulgari
Hon. John V. Lindsay
Billy (William) Baldwin
Sidney Poitier
Mick Jagger
Harry Belafonte
Lord Snowdon (Antony Armstrong-Jones)
Robert Redford
Marques de Villaverde
Thomas Schippers
Frank Gifford
1972 Gianni Bulgari
Mayor John V. Lindsay
Billy Baldwin
David Mahoney
Robert Evans
Mick Jagger
John Galliher
Fred Hughes
Armando Orsini
Richard Roundtree
1973 Count Brando Brandolini
Reinaldo Herrera, Jr.
Hon. David Bruce
Luiz Gastal
Senator Barry Goldwater
Horace Kelland
Peter Revson
David Rothschild
Valerian Stux-Rybar
Yves Vidal
Billy Dee Williams
Michael York
1974 President Valery Giscard d'Estaing
Charles, The Prince of Wales
Guy Burgos
Angelo Donghia
Frank Gifford
J.J. Hooker
Johnny Miller
Thomas Schippers
Telly Savalas
Senator John Tunney
Yves Vidal
Fred Williamson

1975 **Marquis of Bath**
Alistair Cooke
Ahmet Ertegun
President Valery Giscard d'Estaing
George Hamilton
H.I.M. Mohammed Reza Pahlavi, Shah of Iran
Hon. John V. Lindsay
Marcello Mastroianni
Joel Schumacher
O.J. Simpson
Dick van Dyke
Michael York

1976 **Count Brando Brandolini**
Jeffrey Butler
Angelo Donghia
Walt Frazier
Fred Hughes
Governor John Love
Marcello Mastroianni
Marques Anthony de Portago
Roberto Rosellini, Jr.
Joel Schumacher
Valerian Stux-Rybar
Marquis of Tavistock

1977 **Mikhail Baryshnikov**
Earl Blackwell
Jeffrey Burlet
Kim d'Estainville
Arthur Levitt, Jr.
Gov. John Love, Colorado
David Mahoney
Gerry Mulligan
President Anwar Sadat, Egypt
O. J. Simpson
Thomas Tryon
Ambassador Andrew Young

1978-79 **Earl Blackwell**
H.R.H. Prince Charles, Prince of Wales
Gov. Hugh Carey
Vitas Gerulitas
Sir John Gielgud
Reinaldo Herraro, Jr.
Thadde Klosowski
David Mahoney
Dan Rather
President Anwar Sadat
Jay Spectre
John Travolta

1980 **Sen. Charles Percy**
Roger Penske
Gen. Alexander M. Haig
Carlos Ortiz de Rosas
Thomas Ammann
James Hoge
Alastair Cooke
Henry MacElhinney
Pres. Jose Lopez-Portillo
David Hockney
Earl E. T. Smith, Jr.
Jerome Zipkin

SUPPLEMENTAL LIST—WOMEN INVOLVED IN THE FASHION INDUSTRY/FASHION PROFESSIONALS

This category was initially called the "Professional" category, honoring actresses and professional women. Over the years, the category was modified and changed to recognize professionals in the fashion industry (designers, models, retail executives and editors) and women married to men in the fashion industry.

1947 **Mrs. Adam Gimbel**
Mrs. George Schlee (Valentina)
Mrs. Orson D. Munn
Mrs. Gilbert Adrian

1948 **Mrs. Adam Gimbel**
Mrs. George Schlee (Valentina)
Gene Tierney
Janet Gaynor Adrian
Mrs. John C. Wilson

1949 **Valentina** (Mrs. George Schlee)
Mrs. Adam Gimbel
Mrs. John C. Wilson
Janet Gaynor (Mrs. Gilbert Adrian)
Countess Alain de la Falaise

1950 **Janet Gaynor** (Mrs. Gilbert Adrian)
Valentina (Mrs. George Schlee)
Mrs. Adam Gimbel
Mrs. John C. Wilson

1951 **Janet Gaynor** (Mrs. Gilbert Adrian)
Gene Tierney
Gloria Swanson
Valentina (Mrs. George Schlee)
Mrs. Adam Gimbel
Mme. Jacques Fath
Mrs. John C. Wilson
Mrs. Orson D. Munn
Margaret Case
Mrs. Leon Mandel

1952 **Valentina** (Mrs. George Schlee)
Janet Gaynor (Mrs. Gilbert Adrian)
Mrs. Adam Gimbel
Mme. Jacques Fath
Mrs. Orson D. Munn
Mrs. Leon Mandel
Bettina Ballard
Mrs. Andrew Goodman
Gene Tierney

1953 **Sophie Gimbel**
Mrs. Leon Mandel
Mrs. T. Reed Vreeland
Mrs. Walter Hoving
Simonetta Fabiani
Mme. Jacques Fath
Mrs. John C. Wilson
Mrs. Ira Haupt
Valentina (Mrs. George Schlee)

1954 **Margaret Case**
Mrs. Adam Gimbel
Janet Gaynor
Valentina (Mrs. George Schlee)
Mme. Jacques Fath
Mrs. John C. Wilson
Mrs. Orson Munn
Mrs. Andrew Goodman
Margaret Case
Mrs. Leon Mandel

1955 **Mrs. Adam Gimbel**
Simonetta Fabiani
Genevieve Fath
Mrs. Stanley Marcus
Mrs. George Schlee (Valentina)
Mrs. T. Reed Vreeland
Mrs. Carmel Snow
Anne Fogarty
Mrs. Digby Morton
Mrs. Andrew Goodman

1956 **Mme. Henri Bonnet**
Vicomtesse de Ribes
Mrs. Carmel Snow
Katherine McManus

Mrs. Leon Mandel
Mrs. Hector Escoboza
Phyllis Digby-Morton
Valentina Schlee
Signora Simonetta Fabiani
Mrs. Stanley Marcus

1957 Gabrielle Chanel
Signora Simonetta Fabiani
Mrs. Carmel Snow
Helene Arpels
Mrs. Earl E. T. Smith
Mrs. T. Reed Vreeland
Mrs. Stanley Marcus
Mrs. Ira Haupt
Sybil Connolly
Pauline Trigere
Margaret Case

1958 Sophie Gimbel
Simonetta Fabiani
Gabrielle Chanel
Pauline Trigere
Carmel Snow
Enid Haupt
Sybil Connolly
Janet Gaynor (Mrs. Gilbert Adrian)
Mrs. Stanley Marcus
Mrs. Leon Mandel
Mrs. Tom May
Helene Arpels

1959 Gabrielle Chanel
Simonetta Fabiani
Princess Irene Galitzine
Sophie Gimbel
Mrs. Leon Mandel
Mrs. Lawrence Marcus
Mrs. Tom May
Geraldine Stutz
Mrs. Carmel Snow
Pauline Trigere

1960 Pauline Trigere
Simonetta Fabiani
Gabrielle Chanel
Sophie Gimbel
Mrs. Stanley Marcus
Mrs. T. Reed Vreeland
Enid Haupt
Mrs. Carmel Snow
Sybil Connolly
Helene Rochas

1961 Pauline Trigere
Simonetta Fabiani
Gabrielle Chanel
Mrs. T. Reed Vreeland
Mrs. Adam Gimbel
Sybil Connolly
Helene Rochas
Helene Arpels
Mrs. Tom May
Mrs. Lawrence Marcus

1962 Mrs. T. Reed Vreeland
Gabrielle Chanel
Simonetta Fabiani
Pauline Trigere
Anita Colby
Helene Rochas
Enid Haupt
Mrs. Samuel I. Newhouse
Mrs. Stanley Marcus
Mrs. Adam Gimbel
Sybil Connolly
Mrs. Tom May

1963 Gabrielle Chanel
Diana Vreeland
Pauline Trigere
Donna Simonetta Fabiani
Mrs. Adam Gimbel
Mrs. Stanley Marcus
Mrs. S. I. Newhouse
Geraldine Stutz
Princess Irene Galitzine
Margaret Case
Mrs. David Evins
Mrs. Milton Greene

1964 Mrs. Richard Rodgers
Mrs. S. I. Newhouse
Mrs. Frederick Eberstadt
Helena Rubinstein
Geraldine Stutz
Mrs. William Rose
Mrs. Milton Greene
Mollie Parnis
Mary Quant
Mrs. David Evins
Mrs. Robin Butler
Gloria Schiff

1965 Marisa Berenson
Mrs. Richard Rodgers
Mrs. Frederick Eberstadt
Mrs. Robin Butler
Mrs. David Evins
Mary Quant
Amy Greene
Mollie Parnis
Emanuelle Khanh
Mrs. William Rose
Caterine Milinaire
Mrs. Mark Miller

1966 Mrs. Robin Butler
Princess Luciana Pignatelli
Mrs. David Evins
Mollie Parnis Livingston
Mrs. Frank Schiff
Mrs. Frederick Eberstadt
Baroness Fiona Thyssen-Bornemisza
Mrs. Montague Hackett
Francoise de Langlade
Mrs. Thomas (Nan) Kempner
Caterine Milinaire
Marisa Berenson

1967 Mrs. David Evins
Mrs. Oscar de la Renta
Princess Luciana Pignatelli
Mrs. Thomas (Nan) Kempner
Marisa Berenson
Mrs. Frank (Gloria) Schiff
Countess Vera Lehndorff (Verouschka)
Mrs. Montagne Hackett
Elieth Roux
Mary Quant
Mme. Bernard Lanvin
Mrs. Renny (Ellen) Saltzman

1968 No list

1969 Marisa Berenson
Berry Berenson
Mrs. Robin Butler
Mrs. Oscar de la Renta (Francoise de Langlade)
Mrs. David Evins
Pamela, Lady Harlech
Mrs. Thomas (Nan) Kempner
Mme. Minouche Le Blan

Miss Eve Orton
Mrs. Renny Saltzman
Mrs. Frank Schiff
Countess Vera von Lehndorff (Verouschka)

1970 Marisa Berenson
Pilar Crespi
Mrs. David Evins
Pamela, Lady Harlech
Mrs. Thomas (Nan) Kempner
Anne Klein (Mrs. Matthew Rubenstein)
Eve Orton
Sonia Rykiel
Mrs. Robert Sackowitz
Mrs. Renny Saltzman
Naomi Sims

1971 Mrs. Bruce Addison
Marisa Berenson
Francoise (Mrs. Oscar) la Renta
Diane (Princess Egon) von Furstenberg
Mary McFadden
Mrs. Even Orton
Elsa Peretti
Mrs. Robert Sackowitz
Mrs. Renny Saltzman
Mrs. Frank (Gloria) Schiff
Naomi Sims

1972 Naomi Sims
Princess Diane von Furstenberg
Mary McFadden
Elsa Peretti
Jean Muir
Contessa Lulu de la Falaise
Maxime de la Falaise McKendry
Mrs. Bruce Addison
Francoise de la Renta
Mrs. Renny Saltzman
Grace Mirabella
Eve Orton

1973 Contessa Lulu de la Falaise
Countess Alessandro di Montezemolo (Catherine Murray)
Carrie Donovan
Princess Diane von Furstenberg
Angelica Huston
Grace Mirabella
Jean Muir
Audrey Smaltz
Mrs. Robert Sackowitz

1974 Carrie Donovan
Princess Diane von Furstenberg
Mary McFadden
Marchesa Catherine de Montezemolo
Grace Mirabella (Mrs. William Cahan)
Mrs. David Neusteter
Mme. Jacques Rouet
Mary Russell
Mrs. Robert Sackowitz
Marina Schiano
Audrey Smaltz
Baroness Hubert (Lorna) de Wangen

1975 Mrs. Bernard Camu
Contessa Lulu de la Falaise
Carrie Donovan
Sra. Gabriel Echaverria (Pilar Crespi)
Donna Karan
Mary McFadden
Mme. Jacques Rouet
Naomi Sims

1976 Mary McFadden
Mrs. Herbert (Minnie) Marcus
Ellen Saltzman
Naomi Sims
Marina Schiano
Contessa Donina Cicogna

1977 Grace Cuddington
Countess Donina Cicogna
Contessa Lulu de la Falaise
Carrie Donovan
Pilar Crespi Echevarria
Muriel Grateau
Norma Kamali
Donna Karan
Elsa Klensch
Mme. Jacques Rouet
Mme. Elie Thoux
Diane von Furstenburg

1978-79 Muriel Grateau
Marina Schiano
Grace Cuddington
Pat Cleveland
Barbara Allen
Countess Donina Cicogna Mozzani
Norma Kamali
Anna Tiggia
Lacey Neuhaus
Ellin Saltzman

1980 Ellin Saltzman
Marina Schiano
Jean Muir
Princess Anne Carraciolo
Countess Donina Cicogna Mozzani
Norma Kamali
Francine Crescent
Countess Hubert d'Orofana

MEN INVOLVED IN THE FASHION INDUSTRY/FASHION PROFESSIONALS

1966 Pierre Cardin
Norman Parkinson
Bill Blass
John Weitz
I.S.V. Patcevitch
Patrick O'Higgins

1967 No list

1968 No separate category; several men in the fashion field were included in the year's Best-Dressed List.

1969 Bill Blass
Hubert de Givenchy
Luis Estevez
Robert L. Green
Baron Nicolas de Gunzberg
Walter Halle
Sixten Herrgard
Bernard Lanvin
Patrick, Earl of Litchfield
Robert Sakowitz
Philippe Venet
John Weitz

1970 Hardy Amies
Antonia Cerutti
Baron Nicolaus de Gunzburg
Kenneth Jay Lane
Oscar de la Renta
Thomas Nutter
Andre Oliver
Robert Sakowitz
Alexander Shields
Chip Tolbert
Philippe Venet

Daniel Zaren
1971 Oscar de la Renta
Philippe Venet
Hardy Amies
Robert Sakowitz
Andre Oliver
Robert L. Green
Chip Tolbert
Daniel Zarem
Thomas Nutter
Kenneth Jay Lane
1972 Oscar de la Renta
Hardy Amies
Thomas Nutter
Andre Olivier
Philippe Venet
Kenneth Jay Lane
Halston Frowick
James Galanos
Yves Saint-Laurent
Joel Schumacher
Max Evans
Henry Sell
1973 Max Evans
James Galanos
Giancarlo Giametti
Kenneth Jay Lane
Ralph Lauren
Piero Nuti
Carlo Palazzi
Anthony Nutter
Jose Mildano
Yves Saint-Laurent
Chip Tolbert
Daniel Zarem
1974 Giorgio Armani
Robert Bryan
Aldo Cipullo
James Galanos
Uva Harden
Jose Maldonado
Nando Miglio
Ottavio Missoni
Anthony Thomas Nutter
Yves Saint-Laurent
Robert Sakowitz
Joel Schumacher
1975 Giorgio Armani
James Galanos
Calvin Klein
Ralph Lauren
Jerry Magnin
Ottavio Missoni
Anthony Nutter
Carlo Palazzi
Daniel Zarem
1976 Giorgio Armonai
James Galanos
Calvin Klein
Ralph Lauren
Jerry Magnin
Ottavio Missoni
1977 Giorgio Armani
Ted Dawson
Tom Fallon
James Galanos
Alexander Julian
Calvin Klein
Robert Lycett-Green
Jerry Magnin
Ottavio Missoni
Daniel Zarem
1978-79 Wilkes Bashford
Giorgio Armani
Ted Dawson
Tom Fallon
Charles Hix
Alexander Julian
Robert Lycett-Green
Ottavio Missoni
Prince Egon von Furstenberg
Lee Wright
1980 Giorgio Armani
Tom Fallon
Wilkes Bashford
Robert Lycett-Green
Alexander Julian
Count Angelor Zegna
Jean-Baptiste Caumont
Manolo Blanaik

To honor individuals who have consistently been voted to the Best Dressed List—and to make room for new names on the List—the Hall of Fame was instituted as a permanent honor. The Hall of Fame designation is sometimes also given to individuals whose affect on fashion has been great, even though they have not been voted Best Dressed.

SUPER DRESSER OF OUR TIME

1974 Mrs. William Paley

TRENDSETTERS

1978-79 Fred Astaire
Diana Vreeland
Lauren Bacall

WOMEN

1958 Duchess of Windsor
Mrs. William Paley
Countess Edward Von Bismarck
Queen Elizabeth II
Mme. Jacques Balsan
Mary Martin
Irene Dunne
Claudette Colbert
1959 Countess Consuelo Crespi
Mrs. Henry Ford II
Mrs. Winston Guest
Mrs. William Randolph Hearst, Jr.
1960 The Duchess of Kent
Mrs. Bruno Pagliai
Princess Grace of Monaco
Mme. Arturo Lopez-Willshaw
1961 Audrey Hepburn
Mrs. Norman K. Winston
1962 Vicomtesse Jacqueline de Ribes
Countess Aline Quintanilla
1963 Signora Gianni Agnelli
Mme. Herve Alphand
Mrs. John Barry Ryan III
1964 Mrs. Loel Guinness
Mrs. David Bruce
Mrs. Walther Moreira Salles
Mrs. T. Charlton Henry
Rosalind Russell
1965 Mrs. John F. Kennedy
Mrs. Charles Wrightsman
Queen Sirikit of Thailand

Dame Margot Fonteyn
Dina Merrill
Mrs. Gilbert Miller
1966 Mrs. Joseph P. Kennedy
1967 No award
1968 No award
1969 Baronesse Philippe Rothschild
1970 Mrs. William McCormick Blair, Jr.
Mrs. Alfred Bloomingdale
Mrs. Wyatt Cooper (Gloria Vanderbilt)
Mrs. Kirk Douglas
Mrs. Patrick Guinness
1971 Mrs. Charles Revson
Betsy Pickering Theodoracopulos
Mrs. Thomas (Nan) Kempner
Mrs. Ahmet (Mica) Ertegun
Mrs. William (Chessie) Rayner
1972 Mrs. Charles Engelhard, Jr.
Mrs. Graham Mattison
Mrs. David Evins
Mme. Gres
Mrs. Richard Pistell
1973 Mrs. Oscar (Francoise) de la Renta
Mrs. Henry Ford II
Princess Salima Aga Kahn
Elsa Peretti
Mrs. Ronald Reagan
Mrs. Samuel P. Reed
1974 Mrs. Paley voted "Super Dresser of Our Time"
1975 Mme. Ahmed Benhima
Mrs. William F. Buckley, Jr.
Countess Brando Brandolini
Mrs. Kingman Douglas (Adele Astaire)
Mrs. Prestis Cobb Hale
Mrs. Paul Mellon
Grace Mirabella (Mrs. William Cahan)
Mrs. Pierre Schlumberger
1976 Mrs. Frederick (Louise) Melhado
Mrs. Mick (Bianca) Jagger
Mrs. Robin Hambro
1977 Empress Farah Diba, Iran
Mary Wells Lawrence
Mary McFadden
Princess Edouard de Lobkowicz
Mrs. Oscar Wyatt, Jr.
1978-79 Francoise Catroux
Mme. Manuel Machado-Macedo
Pilar Crespi Echevarria
Alexis Smith
Barone Thierry van Zuylen
1980 Lily Auchincloss
Mrs. Reinaldo Herrara, Jr.
Olive Behrendt
Mrs. T. Suffern Tailer

PROFESSIONALS

1964 Gabrielle Chanel
Diana Vreeland
Pauline Trigere
Mrs. Sophie Gimbel
Mrs. Tom May
Mme. Helene Rochas
Donna Simonetta Fabiani
Miss Margaret Case
Mrs. Stanley Marcus
1965 Sybil Connolly
Enid Haupt
Mrs. S. I. Newhouse
Geraldine Stutz Gibbs
Anita Colby
Princess Irene Galitzine
1967 Mollie Parnis Livingston
Mrs. Robin Butler
Mrs. Frederick Eberstadt

MEN

1968 Duke of Windsor
1969 Prince Philip, Duke of Edinburgh
Angier Biddle Duke
Douglas Fairbanks
Cary Grant
Dean Acheson
1970 No award
1971 No award
1972 Patrick, Earl of Licthfield
Baron Nicolas Gunzburg
1973 Earl of Airlie
Hon. Angus Ogilvy
Harry Belafonte
Sidney Poitier
Baron Alexis de Rede
Robert L. Green
1974 Oscar de La Renta
Nino Cerutti
Hernando Courtwright
John Galliher
Andre Oliver
Philippe Venet
1975 Hardy Amies
Billy Baldwin
Max Evans
Kenneth Jay Lane
Chip Tolbert
Van Day Truex
1976 Gianni Bulgari
Robert Evans
Frank Gifford
Prince Philip, Duke of Edinburgh
Horace Kelland
Yves Saint-Laurent
Robert Sakowitz
1977 Angelo Donghia
Yves Vidal
Joel Schumacher
Michael York
1978-79 Jeffrey Butler
O. J. Simpson
Kim d'Estainville
Daniel Zarem
1980 H.R.H. Prince Charles, Prince of Wales
Earl Blackwell
Count Brando Brandolini

Coty American Fashion Critics Awards

COTY INC.
235 E. 42nd St., New York, N.Y. 10017 (212/573-2730)

The Coty American Fashion Critics Awards are presented annually to American designers whose work during the previous year has had a significant effect on American dress. A nominating committee composed of fashion editors of national magazines, newspaper syndicates and newspapers makes recommendations which are submitted to a 400-judge panel, which makes the final selections

The Winnie Award, which is a sculpture by Malvina Hoffman, is given annually to the individual selected as the leading designer of American women's fashion. In addition, a Winnie is presented to the winner of the Return Award, given to a designer whose work merits a top award for a second time.

WINNIE

1943 Norman Norell
1944 Claire MacCardell
1945 Gilbert Adrian
Tina Leser
Emily Wilkens
1946 Clare Potter
Omar Kiam of Ben Reig
Vincent Monte-Sano
1947 Nettie Rosenstein
Mark Morring
Jack Horwitz
Adele Simpson
1948 Hattie Carnegie
1949 Pauline Trigere
1950 Bonnie Cashin
Charles James
1951 Jane Derby
1952 Ben Zuckerman
Ben Sommers
1953 Thomas F. Brigance
1954 James Galanos
1955 Jeanne Campbell
Anne Klein
Herbert Kasper
1956 Luis Estevez
Sally Victor
1957 Leslie Morris
Sydney Wragge
1958 Arnold Scaasi
1959 No award
1960 Ferdinando Sarmi
Jacques Tiffeau
1961 Bill Blass
Gustave Tassell
1962 Donald Brooks
1963 Rudi Gernreich
1964 Geoffrey Beene
1965 No award
1966 Dominic
1967 Oscar de la Renta
1968 George Halley
Luba
1969 Stan Herman
Victor Joris
1970 Giorgio Di Sant'Angelo
Chester Weinberg
1971 Halston
Betsey Johnson
1972 John Anthony
1973 Stephen Burrows
Calvin Klein
1974 Ralph Lauren
1975 Carol Horn
1976 Mary McFadden
1977 Donna Karan and Louis Dell'Olio
Stephen Burrows
1978 Bill Atkinson
Charles Suppon
1979 Perry Ellis
1980 Michaele Vollbracht

RETURN AWARD

1951 Norman Norell
1952 No award
1953 No award
1954 No award
1955 No award
1956 James Galanos
1957 No award
1958 Ben Zuckerman
1959 No award
1960 No award
1961 No award
1962 No award
1963 Bill Blass
1964 Jacques Tiffeau
Sylvia Pedlar
1965 No award
1966 Rudi Gernreich
Geoffrey Beene
1967 Donald Brooks
1968 Oscar de la Renta
1969 Anne Klein
1970 Herbert Kasper
1971 No award
1972 Halston
1973 No award
1974 Calvin Klein
1975 No award
1976 Ralph Lauren
1977 No award
1978 Mary McFadden
1979 No award
1980 Perry Ellis

Special Awards are given as merited to honor noteworthy contributions to fashion ideas. The award consists of a bronze plague decorated with a bas-relief Malvina Hoffman figurine.

1943 Lilly Dache
John Frederics
1944 Sally Victor
Phelps Associates
1945 No award
1946 No award
1947 No award
1948 Ester Dorothy
Joseph De Leo
Maximilian
1949 Toni Owen
David Evins
1950 Mabel and Charles Julianelli
Nancy Melcher
1951 Vera Maxwell
Anne Fogarty
Sylvia Pedlar
1952 Harvey Berin and Karen Stark
Sydney Wragge
1953 Helen Lee
Mattie Talmack and John Moore
1954 Charles James
1955 Adolfo
1956 Gertrude and Robert Goldworm
1957 Emeric Partos
1958 Donald Brooks
Jean Schlumberger
1959 No award
1960 Rudi Gernreich
Sol Klein
Roxane
1961 Bonnie Cashin

Mr. Kenneth
1962 Halston
1963 Arthur and Theodora Edelman
Betty Yokova
1964 David Webb
1965 Anna Potok
Tzaims Luksus
Gertrude Seperack
Pablo
Joint Special Award: Sylvia de Gay, Bill Smith, Victor Joris, Leo Narducci, Don Simonelli, Gayle Kirkpatrick, Stanley Herman, Edie Gladstone and Deanna Littell
1966 Kenneth Jay Lane
1967 Beth and Herbert Levine
1968 Count Giorgio di Sant'Angelo
1969 Adolfo
Halston
Julian Tomchin
1970 Will and Eileen Richardson
Joint Special Awards for Costume Jewlery: Alexis Kirk, Cliff Nicholson, Marty Ruza, Bill Smith, and Daniel Stoenescu and Eileen Richardson
1971 John Kloss of Cira
Nancy Knox of Renegades
Elsa Peretti
Levi Strauss
1972 Dorothy Weatherford
Special Men's Fashion Awards: Alexander Sheilds,
Pinky Wolman and Dianne Beaudry, Alan Rosanes and Robert Margolis
1973 Clovis Ruffin
Special Accessory Awards: Michael Moraux, Joe Famolare, Don Kline, Herbert and Beth Levine, Judith Leiber and Celia Sebiri
1974 Special Menswear Award for Jewelry: Bill Kaiserman for Rafael
Special Lingerie Awards: Fernando Sanchez, Stan Herman, John Kloss, Bill Tice and Stephen Burrows
Special Menswear Awards: Sal Cesarani and John Weitz
1975 Special Award for Swimsuits: Monika Tilley
Special Menswear Award for Leather Design: Nancy Knox
Special Awards for Fur Design: Bill Blass, Fernando Sanchez, Calvin Klein and Viola Sylbert
1976 Special Menswear Award for Neckwear: Vicky Davis
Special Menswear Award for Loungewear: Robert Schafer, Lowell Judson and Ronald Kolodzie
Barbara Dulien
Special Citations: Abercrombie & Fitch, Miller's Riding Clothes, L.L. Bean, Eddie Bauer and Gokey's
1977 Special Award for Jewelry Design: Ted Muehling
Special Award for Lingerie Design: Fernando Sanchez
Special Menswear Award for Hats: Marsha Akens
Special Menswear Award for Furs: Jeffrey Banks
1978 Danskin
Joan Halpern for Joan & David Shoes
Special Menswear Award: Head Sports Wear
1979 Special Award for Creative Knits: Joan Vass
Special Award for Jewelry: Barry Kieselstein Cord
Special Award for Men's Furs: Conrad Bell
Special Award for Men's Shoes: Gil Truedson
1980 Special Award for Women's Jewelry: Alex Mate and Lee Brooks
Special Menswear Award for Ties and Scarves: Jeffrey Aronoff
Special Menswear Award for Sweater Designs: Ron Chereskin

The Coty Menswear Fashion Award designed by Forrest Myers is a free-form aluminum sculpture.

1968 Bill Blass
1969 No award
1970 Ralph Lauren
1971 Larry Kane
1972 No award
1973 Piero Dimitri
1974 Bill Kaiserman
1975 Chuck Howard and Peter Wrigley
1976 Sal Ceserani
1977 Alexander Julian
1978 Robert Stock
1979 Lee Wright
Gil Truedson
1980 Jhane Barnes

MENSWEAR RETURN AWARD

1973 Ralph Lauren
1974 No award
1975 Bill Kaiserman
1976 No award
1977 No award
1978 No award
1979 Alexander Julian
1980 No award

The Hall of Fame Award, which consists of a gold medallion, was established as a higher accolade for the Winnie designer chosen three times as the best of the year.

1956 Norman Norell
1957 No award
1958 Claire McCardell
1959 Pauline Trigere
James Galanos
1960 No award
1961 Ben Zuckerman
1962 No award
1963 No award
1964 No award
1965 No award
1966 No award
1967 Rudi Gernreich
1968 No award
1969 No award
1970 Bill Blass
1971 Bill Blass
Anne Klein
1972 Bonnie Cashin
1973 Oscar de la Renta
1974 Geoffrey Beene
Halston
1975 Geoffrey Beene (Hall of Fame Citation)
Calvin Klein
Hall of Fame for Menswear: Bill Kaiserman
1976 Kasper
Hall of Fame for Menswear: Bill Kaiserman
Hall of Fame for Menswear: Ralph Lauren
1977 No award
1978 Bill Kaiserman
1979 Mary McFadden

1980 **Alexander Julian**

Lulu Award

MEN'S FASHION ASSOCIATION OF AMERICA
1290 Ave. of the Americas, New York, N.Y. 10019
(212/581-8210)

The Lulu Awards are given annually to journalists for covering men's fashions in an outstanding way. Print and broadcast reporters and commentators are considered in up to about 10 categories, the exact criteria for which are not available. The awards have been given since 1959, but only the last few years are available. In addition to the winners listed here, first and second runner-up honors are also made.

1972 **Hope Strong,** *Lima* (Ohio) *News*
Mildred Whiteaker, *San Antonio* (Tex.) *Express and News*
Esther Walker, *San Jose* (Calif.) *Mercury-News*
Robert Heilman, *Seattle Times*
Marji Kunz, *Detroit Free Press*
Yvonne Petrie, *Detroit News*
Berta Mohr, Berta Mohr Fashion Syndicate, New York
John Camposa, *New York Times Magazine* (two awards)
Nancy Welch, *Nancy Welch Show,* WSPA-TV (Spartanburg, S. Ca.)
Bob Carr, *Midday,* WDSU-TV (New Orleans, La.)

1973 **Elviretta Walker,** *Oklahoma Journal* (Oklahoma City)
Mildred Whiteaker, *San Antonio* (Tex.) *Express-News*
Esther Walker, *San Jose* (Calif.) *Mercury-News*
Jason Thomas, *Cleveland Plain Dealer*
Genevieve Buck, *Chicago Tribune*
Walter Logan, United Press International (New York)
John Camposa, *New York Times Magazine* (two awards)
Rita Davenport, *Phoenix at Midday/Open House,* KPHO-TV (Phoenix, Ariz.)
Barbara Walters, *Not for Women Only,* NBC-TV (New York)
Mike Douglas, *The Mike Douglas Show,* syndicated (Philadelphia)

1974 **Elviretta Walker,** *Oklahoma Journal* (Oklahoma City)
Charles F. Hoch, *Corpus Christi* (Tex.) *Caller-Times*
Esther Walker, *San Jose* (Calif.) *Mercury-News*
Jason Thomas, *Cleveland Plain Dealer*
Genevieve Buck, *Chicago Tribune* (two awards)
Walter Logan, United Press International (New York)
John Camposa, *New York Times Magazine*
Kity Broman, *Kitty Today,* WWLP-TV (Springfield, Mass.)
Pia Lindstrom, "Newscenter 4 Lifestyles," WNBC-TV (New York)
Hazel Stebbins, *Hazel Stebbins Show,* KFOR-Radio (Lincoln, Neb.)
Arlene Sachs, WINS Radio (New York)

1975 **Barbara Schuler,** *Arizona Daily Star* -Tucson, Ariz.)
Sarah C. Teague, *Birmingham* (Ala.) *Post Herald*
Mary C. Jackson, *Sacramento* (Calif.) *Bee*
Genevieve Buck, *Chicago Tribune* (two awards)
Jason Thomas, *Chicago Sun-Times*
Addis Durning, *New York News*
Audrey West, *Ask Audrey/Montage,* WKNO-TV (Memphis, Tenn.)
Larry Angelo, *Larry Angelo Show,* WJZO-TV (Baltimore)
Barbara Walters, *Not For Women Only,* NBC-TV (New York)
Pat DiSalvo, *Feminine Angle,* WIOU-Radio (Kokomo, Ind.)
Richard Pyatt, *Fashions for Males,* WNYC-Radio (New York)

1976 **Sarah Teague,** *Birmingham* (Ala.) *Post-Herald*
Dois Hjorth, *Oakland* (Calif.) *Tribune*
Esther Walker, *San Jose* (Calif.) *Mercury-News*
Addis Durning, *New York News* (two awards)
Charles Hix, Newspaper Enterprise Association (New York)
MaeBelle Pendergast, *Sacramento* (Calif.) *Union*
Leta Powell Drake, *The Morning Show,* KOLN-TV (Lincoln, Neb.)
Eyewitness News, WABC-TV (New York)
Pat DiSalvo, *Feminine Angle,* WIOU-Radio (Kokomo, Ind.)
Paige Palmer, *Paige Palmer Show,* WELW-Radio (Bath, Ohio)

1977 **Doris Dale Paysour,** *Greensboro* (N. C.) *Record*
Elviretta Walker, *Oklahoma Journal* (Oklahoma City)
Judy Jeannin, *The Record* (Hackensack, N.J.)
Janice Munson, *Cleveland Plain Dealer*
Marji Kinz, *Detroit News*
Charles Hix, Newspaper Enterprise Association (New York)
MaeBelle Pendergast, *Sacramento* (Calif.) *Union*
Becky Livas, *People, Places and Things,* WTAR-TV (Norfolk, Va.)
Anna Bond, *Eyewitness News,* WABC-TV (New York
Pat DiSalvo, *Feminine Angle,* WIOU-Radio (Kokomo, Ind.)
Sally Jessy Raphael, *The Sally Jessy Raphael Show,* WMCA-Radio, New York

1978 **Doris Dale Paysour,** *Greensboro* (N.C.) *Record*
Charles Hoch, *Corpus Christi* (Tex.) *Caller Times*
Judy Jeannin, *The Record,* Hackensack, N.J.
Lana Ellis, *Dallas Times-Herald*
Marji Kunz, *The Detroit News*
Charles Hix, Newspaper Enterprise Ass., New York
Janet Ghent, *Contra Costa Times* (Walnut Creek, Calif.)
Nancy Hart, *Action News*, Memphis
Marvin Scott, *The 10 O'Clock News*, New York
Dinah Shore, *Dinah!,* Hollywood, Calif.
Merv Griffin, *Merv Griffin Show,* Hollywood, Calif.
Milton Metz, *Metz Here,* Louisville, Ky.
Mitch Lebe, *Getting To Know You,* New York

1979 **Barbara Bernard,** *Holyoke* (Mass.) *Transcript-Telegram*
Beverly Gilmore, *Staten Island* (N.Y.) *Advance*
Jackie White, *Louisville* (Ky.) *Courier- Journal*
Lana Ellis, *Dallas Times Herald*
Timothy Hawkins, *Los Angeles Times*
John Moody, United Press International
Jerry Bishop, *Sun-Up,* KFMC-TV (San Diego)
Steve Baskerville, *Morning Show,* KYW-TV (Philadelphia)
Dinah Shore, *Dinah!,* syndicated
Mitch Lebe, *Getting To Know You,* WNBC-Radio (New York)

1980 **Micki Van Deventer,** *Stillwater* (Okla.) *News Press*
Beryl Ann Brownell, *Gary* (Ind.) *Post-Tribune*

Bonnie D. Haliczer, *Tampa Tribune*
Lana Ellis, *Dallas Times Herald* (two awards)
Nine Hyde, *Washington Post*
Charles Hix, United Feature Syndicate
Mary Mauldin Brown, Patricia Culligan, Daina Hulet and Maggie Miller, *Santa Ana* (Calif.) *Register*
Charlie Rose, *The Charlie Rose Show* WRC-TV (Washington)
Joe Vincent, *Everywhere,* KNBC-TV (Burbank, Calif.)
Vivian Harris, *Top o' the Day,* WBTV (Charlotte, N. C.)
Regis Philbin and Cyndy Garvey, *A. M. Los Angeles* (KABC-TV)
Merv Griffin, *The Merv Griffin Show*
Dorothy Shank, *The Dorothy Shank Show,* WJJL/Mutual Network (Niagara Falls, N.Y.)
Melton Metz, *Metz Here!,* WHAS (Louisville, Ky.)
Pracesca Cappucci, *KIQQ Interviews,* KIQQ-FM (Hollywood, Calif.)
Paige Palmer, *Paige Palmer Show,* WELW (Willoughby, Ohio)

Worst Dressed List

MR. BLACKWELL
719 S. Los Angeles St., Los Angeles, Calif. 90014
(213/627-5202)

Richard Blackwell, known professionally as Mr. Blackwell, annually issues a Worst Dressed List, to cite women who he feels have violated "fashion's prime purpose, to glorify womanhood." While the list has been issued each year since 1959, only the most recent are available, and of these just the last three years are complete. We are including as many of Mr. Blackwell's acerbic reasons for his selections as he shared with us.

1970 **Sophia Loren**
Angie Dickinson
Gloria Vanderbilt
1971 **Ali MacGraw**
Jacqueline Onassis
Princess Anne
1972 **Racquel Welch**
Julie Andrews
Mia Farrow
1973 **Bette Midler**
Princess Anne
Racquel Welch
1974 **Helen Reddy**
Princess Elizabeth of Yugoslavia
Fanne Fox
1975 **Caroline Kennedy,** "A shaggy dog in pants"
Helen Reddy, "She spent the year proving I was right . . . she should have saved her costumes for the Bicentennial explosion!"
Nancy Kissinger, "A traveling fashion stew!"
Bette Midler, "Betsy Bloomer . . . didn't pantaloons go out with the hoopskirt?"
Sally Struthers, "Certainly not in the 'fashion family' "
Princess Anne, "A royal auto mechanic"
Tammy Wynette and Donna Fargo, Both for "country music dressed in a circus tent"
Tatum O'Neal, "Twelve going on forty"
Sonia Rykiel, "She put the 'Fanny Wrap' back in and out of fashion"
Elton John, "Would be the campiest spectacle in the Rose Parade"
1976 **Louise Lasser,** "Mary Hartman, Mary Hartman . . . last summer's Tumble Weed, Tumble Weed!"
Maralin Niska, "Carmen dressed like Sadie Thompson!"
Angie Dickinson, "The policewoman that has caught everything but fashion!"
Charo, "A rumble seat with a pushed-up front!"
Ann Miller, "A 1937 screen test!"
Queen Juliana, "All the Queen's horse's and all of the Queen's men couldn't make Julie look good again!"
Lee Radziwill, "Did Lee's designer go down with the *Titanic*?"
Loretta Lynn, "The right dress in the wrong century!"
Nancy Walker, "Vacuum cleaners have better covers!"
Dinah Shore, "Wild again, beguiled again and constantly contrived again!"
1977 **Farrah Fawcett-Majors,** "Enough splits in her dress for an earthquake!"
Linda Ronstadt, "Bought her entire wardrobe during a five minute bus stop!"
Charo, "Cuchi, Cuchi . . . is that a dress or a bug killer?"
Anita Bryant, "She should go to the 'Queen's' dressmaker!"
Diane Keaton, "Ash Can fashions from her local alley!"
Dolly Parton, "Scarlet O'Hara dressed like Mae West in *My Little Chickadee!*"
Marie Osmond, "Over-done and over-dressed. *The Good Ship Lollipop* in dry dock!"
Dyan Cannon, "Looks like she was blown out of one in a circus!"
Chris Evert, "If tailored is in . . . so is boring!"
Margaret Trudeau, "Canada's loss is New York's loss!"
1978 **Dolly Parton**
Suzanne Somers
Christina Onassis Kauzov
1979 **Bo Derek**
Jill Clayburgh
Loni Anderson
1980 **Brooke Shields,** "Looks like a Halloween trick without a treat!"
Elizabeth Taylor, "Forever Amber in drag!"
Suzanne Somers, "Recycled spaghette!"
Bo Derek, "A butterfly wearing her cocoon!"
Charlene (*Dallas*) Tilton, "A pinup for Frederick's of Hollywood!"
Queen Beatrix of the Netherlands, "Cinderella after midnight!"
Susan Anton, "Looks like an ad for a swap meet!"
Nancy Lopez, "A swinging fashion tragedy."
Princess Grace of Monaco, "Dowdy, not Royal!"
Marie Osmond, "Someone should unplug this Christmas tree!"

MR. BLACKWELL'S LIST OF FABULOUS FASHION INDEPENDENTS

1975 **Marisa Berenson**
Nancy Reagan
Mary Tyler Moore
Rose Kennedy
Princess Caroline of Monaco
Diana Ross
1976 **Judy Collins**
Farrah Fawcett-Majors
Vivian Reed

Jacqueline Bissett
Princess Caroline of Monaco
Mary Tyler Moore
Marthe Keller

1977 Princess Grace of Monaco
Meg Newhouse
Suzanne Summers
Lady Lichfield
Natalie Wood
Contessa Chon
Princess Yasmin Khan
Gena Rowlands

1980 Sophia Loren
Catherine Deneuve
Princess Yasmin Khan
Priscilla Presley
Vivian Blaine
Mary Lazar
Rona Barrett

HALL OF FAME

Elizabeth Taylor
Zsa Zsa Gabor
Barbra Steisand
Racquel Welch

Lord & Taylor Creative Design Award

LORD & TAYLOR, INC.
424 Fifth Ave., New York, N.Y. 10018 (212/391-3344)

The Lord & Taylor Creative Design Award, a Tiffany crystal trophy, honors excellence and creativity in the field. A panel of the department store's creative executives selects the winner.

1977 Harriet Selwyn
1978 Julio
1979 Bill Blass
1980 No award

Culinary

Arts & Homemaking

Contents

Related Awards

National Mother of the Year

AMERICAN MOTHERS COMMITTEE
The Waldorf-Astoria, 301 Park Ave., New York, N.Y. 10022
(212/755-2755)

The American Mothers Committee, which seeks to "strengthen the moral and spiritual foundations of the home," annually selects a woman who sets a high standard for family life as the National Mother of the Year from mothers representing each state and the District of Columbia.

1935 **Lucy Keen Johnson,** Georgia
1936 **Frances Eleanor Smith,** California
1937 **Henriette Flora Gray,** Nebraska
1938 **Grace Noll Crowell,** Texas
1939 **Otelia K. Compton,** Ohio
1940 **Edith Graham Mayo,** Minnesota
1941 **Dena Shelby Diehl,** Kentucky
1942 **Elizabeth Vize Berry,** North Carolina
1943 **Mary Dabney Thompson,** Ohio
1944 **Harriet Duff Phillips,** Pennsylvania
1945 **Georgiana Farr Sibley,** New York
1946 **Emma Clarissa Clement,** Kentucky
1947 **Janette Stevenson Murray,** Iowa
1948 **Helen Gartside Hines,** Illinois
1949 **Pearl Owens Gillis,** Texas
1950 **Elizabeth Roe Cloud,** Oregon
1951 **Mary Martin Sloop,** North Carolina
1952 **Toy Lin Goon,** Maine
1953 **Ethlyn Wisengarver Bott,** Illinois
1954 **Love McDuffie Tolbert,** Georgia
1955 **Lavina Christensen Fugal,** Utah
1956 **Jane Maxwell Pritchard,** Michigan
1957 **Hazel Hempel Abel,** Nebraska
1958 **May Roper Coker,** South Carolina
1959 **Jennie Loitman Barron,** Massachusetts
1960 **Emerald Barman Arbogast,** California
1961 **Louis Giddings Currey,** Tennessee
1962 **Mary Celesta Weatherly,** Alabama
1963 **Olga Pearson Engdahl,** Nebraska
1964 **Cora Hjertaas Stavig,** South Dakota
1965 **Lorena Chipman Fletcher,** Utah
1966 **Bertha Holt,** Oregon
1967 **Minnie Knoop Guenther,** Arizona
1968 **E. Grossman Bodine,** North Dakota
1969 **E. Peterson Le Tourneau,** Texas
1970 **Dorothy Lee Wilson,** Tennessee
1971 **Betty Anthony Zahn,** Oklahoma
1972 **Esther Hunt Moore,** North Carolina
1973 **Ruth Youngdahl Nelson,** Minnesota
1974 **Phyllis Brown Marriott,** District of Columbia
1975 **Josephine Wainman Burson,** Tennessee
1976 **M. Garnett Grindstaff,** New Mexico
1977 **Gloria Berry Landon,** Oklahoma
1978 **Ellen McCall,** Tennessee
1979 **Frances Burten Shaw,** Utah
1980 **Bessie Lieder,** Iowa

WORLD MOTHER

1962 **Clara Sproat Glenn,** Ohio

Bake-Off Contest Grand Prize

THE PILLSBURY CO.
608 Second Ave. S., Minneapolis, Minn. 55402
(612/330-4719)

The Pillsbury Bake-Off is an annual contest now offering one $40,000 Grand Prize and 10 other cash prizes. Any resident of the United States 10 years of age or older may enter the contest. Initial participation is by mail. A professional judging agency, home economists and a consumer panel narrow the field to 100 finalists, who are invited to the Bake-Off site to prepare their entries for evaluation by another panel of judges. Each recipe entered requires the use of at least one Pillsbury brand product.

1949 **Mrs. Ralph E. Smafield,** Rockford, Ill., Water-Rising Twists
1950 **Mrs. Peter Wuebel,** Menlo Park, Calif., Orange Kiss Me Cake
1951 **Mrs. Samuel P. Weston,** La Jolla, Calif., Starlight Double Delight Cake
1952 **Mrs. Peter Harlib,** Chicago, Ill., Snappy Turtle Cookies
1953 **Mrs. Bernard Kanago,** Denver, Colo., My Inspiration Cake
1954 **Mrs. Bernard A. Koteen,** Washington, D.C., Open Sesame Pie
1955 **Mrs. Henry Jorgenson,** Portland, Ore., Ring-A-Lings
1956 **Mrs. Hildreth H. Hatheway,** Santa Barbara, Calif., California Casserole
1957 **Gerda Roderer,** Hayward, Calif., Accordian Treats
1958 **Mrs. Donald DeVault,** Delaware, Ohio, Spicy Apple Twists
1959 **Eunice Surles,** Lake Charles, La., Mardi Gras Party Cake
1960 **Leona P. Schnuelle,** Beatrice, Neb., Dilly Casserole Bread
1961 **Mrs. Vernon Resse,** Minneapolis, Minn., Candy Bar Cookies
1962 **Mrs. Erwin J. Smogor,** South Bend, Ind., Apple Pie '63
1963 **Mrs. Roman Walilko,** Detroit, Mich, Hungry Boys' Casserole
1964 **Janis Boykin Risley,** Sarasota, Fla., Peacheesy Pie
1965 **No award**
1966 **Mrs. John Petrelli,** Ely, Nev., Golden Gate Snack Bread
1967 **Mrs. Carol Bullock,** Spring City, Tenn., Muffin Mix Buffet Bread
1968 **Phillis Lidert,** Fort Lauderdale, Fla., Buttercream Pound Cake
1969 **Edna Holmgren,** Hopkins, Minn., Magic Marshmallow Crescent Puffs
1970 **Nan Robb,** Huachuca City, Ariz., Onion Lover's Twist
1971 **Pearl Hall,** Snohomish, Wash., Pecan Surprise Bars

REFRIGERATED

1972 **Mrs. Gerald Collins,** Elk River, Minn., Quick 'n Chewy Crescent Bars
1973 **Mrs. Jerome Flieller, Jr.,** Floresville, Tex., Quick Crescent Pecan Pie Bars
1974 **Mrs. James S. Castle,** River Forest, Ill., Savory Crescent Chicken Squares
1975 **Barbara Gibson,** Ft. Wayne, Ind., Easy Crescent Danish Rolls
1976 **Mrs. Bert Groves,** San Antonio, Tex., Crescent Caramel Swirl

1977 No award
1978 **Linda Wood,** Indianapolis, Chicken-n-Broccoli Pot Pie

GROCERY

1972 **Mrs. Carl DeDominicis,** Verona, Pa., Streusel Spice Cake
1973 **Mrs. Ronald L. Brooks,** Salisbury, Md., Banana Crunch Cake
1974 **Mrs. Emil Jerzak,** Porter, Minn., Chocolate Cherry Bars
1975 **Luella Maki,** Ely, Minn., Sour Cream Apple Squares
1976 **Mrs. Edward F. Smith,** Harahan, La., Whole Wheat Raisin Loaf
1977 No award
1978 **Esther V. Tomich,** San Pedro, Cal., Nutty Graham Picnic Cake

GRAND PRIZE

1979 No award
1980 **Millicent Caplan,** Tamarac, Fla., Italian Zucchini Crescent Pie

Tableau D'Honneur des Concours Culinaires

SOCIETE CULINAIRE PHILANTHROPIQUE
250 W. 57th St., New York, N.Y. 10019 (212/246-6754)

The winner of the annual Tableau d'Honneur des Concours Culinaires is awarded a medal by the Government of France for outstanding achievement in the culinary arts. The 1977 competition was part of the 109th annual Salon of Culinary Art in New York. In addition to the Grand Prize winners listed here, individual honors are given in 27 other fields, including cooking, artistic preparation of food, pastry, management and service. These are too numerous to mention here.

1912 **O. Gentsch**
1913 **L. Canal**
1914 **A. Foussat**
1915-20 **No awards**
1921 **E. Miserez**
1922 **L. Paquet**
1923 **Ed. Maitre**
1924 **Ch. Scotto**
1925 **P. Bedard**
1926 **A. Gamard**
1927 **A. Paschetto**
1928 **G. Brusati**
1929 **Ch. Champion**
1930 **G. K. Waldner**
1931 **J. Chiarle**
1932 **E. Griesshaber**
1933 **V. Fattori**
1934 **G. Banino**
1935 **J. Dincauze**
1936 **J. Gruny**
1937 **G. Hertrich**
1938 **E. Banino**
1939 **Waldorf Astoria Hotel**
1940-46 **No awards**
1947 **Paul Jourcin**
1948 **Plaza Hotel**
1949 **Aime Patran**
Hermann G. Rusch
1950 **Paul Laesecke**
1951 **Robert Audelan**
1952 **Arthur Irminger**
1953 **Traugott Schneider**
1954 **Humbert Gatti**
1955 **Manuel Orta**
1956 **Clement Grangier**
1957 **Georges Blanc**
1958 **Henri P. Sidoli**
1959 **Joseph Castaybert**
1960 **Henry Haller**
1961 **Greenbrier Hotel**
1962 **Marcel Haentzler**
1963 **Andre Rene**
1964 **Andre Pujol**
1965 **Herbert Barath**
1966 **Andre Soltner**
1967 **Ferdinand Metz**
1968 **Willy Ritz**
1969 **Claude Swartvagher**
Joseph Tarantino
1970 **Culinary Institute of America**
1971 **William Spry**
1972 **New York City Community College**
1973 **Jean-Jacques Rachou**
1974 **Matthew Ryan**
1975 **Joseph Trombetti**
1976 **Gerold Berger**
1977 **Jean Jacques Dietrich**
1978 **Long Island Culinary Association**
1979 **Karl Baumgartner**
1980 **Edmond Kaspar**

Tastemaker Awards

R.T. FRENCH CO.
1 Mustard St., Box 23450, Rochester, N.Y. 14609
(716/482-8000 Ext. 2440)

The $500 Tastemaker Awards are given annually for the best American cookbooks of the previous year, as selected by a panel of magazine, newspaper and cookbook writers, editors and publishers.

1967 **Gloria Bley Miller,** *The Thousand Recipe Chinese Cookbook*
1968 **Anne Seranne,** *America Cooks* ("best of show")
Jose Wilson, *House and Garden's New Cook Book* (basic)
Elizabeth Lambert Ortiz, *The Complete Book of Mexican Cooking* (foreign or regional)
Helen McCully, *Nobody Ever Tells You These Things About Food and Drink* (specialty)
Clementine Paddleford, *Clementine Paddleford's Cook Young* (soft cover)
1969 **Jean Hewitt,** *New York Times Large Type Cookbook* ("best of show" and basic)
Dale Brown, *American Cooking* (foreign or American regional)
Annemarie Huste, *Annemarie's Personal Cookbook* (specialty)
Better Homes and Gardens Cooking for Two (specialty)
Sunset Cook Book of Desserts (soft cover)
1970 **Craig Claiborne,** *Kitchen Primer* (basic)
Adi Boni, *Italian Regional Cooking* (foreign or American regional)
Better Homes and Gardens Ground Meat Cook Book (specialty)
Jean Hewitt, *The New York Times Main Dish Cookbook* (soft cover)

1971 **Albert Stockli,** *Splendid Fare* ("best of show" and basic)
Jeanne Voltz, *California Cookbook* (foreign or American regional)
Michael Field, *All Manner of Food* (specialty)
***Sunset* Magazine Editors,** *Sunset Oriental Cook Book* (soft cover)

1972 **Craig Claiborne,** *The New York Times International Cookbook* ("best of show" and foreign or American regional)
Charlotte Adams, *The Four Seasons Cookbook* (basic)
Jean Hewitt, *The New York Times Natural Foods Cookbook* (specialty)
Helen Worth, *Hostess Without Help* (entertaining)
Alan Hooker, *Herb Cookery* (soft cover)

1973 **James Beard,** *American Cookery* ("best of show" and basic)
Craig Claiborne and Virginia Lee, *The Chinese Cookbook* (foreign or American regional)
Dorothy Ivens, *Pates and Other Marvelous Meat Loves* (specialty)
Marian Burros and Lois Levine, *Summertime Cookbook* (entertaining)
Beatrice Trum Hunter, *The Natural Foods Primer* (organic)
Nancy Bryal, *Better Homes and Gardens Low-Calorie Desserts* (specialty diet)
***Sunset* Magazine Editors,** *Cooking With Wine* (soft cover)

1974 **Perla Myers,** *The Seasonal Kitchen* ("best of show," basic and best first cookbook)
Marcella Hazan, *The Classic Italian Cookbook* (foreign or American regional)
Madeleine Kamman, *Dinner Against the Clock* (specialty)
Diana Collier and Joan Weiner, *Bread: Making It the Natural Way* (organic)
Paul Rubinstein, *Feasts for Two* (entertaining)
Anne Seranne, *Anne Seranne's Good Food Without Meat* (specialty diet)
***Sunset* Magazine Editors,**
Sunset Ideas for Cooking Vegetables (soft cover)

1975 **Nika Hazelton,** *I Cook as I Please* (basic)
Richard Olney, *Simple French Food* ("best of show" and foreign or American regional)
Bernard Clayton, Jr., *The Complete Book of Breads* (specialty and best first cookbook)
Helen Corbitt, *Helen Corbitt Cooks for Company* (entertaining)
Beryl M. Marton, *Dinner for One and All* (health and diet)
Daphne Metaxas, *Classic Greek Cooking* (soft cover)

1976 **Jean Anderson and Elaine Hanna,** *The Doubleday Cookbook* ("best of show" and basic)
Nancy Morton, *Better Homes and Gardens Heritage Cook Book* (foreign or American regional)
Craig Claiborne, *Craig Claiborne's Favorites from the New York Times* (specialty)
Jean Hewitt, *The New York Times Weekend Cookbook* (entertaining)
June Roth, *Salt Free Cooking with Herbs and Spices* (natural and specialty diet)
Mable Hoffman, *Crockery Cookery* (soft cover)
Evan Jones, *American Food, The Gastronomic Story* (best first cookbook)

1977 **Michel Guerard,** *Michel Guerard's Cuisine Minceur* ("best of show," best first cookbook and foreign or American regional)
Carol Cutler, *The Six-Minute Souffle and Other Culinary Delights* (basic)
Nika Hazelton, *The Unabridged Vegetable Cookbook* (specialty)
Diana and Paul von Welanetz, *The Pleasure of Your Company* (entertaining)
Barbara Gibbons, *The Slim Gourmet* (health)
Mable Hoffman, *Crepe Cookery* (soft cover)

1978 **Julia Child,** *Julia Child and Company* ("best of show")
Marcella Hazan, *More Classic Italian Cooking* (foreign)
Time-Life Books editors, *The Time-Life American-Regional Cookbook* (American/regional)
Anne Seranne, *The Joy of Giving Homemade Food* (specialty)
***Sunset* Magazine and Book Editors,** *Cooking for Two . . . Or Just for You* (original soft cover)
Craig Claiborne and Pierre Franey, *Veal Cookery* (single subject)
Marion Burros, *Pure and Simple: Delicious Recipes for Additive-Free Cooking* (natural foods)
Barbara Gibbons, *The International Slim Gourmet Cookbook* (special diet)

1979 **James Beard,** *James Beard's Original Fowl and Gamebird Cookery* (original soft cover)
Jacques Pepin, *La Methode* (best cookbook of year/basic general)
Helen Mitty and Elizabeth Schneider, *Better than Store-Bought,* (specialty)
Jean Yueh, *The Great Tastes of Chinese Cooking* (oriental)
Elizabeth Lambert Ortiz, *The Book of Latin American Cooking* (Europe and the Americas)
Walter Slezak, *My Stomach Goes Traveling* (international)
Helen Corbitt, *Helen Corbitt's Greenhouse Cookbook* and **Martha Rose Shulman** *The Vegetarian Feast* (natural food and special diet)

1980 **Maida Heatter,** *Maida Heatter's Book of Great Chocolate Desserts* (single subject)
Craig Claiborne, *Craig Claiborne's Gourmet Diet* (top cookbook of year, overall foods and special diet)
Tom Margittai and Paul Kovi, *The Four Seasons* (basic/general)
Nika Hazelton, *American Home Cooking* (American regional and international)
Jean Anderson and Andrew Buchan, *Half A Can of Tomato Paste & Other Culinaries* (specialty)
Anne Willan, *La Varenne's Basic French Cookery* (original soft cover/American regional and international)
Colin Tudge, *Future Food* (original soft cover/ specialty)
Walter and Nancy Hall, *The Wild Palate* (original soft cover/single subject)
Sheryl and Mel London, *The Fish Lovers' Cookbook* (meat, fish and dairy)

Award of Merit

AMERICAN WINE SOCIETY
4218 Rosewold, Royal Oak, Mich. 48073 (313/549-2303)

The Award of Merit is given annually for significant contribution to the advancement of knowledge of American wine.

1971 **Konstantin Frank,** Growing vinifera
1972 **Charles Fournier,** Contributions to vinifera

1973 **Leon D. Adams,** Author and founder of the Wine Institute

1974 **Willard Robinson,** Chairman, Department of Enology, State University of New York at Geneva

1975 **Philip and Jocelyn Wagner,** Authors and French hybrid researchers

1976 **Maynard Amerine,** Professor, University of California at Davis, for 20 point scale research

1977 **G. H. Mowbray,** Montbray Winery, for pioneering research with vinifera and hybrids

1978 **Harold Olmo,** University of California/Davis, for grape hybridizing

1979 **George Hostetter,** introducing vinifera to North America after Porhition

1980 **Andre Telistcheff,** contributions to wine-making

Humoro

us & Satirical Awards

Contents

Related Awards

National Hollerin' Contest Winner

SPIVEY'S CORNER VOLUNTEER FIRE DEPARTMENT
Box 332, Dunn, N.C. 28334 (919/567-2156)

A 12-inch trophy is presented to the winner of the annual Spivey's Corner National Hollerin' Contest, which is open to any male aged 13 or above. The event is held on the third Sunday of June, and judging is on the basis of excellence in "old time-type hollerin'." Although the contest has been held since 1969, only the most recent winners' names are available.

1979 **Robey Morgan,** Wendell, N.C.
1980 **Treetop Lemon,** Address unknown

COMA Top Ten Awards

"COMMITTEE ON MERIT AND AWARDS"
Tom Wicker, *New York Times,* 229 W. 43rd St., New York, N.Y. 10036 (212/556-1234)

Columnist Tom Wicker compiled a list of COMA Top Ten Awards to public figures and organizations for performance, statements and other actions during 1979, which elicited "COMA's thanks for being rid of such a year."

1980 **Sen. Larry Pressler** of South Dakota and **Gov. Cliff Finch** of Mississippi, joint award of the "the Goldwater-McGovern Cup for Smallest Ripples on the Largest Pond," when they declared their presidential candidacies

Harold Stassen, "Goldwater-McGovern Cup Emeritus"

Apocalypse Now, "the Warren E. Burger Memorial Plaque for the Fanciest Wrapping on the Smallest Package," for being a movie "with two endings, no story and a second half longer than *Gone With the Wind*"

Three Mile Island Generator, "the Richard Nixon Scholarship for the Single Greatest Achievement" for "reshaping the whole nuclear picture without quite melting down."

Henry Kissinger, "the Pits Award for the Longest Fall from Grace" for "declining from Super K through Cambodia and Iran to Feet of Clay in a single year"

Sen. Edward M. Kennedy, "the Safire Prize for Nattering Nabob of the year," for his reply to Roger Mudd who asked why the Senator wanted to be President: "The reasons I would run are because I have great belief in this country, that is—there's more natural resources than any other nation of the world, there's the greatest educated population in the world . . . and the greatest political system in the world. It just seems to me that this nation can cope and deal with the problem in a way it has done in the past. . . and I would basically feel that it's imperative for the country to either move forward, that it can't stand still or otherwise it moves backward."

John Connally, "the Gerald Ford Foot-in-Mouth Competition" for his Middle East program

The question: "Why Did They Let the Shah in Here in the First Place?", the "Chase Manhattan Bank's Silver Question Mark for the Deepest Mystery of the Year"

Supreme Court for ruling that "courts can or cannot be closed, whichever comes first"; **President Jimmy Carter** for calling for the resignations of all Cabinet members after deciding to fire three of them" and to **Congress,** "the Federal Reserve Board Ribbon for the Most Confused Situation of the Year"

President Jimmy Carter, "The Hamilton Jordan Citation for the Most Greivous Gunshot Wound Inflicted on One's Own Foot" for "his singular handling of the Soviet combat brigade in Cuba"

New York Yankees, Chrysler Corp., Boston Red Sox, Carter Administration anti-inflation guidelines, **Los Angeles Dodgers, President Carter's** energy speech, **Senator Kennedy's** poll standing, **Congress,** the **windfall profits tax** and **President Carter** as a road runner, "the J. Edgar Hoover Medal for Bust of the Year"

Ayatollah Ruhollah Khomeini, "Prime Time's Man of the Year"

Preceptorial Accolade
Sweet Fanny Award

ARCANE ORDER
c/o Studio of Contemplation, 5340 Weller Ave., Jacksonville, Fla. 32211 (904/724-4185)

The Preceptorial Accolade is given semiannually ("unless no one is deemed worthy") to the individual who has "done the most for the order and to prominent speakers, artists, etc., who conduct programs for the order."

1970 **Lorraine Albert,** Oil on canvas
Peggy Mohrer, Service
1971 **Steve Lotz,** Pen and ink drawing
1972 **Leonard Mather,** Collage
1973 **Elihu Edelson,** Lecture
1974 **Carl Begley,** Lecture
Sandy Merriman, Serigraph
1975 **Virginia Cathey,** Poem
1976 **Faith Britton,** Produced ceremony
John Darling, Lecture
1977 **Fielding West,** Lecture
Jean Marie Cornwell, Lecture

Current Status Unknown

The Sweet Fanny Award is given "as specified in 'Academic Research Centograph,' Vol. XXIII, No. 3 (1973), including a callipygian classification chart." The name of the winner is inscribed on a "sublime pot" and a certificate is awarded by judges' decision to male and female members of the order.

1975 **Barbara Nagle**
1976 **Nancy Redfern**
1977 **Harriet Smith**

Current Status Unknown

Dame Maria Van Slyke Medal

INTERNATIONAL CONFEDERATION OF BOOK ACTORS
1364 Rockrimmon Rd., Stamford, Conn. 06903 (203/322-6186)

A Dame Maria Van Slyke Medal, which is actually a scroll, awarded quadriennially, for "exceptional achievement in protean portrayals in works of fiction where characters are assigned names of living persons.

The living person must be represented in works of living authors. . . . Membership in ICOBA gives preferred status in consideration." Winners are selected "by a select committee of members selected by the president." (ICOBA also indicates that it offers the Fiona Wergel Citation for Canine Achievement, which has never been awarded.)

1959 **Dame Maria Van Slyke,** *The Manchurian Candidate,* by Richard Condon

1966 **Bennett Reyes,** *Any God Will Do,* by Richard Condon

1970 **Abraham Weiler,** *The Ecstasy Business,* by Richard Condon

1974 **Norman Keifetz,** *Winter Kills,* by Richard Condon
Franklin Heller, *The Star Spangled Crunch,* by Richard Condon

Current Status Unknown

Bore of the Year

SHOW MAGAZINE
708 Third Ave., New York, N.Y. 10017 (212/687-2545)

The readers of *Show* are invited to fill out a ballot to select the Bore of the Year in six categories. The editors select nominees from whom the readers choose. Space is allowed for write-in votes as well.

1977 Television: **Lee Majors,** "For the best imitation of a robot on-screen and off"
Movies: **Elizabeth Taylor,** "For John Warner"
Sports: **Muhammad Ali,** "For not being more retiring"
Music: **Anita Bryant,** "For obvious reasons"
Publishing: **Larry Flynt,** "For being the biggest hustler of them all"
Broadcast: **Barbara Walters,** "For proving that a million dollars doesn't buy what it used to"

Current Status Unknown

Doublespeak Award

NATIONAL COUNCIL OF TEACHERS OF ENGLISH
1111 Kenyon Rd., Urbana, Ill. 61820 (217/328-3870)

The Doublespeak Award is made annually to cite "outstanding examples of misuse of public language" by government, media, advertising or other organizations. Examples of obscure language and euphemistic downplaying in communications to the public are sought as nominees for the Doublespeak Award. The Committee on Public Doublespeak selects the winners, who now must be Americans.

1974 **Col. Opfer,** U.S. Air Force Press Officer in Cambodia, after a U.S. bombing raid for telling reporters, "You always write it's bombing, bombing, bombing. It's *not* bombing! It's air support." (Award in Misuse of Euphemisms category)
Ron Ziegler, Press Secretary to President Richard M. Nixon, for replying to a question on whether a batch of Watergate tapes were all intact, which required a "yes" or "no" answer, by saying the following:
"I would feel that most of the conversations that took place in those areas of the White House that did have the recording system would in almost their entirety be in existence but the special prosecutor, the court, and, I think, the American people are sufficiently familiar with the recording system to know where the recording devices existed and to know the situation in terms of the recording process but I feel, although the process has not been undertaken yet in preparation of the material to abide by the court decision, really, what the answer to that question is." (Award in Gobbledygook category)
Don J. Willower of Pennsylvania State University for the following remarks in the presidential address to the University Council for Education Administration:
1. "The point in all this is not that frameworks that stress the individual and commonly exhibit a psychological orientation are full of error. They are not. To the contrary, they often furnish important insights. But such modes have dominated the thinking of many educators; a state of affairs reinforced by the tangibility of the person as an object of analysis as contrasted with the misty, obstruse quality of system concepts."
2. "Yet, the most basic problems that arise in connection with knowledge utilization may be those that stem from the social and organizational character of educational institutions. A few university adaptations already have been highlighted. Public schools display a myriad of normative and other regulatory structures that promote internal predictability, as well as a host of adaptive mechanisms that reduce external uncertainties." (Award in Educationeze category)
M&M/Mars Candy Co., for a commercial aimed at children which it claimed in a press release was reviewed by the American Dental Association. The company failed to say that the ADA refused M&M/Mars permission to use the ADA's "statement of scientific accuracy," because the commericial claimed that the "bad guy" in tooth decay is plaque rather than the interaction between plaque and sugar. (Award in Language of Silence category)

1975 **Yasir Arafat,** leader of the Palestinian Liberation Organization for replying to an interviewer's comment that "the Israelis say this means you want to destroy their state over the long term instead of the short term," by saying, "They are wrong. We do not want to destroy any people. It is precisely because we have been advocating coexistence that we have already shed so much blood."

1976 **Government employee** who drew up a job description for the position of Consumer Affairs Coordinator for the State Department. One portion reads, "The purpose of the Department's plan is two-fold, to confirm and reinforce the Department's sensitivity to consumer rights and interests as they impact upon the Department and to take those steps necessary to promote and channel these rights and interests with respect to the maintenance and expansion of an international dialogue and awareness." A second passage states that the job would be "to review existing mechanisms of consumer input, thruput and output, and seek ways of improving these linkages via the consumer communication channel."

1977 **Pentagon and Energy Research and Development Agency** for attempting to slip through the appropriations for the neutron bomb by means of euphemistic jargon and by hiding the item in an obscure section of ERDA's budget request. In Pentagon slang, the weapon which kills people but leaves buildings intact is called the "cookie cutter."

1978 **Earl Clinton Bolton,** for a memorandum written by Bolton for the CIA in 1968 and recently declassified, entitled, "Agency-Academic Relations," which began by suggesting that those assisting the agency "may be put on the defensive." The memo advises academics to defend themselves by explaining their CIA involvement "as a contribution to . . . proper academic goals. . . . It should be stressed that when an apologia is necessary it can best be made: (1) by some distant academic who is not under attack, (2) in a 'respectable' publication of general circulation (e.g., *Harper's, Saturday Review, Vital Speeches*, etc.) and (3) with full use of the jargon of the academy (as illustrated below). . . . Two doctrines fiercely protected by the academy are 'academic freedom' and 'privilege and tenure.' . . . When attacked for aiding the Agency the academic (or institution) should base a rejoinder on these sacred doctrines." Bolton concludes by encouraging the Agency to "have an insulator such as Rand or IDA. Such entities have quite good acceptance in academia. . . . Such an independent corporation should of course have a ringing name (e.g., Institute for a Free Society) . . ."

1979 Nuclear power industry, "for inventing a whole lexicon of jargon and euphemisms used before, during, and after the Three Mile Island accident and serving to downplay the dangers of nuclear accidents. An explosion is called 'energetic disassembly' and a fire, 'rapid oxidation.' A reactor accident is an 'event,' an 'incident,' an 'abnormal evolution,' a 'normal aberration' or a 'plant transient.' Plutonium contamination is 'infiltration,' or 'plutonium has taken up residence.' " —William Lutz, 1979 chair, Committee on Public Doublespeak

1980 Ronald Reagan, for campaign oratory filled with inaccurate assertions and statistics and misrepresentations of his past record. The *Los Angeles Times* and *Time* magazine listed some 18 untrue or inaccurate public statements by Mr. Reagan. As the *New York Times* noted, Mr. Reagan "doesn't let the truth spoil a good anecdote or effective symbol. . . . Mr. Reagan's speeches are peppered with . . . omissions, exaggerations and reinterpretations of his experiences as governor of California and as a candidate." Mr. Reagan, for example, mentioned that he refunded $5.7 billion in property taxes to Californians. But he never mentioned that as governor he raised taxes by a total of $21 billion. He also claimed that General Motors "has to employ 23,300 fulltime employees to comply with government-required paperwork." A General Motors executive pointed out, however, that the firm only has 4,900 persons to do all its paperwork. And even after it was disproved, Mr. Reagan continued to claim that Alaska has more oil than Saudi Arabia. Mr. Reagan continued his omissions, misstatements, misrepresentations and exaggerations throughout his campaign. As *Time* magazine commented, "The misstatements have proven effective; the crowds have cheered, and the voters have pulled the Reagan lever. The big question is: Do the facts, after all, really matter?"

Fleece of the Month
Fleece of the Year

SENATOR WILLIAM PROXMIRE
5241 Dirksen Senate Office Building, Washington, D.C.
(202/224-5653)

The Fleece of the Month is given "for the biggest, most ridiculous or ironic example of waste of the taxpayers' money or government activity which fleeces the taxpayer for the month." It culminates in a Fleece of the Year designation each December. While we have not generally reported monthly honors — or dishonors — in this volume, the amount of money involved in activities which make the monthly list are frequently great enough to warrant their inclusion. Furthermore, the activity is frequently national in scope, or at least, according to the Senator, affects all American taxpayers. Occasionally, Awards of Merit are made to honor praiseworthy actions. The selections are named from activities by the federal government, or a federal government-sponsored program, that come to the attention of the Senator's staff, which selects the winner and makes a public statement concerning its selection.

GOLDEN FLEECE AWARD

March 1975 National Science Foundation, "For squandering $84,000 to try to find out why people fall in love." Other citations to the NSF go for a $15,000 study on hitchhiking, an $81,000 study on the social behavior of the Alaskan brown bear, $25,000 to study primate teeth and $112,000 to study the African climate during the last Ice Age.

April 1975 National Science Foundation, National Aeronautics and Space Administration and Office of Naval Research, "For spending over $500,000 in the last seven years to determine under what conditions rats, monkeys and humans bite and clench their jaws, of which more than $100,000 were federal funds."

May 1975 Selective Service System, "For a $98,029 contract it awarded Mr. Kenneth Coffey to study the all-volunteer army concept in a number of foreign countries two years after the all-volunteer army had been put into effect in the U.S."

Army Corps of Engineers, "For their back-door attempt to commit $6- to $10- billion to build a series of new locks and dams on the Mississippi River under a little-known law designed merely for the maintenance, repair or replacement of existing structures . . . If [they] get by with this action, they can replace any of the other 27 locks and dams on the Mississippi and the seven locks and dams on the Illinois River without specific approval."

June 1975 U.S. Congress, "For living high off the hog while much of the rest of the country is suffering economic disaster." Cited were approval of up to three new committee staffers per senator at a $33,975 each salary, increase of House travel allowances by $23,000 per member, the construction of a new $85-million office building and the installation of 19 automatic elevators at $1.3 million in the House Office Building, while retaining operators to run them.

July 1975 Bureau of Land Management, "For requiring useless paperwork on a contract that resulted in a $4,000 piece of equipment costing over $15,000." The equipment: fire equipment to be placed on two pick-up trucks.

August 1975 Federal Aviation Administration, "For a $57,800, 103-page study of body measurements of airline stewardess trainees."

September 1975 Department of the Navy, "For using 64 aircraft to fly 1,334 officers to the Hilton Hotel in Las Vegas for a reunion of a private organization during the height of the energy crisis."

October 1975 National Institute on Alcohol Abuse and Alcoholism, "For spending millions of dollars to find out if drunk fish are more aggressive than sober fish, if young rats are more likely than adult rats to drink booze in order to reduce anxiety and if rats can be systematically turned into alcoholics."

November 1975 Frank Zarb, Administrator of the Federal Energy Administration, "For spending $25,000 and using almost 19,000 gallons of fuel in 10 months since January 1, 1975, jetting about the country in chartered aircraft urging businessmen and civic groups to economize on energy resources."

December 1975 The White House, "For its efforts to add to its empire through increased funds for consultants, contingencies, travel and high-level personnel while calling for austerity from the rest of the government." Specifically cited were an increase of $1.6 million in consultants fees in the Ford Administration, a 100 per cent increase to $1 million of the discretionary contingency fund, an increase of $60,000 in White House staff travel funds without legislative authorization and for having on staff 54 White House aides earning between $37,800 and $44,600 a year.

January 1976 National Endowment for the Humanities, "For grants to well-heeled doctors, lawyers and school administrators to attend tuition-free, vacation-like, month-long humanistic bull sessions at some of the choicest watering holes in the country next summer. This boon-doggle will cost the hard-pressed taxpayer at least $750,000 this year."

February 1976 Department of the Navy, "For exploding an expected $15,000 in repair and maintenance of Vice President Rockefeller's temporary home to a $537,000 expenditure."

March 1976 National Science Foundation, "For a study supported by an NSF grant on 'Environmental Determinants of Human Aggression.' The method of operation: the researcher's assistant would pull his car to a stop at a red light. . . . When the light turned green, the assistant would refuse to move the car for about 15 seconds . . . to determine when and and how often the driver immediately behind would become impatient and aggressive enough to honk his horn."

April 1976 National Aeronautics and Space Administration, "For requesting $2.8 million to construct an addition to the existing Lunar Receiving Laboratory at the Johnson Space Center to house 100 pounds of moon rocks."

May 1976 Federal Aviation Administration, "The FAA, according to its own Public Affairs Office newsletter, spent over $417,000 for 95 new meteorological instruments so that its employees can make rain predictions while remaining indoors despite the fact that existing instruments perform the same function but must be read outdoors."

June 1976 National Center for Health Services, "An examination of over $20 million of their grants and demonstration contracts indicates that routinely they were not completed on time, cost up to five times the original contract and contained low quality and highly questionable results."

July 1976 National Science Foundation's Research Applied to National Needs program, "RANN awarded a $397,000 contract allegedly to perform an unbiased and scientific study of consumer legislation and services to a principal investigator and research center having an overwhelming bias in favor of the credit industry."

August 1976 General Services Adminstration, "For spending $1,015,000 for 15 statues, murals or works of art at federal buildings under the Art in Architecture program." Works included: a $100,000 80- to 100-foot red-painted steel baseball bat.

September 1976 National Aeronautics and Space Administration, "For a sole source contract award of $140,000 for a 6,000-word article and a follow-up book-length history of the Viking Mars Landing project."

October 1976 Housing and Urban Development Department, "For a $245,000 study of New Towns. Over the last decade New Towns and New Communities have been studied to death while most New Towns are dead or dying."

November 1976 Treasury Department, "For its failure to collect as much as $4.8 million in taxes owed by government big shots who are chauffered to and from home in government cars. As much as $17-$18 million in costs to the taxpayer and taxes not collected have been lost because of the Treasury's inaction."

December 1976 Army Corps of Engineers, "For the worst record of cost overruns in the entire federal government . . . [which] cannot be explained away by inflation."

January 1977 Agriculture Department, "For spending nearly $46,000 to find out how long it takes to cook breakfast."

February 1977 Law Enforcement Assistance Administration, "For spending nearly $27,000 to determine why inmates want to escape from prison."

March 1977 In lieu of a Fleece of the Month Award, a Special Merit Award to Max Cleland, Veterans Administration Director, "Notwithstanding the fact that he is a triple amputee, he is driving himself to and from work in his own car, thereby saving taxpayers at least $16,000 a year."

April 1977 Smithsonian Institute, "For spending $89,000 of public funds in producing a dictionary of Tzotzil, an obscure and unwritten Mayan language spoken by 120,000 corn-farming peasants in southern Mexico."

May 1977 National Endowment for the Humanities, "For making a $2,500 grant through the state to Arlington County, Va., to study why people are rude, cheat and lie on local tennis courts" and "for $132 million of taxpayers' money this year to determine why tennis players hog the courts, become frustrated when they have to wait to play for hours or go from court to court to find one with which to play."

June 1977 In lieu of a Fleece of the Month Award, Merit Awards were made to the following:

Smithsonian Institution, "For building its Air and Space Museum on time, for less money than originally requested and for an improvement rather than a reduction of its quality."

Farmers Home Administration, "For the 1972-76 period the FHA had a 32 per cent increase in the weighted total of the loans and grants it made and serviced with a 3 per cent reduction in the number of persons doing the job."

National Science Foundation, "For funding work to build a man-made working gene . . . which may pave the way for supplies of infection-fighting chemicals, insulin or other medically important substances, . . . to find methods to improve on nature's own way of replenishing nitrogen in the soil . . . and pioneering research on how the brain recovers after being damaged."

July 1977 U. S. Postal Service, "For spending over $3.4 million on a Madison Avenue ad campaign to write more letters . . . [and] almost $775,000 more in a seemingly futile effort to test whether the campaign works."

August 1977 Transportation Department, "For spending $225,000 on a report which forecasts transportation needs in the year 2025 under four separate science fiction 'scenarios'—where the United States undergoes an

Ice Age, becomes a dictatorship, is transformed into a hippie culture or blossoms into a society the authors term 'the American Dream.' "

September 1977 **National Endowment for the Arts,** "For making a $6,025 grant to an artist to film the throwing of crepe paper and burning gases out of high-flying airplanes . . . 'to document on film an event designed to alter an audiences immediate environment for a short period of time.' "

October 1977 **Labor Department,** "For granting a $384,948 contract to hire 101 persons under the Comprehensive Employment and Training Act to do a door-to-door survey to count the dogs, cats and horses at the 160,000 houses and apartments in Ventura County, Calif."

November 1977 **Pentagon civilian and military brass,** "For misusing military aircraft on a massive scale at a cost of at least $52.3 million, including support and personal flights instead of combat training and for flights where commercial transportation was many times cheaper."

December 1977 **Federal Deposit Insurance Corp.,** "For a series of outrageous expenditure's for its former Chairman's personal use as revealed in a General Accounting Office report," including travel expenses of Robert E. Barnett's wife who accompanied him on seven trips to such exotic places as Puerto Rico, Manila and Mexico, billing the FDIC over $6,000; using agency vehicles to transport Mrs. Barnett to her doctor and Mrs. Barnett and her children to visit the Hirschhorn Museum. In one case the Barnett children were chauffeured to Rehobeth Beach by two FDIC employees using an agency car. The FDIC also paid Mr. Barnett's membership fees in a private tennis club in Virginia."

January 1977-July 1980 **Not available**

August 1980 **Government National Mortgage Assn.** (Ginny Mae), "For spending $6,918 to buy 1,200 9×12-in. simulated-leather binders which it sent out to savings and loan associations to commemorate the issue of a total of $100 billion in mortgage-backed securities."

September 1980 **Department of Labor,** "For funding a summer youth employment program in Tucson, Ariz., in which 14 junior college track athletes were paid for twice-a-day training sessions, weekly trips to compete in races and week-long journeys to Flagstaff, Ariz., and Reno, Nev., to train, compete and meet with other runners."

October 1980 **Department of Defense,** "For understating by $1.5 million various excessive costs in operating public housing for high-ranking generals and admirals. The next time the generals and admirals come to Congress asking for more money they should be reminded that 'economy begins at home.' "

November 1980 **Department of Educations's Institute of Museum Services,** "For a $35,000 federal grant to a California zoo, part of which was used to send two animal keepers halfway across the country to attend a three-day elephant workshop in Tulsa, Okla."

December 1980 **Federal Highway Administration,** "For spending $241,764 to produce a computerized system that gives local travel directions to people who can't or won't read maps. This complex system is no substitute for asking at the nearest gas station."

FLEECE OF THE YEAR

1975 **U.S. Air Force,** "For operating a $66 million fleet of 23 plush jets used solely to transport top government officials at a cost to the taxpayers of over $6 million a year. This little-known airline is called the 89th Military Aircraft Wing and is based at Andrews Air Force Base near Washington, D.C."

1976 **No award**

1977 **Treasury Department,** "For its zealous support of an end-of-the-year, end-run attempt to amend the tax laws at a cost to the taxpayers of over $400 million this year," by continuing to exempt U.S. residents abroad $20,000 of earned-income on their federal income tax base

1978-80 **No awards**

Lefthander of the Year
All-Lefty Pro Baseball Team

LEFTHANDERS INTERNATIONAL
3601 SW 29th St., Topeka, Kans. 66614 (913/273-0680)

The Lefthander of the Year is a new award that will be given annually for outstanding achievement by left-handed public personalities, entertainers and athletes. A plaque is presented to the winner, who is selected by membership vote.

1977 **Gerald R. Ford,** public figure
1978 **Bruce Jenner,** sports
1979 **Gerald R. Ford,** public figure
1980 **Herb Brooks,** sports

Favorite lefthanders are now also chosen in addition to the top Lefthander of the Year Honor.

1980 **Michael Landon and Kristy McNichol,** entertainment
Crystal Gayle, music
Ken Stabler, Reggie Jackson, Larry Bird, and Dorothy Hamill, sports
Gerald Ford, public figure
Harry S. Truman, historical lefthander

All-Lefty Pro Baseball Team selections receive a plaque for members of the team, who are chosen periodically by a vote of the membership of Lefthanders International.

1976 **Ted Simmons,** (St. Louis Cardinals), catcher
Vida Blue, (Oakland As), Pitcher
Randy Jones, (San Diego Padres), Pitcher
Al Hrabosky, (St. Louis Cardinals), Pitcher
John Mayberry, (Kansas City Royals), First Base
Rod Carew, (Minnesota Twins), Second Base
George Brett, (Kansas City Royals), Third Base
Joe Morgan, (Cincinnati Reds), Shortstop
Lou Brock, (St. Louis Cardinals), Left Fielder
Fred Lynn, (Boston Red Sox), Center Fielder
Dave Parker, (Pittsburgh Pirates), Right Fielder

1977-80 **No awards**

Procrastinator of the Year Award

PROCRASTINATORS CLUB OF AMERICA
111 Broad-Locust Bldg., Philadelphia, Pa. 19102 (215/KI 6-3861)

The Procrastinator of the Year Award, which consists of a "plaque to be inscribed later," is given annually, more or less, to honor recognizable fulfillment in the art of procrastination—not too recently. An awards committee selects the recipient.

1969 **Unnamed topless dancer,** For putting things off

1970 **Jack Benny,** For never getting around to turning 40
1971 **Dean Martin and Jerry Lewis,** "Comedy Team of the Year"
1972 **Methodist Hospital,** Philadelphia, "For placing their cornerstone, dated 1968, in 1972
1973 **Murray Rappaport,** Breaking the world record for an overdue library book
1974 **Illinois Central Railroad,** Latest train: departed 1903, still not arrived
1975 **Postmaster General Elmer T. Klassen,** Late delivery of mail
1976-79 **No awards,** Committee didn't select in time
1980 **Committee hasn't responded to questionnaire yet**

Sour Apple Award

HOLLYWOOD WOMEN'S PRESS CLUB
9000 Sunset Blvd., Ste. 304, Hollywood, Calif. 91602
(213/769-2506)

The Sour Apple Award was established originally to "chastise" the "least cooperative" stars at the time when the Hollywood Women's Press Club had a membership largely of correspondents and reporters. By 1970, when more press agents had joined the association and might be reluctant to have their own clients so cited, the criteria changed to rap the individual or group who had presented an unfavorable image of Hollywood. At the same time, the name of the award officially became the Sour Apple, to balance the Golden Apple given to the Star of the Year. A committee nominates and the membership votes on the recipient.

LEAST COOPERATIVE MALE

1941 **Fred Astaire**
1942 **George Sanders**
1943 **Errol Flynn**
1944 **Walter Pidgeon**
1945 **Fred MacMurray**
1946 **Frank Sinatra**
1947 **Gary Cooper**
1948 **Eroll Flynn**
1949 **Humphrey Bogart**
1950 **Robert Mitchum**
1951 **Frank Sinatra**
1952 **Mario Lanza**
1953 **Dale Robertson**
1954 **Edmund Purdom**
1955 **No awards**
1960 **Elvis Presley**
1961 **Marlon Brando**
1962 **Warren Beatty**
1963 **James Franciscus**
1964 **Tony Curtis**
1965 **Vince Edwards**
1966 **Elvis Presley**

LEAST COOPERATIVE FEMALE

1941 **Ginger Rogers**
1942 **Jean Arthur**
1943 **Joan Fontaine**
1944 **Sonja Henie**
1945 **Greer Garson**
1946 **Ingrid Bergman**
1947 **Jennifer Jones**
1948 **Rita Hayworth**
1949 **Hedy Lamar**
1950 **Olivia de Havilland**
1951 **Esther Williams**
1952 **Rita Hayworth**
1953 **Esther Williams**
1954 **Doris Day**
1955 **No awards**
1960 **Debbie Reynolds**
1961 **Debbie Reynolds**
1962 **Doris Day**
1963 **Ann-Margret**
1964 **Doris Day**
1965 **Ann-Margret**
1966 **Natalie Wood**

SOUR APPLE

1970 **Jane Fonda**
1971 **No award**
1972 **No award**
1973 **Norman Mailer**
1974 **Frank Sinatra**
1975 **No award**
1976 **Porno film producers**
1977 **Truman Capote**
1978 **Paul Michael Glaser**
David Soul
1979 **Chuck Barris**
1980 **Erik Estrada**

iscellaneous Awards

Contents

Johnny Appleseed Award
Silver Medal
Gold Medal
Woodson K. Jones Memorial Plaque

MEN'S GARDEN CLUBS OF AMERICA
5560 Merle Hay Rd., Des Moines, Iowa 50323
(515/278-0295)

The Johnny Appleseed Award, which consists of a medal, is given annually to a man who in a local, regional or national sense has pioneered in some branch of horticulture in a spirit of service, as exemplified by John Chapman, known as Johnny Appleseed. Any member of MGCA may nominate candidates for consideration by the Awards Committee.

1939 Carleton Morse
John Marvin Yoste
1940 John McLaren
August Kock
1941 Adolph Mueller
1942 Henry Hicks
Jens Jenson
1943 No award
1944 No award
1945 John Bacher
Adolph Jaenicke
1946 Fred Edmunds
Lester Morris
1947 No award
1948 Liberty Hyde Bailey
1949 David Fairchild
1950 E. J. Kraus
1951 Arie den Boer
1952 No award
1953 George Terziev
1954 George W. Kelly
1955 James Henry, Jr.
1956 Henry J. Benninger
1957 A. H. Hermann
1958 No award
1959 Herbert Ferris Crisler
1960 Arthur W. Solomon, Sr.
1961 Harvey Foster Stoke
1962 Wister Henry
1963 No award
1964 George Redlow
1965 David Cowan
1966 Clarence E. Godshalk
1967 Rupert Streets
1968 Perry Davis
1969 Frank Curto
1970 Leo F. Simon
1971 Barnie Kennedy
1972 George E. Allen
1973 Edgar Friedrich
1974 Robert Vines
1975 No award
1976 No award
1977 George E. Hughes
1978 William G. "Turk" Jones
1979 C. C. McDonald
1980 No award

The Silver Medal is awarded annually to a member of the Men's Garden Clubs of America who has rendered outstanding service to the organization. Any member may nominate candidates for consideration by the awards committee.

1953 Charles Hudson, Jr.
1954 Milton Carleton
W. H. Thorne
1955 Clair Johnson
1956 No award
1957 A. Ray Tillman
1958 Herbert E. Kahlert
1959 Harold Laing
1960 Larry Hubbard
1961 Raymond C. Allen
1962 Leo C. Nack
1963 Edgar Weikhorst
1964 J. Bryant Horne
1965 Robert L. Waln
1966 William L. Hull
1967 Frank Leech
1968 C. Hal Nelson
1969 Edwin Engelbrecht
1970 Harold J. Parnham
1971 W. O. Ezell
1972 Carroll Greenman
1973 Larry Grove
1974 George Spader
1975 Leland Fetzer
1976 Sam Fairchild
1977 Ray Cheetham
1978 George Mines
1979 Stan Munro
1980 Delbert Dunbar

The Gold Medal is awarded annually to a man who has made outstanding achievements in the field of horticulture. Any MGCA member may nominate candidates for consideration by the awards committee.

1949 C. Eugene Pfister
1950 No award
1951 William Lathrop
1952 No award
1953 No award
1954 No award
1955 Fred Rockwell
1956 Arno Nehrling
1957 Jan De Graff
1958 Edgar Anderson
1959 George Lewis Slate
1960 Clement Bowers
1961 George Pring
1962 Eugene S. Boerner
1963 Leon C. Snyder
1964 Grant Mitsch
1965 Glen W. Burton
1966 Connie, Robert
Barnard Schreiner
1967 Max Watson
1968 No award
1969 John Nash Ott
1970 No award
1971 Arvil L. Stark
1972 Albert Wilson
1973 No award
1974 Clarence Barbre
1975 Wheelock Wilson
1976 Paul Mangelsdorf
1977 No award
1978 William H. Thompson
1979 No award
1980 Joe Woodard

The Woodson K. Jones Memorial Plaque is awarded to an affiliated club for outstanding projects and service to the community, region and MGCA. Clubs may submit records of their accomplisments for consideration.

1959 **Jackson,** Miss.
1960 **Findlay,** Ohio
1961 **North Shore,** Highland Park, Ill.
1962 **Beaumont,** Tex.
1963 **Spartanburg,** S.C.
1964 **Reidsville,** N.C.
1965 **Reidsville,** N.C.
1966 **East Jefferson,** Colo.
1967 **Spartanburg,** S.C.
1968 **East Jefferson,** Colo.
1969 **Spartanburg,** S.C.
1970 **Marietta,** Ga.
1971 **Marietta,** Ga.
1972 **Grosse Pointe,** Mich.
1973 **Austin,** Tex.
1974 **Austin,** Tex.
1975 **Fort Worth,** Tex.
1976 **Libertyville-Mundelein,** Ill.
1977 **San Antonio,** Tex.
1978 **Dallas,** Tex.
1979 **Libertyville/Mundelein,** Ill.
1980 **Van Wert,** Ohio

All-America Rose Selection Award

ALL-AMERICA ROSE SELECTIONS, INC.
Box 218, 513 W. Sheridan Ave., Shenandoah, Iowa 51601
(712/246-2884)

The All-America Rose Selection Award, which consists of a plaque and assistance in distributing the winning rose, honors the variety of the flower which shows outstanding performance in official gardens through the U.S. during a two-year period. Official judges check entries during the two-year trial and score them on a point basis to determine the winner(s). The list below includes the name of the winning rose, its color and type and its originator.

1940 **Dickson's Red** (Scarlet hybrid tea), A. Dickson
Flash (Oriental red climbing bybrid tea), Hatton
The Chief (Salmon red hybrid tea), Lammerts
World's Fair (Deep red floribunda), Minna Kordes
1941 **Apricot Queen** (Apricot hybrid tea), F.H. Howard
California (Golden yellow hybrid tea), F.H. Howard
Charlotte Armstrong (Cerise red hybrid tea), Lammerts
1942 **Heart's Desire** (Deep rose pink hybrid tea), F.H. Howard
1943 **Grand Duchess Charlotte** (Wine red hybrid tea), Ketten Brothers
Mary Margaret McBride (Rose pink hybrid tea), Nicolas
1944 **Fred Edmunds** (Apricot hybrid tea), F. Meilland
Katherine T. Marshall (Deep pink hybrid tea), Boerner
Lowell Thomas (Butter yellow hybrid tea), Mallerin
Mme. Chiang Kai-Shek (Light yellow hybrid tea), Duehrsen
Mme. Marie Curie (Golden yellow hybrid tea), Gaujard
1945 **Floradora** (Salmon rose floribunda), Tantau
Horace McFarland (Buff pink hybrid tea), Mallerin
Mirandy (Crimson hybrid tea), Lammerts
1946 **Peace** (Pale gold hybrid tea), Mme. A. Meilland
1947 **Rubaiyat** (Cerise red hybrid tea), McGredy
1948 **Diamond Jubilee** (Buff hybrid tea), Boerner
High Noon (Yellow climbing hybrid tea), Lammerts
Nocturne (Dark red hybrid tea), H.C. Swim
Pinkie (Light rose pink floribunda), H.C. Swim
San Fernando (Currant red hybrid tea), Morris
Taffeta (Carmine hybrid tea), Lammerts
1949 **Forty-Niner** (Red and yellow hybrid tea), H.C. Swim
Tallyho (Two-tone pink hybrid tea), H.C. Swim
1950 **Capistrano** (Pink hybrid tea), Morris
Fashion (Coral pink floribunda), Boerner
Mission Bells (Salmon hybrid tea), Morris
Sutters Gold (Golden yellow hybrid tea), H.C. Swim
1951 **No awards**
1952 **Fred Howard** (Yellow, pencilled-pink hybrid tea), F.H. Howard
Helen Traubel (Apricot pink hybrid tea), H.C. Swim
Vogue (Cherry coral floribunda), Boerner
1953 **Chrysler Imperial** (Crimson red hybrid tea), Lammerts
Ma Perkins (Coral-shell pink floribunda), Boerner
1954 **Lilibet** (Dawn pink floribunda), Lindquist
Mojave (Apricot orange hybrid tea), H.C. Swim
1955 **Jiminy Cricket** (Coral orange floribunda), Boerner
Queen Elizabeth (Clear pink grandiflora), Lammerts
Tiffany (Orchid Pink hybrid tea), Lindquist
1956 **Circus** (Multicolored floribunda), H.C. Swim
1957 **Golden Showers** (Daffodil yellow climber), Lammerts
White Bouquet (White floribunda), Boerner
1958 **Fusilier** (Orange-red Floribunda), Morey
Gold Cup (Golden yellow floribunda), Boerner
White Knight (White hybrid tea), F. Meilland
1959 **Ivory Fashion** (Ivory floribunda), Boerner
Starfire (Cherry red grandiflora), Lammerts
1960 **Fire King** (Vermillion floribunda), F. Meilland
Garden Party (White hybrid tea), H.C. Swim
Sarabande (Scarlet orange floribunda), F. Meilland
1961 **Duet** (Salmon pink and orange-red hybrid tea), H.C. Swim
Pink Parfait (Dawn pink grandiflora), H.C. Swim
1962 **Christian Dior** (Crimson-scarlet hybrid tea), F. Meilland
Golden Slippers (Orange gold floribunda), Von Abrams
John S. Armstrong (Deep red grandiflora), H.C. Swim
King's Ransom (Chrome yellow hybrid tea), Morey
1963 **Royal Highness** (Clear pink hybrid tea), H.C. Swim and O.L. Weeks
Tropicana (Orange-red hybrid tea), Matthias Tantau
1964 **Granada** (Scarlet, nasturtium and yellow hybrid tea), Lindquist
Saratoga (White floribunda), Boerner
1965 **Camelot** (Shrimp pink grandiflora), H.C. Swim and O.L. Weeks
Mister Lincoln (Deep red hybrid tea), H.C. Swim and O.L. Weeks
1966 **American Heritage** (Ivory-tinged carmine hybrid tea), Lammerts
Apricot Nectar (Apricot floribunda), Boerner
Matterhorn (White hybrid tea), D.L. Armstrong and H.C. Swim
1967 **Bewitched** (Clear, phlox-pink hybrid tea), Lammerts
Gay Princess (Sheel pink floribunda), Boerner
Lucky Lady (Creamy shrimp-pink grandiflora), D.L. Armstrong and H.C. Swim
Roman Holiday (Orange-red floribunda), Lindquist
1968 **Europeana** (Red floribunda), G. deRuiter

Miss All-American Beauty (Pink hybrid tea), Meilland
Scarlet Knight (Scarlet red grandiflora), Meilland
1969 **Angel Face** (Lavender floribunda), H.C. Swim and O.L. Weeks
Comanche (Scarlet-orange grandiflora), H.C. Swim and O.L. Weeks
Gene Boerner (Pink floribunda), Boerner
Pascali (White hybrid tea), Louis Lens
1970 **First Prize** (Rose-red hybrid tea), Boerner
1971 **Aquarius** (Pink blend grandiflora), D.L. Armstrong
Command Performance (Orange-red hybrid tea), Lindquist
Redgold (Red edge on yellow floribunda), Dickson
1972 **Apollo** (Sunrise yellow hybrid tea), D.L. Armstrong
Portrait (Pink hybrid tea), Carl Meyer
1973 **Electron** (Rose-pink hybrid tea), Sam McGredy IV
Gypsy (Orange-red hybrid tea), O.L. Weeks
Medallion (Apricot pink hybrid tea), William Warriner
1974 **Bahia** (Orange-pink floribunda), Lammerts
Bon Bon (Pink and white bi-color floribunda), William Warriner
Perfume Delight (Clear pink hybrid tea), O.L. Weeks
1975 **Arizona** (Bronze-copper grandiflora), O.L. Weeks
Oregold (Pure yellow hybrid tea), Matthias Tantau
Rose Parade (Pink floribunda), J. Benjamin Williams
1976 **America** (Salmon climber), William Warriner
Cathedral (Golden apricot floribunda), Sam McGredy IV
Seashell (Peach and salmon hybrid tea), Reimer Kordes
Yankee Doodle (Sherbet-orange hybrid rea), Reimer Kordes
1977 **Double Delight** (Red and white bi-color hybrid tea), H.C. Swim
First Edition (Coral floribunda), Georges Delbard
Prominent (Hot organe grandiflora), Reimer Kordes
1978 **Charisma**
Color Magic
1979 **Friendship**
Paradise
Sundowner
1980 **Love Honor Cherish**

Honorary Globetrotter

HARLEM GLOBETROTTERS
5746 Sunset Blvd., Los Angeles, Calif. 90028
(213/464-3111)

The comedy-oriented basketball team known as the Harlem Globetrotters annually honors a well-traveled public figure with a lifetime honorary membership in the Globetrotter organization. The recipient is presented with a personalized uniform.

1976 **Henry Kissinger**
1977 **Bob Hope**
1978 **No award**
1979 **No award**
1980 **No award**

Harry S. Truman Good Neighbor Award

HARRY S. TRUMAN GOOD NEIGHBOR AWARD FOUNDATION
Box 6566, Leawood, Kans. 66206 (913/782-7500)

The Harry S. Truman Good Neighbor Award is annually presented on May 8, the late President's birthday, to an individual for meritorious public service. A committee selects the recipient, who is honored at a luncheon.

1973 **Earl Warren**
1974 **Thomas F. Eagleton**
1975 **Lt. Gen. Louis W. Truman,** USA (Ret.)
1976 **Clarence M. Kelley**
1977 **Gerald R. Ford**
1978 **Vice President Nelson A. Rockefeller**
1979 **Adm. Hyman G. Rickover**
Gen. Omar N. Bradley
1980 **W. Averell Harriman**

Western Heritage Awards

NATIONAL COWBOY HALL OF FAME
1700 NE 63, Oklahoma City, Okla. 73111 (405/478-2252)

After several years of annual presentation, the Western Heritage Awards are now given biennially to recognize the drama and heritage of the Old West in art, literature, music, film and theater which depict the history and legends of America's West. Winners, who are selected by the board of trustees which reviews entries, receive the Wrangler Trophy, a replica of Charles Russell's painting *Night Herder*. Western heritage Awards for novels, non-fiction books, and children's and art books appear elsewhere in this edition.

THEATRICAL MOTION PICTURES

1961 ***The Alamo***
1962 ***The Comancheros***
1963 ***The Man Who Shot Liberty Valance***
1964 ***How The West Was Won***
1965 ***Cheyenne Autumn***
1966 ***Sons of Katie Elder***
1967 ***Appaloosa***
1968 ***The War Wagon***
1969 ***Will Penny***
1970 ***True Grit***
1971 ***A Man Called Horse***
1972 ***The Cowboys***
1973 ***Jeremiah Johnson***
1974 ***The New Land***
1975 **No award**
1976 ***Bite the Bullet***
1977 **No award**
1978 **No award**
1979 **No award**
1980 **No award**

FACTUAL TELEVISION PROGRAMS

1961 **"The Greatest Lounsberry Scoop,"** ***Death Valley Days***
1962 **"The Real West,"** ***Project Twenty***
1963 **"The Hat That Wore The West,"** ***Death Valley Days***
1964 **"The American Cowboy,"** ***Discovery '63***

1965 **"The Hanging Judge"**
"They Went That-a-Way"
1966 **"Custer to the Little Big Horn"**
"The Journals of Lewis and Clark"
1967 **"An Iron Horse In Silver Pastures," *Discovery***
1968 **"The End of the Trail," *Project Twenty***
1969 **"The Bonanza Years"**
1970 **"The West of Charles Russell," *Project Twenty***
1971 **"The Last of the Westerners," ABC News**
1972 **No award**
1973 **"Gone West," *The America Series***
1974 **"Conrad Schwiering—Mountain Painter"**
1975 **"The American Parade: The 34th Star"**
1976 **"I Will Fight No More Forever"**
1977 **No award**
1978 **"The American Idea: The Glory Road West"**
1979 **"Ishi, the Last of His Tribe"**
1980 **"John Denver's Rocky Mountain Reunion"**

FICTION TELEVISION PROGRAMS

1961 **"Incident At Dragoon Crossing,"** *"Rawhide*
1962 **"The Sendoff,"** *Rawhide*
1963 **"The Contender,"** *Stoney Burke*
1964 **"Incident of Iron Bull"** *Rawhide*
1965 **"Corporal Dasovik,"** *Rawhide*
1966 **"The Horse Fighter,"** *The Virginian*
1967 **"The Intruders,"** *The Monroes*
"Deathwatch," *Gunsmoke*
1968 **"Bitter Autumn,"** *The Virginian*
1969 **"The Buffalo Soldiers,"** *The High Chaparral*
1970 **"The Wish,"** *Bonanza*
1971 **"Run, Simon, Run,"** *Movie of the Week*
1972 **"Pike,"** *Gunsmoke*
1973 **"Hec,"** *Hec Ramsey*
1974 **"Pioneer Woman,"** *Movie of the Week*
1975 ***The Little House on the Prairie***
1976 **"The Macahans"**
1977 **No award**
1978 ***Peter Lundy and the Medicine Hat Stallion***
1979 ***Centennial***
1980 ***The Last Ride of the Daltons***

WESTERN DOCUMENTARY FILMS

1961 ***Four Seasons West***
1962 ***101***
1963 ***Appaloosa***
1964 ***Pioneer Painter***
1965 ***Age of the Buffalo***
1966 ***The Beautiful Tree, Chishkale***
1967 ***The Five Civilized Tribes***
1968 ***Colorado: Prehistoric Man***
Time Of The West
1969 ***Born To Buck***
1970 ***The Golden Spike***
1971 ***Rodeo***
1972 ***The Last of the Wild Mustang***
1973 ***Bighorn***
1974 ***The Great American Cowboy***
1975 ***Going Down The Road***
1976 ***Red Sunday: The Battle of the Little Bighorn***
1977 **No award**
1978 ***No More than Bows and Arrows***
1979 ***Lucy Covington: Native American Indian***
1980 ***Art in Taos: The Early Years***

MAGAZINE ARTICLES, SHORT STORIES OR POETRY

1961 **"The Old Chisholm Trail," W. Bruce Bell,** Article in *Kiwanis Magazine*
"All Legal And Proper," Steve Frazee, Short Story in *Ellery Queen Magazine*
1962 **"Comanche Son," Fred Grove,** Short Story in *Boys' Life*
"The Look Of The Last Frontier," Mari Sandoz, Article in *American Heritage*
1963 **"The Prairie Schooner Got Them There," George Stewart,** Article in *American Heritage*
1964 **"Nine Years Among The Indians," Herman Lehmann,** Article in *Frontier Times*
1965 **"Titans Of Western Art," J. Frank Dobie,** Article in *American Heritage*
1966 **"How Lost Was Zebulon Pike," Donald Jackson,** Article in *American Heritage*
1967 **"The Red Man's Last Struggle," Jack Guinn,** Article in *Empire Magazine*
1968 **"The Snows Of Rimrock Ridge," Carolyn Woirhaye,** Article in *The Farm Quarterly*
1969 **"W. R. Leigh: The Artist's Studio Collection," Donnie D. Good,** Article in *The American Scene*
1970 **"Bennett Howell's Cow Country," May Howell Dodson,** Article in *Frontier Times*
1971 **"Cattle, Guns, and Cowboys," James E. Serven,** Article in *Arizona Highways Magazine*
1972 **"Echoes of the Little Bighorn," David Humphreys Miller,** Article in *American Heritage*
1973 **"Horses of the West," James E. Serven,** Article in *Arizona Highways Magazine*
"The Donner Party," George Keithley, George Braziller, Inc.
1974 **"40 Years Gatherins'," Spike Van Cleve,** Article in *The Dude Rancher Magazine*
1975 **"George Humphreys, Half Century With 6666," Jim Jennings,** Article in *Quarter Horse Journal*
1976 **"The Pioneer Woman: Image of Bronze," Patricia J. Broder,** *American Art Review*

MUSIC

1961 ***The Alamo,* Dmitri Tiomkin,** Motion picture score
1962 ***Charles Russell Contata,*** *William J. May for Historical Society of Montana*
1963 **No award**
1964 ***How the West Was Won,*** *Alfred Newman and Ken Darby,* Motion picture score
1965 ***Damon's Road,*** Herschel Burke Gilbert, From "Corporal Dasovik" (*Rawhide*), television program
1966 ***Hallelujah Trail,* Elmer Bernstein,** Motion picture score
1967 **No award**
1968 ***The End Of The Trail,*** Robert Russell Bennett, *Project Twenty* television score
1969 **No award**
1970 ***True Grit,*** Elmer Bernstein and Don Black, Motion picture score
1971 ***Snow Train,*** John Parker, From *Gunsmoke* "Snow Train" television program
1972 ***The Cowboys,*** John Williams, Motion picture score.
1973 ***The Train Robbers,*** Dominic Frontiere, Motion picture score
1974 ***Cahill U.S. Marshall,*** Elmer Bernstein, Motion picture score
1975 ***Little House on the Prairie,*** David Rose, NBC television program
1976 **"Bite the Bullet,"** Alex North, motion picture score
1977 **No award**
1978 ***The Outlaw,* Jerry Field,** Motion picture score
1979 ***Comes a Horseman,* Michael Small,** Motion picture score
1980 ***The Last Ride of the Daltons,* Bob Cobert,** Television score

SPECIAL AWARDS

1970 ***Arizona Highways* Magazine;**
***Death Valley Days;* Swiss National Television Network,**
Far West: The Indians
1971 ***The Autobiography Of Charles Francis Colcord, 1859-1934***
Yakima Canutt, rodeo performer and Western Film actor
The Marlboro Man
The Sons Of The Pioneers
"Survival On The Prairie," NBC News documentary
1972 **John Ford, film director**
Dorthy Harmsen, *Harmsen's Western Americana*
Wyoming Stock Growers Association
Winchester-Western Co.
1973 **William H. Clother**, cinematographer
Ben K. Green, *Some More Horse Tradin'*
Agnes Wright Spring, librarian and historian
Dale Robertson, actor
1974 **Alfred Y. Allee**, Texas ranger
Howard Hawks, film director
Luke Short, author
Dmitri Tiomkin, composer and conductor
Korczak Ziolkowski, mountain carver
National Park Service documentary, *The Excavation of Mound Seven*
1975 **Bob Wills and His Texas Playboys, *For The Last Time*** record album
Delmer Daves, film director
James Whitmore, actor, portayal of Will Rogers
Watt R. Matthews, sponsor of Fandorgle folk festival
Robert Adams, author, *The Architecture and Art of Early Hispanic Colorado*
***Oklahoma Today* Magazine**
1976 ***Mustang Country,*** TV short starring Joel McCrea
W. C. Lawrence, historian of the fur trade
George O'Brien, Western film actor
Spike Van Cleeve: An American Portrait, TV short
Margaret Harper, founder, Texas pageant
George Shirk, leader in historical preservation
1977 **No award**
1978 **Seuil Audiovisual** (prod.), *Frontier Heritage*
Claude Fleouter, writer-director
Denys Limon, writer
Harold Warp, creator of Pioneer Village, Minden, Neb.
Paul Aaron, host of *Cowboy Joe's Radio Ranch* and *Prairie Echoes*
1980 **James A. Michener,** author
Ed Rutherford, collector of Western artifacts

Index

A

B

C

D

E

F

I

J

K

L

M

N

O

P

Q

S

T

U

W

X

Y

Z